2002
WRITER'S

8,000 *EDITORS WHO*
BUY WHAT YOU WRITE

MARKET®

EDITED BY **KIRSTEN HOLM**

WRITER'S DIGEST BOOKS
CINCINNATI, OH

Praise for *Writer's Market*

"No writer should be without the *Writer's Market* . . . This is the biggest and best book in the industry for American markets." **—American Markets Newsletter**

"The *Writer's Market* is by far and away the premier source for [finding a publication or publisher] for writers in all stages in ther career(s)." **—John Austin, Book of the Month**

"The *Writer's Market* is another must-have book for writers seeking to profit from their writing endeavors." **—Writer's Write, The Internet Writing Journal**

"An invaluable resource that lays out the nuts and bolts of getting published." **—Library Journal**

"The writer's bible and best friend. If you're serious about selling what you write and submit material regularly, you need a new copy every year." **—Freelance Writer's Report**

"This volume is a freelancer's working tool, as important as the basic computer or typewriter." **—The Bloomsbury Review**

If your company or contest would like to be considered for a listing in the next edition of *Writer's Market* or www.WritersMarket.com, send a message specifying which section of the book you wish to be in by e-mail to writersmarket.com or by mail to Writer's Market—Questionnaire, 1507 Dana Ave., Cincinnati OH 45207.

All listings in *Writer's Market* are paying markets.

Managing Editor, Annuals Department: Doug Hubbuch
Editorial Director, Annuals Department: Barbara Kuroff
Production Editor: Sarah Spears

Writer's Market Website: www.WritersMarket.com

Writer's Digest Website: www.writersdigest.com

Library of Congress Catalog Number 31-20772
International Standard Serial Number 0084-2729
International Standard Book Number 1-58297-044-0
International Standard Book Number 1-58297-049-1 (Writer's Market Online)

Attention Booksellers: This is an annual directory of F&W Publications. Return deadline for this edition is December 31, 2002.

contents at a glance

Contents

GETTING PUBLISHED

Thinking up great article ideas is a skill you can develop. A successful magazine editor and freelancer suggests some ways to jump start your thinking and insight into how editors evaluate the ideas they receive.

Six new, real-life examples of queries that succeeded and queries that failed, with plenty of comments to help you understand why. Two checklists—what not do in your query and a quick review before you mail it—help you fine tune that letter.

Success is in the "e-tails." Eleven pointers on how to write—and send—e-queries that sell.

Specializing in niche markets is the secret to real and lasting success, offering writers steady work flow and the opportunity to write in the fields they love. Interviews appear in the Consumer Magazines section on pages 368, 432, 443, 462, 708 and 782.

PERSONAL VIEWS

Rejection is a fact of life, even for a successful author. Viewing it with a sense of humor—and moving on—is how George Singleton deals with the realities of publishing.

The key to sportswriting is the same as for any kind of writing, as far as MacGregor is concerned: make it brand-new, every time.

790 Trade, Technical & Professional Journals

Magazines listed in this section serve a wide variety of trades and professions. The introduction tells how to break in and establish yourself in the trades.

917 Scriptwriting

Markets for film and television scripts and stageplays are listed here.

COMPLAINT PROCEDURE

If you feel you have not been treated fairly by a listing in **Writer's Market**, we advise you to take the following steps:

• First try to contact the listing. Sometimes one phone call or a letter can quickly clear up the matter.

• Document all your correspondence with the listing. When you write to us with a complaint, provide the details of your submission, the date of your first contact with the listing and the nature of your subsequent correspondence.

• We will enter your letter into our files and attempt to contact the listing.

• The number and severity of complaints will be considered in our decision whether or not to delete the listing from the next edition.

From the Editor

When I was little, I lived around the corner from a boy genius. Ethan Uggacione was extremely smart. And the most memorable evidence of his intelligence was a science fair project he did one year. He bought a whole chicken, boiled it down, and then assembled the bones with wire to reconstruct the chicken's body. I thought that was the coolest thing.

For the past year and a half the staff of *Writer's Market* have been boiling down the body of Writer's Market, and then reassembling it to construct the print *Writer's Market* you have in your hand, as well as the online service WritersMarket.com. As Ethan did with his chicken, we've learned a lot about how the information contained in the book comes together. But we've been able to go even farther than Ethan.

In the *2002 Writer's Market*, you'll find about **4,000 markets, over 1,000 of them new to this edition**, as well as **reliable advice** on nuts and bolts issues such as query letters, manuscript submission and copyright. This year we have **new articles** on how to break into public relations writing, construct a script treatment, syndicate your column. We introduce a **brand new section on electronic publishing**, with advice from experts on finding and evaluating online markets, how to tailor your writing to their different requirements, and how to protect your writing before it hits the screen.

In the WritersMarket.com, however, we've been able to flesh out the information, and even give it some feathers. Every year we work hard to gather as many listings as possible. Then we have to cut so many to make it all fit in the space of the book. It's as thick as it can be, and we'd have to include complimentary magnifying glasses if the print got any smaller. So WritersMarket.com starts out with about **300 additional listings** for book publishers, magazines and contests over the print edition, including the Small Press section which appears in its entirety on the website, and we will be adding hundreds more over the coming year.

Even more exciting, WritersMarket.com contains **over 400 agent listings from the *Guide to Literary Agents*** as well as several articles and interviews from the current edition.

But wait, there's more! The popular **Submission Tracker** debuted a few months ago, to rave reviews. Based on the program on the previous CD edition, the new online version goes even farther in helping you manage your work. Folders for your favorite markets, alerts when there's been a change in a market, and up-to-the-minute information all combine to make this resource the best available.

There have been a lot of people helping WritersMarket.com to fly this year. I've been grateful to all the readers who've dropped me a quick e-mail to alert me to recent changes at a market, or suggested new markets to pursue. This project has truly been a collaborative effort, and I'd like to thank everyone that has played a part in getting this bird up in the air.

Wishing you the best of luck and a successful year,

Kirsten Campbell Holm

Kirsten Campbell Holm, Editor, *Writer's Market*
WritersMarket@fwpubs.com

Using Your *Writer's Market* to Sell Your Writing

Writer's Market is here to help you decide where and how to submit your writing to appropriate markets. Each listing contains information about the editorial focus of the market, how it prefers material to be submitted, payment information and other helpful tips.

WHAT'S INSIDE?

Writer's Market has always given you the important information you need to know in order to approach a market knowledgeably. We've continued to search out improvements to help you access that information more efficiently.

Symbols. Scanning through the listings to find the right publisher for your book manuscript just got easier. In book publishers, the ⛏ quickly sums up a publisher's interests, along with information on what subjects are currently being emphasized or phased out. In Consumer Magazines the ⛏ zeroes in on what areas of that market are particularly open to freelancers to help you break in. Other symbols let you know whether a listing is new (ℕ), a book publisher accepts only agented writers (🅐), comparative pay rates for a magazine (**$-$$$$**), and more. A key to the symbols appears on the front and back inside covers.

Literary agents. Recognizing the increasing importance of literary agents in the book publishing field, we've researched and included 75 literary and script agents at the beginning of the listings on page 89. All of these agents have indicated a willingness to work with new, previously unpublished writers as well as more established authors. Most are members of the Association of Authors' Representatives (AAR), or the Writers Guild of America (WGA).

More names, royalty rates and advances highlighted. In the Book Publishers section we identify acquisition editors with the word **Acquisitions** to help you get your manuscript to the right person. Royalty rates and advances are highlighted in boldface, as well as important information on the percentage of first-time writers, unagented writers, the number of books published and manuscripts received.

Names, pay rates and percentage freelance-written highlighted. In Consumer Magazines, who to send your article to at each magazine is identified by the boldface word **Contact**. In addition, the percentage of a magazine that is freelance written, the number of articles and pay rates for features, columns and departments, and fillers are also highlighted, quickly identifying the information you need to know when considering whether or not to submit your work.

New query formats. Can you send an editor a query by e-mail? We asked editors if they accept e-queries as well as queries by mail, fax or phone.

New articles. Be sure to check out the new articles geared to more experienced writers in Minding the Details. In Breaking and Entering, John Clausen discusses how to translate your writing skills into the world of Public Relations. Monica McCabe Cardoza discusses strategies for getting a regular byline in Setting Your Sights on Syndicating Your Column. Academy award-winning screenwriter Pamela Wallace de-mystifies script treatments, outlines and synopses.

New electronic publishing section. Many writers are finding lucrative markets on the Web. Debbie Ridpath Ohi, author of *Writer's Online Marketplace*, offers Ten Tips for Finding Markets Online. In E-query Etiquette, Greg Daugherty tells you how to write e-mail queries that get assignments. Anthony Tedesco, author of *Online Markets for Writers*, clues you in to how to tailor your writing to the online environment, details some basic HTML to help you look good, and throws in a number of online markets for good measure. For both magazine writers and book authors, the issue of electronic rights is increasingly important. Moira Allen, author of *Writing.com: Creative Internet Strategies to Advance Your Career*, gives you tips on preserving your rights now and in the future. And M.J. Rose, the Internet publishing pioneer, discusses how e-publishers must master the art of marketing to succeed.

As always, all of the listings have been checked and verified, with more e-mail addresses and websites added, and inside tips straight from the editors.

IF *WRITER'S MARKET* IS NEW TO YOU . . .

A quick look at the Table of Contents will familiarize you with the arrangement of *Writer's Market*. The three largest sections of the book are the market listings of Book Publishers; Consumer Magazines; and Trade, Technical & Professional Journals. You will also find other sections of market listings for Scriptwriting, Syndicates, Greeting Cards and Contests & Awards. The section introductions contain specific information about trends, submission methods and other helpful resources for the material included in that section.

The articles in the first section, Getting Published, are included with newer, unpublished writers in mind. In Where to Get Great Ideas, Greg Daugherty looks at how to generate your own salable ideas. Query Letter Clinic shows you six real-life examples of letters that hit the mark and those that missed it. In Breaking Into Niche Markets Kelly Milner Halls interviews freelancers active in magazine areas as diverse as electronic games, women's interest and sports, and discovers that sometimes narrowing the field broadens your prospects.

Narrowing your search

After you've identified the market categories you're interested in, you can begin researching specific markets within each section.

Book Publishers are categorized, in the Book Publishers Subject Index, according to types of books they are interested in. If, for example, you plan to write a book on a religious topic, simply turn to the Book Publishers Subject Index and look under the Religion subhead in Nonfiction for the names and page numbers of companies that publish such books.

Consumer Magazines and Trade, Technical & Professional Journals are categorized by subject to make it easier for you to identify markets for your work. If you want to publish an article dealing with some aspect of retirement, you could look under the Retirement category of Consumer Magazines to find an appropriate market. You would want to keep in mind, however, that magazines in other categories might also be interested in your article (for example, women's magazines publish such material as well). Keep your antennae up while studying the markets: less obvious markets often offer the best opportunities.

Interpreting the markets

Once you've identified companies or publications that cover the subjects you're interested in, you can begin evaluating specific listings to pinpoint the markets most receptive to your work and most beneficial to you.

In evaluating an individual listing, first check the location of the company, the types of material it is interested in seeing, submission requirements, and rights and payment policies. Depending upon your personal concerns, any of these items could be a deciding factor as you determine which markets you plan to approach. Many listings also include a reporting time, which lets you know how long it will typically take for the publisher to respond to your initial query or submission. (We suggest that you allow an additional month for a response, just in case your submission is under further review or the publisher is backlogged.)

Check the Glossary at the back of the book for unfamiliar words. Specific symbols and abbreviations are explained in the key appearing on the front and back inside covers. The most important abbreviation is SASE—self-addressed, stamped envelope. Always enclose one when you send unsolicited queries, proposals or manuscripts. This requirement is not included in most of the individual market listings because it is a "given" that you must follow if you expect to receive a reply.

A careful reading of the listings will reveal that many editors are very specific about their needs. Your chances of success increase if you follow directions to the letter. Often companies do not accept unsolicited manuscripts and return them unread. Read each listing closely, heed the tips given, and follow the instructions. Work presented professionally will normally be given more serious consideration.

Whenever possible, obtain writer's guidelines before submitting material. You can usually obtain them by sending a SASE to the address in the listing. Magazines often post their guidelines on their website as well. You should also familiarize yourself with the company's publications. Many of the listings contain instructions on how to obtain sample copies, catalogs or market lists. The more research you do upfront, the better your chances of acceptance, publication and payment.

Additional help

The book contains many articles on a variety of helpful topics. Insider Reports—interviews with writers, editors, and publishers—offer advice and an inside look at publishing. Some listings contain editorial comments, indicated by a bullet (●), that provide additional information discovered during our compilation of this year's *Writer's Market*. E-mail addresses and websites have been included for many markets. The Resources section includes some, but by no means all, trade magazines, directories and sources of information on writing-related topics. The Websites section points you to writing-related material on the Web.

Newer or unpublished writers should be sure to read Before Your First Sale. Minding the Details offers valuable information about rights, taxes and other practical matters. There is also a helpful section titled How Much Should I Charge? that offers guidance for setting your freelance fees.

Important Listing Information

- Listings are based on editorial questionnaires and interviews. They are not advertisements; publishers do not pay for their listings. The markets are not endorsed by *Writer's Market* editors. F&W Publications, Inc., Writer's Digest Books and its employees go to great effort to ascertain the validity of information in this book. However, transactions between users of the information and individuals and/or companies are strictly between those parties.
- All listings have been verified before publication of this book. If a listing has not changed from last year, then the editor told us the market's needs have not changed and the previous listing continues to accurately reflect its policies.
- *Writer's Market* reserves the right to exclude any listing.
- When looking for a specific market, check the index. A market may not be listed for one of these reasons:
   1. It doesn't solicit freelance material.
   2. It doesn't pay for material.
   3. It has gone out of business.
   4. It has failed to verify or update its listing for this edition.
   5. It was in the middle of being sold at press time, and rather than disclose premature details, we chose not to list it.
   6. It hasn't answered *Writer's Market* inquiries satisfactorily. (To the best of our ability, and with our readers' help, we try to screen out fraudulent listings.)
   7. It buys few manuscripts, constituting a very small market for freelancers.
- Individual markets that appeared in last year's edition but are not listed in this edition are included in the General Index, with a notation giving the basis for their exclusion.

Getting Published
Before Your First Sale

Many writers new to the craft feel that achieving publication—and getting paid for their work—is an accomplishment so shrouded in mystery and magic that there can be little hope it will ever happen to *them*. Of course, that's nonsense. All writers were newcomers once. Getting paid for your writing is not a matter of insider information or being handed the one "key" to success. There's not even a secret handshake.

Making money from your writing will require three things of you:
- Good writing
- Knowledge of writing markets (magazines and book publishers) and how to approach them professionally
- Persistence

Good writing without marketing know-how and persistence might be art, but who's going to know if it never sells? A knowledge of markets without writing ability or persistence is pointless. And persistence without talent and at least a hint of professionalism is simply irksome. But a writer who can combine the above-mentioned virtues stands a good chance of not only selling a piece occasionally, but enjoying a long and successful writing career.

You may think a previously unpublished writer has a difficult time breaking into the field. As with any profession, experience is valued, but that doesn't mean publishers are closed to new writers. While it is true some editors prefer working with established writers, most are open to professional submissions and good ideas from any writer, and quite a few magazine editors like to feature different styles and voices.

In nonfiction book publishing, experience in writing or in a particular subject area is valued by editors as an indicator of the author's ability and expertise in the subject. As with magazines, the idea is paramount, and new authors break in every year with good, timely ideas.

As you work in the writing field, you may read articles or talk to writers and editors who give conflicting advice. There are some norms in the business, but they are few. You'll probably hear as many different routes to publication as writers you talk to.

The following information on submissions has worked for many writers, but it's not the *only* method you can follow. It's easy to get wrapped up in the specifics of submitting (should my name go at the top left or right of the manuscript?) and fail to consider weightier matters (is this idea appropriate for this market?). Let common sense and courtesy be your guides as you work with editors, and eventually you'll develop your own most effective submission methods.

DEVELOP YOUR IDEAS, THEN TARGET THE MARKETS

Writers often think of an interesting story, complete the manuscript and then begin the search for a suitable publisher or magazine. While this approach is common for fiction, poetry and screenwriting, it reduces your chances of success in many other writing areas. Instead, try choosing categories that interest you and study those sections in *Writer's Market*. Select several listings that you consider good prospects for your type of writing. Sometimes the individual listings will even help you generate ideas.

Next, make a list of the potential markets for each idea. Make the initial contact with markets using the method stated in the market listings. If you exhaust your list of possibilities, don't give up. Reevaluate the idea or try another angle. Continue developing ideas and approaching markets with them. Identify and rank potential markets for an idea and continue the process.

As you submit to the various periodicals listed in *Writer's Market*, it's important to remember that every magazine is published with a particular slant and audience in mind. Probably the number one complaint we hear from editors is that writers often send material and ideas that are completely wrong for their magazines. The first mark of professionalism is to know your market well. That knowledge starts here in *Writer's Market*, but you should also search out back issues of the magazines you wish to write for and learn what specific subjects they have published in past issues and how those subjects have been handled. Websites can be an invaluable source. Not only do many magazines post their writer's guidelines on their site, many publish some or all of the current issue, as well as an archive of past articles. This will give you clues as to what they're interested in and what they've already published.

Prepare for rejection and the sometimes lengthy wait. When a submission is returned, check your file folder of potential markets for that idea. Cross off the market that rejected the idea and immediately mail an appropriate submission to the next market on your list. If the editor has given you suggestions or reasons as to why the manuscript was not accepted, you might want to incorporate these when revising your manuscript.

About rejection. Rejection is a way of life in the publishing world. It's inevitable in a business that deals with such an overwhelming number of applicants for such a limited number of positions. Anyone who has published has lived through many rejections, and writers with thin skin are at a distinct disadvantage. The key to surviving rejection is to remember that it is not a personal attack—it's merely a judgment about the appropriateness of your work for that particular market at that particular time. Writers who let rejection dissuade them from pursuing their dream or who react to each editor's "No" with indignation or fury do themselves a disservice. Writers who let rejection stop them do not publish. Resign yourself to facing rejection now. You will live through it, and you will eventually overcome it.

QUERY AND COVER LETTERS

A query letter is a brief but detailed letter written to interest an editor in your manuscript. It is a tool for selling both nonfiction magazine articles and nonfiction books. With a magazine query you are attempting to interest an editor in buying your article for her periodical. A book query's job is to get an editor interested enough to ask you for either a full proposal or the entire manuscript. (Note: Some book editors accept proposals on first contact. Refer to individual listings for contact guidelines.) Some beginners are hesitant to query, thinking an editor can more fairly judge an idea by seeing the entire manuscript. Actually, most nonfiction editors prefer to be queried.

There is no query formula that guarantees success, but there are some points to consider when you begin. Queries should:

- Be limited to one page, single-spaced, and address the editor by name (Mr. or Ms. and the surname).
- Grab the editor's interest with a strong opening. Some magazine queries begin with a paragraph meant to approximate the lead of the intended article.
- Indicate how you intend to develop the article or book. Give the editor some idea of the work's structure and content.
- Let the editor know if you have photos available to accompany your magazine article (never send original photos—send photocopies or duplicates).
- Mention any expertise or training that qualifies you to write the article or book. If you've published before, mention it; if not, don't.
- End with a direct request to write the article (or, if you're pitching a book, ask for the go-ahead to send in a full proposal or the entire manuscript). Give the editor an idea of the expected length and delivery date of your manuscript.

Some writers state politely in their query letters that after a specified date (slightly beyond the listed reporting time), they will assume the editor is not currently interested in their topic and will submit the query elsewhere. It's a good idea to do this only if your topic is a timely one that will suffer if not considered quickly.

A brief single-spaced cover letter enclosed with your manuscript is helpful in personalizing a submission. If you have previously queried the editor on the article or book, the cover letter should be a brief reminder, not a sales pitch. "Here is the piece on goat herding, which we discussed previously. I look forward to hearing from you at your earliest convenience."

If you are submitting to a market that considers unsolicited complete manuscripts, your cover letter should tell the editor something about your manuscript and about you—your publishing history and any particular qualifications you have for writing the enclosed manuscript.

Once your manuscript has been accepted, you may offer to get involved in the editing process, but policy on this will vary from magazine to magazine. Most magazine editors don't send galleys to authors before publication, but if they do, you should review the galleys and return them as soon as possible. Book publishers will normally involve you in rewrites whether you like it or not.

The Query Letter Clinic on page 19 presents several specific real-life query letters, some that worked (and some that didn't), along with editors' comments on why the letter was successful or where the letter failed to garner an assignment.

For more information about writing query letters, read *How to Write Irresistible Query Letters*, by Lisa Collier Cool, or *How To Write Attention-Grabbing Query & Cover Letters*, by John Wood (both Writer's Digest Books).

Querying for fiction

Fiction is sometimes queried, but most fiction editors don't like to make a final decision until they see the complete manuscript. Most editors will want to see a synopsis and sample chapters for a book, or a complete short story manuscript. Consult individual listings for specific fiction guidelines. If a fiction editor does request a query, briefly describe the main theme and story line, including the conflict and resolution. For more information on what goes into a novel synopsis, see *The Marshall Plan for Novel Writing*, or *Your Novel Proposal: From Creation to Contract*, by Blythe Camenson and Marshall J. Cook (both by Writer's Digest Books).

BOOK PROPOSALS

Most nonfiction books are sold by book proposal, a package of materials that details what your book is about, who its intended audience is, and how you intend to write it. Most fiction is sold either by complete manuscript, especially for first-time authors, or by two or three sample chapters. Take a look at individual listings to see what submission method editors prefer.

The nonfiction book proposal includes some combination of a cover or query letter, an overview, an outline, author's information sheet and sample chapters. Editors also want to see information about the audience for your book and about titles that compete with your proposed book.

If a listing does not specify, send as much of the following information as you can.
- The cover or query letter should be a short introduction to the material you include in the proposal.
- An overview is a brief summary of your book. For nonfiction, it should detail your book's subject and give an idea of how that subject will be developed. If you're sending a synopsis of a novel, cover the basic plot.
- An outline covers your book chapter by chapter. The outline should include all major points covered in each chapter. Some outlines are done in traditional outline form, but most are written in paragraph form.
- An author's information sheet should—as succinctly and clearly as possible—acquaint the editor with your writing background and convince her of your qualifications to write about the subject.
- Many editors like to see sample chapters, especially for a first book. In fiction it's essential.

COVER LETTER

COVER PAGE

OVERVIEW

MARKETING INFORMATION

COMPETITION

AUTHOR INFORMATION

CHAPTER OUTLINE

SAMPLE CHAPTERS

ATTACHMENTS

A nonfiction book proposal will usually consist of the elements illustrated above. Their order is less important than the fact that you have addressed each component.

In nonfiction, sample chapters show the editor how well you write and develop the ideas from your outline.

- Marketing information—i.e., facts about how and to whom your book can be successfully marketed—is now expected to accompany every book proposal. If you can provide information about the audience for your book and suggest ways the book publisher can reach those people, you will increase your chances of acceptance.
- Competitive title analysis is an integral part of the marketing information. Check the *Subject Guide* to *Books in Print* for other titles on your topic. Write a one- or two-sentence synopsis of each. Point out how your book differs and improves upon existing titles.

For more detailed information on what your book proposal should contain, see *How to Write a Book Proposal*, by Michael Larsen (Writer's Digest Books).

A WORD ABOUT AGENTS

Recognizing the importance of literary agents in publishing today, we've included a section of 75 agents, 50 handling books and 25 handling scripts, beginning on page 89. We've selected agents who describe themselves as open to both previously published and newer writers and who do not charge a fee to look at work. The literary agents belong to the Association of Authors' Representatives (AAR), a voluntary professional organization. We've also included a few who are not members of AAR but have come to agenting after a notable career in editing and publishing. The script agents are all signatory agencies of The Writers Guild of America.

An agent represents a writer's work to buyers, negotiates contracts, follows up to see that contracts are fulfilled and generally handles a writer's business affairs, leaving the writer free to write. Effective agents are valued for their contacts in the publishing industry, their savvy about which publishers and editors to approach with which ideas, their ability to guide an author's career, and their business sense.

While most book publishers listed in *Writer's Market* publish books by unagented writers, some of the larger ones are reluctant to consider submissions that have not reached them through a literary agent. Companies with such a policy are noted by a symbol (🅰) at the beginning of the listing, as well as in the submission information within the listing.

For more information about finding and working with a literary agent, as well as over 500 listings of literary and script agents, see *Guide to Literary Agents* (Writer's Digest Books). The *Guide* offers listings similar to those presented here, as well as a wealth of informational articles on the author-agent relationship and publishing processes.

PROFESSIONALISM AND COURTESY

Publishers are as crunched for time as any other business professional. Between struggling to meet deadlines without exceeding budgets and dealing with incoming submissions, most editors find that time is their most precious commodity. This state of affairs means an editor's communications with new writers, while necessarily a part of his job, have to be handled efficiently and with a certain amount of bluntness.

But writers work hard, too. Shouldn't editors treat them nicely? Shouldn't an editor take the time to point out the *good* things about the manuscript he is rejecting? Is that too much to ask? Well, in a way, yes. It *is* too much to ask. Editors are not writing coaches; much less are they counselors or therapists. Editors are in the business of buying workable writing from people who produce it. This, of course, does not excuse editors from observing the conventions of common business courtesy. Good editors know how to be polite (or they hire an assistant who can be polite for them).

The best way for busy writers to get along with (and flourish among) busy editors is to develop professional business habits. Correspondence and phone calls should be kept short and to the point. Don't hound editors with unwanted calls or letters. Honor all agreements, and give every assignment your best effort. Pleasantness, good humor, honesty and reliability will serve you as well in publishing as they will in any other area of life.

You will occasionally run up against editors and publishers who don't share your standard of business etiquette. It is easy enough to withdraw your submissions from such people and avoid them in the future.

WRITING TOOLS

Typewriters and computers. For many years, *the* tool of the writer's trade was the typewriter. While many writers continue to produce perfectly acceptable material on their manual or electric typewriters, more and more writers have discovered the benefits of writing on a computer. Editors, too, have benefited from the change; documents produced on a computer are less likely to present to the editor such distractions as typos, eraser marks or globs of white correction fluid. That's because writing composed on a computer can be corrected before it is printed out.

If you think computers are not for you, you should reconsider. A desktop computer, running a good word processing program, can be the greatest boon to your writing career since the dictionary. For ease of manipulating text, formatting pages and correcting spelling errors, the computer handily outperforms the typewriter. Many word processing programs will count words for you, offer synonyms from a thesaurus, construct an index and give you a choice of typefaces to print out your material. Some will even correct your grammar (if you want them to). When you consider that the personal computer is also a great way of tracking your submissions and staying on top of all the other business details of a writing career—and a handy way to do research if you have a modem—it's hard to imagine how we ever got along without them.

Many people considering working with a computer for the first time are under the mistaken impression that they face an insurmountable learning curve. That's no longer true. While learning computer skills once may have been a daunting undertaking, today's personal computers are much more user-friendly than they once were. And as prices continue to fall, good systems can be had for under $1,000.

Whether you're writing on a computer or typewriter, your goal should be to produce pages of clean, error-free copy. Stick to standard typefaces, avoiding such unusual styles as script or italic. Your work should reflect a professional approach and consideration for your reader. If you are printing from a computer, avoid sending material printed from a low-quality dot-matrix printer, with hard-to-read, poorly shaped characters. Many editors are unwilling to read these manuscripts. New laser and ink jet printers, however, produce high-quality pages that *are* acceptable to editors. Readability is the key.

Electronic submissions. Many publishers are accepting or even requesting that final manuscript submissions be made on computer disk. This saves the magazine or book publisher the expense of having your manuscript typeset, and can be helpful in the editing stage. The publisher will simply download your finished manuscript into the computer system they use to produce their product. Be sure to mention if you are able to submit the final manuscript on disk. The editors will let you know what computer format they use and how they would like to receive your material.

Some publishers who accept submissions on disk also will accept electronic submissions by e-mail. It is an extremely fast way to get your manuscript to the publisher. However, you must work out submission information with the editor *before* you send something via e-mail. Causing the editor's system to crash, or unwittingly infecting his system with a virus, does not make for a happy business relationship.

Fax machines and e-mail. Fax machines transmit copy across phone lines. E-mail addresses are for receiving and sending electronic mail over a computer network, most commonly the Internet. Those publishers who wanted to list their fax machine numbers and e-mail addresses have done so.

Between businesses, the fax has come into standard daily use for materials that have to be sent quickly. Fax machines are in airports, hotels, libraries and even grocery stores. Many libraries, schools, copy shops and even "cyber cafés" offer computer time for free or for a low hourly rate. However, do not fax or e-mail queries, proposals or entire manscripts to editors unless they indicate they are willing to receive them. A proposal on shiny fax paper curling into itself on the editor's desk makes an impression—but not the one you want. If your proposal is being considered, it will probably be routed to a number of people for their reactions. Fax paper won't stand up well to that amount of handling. Writers should continue to use traditional means for sending manuscripts and queries and use the fax number or e-mail address we list only when an editor asks to receive correspondence by this method.

Letters and manuscripts sent to an editor for consideration should be neat, clean and legible. That means typed (or computer-printed), double spaced, on $8\frac{1}{2} \times 11$ inch paper. Handwritten materials will most often not be considered at all. The typing paper should be at least 16 lb. bond (20 lb. is preferred).

The first impression an editor has of your work is its appearance on the page. Why take the chance of blowing that impression with a manuscript or letter that's not as appealing as it could be?

You don't need fancy letterhead for your correspondence with editors. Plain bond paper is fine. Just type your name, address, phone number and the date at the top of the page—centered or in the right-hand corner. If you want letterhead, make it as simple and businesslike as possible. Keep the cute clip art for the family newsletter. Many quick print shops have standard typefaces and can supply letterhead stationery at a relatively low cost. Never use letterhead for typing your manuscripts. Only the first page of queries, cover letters and other correspondence should be typed on letterhead.

MANUSCRIPT FORMAT

When submitting a manuscript for possible publication, you can increase its chances of making a favorable impression by adhering to some fairly standard matters of physical format. Many professional writers use the format described here. Of course, there are no "rules" about what a manuscript must look like. These are just guidelines—some based on common sense, others more a matter of convention—that are meant to help writers display their work to best advantage. Strive for easy readability in whatever method you choose and adapt your style to your own personal tastes and those of the editors to whom you submit.

Most manuscripts do not use a cover sheet or title page. Use a paper clip to hold pages together, not staples. This allows editors to separate the pages easily for editing. Scripts should be submitted with plain cardstock covers front and back, held together by Chicago or Revere screws.

The upper corners of the first page of an article manuscript contain important information about you and your manuscript. This information should be single-spaced. In the upper *left* corner list your name, address and phone number. If you are using a pseudonym for your byline, your legal name still should appear in this space. In the upper *right* corner, indicate the approximate word count of the manuscript, the rights you are offering for sale and your copyright notice (© 2002 Ralph Anderson). A handwritten copyright symbol is acceptable. (For more information about rights and copyright, see Minding the Details on page 57.) For a book manuscript include the same information with the exception of rights. Do not number the first page of your manuscript.

Center the title in capital letters one-third of the way down the page. Set the spacing to double-space. Type "by" and your name or pseudonym centered one double-space beneath that.

After the title and byline, drop down two double-spaces, paragraph indent, and begin the body of your manuscript. Always double-space your manuscript and use standard paragraph indentations of five spaces. Margins should be about $1\frac{1}{4}$ inches on all sides of each full page of the manuscript.

On every page after the first, type your last name, a dash and the page number in either the upper left or right corner. The title of your manuscript may, but need not, be typed on this line or beneath it. Page number two would read: Anderson—2. Follow this format throughout.

If you are submitting novel chapters, leave the top one-third of the first page of each chapter blank before typing the chapter title. Subsequent pages should include the author's last name, the page number, and a shortened form of the book's title: Anderson—2—Skating. (In a variation on this, some authors place the title before the name on the left side and put the page number on the right-hand margin.)

When submitting poetry, the poems should be typed single-spaced (double-space between stanzas), one poem per page. For a long poem requiring more than one page, paper clip the pages together. You may want to write "continued" at the bottom of the page, so if the pages are separated, editors, typesetters and proofreaders won't assume your poem ends at the bottom of the first page.

For more information on manuscript formats, see *Formatting & Submitting Your Manuscript*, by Jack and Glenda Neff and Don Prues (Writer's Digest Books).

ESTIMATING WORD COUNT

Many computers will provide you with a word count of your manuscript. Your editor will count again after editing the manuscript. Although your computer is counting characters, an editor or production editor is more concerned with the amount of space the text will occupy on a page. Several small headlines, or subheads, for instance, will be counted the same by your computer as any other word of text. An editor may count them differently to be sure enough space has been estimated for larger type.

For short manuscripts, it's often quickest to count each word on a representative page and multiply by the number of pages. You can get a very rough count by multiplying the number of pages in your manuscript by 250 (the average number of words on a double-spaced typewritten page). Do not count words for a poetry manuscript or put the word count at the top of the manuscript.

To get a more precise count, add the number of characters and spaces in an average line and divide by six for the average words per line. Then count the number of lines of type on a representative page. Multiply the words per line by the lines per page to find the average number of words per page. Then count the number of manuscript pages (fractions should be counted as fractions, except in book manuscript chapter headings, which are counted as a full page). Multiply the number of pages by the number of words per page you already determined. This will give you the approximate number of words in the manuscript.

PHOTOGRAPHS AND SLIDES

The availability of good quality photos can be a deciding factor when an editor is considering a manuscript. Many publications also offer additional pay for photos accepted with a manuscript. Check the magazine's listing when submitting black & white prints for the size an editor prefers to review. The universally accepted format for transparencies is 35mm; few buyers will look at color prints. Don't send any transparencies or prints with a query; wait until an editor indicates interest in seeing your photos.

On all your photos and slides, you should stamp or print your copyright notice and "Return to:" followed by your name, address and phone number. Rubber stamps are preferred for labeling photos since they are less likely to cause damage. You can order them from many stationery or office supply stores. If you use a pen to write this information on the back of your photos, be careful not to damage the print by pressing too hard or by allowing ink to bleed through the paper. A felt tip pen is best, but you should take care not to put photos or copy together before the ink dries.

Captions can be typed on adhesive labels and affixed to the back of the prints. Some writers, when submitting several transparencies or photos, number the photos and type captions (numbered accordingly) on a separate $8\frac{1}{2} \times 11$ sheet of paper.

Submit prints rather than negatives or consider having duplicates made of your slides or transparencies. Don't risk having your original negative or slide lost or damaged when you submit it.

PHOTOCOPIES

Make copies of your manuscripts and correspondence before putting them in the mail. Don't learn the hard way, as many writers have, that manuscripts get lost in the mail and that publishers sometimes go out of business without returning submissions. You might want to make several good quality copies of your manuscript while it is still clean and submit them while keeping the original manuscript as a file copy.

Some writers include a self-addressed postcard with a photocopied submission and suggest in the cover letter that if the editor is not interested in the manuscript, it may be tossed out and a reply returned on the postcard. This practice is recommended when dealing with international markets. If you find that your personal computer generates copies more cheaply than you can pay to have them returned, you might choose to send disposable manuscripts. Submitting a disposable manuscript costs the writer some photocopy or computer printer expense, but it can save on large postage bills.

MAILING SUBMISSIONS

No matter what size manuscript you're mailing, always include a self-addressed, stamped envelope (SASE) with sufficient return postage that is large enough to contain your manuscript if it is returned. The website for the U.S. Postal Service, www.usps.gov, and the website for the Canadian Postal Service, www.canadapost.ca, both have handy postage calculators if you are unsure of how much you'll need.

A manuscript of fewer than six pages may be folded in thirds and mailed as if it were a letter using a #10 (business-size) envelope. The enclosed SASE can be a #10 folded in thirds or a #9 envelope which will slip into the mailing envelope without being folded. Some editors also appreciate the convenience of having a manuscript folded into halves in a 6×9 envelope. For manuscripts of six pages or longer, use 9×12 envelopes for both mailing and return. The return SASE may be folded in half.

A book manuscript should be mailed in a sturdy, well-wrapped box. Enclose a self-addressed mailing label and paper clip your return postage to the label. Unfortunately, new mailing restrictions make it more difficult to mail packages of 12 ounces and over, causing some publishers to discontinue returning submissions of this size.

Always mail photos and slides First Class. The rougher handling received by standard mail could damage them. If you are concerned about losing prints or slides, send them certified or registered mail. For any photo submission that is mailed separately from a manuscript, enclose a short cover letter of explanation, separate self-addressed label, adequate return postage and an envelope. Never submit photos or slides mounted in glass.

To mail up to 20 prints, you can buy photo mailers that are stamped "Photos—Do Not Bend" and contain two cardboard inserts to sandwich your prints. Or use a 9×12 manila envelope, write "Photos—Do Not Bend" and make your own cardboard inserts. Some photography supply shops also carry heavy cardboard envelopes that are reusable.

When mailing a number of prints, say 25-50 for a book with illustrations, pack them in a sturdy cardboard box. A box for typing paper or photo paper is an adequate mailer. If, after packing both manuscript and photos, there's empty space in the box, slip in enough cardboard inserts to fill the box. Wrap the box securely.

To mail transparencies, first slip them into protective vinyl sleeves, then mail as you would prints. If you're mailing a number of sheets, use a cardboard box as for photos.

Types of mail service

- **First Class** is an expensive way to mail a manuscript, but many writers prefer it. First Class mail generally receives better handling and is delivered more quickly. Mail sent First Class is also forwarded for one year if the addressee has moved, and is returned automatically if it is undeliverable.
- **Priority mail** reaches its destination within two to three days. To mail a package of up to 2 pounds costs $3.95, less than either United Parcel Service or Federal Express. First Class mail over 11 ounces is classified Priority. Confirmation of delivery is an additional 35¢.
- **Standard mail** rates are available for packages, but be sure to pack your materials carefully because they will be handled roughly. To make sure your package will be returned to you if it is undeliverable, print "Return Postage Guaranteed" under your address.

- **Certified Mail** must be signed for when it reaches its destination. If requested, a signed receipt is returned to the sender. There is a $2.10 charge for this service, in addition to the required postage, and a $1.50 charge for a return receipt.
- **Registered Mail** is a high-security method of mailing where the contents are insured. The package is signed in and out of every office it passes through, and a receipt is returned to the sender when the package reaches its destination. The cost depends on the weight, destination and whether you obtain insurance.
- If you're in a hurry to get your material to your editor, you have a lot of choices. In addition to fax and computer technologies mentioned earlier, overnight and two-day mail services are provided by both the U.S. Postal Service and several private firms. More information on next day service is available from the U.S. Post Office or check your Yellow Pages under "Delivery Services."

Other correspondence details

Use money orders if you are ordering sample copies or supplies and do not have checking services. You'll have a receipt, and money orders are traceable. Money orders for up to $700 can be purchased from the U.S. Postal Service for a 90¢ service charge. Banks, savings and loans, and some commercial businesses also carry money orders; their fees vary. *Never* send cash through the mail for sample copies.

Insurance is available for items handled by the U.S. Postal Service but is payable only on typing fees or the tangible value of the item in the package—such as typing paper—so your best insurance when mailing manuscripts is to keep a copy of what you send. Insurance is $1.10 for $50 or less and goes up to a $50 plus postage maximum charge for $5,000.

When corresponding with publishers in other countries, International Reply Coupons (IRCs) must be used for return postage. Surface rates in other countries differ from those in the U.S., and U.S. postage stamps are of use only within the U.S.

U.S. stamps can be purchased online with a credit card at www.usps.gov or by calling 1-800-STAMP24. Non-U.S. residents can call (816)545-1000 or (816)545-1011 to order stamps. Canadian postage can be purchased online at www.canadapost.ca.

Because some post offices don't carry IRCs (or because of the added expense), many writers dealing with international mail send photocopies and tell the publisher to dispose of them if the manuscript is not appropriate. When you use this method, it's best to set a deadline for withdrawing your manuscript from consideration, so you can market it elsewhere.

International money orders are also available from the post office for a charge of $3 or $7.50, depending on the destination.

RECORDING SUBMISSIONS

Once you begin submitting manuscripts, you'll need to manage your writing business by keeping copies of all manuscripts and correspondence, and by recording the dates of submissions.

One way to keep track of your manuscripts is to use a record of submissions that includes the date sent, title, market, editor and enclosures (such as photos). You should also note the date of the editor's response, any rewrites that were done, and, if the manuscript was accepted, the deadline, publication date and payment information. You might want to keep a similar record just for queries.

Also remember to keep a separate file for each manuscript or idea along with its list of potential markets. You may want to keep track of expected reporting times on a calendar, too. Then you'll know if a market has been slow to respond and you can follow up on your query or submission. It will also provide you with a detailed picture of your sales over time.

Where to Get Great Article Ideas

BY GREG DAUGHERTY

More than paper, more than ink, more even than those annoying subscription cards that tumble out at every opportunity, magazines are made of ideas.

Behind every magazine is an idea. Behind every article within the magazine is an idea. Behind every sentence within an article is—or darn well ought to be—an idea.

And where do all those ideas come from? Many come from writers.

Thinking up salable article ideas is a skill that some lucky writers may be born with but that most, I believe, develop over time. When you are first starting out as a writer, you may worry that you'll run out of ideas any day now. By the time you've been at it for a few years, you'll be producing more ideas than you'll ever be able to use.

SIX WAYS TO GENERATE MORE IDEAS

1. Take a lot of showers. Ask any twenty successful freelance writers where they get their best ideas, and I'll bet nineteen of them will say, "in the shower." There's even some science to back them up—something about negative ions, as I recall. But who cares, as long as it works? Keep your brain focused on story ideas rather than letting it wander all over the place. Otherwise you may waste whole showers making grocery lists or thinking up new ways to clean the shower curtain.

2. Put your subconscious to work. Remember that one writer in twenty who doesn't get ideas in the shower? Odds are he or she would tell you that the best ideas seem to bubble up out of nowhere. That, some say, is the subconscious mind at work. You don't have to sit back and wait for your subconscious to start bubbling, either. You can give it an assignment. That, anyhow, was the claim of Napoleon Hill, one of the founders of *Success* magazine. Once, when Hill was trying to come up with a title for a new book, he had a little talk with his subconscious before he went to bed. "I've got to have a million-dollar title, and I've got to have it tonight," he said." (And he said it out loud, yet.) "Do you understand that?"

Apparently his subconscious got the message, because at 2 a.m., Hill woke up, bounded to his typewriter and banged out the title. Hill's book, *Think and Grow Rich*, went on to sell more than twenty million copies and remains in print to this day.

When I've tried Hill's technique the results have been mixed. Some mornings I'll wake up with an idea I've asked for. Other days I'll wake up with a good idea but on an entirely different subject. The rest of the time I just wake up.

Since your subconscious mind has a mind of its own and can spit out ideas any hour of the day or night, keep pen and paper in your pocket, in your car, on your night stand and any other place a brainstorm is likely to strike.

3. Read everything you can get your hands or eyes on. The best writers I know not only try to keep up with the fields they cover but read just about anything in sight. Few of the things

---

GREG DAUGHERTY *has been a successful freelance writer and magazine editor for more than 20 years. His writing has appeared in many magazines, from trade journals to general interest publications, and he has held senior editorial positions for* Reader's Digest, Money, Consumer Reports, *and* Success *magazines. Currently Daugherty is editor-in-chief of* New Choices *and a correspondent for* Writer's Digest.

you read will pay off in an immediate story, but they all help feed that mysterious idea machine in your head.

Books. Poke around the library. Let your self get lost in unfamiliar aisles. Check out the new releases at your local bookstore. Many of the freshest ideas these days appear first as book titles, then make their way into magazines.

Magazines. Read the ones you want to write for, of course, but look at others, too. You'll learn some new things and maybe discover new ways to tell a story. And you may even surprise yourself and stumble on a promising market or two.

Old magazines are another good source of idea fodder. Check out some of the great magazines someday when you're in the library and have nothing else to do: *Holiday*, *Look*, *Saturday Review*, to name a few. Beware, though: You can waste a lot of time in the old magazine stacks, reliving other writers' past glories when you could be at the keyboard creating your own.

Newspapers. Your local paper can be a terrific source of article ideas, especially if it's not a paper that magazine editors regularly follow like *The New York Times*. You may see a story in your local paper that's ripe for telling practically as is in a national magazine. More often, though, you'll find hints of a possible national story. It may be a local trend that's yet to be widely written about or a local person whose tale could be one of several in an article reported from a national perspective. So keep your scissors handy. When you travel, scoop up the local papers there, too.

Online. The Internet may be both the biggest time-saver and the biggest time-waster ever invented. I've found it an incredibly useful research tool but seldom discover any worthwhile article ideas, no matter how many hours I spend browsing. One possible exception: Websites sponsored by local newspapers; they're rarely as rich in detail as the papers themselves, but they offer a window on the goings-on in different parts of the country. And also unlike the papers themselves, they're mostly free (at least as of this writing).

4. Listen up. I find some of the best story ideas come from listening to my friends, neighbors and co-workers talk about their concerns of the moment. Magazines pay a lot of money to convene so-called "focus groups" of everyday people who sit around for an hour talking about their likes, dislikes and whatever else they're asked to discuss. You can accomplish much the same thing for free by paying attention when someone starts griping about X, singing the praises of Y or asking why no magazine has ever told the truth about Z.

For example, I once heard one of my neighbors asking another about the best way to send money to a family member traveling overseas. Until that moment, I'd never given the matter much through. But I checked it out, and a few months later not only did I know the answer but several million magazine readers did as well.

5. Tap into your own experience. Forget for a moment that you're a writer. What's on your mind, just as a human being? If you've wondered about something, chances are other people have, too. The difference is you're a writer and can go out, investigate the matter and maybe even get paid for coming back with the answer. The beauty of your own personal experience is that it's forever changing. Have a baby, and you'll find yourself jotting down child-related story ideas. Switch jobs, change homes, get a divorce, get a disease, win a trip for two to exotic Bora Bora—all of life's amazing twists and turns can supply you with fresh ideas.

My friend Steve Fishman turned a brain hemorrhage into an award-winning magazine article, then into a widely acclaimed book called *A Bomb in the Brain*. I know at least three writers who have gotten stories out of the aggravation they went through after their wallets were stolen.

I'm not saying to lose your wallet or to lust after any other sort of misfortune. But do remember that the events of your life—the good ones and the bad ones—are all part of your material as a writer.

6. Get to know some PR people. Public relations men and women often have great ideas for stories before anybody else does. Many of them are former magazine or newspaper writers themselves. The trouble, of course, is that it's their job to put a spin on the idea that benefits their clients. The other trouble is that they're out to get their clients as much positive publicity as possible, so if you got their story tip, a few dozen other writers probably did, too. That said, I've found PR people worth paying attention to over the years. If nothing else, they can sometimes get you access to key experts and provide background information that you'd otherwise spend a lot of time digging up on your own. Just remember that their agendas and yours aren't identical.

WILL EDITORS SWIPE YOUR IDEAS?

Beginning writers often ask if magazines will steal their ideas. The best answer I can think of: Maybe, but it's not worth worrying about.

In more than 20 years as an editor, I have never stolen an idea from a writer—and I don't think I'm necessarily a shoo-in for sainthood. And in my 20 years as a writer, no magazine has ever stolen an idea of mine (as far as I know, anyhow).

Yes, I've heard a few horror stories along the way, but I don't think idea theft is a crime to lose a whole lot of sleep over. For one thing, a good writer is always generating ideas—far more than he or she can begin to use. For another, if a magazine wants to steal your idea, there is not much you can do about it.

I've seen writers try, though. Some are deliberately vague in their queries, hoping to tease the editor into giving them the assignment simply on faith. Others practically make editors sign formal nondisclosure agreements. All a writer really accomplishes by such amateurish legal tactics is to insult the editor's integrity—a dumb marketing move if there ever was one.

Occasionally you'll see an idea you pitched to a magazine (and the magazine threw back) appear in that very magazine a month, a year or a decade later. Did somebody swipe your idea? Possibly, but more likely the idea came from another writer with a somewhat different approach. Few ideas are so unusual that only one writer will think of them. So chalk it up to coincidence or to just being ahead of your time. (And maybe avoid that magazine in the future.) Then move on. You'll probably have better ideas tomorrow anyway.

WHAT TO DO WITH AN IDEA ONCE YOU HAVE ONE

Ideas are the writer's raw material. And like any other raw material, they're far more valuable once they've been refined.

The most common problem that beginning writers seem to have is grasping the difference between a story idea and what's simply an interesting subject. Here's an illustration: Undersea exploration is an interesting subject, but it's way too broad for a magazine article.

You might, however, be able to see a piece on how undersea exploration is raising some tough new ethical questions. For example, is the wreck of the *Titanic* fair game for souvenir hunters or a sacred resting-place for its victims?

One useful test is to try to write a headline for your proposed article. If it sounds like a book title or a fourteen-part PBS series, you need to bring your idea into sharper focus. But if it sounds like a headline you might see in a magazine—particularly in the magazine you want to propose it to—you're probably on track.

HOW EDITORS LOOK AT IDEAS

You can boost your ideas' odds of success if you learn to step back and look at them the way an editor does. Not all editors think alike, of course, but if you could cut an editor's head open (and wouldn't we all like to sometimes?), you'd probably see a thought process that works something like this:

1. "Does this idea belong in this magazine?" Sometimes the answer is pretty obvious: A magazine about dogs probably won't be interested in a story about cats. Other times, it's far more subtle: A dog magazine that last year ran a story called "Rottweilers: Those Gentle Giants" is an unlikely market for your proposed piece on "Rottweilers: Four-Legged Psychopaths from Hell."

What can you do? Look up what the magazine has run in the past year or two in the *Readers' Guide to Periodical Literature* or on a computerized magazine database at your library. Not all magazines are indexed in this way, but some surprisingly obscure ones are. If you can't find out whether your idea conflicts with one the magazine has already done, just give it a shot. There's no shame in approaching a magazine with an idea that's just slightly off the mark.

2. "Have we done this story before?" And if so, how recently? Some magazines will return to the same topic month after month, as long as they can put at least the illusion of a fresh spin on it. Some women's magazines, for example, run a diet story in every issue, for the simple reason that such stories, however unbelievable, sell copies. Other magazines won't touch a topic that they've covered in the past five or ten years.

3. "Have our competitors already done the story?" Even if the magazine itself hasn't touched the topic, an editor may consider the idea old stuff if one or more of the magazine's competitors has. Magazines differ considerably in what they consider their competition. Some will look only to their specific category (boating magazines, decorating magazines, teen magazines and so forth), while others will consider newspapers, television and every other type of media. Generally speaking, you stand the best chance with ideas that have received no coverage or only very local coverage.

4. "Is this the best way to approach this story?" Sometimes a fresh approach can inject life into a tired topic. For example, "Six Ways to Childproof Your Home" would be a familiar approach to most editors of parenting magazines. But something like "How Professional Childproofers Rip You Off" or "Childproof Accessories That Could Injury Your Child" might get their attention.

5. "Is this the best writer for the job?" As I said earlier, magazines will seldom steal your ideas. But in some cases they may turn a perfectly fine idea down if you don't seem like the right writer. In rare instances, they may offer to buy the idea from you and assign it to another writer.

What may make you inappropriate? Distance is one thing. If you come across a great story in Australia, but you happen to live in Albuquerque, the magazine may not have the budget to send you there. Or, if you are obviously a beginning writer, the magazine may hesitate to assign you what's sure to be a complex, ambitious story.

A magazine is most likely to take a chance on you if an editor there has worked with you elsewhere or knows your work from other publications. A powerful query and strong clips can also make a difference.

6. "Even if this idea isn't right, is the writer someone worth encouraging?" Some editors are too busy or too self-important to send personal notes to writers whose ideas may have just missed the mark. So don't automatically assume the worst if you receive a terse form letter in reply. Other editors will suggest a way an idea might be reshaped or urge you to try again with another one. If your query is impressive enough, an editor may come back at you with a story idea of his or her own.

Query Letter Clinic

BY DON PRUES AND CINDY LAUFENBERG

The most indispensable companion to an unsold piece of writing is its query letter. Whether you're trying to sell a 100-word sidebar, a 4,000-word feature article, a 60,000-word nonfiction book or a 100,000-word novel, you need a darn good query letter to go with it. Period.

The *Writer's Encyclopedia* defines a query letter as "a sales letter to an editor that is designed to interest him in an article or book idea." With so many submissions to evaluate, editors tend to make fast judgments. So you must pitch a tight and concise query that explains the gist of your piece, why readers will want to read it, and why you're the perfect person to write it.

PRE-QUERY PROVISIONS

Identifying what to omit and what to include in your query can mean the difference between earning a sale or receiving a rejection, so take precautions before submitting.

Trust the editor and suppress your paranoia. Some writers exclude important information from a query fearing the editor will "steal" their idea. Bad move. Editors aren't thieves, and leaving important information out of your query will only increase your chances of keeping yourself out of print. As will mentioning fees in your query; it will send your query straight to the can. If you're an unpublished writer, don't mention that either. Finally, never include a separate cover letter with your query letter. The query is your cover letter, your letter of inquiry, and your letter of intent—all packed into one tightly-wrapped, single-spaced page.

While some rules are meant to be broken, the rule of keeping a query to one page remains intact. If you can't explain your idea in less than a page, you're probably not too clear about the idea itself.

Just because a query is simply one page don't assume it is simple to compose. A saleable query demands you include all the right information in a small space. Addressing your query to the appropriate editor is most important. Ensure this by calling the editorial office and asking who handles the type of material you're submitting. If you want to write a travel piece for a magazine, call and ask for the name and title of the travel editor. That's it. Don't ask to speak with the travel editor; merely get the correct spelling of his name. Always type or word process your query and put it on simple letterhead—editors want good ideas, not fancy fonts and cute clip art. Make your salutation formal; no "Dear Jim" or "Hello" (just today I saw two queries with these exact salutations!). And always offer an estimated word count and delivery date.

COMPOSING THE QUERY

You're ready to write your letter. Introduce your idea in a sentence or two that will make the editor curious, such as an interesting fact, an intriguing question, or maybe something humorous. Then state your idea in one crisp sentence to grab the editor's attention. But don't stop there. Reel in the editor with one or two paragraphs expounding upon your idea. Walk through the

DON PRUES *is the co-author of* Formatting & Submitting Your Manuscript *(Writer's Digest Books).*

CINDY LAUFENBERG *is a freelance writer and former Managing Editor of Writer's Digest Books. She lives in Princeton, New Jersey.*

Query Letter Checklist

Before sending queries, ask yourself:

- Have I addressed the query to the right person at the magazine, and have I double-checked spellings, particularly of all proper nouns?
- Is my query neatly typed and free of errors?
- Is my idea to the point?
- Have I outlined the story or given at least a good idea of the direction the story will take?
- Have I included sources I have interviewed or plan to interview?
- Do I know which department or section my piece best fits and have I told the editor?
- Have I included clips that show my talent?
- Have I noted why I'm the right writer for this story?
- Have I included a self-addressed, stamped envelope (SASE) for reply?
- Does my letter note my address, telephone and fax numbers and e-mail address?
- Have I recorded the query's topic, the date and the target publication in a log?
  (If I don't hear back in six to twelve weeks, I can follow up with a letter reminding the editor about my query or a postcard withdrawing the idea.)

from *The Writer's Market Companion*, by Joe Feiertag and Mary Cupito (Writer's Digest Books)

steps of your project and explain why you're the perfect person to write what you're proposing. List your sources, particularly if you have interviews lined up with specialists on your topic, as this will help establish the credibility of your work.

The tone of your writing is also important. Create a catchy query laden with confidence but devoid of cockiness. Include personal information only if it will help sell your piece, such as previous writing experience with the topic and relevant sample clips. And never forget a SASE.

Most questions about queries revolve around whether to send simultaneous submissions. Sending simultaneous queries to multiple editors is typically okay if you inform all editors you're doing so. But some editors refuse to read simultaneous queries because they want an exclusive option to accept or reject your submission. This can be a problem if editors do not respond quickly; it keeps you from submitting to other markets. The two clear advantages to sending simultaneous queries are that you have many lines in the water at once and it prompts a rapid reply—an editor excited by your query will be more apt to get back to you knowing the competition could get to you first.

WHAT THE CLINIC SHOWS YOU

Unpublished writers wonder how published writers break into print. It's not just a matter of luck; published writers construct compelling queries. What follows are six actual queries submitted to editors (names and addresses have been altered). Three queries are strong; three are not. Detailed comments from the editors show what the writer did and did not do to secure a sale. As you'll see, there's no such thing as a boilerplate "good" query; every winning query works its own magic.

ALWAYS SUBMIT unsolicited manuscripts or queries with a self-addressed, stamped envelope (SASE) within your country or a self-addressed envelope with International Reply Coupons (IRC) purchased from the post office for other countries.

Fourteen Things Not to Do In Your Query Letter

1. Don't try any cute attention-getting devices, like marking the envelope "Personal." This also includes fancy stationery that lists every publication you've ever sold to, or "clever" slogans. As Jack Webb used to say on Dragnet, "Just the facts, ma'am."

2. Don't talk about fees. If the fee you mention is too high, it will turn the editor off. If it's too low, he'll think you don't value your work.

3. Keep your opinions to yourself. If you're proposing an article on some public figure, for instance, your personal views are not relevant. Bear in mind that you're offering your services as a reporter, not the author of an editorial or personal opinion column.

4. Don't tell the editors what others you've shown the idea to think of it. ("Several of my friends have read this and think it's marvelous . . ." is a certain sign of the amateur writer.) The same goes for comments from other editors. Sometimes you'll hear from an editor who wanted to buy your idea, but was over-ruled, and that editor might say nice things about it and might even offer the suggestion that "It might be just right for Magazine X." Don't pass that praise along. Let Magazine X decide for itself.

5. Don't name drop. Editors will not be impressed that you once babysat for the state governor or had dinner with Bill and Hillary. However, if you do know somebody who works for that magazine, or writes for it, or if you know an editor on another magazine who has bought your work and likes it, say so. Contacts are valuable; dropping names to show what a big deal you are isn't.

6. Don't try to soft soap the editor by telling him or her how great the magazine is, but definitely make it clear that you read it. You could say that you particularly enjoyed a certain article, to show that you're paying attention, but too much praise sounds phony.

7. Don't send in any unnecessary enclosures, such as a picture of yourself (or your prize-winning Labrador Retriever). Just send in material that will sell the idea, which is usually nothing more than the query itself.

8. Don't offer irrelevant information about yourself. Simply tell the editor what there might be in your background that qualifies you to write this story.

9. Don't offer such comments as "I never read your magazine, but this seems to be a natural . . ." or "I know you don't usually publish articles about mountain-climbing, but . . ." Know the magazine, and send only those ideas that fit the format.

10. Don't ask for a meeting to discuss your idea further. If the editor feels this is necessary, he or she will suggest it.

11. Don't ask for advice, such as "If you don't think you can use this, could you suggest another magazine that could?" Or, "If you don't think this works as it is, do you have any suggestions for ways in which I could change it?" Editors are paid to evaluate ideas and to offer suggestions for revision; they'll do this without your prompting. What they won't do is offer extensive advice on pieces they don't want.

12. Don't offer to rewrite, as this implies you know it's not good enough as you have submitted it. Again, editors will ask for rewrites if necessary, and they usually are.

13. Don't make threats such as, "If I don't hear from you within four weeks I'll submit it elsewhere." If the editor is dubious about the idea anyway, that takes away any reason to make a decision.

14. Don't include a multiple-choice reply card, letting the editor check a box to indicate whether he likes it or not. I never got one of those that accompanied an idea I wanted to encourage.

*From *Magazine Writing That Sells*, by Don McKinney (Writer's Digest Books)

Obviously didn't familiarize herself with our publication. American Profile celebrates home-town American life and is a heartfelt reminder of what's good about who we are and the places many of us still call home. The magazine's philosophy and its range of stories easily can be found at our website at www.americanprofile.com.

Has no relevance to this query.

Would like to know what this book is about.

Clips should have been sent with the query, to show the writer's style. That's imperative when an editor is deciding whether to give a writer an assignment.

Again, there appears to be no familiarity with American Profile, because these subjects don't fit our publication.

I can appreciate her accomplishments, but the question still remains: Can she write?

Bad

American Profile
Publishing Group of America
701 Murfreesboro Road
Nashville, TN 37210

This letter was addressed in late January; our offices had moved in November, so the address was incorrect.

Ms. Davis,

Incorrect punctuation and missing word. Didn't proof her letter. Should be 12-year-old nephew.

I have manuscripts within your guidelines on the following subjects: The Reliable Coyote. A personal experience with a wild coyote that includes research and experiences of others. Photos are available. I Think I Can. A personal inward search involving the mentally and physically challenged 12 year old nephew of a friend. Don't Give Up. A motivational article for writers. I Don't Have Time to Cook! An early morning alternative to on-the-go, empty calorie breakfasts for busy working people. Includes annotated food facts and recipe. Other subjects include, excerpts from by book I'm Not too Old! chronicling my solo 1,800-mile walk, swim and running odyssey during the spring of 1998 to celebrate my 55th birthday and all topics listed below.

My personal objective is to write two pieces per day, 3 days a week.

I have an already established Northeast readership.

I have a book now being final edited that will be sold on CD with pictures, in paperback, in the future translated to German and available in Braille for the sight impaired.

I have written for The Bunnvale Beacon, The Warren Grove Times, Garden State, Flemington Register, Ocean Exposure, Roosevelt Register, Native New Jerseyan, Passaic County Times, In-Flight Magazine, Holiday Hotels of the Northeast (in-house publications) among others.

I have written on the following subjects:
Holistic health, walking, motorcycling, canoeing, triathalon, motorcycle racing, macrobiotic diets, yoga, psychology, TV, UFOs, comedy, travel, interviews, local profiles, swimming, hunting, gardening, adventure and personal opinion. Clips are available.

I have all my own electronics for e-mail, scanning and soon digital photos. I have worked with photographers and illustrators.

I can write from a personal information base on professional athletics, the sportswoman's point of view, professional motorcycle race driver, mother of the year, New Jersey, health over 50 (or 40), adventure, independent business-woman, human being, corporate vice president and CFO, wife, mother and poet.

Thank you for your time.

Sincerely,

Writers who familiarize themselves with American Profile and who send good, relevant ideas and good clips are the first to get assignments. This query letter had none of the above. Tossing out multiple story titles and a one-sentence explanation of each is not enough information for an editor. The old axiom, "Show, don't tell" also applies to query letters. Show me you're qualified to write for us, don't tell me.

Alice Amateur

Comments provided by Carol Davis, national editor of *American Profile*

Good

Dick Matthews
American Profile Magazine
341 Cool Springs Blvd., Suite 400
Franklin, TN 37067

Gives the title of the proposed story immediately. Good start.

Re: Mustard Seed Kitchen: Where Snacks and Service Come Together

Dear Mr. Matthews,

I live in Wellfleet on Cape Cod, an over-the-river-and-through-the-woods type of town. The biggest industry is tourism. After Labor Day, the town shrinks from 20,000 plus to 3,000. There's not much going on, especially for young people. Teenagers used to hang out in front of town hall, displaying skateboards, cigarettes and surly expressions. Parents worried that juvenile delinquency might become a problem. Where could the kids go to stay warm? What would help them take an active interest in life and in their community?

Two mothers of teenage boys came up with the answer. In 1998, Sharyn Lindsay and Ellen Webb started the Mustard Seed Kitchen. The women worked out of their homes until the First Congregational Church offered its basement. The whole town has embraced Mustard Seed. Even the Town Administrator likes to stop by for a brownie or a taste of Lindsay's famous grilled-cheese sandwiches.

Lindsay and Webb prepare food for anyone who calls with an emergency request for a meal, due to sickness, ill health or crisis in the family. The children pack and deliver these care packages. They spend the rest of the afternoon cooking snacks for immediate consumption or playing ping pong with friends in an adjoining room. The two women make the teenagers feel welcome while teaching them community service. This non-profit project is sponsored by the town's Friends of Our Recreation. Mustard Seed Kitchen: Where Snacks and Service Come Together. Interested?

I'm a freelance writer based on Cape Cod and a member of the National Writers Union. I heard on the hotline that you are looking for articles. I enclose clips, a resume, and a SASE, and look forward to hearing from you.

Sincerely,

Good, professional ending.

Everything is included, which allows an editor to immediately determine whether the writer is qualified.

Alexandra Goode

This writer did everything correctly. She familiarized herself with American Profile, queried a story that fits our editorial content, provided enough detail to pique our interest and show she was familiar with the subject, included clips, and kept the letter concise. As a result, she was assigned the story.

This information serves two purposes: it immediately shows that the writer is familiar with our market, and provides a quick overview of the town.

This setup outlines this town's particular challenge, followed by the solution—the good news—and that's what American Profile is all about. Shows familiarity with our content.

The writer shows immediately that this program is legitimate and successful by providing concrete examples of how the town has embraced it.

Provides specifics on what, exactly, the program offers these teenagers.

More good news.

She reiterates the title and asks if we're interested. Nice touch.

It's helpful to an editor, especially at a young publication, to know how a writer came to contact them.

Tells us a little about herself as a writer (We'll find out more from the clips).

Comments provided by Carol Davis, national editor of *American Profile*

Bad

June 5, 2001

Sam Notgood
634 Amateur Blvd.
Needswork, SC 29806

NEW MARKET PRESS
18 East 48th Street.
New York, NY 10017

Dear Ms. Altman,

I self published a book titled *A Yankee Doodle Son* and established an ISBN because I felt the story had possibilities. I've sold enough copies myself to know it is engrossing and marketable. Many of my readers declared: "I couldn't put your book down." "Your story would make a great movie or TV show with Brad Pitt playing the lead." "This book belongs in a college library." Because of this enthusiastic response I feel there is a wider market than I had anticipated. My expertise is medicine not marketing. I need a publisher to market this book properly.

The story begins when a starving Polish village sends my fifteen year old father to America in 1921. Father clears Ellis Island and is dying on the streets of Philadelphia from tuberculosis when he is rescued by the director of a street mission. Soon father is sent to Kansas to an unknown benefactor with a name and an address pinned to the front of his shirt.

Twelve years later my eighteen year old mother is sent by the same village to be father's bride. She is delayed in Italy for a year by greedy immigration officers and father rescues her via the International Red Cross.

Seven years later I am born in North Dakota but I have to rescue myself from my parents' "old country" culture to become a real American.

I am a medical doctor who has written extensively throughout my career. I originally wrote *A Yankee Doodle Son* for my siblings, children and grandchildren. But their friends who read the book were buying their own copies and telling me how they identified with my story and were deeply touched.

I would be happy to send a copy of the book for your perusal. Thank you for reading my letter and I hope to hear from you soon.

Sincerely yours,

Sam Notgood

Handwritten annotations:

Why has he established an ISBN? This seems unnecessary, and it fact it could prove to be a hindrance for a publisher, who will have to issue a new ISBN. It comes across as unprofessional.

How many copies?

These reader responses, while certainly glowing, aren't of use to an editor. What else are his family and friends going to say? I'd rather read it myself and make my own judgments.

This recap of the events is not bad, but it should be shorter—one paragraph.

I would have preferred to see a copy of the book with this submission, or at least some materials like a sample chapter, a table of contents, or a synopsis. Something to give me a sense of the writer's style, which is so important in memoir.

The name of my company is spelled wrong—an inauspicious start.

This editor is no longer at the company, and hasn't been for some time. It's not a big deal, but I always perk up when a writer addresses a letter directly to me.

Shouldn't his expertise be in writing?

Something's missing in this letter. There are so many memoirs out there these days—what books is this story like? In what ways is this tale different or unique? In addition to telling me the facts of the story, I want to know what this story is REALLY about—the larger issues of his memoir. If a book in this genre doesn't have these qualities, it would be impossible for us to publish it.

Comments provided by Michelle Howry, editor with Newmarket Press

Suzanne Goodquery
800 Professional Lane
Success, NY 12254

Good

April 26, 2001

Michelle Howry, Editor
Newmarket Press
Suite 1501, 18 East 48th Street
New York, NY 10017

— Spells my name, and the name of the company, correctly. It matters.

Dear Ms. Howry,

Re: Proposed Non-Fiction Book: I'm Not Crazy: Living with an Anxiety Disorder

More than 19 million Americans suffer from Anxiety Disorders (AD). These people experience recurrent, unwanted and intrusive episodes of intense fear that often lead to the panic attacks and the inability to complete normal, everyday tasks.

Good, solid facts, and a good general introduction to the topic.

I have been suffering from AD for thirteen years. In my non-fiction work, I'm Not Crazy: Living with an Anxiety Disorder, I detail, honestly and often amusingly, erratic behaviors that I have exhibited since childhood and my gradual understanding of the disease, refusal to share this secret with others, numerous attempts to cure myself and eventual pursuance of treatment. My book is unique as I describe the steps of treatment as I go through them, instead of from memory. I have attached the book's short Introduction.

Now we learn about her personal relation to the topic.

A writing sample— good. I can get a feeling for her writing style.

In my long quest for an understanding of AD, I have come across many books on the subject, mainly written with a medical or treatment slant and describing the behaviors of the most severely affected individuals, those who cannot function in daily life. I have found it difficult to find non-fiction books written by "secret" AD sufferers who managed to become highly functioning and educated members of society. My work will fill this niche.

Including a brief discussion of the competitive titles is good. She doesn't trash the competition, but simply tells me what her book offers that none of the others do. Of course, I'll do some research for myself on what other titles are out there, but this is helpful.

I believe that my book will be of interest to fellow AD sufferers, the millions of individuals who have personalities teetering on AD, medical researchers and general readers of non-fiction interested in a realistic portrayal of life with this disease. Further, I feel that there is a large international market for my book as AD knows no geographical bounds.

I am a practicing veterinarian and have written many research papers, medical memoranda and presentations. As a medical student, I was at the top of my class and my writing was published in the University of Wisconsin's medical journal. I will also have my work published in the upcoming semi-annual publication of one of Canada's mental health societies. Finally, I run my own editing business in which I edit medical students' papers.

Well thought out. Convinces me that there's a potential market of real readers out there for a title like this.

I believe that publishing my work could be a profitable endeavor for your company. I look forward to hearing from you at your earliest opportunity. Thank you for your time.

Sincerely,

Useful background information about the author that is relevant to writing and this book.

A polite and businesslike closing.

Linda Goodquery

Encl:SASE
Résumé
Introduction

Overall, I was very impressed with this letter. The author seemed confident, competent, and interesting. She provided the information I needed to evaluate this project, and I was intrigued enough to ask her to send me some more materials.

Comments provided by Michelle Howry, editor with Newmarket Press

Bad

April 15, 2001
P.O. Box 123
Clay City, KY 42782

Spelling error in address is a red flag immediately, especially for a large US city.

Writer's Digest
Melanie Rigney, editor
1507 Dana Avenue
Cincinnatti, Ohio 45207

Her age has nothing to do with whether or not I'm interested in her writing, and a "writer of sorts" doesn't imply a professional.

Ms. Rigney:

I wonder who published this? Doesn't name a publisher, and doesn't give book title.

I am an 85 year old senior citizen living in scenic Central Kentucky, and I am also a non-fiction writer of sorts.

I have just had published a 100 page collection of silly, strange, humorous, out-of-this world and hysterical wills - I call it "Famous Last Words".

I'm wary of anyone describing their own work as "hysterical." Best to let the reader (me) be the judge of that.

This collection is the result of over forty five years of visits to hundreds of law firms, libraries and municipal city halls in the USA, France and Germany.

This collection of last will and testament prose, joviality on paper and last words of wisdom also includes some bizarre and comical funeral arrangements and body removals, as reported by anonymous funeral directors and morticians.

Okay, she obviously hasn't read our guidelines. We don't buy anything like this. And "anonymous"? How do I know she didn't make it all up?

I am taking the liberty of sending you newspaper clips and a few samaple pages of "Famous Last Words". If you would want to make an entry in your magazone as something different, I will appreciate it. If you can use as such, I will be happy to send you a complimentary copy of same.

I'm unsure of what she's proposing here. Does she want us to publish an excerpt? We don't do that, as a general rule. Again guidelines.

While I have your attention I'm taking further liberties - I'm sending you a combination query on 35 different articles which I have either finished or am doing further research on - if, on looking over, you find any one of them interesting, I can furnish the article within three weeks with drawings and photos. Check those you might want on spec. - I enclose a SASE for your convenience. *Oh, jeeze. This is taking a multi-topic query way too far.*

I don't need any of the copy returned as I have copies.

I'd be happy to send them back.

Respectfully,

If she were familiar with our layout and design, she'd know not to suggest this.

Editorial has nothing to do with advertising. Plus she should have read sample copies (either at the library or purchased at bookstore, not free) before submitting.

Nancy Novice
(555)555-1212

P.S. Send a sample copy so I can check advertising rates.

Comments provided by Dawn Ramirez, former senior editor of *Writer's Digest*

Good

From:	**Meilleuremail@aol.com**
Sent:	**Friday, May 25, 2001**
To:	**WDSubmissions@fwpubs.com**
Subject:	**Hot to Make it to the Movies-Query**

At Writer's Digest we like getting e-mail submissions.

Dear Ms. Ramirez: *This is a hot topic for our readers.*

What gives a book movie potential? To many writers it's a mystery, and while good storytelling will get you a long way, knowing how to get in with a story-analyst at a film studio and what they are looking for is even better. As a longtime subscriber to *Writer's Digest* I know how-to articles are important to your readership. *Good to know she's a reader.*

She's gotten my attention by being very specific; I like the fact that she jumps right in, too.

"How to Make it to the Movies" would be an article of approximately 1,000 words giving *Writer's Digest* readers the low down on what story-analysts at film companies do, how you can get your story to them, what common elements they find in novels that they select for movie consideration and how to make your story more appealing for the movie industry. My primary sources would include a story-analyst at Warner Brothers, who has been analyzing novels for movie potential for nearly 20 years.

She knows we need short pieces.

This would be very helpful to our readership; it's packed with useful information.

My writing credits include *Phoenix Magazine*, *Cat Fancy*, *Dog Fancy*, *Pet Product News*, *American Cheerleader*, *Tribune Newspapers*, a daily multi-paper publisher in the Phoenix metro area, *The News-Register*, a daily paper in McMinnville, Oregon, and many others. In addition, I am a member of the National Writers' Union and the International Association of Business Communicators. *She's up on the industry and "who's who."*

Good source. I can have confidence this will be reliable information.

Good credentials.

I was particularly pleased to see "How to Write a Breakout Novel" by Donald Maass in your latest issue, since his agency represents my fiction work.

If you would like to see copy from some of my other how-to articles, you can find them on my website at www.theresameyers.com. In advance, thank you for your time and consideration of this query. I would be delighted with the opportunity to write for a magazine I have so long enjoyed as a reader.

Best Regards, *A smooth compliment never hurts!*

Theresa D. Meilleur
Meilleuremail@aol.com
555-555-1212

We couldn't accept this at the time because we were overbooked in editorial, but this is an excellent query.

Comments provided by Dawn Ramirez, former senior editor of *Writer's Digest*

E-query Etiquette

BY GREG DAUGHERTY

Something strange has happened to my inbox and that of every other magazine editor I know. Instead of being piled high with manila envelopes, our boxes are all but empty. We only have to switch on our computers to know the reason. For there, each morning, will be a stack of fresh e-mail queries, with more to arrive throughout the day.

About a year ago e-mail queries started to overtake paper ones at the magazine I edit. Since then I've seen some beginning writers win assignments with lively queries sent practically by return e-mail. I've also seen otherwise terrific writers flub it by making mistakes they never would have made in conventional paper queries. So what was the difference? With e-queries, success is often in the e-tails. Here are 11 pointers for writing—and sending—e-queries that sell:

1. **First, find out if the magazine accepts e-mail queries**. This may seem too basic even to mention, but there's no point sending out e-mail queries to publications that won't consider them. So check *Writer's Market* (the print edition or online at www.writersmarket.com) or send a quick e-mail to the magazine and ask. Or use that quaint old tool, the telephone. Many magazines also spell out whether they take e-mail queries and where to send them in the writer's guidelines posted on their websites. The *Harper's Magazine* site (www.harpers.org), for example, asks that queries be sent by regular mail; *Travel + Leisure*'s (www.travelandleisure.com) says the magazine accepts e-queries and gives a special address to send them to.

2. **Remember that most basic of basics**. The job of a query letter is to persuade a publication to give you an assignment. So whether it's printed on paper or glowing on a cathode-ray tube, any query you send should be built around a solid idea—one that's right for the publication and for which you are, of course, the ideal writer.

3. **Be a little formal**. E-mail is often more casual than conventional letters. But if you wouldn't call an editor by his or her first name in a letter, don't do it in an e-mail. An editor accustomed to being addressed by strangers as Robert So-and-So may not appreciate an e-mail that begins "Hi, Robert," or "Yo, Bobbo."

4. **Watch your spelling**. Even in the brave new world of e-mail, editors still expect you to know how to spell. Your e-mail program may have a spell-check feature just as your word processing software does. If it doesn't, one option is to write queries on your word processor, spell-check them there, and then paste them into an e-mail.

5. **Make good use of the SUBJECT: line**. The last thing you want to do is carefully write and polish a query and then have some harried editor delete it unread because it looks like spam. One simple way to prevent that is to put the word "query" prominently in the subject line of your e-mail, such as "Query about a new way to garden" or "Query for your Upfront section."

6. **Provide enough contact information**. Put your phone number and snail mail address on your e-mail. If you have a fax number, you might as well toss that in too. Anything that

---

GREG DAUGHERTY *is editor-in-chief of* Reader's Digest New Choices *magazine and the author of* You Can Write for Magazines *(Writer's Digest Books).*

makes it easier for an editor to reply to your query increases the odds that one may actually do so.

7. **Offer to supply samples of your work on request**. But don't load up your e-mail with attachments. Some editors won't even open attachments from strangers for fear of viruses. If samples of your work are available at your own website or elsewhere online, by all means mention that, but don't count on the editor to spend a leisurely afternoon reading them. In most cases you're still better off sending your samples in as plain old photocopies. That gives editors something they can scan quickly, pass around to their colleagues, and spill coffee on.

8. **Save your résumé for job applications**. Just because you can easily attach your résumé to an e-mail doesn't mean you should. As with any writing samples you attach, many editors won't give your résumé so much as a click. Far more effective is a paragraph somewhere near the end of your letter in which you sum up any experience and publishing credits you have that would be relevant to the story you're proposing. And while it may take a little longer, try to adapt that paragraph for each query rather that treating it as interchangeable boilerplate.

9. **Go easy on multiple submissions**. Pitching the same idea to different magazines at the same time couldn't be easier than with e-mail. But unless your idea is so newsy that it can't wait, think twice. Even editors who are willing to look at simultaneous submissions (and many aren't) may be put off by a TO: line with the e-mail addresses of all their competitors. When I get those, I often just delete them, figuring that any writer who wrote to that many publications will never notice whether I replied or not. If you want to try that kind of scattershot approach, be sure to mention that it's a simultaneous submission, but send out separate e-mails with just one addressee each or use the BCC: option.

10. **Don't expect an instant answer**. E-mail can make it easier to churn out queries, but editors still need time to think about your ideas and respond, just as they would with a paper query. An idea is an idea, whether it arrives via modem or mailbag. If you haven't heard anything after a couple of weeks, there's no harm in e-mailing back with a gentle inquiry. But whatever you do, don't get testy about it. Editors felt overwhelmed long before e-mail, and it has only added to their burdens. Remember that the easiest thing any editor can do with your query is hit the delete key.

11. **And finally, be sure to save your old queries on your computer**. Even if a query didn't sell the first time around, hang onto it. A new market may open up or an editor who turned your idea down because it was too close to something the magazine recently ran may have a change of heart a year from now. You'll save yourself a lot of wasted motion if you can retrieve your old queries, update them as needed, and shoot them off again. Just don't address the editor as ''Yo, Bobbo.''

Walking the Beat:
Breaking Into Niche Markets

BY KELLY MILNER HALLS

Independent writers who blaze the freelance trails seem like free-spirited rebels. These highly energized professionals write hard and well for the highest bidder, but work largely for themselves. The best among their ranks are invaluable to editors, and they name their own terms. But while they are free to conduct business as they please, freelancers also face tough circumstances—cash flow issues, stiff competition and the endless need for self-promotion.

So how do these writers make a living without being "on staff?" Specialization in niche markets, answer many freelance experts. For the six writing renegades featured in this section, narrowing the field is the secret to real and lasting success. Focusing their writing to fit their respective niche markets—pets, books and authors, entertainment, gaming, sports, women's—has kept them a few steps ahead of the pack, with the comfort of a steady work flow and the luxury of writing in fields they love.

Throughout the Consumer Magazines section, you'll find the stories behind these freelancers success in their niche markets. You'll hear from Moira Anderson Allen on writing about pets in Animals on page 368; Kelly Milner Halls on writing about books and authors in Contemporary Culture on page 432; Mark Ebner on writing about the entertainment industry in Entertainment on page 443; John Misak on writing about electronic gaming in Games & Puzzles on page 462; Fran Harris on writing about sports in Sports on page 708; and Deanna Pease on writing for women's service magazines in Women's on page 782.

Regardless of the subject matter, all freelancing requires perseverance, the ability to juggle several projects at one time, flexibility and resourcefulness. But for these niche markets, there are some other requirements as well. Throughout these six interviews, our freelance experts will share insights and advice from the trail: how to break in, what editors are looking for now, and how you can sidestep the pitfalls many rookies fall into.

KELLY MILNER HALLS *is a full-time freelancer in Spokane, Washington. Her work has appeared in* Writer's Digest, FamilyFun, Teen PEOPLE, New Jersey Monthly, Booklist, Book Magazine, Highlights for Children, Guidepost for Teens, *the* Washington Post, *the* Chicago Tribune, *the* Denver Post *and many other publications. She also interviews celebrity authors for iUniverse. Her latest children's picture book is* I Bought a Baby Chicken *(Boyds Mills Press).*

Persistence pays off for author George Singleton

BY WILL ALLISON

George Singleton doesn't let rejection bother him. He can't afford to. Before the publication of his first book, the short-story collection *These People Are Us* (River City Publishing), he'd been sending off book manuscripts to agents and publishers—and getting turned down—for 16 years.

And though Singleton has published an astonishing 70 short stories over the past decade or so, he's collected some 1,500 rejection slips in the process. *The Atlantic* passed on 90 of his stories before finally accepting one earlier this year. He had better luck with *Harper's*, sending 29 stories over the course of eight years before they published "The Half-Mammals of Dixie" in their February 2001 issue.

George Singleton

Photo by Glenda Guion

"Sometimes an editor will tell me, 'I love the beginning but hate the ending,' then another editor will read the same story and tell me, 'I love the ending but hate the beginning,' " says 42-year-old Singleton, a resident of Dacusville, South Carolina, and a creative-writing teacher at the South Carolina Governor's School for the Arts & Humanities. "I don't stew over any of this. I just keep sending the story out. Sooner or later an editor will take it, or I'll come to the conclusion that the story doesn't work."

To deal with the long odds of publishing, it helps to have a sense of humor—a prominent aspect of Singleton's work. His stories—described by *Playboy* as "mad crazy fun"—are peopled by hard-luck Southerners who gamely confront life's questions: How do you find a black-market sonogram so your pregnant wife won't discover you accidentally taped over the original? How do you help your father—and everyone else in town—fake tornado damage in order to collect emergency government funds? Why should you avoid the local recycling center when you're looking for your next wife? Ultimately, the questions posed by Singleton's stories are no more absurd than the one he's faced every day of his writing career: Why keep at it when the reward is usually rejection?

When did you begin writing?

I started off writing long, long, bad, bad novels from the age of 21 until the age of 28 or thereabouts. Every writing instructor told me, "After you've written 1,000 pages, you'll be ready." Me, I was a snot-nosed punk—still am, really—and I thought I could beat the system. I didn't. I wrote a bad 450-page third-person novel, another one that was 250 pages, and a third that was 300. Then I started writing short stories, mostly in first person.

Do you have an agent?

No. Early on I got letters from agents saying, "Have you ever thought about writing a novel?" Way later on I got letters saying, "Have you ever thought about writing a novel?" Listen, I've written some bad novels, even after those first three. So I've sent some bad novels to said agents,

WILL ALLISON *is editor-at-large for* Zoetrope: All Story *and former executive editor of* Story.

and they wrote back things like, "Write another—don't write stories. There's no money in stories." And then I get all bowed up and think about how I don't like people telling me what to write, and continue with what I want to do.

Agents started coming out of the woodwork when I sold a story to *Harper's*. I went ahead and told them all, "I will never write a novel. Don't ask me to write a novel." What the hell. I don't want them to waste their time or mine, really.

When you first began submitting your work, did you have a strategy?

I had no clue how to send off manuscripts. I came up before writing instructors started making third-graders send off their work to literary magazines. I sent to *Sou'wester* and *The Chariton Review* early on, but also to *Playboy*. It took about four years before I had a story accepted at *Playboy*. Understand, this was over-the-transom. Slush pile. But I lucked up. This old boy named Chris Napolitano—who wasn't more than 25 at the time—took a liking to what I wrote. He said send more. I did.

Whenever a magazine editor wrote back, "Send more," I did as soon as possible. Hell, if a magazine didn't say anything, I sent more, too.

How did you get involved with River City Publishing?

I have this buddy named Marlin Barton who brings me down to Alabama once a year to teach at a prison for teenage boys outside of Montgomery, and Bart has this buddy named Wayne Greenshaw who was involved with Black Belt Publishing [now River City Publishing]. Wayne pretty much asked if I was waiting for a New York publisher to come along. We sat in a bar called the 1048. I said, "Yeah." He said for me to send him a manuscript anyway. I did. They took it.

Are you happy working with a small press?

Yes. I don't have to worry about my book being out of print in six weeks.

What do you see as the difference between a short story and a novel?

For me, a novel is a big old shaggy dog running around aimlessly, sniffing whatever it wants to sniff for however long it wants to sniff it. A short story is a small cur, backed into a corner, showing its teeth.

Or: A novel is a long, wide river that narrows at points, turns to rapids, slows again, meanders all over the place, and sometimes turns stagnant for brief periods of time. A short story is a guy with a water hose who squirts you when you walk past him.

Do you enjoy working with editors?

When an editor asks for some changes, I revise to his or her specifications. In my opinion, the editor knows what's right, for the most part. The end result should be the best possible short story, not "But it came out of my brain this way and therefore it needs to remain intact."

What do you think, over the years, has been your strongest asset?

That I'm stupid. An intelligent, sane person doesn't like to be rejected every day for years on end. A smart person will either find success early on in writing or quit altogether.

I'm stupid enough to have kept going—and if a person keeps writing, he won't, for the most part, get worse. It's like running. If I go out and run today, then wait a year to run again, I probably won't run any farther than the first time. If I run today and then run every day for a year, I'll be able to show a marked improvement in both distance and speed.

I've written pretty much daily for a number of years. When I get a rejection, I go on. It's like getting a cramp in your side. It doesn't mean you should quit altogether. Keep going. Watch your step. Avoid potholes. Know that a second wind will come.

For more information on River City Publishing, publisher of George Singleton's These People Are Us, *please see the listing on page 281.*

For Jeff MacGregor, Sportswriting Is Writing First, Sports Second

BY WILL ALLISON

Until he covered a rattlesnake hunt for *Sports Illustrated* in 1998, Jeff MacGregor had never before written about sports. Now, only three years later, he's well established in the big leagues of American sportswriting. He has a contract with *Sports Illustrated*. His work appears in *The Best American Sportswriting 2000*. He's even been nominated for the National Magazine Award for each of the past three years.

The secret to his sportswriting success? Make it brand-new, every time.

"Sportswriting is no different than fashion writing or movie writing or technical journal writing in the field of gas chromatographics," says MacGregor. "It's bad when it does nothing more than channel a series of clichés about its subject. It's good when it is bright and vibrant and it transcends the conventional."

MacGregor has taken a decidedly unconventional path to his present post as a 44-year-old freelance writer living in Manhattan. After dropping out of the University of Minnesota, he spent 17 years as a television reporter before writing a piece for *The Los Angeles Times* in 1993. The following year, he attended the Summer Writing Workshop at Yale University (he now teaches in the same program), then holed up in a farmhouse in rural Pennsylvania and did nothing for a year but write. He subsequently attended the MFA Creative Writing Program at The Ohio State University on a fellowship, then moved to Manhattan in 1996. But it wasn't until *Sports Illustrated* offered him a contract on the strength of his first sports piece that MacGregor made the leap, leaving his lucrative job as an ABC network correspondent to write full time.

It was 1998, and though he was new to sportswriting, MacGregor was no rookie reporter. He'd already made a name for himself as a humorist and cultural critic, publishing in *The New Yorker*, *Details*, *Los Angeles Magazine*, and *The New York Times*, for whom he still writes about ten pieces each year. He'd even published short stories in *Story* and *Esquire*.

Fiction or nonfiction, humor or sports, MacGregor believes the elements of fine writing cross all genres: wit, elegance of argumentation, the color and music of language, the world freshly and sharply observed, the unspooling of conflict and its final resolution, honesty, modesty, economy.

"I think that's what I shoot for anyway," he says. "Sports in general are a beautifully compact theater of human experience. Good sportswriting is not just well-crafted writing about sports; rather, it finds in our games the central metaphors of our common struggle, without losing sight of the fact that they are, after all, still games."

How did you first get started in sportswriting?

I had been writing professionally for about five years when an editor I knew from another magazine moved over to *Sports Illustrated*. He suggested that I try a piece for them. I was hesitant, because prior to that I had been publishing mostly humor and fiction and cultural criticism; I had never written sports before, even in high school, which seems to be where most of my colleagues started.

WILL ALLISON *is editor-at-large for* Zoetrope: All Story *and former executive editor of* Story.

So, rather than cover a conventional sporting event (about which the *SI* editors might know a few things), I went to Oklahoma and covered a rattlesnake hunt (about which nobody anywhere knows anything). Since no one had ever seen a long, or even itty-bitty, snake-hunting story before, my piece could only be compared to itself, which is the one comparison it could bear. Thus buffaloed, the editors at *Sports Illustrated* offered me a contract. I've stayed as far away from conventional sports stories as I could ever since.

What prepared you for work as a sportswriter?

As a generalist (or generalissimo), I think every writer everywhere should be able to write about everything. The attributes of a good writer remain the same no matter the field: curiosity, sensitivity, invention, and devotion to the craft. If you are a good observer and an accurate reporter and a thoughtful author of your own ideas, then you should be able to approach any subject and write well about it.

It helps a writer more to know a little bit about everything than it does to know everything about one thing. Being a rabid sports fan isn't necessary to writing about sports, for example, nor is it even desirable, I think, in the many cases where some skepticism about the corporate oligarchy of pro sports or the overwrought mythologies of amateur athletics may be the only way to get at the truest core of the story.

That said, I think my best preparation for the work has been my lifelong love of good writing, my curiosity about why people do what they do, and my willingness to write every day. Also, I can sit for long periods without fidgeting.

Has your experience as a fiction writer been useful to you as a sportswriter?

Yes. I make my living writing nonfiction, but I write at least that much fiction. The intention and the architecture and the techniques are largely interchangeable; in the case of nonfiction, though, the setting, the plot, and the characters have been chosen for you by circumstance. Where the habit of fiction comes in handy is in understanding and revealing the essence of those things. I think fiction writing (and to an even greater extent, the writing of poetry) liberates a writer's imagination in the best possible way and helps to hone a regard for lyric and a willingness to strive for a vivid and original imagery and language.

As a sportswriter, you deal with athletes, many of them famous and rich. Does this present special challenges?

They don't want to talk to me. I think the hardest and worst part of the job is trying to hack my way through the dense thicket of protective cliché in which all professional athletes now hide. If you wait around long enough though—and I mean on the order of *months*—you might eventually catch one of them saying something that doesn't sound like it came from an embroidered sampler or the benediction at a high-school sports banquet.

What's the most difficult aspect of sportswriting?

Finding new ways to see and understand and write about the overexposed and the overfamiliar.

What's the biggest mistake you've ever made on an assignment?

This is a tough one. Because I try to do different kinds of stories every time I write for *Sports Illustrated*, I always make brand-new and often dimwitted mistakes. I sort of learn how to do each story as I'm doing it, which means I do a lot of useless research and write a lot of bad drafts before I figure out how the story should come together. A smart person would just ask at the office, "Say, Frank DeFord, how do I write a profile?" or something and save himself many months of self-loathing and several reams of paper. I prefer to fail my way into and out of every story.

There are two mistakes I make over and over again and warn young writers about. Don't over-research. It can add months to a project. There's a point at which you've trailed the story too far back in time and are simply doing more research because it's easier than actually writing the story. Tip #2? Never order the eggs benedict. Trust me.

How much time do you spend writing a feature?

Between the research and the reporting and the writing I've spent over a year on some stories.

What sportswriters do you like to read?

My friend W.C. Heinz. Red Smith. Tom McGuane on fishing. Frank DeFord and Gary Smith at *Sports Illustrated*, and Charles Pierce at *Esquire* and *GQ*. Hemingway doesn't stink. Roger Angell on baseball. I think Serena Roberts at *The New York Times* is one of the best writers in newspapering. Ring Lardner still holds up. Tom Wolfe and Hunter Thompson.

Do some sports better lend themselves to sportswriting than others?

Common wisdom has it that "the smaller the ball, the better the writing." I'm not so sure that common wisdom is right, except insofar as golf and baseball are pastoral and play out v-e-r-y s-l-o-w-l-y. They're easier to keep track of and write about. They're also much older and have more tradition to invoke. Football, basketball, and hockey are explosive and harder to follow. They're much more recent as well, with less (literary) history to rely on. Things always change, though. Fifty years ago the best writing in sports was about boxing and horse racing, both long since marginalized by the public. At the end of the day the only meaningful issue is who's doing the writing.

Don't Write for a Market, Says Novelist Susan Trott; Let the Market Find You

BY WILL ALLISON

As a college freshman in 1956, ten years before she would sell her first story, Susan Trott already knew that she would be a writer.

"Hemingway was my hero, and I went to Spain to watch bull-fights, get laid, drink absinthe, dance flamenco, and learn Spanish," says Trott, a native of Andover, Massachusetts, who attended private schools in Boston and Providence. "In Spain I met a famous photographer who told me I was not going to learn to be a writer by sitting around in cafés drinking; I had to work at it ten hours a day."

Susan Trott

Impressed, Trott returned to the United States, dropped out of Bennington, was cut off without a penny by her father, and supported herself with odd jobs while she practiced writing.

Trott was still writing when she married, moved to California, had three children, and then divorced. At 50, she took a Norwegian freighter to South America and fell in love with Roy Christensen, the ship's chief engineer. When they married, it seemed natural to live on the water, so they soon bought a houseboat in Sausalito, where they live today.

Trott's work falls under the broad umbrella of literary fiction, though over the years she has also written children's fiction and mysteries. Mainly, publishers and bookstores have found her work difficult to classify. Consider her 1995 national bestseller, *The Holy Man* (Riverhead Press), which was described as "endlessly entertaining and gently profound" by *Kirkus Reviews*. The novel reads something like a Buddhist reworking of Chaucer's *The Canterbury Tales* with sprinklings of Woody Allen and Samuel Beckett thrown in. Riverhead marketed the book as "inspiration/fiction," though it might just as easily go under the headings of literature, philosophy, or religion.

While Trott is best known for *The Holy Man* and its sequel, *The Holy Man's Journey*, she considers *Sightings* to be her finest novel. Originally published by Simon & Schuster in 1987, *Sightings* is being reissued by Storyline Press in fall 2002. *Divorcing Daddy*, another of Trott's novels, will be reissued in spring 2003.

These days, Trott's husband is retired from the Norwegian merchant marine and has a boat he ties up to the houseboat with which he goes fishing for salmon. And Susan?

"I will never retire," says Trott, "but now, at 63, with 15 novels published, I feel I can sit around in cafés whenever I want to."

Tell us the story of your first publishing success.

I was a lone writer in the late sixties. I'd been sending out novels and short stories for ten years and getting rejections. An editor advised me to get an agent. Agents were mysterious figures in

---

WILL ALLISON *is editor-at-large for* Zoetrope: All Story *and former executive editor of* Story.

those days. The editor told me who to try. When I got the agent, he sold two stories in one blow, to *Mademoiselle*, which published fine stories then and paid about $2,000 per. I was thrilled. I went on to publish around 50 stories here and in the United Kingdom. I sold two children's novels, but it wasn't until 1978 that I sold my first adult novel, *The Housewife and the Assassin*. By then I'd been writing seriously for 20 years. The editor remarked that it didn't read like a first novel. It was probably my sixth.

How many drafts do you typically write?

I write the first draft in a creative burst, getting the story down. Then I rewrite to expand on the characters and situations, get the timeline right, add weather, atmosphere, dialogue, etc. The third and final draft is to get every sentence, every word, right.

How do you know when a book is finished?

The ending is the hardest part of writing for me. I want it to be great and satisfying and absolutely right. When I've got the ending, I'm done.

Do you rely on feedback from outside readers before you hand over a manuscript to your agent?

When I've finished a book to my satisfaction, I give it to my three brilliant children who have always been true-blue readers, totally trustworthy, extremely helpful. Now my second husband reads insightfully, too. Don't ask about my first husband.

Over the years and books, have you found that writing gets harder, or easier?

Two quotes. Chaucer: "The lyf so short, the craft so long to lerne." Woody Allen: "If you're not failing now and again, it means you're playing it safe." After I wrote my best novel, *Sightings*, I told myself, "Now I know how to write a novel." I was astonished when my next novel was a dreadful unpublishable mess. The thing is, you can never rest. You always have to try something different, challenge yourself anew, fail.

What role does reading play in your life as a writer?

I read about five books a week. Writers should read everything under the sun. But, when starting out, don't read a writer with a strong style while you're writing or you'll be influenced. You want to find your own voice.

How important is a regular writing schedule to you?

It's essential. I write from eight to twelve at least five days a week. As little as a half-hour every day is better than a burst of six hours every fifth day because it gets your subconscious working on the story. When my kids were little, and time was scarce, I wrote in my head so that when I sat down I was ready with the words. I didn't have to do my thinking in the precious time allotted to me. I still write a lot in my head.

Do you ever abandon projects? If so, how do you know when to pull the plug?

I abandon a book or story if it doesn't sell. I shelve it for a year or two to look at later and see if it's really rotten or has promise. I believe it's better to start a new book than to keep rewriting a book that isn't working. You learn the craft with each book you write.

To what extent do commercial and genre considerations affect your approach to writing?

If you want to be a serious, non-genre novelist, an original storyteller, don't ever think commercially. Don't write for a market, let the market find you. I have been cursed by being called a non-catagorizable writer, and getting published has always been hard for me because of it.

("What in hell shelf does this book go on?") Finally a book reviewer said, "Trott is a genre unto herself," and I was very proud. Publishers have also complained that I have a cult following—that is, not a wide readership. One editor said, "You know, Susan, usually if a writer gets a fan letter, we say that letter probably stands for 5,000 readers from that area. But, with you, it really stands for one reader."

How has *The Holy Man*'s bestseller status affected your life as a writer?

Finally I get royalty checks. I live solely by my writing, and, until *The Holy Man*, most of my earnings have come from Hollywood options. I have had 29 of them. One book, *When Your Lover Leaves*, was an NBC movie of the week.

What's your best advice for a budding novelist?

When Nobel prizewinner Romain Rolland was a young aspiring writer, he decided to go to Russia to learn from Tolstoy. He found him and tailed around after him. Finally Tolstoy wheeled upon Rolland and asked him what he wanted. "I want to be a writer," Rolland said. Tolstoy replied, "If you want to be a writer, then write." I would add: read; exercise an hour a day; live fully; develop as a person; stop, look, and listen; and keep your mind free from dogma, creeds, and thoughts of revenge.

Tolstoy also said he wanted to make his readers "laugh and cry and love life more." That has been my aim. You want your work to reverberate, and you want to tell a terrific story and invent a character your reader will never forget. All this is hard to do, but it's fun trying. There is nothing more fun in the world than writing!

Ten Tips for Finding Markets Online

BY DEBBIE RIDPATH OHI

The frenzy of the dot-com gold rush may have subsided, but the Internet remains a rich resource of market research information and paying opportunities for writers.

Print publications. Many print publications now have an online presence, some with content not included in the print edition.

Electronic publications. Publications which exist solely online sometimes pay for editorial content, although pay rates are generally lower than for print publications.

Web guides and portals. These types of sites occasionally hire freelancers to provide content and maintain specific areas.

Other online opportunities. Additional ways a writer can earn money include copy editing and proofreading, writing press releases, online journalism, teaching online courses, and providing content for corporate websites.

How does one find these opportunities online? Here are ten tips that can help you find paying markets:

1. Use search engines and website analysis.

Most writers know the basics of using a search engine, but very few realize how much time and effort they could save in their writing research with advanced search features.

Just entering the term "submission guidelines" in a standard search engine, for example, will turn up thousands of entries. Adding the term "writer" will help narrow down the search, as will the word "pay". Many search engines will also allow you to specify terms you *don't* want (e.g. "does not pay"), which can further narrow your search.

If the guidelines of the resulting websites don't give a clear indication of whether or not they pay freelance writers, you can get some idea by asking yourself the following questions:

Is it a commercial site? Do they look like they're making money, or is this a non-profit organization run by volunteers? If non-commercial, is the site supported by a well-funded organization?

Does most of the material appear to be produced by in-house staff? Examine editorial content and names of the writers. Do some change every issue, or do the names always remain the same?

2. Learn how to verify a market information source.

Confirm payment and copyright policies. Editors and policies change more quickly online, so be sure to get written confirmation.

Ask around. If you're still unsure, ask other writers whether they have had problems with a particular publication.

Check Web resources. Ease of communication through the Internet has provided writers with increased ability to share information. Some useful sites:

Preditors & Editors—www.sfwa.org/prededitors/

DEBBIE RIDPATH OHI *is the author of* The Writer's Online Marketplace *(Writer's Digest Books, Jan/ 2001) and the creator of Inkspot, a Web resource and community for writers. More info at http://www.electricpenguin.com.*

Writer Beware—www.sfwa.org/beware/

3. Take advantage of online networking opportunities.

According to the results of a survey I sent out to hundreds of online writers, most of those with regular assignments said they found the work through contacts. Many networking opportunities exist online, including chat rooms, message forums, author organizations and groups, job boards, discussion lists and, of course, e-mail.

4. Investigate third-party market information resources.

One of the biggest advantages that the Internet offers writers is access to market information which can be more frequently updated than in a print version, typically in the form of guidelines databases, resource websites for writers, and electronic newsletters.

Quality control. When using a third-party resource, you should ask yourself the following questions:

How reliable is the source? What kind of reputation do they have? Have they been around for several years, or are they relatively new?

How is their market research conducted? Do they get their market information from third-party resources themselves or do they contact publishers and editors directly?

How current is their information? Is there any indication of a "last verified" date? If not, you have no idea whether the info is one week old or two years old. How often is the database or newsletter updated?

Types of third-party resources:

Guidelines databases. Several websites offer free guidelines databases for writers. Most are searchable, allowing you to browse listings by general category. Examples:

Writer's Digest—www.writersdigest.com

Writers Write—www.writerswrite.com/guidelines/

The Writer's Place—www.awoc.com/Guidelines.cfm

Writers' Guideline Database—www.mav.net/guidelines/

Websites and electronic newsletters. Many excellent market resources are available online for writers. Here are just a few:

Inscriptions—www.inscriptionsmagazine.com

Writing-World.com—www.writing-world.com

WritersWeekly.com—www.writersmarkets.com/index-twmr.htm

The Write Market Webzine—www.writemarket.com

The Market List—www.marketlist.com

Spicy Green Iguana—www.spicygreeniguana.com

Ralan.com—www.ralan.com

5. Browse electronic newsstands.

Electronic newsstands are websites where users can browse descriptions of hundreds of publications. The main purpose of electronic newsstands is to sell subscriptions, but they can also be used as a valuable source of market information for writers.

Most are searchable by publication title or category.

Enews.com—www.enews.com

Newsdirectory.com—www.newsdirectory.com

The Multimedia Newsstand—www.mmnews.com

6. Browse publisher websites.

Most book publishers these days have submission guidelines on their websites, saving you the cost of a SASE. Even if there are no guidelines available online, you can still learn a great deal by browsing through the site. Things to look for:

A list of current titles. Some websites will have a searchable online catalog. This can give you a better idea of what kind of topics the publisher is interested in as well as specific topics which have already been thoroughly covered.

Editorial contacts. Find out the name (and correct spelling) of the editor who will be looking at your query or submission.

Newsletter. Some publishers offer free updates or newsletters by electronic mail. This is another way of finding out about recent acquisitions, current needs, and industry news.

7. Get into the habit of checking job boards.

Combing job boards is one of the best ways to find openings for regular online writing assignments. New websites will often post job listings for columnists, editors, and freelance writers. Some offer other career resources.

8. Keep on the lookout for new online content websites.

Look for sites and newsletters that announce launchings of new websites as well as publishing news. Often these sites will be looking for new staff writers even if their submission guidelines aren't online.

9. Research hardcopy sources.

Writer's Market includes publications which pay for online content, and other market guides also carry information about online markets as well as regular print publications. Other hardcopy resources include *The Writer's Online Marketplace* (my book, published by Writer's Digest) and Anthony Tedesco's book, *Online Markets For Writers: How to Make Money by Selling Your Writing on the Internet* (Owl Books/Henry Holt & Co.)

10. Investigate other paying opportunities for writers.

Writers can earn money online in other ways, such as teaching online courses, either on your own or through a third party. If you have a strong interest and experience in a particular subject as well as an aptitude for teaching, you could combine this knowledge with your writing skills by developing a course that can be taught online. Many formats and methods exist for online instruction. Before developing your own, you should research to see what's available. In teaching writing-related courses, for example, some opt to work with an established organization (like WritingClasses.com or Writers.com) so they don't have to worry as much about administration and marketing.

Use the tips above to increase your current writing sales as well as find additional markets and market resources online. Despite the end of "dot-com frenzy," writers can still find many paying opportunities online, if they know where to look.

Writing for Online Markets

BY ANTHONY TEDESCO

There's one thing we should get straight. If you're looking to learn all those geek-speak emoticon hieroglyphic winkey-smiley code symbols, you've come to the wrong article. This is not about cyber-centric parlance. There will be no 12-letter acronyms in lieu of conversational phrases. There will be no obscure technical references ending with three exclamation points denoting excitement about said obscure technical references.

Sure, there are some Net users who communicate almost exclusively in this cryptic high-tech vernacular. But they're a minority. An astute little space-alien minority.

Point is: Most online editors and writers aren't techies writing for techies about techie things. We're just opportunists who've tapped a new market—374 million online readers strong, according to eTForecasts, and growing faster than any other mass medium. For us, technology is a means, not an end. We've supplemented our newsstand options with the Net, but we're still writing and selling the same cultural/comical/whatever-ical pieces we've been writing for traditional media.

Not *exactly* the same. The same topics, yes. But writing for the Internet and the Internet's audience does have its distinct nuances, and knowing these nuances will help you sell articles online. Here are some tips, traps and tricks (try saying that ten times fast) that I've learned from being on both sides of the online magazine query letter for the last nine years.

KNOW YOUR READERS

Online readers are really whoever you want them to be. With personal Net access costing less than $20 per month, and free access being provided by everyone from public and private schools to public libraries and employers, there are just so many different people online—people of all ages, all academic backgrounds, all incomes, all cultures—that you can easily find readers interested in topics that interest you, as well as online magazines catering to those interests.

FIND YOUR TARGET MAGAZINES

The trick, of course, is finding online magazines catering to your interests which also pay writers for content. A few of those markets are listed with submission guidelines in the second half of this article. Other resources include (shameless-yet-pertinent plugs) my free Web resource for writers, MarketsForWriters.com, and my book, *Online Markets for Writers* (Holt). Writer's Digest Books also publishes an excellent resource entitled *Writer's Online Marketplace*, by Debbie Ridpath Ohi. (See Debbie Ridpath Ohi's article "Ten Tips for Finding Online Markets.")

With a little online foraging, however, you can customize your very own list of potential online publications. A good place to start is on the pages of the very same markets you've targeted in traditional media. Most print publications have companion online magazines that feature high-percentages of original online writing. Check the masthead page for their corresponding URL (Internet address), or peruse the advertising pages for website promotions. Even publishing companies with the resources of many magazines usually opt for creating original

ANTHONY TEDESCO *is co-author of* Online Markets for Writers: How to Make Money By Selling Your Writing on the Internet *(Holt), with free e-mail updates, and publisher of* www.MarketsforWriters.com, *a free web resource to help writers live off the writing they love.*

online brands merely rooted in their print counterparts. Condé Nast, for example, publishes the "online versions" of its magazines *Gourmet* and *Bon Appetit* under the online brand Epicurious Food (www.epicurious.com), with primarily original online content.

You can occasionally find a print publication's online version by simply typing the publication's title into the Internet address (www.thetitle.com). If that fails, try entering the title into one of the Internet's many search engines.

Here are a few pervasive print publications with sister online ventures:
* *Boston Globe* online (www.boston.com)
* *USA Today* online (www.usatoday.com)
* *Advertising Age* online (www.adage.com)
* The *Village Voice* online (www.villagevoice.com)
* *Playboy* online (www.playboy.com)

Another way to locate online magazines with your target readers is through directories and electronic newsstands, though there are so many online magazines on the Internet that it's easy to get overwhelmed with options, and often difficult to discern whether or not they pay their freelancers without actually querying the editor. The good news: If you can muster the perseverance, the Internet is your best shot at securing a patron publication for your most idiosyncratic of interests. Here are some resources:
* Etext Archives (www.etext.org) is home to electronic texts of all kinds.
* Ezine Newsgroup (alt.ezines) is a good place to query the e-zine community about any genre of magazine.
* Chip Rowe's Zine Resource Start Page (www.zinebook.com/main.html) is a clearinghouse for all things zine and e-zine.
* Zinos (www.zinos.com/) is a digest of some of the top e-zines on the web.
* The Well's Publications Area (gopher://gopher.well.com/11/Publications) offers information on the full gamut of online magazines.

ADAPTING YOUR WRITING TO THE WEB

Once you're armed/dangerous with your target list of online markets, you can greatly improve your sales by adapting the muse and mechanics of your writing to the nuances of the World Wide Web.

Local writing for a global audience

The words "World" and "Wide" in World Wide Web make this first tip so obvious that writers often overlook it. Readers on the Internet hail from all over the world. English is still the standard, but English doesn't mean U.S.-centric. It's just as easy for someone in Seattle to read a particular online magazine as it is for someone from Sri Lanka. Your articles should reflect that diversity—without watering down the distinctions that make it real. Think local details with global appeal.

Take, for example, one of our past columns at *Crisp* (www.crispzine.com) entitled "Actor's Journal: Amy Carle rants and rambles about trying to balance her office day job with her theater-group dream job." Carle's writing is so engaging because (a) she's an engaging writer/person, and (b) she infuses her journal entries with personal details such as her coworker's compulsion with keeping the workplace temperature a brisk sub-zero, or the high, clunky, and undoubtedly dangerous heels that she's agreed to dance in for the full run of Chicago-based Roadwork's rendition of *Orestes*.

Is Mr. Sri Lanka going to make it to the show to see the heels? Probably not (his loss). Is it cold in your workplace? I don't know, I don't work with you. But Carle balances these animated details with the bigger picture that people all around the world can relate to: making sacrifices in the pursuit of your passions; dealing with quirky (freaky) coworkers at a job that means little more to you than money for bills while pursuing those passions.

Use your own voice

Along the same lines of personal details, Net readers have a penchant for wanting to know people, real people, real regular Joe/Jody individuals, you. I think it stems from the fact that regular Joe/Jody has always had equal billing to corporate behemoths on the Internet. Basic home pages are as accessible as highfalutin sites, and Net users still prize themselves as anti-establishment, give or take an establishment.

Also, although the Internet is a global gathering, it's a gathering that empowers and connects individuals. This subtle dichotomy was best demonstrated in a *Details* article I read about a Net-spawned amateur exhibitionist who was adamant about her being shy, despite her nude pictures posted on her site. She explained that the only reason she was able to, um, exhibit herself in front of so many people was that she wasn't doing it in front of all those people at once. Each person experienced her "art" individually, at his or her own computer.

Okay, that was a dangerous example, but it's worth illustrating this most pivotal aspect of interactive writing: Although it feels like you're writing for a mass audience called Net users, you're actually communicating with people on a one-to-one basis.

So stay away from third person, which says "distanced," "corporate," "disinterested." Or the collective "We" addressing the collective "You." Opt instead for first person, and don't shy away from your opinions (not that you have to bash them with your cyber-soapbox either; impassioned doesn't have to mean belligerent).

Write in your own voice, not standard written English. Let your vernacular and personality show through, even if you're pitching a service-oriented piece such as a book review or an interview. I want to know less about the book and more about how the book made you feel. (Different markets require different nuances, so confirm this voice with your particular editor—but generally it's the case.)

Were you reading the book at your desk or in a hammock sipping makeshift coladas? Why did you choose the book? Were you feeling down about your best friend, Frank Botts, who gave your Yankees seat to some girl-of-the-week he's trying to impress, as if she'll stick around after watching him inhale eight hot dogs? Were you extra-nervous interviewing Paul Newman not only because of his epic celebrity status but because you spent much of your younger days gazing into his dreamy blue eyes on the Cool Hand Luke poster? Do you still have the poster safely stashed away in your room?

Again, study the nuances of your particular market but, far more so than with print readers, Net readers want—even expect—to connect with you as well as your story. Let your article be a window into you as a person and not as a press release.

Brevity and pace

Fast-paced and brief writing is more effective because Net users have so many other options online and it's just so easy to click away—you have to hook them and hook them fast, complementing the visually-oriented medium with soundbite-esque copy. Furthermore, computer screens are more difficult to read than traditional paper pages. The screen is usually small and the area for your text is even smaller. Net users don't want to scroll and scroll to finish a piece—they even go so far as to liken excessive scrolling to a drowning feeling, having to go deeper and deeper into a Web page. (You wouldn't want to drown cute little Net users, now would you?) Brevity is also important to keep download times low (the time readers have to sit around waiting for a page to load onto their screens). Text is data, and while not as cumbersome as images, video, or sound, long text files can cause similar delays.

Getting involved

Interactivity is a buzzword for all publishers. Netizens want to be vehicles, not just voyeurs. Writers must find ways to let their audience participate in their content because they can. The Web provides and promotes immediate interaction, whether readers contribute opinion posts,

---

Crash Course

Public Service Announcement: Go back up your computer now. (I'll wait.) My hard drive crashed while working on this article and I hadn't saved copies of my files for over four months (traveling, quirky back-up disks, blah-blah-blah). Like all writers, I have an inordinate need for my personal computer. It doubles as my professional means for writing and Internet research and professional e-mail correspondence, and it also stores all of my professional toils—grunt writing, one-time muse-inspired masterpieces, ev-er-y-thing. Without my computer, I'm less a writer and more a guy sitting in front of an empty desk, desperately phoning tech people for three weeks straight to save his love/livelihood.

Here's what I learned/what you should know when (not "if") your computer drive crashes:

1. Purchasing and using over-the-counter file recovery software can (and did in my case) cause more damage by overwriting drive information when it "fixes" the problem;

2. There are roughtly 5 gazillion data recovery services, but only one (as in, one) is author-ized to work on Macintosh drives (and every PC drive) without voiding your computer's warranty: DriveSavers (www.drivesavers.com). I found them after 4 gazillion phone calls and, of course, two—legit (authorized but warranty voiding)—companies worked on my computer.

3. Forget "3" and go back up your computer. (Again.)

—AT

---

additional resources and links, instant surveys and form responses, or actual real-time chats with writers.

Incorporating technology

It's important to know what sets this new medium apart from print, and how to incorporate those differences into your creative process and editor pitches.

Note: You don't have to know the mechanisms that make the technologies work. All you have to know is what's out there—what available technology could be used to enhance your article. (And how much fatter your freelance check should be for coming up with such a tech-savvy sidebar.)

Here are a few technologies that could enhance your article:

Audio and Video. Yes, you can incorporate high-quality audio and video right into online articles. Although streaming advantages are cutting the waiting time for readers, your best bet is to limit yourself to short clips. An article about dining on the Italian Riviera could include not only key phrases for ordering, but actual audio clips of the phrases so readers can hear how they are pronounced. At *Crisp*, instead of merely including photos of clothing from the innova-tive, up-and-coming designers of Space Girl, we added short video clips from their fashion show so readers could see how the clothes move on the body.

Hyperlinks. Hyperlinks are words or images that can be clicked on to send Net users to another page or site. Almost every company and institution is on the Web now, so if you refer to one, you can link its name to its site. This concept also goes for references and official home pages of celebrities. If you're writing about it, chances are that there is another relevant article or image out on the Web somewhere that can be linked to, so just as you would do conventional research for any article, search the Web for sites or pages that are relevant to your own piece. The Web is an extremely large database that can be accessed and utilized by the click of a button for the good of humankind, or at least for your freelance check. For example: An interview with

Pamela Anderson could include a sidebar of links to all 14 billion of her fan sites. An article on gingerroot could include links to recipes with ginger available at the many food sites on the Internet.

Chats and Bulletin Boards. Chats and bulletin boards are two of the most widely used aspects of the Web because, at the root of it all, the Web is chock full of people who like to talk and share and complain with other people. If you interview someone, consider asking them to participate in a live chat with readers/fans for a half hour or field questions over a short period on a bulletin board (to plug their latest starry project, of course). Or even just make yourself available to readers with follow-up questions. That sort of access and personal connection means a lot to online readers—which means a lot to online editors.

Java. Java is still so quirky that many sites don't include it. Readers don't like to have their computers crash. Keep an eye out as its usage becomes more stable. An example of incorporating Java into a story is doing a piece on stocks featuring a real-time stock ticker.

Cybercasts. You can not only review a concert or band, you can broadcast it live over the Internet with your article. Check out SonicNet (www.sonicnet.com) for inspiration.

The Only HTML You Actually Need to Know

A few online editors will request (and the rest will emphatically appreciate) your including basic HTML tags in your text. They never want you to design the whole story—just to apply basic formatting. Many e-mail applications give you the option of automatically translating the body of your text message into HTML. In that case, use it. If your e-mail application doesn't provide that option, get one that does. If, like me, you're too broke and/or lazy to upgrade your e-mail application, here's all the HTML you need to know. Before saving your article as "text only," insert these tags where it's appropriate:

To bold text:
<B>the bold words</B>

To italicize text:
<I>the italic words</I>

For a line break:
Insert a
where you want the break

To set a new paragraph:
<P> at the end of a paragraph starts you on the next paragraph by adding the equivalent of two line breaks—one break, then one return line before the next sentence.

To create a text link: <A HREF="http://www.marketsforwriters.com"> This is the text that will be linked, sending people who click on it to http://www.marketsforwriters.com—don't forget those quotation marks.

That's it. Really. The site will handle the forms and graphics and jargon. You're a hero/heroine for handling the above tags, making your text-only article more accurate to the text you want stylized (without the tags in your text-only article, the editor wouldn't know what was supposed to be bold, italic, the end of a paragraph, or a link to another site or page for more information), and making it easier to read for the editor and easier to format for the designer.

QUERYING ONLINE EDITORS

Okay, you've found the online market that makes your heart go "pitter-patter," and you've honed the piece you consider your Pulitzer Prize-winner. Now what?

At the risk of sounding redundant: Remember to read through the online market that made your heart go "pitter-patter" before sending your article. Online editors are just like print editors, only a little cooler (kidding): They don't want a 12,000-word fiction book excerpt if all they publish is breaking news.

Query an editor first with a short e-mail. Electronic querying definitely has its advantages: You don't have to pay postage and you don't have to wait for delivery. It still may take a few days for an editor to respond, but the entire process usually takes much less time than with print queries.

Obviously it's best to send your e-mail directly to the appropriate editor. Sometimes, however, his or her e-mail isn't listed on the masthead of the magazine. Fret not. You still have a few options.

You can rummage through the site until you find a general editorial e-mail address (e.g., "editorial@thetitle.com" or "feedback@thetitle.com") or even the ubiquitous e-mail address of the site's Webmaster (technical overseer) who will probably do you the favor of forwarding your query—unless he or she is particularly busy or he or she just doesn't feel like it. Let's face it, with a title like Webmaster and the perceived power to crash your computer and then charge a celebratory bottle of Dom to your credit card, he or she can do whatever he or she wants, whenever he or she wants to.

Option Two shows a little resourcefulness of your own, though don't tell anyone I showed you. Even though an editor's e-mail address might not be listed in the magazine's masthead, it doesn't mean it doesn't exist, and it doesn't mean you can't find it. Sites such as WhoWhere? (www.whowhere.lycos.com/) and Yahoo People Search (http://people.yahoo.com/) have gathered millions of e-mail addresses from the Internet so you can get in touch with your long-lost best high school pal or fave celebrity. As well as, of course, the editor who's going to jump for joy after reading your revolutionary query.

Yes, the non-joy-jumping editor in me says you shouldn't send me e-mails directly, I'm busy, you shouldn't risk simultaneous submissions, and you shouldn't pitch to me over the phone. But then I'm also a freelance writer doing all of those things for the advantages they provide.

Make your own decision. And mum's the word.

STYLE MANUAL

Despite lofty intentions toward a universal Net style, each publication usually exercises its right to reek of quirkiness (I mean, branding), a lot more so than in print media. The bottom line is that it's tough to look bad grammatically. The onus is usually on the editor because there's really no AP Style Manual-esque rulebook governing Net publishing. (Yet.) Of course, if someone could pull it off, I'd put my little e-dollars on those gifted techno geek guru digerati at *Wired* magazine, revered keepers of all cryptic netspeak, purveyors of digi-panache, and (you get the picture but I'm still going) undisputed virtual-weight champs of neo-neologisms. Although your editor-to-hopefully-be should be the one purchasing *Wired*'s book as a style manual, you could definitely score some tech-savvy points with him or her by perusing your own copy (especially if you're targeting online publications focused on technology). Their book is called, *Wired Style: Principles of English Usage in the Digital Age* (HardWired), and it's edited by Constance Hale, with the editors of *Wired*.

SENDING YOUR QUERY

When you do finally send the article, plee-ease don't send those 12,000 words as an e-mail attachment unless it's been requested. You could be that one writer with one jumbled photo attachment that crashes the editor's computer and all the files that hadn't been backed up, a.k.a., all the files. It could take three days, lots of cash, and numerous sacrifices to the hard-drive deities to get things working again.

Even big attachments that don't crash the system may take years-or-so to come across a humble Internet connection, which means, for years-or-so, someone has to watch that little "percentage completed" line inch and inch (and inch) its way to completion in the middle of morning e-mails. Instead, insert HTML tags, save the article in "text only" format, copy the text and paste it into your e-mail message. Or at least get permission to send it as an attachment. But your best bet with editors is to send your query without clips. Instead, offer to send clips and ask for his or her—greatly varying and often vehement—preferred method of receiving clips (as attachments, as e-mail text, or as URLs pointing to clips on the Web). If you don't have online clips yet, you can offer to mail or fax hard-copy clips.

If the editor does choose to have online clips sent as e-mail text, remember to copy and paste only the text of the article into your e-mail message and double-check the format. Many writers forget, sending formatted articles (with bolds, italics, indents, accents, smart/hooked quotation marks, etc.) via e-mail that is text only. The result is that the aforementioned article arrives spotted with awry symbols—not awry enough to make the e-mail illegible, just enough to make the editor crazy trying to read it. And don't forget to send all e-mails to yourself first to make sure they're formatted how you want them.

AND IN THE END . . .

Best of luck with the freelance process. A little extra effort understanding the Internet and the Internet's readers (and editors) will go a long way to tapping this promising new market.

Online Markets

CLEAN SHEETS MAGAZINE, www.cleansheets.com
E-mail for general information: editor@cleansheets.com. Clean Sheets is a weekly magazine devoted to encouraging and publishing quality erotic writing, along with providing honest information and thoughtful commentary on sexuality to the public. A new issue of the magazine is published every Wednesday, showcasing articles, exotica, fiction, art, poetry and reviews. Estab. October 1998. Circ. 70,000. Pays on publication. Byline given. Buys one-time electronic publication rights; archival rights optional. Accepts simultaneous and previously published submissions (if disclosed). Responds in 2 weeks to queries, 2 months to mss. Submission guidelines online.
Editorial Needs: Book reviews, articles, erotic fiction, poetry. Send complete ms. Length: for fiction prefers less than 4,000 words; poetry prefers fewer than 100 lines. **Pays $50/story; $10/poem.**
Tips: See submission guidelines at www.cleansheets.com.

CYBER AGE ADVENTURES, www.cyberageadventures.com
Cyber Age Adventures, 2403 NW 27th Ave., Boynton Beach FL 33436. (561)742-3634. Frank Fradella, president. **40% freelance written.** Award-winning monthly magazine of superhero fiction. "We provide ground-breaking, thought-provoking fiction in a superhero setting." Estab. January 1999. Circ. 30,000. Pays on publication. Byline given. Buys nonexclusive electronic and print rights. Story will appear on Website for 90 days and may be included in a print anthology with an e-book counterpart. No longer accepts reprints. Responds within 1 month to queries, 2 months to mss. E-mail for submissions: Submissions@cyberageadventures.com. Send complete ms as text file in body of the e-mail. Complete guidelines online.
Editorial Needs: Fiction. Length: 3,000 words for short stories, 1,500 words for short-shorts. **Pays 5-7¢/word.**
Tips: "Our complete submission guidelines and tutorials can be found on our website at www.cyberageadventures.com. The most common error that we see in writers' submissions is not following these guidelines closely enough. Beyond that, we strongly recommend that you actually read our magazine before submitting. The most important thing to realize is that there is no such thing as a superhero story. There is only a story with superheroes in it. If you understand the distinction, you've got a good shot at getting published with us."

GFN.com
111 Broadway, 12th floor, New York NY 10006. (212)349-1659. Fax: (212)349-6100. E-mail for submissions: editor@gfn.com. "The leading online news site of financial and business news tailored to the gay and lesbian community." Estab. April 1998. **60% freelance written.** Circ. 750,000. Pays on publication. Byline given. "Prefers exclusive rights, but not necessary." Accepts simultaneous and previously published submissions.
Editorial Needs: All articles must have a clear gay and lesbian p.o.v.: Business and finance pieces, legal issues, tax

articles, gay parenting/adoption, book excerpts/reviews, gay/lesbian health issues, personal experience, technology. Query. Length: 700-1,000 words. **Pays $75-500.**
Photos/Art/Graphics: State availability of photos with submission. No additional payment.

GORP.com, Great Outdoor Recreation Pages, www.gorp.com

22 West 19th St., 8th Floor, New York NY 10011 (212)675-6555. Fax: (212)675-8114. E-mail for queries: roba@gorp.com. Bryan Oettel, managing editor. **Contact:** Rob Andrejewski, editor. **33% freelance written.** "GORP is the Web's core resource for information on outdoor recreation and adventure travel. We are dedicated to providing our readers with practical information on outdoor destinations and activities while highlighting the gear and skills that make exploring nature more enjoyable. We publish articles on hiking, biking, paddling, fishing, camping, scenic driving, climbing, trekking, and other aspects of outdoor recreation and active travel." Estab. January 1995. Circ. 4 million. **Pays on acceptance.** Byline given. Buys nonexclusive, permanent electronic rights. Accepts simultaneous and previously published submissions. Responds in 10 weeks to queries and mss. Due to the volume of submissions, not all queries are answered.
Editorial Needs: Active travel, as described above. Query with published clips, or send complete ms. Length: 1,000-3,000 words. **Pays $100-300 and up.**
Photos/Art: State availability of photos with submission. Requires captions, identification of subjects. Buys nonexclusive permanent electronic rights.
Tips: See www.gorp.com/gorp/freelance/guide.htm for the whole story.

GOWANUS: An International Online Journal of Idea & Observation, www.gowanusbooks.com

473 17th St. #6, Brooklyn NY 11215-6226. (718)965-3756. E-mail for submissions: tom@gowanusbooks.com. Publisher: Thomas J. Hubschman. **75% freelance written.** "Gowanus is primarily a vehicle for writers in Third World countries. Emphasis is on the personal point of view, though all prose forms are welcome: essay, article, short story. Our readers are worldwide." Estab. June 1997. Circ. in the thousands. Pays on publication. Byline given. Buys electronic publication and archiving, plus one-time print rights (such as in an anthology). Print anthology scheduled for publication June, 2001. Accepts simultaneous and previously published submissions (all assuming copyright is the author's). Responds in days to queries, weeks to mss.
Editorial Needs: Short stories, essays, book excerpts. Articles/personal essays about politics and culture in the author's home country/region; reviews of books and indigenous periodicals. Query for nonfiction; send complete ms for fiction. Length 1,000-4,000 words. **Pays $15-25.**
Photos/Art: State availability of photos with submission. Negotiates payment individually. Requires identification of subjects. Buys same rights as on mss.
Tips: "As always, the best guidelines come from reading the publication itself. We deal with writers whose first language frequently is not English. If the submission is a good one and appropriate to the publication, we do in-depth work to help the author realize her or his idea/story. Most common mistake made by submitters: Sending inappropriate material because they have not actually read the publication but are attracted by the fact that we are a paying market." See www.gowanusbooks.com/response.htm for more information.

NATIONALGEOGRAPHIC.COM, www.nationalgeographic.com

National Geographic Society, 1145 17th St. NW, Washington DC 20036. (202)857-7000. E-mail for queries only ("unsolicited submissions are not welcome"): editor@nationalgeographic.com. **Contact:** Ted Chamberlain, senior writer/editor. **20% freelance written.** This market describes itself as "interactive features, photo galleries, forums, news site, education site, travel, NG store, maps, promotion and editorial content for NGM, World, Traveler, Adventure, Books, TV." Estab. June 1996. Circ. 3.5 million. **Pays on acceptance.** Byline given.
Editorial Needs: Book excerpts, entertainment, essays, health/ fitness, general interest,historical, interview, music, new product, personal experience, technology, travel, sports. Query with published clips. Length: depends on the type of feature. **Pays 30¢-$1/word; "varies according to type of article and writer's experience. Range is more or less."** Sometimes pays expenses of writers on assignment.
Photos/Art: State availability of photos with submission or send photos with submission. Requires captions, model releases, identification of subjects.
Tips: "Let me reiterate, we do not encourage unsolicited [submissions]. Queries may be addressed to editor@nationalgeographic.com."

RECURSIVE ANGEL, www.recursiveangel.com

Aslan Enterprises, 25 Acacia Dr., Hopewell NY 12533. (845)223- 4831. E-mail for administration: David Sutherland at dsutherland@calldei.com. E-mail for poetry submissions: Gene Doty at gdoty@umr.edu. E-mail for fiction submissions: Paul Kloppenborg at paulk@library.lib.rmit.edu.au. E-mail for art submissions: recangel@calldei.com. Managing Editor: David Hunter Sutherland. **100% freelance written.** "*Recursive Angel* is one of the first creative writing/arts publications to have made its presence on the Internet. We feature cutting-edge fiction, poetry, and art, and have received noteworthy commentary from the New York Times on the Web, *The Boston Review*, *Poets & Writers*, and many others. Our goal is to continue to find and publish the best new writers of today and tomorrow." Estab. October 1991. Circ. 16,000. Pays on publication. Buys first rights. Accepts simultaneous submissions. Responds in 1 month to queries and mss.
Editorial Needs: Fiction, poetry, art. Send complete ms. Sometimes pays the expenses of writers on assignment. Length: fiction, 1,500 words; poetry, 40 lines maximum; art, size varies. **Pays $10/poem; $15 poetry w/RealAudio**

recording; $15/piece fiction; art negotiated at time of acceptance (minimum $30). "Oh, and of course you can check our pay rates out at www.RecursiveAngel.com/pay.htm."

Photos/Art: State availability of photos with submission. Negotiates payment individually. Requires identification of subjects. Buys one-time rights.

Tips: "It can't be overstated that future contributors should follow the guidelines to a T. This, in essence, increases the chances of having the work properly read and reviewed."

SALON, www.salon.com

Salon Internet, Inc., 22 Fourth St, 16th Floor, San Francisco CA 94103. Fax: (415)645-9204. E-mail for queries: See www.salon.com/about/staff/index.html for email addresses of each section editor. Laura Miller, New York editorial director. **50% freelance written.** "Every day, Salon publishes stories about books, arts, entertainment, politics, and society. Featuring original reviews, interviews, and commentary on topics ranging from technology and travel to parenting and sex." Estab. November 1995. Circ. 300,000. Pays on publication. Byline given. Purchases exclusive rights for 60 days from the date of the initial publication, unless otherwise negotiated. Editorial lead time varies. Responds in 3 weeks to mss.

Editorial Needs: Book excerpts, health, family, academia, humor, personal experience, essays, expose, interview/profile, religious, general interest, technical, opinion, travel, high-tech, politics, media, news-related, book reviews, music reviews. Length: 500-2,000 words. Query with published clips. **Pays $100-1000 for assigned articles**. Sometimes pays expenses of writers on assignment.

Photos/Art: State availability of photos with submission. Reviews prints. Pays $25-75/photo. Captions, model releases, identification of subjects required. Buys one-time rights.

Tips: "Additional information on how to query or submit articles is available at www.salon.com/contact/submissions/ . For subjects covered, you ought to visit that page on the site and check out the masthead (www.salon.com/about/staff/index.html) to find out what we publish and who edits it. Salon is in perpetual flux, with new sections starting and others being cut all the time."

TRIP.com, Newsstand Section, www.trip.com/completetraveler

6436 S. Racine Circle, Englewood CO 80111. (303)790-9360. Fax: (303)790-9350. E-mail for queries: editor@TRIP.com. **Contact:** Chris Martin, newsletter editor. Newsletter and NewsStand content primarily addresses travel and travel-related issues of the mobile professional market, whether traveling for business or pleasure. Estab. September 1996. Pays on publication. Byline given. Buys online and offline (negotiable) rights.

Editorial Needs: Business and leisure travel. Query with published clips. Length: 800 words. **Payment varies.**

WOMEN.COM, www.women.com

Women.Com Networks, Inc., 1820 Gateway Dr., Suite 200, San Mateo CA 94404. E-mail for queries: editor@women.com. Lisa Stone, editor-in-chief, Channels; Steven Wagner, editor-in-chief, Magazines. **30% freelance written.** "Women.com is the leading online network for women. It includes 18 channels, including Career, Entertainment, Money, Small Business, Travel, Weddings, plus 12 magazine sites, including *Cosmopolitan*, *Redbook*, and *Prevention*. Updated daily." Estab. August 1995. Circ. 9.3 million. **Pays on acceptance.** Byline given sometimes. Buys all rights. Editorial lead time is 3 months. Responds in a few weeks to queries. "Unsolicited manuscripts not accepted."

Editorial Needs: Personal experience (first-person Op-Eds), essays, interview/profile (female movers and shakers, celebrity and otherwise), general interest (features). No long articles. Query with published clips. Length: 300-1,000 words. **Negotiates payment individually.**

Tips: "Be sure to visit Women.com at www.women.com before you make any queries. See what kinds of things are featured already. When pitching an idea, make Web-specific suggestions, i.e., about how you'd lay it out or illustrate it, how it's interactive. Think very visually about your piece. Note that unsolicited manuscripts are not accepted. And note that Women.com is flooded with inquiries; editors look for published writers who have written for national publications and who have Web experience, great clips, and original ideas."

WRITING FOR DOLLARS!, www.writingfordollars.com

AWOC.COM, PMB 225, 2436 S I-35E, Suite 376, Denton TX 76205. E-mail for queries: editor@writingfordollars.com. **Contact:** Dan Case, editor. **95% freelance written.** "Writing for Dollars! is a free, monthly newsletter for writers who want to start selling their work or to increase their present writing income. How to sell to specific markets, interviews with successful writers, and new ways to make money as a writer are some of the themes in each issue. WFD is distributed by e-mail. Back issues can be found at www.writingfordollars.com." Estab. December 1997. Circ. 20,000. **Pays on acceptance.** Byline given. Buys exclusive first-use one-time rights in the e-mail newsletter, Writing for Dollars!, after which AWOC.COM retains the nonexclusive right to archive and display the article online on its website. Responds in 1 week by e-mail, 6 weeks by snail mail to queries and mss.

Editorial Needs: Book excerpts, how-to, interview. Query. Length: 500-1,000 words. **Pays $15.**

Tips: "To subscribe for free, send a message to subscribe@writingfordollars.com. Contact editor@writingfordollars.com for our writers' guidelines by e-mail. We prefer to be queried by e-mail. Read a few back issues at www.writingfordollars.com and the writers' guidelines before you query. We rarely buy unsolicited manuscripts. Do yourself a favor and query us with your idea before you write the article. We can help you get the right slant. We don't do articles on 'How to Overcome Writer's Block,' or 'How I Got Shafted by XYZ Magazine.' The most common reasons for rejection is 'not the right subject or slant' and 'not the correct number of words' (500-1,000)."

Protecting Your Electronic Rights, Online and Off

BY MOIRA ANDERSON ALLEN

The summer of 2001 may prove critical to writers' efforts to control the electronic distribution of their work. Two ongoing lawsuits (neither of which are likely to be resolved by the time this goes to print) have the potential to radically change the way electronic rights are handled. The *Tasini v. New York Times* lawsuit could have a profound impact on the use of electronic rights by periodicals; the *Random House v. Rosetta Books* lawsuit could have an equally profound effect on the electronic rights that can be claimed by book publishers.

The Tasini lawsuit, originally filed in 1993, seeks to bar publishers from reusing or reselling print articles in electronic format, unless the publisher has specifically obtained electronic rights. In particular, it addresses the issue of selling such material to online databases. The original decision (in 1997) went against the plaintiffs, but was overturned on appeal in 1999, and the case is now before the Supreme Court.

In 2001, Random House sued e-publisher Rosetta Books for publishing several titles originally issued in print by Random House. Random House claims the right to issue those works in any "book format"—print or electronic—even though the original contracts did not mention "electronic" rights. Rosetta Books contests that when the contracts were written, e-books did not exist and had not been foreseen, and were therefore not covered by the term "book." At stake in this suit is nothing less than the definition of what constitutes a "book"—its format, or its content—and whether electronic rights can be claimed by a publisher even when they are not explicitly mentioned.

Even if these cases are settled in "favor" of writers, that doesn't mean writers will benefit. Scores of publishers reacted to the Tasini case by demanding all rights instead of the more traditional "First North American Serial Rights (FNASR)," and some even imposed retroactive contracts, demanding all rights not only to future contributions but to materials previously purchased and published.

In this quickly shifting arena, an author's only defense is knowledge and vigilance. Before you sign a contract, be sure you know what rights you're granting—and how that may affect your control of your material.

E-RIGHTS AND PERIODICALS

Rare is the U.S. print publication that does not have a Web presence, even if it's only a subscription page. Many magazines post representative articles from each issue; others post their entire contents; still others offer content not available in the print edition. Hundreds of U.S. newspapers post each day's edition online. Many publications archive material online indefinitely.

Equally rare, therefore, is the U.S. print publication that does not seek some license of elec-

---

MOIRA ANDERSON ALLEN *is the author of* Writing.com: Creative Internet Strategies to Advance Your Internet Career *(Allworth Press, 1999) and* The Writer's Guide to Queries, Pitches and Proposals *(Allworth Press, 2001). She has been writing and editing for more than 20 years, and currently hosts a website and e-mail newsletter for writers at www.writing-world.com.*

tronic rights. Some ask only for what they plan to use; others, however, attempt to grab as many e-rights as they can. Increasingly, writers find themselves facing complex, multi-page contracts written in dense legalese—and inflexible editors who refuse to negotiate.

Most electronic publications are less demanding. Very few electronic publications have a print edition—so most e-zines, e-mail newsletters and "content" sites don't ask for print rights. Some, however, impose a generic exclusivity clause that prevents you from republishing the material anywhere for a period of time, or a "first rights" clause that precludes you from publishing the material in print before it appears electronically. Both print and electronic publications tend to treat previously published material as a reprint, regardless of the medium in which it "first" appeared.

Print and electronic publications are still struggling to develop a "standard" language for electronic rights. Following are some of the terms you're most likely to see in contracts from either medium:

- **First electronic rights**. This frees you to sell reprints in any medium, once the material is initially published.
- **One-time electronic rights**. While this term doesn't specify any time-limit on a publication's use of your material, it does free you to market your work elsewhere.
- **Nonexclusive electronic rights**. This enables you to reuse your material electronically at any time. Most publications ask for such rights either in perpetuity, or "indefinitely."
- **Exclusive electronic rights for (term)**. Often, a publisher will ask for a period of exclusivity (usually three to six months), followed by the nonexclusive right to archive your material indefinitely.
- **Archival rights**. Many print publications, and most electronic publications, expect to archive material online indefinitely or in perpetuity. Make sure this request is "nonexclusive."
- **First/exclusive worldwide electronic rights**. Since "FNASR" has little meaning online, many publications are using a clause that reflects the international nature of electronic publication.

Beware of the following terms:

- **The nonexclusive right to reproduce and distribute the article online or on microfilm, microfiche, electronic databases, CD-ROM, and any other similar system now existing or hereafter developed**. This sounds fairly innocent, but actually grants a publisher the right to distribute and *sell* your material to and through other electronic venues. For example, this clause entitles a publication to sell your work to an electronic database, which can then offer it for sale to the public—and you'll never receive a penny from either transaction.
- **First North American Serial Rights, which includes the right to use the material online**. Some publishers try to sneak electronic rights into the FNASR clause, by claiming that this clause "includes" electronic rights. It does not. The 1997 Tasini decision established that "first" does not mean "first in any medium," and that each medium must be treated separately with respect to "first use."
- **Exclusive worldwide online and multimedia rights**. This is another way of saying "all electronic rights," and enables a publisher to distribute your work in any electronic format, including CD-ROM, electronic database, etc.—while precluding you from reusing the material in any electronic medium.

What you sell today influences what you can sell tomorrow. If, for example, you license "all" electronic rights to one print periodical, you may lose the ability to sell a reprint to another print publication that also wants some form of e-rights—and you'll lose entirely your ability to sell the same material to an e-zine (or even to post it on your own website).

E-RIGHTS AND BOOKS

Just a few years ago, print publishers didn't consider electronic rights terribly important. Today, you'll be hard-pressed to find a publisher who isn't intent on locking up those rights as tightly as possible. Since it's now virtually impossible to retain those rights, the key is to determine the terms under which they are licensed.

The Random House/Rosetta Books debate over what constitutes a "book" may have far-reaching implications. If the term "book" can apply to any format, publishers may gain greater leeway in how they compensate writers for such rights. If, for example, an e-book is considered "just the same" as a print book, authors may be offered the same royalties for print and electronic editions—despite the vast differences in format, costs, and distribution channels. (It should be noted that Random House currently offers the highest electronic royalties of any mainstream commercial publisher.)

One way to avoid this is to ensure that electronic rights are listed under "subsidiary rights," for which an author usually receives 50 percent of revenues. It's also important to try to define, as narrowly as possible, just what is meant by "electronic rights"—and avoid terms that grant rights to "all mechanisms currently known or hereafter to be invented."

Another important consideration is the "reversion" clause. This clause enables an author to reclaim rights to a book after it has gone out of print. If a book is also issued in electronic and/or print-on-demand editions, however, a publisher may claim that it is never "out of print." One way to handle this is to negotiate a minimum annual sales figure, and stipulate a reversion of rights when combined sales of all editions of the book fall below that figure.

Unlike print publishers, many electronic publishers (including print-on-demand and electronic subsidy publishers) are known for their author-friendly contracts. Most claim no print rights, and many will even release an author from a contract on as little as a month's notice if the author finds a print publisher for the book. E-publishing contracts are usually time-limited and renewable, rather than relying on "out of print reversion" clauses.

There are plenty of sharks cruising the e-publishing waters, however. Following are some contract terms that are definite warning flags:

- **Low royalties**. E-publishing and print-on-demand royalties range anywhere from 35-70 percent, so be wary of any e-publisher who tries to claim that royalties of 10-15 percent are "industry standard." Such royalties are standard only for print books, not for e-books.
- **Claims to non-electronic rights**. Most e-publishers don't have any means to exploit anything other than electronic rights, so be wary of any publisher who tries to claim "subsidiary" rights (such as movie rights, translation rights, audio-book rights, or even print rights).
- **A long-term or indefinite contract**. Most e-publishers issue one- to three-year contracts, which can be renewed or cancelled by either party. Many also include clauses whereby an author can cancel the contract before its term has expired. Be wary, therefore, of anyone who attempts to lock up rights for a longer period of time, such as seven to ten years—or worse, "in perpetuity."
- **Claims to copyright**. As the author, you should retain copyright. An e-publisher should not acquire the right to modify the work, publish it in part, publish it as part of a collection of other works, or publish derivative works, without your permission.
- **Claims to monies from other rights sales**. If a publisher doesn't own a particular set of rights, it should derive no income from the sale of those rights. Never sign a contract that grants your publisher a share of revenue from rights that you retain!
- **Claims to earnings after a contract has been terminated**. When a contract is over, it's over. Don't accept a contract that grants an e-publisher ongoing revenues from sales of your book (in any format) after the contract itself has been terminated.
- **Hidden costs**. If a publisher claims to be non-subsidy, make sure you won't be charged

for any "extra" services, such as editing, proofreading, cover design, pages over a certain base number, etc.

If you find any of these danger areas in a contract, don't try to negotiate them away. Instead, continue your search for a more reputable publisher who isn't trying to take advantage of you in the first place.

Electronic rights can be a minefield for the unwary. Understanding the issues and terminology involved won't protect you from every rights-hungry publisher—but it will at least help you recognize where the mines are buried!

Publishing on the web: Marketing makes all the difference

If you had told M.J. Rose a few years ago she'd have three novels published by Pocket Books, a nonfiction title published by St. Martin's, and be recognized as an Internet self-publishing pioneer, she most likely would have laughed in disbelief. But thanks to a combination of solid writing, marketing savvy, and the power of the Internet, Rose has indeed accomplished all of the above, and it all started with her decision to self-publish her second novel, *Lip Service*.

M.J. Rose

Rose was a New York advertising executive with two unpublished novels under her belt, and had an agent actively shopping *Lip Service*. Every time a publisher expressed an interest, the marketing department would reject it because they found Rose's smart mix of romance, erotica and suspense too hard to categorize, and therefore, too hard to market. After a while, Rose decided it was time to take matters into her own hands. "I got frustrated," she says, "and decided to write a nonfiction book, and break through that way. The nonfiction book required Web research, and while doing research I realized that the Web was an incredible marketing tool."

Rose decided to put *Lip Service* on the Web, with the goal of self-publishing and marketing it online "and get maybe 2,000 copies," she says. "Then my agent could go back to a publisher and say, 'Look, this is how to market her stuff. She's showing you how to do it.' So I got a website and I did a cover for the book." She set it up as an electronic download along with a photocopied version of the book for sale. "I had the e-book and the print book on the website, but nobody was buying it because nobody knew it existed. It took me about six months to figure out how to market it, so in the first six months I sold only 150 copies. But once the marketing effort got under way, I sold 1,500 copies."

To Rose's surprise, for every one person who wanted to download the book, ten more wanted to buy the photocopied version. Since she couldn't keep up with the demand, she had 3,000 copies of the book printed and sold them on the website. And soon after, Pocket Books came calling, offering Rose a deal to publish *Lip Service* in a traditional hardcover version.

After the publication of *Lip Service*, Rose was interviewed in business magazines such as *Forbes* and *Business 2.0*, as well as mainstream news magazines like *Time*, as being a poster child for the power of Internet self-publishing. And with the recent influx of new e-publishers all over the Web, her story could very well be any writer's story. But Rose cautions writers not to think of the Internet as a sure way to get published. "Getting your work up on the Internet is really easy," she says. "But how you get people to the work is where the real challenge is.

And unfortunately the challenge has gotten exponentially harder, because by the end of 2001, there will be more than 100,000 books available [on the Web] that were previously unpublished. If there are all those titles, how are you going to get readers to know you exist? So the marketing challenge becomes even greater. It will come down to how clever you can be at marketing your book."

Rose is definitely talking from experience, and that experience led her to write *How to Publish and Promote Online* with Angela Adair-Hoy (who has written several how-to books for freelance writers and self-published authors herself), published by St. Martin's in both print and electronic versions. Self-published on the Web and then picked up by a major publisher, *How to Publish and Promote Online* covers all aspects of self-publishing on the Internet, with inside information on public relations and advertising, e-publishers, self-promotion, cover design—basically, everything a writer needs to know to become self-published on the Internet.

But just posting your book on the Internet doesn't guarantee success. Rose encourages writers to make sure their books are in the best possible shape before even thinking about self-publishing. "The marketplace is so competitive," she says, "and to go out there with your book not being the best book it can be is not making the best use of your time. Anything you can do to get to an agent with the best book you can is beneficial." With *Lip Service*, Rose found the best freelance book editor she could find in New York to help polish her prose. "I did freelance jobs to make enough money to hire a book editor," she says. "I know no author has money, but everyone can get another job. You can't just sit in your room and think that all the work is the book. The most important work is the book, but then there's all the work after the book."

Ever since the publication of *Lip Service*, there's been no rest for Rose. She just sold another novel, *In Fidelity*, to Pocket Books; an excerpt from *Lip Service* was chosen to appear in the *Best American Erotica 2001*; and she's currently working on her third novel. "I was recently interviewed for *Time* magazine," Rose says, "and I'm standing in Central Park having my photograph taken when I realize it was exactly one year ago that I sold *Lip Service*, that started all this. And I thought, in one year, four titles have been sold and all this press and all this stuff has happened—I had no idea. I was three months away from going back into advertising because I had to make a living. I had gone through whatever money I had saved to get to that point and I was ready to give up. I think that's why it happened. It wasn't my goal; my goal was to get a few people to read *Lip Service*."

Even with all the excitement about e-publishing being the next big revolution for writers, there is one thing that Rose agrees will never change about the book publishing business. "You have to write a really, really good book, and I don't think that's ever going to change," she says. "There are no shortcuts to a good book."

—*Cindy Laufenberg*

The Business of Writing

Minding the Details

Writers who have had some success in placing their work know that the effort to publish requires an entirely different set of skills than does the act of writing. A shift in perspective is required when you move from creating your work to selling it. Like it or not, successful writers—*career* writers—have to keep the business side of the writing business in mind as they work.

Each of the following sections discusses a writing business topic that affects anyone selling his writing. We'll take a look at contracts and agreements—the documents that license a publisher to use your work. We'll consider your rights as a writer and sort out some potentially confusing terminology. We'll cover the basics of copyright protection—a topic of perennial concern for writers. And for those of you who are already making money with your writing, we'll offer some tips for keeping track of financial matters and staying on top of your tax liabilities.

Our treatment of the business topics that follow is necessarily limited. Look for complete information on each subject at your local bookstore or library—both in books (some of which we mention) and periodicals aimed at writers. Information is also available from the federal government, as indicated later in this article.

CONTRACTS AND AGREEMENTS

If you've been freelancing even a short time, you know that contracts and agreements vary considerably from one publisher to another. Some magazine editors work only by verbal agreement; others have elaborate documents you must sign in triplicate and return before you begin the assignment. As you evaluate any contract or agreement, consider carefully what you stand to gain and lose by signing. Did you have another sale in mind that selling all rights the first time will negate? Does the agreement provide the publisher with a number of add-ons (electronic rights, advertising rights, reprint rights, etc.) for which they won't have to pay you again?

In contract negotiations, the writer is usually interested in licensing the work for a particular use but limiting the publisher's ability to make other uses of the work in the future. It's in the publisher's best interest, however, to secure rights to use the work in as many ways as possible, both now and later on. Those are the basic positions of each party. The negotiation is a process of compromise and capitulation on questions relating to those basic points—and the amount of compensation to be given the writer for his work.

A contract is rarely a take-it-or-leave-it proposition. If an editor tells you that his company will allow *no* changes on the contract, you will then have to decide how important the assignment is to you. But most editors are open to negotiation, and you should learn to compromise on points that don't matter to you while maintaining your stand on things that do.

When it's not specified, most writers assume that a magazine publisher is buying first rights. Some writers' groups can supply you with a sample magazine contract to use when the publisher doesn't supply one, so you can document your agreement in writing. Members of The Authors

Guild are given a sample book contract and information about negotiating when they join. For more information about contracts and agreements, see *Business and Legal Forms for Authors & Self-Publishers*, by Tad Crawford (Allworth Press, 1990); *From Printout to Published*, by Michael Seidman (Carroll & Graf, 1992) or *The Writer's Guide to Contract Negotiations*, by Richard Balkin (Writer's Digest Books, 1985), which is out of print but should be available in libraries.

RIGHTS AND THE WRITER

A creative work can be used in many different ways. As the originator of written works, you enjoy full control over how those works are used; you are in charge of the rights that your creative works are "born" with. When you agree to have your work published, you are giving the publisher the right to use your work in one or more ways. Whether that right is simply to publish the work for the first time in a periodical or to publish it as many times as he likes and in whatever form he likes is up to you—it all depends on the terms of the contract or agreement the two of you arrive at. As a general rule, the more rights you license away, the less control you have over your work and the more money you should be paid for the license. We find that writers and editors sometimes define rights in different ways. For a classification of terms, read Types of Rights, below.

Sometimes editors don't take the time to specify the rights they are buying. If you sense that an editor is interested in getting stories but doesn't seem to know what his and the writer's responsibilities are regarding rights, be wary. In such a case, you'll want to explain what rights you're offering (preferably one-time or first serial rights only) and that you expect additional payment for subsequent use of your work.

You should strive to keep as many rights to your work as you can from the outset, otherwise, your attempts to resell your writing may be seriously hampered.

The Copyright Law that went into effect January 1, 1978, said writers were primarily selling one-time rights to their work unless they—and the publisher—agreed otherwise in writing. Book rights are covered fully by the contract between the writer and the book publisher.

TYPES OF RIGHTS

- **First Serial Rights**—First serial rights means the writer offers a newspaper or magazine the right to publish the article, story or poem for the first time in any periodical. All other rights to the material remain with the writer. The qualifier "North American" is often added to this phrase to specify a geographical limit to the license.

    When material is excerpted from a book scheduled to be published and it appears in a magazine or newspaper prior to book publication, this is also called first serial rights.
- **One-Time Rights**—A periodical that licenses one-time rights to a work (also known as simultaneous rights) buys the *nonexclusive* right to publish the work once. That is, there is nothing to stop the author from selling the work to other publications at the same time. Simultaneous sales would typically be to periodicals without overlapping audiences.
- **Second Serial (Reprint) Rights**—This gives a newspaper or magazine the opportunity to print an article, poem or story after it has already appeared in another newspaper or magazine. Second serial rights are nonexclusive—that is, they can be licensed to more than one market.
- **All Rights**—This is just what it sounds like. If you license away all rights to your work, you forfeit the right to ever use it again. If you think you'll want to use the material later, you must avoid submitting to such markets or refuse payment and withdraw your material. Ask the editor whether he is willing to buy first rights instead of all rights before you agree to an assignment or sale. Some editors will reassign rights to a writer after a given period, such as one year. It's worth an inquiry in writing.
- **Electronic Rights**—These rights cover usage in a broad range of electronic media, from

online magazines and databases to CD-ROM magazine anthologies and interactive games. The magazine contract should specify if—and which—electronic rights are included. The presumption is that unspecified rights are kept by the writer.

- **Subsidiary Rights**—These are the rights, other than book publication rights, that should be covered in a book contract. These may include various serial rights; movie, television, audiotape and other electronic rights; translation rights, etc. The book contract should specify who controls these rights (author or publisher) and what percentage of sales from the licensing of these sub rights goes to the author.

- **Dramatic, Television and Motion Picture Rights**—This means the writer is selling his material for use on the stage, in television or in the movies. Often a one-year option to buy such rights is offered (generally for 10 percent of the total price). The interested party then tries to sell the idea to other people—actors, directors, studios or television networks, etc. Some properties are optioned over and over again, but most fail to become dramatic productions. In such cases, the writer can sell his rights again and again—as long as there is interest in the material. Though dramatic, TV and motion picture rights are more important to the fiction writer than the nonfiction writer, producers today are increasingly interested in nonfiction material; many biographies, topical books and true stories are being dramatized.

SELLING SUBSIDIARY RIGHTS

The primary right in the world of book publishing is the right to publish the book itself. All other rights (such as movie rights, audio rights, book club rights, electronic rights and foreign

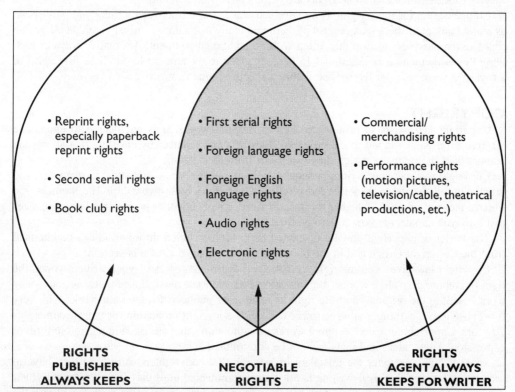

- Reprint rights, especially paperback reprint rights

- Second serial rights

- Book club rights

- First serial rights

- Foreign language rights

- Foreign English language rights

- Audio rights

- Electronic rights

- Commercial/ merchandising rights

- Performance rights (motion pictures, television/cable, theatrical productions, etc.)

RIGHTS PUBLISHER ALWAYS KEEPS

NEGOTIABLE RIGHTS

RIGHTS AGENT ALWAYS KEEPS FOR WRITER

Some subsidiary rights are always granted to the publisher. Some should always be retained by the author. The remainder are negotiable, and require knowledgeable advice from a literary agent or attorney in deciding whether it is more advantageous to grant them to the publisher or reserve them.

rights) are considered secondary, or subsidiary, to the right to print publication. In contract negotiations, authors and their agents traditionally try to avoid granting the publisher subsidiary rights that they feel capable of marketing themselves. Publishers, on the other hand, typically hope to obtain control over as many of the sub rights as they can. Philosophically speaking, subsidiary rights will be best served by being left in the hands of the person or organization most capable of—and interested in—exploiting them profitably. Sometimes that will be the author and her agent, and sometimes that will be the publisher.

Larger agencies have experience selling foreign rights, movie rights and the like, and many authors represented by such agents prefer to retain those rights and let their agents do the selling. Book publishers, on the other hand, have subsidiary rights departments, which are responsible for exploiting all sub rights the publisher was able to retain during the contract negotiation.

That job might begin with a push to sell foreign rights, which normally bring in advance money which is divided among author, agent and publisher. Further efforts then might be made to sell the right to publish the book as a paperback (although many book contracts now call for hard/soft deals, in which the original hardcover publisher buys the right to also publish the paperback version).

Any other rights which the publisher controls will be pursued, such as book clubs and magazines. Publishers usually don't control movie rights to a work, as those are most often retained by author and agent.

The marketing of electronic rights to a work, in this era of rapidly expanding capabilities and markets for electronic material, can be tricky. With the proliferation of electronic and multimedia formats, publishers, agents and authors are going to great pains these days to make sure contracts specify exactly *which* electronic rights are being conveyed (or retained).

Compensation for these rights is a major source of conflict between writers and publishers, as many book publishers seek control of them and many magazines routinely include electronic rights in the purchase of all rights, often with no additional payment. Alternative ways of handling this issue include an additional 15 percent added to the amount to purchase first rights to a royalty system or a flat fee for use within a specified time frame, usually one year.

COPYRIGHT

Copyright law exists to protect creators of original works. It is engineered to encourage creative expression and aid in the progress of the arts and sciences by ensuring that artists and authors hold the rights by which they can profit from their labors.

Copyright protects your writing, unequivocally recognizes you (its creator) as its owner, and grants you all the rights, benefits and privileges that come with ownership. The moment you finish a piece of writing—whether it is a short story, article, novel or poem—the law recognizes that only you can decide how it is to be used.

The basics of copyright law are discussed here. More detailed information can be obtained from the Copyright Office and in the books mentioned at the end of this section.

Copyright law gives you the right to make and distribute copies of your written works, the right to prepare derivative works (dramatizations, translations, musical arrangements, etc.—any work based on the original) and the right to perform or publicly display your work. With very few exceptions, anything you write today will enjoy copyright protection for your lifetime plus 70 years. Copyright protects "original works of authorship" that are fixed in a tangible form of expression. Titles, ideas and facts can *not* be copyrighted.

Some people are under the mistaken impression that copyright is something they have to send away for, and that their writing is not properly protected until they have "received" their copyright from the government. The fact is, you don't have to register your work with the Copyright Office in order for your work to be copyrighted; any piece of writing is copyrighted the moment it is put to paper. Registration of your work does, however, offer some additional protection (specifically, the possibility of recovering punitive damages in an infringement suit) as well as legal proof of the date of copyright.

Registration is a matter of filling out an application form (for writers, that's generally Form TX) and sending the completed form, a nonreturnable copy of the work in question and a check for $30 to the Library of Congress, Copyright Office, Register of Copyrights, 101 Independence Ave. SE, Washington DC 20559-6000. If the thought of paying $30 each to register every piece you write does not appeal to you, you can cut costs by registering a group of your works with one form, under one title for one $30 fee.

Most magazines are registered with the Copyright Office as single collective entities themselves; that is, the individual works that make up the magazine are *not* copyrighted individually in the names of the authors. You'll need to register your article yourself if you wish to have the additional protection of copyright registration. It's always a good idea to ask that your notice of copyright (your name, the year of first publication, and the copyright symbol ©) be appended to any published version of your work. You may use the copyright notice regardless of whether or not your work has been registered.

One thing writers need to be wary of is "work for hire" arrangements. If you sign an agreement stipulating that your writing will be done as work for hire, you will not control the copyright of the completed work—the person or organization who hired you will be the copyright owner. Work for hire arrangements and transfers of exclusive rights must be in writing to be legal, but it's a good idea to get every publishing agreement in writing before the sale.

You can obtain more information about copyright from the Copyright Office, Library of Congress, Washington DC 20559. To get answers to specific questions about copyright, call the Copyright Public Information Office at (202)707-3000 weekdays between 8:30 a.m. and 5 p.m. eastern standard time. To order copyright forms by phone, call (202)707-9100. Forms can also be downloaded from the Library of Congress website at http://lcweb.loc.gov/copyright. The website also includes information on filling out the forms, general copyright information and links to other websites related to copyright issues. A thorough (and thoroughly enjoyable) discussion of the subject of copyright law as it applies to writers can be found in Stephen Fishman's *The Copyright Handbook: How to Protect and Use Written Works* (Nolo Press, 1994). A shorter but no less enlightening treatment is Ellen Kozak's *Every Writer's Guide to Copyright & Publishing Law* (Henry Holt, 1990).

FINANCES AND TAXES

As your writing business grows, so will your obligation to keep track of your writing-related finances and taxes. Keeping a close eye on these details will help you pay as little tax as possible and keep you apprised of the state of your freelance business. A writing business with no systematic way of tracking expenses and income will soon be no writing business at all. If you dislike handling finance-related tasks, you can always hire someone else to handle them for a fee. If you do employ a professional, you must still keep the original records with an eye to providing the professional with the appropriate information.

If you decide to handle these tasks yourself—or if you just want to know what to expect of the person you employ—consider these tips:

Accurate records are essential, and the easiest way to keep them is to separate your writing income and expenses from your personal ones. Most professionals find that separate checking accounts and credit cards help them provide the best and easiest records.

Get in the habit of recording every transaction (both expenses and earnings) related to your writing. You can start at any time; you don't need to begin on January 1. Because you're likely to have expenses before you have income, start keeping your records whenever you make your first purchase related to writing—such as this copy of *Writer's Market*.

Any system of tracking expenses and income will suffice, but the more detailed it is, the better. Be sure to describe each transaction clearly—including the date; the source of the income (or the vendor of your purchase); a description of what was sold or bought; whether the payment was by cash, check or credit card; and the amount of the transaction.

The other necessary component of your financial record-keeping system is an orderly way to store receipts related to your writing. Check stubs, receipts for cash purchases, credit card receipts and similar paperwork should all be kept as well as recorded in your ledger. Any good book about accounting for small business will offer specific suggestions for ways to track your finances.

Freelance writers, artists and photographers have a variety of concerns about taxes that employees don't have, including deductions, self-employment tax and home office credits. Many freelance expenses can be deducted in the year in which they are incurred (rather than having to be capitalized, or depreciated, over a period of years). For details, consult the IRS publications mentioned later.

There also is a home office deduction that can be claimed if an area in your home is used *exclusively* and *regularly* for business and you have no other fixed location where you conduct substantial activities for your business. Contact the IRS for information on requirements and limitations for this deduction. If your freelance income exceeds your expenses, regardless of the amount, you must declare that profit. If you make $400 or more after deductions, you must pay Social Security tax and file Schedule SE, a self-employment form, along with your Form 1040 and Schedule C tax forms.

While we cannot offer you tax advice or interpretations, we can suggest several sources for the most current information.

- Check the IRS website, http://www.irs.ustreas.gov/. Full of helpful tips and information, the site also provides instant access to important IRS forms and publications.
- Call your local IRS office. Look in the white pages of the telephone directory under U.S. Government—Internal Revenue Service. Someone will be able to respond to your request for IRS publications and tax forms or other information. Ask about the IRS Tele-tax service, a series of recorded messages you can hear by dialing on a touch-tone phone. If you need answers to complicated questions, ask to speak with a Taxpayer Service Specialist.
- Obtain the basic IRS publications. You can order them by phone or mail from any IRS office; most are available at libraries and some post offices. Start with *Your Federal Income Tax* (Publication 17) and *Tax Guide for Small Business* (Publication 334). These are both comprehensive, detailed guides—you'll need to find the regulations that apply to you and ignore the rest. There are many IRS publications relating to self-employment and taxes; Publication 334 lists many of these publications—such as *Business Use of Your Home* (Publication 587) and *Self-Employment Tax* (Publication 533).
- Consider other information sources. Many public libraries have detailed tax instructions available on tape. Some colleges and universities offer free assistance in preparing tax returns. And if you decide to consult a professional tax preparer, the fee is a deductible business expense on your tax return.

Breaking and Entering:
Public Relations Writing

BY JOHN CLAUSEN

I've heard many veteran reporters say that if the newspaper business ever became unbearable, they could always turn to public relations writing. This is usually said in a tone that implies the switch from journalist to publicist entails nothing more strenuous than a massive lowering of standards and a willingness to accept tons of money for "doing lunch."

This is patent nonsense of course. Writing for public relations is as demanding as any other kind of freelance writing—perhaps more so. For starters, you are not simply reporting the news and letting the chips fall where they may. You are writing for effect. You are attempting, through your writing, to make your client more successful. You have to put together story ideas and articles that do more than find a sympathetic editor. You have to come up with ideas and writing that please your client and still get recognized as a legitimate news or feature story. This can be more difficult than you anticipated.

It's best to approach the selling of your PR services as though you were a media consultant rather than a writer. That way, your experience as a reporter or freelance journalist becomes an asset rather than a liability. That's right, a liability. A lot of businesspeople have a profound distrust for anyone in the press, even freelancers. If they think you're more interested in journalism than in business, you won't get the job. They're much more likely to hire you if they think they're hiring an insider with major contacts. This does not mean that you have to kiss your journalistic ethics goodbye the day you sign up as a PR writer. It simply means that you will have to be conscious of your clients' attitudes and prejudices and work within them. Your value to your client is your experience in the world of assignment editors and hostile reporters. Your job is to help your client present his or her information to a sometimes skeptical audience of journalists. It's not your job to lie on behalf of your client or to mislead the press. If your client asks you to do anything unethical, you really have to decline. If the client persists, find a new client.

Clear, concise, accurate writing will benefit your client more than anything else. Your writing skills will be the most important when you are putting together press releases. This standby of the PR field attempts to do the same thing as a query letter—entice the editor. Make sure your information is correct and verifiable. Your headline has to attract attention and reveal what the story is all about. The information in the first paragraph must stand alone. In journalism this is what is called the inverted pyramid. In other words, the information in your press release begins with the most important and descends in importance. Here's an example of a press release I did for a local car dealership:

Note that the headline and the first paragraph tell the important parts of the story, while the rest of the piece fills in background and offers the clients a chance to utter a few self-serving

JOHN CLAUSEN *has published hundreds of articles in leading magazines and newspapers, including* Harper's *and* Rolling Stone. *He has edited numerous city magazines, worked as a freelance editor for McGraw-Hill, Time-Life Books, and others, written public relations and advertising copy, and runs his own freelance writing/editing service. For several years Clausen has published a writer's newsletter called* Writing for Money, *and is the author of* Too Lazy to Work, Too Nervous to Steal *(Writer's Digest Books).*

lines about customer service and the secret of his success. The -30- at the end is just a convention of newspaper people. It signifies "the end" and can also be expressed as ###.

Very little of a press release like this one will see publication. Editors will cut from the bottom and fit the piece into whatever space or format they feel is appropriate. Sometimes they don't print it at all. To overcome that problem, my client will sometimes buy advertising space and run his releases the way he wants them. Since this is considerably more expensive than sending out a press release, he does it sparingly and only when something at his dealership merits more elaborate exposure.

As a PR practitioner, you will also be called upon to write speeches, set up interviews, plan and execute events, plan overall media strategy and generally advise your client in the ways of the press.

PR services get sold much the same way as any other service. You have to make it happen. If you're working alone, you'll have to be the sales force, the writer, the media consultant and the janitor.

In my opinion, the best way to break into PR writing is to hire yourself first. Put together a media plan for your own company. If you can make yourself well known, there's a pretty good chance you can do the same for other clients. But how will you go about this?

First, place yourself as far as you can into the local circle of movers and shakers. Attend charity functions. Volunteer to help stage events and promotions for nonprofit organizations. Write guest editorials in the paper every chance you get. Write local news and feature stories even if they pay poorly. Getting your byline in front of the public is the important thing. Cultivate relationships with media folks. Let them know you're opening a PR shop and ask them how you can help them.

Figure out what companies you want to work for and go after their business. Make no secret of it. If you run into the CEO of your target company let him or her know how much you admire the work they do and how much you would appreciate an opportunity to help them publicize that good work. Make sure you have your business cards handy. Attend networking parties and chamber of commerce functions.

Whenever you land a new client, make sure you send out a press release to publicize your new business relationship. You'll have to get permission from your client, of course, before you send out the release. Most will be flattered that you consider their business newsworthy. Others may consider the press release just that much more publicity for them. You should encourage that line of thinking. Be aware, though, that a small number of your clients may consider their public relations efforts to be covert and ask you to refrain from publicizing your deal with them.

Most of all, be ready when you get the telephone call (and you will) from a potentially big client. Go to the meeting with a professional attitude. You're not there with your hat in your hand. You're there to help these people achieve better media relations. You are more valuable to them than you may imagine.

And one last thing: Make sure you charge enough. This goes beyond mere avarice. People in business, especially the people at the top of the local food chain, are used to dealing with people of means. They are not going to respect you if you come with a low-ball offer. Dream big. These folks have money and are willing to spend it lavishly if they think they are getting the best available. As a general range for projects such as press releases, catalog copywriting or event promotions, PR freelancers can earn $25 to $60/hour. Ad copywriting can bring $50 to $100/hour.

Of course, it's a fine thing to say "feel the top" and "charge enough," but how does a freelancer go about finding out what the top really is? I'm reminded of the *Austin Powers* film where Dr. Evil, who has been freeze-dried since the sixties, tells his minions that he is planning to hold the world ransom for "one million dollars." His minions squirm and finally tell him that his legitimate businesses are making billions all by themselves.

The trick, whether you are Dr. Evil or just a freelancer trying to maximize profits, is to find

For Immediate Release   Contact: Frank Glashan
March 4, 2000   Telephone: (828)555-5555

Hunter Chevrolet Names Randy McCrory
1999 Salesman of the Year

Hendersonville, NC-Randy McCrory has been named 1999 Salesman of the Year at Hunter Chevrolet, Volvo, Subaru and Hyundai.

Mr. McCrory, whose track record in customer satisfaction and sales volume prompted the award, is a retired mechanical engineer who worked for DuPont for twenty-two years.

His training in corporate management has helped him as an automobile salesman. "I try to keep a positive attitude with the objective of helping people," he said. "It's very easy for me to be professional with people because I have a professional background.

"I wasn't sure at first if I wanted to get into the car business, but then I interviewed at Hunter, and I came away impressed with the way they did business. Now I'd have to say that back in 1965 when I was starting college, if I'd known what I know now I probably would have skipped college and gone right into the car business. I love the business; it's the most fun I've ever had. Interesting people, never dull . . . no two sales are ever the same. Plus, I think I've helped a lot of people."

His customers apparently agree. Fully 50 percent of his sales come from referrals and repeat customers. "I work very hard," he said. "I try to be very diligent and take this as my own personal business."

Diligence is definitely the key to success, he explained. "I do a huge amount of follow-up. I have a file on every car I've ever sold. I communicate with my customers at least eight times during the year, mostly through telephone calls and follow-up mailings."

Mr. McCrory has two grown children and three grandchildren. He lives in Maggie Valley at the Ketner Inn & Farm, a bed and breakfast inn he bought in 1995.

Hunter Chevrolet, Volvo, Subaru and Hyundai, located at 9999 Acme Highway, offers new and used cars, service on all makes and models, a parts store, a body shop and a tire outlet. Mr. McCrory can be reached at (828)555-5555.

-30-

out what the going rate is and then nudge it up just a bit. You can do this in a covert fashion by calling up an ad agency and asking what they charge for copywriting. Or you can be upfront about the whole thing and simply call other copywriters and ask what they charge. People will usually help you if you ask them nicely.

You might also consider joining the local advertising and public relations club. Almost every city has one. They get together, talk about ad and PR issues and usually hold an annual awards dinner. Get to know your fellow copy scribes, and pretty soon you'll be swapping war stories and pricing info. You might even get some overflow work passed your way.

Once you've established your rates, make sure you keep track of the time you spend and the money you net. Don't be afraid to raise your prices if you're doing good work, the client is happy and you have plenty of assignments. Be proud of what you do—proud enough so that you don't feel awkward asking for fair compensation. You're providing a great service to somebody who can't do the work for himself. That's worth some money.

Some writers tell me they set a specific number of rewrites and revisions they will include with their bid. Any additional work, after those revisions have been spent, will be billed at an hourly rate. I suppose this is a good deal if you have a nitpicky client who likes to see copywriters squirm. However, I prefer to include all necessary revisions in the base price. It seems to me that the client is paying for a completed product, not for the process by which that product is produced. If the brochure is worth $5,000, then that's all the client should have to pay, no matter how much effort it takes on your part. Billing for revisions gives the whole deal a sort of open-ended feel that I wouldn't appreciate if I were the client.

Of course, that doesn't mean you should cave in every time you are challenged on a copy point. You are a professional hired to do a professional job. You deserve professional courtesy and a working environment free of petty harassment and game playing. With my 50 percent deposit up front, if the client becomes too obstreperous, I can always fire him or her and back away with at least some compensation. It's worth noting that, in the last 20 years, I've never had to do that.

So my basic point is this: Whether you're writing magazine pieces, press releases or handling any other freelance assignment, make sure both you and your client understand the ground rules completely—and that you can live with those rules.

Setting Your Sights on Syndicating Your Column

BY MONICA McCABE CARDOZA

For some, writing a column is a hobby and having it placed in a local newspaper for little or no compensation is satisfaction enough. For others, a national publication is their focus and a three-figure payment per column is their goal. Still others aspire to be picked up by a large national syndicate, appear in at least one hundred newspapers and quit their day job.

From my discussions with syndicated columnists, it would appear that the majority of aspiring columnists seem intent on accomplishing the latter goal. Unfortunately, few writers grasp the realities of syndication.

One columnist I interviewed told me of an aspiring columnist who called her for advice. The caller wanted to syndicate a column targeted to Generation Xers. Unfortunately, she had not yet written even a single column and had no idea of the economic realities of syndication. Sure, some writers of nationally syndicated columns may earn fifty thousand dollars or more a year, but most syndicated columnists earn much less. That said, before you set your sights on syndication, understand what it is and how it works.

In general, syndication, whether done by the columnist or by a syndicate, involves selling a column simultaneously to different newspapers or magazines, usually for a commission on the sale price. Syndicated columns are promoted and sold to publications that pay for them according to the size of their circulation. The larger the circulation, the more the publication pays. However, according to one self-syndicated columnist, circulation has become a less reliable predictor of payment. She says some of her biggest newspaper clients pay less than some of her small newspaper clients. If this columnist was represented by a syndicate, it would take a commission of 40 to 60 percent of the net proceeds of the column (gross receipts less the cost of salespeople, promotion, mailing, etc.).

SELF-SYNDICATION

Self-syndication is the starting point for most columnists. It involves submitting completed pieces to editors at publications that do not compete with the one in which you're already published. If your local paper runs your column, you probably couldn't sell it to the competing paper, unless your editor gave you the OK, in which case there would probably be certain restrictions, such as the competing paper cannot run your column until after it has appeared in the first paper. In any case, before selling your column to other publications, run the idea by your editor, who can quickly tell you the ground rules for selling to other publications. Also, expect that other editors will want the same sort of exclusivity.

Beyond selecting suitable publications for your work, a self-syndicated columnist is also responsible for promoting and selling the column idea, establishing payment rates and billing publications. It's a lot of work, involving tasks seemingly unrelated to the reason you started

MONICA McCABE CARDOZA *edited columns for six years for* The New York Times Syndicate, *working with writers such as Leo Buscaglia and Joyce Maynard across a variety of subjects, from relationships to the environment to Hollywood celebrities. She also has written numerous columns throughout her career, including an ongoing one for* Printing Manager.

writing columns in the first place. However, it ensures that the writer earns 100 percent of the proceeds.

Though self-syndication would seem a fairly straightforward endeavor, it's not. Jim Toler, a former United Media sales executive, opened his own syndicate, Toler Media Services, in 1997. In addition to representing six clients, including four columnists, he offers consulting for columnists interested in self-syndication.

Toler uses several criteria when considering whether to take on a consulting job: The columnist's material must be unique, it must fill a niche and it must be able to be localized. In addition, the columnist must have a fairly large ego. "A big part of my consulting is advising clients on various aspects of syndication, then turning them loose," says Toler. "They must be able to take rejection."

According to Toler, if a column is well written and meets the previous criteria, there is hope. "One thing you must make sure you're clear on is that this is not a get-rich-quick business," he says, "but a gut-grinding selling business."

One of Toler's clients echoes his sentiments. "It's a labor-intensive process," says self-syndicated columnist Azriela Jaffe. "It's basically a numbers game. I may be rejected nine times, but on the tenth time, I make a sale."

Jaffe, whose column *Advice from A-Z* offers guidance for the self-employed and home-based professional, says it's not necessarily what your column is about and whether it's well written—that's a given, she says. "It's about timing," she adds.

If you're lucky enough to get an editor on the phone, Jaffe recommends having a prepared description of your column that takes all of one minute to deliver, and delivering it in such a way that the editor knows you've done your homework. "You want to say something like: 'My name is Azriela Jaffe, and I'm known as the Ann Landers of the small business market. I write a small business column, and what's unique about it is that it focuses on the emotional and relationship concerns that small businesses have. I understand you have a Monday business section, and I believe my column would fit in well there.' "

She continues: "You don't want to say: 'I write a column, and everybody who reads it really loves it.' "

Jaffe adds that after three years of writing a column, she still needs to support herself with other freelance writing work. That's why she says you must think of column writing as a long-term process, one that may take as long as three to five years just to make a name for yourself.

Jaffe agrees with Toler's statement that columnists need to be able to take rejection. In fact, she feels it's so important that she's written a book on the topic: *Starting From "No": Ten Strategies to Overcome Your Fear of Rejection and Succeed in Business* (Upstart Publishing, 1999).

BEATING THE ODDS

Aspiring to be picked up by a syndicate is a lofty goal, one that requires a tremendous amount of skill, timing, persistence and even luck. According to an October 3, 1998 article, in *Editor & Publisher* magazine, the biggest syndicates receive seventy-five hundred to ten thousand submissions a year and sign fewer than ten of them.

Of the lucky few chosen for syndication, there's no guarantee it will last. Some syndicates are satisfied to have 50 percent of their new offerings stick around for at least five years. Sometimes the half-decade success rate is more like 30 percent. Columns are generally considered successful when they appear in 25 papers by their first anniversary.

Jim Toler explains that most large syndicates have systems in place to review column submissions and may acquire as many as one or two per quarter. Others may acquire far fewer. For example, the Washington Post Writers Group launched only about 20 features from 1990 to 1998, with about 75 percent of them still in syndication.

Syndicates that take on new columns often don't have the luxury of promoting them over the long term. According to one former salesperson, syndicate salespeople will push newspapers to carry the columns just taken on by the syndicate. But the next quarter, when one or two newer columns are taken on, the columns taken on the previous quarter get less promotion, and on and on until the columns selected the prior year hardly get a mention to editors.

One way to avoid becoming lost in the crowd is to hook up with a syndicate that specializes in a particular subject. If you write an automotive column, consider soliciting a syndicate that sells only columns about cars. Specialized syndicates tend to take on fewer columns than large newspaper syndicates and, therefore, can devote more attention to selling its columns.

If you think your column has international appeal, look for a syndicate that is involved overseas. Indeed, with fewer U.S. dailies, fewer multipaper markets (hence less bidding for columns) and smaller news holes, syndicates are going global, increasing international sales thanks in part to the Internet, which has made delivery to foreign papers easier and cheaper.

Syndicates are also selling more of their columns and features to online papers and other sites. While electronic sales represent the fastest-growing part of the syndicate business, in many cases syndicates charge online clients up to 80 percent less than print clients, reflecting the fact that many newspaper websites still are not profitable. However, considering that online sales constitute a business that barely existed six years ago, pursuing such a market now may ensure your success there later when these sites are making profits.

But newspaper websites aren't the only online entities buying columns. TV networks, radio stations, online magazines, associations and corporations are just a few of the other organizations with websites. These non-newspaper sites often have more revenue available for content and therefore tend to pay more for columns than newspaper websites.

Demand by non-newspaper websites for columns and other material is so strong that it has sparked the creation of companies syndicating exclusively to websites. One of these companies is iSyndicate, which delivers material to corporate, small business, e-commerce, media and other websites. Founded in 1996, the company amassed more than 17,500 clients just two years later. And while iSyndicate began by buying its columns from newspaper syndicates, as well as Web publishers and news services, it intends to eventually take on self-syndicated columnists. The company Web address is www.iSyndicate.com

Despite a market that's dominated by ten big and many small syndicates selling columns to a decreasing number of newspapers with less space available for columns, more syndicates continue to open, finding creative ways to bring well-written, informative material to new readers. Such activity should spark optimism in aspiring columnists. Rather than viewing the market as in decline, columnists must see it for all its opportunities. Indeed, if you can look outside the traditional means of syndication, you will find entirely new opportunities.

How Much Should I Charge?

BY LYNN WASNAK

If you are reading this article with serious intent, chances are you agree with Dr. Samuel Johnson when he said, "No man but a blockhead ever wrote except for money." He knew in the 1700s what we have to remind ourselves in the 21st century—while it is not at all easy to get rich being a writer, it is definitely possible to earn a living freelancing. You may not be able to afford that vacation home you dreamed of or the 30-foot yacht. But every year, real people not much different from you put food on the table, a roof overhead and even pay for the kids' dental bills with their freelance writing income.

This is said despite the well-established reality that writers in general are underpaid and, according to surveys conducted by the Author's Guild and others, writer's wages on the whole are stagnant or declining. Most recent information from the National Writers Union says only 15 percent of working writers make more than $30,000 annually. There is no doubt this is a problem, and writers need to band together through organizations such as the NWU, American Society of Journalists and Authors and others to rattle corporate cages everywhere and give professional writers more respect and more cash.

But we take the glass-is-half-full side of the argument here, because there is data from *Writer's Market*'s newest survey of freelance income that shows a substantial number of writers earn $30,000 to $40,000 and more (sometimes well into 6 figures) by freelance writing activities.

So how are some writers able to "make it" while others are stewing in credit card juice? The money-making writers have certain traits in common. Most are solid, experienced writers who spent some time learning their craft, either independently or as employees in PR departments, ad agencies, magazines, newspapers or book publishers. They have talent, they are reliable professionals who respect deadlines, and most of the better earners specialize in subjects or types of writing in which they have developed "insider" knowledge and expertise. There appears to be more money for more writers in business and technology markets (including advertising and PR) than there is in magazine or book publishing/editing, though some writers prefer the variety and/or prestige offered in traditional publishing arenas. For most freelancers, newspapers are not the way to go if income is a priority. However, they may be useful as a source of initial clips to promote work in better-paying markets, and they may be helpful to specialists or self-publishers who benefit from the publicity.

But the real difference between the haves and the have-nots among freelancers is sheer, unglamorous business savvy. In short, the money-earning freelancer puts effort into developing and refining all small business skills, especially the key element: marketing. There is reason to argue that writers' pay in general is low partly because so few writers care much about the business aspects of this occupation. In this, freelance writing is similar to other creative fields. Hobby artists, photographers, potters and musicians love what they're doing and get paid "hobby" rates, if at all. Professionals in those fields, if they also have good business sense, earn a living with what they do.

So let's assume you are an aspiring freelancer with fairly well-developed writing skills, or

---

LYNN WASNAK *has been a full-time freelancer for more than 20 years. She is intimately acquainted with the peaks, valleys and sinkholes of this fascinating business, and looks forward to making more mistakes (and learning from them) as time goes on.*

an active freelancer who wants to earn more or break into new areas. We'll also assume you would like to be (sooner rather than later) in that giddy realm of the NWU's top 15 percent who earn more than $30,000. The meat of this article is in the rates that follow (gleaned, as previously mentioned, from our survey participants and other writing income analysis). But before you get to the meat, let's tackle the bread-making ingredients of the freelance business.

WHERE THE JOBS ARE

Where do freelancers find their jobs? According to our survey participants, the top job-getter is a toss-up between networking with fellow writers and prior contact with the editor/writing buyer. Both score high. Other strong job leads come from e-mail and/or hard-copy queries, networking with businesses (through Chambers of Commerce and specialized industry meetings), and of course, *Writer's Market*, *Writer's Digest* and topic-specific publications such as *The Travelwriter Marketletter*. Some writers send samples and résumés out cold to potential clients, or do cold-calling on the phone to set up interviews or present samples. (Cold-calling is more acceptable among general business and technology firms than in magazine and book publishing.) Some writers have used direct mail self-promotions successfully, though others said they found it a waste of money.

Obviously, you'll want to stay abreast of developments in the particular industries that you focus on (or would like to enter). Book writers/editors find *Publishers Weekly* a must-read, and business writers of most every stripe will find possible stories or clients in *The Wall Street Journal*. (Both publications and many others have classified want ads that sometimes seek writing or creative talent.) If you have access to press events or conferences where editors and writers mingle, by all means take full advantage. Don't forget to carry a few samples along with your nicely printed brochure and business cards (you *do* have them, don't you?)

But whether or not you have access to the editorial party scene, don't miss the newest wave of writers' marketing opportunities on the Internet. If your freelance activities don't yet include a computer (you need this ASAP, plus fax machine, organized file cabinets etc.), visit your local library, log on and take a peek at websites such as http://www.inkspot.com. This site and several others provide information on both contract (freelance) and staff jobs for writers.

But by far, the most credible referrals for future jobs come about when a past client tells someone you're a top-notch writer. So as you do each assignment, even the most tedious, give your absolute best effort. That person you're writing for might become the best job recruiter you've ever had!

HOW TO CHOOSE YOUR OWN SALARY

Can you really choose your own salary? As an independent business person, unlike an employee, you not only can, you *must* set your own goals. That includes income. You may also set a time frame in which you either expect to meet or exceed these goals—or rethink your business plan. (And yes, it's a very good idea to set down a written plan for your freelancing activity. It doesn't have to be as formal as the business plan for a bank or a retail store, but if you want to earn money, you have to figure out what writing skills you have to sell, who might want them and how you will persuade them that you are the best writer for the job.)

To determine your income requirements, start off with your required annual income and add 30 percent for current expenses and the additional expenses you may have to incur as a new freelancer. Don't forget to figure in approximately another 30 percent for health insurance, social security, retirement and other benefits that may be paid in whole or in part by your present employer. (If you need to get health insurance, check out some of the writers' organizations which offer insurance as a membership option.) This number is your basic income requirement.

Next, figure a standard hourly rate, or rate range. Some business plans suggest arriving at an hourly rate by dividing the basic income requirement above by 2,080 (the number of hours in a 40-hour work week, 52 weeks a year). But this calculation is not too helpful for freelance

Figuring an Hourly Rate

$$\frac{\text{required annual income} + \overset{30\%}{(\text{expenses})} + \overset{30\%}{(\text{benefits})}}{\text{billable hours worked per year}}$$

For example,

$$\frac{\$30,000 + \$9,000 + \$9,000}{1,500 \text{ hours}} = \$32/\text{hour}$$

writers, most of whom are set up as sole proprietorships, unless you plan to work more hours. That's because, as a sole proprietor, you are not likely to bill clients for 40 hours each week, unless you put in a lot of overtime. Full-time freelancers may bill as few as 800 hours annually, because running a writing business means doing it *all*. Researching markets, preparing samples, interviewing prospective clients, putting together proposals, creating your webpage, network-ing—all these vital tasks eat up time. (Occasionally the office needs a good vacuuming, too. Without a helpful partner, the crumbs will stay unless *you* sweep them up.) Few writers have secretaries to do their filing, or accountants to handle the routine jobs of invoicing and check writing. (Many writers do employ outside accountants to handle their taxes, including the some-what cumbersome Business Schedule C. These suppliers may also serve as on-the-fly financial consultants and an accountant might be a useful critic for your business plan.) Most of us who freelance also want a few days of vacation here or there. So subtract these nonbillable hours to get a more realistic number. Divide the realistic billable number into your income goal to come up with a basic hourly rate that will allow you to hit your income target.

When you look at that rate, it may seem extremely high. Maybe it is, maybe it isn't. Your next step is to study the rate guidelines that follow this introduction to see if your hourly fee is in the ballpark. Then do more job-specific research on your own. Ask other writers in your locale (or those who work for the same kind of organization, if it is elsewhere) what they charge. You'll need to factor the competitive rate into your personal equation.

If you follow the job hunting and income guidelines, with a little luck you will be asked to bid on a job. Nearly every one of the freelancers who were earning adequate income stressed the requirement: "Don't sell yourself short!" Most professional freelancers suggest starting your estimate somewhere in the middle range, and being willing to negotiate. They say it is far easier to negotiate your fee downward than the reverse.

HOW LONG DOES IT TAKE?

Hourly rates are a good place to start your process of estimates and billing, but sometimes it's hard to get a handle on how long a project will take. In our survey, we asked participants to estimate the time it takes them to complete various writing assignments. The results pointed out, once again, what wide variables there are among writers, both in the type of work they commonly produce and in the speed of their writing.

This is not a scientific sample by any means, but it may give you some clues to the amount of work time to expect. Of course the best way to figure your own hours once you're active is to keep a detailed work log per project—and don't omit any part of it. (If you have to have

Project Time Guidelines

(Writing time estimates, assuming research at hand)

4-page brochure:
Extremes: 2 hours, low/15 days, high; Typical: 1-2 days

700-word technical article:
Extremes: 45 minutes, low/6 weeks, high; Typical: 2-4 hours

Feature article (2,000 words):
Extremes: 2 hours, low/12 weeks, high; Typical: 10 hours to 1 week

2-page PR release:
Extremes: 20 minutes, low/1 week, high; Typical: 2-4 hours

Speech for corporate executive:
Extremes: 2 hours, low/3 weeks, high; Typical: 3-5 days

8-page newsletter:
Extremes: 4 hours, low/5 weeks, high; Typical: 2-4 days

"thinking time," put that on the log, even if you don't bill the client the full amount.) By keeping good time records of specific project types, before too long you will be able to discern a pattern. Some writers use this pattern to determine their "per project" fees, multiplying their usual hours times their hourly rate (often adding a cushion to cover extraordinary circumstances). Writers who prefer "project fees" may gain speed with experience, and thereby earn higher hourly rates without the client feeling any pain.

Again, the following work times are given as a very rough guideline, not gospel. You've got to take the time it takes you to do the job properly, while keeping the market rates in mind.

ADVERTISING, COPYWRITING & PR

Advertising copywriting: $400 low, $1,000 mid-range, $2,000 high/full page ad depending on the size and kind of client; $50 low, $75 mid-range, $100 high/hour; $250 and up/day; $500 and up/week; $1,000-2,000 as a monthly retainer. In Canada, rates range from $40-80/hour.

Advertorials: $25-35/hour; up to $1/word or by flat fee ($300/700 words is typical). In Canada, 40-80¢/word; $35-75/hour.

Book jacket copywriting: $100-600/front cover jacket plus flaps and back jacket copy summarizing content and tone of the book.

Campaign development or product launch: $3,500 low, $7,000 mid-range, $12,000 high/project.

Catalog copywriting: $25-$45/hour or $85 and up/project.

Copyediting for advertising: $25-35/hour.

Direct mail copywriting: $25-45/hour; $75 and up/item or $400-800/page.

Direct mail packages: This includes copywriting direct mail letter, response card and advertising materials. $50 low, $75 mid-range, $115 high/hour; $2,500-10,000/project, depending on complexity. Additional charges for production such as desktop publishing, addressing, etc.

Direct mail response card for a product: $250-500/project.

Direct mail production (DTP): $50-60/hour.

Event promotions/publicity: $40 low, $60 mid-range, $70 high/hour; $500-750/day.

Fundraising campaign brochure: $50-75 for research (20 hours) and copywriting (30 hours); up to $5,000 for major campaign brochure, including research, writing and production (about 50 hours of work).

High-tech marketing materials: $85 low, $125 mid-range, $250 high/hour.

New product release: $20-35/hour or $300-500/release.

News release: *See Press/news release.*

Political campaigns, public relations: Small town or state campaigns, $10-50/hour; congressional, gubernatorial or other national campaigns, $25-100/hour or up to 10% of campaign budget.

Promotion for events: $20-30/hour. For conventions and longer events, payment may be per diem or a flat fee of $500-2,500. *See also Press/news release.*

Press kits: $50 low, $70 mid-range, $125 high/hour; $1,000-5,000/project.

Press/news release: $40 low, $70 mid-range, $150 high/hour; $150 low, $350 mid-range, $500 high/project.

Print advertisement: $200-500/project. In Canada, $100-200/concept. *See also Advertising copywriting.*

Product information: $30-60/hour; $400-500/day or $100-300/page. *See also Sales and services brochures and fliers.*

Promotion for tourism, museums, art shows, etc.: $20-$50 and up/hour for writing or editing promotion copy. Additional charges for production, mailings, etc.

Public relations for businesses: $250-600/day plus expenses average—more for large corporations.

Public relations for government: $25-50/hour or a monthly retainer based on number of hours per period. Lower fees for local government agencies, higher for state-level and above.

Public relations for organizations or nonprofits: $15-35/hour. If working on a monthly retainer, $100-500/month.

Public relations for schools or libraries: $15-20/hour for small districts or libraries; up to $35/hour for larger districts.

Public relations monthly retainers: $500 low, $800 mid-range, $1,000 high (fee includes press releases, modest events etc.).

Radio advertisement: $50 low, $75 mid-range, $125 high/hour; $400 low, $750 mid-range, $2,000 high/spot; $200-400/week for part-time positions writing radio ads, depending on the size of the city (and market).

Sales and services brochures and fliers: $30 low, $65 mid-range, $100 high/hour; $500 low, $1,000 mid-range, $2,500 high/4-page project depending on size and type of business (small nonprofit organization to a large corporation), the number of pages (usually from 1-16) and complexity of the job.

Sales letters: $2/word; $40 low, $70 mid-range, $125 high/hour; $400 low, $750 mid-range, $2,000 high/project.

Speech editing or evaluation: $50 low, $90 mid-range, $125/high, $200 very high/finished minute. In Canada, $75-125/hour or $70-100/minute of speech.

Speechwriting (general): $50 low, $90 mid-range, $125 high, $200 very high/finished minute. In Canada, $75-125/hour or $70-100/minute of speech.

Speechwriting for business owners or executives: Up to $80/hour or a flat fee of about $100 for a short (6- or 7-minute speech); $500-3,000 for up to 30 minutes. Rates also depend on size of the company and the event.

Speechwriting for government officials: $4,000/20 minutes plus up to $1,000 for travel and expenses.

Speechwriting for political candidates: $250 and up for local candidates (about 15 minutes); $375-800 for statewide candidates and $1,000 or more for national congressional candidates.

TV commercial: 30 second spot: $950-1,500. In Canada, $60-130/minute of script (CBC pays Writers Guild rates, CTV pays close to that and others pay less. For example, TV Ontario pays $70-100/script minute).

AUDIOVISUALS & ELECTRONIC COMMUNICATIONS
(See Technical for computer-related services)

Audiocassette scripts: $10-50/scripted minute, assuming written from existing client materials, with no additional research or meetings; otherwise $85-100/minute, $750 minimum.

Audiovisuals: For writing, $250-350/requested scripted minute; includes rough draft, editing conference with client, and final shooting script. For consulting, research, producing, directing, soundtrack oversight, etc. $400-600/day plus travel and expenses. Writing fee is sometimes 10% of gross production price as billed to client. Some charge flat fee of $1,500-2,100/package.

Book summaries for film producers: $50-100/book. *Note: You must live in the area where the business is located to get this kind of work.*

Business film scripts (training and information): $50 low, $85 mid-range, $200 high/hour; $75 low, $100 mid-range, $175 high/finished minute.

Copyediting audiovisuals: $20-25/hour.

Educational/training film scripts: $50 low, $85 mid-range, $200 high/hour; $100/finished minute.

Industrial product film: $125-150/minute; $500 minimum flat fee.

Novel synopsis for film producer: $150-300/5-10 pages typed, single spaced.

Options (feature films): $1,500 low, $15,000 mid-range, $50,000 high, $400,000 very high/project.

Radio continuity writing: $5/page to $150/week, part-time. In Canada, $40-80/minute of script; $640/show for a multi-part series.

Radio copywriting: *See Advertising, Copywriting & PR.*

Radio documentaries: $258/60 minutes, local station.

Radio editorials: $10-30/90-second to 2-minute spots.

Radio interviews: For National Public Radio, up to 45 seconds, $25; 2 minutes and longer, $62/minute. Small radio stations would pay approximately 50% of the NPR rate; large stations, double the NPR rate.

Script synopsis for business: $40/hour.

Script synopsis for agent or film producer: $75/2-3 typed pages, single-spaced.

Scripts for nontheatrical films for education, business, industry: Prices vary among producers, clients, and sponsors and there is no standardization of rates in the field. Fees include $75-120/minute for one reel (10 minutes) and corresponding increases with each successive reel; approximately 10% of the production cost of films that cost the producer more than $1,500/release minute.

Screenwriting: $6,000 and up/project.

Slide presentation: Including visual formats plus audio, $150-600/10-15 minutes.

Slide/single image photos: $75 flat fee.

Slide/tape script: $50 low, $75 mid-range, $100 high/hour; $100 low, $300 high/finished minute; $1,500-3,000/finished project.

TV commercial: *See Advertising, Copywriting & PR.*

TV documentary: 30-minute 5-6 page proposal outline, $1,839 and up; 15-17 page treatment, $1,839 and up; less in smaller cities. In Canada research for a documentary runs about $6,500.

TV editorials: $35 and up/1-minute, 45 seconds (250-300 words).

TV filmed news and features: From $10-20/clip for 30-second spot; $15-25/60-second clip; more for special events.

TV information scripts: Short 5- to 10-minute scripts for local cable TV stations, $10-15/hour.

TV, national and local public stations: For programs, $35-100/minute down to a flat fee of $5,000 and up/30- to 60-minute script.

TV news film still photo: $3-6 flat fee.

TV news story/feature: $60 low, $95 mid-range, $140 high.

TV scripts: (non-theatrical): $50 low, $75 mid-range, $85 high/hour; $300 per finished minute; $3,000/project.

TV scripts: (Teleplays/mow): $15,000/30-minute sitcom.

BOOK PUBLISHING

Abstracting and abridging: $40 low, $60 mid-range, $85 high/hour; $30-35/hour for reference and professional journals; $600/5,000 word book summary.

Anthology editing: Variable advance plus 3-15 percent of royalties. Advance should cover reprint fees or fees are handled by the publisher. Flat-fee-per-manuscript rates range from $500-5,000 and up.

Book jacket copywriting: *See Advertising, Copywriting & PR.*

Book proposal consultation: $20-75/hour or a flat rate of $100-250.

Book proposal writing: 50¢/word; $45 low, $65 mid-range, $85 high/hour: $2,000-3,500/project, depending on length and whether the client provides full information or the writer must do research, and whether a sample chapter is required.

Book query critique: $50 for critique of letter to the publisher and outline.

Book summaries for book clubs: $50-100/book.

Book writing (own): $20 low, $40 mid-range, $50 high/hour; (advances) $15 low, $35 mid-range, $45 high/hour.

Content editing (scholarly): $14 low, $22 mid-range, $32 high, $100 very high/hour.

Content editing (textbook): $14 low, $35 mid-range, $65 high, $100 very high/hour.

Content editing (trade): $30 low, $60 mid-range, $100 high/hour; $800 low, $1,200 mid-range, $6,000 high/project.

Copyediting: $17 low, $30 mid-range, $50 high, $75 very high/hour; $3-5/page. Lower-end rates charged for light copyedit (3-10 pages/hour) of general, trade material. Higher-end rates charged for substantive copyediting or for textbooks and technical material (2-5 pages/hour).

Ghostwriting, as told to: This is writing for a celebrity or expert either for a self-published book or for a publisher. Author gets full advance plus 50 percent of royalties, typically $15,000 low, $25,000 high/project plus a percentage of ownership and 'with' credit line. Hourly rates for subjects who are self-publishing are $25 low, $55 mid-range, $85 high/hour; $125 low, $175 high/book page. In Canada, author also gets full advance and 50 percent of royalties or $10,000-20,000 flat fee per project. Research time is charged extra.

Ghostwriting, no credit: Projects may include writing for an individual planning to self publish or for a book packager, book producer, publisher, agent or corporation. Rates range from $5,000 very low, $15,000 low, $25,000 mid-range, $50,000 high/project (plus expenses); packagers pay flat fee or combination of advance plus royalties. For self-published clients, ask for one-fourth down payment, one-fourth when book is half-finished, one-fourth at the three-quarters mark and one-fourth upon completion.

Indexing: $15 low, $25 mid-range, $40 high, $95 very high/hour; charge higher hourly rate if using a computer index program that takes fewer hours. Also can charge $2-6/indexable page; 40-70¢/line of index or a flat fee of $250-500 depending on length.

Manuscript evaluation and critique: $150-200/outline and first 20,000 words; $300-500/up to 100,000 words. Also $15-35/hour for trade books, slightly less for nonprofits. Page rates run from $1.50-2.50/page.

Movie novelization: $3,500-15,000 depending on writer's reputation, amount of work to be done and amount of time writer is given.

Novel synopsis for a literary agent: $150/5-10 pages typed, single-spaced.

Page layout (desktop publishing/camera-ready copy): $25 low, $40 mid-range, $50 high/hour. Higher per-page rates may be charged if material involves complex technical material and graphics.

Production editing/project management: $15 low, $30 mid-range, $75 high, $150 very high/ hour. This is overseeing the production of a project, coordinating editing and production stages, etc.

Proofreading: $15 low, $30 mid-range, $55 high/hour; $4-6/page. High-end rates are charged for technical, scientific and reference material.

Research for writers or book publishers: $20-40/hour and up; $150 and up/day plus expenses. A flat rate of $300-500 may be charged, depending on complexity of the job.

Rewriting: $18-50/hour; $5-7/page. Some writers receive royalties on book projects.

Summaries for book clubs/catalogues: $20 low, $40 mid-range, $75 high/hour.

Textbooks: $20 low, $40 mid-range, $60 high/hour.

Translation (literary): 10¢/word, $30-35/hour; also $95-125/1,000 English words.

Typesetting: $20-45/hour or $5-10/page.

BUSINESS

Annual reports: A brief report with some economic information and an explanation of figures, $35 low, $70 mid-range, $100 high, $150 very high/hour; $300 low, $600 high/page; $500/ day; $3,000 low, $6,000 mid-range, $12,000 high/project if extensive research and/or writing is involved in a large project. A report that must meet Securities and Exchange Commission (SEC) standards and reports requiring legal language could bill $75-150/hour. Bill separately if desktop publication (typesetting, page layout, etc.) is involved (some smaller firms and nonprofits may ask for writing/production packages).

Associations and organizations (writing for): $15-25/hour for small organizations; up to $50/ hour for larger associations or a flat fee depending on the length and complexity of the project. For example, $500-1,000 for an association magazine article (2,000 words) or $1,000-1,800 for a 10-page informational booklet.

Audiovisuals/audiocassette scripts: *See Audiovisuals & Electronic Communications.*

Book summaries for businesses: $25-50/page or $20-35/hour.

Brochures, fliers, booklets for business: $25-40/hour for writing or from $500-$4,000 and up/ project (12-16 pages and more). Additional charges for desktop publishing, usually $20-40/ hour; $20-30/page or a flat fee per project. *See also Copyediting for business or Manuscript editing/evaluation for trade journals.*

Business editing (general): $25 low, $40 mid-range, $85 high/hour.

Business letters: $25 low, $65 mid-range, $100 high/hour, depending on the size of the business and the length/complexity of the material, or $2/word.

Business plan: $1/word; $200/manuscript page or up to $1,500/project. High-end rates are charged if extensive research is involved. Sometimes research is charged separately per hour or per day.

Business writing (general): $30-80/hour. In Canada, $1-2/word or $50-100/hour. *See other entries in this section and in Advertising, Copywriting & PR for specific projects such as brochures, copywriting, speechwriting, brochures or business letters. For business film script-writing see Audiovisuals & Electronic Communications.*

Business writing seminars: $500 for a half-day seminar, plus travel expenses or $1,000-5,000/ day. Rates depend on number of participants as well as duration. Average per-person rate is $50/person for a half-day seminar. *See also Educational and Literary Services.*

Catalogs for business: $25-40/hour or $25-600/printed page; more if tables or charts must be reworked for readability or consistency. Additional charges for desktop publishing ($20-40/ hour is average).

Collateral materials for business: *See individual pieces (brochures, catalogs, etc.) in this section and in Advertising, Copywriting & PR.*

Commercial reports for business, insurance companies, credit agencies: $6-15/page.

Consultation on communications: $25 low, $50 mid-range, $85 high/hour; $600 low, $2,000 high/day (includes travel). Lower-end fees charged to nonprofits and small businesses.

Consumer complaint letters (answering): $25-30/letter.

Copyediting for business: $20-40/hour or $20-50/manuscript page, up to $40/hour for business proposals. Charge lower-end fees ($15-25/hour) to nonprofits and very small businesses.

Corporate histories: $30 low, $70 mid-range, $100 high/hour; $500/day; $7,500/project.

Corporate periodicals, editing: $20 very low, $40 low, $60 mid-range, $85 high/hour.

Corporate periodicals, writing: $25 very low, $40 low, $70 mid-range, $120 high/hour, depending on size and nature of the corporation. Also $1-3/word. In Canada, $1-2/word or $40-90/hour.

Corporate profile: $1,250-2,500 flat fee for up to 3,000 words or charge on a per word basis, up to $1/word.

Financial presentation: $1,500-4,500 for a 20-30 minute presentation.

Fundraising campaign brochure: *See Advertising, Copywriting & PR.*

Ghostwriting for business (usually trade magazine articles or business columns): $25-100/hour; $200 or more/day plus expenses (depending on amount of research involved, length of project).

Government research: $35-50/hour.

Government writing: $30-50/hour. In Canada, $50-80/hour.

Grant proposal writing for nonprofits: $30-100/hour or flat fee.

Indexing for professional journals: $20-40/hour.

Industrial/service business training manual: $25-40/hour; $50-100/manuscript page or a flat fee, $1,000-4,000, depending on number of pages and complexity of the job.

Industry training film scripts: *See Business film scripts in Audiovisuals & Electronic Communications.*

Industrial product film script: *See Audiovisuals & Electronic Communications.*

Job application letters: $20-40/letter.

Manuals/documentation: $25-60/hour. *See also Computers, Scientific & Technical.*

Manuscript editing/evaluation for trade journals: $20-40/hour.

Market research survey reports: $25-50/hour or $500-1,500/day; also flat rates of $500-2,000/project.

Newsletters, abstracting: $30/hour.

Newsletters, desktop publishing/production: $25 low, $40 mid-range, $85 high/hour. Higher-end rates for scanning photographs, advertising layout, illustration or design. Editing charged extra.

Newsletters, editing: $25 low, $45 mid-range, $85 high/hour; $200-500/issue; $2/word. Higher-end fees charged if writing or production is included. Editors who produce a regular newsletter on a monthly or quarterly basis tend to charge per month or per issue—and find them easier to do after initial set up.

Newsletters, writing: $35 low, $50 mid-range, $100 high/hour; $500 low, $1,350 mid-range, $2,500 high/project; $200 and up/page. In Canada, $45-70/hour.

Nonprofit editing: $15 low, $30 mid-range, $55 high/hour.

Nonprofit writing: $15 very low, $25 low, $50 mid-range, $70 high/hour.

Programmed instruction consultation fees: *See Educational & Literary Services.*

Programmed instruction materials for business: *See Educational & Literary Services.*

Proofreading for business: $15-50/hour; low-end fees for nonprofits.

Public relations: *See Advertising, Copywriting and PR.*

Résumé writing: $30 low, $55 mid-range, $100 high.

Retail newsletters for customers: Charge regular newsletter rates or $175-300/4-page project. Additional charges for desktop publishing.

Sales brochures, fliers, letters, other advertising materials: *See Advertising, Copywriting & PR.*

Scripts for business/training films: *See Audiovisuals & Electronic Communications.*

Translation, commercial: $30-45/hour; $115-125/1,000 words. Higher-end fees for non-European languages into English.

Translation for government agencies: $30-45; up to $125/1,000 words. Higher-end fees for non-European languages into English.

Translation through translation agencies: Agencies pay 33⅓% average less than end-user clients and mark up translator's prices by as much as 100% or more.

Translation, technical: $30-45/hour; $125 and up/1,000 words, depending on complexity of the material.

COMPUTER, SCIENTIFIC & TECHNICAL

Abstracting, CD-ROM: $50/hour.

Abstracting, online: $40/hour.

Computer documentation, general (print): $35 low, $60 mid-range, $100 high/hour; $100-150/page. *See also Software manual writing.*

Computer documentation (online): $20 low, $50 mid-range, $85 high/hour.

Demonstration software: $70 and up/hour.

Legal/government editing: $15 very low, $25 low, $50 mid-range, $65 high/hour.

Legal/government writing: $15 very low, $30 low, $50 mid-range, $65 high/hour.

Medical and science editing: $20 low, $60 mid-range, $85 high/hour, depending on the complexity of the material and the expertise of the editor.

Medical and science proofreading: $15-30/hour.

Medical and science writing: $35 low, $70 mid-range, $150 high/hour; $1-3/word, depending on the complexity of the project and the writer's expertise.

Online editing: $25 low, $40 mid-range, $68 high/hour.

Software manual writing: $15 low, $50 mid-range, $100 high/hour for research and writing.

Technical editing: $20-60/hour or $150-1,000/day.

Technical typesetting: $4-7/page; $25-35/hour; more for inputting of complex material.

Technical writing: $30-75/hour; $20-30/page. *See also Computer documentation and Software manual writing.*

Technical translation: *See item in Business.*

Webpage design: $50 low, $85 mid-range, $125 high/hour..

Webpage writing/editing: $50 low, $85 mid-range, $125 high/hour; $170 mid-range, $500 high/page.

EDITORIAL/DESIGN PACKAGES

Business catalogs: *See Business.*

Desktop publishing: For 1,000 dots-per-inch type, $5-15/camera-ready page of straight type; $30/camera-ready page with illustrations, maps, tables, charts, photos; $100-150/camera-ready page for oversize pages with art. Also $25-50/hour depending on graphics, number of photos, and amount of copy to be typeset. Packages often include writing, layout/design, and typesetting services.

Greeting cards ideas (with art included): Anywhere from $30-300, depending on size of company.

Newsletters: *See Desktop publishing (this section) and Newsletters (Business).*

Picture editing: $20-40.

Photo brochures: $700-15,000 flat fee for photos and writing.

Photo research: $15-30/hour.

Photography: $10-150/b&w photo; $25-300/color photo; also $800/day.

EDUCATIONAL & LITERARY SERVICES

Business writing seminars: *See Business.*

Consultation for individuals (in business): $250-1,000/day.

Consultation on communications: *See Business.*

Developing and designing courses for business or adult education: $250-$1,500/day or flat fee.

Editing for individual clients: $10-50/hour or $2-7/page.

Educational consulting and educational grant and proposal writing: $250-750/day or $30-75/hour.

Lectures at national conventions by well-known authors: $2,500-20,000 and up, plus expenses; less for panel discussions.

Lectures at regional writers' conferences: $300 and up, plus expenses.

Lectures to local groups, librarians or teachers: $50-150.

Lectures to school classes: $25-75; $150/day; $250/day if farther than 100 miles.

Manuscript evaluation for theses/dissertations: $15-30/hour.

Poetry manuscript critique: $25/16-line poem.

Programmed instruction consultant fees: $300-1,000/day, $50-75/hour.

Programmed instruction materials for business: $50/hour for inhouse writing and editing; $500-1,000/day plus expenses for outside research and writing. Alternate method: $2,000-5,000/hour of programmed training provided depending on technicality of subject.

Public relations for schools: *See Advertising, Copywriting & PR.*

Readings by poets, fiction writers: $25-600 depending on author.

Scripts for nontheatrical films for education: *See Audiovisuals & Electronic Communications.*

Short story manuscript critique: 3,000 words, $40-60.

Teaching adult education course: $15 low, $45 mid-range, $125 high/hour; $1,750-2,500/continuing education course; fee usually set by school, not negotiated by teachers.

Teaching adult seminar: $20 low, $40 mid-range, $60 high/hour; $750-1,000/3-day course. In Canada, $35-50/hour.

Teaching business writing to company employees: *See Consultation on communications in Business.*

Teaching college course or seminar: $15-70/class hour.

Teaching creative writing in school: $15-70/hour of instruction, or $1,500-2,000/12-15 week semester; less in recessionary times.

Teaching elementary and middle school teachers how to teach writing to students: $75-150/1- to 1½ hour session.

Teaching home-bound students: $5-15/hour.

Tutoring: $25/1- to 1½ hour private session.

TV instruction taping: $150/30-minute tape; $25 residual each time tape is sold.

Workshop instructing: $25 low, $50 mid-range, $75 high/hour; $2,500-3,500/13-week course.

Writer-in-schools: Arts council program, $130/day; $650/week. Personal charges plus expenses vary from $25/day to $100/hour depending on school's ability to pay.

Writer's workshop: Lecturing and seminar conducting, $50-150/hour to $750/day plus expenses; local classes, $35-50/student for 10 sessions.

Writing for individual clients: $25-100/hour, depending on the situation. *See also Business writing in Business.*

Writing for scholarly journals: $75/hour.

MAGAZINES & TRADE JOURNALS

Abstracting: $20-30/hour for trade and professional journals; $20 low, $30 mid-range, $60 high/hour for scholarly journals.

Advertorial: $650 low, $1,000 high/printed page.

Article manuscript critique: $40/3,000 words.

Arts reviewing: $35-100 flat fee or 20-30¢/word, plus admission to events or copy of CD (for music).

Book reviews: $22 low, $50 mid-range, $175 high, $750 very high/piece; 25¢-$1/word.

Consultation on magazine editorial: $1,000-1,500/day plus expenses.

Copyediting magazines: $16-30/hour.

Editing: General, $25-500/day or $250-2,000/issue; religious publications, $200-500/month or $15-30/hour.

Fact checking: $26 low, $50 mid-range, $75 high/hour.

Feature articles: Anywhere from 20¢-$4/word; or $150-2,750/1,500 word article, depending on size (circulation) and reputation of magazine.

Ghostwriting articles (general): Up to $2/word; or $300-3,000/project.

Indexing: $15-40/hour.

Magazine, city, calendar of events column: $50-150/column.

Magazine column: 25¢ low, $1.50 mid-range, $4 high/word; $25 low, $200 mid-range, $2,500 high/piece. Larger circulation publications pay fees related to their regular word rate.

Magazine copyediting: $15 low, $25 mid-range, $50 high, $100 very high/hour.

Magazine editing: $15 low, $30 mid-range, $60 high/hour.

Magazine research: $20 low, $40 mid-range, $75 high/hour.

Manuscript consultation: $25-50/hour.

Manuscript criticism: $40-60/article or short story of up to 3,000 words. Also $20-25/hour.

Picture editing: *See Editorial/Design Packages.*

Permission fees to publishers to reprint article or story: $75-500; 10-15¢/word; less for charitable organizations.

Production editing: $15-30/hour.

Proofreading: $12-25/hour.

Research: $20-25/hour.

Rewriting: Up to $80/manuscript page; also $100/published page.

Science writing for magazines: $2,000-5,000/article. *See also Computer, Scientific & Technical.*

Special news article: For a business's submission to trade publication, $250-500/1,000 words. In Canada, 25-45¢/word.

Stringing: 20¢-$1/word based on circulation. Daily rate: $150-250 plus expenses; weekly rate: $900 plus expenses. Also $10-35/hour plus expenses; $1/column inch.

Trade journal ad copywriting: *See Advertising, Copywriting & PR.*

Trade journal feature article: For business client, $400-1,000. Also $1-2/word.

NEWSPAPERS

Ads for small business: $25/small, one-column ad, or $10/hour and up. *See also Advertising, Copywriting & PR.*

Arts reviewing: For weekly newspapers, $15-50 flat fee; for dailies, $50 and up; for Sunday supplements, $100-400. Also admission to event or copy of CD (for music).

Book reviews: For small newspapers, byline and the book only; for larger publications, $35-200 and a copy of the book.

Column, local: $40 low, $125 mid-range, $300 high/hour, depending on circulation.

Copyediting: $10-30/hour; up to $40/hour for large daily paper.

Copywriting: *See Advertising, Copywriting & PR.*

Dance criticism: $25-400/article.

Drama criticism: Local, newspaper rates; non-local, $50 and up/review.

Editing/manuscript evaluation: $25/hour.

Fact checking: *See Magazines & Trade Journals.*

Feature: $25 low, $200 mid-range, $500 high/piece, depending on circulation. In Canada, $15-40/word, but rates vary widely.

Obituary copy: Where local newspapers permit lengthier than normal notices paid for by the funeral home (and charged to the family), $15-25. Writers are engaged by funeral homes.

Picture editing: *See Editorial/Design Packages.*

Proofreading: $16-20/hour.

Reporting: $25 low, $45 mid-range, $100 high/piece (small circulation); $60 low, $175 high/per piece (large circulation).

Science writing for newspapers: *See Computer, Scientific & Technical.*

Stringing: $10 low, $25 mid-range, $40 high/piece; $1/column inch, sometimes with additional mileage payment.

Syndicted column, self-promoted: $5-10 each for weeklies; $10-25/week for dailies, based on circulation.

MISCELLANEOUS

Comedy writing for nightclub entertainers: Gags only, $5-25 each. Routines, $100-1,000/minute. Some new comics may try to get a 5-minute routine for $150; others will pay $2,500 for a 5-minute bit from a top writer.

Comics writing: $35-50/page and up for established comics writers.

Contest judging: Short manuscripts, $10/entry; with one-page critique, $15-25. Overall contest judging: $100-500.

Corporate comedy skits: $300-800/half-hour skit (used at meetings, conventions).

Craft ideas with instructions: $50-200/project.

Encyclopedia articles: Entries in some reference books, such as biographical encyclopedias, 500-2,000 words; pay ranges from $60-80/1,000 words. Specialists' fees vary.

Family histories: Fees depend on whether the writer edits already prepared notes or does extensive research and writing; and the length of the work, $500-15,000.

Institutional (church, school) history: $200-1,000/15-50 pages, or $20-35/hour.

Manuscript typing: Depending on manuscript length and delivery schedule, $1.25-2/page with one copy; $15/hour.

Party toasts, limericks, place card verses: $1.50/line.

Research for individuals: $5-30/hour, depending on experience, geographic area and nature of work.

Special occasion booklet: Family keepsake of a wedding, anniversary, Bar Mitzvah, etc., $120 and up.

Before the Script: How to Write Outlines and Treatments

BY PAMELA WALLACE

A treatment, which is another word for synopsis, is the backbone of your screenplay. It's your blueprint, just like the blueprint a builder follows in building a house. It keeps you focused and prevents you from wandering off the spine of the story. Simply put, a treatment is a narrative account of your story, written in present tense. For example, a treatment might begin: "A teenage boy in a battered old car pulls up to the curb at a middle-class, suburban house. He leaps out, races to the front door, and desperately pounds on it, screaming, 'Jody, it's me! Let me in!' A beat, then a rather plain teenage girl throws open the door and stares in shock at the boy." Notice that it's important to put as much emotion and sense of action into a treatment as possible. It should be a concise but entertaining read, especially if someone is going to read it before looking at your script.

Aside from coming up with a very good, very commercial idea in the first place, the treatment is the hardest part of the writing process. In it, you lay out the story—the plot and the characters and their arcs. Of the total creative effort involved in completing a screenplay, roughly 75 percent or more goes into working out the story. Who are the main characters? What do they want? Why do they want it? How do they set about accomplishing their goals? What stops them? What are the consequences of their success or failure?

There is a famous story about Agatha Christie, the most successful mystery writer of all time, many of whose books were made into movies. She was walking in her garden with a friend, deep in thought. Suddenly, she exclaimed, "I've just finished my new book!" Her friend asked, "May I read it?" Ms. Christie replied, "Oh, I haven't written it yet." She had simply done the hardest part—figuring out how the story would play out.

Before you can get to where Dame Agatha was at the end of that walk in the garden, you must first determine what kind of movie you want your story to fit into. You've written a logline, encapsulating the essence of your story. But what approach do you want to take? Is this a serious drama? A broad comedy? A romance? The same idea can be developed in any of those genres. For instance, the teen movie *Clueless* was a young, hip romantic comedy take on Jane Austen's classic English novel, *Emma*. Same story, very different approach.

Once you've got your logline and genre, you may still be a little confused as to which aspect of the story to focus on. For instance, in *Witness*, we had many choices. We could have focused the story on police corruption, the relationship between the two cops who were partners, the interaction of the Amish with the outer world, the religious beliefs of the Amish or any number

PAMELA WALLACE *began writing screenplays in the mid-1980s, and in 1985 she won an Academy Award for co-writing the movie* Witness. *She has written or co-written several other films, including the award-winning HBO film* If These Walls Could Talk, *the CBS movie of the week* Borrowed Hearts, *and the ABC movies of the week* Lovers of Deceit *and* Alibi. *This chapter is excerpted from her book* You Can Write a Movie *(Writer's Digest Books).*

of other things. But from the inception of the idea, I wanted this to be a romantic story. I felt that the wide gulf between the Amish and the outside world provided a perfect barrier to keep two people who love each other from getting together. Because it's so hard to come up with a fresh conflict in a love story, that was too good a dramatic opportunity to pass up.

Deciding to make it a love story determined the form of the movie. It meant the plot would focus on the developing relationship between the hero and the heroine. And the subplot, of course, concerned the heroine's son who witnesses a murder.

If you give ten different writers the same logline, they will come up with ten different approaches to the story. Each will bring his own feelings, interests and unique perspective to it. A concept that strikes one writer as a perfect vehicle for hilarious comedy appears to another to be ripe for development as a serious drama.

In doing a treatment, you have an opportunity to find out what's wrong with your story before you actually write the screenplay. You'll be able to tell if you've made the following fatal errors that can prevent even an interesting script from selling:

Fatal flaws in the story:
- A slow setup that doesn't capture the audience's attention quickly enough.
- A confusing beginning that doesn't make it clear to the audience what kind of movie this is, who the protagonist is and what's at stake.
- A sagging middle—a boring Act Two that doesn't have enough twists and turns, barriers and complications, to hold the audience's interest.
- An abrupt ending that feels as if the writer simply got tired of the story and wrapped it up in a hurry.
- A cliched story that has nothing new or fresh about it. This is the "we've seen it before" syndrome.
- Too many intrusive flashbacks that keep stopping the momentum of the story.
- A reliance on voice-overs to get across information, instead of finding a way to show this information through action or dialogue. Show, don't tell.
- Too many warring elements. The writer has thrown in everything he can think of in an effort to make the story exciting. Because so much is going on, none of it is very well developed.
- A reliance on lengthy dialogue, as opposed to action or visual elements.

In a treatment you structure the plot and develop the characters of your movie. Structure determines what happens and when it happens. It is defined by the protagonist's goal. It begins with the initial setup, where you establish the main characters, what the movie's about and what's at stake. It moves on to the inciting incident, which launches the real story. The protagonist finds himself in a new situation, with a change of plans. He makes progress toward his goal, despite serious obstacles and complications. Approximately halfway through the movie, the stakes are raised—more is at stake than the protagonist originally conceived. There is a major setback (the "all is lost" moment), followed by renewed determination by the protagonist to achieve his goal. His efforts culminate in the climax, where he succeeds or fails. At the end there's a very brief resolution.

In your treatment, you should know key things about your main characters, especially the protagonist. Usually the protagonist has a wound (either inner or outer), that is an unresolved source of deep pain, and generally precedes the events of the movie. For instance, in *Message in a Bottle* (based on the bestselling novel by Nicholas Sparks), Kevin Costner is mourning the loss of his beloved wife, who died two years before the movie opens. His attachment to her prevents him from fully accepting the love offered by Robin Wright Penn.

The protagonist in any movie must deal with a deep emotional fear. His inner conflict stems from the fact that this fear is an obstacle to fulfillment. Unless the protagonist can resolve this fear, he won't achieve his goal.

A good treatment usually will resemble the following structure.

Act One: This begins with a strong establishing scene, preferably a "hook" that immediately captures the audience's interest. The hero or heroine is introduced in an interesting way, as is the villain or antagonistic force (for instance, tornadoes in *Twister*). The problem is set before the hero, who accepts the challenge, often with serious reluctance or misgivings.

Act Two: This is the backstory explaining the hero's background or the events preceding the beginning of the movie. The hero is in some way attacked or challenged. There are scenes developing the subplot and dealing with the theme. In a romantic story, there will be romantic interludes. The hero will come up against the villain, and at the end of the act, the hero will appear to be defeated, his goal out of reach.

Act Three: The first part of this act is preparation of the plan the hero has come up with to save the day. The middle part of the act is implementing that plan. And the final part of the act is the climax, the ultimate confrontation between hero and villain, followed by a brief resolution scene.

In working on a treatment, a great place to begin is with the ending. Until you know the ending, you can't write your script. (Some writers disagree with this, and love to discover how the story will play out as they write it. Exceptionally talented or very experienced writers will find this easier to do than will novice writers.) Everything in your movie should lead up to the ending.

In general, Act One should have six to ten scenes to set up the main characters and establish what the story is about. Act Two should be approximately fifteen to thirty scenes, focusing on character development, and introducing complications that create barriers to the protagonist achieving his goal. And Act Three should have anywhere from three to ten scenes that show the climax of the story, and a brief epilogue that in some way suggests the future of the protagonist.

THE STEP OUTLINE

A good way to begin a treatment is with a step outline. This is a scene outline that describes step by step what happens in each scene in just a sentence or two. It shows the order of the scenes and the action that happens in each one. The step outline points toward the direction of your screenplay and helps you decide which sequence, or order of scenes, will be the most dramatic.

Writers commonly use several ways to do a step outline. One is to write a description of each scene on a 3×5 or 5×7 card, then lay out the cards in order (perhaps pinning them to a bulletin board). Many writers like to do this because it's easy to move the cards around and change scenes from one act to another. Some writers even use different colored cards for each scene.

Another way is to list the scenes in sequential order on a legal tablet, numbering them as you go. Or you may take a large sheet of paper, divide it into three separate sections, and briefly outline the scenes to go in each section.

Remember that every scene you include must relate to the spine of the story. Scenes that are not absolutely necessary shouldn't be included. If you're confused about whether or not a scene is necessary, ask yourself two questions: Does the scene contribute to the development of the character? Does it move the story forward? If the answer to both these questions is "no," then the scene should be thrown out. Doing this will ensure that you have a fast-paced, tightly constructed story.

Also, scenes should be organized in a rising sequence, with each scene heightening the tension of the story.

Whatever method you choose is purely a matter of personal choice. The purpose of all these methods is to help you create the best structure for your screenplay, with each scene moving in a cause-and-effect manner toward an exciting and fulfilling climax.

THE TREATMENT

Once you've done a step outline, you're ready to write the actual treatment, a detailed narrative account of your story. The only hard and fast rules about treatments are that they should be double-spaced and written in present tense. The length is flexible, but nowadays, short treatments, between five to ten pages, are considered best. A good, thorough treatment could almost be shot as a movie. All it's lacking is dialogue.

If you're writing the treatment for yourself, and not as a sales tool to show to a prospective buyer, it isn't essential to write it in an exciting and colorful style. But if you're going to show it to a producer or studio or network executive, approach it as if you're writing the Great American Short Story. It should be vivid and emotional, and not only hold the reader's interest but get her excited about the movie that could be made from it. Use strong prose, by having highly descriptive passages and active as opposed to passive verbs. For example, don't describe your protagonist as poorly dressed; say his clothes hang in filthy tatters.

Don't forget to write visually. Picture each scene in your mind as if you're seeing it on a movie screen.

After you've written your treatment, ask yourself the following questions:

- Does your main character change his basic approach to dealing with the problem at the heart of the story? (Example: the Humphrey Bogart character in *Casablanca*, who goes from determined noninvolvement to passionate partisanship.)
- Or (which is more rare), does your main character remain steadfast in the face of overwhelming problems? (Example: the Harrison Ford character in *The Fugitive*.)
- Does he grow by losing a negative character trait and/or gaining a positive one? (Example: Robert De Niro becoming less focused on appearing macho and more in touch with his emotions in *Analyze This*.)
- Does your hero or heroine resolve personal problems? (Example: Robin Williams, who combats his suicidal depression by helping people in *Patch Adams*.)
- Does your protagonist achieve the story goal (which happens in most commercial films)?
- Or, does your protagonist fail in achieving the goal, but accomplish something worthwhile nonetheless (which happens in many "tear-jerkers," like *Stepmom*)?

Still unsure about what a treatment should look like? The following is a treatment for a family film written with my frequent collaborator, Madeline DiMaggio.

This is obviously a simple, G-rated movie, aimed at a young audience. But it's an adventurous, fast-paced and emotionally compelling story. The hero, Jed, is transformed by his experience. His character arc is clear—he goes from being a boy who feels hopeless because of his handicap, to a boy who has come to terms with his situation and proven to himself that there's nothing he can't do. The plot builds in intensity, with ever-greater dangers threatening boy and dog, climaxing in the greatest danger of all, the villainous trapper.

Unfortunately, this story didn't sell because there were simply too many movies at that time about children lost in the wilderness. But if it had sold, it would have been relatively simple to write the screenplay, because the treatment was so well worked out.

THE CHALLENGE

JED COLLINS is a handicapped twelve-year-old. SUNNY is a female Golden Labrador who's been trained to help the disabled. Their unforgettable journey begins when the chartered amphibious plane taking them to visit Jed's grandfather crashes in the Alaska wilderness. To survive, they must struggle against the rugged terrain, wild animals, the weather and even a human predator. Using the knowledge his grandfather taught him, and with Sunny's help, Jed is able to overcome daunting physical challenges. Along the way, he comes to terms with the challenge of his disability, and learns that it was only his belief in his own limitations that kept him down.

The pilot has died in the crash, but Jed and Sunny survive relatively unharmed. As Jed waits for help, Sunny remains obediently at his side, even though Jed wants nothing to do with her. The dog, a recent gift from Jed's parents, is a painful reminder to Jed of his dependency. Before a roller-blading accident seriously injured him, Jed was an energetic, athletic adolescent, the star first baseman on his school baseball team, and an avid hiker and camper with his grandfather, who taught him about nature and surviving in the wilderness. Now, Jed must wear heavy leg braces, and has only limited use of his hands and arms.

He has rejected Sunny, for she embodies his sense of helplessness and what he sees as the bleakness of his future. Now, Jed must learn to not only accept her help, but rely on her, as they battle the forces of nature for their very survival. Neither can prevail without the other. They are each other's only way out. Jed discovers that Sunny is more than just an animal trained to help compensate for his handicap. She is a kindred spirit.

After a couple of lonely, terrifying days waiting to be rescued, Jed realizes he'll either starve to death or freeze before too long. It's fall, and the first heavy storm of the season could come at any time. The meager supplies of food and camping equipment Jed was able to salvage from the wrecked plane won't be enough to help him survive a storm.

Scared to death, but realizing he has no choice, Jed sets out to walk to his grandfather's cabin, about fifty miles away. He knows the right direction— but he also knows how rugged the terrain is, and the dangers he faces, alone in the wilderness, with only Sunny for protection.

Meanwhile, Jed's parents have flown to his grandfather's cabin to be closer to the search for their son. It becomes a race against time, as the weather report shows a big snowstorm approaching. There's no way the boy could possibly survive such a storm.

On the first day, Jed covers only a few miles. His legs are stiff from the cold, and his braces difficult to maneuver. He reaches the top of an icy incline and collapses, grasping a shrub to keep from sliding. Sunny grabs the end of a rope hanging from Jed's waist, and begins to tug. Jed angrily yanks it back, and they begin a humorous tug of war. He yells at her that this is no time to play, but Sunny whines and persists until Jed finally realizes what she's trying to do. Jed takes an end of rope in each hand, and Sunny pulls the slack, which forms a giant loop. With the rope in her mouth, she pulls Jed safely down the treacherous hill on his stomach.

That night, both boy and dog are exhausted. Sunny brings wood so Jed can build a fire. Later, Jed sleeps, but Sunny stands sentinel. She watches over the boy as the embers die out, never taking her eyes off the darkness. Curious wolves come to stare at the boy and the dog. In their eye contact with Sunny is a subtle but powerful invitation to join them in their freedom. But she remains loyal to Jed. At dawn, she curls up next to him to sleep.

The next day they must cross a glacier. Sunny stops, sensing danger, her ears perked to attention. Suddenly the ice begins to crack. She pulls Jed to safety just as the floor of ice beneath them crumbles, revealing a deep crevasse.

When they come to a wide river, it looks as though they've reached an impasse. Not only is the river itself a seemingly insurmountable barrier, but there is a huge grizzly there, feasting on the spawning salmon. Jed finds a canoe that has washed ashore, but there's no oar. He uses a piece of driftwood as a substitute. But as he's getting into the canoe, the grizzly threatens him. Sunny barks at the bear, distracting it long enough for Jed to get into the canoe and push away from shore. Then Sunny dives into the water and paddles over to him. As they cross the river, Jed loses the driftwood oar and Sunny jumps overboard to retrieve it.

Finally, boy and dog face their most deadly adversary—a crazed trapper involved in illegal trapping, who is afraid Jed will turn him into the authorities. When Jed risks his life to save Sunny from the trapper, the bonding of boy and dog is complete. Sunny has suffered a serious injury to one leg from a vicious trap. Jed bandages her leg, then fashions a makeshift travois. He promises Sunny that if she'll just hang in there, he'll get them to safety.

His newfound love for Sunny inspires him to go that extra mile—beyond the limitations of his physical handicap—that ends up saving both of them. Pulling Sunny on the travois, Jed finally gets them both near to his grandfather's cabin, where the search party finds them. They have a tearful, joyous reunion with his family.

Along the way on this remarkable journey, Jed learns that he can do a great deal more than he thought he could. If he could survive this ordeal, he can survive anything. And he isn't alone in the challenges he faces. He has Sunny.

THE END

Literary Agents

The publishing world is never static. There's the quiet ebb and flow of imprints expanding and editors moving, and then there's the cataclysmic explosion when publishing giants collide. Through it all, the literary agent has become an increasingly important mediator, connecting writers, ideas and publishers to form books.

With an increasing emphasis on profit margins, many of the larger publishers have eliminated the entry level editorial assistants primarily responsible for reading manuscripts sent in by writers—"over the transom" to the "slush pile," in the jargon. As a result, agents have taken over some of this task, separating the literary wheat from the chaff and forwarding the promising manuscripts on to possible publishers. Most publishers remain open to receiving at least query letters directly from authors, but some of the largest publishers accept agented submissions only.

As you look through the Book Publishers section of *Writer's Market*, you will see the symbol Ⓐ at the beginning of some listings. This symbol denotes publishers that accept submissions only from agents. If you find a book publisher that is a perfect market for your work but only reads agented manuscripts, contacting an agent is your next logical step.

Finding an agent is *not* easier than finding a publisher. It may even be harder, since there are far fewer agents than publishing companies. However, if you do secure representation, your "reach" into the publishing world has extended to include everyone that agent knows.

CHOOSING AND USING AN AGENT

Literary agents, like authors, come in all shapes and sizes, with different areas of interest and expertise. It's to your advantage to take the time and choose an agent who is most closely aligned to your interests and your manuscript's subject.

The agents listed in this section have all indicated that they are open to working with new, previously unpublished writers as well as published writers. None of the agents listed here charge a reading fee, which is money paid to an agent to cover the time and effort in reading a manuscript or a few sample chapters. While there is nothing wrong with charging a reading fee (after all, agents have to make a living too), we encourage writers to first try agents that do not.

Most of the agents listed here are members of AAR, the Association of Authors' Representatives. The AAR is a voluntary professional organization, whose members agree to abide by a strict code of ethics that prohibits charging fees for reading a manuscript or editorial services or receiving "consideration fees" for successful referrals to third parties.

We also present a small section of script agents, all members of the Writers' Guild of America (WGA). WGA signatory agencies are prohibited from charging fees from WGA members; most do not charge fees of nonmembers, as well.

The listings that follow contain the information you need to determine if an agent is suitable for your work. Read each listing carefully to see if an agency specializes in your subject areas. Or go straight to the Literary Agent Subject Index found after the listings to compile a list of agencies specifically interested in the subjects you write. We've broken the Subject Index into three main categories: Nonfiction, Fiction and Scripts.

Literary & Script Agents: The Listings

This section consists of 75 individual agency listings, followed by a Subject Index of nonfiction and fiction book and script categories which list the names of agencies that have expressed an interest in manuscripts on that subject. We've included listings for both literary and script agents. Literary agents are interested in nonfiction and fiction book manuscripts while script agents read only television and movie scripts.

You can approach the information listed here in two ways. You can skim through the listings and see if an agent stands out as particularly right for your manuscript and proceed from there. Or you can check the Subject Indexes that follow these listings to focus your search more narrowly. Cross-referencing categories and concentrating on those agents interested in two or more aspects of your manuscript might increase your chances of success.

Either way, it is important to carefully read the information contained in the listing. Each agency has different interests, submission requirements and response times. They'll tell you what they want, what they don't want, and how they want to receive it. Try to follow their directions as closely as possible. For these agents in particular, time is extremely important, and wasting theirs won't help your case.

There are several sections to each listing. The first paragraph lists the agency's name, address and contact information. It also includes when the agency was established, how many clients it represents and what percentage of those clients are new/previously unpublished writers. It offers the agency's self-described areas of specialization and a breakdown of the different types of manuscripts it handles (nonfiction, fiction, movie scripts, etc.).

The first subsection is **Members Agents**, which lists the individuals who work at the agency. The next is **Handles**, which outlines the different nonfiction and fiction categories an agency will look at. **How to Contact** specifies how agents want to receive material and how long you should wait for their response. **Needs** identifies subjects they are particularly interested in seeing, as well as what they definitely do not handle and will not look at. **Recent Sales** is pretty self-explanatory. **Terms** offers information on the commission an agent takes (domestic and foreign), if a written contract is offered, and whether and what miscellaneous expenses are charged to an author's account. **Writers' Conferences** identifies conferences that agent attends. And **Tips** presents words of advice an agent might want to give prospective authors.

FOR MORE ON THE SUBJECT . . .

The *Guide to Literary Agents* (Writer's Digest Books) offers 550 agent listings and a wealth of informational articles on the author/agent relationship and other related topics.

LITERARY AGENTS

N **ALTAIR LITERARY AGENCY**, 141 Fifth Ave., Suite 8N, New York NY 10010. (212)505-3320. **Contact:** Nicholas Smith, partner. Estab. 1996. Member of AAR. Represents 75 clients. Currently handles: 95% nonfiction books; 2% novels; 2% story collections; juvenile books; 1% multimedia.
Member Agents: Andrea Pedolsky, partner (nonfiction); Nicholas Smith, partner.
Represents: Nonfiction books. **Considers these nonfiction areas:** Anthropology/archaeology, art/architecture/design, biography/autobiography, business/economics, ethnic/cultural interests, gay/lesbian, government/politics/law, health/

medicine, history, how-to, money/finance, music/dance, nature/environment, photography, popular culture, psychology, religious/inspirational, science/technology, self-help/personal improvement, sociology, sports, women's issues/studies, illustrated books. **Considers these fiction areas:** Historical, literary.

O— This agency specializes in nonfiction with an emphasis on authors who have a direct connection to their topic, and at least a moderate level of public exposure.

How to Contact: Query with SASE. Considers simultaneous queries. Responds in 3 weeks on queries; 1 month on mss. Obtains most new clients through recommendations from others, solicitations, author queries

Needs: Solid, well-informed authors who have or are developing a public platform for the subject specialty true crime, memoirs, romance novels.

Recent Sales: *Women of Discovery*, by Milbry Polk and Mary Tiegreen (Crown/Clarkson Potter); *Building a Business the Zen Way*, by Geri Larkin (Ten Speed/Celestial Arts); *Date Smart!*, by David Coleman and Rick Doyle (Prima).

Terms: Agent receives 15% commission on domestic sales; 20% commission on foreign sales. Offers written contract 1 year; 60-day notice must be given to terminate contract. Charges clients for photocopying (edits of the proposal/chapters/ms to author, copies of proposal for submissions), postage (correspondence to author, proposals for submission), and marketing book for translation rights. May refer writers to outside editor but receives no compensation for referral.

Tips: "Beyond being able to write a compelling book, have an understanding of the market issues that are driving publishing today."

MIRIAM ALTSHULER LITERARY AGENCY, 53 Old Post Rd. N., Red Hook NY 12571. (845)758-9408. Fax: (845)758-3118. E-mail: malalit@ulster.net. **Contact:** Miriam Altshuler. Estab. 1994. Member of AAR. Represents 40 clients.

● Ms. Altshuler has been an agent since 1982.

Represents: Nonfiction books, novels, short story collections, juvenile books. **Considers these nonfiction areas:** Biography/autobiography, ethnic/cultural interests, history, language/literature/criticism, memoirs, multicultural, music/dance, nature/environment, popular culture, psychology, sociology, women's issues/studies. **Considers these fiction areas:** Literary, mainstream/contemporary, multicultural, thriller/espionage.

How to Contact: Query with SASE. No e-mail or fax queries. Responds in 2 weeks on queries; 3 weeks on mss. Returns materials only with SASE. Obtains most new clients through recommendations from others.

Terms: Agent receives 15% commission on domestic sales; 20% commission on foreign sales. No written contract. Charges clients for overseas mailing, photocopies.

Writers' Conference(s): Bread Loaf Writers' Conference (Middlebury, VT, August).

BETSY AMSTER LITERARY ENTERPRISES, P.O. Box 27788, Los Angeles CA 90027-0788. **Contact:** Betsy Amster. Estab. 1992. Member of AAR. Represents over 50 clients. 40% of clients are new/unpublished writers. Currently handles: 65% nonfiction books; 35% novels.

● Prior to opening her agency, Ms. Amster was an editor at Pantheon and Vintage for 10 years and served as editorial director for the Globe Pequot Press for 2 years. "This experience gives me a wider perspective on the business and the ability to give focused editorial feedback to my clients."

Represents: Nonfiction books, novels. **Considers these nonfiction areas:** Business/economics, child guidance/parenting, ethnic/cultural interests, gardening, health/medicine, history, money/finance, psychology, sociology, women's issues/studies. **Considers these fiction areas:** Ethnic, literary.

How to Contact: Query with SASE. Responds in 1 month on queries; 2 months on mss. Obtains most new clients through recommendations from others.

Needs: Actively seeking "outstanding fiction (the next Jane Smiley or Wally Lamb) and high profile self-help/psychology." Does not want to receive poetry, children's books, romances, westerns, science fiction.

Recent Sales: *Esperanza's Box of Saints*, by Maria Amparo Escandon; *The Lake of Palos Verdes*, by Joy Nicholson (St. Martin's); *How to be a Chicano Role Model*, by Michele M. Serros (Riverhead).

Terms: Agent receives 15% commission on domestic sales. Offers written contract 1-2 years; 60 days notice must be given to terminate contract. Charges for photocopying, postage, long distance phone calls, messengers and gallerys and books used in submissions to foreign and film agents and to magazines for first serial rights.

Writers' Conference(s): Squaw Valley.

MEREDITH BERNSTEIN LITERARY AGENCY, 2112 Broadway, Suite 503 A, New York NY 10023. (212)799-1007. Fax: (212)799-1145. Estab. 1981. Member of AAR. Represents 100 clients. 20% of clients are new/unpublished writers.

● Prior to opening her agency, Ms. Bernstein served in another agency for 5 years.

Member Agents: Meredith Bernstein; Elizabeth Cavanaugh.

Represents: Nonfiction books, novels. **Considers these nonfiction areas:** Animals (pets), business/economics, child guidance/parenting, health/medicine, psychology, science/technology, spirituality, narrative nonfiction, e-commerce, politics. **Considers these fiction areas:** Literary, mystery/suspense, romance, women's fiction.

O— This agency does not specialize, "very eclectic."

How to Contact: Query with SASE. Obtains most new clients through recommendations from others, conferences, also develops and packages own ideas.

Recent Sales: *Bone Density Diet Book*, by Dr. George Kessler (Ballantine); *Natural Healing for Dogs and Cats*, by Amy Shujai (Rodale); *Interview with an Angel*, by Linda Nathanson and Stephen Thayer (Dell).

Terms: Agent receives 15% commission on domestic sales; 20% commission on foreign sales. Charges clients $75 disbursement fee per year.

N BOOK DEALS, INC., 417 N. Sangamon St, Chicago IL 60622. (312)491-0030. Fax: (312)491-8091. E-mail: bookdeals@aol.com. Website: www.bookdealsinc.com. **Contact:** Caroline Francis Carney. Estab. 1996. Member of AAR. Represents 50 clients. 25% of clients are new/unpublished writers. Currently handles: 75% nonfiction books; 25% novels.

• Prior to opening her agency, Ms. Carney was editorial director for a consumer book imprint within Times Mirror and held senior editorial positions in McGraw-Hill and Simon & Schuster.

Represents: Nonfiction books, novels. **Considers these nonfiction areas:** Business/economics, child guidance/parenting, ethnic/cultural interests, health/medicine (nutrition), history, how-to, money/finance, popular culture, psychology, science/technology, self-help/personal improvement, spirituality (inspirational). **Considers these fiction areas:** Ethnic, literary, mainstream/contemporary, suspense (white collar crime stories), thriller/espionage (financial and medical thrillers), urban literature; contemporary women's fiction.

O– This agency specializes in highly commercial nonfiction and well-crafted action.

How to Contact: Query with SASE, proposal package, outline, Fiction by referral only. Accepts e-mail queries. Considers simultaneous queries. Responds in 1 month on queries.

Needs: Actively seeking well-crafted fiction and nonfiction from authors with engaging voices and impeccable credentials.

Recent Sales: Sold 15 books in the last year. *Out of the Dark*, by Maurice Possley and Rick Kogan (Putnam/film rights to Warner Bros); *The Most Important Thing I Know*, by Lorne Adrain (Andrews McMeel); *Silver Spoons: How to Raise a Child in an Age of Affluence*, by Jon and Eileen Gallo (Contemporary Books).

Terms: Agent receives 15% commission on domestic sales; 20% commission on foreign sales. Offers written contract. Charges clients for photocopying and postage.

N BRANDT & HOCHMAN LITERARY AGENTS INC., 1501 Broadway, New York NY 10036. (212)840-5760. Fax: (212)840-5776. **Contact:** Carl Brandt, Gail Hochman, Marianne Merola, Charles Schlessiger. Estab. 1913. Member of AAR. Represents 200 clients. Currently handles: nonfiction books; novels; story collections; novellas; juvenile books; scholarly books.

Represents: Nonfiction books, novels, short story collections, novellas, juvenile books, scholarly books. **Considers these nonfiction areas:** Agriculture/horticulture, animals, anthropology/archaeology, art/architecture/design, biography/autobiography, business/economics, child guidance/parenting, cooking/foods/nutrition, current affairs, ethnic/cultural interests, gay/lesbian, government/politics/law, health/medicine, history, hobbies (crafts), language/literature/criticism, military/war, money/finance, music/dance, nature/environment, psychology, science/technology (technology), self-help/personal improvement, sociology, sports, true crime/investigative, women's issues/studies, interior design/decorating; juvenile nonfiction. **Considers these fiction areas:** Action/adventure, detective/police/crime, ethnic, experimental, feminist, gay/lesbian, historical, humor, literary, mainstream/contemporary, mystery/suspense, occult (psychic/supernatural), regional, romance, science fiction, sports, suspense, thriller/espionage, western/frontier, young adult. Charges clients $35 mailing/materials fee with signed agency agreement

How to Contact: Query with SASE. Responds in 1 month on queries. Returns materials only with SASE. Obtains most new clients through recommendations from others.

Recent Sales: Sold 50 books in the last year.

Terms: Agent receives 15% commission on domestic sales; 20% commission on foreign sales. Charges clients for "manuscript duplication or other special expenses agreed to in advance."

Tips: "Write a letter which will give the agent a sense of you as a professional writer, your long-term interests as well as a short description of the work at hand."

SHEREE BYKOFSKY ASSOCIATES, INC., 16 W. 36th St., 13th Floor, New York NY 10018. Website: www.shereebee.com. **Contact:** Sheree Bykofsky. Estab. 1984. Member of AAR, ASJA, WNBA. Represents "a limited number" clients. Currently handles: 80% nonfiction books; 20% novels.

• Prior to opening her agency, Ms. Bykofsky served as executive editor of The Stonesong Press and managing editor of Chiron Press. She is also the author or co-author of more than 10 books.

Represents: Nonfiction books, novels. **Considers these nonfiction areas:** Americana, animals, anthropology/archaeology, art/architecture/design, business/economics, child guidance/parenting, computers/electronic, cooking/foods/nutrition, creative nonfiction, education, ethnic/cultural interests, gardening, gay/lesbian, government/politics/law, health/medicine, history, hobbies, language/literature/criticism, memoirs, military/war, money/finance, multicultural, music/dance, nature/environment, philosophy, photography, psychology, recreation, regional, religious/inspirational, science/technology, sex, sociology, software, spirituality, sports, translation, travel, women's issues/studies. **Considers these fiction areas:** Literary, mainstream/contemporary.

How to Contact: Query with SASE. Considers simultaneous queries. Responds in 1 week on queries; 1 month on mss. Returns materials only with SASE. Obtains most new clients through recommendations from others.

Needs: "I have wide-ranging interests, but it really depends on quality of writing, originality, and how a particular project appeals to me (or not). I take on very little fiction unless I completely love it—it doesn't matter what area or genre." Does not want to receive poetry, material for children, screenplays.

Recent Sales: Sold 50 books in the last year.

Terms: Agent receives 15% commission on domestic sales; 15% commission on foreign sales. Offers written contract 1 year. Charges for postage, photocopying and fax.
Writers' Conference(s): ASJA (NYC).
Tips: "Read the agent listing carefully, and comply with guidelines."

☒ MARIA CARVAINIS AGENCY, INC., 1350 Avenue of the Americas, Suite 2905, New York NY 10019. (212)245-6365. Fax: (212)245-7196. E-mail: mca@mariacarvainisagency.com. **Contact:** Maria Carvainis. Estab. 1977. Member of AAR; signatory of WGA. Represents 35 clients. 10% of clients are new/unpublished writers. Currently handles: 34% nonfiction books; 65% novels; 1% poetry.
 • Prior to opening her agency, Ms. Carvainis spent more than 10 years in the publishing industry as a senior editor with Macmillan Publishing, Basic Books, Avon Books, where she worked closely with Peter Mayer and Crown Publishers. Ms. Carvainis has served as a member of the AAR Board of Directors and AAR Treasurer, as well as serving as chair of the AAR Contracts Committee. She presently serves on the AAR Royalty Committee.
Member Agents: Dana Levin (literary associate); Margarate Mary (literary assistant).
Represents: Nonfiction books, novels. **Considers these nonfiction areas:** Biography/autobiography, business/economics, health/medicine, memoirs, science/technology (pop science), women's issues/studies. **Considers these fiction areas:** Fantasy, historical, literary, mainstream/contemporary, mystery/suspense, romance, suspense, thriller/espionage, young adult.
How to Contact: Query with SASE. Responds in 3 weeks on queries; 3 months on mss. Obtains most new clients through recommendations from others, solicitations, conferences. 60% from conferences/referrals; 40% from query letters.
Needs: Does not want to receive science fiction or children's.
Recent Sales: *The Alibi AND Standoff*, by Sandra Brown (Warner Books); *The Guru Guide to the New Economy*, by Joseph H. Boyett and Jimmie T. Boyett (John Wiley and Sonts); *Bearing Witness*, by Michael Kahn (TOR/Forge).
Terms: Agent receives 15% commission on domestic sales; 20% commission on foreign sales. Offers written contract 2 years "on a book-by-book basis." Charges clients for foreign postage, bulk copying.
Writers' Conference(s): BEA.

☒ CASTIGLIA LITERARY AGENCY, 1155 Camino Del Mar, Suite 510, Del Mar CA 92014. (858)755-8761. Fax: (858)755-7063. **Contact:** Julie Castiglia. Estab. 1993. Member of AAR, PEN. Represents 50 clients. Currently handles: 55% nonfiction books; 45% novels.
Member Agents: Winifred Golden; Julie Castiglia.
Represents: Nonfiction books, novels. **Considers these nonfiction areas:** Animals, anthropology/archaeology, biography/autobiography, business/economics, child guidance/parenting, cooking/foods/nutrition, current affairs, ethnic/cultural interests, health/medicine, history, language/literature/criticism, money/finance, nature/environment, psychology, religious/inspirational, science/technology, self-help/personal improvement, sociology, women's issues/studies, New Age/metaphysics. **Considers these fiction areas:** Ethnic, literary, mainstream/contemporary, mystery/suspense, suspense, women's fiction especially.
How to Contact: Query with SASE. Responds in 2 months on mss. Returns materials only with SASE. Obtains most new clients through recommendations from others, solicitations, conferences.
Needs: Does not want to receive horror, science fiction, screenplays or academic nonfiction.
Recent Sales: Sold 24 books in the last year. *Mothers Work*, by Rebecca Matthias (Doubleday); *Squeeze the Moment*, by Karen O'Connor (Waterbrook/Doubleday); *Outside the Bungalow*, by Doug Keister and Paul Discherer (Penguin).
Terms: Agent receives 15% commission on domestic sales; 20% commission on foreign sales. Offers written contract 6-week notice must be given to terminate contract. notice must be given to terminate contract. Charges clients for excessive postage and copying.
Writers' Conference(s): Southwestern Writers Conference (Albuquerque NM, August).
Tips: "Be professional with submissions. Attend workshops and conferences before you approach an agent."

JOAN DAVES AGENCY, 21 W. 26th St., New York NY 10010. (212)685-2663. Fax: (212)685-1781. **Contact:** Jennifer Lyons, director; Heather Currier, assistant. Estab. 1960. Member of AAR. Represents 100 clients. 10% of clients are new/unpublished writers.
Represents: Nonfiction books, novels. **Considers these nonfiction areas:** Gay/lesbian, translation, women's issues/studies. **Considers these fiction areas:** Ethnic, gay/lesbian, literary, mainstream/contemporary.
 ⚬ This agency specializes in literary fiction and nonfiction, also commercial fiction.
How to Contact: Query with SASE. Considers simultaneous queries. Responds in 3 weeks on queries; 6 weeks on mss. Returns materials only with SASE. Obtains most new clients through recommendations from others, solicitations.
Recent Sales: Sold 70 books in the last year. *Strange Fire*, by Melvin Jules Bukiet (W.W. Norton); *JLVT! Growing Up Female with a Bad Reputation*, by Leora Tannenbaum; Candor and Perversion, by Roger Shattuck (W.W. Norton).
Terms: Agent receives 15% commission on domestic sales; 20% commission on foreign sales. Offers written contract per book basis.. Charges for office expenses.

☒ THE JONATHAN DOLGER AGENCY, 49 E. 96th St., Suite 9B, New York NY 10128. (212)427-1853. **Contact:** Herbert Erinmore. President: Jonathan Dolger. Estab. 1980. Member of AAR. Represents 70 clients. 25% of clients are new/unpublished writers.

• Prior to opening his agency, Mr. Dolger was vice president and managing editor for Simon & Schuster Trade Books.

Represents: Nonfiction books, novels, illustrated books.

○━ This agency specializes in adult trade fiction and nonfiction, and illustrated books.

How to Contact: Query with SASE.

Recent Sales: Sold 15-20 books in the last year.

Terms: Agent receives 15% commission on domestic sales; 25% commission on foreign sales. Charges clients for "standard expenses."

Tips: "Writer must have been previously published if submitting fiction. Prefers to work with published/established authors; works with a small number of new/previously unpublished writers."

JANE DYSTEL LITERARY MANAGEMENT, One Union Square West, Suite 904, New York NY 10003. (212)627-9100. Fax: (212)627-9313. Website: www.dystel.com. **Contact:** Miriam Goderich, Todd Keithley. Estab. 1994. Member of AAR. Represents 300 clients. 50% of clients are new/unpublished writers. Currently handles: 65% nonfiction books; 25% novels; 10% Cookbooks.

Member Agents: Stacey Glick; Jessica Jones; Charlotte Ho (foreign rights); Jane Dystel; Jo Fagan; Kyong Cho.

Represents: Nonfiction books, novels, cookbooks. **Considers these nonfiction areas:** Animals, anthropology/archaeology, business/economics, child guidance/parenting, cooking/foods/nutrition, education, ethnic/cultural interests, gay/lesbian, government/politics/law, health/medicine, history, military/war, money/finance, psychology, religious/inspirational, science/technology, women's issues/studies. **Considers these fiction areas:** Action/adventure, ethnic, gay/lesbian, literary, mainstream/contemporary, suspense, thriller/espionage.

○━ This agency specializes in commercial and literary fiction and nonfiction plus cookbooks.

How to Contact: Query with SASE. Responds in 3 weeks on queries; 6 weeks on mss. Obtains most new clients through recommendations from others, solicitations, conferences.

Recent Sales: *The Sparrow and Children of God*, by Mary Russell; *Water Carry Me*, by Thomas Moran; *Syrup*, by Maxx Barry.

Terms: Agent receives 15% commission on domestic sales; 19% commission on foreign sales. Offers written contract book to book basis. Charges for photocopying. Gallery charges and book charges from the publisher are passed on to the author.

Writers' Conference(s): West Coast Writers Conference (Whidbey Island WA, Columbus Day weekend).

Tips: Jane Dystel Literary Management recently acquired the client list of Bedford Book Works.

⟨N⟩ FELICIA ETH LITERARY REPRESENTATION, 555 Bryant St., Suite 350, Palo Alto CA 94301-1700. (650)375-1276. Fax: (650)375-1277. E-mail: feliciaeth@aol.com. **Contact:** Felicia Eth. Estab. 1988. Member of AAR. Represents 25-35 clients. Currently handles: 85% nonfiction books; 15% novels.

Represents: Nonfiction books, novels. **Considers these nonfiction areas:** Animals, anthropology/archaeology, biography/autobiography, business/economics, child guidance/parenting, current affairs, ethnic/cultural interests, gay/lesbian, government/politics/law, health/medicine, history, nature/environment, popular culture, psychology, science/technology, sociology, true crime/investigative, women's issues/studies. **Considers these fiction areas:** Ethnic, feminist, gay/lesbian, literary, mainstream/contemporary, thriller/espionage.

○━ This agency specializes in "provocative, intelligent, thoughtful nonfiction on a wide array of subjects which are commercial and high-quality fiction; preferably mainstream and contemporary."

How to Contact: Query with SASE, outline. Accepts e-mail queries. Responds in 3 weeks on queries; 1 month on mss.

Recent Sales: Sold 7-10 books in the last year. *Recovering the Power of the Ancestral Mind*, by Dr. Gregg Jacobs (Viking); *The Ulster Path*, by Will Ferguson (Grove/Atlantic); *Socrates Cafe*, by Chris Phillips (W.W. Norton).

Terms: Agent receives 15% commission on domestic sales; 20% commission on foreign sales. Charges clients for photocopying, express mail service—extraordinary expenses.

Writers' Conference(s): Independent Writers of LA (LA).

Tips: "For nonfiction, established expertise is certainly a plus, as is magazine publication—though not a prerequisite. I am highly dedicated to those projects I represent."

JEANNE FREDERICKS LITERARY AGENCY, INC., 221 Benedict Hill Rd., New Canaan CT 06840. (203)972-3011. Fax: (203)972-3011. E-mail: jflainc@ix.netcom.com. **Contact:** Jeanne Fredericks. Estab. 1997. Member of AAR. Represents 80 clients. 10% of clients are new/unpublished writers. Currently handles: 98% nonfiction books; 2% novels.

• Prior to opening her agency, Ms. Fredericks was an agent and acting director with the Susan P. Urstadt Inc. Agency.

Represents: Nonfiction books. **Considers these nonfiction areas:** Animals, anthropology/archaeology, art/architecture/design, business/economics, child guidance/parenting, cooking/foods/nutrition, health/medicine, history, money/finance, nature/environment, photography, psychology, science/technology, sports, women's issues/studies. **Considers these fiction areas:** Historical, literary.

○━ This agency specializes in quality adult nonfiction by authorities in their fields.

How to Contact: Query with SASE, submit proposal package, outline, 1-2 sample chapter(s). Accepts e-mail queries. No fax queries. Considers simultaneous queries. Responds in 3 weeks on queries; 6 weeks on mss. Returns materials only with SASE. Obtains most new clients through recommendations from others, solicitations, conferences.

Recent Sales: Sold 22 books in the last year.

Terms: Agent receives 15% commission on domestic sales; 20% commission on foreign sales. Offers written contract 9 months; 2 months notice must be given to terminate contract. Charges for photocopying of whole proposals and mss, overseas postage, priority mail and Federal Express.
Writers' Conference(s): PEN Women Conference (Williamsburg VA, February).
Tips: "Be sure to research the competition for your work and be able to justify why there's a need for it. I enjoy building an author's career, particularly if s(he) is professional, hardworking, and courteous. Aside from eight years of agenting experience, I've had ten years of editorial experience in adult trade book publishing that enables me to help an author polish a proposal so that it's more appealing to prospective editors. My MBA in marketing also distinguishes me from other agents."

SANFORD J. GREENBURGER ASSOCIATES, INC., 55 Fifth Ave., New York NY 10003. (212)206-5600. Fax: (212)463-8718. **Contact:** Heide Lange. Estab. 1945. Member of AAR. Represents 500 clients.
Member Agents: Faith Hamlin, Beth Vesel, Theresa Park, Elyse Cheney, Dan Mandel, Francis Greenburger.
Represents: Nonfiction books, novels. **Considers these nonfiction areas:** Americana, animals, anthropology/archaeology, art/architecture/design, business/economics, child guidance/parenting, computers/electronic, cooking/foods/nutrition, creative nonfiction, education, ethnic/cultural interests, gardening, gay/lesbian, government/politics/law, health/medicine, history, hobbies, language/literature/criticism, memoirs, military/war, money/finance, multicultural, music/dance, nature/environment, philosophy, photography, psychology, recreation, regional, religious/inspirational, science/technology, sex, sociology, software, spirituality, sports, translation, travel, women's issues/studies. **Considers these fiction areas:** Action/adventure, ethnic, feminist, gay/lesbian, historical, humor, literary, mainstream/contemporary, mystery/suspense, regional, sports, suspense, thriller/espionage.
How to Contact: Query with SASE. Responds in 3 weeks on queries; 2 months on mss.
Needs: Does not want to receive romances or westerns.
Recent Sales: Sold 200 books in the last year.
Terms: Agent receives 15% commission on domestic sales; 20% commission on foreign sales. Charges for photocopying, books for foreign and subsidiary rights submissions.

REECE HALSEY NORTH, 98 Main St., #704, Tiburon CA 94920. (415)789-9191. Fax: (415)789-9177. E-mail: bookgirl@worldnet.att.net. **Contact:** Kimberley Cameron. Estab. 1957. Member of AAR. Represents 40 clients. 30% of clients are new/unpublished writers. Currently handles: 70% nonfiction books; 30% novels.
● The Reece Halsey Agency has an illustrious client list largely of established writers, including the estate of Aldous Huxley and has represented Upton Sinclair, William Faulkner and Henry Miller. Ms. Cameron has opened a Northern California office and all queries should be addressed to her at the Tiburon office.
Represents: Nonfiction books, novels. **Considers these nonfiction areas:** History, language/literature/criticism, memoirs, spirituality, women's issues/studies. **Considers these fiction areas:** Action/adventure, ethnic, historical, literary, mainstream/contemporary, mystery/suspense, science fiction.
○➤ This agency specializes in mystery, literary and mainstream fiction, excellent writing.
How to Contact: Query with SASE. Responds in 3 weeks on queries; 3 months on mss. Obtains most new clients through recommendations from others, solicitations.
Terms: Agent receives 15% commission on domestic sales. Offers written contract binding for 1 year. Requests 6 copies of mss if representing author.
Writers' Conference(s): Maui Writer's Conference.
Tips: "Please send a polite, well-written query and include a SASE with it!"

THE JOY HARRIS LITERARY AGENCY, INC., 156 Fifth Ave., Suite 617, New York NY 10010. (212)924-6269. Fax: (212)924-6609. E-mail: gen.office@jhlitagent.com. **Contact:** Joy Harris. Member of AAR. Represents 150 clients. Currently handles: 50% nonfiction books; 50% novels.
Member Agents: Leslie Daniels.
Represents: Nonfiction books, novels. Considers "adult-type books, not juvenile." **Considers these fiction areas:** Considers all fiction areas except fantasy, juvenile, science fiction and westerns.
How to Contact: Query with SASE, submit proposal package, outline, "No unsolicited manuscripts, just query letter." Responds in 2 months to queries. Obtains most new clients through recommendations from clients and editors.
Needs: Does not want to receive screenplays.
Recent Sales: Sold 15 books in the last year.
Terms: Agent receives 15% commission on domestic sales; 20% commission on foreign sales. Charges clients for some office expenses.

HEACOCK LITERARY AGENCY, INC., P.O. Box 927, Main Branch, Malibu CA 90265-0927. (310)589-1775. Fax: (310)589-2825. E-mail: gracebooks@aol.com. **Contact:** Rosalie Grace Heacock. Estab. 1978. Member of AAR. Represents 60 clients. 10% of clients are new/unpublished writers. Currently handles: 100% nonfiction books.
Represents: Nonfiction books (adult), juvenile books (children's picture books). **Considers these nonfiction areas:** Art/architecture/design, biography/autobiography, how-to, music/dance, nature/environment, psychology, science/technology, self-help/personal improvement, spirituality, women's issues/studies, hiking. **Considers these fiction areas:** Considers limited selection of top children's book authors; no beginners, please.

How to Contact: Query with SASE. Responds in 3 weeks on queries; 2 months on mss. Returns materials only with SASE.
Recent Sales: Sold 22 books in the last year.
Terms: Agent receives 15% commission on domestic sales; 15-25% commission on foreign sales. Offers written contract 1 year. 95% of business is derived from commissions on ms sales. Charges clients for actual expense for telephone, postage, packing, photocopying. "We provide copies of each publisher submission letter and the publisher's response."
Writers' Conference(s): Maui Writers Conference.
Reading List: Reads "all trade journals, also literary magazines and environmental periodicals" to find new clients. Looks for "new ways to solve old problems."
Tips: "Take time to write an informative query letter expressing your book idea, the market for it, your qualifications to write the book, the 'hook' that would make a potential reader buy the book. Always enclose SASE; we cannot respond to queries without return postage. Our primary focus is upon books which make a contribution."

N THE JEFF HERMAN AGENCY LLC, 332 Bleecker St., New York NY 10014. (212)941-0540. E-mail: jeff@jeffherman.com. Website: www.jeffherman.com. **Contact:** Jeffrey H. Herman. Estab. 1985. Member of AAR. Represents 100 clients. 10% of clients are new/unpublished writers.
● Prior to opening his agency, Mr. Herman served as a public relations executive.
Member Agents: Deborah Levine (vice president, nonfiction book doctor); Jeff Herman; Amanda White
Represents: Nonfiction books. **Considers these nonfiction areas:** Business/economics, computers/electronic, government/politics/law, health/medicine, history, how-to, psychology (popular), self-help/personal improvement, spirituality, popular reference; recovery.
O➥ This agency specializes in adult nonfiction.
How to Contact: Query with SASE.
Terms: Agent receives 15% commission on domestic sales. Offers written contract.

JCA LITERARY AGENCY, 27 W. 20th St., Suite 1103, New York NY 10011. (212)807-0888. Fax: (212)807-0461. **Contact:** Jeff Gerecke, Tony Outhwaite. Estab. 1978. Member of AAR. Represents 100 clients. 20% of clients are new/unpublished writers. Currently handles: 20% nonfiction books; 75% novels; 5% scholarly books.
Member Agents: Jeff Gerecke; Tony Outhwaite; Peter Steinberg.
Represents: Nonfiction books, novels. **Considers these nonfiction areas:** Anthropology/archaeology, business/economics, government/politics/law, health/medicine, history, language/literature/criticism, memoirs, military/war, money/finance, music/dance, nature/environment, science/technology, sociology, sports, translation, women's issues/studies. **Considers these fiction areas:** Action/adventure, historical, literary, mainstream/contemporary, mystery/suspense, sports, suspense, thriller/espionage.
How to Contact: Query with SASE. No e-mail or fax queries. Considers simultaneous queries. Responds in 2 weeks on queries; 6 weeks on mss. Returns materials only with SASE. Obtains most new clients through recommendations from others, solicitations, conferences.
Needs: Does not want to receive screenplays, poetry, children's books, science fiction/fantasy, genre romance.
Recent Sales: *The Lost Glass Plates of Wilfred Eng*, by Thomas Orton (Counterpoint); *Sharp Shooter*, by David Healey (The Berkley Publishing Group/Jove); *A Healthy Place to Die*, by Peter King (St. Martin's Press).
Terms: Agent receives 15% commission on domestic sales; 20% commission on foreign sales. No written contract. "We work with our clients on a handshake basis." Charges for postage on overseas submissions, photocopying, mss for submission, books purchased for subrights submission, and bank charges, where applicable. "We deduct the cost from payments received from publishers."
Tips: "We do not ourselves provide legal, accounting, or public relations services for our clients, although some of the advice we give falls somewhat into these realms. In cases where it seems necessary we will recommend obtaining outside advice or assistance in these areas from professionals who are not in any way connected to the agency."

N KIDDE, HOYT & PICARD, 335 E. 51st St., New York NY 10022. (212)755-9461. Fax: (212)223-2501. **Contact:** Katherine Kidde, Laura Langlie. Estab. 1980. Member of AAR. Represents 80 clients. Currently handles: 15% nonfiction books; 80% novels; 5% juvenile books.
● Prior to becoming agents, Ms. Kidde was an editor/senior editor at Harcourt Brace, New American Library and Putnam; Ms. Langlie worked in production and editorial at Kensington and Carroll & Graf.
Member Agents: Kay Kidde (mainstream fiction, general nonfiction, mysteries, romances, literary fiction); Laura Langlie (romances, mysteries, literary fiction, general nonfiction).
Represents: Nonfiction books, novels. **Considers these nonfiction areas:** Art/architecture/design, biography/autobiography, current affairs, ethnic/cultural interests, gay/lesbian, history, language/literature/criticism, memoirs, popular culture, psychology, self-help/personal improvement, sociology, women's issues/studies. **Considers these fiction areas:** Detective/police/crime, feminist, gay/lesbian, historical, humor, literary, mainstream/contemporary, mystery/suspense, romance (contemporary, historical, regency), thriller/espionage.
O➥ This agency specializes in mainstream fiction and nonfiction.
How to Contact: Query with SASE. Considers simultaneous queries. Responds in 3 weeks on queries; 1 month on mss. Returns materials only with SASE. Obtains most new clients through recommendations from others, solicitations, "former authors from when I was an editor, listings in LMP, writers' guides."

Needs: Actively seeking "strong mainstream fiction." Does not want to receive "male adventure, science fiction, juvenile, porn, plays or poetry."
Recent Sales: *The Book of the Lion*, by Michael Cadnum (Viking); *Whose Little Girl Are You?*, by Bethany Campbell (Bantam); *Night Bus*, by Janice Law (Forge/TOR).
Terms: Agent receives 15% commission on domestic sales; 20% commission on foreign sales. Charges clients for photocopying.
Reading List: Reads literary journals and magazines, Harper's, DoubleTake, etc. to find new clients.

THE KNIGHT AGENCY, P.O. Box 550648, Atlanta GA 30355. (404)816-9620. E-mail: knightagency@msn.com. Website: www.knightagency.net. **Contact:** Deidre Knight. Estab. 1996. Member of AAR, RWA, Authors Guild. Represents 30 clients. 40% of clients are new/unpublished writers. Currently handles: 50% nonfiction books; 50% novels.
Represents: Nonfiction books, novels. **Considers these nonfiction areas:** Business/economics, child guidance/parenting, computers/electronic, cooking/foods/nutrition, ethnic/cultural interests, health/medicine, history, money/finance, music/dance, psychology, religious/inspirational, sports. **Considers these fiction areas:** Ethnic, literary, mainstream/contemporary, romance (contemporary, historical, inspirational).
How to Contact: Query with SASE. Considers simultaneous queries. Responds in 2 weeks on queries; 6 weeks on mss.
Needs: "We are looking for a wide variety of fictions and nonfiction. In the nonfiction area, we're particularly eager to find personal finance, business investment, pop culture, self-help/motivational and popular reference books. In fiction, we're always looking for romance; women's fiction; commercial fiction."
Recent Sales: Sold 20 books in the last year. *Panic-Proof Parenting*, by Debra Holtzman (NTC/Contemporary); *Simple Strategies for Electronic Daytrades*, by Tori Turner (Adams Media); *Abbey Road to Zapple Records: A Beatles Encyclopedia*, by Judson Knight (Taylor Publishing).
Terms: Agent receives 15% commission on domestic sales; 25% commission on foreign sales. Offers written contract 1 year; 60 days notice must be given to terminate contract. Charges clients for photocopying, postage, overnight courier expenses.

PINDER LANE & GARON-BROOKE ASSOCIATES, LTD., 159 W. 53rd St., Suite 14E, New York NY 10019-6005. (212)489-0880. **Contact:** Robert Thixton. Member of AAR; signatory of WGA. Represents 80 clients. 20% of clients are new/unpublished writers. Currently handles: 25% nonfiction books; 75% novels.
Member Agents: Nancy Coffey, Dick Duane, Robert Thixton.
Represents: Nonfiction books, novels. **Considers these nonfiction areas:** Child guidance/parenting, gay/lesbian, health/medicine, history, memoirs, military/war, music/dance, psychology. **Considers these fiction areas:** Fantasy, gay/lesbian, literary, mainstream/contemporary, mystery/suspense, romance, science fiction, suspense.
    O— This agency specializes in mainstream fiction and nonfiction.
How to Contact: Query with SASE. Responds in 3 weeks on queries; 2 months on mss. Obtains most new clients through recommendations from others, solicitations.
Needs: Does not want to receive screenplays, TV series teleplays or dramatic plays. Obtains new clients through referrals and from queries.
Recent Sales: Sold 15 books in the last year. *Nobody's Safe*, by Richard Steinberg (Doubleday); *The Kill Box*, by Chris Stewart (M. Evans); *Return to Christmas*, by Chris Heimerdinger (Ballantine).
Terms: Agent receives 15% commission on domestic sales; 30% commission on foreign sales. Offers written contract 3-5 years.
Tips: "With our literary and media experience, our agency is uniquely positioned for the current and future direction publishing is taking. Send query letter first giving the essence of the ms and a personal or career bio with SASE."

MICHAEL LARSON/ELIZABETH POMADA LITERARY AGENTS, 1029 Jones St., San Francisco CA 94109-5023. (415)673-0939. E-mail: larsenpoma@aol.com. Website: www.Larsen-Pomada.com. **Contact:** Mike Larsen or Elizabeth Pomada. Estab. 1972. Member of AAR, Authors Guild, ASJA, NWA, PEN, WNBA, California Writers Club. Represents 100 clients. 40-45% of clients are new/unpublished writers. Currently handles: 70% nonfiction books; 30% novels.
    ● Prior to opening their agency, both Mr. Larsen and Ms. Pomada were promotion executives for major publishing houses. Mr. Larsen worked for Morrow, Bantam and Pyramid (now part of Berkley), Ms. Pomada worked at Holt, David McKay, and The Dial Press.
Member Agents: Michael Larsen (nonfiction); Elizabeth Pomada (fiction, books of interest to women).
Represents: Nonfiction books (adult), novels. **Considers these nonfiction areas:** Anthropology/archaeology, art/architecture/design, business/economics, cooking/foods/nutrition, ethnic/cultural interests, gay/lesbian, government/politics/law, health/medicine, history, language/literature/criticism, memoirs, money/finance, music/dance, nature/environment, photography, psychology, religious/inspirational, science/technology, sociology, sports, travel, women's issues/studies. **Considers these fiction areas:** Action/adventure, ethnic, experimental, fantasy, feminist, gay/lesbian, historical, humor, literary, mainstream/contemporary, mystery/suspense, religious, romance (contemporary, gothic, historical).
How to Contact: Query with SASE, submit outline, sample chapter(s). Responds in 2 months on queries.
Needs: Actively seeking commercial and literary fiction. "Fresh voices with new ideas of interest to major publishers." Does not want to receive children's books, plays, short stories, screenplays, pornography.

Recent Sales: *Black Raven*, by Katharine Kerr (Bantam/Spectra); *If Life Is a Game, These Are the Rules*, by Cherie Carter-Scott (Broadway Books); *The Center at the Edge, Seeking the Inner Meaning of Outer Space*, by Wyn Wachhorst (Basic Books).

Terms: Agent receives 15% commission on domestic sales; 20-30% commission on foreign sales. May charge for printing, postage for multiple submissions, foreign mail, foreign phone calls, galleys, books, and legal fees.

Writers' Conference(s): Book Expo America.

Tips: "We have very diverse tastes. We look for fresh voices and new ideas. We handle literary, commercial and genre fiction, and the full range of nonfiction books."

N. NANCY LOVE LITERARY AGENCY, 250 E. 65th St., New York NY 10021-6614. (212)980-3499. Fax: (212)308-6405. **Contact:** Nancy Love or Daniel Genis. Estab. 1984. Member of AAR. Represents 60-80 clients. Currently handles: 90% nonfiction books; 10% novels.

Member Agents: Nancy Love

Represents: Nonfiction books, novels (mysteries and thrillers only). **Considers these nonfiction areas:** Animals, biography/autobiography, child guidance/parenting, cooking/foods/nutrition, current affairs, ethnic/cultural interests, government/politics/law, health/medicine, history, how-to, memoirs, nature/environment, popular culture, psychology, science/technology, self-help/personal improvement, sociology, spirituality (New Age/metaphysics), travel (armchair only, no how-to travel), true crime/investigative, women's issues/studies. **Considers these fiction areas:** Mystery/suspense, thriller/espionage.

O—π This agency specializes in adult nonfiction and mysteries.

How to Contact: For nonficiton, send a proposal, chapter summary and sample chapter. For fiction, query first. No e-mail or fax queries. Considers simultaneous queries. Responds in 3 weeks on queries; 6 weeks on mss. Returns materials only with SASE. Obtains most new clients through recommendations from others.

Needs: Actively seeking health and medicine (including alternative medicine); parenting, spiritual and inspirational Does not want to receive novels other than mysteries and thrillers.

Recent Sales: Sold 18 books in the last year. *The One-Minute Mediator*, by David Nichols, M.D. and William Circhard (Perseus); *Brotherman Rising: Raising Black Boys*, by Warren Spielberg, Ph.D. and Kirkland Vaughans, Ph.D (Harper-Collins); *Deadly Nightshade*, by Cynthia Riggs (St. Martin's Press).

Terms: Agent receives 15% commission on domestic sales; 20% commission on foreign sales. Offers written contract. Charges clients for photocopying, overseas postage, faxes, phone calls.

N. DONALD MAASS LITERARY AGENCY, 160 W. 95th Street, Suite 1B, New York NY 10025. (212)866-8200. Fax: (212)866-8181. **Contact:** Donald Maass, Jennifer Jackson or Michelle Brummer. Estab. 1980. Member of AAR, SFWA, MWA, RWA. Represents over 100 clients. 5% of clients are new/unpublished writers. Currently handles: 100% novels.

● Prior to opening his agency, Mr. Maass served as an editor at Dell Publishing (NY) and as a reader at Gollancz (London). Maass is the current president of AAR.

Member Agents: Donald Maass (mainstream, literary, mystery/suspense, science fiction); Jennifer Jackson (commercial fiction: especially romance, science fiction, fantasy, mystery/suspense); Michelle Brummer (fiction: literary, contemporary, feminist, science fiction, fantasy).

Represents: Novels. **Considers these fiction areas:** Detective/police/crime, fantasy, historical, horror, literary, mainstream/contemporary, mystery/suspense, occult (psychic, supernatural), romance (historical, paranormal, time travel), science fiction, suspense, thriller/espionage.

O—π This agency specializes in commercial fiction, especially science fiction, fantasy, mystery, romance, suspense.

How to Contact: Query with SASE. Considers simultaneous queries. Responds in 2 weeks on queries; 3 months on mss.

Needs: Actively seeking "to expand the literary portion of our list and expand in romance and women's fiction." Does not want to receive nonfiction, children's or poetry.

Recent Sales: Sold over 100 books in the last year. *Slaves of Obsession*, by Anne Perry (Ballantine); *The Lightstone*, by David Zendell (Warner Aspect); *Midnight Robber*, by Nalo Hopkinson (Warner Aspect).

Terms: Agent receives 15% commission on domestic sales; 20% commission on foreign sales. Charges clients for large photocopying orders and book samples "after consultation with author."

Writers' Conference(s): World Science Fiction Convention.

Tips: "We are fiction specialists, also noted for our innovative approach to career planning. Few new clients are accepted, but interested authors should query with SASE. Subagents in all principle foreign countries and Hollywood. No nonfiction or juvenile works considered."

MANUS & ASSOCIATES LITERARY AGENCY, INC., 375 Forest Ave., Palo Alto CA 94301. (650)470-5151. Fax: (650)470-5159. E-mail: manuslit@manuslit.com. Website: www.manuslit.com. **Contact:** Jillian Manus and Janet Manus. Estab. 1985. Member of AAR. Represents 75 clients. 30% of clients are new/unpublished writers. Currently handles: 55% nonfiction books; 40% novels; 5% juvenile books.

● Prior to becoming agents, Jillian Manus was associate publisher of two national magazines and director of development at Warner Bros. and Universal Studios. Janet Manus has been a literary agent for 20 years.

Member Agents: Jandy Nelson (self-help, health, memoirs, narrative nonfiction, literary fiction, multicultural fiction, thrillers); Jill Maverick (self-help, health, memoirs, dramatic nonfiction, women's fiction, commercial literary fiction, Southern writing, thrillers); Stephanie Lee (self-help, memoirs, dramatic nonfiction, commercial literary fiction, multicultural fiction, quirky/edgy fiction).

Represents: Nonfiction books, novels. **Considers these nonfiction areas:** Business/economics, child guidance/parenting, computers/electronic, ethnic/cultural interests, health/medicine, memoirs, money/finance, nature/environment, psychoion books, novels. **Considers these nonfiction areas:** Business/economics, child guidance/parenting, computers/electronic, ethnic/cultural interests, health/medicine, memoirs, money/finance, nature/environment, psychology, science/technology, women's issues/studies. **Considers these fiction areas:** Literary, mainstream/contemporary, multicultural, suspense, thriller/espionage.

> O━ This agency specializes in commercial literary fiction, narrative nonfiction, thrillers, health, pop psychology, women's empowerment. "Our agency is unique in the way that we not only sell the material, but we edit, develop concepts and participate in the marketing effort. We specialize in large, conceptual fiction and nonfiction, and always value a project that can be sold in the TV/feature film market."

How to Contact: Query with SASE, submit outline, 2-3 sample chapter(s). Accepts e-mail and fax queries. Considers simultaneous queries. Responds in 2 months on queries; 6 weeks on mss. Returns materials only with SASE. Obtains most new clients through recommendations from others, solicitations, conferences.

Needs: Actively seeking high-concept thrillers, commercial literary fiction, women's fiction, celebrity biographies, memoirs, multicultural fiction, popular health, women's empowerment Does not want to receive horror, science fiction/fantasy, romance, westerns, young adult, children's, poetry, cookbooks, magazine articles. Usually obtains new clients through recommendations from editors, clients and others; conferences; and unsolicited materials.

Recent Sales: *Catfish & Mandala*, by Andrew X. Pham (Farrar, Strauss & Giroux); *Jake & Mimi*, by Frank Baldwin (Little, Brown); *Wishing Well*, by Paul Pearsall, Ph.D (Hyperion).

Terms: Agent receives 15% commission on domestic sales; 20-25% commission on foreign sales. Offers written contract 2 years; 60 days notice must be given to terminate contract. Charges for photocopying and postage.

Writers' Conference(s): Maui Writers Conference (Maui HI, Labor Day).

Tips: "Research agents using a variety of sources, including *LMP*, guides, *Publishers Weekly*, conferences and even acknowledgements in books similar in tone to yours."

MARGRET McBRIDE LITERARY AGENCY, 7744 Fay Ave., Suite 201, La Jolla CA 92037. (858)454-1550. Fax: (858)454-2156. Estab. 1980. Member of AAR, Authors Guild. Represents 50 clients. 15% of clients are new/unpublished writers.

> • Prior to opening her agency, Ms. McBride served in the marketing departments of Random House and Ballantine Books and the publicity departments of Warner Books and Pinnacle Books.

Represents: Nonfiction books, novels, Audio, video film rights. **Considers these nonfiction areas:** Business/economics, child guidance/parenting, cooking/foods/nutrition, ethnic/cultural interests, gay/lesbian, government/politics/law, health/medicine, history, money/finance, music/dance, psychology, religious/inspirational, science/technology, sociology, sports, women's issues/studies. **Considers these fiction areas:** Action/adventure, ethnic, historical, humor, literary, mainstream/contemporary, mystery/suspense, suspense, thriller/espionage, western/frontier.

> O━ This agency specializes in mainstream fiction and nonfiction.

How to Contact: Query with SASE, submit outline. Considers simultaneous queries. Responds in 6 weeks on queries. Returns materials only with SASE.

Needs: Does not want to receive screenplays.

Recent Sales: Sold 20 books in the last year. *Special Circumstances*, by Sheldon Siegel (Bantam); *Instant Emotional Healing*, by George Pratt Ph.D (Broadway); *Leadership by the Book*, by Ken Blanchard (Morrow).

Terms: Agent receives 15% commission on domestic sales; 25% commission on foreign sales. Charges for overnight delivery and photocopying.

⦙Ṉ⦙ CLAUDIA MENZA LITERARY AGENCY, 1170 Broadway, Suite 807, New York NY 10001. (212)889-6850. **Contact:** Claudia Menza. Estab. 1983. Member of AAR. Represents 111 clients. 50% of clients are new/unpublished writers. Currently handles: 50% nonfiction books; 30% novels; 1% story collections; 2% juvenile books; 3% scholarly books; 1% poetry; 2% movie scripts; 2% TV scripts; stage plays; 2% photographic books; 5% memoir.

> • Prior to becoming an agent, Ms. Menza was an editor/managing editor at a publishing company.

Represents: Nonfiction books, novels, short story collections, juvenile books, scholarly books, poetry books, movie scripts, TV movie of the week, stage plays. **Considers these nonfiction areas:** Business/economics, current affairs, education, ethnic/cultural interests, health/medicine, history, how-to, multicultural, music/dance, photography, psychology, self-help/personal improvement.

> O━ This agency specializes in African-American fiction and nonfiction, and editorial assistance.

How to Contact: Query with SASE, submit outline, 1 sample chapter(s). Responds in 2 weeks on queries; 4 months on mss. Returns materials only with SASE. Obtains most new clients through recommendations from others, solicitations.

Terms: Agent receives 15% commission on domestic sales; 20% commission on foreign sales. Offers written contract.

NEW ENGLAND PUBLISHING ASSOCIATES, INC., P.O. Box 5, Chester CT 06412-0645. (203)345-READ and (203)345-4976. Fax: (203)345-3660. E-mail: nepa@nepa.com. Website: www.nepa.com. **Contact:** Elizabeth Frost-Knappman, Edward W. Knappman, Kristine Sciavi, Ron Formica, or Victoria Harlow. Estab. 1983. Member of AAR, ASJA, Authors Guild, Connecticut Press Club. Represents 100 clients. 15% of clients are new/unpublished writers. **Represents:** Nonfiction books. **Considers these nonfiction areas:** Business/economics, child guidance/parenting, government/politics/law, health/medicine, history, language/literature/criticism, military/war, money/finance, nature/environment, psychology, science/technology, sociology, women's issues/studies. **Considers these fiction areas:** Mystery/suspense, suspense.

O—¬ This agency specializes in adult nonfiction of serious purpose.

How to Contact: Submit proposal package, outline. Considers simultaneous queries. Responds in 3 weeks on queries; 5 weeks on mss. Returns materials only with SASE.

Recent Sales: Sold 50 books in the last year. *The Woman's Migraine Survival Handbook*, by Christina Peterson and Christine Adamec (HarperCollins); *Dreams in the Key of Blue, A Novel*, by John Philpin (Bantam); *Ice Blink: The Mysterious Fate of Sir John Franklin's Lost Polar Expedition*, by Scott Cookman (Wiley).

Terms: Agent receives 15% commission on domestic sales; 20% commission on foreign sales. Offers written contract 6 months.

Writers' Conference(s): BEA (Chicago, June).

Tips: "Send us a well-written proposal that clearly identifies your audience—who will buy this book and why."

N THE BETSY NOLAN LITERARY AGENCY, 224 W. 29th St., 15th Floor, New York NY 10001. (212)967-8200. Fax: (212)967-7292. **Contact:** Donald Lehr, president. Estab. 1980. Member of AAR. Represents 200 clients. 10% of clients are new/unpublished writers. Currently handles: 90% nonfiction books; 10% novels.

Member Agents: Donald Lehr; Carla Glasser.

Represents: Nonfiction books, novels.

How to Contact: Query with SASE, submit outline. No e-mail or fax queries. Considers simultaneous queries. Responds in 3 weeks on queries; 2 months on mss. Returns materials only with SASE.

Recent Sales: Sold 15 books in the last year. *Mangia*, by Sasha Muniak/Ricardo Diaz (HarperCollins); *The Buttercup Bake Shop Cookbook*, by Jennifer Appel (Simon & Schuster); *Desperation Dinners*, by Beverly Mills & Alicia Ross (Workman).

Terms: Agent receives 15% commission on domestic sales; 20% commission on foreign sales.

N L. PERKINS ASSOCIATES, 5800 Arlington Ave., Riverdale NY 10471. (718)543-5344 or (212)279-6418. Fax: (718)543-5354. E-mail: lperkinsagency@yahoo.com. **Contact:** Lori Perkins. Estab. 1990. Member of AAR. Represents 50 clients. 10% of clients are new/unpublished writers. Currently handles: nonfiction books; novels.

● Ms. Perkins has been an agent for 11 years. Her agency has an affiliate agency, Southern Literary Group. She is also the author of *The Insider's Guide to Getting an Agent* (Writer's Digest Books).

Represents: Nonfiction books, novels. **Considers these nonfiction areas:** Popular culture. **Considers these fiction areas:** Fantasy, horror, literary (dark fiction), science fiction.

O—¬ All of Ms. Perkins's clients write both fiction and nonfiction. "This combination keeps my clients publishing for years. I am also a published author so I know what it takes to write a book."

How to Contact: Query with SASE. Accepts fax queries. Considers simultaneous queries. Responds in 6 weeks on queries; 3 months on mss. Returns materials only with SASE. Obtains most new clients through recommendations from others, solicitations, conferences.

Needs: Actively seeking a Latino *Gone With the Wind* and *Waiting to Exhale*, and urban ethnic horror. Does not want to receive "anything outside of the above categories, i.e., westerns, romance."

Recent Sales: Sold 100 books in the last year. *An Unauthorized Biography of J.K. Rowling*, by Marc Shapiro; *An Unauthorized Guide to Dragonballz*, by Lois and Daniel Gresh; *Strangewood*, by Christopher Goldin.

Terms: Agent receives 15% commission on domestic sales; 20% commission on foreign sales. No written contract. Charges clients for photocopying.

Writers' Conference(s): Maui Writer's Conference.

Tips: "Research your field and contact professional writers' organizations to see who is looking for what. Finish your novel before querying agents. Read my book, *An Insider's Guide to Getting an Agent* to get a sense of how agents operate."

JAMES PETER ASSOCIATES, INC., P.O. Box 772, Tenafly NJ 07670-0751. (201)568-0760. Fax: (201)568-2959. E-mail: bertholtje@compuserve.com. **Contact:** Bert Holtje. Estab. 1971. Member of AAR. Represents 54 clients. 15% of clients are new/unpublished writers. Currently handles: 100% nonfiction books.

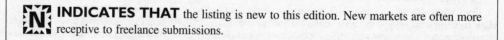

N INDICATES THAT the listing is new to this edition. New markets are often more receptive to freelance submissions.

● Prior to opening his agency, Mr. Holtje was a book packager, and before that, president of advertising agency with book publishing clients.

Represents: Nonfiction books. **Considers these nonfiction areas:** Anthropology/archaeology, art/architecture/design, business/economics, child guidance/parenting, ethnic/cultural interests, gay/lesbian, government/politics/law, health/medicine, history, language/literature/criticism, memoirs (political or business), military/war, money/finance, music/dance, psychology, travel, women's issues/studies.

○➥ This agency specializes in nonfiction, all categories. "We are especially interested in general, trade and reference."

How to Contact: Submit proposal package, outline. Responds in 1 month on queries. Returns materials only with SASE. Obtains most new clients through recommendations from others, solicitations.

Needs: Actively seeking "good ideas in all areas of adult nonfiction." Does not want to receive children's and young adult books, poetry, fiction.

Recent Sales: Sold 34 books in the last year. *Patton on Management*, by Dr. Alan Axelrod (Prentice-Hall); *Out of the Ordinary: A Biographical Dictionary of Women Explorers*, by Sarah Purcell and Edward Purcell (Routledge); *Ace Your Mid Terms and Finals (A 5-book series)*, by The Ian Samuel Group (McGraw-Hill).

Terms: Agent receives 15% commission on domestic sales; 20% commission on foreign sales. Offers written contract on per book basis.

AARON M. PRIEST LITERARY AGENCY, 708 Third Ave., 23rd Floor, New York NY 10017. (212)818-0344. Fax: (212)573-9417. **Contact:** Aaron Priest or Molly Friedrich. Estab. 1974. Member of AAR. Currently handles: 25% nonfiction books; 75% novels.

Member Agents: Lisa Erbach Vance, Paul Cirone.

Represents: Nonfiction books, novels.

How to Contact: Query with SASE. *All unsolicited manuscripts returned unopened.*

Recent Sales: *Absolute Power*, by David Baldacci (Warner); *Three to Get Deadly*, by Janet Evanovich (Scribner); *How Stella Got Her Groove Back*, by Terry McMillan (Viking).

Terms: Agent receives 15% commission on domestic sales. Charges for photocopying, foreign postage expenses.

HELEN REES LITERARY AGENCY, 123 N. Washington St., 2nd Floor, Boston MA 02114. (617)723-5232, ext. 233 or 222. **Contact:** Joan Mazmanian. Estab. 1981. Member of AAR. Represents 50 clients. 50% of clients are new/unpublished writers. Currently handles: 60% nonfiction books; 40% novels.

Represents: Nonfiction books, novels. **Considers these nonfiction areas:** Business/economics, government/politics/law, health/medicine, history, money/finance, women's issues/studies. **Considers these fiction areas:** Historical, literary, mainstream/contemporary, mystery/suspense, suspense, thriller/espionage.

○➥ This agency specializes in general nonfiction, health, business, world politics, autobiographies, psychology, women's issues.

How to Contact: Query with SASE, submit outline, 2 sample chapter(s). Responds in 2 weeks on queries; 3 weeks on mss. Obtains most new clients through recommendations from others, solicitations, conferences.

Recent Sales: *The Mentor*, by Sebastian Stuart (Bantam); *Managing the Human Animal*, by Nigel Nicholson (Times Books); *Just Revenge*, by Alan Dershowitz (Warner).

Terms: Agent receives 15% commission on domestic sales; 20% commission on foreign sales.

ANGELA RINALDI LITERARY AGENCY, P.O. Box 7877, Beverly Hills CA 90212-7877. (310)842-7655. Fax: (310)837-8143. E-mail: e2arinaldi@aol.com. **Contact:** Angela Rinaldi. Estab. 1994. Member of AAR. Represents 50 clients. Currently handles: 50% nonfiction books; 50% novels.

● Prior to opening her agency, Ms. Rinaldi was an editor at New American Library, Pocket Books and Bantam, and the manager of book development of *The Los Angeles Times*.

Represents: Nonfiction books, novels, TV scripts, feature film. **Considers these nonfiction areas:** Business/economics, child guidance/parenting, health/medicine, money/finance, psychology, sociology, women's issues/studies. **Considers these fiction areas:** Literary, mainstream/contemporary.

How to Contact: Query with SASE, submit proposal package, outline, sample chapter(s). Accepts e-mail queries. Considers simultaneous queries. Responds in 6 weeks on queries. Returns materials only with SASE.

Needs: Actively seeking commercial and literary fiction Does not want to receive scripts, category romances, children's books, westerns, science fiction/fantasy and cookbooks.

Recent Sales: *The Starlight Drive-In*, by Marjorie Reynolds (William Morrow & Co); *Twins: Pregnancy, Birth and the First Year of Life*, by Agnew, Klein and Ganon (HarperCollins); *The Thyroid Solution*, by Dr. Ridha Arem.

Terms: Agent receives 15% commission on domestic sales; 20% commission on foreign sales. Offers written contract. Charges for photocopying.

🄽 JANE ROTROSEN AGENCY LLC, 318 E. 51st St., New York NY 10022. (212)593-4330. Fax: (212)935-6985. E-mail: jrotrosen@aol.com. **Contact:** Jane Rotrosen. Estab. 1974. Member of AAR, Authors Guild. Represents over 100 clients. Currently handles: 30% nonfiction books; 70% novels.

Member Agents: Andrea Cirillo; Ruth Kagle; Annelise Robey; Margaret Ruley; Stephanie Tade.

Represents: Nonfiction books, novels. **Considers these nonfiction areas:** Biography/autobiography, business/economics, child guidance/parenting, cooking/foods/nutrition, current affairs, health/medicine, how-to, humor/satire, money/finance, nature/environment, popular culture, psychology, self-help/personal improvement, sports, true crime/investigative, women's issues/studies. **Considers these fiction areas:** Action/adventure, detective/police/crime, historical, horror, mainstream/contemporary, mystery/suspense, romance, thriller/espionage, women's fiction.

How to Contact: Query with SASE. No e-mail or fax queries. Considers simultaneous queries. Responds in 2 weeks on queries; 7 weeks on mss. Returns materials only with SASE.

Recent Sales: Sold 120 books in the last year.

Terms: Agent receives 15% commission on domestic sales; 20% commission on foreign sales. Offers written contract binding for 3 years; 60-days notice must be given to terminate contract notice must be given to terminate contract. Charges clients for photocopying, express mail, overseas postage, book purchase.

N: THE PETER RUBIE LITERARY AGENCY, 240 W. 35th St., Suite 500, New York NY 10001. (212)279-1776. Fax: (212)279-0927. **Contact:** Peter Rubie, Jennifer DeChiarra or June Clark. Estab. 2000. Member of AAR. Represents 130 clients. 30% of clients are new/unpublished writers.

• Prior to opening The Peter Rubie Literary Agency, Mr. Rubie was an agent at Perkins, Rubie & Associates.

Member Agents: June Clark (New Age, pop culture, gay issues); Jennifer DeChiarra (children's books, theatre arts, literary fiction); Peter Rubie (crime, science fiction, fantasy, off-beat mysteries, history, literary fiction, thrillers, narrative nonfiction).

Represents: Nonfiction books, novels. **Considers these nonfiction areas:** Current affairs, ethnic/cultural interests, music/dance, science/technology, narrative nonfiction; commercial academic material; TV. **Considers these fiction areas:** Action/adventure (adventure), detective/police/crime, ethnic, fantasy, historical, literary, mainstream/contemporary, mystery/suspense, science fiction, suspense, thriller/espionage.

How to Contact: Query with SASE. Responds in 2 months on queries; 3 months on mss. Returns materials only with SASE. Obtains most new clients through recommendations from others, solicitations, conferences.

Recent Sales: *Terrorists of Irustan*, by Louise Marley (Berkley); *Shooting at Midnight*, by Gregory Rucka (Bantam); *Violence Proof Your Kids* (Conari Press).

Terms: Agent receives 15% commission on domestic sales; 20% commission on foreign sales. Offers written contract "only if requested" Charges clients for photocopying.

Tips: "We look for writers who are experts and outstanding prose style. Be professional. Read Publishers Weekly and genre-related magazines. Join writers' organizations. Go to conferences. Know your market, and learn your craft."

N: RUSSELL & VOLKENING, 50 W. 29th St., #7E, New York NY 10001. (212)684-6050. Fax: (212)889-3026. **Contact:** Joseph Regal. Estab. 1940. Member of AAR. Represents 140 clients. 10% of clients are new/unpublished writers. Currently handles: 40% nonfiction books; 50% novels; 3% story collections; 2% novella; 5% juvenile books.

Member Agents: Timothy Seldes (nonfiction, literary fiction); Joseph Regal (literary fiction, thrillers, nonfiction); Jennie Dunham (literary fiction, nonfiction, children's books).

Represents: Nonfiction books, novels, short story collections, novellas. **Considers these nonfiction areas:** Anthropology/archaeology, art/architecture/design, biography/autobiography, business/economics, cooking/foods/nutrition, current affairs, education, ethnic/cultural interests, gay/lesbian, government/politics/law, health/medicine, history, language/literature/criticism, military/war, money/finance, music/dance, nature/environment, photography, popular culture, psychology, science/technology, sociology, sports, true crime/investigative, women's issues/studies. **Considers these fiction areas:** Action/adventure, detective/police/crime, ethnic, literary, mainstream/contemporary, mystery/suspense, picture books, sports, suspense, thriller/espionage.

O→ This agency specializes in literary fiction and narrative nonfiction.

How to Contact: Query with SASE. Responds in 1 month on queries; 2 months on mss. Obtains most new clients through recommendations from others. occasionally through query letters.

Recent Sales: *The Many Aspects of Mobile Living*, by Martin Clark (Knopf); *The Special Prisoner*, by Jim Lehrer (Random); *The Visitor*, by Maeve Brennan (Counterpoint).

Terms: Agent receives 15% commission on domestic sales; 20% commission on foreign sales. Charges clients for "standard office expenses relating to the submission of materials of an author we represent, e.g., photocopying, postage."

Tips: "If the query is cogent, well written, well presented and is the type of book we'd represent, we'll ask to see the manuscript. From there, it depends purely on the quality of the work."

VICTORIA SANDERS & ASSOCIATES LITERARY AGENCY, 241 Avenue of the Americas, New York NY 10014-4822. (212)633-8811. Fax: (212)633-0525. **Contact:** Victoria Sanders and/or Diane Dickensheid. Estab. 1993. Member of AAR; signatory of WGA. Represents 75 clients. 25% of clients are new/unpublished writers. Currently handles: 50% nonfiction books; 50% novels.

Represents: Nonfiction books, novels. **Considers these nonfiction areas:** Ethnic/cultural interests, gay/lesbian, government/politics/law, history, language/literature/criticism, music/dance, psychology, translation, women's issues/studies. **Considers these fiction areas:** Action/adventure, ethnic, feminist, gay/lesbian, literary, mainstream/contemporary, suspense, thriller/espionage.

How to Contact: Query with SASE. Considers simultaneous queries. Responds in 1 week on queries; 1 month on mss. Returns materials only with SASE. Obtains most new clients through recommendations from others.

Recent Sales: Sold 15 books in the last year.

Terms: Agent receives 15% commission on domestic sales; 20% commission on foreign sales. Offers written contract at will. Charges for photocopying, ms, messenger, express mail and extraordinary fees. If in excess of $100, client approval is required.
Tips: "Limit query to letter, no calls, and give it your best shot. A good query is going to get a good response."

IRENE SKOLNICK LITERARY AGENCY, 22 W. 23rd St., 5th Floor, New York NY 10010. (212)727-3648. Fax: (212)727-1024. E-mail: sirene35@aol.com. **Contact:** Irene Skolnick. Estab. 1993. Member of AAR. Represents 45 clients. 75% of clients are new/unpublished writers.
Represents: Nonfiction books (adult), novels (adult). **Considers these nonfiction areas:** Biography. **Considers these fiction areas:** Historical, literary, mainstream/contemporary.
How to Contact: Query with SASE, submit outline, sample chapter(s). Accepts fax queries. Considers simultaneous queries. Responds in 1 month on queries. Returns materials only with SASE.
Recent Sales: Sold 15 books in the last year. *An Equal Music*, by Vikram Seth; *Kaaterskill Falls*, by Allegra Goodman; *Taking Lives*, by Michael Pye.
Terms: Agent receives 15% commission on domestic sales; 20% commission on foreign sales. Sometimes offers criticism service. Charges for international postage, photocopying over 40 pages.

N: STEELE-PERKINS LITERARY AGENCY, 26 Island Lane, Canandaigua NY 14424. (716)396-9290. Fax: (716)396-3579. E-mail: pattiesp@aol.com. **Contact:** Pattie Steele-Perkins. Member of AAR, RWA. Currently handles: 100% novels.
• Prior to becoming an agent, Ms. Steele-Perkins was a TV producer/writer for 15 years.
Represents: Novels. **Considers these nonfiction areas:** Sports (specifically sailing). **Considers these fiction areas:** Mainstream/contemporary, multicultural, romance.
O→ The Steele-Perkins Literary Agency takes an active role in marketing their clients work including preparation for media appearances. They also develop with the author individual career plans.
How to Contact: Submit outline, 3 sample chapter(s), SASE. Accepts e-mail queries. Responds in 6 weeks on queries. Returns materials only with SASE. Obtains most new clients through recommendations from others, solicitations.
Needs: Actively seeking romance, women's fiction and multicultural works.
Terms: Agent receives 15% commission on domestic sales. Offers written contract binding for 1 year; 30-day notice must be given to terminate contract notice must be given to terminate contract.
Writers' Conference(s): National Conference of Romance Writer's of America.
Tips: "Be patient. E-mail rather than call. Make sure what you are sending is the best it can be."

N: TOAD HALL, INC., RR 2, Box 2090, Laceyville PA 18623. (570)869-2942. Fax: (570)869-1031. E-mail: toadhall co@aol.com. Website: www.laceyville.com/Toad-Hall. **Contact:** Sharon Jarvis, Anne Pinzow. Estab. 1982. Member of AAR. Represents 35 clients. 10% of clients are new/unpublished writers. Currently handles: 50% nonfiction books; 40% novels; 5% movie scripts; 5% ancillary projects.
• Prior to becoming an agent, Ms. Jarvis was an acquisitions editor.
Member Agents: Sharon Jarvis (fiction, nonfiction); Anne Pinzow (TV, movies); Roxy LeRose (unpublished writers).
Represents: Nonfiction books, novels. **Considers these nonfiction areas:** Animals, anthropology/archaeology, business/economics, child guidance/parenting, cooking/foods/nutrition, health/medicine, hobbies (crafts), how-to, nature/environment, popular culture, religious/inspirational, self-help/personal improvement, spirituality (New Age/metaphysics). **Considers these fiction areas:** Historical, mystery/suspense, romance (contemporary, historical, regency), science fiction, suspense.
O→ This agency specializes in popular nonfiction, some category fiction.
How to Contact: Query with SASE. No e-mail or fax queries. Responds in 3 weeks on queries; 3 months on mss. Obtains most new clients through recommendations from others, solicitations, conferences.
Needs: Actively seeking New Age, paranormal—unusual but popular approaches. "We only handle scripts written by our clients who have published material agented by us." Does not want to receive poetry, short stories, essays, collections, children's books.
Recent Sales: Sold 6 books in the last year. *Against All Odds*, by Barbara Riefe (TOR); *Herbal Medicine*, by Mary Atwood (Sterling); *The Shag Harbour Incident*, by Ledger and Styles (Dell).
Terms: Agent receives 15% commission on domestic sales; 10% commission on foreign sales. Offers written contract binding for 1 year. Charges clients for photocopying, bank fees and special postage (i.e., express mail).
Tips: "Pay attention to what is getting published. Show the agent you've done your homework!"

N: SCOTT TREIMEL NY, 434 Lafayette St., New York NY 10003. (212)505-8353. Fax: (212)505-0664. E-mail: mescottyt@earthlink.net. **Contact:** Scott Treimel. Estab. 1995. Member of AAR. Represents 26 clients. 15% of clients are new/unpublished writers. Currently handles: 100% juvenile books.
• Prior to becoming an agent, Mr. Treimel was a rights agent for Scholastic, Inc.; a book packager and rights agent for United Feature Syndicate; a freelance editor and a rights consultant for HarperCollins Children's Books; and the founding director of Warner Bros. Worldwide Publishing.
Represents: Juvenile books (concept books, picture books, middle grade, first chapter books, young adult). **Considers these nonfiction areas:** Juvenile nonfiction. **Considers these fiction areas:** Juvenile, picture books, young adult, considers all juvenile fiction and nonfiction areas.

○━ This agency specializes in children's books: tightly focused segments of the trade and educational markets.

How to Contact: Query with SASE, "Do not contact if you are 'interviewing' agents." For picture books, send entire ms, no more than two at a time. Returns multiple submissions. Requires a "30-day exclusive on requested manuscripts." Returns materials with SASE or discards upon rejection. referrals and queries.

Needs: Actively seeking picture book illustrators, first chapter books, middle-grade fiction and young adult fiction.

Recent Sales: Sold 21 books in the last year.

Terms: Agent receives 15% commission on domestic sales; 20% commission on foreign sales. Offers verbal or written contract, "binding on a book contract by contract basis." Charges clients for photocopying, overnight/express postage, messengers, and books ordered to sell foreign, film, etc. rights.

Writers' Conference(s): Can You Make a Living from Children's Books, Society of Children's Book Writers & Illustrators (Los Angeles, August).

UNITED TRIBES, 240 W. 35th St., #500, New York NY 10001. (212)534-7646. E-mail: janguerth@aol.com. Website: www.unitedtribes.com. **Contact:** Jan-Erik Guerth. Estab. 1998. Represents 40 clients. 10% of clients are new/unpublished writers. Currently handles: 99% nonfiction books; 1% novels.

● Prior to becoming an agent, Mr. Guerth was a comedian, journalist, radio producer and film distributor.

Represents: Nonfiction books, novels. **Considers these nonfiction areas:** Anthropology/archaeology, art/architecture/design, business/economics, child guidance/parenting, cooking/foods/nutrition, education, ethnic/cultural interests, gay/lesbian, government/politics/law, health/medicine, history, language/literature/criticism, memoirs, money/finance, music/dance, nature/environment, psychology, religious/inspirational, science/technology, sociology, translation, women's issues/studies.

○━ This agency specializes in the "Spirituality of Everyday Life" and ethnic, social, gender and cultural issues, comparative religions, self-help and wellness, science and arts, history and politics, nature and travel, and any fascinating future trends.

How to Contact: Submit outline, 3 sample chapter(s), résumé. Accepts e-mail queries. Responds in 2 weeks on queries; 1 month on mss. Returns materials only with SASE. Obtains most new clients through recommendations from others, solicitations, conferences.

Terms: Agent receives 15% commission on domestic sales; 20% commission on foreign sales.

Ⓝ THE VINES AGENCY, INC., 648 Broadway, Suite 901, New York NY 10012. (212)777-5522. Fax: (212)777-5978. E-mail: jv@vinesagency.com. **Contact:** James C. Vines or Gary Neuwirth. Estab. 1995. Member of AAR; signatory of WGA. Represents 52 clients. 20% of clients are new/unpublished writers. Currently handles: 50% nonfiction books; 50% novels.

● Prior to opening his agency, Mr. Vines served as an agent with the Virginia Literary Agency.

Member Agents: James C. Vines (quality and commercial fiction and nonfiction); Gary Neuwirth; Ali Ryan (women's fiction and nonfiction, mainstream).

Represents: Nonfiction books, novels, TV scripts, feature film. **Considers these nonfiction areas:** Biography/autobiography, business/economics, current affairs, ethnic/cultural interests, history, how-to, humor/satire, memoirs, military/war, money/finance, nature/environment, photography, popular culture, psychology, religious/inspirational, science/technology, self-help/personal improvement, sociology, spirituality (New Age/metaphysics), sports, translation, travel, true crime/investigative, women's issues/studies. **Considers these fiction areas:** Action/adventure, detective/police/crime, ethnic, experimental, feminist, gay/lesbian, historical, horror, humor, literary, mainstream/contemporary, mystery/suspense, occult (psychic, supernatural), regional, romance (contemporary, historical), science fiction, sports, suspense, thriller/espionage, western/frontier, women's fiction. **Considers these script subject areas:** Action/adventure, comedy, detective/police/crime, ethnic, experimental, feminist, gay/lesbian, historical, horror, mainstream, mystery/suspense, romantic comedy, romantic drama, science fiction, teen, thriller/espionage, western/frontier.

○━ This agency specializes in mystery, suspense, mainstream novels, screenplays, teleplays.

How to Contact: Submit outline, 3 sample chapter(s), SASE. Accepts e-mail and fax queries. Considers simultaneous queries. Responds in 2 weeks on queries; 1 month on mss. Returns materials only with SASE. Obtains most new clients through query letters, recommendations from others, reading short stories in magazines, soliciting conferences.

Recent Sales: Sold 46 books and sold 5 scripts in the last year.

Terms: Agent receives 15% commission on domestic sales; 25% commission on foreign sales. Offers written contract binding for 1 year; 30 days cancellation clause notice must be given to terminate contract. Charges clients for foreign postage, messenger services, photocopying.

Writers' Conference(s): Maui Writer's Conference.

Tips: "Do not follow up on submissions with phone calls to the agency. The agency will read and respond by mail only. Do not pack your manuscript in plastic 'peanuts' that will make us have to vacuum the office after opening the package containing your manuscript. Always enclose return postage."

Ⓝ WALES, LITERARY AGENCY, INC., 108 Hayes St., Seattle WA 98109-2808. (206)284-7114. Fax: (206)284-0190. E-mail: waleslit@aol.com. **Contact:** Elizabeth Wales or Nancy Shawn. Estab. 1988. Member of AAR, Book Publishers' Northwest. Represents 60 clients. 10% of clients are new/unpublished writers. Currently handles: 60% nonfiction books; 35% novels; 5% story collections.

● Prior to becoming an agent, Ms. Wales worked at Oxford University Press and Viking Penguin.

Member Agents: Nancy Shawn (foreign rights/reprints); Elizabeth Wales

Represents: Nonfiction books, novels, short story collections, novellas. **Considers these nonfiction areas:** Animals, biography/autobiography, current affairs, ethnic/cultural interests, gay/lesbian, history, memoirs, multicultural, nature/environment, popular culture, science/technology, travel, women's issues/studies, open to creative or serious treatments of almost any nonficiton subject. **Considers these fiction areas:** Erotica, ethnic, feminist, gay/lesbian, literary, mainstream/contemporary, multicultural, regional.

O¬ This agency specializes in mainstream nonfiction and fiction, as well as narrative and literary fiction.

How to Contact: Query with SASE. Accepts e-mail queries. Considers simultaneous queries. Responds in 3 weeks on queries; 6 weeks on mss. Returns materials only with SASE.

Recent Sales: Sold 20 books in the last year. *The Rachel Book*, by Karen Brennan (Norton); *The Stars, the Snow, the Fire*, by John Haines (Graywolf); *Lessons of the Nordstrom Way*, by Robert Spector (John Wiley).

Terms: Agent receives 15% commission on domestic sales; 20% commission on foreign sales. Offers written contract binding on a book-by-book basis.. "We make all our income from commissions. We offer editorial help for some of our clients and help some clients with the development of a proposal, but we do not charge for these services. We do charge clients, after a sale, for express mail, manuscript photocopying costs, foreign postage and outside USA telephone costs."

Writers' Conference(s): Pacific NW Writers Conference (Seattle, July).

Tips: "We are interested in published and non-yet-published writers. Especially encourages writers living in the Pacific Northwest, West Coast, Alaska and Pacific Rim countries to submit work."

SCOTT WAXMAN AGENCY, INC., 1650 Broadway, Suite 1011, New York NY 10019. (212)262-2388. Fax: (212)262-0119. E-mail: gracem@swagency.net. Website: www.swagency.net. **Contact:** Grace Madamba. Estab. 1997. Member of AAR. Represents 60 clients. 50% of clients are new/unpublished writers. Currently handles: 60% nonfiction books; 40% novels.

● Prior to opening his agency, Mr. Waxman was editor for five years at HarperCollins.

Member Agents: Scott Waxman (all categories of nonfiction, commercial fiction); Giles Anderson (literary fiction, commercial fiction).

Represents: Nonfiction books, novels. **Considers these nonfiction areas:** Business/economics, ethnic/cultural interests, health/medicine, history, money/finance, religious/inspirational, sports. **Considers these fiction areas:** Action/adventure, historical, literary, mystery/suspense, religious, romance (contemporary, historical), sports, suspense.

O¬ This agency specializes in "both commercial fiction and nonfiction. We are particularly strong in the areas of crime fiction, sports and religion. Will look at literary fiction."

How to Contact: Query with SASE; *all unsolicited manuscripts returned unopened*. Accepts e-mail queries. Considers simultaneous queries. Responds in 2 weeks on queries; 6 weeks on mss. Returns materials only with SASE. Obtains most new clients through recommendations from others, solicitations, conferences.

Needs: Actively seeking strong, high-concept commercial fiction, narrative nonfiction.

Recent Sales: Sold 40 books in the last year. *Mid-Life Irish*, by Frank Gannon (Wagner); *All Good Things*, by John Reed (Delacorte); *She Got Game*, by Cynthia Cooper (Warner Books).

Terms: Agent receives 15% commission on domestic sales; 20% commission on foreign sales. Offers written contract 60 days notice must be given to terminate contract. Charges for photocopying, express mail, fax, international postage, book orders.

Writers' Conference(s): Celebration of Writing in the Low Country (Beaufort SC, August).

WRITERS HOUSE, 21 W. 26th St., New York NY 10010. (212)685-2400. Fax: (212)685-1781. Estab. 1974. Member of AAR. Represents 280 clients. 50% of clients are new/unpublished writers. Currently handles: 25% nonfiction books; 40% novels; 35% juvenile books.

Member Agents: Albert Zuckerman (major novels, thrillers, women's fiction, important nonfiction); Amy Berkower (major juvenile authors, women's fiction, art and decorating, psychology); Merrilee Heifetz (quality children's fiction, science fiction and fantasy, popular culture, literary fiction); Susan Cohen (juvenile and young adult fiction and nonfiction, Judaism, women's issues); Susan Ginsburg (serious and popular fiction, true crime, narrative nonfiction, personality books, cookbooks); Fran Lebowitz (juvenile and young adult, popular culture); Michele Rubin (serious nonfiction); Karen Solem (contemporary and historical romance, women's fiction, narrative nonfiction, horse and animal books); Robin Rue (commercial fiction and nonfiction, YA fiction); Jennifer Lyons (literary, commercial fiction, international fiction, nonfiction and illustrated).

Represents: Nonfiction books, novels, juvenile books. **Considers these nonfiction areas:** Animals, art/architecture/design, business/economics, child guidance/parenting, cooking/foods/nutrition, health/medicine, history, military/war, money/finance, music/dance, nature/environment, psychology, science/technology, women's issues/studies. **Considers these fiction areas:** Action/adventure, cartoon/comic (,), confession, erotica, ethnic, experimental, fantasy, feminist, gay/lesbian, gothic, hi-lo, historical, horror, humor, juvenile, literary, mainstream/contemporary, military/war, multicultural, multimedia, mystery/suspense, occult, picture books, plays, poetry, poetry in translation, regional, religious, romance, science fiction, short story collections, spiritual, sports, suspense, thriller/espionage, translation, western/frontier, young adult,

O¬ This agency specializes in all types of popular fiction and nonfiction. No scholarly, professional, poetry or screenplays.

How to Contact: Query with SASE. Responds in 1 month on queries. Obtains most new clients through recommendations from others.

Recent Sales: *The New New Thing*, by Michael Lewis (Norton); *The First Victim*, by Ridley Pearson (Hyperion); *Into the Garden*, by V.C. Andrews (Pocket).
Terms: Agent receives 15% commission on domestic sales; 20% commission on foreign sales. Offers written contract 1 year.
Tips: "Do not send mss. Write a compelling letter. If you do, we'll ask to see your work."

THE WRITERS SHOP, 101 Fifth Ave., 11th Floor, New York NY 10003. (212)255-6515. Fax: (212)691-9418. Website: www.thewritersshop.com. **Contact:** Kirstin Lewandowski. Member of AAR; signatory of WGA. Represents 100 clients. Currently handles: 25% nonfiction books; 50% novels; 25% story collections.
Member Agents: Virginia Barber; Jennifer Rudolph Walsh; Jay Mandel.
Represents: Nonfiction books, novels, short story collections, scholarly books.
How to Contact: Query with SASE. Responds in 6 weeks on queries. Returns materials only with SASE. Obtains most new clients through recommendations from others.
Terms: Agent receives 15% commission on domestic sales.
Writers' Conference(s): Bread Loaf.

SCRIPT AGENTS

ABOVE THE LINE AGENCY, 9200 Sunset Blvd., #804, Los Angeles CA 90069. (310)859-6115. Fax: (310)859-6119. Owner: Rima Bauer Greer. **Contact:** Bruce Bartlett. Estab. 1994. Signatory of WGA. Represents 35 clients. 10% of clients are new/unpublished writers. Currently handles: 95% movie scripts; 5% TV scripts.
   • Ms. Greer served as president with Writers & Artists Agency.
Represents: Feature film, TV movie of the week. **Considers these script subject areas:** Cartoon/animation, writers and directors.
How to Contact: Query with SASE.
Recent Sales: Sold 25 scripts in the last year. *3 Stooges*, by Matheson (Columbia); *Charlie's Angels*, by Ryan Rowe (Columbia); *Constantine*, by Frank Cappello (Warner Brothers).
Terms: Agent receives 10% commission on domestic sales; 10% commission on foreign sales.

ABRAMS ARTISTS AGENCY, 275 Seventh Ave., 26th Floor, New York NY 10001. (646)486-4600. Fax: (646)486-0100. **Contact:** Jack Tantleff. Estab. 1986. Member of AAR; signatory of WGA.
Represents: Episodic drama, feature film, sitcom, animation (TV), soap opera, musical. **Considers these script subject areas:** Comedy, contemporary issues, mainstream, mystery/suspense, romantic comedy, romantic drama.
   O━ This agency specializes in theater, film, TV
How to Contact: Query with outline and SASE. Returns material only with SASE. Accepts fax queries.
Terms: Agent receives 10% commission on domestic sales; 10% commission on foreign sales; 10% commission on movie rights.

AGENCY WEST ENTERTAINMENT, 6255 W. Sunset Blvd., #908, Hollywood CA 90028. (323)468-9470. Fax: (323)468-0867. **Contact:** Dackeyia Q. Simmons. Estab. 1995. Signatory of WGA. Represents 10 clients. 25% of clients are new/unpublished writers. Currently handles: 10% nonfiction books; 5% novels; 5% juvenile books; 40% movie scripts; 40% TV scripts.
   • Ms. Simmons was a writer and worked in personal management.
Member Agents: Holly Davis; Nancy Chaidez; Sheba Williams (youth division); J. Renee Colquit (youth division).
Represents: Novels, movie scripts, TV scripts, feature film, TV movie of the week, sitcom, animation, miniseries.
Considers these nonfiction areas: Biography/autobiography, child guidance/parenting, cooking/foods/nutrition, education, ethnic/cultural interests, hobbies, how-to, humor/satire, memoirs, music/dance, religious/inspirational, self-help/personal improvement, sports, true crime/investigative, women's issues/studies, crafts; juvenile nonfiction; inspirational.
Considers these fiction areas: Action/adventure, ethnic, fantasy, humor, juvenile, literary, mainstream/contemporary, religious, sports, young adult, adventure; cartoon/comic; satire; inspirational. **Considers these script subject areas:** Action/adventure, biography/autobiography, cartoon/animation, comedy, ethnic, family saga, fantasy, juvenile, mainstream, religious/inspirational, romantic comedy, romantic drama, science fiction, sports, teen, thriller/espionage.
   O━ This agency specializes in the theatrical development and representation of urban musical and literary artists in television and film.
How to Contact: Query with SASE. Responds in 1 month on queries; 6 weeks on mss. Returns materials only with SASE. Obtains most new clients through recommendations from others, conferences, festivals.
Terms: Agent receives 10% commission on domestic sales; 15% commission on foreign sales. Offers written contract.
Writers' Conference(s): Book Expo America.
Tips: "Make sure your submission is your absolute best work before you send it to us. (No typos, correct grammar, proper script or manuscript format, etc.)."

THE ALPERN GROUP, 15645 Royal Oak Rd., Encino CA 91436. (818)528-1111. Fax: (818)528-1110. **Contact:** Jeff Alpern. Estab. 1994. Represents 50 clients. 10% of clients are new/unpublished writers. Currently handles: 30% movie scripts; 60% TV scripts; 10% stage plays.

● Mr. Alpern served as an agent with Willaim Morris.
Member Agents: Jeff Alpern (president); Liz Wise; Jeff Aghassi
Represents: Episodic drama, movie scripts, TV scripts, feature film, TV movie of the week, miniseries. **Considers these script subject areas:** Considers all script areas.
How to Contact: Query with SASE. Responds in 1 month on queries.
Terms: Agent receives 10% commission on domestic sales. Offers written contract.

KELVIN C. BULGER AND ASSOCIATES, 11 E. Adams St., Suite 604, Chicago IL 60603. (312)692-1002. E-mail: kcbwoi@aol.com. **Contact:** Kelvin C. Bulger. Estab. 1992. Signatory of WGA. Represents 25 clients. 90% of clients are new/unpublished writers. Currently handles: 75% movie scripts; 25% TV scripts.
Represents: Feature film, TV movie of the week, documentary, syndicated material. **Considers these script subject areas:** Action/adventure, cartoon/animation, comedy, contemporary issues, ethnic, family saga, religious/inspirational.
How to Contact: Query with SASE. Responds in 3 weeks on queries; 2 months on mss. Returns materials only with SASE. Obtains most new clients through recommendations from others, solicitations.
Terms: Agent receives 10% commission on domestic sales; 10% commission on foreign sales. Offers written contract binding for 6 months-1 year.
Tips: "Proofread before submitting to agent. We only reply to letter of inquiries if SASE is enclosed."

CIRCLE OF CONFUSION LTD., 666 Fifth Ave., Suite 303, New York NY 10103. (212)969-0653. Fax: (718)997-0521. E-mail: circleltd@aol.com. **Contact:** Rajeev K. Agarwal, Lawrence Mattis. Estab. 1990. Signatory of WGA. Represents 25 clients. 60% of clients are new/unpublished writers. Currently handles: 5% novels; 5% novella; 90% movie scripts.
Member Agents: Annmarie Negretti; John Sherman.
Represents: Nonfiction books, novels, short story collections, novellas, feature film. **Considers these nonfiction areas:** Americana, animals, anthropology/archaeology, art/architecture/design, business/economics, child guidance/parenting, computers/electronic, cooking/foods/nutrition, creative nonfiction, education, ethnic/cultural interests, gardening, gay/lesbian, government/politics/law, health/medicine, history, hobbies, language/literature/criticism, memoirs, military/war, money/finance, multicultural, music/dance, nature/environment, philosophy, photography, psychology, recreation, regional, religious/inspirational, science/technology, sex, sociology, software, spirituality, sports, translation, travel, women's issues/studies. **Considers these fiction areas:** Action/adventure, cartoon/comic, confession, erotica, ethnic, experimental, fantasy, feminist, gay/lesbian, gothic, hi-lo, historical, horror, humor, juvenile, literary, mainstream/contemporary, military/war, multicultural, multimedia, mystery/suspense, occult, picture books, plays, poetry, poetry in translation, regional, religious, romance, science fiction, short story collections, spiritual, sports, suspense, translation, western/frontier, young adult. **Considers these script subject areas:** Action/adventure, biography/autobiography, cartoon/animation, comedy, contemporary issues, detective/police/crime, erotica, ethnic, experimental, family saga, fantasy, feminist, gay/lesbian, glitz, historical, horror, juvenile, mainstream, multicultural, multimedia, mystery/suspense, psychic/supernatural, regional, religious/inspirational, romantic comedy, romantic drama, science fiction, sports, teen, thriller/espionage, western/frontier.
☛ This agency specializes in screenplays for film and TV.
How to Contact: Query with SASE. Responds in 1 month on queries; 2 months on mss. Obtains most new clients through recommendations from others, solicitations, writing contests
Terms: Agent receives 10% commission on domestic sales; 10% commission on foreign sales. Offers written contract binding for 1 year.
Tips: "We look for screenplays and other material for film and television."

CLIENT FIRST-A/K/A LEO P. HAFFEY AGENCY, P.O.Box 128049, Nashville TN 37212-8049. (615)463-2388. E-mail: cl@nashville.net. Website: www.c-1st.com or www.nashville.net/~cl. **Contact:** Robin Swensen. Estab. 1990. Signatory of WGA. Represents 21 clients. 25% of clients are new/unpublished writers. Currently handles: 40% novels; 60% movie scripts.
Member Agents: Leo Haffey (attorney/agent in the motion picture industry).
Represents: Feature film, animation. **Considers these script subject areas:** Action/adventure, cartoon/animation, comedy, contemporary issues, detective/police/crime, family saga, historical, mystery/suspense, romantic drama (contemporary, historical), science fiction, sports, thriller/espionage, western/frontier.
☛ This agency specializes in movie scripts and novels for sale to motion picture industry.
Also Handles: Novels, novellas, short story collections, and self-help books.
How to Contact: Query with SASE. Accepts e-mail queries. Considers simultaneous queries. Responds in 1 week on queries; 2 months on mss. Returns materials only with SASE. Obtains most new clients through recommendations from others. Offers written contract binding for negotiable length of time.
Tips: "The motion picture business is a numbers game like any other. The more you write the better your chances are of success. Please send a SASE along with your query letter."

FILM ARTISTS ASSOCIATES, 13563 Ventura Blvd., 2nd Floor, Sherman Oaks CA 91423. (818)386-9669. Fax: (818)386-9363. E-mail: ronsin@ix.netcom.com. **Contact:** Ron Singer. Signatory of WGA. Represents 6 clients. 75% of clients are new/unpublished writers. Currently handles: 80% movie scripts; 5% multimedia; 15% stage plays.
● Mr. Singer was a manager of writers and performers.

Represents: Movie scripts, feature film, theatrical stage play, stage plays. **Considers these script subject areas:** Action/adventure, biography/autobiography, comedy, historical, horror, mainstream, multimedia, mystery/suspense, romantic comedy, science fiction, military war.

> O⊸ This agency represents writers, new or established, on the basis of their material and how they are able to develop and market it.

How to Contact: Query with SASE. Accepts e-mail queries. Considers simultaneous queries. Responds in 1 week on queries; 1 month on mss. Returns materials only with SASE. Obtains most new clients through recommendations from others.

Recent Sales: Optioned/sold 3 movie/TV MOW scripts scripts in the last year.

Terms: Agent receives 10% commission on domestic sales; 10% commission on foreign sales. Offers written contract binding for 1 year; after 6 months, 1-month notice must be given. Notice must be given to terminate contract. Charges clients for photocopying expenses.

Tips: "Know your craft, know your market, submit accordingly and professionally. Be receptive to criticism and feedback."

THE BARRY FREED CO., 2040 Ave. of the Stars, #400, Los Angeles CA 90067. (310)277-1260. Fax: (310)277-3865. E-mail: blfreed@aol.com. **Contact:** Barry Freed. Signatory of WGA. Represents 15 clients. 95% of clients are new/unpublished writers. Currently handles: 100% movie scripts.

> ● Prior to opening his agency, Mr. Freed worked for ICM.

Represents: Feature film, TV movie of the week. **Considers these script subject areas:** Action/adventure, comedy, contemporary issues, detective/police/crime, ethnic, family saga, horror, mainstream, mystery/suspense.

How to Contact: Query with SASE. Responds in 3 months on mss. Responds immediately. Obtains most new clients through recommendations from others.

Needs: Actively seeking adult drama, comedy, romantic comedy. Does not want to receive period, westerns.

Terms: Offers written contract binding for 2 years.

Tips: "Our clients are a high qualified small roster of writers who write comedy, action adventure/thrillers, adult drama, romantic comedy."

HUDSON AGENCY, 3 Travis Lane, Montrose NY 10548. (914)737-1475. Fax: (914)736-3064. E-mail: hudagency@juno.com. **Contact:** Susan or Pat Giordano. Estab. 1994. Signatory of WGA. Represents 30 clients. 50% of clients are new/unpublished writers. Currently handles: 50% movie scripts; 50% TV scripts.

Member Agents: Sue Giordano (TV animation); Michele Perri (books); Cheri Santone (features and animation); Sunny Bik (Canada contact).

Represents: Feature film, TV movie of the week, sitcom, animation, documentary, miniseries. **Considers these script subject areas:** Action/adventure, cartoon/animation, comedy, contemporary issues, detective/police/crime, family saga, fantasy, juvenile, mystery/suspense, romantic comedy, romantic drama, teen, western/frontier.

> O⊸ This agency specializes in feature film and TV. Also specializes in animation writers

How to Contact: Query with SASE, submit outline, sample chapter(s). Accepts e-mail and fax queries. Responds in 1 week on queries; 3 weeks on mss. Returns materials only with SASE. Obtains most new clients through recommendations from others.

Needs: Actively seeking "writers with television and screenwriting education or workshops under their belts." Does not want to receive "R-rated material, no occult, no one that hasn't taken at least one screenwriting workshop."

Terms: Agent receives 10% commission on domestic sales; 10% commission on foreign sales.

Tips: "Yes, we may be small, but we work very hard for our clients. Any script we are representing gets excellent exposure to producers. Our network has over 1,000 contacts in the business and growing rapidly. We are GOOD salespeople. Ultimately it all depends on the quality of the writing and the market for the subject matter. Do not query unless you have taken at least one screenwriting course and read all of Syd Field's books."

Ñ H.W.A. TALENT REPRESENTATIVE, 3500 W. Olive Ave., Suite 1400, Burbank CA 91505. (818)972-4310. Fax: (818)972-4313. **Contact:** Kimber Wheeler. Estab. 1985. Signatory of WGA. 90% of clients are new/unpublished writers. Currently handles: 10% novels; 90% movie scripts.

Represents: Novels, movie scripts, TV scripts. **Considers these script subject areas:** Action/adventure, biography/autobiography, cartoon/animation, comedy, contemporary issues, detective/police/crime, ethnic, family saga, fantasy, feminist, gay/lesbian, horror, mystery/suspense, psychic/supernatural, romantic comedy, romantic drama, science fiction, sports, thriller/espionage.

How to Contact: Query with SASE, submit proposal package, outline. Accepts fax queries. Considers simultaneous queries.

Terms: Agent receives 10% commission on domestic sales. Offers written contract binding for 1 year; WGA rules on termination apply. Notice must be given to terminate contract.

Tips: "A good query letter is important. Use any relationship you have in the business to get your material read."

Ñ KERIN-GOLDBERG ASSOCIATES, 155 E. 55th St., #5D, New York NY 10022. (212)838-7373. Fax: (212)838-0774. **Contact:** Charles Kerin. Estab. 1984. Signatory of WGA. Represents 29 clients. Currently handles: 30% movie scripts; 30% TV scripts; 40% stage plays.

Represents: Episodic drama, movie scripts, TV scripts, feature film, TV movie of the week, sitcom, variety show, miniseries, stage plays, syndicated material. **Considers these script subject areas:** Considers all script areas.

⊶ This agency specializes in theater plays, screenplays, teleplays.

How to Contact: Query with SASE. Responds in 1 month on queries; 2 months on mss. Obtains most new clients through recommendations from others.

Terms: Agent receives 10% commission on domestic sales; 10% commission on foreign sales. Offers written contract.

N̄ WILLIAM KERWIN AGENCY, 1605 N. Cahuenga, Suite 202, Hollywood CA 90028. (323)469-5155. **Contact:** Al Wood and Bill Kerwin. Estab. 1979. Signatory of WGA. Represents 5 clients. Currently handles: 100% movie scripts.

Represents: Movie scripts. **Considers these script subject areas:** Mystery/suspense, romantic comedy, romantic drama, science fiction, thriller/espionage.

How to Contact: Query with SASE. Responds in 1 day on queries; 1 month on mss. Obtains most new clients through recommendations from others, solicitations.

Terms: Agent receives 10% commission on domestic sales; 10% commission on foreign sales. Offers written contract binding for 1-2 years; 30 days notice must be given to terminate contract. Free criticism service.

Tips: "Listen. Be nice."

N̄ KICK ENTERTAINMENT, 1934 E. 123rd St., Cleveland OH 44106-1912. Phone/fax: (216)791-2515. **Contact:** Sam Klein. Estab. 1992. Signatory of WGA. Represents 8 clients. 100% of clients are new/unpublished writers. Currently handles: 100% movie scripts.

Member Agents: Geno Trunzo (president-motion picture division); Ms. Palm Trunzo (director-creative affairs); Fred Landsmann (TV); Gia Leonardi (creative executive).

Represents: Movie scripts, feature film. **Considers these script subject areas:** Action/adventure, comedy, detective/police/crime, fantasy, horror, mainstream, mystery/suspense, psychic/supernatural, romantic comedy, romantic drama, science fiction, thriller/espionage.

How to Contact: Query with SASE. Responds in 2 weeks on queries; 2 months on mss.

Terms: Agent receives 10% commission on domestic sales; 10% commission on foreign sales. Offers written contract binding for 1-2 years.

Tips: "Always send a query letter first, and enclose a SASE. We now presently represent clients in six states."

N̄ THE CANDACE LAKE AGENCY, 9200 Sunset Blvd., Suite 820, Los Angeles CA 90069. (310)247-2115. Fax: (310)247-2116. E-mail: clagency@earthlink.net. **Contact:** Candace Lake. Estab. 1977. Member of DGA; signatory of WGA. 50% of clients are new/unpublished writers. Currently handles: 20% novels; 40% movie scripts; 40% TV scripts.

Member Agents: Candace Lake (president/agent)

Represents: Novels, episodic drama, feature film, TV movie of the week, sitcom. **Considers these fiction areas:** Considers all fiction types. **Considers these script subject areas:** Considers all script areas.

⊶ This agency specializes in screenplay and teleplay writers Charges clients for expenses associated with manuscript submissions (postage, photocopy).

How to Contact: Query with SASE. No unsolicited material. Accepts fax queries. Considers simultaneous queries. Responds in 1 month on queries; 3 months on mss. Returns materials only with SASE. Obtains most new clients through recommendations from others.

Terms: Agent receives 10% commission on domestic sales; 10% commission on foreign sales. Offers written contract binding for 2 years. Charges clients for photocopying.

N̄ DEE MURA ENTERPRISES, INC., 269 W. Shore Dr., Massapequa NY 11758-8225. (516)795-1616. Fax: (516)795-8797. E-mail: samurai5@ix.netcom.com. **Contact:** Dee Mura, Ken Nyquist. Estab. 1987. Signatory of WGA. 50% of clients are new/unpublished writers. Currently handles: 25% nonfiction books; 25% novels; 15% juvenile books; 10% scholarly books; 25% movie scripts.

• Prior to opening her agency, Ms. Mura was a public relations executive with a roster of film and entertainment clients; and worked in editorial for major weekly news magazines.

Represents: Nonfiction books, juvenile books, scholarly books, episodic drama, feature film, TV movie of the week, sitcom, animation, documentary, variety show, miniseries. **Considers these nonfiction areas:** Agriculture/horticulture, animals, anthropology/archaeology, biography/autobiography, business/economics, child guidance/parenting, computers/electronic, current affairs, education, ethnic/cultural interests, gay/lesbian, government/politics/law, health/medicine, history, how-to, humor/satire, memoirs, military/war, money/finance, nature/environment, science/technology, self-help/personal improvement, sociology, sports, travel, true crime/investigative, women's issues/studies, juvenile nonfiction. **Considers these fiction areas:** Action/adventure, detective/police/crime, ethnic, experimental, fantasy, feminist, gay/lesbian, historical, humor, juvenile, literary, mainstream/contemporary, mystery/suspense, occult (psychic/supernatural), regional, romance (contemporary, gothic, historical, regency), science fiction, sports, thriller/espionage, western/frontier, young adult. **Considers these script subject areas:** Action/adventure, cartoon/animation, comedy, contemporary issues, detective/police/crime, family saga, fantasy, feminist, gay/lesbian, glitz, historical, horror, juvenile, mainstream, mystery/suspense, psychic/supernatural, religious/inspirational, romantic comedy, romantic drama, science fiction, sports, teen, thriller/espionage, western/frontier.

⊶ "We work on everything, but are especially interested in literary fiction, commercial fiction and nonfiction, thrillers and espionage, true life stories, true crime, women's stories and issues."

How to Contact: Query with SASE. Accepts e-mail queries. Considers simultaneous queries. Responds in 2 weeks on queries. Returns materials only with SASE. Obtains most new clients through recommendations from others, solicitations.

Needs: Actively seeking "unique nonfiction manuscripts and proposals; novelists who are great storytellers; contemporary writers with distinct voices and passion." Does not want to receive "ideas for sitcoms, novels, film, etc. or queries without SASEs."

Recent Sales: Sold over 40 books and sold 35 scripts in the last year.

Terms: Agent receives 15% commission on domestic sales; 20% commission on foreign sales. Offers written contract. Charges clients for photocopying, mailing expenses, overseas and long distance phone calls and faxes.

Tips: "Please include a paragraph on writer's background even if writer has no literary background and a brief synopsis of the project. We enjoy well-written query letters that tell us about the project and the author."

PANDA TALENT, 3721 Hoen Ave., Santa Rosa CA 95405. (707)576-0711. Fax: (707)544-2756. **Contact:** Audrey Grace. Estab. 1977. Member of SAG, AFTRA, Equity; signatory of WGA. Represents 10 clients. 80% of clients are new/unpublished writers. Currently handles: 5% novels; 50% movie scripts; 40% TV scripts; 5% stage plays.

Member Agents: Steven Grace (science fiction/war/action); Vicki Lima (mysteries/romance); Cleo West (western/true stories).

Represents: Episodic drama, feature film, TV movie of the week, sitcom. **Considers these script subject areas:** Action/adventure, comedy, detective/police/crime, ethnic, family saga, mystery/suspense, romantic comedy, romantic drama, science fiction, thriller/espionage, western/frontier.

How to Contact: Query with SASE. Responds in 3 weeks on queries; 2 months on mss. Returns materials only with SASE.

Terms: Agent receives 10% commission on domestic sales; 10% commission on foreign sales.

[N] BARRY PERELMAN AGENCY, 9200 Sunset Blvd., #1201, Los Angeles CA 90069. (310)274-5999. Fax: (310)274-6445. **Contact:** Marina D'Amico. Estab. 1982. Member of DGA; signatory of WGA. Represents 40 clients. 15% of clients are new/unpublished writers. Currently handles: 99% movie scripts; 1% TV scripts.

Member Agents: Barry Perelman (motion picture/packaging); Marina D'Amico (television)

Represents: Movie scripts. **Considers these script subject areas:** Action/adventure, biography/autobiography, contemporary issues, detective/police/crime, historical, horror, mystery/suspense, romantic comedy, romantic drama, science fiction, thriller/espionage.

○➤ This agency specializes in motion pictures/packaging.

How to Contact: Query with SASE, submit proposal package, outline. Responds in 1 month on queries. Obtains most new clients through recommendations from others, solicitations.

Terms: Agent receives 10% commission on domestic sales; 10% commission on foreign sales. Offers written contract binding for 1-2 years. Charges clients for postage and photocopying.

[N] SILVER SCREEN PLACEMENTS, 602 65th St., Downers Grove IL, 60516-3020. (630)963-2124. Fax: (630)963-1998. E-mail: silverscreen@mediaone.net. **Contact:** William Levin. Estab. 1990. Signatory of WGA. Represents 11 clients. 100% of clients are new/unpublished writers. Currently handles: 10% novels; 10% juvenile books; 80% movie scripts.

● Prior to opening his agency Mr. Levin did product placement for motion pictures/TV.

Represents: Novels, juvenile books, movie scripts, feature film. **Considers these nonfiction areas:** Education, juvenile nonfiction. **Considers these fiction areas:** Action/adventure (adventure), detective/police/crime, fantasy, historical, humor (satire), juvenile, mainstream/contemporary, mystery/suspense (suspense), science fiction, thriller/espionage, young adult. **Considers these script subject areas:** Action/adventure, comedy, contemporary issues, detective/police/crime, family saga, fantasy, historical, juvenile, mainstream, mystery/suspense, science fiction, thriller/espionage, young adult.

How to Contact: Query with SASE, submit proposal package, outline. Responds in 2 weeks on queries; 2 months on mss. Obtains most new clients through recommendations from others, listings with WGA and *Guide to Literary Agents*.

Needs: "Screenplays for young adults, 17-30." Does not want "horror, religious, X-rated."

Recent Sales: Sold 3 projects plus 2 options in the last year.

Terms: Agent receives 15% commission on foreign sales; 10% (screenplay/teleplay sales) commission on movie rights. Offers written contract binding for 2 years.

Tips: May make referrals to freelance editors. Use of editors does not ensure representation. 0% of business is derived from referrals to editing service. "Advise against 'cutsie' inquiry letters."

SYDRA TECHNIQUES CORP., 481 Eighth Ave. E 24, New York NY 10001. (212)631-0009. Fax: (212)631-0715. E-mail: sbuck@virtualnews.com. **Contact:** Sid Buck. Estab. 1988. Signatory of WGA. Represents 30 clients. 80% of clients are new/unpublished writers. Currently handles: 10% nonfiction books; 10% novels; 30% movie scripts; 30% TV scripts; 10% multimedia; 10% stage plays.

● Prior to opening his agency, Mr. Buck was an artist's agent.

Represents: Episodic drama, feature film, TV movie of the week, sitcom. **Considers these script subject areas:** Action/adventure, cartoon/animation, comedy, contemporary issues, detective/police/crime, family saga, mainstream, mystery/suspense, science fiction, sports.
How to Contact: Query with SASE, submit proposal package, outline. Responds in 1 month on queries. Obtains most new clients through recommendations from others.
Needs: "We are open."
Terms: Agent receives 10% commission on domestic sales; 15% commission on foreign sales. Offers written contract binding for 2 years; 120 days notice must be given to terminate contract.

TALENT SOURCE, 107 E. Hall St., P.O. Box 14120, Savannah GA 31416-1120. (912)232-9390. Fax: (912)232-8213. E-mail: mshortt@ix.netcom.com. Website: www.talentsource.com. **Contact:** Michael L. Shortt. Estab. 1991. Signatory of WGA. 35% of clients are new/unpublished writers. Currently handles: 75% movie scripts; 25% TV scripts.
● Prior to becoming an agent, Mr. Shortt was a television program producer.
Represents: Episodic drama, feature film, TV movie of the week, sitcom. **Considers these script subject areas:** Comedy, contemporary issues, detective/police/crime, erotica, family saga, horror, juvenile, mainstream, mystery/suspense, romantic comedy, romantic drama, teen.
How to Contact: Query with SASE, submit outline. Responds in 10 weeks on queries. Obtains most new clients through recommendations from others.
Needs: Actively seeking "character-driven stories (e.g., *Sling Blade*, *Sex Lies & Videotape*)." Does not want to receive "big budget special effects science fiction."
Terms: Agent receives 10% commission on domestic sales; 15% commission on foreign sales. Offers written contract.

PEREGRINE WHITTLESEY AGENCY, 345 E. 80 St., New York NY 10021. (212)737-0153. Fax: (212)734-5176. **Contact:** Peregrine Whittlesey. Estab. 1986. Signatory of WGA. Represents 30 clients. 50% of clients are new/unpublished writers. Currently handles: 20% movie scripts; 80% stage plays.
Represents: Feature film, stage plays.
O→ This agency specializes in playwrights who also write for screen and TV
How to Contact: Query with SASE. Responds in 1 week on queries; 1 month on mss. Obtains most new clients through recommendations from others.
Terms: Agent receives 10% commission on domestic sales; 15% commission on foreign sales. Offers written contract binding for 2 years.

THE WRIGHT CONCEPT, 1612 W. Olive Ave., Suite 205, Burbank CA 91506. (818)954-8943. Fax: (818)954-9370. E-mail: mrwright@wrightconcept.com. Website: www.wrightconcept.com. **Contact:** Marcie Wright. Estab. 1985. Member of DGA; signatory of WGA. Currently handles: 50% movie scripts; 50% TV scripts.
Represents: Episodic drama, movie scripts, TV scripts, feature film, TV movie of the week, sitcom, animation, variety show, syndicated material. **Considers these script subject areas:** Action/adventure, teen, thriller/espionage.
O→ This agency specializes in TV comedy writers and feature comedy writers.
How to Contact: Query with SASE. Responds in 2 weeks on queries. Obtains most new clients through recommendations from others, solicitations.
Terms: Agent receives 10% commission on domestic sales. Offers written contract binding for 1 year; 90 days notice must be given to terminate contract.
Writers' Conference(s): Southwest Writers Workshop (Albequerque, August).

N¦ ANN WRIGHT REPRESENTATIVES, 165 W. 46th St., Suite 1105, New York NY 10036-2501. (212)764-6770. Fax: (212)764-5125. **Contact:** Dan Wright. Estab. 1961. Signatory of WGA. Represents 23 clients. 30% of clients are new/unpublished writers. Currently handles: 50% novels; 40% movie scripts; 10% TV scripts.
● Mr. Wright was a writer, producer and production manager for film and television (alumnus of CBS Television).
Represents: Novels, episodic drama, feature film, TV movie of the week, sitcom. **Considers these fiction areas:** Action/adventure (adventure), detective/police/crime, feminist, gay/lesbian, humor (satire), literary, mainstream/contemporary, mystery/suspense (suspense), romance (contemporary, historical, regency), sports, thriller/espionage, western/frontier (frontier). **Considers these script subject areas:** Action/adventure, comedy, detective/police/crime, gay/lesbian, historical, horror, mainstream, mystery/suspense, psychic/supernatural, romantic comedy, romantic drama, sports, thriller/espionage, western/frontier.
O→ This agency specializes in "books or screenplays with strong motion picture potential." Prefers to work with published/established authors; works with a small number of new/previously unpublished authors. "Eager to work with any author with material that we can effectively market in the motion picture business worldwide."
How to Contact: Query with SASE, submit outline, Does not read unsolicited mss. Responds in 3 weeks on queries; 4 months on mss. Returns materials only with SASE.
Needs: "Stong competitive novelists and screen writers." "Fantasy or science fiction projects at this time."
Recent Sales: Sold Sold 7 projects in the last year scripts in the last year.
Terms: Agent receives 10% commission on domestic sales; 15-20% commission on foreign sales; 10% on dramtic sales; 20% on packaging commission on movie rights. Offers written contract binding for 2 years. Critiques only works of signed clients. Charges clients for photocopying expenses.
Tips: "Send a letter with SASE. Something about the work, something about the writer."

⬤ ⬛ **WRITER STORE**, 2004 Rockledge Rd., Atlanta GA 30324. (404)874-6260. Fax: (404)874-6330. E-mail: writerstore@mindspring.com. **Contact:** Rebecca Shrager or Brenda Eanes. Signatory of WGA. Represents 16 clients. 80% of clients are new/unpublished writers. Currently handles: 10% novels; 90% movie scripts.

Member Agents: Rebecca Shrager; Brenda Eanes

Represents: Novels, movie scripts, TV scripts, feature film, TV movie of the week, animation, miniseries. **Considers these fiction areas:** Action/adventure (adventure), cartoon/comic, detective/police/crime, fantasy, historical, humor (satire), literary, mainstream/contemporary, multicultural, mystery/suspense (suspense), regional, romance, science fiction, sports, thriller/espionage, young adult, glitz; New Age/metaphysical; psychic/supernatural. **Considers these script subject areas:** Action/adventure, biography/autobiography, cartoon/animation, comedy, contemporary issues, detective/police/crime, ethnic, family saga, fantasy, glitz, historical, mainstream, multicultural, mystery/suspense, psychic/supernatural, regional, romantic comedy, romantic drama, science fiction, sports, teen, thriller/espionage.

    O━ This agency makes frequent trips to Los Angeles to meet with producers and development directors. "We make it a priority to know what the buyers are looking for. People Store, the sister company of Writer Store, has been in business since 1983 and is one of the oldest, largest, and most well respected SAG talent agencies in the southeast. Writer Store reaps the benefits of a wide variety of contacts in the industry developed over a number of years by People Store."

How to Contact: Query with SASE, submit synopsis. Accepts e-mail and fax queries. Considers simultaneous queries. Responds in a few days on queries; 2 months on mss. Returns materials only with SASE. Obtains most new clients through solicitations.

Needs: Action-adventure, urban (dramas and comedies), thrillers, GOOD comedies of all types, GOOD science fiction, Native American, MOWs, sports, music related, based on a true story pieces, big budget Disgusting horror, toilet humor, short stories (unless it'a an anthology), children's books

Terms: Agent receives 10-15% commission on domestic sales; 15-20% commission on foreign sales. Offers written contract binding for generally 2 years.

Writers' Conference(s): Words Into Pictures (Los Angeles, June).

Tips: "Do not send unsolicited manuscripts. They will not be read. Send brief, concise query letter and synopses. No pictures please. Be sure you understand the craft of screenwriting and are using the proper format."

FOR LISTINGS OF OVER 500 literary and script agents, consult the *Guide to Literary Agents* (Writer's Digest Books).

Subject Index

LITERARY AGENTS SUBJECT INDEX/FICTION

Action/Adventure: Agency West; Brandt & Hochman; Circle of Confusion; Jane Dystel; Sanford J. Greenburger Assoc.; Reese Halsey North; JCA; Michael Larsen/Elizabeth Pomada; Margaret McBride; Dee Mura; Jane Rotrosen; Peter Rubie; Russell & Volkening; Victoria Sanders & Assoc.; Silver Screen Placements; Vines Agency; Scott Waxman; Ann Wright; Writer Store; Writers House

Cartoon/comic: Circle of Confusion; Writer Store; Writer's House

Comedy: Silver Screen Placements

Confession: Circle of Confusion; Writer's House

Contemporary Issues: Silver Screen Placements

Detective/Police/Crime: Brandt & Hochman; Kidde Hoyt & Picard; Donald Maass; Dee Mura; Jane Rotrosen; Peter Rubie; Russell & Volkening; Silver Screen Placements; Vines Agency; Ann Wright; Writer Store

Erotica: Circle of Confusion; Wales Literary Agency; Writers House

Ethnic: Agency West; Betsy Amster; Book Deals; Brandt & Hochman; Castiglia Literary Agency; Circle of Confusion; Joan Daves; Jane Dystel; Felicia Eth; Sanford J. Greenburger Assoc.; Reese Halsey North; Knight Agency; Michael Larsen/Elizabeth Pomada; Margaret McBride; Dee Mura; Peter Rubie; Russell & Volkening; Victoria Sanders & Assoc.; Vines Agency; Wales Literary Agency; Writers House

Experimental: Brandt & Hochman; Circle of Confusion; Michael Larsen/Elizabeth Pomada; Vines Agency; Writers House

Fantasy: Agency West; Maria Carvainis; Circle of Confusion; Pinder Lane & Garon Brooke Assoc.; Michael Larsen/Elizabeth Pomada; Donald Maass; Dee Mura; L. Perkins Assoc.; Peter Rubie; Silver Screen Placements; Writer Store; Writers House

Feminist: Brandt & Hochman; Circle of Confusion; Felicia Eth; Sanford J. Greenburger Assoc.; Kidde Hoyt & Picard; Michael Larsen/Elizabeth Pomada; Dee Mura; Victoria Sanders & Assoc.; Vines Agency; Wales Literary Agency; Ann Wright; Writers House

Gay/Lesbian: Brandt & Hochman; Circle of Confusion; Joan Daves; Jane Dystel; Felicia Eth; Sanford J. Greenburger Assoc.; Kidde Hoyt & Picard; Pinder Lane & Garon Brooke Assoc.; Michael Larsen/Elizabeth Pomada; Dee Mura; Victoria Sanders & Assoc.; Vines Agency; Wales Literary Agency; Ann Wright; Writers House

Gothic: Circle of Confusion; Writer's House

Hi-lo: Circle of Confusion; Writer's House

Historical: Altair; Brandt & Hochman; Maria Carvainis; Circle of Confusion; Sanford J. Greenburger Assoc.; Reese Halsey North; Irene Skolnick; JCA; Jeanne Fredericks; Kidde Hoyt & Picard; Kidde Hoyt & Picard; Michael Larsen/Elizabeth Pomada; Donald Maass; Margaret McBride; Dee Mura; Helen Rees; Jane Rotrosen; Peter Rubie; Silver Screen Placements; Toad Hall; Toad Hall; Vines Agency; Scott Waxman; Writer Store; Writers House

Horror: Circle of Confusion; Donald Maass; L. Perkins Assoc.; Jane Rotrosen; Vines Agency; Writers House

Humor: Agency West; Brandt & Hochman; Circle of Confusion; Sanford J. Greenburger Assoc.; Kidde Hoyt & Picard; Michael Larsen/Elizabeth Pomada; Margaret McBride; Dee Mura; Silver Screen Placements; Vines Agency; Ann Wright; Writer Store; Writers House

Juvenile: Agency West; Circle of Confusion; Heacock Literary Agency; Dee Mura; Silver Screen Placements; Scott Treimel NY; Writers House

Literary: Agency West; Altair; Miriam Altshuler; Betsy Amster; Meredith Bernstein; Book Deals; Brandt & Hochman; Sheree Bykofsky; Maria Carvainis; Castiglia Literary Agency; Circle of Confusion; Joan Daves; Jane Dystel; Felicia Eth; Sanford J. Greenburger Assoc.; Reese Halsey North; Irene Skolnick; JCA; Jeanne Fredericks; Kidde Hoyt & Picard; Knight Agency; Pinder Lane & Garon Brooke Assoc.; Michael Larsen/Elizabeth Pomada; Donald Maass; Manus & Assoc.; Margaret McBride; Dee Mura; L. Perkins Assoc.; Helen Rees; Angela Rinaldi; Peter Rubie; Russell & Volkening; Victoria Sanders & Assoc.; Vines Agency; Wales Literary Agency; Scott Waxman; Ann Wright; Writer Store; Writers House

Mainstream/Contemporary: Agency West; Miriam Altshuler;Book Deals; Brandt & Hochman; Sheree Bykofsky; Maria Carvainis; Castiglia Literary Agency; Circle of Confusion; Joan Daves; Jane Dystel; Felicia Eth; Sanford J. Greenburger Assoc.; Reese Halsey North; Irene Skolnick; JCA; Kidde Hoyt & Picard; Knight Agency; Pinder Lane & Garon Brooke Assoc.; Michael Larsen/Elizabeth Pomada; Donald Maass; Manus & Assoc.; Margaret McBride; Dee Mura; Helen Rees; Angela Rinaldi; Jane Rotrosen; Peter Rubie; Russell & Volkening; Victoria Sanders & Assoc.; Silver Screen Placements; Steele-Perkins; Vines Agency; Wales Literary Agency; Ann Wright; Writer Store; Writers House

Military/War: Circle of Confusion; Writers House

Multicultural: Miriam Altshuler; Circle of Confusion; Manus & Assoc.; Steele-Perkins; Wales Literary Agency; Writer Store; Writers House

Multimedia: Circle of Confusion; Writers House

Mystery/Suspense: Meredith Bernstein; Brandt & Hochman; Maria Carvainis; Castiglia Literary Agency; Circle of Confusion; Sanford J. Greenburger Assoc.; Reese Halsey North; JCA; Kidde Hoyt & Picard; Pinder Lane & Garon Brooke Assoc.; Michael Larsen/Elizabeth Pomada; Nancy Love; Donald Maass; Margaret McBride; New England Publishing Assoc.; Helen Rees; Jane Rotrosen; Peter Rubie; Russell & Volkening; Silver Screen Placements; Toad Hall; Vines Agency; Scott Waxman; Ann Wright; Writer Store; Writers House

Occult: Brandt & Hochman; Circle of Confusion; Donald Maass; Dee Mura; Vines Agency; Writers House

Picture Books: Circle of Confusion; Russell & Volkening; Scott Treimel NY; Writers House

Plays: Circle of Confusion; Writer's House

Poetry: Circle of Confusion; Writer's House

Poetry in Translation: Circle of Confusion; Writer's House

Regional: Brandt & Hochman; Circle of Confusion; Sanford J. Greenburger Assoc.; Dee Mura; Vines Agency; Wales Literary Agency; Writer Store; Writers House

Religious: Agency West; Circle of Confusion; Michael Larsen/Elizabeth Pomada; Scott Waxman; Writers House

Romance: Meredith Bernstein; Brandt & Hochman; Maria Carvainis; Circle of Confusion; Kidde Hoyt & Picard; Knight Agency; Pinder Lane & Garon Brooke Assoc.; Michael Larsen/Elizabeth Pomada; Donald Maass; Dee Mura; Jane Rotrosen; Steele-Perkins; Toad Hall; Vines Agency; Scott Waxman; Ann Wright; Writer Store; Writers House

Science Fiction: Brandt & Hochman; Circle of Confusion; Reese Halsey North; Pinder Lane & Garon Brooke Assoc.; Donald Maass; Dee Mura; L. Perkins Assoc.; Peter Rubie; Silver Screen Placements; Toad Hall; Vines Agency; Writer Store; Writers House

Short Story Collections: Circle of Confusion; Writers House

Sports: Agency West; Brandt & Hochman; Circle of Confusion; Sanford J. Greenburger Assoc.; JCA; Dee Mura; Russell & Volkening; Vines Agency; Scott Waxman; Ann Wright; Writer Store; Writers House

Suspense: Book Deals; Brandt & Hochman; Maria Carvainis; Castiglia Literary Agency; Circle of Confusion; Jane Dystel; Sanford J. Greenburger Assoc.; JCA; Pinder Lane & Garon Brooke Assoc.; Donald Maass; Manus & Assoc.; Margaret McBride; New England Publishing Assoc.; Helen Rees; Peter Rubie; Russell & Volkening; Victoria Sanders & Assoc.; Toad Hall; Vines Agency; Scott Waxman; Writers House

Thriller/Espionage: Book Deals; Miriam Altshuler;Brandt & Hochman; Maria Carvainis; Jane Dystel; Felicia Eth; Sanford J. Greenburger Assoc.; JCA; Kidde Hoyt & Picard; Nancy Love; Donald Maass; Manus & Assoc.; Margaret McBride; Dee Mura; Helen Rees; Jane Rotrosen; Peter Rubie; Russell & Volkening; Victoria Sanders & Assoc.; Silver Screen Placements; Vines Agency; Ann Wright; Writer Store; Writers House

Western/Frontier: Brandt & Hochman; Circle of Confusion; Margaret McBride; Dee Mura; Vines Agency; Ann Wright; Writers House

Women's Fiction: Meredith Bernstein; Book Deals; Castiglia Literary Agency; Jane Rotrosen; Vines Agency

Young Adult: Agency West; Brandt & Hochman; Maria Carvainis; Circle of Confusion; Dee Mura; Silver Screen Placements; Scott Treimel NY; Writer Store; Writers House

LITERARY AGENTS SUBJECT INDEX/NONFICTION

Agriculture/horticulture: Brandt & Hochman; Dee Mura

Americana: Sheree Bykofsky; Circle of Confusion; Greenburger Assoc

Animals: Meredith Bernstein; Brandt & Hochman; Sheree Bykofsky; Castiglia Agency; Circle of Confusion; Jane Dystel; Felicia Eth; Jeanne Fredericks; Greenburger Assoc.; Nancy Love; Dee Mura; Toad Hall; Wales Agency; Writers House

Anthropology/archaeology: Altair; Brandt & Hochman; Sheree Bykofsky; Castiglia Agency; Circle of Confusion; Jane Dystel; Felicia Eth; Jeanne Fredericks; Greenburger Assoc.; JCA; Michael Larsen/Elizabeth Pomada; Dee Mura; James Peter; Russell & Volkening; Toad Hall; United Tribes

Art/architecture/design: Altair; Brandt & Hochman; Sheree Bykofsky; Circle of Confusion; Jeanne Fredericks; Greenburger Assoc.; Heacock; Kidde Hoyt & Picard; Michael Larsen/Elizabeth Pomada; James Peter; Russell & Volkening; United Tribes; Writers House

Biography/autobiography: Agency West; Altair; Miram Altshuler; Brandt & Hochman; Maria Carvainis; Castiglia Agency; Felicia Eth; Heacock; Kidde Hoyt & Picard; Nancy Love; Dee Mura; Jane Rotrosen; Russell & Volkening; Irene Skolnick; Vines Agency; Wales Agency

Business/economics: Altair; Betsy Amster; Meredith Bernstein; Book Deals; Brandt & Hochman; Sheree Bykofsky; Maria Carvainis; Castiglia Agency; Circle of Confusion; Jane Dystel; Felicia Eth; Jeanne Fredericks; Greenburger Assoc.; Jeff Herman; JCA; Knight Agency; Michael Larsen/Elizabeth Pomada; Manus & Assoc.; Margaret McBride; Claudia Menza; Dee Mura; New England Pub. Assoc.; James Peter; Helen Rees; Angela Rinaldi; Jane Rotrosen; Russell & Volkening; Toad Hall; United Tribes; Vines Agency; Scott Waxman; Writers House

Child guidance/parenting: Agency West; Betsy Amster; Meredith Bernstein; Book Deals; Brandt & Hochman; Sheree Bykofsky; Castiglia Agency; Circle of Confusion; Jane Dystel; Felicia Eth; Jeanne Fredericks; Greenburger Assoc.; Knight Agency; Pinder Lane & Garon Brooke Assoc.; Nancy Love; Manus & Assoc.; Margaret McBride; Dee Mura; New England Pub. Assoc.; James Peter; Angela Rinaldi; Jane Rotrosen; Toad Hall; United Tribes; Writers House

Computers/electronic: Sheree Bykofsky; Circle of Confusion; Greenburger Assoc.; Jeff Herman; Knight Agency; Manus & Assoc.; Dee Mura

Cooking/Foods/Nutrition: Agency West; Brandt & Hochman; Sheree Bykofsky; Castiglia Agency; Circle of Confusion; Jane Dystel; Jeanne Fredericks; Greenburger Assoc.; Knight Agency; Michael Larsen/Elizabeth Pomada; Nancy Love; Margaret McBride; Jane Rotrosen; Russell & Volkening; Toad Hall; United Tribes; Writers House

Creative Nonfiction: Sheree Bykofsky; Circle of Confusion; Greenburger Assoc

Current Affairs: Brandt & Hochman; Castiglia Agency; Felicia Eth; Reese Halsey North; Kidde Hoyt & Picard; Nancy Love; Claudia Menza; Dee Mura; Jane Rotrosen; Peter Rubie; Russell & Volkening; Vines Agency; Wales Agency

Education: Agency West; Sheree Bykofsky; Circle of Confusion; Jane Dystel; Greenburger Assoc.; Claudia Menza; Dee Mura; Russell & Volkening; Silver Screen Placements; United Tribes

Ethnic/Cultural Interests: Agency West; Altair; Miram Altshuler; Betsy Amster; Book Deals; Brandt & Hochman; Sheree Bykofsky; Castiglia Agency; Circle of Confusion; Jane Dystel; Felicia Eth; Greenburger Assoc.; Kidde Hoyt & Picard; Knight Agency; Michael Larsen/Elizabeth Pomada; Nancy Love; Manus & Assoc.; Margaret McBride; Claudia Menza; Dee Mura; James Peter; Peter Rubie; Russell & Volkening; Victoria Sanders & Assoc.; United Tribes; Vines Agency; Wales Agency; Scott Waxman

Gardening: Betsy Amster; Sheree Bykofsky; Circle of Confusion; Greenburger Assoc

Gay/Lesbian: Altair; Brandt & Hochman; Sheree Bykofsky; Circle of Confusion; Joan Daves; Jane Dystel; Felicia Eth; Greenburger Assoc.; Kidde Hoyt & Picard; Pinder Lane & Garon Brooke Assoc.; Michael Larsen/Elizabeth Pomada; Margaret McBride; Dee Mura; James Peter; Russell & Volkening; Victoria Sanders & Assoc.; United Tribes; Wales Agency

Government/Politics/Law: Altair; Brandt & Hochman; Sheree Bykofsky; Circle of Confusion; Jane Dystel; Felicia Eth; Greenburger Assoc.; Jeff Herman; JCA; Michael Larsen/Elizabeth Pomada; Nancy Love; Margaret McBride; Dee Mura; New England Pub. Assoc.; James Peter; Helen Rees; Russell & Volkening; Victoria Sanders & Assoc.; United Tribes

Health/Medicine: Book Deals; Altair; Betsy Amster; Meredith Bernstein; Brandt & Hochman; Sheree Bykofsky; Maria Carvainis; Castiglia Agency; Circle of Confusion; Jane Dystel; Felicia Eth; Jeanne Fredericks; Greenburger Assoc.; Jeff Herman; JCA; Knight Agency; Pinder Lane & Garon Brooke Assoc.; Michael Larsen/Elizabeth Pomada; Manus & Assoc.; Margaret McBride; Claudia Menza; Dee Mura; New England Pub. Assoc.; James Peter; Helen Rees; Angela Rinaldi; Jane Rotrosen; Russell & Volkening; Toaericks; Greenburger Assoc.; Reese Halsey North; Jeff Herman; JCA; Kidde Hoyt & Picard; Knight Agency; Pinder Lane & Garon Brooke Assoc.; Michael Larsen/Elizabeth Pomada; Nancy Love; Margaret McBride; Claudia Menza; Dee Mura; New England Pub. Assoc.; James Peter; Helen Rees; Russell & Volkening; Victoria Sanders & Assoc.; United Tribes; Vines Agency; Wales Agency; Scott Waxman; Writers House

Hobbies/Crafts: Agency West; Brandt & Hochman; Sheree Bykofsky; Circle of Confusion; Greenburger Assoc.; Toad Hall

How-To: Agency West; Altair; Book Deals; Heacock; Jeff Herman; Nancy Love; Claudia Menza; Dee Mura; Jane Rotrosen; Toad Hall; Vines Agency

Humor/Satire: Agency West; Dee Mura; Jane Rotrosen; Vines Agency

Illustrated Books: Altair

Interior Design/Decorating: Brandt & Hochman

Juvenile Nonfiction: Agency West; Brandt & Hochman; Dee Mura; Silver Screen Placements; Irene Skolnick

Language/Literature/Criticism: Miram Altshuler; Brandt & Hochman; Sheree Bykofsky; Castiglia Agency; Circle of Confusion; Greenburger Assoc.; Reese Halsey North; JCA; Kidde Hoyt & Picard; Michael Larsen/Elizabeth Pomada; New England Pub. Assoc.; James Peter; Russell & Volkening; Victoria Sanders & Assoc.; United Tribes

Memoirs: Agency West; Miram Altshuler; Sheree Bykofsky; Maria Carvainis; Circle of Confusion; Greenburger Assoc.; JCA; Kidde Hoyt & Picard; Pinder Lane & Garon Brooke Assoc.; Michael Larsen/Elizabeth Pomada; Nancy Love; Manus & Assoc.; Dee Mura; James Peter; United Tribes; Vines Agency; Wales Agency

Military/War: Brandt & Hochman; Sheree Bykofsky; Circle of Confusion; Jane Dystel; Greenburger Assoc.; JCA; Pinder Lane & Garon Brooke Assoc.; Dee Mura; New England Pub. Assoc.; James Peter; Russell & Volkening; Vines Agency; Writers House

Money/Finance: Altair; Betsy Amster; Book Deals; Brandt & Hochman; Sheree Bykofsky; Castiglia Agency; Circle of Confusion; Jane Dystel; Jeanne Fredericks; Greenburger Assoc.; JCA; Knight Agency; Michael Larsen/Elizabeth Pomada; Manus & Assoc.; Margaret McBride; Dee Mura; New England Pub. Assoc.; James Peter; Helen Rees; Angela Rinaldi; Jane Rotrosen; Russell & Volkening; United Tribes; Vines Agency; Scott Waxman; Writers House

Multicultural: Miram Altshuler; Sheree Bykofsky; Circle of Confusion; Greenburger Assoc.; Claudia Menza; Wales Agency

Music/Dance: Agency West; Altair; Miram Altshuler; Brandt & Hochman; Sheree Bykofsky; Circle of Confusion; Greenburger Assoc.; Heacock; JCA; Knight Agency; Pinder Lane & Garon Brooke Assoc.; Michael Larsen/Elizabeth Pomada; Margaret McBride; Claudia Menza; James Peter; Peter Rubie; Russell & Volkening; Victoria Sanders & Assoc.; United Tribes; Writers House

Narrative Nonfiction: Meredith Bernstein; Peter Rubie

Nature/Environment: Altair; Miram Altshuler; Brandt & Hochman; Sheree Bykofsky; Castiglia Agency; Circle of Confusion; Felicia Eth; Jeanne Fredericks; Greenburger Assoc.; Heacock; JCA; Michael Larsen/Elizabeth Pomada; Nancy Love; Manus & Assoc.; Dee Mura; New England Pub. Assoc.; Jane Rotrosen; Russell & Volkening; Toad Hall; United Tribes; Vines Agency; Wales Agency; Writers House

New Age/Metaphysics: Castiglia Agency

Philosophy: Sheree Bykofsky; Circle of Confusion; Greenburger Assoc

Photography: Altair; Sheree Bykofsky; Circle of Confusion; Jeanne Fredericks; Greenburger Assoc.; Michael Larsen/Elizabeth Pomada; Claudia Menza; Russell & Volkening; Vines Agency

Politics: Meredith Bernstein

Popular Culture: Altair; Miram Altshuler; Book Deals; Felicia Eth; Reese Halsey North; Kidde Hoyt & Picard; Nancy Love; L. Perkins Assoc.; Jane Rotrosen; Russell & Volkening; Toad Hall; Vines Agency; Wales Agency

Popular Reference: Jeff Herman

Psychology: Altair; Miram Altshuler; Betsy Amster; Meredith Bernstein; Book Deals; Brandt & Hochman; Sheree Bykofsky; Castiglia Agency; Circle of Confusion; Jane Dystel; Felicia Eth; Jeanne Fredericks; Greenburger Assoc.; Heacock; Jeff Herman; Kidde Hoyt & Picard; Knight Agency; Pinder Lane & Garon Brooke Assoc.; Michael Larsen/Elizabeth Pomada Literary Agents; Nancy Love; Manus & Assoc.; Margaret McBride; Claudia Menza; New England Pub. Assoc.; James Peter; Angela Rinaldi; Jane Rotrosen; Russell & Volkening; Victoria Sanders & Assoc.; United Tribes; Vines Agency; Writers House

Recreation: Sheree Bykofsky; Circle of Confusion; Greenburger Assoc.

Regional: Sheree Bykofsky; Circle of Confusion; Greenburger Assoc.

Religious/Inspirational: Agency West; Altair; Sheree Bykofsky; Castiglia Agency; Circle of Confusion; Jane Dystel; Greenburger Assoc.; Knight Agency; Michael Larsen/Elizabeth Pomada; Margaret McBride; Toad Hall; United Tribes; Vines Agency; Scott Waxman

Science/Technology: Altair; Meredith Bernstein; Book Deals; Brandt & Hochman; Sheree Bykofsky; Maria Carvainis; Castiglia Agency; Circle of Confusion; Jane Dystel; Felicia Eth; Jeanne Fredericks; Greenburger Assoc.; Heacock; JCA; Michael Larsen/Elizabeth Pomada; Nancy Love; Manus & Assoc.; Margaret McBride; Dee Mura; New England Pub. Assoc.; Peter Rubie; Russell & Volkening; United Tribes; Vines Agency; Wales Agency; Writers House

Self-Help/Personal Improvement: Agency West; Altair; Book Deals; Brandt & Hochman; Castiglia Agency; Heacock; Jeff Herman; Kidde Hoyt & Picard; Nancy Love; Claudia Menza; Dee Mura; Jane Rotrosen; Toad Hall; Vines Agency

Sex: Sheree Bykofsky; Circle of Confusion; Greenburger Assoc

Sociology: Altair; Miram Altshuler; Betsy Amster; Brandt & Hochman; Sheree Bykofsky; Castiglia Agency; Circle of Confusion; Felicia Eth; Greenburger Assoc.; JCA; Kidde Hoyt & Picard; Michael Larsen/Elizabeth Pomada; Nancy Love; Margaret McBride; Dee Mura; New England Pub. Assoc.; Angela Rinaldi; Russell & Volkening; United Tribes; Vines Agency

Software: Sheree Bykofsky; Circle of Confusion; Greenburger Assoc

Spirituality: Meredith Bernstein; Book Deals; Sheree Bykofsky; Circle of Confusion; Greenburger Assoc.; Heacock; Jeff Herman; Nancy Love; Toad Hall; Vines Agency

Sports: Agency West; Altair; Brandt & Hochman; Sheree Bykofsky; Circle of Confusion; Jeanne Fredericks; Greenburger Assoc.; JCA; Knight Agency; Michael Larsen/Elizabeth Pomada; Margaret McBride; Dee Mura; Jane Rotrosen; Russell & Volkening; Steele-Perkins Agency; Vines Agency; Scott Waxman

Translation: Sheree Bykofsky; Circle of Confusion; Joan Daves; Greenburger Assoc.; JCA; Victoria Sanders & Assoc.; United Tribes; Vines Agency

Travel: Sheree Bykofsky; Circle of Confusion; Greenburger Assoc.; Michael Larsen/Elizabeth Pomada; Nancy Love; Dee Mura; James Peter; Vines Agency; Wales Agency

True Crime/Investigative: Agency West; Brandt & Hochman; Felicia Eth; Reese Halsey North; Nancy Love; Dee Mura; Jane Rotrosen; Russell & Volkening; Vines Agency

Women's Issues/Studies: Agency West; Altair; Miram Altshuler; Betsy Amster; Brandt & Hochman; Sheree Bykofsky; Maria Carvainis; Castiglia Agency; Circle of Confusion; Joan Daves; Jane Dystel; Felicia Eth; Jeanne Fredericks;Greenburger Assoc.; Reese Halsey North; Heacock; JCA; Kidde Hoyt & Picard; Michael Larsen/Elizabeth Pomada; Nancy Love; Manus & Assoc.; Margaret McBride; Dee Mura; New England Pub. Assoc.; James Peter; Helen Rees; Angela Rinaldi; Jane Rotrosen; Russell & Volkening; Victoria Sanders & Assoc.; United Tribes; Vines Agency; Wales Agency; Writers House

SCRIPT AGENTS SUBJECT INDEX

Action/Adventure: Agency West; Bulger & Assoc.; Circle of Confusion; Client First; Film Artists; Barry Freed; H.W.A.; Hudson Agency; Kick Entertainment; Dee Mura Enterprises; Panda Talent; Barry Perelman; Silver Screen Placements; Sydra Techniques; Wright Concept; Ann Wright; Writer Store

Animation: Abrams Artists; Client First; Agency West; Hudson Agency; Wright Concept; Writer Store

Biography/Autobiography: Agency West; Circle of Confusion; Film Artists; H.W.A.; Barry Perelman; Writer Store

Cartoon/Animation: Above the Line; Agency West; Bulger & Assoc.; Circle of Confusion; Client First; H.W.A.; Hudson Agency; Dee Mura Enterprises; Sydra Techniques; Writer Store

Comedy: Abrams Artists; Agency West; Bulger & Assoc.; Circle of Confusion; Client First; Film Artists; Barry Freed; H.W.A.; Hudson Agency; Kick Entertainment; Dee Mura Enterprises; Panda Talent; Silver Screen Placements; Sydra Techniques; Talent Source; Ann Wright; Writer Store

Contemporary Issues: Abrams Artists; Bulger & Assoc.; Circle of Confusion; Client First; Barry Freed; H.W.A.; Hudson Agency; Dee Mura Enterprises; Barry Perelman; Silver Screen Placements; Sydra Techniques; Talent Source; Writer Store

Detective/Police/Crime: Circle of Confusion; Client First; Barry Freed; H.W.A.; Hudson Agency; Kick Entertainment; Dee Mura Enterprises; Panda Talent; Barry Perelman; Silver Screen Placements; Sydra Techniques; Talent Source; Ann Wright; Writer Store

Documentary: Bulger & Assoc.; Hudson Agency

Episodic Drama: Abrams Artists; Alpern Group; Kerin-Goldberg Assoc.; Panda Talent; Sydra Techniques; Talent Source; Wright Concept; Ann Wright

Erotica: Circle of Confusion; Talent Source

Ethnic: Agency West; Bulger & Assoc.; Circle of Confusion; Barry Freed; H.W.A.; Panda Talent; Writer Store

Experimental: Circle of Confusion

Family Saga: Agency West; Agency West; Circle of Confusion; H.W.A.; Hudson Agency; Kick Entertainment; Dee Mura Enterprises; Silver Screen Placements; Writer Store

Feature Film: Above the Line; Abrams Artists; Agency West; Alpern Group; Bulger & Assoc.; Client First; Film Artists; Barry Freed; Hudson Agency; Kerin-Goldberg Assoc.; Kick Entertainment; Panda Talent; Silver Screen Placements; Sydra Techniques; Talent Source; Peregrine Whittlesey; Wright Concept; Ann Wright; Writer Store

Feminist: Circle of Confusion; H.W.A.; Dee Mura Enterprises

Gay/Lesbian: Circle of Confusion; H.W.A.; Dee Mura Enterprises; Ann Wright

Glitz: Circle of Confusion; Dee Mura Enterprises; Writer Store

Historical: Circle of Confusion; Client First; Film Artists; Dee Mura Enterprises; Barry Perelman; Silver Screen Placements; Ann Wright; Writer Store

Horror: Circle of Confusion; Film Artists; Barry Freed; H.W.A.; Kick Entertainment; Dee Mura Enterprises; Barry Perelman; Talent Source; Ann Wright

Juvenile: Agency West; Circle of Confusion; Hudson Agency; Dee Mura Enterprises; Silver Screen Placements; Talent Source

Mainstream: Abrams Artists; Agency West; Circle of Confusion; Film Artists; Barry Freed; Kick Entertainment; Dee Mura Enterprises; Silver Screen Placements; Sydra Techniques; Talent Source; Ann Wright; Writer Store

Military/War: Film Artists

Miniseries: Agency West; Alpern Group; Hudson Agency; Kerin-Goldberg Assoc.; Writer Store

Movie Scripts: Agency West; Alpern Group; Film Artists; H.W.A.; Kerin-Goldberg Assoc.; Kerwin, William; Kick Entertainment; Silver Screen Placements; Wright Concept; Writer Store

Multicultural: Circle of Confusion; Writer Store

Multimedia: Circle of Confusion; Film Artists

Musical: Abrams Artists

Mystery/Suspense: Abrams Artists; Circle of Confusion; Client First; Film Artists; Barry Freed; H.W.A.; Hudson Agency; Kerwin, William; Kick Entertainment; Dee Mura Enterprises; Panda Talent; Barry Perelman; Silver Screen Placements; Sydra Techniques; Talent Source; Ann Wright; Writer Store

Open to All Script Areas: Alpern Group; Candace Lake; Kerin-Goldberg Assoc

Psychic/Supernatural: Circle of Confusion; H.W.A.; Kick Entertainment; Dee Mura Enterprises; Ann Wright; Writer Store

Regional: Circle of Confusion; Writer Store

Religious/Inspirational: Agency West; Bulger & Assoc.; Circle of Confusion; Dee Mura Enterprises

Romantic Comedy: Abrams Artists; Agency West; Circle of Confusion; Film Artists; ; H.W.A.; Hudson Agency; Kerwin, William; Kick Entertainment; Dee Mura Enterprises; Panda Talent; Barry Perelman; Talent Source; Ann Wright; Writer Store

Romantic Drama: Abrams Artists; Agency West; Circle of Confusion; Client First; H.W.A.; Hudson Agency; Kerwin, William; Kick Entertainment; Dee Mura Enterprises; Panda Talent; Barry Perelman; Talent Source; Ann Wright; Writer Store

Science Fiction: Agency West; Circle of Confusion; Client First; Film Artists; H.W.A.; Kerwin, William; Kick Entertainment; Dee Mura Enterprises; Panda Talent; Barry Perelman; Silver Screen Placements; Sydra Techniques; Writer Store

Sitcom: Abrams Artists; Agency West; Hudson Agency; Kerin-Goldberg Assoc.; Panda Talent; Sydra Techniques; Talent Source; Wright Concept; Ann Wright

Soap Opera: Abrams Artists

Sports: Agency West; Circle of Confusion; Client First; H.W.A.; Dee Mura Enterprises; Sydra Techniques; Ann Wright; Writer Store

Stage Plays: Film Artists; Kerin-Goldberg Assoc.; Peregrine Whittlesey

Syndicated Material: Bulger & Assoc.; Kerin-Goldberg Assoc.; Wright Concept

Teen: Agency West; Circle of Confusion; Hudson Agency; Dee Mura Enterprises; Talent Source; Wright Concept; Writer Store

Theatrical Stage Play: Film Artists

Thriller/Espionage: Agency West; Circle of Confusion; Client First; H.W.A.; Kerwin, William; Kick Entertainment; Dee Mura Enterprises; Panda Talent; Barry Perelman; Silver Screen Placements; Wright Concept; Ann Wright; Writer Store

TV Movie of the Week: Above the Line; Agency West; Alpern Group; Bulger & Assoc.; Barry Freed; Hudson Agency; Kerin-Goldberg Assoc.; Panda Talent; Sydra Techniques; Talent Source; Wright Concept; Ann Wright; Writer Store

TV Scripts: Agency West; Alpern Group; H.W.A.; Kerin-Goldberg Assoc.; Wright Concept; Writer Store

Variety Show: Kerin-Goldberg Assoc.; Wright Concept

Western/Frontier: Circle of Confusion; Client First; Hudson Agency; Dee Mura Enterprises; Panda Talent; Ann Wright

Young Adult: Silver Screen Placements

The Markets
Book Publishers

The book business, for the most part, runs on hunches. Whether the idea for a book comes from a writer, an agent or the imagination of an acquiring editor, it is generally expressed in these terms: "This is a book that I *think* people will like. People will *probably* want to buy it." The decision to publish is mainly a matter of the right person, or persons, agreeing that those hunches are sound.

THE PATH TO PUBLICATION

Ideas reach editors in a variety of ways. They arrive unsolicited every day through the mail. They come by phone, sometimes from writers but most often from agents. They arise in the editor's mind because of his daily traffic with the culture in which he lives. The acquisitions editor, so named because he is responsible for securing manuscripts for his company to publish, sifts through the deluge of possibilities, waiting for a book idea to strike him as extraordinary, inevitable, profitable.

In some companies, acquisitions editors possess the authority required to say, "Yes, we will publish this book." In most publishing houses, though, the acquisitions editor must prepare and present the idea to a proposal committee made up of marketing and administrative personnel. Proposal committees are usually less interested in questions of extraordinariness and inevitability than they are in profitability. The editor has to convince them that it makes good business sense to publish this book.

Once a contract is signed, several different wheels are set in motion. The author, of course, writes the book if he hasn't done so already. While the editor is helping to assure that the author is making the book the best it can be, promotion and publicity people are planning mailings of review copies to influential newspapers and review periodicals, writing catalog copy that will help sales representatives push the book to bookstores, and plotting a multitude of other promotional efforts (including interview tours and bookstore signings by the author) designed to dangle the book attractively before the reading public's eye.

When the book is published, it usually receives a concerted promotional push for a month or two. After that, the fate of the book—whether it will "grow legs" and set sales records or sit untouched on bookstore shelves—rests in the hands of the public. Publishers have to compete with all of the other entertainment industries vying for the consumer's money and limited leisure time. Successful books are reprinted to meet the demand. Unsuccessful books are returned from bookstores to publishers and are sold off cheaply as "remainders" or are otherwise disposed of.

THE STATE OF THE BUSINESS

The book publishing industry is beginning to recover from the difficulties experienced in the last few years. Publishers sell their products to bookstores on a returnable basis, which means the stores usually have 120 days to either pay the bill or return the order. With independent bookstores continuing to close and superstores experiencing setbacks as well, many publishers were hit with staggering returns. This has slowed somewhat, but continues to be a concern. While there are many more outlets to *buy* books, including online bookstores such as Amazon.com,

Borders.com and Barnesandnoble.com, this doesn't necessarily translate into more books being *bought*. Some feel the superstore phenomenon has proved a mixed blessing. The greater shelf area means there are more materials available, but also drives a need for books as "wallpaper" that is continually refreshed by returning older books and restocking with newer ones.

But that's not to say publishers are rushing to bring esoteric or highly experimental material to the marketplace. The blockbuster mentality—publishing's penchant for sticking with "name brand" novelists—still drives most large publishers. It's simply a less risky venture to continue publishing authors whom they know readers like. On the other hand, the prospects for nonfiction authors are perhaps better than they have been for years. The boom in available shelf space has provided entree to the marketplace for books on niche topics that heretofore would not have seen the light of day in most bookstores. The superstores position themselves as one-stop shopping centers for readers of every stripe. As such, they must carry books on a wide range of subjects.

The publishing community as a whole is stepping back from the multimedia hype and approaching the market more cautiously, if not abandoning it entirely. While the possibilities offered by CD-ROM technology still exist, publishers realize that marrying format and content are crucial for a successful, profitable product. Online publishing seems to offer promise, if only publishers can figure out how to make money from this new and different format.

HOW TO PUBLISH YOUR BOOK

The markets in this year's Book Publishers section offer opportunities in nearly every area of publishing. Large, commercial houses are here as are their smaller counterparts; large and small "literary" houses are represented as well. In addition, you'll find university presses, industry-related publishers, textbook houses and more.

The Book Publishers Subject Index is the place to start. You'll find it in the back of the book, before the General Index. Subject areas for both fiction and nonfiction are broken out for the over 1,200 total book publisher listings. Not all of them buy the kind of book you've written, but this Index will tell you which ones do.

When you have compiled a list of publishers interested in books in your subject area, read the detailed listings. Pare down your list by cross-referencing two or three subject areas and eliminating the listings only marginally suited to your book. When you have a good list, send for those publishers' catalogs and any manuscript guidelines available or check publishers' websites, which often contain catalog listings, manuscript preparation guidelines, current contact names and other information helpful to prospective authors. You want to make sure your book idea is in line with a publisher's list but is not a duplicate of something already published. Visit bookstores and libraries to see if their books are well represented. When you find a couple of books they have published that are similar to yours, write or call the company to find out who edited these books. This last, extra bit of research could be the key to getting your proposal to precisely the right editor.

Publishers prefer different kinds of submissions on first contact. Most like to see a one-page query with SASE, especially for nonfiction. Others will accept a brief proposal package that might include an outline and/or a sample chapter. Some publishers will accept submissions from agents only. Virtually no publisher wants to see a complete manuscript on initial contact, and sending one when they prefer another method will signal to the publisher "this is an amateur's submission." Editors do not have the time to read an entire manuscript, even editors at small presses who receive fewer submissions. Perhaps the only exceptions to this rule are children's picture book manuscripts and poetry manuscripts, which take only as much time to read as an outline and sample chapter anyway.

In your one-page query, give an overview of your book, mention the intended audience, the competition (check *Books in Print* and local bookstore shelves), and what sets your book apart. Detail any previous publishing experience or special training relevant to the subject of your book. All of this information will help your cause; it is the professional approach.

Only one in a thousand writers will sell a book to the first publisher they query, especially if the book is the writer's first effort. Make a list of a dozen or so publishers that might be interested in your book. Try to learn as much about the books they publish and their editors as you can. Research, knowing the specifics of your subject area, and a professional approach are often the difference between acceptance and rejection. You are likely to receive at least a few rejections, however, and when that happens, don't give up. Rejection is as much a part of publishing, if not more, than signing royalty checks. Send your query to the next publisher on your list. Multiple queries can speed up the process at this early stage.

Personalize your queries by addressing them individually and mentioning what you know about a company from its catalog or books you've seen. Never send a form letter as a query. Envelopes addressed to "Editor" or "Editorial Department" end up in the dreaded slush pile.

If a publisher offers you a contract, you may want to seek advice before signing and returning it. An author's agent will very likely take 15% if you employ one, but you could be making 85% of a larger amount. Some literary agents are available on an hourly basis for contract negotiations only. For more information on literary agents, contact the Association of Authors' Representatives, 10 Astor Place, 3rd Floor, New York NY 10003, (212)353-3709. Also check the current edition of *Guide to Literary Agents* (Writer's Digest Books). Attorneys will only be able to tell you if everything is legal, not if you are getting a good deal, unless they have prior experience with literary contracts. If you have a legal problem, you might consider contacting Volunteer Lawyers for the Arts, 1 E. 53rd St., 6th Floor, New York NY 10022, (212)319-2787.

AUTHOR-SUBSIDY PUBLISHER'S LISTINGS NOT INCLUDED

Writer's Market is a reference tool to help you sell your writing, and we encourage you to work with publishers that pay a royalty. Subsidy publishing involves paying money to a publishing house to publish a book. The source of the money could be a government, foundation or university grant, or it could be the author of the book. Publishers offering nonauthor-subsidized arrangements have been included in the appropriate section. If one of the publishers listed here offers you an author-subsidy arrangement (sometimes called "cooperative publishing," "co-publishing" or "joint venture"), asks you to pay for all or part of the cost of any aspect of publishing (printing, advertising, etc.) or to guarantee the purchase of any number of the books yourself, we would like you to let us know about that company immediately.

Sometimes newer publishers will offer author-subsidy contracts to get a leg up in the business and plan to become royalty-only publishers once they've reached a firm financial footing. Some publishers feel they must offer subsidy contracts to expand their lists beyond the capabilities of their limited resources. This may be true, and you may be willing to agree to it, but we choose to list only those publishers paying a royalty without requiring a financial investment from the author. In recent years, several large subsidy publishers have suddenly gone out of business, leaving authors without their money, their books, and in some cases, without the copyright to their own manuscripts.

WHAT'S NEW

We've added several features to make *Writer's Market* even more helpful in your search for the right publisher for your work, features you won't find in any other writer's guide.

The "key" to successful submissions

You may have written the most wonderful historical romance to ever grace the page. But if you submit it to a publisher of history textbooks, you're not likely to get too far. To help you quickly skim the listings for the right publisher, we've added a key symbol (⚷) with a brief summary of what that publisher does produce, as well as areas of interest they are currently emphasizing and areas they are de-emphasizing.

Information at a glance

Most immediately noticeable, we've added a number of symbols at the beginning of each listing to quickly convey certain information at a glance. In the Book Publisher sections, these symbols identify new listings (🅽), "opportunity" markets that buy at least 50 percent from unagented or first-time writers (🅇), and publishers that accept agented submissions only (🅐). Different sections of *Writer's Market* include other symbols; check the front and back inside covers for an explanation of all the symbols used throughout the book.

How much money? What are my odds?

We've also highlighted important information in boldface, the "quick facts" you won't find in any other market guide but should know before you submit your work. This includes: how many manuscripts a publisher buys per year; how many from first-time authors; how many from unagented writers; the royalty rate a publisher pays; and how large an advance is offered.

Publishers, their imprints and how they are related

In this era of big publishing—and big mergers—the world of publishing has grown even more intertwined. A "family tree" on page 89 lists the imprints and often confusing relationships of the largest conglomerate publishers.

In the listings, "umbrella" listings for these larger houses list the imprints under the company name. Imprint names in boldface indicate a separate, individual listing, easily located alphabetically, which provides much more detailed information about that imprint's specific focus, needs and contacts.

Each listing includes a summary of the editorial mission of the house, an overarching principle that ties together what they publish. Under the heading **Acquisitions:** we list many more editors, often with their specific areas of expertise. We have also increased the number of recent titles to help give you an idea of the publishers' scope. We have included the royalty rates for those publishers willing to disclose them, but contract details are closely guarded and a number of larger publishers are reluctant to publicly state these terms. Standard royalty rates for paperbacks generally range from 7½ to 12½ percent, for hardcovers from 10 to 15 percent. Royalty rates for children's books are often lower, generally ranging from 5 to 10 percent.

Finally, we have listed a number of publishers who only accept agented submissions. This benefits the agents who use *Writer's Market*, those writers with agents who use the book themselves, and those as yet unagented writers who want to know more about a particular company.

For a list of publishers according to their subjects of interest, see the nonfiction and fiction sections of the Book Publishers Subject Index. Information on book publishers and producers listed in the previous edition of *Writer's Market* but not included in this edition can be found in the General Index.

🅽 **A CAPPELLA**, Chicago Review Press, 814 N. Franklin St., Chicago IL 60610. (312)337-0747. Fax: (312)640-0342. Website: www.ipgbook.com. **Acquisitions:** Yuval Taylor, editor (music, film). Publishes hardcover originals, trade paperback originals and reprints. **Publishes 3-12 titles/year. 30-40% of books from first-time authors; 50% from unagented writers. Pays 7½-12½% royalty on retail price. Offers $1,500-7,500 advance.** Publishes book 11 months after acceptance of ms. Accepts simultaneous submissions. Responds in 1 month to queries, proposals and mss. Book catalog free.
Nonfiction: Biography, illustrated book, reference. Music/dance, film subjects. Submit 2 sample chapter(s), SASE.
Recent Title(s): *Bossa Nova*, by Ruy Castro; *Movie Wars*, by Jonathan Rosenbaum.
Tips: "A Cappella caters to an audience of music fans and film buffs."

A&B PUBLISHERS GROUP, 1000 Atlantic Ave., Brooklyn NY 11238. (718)783-7808. Fax: (718)783-7267. E-mail: maxtay@webspan.net. **Acquisitions:** Maxwell Taylor, production manager (children's, adult nonfiction); Wendy Gift, editor (fiction). Estab. 1992. Publishes hardcover originals, trade paperback originals and reprints. **Publishes 12 titles/ year. Receives 120 queries and 150 mss/year. 30% of books from first-time authors; 30% from unagented writers. Pays 5-12% royalty on net receipts. Offers $500-2,500 advance.** Publishes book 18 months after acceptance of ms. Accepts simultaneous submissions. Responds in 2 months to queries and proposals; 5 months to mss. Book catalog free.

O→ The audience for A&B Publishers Group is African-Americans. Currently emphasizing children's books.
Nonfiction: Children's/juvenile, coffee table book, cookbook, illustrated book. Subjects include cooking/foods/nutrition, history. Query with SASE. Reviews artwork/photos as part of ms package. Send photocopies.
Fiction: Query with SASE.
Recent Title(s): *Baggage Check* (fiction).
Tips: "Read, read, read. The best writers are developed from good reading. There is not enough attention to quality. Read, write and revise until you get it almost right."

A-R EDITIONS, INC., 8551 Research Way, Suite 180, Middleton WI 53562. (608)836-9000. Fax: (608)831-8200. Website: www.areditions.com. **Acquisitions:** Paul L. Ranzini, managing editor (Recent Researches music editions); James L. Zychowicz, managing editor (Computer Music and Digital Audio Series). Estab. 1962. **Publishes 30 titles/ year. Receives 40 queries and 30 mss/year. 75% of books from first-time authors; 100% from unagented writers. Pays royalty or honoraria.** Responds in 1 month to queries; 3 months to proposals; 6 months to mss. Book catalog and ms guidelines online.

O→ A-R Editions publishes modern critical editions of music based on current musicological research. Each edition is devoted to works by a single composer or to a single genre of composition. The contents are chosen for their potential interest to scholars and performers, then prepared for publication according to the standards that govern the making of all reliable, historical editions.
Nonfiction: Subjects include computers/electronic, music/dance, software, historical music editions. Computer Music and Digital Audio titles deal with issues tied to digital and electronic media, and include both textbooks and handbooks in this area. Query with SASE or submit outline.
Recent Title(s): *Fundamentals of Digital Audio*, by Alan Kefauver.

ABDO PUBLISHING COMPANY, 4940 Viking Dr., Edina MN 55435. (952)831-1317. Fax: (952)831-1632. E-mail: info@abdopub.com. Website: www.abdopub.com. **Acquisitions:** Paul Abdo, editor-in-chief (nonfiction, sports, history); Bob Italia, senior editor (science, history). Publishes hardcover originals. **Publishes 120 titles/year; imprint publishes 40 titles/year. Receives 300 queries and 100 mss/year. 10% of books from first-time authors; 90% from unagented writers. Makes outright purchase of $500-1,200.** Publishes book 6 months after acceptance of ms. Accepts simultaneous submissions. Responds in 2 months to queries; 4 months to proposals; 6 months to mss. Book catalog can be ordered online.
Imprints: ABDO & Daughters, Buddy Books, Checkerboard Library, SandCastle

O→ ABDO publishes nonfiction children's books (pre-kindergarten to 6th grade) for school and public libraries— mainly history, sports and biography.
Nonfiction: Biography, children's/juvenile, how-to. Subjects include animals, history, sports. Query with SASE.
Recent Title(s): *Civil War*, by Ann Guines (children's nonfiction); *Ricky Martin*, by Paul Joseph (children's biography).

ABINGDON PRESS, The United Methodist Publishing House, 201 Eighth Ave. S., Nashville TN 37203. (615)749-6000. Fax: (615)749-6512. Website: www.abingdon.org. President/Publisher: Neil M. Alexander. Senior Vice President/ Publishing: Harriett Jane Olson. **Acquisitions:** Robert Ratcliff, senior editor (professional clergy); Peg Augustine, editor (children's); Joseph A. Crowe, editor (general interest). Estab. 1789. Publishes hardcover and paperback originals; church supplies. **Publishes 120 titles/year. Receives 3,000 queries and 250 mss/year. Small% of books from first-time authors; 85% from unagented writers. Pays 7½% royalty on retail price. Offers advance.** Publishes book 2 years after acceptance of ms. Responds in 2 months to queries. Book catalog free; ms guidelines for #10 SASE.
Imprints: Dimensions for Living, Cokesbury, Abingdon Press

O→ Abingdon Press, America's oldest theological publisher, provides an ecumenical publishing program dedicated to serving the Christian community—clergy, scholars, church leaders, musicians and general readers—with quality resources in the areas of Bible study, the practice of ministry, theology, devotion, spirituality, inspiration, prayer, music and worship, reference, Christian education and church supplies.
Nonfiction: Children's/juvenile, gift book, reference, textbook, religious-lay and professional, scholarly. Subjects include education, music/dance, religion. Query with outline and samples only.
Recent Title(s): *Celtic Praise*, by Van de Weyer (gift).

HARRY N. ABRAMS, INC., La Martiniere Groupe, 100 Fifth Ave., New York NY 10011. (212)206-7715. Fax: (212)645-8437. Website: www.abramsbooks.com. Publisher: Mark McGowan. **Acquisitions:** Eric Himmel, editor-in-chief. Estab. 1949. Publishes hardcover and "a few" paperback originals. **Publishes 150 titles/year. Pays royalty. Offers variable advance.** Publishes book 2 years after acceptance of ms. Responds in 3 months to queries. Book catalog for $5.

O→ "We publish *only* high-quality illustrated art books, i.e., art, art history, museum exhibition catalogs, written by specialists and scholars in the field."

Nonfiction: Illustrated book. Subjects include art/architecture, nature/environment, recreation (outdoor). Requires illustrated material for art and art history, museums. Submit outline, sample chapter(s), illustrations. Reviews artwork/photos as part of ms package.

Tips: "We are one of the few publishers who publish almost exclusively illustrated books. We consider ourselves the leading publishers of art books and high-quality artwork in the U.S. Once the author has signed a contract to write a book for our firm the author must finish the manuscript to agreed-upon high standards within the schedule agreed upon in the contract."

ABSEY & CO., 23011 Northcrest Dr., Spring TX 77389. (281)257-2340. E-mail: abseyandco@aol.com. Website: www.absey.com. **Acquisitions:** Trey Hall, editor-in-chief. Publishes hardcover, trade paperback and mass market paperback originals. **Publishes 6-10 titles/year. 50% of books from first-time authors; 50% from unagented writers. Royalty and advance vary.** Publishes book 1 year after acceptance of ms. Responds in 3 months to queries; 9 months to mss. Manuscript guidelines online.

O→ "Our goal is to publish original, creative works of literary merit." Currently emphasizing educational, young adult literature. De-emphasizing self-help.

Nonfiction: Subjects include education, language/literature (language arts), general nonfiction. Query with SASE.

Fiction: "Since we are a small, new press, we are looking for book-length manuscripts with a firm intended audience." Query with SASE.

Poetry: Publishes the "Writers and Young Writers Series." Interested in thematic poetry collections of literary merit. Query.

Recent Title(s): *Dragonfly*, by Alice McLerran (fiction); *Where I'm From*, by George Ella Lyon (poetry).

Tips: "We work closely and attentively with authors and their work." Does not accept e-mail submissions.

ACADEMY CHICAGO PUBLISHERS, 363 W. Erie St., Chicago IL 60610-3125. (312)751-7300. Fax: (312)751-7306. E-mail: academy363@aol.com. Website: www.academychicago.com. **Acquisitions:** Anita Miller, editorial director/senior editor. Estab. 1975. Publishes hardcover originals and trade paperback reprints. **Publishes 15 titles/year. Receives 2,000 submissions/year. Pays 7-10% royalty on wholesale price. Offers modest advance.** Publishes book 18 months after acceptance of ms. Responds in 2 months to queries. Book catalog for 9×12 SAE with 6 first-class stamps; ms guidelines for #10 SASE.

O→ "We publish quality fiction and nonfiction. Our audience is literate and discriminating. No novelized biography, history or science fiction."

Nonfiction: Biography. Subjects include history, travel. No religion. Submit proposal package including outline, 3 sample chapter(s), author bio.

Fiction: Historical, mainstream/contemporary, military/war, mystery. "We look for quality work, but we do not publish experimental, avant garde novels." No science fiction. Submit proposal package including 3 sample chapter(s), synopsis.

Recent Title(s): *Food & Drink in Britain*, by C. Ann Nelson; *Cutters' Island*, by Vincent Panella.

Tips: "At the moment, we are looking for good nonfiction; we certainly want excellent original fiction, but we are swamped. No fax queries, no disks. No electronic submissions. We are always interested in reprinting good out-of-print books."

ACE SCIENCE FICTION AND FANTASY, The Berkley Publishing Group, Penguin Putnam Inc., 375 Hudson St., New York NY 10014. (212)366-2000. Website: www.penguinputnam.com. **Acquisitions:** Anne Sowards, editor. Estab. 1953. Publishes hardcover, paperback and trade paperback originals and reprints. **Publishes 75 titles/year. Pays royalty. Offers advance.** Responds in 6 months to queries. Manuscript guidelines for #10 SASE.

O→ Ace publishes science fiction and fantasy exclusively.

Fiction: Fantasy, science fiction. *Accepts agented submissions only.* Query first with SASE.

Recent Title(s): *Forever Peace*, by Joe Haldeman; *Necromancer*, by William Gibson.

ACTA PUBLICATIONS, 4848 N. Clark St., Chicago IL 60640-4711. Fax: (773)271-7399. E-mail: actapublications@aol.com. **Acquisitions:** Gregory F. Augustine Pierce. Estab. 1958. Publishes trade paperback originals. **Publishes 12 titles/year. Receives 50 queries and 15 mss/year. 50% of books from first-time authors; 90% from unagented writers. Pays 10-12% royalty on wholesale price.** Publishes book 1 year after acceptance of ms. Responds in 1 month to proposals. Book catalog and ms guidelines for #10 SASE.

O→ ACTA publishes non-academic, practical books aimed at the mainline religious market.

Nonfiction: Self-help. Subjects include religion, spirituality. Submit outline, 1 sample chapter(s). Reviews artwork/photos as part of ms package. Send photocopies.

Recent Title(s): *Memories of Grace: Portraits from the Monastery*, by James Stephen Behrens, OCSO; *Protect Us from All Anxiety: Meditations for the Depressed*, by William Burke (self-help).

Tips: "Don't send a submission unless you have read our catalog or one of our books."

ADAMS MEDIA CORPORATION, 260 Center St., Holbrook MA 02343. (781)767-8100. Fax: (781)767-0994. E-mail: editors@adamsmedia.com. Website: www.adamsmedia.com. **Acquisitions:** Claire Gerus, executive editor; Jennifer Lantagne, project editor; Elizabeth Gilbert, editorial assistant; Pamela Liflander, executive editor (*Everything* series);

Cheryl Kimball, acquisitions editor (*Everything Kids* series); Leah Bloom, editorial assistant. Estab. 1980. Publishes hardcover originals, trade paperback originals and reprints. **Publishes 200 titles/year. Receives 5,000 queries and 1,500 mss/year. 25% of books from first-time authors; 25% from unagented writers. Pays standard royalty or makes outright purchase. Offers variable advance.** Publishes book 1 year after acceptance of ms. Accepts simultaneous submissions. Responds in 3 months to queries.

○━ Adams Media publishes commercial nonfiction, including career titles, innovative business and self-help books.
Nonfiction: Biography, cookbook, gift book, how-to, humor, illustrated book, reference, self-help. Subjects include Americana, animals, business/economics, child guidance/parenting, cooking/foods/nutrition, gardening, government/politics, health/medicine, history, hobbies, humor, language/literature, military/war, money/finance, nature/environment, psychology, regional, science, sports, women's issues/studies. Submit outline. Does not return unsolicited materials.
Recent Title(s): *Dream Big*, by Cynthia Stewart-Copier; *Heart Warmers*, by Azriela Jaffe.

◼ **ADAMS-BLAKE PUBLISHING**, 8041 Sierra St., Fair Oaks CA 95628. (916)962-9296. Website: www.adams-blake.com. Vice President: Paul Raymond. **Acquisitions:** Monica Blane, senior editor. Estab. 1992. Publishes trade paperback originals and reprints. **Publishes 10-15 titles/year. Receives 150 queries and 90 mss/year. 90% of books from first-time authors; 90% from unagented writers. Pays 15% royalty on wholesale price.** Publishes book 6 months after acceptance of ms. Accepts simultaneous submissions. Responds in 3 months to mss.

○━ Adams-Blake Publishing is looking for business, technology and finance titles as well as data that can be bound/packaged and sold to specific industry groups at high margins. "We publish technical and training material we can sell to the corporate market. We are especially looking for 'high ticket' items that sell to the corporate market for prices between $100-300." Currently emphasizing technical, computers, technology. De-emphasizing business, management.
Nonfiction: How-to, technical. Subjects include business/economics, computers/electronic, health/medicine, money/finance, software. Query with sample chapters or complete ms. Reviews artwork/photos as part of ms package. Send photocopies.
Recent Title(s): *Success From Home*, by Alan Canton.
Tips: "We will take a chance on material the big houses reject. Since we sell the majority of our material directly, we can publish material for a very select market. This year we seek niche market material that we can Docutech and sell direct to the corporate sector. Author should include a marketing plan. Sell us on the project!"

◼ **ADDAX PUBLISHING GROUP, INC.**, 8643 Hauser Dr., Suite 235, Lenexa KS 66215. (913)438-5333. Fax: (913)438-2079. E-mail: addax1@addaxpublishing.com. Website: www.addaxpublishing.com. **Acquisitions:** Submissions Editor. Estab. 1992. Publishes hardcover and trade paperback originals. **Publishes 20 titles/year. 50% of books from first-time authors; 75% from unagented writers. Pays royalty.** Publishes book 1 year after acceptance of ms. Accepts simultaneous submissions.

○━ Addax Publishing Group publishes sports books on and with athletes and teams in both professional and college sports. "In addition, we publish children's books for holidays, goal-oriented children's books with sports themes, select inspiration, motivation, how-to, and humor books. Our titles have both regional and national emphasis."
Nonfiction: Biography, children's/juvenile, coffee table book. Sports, entertainment subjects. Submit complete ms.
Recent Title(s): *The Greatest*, by Kenny Rogers.
Tips: "We have a fairly tightly defined niche in sports-related areas."

◼ **ADDICUS BOOKS, INC.**, P.O. Box 45327, Omaha NE 68145. (402)330-7493. Website: www.AddicusBooks.com. **Acquisitions:** Rod Colvin, president. Estab. 1994. Publishes trade paperback originals. **Publishes 8-10 titles/year. 70% of books from first-time authors; 60% from unagented writers. Pays royalty on retail price. Offers advance.** Publishes book 9 months after acceptance of ms. Accepts simultaneous submissions. Responds in 1 month to proposals. Manuscript guidelines for #10 SASE.

○━ Addicus Books, Inc. seeks manuscripts with strong national or regional appeal.
Nonfiction: How-to, self-help. Subjects include Americana, business/economics, health/medicine, psychology, regional, true crime, true crime. "No electronic submissions please." Query with outline and 3-4 sample chapters. Do not send entire ms unless requested.
Recent Title(s): *Living with PCOS—Polycystic Ovary Syndrome*; *Colon and Rectal Cancer—A Patient's Guide to Treatment*.
Tips: "We are looking for quick-reference books on health topics. Do some market research to make sure the market is not already flooded with similar books. We're also looking for good true-crime manuscripts, with an interesting story, with twists and turns, behind the crime."

◼ **ADIRONDACK MOUNTAIN CLUB, INC.**, 814 Goggins Rd., Lake George NY 12845-4117. (518)668-4447. Fax: (518)668-3746. E-mail: pubs@adk.org. Website: www.adk.org. **Acquisitions:** Andrea Masters, editor (all titles); Neal Burdick, editor (*Adirondac* magazine, published bimonthly). Publishes hardcover and trade paperback originals and reprints. **Publishes 34 titles/year. Receives 36 queries and 12 mss/year. 95% of books from first-time authors; 95% from unagented writers. Pays 6-10% royalty on retail price. Offers $250-1,000 advance.** Publishes book 1 year after acceptance of ms. Responds in 3 months to queries; 4 months to proposals and mss. Book catalog and ms guidelines free.

☛ "Our main focus is recreational guides to the Adirondack and Catskill Parks; however, our titles continue to include natural, cultural and literary histories of these regions. Our main interest is in protecting the resource through environmental education. This is the focus of our magazine, *Adirondack*, as well."

Nonfiction: Reference. Subjects include nature/environment, recreation, regional, sports, travel, trail maps. Query with SASE or submit proposal package including outline, 1-2 sample chapter(s), with proposed illustrations and visuals. Reviews artwork/photos as part of ms package. Send photocopies.

Recent Title(s): *Trailside Notes: A Naturalist's Companion to Adirondack Plants*, by Ruth Schottman; *Kids on the Trail! Hiking with Children in the Adirondacks*, by Rose Rivezzi and David Trithart.

Tips: "Our audience consists of outdoors people interested in muscle-powered recreation, natural history, and 'armchair traveling' in the Adirondacks and Catskills. Bear in mind the educational mandate implicit in our organization's mission. Note range of current ADK titles."

N: AEGIS PUBLISHING GROUP, 796 Aquidneck Ave., Newport RI 02842-7246. (401)849-4200. Fax: (401)849-4231. E-mail: aegis@aegisbooks.com. Website: www.aegisbooks.com. **Acquisitions:** Robert Mastin, publisher. Estab. 1992. Publishes trade paperback originals and reprints. **Publishes 6 titles/year. Pays 12% royalty on net receipts. Offers $1,000-4,000 advance.** Responds in 2 months to queries.

☛ "Our specialty is telecommunications books targeted to small businesses, entrepreneurs and telecommuters—how they can benefit from the latest telecom products and services. Our goal is to become the primary publisher of nontechnical telecommunications books for small organizations, end users, new entrants to the industry and telecom managers." Currently emphasizing data networks and the Internet.

Nonfiction: Reference, business. Telecommunications, data networking subjects. "Author must be an experienced authority in the subject, and the material must be very specific with helpful step-by-step advice." Query with SASE.

Recent Title(s): *Digital Convergence*, by Andy Covell; *Office Emails That Really Click*, by Maureen Chase and Sandy Trupp.

N: AKTRIN FURNITURE INFORMATION CENTER, 164 S. Main St., P.O. Box 898, High Point NC 27261. (336)841-8535. Fax: (336)841-5435. E-mail: aktrin@aktrin.com. Website: www.furniture-info.com. Wayne Damba, director of operations. Estab. 1985. Publishes trade paperback originals. **Publishes 8 titles/year. Receives 5 queries/year. 20% of books from first-time authors; 20% from unagented writers. Makes outright purchase of $1,500 minimum. Offers $300-600 advance.** Publishes book 2 months after acceptance of ms. Accepts simultaneous submissions. Responds in 1 month. *Writer's Market* recommends allowing 2 months for reply to queries. Book catalog free.

Imprints: AKTRIN Furniture Information Center-Canada (151 Randall St., Oakville, Ontario L6J 1P5 Canada. (905)845-3474. Contact: Stefan Wille)

☛ AKTRIN is a full-service organization dedicated to the furniture industry. "Our focus is on determining trends, challenges and opportunities, while also identifying problems and weak spots." Currently emphasizing the wood industry.

Nonfiction: Reference. Subjects include business/economics. "We are writing only about the furniture industry. Have an understanding of business/economics." Query.

Recent Title(s): *The American Demand for Household Furniture and Trends*, by Thomas McCormick (in-depth analysis of American household furniture market).

Tips: Audience is executives of furniture companies (manufacturers and retailers) and suppliers and consultants to the furniture industry.

ALASKA NORTHWEST BOOKS, Graphic Arts Center Publishing, P.O. Box 10306, Portland OR 97296-0306. (503)226-2402. Fax: (503)223-1410. Website: www.gacpc.com. **Acquisitions:** Tricia Brown. Estab. 1959. Publishes hardcover and trade paperback originals and reprints. **Publishes 12 titles/year. Receives hundreds submissions/year. 10% of books from first-time authors; 90% from unagented writers. Pays 10-14% royalty on net revenues. Buys mss outright (rarely). Offers advance.** Publishes book an average of 2 years after acceptance of ms. Accepts simultaneous submissions. Responds in 6 months to queries. Book catalog for 9 × 12 SAE with 6 first-class stamps; ms guidelines online.

☛ "Our book needs are as follows: one-half Alaskan focus, one-quarter Northwest, one-eighth Pacific coast, one-eighth national (looking for logical extensions of current subjects)."

Nonfiction: Children's/juvenile, cookbook. Subjects include nature/environment, recreation, sports, travel, Native American culture, adventure, the arts. "All written for a general readership, not for experts in the subject." Submit outline, sample chapter(s).

Recent Title(s): *Through Yup'ik Eyes*, by Colin Chisholm (memoir); *Neeluk: An Eskimo Boy in the Days of the Whaling Ships* (historical).

Tips: "Book proposals that are professionally written and polished with a clear market receive our most careful consideration. We are looking for originality. We publish a wide range of books for a wide audience. Some of our books are clearly for travelers, others for those interested in outdoor recreation or various regional subjects. If I were a writer trying to market a book today, I would research the competition (existing books) for what I have in mind, and clearly (and concisely) express why my idea is different and better. I would describe the book buyers (and readers)—where they are, how many of them are there, how they can be reached (organizations, publications), why they would want or need my book."

ALBA HOUSE, 2187 Victory Blvd., Staten Island NY 10314-6603. (718)761-0047. Fax: (718)761-0057. E-mail: albabooks@aol.com. Website: www.albahouse.org. **Acquisitions:** Edmund C. Lane, S.S.P., editor. Estab. 1961. Publishes hardcover, trade paperback and mass market paperback originals. **Publishes 24 titles/year. Receives 300 queries and 150 mss/year. 20% of books from first-time authors; 100% from unagented writers. Pays 7-10% royalty.** Publishes book 9 months after acceptance of ms. Responds in 1 month to queries and proposals; 2 months to mss. Book catalog and ms guidelines free.

O─┐ Alba House is the North American publishing division of the Society of St. Paul, an International Roman Catholic Missionary Religious Congregation dedicated to spreading the Gospel message.

Nonfiction: Manuscripts which contribute, from a Roman Catholic perspective, to the personal, intellectual and spiritual growth of individuals in the following areas: Scripture, theology and the Church, saints (their lives and teachings), spirituality and prayer, religious life, marriage and family life, liturgy and homily preparation, pastoral concerns, religious education, bereavement, moral and ethical concerns. Reference, textbook. Subjects include education, philosophy, psychology, religion, spirituality. Reviews artwork/photos as part of ms package. Send photocopies.
Recent Title(s): *Christian Spirituality*, by Charles J. Healey, S.J.

ALBURY PUBLISHING, P.O. Box 470406, Tulsa OK 74147. **Acquisitions:** Elizabeth Sherman, senior acquisitions editor. Publishes hardcover and trade paperback originals and reprints. **Publishes 20-30 titles/year. Receives 200 queries and 600 mss/year. 1% of books from first-time authors; 50% from unagented writers. Pays royalty or outright purchase. Offers advance.** Publishes book 2-3 years after acceptance of ms. Responds in 3 months to queries. Book catalog for 9×12 SAE; ms guidelines for #10 SASE.

O─┐ "We are a Christian publisher with an upbeat presentation."

Nonfiction: Humor, self-help, Bible teaching, compilations of historic Christian leaders and devotionals. Subjects include humor, religion. "Most of our authors are established ministers and friends of the house. In order to break into our market, writers must exhibit a clearly defined, professionally presented proposal that shows they know and understand our market." Query with SASE.
Fiction: Juvenile, young adult, adult. Query with SASE.
Recent Title(s): *Jesus Freaks*, by dc Talk; *Voice of the Martyrs*.

ALEXANDER BOOKS, Creativity, Inc., 65 Macedonia Rd., Alexander NC 28701. (828)252-9515. Fax: (828)255-8719. E-mail: sales@abooks.com. Website: abooks.com. **Acquisitions:** Pat Roberts, acquisitions editor. Publishes hardcover originals and trade and mass market paperback originals and reprints. **Publishes 15-20 titles/year. Receives 200 queries and 100 mss/year. 10% of books from first-time authors; 75% from unagented writers. Pays 12-15% royalty on wholesale price. Offers rare (minimum $100) advance.** Publishes book 18 months after acceptance of ms. Book catalog for 9×12 SASE with 5 ounces postage; ms guidelines for #10 SASE.
Imprints: Farthest Star (classic science fiction, very few new titles), Mountain Church (mainline Protestant material)

O─┐ Alexander Books publishes mostly nonfiction national titles, both new and reprints.

Nonfiction: Biography, how-to, reference, self-help. Subjects include computers/electronic, government/politics, history, regional, religion, travel, collectibles. "We are interested in large niche markets." Query or submit 3 sample chapters and proposal package, including marketing plans with SASE. Reviews artwork/photos as part of ms package. Send photocopies.
Fiction: Historical, mainstream/contemporary, mystery, science fiction, western. "We prefer local or well-known authors or local interest settings." Query with SASE or submit 3 sample chapter(s), synopsis.
Recent Title(s): *Sanders Price Guide to Autographs, 5th ed*, by Sanders and Roberts; *Birthright*, by Mike Resnick.
Tips: "Send well-proofed manuscripts in final form. We will not read first rough drafts. Know your market."

N: ALGORA PUBLISHING, 222 Riverside Dr., 16th Floor, New York NY 10025-6809. (212)678-0232. Fax: (212)663-9805. E-mail: editors@algora.com. Website: www.algora.com. **Acquisitions:** Martin DeMers, editor (sociology/philosophy/economics); Claudiu A. Secara, publisher (philosophy/international affairs). Publishes trade paperback originals and reprints. **Publishes 15 titles/year. Receives 100 queries and 75 mss/year. 20% of books from first-time authors; 85% from unagented writers. Pays 7½-12% royalty on wholesale price. Offers $0-1,000 advance.** Publishes book 10 months after acceptance of ms. Accepts simultaneous submissions. Responds in 2 weeks to queries and proposals; 1 month to mss. Book catalog and ms guidelines online.

O─┐ Algora Publishing is an academic-type press, focusing on works by mostly (but not exclusively) American and European authors for the educated general reader.

Nonfiction: General nonfiction for the educated reader. Subjects include anthropology/archeology, business/economics, creative nonfiction, education, government/politics, health/medicine, history, language/literature, military/war, money/finance, music/dance, nature/environment, philosophy, psychology, religion, science, sociology, translation, travel, women's issues/studies. Query by e-mail (preferred) or submit proposal package including outline, 3 sample chapers or complete ms.
Recent Title(s): *Soul Snatchers—The Mechanics of Cults*, by Jean-Marie Abgrall (sociology); *Russian Intelligence Services*, by Vladimir Plougin (history).
Tips: "We welcome first-time writers; we have a special program to help them outline their project, crafting an author's raw manuscript into a literary work."

ALLIGATOR PRESS, INC., P.O. Box 221528, El Paso TX 79913. (915)585-3426. Fax: (915)585-7576. E-mail: kkimball@alligatorpress.com. Website: www.alligatorpress.com. **Acquisitions:** Kirk Markin, editor (literature, fiction, humor); Wendy Broadwater, editor (gay/lesbian). Publishes hardcover, trade paperback and mass market paperback originals. **Publishes 8 titles/year. Pays 5-10% royalty on retail price. Offers $500-5,000 advance.** Publishes book 8 months after acceptance of ms. Accepts simultaneous submissions. Manuscript guidelines online.
Nonfiction: Self-help. Subjects include gay/lesbian, language/literature. Query with SASE.
Fiction: Adventure, erotica, ethnic, feminist, gay/lesbian, horror, literary, mainstream/contemporary, military/war, multi-cultural, mystery, romance, science fiction, suspense. Query with SASE.
Recent Title(s): *Cuando cantan los lagartos*, by Miguel Santana (historical romance); *Cloven*, by Chae Waters (mystery/suspense).

■ **ALLISONE PRESS**, Star Rising Publishers. P.O. Box 494, Mt. Shasta CA 96067. (877)249-6894. Fax: (877)249-6894. E-mail: publisher@allisonepress.com or editor@allisonepress.com. Website: www.allisonepress.com. **Acquisitions:** Kristen B. May, editor (poetry, fiction); Leondra, editor (New Age, Earth-based religions, occult, paranormal); Robin May, publisher (New Age, spiritual). Publishes trade paperback originals. **Publishes 5-6 titles/year; imprint publishes 2-3 titles/year. Receives 100 queries and 75 mss/year. 90% of books from first-time authors; 90% from unagented writers. Pays 10-20% royalty on retail price or makes outright purchase of $500-5,000.** Publishes book 18 months after acceptance of ms. Accepts simultaneous submissions. Responds in 1 month to queries and proposals; 4 months to mss. Book catalog and ms guidelines for #10 SASE or online.
Imprints: Allisone (contact Robin May), Star Rising (contact Kristen May)
   O→ Allisone Press publishes New Age and spirituality. "We cater to the New Age consumer, from the layperson to the expert." Currently emphasizing Earth-based religions: New Age, Wiccan, pagan. De-emphasizing science fiction, poetry, children's titles.
Nonfiction: How-to, self-help. Subjects include creative nonfiction, health/medicine, nature/environment, New Age, philosophy, religion, spirituality, astrology, New Age, channeling, metaphysical, occult, witchcraft, Earth religions. Submit complete ms. *Writer's Market recommends query with SASE first.*
Fiction: Fantasy, occult, poetry, religious, short story collections, spiritual. "We are looking for 'new writers' with that creative flow and uninhibited expression." Submit complete ms. *Writer's Market recommends query with SASE first.*
Poetry: Submit complete ms.
Recent Title(s): *Walk Like an Egyptian*, by Ramona Louise Wheeler (religion); *A Place Called the Light*, Arlean Thornton (fiction); *From the Beats to the B Sides*, by John Hulse (poetry).
Tips: "Be creative and don't judge your work too harshly. Free up the creativity that we all possess."

ALLWORTH PRESS, 10 E. 23rd St., Suite 510, New York NY 10010-4402. Fax: (212)777-8261. E-mail: pub@allworth.com. Website: www.allworth.com. Tad Crawford, publisher. **Acquisitions:** Nicole Potter, senior editor. Estab. 1989. Publishes hardcover and trade paperback originals. **Publishes 36-40 titles/year. Offers advance.** Responds in 1 month to queries and proposals. Book catalog and ms guidelines free.
   O→ Allworth Press publishes business and self-help information for artists, designers, photographers, authors and film and performing artists, as well as books about business, money and the law for the general public. The press also publishes the best of classic and contemporary writing in art and graphic design. Currently emphasizing photography, film, video and theater.
Nonfiction: How-to, reference. Subjects include art/architecture, business/economics, film/cinema/stage, music/dance, photography, film, television, graphic design, performing arts, writing, as well as business and legal guides for the public. Query.
Recent Title(s): *Emotional Branding*, by Marc Gobé; *Career Solutions for Creative People*, by Dr. Ronda Ormont.
Tips: "We are trying to give ordinary people advice to better themselves in practical ways—as well as helping creative people in the fine and commercial arts."

■ **ALYSON PUBLICATIONS, INC.**, 6922 Hollywood Blvd., Suite 1000, Los Angeles CA 90028. (323)860-6065. Fax: (323)467-0152. E-mail: mail@alyson.com. Website: www.alyson.com. **Acquisitions:** Attn. Editorial Dept.; Scott Brassart, associate publisher (fiction, science); Angela Brown, associate editor (women's fiction, arts). Estab. 1979. Publishes trade paperback originals and reprints. **Publishes 40 titles/year. Receives 1,500 submissions/year. 40% of books from first-time authors; 70% from unagented writers. Pays 8-15% royalty on net receipts. Offers $1,500-15,000 advance.** Publishes book 18 months after acceptance of ms. Responds in 2 months to queries. Book catalog and ms guidelines for 6×9 SAE with 3 first-class stamps.
Imprints: Alyson Wonderland, Alyson Classics Library
   O→ Alyson Publications publishes books for and about gay men and lesbians from all economic and social segments of society, and explores the political, legal, financial, medical, spiritual, social and sexual aspects of gay and lesbian life, and contributions to society. They also consider bisexual and transgender material. Emphasizing medical, legal and financial nonfiction titles. De-emphasizing children's books.
Nonfiction: Subjects include gay/lesbian. "We are especially interested in nonfiction providing a positive approach to gay/lesbian/bisexual issues." Accepts nonfiction translations. No dissertations. Submit 2-page outline with SASE. Reviews artwork/photos as part of ms package.
Fiction: Gay novels. Accepts fiction translations. No short stories or poetry. Submit 1-2 page synopsis with SASE.
Recent Title(s): *The Greatest Taboo*, by Delroy Constantine-Simms; *Under the Mink*, by Lisa Davis.

Tips: "We publish many books by new authors. The writer has the best chance of selling to our firm well-researched, popularly written nonfiction on a subject (e.g., some aspect of gay history) that has not yet been written about much. With fiction, create a strong storyline that makes the reader want to find out what happens. With nonfiction, write in a popular style for a nonacademic audience."

AMACOM BOOKS, American Management Association, 1601 Broadway, New York NY 10019-7406. (212)903-8417. Fax: (212)903-8083. Website: www.amanet.org. CEO: Weldon P. Rackley. President and Publisher: Hank Kennedy. **Acquisitions:** Adrienne Hickey, executive editor (management, human resources development, organizational effectiveness, strategic planning); Ellen Kadin, senior acquisitions editor (marketing, sales, customer service, personal development); Ray O'Connell, senior acquisitions editor (finance, project management); Jacquie Flynn, senior acquisitions editor (information technology, training); Neil Levine, senior acquisitions editor (manufacturing, supply chain management operations and facilities management). Estab. 1923. Publishes hardcover and trade paperback originals, professional books in various formats. **Publishes 80-90 titles/year. Receives 800 submissions/year. 50% of books from first-time authors; 70% from unagented writers. Pays 10-15% royalty on net receipts. Offers advance.** Publishes book 9 months after acceptance of ms. Responds in 2 months to queries. Book catalog and ms guidelines free.

  O→ Amacom is the publishing arm of the American Management Association, the world's largest training organization for managers and executives. Amacom publishes books on business issues, strategies and tasks to enhance organizational and individual effectiveness. Currently emphasizing technology applications. De-emphasizing small-business management, job-finding.

Nonfiction: Subjects include money/finance, business management. Publishes business books of all types, including management, marketing, training, technology applications, finance, career, professional skills for retail, direct mail, college and corporate markets. Query or submit outline/synopsis, sample chapters, résumé.
Recent Title(s): *Leading at the Edge*, by Dennis N.T. Perkins; *The E-Aligned Enterprise*, by Jac Fitzenz; *The Nokia Revolution*, by Dan Steinbock.

AMERICA WEST PUBLISHERS, P.O. Box 2208, Carson City NV 89702-2208. (775)585-0700. Fax: (877)726-2632. E-mail: global@nohoax.com. Website: www.nohoax.com. **Acquisitions:** George Green, president. Estab. 1985. Publishes hardcover and trade paperback originals and reprints. **Publishes 20 titles/year. Receives 150 submissions/year. 90% of books from first-time authors; 90% from unagented writers. Pays 10% royalty on wholesale price. Offers $300 average advance.** Publishes book 6 months after acceptance of ms. Accepts simultaneous submissions. Responds in 1 month to queries. Book catalog and ms guidelines free.
Imprints: Bridger House Publishers, Inc.

  O→ America West seeks the "other side of the picture," political cover-ups and new health alternatives.
Nonfiction: Subjects include business/economics, government/politics, health/medicine (holistic self-help), New Age, UFO-metaphysical. Submit outline, sample chapter(s). Reviews artwork/photos as part of ms package.
Recent Title(s): *Psychokinesiology*, by Dr. Alec Halub.
Tips: "We currently have materials in all bookstores that have areas of UFOs; also political and economic nonfiction."

AMERICAN ASTRONAUTICAL SOCIETY, Univelt, Inc., Publisher, P.O. Box 28130, San Diego CA 92198. (760)746-4005. Fax: (760)746-3139. Website: univelt.staigerland.com. **Acquisitions:** Robert H. Jacobs, editorial director. Estab. 1970. Publishes hardcover originals. **Publishes 8 titles/year. Receives 12-15 submissions/year. 5% of books from first-time authors; 5% from unagented writers. Pays 10% royalty on actual sales. Offers advance.** Publishes book 4 months after acceptance of ms. Accepts simultaneous submissions. Responds in 1 month to queries. Book catalog and ms guidelines for 9 × 12 SAE with 3 first-class stamps.

  O→ "Our books must be space-oriented or space-related. They are meant for technical libraries, research establishments and the aerospace industry worldwide."
Nonfiction: Proceedings or monographs in the field of astronautics, including applications of aerospace technology to Earth's problems. Subjects include science. Call first, then submit outline and 1-2 sample chapters. Reviews artwork/photos as part of ms package.
Recent Title(s): *Space Access and Utilization Beyond 2000*.

AMERICAN BAR ASSOCIATION BOOK PUBLISHING, 750 N. Lake Shore Dr., Chicago IL 60611. (312)988-5000. Fax: (312)988-6030. E-mail: rockwelm@staff.abanet.org. Website: www.ababooks.org. **Acquisitions:** Mary Kay Rockwell, Esq., publisher/director; Adrienne Cook, Esq., director of new product development. Estab. 1878. Publishes hardcover and trade paperback originals. **Publishes 100 titles/year. Receives 50 queries/year. 20% of books from first-time authors; 95% from unagented writers. Pays 5-15% royalty on net receipts.** Publishes book 18 months after acceptance of ms. Accepts simultaneous submissions. Responds in 1 month to queries and proposals; 3 months to mss. Book catalog and ms guidelines online.

  O→ "We are interested in books that will help lawyers practice law more effectively whether it's help in handling clients, structuring a real estate deal or taking an antitrust case to court."
Nonfiction: All areas of legal practice. How-to (in the legal market), reference, technical. Subjects include business/economics, computers/electronic, money/finance, software, legal practice. "Our market is not, generally, the public. Books need to be targeted to lawyers who are seeking solutions to their practice problems. We rarely publish scholarly treatises." Query with SASE.

Recent Title(s): *The Effective Estate Planning Practice*; *The Supreme Court and Its Justices (2nd ed.)*; *Sexual Harassment in the Public Workplace*.

Tips: "ABA books are written for busy, practicing lawyers. The most successful books have a practical, reader-friendly voice. If you can build in features like checklists, exhibits, sample contracts, flow charts, and tables of cases, please do so." The Association also publishes over 50 major national periodicals in a variety of legal areas. Contact Susan Yessne, executive editor, at the above address for guidelines.

AMERICAN CHEMICAL SOCIETY, 1155 16th St. NW, Washington DC 20036. (202)452-2120. Fax: (202)452-8913. E-mail: k_dennis@acs.org. Website: pubs.acs.org/books/. **Acquisitions:** Kelly Dennis, associate acquisitions editor. Estab. 1876. Publishes hardcover originals. **Publishes 35 titles/year. Pays royalty.** Accepts simultaneous submissions. Responds in 2 months to proposals. Book catalog free.

O─▪ American Chemical Society publishes symposium-based books for chemistry.

Nonfiction: Technical, semi-technical. Subjects include science. "Emphasis is on meeting-based books."

Recent Title(s): *Infrared Analysis of Peptides and Proteins*, edited by Singh.

AMERICAN COLLEGE OF PHYSICIAN EXECUTIVES, (ACPE PUBLICATIONS), 4890 W. Kennedy Blvd., Suite 200, Tampa FL 33609. (813)287-2000. E-mail: wcurry@acpe.org. Website: www.acpe.org. **Acquisitions:** Wesley Curry, managing editor. Estab. 1975. Publishes hardcover and trade paperback originals. **Publishes 12-15 titles/year. Receives 6 queries and 3 mss/year. 80% of books from first-time authors; 100% from unagented writers. Pays 10-15% royalty on wholesale price or makes outright purchase of $1,000-4,000. Offers advance.** Publishes book 8 months after acceptance of ms. Responds in 1 month to queries and mss; 2 months to proposals. Book catalog and ms guidelines free.

O─▪ "Our books are aimed at the professional information needs of physicians in management roles."

Nonfiction: Technical, textbook. Subjects include business/economics, health/medicine. Query and submit outline. Reviews artwork/photos as part of ms package. Send photocopies.

Recent Title(s): *The Last Sick Generation*, by Joanne Magda Polenz; *Practicing Medicine Profitably*, by Barry Verkauf; *Leading Physicians through Change*, by Jack Silversin and Mary Jane Kornacki.

AMERICAN CORRECTIONAL ASSOCIATION, 4380 Forbes Blvd., Lanham MD 20706. (301)918-1800. Fax: (301)918-1896. E-mail: afins@aca.org. Website: www.corrections.com/aca. **Acquisitions:** Alice Fins, managing editor. Estab. 1870. Publishes hardcover and trade paperback originals. **Publishes 18 titles/year. Receives 40 submissions/year. 90% of books from first-time authors; 100% from unagented writers. Pays 10% royalty on net receipts.** Publishes book 1 year after acceptance of ms. Responds in 4 months to queries. Book catalog and ms guidelines free.

O─▪ American Correctional Association provides practical information on jails, prisons, boot camps, probation, parole, community corrections, juvenile facilities and rehabilitation programs, substance abuse programs and other areas of corrections.

Nonfiction: "We are looking for practical, how-to texts or training materials written for the corrections profession." How-to, reference, technical, textbook, correspondence courses. Subjects include corrections and criminal justice. No autobiographies or true-life accounts by current or former inmates or correctional officers, theses, or dissertations. No fiction or poetry. Query with SASE. Reviews artwork/photos as part of ms package.

Recent Title(s): *No Time to Play: Youthful Offenders in Adult Correctional Systems*, by Barry Glick, Ph.D., William Sturgeon with Charles Venator-Santiago.

Tips: Authors are professionals in the field and corrections. "Our audience is made up of corrections professionals and criminal justice students. No books by inmates or former inmates." This publisher advises out-of-town freelance editors, indexers and proofreaders to refrain from requesting work from them.

AMERICAN COUNSELING ASSOCIATION, 5999 Stevenson Ave., Alexandria VA 22304-3300. (703)823-9800. **Acquisitions:** Carolyn C. Baker, director of publications. Estab. 1952. Publishes paperback originals. **Publishes 10-15 titles/year. Receives 200 queries and 125 mss/year. 5% of books from first-time authors; 90% from unagented writers. Pays 10-15% royalty on net receipts.** Publishes book 7 months after acceptance of ms. Accepts simultaneous submissions. Responds in 2 months to queries and proposals; 4 months to mss. Manuscript guidelines free.

O─▪ The American Counseling Association is dedicated to promoting public confidence and trust in the counseling profession. "We publish scholarly texts for graduate level students and mental health professionals. We do not publish books for the general public."

Nonfiction: Reference, textbook (for professional counselors). Subjects include education, gay/lesbian, health/medicine, psychology, religion, sociology, women's issues/studies. ACA does not publish self-help books or autobiographies. Query with SASE or submit proposal package including outline, 2 sample chapter(s), vitae.

Recent Title(s): *Critical Incidents in School Counseling*, by Paul Pedersen and Lawrence Tyson.

Tips: "Target your market. Your books will not be appropriate for everyone across all disciplines."

AMERICAN NURSES PUBLISHING, American Nurses Foundation, an affiliate of the American Nurses Association, 600 Maryland Ave. SW, #100 West, Washington DC 20024-2571. (202)651-7213. Fax: (202)651-7003. **Acquisitions:** Rosanne O'Connor, publisher; Eric Wurzbacher, editor/project manager. Publishes professional paperback originals and reprints. **Publishes 15-20 titles/year. Receives 300 queries and 10 mss/year. 75% of books from first-time**

authors; **100% from unagented writers. Pays 10% royalty on retail price. Offers negotiable advance.** Publishes book 4 months after acceptance of ms. Responds in 4 months to proposals and mss. Book catalog online; ms guidelines free.

O— American Nurses publishes books designed to help professional nurses in their work and careers. Through the publishing program, the Foundation fulfills one of its core missions—to provide nurses in all practice settings with publications that address cutting-edge issues and form a basis for debate and exploration of this century's most critical health care trends.

Nonfiction: Reference, technical, textbook. Subjects include health/medicine. Subjects include advanced practice, computers, continuing education, ethics, human rights, health care policy, managed care, nursing administration, psychiatric and mental health, quality, research, workplace issues, key clinical topics. Submit outline, 1 sample chapter, cv. Reviews artwork/photos as part of ms package. Send photocopies.

Recent Title(s): *ANA Workplace Health and Safety Guide for Nurses*; *Developing TeleHealth Protocols*; *Public Health Nursing Leadership*.

AMERICAN PRESS, 28 State St., Suite 1100, Boston MA 02109. (617)247-0022. Fax: (617)247-0022. **Acquisitions:** Jana Kirk, editor. Estab. 1911. Publishes college textbooks. **Publishes 25 titles/year. Receives 350 queries and 100 mss/year. 50% of books from first-time authors; 90% from unagented writers. Pays 5-15% royalty on wholesale price.** Publishes book 9 months after acceptance of ms. Responds in 3 months to queries. Book catalog free.

Nonfiction: Technical, textbook. Subjects include agriculture/horticulture, anthropology/archeology, art/architecture, business/economics, education, government/politics, health/medicine, history, music/dance, psychology, science, sociology, sports. "We prefer that our authors actually teach courses for which the manuscripts are designed." Query or submit outline with tentative table of contents. No complete mss.

Recent Title(s): *Basic Communications Course Annual 2001*; *Beginning Swimming*.

■ **AMERICAN QUILTER'S SOCIETY**, Schroeder Publishing, P.O. Box 3290, Paducah KY 42002-3290. (270)898-7903. Fax: (270)898-8890. E-mail: meredith@aqsquilt.com or editor@aqsquilt.com. Website: www.AQSquilt.com. **Acquisitions:** Barbara Smith, executive book editor (primarily how-to and patterns, but other quilting books sometimes published). Estab. 1984. Publishes hardcover and trade paperback originals. **Publishes 18 titles/year. Receives 300 queries/year. 60% of books from first-time authors; 100% from unagented writers. Pays 5% royalty on retail price.** Publishes book 11 months after acceptance of ms. Accepts simultaneous submissions. Responds in same day to queries to queries; 2 months to proposals. Book catalog and ms guidelines free.

O— American Quilter's Society publishes how-to and pattern books for quilters (beginners through intermediate skill level).

Nonfiction: Coffee table book, how-to, reference, technical (about quilting). Subjects include creative nonfiction, hobbies (about quilting). Query with SASE or submit proposal package including outline, 2 sample chapter(s), photos and patterns (if available). Reviews artwork/photos as part of ms package. Send photocopies; slides and drawings are also acceptable for a proposal.

Recent Title(s): *Favorite Redwork Designs*, by Betty Alderman (embroidery and applique patterns).

AMERICAN SOCIETY OF CIVIL ENGINEERS PRESS, 1801 Alexander Bell Dr., Reston VA 20191-4400. (703)295-6275. Fax: (703)295-6278. E-mail: ascepress@asce.org. Website: www.pubs.asce.org. **Acquisitions:** Joy E. Bramble, acquisitions editor. Estab. 1988. **Publishes 15-20 titles/year. 50% of books from first-time authors; 100% from unagented writers. Pays 10% royalty.** Accepts simultaneous submissions. Request ASCE book proposal submission guidelines.

O— ASCE Press publishes technical volumes that are useful to both practicing civil engineers and graduate level civil engineering students. "We publish books by individual authors and editors to advance the civil engineering profession." Currently emphasizing geotechnical, hydrology, structural engineering and bridge engineering. De-emphasizing highly specialized areas with narrow scope.

Nonfiction: "We are looking for topics that are useful and instructive to the engineering practitioner." Subjects include civil engineering. Query with outline, sample chapters and cv.

Recent Title(s): *Design of Shallow Foundations*, by Samuel French.

Tips: "ASCE Press is a book publishing imprint of ASCE and produces authored and edited applications-oriented books for practicing civil engineers and graduate level civil engineering students. All proposals and manuscripts undergo a vigorous review process."

AMERICAN WATER WORKS ASSOCIATION, 6666 W. Quincy Ave., Denver CO 80235. (303)794-7711. Fax: (303)794-7310. E-mail: cmurcray@awwa.org. Website: www.awwa.org. **Acquisitions:** Colin Murcray, senior acquisitions editor; Mindy Burke, senior technical editor. Estab. 1881. Publishes hardcover and trade paperback originals. **Publishes 100 titles/year. Receives 200 queries and 35 mss/year. 30% of books from first-time authors; 100% from unagented writers. Pays 15% royalty on wholesale or retail price.** Publishes book 1 year after acceptance of ms. Responds in 3 months to queries. Book catalog and ms guidelines free.

O— AWWA strives to advance and promote the safety and knowledge of drinking water and related issues to all audiences—from kindergarten through post-doctorate.

Nonfiction: Subjects include nature/environment, science, software, drinking water-related topics. Query with SASE or submit outline, 3 sample chapter(s), author bio. Reviews artwork/photos as part of ms package. Send photocopies.

Recent Title(s): *The Drinking Water Dictionary*, by Jim Symons, et al.

[N] AMG PUBLISHERS, 6815 Shallowford Rd., Chattanooga TN 37421-1755. (423)894-6060. Fax: (423)894-9511. E-mail: info@amgpublishers.com. Website: www.amgpublishers.com. **Acquisitions:** Dr. Warren Baker, managing editor (Biblical languages, reference, study Bibles, educational); Richard Steele, Jr., associate editor (Bible study, workbooks and educational). Publishes hardcover and trade paperback originals and trade paperback reprints. **Publishes 12-15 titles/year; imprint publishes 1-2 titles/year. Receives 225 queries and 75 mss/year. 15% of books from first-time authors; 85% from unagented writers. Pays 8-15% royalty on wholesale price.** Publishes book 4 months after acceptance of ms. Accepts simultaneous submissions. Responds in 1 month to queries; 2 months to proposals; 4 months to mss. Book catalog online; ms guidelines free.

Imprints: Future Events Publications

  O── Currently emphasizing workbooks (*Following God* series); de-emphasizing devotional books.

Nonfiction: Reference, textbook, workbook, Bibles, commentaries. Subjects include education, language/literature, religion, spirituality, translation. Note our *Following God* series (www.followinggod.com) which provides a personal look at the lives of key characters found in the Bible. This Bible study is designed in an interactive format. Query with SASE. Reviews artwork/photos as part of ms package. Send photocopies.

Recent Title(s): *The Tim LaHaye Prophecy Study Bible*, edited by Tim LaHaye et, al (study Bible); *The Sword of Suffering*, by Stephen Olford (spiritual).

Tips: "The AMG readership consists largely of adults involved in personal Bible study. We rarely accept books outside of our current genres, so be sure what you're submitting will fit in with our current works."

AMHERST MEDIA, INC., 155 Rano St., Suite 300, Buffalo NY 14207. (716)874-4450. Fax: (716)874-4508. E-mail: amherstmed@aol.com. Website: www.AmherstMedia.com. **Acquisitions:** Craig Alesse, publisher. Estab. 1974. Publishes trade paperback originals and reprints. **Publishes 30 titles/year. Receives 50 submissions/year. 80% of books from first-time authors; 100% from unagented writers. Pays 6-8% royalty on retail price. Offers advance.** Publishes book 1 year after acceptance of ms. Accepts simultaneous submissions. Responds in 2 months to queries. Book catalog and ms guidelines free.

  O── Amherst Media publishes how-to photography books.

Nonfiction: How-to. Photography subjects. "Looking for well-written and illustrated photo books." Query with outline, 2 sample chapters and SASE. Reviews artwork/photos as part of ms package.

Recent Title(s): *Portrait Photographer's Handbook*, by Bill Horter.

Tips: "Our audience is made up of beginning to advanced photographers. If I were a writer trying to market a book today, I would fill the need of a specific audience and self-edit in a tight manner."

ANCESTRY INCORPORATED, 360 W. 4800 North, Provo UT 84064. (801)705-7000. Fax: (801)705-7120. E-mail: mwright@ancestry.com. Loretto Szucs, executive editor. **Acquisitions:** Matthew Wright, book editor; Jennifer Utley, *Ancestry* magazine editor. Estab. 1983. Publishes hardcover, trade and paperback originals and *Ancestry* magazine. **Publishes 12-20 titles/year. Receives over 100 submissions/year. 70% of books from first-time authors; 100% from unagented writers. Pays 8-12% royalty or makes outright purchase.** Accepts simultaneous submissions. Responds in 2 months to queries. Book catalog for 9×12 SAE with 2 first-class stamps.

  O── "Our publications are aimed exclusively at the genealogist. We consider everything from short monographs to book length works on topics such as immigration, migration, record collections and heraldic topics, among others."

Nonfiction: How-to, reference, genealogy. Subjects include Americana, hobbies, histercial methodology and genealogical research techniques. No mss that are not genealogical or historical. Query with SASE or submit outline, sample chapter(s). Reviews artwork/photos as part of ms package.

Recent Title(s): *Finding Your African-American Ancestors*.

Tips: "Genealogical and historical reference, how-to, and descriptions of source collections have the best chance of selling to our firm. Be precise in your description. Please, no family histories or genealogies."

ANCHORAGE PRESS PLAYS, INC., P.O. Box 2901, Louisville KY 40201. (502)583-2288. Fax: (502)583-2281. E-mail: applays@bellsouth.net. Website: www.applays.com. **Acquisitions:** Marilee Miller, publisher. Estab. 1935. Publishes hardcover originals. **Publishes 10 titles/year. Receives 45-90 submissions/year. 50% of books from first-time authors; 80% from unagented writers. Pays 10-15% royalty on retail price. Playwrights also receive 50-75% royalties.** Publishes book 1-2 years after acceptance of ms. Responds in 1 month to queries; 6 months to mss. Book catalog and ms guidelines free.

  O── "We are an international agency for plays for young people. First in the field since 1935."

Nonfiction: Textbook, plays. Subjects include education, language/literature, plays. "We are looking for play anthologies; and texts for teachers of drama/theater (middle school and high school.)" Query. Reviews artwork/photos as part of ms package.

Recent Title(s): *The Oldest Story Ever Told*, by David F. Ebet; *Bushveld Bibble-Babble*, by Malcolm Welfson; *Invisible People*, by William Lavender.

A **ANDREWS McMEEL UNIVERSAL**, 4520 Main St., Kansas City MO 64111-7701. (816)932-6700. Website: www.uexpress.com. **Acquisitions:** Christine Schillig, vice president/editorial director. Estab. 1973. Publishes hardcover and paperback originals. **Publishes 300 titles/year. Pays royalty on retail price. Offers advance**.

O⊸ Andrews McMeel publishes general trade books, humor books, miniature gift books, calendars, greeting cards, and stationery products.

Nonfiction: How-to, humor. Subjects include general trade, pop culture. Also produces gift books, posters and kits. *Accepts agented submissions only.*

Recent Title(s): *The Blue Day Book*, by Bradley Trevor Greive.

N **APDG PUBLISHING, INC.**, 202 Main St., Fuguay-Varina NC 27526-1936. (919)557-2260. Fax: (919)557-2261. E-mail: info@apdg-inc.com. Website: www.apdg-inc.com. Publisher: Lawrence Harte. **Acquisitions:** Dave Richardson, project manager. Publishes hardcover and trade paperback originals. **Publishes 10 titles/year. Receives 50 queries/ year. Pays 5-15% royalty on retail price.** Publishes book 6 months after acceptance of ms. Responds in 3 months to proposals; 6 months to mss. Book catalog online; ms guidelines free.

O⊸ APDG supplies expertise and services to telecommunications and consumer electronics companies not only through publishing but consulting, research, training and techno-media as well.

Nonfiction: Textbook. Telecommunications subjects. Query with SASE. Reviews artwork/photos as part of ms package. Send photocopies.

APPALACHIAN MOUNTAIN CLUB BOOKS, 5 Joy St., Boston MA 02108. Fax: (617)523-0722. Website: www.o utdoors.org. **Acquisitions:** Beth Krusi, publisher/editor. Estab. 1897. Publishes hardcover and trade paperback originals. **Publishes 10-15 titles/year. Receives 200 queries and 20 mss/year. 30% of books from first-time authors; 90% from unagented writers. Pays 7-10% royalty on retail price. Offers modest advance.** Publishes book 1 year after acceptance of ms. Accepts simultaneous submissions. Responds in 3 months to proposals. Manuscript guidelines online.

O⊸ Appalachian Mountain Club publishes hiking guides, water-recreation guides (non-motorized), nature, conservation and mountain-subject guides for America's Northeast. "We connect recreation to conservation and education."

Nonfiction: How-to, guidebooks. Subjects include history (mountains, Northeast), nature/environment, recreation, regional (Northeast outdoor recreation). "Writers should avoid submitting: proposals on Appalachia (rural southern mountains); not enough market research; too much personal experience—autobiography." Query. Reviews artwork/ photos as part of ms package. Send photocopies or transparencies.

Recent Title(s): *Not Without Peril*; *Journey North*.

Tips: "Our audience is outdoor recreationalists, conservation-minded hikers and canoeists, family outdoor lovers, armchair enthusiasts. Our guidebooks have a strong conservation message. Visit our website for proposal submission guidelines and more information."

ARABESQUE, BET Books, 850 Third Ave., 16th Floor, New York NY 10022. (212)407-1500. Website: www.bet. com. **Acquisitions:** Karen Thomas, executive editor; Chandra Taylor, consulting editor. Publishes mass market paperback originals. **Publishes 60 titles/year. 30-50% of books from first-time authors; 50% from unagented writers. Pays royalty on retail price, varies by author. Offers varying advance.** Publishes book 18 months after acceptance of ms. Accepts simultaneous submissions. Responds in 3 months to mss. Book catalog for #10 SASE.

O⊸ Arabesque publishes contemporary romances about African-American couples.

Fiction: Multicultural (romance). Query with synopsis and SASE. *No unsolicited mss.*

Recent Title(s): *His 1-800 Wife*, by Shirley Hailstock.

A **ARCADE PUBLISHING**, 141 Fifth Ave., New York NY 10010. (212)475-2633. Publisher/editor-in-chief: Richard Seaver. Publisher/executive editor: Jeannette Seaver. **Acquisitions:** Webb Younce, senior editor. Estab. 1988. Publishes hardcover originals, trade paperback originals and reprints. **Publishes 45 titles/year. 5% of books from first-time authors. Pays royalty on retail price. Offers $3,000-50,000 advance.** Publishes book within 18 months after acceptance of ms. Responds in 3 months to queries.

O⊸ Arcade prides itself on publishing top-notch commercial nonfiction and literary fiction, with a significant proportion of foreign writers.

Nonfiction: Biography, cookbook, general nonfiction. Subjects include cooking/foods/nutrition, general, government/ politics, history, nature/environment, travel. *Accepts agented submissions only.* Reviews artwork/photos as part of ms package. Send photocopies.

Fiction: Ethnic, historical, humor, literary, mainstream/contemporary, mystery, short story collections, suspense. *Accepts agented submissions only.*

Recent Title(s): *The Banyan Tree*, by Christopher Nolan.

ARCADIA PUBLISHING, Tempus Publishing, 2-A Cumberland St., Charleston SC 29401. (843)853-2070. Fax: (843)853-0044. E-mail: sales@arcadiapublishing.com. Website: www.arcadiapublishing.com. **Acquisitions:** Keith Ulrich, publisher (Midwest and West); Amy Sutton, publisher (North); Christine Riley, publisher (South); Mark Berry, publisher (narrative local history). Publishes mass market paperback originals. **Publishes 800 titles/year; imprint**

publishes 350 titles/year. Receives 100 queries and 20 mss/year. 80% of books from first-time authors; 95% from unagented writers. Pays 10% royalty. Accepts simultaneous submissions. Responds in 1 month to queries. Book catalog online; ms guidelines for #10 SASE.

O→ Arcadia publishes photographic regional histories. "We have more than 1,000 in print in our 'Images of America' series. We have expanded our program to include Midwest and West Coast locations." Currently emphasizing local history, oral history, Civil War history, college histories, African-American history.

Nonfiction: Coffee table book, gift book. Subjects include history, military/war, regional, sports, pictorial history, local history, African-American history, postcard history, sports history, college history, oral history, Civil War history, local, national and regional publications. Query with SASE. Reviews artwork/photos as part of ms package. Send photocopies.

Recent Title(s): *Charleston: Alone Among the Cities*, by The South Carolina Historical Society.

Tips: "Writers should know that we only publish history titles. The majority of our books are on a city or region, and are pictorial in nature. We are beginning new series, including oral histories, sports histories, black histories and college histories."

A ARCHWAY PAPERBACKS, Pocket Books for Young Readers, Simon & Schuster, 1230 Avenue of the Americas, New York NY 10020. (212)698-7669. Website: www.simonsayskids.com. Publishes mass market paperback originals and reprints. **Publishes approximately 100 titles/year. Receives over 1,000 submissions/year. Pays 6-8% royalty on retail price. Offers advance.** Publishes book 2 years after acceptance of ms. Responds in 3 months to queries.

O→ Archway Paperbacks publishes fiction and current nonfiction for young adult readers ages 12-18.

Nonfiction: Young adult, ages 12-18. Subjects include sports, current popular subjects or people. *Accepts agented submissions only.*

Fiction: Young adult horror, mystery, suspense thrillers, contemporary fiction, romances for YA, ages 12-18. *Accepts agented submissions only.*

Recent Title(s): *Buffy the Vampire Slayer; Dawson's Creek* (TV-tie-in titles).

ARDSLEY HOUSE PUBLISHERS, INC., Rowman & Littlefield, 4720 Boston Way, Lanham MD 20706. (301)459-3366. Fax: (301)429-5748. Website: www.rowmanlittlefield.com. **Acquisitions:** Jon Sisk. Estab. 1982. Publishes hardcover and trade paperback originals and reprints. **Publishes 5-8 titles/year. 25% of books from first-time authors; 100% from unagented writers. Pays generally by royalty. Offers advance.** Publishes book 1 year after acceptance of ms. Responds in 1 month to queries; 2 months to proposals; 3 months to mss.

O→ Ardsley House publishes only college-level textbooks in mathematics and economics.

Nonfiction: Textbook (college). Subjects include business/economics, mathematics. "We don't accept any other type of manuscript." Query with SASE or submit proposal package including outline, 2-3 sample chapter(s), résumé, author bio, prospectus. Send photocopies.

Recent Title(s): *A Mathemataics Sampler; Invention and the Rise of Techno-Capitalism*, by Suarez-Villa.

ARKANSAS RESEARCH, INC., P.O. Box 303, Conway AR 72033. (501)470-1120. Fax: (501)470-1120. E-mail: desmond@ipa.net. **Acquisitions:** Desmond Walls Allen, owner. Estab. 1985. Publishes hardcover originals and trade paperback originals and reprints. **Publishes 20 titles/year. 90% of books from first-time authors; 100% from unagented writers. Pays 5-10% royalty on retail price.** Publishes book 6 months after acceptance of ms. Responds in 1 month to queries. Book catalog for $1; ms guidelines free.

Imprints: Research Associates

O→ "Our company opens a world of information to researchers interested in the history of Arkansas."

Nonfiction: All Arkansas-related subjects. How-to (genealogy), reference, self-help. Subjects include Americana, ethnic, history, hobbies (genealogy), military/war, regional. "We don't print autobiographies or genealogies about one family." Query with SASE. Reviews artwork/photos as part of ms package. Send photocopies.

Recent Title(s): *Life & Times from The Clay County Courier Newspaper Published at Corning, Arkansas, 1893-1900.*

JASON ARONSON, INC., 230 Livingston St., Northvale NJ 07647-1726. (201)767-4093. Fax: (201)767-4330. Website: www.aronson.com. Editor-in-chief: Arthur Kurzweil. **Acquisitions:** Arthur Kurzweil, vice president/editor-in-chief (Judaica). Estab. 1967. Publishes hardcover and trade paperback originals and reprints. **Publishes 100 titles/year. 50% of books from first-time authors; 95% from unagented writers. Pays 10-15% royalty on retail price.** Publishes book an average of 2 years after acceptance of ms. Responds in 1 month to queries. Book catalog and ms guidelines free.

O→ "We are looking for high quality, serious, scholarly books in two fields: psychotherapy and Judaica."

Nonfiction: Subjects include history, philosophy, psychology, religion, translation. Query or submit outline and sample chapters. Reviews artwork/photos as part of ms package. Send photocopies.

Recent Title(s): *The Candle of God*, by Adin Steinsaltz (Judaica).

N ART DIRECTION BOOK COMPANY, INC., 456 Glenbrook Rd., Glenbrook CT 06096-1800. (203)353-1441. Fax: (203)353-1371. **Acquisitions:** Don Barron, editorial director. Estab. 1959. Publishes hardcover and paperback originals. **Publishes 8 titles/year. Pays 10% royalty on retail price. Offers average $1,000 advance.** Publishes book 1 year after acceptance of ms. Responds in 3 months to queries. Book catalog for 6×9 SAE.

Imprints: Infosource Publications

O⊸ Art Direction Book Company is interested in books for the professional advertising art field—books for art directors, designers, etc.; also entry level books for commercial and advertising art students in such fields as typography, photography, paste-up, illustration, clip-art, design, layout and graphic arts.

Nonfiction: Textbook, commercial art, ad art how-to. Subjects include art/architecture. Query with outline and 1 sample chapter. Reviews artwork/photos as part of ms package.

Recent Title(s): *Black, White and Gray Illustration*, by Stephen Kidd.

ARTE PUBLICO PRESS, University of Houston, Houston TX 77204-2174. (713)743-2841. Fax: (713)743-2847. Website: www.arte.uh.edu. **Acquisitions:** Nicolas Kanellos, editor. Estab. 1979. Publishes hardcover originals, trade paperback originals and reprints. **Publishes 36 titles/year. Receives 1,000 queries and 500 mss/year. 50% of books from first-time authors; 80% from unagented writers. Pays 10% royalty on wholesale price. Offers $1,000-3,000 advance.** Publishes book 2 years after acceptance of ms. Accepts simultaneous submissions. Responds in 1 month to queries and proposals; 4 months to mss. Book catalog free; ms guidelines for #10 SASE.

Imprints: Piñata Books

O⊸ "We are a showcase for Hispanic literary creativity, arts and culture. Our endeavor is to provide a national forum for Hispanic literature."

Nonfiction: Children's/juvenile, reference. Subjects include ethnic, language/literature, regional, translation, women's issues/studies. "Nonfiction is definitely not our major publishing area." Query with SASE or submit outline, 2 sample chapter(s). "Include cover letter explaining why your manuscript is unique and important, why we should publish it, who will buy it, etc."

Fiction: Ethnic, literary, mainstream/contemporary. Query with SASE or submit 2 sample chapter(s), synopsis.

Poetry: Submit 10 sample poems.

Recent Title(s): *Chicano! The History of the Mexican American Civil Rights Movement*, by F. Arturo Rosales (history/nonfiction); *Project Death*, by Richard Bertematti (novel/mystery); *I Used to Be a Superwoman*, by Gloria Velasquez (poetry collection/inspirational).

ASA, AVIATION SUPPLIES & ACADEMICS, 7005 132nd Place SE, Newcastle WA 98059. (425)235-1500. Fax: (425)235-0128. Website: www.asa2fly.com. Director of Operations: Mike Lorden. Editor: Jennifer Trerise. **Acquisitions:** Fred Boyns, controller; Jacqueline Spanitz, curriculum director and technical advisor (pilot and aviation educator). **Publishes 25-40 titles/year. 100% from unagented writers.** Publishes book 9 months or more after acceptance of ms. Book catalog free.

O⊸ ASA is an industry leader in the development and sales of aviation supplies, publications, and software for pilots, flight instructors, flight engineers and aviation technicians. All ASA products are developed by a team of researchers, authors and editors.

Nonfiction: All subjects must be related to aviation education and training. How-to, technical. Subjects include education. "We are primarily an aviation publisher. Educational books in this area are our specialty; other aviation books will be considered." Query with outline. Send photocopies.

Recent Title(s): *The Savvy Flight Instructor: Secrets of the Successful CFI*, by Greg Brown.

Tips: "Two of our specialty series include ASA's *Focus Series*, and ASA *Aviator's Library*. Books in our *Focus Series* concentrate on single-subject areas of aviation knowledge, curriculum and practice. The *Aviator's Library* is comprised of titles of known and/or classic aviation authors or established instructor/authors in the industry, and other aviation specialty titles."

ASIAN HUMANITIES PRESS, Jain Publishing Co., P.O. Box 3523, Fremont CA 94539. (510)659-8272. Fax: (510)659-0501. E-mail: mail@jainpub.com. Website: www.jainpub.com. **Acquisitions:** M.K. Jain, editor-in-chief. Estab. 1989. Publishes hardcover and trade paperback originals and reprints. **Publishes 6 titles/year. Receives 200 submissions/year. 100% from unagented writers. Pays up to 15% royalty on net receipts. Offers occasional advance.** Publishes book 1-2 years after acceptance of ms. Responds in 3 months to mss. Book catalog and ms guidelines online.

O⊸ Asian Humanities Press publishes in the areas of Asian religions, philosophies, languages and literature. Currently emphasizing undergraduate-level textbooks.

Nonfiction: Reference, textbook, general trade books. Subjects include language/literature (Asian), philosophy (Asian and East-West), psychology (Asian and East-West), religion (Asian and East-West), spirituality (Asian and East-West), Asian classics, Asian art/culture. Submit proposal package including vita, list of prior publications. Reviews artwork/photos as part of ms package. Send photos; does not return proposal material.

Recent Title(s): *The Upanishads*, by Shyam N. Shukla.

ASLAN PUBLISHING, 2490 Black Rock Turnpike, #342, Fairfield CT 06432. (203)372-0300. Fax: (203)374-4766. E-mail: info@aslanpublishing.com. Website: www.aslanpublishing.com. **Acquisitions:** Barbara H. Levine, creative director. **Publishes 3-6 titles/year. Receives 75 queries and 50 mss/year. 75% of books from first-time authors; 90% from unagented writers. Pays 8-10% royalty on wholesale price.** Publishes book 18-24 months after acceptance of ms. Accepts simultaneous submissions. Responds in 2 months to queries; 5 months to proposals. Book catalog and ms guidelines online.

O⊸ "Aslan Publishing offers readers a window to the soul via well-crafted and practical self-help books, inspirational books and modern day parables. Our mission is to publish books that uplift one's mind, body and spirit."

Nonfiction: Biography, how-to, humor, self-help. Subjects include business/economics, child guidance/parenting, education (non-textbook), ethnic, gay/lesbian, health/medicine, memoirs, military/war, multicultural, music/dance, psychology, religion, sex, spirituality, women's issues/studies, adoption, relationships, open to unusual ideas. "We want authors who will do their own promotion in addition to our own. Self-help books must include personal exmaples." No fiction. Query with SASE or submit proposal package including outline, 3 sample chapter(s), author bio, 1-2 page synopsis, chapter outlines, table of contets, author's e-mail address.

Recent Title(s): *Candida Control Cookbook*; *The Gift of Wounding*; *How Loving Couples Fight*.

Tips: Audience is general mainstream America, plus New Age, religious, spiritual seekers. "No agent necessary. Include e-mail address phone number, word count. Be patient. Show me your passion. Use large type and short paragraphs. If possible, have the manuscript professionally edited before submitting."

ASM INTERNATIONAL, 9639 Kinsman Rd., Materials Park OH 44073-0002. (440)338-5151. Fax: (440)338-4634. E-mail: cust-srv@po.asm-intl.org. Website: www.asm-intl.org. **Acquisitions:** Veronica Flint, manager of book acquisitions (metallurgy/materials). Publishes hardcover originals. **Publishes 15-20 titles/year. Receives 50 queries and 10 mss/year. 50% of books from first-time authors; 100% from unagented writers. Pays royalty on wholesale price or makes outright purchase.** Responds in 1 month to queries; 4 months to proposals; 2 months to mss. Book catalog and ms guidelines free.

   O— "We focus on practical information related to materials selection and processing."

Nonfiction: Reference, technical, textbook. Subjects include engineering reference. Submit proposal package including outline, 1 sample chapter(s), author credentials. Reviews artwork/photos as part of ms package. Send photocopies.

Recent Title(s): *Properties of Aluminum Alloys*, by J.G. Kaufman; *Titanium: A Technical Guide, 2nd edition*, by M.J. Donachie, Jr.

Tips: "Our audience consists of technically trained people seeking practical information on metals and materials to help them solve problems on the job."

ASSOCIATION FOR SUPERVISION AND CURRICULUM DEVELOPMENT, 1703 N. Beauregard St., Alexandria VA 22311. (703)578-9600. Fax: (703)575-5400. Website: www.ascd.org. **Acquisitions:** John O'Neil, acquisitions director. Estab. 1943. Publishes trade paperback originals. **Publishes 24-30 titles/year. Receives 100 queries and 100 mss/year. 50% of books from first-time authors; 100% from unagented writers. Pays negotiable royalty on actual monies received.** Publishes book 1 year after acceptance of ms. Accepts simultaneous submissions. Responds in 3 months to proposals. Book catalog and ms guidelines online.

   O— ASCD publishes high-quality professional books for educators.

Nonfiction: Subjects include education (for professional educators). Submit outline, 2 sample chapter(s). Reviews artwork/photos as part of ms package. Send photocopies.

Recent Title(s): *Transforming Classroom Grading*, by Robert J. Marzano.

ASTRAGAL PRESS, P.O. Box 239, Mendham NJ 07945. (973)543-3045. Fax: (973)543-3044. E-mail: astragalpress@attglobal.net. Website: www.astragalpress.com. **Acquisitions:** Lisa Pollak, president. Estab. 1983. Publishes hardcover and trade paperback originals and reprints. **Publishes 4-6 titles/year. Receives 50 queries/year. Pays 10% royalty on net receipts.** Publishes book 1 year after acceptance of ms. Responds in 1 month to queries. Book catalog and ms guidelines free.

   O— "Our primary audience includes those interested in collecting and working with old tools (hand tools especially) and working in traditional early trades (metalworking especially)."

Nonfiction: Books on early tools, trades or technology. Query. Send photocopies.

Recent Title(s): *A Price Guide to Antique Tools, 3rd ed*, by Herbert P. Kean.

Tips: "We sell to niche markets. We are happy to work with knowledgeable amateur authors in developing titles."

ATHENEUM BOOKS FOR YOUNG READERS, Simon & Schuster, 1230 Avenue of the Americas, New York NY 10020. (212)698-2715. Website: www.simonsayskids.com. Associate Publisher/Vice President: Ginee Seo. **Acquisitions:** Anne Schwartz, editorial director, Anne Schwartz Books; Caitlyn Dlouhy, senior editor. Estab. 1960. Publishes hardcover originals. **Publishes 70 titles/year. Receives 15,000 submissions/year. 8-12% of books from first-time authors; 50% from unagented writers. Pays 10% royalty on retail price. Offers $2,000-3,000 average advance.** Publishes book 18 months after acceptance of ms. Responds in 3 months to queries. Manuscript guidelines for #10 SASE.

   O— Atheneum Books for Young Readers publishes books aimed at children from pre-school age, up through high school.

Nonfiction: Biography, children's/juvenile, humor, self-help. Subjects include Americana, animals, art/architecture, business/economics, government/politics, health/medicine, history, humor, music/dance, nature/environment, photography, psychology, recreation, religion, science, sociology, sports, travel. "Do remember, most publishers plan their lists as much as two years in advance. So if a topic is 'hot' right now, it may be 'old hat' by the time we could bring it out. It's better to steer clear of fads. Some writers assume juvenile books are for 'practice' until you get good enough to write adult books. Not so. Books for young readers demand just as much professionalism in writing as adult books. So save those 'practice' manuscripts for class, or polish them before sending them. *Query letter only for all submissions. We do not accept unsolicited mss.*"

Fiction: All in juvenile versions. Adventure, ethnic, experimental, fantasy, gothic, historical, horror, humor, mainstream/contemporary, mystery, science fiction, suspense, western. "We have few specific needs except for books that are fresh, interesting and well written. Again, fad topics are dangerous, as are works you haven't polished to the best of your ability. (The competition is fierce.) Other things we don't need at this time are safety pamphlets, ABC books, coloring books and board books. In writing picture book texts, avoid the coy and 'cutesy,' such as stories about characters with alliterative names. *Query letter only for all submissions.* We do not accept unsolicited mss." Send art samples under separate cover to Ann Bobco at the above address.
Recent Title(s): *The Century That Was*, by Giblin (nonfiction); *Horace and Morris But Mostly Dolores*, by Howe (fiction); *Doodle Dandies*, by Lewis (poetry).

ATL PRESS, INC., P.O. Box 4563, Shrewsbury MA 01545. (508)898-2290. E-mail: atlpinc@aol.com. Website: www.a tlpress.com. **Acquisitions:** Paul Lucio, acquisitions manager. Estab. 1992. Publishes hardcover and trade paperback originals. **Publishes 8-12 titles/year. Receives 100 queries/year. 25% of books from first-time authors. Pays royalty on retail price.** Publishes book 3 months after acceptance of ms. Responds in 2 months to queries. Book catalog and ms guidelines for #10 SASE.
O→ "ATL specializes in science and technology publications for both the professional and the popular audience."
Nonfiction: Children's/juvenile, multimedia (CD-ROM), reference, technical, textbook. Subjects include business/economics, education, health/medicine, money/finance, nature/environment, science. "We look for well-written manuscripts in subjects with either broad, general interest topics of leading-edge professional topics. Avoid too narrow a focus." Submit outline, 3-4 sample chapter(s), SASE.
Recent Title(s): *Misinformed Consent*, by Lise Cloutier-Steele.
Tips: "Audience is educated, open-minded adults, juveniles, parents, educators, professionals. Realistically evaluate your manuscript against competition. We publish only titles for which there is an actual demand. We are committed to produce authoritative and thought-provoking titles that are distinguished both in their content and appearance."

AUBURN HOUSE, Greenwood Publishing Group, 88 Post Rd. W., Westport CT 06881. (203)226-3571. Fax: (203)222-1502. Website: www.greenwood.com. **Acquisitions:** Lynn Taylor, executive editor. Publishes hardcover and trade paperback originals. **Publishes 16 titles/year. Pays variable royalty of net price.** Publishes book 1 year after acceptance of ms. Accepts simultaneous submissions. Responds in 6 months to queries and proposals. Book catalog and ms guidelines online.
O→ "Auburn publishes books and advanced texts in health studies, education and social policy."
Nonfiction: Subjects include business/economics, government/politics, health/medicine. *No unsolicited mss.* Query with proposal package, including scope, whether a complete ms is available or when it will be, cv or résumé and SASE.
Recent Title(s): *Adoption Policy and Special Needs Children*, edited by Rosemary Avery (sociology).
Tips: Greenwood Publishing maintains an excellent website offering catalog, ms guidelines and editorial contacts.

N AUGSBURG BOOKS, Augsburg Fortress Publishers, P.O. Box 1209, Minneapolis MN 55440-1209. (612)330-3300. Website: www.augsburgfortress.org. Director of Publications: Tia Simons. **Acquisitions:** Robert Klausmeier, Martha Rosenquist, acquisitions editors. Publishes trade and mass market paperback originals and reprints, hardcover picture books. **Publishes 40 titles/year. 2-3% of books from first-time authors. Pays royalty.** Publishes book 18 months after acceptance of ms. Responds in 3 months to queries. Book catalog for 9×12 SAE with 3 first-class stamps; ms guidelines for #10 SASE.
O→ Augsburg Books publishes for the mainline Christian market.
Nonfiction: Children's/juvenile, self-help. Subjects include religion, spirituality (adult), grief/healing/wholeness, parenting, interactive books for children and families, seasonal and picture books. Submit outline, 1-2 sample chapters (if requested).
Recent Title(s): *The Christmas Bird*, by Sallie Ketcham; *A Prayerbook for Husbands and Wives*, by Ruthanne and Walter Wangerin, Jr.

AUSTIN & WINFIELD PUBLISHERS, The University Press of America, 4720 Boston Way, Lanham MD 20706. (301)459-3366. Fax: (301)429-5748. E-mail: lraimond@univpress.com. Website: www.univpress.com. **Acquisitions:** Acquisitions Department. Estab. 1992. Publishes hardcover and paperback originals and reprints. **Publishes 120 titles/year; imprint publishes 41 titles/year. Receives 300 queries and 180 mss/year. 60% of books from first-time authors; 100% from unagented writers. Pays royalty.** Publishes book 5 months after acceptance of ms. Accepts simultaneous submissions. Responds in 1 month to queries. Book catalog and ms guidelines for #10 SASE or online.
O→ Austin & Winfield is an international scholarly publisher specializing in law, criminal justice and legal policy. "We publish monographs and revised dissertations—this is what we are seeking."
Nonfiction: Reference, technical, textbook. Subjects include government/politics, philosophy, sociology. Submit proposal package including outline, 2 sample chapter(s), résumé.
Recent Title(s): *Constitutional Law in the United States, 3rd ed*, by Randall Bland and Joseph Brogan.
Tips: "Scholarly/library market is our main focus—we are like a university press in standards and expectations."

AUTONOMEDIA, P.O. Box 568, Williamsburgh Station, Brooklyn NY 11211. (718)963-2603. Fax: (718)963-2603. E-mail: info@autonomedia.org. Website: www.autonomedia.org. **Acquisitions:** Kevin Coogan, acquisitions editor. Estab. 1984. Publishes trade paperback originals and reprints. **Publishes 25 titles/year. Receives 350 queries/year. 30%**

of books from first-time authors; 90% from unagented writers. **Pays variable royalty. Offers $100 advance. Publishes book 6 months after acceptance of ms. Accepts simultaneous submissions. Responds in 2 months to queries. Book catalog for $1; ms guidelines online.**

O→ Autonomedia publishes radical and marginal books on culture, media and politics.

Nonfiction: Subjects include anthropology/archeology, art/architecture, business/economics, computers/electronic, gay/lesbian, government/politics, history, multicultural, nature/environment, philosophy, religion, sex, translation, women's issues/studies, world affairs, general nonfiction. Submit outline, SASE. Reviews artwork/photos as part of ms package. Send photocopies.

Fiction: Erotica, experimental, feminist, gay/lesbian, literary, mainstream/contemporary, occult, science fiction, short story collections. Submit synopsis, SASE.

Recent Title(s): *The Anarchists*, by John Henry MacKay.

AVALON BOOKS, Thomas Bouregy & Co., Inc., 160 Madison Ave., New York NY 10016. (212)598-0222. Fax: (212)223-5251. E-mail: avalon-books@att.net. Website: www.avalonbooks.com. **Acquisitions:** Erin Cartwright, senior editor; Mira Son, assistant editor. Estab. 1950. **Publishes 60 titles/year. Receives 2,000 queries and 1,200 mss/year. 65% of books from first-time authors; 80% from unagented writers. Pays 5-15% royalty. Offers $1,000+ advance.** Publishes book 6-10 months after acceptance of ms. Responds in 1 month to queries; 4 months to mss. Book catalog online; ms guidelines for #10 SASE.

O→ "We publish wholesome fiction. We're the 'Family Channel' of publishing. We try to make what we publish suitable for anybody in the family." Currently seeking contemporary romances, career romances, mysteries, series, westerns, good writing, developed characters, interesting story lines. De-emphasizing romantic suspense.

Fiction: Historical, mystery, romance, western. "We publish wholesome contemporary romances, mysteries, historical romances (coming in 2001) and westerns. Our books are read by adults as well as teenagers, and the characters are all adults. All mysteries are contemporary. We publish: hardcover career romances (two every two months); contemporary romances (four every two months—changing in 2002 to two every two months), mysteries (two every two months) and westerns (two every two months). In February 2002 we will begin publishing two historical romances every two months." Submit first 3 sample chapters, a 2-3 page synopsis and SASE. Starting March 1, 2001, we will accept outlines and the first three chapters for historical romances of every genre. The manuscripts should be between 50,000 to 60,000 words. Manuscripts that are too long will not be considered. Time period and setting are the author's preference. The historical romances will maintain the high level of reading expected by our readers. The books shall be wholesome fiction, without graphic sex, violence or strong language."

Recent Title(s): *Chasing Charlie*, by Kathy Carmichael (romance); *Foundation of the Law*, by Johnny D. Boggs (western); *One Last Goodbye*, by Joyce and Jim Lavene (mystery).

Tips: "We are looking for love stories, heroines who have interesting professions, and we are actively seeking new authors. We do accept unagented manuscripts, and we do publish first novels. Right now we are concentrating on finding talented new mystery and historical romance writers with solid story-telling skills. Read our guidelines carefully before submitting."

AVALON TRAVEL PUBLISHING, Avalon Publishing Group, 5855 Beaudry St., Emeryville CA 94608. (510)595-3664. E-mail: acquisitions@avalonpub.com. Website: www.travelmatters.com. Publisher: Bill Newlin. **Acquisitions:** Pauli Galin, acquisitions director. Estab. 1973. Publishes trade paperback originals. **Publishes 100 titles/year. Receives 100-200 submissions/year. 50% of books from first-time authors; 95% from unagented writers. Pays royalty on net receipts. Offers up to $10,000 advance.** Publishes book an average of 9 months after acceptance of ms. Accepts simultaneous submissions. Responds in 2 months to queries. Book catalog and ms guidelines for 7½×10½ SAE with 2 first-class stamps.

Imprints: *Series:* Adapter Kit; City Smart; Dog Lover's Companion; Moon Handbooks; Rick Steves; Road Trip USA; Travel Smart

O→ "Avalon Travel Publishing publishes comprehensive, articulate travel information to North and South America, Asia and the Pacific. We have an interest in niche markets such as families, older travelers, Afro-American, disabled, outdoor recreation including camping/hiking/biking."

Nonfiction: Subjects include regional, travel. "We specialize in travel guides to Asia and the Pacific Basin, the United States, Canada, the Caribbean, Latin America and South America, but are open to new ideas." Query with SASE or submit proposal package including outline, table of contents, writing sample. Reviews artwork/photos as part of ms package.

Tips: "Avalon Travel Publishing produces books that are designed by and for independent travelers seeking the most rewarding travel experience possible. Check our website."

AVIATION PUBLISHERS, 1 Oakglade Circle, Hummelstown PA 17036-9525. (717)566-0468. Fax: (717)566-6423. E-mail: avipub@excite.com. **Acquisitions:** Michael A. Markowski, editor-in-chief. Manuscript guidelines for #10 SAE with 2 first-class stamps.

O→ Aviation Publishers publishes books to help people learn more about aviation and model aviation through the written word.

Nonfiction: How-to, technical. Subjects include history, hobbies, recreation, radio control, free flight, indoor models, electric flight, rubber powered flying models, micro radio control, aviation history, homebuilt aircraft, ultralights and hang gliders.

Recent Title(s): *Birdflight as the Basis of Aviation*, by Otto Lilrenthal.
Tips: "Our focus is on books of short to medium length that will serve the emerging needs of the hobby. We want to help youth get started and enhance everyone's enjoyment of the hobby."

AVISSON PRESS, INC., 3007 Taliaferro Rd., Greensboro NC 27408. Fax: (336)288-6989. **Acquisitions:** M.L. Hester, editor. Estab. 1994. Publishes hardcover originals and trade paperback originals and reprints. **Publishes 9-10 titles/year. Receives 600 queries and 400 mss/year. 5% of books from first-time authors; 90% from unagented writers. Pays 8-10% royalty on wholesale price. Offers occasional small advance.** Publishes book 15 months after acceptance of ms. Accepts simultaneous submissions. Responds in 1 week to queries and proposals; 3 months to mss. Book catalog for #10 SASE.
    O⊸ Avisson Press publishes helpful nonfiction for senior citizens, minority topics and young adult biographies (African-American, women). Currently emphasizing young-adult biography only. No fiction or poetry.
Nonfiction: Biography, reference, self-help (senior citizens and teenagers), textbook (creative writing text). Subjects include ethnic, history (Southeast or North Carolina), language/literature, psychology, regional (or North Carolina), sports, women's issues/studies. Query with SASE or submit outline, 1-3 sample chapter(s).
Recent Title(s): *Go, Girl!: Young Women Superstars of Pop Music*, by Jacqueline Robb; *The Experimenters: Eleven Great Chemists*, by Margery Everden.
Tips: Audience is primarily public and school libraries.

AZTEX CORP., P.O. 50046, Tucson AZ 85703-1046. (520)882-4656. Website: www.aztexcorp.com. **Acquisitions:** Elaine Jordan, editor. Estab. 1976. Publishes hardcover and paperback originals. **Publishes 10 titles/year. Receives 250 submissions/year. 100% from unagented writers. Pays 10% royalty.** Publishes book 18 months after acceptance of ms. Responds in 3 months to queries.
Nonfiction: How-to. Subjects include history, transportation, motor sports, automobiles. "We specialize in transportation subjects (how-to and history)." Biographies and autobiographies are of less interest. Accepts nonfiction translations. Submit outline, 2 sample chapter(s). Reviews artwork/photos as part of ms package.
Tips: "We look for accuracy, thoroughness and interesting presentation."

BACKCOUNTRY GUIDES, (formerly Backcountry Publications), The Countryman Press, P. O. Box 748, Woodstock VT 05091-0748. (802)457-4826. Fax: (802)457-1678. E-mail: countrymanpress@wwnorton.com. Website: www.countrymanpress.com. **Acquisitions:** Kermit Hummell, editorial director; Ann Kraybill, managing editor. Publishes trade paperback originals. **Publishes 15 titles/year. Receives 1,000 queries and a few mss/year. 25% of books from first-time authors; 75% from unagented writers. Pays 7-10% royalty on retail price. Offers $1,500-2,500 advance.** Publishes book 18 after acceptance of ms. Accepts simultaneous submissions. Responds in 2 months to proposals. Book catalog free; ms guidelines for #10 SASE.
    O⊸ Backcountry Guides publishes guidebooks that encourage physical fitness and appreciation for and understanding of the natural world, self-sufficiency and adventure. "We publish several series of regional destination guidebooks to outdoor recreation. They include: the 50 Hikes series; Backroad Bicycling series; Trout Streams series; Bicycling America's National Parks series; and a paddling (canoeing and kayaking) series."
Nonfiction: Subjects include nature/environment, recreation (bicycling, hiking, canoeing, kayaking, fly fishing, walking, guidebooks and series), sports. Query with SASE or submit proposal package including outline, market analysis, 50 sample pages.
Recent Title(s): *Bicycling America's National Parks: California*, by David Story; *Kayaking the Maine Coast*, by Dorcas Miller.
Tips: "Look at our existing series of guidebooks to see how your proposal fits in."

BAEN PUBLISHING ENTERPRISES, P.O. Box 1403, Riverdale NY 10471-0671. (718)548-3100. Website: baen.com. **Acquisitions:** Jim Baen, editor-in-chief; Toni Weisskopf, executive editor. Estab. 1983. Publishes hardcover, trade paperback and mass market paperback originals and reprints. **Publishes 120 titles/year. Receives 5,000 submissions/year. 5% of books from first-time authors; 50% from unagented writers. Pays royalty on retail price. Offers advance.** Responds in 8 months to queries and proposals; 1 year to mss. Book catalog free; ms guidelines for #10 SASE.
    O⊸ "We publish books at the heart of science fiction and fantasy."
Fiction: Fantasy, science fiction. Submit outline, sample chapter(s), synopsis or submit complete ms.
Recent Title(s): *Ashes of Victory*, by David Weber.
Tips: "See our books before submitting. Send for our writers' guidelines."

BAKER BOOKS, Baker Book House Company, P.O. Box 6287, Grand Rapids MI 49516-6287. (616)676-9185. Fax: (616)676-9573. Website: www.bakerbooks.com. Director of Publications: Don Stephenson. **Acquisitions:** Rebecca Cooper, assistant editor. Estab. 1939. Publishes hardcover and trade paperback originals and trade paperback reprints. **Publishes 80 titles/year. 10% of books from first-time authors; 85% from unagented writers. Pays 14% royalty on net receipts.** Publishes book within 1 year after acceptance of ms. Accepts simultaneous submissions. Responds in 2 months to proposals. Book catalog for 8½×11 SAE with 6 first-class stamps or online; ms guidelines for #10 SASE or online.
Imprints: Hamewith, Hourglass, Labyrinth, Raven's Ridge, Spire Books

O–π "Baker Books publishes popular religious nonfiction and fiction, children's books, academic and reference books, and professional books for church leaders. Most of our authors and readers are evangelical Christians, and our books are purchased from Christian bookstores, mail-order retailers, and school bookstores."

Nonfiction: Biography, children's/juvenile, gift book, illustrated book, multimedia, reference, self-help, textbook, CD-ROM. Subjects include anthropology/archeology, child guidance/parenting, psychology, religion, women's issues/ studies, Christian doctrine, books for pastors and church leaders, seniors' concerns, singleness, contemporary issues. Query with SASE or submit proposal package including outline, sample chapter(s), résumé. Reviews artwork/photos as part of ms package. Send 1-2 photocopies.

Fiction: Juvenile, literary, mainstream/contemporary, mystery, picture books, religious, young adult. Query with SASE or submit outline, sample chapter(s), résumé, synopsis.

Recent Title(s): *The Last Days According to Jesus*, by R.C. Sproul (theology); *Resting in the Bosom of the Lamb*, by Augusta Trobaugh (southern fiction).

BALE BOOKS, Bale Publications, 5121 St. Charles Ave., Suite #13, New Orleans LA 70115. **Acquisitions:** Don Bale, Jr, editor-in-chief. Estab. 1963. Publishes hardcover and paperback originals and reprints. **Publishes 10 titles/ year. Receives 25 submissions/year. 50% of books from first-time authors; 90% from unagented writers. Offers standard 10-12½% royalty contract on wholesale or retail price; sometimes makes outright purchases of $500.** Publishes book 3 years after acceptance of ms. Responds in 3 months to queries. Book catalog for #10 SAE with 2 first-class stamps.

O–π "Our mission is to educate numismatists about coins, coin collecting and investing opportunities."

Nonfiction: Numismatics. Subjects include hobbies, money/finance. "Our specialties are coin and stock market investment books; especially coin investment books and coin price guides." Submit outline, 3 sample chapter(s).

Recent Title(s): *How to Find Valuable Old & Scarce Coins*, by Jules Penn.

Tips: "Most of our books are sold through publicity and ads in the coin newspapers. We are open to any new ideas in the area of numismatics. Write for a teenage through adult level. Lead the reader by the hand like a teacher, building chapter by chapter. Our books sometimes have a light, humorous treatment, but not necessarily. We look for good English, construction and content, and sales potential."

A **BALLANTINE BOOKS**, Random House, Inc., 1540 Broadway, New York NY 10036. (212)782-9000. Website: www.randomhouse.com/BB. Publisher: Gina Centrello. Senior VP/Editor-in-Chief: Nancy Miller. VP/Editorial Director: Linda Marrow. **Acquisitions:** Joe Blades, vice president/executive editor (*fiction*: suspense, mystery, *nonfiction*: pop culture, film history and criticism, travel); Peter Borland, vice president/editorial director (*fiction*: commerical and literary, *nonfiction*: narrative, popular culture, social history); Tracy Brown, senior editor (*fiction*: literary, quality commerical, paperback reprint *nonfiction*: history, travel, issue-oriented, nature, narrative, biography, paperback reprint); Allison Dickens, assistant editor (*fiction*: literary, women's fiction, commercial, *nonfiction*: biography, narrative, history (art, culinary, travel); Anita Diggs, One World imprint, senior editor (*fiction*: literary, mystery, commerical, romance, *nonfiction*: autobiography, African-American studies, contemporary affairs, humor, essay, travel, performing arts and film); Charlotte Herscher, associate editor (*fiction*: historical and contemporary romance); Linda Marrow, vice president/ editorial director (*fiction*: suspense, women's, crime); Leslie Meredith, Wellspring imprint, vice president/executive editor (*nonfiction*: holistic health and nutrition, women's health and spirituality, psychological spirituality, popular religion, popular science and psychology, psychological astrology, self-help and how-to). Estab. 1952. Publishes hardcover, trade paperback, mass market paperback originals.

O–π Ballantine Books publishes a wide variety of nonfiction and fiction.

Nonfiction: How-to, humor, self-help. Subjects include animals, child guidance/parenting, cooking/foods/nutrition, general, health/medicine, religion, true crime. *Accepts agented submissions only.*

Fiction: Historical, mainstream/contemporary (women's), multicultural, general fiction. *Accepts agented submissions only.*

BANTAM DOUBLEDAY DELL BOOKS FOR YOUNG READERS, Random House Children's Publishing, Random House, Inc., 1540 Broadway, New York NY 10036. (212)782-9000. Fax: (212)782-9452. Website: www.random house.com/kids. Vice President/Publisher: Beverly Horowitz. **Acquisitions:** Michelle Poploff, editorial director. Publishes hardcover, trade paperback and mass market paperback series originals, trade paperback reprints. **Publishes 300 titles/year. Receives thousands queries/year. 10% of books from first-time authors; small% from unagented writers. Pays royalty. Offers varied advance.** Publishes book 2 years after acceptance of ms. Responds in 2 months to queries. Book catalog for 9×12 SASE.

Imprints: Delacorte Press Books for Young Readers, Doubleday Books for Young Readers, Laurel Leaf (ya), Picture Yearling, Skylark, Starfire, Yearling (middle grade)

O–π "Bantam Doubleday Dell Books for Young Readers publishes award-winning books by distinguished authors and the most promising new writers." The best way to break in to this market is through its two contests, the Marguerite de Angeli Contest and the Delacorte Press Contest for a First Young Adult Novel, listed in the Contests & Awards section of this book.

Nonfiction: Children's/juvenile. "Bantam Doubleday Dell Books for Young Readers publishes a very limited number of nonfiction titles."

Fiction: Adventure, fantasy, humor, juvenile, mainstream/contemporary, mystery, picture books, suspense, young adult. *No unsolicited mss.*

Recent Title(s): *Bud, Not Buddy*, by Christopher Paul Curtis (Newbery Award winner); *My Friend John*, by Charlotte Zolotow (picture book); *Ties That Bind, Ties That Break*, by Lensey Namiska (fiction).

BARBOUR PUBLISHING, INC., P.O. Box 719, Uhrichsville OH 44683. (740)922-6045. Website: www.barbour books.com. **Acquisitions:** Paul Muckley, senior editor (all areas); Rebecca Germany, managing editor (fiction). Estab. 1981. Publishes hardcover, trade paperback and mass market paperback originals and reprints. **Publishes 100 titles/ year. Receives 520 queries and 625 mss/year. 40% of books from first-time authors; 95% from unagented writers. Pays 0-12% royalty on net price or makes outright purchase of $500-5,000. Offers $500-2,500 advance.** Publishes book 2 years after acceptance of ms. Accepts simultaneous submissions. Responds in 1 month to queries; 3 months to proposals and mss. Book catalog online for 9 × 12 SAE with 2 first-class stamps; ms guidelines for #10 SASE or online. **Imprints:** Heartsong Presents (contact Rebecca Germany, managing editor), Promise Press (contact Susan Schlabach, senior editor)
  O-π Barbour Books publishes mostly devotional material that is non-denominational and evangelical in nature; Heartsong Presents publishes Christian romance. "We're a Christian evangelical publisher."
Nonfiction: Biography, children's/juvenile, cookbook, gift book, humor, illustrated book, reference. Subjects include child guidance/parenting, cooking/foods/nutrition, humor, money/finance, religion (evangelical Christian), women's issues/studies. "We are always looking for biographical material for adults and children on heroes of the faith. Always looking for humor! Some writers do not explain their purpose for writing the book and don't specify who their audience is. Many proposals are sketchy, non-specific and difficult to understand. If I can't decipher the proposal, I certainly won't accept a manuscript." Submit outline, 3 sample chapter(s), SASE. Reviews artwork/photos as part of ms package. Send photocopies.
Fiction: Historical, humor, mainstream/contemporary, religious, romance, short story collections, western. "All of our fiction is 'sweet' romance. No sex, no bad language, etc. Audience is evangelical/Christian, and we're looking for wholesome material for young as well as old. Common writer's mistakes are a sketchy proposal, an unbelievable story and a story that doesn't fit our guidelines for inspirational romances." Submit 3 sample chapter(s), synopsis, SASE.
Recent Title(s): *God Is in the Small Stuff*, by Bruce Bickel and Stan Jantz (nonfiction); *Short Stories for Long Rainy Days*, by Katherine Douglas (fiction).
Tips: "Audience is evangelical/Christian conservative, non-denominational, young and old. We're looking for *great concepts*, not necessarily a big name author or agent. We want to publish books that will sell millions, not just 'flash in the pan' releases. Send us your ideas!"

BARRICADE BOOKS INC., 185 Bridge Plaza N., Suite 308A, Fort Lee NJ 07024-5900. (201)944-7600. Fax: (201)944-6363. **Acquisitions:** Carole Stuart, publisher. Estab. 1991. Publishes hardcover and trade paperback originals, trade paperback reprints. **Publishes 30 titles/year. Receives 200 queries and 100 mss/year. 80% of books from first-time authors; 50% from unagented writers. Pays 10-12% royalty on retail price for hardcover. Offers advance.** Publishes book 18 months after acceptance of ms. Responds in 1 month to queries. Book catalog for $3.
  O-π Barricate Books publishes nonfiction, "mostly of the controversial type, and books we can promote with authors who can talk about their topics on radio and television and to the press."
Nonfiction: Biography, how-to, reference, self-help. Subjects include business/economics, ethnic, gay/lesbian, govern-ment/politics, health/medicine, history, nature/environment, psychology, sociology, women's issues/studies. Query with SASE or submit outline, 1-2 sample chapter(s). Material will not be returned without SASE. Reviews artwork/photos as part of ms package. Send photocopies.
Recent Title(s): *The Animal in Hollywood*, by John L. Smith (crime/mafia).
Tips: "Do your homework. Visit bookshops to find publishers who are doing the kinds of books you want to write. Always submit to a *person*—not just 'Editor.' Always enclose SASE or you may not get a response."

BARRON'S EDUCATIONAL SERIES, INC., 250 Wireless Blvd., Hauppauge NY 11788. (631)434-3311. Fax: (631)434-3217. Website: barronseduc.com. **Acquisitions:** Wayne Barr, managing editor/director of acquisitions. Estab. 1941. Publishes hardcover, paperback and mass market originals and software. **Publishes 400 titles/year. Receives 2,000 queries and 1,000 submissions/year. 40% of books from first-time authors; 75% from unagented writers. Pays 12-14% royalty on both wholesale and retail price or makes outright purchase of $2,500-5,000. Offers $3,000 advance.** Publishes book 18 months after acceptance of ms. Accepts simultaneous submissions. Responds in 2 months to queries; 8 months to mss. Book catalog free.
  O-π Barron's tends to publish series of books, both for adults and children. "We are always on the lookout for creative nonfiction ideas for children and adults."
Nonfiction: Children's/juvenile, cookbook, textbook, student test prep guides. Subjects include animals, art/architec-ture, business/economics, child guidance/parenting, cooking/foods/nutrition, education, health/medicine, hobbies, lan-guage/literature, sports, translation, travel, adult education, crafts, foreign language, review books, guidance, pet books, literary guides, young adult sports. Query with SASE or submit outline, 2-3 sample chapter(s). Reviews artwork/photos as part of ms package.
Fiction: Juvenile. Submit complete ms.
Recent Title(s): *A Book of Magical Herbs*, by Margaret Picton; *Family Gardener*, by Lucy Peel.
Tips: "Audience is mostly educated self-learners and hobbyists. The writer has the best chance of selling us a book that will fit into one of our series. Children's books have less chance for acceptance because of the glut of submissions. SASE must be included for the return of all materials. Please be patient for replies."

BATTELLE PRESS, Battelle Memorial Institute, 505 King Ave., Columbus OH 43201. (614)424-6393. Fax: (614)424-3819. E-mail: press@battelle.org. Website: www.battelle.org/bookstore. **Acquisitions:** Joe Sheldrick. Estab. 1980. Publishes hardcover and paperback originals and markets primarily by direct mail. **Publishes 15 titles/year. Pays 10% royalty on wholesale price.** Publishes book 6 months after acceptance of ms. Accepts simultaneous submissions. Responds in 1 month to queries. Book catalog free.
   Oー Battelle Press strives to be a primary source of books and software on science and technology management.
Nonfiction: Subjects include science. "We are looking for management, leadership, project management and communication books specifically targeted to engineers and scientists." Query with SASE. Returns submissions with SASE only by writer's request. Reviews artwork/photos as part of ms package. Send photocopies.
Recent Title(s): *Managing the Industry/University Cooperative Research Center*; *Project Manager's Survival Guide*.
Tips: Audience consists of engineers, researchers, scientists and corporate researchers and developers.

BAYWOOD PUBLISHING CO., INC., 26 Austin Ave., Amityville NY 11701. (631)691-1270. Fax: (631)691-1770. E-mail: baywood@baywood.com. Website: www.baywood.com. **Acquisitions:** Stuart Cohen, managing editor. Estab. 1964. **Publishes 25 titles/year. Pays 7-15% royalty on retail price. Offers advance.** Publishes book within 1 year after acceptance of ms. Book catalog and ms guidelines free.
   Oー Baywood Publishing publishes original and innovative books in the humanities and social sciences, including areas such as health sciences, gerontology, death and bereavement, psychology, technical communications and archaeology.
Nonfiction: Technical, scholarly. Subjects include anthropology/archeology, computers/electronic, education, health/medicine, nature/environment, psychology, sociology, women's issues/studies, gerontology, imagery, labor relations, death/dying, drugs. Submit outline, sample chapter(s).
Recent Title(s): *Eighteenth-Century British Aesthetics*, by Dabney Townsend.

BEACHWAY PRESS, 300 W. Main St., Suite A, Charlottesville VA 22903. (804)245-6800. Fax: (804)297-0569. E-mail: writers@beachway.com. Website: www.outside-america.com. **Acquisitions:** Scott Adams, publisher. **Publishes 10-15 titles/year. Pays 7-10% royalty on wholesale price. Offers $2,500 advance.** Publishes book 1 year after acceptance of ms. Responds in 2 months to queries and proposals. Manuscript guidelines for #10 SASE or online.
   Oー Beachway Press publishes books designed to open up new worlds of experiences for those anxious to explore, and to provide the detailed information necessary to get them started.
Nonfiction: Subjects include nature/environment, recreation, sports, travel. "We welcome ideas that explore the world of adventure and wonder; from day hikes to mountain bikes, from surf to skis." Query with SASE or submit outline, 2 sample chapter(s), methods of research. Reviews artwork/photos as part of ms package.
Recent Title(s): *Hike America*; *Ski & Snowboard America*.
Tips: "Someone interested in writing for us should be both an avid outdoors person and an expert in their area of interest. This person should have a clear understanding of maps and terrain and should enjoy sharing their adventurous spirit and enthusiasm with others. E-mail queries get fastest response."

N: BEACON HILL PRESS OF KANSAS CITY, Nazarene Publishing House, P.O. Box 419527, Kansas City KS 64141. (816)931-1900. Fax: (816)753-4071. **Acquisitions:** Bonnie Perry, editorial director. Estab. 1912. Publishes hardcover and paperback originals. **Publishes 30 titles/year. Pays 12% royalty on net sales for first 10,000 copies and 14% on subsequent copies. Sometimes makes flat rate purchase.** Publishes book 1 year after acceptance of ms. Responds in 3 months to queries.
Imprints: Crystal Sea Books, Lillenas Publishing
   Oー "Beacon Hill Press is a Christ-centered publisher that provides authentically Christian resources that are faithful to God's word and relevant to life."
Nonfiction: Doctrinally must conform to the evangelical, Wesleyan tradition. Accent on holy living; encouragement in daily Christian life. Subjects include applied Christianity, spiritual formation, leadership resources, contemporary issues. No fiction, autobiography, poetry, short stories or children's picture books. Query with SASE or submit proposal package. Average ms length: 30,000-60,000.
Recent Title(s): *Leading with Vision*, by Dale Galloway.

N: BEHR PUBLISHING, Behr Enterprises, LLC, 9 Trapper Rd., Sewell NJ 08080-3315. (856)881-0500. Fax: (856)582-2313. E-mail: TGBehr@cs.com. Website: www.Behrpublishing.com. **Acquisitions:** Donna Hedley, editor (nonfiction); Laura Mitchell, assistant editor (fiction); Mike Dexter, assistant editor (science fiction). Publishes trade paperback originals. **Publishes 10 titles/year. 50% of books from first-time authors; 100% from unagented writers. Pays 10-50% royalty on wholesale price. Offers $1,000-3,000 advance.** Publishes book 9 months after acceptance of ms. Responds in 1 month to queries and proposals.
   Oー "Our publishing plans include books with an emphasis on: Career change, career development networking, and how to books for managers, marketers and consultants."
Nonfiction: How-to, self-help. Subjects include business/economics, child guidance/parenting, education, career change. Query with SASE.
Fiction: Modern political thrillers. "We are very interested in fiction by New Jersey authors. We hope to publish the work of at least two new writers every year. Our special interests include: adventure, espionage, mystery and sports fiction." Query with SASE.

Recent Title(s): *Retro Boomers*, by William Fogerty (career transition); *A Laugh and a Tear*, by Herb Packer (parenting); *Fiddler's Elbow*, by Ron Kase (conspiracy-fiction).
Tips: Behr Publishing's nonfiction books are marketed toward "readers ready for career changes due to retirement or downsizing of companies. Also active people in business interested in becoming business consultants. Please send only a letter of inquiry and a SASE. We have limited staff, and can only consider material that fits our goals."

BEHRMAN HOUSE INC., 11 Edison Place, Springfield NJ 07081. (973)379-7200. Fax: (973)379-7280. E-mail: webmaster@behrmanhouse.com. Website: www.behrmanhouse.com. **Acquisitions:** David Behrman. Estab. 1921. **Publishes 20 titles/year. Receives 200 submissions/year. 20% of books from first-time authors; 95% from unagented writers. Pays 2-10% on wholesale price or retail price or makes outright purchase of $500-10,000. Offers $1,000 average advance.** Publishes book 18 months after acceptance of ms. Accepts simultaneous submissions. Responds in 2 months to queries. Book catalog free.
  O→ "Behrman House publishes quality books of Jewish content—history, Bible, philosophy, holidays, ethics, Israel, Hebrew—for children and adults."
Nonfiction: Children's/juvenile (ages 1-18), reference, textbook. Subjects include ethnic, philosophy, religion. "We want Jewish textbooks for the el-hi market." Query with SASE.
Recent Title(s): *Living As Partners with God*, by Gila Gevirtz (theology).

FREDERIC C. BEIL, PUBLISHER, INC., 609 Whitaker St., Savannah GA 31401. (912)233-2446. Fax: (912)233-6456. E-mail: beilbook@beil.com. Website: www.beil.com. **Acquisitions:** Mary Ann Bowman, editor. Estab. 1982. Publishes hardcover originals and reprints. **Publishes 13 titles/year. Receives 1,800 queries and 13 mss/year. 80% of books from first-time authors; 100% from unagented writers. Pays 7½% royalty on retail price.** Publishes book 20 months after acceptance of ms. Accepts simultaneous submissions. Responds in 2 weeks to queries. Book catalog free.
Imprints: The Sandstone Press, Hypermedia, Inc
  O→ Frederic C. Beil publishes in the fields of history, literature, biography, books about books, and the book arts.
Nonfiction: Biography, children's/juvenile, illustrated book, reference, general trade. Subjects include art/architecture, general, history, language/literature, book arts. Query with SASE. Reviews artwork/photos as part of ms package. Send photocopies.
Fiction: Historical, literary. Query with SASE.
Recent Title(s): *Joseph Jefferson: Dean of the American Theatre*, by Arthur Bloom; *Goya, Are You With Me Now?*, by H.E. Francis.
Tips: "Our objectives are (1) to offer to the reading public carefully selected texts of lasting value; (2) to adhere to high standards in the choice of materials and in bookmaking craftsmanship; (3) to produce books that exemplify good taste in format and design; and (4) to maintain the lowest cost consistent with quality."

BELLWETHER-CROSS PUBLISHING, 18319 Highway 20 W., East Dubuque IL 61025. (815)747-6255 or (888)516-5096. Fax: (815)747-3770. E-mail: jwhite@bellwethercross.com. **Acquisitions:** Janet White, senior developmental editor. Publishes college textbooks. **Publishes 18 titles/year. Receives 100 mss/year. 80% of books from first-time authors; 100% from unagented writers. Pays 10% royalty on wholesale price.** Publishes book 6 months after acceptance of ms. Responds in 1 month to queries. Manuscript guidelines available.
  O→ Bellwether-Cross concentrates on college environmental books and nontraditional textbooks with mainstream possibilities.
Nonfiction: Textbook. Submit cover letter and complete ms with SASE. Reviews artwork/photos as part of ms package. Send photocopies.
Recent Title(s): *Fire Mists in the Sky*, by Dr. Edward Ortell and Coary Fugman.

THE BENEFACTORY, INC., 925 N. Milwaukee, Suite 1010, Wheeling IL 60090. (847)919-1777. Fax: (847)919-2777. E-mail: benfactory@aol.com. Website: www.readplay.com. **Acquisitions:** Cynthia A. Germain, senior manager, product development. Estab. 1990. Publishes hardcover and trade paperback originals and reprints. **Publishes 9 titles/year. 50% of books from first-time authors; 50% from unagented writers. Pays 3-5% royalty on wholesale price. Offers $3,000-5,000 advance.** Publishes book 1 year after acceptance of ms. Accepts simultaneous submissions. Responds in 6 months to queries; 1 year to proposals and mss. Book catalog and ms guidelines free.
  O→ The Benefactory's mission is to foster animal protection, motivate reading, teach core values and encourage children to become creative, responsible individuals. Emphasizing true stories about real animals for children ages 5-9. Will not read or return any mss that are not true stories about real animals.
Nonfiction: Children's/juvenile. Subjects include animals, nature/environment. "Each story must be a true story about a real animal and contain educational details. Both prose and verse are accepted." Submit outline, SASE. Reviews artwork/photos as part of ms package. Send photocopies.
Recent Title(s): *Caesar, On Deaf Ears*, by Loren Spiotta DiMare; *Freefall*, by Lyn Littlefield Hoopes.

BENTLEY PUBLISHERS, Automotive Publishers, 1734 Massachusetts Ave., Cambridge MA 02138-1804. (617)547-4170. **Acquisitions:** Janet Barnes, senior editor; Albert Dalia, editor; Jonathan Stein, editor. Estab. 1949. Publishes hardcover and trade paperback originals and reprints. **Publishes 15-20 titles/year. 20% of books from first-time**

authors; **95% from unagented writers. Pays 10-15% royalty on net price or makes outright purchase. Offers negotiable advance.** Publishes book 1 year after acceptance of ms. Responds in 6 weeks to queries. Book catalog and ms guidelines for 9×12 SAE with 4 first-class stamps.

O— Bentley Publishers publishes books for automotive enthusiasts.

Nonfiction: Automotive subjects only. Coffee table book, how-to, technical, theory of operation. Subjects include sports (motor sports), Query with SASE or submit outline, sample chapter(s). Reviews artwork/photos as part of ms package.

Recent Title(s): *Road and Track Illustrated Dictionary,* by John Dinkel (reference).

Tips: "Our audience is composed of serious, intelligent automobile, sports car, and racing enthusiasts, automotive technicians and high-performance tuners."

BERGIN & GARVEY, Greenwood Publishing Group, 88 Post Rd. W., Westport CT 06881. (203)226-3571. Fax: (203)222-1502. Website: www.greenwood.com. **Acquisitions:** Jane Garry, senior editor. Publishes hardcover and trade paperback originals. **Publishes 50 titles/year. Receives 1000s queries/year. 50% of books from first-time authors. Pays variable royalty on net price.** Publishes book 1 year after acceptance of ms. Accepts simultaneous submissions. Responds in 6 months to queries and proposals. Book catalog and ms guidelines online.

O— Bergin & Garvey publishes nonfiction in the areas of education, anthropology, alternative medicine and parenting for libraries, educational groups and university scholars.

Nonfiction: Subjects include anthropology/archeology, child guidance/parenting, education. *No unsolicited mss.* Query with SASE or submit proposal package including résumé, scope, organization, length of project, whether a complete ms is available or when it will be, cv.

THE BERKLEY PUBLISHING GROUP, Penguin Putnam, Inc., 375 Hudson St., New York NY 10014. (212)366-2000. Website: www.penguinputnam.com. **Acquisitions:** Denise Silvestro, senior editor (general nonfiction, business); Tom Colgan, senior editor (history, business, inspiration, biography, suspense/thriller, mystery, adventure); Gail Fortune, senior editor (women's fiction, romance, mystery); Martha Bushko, associate editor (mystery, literary fiction, narrative nonfiction, history, suspense/thriller); Kimberly Waltemyer, editor (adult western, romance, mystery); Christine Zika, senior editor (women's fiction, romance, mystery, health, diet, parenting, self-help, New Age, relationships); Allison McCabe, senior editor (women's fiction, literary fiction, narrative nonfiction, suspense/thriller, romance). Estab. 1954. Publishes paperback and mass market originals and reprints. **Publishes approximately 800 titles/year. Small % of books from first-time authors; 1% from unagented writers. Pays 4-15% royalty on retail price. Offers advance.** Publishes book 2 years after acceptance of ms. Responds in 6 weeks to queries.

Imprints: Ace Science Fiction, Berkley, Boulevard, Jove, Prime Crime

O— The Berkley Publishing Group publishes a variety of general nonfiction and fiction including the traditional categories of romance, mystery and science fiction.

Nonfiction: Biography, how-to, reference, self-help. Subjects include business/economics, child guidance/parenting, creative nonfiction, gay/lesbian, general, health/medicine, history, New Age, psychology, true crime, women's issues/studies, job-seeking communication, positive thinking, general commercial publishing. No memoirs or personal stories. Query with SASE. *Prefers agented submissions.*

Fiction: Adventure, historical, literary, mystery, romance, spiritual, suspense, western, young adult. No occult fiction. Query with SASE. *Prefers agented submissions.*

Recent Title(s): *Tom Clancy's Rainbow Six,* by Tom Clancy (novel); *Meditations from Conversations with God,* by Neale Donald Walsch (inspiration).

BERKSHIRE HOUSE PUBLISHERS, INC., 480 Pleasant St., Suite #5, Lee MA 01238. (413)243-0303. Fax: (413)243-4737. E-mail: info@berkshirehouse.com. Website: www.berkshirehouse.com. President: Jean J. Rousseau. **Acquisitions:** Philip Rich, editorial director. Estab. 1966. **Publishes 10-15 titles/year. Receives 100 queries and 6 mss/year. 50% of books from first-time authors; 80% from unagented writers. Pays 5-10% royalty on retail price. Offers $500-5,000 advance.** Publishes book 18 months after acceptance of ms. Accepts simultaneous submissions. Responds in 1 month to proposals. Book catalog free.

O— "We publish a series of travel guides, the Great Destinations Series, about specific U.S. destinations, guides to appeal to discerning travelers. We also specialize in books about our own region (the Berkshires and New England), especially recreational activities such as outdoor exploration and gardening. We occasionally publish cookbooks related to New England or country living/country inns in general. We offer books of historical interest in our American Classics Series." Currently emphasizing Great Destinations series, outdoor recreation. De-emphasizing cookbooks except those related to New England or country living and country inns. Please refer to website for more information.

Nonfiction: Cookbook (relating to country inns, travel, especially in New England). Subjects include Americana, history, nature/environment, recreation, regional, travel. "To a great extent, we choose our topics then commission the authors, but we don't discourage speculative submissions. We just don't accept many. Don't overdo it; a well-written outline/proposal is more useful than a full manuscript. Also, include a cv with writing credits."

Recent Title(s): *The Finger Lakes Book: A Complete Guide,* by Katherine Delavan Dyson.

Tips: "Our readers are literate, active, interested in travel, especially in selected 'Great Destinations' areas and outdoor activities and cooking."

BETHANY HOUSE PUBLISHERS, 11400 Hampshire Ave. S., Minneapolis MN 55438. (952)829-2500. Fax: (952)829-2768. Website: www.bethanyhouse.com. Publisher: Gary Johnson. **Acquisitions:** Sharon Madison, manuscript review editor; Steve Laube, senior editor (nonfiction); David Horton, senior editor (adult fiction); Barbara Lilland, senior editor (adult fiction); Rochelle Gloege, senior editor (children and youth). Estab. 1956. Publishes hardcover and trade paperback originals, mass market paperback reprints. **Publishes 120-150 titles/year. 2% of books from first-time authors; 93% from unagented writers. Pays negotiable royalty on net price. Offers negotiable advance.** Publishes book 1 year after acceptance of ms. Accepts simultaneous submissions. Responds in 3 months to queries. Manuscript guidelines for 9×12 SAE with 5 first-class stamps.

O→ Bethany House Publishers specializes in books that communicate Biblical truth and assist people in both spiritual and practical areas of life. New interest in contemporary fiction.

Nonfiction: Biography, gift book, how-to, reference, self-help. Subjects include child guidance/parenting, ethnic, psychology, religion, sociology, women's issues/studies, personal growth, devotional, contemporary issues, marriage and family, applied theology, inspirational. Query with SASE or submit proposal package including outline, 3 sample chapter(s), author bio. "Prospective authors must have credentials, credibility and well-honed writing." Reviews artwork/photos as part of ms package. Send photocopies.

Fiction: Adventure, historical, juvenile, young adult, children's fiction series (ages 8-12) and Bethany Backyard (ages 6-12). Send SASE for guidelines.

Recent Title(s): *Unshakable Foundations*, by Dr. Norman Geisler & Peter Bocchino (Christian living); *Serenity Bay*, by Bette Nordberg (fiction); *God's Will, God's Best—for Your Life*, by Josh McDowell and Kevin Johnson (teen Christian living).

Tips: "Bethany House Publishers' publishing program relates Biblical truth to all areas of life—whether in the framework of a well-told story, of a challenging book for spiritual growth, or of a Bible reference work. We are seeking high quality fiction and nonfiction that will inspire and challenge our audience."

BETTERWAY BOOKS, F&W Publications, 1507 Dana Ave., Cincinnati OH 45207. (513)531-2690. **Acquisitions:** Jack Heffron (genealogy, small business; lifestyle, including time management and home organization). Estab. 1982. Publishes hardcover and trade paperback originals, trade paperback reprints. **Publishes 30 titles/year. Pays 10-20% royalty on net receipts. Offers $3,000-5,000 advance.** Publishes book an average of 18 months after acceptance of ms. Accepts simultaneous submissions. Responds in 6 weeks to queries. Book catalog for 9×12 SAE with 6 first-class stamps.

O→ Betterway books are practical instructional books that are to be *used*. "We like specific step-by-step advice, charts, illustrations, and clear explanations of the activities and projects the books describe."

Nonfiction: How-to, illustrated book, reference, self-help. Subjects include business/economics, film/cinema/stage, hobbies, money/finance, music/dance, recreation. "Genealogy and family traditions are topics that we're particularly interested in. We are interested mostly in original material, but we will consider republishing self-published nonfiction books and good instructional or reference books that have gone out of print before their time. Send a sample copy, sales information, and reviews, if available. If you have a good idea for a reference book that can be updated annually, try us. We're willing to consider freelance compilers of such works." No cookbooks, diet/exercise, psychology self-help, health or parenting books. Submit outline, sample chapter(s). Reviews artwork/photos as part of ms package.

Recent Title(s): *Jump Start Your Business Brain*, by Doug Hall (business).

Tips: "Keep the imprint name well in mind when submitting ideas to us. What is the 'better way' you're proposing? How will readers benefit *immediately* from the instruction and information you're giving them?"

N: BEYOND WORDS PUBLISHING INC., 20827 NW Cornell Rd., Suite 500, Hillsboro OR 97124. (503)531-8700. Fax: (503)531-8773. E-mail: info@beyondword.com. Website: www.beyondword.com. **Acquisitions:** Cynthia Black, editor-in-chief (adult books); Michelle Rochim, acquisitions editor (children's books). Publishes hardcover and trade paperback originals. **Publishes 20-25 titles/year. Receives 4,000 queries and 2,000 mss/year. 65% of books from first-time authors; 50% from unagented writers. Pays 10-15% royalty on publishers proceeds. Offers advance.** Publishes book 12-18 months after acceptance of ms. Accepts simultaneous submissions. Responds in 4 months to queries, proposals and mss. Book catalog and ms guidelines for #10 SASE or online.

Nonfiction: Children's/juvenile, coffee table book, gift book, how-to, self-help. Subjects include animals, child guidance/parenting, health/medicine, photography (selectively), psychology, spirituality, women's issues/studies. Query with SASE or submit proposal package including outline, 3 sample chapter(s). Reviews artwork/photos as part of ms package. Send photocopies.

Tips: "*Beyond Words* markets to cultural, creative people, mostly women ages 30-60. Study our list before you submit and check out our website to make sure your book is a good fit for our list."

BLACK DOG & LEVENTHAL PUBLISHERS INC., 151 W. 19th St., 12th Floor, New York NY 10011. (212)647-9336. Fax: (212)647-9332. Publishes hardcover originals and reprints. **Publishes 30-40 titles/year. Receives 12 queries and 12 mss/year. Pays royalty on retail price or on net receipts or makes outright purchase. Offers $1,500-20,000 advance.** Publishes book 6 months after acceptance of ms. Accepts simultaneous submissions. Responds in 6 months to queries.

O→ "We look for very commercial books that will appeal to a broad-based audience."

Nonfiction: Coffee table book, cookbook, gift book, how-to, humor, illustrated book, reference. Subjects include Americana, animals, art/architecture, cooking/foods/nutrition, gardening, health/medicine, hobbies, humor, photography, regional, sports, travel. Query with SASE. Reviews artwork/photos as part of ms package.
Recent Title(s): *Moments: The Pulitzer Prize Photographs*, by Hal Buell (photo journalism); *Skyscrapers*, by Judith Dupre (architecture).
Tips: "We look for books that are very commercial and that can be sold in an array of outlets such as bookstores, catalogs, warehouse clubs, K-mart, Costco, book clubs, etc."

BLACKBIRCH PRESS, INC., P.O. Box 3573, Woodbridge CT 06525. (203)387-7525. E-mail: staff@blackbirch. com. Website: www.blackbirch.com. **Acquisitions:** Scott Ingram, editorial director. Estab. 1990. Publishes hardcover and trade paperback originals. **Publishes 70-90 titles/year. Receives 400 queries and 75 mss/year. 100% from unagented writers. Pays 4-8% royalty on net price or makes outright purchase. Offers $1,000-5,000 advance.** Publishes book 1 year after acceptance of ms. Accepts simultaneous submissions. Replies only if interested to queries. Manuscript guidelines free.
O➤ Blackbirch Press publishes juvenile and young adult nonfiction and fiction titles.
Nonfiction: Biography, children's/juvenile, illustrated book, reference. Subjects include animals, anthropology/archeology, art/architecture, education, health/medicine, history, nature/environment, science, sports, travel, women's issues/studies. Publishes in series—6-8 books at a time. "No proposals for adult readers, please." *No unsolicited mss or proposals. No phone calls.* Query with SASE. Cover letters and résumés are useful for identifying new authors. Reviews artwork/photos as part of ms package. Send photocopies.
Recent Title(s): *A Whale on Her Own: The True Story of Wilma the Whale*, by Brian Skerry; *Flies*, by Elaine Pascoe.
Tips: "We cannot return submissions or send guidelines/replies without an enclosed SASE."

JOHN F. BLAIR, PUBLISHER, 1406 Plaza Dr., Winston-Salem NC 27103-1470. (336)768-1374. Fax: (336)768-9194. President: Carolyn Sakowski. **Acquisitions:** Acquisitions Committee. Estab. 1954. Publishes hardcover originals and trade paperbacks. **Publishes 20 titles/year. Receives 2,000 submissions/year. 20-30% of books from first-time authors; 90% from unagented writers. Royalty negotiable. Offers advance.** Publishes book 18 months after acceptance of ms. Responds in 3 months to queries. Book catalog and ms guidelines for 9×12 SAE with 5 first-class stamps.
O➤ John F. Blair publishes in the areas of travel, history, folklore and the outdoors for a general trade audience, most of whom live or travel in the Southeastern U.S.
Nonfiction: Subjects include Americana, history, nature/environment, regional, travel, women's issues/studies. Especially interested in travel guides dealing with the Southeastern U.S. Also interested in Civil War, outdoors, travel and Americana; query on other nonfiction topics. Looks for utility and significance. Submit outline, 3 sample chapter(s). Reviews artwork/photos as part of ms package.
Fiction: "We publish one work of fiction per season relating to the Southeastern U.S." No category fiction, juvenile fiction, picture books, short story collections or poetry. Query with SASE.

BLOOMBERG PRESS, Bloomberg L.P., 100 Business Park Dr., P.O. Box 888, Princeton NJ 08542-0888. Website: www.bloomberg.com/books. **Acquisitions:** Kathleen Peterson, senior acquisitions editor. Estab. 1995. Publishes hardcover and trade paperback originals. **Publishes 18-22 titles/year. Receives 90 queries and 17 mss/year. 45% from unagented writers. Pays negotiable, competitive royalty. Offers negotiable advance.** Publishes book 9 months after acceptance of ms. Accepts simultaneous submissions. Responds in 1 month to queries. Book catalog for 10×13 SAE with 5 first-class stamps.
Imprints: Bloomberg Personal Bookshelf, Bloomberg Professional Library, Bloomberg Entrepreneur
O➤ Bloomberg Press publishes professional books for practitioners in the financial markets, and finance and investing books for informed personal investors, entrepreneurs, and consumers. "We publish commercially successful, very high-quality books that stand out clearly from the competition by their brevity, ease of use, sophistication, and abundance of practical tips and strategies; books readers need, will use and appreciate."
Nonfiction: How-to, reference, technical. Subjects include business/economics, money/finance, small business, current affairs, new economy, personal finance and investing for consumers, professional books on finance, investment and financial services. "We are looking for authorities and experienced service journalists. We are looking for original solutions to widespread problems and books offering fresh investment opportunities. Do not send us management books—we don't publish them—or unfocused books containing general information already covered by one or more well-established backlist books in the marketplace." Submit outline, sample chapter(s), SAE with sufficient postage.
Recent Title(s): *Investing in IPOs*, by Tom Taulli; *The Angel Investor's Handbook*, by Gerald A. Benjamin and Joel Margulis; *In Defense of Free Capital Markets*, by David F. DeRosa.
Tips: "*Bloomberg Professional Library*: Audience is upscale financial professionals—traders, dealers, brokers, planners and advisors, financial managers, money managers, company executives, sophisticated investors. *Bloomberg Personal Bookshelf*: audience is upscale consumers and individual investors. Authors are experienced business and financial journalists and/or financial professionals nationally prominent in their specialty for some time who have proven an ability to write a successful book. Research Bloomberg and look at our specially formatted books in a library or bookstore, read *Bloomberg Personal Finance* and *Bloomberg* magazines and peruse our website."

BLUE HERON PUBLISHING, 1234 SW Stark St., Portland OR 97205. (503)221-6841. Fax: (503)221-6843. E-mail: publisher@blueheronpublishing.com. Website: www.blueheronpublishing.com. **Acquisitions:** Dennis Stovall, publisher. Estab. 1985. Publishes trade paperback originals and reprints. **Publishes 12 titles/year. Offers advance.** Responds in 6 weeks to queries. Book catalog for #10 SASE.

> Blue Heron publishes books on writing and the teaching of writing, young adult and adult literature, western outdoor photography, and left-wing novels of mystery and suspense. Now considering ethnic cookbooks. Currently emphasizing books on writing and the teaching of writing, mysteries. De-emphasizing young adult.

Nonfiction: Education subjects. Looking for books that sell in educational markets as well as trade. Query with SASE.

Recent Title(s): *A Story Is a Promise*, by Bill Johnson (nonfiction); *Boomboom*, by Joe Ferone (fiction).

Tips: "We publish in several overlapping markets from an editorial perspective of fostering cultural diversity, encouraging new literary voices, and promulgating progressive positions on social and political issues through fine fiction and nonfiction."

BLUE POPPY PRESS, 5441 Western Ave., #2, Boulder CO 80301-2733. (303)447-8372. Fax: (303)245-8362. E-mail: info@bluepoppy.com. Website: www.bluepoppy.com. **Acquisitions:** Bob Flaws, editor-in-chief. Estab. 1981. Publishes hardcover and trade paperback originals. **Publishes 9-12 titles/year. Receives 50-100 queries and 20 mss/year. 40-50% of books from first-time authors; 100% from unagented writers. Pays 10-15% royalty. Offers advance.** Publishes book 1 year after acceptance of ms. Responds in 1 month to queries. Book catalog and ms guidelines free.

> Blue Poppy Press is dedicated to expanding and improving the English language literature on acupuncture and Asian medicine for both professional practitioners and lay readers.

Nonfiction: Self-help, technical, textbook (related to acupuncture and Oriental medicine). Subjects include ethnic, health/medicine. "We only publish books on acupuncture and Oriental medicine by authors who can read Chinese and have a minimum of five years clinical experience. We also require all our authors to use Wiseman's *Glossary of Chinese Medical Terminology* as their standard for technical terms." Query with SASE or submit outline, 1 sample chapter(s).

Recent Title(s): *Chinese Medical Psychiatry*, by Bob Flaws & James Lake, MD.

Tips: Audience is "practicing acupuncturists, interested in alternatives in healthcare, preventive medicine, Chinese philosophy and medicine."

BLUEWOOD BOOKS, The Siyeh Group, Inc., P.O. Box 689, San Mateo CA 94401. (650)548-0754. Fax: (650)548-0654. E-mail: bluewoodb@aol.com. **Acquisitions:** Richard Michaels, director. Publishes trade paperback originals. **Publishes 8 titles/year. 20% of books from first-time authors; 100% from unagented writers. Makes work for hire assignments—fee depends upon book and writer's expertise. Offers ⅓ fee advance.**

> "We are looking for qualified writers for nonfiction series—history and biography oriented."

Nonfiction: Biography, illustrated book. Subjects include Americana, anthropology/archeology, art/architecture, business/economics, government/politics, health/medicine, history, military/war, multicultural, science, sports, women's issues/studies. Query with SASE.

Recent Title(s): *American Politics in the 20th Century*, by J. Bonasia (political history); *100 Families Who Shaped World History*, by Samuel Crompton (world history).

Tips: "Our audience consists of adults and young adults. Our books are written on a newspaper level—clear, concise, well organized and easy to understand. We encourage potential writers to send us a résumé, providing background, qualifications and references."

BNA BOOKS, The Bureau of National Affairs, Inc., 1231 25th St. NW, Washington DC 20037-1165. (202)452-4343. Fax: (202)452-4997. E-mail: books@bna.com. Website: www.bnabooks.com. **Acquisitions:** Jim Fattibene, acquisitions manager. Estab. 1929. Publishes hardcover and softcover originals. **Publishes 35 titles/year. Receives 200 submissions/year. 20% of books from first-time authors; 95% from unagented writers. Pays 5-15% royalty on net receipts. Offers $500 average advance.** Publishes book 1 year after acceptance of ms. Accepts simultaneous submissions. Responds in 3 months to queries. Book catalog and ms guidelines free.

> BNA Books publishes professional reference books written by lawyers, for lawyers. Currently emphasizing health law.

Nonfiction: Reference. Subjects include labor and employment law, health law, legal practice, labor relations law, intellectual property law. No fiction, biographies, bibliographies, cookbooks, religion books, humor or trade books. Submit detailed table of contents or outline.

Recent Title(s): *Fair Labor Standards Act; Intellectual Property Law in Cyberspace*.

Tips: "Our audience is made up of practicing lawyers and business executives; managers, federal, state, and local government administrators; unions; and law libraries. We look for authoritative and comprehensive works that can be supplemented or revised every year or two on subjects of interest to those audiences."

BOA EDITIONS, LTD., 260 East Ave., Rochester NY 14604. (716)546-3410. Fax: (716)546-3913. E-mail: boaedit@frontiernet.net. Website: www.boaeditions.org. **Acquisitions:** Steven Huff, publisher/managing editor; Thom Ward, editor. Estab. 1976. Publishes hardcover and trade paperback originals. **Publishes 10 titles/year. Receives 1,000 queries and 700 mss/year. 15% of books from first-time authors; 90% from unagented writers. Pays 8-10% royalty on retail price. Offers $500 advance.** Publishes book 18 months after acceptance of ms. Accepts simultaneous submissions. Responds in 1 week to queries; 4 months to mss. Manuscript guidelines free.

O→ BOA Editions publishes distinguished collections of poetry and poetry in translation. "Our goal is to publish the finest American contemporary poetry and poetry in translation."

Poetry: Accepting mss for publication in 2002 and beyond. Query.

Recent Title(s): *Tell Me*, by Kim Addonizio; *Blessing the Boats*, by Lucille Clifton.

Tips: "Readers who, like Whitman, expect of the poet to 'indicate more than the beauty and dignity which always attach to dumb real objects... They expect him to indicate the path between reality and their souls,' are the audience of BOA's books."

[N] THE BOLD STRUMMER LTD., 20 Turkey Hill Circle P.O. Box 2037, Westport CT 06880-2037. (203)259-3021. Fax: (203)259-7369. Website: www.boldstrummerltd.com. **Acquisitions:** Nicholas Clarke. Estab. 1974. Publishes hardcover and trade paperback originals and reprints. **Publishes 6-8 titles/year. Receives 5 queries and 2 mss/year. 50% of books from first-time authors; 100% from unagented writers. Pays 10% royalty on retail price.** Publishes book 1 year after acceptance of ms. Book catalog and ms guidelines free.

O→ "The Bold Strummer Ltd., or our associate publisher Pro/Am Music resources, publishes most good quality work that is offered in our field(s). BSL publishes guitar and related instrument books (guitar, violin, drums). We are now the sole distributor of Pro/Am's publications."

Nonfiction: Subjects include music/dance (guitar and piano-related books). Query with SASE. Reviews artwork/photos as part of ms package. Send photocopies.

Tips: "Bold Strummer has also become a leading source of books about Flamenco Gypsies. Pro/AM specializes in piano books, composer biography, etc. Very narrow niche publishers."

BOOKWORLD, INC./BLUE STAR PRODUCTIONS, 9666 E. Riggs Rd., #194, Sun Lakes AZ 85248. (480)895-7995. Fax: (480)895-6991. E-mail: bookworldinc@earthlink.net. Website: www.bkworld.com. **Acquisitions:** Barbara DeBolt, editor. Publishes trade and mass market paperback originals. **Publishes 10-12 titles/year. Receives thousands of submissions/year. 75% of books from first-time authors; 90% from unagented writers. Pays royalty.** Responds in 8 months to queries; 16 or more months to mss. Book catalog online; ms guidelines for #10 SASE or online.

O→ Book World, Inc. publishes mainstream and specialty books. Blue Star Productions focuses on UFOs, the paranormal, metaphysical, angels, psychic phenomena, visionary fiction, spiritual—both fiction and nonfiction.

Nonfiction: Subjects include New Age, philosophy, religion, UFO-related subjects, anything pertaining to the paranormal. "To save time and reduce the amount of paper submissions, we are encouraging e-mail queries and submissions (no downloads or attachments), or disk submissions formatted for Windows 95, using Word Perfect or Microsoft Word. Our response will be via e-mail so no SASE will be needed in these instances, unless the disk needs to be returned. For those without computer access, a SASE is a must and we prefer seeing the actual manuscript, a query letter. *No phone queries.*"

Fiction: Fantasy.

Recent Title(s): *Return of the Giants*, by Barry Chamisk; *The Raven's Way*, by Michael Patton.

Tips: "Know our guidelines. We are now accepting manuscripts on disk using WordPerfect 6.0 and higher."

[A] BOULEVARD, Penguin Putnam Inc., 375 Hudson St., New York NY 10014. (212)366-2000. Website: www.penguinputnam.com. **Acquisitions:** Acquisitions Editor. Estab. 1995. Publishes trade paperback and mass market paperback originals and reprints. **Publishes 85 titles/year. Offers advance.** *Accepts agented submissions only.*

BOWLING GREEN STATE UNIVERSITY POPULAR PRESS, Bowling Green State University, Bowling Green OH 43403-1000. (419)372-7866. Fax: (419)372-8095. E-mail: abrowne@bgnet.bgsu.edu. Website: www.bgsu.edu/offices/press/. **Acquisitions:** (Ms.) Pat Browne, director (popular culture). Estab. 1967. Publishes hardcover originals and trade paperback originals. **Publishes 20 titles/year. Receives 350 queries and 75 mss/year. 50% of books from first-time authors; 100% from unagented writers. Pays 5-12% royalty on wholesale price or makes outright purchase. Offers advance.** Publishes book 9 months after acceptance of ms. Responds in 3 months to queries. Book catalog and ms guidelines free.

O→ Bowling Green publishes books on literature and popular culture for an academic audience.

Nonfiction: Biography, reference, textbook. Subjects include Americana, art/architecture, ethnic, history, language/literature, regional, sports, women's issues/studies. Submit outline, 3 sample chapter(s).

Recent Title(s): *Stephen King's America*, by Jonathan Davis.

Tips: "Our audience includes university professors, students, and libraries."

BOYDS MILLS PRESS, *Highlights for Children*, 815 Church St., Honesdale PA 18431-1895. (570)253-1164. Website: www.boydsmillspress.com. Publisher: Kent L. Brown. **Acquisitions:** Larry Rosler, editorial director. Estab. 1990. Publishes hardcover originals and trade paperback reprints. **Publishes 50 titles/year; imprint publishes 2-6 titles/year. Receives 10,000 queries and 7,500 mss/year. 20% of books from first-time authors; 20% from unagented writers. Pays 5-15% royalty on retail price. Offers varying advance.** Accepts simultaneous submissions. Responds in 1 month to queries and mss. Book catalog for $2 postage and SAE; ms guidelines for #10 SASE.

Imprints: Wordsong (poetry)

O→ Boyds Mill Press, the book publishing arm of *Highlights for Children*, publishes a wide range of children's books of literary merit, from preschool to young adult. Currently emphasizing picture books and novels (but no fantasy, romance or horror).

Nonfiction: Children's/juvenile. Subjects include agriculture/horticulture, animals, ethnic, history, nature/environment, sports, travel. "Nonfiction should be accurate, tailored to young audience. Accompanying art is preferred, as is simple, narrative style, but in compelling, evocative language. Too many authors overwrite for the young audience and get bogged down in minutiae. Boyds Mills Press is not interested in manuscripts depicting violence, explicit sexuality, racism of any kind or which promote hatred. We also are not the right market for self-help books." Query with SASE or submit proposal package including outline, 1 sample chapter(s), art samples (photos, drawings). Reviews artwork/ photos as part of ms package.

Fiction: Adventure, ethnic, historical, humor, juvenile, mystery, picture books, young adult. "Don't let a personal agenda dominate to the detriment of plot. In short, tell a good story. Too many writers miss the essence of a good story: beginning, middle, end; conflict and resolution because they're more interested in making a sociological statement." Submit outline/synopsis and 3 sample chapters for novel or complete ms for picture book.

Poetry: "Poetry should be appropriate for young audiences, clever, fun language, with easily understood meaning. Too much poetry is either too simple and static in meaning or too obscure." Collections should have a unifying theme. Submit 6 sample poems.

Recent Title(s): *Sharks! Strange and Wonderful*, by Laurence Pringle; *Groover's Heart*, by Carole Crowe; *Storm Coming!*, by Audrey B. Baird.

Tips: "Our audience is pre-school to young adult. Concentrate first on your writing. Polish it. Then—and only then— select a market. We need primarily picture books with fresh ideas and characters—avoid worn themes of 'coming-of-age,' 'new sibling,' and self-help ideas. We are always interested in multicultural settings. Please—no anthropomorphic characters."

BRANDEN PUBLISHING CO., INC., P.O. Box 812094, Wellesley MA 02482. Fax: (781)790-1056. Website: www.branden.com. **Acquisitions:** Adolph Caso, editor. Estab. 1965. Publishes hardcover and trade paperback originals, reprints and software. **Publishes 15 titles/year. Receives 1,000 submissions/year. 80% of books from first-time authors; 90% from unagented writers. Pays 5-10% royalty on net receipts. Offers $1,000 maximum advance.** Publishes book 10 months after acceptance of ms. Responds in 1 month to queries.

Imprints: International Pocket Library and Popular Technology, Four Seas and Brashear

○── Branden publishes books by or about women, children, military, Italian-American or African-American themes.

Nonfiction: Biography, children's/juvenile, illustrated book, reference, technical, textbook. Subjects include Americana, art/architecture, computers/electronic, government/politics, health/medicine, history, music/dance, photography, sociology, software, classics. Especially looking for "about 10 manuscripts on national and international subjects, including biographies of well-known individuals." No religion or philosophy. *No unsolicited mss.* Paragraph query only with author's vita and SASE. No telephone inquiries, e-mail or fax inquiries. Reviews artwork/photos as part of ms package.

Fiction: Ethnic (histories, integration), religious (historical-reconstructive). No science, mystery or pornography. *No unsolicited mss.* Paragraph query only with author's vita and SASE. No telephone inquiries, e-mail or fax inquiries.

Recent Title(s): *Understanding Surgery*, by Joe Berman; *One Ethereal Winter*, by Marilyn Seguin.

BRASSEY'S INC., 22841 Quicksilver Dr., Dulles VA 20166. (703)661-1548. Fax: (703)661-1547. E-mail: djacobs@bo oksintl.com. Website: www.brasseysinc.com. **Acquisitions:** Don McKeon, publisher (military history, national and international affairs, defense, sports); Don Jacobs, senior assistant editor (general inquiries). Estab. 1984. Publishes hardcover and trade paperback originals and reprints. **Publishes 80 titles/year. Receives 900 queries/year. 30% of books from first-time authors; 80% from unagented writers. Pays 6-12% royalty on wholesale price. Offers $20,000 maximum advance.** Publishes book 1 year after acceptance of ms. Accepts simultaneous submissions. Responds in 2 months to queries. Book catalog free; ms guidelines for 9 × 12 SAE with 4 first-class stamps.

Imprints: Brassey's Sports

○── Brassey's specializes in national and international affairs, military history, biography, intelligence, foreign policy, defense, transportation, reference and sports "We are seeking to build our biography, military history and national affairs lists."

Nonfiction: Biography, coffee table book, reference, textbook. Subjects include government/politics, history, military/ war, sports, world affairs, national and international affairs, intelligence studies. When submitting nonfiction, be sure to include sufficient biographical information (e.g., track records of previous publications), and "make clear in the proposal how your work might differ from other such works already published and with which yours might compete." Query with SASE or submit proposal package including outline, 2 sample chapter(s), author bio, analysis of book's competition. Reviews artwork/photos as part of ms package. Send photocopies.

Recent Title(s): *Legacy of Discord: Voices of the Vietnam War Era*, by Gil Dorland; *Aces in Command: Fighter Pilots as Combat Leaders*, by Walter I. Boyne.

Tips: "Our audience consists of military personnel, government policymakers, and general readers with an interest in military history, biography, national/international affairs, defense issues, intelligence studies and sports."

BRASSEY'S SPORTS, Brassey's Inc., 22841 Quicksilver Dr., Dulles VA 20166. (703)661-1548. Fax: (703)661-1547. E-mail: djacobs@booksintl.com. Website: www.brasseysinc.com. **Acquisitions:** Don McKeon, publisher. Publishes hardcover and trade paperback originals and reprints. **Publishes 80 titles/year. Receives 900 queries/year. 30% of**

books from first-time authors; 80% from unagented writers. Pays 6-12% royalty on wholesale price. Offers maximum $20,000 advance. Publishes book 1 year after acceptance of ms. Accepts simultaneous submissions. Responds in 2 months to queries. Book catalog free; ms guidelines for 9×12 SAE with 4 first-class stamps.

Nonfiction: Sports subjects. Query with SASE. Reviews artwork/photos as part of ms package. Send photocopies.

Recent Title(s): *Baseball Prospectus 2001 Edition*, by Joseph Sheehan, Chris Kahrl, et al (annual reference); *Football's Most Wanted*, by Floyd Conner.

BREAKAWAY BOOKS, P.O. Box 24, Halcottsville NY 12438. (212)898-0408. E-mail: mail@breakawaybooks.c om. Website: www.breakawaybooks.com. **Acquisitions:** Garth Battista, publisher. Publishes hardcover and trade paperback originals. **Publishes 8-10 titles/year. Receives 400 queries and 100 mss/year. 35% of books from first-time authors; 75% from unagented writers. Pays 6-15% royalty on retail price. Offers $2,000-3,000 advance.** Publishes book 9 months after acceptance of ms. Accepts simultaneous submissions. Responds in 1 month to queries and proposals; 2 months to mss. Book catalog and ms guidelines free.

　　O→ "Breakaway Books is a sports literature specialty publisher—only fiction and narrative nonfiction. No how-tos."

Nonfiction: Sports subjects (narrative only, not how-to). Query with SASE or by e-mail.

Fiction: Short story collections (sports stories), sports. Query with SASE or by e-mail.

Recent Title(s): *Metal Cowboy*, by Joe Kurmashie; *Hockey Sur Glace*, by Peter LaSalle (short stories).

Tips: Audience is intelligent, passionately committed to athletes.

BREAKOUT PRODUCTIONS, P.O. Box 1643, Port Townsend WA 98368. (360)379-1965. Fax: (360)379-3794. **Acquisitions:** Gia Cosindas, editor. Publishes trade paperback originals and reprints. **Publishes 6 titles/year. Pays 10-15% royalty on wholesale price. Offers 500-1,500 advance.** Publishes book 6 months after acceptance of ms. Accepts simultaneous submissions. Responds in 1 month to queries; 3 months to proposals and mss. Book catalog and ms guidelines free.

Nonfiction: How-to, self-help, technical. Subjects include agriculture/horticulture, Americana, anthropology/archeology, computers/electronic, creative nonfiction, education, gardening, health/medicine, history, hobbies, military/war, philosophy, psychology, religion, science, sex, travel, unusual jobs, privacy. Query with SASE or submit proposal package including outline, sample chapter(s) or submit complete ms. Reviews artwork/photos as part of ms package. Send photocopies.

Recent Title(s): *Be Your Own Dick—Private Investigation Made Easy*, by John Newman (how-to); *Think Free to Be Free*, by Claire Wolfe (self help).

Tips: "We like the unusual 'take' on things. The author who presents his ideas from an unusual 'road less taken' viewpoint has a better chance than someone who recycles old ideas. We never publish fiction or poetry."

BREVET PRESS, INC., P.O. Box 1404, Sioux Falls SD 57101. **Acquisitions:** Donald P. Mackintosh, publisher (business); Peter E. Reid, managing editor (technical); A. Melton, editor (Americana); B. Mackintosh, editor (history). Estab. 1972. Publishes hardcover and paperback originals and reprints. **Publishes 15 titles/year. Receives 40 submissions/year. 50% of books from first-time authors; 100% from unagented writers. Pays 5% royalty. Offers $1,000 average advance.** Publishes book 1 year after acceptance of ms. Accepts simultaneous submissions. Responds in 2 months to queries. Book catalog free.

　　O→ Brevet Books seeks nonfiction with "market potential and literary excellence."

Nonfiction: Technical. Subjects include Americana, business/economics, history. Query with SASE. "After query, detailed instructions will follow if we are interested." Reviews artwork/photos as part of ms package. Send photocopies.

Tips: "Keep sexism out of the manuscripts."

BREWERS PUBLICATIONS, Association of Brewers, 736 Pearl St., Boulder CO 80302. (303)447-0816. Fax: (303)447-2825. E-mail: bp@aob.org. Website: beertown.org. **Acquisitions:** Toni Knapp, publisher. Estab. 1986. Publishes hardcover and trade paperback originals. **Publishes 8 titles/year. 50% of books from first-time authors; 50% from unagented writers. Pays royalty on net receipts. Offers negotiated advance.** Publishes book 18 months after acceptance of ms. Accepts simultaneous submissions. Responds in 3 months to queries.

　　O→ Brewers Publications is the largest publisher of books on beer-related subjects.

Nonfiction: Biography, humor. Subjects include art/architecture, cooking/foods/nutrition, health/medicine, history, hobbies, language/literature, science. "We publish books on history, art, culture, literature, brewing and science of beer. In a broad sense, this also includes biographies, humor, cooking." Query first with brief proposal and SASE.

Recent Title(s): *Independence Days: Still Just Boys and Other Stories*, by Justin Matott; *Bike and Brew America*, by Todd Mercer (series).

BRIDGE WORKS PUBLISHING CO., Box 1798, Bridge Lane, Bridgehampton NY 11932. (516)537-3418. Fax: (516)537-5092. E-mail: bap@hamptons.com. **Acquisitions:** Barbara Phillips, editor/publisher. Estab. 1992. Publishes hardcover originals and reprints. **Publishes 6-9 titles/year. Receives 1,000 queries and 1,000 mss/year. 50% of books from first-time authors; 50% from unagented writers. Pays 10% royalty on retail price. Offers $1,000 advance.** Publishes book 1 year after acceptance of ms. Responds in 1 month to queries and proposals; 2 months to mss. Book catalog and ms guidelines for #10 SASE.

O➛ "Bridge Works is a small press dedicated to mainstream quality fiction and nonfiction. We have no niche other than the propagation of information, education and entertainment."

Nonfiction: Biography. Subjects include history, language/literature, public policy. "We do not accept multiple submissions. We prefer a query first." Query with SASE or submit proposal package including outline.

Fiction: Literary, mystery, short story collections. "Query with SASE before submitting ms. First-time authors should have manuscripts vetted by freelance editors before submitting. We do not accept or read multiple submissions." Query with SASE or submit 2 sample chapter(s), synopsis.

Poetry: "We publish only *one* collection every five years." Query.

Recent Title(s): *Duty*, by Jim R. Lane; *A Window Facing West*, by John L. Tarlton.

Tips: "Query letters should be one page, giving general subject or plot of the book and stating who the writer feels is the audience for the work. In the case of novels or poetry, a portion of the work could be enclosed. We *do not* publish how-to's, self-help, romances or cookbooks."

BRISTOL FASHION PUBLICATIONS, INC., P.O. Box 20, Enola PA 17025. Website: www.BFPBOOKS.com. **Acquisitions:** John Kaufman, publisher. Publishes trade paperback originals. **Publishes 25 titles/year. Receives 250 queries and 200 mss/year. 50% of books from first-time authors; 100% from unagented writers. Pays 7-11% royalty on retail price.** Publishes book 3 months after acceptance of ms. Responds in 1 month to queries. Book catalog for 6½×9 SAE and 99¢ postage; ms guidelines for #10 SASE.

O➛ Bristol Fashion publishes books on boats and boating.

Nonfiction: General interest relating to boats and boating. How-to, reference. Subjects include history. "We are interested in any title which relates to these fields. Query with a list of ideas. Include phone number. This is a fast changing market. Our title plans rarely extend past 6 months, although we know the type and quantity of books we will publish over the next 2 years. We prefer good knowledge with simple to understand writing style containing a well-rounded vocabulary." Query with SASE. Reviews artwork/photos as part of ms package. Send photocopies or JPEG files on CD.

Fiction: Adventure.

Recent Title(s): *White Squall*; *Complete Guide to Diesel Marine Engines*; *Living Abroad*.

Tips: "All of our staff and editors are boaters. As such, we publish what we would want to read relating to boats. Our audience is generally boat owners or expected owners who are interested in learning about boats, boat repair and boating. Keep it easy and simple to follow. Use nautical terms where appropriate. Do not use complicated technical jargon, terms or formulas without a detailed explanation of same. Use experienced craftsmen as a resource for knowledge."

BRISTOL PUBLISHING ENTERPRISES, 14692 Wicks Blvd., San Leandro CA 94577. Fax: (510)895-4459. Website: bristolcookbooks.com. **Acquisitions:** Pat Hall. Estab. 1988. Publishes trade paperback originals. **Publishes 10-20 titles/year. Receives 100-200 queries/year. 25% of books from first-time authors; 100% from unagented writers. Pays 6% royalty on net proceeds or makes outright purchase. Offers small advance.** Publishes book 1 year after acceptance of ms. Accepts simultaneous submissions. Responds in 4 months to queries. Book catalog online.

Imprints: Nitty Gritty cookbooks, The Best 50 Recipe Series, Pet Care Series

Nonfiction: Cookbook, craft books, pet care books. Subjects include cooking/foods/nutrition. Send a proposal or query with possible outline, brief note about author's background, sample of writing or chapter from ms.

Recent Title(s): *Gourmet Dog Biscuits*; *Cooking With Your Kids*; *The Barbecue Cookbook*.

Tips: Readers of cookbooks are novice cooks. "Our books educate without intimidating. We require our authors to have some form of background in the food industry."

BROADCAST INTERVIEW SOURCE, INC., Free Library, 2233 Wisconsin Ave., NW #301, Washington DC 20007. (202)333-4904. Fax: (202)342-5411. E-mail: davis@yearbooknews.com. Website: www.freelibrary.com. **Acquisitions:** Randal Templeton, travel editor; Simon Goldfarb, information-oriented titles. Estab. 1984. Publishes trade paperback originals and reprints. **Publishes 14 titles/year. Receives 750 queries and 110 mss/year. 20% of books from first-time authors; 40% from unagented writers. Pays 5-15% royalty on wholesale price or makes outright purchase of $2,000-10,000. Offers $2,000 advance.** Publishes book 1 month after acceptance of ms. Accepts simultaneous submissions. Responds in 1 month to queries. Book catalog and ms guidelines free or online.

O➛ Broadcast Interview Source develops and publishes resources for publicists and journalists. Currently emphasizing information/reference. Does not want fiction.

Nonfiction: Biography, cookbook, gift book, how-to, humor, multimedia, reference, self-help, technical, textbook, catalogs, almanacs. Subjects include agriculture/horticulture, Americana, business/economics, computers/electronic, cooking/foods/nutrition, education, history, hobbies, humor, military/war, money/finance, psychology, recreation, religion, translation. Submit proposal package including outline, 3 sample chapter(s).

Recent Title(s): *Baseball Goes to War*.

Tips: "We expect authors to be available for radio interviews at www.radiotour.com."

BROADMAN & HOLMAN, 127 Ninth Ave. N., Nashville TN 37234. (615)251-2392. Fax: (615)251-3752. Publisher: David Shepherd. **Acquisitions:** Leonard G. Goss, editorial director. Estab. 1934. Publishes hardcover and paperback originals. **Publishes 70 titles/year. Pays negotiable royalty.** Responds in 3 months to queries.

Broadman & Holman publishes books that provide biblical solutions that spiritually transform individuals and cultures. Currently emphasizing inspirational/gift books, general Christian living and books on Christianity and society.

Nonfiction: Biography, children's/juvenile, coffee table book, gift book, humor, reference, self-help, textbook. Subjects include anthropology/archeology, business/economics, creative nonfiction, history, memoirs, philosophy, religion (Protestant Evangelical), spirituality. "We are open to freelance submissions in all areas. Materials in these areas must be suited for an evangelical Christian readership." No poetry, biography or sermons. Query with SASE.

Fiction: Religious. "We publish fiction in all the main genres. We want not only a very good story, but also one that sets forth Christian values. Nothing that lacks a positive Christian emphasis (but do NOT preach, however); nothing that fails to sustain reader interest." Query with SASE.

Recent Title(s): *Payne Stewart: The Authorized Biography*, by Tracey Stewart (nonfiction); *To Live is Christ*, by Beth Moore; *In the Shadow of the Cross*, by Ray Pritchard.

BROADWAY BOOKS, Doubleday Broadway Publishing Group, Random House, Inc., 1540 Broadway, New York NY 10036. (212)782-9000. Fax: (212)782-8338. Website: www.broadwaybooks.com. **Acquisitions:** Lauren Marino, executive editor (pop culture, entertainment, spirituality); Suzanne Oaks, senior editor (business); Charles Conrad, vice president and executive editor (general nonfiction); Gerald Howard, vice president/editorial director; Jennifer Josephy (cookbooks); Luke Dempsey, senior editor (sports, media, fiction); Ann Campbell, editor (psychology/self-help, parenting, health). Estab. 1995. Publishes hardcover and trade paperback originals and reprints.

Broadway publishes general interest nonfiction and fiction for adults.

Nonfiction: Biography, cookbook, illustrated book, reference, General interest adult books. Subjects include business/economics, child guidance/parenting, cooking/foods/nutrition, gay/lesbian, general, government/politics, health/medicine, history, memoirs, money/finance, multicultural, New Age, psychology, sex, spirituality, sports, travel (narrative), women's issues/studies, current affairs, motivational/inspirational, popular culture, consumer reference, golf. *Accepts agented submissions only.*

Fiction: Publishes a limited list of commercial literary fiction.

Recent Title(s): *I'm a Stranger Here Myself*, by Bill Bryson; *Bella Tuscany*, by Frances Mayes.

BRYANT & DILLON PUBLISHERS, INC., 100 N. Wyoming Ave., S, Orange NJ 07079. (973)763-1470. Fax: (973)763-2533. E-mail: tatajb@aol.com. **Acquisitions:** James Bryant, editor (women's issues, film, photography). Estab. 1993. Publishes hardcover and trade paperback originals. **Publishes 8-10 titles/year. Receives 500 queries and 700 mss/year. 100% of books from first-time authors; 90% from unagented writers. Pays 6-10% royalty on retail price. Offers advance.** Publishes book 1 year after acceptance of ms. Accepts simultaneous submissions. Responds in 3 months to proposals.

Bryant & Dillon publishes books that speak to an African-American audience and others interested in the African-American experience.

Nonfiction: Biography, how-to, self-help. Subjects include business/economics, education, ethnic, film/cinema/stage, government/politics, history, language/literature, money/finance, women's issues/studies, Black studies, film. "Must be on subjects of interest to African-Americans." No poetry or children's books. Submit cover letter, author's information sheet, marketing information, outline and 3 sample chapters with SASE (envelope large enough for contents sent).

BUCKNELL UNIVERSITY PRESS, Lewisburg PA 17837. (570)577-3674. Fax: (570)577-3797. E-mail: clingham@bucknell.edu. Website: www.departments.bucknell.edu/univ_press. **Acquisitions:** Greg Clingham, director. Estab. 1969. Publishes hardcover originals. **Publishes 35-40 titles/year. Receives 400 submissions/year. 20% of books from first-time authors; 99% from unagented writers. Pays royalty.** Publishes book 12-18 months after acceptance of ms. Responds in 1 month to queries. Book catalog free.

"In all fields, our criteria are scholarly excellence, critical originality, and interdisciplinary and theoretical expertise and sensitivity."

Nonfiction: Subjects include art/architecture, ethnic, government/politics, history, language/literature, philosophy, psychology, religion, sociology, English and American literary criticism, literary theory and cultural studies, historiography (including the history of law, medicine and science), art history, modern languages, classics, anthropology, ethnology, cultural and political geography. Series: Bucknell Studies in Eighteenth-Century Literature and Culture, Bucknell Studies in Latin American Literature and Theory. Eighteenth-Century Scotland. Biannual Journal: *The Bucknell Review: A Scholarly Journal of Letters, Arts, and Science*. Query with SASE.

Recent Title(s): *Interculturalism and Resistance in the London Theatre 1660-1800: Identity, Performance, Empire*, by Mita Choudhury; *Retelling Dostoyevsky: Literary Responses and Other Observations*, by Gary Adelman.

Tips: "An original work of high-quality scholarship has the best chance. We publish for the scholarly community."

BULFINCH PRESS, Little, Brown & Co., 3 Center Plaza, Boston MA 02108. (617)263-2797. Fax: (617)263-2857. Website: www.bulfinchpress.com. Publisher: Carol Judy Leslie. **Acquisitions:** Emily Martin, department assistant. Publishes hardcover and trade paperback originals. **Publishes 60-70 titles/year. Receives 500 queries/year. Pays variable royalty on wholesale price. Offers varies advance.** Publishes book 18 months after acceptance of ms. Accepts simultaneous submissions. Responds in 2 months to proposals.

Bulfinch Press publishes large format art books.

Nonfiction: Coffee table book, gift book, illustrated book. Subjects include art/architecture, gardening, photography. Query with SASE or submit outline, sample artwork. Reviews artwork/photos as part of ms package. Send color photocopies or laser prints.
Recent Title(s): *Ansel Adams at 100*; *Alive*, by Mario Testino.

THE BUREAU FOR AT-RISK YOUTH, P.O. Box 760, Plainview NY 11803-0760. (516)349-5520. Fax: (516)349-5521. E-mail: info@at-risk.com. Website: www.at-risk.com. **Acquisitions:** Sally Germain, editor-in-chief. Estab. 1988. **Publishes 25-50 titles/year. Receives hundreds submissions/year. 100% from unagented writers. Pays 10% maximum royalty on selling price. Offers varies advance.** Publishes book 1 year after acceptance of ms. Accepts simultaneous submissions. Responds in 8 months to queries. Book catalog free if appropriate after communication with author.
    O─┐ Publishes materials on youth guidance topics, such as drugs and violence prevention, character education and life skills for young people in grades K-12, and the educators, parents, mental health and juvenile justice professionals who work with them. "We prefer a workbook/activity book, curriculum, or book/booklet series format."
Nonfiction: Educational materials for parents, educators and other professionals who work with youth. Subjects include child guidance/parenting, education. "The materials we publish are curriculum, book series, workbook/activity books or how-to-oriented pieces tailored to our audience. They are generally not single book titles and are rarely book length." Query with SASE.
Recent Title(s): *Youthlink: Developing Effective Mentoring Programs Curriculum*, by Dr. Nathan Arani.
Tips: "Publications are sold exclusively through direct mail catalog. We do not publish book-length pieces. Writers whose expertise is appropriate to our customers should send query or proposal since we tailor everything very specifically to meet our audience's needs."

BURFORD BOOKS, P.O. Box 388, Short Hills NJ 07078. (973)258-0960. Fax: (973)258-0113. **Acquisitions:** Peter Burford, publisher. Estab. 1997. Publishes hardcover originals, trade paperback originals and reprints. **Publishes 25 titles/year. Receives 300 queries and 200 mss/year. 30% of books from first-time authors; 60% from unagented writers. Pays royalty on wholesale price.** Publishes book 18 months after acceptance of ms. Accepts simultaneous submissions. Responds in 1 month to queries and proposals; 2 months to mss. Book catalog and ms guidelines free.
    O─┐ Burford Books publishes books on all aspects of the outdoors, from gardening to sports, practical and literary.
Nonfiction: How-to, illustrated book. Subjects include agriculture/horticulture, animals, cooking/foods/nutrition, gardening, hobbies, military/war, nature/environment, recreation, sports, travel. Query with SASE or submit outline. Reviews artwork/photos as part of ms package. Send photocopies.
Recent Title(s): *Three-Shot Golf for Women*, by Janet Coles; *Simply Grande Gardening Cookbook*, by Pollard.

BURNHAM PUBLISHERS, (formerly Nelson-Hall Publishers) 111 N. Canal St., Chicago IL 60606. (312)930-9446. Senior Editor: Richard O. Meade. **Acquisitions:** Editorial Director. Estab. 1999. Publishes hardcover and paperback originals. **Publishes 30 titles/year. Receives 200 queries and 20 mss/year. 90% from unagented writers. Pays 5-15% royalty on wholesale price.** Publishes book 1 year after acceptance of ms. Accepts simultaneous submissions. Responds in 1 month to queries.
    O─┐ Burnham publishes college textbooks and, more rarely, general scholarly books in the social sciences.
Nonfiction: Subjects include anthropology/archeology, government/politics, psychology, sociology, criminology. Query with SASE or submit outline, 2 sample chapters, cv.
Recent Title(s): *Cities in the Third Wave*, by Leonard Ruchelman.

N. **BUTTE PUBLICATIONS, INC.**, P.O. Box 1328, Hillsboro OR 97123-1328. (503)648-9791. Fax: (503)693-9526. Website: www.buttepublications.com. **Acquisitions:** M. Brink, president. Estab. 1992. **Publishes 6-8 titles/year. Receives 30 queries and 20 mss/year. 50% of books from first-time authors; 100% from unagented writers. Pays 8-12% royalty on net receipts.** Publishes book 1 year after acceptance of ms. Accepts simultaneous submissions. Responds in 1 month to queries; 4 months to proposals; 6 months to mss. Book catalog and ms guidelines for #10 SASE or online.
    O─┐ Butte publishes classroom books related to deafness and language.
Nonfiction: Children's/juvenile, textbook. Subjects include education (all related to field of deafness and education). Submit proposal package, including author bio, synopsis, market survey and complete ms, if completed. Reviews artwork/photos as part of ms package. Send photocopies.
Recent Title(s): *Fables*, by Paris and Tracy; *Living Legends III*, by Toole.
Tips: "Audience is students, teachers, parents and professionals in the arena dealing with deafness and hearing loss."

C&T PUBLISHING, 1651 Challenge Dr., Concord CA 94520. (925)677-0377. Fax: (925)677-0374. E-mail: ctinfo@ct pub.com. Website: www.ctpub.com. **Acquisitions:** Jan Grigsby, editor. Estab. 1983. Publishes hardcover and trade paperback originals. **Publishes 32 titles/year. Receives 120 submissions/year. 20% of books from first-time authors; 100% from unagented writers. Pays 5-10% royalty on retail price. Offers $1,000 average advance.** Accepts simultaneous submissions. Responds in 3 months to queries. Book catalog and ms guidelines free.
    O─┐ "C&T publishes well-written, beautifully designed books on quilting, dollmaking, fiber arts and ribbonwork."

Nonfiction: How-to (quilting), illustrated book. Subjects include art/architecture, hobbies, quilting books, primarily how-to, occasional quilt picture books, quilt-related crafts, wearable art, needlework, fiber and surface embellishments, other books relating to fabric crafting. "Please call or write for proposal guidelines." Extensive proposal guidelines are also available on their website.
Recent Title(s): *Laurel Burch Quilts*, by Laurel Burch; *Machine Embroidery and More*, by Kristen Dibbs.
Tips: "In our industry, we find that how-to books have the longest selling life. Quiltmakers, sewing enthusiasts, needle artists and fiber artists are our audience. We like to see new concepts or techniques. Include some great examples and you'll get our attention quickly. Dynamic design is hard to resist, and if that's your forte, show us what you've done."

CADENCE JAZZ BOOKS, Cadence Building, Redwood NY 13679. (315)287-2852. Fax: (315)287-2860. E-mail: cjb@cadencebuilding.com. Website: www.cadencebuilding.com. **Acquisitions:** Bob Rusch, Carl Ericson. Estab. 1992. Publishes trade paperback and mass market paperback originals. **Publishes 15 titles/year. Receives 10 queries and 10 mss/year. 90% of books from first-time authors; 100% from unagented writers. Pays royalty or makes outright purchase. Offers advance.** Publishes book 6 months after acceptance of ms. Responds in 1 month to queries.
　　○➤ Cadence publishes jazz histories and discographies.
Nonfiction: Biography, reference. Subjects include music/dance, jazz music biographies, discographies and reference works. Submit outline, sample chapter(s), SASE. Reviews artwork/photos as part of ms package. Send photocopies.
Recent Title(s): *The Earthly Recordings of Sun Ra*, by Robert L. Campbell (discography).

CAMBRIDGE EDUCATIONAL, P.O. Box 931, Monmouth Junction NJ 08852-0931. (888)744-0100. Fax: (304)744-9351. Website: www.cambridgeeducational.com. President: Betsy Sherer. Subsidiaries include: Cambridge Parenting and Cambridge Job Search. **Acquisitions:** Frank Batavick, VP acquisitions. Estab. 1981. Publishes supplemental educational products. **Publishes 30-40 titles/year. Receives 200 submissions/year. 20% of books from first-time authors; 90% from unagented writers. Makes outright purchase of $1,500-4,000. Occasional royalty arrangement.** Publishes book 8 months after acceptance of ms. Accepts simultaneous submissions.
　　○➤ "We are known in the education industry for guidance-related and career search programs." Currently emphasizing social studies and science.
Nonfiction: Subjects include child guidance/parenting, cooking/foods/nutrition, education, health/medicine, money/finance, science, career guidance, social studies. "We are looking for scriptwriters in the same subject areas and age group. We only publish books written for young adults and primarily sold to libraries, schools, etc. We do not seek books targeted to adults or written at high readability levels." Query or submit outline/synopsis and sample chapters. Does not respond unless interested. Reviews artwork/photos as part of ms package.
Recent Title(s): *6 Steps to Getting a Job for People with Disabilities*, by Wayne Forster.
Tips: "We encourage the submission of high-quality books on timely topics written for young adult audiences at moderate to low readibility levels. Call and request a copy of all our current catalogs, talk to the management about what is timely in the areas you wish to write on, thoroughly research the topic, and write a manuscript that will be read by young adults without being overly technical. Low to moderate readibility yet entertaining, informative and accurate."

CAMINO BOOKS, INC., P.O. Box 59026, Philadelphia PA 19102. (215)413-1917. Fax: (215)413-3255. Website: www.caminobooks.com. **Acquisitions:** E. Jutkowitz, publisher. Estab. 1987. Publishes hardcover and trade paperback originals. **Publishes 8 titles/year. Receives 500 submissions/year. 20% of books from first-time authors. Pays 6-12% royalty on net receipts. Offers $1,000 average advance.** Publishes book 1 year after acceptance of ms. Responds in 2 weeks to queries.
　　○➤ Camino publishes nonfiction of regional interest to the Mid-Atlantic states.
Nonfiction: Biography, children's/juvenile, cookbook, how-to. Subjects include agriculture/horticulture, Americana, art/architecture, child guidance/parenting, cooking/foods/nutrition, ethnic, gardening, government/politics, history, regional, travel. Query with SASE or submit outline, sample chapter(s).
Tips: "The books must be of interest to readers in the Middle Atlantic states, or they should have a clearly defined niche, such as cookbooks."

CANDLEWICK PRESS, 2067 Massachusetts Ave., Cambridge MA 02140. (617)661-3330. Fax: (617)661-0565. President/Publisher: Karen Lotz. **Acquisitions:** Yolanda Leroy, editor; Jamie Michalak, associate editor; Joan Powers, editorial director (novelty); Liz Bicknell, editorial director/associate publisher (poetry, picture books, fiction); Mary Lee Donovan, executive editor (nonfiction/fiction); Gale Pryor, editor (nonfiction/fiction); Amy Ehrlich, editor-at-large (picture books). Estab. 1991. Publishes hardcover originals, trade paperback originals and reprints. **Publishes 200 titles/year. Receives 12,000-15,000 submissions/year. 5% of books from first-time authors; 40% from unagented writers. Pays 10% royalty on retail price. Offers varying advance.** Publishes book 1-3 years after acceptance of ms. Accepts simultaneous submissions. Responds in 10 weeks to mss.

FOR INFORMATION on book publishers' areas of interest, see the nonfiction and fiction sections in the Book Publishers Subject Index.

O━ Candlewick Press publishes high-quality, illustrated children's books for ages infant through young adult. "We are a truly child-centered publisher."

Nonfiction: Children's/juvenile. "Good writing is essential; specific topics are less important than strong, clear writing."

Fiction: Juvenile, picture books.

Recent Title(s): *It's So Amazing*, by Robie Harris, illustrated by Michael Emberley (nonfiction); *Because of Winn-Dixie*, by Kate DiCamillo (Newberry Honor Winner); *Weslandia*, by Paul Fleischman, illustrated by Kevin Hawkes (picture book).

CANDYCANE PRESS, Ideals Publications, 535 Metroplex Dr., Suite 250, Nashville TN 37211. (615)333-0478. Publisher: Patricia Pingry. **Acquisitions:** Assistant Editor. **Publishes 20 titles/year. Offers varied advance.** Responds in 2 months to queries.

O━ CandyCane publishes board books and picture books for children ages 3-8.

Fiction: Juvenile, religious, holiday, patriotic themes. Submit complete ms.

Recent Title(s): *Barefoot Days* (children's poetry); *The Story of David* (board book); *Jolly Old Santa Claus*.

CAPSTONE PRESS, P.O. Box 669, Mankato MN 56002. (507)388-6650. Fax: (507)625-4662. Website: www.capstone-press.com. **Acquisitions:** Helen Moore, product planning editor (nonfiction for students grades K-12). Publishes hardcover originals. **Publishes 250-300 titles/year. Receives 100 queries/year. 5% of books from first-time authors. Makes outright purchase; payment varies by imprint. Offers advance.** Responds in 3 months to queries. Book catalog online.

Imprints: Capstone Books, Blue Earth Books, Bridgestone Books, Pebble Books, LifeMatters

O━ Capstone publishes nonfiction children's books for schools and libraries.

Nonfiction: Children's/juvenile. Subjects include Americana, animals, child guidance/parenting, cooking/foods/nutrition, health/medicine, history, military/war, multicultural, nature/environment, recreation, science, sports. "We do not accept proposals or manuscripts. Authors interested in writing for Capstone Press can request an author's brochure." Query with SASE.

Recent Title(s): *Downhill In-Line Skating*, by Nick Cook; *The Nez Perce Tribe*, by Allison Lassieur.

Tips: Audience is made up of elementary, middle school, and high school students who are just learning how to read, who are experiencing reading difficulties, or who are learning English. Capstone Press does not publish unsolicited mss submitted by authors, and it rarely entertains proposals. Instead, Capstone hires freelance authors to write on nonfiction topics selected by the company. Authors may send an SASE to request a brochure.

THE CAREER PRESS, INC., Box 687, 3 Tice Rd., Franklin Lakes NJ 07417. (201)848-0310. Fax: (201)848-1727. Website: www.careerpress.com. President: Ronald Fry. **Acquisitions:** Michael Lewis, acquisitions editor. Estab. 1985. Publishes hardcover and paperback originals. **Publishes 70 titles/year. Receives 300 queries and 1,000 mss/year. 10% of books from first-time authors; 10% from unagented writers. Offers advance.** Publishes book up to 6 months after acceptance of ms.

Imprints: New Page Books

O━ Career Press publishes books for adult readers seeking practical information to improve themselves in careers, college, finance, parenting, retirement, spirituality and other related topics, as well as management philosophy titles for a small business and management audience. New Page Books publishes in the areas of New Age, health, parenting, and weddings/entertaining. Currently de-emphasizing Judaica.

Nonfiction: How-to, reference, self-help. Subjects include business/economics, money/finance, recreation, nutrition. "Look through our catalog; become familiar with our publications. We like to select authors who are specialists on their topic." Query with SASE or submit outline, 1-2 sample chapter(s).

Recent Title(s): *Hollywood Urban Legends*, by Richard Roeper; *100 Ways to Motivate Yourself*, by Steve Chandler.

[N]̃ CAREER PUBLISHING, INC., P.O. Box 5486, Orange CA 92863-5486. (714)771-5155. Fax: (714)532-0180. E-mail: info@careerpubinc.com. Website: www.careerpubinc.com. **Acquisitions:** Christine Blakley, project manager (allied health); Harold Haase, publisher (transportation). Estab. 1972. Publishes paperback originals and reprints and software. **Publishes 5-7 titles/year. Receives 300 submissions/year. 80% of books from first-time authors; 100% from unagented writers. Pays 7½-10% royalty on actual amount received.** Publishes book 1 year after acceptance of ms. Accepts simultaneous submissions. Responds in 2 months to queries. Book catalog and ms guidelines for 9 × 12 SAE with 2 first-class stamps.

O━ Career publishes educational, career-related texts and software for vocational schools and community colleges.

Nonfiction: Textbook. Subjects include computers/electronic, health/medicine, software. "Textbooks should provide core upon which class curriculum can be based: textbook, workbook or kit with 'hands-on' activities and exercises, and teacher's guide. Should incorporate modern and effective teaching techniques. Should lead to a job objective. We also publish support materials for existing courses and are open to unique, marketable ideas with schools (secondary and post secondary) in mind. Reading level should be controlled appropriately—usually 7th-10th grade equivalent for vocational school and community college level courses. Any sign of sexism or racism will disqualify the work. No career awareness masquerading as career training." Submit outline, 2 sample chapter(s), table of contents. Reviews artwork/photos as part of ms package. If material is to be returned, enclose SAE and return postage.

Recent Title(s): *Clinical Laboratory Assistant/Phlebotomist*; *Mental Health Worker: Psychiatric Aide*; *Electrocardiography Essentials.*

Tips: "Authors should be aware of vocational/career areas with inadequate or no training textbooks and submit ideas and samples to fill the gap. Trends in book publishing that freelance writers should be aware of include education—especially for microcomputers."

CAROLRHODA BOOKS, INC., Lerner Publishing Group, 241 First Ave. N., Minneapolis MN 55401. (612)332-3344. Fax: (612)332-7615. Website: www.lernerbooks.com. **Acquisitions:** Rebecca Poole, submissions editor. Estab. 1969. **Publishes 50-60 titles/year. Receives 2,000 submissions/year. 10% of books from first-time authors; 90% from unagented writers. Offers varied advance.** Book catalog for 9 × 12 SAE with $3.50 postage; ms guidelines for #10 SASE.

> O—π Carolrhoda Books is a children's publisher focused on producing high-quality, socially conscious nonfiction and fiction books with unique and well-developed ideas and angles for young readers that help them learn about and explore the world around them.

Nonfiction: Carolrhoda Books seeks creative children's nonfiction. Biography, children's/juvenile, picture books. Subjects include ethnic, nature/environment, science, sports. "We are always interested in adding to our biography series. Books on the natural and hard sciences are also of interest." Query with SASE. Reviews artwork/photos as part of ms package. Send photocopies.

Fiction: Historical, juvenile, picture books, young reader fiction. Query with SASE, send complete ms for picture books.

Recent Title(s): *The War*, by Anais Vaugelade; *Little Wolf's Haunted Hall for Small Horrors*, by Ian Whybrow.

> • Accepts submissions from March 1-31 and October 1-31 only. Submission received at other times of the year will be returned to sender. No phone calls.

Tips: Carolrhoda does not publish alphabet books, puzzle books, songbooks, textbooks, workbooks, religious subject matter or plays.

A CARROLL & GRAF PUBLISHERS INC., Avalon Publishing Group, 161 William St., New York NY 10038. (646)375-2570. Fax: (646)375-2571. Website: www.avalonpub.com. **Acquisitions:** Herman Graf, publisher; Phillip Turner, executive editor; Tina Pholman, senior editor. Estab. 1983. Publishes hardcover and trade paperback originals. **Publishes 120 titles/year. 10% of books from first-time authors. Pays 10-15% royalty on retail price for hardcover, 7½% for paperback. Offers advance commensurate with the work.** Publishes book 9-18 months after acceptance of ms. Responds in a timely fashion to queries. Book catalog free.

> O—π Carroll and Graf Publishers offers quality fiction and nonfiction for a general readership. Carroll and Graf was acquired by Avalon Publishing Group.

Nonfiction: Publish general trade books; interested in developing long term relations with authors. Biography, reference, self-help. Subjects include business/economics, health/medicine, history, memoirs, military/war, psychology, sports, true crime, contemporary culture, true crime. *Accepts agented submissions only.*

Fiction: Literary, mystery, science fiction, suspense, thriller. *Accepts agented submissions only.*

Recent Title(s): *The Last Battle: The Mayaguez Incident and the End of the Vietnam War*, by Ralph Wetterhahn; *According to Queeny*, by Beryl Bainbridge.

N ⊡ CARSON-DELLOSA PUBLISHING CO., INC., P.O. Box 35665, Greensboro NC 27425-5665. (336)632-0084. Fax: (336)632-0087. Website: www.carson-dellosa.com. **Acquisitions:** Wolfgang D. Hoelscher, senior editor. **Publishes 20-30 titles/year. Receives 100 submissions/year. 50% of books from first-time authors; 95% from unagented writers. Makes outright purchase.** Publishes book 1 year after acceptance of ms. Accepts simultaneous submissions. Responds in 2 months to proposals. Book catalog online; ms guidelines free.

Nonfiction: We publish supplementary educational materials, such as teacher resource books, workbooks, and activity books. Subjects include education. No textbooks or trade children's books, please. Submit proposal package including SASE, sample chapters or pages. Reviews artwork/photos as part of ms package. Send photocopies.

Tips: "Our audience consists of pre-K through 8 educators, parents and students. Ask for our submission guidelines and a catalog before you send us your materials. We do not publish fiction or nonfiction storybooks."

CARSTENS PUBLICATIONS, INC., Hobby Book Division, P.O. Box 700, Newton NJ 07860-0700. (973)383-3355. Fax: (973)383-4064. Website: www.carstens-publications.com. **Acquisitions:** Harold H. Carstens, publisher. Estab. 1933. Publishes paperback originals. **Publishes 8 titles/year. 100% from unagented writers. Pays 10% royalty on retail price. Offers advance.** Publishes book 1 year after acceptance of ms. Responds in 2 months to queries. Book catalog for #10 SASE.

> O—π Carstens specializes in books about railroads, model railroads and airplanes for hobbyists.

Nonfiction: Subjects include hobbies, model railroading, toy trains, model aviation, railroads and model hobbies. "Authors must know their field intimately because our readers are active modelers. Writers cannot write about somebody else's hobby with authority. If they do, we can't use them. Our railroad books presently are primarily photographic essays on specific railroads." Query with SASE. Reviews artwork/photos as part of ms package.

Recent Title(s): *150 Years of Train Models*, by Harold H. Carstens; *B&O Thunder on the Alleghenies*, by Dean Mellander.

Tips: "We need lots of good photos. Material must be in model, hobby, railroad and transportation field only."

A CARTWHEEL BOOKS, Scholastic, Inc., 555 Broadway, New York NY 10012. (212)343-6100. Fax: (212)343-4444. Website: www.scholastic.com. Vice President/Editorial Director: Bernette Ford. **Acquisitions:** Grace Maccarone, executive editor; Sonia Black, senior editor; Jane Gerver, executive editor; Sonali Fry, editor. Estab. 1991. Publishes hardcover originals. **Publishes 85-100 titles/year. Receives 250 queries and 1,200 mss/year. 1% of books from first-time authors; 50% from unagented writers. Pays royalty on retail price. Offers advance.** Publishes book 2 years after acceptance of ms. Accepts simultaneous submissions. Responds in 1 month to queries; 4 months to proposals; 6 months to mss. Book catalog for 9×12 SAE; ms guidelines free.

  O→ Cartwheel Books publishes innovative books for children, up to age 8. "We are looking for 'novelties' that are books first, play objects second. Even without its gimmick, a Cartwheel Book should stand alone as a valid piece of children's literature."

Nonfiction: Children's/juvenile. Subjects include animals, history, music/dance, nature/environment, recreation, science, sports. "Cartwheel Books publishes for the very young, therefore nonfiction should be written in a manner that is accessible to preschoolers through 2nd grade. Often writers choose topics that are too narrow or 'special' and do not appeal to the mass market. Also, the text and vocabulary are frequently too difficult for our young audience." *Accepts agented submissions only.* Reviews artwork/photos as part of ms package.

Fiction: Humor, juvenile, mystery, picture books. "Again, the subject should have mass market appeal for very young children. Humor can be helpful, but not necessary. Mistakes writers make are a reading level that is too difficult, a topic of no interest or too narrow, or manuscripts that are too long." *Accepts agented submissions only.*

Recent Title(s): *Clifford's Furry Friends*; *Too Many Rabbits*, by Judith Moffatt.

Tips: Audience is young children, ages 3-9. "Know what types of books the publisher does. Some manuscripts that don't work for one house may be perfect for another. Check out bookstores or catalogs to see where your writing would 'fit' best."

CATHOLIC UNIVERSITY OF AMERICA PRESS, 620 Michigan Ave. NE, Washington DC 20064. (202)319-5052. Fax: (202)319-4985. E-mail: cua-press@cua.edu. Website: cuapress.cua.edu. **Acquisitions:** Dr. David J. McGonagle, director. Estab. 1939. **Publishes 20-25 titles/year. Receives 100 submissions/year. 50% of books from first-time authors; 100% from unagented writers. Pays variable royalty on net receipts.** Publishes book 2 years after acceptance of ms. Responds in 6 months to queries. Book catalog for #10 SASE.

  O→ The Catholic University of America Press publishes in the fields of history (ecclesiastical and secular), literature and languages, philosophy, political theory, social studies, and theology. "We have interdisciplinary emphasis on patristics, medieval studies and Irish studies. Our principal interest is in works of original scholarship intended for scholars and other professionals and for academic libraries, but we will also consider manuscripts whose chief contribution is to offer a synthesis of knowledge of the subject which may be of interest to a wider audience or suitable for use as supplementary reading material in courses."

Nonfiction: Subjects include government/politics, history, language/literature, philosophy, religion, Church-state relations. No unrevised doctoral dissertations. Length: 80,000-200,000 words. Query with outline, sample chapter, cv and list of previous publications.

Recent Title(s): *Mediapolitik: How the Mass Media Have Transformed World Politics*, by Lee Edwards.

Tips: "Scholarly monographs and works suitable for adoption as supplementary reading material in courses have the best chance."

CATO INSTITUTE, 1000 Massachusetts Ave. NW, Washington DC 20001. (202)842-0200. Website: www.cato.org. **Acquisitions:** David Boaz, executive vice president. Estab. 1977. Publishes hardcover originals, trade paperback originals and reprints. **Publishes 12 titles/year. Receives 50 submissions/year. 25% of books from first-time authors; 90% from unagented writers. Makes outright purchase of $1,000-10,000. Offers advance.** Publishes book 9 months after acceptance of ms. Accepts simultaneous submissions. Responds in 3 months to queries. Book catalog free.

  O→ Cato Institute publishes books on public policy issues from a free-market or libertarian perspective.

Nonfiction: Subjects include business/economics, education, government/politics, health/medicine, money/finance, sociology, public policy, foreign policy, monetary policy. Query with SASE.

Recent Title(s): *After Prohibition: An Adult Approach to Drug Policies*, by Lynch; *Global Fortune: The Stumble & Rise of World Capitalism*, by Vasquez.

CAXTON PRESS, 312 Main St., Caldwell ID 83605-3299. (208)459-7421. Fax: (208)459-7450. Website: caxtonpress.com. President: Scott Gipson. **Acquisitions:** Wayne Cornell, managing acquisitions editor (Western Americana, regional nonfiction). Estab. 1907. Publishes hardcover and trade paperback originals. **Publishes 6-10 titles/year. Receives 250/year submissions/year. 50% of books from first-time authors; 60% from unagented writers. Pays royalty. Offers advance.** Publishes book 18 months after acceptance of ms. Accepts simultaneous submissions. Responds in 3 months to queries. Book catalog for 9×12 SAE.

  O→ "Western Americana nonfiction remains our focus. We define Western Americana as almost any topic that deals with the people or culture of the west, past and present." Currently emphasizing regional issues—primarily Pacific Northwest. De-emphasizing "coffee table" or photographic intensive books.

Nonfiction: Biography, children's/juvenile, cookbook, scholarly. Subjects include Americana, history, regional. "We need good Western Americana, especially the Northwest, emphasis on serious, narrative nonfiction." Query. Reviews artwork/photos as part of ms package.

Recent Title(s): *Outlaws of the Pacific Northwest*, by Bill Gulick.

Tips: "Books to us never can or will be primarily articles of merchandise to be produced as cheaply as possible and to be sold like slabs of bacon or packages of cereal over the counter. If there is anything that is really worthwhile in this mad jumble we call the twenty-first century, it should be books."

CCC PUBLICATIONS, LLC, 9725 Lurline Ave., Chatsworth CA 91311. (818)718-0507. **Acquisitions:** Cliff Carle, editorial director. Estab. 1983. Publishes trade paperback originals. **Publishes 40 titles/year. Receives 1,000 mss/year. 30% of books from first-time authors; 50% from unagented writers. Pays 8-12% royalty on wholesale price. Offers variable advance.** Publishes book 6 months after acceptance of ms. Accepts simultaneous submissions. Responds in 3 months to queries. Book catalog for 10×13 SAE with 2 first-class stamps.

> O━ CCC publishes humor that is "today" and will appeal to a wide demographic. Currently emphasizing "short, punchy pieces with *lots* of cartoon illustrations, or very well-written text if long form."

Nonfiction: How-to, humor, self-help. "We are looking for *original*, *clever* and *current* humor that is not too limited in audience appeal or that will have a limited shelf life. All of our titles are as marketable five years from now as they are today. No rip-offs of previously published books, or too special interest manuscripts." Query with SASE or submit complete ms. Reviews artwork/photos as part of ms package.

Recent Title(s): *Your Computer Thinks You're An Idiot*, by Randy Glasbergen.

Tips: "Humor—we specialize in the subject and have a good reputation with retailers and wholesalers for publishing super-impulse titles. SASE is a must!"

N: CELESTIAL ARTS, Ten Speed Press, P.O. Box 7123, Berkeley CA 94707. (510)559-1600. Fax: (510)524-1052. **Acquisitions:** Jo Ann Deck, publisher; Veronica Randall, managing editor/interim publisher. Estab. 1966. Publishes hardcover and trade paperback originals, trade paperback reprints. **Publishes 40 titles/year. Receives 500 queries and 200 mss/year. 30% of books from first-time authors; 10% from unagented writers. Pays 15% royalty on wholesale price. Offers modest advance.** Accepts simultaneous submissions. Responds in 6 weeks to queries. Book catalog and ms guidelines free.

> O━ Celestial Arts publishes nonfiction for a forward-thinking, open-minded audience interested in psychology, self-help, spirituality, health and parenting.

Nonfiction: Cookbook, how-to, reference, self-help. Subjects include child guidance/parenting, cooking/foods/nutrition, education, gay/lesbian, health/medicine, New Age, psychology, women's issues/studies. "We specialize in parenting, women's issues and health. On gay/lesbian topics, we publish nonfiction only. And please, no poetry!" Submit proposal package including outline, 1-2 sample chapter(s), author bio, SASE. Reviews artwork/photos as part of ms package. Send photocopies.

Recent Title(s): *Uncommon Sense for Parents with Teenagers*, by Mike Riera.

Tips: Audience is fairly well-informed, interested in psychology and sociology-related topics, open-minded, innovative, forward-thinking. "The most completely thought-out (developed) proposals earn the most consideration."

CENTERSTREAM PUBLICATIONS, P.O. Box 17878, Anaheim Hills CA 92807. (714)779-9390. Fax: (714)779-9390. E-mail: centerstrm@aol.com. Website: centerstream-usa.com. **Acquisitions:** Ron Middlebrook, Cindy Middlebrook, owners. Estab. 1980. Publishes hardcover and mass market paperback originals, trade paperback and mass market paperback reprints. **Publishes 12 titles/year. Receives 15 queries and 15 mss/year. 80% of books from first-time authors; 100% from unagented writers. Pays 10-15% royalty on wholesale price. Offers $300-3,000 advance.** Publishes book 8 months after acceptance of ms. Accepts simultaneous submissions. Responds in 3 months to queries. Book catalog and ms guidelines for #10 SASE.

> O━ Centerstream publishes music history and instructional books.

Nonfiction: How-to. Subjects include history, music/dance. Query with SASE.

Recent Title(s): *History of Dobro Guitars*.

CHALICE PRESS, P.O. Box 179, St. Louis MO 63166. (314)231-8500. Fax: (314)231-8524. E-mail: chalice@cbp21.com. **Acquisitions:** Dr. David P. Polk, editor-in-chief (religion: general); Dr. Jon L. Berquist, academic editor (religion: academic). Publishes hardcover and trade paperback originals. **Publishes 50 titles/year. Receives 500 queries and 400 mss/year. 15% of books from first-time authors; 100% from unagented writers. Pays 14-18% royalty on wholesale price. Offers $500 advance.** Publishes book 1 year after acceptance of ms. Accepts simultaneous submissions. Responds in 1 month to queries; 2 months to proposals; 3 months to mss. Book catalog and ms guidelines online.

Nonfiction: Textbook. Subjects include religion, spirituality. Submit proposal package including outline, 1-2 sample chapter(s).

Recent Title(s): *Touchstones*, by Scott Colglazier (spirituality).

Tips: "We publish for both professional and lay Christian readers."

N: THE CHARLES PRESS, PUBLISHERS, 117 S. 17th St., Suite 310, Philadelphia PA 19103. (215)496-9616. Fax: (215)496-9637. E-mail: mailbox@charlespresspub.com. Website: www.charlespresspub.com. **Acquisitions:** Lauren Meltzer, publisher. Estab. 1982. Publishes hardcover and trade paperback originals. **Publishes 12-16 titles/year. Receives 2,500 queries and 800 mss/year. Pays 7½-12% royalty. Offers $1,000-8,000 advance.** Publishes book 1 year after acceptance of ms. Accepts simultaneous submissions. Responds in 1 month to queries; 2 months to proposals and mss. Book catalog and ms guidelines free.

> O━ Currently emphasizing true crime, criminology, psychology, suicide and violence.

Nonfiction: Subjects include child guidance/parenting, health/medicine, psychology, religion, sociology, spirituality, counseling, criminology, true crime. No fiction or poetry. Query or submit proposal package, including description of book, intended audience, reasons people will buy it and SASE. Reviews artwork/photos as part of ms package. Send photocopies or transparencies.
Recent Title(s): *How to Identify Suicidal People: A Systematic Approach to Risk Assessment*, by Thomas White.

CHARLES RIVER MEDIA, 20 Downer Ave., Suite 3, Hingham MA 02043-1132. (781)740-0400. Fax: (781)740-8816. E-mail: info@charlesriver.com. Website: www.charlesriver.com. **Acquisitions:** David Pallai, president (networking, Internet related); Jennifer Niles, publisher (computer graphics, animation, game programming). Publishes hardcover and trade paperback originals. **Publishes 30 titles/year. Receives 1,000 queries and 250 mss/year. 20% of books from first-time authors; 90% from unagented writers. Pays 5-30% royalty on wholesale price. Offers $3,000-20,000 advance.** Publishes book 4 months after acceptance of ms. Accepts simultaneous submissions. Responds in 1 month to queries. Book catalog for #10 SASE; ms guidelines online.
> **O—** "Our publishing program concentrates on 3 major areas: Internet, networking, and graphics. The majority of our titles are considered intermediate, not high level research monographs, and not for lowest-level general users."

Nonfiction: Multimedia (Win/Mac format), reference, technical. Subjects include computers/electronic. Query with SASE or submit proposal package including outline, 2 sample chapter(s), résumé. Reviews artwork/photos as part of ms package. Send photocopies or GIF, TIFF or PDF files.
Recent Title(s): *Game Programming Gems*, by Mark DeLoura; *Web Design and Development*, by Kelly Valqui.
Tips: "We are very receptive to detailed proposals by first-time or non-agented authors. Consult our website for proposal outlines. Manuscripts must be completed within 6 months of contract signing."

CHARLESBRIDGE PUBLISHING, School Division, 85 Main St., Watertown MA 02472. (617)926-0329. Fax: (617)926-5720. E-mail: books@charlesbridge.com. Website: www.charlesbridge.com. **Acquisitions:** Elena Dworkin Wright, vice president school division. Estab. 1980. Publishes hardcover and trade paperback nonfiction children's picture books (80%) and fiction picture books for school programs and supplementary materials, trade bookstores, clubs and mass market. **Publishes 20 titles/year. Receives 2,500 submissions/year. 10-20% of books from first-time authors; 80% from unagented writers. Royalty and advance vary.** Publishes book 2 years after acceptance of ms.
> **O—** "We're looking for fiction and nonfiction with literary quality for children grades K-6 (ages 3-12)."

Nonfiction: Children's/juvenile, textbook. Subjects include education, multicultural, nature/environment, science. School or craft books that involve problem solving, building, projects, books written with humor and expertise in the field. Submit complete ms.
Fiction: Non-rhyming stories.
Recent Title(s): *The Ugly Vegetables*, written and illustrated by Grace Lin; *Sir Cumference and the Great Knight of Angleland*, by Cindy Neuschwander.

CHARLESBRIDGE PUBLISHING, Trade Division, 85 Main St., Watertown MA 02472. (617)926-0329. Fax: (617)926-5720. E-mail: tradeeditorial@charlesbridge.com. Website: www.charlesbridge.com. **Acquisitions:** Harold Underdown, editorial director; Yolanda LeRoy, editor. Estab. 1980. Publishes hardcover and trade paperback nonfiction children's picture picture books (80%) and fiction picture books for the trade and library markets, as well as school programs and supplementary materials. **Publishes 30 titles/year. Receives 2,500 submissions/year. 10-20% of books from first-time authors; 80% from unagented writers. Pays royalty. Offers advance.** Publishes book 2-4 years after acceptance of ms.
Imprints: Charlesbridge (8 nonfiction titles/season); Talewinds (2 fiction titles/season); Whispering Coyote (3 fiction titles/season)
> **O—** "We're always interested in innovative approaches to a difficult genre, the nonfiction picture book. No novels or books for older children." Currently emphasizing nature, science, multiculturalism.

Nonfiction: Children's/juvenile. Subjects include animals, creative nonfiction, history, multicultural, nature/environment, science, social science. Strong interest in nature, environment, social studies and other topics for trade and library markets. *Exclusive submissions only.*
Fiction: "Strong, realistic stories with enduring themes." *Exclusive submissions only.*
Recent Title(s): *Footprints on the Moon*, by Alexandra Siy; *Scatterbrain Sam*, by Ellen Jackson, illustrated by Matt Faulkner; *Looking Out for Sarah*, by Glenna Long.

⦿ CHATHAM PRESS, Box A, Greenwich CT 06870. **Acquisitions:** Jane Andrassi. Estab. 1971. Publishes hardcover and paperback originals, reprints and anthologies. **Publishes 10 titles/year. Receives 50 submissions/year. 25% of books from first-time authors; 75% from unagented writers.** Publishes book 6 months after acceptance of ms. Responds in 2 months to queries. Book catalog and ms guidelines for 6×9 SAE with 6 first-class stamps.
> **O—** Chatham Press publishes "books that relate to the U.S. coastline from Maine to the Carolinas and which bring a new insight, visual or verbal, to the nonfiction topic."

Nonfiction: Illustrated book. Subjects include history, nature/environment, regional (Northeast seaboard), translation (from French and German), natural history. Query with SASE. Reviews artwork/photos as part of ms package.
Recent Title(s): *Exploring Old Martha's Vineyard*.

Tips: "Illustrated New England-relevant titles have the best chance of being sold to our firm. We have a slightly greater (15%) skew towards cooking and travel titles."

CHELSEA GREEN PUBLISHING COMPANY, P.O. Box 428, #205 Gates-Briggs Bldg., White River Junction VT 05001-0428. (802)295-6300. Fax: (802)295-6444. Website: www.chelseagreen.com. **Acquisitions:** Alan Berolzheimer, acquisitions editor. Estab. 1984. Publishes hardcover and trade paperback originals and reprints. **Publishes 16-20 titles/ year; imprint publishes 3-4 titles/year. Receives 300-400 queries and 200-300 mss/year. 30% of books from first-time authors; 80% from unagented writers. Pays royalty on publisher's net. Offers $2,500-10,000 advance.** Publishes book 18 months after acceptance of ms. Responds in 1 week to queries; 1 month to proposals and mss. Book catalog and ms guidelines free or online.

Imprints: Real Goods Solar Living Book series

○→ Chelsea Green publishes and distributes books relating to issues of sustainability with a special concentration on books about nature, the environment, independent living and enterprise, organic gardening, renewable energy and alternative or natural building techniques. The books reflect positive options in a world of environmental turmoil. Emphasizing food/agriculture/gardening, innovative shelter and natural building, renewable energy, sustainable business and enterprise. De-emphasizing nature/natural history.

Nonfiction: Biography, cookbook, how-to, reference, self-help, technical. Subjects include agriculture/horticulture, art/ architecture, cooking/foods/nutrition, gardening, health/medicine, memoirs, money/finance, nature/environment, regional, forestry. Query with SASE or submit proposal package including outline, 1-2 sample chapter(s). Reviews artwork/ photos as part of ms package.

Recent Title(s): *The Natural House*, by Daniel D. Chiras; *The Neighborhood Forager*, by Robert K. Henderson; *Grassroots Marketing*, by Shel Horowitz.

Tips: "Our readers are passionately enthusiastic about ecological solutions for contemporary challenges in construction, energy harvesting, agriculture and forestry. Our books are also carefully and handsomely produced to give pleasure to bibliophiles of a practical bent. It would be very helpful for prospective authors to have a look at several of our current books, as well as our catalog and website. For certain types of book, we are the perfect publisher, but we are exceedingly focused on particular areas."

CHELSEA HOUSE PUBLISHERS, Haights Cross Communications, 1974 Sproul Rd., Suite 400, Broomall PA 19008-0914. (610)353-5166. Fax: (610)353-5191. E-mail: chelseahouse@att.net. Website: www.chelseahouse.com. **Acquisitions:** Sarah Bloom, editorial assistant. Publishes hardcover originals and reprints. **Publishes 350 titles/year. Receives 1,000 queries and 500 mss/year. 25% of books from first-time authors; 98% from unagented writers. Makes outright purchase of $1,500-3,500.** Publishes book 16 months after acceptance of ms. Accepts simultaneous submissions. Responds in 1 month to queries; 2 months to proposals and mss. Book catalog online; ms guidelines for #10 SASE.

○→ "We publish education series primarily for the library market/schools."

Nonfiction: Biography (must be common format, fitting under a series umbrella), children's/juvenile. Subjects include Americana, animals, anthropology/archeology, ethnic, gay/lesbian, government/politics, health/medicine, history, hobbies, language/literature, military/war, multicultural, music/dance, nature/environment, recreation, regional, religion; science, sociology, sports, travel, women's issues/studies. "We are interested in expanding our topics to include more on the physical, life and environmental sciences." Query with SASE or submit proposal package including outline, 2-3 sample chapter(s), résumé. Reviews artwork/photos as part of ms package. Send photocopies.

Recent Title(s): *The History of Motown*, by Virginia Aronson (African American Achievers series); *Cameron Diaz*, by Anne E. Hill (Galaxy of Superstars series); *Catch-22*, edited by Harold Bloom (literary criticism).

Tips: "Know our product. Do not waste your time or ours by sending something that does not fit our market. Be professional. Send clean, clear submissions that show you read the preferred submission format."

CHEMICAL PUBLISHING COMPANY, INC., 527 Third Ave., #427, New York NY 10016-4168. (212)779-0090. Fax: (212)889-1537. E-mail: chempub@aol.com. Website: www.chemicalpublishing.com. **Acquisitions:** Ms. S. Soto-Galicia, publisher. Estab. 1934. Publishes hardcover originals. **Publishes 8 titles/year. Receives 20 queries/year. 50% of books from first-time authors; 100% from unagented writers. Pays 10% royalty on retail price or makes negotiable outright purchase. Offers negotiable advance.** Publishes book 8 months after acceptance of ms. Responds in 3 weeks to queries; 5 weeks to proposals; 2 months to mss. Book catalog and ms guidelines free.

○→ Chemical publishes professional chemistry-technical titles aimed at people employed in the chemical industry, libraries and graduate courses.

Nonfiction: How-to, reference, applied chemical technology (cosmetics, cement, textiles). Subjects include agriculture/ horticulture, cooking/foods/nutrition, health/medicine, nature/environment, science, analytical methods, chemical technology, cosmetics, dictionaries, engineering, environmental science, food technology, formularies, industrial technology, medical, metallurgy, textiles. Submit outline, few pages of 3 sample chapter(s), SASE. Reviews artwork/photos as part of ms package.

Recent Title(s): *Cooling Water Treatment, Principles and Practice*; *Harry's Cosmeticology, 8th Edition*; *Library Handbook for Organic Chemists*.

Tips: Audience is professionals in various fields of chemistry, corporate and public libraries, college libraries.

CHICAGO REVIEW PRESS, 814 N. Franklin, Chicago IL 60610-3109. (312)337-0747. Fax: (312)337-5985. E-mail: csherry@ipgbook.com or yuval@ipgbook.com. Website: www.ipgbook.com. **Acquisitions:** Cynthia Sherry, executive editor (general nonfiction, children's); Yuval Taylor, editor (African, African-American and performing arts). Estab. 1973. Publishes hardcover and trade paperback originals and trade paperback reprints. **Publishes 30-35 titles/year. Receives 200 queries and 600 mss/year. 50% of books from first-time authors; 50% from unagented writers. Pays 7-12½% royalty. Offers $1,500-5,000 average advance.** Publishes book 18 months after acceptance of ms. Accepts simultaneous submissions. Responds in 3 months to queries. Book catalog for $3.50; ms guidelines for #10 SASE or online.

Imprints: Lawrence Hill Books, A Capella Books (contact Yuval Taylor)

O─╾ Chicago Review Press publishes intelligent nonfiction on timely subjects for educated readers with special interests.

Nonfiction: Children's/juvenile (activity books only), cookbook (specialty only), how-to. Subjects include art/architecture, child guidance/parenting, cooking/foods/nutrition, creative nonfiction, education, ethnic, gardening (regional), health/medicine, history, hobbies, memoirs, multicultural, music/dance, nature/environment, recreation, regional. Query with outline, toc and 1-2 sample chapters. Reviews artwork/photos as part of ms package.

Recent Title(s): *The Civil War for Kids*, by Janis Herbert.

Tips: "Along with a table of contents and 1-2 sample chapters, also send a cover letter and a list of credentials with your proposal. Also, provide the following information in your cover letter: audience, market and competition—who is the book written for and what sets it apart from what's already out there."

CHILD WELFARE LEAGUE OF AMERICA, 440 First St. NW, 3rd Floor, Washington DC 20001. (202)638-2952. Fax: (202)638-4004. E-mail: books@cwla.org. Website: www.cwla.org. **Acquisitions:** Acquisitions Editor. Publishes hardcover and trade paperback originals. **Publishes 30-50 titles/year. Receives 300 submissions/year. 95% from unagented writers. Pays 0-10% royalty on net domestic sales.** Publishes book 1 year after acceptance of ms. Responds in 3 months to queries. Book catalog and ms guidelines free.

Imprints: CWLA Press (child welfare professional publications), Child & Family Press (children's books and parenting books for the general public)

O─╾ CWLA is a privately supported, nonprofit, membership-based organization committed to preserving, protecting and promoting the well-being of all children and their families.

Nonfiction: Children's/juvenile. Subjects include child guidance/parenting, sociology. Submit complete ms.

Recent Title(s): *An American Face* (children's book); *Seven Sensible Strategies for Drug Free Kids*.

Tips: "We are looking for positive, kid friendly books for ages 3-9. We are looking for books that have a positive message... a feel-good book."

CHILDREN'S PRESS, Scholastic, Inc., 90 Sherman Turnpike, Danbury CT 06816. (203)797-3500. Fax: (203)797-6986. Website: www.grolier.publishing.com. Publisher: John Selfridge. **Acquisitions:** Dina Rubin, managing editor; Andrew Hudak, editor (reference); Wendy Mead, editor (general fiction and nonfiction); Christina Gardeski, editor (emergent and early reading). Estab. 1946. Publishes nonfiction hardcover originals. **Publishes 300 titles/year. Makes outright purchase of $500-1,000.** Publishes book 20 months after acceptance of ms. Book catalog and ms guidelines for #10 SASE.

O─╾ Children's Press publishes 90% nonfiction for the school and library market, and 10% emergent reader fiction and nonfiction. "Our books support textbooks and closely relate to the elementary and middle-school curriculum."

Nonfiction: Biography, children's/juvenile, cookbook, reference. Subjects include animals, anthropology/archeology, art/architecture, ethnic, health/medicine, history, hobbies, multicultural, music/dance, nature/environment, science, sports, general children's nonfiction. "We publish nonfiction books that supplement the elementary school curriculum." No fiction, poetry, folktales, cookbooks or novelty books. Query with SASE.

Recent Title(s): *Extraordinary People of the Harlem Renaissance*, by Hardy and Hardy; *My Book of Me*, by Dana Meachen Rau.

Tips: Most of this publisher's books are developed inhouse; less than 5% come from unsolicited submissions. However, they publish several series for which they always need new books. Study catalogs to discover possible needs.

N **CHILDSWORK/CHILDSPLAY, LLC**, The Guidance Channel, 135 Dupont St., P.O. Box 760, Plainview NY 11803-0760. (516)349-5520. Website: www.childswork.com. **Acquisitions:** Constance Hallinan Lagan, product development coordinator (psychological books and games for use with children). Publishes trade paperback originals and reprints. **Publishes 10-12 titles/year. Receives 250 queries and 50 mss/year. 5% of books from first-time authors; 100% from unagented writers. Makes outright purchase of $500-3,000.** Publishes book 9 months after acceptance of ms. Accepts simultaneous submissions. Responds in 1 month to queries and proposals; 3 months to mss. Book catalog and ms guidelines for 9×12 SAE with 4 first-class stamps.

O─╾ Our target market includes therapists, counselors and teachers working with children who are experiencing behavioral, emotional and social difficulties.

Nonfiction: Psychological storybooks and workbooks, psychological games. Subjects include child guidance/parenting, education, health/medicine, psychology. All books and games are psychologically based and well researched. Query with SASE.

Fiction: Children's storybooks must deal with some aspect of psychological development or difficulty (e.g., ADHD, anger management, social skills, OCD, etc.) "Be in our files (résumé, writing samples) and we will contact you when we develop new projects." Submit complete ms.

Recent Title(s): *Forms for Helping the Socially Fearful Child*, by Hennie M. Shore.

Tips: "Our market is comprised of mental health and education professionals who are primarily therapists, guidance counselors and teachers. A majority of our projects are assignments rather than over-the-transit submissions. Impress us with your writing ability and your background in psychology and education. If submitting rather seeking work on assignment, demonstrate that your work is marketable and profitable."

CHITRA PUBLICATIONS, 2 Public Ave., Montrose PA 18801. (570)278-1984. Fax: (570)278-2223. E-mail: chitra@epix.net. Website: www.Quilttownusa.com. **Acquisitions:** Joyce Libal, senior editor (articles, how-to); Connie Ellsworth, production (patterns, articles); Shalane Weidow, editorial assistant (shows, exhibits, articles). Publishes trade paperback originals. **Publishes 6 titles/year. Receives 70-80 queries and 10-20 mss/year. Pays royalty.** Publishes book 6-12 months after acceptance of ms. Responds in 2 weeks to queries; 3 weeks to proposals; 1 month to mss. Book catalog and ms guidelines for #10 SASE.

О—¬ "We publish quality quilting magazines and pattern books that recognize, promote, and inspire self expression."

Nonfiction: How-to. Subjects include quilting. Query with SASE. Reviews artwork/photos as part of ms package. Send transparencies.

CHOSEN BOOKS PUBLISHING CO., LTD., 3985 Bradwater St., Fairfax VA 22031-3702. (703)764-8250. Fax: (703)764-3995. E-mail: jecampbell@aol.com. Website: www.bakerbooks.com. **Acquisitions:** Jane Campbell, editorial director. Estab. 1971. Publishes hardcover and trade paperback originals. **Publishes 12 titles/year. Receives 500 submissions/year. 15% of books from first-time authors; 99% from unagented writers. Offers small advance.** Publishes book 12-18 months after acceptance of ms. Accepts simultaneous submissions. Responds in 3 months to queries. Manuscript guidelines for #10 SASE.

О—¬ "We publish well-crafted books that recognize the gifts and ministry of the Holy Spirit, and help the reader live a more empowered and effective life for Jesus Christ."

Nonfiction: Subjects include religion. "We publish books reflecting the current acts of the Holy Spirit in the world, books with a charismatic Christian orientation." No New Age, poetry, fiction, autobiographies, biographies, compilations, Bible studies, booklets, academic or children's books. Submit synopsis, chapter outline, résumé, 2 chapters and SASE. No computer disks or e-mail submissions; brief query only by e-mail.

Recent Title(s): *Healing the Nations: A Call to Global Intercession*, by John Sandford.

Tips: "We look for solid, practical advice for the growing and maturing Christian from authors with professional or personal experience platforms. No conversion accounts or chronicling of life events, please. State the topic or theme of your book clearly in your cover letter."

CHRISTIAN ED. PUBLISHERS, P.O. Box 26639, San Diego CA 92196. (858)578-4700. Fax: (858)578-2431. E-mail: lackelson@aol.com. Website: www.christianedwarehouse.com. **Acquisitions:** Dr. Lon Ackelson, senior editor. **Publishes 64 titles/year. Makes outright purchase of 3¢/word.** Responds in 3 months on assigned material to mss. Book catalog for 9×12 SAE with 4 first-class stamps; ms guidelines for #10 SASE.

О—¬ Christian Ed. Publishers is an independent, non-denominational, evangelical company founded nearly 50 years ago to produce Christ-centered curriculum materials based on the Word of God for thousands of churches of different denominations throughout the world. "Our mission is to introduce children, teens, and adults to a personal faith in Jesus Christ and to help them grow in their faith and service to the Lord. We publish materials that teach moral and spiritual values while training individuals for a lifetime of Christian service." Currently emphasizing Bible curriculum for preschool through preteen ages.

Nonfiction: Children's/juvenile. Education, religion subjects. "All subjects are on assignment." Query with SASE.

Fiction: "All writing is done on assignment." Query with SASE.

Recent Title(s): *All-Stars for Jesus: Bible Curriculum for Juniors*.

Tips: "Read our guidelines carefully before sending us a manuscript. All writing is done on assignment only and must be age appropriate (preschool-6th grade)."

CHRISTIAN PUBLICATIONS, INC./HORIZON BOOKS, 3825 Hartzdale Dr., Camp Hill PA 17011. (717)761-7044. Fax: (717)761-7273. E-mail: editors@cpi-horizon.com. Website: www.cpi-horizon.com. **Acquisitions:** David E. Fessenden, managing editor. Estab. 1883. Publishes hardcover, mass market and trade paperback originals. **Publishes 35 titles/year. Receives 300 queries and 600 mss/year. 25% of books from first-time authors; 90% from unagented writers. Pays 5-10% royalty on retail price or makes outright purchase. Offers varying advance.** Publishes book 18 months after acceptance of ms. Accepts simultaneous submissions. Responds in 1 month to queries; 3 months to proposals and mss. Book catalog for 9×12 SAE with 7 first-class stamps; ms guidelines for #10 SASE or online.

Imprints: Horizon Books

О—¬ "Our purpose is to propagate the gospel of Jesus Christ through evangelistic, deeper life and other publishing, serving our denomination and the wider Christian community. All topics must be from an evangelical Christian viewpoint."

Nonfiction: Biography, gift book, how-to, humor, reference (reprints only), self-help, textbook, teen/young adult. Subjects include Americana, child guidance/parenting, humor, religion (Evangelical Christian perspective), spirituality. Query with SASE or submit proposal package, including chapter synopsis, 2 sample chapters (including chapter 1), audience and market ideas, author bio. Reviews artwork/photos as part of ms package. Send photocopies.
Fiction: Historical, humor, mainstream/contemporary, mystery, religious, spiritual, young adult. "We are not considering unsolicited fiction at this time. No poetry."
Recent Title(s): *Reality Check*, by Verla Gillmor (devotional); *Enjoying the Journey*, by Lois Olmstead (Christian living).
Tips: "Please do not send manuscripts without a complete proposal. We do *not* reprint other publishers' material. We are owned by The Christian and Missionary Alliance denomination; while we welcome and publish authors from various denominations, their theological perspective must be compatible with The Christian and Missionary Alliance. We are especially interested in fresh, practical approaches to deeper life—sanctification with running shoes on. Readers are evangelical, regular church-goers, mostly female, usually leaders in their church. Your book should grow out of a thorough and faithful study of Scripture. You need not be a 'Bible scholar,' but you should be a devoted student of the Bible."

CHRONICLE BOOKS FOR CHILDREN, 85 Second St., 6th Floor, San Francisco CA 94105. (415)537-3730. Fax: (415)537-4420. E-mail: frontdesk@chroniclebooks.com. Website: www.chroniclebooks.com/Kids. **Acquisitions:** Victoria Rock, director of Children's Books; Beth Weber, managing editor; Jennifer Vetter, editor; Samantha Dilday, editorial assistant. Publishes hardcover and trade paperback originals. **Publishes 40-50 titles/year. Receives 20,000 submissions/year. 5% of books from first-time authors; 25% from unagented writers. Pays 8% royalty. Offers variable advance.** Publishes book 18 months after acceptance of ms. Accepts simultaneous submissions. Responds in 2-18 weeks to queries; 5 months to mss. Book catalog for 9 × 12 SAE with 3 first-class stamps; ms guidelines for #10 SASE.
- Chronicle Books for Children publishes an eclectic mixture of traditional and innovative children's books. "Our aim is to publish books that inspire young readers to learn and grow creatively while helping them discover the joy of reading. We're looking for quirky, bold artwork and subject matter." Currently emphasizing picture books. De-emphasizing young adult.
Nonfiction: Biography, children's/juvenile (for ages 8-12), illustrated book, picture books (for ages up to 8 years). Subjects include animals, art/architecture, multicultural, nature/environment, science. Query with synopsis and SASE. Reviews artwork/photos as part of ms package.
Fiction: Mainstream/contemporary, multicultural, young adult, picture books, middle grade fiction, young adult projects. Query with synopsis and SASE. Send complete ms for picture books.
Recent Title(s): *The Sketchbook of Thomas Blue Eagle*; *Pet Boy*.
Tips: "We are interested in projects that have a unique bent to them—be it in subject matter, writing style, or illustrative technique. As a small list, we are looking for books that will lend our list a distinctive flavor. Primarily we are interested in fiction and nonfiction picture books for children ages up to eight years, and nonfiction books for children ages up to twelve years. We publish board, pop-up, and other novelty formats as well as picture books. We are also interested in early chapter books, middle grade fiction, and young adult projects."

CHRONICLE BOOKS, 85 Second St., San Francisco CA 94105. (415)537-3730. Fax: (415)537-4440. E-mail: frontdesk@chroniclebooks.com. Website: www.chroniclebooks.com. President: Jack Jensen. **Acquisitions:** Bill LeBlond, editor (cookbooks); Leslie Jonath, editor (lifestyle); Alan Rapp, editor (art and design); Sarah Malarky (licensing and popular culture); Mikyla Bruder, editor (lifestyle); Steve Mockus, editor (popular culture); Debra Lande, editor (gift books); Beth Weber, managing editor (children's). Estab. 1966. Publishes hardcover and trade paperback originals. **Publishes 200 titles/year.** Publishes book 18 months after acceptance of ms. Accepts simultaneous submissions. Responds in 3 months to queries. Book catalog for 11 × 14 SAE with 5 first-class stamps; ms guidelines online.
Imprints: Chronicle Books for Children, GiftWorks (ancillary products, such as stationery, gift books)
- "Inspired by the enduring magic and importance of books, our objective is to create and distribute exceptional publishing that is instantly recognizable for its spirit, creativity and value. This objective informs our business relationships and endeavors, be they with customers, authors, suppliers or colleagues."
Nonfiction: Coffee table book, cookbook, gift book. Subjects include art/architecture, cooking/foods/nutrition, gardening, nature/environment, photography, recreation, regional, design, pop culture, interior design. Query or submit outline/synopsis with artwork and sample chapters.
Recent Title(s): *The Beatles Anthology*, by The Beatles; *Worst-Case Scenario Survival Handbook*, by David Borgenicht and Joshua Piven.

CIRCLET PRESS INC., 1770 Massachusetts Ave., #278, Cambridge MA 02140. (617)864-0492. Fax: (617)864-0663. E-mail: circlet-info@circlet.com. Website: www.circlet.com. **Acquisitions:** Cecilia Tan, publisher/editor. Estab. 1992. Publishes hardcover and trade paperback originals. **Publishes 8-12 titles/year. Receives 50-100 queries and 500 mss/year. 90% from unagented writers. Pays 4-12% royalty on retail price or makes outright purchase Also pays in books, if author prefers.** Publishes book 18 months after acceptance of ms. Accepts simultaneous submissions. Responds in 1 months to queries; 6-18 months to mss. Book catalog and ms guidelines online.
Imprints: The Ultra Violet Library (gay and lesbian science fiction and fantasy "these books will not be as erotic as our others"); Circumflex (erotic and sexual nonfiction titles, how-to and essays)

O— "Circlet Press publishes science fiction/fantasy short stories which are too erotic for the mainstream and to promote literature with a positive view of sex and sexuality, which celebrates pleasure and diversity. We also publish other books celebrating sexuality and imagination with our imprints: The Ultra Violet Library and Circumflex."

Fiction: Erotica, fantasy, gay/lesbian, science fiction, short story collections. "Fiction must combine both the erotic and the fantastic. The erotic content needs to be an integral part of a science fiction story, and vice versa. Writers should not assume that any sex is the same as erotica." Submit full short stories up to 10,000 words between April 15 and August 31. Manuscripts received outside this reading period are discarded. Queries only via e-mail.

Recent Title(s): *Nymph*, by Francesca Lia Block; *Through A Brazen Mirror*, by Delia Sherman.

Tips: "Our audience is adults who enjoy science fiction and fantasy, especially the works of Anne Rice, Storm Constantine, Samuel Delany, who enjoy vivid storytelling and erotic content. Seize your most vivid fantasy, your deepest dream and set it free onto paper. That is at the heart of all good speculative fiction. Then if it has an erotic theme as well as a science fiction one, send it to me. No horror, rape, death or mutilation! I want to see stories that *celebrate* sex and sexuality in a positive manner. Please write for our guidelines as each year we have a specific list of topics we seek."

CITY & COMPANY, 22 W. 23rd St., New York NY 10010. (212)366-1988. Fax: (212)242-0415. E-mail: cityco@ mindspring.com. Website: cityandcompany.com. **Acquisitions:** Helene Silver, publisher. Estab. 1994. Publishes hardcover and trade paperback originals. **Publishes 10 titles/year. Receives 75 queries and 10 mss/year. 50% of books from first-time authors; 75% from unagented writers. Pays 5-10% royalty on wholesale price. Offers advance.** Publishes book 6 months after acceptance of ms. Accepts simultaneous submissions. Responds in 3 months to queries. Book catalog free.

O— City & Company specializes in single subject New York city guide books.

Nonfiction: Gift book, illustrated book, reference. Subjects include child guidance/parenting, gardening, music/dance, nature/environment, recreation, regional, sports, travel, single subject city guide. Must have New York focus. Submit proposal package including outline, 3 sample chapter(s), author bio. Reviews artwork/photos as part of ms package.

CLARION BOOKS, 215 Park Ave. S., New York NY 10003. **Acquisitions:** Dinah Stevenson, editorial director. Estab. 1965. Publishes hardcover originals for children. **Publishes 50 titles/year. Pays 5-10% royalty on retail price. Offers minimum of $4,000 advance.** Publishes book 2 years after acceptance of ms. Responds in 2 months to queries. Prefers no multiple submissions to mss. Manuscript guidelines for #10 SASE.

O— Clarion Books publishes picture books, nonfiction, and fiction for infants through grade 12. Avoid telling your stories in verse unless you are a professional poet.

Nonfiction: Biography, children's/juvenile, photo essay. Subjects include Americana, history, language/literature, nature/environment, photography, holiday. *No unsolicited mss.* Query with SASE or submit proposal package including sample chapter(s), SASE. Reviews artwork/photos as part of ms package. Send photocopies.

Fiction: Adventure, historical, humor, mystery, suspense, strong character studies. Clarion is highly selective in the areas of historical fiction, fantasy, and science fiction. A novel must be superlatively written in order to find a place on the list. Manuscripts that arrive without an SASE of adequate size will *not* be responded to or returned. Accepts fiction translations. *No unsolicited mss.* Submit complete ms.

Recent Title(s): *In the Days of the Vaqueros: America's First True Cowboys*, by Russell Freedman (nonfiction); *Matilda Bone*, by Karen Cushman (fiction); *Toasting Marshmallows*, by Kristine O'Connell George (poetry).

Tips: Looks for "freshness, enthusiasm—in short, life."

CLEAR LIGHT PUBLISHERS, 823 Don Diego, Santa Fe NM 87501-4224. (505)989-9590. E-mail: clpublish@aol.c om. **Acquisitions:** Harmon Houghton, publisher. Estab. 1981. Publishes hardcover and trade paperback originals. **Publishes 20-24 titles/year. Receives 100 queries/year. 10% of books from first-time authors; 50% from unagented writers. Pays 10% royalty on wholesale price. Offers advance, a percent of gross potential.** Publishes book 1 year after acceptance of ms. Accepts simultaneous submissions. Responds in 3 months to queries. Book catalog free.

O— Clear Light publishes books that "accurately depict the positive side of human experience and inspire the spirit."

Nonfiction: Biography, coffee table book, cookbook. Subjects include Americana, anthropology/archeology, art/architecture, cooking/foods/nutrition, ethnic, history, nature/environment, philosophy, photography, regional (Southwest). Query with SASE. Reviews artwork/photos as part of ms package. Send photocopies.

Recent Title(s): *Utopian Legacies*, by John Mohawk; *Native Science*, by Gregory Cajete.

CLEIS PRESS, P.O. Box 14684, San Francisco CA 94114-0684. (415)575-4700. Fax: (415)575-4705. Website: www.cl eispress.com. **Acquisitions:** Frederique Delacoste. Estab. 1980. Publishes trade paperback originals and reprints. **Publishes 20 titles/year. 10% of books from first-time authors; 90% from unagented writers. Pays variable royalty on retail price.** Publishes book 2 years after acceptance of ms. Responds in 1 month to queries. Book catalog for #10 SAE with 2 first-class stamps.

O— Cleis Press specializes in gay/lesbian fiction and nonfiction.

Nonfiction: Subjects include ethnic, gay/lesbian, government/politics, sociology, women's issues/studies, Human Rights. "We are interested in books by and about women in Latin America; on lesbian and gay rights; on sexuality;

topics which have not already been widely documented. We do not want religious/spiritual tracts; we are not interested in books on topics which have been documented over and over, unless the author is approaching the topic from a new viewpoint." Query or submit outline and sample chapters.

Fiction: Feminist, gay/lesbian, literary. "We are looking for high quality fiction by women and men." No romances. Submit complete ms. *Writer's Market* recommends sending a query with SASE first.

Recent Title(s): *Gore Vidal: Sexually Speaking* (nonfiction); *The Woman Who Rode to the Moon*, by Bett Reece Johnson (fiction).

Tips: "Be familiar with publishers' catalogs; be absolutely aware of your audience; research potential markets; present fresh new ways of looking at your topic; avoid 'PR' language and include publishing history in query letter."

CLOUD PEAK, 730 W. 51st St., Casper WY 82601. E-mail: pharwitz@isis-intl.com. **Acquisitions:** Paul Harwitz. Publishes hardcover, trade paperback and mass market paperback originals and reprints. **Publishes 36 titles/year. Receives 200 queries and 80 mss/year. 10% of books from first-time authors; 50% from unagented writers. Pays 10% royalty for nonfiction; percentage for fiction varies.** Publishes book 1-2 years after acceptance of ms. Accepts simultaneous submissions. Responds in 2 months to queries and mss; 3 months to proposals. Book catalog and ms guidelines for #10 SASE or online.

    O— Cloud Peak is currently emphasizing nonfiction books about Indians, African-Americans, Asians, Hispanics and other "minorities" in the West.

Nonfiction: Biography, children's/juvenile, how-to, humor. Subjects include Americana (Western), education, history, humor, military/war, multicultural, sports, women's issues/studies. "Submissions to our 'Women of the West' line of nonfiction will receive special consideration." Query with SASE. *All unsolicited mss returned unopened.* Reviews artwork/photos as part of ms package. Send photocopies, transparencies or computer files on 3.5-inch disk.

Fiction: Adventure, fantasy, historical, horror, humor, juvenile, military/war, multicultural, multimedia, mystery, poetry, science fiction, suspense, western, Native American. "Do everything you can to make the book a real 'page-turner,' Plots and sub-plots must be plausible and suited to the locale(s). Main and secondary characters must speak dialog which matches their respective personality traits. Blacks, Spanish-speaking people and other 'minorities' must *not* be portrayed stereotypically. Historical accuracy is important." Query with SASE. *All unsolicited mss returned unopened.*

Poetry: "We publish Western/cowboy/Indian poetry in single-author collections and multi-author anthologies." Query or submit 3 sample poems or submit complete ms.

Recent Title(s): *Soldiers Falling Into Camp: The Battles at the Rosebud and Little Bighorn*, by Robert Kammen, Frederick Lefthand and Joe Marshall (military history); *The Watcher*, by Robert Kammen (Western/supernatural/ecological); *Riders of the Leafy Spurge*, by Bill Lowman (cowboy poetry).

Tips: "Buy, read and study the *Writer's Market* each year. Writing must flow. Imagine you are a reader visiting a bookstore. Write the first page of the book in such a way that the reader feels *compelled* to buy it. It helps a writer to work from an outline. When we solicit a manuscript for consideration, we like to receive both a hard copy and a floppy disk."

COACHES CHOICE, P.O. Box 1828, Monterey CA 93942. (888)229-5745. Fax: (831)372-6075. E-mail: info@healthylearning.com. Website: www.coacheschoiceweb.com. **Acquisitions:** Sue Peterson, general manager (sports); Jim Peterson, director of acquisitions (sports); Shannon Koprowski, director of operations. Publishes trade paperback originals and reprints. **Publishes 40 titles/year. Receives 100 queries and 60 mss/year. 50% of books from first-time authors; 95% from unagented writers. Pays 10-15% royalty.** Publishes book 1 year after acceptance of ms. Accepts simultaneous submissions. Responds in 2 months to queries. Book catalog and ms guidelines free.

    O— "We publish books for anyone who coaches a sport or has an interest in coaching a sport—all levels of competition."

Nonfiction: How-to, reference. Subjects include sports, sports specific training, general physical conditioning. Submit proposal package including outline, 2 sample chapter(s), résumé. Reviews artwork/photos as part of ms package. Send photocopies or diagrams.

Recent Title(s): *Coaching the Multiple West Coast Offense*, by Ron Jenkins.

COASTAL CAROLINA PRESS, 2231 Wrightsville Ave., Wilmington NC 28403. (877)817-9900. E-mail: books@coastalcarolinapress.org. Website: www.coastalcarolinapress.org. **Acquisitions:** Editorial Department. Publishes hardcover, trade and mass market paperback originals and reprints. **Publishes 6-8 titles/year. 70% of books from first-time authors; 100% from unagented writers. Pays royalty.** Book catalog and ms guidelines online.

    O— "We are a nonprofit corporation dedicated to publishing materials about the history, culture and activities of coastal North and South Carolina. We do not publish poetry or religious titles."

Nonfiction: Publishes books with a regional niche. Cookbook, folklore. Subjects include education, ethnic, gardening, history, nature/environment, photography, recreation, essays, guides, film. Query with SASE.

Fiction: Publishes books with a regional niche. Humor, juvenile, mystery, regional, young adult. Query with SASE.

Recent Title(s): *Coastal Waters: Images of North Carolina*, by Scott Taylor; *Island Murders*, by Wanda Canada.

COFFEE HOUSE PRESS, 27 N. Fourth St., Suite 400, Minneapolis MN 55401. Fax: (612)338-4004. Publisher: Allan Kornblum. **Acquisitions:** Chris Fischbach, managing editor. Estab. 1984. Publishes hardcover and trade paperback originals. **Publishes 14 titles/year. Receives 5,000 queries and 3,000 mss/year. 75% from unagented writers. Pays 8% royalty on retail price.** Publishes book 18 months after acceptance of ms. Responds in 1 month to queries; up to 6 months to mss. Book catalog and ms guidelines for #10 SASE with 2 first-class stamps.

Fiction: Literary, short story collections, novels. No genre. Query first with samples and SASE.

Poetry: Full-length collections.

Recent Title(s): *Our Sometime Sister*, by Norah Labiner (fiction); *Avalanche*, by Quincy Troupe (poetry).

Tips: "Look for our books at stores and libraries to get a feel for what we publish. No phone calls, e-mails, or faxes."

COLLECTORS PRESS, INC., P.O. Box 230986, Portland OR 97281-0986. (503)684-3030. Fax: (503)684-3777. Website: www.collectorspress.com. **Acquisitions:** Richard Perry, publisher. Estab. 1992. Publishes hardcover and trade paperback originals. **Publishes 20 titles/year. Receives 500 queries and 200 mss/year. 75% of books from first-time authors; 75% from unagented writers. Pays royalty.** Publishes book 1 year after acceptance of ms. Responds in 1 month to queries. Book catalog and ms guidelines free.

    O⌐ Collectors Press Inc. publishes award-winning popular-culture coffee table and gift books on 20th century and modern collections and interests.

Nonfiction: Illustrated book, reference. Subjects include art/architecture, photography, science-fiction art, fantasy art, graphic design, comic art, magazine art, historical art, poster art, genre specific art. Submit proposal package, including market research, outline, 2 sample chapters and SASE. Reviews artwork/photos as part of ms package. Send transparencies or *very* clear photos.

Recent Title(s): *Science Fiction of the 20th Century: An Illustrated History.*

Tips: "Your professional package must be typed. No computer disks accepted."

N: THE COLLEGE BOARD, College Entrance Examination Board, 45 Columbus Ave., New York NY 10023-6992. (212)713-8000. Website: www.collegeboard.com. **Acquisitions:** Thomas Vanderberg, director of publications. Publishes trade paperback originals. **Publishes 30 titles/year. Receives 60 submissions/year. 25% of books from first-time authors; 50% from unagented writers. Pays royalty on retail price. Offers advance.** Publishes book 9 months after acceptance of ms. Responds in 2 months to queries. Book catalog free.

    O⌐ The College Board publishes guidance information for college-bound students.

Nonfiction: "We want books to help students make a successful transition from high school to college." Humor, reference. Subjects include education, college guidance. Query with SASE or submit outline, sample chapter(s), SASE.

Recent Title(s): *Paying for College*, by Gerald Krefetz.

COLLEGE PRESS PUBLISHING COMPANY, P.O. Box 1132, Joplin MO 64802. (417)623-6280. Website: www.collegepress.com. **Acquisitions:** Acquisitions Editor. Estab. 1959. Publishes hardcover and trade paperback originals and reprints. **Publishes 25-30 titles/year. Receives 400 queries and 300 mss/year. 25% of books from first-time authors; 90% from unagented writers. Pays 5-15% royalty on wholesale price.** Publishes book 6 months after acceptance of ms. Accepts simultaneous submissions. Responds in 3 months to proposals. Book catalog for 9×12 SAE with 5 first-class stamps; ms guidelines for #10 SASE.

    O⌐ "College Press is an evangelical Christian publishing house primarily associated with the Christian churches/Church of Christ."

Nonfiction: "We seek textbooks used in Christian colleges and universities—leaning toward an Arminian and an amillennial mindset." Textbook (Christian textbooks and small group studies). Subjects include religion, Christian apologetics. Query with SASE or submit proposal package including 3 sample chapter(s), author bio, synopsis.

Recent Title(s): *Making Your Church a Place to Serve*, by Don Waddell.

Tips: "Our core market is Christian Churches/Churches of Christ and conservative evangelical Christians. Have your material critically reviewed prior to sending it. Make sure that it is non-Calvinistic and that it leans more amillennial (if it is apocalyptic writing)."

COMBINED PUBLISHING, INC., Perseus Publishing, 476 W. Elm St., P.O. Box 307, Conshohocken PA 19428. (610)828-2595. Fax: (610)828-2603. E-mail: combined@combinedpublishing.com. Website: www.combinedpublishing.com. President: Robert Pigeon. **Acquisitions:** Kenneth S. Gallagher, senior editor. Estab. 1985. Publishes hardcover originals and trade paperback reprints. **Publishes 12-14 titles/year. 30% of books from first-time authors; 100% from unagented writers. Pays 8-10% royalty on wholesale price. Offers $1,000-1,500 advance.** Publishes book 1 year after acceptance of ms. Responds in 4 months to queries. Book catalog free.

    O⌐ "Our focus is military nonfiction, usually books of about 75,000 words. Civil War and World War II are the periods most heavily covered. We publish a series called Great Campaigns. Authors should be aware of the editorial formula of this series."

Nonfiction: Subjects include military/war (military history). Submit outline, 1 sample chapter(s), SASE. Reviews artwork/photos as part of ms package. Send photocopies.

    ● Combined Publishing has been purchased by Perseus Publishing.

Recent Title(s): *Joshua Chamberlain*, by Edward G. Longacre.

◼ COMMON COURAGE PRESS, One Red Barn Rd., Box 702, Monroe ME 04951. (207)525-0900 or (800)497-3207. Fax: (207)525-3068. E-mail: orders-info@commoncouragepress.com. Website: www.commoncouragepress.com. **Acquisitions:** Ms. Flic Shooter, publisher (leftist political literature). Publishes hardcover and trade paperback originals and trade paperback reprints. **Publishes 12 titles/year. Receives 50 queries and 200 mss/year. 50% of books from first-time authors; 100% from unagented writers. Pays 10% royalty on wholesale price. Offers advance.** Publishes book 9 months after acceptance of ms. Accepts simultaneous submissions. Responds in 1 month to queries. Book catalog and ms guidelines online.

○┓ "Nonfiction leftist, activist, political, history, feminist, media issues are our niche."

Nonfiction: Biography, humor, illustrated book, reference, textbook. Subjects include anthropology/archeology, creative nonfiction, ethnic, gay/lesbian, government/politics, health/medicine, history, humor, military/war, multicultural, nature/environment, science, spirituality. Query with SASE or submit proposal package, including outline or submit completed ms. Reviews artwork/photos as part of ms package.

Poetry: Activist only. Submit 10 sample poems or submit complete ms.

Recent Title(s): *New Military Humanism*, by Noam Chomsky (leftist political); *Habits of Highly Deceptive Media*, by Norman Solomon (media bias).

Tips: Audience consists of left-wing activists, college audiences.

[N] CONARI PRESS, 2550 Ninth St., Suite 101, Berkeley CA 94710. (510)649-7175. Fax: (510)649-7190. E-mail: conari@conari.com. Website: www.conari.com. **Acquisitions:** Julie Kessler, editorial assistant (spirituality, personal growth relationships, women's issues, family, inspiration). Publishes hardcover and trade paperback originals and trade paperback reprints. **Publishes 35 titles/year. Receives 600 queries and 500 mss/year. Pays royalty.** Publishes book 6-12 months after acceptance of ms. Accepts simultaneous submissions. Responds in 3 months to queries, proposals and mss. Book catalog and ms guidelines free.

Nonfiction: Cookbook, gift book, self-help. Subjects include animals, child guidance/parenting, cooking/foods/nutrition, education, ethnic, gardening, gay/lesbian, health/medicine, history, hobbies, memoirs, money/finance, multicultural, nature/environment, psychology, religion, science, sex, sociology, spirituality, travel, women's issues/studies. Submit proposal package including outline, 2-3 sample chapter(s), SASE.

Recent Title(s): *Memoirs of a Spiritual Outsider*, by Suzanne Clores (memoir); *The Book of Awakening*, by Mark Nepo (spirituality).

CONCORDIA PUBLISHING HOUSE, 3558 S. Jefferson Ave., St. Louis MO 63118-3968. (314)268-1187. Fax: (314)268-1329. E-mail: Brandy.overton@cph.org. Website: www.cph.org. **Acquisitions:** Jane Wilke, acquisitions editor (children's product, adult devotional, teaching resources); Ken Wagener, acquistions editor (adult nonfiction on Christian spirituality and culture, academic works of interest in Lutheran markets). Estab. 1869. Publishes hardcover and trade paperback originals. **Publishes 75 titles/year. Receives 2,500 submissions/year. 10% of books from first-time authors; 95% from unagented writers. Pays royalty or makes outright purchase.** Publishes book 15 months after acceptance of ms. Responds in 3 months to queries.

○┓ Concordia publishes Protestant, inspirational, theological, family and juvenile material. All manuscripts must conform to the doctrinal tenets of The Lutheran Church—Missouri Synod. Currently emphasizing practical parenting books. No longer publishes fiction.

Nonfiction: Children's/juvenile, how-to, humor, adult. Subjects include child guidance/parenting (in Christian context), religion, inspirational. Query with SASE.

Recent Title(s): *Every Day is Saturday*, by L. James and Jackie Harvey (nonfiction); *The Sermon on the Mount*, by David Scaer (academic).

Tips: "Our needs have broadened to include writers of books for lay adult Christians."

CONSORTIUM PUBLISHING, 640 Weaver Hill Rd., West Greenwich RI 02817-2261. (401)397-9838. Fax: (401)392-1926. John M. Carlevale, chief of publications. Estab. 1990. Publishes trade paperback originals and reprints. **Publishes 12 titles/year. Receives 150 queries and 50 mss/year. 50% of books from first-time authors; 95% from unagented writers. Pays 10-15% royalty.** Publishes book 3 months after acceptance of ms. Responds in 2 months to queries. Book catalog and ms guidelines for #10 SASE.

○┓ Consortium publishes books for all levels of the education market.

Nonfiction: How-to, humor, illustrated book, reference, self-help, technical, textbook. Subjects include business/economics, child guidance/parenting, education, government/politics, health/medicine, history, music/dance, nature/environment, psychology, science, sociology, women's issues/studies. Query or submit proposal package, including table of contents, outline, 1 sample chapter and SASE. Reviews artwork/photos as part of ms package. Send photocopies.

Recent Title(s): *Teaching the Child Under Six, 4th edition*, by James L. Hymes, Jr (education).

Tips: Audience is college and high school students and instructors, elementary school teachers and other trainers.

CONTEMPORARY BOOKS, McGraw-Hill Company, 4255 W. Touhy Ave., Lincolnwood IL 60712. (847)679-5500. Fax: (847)679-2494. Website: www.mcgraw-hill.com. Vice President and Publisher-Trade Division: John T. Nolan. **Acquisitions:** Danielle Egan-Miller, business editor; Rob Taylor, associate editor; Denise Betts, assistant editor; Betsy Lancefield, senior editor. Estab. 1947. Publishes hardcover originals and trade paperback originals and reprints. **Publishes 300 titles/year. Receives 5,000 submissions/year. 10% of books from first-time authors; 25% from unagented writers. Pays 6-15% royalty on retail price. Offers advance.** Publishes book 1 year after acceptance of ms. Accepts simultaneous submissions. Responds in 2 months to queries. Manuscript guidelines for #10 SASE.

Imprints: Contemporary Books, Keats Publishing, Lowell House, NTC Business Books, NTC Publishing Group, Passport Books, The Quilt Digest Press, VGM Career Horizons

O— "We are a midsize, niche-oriented, backlist-oriented publisher. We publish exclusively nonfiction in general interest trade categories."

Nonfiction: Biography, cookbook, how-to, reference, self-help. Subjects include business/economics, cooking/foods/ nutrition, health/medicine, money/finance, psychology, sports, women's issues/studies. Query with SASE or submit outline, sample chapter(s). Reviews artwork/photos as part of ms package.

Recent Title(s): *Raising Resilient Children*, by Robert Brooks and Sam Goldstein; *Bob Feller's Little Black Book of Baseball Wisdom.*

COOK COMMUNICATIONS, (formerly Chariot/Victor Publishing), 4050 Lee Vance View, Colorado Springs CO 80918. (719)536-3271. Fax: (719)536-3269. **Acquisitions:** Sheila Lapora, editorial assistant. Estab. 1875. Publishes hardcover and trade paperback originals. **Publishes 150 titles/year. 10% of books from first-time authors; 50% from unagented writers. Pays variable royalty on net price. Offers varied advance.** Publishes book 1-2 years after acceptance of ms. Accepts simultaneous submissions. Responds in 3 months to queries. Book catalog for #10 SASE.

Imprints: Faith Books (children), Rainfall (toys, media, games), Victor, Faith Parenting, Faith Marriage and Faithful Woman

O— Cook Communications publishes children's and family spiritual growth books. Books "must have strong under-lying Christian themes or clearly stated Biblical value."

Nonfiction: Biography, children's/juvenile. Subjects include child guidance/parenting, history, religion. Query with SASE.

Fiction: Juvenile.

Recent Title(s): *Follow Your Heart*, by Judy Peterson (nonfiction); *Loving a Prodigal*, by Norm Wright (family issues).

Tips: "All books must in some way be Bible-related by authors who themselves are evangelical Christians with a platform. Only a small fraction of the manuscripts received can be seriously considered for publication. Most books result from contacts that acquisitions editors make with qualified authors, though from time to time an unsolicited proposal triggers enough excitement to result in a contract. A writer has the best chance of selling Cook a well-conceived and imaginative manuscript that helps the reader apply Christianity to her life in practical ways. Christians active in the local church and their children are our audience."

CORNELL MARITIME PRESS, INC., P.O. Box 456, Centreville MD 21617-0456. (410)758-1075. Fax: (410)758-6849. E-mail: cornell@crosslink.net. **Acquisitions:** Charlotte Kurst, managing editor. Estab. 1938. Publishes hardcover originals and quality paperbacks. **Publishes 7-9 titles/year. Receives 150 submissions/year. 80% of books from first-time authors; 99% from unagented writers.** Publishes book 1 year after acceptance of ms. Responds in 2 months to queries. Book catalog for 10×13 SAE with 5 first-class stamps.

Imprints: Tidewater (regional history, folklore and wildlife of the Chesapeake Bay and the Delmarva Peninsula)

O— Cornell Maritime Press publishes books for the merchant marine and a few recreational boating books for professional mariners and yachtsmen.

Nonfiction: How-to (on maritime subjects), technical, manuals. Subjects include marine subjects (highly technical). Query first, with writing samples and outlines of book ideas.

Recent Title(s): *The Business of Shipping, Seventh Edition*, by Lane C. Kendall and James J. Buckley.

CORNELL UNIVERSITY PRESS, Sage House, 512 E. State St., Ithaca NY 14850. (607)277-2338. Fax: (607)277-2374. Website: www.cornellpress.cornell.edu. **Acquisitions:** Frances Benson, editor-in-chief. Estab. 1869. Publishes hardcover and paperback originals. **Publishes 150 titles/year. Pays royalty. Offers $0-5,000 advance.** Publishes book 1 year after acceptance of ms. Accepts simultaneous submissions. Book catalog and ms guidelines online.

Imprints: Comstock (contact Peter J. Prescott, science editor), ILR Press

O— Cornell Press is an academic publisher of nonfiction with particular strengths in anthropology, Asian studies, biological sciences, classics, history, labor and business, literary criticism, politics and international relations, psychology, women's studies, Slavic studies, philosophy. Currently emphasizing sound scholarships that appeal beyond the academic community.

Nonfiction: Biography, reference, textbook. Subjects include agriculture/horticulture, anthropology/archeology, art/ architecture, business/economics, education, ethnic, gay/lesbian, government/politics, history, language/literature, military/war, music/dance, philosophy, psychology, regional, religion, science, sociology, translation, women's issues/studies. Submit résumé, cover letter and prospectus.

Recent Title(s): *Cathedrals of Europe*, by Anne Prache; *The Working Class Majority*, by Michael Zweig.

Tips: "Cornell University Press is the oldest university press in the country. From our beginnings in 1869, we have grown to be a major scholarly publisher, offering 150 new titles a year in many disciplines."

CORWIN PRESS, INC., 2455 Teller Rd., Thousand Oaks CA 91320. (805)499-9734. Fax: (805)499-5323. E-mail: faye.zucker@corwinpress.com. **Acquisitions:** Faye Zucker, executive editor (teaching, learning, curriculum); Robb Clouse, acquisitions editor (administration, special education, technology); Rachel Livsey, acquisitions editor (staff development, assessment, diversity, education issues); Mark Goldberg, editor-at-large. Estab. 1990. Publishes hardcover and paperback originals. **Publishes 90 titles/year. Pays 10% royalty on net receipts.** Publishes book 7 months after acceptance of ms. Responds in 1 month to queries. Manuscript guidelines for #10 SASE.

O— Corwin Press, Inc. publishes leading-edge, user-friendly publications for education professionals.

Nonfiction: Professional-level publications for administrators, teachers, school specialists, policymakers, researchers and others involved with K-12 education. Subjects include education. Seeking fresh insights, conclusions, and recommendations for action. Prefers theory or research based books that provide real-world examples and practical, hands-on strategies to help busy educators be successful. No textbooks that simply summarize existing knowledge or mass-market books. Query with SASE.
Recent Title(s): *How the Brain Learns*, by David Sousa; *Keys to the Classroom*, by Carol Moran; *Beginning the Principalship*, by John Daresh.

THE COUNTRYMAN PRESS, P.O. Box 748, Woodstock VT 05091-0748. (802)457-4826. Fax: (802)457-1678. E-mail: countrymanpress@wwnorton.com. Website: www.countrymanpress.com. Editorial Director: Kermit Hummel. **Acquisitions:** Ann Kraybill, managing editor. Estab. 1973. Publishes hardcover originals, trade paperback originals and reprints. **Publishes 25 titles/year. Receives 1,000 queries/year. 30% of books from first-time authors; 70% from unagented writers. Pays 5-15% royalty on retail price. Offers $1,000-5,000 advance.** Publishes book 18 months after acceptance of ms. Accepts simultaneous submissions. Responds in 2 months to proposals. Book catalog free; ms guidelines for #10 SASE.
Imprints: Backcountry Guides
 O→ Countryman Press publishes books that encourage physical fitness and appreciation for and understanding of the natural world, self-sufficiency and adventure.
Nonfiction: "We publish several series of regional recreation guidebooks—hiking, bicycling, walking, fly-fishing, canoeing, kayaking—and are looking to expand them. We're also looking for books of national interest on travel, gardening, rural living, nature and fly-fishing." How-to, guidebooks, general nonfiction. Subjects include cooking/foods/nutrition, gardening, general, history (New England), nature/environment, recreation, regional (New England), travel, country living. Submit proposal package including outline, 3 sample chapter(s), author bio, SASE, market information. Reviews artwork/photos as part of ms package. Send photocopies.
Recent Title(s): *The Granite Landscape: A Natural History of America's Mountain Domes, from Arcadia to Yosemite*, by Tom Wessles, illustrated by Brian D. Cohen.

[N] COVENANT COMMUNICATIONS, INC., Box 416, American Fork UT 84003-0416. (801)756-1041. Website: www.covenant-lds.com. **Publishes 50+ titles/year. 35% of books from first-time authors; 100% from unagented writers. Pays 6½-15% royalty on retail price.** Publishes book 6-12 months after acceptance of ms. Responds in 4 months to mss. Manuscript guidelines online.
 O→ Currently emphasizing inspirational, devotional, historical, biography. Our fiction is also expanding, and we are looking for new approaches to LDS literature and storytelling.
Nonfiction: Biography, children's/juvenile, coffee table book, gift book, humor, illustrated book, multimedia (CD-ROM), reference, scholarly. Subjects include child guidance/parenting, creative nonfiction, history, memoirs, religion (LDS or Mormon), spirituality. Submit completed manuscript with synopsis and one-page cover letter.
Fiction: "We publish exclusively to the 'Mormon' (The Church of Jesus Christ of Latter-Day Saints) market. All work must appeal to that audience." Adventure, fantasy, historical, humor, juvenile, literary, mainstream/contemporary, mystery, picture books, regional, religious, romance, science fiction, spiritual, suspense, young adult. Submit completed manuscript with synopsis and one-page cover letter.
Recent Title(s): *Between Husband and Wife*, by Brinley and Lamb (marriage/self-help); *Pillar of Fire*, by Woolley (epic poetry).
Tips: Our audience is exclusively LDS (Latter-Day Saints, "Mormon").

CQ PRESS, 1414 22nd St. NW, Washington DC 20037. (202)887-8500. Fax: (202)822-6583. E-mail: ksuarez@cq.com. Website: www.books.cq.com. **Acquisitions:** David Tarr; Chris Anzalone, Adrian Forman (library/reference); Brenda Carter, Clarisse Kiino (college/political science), acquisitions editors. Estab. 1945. Publishes hardcover and paperback titles. **Publishes 50-70 titles/year. 95% from unagented writers. Pays college or reference royalties or fees. Offers occasional advance.** Publishes book an average of 1 year after acceptance of ms. Accepts simultaneous submissions. Responds in 3 months to queries. Book catalog free.
Imprints: CQ Press; College/Political Science, Library/Reference, Directory
 O→ CQ seeks "to educate the public by publishing authoritative works on American and international government and politics."
Nonfiction: "We are interested in American government, public administration, comparative government, and international relations." Reference, textbook (all levels of college political science texts), information directories (on federal and state governments, national elections, international/state politics and governmental issues). Subjects include government/politics, history (American, reference only). Submit proposal package including outline.
Recent Title(s): *Guide to Congress*.
Tips: "Our books present important information on American government and politics, and related issues, with careful attention to accuracy, thoroughness and readability."

CRAFTSMAN BOOK COMPANY, 6058 Corte Del Cedro, Carlsbad CA 92009-9974. (760)438-7828 or (800)829-8123. Fax: (760)438-0398. E-mail: jacobs@costbook.com. Website: www.craftsman-book.com. **Acquisitions:** Laurence D. Jacobs, editorial manager. Estab. 1957. Publishes paperback originals. **Publishes 12 titles/year. Receives 50 submis-**

sions/year. **85% of books from first-time authors; 98% from unagented writers. Pays 7½-12½% royalty on wholesale price or retail price.** Publishes book 2 years after acceptance of ms. Accepts simultaneous submissions. Responds in 2 months to queries. Book catalog and ms guidelines free.

    O—π Publishes how-to manuals for professional builders. Currently emphasizing construction software.

Nonfiction: All titles are related to construction for professional builders. How-to, technical. Subjects include building, construction. Query with SASE. Reviews artwork/photos as part of ms package.

Recent Title(s): *Steel-Frame House Construction*, by Tim Waite.

Tips: "The book should be loaded with step-by-step instructions, illustrations, charts, reference data, forms, samples, cost estimates, rules of thumb, and examples that solve actual problems in the builder's office and in the field. The book must cover the subject completely, become the owner's primary reference on the subject, have a high utility-to-cost ratio, and help the owner make a better living in his chosen field."

CREATIVE HOMEOWNER, 24 Park Way, Upper Saddle River NJ 07458. (201)934-7100. Fax: (201)934-7541. E-mail: Sharon.Ranftle@creativehomeowner.com. Website: www.creativehomeowner.com. **Acquisitions:** Tim Bakke, editorial director; Miranda Smith, editor (gardening); Bill Brockway, editor (home improvement/repair); Kathie Robitz, senior editor (home decorating/design). Estab. 1978. Publishes trade paperback originals. **Publishes 12-16 titles/year. Receives dozens queries and and mss/year. 50% of books from first-time authors; 98% from unagented writers. Makes outright purchase of $8,000-35,000.** Publishes book 16 months after acceptance of ms. Responds in 6 months to queries. Book catalog free.

    O—π Creative Homeowner Press is the one source for the largest selection of quality how-to books, booklets and project plans.

Nonfiction: How-to, illustrated book. Subjects include gardening, hobbies, home remodeling/building, home repairs, home decorating/design. Query or submit proposal package, including competitive books (short analysis) and outline and SASE. Reviews artwork/photos as part of ms package.

Recent Title(s): *Real-Life Decorating*, by Lyn Peterson; *Foolproof Guide to Roses*, by Field Roebuck; *Yard & Garden Furniture*, by Bill Hylton.

CRICKET BOOKS, 332 S. Michigan Ave., #1100, Chicago IL 60604. (312)939-1500. E-mail: cricketbooks@caruspub .com. Website: www.cricketbooks.net. **Acquisitions:** Carol Saller, editor (picture books, chapter books, middle-grade and young adult fiction); Marc Aronson, editorial director (fiction and nonfiction primarily for teenagers). Estab. 1999. Publishes hardcover originals. **Publishes 24 titles/year. Receives 500 queries and 1,500 mss/year. Open to first-time and unagented authors. Pays up to 10% royalty on retail price. Offers $2,000 and up advance.** Publishes book 18 months after acceptance of ms. Accepts simultaneous submissions. Responds in 3 months to queries and proposals; 4 months to mss. Manuscript guidelines for #10 SASE.

    O—π Cricket Books publishes picture books, chapter books and middle-grade novels for children ages 7-14.

Nonfiction: Children's/juvenile. Send proposal, including sample chapters, table of contents, and description of competition.

Fiction: Juvenile. Submit complete ms.

Recent Title(s): *John Riley's Daughter*, by Kezi Matthews; *Two Suns in the Sky*, by Miriam Bat-Ami.

Tips: Audience is children ages 7-14. "Take a look at the recent titles to see what sort of materials we're interested in."

CROSS CULTURAL PUBLICATIONS, INC., P.O. Box 506, Notre Dame IN 46556. (219)273-6526. Fax: (219)273-5973. E-mail: crosscult@aol.com. Website: www.crossculturalpub.com. **Acquisitions:** Cyriac Pullapilly, general editor. Estab. 1980. Publishes hardcover and trade paperback originals and reprints. **Publishes 5-20 titles/year. Receives 5,000 queries and 2,000 mss/year. 40% of books from first-time authors; 90% from unagented writers. Pays 10% royalty on wholesale price.** Publishes book 6 months after acceptance of ms. Accepts simultaneous submissions. Responds in 2 months to queries; 3 months to proposals; 4 months to mss. Book catalog and ms guidelines online.

    O—π "We publish to promote intercultural and interfaith understanding." Currently emphasizing religious and philosophical books.

Nonfiction: "We publish scholarly books that deal with intercultural topics—regardless of discipline. Books pushing into new horizons are welcome, but they have to be intellectually sound and balanced in judgement." Biography, coffee table book, cookbook, humor, reference, textbook, scholarly. Subjects include anthropology/archeology, business/economics, cooking/foods/nutrition, ethnic, government/politics, history, memoirs, multicultural, nature/environment, philosophy, psychology, religion, sociology, spirituality, translation, travel, women's issues/studies, general nonfiction, New Age, world affairs. Submit proposal package including outline.

Fiction: Historical, religious, romance, science fiction. "Should have a serious plot and message." Query with SASE or submit proposal package including synopsis, SASE.

Poetry: "Exceptionally good poetry with moving message." Query or submit complete ms.

Recent Title(s): *St. John of the Cross and Bhagavad-Gita: Love, Union and Renunciation*, by Thomas Mybadil; *The Cancer Within: Pedophilia and Power in the Catholic Church*, by Patrick Bascio; *A Seed of Hope*, by Anthony David Reid.

[N] **CROSSQUARTER PUBLISHING GROUP**, (formerly Crossquarter Breeze),. P.O. Box 8756, Santa Fe NM 87504. (505)438-9846. Website: www.crossquarter.com. **Acquisitions:** Anthony Ravenscroft. Publishes case and trade paperback originals and reprints. **Publishes 5-10 titles/year. Receives 75 queries/year. 90% of books from first-time authors. Pays 8-10% royalty on wholesale or retail price.** Publishes book 1 year after acceptance of ms. Accepts simultaneous submissions. Responds in 3 months to queries. Book catalog for $1.75; ms guidelines online.

> O➤ "We emphasize personal sovereignty, self responsibility and growth with pagan or pagan-friendly emphasis for young adults and adults."

Nonfiction: How-to, self-help. Subjects include health/medicine, nature/environment, philosophy, religion (pagan only), autobiography. Query with SASE. Reviews artwork/photos as part of ms package. Send photocopies.
Fiction: Science fiction, visionary fiction. Query with SASE.
Recent Title(s): *20 Herbs to Take Outdoors*, by Therese Francis; *Beyond One's Own*, by Gabriel Carstans.
Tips: "Audience is earth-conscious people looking to grow into balance of body, mind, heart and spirit."

CROSSWAY BOOKS, 1300 Crescent St., Wheaton IL 60187-5800. Fax: (630)682-4785. Editorial Director: Marvin Padgett. **Acquisitions:** Jill Carter . Estab. 1938. Publishes hardcover and trade paperback originals. **Publishes 95 titles/ year. Receives 2,500 submissions/year. 2% of books from first-time authors; 75% from unagented writers. Pays negotiable royalty. Offers negotiable advance.** Publishes book 18 months after acceptance of ms. Responds in up to 2 months to queries. Book catalog for 9×12 SAE with 7 first-class stamps; ms guidelines for #10 SASE.

> O➤ "'With making a difference in people's lives for Christ' as its maxim, Crossway Books lists titles written from an evangelical Christian worldview."

Nonfiction: Subjects include religion, spirituality. "Books that provide fresh understanding and a distinctively Christian examination of questions confronting Christians and non-Christians in their personal lives, families, churches, communities and the wider culture. The main types include: (1) Issues books that typically address critical issues facing Christians today; (2) Books on the deeper Christian life that provide a deeper understanding of Christianity and its application to daily life; and, (3) Christian academic and professional books directed at an audience of religious professionals. Be sure the books are from an evangelical Christian worldview. Writers often give sketchy information on their book's content." Query with SASE. No phone queries.
Fiction: "We publish fiction that falls into these categories: (1) Christian realism, or novels set in modern, true-to-life settings as a means of telling stories about Christians today in an increasingly post-Christian era; (2) Supernatural fiction, or stories typically set in the 'real world' but that bring supernatural reality into it in a way that heightens our spiritual dimension; (3) Historical fiction, using historical characters, times and places of interest as a mirror for our own times; (4) Some genre-technique fiction (mystery, western); and (5) Children's fiction. We are not interested in romance novels, horror novels, biblical novels (i.e., stories set in Bible times that fictionalize events in the lives of prominent biblical characters), issues novels (i.e., fictionalized treatments of contemporary issues), and end times/prophecy novels. We do not accept full manuscripts or electronic submissions." Submit synopsis with 2 sample chapters and SASE.
Recent Title(s): *The Hidden Smile of God*, by John Piper (nonfiction); *Cry Freedom*, by Marlo Schalesky (fiction).
Tips: "All of our fiction must have 'Christian' content—combine the Truth of God's Word with a passion to live it out. Writers often submit without thinking about what a publisher actually publishes. They also send full manuscripts without a synopsis. Without a synopsis, the manuscript does not get read."

CROWN BUSINESS, (formerly Times Business) Random House, Inc., 299 Park Ave., New York NY 10171-0002. (212)572-2600. Fax: (212)572-4949. Website: www.crownbusiness.com. **Acquisitions:** John Mahaney, executive editor. Estab. 1995. Publishes hardcover and trade paperback originals. **Publishes 20-25 titles/year. 50% of books from first-time authors; 15% from unagented writers. Pays negotiable royalty on list price; hardcover on invoice price. Offers negotiable advance.** Publishes book 9 months after acceptance of ms. Accepts simultaneous submissions. Responds in 1 month to proposals. Book catalog online.
Nonfiction: Subjects include business/economics, money/finance, management, technology. Query with proposal package including outline, 1-2 sample chapters, market analysis and SASE.
Recent Title(s): *Profit Zone*, by Adrian Zlywotzky and David Morrison.

[N] CSLI PUBLICATIONS, Ventura Hall, Stanford University, Stanford CA 94305-4115. (650)723-1839. Fax: (650)725-2166. E-mail: pubs@csli.stanford.edu. Website: cslipublications.stanford.edu. **Acquisitions:** Dikran Karagueuzian, director (linguistics, philosophy, logic, computer science). Publishes hardcover and scholarly paperback originals. **Publishes 40 titles/year. Receives 200 queries and 50 mss/year. Pays 3-10% royalty; honorarium.** Publishes book 1 year after acceptance of ms. Responds in 1 month to queries; 4 months to proposals; 6 months to mss. Book catalog free.

> O➤ "CSLI Publications, part of the Center for the Studies of Language and Information, specializes in books in the areas of formal linguistics, logic, philosophy, computer science and human-computer interaction." Currently emphasizing human-computer interaction, computers and media, voice technology. De-emphasizing pragmatic linguistics.

Nonfiction: Reference, technical, textbook, scholarly. Subjects include anthropology/archeology, computers/electronic, language/literature (linguistics), science, logic, cognitive science. Query with SASE or by email.
Recent Title(s): *The Significance of Word Lists*, by Brett Kessler.

CUMBERLAND HOUSE PUBLISHING, 431 Harding Industrial Dr., Nashville TN 37211. (615)832-1171. Fax: (615)832-0633. E-mail: cumbhouse@aol.com. **Acquisitions:** Tilly Katz, acquisitions editor. Estab. 1996. Publishes hardcover, trade paperback and mass market originals and reprints. **Publishes 60 titles/year; imprint publishes 5 titles/**

year. Receives 3,000 queries and 500 mss/year. **30% of books from first-time authors; 80% from unagented writers. Pays 10-20% royalty on wholesale price. Offers $1,000-10,000 advance.** Publishes book an average of 12 months after acceptance of ms. Accepts simultaneous submissions. Responds in 1 year to queries, proposals and mss. Book catalog for 8×10 SAE with 4 first-class stamps; ms guidelines free.
Imprints: Cumberland House Hearthside, Highland Books

O─┐ Cumberland House publishes "market specific books. We evaluate in terms of what type book seems to be working for us in our customer avenues at the moment and then the quality or uniqueness of a project." Currently emphasizing "mystery (exceptional only) and general Christian living titles." De-emphasizing "cookbooks and humor."

Nonfiction: Cookbook, gift book, how-to, humor, reference. Subjects include Americana, cooking/foods/nutrition, government/politics, history, humor, military/war, recreation, regional, sports, travel. Query or submit outline. Reviews artwork/photos as part of ms package. Send photocopies only. No originals.
Fiction: Mystery. Writers should know "the odds are really stacked against them." Query with SASE.
Recent Title(s): *Smokehouse Ham, Spoon Bread and Scuppernong Wine*, by Joe Dabney (winner of 1999 James Beard Cookbook of the Year Award); *Airtight Case*, by Beverly Connor (mystery); *Best Little Ironies, Oddities & Mysteries of the Civil War*, by C. Brian Kelly.
Tips: Audience is "adventuresome people who like a fresh approach to things. Writers should tell what their idea is, why it's unique and why somebody would want to buy it—but don't pester us."

[A] CURRENCY, 1540 Broadway, New York NY 10036. (212)782-9730. Fax: (212)782-8911. E-mail: rscholl@randomhouse.com. **Acquisitions:** Roger Scholl, executive editor. Estab. 1989. **Pays 7½-15% royalty on retail price. Offers advance.** Publishes book 1 year after acceptance of ms.

O─┐ Currency publishes "business books for people who want to make a difference, not just a living."
Nonfiction: Subjects include business/economics, marketing, investment. *Accepts agented submissions only.*
Recent Title(s): *The Street.com Guide to Smart Investing in the Internet Era*, by Dave Kansas and the writers of The Street.com; *The Art of Innovation*, by Tom Kelley.

CYPRESS PUBLISHING GROUP, 11835 ROE #187, Leawood KS 66211. (913)681-9875. Fax: (913)681-9875. E-mail: cypressbook@hotmail.com. Website: cypresspublishing.com. Vice President Marketing: Carl Heintz. **Acquisitions:** William S. Noblitt, JoAnn Heinz. Publishes hardcover and trade paperback originals. **Publishes 10 titles/year. 80% of books from first-time authors; 90% from unagented writers. Pays 10-15% royalty on wholesale price.** Publishes book 8 months after acceptance of ms. Responds in 1 month to queries, proposals and mss. Book catalog free.

O─┐ "We are an innovative niche publisher of business and finance books, including training materials." Currently emphasizing business, finance, investing.
Nonfiction: How-to, illustrated book, self-help, technical, textbook. Subjects include business/economics, computers/electronic (business related), money/finance (small business, personal finance, investing, accounting), psychology (business related), software (business related). Query with proposal package, including outline, 1-3 sample chapters, overview of book. Send photocopies.
Recent Title(s): *Money*, by Alex Grant; *Number Sense*, by Carl Heintz.
Tips: "Our editorial plans change—we are always looking for outstanding submissions. Many writers fail to consider what other books on the topics are available. The writer must think about the fundamental book marketing question: Why will a customer *buy* the book?"

[N] THE DANA PRESS, 1001 G St., NW, Suite 1025, Washington DC 20001. (202)737-9200. Fax: (202)737-9204. Website: www.dana.org/books/press. **Acquisitions:** Jane Nevins, editor-in-chief; Andrew Cocke, editorial associate. Publishes hardcover and trade paperback originals. **Publishes 4 titles/year. Receives 10 queries and 3 mss/year. 50% of books from first-time authors; 90% from unagented writers. Pays 14-20% royalty on wholesale price. Offers $10,000-35,000 advance.** Publishes book 1 year after acceptance of ms. Accepts simultaneous submissions. Responds in 2 weeks to queries; 1 month to proposals; 2 months to mss. Book catalog and ms guidelines online.
Nonfiction: Biography, coffee table book, self-help, brain-related health books. Subjects include health/medicine, memoirs, psychology, science. "We focus almost exclusively on the brain." Reviews artwork/photos as part of ms package. Send photocopies.
Recent Title(s): *States of Mind*, by multiple authors (essays); *Longevity Strategy*, by Richard Restak/David Mahoney (self-help); *End of Stress as We Know It*, by Bruce McEwen.
Tips: "Coherent, thought-out proposals are key. What is the scope of the book? Who is the reader? It's important to have an angle."

DANTE UNIVERSITY OF AMERICA PRESS, INC., P.O. Box 812158, Wellesley MA 02482. Fax: (781)790-1056. E-mail: danteu@danteuniversity.org. Website: www.danteuniversity.org/dpress.html. **Acquisitions:** Adolph Caso, president. Estab. 1975. Publishes hardcover and trade paperback originals and reprints. **Publishes 5 titles/year. Receives 50 submissions/year. 50% of books from first-time authors; 50% from unagented writers. Pays royalty. Offers negotiable advance.** Publishes book 10 months after acceptance of ms. Responds in 2 months to queries.

☞ "The Dante University Press exists to bring quality, educational books pertaining to our Italian heritage as well as the historical and political studies of America. Profits from the sale of these publications benefit the Foundation, bringing Dante University closer to a reality."
Nonfiction: Biography, reference, reprints. Subjects include history (Italian-American), translation (from Italian and latin), general scholarly nonfiction, Renaissance thought and letter, Italian language and linguistics, Italian-American culture, bilingual education. Query with SASE. Reviews artwork/photos as part of ms package.
Fiction: Translations from Italian and Latin. Query with SASE.
Poetry: "There is a chance that we would use Renaissance poetry translations."
Recent Title(s): *Trapped in Tuscany*, by Tullio Bertini (World War II nonfiction); *Rogue Angel*, by Carol Damioli (mystery).

DARLINGTON PRODUCTIONS, INC., P.O. Box 5884, Darlington MD 21034. (410)457-5400. E-mail: dpi14@aol .com. Website: www.darlingtonproductions.com. **Acquisitions:** Jeffrey D. McKaughan, president. Publishes hardcover originals, trade paperback originals and reprints. **Publishes 9 titles/year. Receives 20 queries/year. 75% of books from first-time authors; 100% from unagented writers. Pays 10% royalty on retail price.** Publishes book 6 months after acceptance of ms. Accepts simultaneous submissions. Responds in 1 month to queries and proposals; 3 months to mss. Book catalog and ms guidelines free.
☞ Darlington publishes military history/war reference and illustrated titles.
Nonfiction: Illustrated book, reference, technical. Subjects include history, military/war. Query with outline. Reviews artwork/photos as part of ms package. Send photocopies.
Recent Title(s): *Russian/Soviet Armor and Artillery Design Practices 1945-Present*, by Zaloga, Hull and Markov.

JONATHAN DAVID PUBLISHERS, INC., 68-22 Eliot Ave., Middle Village NY 11379-1194. (718)456-8611. Fax: (718)894-2818. E-mail: info@jdbooks.com. Website: www.jdbooks.com. **Acquisitions:** Alfred J. Kolatch, editor-in-chief. Estab. 1948. Publishes hardcover and trade paperback originals and reprints. **Publishes 20-25 titles/year. 50% of books from first-time authors; 90% from unagented writers. Pays royalty or makes outright purchase.** Publishes book 18 months after acceptance of ms. Responds in 1 month to queries and proposals; 2 months to mss. Book catalog online; ms guidelines for #10 SASE or online.
☞ Jonathan David publishes "popular Judaica." Currently emphasizing projects geared toward children.
Nonfiction: Biography, children's/juvenile, coffee table book, cookbook, gift book, how-to, humor, illustrated book, reference, self-help. Subjects include cooking/foods/nutrition, creative nonfiction, ethnic, humor, multicultural, religion, sex, sports. Query with SASE or submit proposal package including outline, 3 sample chapter(s), résumé. Reviews artwork/photos as part of ms package. Send photocopies.
Recent Title(s): *Drawing a Crowd*, by Bill Gallo (sports cartoons/memoir).

DAVIS PUBLICATIONS, INC., 50 Portland St., Worcester MA 01608. (508)754-7201. Fax: (508)753-3834. **Acquisitions:** Helen Ronan, editor-in-chief. Estab. 1901. **Publishes 5-10 titles/year. Pays 10-12% royalty. Offers advance.** Publishes book 1 year after acceptance of ms. Book catalog for 9×12 SAE with 2 first-class stamps; ms guidelines for #10 SASE.
☞ Davis publishes art, design and craft books for the elementary and high school art education markets.
Nonfiction: Illustrated book. Subjects include art/architecture, education, history. Submit outline, sample chapter(s). Reviews artwork/photos as part of ms package.
Recent Title(s): *The Roots of Art Education in Practice*, by Mary Ann Stankiewicz; *Enduring Visions: Women's Artistic Heritage Around the World*, by Abby Remer; *Off the Wall Museum Guide Series*, by Ruthie Knapp and Janice Lehmberg.
Tips: "Keep in mind the intended audience. Our readers are visually oriented. All illustrations should be collated separately from the text, but keyed to the text. Photos should be good quality transparencies and black and white photographs. Well-selected illustrations should explain, amplify, and enhance the text. We average 2-4 photos/page. We like to see technique photos as well as illustrations of finished artwork, by a variety of artists, including students. Recent books have been on museum guides for children, weaving, women artists, art education profession, history through art timeline."

🅽 DAWN PUBLICATIONS, P.O. Box 2010, Nevada City CA 95959. (800)545-7475 or (530)478-0111. Fax: (530)478-0112. E-mail: nature@DawnPub.com. Website: www.dawnpub.com. **Acquisitions:** Glenn Hovemann, editor. Estab. 1979. Publishes hardcover and trade paperback originals. **Publishes 6 titles/year. Receives 550 queries and 2,500 mss/year. 15% of books from first-time authors; 90% from unagented writers. Pays royalty on wholesale price. Offers advance.** Publishes book 1 to 2 years after acceptance of ms. Accepts simultaneous submissions. Responds in 2 months to queries. Book catalog and ms guidelines online.
☞ Dawn Publications' mission is to assist parents and educators to open the minds and hearts of children to the transforming influence of nature. Dawn Publications is dedicated to inspiring in children a sense of appreciation for all life on earth. Dawn looks for nature awareness and appreciation titles that promote a relationship with the natural world and specific habitats, usually through inspiring treatment and nonfiction.
Nonfiction: Children's/juvenile. Subjects include animals, nature/environment. Query with SASE.
Recent Title(s): *Salmon Stream*, by Carol Reed-Jones.
Tips: Publishes mostly nonfiction with lightness and inspiration.

N. DBS PRODUCTIONS, P.O. Box 1894, Charlottesville VA 22903. (800)745-1581. Fax: (804)293-5502. E-mail: robert@dbs-sar.com. Website: www.dbs-sar.com. **Acquisitions:** Bob Adams, publisher. Estab. 1989. Publishes hardcover and trade paperback originals. **Publishes 6 titles/year. Receives 5 queries/year. 5% of books from first-time authors; 100% from unagented writers. Pays 5-20% royalty on retail price.** Publishes book 1 year after acceptance of ms. Responds in 2 months to queries. Book catalog online; ms guidelines for #10 SASE.

O➝ dbs Productions produces search and rescue and outdoor first-aid related materials and courses. It offers a selection of publications, videotapes, management kits and tools and instructional modules.

Nonfiction: Technical, textbook. Subjects include health/medicine. Submit proposal package including outline, 2 sample chapter(s). Reviews artwork/photos as part of ms package. Send photocopies.

Recent Title(s): *Field Operations Guide for Search and Rescue, 2nd Edition*, by R. Koester.

DEARBORN, 155 N. Wacker Dr., Chicago IL 60606-1719. (312)836-4400. Fax: (312)836-1021. E-mail: zigmund@dea rborn.com. Website: www.dearborntrade.com. **Acquisitions:** Cynthia Zigmund, publisher (finance); Jean Iversen, senior acquisitions editor (general business/management); Mary B. Good, acquisitions editor (entrepreneurship, consumer real estate, business biographies). Estab. 1959. Publishes hardcover and paperback originals. **Publishes 50 titles/year. Receives 400 submissions/year. 30% of books from first-time authors; 50% from unagented writers. Pays 10-15% royalty on wholesale price. Offers advance.** Publishes book 6 months after acceptance of ms. Accepts simultaneous submissions. Responds in 1 month to queries. Book catalog and ms guidelines free.

O➝ The trade division of Dearborn publishes practical, solutions-oriented books for individuals and corporations on the subjects of finance, consumer real estate, business and entrepreneurship. Currently emphasizing finance, general business/management, consumer real estate. De-emphasizing small business.

Nonfiction: How-to, reference, textbook. Subjects include business/economics, money/finance. Query with SASE.

Recent Title(s): *The Power of Six Sigma*, by Subir Chowdhury; *The New Retirementality*, by Mitch Anthony; *Real Estate a la Carte*, by Julie Garton-Good.

IVAN R. DEE, INC., The Rowman & Littlefield Publishing Group, 1332 N. Halsted St., Chicago IL 60622-2637. (312)787-6262. Fax: (312)787-6269. E-mail: elephant@ivanrdee.com. Website: www.ivanrdee.com. **Acquisitions:** Ivan R. Dee, president; Hilary Schaefer, associate editor. Estab. 1988. Publishes hardcover originals and trade paperback originals and reprints. **Publishes 60 titles/year. 10% of books from first-time authors; 75% from unagented writers. Pays royalty. Offers advance.** Publishes book 9 months after acceptance of ms. Responds in 1 month to queries. Book catalog free.

Imprints: Elephant Paperbacks, New Amsterdam Books, J.S. Sanders Books

O➝ Ivan R. Dee publishes serious nonfiction for general informed readers. Currently de-emphasizing literary criticism.

Nonfiction: Biography. Subjects include art/architecture, film/cinema/stage, government/politics, history, language/literature, world affairs, contemporary culture, film/cinema/stage, baseball. Submit outline, sample chapter(s). Reviews artwork/photos as part of ms package.

Recent Title(s): *Journal 1935-1944*, by Mihail Sebastian; *Bad News*, by Robert Shogan.

Tips: "We publish for an intelligent lay audience and college course adoptions."

A. DEL REY BOOKS, Ballantine Publishing Group, Random House, Inc., 1540 Broadway, 11th Floor-J, New York NY 10036. (212)782-8393. E-mail: delrey@randomhouse.com. Website: www.randomhouse.com/delrey/. **Acquisitions:** Shelly Shapiro, editorial director (science fiction, fantasy); Steve Saffel, senior editor (fantasy, alternate history); Chris Schluep, assistant editor (science fiction); Christopher Evans (military science fiction and fantasy). Estab. 1977. Publishes hardcover, trade paperback, and mass market originals and mass market paperback reprints. **Publishes 70 titles/year. Receives 1,900 submissions/year. 10% of books from first-time authors; 0% from unagented writers. Pays royalty on retail price. Offers competitive advance.** Publishes book 1 year after acceptance of ms. Responds in 6 months to queries. Manuscript guidelines for #10 SASE.

O➝ Del Rey publishes top level fantasy, alternate history, and science fiction.

Fiction: Fantasy (should have the practice of magic as an essential element of the plot), science fiction (well-plotted novels with good characterizations, exotic locales and detailed alien creatures), alternate history ("novels that take major historical events, such as the Civil War, and bend history in a new direction sometimes through science fiction and fantasy devices"). *Accepts agented submissions only.*

Recent Title(s): *Darwin's Radio*, by Greg Bear; *Voyage of the Jerle Shannara: Ilse Witch*, by Terry Brooks; *Kiss of Shadows*, by Laurell K. Hamilton.

Tips: "Del Rey is a reader's house. Pay particular attention to plotting, strong characters, and dramatic, satisfactory conclusions. It must be/feel believable. That's what the readers like. In terms of mass market, we basically created the field of fantasy bestsellers. Not that it didn't exist before, but we put the mass into mass market."

N. THE DENALI PRESS, P.O. Box 021535, Juneau AK 99802-1535. (907)586-6014. Fax: (907)463-6780. E-mail: info@denalipress.com. Website: www.denalipress.com. **Acquisitions:** Alan Schorr, editorial director; Sally Silvas-Ottumwa, editorial associate. Estab. 1986. Publishes trade paperback originals. **Publishes 5 titles/year. Receives 120 submissions/year. 50% of books from first-time authors; 80% from unagented writers. Pays 10% royalty on wholesale price or makes outright purchase. Offers advance.** Publishes book 1 year after acceptance of ms. Accepts simultaneous submissions. Responds in 1 month to queries.

O— The Denali Press looks for reference works suitable for the educational, professional and library market. "Though we publish books on a variety of topics, our focus is most broadly centered on multiculturalism, public policy, Alaskana, and general reference works."

Nonfiction: Reference. Subjects include Americana, anthropology/archeology, ethnic, government/politics, history, multicultural, recreation, regional. "We need reference books—ethnic, refugee and minority concerns." Query with SASE or submit outline, sample chapter(s). *All unsolicited mss returned unopened.*

Recent Title(s): *Winning Political Campaigns: A Comprehensive Guide to Electoral Success*, by William S. Bike.

THE DESIGN IMAGE GROUP INC., 231 S. Frontage Rd., Suite 17, Burr Ridge IL 60521. (630)789-8991. Fax: (630)789-9013. E-mail: dig@designimagegroup.com. Website: www.designimagegroup.com. **Acquisitions:** Editorial Committee. Estab. 1984. Publishes trade paperback originals. **Publishes 6 titles/year. Receives 400 queries and 800 mss/year. 75% of books from first-time authors; 90% from unagented writers. Pays 10-20% royalty on wholesale (horror line); new mystery line: pays straight royalty only—30% on wholesale. Offers $3,000-3,600 (horror line) advance.** Accepts simultaneous submissions. Responds in 1 month to queries; 2 months to mss. Book catalog for 6×9 SAE with 2 first-class stamps; ms guidelines for #10 SASE.

O— The Design Image Group publishes "traditional supernatural, human form, monster-based horror fiction and neo-noir and retro-pulp flavored dark mysteries."

Fiction: Horror, new neo-noir dark mystery line. "Please, no complete ms. Absolutely no phone queries! Absolutely no fax queries!" Query with SASE or submit 3 sample chapter(s).

Recent Title(s): *Bell, Book & Beyond, An Anthology of Witchy Tales*, by P.D. Cacek.

Tips: "Best advice to understand what we seek: send for our guidelines! They spell out quite clearly what we're looking for... and what we don't want to see. Show us something that's been rejected by the major New York trade publishers, and we might surprise you! Nonetheless, we demand the same quality writing, suspenseful plotting and engaging characters any mass market publisher would; don't confuse the small press with amateur or experimental publishing. We seek mass market appeal for our smaller audience."

DIAL BOOKS FOR YOUNG READERS, Penguin Putnam Inc., 345 Hudson St., 3rd Floor, New York NY 10014. (212)366-2800. President/Publisher: Nancy Paulsen. Editorial Director: Lauri Hornik. **Acquisitions:** Submissions Editor. Publishes hardcover originals. **Publishes 50 titles/year. Receives 5,000 queries/year. 20% of books from first-time authors. Pays royalty. Offers varies advance.** Responds in 3 months to queries.

Imprints: Phyllis Fogelman Books

O— Dial Books for Young Readers publishes quality picture books for ages 18 months-8 years, lively, believable novels for middle readers and young adults, and occasional nonfiction for middle readers and young adults.

Nonfiction: Children's/juvenile, illustrated book. *Accepts agented submissions only.*

Fiction: Adventure, fantasy, juvenile, picture books, young adult. Especially looking for "lively and well-written novels for middle grade and young adult children involving a convincing plot and believable characters. The subject matter or theme should not already be overworked in previously published books. The approach must not be demeaning to any minority group, nor should the roles of female characters (or others) be stereotyped, though we don't think books should be didactic, or in any way message-y. No topics inappropriate for the juvenile, young adult, and middle grade audiences. No plays." *No unsolicited mss. Accepts agented submissions only.*

Recent Title(s): *Asteroid Impact*, by Doug Henderson; *A Year Down Yonder*, by Richard Parl; *The Missing Mitten Mystery*, by Steven Kellogg.

Tips: "Our readers are anywhere from preschool age to teenage. Picture books must have strong plots, lots of action, unusual premises, or universal themes treated with freshness and originality. Humor works well in these books. A very well thought out and intelligently presented book has the best chance of being taken on. Genre isn't as much of a factor as presentation."

DIAL PRESS, Bantam Dell Publishing Group, Random House, Inc., 1540 Broadway, New York NY 10036. (212)354-6500. Fax: (212)782-8414. Website: www.bbd.com. **Acquisitions:** Susan Kamil, vice president, editorial director. Estab. 1924. **Publishes 6-12 titles/year. Receives 200 queries and 450 mss/year. 75% of books from first-time authors. Pays royalty on retail price. Offers advance.** Publishes book 18 months after acceptance of ms. Accepts simultaneous submissions.

O— Dial Press publishes quality fiction and nonfiction.

Nonfiction: Biography. Subjects include Americana, art/architecture, government/politics, health/medicine, history, memoirs, psychology, women's issues/studies. *Accepts agented submissions only.*

Fiction: Literary (general). *Accepts agented submissions only.*

Recent Title(s): *Letters of the Century* (nonfiction); *City of Light* (fiction); *Driving Mr. Albert* (nonfiction).

DIMI PRESS, 3820 Oak Hollow Lane, SE, Salem OR 97302-4774. (503)364-7698. Fax: (503)364-9727. E-mail: dickbook@earthlink.net. Website: www.home.earthlink.net/~dickbook. **Acquisitions:** Dick Lutz, president. Publishes trade paperback originals. **Publishes 5 titles/year. Receives 100-150 queries and 20-25 mss/year. 80% of books from first-time authors; 90% from unagented writers. Pays 10% royalty on net receipts.** Publishes book 9 months after acceptance of ms. Accepts simultaneous submissions. Responds in 2 weeks to queries and proposals; 1 month to mss. Book catalog and ms guidelines for #10 SASE.

O— "We provide accurate information about unusual things in nature." Currently de-emphasizing self-help books.

Nonfiction: Subjects include animals, nature/environment, science. "Soliciting manuscripts on unusual things in nature, such as unusual animals or natural formations. Also natural disasters such as volcanic eruptions, earthquakes, or floods. Preferably of the world's 'worst.' Also related manuscripts on nature/travel/environment. No travel guides." Query with SASE or submit outline, 1 sample chapter(s). Reviews artwork/photos as part of ms package. Send photocopies.
Recent Title(s): *The Running Indians*; *Komodo, The Living Dragon*; *Hidden Amazon*.
Tips: "Audience is adults who wish to learn something and are interested in unusual travel excursions. Guidelines are available at: http://home.earthlink.net/~guidelines. Please check guidelines before submitting."

DIOGENES PUBLISHING, SAN #253-1615, 965 Alamo Dr., Unit 336, Vacaville CA 95687. (707)447-6482. Fax: (707)447-6482. E-mail: sales@diogenespublishing.com. Website: www.diogenespublishing.com. **Acquisitions:** Chris Primi, marketing director. Publishes trade paperback originals. **Publishes 6 titles/year. Receives 150 queries and 50 mss/year. 90% of books from first-time authors; 95% from unagented writers. Pays 10% royalty on wholesale price.** Publishes book 1 year after acceptance of ms. Responds in 1 month to queries, proposals and mss. Book catalog online.
　　O→ Diogenes is a nonfiction publisher seeking "quality writing, original thinking."
Nonfiction: Subjects include creative nonfiction, philosophy, psychology, sociology. Query with SASE. Reviews artwork/photos as part of ms package. Send photocopies.
Recent Title(s): *Happiness & Other Lies*, by Mary Massaro; *Self Esteem for Children*, by John Prosper.

DISCOVERY ENTERPRISES, LTD., 31 Laurelwood Dr., Carlisle MA 07141. (978)287-5401. Fax: (978)287-5402. E-mail: ushistorydocs@aol.com. **Acquisitions:** JoAnne W. Deitch, president (plays for Readers Theatre, on American history). Publishes trade paperback originals. **Publishes 10 titles/year. Receives 50 queries and 20 mss/year. 5% of books from first-time authors; 90% from unagented writers. Pays 20% royalty.** Publishes book 3 months after acceptance of ms. Accepts simultaneous submissions. Responds in 1 month to queries. Book catalog for 6×9 SAE with 3 first-class stamps.
Fiction: "We're interested in 40-minute plays (reading time) for students in grades 4-10 on topics in U.S. history." Historical, plays. Query with SASE or submit complete ms.
Recent Title(s): *Life on the Road: Sojourner Truth*, by Sharon Fennessey; *Salem Witch Hunt*, by Hilary Weisman; *Lewis and Clark: Across a Vast Land*, by Harold Torrance.
Tips: "Call or send query letter on topic prior to sending ms for plays."

[N] DO-IT-YOURSELF LEGAL PUBLISHERS, 60 Park Place, Suite 103, Newark NJ 07102. (973)639-0400. Fax: (973)639-1801. **Acquisitions:** Dan Benjamin, associate editor; Anne Torrey, editorial director. Estab. 1978. Publishes trade paperback originals. **Publishes 6 titles/year; imprint publishes 2 titles/year. Receives 25 queries/year. Pays 15-20% royalty on wholesale price.** Publishes book 1 year after acceptance of ms. Accepts simultaneous submissions. Responds in 1 month to queries and proposals; 3 months to mss.
Imprints: Selfhelper Law Press of America
　　O→ "The fundamental premise underlying our works is that the simplest problems can be effectively handled by anyone with average common sense and a competent guidebook."
Nonfiction: Subject matter should deal with self-help law topics that instruct the lay person on how to undertake legal tasks without the use of attorney or other high cost experts. How-to, self-help. Subjects include law. Query with SASE.
Recent Title(s): *The National Mortgage Qualification Kit*, by Benji O. Anosike, Ph.D.

[A] DOUBLEDAY, Doubleday Broadway Publishing Group, Random House, Inc., 1540 Broadway, New York NY 10036. (212)782-9000. Fax: (212)782-9700. Website: www.randomhouse.com. Vice President/Editor-in-Chief: William Thomas. Estab. 1897. Publishes hardcover and trade paperback originals and reprints. **Publishes 200 titles/year. Receives thousands queries and thousands mss/year. 30% of books from first-time authors. Pays royalty on retail price. Offers advance.** Publishes book 1 year after acceptance of ms.
Imprints: Anchor Books; Currency; Doubleday Religious Division; Image Books; Nan A. Talese
　　O→ Doubleday publishes high-quality fiction and nonfiction.
Nonfiction: Biography, humor. Subjects include Americana, anthropology/archeology, business/economics, computers/electronic, education, ethnic, government/politics, health/medicine, history, humor, language/literature, money/finance, nature/environment, philosophy, religion, science, sociology, software, sports, translation, women's issues/studies. *Accepts agented submissions only.*
Fiction: Adventure, confession, ethnic, experimental, feminist, gay/lesbian, historical, humor, literary, mainstream/contemporary, picture books, religious, short story collections, suspense. *Accepts agented submissions only.*
Recent Title(s): *The Street Lawyer*, by John Grisham (fiction).

[A] DOUBLEDAY RELIGIOUS PUBLISHING, Doubleday Broadway Publishing Group, Random House, Inc., 1540 Broadway, New York NY 10036. (212)354-6500. Fax: (212)782-8911. Website: www.randomhouse.com. **Acquisitions:** Eric Major, vice president, religious division; Trace Murphy, senior editor; Andrew Corbin, editor. Estab. 1897. Publishes hardcover and trade paperback originals and reprints. **Publishes 45-50 titles/year; imprint publishes 12 titles/year. Receives 1,000 queries and 500 mss/year. 3% from unagented writers. Pays 7½-15% royalty. Offers advance.** Publishes book 1 year after acceptance of ms. Accepts simultaneous submissions. Responds in 3 months to proposals. Book catalog for SAE with 3 first-class stamps.

Imprints: Image Books, Anchor Bible Commentary, Anchor Bible Reference, Galilee, New Jerusalem Bible
Nonfiction: Biography, cookbook, gift book, reference, self-help. Subjects include child guidance/parenting, cooking/foods/nutrition, money/finance, religion, sex, spirituality. *Accepts agented submissions only.*
Fiction: Religious. *Accepts agented submissions only.*
Recent Title(s): *The Lamb's Supper*, by Scott Hahn.

DOUBLEDAY/IMAGE, Doubleday Broadway Publishing Group, Random House, Inc., 1540 Broadway, New York NY 10036. (212)782-9000. Fax: (212)782-9735. Website: www.randomhouse.com. **Acquisitions:** Trace Murphy, senior editor. Estab. 1956. Publishes hardcover, trade and mass market paperback originals and reprints. **Publishes 12 titles/year. Receives 500 queries and 300 mss/year. 10% of books from first-time authors. Pays royalty on retail price. Offers varied advance.** Publishes book 18 months after acceptance of ms. Accepts simultaneous submissions. Responds in 3 months to proposals.
　　O→ Image Books has grown from a classic Catholic list to include a variety of current and future classics, maintaining a high standard of quality as the finest in religious paperbacks. Also publishes Doubleday paperbacks/hardcovers for general religion, spirituality, including works based in Buddhism, Islam, Judaism.
Nonfiction: Biography, cookbook, gift book, how-to, humor, illustrated book, reference, self-help. Subjects include cooking/foods/nutrition, humor, philosophy, psychology, religion, women's issues/studies. Query with SASE. Reviews artwork/photos as part of ms package. Send photocopies.
Recent Title(s): *Papal Sin*, by Garry Wills; *Kosher Sex*, by Shumley Boteach; *The Holy Longing*, by Ronald Rolheiser.

DOVER PUBLICATIONS, INC., 31 E. 2nd St., Mineola NY 11501. (516)294-7000. Fax: (516)873-1401. E-mail: dover@inch.com. Website: www.doverpublications.com. **Acquisitions:** Paul Negri, editor-in-chief; John Grafton (math/science reprints). Estab. 1941. Publishes trade paperback originals and reprints. **Publishes 500 titles/year. Makes outright purchase. Offers advance.** Book catalog online.
Nonfiction: Biography, children's/juvenile, coffee table book, cookbook, how-to, humor, illustrated book, textbook. Subjects include agriculture/horticulture, Americana, animals, anthropology/archeology, art/architecture, cooking/foods/nutrition, health/medicine, history, hobbies, humor, language/literature, music/dance, nature/environment, philosophy, photography, religion, science, sports, translation, travel. Publishes mostly reprints. Accepts original paper doll collections, game books, coloring books (juvenile). Query with SASE. Reviews artwork/photos as part of ms package.
Recent Title(s): *The Waning of the Middle Ages*, by John Huizenga.

[N] DOWLING PRESS, INC., 2817 W. End Ave. #126-247, Nashville TN 37203-1453. Website: www.dowlingpress.com. **Acquisitions:** Maryglenn McCombs. Publishes hardcover, trade paperback and mass market paperback originals. **Publishes 5 titles/year.** Responds in 6 months to queries. Manuscript guidelines for #10 SASE.
　　O→ Dowling Press publishes music-related nonfiction.
Nonfiction: Subjects include music/pop culture.
Recent Title(s): *Modern Twang*, by David Goodman (nonfiction); *Fall to Pieces*, by Cecelia Tishy (fiction).
Tips: Audience is 18-40 year olds, middle class. "Please proofread! There is nothing worse than carelessness (especially in a cover letter). Don't call us a day after we've received the manuscript to ask what we think! Be patient. Please no phone calls!"

DOWN EAST BOOKS, Down East Enterprise, Inc., P.O. Box 679, Camden ME 04843-0679. Fax: (207)594-7215. **Acquisitions:** Chris Cornell, editor (Silver Quill); Michael Steere, associate editor (general). Estab. 1967. Publishes hardcover and trade paperback originals, trade paperback reprints. **Publishes 20-24 titles/year. Receives 1,000 submissions/year. 50% of books from first-time authors; 90% from unagented writers. Pays 10-15% royalty on net receipts. Offers $200 average advance.** Publishes book 1 year after acceptance of ms. Accepts simultaneous submissions. Responds in 3 months to queries. Manuscript guidelines for 9×12 SAE with 3 first-class stamps.
Imprints: Silver Quill (fly fishing and wing-shooting market; Chris Cornell, editor, e-mail: ccornell@downeast.com)
　　O→ Down East Books publishes books that capture and illuminate the unique beauty and character of New England's history, culture, and wild places.
Nonfiction: Children's/juvenile. Subjects include Americana, history, nature/environment, recreation, regional, sports. Books about the New England region, Maine in particular. "All of our regional books must have a Maine or New England emphasis." Query with SASE. Reviews artwork/photos as part of ms package.
Fiction: Juvenile, mainstream/contemporary. "We publish 1-2 juvenile titles/year (fiction and nonfiction), and 1-2 adult fiction titles/year." Query with SASE.
Recent Title(s): *Handy to Home*, by Tom Hennessey; *Something in the Water*, by Peter Scott.

[A] LISA DREW BOOKS, Simon & Schuster, 1230 Avenue of the Americas, New York NY 10020. (212)698-7000. Website: www.simonsays.com. **Acquisitions:** Lisa Drew, publisher. Publishes hardcover originals. **Publishes 10-14 titles/year. Receives 600 queries/year. 10% of books from first-time authors. Pays royalty on retail price. Offers varies advance.** Publishes book 1 year after acceptance of ms. Accepts simultaneous submissions. Responds in 1 month to queries. Book catalog free.
　　O→ "We publish *reading* books; nonfiction that tells a story, not '14 ways to improve your marriage.'"
Nonfiction: Subjects include government/politics, history, women's issues/studies. *No unsolicited material. Accepts agented submissions only.*

DRY BONES PRESS, P.O. Box 1437, Roseville CA 95678. (415)707-2129. Fax: (415)707-2129. Website: www.drybo nes.com. **Acquisitions:** J. Rankin, editor/publisher. Publishes hardcover and trade paperback originals and reprints and mass market paperback originals. **Publishes 6-10 titles/year. Pays 6-10% royalty on retail price. Offers advance.** Publishes book 2 years after acceptance of ms. Accepts simultaneous submissions. Responds in 2 months to queries.
Nonfiction: Reference, technical. Subjects include health/medicine, history, philosophy, regional, religion, translation. California Gold Rush, nursing patient waiting. Submit proposal package including outline, 1-2 sample chapter(s), SASE.
Fiction: Historical, humor, mainstream/contemporary, mystery, plays, religious, science fiction. "Looking for unique items, with solid quality. No maudlin sentimentality or failure to develop insight or characters." Submit 1-2 sample chapter(s), synopsis, SASE.
Recent Title(s): *The Tenth House: The Divine and Healing Path* (Catechism); *Mother Julian and the Gentle Vampire* (fiction); *Year of the Smoke Girl* (fiction).
Tips: "We now work with Ingram/LPI, Borders/Sprint, and PublishingOnline.com routinely."

DUFOUR EDITIONS, P.O. Box 7, Chester Springs PA 19425. (610)458-5005. Fax: (610)458-5005. E-mail: dufour802 3@aol.com. Website: go.to/dufour. **Acquisitions:** Thomas Lavoie, associate publisher. Estab. 1948. Publishes hardcover originals, trade paperback originals and reprints. **Publishes 5-6 titles/year. Receives 100 queries and 15 mss/year. 20-30% of books from first-time authors; 50% from unagented writers. Pays 6-10% royalty on net receipts. Offers $500-1,000 advance.** Publishes book 18 months after acceptance of ms. Accepts simultaneous submissions. Responds in 3 months to queries and proposals; 6 months to mss. Book catalog free.
  O— "We publish literary fiction by good writers which is well received and achieves modest sales." De-emphsazing poetry and nonfiction.
Nonfiction: Biography. Subjects include history, translation. Query with SASE. Reviews artwork/photos as part of ms package. Send photocopies.
Fiction: Ethnic, historical, literary, short story collections. Query with SASE.
Poetry: Query.
Recent Title(s): *The Case of the Pederast's Wife*, by Clare Elfman; *Tideland*, by Mitch Cullin; *Collected Poems of Georges Bataille*, translated and edited by Mark Spitzer.
Tips: "Audience is sophisticated, literate readers especially interested in foreign literature and translations, and a strong Irish-Celtic focus. Check to see if the publisher is really a good match for your subject matter."

[A] THOMAS DUNNE BOOKS, St. Martin's Press, 175 Fifth Ave., New York NY 10010. (212)674-5151. **Acquisitions:** Tom Dunne, publisher; Peter J. Wolverton, associate publisher; Ruth Cavin, associate publisher (mysteries). Publishes hardcover originals, trade paperback originals and reprints. **Publishes 90 titles/year. Receives 1,000 queries/ year. 20% of books from first-time authors. Pays royalty Pays 10-15% royalty on retail price for hardcover, 7½% for paperback. Offers varying advance.** Publishes book 1 year after acceptance of ms. Accepts simultaneous submissions. Responds in 2 months to queries.
  O— Thomas Dunne publishes a wide range of fiction and nonfiction.
Nonfiction: Biography. Subjects include government/politics, history, political commentary. "Author's attention to detail is important. We get a lot of manuscripts that are poorly proofread and just can't be considered." *Accepts agented submissions only.* Agents submit query or an outline and 100 sample pages. Reviews artwork/photos as part of ms package. Send photocopies.
Fiction: Mainstream/contemporary, suspense, thrillers, women's. *Accepts agented submissions only.* Agents submit query or submit synopsis and 100 sample pages.
Recent Title(s): *An Ocean Apart*, by Robin Pilcher (commercial fiction).

DUQUESNE UNIVERSITY PRESS, 600 Forbes Ave., Pittsburgh PA 15282-0101. (412)396-6610. Fax: (412)396-5984. Website: www.dupress.duq.edu. **Acquisitions:** Susan Wadsworth-Booth, director. Estab. 1927. Publishes hardcover and trade paperback originals. **Publishes 8-12 titles/year. Receives 500 queries and 75 mss/year. 30% of books from first-time authors; 95% from unagented writers. Pays royalty on net price. Offers (some) advance.** Publishes book 1 year after acceptance of ms. Responds in 1 month to proposals; 3 months to mss. Book catalog and ms guidelines for #10 SASE.
  O— Duquesne publishes scholarly monographs in the fields of literary studies (medieval & Renaissance), philosophy, ethics, religious studies and psychology. "We also publish a series, *Emerging Writers in Creative Nonfiction*, for first-time authors of creative nonfiction for a general readership."
Nonfiction: Scholarly/academic. Subjects include creative nonfiction, language/literature, philosophy, psychology, religion. "We look for quality of scholarship." For scholarly books, query or submit outline, 1 sample chapter and SASE. For creative nonfiction, submit 2 copies of ms.
Recent Title(s): *Walking My Dog, Jane*, by Ned Rozell; *The Last Settler*, by Jennifer Brice and Charles Mason.

[A] DUTTON, Penguin Putnam, Inc., 375 Hudson St., New York NY 10014. (212)366-2000. Website: www.penguinpu tnam.com. President: Clare Ferraro. Estab. 1852. **Publishes 40 titles/year. Accepts no unsolicited manuscripts. Offers negotiable advance.** Responds in 6 months to queries.
  O— Dutton publishes hardcover, original, mainstream, and contemporary fiction and nonfiction in the areas of biography, self-help, politics, psychology, and science for a general readership.

Nonfiction: Biography, humor, reference, self-help. Subjects include general, government/politics, psychology, science. *No unsolicited mss. Accepts agented submissions only.*
Fiction: Adventure, historical, literary, mainstream/contemporary, mystery, short story collections, suspense. Accpts no unsolicited manuscripts. *Accepts agented submissions only.*
Recent Title(s): *The Darwin Awards*, by Wendy Northcutt (humor); *Girl with a Pearl Earring*, by Tracy Chevalier (fiction).
Tips: "Write the complete manuscript and submit it to an agent or agents. They will know exactly which editor will be interested in a project."

DUTTON CHILDREN'S BOOKS, Penguin Putman Inc., 345 Hudson St., New York NY 10014. (212)414-3700. Fax: (212)414-3397. Website: www.penguinputnam.com. **Acquisitions:** Lucia Monfried, associate publisher/editor-in-chief (picture books, easy-to-read books, fiction); Stephanie Owens Lurie, president and publisher (picture books and fiction); Donna Brooks, editorial director (books for all ages with distinctive narrative style); Susan Van Metre, senior editor (character-oriented picture books and middle grade fiction); Tamar Mays, executive editor (novelty, picture books, fiction); Meredith Mundy Wasinger, editor (picture books, fiction and nonfiction). Estab. 1852. Publishes hardcover originals as well as novelty formats. **Publishes 100 titles/year. 15% of books from first-time authors. Pays royalty. Offers advance**.
  ○┓ Dutton Children's Books publishes high-quality fiction and nonfiction for readers ranging from preschoolers to young adults on a variety of subjects. Currently emphasizing picture books and middle-grade fiction that offer a fresh perspective. De-emphasizing photographic nonfiction.
Nonfiction: Children's/juvenile, For preschoolers to young adults. Subjects include animals, history (U.S.), nature/environment, science. Query with SASE.
Fiction: Picture books. Dutton Children's Books has a diverse, general interest list that includes picture books; easy-to-read books; and fiction for all ages, from "first chapter" books to young adult readers. Query with SASE only.
Recent Title(s): *Sun Bread*, by Elsa Kleven (picture book); *Food Rules*, by Bill Haduch (nonfiction); *Dial a Ghost*, by Eve Ibbotson (fiction).

■ **EAKIN PRESS/SUNBELT MEDIA, INC.**, P.O. Box 90159, Austin TX 78709-0159. (512)288-1771. Fax: (512)288-1813. E-mail: eakinpub@sig.net. Website: www.Eakinpress.com. **Acquisitions:** Edwin M. Eakin, editorial director; Virginia Messer, publisher. Estab. 1978. Publishes hardcover and paperback originals and reprints. **Publishes 60 titles/year. Receives 1,500 submissions/year. 50% of books from first-time authors; 90% from unagented writers. Pays 10-12-15% royalty on net sales.** Publishes book 18 months after acceptance of ms. Accepts simultaneous submissions. Responds in 3 months to queries. Book catalog for $1.25; ms guidelines for #10 SASE.
Imprints: Eakin Press, Nortex Press
  ○┓ Eakin specializes in Texana and Western Americana for adults and juveniles. Currently emphasizing women's studies.
Nonfiction: Biography, cookbook (regional). Subjects include Americana (Western), business/economics, cooking/foods/nutrition, ethnic, history, military/war, regional, sports, African American studies, Civil War, Texas history, World War II. Juvenile nonfiction: includes biographies of historic personalities, prefer with Texas or regional interest, or nature studies; and easy-read illustrated books for grades 1-3. Query with SASE.
Fiction: Juvenile fiction for grades K-12, preferably relating to Texas and the Southwest or contemporary. No adult fiction. Query or submit outline/synopsis and sample chapters.
Recent Title(s): *Inside Russia*, by Inez Jeffery; *Black, Buckskin and Blue*, by Art Burton.

■ **EDICIONES NUEVO ESPACIO**. E-mail: ednuevoespacio@aol.com. Website: www.editorial-ene.com. **Acquisitions:** Gustavo Gac-Artigas, senior editor (fiction); Maria C. Cintron, editor (fiction and academia). Publishes trade paperback originals and reprints. **Publishes 100 titles/year. Receives 1,000 queries and 500 mss/year. 30% of books from first-time authors; 100% from unagented writers. Pays 10-15% royalty; on CD books pays 10-18% royalty.** Accepts simultaneous submissions. Responds in 2 weeks to queries; 1 month to proposals; 2 months to mss. Book catalog and ms guidelines online.
Imprints: Gutenberg (traditional books), Platinum (CD books), Academia (scholarly studies)
  ○┓ "We publish book length (108-400 pages) critical studies on subjects related to Spanish, Spanish-American and USA Latino/a literature, and proceedings of conferences on Spanish and Spanish-American literature."
Nonfiction: Reference, scholarly and proceedings of literary conferences. Subjects include language/literature, memoirs, multicultural, translation, women's issues/studies. Query by e-mail to ednuevoespacio@aol.com or submit completed ms including the names of 3 experts in the field to editores@editorial-ene.com.
Fiction: Feminist, historical, literary, multicultural, mystery, plays, poetry, poetry in translation, romance, short story collections, suspense, young adult. Submit an e-mail query, and later, the ms by e-mail in Word or rich-text format.
Poetry: "We publish poetry collections with a minimum of 108 pages in Spanish, English or Bilingual Edition. The quality determines publication. We reprint poetry books." E-mail query to ednuevoespacio@aol.com or submit attached complete ms to editores@editorial-ene.com.
Recent Title(s): *Yo, Alejandro*, by Alejandro Gac-Artigas (Latino, memoir); *Correo electronico para amantes*, by Beatriz Salcedo-Strumpf (Mexico, novel); *Los mosquitos de orixa chango*, by Carlos G. Wilson (Panama, collected short stories and poetry).

Tips: "Be sure that your manuscript is ready to be published, that the minimum length of the book is 108 pages, that you own the rights, and that you send it to the appropriate imprint." Does not return submissions.

EDUCATOR'S INTERNATIONAL PRESS, INC., 18 Colleen Rd., Troy NY 12180. (518)271-9886. Fax: (518)266-9422. E-mail: sarah@edint.com. Website: www.edint.com. **Acquisitions:** Sarah J. Biondello, publisher/acquisitions editor. Estab. 1996. Publishes hardcover and trade paperback originals and reprints. **Publishes 10-12 titles/year. Receives 50 queries and 50 mss/year. 50% of books from first-time authors; 98% from unagented writers. Pays 3-15% royalty on wholesale price.** Publishes book 1 year after acceptance of ms. Accepts simultaneous submissions. Responds in 2 months to queries and proposals; 3 months to mss. Book catalog and ms guidelines free.

  O→ Educator's International publishes books in all aspects of education, broadly conceived, from pre-kindergarten to postgraduate. "We specialize in texts, professional books, videos and other materials for students, faculty, practitioners and researchers. We also publish a full list of books in the areas of women's studies, and social and behavioral sciences."

Nonfiction: Textbook, supplemental texts, conference proceedings. Subjects include education, gay/lesbian, language/literature, philosophy, psychology, software, women's issues/studies. Submit table of contents, outline, 2-3 chapters, résumé with SASE. Reviews artwork/photos as part of ms package.
Recent Title(s): *Our Sons Were Labeled Behavior Disordered*, by Joy-Ruth Mickelson.
Tips: Audience is professors, students, researchers, individuals, libraries.

EDUCATORS PUBLISHING SERVICE, INC., 31 Smith Place, Cambridge MA 02138-1089. (617)547-6706. Fax: (617)547-3805. Website: www.epsbooks.com. **Acquisitions:** Dorothy Miller, vice president and executive editor. Estab. 1952. **Publishes 26 titles/year. Receives 400 queries and 400 mss/year. 50% of books from first-time authors; 100% from unagented writers. Pays 5-12% royalty on retail price.** Publishes book 8 months minimum after acceptance of ms. Accepts simultaneous submissions. Responds in 1 month to queries; 3 months to proposals and mss. Book catalog and ms guidelines free.

  O→ EPS is looking for supplementary materials for the regular K-12 classroom. "We are particularly interested in workbook series, but will gladly consider any proposals for high-quality material that is useful to teachers and students." Currently emphasizing reading comprehension workbooks K-6.

Nonfiction: Workbooks (language arts and math) and some professional books. Subjects include language/literature. Query with SASE. Reviews artwork/photos as part of ms package. Send photocopies.
Recent Title(s): *Claims to Fame: 12 Short Biographies*, by Carol Einstein; *Handprints: An Early Reading Program*, by Ann Staman.
Tips: Teacher, students (K-adult) audiences.

EDUPRESS, INC., 208 Avenida Fabricante #200, San Clemente CA 92673. (949)366-9499. Fax: (949)366-9441. E-mail: info@edupressinc.com. Website: www.edupressinc.com. **Acquisitions:** Ellen Shanahan, production manager. Estab. 1979. Publishes trade paperback originals. **Publishes 40 titles/year. Receives 20 queries and 100 mss/year. 25% of books from first-time authors. Makes outright purchase.** Publishes book 1 year after acceptance of ms. Responds in 2 months to queries; 5 months to mss. Book catalog and ms guidelines free.

  O→ Edupress publishes supplemental resources for classroom curriculum. Currently emphasizing more science, math, writing emphasis than in the past.

Nonfiction: Subjects include education, resources for pre-school through middle school. "We use inhouse artists but will consider submitted art." Submit proposal package, including ms copy, outline, 1 sample chapter and SASE. Reviews artwork/photos as part of ms package. Send photocopies.
Recent Title(s): *Renaissance Activity Book*, by Linda Milliken.
Tips: Audience is classroom teachers and homeschool parents.

EDUTAINMENT MEDIA, P.O. Box 15274, Portland ME 04112. (207)780-1653. E-mail: scribe68@yahoo.com. Website: www.zenhemingway.com. **Acquisitions:** Jason Raschack, publisher (biography, how-to); Celeste McMann, acquisitions editor (photography, political books). Publishes hardcover originals and trade paperback originals and reprints. **Publishes 4 titles/year. 50% of books from first-time authors; 50% from unagented writers. Pays 6-8% royalty on retail price. Offers $1,000 advance.** Publishes book 1 year after acceptance of ms. Accepts simultaneous submissions. Responds in 1 month to queries. Book catalog free; ms guidelines for #10 SASE.

  O→ Future plans call for submissions on the following specific subject areas: welfare reform, education reform and libertarian political philosophy.

Nonfiction: Biography, how-to, illustrated book, self-help. Subjects include business/economics, history, hobbies, photography. Query with SASE. *All unsolicited mss returned unopened.* Reviews artwork/photos as part of ms package. Send photocopies.
Fiction: Comic books, graphic novels. Absolutely no children's books. Submit complete ms.
Recent Title(s): *Comic Book Publishing, A How-to Manual*, by J. Raschack; *Women: A Success Guide for Men; Men: A Success Guide for Women*.
Tips: "Our audience consists of highly educated people that follow all publications on subjects they are interested in."

EERDMANS BOOKS FOR YOUNG READERS, William B. Eerdmans Publishing Co., 255 Jefferson Ave. SE, Grand Rapids MI 49503. (616)459-4591. Fax: (616)459-6540. **Acquisitions:** Judy Zylstra, editor. Publishes picture books and middle reader and young adult fiction and nonfiction. **Publishes 12-15 titles/year. Receives 3,000 submissions/year. Pays 5-7½% royalty on retail price.** Accepts simultaneous submissions. Responds in 6 weeks to queries. Publishes middle reader and YA books 1 year after acceptance. Publishes picture books 2-3 years after acceptance. Book catalog for large SASE.

    Oᴙ "We publish books for children and young adults that deal with spiritual themes—but never in a preachy or heavy-handed way. Some of our books are clearly religious, while others (especially our novels) look at spiritual issues in very subtle ways. We look for books that are honest, wise and hopeful." Currently emphasizing general picture books (also picture book biographies), novels (middle reader and YA). De-emphasizing YA biographies, retellings of Bible stories.

Nonfiction: Children's/juvenile, picture books, middle reader, young adult nonfiction. "Do not send illustrations unless you are a professional illustrator." Submit complete mss for picture books and novels or biographies under 200 pages with SASE. For longer books, send query letter and 3 or 4 sample chapters with SASE. Reviews artwork/photos as part of ms package. Send color photocopies rather than original art.

Fiction: Juvenile, picture books, young adult, middle reader. "Do not send illustrations unless you are a professional illustrator." Submit complete mss for picture books and novels or biographies under 200 pages with SASE. For longer books, send query letter and 3 or 4 sample chapters with SASE.

Recent Title(s): *A Bird or Two: A Story about Henri Matisse*, written and illustrated by Bijou Le Tord; *At Break of Day*, written by Nikki Grimes, illustrated by Paul Morin.

WILLIAM B. EERDMANS PUBLISHING CO., 255 Jefferson Ave. SE, Grand Rapids MI 49503. (616)459-4591. Fax: (616)459-6540. E-mail: sales@eerdmans.com. **Acquisitions:** Jon Pott, editor-in-chief; Charles Van Hof, managing editor (history); Judy Zylstra, children's book editor. Estab. 1911. Publishes hardcover and paperback originals and reprints. **Publishes 120-130 titles/year. Receives 3,000-4,000 submissions/year. 10% of books from first-time authors; 95% from unagented writers. Pays royalty. Offers occasional advance.** Publishes book 1 year after acceptance of ms. Accepts simultaneous submissions. Responds in 6 weeks to queries. Book catalog free.

Imprints: Eerdmans Books for Young Readers (Judy Zylstra, editor)

    Oᴙ "Approximately 80% of our adult publications are religious and most of these are academic or semi-academic in character (as opposed to inspirational or celebrity books), though we also publish books on the Christian life. Our nonreligious titles, most of them in regional history or on social issues, aim, similarly, at an educated audience."

Nonfiction: Children's/juvenile, reference, textbook, monographs. Subjects include history (religious), language/literature, philosophy (of religion), psychology, regional (history), religion, sociology, translation, Biblical studies, theology, ethics. "We prefer that writers take the time to notice if we have published anything at all in the same category as their manuscript before sending it to us." Query with outline, 2-3 sample chapter and SASE for return of ms. Reviews artwork/photos as part of ms package.

Recent Title(s): *Abraham Lincoln: Redeemer President*, by Allen C. Guelzo; *The Book of Marriage: The Wisest Answers to the Toughest Questions*, edited by Dana Mack and David Blankenhorn.

■ **ELECTRIC WORKS PUBLISHING**, 605 Ave. C.E., Bismarck ND 58501. (701)255-0356. E-mail: editors@electricpublishing.com. Website: www.electricpublishing.com. **Acquisitions:** James R. Bohe, editor-in-chief. Publishes digital books. **Publishes 50 titles/year. Receives 30 queries and 250 mss/year. 70% of books from first-time authors; 85% from unagented writers. Pays 36-40% royalty on wholesale price.** Publishes book 3 months after acceptance of ms. Accepts simultaneous submissions. Responds in 5 months to queries. Book catalog and ms guidelines online.

    Oᴙ Digital publisher offering a wide range of subjects.

Nonfiction: Biography, children's/juvenile, cookbook, how-to, humor, illustrated book, multimedia (CD-ROM, disk), reference, self-help, technical. Subjects include agriculture/horticulture, Americana, animals, anthropology/archeology, art/architecture, business/economics, child guidance/parenting, computers/electronic, cooking/foods/nutrition, creative nonfiction, education, ethnic, gardening, government/politics, health/medicine, history, hobbies, humor, language/literature, memoirs, military/war, money/finance, multicultural, music/dance, nature/environment, philosophy, photography, psychology, recreation, regional, religion, science, sociology, software, spirituality, sports, translation, travel, women's issues/studies. *Electronic submissions only.* Submit entire ms in digital format. Reviews artwork/photos as part of ms package.

Fiction: Adventure, ethnic, experimental, fantasy, gothic, historical, horror, humor, juvenile, literary, mainstream/contemporary, military/war, multicultural, multimedia, mystery, occult, plays, poetry in translation, regional, religious, romance, science fiction, short story collections, spiritual, sports, suspense, western, young adult. *Electronic submissions only.* Submit ms in digital format.

Poetry: Submit complete ms.

Recent Title(s): *Felling of the Sons*, by Monette Bebow-Reinhard; *Marzipan*, by George Laidlaw.

ELEPHANT BOOKS, 65 Macedonia Rd., Alexander NC 28701. (828)252-9515. Fax: (828)255-8719. E-mail: sales@abooks.com. Website: abooks.com/elephant. **Acquisitions:** Pat Roberts, acquisitions editor. Publishes trade paperback originals and reprints. **Publishes 8 titles/year. Receives 100 queries and 50 mss/year. 90% of books from first-time authors; 80% from unagented writers. Pays 12-15% royalty on wholesale price Seldom offers advance.** Publishes book 18 months after acceptance of ms. Book catalog and ms guidelines for 9×12 SASE with 5 ounces postage.

Imprints: Blue/Gray Books (contact Ralph Roberts, Civil War history)

Nonfiction: Cookbook. Subjects include cooking/foods/nutrition, history, military/war (Civil War). Query or submit outline with 3 sample chapters and proposal package, including potential marketing plans with SASE. Reviews artwork/photos as part of ms package. Send photocopies.
Recent Title(s): *Rebel Boast*, by Manly Wade Wellman.

◼ EMPIRE PUBLISHING SERVICE, P.O. Box 1344, Studio City CA 91614-0344. (818)789-4980. **Acquisitions:** Joseph Witt. Publishes hardcover reprints and trade paperback originals and reprints. **Publishes 40 titles/year; imprint publishes 15 titles/year. Receives 500 queries and 85 mss/year. 50% of books from first-time authors; 95% from unagented writers. Pays 6-10% royalty on retail price. Offers variable advance.** Publishes book up to 2 years after acceptance of ms. Responds in 1 month to queries; 2 months to proposals; up to 1 year to mss. Book catalog for SAE with 5 first-class stamps; ms guidelines $1 with #10 SASE.
Imprints: Gaslight Publications, Gaslight Books, Empire Publications
  ○━ "Submit only Sherlock Holmes, performing arts and health."
Nonfiction: How-to, humor, reference, technical, textbook. Subjects include health/medicine, humor, music/dance, Sherlock Holmes. Query with SASE. Reviews artwork/photos as part of ms package. Send photocopies.
Fiction: Sherlock Holmes. Query with SASE.
Recent Title(s): *Sherlock Holmes and the Curse of the Mummy's Tomb*, by J. Harries (mystery, music and suspense); *Sherlock Holmes in the Deerstalker*, by T. Mustoo/D. Flack (musical, mystery).

◼ ENCOUNTER BOOKS, 116 New Montgomery St., Suite 206, San Francisco CA 94105-3640. (415)538-1460. Fax: (415)538-1461. Website: www.encounterbooks.com. **Acquisitions:** Peter Collier, publisher. Hardcover originals and trade paperback reprints. **Publishes 12-20 titles/year. Receives 500 queries and 200 mss/year. 40% of books from first-time authors; 60% from unagented writers. Pays 7-10% royalty on retail price. Offers $2,000-25,000 advance.** Publishes book 22 months after acceptance of ms. Accepts simultaneous submissions. Responds in 3 months to queries; 4 months to proposals and mss. Book catalog and ms guidelines online.
  ○━ Encounter Books publishes serious nonfiction—books that can alter our society, challenge our morality, stimulate our imaginations. Currently emphasizing history, culture, social criticism and politics.
Nonfiction: Biography, reference. Subjects include anthropology/archeology, business/economics, child guidance/parenting, education, ethnic, government/politics, health/medicine, history, language/literature, memoirs, military/war, multicultural, nature/environment, philosophy, psychology, religion, science, sociology, women's issues/studies, gender studies. Submit proposal package, including outline and 1 sample chapter.
Recent Title(s): *The Long March: How the Cultural Revolution of the 1960s Changed America*, by Roger Kimball; *Culture of Death: The Assault on Medical Ethics in America*, by Wesley J. Smith.

◼ ENTREPRENEUR PRESS, 245 McCabe Way, Irvine CA 92614. (949)261-2325. Fax: (949)261-7729. E-mail: kwright@entrepreneur.com. Website: www.smallbizbooks.com. **Acquisitions:** Jere Calmes, editorial director; Kaina Wright, assistant editor. Publishes hardcover and trade paperback originals and trade paperback reprints. **Publishes 160 titles/year. Receives 1,200 queries and 600 mss/year. 40% of books from first-time authors; 60% from unagented writers. Pays 2-30% royalty or makes $2,000-15,000 outright purchase.** Accepts simultaneous submissions. Book catalog and ms guidelines free.
Nonfiction: Humor, multimedia (e-book), reference, self-help. Subjects include business/economics, women's issues/studies. Query with SASE or submit proposal package including outline, 2 sample chapter(s), author bio, preface or executive summary, competition. Reviews artwork/photos as part of ms package. Send transparencies.
Recent Title(s): *Start Your Own Business*, by Lesonsky; *How to Be a Teenage Millionaire*, by Beroff and Adams.
Tips: Audience is "people who are thinking about starting their own business and people who have recently started their own business. Also general business skills, including finance, marketing, presentation, leadership, etc."

Ⓐ EOS, (formerly Avon Eos), HarperCollins, 10 E. 53rd St., New York NY 10022. (212)207-7000. Website: www.eos books.com. Publishes hardcover originals, trade and mass market paperback originals and reprints. **Publishes 55-60 titles/year. 10% of books from first-time authors. Pays royalty on retail price. Offers variable advance.** Publishes book 18-24 months after acceptance of ms. Responds in 6 months to queries. Manuscript guidelines for #10 SASE.
  ○━ Eos publishes "quality science fiction/fantasy with broad appeal." .
Fiction: Fantasy, science fiction. No horror or juvenile. *Accepts agented submissions only. All unsolicited mss returned unopened. No unsolicited submissions.*
Recent Title(s): *The Fresco*, by Sheri S. Tepper; *Colony Fleet*, by Susan R. Matthews; *Sky of Swords*, by Dave Duncan.
Tips: "We strongly advise submitting via a literary agent, as good agents know the tastes and needs of individual editors. It is a policy of HarperCollins to return unread all unsolicited manuscripts and proposals for books that the company receives. Unfortunately the volume of these submissions is so large that we cannot give them the attention they deserve. We recommend that you consult your public library for sources that can direct you in preparing a submission and locating an appropriate agent and/or publisher."

◼ EPICENTER PRESS, INC., P.O. Box 82368, Kenmore WA 98028. (425)485-6822. Fax: (425)481-8253. E-mail: info@EpicenterPress.com. Website: www.EpicenterPress.com. **Acquisitions:** Kent Sturgis, publisher. Estab. 1987.

Publishes hardcover and trade paperback originals. **Publishes 10 titles/year. Receives 200 queries and 100 mss/year. 75% of books from first-time authors; 90% from unagented writers.** Publishes book 1-2 years after acceptance of ms. Responds in 2 months to queries. Book catalog and ms guidelines online.

    O→ "We are a regional press founded in Alaska whose interests include but are not limited to the arts, history, environment, and diverse cultures and lifestyles of the North Pacific and high latitudes.

Nonfiction: "Our focus is Alaska. We do not encourage nonfiction titles from outside Alaska." Biography, coffee table book, gift book, humor. Subjects include animals, art/architecture, ethnic, history, humor, nature/environment, photography, recreation, regional, women's issues/studies. Submit outline and 3 sample chapters. Reviews artwork/photos as part of ms package. Send photocopies.

Recent Title(s): *Cold River Spirits*, by Jan Harper-Haines.

ETC PUBLICATIONS, 700 E. Vereda Sur, Palm Springs CA 92262-4816. (760)325-5352. Fax: (760)325-8841. **Acquisitions:** Dr. Richard W. Hostrop, publisher (education and social sciences); Lee Ona S. Hostrop, editorial director (history and works suitable below the college level). Estab. 1972. Publishes hardcover and paperback originals. **Publishes 6-12 titles/year. Receives 100 submissions/year. 75% of books from first-time authors; 90% from unagented writers. Offers 5-15% royalty, based on wholesale and retail price.** Publishes book 9 months after acceptance of ms. *Writer's Market* recommends allowing 2 months for reply to queries.

    O→ ETC publishes works that "further learning as opposed to entertainment."

Nonfiction: Textbook, educational management, gifted education, futuristics. Subjects include education, translation (in above areas). Submit complete ms with SASE. *Writer's Market* recommends query first with SASE. Reviews artwork/photos as part of ms package.

Recent Title(s): *The Internet for Educators and Homeschoolers*, by Steve Jones, Ph.D.

Tips: "Special consideration is given to those authors who are capable and willing to submit their completed work in camera-ready, typeset form. We are particularly interested in works suitable for *both* the Christian school market and homeschoolers; e.g., state history texts below the high school level with a Christian-oriented slant."

EVAN-MOOR EDUCATIONAL PUBLISHERS, 18 Lower Ragsdale Dr., Monterey CA 93940-5746. (831)649-5901. Fax: (831)649-6256. E-mail: editorial@evan-moor.com. Website: www.evan-moor.com. **Acquisitions:** Marilyn Evans, senior editor. Estab. 1979. Publishes teaching materials. **Publishes 50-60 titles/year. Receives 50 queries and 100 mss/year. 1% of books from first-time authors; 100% from unagented writers. Makes outright purchase.** Publishes book 1 year after acceptance of ms. Accepts simultaneous submissions. Responds in 3 months to queries. Book catalog and ms guidelines online.

    O→ "Our books are teaching ideas, lesson plans, and blackline reproducibles for grades PreK-6 in all curriculum areas except music and bilingual." Currently emphasizing writing/language arts, practice materials for home use. De-emphasizing thematic materials. We do not publish children's literature.

Nonfiction: Children's/juvenile. Subjects include education, teaching materials, grade pre-K-6. No children's literature. Submit proposal package, including outline and 3 sample chapters.

Recent Title(s): *How to Plan Your School Year*, by Jill Norris; *Math Practice at Home* (5 book series); *Literacy Centers*, by JoEllen Moore.

Tips: "Writers should know how classroom/educational materials differ from trade publications. They should request catalogs and submissions guidelines before sending queries or manuscripts."

M. EVANS AND CO., INC., 216 E. 49th St., New York NY 10017-1502. Fax: (212)688-2810. E-mail: mevans@sprynet.com. **Acquisitions:** George C. deKay, editor-in-chief (general trade); P.J. Dempsey, senior editor (general nonfiction). Estab. 1960. Publishes hardcover and trade paperback originals. **Publishes 30-40 titles/year. 5% from unagented writers. Pays negotiable royalty.** Publishes book 8 months after acceptance of ms. Responds in 2 months to queries. Book catalog for 9×12 SAE with 3 first-class stamps.

    O→ Evans has a strong line of health and self-help books but is interested in publishing quality titles on a wide variety of subject matters. "We publish a general trade list of adult nonfiction, cookbooks and semi-reference works. The emphasis is on selectivity, publishing commercial works with quality." Currently emphasizing health, relationships, nutrition.

Nonfiction: Cookbook, self-help. Subjects include cooking/foods/nutrition, general, health/medicine, relationships. "Our most successful nonfiction titles have been related to health and the behavioral sciences. No limitation on subject." Query with SASE. *No unsolicited mss.*

Fiction: "Our very small general fiction list represents an attempt to combine quality with commercial potential. We publish no more than one novel per season." Query with SASE. *No unsolicited mss.*

Recent Title(s): *Dr. Atkins' Diet Revolution* (health); *This Is How Love Works*, by Steven Carter.

Tips: "A writer should clearly indicate what his book is all about, frequently the task the writer performs least well. His credentials, although important, mean less than his ability to convince this company that he understands his subject and that he has the ability to communicate a message worth hearing. Writers should review our book catalog before making submissions."

EXCALIBUR PUBLICATIONS, P.O. Box 35369, Tucson AZ 85740-5369. **Acquisitions:** Alan M. Petrillo, editor. Publishes trade paperback originals. **Publishes 6-8 titles/year. Pays royalty or makes outright purchase.** Responds in 2 months to mss.

O→ Excalibur publishes historical and military works from all time periods.

Nonfiction: Subjects include history (military), military/war (strategy and tactics, as well as the history of battles, firearms, arms and armour). "We are seeking well-researched and documented works. Unpublished writers are welcome." Query with outline, first chapter and any 2 additional consecutive chapters with SASE. Include notes on photos, illustrations and maps.

Recent Title(s): *Socket Bayonets of the Great Powers*, by Robert W. Shuey.

Tips: "Know your subject matter, and present it in a clear and precise manner. Please give us a brief description of your background or experience as it relates to your submission."

N: EXCELSIOR CEE PUBLISHING, P.O. Box 5861, Norman OK 73070. (405)329-3909. Fax: (405)329-6886. **Acquisitions:** J.C. Marshall. Estab. 1989. Publishes hardcover and trade paperback originals. **Publishes 8 titles/year. Receives 400 queries/year. Pays royalty or makes outright purchase (both negotiable).** Publishes book 1 year after acceptance of ms. Accepts simultaneous submissions. Responds in 1 month to queries. Book catalog for #10 SASE.

O→ "All of our books speak to the reader through words of feeling—whether they are how-to, educational, humor or whatever genre, the reader comes away with feeling, truth and inspiration." Currently emphasizing how-to, family history, memoirs, inspiration. De-emphasizing childrens.

Nonfiction: Biography, coffee table book, gift book, how-to, humor, self-help, textbook. Subjects include Americana, education, history, hobbies, language/literature, women's issues/studies, general nonfiction, writing. Query with SASE.

Recent Title(s): *How to Write Your Personal Memoirs*; *How to Record Your Family History*; *Letters from the 20th Century—A History in Memories*.

Tips: "We have a general audience, book store browsers interested in nonfiction reading. We publish titles that have a mass appeal and can be enjoyed by a large reading public. We publish very few unsolicited manuscripts, and our publishing calendar is 75% full up to 1 year in advance."

EXECUTIVE EXCELLENCE PUBLISHING, 1366 E. 1120 S., Provo UT 84606. (800)304-9782. Fax: (801)377-5960. E-mail: info@eep.com. Website: www.eep.com. **Acquisitions:** Ken Shelton, editor in chief. Estab. 1984. Publishes hardcover and trade paperback originals and trade paperback reprints. **Publishes 16-20 titles/year. Receives 300 queries and 150 mss/year. 35% of books from first-time authors; 95% from unagented writers. Pays 15% on cash received and 50% of subsidary right proceeds.** Publishes book 6-9 months after acceptance of ms. Accepts simultaneous submissions. Responds in 1 month to queries and proposals; 3 months to mss. Book catalog online.

O→ Executive Excellence publishes business and self-help titles. "We help you—the busy person, executive or entrepreneur—to find a wiser, better way to live your life and lead your organization." Currently emphasizing business innovations for general management and leadership (from the personal perspective). De-emphasizing technical or scholarly textbooks on operational processes and financial management or workbooks.

Nonfiction: Self-help. Subjects include business/economics, leadership/management, entrepreneurship, career, small buisness, motivational. Submit proposal package, including outline, 1-2 sample chapters and author bio, company information.

Recent Title(s): *Spirit of Leadership*, by Robert J. Spitzer; *Traits of Champions*, by Andrew Word.

Tips: "Executive Excellence Publishing is an established publishing house with a strong niche in the marketplace. Our magazines, *Executive Excellence*, *Sales and Marketing Excellence* and *Personal Excellence*, are distributed monthly in twelve countries across the world and give us and our authors massive market exposure. Our authors are on the cutting edge in their fields of leadership, self-help and business and organizational development. We usually publish only the biggest names in the field, but we are always looking for strong new talent with something to say, and a burning desire to say it."

FACTS ON FILE, INC., 11 Penn Plaza, 15th Floor, New York NY 10001. (212)967-8800. Fax: (212)967-9196. E-mail: llikoff@factsonfile.com. Website: www.factsonfile.com. **Acquisitions:** Laurie Likoff, editorial director (science, music, history); Frank Darmstadt (science, nature, multi-volume reference); Nicole Bowen, senior editor (American history, women's studies, young adult reference); James Chambers, trade editor (health, pop culture, sports); Anne Savarese, acquisitions editor (language/literature). Estab. 1941. Publishes hardcover originals and reprints. **Publishes 135 titles/year. 25% from unagented writers. Pays 10% royalty on retail price Offers $7,000-10,000 advance.** Accepts simultaneous submissions. Responds in 2 months to queries. Book catalog free.

Imprints: Checkmark Books

O→ Facts on File produces high-quality reference materials on a broad range of subjects for the school library market and the general nonfiction trade.

Nonfiction: "We publish serious, informational books for a targeted audience. All our books must have strong library interest, but we also distribute books effectively to the trade. Our library books fit the junior and senior high school curriculum." Reference. Subjects include education, health/medicine, history, language/literature, multicultural, recreation, religion, sports, careers, entertainment, natural history, popular culture. No computer books, technical books, cookbooks, biographies (except YA), pop psychology, humor, fiction or poetry. Query or submit outline and sample chapter with SASE. No submissions returned without SASE.

Tips: "Our audience is school and public libraries for our more reference-oriented books and libraries, schools and bookstores for our less reference-oriented informational titles."

FAIRLEIGH DICKINSON UNIVERSITY PRESS, 285 Madison Ave., Madison NJ 07940. (973)443-8564. Fax: (973)443-8364. E-mail: fdupress@fdu.edu. **Acquisitions:** Harry Keyishian, director. Estab. 1967. Publishes hardcover originals. **Publishes 45 titles/year. Receives 300 submissions/year. 33% of books from first-time authors; 95% from unagented writers.** Publishes book 1 year after acceptance of ms. Responds in 2 weeks to queries. *Writer's Market* recommends allowing 2 months for reply.
- "Contract is arranged through Associated University Presses of Cranbury, New Jersey. We are a *selection* committee only." Nonauthor subsidy publishes 2% of books.
- O→ Fairleigh Dickinson publishes books for the academic market.

Nonfiction: Reference, scholarly books. Subjects include art/architecture, business/economics, film/cinema/stage, government/politics, history, music/dance, philosophy, psychology, sociology, women's issues/studies, Civil War, film, Jewish studies, literary criticism. Looking for scholarly books in all fields; no nonscholarly books. Query with outline and sample chapters. Reviews artwork/photos as part of ms package.
Recent Title(s): *The Mental Anatomies of William Godwin and Mary Shelley*, by William D. Brewer.
Tips: "Research must be up to date. Poor reviews result when authors' bibliographies and notes don't reflect current research. We follow *Chicago Manual of Style* (14th edition) style in scholarly citations. We will consider collections of unpublished conference papers or essay collections, if they relate to a strong central theme and have scholarly merit."

FAIRVIEW PRESS, 2450 Riverside Ave., Minneapolis MN 55454. (800)544-8207. Fax: (612)672-4980. E-mail: press@fairview.org. Website: www.fairviewpress.org. **Acquisitions:** Lane Stiles, director; Stephanie Billecke, senior editor. Estab. 1988. Publishes hardcover and trade paperback originals and reprints. **Publishes 8-12 titles/year. Receives 3,000 queries and 1,500 mss/year. 40% of books from first-time authors; 65% from unagented writers. Advance and royalties negotiable.** Publishes book 1 year after acceptance of ms. Accepts simultaneous submissions. Responds in 6 months to proposals. Book catalog and ms guidelines free.
- O→ Fairview Press currently publishes books and related materials emphasizing aging, end-of-life issues, caregiving, grief and bereavement.

Nonfiction: Reference, self-help. Subjects include health/medicine, women's issues/studies, aging, grief and bereavement, patient education, nutrition. "Manuscripts that are essentially one person's story are rarely salable." Submit proposal package including outline, 2 sample chapter(s), author bio, SASE, marketing ideas. Reviews artwork/photos as part of ms package. Send photocopies.
Recent Title(s): *Remembering with Love*, by Elizabeth Levang and Sherokee Isle.
Tips: Audience is general reader, especially families. "Tell us what void your book fills in the market; give us an angle. Tell us who will buy your book. We have moved away from recovery books and have focused on health and medical issues."

[N:] FAITH KIDS BOOKS, Chariot Victor Publishing, 4050 Lee Vance View, Colorado Springs CO 80918. (719)536-3271. Fax: (719)536-3269. **Acquisitions:** Mary McNeil, children's product manager; Heather Gemmen, editor. Publishes hardcover and paperback originals. **Publishes 40-50 titles/year. Receives 500-1,000 mss/year. Pays variable royalty on retail price or flat fee, depending on project.** Publishes book 18 months after acceptance of ms. Accepts simultaneous submissions. Responds in 4 months to queries. Book catalog free; ms guidelines for #10 SASE.
- O→ Faith Kids Books publishes inspirational works for children, ages 1-12, with a strong underlying Christian theme or clearly stated Biblical value, designed to foster spiritual growth in children and positive interaction between parent and child. Currently emphasizing picture books, books for the very young (under 4). De-emphasizing fiction for 8-16-year-olds.

Nonfiction: Biography, children's/juvenile. Subjects include religion (Bible stories, devotionals), picture books on nonfiction subjects. Submit proposal package including SASE, cover letter.
Fiction: Historical, juvenile, picture books, religious, toddler books. No teen fiction. Accepts proposals with SASE from previously published authors or agented authors only.
Recent Title(s): *Devotions from the World of Sports*, by John & Kathy Hillman (nonfiction).

FARRAR, STRAUS & GIROUX BOOKS FOR YOUNG READERS, Farrar Straus Giroux, Inc., 19 Union Square West, New York NY 10003. (212)741-6900. Fax: (212)633-2427. **Acquisitions:** Margaret Ferguson, editorial director. Estab. 1946. Publishes hardcover and trade paperback originals. **Publishes 75 titles/year. Receives 6,000 queries and mss/year. 5% of books from first-time authors; 50% from unagented writers. Pays 3-6% royalty on retail price for paperbacks, 5-10% for hardcovers. Offers $3,000-25,000 advance.** Publishes book 18 months after acceptance of ms. Accepts simultaneous submissions. Responds in 2 months to queries; 3 months to mss. Book catalog for 9×12 SAE with $1.87 postage; ms guidelines for #10 SASE.
Imprints: Aerial Fiction, Frances Foster Books, Melanie Kroupa Books, Mirasol/Libros Juveniles, R&S Books, Sunburst Paperbacks
- O→ "We publish original and well-written material for all ages."

Fiction: Juvenile, picture books, young adult. "We still look at unsolicited manuscripts, but for novels we prefer synopsis and sample chapters. Always enclose SASE for any materials author wishes returned. Query status of submissions in writing—no calls, please." Query with SASE; considers complete ms.
Recent Title(s): *Holes*, by Louis Sachar (Newberry Medal Book, ages 10 and up); *Trolls*, by Polly Horvath; *Snow*, by Uri Shulevitz (Caldecott Honor Book).
Tips: Audience is full age range, preschool to young adult. Specializes in literary fiction.

A **FARRAR, STRAUS & GIROUX PAPERBACKS**, 19 Union Square West, New York NY 10003. (212)741-6900. Publishes trade paperback originals and reprints. **Publishes 70 titles/year. Receives 1,500-2,000 queries and mss/year. Pays 6% royalty on retail price. Advance varies.** Accepts simultaneous submissions. Responds in 2 months to queries; 2 months to proposals. Book catalog and ms guidelines free.

○━ Farrar, Straus & Giroux Paperbacks emphasizes literary nonfiction and fiction, as well as fiction and poetry reprints.

Nonfiction: Biography. Subjects include child guidance/parenting, education, language/literature. *No unsolicited mss.* Query with outline, 2-3 sample chapters, cv, cover letter describing project and SASE.

Fiction: Literary. Mostly reprints of classic authors.

Recent Title(s): *Message from My Father*, by Calvin Trillin (memoir); *Enemies: A Love Story*, by Isaac Bashevis Singer (fiction).

A **FARRAR, STRAUS & GIROUX, INC.**, 19 Union Square West, New York NY 10003. Estab. 1946. Publishes hardcover originals. **Publishes 120 titles/year. Receives 5,000 submissions/year. Pays variable royalty. Offers advance.** Publishes book 18 months after acceptance of ms.

Imprints: Faber & Faber Inc. (UK-originated books), Farrar, Straus & Giroux Paperbacks, Farrar, Straus & Giroux Books for Young Readers, Hill & Wang, North Point Press, Sunburst Books

○━ Farrar, Straus & Giroux is one of the most respected publishers of top-notch commercial-literary fiction and specialized nonfiction, as well as cutting-edge poetry.

FREDERICK FELL PUBLISHERS, INC., 2131 Hollywood Blvd., Hollywood FL 33020. (954)925-5242. Fax: (954)925-5244. E-mail: fellpub@aol.com. Website: www.fellpub.com. **Acquisitions:** Barnara Newman, senior editor. Publishes hardcover and trade paperback originals. **Publishes 25 titles/year. Receives 4,000 queries and 1,000 mss/year. 95% of books from first-time authors; 95% from unagented writers. Pays negotiable royalty on retail price. Offers up to $10,000 advance.** Publishes book 1 year after acceptance of ms. Accepts simultaneous submissions. Responds in 1 month to queries; 3 months to proposals. Manuscript guidelines for #10 SASE.

○━ "Fell has just launched the *Know-It-All* series. We will be publishing over 125 titles in all genres. Prove to us that your title is the best in this new exciting format."

Nonfiction: "We are reviewing in all categories. Advise us of the top three competitive titles for your work and the reasons why the public would benefit by having your book published." How-to, reference, self-help. Subjects include business/economics, child guidance/parenting, education, ethnic, film/cinema/stage, health/medicine, hobbies, money/finance, spirituality. Submit proposal package, including outline, 3 sample chapters, author bio, publicity ideas, market analysis. Reviews artwork/photos as part of ms package. Send photocopies.

Recent Title(s): *Fell's Official Know-It-All Guide to Writing Bestsellers*; *Fell's Official Know-It-All Guide to Diabetes*; *Fell's Official Know-It-All Guide to Hypnosis*.

Tips: "We are most interested in well-written, timely nonfiction with strong sales potential. We will not consider topics that appeal to a small, select audience. Learn markets and be prepared to help with sales and promotion. Show us how your book is unique or better than the competition."

N **THE FEMINIST PRESS AT THE CITY UNIVERSITY OF NEW YORK**, 365 Fifth Ave., Suite 5406, New York NY 10016. (212)817-7915. Fax: (212)817-1593. **Acquisitions:** Jean Casella, publisher/director. Estab. 1970. Publishes hardcover and trade paperback originals and reprints. **Publishes 22 titles/year. Receives 1,000 submissions/year. 10% of books from first-time authors; 50% from unagented writers. Pays royalty on net receipts. Offers $250 advance.** Accepts simultaneous submissions. Responds in 6 months to proposals. Book catalog for 8½×11 SASE; ms guidelines for #10 SASE.

○━ Our primary mission is to publish works of fiction by women which preserve and extend women's literary traditions. We emphasize work by multicultural/international women writers.

Nonfiction: Subjects include ethnic, gay/lesbian, government/politics, health/medicine, history, language/literature, memoirs, multicultural, music/dance, sociology, translation, women's issues/studies. "We look for nonfiction work which challenges gender-role stereotypes and documents women's historical and cultural contributions. Note that we generally publish for the college classroom as well as the trade." Children's (ages 10 and up)/juvenile primary materials for the humanities and social science classroom and general readers, with a special emphasis on multicultural and international characters and settings. No monographs. Send proposal package, including materials requested in guidelines. Reviews artwork/photos as part of ms package. Send photocopies.

Fiction: "The Feminist Press publishes fiction reprints only. No original fiction is considered."

Recent Title(s): *Coming to Birth*, by Marjorie Oludhe Macgoye (1986 Sinclair Prize Winner); *David's Story*, by Zoe Wicomb; *Almost Touching the Skies*, edited by Florence Howe and Jean Casella (women's coming of age stories).

FERGUSON PUBLISHING COMPANY, 200 W. Jackson, 7th Floor, Chicago IL 60606. Website: www.fergpubco.com. **Acquisitions:** Andrew Morkes, managing editor, career publications. Estab. 1940. Publishes hardcover originals. **Publishes 50 titles/year. Pays by project.** Responds in 6 months to queries.

○━ "We are primarily a career education publisher that publishes for schools and libraries. We need writers who have expertise in a particular career or career field, (for possible full-length books on a specific career or field)."

Nonfiction: "We publish work specifically for the elementary/junior high/high school/college library reference market. Works are generally encyclopedic in nature. Our current focus is career encyclopedias. We consider manuscripts that cross over into the trade market." Reference. Subjects include careers. "No mass market, poetry, scholarly, or juvenile books, please." Query or submit an outline and 1 sample chapter.
Recent Title(s): *Ferguson Career Biographies: Colin Powell, Bill Gates, etc* (20 total books in series); *Why Are You Underpaid and What You Can Do About It*, by Roy Dreyfack.
Tips: "We like writers who know the market—former or current librarians or teachers or guidance counselors."
Nonfiction: Subjects include Americana, anthropology/archeology, cooking/foods/nutrition, ethnic, history, memoirs, nature/environment, regional, crafts and crafts people of the Southwest, Women Writers of the West. "We're interested in the history and natural history of the West." Query with outline and SASE. Reviews artwork/photos as part of ms package.
Recent Title(s): *Viva el Amor, A Latino Wedding Planner*, by Dr. Edna Bautista (nonfiction); *Little Fox's Secret*, by Mary Peace Finley (children's fiction); *White Grizzly*, by Mary Peace Finley (mid-grade historical fiction).

N: FINDHORN PRESS, P.O. Box 13939, Tallahassee FL 32317-3939. (850)893-2920. Fax: (850)893-3442. E-mail: info@findhornpress.com. Website: www.findhornpress.com. **Acquisitions:** Thierry Bogliolo, publisher. Publishes trade paperback originals. **Publishes 10 titles/year. Receives 500 queries/year. 50% of books from first-time authors. Pays 10-15% royalty on wholesale price.** Publishes book 1 year after acceptance of ms. Book catalog and ms guidelines online.
Nonfiction: Self-help. Subjects include health/medicine, nature/environment, spirituality. Submit proposal package including outline, 1 sample chapter(s), marketing plan.

FIRE ENGINEERING BOOKS & VIDEOS, PennWell Publishing Co., 1421 S. Sheridan Rd., Tulsa OK 74112-6600. (918)831-9420. Fax: (918)832-9319. E-mail: jaredw@pennwell.com. Website: www.pennwell-store.com. **Acquisitions:** Margaret Shake, publisher; Jared Wicklund, supervising editor. Publishes hardcover and softcover originals. **Publishes 10 titles/year. Receives 24 queries/year. 75% of books from first-time authors; 100% from unagented writers. Pays 15% royalty on net sales.** Publishes book 1 year after acceptance of ms. Responds in 3 months to proposals. Book catalog free.
O─ Fire Engineering publishes textbooks relevant to firefighting and training. Training firefighters and other emergency responders. Currently emphasizing strategy and tactics, reserve training, preparedness for terrorist threats, natural disasters, first response to fires and emergencies.
Nonfiction: Reference, technical, textbook. Subjects include firefighter training, public safety. Submit outline, 2 sample chapter(s), résumé, author bio, SASE, table of contents.
Recent Title(s): *Managing Major Fires*, by Skip Coleman.
Tips: "No human interest stories, technical training only."

FLYING BOOKS, Sky Media, LLC. 121 5th Ave., NW, Suite 399, New Brighton MN 55112. (651)635-0100. Fax: (651)635-0700. E-mail: histaviate@earthlink.net. Website: www.aviationhistory.com. **Acquisitions:** G.E. Herrick, publisher (aviation history). Publishes hardcover and trade paperback originals and reprints. **Publishes 12 titles/year; imprint publishes 2 titles/year. Receives 30 queries and 15 mss/year. 30% of books from first-time authors; 90% from unagented writers. Pays 10% royalty on wholesale price.** Responds in 1 month to queries and proposals; 2 months to mss. Book catalog free.
O─ "Aviation and aviation history are our strong points. Illustrations, photographs and other documentation appeal to our customers. We like to see the story told: how did this aircraft 'fit,' what did it do, how did it impact peoples lives?"
Nonfiction: Subjects include history, military/war, aviation. Reviews artwork/photos as part of ms package. Send photocopies.
Recent Title(s): *Mystery Ship!*, by Edward Phillips (aviation history); *Wings of Stearman*, by Peter Bowers (aviation history).
Tips: "Our buyers are interested in aviation history and aircraft in general. Of particular interest are nonfiction works covering specific aircraft types, manufacturers or military aircraft. Research and accuracy are of paramount importance."

FOCAL PRESS, Butterworth Heinemann, Reed Elsevier (USA) Inc., 225 Wildwood Ave., Woburn MA 01801-2041. Fax: (781)904-2640. E-mail: editors@focalpress.com. Website: www.focalpress.com. **Acquisitions:** Marie Lee, publisher; Terri Jadick, associate editor. Estab. US, 1981; UK, 1938. Publishes hardcover and paperback originals and reprints. **Publishes 60-65 UK-US titles/year; entire firm publishes 200 titles/year. Receives 500-700 submissions/ year. 25% of books from first-time authors; 90% from unagented writers. Pays 10-12% royalty on net receipts. Offers modest advance.** Publishes book 9-12 months after acceptance of ms. Accepts simultaneous submissions. Responds in 2 months to queries. Book catalog and ms guidelines for #10 SASE.
O─ Focal Press publishes reference material in all areas of the media, from audio, broadcasting, and cinematography, through to journalism, radio, television, video, and writing. Currently emphasizing graphics, animation and multimedia.
Nonfiction: Media arts. How-to, reference, technical, textbook. Subjects include film/cinema/stage, photography, film, cinematography, broadcasting, theater and performing arts, audio, sound and media technology. "Our books are text-

oriented, with artwork serving to illustrate and expand on points in the text." High-level scientific/technical monographs are also considered. "We do not publish collections of photographs or books composed primarily of photographs." Query preferred, or submit outline and sample chapters. Reviews artwork/photos as part of ms package.

Recent Title(s): *Adobe Photoshop 6.0 for Photographers*, by Martin Evening (nonfiction).

Tips: "Our advances and royalties are more carefully determined with an eye toward greater profitability for all our publications."

FODOR'S TRAVEL PUBLICATIONS, INC., Random House, Inc., 280 Park Ave., New York NY 10171-0002. Website: www.fodors.com. **Acquisitions:** Karen Cure, editorial director. Estab. 1936. Publishes trade paperback originals. **Publishes 300 titles/year. Receives 100 queries and 4 mss/year. Most titles are collective works, with contributions as works for hire. Most contributions are updates of previously published volumes.** Publishes book 1 year after acceptance of ms. Accepts simultaneous submissions. Responds in 2 months to queries. Book catalog free.

   Oⴖ Fodor's publishes travel books on many regions and countries.

Nonfiction: How-to (travel), illustrated book (travel), travel guide. Subjects include travel. "We are interested in unique approaches to favorite destinations. Writers seldom review our catalog or our list and often query about books on topics that we're already covering. Beyond that, it's important to review competition and to say what the proposed book will add. Do not send originals without first querying as to our interest in the project. We're not interested in travel literature or in proposals for general travel guidebooks." Query or submit outline, sample chapter(s) and proposal package, including competition review and review of market with SASE.

Recent Title(s): *Venice and the Veneto*; *How to Pack*.

Tips: "In preparing your query or proposal, remember that it's the only argument Fodor's will hear about why your book will be a good one and why you think it will sell; and it's also best evidence of your ability to create the book you propose. Craft your proposal well and carefully so that it puts your best foot forward."

Ni FORDHAM UNIVERSITY PRESS, University Box L, Bronx NY 10458. Website: www.bookmasters.com/fordhampress. **Acquisitions:** Mary Beatrice Schulte, executive editor. Publishes hardcover and trade paperback originals and reprints. **Publishes 30 titles/year. Receives 450 queries and 100 mss/year. 25% of books from first-time authors; 100% from unagented writers. Pays 4-7% royalty on retail price.** Publishes book 6-24 months after acceptance of ms. Responds in 2 months to proposals and mss. Book catalog and ms guidelines free.

   Oⴖ "We are a publisher in humanities, accepting scholarly monographs, collections, occasional reprints and general interest titles for consideration."

Nonfiction: Biography, textbook, scholarly. Subjects include Americana, anthropology/archeology, art/architecture, government/politics, history, language/literature, military/war (World War II), philosophy, regional (New York), religion, sociology, translation. No fiction. Submit outline, 2-5 sample chapter(s).

Recent Title(s): *Our Tomorrows Never Came*, by Etunia Bauer Katz.

Tips: "We have an academic and general audience."

Ni FOREIGN POLICY ASSOCIATION, 470 Park Ave. S., New York NY 10016. (212)481-8100. Fax: (212)481-9275. E-mail: info@fpa.org. Website: www.fpa.org. **Acquisitions:** Karen Rohan, editor-in-chief. Publishes 2 periodicals and an occasional hardcover and trade paperback original. **Publishes 5-6 titles/year. Receives 12 queries and 6 mss/year. 99% from unagented writers. Makes outright purchase of $2,500-4,000.** Publishes book 9 months after acceptance of ms. Accepts simultaneous submissions. Responds in 2 months to queries. Book catalog free.

Imprints: Headline Series (quarterly), Great Decisions (annual)

   Oⴖ "The Foreign Policy Association, a nonpartisan, not-for-profit educational organization founded in 1918, is a catalyst for developing awareness, understanding of and informed opinion on U.S. foreign policy and global issues. Through its balanced, nonpartisan publications, FPA seeks to encourage individuals in schools, communities and the workplace to participate in the foreign policy process."

Nonfiction: Reference, textbook. Subjects include government/politics, history, foreign policy, social studies. Query, submit outline.

Recent Title(s): *India: Old Civilization in a New World*, by Barbara Crossette.

Tips: Audience is students and people with an interest, but not necessarily any expertise, in foreign policy and international relations.

FORGE, Tom Doherty Associates, LLC, 175 Fifth Ave. 14th Floor, New York NY 10010. (212)388-0100. Fax: (212)388-0191. E-mail: inquiries@tor.com. Website: www.tor.com. **Acquisitions:** Patrick Nielsen Hayden, senior editor (science fiction and fantasy, techno-thriller, alternate history); Melissa Ann Singer, senior editor (historicals, thrillers with medical, ecological, or biotech elements, contemporary mysteries, women's fiction, nonfiction on women's or health issues, horror/occult); Natalia Aponte, senior editor (biotech and medical thrillers, women's fiction, historicals); Claire Eddy, editor (science fiction and fantasy, mystery, historical, suspense). Publishes hardcover, trade paperback and mass market paperback originals, trade and mass market paperback reprints. **Receives 5,000 mss/year. 2% of books from first-time authors. Paperback: pays 6-8% royalty for first-time authors, 8-10% royalty for established authors; hardcover: pays 10% first 5,000 12½% second 5,000, 15% thereafter. Offers advance.** Responds in 4 months to proposals. Book catalog for 9×12 SAE with 2 first-class stamps.

   Oⴖ "TDA publishes the best of past, present, and future—meaning that we cover all ground in fiction from

historicals set in prehistory to the sharpest contemporary fiction to the acknowledged best in science fiction and fantasy. We are a little more interested in quality horror fiction than we were a year ago. We are less interested in apocalyptic or millennial thrillers, obviously. We're not much interested in serial killers either."
Nonfiction: Subjects include health/medicine, science, women's issues/studies. Query with outline and 3 sample chapters.
Fiction: Historical, horror, mainstream/contemporary, mystery, suspense, thriller, general fiction of all sorts. "We handle a wide range of books; if you're not sure if a project is right for us, phone us and ask." Query with synopsis and 3 sample chapters.
Recent Title(s): *Peace, War & Politics*, by Jack Anderson (nonfiction); *Vengeance*, by Stuart M. Kaminsky (fiction).

FORT ROSS INC. RUSSIAN-AMERICAN PUBLISHING PROJECTS, 26 Arthur Place, Yonkers NY 10701. (914)375-6448. Fax: (914)375-6439. E-mail: ftross@ix.netcom.com. **Acquisitions:** Dr. Vladimir P. Kartsev, executive director (romance, mystery, science fiction, fantasy, nonfiction). Publishes paperback originals. **Publishes 12 titles/year. Receives 100 queries and 100 mss/year. Pays 4-7% royalty on wholesale price or makes outright purchase of $500-1,500. Offers $500 advance.** Publishes book 1 year after acceptance of ms. Accepts simultaneous submissions. Responds in 1 month to queries and proposals; 3 months to mss.
  O→ "Generally, we publish Russia-related books in English or Russian. Sometimes we publish books in collaboration with the Russian publishers in translation. In this case we are looking for the books of 'all-in-one' character, 'how-to' books, books for teens, romance, mystery, science fiction and adventure."
Nonfiction: Biography, illustrated book, technical. Subjects include art/architecture, business/economics, memoirs. Query with SASE. Reviews artwork/photos as part of ms package. Send photocopies.
Fiction: "We are looking for the manuscripts (books) of well-established authors to publish them in Russian and other European languages in collaboration with the publishers in Europe." Adventure, fantasy, horror, mainstream/contemporary, mystery, romance, science fiction, suspense. Query with SASE.
Recent Title(s): *Kiss of Midas*, by Geoge Vainer; *Immigrants*, by Howard Fast.

N: FORTRESS PRESS, Augsburg Fortress Publishers, Box 1209, Minneapolis MN 55440-1209. (612)330-3300. Website: www.fortresspress.com. **Acquisitions:** J. Michael West, editor-in-chief; Dr. K.C. Hanson, acquisitions editor. Estab. 1855. Publishes hardcover and trade paperback originals. **Publishes 60 titles/year. Receives 500-700 queries/year. 5-10% of books from first-time authors. Pays royalty on retail price.** Publishes book 1-2 years after acceptance of ms. Accepts simultaneous submissions. Responds in 3 months to proposals. Book catalog free (call 1-800-328-4648); ms guidelines online.
  O→ Fortress Press publishes academic books in Biblical studies, theology, Christian ethics, church history, and professional books in pastoral care and counseling.
Nonfiction: Subjects include religion, women's issues/studies, church history, African-American studies. Query with annotated toc, brief cv, sample chapter (introduction) and SASE. Please study guidelines before submitting.
Recent Title(s): *Introducing the New Testament*, by John Drane.

FORUM PUBLISHING COMPANY, 383 E. Main St., Centerport NY 11721. (631)754-5000. Fax: (631)754-0630. Website: www.forum123.com. **Acquisitions:** Martin Stevens. Estab. 1981. Publishes trade paperback originals. **Publishes 12 titles/year. Receives 200 queries and 25 mss/year. 75% of books from first-time authors; 75% from unagented writers. Makes outright purchase of $250-750.** Publishes book 4 months after acceptance of ms. Accepts simultaneous submissions. Responds in 1 month to mss. Book catalog free.
  O→ "Forum publishes only business titles."
Nonfiction: Subjects include business/economics, money/finance. Submit outline. Reviews artwork/photos as part of ms package. Send photocopies.
Recent Title(s): *Selling Information By Mail*, by Glen Gilcrest.

FORWARD MOVEMENT PUBLICATIONS, 412 Sycamore St., Cincinnati OH 45202. (513)721-6659. Fax: (513)721-0729. E-mail: esgleason@forwarddaybyday.com. Website: www.forwardmovement.org. **Acquisitions:** The Reverend Dr. Edward S. Gleason, editor and director. Estab. 1934. Publishes trade and mass market paperback originals, trade paperback reprints and tracts. **Publishes 6 titles/year. Receives 1,000 queries and 300 mss/year. 30% of books from first-time authors; 100% from unagented writers. Pays one-time honorarium.** Responds in 1 month to queries and proposals; 2 months to mss. Book catalog and ms guidelines free.
  O→ "Forward Movement was established 'to help reinvigorate the life of the church.' Many titles focus on the life of prayer, where our relationship with God is centered, death, marriage, baptism, recovery, joy, the Episcopal Church and more." Currently emphasizing prayer/spirituality.

ALWAYS ENCLOSE a self-addressed, stamped envelope (SASE) with all your queries and correspondence.

Nonfiction: "We publish a variety of types of books, but they all relate to the lives of Christians. We are an agency of the Episcopal Church." Biography, children's/juvenile, reference, self-help (about religion and prayer). Subjects include religion. Query with SASE or submit complete ms.

Fiction: Episcopal for middle school (ages 8-12) readers. Juvenile. Query with SASE.

Recent Title(s): *God Is Not in the Thesaurus*, by Bo Don Cox (nonfiction); *Dare to Imagine*, by Sydney Von Lehn (fiction).

Tips: Audience is primarily Episcopalians and other Christians.

N WALTER FOSTER PUBLISHING, INC., A Quarto Group Company, 23062 La Cadena Dr., Laguna Hills CA 92653. (949)380-7510. Fax: (949)380-7575. **Acquisitions:** Sydney Sprague, associate publisher. Publishes trade paperback originals. **Publishes 30-40 titles/year. Receives 20-30 queries/year. 50% of books from first-time authors; 100% from unagented writers. Makes outright purchase.** Publishes book 1 year after acceptance of ms. Accepts simultaneous submissions. Responds in 2 months to queries; 6 months to proposals and mss. Book catalog free.

O-π Walter Foster publishes instructional how-to/craft instruction as well as licensed products.

Nonfiction: How-to. Subjects include arts and crafts. Submit proposal package, including query letter, color photos/examples of artwork. Reviews artwork/photos as part of ms package. Send color photocopies or color photos. Samples cannot be returned.

Recent Title(s): *Glass Painting; Ceramic Painting; Paper Crafts* (art instruction).

FOUR WALLS EIGHT WINDOWS, 39 W. 14th St., Room 503, New York NY 10011. Fax: (212)206-8799. E-mail: edit@4w8w.com. Website: www.4w8w.com. Publisher: John Oakes. **Acquisitions:** Acquistions Editor. Estab. 1987. Publishes hardcover originals, trade paperback originals and reprints. **Publishes 28 titles/year. Receives 3,000 submissions/year. 15% of books from first-time authors; 50% from unagented writers. Pays royalty on retail price. Offers variable advance.** Publishes book 1-2 years after acceptance of ms. Responds in 2 months to queries. Book catalog for 6×9 SAE with 3 first-class stamps.

Imprints: No Exit, Axoplasm

O-π Emphasizing fine literature and quality nonfiction, Four Walls Eight Windows has a reputation for carefully edited and distinctive books.

Nonfiction: Subjects include history, nature/environment, science. No New Age. Query with outline and SASE. All mss without SASE discarded.

Fiction: Feminist, gay/lesbian. "No romance, popular." Query first with outline/synopsis and SASE.

Recent Title(s): *Genesis: The Story of Apollo 8*, by Robert Zimmerman (science); *Atom*, by Steve Aylett (fiction); *1927*, by Gerald Leinwand (history).

FOX CHAPEL PUBLISHING, 1970 Broad St., East Petersburg PA 17520. (717)560-4703. Fax: (717)560-4702. E-mail: editors@carvingworld.com. Website: www.carvingworld.com. **Acquisitions:** Alan Giagnocavo, publisher; Ayleen Stellhorn, editor. Publishes hardcover and trade paperback originals and trade paperback reprints. **Publishes 12-20 titles/year. 80% of books from first-time authors; 100% from unagented writers. Pays royalty or makes outright purchase. Offers variable advance.** Publishes book 6-18 months after acceptance of ms. Accepts simultaneous submissions. Responds in 2 months to queries.

O-π Fox Chapel publishes woodworking and woodcarving titles for professionals and hobbyists.

Nonfiction: Subjects include woodworking, wood carving, scroll saw. Write for query submission guidelines. Reviews artwork/photos as part of ms package. Send photocopies.

Recent Title(s): *Carving the Human Face*, by Jeff Phares; *Scroll Saw Workbook*.

Tips: "We're looking for knowledgeable artists, woodworkers first, writers second to write for us. Our market is for avid woodworking hobbyists and professionals."

THE FREE PRESS, Simon & Schuster, 1230 Avenue of the Americas, New York NY 10020. (212)698-7000. Fax: (212)632-4989. Website: www.simonsays.com. **Acquisitions:** Chad Conway, associate editor (history/current events); Robert Wallace, senior editor (business); Bruce Nichols, senior editor (history); Philip Rapapport, editor (psychology/social work/self-help); Steven Morrow, editor (science, math, literature, art). Estab. 1947. **Publishes 120 titles/year. Receives 3,000 submissions/year. 15% of books from first-time authors; 50% from unagented writers. Pays variable royalty. Offers advance.** Publishes book 1 year after acceptance of ms. Responds in 2 months to queries.

O-π The Free Press publishes serious adult nonfiction.

Nonfiction: Textbook, professional texts. Subjects include business/economics, translation, social sciences, humanities. "We look for an identifiable target audience, evidence of writing ability." Query with 1-3 sample chapters, outline before submitting mss. Reviews artwork/photos as part of ms package.

Recent Title(s): *The Educated Child*, by William Bennett; *Eye of the Storm*, by Robert Sneden.

FREE SPIRIT PUBLISHING INC., 217 Fifth Ave. N., Suite 200, Minneapolis MN 55401-1260. (612)338-2068. Fax: (612)337-5050. E-mail: help4kids@freespirit.com. Website: www.freespirit.com. Publisher: Judy Galbraith. **Acquisitions:** Acquisitions Editor. Estab. 1983. Publishes trade paperback originals and reprints. **Publishes 30 titles/year. 25% of books from first-time authors; 75% from unagented writers. Offers advance.** Book catalog and ms guidelines free.

Imprints: Self-Help for Kids, Free Spirited Classroom Series, Self-Help for Teens

O→ "We believe passionately in empowering kids to learn to think for themselves and make their own good choices."

Nonfiction: Children's/juvenile, self-help. Subjects include child guidance/parenting, education (pre-K-12, but not textbooks or basic skills books like reading, counting, etc.), health/medicine (mental/emotional health-*not* physical health-for/about children), psychology (for/about children), sociology (for/about children). "Many of our authors are teachers, counselors or others involved in helping kids." No fiction, poetry or autobiographies. Query with outline, 2 sample chapters, résumé and SASE. Send photocopies.

Recent Title(s): *What Do You Really Want? How to Set a Goal and Go for It!*, by Beverly K. Bachel.

Tips: "Our audience is children, teens, teachers, parents and youth counselors. We are concerned with kids' mental/emotional well-being and are especially looking for books written directly to kids in a language they can understand. We are not looking for academic or religious materials, nor books that analyze problems with the nation's school systems. Instead we want books that offer practical, positive advice so kids can help themselves."

FRONT STREET, 20 Battery Park Ave., #403, Asheville NC 28801. (828)236-3097. Fax: (828)236-3098. E-mail: contactus@frontstreetbooks.com. Website: www.frontstreetbooks.com. **Acquisitions:** Stephen Roxburgh, president and publisher; Joy Neaves, editor. Publishes hardcover originals. **Publishes 12-24 titles/year; imprint publishes 6-12 titles/year. Receives 1,000 queries and 2,000 mss/year. 50% of books from first-time authors; 90% from unagented writers. Pays royalty on retail price. Offers advance.** Publishes book 1 year after acceptance of ms. Accepts simultaneous submissions. Responds in 1 month to queries; 2 months to proposals; 3 months to mss. Book catalog for 6×9 SAE with 78¢ postage or online; ms guidelines for #10 SASE or online.

Imprints: Front Street/Lemniscant Books (Stephen Roxburgh)

O→ "We are an independent publisher of books for children and young adults."

Nonfiction: Biography, children's/juvenile, gift book, humor, illustrated book. Subjects include animals, creative nonfiction, ethnic, gardening, gay/lesbian, history, language/literature, memoirs, philosophy, spirituality, women's issues/studies, film/cinema/stage. Reviews artwork/photos as part of ms package. Send photocopies.

Fiction: Adventure, fantasy, feminist, historical, horror, humor, juvenile, literary, picture books, romance, science fiction, young adult. Query with SASE.

Poetry: Submit 25 sample poems.

Recent Title(s): *Cut*, by Patricia McCormick (YA novel); *Carver: A Life in Poems*, by Marilyn Nelson (poetry); *Many Stones*, by Carolyn Coman (YA novel).

FUTURE HORIZONS, 721 W. Abram St., Arlington TX 76013. (817)277-0727. Fax: (817)277-2270. E-mail: edfuture@onramp.net. Website: www.FutureHorizons-autism.com. **Acquisitions:** R. Wayne Gilpin, president (autism/Asperger's syndrome); David Brown, CEO (sensory issues for special education). Publishes hardcover originals, trade paperback originals and reprints. **Publishes 10 titles/year; imprint publishes 4 titles/year. Receives 250 queries and 125 mss/year. 75% of books from first-time authors; 95% from unagented writers. Pays 10% royalty or makes outright purchase.** Publishes book 2 months after acceptance of ms. Accepts simultaneous submissions. Responds in 1 month to queries; 2 months to proposals. Book catalog and ms guidelines free.

Nonfiction: Children's/juvenile (pertaining to autism), cookbook (for autistic individuals), humor (about autism), self-help (detailing with autism/Asperger's syndrome). Subjects include education (about autism/Asperger's syndrome), autism. Submit proposal package including outline. Reviews artwork/photos as part of ms package. Send photocopies.

Recent Title(s): *Diagnosing Jefferson*, by Norm Ledgin (nonfiction); *Asperger's Syndrome*, by Tony Attwood, Ph.D (nonfiction).

Tips: Audience is parents, teachers, professionals dealing with individuals with autism or Asperger's syndrome. "Books that sell well, have practical and useful information on how to help individuals and/or care givers of individuals with autism. Personal stories, even success stories, are not helpful to others in a practical way."

GATFPress, Graphic Arts Technical Foundation, 200 Deer Run Rd., Sewickley PA 15143-2600. (412)741-6860. Fax: (412)741-2311. E-mail: poresick@gatf.com. Website: www.gatf.org or www.gain.net. **Acquisitions:** Peter Oresick, director of publications; Tom Destree, editor in chief; Amy Woodall, managing editor (graphic arts, communication, book publishing, printing). Estab. 1924. Publishes trade paperback originals and hardcover reference texts. **Publishes 15 titles/year. Receives 25 submissions/year. 50% of books from first-time authors; 100% from unagented writers. Pays 5-15% royalty on retail price.** Publishes book 6 months after acceptance of ms. Responds in 1 month. *Writer's Market* recommends allowing 2 months for reply to queries. Book catalog for 9×12 SAE with 2 first-class stamps; ms guidelines for #10 SASE.

O→ "GATF's mission is to serve the graphic communications community as the major resource for technical information and services through research and education." Currrently emphasizing career guides for graphic communications.

Nonfiction: How-to, reference, technical, textbook. Subjects include printing/graphic communications, electronic publishing. "We primarily want textbook/reference books about printing and related technologies. However, we are expanding our reach into electronic communications." Query with SASE or submit outline, sample chapters and SASE. Reviews artwork/photos as part of ms package.

Recent Title(s): *Practical Proofreading*, by Matthew Willen; *Understanding Graphic Communication*, by Harvey Levenson; *Chemistry for the Graphic Arts*, by Nelson Eldred.

Tips: "We are publishing titles that are updated more frequently, such as *On-Demand Publishing*. Our scope now includes reference titles geared toward general audiences interested in computers, imaging, and Internet as well as print publishing."

GAY SUNSHINE PRESS and LEYLAND PUBLICATIONS, P.O. Box 410690, San Francisco CA 94141-0690. Website: www.gaysunshine.com. **Acquisitions:** Winston Leyland, editor. Estab. 1970. Publishes hardcover originals, trade paperback originals and reprints. **Publishes 6-8 titles/year. Pays royalty or makes outright purchase.** Responds in 6 weeks to queries. Book catalog for $1.

　　O─┓ Gay history, sex, politics, and culture are the focus of the quality books published by Gay Sunshine Press. Leyland Publications publishes books on popular aspects of gay sexuality and culture.

Nonfiction: "We're interested in innovative literary nonfiction which deals with gay lifestyles." How-to. Subjects include gay/lesbian. No long personal accounts, academic or overly formal titles. Query with SASE. *All unsolicited mss returned unopened.*

Fiction: Interested in innovative well-written novels on gay themes; also short story collections. Erotica, experimental, historical, mystery, science fiction. "We have a high literary standard for fiction." Query with SASE. *All unsolicited mss returned unopened.*

Recent Title(s): *Out of the Closet Into Our Hearts: Celebration of Our Gay/Lesbian Family Members.*

GEM GUIDES BOOK COMPANY, 315 Cloverleaf Dr., Suite F, Baldwin Park CA 91706-6510. (626)855-1611. Fax: (626)855-1610. E-mail: gembooks@aol.com. Website: www.gemguidesbooks.com. **Acquisitions:** Kathy Mayerski, editor. Estab. 1965. **Publishes 6-8 titles/year. Receives 20 submissions/year. 60% of books from first-time authors; 100% from unagented writers. Pays 6-10% royalty on retail price.** Publishes book 1 year after acceptance of ms. Accepts simultaneous submissions. Responds in 3 months to queries.

Imprints: Gembooks

　　O─┓ "Gem Guides prefers nonfiction books for the hobbyist in rocks and minerals; lapidary and jewelry-making; travel and recreation guide books for the West and Southwest; and other regional local interest." Currently emphasizing how-to, field guides, West/Southwest regional interest. De-emphasizing stories, history, poetry.

Nonfiction: Subjects include history (Western), hobbies (lapidary and jewelry-making), nature/environment, recreation, regional (Western US), science (earth), travel. Query with outline/synopsis and sample chapters with SASE. Reviews artwork/photos as part of ms package.

Recent Title(s): *Where to Find Gold in Northern California*, by James Klein; *Discover Historic Washington State*, by George and Jan Roberts; *Day Hikes and Trail Rides In and Around Phoenix*, by Roger and Ethel Freeman.

Tips: "We have a general audience of people interested in recreational activities. Publishers plan and have specific book lines in which they specialize. Learn about the publisher and submit materials compatible with that publisher's product line."

LAURA GERINGER BOOKS, HarperCollins Children's Books, 1350 Avenue of the Americas, New York NY 10019. (212)207-7000. Website: www.harperchildrens.com. **Acquisitions:** Laura Geringer, senior vice president/publisher. Publishes hardcover originals. **Publishes 15-20 titles/year. 5% of books from first-time authors; 25% from unagented writers. Pays 10-12½% on retail price. Offers variable advance.** Publishes book 6-12 months for novels; 1-2 years for picture books after acceptance of ms. Responds in 3 months to queries and proposals; 4 months to mss. Book catalog for 8×10 SAE with 5 first-class stamps; ms guidelines for #10 SASE.

　　O─┓ "We look for books that are out of the ordinary, authors who have their own definite take, and artists that add a sense of humor to the text."

Fiction: Adventure, fantasy, humor, juvenile, literary, picture books, young adult. "A mistake writers often make is failing to research the type of books an imprint publishes, therefore sending inappropriate material." Query with SASE for picture books; submit complete ms with SASE for novels.

Recent Title(s): *Take a Mouse to the Movies*, by Laura Nurmeroff; illustrated by Felicia Bond.

GGC, INC./PUBLISHING, 4602 John Hancock Ct., Suite 302, Annandale VA 22003. (703)354-8278. Fax: (703)354-8279. E-mail: gardner@ggcinc.com. Website: www.gogardner.com. **Acquisitions:** Garth Gardner, publisher (computer graphics, aviation); Bonney Ford, editor (GGC, Art, animation). Publishes trade paperback reprints. **Publishes 10 titles/year; imprint publishes 2 titles/year. Receives 50 queries and 25 mss/year. 80% of books from first-time authors; 70% from unagented writers. Pays 10-15% royalty on wholesale price or makes outright purchase.** Publishes book 3 months after acceptance of ms. Accepts simultaneous submissions. Responds in 1 month to queries. Book catalog online.

　　O─┓ GGC publishes books on the subjects of computer graphics, animation, new media, multimedia, art.

Nonfiction: How-to, multimedia, reference, self-help, technical, textbook. Subjects include art/architecture, education, history, computer graphics. Query with SASE or submit proposal package including 2 sample chapter(s), résumé, cover letter. Reviews artwork/photos as part of ms package. Send photocopies.

Recent Title(s): *Gardner's Guide to Animation Scriptwriting: The Writer's Road Map*, by Marilyn Webber; *Gardner's Guide to Screenwriting: The Writer's Road Map*, by M. Webber; *Gardner's Guide to Multimedia and Animation Studios*, by G. Gardner.

GIFTED EDUCATION PRESS, 10201 Yuma Court, P.O. Box 1586, Manassas VA 20109. (703)369-5017. E-mail: mdfish@cais.com. **Acquisitions:** Maurice Fisher, publisher. Estab. 1981. Publishes mass market paperback originals. **Publishes 10 titles/year. Receives 75 queries and 25 mss/year. 90% of books from first-time authors; 100% from unagented writers. Pays 10-12% royalty on retail price.** Publishes book 3 months after acceptance of ms. Accepts simultaneous submissions. Responds in 1 month to queries. Book catalog free; ms guidelines for #10 SASE.

    O— Gifted Education Press publishes books on multiple intelligences, humanities education for gifted children and how to parent gifted children. Currently emphasizing mentoring, multiple intelligences and problems/issues of educating gifted children.

Nonfiction: Reference, textbook, teacher's guides. Subjects include business/economics, child guidance/parenting, computers/electronic, education, language/literature, philosophy, psychology, science. "Writers must indicate their expertise in the subject and propose challenging topics for teachers and gifted students." *All unsolicited mss returned unopened.* Query or submit outline with SASE. Reviews artwork/photos as part of ms package.

Recent Title(s): *Gifted Education Comes Home*, by Lisa Rivero.

Tips: Audience is parents and teachers of gifted students, university professors and graduate students. "We are looking for clear, straight forward and well-organized writing. Expertise in the topical areas is required."

N: GIFTED PSYCHOLOGY PRESS, INC., Anodyne, Inc., P.O. Box 5057, Scottsdale AZ 85261. (602)954-4200. Fax: (602)954-0185. E-mail: giftedbook@earthlink.net. Website: www.GiftedPsychologyPress.com. **Acquisitions:** Janet Gore, editor (gifted curriculum in schools); James Webb, president (social and emotional needs); Lynn Gudhus, editor (mainstream children's issues). Estab. 1986. Publishes trade paperback originals. **Publishes 4-5 titles/year. Receives 10 queries and 10 mss/year. 25% of books from first-time authors; 100% from unagented writers. Pays 9-15% royalty on retail price. Offers $0-750 advance.** Publishes book 6 months after acceptance of ms. Accepts simultaneous submissions. Responds in 2 months to queries; 3 months to proposals; 4 months to mss. Book catalog and ms guidelines online.

    O— Gifted Psychology Press publishes books on the social/emotional/interpersonal/creative needs of gifted and talented children and adults for parents and teachers of gifted and talented youngsters. Currently emphasizing books for gifted and talented children. De-emphasizing research-based books.

Nonfiction: Biography, children's/juvenile, humor, reference, self-help, textbook, assessment scales. Subjects include child guidance/parenting, education, multicultural, psychology, translation, travel, women's issues/studies, gifted/talented children and adults. No research-based books. Submit proposal package, including outline, 3 sample chapters and an explanation of how work differs from similar published books.

Recent Title(s): *Helping Gifted Children Soar*, by Carol Strip, Ph.D.

Tips: "Manuscripts should be clear, cogent, and well-written and should pertain to gifted, talented, and creative persons and/or issues."

THE GLENLAKE PUBLISHING COMPANY, LTD., 1261 W. Glenlake, Chicago IL 60660. (773)262-9765. Fax: (773)262-9436. E-mail: glenlake@ix.netcom.com. **Acquisitions:** Barbara Craig, editor. Estab. 1995. Publishes hardcover originals. **Publishes 20 titles/year. Receives 50 queries and 5 mss/year. 25% of books from first-time authors; 100% from unagented writers. Pays 10-15% royalty on wholesale price. Offers $1,500 average advance.** Publishes book 2 months after acceptance of ms. Accepts simultaneous submissions. Responds in 1 month to queries. Book catalog for #10 SASE.

    O— "Glenlake is an independent book publisher whose primary objective is to promote the advancement of critical thinking in the areas of business, finance, economics, applied statistics, computer applications to business and statistics, and environmental science and engineering."

Nonfiction: Subjects include business/economics, computers/electronic, money/finance (stocks/bonds, insurance), software, technology, risk management. Submit proposal package, including author's bio, outline, 1 sample chapter and SASE.

Recent Title(s): *International Handbook of Convertible Securities*; *Irrational Markets and the Illusion of Prosperity.*

THE GLOBE PEQUOT PRESS, INC., P.O. Box 480, Guilford CT 06437. (203)458-4500. Fax: (203)458-4604. Website: www.globe-pequot.com. President/Publisher: Linda Kennedy. **Acquisitions:** Shelley Wolf, submissions editor. Estab. 1947. Publishes paperback originals, hardcover originals and reprints. **Publishes 500 titles/year. Receives 2,500 submissions/year. 30% of books from first-time authors; 70% from unagented writers. Average print order for a first book is 4,000-7,500. Makes an outright purchase or pays 10% royalty on net price. Offers advance.** Publishes book 1 year after acceptance of ms. Accepts simultaneous submissions. Responds in 3 months to queries.

    ● The Globe Pequot Press recently acquired Falcon Publishing, which will continue as an imprint.

    O— Globe Pequot is the largest publisher of regional travel books and outdoor recreation in the United States and offers the broadest selection of travel titles of any vendor in this market.

Nonfiction: Regional travel guidebooks, outdoor recreation guides, natural history field guides. Subjects include cooking/foods/nutrition (regional), history (popular, regional), nature/environment, recreation, regional, travel. No doctoral theses, fiction, genealogies, memoirs, poetry, or textbooks. Submit brief synopsis of work, table of contents or outline, sample chapter, résumé/vita, definition of target audience, and an analysis of competing titles. Reviews artwork/photos as part of ms package.

Recent Title(s): *Great American Rail Journeys*; *Insider's Guides*; *Northern Rocky Mountain Wildflowers.*

DAVID R. GODINE, PUBLISHER, INC., 9 Hamilton Place, Boston MA 02108. (617)451-9600. Fax: (617)350-0250. E-mail: info@godine.com. Website: www.godine.com. Estab. 1970. Publishes hardcover and trade paperback originals and reprints. **Publishes 35 titles/year. Pays royalty on retail price.** Publishes book 3 years after acceptance of ms. Book catalog for 5×8 SAE with 3 first-class stamps.

    O⇥ "Our particular strengths are books about the history and design of the written word, literary essays, and the best of world fiction in translation. We also have an unusually strong list of children's books, all of them printed in their entirety with no cuts, deletions, or side-stepping to keep the political watchdogs happy."

Nonfiction: Biography, children's/juvenile, coffee table book, cookbook, illustrated book. Subjects include Americana, art/architecture, gardening, nature/environment, photography, literary criticism, current affairs. *No unsolicited mss.* Query with SASE.

Fiction: Juvenile, literary, short story collections. *No unsolicited mss.* Query with SASE.

Recent Title(s): *The Last Buffalo Hunter*, by Jake Mosher (fiction); *Easy To Remember: The Great American Songwriters and Their Songs*, by William Zinsser.

N GOLDEN WEST BOOKS, P.O. Box 80250, San Marino CA 91118-8250. (626)458-8148. Fax: (626)458-8148. E-mail: trainbook@earthlink.net. Website: www.goldenbooks.com. **Acquisitions:** Donald Duke, publisher. Publishes hardcover originals. **Publishes 3-4 titles/year. Receives 8-10 queries and 5 mss/year. 75% of books from first-time authors; 100% from unagented writers. Pays 8-10% royalty on wholesale price. Offers no advance.** Publishes book 3 months after acceptance of ms. Responds in 3 months to queries. Book catalog and ms guidelines free.

    O⇥ Golden West Books specializes in railroad history.

Nonfiction: Illustrated book (railroad history). Subjects include Americana, history. Query with SASE. Reviews artwork/photos as part of ms package.

Recent Title(s): *The Ulster & Delaware Railroad Through the Catskills*, by Gerald M. Best; *The Streamline Era*, by Robert C. Reed; *Electric Railways Around San Francisco Bay*, by Donald Duke.

GOLLEHON PRESS, INC., 6157 28th St., SE, Grand Rapids MI 49546. (616)949-3515. Fax: (616)949-8674. Website: www.gollehonbooks.com. **Acquisitions:** Lori Adams, editor. Publishes hardcover, trade paperback and mass market paperback originals. **Publishes 6-8 titles/year. Receives 100 queries and 30 mss/year. 85% of books from first-time authors; 90% from unagented writers. Pays 7% royalty on retail price. Offers $500-1,000 advance.** Publishes book 6 months after acceptance of ms. Accepts simultaneous submissions. Responds in 1 month to queries and proposals if interested; 2 months to mss. Book catalog and ms guidelines online.

    O⇥ Currently emphasizing how-to, self-help, pets, nutrition, gardening books for seniors. *No unsolicited mss*; brief proposals only.

Nonfiction: How-to, self-help. Subjects include animals, anthropology/archeology, business/economics, gardening, health/medicine, hobbies, humor, money/finance, psychology, pets, nutrition. Submit proposal package. No SASE (we do not return mss). Reviews artwork/photos as part of ms package. Send photocopies only if requested.

Tips: "Mail brief book proposal and few sample pages only. We will request full manuscript if interested. We cannot respond to all queries. Full manuscript will be returned if we requested it and writer provides SASE. We do not return proposals. Simultaneous submissions are encouraged."

THE GRADUATE GROUP, P.O. Box 370351, West Hartford CT 06137-0351. (860)233-2330. Fax: (860)233-2330. E-mail: graduategroup@hotmail.com. Website: www.GraduateGroup.com. **Acquisitions:** Mara Whitman, president; Robert Whitman, vice president. Estab. 1964. Publishes trade paperback originals. **Publishes 50 titles/year. Receives 100 queries and 70 mss/year. 60% of books from first-time authors; 85% from unagented writers. Pays 20% royalty on retail price.** Publishes book 3 months after acceptance of ms. Accepts simultaneous submissions. Responds in 1 month to queries. Book catalog and ms guidelines free.

    O⇥ "The Graduate Group helps college and graduate students better prepare themselves for rewarding careers and helps people advance in the workplace." Currently emphasizing test preparation, career advancement and materials for prisoners, law enforcement, books on unique careers.

Nonfiction: Reference. Subjects include business/economics, education, government/politics, health/medicine, money/finance, law enforcement. Submit complete ms and SASE with sufficient postage.

Recent Title(s): *Real Life 101: Winning Secrets You Won't Find in Class*, by Debra Yergen; *Getting In: Applicant's Guide to Graduate School Admissions*, by David Burrell.

Tips: Audience is career planning offices; college, graduate school and public libraries. "We are open to all submissions, especially those involving career planning, internships and other nonfiction titles. Looking for books on law enforcement, books for prisoners and reference books on subjects/fields students would be interested in. We want books on helping students and others to interview, pass tests, gain opportunity, understand the world of work, networking, building experience, preparing for advancement, preparing to enter business, improving personality and building relationships."

GRANITE PUBLISHING, LLC, (formerly Blue Water Publishing), P.O. Box 1429, Columbus NC 28756. (828)894-8444. Fax: (828)894-8454. E-mail: granitepub@5thworld.com. Website: www.5thworld.com. President: Pam Meyer. **Acquisitions:** Brian Crissey. Publishes hardcover originals and trade paperback originals and reprints. **Publishes 6 titles/year. Receives 50 queries and 25/month mss/year. 80% of books from first-time authors; 90% from unagented writers. Pays 7½-15% royalty.** Publishes book 16 months after acceptance of ms. Accepts simultaneous submissions. Responds in 2 months to mss. Book catalog and ms guidelines for SASE.

Imprints: Wild Flower Press, Swan-Raven & Co., Agents of Change, Isso Press

O—π "Granite Publishing strives to preserve the Earth by publishing books that develop new wisdom about our emerging planetary citizenship, bringing information from the outerworlds to our world." Currently emphasizing natural history, planetary healing.

Nonfiction: Multimedia. Subjects include New Age, planetary paradigm shift. Submit proposal. Reviews artwork/photos as part of ms package. Send photocopies.

Recent Title(s): *Voyagers*, by Ashayana Deane.

GRAYWOLF PRESS, 2402 University Ave., Suite 203, St. Paul MN 55114. (651)641-0077. Fax: (651)641-0036. Website: www.graywolfpress.org. Editor/Publisher: Fiona McCrae. Executive Editor: Anne Czarniecki. **Acquisitions:** Daniel Kos (poetry, nonfiction); Katie Dublinski, editor (fiction). Estab. 1974. Publishes trade cloth and paperback originals. **Publishes 16 titles/year. Receives 2,500 queries/year. 20% of books from first-time authors; 50% from unagented writers. Pays royalty on retail price. Offers $1,000-6,000 advance.** Publishes book 18 months after acceptance of ms. Responds in 3 months to queries. Book catalog free; ms guidelines for #10 SASE.

O—π Graywolf Press is an independent, nonprofit publisher dedicated to the creation and promotion of thoughtful and imaginative contemporary literature essential to a vital and diverse culture.

Nonfiction: Subjects include language/literature, culture. Query with SASE.

Fiction: Literary. "Familiarize yourself with our list first."

Poetry: "We are interested in linguistically challenging work." Query with SASE.

Recent Title(s): *War Memorials*, by Clint McCown; *Halls of Fame*, by John D'Agata; *Some Ether*, by Nick Flynn.

✠ GREEN NATURE BOOKS, 16021 SW 284 St., Homestead FL 33033. (305)242-1317. Fax: (305)246-4101. E-mail: info@greennaturebooks.com. Website: www.greennaturebooks.com. **Acquisitions:** R.C. Paull, publisher (tortoises and orchids). Publishes hardcover and trade paperback originals, trade paperback reprints. **Publishes 9 titles/year. Receives 50 queries/year. 25% of books from first-time authors; 100% from unagented writers. Pays up to 10% royalty on retail price.** Publishes book 6 months after acceptance of ms. Book catalog for #10 SASE.

O—π Green Nature Books specializes in books about tortoises and orchids.

Nonfiction: How-to, illustrated book, technical. Subjects include agriculture/horticulture, animals, hobbies, nature/environment, religion, science, travel. Query with SASE.

Recent Title(s): *Housing Your Turtles and Tortoises Outside*, by Wayne Lebenda.

Tips: "The dedicated tortoise keeper is our audience. If you are expert in herpetology, including care and breeding, contact us."

N ✠ GREENE BARK PRESS, P.O. Box 1108, Bridgeport CT 06601. (203)372-4861. Fax: (203)371-5856. Website: www.greenebarkpress.com. **Acquisitions:** Thomas J. Greene, publisher; Michele Hofbauer, associate publisher. Estab. 1991. Publishes hardcover originals. **Publishes 5 titles/year. Receives 100 queries and 6,000 mss/year. 60% of books from first-time authors; 100% from unagented writers. Pays 10-15% royalty on wholesale price.** Publishes book 1 year after acceptance of ms. Accepts simultaneous submissions. Responds in 1 month to queries; 6 months to mss. Book catalog for $2; ms guidelines for SASE.

O—π Greene Bark Press only publishes books for children and young adults, mainly picture and read-to books. "All of our titles appeal to the imagination and encourage children to read and explore the world through books. We only publish children's fiction—all subjects—but in reading picture book format appealing to ages 3-9 or all ages."

Fiction: Juvenile. Submit complete ms. No queries or ms by e-mail.

Recent Title(s): *Could We Make a Difference*, by Michele Hofbauer.

Tips: Audience is "children who read to themselves and others. Mothers, fathers, grandparents, godparents who read to their respective children, grandchildren. Include SASE, be prepared to wait, do not inquire by telephone."

GREENHAVEN PRESS, INC., P.O. Box 289009, San Diego CA 92198-9009. (858)485-7424. Fax: (858)485-9549. Website: www.greenhaven.com. **Acquisitions:** Scott Barbour, managing editor. Estab. 1970. Publishes approximately 100 anthologies/year; all anthologies are works for hire. **Makes outright purchase of $1,000-3,000.** Publishes book 1 year after acceptance of ms. Book catalog for 9×12 SAE with 3 first-class stamps or online.

O—π Greenhaven Press publishes hard and softcover educational supplementary materials and (nontrade) nonfiction anthologies on contemporary issues, literary criticism and history for high school and college readers. These anthologies serve as supplementary educational material for high school and college libraries and classrooms. Currently emphasizing literary and historical topics, and social-issue anthologies.

Nonfiction: Children's/juvenile. Subjects include education, history. "We produce tightly formatted anthologies on contemporary issues, literary criticism, and history for high school and college-level readers. We are looking for freelance book editors to research and compile these anthologies; we are not interested in submissions of single-author manuscripts. Each series has specific requirements. Potential book editors should familiarize themselves with our catalog and anthologies." Query. No unsolicited ms.

Recent Title(s): *Biomedical Ethics* (Opposing Viewpoints Series).

GREENWILLOW BOOKS, HarperCollins Publishers, 1350 Avenue of the Americas, New York NY 10019. (212)261-6500. Website: www.harperchildrens.com. Senior Editor: Rebecca Davis. **Acquisitions:** Editorial Department,

Greenwillow Books. Estab. 1974. Publishes hardcover originals and reprints. **Publishes 50-60 titles/year. 1% of books from first-time authors; 30% from unagented writers. Pays 10% royalty on wholesale price for first-time authors. Offers variable advance.** Publishes book 2 years after acceptance of ms. Accepts simultaneous submissions. Book catalog for 9×12 SASE with $2.30 postage; ms guidelines for #10 SASE.
   O— Greenwillow Books publishes quality picture books and fiction for young readers of all ages, and nonfiction primarily for children under seven years of age. Reviews artwork/photos as part of ms package.
Fiction: Juvenile. Fantasy, humor, literary, mystery, picture books. Submit complete ms with SASE.
Recent Title(s): *Whale Talk*, by Chris Crutcher.

GREENWOOD PRESS, Greenwood Publishing Group, 88 Post Rd. W., Westport CT 06881. (203)226-3571. Fax: (203)222-1502. Website: www.greenwood.com. **Acquisitions:** Peter Kracht, executive editor. Publishes hardcover originals. **Publishes 200 titles/year. Receives 1,000 queries/year. 25% of books from first-time authors. Pays variable royalty on net price. Offers rare advance.** Publishes book 1 year after acceptance of ms. Accepts simultaneous submissions. Responds in 6 months to queries. Book catalog and ms guidelines online.
   O— Greenwood Press publishes reference materials for the entire spectrum of libraries, as well as scholarly monographs in the humanities and the social and behavioral sciences.
Nonfiction: Reference. Subjects include humanities and the social and behavioral sciences. Query with proposal package, including scope, organization, length of project, whether complete ms is available or when it will be, cv or résumé and SASE. *No unsolicited mss.*
Recent Title(s): *John Grisham: A Critical Companion*, by Mary Beth Pringle.

GREENWOOD PUBLISHING GROUP, Reed-Elsevier (USA) Inc., 88 Post Rd. W, Westport CT 06881. (203)226-3571. Fax: (203)222-1502. Website: www.greenwood.com. **Acquisitions:** Academic, reference and trade—George Butler (anthropology, education, literature, drama and sociology, ext. 3461, gbutler@greenwood.com); Cynthia Harris (history and economics, ext. 3460, charris@greenwood.com); Debbie Carvalko (multicultural and women's studies, gerontology, media, political science and law, psychology, ext. 3842, nromer@greenwood.com); Eric Levy (art and architecture, music and dance, philosophy and religion, popular culture, ext. 3445, elevy@greenwood.com); Interdisciplinary studies, such as African-American studies are handled by all editors—contact js@greenwood.com. Secondary School Reference—Emily Birch (sociology, psychology, arts, religion, sports and recreation, ext. 3448, ebirch@greenwood.com); Jane Garry (library science, pregnancy, parenting, alternative medicine, education, and anthropology, ext. 3480, jgarry@greenwood.com); Barbara Rader (literature, history, women's studies, school librarianship, ext. 3442, brader@greenwood.com); Heather Staines (history and military studies, ext. 3214, hstaines@greenwood.com). Professional Publishing: Eric Valentine (Quorum Books, ext. 3471, evalentine@greenwood.com). **Publishes 700 titles/year. Pays variable royalty on net price. Offers advance rarely. Offers rare advance.** Publishes book 1 year after acceptance of ms. Accepts simultaneous submissions. Book catalog and ms guidelines online.
Imprints: Auburn House, Bergin & Garvey, Greenwood Press, Praeger Publishers, Quorum Books, Ablex, Oryx Books
   O— The Greenwood Publishing Group consists of seven distinguished imprints with one unifying purpose: to provide the best possible reference, professional, text, and scholarly resources in the humanities and the social and behavioral sciences.
Nonfiction: Reference, textbook. Subjects include anthropology/archeology, business/economics, child guidance/parenting, education, government/politics, history, language/literature, music/dance, philosophy, psychology, religion, sociology, sports, women's issues/studies. Query with proposal package, including scope, organization, length of project, whether a complete ms is available or when it will be, cv or résumé and SASE. *No unsolicited mss.*
Recent Title(s): *From the Unthinkable to the Unavoidable*, edited by Carol Rittner and John Roth (religion/Holocaust studies); *The Feminist Encyclopedia of German Literature*, edited by Friederike Eigler and Susanne Kord; *The Fighting Pattons*, by Brian Sobel (military).
Tips: "No interest in fiction, drama, poetry—looking for serious, scholarly, analytical studies of historical problems." Greenwood Publishing maintains an excellent website, providing complete catalog, ms guidelines and editorial contacts.

GROUP PUBLISHING, INC., 1515 Cascade Ave., Loveland CO 80538. (970)669-3836. Fax: (970)679-4370. E-mail: kloesche@grouppublishing.com. Website: www.grouppublishing.com. **Acquisitions:** Kerri Loesche, editorial assistant. Estab. 1974. Publishes trade paperback originals. **Publishes 24 titles/year. Receives 200 queries and 50 mss/year. 40% of books from first-time authors; 95% from unagented writers. Pays up to 10% royalty on wholesale price or makes outright purchase or work for hire. Offers up to $1,000 advance.** Publishes book 18 months after acceptance of ms. Accepts simultaneous submissions. Responds in 1 month to queries; 6 months to proposals and mss. Book catalog for 9×12 SAE with 2 first-class stamps; ms guidelines online.
   O— "Our mission is to encourage Christian growth in children, youth and adults."
Nonfiction: Children's/juvenile, how-to, multimedia, textbook. Subjects include education, religion. "We're an interdenominational publisher of resource materials for people who work with adults, youth or children in a Christian church setting. We also publish materials for use directly by youth or children (such as devotional books, workbooks or Bibles stories). Everything we do is based on concepts of active and interactive learning as described in *Why Nobody Learns Much of Anything at Church: And How to Fix It*, by Thom and Joani Schultz. We need new, practical, hands-on, innovative, out-of-the-box ideas—things that no one's doing... yet." Query with SASE or submit proposal package including outline, 3 sample chapter(s), cover letter, introduction to book, and sample activities if appropriate.

Recent Title(s): *Aqua Church*, by Leonard Sweet (church leadership); *The Dirt on Learning*, by Thom and Joani Schultz (effective teaching and learning).
Tips: "Our audience consists of pastors, Christian education directors and Sunday school teachers."

A **GROVE/ATLANTIC, INC.**, 841 Broadway, New York NY 10003. (212)614-7850. Fax: (212)614-7886. Estab. 1952. Publishes hardcover originals, trade paperback originals and reprints. **Publishes 60-70 titles/year. Receives 1000s queries/year. 10-15% of books from first-time authors. Pays 7½-15% royalty on retail price. Offers considerably variable advance.** Publishes book 1 year after acceptance of ms. Accepts simultaneous submissions. Book catalog free.
Imprints: Grove Press (estab. 1952), Atlantic Monthly Press (estab. 1917)
○─┐ Grove/Atlantic publishes serious nonfiction and literary fiction.
Nonfiction: Biography. Subjects include government/politics, history, travel. Query with SASE. *No unsolicited mss.*
Fiction: Experimental, literary. Query with SASE. *No unsolicited mss.*
Poetry: "We try to publish at least one volume of poetry every list." *No unsolicited mss.* Query.
Recent Title(s): *Black Hawk Dawn: A Story of Modern War*, by Mark Bowden.

ALDINE DE GRUYTER, Walter de Gruyter, Inc., 200 Saw Mill River Rd., Hawthorne NY 10532. (914)747-0110. Fax: (914)747-1326. E-mail: rkoffler@degruyterny.com. Website: www.degruyter.de. **Acquisitions:** Dr. Richard Koffler, executive editor. Publishes hardcover and academic paperback originals. **Publishes 15-25 titles/year. Receives several hundred queries and 100 mss/year. 15% of books from first-time authors; 99% from unagented writers. Pays 7½-10% royalty on net receipts.** Publishes book 9 months after acceptance of ms. Accepts simultaneous submissions. Responds in 2 months to proposals. Book catalog free; ms guidelines only after contract.
○─┐ Aldine de Gruyter is an academic nonfiction publisher.
Nonfiction: Textbook (rare), course-related monographs, edited volumes. Subjects include anthropology/archeology, psychology (evolutionary), sociology, social psychology (not clinical), human services. "Aldine's authors are academics with Ph.D's and strong publication records. No poetry or fiction." Submit proposal package including 1-2 sample chapter(s), cv, market, competing texts, reviews of early work.
Recent Title(s): *The Politics of Medicare*, by Theodore R. Marmor.
Tips: Audience is professors and upper level and graduate students.

N **GRYPHON HOUSE, INC.**, P.O. Box 207, Beltsville MD 20704. (301)595-9500. Fax: (301)595-0051. Website: www.gryphonhouse.com. **Acquisitions:** Kathy Charner, editor-in-chief. Estab. 1971. Publishes trade paperback originals. **Publishes 6 titles/year. Pays royalty on wholesale price.** Responds in 3 months to queries.
○─┐ Gryphon House publishes books of creative educational activities for parents and teachers of young children ages 0-8.
Nonfiction: Children's/juvenile, how-to. Subjects include education. Submit outline, 2-3 sample chapter(s), SASE.
Recent Title(s): *The Big Messy Art Book*, by Maryann Kohl and Jean Potter; *125 Brain Games for Toddlers and Twos*, by Jackie Silberg.

GRYPHON PUBLICATIONS, P.O. Box 209, Brooklyn NY 11228. **Acquisitions:** Gary Lovisi, owner/publisher. Publishes trade paperback originals and reprints. **Publishes 10 titles/year. Receives 500 queries and 1,000 mss/year. 60% of books from first-time authors; 90% from unagented writers. Makes outright purchase by contract, price varies. Offers no advance.** Publishes book 1-2 years after acceptance of ms. Responds in 1 month to queries. *Writer's Market* recommends allowing 2 months for reply to queries. Book catalog and ms guidelines for #10 SASE.
Imprints: Paperback Parade Magazine, Hardboiled Magazine, Gryphon Books, Gryphon Doubles
Nonfiction: Reference, bibliography. Subjects include hobbies, language/literature, book collecting. "We need well-written, well-researched articles, but query first on topic and length. Writers should not submit material that is not fully developed/researched." Query with SASE. Reviews artwork/photos as part of ms package. Send photocopies; slides, transparencies may be necessary later.
Fiction: Crime, hard-boiled fiction. "We want cutting-edge fiction, under 3,000 words with impact!" For short stories, query or submit complete ms. For novels, send 1-page query letter with SASE.
Tips: "We are very particular about novels and book-length work. A first-timer has a better chance with a short story or article. On anything over 6,000 words *do not* send manuscript, send *only* query letter with SASE."

GUILFORD PUBLICATIONS, INC., 72 Spring St., New York NY 10012. (212)431-9800. Fax: (212)966-6708. E-mail: info@guilford.com. Website: www.guilford.com. **Acquisitions:** Seymour Weingarten, editor-in-chief; Rochelle Serwator, editor (neuropsychology, developmental disabilities, speech and language); Kitty Moore, executive editor (psychology/psychiatry, child clinical); Christopher Jennison, senior editor (education, school psychology); Jim Nageotte, senior editor (family, social work, culture, clinical psychology); Kristal Hawkins, editor (geography, communication, social theory). Estab. 1978. Publishes hardcover and trade paperback originals and trade paperback reprints. **Publishes 75 titles/year. Receives 200 queries and 50 mss/year. 15% of books from first-time authors; 90% from unagented writers. Pays 0-15% royalty on wholesale price. Offers $500-5,000 advance.** Publishes book 7 months after acceptance of ms. Accepts simultaneous submissions. Responds in 2 months to queries, proposals and mss. Book catalog and ms guidelines online.

O-¬ Guilford Publications publishes quality professional trade titles in psychology, psychiatry and the behavioral sciences, including addictions, gender issues and child abuse; as well as cultural studies, philosophy, politics, geography, communication and education. Products include books, journals and videos.

Nonfiction: Self-help, technical, textbook. Subjects include child guidance/parenting, education, gay/lesbian, government/politics, health/medicine, philosophy, psychology, sociology, women's issues/studies. Query with SASE or submit proposal package including outline, 2 sample chapter(s), cv.

Recent Title(s): *Take Back Your Marriage*, by William Doherty.

Tips: "Projects must be solidly research-based."

☒ HACHAI PUBLISHING, 156 Chester Ave., Brooklyn NY 11218. (718)633-0100. Website: www.hachai.com. **Acquisitions:** Devorah Leah Rosenfeld, editor. Estab. 1988. Publishes hardcover originals. **Publishes 4 titles/year. Pays $800 outright purchase.** Accepts simultaneous submissions. Responds in 2 months to mss. Book catalog free; ms guidelines for #10 SASE.

O-¬ "Hachai is dedicated to producing high quality Jewish children's literature, ages 2 through 10. Story should promote universal values such as sharing, kindness, etc."

Nonfiction: Children's/juvenile. Subjects include ethnic, religion. Submit complete manuscript, SASE. Reviews artwork/photos as part of ms package. Send photocopies.

Recent Title(s): *Nine Spoons*, by Marci Stillerman (nonfiction); *On the Ball*, by Dina Rosenfeld (fiction).

Tips: "We are looking for books that convey the traditional Jewish experience in modern times or long ago; traditional Jewish observance such as Sabbath and Holidays and mitzvos such as mezuzah, blessings etc.; positive character traits (middos) such as honesty, charity, respect, sharing, etc. We are also interested in biographies of spiritually great men and women in Jewish history; problem novels, historical fiction and tales of adventure for young readers (7-10) written with a traditional Jewish perspective; and highlighting the relevance of Torah in making important choices. Please, no animal stories, romance, violence, preachy sermonizing."

HALF HALT PRESS, INC., P.O. Box 67, Boonsboro MD 21713. (301)733-7119. Fax: (301)733-7408. E-mail: hhpress@aol.com. Website: www.halfhaltpress.com. **Acquisitions:** Elizabeth Carnes, publisher. Estab. 1986. Publishes 90% hardcover and trade paperback originals and 10% reprints. **Publishes 15 titles/year. Receives 150 submissions/ year. 25% of books from first-time authors; 50% from unagented writers. Pays 10-12½% royalty on retail price.** Publishes book 1 year after acceptance of ms. Responds in 1 month. *Writer's Market* suggests allowing 2 months for reply to queries. Book catalog for 6×9 SAE 2 first-class stamps.

O-¬ "We publish high-quality nonfiction on equestrian topics, books that help riders and trainers do something better."

Nonfiction: How-to. Subjects include animals (horses), sports. "We need serious instructional works by authorities in the field on horse-related topics, broadly defined." Query with SASE. Reviews artwork/photos as part of ms package.

Recent Title(s): *Dressage in Harmony*, by Walter Zettl.

Tips: "Writers have the best chance selling us well-written, unique works that teach serious horse people how to do something better. If I were a writer trying to market a book today, I would offer a straightforward presentation, letting the work speak for itself, without hype or hard sell. Allow publisher to contact writer, without frequent calling to check status. They haven't forgotten the writer but may have many different proposals at hand; frequent calls to 'touch base,' multiplied by the number of submissions, become an annoyance. As the publisher/author relationship becomes close and is based on working well together, early impressions may be important, even to the point of being a consideration in acceptance for publication."

HAMPTON ROADS PUBLISHING COMPANY, INC., 1125 Stoney Ridge Rd., Charlottesville VA 22902. (804)296-2772. Fax: (804)296-5096. E-mail: hrpc@hrpub.com. Website: hrpub.com. **Acquisitions:** Frank DeMarco, chief editor (metaphysical/visionary fiction); Robert S. Friedman, president (metaphysical, spiritual, inspirational, self-help); Ellen McKenna, marketing director (spiritual paths/Toltec); Richard Leviton, senior editor (alternative medicine). Estab. 1989. Publishes hardcover and trade paperback originals. **Publishes 35-40 titles/year. Receives 1,000 queries and 1,500 mss/year. 50% of books from first-time authors; 70% from unagented writers. Pays royalty. Offers $1,000-100,000 advance.** Publishes book 1 year after acceptance of ms. Accepts simultaneous submissions. Responds in 2 months to queries and proposals; 6 months to mss.

Imprints: Young Spirit (children's spiritual)

O-¬ "Our reason for being is to impact, uplift and contribute to positive change in the world. We publish books that will enrich and empower the evolving consciousness of mankind."

Nonfiction: How-to, illustrated book, self-help. Subjects include New Age, spirituality. Query with SASE or submit SASE, synopsis. Reviews artwork/photos as part of ms package. Send photocopies.

Fiction: Spiritual. "Fiction should have one or more of the following themes: spiritual, inspirational, metaphysical, i.e., past life recall, out-of-body experiences, near death experience, paranormal." Query with SASE or submit synopsis or submit complete ms.

Recent Title(s): *Moments of Grace*, by Neale Donald Walsch; *Spider World: The Tower*, by Colin Wilson.

◤◢ HANCOCK HOUSE PUBLISHERS, 1431 Harrison Ave., Blaine WA 98230-5005. (604)538-1114. Fax: (604)538-2262. E-mail: david@hancockwildlife.org. Website: www.hancockwildlife.org. David Hancock, publisher. **Acquisitions:** Melanie Clark, promotional manager. Estab. 1971. Publishes hardcover and trade paperback originals and reprints. **Publishes 14 titles/year. Receives 300 submissions/year. 50% of books from first-time authors; 90% from unagented writers. Pays 10% royalty.** Publishes book up to 1 year after acceptance of ms. Accepts simultaneous submissions. Book catalog free; ms guidelines for #10 SASE.

    ○━ Hancock House Publishers is the largest North American publisher of wildlife, and Native Indian titles. "We also cover Pacific Northwest, fishing, history, Canadiana, biographies. We are seeking agriculture, natural history, animal husbandry, conservation and popular science titles with a regional (Pacific Northwest), national or international focus." Currently emphasizing non-fiction wildlife, native history, biography, fishing. De-emphasizing cryptozoology, cowboy poetry, and guide books.

Nonfiction: "Centered around Pacific Northwest, local history, nature guide books, international ornithology and Native Americans." Biography, how-to, reference, technical, Pacific Northwest history and biography. Subjects include agriculture/horticulture, animals, ethnic, history, nature/environment, regional. Submit proposal package including outline, 3 sample chapter(s), SASE, selling points. Reviews artwork/photos as part of ms package. Send photocopies.

Recent Title(s): *Wings Across Desert (Great Motorized Crane Migration)*, by David H. Ellis; *Russell Country*, by Bette Wolf Duncan.

HANSER GARDNER PUBLICATIONS, 6915 Valley Ave., Cincinnati OH 45244. (513)527-8977. Fax: (513)527-8950. Website: www.hansergardner.com. **Acquisitions:** Woody Chapman. Estab. 1993. Publishes hardcover and paperback originals and reprints. **Publishes 5-10 titles/year. Receives 40-50 queries and 5-10 mss/year. 75% of books from first-time authors; 100% from unagented writers. Pays 10-15% royalty on net receipts.** Publishes book 10 months after acceptance of ms. Accepts simultaneous submissions. Responds in 2 weeks to queries; 1 month to proposals and mss. Book catalog and ms guidelines free.

    ○━ Hanser Gardner publishes training and practical application titles for metalworking, machining and finishing shops/plants.

Nonfiction: "Our books are primarily basic introductory-level training books and books that emphasize practical applications. Strictly deal with subjects shown above." How-to, technical, textbook. Subjects include metalworking, machining and finishing shops/plants. Submit outline, sample chapter(s), résumé, preface and comparison to competing or similar titles. Reviews artwork/photos as part of ms package. Send photocopies.

Recent Title(s): *Industrial Painting*, by Norman R. Roobol (industrial reference).

Tips: "Our readers and authors occupy various positions within small and large metalworking, machining and finishing shops/plants. We prefer that interested individuals write, call, or fax us with their queries first, so we can send them our proposal guideline form."

HARBOR PRESS, 5713 Wollochet Dr. NW, Gig Harbor WA 98335. Fax: (253)851-5191. E-mail: info@harborpress.com. Website: www.harborpress.com. President/Publisher: Harry R. Lynn. **Acquisitions:** Deborah Young, senior editor (please direct submissions to Harbor Press, 5 Glen Dr., Plainview NY 11803). Estab. 1985. Publishes hardcover and trade paperback originals and reprints. **Publishes 4-6 titles/year. Negotiates competitive royalties on wholesale price or makes outright purchase.**

    ○━ Harbor Press publishes books that will help readers achieve better health and more successful lives. Currently emphasizing diet and weight loss, parenting, psychology/human relationships, successful living books. Credentialed authors only.

Nonfiction: How-to, self-help. Subjects include child guidance/parenting, cooking/foods/nutrition (diet and weight loss only), health/medicine, psychology. Query with SASE or submit proposal package including outline, 3 sample chapter(s), synopsis. Reviews artwork/photos as part of ms package. Send photocopies.

Recent Title(s): *The Prostate Diet Cookbook*, by Buffy Sanders; *Yes! Your Teen Is Crazy: Loving Your Kid Without Losing Your Mind*, by Michael Bradley.

Ⓐ **HARCOURT INC.**, Trade Division, 525 B St., Suite 1900, San Diego CA 92101. (619)699-6560. Fax: (619)699-5555. Website: www.harcourt.com. **Acquisitions:** David Hough, managing editor; Jane Isay, editor-in-chief (science, math, history, language); Drenka Willen, senior editor (poetry, fiction in translation, history); Walter Bode, editor (history, geography, American fiction). Publishes hardcover and trade paperback originals and trade paperback reprints. **Publishes 120 titles/year. 5% of books from first-time authors; 5% from unagented writers. Pays 6-15% royalty on retail price. Offers $2,000 minimum advance.** Accepts simultaneous submissions.

Imprints: Harvest (contact Andre Bernard)

    ○━ Harcourt Inc. owns some of the world's most prestigious publishing imprints—imprints which distinguish quality products for the juvenile, educational, scientific, technical, medical, professional and trade markets worldwide. Currently emphasizing science and math.

Nonfiction: Biography, children's/juvenile, coffee table book, gift book, illustrated book, multimedia, reference, technical. Subjects include anthropology/archeology, art/architecture, child guidance/parenting, creative nonfiction, education, ethnic, gay/lesbian, general, government/politics, health/medicine, history, language/literature, memoirs, military/war, multicultural, philosophy, psychology, religion, science, sociology, spirituality, sports, translation, travel, women's issues/studies. Published all categories *except* business/finance (university texts), cookbooks, self-help, sex. *No unsolicited mss. Accepts agented submissions only.*

Recent Title(s): *Elvis in the Morning*, by William F. Buckley (fiction); *The Peppered Moth*, by Margaret Drabble (fiction); *The Head Game*, by Roger Kahn (nonfiction).

N A HARPERINFORMATION, HarperCollins Publishers, 10 East 53rd St., New York NY 10022. (212)207-7000. Fax: (212)207-6961. E-mail: adrian.zackheim@harpercollins.com. Website: www.harpercollins.com. **Acquisitions:** Adrian Zackheim, publisher (business); Megan Newman, editorial director (resource); Dave Conti, senior editor (business). Publishes hardcover originals, trade paperback originals and reprints. **10% of books from first-time authors; 0% from unagented writers.** Publishes book 1 year after acceptance of ms. Accepts simultaneous submissions. Responds in 1 month to queries; 1 month to proposals; 1 month to mss. Book catalog online.
Imprints: HarperBusiness (Adrian Zackheim); HarperResource (Megan Newman)
Nonfiction: Coffee table book, cookbook, gift book, how-to, reference, self-help. Subjects include business/economics, child guidance/parenting, computers/electronic, cooking/foods/nutrition, health/medicine, hobbies, language/literature, money/finance, sex, sociology, spirituality. *Accepts agented submissions only.*
Recent Title(s): *The Unfinished Revolution*, by Michael Dertouzos (business); *Emeril's TV Dinners*, by Emeril Lagasse (cookbook); *A Charlie Brown Christmas*, by Charles Schultz (resource).

HARPERSANFRANCISCO, Harper Collins Publishers, 353 Sacramento St., Suite 500, San Francisco CA 94111-3653. (415)477-4400. Fax: (415)477-4444. E-mail: hcsanfrancisco@harpercollins.com. Senior Vice President/Publisher: Stephen Hanselman. **Acquisitions:** Liz Perle, editor-at-large (women's studies, psychology, personal growth, inspiration); John Loudon, executive editor (religious studies, biblical studies, psychology/personal growth, Eastern religions, Catholic, spirituality, inspiration); Gideon Weil, assistant editor (general nonfiction, spiritual fiction, self-help, inspiration, Judaica). Estab. 1977. Publishes hardcover originals, trade paperback originals and reprints. **Publishes 75 titles/year. Receives about 10,000 submissions/year. 5% of books from first-time authors. Pays royalty. Offers advance.** Publishes book within 18 months after acceptance of ms.
 O━ HarperSanFrancisco publishes books that "nurture the mind, body and spirit; support readers in their ongoing self-discovery and personal growth; explore the essential religious and philosophical issues of our time; and present the rich and diverse array of the wisdom traditions of the world to a contemporary audience."
Nonfiction: Biography, how-to, reference, self-help. Subjects include psychology, religion, spirituality. Query with SASE. *No unsolicited mss.*
Recent Title(s): *Why Religion Matters*, by Houston Smith; *The Invitation*, by Oriah Mountain Dreamer; *Touching My Father's Soul*, by Tenzing Norgay.

N HARTMAN PUBLISHING INC., 8529-A Indian School NE, Albuquerque NM 87112. (505)291-1274. Fax: (505)291-1284. E-mail: susan@hartmanonline.com. Website: www.hartmanonline.com. **Acquisitions:** Susan Alvare, managing editor (healthcare education). Publishes trade paperback originals. **Publishes 5-10 titles/year. Receives 50 queries and 25 mss/year. 50% of books from first-time authors; 100% from unagented writers. Pays 6-12% royalty on wholesale or retail price or makes outright purchase of $200-600.** Publishes book 4-12 months after acceptance of ms. Accepts simultaneous submissions. Responds in 1 month to proposals; 3 months to mss. Book catalog and ms guidelines free.
Imprints: Care Spring (Mark Hartman, publisher)
 O━ We publish educational and inspirational books for employees of nursing homes, home health agencies, hospitals, and providers of eldercare.
Nonfiction: Textbook. Subjects include health/medicine. "Writers should request our books wanted list, as well as view samples of our published material." Query with SASE or submit proposal package including outline, 1 sample chapter(s) or submit complete ms. Reviews artwork/photos as part of ms package. Send photocopies or transparencies.

HARVARD BUSINESS SCHOOL PRESS, Harvard Business School Publishing Corp., 60 Harvard Way, Boston MA 02163. (617)783-7400. Fax: (617)783-7489. E-mail: bookpublisher@hbsp.harvard.edu. Website: www.hbsp.harvard.edu. Director: Carol Franco. **Acquisitions:** Marjorie Williams, editorial director; Kirsten Sandberg, executive editor; Melinda Adams Merino, senior editor; Hollis Heimbouch, executive editor; Jeff Kehoe, editor. Estab. 1984. Publishes hardcover originals. **Publishes 35-45 titles/year. Pays escalating royalty on retail price. Advances vary widely depending on author and market for the book.** Accepts simultaneous submissions. Responds in 1 month to proposals and mss. Book catalog and ms guidelines online.
 O━ The Harvard Business School Press publishes books for an audience of senior and general managers and business scholars. HBS Press is the source of the most influential ideas and conversations that shape business worldwide.
Nonfiction: Subjects include business/economics, general management, marketing, finance, digital economy, technology and innovation, human resources. Submit proposal package including outline, sample chapter(s).
Recent Title(s): *The Strategy Focused Organization*, by Robert Kaplan and David P. Norton; *Leading the Revolution*, by Gary Hamel; *Unchained Value*, by Mary J. Cronin.
Tips: "Take care to really look into the type of business books we publish. They are generally not handbooks, how-to manuals, policy-oriented, dissertations, edited collections, or personal business narratives."

THE HARVARD COMMON PRESS, 535 Albany St., Boston MA 02118-2500. (617)423-5803. Fax: (617)423-0679. Website: www.harvardcommonpress.com. Executive Editor: Pamela Hoenig. **Acquisitions:** Bruce P. Shaw, president/publisher. Estab. 1976. Publishes hardcover and trade paperback originals and reprints. **Publishes 16 titles/year. Receives**

1,000 submissions/year. 20% of books from first-time authors; 40% from unagented writers. Pays royalty. Offers average $4,000 advance. Publishes book 1 year after acceptance of ms. Accepts simultaneous submissions. Responds in 2 months to queries. Book catalog for 9×12 SAE with 3 first-class stamps; ms guidelines for #10 SASE.

Imprints: Gambit Books

O→ "We want strong, practical books that help people gain control over a particular area of their lives." Currently emphasizing cooking, child care/parenting, health. De-emphasizing general instructional books, travel.

Nonfiction: Subjects include child guidance/parenting, cooking/foods/nutrition, health/medicine, translation, travel. "A large percentage of our list is made up of books about cooking, child care, and parenting; in these areas we are looking for authors who are knowledgeable, if not experts, and who can offer a different approach to the subject. We are open to good nonfiction proposals that show evidence of strong organization and writing, and clearly demonstrate a need in the marketplace. First-time authors are welcome." Submit outline, 1-3 sample chapter(s). Reviews artwork/photos as part of ms package.

Recent Title(s): *The Bread Lover's Bread Machine Cookbook*, by Beth Hensperger.

Tips: "We are demanding about the quality of proposals; in addition to strong writing skills and thorough knowledge of the subject matter, we require a detailed analysis of the competition."

HATHERLEIGH PRESS, 5-22 46th Ave. #200, Long Island City NY 11101-5215. (212)832-1584. Fax: (212)832-1502. E-mail: info@hatherleigh.com. Website: www.hatherleigh.com. **Acquisitions:** Kevin J. Moran, publisher. Estab. 1995. Publishes hardcover originals, trade paperback originals and reprints. **Publishes 15-20 titles/year. Publishes 20 queries and 20 mss/year. Pays 5-15% royalty on retail price or makes outright purchase. Offers $500-5,000 advance.** Publishes book 6 months after acceptance of ms. Responds in 2 months to queries. Book catalog free.

Imprints: Red Brick Books—new fiction imprint (Kevin J. Moran, acquisitions editor); Getfitnow.com Books

O→ Hatherleigh Press publishes general self-help titles and reference books for mental health professionals. Currently emphasizing fitness, popular medicine. De-emphasizing self-help.

Nonfiction: Reference, self-help, technical. Subjects include health/medicine, psychology. Submit outline, 1 sample chapter(s), SASE. Reviews artwork/photos as part of ms package. Send photocopies.

Recent Title(s): *Living with Juvenile Diabetes*, by Victoria Peurrung.

Tips: Audience is mental health professionals and general trade consumers. Submit a clear outline, including market and audience for your book.

HAWK PUBLISHING GROUP, 6420 S. Richmond Ave., Tulsa OK 74136. Website: www.hawkpub.com. **Acquisitions:** William Bernhardt, publisher. Publishes hardcover and trade paperback originals and reprints. **Publishes 20-30 titles/year. 10% of books from first-time authors; 50% from unagented writers. Pays royalty.** Publishes book 9 months after acceptance of ms. Accepts simultaneous submissions. Responds in 1 month to mss. Manuscript guidelines online.

O→ "The best way to learn what HAWK publishes is to examine previous HAWK books. Search at www.hawkpub.com to see what we've done in the past."

Nonfiction: Biography, children's/juvenile, how-to, self-help. Subjects include anthropology/archeology, business/economics, child guidance/parenting, education, health/medicine, history, hobbies, language/literature, money/finance, nature/environment, philosophy, recreation. Submit proposal package including outline, 3 sample chapter(s). Queries by e-mail are welcome. Reviews artwork/photos as part of ms package. Send photocopies.

Fiction: Adventure, fantasy, historical, horror, humor, juvenile, literary, mainstream/contemporary, mystery, picture books, science fiction, suspense, young adult. Query with SASE or submit 3 sample chapter(s), synopsis. Queries welcome by e-mail.

Poetry: Query or submit complete ms.

Recent Title(s): *A Bus of My Own*, by Jim Lehrer (autobiography); *Murder in Tinseltown*, by Earl Hamner (novel).

THE HAWORTH PRESS, INC., 10 Alice St., Binghamton NY 13904. (607)722-5857. Fax: (607)722-8465. Website: www.haworthpressinc.com. **Acquisitions:** Bill Palmer, managing editor. Estab. 1973. Publishes hardcover and trade paperback originals. **Publishes 100 titles/year. Receives 500 queries and 250 mss/year. 60% of books from first-time authors; 98% from unagented writers. Pays 7½-15% royalty on wholesale price. Offers $500-1,000 advance.** Publishes book 1 year after acceptance of ms. Responds in 2 months to proposals. Manuscript guidelines free.

Imprints: The Harrington Park Press, Haworth Pastoral Press, Haworth Food Products Press

O→ The Haworth Press is primarily a scholarly press.

Nonfiction: Reference, textbook. Subjects include agriculture/horticulture, business/economics, child guidance/parenting, cooking/foods/nutrition, gay/lesbian, health/medicine, money/finance, psychology, sociology, women's issues/studies. "No 'pop' books." Submit proposal package including outline, 1-3 sample chapter(s), author bio. Reviews artwork/photos as part of ms package. Send photocopies.

Recent Title(s): *The Mental Health Diagnostic*, by Carlton Munson; *Straight Talk About Gays in the Workplace*, by Liz Winfield and Susan Spielman; *Health Care in the Black Community*, by Logan and Freeman.

HAY HOUSE, INC., P.O. Box 5100, Carlsbad CA 92018-5100. (760)431-7695. Fax: (760)431-6948. E-mail: stodd@hayhouse.com. Website: www.hayhouse.com. **Acquisitions:** Jill Kramer, editorial director. Estab. 1985. Publishes hardcover and trade paperback originals. **Publishes 45 titles/year. Receives 1,200 submissions/year. 10% of books from first-time authors; 25% from unagented writers. Pays standard royalty.** Publishes book 10-15 months after acceptance of ms. Accepts simultaneous submissions. Responds in 2 months to mss. No e-mail submissions.

Imprints: Astro Room, Hay House Lifestyles, Mountain Movers Press

○⊸ "We publish books, audios and videos that help heal the planet."

Nonfiction: Self-help. Subjects include cooking/foods/nutrition, education, health/medicine, money/finance, nature/environment, New Age, philosophy, psychology, sociology, women's issues/studies. "Hay House is interested in a variety of subjects as long as they have a positive self-help slant to them. No poetry, children's books or negative concepts that are not conducive to helping/healing ourselves or our planet." Query with SASE or submit outline, sample chapter(s).

Recent Title(s): *The Nature of Good and Evil*, by Sylvia Browne.

Tips: "Our audience is concerned with our planet, the healing properties of love, and general self-help principles. If I were a writer trying to market a book today, I would research the market thoroughly to make sure there weren't already too many books on the subject I was interested in writing about. Then I would make sure I had a unique slant on my idea. SASE a must! Simultaneous submissions through the mail only—no e-mail submissions."

HAZELDEN PUBLISHING, P.O. Box 176, Center City MN 55012. (651)257-4010. Website: www.hazelden.org. Rebecca Post, executive editor. Estab. 1954. Publishes hardcover and trade paperback originals and trade paperback reprints. **Publishes 100 titles/year. Receives 2,500 queries and 2,000 mss/year. 30% of books from first-time authors; 50% from unagented writers. Pays 8% royalty on retail price. Offers variable advance.** Publishes book 1 year after acceptance of ms. Accepts simultaneous submissions. Responds in 6 months to queries. Book catalog and ms guidelines online.

○⊸ Hazelden is a trade, educational and professional publisher specializing is psychology, self-help, and spiritual books that help enhance the quality of people's lives. Products include gift books, curriculum, workbooks, audio and video, computer-based products and wellness products. "We specialize in books on addiction/recovery, spirituality/personal growth, chronic illness and prevention topics related to chemical and mental health."

Nonfiction: Gift book, how-to, multimedia, self-help. Subjects include child guidance/parenting, gay/lesbian, health/medicine, memoirs, psychology, sex, spirituality. Query with SASE.

Recent Title(s): *Playing It By Heart*, by Melody Beattie (self-help); *I Closed My Eyes: Revealations of a Battered Woman*, by Michelle Weldon.

Tips: Audience includes "consumers and professionals interested in the range of topics related to chemical and emotional health, including spirituality, self-help and addiction recovery."

HEALTH COMMUNICATIONS, INC., 3201 SW 15th St., Deerfield Beach FL 33442. (954)360-0909. Fax: (954)360-0034. Website: www.hci-online.com. **Acquisitions:** Christine Belleris, editorial director; Susan Tobias, editor; Allison Janse, editor; Lisa Drucker, editor. Estab. 1976. Publishes hardcover and trade paperback originals. **Publishes 40 titles/year. 20% of books from first-time authors; 80% from unagented writers. Pays 15% royalty on net price.** Publishes book 9 months after acceptance of ms. Accepts simultaneous submissions. Responds in 1 month to queries; 3 months to proposals and mss. Book catalog for 8½ × 11 SASE; ms guidelines online.

○⊸ "We are the Life Issues Publisher. Health Communications, Inc., strives to help people grow and improve their lives from physical and emotional health to finances and interpersonal relationships." Currently emphasizing books for a teenage audience with a new interest in books for active senior citizens.

Nonfiction: Gift book, self-help. Subjects include child guidance/parenting, health/medicine, psychology, sex, women's issues/studies. Submit proposal package including outline, 2 sample chapter(s), SASE, vitae, marketing study. *No phone calls.* Reviews artwork/photos as part of ms package. Send photocopies.

Recent Title(s): *Chicken Soup for the Veteran's Soul*, by Canfield and Hansen; *But I Don't Feel Too Old To Be a Mommy*, by Doreen Nagle.

Tips: Audience is composed primarily of women, aged 25-60, interested in personal growth and self-improvement. "Please do your research in your subject area. We publish general self-help books and are expanding to include new subjects such as alternative healing. We need to know why there is a need for your book, how it might differ from other books on the market and what you have to offer to promote your work."

HEALTH PRESS, P.O. Box 1388, Santa Fe NM 87504. (505)474-0303. Fax: (505)424-0444. E-mail: goodbooks@healt hpress.com. Website: www.healthpress.com. **Acquisitions:** K. Frazer, editor. Estab. 1988. Publishes hardcover and trade paperback originals. **Publishes 8 titles/year. 90% of books from first-time authors; 90% from unagented writers. Pays standard royalty on wholesale price.** Publishes book 1 year after acceptance of ms. Accepts simultaneous submissions. Responds in 2 months to proposals. Book catalog free.

○⊸ Health Press publishes books by health care professionals on cutting-edge patient education topics.

Nonfiction: How-to, reference, self-help, textbook. Subjects include education, health/medicine. Submit proposal package including outline, 3 complete sample chapter(s), résumé. Reviews artwork/photos as part of ms package. Send photocopies.

Recent Title(s): *Blueberry Eyes*, by Monica Dorscoll Beatty, illustration by Peg Michel (children's book concerning eye treatment).

N: HEALTH PROFESSIONS PRESS, P.O. Box 10624, Baltimore MD 21285-0624. (410)337-9585. Fax: (410)337-8539. E-mail: acquis@healthpropress.com. Website: www.healthpropress.com. **Acquisitions:** Mary Magnus, director of publications (aging, long-term care, health administration). Publishes hardcover and trade paperback originals. **Publishes 6-8 titles/year. Receives 70 queries and 12 mss/year. 50% of books from first-time authors; 100% from unagented writers. Pays 8-18% royalty on wholesale price.** Publishes book 10 months after acceptance of ms. Accepts simultaneous submissions. Responds in 1 month to queries; 3 months to proposals; 4 months to mss. Book catalog and ms guidelines online.

O→ "We are a specialty publisher. Our primary audiences are professionals, students and educated consumers interested in topics related to aging and eldercare."

Nonfiction: How-to, reference, self-help, textbook. Subjects include health/medicine, psychology. Query with SASE or submit proposal package including outline, 1-2 sample chapter(s), résumé, cover letter.

Recent Title(s): *Rethinking Alzheimer's Care*, by Fazio, Seman, Stansell (professional references); *It Takes More Than Love: A Practical Guide to Taking Care of an Aging Adult*, by Beckerman and Tappen (how-to).

WILLIAM S. HEIN & CO., INC., 1285 Main St., Buffalo NY 14209-1987. (716)882-2600. Fax: (716)883-8100. E-mail: mail@wshein.com. **Acquisitions:** Sheila Jarrett, publications manager. Estab. 1961. **Publishes 50 titles/year. Receives 80 queries and 40 mss/year. 20% of books from first-time authors; 100% from unagented writers. Pays 10-25% royalty on net price.** Publishes book 9 months after acceptance of ms. Accepts simultaneous submissions. Responds in 1 months to queries. Book catalog online.

O→ William S. Hein & Co. publishes reference books for law librarians, legal researchers and those interested in legal writing. Currently emphasizing legal research, legal writing and legal education.

Nonfiction: Law. Reference, scholarly. Subjects include education, government/politics, women's issues/studies, world affairs.

Recent Title(s): *Navigating the Internet: Legal Research on the World Wide Web*, by Herbert Ramy and Samantha Moppett; *Amended Criminal Procedure Law and the Criminal Court Rules of the People's Republic of China*, by Wei Luo.

H: HEINEMANN, Reed Elsevier (USA) Inc., 361 Hanover St., Portsmouth NH 03801. (603)431-7894. Fax: (603)431-7840. Website: www.heinemann.com. **Acquisitions:** Leigh Peake, editorial director (education); Lisa Barnett, senior editor (performing arts); William Varner, acquisitions editor (literacy); Lisa Luedeke, acquisitions editor (Boynton/Cook). Estab. 1977. Publishes hardcover and trade paperback originals. **Publishes 80-100 titles/year. 50% of books from first-time authors; 75% from unagented writers. Pays royalty on wholesale price. Offers variable advance.** Accepts simultaneous submissions. Responds in 2 months to proposals. Book catalog free; ms guidelines online.

Imprints: Boynton/Cook Publishers

O→ Heinemann specializes in theater and education titles. "Our goal is to offer a wide selecton of books that satisfy the needs and interests of educators from kindergarten to college." Currently emphasizing literacy education, social studies, mathematics, science, K-12 education through technology.

Nonfiction: How-to, reference. Subjects include child guidance/parenting, education, film/cinema/stage, gay/lesbian, language/literature, women's issues/studies. "Our goal is to provide books that represent leading ideas within our niche markets. We publish very strictly within our categories. We do not publish classroom textbooks." Query with SASE or submit proposal package including outline, 1-2 sample chapter(s), table of contents.

Recent Title(s): *Word Matters*, by Irene Fountas and Gay-sa Pirrell.

Tips: "Keep your queries (and manuscripts!) short, study the market, be realistic and prepared to promote your book."

HELLGATE PRESS, PSI Research, P.O. Box 3727, Central Point OR 97502-0032. (541)245-6502. Fax: (541)245-6505. Website: www.psi-research.com/hellgate.htm. **Acquisitions:** Emmett Ramey, president. Estab. 1996. **Publishes 20-25 titles/year. Pays royalty.** Publishes book 6 months after acceptance of ms. Accepts simultaneous submissions. Responds in 2 months to queries. Book catalog for catalog envelope with SASE; ms guidelines for #10 SASE.

O→ Hellgate Press specializes in military history, other military topics and travel.

Nonfiction: Subjects include history, military/war, travel. Query with SASE or submit outline, sample chapter(s). Reviews artwork/photos as part of ms package. Send photocopies.

Recent Title(s): *Patriot Dreams*, by Robin Higgins.

HENDRICKSON PUBLISHERS, INC., 140 Summit St., P.O. Box 3473, Peabody MA 01961-3473. Fax: (978)531-8146. E-mail: DPenwell@hendrickson.com. **Acquisitions:** Dan Penwell, manager of trade products. Estab. 1983. Publishes hardcover and trade paperback originals and reprints. **Publishes 35 titles/year. Receives 200 submissions/year. 10% of books from first-time authors; 90% from unagented writers.** Publishes book an average of 1 year after acceptance of ms. Accepts simultaneous submissions. Responds in 2 months to queries. Book catalog and ms guidelines for #10 SASE.

O→ Hendrickson is an Evangelical Christian publisher of books that "give insight into Bible understanding (academically) and encourage spiritual growth (popular trade)." Currently emphasizing Biblical helps and reference, ministerial helps, women's interest and de-emphasizing fiction and biography.

Nonfiction: Reference. Subjects include religion. "We will consider any quality manuscript specifically related to Biblical studies and related fields. Also, nonfiction books in a more popular vein that give a hunger to studying, understanding and applying Scripture; books that encourage spiritual growth, such as personal devotionals." Submit outline, sample chapter(s).
Recent Title(s): *A Woman's Guide to Healing the Heartbreak of Divorce*, by Rose Sweet.

[N] JOSEPH HENRY PRESS, National Academy Press, 2101 Constitution Ave. NW, Washington DC 20418. (202)334-3336. E-mail: smautner@nas.edu. **Acquisitions:** Stephen Mautner, executive editor. Publishes hardcover and trade paperback originals. **Publishes 15-20 titles/year. Receives 200 queries and 60 mss/year. 40% of books from first-time authors; 80% from unagented writers. Pays 10% royalty on net receipts. Offers occasional, varying advance.** Publishes book 18 months after acceptance of ms. Accepts simultaneous submissions. Responds in 1 month to queries.

   O→ "The Joseph Henry Press seeks manuscripts in general science and technology that will appeal to young scientists and established professionals or to interested lay readers within the overall categories of science, technology and health. We'll be looking at everything from astrophysics to the environment to nutrition."
Nonfiction: Technical. Subjects include health/medicine, nature/environment, psychology, science, technology, nutrition. Submit proposal package including author bio, SASE, table of contents, prospectus.
Recent Title(s): *Einstein's Unfinished Symphony: Listening to the Sounds of Space-Time*, by Marcia Bartusiak; *Buzzwords: A Scientist Muses on Sex, Bugs and Rock 'n' Roll*, by May R. Berenbaum.

HENSLEY PUBLISHING, (formerly Virgil Hensley), 6116 E. 32nd St., Tulsa OK 74135-5494. (918)664-8520. E-mail: terri@hensleypublishing.com. Website: www.hensleypublishing.com. **Acquisitions:** Terri Kalfas, editor. Publishes hardcover and paperback originals. **Publishes 5-10 titles/year. Receives 800 submissions/year. 50% of books from first-time authors; 50% from unagented writers.** Publishes book 18 months after acceptance of ms. Responds in 2 months to queries. Manuscript guidelines for #10 SASE.

   O→ Hensley Publishing publishes Bible studies and curriculum that offer the reader a wide range of topics. Currently emphasizing shorter studies.
Nonfiction: Subjects include child guidance/parenting, money/finance, religion, women's issues/studies. "We do not want to see anything non-Christian." No New Age, poetry, plays, sermon collections. Query with synopsis and sample chapters.
Recent Title(s): *Rare and Beautiful Treasures*, by Nolene Niles.
Tips: "Submit something that crosses denominational lines directed toward the large Christian market, not small specialized groups. We serve an interdenominational market—all Christian persuasions. Our goal is to get readers back into studying their Bible instead of studying about the Bible."

HERITAGE BOOKS, INC., 1540-E Pointer Ridge Place, Bowie MD 20716-1859. (301)390-7708. Fax: (301)390-7193. **Acquisitions:** Leslie Towle, editorial supervisor. Estab. 1978. Publishes hardcover and paperback originals and reprints. **Publishes 200 titles/year. Receives 300 submissions/year. 25% of books from first-time authors; 100% from unagented writers. Pays 10% royalty on list price.** Accepts simultaneous submissions. Responds in 1 month. *Writer's Market* recommends allowing 2 months for reply to queries. Book catalog for SAE.

   O→ "Our goal is to celebrate life by exploring all aspects of American life: settlement, development, wars and other significant events, including family histories, memoirs, etc." Currently emphasizing early American life, early wars and conflicts. De-emphasizing ancestries of contemporary people.
Nonfiction: Biography, how-to (genealogical, historical), reference, scholarly. Subjects include Americana, ethnic (origins and research guides), history, memoirs, military/war, regional (history). "Ancestries of contemporary people are not of interest. The titles should be either of general interest or restricted to Eastern U.S. and Midwest, United Kingdom, Germany." Query with SASE or submit outline. Reviews artwork/photos as part of ms package.
Tips: "The quality of the book is of prime importance; next is its relevance to our fields of interest."

[N] HERODIAS, 346 First Ave., New York NY 10009. (212)995-5332. Fax: (212)995-5332. E-mail: greatblue@acninc.net. Website: www.herodias.com. **Acquisitions:** Paul Williams, editor (fiction, biography, arts). Publishes hardcover originals, trade paperback originals and reprints. **Publishes 10 titles/year. Receives 500 queries and 50 mss/year. 25% of books from first-time authors; 75% from unagented writers. Pays 7½-17½% royalty. Offers $500-2,000 advance.** Publishes book 1 year after acceptance of ms. Accepts simultaneous submissions. Responds in 2 weeks to queries; 1 month to proposals; 3 months to mss. Book catalog and ms guidelines online.
Imprints: Herodias Books for Young Readers (young adult); Little Blue Books (kids)
Nonfiction: Favors biographies/memoirs, philosophy and "ideas" books. Biography, children's/juvenile, coffee table book, cookbook, gift book, self-help. Subjects include animals, art/architecture, cooking/foods/nutrition, language/literature, memoirs, philosophy, photography, translation. Query with SASE or submit proposal package including outline. Reviews artwork/photos as part of ms package. Send photocopies.
Fiction: Erotica, fantasy, historical, juvenile, literary, mainstream/contemporary, poetry, poetry in translation, young adult. Query with SASE or submit proposal package including synopsis.
Poetry: Poets "must be widely published in journals/good promoter." Query.
Recent Title(s): *My Lucky Star*, by Zdenka Fantlová (memoir); *The Cuttlefish*, by Maryline Desbiolles (novel); *The Bold Saboteurs*, by Chandler Brassard (novel).

HEYDAY BOOKS, Box 9145, Berkeley CA 94709-9145. Fax: (510)549-1889. E-mail: heyday@heydaybooks.com. Website: www.heydaybooks.com. **Acquisitions:** Malcolm Margolin, publisher; Jeannine Gendar, managing editor. Estab. 1974. Publishes hardcover originals, trade paperback originals and reprints. **Publishes 12-15 titles/year. Receives 200 submissions/year. 50% of books from first-time authors; 90% from unagented writers. Pays 8% royalty on net price.** Publishes book 8 months after acceptance of ms. Responds in 2 months to queries and mss. Book catalog for 7×9 SAE with 3 first-class stamps.

    O—**•** Heyday Books publishes nonfiction books and literary anthologies with a strong California focus. "We publish books about Native Americans, natural history, history, literature, and recreation, with a strong California focus."

Nonfiction: Books about California only. Subjects include Americana, ethnic, history, nature/environment, recreation, regional, travel. Query with outline and synopsis. Reviews artwork/photos as part of ms package.

Recent Title(s): *California Literary Landscapes*, edited by Terry Beers; *Unfinished Message: Selected Works of Toshio Mori*, intro by Lawson Fusao Inada; *How Much Earth: An Anthology of Fresno Poets*, edited by Christopher Buckley, David Oliviera and M.L. Williams (anthology poetry).

HI-TIME PFLAUM, (formerly Hi-Time Publishing), N90 W16890 Roosevelt Dr., Menomonee Falls WI 53051-7933. (262)502-4222. Fax: (262)502-4224. E-mail: kcannizzo@hi-time.com. **Acquisitions:** Karen A. Cannizzo, co-publisher. **Publishes 20 titles/year. Payment may be outright purchase, royalty or down payment plus royalty.** Book catalog and ms guidelines free.

    O—**•** "Hi-time Pflaum, a division of Peter Li, Inc., serves the specialized market of religious education, primarily Roman Catholic. We provide high quality, theologically sound, practical, and affordable resources that assist religious educators of and ministers to children from preschool through senior high school."

Nonfiction: Religious education programs and catechetical resources. Subjects include education. Query with SASE.

Recent Title(s): *Active Learning for Catholic Kids* (series); *Conversations with Teens: Catholic Perspectives* (series).

HIDDENSPRING, 997 Macarthur Blvd., Mahwah NJ 07430. (201)825-7300. Fax: (201)825-8345. Website: www.hiddenspringbooks.com. **Acquisitions:** Jan-Erik Guerth, editorial director (nonfiction/spirituality). Publishes hardcover and trade paperback originals and reprints. **Publishes 10-12 titles/year. 5% of books from first-time authors; 10% from unagented writers. Royalty varies on wholesale or retail price. Offers variable advance.** Accepts simultaneous submissions. Resonds in 1 month to queries. Manuscript guidelines online.

    O—**•** "Books should always have a spiritual angle—nonfiction with a spiritual twist."

Nonfiction: Biography, gift book, how-to, self-help. Subjects include Americana, anthropology/archeology, art/architecture, business/economics, child guidance/parenting, cooking/foods/nutrition, creative nonfiction, ethnic, gardening, gay/lesbian, government/politics, health/medicine, history, money/finance, multicultural, music/dance, nature/environment, philosophy, psychology, regional, religion, science, sex, sociology, travel, women's issues/studies. Submit proposal package including outline, 1 sample chapter(s), SASE.

Recent Title(s): *The Spiritual Traveler: England, Scotland, Wales*; *Francis of Assisi*, by Adrian House; *Your Soul at Work*, by Nicholas Weiler.

N: HIGH PLAINS PRESS, P.O. Box 123, 539 Cassa Rd., Glendo WY 82213. (307)735-4370. Fax: (307)735-4590. E-mail: editor@highplainspress.com. Website: www.highplainspress.com. **Acquisitions:** Nancy Curtis, publisher. Estab. 1986. Publishes hardcover and trade paperback originals. **Publishes 4 titles/year. Receives 300 queries and 200 mss/year. 80% of books from first-time authors; 95% from unagented writers. Pays 10% royalty on wholesale price. Offers $100-600 advance.** Publishes book 2 years after acceptance of ms. Accepts simultaneous submissions. Responds in 1 month to queries and proposals; 3 months to mss. Book catalog and ms guidelines for 9×12 SASE.

    O—**•** "What we sell best is history of the Old West, particularly things relating to Wyoming. We also publish one book of poetry a year in our Poetry of the American West series."

Nonfiction: "We focus on books of the American West, mainly history." Biography. Subjects include Americana, art/architecture, history, nature/environment, regional. Submit outline. Reviews artwork/photos as part of ms package. Send photocopies.

Poetry: "We only seek poetry closely tied to the Rockies. Do not submit single poems." Query or submit complete ms.

Recent Title(s): *Petticoat Prisoners*, by Larry K. Brown; *Bitter Creek Junction*, by Linda Hasselstrom (poetry).

HIGH TIDE PRESS, 3650 W. 183rd St., Homewood IL 60430-2603. (708)206-2054. Fax: (708)206-2044. E-mail: managing.editor@hightidepress.com. Website: www.hightidepress.com. **Acquisitions:** Diane J. Bell, managing editor. Publishes hardcover and trade paperback originals. **Publishes 8 titles/year. Receives 20 queries and 10 mss/year. 50% of books from first-time authors; 80% from unagented writers. Pays 8-12% royalty on wholesale price. Offers $500-30,000 advance.** Publishes book 1 year after acceptance of ms. Accepts simultaneous submissions. Responds in 1 month to queries and proposals; 4 months to mss. Book catalog online; ms guidelines for #10 SASE.

Nonfiction: Coffee table book. Subjects include business/economics, education, health/medicine, photography, psychology, sex. Reviews artwork/photos as part of ms package.

Recent Title(s): *Managed Care & Developmental Disabilities*, by Dale Mitchell, Ph.D; *Making Money While Making a Difference*, by Richard Steckel, Ph.D.

Tips: "Our audience consists of professionals in these fields: mental health/psychology, disabilities, business, marketing, nonprofit leadership and management. You should send us a one-page query with SASE, giving a brief overview of the book, its market and your background. If we are interested, we will request a book proposal. The book proposal outlines the nature of your work, who your market is, and information about your background. Please do not send a complete manuscript unless we request one."

HIGHSMITH PRESS, P.O. Box 800, Fort Atkinson WI 53538-0800. (920)563-9571. Fax: (920)563-4801. E-mail: hpress@highsmith.com. Website: www.highsmith.com. **Acquisitions:** Matt Mulder, director of publications. Estab. 1990. Publishes hardcover and paperback originals. **Publishes 20 titles/year. Receives 500-600 queries and 400-500 mss/year. 30% of books from first-time authors; 100% from unagented writers. Pays 10-12% royalty on net receipts. Offers $250-1,000 advance.** Publishes book 6 months after acceptance of ms. Accepts simultaneous submissions. Responds in 1 month to queries; 2 months to proposals. Book catalog and ms guidelines online.
Imprints: Alleyside Press, Upstart Books (creative supplemental reading, library and critical thinking skills materials designed to expand the learning environment)
    O→ Highsmith Press publishes educational, professional, and informational resources to meet the practical needs of librarians, educators, readers, library users, colleges, media specialists, schools and related institutions, and to help them fulfill their valuable functions.
Nonfiction: Children's/juvenile, reference. Subjects include education, language/literature, multicultural. "We are primarily interested in manuscripts that stimulate or strengthen reading, library and information-seeking skills and foster critical thinking." Query with outline and 1-2 sample chapters. Reviews artwork/photos as part of ms package. Send transparencies.
Fiction: "Our current emphasis is on storytelling collections for preschool-grade 6. We prefer stories that can be easily used by teachers and children's librarians, multicultural topics, and manuscripts that feature fold and cut, flannelboard, tangram, or similar simple patterns that can be reproduced. No longer accepting children's picture book mss.
Recent Title(s): *Library Celebrations*, by Cindy Dingwall; *Literature Online*, by Karen Moran.

LAWRENCE HILL BOOKS, Chicago Review Press, 814 N. Franklin St., Chicago IL 60610. (312)337-0747. Fax: (312)640-0542. **Acquisitions:** Yuval Taylor, editor (black interest). Publishes hardcover originals and trade paperback originals and reprints. **Publishes 3-10 titles/year. Receives 20 queries and 10 mss/year. 40% of books from first-time authors; 50% from unagented writers. Pays 7½-12½% royalty on retail price. Offers $1,500-7,500 advance.** Publishes book 1 year after acceptance of ms. Accepts simultaneous submissions. Responds in 1 month to queries, proposals and mss. Book catalog free.
Nonfiction: Biography, reference, general nonfiction. Subjects include ethnic, government/politics, history, multicultural. All books should appeal directly to an African American readership. Submit proposal package including outline, 2 sample chapter(s).
Fiction: Ethnic, multicultural. Must be African or African-American fiction. Submit proposal package including synopsis or submit complete ms.
Recent Title(s): *Afraid of the Dark*, by Jim Myers (nonfiction); *The Fire of Origins*, by Emmanuel Dangala (fiction).

HILL STREET PRESS, 191 E. Broad St., Suite 209, Athens GA 30601-2848. (706)613-7200. Fax: (706)613-7204. E-mail: info@hillstreetpress.com. **Acquisitions:** Patrick Allen, senior editor; Judy Long. Publishes hardcover originals, trade paperback originals and reprints. **Publishes 40 titles/year. Receives 300 queries/year. 5% of books from first-time authors; 2% from unagented writers. Pays 9-12½% royalty on wholesale price.** Publishes book 1 year after acceptance of ms. Accepts simultaneous submissions. Responds in 1 month to queries; 3 months to proposals; 6 months to mss. Book catalog and ms guidelines online.
    O→ "HSP is a Southern regional press. While we are not a scholarly or academic press, our nonfiction titles must meet the standards of research for an exacting general audience."
Nonfiction: Biography, coffee table book, cookbook, gift book, humor, illustrated book. Subjects include Americana, cooking/foods/nutrition, creative nonfiction, gardening, gay/lesbian, history, memoirs, nature/environment, recreation, regional (Southern), sports, travel. Submit proposal package including outline, 3 sample chapter(s), résumé.
Fiction: Must have a strong connection with the American South. Gay/lesbian, historical, humor, literary, mainstream/contemporary, military/war, religious, sports. Submit proposal package including 3 sample chapter(s), résumé, synopsis, press clips.
Recent Title(s): *Strange Birds in the Tree of Heaven*, by Karen Salyer McElmurray (literary fiction); *My Brother Bill*, by John Faulkner (memoir).
Tips: "Audience is discerning with an interest in the fiction, history, current issues and food of the American South"

HIPPOCRENE BOOKS INC., 171 Madison Ave., New York NY 10016. (212)685-4371. Fax: (212)779-9338. E-mail: hippocre@ix.netcom.com. Website: www.hippocrenebooks.com. President/Publisher: George Blagowidow. **Acquisitions:** Carol Chitnis-Gress, managing editor (cooking, history, travel, nonfiction reference); Caroline Gates, associate editor (foreign language, dictionaries, language guides); Paul Simpson, associate editor (illustrated histories). Estab. 1971. Publishes hardcover and trade paperback originals. **Publishes 100 titles/year. Receives 250 submissions/year. 10% of books from first-time authors; 95% from unagented writers. Pays 6-10% royalty on retail price. Offers $2,000 advance.** Publishes book 16 months after acceptance of ms. Accepts simultaneous submissions. Responds in 2 months to queries. Book catalog for 9×12 SAE with 5 first-class stamps; ms guidelines for #10 SASE.

O→ "We focus on ethnic-interest and language-related titles, particularly on lesser published and often overlooked ones." Currently emphasizing concise foreign language dictionaries. De-emphasizing military history.

Nonfiction: Biography, cookbook, reference. Subjects include cooking/foods/nutrition, ethnic, history, language/literature, multicultural, travel. Submit proposal package including outline, 2 sample chapter(s), table of contents.

Recent Title(s): *Imperial Mongolian Cooking: Recipes from the Kingdoms of Genghis Khan*; *Jews in Old China: Studies by Chinese Scholars*.

Tips: "Our recent successes in publishing general books considered midlist by larger publishers is making us more of a general trade publisher. We continue to do well with reference books like dictionaries, atlases and language studies. We ask for proposal, sample chapter, and table of contents. We then ask for material if we are interested."

N HOBAR PUBLICATIONS, Finney Company, 3943 Meadowbrook Rd., Minneapolis MN 55426. (952)938-9330. Fax: (952)938-7353. E-mail: feedback@finney-hobar.com. Website: www.finney-hobar.com. **Acquisitions:** Alan E. Krysan, president. Publishes trade paperback originals. **Publishes 4-6 titles/year. Receives 30 queries and 10 mss/year. 35% of books from first-time authors; 100% from unagented writers. Pays 10% royalty on wholesale price. Offers advance.** Publishes book 6-12 months after acceptance of ms. Accepts simultaneous submissions. Responds in 3 weeks to queries.

O→ Hobar publishes agricultural and industrial technology educational materials.

Nonfiction: How-to, illustrated book, reference, technical, textbook, handbooks, field guides. Subjects include agriculture/horticulture, animals, business/economics, education, gardening, nature/environment, science, building trades. Query with SASE. Reviews artwork/photos as part of ms package.

Recent Title(s): *Making Dollars and Sense—Value-Added Agriculture*, by the University of Minnesota; *Science South Resource Book*, by Powell.

N HOBBY HOUSE PRESS, 1 Corporate Dr., Grantsville MD 21536. (301)895-3792. Fax: (301)895-5029. Website: www.hobbyhouse.com. Publishes hardcover originals. **Publishes 20 titles/year. Receives 50 queries and 25 mss/year. 85% of books from first-time authors; 100% from unagented writers. Pays 10% royalty on retail price.** Publishes book 6 months after acceptance of ms. Accepts simultaneous submissions. Responds in 2 weeks to queries; 1 month to proposals. Book catalog and ms guidelines free.

Nonfiction: Gift book, how-to, reference, price guides. Subjects include gardening, hobbies (collecting/antiques). Query with SASE or submit outline, 1 sample chapter(s), photos. Reviews artwork/photos as part of ms package. Send prints.

Recent Title(s): *Reflections of Love: An Adoptive Parent's Keepsake Journal* (gift); *The Story of German Doll Making*, by Mary Krembholtz (dolls); *Steiff Identification and Price Guide*, by Linda Mullins.

HOHM PRESS, P.O. Box 2501, Prescott AZ 86302. Fax: (520)717-1779. E-mail: pinedr@goodnet.com. **Acquisitions:** Regina Sara Ryan, managing editor. Estab. 1975. Publishes hardcover and trade paperback originals. **Publishes 6-8 titles/year. 50% of books from first-time authors. Pays 10% royalty on net sales.** Publishes book 18 months after acceptance of ms. Accepts simultaneous submissions. Responds in 3 months to queries.

O→ Hohm Press publishes a range of titles in the areas of transpersonal psychology and spirituality, herbistry, alternative health methods and nutrition. Currently emphasizing health alternatives. Not interested in personal health survival stories.

Nonfiction: Self-help. Subjects include health/medicine, philosophy, religion (Hindu, Buddhist, Sufi or translations of classic texts in major religious traditions), translation. "We look for writers who have an established record in their field of expertise. The best buy of recent years came from two women who fully substantiated how they could market their book. We believed they could do it. We were right." Query with SASE.

Poetry: "We are not accepting poetry at this time except for translations of recognized religious/spiritual classics."

Recent Title(s): *The Yoga Tradition*, by Georg Feuerstein; *Beyond Aspirin*, by Thomas Newmark and Paul Schulick.

HOLIDAY HOUSE INC., 425 Madison Ave., New York NY 10017. (212)688-0085. Fax: (212)421-6134. Editor-in-Chief: Regina Griffin. **Acquisitions:** Suzanne Reinoehl, associate editor. Estab. 1935. Publishes hardcover originals. **Publishes 60 titles/year. Receives 3,000 submissions/year. 2-5% of books from first-time authors; 50% from unagented writers. Pays royalty on list price, range varies. Offers advance.** Publishes book 1-2 years after acceptance of ms. Manuscript guidelines for #10 SASE.

O→ Holiday House publishes children's and young adult books for the school and library markets. "We have a commitment to publishing first-time authors and illustrators. We specialize in quality hardcovers from picture books to young adult, both fiction and nonfiction, primarily for the school and library market." Currently emphasizing literary middle-grade novels.

Nonfiction: Biography, humor. Subjects include Americana, history, science, Judaica. Query with SASE. Reviews artwork/photos as part of ms package. Send photocopies—no originals—to Claire Counihan, art director.

Fiction: Adventure, historical. Query with SASE.

Recent Title(s): *John and Abigail Adams*, by Judith St. George; *A Child's Calendar*, by John Updike, illustrated by Trina Schart Hyman.

Tips: "We are not geared toward the mass market, but toward school and library markets. We need picture book texts with strong stories and writing. We do not publish board books or novelties."

HOLMES & MEIER PUBLISHERS, INC., East Building, 160 Broadway, New York NY 10038. (212)374-0100. Fax: (212)374-1313. E-mail: hmp160@aol.com. Website: www.holmesandmeier.com. Publisher: Miriam H. Holmes. **Acquisitions:** Maggie Kennedy, managing editor. Estab. 1969. Publishes hardcover and paperback originals. **Publishes 20 titles/year. Pays royalty.** Publishes book an average of 18 months after acceptance of ms. Responds in 6 months to queries. Book catalog free.

Imprints: Africana Publishing Company

> O→ "We are noted as an academic publishing house and are pleased with our reputation for excellence in the field. However, we are also expanding our list to include books of more general interest."

Nonfiction: Biography, reference. Subjects include art/architecture, business/economics, ethnic, government/politics, history, regional, translation, women's issues/studies. Query first with outline, sample chapters, cv and idea of intended market/audience.

HOLMES PUBLISHING GROUP LLC, P.O. Box 623, Edmonds WA 98020. E-mail: HPubG@aol.com. CEO: J.D. Holmes. **Acquisitions:** L.Y. Fitzgerald. Estab. 1983. Publishes hardcover and trade paperback originals and reprints. **Publishes 40 titles/year. Receives 120 queries and 80 mss/year. 20% of books from first-time authors; 20% from unagented writers. Pays 10% royalty on net revenue.** Publishes book 4 months after acceptance of ms. Responds in 2 months to queries.

Imprints: Alchemical Press, Alexandrian Press, Contra/Thought, Sure Fire Press

> O→ Holmes publishes informative spiritual titles on philosophy, metaphysical and religious subjects, and alternative medicine and health. Holmes Publishing Group no longer publishes fiction.

Nonfiction: Self-help. Subjects include health/medicine, New Age, philosophy, religion, occult, metaphysical. "We do not publish titles that are more inspirational than informative." Query with SASE; no e-mail queries.

Recent Title(s): *The Geography of the Soul: The Enneagram in Christian Perspective*, by Thomas Garrett Isham.

HENRY HOLT & COMPANY BOOKS FOR YOUNG READERS, Henry Holt & Co., Inc., 115 W. 18th St., New York NY 10011. (212)886-9200. **Acquisitions:** Laura Godwin, associate publisher (picture books, chapter books and middle grade); Christy Ottaviano, executive editor (picture books, chapter books and middle grade); Nina Ignatowicz, senior editor (picture books and chapter books); Reka Simonsen, editor (picture books, chapter books and middle grade). Estab. 1866 (Holt). Publishes hardcover originals. **Publishes 70-80 titles/year. 10% of books from first-time authors; 50% from unagented writers. Pays royalty on retail price. Offers $3,000 and up advance.** Publishes book 18 months after acceptance of ms. Responds in 5 months to queries. Book catalog and ms guidelines for #10 SASE.

Imprints: Books by Michael Hague, Books by Bill Martin Jr. and John Archambault; Owlet Paperbacks; Redfeather Books (chapter books for ages 7-10)

> O→ "Henry Holt Books for Young Readers publishes highly original and cutting-edge fiction and nonfiction for all ages, from the very young to the young adult."

Nonfiction: Children's/juvenile, illustrated book. Submit complete ms.

Fiction: Adventure, fantasy, historical, humor, multicultural, mystery, picture books, sports, suspense, young adult. Juvenile: adventure, animal, contemporary, fantasy, history, humor, multicultural, sports, suspense/mystery. Picture books: animal, concept, history, humor, mulitcultural, sports. Young adult: contemporary, fantasy, history, multicultural, nature/environment, problem novels, sports. Submit complete ms.

Recent Title(s): *Uptown*, by Bryan Collier (picture book); *Pedro and Me: Friendship, Loss and What I Learned*, by Judd Winik (nonfiction).

HOME PLANNERS, LLC, 3275 West Ina Rd., #110, Tucson AZ 85741. (520)297-8200. Fax: (520)297-6219. E-mail: pdague@homeplanners.com. Website: www.homeplanners.com. **Acquisitions:** Paulette Dague, special projects and acquisitions editor. Estab. 1946. Publishes hardcover and trade paperback originals. **Publishes 12-15 titles/year. Receives 8-10 queries and 2-3 mss/year. 80% of books from first-time authors; 100% from unagented writers. Makes outright purchase of $5,000-18,000.** Publishes book 6 months after acceptance of ms. Accepts simultaneous submissions. Book catalog free.

> O→ Home Planners publishes home plan, landscape, interior design books and magazines and construction plans. "We are primarily interested in how-to or reference titles. We may consider personal experience or technical stories but only if unusual and exceptionally well done."

Nonfiction: How-to, reference. Subjects include art/architecture, gardening, homebuilding/home improvement/remodeling. Query with SASE or submit proposal package including outline, sample chapter. Reviews artwork/photos as part of ms package. Send photocopies.

Recent Title(s): *Building Your Country Home*, by Homer C. Emery.

Tips: "Have some experience in architecture, building or remodeling. Previous publishing or magazine writing in the field preferred."

HOUGHTON MIFFLIN BOOKS FOR CHILDREN, Houghton Mifflin Company, 222 Berkeley St., Boston MA 02116. (617)351-5959. Fax: (617)351-1111. E-mail: Childrens_Books@hmco.com. Website: www.hmco.com. **Acquisitions:** Hannah Rodgers, submissions coordinator. Publishes hardcover and trade paperback originals and reprints. **Publishes 100 titles/year. Receives 5,000 queries and 12,000 mss/year. 10% of books from first-time authors; 70%**

from unagented writers. **Pays 5-10% royalty on retail price. Offers variable advance.** Publishes book 18 months after acceptance of ms. Accepts simultaneous submissions. Responds in 4 months to queries. Book catalog for 9×12 SASE with 3 first-class stamps; ms guidelines for #10 SASE.

Imprints: Sandpiper Paperback Books (Eden Edwards, editor)

O─┐ "Houghton Mifflin gives shape to ideas that educate, inform, and above all, delight."

Nonfiction: Biography, children's/juvenile, humor, illustrated book. Subjects include agriculture/horticulture, Americana, animals, anthropology/archeology, art/architecture, ethnic, gardening, history, humor, language/literature, music/dance, nature/environment, recreation, regional, science, sports, travel. Interested in "innovative science books, especially about scientists 'in the field' and what they do." Query with SASE or submit outline, 2 sample chapter(s). Note: Mss not returned without appropriate-sized SASE. Reviews artwork/photos as part of ms package. Send photocopies.

Fiction: Adventure, ethnic, historical, humor, juvenile (early readers), literary, mystery, picture books, suspense, young adult, board books. Submit complete ms with appropriate-sized SASE.

Recent Title(s): *Top of the World*, by Steve Jenkins (nonfiction); *Signs and Wonders*, by Pat Lowery Collins (fiction); *Dutch Sneakers and Flea Keepers*, by Calef Brown (poetry).

Tips: "Faxed or e-mailed manuscripts and proposals are not considered."

[A] HOUGHTON MIFFLIN COMPANY, 222 Berkeley St., Boston MA 02116. (617)351-5000. Fax: (617)351-1202. Website: www.hmco.com. Executive Vice President: Wendy J. Strothman. Editor-in-Chief, Adult Books: Janet Silver. Publisher, Children's Books: Anita Silvey. **Acquisitions:** Submissions Editor. Estab. 1832. Publishes hardcover and trade paperback originals and reprints. **Publishes 90-100 titles/year. 10% of books from first-time authors. Hardcover: pays 10-15% royalty on retail price, sliding scale or flat rate based on sales; paperback: 7½% flat fee, but negotiable. Offers variable advance.** Publishes book 1-2 years after acceptance of ms. Accepts simultaneous submissions. Responds in 3 months to proposals. Book catalog and ms guidelines free.

Imprints: Clarion Books, Walter Lorraine Books, Houghton Mifflin Books for Children, Mariner Paperbacks, Sandpiper Paperbacks, Frances Tenenbaum Books

O─┐ "Houghton Mifflin gives shape to ideas that educate, inform and delight. In a new era of publishing, our legacy of quality thrives as we combine imagination with technology, bringing you new ways to know."

Nonfiction: Biography, children's/juvenile, reference, self-help. Subjects include cooking/foods/nutrition, gardening, history, nature/environment, travel, guidebooks. "We are not a mass market publisher. Our main focus is serious nonfiction. We do practical self-help but not pop psychology self-help." *Accepts agented submissions only.*

Fiction: Literary. "We are not a mass market publisher. Study the current list." *Accepts agented submissions only.*

Poetry: "At this point we have an established roster of poets we use. It is hard for first-time poets to get published by Houghton Mifflin."

Recent Title(s): *The Dying Animal*, by Philip Roth; *Hotel Honolulu*, by Paul Theroux; *Fast Food Nation*, by Eric Schlosser.

HOUSE OF COLLECTIBLES, Crown Publishing Group, Random House, Inc., 299 Park Ave., New York NY 10171. Website: www.randomhouse.com. **Acquisitions:** Dorothy Harris, editor. Publishes trade and mass market paperback originals. **Publishes 25-28 titles/year. Receives 200 queries/year. 1% of books from first-time authors; 85% from unagented writers. Royalty on retail price varies. Offers varied advance.** Publishes book 1 year after acceptance of ms. Book catalog free.

Imprints: Official Price Guide series

O─┐ "One of the premier publishing companies devoted to books on a wide range of antiques and collectibles, House of Collectibles publishes books for the seasoned expert and the beginning collector alike."

Nonfiction: How-to (related to collecting antiques and coins), reference. Subjects include hobbies, recreation.

Recent Title(s): *Official Price Guide to Records*, by Jerry Osborne.

Tips: "We have been publishing price guides and other books on antiques and collectibles for over 35 years and plan to meet the needs of collectors, dealers and appraisers well into the 21st century."

HOWELL PRESS, INC., 1713-2D Allied Lane, Charlottesville VA 22903. (804)977-4006. Fax: (804)971-7204. E-mail: howellpres@aol.com. Website: www.howellpress.com. **Acquisitions:** Ross A. Howell, president; Meghan Mitchell, editor. Estab. 1985. **Publishes 10-13 titles/year. Receives 500 submissions/year. 10% of books from first-time authors; 80% from unagented writers. Pays 5-10% royalty Offers advance.** Publishes book 18 months after acceptance of ms. Book catalog for 9×12 SAE with 4 first-class stamps; ms guidelines for #10 SASE.

O─┐ "While our aviation, history and transportation titles are produced for the enthusiast market, writing must be accessible to the general adult reader." Currently emphasizing regional (Mid-Atlantic and Southeast), travel, ghost stories, gardens, quilts and quilt history. De-emphasizing general garden guides.

Nonfiction: Illustrated book. Subjects include history, regional, aviation, transportation, gourmet, quilts. "Generally open to most ideas, as long as writing is accessible to average adult reader. Our line is targeted, so it would be advisable to look over our catalog before querying to better understand what Howell Press does." Query with SASE or submit outline, sample chapter(s). Does not return mss without SASE. Reviews artwork/photos as part of ms package.

Recent Title(s): *The Virginia Landscape*, by James Kelly and William Rasmussen.

Tips: "Focus of our program has been illustrated books, but we will also consider nonfiction manuscripts that would not be illustrated."

HUDSON HILLS PRESS, INC., 1133 Broadway, Suite 1301, New York NY 10010-8001. (212)929-4994. Fax: (212)929-9051. **Acquisitions:** Paul Anbinder, president/publisher. Estab. 1978. Publishes hardcover and paperback originals. **Publishes 15 titles/year. Receives 50-100 submissions/year. 15% of books from first-time authors; 90% from unagented writers. Pays 4-6% royalty on retail price. Offers $3,500 average advance.** Publishes book 1 year after acceptance of ms. Accepts simultaneous submissions. Responds in 2 months to queries. Book catalog for 6×9 SAE with 2 first-class stamps.

O⊸ Hudson Hills Press publishes books about art and photography, including monographs.

Nonfiction: Subjects include art/architecture, photography. Query first, then submit outline and sample chapters. Reviews artwork/photos as part of ms package.

Recent Title(s): *Hollis Sigler's Breast Cancer Journal*, by Hollis Sigler and Susan M. Love, M.D.

HUMAN KINETICS PUBLISHERS, INC., P.O. Box 5076, Champaign IL 61825-5076. (217)351-5076. Fax: (217)351-2674. E-mail: hk@hkusa.com. Website: www.HumanKinetics.com. Publisher: Rainer Martens. **Acquisitions:** Ted Miller, vice president and director (trade); Martin Barnard, trade senior acquisitions editor (fitness, running, golf, tennis, cycling, fishing); Scott Wikgren, HPERD director (health, physical education, recreation, dance); Mike Bahrke, STM acquisitions editor (scientific, technical, medical); Loarn Robertson, STM acquisitions editor (biomechanics, anatomy, athletic training, cardiac rehab, test/measurement); Judy Wright, HPERD acquisitions editor (dance, motor, learning/behavior/performance/development, gymnastics, adapted physical education, older adults); Amy Pickering, HPERD acquisitions editor (games, health and physical activity promotion, recreation and leisure, sport management). Estab. 1974. Publishes hardcover and paperback text and reference books, trade paperback originals, software and audiovisual. **Publishes 120 titles/year. Receives 300 submissions/year. 30% of books from first-time authors; 90% from unagented writers. Pays 10-15% royalty on net income.** Publishes book an average of 18 months after acceptance of ms. Accepts simultaneous submissions. Responds in 2 months to queries. Book catalog free.

Imprints: HK Trade, HK Academic

O⊸ Human Kinetics publishes books which accurately interpret sport and fitness training and techniques, physical education, sports sciences and sports medicine for coaches, athletes and fitness enthusiasts and professionals in the physical action field.

Nonfiction: How-to, multimedia, reference, self-help, technical, textbook. Subjects include education, health/medicine, psychology, recreation, sports. No sport biographies, sport record or statistics books or regional books. Submit outline, sample chapter(s). Reviews artwork/photos as part of ms package.

Recent Title(s): *Introduction to Kinesiology*, by Shirl J. Hoffman, Ed.D. and Janet C. Harris, Ph.D (academic); *Advanced Marathoning*, by Pete Pfitzinger and Scott Douglas (trade nonfiction).

[N] **HUMANICS LEARNING**, Humanics Publishing Group, P.O. Box 7400, Atlanta GA 30357. (404)874-2176. Fax: (404)874-1976. Website: www.humanicslearning.com. **Acquisitions:** Arthur Blye, editor. Estab. 1976. Publishes hardcover and trade paperback originals and reprints. **Publishes 20 titles/year. Receives 1,500 queries and 1,300 mss/year. 90% from unagented writers. Pays 5-13% royalty on net receipts. Offers $500-1,000 advance.** Publishes book 6 months after acceptance of ms. Accepts simultaneous submissions. Responds in 3 months to queries. Book catalog for 9×12 SAE and 1 55¢ stamp; ms guidelines for #10 SASE or online.

O⊸ "Our goal is to furnish teachers, home schoolers, day care facilitators and other instructors with the best teacher resource guides available to help improve the education of the child."

Nonfiction: How-to (teacher resource guides). Subjects include child guidance/parenting, education, ethnic, health/medicine, language/literature, music/dance, nature/environment, psychology, science, self esteem. "Know our focus. Request a catalog." Query with SASE or submit outline, 3 sample chapter(s). Reviews artwork/photos as part of ms package. Send photocopies.

Recent Title(s): *Super Simple Science*, by Marvin Tollman and Lynn Booth.

HUMANICS PUBLISHING GROUP, P.O. Box 7400, Atlanta GA 30357. (404)874-2176. Fax: (404)874-1976. E-mail: humanics@mindspring.com. Website: humanicspub.com. **Acquisitions:** W. Arthur Bligh, editor. Estab. 1976. Publishes trade paperback originals. **Publishes 20 titles/year; imprint publishes 22 titles/year. Receives 5,000 queries/year. 70% of books from first-time authors. Pays 10% royalty on wholesale price. Offers $500-3,000 advance.** Publishes book 1-12 months after acceptance of ms. Accepts simultaneous submissions. Responds to queries only if interested. Book catalog free; ms guidelines for #10 SASE.

Imprints: Humanics Trade Paperback, Humanics Learning

O⊸ "We publish books which will target the New Age market (i.e., self-help, eastern philosophy, metaphysics, psychology). We also publish teacher resource guides and activity books for early childhood development." Currently emphasizing Feng Shui, Taoism, learning (phonics, reading, parent involvement). De-emphasizing children's books.

Nonfiction: Children's/juvenile, illustrated book, self-help. Subjects include child guidance/parenting, philosophy, psychology, spirituality (e.g., taoism), New Age. Query with SASE or submit outline, 1 sample chapter(s).

Recent Title(s): *Lifestyles for the 21st Century*, by Marcus Wells; *Tao of an Unclutted Life*, by Karen Hicks.

Tips: "For our activity books, audience is parents and educators looking for books which will enrich their children's lives. For our trade books, audience is anyone interested in positive, healthy self-development. We are looking for quality and creativity. As a small publisher, we don't waste our time or an author's time on books that are not of lasting importance or value. Taoism and Zen high interest."

A **HUNGRY MINDS, INC., Consumer Business Group**, (formerly IDG Books Worldwide, Business Group), 645 N. Michigan Ave., Suite 800, Chicago, IL 60611. (312)482-8460. Fax: (312)482-8561. E-mail: kwelton@hungrymin ds.com. Website: www.hungryminds.com. **Acquisitions:** Kathleen A. Welton, vice president/publisher; Mark Butler, executive editor (personal finance, taxes, small business, e-commerce); Holly McGuire, executive editor (technical/how-to, management and skills training, business self-help); Karen Hansen, acquisitions editor (careers); Stacy Collins (sports). Publishes trade paperback originals. **Pays 10-15% royalty. Offers $0-25,000 advance.** Publishes book 3 months after acceptance of ms. Responds in 2 months to queries. Manuscript guidelines free.
> "Hungry Minds dedicates itself to publishing innovative, high-quality titles on the most popular business, self-help and general reference topics."

Nonfiction: How-to, illustrated book, reference, self-help, technical. Subjects include business/economics (small business, e-commerce, careers), education (management and skills training), money/finance (personal finance, taxes), sports. *Accepts agented submissions only.*
Recent Title(s): *Investing For Dummies*, by Eric Tyson.

A **HUNGRY MINDS, INC., Education Group**, (formerly IDG Books Worldwide, Education Group), 10475 Crosspoint Blvd., Indianapolis IN 46256. (317)572-3075. E-mail: dsteele@hungryminds.com. Website: www.hungrymin ds.com. **Acquisitions:** Diane Steele, vice president/publisher. Publishes trade paperback originals. **Contracts negotiated on a title-by-title basis. Offers industry standard advance.** Publishes book 3 months after acceptance of ms. Responds in 2 months to queries. Manuscript guidelines free.
> "Hungry Minds dedicates itself to publishing innovative, high-quality titles on the most popular business, self-help and general topics."

Nonfiction: How-to, reference, self-help. Subjects include education. *Accepts agented submissions only.*

H **HUNTER HOUSE**, P.O. Box 2914, Alameda CA 94501. (510)865-5282. Fax: (510)865-4295. E-mail: acquisition s@hunterhouse.com. Website: www.hunterhouse.com. **Acquisitions:** Jeanne Brondino, acquisitions editor; Kiran S. Rana, publisher. Estab. 1978. Publishes hardcover and trade paperback originals and reprints. **Publishes 18 titles/year. Receives 200-300 queries and 100 mss/year. 50% of books from first-time authors; 80% from unagented writers. Pays 12-15% royalty on net receipts, defined as selling price. Offers $500-3,000 advance.** Publishes book 1-2 years after acceptance of ms. Accepts simultaneous submissions. Responds in 2 months to queries; 3 months to proposals; 6 months to mss. Book catalog and ms guidelines for 8½×11 SAE with 3 first-class stamps.
> Hunter House publishes health books (especially women's health), self-help health, sexuality and couple relationships, violence prevention and intervention. De-emphasizing reference, self-help psychology.

Nonfiction: Subjects include health/medicine, self-help, women's health, fitness, relationships, sexuality, personal growth, and violence prevention. "Health books (especially women's health) should focus on emerging health issues or current issues that are inadequately covered and be written for the general population. Family books: Our current focus is sexuality and couple relationships, and alternative lifestyles to high stress. Community topics include violence prevention/violence intervention. We also publish specialized curricula for counselors and educators in the areas of violence prevention and trauma in children." Query with proposal package, including synopsis, table of contents and chapter outline, sample chapter, target audience information, competition and what distinguishes the book. Reviews artwork/photos as part of ms package. Send photocopies, proposals generally not returned, requested mss returned with SASE. Reviews artwork/photos as part of ms package.
Recent Title(s): *The Complete Guide to Joseph H. Pilates' Techniques of Physical Conditioning*, by Allan Menezes; *Pocket Book of Foreplay*, Richard Craze; *Living Beyond Multiple Sclerosis—A Women's Guide*, by Judith Lynn Nichols.
Tips: Audience is concerned people who are looking to educate themselves and their community about real-life issues that affect them. "Please send as much information as possible about *who* your audience is, *how* your book addresses their needs, and *how* you reach that audience in your ongoing work."

HUNTER PUBLISHING, INC., 130 Campus Dr., Edison NJ 08818. Fax: (561)546-8040. E-mail: hunterp@bellsouth. net. Website: www.hunterpublishing.com. President: Michael Hunter. **Acquisitions:** Kim Andre, editor; Lissa Dailey. Estab. 1985. **Publishes 100 titles/year. Receives 300 submissions/year. 10% of books from first-time authors; 75% from unagented writers. Pays royalty. Offers negotiable advance.** Publishes book 5 months after acceptance of ms. Accepts simultaneous submissions. Responds in 3 weeks to queries; 1 month to mss. Book catalog for #10 SAE with 4 first-class stamps.
Imprints: Adventure Guides, Romantic Weekends Guides, Alive Guides
> Hunter Publishing publishes practical guides for travelers going to the Caribbean, U.S., Europe, South America, and the far reaches of the globe.

Nonfiction: Reference. Subjects include regional, travel (travel guides). "We need travel guides to areas covered by few competitors: Caribbean Islands, South and Central America, regional U.S. from an active 'adventure' perspective." No personal travel stories or books not directed to travelers. Query or submit outline/synopsis and sample chapters. Reviews artwork/photos as part of ms package.
Recent Title(s): *Adventure Guide to Canada's Atlantic Provinces*, by Barbara Radcliffe-Rogers.
Tips: "Guides should be destination-specific, rather than theme-based alone. Thus, 'travel with kids' is too broad; 'Florida with Kids' is OK. Make sure the guide doesn't duplicate what other guide publishers do. We need active adventure-oriented guides and more specialized guides for travelers in search of the unusual."

IBEX PUBLISHERS, P.O. Box 30087, Bethesda MD 20824. (301)718-8188. Fax: (301)907-8707. E-mail: info@ibexp ub.com. Website: www.ibexpub.com. Publishes hardcover and trade paperback originals and reprints. **Publishes 6-10 titles/year. Pay varies.** Accepts simultaneous submissions. Book catalog free.
Imprints: Iranbooks Press
O➤ IBEX publishes books about Iran and the Middle East.
Nonfiction: Biography, cookbook, reference, textbook. Subjects include cooking/foods/nutrition, language/literature. Query with SASE or submit propsal package, including outline and 2 sample chapters.
Poetry: Translations of Persian poets will be considered.

ICON EDITIONS, Westview Press, Perseus Books Group, 5500 Central Ave., Boulder CO 80301-2877. (303)444-3541. **Acquisitions:** Sarah Warner. Estab. 1973. Publishes hardcover and trade paperback originals and reprints. **Publishes 6 titles/year. Receives hundreds of queries/year. 25% of books from first-time authors; 80% from unagented writers. Royalty and advance vary.** Publishes book 18 months after acceptance of ms. Accepts simultaneous submissions. Book catalog free.
O➤ Icon Editions focuses on books in architecture, art history and art criticism for the academic and semi-academic market, college and university market.
Nonfiction: Textbook. Subjects include art/architecture, art history, art criticism. Query with SASE. Reviews artwork/photos as part of ms package.
Recent Title(s): *Italian Renaissance Art*, by Laurie Schneider Adams.

◤ **ICONOGRAFIX, INC.**, 1830A Hanley Rd., P.O. Box 446, Hudson WI 54016. (715)381-9755. Fax: (715)381-9756. E-mail: iconogfx@spacestar.net. **Acquisitions:** Dylan Frautschi, acquisitions manager (transportation). Estab. 1992. Publishes trade paperback originals. **Publishes 24 titles/year. Receives 100 queries and 20 mss/year. 50% of books from first-time authors; 100% from unagented writers. Pays 8-12½% royalty on wholesale price or makes outright purchase of $1,000-3,000. Offers $1,000-3,500 advance.** Publishes book 1 year after acceptance of ms. Accepts simultaneous submissions. Responds in 1 month to queries; 3 months to proposals and mss. Book catalog and ms guidelines free.
O➤ Iconografix publishes special historical interest photographic books for transportation equipment enthusiasts. Currently emphasizing emergency vehicles, buses, trucks, railroads, automobiles, auto racing, construction equipment. De-emphasizing American culture.
Nonfiction: Interested in photo archives. Coffee table book, illustrated book (photographic), photo albums. Subjects include Americana (icons, photos from archives of historic places, objects, people), history, hobbies, military/war, photography, travel, transportation (older photos of specific vehicles). Query with SASE or submit proposal package, including outline. Reviews artwork/photos as part of ms package. Send photocopies.
Recent Title(s): *Greyhound Buses 1914-2000 Photo Archive*, by William A. Luke; *Indianapolis Racing Cars of Frank Kurtis, 1941-1963 Photo Archive*, by Gordon Eliot White; *Pontiac Firebird 1967-2000 Photo History*, by George W. Scala.

IDEALS PUBLICATIONS INC., 535 Metroplex Dr., Suite 250, Nashville TN 37211. (615)333-0478. Publisher: Patricia Pingry. **Acquisitions:** Copy Editor. Estab. 1944. Publishes 8-10 hardbound books, 25-30 childrens titles. **Publishes 33-40 titles/year. Offers varied advance.** Publishes book 18 months after acceptance of ms. Accepts simultaneous submissions. Responds in 2 months only with SASE to queries. Manuscript guidelines for #10 SASE.
Imprints: Candy Cane Press (children's holiday-oriented, Americana, religious)
• Uses short prose and poetry. Accepts previously published material. Send information about when and where the piece previously appeared. Also publishes *Ideals* magazine. Most material from unagented submissions.
O➤ Ideals publishes highly illustrated seasonal, nostalgic, inspirational and patriotic coffee table books, including a travel book series, and children's picture and board books.
Nonfiction: Biography, coffee table book, how-to, self-help. Subjects include history, travel, inspirational, nostalgic, patriotic.
Recent Title(s): *My First Day of School*, by Nancy Skarmaes, illustrated by Meredith Johnson; *The Ideals Guide to the American Revolution*.

◧ **IDYLL ARBOR, INC.**, P.O. Box 720, Ravensdale WA 98051. (425)432-3231. Fax: (425)432-3726. E-mail: editors@idyllarbor.com. **Acquisitions:** Tom Blaschko. Publishes hardcover and trade paperback originals and trade paperback reprints. **Publishes 6 titles/year. 50% of books from first-time authors; 100% from unagented writers. Pays 8-15% royalty on wholesale price or retail price.** Publishes book 1 year after acceptance of ms. Accepts simultaneous submissions. Responds in 1 month to queries; 2 months to proposals; 4 months to mss. Book catalog and ms guidelines free.
Imprints: Issues Press, Pine Woods Press
O➤ Idyll Arbor publishes practical information on the current state and art of health care practice. Currently emphasizing therapies (recreational, occupational, music, horticultural), activity directors in long term care facilities, and social service professionals.
Nonfiction: Reference, technical, textbook. Subjects include agriculture/horticulture (used in long-term care activities or health care-therapy), health/medicine (for therapists, social service providers and activity directors), psychology, recreation (as therapy). "Idyll Arbor is currently developing a line of books under the imprint Issues Press, which treats

emotional issues in a clear-headed manner. The first books will be *Female Sex Offenders: What Therapists, Law Enforcement and Child Protective Services Need to Know* and *Sexual Addiction: Eight Years on Recovery Road.* Another series of *Personal Health* books explains a condition or a closely related set of medical or psychological conditions. The target audience is the person or the family of the person with the condition. We want to publish a book that explains a condition at the level of detail expected of the average primary care physician so that our readers can address the situation intelligently with specialists. We look for manuscripts from authors with recent clinical experience. Good grounding in theory is required, but practical experience is more important." Query preferred with outline and 1 sample chapter. Reviews artwork/photos as part of ms package. Send photocopies.

Recent Title(s): *Long Term Care for Activity and Social Service Professionals, Third Edition*, by Elizabeth Best Martini, Mary Anne Weeks and Priscilla Wirth; *After Natural Disaster: How to Get Back to Normal Life*, by Ilana Singer.

Tips: "The books must be useful for the health practitioner who meets face to face with patients *or* the books must be useful for teaching undergraduate and graduate level classes. We are especially looking for therapists with a solid clinical background to write on their area of expertise."

ILR PRESS, Cornell University Press, Sage House, 512 E. State St., Ithaca NY 14850. (607)277-2338 ext. 232. Fax: (607)277-2374. **Acquisitions:** F. Benson, editor. Estab. 1945. Publishes hardcover and trade paperback originals and reprints. **Publishes 10-12 titles/year. Pays royalty.** Responds in 2 months to queries. Book catalog free.

> ○ "We are interested in manuscripts with innovative perspectives on current workplace issues that concern both academics and the general public."

Nonfiction: Subjects include business/economics, government/politics, history, sociology. All titles relate to industrial relations and/or workplace issues including relevant work in the fields of history, sociology, political science, economics, human resources, and organizational behavior. Query with SASE or submit outline, sample chapter(s), cv.

Recent Title(s): *Manufacturing Advantage: Why High-Performance Systems Pay Off*, by Eileen Appelbaum, et al; *The Working Class Majority: America's Best Kept Secret*, by Michael Zweig.

Tips: "Manuscripts must be well documented to pass our editorial evaluation, which includes review by academics in related fields."

IMAGINART INTERNATIONAL, INC., 307 Arizona St., Bisbee AZ 85603. (520)432-5741. Fax: (520)432-5134. E-mail: imaginart@compuserve.com. Website: www.imaginartonline.com. **Acquisitions:** Cindy Drolert, editor-in-chief. Publishes trade paperback originals. **Publishes 6 titles/year. Receives 30 queries and 10 mss/year. 70% of books from first-time authors; 100% from unagented writers. Pays 8-11% royalty on retail price.** Publishes book 9 months after acceptance of ms. Accepts simultaneous submissions. Responds in 3 months to queries, proposals and mss. Book catalog online; ms guidelines free.

Nonfiction: Hands-on manuals in fields of rehabilitation and special education. Textbook. Subjects include speech pathology, OT, PT, special education (particularly language and autism). It is critical to have an academic degree in teaching or a field in rehabilitation to be an author for us. Does not publish children's storybooks or stories about the lives of people who have a disability. Query with SASE.

Recent Title(s): *Preschool Motor Speech Evalutaion and Intervention*, by Peggy Earnest, M.A., CCC-SLP; *Sensory Motor Activities for the Young Child*, by Donna Staisiunas Hurley, P.T (theraputic activities).

Tips: Audience consists of speech pathologists, occupational therapists, physical therapists, family members of persons with disabilities, special education teachers. "We are mostly intested in down-to-earth, hands-on materials rather than textbooks."

THE IMAGINATION STORE, 2424 Beekman St., Cincinnati OH 45214. (513)471-6060. Fax: (513)251-5239. E-mail: TotalBelief@aol.com. Website: www.theimaginationstore.com. **Acquisitions:** Cliff Carle, editorial director (self-help, how-to). Publishes trade paperback originals. **Publishes 15-20 titles/year. Receives 1,000+ queries and 800+ mss/year. 30% of books from first-time authors; 40% from unagented writers. Pays 10-15% royalty on wholesale price. Offers $500-2,500 advance.** Publishes book 6-9 months after acceptance of ms. Accepts simultaneous submissions. Responds in 2 months to queries and proposals; 3 months to mss. Book catalog online; ms guidelines for #10 SASE.

Nonfiction: "We look for a spiritual (but not religious) approach to all subjects." How-to, self-help. Subjects include health/medicine (natural health, herbal medicine), nature/environment, philosophy, sex, spirituality, nutrition. Query with SASE or submit completed manuscript with SASE. Reviews artwork/photos as part of ms package. Send photocopies.

Fiction: Spiritual. "Will consider spiritual fiction if the story is allegorical and/or contains a valuable (and clear) life lesson." Query with SASE or submit completed manuscript with SASE.

Recent Title(s): *The Lover's Workbook*, by Chuck Francis with Cliff Carle (self-help); *The Helping Hands Technique*, by Chuck Francis (self-help).

Tips: Audience is individuals seeking personal growth and interested in improving any or all aspects of their lives, especially physical, mental/emotional, and spiritual. "Be extremely clear on the particular *need* your book will fulfill. And be sure this need is universal. Our motto explains what we're up to: 'Simple solutions for life's big problems'."

IMAJINN BOOKS, P.O. Box 162, Hickory Corners MI 49060-0162. (616)671-4633. Fax: (616)671-4535. E-mail: imajinn@att.net. Website: www.imajinnbooks.com. **Acquisitions:** Linda Kichline, senior editor. Publishes trade paperback originals and reprints. **Publishes 36-40 titles/year. Receives 1,500 queries and 300 submissions/year. 70%**

of books from first-time authors; 80% from unagented writers. Pays 6-10% royalty on retail price. Offers 25-100 advance. Publishes book 1 year after acceptance of ms. Responds in 3 months to queries and proposals; 4 months to mss. Book catalog and ms guidelines for #10 SASE or online.

Fiction: "We publish only alternative reality romance, i.e., paranormal, supernatural, futuristic, fantasy, time travel and children's science fiction and fantasy, ages 8-12 and 13-17. Juvenile, romance. Query with SASE or submit proposal package including 3 sample chapter(s), synopsis, on request only.

Recent Title(s): *Midnight Shadows*, by Nancy Gideon (vampire romance); *Penelope Quagmire*, by Hal Lanse (children's science fiction).

Tips: "We require certain elements to be in our books. Read several of them to determine how to ensure your book meets our needs."

IMPACT PUBLICATIONS, 9104 Manassas Dr., Suite N, Manassas Park VA 20111-5211. (703)361-7300. Fax: (703)335-9486. E-mail: submit@impactpublications.com. Website: www.impactpublications.com. **Acquisitions:** Caryl Krannich, vice president. Publishes hardcover and trade paperback originals and reprints. **Publishes 15-20 titles/year. Receives 30 queries and 20 mss/year. 30% of books from first-time authors; 100% from unagented writers. Pays 10-15% royalty on wholesale price.** Publishes book 10 months after acceptance of ms. Accepts simultaneous submissions. Responds in 2 months to queries. Book catalog online; ms guidelines for #10 SAE or online.

Imprints: Impact Guides

   ○━ Impact Publications publishes business, career and travel books.

Nonfiction: Reference, self-help. Subjects include business/economics, travel, career. Submit proposal package, including outline, 1 sample chapter and marketing plan. Reviews artwork/photos as part of ms package. Send photocopies.

Recent Title(s): *Savvy Interviewing*, by Ron and Caryl Krannich (career/business); *Take This Job and Thrive*, by Anita Bruzzese (business/career).

IMPACT PUBLISHERS, INC., P.O. Box 6016, Atascadero CA 93423-6016. (805)466-5917. Fax: (805)466-5919. E-mail: info@impactpublishers.com. Website: www.impactpublishers.com. **Acquisitions:** Freeman Porter, acquisitions editor. Estab. 1970. Publishes trade paperback originals. **Publishes 6-10 titles/year. Receives 250 queries and 250 mss/year. 20% of books from first-time authors; 60% from unagented writers. Pays 10% royalty on net receipts. Offers advance.** Publishes book 12-18 months after acceptance of ms. Accepts simultaneous submissions. Responds in 5 months to proposals. Book catalog and ms guidelines free.

Imprints: American Source Books, Little Imp Books, Rebuilding Books, Practial Therapist series

   ○━ "Our purpose is to make the best human services expertise available to the widest possible audience: children, teens, parents, couples, individuals seeking self-help and personal growth, and human service professionals." Currently emphasizing books on divorce recovery for "The Rebuilding Books Series." De-emphasizing children's books.

Nonfiction: "All our books are written by qualified human service professionals and are in the fields of mental health, personal growth, relationships, aging, families, children and professional psychology." Children's/juvenile, self-help. Subjects include child guidance/parenting, health/medicine, psychology (professional), caregiving/eldercare. "We do not publish general fiction for children. We do not publish poetry." Submit proposal package, including short résumé or vita, book description, audience description, outline, 1-3 sample chapters and SASE.

Recent Title(s): *Making Intimate Connections: Seven Guidelines for Great Relationships and Better Communication*, by Albert Ellis, Ph.D., and Ted Crawford.

Tips: "Don't call to see if we have received your submission. Include a self-addressed, stamped postcard if you want to know if manuscript arrived safely. We prefer a non-academic, readable style. We publish only popular psychology and self-help materials written in 'everyday language' by professionals with advanced degrees and significant experience in the human services."

INCENTIVE PUBLICATIONS, INC., 3835 Cleghorn Ave., Nashville TN 37215-2532. (615)385-2934. Fax: (615)385-2967. E-mail: comments@incentivepublications.com. Website: www.incentivepublications.com. **Acquisitions:** Jean K. Signor, editor. Estab. 1970. Publishes paperback originals. **Publishes 25-30 titles/year. Receives 350 submissions/year. 25% of books from first-time authors; 100% from unagented writers. Pays royalty or makes outright purchase.** Publishes book an average of 1 year after acceptance of ms. Responds in 1 month to queries.

   ○━ Incentive publishes developmentally appropriate teacher/parent resource materials and educational workbooks for children in grades K-12. Currently emphasizing primary material. Also interested in character education, English as a second language programs, early learning, current technology, related materials.

Nonfiction: Subjects include education. Teacher resource books in pre-K through 12th grade. Query with synopsis and detailed outline.

Recent Title(s): *The BASIC/Not Boring Grade Book Series*, by Imogene Forte and Marjorie Frank (Grades 1-5); *Can We Eat the Art?*, by Paula Guhin; *Romeo & Juliet Curriculum Guide*, by Laura Maravilla.

INFORMATION TODAY, INC., 143 Old Marlton Pike, Medford NJ 08055. (609)654-6266. Fax: (609)654-4309. E-mail: jbryans@infotoday.com. Website: www.infotoday.com. **Acquisitions:** John B. Bryans, editor-in-chief. Publishes hardcover and trade paperback originals. **Publishes 15-20 titles/year. Receives 100 queries and 30 mss/year. 30% of books from first-time authors; 90% from unagented writers. Pays 10-15% royalty on wholesale price.** Offers

$500-2,500 advance. Publishes book 9 months after acceptance of ms. Accepts simultaneous submissions. Responds in 1 month to queries; 2 months to proposals; 3 months to mss. Book catalog online; ms guidelines free or via e-mail as attachment.

Imprints: ITI (academic, scholarly, library science); CyberAge Books (high-end consumer and business technology books—emphasis on Internet/www topics including online research)

O→ "We look for highly-focused coverage of cutting-edge technology topics, written by established experts and targeted to a tech-savvy readership. Virtually all our titles focus on how information is accessed, used, shared and transformed into knowledge that can benefit people, business and society." Currently emphasizing Internet/online technologies, including their social significance; biography, how-to, technical, reference. De-emphasizing fiction.

Nonfiction: Biography, how-to, multimedia, reference, self-help, technical, scholarly. Subjects include business/economics, computers/electronic, education, science, Internet and cyberculture, library and information science. Query with SASE. Reviews artwork/photos as part of ms package. Send photocopies.

Recent Title(s): *The Invisible Web: Uncovering Information Sources Search Engines*; *Can't See*, by Chris Sherman and Gary Price.

Tips: "Our readers include scholars, academics, indexers, librarians, information professionals (ITI imprint) as well as high-end consumer and business users of Internet/www/online technologies, and people interested in the marriage of technology with issues of social significance (i.e., cyberculture)."

INNER TRADITIONS INTERNATIONAL, P.O. Box 388, 1 Park St., Rochester VT 05767. (802)767-3174. Fax: (802)767-3726. E-mail: info@innertraditions.com. Website: www.innertraditions.com. Managing Editor: Jennie Levitan. **Acquisitions:** Jon Graham, editor . Estab. 1975. Publishes hardcover and trade paperback originals and reprints. **Publishes 60 titles/year. Receives 3,000 submissions/year. 10% of books from first-time authors; 20% from unagented writers. Pays 8-10% royalty on net receipts. Offers $1,000 average advance.** Publishes book 1 year after acceptance of ms. Responds in 3 months to queries; 6 months to mss. Book catalog and ms guidelines free.

Imprints: Destiny Audio Editions, Destiny Books, Destiny Recordings, Healing Arts Press, Inner Traditions, Inner Traditions En Espanol, Inner Traditions India, Park Street Press, Bear & Company, Bear Cub, Bindu Books

O→ Inner Traditions publishes works representing the spiritual, cultural and mythic traditions of the world and works on alternative medicine and holistic health that combine contemporary thought with the knowledge of the world's great healing traditions. Currently emphasizing sacred sexuality, indigenous spirituality, ancient history.

Nonfiction: "We are interested in the relationship of the spiritual and transformative aspects of world cultures." Children's/juvenile, self-help. Subjects include animals, art/architecture, child guidance/parenting, ethnic, health/medicine (alternative medicine), history (ancient history and mythology), music/dance, nature/environment (and environment), philosophy (esoteric), psychology, religion (world religions), sex, spirituality, women's issues/studies, contemporary culture, beauty, New Age, indigenous cultures, ethnobotany. No fiction. Query or submit outline and sample chapters with SASE. Does not return mss without SASE. Reviews artwork/photos as part of ms package.

Recent Title(s): *Transfigurations*, by Alex Grey; *Mystery of Awareness: Living the Agreements*, by Doña Berndadette Vigil with Arlene Broksa, Ph.D.

Tips: "We are not interested in autobiographical stories of self-transformation. We do accept electronic submissions (via e-mail). We are not currently looking at fiction."

N ☒ **INNISFREE PRESS**, 136 Roumfort Rd., Philadelphia PA 19119. (215)247-4085. Fax: (215)247-2343. E-mail: InnisfreeP@aol.com. Website: www.innisfreepress.com. **Acquisitions:** Marcia Broucek, publisher. Estab. 1996. Publishes trade paperback originals. **Publishes 6-8 titles/year. Receives 500 queries and 300 mss/year. 50% of books from first-time authors; 90% from unagented writers. Pays 10% royalty on wholesale price.** Publishes book 1 year after acceptance of ms. Accepts simultaneous submissions. Responds in 2 months to queries; 3 months to proposals; 4 months to mss. Book catalog and ms guidelines free.

O→ "Innisfree's mission is to publish spiritual classics that 'call to the deep heart's core.' " Currently emphasizing women's issues, spirituality. De-emphasizing self-help books.

Nonfiction: Spiritually focused. Subjects include religion, women's issues/studies. No poetry or children's material or fiction please. Query with proposal package, including outline, 2 sample chapters, potential audience, and what makes the book unique, with SASE. Reviews artwork/photos as part of ms package. Send photocopies.

Recent Title(s): *Leading Ladies: Transformative Biblical Images for Women in Leadership*, by Jeanne Porter.

Tips: "Our books respond to the needs of today's seekers—people who are looking for deeper meaning and purpose in their lives, for ways to integrate spiritual depth with religious traditions."

N **INSTITUTE OF POLICE TECHNOLOGY AND MANAGEMENT**, University of North Florida, 12000 Alumni Drive, Jacksonville FL 32224-2678. (904)620-4786. Fax: (904)620-2453. E-mail: rhodge@unf.edu. Website: www.unf.edu/iptm/. **Acquisitions:** Richard C. Hodge, editor. Estab. 1980. Publishes trade paperback originals. **Publishes 8 titles/year. Receives 30 queries and 12 mss/year. 50% of books from first-time authors; 100% from unagented writers. Pays 25% royalty on retail price or makes outright purchase of $300-2,000 (may be some combination of above).** Publishes book 6 months after acceptance of ms. Responds in 2 months to queries.

O→ "Our publications are principally for law enforcement. Our authors are almost all present or retired law enforcement officers with excellent, up-to-date knowledge." Currently emphasizing criminal investigation, management (police), security.

Nonfiction: Illustrated book, reference, technical, textbook. Subjects include law enforcement, criminal investigations, security. "Our authors are not necessarily persons whose works have been published. Manuscripts should *not* be submitted until the author has talked with the editor on the telephone. The best procedure is to have this talk before beginning to write. Articles and short handbooks are acceptable as well as longer manuals." Reviews artwork/photos as part of ms package.

Recent Title(s): *Lines of Defense: Police Ideology and the Constitution*, by Chuck Klein; *Commercial Motor Vehicle Crash Investigation*, by David E. Brill.

Tips: Audience is law enforcement, private investigators, trial attorneys, insurance investigators and adjustors.

INTERCONTINENTAL PUBLISHING, 6451 Steeple Chase Lane, Manassas VA 20111-2611. (703)369-4992. Fax: (703)670-7825. E-mail: icpub@worldnet.att.net. **Acquisitions:** H.G. Smittenaar, publisher. Publishes hardcover and trade paperback originals. **Publishes 6 titles/year. Pays 5% minimum royalty.** Accepts simultaneous submissions. Responds in 2 months to queries and mss.

O→ Intercontinental publishes mystery and suspense novels.

Fiction: Mystery, suspense. Submit proposal package, including 1-3 sample chapters, estimated word count and SASE.

Recent Title(s): *The Cop Was White as Snow*, by Spizer (mystery); *Dekok and Murder in Ecstasy*, by Baantjer (police procedural).

Tips: "Be original, write proper English, be entertaining."

INTERCULTURAL PRESS, INC., P.O. Box 700, Yarmouth ME 04096. (207)846-5168. Fax: (207)846-5181. E-mail: books@interculturalpress.com. Website: www.interculturalpress.com. **Acquisitions:** Judy Carl-Hendrick, managing editor. Estab. 1980. Publishes hardcover and paperback originals. **Publishes 8-12 titles/year. Receives 50-80 submissions/year. 50% of books from first-time authors; 95% from unagented writers. Pays royalty. Offers small advance occasionally.** Publishes book within 2 years after acceptance of ms. Accepts simultaneous submissions. Responds in 1 month to queries. Book catalog and ms guidelines free.

O→ Intercultural Press publishes materials related to intercultural relations, including the practical concerns of living and working in foreign countries, the impact of cultural differences on personal and professional relationships and the challenges of interacting with people from unfamiliar cultures, whether at home or abroad. Currently emphasizing international business.

Nonfiction: "We want books with an international or domestic intercultural or multicultural focus, especially those on business operations (how to be effective in intercultural business activities), education (textbooks for teaching intercultural subjects, for instance) and training (for Americans abroad or foreign nationals coming to the United States)." Reference, textbooks, theory. Subjects include world affairs, business, education, diversity and multicultural, relocation and cultural adaptation, culture learning, training materials, country-specific guides. "Our books are published for educators in the intercultural field, business people engaged in international business, managers concerned with cultural diversity in the workplace, and anyone who works in an occupation where cross-cultural communication and adaptation are important skills. No manuscripts that don't have an intercultural focus." Accepts nonfiction translations. Submit proposals, outline.

Recent Title(s): *Au Contraire! Figuring Out the French*, by Gilles Asselin and Ruth Mastron; *The Third Culture Kid Experience*, by David C. Pillock and Ruth E. Van Reken; *South Africa's 'Black' Market: How to Do Business with Africans*, by Jeffrey A. Fadiman.

INTERLINK PUBLISHING GROUP, INC., 46 Crosby St., Northampton MA 01060. (413)582-7054. Fax: (413)582-7057. E-mail: info@interlinkbooks.com. Website: www.interlinkbooks.com. **Acquisitions:** Michel Moushabeck, publisher. Estab. 1987. Publishes hardcover and trade paperback originals. **Publishes 50 titles/year. Receives 600 submissions/year. 30% of books from first-time authors; 50% from unagented writers. Pays 6-8% royalty on retail price. Offers small advance.** Publishes book 18 months after acceptance of ms. Accepts simultaneous submissions. Responds in 1 month to queries. Book catalog free; ms guidelines online.

Imprints: Crocodile Books, USA; Interlink Books; Olive Branch Press

O→ Interlink publishes a general trade list of adult fiction and nonfiction with an emphasis on books that have a wide appeal while also meeting high intellectual and literary standards.

Nonfiction: Subjects include world travel, world history and politics, ethnic cooking, world music. Submit outline and sample chapters.

Fiction: Ethnic, international. "Adult fiction—We are looking for translated works relating to the Middle East, Africa or Latin America. Juvenile/Picture Books—Our list is full for the next two years." No science fiction, romance, plays, erotica, fantasy, horror. Submit outline/synopsis and sample chapters.

Recent Title(s): *House of the Winds*, by Mia Yun.

Tips: "Any submissions that fit well in our publishing program will receive careful attention. A visit to our website, your local bookstore, or library to look at some of our books before you send in your submission is recommended."

INTERNATIONAL MARINE, The McGraw-Hill Companies, P.O. Box 220, Camden ME 04843-0220. (207)236-4838. Fax: (207)236-6314. Website: www.internationalmarine.com. Jonathan Eaton, editorial director (boating, marine nonfiction). Estab. 1969. Publishes hardcover and paperback originals. **Publishes 50 titles/year. Receives 500-700 mss/ year. 30% of books from first-time authors; 80% from unagented writers. Pays standard royalties based on net price. Offers advance.** Publishes book 1 year after acceptance of ms. Responds in 2 months to queries. Book catalog and ms guidelines for #10 SASE.

Imprints: Ragged Mountain Press (sports and outdoor books that take you off the beaten path)

O—¬ International Marine publishes "good books about boats."

Nonfiction: Publishes "a wide range of subjects include: sea stories, seamanship, boat maintenance, etc." Subjects include marine and outdoor nonfiction. All books are illustrated. "Material in all stages welcome." Query first with outline and 2-3 sample chapters. Reviews artwork/photos as part of ms package.

Recent Title(s): *The Ship and the Storm*, by Jim Carrier; *Nigel Calder's Cruising Handbook.*

Tips: "Writers should be aware of the need for clarity, accuracy and interest. Many progress too far in the actual writing."

INTERNATIONAL MEDICAL PUBLISHING, 1516 Mintwood Drive, McLean VA 22101-0479. (703)356-2037. Fax: (703)734-8987. E-mail: medicalpublishing@ediabetes.com. Website: www.medicalpublishing.com. **Acquisitions:** Thomas Masterson, MD, editor. Estab. 1991. Publishes mass market paperback originals. **Publishes 30 titles/year. Receives 100 queries and 20 mss/year. 5% of books from first-time authors; 100% from unagented writers. Pays royalty on gross receipts.** Publishes book 8 months after acceptance of ms. Responds in 2 months to queries.

O—¬ IMP publishes books to make life easier for doctors in training. "We're branching out to also make life easier for people with chronic medical problems."

Nonfiction: Reference, textbook. Subjects include health/medicine. "We distribute only through medical and scientific bookstores. Think about practical material for doctors-in-training. We are interested in handbooks. Online projects are of interest." Query with outline.

Recent Title(s): *Healthy People 2010*, by the US Department of Health and Human Services.

INTERNATIONAL SCHOLARS PUBLICATIONS, INC., The University Press of America, 4720 Boston Way, Lanham MD 20706. (301)459-3366. Fax: (301)306-5357. E-mail: lraimond@univpress.com. Website: www.univpress.c om. **Acquisitions:** Acquisitions Department. Estab. 1993. Publishes hardcover and trade paperback originals and reprints. **Publishes 32 titles/year. Receives 200 queries and 140 mss/year. 80% of books from first-time authors; 100% from unagented writers. Pays royalty.** Publishes book 5 months after acceptance of ms. Accepts simultaneous submissions. Responds in 1 month to queries. Book catalog and ms guidelines for #10 SASE or online.

Imprints: Catholic Scholars Publications, Christian Universities Press, University Press for West Africa

Nonfiction: Biography, reference, textbook, scholarly. Subjects include art/architecture, education, ethnic, government/ politics, history, language/literature, military/war, money/finance, philosophy, psychology, religion, science, sociology, women's issues/studies, world affairs, Africa. "Research monographs and revised dissertations welcome. Some submissions do not contain enough information or have work condition problems." Query with outline, 2 sample chapters, cv and SASE.

Recent Title(s): *Aspects of Personal Faith*, by Barnett Friel; *Paradoxical Feminism: The Novels of Rebecca West*, by Ann Norton.

Tips: "Audience are upscale readers who enjoy an intellectual challenge. Focus on concept, contents, size of work and why it should be released."

⌸ INTERNATIONAL SOCIETY FOR TECHNOLOGY IN LEARNING (ISTE), 1787 Agate St., Eugene OR 97403-1923. (541)346-0816. E-mail: mmanweller@iste.org. Website: www.iste.org. **Acquisitions:** Mathew Manweller, acquisitions editor. Publishes trade paperback originals. **Publishes 20 titles/year. Receives 150 queries and 50 mss/ year. 75% of books from first-time authors; 100% from unagented writers. Pays 12-15% royalty on retail price.** Publishes book 5 months after acceptance of ms. Accepts simultaneous submissions. Responds in 1 month to queries, proposals and mss. Book catalog and ms guidelines free.

O—¬ Currently emphasizing curriculum and project development books. De-emphasizing how-to books.

Nonfiction: Reference, technical, curriculum. Subjects include computers/electronic, education, software, technology. Submit proposal package including outline, 1 sample chapter(s). Reviews artwork/photos as part of ms package. Send photocopies.

Recent Title(s): *The Best Web Sites for Teachers*, by Vicki Sharp.

Tips: "Our audience is teachers, technology coordinators, administrators."

INTERNATIONAL WEALTH SUCCESS, P.O. Box 186, Merrick NY 11570-0186. (516)766-5850. Fax: (516)766-5919. **Acquisitions:** Tyler G. Hicks, editor. Estab. 1967. **Publishes 10 titles/year. Receives 100 submissions/year. 100% of books from first-time authors; 100% from unagented writers. Pays 10% royalty on wholesale or retail price. Offers usual advance of $1,000, but this varies depending on author's reputation and nature of book. Buys all rights.** Publishes book 4 months after acceptance of ms. Responds in 1 month to queries. Book catalog and ms guidelines for 9×12 SAE with 3 first-class stamps.

O—¬ "We publish nonfiction books and periodicals to help Beginning Wealth Builders choose, start, finance, and succeed in their own home-based or externally-quartered small business. Currently looking for books on making money on the internet and using the internet in a small business, along with real estate, import-export, financing, etc."

Nonfiction: How-to, self-help. Subjects include business/economics, financing, business success, venture capital, etc. "Techniques, methods, sources for building wealth. Highly personal, how-to-do-it with plenty of case histories. Books are aimed at wealth builders and are highly sympathetic to their problems. These publications present a wide range of business opportunities while providing practical, hands-on, step-by-step instructions aimed at helping readers achieve their personal goals in as short a time as possible while adhering to ethical and professional business standards." Length: 60,000-70,000 words. Query. Reviews artwork/photos as part of ms package.

Recent Title(s): *How to Make Fast Cash in Real Estate with No Money Down Deals*, by Rod L. Griffin.

Tips: "With the mass layoffs in large and medium-size companies there is an increasing interest in owning your own business. So we focus on more how-to hands-on material on owning—and becoming successful in—one's own business of any kind. Our market is the BWB—Beginning Wealth Builder. This person has so little money that financial planning is something they never think of. Instead, they want to know what kind of a business they can get into to make some money without a large investment. Write for this market and you have millions of potential readers. Remember—there are a lot more people *without* money than *with* money."

INTERSTATE PUBLISHERS, INC., 510 N. Vermilion St., P.O. Box 50, Danville IL 61834-0050. (217)446-0500. Fax: (217)446-9706. E-mail: info-ipp@ippinc.com. Website: www.interstatepublishers.com. **Acquisitions:** Ronald L. McDaniel, vice president, editorial. Estab. 1914. Publishes hardcover originals. **Publishes 20 titles/year. Receives 100 queries and 25 mss/year. 50% of books from first-time authors; 100% from unagented writers. Pays 10% royalty on net receipts.** Publishes book 6 months after acceptance of ms. Responds in 2 months to proposals. Book catalog for 9 × 12 SAE with 4 first-class stamps (specify high school or college).

O—¬ Interstate Publishers publishes middle school, high school, and college textbooks and related materials that infuse science concepts into agricultural education.

Nonfiction: Textbook. Subjects include ancillary materials for agriculture/horticulure, education. Submit proposal package including outline, 2 sample chapter(s), SASE. Reviews artwork/photos as part of ms package. Send photocopies.

Recent Title(s): *Introduction to Livestock and Companion Animals, 2nd ed*, by Jasper S. Lee, et al; *The Meat We Eat, 14th ed*, by John R. Romans, et al.

Tips: "Our audience is students who are interested in agriculture. They may simply want to become literate in the subject, or they may be preparing for careers in the new science-oriented agriculture. These careers may well be off the farm and in areas such as landscaping, food technology, biotechnology, plant and soil science, etc. Educational texts must demonstrate fair and balanced treatment of the sexes, minorities, and persons with disabilities."

INTERWEAVE PRESS, 201 E. Fourth St., Loveland CO 80537. (970)669-7672. Fax: (970)667-8317. Website: www.interweave.com. **Acquisitions:** Marilyn Murphy, editorial director. Estab. 1975. Publishes hardcover and trade paperback originals. **Publishes 10-15 titles/year. Receives 50 submissions/year. 60% of books from first-time authors; 98% from unagented writers. Pays 10% royalty on net receipts.** Publishes book 1 year after acceptance of ms. Accepts simultaneous submissions. Responds in 2 months to queries. Book catalog and ms guidelines free.

O—¬ Interweave Press publishes instructive and inspirational titles relating to the fiber arts and beadwork topics.

Nonfiction: Subjects limited to fiber arts—basketry, spinning, knitting, dyeing and weaving—and beadwork topics. How-to, technical. Subjects include cooking/foods/nutrition, gardening, hobbies. Submit outline, sample chapter(s). Reviews artwork/photos as part of ms package.

Recent Title(s): *Beading with Brick Stitch*, by Diane Fitzgerald.

Tips: "We are looking for very clear, informally written, technically correct manuscripts, generally of a how-to nature, in our specific fiber and beadwork fields only. Our audience includes a variety of creative self-starters who appreciate inspiration and clear instruction. They are often well educated and skillful in many areas."

N **□** **iPublish.com at TIME WARNER BOOKS**, Time Warner Books. . Website: www.ipublish.com. Publishes ebooks. **Publishes 500 titles/year. Pays competitive rates.** Publishes book 3 months after acceptance of ms. Responds in 3 months to mss. Book catalog and ms guidelines online.

O—¬ iPublish.com at Time Warner Books is uniquely designed to allow an online community of writers to read and rate submissions—the most highly rated will be considered by our editors."

Nonfiction: Biography, how-to, humor, self-help. Subjects include business/economics, government/politics, health/medicine, memoirs, money/finance, spirituality. Follow online submission process.

Fiction: Erotica, fantasy, humor, mainstream/contemporary, mystery, romance, science fiction. Follow online submission process.

Recent Title(s): *Anything Goes!*, by Larry King (politics); *Whispers in the Dark*, by Walter Mosley.

N **IRI/SKYLIGHT TRAINING AND PUBLISHING, INC.**, 2626 Clearbrook Dr., Arlington Heights IL 60005. (800)348-4474. E-mail: info@skylightedu.com. Website: www.skylightedu.com. **Acquisitions:** Chris Jaegi, executive editor. Estab. 1990. **Publishes 20-25 titles/year. Receives 100 queries and 60 mss/year. 40% of books from first-time authors; 100% from unagented writers. Pays 5-10% royalty on retail price.** Publishes book 9 months after acceptance of ms. Responds in 1 months to queries; 4 months to proposals and mss. Book catalog and ms guidelines free.

O—¬ "We seek books that provide a bridge from the theory to practice in the classroom."

Nonfiction: Subjects include education. Educational how-to for K-12 classroom practitioners. Multiple intelligences, integrated curriculum, year-round education, multi-age clasrooms, diversity, inclusion, cooperative learning, higher-level thinking and technology in the classroom. Submit outline, sample chapter(s), brief synopsis of each chapter. Reviews artwork/photos as part of ms package. Send photocopies.

Recent Title(s): *Empowering Students with Technology*, by Alan November.

Tips: "Target K-12 classroom practitioners, staff developers, school administrators, education students. We are interested in research-based books that tell teachers in a clear, friendly, direct manner how to apply educational best practices to their classrooms. We are especially interested in books that give teachers the tools to create lessons on their own, no matter what subject area they teach."

IRON GATE PUBLISHING, P.O. Box 999, Niwot CO 80544-0999. (303)530-2551. Fax: (303)530-5273. E-mail: editor@irongate.com. Website: www.irongate.com. **Acquisitions:** Dina C. Carson, publisher (how-to, genealogy); Risa J. Johnson, editor (reunions). Publishes hardcover and trade paperback originals. **Publishes 6-10 titles/year; imprint publishes 2-6 titles/year. Receives 100 queries and 20 mss/year. 30% of books from first-time authors; 10% from unagented writers. Pays royalty on a case-by-case basis.** Publishes book 1 year after acceptance of ms. Accepts simultaneous submissions. Responds in 2 months to proposals. Book catalog and ms guidelines online.

Imprints: Reunion Solutions Press, KinderMed Press

   O→ "Our readers are people who are looking for solid, how-to advice on planning reunions or self-publishing a genealogy."

Nonfiction: How-to, multimedia, reference. Subjects include child guidance/parenting, health/medicine, hobbies. Query with SASE or submit proposal package, including outline, 2 sample chapters and marketing summary. Reviews artwork/photos as part of ms package. Send photocopies.

Recent Title(s): *The Genealogy and Local History Researcher's Self-Publishing Guide*; *Reunion Solutions: Everything You Need to Know to Plan a Family, Class, Military, Association or Corporate Reunion.*

Tips: "Please look at the other books we publish and tell us in your query letter why your book would fit into our line of books."

ISLAND PRESS, Shearwater Books, 1718 Connecticut Ave. NW, Washington DC 20009. (202)232-7933. Fax: (202)234-1328. E-mail: info@islandpress.org. Website: www.islandpress.org. **Acquisitions:** Barbara Dean, executive editor (ecosystems management); Todd Baldwin, senior editor (business/economics); Heather Boyer, sponsoring editor (land use/community issues). Publishes hardcover and trade paperback originals and reprints. **Publishes 50 titles/year; imprint publishes 10 titles/year. Receives 50-75 queries and 5-10 mss/year. 50% of books from first-time authors; 60% from unagented writers. Pays 10-15% royalty on wholesale price.** Publishes book 1 year after acceptance of ms. Accepts simultaneous submissions. Responds in 1 month to queries and proposals; 2 months to mss. Book catalog and ms guidelines online.

Imprints: Shearwater Books (Jonathan Cobb, editor).

   O→ Island Press specializes in books about environmental problems.

Nonfiction: Biography, reference, textbook, scholarly, professional. Subjects include anthropology/archeology, business/economics, nature/environment, science, land use, planning. Query with SASE or submit proposal package including outline, 2 sample chapter(s). Reviews artwork/photos as part of ms package. Send photocopies.

Recent Title(s): *Earth Rising: American Environmentalism in the 21st Century*, by Philip Shabecoff; *All the Wild and Lonely Places, Journeys in a Desert Landscape*, by Lawrence Hogue.

Tips: "We're looking for solutions-oriented information for professionals, students and concerned citizens working to solve environmental problems."

LEE JACOBS PRODUCTIONS, Box 362, Pomeroy OH 45769-0362. (740)992-5208. Fax: (740)992-0616. E-mail: LJacobs@frognet.net. Website: LeeJacobsProductions.com. **Acquisitions:** Lee Jacobs, president. Publishes hardcover and trade paperback originals and reprints. **Publishes 5 titles/year. Receives 5 queries and 5 mss/year. 10% of books from first-time authors; 90% from unagented writers. Pays 5% royalty or makes outright purchase of $100-5,000.** Publishes book 6 months after acceptance of ms. Responds in 1 month to queries and proposals; 6 months to mss. Book catalog for $5 or online.

   O→ Lee Jacobs Productions publishes books about magic, comedy and entertainment.

Nonfiction: Biography, coffee table book, how-to, humor, illustrated book, reference, technical, textbook. Subjects include history, hobbies, memoirs, money/finance, photography, psychology, recreation. Query with SASE. Reviews artwork/photos as part of ms package.

Tips: Audience is magicians, comedians, pro entertainers, mentalists.

JAIN PUBLISHING CO., P.O. Box 3523, Fremont CA 94539. (510)659-8272. Fax: (510)659-0501. E-mail: mail@jainpub.com. Website: www.jainpub.com. **Acquisitions:** M.K. Jain, editor-in-chief. Estab. 1989. Publishes hardcover and trade paperback originals and reprints. **Publishes 6 titles/year. Receives 300 queries/year. 100% from unagented writers. Pays up to 15% royalty on net sales. Offers occasional advance.** Publishes book 1-2 years after acceptance of ms. Responds in 3 months to mss. Book catalog and ms guidelines online.

Imprints: Asian Humanities Press

○━ Jain Publishing Company is a general trade and college textbook publisher with a diversified list in subjects such as business/management, health/healing and religions/philosophies. Continued emphasis on undergraduate textbooks.

Nonfiction: Reference, textbook. Subjects include business/economics, health/medicine (alternative), philosophy (Eastern), religion (Eastern). "Manuscripts should be thoroughly researched and written in an 'easy to read' format. Preferably between 60,000-100,000 words." Submit proposal package including publishing history. Reviews artwork/photos as part of ms package. Send photocopies.

Recent Title(s): *Hush! Don't Say Anything to God: Passionate Poems of Rumi*, by Shahram Shiva (philosphies/religion).

JAMESON BOOKS INC., 722 Columbus St., P.O. Box 738, Ottawa IL 61350. (815)434-7905. Fax: (815)434-7907. **Acquisitions:** Jameson G. Campaigne, publisher/editor. Estab. 1986. Publishes hardcover originals. **Publishes 12 titles/year. Receives 500 queries and 300 mss/year. 33% of books from first-time authors; 33% from unagented writers. Pays 6-15% royalty on retail price. Offers $1,000-25,000 advance.** Publishes book 1 year after acceptance of ms. Accepts simultaneous submissions. Responds in 6 months to queries. Book catalog for 8×10 SASE.

○━ Jameson Books publishes conservative politics and economics; Chicago area history; and biographies.

Nonfiction: Biography. Subjects include business/economics, government/politics, history, regional (Chicago area). Query with SASE or submit 1 sample chapter(s). Submissions not returned without SASE.

Fiction: Interested in pre-cowboy frontier fiction. Query with SASE or submit 1 sample chapter(s).

Recent Title(s): *Politics as a Noble Calling*, by F. Clifton White (memoirs); *Yellowstone Kelly: Gentleman and Scout*, by Peter Bowen (fiction).

[N] JAYJO BOOKS, L.L.C., The Guidance Channel, P.O. Box 760, 135 Dupont St., Plainview NY 11803-0769. (516)349-5520. Fax: (516)349-5521. **Acquisitions:** Sally Germain, editor-in-chief (health topics for elementary/middle school age youth). Publishes trade paperback originals. **Publishes 8-12 titles/year. Receives 100 queries/year. 25% of books from first-time authors; 100% from unagented writers. Makes outright purchase of $500-1,000.** Publishes book 9 months after acceptance of ms. Accepts simultaneous submissions. Responds in 2 months to queries, proposals and mss. Book catalog and writer's guidelines for #10 SASE.

Imprints: Each book published is for a specific series. Series include: Special Family and Friends, Health Habits for Kids, Substance Free Kids, Special Kids in School. Series publish 1-5 titles/year

Nonfiction: Children's/juvenile, illustrated book. Subjects include health/medicine (issues for children). "JayJo Books is a publisher of nonfiction books to help teachers, parents, and children cope with chronic illnesses, special needs, and health education in classroom, family, and social settings. Each JayJo series has a particular style and format it must follow. Writers should send query letter with areas of expertise or interest and suggested focus of book." No animal character books or illustrated books. Query with SASE.

Tips: "Send query letter—since we only publish books adapted to our special formats—we contact appropriate potential authors and work with them to customize manuscript."

[▲] JEWISH LIGHTS PUBLISHING, LongHill Partners, Inc., P.O. Box 237, Sunset Farms Offices, Rt. 4, Woodstock VT 05091. (802)457-4000. Editor: Stuart Matlins. **Acquisitions:** Acquisitions Editor. Estab. 1990. Publishes hardcover and trade paperback originals, trade paperback reprints. **Publishes 30 titles/year. Receives 500 queries and 250 mss/year. 50% of books from first-time authors; 99% from unagented writers. Pays royalty on net sales, 10% on first printing, then increases.** Publishes book 1 year after acceptance of ms. Accepts simultaneous submissions. Responds in 3 months to queries. Book catalog and ms guidelines free.

○━ "People of all faiths and backgrounds yearn for books that attract, engage, educate and spiritually inspire. Our principal goal is to stimulate thought and help all people learn about who the Jewish people are, where they come from, and what the future may hold."

Nonfiction: Children's/juvenile, illustrated book, reference, self-help, spirituality, inspiration. Subjects include business/economics (with spiritual slant, finding spiritual meaning in one's work), health/medicine, history, nature/environment, philosophy, religion, women's issues/studies, healing/recovery, wellness, aging, life cycle, theology. "We do *not* publish haggadot, biography, poetry, cookbooks or books aiming to be most successfully sold during any specific holiday season." Submit proposal package, including cover letter, table of contents, 2 sample chapters and SASE (postage must cover weight of ms). Reviews artwork/photos as part of ms package. Send photocopies.

Recent Title(s): *Does the Soul Survive?: A Jewish Journey to Belief in Afterlife, Past Lives and Living with Purpose*, by Elie Haplan Spitz; *The Way Into Torah*, by Norman J. Cohen.

Tips: "We publish books for all faiths and backgrounds. Many also reflect the Jewish wisdom tradition."

JIST WORKS, INC., 8902 Otis Ave., Indianapolis IN 46216-1033. (317)613-4200. Fax: (317)613-4309. E-mail: editorial@jist.com. Website: www.jist.com. **Acquisitions:** Susan Pines, senior development editor. Estab. 1981. Publishes trade paperback originals and reprints. **Publishes 60 titles/year. Receives 150 submissions/year. 60% of books from first-time authors. Pays 5-12% royalty on wholesale price or makes outright purchase (negotiable).** Publishes book 1 year after acceptance of ms. Accepts simultaneous submissions. Responds in 3 months to queries. Book catalog and ms guidelines online or for 9×12 SAE with 6 first-class stamps.

Imprints: Park Avenue Publications (business and self-help that falls outside of the JIST topical parameters)

O→ "Our purpose is to provide quality career, job search, and other living skills information, products, and services that help people manage and improve their lives—and the lives of others."

Nonfiction: How-to, multimedia, reference, self-help, textbook, video. Subjects include business/economics, computers/electronic, software, careers. Specializes in job search, self-help and career-related topics., "We want text/workbook formats that would be useful in a school or other institutional setting. We also publish trade titles, all reading levels. Will consider books for professional staff and educators, appropriate software and videos." Query with SASE. Reviews artwork/photos as part of ms package.

Recent Title(s): *The Quick Résumé & Cover Letter Book*, by J. Michael Farr.

Tips: "Institutions and staff who work with people of all reading and academic skill levels, making career and life decisions or people who are looking for jobs are our primary audience, but we're focusing more on business and trade topics for consumers."

JOHNSON BOOKS, Johnson Publishing Co., 1880 S. 57th Court., Boulder CO 80301. (303)443-9766. Fax: (303)443-1106. E-mail: books@jpcolorado.com. **Acquisitions:** Stephen Topping, editorial director. Estab. 1979. Publishes hardcover and paperback originals and reprints. **Publishes 10-12 titles/year. Receives 500 submissions/year. 30% of books from first-time authors; 90% from unagented writers. Royalties vary.** Publishes book 1 year after acceptance of ms. Responds in 3 months to queries. Book catalog for 9×12 SAE with 5 first-class stamps.

Imprints: Spring Creek Press

O→ Johnson Books specializes in books on the American West, primarily outdoor, "useful" titles that will have strong national appeal.

Nonfiction: Guidebooks. Subjects include anthropology/archeology, general, history, nature/environment (environmental subjects), recreation (outdoor), regional, science, translation, travel, general nonfiction, books on the West, natural history, paleontology, geology. "We are primarily interested in books for the informed popular market, though we will consider vividly written scholarly works." Looks for "good writing, thorough research, professional presentation and appropriate style. Marketing suggestions from writers are helpful." Submit outline/synopsis and 3 sample chapters.

Recent Title(s): *Women of Consequence*, by Jeanne Varnell (western biography).

BOB JONES UNIVERSITY PRESS, (formerly Journey Books), 1700 Wade Hampton Blvd., Greenville SC 29614-0001. (864)370-1800. Fax: (864)298-0268. E-mail: jb@bjup.com. Website: www.bjup.com. **Acquisitions:** Nancy Lohr, juvenile fiction editor (ages two through teens); Suzette Jordan, nonficiton editor (adult readers). Estab. 1974. Publishes trade paperback originals and reprints. **Publishes 18 titles/year. Receives 180 queries and 570 mss/year. 10% of books from first-time authors; 100% from unagented writers. Makes outright purchase or pays royalties to established authors.** Publishes book 18 months after acceptance of ms. Accepts simultaneous submissions. Responds in 3 months to mss. Book catalog and ms guidelines free.

O→ The mission of BJU Press is to produce well-written books for readers of varying abilities and interests—books excellent in every facet of their presentation. Currently emphasizing juvenile fiction and biography, adult Christian living titles and Christian education. Not accepting picture books.

Nonfiction: Biography, children's/juvenile. Subjects include animals, history, religion, sports. Adult: Christian living, Christian education, family. Query with SASE.

Fiction: Juvenile, young adult. "We're looking for well-rounded characters and plots with plenty of action suitable for a Christian audience." Submit synopsis and 5 sample chapters or complete ms.

Recent Title(s): *Contending for the Faith*, by Fred Moritz (nonfiction); *God's Prophetic Blueprint*, by Bob Shelton (nonfiction); *Little Bear's Crunch-A-Roo Cookies*, by Kathleen Allan-Meyer (fiction).

Tips: "Our readers are children ages two and up, teens and young adults. We're looking for high-quality writing that reflects a Christian standard of thought and features well-developed characters capable of dynamic changes, in a convincing plot. Most open to first chapter books, adventure, biography."

N̄: JOSSEY-BASS/PFEIFFER, 350 Sansome St., 5th Floor, San Francisco CA 94104. (415)433-1740. Fax: (415)433-1711. Website: www.pfeiffer.com. **Acquisitions:** Samya Sattar, editorial assistant. **Publishes 20-25 titles/year. 25% of books from first-time authors; 95% from unagented writers. Pays 10% royalty. Offers advance.** Publishes book 1 year after acceptance of ms. Accepts simultaneous submissions. Responds in 2 months to queries. Manuscript guidelines online.

Nonfiction: Subjects include management, human resource development, training, both books and instruments. Query with SASE or submit proposal package including outline, sample chapter(s), résumé, author bio, competitive analysis. Detailed proposal guidelines online.

Recent Title(s): *Flawless Consulting*, by Peter Block; *The Business of Consulting*, by Elaine Bleeh.

JUDAICA PRESS, 123 Ditmas Ave., Brooklyn NY 11218. (718)972-6200. Fax: (718)972-6204. E-mail: info@judaicap ress.com. Website: www.judaicapress.com. **Acquisitions:** Nachum Shapiro, managing editor. Estab. 1963. Publishes hardcover and trade paperback originals and reprints. **Publishes 12 titles/year.** Responds in 3 months to queries. Book catalog online.

O→ "We cater to the traditional, Orthodox Jewish market."

Nonfiction: "Looking for very traditional Judaica, especially children's books." Biography, children's/juvenile, cookbook, textbook. Subjects include history, religion. Query with SASE or submit outline, 1 sample chapter(s).

Recent Title(s): *Friend or Foe*, by Eva Vogiel; *Living on the Edge*, by Rabbi David Goldwasser.

JUDSON PRESS, P.O. Box 851, Valley Forge PA 19482-0851. (610)768-2128. Fax: (610)768-2441. E-mail: judsonpres s@juno.com. Website: www.judsonpress.com. Publisher: Kristy Arnesen Pullen. **Acquisitions:** Randy Frame. Estab. 1824. Publishes hardcover and paperback originals. **Publishes 20-30 titles/year. Receives 750 queries/year. Pays royalty or makes outright purchase.** Publishes book 10 months after acceptance of ms. Accepts simultaneous submissions. Responds in 3 months to queries. Book catalog for 9 × 12 SAE with 4 first-class stamps; ms guidelines for #10 SASE.

    ● Judson Press also publishes a quarterly journal, *The African American Pulpit*; call for submission guidelines.

    O─ "Our audience is mostly church members and leaders who seek to have a more fulfilling personal spiritual life and want to serve Christ in their churches and other relationships. We have a large African American readership." Currently emphasizing worship resources/small group resources. De-emphasizing biography, poetry.

Nonfiction: Adult religious nonfiction of 30,000-80,000 words. Subjects include multicultural, religion. Query with SASE or submit outline, sample chapter(s).

Recent Title(s): *Journey Into Day: Meditations for New Cancer Patients*, by Rusty Freeman.

Tips: "Writers have the best chance selling us practical books assisting clergy or laypersons in their ministry and personal lives. Our audience consists of Protestant church leaders and members. Be sensitive to our workload and adapt to the market's needs. Books on multicultural issues are very welcome. Also seeking books that heighten awareness and sensitivity to issues related to the poor and to social justice."

⊠ KALMBACH PUBLISHING CO., 21027 Crossroads Circle, P.O. Box 1612, Waukesha WI 53187-1612. (262)796-8776. Fax: (262)798-6468. E-mail: rchristianson@kalmbach.com. Website: books.kalmbachbooks.com. **Acquisitions:** Dick Christianson, editor-in-chief (model railroading, scale modeling, toy trains, railfanning); Kent Johnson, acquisitions editor (model railroading, toy trains); Philip Martin, acquisitions editor (books on writing). Estab. 1934. Publishes hardcover and paperback originals, paperback reprints. **Publishes 15-20 titles/year. Receives 100 submissions/year. 75% of books from first-time authors; 100% from unagented writers. Pays 10% royalty on net receipts. Offers $1,500 average advance.** Publishes book 18 months after acceptance of ms. Responds in 2 months to queries.

    O─ Kalmbach publishes reference materials and how-to publications for serious hobbyists in the railfan, model railroading, plastic modeling and toy train collecting/operating hobbies as well as books on the art and craft of writing.

Nonfiction: How-to, illustrated book. Subjects include hobbies, science, amateur astronomy, railroading, writing. "Our book publishing effort is in railroading and hobby how-to-do-it titles *only*. I welcome telephone inquiries. They save me a lot of time, and they can save an author a lot of misconceptions and wasted work." Query first. In written query, wants detailed outline of 2-3 pages and a complete sample chapter with photos, drawings, and how-to text. Reviews artwork/photos as part of ms package.

Recent Title(s): *Basics of Ship Modeling*, by Mike Ashey.

Tips: "Our hobby books are about half text and half illustrations. Any hobby author who wants to publish with us must be able to furnish good photographs and rough drawings before we'll consider contracting for his book."

KAMEHAMEHA SCHOOLS PRESS, Kamehameha Schools, 1887 Makuakane St., Honolulu HI 96817-1887. (808)842-8880. Fax: (808)842-8876. E-mail: kspress@ksbe.edu. Website: www.ksbe.edu/pubs/KSPress/catalog.html. **Acquisitions:** Henry Bennett. Publishes hardcover and trade paperback originals and reprints. **Publishes 3-5 titles/year. 10-25% of books from first-time authors; 100% from unagented writers. Makes outright purchase.** Publishes book up to 2 years after acceptance of ms. Responds in 3 months to queries. Book catalog for #10 SASE.

Imprints: Kamehameha Schools, Kamehameha Schools Bishop Estate

    O─ "Only writers with substantial and documented expertise in Hawaiian history, Hawaiian culture, Hawaiian language, and/or Hawaiian studies should consider submitting to Kamehameha Schools Press. We prefer to work with writers available to physically meet at our Honolulu offices."

Nonfiction: Biography, children's/juvenile, reference, textbook. Subjects include education, history, regional, translation. Query with SASE. Reviews artwork/photos as part of ms package. Send photocopies.

KAR-BEN COPIES, INC., 6800 Tildenwood Ln., Rockville MD 20852. (800)452-7236. Fax: (301)881-9195. E-mail: karben@aol.com. Website: www.karben.com. **Acquisitions:** Madeline Wikler, editor (juvenile Judaica). Estab. 1976. Publishes hardcover and trade paperback originals. **Publishes 8-10 titles/year. Receives 50-100 queries and 300-400 mss/year. 5% of books from first-time authors; 100% from unagented writers. Pays 5-8% royalty on net receipts. Offers $500-2,500 advance.** Publishes book 10 months after acceptance of ms. Accepts simultaneous submissions. Responds in 1 month to queries. Book catalog online; ms guidelines for 9 × 12 SAE with 2 first-class stamps.

    O─ Kar-Ben Copies publishes high-quality materials on Jewish themes for young children and families.

Nonfiction: "Jewish themes only!" Children's/juvenile (Judaica only). Subjects include religion. Submit complete ms.

Fiction: "Jewish themes and young kids only!" Juvenile, religious.

Recent Title(s): *Bible Story Crafts for Little Hands*.

Tips: "Do a literature search to make sure similar title doesn't already exist."

N̄ KAYA PRODUCTION, 373 Broadway, Room E-2, New York NY 10013-3939. E-mail: kaya@kaya.com. Website: www.kaya.com. **Acquisitions:** Sunyoung Lee, editor. Publishes hardcover originals and trade paperback originals and reprints. Accepts simultaneous submissions. Responds in 6 months to mss. Book catalog free; ms guidelines for #10 SASE.

O→ "Kaya is an independent literary press dedicated to the publication of innovative literature from the Asian diaspora."

Nonfiction: Subjects include multicultural. "Kaya publishes Asian, Asian American and Asian diasporic materials. We are looking for innovative writers with a commitment to quality literature." Submit proposal package including outline, sample chapter(s), SASE, previous publications. Reviews artwork/photos as part of ms package. Send photocopies.

Fiction: Submit 2-4 sample chapter(s), synopsis, SASE.

Poetry: Submit complete ms.

Recent Title(s): *Where We Once Belonged*, by Sia Figiel (novel); *The Anchored Angel: Selected Writings*, by Jose Garcia Villa, edited by Gileen Tabios.

Tips: Audience is people interested in a high standard of literature and who are interested in breaking down easy approaches to multicultural literature.

A KENSINGTON PUBLISHING CORP., 850 Third Ave., 16th Floor, New York NY 10022. (212)407-1500. Fax: (212)935-0699. Website: www.kensingtonbooks.com. **Acquisitions:** Ann LaFarge, executive editor (romance, fiction); Tracy Bernstein, editorial director (pop culture, spiritual, New Age, parenting, health); Paul Dinas, editor-in-chief (nonfiction, true crime thrillers, epic westerns); Kate Duffy, editorial director (historical romance, regency, romance, ballad, erotica); John Scognamiglio, editorial director (romance, regency, mystery, thrillers, pop culture, gay/lesbian); Clare Gerus, editor (alternative health, general nonfiction); Karen Haas, editor (romance, true crime, westerns); Amy Garvey, editor (romance, regency, Precious Gems historical romances); Tomasita Ortiz, editor (romance, Encanto Hispanic romances); Karen Thomas, senior editor (Arabesque romance, African American fiction and nonfiction); Diane Stockwell, editor (Encanto Hispanic romances); Hillary Sares, editor (Precious Gem romances). Estab. 1975. Publishes hardcover and trade paperback originals, mass market paperback originals and reprints. **Publishes 500 titles/year; imprint publishes 3-20 titles/year. Receives 5,000 queries and 2,000 mss/year. 10% of books from first-time authors; 30% from unagented writers. Pays 8-15% royalty on retail price or makes outright purchase of $1,000-3,000. Offers 2,000-2,000,000 advance.** Publishes book 9 months after acceptance of ms. Accepts simultaneous submissions. Responds in 1 month to queries and proposals; 4 months to mss. Book catalog online; ms guidelines for #10 SASE or online.

● Kensington recently purchased the Carol Publishing Group.

Imprints: Arabesque and Dafina (Karen Thomas, executive editor); Ballad, Brava and Encanto (Kate Duffy, editorial director); Citadel (Claire Gerus, executive editor); Kensington; Pinnacle; Precious Gems; Twin Streams (Elaine Sparber, senior editor); Zebra

O→ Kensington focuses on profitable niches and uses aggressive marketing techniques to support its books.

Nonfiction: Biography, cookbook, gift book, how-to, humor, illustrated book, reference, self-help. Subjects include Americana, animals, business/economics, child guidance/parenting, cooking/foods/nutrition, gay/lesbian, health/medicine (alternative), history, hobbies, humor, memoirs, military/war, money/finance, multicultural, nature/environment, philosophy, psychology, recreation, regional, sex, sports, travel, true crime, women's issues/studies, pop culture, true crime, current events. *No unsolicited mss. Accepts agented submissions only.* Reviews artwork/photos as part of ms package. Send photocopies.

Fiction: Erotica, ethnic, gay/lesbian, historical, horror, mainstream/contemporary, multicultural, mystery, occult, romance, suspense, western (epic), thrillere, women's. *No unsolicited mss. No unagented writers. Accepts agented submissions only.*

Recent Title(s): *Landing It*, by Scott Hamilton (nonfiction); *Celebration*, by Fern Michaels (fiction).

Tips: Agented submissions only, except for submissions to Arabesque, Ballad, Bouquet, Encanto and Precious Gems. For those imprints, query with SASE or submit proposal package including 3 sample chapter(s), synopsis.

KENT STATE UNIVERSITY PRESS, P.O. Box 5190, Kent OH 44242-0001. (330)672-7913. Fax: (330)672-3104. **Acquisitions:** John T. Hubbell, director (history); Joanna H. Craig, editor-in-chief (literary criticism, regional). Estab. 1965. Publishes hardcover and paperback originals and some reprints. **Publishes 30-35 titles/year. Nonauthor subsidy publishes 20% of books. Standard minimum book contract on net sales. Offers advance rarely.** Responds in 3 months to queries. Book catalog free.

O→ Kent State publishes primarily scholarly works and titles of regional interest. Currently emphasizing US history, literary criticism. De-emphasizing European history.

Nonfiction: Biography. Subjects include anthropology/archeology, art/architecture, general, history, language/literature, regional, literary criticism, material culture, textile/fashion studies. Especially interested in "scholarly works in history and literary studies of high quality, any titles of regional interest for Ohio, scholarly biographies, archaeological research, the arts, and general nonfiction. Always write a letter of inquiry before submitting manuscripts. We can publish only a limited number of titles each year and can frequently tell in advance whether or not we would be interested in a particular manuscript. This practice saves both our time and that of the author, not to mention postage costs. If interested we will ask for complete manuscript. Decisions based on inhouse readings and two by outside scholars in the field of study." Enclose return postage.

MICHAEL KESEND PUBLISHING, LTD., 1025 Fifth Ave., New York NY 10028. (212)249-5150. Publisher: Michael Kesend. **Acquisitions:** Judy Wilder, editor. Estab. 1979. Publishes hardcover and trade paperback originals and reprints. **Publishes 4-6 titles/year. Receives 300 submissions/year. 20% of books from first-time authors; 40% from unagented writers. Pays 6% royalty on wholesale price. Offers varying advance.** Publishes book 18 months after acceptance of ms. Responds in 2 months to queries. Manuscript guidelines for #10 SASE.

    ○→ Michael Kesend publishes guidebooks and other nonfiction titles for sale in bookstore chains and independents, in museum stores, parks or similar outlets. Currently emphasizing travel guidebooks. De-emphasizing health/ animals/hobbies.

Nonfiction: Biography, how-to, self-help. Subjects include animals, art/architecture, gardening, health/medicine, history, hobbies, nature/environment, sports, travel (regional and national guides). Needs sports and environmental awareness guides. No photography mss. Submit outline, sample chapter(s). Reviews artwork/photos as part of ms package.

Recent Title(s): *West Coast Garden Walks*, by Alice Joyce.

Tips: "Looking for national guides, outdoor travel guides, sports nonfiction, art or garden-related guides and/or others suitable for museum stores, natural history and national or state park outlets."

N B. KLEIN PUBLICATIONS, P.O. Box 6578, Delray Beach FL 33482. (561)496-3316. Fax: (561)496-5546. **Acquisitions:** Bernard Klein, editor-in-chief. Estab. 1946. Publishes hardcover and paperback originals. **Publishes 5 titles/year. Pays 10% royalty on wholesale price.** Accepts simultaneous submissions. Responds in 2 months to queries. Book catalog for #10 SASE.

    ○→ B. Klein Publications specializes in directories, annuals, who's who books, bibliography, business opportunity, reference books. Markets books by direct mail and mail order.

Nonfiction: How-to, reference, self-help, directories, bibliographies. Subjects include business/economics, hobbies. Query with SASE or submit outline, sample chapter(s).

Recent Title(s): *Guide to American Directories*, by Bernard Klein.

A ALFRED A. KNOPF AND CROWN BOOKS FOR YOUNG READERS, Random House, Inc., 1540 Broadway, New York NY 10036. (212)782-5623. Website: www.randomhouse.com/kids. Vice President/Publishing Director: Simon Boughton. Associate Publishing Director: Andrea Cascardi. Editor: Nancy Siscoe. Senior Editor: Tracy Gates. **Acquisitions:** Crown/Editorial Department. Publishes hardcover originals, trade paperback reprints. **Publishes 60 titles/ year. 10% of books from first-time authors; 40% from unagented writers. Pays 4-10% royalty on retail price. Offers $3,000 and up advance.** Publishes book 1-2 years after acceptance of ms. Accepts simultaneous submissions. Book catalog for 9×12 SASE.

Imprints: Alfred A. Knopf Books for Young Readers, Crown Books for Young Readers, Knopf Paperbacks, Dragonfly

    ○→ Knopf is known for high quality literary fiction, and is willing to take risks with writing styles. It publishes for children ages 4 and up. Crown is known for books young children immediately use and relate to. It focuses on children ages 2-6. Crown also publishes nonfiction for all ages.

Nonfiction: Biography, children's/juvenile. Subjects include ethnic, history, nature/environment, science. This publisher accepts agented submissions only.

Fiction: Juvenile, literary, picture books, young adult. *Accepts agented submissions only.*

Recent Title(s): *Sammy Keyes and the Hotel Thief*, by Wendelin van Draanen (fiction); *Emeline at the Circus*, by Marjorie Priceman (picture book).

ALFRED A. KNOPF, INC., Knopf Publishing Group, Random House, Inc., 299 Park Ave., New York NY 10171. (212)751-2600. Website: www.aaknopf.com. **Acquisitions:** Senior Editor. Estab. 1915. Publishes hardcover and paperback originals. **Publishes 200 titles/year. 15% of books from first-time authors; 30% from unagented writers. Royalty and advance vary.** Publishes book 1 year after acceptance of ms. Accepts simultaneous submissions. Responds in 3 months to queries. Book catalog for 7½×10½ SAE with 5 first-class stamps.

    ○→ Knopf is a general publisher of quality nonfiction and fiction.

Nonfiction: Book-length nonfiction, including books of scholarly merit. Subjects include general, general scholarly nonfiction. "A good nonfiction writer should be able to follow the latest scholarship in any field of human knowledge, and fill in the abstractions of scholarship for the benefit of the general reader by means of good, concrete, sensory reporting." Preferred length: 50,000-150,000 words. Query with SASE. Reviews artwork/photos as part of ms package.

Fiction: Publishes book-length fiction of literary merit by known or unknown writers. Length: 40,000-150,000 words. Query with SASE or submit sample chapter(s).

Recent Title(s): *Time, Love, Memory*, by Jonathan Weiner (nonfiction); *Gertrude and Claudius*, by John Updike (fiction); *Handwriting*, by Michael Ondaatje (poetry).

KRAUSE PUBLICATIONS, 700 E. State, Iola WI 54990. (715)445-2214. Website: www.krause.com. **Acquisitions:** Acquisitions Editor. Publishes hardcover and trade paperback originals. **Publishes 150 titles/year. Receives 300 queries and 30 mss/year. 10% of books from first-time authors; 90% from unagented writers. Pays 9-12½% royalty on net or makes outright purchase of $500-10,000. Offers up to $3,500 advance.** Publishes book 8 months after acceptance of ms. Accepts simultaneous submissions. Responds in 2 months to proposals; 1 month to mss. Book catalog online; ms guidelines free.

    ○→ "We are the world's largest hobby and collectibles publisher."

Nonfiction: Cookbook, how-to, illustrated book, reference, technical. Subjects include Americana, hobbies, recreation, sports, outdoors, hunting, fishing, automotive, coins, stamps, firearms, knives, records, sewing, crafts, toys, colletibles, antiques. Submit proposal package, including outline, 1-3 sample chapters and letter explaining your project's unique contributions. Reviews artwork/photos as part of ms package. Send sample photos.

Recent Title(s): *Golf Collectibles*, by C. Furjamie (reference/price guide); *Outdoor Survival*, by Fears (how-to); *100 Greatest Baby Boomer Toys*, by Mark Rich.

Tips: Audience consists of serious hobbyists. "Your work should provide a unique contribution to the special interest."

KREGEL PUBLICATIONS, Kregel, Inc., P.O. Box 2607, Grand Rapids MI 49501. (616)451-4775. Fax: (616)451-9330. E-mail: kregelbooks@kregel.com. Website: www.kregel.com. **Acquisitions:** Dennis R. Hillman, publisher. Estab. 1949. Publishes hardcover and trade paperback originals and reprints. **Publishes 90 titles/year. Receives 400 queries and 100 mss/year. 10% of books from first-time authors; 90% from unagented writers. Pays 8-16% royalty on wholesale price. Offers $200-2,000 advance.** Publishes book 14 months after acceptance of ms. Accepts simultaneous submissions. Responds in 3 months to queries. Book catalog free; ms guidelines for #10 SASE or online.

Imprints: Editorial Portavoz (contact Luis Seaone)

O→ "Our mission as an evangelical Christian publisher is to provide—with integrity and excellence—trusted, biblically-based resources that challenge and encourage individuals in their Christian lives. Works in theology and biblical studies should reflect the historic, orthodox Protestant tradition."

Nonfiction: "We serve evangelical Christian readers and those in career Christian service." Biography (Christian), gift book, reference. Subjects include religion, spirituality. Query with SASE.

Fiction: Religious. Fiction should be geared toward the evangelical Christian market. Query with SASE.

Recent Title(s): *Eusebius: The Church History*, by Paul L. Maier (church history); *Joy to the World*, by Ken Osbeck (inspirational); *Lethal Harvest*, by William Cutrer (mystery).

Tips: "Our audience consists of conservative, evangelical Christians, including pastors and ministry students. Think through very clearly the intended audience for the work."

KRIEGER PUBLISHING CO., P.O. Box 9542, Melbourne FL 32902-9542. (321)724-9542. Fax: (321)951-3671. E-mail: info@krieger-publishing.com. Website: www.krieger-publishing.com. **Acquisitions:** Elaine Harland, manager/editor (natural history/sciences and veterinary medicine); Sharan Merriam, series editor (adult education); Gordon Patterson, series editor (essays compiled to explore issues and concerns of scholars); Donald M. Waltz, series editor (space sciences); David E. Kyvig, series director (local history); Hans Trefousse, series editor (history); James B. Gardner, series editor (history). Estab. 1969. Publishes hardcover and paperback originals and reprints. **Publishes 30 titles/year. Receives 100 submissions/year. 30% of books from first-time authors; 100% from unagented writers. Pays royalty on net price.** Publishes book 18 months after acceptance of ms. Responds in 3 months to queries. Book catalog free.

Imprints: Anvil Series, Orbit Series, Public History

O→ "We are a short-run niche publisher providing accurate and well-documented scientific and technical titles for text and reference use, college level and higher."

Nonfiction: Reference, technical, textbook, scholarly. Subjects include agriculture/horticulture, animals, education (adult), history, nature/environment, science (space), herpetology, chemistry, physics, engineering, veterinary medicine, natural history, math. Query with SASE. Reviews artwork/photos as part of ms package.

Recent Title(s): *Introduction to Space, 3rd Edition*, by Thomas D. Damon; *Amphibians and Reptiles of Madagascar and the Mascarene, Seychelles and Comoro Islands*, by Friedrich-Wilhelm Henkel and Wolgang Schmidt.

LADYBUGPRESS, 751 Laurel St., San Carlos CA 94070-3113. (650)591-6212. Fax: (650)591-1123. E-mail: Georgia adybugbooks.com. Website: www.ladybugbooks.com. **Acquisitions:** Georgia Jones, publisher. Publishes trade paperback originals. **Publishes 3-4 titles/year. Receives 50 queries and 15 mss/year. 90% of books from first-time authors; 100% from unagented writers. Pays up to 15% royalty on wholesale price.** Publishes book 1 year after acceptance of ms. Accepts simultaneous submissions. Responds in 2 months to queries; 4 months to mss. Book catalog and ms guidelines online.

O→ LadybugPress publishes books focused on women's interests, books to feed the soul and fire the imagination. Currently emphasizing new technologies in book production: CDs, e-books, and multimedia.

Nonfiction: Subjects include anthropology/archeology, art/architecture, business/economics, child guidance/parenting, computers/electronic, creative nonfiction, gay/lesbian, multicultural, sociology, sports, women's issues/studies. Query with SASE and e-mail address. Reviews artwork/photos as part of ms package. Send photocopies.

Fiction: Varied topics. In audio format only. Query with SASE and e-mail address.

Poetry: Audio format only. Query.

Recent Title(s): *Women and Disabilities: It Isn't Them and Us*, by Mona Hughes (nonfiction); *Women on a Wire, electonic edition*, edited by Georgia Jones (poetry).

Tips: "All our books include a nonprofit donation. Our focus is women but we do not discriminate against male authors. We are looking for fresh perspectives and are not afraid of taking chances. Don't send us your 'everyone said I should write a book' manuscript. We are looking for people who have something to say."

LAKE CLAREMONT PRESS, 4650 N. Rockwell St., Chicago IL 60625. (773)583-7800. Fax: (773)583-7877. E-mail: sharon@lakeclaremont.com. Website: www.lakeclaremont.com. **Acquisitions:** Sharon Woodhouse, publisher. Publishes trade paperback originals. **Publishes 5-7 titles/year. Receives 60 queries and 15 mss/year. 50% of books from first-time authors; 100% from unagented writers. Pays 10-15% royalty on wholesale price. Offers $250-2,000 advance.** Publishes book 8 months after acceptance of ms. Accepts simultaneous submissions. Responds in 1 month to queries and mss; 2 months to proposals. Book catalog online.

   O→ "We currently specialize in books on the Chicago area and its history, and are expanding into general nonfiction, especially regional titles for other areas. We also like nonfiction books on ghosts, graveyards and folklore."

Nonfiction: Subjects include Americana, ethnic, history, nature/environment (regional), regional, travel, women's issues/studies, film/cinema/stage (regional), urban studies. Query with SASE or submit proposal package, including outline and 2 sample chapters, or submit complete ms (e-mail queries and proposals preferred).

Recent Title(s): *The Chicago River: A Natural and Unnatural History*, by Libby Hill; *Haunted Michigan: Recent Encounters with Active Spirits*, by Rev. Gerald S. Hunter.

Tips: "Please include a market analysis in proposals (who would buy this book & where?) and an analysis of similar books available for different regions. Please know what else is out there."

LANGENSCHEIDT PUBLISHING GROUP, 46-35 54th Rd., Maspeth NY 11378. (800)432-MAPS. Fax: (718)784-0640. E-mail: spohja@langenscheidt.com. **Acquisitions:** Sue Pohja, acquisitions; Christine Cardone, editor. Estab. 1983. Publishes hardcover and trade paperback originals. **Publishes 200 titles/year. Receives 75 queries and 30 mss/year. 100% from unagented writers. Pays royalty or makes outright purchase.** Publishes book 6 months after acceptance of ms. Accepts simultaneous submissions. Responds in 1 month to proposals. Book catalog free.

Imprints: ADC Map, American Map, Arrow Map, Creative Sales, Hagstrom Map, Hammond Map, Insight Guides, Hammond World Atlas Corp., Trakker Map

   O→ Langenscheidt Publishing Group publishes maps, travel guides, foreign language dictionary products, world atlases and educational materials.

Nonfiction: Reference. Subjects include education, travel, foreign language. "Any potential title that fills a gap in our line is welcome." Submit outline and 2 sample chapters (complete ms preferred).

Recent Title(s): *Pocket Vietnamese*; *Atlas of the 20th Century*.

Tips: "Any item related to our map, foreign language dictionary, atlas and travel lines could have potential for us. Of particular interest are titles that are viable and have little in the way of good competition."

★ LARK, Sterling Publishing, 50 College St., Asheville NC 28801. (828)253-0467. Fax: (828)253-7952. Website: www.larkbooks.com. Director of Publishing: Carol Taylor. **Acquisitions:** Nicole Tuggle, submissions coordinator. Estab. 1976. Publishes hardcover and trade paperback originals and reprints. **Publishes 50 titles/year. Receives 300 queries and 100 mss/year. 80% of books from first-time authors; 90% from unagented writers. Offers up to $4,000 advance.** Publishes book 1 year after acceptance of ms. Accepts simultaneous submissions. Responds in 2 months to queries.

   O→ Lark Books publishes high quality, highly illustrated books, primarily in the crafts/leisure markets celebrating the creative spirit. We work closely with bookclubs. Our books are either how-to, 'gallery' or combination books."

Nonfiction: Children's/juvenile, coffee table book, cookbook, how-to, illustrated book. Subjects include gardening, hobbies, nature/environment, crafts, occasionally cooking. Query first. If asked, submit outline and 1 sample chapter, sample projects, table of contents, visuals. Reviews artwork/photos as part of ms package. Send transparencies.

Recent Title(s): *Complete Book of Floorcloths*, by Cathy Cooper.

Tips: "We publish both first-time and seasoned authors. In either case, we need to know that you have substantial expertise on the topic of the proposed book—that we can trust you to know what you're talking about. If you're great at your craft but not so great as a writer, you might want to work with us as a coauthor or as a creative consultant."

LARSON PUBLICATIONS/PBPF, 4936 Rt. 414, Burdett NY 14818-9729. (607)546-9342. Fax: (607)546-9344. E-mail: larson@lightlink.com. Website: www.larsonpublications.org. **Acquisitions:** Paul Cash, director. Estab. 1982. Publishes hardcover and trade paperback originals. **Publishes 4-5 titles/year. Receives 1,000 submissions/year. 5% of books from first-time authors. Pays variable royalty. Seldom offers advance.** Publishes book 1 year after acceptance of ms. Accepts simultaneous submissions. Responds in 4 months to queries. Visit website for book catalog.

Nonfiction: Subjects include philosophy, psychology, religion, spirituality. Query with SASE and outline.

Recent Title(s): *The Art of Napping at Work*, by William and Camille Anthony.

Tips: "We look for studies of comparative spiritual philosophy or personal fruits of independent (transsectarian viewpoint) spiritual research/practice."

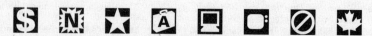

LATIN AMERICAN LITERARY REVIEW PRESS, 121 Edgewood Ave., Pittsburgh PA 15218. (412)371-9023. Fax: (412)371-9025. E-mail: latin@angstrom.net. Website: www.lalrp.org. **Acquisitions:** Maria G. Trujillo, assistant editor (Latin American fiction). Estab. 1980. Publishes trade paperback originals. **Publishes 12 titles/year. Receives 40 queries and 50 mss/year. 25% of books from first-time authors; 75% from unagented writers. Pays 7-10% royalty or makes outright purchase. Offers advance.** Publishes book 14 months after acceptance of ms. Accepts simultaneous submissions. Responds in 6 months to mss. Book catalog and ms guidelines for #10 SASE or online.

   O⊸ "We focus on English translations of works that were originally written in Spanish or Portuguese."

Nonfiction: Children's/juvenile, textbook. Subjects include language/literature, translation, women's issues/studies. Query with SASE. Reviews artwork/photos as part of ms package. Send photocopies.

Fiction: Literary, multicultural, short story collections. Submit complete ms with SASE.

Poetry: "Translated poetry should be by a recognized name." Poetry, poetry in translation. Submit complete ms.

Recent Title(s): *Strange Forces*, by Leopoldo Lugones (fiction); *Scent of Love*, by Elda Van Steen (fiction); *The Island of Cundeamor*, by Rene Vazquez Diaz.

Tips: Publishes for the general adult and college level audiences.

MERLOYD LAWRENCE BOOKS, Perseus Book Group, 102 Chestnut St., Boston MA 02108. **Acquisitions:** Merloyd Lawrence, president. Estab. 1982. Publishes hardcover and trade paperback originals. **Publishes 7-8 titles/year. Receives 400 submissions/year. 25% of books from first-time authors; 20% from unagented writers. Pays royalty on retail price. Offers advance.** Accepts simultaneous submissions.

Nonfiction: Subjects include health/medicine, nature/environment, psychology, child development. *No unsolicited mss.* Query with SASE. *All unsolicited mss returned unopened.*

Recent Title(s): *You Can't Eat GNP*, by Eric Davidson.

LAWYERS & JUDGES PUBLISHING CO., P.O. Box 30040, Tucson AZ 85751-0040. (520)323-1500. Fax: (520)323-0055. E-mail: sales@lawyersandjudges.com. Website: www.lawyersandjudges.com. **Acquisitions:** Steve Weintraub, president. Estab. 1963. Publishes professional hardcover originals. **Publishes 15 titles/year. Receives 200 queries and 30 mss/year. 5% of books from first-time authors; 100% from unagented writers. Pays 7-10% royalty on retail price.** Publishes book 5 months after acceptance of ms. Accepts simultaneous submissions. Responds in 2 months to queries. Book catalog free.

   O⊸ Lawyers & Judges is a highly specific publishing company, reaching the legal and insurance fields and accident reconstruction."

Nonfiction: Reference. Subjects include law, insurance. "Unless a writer is an expert in the legal/insurance areas, we are not interested." Submit proposal package including outline, sample chapter(s).

Recent Title(s): *Forensic Aspects of Vision and Highway Safety, 2nd edition.*

LEARNING PUBLICATIONS, INC., 5351 Gulf Dr., Holmes Beach FL 34217. (941)778-6651. Fax: (941)778-6818. E-mail: info@learningpublications.com. Website: www.learningpublications.com. **Acquisitions:** Ruth Erickson, editor. Estab. 1975. Publishes trade paperback originals and reprints. **Publishes 10-15 titles/year. Receives 150 queries and 50 mss/year. 50% of books from first-time authors; 100% from unagented writers. Pays 5-10% royalty.** Publishes book 1 year after acceptance of ms. Accepts simultaneous submissions. Responds in 1 month to queries and proposals; 4 months to mss. Book catalog and ms guidelines online.

   O⊸ "We specifically market by direct mail to education and human service professionals materials to use with students and clients."

Nonfiction: Reference, textbook. Subjects include education, psychology, sociology, women's issues/studies. "Writers interested in submitting mss should request our guidelines first." Query with SASE or submit proposal package including outline, 1 sample chapter(s), résumé. Reviews artwork/photos as part of ms package. Send photocopies.

Tips: "Learning Publications has a limited, specific market. Writers should be familiar with who buys our books."

LEBHAR-FRIEDMAN BOOKS, Lebhar-Friedman, Inc., 425 Park Ave., New York NY 10022-3556. (212)756-5248. Fax: (212)756-5128. E-mail: kizuriet@lf.com. Website: www.lfbooks.com. **Acquisitions:** Kristen Izurieta, associate editor (cooking, travel); Geoff Golson, publisher. Publishes hardcover and trade paperback originals and reprints. **Publishes 15-20 titles/year. Receives 500 queries and 300 mss/year. 50% of books from first-time authors; 20% from unagented writers. Pays 7½-15% royalty on retail price. Offers competitive advance.** Publishes book 1 year after acceptance of ms. Accepts simultaneous submissions. Responds in 1 month to queries; 2 months to proposals; 3 months to mss. Book catalog free; ms guidelines for #10 SASE.

   O⊸ Lebhar-Friedman publishes quality trade, professional and custom books for the cooking, restaurant and foodservice markets. Currently emphasizing professional cookbooks. De-emphasizing health and home repair.

Nonfiction: Biography, coffee table book, cookbook, gift book, how-to, illustrated book, multimedia, reference, self-help, technical, textbook. Subjects include business/economics, computers/electronic, cooking/foods/nutrition, education, humor, memoirs, money/finance, recreation, regional, travel. Query with SASE or submit proposal package including outline, 2 sample chapter(s). Reviews artwork/photos as part of ms package. Send photocopies.

Recent Title(s): *The Culinary Institute of America Book of Soups* (cookbook); *Time to Make the Donuts*, by Bill Rosenberg (biography).

LEE & LOW BOOKS, 95 Madison Ave., New York NY 10016. (212)779-4400. Fax: (212)683-1894. Website: www.lee andlow.com. **Acquisitions:** Louise May, executive editor. Estab. 1991. **Publishes 12-14 titles/year. Offers advance.** Responds in 5 months to queries and mss. Manuscript guidelines for #10 SASE.

> O→ "Our goals are to meet a growing need for books that address children of color, and to present literature that all children can identify with. We only consider multicultural children's picture books." Currently emphasizing material for 2-10 year olds. Sponsors a yearly New Voices Award for first-time picture book authors of colors. Contest rules online or for SASE.

Nonfiction: Children's/juvenile, illustrated book. Subjects include ethnic, multicultural.
Fiction: Ethnic.
Recent Title(s): *The Secret to Freedom,* by Marcia Vaughan, illustrated by Larry Johnson; *Love to Mama: A Tribute to Mothers,* edited by Pat Mora.
Tips: "Of special interest are stories set in contemporary America. We are interested in fiction as well as nonfiction. We do not consider folktales, fairy tales or animal stories."

N J & L LEE CO., P.O. Box 5575, Lincoln NE 68505. **Acquisitions:** James L. McKee, publisher. Publishes trade paperback originals and reprints. **Publishes 5 titles/year. Receives 25 queries and 5-10 mss/year. 20% of books from first-time authors; 60% from unagented writers. Pays 10% royalty on retail price or makes outright purchase. Offers advance.** Publishes book 18 months after acceptance of ms. Accepts simultaneous submissions. Responds in 6 months to queries and mss; 1 month to proposals. Book catalog free.
Imprints: Salt Creek Press, Young Hearts

> O→ "Virtually everything we publish is of a Great Plains nature."

Nonfiction: Biography, reference. Subjects include Americana, history, regional. Query with SASE.
Recent Title(s): *Lay of the Land,* by Brent Olson.

LEGACY PRESS, Rainbow Publishers, P.O. Box 261129, San Diego CA 92196. (858)271-7600. **Acquisitions:** Christy Allen, editor. Estab. 1997. **Publishes 20 titles/year. Receives 250 queries and 100 mss/year. 50% of books from first-time authors. Pays flat fee or royalty based on wholesale price. Offers negotiable advance.** Publishes book 3 years after acceptance of ms. Accepts simultaneous submissions. Book catalog for 9 × 12 SAE with 2 first-class stamps; ms guidelines for #10 SASE.

> O→ "Legacy Press strives to publish Bible-based materials that contribute to, inspire spiritual growth and develop-
> ment in children and meet the needs of readers in the Christian realm, preferably evangelical." Currently
> emphasizing nonfiction for kids, particularly pre-teens and more specifically girls, although we are publishing
> boys and girls 2-12. De-emphasizing picture books, retold versions of traditional Bible stories and plays.

Nonfiction: Subjects include creative nonfiction, education, hobbies, religion. Query with SASE or submit outline, 3-5 sample chapter(s), market analysis.
Recent Title(s): *The Official Christian Babysitting Guide,* by Rebecca P. Totilo; *The Ponytails,* by Bonnie Compton Hanson (5-book series).
Tips: "We are looking for Christian versions of general market nonfiction for kids, as well as original ideas."

LEHIGH UNIVERSITY PRESS, Linderman Library, 30 Library Dr., Lehigh University, Bethlehem PA 18015-3067. (610)758-3933. Fax: (610)758-6331. E-mail: inlup@lehigh.edu. **Acquisitions:** Philip A. Metzger, director. Estab. 1985. Publishes hardcover originals. **Publishes 10 titles/year. Receives 90-100 queries and 50-60 mss/year. 70% of books from first-time authors; 100% from unagented writers. Pays royalty.** Publishes book 18 months after acceptance of ms. Accepts simultaneous submissions. Responds in 3 months to queries. Book catalog and ms guidelines free.

> O→ "Currently emphasizing works on 18th-century studies, East-Asian studies and literary criticism. Accepts all
> subjects of academic merit."

Nonfiction: Lehigh University Press is a conduit for nonfiction works of scholarly interest to the academic community. Biography, reference, scholarly. Subjects include Americana, art/architecture, history, language/literature, science. Submit proposal package including 1 sample chapter(s).
Recent Title(s): *Separation, the Allies, and the Mafia: The Struggle for Sicilian Independance, 1943-1948,* by Monte S. Finkelstein; *The Nightmare of History: The Fictions of Virginia Woolf and D.H. Lawrence,* by Helen Wussow.

LEISURE BOOKS, Dorchester Publishing Co., 276 Fifth Ave., Suite 1008, New York NY 10001-0112. (212)725-8811. Fax: (212)532-1054. E-mail: dorchedit@dorchesterpub.com. Website: www.dorchesterpub.com. **Acquisitions:** Ashley Keuhl, editorial assistant; Kate Seaver, associate editor; Alicia Condon, editorial director; Don D'Auria, senior editor (westerns, technothrillers, horror); Christopher Keeslar, editor. Estab. 1970. Publishes mass market paperback originals and reprints. **Publishes 160 titles/year. Receives thousands submissions/year. 20% of books from first-time authors; 20% from unagented writers. Pays royalty on retail price. Offers negotiable advance.** Publishes book 18 months after acceptance of ms. Responds in 6 months to queries. Book catalog free (800)481-9191; ms guidelines for #10 SASE or online.
Imprints: Love Spell (romance), Leisure (romance, western, techno, horror)

> O→ Leisure Books is seeking historical and time travel romances.

Fiction: Historical, horror, romance, western, technothrillers. "We are strongly backing historical romance. All historical romance should be set pre-1900. Horrors and westerns are growing as well. No sweet romance, science fiction, erotica, contemporary women's fiction, mainstream or action/adventure." Query with SASE or submit outline, first 3 sample chapter(s), synopsis.
Recent Title(s): *Mine to Take*, by Dara Joy (romance).

LERNER PUBLISHING GROUP, 241 First Ave. N., Minneapolis MN 55401. (612)332-3344. Fax: (612)332-7615. Website: www.lernerbooks.com. Editor-in-Chief: Mary Rodgers. **Acquisitions:** Jennifer Zimian, editor. Estab. 1959. Publishes hardcover originals, trade paperback originals and reprints. **Publishes 150-175 titles/year. Receives 1,000 queries and 300 mss/year. 20% of books from first-time authors; 95% from unagented writers. Offers varied advance.** Accepts simultaneous submissions. Responds in 4 months to proposals. Book catalog for 9×12 SAE with $3.50 postage; ms guidelines for #10 SASE.
Imprints: Carolrhoda Books; First Avenue Editions (paperback reprints for hard/soft deals only); Lerner Publications; Runestone Press, Lerner Sports, Lerner Classroom
  O→ "Our goal is to publish children's books that educate, stimulate and stretch the imagination, foster global awareness, encourage critical thinking and inform, inspire and entertain."
Nonfiction: Biography, children's/juvenile. Subjects include art/architecture, ethnic, history, nature/environment, science, sports. Query with SASE or submit outline, 1-2 sample chapter(s).
Recent Title(s): *Your Travel Guide to Ancient Greece*, by Nancy Day; *Alice Walker*, by Caroline Lazo.

ARTHUR LEVINE BOOKS, Scholastic Inc., 555 Broadway, New York NY 10012. (212)343-4436. **Acquisitions:** Arthur Levine, editorial director. **Publishes 10-14 titles/year. Pays royalty on retail price. Offers varies advance.** Book catalog for 9×12 SASE.
Fiction: Juvenile, picture books. Query with SASE.
Recent Title(s): *The Hickory Chair*, by Lisa Rowe Fraustino; *The Giggler Treatment*, by Roddy Doyle.

■ **LIBRARIES UNLIMITED, INC.**, P.O. Box 6633, Englewood CO 80155. (303)770-1220. Fax: (303)220-8843. E-mail: lu-editorial@lu.com. Website: www.lu.com. **Acquisitions:** Barbara Ittner, acquisitions editor (public library titles); Sharon Coatney (school library titles); Suzanne Barchers (teacher resources); Edward Kurdyla, general manager (academic/reference titles). Estab. 1964. Publishes hardcover originals. **Publishes 75 titles/year. Receives 400 queries and 100 mss/year. 50% of books from first-time authors; 100% from unagented writers. Pays 8-15% royalty on wholesale price. Offers advance.** Publishes book 1 year after acceptance of ms. Accepts simultaneous submissions. Responds in 1 month to queries; 2 months to proposals and mss. Book catalog and ms guidelines online or with SASE.
Imprints: Teacher Ideas Press (Susan Zernial, acquisitions editor); Ukrainian Academic Press
  O→ Libraries Unlimited publishes resources for libraries, librarians and educators. "We are currently emphasizing readers' advisory guides, academic reference works, readers' theatre, storytelling, biographical dictionary, and de-emphasizing teacher books."
Nonfiction: Biography (collections), reference, textbook. Subjects include agriculture/horticulture, anthropology/archeology, art/architecture, business/economics, education, ethnic, health/medicine, history, language/literature, music/dance, philosophy, psychology, religion, science, sociology, women's issues/studies. "We are interested in library applications and tools for all subject areas." Submit proposal package including outline, 1 sample chapter(s), résumé. Reviews artwork/photos as part of ms package. Send photocopies.
Recent Title(s): *Women in U.S. History*, by Lyda Mary Hardy; *The Eagle on the Cactus: Traditional Stories from Mexico*, by Angel Vigil.
Tips: "We welcome any ideas that combine professional expertise, writing ability, and innovative thinking. Audience is librarians (school, public, academic and special) and teachers (K-12)."

LIGUORI PUBLICATIONS, One Liguori Dr., Liguori MO 63057. (636)464-2500. Fax: (636)464-8449. E-mail: jbauer@liguori.org. Website: www.liguori.org. Publisher: Harry Grile. **Acquisitions:** Judith A. Bauer, managing editor (Trade Group); Lauren Borstel, managing editor (Pastorlink, electronic publishing). Estab. 1943. Publishes paperback originals and reprints under the Liguori and Libros Liguori imprints. **Publishes 30 titles/year. Pays royalty or makes outright purchase. Offers varied advance.** Publishes book 2 years after acceptance of ms. Responds in 2 months to queries and proposals; 3 months to mss. Manuscript guidelines online.
Imprints: Faithwarerg, Libros Liguori, Liguori Books, Liguori/Triumph
  O→ Liguori Publications, faithful to the charism of Saint Alphonsus, is an apostolate within the mission of the Denver Province. Its mission, a collaborative effort of Redemptorists and laity, is to spread the gospel of Jesus Christ primarily through the print and electronic media. It shares in the Redemptorist priority of giving special attention to the poor and the most abandoned. Currently emphasizing practical spirituality, prayers and devotions, "how-to" spirituality.
Nonfiction: Manuscripts with Catholic sensibility. Self-help. Subjects include computers/electronic, religion, spirituality. Mostly adult audience; limited children/juvenile. Query with SASE or submit outline, 1 sample chapter(s).
Recent Title(s): *Francis: A Saint's Way*, by James Cowan.

LIMELIGHT EDITIONS, Proscenium Publishers, Inc., 118 E. 30th St., New York NY 10016. Fax: (212)532-5526. E-mail: limelighteditions@earthlink.net. Website: www.limelighteditions.com. **Acquisitions:** Melvyn B. Zerman, president; Roxanna Font, associate publisher. Estab. 1983. Publishes hardcover and trade paperback originals, trade paperback reprints. **Publishes 14 titles/year. Receives 150 queries and 40 mss/year. 15% of books from first-time authors; 20% from unagented writers. Pays 7½-10% royalty on retail price. Offers $500-2,000 advance.** Publishes book 10 months after acceptance of ms. Responds in 1 month to queries and proposals; 3 months to mss. Book catalog and ms guidelines free.

  O─┐ Limelight Editions publishes books on film, theater, music and dance. "Our books make a strong contribution to their fields and deserve to remain in print for many years."

Nonfiction: "All books are on the performing arts *exclusively*." Biography, how-to, humor, illustrated book. Subjects include film/cinema/stage, history, humor, music/dance. Query with SASE or submit proposal package including outline, 2-3 sample chapter(s). Reviews artwork/photos as part of ms package. Send photocopies.

Recent Title(s): *Detours and Lost Highways: A Map of Neo-Noir*, by Foster Hirsch (film); *Actors Talk: Profiles and Stories from the Acting Trade*, by Dennis Brown.

LION BOOKS, 210 Nelson Rd., Scarsdale NY 10583. (914)725-2280. Fax: (914)725-3572. **Acquisitions:** Harriet Ross, editor. Estab. 1966. Publishes hardcover originals and reprints, trade paperback reprints. **Publishes 14 titles/year. Receives 60-150 queries and 100 mss/year. 60% of books from first-time authors. Pays 7-15% royalty on wholesale price. Offers advance.** Publishes book 5 months after acceptance of ms. Responds in 1 week to queries; 1 month to mss.

Nonfiction: Biography, how-to. Subjects include Americana, ethnic, government/politics, history, recreation, sports. No fiction. Submit complete manuscript with SASE.

LIPPINCOTT WILLIAMS & WILKINS, 530 Walnut St., Philadelphia PA 19106. (215)521-8300. Fax: (215)521-8902. Website: www.LWW.com. **Acquisitions:** Doug Symington, publisher (nursing education). Estab. 1792. Publishes hardcover and softcover originals. **Publishes 325 titles/year. Pay rate depends upon various criteria. Offers advance.** Accepts simultaneous submissions. Responds in 3 months to proposals.

  O─┐ Lippincott Williams & Wilkins publishes books on healthcare information, including basic science, for medical and nursing students and ongoing education for practicing nurses and clinicians.

Nonfiction: Reference, textbook. Subjects include health/medicine. "We do not publish for the layperson." Query with SASE or submit proposal package including outline.

Recent Title(s): *Radiology of the Foot and Ankle*; *Problems in Anesthesia*.

Tips: Audience includes physicians, medical scientists, medical and nursing students, and practicing nurses and clinicians.

Ⓐ LISTEN & LIVE AUDIO, INC., P.O. Box 817, Roseland NJ 07068. (201)798-3830. Fax: (201)798-3225. E-mail: alfred@listenandlive.com. Website: www.listenandlive.com. **Acquisitions:** Alisa Weberman, publisher (manuscripts for audio). **Publishes 20 titles/year. Receives 100 mss/year. Offers advance.** Publishes book 6 months after acceptance of ms. Accepts simultaneous submissions. Responds in 3 months to mss. Book catalog online.

Imprints: South Bay Entertainment

  O─┐ Listen & Live publishes fiction and nonfiction books on audio cassette.

Nonfiction: Multimedia (audio format), self-help. Subjects include business/economics. *Accepts agented submissions only.*

Fiction: Young adult. *Accepts agented submissions only.*

Recent Title(s): *Rough Water: Stories of Survival From the Sea*, various authors (audio, outdoor adventure); *The World's Shortest Stories*.

Tips: Agents/publishers only may submit books.

LITTLE SIMON, Simon & Schuster Children's Publishing Division, Simon & Schuster, 1230 Avenue of the Americas, New York NY 10020. (212)698-1295. Fax: (212)698-2794. Website: www.simonsayskids.com. Vice President/Publisher: Robin Corey. **Acquisitions:** Cindy Alvarez, editorial director; Erin Molta, senior editor. Publishes novelty books only. **Publishes 75 titles/year. 5% of books from first-time authors; 5% from unagented writers. Pays 2-5% royalty on retail price. Offers advance.** Publishes book 6 months after acceptance of ms. Responds in 8 months to queries.

  O─┐ "Our goal is to provide fresh material in an innovative format for pre-school to age eight. Our books are often, if not exclusively, format driven."

Nonfiction: "Novelty books include many things that do not fit in the traditional hardcover or paperback format, such as pop-up, board book, scratch and sniff, glow in the dark, lift the flap, etc." Children's/juvenile. No picture books. Query with SASE.

Recent Title(s): *Yay, You!*, by Sandra Boynton; *Easter Bugs*, by David Carter.

Ⓐ LITTLE, BROWN AND CO., CHILDREN'S BOOKS, 3 Center Plaza, Boston MA 02108. (617)227-0730. Website: www.littlebrown.com. Editorial Director/Associate Publisher: Maria Modugno. Editor: Cindy Eagan. **Acquisitions:** Leila Little. Estab. 1837. Publishes hardcover originals, trade paperback reprints. **Publishes 60-70 titles/year. Pays royalty on retail price. Offers negotiable advance.** Publishes book 2 years after acceptance of ms. Accepts simultaneous submissions. Responds in 1 month to queries; 2 months to proposals and mss.

Imprints: Megan Tingley Books (Megan Tingley, executive editor)

O→ Little, Brown and Co. publishes board books, picture books, middle grade fiction and nonfiction YA titles. "We are looking for strong writing and presentation, but no predetermined topics."

Nonfiction: Children's/juvenile. Subjects include animals, art/architecture, ethnic, gay/lesbian, history, hobbies, nature/environment, recreation, science, sports. Writers should avoid "looking for the 'issue' they think publishers want to see, choosing instead topics they know best and are most enthusiastic about/inspired by." *Accepts agented submissions only.*

Fiction: Adventure, ethnic, fantasy, feminist, gay/lesbian, historical, humor, juvenile, mystery, picture books, science fiction, suspense, young adult. "We are looking for strong fiction for children of all ages in any area, including multicultural. We always prefer full manuscripts for fiction." *Accepts agented submissions only.*

Recent Title(s): *I Love You Like Crazy Cakes*, by Rose Lewis, illustrated by Jane Dyer; *All the Blue Moons at the Wallace Hotel*, by Phoebe Stone.

Tips: "Our audience is children of all ages, from preschool through young adult. We are looking for quality material that will work in hardcover—send us your best."

LITTLE, BROWN AND CO., INC., Time Warner Inc., 1271 Avenue of the Americas, New York NY 10020. (212)522-8700. Website: twbookmark.com. Publisher/Editor-in-Chief: Michael Pietsch. **Acquisitions:** Editorial Department, Trade Division. Estab. 1837. Publishes hardcover originals and paperback originals and reprints. **Publishes 100 titles/year. Pays royalty. Offers varying advance.**

Imprints: Back Bay Books; Bulfinch Press; Little, Brown and Co. Children's Books

O→ "The general editorial philosophy for all divisions continues to be broad and flexible, with high quality and the promise of commercial success as always the first considerations."

Nonfiction: Biography, cookbook. Subjects include cooking/foods/nutrition, history, memoirs, nature/environment, science, sports. *No unsolicited mss or proposals.* Query with SASE.

Fiction: Literary, mainstream/contemporary. *No unsolicited mss.* Query with SASE.

Recent Title(s): *The Tipping Point*, by Malcom Gladwell; *A Darkness More Than Night*, by Michael Connelly.

LIVINGSTON PRESS, University of West Alabama, Station 22, Livingston AL 35470. E-mail: jwt@uwa.edu. Website: www.livingstonpress.westal.edu. **Acquisitions:** Joe Taylor, director. Estab. 1984. Publishes hardcover and trade paperback originals. **Publishes 4-6 titles/year. 20% of books from first-time authors; 90% from unagented writers. Pays 12½% royalty. Offers advance.** Publishes book 18 months after acceptance of ms. Accepts simultaneous submissions. Responds in 1 month to queries; 1 year to mss.

Imprints: Swallow's Tale Press

O→ Livingston Press publishes topics such as Southern literature and quirky fiction. Currently emphasizing short stories. De-emphasizing poetry.

Fiction: Experimental, literary, short story collections. Query with SASE.

Poetry: "We publish very little poetry, mostly books we have asked to see." Query.

Recent Title(s): *Partita In Venice*, by Curt Leviant; *Flight From Valhalla*, by Michael Bugeja (poetry); *B. Horror and Other Stories*, by Wendell Mayo.

Tips: "Our readers are interested in literature, often quirky literature."

LLEWELLYN PUBLICATIONS, Llewellyn Worldwide, Ltd., P.O. Box 64383, St. Paul MN 55164-0383. (612)291-1970. Fax: (612)291-1908. E-mail: lwlpc@llewellyn.com. Website: www.llewellyn.com. **Acquisitions:** Nancy J. Mostad, acquisitions manager (New Age, metaphysical, occult, self-help, how-to books); Barbara Wright, acquisitions editor (kits and decks). Estab. 1901. Publishes trade and mass market paperback originals. **Publishes 100 titles/year. Receives 2,000 submissions/year. 30% of books from first-time authors; 90% from unagented writers. Pays 10% royalty on wholesale price or retail price.** Accepts simultaneous submissions. Responds in 3 months to queries. Book catalog for 9×12 SAE with 4 first-class stamps; ms guidelines for #10 SASE.

O→ Llewellyn publishes New Age fiction and nonfiction exploring "new worlds of mind and spirit." Currently emphasizing astrology, wicca, alternative health and healing, tarot. De-emphasizing fiction, channeling.

Nonfiction: How-to, self-help. Subjects include cooking/foods/nutrition, health/medicine, nature/environment, New Age, psychology, women's issues/studies. Submit outline, sample chapter(s). Reviews artwork/photos as part of ms package.

Fiction: "Authentic and educational, yet entertaining." Occult, spiritual (metaphysical).

Recent Title(s): *Understanding the Birth Chart*, by Kevin Burk (nonfiction).

LOCUST HILL PRESS, P.O. Box 260, West Cornwall CT 06796-0260. (860)672-0060. Fax: (860)672-4968. E-mail: locusthill@snet.net. **Acquisitions:** Thomas C. Bechtle, publisher. Estab. 1985. Publishes hardcover originals. **Publishes 12 titles/year. Receives 150 queries and 20 mss/year. 100% from unagented writers. Pays 12-18% royalty on retail price. Offers advance.** Publishes book 6 months after acceptance of ms. Accepts simultaneous submissions. Responds in 1 month to queries. Book catalog free.

O→ Locust Hill Press specializes in scholarly reference and bibliography works for college and university libraries worldwide, as well as monographs and essay collections on literary subjects.

Nonfiction: Reference. Subjects include ethnic, language/literature, women's issues/studies. "Since our audience is exclusively college and university libraries (and the occasional specialist), we are less inclined to accept manuscripts in 'popular' (i.e., public library) fields. While bibliography has been and will continue to be a specialty, our Locust Hill Literary Studies is gaining popularity as a series of essay collections and monographs in a wide variety of literary topics." Query with SASE.

Recent Title(s): *Denise Levertov: New Perspectives*, by Anne C. Little and Susie Paul.

Tips: "Remember that this is a small, very specialized academic publisher with no distribution network other than mail contact with most academic libraries worldwide. Please shape your expectations accordingly. If your aim is to reach the world's scholarly community by way of its libraries, we are the correct firm to contact. But *please*: no fiction, poetry, popular religion, or personal memoirs."

N. LOFT PRESS, INC., P.O. Box 126, Fort Valley VA 22652. (540)933-6210. **Acquisitions:** Ann A. Hunter, editor-in-chief. Publishes hardcover and trade paperback originals and reprints. **Publishes 12-20 titles/year; imprint publishes 2-4 titles/year. Receives 60 queries and 30 mss/year. 20% of books from first-time authors; 100% from unagented writers. Pays royalty on net receipts.** Publishes book 6 months after acceptance of ms.

Imprints: Eschart Press, Far Music Press (both contact Stephen R. Hunter, publisher)

Nonfiction: Biography, coffee table book, how-to, technical, textbook. Subjects include Americana, art/architecture, business/economics, computers/electronic, government/politics, history, language/literature, memoirs, philosophy, regional, religion, science. Submit proposal package including outline, 1 sample chapter(s). Reviews artwork/photos as part of ms package. Send photocopies.

Fiction: Literary, plays, poetry, poetry in translation, regional, short story collections. Submit proposal package including 1 sample chapter(s), synopsis.

Poetry: Submit 5 sample poems.

Recent Title(s): *Manager's Guide to Freight Loss and Damage Claims*, by Colin Barrett (nonfiction); *The Paranoia Factor*, by Alan Peters (adventure fiction); *More Is Not Enough*, by Pieter Greeff (poetry).

LONE EAGLE PUBLISHING CO., 1024 N. Orange Ave., Hollywood CA 90038. (323)308-3411 or 1-800-FILM-BKS. E-mail: Info@loneeagle.com. Website: www.loneeagle.com. **Acquisitions:** Jeff Black, editor. Estab. 1982. Publishes perfectbound and trade paperback originals. **Publishes 15 titles/year. Receives 100 submissions/year. 50% from unagented writers. Pays 10% royalty. Offers $2,500-5,000 average advance.** Publishes book 1 year after acceptance of ms. Accepts simultaneous submissions. Responds quarterly to queries. Book catalog free.

O─m Lone Eagle Publishing Company publishes reference directories that contain comprehensive and accurate credits, personal data and contact information for every major entertainment industry craft. Lone Eagle also publishes many 'how-to' books for the film production business, including books on screenwriting, directing, budgeting and producing, acting, editing, etc. Lone Eagle is broadening its base to include general entertainment titles.

Nonfiction: Biography, how-to, reference, technical. Subjects include film/cinema/stage, entertainment. "We are looking for books in film and television, related topics or biographies." Submit outline, sample chapter(s). Reviews artwork/photos as part of ms package.

Recent Title(s): *Elements of Style for Screenwriters*, by Paul Argentina; *1001: A Video Odyssey*, by Steve Tathan.

Tips: "A well-written, well-thought-out book on some technical aspect of the motion picture (or video) industry has the best chance. Pick a subject that has not been done to death, make sure you know what you're talking about, get someone well-known in that area to endorse the book and prepare to spend a lot of time publicizing the book. Completed manuscripts have the best chance for acceptance."

LONELY PLANET PUBLICATIONS, 150 Linden St., Oakland CA 94607-2538. (510)893-8556. Fax: (510)893-8572. E-mail: info@lonelyplanet.com. Website: www.lonelyplanet.com. **Acquisitions:** Mariah Bear, publishing manager (travel guide books); Roslyn Bullas, publishing manager (Pisces). Estab. 1973. Publishes trade paperback originals. **Publishes 60 titles/year. Receives 500 queries and 100 mss/year. 5% of books from first-time authors; 100% from unagented writers. Work-for-hire: ⅓ on contract, ⅓ on submission, ⅓ on approval. Offers advance.** Accepts simultaneous submissions. Responds in 3 months to queries. Manuscript guidelines for #10 SASE.

O─m Lonely Planet publishes travel guides, atlases, travel literature, diving and snorkeling guides.

Nonfiction: "We only work with contract writers on book ideas that we originate. We do not accept original proposals. Request our writer's guidelines. Send résumé and clips of travel writing." Subjects include travel. "Request our catalog first to make sure we don't already have a similar book or call and see if a similar book is on our production schedule."

Recent Title(s): *Montreal City Guide*; *Toronto City Guide*.

A LONGSTREET PRESS, INC., 2140 Newmarket Parkway, Suite 122, Marietta GA 30067. (770)980-1488. Fax: (770)859-9894. Website: www.longstreetpress.com. President/Editor: Scott Bard. **Acquisitions:** Tysie Whitman, senior editor (general nonfiction, regional interest); John Yow, senior editor (business, self-help, Southern memoir, Southern fiction). Estab. 1988. Publishes hardcover and trade paperback originals. **Publishes 45 titles/year. Receives 2,500 submissions/year. 10% of books from first-time authors. Pays royalty. Offers advance.** Publishes book 1 year after acceptance of ms. Accepts simultaneous submissions. Responds in 3 months to queries. Book catalog for 9×12 SAE with 4 first-class stamps or online; ms guidelines for #10 SASE or online.

O─m Although Longstreet Press publishes a number of genres, their strengths in the future will be general nonfiction such as business, self-help and Southern biography, guidebooks, and fiction. "As Southern publishers, we look for regional material." Currently emphasizing quality nonfiction for a wide audience (memoir, business, self-help). De-emphasizing humor, cookbooks, gift and illustrated books.

Nonfiction: Biography, coffee table book, humor, illustrated book, reference. Subjects include Americana, cooking/foods/nutrition, gardening, history, humor, language/literature, nature/environment, photography, regional, sports, women's issues/studies. "No poetry, scientific or highly technical, textbooks of any kind, erotica." *Accepts agented submissions only.*
Fiction: Literary, mainstream/contemporary (Southern fiction). *Accepts agented submissions only.*
Recent Title(s): *No Such Thing As a Bad Day*, by Hamilton Jordan.

LOOMPANICS UNLIMITED, P.O. Box 1197, Port Townsend WA 98368-0997. Fax: (360)385-7785. E-mail: editorial@loompanics.com. Website: www.loompanics.com. President: Michael Hoy. **Acquisitions:** Gia Cosindas, editor. Estab. 1975. Publishes trade paperback originals. **Publishes 15 titles/year. Receives 500 submissions/year. 40% of books from first-time authors; 100% from unagented writers. Pays 10-15% royalty on wholesale price or retail price or makes outright purchase of $100-1,200. Offers $500 average advance.** Publishes book 1 year after acceptance of ms. Accepts simultaneous submissions. Responds in 2 months to queries. Book catalog for $5, postage paid; ms guidelines free.
    ○┐ "Our motto 'no more secrets-no more excuses-no more limits' says it all. Whatever the subject, our books are somewhat 'edgy'. We are the name in beat-the-system books. From computer hacking to gardening to tax avoision." Currently emphasizing unusual takes on subjects that are controversial and how-to books. Does not want anything that's already been done, New Age.
Nonfiction: "In general, works about outrageous topics or obscure-but-useful technology written authoritatively in a matter-of-fact way. We are looking for how-to books in the fields of espionage, investigation, the underground economy, police methods, how to beat the system, crime and criminal techniques." How-to, reference, self-help, technical. Subjects include agriculture/horticulture, Americana, anthropology/archeology, computers/electronic, government/politics, health/medicine, money/finance, psychology, science, film/cinema/stage. "We are also looking for similarly-written articles for our catalog and its supplements." Query with SASE or submit outline, sample chapter(s). Reviews artwork/photos as part of ms package.
Recent Title(s): *Herbs of the Northern Shaman*, by Steve Andrews; *Sex, Drugs, and the Twinkie Murders*, by Paul Krassner.
Tips: "Our audience is young males looking for hard-to-find information on alternatives to 'The System.' Your chances for success are greatly improved if you can show us how your proposal fits in with our catalog."

LOUISIANA STATE UNIVERSITY PRESS, P.O. Box 25053, Baton Rouge LA 70894-5053. (225)388-6294. Fax: (225)388-6461. **Acquisitions:** L.E. Phillabaum, director; Maureen G. Hewitt, assistant director and editor-in-chief; John Easterly, executive editor; Sylvia Frank, acquisitions editor. Estab. 1935. Publishes hardcover originals, hardcover and trade paperback reprints. **Publishes 70-80 titles/year. Receives 800 submissions/year. 33% of books from first-time authors; 95% from unagented writers. Pays royalty.** Publishes book 1 year after acceptance of ms. Responds in 1 month to queries. Book catalog and ms guidelines free.
Nonfiction: Biography. Subjects include art/architecture, ethnic, government/politics, history, language/literature, music/dance, photography, regional, sociology, women's issues/studies. Query with SASE or submit outline, sample chapter(s).
Poetry: Literary.
Recent Title(s): *The Collected Poems of Robert Penn Warren* (poetry); *Lee and His Generals in War and Memory*, by Gary W. Gallagher (history).
Tips: "Our audience includes scholars, intelligent laymen, general audience."

LOVE SPELL, Dorchester Publishing Co., Inc., 276 Fifth Ave., Suite 1008, New York NY 10001-0112. (212)725-8811. Website: www.dorchesterpub.com. **Acquisitions:** Leah Hultenschmidt, editorial assistant; Kate Seaver, associate editor; Christopher Keeslar, editor. Publishes mass market paperback originals. **Publishes 48 titles/year. Receives 1,500-2,000 queries and 150-500 mss/year. 30% of books from first-time authors; 25-30% from unagented writers. Pays 4% royalty on retail price. Offers $2,000 average advance.** Publishes book 1 year after acceptance of ms. Responds in 6 months to mss. Book catalog free (800)481-9191; ms guidelines for #10 SASE or online.
    ○┐ Love Spell publishes the quirky sub-genres of romance: time-travel, paranormal, futuristic. "Despite the exotic settings, we are still interested in character-driven plots." Love Spell has two humor lines including both contemporary and historical romances.
Fiction: Gothic, historical, science fiction. "Books industry-wide are getting shorter; we're interested in 90,000 words." Query with SASE or submit 3 sample chapter(s), synopsis. No material will be returned without SASE.
Recent Title(s): *Baby, Oh Baby!*, by Robin Wells; *Devil in the Dark*, by Evelyn Rogers.

LOYOLA PRESS, 3441 N. Ashland Ave., Chicago IL 60657-1397. (773)281-1818. Fax: (773)281-0152. E-mail: editorial@loyolapress.com. Website: www.loyolapress.org. **Acquisitions:** Daniel Connor, editorial assistant; Jim Manney, acquisitions editor (religion, spirituality); Linda Schlafer, acquisitions editor (Ignatian spirituality). Estab. 1912. Publishes hardcover and trade paperback originals. **Publishes 30 titles/year. Receives 500 queries/year. 5% of books from first-time authors; 50% from unagented writers. Pays 10% royalty on wholesale price. Offers up to $6,000 advance.** Publishes book 1 year after acceptance of ms. Accepts simultaneous submissions. Responds in 1 month to queries; 3 months to proposals and mss. Book catalog and ms guidelines online.
Imprints: Jesuit Way

Nonfiction: Biography. Subjects include art/architecture, history, regional, religion, spirituality, inspirational, prayer, Catholic life. *Jesuit Way* books focus on Jesuit life and history as well as on Ignatian spirituality and ministry. Query with SASE.

Recent Title(s): *Good People... from a Novelist's Life*, by Jon Hassler; *spirituality@work*, by Gregory F.A. Pierce; *The Book of Catholic Prayer*, by Sean Finnegan.

Tips: "Our audience is general readers of books on spirituality, with Catholic or sacramental interests. We do not publish academic books or books for religious professionals. We do publish in the area of Catholic faith formation. Study our guidelines. We get many inappropriate submissions because authors do not know we are a trade publisher of religion books for a non-professional market."

THE LYONS PRESS, The Globe Pequot Press, Inc., 123 W. 18th St., New York NY 10011. (212)620-9580. Fax: (212)929-1836. Website: www.lyonspress.com. Publisher/President: Tony Lyons. **Acquisitions:** Becky Koh, editor (narrative nonfiction, sports, health, cooking); Richard Rothschild, managing editor; Lilly Golden, editor-at-large; Enrica Gadler, editor (narrative nonfiction, games, nature); Jay Cassell, editor (fishing, hunting); J. McCullogh, associate editor; Brando Skyhorse, assistant editor (travel, camping, gardening). Estab. 1984 (Lyons & Burford), 1997 (The Lyons Press). Publishes hardcover and trade paperback originals and reprints. **Publishes 200 titles/year. 50% of books from first-time authors; 30% from unagented writers. Pays 5-10% royalty on wholesale price Offers $2,000-7,000 advance.** Publishes book 1 year after acceptance of ms. Accepts simultaneous submissions. Responds in 1 month to queries and proposals; 2 months to mss. Book catalog online.
- The Lyons Press has teamed up to develop books with L.L. Bean, *Field & Stream*, The Nature Conservancy and *Golf Magazine*. It was recently purchased by Globe Pequot Press.
- The Lyons Press publishes practical and literary books, chiefly centered on outdoor subjects—natural history, all sports, gardening, horses, fishing. Currently emphasizing adventure, sports. De-emphasizing hobbies, travel.

Nonfiction: Biography, cookbook, how-to, reference. Subjects include agriculture/horticulture, Americana, animals, anthropology/archeology, cooking/foods/nutrition, gardening, health/medicine, history, hobbies, military/war, nature/environment (environment), recreation, science, sports, travel. "Visit our website and note the featured categories." Query with SASE or submit proposal package including outline, 3 sample chapter(s). and marketing description. Reviews artwork/photos as part of ms package. Send photocopies or non-original prints.

Fiction: Historical, military/war, short story collections (fishing, hunting, outdoor, nature), sports. Query with SASE or submit proposal package including outline, 3-5 sample chapter(s).

Recent Title(s): *Doctor on Everest*, by Kenneth Kamler, M.D (sports/adventure); *The Farmer's Market Cookbook*, by Richard Ruben (cooking); *The Snowfly*, by Joseph Heywood (flyfishing novel).

MACADAM/CAGE PUBLISHING INC., 155 Sansome St., Suite 620, San Francisco CA 94104. (415)986-7502. Fax: (415)986-7414. E-mail: info@macadamcage.com. Website: www.macadamcage.com. Publisher: David Poindexter. **Acquisitions:** Patrick Walsh, editor. Publishes hardcover originals. **Publishes 10-20 titles/year. Receives 2,000 queries and 1,500 mss/year. 75% of books from first-time authors; 25% from unagented writers. Pays negotiable royalty.** Publishes book up to 1 year after acceptance of ms. Accepts simultaneous submissions. Responds in 4 months to queries. Manuscript guidelines for #10 SASE.
- MacAdam/Cage publishes quality works of literary fiction that are carefully crafted and tell a bold story. De-emphasizing romance, poetry, Christian or New Age mss.

Nonfiction: Subjects include memoirs. "Narrative nonfiction such as memoirs. Nonfiction that reads like fiction." Submit proposal package including outline, up to 3 sample chapter(s), SASE.

Fiction: Historical, literary, mainstream/contemporary. Submit proposal package including up to 3 sample chapter(s), synopsis, SASE.

Recent Title(s): *Farewell to Prague*, by Miriam Darvas (nonfiction); *Beneath that Starry Place*, by Terry Jordan (fiction).

Tips: "We like to keep in close contact with writers. We publish for readers of quality fiction and nonfiction."

MADISON BOOKS, Rowman and Littlefield Publishing Group, 4720 Boston Way, Lanham MD 20706. (301)459-3366. Fax: (301)429-5748. **Acquisitions:** Alyssa Theodore, acquisitions editor. Estab. 1984. Publishes hardcover originals, trade paperback originals and reprints. **Publishes 40 titles/year. Receives 1,200 submissions/year. 15% of books from first-time authors; 65% from unagented writers. Pays 10-15% royalty on net receipts.** Publishes book 1 year after acceptance of ms. Responds in 2 months to queries. Book catalog and ms guidelines for 9×12 SAE with 4 first-class stamps.

Nonfiction: Biography, reference (trade). Subjects include history, contemporary affairs. *No unsolicited mss.* Query with SASE or submit outline, sample chapter(s).

THE MAGNI GROUP, INC., 7106 Wellington Point Rd., McKinney TX 75070. (972)540-2050. Fax: (972)540-1057. E-mail: info@magnico.com. Website: www.magnico.com. **Acquisitions:** Evan Reynolds, president. Publishes hardcover originals and trade paperback reprints. **Publishes 5-10 titles/year. Receives 20 queries and 10-20 mss/year. 50% of books from first-time authors; 80% from unagented writers. Pays royalty on wholesale price or makes outright purchase. Offers advance.** Publishes book 6 months after acceptance of ms. Responds in 2 months to queries. Book catalog and ms guidelines online.

Imprints: Magni Publishing

Nonfiction: Cookbook, how-to, self-help. Subjects include child guidance/parenting, cooking/foods/nutrition, health/medicine, money/finance, sex. Submit complete ms. Reviews artwork/photos as part of ms package. Send photocopies.
Recent Title(s): *Burn Fat for Fuel.*

N] MAGNUS PRESS, P.O. Box 2666, Carlsbad CA 92018. (760)806-3743. Fax: (760)806-3689. E-mail: magnuspres @aol.com. **Acquisitions:** Warren Angel, editorial director. Publishes trade paperback originals and reprints. **Publishes 3-5 titles/year; imprint publishes 2 titles/year. 62% of books from first-time authors; 100% from unagented writers. Pays 6-11% royalty on retail price.** Publishes book 6 months after acceptance of ms. Accepts simultaneous submissions. Responds in 1 month to queries; 2 months to proposals and mss. Book catalog and ms guidelines for #10 SASE.
Imprints: Canticle Books
Nonfiction: Inspirational, Biblical studies. Subjects include religion (from a Christian perspective.). "Writers must be well-grounded in Biblical knowledge and must be able to communicate effectively with the lay person." Query with SASE or submit proposal package including outline, 3 sample chapter(s).
Tips: Magnus Press's audience is mainly Christian lay persons, but also includes anyone interested in spirituality and/or Biblical studies and the church. "Study our listings and catalog; learn to write effectively for an average reader; read any one of our published books."

N] MAISONNEUVE PRESS, 6423 Adelphi Rd., University Park MD 20782. (301)277-7505. Fax: (301)277-7505. E-mail: editors@maisonneuvepress.com. Website: www.maisonneuvepress.com. **Acquisitions:** Robert Merrill, editor (politics, literature, philosophy); Dennis Crow, editor (architecture, urban studies, sociology). Publishes hardcover and trade paperback originals. **Publishes 6 titles/year. 5% of books from first-time authors; 100% from unagented writers. Pays 2-9% royalty on wholesale price or $2,000 maximum outright purchase.** Publishes book 1 year after acceptance of ms. Accepts simultaneous submissions. Responds in 1 month to queries; 2 months to proposals; 5 months to mss. Book catalog free; send letter for guidelines, individual response.
  O-π "Maisonneuve provides solid, first-hand information for serious adult readers: academics and political activists."
Nonfiction: Biography. Subjects include education, ethnic, gay/lesbian, government/politics, history, language/literature, military/war, philosophy, psychology, sociology, translation, women's issues/studies, literary criticism, social theory, economics, essay collections. "We make decisions on completed mss only. Will correspond on work in progress. Some books submitted are too narrowly focused; not marketable enough." Query with SASE or submit complete ms. Reviews artwork/photos as part of ms package. Send photocopies.
Recent Title(s): *Positively Postmodern: The Multi-Media Muse in America,* edited by Nicholas Zurburgg.

M] MARCH STREET PRESS, 3413 Wilshire, Greensboro NC 27408. (336)282-9754. Fax: (336)282-9754. E-mail: rbixby@aol.com. Website: users.aol.com/marchst. **Acquisitions:** Robert Bixby, editor/publisher. Estab. 1988. Publishes literary chapbooks. **Publishes 6-10 titles/year. Receives 12 queries and 30 mss/year. 50% of books from first-time authors; 100% from unagented writers. Pays 15% royalty. Offers 10 copy advance.** Publishes book 6 months after acceptance of ms. Accepts simultaneous submissions. Responds in 3 months to mss. Book catalog and ms guidelines for #10 SASE.
  O-π March Street publishes poetry chapbooks. "We like unusual, risky, interesting things. We like to be amazed. So do our readers and writers."
Poetry: "My plans are based on the submissions I receive, not vice versa."
Recent Title(s): *Road to Alaska,* by Ray Miller; *Her Bodies,* by Elizabeth Kerlikowske.
Tips: "March Street Press is purely an act of hedonistic indulgence. The mission is to enjoy myself. Just as authors express themselves through writing, I find a creative release in designing, editing and publishing. Audience is extremely sophisticated, widely read graduates of M.A., M.F.A. and Ph.D. programs in English and fine arts. Also lovers of significant, vibrant and enriching verse regardless of field of study or endeavor. Most beginning poets, I have found, think it beneath them to read other poets. This is the most glaring flaw in their work. My advice is to read ceaselessly. Otherwise, you may be published, but you will never be accomplished."

N] MARINE TECHNIQUES PUBLISHING, INC., 126 Western Ave., Suite 266, Augusta ME 04330-7252. (207)622-7984. Fax: (207)621-0821. **Acquisitions:** James L. Pelletier, president/CEO (commercial marine or maritime international); Christopher S. Pelletier, vice president operations (national and international maritime related properties). **Publishes 3-5 titles/year. Receives 5-20 queries and 1-4 mss/year. 15% of books from first-time authors. Pays 25-43% royalty on wholesale or retail price.** Publishes book 6-12 months after acceptance of ms. Accepts simultaneous submissions. Responds in 2 months to queries; 4 months to proposals; 6 months to mss. Book catalog free.
  O-π Publishes only books related to the commercial marine industry.
Nonfiction: Reference, self-help, technical, maritime company directories. Subjects include the commerical maritime industry only. Submit proposal package, including ms., with all photos (photocopies OK).
Fiction: Must be commercial maritime/marine related. Submit complete ms.
Poetry: Must be related to maritime/marine subject matter. Submit complete ms.

Tips: Audience consists of commercial marine/maritime firms, persons employed in all aspects of the marine/maritime commercial and recreational fields, persons interested in seeking employment in the commercial marine industry; firms seeking to sell their products and services to vessel owners, operators, and managers in the commercial marine industry worldwide, etc.

[N] [A] MARINER BOOKS, Houghton Mifflin, 222 Berkeley St., Boston MA 02116. (617)351-5000. Fax: (617)351-1202. Website: www.hmco.com. **Acquisitions:** Susan Canavan, manager. Publishes trade paperback originals and reprints. **Pays royalty. Offers varing advance.** Responds in 2 months to mss.
> Houghton Mifflin books give shape to ideas that educate, inform and delight. Mariner has an eclectic list that notably embraces fiction.

Nonfiction: Biography. Subjects include education, government/politics, history, philosophy, sociology, political thought. *Accepts agented submissions only.*
Fiction: Literary, mainstream/contemporary. *Accepts agented submissions only.*
Recent Title(s): *Kit's Law*, by Donna Morrissey; *The Hallelujah Side*, by Rhoda Huffey; *The Bostos*, by Carolyn Cooke.

[N] MARLOR PRESS, INC., 4304 Brigadoon Dr., St. Paul MN 55126. (651)484-4600. E-mail: marlin.marlor@minn.net. **Acquisitions:** Marlin Bree, publisher. Estab. 1981. Publishes trade paperback originals. **Publishes 6 titles/year. Receives 100 queries and 25 mss/year. Pays 8-10% royalty on wholesale price.** Publishes book 1 year after acceptance of ms. Responds in 6 weeks to queries. Manuscript guidelines for #10 SASE.
> Currently emphasizing general interest nonfiction children's books and nonfiction boating books. De-emphasizing travel.

Nonfiction: Children's/juvenile, how-to. Subjects include travel, boating. "Primarily how-to stuff." *No unsolicited mss.* No anecdotal reminiscences or biographical materials. No fiction or poetry. Query first; submit outline with sample chapters only when requested. Do not send full ms. Reviews artwork/photos as part of ms package.
Recent Title(s): *Going Abroad: The Bathroom Survival Guide*, by Eva Newman; *Wake of the Green Storm: A Survivor's Tale*, by Marlin Bree.

[N] MAUPIN HOUSE PUBLISHING INC., P.O. Box 90148, Gainesville FL 32607-0148. (800)524-0634. E-mail: jgraddy@maupinhouse.com. Website: www.maupinhouse.com. **Acquisitions:** Julia Graddy, co-publisher. Publishes trade paperback originals and reprints. **Publishes 7 titles/year. Pays 5-10% royalty on retail price.** Responds in 2 months to queries.
> Maupin House publishes teacher resource books for language arts teachers K-12.

Nonfiction: How-to. Subjects include education, language/literature. "We are looking for practical, in-classroom resource materials, especially in the field of language arts and writing workshops. Classroom teachers are our top choice as authors." Query with SASE.
Fiction: Juvenile (grades 3-5). "We are interested in fiction that features a child set in historical Florida."
Recent Title(s): *The Writing Menu*, by Melissa Forney (nonfiction).

MAXIMUM PRESS, 605 Silverthorn Rd., Gulf Breeze FL 32561. (850)934-0819.
Acquisitions: Jim Hoskins, publisher. Publishes trade paperback originals. **Publishes 10-12 titles/year. Receives 10 queries and 10 mss/year. 40% of books from first-time authors; 90% from unagented writers. Pays 7½-15% royalty on wholesale price. Offers $1,000-5,000 advance.** Publishes book 3 months after acceptance of ms. Responds in 1 month to queries. *Writer's Market* recommends allowing 2 months for reply to queries. Book catalog free.
> "Maximum Press is a premier publisher of books that help readers apply technology efficiently and profitably. Special emphasis is on books that help individuals and businesses increase revenue and reduce expenses through the use of computers and other low-cost information tools." Currently emphasizing e-business.

Nonfiction: How-to, technical. Subjects include business/economics, computers/electronic, Internet. Query with SASE or submit proposal package including résumé.
Recent Title(s): *Marketing on the Internet*, by Jan Zimmerman (computer/Internet); *101 Ways to Promote Your Web Site*, by Susan Sweeney (e-business).

MBI PUBLISHING, 729 Prospect Ave., P.O. Box 1, Osceola WI 54020-0001. (715)294-3345. Fax: (715)294-4448. E-mail: mbibks@motorbooks.com. Website: www.motorbooks.com. Publishing Director: Zack Miller. **Acquisitions:** Lee Klancher, editor-in-chief; Darwin Holmstrom (motorcycles); Mike Haenggi, acquisitions editor (aviation, military history); Keith Mathiowetz, acquisitions editor (American cars, Americana, railroading collectibles); Paul Johnson, acquisitions editor (automotive how-to, boating); John Adams-Graf, acquisitions editor (foreign cars, vintage racing); Steve Hendrickson, acquisitions editor (hot rods). Estab. 1973. Publishes hardcover and paperback originals. **Publishes 125 titles/year. Receives 200 queries and 50 mss/year. 95% from unagented writers. Pays royalty on net receipts. Offers $5,000 average advance.** Publishes book 1 year after acceptance of ms. Accepts simultaneous submissions. Responds in 3 months to queries. Book catalog free; ms guidelines for #10 SASE.
Imprints: Bay View, Bicycle Books, Crestline, Zenith Books
> MBI is a transportation-related publisher: cars, motorcycles, racing, trucks, tractors, boats, bicycles—also Americana, aviation and military history. Currently emphasizing Americana and the Civil War.

Nonfiction: Transportation-related subjects. Coffee table book, gift book, how-to, illustrated book. Subjects include Americana, history, hobbies, military/war, photography, translation (nonfiction). "State qualifications for doing book." Query with SASE. Reviews artwork/photos as part of ms package. Send photocopies.
Recent Title(s): *America's Special Forces*, by David Bohrer (modern military).

McBOOKS PRESS, 120 W. State St., Ithaca NY 14850. E-mail: mcbooks@mcbooks.com. Website: www.mcbooks.com. Publisher: Alexander G. Skutt.
Acquisitions: (Ms.) S.K. List, editorial director. Estab. 1979. Publishes trade paperback and hardcover originals and reprints. **Publishes 20 titles/year. Pays 5-10% royalty on retail price. Offers $1,000-5,000 advance.** Responds in 1 month to queries; 2 months to proposals.
  • "We are booked nearly solid for the next few years. We can only consider the highest quality projects in our narrow interest areas."
  O₋ Currently emphasizing nautical and military historical fiction.
Nonfiction: Subjects include cooking/foods/nutrition (vegetarianism and veganism), regional (New York state). "Authors' ability to promote a plus." *No unsolicited mss.* Query with SASE.
Fiction: Nautical and military historical. Query with SASE.
Recent Title(s): *Vegan: The New Ethics of Eating*, by Erik Marcus; *Wicked Trade*, by Jan Needle.

McDONALD & WOODWARD PUBLISHING CO., 431-B E. Broadway, Granville OH 43023-1310. (740)321-1140. Fax: (740)321-1141. Website: www.mwpubco.com. **Acquisitions:** Jerry N. McDonald, managing partner/publisher. Estab. 1986. Publishes hardcover and trade paperback originals. **Publishes 8 titles/year. Receives 100 queries and 20 mss/year. 50% of books from first-time authors; 100% from unagented writers. Pays 10% royalty on net receipts.** Publishes book 1 year after acceptance of ms. Accepts simultaneous submissions. Responds in 2 weeks to queries. Book catalog free.
  O₋ "McDonald & Woodward publishes books in natural and cultural history." Currently emphasizing travel, history, natural history. De-emphasizing self-help.
Nonfiction: Biography, coffee table book, illustrated book. Subjects include Americana, animals, anthropology/archeology, ethnic, history, nature/environment, science, travel. Query with SASE or submit outline, sample chapter(s). Reviews artwork/photos as part of ms package. Send photocopies.
Recent Title(s): *The Carousel Keepers: An Oral History of American Carousels*, by Carrie Papa; *The Mammals of Virginia*, by Donald W. Linzey; *Juan Ponce de Leon and the Spanish Discovery of Puerto Rico and Florida*, by Robert H. Fuson.
Tips: "We are especially interested in additional titles in our 'Guides to the American Landscape' series. Should consult titles in print for guidance. We want well-organized, clearly written, substantive material."

MARGARET K. McELDERRY BOOKS, Simon & Schuster Children's Publishing Division, Simon & Schuster, 1230 Sixth Ave., New York NY 10020. (212)698-2761. Fax: (212)698-2796. Website: www.simonsayskids.com. Vice President/Publisher: Brenda Bowen. Editor-at-Large: Margaret K. McElderry.
Acquisitions: Emma D. Dryden, editorial director (books for preschoolers to 16-year-olds); Kristen McCurry, assistant editor. Estab. 1971. Publishes quality material for preschoolers to 16-year-olds, but publishes only a few YAs. **Publishes 25 titles/year. Receives 5,000 queries/year. 10% of books from first-time authors; 50% from unagented writers. Average print order is 4,000-6,000 for a first teen book; 7,500-10,000 for a first picture book. Pays royalty on retail price: 10% fiction; picture book, 5% author, 5% illustrator. Offers $5,000-6,000 advance for new authors.** Publishes book up to 2 years after acceptance of ms. Manuscript guidelines for #10 SASE.
  O₋ "We are more interested in superior writing and illustration than in a particular 'type' of book." Currently emphasizing young picture books. De-emphasizing picture books with a lot of text.
Nonfiction: Biography, children's/juvenile. Subjects include history, adventure. "Read. The field is competitive. See what's been done and what's out there before submitting. Looks for originality of ideas, clarity and felicity of expression, well-organized plot and strong characterization (fiction) or clear exposition (nonfiction); quality. We will accept one-page query letters with SASE for picture books or novels." *No unsolicited mss.*
Fiction: Adventure, fantasy, historical, mainstream/contemporary, mystery, young adult (or middle grade). No unsolicited mss. Send one-page query letter with SASE.
Poetry: Query or submit 3 sample poems.
Recent Title(s): *The Year of Miss Agnes*, by Kirkpatrick Hill (middle grade fiction); *Stowaway*, by Karen Hesse (young adult fiction); *Puff-Puff, Chugga-Chugga*, by Christopher Wormell (picture book fiction).
Tips: "Freelance writers should be aware of the swing away from teen-age novels to books for younger readers and of the growing need for beginning chapter books for children just learning to read on their own."

McFARLAND & COMPANY, INC., PUBLISHERS, Box 611, Jefferson NC 28640. (336)246-4460. Fax: (336)246-5018. E-mail: info@mcfarlandpub.com. Website: www.mcfarlandpub.com. **Acquisitions:** Robert Franklin, president/editor-in-chief (chess, general); Steve Wilson, senior editor (automotive, general); Virginia Tobiassen, editor (general); Marty McGee, assistant editor; Gary Mitchem, assistant editor. Estab. 1979. Publishes hardcover and "quality" paperback originals; a "non-trade" publisher. **Publishes 190 titles/year. Receives 1,400 submissions/year. 70% of books from first-time authors; 95% from unagented writers. Pays 10-12½% royalty on net receipts.** Publishes book 10 months after acceptance of ms. Responds in 1 month to queries.

O— McFarland publishes serious nonfiction in a variety of fields, including general reference, performing arts, sports (particularly baseball); women's studies, librarianship, literature, Civil War, history and international studies. Currently emphasizing medieval history, automotive history. De-emphasizing memoirs.

Nonfiction: Reference (and scholarly), technical, professional monographs. Subjects include art/architecture, business/economics, ethnic, film/cinema/stage, health/medicine, history, music/dance, recreation, sociology, sports (very strong), women's issues/studies (very strong), world affairs, African-American studies (very strong), chess, Civil War, drama/theater, cinema/radio/TV (very strong), librarianship (very strong), pop culture, world affairs (very strong). Reference books are particularly wanted—fresh material (i.e., not in head-to-head competition with an established title). "We prefer manuscripts of 250 or more double-spaced pages." No fiction, New Age, exposés, poetry, children's books, devotional/inspirational works, Bible studies or personal essays. Query with SASE or submit outline, sample chapter(s). Reviews artwork/photos as part of ms package.

Recent Title(s): *Who's Who In the Middle Ages*, by Mary Ellen Snodgrass.

Tips: "We want well-organized knowledge of an area in which there is not information coverage at present, plus reliability so we don't feel we have to check absolutely everything. Our market is worldwide and libraries are an important part." McFarland also publishes the *Journal of Information Ethics*.

McGREGOR PUBLISHING, 4532 W. Kennedy Blvd., Suite 233, Tampa FL 33609. (813)805-2665 or (888)405-2665. Fax: (813)832-6777. E-mail: mcgregpub@aol.com. **Acquisitions:** Dave Rosenbaum, acquisitions editor. Publishes hardcover and trade paperback originals. **Publishes 15-20 titles/year. Receives 150 queries and 40 mss/year. 75% of books from first-time authors; 80% from unagented writers. Pays 10-12% royalty on retail price; 13-16% on wholesale price. Offers varied advance.** Publishes book 1 year after acceptance of ms. Accepts simultaneous submissions. Responds in 2 months to queries and proposals; 3 months to mss. Book catalog and ms guidelines free.

● McGregor no longer publishes fiction.

O— "We specialize in nonfiction books that 'tell the story behind the story'." Currently emphasizing true crime, sports. De-emphasizing self-help.

Nonfiction: "We're always looking for regional nonfiction titles, and especially for sports, biographies, true crime and how-to books." Biography, how-to. Subjects include business/economics, ethnic, history, money/finance, regional, sports, true crime. Query with SASE or submit outline, 2 sample chapter(s).

Recent Title(s): *Home Ice: Reflections on Frozen Ponds and Backyard Rinks*, by Jack Falls (nonfiction).

Tips: "We pride ourselves on working closely with an author and producing a quality product with strong promotional campaigns."

MEADOWBROOK PRESS, 5451 Smetana Dr., Minnetonka MN 55343. (952)930-1100. Fax: (952)930-1940. Website: www.meadowbrookpress.com. **Acquisitions:** Submissions Editor. Estab. 1975. Publishes trade paperback originals and reprints. **Publishes 20 titles/year. Receives 1,500 queries/year. 15% of books from first-time authors. Pays 10% royalty. Offers small advance.** Publishes book 1 year after acceptance of ms. Accepts simultaneous submissions. Responds in 4 months to queries. Book catalog and ms guidelines for #10 SASE.

O— Meadowbrook is a family-oriented press which specializes in parenting and pregnancy books, party planning books and children's poetry and fiction. De-emphasizing joke, quote books, and adult poetry.

Nonfiction: How-to, reference. Subjects include child guidance/parenting, cooking/foods/nutrition, humor, senior citizens, children's activities, relationships. "We prefer a query first; then we will request an outline and/or sample material." Send for guidelines. No academic or biography. Query with SASE or submit outline, sample chapter(s).

Fiction: Anthology. Children's fiction ages 7-12. Query with SASE.

Poetry: Children's humorous poetry. Query.

Recent Title(s): *52 Romantic Evenings to Spice Up Your Love Life*, by Liya Lev Oertel (nonfiction); *Mystery of the Haunted Caves*, by Penny Warner (fiction); *The Aliens Have Landed!*, by Kenn Nesbitt (poetry).

Tips: "Always send for fiction and poetry guidelines before submitting material. We do not accept unsolicited picture book submissions." Meadowbrook has several series, including Newfangled Fairy Tales and Kids Pick the Funniest Poems.

MEDICAL PHYSICS PUBLISHING, 4513 Vernon Blvd., Madison WI 53705. (608)262-4021. Fax: (608)265-2121. E-mail: mpp@medicalphysics.org. Website: www.medicalphysics.org. **Acquisitions:** John Cameron, president; Betsey Phelps, managing editor. Estab. 1985. Publishes hardcover and trade paperback originals and reprints. **Publishes 10-12 titles/year. Receives 10-20 queries/year. 100% from unagented writers. Pays 10% royalty on wholesale price.** Publishes book 6 months after acceptance of ms. Accepts simultaneous submissions. Responds in 6 months to mss. Book catalog online.

O— "We are a nonprofit, membership organization publishing affordable books in medical physics and related fields." Currently emphasizing biomedical engineering. De-emphasizing books for the general public.

Nonfiction: Reference, technical, textbook. Subjects include health/medicine, symposium proceedings in the fields of medical physics and radiology. Submit complete ms. Reviews artwork/photos as part of ms package. Send disposable copies.

Recent Title(s): *The Modern Technology of Radiation Oncology*, edited by Jacob Van Dyk; *Physics of the Body*, by John R. Cameron, James G. Skofronick and Roderick M. Grant.

N̲ **MENASHA RIDGE PRESS**, P.O. Box 43059, Birmingham AL 35243. (205)322-0439. E-mail: bzehmer@menash aridge.com. Website: www.menasharidge.com. **Acquisitions:** Bud Zehmer, senior acquisitions editor (outdoors); Molly Merkle, associate publisher (travel, reference). Publishes hardcover and trade paperback originals. **Publishes 20 titles/ year. Receives 600-800 submissions/year. 30% of books from first-time authors; 85% from unagented writers. Pays varying royalty. Offers varying advance.** Publishes book 1 year after acceptance of ms. Accepts simultaneous submissions. Responds in 2 months to queries. Book catalog for 9×12 SAE with 4 first-class stamps.

O─ Menasha Ridge Press publishes "distinctive books in the areas of outdoor sports, travel and diving. Our authors are among the best in their fields."

Nonfiction: How-to, humor, travel guides. Subjects include recreation (outdoor), sports (adventure), travel, outdoors. "Most concepts are generated in-house, but a few come from outside submissions." Submit proposal package including résumé, synopsis. Reviews artwork/photos as part of ms package.

Recent Title(s): *The Nearly Way of Knowledge*, by William Nealy.

Tips: Audience is 25-60, 14-18 years' education, white collar and professional, $30,000 median income, 75% male, 55% east of the Mississippi River.

MERIWETHER PUBLISHING LTD., 885 Elkton Dr., Colorado Springs CO 80907-3557. (719)594-4422. Fax: (719)594-9916. E-mail: merpcds@aol.com. **Acquisitions:** Arthur Zapel, Theodore Zapel, Rhonda Wray, editors. Estab. 1969. Publishes paperback originals and reprints. **Receives 1,200 submissions/year. 50% of books from first-time authors; 90% from unagented writers. Pays 10% royalty on retail price or makes outright purchase.** Publishes book 6 months after acceptance of ms. Accepts simultaneous submissions. Responds in 1 month to queries. Book catalog and ms guidelines for $2 postage.

O─ Meriwether publishes theater books, games and videos; speech resources; plays, skits and musicals; and resources for gifted students. "We specialize in books on the theatre arts and religious plays for Christmas, Easter and youth activities. We also publish musicals for high school performers and churches." Currently emphasizing how-to books for theatrical arts and church youth activities.

Nonfiction: "We publish unusual textbooks or trade books related to the communication or performing arts and how-to books on staging, costuming, lighting, etc." How-to, humor, reference, textbook. Subjects include film/cinema/ stage, music/dance, recreation, religion, theater/drama. "We prefer mainstream religion titles." Query or submit outline/ synopsis and sample chapters.

Fiction: Humor, mainstream/contemporary, mystery, plays (and musicals), religious, suspense, all in playscript format.

Recent Title(s): *International Plays for Young Audiences*, by Roger Ellis; *Spontaneous Performance*, by Marsh Cassady.

Tips: "Our educational books are sold to teachers and students at college, high school and middle school levels. Our religious books are sold to youth activity directors, pastors and choir directors. Our trade books are directed at the public with a sense of humor. Another group of buyers is the professional theatre, radio and TV category. We focus more on books of plays and short scenes and textbooks on directing, staging, make-up, lighting, etc."

◼ MERRIAM PRESS, 218 Beech St., Bennington VT 05201-2611. (802)447-0313. Fax: (305)847-5978. E-mail: ray@merriam-press.com. Website: www.merriam-press.com. Publishes hardcover originals and reprints and trade paperback originals and reprints. **Publishes 12 titles/year. Receives 50 queries and 30 mss/year. 70-90% of books from first-time authors; 90% from unagented writers. Pays 10% royalty on retail price.** Publishes book 1 year after acceptance of ms. Accepts simultaneous submissions. Responds in 1 month to queries. Book catalog for $3 or online; ms guidelines for #10 SASE or online.

O─ Merriam Press specializes in military subjects, especially World War II.

Nonfiction: Biography, illustrated book, reference, technical. Subjects include military/war. Query with SASE or submit proposal package, including outline and 1 sample chapter or submit complete ms. Reviews artwork/photos as part of ms package. Send photocopies.

Recent Title(s): *Marine Chaplain 1943-1946*, by George W. Wickersham II; *Mount Up! We're Moving Out!*, by Vernon H. Brown Jr.

Tips: "Our books are geared for WWII/military history historians, collectors, model kit builders, wargamers, veterans, general enthusiasts."

METAL POWDER INDUSTRIES FEDERATION, 105 College Rd. E., Princeton NJ 08540. (609)452-7700. Fax: (609)987-8523. E-mail: info@mpif.org. Website: www.mpif.org. **Acquisitions:** Cindy Jablonowski, publications manager; Peggy Lebedz, assistant publications manager. Estab. 1946. Publishes hardcover originals. **Publishes 10 titles/ year. Pays 3-12½% royalty on wholesale or retail price. Offers $3,000-5,000 advance.** Responds in 1 month to queries.

O─ Metal Powder Industries publishes monographs, textbooks, handbooks, design guides, conference proceedings, standards, and general titles in the field of powder metullary or particulate materials.

Nonfiction: Work must relate to powder metallurgy or particulate materials. Technical, textbook.

Recent Title(s): *Advances in Powder Metallurgy and Particulate Materials* (conference proceeding).

N̲ **METAMORPHOUS PRESS**, P.O. Box 10616, Portland OR 97296-0616. (503)228-4972. Fax: (503)223-9117. E-mail: metabooks@metamodels.com. Website: www.metamodels.com/meta/meta.html. Publisher: David Balding. Editorial Director: Lori Vannorsdel. **Acquisitions:** Nancy Wyatt-Kelsey, acquisitions editor. Estab. 1982. Publishes trade paperback originals and reprints. **Publishes 4-5 titles/year. Receives 2,500 submissions/year. 90% of books from first-time authors; 90% from unagented writers. Pays minimum 10% profit split on wholesale prices.** Publishes book 1 year after acceptance of ms. Accepts simultaneous submissions. Responds in 3 months to queries. Book catalog and ms guidelines for 9×12 SAE with 3 first-class stamps or online.

Imprints: Grinder & Associates (Lori Vannorsdel, editorial director)

O→ "Our primary editorial screen is 'will this (behavioral science) book further define, explain or support the concept that we are responsible for our reality or assist people in gaining control of their lives?'" Currently emphasizing NLP, enneagram, Ericksonian hypnosis. De-emphasizing New Age.

Nonfiction: How-to, reference, self-help, technical, textbook, (all related to behavioral science and personal growth). Subjects include business/economics (and sales), education, health/medicine, psychology, science, sociology, relationships, new ideas in behavioral science. "We are interested in any well-proven new idea or philosophy in the behavioral science areas." Submit idea, outline and table of contents only. Reviews artwork/photos as part of ms package.

Recent Title(s): *Enneagram Spectrum of Personality Styles*, by Wagner; *Framework of Excellence*, by C. Miliner; *Patterns of Therapeutic Technology of Milton Erickson, vols 1-2*, by Bandler & Grinder (hypnotherapy).

MEYERBOOKS, PUBLISHER, P.O. Box 427, Glenwood IL 60425-0427. (708)757-4950. **Acquisitions:** David Meyer, publisher. Estab. 1976. Publishes hardcover and trade paperback originals and reprints. **Publishes 5 titles/year. Pays 10-15% royalty on wholesale or retail price.** Responds in 3 months to queries.

Imprints: David Meyer Magic Books, Waltham Street Press

O→ "We are currently publishing books on stage magic history. We only consider subjects which have never been presented in book form before. We are not currently considering books on health, herbs, cookery or general Americana."

Nonfiction: Reference. Subjects include history of stage magic. Query with SASE.

Recent Title(s): *Blackstone: A Magician's Life. The World and Magic Show of Harry Blackstone, 1885-1965*, by Daniel G. Waldron (theatrical biography).

MICHIGAN STATE UNIVERSITY PRESS, 1405 S. Harrison Rd. Manly Miles Bldg., Suite 25, East Lansing MI 48823-5202. (517)355-9543. Fax: (517)432-2611. E-mail: msupress@msu.edu. Website: www.msupress.edu/unit/msupress. **Acquisitions:** Martha Bates, acquisitions editor. Estab. 1947. Publishes hardcover and softcover originals. **Publishes 35 titles/year. Receives 2,400 submissions/year. 75% of books from first-time authors; 100% from unagented writers. Pays variable royalty.** Publishes book 18 months after acceptance of ms. Book catalog and ms guidelines for 9×12 SASE.

Imprints: Lotus, Colleagues

O→ Michigan State University publishes scholarly books that further scholarship in their particular field. In addition they publish nonfiction that addresses, in a more contemporary way, social concerns, such as diversity, civil rights, the environment.

Nonfiction: Subjects include Americana (American studies), business/economics, creative nonfiction, ethnic (Afro-American studies), government/politics, history (contemporary civil rights), language/literature, regional (Great Lakes regional, Canadian studies), women's issues/studies. Reviews artwork/photos as part of ms package.

Recent Title(s): *This Is the World*, by W.S. Penn (fiction).

MID-LIST PRESS, Jackson, Hart & Leslie, 4324 12th Ave S., Minneapolis MN 55407-3218. Website: www.midlist.org. Publisher: Marianne Nora. **Acquisitions:** Lane Stiles, senior editor. Estab. 1989. Publishes hardcover and trade paperback originals. **Publishes 4 titles/year. Pays 40-50% royalty.** SASE for First Series guidelines and/or general submission guidelines; also available online.

O→ Mid-List Press publishes books of high literary merit and fresh artistic vision by new and emerging writers.

Recent Title(s): *Objects and Empathy*, by Arthur Saltzman (nonfiction); *Leaving the Neighborhood and Other Stories*, by Lucy Ferriss (fiction); *Jonah's Promise*, by Adam Sol (poetry).

Tips: Mid-List Press is an independent press. In addition to publishing the annual winners of the Mid-List Press First Series Awards, Mid-List Press publishes fiction, poetry, and creative nonfiction by first-time and established writers.

THE MIDKNIGHT CLUB, P.O. Box 25, Brown Mills NJ 08015. (609)735-9043. E-mail: info@midknightclub.net. Website: www.midknightclub.net. **Acquisitions:** Faith Ann Hotchkin, editor-in-chief. Publishes trade paperback originals and reprints. **Publishes 4-6 titles/year. Receives 300 queries and 200 mss/year. 65% of books from first-time authors; 100% from unagented writers. Pays 10-12% royalty on wholesale price. Offers advance.** Publishes book 8 months after acceptance of ms. Accepts simultaneous submissions. Responds in 1 month to queries; 2 months to proposals. Book catalog online; ms guidelines for #10 SASE and online.

O→ "We're interested in religions of the ages and occult matters that have existed for a long time. No New Age fads."

Nonfiction: How-to, self-help. Subjects include philosophy, religion, spirituality. Reviews artwork/photos as part of ms package. Send photocopies.

Recent Title(s): *Demonology*, Michael Szul.

MILKWEED EDITIONS, 1011 Washington Ave. S., Suite 300, Minneapolis MN 55415. (612)332-3192. Fax: (612)215-2550. Website: www.milkweed.org and www.worldashome.org. **Acquisitions:** Emilie Buchwald, publisher;

Elisabeth Fitz, first reader (fiction, children's fiction, poetry); City as Home editor (literary writing about cities); World as Home editor (literary writing about the natural world). Estab. 1980. Publishes hardcover originals and paperback originals and reprints. **Publishes 15 titles/year. Receives 3,000 submissions/year. 30% of books from first-time authors; 70% from unagented writers. Pays 7½% royalty on retail price. Offers varied advance.** Publishes book 1-2 years after acceptance of ms. Accepts simultaneous submissions. Responds in 2 months to queries; 6 months to mss. Book catalog for $1.50; ms guidelines for #10 SASE.

- Milkweed Editions publishes literary fiction for adults and middle grade readers, nonfiction, memoir and poetry. "Our vision is focused on giving voice to writers whose work is of the highest literary quality and whose ideas engender personal reflection and cultural action." Currently emphasizing nonfiction about the natural world.

Nonfiction: Literary. Subjects include nature/environment, human community. Submit complete ms.

Fiction: Literary. Novels for adults and for readers 8-13. High literary quality. Submit complete ms.

Recent Title(s): *The Prairie in Her Eyes*, by Ann Daum (nonfiction); *My Lord Bag of Rice*, by Carol Bly (fiction); *Turning Over the Earth*, by Ralph Black (poetry).

Tips: "We are looking for excellent writing in fiction, nonfiction, poetry, and children's novels, with the intent of making a humane impact on society. Send for guidelines. Acquaint yourself with our books in terms of style and quality before submitting. Many factors influence our selection process, so don't get discouraged. Nonfiction is focused on literary writing about the natural world, including living well in urban environments. We no longer publish children's biographies. We read poetry in January and June only."

MILKWEEDS FOR YOUNG READERS, 1011 Washington Ave. S., Suite 300, Minneapolis MN 55415. (612)332-3192. Fax: (612)215-2550. Website: www.milkweed.org. **Acquisitions:** Elizabeth Fitz, children's reader. Estab. 1984. Publishes hardcover and trade paperback originals. **Publishes 1-2 titles/year. 25% of books from first-time authors; 70% from unagented writers. Pays 7½% royalty on retail price. Offers varies advance.** Publishes book 1 year after acceptance of ms. Accepts simultaneous submissions. Responds in 2 months to queries. Book catalog for $1.50; ms guidelines for #10 SASE.

- "We are looking first of all for high-quality literary writitng. We publish books with the intention of making a humane impact on society." Currently emphasizing literary nonfiction about the natural world.

Fiction: For ages 8-12. Adventure, fantasy, historical, humor, mainstream/contemporary, animal, environmental. Query with SASE.

Recent Title(s): *Eccentric Islands*, by Bill Holm (nonfiction); *My Lord Bag of Rice*, by Carol Bly (fiction); *Turning Over the Earth*, by Ralph Black (poetry).

A THE MILLBROOK PRESS INC., 2 Old New Milford Rd., Brookfield CT 06804. Fax: (203)775-5643. Website: www.millbrookpress.com. Senior Vice President/Publisher: Jean Reynolds. Editor in Chief: Amy Shields. Senior Editors: Laura Walsh, Anita Holmes, Kristen Bettcher. **Acquisitions:** Kristen Vibbert, manuscript coordinator. Estab. 1989. Publishes hardcover and paperback originals. **Publishes 200 titles/year. Pays varying royalty on wholesale price or makes outright purchase. Offers variable advance.** Publishes book 1 year after acceptance of ms.

Imprints: Twenty-First Century Books, Roaring Brook

- "We no longer accept unsolicited mss. *Accepts agented submissions only.*"
- Millbrook Press publishes quality children's books of curriculum-related nonfiction for the school/library market.

Nonfiction: Children's/juvenile. Subjects include animals, anthropology/archeology, ethnic, government/politics, health/medicine, history, hobbies, multicultural, nature/environment, science, sports. Specializes in general reference, social studies, science, arts and crafts, multicultural and picutre books. *Accepts agented submissions only.*

Recent Title(s): *Let's Celebrate Earth Day*; *Space Mission Patches*; *50 American Heroes Every Kid Should Meet.*

MINNESOTA HISTORICAL SOCIETY PRESS, Minnesota Historical Society. 345 Kellogg Blvd. W., St. Paul MN 55102-1906. (651)296-2264. Fax: (651)297-1345. Website: www.mnhs.org/mhspress. Managing Editor: Ann Regan. **Acquisitions:** Gregory M. Britton, director. Estab. 1849. Publishes hardcover and trade paperback originals, trade paperback reprints. **Publishes 20 titles/year; imprint publishes 1-4 titles/year. Receives 100 queries and 25 mss/year. 50% of books from first-time authors; 100% from unagented writers. Royalties are negotiated. Offers advance.** Publishes book 14 months after acceptance of ms. Responds in 1 month. *Writer's Market* recommends allowing 2 months for reply to queries. Book catalog free.

Imprints: Borealis Books (reprints only); Midwest Reflections (memoir and personal history); Native Voices (works by American Indians)

- Minnesota Historical Society Press publishes both scholarly and general interest books that contribute to the understanding of Minnesota and Midwestern history.

Nonfiction: Regional works only. Biography, coffee table book, cookbook, illustrated book, reference. Subjects include anthropology/archeology, art/architecture, cooking/foods/nutrition, ethnic, history, memoirs, photography, regional, women's issues/studies. Query with SASE or submit proposal package including outline, 1 sample chapter(s). Reviews artwork/photos as part of ms package. Send photocopies.

Recent Title(s): *Packinghouse Daughter: A Memoir*, by Cherie Register; *The Everlasting Sky*, by Gerald Vizenor; *Last Full Measure*, by Richard Moe.

Tips: A regional connection is required.

A MINSTREL BOOKS, Pocket Books for Young Readers, Simon & Schuster, 1230 Avenue of the Americas, New York NY 10020. (212)698-7669. Website: www.simonsayskids.com. Editorial Director: Patricia MacDonald. **Acquisitions:** Attn: Manuscript proposals. Estab. 1986. Publishes hardcover originals and reprints, trade paperback originals. **Publishes 125 titles/year. Receives 1,200 queries/year. 25% of books from first-time authors. Pays 6-8% royalty on retail price. Offers variable advance.** Publishes book 2 years after acceptance of ms. Accepts simultaneous submissions. Book catalog online; ms guidelines free.

O─ "Minstrel publishes fun, kid-oriented books, the kinds kids pick for themselves, for middle grade readers, ages 8-12."

Nonfiction: Children's juvenile—middle grades, ages 8-12. Biography, children's/juvenile. Subjects include TV shows. *Accepts agented submissions only.*

Fiction: Adventure, fantasy, humor, juvenile, mystery, science fiction, suspense, animal. "Thrillers are very popular, and 'humor at school' books." No picture books.

Recent Title(s): *Snow Day*, by Mel Odom; *I Was a Sixth Grade Alien, series*, by Bruce Coville.

Tips: "Hang out with kids to make sure your dialogue and subject matter are accurate."

MITCHELL LANE PUBLISHERS, INC., P.O. Box 619, Bear DE 19701. (302)834-9646. Fax: (302)834-4164. **Acquisitions:** Barbara Mitchell, publisher. Estab. 1993. Publishes hardcover and trade paperback originals. **Publishes 22-27 titles/year. Receives 100 queries and 5 mss/year. 0% of books from first-time authors; 100% from unagented writers. Makes outright purchase on work-for-hire basis.** Publishes book 1 year after acceptance of ms. Responds to queries and proposals only if interested. Book catalog free.

O─ "Mitchell Lane publishes multicultural biographies for children and young adults."

Nonfiction: Biography, children's/juvenile. Subjects include ethnic, multicultural. *All unsolicited mss returned unopened.*

Recent Title(s): *Britney Spears*, by Ann Gaines; *Ricky Martin*, by Valerie Menard (Real-Life Reader Biographies).

Tips: "We hire writers on a 'work-for-hire' basis to complete book projects we assign. Send résumé and writing samples that do not need to be returned."

MODERN LANGUAGE ASSOCIATION OF AMERICA, 26 Broadway, 3rd Floor, New York NY 10004-1789. (646)576-5000. Fax: (646)458-0030. Director of MLA Book Publications: Martha Evans. **Acquisitions:** Joseph Gibaldi, director of book acquisitions and development. Estab. 1883. Publishes hardcover and paperback originals. **Publishes 15 titles/year. Receives 125 submissions/year. 100% from unagented writers. Pays 5-10% royalty on net receipts. Offers advance.** Publishes book 1 year after acceptance of ms. Responds in 2 months to mss. Book catalog free.

O─ The MLA publishes on current issues in literary and linguistic research and teaching of language and literature at postsecondary level.

Nonfiction: Scholarly, professional. Subjects include education, language/literature. No critical monographs. Query with SASE or submit outline.

◪ MOMENTUM BOOKS, LTD., 1174 E. Big Beaver Rd., Troy MI 48083-1934. (248)689-0936. Fax: (248)689-0956. E-mail: momentumbooks@glis.net. Website: www.momentumbooks.com. **Acquisitions:** Franklin Foxx, editor. Estab. 1987. **Publishes 6 titles/year. Receives 100 queries and 30 mss/year. 95% of books from first-time authors; 100% from unagented writers. Pays 10-15% royalty.**

O─ Momentum Books publishes regional books and general interest nonfiction.

Nonfiction: Biography, cookbook, guides. Subjects include cooking/foods/nutrition, government/politics, history, memoirs, military/war, sports, travel, women's issues/studies. Submit proposal package including outline, 3 sample chapter(s), marketing outline.

Recent Title(s): *Thus Spake David E*, by David E. Davis, Sr (automotive); *Rockin' Down the Dial*, by David Carson (regional history).

MONACELLI PRESS, 10 E. 92nd St., New York NY 10128. (212)831-0248. **Acquisitions:** Andrea Monfried, editor. Estab. 1994. Publishes hardcover and trade paperback originals. **Publishes 25-30 titles/year. Receives 100 submissions/year. 10% of books from first-time authors; 90% from unagented writers. Pays royalty on retail price. Offers occasional negotiable advance.** Publishes book 18 months after acceptance of ms. Accepts simultaneous submissions. Book catalog free.

O─ Monacelli Press produces high-quality illustrated books in architecture, fine arts, decorative arts, landscape and photography.

Nonfiction: Coffee table book. Subjects include art/architecture, photography. Query with SASE or submit outline, 1 sample chapter(s). Reviews artwork/photos as part of ms package. Send transparencies or duplicate slides best (Monacelli does not assume responsibility for unsolicited artwork; call if you are uncertain about what to send.).

Recent Title(s): *Le Corbusier and the Continual Revolution in Architecture*, by Charles Jencks; *Eric Fischl: 1970-2000*, by Robert Enright.

A MOODY PRESS, Moody Bible Institute, 820 N. LaSalle Blvd., Chicago IL 60610. (800)678-8001. Fax: (800)678-0003. Website: www.moodypress.org. Vice President/Executive Editor: Greg Thornton **Acquisitions:** Michele Straubel, acquisitions coordinator. Estab. 1894. Publishes hardcover, trade and mass market paperback originals and hardcover and mass market paperback reprints. **Publishes 60 titles/year; imprint publishes 5-10 titles/year. Receives 1,500**

queries and 2,000 mss/year. 1% of books from first-time authors; 99% from unagented writers. Royalty varies. Offers $500-5,000 advance. Publishes book 9-12 months after acceptance of ms. Responds in 2 months to queries. Book catalog for 9×12 SAE with 4 first-class stamps; ms guidelines for #10 SASE.

Imprints: Northfield Publishing, Moody Children & Youth

O⊸ "The mission of Moody Press is to educate and edify the Christian and to evangelize the non-Christian by ethically publishing conservative, evangelical Christian literature and other media for all ages around the world; and to help provide resources for Moody Bible Institute in its training of future Christian leaders."

Nonfiction: Children's/juvenile, gift book, general Christian living. Subjects include child guidance/parenting, money/ finance, religion, spirituality, women's issues/studies. "Look at our recent publications, and convince us of what sets your book apart from all the rest on bookstore shelves and why it's consistent with our publications. Many writers don't do enough research of the market or of our needs. We are no longer reviewing queries or unsolicited manuscripts unless they come to us through an agent. Unsolicited proposals will be returned only if proper postage is included. We are not able to acknowledge the receipt of your unsolicited proposal." *Accepts agented submissions only.*

Recent Title(s): *Lies Women Believe*, by Nancy Leigh DeMoss; *The New Sugar Creek Gang series*, by Pauline Hutchene Wilson and Sandy Dengler.

Tips: "Our audience consists of general, average Christian readers, not scholars. Know the market and publishers. Spend time in bookstores researching."

THOMAS MORE PUBLISHING, Resources for Christian Living,200 E. Bethany Dr., Allen TX 75002. (972)390-6923. Fax: (972)390-6620. E-mail: dhampton@rcl-enterprises.com. Website: www.thomasmore.com. **Acquisitions:** Debra Hampton, marketing and sales director (religious publishing). Publishes hardcover, trade paperback and mass market paperback originals and reprints. **Publishes 25 titles/year. Receives 250 queries and 150 mss/year. 25% of books from first-time authors; 50% from unagented writers. Pays 8-12% royalty on wholesale price. Offers $2-10,000 advance.** Publishes book 8 months after acceptance of ms. Accepts simultaneous submissions. Responds in 3 months to proposals and mss. Book catalog free.

Imprints: Christian Classics (contact: Debra Hampton)

O⊸ Thomas More specializes in self-help and religious titles.

Nonfiction: Self-help. Subjects include religion, spirituality, women's issues/studies. Submit proposal package including outline, 3 sample chapter(s). Reviews artwork/photos as part of ms package. Send photocopies.

Recent Title(s): *Forever Young: The Authorized Biography of Loretta Young*, by Joan Webster-Anderson; *Good Marriages Don't Just Happen*, by Catherine Musco Garcia-Prats and Joseph A. Garcia-Prats, M.D.

MOREHOUSE PUBLISHING CO., 4475 Linglestown Rd., Harrisburg PA 17112. (717)541-8130. Fax: (717)541-8136. E-mail: morehouse@morehousegroup.com. Website: www.morehousepublishing.com. **Acquisitions:** Debra Farrington, editorial director. Estab. 1884. Publishes hardcover and paperback originals. **Publishes 35 titles/year. 50% of books from first-time authors. Pays 10% royalty on net receipts. Offers small advance.** Publishes book 18 months after acceptance of ms. Accepts simultaneous submissions. Responds in 2 months to queries. Manuscript guidelines free.

O⊸ Morehouse Publishing publishes mainline Christian books, particularly Episcopal/Anglican works. Currently emphasizing Christian spiritual direction.

Nonfiction: Children's/juvenile (religious, ages 1-6 only). Subjects include religion (Christian), women's issues/studies, Christian spirituality, Bibical studies, Liturgies, congregational resources, devotions, meditations, issues around Christian life. "In addition to its line of books for the Episcopal church, it also publishes books of practical value from within the Christian tradition for clergy, laity, academics, professionals, and seekers." Submit outline, 1-2 sample chapter(s), résumé, market analysis.

Recent Title(s): *Echo of the Soul*, by Philip Newell; *Meditations for Church School Teachers*, by Nell and Noonan.

MORNINGSIDE HOUSE, INC., Morningside Bookshop,260 Oak St., Dayton OH 45410. (937)461-6736. Fax: (937)461-4260. E-mail: msbooks@erinet.com. Website: www.morningsidebooks.com. **Acquisitions:** Robert J. Younger, publisher. Publishes hardcover and trade paperback originals. **Publishes 10 titles/year; imprint publishes 5 titles/year. Receives 30 queries and 10 mss/year. 20% of books from first-time authors; 80% from unagented writers. Pays 10% royalty on retail price. Offers $1,000-2,000 advance.** Publishes book 15 months after acceptance of ms. Accepts simultaneous submissions. Book catalog for $4 or online.

Imprints: Morningside Press, Press of Morningside Bookshop

O⊸ Morningside publishes books for readers interested in the history of the American Civil War.

Nonfiction: Subjects include history, military/war. Query with SASE or submit complete ms. Reviews artwork/photos as part of ms package. Send photocopies.

Recent Title(s): *The Mississippi Brigade of Brig. Gen. Joseph R. Davis*, by T.P. Williams.

Tips: "We are only interested in previously unpublished material."

A⃞ **WILLIAM MORROW**, HarperCollins,10 E. 53rd St., New York NY 10022. (212)207-7000. Fax: (212)207-7145. Website: www.harpercollins.com. **Acquisitions:** Acquisitions Editor. Estab. 1926. **Publishes 200 titles/year. Receives 10,000 submissions/year. 10% of books from first-time authors. Pays standard royalty on retail price. Offers varying advance.** Publishes book 2 years after acceptance of ms.

O┓ William Morrow publishes a wide range of titles that receive much recognition and prestige. A most selective house.

Nonfiction: Biography, cookbook, how-to. Subjects include art/architecture, cooking/foods/nutrition, general, history. Length 50,000-100,000 words. *No unsolicited mss or proposals. This publisher accepts agented submissions only.*
Fiction: Publishes adult ficiton. Length 50,000-100,000 words. *No unsolicited mss or proposals. This publisher accepts agented submissions only.*
Recent Title(s): *From This Day Forward*, by Cokie and Steve Roberts; *Stiffed*, by Susan Faludi.

MORROW/AVON BOOKS, HarperCollins,10 E. 53rd St., New York NY 10022. Website: www.avonbooks.com.
Acquisitions: Editorial Submissions. Estab. 1941. Publishes hardover and mass market paperback originals and reprints.
Publishes 400 titles/year. Royalty negotiable. Offers advance. Publishes book 2 years after acceptance of ms. Accepts simultaneous submissions. Responds in 3 months to queries. Manuscript guidelines for #10 SASE.
Imprints: Eos, HarperEntertainment, HarperTorch
Nonfiction: Biography, how-to, self-help. Subjects include business/economics, government/politics, health/medicine, history, military/war, psychology (popular), sports. No textbooks. Query with SASE.
Fiction: Fantasy, mystery, romance (contemporary, historical), science fiction, suspense. Query with SASE.
Recent Title(s): *Joining*, by Johanna Lindsey.

◤◢ MOUNTAIN N'AIR BOOKS, P.O. Box 12540, La Crescenta CA 91224. (818)951-4150. Website: www.mount ain-n-air.com. **Acquisitions:** Gilberto d'Urso, owner. Publishes trade paperback originals. **Publishes 6 titles/year. Receives 50 queries and 35 mss/year. 75% of books from first-time authors; 100% from unagented writers. Pays 5-10% royalty on retail price or makes outright purchase.** Publishes book 6 months after acceptance of ms. Responds in 2 weeks to queries; 2 months to mss. Manuscript guidelines online or #10 SASE.
Imprints: Bearly Cooking
O┓ Mountain N'Air publishes books for those generally interested in the outdoors and travel.
Nonfiction: Biography, cookbook, how-to. Subjects include cooking/foods/nutrition, nature/environment, recreation, travel. Submit outline, 2 sample chapter(s). Reviews artwork/photos as part of ms package. Send photocopies.
Recent Title(s): *Thinking Out Loud Through the American West*; *An Explorer's Adventures in Tibet: An 1897 Epic*.

◤◢ MOUNTAIN PRESS PUBLISHING COMPANY, P.O. Box 2399, Missoula MT 59806-2399. (406)728-1900.
Fax: (406)728-1635. E-mail: mtnpress@montana.com. Website: www.mountainpresspublish.com. **Acquisitions:** Kathleen Ort, editor-in-chief (natural history/science/outdoors); Gwen McKenna, editor (history); Jennifer Carey, assistant editor (Roadside Geology and Tumblweed Series). Estab. 1948. Publishes hardcover and trade paperback originals.
Publishes 15 titles/year. Receives 250 submissions/year. 50% of books from first-time authors; 90% from unagented writers. Pays 7-12% royalty on wholesale price. Publishes book 2 years after acceptance of ms. Responds in 3 months to queries. Book catalog online.
O┓ "We are expanding our Roadside Geology, Geology Underfoot and Roadside History series (done on a state by state basis). We are interested in well-written regional field guides—plants, flowers and birds—and readable history and natural history."
Nonfiction: How-to. Subjects include animals, creative nonfiction, history (Western), nature/environment, regional, science (Earth). "No personal histories or journals." Query with SASE or submit outline, sample chapter(s). Reviews artwork/photos as part of ms package.
Recent Title(s): *From Earth to Herbalist: An Earth Conscious Guide to Medicinal Plants*, by Gregory Tilford; *William Henry Jackson: Framing the Frontier*, by Douglas Waitley.
Tips: "Find out what kind of books a publisher is interested in and tailor your writing to them; research markets and target your audience. Research other books on the same subjects. Make yours different. Don't present your manuscript to a publisher—*sell* it to him. Give him the information he needs to make a decision on a title. Please learn what we publish before sending your proposal. We are a 'niche' publisher."

THE MOUNTAINEERS BOOKS, 1001 SW Klickitat Way, Suite 201, Seattle WA 98134-1162. (206)223-6303.
Fax: (206)223-6306. E-mail: mbooks@mountaineers.org. Website: www.mountaineersbooks.org. **Acquisitions:** David Emblidge, editor-in-chief. Estab. 1961. Publishes 95% hardcover and trade paperback originals and 5% reprints. **Publishes 40 titles/year. Receives 150-250 submissions/year. 25% of books from first-time authors; 98% from unagented writers. Pays royalty on net receipts. Offers advance.** Publishes book 1 year after acceptance of ms. Responds in 3 months to queries. Book catalog for 9×12 SAE with $1.33 postage first-class stamps.
● See the Contests and Awards section for information on the Barbara Savage/"Miles From Nowhere" Memorial Award for outstanding adventure narratives offered by Mountaineers Books.
O┓ Mountaineers Books specializes in expert, authoritative books dealing with mountaineering, hiking, backpacking, skiing, snowshoeing, kayaking, canoeing, bicycling, etc. These can be either how-to-do-it or where-to-do-it (guidebooks). Currently emphasizing regional conservation and natural history.
Nonfiction: Children's/juvenile, how-to (outdoor), guidebooks for national and international adventure travel. Subjects include nature/environment, recreation, regional, sports (non-competitive self-propelled), translation, travel, natural history, conservation. Accepts nonfiction translations. Looks for "expert knowledge, good organization." Also interested in nonfiction adventure narratives. Does *not* want to see "anything dealing with hunting, fishing or motorized travel." Submit outline, 2 sample chapter(s), author bio.

Recent Title(s): *100 Classic Hikes in Colorado*, by Warren; *Climbing: From Gym to Crag: Building Skills for Real Rock*, by Lewis and Cauthorn.
Tips: "The type of book the writer has the best chance of selling to our firm is an authoritative guidebook (*in our field*) to a specific area not otherwise covered; or a how-to that is better than existing competition (again, *in our field*)."

[A] MULTNOMAH PUBLISHERS, INC., P.O. Box 1720, Sisters OR 97759. (541)549-1144. Website: www.multnomahbooks.com. **Acquisitions:** Rod Morris, editor (general fiction). Estab. 1987. Publishes hardcover and trade paperback originals. **Publishes 100 titles/year. 2% of books from first-time authors; 50% from unagented writers. Pays royalty on wholesale price. Offers advance.** Publishes book 1-2 years after acceptance of ms. Accepts simultaneous submissions. Manuscript guidelines online or for #10 SASE.
Imprints: Multnomah Books, Multnomah Gifts, Multnomah Fiction
 • Multnomah is currently not accepting unsolicited queries, proposals or manuscripts. Queries will be accepted thruogh agents and at writers' conferences at which a Multnomah representative is present.
 O→ Multnomah publishes books on Christian living and family enrichment, devotional and gift books and fiction.
Nonfiction: Children's/juvenile, coffee table book, gift book, humor, illustrated book. Subjects include child guidance/parenting, humor, religion, Christian living. *Accepts agented submissions only.*
Fiction: Adventure, historical, humor, mystery, religious, romance, suspense, western. *Accepts agented submissions only.*
Recent Title(s): *The Prayer of Jabez*, by Bruce Wilkinson (nonfiction); *The Veritas Conflict*, by Shaunti Feldhahn (fiction); *Diary of a Teenage Girl*, by Melody Carlson (fiction).

MUSTANG PUBLISHING CO., P.O. Box 770426, Memphis TN 38177-0426. Website: www.mustangpublishing.com. **Acquisitions:** Rollin Riggs, editor. Estab. 1983. Publishes hardcover and trade paperback originals. **Publishes 10 titles/year. Receives 1,000 submissions/year. 50% of books from first-time authors; 90% from unagented writers. Pays 6-8% royalty on retail price. Offers advance.** Publishes book 1 year after acceptance of ms. Accepts simultaneous submissions. Responds in 1 month. *Writer's Market* recommends allowing 2 months for reply to queries. Book catalog for $2 and #10 SASE. No phone calls, please.
 O→ Mustang publishes general interest nonfiction for an adult audience.
Nonfiction: How-to, humor, self-help. Subjects include Americana, general, hobbies, humor, recreation, sports, travel. "Our needs are very general—humor, travel, how-to, etc.—for the 18-to 60-year-old market." Query with SASE or submit outline, sample chapter(s). Reviews artwork/photos as part of ms package. Send photocopies.
Recent Title(s): *Medical School Admissions: The Insider's Guide*, by Zebala (career); *The Complete Book of Golf Games*, by Johnston (sports).
Tips: "From the proposals we receive, it seems that many writers never go to bookstores and have no idea what sells. Before you waste a lot of time on a nonfiction book idea, ask yourself, 'How often have my friends and I actually *bought* a book like this?' We are not interested in first-person travel accounts or memoirs."

[A] THE MYSTERIOUS PRESS, Warner Books, 1271 Avenue of the Americas, New York NY 10020. (212)522-7200. Fax: (212)522-7990. Website: www.twbookmark. **Acquisitions:** Sara Ann Freed, editor-in-chief. Estab. 1976. Publishes hardcover, trade paperback and mass market editions. **Publishes 36-45 titles/year. Pays standard, but negotiable, royalty on retail price. Offers negotiable advance.** Publishes book an average of 1 year after acceptance of ms. Responds in 2 months to queries.
 O→ The Mysterious Press publishes well-written crime/mystery/suspense fiction.
Fiction: Mystery, suspense, Crime/detective novels. No short stories. *Accepts agented submissions only.*
Recent Title(s): *Bad News*, by Donald Westlake; *The Red Room*, by Nicci French.

[N] MYSTIC SEAPORT MUSEUM, 75 Greenmanville Ave., Mystic CT 06355-0990. (860)572-0711. Fax: (860)572-5326. **Acquisitions:** Joseph Gribbins, publications director. Estab. 1970. Publishes hardcover and trade paperback originals and reprints. **Publishes 3-4 titles/year. Pays 15% royalty on wholesale price. Offers advance.** Responds in 3 months to proposals.
Imprints: American Maritime Library
 O→ "We strive to publish significant new work in the areas of American maritime, yachting and small-craft history and biography." Mystic Seaport Museum has enlarged its focus from New England to North America.
Nonfiction: Biography, how-to, reference, studies of economic, social, artistic, or musical elements of American maritime (not naval) history; books on traditional boat and ship types and construction (how to). Subjects include Americana, art/architecture, history. "We need serious, well-documented biographies, studies of economic, social, artistic, or musical elements of American maritime (not naval) history; books on traditional boat and ship types and construction (how-to). We are now interested in all North American maritime history—not, as in the past, principally New England. We like to see anything and everything, from queries to finished work." Query with SASE or submit outline, 3 sample chapter(s).
Recent Title(s): *America and the Sea: A Maritime History*, Benjamin W. Labaree, et. al.

THE NAIAD PRESS, INC., P.O. Box 10543, Tallahassee FL 32302. (850)539-5965. Fax: (850)539-9731. Website: www.naiadpress.com. **Acquisitions:** Barbara Grier, editorial director. Estab. 1973. Publishes paperback originals. **Pub-**

lishes 32 titles/year. Receives 1,500 submissions/year. 20% of books from first-time authors; 99% from unagented writers. Pays 15% royalty on wholesale or retail price. Publishes book 2 years after acceptance of ms. Responds in 4 months to queries. Book catalog for 6×9 SAE with $1.50 first-class stamps.

O-π The Naiad Press publishes lesbian fiction, preferably lesbian/feminist fiction.

Fiction: Fantasy (lesbian theme), gay/lesbian, mystery (lesbian theme), short story collections (lesbian themes). "We are not impressed with the 'oh woe' school and prefer realistic (i.e., happy) novels. We emphasize fiction and are now heavily reading manuscripts in that area. We are working in a lot of genre fiction—mysteries, short stories, fantasy—all with lesbian themes, of course. We have instituted an inhouse anthology series, featuring short stories only by our own authors (authors who have published full length fiction with us or those signed to do so)." Query with SASE.

Recent Title(s): *She Walks in Beauty*, by Nicole Conn.

Tips: "There is tremendous world-wide demand for lesbian mysteries from lesbian authors published by lesbian presses, and we are doing several such series. We are no longer seeking science fiction. Manuscripts under 50,000 words have twice as good a chance as over 50,000."

NARWHAL PRESS, INC., 1629 Meeting St., Charleston SC 29405-9408. (843)853-0510. Fax: (843)853-2528. E-mail: shipwrex@aol.com. Website: www.shipwrecks.com. **Acquisitions:** Dr. E. Lee Spence, chief editor (marine archaeology, shipwrecks); Dr. Robert Stockton, managing editor (novels, marine histories, military). Estab. 1994. Publishes hardcover and quality trade paperback originals. **Publishes 10 titles/year. Receives 100 queries and 50 mss/year. 75% of books from first-time authors; 95% from unagented writers. Pays 10-15% royalty on wholesale price. Offers $1,000-2,000 advance.** Publishes book at least 3 months, depending on revisions and other considerations after acceptance of ms. Accepts simultaneous submissions. Responds in 2 weeks to queries; 1 month to mss.

O-π Narwhal Press specializes in books about shipwrecks and marine archaeology and military history.

Nonfiction: "We are constantly searching for titles of interest to shipwreck divers, marine archaeologists, Civil War buffs, etc., but we are expanding our titles to include novels, children's books, modern naval history, World War II, Korea, Vietnam and personal memoirs." Biography, children's/juvenile, how-to, reference. Subjects include Americana, anthropology/archeology, art/architecture, history, memoirs, military/war, Civil War. Query with SASE or submit outline, 3 sample chapter(s). Reviews artwork/photos as part of ms package. Send photocopies.

Fiction: Historical, juvenile, mainstream/contemporary, military/war, young adult, dive related. "We prefer novels with a strong historical context. We invite writers to submit fiction about undersea adventures. Best to call or write first." Query with SASE or submit 3 sample chapter(s), synopsis.

Recent Title(s): *The Collector*, by William Kerr; *The Hunley*, by Mark Rogan.

Tips: "Become an expert in your subject area. Polish and proofread your writing."

NATUREGRAPH PUBLISHERS, INC., P.O. Box 1047, Happy Camp CA 96039. (530)493-5353. Fax: (530)493-5240. E-mail: nature@sisqtel.net or naturgraph@aol.com. Website: naturegraph.com. Keven Brown, editor.**Acquisitions:** Barbara Brown, editor-in-chief. Estab. 1946. Publishes trade paperback originals. **Publishes 5 titles/year. Pays 8-10% royalty on wholesale price.** Responds in 1 month to queries; 2 months to mss. Book catalog free.

O-π "Naturegraph publishes books to help people learn about the natural world and Native American culture. Not so technically written to scare away beginners." Emphasizing natural history and Native American history (but not political).

Nonfiction: Primarily publishes nonfiction for the layman in natural history (biology, geology, ecology, astronomy); American Indian (historical and contemporary); outdoor living (backpacking, wild edibles, etc.). How-to. Subjects include ethnic, nature/environment, science (natural history: biology, geology, ecology, astronomy), crafts. "Our primary niches are nature and Native American subjects with adult level, non-technical language and scientific accuracy. First, send for our free catalog. Study what kind of books we have already published." Query with SASE or submit outline, 2 sample chapter(s).

Recent Title(s): *Anasazi Legends*, by Lou Cuevas.

Tips: "Please—always send a stamped reply envelope. Publishers get hundreds of manuscripts yearly; not just yours."

THE NAUTICAL & AVIATION PUBLISHING CO., 1250 Fairmont Ave., Mt. Pleasant SC 29464. (843)856-0561. Fax: (843)856-3164. E-mail: nautical.aviation.publishing@worldnet.att.net. Website: www.nauticalaviation.com. **Acquisitions:** Heather Parker, acquisitions editor. Estab. 1979. Publishes hardcover originals and reprints. **Publishes 10-12 titles/year. Receives 500 submissions/year. Pays 10-14% royalty on net receipts. Offers rare advance.** Accepts simultaneous submissions. Book catalog free.

O-π The Nautical & Aviation Publishing Co. publishes naval and military history fiction and reference.

Nonfiction: Reference. Subjects include military/war (American), naval history. Query with SASE or submit 3 sample chapter(s), synopsis. Reviews artwork/photos as part of ms package.

Fiction: Historical. Submit outline, synopsis.

Recent Title(s): *Sea of Glory*, by Nathan Miller.

Tips: "We are primarily a nonfiction publisher, but will review historical fiction of military interest with strong literary merit."

✦ NAVAL INSTITUTE PRESS, US Naval Institute, 291 Wood Ave., Annapolis MD 21402-5035. (410)268-6110. Fax: (410)295-1084. E-mail: esecunda@usni.org. Website: www.usni.org. Press Director: Ronald Chambers.**Acquisitions:** Paul Wilderson, executive editor; Tom Cutler, senior acquisitions editor; Eric Mills, acquisitions editor. Estab.

1873. **Publishes 80-90 titles/year. Receives 700-800 submissions/year. 50% of books from first-time authors; 85% from unagented writers. Pays 5-10% royalty on net receipts. Offers advance.** Publishes book 1 year after acceptance of ms. Book catalog for 9×12 SASE; ms guidelines for #10 SASE.
Imprints: Bluejacket Books (paperback reprints)
○→ The U.S. Naval Institute Press publishes general and scholarly books of professional, scientific, historical and literary interest to the naval and maritime community.
Nonfiction: "We are interested in naval and maritime subjects and in broad military topics, including government policy and funding." Biography. Subjects include government/politics, history, science, women's issues/studies, tactics, strategy, navigation, aviation, technology and others. Query with SASE.
Fiction: Historical, military/war. Limited to fiction on military and naval themes.
Recent Title(s): *Punk's War*, by Ward Carroll (fiction); *Nelson Speaks*, by Joseph Callo (nonfiction).

[N] NAVPRESS PUBLISHING GROUP, P.O. Box 35001, Colorado Springs CO 80935. Website: www.navpress.com. Publishes hardcover, trade paperback and mass market paperback originals and reprints. **Publishes 45 titles/year. 25% of books from first-time authors; 90% from unagented writers. Pays royalty.** Book catalog free.
Imprints: Pinion Press
Nonfiction: Reference, self-help, inspirational/Christian living/Bible studies. Subjects include business/economics, child guidance/parenting, religion, spirituality, marriage. "We do not accept unsolicited mss. Unsolicited mss will not be responded to without an SASE."

[X] NEAL-SCHUMAN PUBLISHERS, INC., 100 Varick St., New York NY 10013. (212)925-8650. Fax: (212)219-8916. E-mail: charles@neal-schuman.com. Website: www.neal-schuman.com. **Acquisitions:** Charles Harmon, director of publishing. Estab. 1976. Publishes hardcover and trade paperback originals. **Publishes 30 titles/year. Receives 500 submissions/year. 75% of books from first-time authors; 90% from unagented writers. Pays 10% royalty on net receipts. Offers infrequent advance.** Publishes book 4 months after acceptance of ms. Responds in 1 month to proposals. Book catalog and ms guidelines free.
○→ "Neal-Schuman publishes books about libraries, information science and the use of information technology, especially in education and libraries."
Nonfiction: Reference, technical, textbook, professional. Subjects include computers/electronic, education, software, Internet guides, library and information science. "We are looking for many books about the Internet." Submit proposal package including outline, sample chapter(s), résumé, preface.
Recent Title(s): *Internet Power Searching*, by Phil Bradley.

THOMAS NELSON PUBLISHERS, Nelson Word Publishing Group, Box 141000, Nashville TN 37214-1000. (615)889-9000. Website: www.thomasnelson.com. **Acquisitions:** Acquisitions Editor. **Publishes 150-200 titles/year. Pays royalty on net receipts Rates negotiated for each project. Offers advance.** Publishes book 1-2 years after acceptance of ms. Accepts simultaneous submissions. Responds in 3 months to queries.
Imprints: Janet Thoma Books, Oliver-Nelson Books, Nelson Books, Word Publishing, Rutledge-Hill, J. Countryman
• Corporate address does not accept unsolicited mss; no phone queires.
○→ Thomas Nelson publishes Christian lifestyle nonfiction and fiction.
Nonfiction: Reference, self-help. Subjects include religion, spirituality, adult inspirational, motivational, devotional, Christian living, prayer and evangelism, Bible study. Query with SASE or submit 1 sample chapter(s), résumé, 1-page synopsis.
Fiction: Seeking successfully published commercial fiction authors who write for adults from a Christian perspective. Query with SASE or submit 1 sample chapter(s), résumé, synopsis.
Recent Title(s): *Success God's Way*, by Charles Stanley; *The Death of Innocence*, by John and Patsy Ramsey.

TOMMY NELSON, Thomas Nelson, Inc., P.O. Box 141000, Nashville TN 37214-1000. (615)889-9000. Fax: (615)902-3330. Website: www.tommynelson.com. Publishes hardcover and trade paperback originals. **Publishes 50-75 titles/year. Receives 1,000 mss/year. 5% of books from first-time authors; 50% from unagented writers. Pays royalty on wholesale price or makes outright purchase. Offers $1,000 minimum advance.** Publishes book 18 months after acceptance of ms.
Imprints: Word Kids
○→ Tommy Nelson publishes children's Christian nonfiction and fiction for boys and girls up to age 14. "We honor God and serve people through books, videos, software and Bibles for children that improve the lives of our customers."
Nonfiction: Children's/juvenile. Subjects include religion (Christian evangelical). *No unsolicited submissions.*
Fiction: Adventure, juvenile, mystery, picture books, religious. "No stereotypical characters without depth." No unsolicited submissions.
Recent Title(s): *Hangman's Curse*, by Frank Paretti; *Small Gifts in God's Hands*, by Max Lucado.
Tips: "Know the CBA market. Check out the Christian bookstores to see what sells and what is needed."

[A] NEW AMERICAN LIBRARY, Penguin Putnam Inc., 375 Hudson St., New York NY 10014. (212)366-2000. Website: www.penguinputnam.com. Publisher: Louise Burke. Executive Director: Carolyn Nichols. **Acquisitions:** Ellen Edwards, executive editor (commercial women's fiction—mainstream novels and contemporary romances; mysteries in

a series and single title suspense; nonfiction of all types for a general audience and historical); Laura Anne Gilman, executive editor (science fiction/fantasy/horror, mystery series, New Age); Jennifer Heddle, associate editor (science fiction/fantasy, pop culture and general nonfiction, historical fiction, erotica); Audrey LaFehr, executive editor (contemporary and historical romance, women's suspense, multicultural fiction); Hilary Ross, associate executive editor (romances, Regencies); Doug Grad, senior editor (thrillers, suspense novels, international intrigue, technothrillers, military fiction and nonfiction, adventure nonfiction); Genny Ostertag, senior editor (mysteries, suspense, commerical women's fiction); Dan Slater, senior editor (historical fiction, adult westerns, thrillers, military fiction and nonfiction, true crime, media tie-ins); Cecilia Oh, associate editor (romance, Regency, commercial women's fiction, inspirational nonfiction); Jennifer Jahner, assistant editor (suspense, multicultural commercial fiction, women's fiction); Marie Timell, senior editor (practical nonfiction, self-help, health, nutrition, New Age, inspirational, visionary fiction). Publishes mass market paperback originals and reprints. **Publishes 500 titles/year. Receives 20,000 queries and 10,000 mss/year. 30-40% of books from first-time authors; 5% from unagented writers. Pays negotiable royalty. Offers negotiable advance.** Publishes book 1-2 years after acceptance of ms. Responds in 6 months to queries.
Imprints: Mentor, Onyx, ROC, Signet, Signet Classic, Signet Reference

  O→ NAL publishes commercial fiction and nonfiction for the popular audience.

Nonfiction: Biography, how-to, reference, self-help. Subjects include animals, child guidance/parenting, cooking/foods/nutrition, ethnic, health/medicine, language/literature, military/war, money/finance, psychology, sports, women's issues/studies. "Looking for reference and annual books." *Accepts agented submissions only.*
Fiction: Erotica, ethnic, fantasy, historical, horror, literary, mainstream/contemporary, mystery, occult, romance, science fiction, suspense, western. "Looking for writers who can deliver a book a year (or faster) of consistent quality." *Accepts agented submissions only.*
Recent Title(s): *Suspicion of Betrayal*, by Barbara Parker; *The Medusa Stone*, by Jack DuBrul.

NEW CANAAN PUBLISHING COMPANY, INC., P.O. Box 752, New Canaan CT 06840. (203)966-3408. Fax: (203)966-3408. E-mail: info@newcanaanpublishing.com. Website: www.newcanaanpublishing.com. **Acquisitions:** Kathy Mittelstadt, vice president (children's fiction). Publishes hardcover trade and paperback originals and reprints. **Publishes 4 titles/year. Receives 500 queries and 500 mss/year. 50% of books from first-time authors; 90% from unagented writers. Pays 8-10% royalty on wholesale price. Offers occasional advance.** Publishes book 1 year after acceptance of ms. Responds in 3 months to queries and proposals; 4 months to mss. Book catalog and ms guidelines online or #10 SASE.

  O→ New Canaan publishes children's, young adult, and Christian titles. "We are developing two lists (1)children's/young adult titles, fiction or educational (science/history/religion); and (2) Christian titles (fiction or nonfiction)."

Nonfiction: Children's/juvenile. Subjects include education, religion, science. Submit proposal package including outline, 2 sample chapter(s) or submit complete ms. "We no longer return submissions." Reviews artwork/photos as part of ms package. Send photocopies.
Fiction: Juvenile, religious (Christian), young adult. Query with SASE or submit proposal package including 2 sample chapter(s), synopsis, SASE, or submit complete ms.
Recent Title(s): *Rock Your World*, by Bill Scott; *Rainbows and Other Promises*, by Laurie Swinwood.

THE NEW ENGLAND PRESS, INC., P.O. Box 575, Shelburne VT 05482. (802)863-2520. Fax: (802)863-1510. E-mail: nep@together.net. Website: www.nepress.com. **Acquisitions:** Mark Wanner, managing editor. Estab. 1978. Publishes hardcover and trade paperback originals. **Publishes 6-8 titles/year. Receives 500 queries and 200 mss/year. 50% of books from first-time authors; 90% from unagented writers. Pays royalty on wholesale price.** Publishes book 15 months after acceptance of ms. Accepts simultaneous submissions. Responds in 3 months to queries. Book catalog free.

  O→ The New England Press publishes high-quality trade books of regional northern New England interest. Currently emphasizing young adult biography. De-emphasizing railroading.

Nonfiction: Biography, illustrated book, young adult. Subjects include history, nature/environment, regional, world affairs, Vermontiana. "Nonfiction submissions must be based in Vermont and have northern New England topics. No memoirs or family histories. Identify potential markets and ways to reach them in cover letter." Query with SASE or submit outline, 2 sample chapter(s). Reviews artwork/photos as part of ms package. Send photocopies.
Fiction: Historical (Vermont, New Hampshire, Maine). "We look for very specific subject matters based on Vermont history and heritage. We are also interested in historical novels for young adults based in New Hampshire and Maine. We do not publish contemporary adult fiction of any kind." Query with SASE or submit 2 sample chapter(s), synopsis.
Recent Title(s): *Vermont Owner's Manual*, by Frank Bryan and Bill Mares (nonfiction); *Robert Frost: The People, Places, and Stones Behind His New England Poetry*, by Lea Newman (poetry).
Tips: "Our readers are interested in all aspects of Vermont and northern New England, including hobbyists (railroad books) and students (young adult fiction and biography). No agent is needed, but our market is extremely specific and our volume is low, so send a query or outline and writing samples first. Sending the whole manuscript is discouraged. We will not accept projects that are still under development or give advances."

NEW HARBINGER PUBLICATIONS, 5674 Shattuck Ave., Oakland CA 94609. (510)652-0215. Fax: (510)652-5472. E-mail: nhelp@newharbinger.com. Website: www.Newharbinger.com. **Acquisitions:** Catharine Sutker, acquisitions manager; Jeuli Gastwirth, senior acquisitions editor. Estab. 1979. **Publishes 50 titles/year. Receives 1,000 queries**

and 300 mss/year. **60% of books from first-time authors; 80% from unagented writers. Pays 12% royalty on net receipts. Offers $0-5,000 advance.** Publishes book 1 year after acceptance of ms. Accepts simultaneous submissions. Responds in 1 month to queries and proposals; 2 months to mss. Book catalog and ms guidelines free.

> **O⊸** "We look for self-help titles on psychology, health and balanced living titles that teach the average reader how to master essential skills. Our books are also read by mental health professionals who want simple, clear explanations of important psychological techniques and health issues."

Nonfiction: Self-help (psychology/health). Subjects include gay/lesbian, health/medicine, psychology, women's issues/studies, balanced living, anger management, anxiety, coping. "Authors need to be a qualified psychotherapist or health practitioner to publish with us." Submit proposal package including outline, 2 sample chapter(s), competing titles and a compelling, supported reason why the book is unique.

Recent Title(s): *The Anxiety & Phobia Workbook, 3rd edition*, by Edmund J. Bourne; *Rosacea: A Self-Help Guide*, by Arlen Brownstein; *Undefended Love*, by Jett Psaris and Marlena Lyons.

Tips: Audience includes psychotherapists and lay readers wanting step-by-step strategies to solve specific problems. "Our definition of a self-help psychology or health book is one that teaches essential life skills. The primary goal is to train the reader so that, after reading the book, he or she can deal more effectively with health and/or psychological challenges."

NEW HOPE PUBLISHERS, Women's Missionary Union, P.O. Box 12065, Birmingham AL 35202-2065. (205)991-8100. Fax: (205)991-4015. E-mail: new_hope@wmu.org. Website: www.newhopepubl.com. **Acquisitions:** Acquisitions Editor. **Publishes 18-24 titles/year. Receives several hundred queries/year. Large% of books from first-time authors; large% from unagented writers. Pays royalty on net receipts.** Publishes book 2 years after acceptance of ms. Responds in 6 weeks to mss. Book catalog for 9×12 SAE with 3 first-class stamps; ms guidelines for #10 SASE.

Imprints: New Hope

> **O⊸** "Our goal is to create unique books that help women and families to grow in Christ and share His hope."

Nonfiction: "We publish books dealing with all facets of Christian life for women and families, including health, discipleship, missions, ministry, Bible studies, spiritual development, parenting, and marriage. We currently do not accept adult fiction or children's picture books. We are particularly interested in niche categories (such as mission trips, domestic violence, practicing forgiveness) and books on lifestyle development and change (blended families, retirement, etc)." Children's/juvenile (religion). Subjects include child guidance/parenting (from Christian perspective), education (Christian church), health/medicine (Christian), multicultural, religion (spiritual development, Bible study, life situations from Christian perspective, ministry), women's issues/studies (Christian), church leadership, evangelism (Christian faith—must relate to missions work, cultural or multicultural issues). Prefers a query and prospectus but will evaluate a complete ms.

Recent Title(s): *A Woman's Guide to True Contentment*, by Rhonda H. Kelley; *Growing Weary Doing Good? Encouragement for Exhausted Women*, by Karla Worley; *Extraordinary Living: What Happens When God Works Through You*, by Andrea Mullins.

▐▲ NEW HORIZON PRESS, P.O. Box 669, Far Hills NJ 07931. (908)604-6311. Fax: (908)604-6330. E-mail: nhp@newhorizonpressbooks.com. Website: www.newhorizonpressbooks.com. **Acquisitions:** Dr. Joan S. Dunphy, publisher (nonfiction, social cause, true crime). Estab. 1983. Publishes hardcover and trade paperback originals. **Publishes 12 titles/year. 90% of books from first-time authors; 50% from unagented writers. Pays standard royalty on net receipts. Offers advance.** Publishes book 2 years after acceptance of ms. Accepts simultaneous submissions. Book catalog and ms guidelines free.

Imprints: Small Horizons

> **O⊸** New Horizon publishes adult nonfiction featuring true stories of uncommon heroes, true crime, social issues and self help. Introducing a new line of children's self-help.

Nonfiction: Biography, children's/juvenile, how-to, self-help. Subjects include child guidance/parenting, creative nonfiction, government/politics, health/medicine, nature/environment, psychology, women's issues/studies, true crime. Submit proposal package including outline, 3 sample chapter(s), résumé, author bio, photo, marketing information.

Recent Title(s): *Deadly Deception*, by Brenda Gunn and Shannon Richardson.

Tips: "We are a small publisher, thus it is important that the author/publisher have a good working relationship. The author must be willing to sell his book."

▐▲ NEW VICTORIA PUBLISHERS, P.O. Box 27, Norwich VT 05055-0027. (802)649-5297. Fax: (802)649-5297. E-mail: newvic@aol.com. Website: www.opendoor.com/NewVic/. Editor: ReBecca Beguin. **Acquisitions:** Claudia Lamperti, editor. Estab. 1976. Publishes trade paperback originals. **Publishes 8-10 titles/year. Receives 100 submissions/year. 50% of books from first-time authors; large% from unagented writers. Pays 10% royalty. Offers advance.** Publishes book 1 year after acceptance of ms. Book catalog free.

> **O⊸** "New Victoria is a nonprofit literary and cultural organization producing the finest in lesbian fiction and nonfiction." Emphasizing fantasy. De-emphasizing coming-of-age stories.

Nonfiction: Biography. Subjects include gay/lesbian, history (feminist), women's issues/studies. "We are interested in feminist history or biography and interviews with or topics relating to lesbians." No poetry. Submit outline, sample chapter(s).

Fiction: Adventure, erotica, fantasy, feminist, historical, humor, mystery, romance, science fiction, western. "We will consider most anything if it is well written and appeals to lesbian/feminist audience. Hard copy only—no disks." Submit outline, sample chapter(s), synopsis.

Recent Title(s): *Queer Japan*, by Barbara Summerhawk (nonfiction); *Talk Show*, by Melissa Hartman (fiction).

Tips: "Try to appeal to a specific audience and not write for the general market. We're still looking for well-written, hopefully humorous, lesbian fiction and well-researched biography or nonfiction."

NEW WORLD LIBRARY, 14 Pamaron Way, Novato CA 94949. (415)884-2100. Fax: (415)884-2199. E-mail: escort@ nwlib.com. Website: www.newworldlibrary.com. Publisher: Marc Allen. Senior Editor: Jason Gardner. **Acquisitions:** Georgia Hughes, editorial director. Estab. 1979. Publishes hardcover and trade paperback originals and reprints. **Publishes 35 titles/year. 10% of books from first-time authors; 50% from unagented writers. Pays 12-20% royalty on wholesale price for hardcover. Offers $0-30,000 advance.** Publishes book 18 months after acceptance of ms. Accepts simultaneous submissions. Responds in 3 months to queries. Book catalog and ms guidelines free.

Imprints: Nataraj, H.J. Kramer

   ○→ NWL is dedicated to publishing books that inspire and challenge us to improve the quality of our lives and our world.

Nonfiction: Gift book, self-help. Subjects include business/economics (prosperity), ethnic (African/American, Native American), health/medicine (natural), money/finance, nature/environment, psychology, religion, women's issues/studies, nutrition, personal growth, parenting. Query with SASE or submit outline, 1 sample chapter(s), author bio. Reviews artwork/photos as part of ms package. Send photocopies.

Recent Title(s): *A Toolbox for Our Daughters*, by Annette Geffert and Diane Brown; *The Power of Now*, by Eckhart Tolle; *The Mystic Heart*, by Wayne Teasdale.

NEW YORK UNIVERSITY PRESS, 838 Broadway, New York NY 10003. (212)998-2575. Fax: (212)995-3833. Website: www.nyupress.nyu.edu. **Acquisitions:** Eric Zinner (cultural studies, literature, media, history); Jennifer Hammer (Jewish studies, psychology, religion, women's studies); Stephen Magro (social sciences). Estab. 1916. Hardcover and trade paperback originals. **Publishes 150 titles/year. Receives 800-1,000 queries/year. 30% of books from first-time authors; 90% from unagented writers. Pays royalty on net receipts.** Publishes book 8 months after acceptance of ms. Accepts simultaneous submissions. Responds in 1 month (peer reviewed) to proposals.

   ○→ New York University Press embraces ideological diversity. "We often publish books on the same issue from different poles to generate dialogue, engender and resist pat categorizations."

Nonfiction: Subjects include anthropology/archeology, business/economics, ethnic, gay/lesbian, government/politics, history, language/literature, military/war, psychology, regional, religion, sociology, sports, women's issues/studies. Query with SASE or submit proposal package including outline, 1 sample chapter(s). Reviews artwork/photos as part of ms package. Send photocopies.

NEWJOY PRESS, P.O. Box 3437, Ventura CA 93006. (800)876-1373. Fax: (805)984-0503. E-mail: njpublish@earthlin k.com. **Acquisitions:** Joy Nyquist, publisher. Estab. 1993. Publishes trade paperback originals. **Publishes 4 titles/year. 95% of books from first-time authors. Pays 10-20% royalty on retail price.** Publishes book 8-12 months after acceptance of ms. Responds in 2 months to queries. Book catalog and ms guidelines free.

   ○→ Newjoy Press focuses on books that offer clear and usable information about travel, history, self-help and chemical dependency.

Nonfiction: Subjects include history (told in a story fashion that is easy to follow and read), travel, self-help, health, chemical dependency. A detailed marketing plan is essential to acceptance of a proposed book and it will be part of a contract between author and publisher. Submissions must be on disk. Submit proposal package including outline, sample chapter(s), SASE, author's qualifications.

Recent Title(s): *The Frugal Traveler: How to See More of the World for Less*; *Travel Light: How to Go Anywhere in the World with Only One Suitcase*.

Tips: "Experience in public speaking and marketing are big pluses."

[N] NEWMARKET PRESS, 18 E. 48th St., New York NY 10017. (212)832-3575. Fax: (212)832-3629. E-mail: mailbox@newmarketpress.com. President/Publisher: Esther Margolis. **Acquisitions:** Keith Hollaman, managing editor; Michelle Howry, editor. Publishes hardcover and trade paperback originals and reprints. **Publishes 25-30 titles/year. 10% of books from first-time authors; 20% from unagented writers. Pays royalty. Offers varied advance.** Publishes book 1 year after acceptance of ms. Accepts simultaneous submissions. Responds in 3 months to queries, proposals and mss. Manuscript guidelines for #10 SASE.

   ○→ Currently emphasizing movie tie-in/companion books, health, psychology, parenting. De-emphasizing fiction.

Nonfiction: "Our focus is on parenting and health titles, and on finance books." Biography, coffee table book, self-help. Subjects include child guidance/parenting, cooking/foods/nutrition, general, health/medicine, history, memoirs, personal finance, film/performing arts. Query with SASE or submit proposal package including outline, 1-3 sample chapter(s), author info explaining why you're the best person to write this book.

Recent Title(s): *Mommy, My Head Hurts: A Doctor's Guide to Your Child's Headache*, by Sarah Cheyette, MD (parenting/childcare); *The Art of the Matrix*, edited by Spencer Lamm (film).

NICHOLS PUBLISHING, P.O. Box 6036, E. Brunswick NJ 08816. (732)297-2862. Fax: (732)940-0549. **Acquisitions:** Fran Lubrano, editorial director. Estab. 1979. Publishes training and management reference books. Publishes hardcover and paperback originals. **Publishes 50 titles/year. 98% from unagented writers. Pays negotiable royalty. Offers negotiable advance.** Publishes book 9 months after acceptance of ms. Accepts simultaneous submissions. Responds in 1 month. *Writer's Market* recommends allowing 2 months for reply to queries. Book catalog free.
Nonfiction: Reference, technical. Subjects include business/economics, education, management, training. Submit outline, sample chapter(s).
Recent Title(s): *Assembling Course Materials*, by Nicolay and Barrett.
Tips: "No longer seeking books on architecture, computers/electronics, or engineering."

NO STARCH PRESS, 555 De Haro St., Suite 250, San Francisco CA 94107. (415)863-9900. Fax: (415)863-9950. E-mail: info@nostarch.com. Website: www.nostarch.com. **Acquisitions:** William Pollock, publisher. Estab. 1994. Publishes trade paperback originals. **Publishes 10-12 titles/year. Receives 100 queries and 5 mss/year. 80% of books from first-time authors; 90% from unagented writers. Pays 10-15% royalty on wholesale price. Offers advance.** Publishes book 4 months after acceptance of ms. Accepts simultaneous submissions. Book catalog free.
Imprints: Linux Journal Press
   O–π No Starch Press publishes informative, easy to read computer books for non-computer people to help them get the most from their hardware and software. Currently emphasizing Linux, computer graphics and Internet security. "More stuff, less fluff."
Nonfiction: How-to, reference, technical. Subjects include computers/electronic, hobbies, software (Linux). Submit outline, 1 sample chapter(s), author bio, market rationale. Reviews artwork/photos as part of ms package. Send photocopies.
Recent Title(s): *Steal This Computer Book 2*, by Wallace Wang; *Linux Music and Sound*, by Dave Phillips.
Tips: "No fluff—content, content, content or just plain fun. Understand how your book fits into the market. Tell us why someone, anyone, will buy your book. Be enthusiastic."

Ⓝ NODIN PRESS, Micawber's Inc., 525 N. Third St., Minneapolis MN 55401. (612)333-6300. Fax: (612)359-5737. E-mail: ardye@bookmen.com. **Acquisitions:** Norton Stillman, publisher. Publishes hardcover and trade paperback originals. **Publishes 4 titles/year. Receives 20 queries and 20 mss/year. 75% of books from first-time authors; 100% from unagented writers. Pays 10% royalty. Offers $250-1,000 advance.** Publishes book 20 months after acceptance of ms. Accepts simultaneous submissions. Responds in 6 months to queries. Book catalog and ms guidelines free.
   O–π Nodin Press publishes Minnesota regional titles: nonfiction, memoir, sports, poetry.
Nonfiction: Biography, regional guide book. Subjects include history (ethnic), regional, sports, travel. Query with SASE.
Recent Title(s): *Frozen Memories: Celebrating a Century of Minnesota Hockey*, by R. Bernstein (nonfiction); *Downtown: A History of Downtown Minneapolis and St. Paul*, by D. Anderson (anthology); *33 Minnesota Poets*, by D.E. Grazi (anthology).

NOLO.COM, 950 Parker St., Berkeley CA 94710. (510)549-1976. Fax: (510)548-5902. E-mail: info@nolo.com. Website: www.nolo.com. **Acquisitions:** Barbara Kate Repa, senior editor. Estab. 1971. Publishes trade paperback originals. **Publishes 25 titles/year. 10% of books from first-time authors; 98% from unagented writers. Pays 10-12% royalty on net receipts.** Accepts simultaneous submissions. Responds in 2 weeks to proposals.
   O–π "Our goal is to publish 'plain English' self-help law books, software and various electronic products for our consumers."
Nonfiction: How-to, reference, self-help. Subjects include business/economics, general, money/finance, legal guides in various topics including employment, consumer, small business, intellectual property landlord/tenant and estate planning. "We do some business and finance titles, but always from a legal perspective, i.e., bankruptcy law." Query with SASE or submit outline, 1 sample chapter(s). Welcome queries but majority of titles are produced inhouse.
Recent Title(s): *Avoid Employee Lawsuits*, by Barbara Kate Repa; *Using Divorce Mediation*, by Katherine E. Stoner.

Ⓝ NORTH CAROLINA DIVISION OF ARCHIVES AND HISTORY, Historical Publications Section, 4622 Mail Service Center, Raleigh NC 27699-4622. (919)733-7442. Fax: (919)733-1439. E-mail: jmobley@ncsl.der.state.nc.us. Website: www.ah.dcr.state.nc.us/sections/hp. **Acquisitions:** Joe A. Mobley, administrator (North Carolina and southern history). Publishes hardcover and trade paperback originals. **Publishes 4 titles/year. Receives 20 queries and 25 mss/year. 5% of books from first-time authors; 100% from unagented writers. Makes one-time payment upon delivery of completed manuscript.** Publishes book 2 years after acceptance of ms. Accepts simultaneous submissions. Responds in 1 week to queries and proposals; 2 months to mss. Manuscript guidelines for $3.
   O–π "We publish *only* titles that relate to North Carolina. The North Carolina Division of Archives and History also publishes the *North Carolina Historical Review*, a scholarly journal of history."
Nonfiction: Hardcover and trade paperback books relating to North Carolina. Subjects include history (related to NC), military/war (related to NC), regional (NC and southern history). Query with SASE. Reviews artwork/photos as part of ms package. Send photocopies.
Recent Title(s): *Tar Heels: How North Carolinians Got Their Nickname*, by Michael Taylor; *Recollections of My Slavery Days*, edited by Katherine Mellen Charron and David Cecelski (edited slave narrative).

Tips: Audience is public school and college teachers and students, librarians, historians, genealogists, NC citizens, tourists.

NORTH LIGHT BOOKS, F&W Publications, 1507 Dana Ave., Cincinnati OH 45207. Editorial Director: Greg Albert. **Acquisitions:** Acquisitions Coordinator. Publishes hardcover and trade paperback how-to books. **Publishes 40-45 titles/ year. Pays 10% royalty on net receipts. Offers $4,000 advance.** Accepts simultaneous submissions. Responds in 1 month to queries. Book catalog for 9×12 SAE with 6 first-class stamps.

    ○┱ North Light Books publishes art, craft and design books, including watercolor, drawing, colored pencil and decorative painting titles that emphasize illustrated how-to art instruction. Currently emphasizing table-top crafts using materials found in craft stores like Michael's, Hobby Lobby.

Nonfiction: Art. How-to. Subjects include computers/electronic, hobbies, watercolor, drawing, colored pencil, decorative painting, craft and graphic design instruction books. Interested in books on watercolor painting, basic drawing, pen and ink, colored pencil, decorative painting, table-top crafts, basic design, computer graphics, layout and typography. Do not submit coffee table art books without how-to art instruction. Query with SASE or submit outline. Send photocopies or transparencies.

Recent Title(s): *Crafting Your Own Heritage Album*, by Bev Kirschner Braun.

NORTH POINT PRESS, Farrar Straus & Giroux, Inc., 19 Union Square W., New York NY 10003. (212)741-6900. Fax: (212)633-9385. **Acquisitions:** Rebecca Saletan, editorial director; Ethan Nosowsky, editor; Karen Wilder, assistant editor. Estab. 1980. Publishes hardcover and paperback originals. **Publishes 25 titles/year. Receives 100 queries and 100 mss/year. 20% of books from first-time authors. Pays standard royalty. Offers varied advance.** Publishes book 18 months after acceptance of ms. Accepts simultaneous submissions. Responds in 2 months to queries; 3 months to proposals and mss. Manuscript guidelines for #10 SASE.

    ○┱ "We are a broad-based literary trade publisher—high quality writing only."

Nonfiction: Biography. Subjects include gardening, history, memoirs, nature/environment, religion (no New Age), sports, travel, music, cooking/food. "Be familiar with our list. No genres." Query with SASE or submit outline, 1-2 sample chapter(s).

Recent Title(s): *On the Other Side of Eden*, by Hugh Brady; *The Geometry of Love*, by Margaret Visser.

🅐 NORTH-SOUTH BOOKS, Nord-Sud Verlag AG, 1123 Broadway, Suite 800, New York NY 10010. (212)706-4545. Website: www.northsouth.com. **Acquisitions:** Julie Amper. Estab. 1985. **Publishes 100 titles/year. Receives 5,000 queries/year. 5% of books from first-time authors. Pays royalty on retail price. Offers advance.** Publishes book an average of 2 years after acceptance of ms. Does not respond unless interested to proposals.

    ○┱ "The aim of North-South is to build bridges—bridges between authors and artists from different countries and between readers of all ages. We believe children should be exposed to as wide a range of artistic styles as possible with universal themes."

Fiction: Picture books, easy-to-read. "We are currently accepting only picture books; all other books are selected by our German office." *Accepts agented submissions only. All unsolicited mss returned unopened.*

Recent Title(s): *The Rainbow Fish & the Big Blue Whale*, by Marcus Pfister (picture).

NORTHEASTERN UNIVERSITY PRESS, 360 Huntington Ave., 416CP, Boston MA 02115. (617)373-5480. Fax: (617)373-5483. Website: www.neu.edu/nupress. **Acquisitions:** William Frohlich, director (music, criminal justice); John Weingartner, senior editor (history, law and society); Elizabeth Swayze, editor (women's studies). Estab. 1977. Publishes hardcover originals and trade paperback originals and reprints. **Publishes 40 titles/year. Receives 500 queries and 100 mss/year. 50% of books from first-time authors; 90% from unagented writers. Pays 5-15% royalty on wholesale price. Offers $500-5,000 advance.** Publishes book 1 year after acceptance of ms. Accepts simultaneous submissions. Book catalog and ms guidelines free.

    ○┱ Northeastern University Press publishes scholarly and general interest titles in the areas of American history, criminal justice, law and society, women's studies, African-American literature and music. Currently emphasizing American studies. De-emphasizing literary studies.

Nonfiction: Biography, adult trade scholarly monographs. Subjects include Americana, history, regional, women's issues/studies, music, criminal justice, law/society. Query with SASE or submit proposal package including outline, 1-2 sample chapter(s). Reviews artwork/photos as part of ms package. Send photocopies.

Recent Title(s): *The Hub: Boston Past and Present*, by Thomas H. O'Connor; *Women Pioneers for the Environment*, by Mary Joy Breton.

NORTHERN ILLINOIS UNIVERSITY PRESS, 310 N. Fifth St., DeKalb IL 60115-2854. (815)753-1826. Fax: (815)753-1845. Director/Editor-in-Chief: Mary L. Lincoln. **Acquisitions:** Martin Johnson, acquisitions editor (history, politics). Estab. 1965. **Publishes 18-20 titles/year. Pays 10-15% royalty on wholesale price. Offers advance**. Book catalog free.

    ○┱ NIU Press publishes both specialized scholarly work and books of general interest to the informed public. "We publish mainly history, politics, anthropology, and other social sciences. We are interested also in studies on the Chicago area and midwest and in literature in translation." Currently emphasizing history, the social sciences and cultural studies.

Nonfiction: "Publishes mainly history, political science, social sciences, philosophy, literary criticism and regional studies." Subjects include anthropology/archeology, government/politics, history, philosophy, regional, translation, cultural studies. No collections of previously published essays, no unsolicited poetry. Query with SASE or submit outline, 1-3 sample chapter(s).
Recent Title(s): *Possessed: Women, Witches and Demons in Imperial Russia.*

A NORTHFIELD PUBLISHING, Moody Press, 215 W. Locust St., Chicago IL 60610. (800)678-8001. Fax: (312)329-2019. **Acquisitions:** Acquisitions Coordinator. **Publishes 5-10 titles/year. 1% of books from first-time authors. Pays royalty on net receipts. Offers $500-50,000 advance.** Publishes book 1 year after acceptance of ms. Book catalog for 9×12 SAE with 2 first-class stamps.
  O— "Northfield publishes a line of books for non-Christians or those exploring the Christian faith. While staying true to Biblical principles, we eliminate some of the Christian wording and Scriptual references to avoid confusion."
Nonfiction: Biography (classic). Subjects include business/economics, child guidance/parenting, money/finance, religion. *Accepts agented submissions only.*
Recent Title(s): *The World's Easiest Guide to Finances*, by Larry Burkett with Randy Southern.

NORTHLAND PUBLISHING, LLC, P.O. Box 1389, Flagstaff AZ 86002-1389. (520)774-5251. Fax: (520)774-0592. E-mail: editorial@northlandpub.com. Website: www.northlandpub.com. **Acquisitions:** Brad Melton, adult editor (Native American and Western history, popular culture, lifestyle and cookery); Aimee Jackson, kids editor (picture books, especially humor). Estab. 1958. Publishes hardcover and trade paperback originals. **Publishes 25 titles/year; imprint publishes 10-12 titles/year. Receives 4,000 submissions/year. 20% of books from first-time authors; 20% from unagented writers. Pays royalty. Offers advance.** Publishes book 2 years after acceptance of ms. Accepts simultaneous submissions. Responds in 3 months to queries. Call for book catalog and ms guidelines.
Imprints: Rising Moon (books for young readers)
  • Rising Moon, the children's imprint of Northland Publishing, has temporarily suspended consideration of unsolicited manuscripts.
  O— "Northland has an excellent reputation for publishing quality nonfiction books that emphasize the American West. Our strengths include Native American and Western history, culture, art and cookbooks. Under our imprint, Rising Moon, we publish picture books for children, with universal themes and national appeal." Currently emphasizing popular culture, lifestyle, (cookery, architecture, interior design, gardening), Southwest or West in general, regional sports and women's history. De-emphasizing animals for adult line.
Nonfiction: Biography, children's/juvenile, coffee table book, cookbook, gift book, illustrated book. Subjects include anthropology/archeology (Native American), art/architecture, cooking/foods/nutrition (Southwest cookbooks), ethnic (Native American, Hispanic), gardening, history (natural, military and Native American), hobbies (collecting/arts), military/war (history), nature/environment (picture books), photography, regional (Southwestern, Western US), travel, popular culture (film, nostalgia). Query with SASE or submit outline, 2-3 sample chapter(s). No fax or e-mail submissions. Reviews artwork/photos as part of ms package.
Fiction: Picture books. Submit complete ms.
Recent Title(s): *Southwest Style: A Home-Lovers Guide to Architecture and Design*, by Linda Mason Hunter; *Trailblazers: Twenty Great Western Women*, by Karen Surina Mulford; *When Elephant Goes to a Party*, by Sonia Levitin and Jeff Seaver (children's).
Tips: "Our audience is composed of general interest readers."

NORTHWORD PRESS, Creative Publishing International, Inc., 5900 Green Oak Dr., Minnetonka MN 55343. (612)936-4700. Fax: (612)933-1456. **Acquisitions:** Barbara K. Harold, editorial director. Estab. 1984. Publishes hardcover and trade paperback originals. **Publishes 15-20 titles/year. Receives 600 submissions/year. 50% of books from first-time authors; 90% from unagented writers. Pays 10-12% royalty on wholesale price. Offers $2,000-10,000 advance.** Publishes book 1 year after acceptance of ms. Accepts simultaneous submissions. Responds in 3 months to queries. Manuscript guidelines for #10 SASE.
  O— NorthWord Press publishes exclusively nature and wildlife titles for adults, teens, and children.
Nonfiction: Children's/juvenile, coffee table book, illustrated book, introductions to wildlife and natural history. Subjects include animals, nature/environment. Query with SASE or submit outline, sample chapter(s).
Recent Title(s): *Daybreak 2000*, by Roger Tefft; *Greenland Expedition*, by Lonnie Dupre; *Water: The Drop of Life*, by Peter Swanson.
Tips: "No poetry, fiction or memoirs. We have expanded to include exotic and non-North American topics."

W.W. NORTON CO., INC., 500 Fifth Ave., New York NY 10110. Fax: (212)869-0856. Website: www.wwnorton.com. **Acquisitions:** Starling Lawrence, editor-in-chief; Robert Weil, executive editor; Edwin Barber; Jill Bialosky (literary fiction, biography, memoirs); Amy Cherry (history, biography, women's issues, African-American, health); Carol Houck-Smith (literary fiction, travel memoirs, behavioral sciences, nature); Angela von der Leppe (trade nonfiction, behavioral sciences, earth sciences, astronomy, neuro-science, education); Jim Mairs (history, biography, illustrated books); Alane Mason (serious nonfiction cultural and intellectual history, illustrated books, literary fiction and memoir); W. Drake McFeely, president (nonfiction, particularly science and social science). Estab. 1923. Publishes hardcover and paperback originals and reprints. **Publishes 300 titles/year. Pays royalty. Offers advance.** Responds in 2 months to queries.

Imprints: Backcountry Publication, Countryman Press, W.W. Norton

○┯ General trade publisher of fiction, poetry and nonfiction, educational and professional books. "W. W. Norton Co. strives to carry out the imperative of its founder to 'publish books not for a single season, but for the years' in the areas of fiction, nonfiction and poetry."

Nonfiction: Biography, reference, self-help. Subjects include agriculture/horticulture, art/architecture, business/economics, child guidance/parenting, computers/electronic, cooking/foods/nutrition, government/politics, health/medicine, history, hobbies, language/literature, memoirs, music/dance, nature/environment, photography, psychology, religion, science, sports, travel, antiques and collectibles, current affairs, family, games, law, mystery, nautical subjects, poetry, political science, sailing, transportation. College Department: Subjects include biological sciences, economics, psychology, political science and computer science. Professional Books specializes in psychotherapy. "We are not interested in considering books from the following categories: juvenile or young adult, religious, occult or paranormal, and arts and crafts." Query with SASE or submit 2-3, one of which should be the first chapter sample chapter(s). Please give a brief description of your submission, your writing credentials, and any experience, professional or otherwise, which is relevant to your submission. No phone calls. Address envelope and letter to The Editors.

Fiction: Literary, poetry, poetry in translation, religious. "We are not interested in considering books from the following categories: juvenile or young adult, religious, occult or paranormal, genre fiction (formula romances, sci-fi or westerns)." Query with SASE or submit 2-3, one of which should be the first chapter sample chapter(s). Please give a brief description of your submission, your writing credentials, and any experience, professional or otherwise, which is relevant to your submission. No phone calls. Address envelope and letter to The Editors.

Recent Title(s): *Guns, Germs and Steel*, by Jared Diamond; *Island*, by Alistir MacLeod.

N: NOVA PRESS, 11659 Mayfield Ave., Suite 1, Los Angeles CA 90049. (310)207-4078. Fax: (310)571-0908. E-mail: novapress@aol.com. Website: www.novapress.net. **Acquisitions:** Jeff Kolby, president. Estab. 1993. Publishes trade paperback originals. **Publishes 4 titles/year. Pays 10-22½% royalty on net receipts. Offers advance.** Publishes book 6 months after acceptance of ms. Book catalog free.

○┯ Nova Press publishes only test prep books for college entrance exams (SAT, GRE, GMAT, LSAT, etc.), and closely related reference books, such as college guides and vocabulary books.

Nonfiction: How-to, self-help, technical, test prep books for college entrance exams. Subjects include education, software.

Recent Title(s): *The MCAT Chemistry Book*, by Ajikumar Aryangat.

OAK KNOLL PRESS, 310 Delaware St., New Castle DE 19720. (302)328-7232. Fax: (302)328-7274. E-mail: oakknoll @oakknoll.com. Website: www.oakknoll.com. Estab. 1976. Publishes hardcover and trade paperback originals and reprints. **Publishes 40 titles/year. Receives 250 queries and 100 mss/year. 50% of books from first-time authors; 100% from unagented writers.** Publishes book 12 months after acceptance of ms. Accepts simultaneous submissions.

○┯ Oak Knoll specializes in books about books—preserving the art and lore of the printed word.

Nonfiction: How-to. Subjects include book arts, printing, papermaking, bookbinding, book collecting, etc. Reviews artwork/photos as part of ms package. Send photocopies.

Recent Title(s): *Historical Scripts*, by Stan Knight; *The Great Libraries*, by Stan Staikos.

N: THE OAKLEA PRESS, 6912-B Three Chopt Road, Richmond VA 23226. (804)281-5872. Fax: (804)281-5686. E-mail: jgots@oakleapress.com. Website: www.oakleapress.com. **Acquisitions:** Jim Johns, vice president (business); John Gotschalk, editor (visionary fiction); S.H. Martin, publisher (self-help). Publishes hardcover and trade paperback originals. **Receives 50 queries and 25 mss/year. 25% of books from first-time authors; 100% from unagented writers. Pays 10-20% royalty on wholesale price.** Publishes book 6 months after acceptance of ms. Accepts simultaneous submissions. Responds in 1 month to queries and proposals; 3 months to mss. Book catalog online.

Nonfiction: How-to, self-help. Subjects include business/economics, psychology, spirituality. "Currently we are looking for books on lean enterprise and e-commerce." Submit proposal package including outline, 1 sample chapter(s).

Fiction: Mystery, occult, suspense, visionary fiction. "We like fast-paced adventure, suspense, and mystery stories that have an underpinning of metaphysics/spirituality." Submit proposal package including 1 sample chapter(s), synopsis.

Recent Title(s): *Under a Lemon Moon*, by David Martin (fiction).

OASIS PRESS, P.O. Box 3727, Central Point OR 97502. (541)245-6502. **Acquisitions:** Emmett Ramey, president. Estab. 1975. Publishes hardcover, trade paperback and binder originals. **Publishes 20-30 titles/year. Receives 90 submissions/year. 60% of books from first-time authors; 90% from unagented writers. Pays 10% royalty on the net received.** Publishes book 6 months after acceptance of ms. Accepts simultaneous submissions. Responds in 2 months (initial feedback) to queries. Book catalog and ms guidelines for #10 SASE.

Imprints: Hellgate Press

○┯ Oasis Press publishes books for small business or individuals who are entrepreneurs or owners or managers of small businesses (1-300 employees).

Nonfiction: How-to, reference, textbook. Subjects include business/economics, computers/electronic, education, money/finance, nature/environment, retirement, exporting, franchise, finance, marketing/public relations, relocations, environment, taxes, business start up and operation. Needs information-heavy, readable mss written by professionals in their subject fields. Interactive where appropriate. Authorship credentials less important than hands-on experience qualifications. Submit outline, sample chapter(s). Query for unwritten material or to check current interest in topic and orientation. Reviews artwork/photos as part of ms package.

Recent Title(s): *What's It Worth*, by Lloyd Manning.

Tips: "Best chance is with practical, step-by-step manuals for operating a business, with worksheets, checklists. The audience is made up of entrepreneurs of all types: Small business owners and those who would like to be; attorneys, accountants and consultants who work with small businesses; college students; dreamers. Make sure your information is valid and timely for its audience, also that by virtue of either its content quality or viewpoint, it distinguishes itself from other books on the market."

OCTAMERON ASSOCIATES, 1900 Mount Vernon Ave., Alexandria VA 22301. (703)836-5480. Website: www.octameron.com. **Acquisitions:** Karen Stokstad, editor. Publishes trade paperback originals. **Publishes 17 titles/ year. Receives 100 submissions/year. 15% of books from first-time authors; 100% from unagented writers. Pays 7½% royalty on retail price. Offers $500-1,000 advance.** Publishes book 9 months after acceptance of ms. Accepts simultaneous submissions. Responds in 2 months to proposals. Book catalog free.

Nonfiction: Reference. Subjects include education. Submit proposal package including 2 sample chapter(s), table of contents.

Recent Title(s): *Majoring in Success*, by Anthony Arcieri and Marianne Green; *The Best 201 Colleges*, by Michael Viollt.

Tips: Audience is high school students and their parents, high school guidance counselors. "Keep the tone light."

OHIO STATE UNIVERSITY PRESS, 1070 Carmack Rd., Columbus OH 43210-1002. (614)292-6930. Fax: (614)292-2065. E-mail: ohiostatepress@osu.edu. Website: www.ohiostatepress.org. **Acquisitions:** Malcolm Litchfield, director; Heather Miller, acquisitions editor. Estab. 1957. **Publishes 30 titles/year. Pays royalty. Offers advance.** Responds in 3 months to queries.

○┐ Ohio State University Press publishes scholarly nonfiction, and offers short fiction and short poetry prizes. Currently emphasizing history, literary studies, political science, women's health.

Nonfiction: Scholarly. Subjects include business/economics, education, general, government/politics, history (American), language/literature, multicultural, regional, sociology, women's issues/studies, criminology, literary criticism, women's health. Query with SASE.

Recent Title(s): *Saving Lives*, by Albert Goldbarth (poetry); *Visions of Place: The City, Neighborhoods, Suburbs, and Cincinnati's Clifton 1850-2000*, by Zane L. Miller (nonfiction).

Tips: "Publishes some poetry and fiction in addition to the prizes. Query first."

OHIO UNIVERSITY PRESS, Scott Quadrangle, Athens OH 45701. (740)593-1155. Fax: (740)593-4536. Website: www.ohiou.edu/oupress/. **Acquisitions:** Gillian Berchowitz, senior editor (contemporary history, African studies, Appalachian studies); David Sanders, director (literature, literary criticism, midwest and frontier studies, Ohioana). Estab. 1964. Publishes hardcover and trade paperback originals and reprints. **Publishes 45-50 titles/year. Receives 500 queries and 50 mss/year. 20% of books from first-time authors; 95% from unagented writers. Pays 7-10% royalty on net receipts.** Publishes book 1 year after acceptance of ms. Responds in 1 month to queries and proposals; 2 months to mss. Book catalog free; ms guidelines for #10 SASE.

Imprints: Ohio University Research International Studies (Gillian Berchowitz); Swallow Press (David Sanders, director)

○┐ Ohio University Press publishes and disseminates the fruits of research and creative endeavor, specifically in the areas of literary studies, regional works, philosophy, contemporary history, African studies and frontier Americana. Its charge to produce books of value in service to the academic community and for the enrichment of the broader culture is in keeping with the university's mission of teaching, research and service to its constituents.

Nonfiction: Biography, reference, scholarly. Subjects include agriculture/horticulture, Americana, animals, anthropology/archeology, art/architecture, ethnic, gardening, government/politics, history, language/literature, military/war, nature/environment, philosophy, regional, sociology, travel, women's issues/studies, African studies. "We prefer queries or detailed proposals, rather than manuscripts, pertaining to scholarly projects that might have a general interest. Proposals should explain the thesis and details of the subject matter, not just sell a title." Query with SASE. Reviews artwork/photos as part of ms package. Send photocopies.

Recent Title(s): *Set the Ploughshare Deep: A Prairie Memoir*, by Timothy Murphy; *The Selected Letters of Yvor Winters*, edited by R.L. Barth; *Midland: Poems*, by Kwame Dawes.

Tips: "Rather than trying to hook the editor on your work, let the material be compelling enough and well-presented enough to do it for you."

THE OLIVER PRESS, INC., 5707 W. 36th St., Minneapolis MN 55416-2510. (952)926-8981. Fax: (952)926-8965. E-mail: queries@oliverpress.com. Website: www.oliverpress.com. **Acquisitions:** Denise Sterling, editor. Estab. 1991. Publishes hardcover originals. **Publishes 10 titles/year. Receives 100 queries and 20 mss/year. 10% of books from first-time authors; 100% from unagented writers.** Publishes book up to 2 years after acceptance of ms. Accepts simultaneous submissions. Responds in 6 months to queries. Book catalog for 9×12 SAE with 4 first-class stamps; ms guidelines for #10 SASE.

O→ "We publish collective biographies for ages 10 and up. Although we cover a wide array of subjects, all are published in this format. We are looking for titles for our Innovators series (history of technology) and Business Builders series."

Nonfiction: Collective biographies only. Children's/juvenile. Subjects include business/economics, ethnic, government/politics, health/medicine, history (history of technology), military/war, nature/environment, science. Query with SASE.
Recent Title(s): *Business Builders in Fast Food*, by Nathan Aaseng; *Women with Wings*, by Jacqueline McLean.
Tips: "Audience is primarily junior and senior high school students writing reports."

ONE ON ONE COMPUTER TRAINING, Mosaic Media, 2055 Army Trail Rd., Suite 100, Addison IL 60101. (630)628-0500. Fax: (630)628-0550. E-mail: oneonone@pincom.com. Website: www.ooootraining.com. **Acquisitions:** Natalie Young, manager product development. Estab. 1976. **Publishes 10-20 titles/year. 100% from unagented writers. Makes outright purchase of $3,500-10,000 Pays 5-10% royalty (rarely). Advance offer depends on purchase contract.** Publishes book 3 months after acceptance of ms. Responds in 1 month to queries. Book catalog free.
Imprints: OneOnOne Computer Training, Working Smarter, Professional Training Associates
O→ OneOnOne Computer Training publishes ongoing computer training for computer users and office professionals. Currently emphasizing soft skills for IT professionals.
Nonfiction: How-to, self-help, technical. Subjects include computers/electronic, software, IT, Internet programming, software certification and computer security. *All unsolicited mss returned unopened.* Query.
Recent Title(s): *Problem Solving with Visual Basic*; *Managing People at Work.*

N A ONE WORLD BOOKS, Ballantine Publishing Group, Inc., 1540 Broadway, 11th Floor, New York NY 10036. (212)782-8378. Fax: (212)782-8442. E-mail: adiggs@randomhouse.com. **Acquisitions:** Anita Diggs, senior editor. Publishes hardcover, trade and mass market paperback originals and trade paperback reprints. **Publishes 24 titles/year. Receives 350 queries and 500 submissions/year. 50% of books from first-time authors; 5% from unagented writers. Pays 7½-15% royalty on retail price. Offers 40,000-200,000 advance.** Publishes book 18 months after acceptance of ms. Accepts simultaneous submissions. Responds in 1 month to queries and proposals; 2 months to mss.
Fiction: "All One World Books must be specifically written for either an African-American, Asian or Hispanic audience. Absolutely no exceptions!" Adventure, confession, erotica, ethnic, historical, humor, literary, mainstream/contemporary, multicultural, mystery, regional, romance, short story collections, suspense, strong need for commercial women's fiction. No poetry. *Accepts agented submissions only.*
Recent Title(s): *Brotherman*, by Herb Boyd and Robert L. Allen (anthology); *Cookie Cutter*, by Sterling Anthony (mystery).
Tips: Targets African-American, Asian and Hispanic readers. All books must be written in English.

ONJINJINKTA PUBLISHING, The Betty J. Eadie Press, 909 S.E. Everett Mall Way, Suite A-120, Everett WA 98208. (425)290-7809. Fax: (425)290-7789. E-mail: peter@onjinjinkta.com. Website: www.onjinjinkta.com. **Acquisitions:** Peter Orullian, senior editor (fiction: redemptive, engaging stories; spirituality nonfiction); Bret Sable, associate editor (nonfiction). Publishes hardcover, trade paperback and mass market paperback originals and reprints. **Publishes 8-12 titles/year. Receives 2,000 queries and 600 mss/year. 50% of books from first-time authors; 80% from unagented writers. Pays 5-15% royalty on retail price. Offers $1,000-10,000 advance.** Publishes book 18 months after acceptance of ms. Accepts simultaneous submissions. Responds in 2 months to queries and proposals; 3 months to mss. Manuscript guidelines for #10 SASE.
O→ "We primarily publish books intended to bring the reader closer to God, or to truth generally. We want to see books on spirituality and redeeming principles. De-emphasizing new age subjects."
Nonfiction: Children's/juvenile, humor, self-help. Subjects include Americana, anthropology/archeology, creative non-fiction, health/medicine, history, humor, language/literature, military/war, music/dance, nature/environment, philosophy, psychology, regional, religion, sociology, spirituality. Submit proposal package including outline, 1 sample chapter(s), author bio, SASE.
Fiction: Adventure, fantasy, humor, mainstream/contemporary, military/war, regional, religious, spiritual, suspense. Submit proposal package including 1 sample chapter(s), synopsis.
Recent Title(s): *The Ripple Effect*, by Betty J. Eadie.
Tips: "Nonfiction audience is thoughtful, hopeful individuals who seek self-awareness. Fiction audience is readers who desire to be engaged in the high art of escapism. We can only publish a short list each year; your book must target its market forcefully, and its story must express and invoke fresh ideas on the ancient themes."

OPEN ROAD PUBLISHING, P.O. Box 284, Cold Spring Harbor NY 11724. (631)692-7172. Fax: (631)692-7193. E-mail: Jopenroad@aol.com. Website: openroadpub.com. Publisher: Jonathan Stein. Publishes trade paperback originals. **Publishes 22-27 titles/year. Receives 100 queries and 50 mss/year. 30% of books from first-time authors; 98% from unagented writers. Pays 5-6% royalty on retail price. Offers $1,000-5,000 advance.** Publishes book 3 months after acceptance of ms. Accepts simultaneous submissions. Responds in 1 month to queries; 2 months to proposals. Book catalog and ms guidelines free.
O→ Open Road publishes travel guides.
Nonfiction: How-to. Subjects include travel. *No unsolicited mss.* Query with SASE.
Recent Title(s): *England & Wales Guide*, by Paul Tarrant; *Caribbean Guide*, by Janet Groene; *Las Vegas with Kids*, by Paris Permenter.

ORANGE FRAZER PRESS, INC., P.O. Box 214, Wilmington OH 45177. (937)382-3196. Fax: (937)383-3159. Website: www.orangefrazer.com. **Acquisitions:** Marcy Hawley, editor. Publishes hardcover and trade paperback originals and reprints. **Publishes 20 titles/year. Receives 50 queries and 40 mss/year. 50% of books from first-time authors; 99% from unagented writers. Pays 10-12% royalty on wholesale price. Offers advance.** Publishes book 18 months after acceptance of ms. Accepts simultaneous submissions. Responds in 2 months to queries; 1 month to proposals and mss. Book catalog free.

O── Orange Frazer Press accepts Ohio-related nonfiction only.

Nonfiction: Accepts Ohio nonfiction only! Biography, coffee table book, cookbook, gift book, humor, illustrated book, reference, textbook. Subjects include art/architecture, cooking/foods/nutrition, education, history, memoirs, nature/environment, photography, recreation, regional (Ohio), sports, travel, women's issues/studies. Submit proposal package including outline, 1 sample chapter(s), SASE. Reviews artwork/photos as part of ms package. Send photocopies or transparencies.

Recent Title(s): *Ohio Nature Almanac*; *Earle, A Coach's Story*; *Indians Illustrated, 100 Years of Cleveland Indians Photos*.

ORCHARD BOOKS, A Grolier Company, 95 Madison Ave., New York NY 10016. (212)951-2600. Fax: (212)213-6435. E-mail: jwilson@Grolier.com. Website: www.grolier.com. President/Publisher: Judy V. Wilson. **Acquisitions:** Rebecca Davis, senior editor; Ana Cerro, editor; Lisa Hammond, assistant editor; Tamson Weston, assistant editor. Estab. 1987. Publishes hardcover and trade paperback originals. **Publishes 60-70 titles/year. Receives 3,000 queries/year. 25% of books from first-time authors; 50% from unagented writers. Pays 6-10% royalty on retail price. Offers varied advance.** Publishes book 1 year after acceptance of ms. Responds in 3 months to queries.

• Grolier was recently purchased by Scholastic, Inc.

O── Orchard specializes in children's picture books. Currently emphasizing picture books and middle grade novels (ages 8-12). De-emphasizing young adult.

Nonfiction: Children's/juvenile, illustrated book. Subjects include animals, history, nature/environment. "*No unsolicited mss at this time*. Queries only! Be as specific and enlightening as possible about your book." Query with SASE. Reviews artwork/photos as part of ms package. Send photocopies.

Fiction: Picture books, young adult, middle reader, board book, novelty. *No unsolicited mss.* Query with SASE.

Recent Title(s): *Wolf!*, by Bloom and Piet; *Mouse in Love*, by Aruego and Dewey.

Tips: "Go to a bookstore and read several Orchard Books to get an idea of what we publish. Write what you feel and query us if you think it's 'right.' It's worth finding the right publishing match."

ORCHISES PRESS, P.O. Box 20602, Alexandria VA 22320-1602. (703)683-1243. E-mail: rlathbur@osfl.gmu.edu. Website: mason.gmu.edu/~rlathbur. **Acquisitions:** Roger Lathbury, editor-in-chief. Estab. 1983. Publishes hardcover and trade paperback originals and reprints. **Publishes 4-5 titles/year. Receives 600 queries and 200 mss/year. 1% of books from first-time authors; 95% from unagented writers. Pays 36% of receipts after Orchises has recouped its costs.** Publishes book 1 year after acceptance of ms. Accepts simultaneous submissions. Responds in 3 months to queries. Book catalog for #10 SASE.

O── Orchises Press is a general literary publisher specializing in poetry with selected reprints and textbooks. No new fiction or children's books.

Nonfiction: Biography, how-to, humor, reference, technical, textbook. Subjects include literary. No real restrictions on subject matter. Query with SASE. Reviews artwork/photos as part of ms package. Send photocopies.

Poetry: Poetry must have been published in respected literary journals. Publishes free verse, but has strong formalist preferences. Query or submit 5 sample poems.

Recent Title(s): *College*, by Stephen Akey (nonfiction); *Chokecherries, New and Selected Poems 1966-1999*, by Peter Klappert (poetry).

Tips: "Show some evidence of appealing to a wider audience than simply people you know. Publication in a nationally prominent venue is not required, but it helps."

OREGON STATE UNIVERSITY PRESS, 101 Waldo Hall, Corvallis OR 97331-6407. (541)737-3166. Fax: (541)737-3170. Website: osu.orst.edu/dept/press. **Acquisitions:** Mary Braun, acquiring editor. Estab. 1965. Publishes hardcover and paperback originals. **Publishes 15-20 titles/year. Receives 100 submissions/year. 75% of books from first-time authors; 100% from unagented writers. Pays royalty on net receipts.** Publishes book 1 year after acceptance of ms. Responds in 3 months to queries. Book catalog and ms guidelines online or for 6×9 SAE with 2 first-class stamps.

O── Oregon State University Press publishes several scholarly and specialized books and books of particular importance to the Pacific Northwest. "OSU Press plays an essential role by publishing books that may not have a large audience, but are important to scholars, students and librarians in the region."

Nonfiction: Publishes scholarly books in history, biography, geography, literature, natural resource management, with strong emphasis on Pacific or Northwestern topics. Subjects include regional, science. Submit outline, sample chapter(s).

Recent Title(s): *Linus Pauling: Scientist and Peacemaker*, by Clifford Mead and Thomas Hager.

Tips: Send for an authors' guidelines pamphlet.

ORYX PRESS, 4041 N. Central Ave., Suite 700, Phoenix AZ 85012. (602)265-2651. Fax: (602)265-6250. E-mail: info@oryxpress.com. Website: www.oryxpress.com. Publisher: Susan Stesinger. **Acquisitions:** Eleanora Von Dehsen, acquisitions editor. Estab. 1975. **Publishes 50 titles/year. Receives 500 submissions/year. 40% of books from first-time authors; 80% from unagented writers. Pays 10% royalty on net receipts. Offers moderate advance.** Publishes book 9 months after acceptance of ms. Responds in 1 month to queries. Book proposals via Internet welcomed; Book catalog and ms guidelines online.

O─π Oryx Press publishes print and/or electronic reference resources for public, college and university, K-12 school, business and medical libraries, and professionals. Currently emphasizing social sciences, humanities, science. De-emphasizing law and medicine.

Nonfiction: Reference, scholarly, directories, dictionaries, encyclopedias, in print and electronic formats (online and CD-ROM). Subjects include anthropology/archeology, art/architecture, business/economics, education, government/politics, health/medicine, history, language/literature, multicultural, science, women's issues/studies, contemporary culture, world affairs, gerontology, social sciences. Queries may be routed to other editors in the publishing group. Query with SASE or submit outline, samples.

Recent Title(s): *Chronological Encyclopedia of Discoveries in Space*, by Robert Zimmerman; *Encyclopedia of Birth Control*, by Marian Rengel.

Tips: "We are accepting and promoting more titles over the Internet. We are also looking for up-to-date, relevant ideas to add to our established line of print and electronic works."

OSBORNE/MCGRAW HILL, The McGraw-Hill Companies, 2600 10th St., Berkeley CA 94710. (510)549-6600. Website: www.osborne.com. **Acquisitions:** Scott Rogers, editor-in-chief/vice president; Wendy Rinaldi, editorial director (programmaing and web development); Gareth Hancock, editorial director (certification); Roger Stewart, editorial director (consumer and hardware applications); Tracey Dunkleberger, director of networking. Estab. 1979. Publishes computer trade paperback originals. **Publishes 250 titles/year. Receives 500 submissions/year. 25% of books from first-time authors; 25% from unagented writers. Pays 7½-15% royalty on net receipts. Offers varying advance.** Publishes book 6-9 months after acceptance of ms. Accepts simultaneous submissions. Responds in 2 weeks to proposals. Book catalog and ms guidelines online.

O─π Publishes technical computer books and software with an emphasis on emerging technologies.

Nonfiction: Reference, technical. Subjects include computers/electronic, software. Query with SASE or submit proposal package including outline, sample chapter(s), SASE. Reviews artwork/photos as part of ms package.

Recent Title(s): *All-in-One A+ Exam Guide*, by Meyers.

Tips: "A leader in self-paced training and skills development tools on information technology and computers."

OSPREY PUBLISHING LIMITED, SBM Inc., % Specialty Book Marketing, Inc., 443 Park Ave. S. #801, New York NY 10016. (212)685-5560. Fax: (212)685-5836. E-mail: ospreyusa@aol.com. Website: www.ospreypublishing.com. **Acquisitions:** Jane Penrose, managing editor (military, uniforms, battles). Publishes hardcover and trade paperback originals. **Publishes 78 titles/year. 25% of books from first-time authors; 100% from unagented writers. Makes outright purchase of $1,000-5,000. Offers advance.** Publishes book 1 year after acceptance of ms. Responds in 3 months to queries. Book catalog free or online.

O─π Osprey Publishing produces high-quality illustrated nonfiction series in the areas of military and aviation history. Lines include Air Combat, Aircraft of the Aces, Campaign, Elite, Men at Arms, New Vanguard, Warrior. No longer publishes automotive titles.

Nonfiction: Biography, illustrated book. Subjects include history, hobbies, military/war, aviation. Query with SASE. Reviews artwork/photos as part of ms package. Send photocopies.

Recent Title(s): *Iwo Jima: Marines Raise the Flag on Mount Suribachi*, by Derrick Wright.

Tips: "Osprey history books appeal to everyone with an interest in history: Teachers, students, history buffs, re-enactors, model makers, researchers, writers, movie production companies, etc. Known for meticulous research and attention to detail, our books are considered accurate and informative. Please do not send manuscript. We publish mainly in series in specific monographic format. Please provide academic credentials and subject matter of work. Artist references must be provided by author."

OUR SUNDAY VISITOR PUBLISHING, 200 Noll Plaza, Huntington IN 46750-4303. (219)356-8400. Fax: (219)359-9117. E-mail: booksed@osv.com. Website: osv.com. President/Publisher: Greg Erlandson. **Acquisitions:** Jacquelyn Lindsey, Michael Dubruiel, Beth McNamara, acquisitions editors. Estab. 1912. Publishes paperback and hardbound originals. **Publishes 30-40 titles/year. Receives 500 submissions/year. 10% of books from first-time authors; 90% from unagented writers. Pays variable royalty on net receipts. Offers $1,500 average advance.** Publishes book 1-2 years after acceptance of ms. Responds in 3 months to queries. Book catalog for 9×12 SAE; ms guidelines for #10 SASE or online.

O─π "We are a Catholic publishing company seeking to educate and deepen our readers in their faith." Currently emphasizing reference, apologetics and catechetics. De-emphasizing inspirational.

Nonfiction: Catholic viewpoints on family, prayer and devotional books, and Catholic heritage books. Reference. Subjects include religion. Prefers to see well-developed proposals as first submission with annotated outline and definition of intended market. Reviews artwork/photos as part of ms package.

Recent Title(s): *Our Sunday Visitor's Treasury of Catholic Stories*, by Gerald Costello.

Tips: "Solid devotional books that are not first-person, or lives of the saints and catechetical books have the best chance of selling to our firm. Make it solidly Catholic, unique, without pious platitudes."

A **THE OVERLOOK PRESS**, Distributed by Penguin Putnam, 386 W. Broadway, New York NY 10012. (212)965-8400. Fax: (212)965-9839. Publisher: Peter Mayer. **Acquisitions:** (Ms.) Tracy Carns, editor. Estab. 1971. Publishes hardcover and trade paperback originals and hardcover reprints. **Publishes 40 titles/year. Receives 300 submissions/year. Pays 3-15% royalty on wholesale price or retail price. Offers advance.** Responds in 5 months to queries. Book catalog free.
Imprints: Elephant's Eye, Tusk Books
○➤ Overlook Press publishes fiction, children's books and nonfiction.
Nonfiction: Biography. Subjects include art/architecture, film/cinema/stage, history, current events, design, film, health/fitness, how-to, lifestyle, material arts, music, popular culture, New York State regional. No pornography. *Accepts agented submissions only.*
Fiction: Fantasy, literary, foreign literature in translation. *Accepts agented submissions only.*

A **THE OVERMOUNTAIN PRESS**, P.O. Box 1261, Johnson City TN 37605. (423)926-2691. Fax: (423)929-2464. E-mail: bethw@overmtn.com. Website: www.overmtn.com. **Acquisitions:** Elizabeth L. Wright, managing editor. Estab. 1970. Publishes hardcover and trade paperback originals and reprints. **Publishes 15-20 titles/year. Receives 500 queries and 100 mss/year. 50% of books from first-time authors; 100% from unagented writers. Pays 7½-15% royalty on wholesale price.** Publishes book 1 year after acceptance of ms. Accepts simultaneous submissions. Responds in 6 months to proposals and mss. Book catalog and ms guidelines free.
Imprints: Silver Dagger Mysteries
○➤ The Overmountain Press publishes primarily Appalachian history. Audience is people interested in history of Tennessee, Virginia, North Carolina, Kentucky, and all aspects of this region—Revolutionary War, Civil War, county histories, historical biographies, etc. Currently emphasizing regional (Southern Appalachian) children's books, regional nonfiction, children's regional history. De-emphasizing general interest children's fiction, poetry.
Nonfiction: Regional works only. Biography, children's/juvenile, coffee table book, cookbook. Subjects include Americana, cooking/foods/nutrition, ethnic, history, military/war, nature/environment, photography, regional, women's issues/studies, Native American. Submit proposal package including outline, 3 sample chapter(s), marketing suggestions. Reviews artwork/photos as part of ms package. Send photocopies.
Fiction: Picture books.
Recent Title(s): *Textile Art from Southern Appalachia*, by Kathleen Curtis Wilson; *Soapy-Dope*, by Denvil Mullins (children's fiction).
Tips: "Please submit a proposal. Please no phone calls."

RICHARD C. OWEN PUBLISHERS INC., P.O. Box 585, Katonah NY 10536. (914)232-3903. Website: www.RCOwen.com. **Acquisitions:** Janice Boland, director of children's books; Amy Finney, project editor (professional development, teacher-oriented books). Estab. 1982. Publishes hardcover and paperback originals. **Publishes 23 titles/year. Receives 50 queries and 1,000 mss/year. 99% of books from first-time authors; 100% from unagented writers.** Publishes book 2-5 years after acceptance of ms. Accepts simultaneous submissions. Responds in 1 month to queries and proposals; 5 months to mss. Manuscript guidelines for SASE with 52¢ postage.
○➤ "In addition to publishing good literature, meaningful stories for 5-7-year-old children, we are also seeking mss for short, snappy stories to be included in anthologies for 7-8-year-old children. Subjects include humor, careers, mysteries, science fiction, folktales, women, fashion trends, sports, music, myths, journalism, history, inventions, planets, architecture, plays, adventure, technology, vehicles."
Nonfiction: Children's/juvenile, humor, illustrated book. Subjects include animals, art/architecture, fashion/beauty, gardening, history, humor, music/dance, nature/environment, recreation, science, sports, women's issues/studies, contemporary culture. "Our books are for kindergarten, first and second grade children to read on their own. The stories are very brief—under 200 words—yet well structured and crafted with memorable characters, language and plots." Send for ms guidelines, then submit complete ms with SASE via mail only.
Fiction: Adventure, picture books. "Brief, strong story line, believable characters, natural language, exciting—child-appealing stories with a twist. No lists, alphabet or counting books." Send for ms guidelines, then submit full ms with SASE via mail only.
Poetry: "Poems that excite children are fun, humorous, fresh and interesting. If rhyming, must be without force or contrivance. Poems should tell a story or evoke a mood and have rhythmic language." No jingles. Submit complete ms.
Recent Title(s): *Strange Plants*, by Nic Bishop (nonfiction); *Archie's Dollar*, by Nathan Zimclman (fiction); *Dogs Love to Play Ball*, by Suzanne Hardin (limerick).
Tips: "We don't respond to queries. Please do *not* fax or e-mail us. Because our books are so brief it is better to send entire ms. We publish books with inherent educational value for young readers—books they can read with enjoyment and success. We believe students become enthusiastic, independent, life-long learners when supported and guided by skillful teachers. The professional development work we do and the books we publish support these beliefs."

N **OXFORD UNIVERSITY PRESS**, 198 Madison Ave., New York NY 10016. (212)726-6000. Website: www.oup-usa.org. **Acquisitions:** Joan Bossert, vice president/editorial director; Laura Brown, president. Publishes hardcover and trade paperback originals and reprints. **Publishes 1,500 titles/year. 40% of books from first-time authors; 80% from**

unagented writers. Pays 0-15% royalty on wholesale price or retail price. Offers $0-40,000 advance. Publishes book 10 months after acceptance of ms. Accepts simultaneous submissions. Responds in 3 months to proposals. Book catalog free.

O→ "We publish books that make a significant contribution to the literature and research in a number of disciplines, which reflect the departments at the University of Oxford."

Nonfiction: Oxford is an academic, scholarly press. Biography, children's/juvenile, reference, technical, textbook. Subjects include anthropology/archeology, art/architecture, business/economics, computers/electronic, gay/lesbian, government/politics, health/medicine, history, language/literature, military/war, money/finance, music/dance, nature/environment, philosophy, psychology (and psychiatry), religion, science, sociology, women's issues/studies, law. Submit outline, sample chapter(s), cv. Reviews artwork/photos as part of ms package.

PACIFIC BOOKS, PUBLISHERS, P.O. Box 558, Palo Alto CA 94302-0558. (650)965-1980. **Acquisitions:** Henry Ponleithner, editor. Estab. 1945. **Publishes 6-12 titles/year. Pays 7½-15% royalty.** Responds in 1 month to queries. Book catalog and ms guidelines for 9×12 SAE.

O→ Pacific Books publishes general interest and scholarly nonfiction including professional and technical books, and college textbooks.

Nonfiction: General interest, professional, technical and scholarly nonfiction trade books. Reference, technical, textbook. Subjects include Americana (western), general, regional, translation, Hawaiiana. Looks for "well-written, documented material of interest to a significant audience." Also considers text and reference books for high school and college. Query with SASE or submit outline. Reviews artwork/photos as part of ms package.

Recent Title(s): *How to Choose a Nursery School: A Parents' Guide to Preschool Education*, by Ada Anbar.

PACIFIC PRESS PUBLISHING ASSOCIATION, Book Division, P.O. Box 5353, Nampa ID 83653-5353. (208)465-2570. Fax: (208)465-2531. E-mail: booksubmissions@pacificpress.com. Website: www.pacificpress.com. **Acquisitions:** Tim Lale (children's stories, devotional, biblical). Estab. 1874. Publishes hardcover and trade paperback originals and reprints. **Publishes 35 titles/year. Receives 600 submissions/year. 35% of books from first-time authors; 100% from unagented writers. Pays 8-16% royalty. Offers $300-1,500 average advance depending on length advance.** Publishes book 10 months after acceptance of ms. Responds in 3 months to queries. Manuscript guidelines online or send #10 SASE.

O→ Pacific Press is an exclusively religious publisher of the Seventh-Day Adventist denomination. "We are looking for practical, how-to oriented manuscripts on religion, health, and family life that speak to human needs, interests and problems from a Biblical perspective. We publish books that promote a stronger relationship with God, deeper Bible study, and a healthy, helping lifestyle."

Nonfiction: Biography, children's/juvenile, cookbook (vegetarian), how-to, self-help. Subjects include cooking/foods/nutrition (vegetarian only), health/medicine, nature/environment, religion, family living. "We can't use anything totally secular or written from other than a Christian perspective." Query or request information on how to submit a proposal. Reviews artwork/photos as part of ms package.

Recent Title(s): *Walking with Angel*, by Lonnie Melashenko and Brian Jones; *Anticipation*, by Hyveth Williams.

Tips: "Our primary audience is members of the Seventh-Day Adventist denomination. Almost all are written by Seventh-Day Adventists. Books that are doing well for us are those that relate the Biblical message to practical human concerns and those that focus more on the experiential rather than theoretical aspects of Christianity. We are assigning more titles, using less unsolicited material—although we still publish manuscripts from freelance submissions and proposals."

PALADIN PRESS, P.O. Box 1307, Boulder CO 80306-1307. (303)443-7250. Fax: (303)442-8741. E-mail: editorial@paladin-press.com. Website: www.paladin-press.com. President/Publisher: Peder C. Lund. **Acquisitions:** Jon Ford, editorial director. Estab. 1970. Publishes hardcover originals and paperback originals and reprints. **Publishes 50 titles/year. 50% of books from first-time authors; 100% from unagented writers. Pays 10-15% royalty on net receipts. Offers advance.** Publishes book 1 year after acceptance of ms. Accepts simultaneous submissions. Responds in 2 months to proposals. Book catalog free.

Imprints: Sycamore Island Books, Flying Machines Press

O→ Paladin Press publishes the "action library" of nonfiction in military science, police science, weapons, combat, personal freedom, self-defense, survival, "revenge humor." Currently emphasizing personal freedom, financial freedom.

Nonfiction: "Paladin Press primarily publishes original manuscripts on military science, weaponry, self-defense, personal privacy, financial freedom, espionage, police science, action careers, guerrilla warfare, fieldcraft and 'creative revenge' humor." How-to, reference. Subjects include government/politics, humor, military/war, money/finance, science, women's issues/studies. "If applicable, send sample photographs and line drawings with complete outline and sample chapters." Query with SASE.

Recent Title(s): *Techniques of Medieval Armour Reproduction*, by Brian Price.

Tips: "We need lucid, instructive material aimed at our market and accompanied by sharp, relevant illustrations and photos. As we are primarily a publisher of 'how-to' books, a manuscript that has step-by-step instructions, written in a clear and concise manner (but not strictly outline form) is desirable. No fiction, first-person accounts, children's, religious or joke books. We are also interested in serious, professional videos and video ideas (contact Michael Janich)."

PALGRAVE, St. Martin's Press, 175 Fifth Ave., New York NY 10010. (212)982-3900. Fax: (212)777-6359. **Acquisitions:** Michael Flamini, vice president and editorial director (history, politics, education, religion); Karen Wolny, senior editor (politics); Kristi Long, editor (literary criticism, biography, gender studies, anthropology); Anthony Wahl, editor (political economy, political theory, business, Asian studies); Gavatri Patnaik, editor (religion, Latino and Latin American studies, queer studies); Deborah Gershenowitz, editor (American history). Publishes hardcover and trade paperback originals. **Publishes 700 titles/year. Receives 500 queries and 600 mss/year. 25% of books from first-time authors; 50% from unagented writers. Pays royalty: trade, 10-15% list; other, 7-10% net. Offers varying advance.** Publishes book 7-10 months after acceptance of ms. Accepts simultaneous submissions. Responds in 1 month to proposals. Book catalog and ms guidelines free.

- St. Martin's Press, Scholarly and Reference Division joined with Macmillan UK and is now called Palgrave.
- O→ Palgrave wishes to "expand on our already successful academic, trade, and reference programs so that we will remain at the forefront of publishing in the global information economy of the 21st century. We publish high-quality academic works and a distinguished range of reference titles, and we expect to see many of our works available in electronic form."

Nonfiction: Biography, reference, scholarly. Subjects include business/economics, creative nonfiction, education, ethnic, gay/lesbian, government/politics, history, language/literature, military/war, money/finance, multicultural, music/dance, philosophy, regional, religion, sociology, spirituality, translation, women's issues/studies, humanities, social studies, film/cinema/stage, contemporary culture, general nonfiction, world affairs. "We are looking for good solid scholarship." Query with proposal package including outline, 3-4 sample chapters, prospectus, cv and SASE. Reviews artwork/photos as part of ms package.
Recent Title(s): *The Man Who Was Dorian Gray*, by Jerusha Hull McCormack; *The Actor Speaks*, by Patsy Rodenburg.

PANTHEON BOOKS, Knopf Publishing Group, Random House, Inc., 299 Park Ave., New York NY 10171. (212)751-2600. Fax: (212)572-6030. Website: www.pantheonbooks.com. Editorial Director: Dan Frank. Senior Editors: Shelley Wanger, Deborah Garrison. Executive Editor: Erroll McDonald. **Acquisitions:** Adult Editorial Department. Estab. 1942. **Pays royalty. Offers advance**.

- O→ Pantheon Books publishes both Western and non-Western authors of literary fiction and important nonfiction.
Nonfiction: Biography, literary, international. Subjects include general, government/politics, history, memoirs, science, travel.
Recent Title(s): *The Feast of Love*, by Charles Baxter; *The Diagnosis*, by Alan Lightman.

PARACLETE PRESS, P.O. Box 1568, Orleans MA 02653. (508)255-4685. Fax: (508)255-5705. **Acquisitions:** Editorial Review Committee. Estab. 1981. Publishes hardcover and trade paperback originals. **Publishes 16 titles/year. Receives 250 mss/year.** Publishes book up to 2 years after acceptance of ms. Accepts simultaneous submissions. Responds in 2 months to queries and mss. Book catalog for 8½×11 SAE with 4 first-class stamps; ms guidelines for #10 SASE.

- O→ Publisher of Christian classics, personal testimonies, devotionals, new editions of classics, compact discs and videos.
Nonfiction: Subjects include religion. No poetry or children's books. Query with SASE or submit 2-3 sample chapter(s), table of contents, chapter summaries.
Recent Title(s): *Mystery of the Cross*, by Cardinal Basil Home; *A Season in the Desert*, by W. Paul Jones; *Tell Me a Story*, by Lisa Suhay.

⟦N⟧ PARADISE CAY PUBLICATIONS, P.O. Box 29, Arcata CA 95518-0029. (707)822-9063. Fax: (707)822-9163. E-mail: paracay@humboldt1.com. Website: www.paracay.com. **Acquisitions:** Matt Morehouse, publisher (nautical). Publishes hardcover and trade paperback originals and reprints. **Publishes 5 titles/year; imprint publishes 2 titles/year. Receives 30-40 queries and 20-30 mss/year. 10% of books from first-time authors; 100% from unagented writers. Pays 10-15% royalty on wholesale price or makes outright purchase of $1,000-10,000. Offers $0-2,000 advance.** Publishes book 4 months after acceptance of ms. Responds in 1 month to queries and proposals; 2 months to mss. Book catalog and ms guidelines online.
Imprints: Parday Books
Nonfiction: Cookbook, how-to, illustrated book, reference, technical, textbook. Subjects include cooking/foods/nutrition, recreation, sports, travel. Query with SASE or submit proposal package including 2-3 sample chapter(s), call first. Reviews artwork/photos as part of ms package. Send photocopies.
Fiction: Adventure (nautical, sailing), sports. All fiction must have a nautical theme. Query with SASE or submit proposal package including 2-3 sample chapter(s), synopsis.
Recent Title(s): *Heavy Weather Tactics Using Sea Anchors and Drogues*, by Earl R. Hinz (nonfiction); *Green Flash*, by L.M. Lanison (mystery).
Tips: Audience is recreational sailors and powerboaters. Call Matt Morehouse (publisher) before submitting anything.

PARAGON HOUSE PUBLISHERS, 2700 University Ave. W., Suite 200, St. Paul MN 55114-1016. (651)644-3087. Fax: (651)644-0997. E-mail: paragon@paragonhouse.com. Website: www.paragonhouse.com. **Acquisitions:** Laureen Enright, acquisitions editor. Estab. 1962. Publishes hardcover and trade paperback originals and trade paperback reprints.

Publishes 12-15 titles/year; imprint publishes 2-5 titles/year. Receives 1,500 queries and 150 mss/year. 7% of books from first-time authors; 90% from unagented writers. Offers $500-1,500 advance. Publishes book 1 year after acceptance of ms. Accepts simultaneous submissions.

Imprints: PWPA Books (Dr. Gordon L. Anderson); Althena Books; New Era Books; ICUS Books

O—π "We publish general interest titles and textbooks that provide the readers greater understanding of society and the world." Currently emphasizing religion, philosophy.

Nonfiction: Biography, reference, textbook. Subjects include child guidance/parenting, government/politics, memoirs, multicultural, nature/environment, philosophy, religion, sex, sociology, women's issues/studies, world affairs. Submit proposal package including outline, 2 sample chapter(s), SASE, market breakdown.

Recent Title(s): *Wisdom's Book: The Sophia Anthology*, by Dr. Arthur Versluis; *From Ruge to Responsibility: Black Conservative Jesse Lee Peterson and America Today*, by Jesse Lee Peterson with Brad Stetson; *Philosophy of Human Rights: Readings in Context*, by Patrick Hayden.

N PARKWAY PUBLISHERS, INC., Box 3678, Boone NC 28607. (828)265-3993. Fax: (828)265-3993. E-mail: parkwaypub@hotmail.com. Website: www.parkwaypublishers.com. **Acquisitions:** Rao Aluri, president. Publishes hardcover and trade paperback originals. **Publishes 4-6 titles/year. Receives 15-20 queries and 10 mss/year. 75% of books from first-time authors; 100% from unagented writers.** Publishes book 8 months after acceptance of ms.

O—π Parkway publishes books on the local history and culture of Western North Carolina. "We are located on Blue Ridge Parkway and our primary industry is tourism. We are interested in books which present the history and culture of western North Carolina to the tourist market." Will consider fiction if it highlights the region. De-emphasizing academic books and poetry books.

Nonfiction: Technical. Subjects include history, psychology, regional. Query with SASE or submit complete ms.

Recent Title(s): *Letter from James*, by Ruth Layng (historical fiction).

PARLAY INTERNATIONAL, P.O. Box 8817, Emeryville CA 94662-0817. (510)601-1000. Fax: (510)601-1008. E-mail: info@parlay.com. Website: www.parlay.com. **Acquisitions:** Maria Sundeen, director of product development. Publishes hardcover, trade paperback, mass market paperback originals and trade paperback reprints. **Publishes 6-10 titles/year. Offers advance.** Publishes book 10 months after acceptance of ms. Accepts simultaneous submissions.

O—π Parlay International specializes in health, safety and productivity subjects.

Nonfiction: Reference, self-help, technical. Subjects include child guidance/parenting, health/medicine, money/finance, business, nutrition, productivity, safety and leadership, interpersonal skills. Query with SASE or submit proposal package including outline, 2 sample chapter(s).

Recent Title(s): *Aging & Elder Care* (book/Kopy Kit/CD-ROM packages); *Managing Work & Family* (book/Kopy Kit/CD-ROM packages).

Tips: "Parlay International publishes books for training, education and communication. Our three primary areas of information include health, safety and productivity topics. We have historically been providers of materials for educators, healthcare providers, business professionals, newsletters and training specialists. We are looking to expand our customer base to include not only business to business sales but mass market and consumer trade sales as well. Any suggested manuscript should be able to sell equally to our existing customer base as well as to the mass market, while retaining a thematic connection to our three specialty areas. Our customer base and specialty areas are very specific. Please review our website or catalogs before submitting a query."

PASSEGGIATA PRESS, 222 W. B St., Pueblo CO 81003-3404. (719)544-1038. Fax: (719)544-7911. E-mail: Passeggiata@compuserv.com. **Acquisitions:** Donald E. Herdeck, publisher/editor-in-chief, Harold Ames, Jr., general editor. Estab. 1973. Publishes hardcover and paperback originals. **Publishes 10-20 titles/year. Receives 200 submissions/year. 15% of books from first-time authors; 99% from unagented writers. Pays 10% royalty. Offers advance.** Accepts simultaneous submissions. Responds in 1 month to queries.

O—π "We search for books that will make clear the complexity and value of non-Western literature and culture. Mostly we do fiction in translation." Currently emphasizing criticism of non-Western writing (Caribbean, Latin American, etc.). De-emphasizing poetry.

Nonfiction: Subjects include ethnic, history, language/literature, multicultural, regional, translation. Specializes in African, Caribbean, Middle Eastern (Arabic and Persian) and Asian-Pacific literature, criticism and translation, Third World literature and history. Query with outline, table of contents. Reviews artwork/photos as part of ms package. Send State availability of photos/illustrations.

Fiction: Query with synopsis, plot summary (1-3 pages).

Poetry: Submit 5-10 sample poems.

Recent Title(s): *History of Syriac Literature and Sciences*; *Ghost Songs: A Palestinian Love Story*.

Tips: "We are always interested in genuine contributions to understanding non-Western culture. We need a *polished* translation, or original prose or poetry by non-Western authors *only*. Critical and cross-cultural studies are accepted from any scholar from anywhere."

N PASSPORT PRESS, P.O. Box 1346, Champlain NY 12919-1346. **Acquisitions:** Jack Levesque, publisher. Estab. 1975. Publishes trade paperback originals. **Publishes 4 titles/year. 25% of books from first-time authors; 100% from unagented writers. Pays 6% royalty on retail price. Offers advance.** Publishes book 9 months after acceptance of ms.

Imprints: Travel Line Press

○₋ Passport Press publishes practical travel guides on specific countries. Currently emphasizing offbeat countries.

Nonfiction: Subjects include travel. Especially looking for mss on practical travel subjects and travel guides on specific countries. No travelogues. Send 1-page query only. Reviews artwork/photos as part of ms package.

Recent Title(s): *Costa Rica Guide: New Authorized Edition*, by Paul Glassman.

PATHFINDER PUBLISHING OF CALIFORNIA, 3600 Harbor Blvd., #82, Oxnard CA 93035. (805)984-7756. Fax: (805)985-3267. E-mail: bmosbrook@earthlink.net. Website: www.pathfinderpublishing.com. Publishes hardcover and trade paperback originals. **Publishes 4 titles/year. Receives 100 queries and 75 mss/year. 80% of books from first-time authors; 70% from unagented writers. Pays 9-15% royalty on wholesale price. Offers $200-1,000 advance.** Publishes book 4 months after acceptance of ms. Responds in 1 month to queries. Book catalog online.

○₋ Pathfinder Publishing of California was founded to seek new ways to help people cope with psychological and health problems resulting from illness, accidents, losses or crime.

Nonfiction: Self-help. Subjects include creative nonfiction, health/medicine, hobbies, psychology, sociology. Submit complete ms. Reviews artwork/photos as part of ms package. Send photocopies.

Recent Title(s): *Unleash the Power of Your Mind*.

PAULINE BOOKS & MEDIA, Daughters of St. Paul, 50 St. Paul's Ave., Jamaica Plain MA 02130-3491. (617)522-8911. Fax: (617)541-9805. Website: www.pauline.org. **Acquisitions:** Sister Mary Mark Wickenheiser, FSP, acquisitions (adult); Sister Patricia Edward Jablonski, acquisitions (children); Sister Madonna Ratliff, FSP, acquisitions editor (adult). Estab. 1948. Publishes trade paperback originals and reprints. **Publishes 25-35 titles/year. Receives 1,300 submissions/ year. Pays 8-12% royalty on net receipts. Offers advance.** Publishes book 2-3 years after acceptance of ms. Responds in 3 months to queries. Book catalog for 9×12 SAE with 4 first-class stamps.

○₋ "As a Catholic publishing house, Pauline Books and Media publishes in the areas of faith and moral values, family formation, spiritual growth and development, children's faith formation, instruction in the Catholic faith for young adults and adults. Works consonant with Catholic theology are sought." Currently emphasizing saints/biographies, popular presentation of Catholic faith, biblical prayer. De-emphasizing pastoral ministry, teen fiction.

Nonfiction: Biography (saints), children's/juvenile, self-help, spiritual growth, faith development. Subjects include child guidance/parenting, religion (teacher resources), Scripture. No strictly secular mss. *No unsolicited mss.* Query with SASE.

Fiction: Juvenile. *No unsolicited mss.* Query only with SASE.

Recent Title(s): *Testimony of Hope*, by Cardinal F.X. Van Thuan (spirituality/biography); *Man of the Millennium, John Paul II*, by Luigi Accatoli (biography); *Poetry as Prayer Series*.

PAULIST PRESS, 997 MacArthur Blvd., Mahwah NJ 07430. (201)825-7300. Fax: (201)825-8345. E-mail: info@paulis tpress.com. Website: www.paulistpress.com. **Acquisitions:** Donna Crilly, editor (liturgy and catechetics); Joseph Scott, editor (adult theology, Catholic faith issues); Kathleen Walsh, editor (classics of Western spirituality); Donald Brophy, editor (general spirituality, special projects); Susan O'Keefe, editor (children's books). Estab. 1865. Publishes hardcover and paperback originals and paperback reprints. **Publishes 90-100 titles/year. Receives 500 submissions/year. 5-8% of books from first-time authors; 95% from unagented writers. Usually pays royalty on net, but occasionally on retail price. Offers advance.** Publishes book 10 months after acceptance of ms. Responds in 2 months to queries.

○₋ "The editorial mission of the Paulist Press is to publish books in the area of religious thought, especially but not exclusively Catholic religious thought. The major topics would be religious children's books, college theological textbooks, spirituality of prayer and religious classical works." Current areas of special interest are books that appeal to the religious and spiritual searching of unchurched people, children's books on Catholic subjects, and theology textbooks for college courses in religion. Less desired at this time are books in philosophy and biography, poetry and fiction.

Nonfiction: Self-help, textbook (religious). Subjects include philosophy, religion. "We would like to see theology (Catholic and ecumenical Christian), popular spirituality, liturgy, and religious education texts." Submit outline, 2 sample chapter(s). Reviews artwork/photos as part of ms package.

Recent Title(s): *Soul Wilderness*, by Kerry Walters; *The Nurse's Calling*, by Mary Elizabeth O'Brien.

PBC INTERNATIONAL INC., 1 School St., Glen Cove NY 11542. (516)676-2727. Fax: (516)676-2738. Publisher: Mark Serchuck. **Acquisitions:** Annette Dippolito, project manager. Estab. 1980. Publishes hardcover and paperback originals. Most of books from first-time authors and unagented writers done on assignment. **Publishes 20 titles/year. Receives 100-200 submissions/year. Pays royalty and/or flat fees. Offers advance.** Accepts simultaneous submissions. Responds in 3 months to proposals. Book catalog for 9×12 SASE.

Nonfiction: Coffee table book, gift book, illustrated book. Subjects include art/architecture, gardening, hobbies, photography, travel, graphic art, design, packaging design, marketing design, product design, fashion, film/cinema/stage, interior design, lifestyle, crafts. No submissions not covered in the above listed topics. Query with SASE or submit outline, sample chapter(s). Reviews artwork/photos as part of ms package.

Recent Title(s): *Designing with Spirituality: The Creative Touch*.

PEACHTREE PUBLISHERS, LTD., 1700 Chattahoochee Avenue, Atlanta GA 30318-2112. (404)876-8761. Fax: (404)875-2578. E-mail: hello@peachtree-online.com. Website: www.peachtree-online.com. **Acquisitions:** Helen Harriss, submissions editor. Estab. 1978. Publishes hardcover and trade paperback originals. **Publishes 20-25 titles/year. Receives 18,000 submissions/year. 25% of books from first-time authors; 75% from unagented writers. Royalty varies. Offers advance.** Publishes book 2 years or more after acceptance of ms. Responds in 6 months to queries. Book catalog for 9×12 SAE with 3 first-class stamps.

Imprints: Peachtree Children's Books (Peachtree Jr., Free Stone)

O━ Peachtree Publishers specializes in children's books, juvenile chapter books, young adult, regional guidebooks, parenting and self-help. Currently emphasizing young adult, self-help, children's, juvenile chapter books. De-emphasizing cooking, gardening, adult fiction.

Nonfiction: Biography, children's/juvenile, gift book, self-help. Subjects include general, health/medicine, history, humor, recreation. No technical or reference. Submit outline, sample chapter(s). Reviews artwork/photos as part of ms package. Send photocopies.

Fiction: Juvenile, literary, young adult. No fantasy, science fiction or romance. Submit sample chapter(s), synopsis. Inquires/submissions by US Mail only. E-mail and fax will not be answered.

Recent Title(s): *Around Atlanta with Children*, by Denise Black and Janet Schwartz; *Yellow Star*, by Carhen Agra Deedy; *Surviving Jamestown: The Adventures of Young Sam Collier*, by Gail Langer Karwoski.

PELICAN PUBLISHING COMPANY, P.O. Box 3110, Gretna LA 70054. (504)368-1175. Website: www.pelicanpub. com. **Acquisitions:** Nina Kooij, editor-in-chief. Estab. 1926. Publishes hardcover, trade paperback and mass market paperback originals and reprints. **Publishes 70 titles/year. Receives 5,000 submissions/year. 10% of books from first-time authors; 90% from unagented writers. Pays royalty on actual receipts. Offers advance.** Publishes book 9-18 months after acceptance of ms. Responds in 1 month to queries. Writer's guidelines for SASE or online.

O━ "We believe ideas have consequences. One of the consequences is that they lead to a bestselling book. We publish books to improve and uplift the reader." Currently emphasizing business titles.

Nonfiction: Biography, children's/juvenile, coffee table book (limited), cookbook, gift book, illustrated book, self-help. Subjects include Americana (especially Southern regional, Ozarks, Texas, Florida and Southwest), art/architecture, ethnic, government/politics, history (popular), multicultural, music/dance (American artforms, but will consider others: jazz, blues, Cajun, R&B), regional, religion (for popular audience mostly, but will consider others), sports, travel (regional and international), motivational (with business slant), inspirational (author must be someone with potential for large audience), Scottish, Irish, editorial cartoon. "We look for authors who can promote successfully. We require that a query be made first. This greatly expedites the review process and can save the writer additional postage expenses." No multiple queries or submissions. Query with SASE. Reviews artwork/photos as part of ms package.

Fiction: Historical, juvenile. "We publish maybe one novel a year, usually by an author we already have. Almost all proposals are returned. We are most interested in historical Southern novels." No young adult, romance, science fiction, fantasy, gothic, mystery, erotica, confession, horror, sex or violence. Submit outline, 2 sample chapter(s), synopsis, SASE.

Recent Title(s): *Black Knights: The Story of the Tuskegee Airmen*, by Lynn Homan and Thomas Reilly (history).

Tips: "We do extremely well with cookbooks, travel, popular histories, and some business. We will continue to build in these areas. The writer must have a clear sense of the market and knowledge of the competition. A query letter should describe the project briefly, give the author's writing and professional credentials, and promotional ideas."

PENCIL POINT PRESS, INC., 277 Fairfield Rd., Fairfield NJ 07004. **Acquisitions:** Gene Garone, publisher (all areas). **Publishes 4-12 titles/year. Receives 4-12 queries and 12 mss/year. 100% of books from first-time authors. Pays 5-16% royalty Pays 5-16% royalty or makes outright purchase by contract.** Publishes book 1 year after acceptance of ms. Accepts simultaneous submissions. Responds in 2 months to proposals. Book catalog free.

O━ Pencil Point publishes educational supplemental materials for teachers of all levels. Currently emphasizing mathematics and science. De-emphasizing language arts.

Nonfiction: Prefers supplemental resource materials for teachers grades K-12 and college (especially mathematics). Reference, technical, textbook. Subjects include education, language/literature, music/dance, science. Education subjects, including professional reference, music, science, mathematics, language arts, ESL and special needs. Submit proposal package including outline, 2 sample chapter(s), memo stating rationale and markets.

Recent Title(s): *Earthscope: Exploring Relationships Affecting Our Global Environment*, by Wright H. Gwyn.

Tips: Audience is K-8 teachers, 9-12 teachers and college-level supplements. No children's trade books or poetry.

PENGUIN PUTNAM INC., 375 Hudson St., New York NY 10014. Website: www.penguinputnam.com.

O━ General interest publisher of both fiction and nonfiction.

Imprints: *Adult Division*: Ace Books; Avery; Berkley Books; BlueHen Books; Dutton; G.P. Putnam's Sons; HPBooks; Jeremy P. Tarcher; Jove; New American Library [Mentor, Onyx, Signet, Signet Classics, Signet Reference]; Penguin; Putnam; Perigee; Plume; Riverhead Books; Viking; Viking Studio. *Children's Division*: AlloyBooks; Dial Books for Young Readers; Dutton Children's Books; Frederick Warne; G.P. Putnam's Sons; Grosset & Dunlap; Philomel; Phyllis Fogelman Books; Planet Dexter; Price Stern Sloan; Puffin Books; Viking Children's Books.

PENNSYLVANIA HISTORICAL AND MUSEUM COMMISSION, Commonwealth of Pennsylvania. Keystone Building, 400 North St., Harrisburg PA 17120-0053. (717)787-8099. Fax: (717)787-8312. Website: www.phmc.state.pa.

us. **Acquisitions:** Diane B. Reed, chief, publications and sales division. Estab. 1913. Publishes hardcover and paperback originals and reprints. **Publishes 6-8 titles/year. Receives 25 submissions/year. Pays 5-10% royalty on retail price or makes outright purchase; sometimes makes special assignments.** Publishes book 18 months after acceptance of ms. Accepts simultaneous submissions. Responds in 4 months to queries. Prepare ms according to the *Chicago Manual of Style.*

O─╖ "We are a public history agency and have a tradition of publishing scholarly and reference works, as well as more popularly styled books that reach an even broader audience interested in some aspect of Pennsylvania."

Nonfiction: All books must be related to Pennsylvania, its history or culture. "The Commission seeks manuscripts on Pennsylvania, specifically on archaeology, history, art (decorative and fine), politics and biography." Biography, illustrated book, reference, technical. Subjects include anthropology/archeology, art/architecture, government/politics, history, regional, travel (historic). Guidelines and proposal forms available. No fiction. Query with SASE or submit outline, sample chapter(s).

Recent Title(s): *Pennsylvannia Architecture,* by Richard Webster and Deborah Stephens Burns.

Tips: "Our audience is diverse—students, specialists and generalists—all of them interested in one or more aspects of Pennsylvania's history and culture. Manuscripts must be well researched and documented (footnotes not necessarily required depending on the nature of the manuscript) and interestingly written. Manuscripts must be factually accurate, but in being so, writers must not sacrifice style."

PERFECTION LEARNING CORPORATION, 10520 New York Ave., Des Moines IA 50322-3775. (515)278-0133. Fax: (515)278-2980. Website: perfectionlearning.com. **Acquisitions:** Sue Thies, editorial director (books division), Rebecca Christian, senior editor (curriculum division). Estab. 1926. Publishes hardcover and trade paperback originals. **Publishes 50-100 fiction and informational; 25 workbooks titles/year. Pays 5-7% royalty on retail price. Offers $300-500 advance.** Responds in 2 months to proposals.

Imprints: Cover-to-Cover, Summit Books

O─╖ "Perfection Learning is dedicated to publishing books and literature-based materials that enhance teaching and learning in pre-K-12 classrooms and libraries." Emphasizing hi/lo fiction and nonfiction books for reluctant readers (extreme sports, adventure fiction, etc.), high-interest novels with male protagonists.

Nonfiction: Publishes nonfiction and curriculum books, including workbooks, literature anthologies, teacher guides, literature tests, and niche textbooks for grades 3-12. "We are publishing hi-lo informational books for students in grades 2-12, reading levels 1-6." Biography. Subjects include science, social studies, high-interest topics. Query with SASE or submit outline. For curriculum books, submit proposal and writing sample with SASE.

Fiction: "We are publishing hi-lo informational books for students in grades 2-12, reading levels 1-6." No picture books. Submit 2-3 sample chapter(s), SASE.

Recent Title(s): *Into the Abyss: A Tour of Inner Peace,* by Ellen Hopkins.

PERIGEE BOOKS, Penguin Putnam Inc. 375 Hudson St., New York NY 10014. (212)366-2000. Publisher: John Duff. **Acquisitions:** Sheila Curry Oakes, executive editor (child care, health); Jennifer Repo, editor (spirituality, personal growth, personal finance, women's issues). Publishes trade paperback originals and reprints. **Publishes 55-60 titles/ year. Receives hundreds queries and 300+ submissions/year. 30% of books from first-time authors; 10% from unagented writers. Pays 6-7½% royalty. Offers $5,000-150,000 advance.** Publishes book 18 months after acceptance of ms. Accepts simultaneous submissions. Responds in 2 months to queries. Book catalog free; ms guidelines given on acceptance of ms.

O─╖ Publishes in all areas of self-help and how-to with particular interest in health and child care. Currently emphasizing popular psychology, trend watching, accessible spirituality; de-emphasizing games.

Nonfiction: How-to, reference (popular), self-help, prescriptive books. Subjects include animals, business/economics, child guidance/parenting, cooking/foods/nutrition, health/medicine, hobbies, money/finance, nature/environment, psychology, sex, spirituality, sports, women's issues/studies, fashion/beauty, film/cinema/stage. Prefers agented mss, but accepts unsolicited queries. Query with SASE or submit outline.

THE PERMANENT PRESS/SECOND CHANCE PRESS, 4170 Noyac Rd., Sag Harbor NY 11963. (631)725-1101. Fax: (631)725-8215. E-mail: thepermanentpress.com. Website: www.thepermanentpress.com. **Acquisitions:** Judith Shepard, editor. Estab. 1978. Publishes hardcover originals. **Publishes 12 titles/year. Receives 7,000 submissions/ year. 60% of books from first-time authors; 60% from unagented writers. Pays 10-15% royalty on wholesale price. Offers $1,000 advance for Permanent Press books; royalty only on Second Chance Press titles.** Publishes book 18 months after acceptance of ms. Accepts simultaneous submissions. Responds in 6 months to mss. Book catalog for 8×10 SAE with 7 first-class stamps; ms guidelines for #10 SASE.

O─╖ Permanent Press publishes literary fiction. Second Chance Press devotes itself exclusively to re-publishing fine books that are out of print and deserve continued recognition. "We endeavor to publish quality writing—primarily fiction—without regard to authors' reputations or track records." Currently emphasizing literary fiction. No poetry, short story collections.

Nonfiction: Biography, autobiography. Subjects include history, memoirs. No scientific and technical material, academic studies. Query with SASE.

Fiction: Literary, mainstream/contemporary, mystery. Especially looking for high line literary fiction, "artful, original and arresting." Query with first 20 pages.

Recent Title(s): *The Cosmology of Bing,* by Mitch Cullin; *Piper,* by John Keegan.

Tips: "Audience is the silent minority—people with good taste. We are interested in the writing more than anything and dislike long outlines. The SASE is vital to keep track of things, as we are receiving ever more submissions. No fax queries will be answered. We aren't looking for genre fiction but a compelling, well-written story." Permanent Press does not employ readers and the number of submissions it receives has grown. If the writer sends a query or manuscript that the press is not interested in, a reply may take six weeks. If there is interest, it may take 3 to 6 months.

PERSPECTIVES PRESS, P.O. Box 90318, Indianapolis IN 46290-0318. (317)872-3055. E-mail: ppress@iquest.n et. Website: www.perspectivespress.com. **Acquisitions:** Pat Johnston, publisher. Estab. 1982. Publishes hardcover and trade paperback originals. **Publishes 4 titles/year. Receives 200 queries/year. 95% of books from first-time authors; 95% from unagented writers. Pays 5-15% royalty on net receipts.** Publishes book 1 year after acceptance of ms. Responds in 1 month to queries. Book catalog for #10 SAE and 2 first-class stamps or online; ms guidelines online.
- "Our purpose is to promote understanding of infertility issues and alternatives, adoption and closely-related child welfare issues, and to educate and sensitize those personally experiencing these life situations, professionals who work with such clients, and the public at large."

Nonfiction: Children's/juvenile, how-to, self-help. Subjects include health/medicine, psychology, sociology. Must be related to infertility, adoption, alternative routes to family building. "No adult fiction!" Query with SASE.
Recent Title(s): *PCOS: The Hidden Epidemic*, by Samuel Thatcher MD; *Inside Transracial Adoption*, by Gail Steinberg and Beth Hall; *Adoption is a Family Affair*, by Patricia Lorsin Johnston.
Tips: "For adults, we are seeking infertility and adoption decision-making materials, books dealing with adoptive or foster parenting issues, books to use with children, books to share with others to help explain infertility, adoption, foster care, third party reproductive assistance, special programming or training manuals, etc. For children, we will consider adoption or foster care-related fiction manuscripts that are appropriate for preschoolers and early elementary school children. We do not consider YA. Nonfiction manuscripts are considered for all ages. No autobiography, memoir or adult fiction. While we would consider a manuscript from a writer who was not personally or professionally involved in these issues, we would be more inclined to accept a manuscript submitted by an infertile person, an adoptee, a birthparent, an adoptive parent or a professional working with any of these."

PETER PAUPER PRESS, INC., 202 Mamaroneck Ave., White Plains NY 10601-5376. E-mail: lkaufman@peterp auper.com. **Acquisitions:** Elizabeth Poyet, editorial director. Estab. 1928. Publishes hardcover originals. **Publishes 40-50 titles/year. Receives 700 queries and 300 mss/year. 5% of books from first-time authors; 90% from unagented writers. Makes outright purchase only. Offers advance.** Publishes book 1 year after acceptance of ms. Responds in 1 month to queries. Manuscript guidelines for #10 SASE or may request via e-mail for a faxed copy (include fax number in e-mail request).
- PPP publishes small and medium format, illustrated gift books for occasions and in celebration of specific relationships such as Mom, sister, friend, teacher, grandmother, granddaughter. PPP has expanded into the following areas: books for teens and tweens, books on popular topics of nonfiction for adults and licensed books by bestselling authors.

Nonfiction: Gift book. Subjects include specific relationships or special occasions (graduation, Mother's Day, Christmas, etc.). "We do publish interactive journals and workbooks but not narrative manuscripts or fiction. We publish brief, original quotes, aphorisms, and wise sayings. *Please do not send us other people's quotes*." Query with SASE.
Recent Title(s): *The Essential Writer's Notebook*, by Natalie Goldberg; *The Feng Shui Journal*, by Teresa Polance; *My Llife as a Baby*.
Tips: "Our readers are primarily female, age 10 and over, who are likely to buy a 'gift' book or gift book set in a stationery, gift, book or boutique store or national book chain. Writers should become familiar with our previously published work. We publish only small- and medium-format illustrated hardcover gift books and sets of between 750-4,000 words. We have no interest in work aimed at men."

PETERSON'S, 2000 Lenox Dr., Princeton Pike Corporate Center, Lawrenceville NJ 08648. (800)338-3282. Fax: (609)896-1800. Website: www.petersons.com. **Acquisitions:** Denise Rance, executive assistant, editorial. Estab. 1966. Publishes trade and reference books. **Publishes over 200 titles/year. Receives 250-300 submissions/year. 60% of books from first-time authors; 90% from unagented writers. Pays royalty. Offers advance.** Publishes book 1 year after acceptance of ms. Responds in 3 months to queries. Book catalog free.
- "Peterson's publishes guides to graduate and professional programs, colleges and universities, financial aid, distance learning, private schools, summer programs, international study, executive education, job hunting and career opportunities, educational and career test prep, as well as online products and services offering educational and career guidance and information for adult learners and workplace solutions for education professionals."

MARKETS THAT WERE listed in the 2001 edition of *Writer's Market* but do not appear this year are listed in the General Index with a notation explaining why they were omitted.

Nonfiction: Authored titles, education directories, career directories. Subjects include business/economics, education, careers. Looks for "appropriateness of contents to our markets, author's credentials, and writing style suitable for audience." Submit complete ms or table of contents, introduction and 2 sample chapters with SASE.
Recent Title(s): *The Insider's Guide to Study Abroad*, by Ann M. Moore.
Tips: Many of Peterson's reference works are updated annually. Peterson's markets strongly to libraries and institutions, as well as to the corporate sector.

PHAIDON PRESS, 180 Varick St., 14th Floor, New York NY 10014. (212)652-5410. Fax: (212)652-5419. Website: www.phaidon.com. **Acquisitions:** Karen Stein, editorial director (art and architecture, design, photography). Publishes hardcover and trade paperback originals and reprints. **Publishes 100 titles/year. Receives 500 mss/year. 20% of books from first-time authors; 80% from unagented writers. Pays royalty on wholesale price. Offers advance.** Publishes book 1 year after acceptance of ms. Accepts simultaneous submissions. Responds in 3 months to proposals. Book catalog free.
Imprints: Phaidon
Nonfiction: Subjects include art/architecture, photography. Submit proposal package including outline or submit complete ms. Reviews artwork/photos as part of ms package. Send photocopies.

PHI DELTA KAPPA EDUCATIONAL FOUNDATION, P.O. Box 789, Bloomington IN 47402. (812)339-1156. Fax: (812)339-0018. E-mail: special.pubs@pdkintl.org. Website: www.pdkintl.org. **Acquisitions:** Donovan R. Walling, director of publications and research. Estab. 1906. Publishes hardcover and trade paperback originals. **Publishes 24-30 titles/year. Receives 100 queries and 50-60 mss/year. 50% of books from first-time authors; 100% from unagented writers. Pays honorarium of $500-5,000.** Publishes book 9 months after acceptance of ms. Responds in 3 months to proposals. Book catalog and ms guidelines free.
 O─┰ "We publish books for educators—K-12 and higher education. Our professional books are often used in college courses but are never specifically designed as textbooks."
Nonfiction: How-to, reference, essay collections. Subjects include child guidance/parenting, education, legal issues. Query with SASE or submit outline, 1 sample chapter(s). Reviews artwork/photos as part of ms package.
Recent Title(s): *The ABC's of Behavior Change*, by Frank J. Sparzo; *American Overseas Schools*, edited by Robert J. Simpson and Charles R. Duke.

PHILOMEL BOOKS, Penguin Putnam Inc., 345 Hudson St., New York NY 10014. (212)414-3610. **Acquisitions:** Patricia Lee Gauch, editorial director, Michael Green, senior editor. Estab. 1980. Publishes hardcover originals. **Publishes 20-25 titles/year. Receives 2,600 submissions/year. 15% of books from first-time authors; 30% from unagented writers. Pays royalty. Offers advance.** Publishes book 1-2 years after acceptance of ms. Accepts simultaneous submissions. Book catalog for 9×12 SAE with 4 first-class stamps.
 O─┰ "We look for beautifully written, engaging manuscripts for children and young adults."
Fiction: Historical. Children's picture books (ages 3-8); middle-grade fiction and illustrated chapter books (ages 7-10); young adult novels (ages 10-15). Particularly interested in picture book mss with original stories and regional fiction with a distinct voice. No series or activity books. Query with SASE. *No unsolicited mss,.*
Recent Title(s): *Castaways of the Flying Dutchman*, by Brian Jacques; *Betty Doll*, by Patricia Palacco; *I am Morgan Le Fay*, by Nancy Springer.
Tips: "We prefer a very brief synopsis that states the basic premise of the story. This will help us determine whether or not the manuscript is suited to our list. If applicable, we'd be interested in knowing the author's writing experience or background knowledge. We try to be less influenced by the swings of the market than in the power, value, essence of the manuscript itself."

PICADOR USA, 175 Fifth Ave., New York NY 10010. Website: www.picadorusa.com. Estab. 1994. Publishes hardcover originals and trade paperback originals and reprints. **Publishes 70-80 titles/year. 30% of books from first-time authors; small% from unagented writers. Pays 7½-15% royalty on retail price. Offers varies advance.** Publishes book 18 months after acceptance of ms. Accepts simultaneous submissions. Responds in 2 months to queries. Book catalog for 9×12 SASE and $2.60 postage; ms guidelines for #10 SASE or online.
 O─┰ Picador publishes high-quality literary fiction and nonfiction. "We are open to a broad range of subjects, well written by authoritative authors."
Nonfiction: Biography, illustrated book. Subjects include language/literature, philosophy, cultural history, narrative books with a point of view on a particular subject. "When submitting queries, be aware of things outside the book, including credentials, that may affect our decision." Query only with SASE. No phone queries.
Fiction: Literary. Query only with SASE.
Recent Title(s): *The Amazing Adventures of Kavalier and Cly*, by Michael Chabon; *Being Dead*, by Jim Crace.

■ PICCADILLY BOOKS LTD., P.O. Box 25203, Colorado Springs CO 80936-5203. (719)550-9887. Website: www.piccadillybooks.com. Publisher: Bruce Fife. **Acquisitions:** Submissions Department. Estab. 1985. Publishes hardcover originals and trade paperback originals and reprints. **Publishes 5-8 titles/year. Receives 120 submissions/year. 70% of books from first-time authors; 95% from unagented writers. Pays 10% royalty on retail price.** Publishes book 1 year after acceptance of ms. Accepts simultaneous submissions. Responds to queries only if interested, unless accompanied by a SASE.

O— Picadilly publishes books on humor, entertainment, performing arts, skits and sketches, and writing.

Nonfiction: How-to (on entertainment). Subjects include film/cinema/stage, humor, performing arts, writing, small business. "We have a strong interest in subjects on clowning, magic, puppetry and related arts, including comedy skits and dialogs." Query with SASE or submit sample chapter(s).

Recent Title(s): *The Sherlock Holmes Book of Magic*, by Jeff Brown.

Tips: "Experience has shown that those who order our books are either kooky or highly intelligent or both. If you like to laugh, have fun, enjoy games, or have a desire to act like a jolly buffoon, we've got the books for you."

PICTON PRESS, Picton Corp., P.O. Box 250, Rockport ME 04856-0250. (207)236-6565. Fax: (207)236-6713. E-mail: sales@pictonpress.com. Website: www.pictonpress.com. Publishes hardcover and mass market paperback originals and reprints. **Publishes 30 titles/year. Receives 30 queries and 15 mss/year. 50% of books from first-time authors; 100% from unagented writers. Pays 0-10% royalty on wholesale price or makes outright purchase. Offers advance.** Publishes book 6 months after acceptance of ms. Responds in 2 months to queries and proposals; 3 months to mss. Book catalog free.

Imprints: Cricketfield Press, New England History Press, Penobscot Press, Picton Press

O— "Picton Press is one of America's oldest, largest and most respected publishers of genealogical and historical books specializing in research tools for the 17th, 18th and 19th centuries."

Nonfiction: Reference, textbook. Subjects include Americana, history, hobbies, genealogy, vital records. Query with SASE or submit outline.

Recent Title(s): *Nemesis At Potsdam*, by Alfred de Zayas.

THE PILGRIM PRESS, United Church of Christ, United Church Press, 700 Prospect Ave. E., Cleveland OH 44115-1100. (216)736-3764. Fax: (216)736-3703. E-mail: stavet@ucc.org. Website: www.pilgrimpress.com. **Acquisitions:** Timothy G. Staveteig, publisher. Publishes hardcover and trade paperback originals. **Publishes 25 titles/year. 30% of books from first-time authors; 80% from unagented writers. Pays standard royalties. Offers advance.** Publishes book an average of 18 months after acceptance of ms. Responds in 3 months to queries. Book catalog and ms guidelines online.

Nonfiction: Subjects include business/economics, gay/lesbian, government/politics, health/medicine, nature/environment, religion, ethics, social issues with a strong commitment to justice—addressing such topics as public policy, sexuality and gender, human rights and minority liberation—primarily in a Christian context, but not exclusively.

Recent Title(s): *Coming Out Young and Faithful*, by Leanne McCall and Timothy Brown.

Tips: "We are concentrating more on academic and trade submissions. Writers should send books about contemporary social issues. Our audience is liberal, open-minded, socially aware, feminist, church members and clergy, teachers and seminary professors."

PIÑATA BOOKS, Arte Publico Press, University of Houston, Houston TX 77204-2174. (713)743-2841. Fax: (713)743-2847. Website: www.arte.uh.edu. **Acquisitions:** Nicolas Kanellos, director. Estab. 1994. Publishes hardcover and trade paperback originals. **Publishes 10-15 titles/year. 60% of books from first-time authors. Pays 10% royalty on wholesale price. Offers $1,000-3,000 advance.** Publishes book 2 years after acceptance of ms. Accepts simultaneous submissions. Responds in 1 month to queries; 6 months to mss. Book catalog and ms guidelines online or with #10 SASE.

O— Pinata Books is dedicated to the publication of children's and young adult literature focusing on US Hispanic culture.

Nonfiction: "Piñata Books specializes in publication of children's and young adult literature that authentically portrays themes, characters and customs unique to U.S. Hispanic culture." Children's/juvenile. Subjects include ethnic. Query with SASE or submit outline, 2 sample chapter(s), synopsis.

Fiction: Adventure, juvenile, picture books, young adult. Query with synopsis, 2 sample chapters and SASE.

Poetry: Appropriate to Hispanic theme. Submit 10 sample poems.

Recent Title(s): *Tun-ta-ca-tun*, by Sylvia Pena (children's poetry, preschool to young adult).

Tips: "Include cover letter with submission explaining why your manuscript is unique and important, why we should publish it, who will buy it, etc."

PINEAPPLE PRESS, INC., P.O. Box 3899, Sarasota FL 34230. (941)359-0886. **Acquisitions:** June Cussen, editor. Estab. 1982. Publishes hardcover and trade paperback originals. **Publishes 20 titles/year. Receives 1,500 submissions/year. 20% of books from first-time authors; 80% from unagented writers. Pays 6½-15% royalty on net receipts. Offers rare advance.** Publishes book 18 months after acceptance of ms. Accepts simultaneous submissions. Responds in 3 months to queries. Book catalog for 9×12 SAE with $1.25 postage.

O— "We are seeking quality nonfiction on diverse topics for the library and book trade markets."

Nonfiction: Biography, how-to, reference. Subjects include animals, gardening, history, nature/environment, regional (Florida). "We will consider most nonfiction topics. Most, though not all, of our fiction and nonfiction deals with Florida." No pop psychology or autobiographies. Query or submit outline/brief synopsis, sample chapters and SASE.

Fiction: Historical, literary, mainstream/contemporary, regional (Florida). No romance or science fiction. Submit outline/brief synopsis and sample chapters.

Recent Title(s): *Seasons of the Sea*, by Jay Humphreys.

Tips: "Learn everything you can about book publishing and publicity and agree to actively participate in promoting your book. A query on a novel without a brief sample seems useless."

N PIPPIN PRESS, 229 E. 85th St., P.O. Box 1347, Gracie Station, New York NY 10028. (212)288-4920. Fax: (732)225-1562. **Acquisitions:** Barbara Francis, president and editor-in-chief; Joyce Segal, senior editor. Estab. 1987. Publishes hardcover originals. **Publishes 4-6 titles/year. Receives 1,500 queries/year. 80% from unagented writers. Pays royalty. Offers advance.** Publishes book 2 years after acceptance of ms. Responds in 3 weeks to queries. Book catalog for 6×9 SASE; ms guidelines for #10 SASE.
○→ Pippin publishes general nonfiction and fiction for children ages 4-12.
Nonfiction: Biography, children's/juvenile, humor, illustrated book, autobiography. Subjects include animals, history, language/literature, memoirs, nature/environment, science, general nonfiction for children ages 4-12. *No unsolicited mss.* Query with SASE only. Reviews artwork/photos as part of ms package. Send photocopies.
Fiction: Historical, humor, mystery, picture books. "We're especially looking for small chapter books for 7- to 11-year olds, especially by people of many cultures." Also interested in humorous fiction for ages 7-11. Query with SASE only.
Recent Title(s): *A Visit from the Leopard: Memories of a Ugandan Childhood*, by Catherine Mudiko-Piwang and Edward Frascino; *Abigail's Drum*, by John A. Minahan, illustrated by Robert Quackenbush (historical fiction).
Tips: "Read as many of the best children's books published in the last five years as you can. We are looking for multi-ethnic fiction and nonfiction for ages 7-10, as well as general fiction for this age group. I would pay particular attention to children's books favorably reviewed in *School Library Journal*, *The Booklist*, *The New York Times Book Review*, and *Publishers Weekly*."

N PLANNERS PRESS, American Planning Association, 122 S. Michigan Ave., Chicago IL 60603. Fax: (312)431-9985. E-mail: slewis@planning.org. Website: www.planning.org. **Acquisitions:** Sylvia Lewis, director of publications. Estab. 1978. Publishes hardcover and trade paperback originals. **Publishes 4-6 titles/year. Receives 20 queries and 6-8 mss/year. 50% of books from first-time authors; 100% from unagented writers. Pays 7½-12% royalty on retail price. Offers advance.** Publishes book 1 year after acceptance of ms. Responds in 1 month to queries; 2 months to proposals and mss. Book catalog and ms guidelines free.
○→ "Our books have a narrow audience of city planners and often focus on the tools of city planning."
Nonfiction: Technical (public policy and city planning). Subjects include government/politics. Submit 2 sample chapters and table of contents. Reviews artwork/photos as part of ms package. Send photocopies.
Recent Title(s): *Sprawl Busting: State Programs to Guide Growth*; *SafeScape*; *Planning in Plain English*.

PLANNING/COMMUNICATIONS, 7215 Oak Ave., River Forest IL 60305. (708)366-5200. E-mail: dl@jobfinders online.com. Website: jobfindersonline.com. **Acquisitions:** Daniel Lauber, president. Estab. 1979. Publishes hardcover, trade and mass market paperback originals, trade paperback reprints. **Publishes 3-6 titles/year. Receives 30 queries and 3 mss/year. 50% of books from first-time authors; 100% from unagented writers. Pays 10-16% royalty on net receipts.** Publishes book 1 year after acceptance of ms. Accepts simultaneous submissions. Responds in 3 months to queries. Book catalog and ms guidelines for $2 or online.
○→ Planning Communications publishes books on careers, improving your life, ending discrimination, sociology, urban planning and politics.
Nonfiction: Self-help. Subjects include business/economics (careers), education, government/politics, money/finance, sociology, ending discrimination, careers, résumés, cover letters, interviewing. Submit outline, 3 sample chapter(s), SASE. Reviews artwork/photos as part of ms package. Send photocopies.
Recent Title(s): *International Job Finder*, by Daniel Lowber.
Tips: "Our editorial mission is to publish books that can make a difference in people's lives—books of substance, not glitz."

PLAYERS PRESS, INC., P.O. Box 1132, Studio City CA 91614-0132. (818)789-4980. **Acquisitions:** Robert W. Gordon, vice president, editorial. Estab. 1965. Publishes hardcover originals and trade paperback originals and reprints. **Publishes 35-70 titles/year. Receives 200-1,000 submissions/year. 15% of books from first-time authors; 80% from unagented writers. Pays royalty on wholesale price. Offers advance.** Publishes book 3 months-2 years after acceptance of ms. Book catalog for #10 SASE; ms guidelines for 9×12 SAE with 5 first-class stamps.
○→ Players Press publishes support books for the entertainment industries: theater, film, television, dance and technical. Currently emphasizing plays for all ages, theatre crafts, monologues and short scenes for ages 5-9, 11-15.
Nonfiction: Children's/juvenile, theatrical drama/entertainment industry. Subjects include film/cinema/stage, performing arts, costume, theater crafts, film crafts, dance. Needs quality plays and musicals, adult or juvenile. Query with SASE. Reviews music as part of ms package.
Fiction: Plays: Subject matter includes adventure, confession, ethnic, experimental, fantasy, historical, horror, humor, mainstream, mystery, religious romance, science fiction, suspense, western. Submit complete ms for theatrical plays only. Plays must be previously produced. "No novels or story books are accepted."
Recent Title(s): *Monologues for Teens*, by Vernon Howard; *Moments*, by David Crawford.
Tips: "Plays, entertainment industry texts, theater, film and TV books have the only chances of selling to our firm."

[N] PLAYHOUSE PUBLISHING, 1566 Akron-Peninsula Road, Akron OH 44313. (330)926-1313. Fax: (330)926-1315. Website: www.playhousepublishing.com. **Acquisitions:** Deborah D'Andrea, publisher (children's fiction). Publishes hardcover originals. **Publishes 10-15 titles/year; imprint publishes 3-5 titles/year. Work-for-hire. Makes $150-350 outright purchase.** Publishes book 1 year after acceptance of ms. Accepts simultaneous submissions. Responds in 2 months to mss. Book catalog online.

Imprints: Picture Me Books (board books with photos) and Nibble Me Books (board books with candy)

 O→ "We publish juvenile fiction appropriate for children from pre-school to third grade. All Picture Me Books titles incorporate the 'picture me' concept. All Nibble Me Books titles incorporate snack foods or candy."

Fiction: Juvenile. Submit complete ms with SASE for return.

Recent Title(s): *Picture Me as Dad's Little Helper*, by Catherine McCafferty; *Picture Me Cuddly as a Bunny*, by Kaycee Hoffman; *Reese's Pieces Math Fun*, by Mary Bono and Craig Strasshofer (Nibble Me Books).

[■] PLEASANT COMPANY PUBLICATIONS, 8400 Fairway Pl., Middleton WI 53562. Fax: (608)828-4768. Website: www.americangirl.com. **Acquisitions:** Erin Falligant, submissions editor. Estab. 1986. Publishes hardcover and trade paperback originals. **Publishes 50-60 titles/year. Receives 500 queries and 800 mss/year. 90% from un-agented writers. Offers varying advance.** Accepts simultaneous submissions. Responds in 3 months to queries. Book catalog for #10 SASE.

Imprints: The American Girls Collection, American Girl Library, AG Fiction, History Mysteries

 O→ Pleasant Company publishes fiction and nonfiction for girls 7-12.

Nonfiction: Children's/juvenile (for girls 7-12), how-to. Subjects include Americana, history, contemporary lifestyle, activities. Query with SASE.

Fiction: Historical, juvenile (for girls, ages 7-12), mystery, contemporary. "We are seeking strong, well-written fiction, historical and contemporary, told from the perspective of a middle-school-age girl. No romance, picture books, poetry." Query with SASE or submit complete ms.

Recent Title(s): *Smoke Screen*, by Amy Goldman Koss; *Trouble at Fort La Pointe*, by Kathleen Ernst.

PLEXUS PUBLISHING, INC., 143 Old Marlton Pike, Medford NJ 08055-8750. (609)654-6500. Fax: (609)654-4309. E-mail: jbryans@infotoday.com. **Acquisitions:** John B. Bryans, editor-in-chief. Estab. 1977. Publishes hardcover and paperback originals. **Publishes 4-5 titles/year. Receives 30-60 submissions/year. 70% of books from first-time authors; 90% from unagented writers. Pays 17½% royalty on wholesale price or makes outright purchase of $250-1,000. Offers $500-1,000 advance.** Accepts simultaneous submissions. Responds in 3 months to proposals. Book catalog and ms guidelines for 10×13 SAE with 4 first-class stamps.

 O→ Plexus publishes mainly regional-interest (southern NJ) fiction and nonfiction including mysteries, field guides, history. Also health/medicine, biology, ecology, botony, astronomy.

Nonfiction: Coffee table book, how-to, illustrated book, reference, textbook, natural, historical references, and scholarly. Subjects include agriculture/horticulture, education, gardening, health/medicine, history (southern New Jersey), nature/environment, recreation, regional (southern NJ), science, botany, medicine, biology, ecology, astronomy. "We will consider any book on a nature/biology subject, particularly those of a reference (permanent) nature that would be of lasting value to high school and college audiences, and/or the general reading public (ages 14 and up). Authors should have authentic qualifications in their subject area, but qualifications may be by experience as well as academic training." Also interested in mss of about 20-40 pages in length for feature articles in *Biology Digest* (guidelines available for SASE). No gardening, philosophy or psychology; generally not interested in travel but will consider travel that gives sound ecological information. Query with SASE. Reviews artwork/photos as part of ms package. Send photocopies.

Fiction: Mysteries and literary novels with a strong regional (southern NJ) angle. Query with SASE.

Recent Title(s): *Down Barnegat Bay: A Nor'easter Midnight Reader*, by Robert Jahn.

[A] POCKET BOOKS, Simon & Schuster, 1230 Avenue of the Americas, New York NY 10020. (212)698-7000. Website: www.simonsays.com. Vice President/Editorial Director: Tracy Behar. Publishes paperback originals and reprints, mass market and trade paperbacks and hardcovers. **Publishes 250 titles/year. Receives 2,500 submissions/year. 25% of books from first-time authors; 5% from unagented writers. Pays 6-8% royalty on retail price. Offers advance.** Publishes book an average of 2 years after acceptance of ms. Book catalog free; ms guidelines online.

 O→ Pocket Books publishes general interest nonfiction and adult fiction.

Nonfiction: Biography, reference. Subjects include cooking/foods/nutrition, general, history, humor. *Accepts agented submissions only.*

Fiction: Adult (mysteries, thriller, psychological suspense, *Star Trek* novels, romance, westerns). *Accepts agented submissions only.*

Recent Title(s): *Talking Dirty with the Queen of Clean*, by Linda Cobb.

[■] POPULAR CULTURE INK, P.O. Box 110, Harbor Springs MI 49740-0110. (231)439-9767. **Acquisitions:** Tom Schultheiss, publisher. Estab. 1989. Publishes hardcover originals and reprints. **Publishes 4-6 titles/year. Receives 50 queries and 20 mss/year. 100% of books from first-time authors; 100% from unagented writers. Pays variable royalty on wholesale price. Offers variable advance.** Publishes book 2 years after acceptance of ms. Accepts simultaneous submissions. Responds in 1 month to queries. Book catalog and ms guidelines free.

 O→ Popular Culture Ink publishes directories and reference books for radio, TV, music and other entertainment subjects.

Nonfiction: Reference. Subjects include music/dance, popular entertainment. Query with SASE.
Recent Title(s): *Surfin' Guitars*, by Robert Dalley (1960s surf music).
Tips: Audience is libraries, avid collectors. "Know your subject backwards. Make sure your book is unique."

POPULAR WOODWORKING BOOKS, F&W Publications, 1507 Dana Ave., Cincinnati OH 45207. (513)531-2690. **Acquisitions:** Jim Stack, acquisitions editor. Publishes trade paperback originals and reprints. **Publishes 10-12 titles/year. Receives 30 queries and 10 mss/year. 50% of books from first-time authors; 95% from unagented writers. Pays 10-20% royalty on net receipts. Offers $3,000-5,000 advance.** Publishes book 1 year after acceptance of ms. Accepts simultaneous submissions. Responds in 1 month to queries. Book catalog and ms guidelines for 9 × 12 SAE with 6 first-class stamps.

  O— Popular Woodworking publishes how-to woodworking books that use photos with captions to show and tell the reader how to build projects. Technical illustrations and materials lists supply all the rest of the information needed. Currently emphasizing woodworking jigs and fixtures, furniture and cabinet projects, smaller finely crafted boxes, all styles of furniture. De-emphasizing woodturning, woodcarving, scroll saw projects.

Nonfiction: "We publish heavily illustrated how-to woodworking books that show, rather than tell, our readers how to accomplish their woodworking goals." How-to, illustrated book. Subjects include hobbies, woodworking/wood crafts. Query with SASE or submit proposal package including outline, transparencies. Reviews artwork/photos as part of ms package.
Recent Title(s): *Fast Furniture*, by Armand Sussman; *25 Essential Projects for Your Workshop*, by the editors of *Popular Woodworking*.
Tips: "Our books are for 'advanced beginner' woodworking enthusiasts."

▲ POSSIBILITY PRESS, One Oakglade Circle, Hummelstown PA 17036-9525. (717)566-0468. Fax: (717)566-6423. E-mail: posspress@excite.com. Website: www.possibilitypress.com. **Acquisitions:** Mike Markowski, publisher, Marjorie L. Markowski, editor-in-chief. Estab. 1981. Publishes trade paperback originals. **Publishes 10-20 titles/year. Receives 1,000 submissions/year. 90% of books from first-time authors; 95% from unagented writers. Royalties vary.** Publishes book approximately 1 year after acceptance of ms. Responds in 2 months to queries. Manuscript guidelines for #10 SAE with 2 first-class stamps.
Imprints: Aviation Publishers, Possibility Press

  O— "Our mission is to help the people of the world grow and become the best they can be, through the written and spoken word." No longer interested in health issues.

Nonfiction: How-to, self-help, inspirational. Subjects include business, current significant events, pop-psychology, success/motivation, inspiration, entrepreneurship, sales marketing, network and homebased business topics, and human interest success stories.
Recent Title(s): *If It Is to Be, It's Up to Me*, by Thomas B. Smith.
Tips: "Our focus is on creating and publishing short to medium length bestsellers written by authors who speak and consult. We're looking for authors who are serious about making a difference in the world."

PRAEGER PUBLISHERS, The Greenwood Publishing Group, Inc., 88 Post Road W., Westport CT 06881. (203)226-3571. Fax: (203)226-6009. Publisher: Peter Kracht. **Acquisitions:** Heather Stainer (history, military); Debbie Carvalko (psychology); Suzanne Staszak-Silva (sociology); Cynthia Harris (economics); Eric Levy (cultural studies, media); James Sabin (politics). Estab. 1949. Publishes paperback originals. **Publishes 250 titles/year. Receives 1,200 submissions/year. 5% of books from first-time authors; 90% from unagented writers. Pays 6½-12% royalty on net receipts. Offers rare advance.** Publishes book an average of 1 year after acceptance of ms. Accepts simultaneous submissions. Responds in 1 month to queries. Book catalog and ms guidelines online.

  O— Praeger publishes scholarly trade and advanced texts in the the social and behavioral sciences and communications, international relations and military studies.

Nonfiction: Subjects include business/economics, government/politics, history, psychology, sociology, women's issues/studies. "We are looking for scholarly works in women's studies, sociology, psychology, contemporary history, military studies, political science, economics, international relations. No language and literature." Query with proposal package, including: scope, organization, length of project; whether a complete ms is available, or when it will be; cv or résumé with SASE. *No unsolicited mss.*
Recent Title(s): *An American Paradox: Censorship in a Nation of Free Speech*, Patrick Garry; *Pharmacracy: Medicine and Politics in America*, edited by Thomas Szasz.

PRAIRIE OAK PRESS, 821 Prospect Place, Madison WI 53703. (608)255-2288. Fax: (608)255-4204. E-mail: popjama@aol.com. **Acquisitions:** Jerry Minnich, president. Estab. 1991. Publishes hardcover originals, trade paperback originals and reprints. **Publishes 6-8 titles/year. Pays royalty. Offers $500-1,000 advance.** Responds in 3 months to proposals.
Imprints: Prairie Classics, Acorn Guides

  O— Prairie Oak publishes exclusively Upper Great Lakes regional nonfiction. Currently emphasizing travel, sports, recreation.

Nonfiction: "Any work considered must have a strong tie to Wisconsin and/or the Upper Great Lakes region." Subjects include art/architecture, gardening, general, history, regional, sports, travel, folklore, general trade subjects. No poetry, fiction or juvenile. Query with SASE or submit outline, 1 sample chapter(s).
Recent Title(s): *Wisconsin Lighthouses*, by Ken and Barb Wardius.

Tips: "When we say we publish regional works only, we mean Wisconsin, Minnesota, Michigan, Illinois. Please do not submit books of national interest. We cannot consider them."

⚑ PRB PRODUCTIONS, 963 Peralta Ave., Albany CA 94706-2144. (510)526-0722. Fax: (510)527-4763. E-mail: PRBPrdns@aol.com. Website: www.prbpro.com. **Acquisitions:** Peter R. Ballinger, publisher (early and contemporary music for instruments and voices). **Publishes 10-15 titles/year. Pays 10-15% royalty on retail price.** Publishes book 3 months after acceptance of ms. Accepts simultaneous submissions. Responds in 1 month to queries; 3 months to mss. Book catalog online.
Nonfiction: Textbook, sheet music. Subjects include music/dance. Query with SASE or submit complete ms.
Recent Title(s): *Six Sonatas for Violincello and Basso Continuo*, by Francesco Guerini, edited by Sarah Freiberg (music score and parts).
Tips: Audience is music schools, universities, libraries, professional music educators, and amateur/professional musicians.

PRECEPT PRESS, Bonus Books, 160 E. Illinois St., Chicago IL 60611. (312)467-0580. Fax: (312)467-9271. E-mail: bb@bonus-books.com. Website: www.bonus-books.com. **Acquisitions:** Erin Kahl, acquisitions editor. Estab. 1970. Publishes hardcover and trade paperback originals. **Publishes 5-10 titles/year. Receives 300 queries and 100 mss/ year. 25% of books from first-time authors; 90% from unagented writers. Pays royalty. Offers advance.** Publishes book 1 year after acceptance of ms. Accepts simultaneous submissions. Responds in 3 months to proposals. Manuscript guidelines for #10 SASE.
○━ Precept Press features a wide variety of books for the technical community. Currently emphasizing cultural and film theory.
Nonfiction: Reference, technical, textbook. Subjects include business/economics, film/cinema/stage, health/medicine (clinical medical, oncology texts), science. Query with SASE.
Recent Title(s): *Nutritional Care for High-Risk Newborns*, ed. by Groh-Wargo, Thompson & Cox.

PRESIDIO PRESS, 505B San Marin Dr., Suite 160, Novato CA 94945-1340. (415)898-1081 ext. 25. Fax: (415)898-0383. **Acquisitions:** Mr. E.J. McCarthy, executive editor. Estab. 1974. Publishes hardcover originals and reprints. **Publishes 24 titles/year. Receives 1,600 submissions/year. 35% of books from first-time authors; 65% from unagented writers. Pays 15-20% royalty on net receipts. Offers varies advance.** Publishes book 18 months after acceptance of ms. Responds in 1 month to queries. Book catalog and ms guidelines for 7½×10½ SAE with 4 first-class stamps.
○━ "We publish the finest and most accurate military history and military affairs nonfiction, plus entertaining and provocative fiction related to military affairs."
Nonfiction: Subjects include history, military/war (military history and military affairs). Query with SASE. Reviews artwork/photos as part of ms package. Send photocopies.
Fiction: Military/war. Query with SASE.
Recent Title(s): *Somalia on $5 a Day*, by Martin Stanton; *Beyond the Rhine*, by Donald R. Burgett (military fiction).
Tips: "Study the market. Find out what publishers are publishing, what they say they want and so forth. Then write what the market seems to be asking for, but with some unique angle that differentiates the work from others on the same subject. We feel that readers of hardcover fiction are looking for works of no less than 80,000 words."

THE PRESS AT THE MARYLAND HISTORICAL SOCIETY, 201 W. Monument St., Baltimore MD 21201. (410)685-3750. Fax: (410)385-2105. E-mail: rcottom@mdhs.org. Website: www.mdhs.org. **Acquisitions:** Robert I. Cottom, publisher (MD/Chesapeake history); Donna B. Shear, senior editor (Maryland-Chesapeake history). Publishes hardcover and trade paperback originals and trade paperback reprints. **Publishes 6-8 titles/year. Receives 12-15 queries and 8-10 mss/year. 50% of books from first-time authors; 100% from unagented writers. Pays 6-10% royalty on retail price.** Publishes book 1 year after acceptance of ms. Accepts simultaneous submissions. Responds in 1 month to queries and proposals; 6 months to mss. Book catalog online.
○━ The Press at the Maryland Historical Society specializes in Maryland state and Chesapeake regional subjects.
Nonfiction: Biography, children's/juvenile, illustrated book, scholarly textbook. Subjects include anthropology/archeology, art/architecture, history. Query with SASE or submit proposal package including outline, 1-2 sample chapter(s).
Recent Title(s): *Troubled Waters: An Environmental History of Chesapeake Bay*, by John R. Wennersten.
Tips: "Our audience consists of intelligent readers of Maryland/Chesapeake regional history and biography."

⚑ PRESSFORWARD PUBLISHING HOUSE LLC, 4341 Doncaster Dr., Madison WI 53711-3717. (877)894-4015. E-mail: PressForward@msn.com. **Acquisitions:** Arthur W. Cran, publisher. Publishes hardcover, trade paperback and mass market paperback originals. **Publishes 3-5 titles/year. Receives 20 queries and 15 mss/year. 75% of books from first-time authors; 100% from unagented writers. Pays 10-20% royalty on retail price.** Publishes book 9 months after acceptance of ms. Accepts simultaneous submissions. Responds in 1 month to queries, proposals and mss. Book catalog and ms guidelines free.
○━ "We address mental health providers and consumers, as well as their families. We are beginning to accept compelling life stories of consumers."

Nonfiction: Biography, coffee table book, self-help. Subjects include education, health/medicine, nature/environment, psychology. "We like writers who have compelling life stories of overcoming disabilities of psychological or psychiatric in nature. We especially like to hear from educated mental health consumers who have new insights to share." Query with SASE or submit complete ms. Reviews artwork/photos as part of ms package. Send photocopies.

Recent Title(s): *Child Sexual Abuse: Making the Tactics Visible*, by Sam Warner.

Tips: Our audience is mental health professionals of all types; also family groups, and mental health consumers. "We want mental health consumers who have 'been through' the system and who have new stories to tell and insight to share. They should contact the publisher here at (877)894-4015. Potential writers should be skilled, well read generally and specifically and have valuable ideas about mental health treatment and recovery."

N: PRESTWICK HOUSE, INC., 605 Forest St., Dover DE 19904. (302)736-5614. Website: www.prestwickhouse.com. **Acquisitions:** Paul Moliken, editor. **Publishes 5 titles/year. Makes outright purchase of $200-1,500.**

Nonfiction: Reference, textbook, teaching supplements. Subjects include grammar, writing, test taking. Submit proposal package including outline, 1 sample chapter(s), résumé.

Recent Title(s): *Understanding the Language of Shakespeare*, by B. Kampa; *Notetaking and Outlining*, by J. Scott.

Tips: "We market our books primarily for high school English teachers. Submissions should address a direct need of grades 7-12 language arts teachers. Current and former English teachers are encouraged to submit materials developed and used by them successfully in the classroom."

PRICE STERN SLOAN, INC., Penguin Putnam Inc., 345 Hudson, New York NY 10014. (212)414-3610. Fax: (212)414-3396. **Acquisitions:** Jon Anderson, publisher. Estab. 1963. **Publishes 80 titles/year. Makes outright purchase. Offers advance.** Responds in 3 months to queries. Book catalog for 9×12 SAE with 5 first-class stamps; ms guidelines for #10 SASE. Address to Book Catalog or Manuscript Guidelines.

Imprints: Doodle Art, Mad Libs, Mr. Men & Little Miss, Plugged In, Serendipity, Troubador Press, Wee Sing

○── Price Stern Sloan publishes quirky mass market novelty series for children.

Nonfiction: Children's/juvenile, humor. "Most of our titles are unique in concept as well as execution." Do not send *original* artwork or ms. *No unsolicited mss.*

Fiction: "We publish very little in the way of fiction."

Recent Title(s): *Who's Got Mail?*, by Charles Reasoner (preschool); *What Do You Want On Your Pizza?*, by William Boniface (preschool); *Growing-Money*, by Gail Karlitz (nonfiction).

Tips: "Price Stern Sloan has a unique, humorous, off-the-wall feel."

PRIMA PUBLISHING, Random House Inc., P.O. Box 1260, Rocklin CA 95677-1260. (916)632-4400. Website: www.primapublishing.com. President/Founder: Ben Dominitz. **Acquisitions:** *Lifestyles Division:* Alice Feinstein, editorial director; Steve Martin, Forum publisher; Susan Silva, acquisitions; Jamie Miller, acquisitions; Denise Sternad, acquisitions (girls, weddings, home, crafts); Lorna Dolley, acquisitions (brain performance, creativity, pets); David Richardson, acquisitions (high-end business, money, investing); Lorna Eby, acquisitions. *Prima Games Division:* Debra Kempker, publisher; Stacy DeFoe, product manager; Amy Raynor, product manager. Estab. 1984. Publishes hardcover originals and trade paperback originals and reprints. **Publishes 300 titles/year. Receives 750 queries/year. 10% of books from first-time authors; 30% from unagented writers. Pays 15-20% royalty on wholesale price. Offers variable advance.** Publishes book 18 months after acceptance of ms. Accepts simultaneous submissions. Responds in 3 months to queries. Book catalog for 9×12 SAE with 8 first-class stamps; ms guidelines for #10 SASE.

● Prima was acquired by Random House. PrimaTech will be sold or fold; other divisions will be incorporated. Editorial offices will remain in California.

Nonfiction: Biography, self-help. Subjects include business/economics, child guidance/parenting, cooking/foods/nutrition, education, health/medicine (alternative and traditional), history, psychology, sports, entertainment, writing, crafts, pets, politics, current affairs, network marketing. "We want books with originality, written by highly qualified individuals. No fiction at this time." Query with SASE.

Recent Title(s): *Emergency Animal Rescue Stories*, by Terri Crisp; *Sacred Dying*, by Megory Anderson.

Tips: "Prima strives to reach the primary and secondary markets for each of its books. We are known for promoting our books aggressively. Books that genuinely solve problems for people will always do well if properly promoted. Try to picture the intended audience while writing the book. Too many books are written to an audience that doesn't exist."

PROMETHEUS BOOKS, 59 John Glenn Dr., Amherst NY 14228-2197. (716)691-0133 ext. 207. Fax: (716)564-2711. E-mail: slmitchell@prometheusmail.com. Website: www.prometheusbooks.com. **Acquisitions:** Steven L. Mitchell, editor-in-chief (Prometheus/Humanity Books, philosophy, social science, political science, general nonfiction); Eugene O'Connor, acquisitions editor (Humanity Books, scholarly and professional works in philosophy, social science); Linda Greenspan Regan, executive editor (Prometheus, popular science, health, psychology, criminology). Estab. 1969. Publishes hardcover originals, trade paperback originals and reprints. **Publishes 85-100 titles/year. Receives 2,500 submissions/year. 25% of books from first-time authors; 50% from unagented writers. Pays 10-15% royalty on wholesale price. Offers $0-3,000 advance.** Publishes book 18 months after acceptance of ms. Accepts simultaneous submissions. Responds in 1 month to queries; 2 months to proposals; 4 months to mss. Book catalog online; ms guidelines for #10 SASE.

Imprints: Humanity Books (scholarly and professionals monographs in philosophy, social science, sociology, archaeology, Marxist studies, etc.)

O— "Prometheus Books is a leading independent publisher in philosophy, popular science and critical thinking. We publish authoritative and thoughtful books by distinguished authors in many categories. We are a niche, or specialized, publisher that features *critiques* of the paranormal and pseudoscience, critiques of religious extremism and right wing fundamentalism and creationism; Biblical and Koranic criticism: human sexuality, etc. Currently emphasizing popular science, health, psychology, social science."

Nonfiction: Biography, children's/juvenile, reference, self-help. Subjects include education, government/politics, health/medicine, history, language/literature, New Age, philosophy, psychology, religion (not religious, but critiquing), contemporary issues, current events, Islamic studies, law, popular science, critiques of the paranormal and UFO sightings, sexuality. "Ask for a catalog, go to the library, look at our books and others like them to get an idea of what our focus is." Submit proposal package including outline, synopsis and a well-developed query letter with SASE. Reviews artwork/photos as part of ms package. Send photocopies.

Recent Title(s): *Overcoming Destructive Beliefs, Feelings and Behavior*, by Albert Ellis.

Tips: "Audience is highly literate with multiple degrees; an audience that is intellectually mature and knows what it wants. They are aware, and we try to provide them with new information on topics of interest to them in mainstream and related areas."

PROSTAR PUBLICATIONS INC., 3 Church Circle, #109, Annapolis MD 21401. (800)481-6277. Fax: (800)487-6277. Website: www.nauticalbooks.com. **Acquisitions:** Peter Griffes, president (marine-related/how-to/business/technical); Susan Willson, editor (history/memoirs). Estab. 1965. Publishes trade paperback originals. **Publishes 150 titles/year; imprint publishes 10-15 titles/year. Receives 60 queries and 25 mss/year. 50% of books from first-time authors; 100% from unagented writers. Pays 15% royalty on wholesale price. Rarely offers advance.** Publishes book 1 year after acceptance of ms. Accepts simultaneous submissions. Responds in 3 months to queries and proposals. Book catalog online.

Imprints: Lighthouse Press (Peter Griffes)

O— "Originally, ProStar published only nautical books. At present, however, we are expanding. Any quality nonfiction book would be of interest."

Nonfiction: Coffee table book, how-to, illustrated book, technical. Subjects include history, memoirs, nature/environment, travel, nautical. Query with SASE. Reviews artwork/photos as part of ms package. Send photocopies.

Recent Title(s): *The Steeples of Old New England*, by Kirk Chivell; *Memories, Memories*, by Lily Marguless.

Tips: "We prefer to work directly with the author; we seldom work with agents. Send in a well-written query letter, and we will give your book serious consideration."

PRUETT PUBLISHING, 7464 Arapahoe Rd., Suite A-9, Boulder CO 80303. (303)449-4919. Fax: (303)443-9019. E-mail: pruettbks@aol.com. **Acquisitions:** Jim Pruett, publisher. Estab. 1959. Publishes hardcover and trade paperback originals and reprints. **Publishes 10-15 titles/year. 60% of books from first-time authors; 95% from unagented writers. Pays 10-12% royalty on net receipts. Offers advance.** Publishes book 18 months after acceptance of ms. Accepts simultaneous submissions. Responds in 2 months to queries. Book catalog and ms guidelines free.

O— "Pruett Publishing strives to convey to our customers and readers a respect of the American West, in particular the spirit, traditions, and attitude of the region. We publish books in the following subject areas: outdoor recreation, regional history, environment and nature, travel and culture. We especially need books on outdoor recreation."

Nonfiction: "We are looking for nonfiction manuscripts and guides that focus on the Rocky Mountain West." Guidebooks. Subjects include Americana (Western), anthropology/archeology (Native American), cooking/foods/nutrition (Native American, Mexican, Spanish), ethnic, history (Western), nature/environment, recreation (outdoor), regional, sports (cycling, hiking, fly fishing), travel. Submit proposal package. Reviews artwork/photos as part of ms package.

Recent Title(s): *Flyfishing the Texas Coast: Back Country Flats to Bluewater*, by Chuck Scales and Phil Shook, photography by David J. Sams; *Trout Country: Reflections on Rivers, Flyfishing & Related Addictions*, by Bob Saile; *Rocky Mountain Christmas*, by John H. Monnett.

Tips: "There has been a movement away from large publisher's mass market books and towards small publisher's regional interest books, and in turn distributors and retail outlets are more interested in small publishers. Authors don't need to have a big name to have a good publisher. Look for similar books that you feel are well produced—consider design, editing, overall quality and contact those publishers. Get to know several publishers, and find the one that feels right—trust your instincts."

PRUFROCK PRESS INC., P.O. Box 8813, Waco TX 76714. (254)756-3337. Fax: (254)756-3339. E-mail: mcintosh@prufrock.com. Website: www.prufrock.com. **Acquisitions:** Joel McIntosh, publisher. Publishes trade paperback originals and reprints. **Publishes 10 titles/year. Receives 150 queries and 50 mss/year. 50% of books from first-time authors; 100% from unagented writers. Pays 10% royalty on sale price. Offers advance.** Publishes book 9 months after acceptance of ms. Responds in 2 months to queries. Book catalog and ms guidelines free.

O— "Prufrock Press publishes exciting, innovative and current resources supporting the education of gifted and talented learners."

Nonfiction: How-to, textbook, scholarly. Subjects include child guidance/parenting, education. "We publish for the education market. Our readers are typically teachers or parents of gifted and talented children. Our product line is built around professional development books for teachers and activity books for gifted children. Our products support innovative ways of making learning more fun and exciting for gifted and talented children." Request query package from publisher.

Recent Title(s): *Philosophy for Kids*, by David A. White, Ph.D; *On the Social and Emotional Lives of Gifted Children*, by Tracy L. Cross, Ph.D; *Alien Math*, by Nick Bellow, Rita Beng and Marya Tyler.

Tips: "We are looking for practical, classroom-ready materials that encourage children to creatively learn and think."

PUFFIN BOOKS, Penguin Putnam Inc., 345 Hudson St., New York NY 10014-3657. (212)414-2000. Website: www.penguinputnam.com. President/Publisher: Tracy Tang. **Acquisitions:** Sharyn November, senior editor, Kristin Gilson, executive editor. Publishes trade paperback originals and reprints. **Publishes 175-200 titles/year. Receives 300 queries and 300 mss/year. 1% of books from first-time authors; 5% from unagented writers. Royalty varies. Offers varies advance.** Publishes book 1 year after acceptance of ms. Responds in 3 months to mss. Book catalog for 9×12 SAE with 7 first-class stamps; send request to Marketing Department.

○━ Puffin Books publishes high-end trade paperbacks and paperback reprints for preschool children, beginning and middle readers, and young adults.

Nonfiction: Biography, children's/juvenile, illustrated book, Young children's concept books (counting, shapes, colors). Subjects include education (for teaching concepts and colors, not academic), history, women's issues/studies. " 'Women in history' books interest us." *No unsolicited mss.* Query with SASE.

Fiction: Picture books, young adult, Middle Grade, Easy-to-Read Grades 1-3. "We publish mostly paperback reprints. We do very few original titles." *No unsolicited mss.*

Tips: "Our audience ranges from little children 'first books' to young adult (ages 14-16). An original idea has the best luck."

PURDUE UNIVERSITY PRESS, 1207 South Campus Courts, Bldg. E, West Lafayette IN 47907-1207. (765)494-2038. Website: www.thepress.purdue.edu. **Acquisitions:** Thomas Bacher, director (technology, business, veterinary medicine, philosophy); Margaret Hunt, managing editor (Central European studies, regional, literature). Estab. 1960. Publishes hardcover and trade paperback originals and trade paperback reprints. **Publishes 14-20 titles/year. Receives 600 submissions/year. Pays 7½-15% royalty. Offers advance.** Publishes book 9 months after acceptance of ms. Responds in 2 months to queries. Book catalog and ms guidelines for 9×12 SASE.

○━ "We look for books that look at the world as a whole and offer new thoughts and insights into the standard debate." Currently emphasizing technology, human-animal issues, business. De-emphasizing literary studies.

Nonfiction: "We publish work of quality scholarship and titles with regional (Midwest) flair. Especially interested in innovative contributions to the social sciences and humanities that break new barriers and provide unique views on current topics. Expanding into veterinary medicine, engineering and business topics." Biography. Subjects include agriculture/horticulture, Americana, business/economics, government/politics, health/medicine, history, language/literature, philosophy, regional, science, sociology. "Always looking for new authors who show creativity and thoroughness of research." Print and electronic projects accepted. Query before submitting.

Recent Title(s): *Route Across the Rocky Mountains*, edited by Angela Firkus; *Bitter Prerequisites: A Faculty for Survival from Nazi Terror*, by Laird Kleine-Ahlbrandt; *A Story for All Americans: Vietnam, Victims and Veterans*, by Frank Grzyb.

Ⓐ **G.P. PUTNAM'S SONS**, (Adult Trade), Penguin Putnam, Inc., 375 Hudson, New York NY 10014. (212)366-2000. Fax: (212)366-2666. Website: www.penguinputnam.com. Publisher: Neil Nyren. Vice President: Marian Woods. Publishes hardcover and trade paperback originals. **5% from unagented writers. Pays royalty. Offers advance.** Accepts simultaneous submissions. Responds in 6 months to queries. Request book catalog through mail order department; ms guidelines free.

Nonfiction: Biography, cookbook, self-help, celebrity-related topics, contemporary issues. Subjects include animals, business/economics, child guidance/parenting, cooking/foods/nutrition, health/medicine, military/war, nature/environment, religion, science, sports, travel, women's issues/studies. *Accepts agented submissions only.*

Fiction: Adventure, literary, mainstream/contemporary, mystery, suspense, Women's. *Accepts agented submissions only.*

Recent Title(s): *Lindbergh*, A. Scott Berg (nonfiction); *Rainbow Six*, Tom Clancy (adventure).

QUE, Pearson Education, Indianapolis IN 46290. (317)581-3500. Website: www.quepublishing.com. Publisher: Rob Linksy. **Acquisitions:** Angelina Ward, Heather Kane, Jenny Watson, Michelle Newcomb, Loretta Yates, Todd Green, Lloyd Black, acquisitions editors. Publishes hardcover, trade paperback and mass market paperback originals and reprints. **Publishes 200 titles/year. 85% from unagented writers. Pays variable royalty on wholesale price or makes work-for-hire arrangements. Offers varying advance.** Accepts simultaneous submissions. Responds in 1 month to proposals. Book catalog and ms guidelines online.

Nonfiction: Subjects include computers and technology.

Recent Title(s): *Upgrading and Repairing PCs, 13th edition*, by Scott Mueller.

G.P. PUTNAM'S SONS BOOKS FOR YOUNG READERS, Penguin Putnam Books for Young Readers, Penguin Putnam Inc., 345 Hudson St., 14th Floor, New York NY 10014. (212)414-3610. Website: www.penguinputnam.com.

Publishes hardcover originals. **Publishes 45 titles/year. Receives 8,000 submissions/year. 20% of books from first-time authors; 30% from unagented writers. Pays standard royalty. Offers negotiable advance.** Publishes book 2 years after acceptance of ms. Responds in 2 months to queries and mss. Manuscript guidelines for SASE.

Fiction: Children's picture books (ages 0-8), middle-grade fiction and illustrated chapter books (ages 7-10), older middle-grade fiction (ages 10-14), some young adult (14-18). Particularly interested in middle-grade fiction with strong voice, literary quality, high interest for audience, poignancy, humor, unusual settings or plots. Historical fiction OK. No series or activity books, no board books. Always include SASE or no response. Query with SASE. Submit proposal package, including outline, table of contents and 3 sample chapters.

Recent Title(s): *Hope Was Here*, by Joan Bauer; *What a Trip, Amber Brown*, by Paula Danziger; *Car Wash*, by Susan Steen and Sandra Steen.

QUEST BOOKS, Theosophical Publishing House. 360 West Geneva Rd., Wheaton IL 60187. (630)665-0130. Fax: (630)665-8791. E-mail: questbooks@theosmail.net. Website: www.theosophical.org. **Acquisitions:** Nicole Krier. Publishes hardcover originals and trade paperback originals and reprints. **Publishes 12-15 titles/year. Receives 500 submissions/year. 75% of books from first-time authors; 90% from unagented writers. Pays royalty. Offers varying advance.** Publishes book 20 months after acceptance of ms. Accepts simultaneous submissions. Responds in 1 month to queries. Book catalog and ms guidelines free.

    O── "Quest Books is the imprint of the Theosophical Publishing House, the publishing arm of the Theosophical Society of America. Since 1965, Quest books has sold millions of books by leading cultural thinkers on such increasingly popular subjects as transpersonal psychology, comparative religion, deep ecology, spiritual growth, the development of creativity and alternative health practices."

Nonfiction: Biography, illustrated book, self-help. Subjects include anthropology/archeology, art/architecture, health/medicine, music/dance, nature/environment, New Age, philosophy (holistic), psychology (transpersonal), religion (Eastern and Western), science, sex, spirituality (men, women, Native American), travel, women's issues/studies, theosophy, comparative religion, men's and women's spirituality, holistic implications in science, health and healing, yoga, meditation, astrology. "Our speciality is high-quality spiritual nonfiction with a self-help aspect. Great writing is a must. We seldom publish 'personal spiritual awakening' stories. No submissions accepted that do not fit the needs outlined above." Accepts nonfiction translations. No fiction, poetry, children's books or any literature based on channeling or personal psychic impressions. Query with SASE or submit proposal package including sample chapter(s), author bio, toc. Reviews artwork/photos as part of ms package. Send photocopies.

Recent Title(s): *Unconditional Bliss*; *The Zen of Listening*; *When Oracles Speak*.

Tips: "Our audience includes the 'New Age' community, seekers in all religions, general public, professors, and health professionals. Read a few recent Quest titles. Know our books and our company goals. Explain how your book or proposal relates to other Quest titles. Quest gives preference to writers with established reputations/successful publications."

QUILL DRIVER BOOKS/WORD DANCER PRESS, 8386 N. Madsen Ave., Clovis CA 93611. (559)322-5917. Fax: (559)322-5967. E-mail: sbm12@csufresno.edu. **Acquisitions:** Stephen Blake Mettee, publisher. Publishes hardcover and trade paperback originals and reprints. **Publishes 10-12 (Quill Driver Books: 4/year, Word Dancer Press: 6-8/year) titles/year. 50% of books from first-time authors; 95% from unagented writers. Pays 4-10% royalty on retail price. Offers $500-5,000 advance.** Publishes book 9 months after acceptance of ms. Accepts simultaneous submissions. Responds in 1 month to queries and proposals; 3 months to mss. Book catalog and ms guidelines for #10 SASE.

    O── "We publish a modest number of books per year, each of which, we hope, makes a worthwhile contribution to the human community, and we have a little fun along the way. We are strongly emphasizing our two new book series: The Best Half of Life series—on subjects which will serve to enhance the lifestyles, life skills, and pleasures of living for those over 50. The Fast Track Course series—short how-to or explanatory books on any subject."

Nonfiction: Biography, how-to, reference, general. Subjects include general, regional (California), writing, aging. Query with SASE or submit proposal package. Reviews artwork/photos as part of ms package. Send photocopies.

Recent Title(s): *Damn! Why Didn't I Write That?: How Ordinary People are Raking in $100,000.00 or More Writing Nonfiction Books & How You Can Too!*, by Marc McClutcheon; *The Fast Track Course on How to Write a Nonfiction Book Proposal*, by Stephen Blake Mettee.

QUITE SPECIFIC MEDIA GROUP LTD., 7 Old Fulton St., Brooklyn Heights NY 11201. (212)725-5377. Fax: (212)725-8506. E-mail: info@quitespecificmedia.com. Website: www.quitespecificmedia.com. **Acquisitions:** Ralph Pine, editor-in-chief. Estab. 1967. Publishes hardcover originals, trade paperback originals and reprints. **Publishes 12 titles/year. Receives 300 queries and 100 mss/year. 75% of books from first-time authors; 85% from unagented writers. Pays royalty on wholesale price. Offers varies advance.** Publishes book 18 months after acceptance of ms. Accepts simultaneous submissions. Responds to queries. Book catalog online; ms guidelines free.

Imprints: Costume & Fashion Press, Drama Publishers, By Design Press, Entertainment Pro, Jade Rabbit

    • Recently co-published books with the Victoria and Albert Museum, London.

    O── Quite Specific Media Group is an umbrella company of five imprints specializing in costume and fashion, theater and design.

Nonfiction: For and about performing arts theory and practice: acting, directing; voice, speech, movement; makeup, masks, wits; costumes, sets, lighting, sound; design and execution; technical theater, stagecraft, equipment; stage management; producing; arts management, all varieties; business and legal aspects; film, radio, television, cable, video; theory, criticism, reference; theater and performance history; costume and fashion. How-to, multimedia, reference, textbook, guides, manuals, directories. Subjects include fashion/beauty, film/cinema/stage, history, translation. Accepts nonfiction and technical works in translations also. Query with SASE or submit 1-3 sample chapter(s). No complete ms. Reviews artwork/photos as part of ms package.

QUORUM BOOKS, Greenwood Publishing Group, 88 Post Rd. W., Westport CT 06881. (203)226-3571. Fax: (203)222-1502. E-mail: er@greenwood.com. Website: www.greenwood.com. **Acquisitions:** Eric Valentine, publisher. **Publishes 75 titles/year. 50% of books from first-time authors. Pays 8-15% royalty on net receipts. Offers occasional advance.** Publishes book 9-12 months after acceptance of ms. Accepts simultaneous submissions. Responds in 2 weeks to queries; 1 month to proposals. Book catalog and ms guidelines online.
Nonfiction: Scholarly and professional books. Subjects include business/economics, finance, applied economics, business law. *No unsolicited mss.* Query with proposal package, including content scope, organization, length of project, table of contents, intended markets, competing books, whether a complete ms is available or when it will be, cv or résumé and SASE.
Tips: "We are not a trade publisher. Our products are sold almost entirely by mail, in hardcover and at relatively high list prices, and to scholars, graduate level students and skilled professionals throughout the public and private sectors."

RAGGED MOUNTAIN PRESS, P.O. Box 220, Camden ME 04843-0220. (207)236-4837. Fax: (207)236-6314. Website: www.raggedmountainpress.com. **Acquisitions:** Jonathan Eaton, editorial director. Estab. 1969. Publishes hardcover and trade paperback originals and reprints. **Publishes 40 titles/year; imprint publishes 15 titles/year. Receives 200 queries and 100 mss/year. 30% of books from first-time authors; 90% from unagented writers. Pays 10-15% royalty on net receipts. Offers advance.** Publishes book 1 year after acceptance of ms. Accepts simultaneous submissions. Responds in 1 month to queries. Book catalog for 9×12 SAE with 10 first-class stamps; ms guidelines for #10 SASE.
  O➛ Ragged Mountain Press publishes books that take you off the beaten path.
Nonfiction: "Ragged Mountain publishes nonconsumptive outdoor and environmental issues books of literary merit or unique appeal." How-to (outdoor-related), humor, guidebooks, essays. Subjects include cooking/foods/nutrition, humor, nature/environment, recreation, sports, adventure, camping, fly fishing, snowshoeing, backpacking, canoeing, outdoor cookery, skiing, snowboarding, survival skills, wilderness know-how, birdwatching, natural history, climbing, kayaking. "Be familiar with the existing literature. Find a subject that hasn't been done or has been done poorly, then explore it in detail and from all angles." Query with SASE or submit outline, 1 sample chapter(s). Reviews artwork/photos as part of ms package. Send photocopies.
Recent Title(s): *Alberto Salazar's Guide to Running*; *Coaching Softball: The Baffled Parent's Guide*, by Jacquie Joseph.

Ⓐ RANDOM HOUSE BOOKS FOR YOUNG READERS, Random House, Inc., 201 E. 50th St., New York NY 10022. (212)751-2600. Fax: (212)940-7685. Website: www.randomhouse/com/kids. Vice President/Publishing Director: Kate Klimo. **Acquisitions:** Mallory Loehr, senior editor/licensing director (Stepping Stones); Heidi Kilgras, editor (Step into Reading); Naomi Kleinberg, senior editor (Picturebacks). Estab. 1935. Publishes hardcover, trade paperback, and mass market paperback originals and reprints. **Publishes 200 titles/year. Receives 1,000 queries/year. Pays 1-6% royalty or makes outright purchase. Offers variable advance.** Accepts simultaneous submissions. Book catalog free.
Imprints: Random House Books for Young Readers, Alfred A. Knopf and Crown Children's Books, Bantam, Delacorte, Dell, Disney, Doubleday, Luarel-Leaf, Yearling
  O➛ "Random House Books aim to create books that nurture the hearts and minds of children, providing and promoting quality books and a rich variety of media that entertain and educate readers from 6 months to 12 years."
Nonfiction: Children's/juvenile. Subjects include animals, history, nature/environment, science, sports, popular culture. *No unsolicited manuscripts. Accepts agented submissions only.*
Fiction: Horror, juvenile, mystery, picture books, young adult. "Familiarize yourself with our list. We look for original, unique stories. Do something that hasn't been done." *Accepts agented submissions only. No unsolicited manuscripts.*
Recent Title(s): *Gerald McBoing Boing*, by Dr. Seuss.

Ⓐ RANDOM HOUSE, TRADE PUBLISHING GROUP, Random House, Inc., 201 E. 50th St., 11th Floor, New York NY 10022. (212)751-2600. Website: www.randomhouse.com. Estab. 1925. **Publishes 120 titles/year. Receives 3,000 submissions/year. Pays royalty on retail price. Offers advance.** Accepts simultaneous submissions. Responds in 2 months to queries. Book catalog free; ms guidelines for #10 SASE.
Imprints: Modern Library, Random House Trade Books, Villard
  ● *"Accepts agented submissions only."*
  O➛ "Random House is the world's largest English-language general trade book publisher. It includes an array of prestigious imprints that publish some of the foremost writers of our time—in hardcover, trade paperback, mass market paperback, electronic, multimedia and other formats."
Nonfiction: Biography, cookbook, humor, illustrated book, self-help. Subjects include Americana, art/architecture, business/economics, cooking/foods/nutrition, health/medicine, history, humor, music/dance, nature/environment, New Age, photography, psychology, religion, sociology, sports, classics, politics, No juveniles or textbooks (separate divisions). *Accepts agented submissions only.*

Fiction: Adventure, confession, experimental, fantasy, historical, horror, humor, mainstream/contemporary, mystery, suspense. *Accepts agented submissions only.*
Recent Title(s): *Sex On Campus*, by Elliott and Brantley; *The Gospel According to the Son*, by Norman Mailer.

RANDOM HOUSE, INC., 201 E. 50th St., New York NY 10022. (212)751-2600. Website: www.randomhouse.com.
Pays royalty. Offers advance.
Imprints: *Ballantine Publishing Group:* Ballantine Books, Del Rey, Fawcett, Ivy, Library of Contemporary Thought, One World. Wellspring. *The Bantam Dell Publishing Group:* Bantam, Delacorte Press, Dell, Delta, The Dial Press, DTP (Dell Trade Paperbacks), Island. *The Crown Publishing Group:* Bell Tower, Clarkson Potter, Crown Business, Crown Publishers, Discovery Books, Harmony Books, House of Collectibles, Prima Lifestyle Group, Sierra Club Books, Three Rivers Press, Times Books. *The Doubleday Broadway Publishing Group*: Broadway Books, Currency, Doubleday, Doubleday Religious Publishing, Doubleday/Image, Nan A. Talese, Waterbrook Press. *The Knopf Publishing Group:* Alfred A. Knopf, Everyman's Library, Pantheon Books, Schocken Books, Vintage Anchor Publishing. *Random House Audio Publishing Group:* Bantam Doubleday Dell Audio Publishing, Listening Library, Random House AudioBooks. *Random House Children's Media Group:* Alfred A. Knopf Books for Young Readers, Bantam Books for Young Readers, Crown Books for Young Readers, CTW Books (Children's Television Workshop), Delacorte Press Books for Young Readers, Doubleday Books for Young Readers, Dragonfly Books, Laurel-Leaf Books, Random House Books for Young Readers, Yearling Books, Random House Home Video. *Random House Diversified Publishing Group:* Random House Large Print Publishing, Random House Value Publishing. *Random House Information Group:* Fodor's Travel Publications, Living Language, Prima Games, Princeton Review, Random House Puzzles & Games, Random House Reference & Information Publishing. *The Random House Trade Publishing Group:* Random House Trade Books, Villard Books, The Modern Library.

N: REALLY GREAT BOOKS, P.O. Box 861302, Los Angeles CA 90086. (213)624-8555. Fax: (213)624-8666. E-mail: info@reallygreatbooks.com. Website: www.reallygreatbooks.com. **Acquisitions:** Nina Wiener, editor (Los Angeles-oriented nonfiction and fiction). Publishes hardcover and trade paperback originals and trade paperback reprints. **Publishes 4 titles/year; imprint publishes 2 each titles/year. Receives 100 queries and 40 mss/year. 50% of books from first-time authors; 25% from unagented writers. Pays 5-15% royalty.** Publishes book 15 months after acceptance of ms. Accepts simultaneous submissions. Responds in 1 month to queries; 4 months to proposals and mss. Book catalog for #10 SASE or online; ms guidelines for #10 SASE.
Imprints: Really Great Books, Glove Box Guides, Red Line Press (literary fiction and creative nonfiction), Spring Street (architecture)
Nonfiction: Subjects include art/architecture, creative nonfiction, ethnic, gay/lesbian, history, photography, regional, travel. "All titles we publish represent what we like to call 'the real Los Angeles.' We're interested in the city behind the facade, drawn in a compelling enough manner to appeal to a national—even a international audience." Request submission guidelines and use them to submit proposal package, including outline, 2 sample chapters and marketing proposal. Reviews artwork/photos as part of ms package. Send photocopies.
Fiction: Ethnic, gay/lesbian, literary, regional. "We are only able to publish one or two fiction titles/year, and only consider edgy novels set against the backdrop of the 'real Los Angeles.' Think Hector Tobar, Rachel Resnick, Jervey Tervalon." Request submission guidelines and use them to submit proposal package, including 3 sample chapters and marketing proposal.
Recent Title(s): *Plots and Characters*, by Millard Kaufman (screenwriting/Hollywood history); *Popcorn: Hollywood Stories*, by Julia Cameron (Hollywood/literary fiction).
Tips: Our audience is "Gen-X and Y culture vultures hungry for looks at a Los Angeles the power structure of New York publishing just doesn't seem to 'get.' We are a very small company and sometimes get overwhelmed by the task at hand—please be patient if we take a while getting back to you."

RED HEN PRESS, P.O. Box 3537, Granada Hills CA 91394. (818)831-0649. Fax: (818)831-6659. E-mail: editor@redh en.org. Website: www.redhen.org. **Acquisitions:** Mark E. Cull, publisher/editor (fiction), Katherine Gale, poetry editor (poetry, literary fiction). Estab. 1993. Publishes trade paperback originals. **Publishes 10 titles/year. Receives 2,000 queries and 500 mss/year. 10% of books from first-time authors; 90% from unagented writers.** Publishes book 1 year after acceptance of ms. Accepts simultaneous submissions. Responds in 1 month to queries; 2 months to proposals; 3 months to mss. Book catalog and ms guidelines online.
   O→ Red Hen Press is a nonprofit organization specializing in literary fiction and nonfiction. Currently de-emphasizing poetry.
Nonfiction: Biography, children's/juvenile, cookbook. Subjects include anthropology/archeology, cooking/foods/nutrition, ethnic, gay/lesbian, language/literature, memoirs, travel, women's issues/studies, political/social interest. Query with SASE. Reviews artwork/photos as part of ms package. Send photocopies.
Fiction: "We prefer high-quality literary fiction." Ethnic, experimental, feminist, gay/lesbian, historical, literary, mainstream/contemporary, poetry, poetry in translation, short story collections. Query with SASE.
Poetry: Query or submit 5 sample poems.
Recent Title(s): *Letters from the Underground*, by Abbie and Anita Hoffman; *Tisch*, by Stephen Dixon.
Tips: "Audience reads poetry, literary fiction, intelligent nonfiction. If you have an agent, we may be too small since we don't pay advances. Write well. Send queries first. Be willing to help promote your own book."

[N] REFERENCE PRESS INTERNATIONAL, P.O. Box 4126, Greenwich CT 06831. (203)622-6860. Fax: (707)929-0282. E-mail: ckl1414@aol.com. **Acquisitions:** Cheryl Lacoff, senior editor. Publishes hardcover and trade paperback originals. **Publishes 6 titles/year. Receives 50 queries and 20 mss/year. 75% of books from first-time authors; 90% from unagented writers. Pays royalty or makes outright purchase. Offers determined by project advance.** Publishes book 6 months after acceptance of ms. Accepts simultaneous submissions. Responds in 3 months to queries.

Oー Reference Press specializes in gift books, instructional, reference and how-to titles.

Nonfiction: Gift book, how-to, illustrated book, multimedia (audio, video, CD-ROM), reference, technical, instructional. Subjects include Americana, art/architecture, business/economics, education, gardening, hobbies, money/finance, photography, anything related to the arts or crafts field. "Follow the guidelines as stated concerning subjects and types of books we're looking for." Query with SASE or submit outline, 1-3 sample chapter(s). Reviews artwork/photos as part of ms package. Send photocopies.

Recent Title(s): *Who's Who in the Peace Corps* (alumni directory).

REFERENCE SERVICE PRESS, 5000 Windplay Dr., Suite 4, El Dorado Hills CA 95762. (916)939-9620. Fax: (916)939-9626. E-mail: findaid@aol.com. Website: www.rspfunding.com. **Acquisitions:** Stuart Hauser, acquisitions editor. Estab. 1977. Publishes hardcover originals. **Publishes 10-20 titles/year. 100% from unagented writers. Pays 10% royalty. Offers advance.** Publishes book 6 months after acceptance of ms. Accepts simultaneous submissions. Responds in 2 months to queries. Book catalog for #10 SASE.

Oー Reference Service Press focuses on the development and publication of financial aid resources in any format (print, electronic, e-book, etc.). We are interested in financial aid publications aimed at specific groups (e.g., minorities, women, veterans, the disabled, undergraduates majoring in specific subject areas, specific types of financial aid, etc.).

Nonfiction: Specializes in financial aid opportunities for students in or having these characteristics: women, minorities, veterans, the disabled, etc. Reference. Subjects include agriculture/horticulture, art/architecture, business/economics, education, ethnic, health/medicine, history, religion, science, sociology, women's issues/studies, disabled. Submit outline, sample chapter(s).

Recent Title(s): *Financial Aids for African Americans, 2001-2003.*

Tips: "Our audience consists of librarians, counselors, researchers, students, re-entry women, scholars and other fund-seekers."

[A] REGNERY PUBLISHING, INC., Eagle Publishing, One Massachusetts Ave., NW, Washington DC 20001. (202)216-0600. Website: www.regnery.com. Publisher: Alfred S. Regnery. **Acquisitions:** Harry Crocker, executive editor (bestsellers); Brian Robertson, editor; Jed Donahue, editor (biography, American history). Estab. 1947. Publishes hardcover and paperback originals and reprints. **Publishes 30 titles/year. 0% from unagented writers. Pays 8-15% royalty on retail price. Offers $0-50,000 advance.** Publishes book 1 year after acceptance of ms. Responds in 3 months to queries, proposals and mss.

Imprints: Gateway Editions, LifeLine Health, Capital Press

Oー Regnery publishes conservative, well-written, well-produced, sometimes controversial books. Currently emphasizing health and business books.

Nonfiction: Biography, current affairs. Subjects include business/economics, government/politics, health/medicine, history, money/finance. *Accepts agented submissions only. No unsolicited mss.*

Recent Title(s): *Sellout*, by David P. Schippers; *God, Guns & Rock 'n' Roll*, by Ted Nugent; *The China Threat*, by Bill Gertz.

Tips: "We seek high-impact, headline-making, bestseller treatments of pressing current issues by established experts in the field."

REPUBLIC OF TEXAS PRESS, Wordware Publishing, Inc., 2320 Los Rios Blvd., Suite 200, Plano TX 75074. (972)423-0090. Fax: (972)881-9147. E-mail: gbivona@republicoftexaspress.com. Website: www.republicoftexaspress.com. **Acquisitions:** Ginnie Bivona, acquisitions editor. Publishes trade and mass market paperback originals. **Publishes 28-32 titles/year. Receives 400 queries and 300 mss/year. 95% from unagented writers. Pays 8-10% royalty on net receipts. Offers advance.** Publishes book within 6 months after acceptance of ms. Responds in 2 months to queries. Book catalog and ms guidelines for #10 SASE.

Oー Republic of Texas Press specializes in Texas history and general Texana.

Nonfiction: Biography, humor. Subjects include cooking/foods/nutrition, ethnic, general, history, humor, nature/environment, regional, sports, travel, women's issues/studies, Old West, cuisine, Texas military, ghost and mystery stories, trivia. Submit table of contents, 2 sample chapters, target audience, author bio and SASE.

Recent Title(s): *The Alamo Story: From Early History to Current Conflicts*, by J.R. Edmondson; *Exploring Houston with Children*, by Elaine Galit and Vikk Simmons.

Tips: "We are interested in anything relating to Texas. From the wacky to the most informative, any nonfiction concept will be considered. Our market is primarily adult, but we will consider material for children aged 10-14."

[N] RESURRECTION PRESS, LTD., 77 W. End Rd., Totowa NJ 07512-1405. (516)742-5686. Fax: (516)746-6872. **Acquisitions:** Emilie Mackney, publisher. Publishes trade paperback originals and reprints. **Publishes 6-8 titles/year; imprint publishes 4 titles/year. Receives 100 queries and 100 mss/year. 25% of books from first-time authors;**

100% from unagented writers. Pays 5-10% royalty. Offers $250-2,000 advance. Publishes book 1 year after acceptance of ms. Accepts simultaneous submissions. Responds in 1 month to queries and proposals; 2 months to mss. Book catalog and ms guidelines free.

Imprints: Spirit Life Series

   O→ Resurrection Press publishes religious, devotional and inspirational titles.

Nonfiction: Self-help. Subjects include religion. Query with SASE or submit outline, 2 sample chapter(s). Reviews artwork/photos as part of ms package. Send photocopies.

Recent Title(s): *Praying with John Paul II in the Holy Land*, by Keeler/Moses.

FLEMING H. REVELL PUBLISHING, Baker Book House, P.O. Box 6287, Grand Rapids MI 49516. Fax: (616)676-2315. Website: www.bakerbooks.com. **Acquisitions:** Lonnie Hull DuPont, interim editorial director; Bill Petersen, senior acquisitions editor; Jane Campbell, senior editor (Chosen Books); Jennifer Leep, acquisitions editor. Estab. 1870. Publishes hardcover, trade paperback and mass market paperback originals and reprints. **Publishes 50 titles/year; imprint publishes 10 titles/year. Receives 750 queries and 1,000 mss/year. 1% of books from first-time authors; 75% from unagented writers. Pays 14-18% royalty on wholesale price. Offers advance.** Publishes book 1 year after acceptance of ms. Accepts simultaneous submissions. Responds in 3 months to queries. Manuscript guidelines for #10 SASE.

Imprints: Chosen Books, Spire Books

   O→ Revell publishes to the heart (rather than to the head). For 125 years, Revell has been publishing evangelical books for the personal enrichment and spiritual growth of general Christian readers.

Nonfiction: Biography, coffee table book, how-to, self-help. Subjects include child guidance/parenting, religion, Christian living. Query with SASE or submit outline, 2 sample chapter(s).

Fiction: Religious. Submit 2 sample chapter(s), synopsis.

Recent Title(s): *Making Children Mind Without Losing Yours*, by Dr. Kevin Leman (nonfiction); *Woman of Grace*, by Kathleen Morgan (fiction).

■▲ **REVIEW AND HERALD PUBLISHING ASSOCIATION**, 55 W. Oak Ridge Dr., Hagerstown MD 21740. (301)393-4050. E-mail: jjohnson@rhpa.org. **Acquisitions:** Jeannette R. Johnson, acquisitions editor. Estab. 1861. Publishes hardcover, trade paperback and mass market paperback originals and reprints. **Publishes 40-50 titles/year. Receives 200 queries and 600 mss/year. 50% of books from first-time authors; 95% from unagented writers. Pays 7-16% royalty. Offers $500-1,000 advance.** Publishes book 18-24 months after acceptance of ms. Accepts simultaneous submissions. Responds in 1 month to queries and proposals; 2 months to mss. Book catalog and ms guidelines for 10×13 SAE.

   O→ "Through print and electronic media, the Review and Herald Publishing Association nurtures a growing relationship with God by providing products that teach and enrich people spiritually, mentally, physically and socially as we near Christ's soon second coming. We belong to the Seventh-Day Adventist denomination."

Nonfiction: Biography, children's/juvenile, cookbook, gift book, humor, multimedia, reference, self-help, textbook, Christian lifestyle, inspirational. Subjects include animals, anthropology/archeology, child guidance/parenting, cooking/foods/nutrition, education, health/medicine, history, humor, nature/environment, philosophy, religion, women's issues/studies. Submit 3 sample chapters and cover letter with SASE.

Fiction: Adventure, historical, humor, juvenile, mainstream/contemporary, religious. All Christian-living related. Submit 3 sample chapter(s), synopsis.

Recent Title(s): *The Case of the Stolen Red Mary*, by Maylan Schurch (children's); *Ten Christian Values Every Kid Should Know*, by Donna Habenicht (child guidance); *The Intimate Marriage*, by Alberta Mazat (marriage).

■▲ **MORGAN REYNOLDS PUBLISHING**, 620 S. Elm St., Suite 223, Greensboro NC 27406. Fax: (336)275-1152. E-mail: info@morganreynolds.com. Website: www.morganreynolds.com. **Acquisitions:** Laura Shoemaker, editor. Publishes hardcover originals. **Publishes 20-24 titles/year. Receives 250-300 queries and 100-150 mss/year. 50% of books from first-time authors; 100% from unagented writers. Pays 5-9% royalty on wholesale price. Offers $500 advance.** Publishes book 8 months after acceptance of ms. Accepts simultaneous submissions. Responds in 3 months to queries.

   O→ Morgan Reynolds publishes nonfiction books for juvenile and young adult readers. "We prefer lively, well-written biographies of interesting contemporary and historical figures for our biography series. Books for our Great Events series should be insightful and exciting looks at critical periods. We are interested in more well-known subjects rather than the esoteric." Currently emphasizing great scientists, composers, philosophers, world writers. De-emphasizing sports figures.

Nonfiction: "We do not always publish the obvious subjects. Don't shy away from less popular subjects. We also publish nonfiction related to great events." Biography. Subjects include Americana (young adult/juvenile oriented), business/economics, government/politics, history, language/literature, military/war, money/finance, women's issues/studies, young adult. No children's books, picture books or fiction. Query with SASE.

Recent Title(s): *The Firing on Fort Sumter: A Splintered Nation Goes to War*, by Nancy Colbert.

Tips: "Research the markets before submitting. We spend too much time dealing with manuscripts that shouldn't have been submitted. Request our writer's guidelines and visit our website. We will be happy to send a catalog if provided with 77 cents postage."

N: RFF PRESS, Resources for the Future, 1616 P St., NW, Washington DC 20036. (202)328-5086. Fax: (202)939-3460. E-mail: rffpress@rff.org. Website: www.rff.org. **Acquisitions:** Don Reisman, director. Publishes hardcover, trade paperback and electronic originals. **Publishes 20 titles/year. 10% of books from first-time authors. Pays royalty on wholesale price.** Publishes book 6 months after acceptance of ms. Accepts simultaneous submissions. Responds in 1 month to queries and proposals; 2 months to mss. Book catalog online; ms guidelines free.
Nonfiction: "We focus on social science approaches to environmental and natural resource issues." Reference, technical, textbook. Subjects include agriculture/horticulture, business/economics, government/politics, history, nature/environment, science. "We do not publish works that are purely opinion driven. Inquire via e-mail or letter; no phone calls." Submit proposal package including outline. Reviews artwork/photos as part of ms package. Send photocopies.
Recent Title(s): *People Managing Forests: The Links Between Human Well-Being and Sustainability*; *Climate Change Economics and Policy* (anthology).
Tips: Audience is scholars, policy makes, activists, businesses, the general public.

RISING TIDE PRESS, P.O. Box 30457, Tucson AZ 85751-0457. (520)888-1140. Fax: (520)888-1123. Website: www.risingtidepress.com. **Acquisitions:** Debra Tobin, partner (mystery, adventure, nonfiction), Brenda Kazen, partner (science fiction, young adult fiction). Estab. 1991. Publishes trade paperback originals. **Publishes 10-15 titles/year. Receives 1,000 queries and 600 mss/year. 75% of books from first-time authors; 100% from unagented writers. Pays royalty on wholesale price.** Publishes book 15 months after acceptance of ms. Responds in 2 months to queries and proposals; 3 months to mss. Book catalog for $1; ms guidelines for #10 SASE.
   O— "We are committed to publishing books by, for and about strong women and their lives.
Nonfiction: Subjects include women's issues/studies, lesbian nonfiction. Query with outline, entire ms and large SASE. Reviews artwork/photos as part of ms package. Send photocopies.
Fiction: Women's fiction only. Adventure, fantasy, historical, horror, humor, literary, mainstream/contemporary, mystery, occult, romance, science fiction, suspense, mixed genres. "Major characters must be women and stories must depict strong women characters." Query with SASE or submit synopsis or submit complete ms.
Recent Title(s): *Feathering Your Nest: An Interactive Workbook & Guide to a Loving Lesbian Relationship*, by Gwen Leonhard and Jennie Mast (nonfiction); *Agenda for Murder*, by Joan Alberella (fiction); *Storm Rising*, by Linda Kay Silva (fiction).
Tips: "We welcome unpublished authors. 2 cash prizes awarded annually. Any material submitted should be proofed. No multiple submissions."

N: RIVER CITY PUBLISHING, River City Publishing, LLC, 610 N. Perry St., Montgomery AL 36104. (334)265-6753. Fax: (334)265-8880. E-mail: info@rivercitypublish.com. Website: rivercitypublishing.com. **Acquisitions:** Jim Davis, managing editor; Tina Tatum, general manager; Al Newman, owner. Publishes hardcover and trade paperback originals and reprints. **Publishes 12 titles/year; imprint publishes 10 titles/year. Receives 50 queries and 300 mss/year. 20% of books from first-time authors; 90% from unagented writers. Pays 10-15% royalty on retail price. Offers 500-5,000 advance.** Publishes book 6 months after acceptance of ms. Accepts simultaneous submissions. Responds in 3 months to queries; 4 months to proposals; 1 year to mss. Book catalog and ms guidelines free.
Imprints: Starrhill Press, Black Belt Press
Nonfiction: Biography, coffee table book, illustrated book, multimedia, self-help. Subjects include art/architecture, child guidance/parenting, creative nonfiction, ethnic, gardening, gay/lesbian, government/politics, health/medicine, history, language/literature, memoirs, multicultural, music/dance, photography, regional, sports, travel. Submit proposal package including outline, 2 sample chapter(s). Reviews artwork/photos as part of ms package. Send photocopies.
Fiction: Ethnic, gay/lesbian, historical, literary, mainstream/contemporary, multicultural, poetry, regional, short story collections. Submit proposal package including 2 sample chapter(s), synopsis.
Poetry: Query.
Recent Title(s): *Turnaround*, by Tom Stoddard (sports/bio/inspirational); *These People Are Us*, by George Singleton (short stories); *The Map That Lies Between Us*, by Anne C. George (poetry).

RIVER OAK PUBLISHING, Eagle Communication International, 2448 E. 81 St., Suite 4800, Tulsa OK 74137. (918)523-5600. Fax: (918)523-5644. E-mail: info@riveroakpublishing.com. Website: www.riveroakpublishing.com. **Acquisitions:** Jeff Dunn, editorial director (Christian living/fiction). Publishes hardcover, trade paperback and mass market paperback originals and reprints. **Publishes 40-50 titles/year. Receives 1,000 queries and 500 mss/year. 5% of books from first-time authors; 80% from unagented writers. Pays royalty on wholesale price. Offers negotiable advance.** Publishes book 18 months after acceptance of ms. Accepts simultaneous submissions. Responds in 1 month to queries; 6 months to proposals. Manuscript guidelines for #10 SASE.
Nonfiction: Gift book, humor, multimedia (CD-ROM, audio), self-help. Subjects include money/finance, religion, spirituality. Query with SASE.
Fiction: "We are looking for the best in various genres of Christian fiction." Adventure, fantasy, historical, humor, mystery, religious, romance, spiritual, sports, western. Query with SASE.
Recent Title(s): *Who Moved My Church?*, by Mike Nappa; *The Ultimate Gift*, by Jim Stovall; *Mighty Mom's Secrets for Raising Super Kids*, by Gwendolyn Mitchell Diaz.
Tips: "Our books are written for Christian readers desiring to strengthen their walk with God. We look for what you believe, not what you are against. We like creative ways to present biblically-correct inspirational stories."

ROC BOOKS, Penguin Putnam Inc., 375 Hudson St., New York NY 10014. (212)366-2000. Website: www.penguinput nam.com. **Acquisitions:** Laura Anne Gilman, executive editor, Jennifer Heddle, assistant editor. Publishes mass market, trade and hardcover originals. **Publishes 36 titles/year. Receives 500 queries/year. Pays royalty. Offers negotiable advance.** Accepts simultaneous submissions. Responds in 3 months to queries.

O—¬ "We're looking for books that are a good read, that people will want to pick up time and time again."

Fiction: Fantasy, horror, science fiction. "Roc tries to strike a balance between fantasy and science fiction." "We discourage unsolicited submissions." Query with SASE or submit 1-2 sample chapter(s), synopsis.

Recent Title(s): *Queen of the Darkness*, by Anne Bishop; *On the Oceans of Eternity*, by S.M. Stirling.

RONIN PUBLISHING, INC., P.O. Box 522, Berkeley CA 94701. (510)420-3669. Fax: (510)420-3672. E-mail: info@roninpub.com. Website: www.roninpub.com. **Acquisitions:** Beverly Potter, publisher; Dan Joy, editor. Estab. 1983. Publishes trade paperback originals and reprints. **Publishes 8 titles/year; imprint publishes 1-2 titles/year. Receives 10 queries and 10 mss/year. Pays royalty on net only. Offers $500-1,000 advance.** Publishes book 1 year after acceptance of ms. Responds in 3 months to queries; 6 months to proposals and mss. Book catalog free.

Imprints: 20th Century Alchemist

O—¬ "Ronin publishes book as tools for personal development, visionary alternatives and expanded consciousness."

Nonfiction: Biography, reference, self-help. Subjects include agriculture/horticulture, business/economics, cooking/foods/nutrition, gardening, health/medicine, psychology, spirituality, counterculture/psychedelia. "Our publishing purview is highly specific, as indicated in our catalog. We have rarely if ever published a book which initially arrived as an unsolicited manuscript. Please send queries only." Query with SASE. *No unsolicited mss.*

Recent Title(s): *Timothy Leary: Turn on, Tune in, Drop Out.*

Tips: "Our audience is interested in hard information and often buys several books on the same subject. Please submit query only. If on the basis of the query, we are interested in seeing the proposal or manuscript, we will let you know. No response to the query indicates that we have no interest. Become familiar with our interests through our catalog."

ROSE PUBLISHING, 4455 Torrance Blvd., #259, Torrance CA 90503. (310)370-8962. Fax: (310)370-7492. E-mail: rosepubl@aol.com. Website: www.rose-publishing.com. **Acquisitions:** Carol R. Witte, editor. **Publishes 5-10 titles/year. 5% of books from first-time authors; 100% from unagented writers. Makes outright purchase.** Publishes book 18 months after acceptance of ms. Accepts simultaneous submissions. Responds in 3 months to proposals; 2 months to mss. Book catalog free.

O—¬ "We publish only Bible-based materials in chart, poster or pamphlet form, easy-to-understand and appealing to children, teens or adults on Bible study, prayer, basic beliefs, Scripture memory, salvation, sharing the gospel and worship."

Nonfiction: Reference, pamphlets, group study books. Subjects include anthropology/archeology, religion, science, sex, spirituality, Bible studies, christian history, counseling aids, cults/occult, curriculum, Christian discipleship, evangelism/witnessing, Christian living, marriage, prayer, prophecy, creation, singles issues. Submit proposal package including outline, 3 sample chapter(s), photocopies of chart contents or poster artwork. Reviews artwork/photos as part of ms package. Send photocopies.

Recent Title(s): *Far Views of the Millennium* (chart); *Bible Time Line* (pamphlet).

Tips: Audience includes both church (Bible study leaders, Sunday school teachers [all ages], pastors, youth leaders) and home (parents, home schoolers, children, youth, high school and college). Open to topics that supplement Sunday School curriculum or Bible study.

THE ROSEN PUBLISHING GROUP, 29 E. 21st St., New York NY 10010. **Acquisitions:** Iris Rosoff, editorial director. Estab. 1950. Publishes nonfiction hardcover originals. **50% of books from first-time authors; 95% from unagented writers. Makes outright purchase of $175-1,200. Offers advance.** Publishes book 9 months after acceptance of ms. Responds in 2 months to proposals. Book catalog and ms guidelines free.

Imprints: PowerKids Press (Nonfiction for grades K-4 that are supplementary to the curriculum. Topics include conflict resolution, character-building, health, safety, drug abuse prevention, history, self-help, religion, science and multicultural titles. Contact: Kristen Eck, PowerKids Press editorial division leader). Rosen Central (Nonfiction for grades 5-8 on a wide range of topics, guidance topics or material related to the curriculum. Topics include social issues, health, sports, self-esteem, history and science. Contact: Erin M. Hovanec, young adult editorial division.)

O—¬ The Rosen Publishing Group publishes young adult titles for sale to school and public libraries. Each book is aimed at teenage readers and addresses them directly.

Nonfiction: Children's/juvenile, reference, self-help, textbook, young adult. Subjects include ethnic, health/medicine, multicultural, religion, science. Areas of particular interest include ethnographic studies; careers; coping with social, medical and personal problems; values and ethical behavior; drug abuse prevention; self-esteem; social activism; religion; social studies. Submit outline, 1 sample chapter(s).

Recent Title(s): *The Divorce Resource Series*; *Psyched for Science* (series).

Tips: "The writer has the best chance of selling our firm a book on vocational guidance or personal social adjustment, or high-interest, low reading-level material for teens."

ROWMAN & LITTLEFIELD PUBLISHING GROUP, 4720 Boston Way, Lanham MD 20706. (301)459-3366. Website: www.rowmanlittlefield.com. Publishes hardcover and trade paperback originals and reprints. **Publishes 1,000 titles/year. Offers advance.**

Imprints: AltaMira Press, Ivan R. Dee, Derrydale Press, Lexington Books, New Amsterdam Books, Rowman & Littlefield Publishers, Madison Books, Scarecrow Press, University Press of America, Vestal Press.
Tips: "We have a scholarly audience."

ROXBURY PUBLISHING CO., P.O. Box 491044, Los Angeles CA 90049. (310)473-3312. **Acquisitions:** Claude Teweles, publisher. Estab. 1981. Publishes hardcover and paperback originals and reprints. **Publishes 15-20 titles/year. Pays royalty. Offers advance.** Accepts simultaneous submissions. Responds in 2 months to queries.
○➔ Roxbury publishes college textbooks in the humanities and social sciences only.
Nonfiction: Textbook (college-level textbooks and supplements only). Subjects include sociology, speech, communication, political science, family studies, criminology, criminal justice. Query with SASE or submit outline, sample chapter(s), synopsis or submit complete ms.

RUMINATOR BOOKS, 1648 Grand Ave., St. Paul MN 55105. (651)699-7038. Fax: (651)699-7190. E-mail: books@ruminator.com. Website: www.ruminator.com. **Acquisitions:** Pearl Kilbride. Publishes hardcover originals, trade paperback originals and reprints. **Publishes 10-12 titles/year. Receives 300 queries and 500 mss/year. 40% from unagented writers. Royalty varies. Offers varying advance.** Publishes book 1 year after acceptance of ms. Accepts simultaneous submissions. Responds in 4 months to proposals. Book catalog for 9×12 SAE with 2 first-class stamps; ms guidelines for #10 SASE.
○➔ Ruminator Books is an independent press dedicated to publishing nonfiction and fiction literary works from diverse voices, books that bring political, social, or cultural ideas to a wide and varied readership. Currently emphasizing culture studies, political, travel, memoirs, nature novels, history, world views. De-emphasizing spirituality, cooking, romance, mysteries, how-to, business, poetry.
Nonfiction: Subjects include government/politics, history, language/literature, memoirs, nature/environment, travel, worldviews, culture studies. No how-to or self-help/instructional mss. Submit proposal package, including letter, outline and at least one sample chapter with SASE.
Fiction: Literary, adult fiction. Query with SASE or submit proposal package including outline, sample chapter(s).
Recent Title(s): *Facing the Congo*, by Jeffrey Taylor; *Natural Prayers*, by Chet Raymo.

RUNNING PRESS BOOK PUBLISHERS, 125 S. 22nd St., Philadelphia PA 19103. (215)567-5080. Fax: (215)568-2919. President/Publisher: Stuart Teacher. **Acquisitions:** Carlo DeVito, associate publisher; Jennifer Worick, editorial director; Sam Caggiula, publicity director; Bill Jones, design director; John Whalen, sales director; Peter Horodowich, production director. Estab. 1972. Publishes hardcover originals, trade paperback originals and reprints. **Publishes 150 titles/year. Receives 600 queries/year. 50% of books from first-time authors; 30% from unagented writers. Offers varies advance.** Publishes book 6-18 months after acceptance of ms. Accepts simultaneous submissions. Responds in 2 months to queries. Book catalog free; ms guidelines for #10 SASE.
Imprints: Courage Books
○➔ "Running Press and Courage Books publish nonfiction trade and promotional titles, including pop culture books, cookbooks, quote books, children's learning kits, photo-essay books, journals, notebooks, literary classics, inspirational, crossword puzzles."
Nonfiction: Children's/juvenile, how-to, self-help. Subjects include art/architecture, cooking/foods/nutrition, health/medicine, recreation, science, craft. Query with SASE or submit outline, table of contents, synopsis. Reviews artwork/photos as part of ms package. Send photocopies.
Recent Title(s): *Strange Fruit*, by David Margolick; *It's Slinky!*, by Lou Harry; *I Feel Great*, by Pat Croce.

RUTGERS UNIVERSITY PRESS, 100 Joyce Kilmer Ave., Piscataway NJ 08854-8099. (732)445-7762. Fax: (732)445-7039. E-mail: tliv@rci.rutgers.edu. Website: rutgerspress.rutgers.edu. **Acquisitions:** Leslie Mitchner, editor-in-chief/associate director (humanities); David Myers, acquiring editor (social sciences); Helen Hsu, senior editor (science, regional books). Estab. 1936. Publishes hardcover originals and trade paperback originals and reprints. **Publishes 80 titles/year. Receives 1,500 queries and 300 mss/year. 30% of books from first-time authors; 70% from unagented writers. Pays 7½-15% royalty. Offers $1,000-10,000 advance.** Publishes book 1 year after acceptance of ms. Responds in 1 month to proposals. Book catalog and ms guidelines online or with SASE.
○➔ "Our press aims to reach audiences beyond the academic community with accessible scholarly and regional books."
Nonfiction: Reference. Subjects include art/architecture (art history), ethnic, film/cinema/stage, gay/lesbian, government/politics, health/medicine, history, multicultural, nature/environment, regional, religion, sociology, women's issues/studies, African-American studies, Asian-American studies, history of science and technology, literature, literary criticism, human evolution, ecology, media studies. Books for use in undergraduate courses. Submit outline, 2-3 sample chapter(s). Reviews artwork/photos as part of ms package. Send photocopies.
Recent Title(s): *The Great Communication Gap: Why Americans Feel So Alone*, by Laura Pappano.
Tips: Both academic and general audiences. "Many of our books have potential for undergraduate course use. We are more trade-oriented than most university presses. We are looking for intelligent, well-written and accessible books. Avoid overly narrow topics."

RUTLEDGE HILL PRESS, Thomas Nelson, P.O. Box 141000, Nashville TN 37214-1000. (615)902-2333. Fax: (615)902-2340. Website: www.rutledgehillpress.com. **Acquisitions:** Lawrence Stone, publisher. Estab. 1982. Publishes hardcover and trade paperback originals and reprints. **Publishes 40-50 titles/year. Receives 1,000 submissions/year. 40% of books from first-time authors; 80% from unagented writers. Pays royalty. Offers advance.** Publishes book 10 months after acceptance of ms. Responds in 8 months to queries. Book catalog for 9×12 SAE with 4 first-class stamps; ms guidelines for #10 SASE.

• Rutledge Hill was acquired last year by the large Christian publisher Thomas Nelson.

O→ "We are a publisher of market-specific books, focusing on particular genres or regions."

Nonfiction: Biography, cookbook, humor. Subjects include cooking/foods/nutrition, humor, sports, travel (regional), women's issues/studies, Civil War history. "The book should have a unique marketing hook other than the subject matter itself. Books built on new ideas and targeted to a specific U.S. region are welcome. Please, no fiction, children's, academic, poetry or religious works, and we won't even look at *Life's Little Instruction Book* spinoffs or copycats." Submit cover letter that includes brief marketing strategy and author bio, outline and sample chapters. Reviews artwork/photos as part of ms package.

Recent Title(s): *A Gentleman Entertains,* by John Bridges and Bryan Curtis; *101 Secrets a Good Dad Knows,* by Walter Browder and Sue Ellen Browder; *Pilgrims: Sinners, Saints and Prophets,* by Marty Stuart.

N¡ SAE INTERNATIONAL, Society of Automotive Engineers. 400 Commonwealth Dr., Warrendale PA 15096. (724)776-4841. **Acquisitions:** Jeff Worsinger, product manager; Edward Manns, product manager; Martha Swiss, product manager; Lisa Moses, product manager; Kris Hattman, product manager; Tracy Fedkoe, product developer; Ed Manns, manager, product development division. Estab. 1905. Publishes hardcover and trade paperback originals, web and CD-ROM based electronic products. **Publishes 30-40 titles/year. Receives 250 queries and 75 mss/year. 30-40% of books from first-time authors; 100% from unagented writers. Pays royalty. Offers possible advance.** Publishes book 8 months after acceptance of ms. Accepts simultaneous submissions. Responds in 2 months to queries. Book catalog and ms guidelines free.

O→ "Automotive means anything self-propelled. We are a professional society serving this area, which includes aircraft, spacecraft, marine, rail, automobiles, trucks and off-highway vehicles." Currently emphasizing automotive history and engineering, aerospace history and engineering.

Nonfiction: Biography, multimedia (CD-ROM, web-based), reference, technical, textbook. Subjects include automotive and aerospace subjects. Query with SASE. Reviews artwork/photos as part of ms package. Send photocopies.

Recent Title(s): *The Future of the Automotive Industry, Race Car Engineering and Mechanics.*

Tips: "Audience is automotive engineers, technicians, car buffs, aerospace engineers, technicians and historians."

SAFARI PRESS, INC., 15621 Chemical Lane, Building B, Huntington Beach CA 92649-1506. (714)894-9080. Fax: (714)894-4949. E-mail: info@safaripress.com. Website: www.safaripress.com. **Acquisitions:** Jacqueline Neufeld, editor. Estab. 1984. Publishes hardcover originals and reprints and trade paperback reprints. **Publishes 20-25 titles/year. 50% of books from first-time authors; 99% from unagented writers. Pays 8-15% royalty on wholesale price.** Book catalog for $1.

• The editor notes that she receives many manuscripts outside the areas of big-game hunting, wingshooting, and sporting firearms, and these are always rejected.

O→ Safari Press publishes books only on big-game hunting, sporting, firearms, and wingshooting; this includes African, North American, European, Asian, and South American hunting and wingshooting. Does not want books on 'outdoors' topics (hiking, camping, canoeing, etc.).

Nonfiction: Biography (of hunters), how-to (hunting and wingshooting stories), hunting adventure stories. Subjects include hunting, firearms, wingshooting, "We discourage autobiographies, unless the life of the hunter or firearms maker has been exceptional. We routinely reject manuscripts along the lines of 'Me and my buddies went hunting for... and a good time was had by all!'" No outdoors topics (hiking, camping, canoeing, fishing, etc.). Query with SASE or submit outline.

Recent Title(s): *Fine European Gunmakers; Greatest Elk.*

SAFER SOCIETY PRESS, P.O. Box 340, Brandon VT 05733. (802)247-3132. Fax: (802)247-4233. Website: www.safersociety.org. **Acquisitions:** Lynne Porter, executive director. Estab. 1985. Publishes trade paperback originals. **Publishes 4-6 titles/year. Receives 15-20 queries and 15-20 mss/year. 90% of books from first-time authors; 100% from unagented writers. Pays 5% royalty on retail price.** Publishes book 1 year after acceptance of ms. Accepts simultaneous submissions. Book catalog free.

O→ "Our mission is the prevention and treatment of sexual abuse."

Nonfiction: Self-help (sex abuse prevention and treatment). Subjects include psychology (sexual abuse). "We are a small, nonprofit, niche press." Query with SASE, submit proposal package or complete ms. Reviews artwork/photos as part of ms package. Send photocopies.

Recent Title(s): *Healthy Thinking/Feeling/Doing from the Inside Out,* by Pransky and Carpenos.

Tips: Audience is persons working in mental health/persons needing self-help books. Pays small fees or low royalties.

SAGAMORE PUBLISHING, 804 N. Neil St., Suite 100, Champaign IL 61820. (217)363-2072. Fax: (217)363-2073. E-mail: books@sagamorepub.com. Website: www.sagamorepub.com. **Acquisitions:** Joseph Bannon, CEO (parks, recreation, leisure). Estab. 1974. Publishes hardcover and trade paperback originals. **Publishes 10-12 titles/year. Re-**

ceives 30-40 queries and 25-30 mss/year. **40% of books from first-time authors; 100% from unagented writers. Pays 7-15% royalty.** Publishes book 6 months after acceptance of ms. Accepts simultaneous submissions. Responds in 1 month to queries. Book catalog and ms guidelines free or online.

> O→ "Sagamore Publishing has been a leader in the parks and recreation field for over 20 years. We are now expanding into the areas of tourism and recreation for special populations such as people with autism or ADD/ADHD, and outdoor adventure and wildlife."

Nonfiction: Reference, textbook. Subjects include education, health/medicine, nature/environment, recreation, outdoor adventure, tourism. Submit proposal package, including outline, 1 sample chapter and market projections. Reviews artwork/photos as part of ms package. Send photocopies.
Recent Title(s): *Outdoor Recreation in American Life*, by Ken Cordell (textbook/reference).
Tips: "We strongly encourage potential authors to submit a marketing prospective with any manuscript they submit."

SALEM PRESS, INC., Magill's Choice, 131 N. El Molino, Suite 350, Pasadena CA 91101. (626)584-0106. Fax: (626)584-1525. Website: www.salempress.com. **Acquisitions:** Dawn P. Dawson. **Publishes 20-22 titles/year. Receives 15 queries/year. Work-for-hire pays 5-15 cents/word.** Responds in 1 month to queries, proposals and mss. Book catalog online.
Nonfiction: Reference. Subjects include business/economics, ethnic, government/politics, health/medicine, history, language/literature, military/war, music/dance, nature/environment, philosophy, psychology, science, sociology, women's issues/studies. "We accept vitas only of wrters interested in supplying articles/entries for encyclopedia-type entries in library reference books. Will also accept multi-volume book ideas from people interested in being a general editor." Query with SASE.

SALINA BOOKSHELF, 624 ½ North Beaver Street, Flagstaff AZ 86001. (520)527-0070. Website: www.salinabookshelf.com. **Acquisitions:** Louise Lockard, editor. Publishes trade paperback originals and reprints. **Publishes 4-5 titles/year. 0% of books from first-time authors; 100% from unagented writers. Pays 20% minimum royalty. Offers advance.** Publishes book 6 months after acceptance of ms. Accepts simultaneous submissions. Responds in 3 months to queries.
Nonfiction: Children's/juvenile, textbook (Navajo language). Subjects include education, ethnic, science. "We publish childrens' bilingual readers. Nonfiction should be appropriate to science and social studies curriculum grades 3-8." Query with SASE. Reviews artwork/photos as part of ms package. Send photocopies.
Fiction: Juvenile. "Submissions should be in English or a language taught in Southwest classrooms." Query with SASE.
Poetry: "We accept poetry in English/Southwest language for children." Submit 3 sample poems.
Recent Title(s): *Dine Bizaad: Speak, Read, Write Navajo*, by Irvy W. Goossen.

SALVO PRESS, P.O. Box 9095, Bend OR 97708. (541)330-8746. Fax: (541)330-8746. E-mail: info@salvopress.com. Website: www.salvopress.com. **Acquisitions:** Scott Schmidt, publisher. Publishes hardcover and trade paperback originals and e-books. **Publishes 6 titles/year. Receives 500 queries and 100 mss/year. 50% of books from first-time authors; 50% from unagented writers. Pays 8-15% royalty on retail price.** Publishes book 9 months after acceptance of ms. Responds in 1 month to queries; 2 months to mss. Book catalog and ms guidelines online.
Fiction: Mystery, suspense, espionage, thriller. "Our needs change. Check our website." Query with SASE.
Recent Title(s): *Kafka's Fedora*, by A.J. Adler (mainstream); *Hypershot*, by Trevor Scott.
Tips: "Salvo Press also sponsors the annual Mystery Novel Award. Send SASE for guidelines or check the website for them."

SAMS, Pearson Education, 201 W. 103rd St., Indianapolis IN 46290. (317)581-3500. Website: www.samspublishing.com. Publisher: Paul Boger. **Acquisitions:** Jeff Kock, acquisitions editor (operating systems, certification, professional programming), Mark Taber, associate publisher (web development), Linda Engelman, associate publisher (programming technologies). Estab. 1951. Publishes trade paperback originals. **Publishes 160 titles/year. 30% of books from first-time authors; 95% from unagented writers. Pays negotiable royalty on wholesale price. Offers negotiable advance.** Publishes book 1 year after acceptance of ms. Responds in 6 weeks to queries. Manuscript guidelines online.

> O→ Sams has made a major commitment to publishing books that meet the needs of computer users, programmers, administrative and support personnel, and managers.

Nonfiction: Technical. Subjects include computers and related technologies. Accepts simultaneous submissions if noted; "however once contract is signed, Sams Publishing retains first option rights on future works on same subject." Query with SASE.
Recent Title(s): *Wireless Java Programming*; *Teach Yourself in 24 Hours*.

SANDLAPPER PUBLISHING CO., INC., P.O. Box 730, Orangeburg SC 29116-0730. E-mail: agallmanl@mindspring.com. **Acquisitions:** Amanda Gallman, managing editor. Estab. 1982. Publishes hardcover and trade paperback originals and reprints. **Publishes 6 titles/year. Receives 200 submissions/year. 80% of books from first-time authors; 95% from unagented writers. Pays 15% maximum royalty on net receipts. Offers advance.** Publishes book 20 months after acceptance of ms. Responds in 3 months to queries. Book catalog and ms guidelines for 9×12 SAE with 4 first-class stamps.

O-- "We are an independent, regional book publisher specializing in educational nonfiction relating to South Carolina." Emphasizing history and travel.

Nonfiction: Biography, children's/juvenile (ages 9-14), cookbook, humor, illustrated book, reference, textbook. Subjects include cooking/foods/nutrition, history, humor, regional, culture and cuisine of the Southeast especially South Carolina. "We are looking for manuscripts that reveal under-appreciated or undiscovered facets of the rich heritage of our region. If a manuscript doesn't deal with South Carolina or the Southeast, the work is probably not appropriate for us. We don't do self-help books, children's books about divorce, kidnapping, etc., and absolutely no religious manuscripts." No phone calls. Query with SASE or submit outline, sample chapter(s). Reviews artwork/photos as part of ms package.

Recent Title(s): *Lowcountry Scenes*, by Jon Wongrey.

Tips: "Our readers are South Carolinians, visitors to the region's tourist spots, and friends and family that live out-of-state. We are striving to be a leading regional publisher for South Carolina. We will be looking for more history, travel and biography."

SANTA MONICA PRESS LLC, P.O. Box 1076, Santa Monica CA 90406. Website: www.santamonicapress.com. **Acquisitions:** Acquistions Editor. Estab. 1991. Publishes trade paperback originals. **Publishes 6-10 titles/year. Receives 500+ submissions/year. 10% of books from first-time authors; 50% from unagented writers. Pays 4-10% royalty on wholesale price. Offers $500-2,500 advance.** Publishes book 6-18 months after acceptance of ms. Accepts simultaneous submissions. Responds in 2 months to proposals. Book catalog for 9×12 SASE with 76¢ postage; ms guidelines for #10 SASE.

O-- "At Santa Monica Press, we're not afraid to cast a wide editorial net. Our vision extends from lively and modern how-to books to offbeat looks at popular culture, from fiction to new age."

Nonfiction: Biography, gift book, how-to, humor, illustrated book, reference. Subjects include Americana, creative nonfiction, film/cinema/stage, health/medicine, language/literature, memoirs, music/dance, spirituality, sports, travel, contemporary culture, film/cinema/stage, general nonfiction, New Age. *All unsolicited mss returned unopened.* Submit proposal package, including outline, 2-3 sample chapters, biography, marketing and publicity plans, analysis of competitive titles, SASE. Reviews artwork/photos as part of ms package. Send photocopies.

Recent Title(s): *Quack! Tales of Medical Fraud from the Museum of Questionable Medical Devices*, by Bob McCoy; *Cafe Nation: Coffee Folklore, Magick, and Divination*, by Sandra Mizumoto Posey.

Tips: "Visit our website before submitting to get a clear idea of the types of books we publish. Carefully analyze your book's competition and tell us what makes your book different—and what makes it better. Also let us know what promotional and marketing opportunities you, as the author, bring to the project."

SARABANDE BOOKS, INC., 2234 Dundee Rd., Suite 200, Louisville KY 40205. (502)458-4028. Fax: (502)458-4065. E-mail: sarabandeb@aol.com. Website: www.sarabandebooks.org. **Acquisitions:** Sarah Gorham, editor-in-chief. Publishes hardcover and trade paperback originals. **Publishes 8 titles/year. Receives 500 queries and 2,000 mss/year. 35% of books from first-time authors; 75% from unagented writers. 10% on actual income received. Offers $500-1,000 advance.** Publishes book 18 months after acceptance of ms. Accepts simultaneous submissions. Responds in 3 months to queries; 6 months to mss. Book catalog free; ms guidelines for #10 SASE.

O-- "Sarabande Books was founded to publish poetry and short fiction, as well as the occasional literary essay collection. We look for works of lasting literary value. We are actively seeking novellas, as well as essays on the writing life."

Fiction: Literary, short story collections, novellas. Queries in September only. "We do not publish novels." Query with 1 sample story, 1 page bio, listing of publishing credits and SASE.

Poetry: "Poetry of superior artistic quality. Otherwise no restraints or specifications." Submissions in September only. Query or submit 10 sample poems.

Recent Title(s): *Head*, by William Tester (fiction); *Multitudes: Poems Selected and New*, by Afaa Michael Weaver (poetry).

Tips: Sarabande publishes for a general literary audience. "Know your market. Read—and buy—books of literature." Sponsors contests.

SARPEDON PUBLISHERS, 49 Front St., Rockville Centre NY 11570. (800)207-8045. Fax: (516)255-0334. Website: www.combinedpublishing.com/sarpedon. **Acquisitions:** Steven Smith. Estab. 1991. Publishes hardcover originals and trade paperback reprints. **Publishes 15 titles/year. Receives 100 queries/year. 14% of books from first-time authors; 20% from unagented writers. Pays royalty. Offers $250-1,250 advance.** Publishes book 6-9 months after acceptance of ms. Accepts simultaneous submissions. Responds in 1 month to queries; 2 months to proposals; 3 months to mss. Book catalog and ms guidelines for #10 SASE.

Nonfiction: Biography. Subjects include Americana, government/politics, history (European), military/war, exploration. Submit outline, 2 sample chapter(s), synopsis. Reviews artwork/photos as part of ms package. Send photocopies.

Recent Title(s): *Refuge from the Reich*, by Stephen Tanner; *Robbing Banks*, by L.R. Kirchner.

SAS PUBLISHING, SAS Campus Dr., Cary NC 27513-2414. (919)677-8000. Fax: (919)677-4444. E-mail: sasbbu@sas.com. Website: www.sas.com. **Acquisitions:** Julie M. Platt, editor-in-chief. Estab. 1976. Publishes hardcover and trade paperback originals. **Publishes 40 titles/year. Receives 30 submissions/year. 50% of books from first-time authors; 100% from unagented writers. Payment negotiable. Offers negotiable advance.** Responds in 2 weeks to queries. Book catalog and ms guidelines online or with SASE.

    O➤ SAS publishes books for SAS software users, "both new and experienced."

Nonfiction: Technical, textbook. Subjects include software, statistics. "SAS Publishing develops and writes books inhouse. Through Books by Users Press, we also publish books by SAS users on a variety of topics relating to SAS software. We want to provide our users with additional titles to supplement our primary documentation and to enhance the users' ability to use SAS effectively. We're interested in publishing manuscripts that describe or illustrate using any of SAS products. Books must be aimed at SAS users, either new or experienced. Tutorials are particularly attractive, as are descriptions of user-written applications for solving real-life business, industry or academic problems. Books on programming techniques using SAS are also desirable. Manuscripts must reflect current or upcoming software releases, and the author's writing should indicate an understanding of SAS and the technical aspects covered in the manuscript." Query with SASE or submit outline, sample chapter(s). Reviews artwork/photos as part of ms package.

Recent Title(s): *The Little SAS Book: A Primer, Second Edition*, by Lora D. Delwiche and Susan J. Slaughter.

Tips: "If I were a writer trying to market a book today, I would concentrate on developing a manuscript that teaches or illustrates a specific concept or application that SAS users will find beneficial in their own environments or can adapt to their own needs."

SASQUATCH BOOKS, 615 Second Ave., Suite 260, Seattle WA 98104. (206)467-4300. Fax: (206)467-4301. E-mail: books@sasquatchbooks.com. Website: www.sasquatchbooks.com. President: Chad Haight. **Acquisitions:** Kate Rogers, senior editor (travel, Alaska, women's issues); Jennie McDonald, senior editor (California subjects: food and wine, gardening, history); Novella Carpenter, assistant editor (urban lifestyle, humor, women's issues). Estab. 1986. Publishes regional hardcover and trade paperback originals. **Publishes 30 titles/year. 20% of books from first-time authors; 75% from unagented writers. Pays royalty on cover price. Offers wide range advance.** Publishes book 6 months after acceptance of ms. Responds in 3 months to queries. Book catalog for 9×12 SAE with 2 first-class stamps.

    O➤ Sasquatch Books publishes books for a West Coast regional audience. Currently emphasizing outdoor recreation, cookbooks and history.

Nonfiction: "We are seeking quality nonfiction works about the Pacific Northwest and West Coast regions (including Alaska to California). The literature of place includes how-to and where-to as well as history and narrative nonfiction." Reference. Subjects include animals, art/architecture, business/economics, cooking/foods/nutrition, gardening, history, nature/environment, recreation, regional, sports, travel, women's issues/studies, outdoors. Query first, then submit outline and sample chapters with SASE.

Recent Title(s): *The Secret Knowledge of Water*, by Craig Charles; *Best Places: Northern California*; *Artists in Their Gardens*, by Valerie Easton and David Laskin.

Tips: "We sell books through a range of channels in addition to the book trade. Our primary audience consists of active, literate residents of the West Coast."

SCARECROW PRESS, INC., Rowman & Littlefield Publishing Company, 4720 Boston Way, Lanham MD 20706. (301)459-3366. Fax: (301)459-2118. Website: www.scarecrowpress.com. **Acquisitions:** Sue Easun, acquisitions editor (information studies, interdisciplinary studies, general reference); Bruce Phillips, acquisitions editor (music, film and theatre); Tom Koerner, editorial director (educational practice and policy). Estab. 1950. Publishes hardcover originals. **Publishes 165 titles/year. Receives 600-700 submissions/year. 70% of books from first-time authors; 99% from unagented writers. Pays 8% royalty on net of first 1,000 copies; 10% of net price thereafter.** Publishes book 18 months after acceptance of ms. Responds in 2 months to queries. Book catalog for 9×12 SAE with 4 first-class stamps.

    O➤ Scarecrow Press publishes several series: Historical Dictionaries, which include countries, religions, international organizations and area studies; Studies and Documentaries on the History of Popular Entertainment (forthcoming); Society, Culture and Libraries. "Emphasis is on any title likely to appeal to libraries." Currently emphasizing jazz, Africana, and educational issues of contemporary interest.

Nonfiction: Reference (criminology, curriculum resource guides, military history). Subjects include film/cinema/stage, language/literature, religion, sports, annotated bibliographies, handbooks and biographical dictionaries in the areas of women's studies and ethnic studies, parapsychology, fine arts and handicrafts, genealogy, sports history, music, movies, stage, library and information science. Query with SASE.

Recent Title(s): *A White Teacher Talks About Race*, by Julie Landsman; *The Twentieth Century String Quartet*, by Ian Lawrence.

N FRANK SCHAFFER PUBLICATIONS FAMILY OF COMPANIES, 23740 Hawthorne Blvd., Torrance CA 90505. (310)378-1133. Fax: (310)791-5468. E-mail: FSPEditor@aol.com. Website: frankschaffer.com. **Acquisitions:** Stephanie Oberc, editorial director (Judy/Instructo, Pre-K-1); Kathleen Hex, editorial director (Good Apple, 4 to 8); Jeanine Manfro, editorial director (FSP Products, Grade K-6); Hanna Hotero, editorial director (Feron, K-3 and Totline, pre-K-1). Imprint publishes mass market paperback originals and reprints. **Publishes 500 titles/year; imprint publishes 200 titles/year. Receives 500 queries and 250 mss/year. 25% of books from first-time authors; 10% from unagented writers. Pays 5% royalty on retail price Outright purchase varies.** Publishes book 1-2 years after acceptance of ms. Accepts simultaneous submissions. Responds in 3 months to queries. Book catalog and ms guidelines online.

Imprints: Fearon, Good Apple, Totline, Shining Star, Grade Publications and Judy/Instructo

Nonfiction: Subjects include education. "We publish educational (supplemental) materials from pre-school to grade 8 and a limited amount for grades 9 to 12." Query with SASE or submit complete ms. Reviews artwork/photos as part of ms package. Send photocopies or transparencies to Art Department.

Tips: Audience is parents and teachers for children from pre-school to grade 8—some for grades 9-12. "Be concise and to the point. Make sure your spelling and grammar is correct in your submission letter."

SCHENKMAN BOOKS, INC., 118 Main Street, Rochester VT 05767. (802)767-3702. Fax: (802)767-9528. E-mail: schenkma@sover.net. Website: www.sover.net/~schenkma/. **Acquisitions:** Joe Schenkman, editor. Estab. 1961. Publishes hardcover and trade paperback originals and reprints. **Publishes 6 titles/year. Receives 100 queries and 25 mss/year. 80% of books from first-time authors; 95% from unagented writers. Pays 10% royalty on net receipts.** Accepts simultaneous submissions. Book catalog and ms guidelines free.

    O—π "Schenkman Books specializes in publishing scholarly monographs for the academic community. For almost forty years we have brought revolutionary works to the public to fuel discourse on important issues. It is our hope that the material we make available contributes to the efforts toward peace and humanitarianism throughout the world."

Nonfiction: Biography, self-help, textbook, scholarly monographs. Subjects include anthropology/archeology, ethnic, government/politics, history, music/dance, philosophy, psychology, sociology, women's issues/studies, African studies, African-American studies, Asian studies, Caribbean studies. Query with SASE or submit outline. Reviews artwork/photos as part of ms package. Send photocopies.

Recent Title(s): *Work Abuse*, by Judith Wyatt and Chauncey Hare (self-help/management relations).

Ⓐ SCHOCKEN BOOKS, Knopf Publishing Group, Random House, Inc., 299 Park Ave., New York NY 10171. (212)572-2559. Fax: (212)572-6030. Website: www.schocken.com. **Acquisitions:** Susan Ralston, editorial director, Altie Karper, editor. Estab. 1931. Publishes hardcover and trade paperback originals and reprints. **Publishes 12-15 titles/year. Small % of books from first-time authors; small % from unagented writers. Offers varied advance.** Accepts simultaneous submissions.

    O—π "Schocken publishes a broad list of serious, solid fiction and nonfiction books with commercial appeal, as well as reprints of classics." Schocken has a commitment to publishing Judaica, and also specializes in the areas of cultural and historical studies.

Nonfiction: Subjects include history, philosophy, women's issues/studies, cultural studies, Judaica. *Accepts agented submissions only.*

Recent Title(s): *How To Be a Jewish Parent*, by Anita Diamont; *The Funeral Party*, by Ludmila Ulitskaya.

SCHOLASTIC INC., Book Group, 555 Broadway, New York NY 10012. (212)343-6100. Website: www.scholastic.com. **Acquisitions:** Vice President/Publisher: Jean Feiwel. Estab. 1920. Publishes trade paperback originals for children ages 4-young adult, juvenile hardcover picture books, novels and nonfiction. **Pays royalty on retail price. Offers advance.** Responds in 6 months to queries. Manuscript guidelines for #10 SASE.

Imprints: Blue Sky Press (contact Bonnie Verburg), Cartwheel Books (contact Bernette Ford), Arthur Levine Books (contact Arthur Levine), Mariposa (contact Susanna Pasternac), Scholastic Press (contact Elizabeth Szabla), Scholastic Reference & Gallimard (contact Kate Walters), Scholastic Trade Paperback (contact Craig Walker), Orchard Books (contact Amy Griffin)

    ● Scholastic recently purchsed Grolier, Inc.

    O—π "We are proud of the many fine, innovative materials we have created—such as classroom magazines, book clubs, book fairs, and our new literacy and technology programs. But we are most proud of our reputation as 'The Most Trusted Name in Learning.'"

Nonfiction: Children's/juvenile (ages 4 to teen). Query with SASE.

Fiction: Juvenile, mystery, romance, young adult. Hardcover—open to all subjects suitable for children. Paperback—family stories, mysteries, school, friendships for ages 8-12, 35,000 words. YA fiction, romance, family and mystery for ages 12-15, 40,000-45,000 words for average to good readers. *No unsolicited mss.* Queries welcome.

Recent Title(s): *The Great Fire*, by Jim Murphy; *Out of the Dust*, by Karen Hesse.

Tips: New writers for children should study the children's book field before submitting.

Ⓐ SCHOLASTIC PRESS, Scholastic Inc., 555 Broadway, New York NY 10012. (212)343-6100. Website: www.scholastic.com. **Acquisitions:** Elizabeth Szabla, editorial director. Publishes hardcover originals. **Publishes 50 titles/year. Receives 2,500 queries/year. 5% of books from first-time authors. Pays royalty on retail price. Offers varies advance.** Publishes book 18-24 months after acceptance of ms. Responds in 6 months to queries.

    O—π Scholastic Press publishes "fresh, literary picture book fiction and nonfiction; fresh, literary non-series or genre-oriented middle grade and young adult fiction." Currently emphasizing "subtly handled treatments of key relationships in children's lives; unusual approaches to commonly dry subjects, such as biography, math, history or science." De-emphasizing fairy tales (or retellings), board books, genre or series fiction (mystery, fantasy, etc.).

Nonfiction: Children's/juvenile, general interest. *Accepts agented submissions only.*

Fiction: Juvenile, picture books. *Accepts agented submissions only.*

Recent Title(s): *The Greatest: Muhammad Ali*, by Walter Dean Myers; *Learning to Swim*, by Ann Turner; *Esperanza Rising*, by Pam Munoz Ryan.

SCHOLASTIC PROFESSIONAL PUBLISHING, Scholastic Inc. 555 Broadway, New York NY 10012. Website: www.scholastic.com. Vice President/Editor-in-Chief: Terry Cooper. **Acquisitions:** Liza Charlesworth, editorial director (pre-K-grade 4 teacher resource books and materials); Virginia Dooley, editorial director (grade 4-8 teacher resource books); Wendy Murray, executive editor (teaching strategy, professional development and theory-based books). Estab. 1989. **Publishes 140+ titles/year. Offers advance.** Responds in 3 months to queries. Book catalog for 9 × 12 SASE.

O—≖ "We publish a line of teacher resources to help enrich classrooms, to help meet teachers' needs." Currently emphasizing multiple intelligences, differentiated curriculum, standards, testing.

Nonfiction: Subjects include education. Elementary and middle-school level enrichment—all subject areas, including math and science and theme units, integrated materials, writing process, management techniques, teaching strategies based on personal/professional experience in the clssroom and technology ideas. Production is limited to printed matter: resource and activity books, professional development materials, reference titles. Length: 6,000-12,000 words. Offers standard contract. Query with table of contents, outline and sample chapter.

Recent Title(s): *Getting the Most Out of Morning Message & Other Shared Writing Lessons*, by Carleen DaCruz Payne and Mary Browning Schulman; *150 Totally Terrific Writing Prompts*, by Justin Martin.

Tips: "Writer should have background working in the classroom with elementary or middle school children, teaching pre-service students, and/or solid background in developing supplementary educational materials for these markets."

N. SCHREIBER PUBLISHING, INC., 51 Monroe St., Suite 101, Rockville MD 20850. (301)424-7737 ext. 28. Fax: (301)424-2336. E-mail: spbooks@aol.com. Website: www.schreibernet.com. President: Morry Schreiber. **Acquisitions:** Linguistics Editor; Judaica Editor. Publishes hardcover and trade paperback originals and reprints. **Publishes 8 titles/ year. Receives 40 queries and 12 mss/year. 80% of books from first-time authors; 95% from unagented writers. Pays negotiable royalty on retail price.** Publishes book 6 months after acceptance of ms. Accepts simultaneous submissions. Responds in 1 month to queries, proposals and mss. Book catalog online; ms guidelines free.

O—≖ Publishes reference books and dictionaries for better language and translation work, as well as Judaica books emphasizing Jewish culture and religion. Currently emphasizing multicultural dictionaries and parochial books.

Nonfiction: Biography, children's/juvenile, coffee table book, gift book, humor, multimedia (CD-ROM), reference, textbook. Subjects include history, language/literature, memoirs, money/finance, multicultural, religion, science, translation. Query with SASE; or submit proposal package, including: outline, 1 sample chapter and table of contents. Reviews artwork/photos as part of ms package. Send photocopies.

Recent Title(s): *Saving the Jews*, by Mordecai Paldiel (history/religion).

A. SCRIBNER, Simon & Schuster, 1230 Avenue of the Americas, New York NY 10020. (212)698-7000. Website: www.simonsays.com. Publishes hardcover originals. **Publishes 70-75 titles/year. Receives thousands queries/year. 20% of books from first-time authors; 0% from unagented writers. Pays 7½-15% royalty. Offers varies advance.** Accepts simultaneous submissions. Responds in 3 months to queries.

Imprints: Rawson Associates; Lisa Drew Books; Scribner Classics (reprints only); Scribner Poetry (by invitation only); Simple Abundance Press

Nonfiction: Biography. Subjects include education, ethnic, gay/lesbian, health/medicine, history, language/literature, nature/environment, philosophy, psychology, religion, science, criticism. *Accepts agented submissions only.*

Fiction: Literary, mystery, suspense. *Accepts agented submissions only.*

Recent Title(s): *Dreamcatcher*, by Stephen King; *The Constant Gardener*, by John le Carre; *Fatal Voyage*, by Kathy Reichs.

SCRIVENERY PRESS, P.O. Box 740969-1003, Houston TX 77274-0969. (713)665-6760. Fax: (713)665-8838. E-mail: books@scrivenery.com. Website: www.scrivenery.com. **Acquisitions:** Kevin Miller, associate editor (nonfiction); Chris Coleman, associate editor (fiction/general); Leila B. Joiner, editor (fiction/literary). Publishes hardcover originals and trade paperback originals and reprints. **Publishes 10 titles/year. Receives 2,000 queries and 30 mss/year. 25% of books from first-time authors; 50% from unagented writers. Pays 8½-15% royalty on retail price Electronic and other subsidiary rights at 50% publisher's net; motion picture rights remain with author. Offers rare advance.** Publishes book 10 months after acceptance of ms. Accepts simultaneous submissions. Responds in 3 months to queries and proposals; 4 months to mss. Book catalog for $2 or online; ms guidelines for #10 SASE or online.

O—≖ "Our primary needs are in the humanities: English literatuare (history and/or analyses); literary theory (for a general, educated audience); science, technology, and culture, and natural history (e.g., Edward O. Wilson, Stephen Jay Gould); and history, targeted at an adult, well-educated audience who seek the pleasure of expertly-wielded language. Biography (no memoirs or autobiography) is also needed; we prefer figures from arts, letters and science rather than political/military figures."

Nonfiction: Biography, how-to, self-help, humanities. Subjects include Americana, creative nonfiction, history, hobbies, language/literature, nature/environment, philosophy, science, translation. Submit proposal package including outline, 3 sample chapter(s). *All unsolicited mss returned unopened.* Reviews artwork/photos as part of ms package. Send photocopies or line-art only; no photos.

Fiction: Adventure, experimental, historical, literary, mainstream/contemporary, regional, short story collections, suspense. "Our greatest interest is in mainstream and literary fiction; we prefer literary crossover in all genres." Submit proposal package including 3 sample chapter(s), synopsis. *All unsolicited mss returned unopened.*

Recent Title(s): *Next Year in Cuba*; *Easy Reading Writing*.

Tips: "In both fiction and nonfiction, we market to an adult, educated audience who seek the pleasure of expertly-wielded language in addition to well-crafted story. Scrivenery Press is open to unpublished talent, but not writers new to the craft. Polish your manuscript as best you can; expect to be judged against seasoned pros. In fiction, we prefer polished, literate work that could be construed as a crossover between genre and literary fiction; examples would be, in mystery, Umberto Eco's *The Name of the Rose*; in mainstream, David Guterson's *Snow Falling on Cedars* or Annie Proulx's *The Shipping News*; in the history genre, Charles Frazier's *Cold Mountain*, or our recent release by E.A. Blair, *A Journey to the Interior*. In nonfiction we seek thoughtful work, but material not specifically geared to an academic market."

SEAL PRESS, 3131 Western Ave., Suite 410, Seattle WA 98121. Fax: (206)285-9410. E-mail: sealpress@sealpress.com. Website: www.sealpress.com. **Acquisitions:** Faith Conlon, editor/publisher; Leslie Miller, senior editor; Anne Mathews, managing editor. Publishes hardcover and trade paperback originals. **Publishes 15 titles/year. Receives 1,000 queries and 750 mss/year. 25% of books from first-time authors; 70% from unagented writers. Pays 7-10% royalty on retail price. Offers $500-2,000 advance.** Publishes book 18 months after acceptance of ms. Accepts simultaneous submissions. Responds in 2 months to queries. Book catalog and ms guidelines for SASE.
Imprints: Adventura Books (travel/outdoors), Live Girls (Third-Wave, young feminist)
> ⚬╍ "Seal Press is an independent feminist book publisher interested in original, lively, radical, empowering and culturally diverse nonfiction by women addressing contemporary issues from a feminist perspective or speak positively to the experience of being female." Currently emphasizing women outdoor adventurists, young feminists. De-emphasizing fiction.

Nonfiction: Biography (women only), literary nonfiction essays. Subjects include Americana, child guidance/parenting, creative nonfiction, ethnic, gay/lesbian, memoirs, multicultural, nature/environment, sex, travel, women's issues/studies, popular culture. Query with SASE. Reviews artwork/photos as part of ms package. Send photocopies.
Fiction: Ethnic, feminist, gay/lesbian, literary. Must fall within Adventura or Live Girls imprints. "We are interested in alternative voices." *No unsolicited mss.* Query with SASE or submit synopsis.
Recent Title(s): *Breeder: Real-Life Stories from the New Generation of Mothers*, edited by Ariel Gore and Bee Lavender (nonfiction); *Bruised Hibiscus*, Elizabeth Nunez (fiction).
Tips: "Our audience is generally composed of women interested in reading about contemporary issues addressed from a feminist perspective."

⟦N⟧ SEAWORTHY PUBLICATIONS, INC., 215 S. Park St., Suite #1, Port Washington WI 53074. (262)268-9250. Fax: (262)268-9208. E-mail: publisher@seaworthy.com. Website: www.seaworthy.com. **Acquisitions:** Joseph F. Janson, publisher. Publishes trade paperback originals, hardcover originals and reprints. **Publishes 8 titles/year. Receives 150 queries and 40 mss/year. 60% of books from first-time authors; 100% from unagented writers. Pays 15% royalty on wholesale price. Offers $1,000 advance.** Publishes book 6 months after acceptance of ms. Responds in 1 month to queries. Book catalog and ms guidelines online or for #10 SASE.
> ● Seaworthy Publications is not accepting fiction or poetry at this time.
> ⚬╍ Seaworthy Publications is a nautical book publisher that primarily publishes books of interest to recreational boaters and serious bluewater cruisers, including cruising guides, how-to and first-person adventure. Currently emphasizing guidebooks, how-to. De-emphasizing first-person adventure.

Nonfiction: Illustrated book, reference, technical. Subjects include history (nautical), hobbies (sailing, boating), regional (boating guide books), sports (sail racing), travel (world, circumnavigation). Regional guide books, first-person adventure, illustrated book, reference, technical—all dealing with boating. Query with SASE or submit 3 sample chapter(s), table of contents. Prefers electronic query via e-mail. Reviews artwork/photos as part of ms package. Send photocopies or color prints.
Recent Title(s): *Financial Freedom Afloat*, by Charles Tuller.
Tips: "Our audience consists of sailors, boaters, and those interested in the sea, sailing or long distance cruising and racing."

⟦△⟧ SEEDLING PUBLICATIONS, INC., 4522 Indianola Ave., Columbus OH 43214-2246. (614)267-7333. Fax: (614)267-4205. E-mail: sales@seedlingpub.com. Website: www.seedlingpub.com. **Acquisitions:** Josie Stewart, vice president. Estab. 1992. Publishes in an 8-, 12-, or 16-page format for beginning readers. **Publishes 8-10 titles/year. Receives 50 queries and 450 mss/year. 50% of books from first-time authors; 100% from unagented writers. Pays royalty or makes outright purchase. Offers advance.** Publishes book 1 year after acceptance of ms. Accepts simultaneous submissions. Responds in 6 months to queries. Book catalog for #10 SAE with 3 first-class stamps; ms guidelines for #10 SASE.
> ⚬╍ "We are an education niche publisher, producing books for beginning readers. Stories must include language that is natural to young children and story lines that are interesting to 5-7-year-olds and written at their beginning reading level."

Nonfiction: Children's/juvenile. Subjects include animals. Science, math or social studies concepts are considered. Does not accept mss or queries via fax or e-mail. Submit outline, SASE. Reviews artwork/photos as part of ms package. Send photocopies.
Fiction: Juvenile. Query with SASE or submit outline or submit complete ms.
Recent Title(s): *Zebras*, by Lynn Salem, Josie Stewart; *Treasure in the Attic*, by Linda Kulp.

Tips: "Follow our guidelines. Do not submit full-length picture books or chapter books. We are an education niche publisher. Our books are for children, ages 5-7, who are just beginning to read independently. We do not accept stories that rhyme or poetry at this time. Try a manuscript with young readers. Listen for spots in the text that don't flow when the child reads the story. Rewrite until the text sounds natural to beginning readers." Does not accept manuscripts or queries via email or fax.

■ ■ **SERENDIPITY SYSTEMS**, P.O. Box 140, San Simeon CA 93452. (805)927-5259. E-mail: bookware@thegr id.net. Website: www.s-e-r-e-n-d-i-p-i-t-y.com. **Acquisitions:** John Galuszka, publisher. Estab. 1986. "We publish on disks, the Internet and CD-ROMs, plus Rocket Editions for Gemstar's RCA Reb1100 eBook reader device." **Publishes 6-12 titles/year; imprint publishes 0-6 titles/year. Receives 600 queries and 150 mss/year. 95% from unagented writers. Pays 33% royalty on wholesale price or on retail price, depending on how the books goes out.** Publishes book 2 months after acceptance of ms. Accepts simultaneous submissions. Responds in 1 month to mss. Book catalog online; ms guidelines for #10 SASE or online.
Imprints: Books-on-Disks, Bookware
　○┅ "Serendipity Systems publishes electronic books for IBM-PC compatible computers."
Nonfiction: Multimedia, reference. Subjects include computers/electronic, language/literature, software. "We only publish reference books on literature, writing and electronic publishing." Queries by e-mail; mss, summaries with sample chapters and long documents should be sent by postal mail. No religious, occult, New Age or children's mss. Submit entire ms on disk in ASCII or HTML files.
Fiction: "We want to see *only* works which use (or have a high potential to use) hypertext, multimedia, interactivity or other computer-enhanced features." No romance, religious, occult, New Age, fantasy, or children's mss. Submit entire ms on disk in ASCII or HTML files. Query first.
Recent Title(s): *Science Fiction Six-Pack*, by M.Allen, T. Easton, J. Dacy II, and J. Peter; *The Electronic Publishing Forum* (nonfiction).
Tips: "We publish on disks, the Internet and CD-ROMs, plus Rocket Editions for Nuvo Media's Rocket eBook reader device. Check our guidelines on the Internet for the latest information."

■ **SERGEANT KIRKLAND'S PRESS**, 8 Yakama Trail, Spotsylvania VA 22553-2422. (540)582-6296. Fax: (540)582-8312. E-mail: seagraver@kirklands.org. **Acquisitions:** Pia S. Seagrave, Phd.D., editor-in-chief. Publishes hardcover and trade paperback originals, hardcover reprints. **Publishes 28 titles/year. Receives 200 queries and 150 mss/year. 70% of books from first-time authors; 90% from unagented writers. Pays 10% royalty.** Publishes book 6 months after acceptance of ms. Responds in 3 months to queries and proposals; 4 months to mss. Book catalog and ms guidelines online.
　○┅ Currently emphasizing American history of academic and regional interest—colonial, Civil War, WWII and Vietnam periods.
Nonfiction: Biography, reference. Subjects include Americana, anthropology/archeology, government/politics, history, military/war, Jewish-Holocaust. Query with SASE or submit complete ms. Reviews artwork/photos as part of ms package. Send photocopies.
Recent Title(s): *Sara's Children: The Destruction of the Chmielnik*, by Suzan Hagstrom (Holocaust).
Tips: "Have your work professionally edited and be sure it meets the general standards of the *Chicago Manual of Style*."

SEVEN STORIES PRESS, 140 Watts St., New York NY 10013. (212)226-8760. Fax: (212)226-1411. E-mail: info@se venstories.com. Website: www.sevenstories.com. **Acquisitions:** Daniel Simon; Greg Ruggiero; Michael Manekin; Vi daine Husman; Jill Schoolman; Violane Huisman. Estab. 1995. Publishes hardcover and trade paperback originals. **Publishes 20-25 titles/year. 15% of books from first-time authors; 15% from unagented writers. Pays 7-15% royalty on retail price. Offers advance.** Publishes book 1-3 years after acceptance of ms. Accepts simultaneous submissions. Responds in 3 months to queries. Book catalog and ms guidelines free.
　○┅ Seven Stories Press publishes literary/activist fiction and nonfiction "on the premise that both are works of the imagination and that there is no contradiction in publishing the two side by side." Currently emphasizing politics, social justice, biographies, foreign writings.
Nonfiction: Biography. Subjects include general nonfiction. Responds only if interested. *No unsolicited mss.* Query only.
Fiction: Literary. *No unsolicited mss.* Query only. SASE required.
Recent Title(s): *All Things Censored*, by Mumia Abu Jamal (nonfiction); *Algerian White*, by Assia Djebar (fiction); *Poems for the Nation*, edited by Allen Ginsberg (poetry).

SHAW BOOKS, Waterbrook Press, 2375 Telstar Dr. #160, Colorado Springs CO 80920-1029. (719)590-4999. Fax: (719)590-8977. **Acquisitions:** Elisa Fryling, editor. Estab. 1967. Publishes mostly trade paperback originals and reprints. **Publishes 30 titles/year. Receives 1,000 submissions/year. 10-20% of books from first-time authors; 60% from unagented writers. Pays 10-12% royalty on net receipts Sometimes makes outright purchase of $375-2,500 for Bible studies and compilations. Offers advance.** Publishes book 18 months after acceptance of ms. Responds in 6 months to queries.

O─ "We are looking for unique mss from a Christian perspective on the topics below. Queries accepted but not unsolicited mss." Currently emphasizing health and wellness, family and education, literary nonfiction, Bible study guides.

Nonfiction: Subjects include cooking/foods/nutrition, creative nonfiction, education, general, language/literature, parenting, health and wellness, Bible study, literary topics all from a Christian perspective. "We are looking for adult nonfiction with different twists—self-help manuscripts with fresh insight and colorful, vibrant writing style." No fiction, poetry or unsolicited mss. Query with SASE.

Recent Title(s): *Madeleine L'Engle Herself*, by Madeleine L'Engle; *The Contemplative Mom*, by Ann Kroeker.

SHEED & WARD BOOK PUBLISHING, 7373 S. Lovers Lane Rd., Franklin WI 53132. (800)558-0580. Fax: (800)369-4448. E-mail: sheed@execpc.com. Website: www.sheedandward.com. **Acquisitions:** Jeremy W. Langford, editor-in-chief (Catholicism). Publishes hardcover and trade paperback originals. **Publishes 25-30 titles/year. Receives 600-1,000 queries and 600-1,000 mss/year. 25% of books from first-time authors; 90% from unagented writers. Pays 6-12% royalty on retail price. Offers $500-2,000 advance.** Publishes book 8 months after acceptance of ms. Responds in 1 month to queries; 2 months to proposals and mss. Book catalog and ms guidelines online.

O─ "We are looking for books that help our readers, most of whom are college educated, gain access to the riches of the Catholic/Christian tradition. We publish in the areas of history, biography, spirituality, prayer, ethics, ministry, justice, liturgy."

Nonfiction: Biography, gift book, reference. Subjects include religion, sex, spirituality. Submit proposal package including outline, 2 sample chapter(s), strong cover letter indicating why the project is unique and compelling. Reviews artwork/photos as part of ms package. Send photocopies.

Recent Title(s): *Why Do We Suffer? A Scriptural Approach to the Human Condition*, by Daniel Harrington; *Job: And Death No Dominion*, by Daniel Berrigan.

Tips: "We prefer that writers get our author guidelines either from our website or via mail before submitting proposals."

N SHEEP MEADOW PRESS, P.O. Box 1345, Riverdale NY 10471. (718)548-5547. Fax: (718)884-0406. E-mail: sheepmdwpr@aol.com. **Acquisitions:** Stanley Moss, publisher. Publishes hardcover and trade paperback originals and reprints. **Publishes 10-12 titles/year. Pays 7-10% royalty on retail price.** Book catalog free.

Poetry: Submit complete ms.

SIERRA CLUB BOOKS, 85 Second St., San Francisco CA 94105. (415)977-5500. Fax: (415)977-5793. E-mail: danny.moses@sierraclub.org. Website: www.sierraclub.org/books. **Acquisitions:** Danny Moses, editor-in-chief; James Cohee, senior editor; Linda Gunnarson, editor. Estab. 1962. Publishes hardcover and paperback originals and reprints. **Publishes 20-30 titles/year. Receives 1,000 submissions/year. 50% from unagented writers. Pays 10-12% royalty on wholesale price. Offers $3,000-10,000 average advance.** Publishes book 10 months after acceptance of ms. Responds in 1 month to queries; 2 months to proposals; 3 months to mss. Book catalog online.

O─ The Sierra Club was founded to help people to explore, enjoy and preserve the nation's forests, waters, wildlife and wilderness. The books program publishes quality trade books about the outdoors and the protection of natural resources.

Nonfiction: Subjects include general, nature/environment. A broad range of environmental subjects: outdoor adventure, descriptive and how-to, women in the outdoors; landscape and wildlife pictorials; literature, including travel and works on the spiritual aspects of the natural world; travel and trail; natural history and current environmental issues, including public health and uses of appropriate technology; gardening; general interest. "Specifically, we are interested in literary natural history, environmental issues such as nuclear power, self-sufficiency, politics and travel." Does *not* want "proposals for large color photographic books without substantial text; how-to books on building things outdoors; books on motorized travel; or any but the most professional studies of animals." No fiction or poetry. Query with SASE. Reviews artwork/photos as part of ms package. Send photocopies.

Recent Title(s): *Seven Wonders: Timeless Travels for a Healthier Planet.*

SILHOUETTE BOOKS, 300 E. 42nd St., New York NY 10017. (212)682-6080. Fax: (212)682-4539. Website: www.eHarlequin.com. Editorial Director, Silhouette Books, Harlequin Historicals: Tara Gavin. **Acquisitions:** Mary Theresa Hussey, senior editor (Silhouette Romance); Karen Taylor Richman, senior editor (Silhouette Special Editions); Joan Marlow Golan, senior editor (Silhouette Desires); Leslie Wainger, executive senior editor (Silhouette Intimate Moments); Tracy Farrell, senior editor/editorial coordinator (Harlequin Historicals). Estab. 1979. Publishes mass market paperback originals. **Publishes over 350 titles/year. Receives approximately 4,000 submissions/year. Pays royalty. Offers advance.** Publishes book 1-3 years after acceptance of ms. Manuscript guidelines for #10 SASE.

Imprints: *Silhouette Romance* (contemporary adult romances, 53,000-58,000 words); *Silhouette Desire* (contemporary adult romances, 55,000-60,000 words); *Silhouette Intimate Moments* (contemporary adult romances, 80,000 words); *Harlequin Historicals* (adult historical romances, 95,000-105,000 words); *Silhouette Special Edition* (contemporary adult romances, 75,000-80,000 words)

O─ Silhouette publishes contemporary adult romances.

Fiction: Romance (contemporary and historical romance for adults). "We are interested in seeing submissions for all our lines. No manuscripts other than the types outlined. Manuscript should follow our general format, yet have an individuality and life of its own that will make it stand out in the readers' minds." *No unsolicited mss.* Send query letter, 2 page synopsis and SASE to head of imprint.

Recent Title(s): *Considering Kate*, by Nora Roberts.
Tips: "The romance market is constantly changing, so when you read for research, read the latest books and those that have been recommended to you by people knowledgeable in the genre. We are actively seeking new authors for all our lines, contemporary and historical."

N SILMAN-JAMES PRESS, 3624 Shannon Rd., Los Angeles CA 90027. (303)661-9922. E-mail: silmanjamespress @earthlink.net. **Acquisitions:** Gwen Feldman, Jim Fox, publishers. Publishes trade paperback originals and reprints. **Publishes 6-10 titles/year. Receives 50 queries and 40 mss/year. 50% of books from first-time authors; 80% from unagented writers. Pays 6-12% royalty on retail price.** Responds in 1 month to queries; 2 months to proposals; 3 months to mss. Book catalog free.
Nonfiction: Pertaining to film, theatre, music, peforming arts. Biography, how-to, reference, technical, textbook. Submit proposal package including outline, 1+ sample chapter(s) or submit complete ms. Reviews artwork/photos as part of ms package. Send photocopies.
Recent Title(s): *Comic Insights: The Art of Stand-Up Comedy*, by Franklyn Ajaye.
Tips: "Our audience ranges from people with a general interest in film (fans, etc.) to students of film and performing arts to industry professionals. We will accept 'query' phone calls."

SILVER DAGGER MYSTERIES, The Overmountain Press, P.O. Box 1261, Johnson City TN 37605. (423)926-2691. Fax: (423)929-2464. E-mail: alexfoster@silverdaggerstore.com. Website: www.silverdaggerstore.com. **Acquisitions:** Alex Foster, acquisitions editor. Publishes hardcover and trade paperback originals and reprints. **Publishes 30 titles/year; imprint publishes 15 titles/year. Receives 100 queries and 50 mss/year. 50% of books from first-time authors; 50% from unagented writers. Pays 15% royalty on wholesale price.** Publishes book 1 year after acceptance of ms. Accepts simultaneous submissions. Responds in 1 month to queries; 3 months to proposals; 6 months to mss. Book catalog and ms guidelines online.
    O→ Silver Dagger publishes mysteries that take place in the American South. Emphasizing cozies, police procedurals, hard-boiled detectives.
Fiction: Mystery. "We look for average-length books of 60-80,000 words." No horror or science fiction. Query with SASE or submit proposal package including 2 sample chapter(s), synopsis, author bio. *All unsolicited mss returned unopened.*
Recent Title(s): *Death's Favorite Child*, by Frankie Y. Bailey; *Voices in the Sand*, by Anne Underwood Grant.
Tips: "We publish cozies, hard-boiled and police procedural mysteries. Check the website for specific guidelines and submission dates. Due to a large number of submissions, we only review at certain times of the year."

N SILVER MOON PRESS, 160 Fifth Ave., New York NY 10010. (212)242-6499. Fax: (212)242-6799. **Acquisitions:** Carmen McCain, managing editor. Publishes hardcover originals. **Publishes 5-8 titles/year. Receives 600 queries and 400 mss/year. 60% of books from first-time authors; 70% from unagented writers. Pays 7-10% royalty.** Offers 500-1,000 advance. Publishes book 18 months after acceptance of ms. Accepts simultaneous submissions. Responds in 2 months to queries and proposals; 6 months to mss. Book catalog for 9 × 12 SAE with 2 first-class stamps; ms guidelines for #10 SAE.
    O→ Publishes educational material for grades 3-8.
Nonfiction: Biography, test prep material. Subjects include education, history, language/literature, multicultural. Query with SASE or submit proposal package including outline, 1-3 sample chapter(s).
Fiction: Historical, multicultural, biographical. Query with SASE or submit proposal package including 1-3 sample chapter(s), synopsis.
Recent Title(s): *Thunder on the Sierra*, by Kathy Balmes (social studies, historical fiction); *Raid at Red Mill*, by Mary McGahan (historical fiction).

SIMON & SCHUSTER, 1230 Avenue of the Americas, New York NY 10020. (212)698-7000. Website: www.simonsay s.com.
Imprints: *Simon & Schuster Adult Publishing Group*: Simon & Schuster, Scribner (Scribner, Lisa Drew, Rawson Associates, Simple Abundance Press), The Free Press, Kaplan, Touchstone, Scribner Paperback Fiction, S&S Librow en Espanol, Simon & Schuster Source, Wall Street Journal Books, Pocket Books (Pocket Star, Washington Square Press, MTV Books, Sonnet Books, Star Trek, The New Folger Shakespeare, VH-1 Books). *Simon & Schuster Children's Publishing* Aladdin Paperbacks, Atheneum Books for Young Readers (Anne Schwartz Books, Richard Jackson Books) Little Simon (Simon Spotlight, Rabbit Ears Books & Audio), Margaret K. McElderry Books, Pocket Books for Young Readers (Archway Books, Minstreal Books, Pocket Pulse), Simon & Schuster Books for Young Readers. *Simon & Schuster New Media*: Simon & Schuster Audio (Simon & Schuster Audio Works, Simon & Schuster Sound Ideas, Pimsleur, Success), Simon & Schuster Interactive.

SIMON & SCHUSTER BOOKS FOR YOUNG READERS, Simon & Schuster Children's Publishing Division, 1230 Avenue of the Americas, New York NY 10020. (212)698-2851. Fax: (212)698-2796. Website: www.simonandschus ter.com. **Acquisitions:** Stephen Geck, vice president/associate publisher (humorous picture books, fiction, nonfiction); Kevin Lewis, senior editor (African-American/multicultural picture books, humorous picture books, middle-grade); David Gale, editorial director (young adult/middle grade novels); Jessica Schulte, editor (picture books, young adult); Amy Hampton-Knight, editor (character-centered picture books and poetry). Publishes hardcover originals. **Publishes**

80-90 titles/year. Receives 2,500 queries and 10,000 mss/year. 5-10% of books from first-time authors; 40% from unagented writers. Pays 4-12% royalty on retail price. Offers varied advance. Publishes book 1-3 years after acceptance of ms. Accepts simultaneous submissions. Responds in 2 months to queries. Manuscript guidelines for #10 SASE.

O─ "The three adjectives we use to describe our imprint are fresh, family-oriented and accessible. We're looking for writing-edge fiction, family-oriented picture books that are character-oriented." Currently emphasizing middle grade humor/adventure stories. De-emphasizing nonfiction.

Nonfiction: Children's/juvenile. Subjects include animals, ethnic, history, nature/environment. "We're looking for innovative, appealing nonfiction especially for younger readers. Please don't submit education or textbooks." *All unsolicited mss returned unopened.* Query with SASE only.

Fiction: Fantasy, historical, humor, juvenile, mystery, picture books, science fiction, young adult. "Fiction needs to be fresh, unusual and compelling to stand out from the competition. We're not looking for problem novels, stories with a moral, or rhymed picture book texts." *All unsolicited mss returned unopened.* Query with SASE only.

Poetry: "Most of our poetry titles are anthologies; we publish very few stand-alone poets." No picture book ms in rhymed verse. Query.

Recent Title(s): *Click, Clack, Moo,* by Doreen Cronin; *A Boy at War,* by Harry Mazer; *My America,* edited by Lee Bennett Hopkins (poetry).

Tips: "We're looking for fresh, original voices and unexplored topics. Don't do something because everyone else is doing it. Try to find what they're *not* doing. We publish mainly for the bookstore market, and are looking for books that will appeal directly to kids."

SKINNER HOUSE BOOKS, The Unitarian Universalist Association, 25 Beacon St., Boston MA 02108. (617)742-2100 ext. 601. Fax: (617)742-7025. Website: www.uua.org/skinner. **Acquisitions:** Kirstie Anderson, marketing coordinator. Estab. 1975. Publishes trade paperback originals and reprints. **Publishes 8-10 titles/year. 50% of books from first-time authors; 100% from unagented writers. Pays 5-10% royalty on net receipts.** Publishes book 1 year after acceptance of ms. Responds in 3 months to queries. Book catalog for 6×9 SAE with 3 first-class stamps; ms guidelines for #10 SASE.

O─ "We publish titles in Unitarian Universalist faith, liberal religion, history, biography, worship, and issues of social justice. We also publish a selected number of inspirational titles of poetic prose and meditations. Writers should know that Unitarian Universalism is a liberal religious denomination committed to progressive ideals." Currently emphasizing spiritual memoir. De-emphasizing juvenile.

Nonfiction: Biography, self-help. Subjects include gay/lesbian, religion, women's issues/studies, inspirational, church leadership. Query with SASE. Reviews artwork/photos as part of ms package. Send photocopies. Query with SASE.

Recent Title(s): *Get a God! More Conversations with Coyote,* by Webster Kitchell; *Swingin on the Garden Gate: A Spiritual Memoir,* by Elizabeth Andrew; *Standing Before Us: Unitarian Universalist Women and Social Reform, 1776-1936,* ed. by Dorothy May Emerson.

Tips: "From outside our denomination, we are interested in manuscripts that will be of help or interest to liberal churches, Sunday School classes, parents, ministers and volunteers. Inspirational/spiritual and children's titles must reflect liberal Unitarian Universalist values. Fiction for youth is being considered."

SKY PUBLISHING CORP., 49 Bay State Rd., Cambridge MA 02138. (617)864-7360. Fax: (617)864-6117. E-mail: postmaster@skypub.com. Website: www.skypub.com. President/Publisher: Susan B. Lit. **Acquisitions:** Richard Tresch Fienberg, editor-in-chief. Estab. 1941. Publishes hardcover and trade paperback originals on topics of interest to serious amateur astronomers as well as *Sky & Telescope: The Essential Magazine of Astronomy* and *Skywatch: Your Guide to Stargazing and Space Exploration.* **Publishes 4 titles/year. Pays 10% royalty on net receipts Magazine articles: pays 5 cents/word. Offers advance.** Book catalog free; magazine author and book proposal guidelines available.

O─ Sky Publishing Corporation will be an advocate of astronomy and space science through its products and services and will aggressively promote greater understanding of these disciplines among laypeople.

Nonfiction: Technical. Subjects include science (astronomy). No fiction.

Recent Title(s): *Sky Atlas 2000.0,* 2nd edition, by Wil Tirion and Roger W. Sinnott; *Deep-Sky Wonder,* by Walter Scott Houston, edited by Stephen James O'Meara.

SLACK INC., 6900 Grove Rd., Thorofare NJ 08086. (856)848-1000. Fax: (856)853-5991. E-mail: adrummond@slackinc.com. Website: www.slackinc.com. **Acquisitions:** Amy E. Drummond, editorial director. Estab. 1960. Publishes hardcover and softcover originals. **Publishes 32 titles/year. Receives 80 queries and 23 mss/year. 75% of books from first-time authors; 100% from unagented writers. Pays 10% royalty. Offers advance.** Publishes book 8 months after acceptance of ms. Accepts simultaneous submissions. Responds in 4 months to queries; 1 month to proposals; 3 months to mss. Book catalog and ms guidelines free.

O─ Slack publishes academic textbooks and professional reference books on various medical topics in an expedient manner. Emphasizing more athletic training than in previous years.

Nonfiction: Multimedia (CD-ROMs), textbook (medical). Subjects include health/medicine, ophthalmology, athletic training, physical theraphy, occupational therapy, orthopedics, gastroenterology. Submit proposal package including outline, 2 sample chapter(s), market profile and cv. Reviews artwork/photos as part of ms package. Send photocopies.

Recent Title(s): *Ryan's Occupational Therapy Assistant, 3rd Edition,* by Ryan and Sladyk.

SMITH AND KRAUS PUBLISHERS, INC., P.O. Box 127, Lyme NH 03768. (603)643-6431. Fax: (603) 643-1831. **Acquisitions:** Marisa Smith, president/publisher. Estab. 1990. Publishes hardcover and trade paperback originals. **Publishes 35-40 titles/year. 10% of books from first-time authors; 10-20% from unagented writers. Pays 7% royalty on retail price. Offers $500-2,000 advance.** Publishes book 1 year after acceptance of ms. Responds in 1 month to queries; 2 months to proposals; 4 months to mss. Book catalog free.

Nonfiction: Subjects include film/cinema/stage, drama, theater. Does not return submissions. Query with SASE.

Fiction: Drama, theater. Does not return submissions. Query with SASE.

Recent Title(s): *A Shakespearean Actor Prepares*, by Adrian Brine and Michael York; *Humana Festival 2000: The Complete Plays*.

GIBBS SMITH, PUBLISHER, P.O. Box 667, Layton UT 84041. (801)544-9800. Fax: (801)544-5582. E-mail: info@gibbs-smith.com. Website: www.gibbs-smith.com. **Acquisitions:** Madge Baird, editorial director (humor, western); Gail Yngve, editor (gift books, architecture, interior decorating, poetry); Suzanne Taylor, editor (children's, rustic living, outdoor activities and picture); Linda Nimori, editor. Estab. 1969. Publishes hardcover and trade paperback originals. **Publishes 50 titles/year. Receives 1,500-2,000 submissions/year. 8-10% of books from first-time authors; 50% from unagented writers. Pays 8-14% royalty on gross receipts. Offers $2,000-3,000 advance.** Publishes book 1-2 years after acceptance of ms. Responds in 1 month to queries; 10 weeks to proposals and mss. Book catalog for 9×12 SAE and $2.13 in postage; ms guidelines free.

Imprints: Gibbs Smith Junior

○━ "We publish books that enrich and inspire humankind." Currently emphasizing interior decorating and design, home reference. De-emphasizing novels and short stories.

Nonfiction: Humor, illustrated book, textbook, children's. Subjects include art/architecture, humor, nature/environment, regional, interior design. Query with SASE or submit outline, several completed sample chapter(s), author's cv. Reviews artwork/photos as part of ms package. Send sample illustrations if applicable.

Fiction: Only short works oriented to gift market. No novels or short stories. Submit synopsis with sample illustrations, if applicable.

Poetry: "Our annual poetry contest accepts entries only in April. Charges $20 fee. Prize: $1,000." Submit complete ms.

Recent Title(s): *Timberframe Interiors* (nonfiction); *A Strong Man*, by Carol Lynn Pearson (fiction).

⟦N⟧ SOCIAL SCIENCE EDUCATION CONSORTIUM, P.O. Box 21270, Boulder CO 80308-4270. (303)492-8154. Fax: (303)449-3925. E-mail: singletl@stripe.colorado.edu. Website: www.ssecinc.org. **Acquisitions:** Laurel R. Singleton, managing editor. Estab. 1963. Publishes trade paperback originals. **Publishes 8 titles/year. 25% of books from first-time authors; 100% from unagented writers. Pays 8-12% royalty on net receipts.** Publishes book 6 months after acceptance of ms. Accepts simultaneous submissions. Responds in 1 month to proposals.

○━ "We publish materials to help K-12 social studies teachers enrich their curriculum—through lessons on new topics, units that take students deeper than a traditional text would, or lessons that involve innovative teaching strategies. We also serve collegiate programs that train teachers. We publish resource materials, not textbooks or scholarly treatises." Currently emphasizing history, geography, economics and civics education.

Nonfiction: "We publish titles of interest to social studies teachers particularly; we do not generally publish on such broad educational topics as discipline, unless there is a specific relationship to the social studies/social sciences." Teacher resources. Subjects include computers/electronic (use in social science education), education, government/politics, history, Asian studies. Must include teaching applications. Submit outline, 1-2 sample chapter(s).

Recent Title(s): *New Horizons in the Social Sciences: Implications for Educaton*, by Sara Bednarz and Robert Bednarz; *Latin America and Japan: Crossing Borders and Making Connections*, by Charlotte Anderson and Marcel Lewinski.

Tips: "The mission of the Social Science Education Consortium is to improve social science education at all levels by promoting collaboration among social scientists and social studies educators. SSEC will accomplish this mission by: (1) Developing and disseminating exemplary social science curricula, materials, and teaching approaches. (2) Promoting and conducting research that points the way to more effective social science teaching and learning. (3) Representing and promoting social science education within the education community and to the public at large."

⟦N⟧ SOCIETY OF MANUFACTURING ENGINEERS, One SME Dr., P.O. Box 930, Dearborn MI 48121. (313)271-1500. Fax: (313)271-2861. E-mail: kingbob@sme.org. Website: www.sme.org. **Acquisitions:** Robert King, manager; Phillip Mitchell, senior editor. Publishes hardcover and trade paperback originals. **Publishes 10 titles/year. Receives 20 queries and 10 mss/year. 90% of books from first-time authors; 100% from unagented writers. Pays 5-15% royalty on wholesale price or retail price.** Publishes book 8 months after acceptance of ms. Responds in 1 month to queries, proposals and mss. Book catalog and ms guidelines online.

Nonfiction: "Seeking manuscripts that would assist manufacturing practitioners in increasing their productivity, quality and/or efficiency." Technical, textbook. Subjects include engineering, industry. Query with SASE. Reviews artwork/photos as part of ms package. Send photocopies.

Recent Title(s): *Lean Manufacturing for Small Business*; *Electorial Discharge Machining*.

Tips: Audience is "manufacturing practitioners and management, indivuduals wishing to advance their careers in the industry or to enhance productivity, quality, and efficiency within a manufacturing operation."

■ **SOFT SKULL PRESS INC.**, 98 Suffolk, #3A, New York NY 10002. (212)673-2502. Fax: (212)673-0787. E-mail: sander@softskull.com. Website: www.softskull.com. **Acquisitions:** Nick Mamatas, editor (political science), Sander Hicks, editor-in-chief (everything). Publishes hardcover and trade paperback originals. **Publishes 12-15 titles/ year. Receives 100 queries and 100 mss/year. 80% of books from first-time authors; 50% from unagented writers. Pays 7-10% royalty. Offers $100-15,000 advance.** Publishes book 6 months after acceptance of ms. Responds in 2 months to proposals; 3 months to mss. Book catalog and ms guidelines online.

○➤ "We're always interested in receiving work from new writers but are not accepting mss until August 2001."

Nonfiction: Biography. Subjects include art/architecture, gay/lesbian, government/politics, military/war, music/dance, philosophy. Agented submissions are encouraged. Query with SASE or submit proposal package including outline, 2 sample chapter(s).

Fiction: Confession, experimental, historical, literary, mainstream/contemporary, multicultural, short story collections. "We love Richard Ford, Hemmingway, Dennis Cooper and Denis Johnson." Agented submissions encouraged. Query with SASE or submit proposal package including 1 sample chapter(s), synopsis.

Poetry: "We're not doing as much as we used to. Must be exceptional." Query or submit with no more than 10 sample poems.

Recent Title(s): *Cool For You*, by Eileen Myles (literary); *Why Things Burn*, by Daphne Gottlieb (poetry).

Tips: "Our audience is passionate, radical, angry, dissatisfied with the current political and cultural status quo."

SOHO PRESS, INC., 853 Broadway, New York NY 10003. (212)260-1900. Website: www.sohopress.com. **Acquisitions:** Juris Jurjevics, publisher/editor-in-chief; Laura Hruska, associate publisher; Melanie Fleishman, editor/director of marketing. Estab. 1986. Publishes hardcover and trade paperback originals. **Publishes 40 titles/year. Receives 7,000 submissions/year. 75% of books from first-time authors; 40% from unagented writers. Pays 10-15% royalty on retail price. Offers advance.** Publishes book within 1 year after acceptance of ms. Accepts simultaneous submissions. Responds in 2 months to queries. Book catalog for 6×9 SAE with 2 first-class stamps.

○➤ Soho Press publishes literate fiction and nonfiction.

Nonfiction: Biography, autobiography, literary. Subjects include memoirs, travel. No self-help, how-to or cookbooks. Submit outline, sample chapter(s).

Fiction: Adventure, ethnic, feminist, historical, literary, mainstream/contemporary, mystery, suspense. Query with SASE or submit complete ms.

Recent Title(s): *23rd Precinct*, by Arlene Schulman (nonfiction); *Deceit*, by Clare Francis (fiction); *Smell*, by Radhika Jha (fiction).

Tips: "Soho Press publishes discerning authors for discriminating readers, finding the strongest possible writers and publishing them." Soho Press also publishes two book series: Hera (historical fiction reprints with accurate and strong female lead characters) and Soho Crime (mysteries set overseas, noir, procedurals).

SOUNDPRINTS, The Trudy Corp., 353 Main Ave., Norwalk CT 06851. (203)846-2274. Fax: (203)846-1776. E-mail: sndprnts@ix.netcom.com. Website: www.soundprints.com. **Acquisitions:** Chelsea Shriver, assistant editor. Estab. 1988. Publishes hardcover originals. **Publishes 12-14 titles/year. Receives 200 queries/year. 90% from unagented writers. Makes outright purchase.** Publishes book 2 years after acceptance of ms. Accepts simultaneous submissions. Responds in 1 month to queries. Book catalog online; ms guidelines for #10 SASE.

○➤ Soundprints publishes picture books that portray a particular animal and its habitat. All books are reviewed for accuracy by curators from the Smithsonian Institution and other wildlife experts.

Nonfiction: Children's/juvenile, illustrated book. Subjects include animals, nature/environment. "We focus on world-wide wildlife and habitats. Subject animals must be portrayed realistically and must not be anthropomorphic. Meticulous research is required. All books are illustrated in full color." Query with SASE.

Fiction: Juvenile. "Most of our books are under license from the Smithsonian Institution and are closely curated fictional stories based on fact. We never do stories of anthropomorphic animals. When we publish juvenile fiction, it will be about wildlife or history and all information in the book *must* be accurate." Query with SASE.

Recent Title(s): *Bumblebee at Apple Tree Lane*, by Laura Gates Galvin; *Sockeye's Journey Home: The Story of a Pacific Salmon*, by Barbara Gaines Winkelman.

Tips: "Our books are written for children from ages four through eight. Our most successful authors can craft a wonderful story which is derived from authentic wildlife or historic facts. First inquiry to us should ask about our interest in publishing a book about a specific animal or habitat."

SOURCEBOOKS, INC., P.O. Box 4410, Naperville IL 60567. (630)961-3900. Fax: (630)961-2168. Website: www.sourcebooks.com. Publisher: Dominique Raccah. **Acquisitions:** Todd Stocke, editorial director (nonfiction trade); Deborah Werksman (Sourcebooks Hysteria). Estab. 1987. Publishes hardcover and trade paperback originals. **Publishes 120 titles/year. 30% of books from first-time authors; 25% from unagented writers. Pays royalty on wholesale price. Offers advance.** Publishes book 1 year after acceptance of ms. Accepts simultaneous submissions. Responds in 3 months to queries. Book catalog and ms guidelines for 9×12 SASE.

Imprints: Sourcebooks Casablanca Press (love/relationships), Sphinx Publishing (self-help legal), Sourcebooks Hysteria (women's humor/gift book), Sourcebooks Media Fusion

○➤ Sourcebooks publishes many forms of nonfiction titles, generally in the how-to and reference areas, including books on parenting, self-help/psychology, business and health. Focus is on practical, useful information and skills. It also continues to publish in the reference, New Age, history, current affairs and travel categories. Currently emphasizing humor, gift, women's interest, New Age.

Nonfiction: "We seek unique books on traditional subjects and authors who are smart and aggressive." Biography, gift book, how-to, illustrated book, multimedia, reference, self-help, technical, textbook. Subjects include art/architecture, business/economics, child guidance/parenting, money/finance, psychology, sports, women's issues/studies, contemporary culture. Books for small business owners, entrepreneurs and students. "A key to submitting books to us is to explain how your book helps the reader, why it is different from the books already out there (please do your homework) and the author's credentials for writing this book. Books likely to succeed with us are self-help, art books, parenting and childcare, psychology, women's issues, how-to, house and home, humor, gift books or books with strong artwork." Query with SASE. 2-3 sample chapters (not the first). No complete mss. Reviews artwork/photos as part of ms package.

Recent Title(s): *How to Think Like Einstein*, by Scott Thorpe (self-help).

Tips: "Our market is a decidedly trade-oriented bookstore audience. We also have very strong penetration into the gift store market. Books which cross over between these two very different markets do extremely well with us. Our list is a solid mix of unique and general audience titles and series-oriented projects. In other words, we are looking for products that break new ground either in their own areas or within the framework of our series of imprints. We love to develop books in new areas or develop strong titles in areas that are already well developed."

SOUTH END PRESS, 7 Brookline St., Cambridge MA 02139. (617)547-4002. Fax: (617)547-1333. E-mail: southend @southendpress.org. Website: www.southendpress.org. **Acquisitions:** Acquisitions Department. Estab. 1977. Publishes library and trade paperback originals and reprints. **Publishes 10 titles/year. Receives 400 queries and 100 mss/year. 30% of books from first-time authors; 95% from unagented writers. Pays 11% royalty on wholesale price. Offers occasionally $500-2,500 advance.** Publishes book 9 months after acceptance of ms. Accepts simultaneous submissions. Responds in up to 3 months to queries and proposals. Book catalog and ms guidelines free.

O-π South End Press publishes nonfiction political books with a left/feminist/multicultural perspective.

Nonfiction: Subjects include ethnic, gay/lesbian, government/politics, health/medicine, history, nature/environment (environment), philosophy, science, sociology, women's issues/studies, economics, world affairs. Query with SASE or submit 2 sample chapter(s), intro or conclusion and annotated toc. Reviews artwork/photos as part of ms package. Send photocopies.

Recent Title(s): *Marx in Soho*, by Howard Zinn; *Rogue States*, by Noam Chomsky.

SOUTHERN ILLINOIS UNIVERSITY PRESS, P.O. Box 3697, Carbondale IL 62902-3697. (618)453-2281. Fax: (618)453-1221. Website: www.siu.edu/-siupress. **Acquisitions:** Rick Stetter, director (film, criminology, trade nonfiction); Karl Kageff, senior sponsoring editor (composition, rhetoric, sports); Elizabeth Bryer, sponsoring editor (theater); Susan Wilson, associate director (American history, women's studies). Estab. 1956. Publishes hardcover and trade paperback originals and reprints. **Publishes 50-60 titles/year; imprint publishes 4-6 titles/year. Receives 800 queries and 300 mss/year. 45% of books from first-time authors; 100% from unagented writers. Pays 5-10% royalty on wholesale price. Offers rarely advance.** Publishes book 1 year after receipt of a final ms after acceptance of ms. Responds in 3 months to queries. Book catalog and ms guidelines free.

Imprints: Shawnee Books, Shawnee Classics (regional reprint series)

O-π "Scholarly press specializes in film and theater studies, rhetoric and composition studies, American history, aviation studies, regional and nonfiction trade, women's studies. No fiction." Currently emphasizing theater, film, American history. De-emphasizing literary criticism.

Nonfiction: Biography, reference (scholarly), textbook. Subjects include Americana, military/war, nature/environment, film/cinema/stage, true crime. Query with SASE or submit proposal package including including synopsis, table of contents, author's vita.

Recent Title(s): *The International Movie Industry*, by Gorham Kindem (film studies); *Dario Fo: Stage, Text, and Tradition*, by J. Farrell and A. Scuderi (theater); *With Lincoln in the White House*, by Michael Burlingame (American history).

SOUTHERN METHODIST UNIVERSITY PRESS, P.O. Box 750415, Dallas TX 75275-0415. Fax: (214)768-1432. Website: www.tamu.edu/upress. **Acquisitions:** Kathryn Lang, senior editor. Estab. 1937. Publishes hardcover and trade paperback originals and reprints. **Publishes 10-12 titles/year. Receives 500 queries and 500 mss/year. 75% of books from first-time authors; 95% from unagented writers. Pays up to 10% royalty on wholesale price. Offers $500 advance.** Publishes book 1 year after acceptance of ms. Responds in 1 month to queries, proposals and mss.

O-π Southern Methodist University publishes for the general, educated audience in the fields of literary fiction, ethics and human values, film and theater, regional studies and theological studies. Currently emphasizing literary fiction. De-emphasizing scholarly, narrowly focused academic studies.

Nonfiction: Subjects include creative nonfiction, medical, ethics/human values, film/theater, regional history, theology. Query with SASE or submit outline, 3 sample chapter(s), author bio, table of contents. Reviews artwork/photos as part of ms package. Send photocopies.

Fiction: Literary (novels), short story collections. Query with SASE.

Recent Title(s): *La Scala West*, by Ronald L. Davis; *You Can Sleep While I Drive*, by Liza Wieland.

N. SOUTHFARM PRESS, P.O. Box 1296, Middletown CT 06457. (860)346-8798. Fax: (860)347-9931. E-mail: southfar@ix.netcom.com. Website: www.war-books.com. Publisher: Walter J. Haan. **Acquisitions:** Wanda P. Haan, editor-in-chief. Estab. 1983. Publishes trade hardcover and paperback originals. **Publishes 5 titles/year. 90% of books from first-time authors; 100% from unagented writers. Pays 5-10% royalty on retail price.** Publishes book 1 year after acceptance of ms. Accepts simultaneous submissions. Responds in 1 month to queries.

    O⊶ Southfarm publishes primarily history and military/war nonfiction. Currently emphasizing air wars, Civil War. No longer publishing on dog breeds.

Nonfiction: Subjects include history, military/war, women's issues/studies. Submit outline, sample chapter(s), synopsis.

Recent Title(s): *The Emperor's Angry Guest*, by Ralph Knox (nonfiction); *Abe Lincoln and the Frontier Folk of New Salem*, by Thomas Reep.

THE SPEECH BIN, INC., 1965 25th Ave., Vero Beach FL 32960-3062. (561)770-0007. **Acquisitions:** Jan J. Binney, senior editor. Estab. 1984. Publishes trade paperback originals. **Publishes 10-20 titles/year. Receives 500 mss/year. 50% of books from first-time authors; 90% from unagented writers. Pays negotiable royalty on wholesale price. Offers advance.** Publishes book 1 year after acceptance of ms. Responds in 3 months to queries. Book catalog for 9×12 SASE and $1.48.

    O⊶ Publishes professional materials for specialists in rehabilitation, particularly speech-language pathologists and audiologists, special educators, occupational and physical therapists, and parents and caregivers of children and adults with developmental and post-trauma disabilities."

Nonfiction: Children's/juvenile (preschool-teen), how-to, illustrated book, reference, textbook, games for children and adults. Subjects include education, health/medicine, communication disorders, education for handicapped persons. Query with SASE or submit outline, sample chapter(s). Reviews artwork/photos as part of ms package. Send photocopies.

Fiction: "Booklets or books for children and adults about handicapped persons, especially with communication disorders. This is a potentially new market for The Speech Bin." Query with SASE or submit outline, sample chapter(s), synopsis.

Recent Title(s): *Is My Child Really Stuttering?*; *Sound Corrections*.

Tips: "Books and materials must be clearly presented, well written and competently illustrated. We have added books and materials for use by other allied health professionals. We are also looking for more materials for use in treating adults and very young children with communication disorders. Please do not fax manuscripts to us." The Speech Bin is increasing their number of books published per year and is especially interested in reviewing treatment materials for adults and adolescents.

SPENCE PUBLISHING COMPANY, 111 Cole St., Dallas TX 75207. (214)939-1700. Fax: (214)939-1800. E-mail: muncy@spencepublishing.com. Website: www.spencepublishing.com. **Acquisitions:** Mitchell Muncy, editor-in-chief. Estab. 1995. Publishes hardcover and trade paperback originals. **Publishes 8-10 titles/year. Pays 12% royalty on net receipts.** Accepts simultaneous submissions. Responds in 1 month to queries; 2 months to proposals. Book catalog online; ms guidelines for #10 SASE.

    O⊶ "We look for original works of commentary and analysis on culture and society. Originality, uniqueness and historical perspective are especially desired." Currently de-emphasizing narratives, very broad "world view" books, exposés of "political corretness" in universities.

Nonfiction: Subjects include education, government/politics, philosophy, religion, sociology, women's issues/studies, contemporary culture, film/cinema/stage. No proposal accepted without prior request for guidelines. Under no circumstances send ms before query.

Recent Title(s): *All Shook Up: Music, Passion and Politics*, by Carson Holloway.

Tips: "We publish books on culture and society from a generally (though not exclusively) conservative point of view. We seek books with a fresh approach to serious questions of public and private life that propose constructive alternatives to the status quo."

SPINSTERS INK, P.O. Box 22005, Denver CO 80222. (303)761-5552. Fax: (303)761-5284. E-mail: spinster@spinsters-ink.com. Website: www.spinsters-ink.com. Publisher: Kathy Hovis. **Acquisitions:** Sharon Silvas, editor. Estab. 1978. Publishes trade paperback originals and reprints. **Publishes 6 titles/year. Receives 400 submissions/year. 50% of books from first-time authors; 95% from unagented writers. Pays 7-11% royalty on retail price.** Publishes book 18 months after acceptance of ms. Responds in 4 months to queries. Book catalog free; ms guidelines for SASE or online.

    • Spinsters Ink was sold to Hovis Publishing, publisher of the monthly newspaper *Colorado Woman News*. The company plans to publish two books in 2001, six in 2002, and grow from there.

    O⊶ "Spinsters Ink publishes novels and nonfiction works that deal with significant issues in women's lives from a feminist perspective: Books that not only name these crucial issues, but—more important—encourage change and growth. We are committed to publishing works by women writing from the periphery, fat women, Jewish women, lesbians, old women, poor women, rural women, women examining classism, women of color, women with disabilities, women who are writing books that help make the best in our lives more possible."

Nonfiction: Feminist analysis for positive change. Subjects include women's issues/studies. "We do not want to see work by men or anything that is not specific to women's lives (humor, children's books, etc.)." Query with SASE. Reviews artwork/photos as part of ms package.

Fiction: Ethnic, gay/lesbian, women's. "We do not publish poetry or short fiction. We are interested in fiction that challenges, women's language that is feminist, stories that treat lifestyles with the diversity and complexity they deserve. We are also interested in genre fiction, especially mysteries." Submit outline, sample chapter(s), synopsis.

Recent Title(s): *Those Jordan Girls*, by Jan Drury (fiction); *Deadly Embrace*, by Trudy Labovitz (murder mystery).

N SQUARE ONE PUBLISHERS, INC., 16 First St., Garden City Park NY 11040. (516)535-2010. Fax: (516)535-2014. Website: www.squareonepublishers.com. Publisher: Rudy Shur. **Acquisitions:** Acquisitions Editor. Publishes trade paperback originals. **Publishes 20 titles/year. Receives 500 queries and 100 mss/year. 95% of books from first-time authors; 95% from unagented writers. Pays 10-15% royalty on wholesale price. Offers varying advance.** Publishes book 10 months after acceptance of ms. Accepts simultaneous submissions. Responds in 1 month to queries, proposals and mss. Book catalog and ms guidelines online.

Nonfiction: Cookbook, how-to, reference, self-help. Subjects include animals, art/architecture, business/economics, child guidance/parenting, hobbies, money/finance, nature/environment, psychology, regional, religion, spirituality, sports, travel, writers' guides, cooking/foods, gaming/gambling. Query with SASE or submit proposal package including outline, author bio, SASE, introduction, synopsis. Reviews artwork/photos as part of ms package. Send photocopies.

Recent Title(s): *Losing Paradise*, by Paul Irwin (environmental/animal welfare); *Retiring Right*, by Lawrence Kaplan (personal finance); *How To Publish Your Nonfiction Book*, by Rudy Shur (writers' reference).

Tips: "We focus on making our books accessible, accurate, and interesting. They are written for people who are looking for the best place to start, and who don't appreciate the terms 'dummy,' 'idiot,' or 'fool' on the cover of their books. We look for smartly written, informative books that have a strong point of view, and that are authored by people who know their subjects well."

ST. ANTHONY MESSENGER PRESS, 1615 Republic St., Cincinnati OH 45210-1298. (513)241-5615. Fax: (513)241-0399. E-mail: stanthony@americancatholic.org. Website: www.americancatholic.org. Publisher: The Rev. Jeremy Harrington, O.F.M. **Acquisitions:** Lisa Biedenbach, managing editor; Katie Carroll, book editor (children's); April Bolton, book editor (prayer/spirituality). Estab. 1970. Publishes trade paperback originals. **Publishes 15-25 titles/year. Receives 200 queries and 50 mss/year. 5% of books from first-time authors; 99% from unagented writers. Pays 10-12% royalty on net receipts. Offers $1,000 average advance.** Publishes book 18 months after acceptance of ms. Responds in 1 month to queries; 2 months to proposals and mss. Book catalog for 9 × 12 SAE with 4 first-class stamps; ms guidelines free.

O─ "St. Anthony Messenger Press/Franciscan Communications seeks to communicate the word that is Jesus Christ in the styles of Saints Francis and Anthony. Through print and electronic media marketed in North America and worldwide, we endeavor to evangelize, inspire and inform those who search for God and seek a richer Catholic, Christian, human life. Our efforts help support the life, ministry and charities of the Franciscan Friars of St. John the Baptist Province, who sponsor our work." Currently emphasizing prayer/spirituality. De-emphasizing children's.

Nonfiction: Family-based religious education programs. Subjects include education, history, religion, sex, Catholic identity and teaching, prayer and spirituality resources, Scripture study. Query with SASE or submit outline. Reviews artwork/photos as part of ms package.

Recent Title(s): *Mary's Flowers: Gardens, Legends and Meditations*, by Vincenzina Krymow; *Sun & Moon Over Assisi—A Personal Encounter with Francis & Clare*, by Gerard Thomas Straub.

Tips: "Our readers are ordinary 'folks in the pews' and those who minister to and educate these folks. Writers need to know the audience and the kind of books we publish. Manuscripts should reflect best and current Catholic theology and doctrine." St. Anthony Messenger Press especially seeks books which will sell in bulk quantities to parishes, teachers, pastoral ministers, etc. They expect to sell at least 5,000 to 7,000 copies of a book.

ST. AUGUSTINE'S PRESS, P.O. Box 2285, South Bend IN 46680-2285. (219)-291-3500. Fax: (219)291-3700. E-mail: bruce@staugustine.net. Website: wwwstaugustine.net. **Acquisitions:** Bruce Fingerhut, president (philosophy). Publishes hardcover originals and trade paperback originals and reprints. **Publishes 50 titles/year. Receives 200 queries and 100 mss/year. 5% of books from first-time authors; 95% from unagented writers. Pays 6-20% royalty. Offers $500-5,000 advance.** Publishes book 8 months after acceptance of ms. Accepts simultaneous submissions. Responds in 2 months to queries; 3 months to proposals; 4 months to mss. Book catalog free.

Imprints: Carthage Reprints

O─ "Our market is scholarly in the humanities. We publish in philosophy, religion, cultural history, and history of ideas only."

Nonfiction: Biography, textbook. Subjects include history (of ideas), philosophy, religion. Query with SASE. Reviews artwork/photos as part of ms package. Send photocopies.

Recent Title(s): *Plato's Symposium*, by Stanley Rosen (philosophy); *Xanthippic Dialogues*, by Roger Scruton (philosophy).

Tips: Scholarly and student audience.

ST. BEDE'S PUBLICATIONS, St. Scholastica Priory, P.O. Box 545, Petersham MA 01366-0545. (978)724-3213. Fax: (978)724-3216. President: Mother Mary Clare Vincent. **Acquisitions:** Acquisitions Editor. Estab. 1977. Publishes hardcover originals, trade paperback originals and reprints. **Publishes 3-4 titles/year. Receives 100 submissions/year.**

30-40% of books from first-time authors; 98% from unagented writers. Pays 5-10% royalty on wholesale price or retail price. Publishes book 2 years after acceptance of ms. Accepts simultaneous submissions. Responds in 2 months to queries. Book catalog and ms guidelines for 9 × 12 SAE with 2 first-class stamps.

> O━ St. Bede's Publications is owned and operated by the Roman Catholic nuns of St. Scholastica Priory. The publications are seen as apostolic outreach. Their mission is to make available to everyone quality books on spiritual subjects such as prayer, scripture, theology and the lives of holy people.

Nonfiction: Textbook (theology). Subjects include history, philosophy, religion, sex, spirituality, translation, prayer, hagiography, theology, Church history, related lives of saints. No submissions unrelated to religion, theology, spirituality, etc., and no poetry, fiction or children's books. Does not return submissions without adequate postage. Query or submit outline and sample chapters with SASE.

Recent Title(s): *Memoirs, From Grace to Grace*, by Jean Leclercq; *Out of Darkness*, by Marcus Rome; *Love Strong as Death*, by Father Ronald Walls.

Tips: "There seems to be a growing interest in monasticism among lay people, and we will be publishing more books in this area. For our theology/philosophy titles our audience is scholars, colleges and universities, seminaries, etc. For our other titles (i.e. prayer, spirituality, lives of saints, etc.) the audience is above-average readers interested in furthering their knowledge in these areas."

A **ST. MARTIN'S PRESS**, 175 Fifth Ave., New York NY 10010. (212)674-5151. Fax: (212)420-9314. Website: www.stmartins.com. Estab. 1952. Publishes hardcover, trade paperback and mass market originals. **Publishes 1,500 titles/year. Pays royalty. Offers advance**.

Imprints: Bedford Books, Buzz Books, Dead Letter, Thomas Dunne Books, Forge, Picador USA, St. Martin's Press Scholarly & Reference, Stonewall Inn Editions, TOR Books, Minotaur, LA Weekly, Palgrave

> O━ General interest publisher of both fiction and nonfiction.

Nonfiction: Biography, cookbook, reference, self-help, textbook, scholarly. Subjects include business/economics, cooking/foods/nutrition, sports, true crime, general nonfiction, contemporary culture, true crime. *Accepts agented submissions only. No unsolicited mss.*

Fiction: Fantasy, historical, horror, literary, mainstream/contemporary, mystery, science fiction, suspense, western (contemporary), general fiction, thriller. *Accepts agented submissions only. No unsolicited mss.*

STA-KRIS, INC., P.O. Box 714, Gantsburg, WI 54840. (715)463-2907. E-mail: stakris@grantsburgtelcom.net. Website: www.stakris.com. **Acquisitions:** Kathy Wagoner, president. Publishes hardcover and trade paperback originals. **Publishes 4 titles/year. Pays negotiated royalty on wholesale price or makes outright purchase. Offers advance.** Publishes book 1 year after acceptance of ms. Accepts simultaneous submissions. Responds in 2 months to queries and proposals; 4 months to mss. Book catalog free.

Nonfiction: Coffee table book, gift book, illustrated book, self-help. "We publish nonfiction gift books that portray universal feelings, truths and values or have a special occasion theme, plus small format compilations of statements about professions, issues, attitudes, etc." Query with SASE. Submit proposal package including synopsis, bio, published clips.

Recent Title(s): *The Grandparents' Memory Book*, by Teri Harrison.

Tips: "Our audience tends to be women ages 20 and older. We are an independent publisher who supports the marketing of their books with great energy and knowledge. We are currently looking for projects that would fit nicely in the gift store market."

STACKPOLE BOOKS, 5067 Ritter Rd., Mechanicsburg PA 17055. Fax: (717)796-0412. E-mail: jschnell@stackpolebooks.com. Website: www.stackpolebooks.com. **Acquisitions:** Judith Schnell, editorial director (fly fishing, sports); William C. Davis, editor (history); Mark Allison, editor (nature, photography); Ed Skender, editor (military guides); Kyle Weaver, editor (Pennsylvania). Estab. 1935. Publishes hardcover and paperback originals and reprints. **Publishes 75 titles/year. Offers industry standard advance.** Publishes book 1 year after acceptance of ms. Responds in 1 month to queries.

> O━ "Stackpole maintains a growing and vital publishing program by featuring authors who are experts in their fields, from outdoor activities to Civil War history."

Nonfiction: Subjects include history (especially Civil War), military/war, nature/environment, photography, recreation, sports, wildlife, outdoor skills, fly fishing, paddling, climbing. Query with SASE. Does not return unsolicited mss. Reviews artwork/photos as part of ms package.

Recent Title(s): *Exploring the Appalachian Trail Guides* (5-book hiking series).

Tips: "Stackpole seeks well-written, authoritative manuscripts for specialized and general trade markets. Proposals should include chapter outline, sample chapter and illustrations and author's credentials."

STANDARD PUBLISHING, Standex International Corp., 8121 Hamilton Ave., Cincinnati OH 45231. (513)931-4050. Website: www.standardpub.com. Vice President, Church Resources: Mark Taylor. Managing Director, Church Resources: Paul Learned. Managing Director, Children's Publishing: Diane Stortz. **Acquisitions:** Ruth Frederick (children's ministry resources); Dale Reeves (Empowered Youth Products). Estab. 1866. Publishes hardcover and paperback originals and reprints. **Pays royalty.** Publishes book 18 months after acceptance of ms. Responds in 3 months to queries. Manuscript guidelines for #10 SASE, send request to Tamara Neuenschwander.

> O━ Standard specializes in religious books for children and religious education. De-emphasizing board books.

Nonfiction: Children's/juvenile, illustrated book, reference. Subjects include education, religion, picture books, Christian education (teacher training, working with volunteers), quiz, puzzle, crafts (to be used in Christian education). Query with SASE.

Recent Title(s): *My Good Night Bible*, by Susan Lingo (nonfiction); *Can God See Me?*, by JoDee McConnaughhay (fiction); *Edible Object Talks*, by Susan Lingo.

STANFORD UNIVERSITY PRESS, Stanford CA 94305-2235. (650)723-9434. Fax: (650)725-3457. Website: www.sup.org. Senior Editor: Muriel Bell. Humanities Editor: Helen Tartar. **Acquisitions:** Norris Pope, director. Estab. 1925. **Publishes 120 titles/year. Receives 1,500 submissions/year. 40% of books from first-time authors; 95% from unagented writers. Pays up to 14% royalty (typically 10%, sometimes none). Offers occasional advance.** Publishes book 1 year after acceptance of ms. Responds in 6 weeks to queries.
  O— Stanford University Press publishes scholarly books in the humanities and social sciences, along with professional books in business and management science; also high-level textbooks and some books for a more general audience.

Nonfiction: Textbook, scholarly books, professional books. Subjects include anthropology/archeology, business/economics, ethnic (studies), gay/lesbian, government/politics, history, language/literature, nature/environment, philosophy, psychology, religion, science, sociology, history and culture of China, Japan and Latin America; literature, criticism, and literary theory; European history; linguistics; geology; medieval and classical studies. Query with prospectus and an outline. Reviews artwork/photos as part of ms package.

Recent Title(s): *The Selected Poetry of Robinson Jeffers*.

Tips: "The writer's best chance is a work of original scholarship with an argument of some importance."

STARBURST PUBLISHERS, P.O. Box 4123, Lancaster PA 17604. (717)293-0939. Fax: (717)293-1945. E-mail: editorial@starburstpublishers.com. Website: www.starburstpublishers.com. **Acquisitions:** Editorial Department. Estab. 1982. Publishes hardcover and trade paperback originals. **Publishes 15-20 titles/year. Receives 1,000 submissions/year. 50% of books from first-time authors; 75% from unagented writers. Pays 6-16% royalty on wholesale price. Offers varies advance.** Publishes book 1 year after acceptance of ms. Accepts simultaneous submissions. Responds in 1 month to queries. Book catalog for 9×12 SAE with 4 first-class stamps; ms guidelines for #10 SASE.
  O— Starburst publishes quality self-help, health and inspirational titles for the trade and religious markets. Currently emphasizing inspirational gift, Bible study and Bible reference, how-to and health books. De-emphasizing fiction.

Nonfiction: "We are looking for books that inspire, teach and help today's average American." Cookbook, gift book, how-to, self-help, Christian, general nonfiction. Subjects include business/economics, child guidance/parenting, cooking/foods/nutrition, education, gardening, general, health/medicine, money/finance, nature/environment, psychology, recreation, religion, counseling/career guidance, home, real estate. Submit proposal package including outline, 3 sample chapter(s), author bio. Reviews artwork/photos as part of ms package. Send photocopies.

Fiction: Inspirational. "We are only looking for good wholesome fiction that inspires or fiction that teaches self-help principles." Submit outline, 3 sample chapter(s), author bio.

Recent Title(s): *What's in the Bible for Teens*, by Mark Littleton (nonfiction); *Cheap Talk with the Frugal Friends*, by Deana Ricks (nonfiction).

Tips: "Fifty percent of our line goes into the Christian marketplace, fifty percent into the general marketplace. We have direct sales representatives in both the Christian and general (bookstore, catalog, price club, mass merchandiser, library, health and gift) marketplace. Write on an issue that slots you on talk shows and thus establishes your name as an expert and writer."

STEEL PRESS PUBLISHING, P.O. Box 205, West Mifflin PA 15122. (412)469-8293. E-mail: publisher@steelpress.com. Website: www.steelpress.com. **Acquisitions:** Jerome Edward Laycak, publisher. Publishes hardcover and trade paperback originals. **Publishes 120 titles/year. Receives 1,500 queries/year. 75% of books from first-time authors; 85% from unagented writers. Pays 10-20% royalty on retail price.** Publishes book 5 months after acceptance of ms. Accepts simultaneous submissions. Responds in 1 month to queries; 2 months to mss. Book catalog and ms guidelines online.
  O— Steel Press publishes a wide array of titles that are of interest to an eclectic readership.

Nonfiction: Biography, how-to, humor, self-help, technical. Subjects include computers/electronic, creative nonfiction, education, government/politics, history, hobbies, language/literature, memoirs, military/war, philosophy, psychology, science, software. "Know your subject. Have plenty of references." Query with SASE. Reviews artwork/photos as part of ms package. Send photocopies.

Fiction: Adventure, fantasy, gothic, historical, horror, humor, literary, mainstream/contemporary, military/war, mystery, poetry, romance, science fiction, suspense. "Always looking for a fine story." Query with SASE.

Recent Title(s): *Michael Patrick*, by Victoria Thompson (fantasy); *The Abandoned*, by R.B. Campbell (military); *Bangkok Magic*, by Patsy Robson (romance).

Tips: Prefers queries sent via e-mail to submissions@steelpress.com.

STEEPLE HILL, Harlequin Enterprises, 300 E. 42nd St., New York NY 10017. Website: www.@harlequin.com. **Acquisitions:** Tara Gavin, editorial director; Tracy Farrell, senior editor; Ann Leslie Tuttle, associate editor; Melissa Endlich, associate editor; Kim Nadelson, all Silhouette/Harlequin Historicals editors. Estab. 1997. Publishes mass market paperback originals. **Pays royalty. Offers advance.** Manuscript guidelines for #10 SASE.
Imprints: Love Inspired
○━ "This series of contemporary, inspirational love stories portrays Christian characters facing the many challenges of life, faith and love in today's world."
Fiction: Romance (Christian, 70,000 words). Query with SASE or submit 3 sample chapter(s), synopsis.
Recent Title(s): *Redeeming Claire*, by Cynthia Rutledge.
Tips: "Drama, humor and even a touch of mystery all have a place in this series. Subplots are welcome and should further the story's main focus or intertwine in a meaningful way. Secondary characters (children, family, friends, neighbors, fellow church members, etc.) may all contribute to a substantial and satisfying story. These wholesome tales of romance include strong family values and high moral standards. While there is no premarital sex between characters, a vivid, exciting romance that is presented with a mature perspective, is essential. Although the element of faith must clearly be present, it should be well integrated into the characterizations and plot. The conflict between the main characters should be an emotional one, arising naturally from the well-developed personalities you've created. Suitable stories should also impart an important lesson about the powers of trust and faith."

STENHOUSE PUBLISHERS, 477 Congress St., Suite 4B, Portland ME 04101-3417. (207)253-1600. Fax: (207)253-5121. E-mail: philippa@stenhouse.com. Website: www.stenhouse.com. **Acquisitions:** Philippa Stratton, editorial director. Estab. 1993. Publishes paperback originals. **Publishes 15 titles/year. Receives 300 queries/year. 30% of books from first-time authors; 99% from unagented writers. Pays royalty on wholesale price. Offers very modest advance.** Responds in 1 month to queries; 3 months to mss. Book catalog and ms guidelines online.
○━ Stenhouse publishes exclusively professional books for teachers, K-12.
Nonfiction: Subjects include education (specializing in literacy). "All our books are a combination of theory and practice." No children's books or student texts. Query with SASE or submit outline. Reviews artwork/photos as part of ms package. Send photocopies.
Recent Title(s): *Read it Again*, by Brenda Parkes; *Strategies That Work: Teaching Comprehension to Enhance Understanding*, by Stephanie Harvey and Anne Goudvis.

STERLING PUBLISHING, 387 Park Ave. S., New York NY 10016. (212)532-7160. Fax: (212)213-2495. Website: www.sterlingpub.com. **Acquisitions:** Sheila Anne Barry, acquisitions editor. Estab. 1949. Publishes hardcover and paperback originals and reprints. **Publishes 350 titles/year. Pays royalty. Offers advance.** Publishes book 1 year after acceptance of ms. Responds in 4 months to queries. Manuscript guidelines for #10 SASE.
Imprints: Sterling/Chapelle, Lark, Sterling/Tamos, Sterling/Silver, Sterling/Godsfield, Sterling/SIR
○━ Sterling publishes highly illustrated, accessible, hands-on, practical books for adults and children.
Nonfiction: Children's/juvenile, how-to, humor, reference. Subjects include animals, art/architecture, ethnic, gardening, health/medicine, hobbies, humor, New Age, recreation, science, sports, fiber arts, games and puzzles, children's humor, children's science, nature and activities, pets, wine, home decorating, dolls and puppets, ghosts, UFOs, woodworking, crafts, medieval, Celtic subjects, alternative health and healing, new consciousness. Query with SASE or submit outline, 2 sample chapter(s), SASE. Reviews artwork/photos as part of ms package.
Recent Title(s): *The Great Rubber Stamp Book*, by Dee Gruenig.

STIPES PUBLISHING CO., P.O. Box 526, Champaign IL 61824-9933. (217)356-8391. Fax: (217)356-5753. E-mail: stipes@soltec.com. Website: www.stipes.com. **Acquisitions:** Benjamin H. Watts, (engineering, science, business); Robert Watts (agriculture, music and physical education). Estab. 1925. Publishes hardcover and paperback originals. **Publishes 15-30 titles/year. Receives 150 submissions/year. 50% of books from first-time authors; 95% from unagented writers. Pays 15% maximum royalty on retail price. Offers advance.** Publishes book 4 months after acceptance of ms. Responds in 2 months to queries.
○━ Stipes Publishing is "oriented towards the education market and educational books with some emphasis in the trade market."
Nonfiction: Technical (some areas), textbook (on business/economics, music, chemistry, CADD, agriculture/horticulture, environmental education, recreation, physical education). Subjects include agriculture/horticulture, business/economics, music/dance, nature/environment, recreation, science. "All of our books in the trade area are books that also have a college text market. No books unrelated to educational fields taught at the college level." Submit outline, 1 sample chapter(s).
Recent Title(s): *The Microstation J Workbook*, by Michael Ward.

STOEGER PUBLISHING COMPANY, 17603 Indian Head Hwy., Suite 300, Accokeek MD 20607. (301)283-6300. Fax: (301)283-6986. Website: www.StoegerIndustries.com. **Acquisitions:** Stephen McKelvain, director of marketing communicatins. Estab. 1925. Publishes trade paperback originals. **Publishes 12-15 titles/year. Royalty varies, depending on ms. Offers advance.** Accepts simultaneous submissions. Responds in 1 month to queries. Book catalog online.
○━ Stoeger publishes books on hunting, shooting sports, fishing, cooking, nature and wildlife.
Nonfiction: Specializes in reference and how-to books that pertain to hunting, fishing and appeal to gun enthusiasts. How-to, reference. Subjects include sports. Submit outline, sample chapter(s).

Recent Title(s): *Complete Book of Whitetail Hunting*, by Toby Bridges; *Complete Guide to Modern Rifles*, by Gene Gangarosa, Jr.

STONE BRIDGE PRESS, P.O. Box 8208, Berkeley CA 94707. (510)524-8732. Fax: (510)524-8711. E-mail: sbp@ston ebridge.com. Website: www.stonebridge.com/. **Acquisitions:** Peter Goodman, publisher. Estab. 1989. Publishes hard-cover and trade paperback originals. **Publishes 8 titles/year; imprint publishes 2 titles/year. Receives 100 queries and 75 mss/year. 15-20% of books from first-time authors; 90% from unagented writers. Pays royalty on wholesale price. Offers varying advance.** Publishes book 2 years after acceptance of ms. Accepts simultaneous submissions. Responds in 2 month to queries; 3 month to proposals; 4 months to mss. Book catalog free.
Imprints: The Rock Spring Collection of Japanese Literature
> ○→ Stone Bridge Press strives "to publish and distribute high-quality informational tools about Japan." Currently emphasizing art/design, spirituality. De-emphasizing business, current affairs.

Nonfiction: How-to, reference. Subjects include art/architecture, business/economics, ethnic, language/literature, phi-losophy, translation, travel, women's issues/studies. "We publish Japan- (and some Asia-) related books only." Query with SASE. Reviews artwork/photos as part of ms package. Send photocopies.
Fiction: Experimental, fantasy, gay/lesbian. Query with SASE.
Recent Title(s): *Hayao Miyazaki: Master of Japanese Animation*; *Japanese Yoga*; *The Japanese Way of the Flower*.
Tips: Audience is "intelligent, worldly readers with an interest in Japan based on personal need or experience. No children's books or commercial fiction. Realize that interest in Japan is a moving target. Please don't submit yesterday's trends or rely on a view of Japan that is outmoded. Stay current!"

STONEWALL INN, St. Martins Press, 175 Fifth Ave., New York NY 10010. (212)674-5151. Website: www.stonewalli nn.com. **Acquisitions:** Keith Kahla, general editor. Publishes trade paperback originals and reprints. **Publishes 20-23 titles/year. Receives 3,000 queries/year. 40% of books from first-time authors; 25% from unagented writers. Pays standard royalty on retail price. Offers varies advance.** Publishes book 1 year after acceptance of ms. Accepts simultaneous submissions. Responds in 6 months to queries.
> ○→ Stonewall Inn is an imprint for gay and lesbian themed fiction, nonfiction and mysteries. Currently emphasizing literary fiction. De-emphasizing mysteries.

Nonfiction: Subjects include gay/lesbian, philosophy, sociology. Subjects include nearly every aspect of gay/lesbian studies. "We are looking for well-researched sociological works; author's credentials count for a great deal." Query with SASE.
Fiction: Gay/lesbian, literary, mystery. "Anybody who has any question about what a gay novel is should go out and read half a dozen. For example, there are hundreds of 'coming out' novels in print." Query with SASE.
Recent Title(s): *The Coming Storm*, by Paul Russell; *Trouble Maker*, by Brian Pera.
Tips: Address queries to "Stonewall Inn, an Imprint of St. Martins."

STONEYDALE PRESS, 523 Main St., Stevensville MT 59870. (406)777-2729. Fax: (406)777-2521. E-mail: daleburk @montana.com. **Acquisitions:** Dale A. Burk, publisher. Estab. 1976. Publishes hardcover and trade paperback originals. **Publishes 4-6 titles/year. Receives 40-50 queries and 6-8 mss/year. 90% from unagented writers. Pays 12-15% royalty. Offers advance.** Publishes book 18 months after acceptance of ms. Responds in 2 months to queries. Book catalog available.
> ○→ "We seek to publish the best available source books on big game hunting, historical reminiscence and outdoor recreation in the Northern Rocky Mountain region."

Nonfiction: How-to (hunting books). Subjects include regional, sports, historical reminiscences. Query with SASE.
Recent Title(s): *Lewis & Clark on the Upper Missouri*, by Jeanne O'Neil; *Montana's Bitterroot Valley*, by Russ Lawrence.

STOREY PUBLISHING, Workman Publishing, 210 MASS MoCA Way, North Adams MA 01247. (413)346-2100. Fax: (413)346-2196. Website: www.storey.com. **Acquisitions:** Deborah Balmuth, editorial director (natural beauty and healing/health, crafts, herbs); Deborah Burns (horses, farming); Gwen Steege (gardening, crafts); Nancy Ringer (animals, nature); Dianne Cutillo (cooking). Estab. 1983. Publishes hardcover and trade paperback originals and reprints. **Publishes 45 titles/year. Receives 600 queries and 150 mss/year. 25% of books from first-time authors; 80% from unagented writers. Pays royalty or makes outright purchase. Offers advance.** Publishes book within 2 years after acceptance of ms. Accepts simultaneous submissions. Responds in 1 month to queries; 3 months to proposals and mss. Book catalog and ms guidelines online.
> ○→ "We publish practical information that encourages personal independence in harmony with the environment."

Nonfiction: Subjects include animals, cooking/foods/nutrition, fashion/beauty, gardening, health/medicine, nature/environment, home, herbs, natural health and beauty, birds, beer and wine, crafts, building. Reviews artwork/photos as part of ms package.
> • Storey was acquired by Workman Publishing, which has distributed its books.

Recent Title(s): *The Handcrafted Letter*, by Diane Maurer-Mathison; *Renovating Barns, Sheds and Outbuildings*, by Nick Engler; *The Vegetable Gardener's Bible*, by Edward C. Smith.

STORY LINE PRESS, Three Oaks Farm, P.O. Box 1240, Ashland OR 97520-0055. (541)512-8792. Fax: (541)512-8793. E-mail: mail@storylinepress.com. Website: www.storylinepress.com. **Acquisitions:** Robert McDowell, publisher/

editor. Estab. 1985. Publishes hardcover and trade paperback originals. **Publishes 12-16 titles/year. Receives 500 queries and 1,000 mss/year. 10% of books from first-time authors. Pays 10-15% royalty on net retail price or makes outright purchase of $250-1,500. Offers $0-3,000 advance.** Publishes book 1-2 years after acceptance of ms. Accepts simultaneous submissions. Responds in 1 month to queries; 3 months to mss. Book catalog free; ms guidelines for #10 SASE.

O— "Story Line Press exists to publish the best stories of our time in poetry, fiction and nonfiction. Seventy-five percent of our list includes a wide range of poetry and books about poetry. Our books are intended for the general and academic reader. We are working to expand the audience for serious literature."

Nonfiction: Literary. Subjects include language/literature, authors. Query with SASE.

Fiction: Literary. No popular genres. Query with SASE.

Poetry: Query with SASE.

Recent Title(s): *New Expansive Poetry*, by R.S. Gwynn, editor (nonfiction); *Quit Monks Or Die!*, by Maxine Kumin (fiction); *Questions for Ecclesiastes*, by Mark Jarman (poetry).

Tips: "We strongly recommend that first-time poetry authors submit their book-length manuscripts in the Nicholas Roerich Poetry Contest, and first-time fiction authors send to the Three Oaks Fiction Contest." See the Contests & Awards section for details.

■■ **STYLUS PUBLISHING, LLC**, 22883 Quicksilver Dr., Sterling VA 20166. Website: styluspub.com. **Acquisitions:** John von Knorring, publisher. Estab. 1996. Publishes hardcover and trade paperback originals. **Publishes 6-10 titles/year. Receives 50 queries and 6 mss/year. 50% of books from first-time authors; 100% from unagented writers. Pays 5-10% royalty on wholesale price. Offers advance.** Publishes book 6 months after acceptance of ms. Responds in 1 month to queries. Book catalog free; ms guidelines online.

O— "We publish in higher education (professional development, distance education, teaching, administration) and training (training and development for corporate, nonprofit and government organizations)."

Nonfiction: Subjects include business/economics, education, training. Query or submit outline, 1 sample chapter with SASE. Reviews artwork/photos as part of ms package. Send photocopies.

Recent Title(s): *Learning from Change*; *Training with a Beat*.

SUCCESS PUBLISHING, 3419 Dunham Rd., Warsaw NY 14569-9735. (716)786-5663. **Acquisitions:** Allan H. Smith, president (home-based business); Ginger Smith (business); Dana Herbison (home/craft); Robin Garretson (fiction). Estab. 1982. Publishes mass market paperback originals. **Publishes 6 titles/year. Receives 175 submissions and 10 mss/year. 90% of books from first-time authors; 100% from unagented writers. Pays 7-12% royalty. Offers $500-1,000 advance.** Publishes book 10 months after acceptance of ms. Accepts simultaneous submissions. Responds in 2 months to queries. Book catalog and ms guidelines for #10 SAE with 2 first-class stamps.

● Success Publishing notes that it is looking for ghostwriters.

O— Success publishes guides that focus on the needs of the home entrepreneur to succeed as a viable business. Currently emphasizing starting a new business. De-emphasizing self-help/motivation books.

Nonfiction: Children's/juvenile, how-to, self-help. Subjects include business/economics, child guidance/parenting, hobbies, money/finance, craft/home-based business. "We are looking for books on how-to subjects such as home business and sewing." Query with SASE.

Recent Title(s): *How to Find a Date/Mate*, by Dana Herbison.

Tips: "Our audience is made up of housewives, hobbyists and owners of home-based businesses."

Ñ **SUN BOOKS/SUN PUBLISHING**, P.O. Box 5588, Santa Fe NM 87502-5588. (505)471-5177. E-mail: info@sunbooks.com. Website: www.sunbooks.com. **Acquisitions:** Skip Whitson, director. Publishes trade paperback originals and reprints. **Publishes 10-15 titles/year. Receives hundreds submissions/year. 30% of books from first-time authors; 90% from unagented writers. Pays 5% royalty on retail price or makes outright purchase.** Publishes book 16 months after acceptance of ms. Responds in 2 months to queries and proposals; 6 months to mss. Book catalog online.

Nonfiction: Biography, cookbook, how-to, humor, illustrated book, reference, self-help, technical. Subjects include Americana, anthropology/archeology, business/economics, cooking/foods/nutrition, creative nonfiction, education, government/politics, health/medicine, history, language/literature, memoirs, money/finance, multicultural, nature/environment, philosophy, psychology, regional, religion, sociology, travel, women's issues/studies, metaphysics, motivational, inspirational, Oriental studes. Query with SASE or submit proposal package including outline, sample chapter(s). Reviews artwork/photos as part of ms package. Send photocopies.

Recent Title(s): *Semakanda: Threshold Memories*; *This Mystical Life of Ours*.

Ñ **SUNBELT PUBLICATIONS**, 1250 Fayette St., El Cajon CA 92020. (619)258-4911. Fax: (619)258-4916. E-mail: sunbeltpub@prodigy.net. Website: www.sunbeltpub.com. **Acquisitions:** Jennifer Redmond, publications coordinator; Lowell Lindsay, publisher (natural history). Publishes hardcover and trade paperback originals and reprints. **Publishes 6-10 titles/year. Receives 30 queries and 20 mss/year. 80% of books from first-time authors; 100% from unagented writers. Pays 10-14% royalty.** Accepts simultaneous submissions. Responds in 1 month to queries and proposals; 3 months to mss. Book catalog and ms guidelines online.

O— "We are interested in the cultural and natural history of the 'The Californias' in the U.S. and Mexico."

Nonfiction: "We publish multi-language pictorials, natural science and outdoor guidebooks, regional references and stories that celebrate the land and its people." Coffee table book, how-to, reference, guidebooks. Subjects include anthropology/archeology, history (regional), nature/environment (natural history), recreation, regional, travel. Query with SASE or submit proposal package including outline, 1-2 sample chapter(s) or submit complete ms. Reviews artwork/photos as part of ms package. Send photocopies.

Recent Title(s): *Journey with a Baja Burro*, by Graham MacKintosh (adventure travel); *Mission Memoirs*, by Terry Rascin (photo essay).

Tips: "Our audience is interested in natural science or the culture history of California and Baja California, Mexico. They want specific information that is accurate and up-to-date. Our books are written for an adult audience that is primarily interested in adventure and the outdoors. Our guidebooks lead to both personal and armchair adventure and travel. Authors must be willing to actively promote their book through book signings, the media, and lectures/slide shows for intended audiences."

SWEDENBORG FOUNDATION PUBLISHERS, 320 North Church St., West Chester PA 19380. (610)430-3222. Fax: (610)430-7982. E-mail: editor@swedenborg.com. Website: www.swedenborg.com. **Acquisitions:** Mary Lou Bertucci, senior editor. Estab. 1849. Publishes hardcover and trade paperback originals and reprints. **Publishes 10 titles/ year. Pays 10% royalty on net receipts or makes outright purchase. Offers $1000 minimum advance.** Responds in 1 month to queries; 3 months to proposals and mss. Book catalog and ms guidelines free.

Imprints: Chrysalis Books, Swedenborg Foundation Press

- ○→ "The Swedenborg Foundation publishes books by and about Emanuel Swedenborg (1688-1772), his ideas, how his ideas have influenced others, and related topics. A Chrysalis book is an adventurous, spiritually focused book presented with a nonsectarian perspective that appeals to open-minded, well-educated seekers of all traditions. Appropriate topics include—but are not limited to—science, mysticism, spiritual growth and development, wisdom traditions, healing and spirituality, as well as subjects that explore Swedenborgian concepts, such as: near-death experience, angels, biblical interpretation, mysteries of good and evil, etc. These books will foster a searching approach to the spiritual basis of reality."

Nonfiction: Self-help, spiritual growth and development. Subjects include philosophy, psychology, religion, science. Query with SASE or submit proposal package including outline, sample chapter(s), synopsis. Reviews artwork/photos as part of ms package. Send photocopies.

Recent Title(s): *Sacred Quest*, by L. Robert Keck.

Tips: "Readers of our books are thoughtful, well-read individuals seeking resources for their philosophical, spiritual or religious growth. Especially sought are nonfiction works that bridge contemporary issues to spiritual insights and that relate Swedenborgian thought to these."

SYBEX, INC., 1151 Marina Village Pkwy., Alameda CA 94501. (510)523-8233. Fax: (510)523-2373. E-mail: proposals @sybex.com. Website: www.sybex.com. VP/Publisher: Jordan Gold. **Acquisitions:** Kristine O'Callaghan, contracts and licensing manager. Estab. 1976. Publishes paperback originals. **Publishes 180 titles/year. Pays standard royalties. Offers competitive advance.** Publishes book 3 months after acceptance of ms. Accepts simultaneous submissions. Responds in 1 month to queries. Book catalog online.

- ○→ Sybex publishes computer and software titles.

Nonfiction: "Manuscripts most publishable in the field of PC applications software, hardware, programming languages, operating systems, computer games, Internet/Web certification and networking." Technical. Subjects include computers/ electronic, software. Looks for "clear writing, logical presentation of material; and good selection of material such that the most important aspects of the subject matter are thoroughly covered; well-focused subject matter; clear understanding of target audience; and well thought-out organization that helps the reader understand the material." Submit outline, 2-3 sample chapter(s), résumé. Reviews artwork/photos as part of ms package. Send disk/CD.

Recent Title(s): *Mastering Photoshop 6*, by Stephen Romanelli; *The Complete PC Upgrade and Maintenance Guide*, 10th edition, by Mark Minasi; *CCNA: Cisco Certified Network Associate Study Guide*, by Todd Lammle.

Tips: "Queries/mss may be routed to other editors in the publishing group. Also seeking freelance writers for revising existing works and as contributors in multi-author projects, and freelance editors for editing works in progress."

SYRACUSE UNIVERSITY PRESS, 621 Skytop Road, Suite 110, Syracuse NY 13244-5290. (315)443-5534. Fax: (315)443-5545. Website: sumweb.syr.edu/su_press/. **Acquisitions:** John J. Freuhwirth, acting director. Estab. 1943. **Publishes 80 titles/year. Receives 600-700 submissions/year. 25% of books from first-time authors; 75% from unagented writers. Pays royalty on net receipts. Offers advance.** Publishes book an average of 15 months after acceptance of ms. Book catalog for 9×12 SAE with 3 first-class stamps.

- ○→ Currently emphasizing television, Jewish studies, Middle East topics. De-emphasizing peace studies.

Nonfiction: Subjects include regional. "Special opportunity in our nonfiction program for freelance writers of books on New York state, sports history, Jewish studies, the Middle East, religious studies, television and popular culture.

WRITERSMARKET.COM at http://www.WritersMarket.com features streamlined searches, personalized market information as well as new markets, daily updates and more.

Provide precise descriptions of subjects, along with background description of project. The author must make a case for the importance of his or her subject." Query with SASE or submit outline, 2 sample chapter(s). Reviews artwork/photos as part of ms package.

Recent Title(s): *Second Generation Voices: The Reflections by Children of Holocaust Survivors and Perpetrators*, by Alan L. Berger and Naomi Berger (Jewish Studies); *Crossing Highbridge*, by Maureen Waters (Irish studies); *The Forgotten: Catholics of the Soviet Empire from Lenin through Stalin*, by Rev. Christopher Lawrence Zugger (religion).
Tips: "We're seeking well-written and well-researched books that will make a significant contribution to the subject areas listed above and will be well-received in the marketplace."

N. SYSTEMS CO., INC., P.O. Box 339, Carlsborg WA 98324. (360)683-6860. **Acquisitions:** Richard H. Peetz, Ph.D., president. Estab. 1981. Publishes hardcover and trade paperback originals. **Publishes 3-5 titles/year. 50% of books from first-time authors; 100% from unagented writers. Pays 20% royalty on wholesale price after costs.** **Offers advance.** Publishes book 6 months after acceptance of ms. Accepts simultaneous submissions. Responds in 2 months to queries. Book catalog free; ms guidelines for $1.
O— "We publish succinct and well-organized technical and how-to-do-it books with minimum filler." De-emphasizing business/economics, health/medicine.
Nonfiction: How-to, self-help, technical, textbook. Subjects include business/economics, health/medicine, money/finance, nature/environment, science (engineering), automotive. Submit outline, 2 sample chapter(s), SASE. Reviews artwork/photos as part of ms package. Send photocopies.
Recent Title(s): *Existentialism & Folklore*, by J.S. Hescher, M.D.
Tips: "Our audience consists of people in technical occupations, people interested in doing things themselves. In submitting nonfiction, writers often make the mistake of picking a common topic with lots of published books in print."

A. NAN A. TALESE, Random House, Inc., 1540 Broadway, New York NY 10036. (212)782-8918. Fax: (212)782-9261. Website: www.nantalese.com. **Acquisitions:** Nan A. Talese, editorial director. Publishes hardcover originals. **Publishes 15 titles/year. Receives 400 queries and 400 mss/year. Pays variable royalty on retail price. Offers varying advance.** Publishes book 1 year after acceptance of ms. Accepts simultaneous submissions. Responds in 1 week to queries; 2 weeks to proposals and mss.
O— Nan A. Talese publishes nonfiction with a powerful guiding narrative and relevance to larger cultural interests, and literary fiction of the highest quality. Currently emphasizing literary fiction; de-emphasizing literary biography.
Nonfiction: Biography. Subjects include history, philosophy, sociology. *Accepts agented submissions only.*
Fiction: Well written narratives with a compelling story line, good characterization and use of language. We like stories with an edge. *Accepts aented submissions only.*
Recent Title(s): *The Blind Assassin*, by Margaret Atwood (fiction).
Tips: "Audience is highly literate people interested in story, information and insight. We want well-written material. See our website."

N. JEREMY P. TARCHER, INC., Penguin Putnam, Inc., 375 Hudson St., New York NY 10014. (212)366-2000. Website: www.penguinputnam.com. Publisher: Joel Fotinos. **Acquisitions:** Mitch Horowitz, senior editor; Wendy Hubbert, senior editor; Sara Carder, editor; Joel Fotinos, publisher. Estab. 1972. Publishes hardcover and trade paperback originals and reprints. **Publishes 40-50 titles/year. Receives 750 queries and 750 mss/year. 10% of books from first-time authors; 5% from unagented writers. Pays royalty. Offers advance.** Accepts simultaneous submissions. Book catalog free.
O— Tarcher's vision is to publish ideas and works about human consciousness that were large enough to include all aspects of human experience.
Nonfiction: How-to, self-help. Subjects include business/economics, child guidance/parenting, gay/lesbian, health/medicine, nature/environment, philosophy, psychology, religion, women's issues/studies. Query with SASE.
Recent Title(s): *The Lost Daughters of China*, by Karin Evans; *Trust Us, We're Experts*, by Sheldon Rampton & John Stauber.
Tips: "Our audience seeks personal growth through books. Understand the imprint's focus and categories. We stick with the tried and true."

TAYLOR PUBLISHING COMPANY, 1550 W. Mockingbird Lane, Dallas TX 75235. (214)819-8334. Fax: (214)819-8580. Publisher: Lynn Brooks. **Acquisitions:** Michael Emmerich, acquistions director. Estab. 1980. Publishes hardcover and softcover originals. **Publishes 35 titles/year. Receives 1,500 submissions/year. 25% of books from first-time authors; 25% from unagented writers. Offers advance.** Publishes book 1-2 years after acceptance of ms. Accepts simultaneous submissions. Responds in 3 months to queries. Book catalog and ms guidelines for 10×13 SASE.
O— "We publish solid, practical books that should backlist well. We look for authors who are experts in their field and already have some recognition through magazine articles, radio appearances or their own TV or radio show. We also look for speakers or educators."
Nonfiction: Biography. Subjects include child guidance/parenting, gardening, general, health/medicine, history, sports, popular history, miscellaneous nonfiction. Submit outline, sample chapter(s), author bio, two-page summary of work, overveiw of market and competition. Reviews artwork/photos as part of ms package.
Recent Title(s): *Fixed*, by David Porter.

TCU PRESS, P.O. Box 298300, TCU, Fort Worth TX 76129. (817)257-7822. Fax: (817)257-5075. **Acquisitions:** Judy Alter, director; James Ward Lee, acquisitions consultant; A.T. Row, editor. Estab. 1966. Publishes hardcover originals, some reprints. **Publishes 12-15 titles/year. Receives 100 submissions/year. 10% of books from first-time authors; 75% from unagented writers. Pays 10% royalty on net receipts.** Publishes book 16 months after acceptance of ms. Responds in 3 months to queries.

○→ TCU publishes "scholarly works and regional titles of significance focusing on the history and literature of the American West." Currently emphasizing women's studies.

Nonfiction: Subjects include Americana, language/literature, regional, women's issues/studies, American studies, criticism. Query with SASE. Reviews artwork/photos as part of ms package.

Recent Title(s): *Forging the Tortilla Curtain*; *The Devil's Tiger*.

Tips: "Regional and/or Texana nonfiction has best chance of breaking into our firm."

TEACHING & LEARNING COMPANY, 1204 Buchanan St., P.O. Box 10, Carthage IL 62321-0010. (217)357-2591. Fax: (217)357-6789. E-mail: customerservice@TeachingLearning.com. Website: www.TeachingLearning.com. **Acquisitions:** Jill Eckhardt, managing editor. Estab. 1994. **Publishes 60 titles/year. Receives 25 queries and 200 mss/year. 25% of books from first-time authors; 98% from unagented writers. Pays royalty.** Accepts simultaneous submissions. Responds in 3 months to queries; 9 months to proposals and mss. Book catalog and ms guidelines free.

○→ Teaching & Learning Company publishes teacher resources (supplementary activity/idea books) for grades pre K-8. Currently emphasizing "more math for all grade levels, more primary science material."

Nonfiction: Children's/juvenile. Subjects include art/architecture, education, language/literature, science, teacher resources in language arts, reading, math, science, social studies, arts and crafts, responsibility education. No picture books or storybooks. Submit table of contents, introduction, 3 sample chapters with SASE. Reviews artwork/photos as part of ms package. Send photocopies.

Recent Title(s): *Group Project Student Role Sheets*, by Christine Boardman Moen (nonfiction); *Poetry Writing Handbook*, by Greta Barclay Upson, Ed.D (poetry); *Four Square Writing Methods (3 books)*, by Evan and Judith Gould.

Tips: "Our books are for teachers and parents of pre K-8th grade children."

TEMPLE UNIVERSITY PRESS, USB, 1601 N. Broad St., Philadelphia PA 19122-6099. (215)204-8787. Fax: (215)204-4719. E-mail: tempress@astro.ocis.temple.edu. Website: www.temple.edu/tempress/. **Acquisitions:** Janet Francendese, editor-in-chief; Peter Wissoker, senior acquisitions editor (communications, urban studies, geography, law); Micah Kleit, senior acquisitions editor. Estab. 1969. **Publishes 60 titles/year. Pays 10% royalty on wholesale price. Offers advance.** Publishes book 10 months after acceptance of ms. Responds in 2 months to queries. Book catalog free.

○→ "Temple University Press has been publishing useful books on Asian-Americans, law, gender issues, film, women's studies and other interesting areas for nearly 30 years for the goal of social change."

Nonfiction: Subjects include ethnic, government/politics, health/medicine, history (American), photography, regional (Philadelphia), sociology, women's issues/studies, labor studies, urban studies, Latin American, Asian American, African American, public policy. "No memoirs, fiction or poetry." Query with SASE. Reviews artwork/photos as part of ms package.

Recent Title(s): *Critical Race Theory: The Cutting Edge*, second edition, edited by Richard Delgado and Jean Stefancie.

TEN SPEED PRESS, P.O. Box 7123, Berkeley CA 94707. (510)559-1600. Fax: (510)524-1052. E-mail: info@tenspeed.com. Website: www.tenspeed.com. **Acquisitions:** Kirsty Melville, publisher; Lorena Jones, editorial director. Estab. 1971. Publishes trade paperback originals and reprints. **Publishes 100 titles/year; imprint publishes 70 titles/year. 25% of books from first-time authors; 50% from unagented writers. Pays 15-20% royalty on net receipts. Offers $2,500 average advance.** Publishes book 1 year after acceptance of ms. Accepts simultaneous submissions. Responds in 3 months to queries. Book catalog for 9×12 SAE with 6 first-class stamps; ms guidelines for #10 SASE or online.

Imprints: Celestial Arts, Tricycle Press

○→ Ten Speed Press publishes authoritative books for an audience interested in innovative, proven ideas. Currently emphasizing cookbooks, career, business, alternative education, and offbeat general nonfiction gift books.

Nonfiction: "We mainly publish innovative how-to books. We are always looking for cookbooks from proven, tested sources—successful restaurants, etc. *Not* 'Grandma's favorite recipes.' Books about the 'new science' interest us." Cookbook, gift book, how-to, humor, reference, self-help. Subjects include business/economics, child guidance/parenting, cooking/foods/nutrition, gardening, health/medicine, money/finance, nature/environment, recreation, science. "No biographies or autobiographies, first-person travel narratives, fiction or humorous treatments of just about anything." Query with SASE or submit outline, sample chapter(s).

Recent Title(s): *Charlie Trotter Cooks at Home*, by Charlie Trotter.

Tips: "We like books from people who really know their subject, rather than people who think they've spotted a trend to capitalize on. We like books that will sell for a long time, rather than nine-day wonders. Our audience consists of a well-educated, slightly weird group of people who like food, the outdoors and take a light but serious approach to business and careers. Study the backlist of each publisher you're submitting to and tailor your proposal to what you perceive as their needs. Nothing gets a publisher's attention like someone who knows what he or she is talking about, and nothing falls flat like someone who obviously has no idea who he or she is submitting to."

TEXAS A&M UNIVERSITY PRESS, College Station TX 77843-4354. (979)845-1436. Fax: (979)847-8752. E-mail: fdl@tampress.tamu.edu. Website: www.tamu.edu/upress. **Acquisitions:** Mary Lenn Dixon, editor-in-chief (political science, presidential studies, anthropology, borderlands, western history); Jim Sadkovich, associate editor (military, eastern Europe, natural history, agriculture, nautical archaeology). Estab. 1974. **Publishes 50 titles/year. Pays royalty. Offers advance.** Publishes book 1 year after acceptance of ms. Responds in 1 month to queries. Book catalog free.

> O→ Texas A&M University Press publishes a wide range of nonfiction, scholarly trade and crossover books of regional and national interest, "reflecting the interests of the university, the broader scholarly community, and the people of our state and region."

Nonfiction: Subjects include agriculture/horticulture, anthropology/archeology, art/architecture, business/economics, government/politics, history (American and Western), language/literature (Texas and western), military/war, nature/environment, photography, regional (Texas and the Southwest), women's issues/studies, Mexican-US borderlands studies, nautical archaeology, ethnic studies, natural history, presidential studies, business history, veterinary medicine. Query with SASE.

Recent Title(s): *Lighthouses of Texas*, by T. Lindsay Baker.

Tips: Proposal requirements are posted on the website.

TEXAS STATE HISTORICAL ASSOCIATION, 2.306 Richardson Hall, University Station, Austin TX 78712. (512)471-1525. Website: www.tsha.utexas.edu. **Acquisitions:** George B. Ward, assistant director. Estab. 1897. Publishes hardcover and trade paperback originals and reprints. **Publishes 8 titles/year. Receives 50 queries and 50 mss/year. 10% of books from first-time authors; 95% from unagented writers. Pays 10% royalty on net cash proceeds.** Publishes book 1 year after acceptance of ms. Responds in 3 months to mss. Book catalog and ms guidelines free.

> O→ "We are interested in scholarly historical articles and books on any aspect of Texas history and culture."

Nonfiction: Biography, coffee table book, illustrated book, reference. Subjects include history. Query with SASE. Reviews artwork/photos as part of ms package. Send photocopies.

Recent Title(s): *El Llano Estacado: Exploration and Imagination on the High Plains of Texas and New Mexico, 1536-1860*, by John Miller Morris (history).

TEXAS WESTERN PRESS, The University of Texas at El Paso, El Paso TX 79968-0633. (915)747-5688. Fax: (915)747-7515. E-mail: twp@utep.edu. Website: www.utep.edu/~twpress. Director: John Bristol. **Acquisitions:** Bobbi McConaughey Gonzales. Estab. 1952. Publishes hardcover and paperback originals. **Publishes 7-8 titles/year. Pays standard 10% royalty. Offers advance.** Responds in 2 months to queries. Book catalog and ms guidelines free.

Imprints: Southwestern Studies

> O→ Texas Western Press publishes books on the history and cultures of the American Southwest, especially historical and biographical works about West Texas, New Mexico, northern Mexico and the US-Mexico borderlands. Currently emphasizing developing border issues, economic issues of the border. De-emphasizing coffee table books.

Nonfiction: Technical, scholarly. Subjects include education, health/medicine, history, language/literature, nature/environment, regional, science. Historic and cultural accounts of the Southwest (West Texas, New Mexico, northern Mexico and Arizona). Also art, photographic books, Native American and limited regional ficiton reprints. Occasional technical titles. "Our *Southwestern Studies* use manuscripts of up to 30,000 words. Our hardback books range from 30,000 words up. The writer should use good exposition in his work. Most of our work requires documentation. We favor a scholarly, but not overly pedantic, style. We specialize in superior book design." Query with SASE or submit outline. Follow *Chicago Manual of Style*.

Recent Title(s): *Frontier Cavalryman*, by Marcos Kinevan; *James Wiley Magoffin*, by W.H. Timmons.

Tips: Texas Western Press is interested in books relating to the history of Hispanics in the US, will experiment with photo-documentary books, and is interested in seeing more 'popular' history and books on Southwestern culture/life. "We try to treat our authors professionally, produce handsome, long-lived books and aim for quality, rather than quantity of titles carrying our imprint."

THIRD WORLD PRESS, P.O. Box 19730, Chicago IL 60619. (773)651-0700. Fax: (773)651-7286. E-mail: TWPress3@aol.com. Publisher: Haki R. Madhubuti. **Acquisitions:** Gwendolyn Mitchell, editor. Estab. 1967. Publishes hardcover and trade paperback originals and reprints. **Publishes 20 titles/year. Receives 200-300 queries and 200 mss/year. 20% of books from first-time authors; 80% from unagented writers. Pays royalty on retail price. Offers advance.** Publishes book 18 months after acceptance of ms. Accepts simultaneous submissions. Responds in 6 months to queries. Book catalog free; ms guidelines for #10 SASE.

> ● Third World Press is open to submissions in January and July.

Nonfiction: Children's/juvenile, illustrated book, reference, self-help, textbook, African-centered, African-American materials. Subjects include anthropology/archeology, education, ethnic, government/politics, health/medicine, history, language/literature, philosophy, psychology, regional, religion, sociology, women's issues/studies, Black studies, literary criticism. Query with SASE or submit outline, 5 sample chapter(s). Reviews artwork/photos as part of ms package. Send photocopies.

Fiction: Ethnic, feminist, historical, juvenile, literary, mainstream/contemporary, picture books, plays, short story collections, young adult, African-centered, African-American materials. Query with SASE or submit 5 sample chapter(s), synopsis.

Poetry: African-centered and African-American materials. Submit complete ms.

Recent Title(s): *Breaking Through the Wall: A Marathoner's Story*, by Delores E. Cross; *In the Shadow of the Son*, by Michael Simanga.

THORNDIKE PRESS, The Gale Group, P.O Box 159, Thorndike ME 04986. (207)948-2962. Fax: (207)948-2863. E-mail: Hazel.Rumney@galegroup.com. **Acquisitions:** Hazel Rumney, editor (romance, western, women's fiction); Mary Smith, senior editor (mystery); Jamie Knobloch, editorial director. Publishes hardcover originals, reprints and large print reprints. **Publishes 96 titles/year. Receives 1,000 queries and 1,000 mss/year. 60% of books from first-time authors; 75% from unagented writers. Pays royalty on wholesale price. Offers $1,000-2,000 advance.** Publishes book 8 months after acceptance of ms. Accepts simultaneous submissions. Responds in 2 months to queries and proposals; 4 months to mss. Book catalog free; ms guidelines for #10 SASE.
Imprints: Five Star (contact: Hazel Rumney).
Fiction: Mystery, romance, western, women's. Submit proposal package including 3 sample chapter(s), synopsis.
Recent Title(s): *Friends and Enemies*, by Susan Oleksiw (mystery); *Desparate Acts*, by Jane Candia Coleman (romance).
Tips: Audience is intelligent readers looking for something different and satisfying. "We want highly original material that contains believable motivation, with little repetitive introspection. Show us how a character feels, rather than tell us. Humor is good; cliches are not."

THREE FORKS BOOKS, The Globe Pequot Press, P.O. Box 1718, Helena MT 59624. (406)442-6597. Fax: (406)442-0384. Website: www.falcon.com. **Acquisitions:** Megan Hiller, senior editor. Publishes hardcover and trade paperback originals. **Publishes 4 titles/year. 80% of books from first-time authors; 80% from unagented writers. Pays variable royalty.** Responds in 2 months to queries. Book catalog and ms guidelines free.
   O─► Three Forks specializes in regional cookbooks *or* cookbooks with a unique, non-food theme. We do not publish single-food themed cookbooks.
Nonfiction: Cookbook. Subjects include regional. Query with SASE or submit proposal package. Reviews artwork/photos as part of ms package. Send photocopies. Do not send originals.
Recent Title(s): *Whistleberries, Stirabout, & Depression Cake* (food history); *Chocolate Snowball* (cookbook).

TIARE PUBLICATIONS, P.O. Box 493, Lake Geneva WI 53147-0493. Fax: (262)249-0299. E-mail: info@tiare.com. Website: www.tiare.com. **Acquisitions:** Gerry L. Dexter, president. Estab. 1986. Publishes trade paperback originals. **Publishes 6-12 titles/year. Receives 25 queries and 10 mss/year. 40% of books from first-time authors; 100% from unagented writers. Pays 15% royalty on wholesale price or retail price. Offers advance.** Publishes book 3 months after acceptance of ms. Responds in 1 month to queries. Book catalog for $1.
Imprints: LimeLight Books, Balboa Books
   O─► Tiare offers a wide selection of books for the radio communications enthusiast. LimeLight publishes general nonfiction on subjects ranging from crime to root beer. Balboa offers big band and jazz titles.
Nonfiction: How-to, technical, general. Subjects include computers/electronic, general, music/dance, jazz/big bands. Query with SASE.
Recent Title(s): *Air-Ways—The Insider's Guide to Air Travel*.

TIDEWATER PUBLISHERS, Cornell Maritime Press, Inc., P.O. Box 456, Centreville MD 21617-0456. (410)758-1075. Fax: (410)758-6849. **Acquisitions:** Charlotte Kurst, managing editor. Estab. 1938. Publishes hardcover and paperback originals. **Publishes 7-9 titles/year. Receives 150 submissions/year. 41% of books from first-time authors; 99% from unagented writers. Pays 7½-15% royalty on retail price. Offers advance.** Publishes book 1 year after acceptance of ms. Responds in 2 months to queries. Book catalog for 10×13 SAE with 5 first-class stamps.
   O─► Tidewater Publishers issues adult nonfiction works related to the Chesapeake Bay area, Delmarva or Maryland in general. "The only fiction we handle is juvenile and must have a regional focus."
Nonfiction: Regional subjects only. Children's/juvenile, cookbook, illustrated book, reference. Subjects include cooking/foods/nutrition, history, regional. Query with SASE or submit outline, sample chapter(s). Reviews artwork/photos as part of ms package.
Fiction: Regional juvenile fiction only. Query with SASE or submit outline, sample chapter(s), synopsis.
Recent Title(s): *Chesapeake ABC*, by Priscilla Cummings, illustrated by David Aiken; *Lost Towns of Tidewater Maryland*, by Donald G. Shomette.
Tips: "Our audience is made up of readers interested in works that are specific to the Chesapeake Bay and Delmarva Peninsula area. We do not publish personal narratives, adult fiction or poetry."

TIMBERWOLF PRESS, INC., 202 N. Allen Dr., Suite A, Allen TX 75013. (972)359-0911. Fax: (972)359-0525. E-mail: submissions@timberwolfpress.com. Website: www.timberwolfpress.com. **Acquisitions:** Carol Woods, senior editor. Publishes trade paperback originals. **Publishes 24-30 titles/year. Receives 300+ queries and 100+ mss/year. 33% of books from first-time authors; 84% from unagented writers. Pays royalty on wholesale price. Offers industry standard advance or better.** Publishes book 6 months after acceptance of ms. Accepts simultaneous submissions. Responds in 1 month to queries; 3 months to mss. Book catalog and ms guidelines online.

Fiction: Fantasy, military/war, mystery, science fiction, suspense. "In addition to the p-book, we present each title in fully-cast, dramatized, unabridged audio, available in the usual formats; and downloadable in all formats from our website. We also stream this audio in 30-minute episodes on our website. So our stories must maintain tension and pace. Think exciting. Think breathless. Think terrific story, terrific characters, terrific writing." Query via e-mail only.
Recent Title(s): *All the Tea*, by Ken Carodine (technothriller); *Calculated Risk*, by Denise Tiller (mystery).
Tips: "We accept e-queries and e-submissions only: *submissions@timberwolfpress.com* And polish that query. Grammar, punctuation, and spelling are as important in e-queries and e-submissions as they are in p-queries."

A MEGAN TINGLEY BOOKS, Little, Brown & Co., Three Center Plaza, Boston MA 02108. (617)227-0730. Fax: (617)263-2864. Website: www.twbookmark.com. **Acquisitions:** Megan Tingley, editorial director; Alvina Ling, editorial assistant; Mary Gruetzke, assistant editor. Publishes hardcover and trade paperback originals. **Publishes 80-100 titles/year; imprint publishes 10-20 titles/year. Pays 0-15% royalty on retail price. Offers advance.** Accepts simultaneous submissions.
  ○→ Megan Tingley Books is a new imprint of the children's book department of Little, Brown and Company. Currently emphasizing picture books for the very young. Does not want genre novels (mystery, science fiction, romance).
Nonfiction: Children's/juvenile. Subjects include all juvenile interests. *Accepts agented submissions only*, but unsolicited queries are okay. Query with SASE.
Fiction: Juvenile, picture books, young adult. *Accepts agented submissions only*, but unsolicited queries are okay.
Recent Title(s): *Twin Tales: The Magic and Mystery of Multiple Birth*, by Donna Jackson (nonfiction); *Blossom and Boo: A Story About Best Friends*, by Dawn Apperley.

N TODD PUBLICATIONS, P.O. Box 635, Nyack NY 10960. (845)358-6213. E-mail: toddpub@aol.com. Website: www.toddpublications.com. **Acquisitions:** Barry Klein, president. Estab. 1973. Publishes hardcover and trade paperback originals. **Publishes 5 titles/year. 1% of books from first-time authors. Pays 10-15% royalty on wholesale price. Offers advance.** Publishes book 3 months after acceptance of ms. Accepts simultaneous submissions. Responds in 1 month to proposals. Book catalog online or with SASE; ms guidelines for #10 SASE.
  ○→ Todd publishes and distributes reference books and directories of all types.
Nonfiction: How-to, reference, self-help, directories. Subjects include business/economics, ethnic, health/medicine, money/finance, travel. Submit 2 sample chapter(s).
Recent Title(s): *Directory Of Mastercard & Visa Credit Card Sources*; *Insider's Guide To Bank Cards With No Credit Check*; *Indian Country Address Book*.

TOR BOOKS, Tom Doherty Associates, 175 Fifth Ave., New York NY 10010. (212)388-0100. Fax: (212)388-0191. E-mail: inquiries@tor.com. Website: www.tor.com. **Acquisitions:** Patrick Nielsen Hayden, senior editor. Estab. 1980. Publishes hardcover originals and trade and mass market paperback originals and reprints. **Publishes 150-200 titles/year. 2-3% of books from first-time authors; 3-5% from unagented writers. Pays royalty on retail price. Offers advance.** Publishes book 1-2 years after acceptance of ms. Responds in 4 months to queries; 6 months to proposals; 2 months to mss. Book catalog for 9×12 SAE with 2 first-class stamps; ms guidelines for #10 SASE.
  ○→ "Tor Books publishes what is arguably the largest and most diverse line of science fiction and fantasy ever produced by a single English-language publisher."
Fiction: Adventure, fantasy, historical, horror, science fiction. Submit 3 sample chapter(s), synopsis.
Recent Title(s): *Winter's Heart*, Robert Jordan (fantasy).
Tips: "We're never short of good sf or fantasy, but we're always open to solid, technologically knowledgeable hard science fiction or thrillers by writers with solid expertise."

TOWER PUBLISHING, 588 Saco Rd., Standish ME 04084. (207)642-5400. Fax: (207)642-5463. E-mail: info@tower pub.com. Website: www.towerpub.com. **Acquisitions:** Michael Lyons, president. Estab. 1772. Publishes hardcover originals and reprints, trade paperback originals. **Publishes 15 titles/year. Receives 60 queries and 30 mss/year. 10% of books from first-time authors; 90% from unagented writers. Pays royalty on net receipts.** Publishes book 6 months after acceptance of ms. Accepts simultaneous submissions. Responds in 1 month to queries; 2 months to proposals and mss. Book catalog and ms guidelines online.
  ○→ Tower Publishing specializes in business and professional directories and legal books.
Nonfiction: Reference. Subjects include business/economics. Looking for legal books of a national stature. Query with SASE or submit outline.

TOWLEHOUSE PUBLISHING CO., 1312 Bell Grimes Lane, Nashville TN 37207. (615)612-3005. Fax: (615)612-0067. E-mail: vermonte@aol.com. Website: www.Towlehouse.com. **Acquisitions:** Mike Towle, president/publisher (nonfiction, sports, gift books, pop culture, cookbooks, Christianity). Publishes hardcover, trade paperback and mass market paperback originals, hardcover and trade paperback reprints. **Publishes 8-10 titles/year. Receives 100-250 mss/year. 75% of books from first-time authors; 80% from unagented writers. Pays 8-20% royalty on wholesale price. Offers $500-2,000 advance.** Publishes book 9 months after acceptance of ms. Accepts simultaneous submissions. Responds in 2 months to queries.
  ○→ "We publish nonfiction books about America that are informative and entertaining." Currently emphasizing sports books, especially golf, and books generated by headlines. De-emphasizing cookbooks and poetry.

Nonfiction: Biography, cookbook, gift book, humor. Subjects include Americana, cooking/foods/nutrition, creative nonfiction, government/politics, history, military/war, regional, religion, sports, insta-books dictated by headlines and milestone anniversaries of significant events. "I don't solicit children's books, poetry or non-Christian religious titles. Authors using profanity, obscenities or other vulgar or immoral language in their books need not contact me." Query with SASE or submit proposal package including outline, 2 sample chapter(s), author bio, letter containing marketing plan. Reviews artwork/photos as part of ms package. Send photocopies.

Recent Title(s): *The Book of Landry*, by Jennifer Briggs Kaski (sports); *Quotable Joe*, by L. Budd Thalman (sports).

Tips: "Send one proposal for one book at a time. If you send me a query listing three, four or more 'ideas' for books, I will immediately know that you lack the commitment needed to author a book. Send a SASE for anything you send me. I don't accept fiction unless you're a bestselling fiction author."

TRAFALGAR SQUARE PUBLISHING, P.O. Box 257, N. Pomfret VT 05053-0257. (802)457-1911. Fax: (802)457-1913. E-mail: tsquare@sover.net. Website: www.horseandriderbooks.com. Publisher: Caroline Robbins. **Acquisitions:** Martha Cook, managing editor. Estab. 1987. Publishes hardcover and trade paperback originals and reprints. **Publishes 10 titles/year. Pays royalty. Offers advance.** Responds in 2 months to queries.

○━ "We publish high quality instructional books for horsemen and horsewomen, always with the horse's welfare in mind."

Nonfiction: "We publish books for intermediate to advanced riders and horsemen." Subjects include animals (horses). "No stories, children's books or horse biographies." Query with SASE or submit proposal package including outline, 1-2 sample chapter(s), Letter of writer's qualifications and audience for book's subject.

Recent Title(s): *Resistance Free Training*, by Richard Shrake; *You Can Train Your Horse to Do Anything!*, by Shawna and Vinton Karrasch.

TRANSNATIONAL PUBLISHERS, INC., 410 Saw Mill River Rd., Ardsley NY 10502. (914)693-5100. Fax: (914)693-4430. E-mail: info@transnationalpubs.com. Website: www.transnationalpubs.com. Publisher: Heike Fenton. **Acquisitions:** John Berger, VP/publishing director. Estab. 1980. **Publishes 15-20 titles/year. Receives 40-50 queries and 30 mss/year. 60% of books from first-time authors; 95% from unagented writers. Pays royalty.** Publishes book 6-9 months after acceptance of ms. Accepts simultaneous submissions. Responds in 1 month to queries. Book catalog and ms guidelines free.

○━ "We provide specialized international law publications for the teaching of law and law-related subjects in law school classroom, clinic and continuing legal education settings." Currently emphasizing any area of international law that is considered a current issue/event.

Nonfiction: Reference, technical, textbook. Subjects include business/economics, government/politics, women's issues/studies, international law. Query with SASE or submit proposal package including sample chapter(s), table of contents and introduction.

Recent Title(s): *Reconciling Environment and Trade*, edited by Edith Brown Weiss and John J. Jackson.

TRICYCLE PRESS, Ten Speed Press, P.O. Box 7123, Berkeley CA 94707. (510)559-1600. Fax: (510)559-1637. Website: www.tenspeed.com. **Acquisitions:** Nicole Geiger, publisher; Abigail Samoun, editorial assistant. Publishes hardcover and trade paperback originals. **Publishes 14-16 titles/year. 20% of books from first-time authors; 60% from unagented writers. Pays 15-20% royalty on wholesale price (lower if books is illustrated). Offers $0-9,000 advance.** Publishes book 1 year after acceptance of ms. Accepts simultaneous submissions. Responds in 4 months to mss. Book catalog and ms guidelines for 9×12 SAE with 3 first-class stamps.

○━ "Tricycle Press looks for something outside the mainstream; books that encourage children to look at the world from a possibly alternative angle. We have been trying to expand into the educational market and middle grade fiction."

Nonfiction: Children's/juvenile, how-to, self-help, picture books, activity books. Subjects include art/architecture, gardening, health/medicine, nature/environment, science, geography, math. Submit complete ms for activity books; 2-3 chapters or 20 pages for others. Reviews artwork/photos as part of ms package. Send photocopies.

Fiction: Picture books. Picture books: Submit complete ms. Middle grade books: Send complete outline and 2-3 sample chapters (ages 8-12). Query with synopsis and SASE for all others.

Recent Title(s): *Born to Be a Cowgirl*, by Candare Savage; *Danger Boy #1: Ancient Fire*, by Mark London Williams.

N: THE TRINITY FOUNDATION, P.O. Box 68, Unicoi TN 37692. (423)743-0199. Fax: (423)743-2005. Website: www.trinityfoundation.org. **Acquisitions:** John Robbins. Publishes hardcover and paperback originals and reprints. **Publishes 5 titles/year. Receives 12 queries and 2 submissions/year. 100% from unagented writers. Makes outright purchase of $1-1,500.** Publishes book 9 months after acceptance of ms. Responds in 1 month to queries and proposals; 3 months to mss. Book catalog online.

Nonfiction: "Only books that confirm to the philosophy and theology of the Westminster Confession of Faith." Textbook. Subjects include business/economics, education, government/politics, history, philosophy, religion, science. Query with SASE. Reviews artwork/photos as part of ms package.

TRINITY PRESS INTERNATIONAL, 4775 Linglestown Rd., Harrisburg PA 17112. **Acquisitions:** Henry Carrigan, editorial director. Estab. 1989. Publishes trade paperback originals and reprints. **Publishes 40 titles/year. Pays 10% royalty on wholesale price. Offers advance.** Publishes book 9 months after acceptance of ms. Accepts simultaneous submissions. Book catalog free.
  0→ Trinity Press International is an ecumenical publisher of serious books on theology and the Bible for the religious academic community, religious professionals, and serious book readers. Currently emphasizing religion and science, ethics, Biblical studies, film and religion, and religion and culture books.
Nonfiction: Textbook. Subjects include history (as relates to the Bible), religion, Christian/theological studies. Submit outline, 1 sample chapter(s).
Recent Title(s): *God and Globalization*, by Max Stackhouse.

N: TRIUMPH BOOKS, 601 S. LaSalle St., Suite 500, Chicago IL 60605. (312)939-3330. Fax: (312)663-3557. **Acquisitions:** Thomas Bast, editorial director (sports). Publishes hardcover originals and trade paperback originals and reprints. **Publishes 24-30 titles/year. Receives 300 queries and 150 mss/year. 25% of books from first-time authors; 40% from unagented writers. Pays 10-20% royalty on wholesale price. Offers $3,000-50,000 advance.** Publishes book 1 year after acceptance of ms. Accepts simultaneous submissions. Responds in 1 month to queries; 2 months to proposals and mss. Book catalog free.
Nonfiction: Biography, coffee table book, gift book, humor, illustrated book. Subjects include business/economics, health/medicine, recreation, sports. Query with SASE or submit proposal package including outline, 1-2 sample chapter(s). Reviews artwork/photos as part of ms package. Send photocopies.
Recent Title(s): *Southern Fried Football*, by Tony Barnhart; *Best of Frank Deford*, by Frank Deford.

TRUMAN STATE UNIVERSITY PRESS, 100 E. Normal St., Kirksville MO 63501-4221. (660)785-7199. Fax: (660)785-4480. E-mail: tsup@truman.edu. Website: www2.truman.edu/tsup. **Acquisitions:** Paula Presley, director/editor-in-chief (reference works/bibliography/history); Nancy Reschly, poetry editor (contemporary narrative poetry); Raymond Mentzer, general editor (early modern history, literature, biography). **Publishes 8-10 titles/year. Pays 7% royalty on net receipts.**
Nonfiction: Biography, illustrated book, textbook, monographs. Subjects include Americana, history (early modern), art history, literature.
Recent Title(s): *When the Railroad Leaves Town*, by Joseph P. Schwieterman (nonfiction); *Sun Symbolism and Cosmology in Michelangelo's Last Supper*, by Valerie Shrimplin (nonfiction); *After Greece*, by Christopher Bakken (poetry).

TURTLE BOOKS, 866 United Nations Plaza, Suite #525, New York NY 10017. (212)644-2020. Fax: (212)223-4387. Website: www.turtlebooks.com. **Acquisitions:** John Whitman, publisher (children's picture books). Publishes hardcover and trade paperback originals. **Publishes 6-8 titles/year. Receives 1,000 mss/year. 25% of books from first-time authors; 50% from unagented writers. Pays royalty on retail price. Offers advance.** Publishes book 12 months after acceptance of ms. Accepts simultaneous submissions.
  0→ Turtle Books publishes children's picture books.
Nonfiction: Children's/juvenile, illustrated book. Subjects include animals, education, history, language/literature, multicultural, nature/environment, regional, Any subject suitable for a children's picture book. Submit complete ms. Reviews artwork/photos as part of ms package. Send photocopies. Do not send original art.
Fiction: Adventure, ethnic, fantasy, historical, multicultural, regional, sports, western. Subjects suitable for children's picture books. "We are looking for good stories which can be illustrated as children's picture books." Submit complete ms.
Poetry: Must be suitable for an illustrated children's book format. Submit complete ms.
Recent Title(s): *Keeper of the Swamp*, by Ann Garrett; *The Crab Man*, by Patricia Van West; *Alphabet Fiesta*, by Anne Miranda.
Tips: "Our preference is for stories rather than concept books. We will consider only children's picture book manuscripts."

TURTLE PRESS, S.K. Productions, P.O. Box 290206, Wethersfield CT 06129-0206. (860)529-7770. Fax: (860)529-7775. E-mail: editorial@turtlepress.com. Website: www.turtlepress.com. **Acquisitions:** Cynthia Kim, editor. Publishes hardcover originals, trade paperback originals and reprints. **Publishes 4-8 titles/year. Pays 8-10% royalty. Offers $500-1,500 advance.** Responds in 1 month to queries.
  0→ Turtle Press publishes sports and martial arts nonfiction for a specialty niche audience. Currently emphasizing martial arts, eastern philosophy. De-emphasizing self-help.
Nonfiction: How-to, self-help. Subjects include philosophy, sports, martial arts. "We prefer tightly targeted topics on which there is little or no information available in the market, particularly for our sports and martial arts titles." Query with SASE.
Recent Title(s): *Warrior Speed*, by Ted Weimann.

TUTTLE PUBLISHING, 153 Milk St., 5th Floor, Boston MA 02109. **Acquisitions:** Editorial Acquisitions. Estab. 1832. Publishes hardcover and trade paperback originals and reprints. **Publishes 125 titles/year. Receives 1,000 queries/**

year. **20% of books from first-time authors; 40% from unagented writers. Pays 5-10% royalty on net or retail price, depending on format and kind of book. Offers advance.** Publishes book 18 months after acceptance of ms. Accepts simultaneous submissions. Responds in 4 months to proposals.

O⌐ "Tuttle is America's leading publisher of books on Japan and Asia."

Nonfiction: Self-help. Subjects include ethnic, health/medicine, philosophy (Eastern), religion (Eastern), Taoist. Query with SASE or submit outline. Cannot guarantee return of ms.

Recent Title(s): *St. Nadie in Winter*, by Terrance Keenan; *Bruce Lee: The Celebrated Life of the Golden Dragon*, by John Little.

N. TWAYNE PUBLISHERS, MacMillan Library Reference. 1633 Broadway, 23rd Floor, New York NY 10019. (646)756-2666. Fax: (646)756-2654. **Acquisitions:** Amanda Materne, editor. Publishes hardcover and paperback originals. **Receives 100 submissions/year. 5% of books from first-time authors; 90% from unagented writers. Pays royalty.**

O⌐ Publishes concise, introductory, scholary books and volumes in series for the general and academic reader.

Nonfiction: Literary criticism. Query with SASE. *No unsolicited mss.*

A. TWENTY-FIRST CENTURY BOOKS, Millbrook Press, 2 Old New Milford Rd., Brookfield CT 06804. (203)740-2220. Senior Vice President/Publisher: Jean Reynolds. Editor in Chief: Amy Shields. Senior Editors: Laura Walsh, Anita Holmes, Kristen Bettcher. **Acquisitions:** Kirsten Vibbert, manuscript coordinator. Publishes hardcover originals. **Publishes 30 titles/year. Receives 200 queries and 50 mss/year. 20% of books from first-time authors. Pays 5-8% royalty. Offers advance.** Publishes book 18 months after acceptance of ms.

O⌐ Twenty-First Century Books publishes nonfiction science, technology and social issues titles for children and young adults. "We no longer accept unsolicited manuscripts." *Accepts agented submissions only.*

Nonfiction: Children's/juvenile, young adult. Subjects include government/politics, health/medicine, history, military/war, nature/environment, science, current events, social issues. "We publish primarily in series of four or more titles, for ages 12 and up, and single titles for grades 7 and up. No picture books, fiction or adult books." *Accepts agented submissions only.*

Recent Title(s): *The Civil War at Sea*; *101 Questions About Blood and Circulation.*

Tips: "We are now accepting single titles for young adult readers."

TWO DOT, The Globe Pequot Press, Box 1718, Helena MT 59624. (406)442-6597. Fax: (406)442-0384. Website: www.twodotbooks.com. **Acquisitions:** Megan Hiller, editor; Charlene Patterson, editor (series nonfiction, regional history). Publishes hardcover and trade paperback originals. **Publishes 10 titles/year. 30% of books from first-time authors; 90% from unagented writers. Pays royalty on net price.** Accepts simultaneous submissions. Responds in 3 months to queries. Book catalog for 9 × 12 SAE with 3 first-class stamps; ms guidelines for #10 SASE.

O⌐ "Two Dot looks for lively writing for a popular audience, well-researched, on regional themes." Currently emphasizing popular history, western history, regional history, western Americana. De-emphasizing scholarly writings, children's books, fiction, poetry.

Nonfiction: Coffee table book. Subjects include Americana (western), history, regional. Three state by state series of interest: *More than Petticoats* (notable women); *It Happened In ...* (state histories); and *Outlaw Tales* (by state). Submit outline, 1 sample chapter(s), SASE. Reviews artwork/photos as part of ms package. Send photocopies.

Recent Title(s): *Toward the Setting Sun: Pioneer Girls Traveling the Overland Trails*; *Montana Behind the Scenes*, by Durral and John Johanek.

TYNDALE HOUSE PUBLISHERS, INC., 351 Executive Dr., Carol Stream IL 60188. (630)668-8300. Website: www.tyndale.com. **Acquisitions:** Ron Beers Publishing Division. Estab. 1962. Publishes hardcover and trade paperback originals and mass paperback reprints. **Publishes 125-150 titles/year. 5% of books from first-time authors. Pays negotiable royalty. Offers negotiable advance.** Publishes book 9 months after acceptance of ms. Responds in 3 months to queries. Manuscript guidelines for #10 SASE.

O⌐ Tyndale House publishes "practical, user-friendly Christian books for the home and family."

Nonfiction: Children's/juvenile, self-help (Christian growth). Subjects include child guidance/parenting, religion, devotional/inspirational, theology/Bible doctrine, contemporary/critical issues. Query with SASE or submit outline. *No unsolicited mss.*

Fiction: Romance. "Biblical historical and other Christian themes. No short story collections. Youth books: character building stories with Christian perspective. Especially interested in ages 10-14." No short story collections. Query with SASE or submit synopsis. *No unsolicited mss.*

Recent Title(s): *Unspoken*, by Francine Rivers (fiction); *Safely Home*, by Randy Alcorn; *Adolescence Isn't Terminal*, by Kevin Leman.

UCLA AMERICAN INDIAN STUDIES CENTER, 3220 Campbell Hall. Box 951548, UCLA, Los Angeles CA 90095-1548. (310)825-7315. Fax: (310)206-7060. E-mail: aiscpubs@ucla.edu. Website: www.sscnet.ucla.edu/esp/aisc/index.html. **Acquisitions:** Duane Champagne, director/editor. Publishes hardcover and trade paperback originals. **Publishes 4 titles/year. Receives 10 queries and 8 mss/year. 60% of books from first-time authors; 100% from unagented writers. Pays 8% royalty on retail price.** Publishes book 7 months after acceptance of ms. Accepts simultaneous submissions. Responds in 2 months to queries; 3 months to mss. Book catalog and ms guidelines free.

O— "We publish nonfiction, fiction and poetry by and about Native Americans. We publish the *American Indian Culture and Research Journal*, which accepts poetry submissions.

Nonfiction: Reference, scholarly. Subjects include Americana, anthropology/archeology, ethnic, government/politics, health/medicine, history, language/literature, multicultural, religion, sociology, contemporary culture. Submit proposal package including outline, 2 sample chapter(s). Reviews artwork/photos as part of ms package. Send photocopies.

Fiction: Ethnic, plays, poetry, religious. Submit proposal package including synopsis.

Poetry: Query or submit complete ms.

Recent Title(s): *Songs from an Outcast*; *Indian Gaming: Who Wins?*; *A Sacred Path: The Way of the Muscogee Creeks.*

UNITY HOUSE, Unity School of Christianity, 1901 NW Blue Parkway, Unity Village MO 64065-0001. (816)524-3550 ext. 3190. Fax: (816)251-3552. Website: www.unityworldhq.org. **Acquisitions:** Michael Maday, editor; Raymond Teague, associate editor. Estab. 1889. Publishes hardcover and trade paperback originals and reprints. **Publishes 16 titles/year. Receives 500 submissions/year. 30% of books from first-time authors; 95% from unagented writers. Pays 10-15% royalty on net receipts. Offers advance.** Publishes book 13 months after acceptance of ms. Responds in 1 month to queries and proposals; 2 months to mss. Book catalog free; ms guidelines online.

O— "Unity House publishes metaphysical Christian books based on Unity principles, as well as inspirational books on metaphysics and practical spirituality. All manuscripts must reflect a spiritual foundation and express the Unity philosophy, practical Christianity, universal principles, and/or metaphysics."

Nonfiction: "Writers should be familiar with principles of metaphysical Christianity but not feel bound by them. We are interested in works in the related fields of holistic health, spiritual psychology and the philosophy of other world religions." Reference (spiritual/metaphysical), self-help, inspirational. Subjects include health/medicine (holistic), philosophy (perennial/New Thought), psychology (transpersonal), religion (spiritual/metaphysical Bible interpretation/modern Biblical studies). Query with book proposal, including cover letter, summarizing unique features and suggested sales and marketing strategies, toc or project outline and 1-3 sample chapters with SASE. Reviews artwork/photos as part of ms package. Send photocopies.

Fiction: Juvenile, picture books, young adult. Query with SASE.

Recent Title(s): *Ordinary Enlightenment*, by John C. Robinson, Ph.D.

N: UNIVELT, INC., P.O. Box 28130, San Diego CA 92198. (760)746-4005. Fax: (760)746-3139. Website: univelt.staigerland.com. **Acquisitions:** Robert H. Jacobs, publisher. Estab. 1970. Publishes hardcover originals. **Publishes 8 titles/year. Receives 20 submissions/year. 5% of books from first-time authors; 5% from unagented writers. Pays 10% royalty on actual sales.** Publishes book 4 months after acceptance of ms. Responds in 1 month to queries. Book catalog and ms guidelines for #10 SASE.

Imprints: American Astronautical Society, National Space Society

O— Univelt publishes astronautics, spaceflight, aerospace technology and history titles.

Nonfiction: Publishes in the field of aerospace, especially astronautics, including application of aerospace technology to Earth's problems. Technical. Subjects include science. Call, then submit outline and 1-2 chapters. Reviews artwork/photos as part of ms package.

Recent Title(s): *The Case for Mars VI: Making Mars an Affordable Destination*, edited by Kelly R. McMillen.

Tips: "Writers have the best chance of selling manuscripts on the history of astronautics (we have a history series) and astronautics/spaceflight subjects. We publish for the American Astronautical Society."

THE UNIVERSITY OF AKRON PRESS, 374B Bierce Library, Akron OH 44325-1703. (330)972-5342. Fax: (330)972-8364. E-mail: uapress@uakron.edu. Website: www.uakron.edu/uapress. **Acquisitions:** Michael Carley, director. Estab. 1988. Publishes hardcover and trade paperback originals. **Publishes 8-12 titles/year. Receives 400-500 queries and 100 mss/year. 40% of books from first-time authors; 100% from unagented writers. Pays 5-10% royalty. Offers (possible) advance.** Publishes book 10-12 months after acceptance of ms. Responds in 2 months to queries and proposals; 3 months to mss. Book catalog free; ms guidelines for #10 SASE.

O— "The University of Akron Press strives to be the University's ambassador for scholarship and creative writing at the national and international levels." Currently emphasizing technology and the environment, Ohio history and culture, poetry, history of law, political science, and international, political, and economic history. De-emphasizing fiction.

Nonfiction: Scholarly. Subjects include history, regional, science, environment, technology, law, political science. "We publish mostly in our four nonfiction series: Technology and the Environment; Ohio History and Culture; Law, Politics and Society; and International, Political, and Economic History." Query with SASE. Reviews artwork/photos as part of ms package. Send photocopies.

Poetry: Follow the guidelines and submit manuscripts only for the contest. www.uakron.edu/uapress/poetry.html.

Recent Title(s): *Murder, Culture, and Injustice*, by Walter L. Hixson; *When Giants Roamed the Sky*, by Dale Topping.

Tips: "We have mostly an audience of general educated readers, with a more specialized audience of public historians, sociologists and political scientists for the scholarly series."

UNIVERSITY OF ALABAMA PRESS, P.O. Box 870380, Tuscaloosa AL 35487-0380. (205)348-5180. Fax: (205)348-9201. Website: www.uapress.ua.edu. **Acquisitions:** Nicole Mitchell, director (history, political science, regional interest); Curtis Clark, assistant director/editor-in-chief (American literature, communications, Jewish studies,

public administration); Judith Knight, acquisition editor (archaeology). Estab. 1945. Publishes nonfiction hardcover and paperbound originals and fiction paperback reprints. **Publishes 45-50 titles/year. Receives 300 submissions/year. 70% of books from first-time authors; 95% from unagented writers. Offers advance.** Publishes book 1 year after acceptance of ms. Responds in 2 weeks to queries. Book catalog free; ms guidelines for #10 SASE.
Nonfiction: Biography. Subjects include anthropology/archeology, government/politics, history, language/literature, religion, translation. Considers upon merit almost any subject of scholarly interest, but specializes in communications, political science and public administration, literary criticism and biography, history, Jewish studies and archaeology of the Southeastern US. Accepts nonfiction translations. Query with SASE. Reviews artwork/photos as part of ms package.
Fiction: Reprints of works by contemporary Southern writers.
Tips: University of Alabama Press responds to an author within 2 weeks upon receiving the manuscript. If they think it is unsuitable for Alabama's program, they tell the author at once. If the manuscript warrants it, they begin the peer-review process, which may take two to four months to complete. During that process, they keep the author fully informed.

THE UNIVERSITY OF ARKANSAS PRESS, 201 Ozark Ave., Fayetteville AR 72701-1201. (501)575-3246. Fax: (501)575-6044. E-mail: uaprinfo@cavern.uark.edu. Website: www.uapress.com. **Acquisitions:** Lawrence J. Malley, director and editor-in-chief. Estab. 1980. Publishes hardcover and trade paperback originals and reprints. **Publishes 30 titles/year. Receives 1,000 submissions/year. 30% of books from first-time authors; 95% from unagented writers. Pays royalty on net receipts. Offers advance.** Publishes book 1 year after acceptance of ms. Responds in 3 months to proposals. Book catalog online or for 9×12 SAE with 5 first-class stamps; ms guidelines for #10 SASE.
O→ The University of Arkansas Press publishes books on Ozark studies, Civil War in the West, black community studies, American music forms, literary studies and poetics, and sport and society.
Nonfiction: Subjects include Americana, government/politics, history (Southern), language/literature, nature/environment, regional, Arkansas, African-American studies, Middle Eastern studies. Accepted mss must be submitted on disk. "Our current needs include African-American studies and history. We won't consider manuscripts for general textbooks, juvenile or anything requiring a specialized or exotic vocabulary." Query with SASE or submit outline, sample chapter(s), résumé.
Recent Title(s): *A Muslim Primer*, by Ira G. Zepp; *All Shook Up: Collected Poems About Elvis*, by Will Clemons; *Leaving Readers Behind: The Age of Corporate Newspapering*, by Gene Roberts.

UNIVERSITY OF CALIFORNIA PRESS, 2120 Berkeley Way, Berkeley CA 94720. (510)642-4247. Website: www.ucpress.edu. Director: James H. Clark., Associate Director: Lynne E. Withey. **Acquisitions:** Reed Malcolm, editor (religion); Doris Kretschmer, executive editor (natural history, biology); Deborah Kirshman, editor (art); Kate Toll, editor (classics); Sheila Levine, editorial director (Asian studies, history); Monica McCormick, editor (African studies, American history); Naomi Schneider, executive editor (sociology, politics, gender studies); Blake Edgar, editor (science); Linda Norton, editor (literature, poetry); Stephanie Fay, editor (art); Stan Holwitz, assistant director (anthropology, sociology); Eric Smoodin, editor (film, philosophy); Lynne Withey, associate director (music, Middle Eastern studies). Estab. 1893. Publishes hardcover and paperback originals and reprints. **Publishes 180 titles/year. Offers advance.** Response time varies, depending on the subject. Enclose return postage to queries.
O→ University of California Press publishes mostly hardcover nonfiction written by scholars.
Nonfiction: Subjects include art/architecture, history, language/literature, nature/environment, translation, literary studies, social sciences, natural sciences, some high-level popularizations. No length preference. Query with SASE.
Fiction: Publishes fiction only in translation.
Poetry: Publishes poetry only in translation.
Recent Title(s): *Los Angeles A to Z*, by Leonard and Dale Pitt (reference); *The Transformation of the Roman World*, edited by Leslie Webster and Michelle Brown; *Schubert: The Music and the Man*, by Brian Newbould.

UNIVERSITY OF GEORGIA PRESS, 330 Research Dr., Athens GA 30602-4901. (706)369-6130. Fax: (706)369-6131. E-mail: books@ugapress.uga.edu. Website: www.uga.edu/ugapress. **Acquisitions:** Barbara Ras, executive editor. Estab. 1938. Publishes hardcover originals, trade paperback originals and reprints. **Publishes 85 titles/year. Receives 600 queries/year. 33% of books from first-time authors; 66% from unagented writers. Pays 7-10% royalty on net receipts. Offers rare, varying advance.** Publishes book 1 year after acceptance of ms. Responds in 2 months to queries. Book catalog and ms guidelines for #10 SASE.
Nonfiction: Subjects include government/politics, history (American), nature/environment, regional, environmental studies, literary nonfiction, biography. Query with SASE or submit 1 sample chapter(s), author bio, Reviews artwork/photos as part of ms package. Send if essential to book.
Fiction: Short story collections published in Flannery O'Connor Award Competition. Query #10 SASE for guidelines and submission periods. Charges $15 submission fee.
Poetry: Published only through contemporary poetry series competition. Query first for guidelines and submission periods. Charges $15 submission fee. #10 SASE for guidelines.
Recent Title(s): *Deep in Our Hearts: Nine White Women in the Freedom Movement*, by Connie Curry et al; *As Eve Said to the Serpent: On Landscape, Gender and Art*, by Rebecca Solnit; *Big Bend*, by Bill Roorbach.

UNIVERSITY OF IDAHO PRESS, 16 Brink Hall, Moscow ID 83844-1107. (208)885-6245. Fax: (208)885-9059. E-mail: uipress@uidaho.edu. Website: www.uidaho.edu/~uipress. **Acquisitions:** Ivar Nelson, director. Estab. 1972. Publishes hardcover and trade paperback originals and reprints. **Publishes 8-10 titles/year. Receives 150-250 queries and 25-50 mss/year. 100% from unagented writers. Pays up to 10% royalty on net sales. Offers occasional advance.** Publishes book 1 year after acceptance of ms. Responds in 6 months to queries. Book catalog and ms guidelines free.

Imprints: Idaho Yesterdays; Northwest Naturalist Books; Living the West

> O— Major genre published by the Press include the history of Idaho, the northern Rocky Mountains and the region; the natural history of the same area; Native American culture and history; mining history; Hemingway studies; ecological literary criticism, resource and policy studies; and literature of the region and the West.

Nonfiction: Biography, reference, technical, textbook. Subjects include agriculture/horticulture, Americana, anthropology/archeology, ethnic, history, language/literature, nature/environment, recreation, regional, women's issues/studies, folklore. "Writers should contact us to discuss projects in advance. Be aware of the constraints of scholarly publishing, and avoid submitting queries and manuscripts in areas in which the press doesn't publish." Query with SASE or submit proposal package including sample chapter(s), contents and vita. Reviews artwork/photos as part of ms package. Send photocopies.

Recent Title(s): *For Wood River or Bust*, by Clark E. Spence (nonfiction); *Women on the Run*, by Janet Campbell Hale (fiction).

UNIVERSITY OF ILLINOIS PRESS, 1325 S. Oak St., Champaign IL 61820-6903. (217)333-0950. Fax: (217)244-8082. E-mail: uipress@uiuc.edu. Website: www.press.uillinois.edu. **Acquisitions:** Willis Regier, director; Joan Catapano, associate director and editor-in-chief (women's studies, film, African American studies); Judy McCullon, assistant director (music, folklore, dance); Richard Martin, executive editor (philosophy, architecture). Estab. 1918. Publishes hardcover and trade paperback originals and reprints. **Publishes 150 titles/year. 50% of books from first-time authors; 95% from unagented writers. Pays 0-10% royalty on net receipts. Offers $1,000-1,500 (rarely) advance.** Publishes book 1 year after acceptance of ms. Responds in 1 month to queries. Book catalog for 9×12 SAE with 2 first-class stamps.

> O— University of Illinois Press publishes "scholarly books and serious nonfiction" with a wide range of study interests. Currently emphasizing American history, especially immigration, labor, African American, and military; American religion, music, women's studies, and film.

Nonfiction: Biography, reference, scholarly. Subjects include Americana, animals, cooking/foods/nutrition, government/politics, history (especially American history), language/literature, military/war, music/dance (especially American music), philosophy, regional, sociology, sports, translation, film/cinema/stage. Always looking for "solid, scholarly books in American history, especially social history; books on American popular music, and books in the broad area of American studies." Query with SASE or submit outline.

Fiction: Experimental. Query with SASE.

Recent Title(s): *Thermin: Ether Music and Espionage*, by Albert Glinsky (nonfiction); *Fanny Herself*, by Edna Ferber (fiction); *Songs from Michael Tree*, by Michael Harper (poetry).

Tips: "Serious scholarly books that are broad enough and well-written enough to appeal to nonspecialists are doing well for us in today's market."

UNIVERSITY OF IOWA PRESS, 119 W. Park Rd., Iowa City IA 52242-1000. (319)335-2000. Fax: (319)335-2055. Website: www.uiowa.edu/~uipress. **Acquisitions:** Holly Carver, director; Prasenjit Gupta, acquisitions editor. Estab. 1969. Publishes hardcover and paperback originals. **Publishes 35 titles/year. Receives 300-400 submissions/year. 30% of books from first-time authors; 95% from unagented writers. Pays 7-10% royalty on net receipts.** Publishes book 1 year after acceptance of ms. Responds in within 6 months to queries. Book catalog online; ms guidelines free.

> O— "We publish authoritative, original nonfiction that we market mostly by direct mail to groups with special interests in our titles and by advertising in trade and scholarly publications."

Nonfiction: Subjects include anthropology/archeology, creative nonfiction, history (US autobiography natural), language/literature, nature/environment, American literary studies. Looks for evidence of original research; reliable sources; clarity of organization; complete development of theme with documentation, supportive footnotes and/or bibliography; and a substantive contribution to knowledge in the field treated. Use *Chicago Manual of Style*. Query with SASE or submit outline. Reviews artwork/photos as part of ms package.

Fiction: Currently publishes the Iowa Short Fiction Award selections. Competition guidelines available online.

Poetry: Currently publishes winners of the Iowa Poetry Prize Competition. Competition guidelines available online.

Recent Title(s): *Memoirs of a Cold War Sun*, by Gaines Post, Jr.

Tips: "Developing a series in creative nonfiction."

UNIVERSITY OF MAINE PRESS, 126A College Ave., Orono ME 04473. (207)866-0573. Fax: (207)866-2084. E-mail: umpress@umit.maine.edu. Website: umaine.edu/umpress. **Acquisitions:** Editorial Director. Publishes hardcover and trade paperback originals and reprints. **Publishes 4 titles/year. Receives 50 queries and 25 mss/year. 10% of books from first-time authors; 90% from unagented writers.** Publishes book 1 year after acceptance of ms.

Nonfiction: Subjects include history, regional, science. "We are an academic book publisher, interested in scholarly works on regional history, regional life sciences, Franco-American studies. Authors should be able to articulate their ideas on the potential market for their work." Query with SASE.

Recent Title(s): *Maine Amphibians and Reptiles*, by Hunter, Calhoun, et al.

UNIVERSITY OF MISSOURI PRESS, 2910 LeMone Blvd., Columbia MO 65201. (573)882-7641. Fax: (573)884-4498. Website: www.system.missouri.edu/upress. **Acquisitions:** (Mr.) Clair Willcox, acquisitions editor (literary criticism, short fiction, American history); Maurice Manring acquisitions editor (American history, political philosophy, general nonfiction); Beverly Jarrett, director (intellectual history, women's studies, African-American studies). Estab. 1958. Publishes hardcover and paperback originals and paperback reprints. **Publishes 55 titles/year. Receives 500 submissions/year. 40-50% of books from first-time authors; 90% from unagented writers. Pays up to 10% royalty on net receipts.** Publishes book 1 year after acceptance of ms. immediately to queries. Book catalog free.

　　O→ University of Missouri Press publishes primarily scholarly nonfiction in the humanities and social sciences and also some short fiction collections. Currently emphasizing American history, political philosophy, literary criticism, African-American studies, women's studies. De-emphasizing art history and journalism.

Nonfiction: Scholarly publisher interested in history, literary criticism, political science, journalism, social science, regional works. Subjects include government/politics, history, regional (Missouri and the Midwest). Consult *Chicago Manual of Style*. No mathematics or hard sciences. Query with SASE or submit outline, sample chapter(s).

Fiction: "Collections of short fiction are considered throughout the year; the press does not publish novels. Queries should include sample story, a table of contents and a brief description of the manuscript that notes its length."

Recent Title(s): *Women Escaping Violence*, by Elaine Lawless; *The Voice of America and the Domestic Propaganda Battles 1945-1953*, by David Krugler.

N: UNIVERSITY OF NEBRASKA PRESS, 233 N. 8th St., Lincoln NE 68588-0225. (402)472-3581. Fax: (402)472-0308. E-mail: pressmail@unl.edu. Website: nebraskapress.unl.edu. **Acquisitions:** Gary Dunham, editor-in-chief (Native American studies); Ladette Randolph, acquisitions editor (creative nonfiction); Daniel Ross, director (sports history and culture). Publishes hardcover and trade paperback originals and trade paperback reprints. **Publishes 140 titles/year. Receives 1,000 queries and 100 mss/year. 60% of books from first-time authors; 95% from unagented writers. Pays 5-10% royalty on wholesale price. Offers 500-1,000 advance.** Publishes book 1 year after acceptance of ms. Responds in 1 month to queries and proposals; 2 months to mss. Book catalog and ms guidelines free.

Imprints: Bison Books

Nonfiction: Biography, cookbook, reference, textbook. Subjects include agriculture/horticulture, animals, anthropology/archeology, creative nonfiction, history, memoirs, military/war, multicultural, nature/environment, religion, sports, translation, women's issues/studies, Native American studies. Query with SASE.

Recent Title(s): *Quilting Lessons*, by Janet Berlo (creative nonfiction); *The Midsummer Classic*, by David Vincent (sports); *Sarah Winnemucca*, by Sally Zanjani (Native American memoir).

UNIVERSITY OF NEVADA PRESS, MS 166, Reno NV 89557. (775)784-6573. Fax: (775)784-6200. E-mail: rlatimer@unr.edu, crooms@scs.unr.edu. **Acquisitions:** Ronald Latimer, director (Environmental Arts & Humanities series, western geography); Sandy Crooms, assistant director (western history, mining history, ethnic studies [Western US]); Sara Velez Mallea, editor (Basque Studies). Estab. 1961. Publishes hardcover and paperback originals and reprints. **Publishes 35 titles/year. 20% of books from first-time authors; 99% from unagented writers. Pays 10% royalty on net receipts. Offers advance.** Publishes book 18 months after acceptance of ms. Responds in 2 months to queries. Book catalog and ms guidelines free.

　　O→ "We are the first university press to sustain a sound series on Basque studies—New World and Old World."

Nonfiction: Biography. Subjects include anthropology/archeology, ethnic (studies), history (regional and natural), language/literature, nature/environment, regional (history and geography), current affairs, ethno-nationalism, gambling and gaming, Basque studies. No juvenile books. Submit complete ms. *Writer's Market* recommends a query with SASE first. Reviews artwork/photos as part of ms package. Send photocopies.

Recent Title(s): *Down by the Lemonade Springs: Essays on Wallace Stegner*, by Jackson J. Benson; *Travels with My Royal: A Memoir of the Writing Life*, by Robert Laxalt; *Flight and Other Stories*, by Jose Skinner.

UNIVERSITY OF NEW MEXICO PRESS, 1720 Lomas Blvd. NE, Albuquerque NM 87131-1591. (505)277-2346. E-mail: unmpress@unm.edu. **Acquisitions:** Evelyn Schlater, acquisitions (anthropology, archaeology, multicultural); David Holtby, acquisitions editor (history, Latin America); Dawn Hall, managing editor. Estab. 1929. Publishes hardcover originals and trade paperback originals and reprints. **Publishes 70 titles/year. Receives 600 submissions/year. 12% of books from first-time authors; 90% from unagented writers. Pays variable royalty. Offers advance.** *Writer's Market* recommends allowing 2 months for reply to queries. Book catalog free.

　　O→ "The Press is well known as a publisher in the fields of anthropology, archeology, Latin American studies, photography, architecture and the history and culture of the American West, fiction, some poetry, Chicano/a studies and works by and about American Indians."

Nonfiction: Biography, children's/juvenile, illustrated book, multimedia, scholarly. Subjects include Americana, anthropology/archeology, art/architecture, creative nonfiction, ethnic, gardening, gay/lesbian, government/politics, history, language/literature, memoirs, military/war, multicultural, music/dance, nature/environment, photography, regional, religion, science, spirituality, translation, travel, women's issues/studies, contemporary culture, film/cinema/stage, true crime, New Age, general nonfiction. "No how-to, humor, juvenile, self-help, software, technical or textbooks." Query with SASE. Reviews artwork/photos as part of ms package. Send photocopies.

Recent Title(s): *Going Native*, by Tom Harmer; *Vanishing Point*, by Judith van Gieson.

N: THE UNIVERSITY OF NORTH CAROLINA PRESS, P.O. Box 2288, Chapel Hill NC 27515-2288. (919)966-3561. Fax: (919)966-3829. E-mail: uncpress@unc.edu. Website: www.uncpress.unc.edu. **Acquisitions:** Kate Torrey, director (women's history, gender studies); David Perry, editor-in-chief (regional trade, Civil War); Charles Grench, senior editor (American history, European history, law and legal studies, business and economic history, classics, political or social science); Elaine Maisner, editor (Latin American studies, religious studies, anthropology, regional trade, folklore); Sian Hunter, editor (literary studies, American studies, African American studies, social medicine, Appalachian studies, media studies); Mark Simpson-Vos, associate editor (electronic press). Publises hardcover originals, trade paperback originals and reprints. **Publishes 90 titles/year. Receives 300 queries and 200 mss/year. 50% of books from first-time authors; 98% from unagented writers. Pays 5-15% royalty on wholesale price. Offers $1,000-10,000 advance.** Publishes book 1 year after acceptance of ms. Responds in 3 weeks to queries; 2 weeks to proposals and mss. Book catalog and ms guidelines online.

O→ "UNC Press publishes nonfiction books for academic and general audiences. We have a special interest in trade and scholarly titles about our region. We do not, however, publish memoirs of living persons or festshriften.

Nonfiction: Biography, cookbook, multimedia (CD-ROM). Subjects include Americana, anthropology/archeology, art/architecture, cooking/foods/nutrition, gardening, government/politics, health/medicine, history, language/literature, military/war, multicultural, music/dance, nature/environment, philosophy, photography, regional, religion, translation, African American studies, American studies, cultural studies, Latin American studies, media studies, gender studies, social medicine, Appalachian studies. Submit proposal package including outline, c.v., cover letter, abstract, and table of contents. Reviews artwork/photos as part of ms package. Send photocopies.

UNIVERSITY OF NORTH TEXAS PRESS, P.O. Box 311336, Denton TX 76203-1336. Fax: (940)565-4590. E-mail: rchrisman@unt.edu or kdevinney@unt.edu. Website: www.unt.edu/untpress. Director: Ronald Chrisman. **Acquisitions:** Karen DeVinney, managing editor. Estab. 1987. Publishes hardcover and trade paperback originals and reprints. **Publishes 15-20 titles/year. Receives 500 queries and and mss/year. 95% from unagented writers. Pays 7½-10% royalty on net receipts.** Publishes book 2 years after acceptance of ms. Responds in 3 months to queries. Book catalog for 8½×11 SASE.

O→ We are dedicated to producing the highest quality scholarly, academic and general interest books. We are committed to serving all peoples by publishing stories of their cultures and experiences that have been overlooked. Currently emphasizing military history, Texas history and Texas literature. De-emphasizing memoirs and fiction.

Nonfiction: Subjects include agriculture/horticulture, Americana, ethnic, government/politics, history, language/literature, military/war, nature/environment, regional, women's issues/studies. Query with SASE. Reviews artwork/photos as part of ms package. Send photocopies.

Poetry: The only poetry we publish is the winner of the Vassar Miller Prize in Poetry, an annual, national competition with a $1,000 prize and publication of the winning manuscript each fall. Query.

Recent Title(s): *The Best of Helen Corbitt's Kitchens* (cookbook); *Combat Chaplain* (military).

Tips: "We publish series called War and the Southwest; Texas Folklore Society Publications; the Western Life Series; Literary Biographies of Texas Writers."

UNIVERSITY OF OKLAHOMA PRESS, 1005 Asp Ave., Norman OK 73019-6051. (405)325-2000. Fax: (405)325-4000. E-mail: oupress@ou.edu. Website: www.ou.edu/oupress. **Acquisitions:** Chuck Rankin, editor-in-chief (American Indian studies, Latin American studies, Mesoamerican studies); Jean Hurtado, acquisitions editor (political science, women's studies); Daniel Simon, acquisitions editor (literary studies, paperbacks, military history); JoAnn Reece, acquisitions editor (American Indian studies). Estab. 1928. Publishes hardcover and paperback originals and reprints. **Publishes 100 titles/year. Standard royalty for comparable books. Offers advance.** Publishes book 18 months after acceptance of ms. Responds in 3 months to queries. Book catalog for $1 and 9×12 SAE with 6 first-class stamps.

Imprints: Red River Books (paperbacks), Plains Reprints

O→ University of Oklahoma Press publishes books for both a scholarly and general audience.

Nonfiction: Subjects include Americana, ethnic, government/politics, history (natural, military), language/literature, military/war (history), regional (Western US history), science (political), women's issues/studies, American Indian studies, literary theory, classical studies, Mesoamerican studies. No unsolicited poetry or fiction. Query with SASE or submit outline, 1-2 sample chapter(s), résumé. Use *Chicago Manual of Style* for ms guidelines. Reviews artwork/photos as part of ms package.

Recent Title(s): *I Hear the Train*, by Louis Owens (American Indian literature); *Frontier Children*, by Linda Peavy and Ursula Smith (western history).

UNIVERSITY OF PENNSYLVANIA PRESS, 4200 Pine St., Philadelphia PA 19104-4011. (215)898-6261. Fax: (215)898-0404. Website: www.upenn.edu/pennpress. Director: Eric Halpern. **Acquisitions:** Jerome Singerman, humanities editor; Walda Metcalf and Peter Agree, social sciences editors; Jo Joslyn, art and architecture editor; Robert Lockhart, history editor. Estab. 1890. Publishes hardcover and paperback originals and reprints. **Publishes 75 titles/year. Receives 1,000 submissions/year. 10-20% of books from first-time authors; 95% from unagented writers. Royalty determined on book-by-book basis. Offers advance.** Publishes book 10 months after delivery of ms after acceptance of ms. Responds in 3 months to queries. Book catalog online.

Nonfiction: "Serious books that serve the scholar and the professional, student and general reader." Subjects include Americana, anthropology/archeology, art/architecture, business/economics, history (American, art), language/literature, sociology, literary criticism, cultural studies, ancient studies, medieval studies. Follow the *Chicago Manual of Style. No unsolicited mss.* Query with SASE or submit outline, résumé. Reviews artwork/photos as part of ms package. Send photocopies.

Recent Title(s): *The London Monster*, by Patricia Tyson Stroud.

N: UNIVERSITY OF SCRANTON PRESS, University of Scranton, Linden and Monroe, Scranton PA 18510-4660. (570)941-4228. Fax: (570)941-4309. E-mail: richard.rousseau@scranton.edu. Website: www.scrantonpress.com. **Acquisitions:** Richard Rousseau, director. Estab. 1981. Publishes paperback originals. **Publishes 5 titles/year. Receives 200 queries and 45 mss/year. 60% of books from first-time authors; 100% from unagented writers. Pays 10% royalty.** Publishes book within 1 year after acceptance of ms. Book catalog and ms guidelines free.
Imprints: Ridge Row Press

O— The University of Scranton Press, a member of the Association of Jesuit University Presses, publishes primarily scholarly monographs in theology, philosophy, and the culture and history of northeast Pennsylvania.

Nonfiction: Looking for clear editorial focus: theology/religious studies; philosophy/philosophy of religion; scholarly treatments; the culture of northeast Pennsylvania. Scholarly monographs. Subjects include art/architecture, language/literature, philosophy, regional, religion, sociology. Query with SASE or submit outline, 2 sample chapter(s).
Poetry: Only poetry related to northeast Pennsylvania.
Recent Title(s): *Listen to Voices from the Sea*, translated by M. Yamanouchi and J. Quinn (Japanese translation).

UNIVERSITY OF SOUTH CAROLINA PRESS, 937 Assembly St., Carolina Plaza, 8th Floor, Columbia SC 29208. (803)777-5243. Fax: (803)777-0160. Website: www.sc.edu/uscpress. **Acquisitions:** Linda Fogle, assistant director (trade books); Barry Blose, acquisitions editor (literature, religious studies, rhetoric, communication, social work); Alexander Moore, acquisitions editor (history, regional studies). Estab. 1944. Publishes hardcover originals, trade paperback originals and reprints. **Publishes 50-55 titles/year. Receives 1,000 queries and 250 mss/year. 30% of books from first-time authors; 95% from unagented writers.** Publishes book 12-15 months after acceptance of ms. Accepts simultaneous submissions. Responds in 3 months to mss. Book catalog and ms guidelines free.

O— "We focus on scholarly monographs and regional trade books of lasting merit."

Nonfiction: Biography, illustrated book, monograph. Subjects include art/architecture, history (American, Civil War, culinary, maritime, women's), language/literature, regional, religion, world affairs, rhetoric, communication. "Do not submit entire unsolicited manuscripts or projects with limited scholarly value." Query with SASE or submit proposal package and outline and 1 sample chapter and résumé with SASE. Reviews artwork/photos as part of ms package. Send photocopies.
Recent Title(s): *Crossing the Color Line: Readings in Black and White*, edited by Suzanne W. Jones; *Heaven Is a Beautiful Place: A Memoir of the South Carolina Coast*, by Genevieve C. Peterkin in conjunction with William P. Baldwin.

THE UNIVERSITY OF TENNESSEE PRESS, 110 Conference Center, Knoxville TN 37996-4108. (865)974-3321. Fax: (865)974-3724. E-mail: utpress2@utk.edu. Website: www.sunsite.utk.edu/utpress/. **Acquisitions:** Joyce Harrison, acquisitions editor (scholarly books); Jennifer Siler, director (regional trades, fiction). Estab. 1940. **Publishes 30 titles/year. Receives 450 submissions/year. 35% of books from first-time authors; 99% from unagented writers. Pays negotiable royalty on net receipts.** Book catalog for 12×x16 SAE with 2 first-class stamps; ms guidelines for #10 SASE.

O— "Our mission is to stimulate scientific and scholarly research in all fields; to channel such studies, either in scholarly or popular form, to a larger number of people; and to extend the regional leadership of the University of Tennessee by stimulating research projects within the South and by non-university authors."

Nonfiction: American studies only. Subjects include Americana, anthropology/archeology (historical), art/architecture (vernacular), ethnic, history, language/literature, regional, religion (history sociology, anthropology, biography only), women's issues/studies, African-American studies, Appalachian studies, folklore/folklife, material culture. Prefers "scholarly treatment and a readable style. Authors usually have Ph.D.s." Submissions in other fields, and submissions of poetry, textbooks, plays and translations are not invited. Submit outline, 2 sample chapter(s), author bio. Reviews artwork/photos as part of ms package.
Fiction: Query with SASE or submit synopsis, author bio.
Recent Title(s): *Blood Feud*, by Annabel Thomas (fiction).
Tips: "Our market is in several groups: scholars; educated readers with special interests in given scholarly subjects; and the general educated public interested in Tennessee, Appalachia and the South. Not all our books appeal to all these groups, of course, but any given book must appeal to at least one of them."

UNIVERSITY OF TEXAS PRESS, P.O. Box 7819, Austin TX 78713-7819. (512)471-7233. Fax: (512)252-7178. E-mail: utpress@uts.cc.utexas.edu. Website: www.utexas.edu/utpress/. **Acquisitions:** Theresa May, assistant director/executive editor (social sciences, Latin American studies); James Burr, acquisition editor (humanities, classics); William Bishel (sciences). Estab. 1952. **Publishes 90 titles/year. Receives 1,000 submissions/year. 50% of books from first-time authors; 99% from unagented writers. Pays royalty on net receipts. Offers occasional advance.** Publishes book 18 months after acceptance of ms. Responds in 3 months to queries. Book catalog and ms guidelines free.

O⟶ "In addition to publishing the results of advanced research for scholars worldwide, UT Press has a special obligation to the people of its state to publish authoritative books on Texas. We do not publish fiction or poetry, except for some Latin American and Middle Eastern literature in translation."

Nonfiction: Biography. Subjects include anthropology/archeology, art/architecture, ethnic, film/cinema/stage, history, language/literature, nature/environment, regional, science, translation, women's issues/studies, natural history; American, Latin American, Native American, Chicano and Middle Eastern studies; classics and the ancient world, film, contemporary regional architecture, geography, ornithology, biology, linguistics. Also uses specialty titles related to Texas and the Southwest, national trade titles and regional trade titles. Query with SASE or submit outline, 2 sample chapter(s). Reviews artwork/photos as part of ms package.

Fiction: Latin American and Middle Eastern translation. No poetry.

Recent Title(s): *American Films of the '70s*, by Peter Lev; *Places for Dead Bodies*, by Gary Hausladen.

Tips: "It's difficult to make a manuscript over 400 double-spaced pages into a feasible book. Authors should take special care to edit out extraneous material. We look for sharply focused, in-depth treatments of important topics."

UNIVERSITY PRESS OF COLORADO, 5589 Arapahoe, Suite 206C, Boulder CO 80303. (720)406-8849. Fax: (720)406-3443. Director: Darrin Pratt. **Acquisitions:** David Archer, assistant editor. Estab. 1965. Publishes hardcover and paperback originals. **Publishes 15-20 titles/year. Receives 1,000 submissions/year. 50% of books from first-time authors; 95% from unagented writers. Pays 5-15% royalty on net receipts. Offers advance.** Publishes book 2 years after acceptance of ms. Responds in 6 months to queries. Book catalog free.

O⟶ "We are a university press that publishes scholarly nonfiction in the disciplines of the American West, Native American studies, archeology, environmental studies and regional interest titles." Currently de-emphasizing fiction, poetry, biography.

Nonfiction: Scholarly. Subjects include nature/environment, regional. Length: 250-500 pages. Query with SASE. Reviews artwork/photos as part of ms package.

Recent Title(s): *Sacred Objects and Sacred Places*, by Andrew Gulliford; *Exotic Deviance*, by Robert E. Bartholomew.

Tips: "We have series on the Women's West and on Mesoamerican worlds."

UNIVERSITY PRESS OF KANSAS, 2501 W. 15th St., Lawrence KS 66049-3905. (785)864-4154. Fax: (785)864-4586. E-mail: mail@newpress.upress.ukans.edu. Website: www.kansaspress.ku.edu. **Acquisitions:** Michael J. Briggs, editor-in-chief (military history, political science, law); Nancy Scott Jackson, acquisitions editor (western history, American studies, environmental studies, women's studies, philosophy); Fred M. Woodward, director, (political science, presidency, regional). Estab. 1946. Publishes hardcover originals, trade paperback originals and reprints. **Publishes 50 titles/year. Receives 600 queries/year. 20% of books from first-time authors; 98% from unagented writers. Pays 5-15% royalty on net receipts. Offers selective advance.** Publishes book 10 months after acceptance of ms. Responds in 1 month to proposals. Book catalog and ms guidelines free.

O⟶ The University Press of Kansas publishes scholarly books that advance knowledge and regional books that contribute to the understanding of Kansas, the Great Plains and the Midwest. Currently emphasizing military history.

Nonfiction: Biography. Subjects include Americana, anthropology/archeology, government/politics, history, military/war, nature/environment, philosophy, regional, sociology, women's issues/studies. "We are looking for books on topics of wide interest based on solid scholarship and written for both specialists and informed general readers. Do not send unsolicited complete manuscripts." Submit outline, sample chapter(s), cover letter, cv, prospectus. Reviews artwork/photos as part of ms package. Send photocopies.

Recent Title(s): *States' Rights and the Union: Imperium in Imperio*, by Forrest McDonald.

UNIVERSITY PRESS OF KENTUCKY, 663 S. Limestone, Lexington KY 40508-4008. (859)257-2951. Fax: (859)323-1873. Website: www.kentuckypress.com. **Acquisitions:** Kenneth Cherry, director and editor. Estab. 1943. Publishes hardcover and paperback originals and reprints. **Publishes 60 titles/year. Royalty varies.** Publishes book 1 year after acceptance of ms. Responds in 2 months to queries. Book catalog free.

O⟶ "We are a scholarly publisher, publishing chiefly for an academic and professional audience, as well as books about Kentucky, the upper South, Appalachia, and the Ohio Valley."

Nonfiction: Biography, reference, monographs. Subjects include Americana, ethnic, history (American), language/literature, military/war (history), regional, women's issues/studies, film studies, American and African-American studies, folklore, Kentuckiana and regional books, Appalachian studies. "No textbooks, genealogical material, lightweight popular treatments, how-to books or books unrelated to our major areas of interest. The Press does not consider original works of fiction or poetry." Query with SASE.

Recent Title(s): *Encyclopedia of Louisville*, edited by John Kleber; *Rare Birds*, by Dan Bessie.

UNIVERSITY PRESS OF MISSISSIPPI, 3825 Ridgewood Rd., Jackson MS 39211-6492. (601)432-6205. Fax: (601)432-6217. E-mail: press@ihl.state.ms.us. **Acquisitions:** Craig Gill, editor-in-chief (regional studies, anthropology, military history); Seetha Srinivasan, director (art, literature). Estab. 1970. Publishes hardcover and paperback originals and reprints. **Publishes 60 titles/year. Receives 750 submissions/year. 20% of books from first-time authors; 90% from unagented writers. Competitive royalties and terms. Offers advance.** Publishes book 1 year after acceptance of ms. Responds in 3 months to queries. Book catalog for 9×12 SAE with 3 first-class stamps.

Imprints: Muscadine Books (regional trade), Banner Books (literary reprints)

O— "University Press of Mississippi publishes scholarly and trade titles, as well as special series, including: American Made Music; Conversations with Public Intellectuals; Interviews with Film Makers; Faulkner and Yoknapatawpha; Fiction Series; Folk Art and Artists; Folklife in the South; Literary Conversations; Natural History; Performance Studies; Studies in Popular Culture; Understanding Health and Sickness; Writers and Their Work."

Nonfiction: Biography. Subjects include Americana, art/architecture, ethnic (minority studies), government/politics, health/medicine, history, language/literature, music/dance, photography, regional (Southern), folklife, literary criticism, popular culture with scholarly emphasis, literary studies. "We prefer a proposal that describes the significance of the work and a chapter outline." Submit outline, sample chapter(s).

Fiction: Commissioned trade editions by prominent writers.

Recent Title(s): *German Boy: A Refugee's Story*, by Wolfgang W.E. Samuel; *Kangaroo Hollow*, by Thomas Hal Phillips.

UNIVERSITY PRESS OF NEW ENGLAND, 23 S. Main St., Hanover NH 03755-2048. (603)643-7100. Fax: (603)643-1540. E-mail: university.press@dartmouth.edu. Website: www.upne.com. Director: Richard Abel. **Acquisitions:** Phil Pochoda, editorial director (American/northeastern studies, fiction, biography, cultural studies); Phyllis Deutsch, editor (Jewish studies, art, biography, American studies, French studies); Ellen Wicklum, assistant editor (nature, American/regional studies). Estab. 1970. Publishes hardcover and trade paperback originals, trade paperback reprints. **Publishes 75-80 titles/year. Pays standard royalty. Offers occasional advance.** Responds in 2 months to queries. Book catalog and ms guidelines for 9×12 SASE and 5 first-class stamps.

O— "University Press of New England is a consortium of university presses. Some books—those published for one of the consortium members—carry the joint imprint of New England and the member: Dartmouth, Brandeis, Tufts, University of New Hampshire and Middlebury College. We publish academic studies for an academic audience (mostly American studies and Jewish studies) as well as nonfiction aimed at the educated reader/intellectual. We also encourage regional (New England) work (academic, fiction, poetry or otherwise)." Currently emphasizing American studies, cultural studies. De-emphasizing fiction.

Nonfiction: Biography. Subjects include Americana (New England), art/architecture, music/dance, nature/environment, regional (New England), American studies, Jewish studies, performance studies. No festschriften, unrevised doctoral dissertations, or symposium collections. Submit outline, 1-2 sample chapter(s). No electronic submissions.

Fiction: Only New England novels and reprints.

Recent Title(s): *Hard Bottom*, by G.F. Michelson (fiction); *Generation Exodus: The Fate of Young Jewish Refugees from Nazi Germany.*

THE URBAN LAND INSTITUTE, 1025 Thomas Jefferson St. NW, Washington DC 20007-5201. (202)624-7000. Fax: (202)624-7140. E-mail: rlevit@uli.org. Website: www.uli.org. **Acquisitions:** Rachelle Levitt, senior vice president/publisher. Estab. 1936. Publishes hardcover and trade paperback originals. **Publishes 15-20 titles/year. Receives 20 submissions/year. 2% of books from first-time authors; 100% from unagented writers. Pays 10% royalty on gross sales. Offers $1,500-2,000 advance.** Publishes book 6 months after acceptance of ms. Book catalog and ms. guidelines online or 9×12 SAE.

O— The Urban Land Institute publishes technical books on real estate development and land planning.

Nonfiction: Technical. Subjects include money/finance. "The majority of manuscripts are created inhouse by research staff. We acquire two or three outside authors to fill schedule and subject areas where our list has gaps. We are not interested in real estate sales, brokerages, appraisal, making money in real estate, opinion, personal point of view, or mauscripts negative toward growth and development." Query with SASE. Reviews artwork/photos as part of ms package.

Recent Title(s): *Active Adult Retirement Communities.*

UTAH STATE UNIVERSITY PRESS, 7800 Old Main Hill, Logan UT 84322-7800. (435)797-1362. Fax: (435)797-0313. Website: www.usu.edu/usupress. **Acquisitions:** Michael Spooner, director (composition, poetry); John Alley, editor (history, folklore, fiction). Estab. 1972. Publishes hardcover and trade paperback originals and reprints. **Publishes 18 titles/year. Receives 250 submissions/year. 8% of books from first-time authors. Pays royalty on net receipts.** Publishes book 18 months after acceptance of ms. Responds in 1 month to queries. Book catalog free; ms guidelines online.

O— Utah State University Press publishes scholarly works in the academic areas noted below. Currently interested in book-length scholarly manuscripts dealing with folklore studies, composition studies, Native American studies and history.

Nonfiction: Biography, reference, textbook. Subjects include history (of the West), regional, folklore, the West, Native American studies, studies in composition and rhetoric. Query with SASE. Reviews artwork/photos as part of ms package. Send photocopies.

Recent Title(s): *World Views and the American West*, edited by Polly Stewart, et al; *Sagwitch*, by Scott R. Christensen; *Mine Work*, by Jim Davidson (fiction).

Tips: Utah State University Press also sponsors the annual May Swenson Poetry Award.

N̈ VAN DER PLAS PUBLICATIONS, 1282 Seventh Ave., San Francisco CA 94122-2526. (415)665-8214. Fax: (415)753-8572. **Acquisitions:** Rob van der Plas, publisher/editor. Estab. 1997. Publishes hardcover and trade paperback

originals. **Publishes 6 titles/year. Receives 15 submissions/year. 10% of books from first-time authors; 100% from unagented writers. Pays 12% royalty on net receipts.** Publishes book an average of 1 year after acceptance of ms. Accepts simultaneous submissions. Responds in 3 months to queries. Book catalog and ms guidelines for #10 SASE.
Nonfiction: How-to, technical. Subjects include recreation, sports, travel. Submit complete ms. Reviews artwork/photos as part of ms package.
Recent Title(s): *Lance Armstrong's Comeback from Cancer*; *Buying a Manufactured Home.*
Tips: "Writers have a good chance selling us books with better and more illustrations and a systematic treatment of the subject. First check what is on the market and ask yourself whether you are writing something that is not yet available and wanted."

VANDAMERE PRESS, AB Associates International, Inc., P.O. Box 17446, Clearwater FL 33762. (727)556-0950. Fax: (727)556-2560. **Acquisitions:** Jerry Frank, senior acquistions editor. Estab. 1984. Publishes hardcover and trade paperback originals and reprints. **Publishes 8-15 titles/year. Receives 750 queries and 2,000 mss/year. 25% of books from first-time authors; 90% from unagented writers. Pays royalty on revenues generated. Offers advance.** Publishes book 1-3 years after acceptance of ms. Accepts simultaneous submissions. Responds in 6 months to queries.
   O—¬ Vandamere publishes high-quality work with solid, well-documented research and minimum author/political bias.
Nonfiction: Biography, coffee table book, illustrated book, reference. Subjects include Americana, education, health/medicine, history, military/war, photography, regional (Washington D.C./Mid-Atlantic), women's issues/studies, disability/healthcare issues. No New Age. Submit outline, 2-3 sample chapter(s). Send photocopies.
Fiction: Adventure, erotica, humor, mystery, suspense. Submit 5-10 sample chapter(s), synopsis.
Recent Title(s): *Unheralded Victory*, by Mark Woodruff (nonfiction); *Cry Me a River*, by Patricia Hagan (fiction).
Tips: "Authors who can provide endorsements from significant published writers, celebrities, etc., will *always* be given serious consideration. Clean, easy-to-read, *dark* copy is essential. Patience in waiting for replies is essential. All unsolicited work is looked at, but at certain times of the year our review schedule will stop. No response without SASE."

VANDERBILT UNIVERSITY PRESS, Box 1813, Station B, Nashville TN 37235. (615)322-3585. Fax: (615)343-8823. E-mail: vupress@vanderbilt.edu. Website: www.vanderbilt.edu/vupress. **Acquisitions:** Michael Amos, director. Publishes hardcover originals and trade paperback originals and reprints. **Publishes 20-25 titles/year. Receives 500 queries/year. 25% of books from first-time authors; 90% from unagented writers. Pays 8% royalty on net receipts. Offers rare advance.** Publishes book 10 months after acceptance of ms. Responds in 3 weeks to proposals. Book catalog free.
   ● Also distributes for and co-publishes Country Music Foundaiton.
   O—¬ "Vanderbilt University Press publishes books on health care, social sciences, education and regional studies, for both academic and general audiences that are intellectually significant, socially relevant and of practical importance."
Nonfiction: Biography, textbook, scholarly. Subjects include Americana, anthropology/archeology, education, ethnic, government/politics, health/medicine, history, language/literature, multicultural, music/dance, nature/environment, philosophy, women's issues/studies. Submit prospectus, sample chapter, cv. Reviews artwork/photos as part of ms package. Send photocopies.
Recent Title(s): *A Good-Natured Riot: The Birth of the Grand Ole Opry*, by Charles K. Wolfe.
Tips: "Our audience consists of scholars and educated general readers."

VENTURE PUBLISHING, INC., 1999 Cato Ave., State College PA 16801. (814)234-4561. Fax: (814)234-1561. E-mail: vpublish@venturepublish.com. Website: www.venturepublish.com. **Acquisitions:** Geof Godbey, editor. Estab. 1979. Publishes hardcover and paperback originals and reprints. **Publishes 10-12 titles/year. Receives 50 queries and 20 mss/year. 40% of books from first-time authors; 100% from unagented writers. Pays royalty on wholesale price. Offers advance.** Publishes book 9 months after acceptance of ms. Responds in 1 month to queries; 2 months to proposals and mss. Book catalog and ms guidelines for SASE or online.
   O—¬ Venture Publishing produces quality educational publications, also workbooks for professionals, educators, and students in the fields of recreation, parks, leisure studies, therapeutic recreation and long term care.
Nonfiction: Textbook, college academic, professional. Subjects include nature/environment (outdoor recreation management and leadership texts), recreation, sociology (leisure studies), long-term care nursing homes, therapeutic recreation. "Textbooks and books for recreation activity leaders high priority." Submit outline, 1 sample chapter(s).
Recent Title(s): *Adventure Programming*, edited by John Miles and Simon Priest; *Leisure in Your Life*, by Geof Godbey.

VERSO, 180 Varick St., 10th Floor, New York NY 10014. (212)807-9680. Fax: (212)807-9152. E-mail: versoinc@aol.com. Website: www.versobooks.com. **Acquisitions:** Colin Robinson, managing director. Estab. 1970. Publishes hardcover and trade paperback originals. **Publishes 40-60 titles/year. Receives 300 queries and 150 mss/year. 10% of books from first-time authors; 95% from unagented writers. Pays royalty. Offers advance.** Publishes book 1 year after acceptance of ms. Accepts simultaneous submissions. Responds in 5 months to queries. Book catalog free.
   O—¬ "Our books cover economics, politics, cinema studies, and history (among other topics), but all come from a critical, Leftist viewpoint, on the border between trade and academic."

Nonfiction: Illustrated book. Subjects include business/economics, government/politics, history, philosophy, sociology, women's issues/studies. "We are loosely affiliated with *New Left Review* (London). We are not interested in academic monographs." Submit proposal package including 1 sample chapter(s).
Recent Title(s): *Late Victorian Holocausts*, by Mike Davis.

VGM CAREER BOOKS, NTC/Contemporary Publishing Group, 4255 W. Touhy Ave., Lincolnwood IL 60712. (847)679-5500. Fax: (847)679-2494. **Acquisitions:** Denise Betts. Estab. 1963. Publishes hardcover and paperback originals. **Publishes 35 titles/year. Receives 50-100 submissions/year. 15% of books from first-time authors; 95% from unagented writers. Pays royalty or makes outright purchase. Offers $1,000-5,000 advance.** Publishes book 1 year after acceptance of ms. Accepts simultaneous submissions. Responds in 3 months to queries. Book catalog and ms guidelines for 9×12 SAE with 5 first-class stamps.
   O— VGM publishes career-focused titles for job seekers, career planners, job changers, students and adults in education and trade markets.
Nonfiction: Textbook, general trade. Subjects include business/economics, health/medicine, nature/environment. Query with SASE or submit outline, sample chapter(s).
Recent Title(s): *Career Change*, by Dr. David P. Helfand.
Tips: VGM also hires revision authors to handle rewrites and new editions of existing titles.

N VIA DOLOROSA PRESS, 701 E. Schaaf Rd., Cleveland OH 44131. (216)459-0896. Fax: (216)459-0896. E-mail: hyacinthe@disinfo.net. Website: www.angelfire.com/oh2/dolorosa/. **Acquisitions:** Hyacinthe L. Raven, editor. Estab. 1994. Publishes mostly chapbooks, some trade paperbacks. **Publishes 2-10 titles/year. Receives 100 queries and 60 mss/year. 25% of books from first-time authors; 100% from unagented writers. Pays 25% royalty and 10% of first print run.** Publishes book 3 months after acceptance of ms. Responds in 1 month to queries, proposals and mss. Book catalog online.
   O— We are a small press, and publish chapbooks and chapbook-sized works. VDP concentrates on helping those who are suicidal and depressed by publishing works of catharsis. All works we publish are dark, painful, anguished. Currently emphasizing scholarly nonfiction, essays and literary criticism.
Nonfiction: Biography, reference, self-help, textbook, essays, literary criticism. Subjects include creative nonfiction, education, gay/lesbian (if they adhere to our theme), history, language/literature, memoirs, multicultural, philosophy, religion, spirituality, translation, contemporary culture (alternative, college-aged youth). "Write to us for our guidelines; they spell out exactly what we will and won't accept." Submit complete ms. Reviews artwork/photos as part of ms package. Send photocopies.
Fiction: Confession, experimental, historical, literary, plays, poetry, poetry in translation, short story collections, philosophical. "Consider and examine our influences: Albert Camus, Par Lagerkvist, Nathanael West. If you think someone who likes those writers would like your work, then submit it." Submit complete ms.
Poetry: Because of our theme, it is essential to request our submission guidelines. We also greatly suggest ordering a book or journal to see the style we prefer. Submit complete ms.
Recent Title(s): *The Cross*, by Paola Sorrentino (history/religion); *Lacrymosa Dies Illa*, by Hyacinthe L. Raven (short stories); *Seasons of Rust*, by John Sweet (free verse poetry).
Tips: Our audience is college-aged/educated adults. Many readers of ours prefer counter-culture styles, music and ideologies, and they are particularly in the Goth scene. Check out our background. We are strict about our theme and style. All of the work we print has a dark nature and we insist that writers send only introspective, personal works. We are not a Christian publisher and will not accept works which glorify any particular religion. No fax or e-mail submissions."

A VIKING, Penguin Putnam Inc., 375 Hudson St., New York NY 10014. (212)366-2000. Publisher: Clare Ferraro. Publishes hardcover and trade paperback originals. **Pays royalty. Offers advance.** Publishes book 1 year after acceptance of ms. Accepts simultaneous submissions. Responds in 6 months to queries.
   O— Viking publishes a mix of academic and popular fiction and nonfiction.
Nonfiction: Biography. Subjects include business/economics, child guidance/parenting, cooking/foods/nutrition, health/medicine, history, language/literature, music/dance, philosophy, women's issues/studies. *Accepts agented submissions only.*
Fiction: Literary, mainstream/contemporary, mystery, suspense. *Accepts agented submissions only.*
Recent Title(s): *A Common life*, by Jan Karon (novel); *A Day Late and a Dollar Short*, by Terry McMillan (novel); *In the Heart of the Sea*, by Nathaniel Philbrick (National Book Award winner).

VIKING CHILDREN'S BOOKS, Penguin Putnam Inc., 345 Hudson St., New York NY 10014. (212)366-2000. Regina Hayes, president/publisher. **Acquisitions:** Melanie Cecka, Elizabeth Law. Publishes hardcover originals. **Publishes 80 titles/year. Receives 7,500 queries/year. 25% of books from first-time authors; 33% from unagented writers. Pays 10% royalty on retail price. Offers negotiable advance.** Publishes book 1 year after acceptance of ms. Responds in 4 months to queries.
   O— Viking Children's Books publishes high-quality trade books for children including fiction, nonfiction, picture books and novelty books for pre-schoolers through young adults.
Nonfiction: Children's/juvenile. Query with SASE or submit outline, 3 sample chapter(s), SASE.
Fiction: Juvenile, picture books, young adult. Submit complete ms. for novels, picture books, chapter books with SASE.

Recent Title(s): *Joseph Had a Little Overcoat*, by Simms Taback; *Someone Like You*, by Sarah Dessen.

VIKING STUDIO, Penguin Putnam, Inc., 375 Hudson St., New York NY 10014. (212)366-2000. Fax: (212)366-2011. Website: www.penguinputnam.com. **Acquisitions:** Christopher Sweet, executive editor (art, music, history, photography, fashion, religion), Cyril Nelson, senior editor (arts & crafts, decorative arts). Publishes hardcover originals. **Publishes 35-40 titles/year. Pays royalty. Offers advance.** Responds in 2 months to queries.

    ○→ Viking publishes high production value, quality designed books on subjects of mainstream interest that allow a compelling visual treatment. Currently emphasizing reference, history, religion.

Nonfiction: Subjects include Americana, art/architecture, hobbies, philosophy, photography, New Age/metaphysics, popular culture, fashion, astrology. Reviews artwork/photos as part of ms package. Send photocopies.

Recent Title(s): *Vanity Fair's Hollywood*; *Martin Luther King*.

A **VILLARD BOOKS**, Random House, 299 Park Ave., New York NY 10171-0002. (212)572-2600. Website: www.at random.com. Publisher: Ann Godoff. Estab. 1983. Publishes hardcover and trade paperback originals. **Publishes 55-60 titles/year. 5% from unagented writers. Pays negotiable royalty. Offers negotiable advance.** Accepts simultaneous submissions.

    ○→ "Villard Books is the publisher of savvy and sometimes quirky bestseller hardcovers and trade paperbacks."

Nonfiction: Subjects include general, commercial nonfiction. *Accepts agented submissions only.*

Fiction: Commercial fiction. *Accepts agented submissions only.*

Recent Title(s): *Never Die Easy*, by Walter Payton; *The Truth Is*, by Melissa Etheridge.

N: A **VINTAGE ANCHOR PUBLISHING**, Knopf Publishing Group, Random House Inc., 299 Park Ave., New York NY 10171. Website: www.randomhouse.com. Vice President: LuAnn Walther. Editor-in-Chief: Martin Asher. **Acquisitions:** Submissions Department. Publishes trade paperback originals and reprints. **Publishes 200 titles/year. Receives 700 queries/year. 5% of books from first-time authors; less than 1% from unagented writers. Pays 4-8% royalty on retail price. Offers $2,500 and up advance.** Publishes book 1 year after acceptance of ms. Accepts simultaneous submissions. Responds in 6 months to queries.

Nonfiction: Biography. Subjects include anthropology/archeology, business/economics, child guidance/parenting, education, ethnic, gay/lesbian, government/politics, health/medicine, history, language/literature, military/war, nature/environment, philosophy, psychology, regional, science, sociology, translation, travel, women's issues/studies. *Accepts agented submissions only.*

Fiction: Literary, mainstream/contemporary, short story collections. *Accepts agented submissions only.*

Recent Title(s): *Snow Falling on Cedars*, by David Guterson.

VINTAGE IMAGES, P.O. Box 4699, Silver Spring MD 20914. (301)879-6522. Fax: (301)879-6524. E-mail: vimages@ erols.com. Website: www.vintageimages.com. **Acquisitions:** Brian Smolens, president. Publishes trade paperback originals. **Publishes 8 titles/year. Pays 4-8% royalty on wholesale price.** Publishes book 5 months after acceptance of ms. Manuscript guidelines online.

    ○→ "We publish photographic poster books and need writers who are exceptionally creative. This is truly a creative writing exercise."

Nonfiction: Gift book, humor, illustrated book, poster books. Subjects include Americana, photography.

Recent Title(s): *Fishing Tales: A Vintage Images Poster Book*.

Tips: "We are interested in creative writers who can weave a humorous/dramatic theme around 36 vintage photos (early 1900s)."

VISTA PUBLISHING, INC., 422 Morris Ave., Suite #1, Long Branch NJ 07740. (732)229-6500. Fax: (732)229-9647. E-mail: czagury@vistapubl.com. Website: www.vistapubl.com. **Acquisitions:** Carolyn Zagury, president. Estab. 1991. Publishes trade paperback originals. **Publishes 12 titles/year. Receives 200 queries and 125 mss/year. 75% of books from first-time authors; 100% from unagented writers. Pays 50% royalty on wholesale price or retail price.** Publishes book 2-3 years after acceptance of ms. Accepts simultaneous submissions. Responds in 3 months to mss. Book catalog and ms guidelines free.

    ○→ Vista publishes books by nurses and allied health professionals. Currently emphasizing clinical topics. De-emphasizing fiction.

Nonfiction: Nursing, career related. Subjects include business/economics, child guidance/parenting, creative nonfiction, health/medicine, women's issues/studies (specific to nursing and allied health professionals). Submit complete ms with SASE. Reviews artwork/photos as part of ms package. Send photocopies.

Fiction: "We specialize in nurse and allied health professional authors." Horror, multicultural, mystery, poetry, short story collections, nursing, medical. Submit complete ms with SASE.

Poetry: Nursing related. Submit complete ms.

Recent Title(s): *Basics of Computers and Nursing Informatics*, by Donna Gloe, RN, Ed.D (nonfiction); *Error in Judgement*, by Dr. Gary Birken (fiction).

Tips: "It's always worth the effort to submit your manuscript."

VOLCANO PRESS, INC., P.O. Box 270, Volcano CA 95689-0270. (209)296-4991. Fax: (209)296-4995. E-mail: ruth@volcanopress.com. Website: www.volcanopress.com. **Acquisitions:** Ruth Gottstein, publisher. Estab. 1969. Publishes trade paperback originals. **Publishes 4-6 titles/year. Pays royalty on net receipts. Offers $500-1,000 advance.** Responds in 1 month to queries. Book catalog free.

    O━ "We believe that the books we are producing today are of even greater value than the gold of yesteryear and that the sybolism of the term 'Mother Lode' is still relevant to our work."

Nonfiction: Self-help. Subjects include health/medicine, multicultural, women's issues/studies. "We publish women's health and social issues, particularly in the field of domestic violence." Query with SASE or submit outline. No e-mail or fax submissions.

Recent Title(s): *Ghost Towns of Amador*, by Andrews; *Journal and Letters from the Mines*, John Doble.

Tips: "Look at our titles on the Web or in our catalog, and submit materials consistent with what we already publish."

VOYAGEUR PRESS, 123 N. Second St., Stillwater MN 55082. (651)430-2210. Fax: (651)430-2211. E-mail: mdregni @voyageurpress.com. **Acquisitions:** Michael Dregni, editorial director. Estab. 1972. Publishes hardcover and trade paperback originals. **Publishes 50 titles/year. Receives 1,200 queries and 500 mss/year. 10% of books from first-time authors; 90% from unagented writers. Pays royalty. Offers advance.** Publishes book 1 year after acceptance of ms. Accepts simultaneous submissions. Responds in 3 months to queries.

    O━ "Voyageur Press is internationally known as a leading publisher of quality natural history, wildlife and regional books."

Nonfiction: Coffee table book (smaller format photographic essay books), cookbook. Subjects include Americana, cooking/foods/nutrition, history (natural), hobbies, nature/environment, regional, collectibles, outdoor recreation. Query with SASE or submit outline. Reviews artwork/photos as part of ms package. Send transparencies (duplicates and tearsheets only).

Recent Title(s): *This Old Tractor* (stories and photos about farm tractors); *Last Standing Woman* (Native American novel).

Tips: "We publish books for a sophisticated audience interested in natural history and cultural history of a variety of subjects. Please present as focused an idea as possible in a brief submission (one page cover letter; two page outline or proposal). Note your credentials for writing the book. Tell all you know about the market niche and marketing possibilities for proposed book."

J. WESTON WALCH, PUBLISHER, P.O. Box 658, Portland ME 04104-0658. (207)772-2846. Fax: (207)774-7167. Website: www.walch.com. **Acquisitions:** Susan Blair, editor-in-chief. Estab. 1927. **Publishes 100 titles/year. Receives 300 submissions/year. 10% of books from first-time authors; 95% from unagented writers. Pays 8-10% royalty on gross receipts. Offers negotiable advance.** Publishes book 18 months after acceptance of ms. Responds in 4 months to queries. Book catalog for 9×12 SAE with 5 first-class stamps; ms guidelines for #10 SASE.

    O━ "We focus on English/language arts, math, social studies and science teaching resources for middle school through adult assessment titles."

Nonfiction: Formats include teacher resources, reproducibles, posters and mixed packages. Subjects include education, government/politics, history, language/literature, science, technology, mathematics, middle school, social studies, remedial and special education. Most titles are assigned by us, though we occasionally accept an author's unsolicited submission. We have a great need for author/artist teams and for authors who can write at third- to seventh-grade levels. Looks for sense of organization, writing ability, knowledge of subject, skill of communicating with intended audience. We do *not* want textbooks or anthologies. All authors should have educational experience at the secondary level. *Query first. No unsolicited mss.* Query with SASE. Reviews artwork/photos as part of ms package.

Recent Title(s): *Document-Based Assessment Activities for Global History*, by Theresa C. Noonan; *Bridges: Making the Transition from School to Work*, by Kathleen Zeien and Beverly Anderson; *Assessment Strategies for Science*, by Carl Raab.

WALKER AND CO., Walker Publishing Co., 435 Hudson St., New York NY 10014. Fax: (212)727-0984. Publisher: George Gibson. Editors: Jacqueline Johnson, Michael Seidman. Juvenile Publisher: Emily Easton. Juvenile Editor: Tim Travaglini. **Acquisitions:** Submissions Editor or Submissions Editor-Juvenile. Estab. 1959. Publishes hardcover and trade paperback originals. **Publishes 70 titles/year. Receives 3,500 submissions/year. Pays 7½-12% on paperback, 10-15% on hardcover. Offers competitive advance.** Responds in 3 months to queries. Book catalog for 9×12 SAE with 3 first-class stamps.

    O━ Walker publishes general nonfiction on a variety of subjects as well as mysteries, children's books and large print religious reprints. Currently emphasizing science, history, technology, math. De-emphasizing music, self-help, sports.

Nonfiction: Biography, children's/juvenile, reference, self-help. Subjects include health/medicine, history (natural), music/dance, nature/environment, science (popular), sports (baseball). Query with SASE. No phone calls.

Fiction: Juvenile, mystery (adult), picture books. Query with SASE.

Recent Title(s): *Galileo's Daughter*, by Dava Sobel (history/biography/science); *Testing Miss Malarky* (juvenile); *The Basque History of the World*, by Mark Kurlansky (history).

■ **WALSWORTH PUBLISHING CO.**, Donning Co. Publishers, 306 N. Kansas Ave., Marceline MO 64658. (800)369-2646. Fax: (660)258-7798. E-mail: steve.mull@walsworth.com. Website: www.donning.com. **Acquisitions:**

Steve Mull, general manager. Publishes hardcover originals and reprints. **Publishes 40-50 titles/year. Receives 25 queries and 50 mss/year. 70% of books from first-time authors; 99% from unagented writers. Pays 5-15% royalty on wholesale price. Offers advance**. Manuscript guidelines free.

○┐ Publishes coffee table books.

Nonfiction: Coffee table book. Subjects include agriculture/horticulture, business/economics, ethnic, history (community, college, agricultural, business/economic), military/war, sports. Query with SASE.

WALTSAN PUBLISHING, LLC, 5000 Barnett St., Fort Worth TX 76103-2006. (817)654-2978. E-mail: sandra @waltsan.com. Website: www.waltsan.com. **Publishes 10-20 titles/year. Receives 150 queries and 100 mss/year. 95% of books from first-time authors; 95% from unagented writers. Pays 20% royalty on wholesale price.** Publishes book 9 months after acceptance of ms. Accepts simultaneous submissions. Responds in 1 month to queries and proposals; 2 months to mss. Book catalog and ms guidelines online.

Nonfiction: Subjects include general nonfiction. "We look at any nonfiction subject." Query with SASE or via website or submit proposal package, including outline and 3 sample chapters or submit complete ms. Reviews artwork/photos as part of ms package. Send photocopies.

Fiction: "We look at all fiction." Full-length or collections equal to full-length only. "We would like to have more queries for fiction that appeals to the youth (12-18) and juvenile (8-11) age groups." Query with SASE or submit proposal package including 3 sample chapter(s), synopsis or submit complete ms.

Recent Title(s): *Getting Yourself Together*, by Marilyn Komechak, Ph.D (self-help psychological); *Tales by Mail*, by Karen Carter (fairy tale).

Tips: Audience is computer literate, generally higher income and intelligent. "When possible, authors record their manuscript to include audio on the CD. Check our website for guidelines and sample contract."

WARNER ASPECT, Warner Books, 1271 Avenue of the Americas, New York NY 10020. (212)522-7200. Website: twbookmark.com. Editor-in-Chief: Betsy Mitchell. Publishes hardcover, trade paperback, mass market paperback originals and mass market paperback reprints. **Publishes 30 titles/year. Receives 500 queries and 350 mss/year. 5-10% of books from first-time authors; 1% from unagented writers. Pays royalty on retail price. Offers $5,000-up advance.** Publishes book 1 year after acceptance of ms. Responds in 3 months to mss.

○┐ "We're looking for 'epic' stories in both fantasy and science fiction. Also seeking writers of color to add to what we've already published by Octavia E. Butler, Nalo Hopkinson, Walter Mosley, etc." .

Fiction: Fantasy, science fiction. "Sample our existing titles—we're a fairly new list and pretty strongly focused." Mistake writers often make is "hoping against hope that being unagented won't make a difference. We simply don't have the staff to look at unagented projects." *Accepts agented submissions only.*

Recent Title(s): *Dark Matter: A Century of Speculative Fiction from the African Diaspora*, edited by Sheree R. Thomas (science fiction anthology).

WARNER BOOKS, Time & Life Building, 1271 Avenue of the Americas, New York NY 10020. (212)522-7200. Website: www.twbookmark.com. President: Maureen Egen. **Acquisitions:** (Ms.) Jamie Raab, senior vice president/ publisher (general nonfiction and fiction); Les Pockell, associate publisher (general nonfiction); Rick Horgan, vice president/executive editor (general nonfiction and fiction, thrillers); Amy Einhorn, editorial director, trade paperback (popular culture, business, fitness, self-help); Beth de Guzman, editorial director, mass market (fiction and nonfiction); Rick Wolff, executive editor (business, humor, sports); Betsy Mitchell, executive editor (science fiction); Sara Ann Freed, editor-in-chief, Mysterious Press (mysteries, suspense); Caryn Karmatz Rudy, senior editor (fiction, general nonfiction, popular culture); Rob McMahon, editor (fiction, business, sports); Diana Baroni, editor (health, fitness); John Aherne, associate editor (popular culture, fiction, general nonfiction); Jackie Joiner, associate editor (commercial fiction, spiritual/new age, memoir/biography); Rolf Aettersten, vice president (books for the CBA market). Estab. 1960. Publishes hardcover, trade paperback and mass market paperback originals and reprints. **Publishes 250 titles/year. Pays variable royalty. Offers variable advance.** Publishes book 2 years after acceptance of ms. Responds in 4 months to queries.

Imprints: Mysterious Press (mystery/suspense), Warner Aspect (science fiction and fantasy), Warner Vision, Warner Business, Walk Worthy Press

○┐ Warner publishes general interest fiction and nonfiction.

Nonfiction: Biography, humor, reference, self-help. Subjects include business/economics, cooking/foods/nutrition, health/medicine, history, humor, psychology, spirituality, sports, current affairs, home, popular culture, human potential. *No unsolicited mss.*

Fiction: Fantasy, horror, mainstream/contemporary, mystery, romance, science fiction, suspense, thrillers. *No unsolicited mss.*

Recent Title(s): *The Lion's Game*, by Nelson DeMille; *Ten Things I Wish I'd Known Before I Went Out into the Real World*, by Maria Shriver; *Reason for Hope*, by Jane Goodall.

Tips: "We do not accept unsolicited manuscripts."

WASHINGTON STATE UNIVERSITY PRESS, Pullman WA 99164-5910. (800)354-7360. Fax: (509)335-8568. E-mail: wsupress@wsu.edu. Website: www.wsu.edu/wsupress. Director: Thomas H. Sanders. **Acquisitions:** Glen Lindeman, editor. Estab. 1928. Publishes hardcover originals, trade paperback originals and reprints. **Publishes 8-10 titles/**

year. Receives 300-400 submissions/year. 50% of books from first-time authors. Most books from unagented writers. Pays 5% royalty graduated according to sales. Publishes book 18 months after acceptance of ms. Responds in 2 months to queries.

O→ WSU Press publishes books on the history, pre-history, culture, and politics of the West, particularly the Pacific Northwest.

Nonfiction: Biography. Subjects include Americana, anthropology/archeology, art/architecture, cooking/foods/nutrition, ethnic (studies), government/politics, history (especially of the American West and the Pacific Northwest), nature/environment, regional, essays. "We seek manuscripts that focus on the Pacific Northwest as a region. No romance novels, how-to books, gardening books or books used specifically as classroom texts. We welcome innovative and thought-provoking titles in a wide diversity of genres, from essays and memoirs to history, anthropology and political science." Submit outline, sample chapter(s). Reviews artwork/photos as part of ms package.

Recent Title(s): *Railroad Shutterbug: Jim Fredrickson's Northern Pacific.*

Tips: "We have developed our marketing in the direction of regional and local history and have attempted to use this as the base upon which to expand our publishing program. In regional history, the secret is to write a good narrative—a good story—that is substantiated factually. It should be told in an imaginative, clever way. Have visuals (photos, maps, etc.) available to help the reader envision what has happened. Tell the regional history story in a way that ties it to larger, national, and even international events. Weave it into the large pattern of history."

FRANKLIN WATTS, Grolier Publishing, 90 Sherman Turnpike, Danbury CT 06816. (203)797-6802. Fax: (203)797-6986. Website: www.grolier.com. Publisher: John Selfridge. **Acquisitions:** Dina Rubin, executive editor. Estab. 1942. Publishes hardcover and softcover originals. **Publishes 150 titles/year. 5% of books from first-time authors; 95% from unagented writers. Offers advance.** Publishes book 18 months after acceptance of ms. Accepts simultaneous submissions. Responds in 4 months to queries. Book catalog for #10 SASE; ms guidelines for #10 SASE.

● Grolier was recently purchased by Scholastic, Inc.

O→ Franklin Watts publishes nonfiction books for the library market (K-12) to supplement textbooks.

Nonfiction: Biography, children's/juvenile. Subjects include education, government/politics, history (American, world), language/literature, multicultural, nature/environment, science (natural, physical), sociology, social issues. Multicultural, curriculum-based nonfiction lists published twice a year. Strong also in the area of contemporary problems and issues facing young people. No humor, coffee table books, fiction, picture books, poetry, cookbooks or gardening books. Query with SASE or submit outline, SASE, writing sample. *No unsolicited mss.* No phone calls. Prefers to work with unagented authors.

Recent Title(s): *Sleep and Dreams*, by Andrew T. McPhee; *Autism*, by Elaine Landau.

Tips: Most of this publisher's books are developed inhouse; less than 5% come from unsolicited submissions. However, they publish several series for which they always need new books. Study catalogs to discover possible needs.

WEATHERHILL, INC., 41 Monroe Turnpike, Trumbull CT 06611. (203)459-5090. Fax: (203)459-5095. E-mail: weatherhill@weatherhill.com. Website: www.weatherhill.com. **Acquisitions:** Raymond Furse, editorial director. Estab. 1962. Publishes hardcover and trade paperback originals and reprints. **Publishes 36 titles/year. Receives 250 queries and 100 mss/year. 20% of books from first-time authors; 95% from unagented writers. Pays 12-18% royalty on wholesale price. Offers up to $10,000 advance.** Publishes book 8 months after acceptance of ms. Accepts simultaneous submissions. Responds in 1 month to proposals. Book catalog and ms guidelines free.

Imprints: Weatherhill, Tengu Books

O→ Weatherhill publishes exclusively Asia-related nonfiction and Asian fiction and poetry in translation.

Nonfiction: Asia related topics only. Biography, coffee table book, cookbook, gift book, how-to, humor, illustrated book, reference, self-help. Subjects include anthropology/archeology, art/architecture, cooking/foods/nutrition, gardening, history, humor, language/literature, music/dance, nature/environment, photography, regional, religion, sociology, translation, travel, martial arts. Submit outline, 2 sample chapter(s), and sample illustrations (if applicable). Reviews artwork/photos as part of ms package. Send photocopies.

Fiction: "We publish only important Asian writers in translation. Asian fiction is a hard sell. Authors should check funding possibilities from appropriate sources: Japan Foundation, Korea Foundation, etc." Submit synopsis.

Poetry: Only Asian poetry in translation. Query.

Recent Title(s): *Buddha and Christ*, by Hapkido.

WEIDNER & SONS PUBLISHING, P.O. Box 2178, Riverton NJ 08077. (856)486-1755. Fax: (856)486-7583. E-mail: weidner@waterw.com. Website: www.weidnerpublishing.com. **Acquisitions:** James H. Weidner, president. Estab. 1967. Publishes hardcover and trade paperback originals and reprints. **Publishes 10-20 titles/year; imprint publishes 10 titles/year. Receives hundreds queries and 50 mss/year. 100% of books from first-time authors; 90% from unagented writers. Pays 10% royalty on wholesale price. Offers advance.** Accepts simultaneous submissions. Responds in 1 month to queries.

Imprints: Bird Sci Books, Delaware Estuary Press, Hazlaw Books, Medlaw Books, Pulse Publications, Tycooly Publishing USA

O→ Weidner & Sons publishes primarily science, text and reference books for scholars, college students and researchers.

Nonfiction: Reference, technical, textbook. Subjects include agriculture/horticulture, animals, business/economics, child guidance/parenting, computers/electronic, education, gardening, health/medicine, hobbies (electronic), language/

literature, nature/environment, psychology, science, ecology/environment. "We do not publish fiction; never poetry. No topics in the 'pseudosciences': occult, astrology, New Age and metaphysics, etc. Suggest 2 copies of ms, double spaced, along with PC disk in Word, Write or Pagemaker." Query with SASE or submit outline, sample chapter(s), SASE, include e-mail address for faster response. Reviews artwork/photos as part of ms package. Send photocopies.

Recent Title(s): *The Huntington Sexual Behavior Scale*, by Vince Huntington (Perspectives in Psychology series).

WELCOME ENTERPRISES, INC., 588 Broadway, New York NY 10012. (212)343-9430. Fax: (212)343-9434. **Acquisitions:** Leah Tabori, editor; Natasha Tabori Freed, editor; Alice Wong, editor. **Publishes 10 titles/year. Pays 4-10% royalty on retail price.**

Nonfiction: Children's/juvenile, illustrated book. Art/architecture, language/literature subjects. Query with SASE.

Recent Title(s): *The Little Big Book for Dads*; *The Little Big Book for Moms*; *The Little Big Organizer for Moms*.

WESCOTT COVE PUBLISHING CO., P.O. Box 130, Stamford CT 06904. (203)322-0998. Fax: (203)322-1388. **Acquisitions:** Julius M. Wilensky, president. Estab. 1968. Publishes trade paperback originals and reprints. **Publishes 4 titles/year. Receives 15 queries and 10 mss/year. 25% of books from first-time authors; 95% from unagented writers. Pays 5-10% royalty on retail price. Offers $1,000-1,500 advance.** Publishes book 1 year after acceptance of ms. Accepts simultaneous submissions. Responds in 1 week to queries. Book catalog free.

○─ "We publish the most complete cruising guides, each one an authentic reference for the area covered."

Nonfiction: "All titles are nautical books; half of them are cruising guides. Mostly we seek out authors knowledgeable in sailing, navigation, cartography and the area we want covered. Then we commission them to write the book." How-to, humor, illustrated book, reference. Subjects include history, hobbies, regional, travel, nautical. Query with SASE or submit outline, 1-2 sample chapter(s), SASE.

Recent Title(s): *Chesapeake Bay Cruising Guide Volume I, Upper Bay*, by Tom Neale.

WESLEYAN UNIVERSITY PRESS, 110 Mount Vernon St., Middletown CT 06459. (860)685-2420. Director: Tom Radko. **Acquisitions:** Suzanna Tamminen, editor-in-chief. Estab. 1957. Publishes hardcover originals and paperbacks. **Publishes 25-30 titles/year. Receives 1,500 queries and 1,000 mss/year. 10% of books from first-time authors; 80% from unagented writers. Pays 0-10% royalty. Offers up to $3,000 advance.** Publishes book 1-3 years after acceptance of ms. Accepts simultaneous submissions. Responds in 1 month to queries; 2 months to proposals; 3 months to mss. Book catalog free; ms guidelines for #10 SASE.

○─ Wesleyan University Press is a scholarly press with a focus on poetry, music, dance and cultural studies.

Nonfiction: Biography, textbook, scholarly. Subjects include ethnic, film/cinema/stage, gay/lesbian, history, language/literature, music/dance, philosophy. Submit proposal package including outline, introductory letter, curriculum vitae, table of contents. Reviews artwork/photos as part of ms package. Send photocopies.

Fiction: Science fiction. "We publish very little fiction, less than 3% of our entire list."

Poetry: "Writers should request a catalog and guidelines." Submit 5-10 sample poems.

Recent Title(s): *Pleasure Dome: New and Collected Poems*, by Yusef Kommunyakaa (poetry).

WESTCLIFFE PUBLISHERS, P.O. Box 1261, Englewood CO 80150. (303)935-0900. Fax: (303)935-0903. E-mail: editor@westcliffepublishers.com. Website: www.westcliffepublishers.com. Linda Doyle, associate publisher. **Acquisitions:** Jenna Samelson, managing editor. Estab. 1981. Publishes hardcover originals, trade paperback originals and reprints. **Publishes 18 titles/year. Receives 100 queries and 60 mss/year. 50% of books from first-time authors; 100% from unagented writers. Pays royalty on retail price. Offers advance.** Publishes book 18 months after acceptance of ms. Accepts simultaneous submissions. Responds in 1 month to queries. Book catalog free; ms guidelines online.

○─ "Westcliffe Publishers produces the highest quality in regional photography and essays for our outdoor guide-books, coffee table-style books, and calendars. As an eco-publisher our mission is to foster environmental awareness by showing the beauty of the natural world." Strong concentration on color guide books, outdoor sports, history.

Nonfiction: Coffee table book, gift book, illustrated book, reference. Subjects include Americana, animals, gardening, history, nature/environment, photography, regional, sports (outdoor), travel. "Writers need to do their market research to justify a need in the marketplace." Submit proposal package including outline. Westcliffe will contact you for photos, writing samples.

Recent Title(s): *Colorado: 1870-2000*, by John Fielder; *Haunted Texas Vacations*, by Lisa Farwell.

Tips: Audience are nature and outdoors enthusiasts and photographers. "Just call us!"

WESTERN PSYCHOLOGICAL SERVICES, Manson Western Corp., 12031 Wilshire Blvd., Los Angeles CA 90025. (310)478-2061. Fax: (310)478-2061. E-mail: smanson@wpspublish.com. Website: www.wpspublish.com. **Acquisitions:** Susan Madden, director of marketing. Estab. 1948. Publishes trade paperback originals. **Publishes 6 titles/year. Receives 6 queries and 12 mss/year. 75% of books from first-time authors; 80% from unagented writers. Pays 5-10% royalty on wholesale price.** Publishes book 1 year after acceptance of ms. Accepts simultaneous submissions. Responds in 1 month to queries. Book catalog free.

○─ Western Psychological Services publishes practical books used by therapists, counselors, social workers and others in the helping field working with children and adults.

Nonfiction: Self-help. Subjects include child guidance/parenting, education, multicultural, psychology. Submit complete ms. *Writer's Market* recommends a query first. Reviews artwork/photos as part of ms package. Send photocopies.
Fiction: Expressing feelings, understanding and dealing with emotional problems. Submit complete ms. *Writer's Market* recommends query first.
Recent Title(s): *Psychodiagnostics and Personality Assessment: Third Edition*, by Donald P. Ogden.

WESTERNLORE PRESS, P.O. Box 35305, Tucson AZ 85740. (520)297-5491. Fax: (520)297-1722. **Acquisitions:** Lynn R. Bailey, editor. Estab. 1941. **Publishes 6-12 titles/year. Pays standard royalty on retail price. Offers advance.** Responds in 2 months to queries.
○┉ Westernlore publishes Western Americana of a scholarly and semischolarly nature.
Nonfiction: Biography. Subjects include Americana, anthropology/archeology, history, regional, historic sights, restoration, ethnohistory pertaining to the American West. Re-publication of rare and out-of-print books. Length: 25,000-100,000 words. Query with SASE.
Recent Title(s): *The Apache Kid*, by de la Gaza (Western history).

WESTMINSTER JOHN KNOX PRESS, Presbyterian Publishing Corporation, 100 Witherspoon St., Louisville KY 40202-1396. (502)569-5342. Fax: (502)569-5113. Website: www.wjkacademic.com. Stephanie Egnotovich, executive editor. **Acquisitions:** Angela D. Jackson. Publishes hardcover and trade paperback originals and reprints. **Publishes 160 titles/year. Receives 2,500 queries and 750 mss/year. 10% of books from first-time authors. Pays royalty on retail price. Offers advance.** Publishes book up to 18 months after acceptance of ms. Accepts simultaneous submissions. Book catalog and ms guidelines for #10 SASE.
○┉ "All WJK books have a religious/spiritual angle, but are written for various markets—scholarly, professional, and the general reader." Westminster John Knox is affiliated with the Presbyterian Church USA.
Nonfiction: Biography, gift book, how-to, humor, illustrated book, multimedia, reference, self-help, textbook. Subjects include anthropology/archeology, child guidance/parenting, education, ethnic, gay/lesbian, history, humor, multicultural, philosophy, psychology, religion, sociology, spirituality, women's issues/studies. Submit proposal package including according to WJK book proposal guidelines.

WESTWINDS PRESS, Graphic Arts Center Publishing, P.O. Box 10306, Portland OR 97296-0306. (503)226-2402. Fax: (503)223-1410. Website: www.gacpc.com. **Acquisitions:** Tricia Brown, acquisitions editor. Estab. 1999. Publishes hardcover and trade paperback originals and reprints. **Publishes 5-7 titles/year. Receives hundreds submissions/year. 10% of books from first-time authors; 90% from unagented writers. Pays 10-14% royalty on net receipts or makes outright purchase. Offers advance.** Publishes book an average of 2 years after acceptance of ms. Accepts simultaneous submissions. Responds in 6 months to queries. Book catalog and ms guidelines for 9×12 SAE with 6 first-class stamps.
Nonfiction: Children's/juvenile, cookbook. Subjects include history, memoirs, regional (Western regional states—nature, travel, cookbooks, Native American culture, adventure, outdoor recreation, sports, the arts and children's books), guidebooks.
Recent Title(s): *San Francisco's Golden Gate Park* (guidebook); *The Great Arizona Almanac: Facts About Arizona*.
Tips: "Book proposals that are professionally written and polished with a clear market receive our most careful consideration. We are looking for originality. We publish a wide range of books for a wide audience. Some of our books are clearly for travelers, others for those interested in outdoor recreation or various regional subjects. If I were a writer trying to market a book today, I would research the competition (existing books) for what I have in mind, and clearly (and concisely) express why my idea is different and better. I would describe the book buyers (and readers)—where they are, how many of them are there, how they can be reached (organizations, publications), why they would want or need my book."

WHAT'S INSIDE PRESS, P.O. Box 16965, Beverly Hills CA 90209. (800)269-7757. Fax: (800)856-2160. E-mail: whatsin@aol.com. Website: www.whatsinsidepress.com. **Acquisitions:** Shalane Fulton, acquisitions editor (young adult); Jenna Silver, acquisitions editor (children's picture). Publishes hardcover and trade paperback originals. **Publishes 8-12 titles/year. Receives 3,000 queries/year. 50% of books from first-time authors; 100% from unagented writers. Pays 8-15% royalty. In addition to author royalty, 10% of net book sales goes to a children's charity of the author's choice.** Publishes book 2 years after acceptance of ms. Responds in 1 month to queries; 2 months to mss. Book catalog and ms guidelines online.
○┉ Publisher of children's and YA fiction and picture books. Currently de-emphasizing animal stories, religious, and rhyme. Sponsors annual literary contest for unpublished writers, Brant Point Prize. Proceeds for charity.
Fiction: Juvenile, picture books, young adult, illustrated book. E-mail queries only.
Recent Title(s): *The Tree in the Field of Mathingamy Thame*, by Walter Caldwell (children's picture books); *Kitty in the City, Mind Your Manners, S'il Vous Plait*, by Kinsley Foster (children's picture book).
Tips: "Please do not send a résumé of past publication or writing experience. For the writer's convenience, a detailed explanation of submission procedures is available on our website." Brief e-mail queries only. No phone calls please.

WHITE CLIFFS MEDIA, INC., Editorial Dept., PMB 208, 5150 Mae Anne Ave., Suite 213, Reno NV 89523-1892. **Acquisitions:** Lawrence Aynesmith. Estab. 1985. Publishes hardcover and trade paperback originals. **Publishes**

5-10 titles/year. **50% of books from first-time authors; 50% from unagented writers. Pays 5-12% royalty or makes outright purchase.** Publishes book 1 year after acceptance of ms. Responds in 2 months to queries; 4 months to proposals; 6 months to mss. Book catalog for #10 SASE.

Oⲡ Publishes music titles for an academic and general audience.

Nonfiction: Biography, textbook. Subjects include anthropology/archeology, ethnic, music/dance. Query. Reviews artwork/photos as part of ms package. Send photocopies.

Recent Title(s): *Drum Circle Spirit*, by Arthur Hull.

Tips: "Distribution is more difficult due to the large number of publishers. Writers should send proposals that have potential for mass markets as well as college texts, and that will be submitted and completed on schedule. Our audience reads college texts, general interest trade publications. If I were a writer trying to market a book today, I would send a book on music comparable in quality and mass appeal to a book like Stephen Hawking's *A Brief History of Time*."

WHITE MANE BOOKS, White Mane Publishing Company Inc., 63 W. Burd St., P.O. Box 152, Shippensburg PA 17257. (717)532-2237. Fax: (717)532-6110. E-mail: editorial@whitemane.com. Website: www.whitemane.com. **Acquisitions:** Harold Collier, vice president; Alexis Handerahan, associate editor. Estab. 1987. Publishes hardcover, and trade paperback originals and reprints. **Publishes 60 titles/year; imprint publishes 12-18 titles/year. Receives 300 queries and 50 mss/year. 50% of books from first-time authors; 75% from unagented writers. Pays royalty on monies received. Offers advance.** Publishes book 18 months after acceptance of ms. Accepts simultaneous submissions. Responds in 1 month to queries; 1 month to proposals; 3 months to mss. Book catalog and ms guidelines free.

Imprints: Burd Street Press (military history, emphasis on American Civil War); Ragged Edge Press (religious); WMkids (historically based children's fiction)

Oⲡ "White Mane Publishing Company, Inc., continues its tradition of publishing the finest military history, regional, religious and children's historical fiction books." Currently emphasizing American Civil War, World War II, children's historical fiction.

Nonfiction: Children's/juvenile, reference (adult), scholarly. Subjects include history, military/war, women's issues/studies. Query with SASE. Reviews artwork/photos as part of ms package. Send photocopies.

Fiction: Historical, juvenile. Query with SASE.

Recent Title(s): *Civil War Hostages: Hostage Taking in the Civil War*, by Webb Garrison (nonfiction); *Retreat From Gettysburg*, by Kathleen Ernst (fiction).

WHITE STONE CIRCLE PRESS, P.O. Box 4546, Tubac AZ 85646. (877)424-7253. Fax: (520)398-1243. E-mail: wscpress@hotmail.com. Website: www.carethere.com. **Acquisitions:** Wayne A. Ewing, Ph.D., publisher (inspirational, devotional). Publishes hardcover originals. **Publishes 1-5 titles/year. Receives 25 queries and 10-15 mss/year. 100% of books from first-time authors; 100% from unagented writers. Pays 10-25% royalty on wholesale price. Offers advance.** Publishes book 18 months after acceptance of ms. Accepts simultaneous submissions. Responds in 2 months to queries, proposals and mss. Manuscript guidelines for #10 SASE.

Oⲡ White Stone Circle Press specializes in caregivers' literature.

Nonfiction: Devotional works. Subjects include religion, spirituality. Query with SASE. Reviews artwork/photos as part of ms package. Send photocopies.

Poetry: Interested in poetry of caregivers for future series. Query.

Recent Title(s): *Tears in God's Bottle: Reflections on Alzheimers Caregiving*, by W. Ewing (inspirational).

Tips: Audience is caregivers, hospice workers, clergy and chaplains. "We're interested only in work from the experienced heart; absolutely no schlock; not at all interested in ideological religious writing."

WHITEHORSE PRESS, P.O. Box 60, North Conway NH 03860-0060. (603)356-6556. Fax: (603)356-6590. **Acquisitions:** Dan Kennedy, publisher. Estab. 1988. Publishes trade paperback originals. **Publishes 6-8 titles/year. Pays 10% royalty on wholesale price.** Responds in 1 month to queries.

Nonfiction: "We are actively seeking nonfiction books to aid motorcyclists in topics such as motorcycle safety, restoration, repair and touring. We are especially interested in technical subjects related to motorcycling." How-to, reference. Subjects include travel. Query with SASE.

Recent Title(s): *How to Set Up Your Motorcycle Workshop*, by Charlie Masi (trade paperback).

Tips: "We like to discuss project ideas at an early stage and work with authors to develop those ideas to fit our market."

ALBERT WHITMAN AND CO., 6340 Oakton St., Morton Grove IL 60053-2723. (847)581-0033. Website: www.awhitmanco.com. **Acquisitions:** Kathleen Tucker, editor-in-chief. Estab. 1919. Publishes hardcover originals and paperback reprints. **Publishes 30 titles/year. Receives 5,000 submissions/year. 20% of books from first-time authors; 70% from unagented writers. Pays 10% royalty for novels; 5% for picture books. Offers advance.** Publishes book an average of 18 months after acceptance of ms. Accepts simultaneous submissions. Responds in 6 weeks to queries; 4 months to mss. Book catalog for 8×10 SAE with 3 first-class stamps; ms guidelines for #10 SASE.

Oⲡ Albert Whitman publishes good books for children on a variety of topics: holidays (i.e., Halloween), special needs (such as diabetes) and problems like divorce. The majority of our titles are picture books with less than 1,500 words." De-emphasizing folk tales and bedtime stories.

Nonfiction: All books are for ages 2-12. Children's/juvenile, illustrated book. Subjects include animals, anthropology/archeology, art/architecture, computers/electronic, cooking/foods/nutrition, ethnic, gardening, health/medicine, history, hobbies, language/literature, music/dance, nature/environment, photography, recreation, religion, science, sports, travel, social studies, math. Submit complete ms. if it is picture book length; otherwise query with SASE.

Fiction: "All books are for ages 2-12. We need easy historical fiction and picture books." Adventure, ethnic, fantasy, historical, humor, mystery, holiday, concept books (to help children deal with problems). No young adult and adult books. Submit complete ms. for picture books; for longer works submit query with outline and sample chapters.

Recent Title(s): *Jungle Halloween*, by Maryann Cocca-Leffler.

Tips: "We sell mostly to libraries, but our bookstore sales are growing. We recommend you study our catalog or visit our website before submitting your work."

WHITSTON PUBLISHING CO., INC., 1717 Central Ave., Suite 201, Albany NY 12205. (518)452-1900. Fax: (518)452-1777. E-mail: whitson@capital.net. Website: www.whitston.com. **Acquisitions:** Michael Laddin, editorial director. Estab. 1969. Publishes hardcover originals. **Publishes 12 titles/year. Receives 100 submissions/year. 50% of books from first-time authors; 100% from unagented writers. Pays royalties after sale of 500 copies.** Publishes book 1 year after acceptance of ms. Responds in 6 months to queries.

O─┐ Whitston focuses on Modern American and English literature and bibliographies.

Nonfiction: "We publish nonfiction and scholarly books in the humanities. We also publish bibliographies and indexes." Scholarly, critical, bibliographies, indexes, collections of essays. Subjects include art/architecture, health/medicine, history, language/literature. Query with SASE. Reviews artwork/photos as part of ms package.

Recent Title(s): *Understanding Toni Morrison's Beloved and Sula*, edited by Solomon and Marla Iyasere; *The Living Underground: Prose from America's Finest Unheralded Writers, 1970-1999*, edited by Hugh Fox.

MARKUS WIENER PUBLISHERS INC., 231 Nassau St., Princeton NJ 08542. (609)921-1141. **Acquisitions:** Shelley Frisch, editor-in-chief. Estab. 1981. Publishes hardcover originals and trade paperback originals and reprints. **Publishes 20 titles/year; imprint publishes 5 titles/year. Receives 50-150 queries and 50 mss/year. Pays 10% royalty on net receipts.** Publishes book 1 year after acceptance of ms. Responds in 2 months to queries and proposals. Book catalog free.

Imprints: Princeton Series on the Middle East, Topics in World History

O─┐ Markus Wiener publishes textbooks in history subjects and regional world history.

Nonfiction: Textbook. Subjects include history, world affairs, Caribbean studies, Middle East, Africa.

Recent Title(s): *Afro-Cuban Music*, by Miguel Barnet (Middle East studies); *Land of the Enchanters: Egyptian Short Stories from Antiquities to Modern Times*, ed. by Bernard Lewis and Stanley Burstein; *Bitter Bonds: 17th Century Colonial Divorce Drama*, by Leonard Blusse.

[N] MICHAEL WIESE PRODUCTIONS, 11288 Ventura Blvd., Suite 821, Studio City CA 91604. (818)379-8799. E-mail: kenlee@mwp.com. Website: www.mwp.com. **Acquisitions:** Ken Lee, vice president. Estab. 1981. Publishes trade paperback originals. **Publishes 4-6 titles/year. Receives 10-15 queries/year. 90% of books from first-time authors. Pays 7-10% royalty on retail price. Offers $500-1,000 advance.** Publishes book 10 months after acceptance of ms. Accepts simultaneous submissions. Responds in 1 month to queries and proposals; 2 months to mss. Book catalog online.

O─┐ Michael Wiese publishes how-to books for professional film or video makers, film schools and bookstores.

Nonfiction: How-to. Subjects include professional film and videomaking. Submit outline, 3 sample chapter(s). Call before submitting.

Recent Title(s): *Scripts Magic*, by Marisa D'Vari; *Freelance Writing for Hollywood*, by Scott Essman.

Tips: Audience is professional filmmakers, writers, producers, directors, actors and university film students.

WILDCAT CANYON PRESS, Circulus Publishing Group, Inc., 2716 Ninth St., Berkeley CA 94710. (510)848-3600. Fax: (510)848-1326. E-mail: info@wildcatcanyon.com. Website: www.wildcatcanyon.com. **Acquisitions:** Tamara Traeder, publisher (relationships/gift books); Roy M. Carlisle, editorial director (psychology/relationships). Publishes trade paperback originals. **Publishes 10-12 titles/year. Receives 500 queries and 300 mss/year. Pays 10-16% royalty on wholesale price. Offers $1,000-3,000 advance.** Publishes book 9 months after acceptance of ms. Accepts simultaneous submissions. Responds in 3 months to queries. Book catalog and ms guidelines free.

● Now accepting mss on behalf of Pagemill Press

O─┐ Wildcat Canyon Press publishes books that embrace and enhance such relationship subjects as friendship, spirituality, women's issues, and home and family, all with a focus on self-help and personal growth.

Nonfiction: Gift book, self-help. Subjects include psychology, women's issues/studies, relationships. Query with SASE or submit proposal package including outline, SASE. E-queries are accepted. Reviews artwork/photos as part of ms package. Send photocopies.

Recent Title(s): *Bountiful Women: Large Women's Secrets for Living the Life They Desire*, by Bonnie Bernell; *Life Is Not Work, Work Is Not Life: Simple Reminders for Finding Balance in a 24-7 World*, by Robert K. Johnson and J. Walker Smith.

Tips: "As a proactive publishing house we commission most of our titles and we are primarily interested in solicited queries and proposals."

[N:] **WILDER PUBLISHING CENTER**, 919 Lafond Ave., St. Paul MN 55104. (612)659-6013. Fax: (612)642-2061. E-mail: vlh@wilder.org. Website: www.wilder.org. **Acquisitions:** Vincent Hyman, director. Publishes trade paperback originals. **Publishes 6 titles/year. Receives 30 queries and 15 mss/year. 75% of books from first-time authors; 100% from unagented writers. Pays 10% royalty on net receipts Books are sold through direct mail; average discount is 20%. Offers $1,000-3,000 advance.** Publishes book 1 year after acceptance of ms. Responds in 1 month to queries and proposals; 3 months to mss. Book catalog and ms guidelines online.

O-- Wilder Publishing Center emphasizes community and nonprofit organization management and development.

Nonfiction: Subjects include nonprofit management, organizational development, community building. "We are in a growth mode and welcome proposals in these areas. We are seeking manuscripts that report 'best practice' methods using handbook or workbook formats." Submit 3 sample chapter(s). Phone query OK before submitting proposal with detailed chapter outline, SASE, statement of unique selling points, identification of audience.

Recent Title(s): *Resolving Conflict in Nonprofit Organizations: The Leader's Guide to Finding Creative Solutions.*

Tips: "Writers must be practitioners with a passion for their work in nonprofit management or community building and experience presenting their techniques at conferences. Freelance writers with an interest in our niches could do well searching out and teaming up with such practitioners as our books sell very well to a tightly-targeted market."

WILDERNESS PRESS, 1200 Fifth St., Berkley CA 94710. (510)558-1666. Fax: (510)558-1696. E-mail: mail@wilder nesspress.com. Website: www.wildernesspress.com. **Acquisitions:** Jannie Dresser, managing editor. Estab. 1967. Publishes paperback originals. **Publishes 12 titles/year. Receives 75 submissions/year. 20% of books from first-time authors; 95% from unagented writers. Pays 8-10% royalty on retail price. Offers $1,000 average advance.** Publishes book 8 months after acceptance of ms. Responds in 2 months to queries. Book catalog and ms guidelines online.

O-- "We seek to publish the most accurate, reliable and useful outdoor books and maps for self-propelled outdoor activities for hikers, kayakers, skiers, snowshoers, backpackers, mountain biking."

Nonfiction: How-to (outdoors). Subjects include nature/environment, recreation, trail guides for hikers and backpackers. "We publish books about the outdoors. Most are trail guides for hikers and backpackers, but we also publish how-to books about the outdoors. The manuscript must be accurate. The author must research an area in person. If writing a trail guide, you must walk all the trails in the area your book is about. Outlook must be strongly conservationist. Style must be appropriate for a highly literate audience." Request proposal guidelines.

Recent Title(s): *Backpacking California*, by Paul Backhurst; *Sea Kayaking: Safety and Rescue*, by John Lull.

JOHN WILEY & SONS, INC., 605 Third Ave., New York NY 10158. Website: www.wiley.com. Publisher: G. Helferich. **Acquisitions:** Editorial Department. Estab. 1807. Publishes hardcover originals, trade paperback originals and reprints. **Pays competitive rates. Offers advance.** Accepts simultaneous submissions. Book catalog and ms guidelines for #10 SASE.

O-- "The General Interest group publishes books for the consumer market."

Nonfiction: Biography, children's/juvenile, reference, narrative nonfiction. Subjects include history, memoirs, psychology, science (popular), African American interest, health/self-improvement. Query with SASE.

Recent Title(s): *Carl Sagan*, by Keay Davidson; *The Carbohydrate Addict's Cookbook*, by Dr. Richard F. Heller and Dr. Rachel F. Heller.

[■] **WILLIAMSON PUBLISHING CO.**, P.O. Box 185, Church Hill Rd., Charlotte VT 05445. Website: www.willia msonbooks.com. **Acquisitions:** Susan Williamson, editorial director. Estab. 1983. Publishes trade paperback originals. **Publishes 20 titles/year. Receives 1,000 queries/year. 75% of books from first-time authors; 90% from unagented writers. Pays royalty on net receipts or makes outright purchase. Offers standard advance.** Publishes book 18 months after acceptance of ms. Responds in 4 months to queries. Book catalog for 8½×11 SAE with 4 first-class stamps; ms guidelines online.

● Williamson's big success is its *Kids Can* and *Kaleidoscope Kids*. *Pyramids*, *Knights & Castles* and *Mexico* were all chosen American Bookseller Pick of the Lists; *Pyramids* and *Knights & Castles* were selected as Children's Book Council Notable Books.

O-- "Our mission is to help every child fulfull his/her potential and experience personal growth through active learning. We want 'our kids' to be able to work toward a culturally rich, ethnically diverse, peaceful nation and global community." Currently emphasizing creative approaches to specific areas of science, history, cultural experiences, diversity.

Nonfiction: Subjects include art/architecture, child guidance/parenting, cooking/foods/nutrition, ethnic, history, nature/environment, psychology, science, geography, early learning skills, careers, arts, crafts. "Williamson has five very successful children's book series: *Little Hands* (ages 2-6), *Kids Can* (ages 6-12), *Starts Quick for Kids* (64 pages, ages 8 and up), *Tales Alive* (folktales plus activities, ages 4-10) and *Kaleidoscope Kids* (96 pages, single subject, ages 8-14). They must incorporate learning through doing. *No picture books, story books, or fiction please!* Please don't call concerning your submission. It never helps your review, and it takes too much of our time. With an SASE, you'll hear from us." Query with SASE or submit 1-2 sample chapter(s), SASE, toc.

Recent Title(s): *Skyscrapers*, by Carol Johnmann; *Kids Book of Natural History*, by Judy Press.

Tips: "Our children's books are used by kids, their parents, and educators. They encourage self-discovery, creativity and personal growth. Our books are based on the philosophy that children learn best by doing, by being involved. Our authors need to be excited about their subject area and equally important, excited about kids. Please, please, please no storybooks of any kind."

WILLOW CREEK PRESS, P.O. Box 147, 9931 Highway 70 W., Minocqua WI 54548. (715)358-7010. Fax: (715)358-2807. E-mail: andread@willowcreekpress.com. Website: www.willowcreekpress.com. **Acquisitions:** Andrea Donner, managing editor. Estab. 1986. Publishes hardcover and trade paperback originals and reprints. **Publishes 25 titles/year. Receives 400 queries and 150 mss/year. 15% of books from first-time authors; 50% from unagented writers. Pays 6-15% royalty on wholesale price. Offers $2,000-5,000 advance.** Publishes book within 18 months after acceptance of ms. Accepts simultaneous submissions. Responds in 2 months to queries.

O⇢ "We specialize in nature, outdoor, and sporting topics, including gardening, wildlife and animal books. Pets, cookbooks, and a few humor books and essays round out our titles." Currently emphasizing pets (mainly dogs and cats), wildlife, outdoor sports (hunting, fishing). De-emphasizing essays, fiction.

Nonfiction: Coffee table book, cookbook, how-to, humor, illustrated book, reference. Subjects include animals, cooking/foods/nutrition, gardening, humor, nature/environment, recreation, sports, travel, wildlife, pets. Submit outline, 1 sample chapter(s), SASE. Reviews artwork/photos as part of ms package.

Recent Title(s): *What Dogs Teach Us*, by Glenn Dromgoole; *The American Mustang Guidebook*, by Lisa Dines; *Bear vs. Man*, by Brad Garfield.

WILLOWGATE PRESS, P.O. Box 6529, Holliston MA 01746. (508)429-8774. E-mail: willowgatepress@yahoo.com. Website: www.willowgatepress.com. **Acquisitions:** Robert Tolins, editor. Publishes trade paperback and mass market paperback originals. **Publishes 3-5 titles/year. 50% of books from first-time authors; 100% from unagented writers. Pays 5-15% royalty on retail price. Offers $500 advance.** Publishes book 6 months after acceptance of ms. Accepts simultaneous submissions. Responds in 2 months to queries; 6 months to mss. Book catalog and ms guidelines online.

O⇢ "Willowgate is a small, independent press established for the purpose of publishing good writing of the sort that the public is currently not receiving. Fundamentally, we seek to provide quality book-length fiction in all categories, and to see our titles widely promoted and kept available for longer than the brief shelf life allowed by the traditional houses. We believe that there is a need for a press whose goal is to publish quality works by new and established writers, without regard for the 'blockbuster' mentality that presently prevents more established houses from taking on such projects."

Fiction: Confession, erotica, ethnic, experimental, fantasy, feminist, gay/lesbian, gothic, hi-lo, historical, horror, humor, literary, mainstream/contemporary, military/war, multicultural, multimedia, mystery, occult, regional, romance, science fiction, short story collections, sports. Query with SASE or submit outline, plus the first ten pages and ten pages of the aurthor's choosing. Submit a complete, edited, revised and polished manuscript.

Tips: "If a manuscript is accepted for publication, we will make every effort to avoid lengthy delays in bringing the product to market. The writer will be given a voice in all aspects of publishing, promotion, advertising and marketing, including cover art, copy, promotional forums, etc. The writer will be expected to be an active and enthusiastic participant in all stages of the publication process. We hope to attract the finest writers of contemporary fiction and to help generate similar enthusiasm in them and in their readers. Please don't send cash or a check in lieu of stamps for return postage."

◼ **WILSHIRE BOOK CO.**, 12015 Sherman Rd., North Hollywood CA 91605-3781. (818)765-8579. Fax: (818)765-2922. E-mail: mpowers@mpowers.com. Website: www.mpowers.com. Publisher: Melvin Powers. **Acquisitions:** Marcia Grad, senior editor. Estab. 1947. Publishes trade paperback originals and reprints. **Publishes 25 titles/year. Receives 2,500 submissions/year. 80% of books from first-time authors; 75% from unagented writers. Pays standard royalty. Offers advance.** Publishes book 6 months after acceptance of ms. Responds in 2 months to queries. Welcomes telephone calls to discuss mss or book concepts.

Nonfiction: How-to, self-help, motivational/inspiration, recovery. Subjects include psychology, personal success, entrepreneurship, humor, Internet marketing, mail order, horsmanship, trick training for horses. Minimum 50,000 words. Query with SASE or submit outline, 3 sample chapter(s), author bio, analysis of book's competition, or submit complete ms. Reviews artwork/photos as part of ms package. Send photocopies.

Fiction: Allegories that teach principles of psychological growth or offer guidance in living. Minimum 25,000 words. Submit 3 sample chapter(s), synopsis or submit complete ms.

Recent Title(s): *The Secret of Overcoming Verbal Abuse*, by Dr. Albert Ellis and Marcia Grad Powers.

Tips: "We are vitally interested in all new material we receive. Just as you hopefully submit your manuscript for publication, we hopefully read every one submitted, searching for those that we believe will be successful in the marketplace. Writing and publishing must be a team effort. We need you to write what we can sell. We suggest that you read the successful books mentioned above or others that are similar to the manuscript you want to write. Analyze them to discover what elements make them winners. Duplicate those elements in your own style, using a creative new approach and fresh material, and you will have written a book we can catapult onto the bestseller list."

N̳ WINDSOR BOOKS, Windsor Marketing Corp., P.O. Box 280, Brightwaters NY 11718-0280. (631)321-7830. Website: www.windsorpublishing.com. **Acquisitions:** Jeff Schmidt, managing editor. Estab. 1968. Publishes hardcover and trade paperback originals, reprints, and very specific software. **Publishes 6 titles/year. Receives approximately 40 submissions/year. 60% of books from first-time authors; 90% from unagented writers. Pays 10% royalty on retail price; 5% on whoelsale price (50% of total cost). Offers variable advance.** Publishes book an average of 6 months after acceptance of ms. Accepts simultaneous submissions. Responds in 2 weeks to queries. Book catalog and ms guidelines free.

O⇢ "Our books are for serious investors."

Nonfiction: Interested in books on strategies, methods for investing in the stock market, options market and commodities markets. How-to, technical. Subjects include business/economics (investing in stocks and commodities), money/finance, software. Query with SASE or submit outline, sample chapter(s). Reviews artwork/photos as part of ms package.
Tips: "We sell through direct mail to our mailing list and other financial lists. Writers must keep their work original; this market tends to have a great deal of information overlap among publications."

WINDSTORM CREATIVE LTD, (formerly Pride & Imprints), 7419 Ebbert Dr. SE, Port Orchard WA 98367. Website: www.windstormcreative.com. **Acquisitions:** (Ms.) Cris Newport, senior editor. Estab. 1989. Publishes trade paperback originals and reprints. **Publishes 50 titles/year. Receives 5,200 queries and 15,000 mss/year. Pays 10-15% royalty on wholesale price.** Publishes book 1-2 years after acceptance of ms. Responds in 6 months to mss.
O— Publisher of fiction and poetry.
Fiction: Adventure, erotica, experimental, fantasy, gay/lesbian, gothic, historical, humor, literary, science fiction, young adult. No children's books, horror, "bestseller" fiction, spy or espionage novels, "thrillers," any work which describes childhood sexual abuse or in which this theme figures prominently. Query with cover letter and a one page synopsis of the ms which details the major plot developments. SASE required.
Recent Title(s): *Bones Become Flowers*, by Jess Mowry (contemporary); *Annabel and I*, by Chris Anne Wolfe (lesbian); *Journey of a Thousand Miles*, by Peter Kasting (gay).
Tips: "Visit website for detailed submission instructions."

WINDSWEPT HOUSE PUBLISHERS, P.O. Box 159, Mount Desert ME 04660-0159. (207)244-5027. Fax: (207)244-3369. E-mail: winswept@acadia.net. Website: www.booknotes.com/windswept. **Acquisitions:** Mavis Weinberger, owner. Publishes hardcover and trade paperback originals. **Publishes 4 titles/year. Pays up to 10% royalty.** Responds in 1 month to queries. Book catalog online; ms guidelines for #10 SASE.
Nonfiction: Biography, children's/juvenile, illustrated book. Subjects include animals, history, memoirs, nature/environment, regional. *All unsolicited mss returned unopened.* Reviews artwork/photos as part of ms package. Send photocopies.
Recent Title(s): *Tulips Under the Quarter Moon*, by Grant Judd (poetry with illustrations).

WINDWARD PUBLISHING, INC., 3943 Meadowbrook Road, Minneapolis MN 55426. (952)938-9330. Fax: (952)938-7353. E-mail: feedback@finney-hobar.com. Website: www.finney-hobar.com. **Acquisitions:** Alan E. Kryson, president. Estab. 1973. Publishes trade paperback originals. **Publishes 6-10 titles/year. Receives 50 queries and 10 mss/year. 35% of books from first-time authors; 100% from unagented writers. Pays 10% royalty on wholesale price. Offers advance.** Publishes book 6-12 months after acceptance of ms. Accepts simultaneous submissions. Responds in 3 weeks to queries.
O— Windward publishes illustrated natural history and recreation books.
Nonfiction: Illustrated book, handbooks, field guides. Subjects include agriculture/horticulture, animals, gardening, nature/environment, recreation, science, sports, natural history. Query with SASE. Reviews artwork/photos as part of ms package.
Recent Title(s): *Birds of the Water, Sea, and Shore*, by Romashko; *Mammals of Florida*, by Brown.

WINSLOW PRESS, 115 E. 23rd St., 10th Floor, New York NY 10010. (212)254-2025. Fax: (212)254-2410. E-mail: winslow@winslowpress.com. Website: www.winslowpress.com. Publishes hardcover originals. **Publishes 30 titles/year. Receives 2,000 mss/year. 20% of books from first-time authors; 30% from unagented writers. Pays royalty. Offers advance.** Accepts simultaneous submissions. Responds in 4 months to queries. Book catalog for 8×10 SAE with 75¢ first-class stamps.
Nonfiction: Children's/juvenile only. Subjects include all but inspirational. Query with SASE. Reviews artwork/photos as part of ms package. Send photocopies.
Fiction: All juvenile subjects, except inspirational Not accepting picture books at this time.
Poetry: Children's/juvenile only.
Tips: "We publish books for children from pre-K to young adult. We have an innovative Web program which all of our books are a part of."

WISDOM PUBLICATIONS, 199 Elm St., Somerville MA 02144. (617)776-7416 ext. 25. Fax: (617)776-7841. E-mail: editorial@wisdompubs.org. Website: www.wisdompubs.org. Publisher: Timothy McNeill. **Acquisitions:** E. Gene Smith, acquisitions editor. Estab. 1976. Publishes hardcover originals, trade paperback originals and reprints. **Publishes 12-15 titles/year. Receives 240 queries/year. 50% of books from first-time authors; 95% from unagented writers. Pays 4-8% royalty on wholesale price. Offers advance.** Publishes book within 2 years after acceptance of ms. Book catalog and ms guidelines online.
O— Wisdom Publications is dedicated to making available authentic Buddhist works for the benefit of all. "We publish translations, commentaries and teachings of past and contemporary Buddhist masters and original works by leading Buddhist scholars." Currently emphasizing popular applied Buddhism, scholarly titles.
Nonfiction: Reference, self-help, textbook (Buddhist). Subjects include philosophy (Buddhist or comparative Buddhist/Western), psychology, religion, Buddhism, Tibet. Query with SASE. Reviews artwork/photos as part of ms package. Send photocopies.
Poetry: Buddhist. Query.

Recent Title(s): *Engaged Buddhism in the West*, by Christopher S. Queen.
Tips: "We are basically a publisher of Buddhist books—all schools and traditions of Buddhism. Please see our catalog or our website *before* you send anything to us to get a sense of what we publish."

N **WISH PUBLISHING**, P.O. Box 10337, Terre Haute IN 47801. (812)478-3529. Fax: (812)447-1836. E-mail: holly@wishpublishing.com. Website: www.wishpublishing.com. **Acquisitions:** Holly Kondras, president. Publishes hardcover and trade paperback originals. **Publishes 5-10 titles/year. Pays 10-18% royalty on wholesale price.** Accepts simultaneous submissions. Responds in 2 months to queries, proposals and mss. Book catalog and ms guidelines online.
Nonfiction: Biography, children's/juvenile, reference. Subjects include health/medicine, sports, women's issues/studies. Query with SASE or submit proposal package including outline, 2 sample chapter(s), author bio. Reviews artwork/photos as part of ms package. Send photocopies.
Recent Title(s): *Entering the Mother Zone* (parenting); *Tae Kwon Do for Women* (sports).
Tips: Audience is women and girls who play sports and their coaches, parents and supporters.

WIZARDS OF THE COAST, P.O. Box 707, Renton WA 98057-0707. (425)226-6500. Website: www.wizards.com. Executive Editor: Mary Kirchoff. **Acquisitions:** Peter Archer, editorial director. Publishes hardcover and trade paperback originals and trade paperback reprints. **Publishes 50-60 titles/year. Receives 600 queries and 300 mss/year. 25% of books from first-time authors; 35% from unagented writers. Pays 4-8% royalty on retail price. Offers $4,000-6,000 average advance.** Publishes book 1 year after acceptance of ms. Accepts simultaneous submissions. Responds in 4 months to queries. Manuscript guidelines for #10 SASE.
Imprints: Dragonlance Books; Forgotten Realms Books; Greyhawk Novels; Magic: The Gathering Books; Legend of the Five Rings Novels; Star*Drive Books
   Oᴙ Wizards of the Coast publishes science fiction and fantasy shared world titles. Currently emphasizing solid fantasy writers. De-emphasizing gothic fiction.
Nonfiction: "All of our nonfiction books are generated inhouse."
Fiction: Fantasy, gothic, science fiction, short story collections. "We currently publish only work-for-hire novels set in our trademarked worlds. No violent or gory fantasy or science fiction." Request guidelines, then query with outline/synopsis and 3 sample chapters.
Recent Title(s): *Dragons of a Lost Star*, by Margaret Weis and Tracy Hickman.
Tips: "Our audience largely is comprised of highly imaginative 12-30 year-old males."

WOODBINE HOUSE, 6510 Bells Mill Rd., Bethesda MD 20817. (301)897-3570. Fax: (301)897-5838. E-mail: gray@woodbinehouse.com. **Acquisitions:** Mary Gray, assistant editor. Estab. 1985. Publishes hardcover and trade paperback originals and reprints. **Publishes 10 titles/year. 90% from unagented writers. Pays 10-12% royalty. Offers advance.** Publishes book 18 months after acceptance of ms. Accepts simultaneous submissions. Responds in 8 months to queries. Book catalog and ms guidelines for 6×9 SAE with 3 first-class stamps.
   Oᴙ Woodbine House publishes books for or about individuals with disabilities to help those individuals and their families live fulfilling and satisfying lives in their communities.
Nonfiction: Publishes books for and about children and adults with disabilities. Reference. Subjects include health/medicine. No personal accounts or general parenting guides. Submit outline, 3 sample chapter(s). Reviews artwork/photos as part of ms package.
Fiction: Picture books (children's). Submit complete ms. with SASE.
Recent Title(s): *Children with Autism: A Parent's Guide, 2nd ed.*, by Michael D. Powers, Ed; *How Many Days Until Tomorrow?*, by Caroline Janover.
Tips: "Do not send us a proposal on the basis of this description. Examine our catalog and a couple of our books to make sure you are on the right track. Put some thought into how your book could be marketed (aside from in bookstores). Keep cover letters concise and to the point; if it's a subject that interests us, we'll ask to see more."

WOODLAND PUBLISHING INC., P.O. Box 160, Pleasant Grove UT 84062. (801)785-8100. Fax: (801)785-8511. Website: www.woodlandpublishing.com. Publisher: Calvin Harper. **Acquisitions:** Cord Udall, editor. Estab. 1974. Publishes perfect bound and trade paperback originals. **Publishes 20 titles/year. Receives 100 queries and 60 mss/year. 50% of books from first-time authors; 100% from unagented writers. Offers advance.** Publishes book 6 months after acceptance of ms. Accepts simultaneous submissions. Responds in 1 month. *Writer's Market* recommends allowing 2 months for reply to proposals. Book catalog and ms guidelines for #10 SASE or online.
   Oᴙ "Our readers are interested in herbs and other natural health topics. Most of our books are sold through health food stores."
Nonfiction: Subjects include health/medicine (alternative). Query with SASE.
Recent Title(s): *Soy Smart Health*, by Neil Soloman, M.D.
Tips: "Our readers are interested in herbs and other natural health topics. Most of our books are sold through health food stores."

WORDWARE PUBLISHING, INC., 2320 Los Rios Blvd., Suite 200, Plano TX 75074. (972)423-0090. Fax: (972)881-9147. E-mail: jhill@wordware.com. Website: www.wordware.com. President: Russell A. Stultz. **Acquisitions:** Jim Hill, publisher. Estab. 1983. Publishes trade paperback and mass market paperback originals. **Publishes 50-60 titles/**

year. **Receives 100-150 queries and 50-75 mss/year. 40% of books from first-time authors; 95% from unagented writers. Pays 8% royalty on wholesale price. Offers advance.** Publishes book 6 months after acceptance of ms. Accepts simultaneous submissions. Responds in 2 months to queries. Book catalog free; ms guidelines online.
Imprints: Republic of Texas Press
    O→ Wordware publishes computer/electronics books covering a broad range of technologies for professional programmers and developers.
Nonfiction: Reference, technical, textbook. Subjects include computers/electronic. "Wordware publishes advanced titles for developers and professional programmers." Submit proposal package including 2 sample chapter(s), table of contents, target audience summation, competing books.
Recent Title(s): *The Tomes of Delphi Win32 Database Developers Guide*, by Warren Rachele; *Search Engine Positioning*, by Frederick Marckini.

WORKMAN PUBLISHING CO., 708 Broadway, New York NY 10003. (212)254-5900. Fax: (212)254-8098. Website: www.workman.com. Editor-in-chief: Susan Bolotin. **Acquisitions:** Suzanne Rafer, executive editor (cookbook, child care, parenting, teen interest); Ruth Sullivan, senior editor (humor, fashion, health); Liz Carey, senior editor (crafts, children, humor). Estab. 1967. Publishes hardcover and trade paperback originals. **Publishes 40 titles/year. Receives thousands queries/year. Open to first-time authors. Pays variable royalty on retail price. Offers varying advance.** Publishes book 1 year after acceptance of ms. Accepts simultaneous submissions. Responds in 5 months to queries. Book catalog free.
Imprints: Algonquin Books of Chapel Hill, Artisan
    O→ "We are a trade paperback house specializing in a wide range of popular nonfiction. We publish no adult fiction and very little children's fiction. We also publish a full range of full color wall and Page-A-Day calendars."
Nonfiction: Cookbook, gift book, how-to, humor. Subjects include child guidance/parenting, cooking/foods/nutrition, gardening, health/medicine, humor, sports, travel. Query with SASE first for guidelines. Reviews artwork/photos as part of ms package.
Recent Title(s): *Antiques Roadshow Primer*, by Carol Prisant; *The Cake Mix Doctor*, by Anne Byrn.
Tips: "No phone calls please. We do not accept submissions via fax or e-mail."

WORLD LEISURE, P.O. Box 160, Hampstead NH 03841. (617)569-1966. Fax: (617)561-7654. E-mail: wleisure @aol.com. Website: www.worldleisure.com. **Acquisitions:** Charles Leocha, president. Estab. 1977. Publishes trade paperback originals. **Publishes 3-5 titles/year. Pays royalty or makes outright purchase.** Responds in 2 months to queries. Book catalog and ms guidelines online.
    O→ World Leisure specializes in travel books, activity guidebooks and self-help titles.
Nonfiction: Self-help. Subjects include recreation, sports (skiing), travel. "We will be publishing annual updates to *Ski Europe* and *Skiing America*. Writers planning any ski stories should contact us for possible add-on assignments at areas not covered by our staff. We also will publish general travel titles such as *Travelers' Rights*, Family travel guides, guidebooks about myths and legends, the *Cheap Dates* (affordable activity guidebooks) series and self-help books such as *Getting To Know You*, and *A Woman's ABCs of Life*." Submit outline, intro sample chapter(s), SASE, annotated table of contents.
Recent Title(s): *Millionaires Handbook*, by Peter Miller.

WRITE WAY PUBLISHING, P.O. Box 441278, Aurora CO 80044. (303)617-0497. Fax: (303)617-1440. E-mail: staff@writewaypub.com. Website: www.writewaypub.com. **Acquisitions:** Dorrie O'Brien, owner/editor. Estab. 1993. Publishes hardcover and trade paperback originals. **Publishes 10-15 titles/year. Receives 1,000 queries and 350 mss/year. 50% of books from first-time authors; 5% from unagented writers. Pays 8-10% royalty on wholesale price.** Publishes book within 3 years after acceptance of ms. Accepts simultaneous submissions. Responds in 1 month to queries; 9 months to mss. Book catalog and ms guidelines for #10 SASE.
    O→ Write Way is a fiction-only small press concentrating on mysteries, soft science fiction and fairy tale/fantasys. Currently emphasizing adult (whodunit?) mysteries/science fiction/fantasy. De-emphasizing suspense, spy, adventure, literature, romance, et al.
Fiction: Fantasy, horror, mystery, science fiction. "We only consider completed works." Query with SASE or submit first 1-2 sample chapter(s), synopsis, postage with proper sized box or envelope.
Recent Title(s): *The Music Box Mysteries*, by Larry Karp; *The Deadline*, by Ron Franscell.
Tips: "We find that lengthy outlines and/or synopsis are unnecessary and much too time-consuming for our editors to read. We prefer a very short plot review and one to two chapters to get a feel for the writer's style. If we like what we read, then we'll ask for the whole manuscript."

WRITER'S DIGEST BOOKS, F&W Publications, 1507 Dana Ave., Cincinnati OH 45207. (513)531-2690. Fax: (513)531-7107. Website: www.writersdigest.com. **Acquisitions:** Jack Heffron. Estab. 1920. Publishes hardcover and paperback originals. **Publishes 28 titles/year. Receives 500 queries and 100 mss/year. 20% from unagented writers. Pays 10-20% royalty on net receipts. Offers average $5,000 and up advance.** Publishes book 18 months after acceptance of ms. Accepts simultaneous submissions. Responds in 2 months to queries. Book catalog for 9×12 SAE with 6 first-class stamps.
Imprints: Walking Stick (journaling and self-discovery)

O─┐ Writer's Digest Books is the premiere source for books about writing, publishing instructional and reference books for writers that concentrate on the creative technique and craft of writing rather than the marketing of writing.

Nonfiction: How-to, reference, instructional, creativity books for writers. Subjects include language/literature, music/dance, photography. "Our instruction books stress results and how specifically to achieve them. Should be well-researched, yet lively and readable. Our books concentrate on writing techniques over marketing techniques. We do *not* want to see books telling readers how to crack specific nonfiction markets: *Writing for the Computer Market* or *Writing for Trade Publications*, for instance. Concentrate on broader writing topics. We are continuing to grow our line of reference books for writers with titles such as the *Writer's Book of Character Trains* and *Careers for Characters*. References must be usable, accessible, and, of course, accurate. Be prepared to explain how the proposed book differs from existing books on the subject." No fiction or poetry. Query with SASE or submit outline, sample chapter(s), SASE.

Recent Title(s): *Guerilla Marketing for Writers*, by Jay Conrad Levinson and Michael Larsen.

Tips: "Writer's Digest Books also publishes instructional books for photographers and songwriters, but the main thrust is on writing books. The same philosophy applies to songwriting and photography books: they must instruct about the creative craft, as opposed to instructing about marketing."

YALE UNIVERSITY PRESS, 302 Temple St., New Haven CT 06511. (203)432-0960. Fax: (203)432-0948. Website: www.yale.edu/yup. **Acquisitions:** Jonathan Brent, editorial director (literature, philosophy, poetry, Annals of Communism, Cold War studies, Judaic studies); Susan C. Arellano (behavioral and social sciences, education); Jean E. Thomson Black (science and medicine); Alex Schwartz (reference books); Harry Haskell (archaeology, classics, music and performing arts); Lara Heimert (English-language literary studies); Patricia Fidler (art and architectural history, geography, landscape studies); Mary Jane Peluso (languages); Tamara Belknap (Yale Series of Younger Poets). Estab. 1908. Publishes hardcover and trade paperback originals. **Publishes 250 titles/year. Receives 8,000 queries and 400 mss/year. 15% of books from first-time authors; 85% from unagented writers. Pays 0-15% royalty on net receipts. Offers $500-50,000 (based on expected sales) advance.** Publishes book 1 year after acceptance of ms. Accepts simultaneous submissions. Responds in 1 month to queries; 2 months to proposals; 3 months to mss. Book catalog and ms guidelines for #10 SASE.

O─┐ Yale University Press publishes scholarly and general interest books.

Nonfiction: Biography, illustrated book, reference, textbook, scholarly works. Subjects include Americana, anthropology/archeology, art/architecture, business/economics, education, health/medicine, history, language/literature, military/war, music/dance, philosophy, psychology, religion, science, sociology, women's issues/studies. "Our nonfiction has to be at a very high level. Most of our books are written by professors or journalists, with a high level of expertise. Submit proposals only. We'll ask if we want to see more. *No unsolicited mss.* We won't return them." Query with SASE. Reviews artwork/photos as part of ms package. Send photocopies.

Poetry: Publishes 1 book each year. Submit to Yale Series of Younger Poets Competition. Open to poets under 40 who have not had a book previously published. Submit ms of 48-64 pages in February only! Entry fee: $15. Rules and guidelines available online or via SASE. Submit complete ms.

Recent Title(s): *Bill Evans: How My Heart Sings*, by Peter Pettinger.

Tips: "Audience is scholars, students and general readers."

YMAA PUBLICATION CENTER, 4354 Washington St., Roslindale MA 02131. (617)323-7215. Fax: (617)323-7417. E-mail: ymaa@aol.com. Website: www.ymaa.com. **Acquisitions:** David Ripianzi, director. Estab. 1982. Publishes hardcover and trade paperback originals and reprints. **Publishes 10 titles/year. Receives 50 queries and 20 mss/year. 25% of books from first-time authors; 100% from unagented writers. Pays 7-10% royalty on net receipts.** Publishes book 18 months after acceptance of ms. Accepts simultaneous submissions. Responds in 3 months to proposals. Book catalog online; ms guidelines free.

O─┐ "YMAA publishes books on Chinese Chi Kung (Qigong), Taijiquan, Tai Chi and Asian martial arts. We are expanding our focus to include books on healing, wellness, meditation and subjects related to Asian culture and Asian medicine." De-emphasizing fitness books.

Nonfiction: "We are most interested in Asian martial arts, Chinese medicine and Chinese Qigong. We publish Eastern thought, health, meditation, massage and East/West synthesis." How-to, multimedia, self-help. Subjects include ethnic, health/medicine (Chinese), history, philosophy, spirituality, sports, Asian martial arts, Chinese Qigong. "We no longer publish or solicit books for children. We also produce instructional videos to accompany our books on traditional Chinese martial arts, meditation, massage and Chi Kung." Submit proposal package including outline, 1 sample chapter(s), author bio, SASE. Reviews artwork/photos as part of ms package. Send photocopies and 1-2 originals to determine quality of photo/line art.

Recent Title(s): *A Woman's Qigong Guide*, by Yanling Johnson.

Tips: "If you are submitting health-related material, please refer to an Asian tradition. Learn about author publicity options as your participation is mandatory."

YUCCA TREE PRESS, 2130 Hixon Dr., Las Cruces NM 88005-3305. (505)524-2357. Fax: (505)523-8935. E-mail: yuccatree@zianet.com. Website: www.yuccatree.com. **Acquisitions:** Janie Matson, publisher. Publishes hardcover and trade paperback originals and trade paperback reprints. **Publishes 3-6 titles/year. Receives 15 queries and 10 mss/**

year. 75% of books from first-time authors; 100% from unagented writers. Pays 10-20% royalty on wholesale price. Publishes book 1 year after acceptance of ms. Responds in 1 month to queries. Book catalog online; ms guidelines for #10 SASE.

Nonfiction: Military and Southwestern history only. Subjects include history (Southwestern), military/war. No fiction or historical fiction. Query with SASE. Reviews artwork/photos as part of ms package. Send photocopies.

Tips: Targets adult readers of quality history.

ZEBRA BOOKS, Kensington, 850 Third Ave., 16th Floor, New York NY 10022. (212)407-1500. Website: www.kensin gtonbooks.com. **Acquisitions:** Ann Lafarge, executive editor; Kate Duffy, senior editor (historical, regency, romance); John Scognamiglio, senior editor (romance, mystery, thrillers, pop culture); Hillary Sares (Precious Gem contemporary romances); Amy Garvey, editor (Precious Gem historical romances); Karen Thomas, editorial director(Arabesque, Dafina); Elaine Sparber, senior editor (health and alternative health). Publishes hardcover originals, trade paperback and mass market paperback originals and reprints. **Publishes 140-170 titles/year. 5% of books from first-time authors; 30% from unagented writers. Pays variable royalty. Offers variable advance.** Publishes book 18 months after acceptance of ms. Accepts simultaneous submissions. Responds in 1 month to queries; 3 months to mss. Book catalog online.

O→ Zebra Books is dedicated to women's fiction, which includes, but is not limited to romance.

Fiction: Romance, women's fiction. *No unsolicited mss.* Query with SASE or submit synopsis, SASE.

ZOLAND BOOKS, INC., 384 Huron Ave., Cambridge MA 02138. (617)864-6252. Fax: (617)661-4998. **Acquisitions:** Roland Pease, Jr., publisher/editor. Estab. 1987. Publishes hardcover and trade paperback originals. **Publishes 14 titles/year. Receives 700 submissions/year. 15% of books from first-time authors; 40% from unagented writers. Pays 7½% royalty on retail price. Offers advance.** Publishes book 18 months after acceptance of ms. Responds in 3 months to queries. Book catalog for 6½×9½ SAE with 2 first-class stamps.

O→ Zoland Books is an independent publishing company producing fiction, poetry and art books of literary interest.

Nonfiction: Biography. Subjects include art/architecture, language/literature, nature/environment, photography, regional, translation, travel, women's issues/studies. Query with SASE. Reviews artwork/photos as part of ms package.

Fiction: Literary, short story collections. Submit complete ms. *Writer's Market* recommends querying with SASE first.

Recent Title(s): *Children of Pithiviers*, by Sheila Kohler; *To Repel Ghosts*, by Kevin Young; *In the Pond*, Ha Jin.

Tips: "We are most likely to publish books which provide original, thought-provoking ideas, books which will captivate the reader and are evocative."

ZONDERVAN, HarperCollins Publishers, 5300 Patterson Ave. SE, Grand Rapids MI 49530-0002. (616)698-6900. E-mail: zpub@zondervan.com. Website: www.zondervan.com. Executive VP: Scott Bolinder. **Acquisitions:** Manuscript Review Editor. Estab. 1931. Publishes hardcover and trade paperback originals and reprints. **Publishes 120 titles/year. Receives 3,000 submissions/year. 10% of books from first-time authors; 60% from unagented writers. Pays 14% royalty on net amount received on sales of cloth and softcover trade editions; 12% royalty on net amount received on sales of mass market paperbacks. Offers variable advance.** Responds in 3 months to proposals. Manuscript guidelines for #10 SASE.

Imprints: Zonderkidz, Inspiro (includes Bible covers, devotional calendars)

O→ "Our mission is to be the leading Christian communications company meeting the needs of people with resources that glorify Jesus Christ and promote biblical principles."

Nonfiction: All religious perspective (evangelical). Biography, children's/juvenile, reference, self-help, textbook. Subjects include history, memoirs, religion, Christian living, devotional, Bible study resources, preaching, counseling, college and seminary textbooks, discipleship, worship, and church renewal for pastors, professionals and lay leaders in ministry; theological and biblical reference books. Query with SASE or submit outline, 1 sample chapter(s).

Fiction: Some adult fiction. Refer to nonfiction. Query with SASE or submit outline, 1 sample chapter(s), synopsis.

Recent Title(s): *Soul Salsa*, by Leonard Sweet (nonfiction); *Blood of Heaven*, by Bill Myers (fiction).

MARKET CONDITIONS are constantly changing! If this is 2003 or later, buy the newest edition of *Writer's Market* at your favorite bookstore or order directly from Writer's Digest Books at (800)289-0963.

Canadian Book Publishers

Canadian book publishers share the same mission as their U.S. counterparts—publishing timely books on subjects of concern and interest to a targetable audience. Most of the publishers listed in this section, however, differ from U.S. publishers in that their needs tend toward subjects that are specifically Canadian or intended for a Canadian audience. Some are interested in submissions from Canadian writers only. There are many regional Canadian publishers that concentrate on region-specific subjects, and many Quebec publishers will consider only works in French.

U.S. writers hoping to do business with Canadian publishers should take pains to find out as much about their intended markets as possible. The listings will inform you about what kinds of books the companies publish and tell you whether they are open to receiving submissions from nonCanadians. To further target your markets and see very specific examples of the books they are publishing, send for catalogs from publishers or check their websites.

There has always been more government subsidy of publishing in Canada than in the U.S. However, with continued cuts in such subsidies, government support is on the decline. There are a few author-subsidy publishers in Canada and writers should proceed with caution when they are made this offer.

Publishers offering author-subsidy arrangements (sometimes referred to as "joint venture," "co-publishing" or "cooperative publishing") are not listed in *Writer's Market*. If one of the publishers in this section offers you an author-subsidy arrangement or asks you to pay for all or part of the cost of any aspect of publishing (printing, marketing, etc.) or asks you to guarantee the purchase of a number of books yourself, please let us know about that company immediately.

Despite a healthy book publishing industry, Canada is still dominated by publishers from the U.S. Two out of every three books found in Canadian bookstores are published in the U.S. These odds have made some Canadian publishers even more determined to concentrate on Canadian authors and subjects. Canadian publishers that accept manuscripts only from Canadian authors are indicated by the 🗺 symbol. Writers interested in additional Canadian book publishing markets should consult *Literary Market Place* (R.R. Bowker & Co.), and *The Canadian Writer's Market* (McClelland & Stewart).

INTERNATIONAL MAIL

U.S. postage stamps are useless on mailings originating outside of the U.S. When enclosing a self-addressed envelope for return of your query or manuscript from a publisher outside the U.S., you must include International Reply Coupons (IRCs) or postage stamps from that country. Canadian stamps are sold online at http://www.canadapost.ca. IRCs are available at your local post office and can be redeemed for stamps of any country. You can cut a substantial portion of your international mailing expenses by sending disposable proposals and manuscripts (i.e., photocopies or computer printouts which the recipient can recycle if she is not interested), instead of paying postage for the return of rejected material. Please note that the cost for items such as catalogs is expressed in the currency of the country in which the publisher is located.

For a list of publishers according to their subjects of interest, see the nonfiction and fiction sections of the Book Publishers Subject Index. Information on book publishers and producers listed in the previous edition of *Writer's Market* but not included in this edition can be found in the General Index.

N ◼ **ADVENTURE BOOK PUBLISHERS**, Durksen Enterprises Ltd. #712-3545-32 Ave. NE, Calgary, Alberta T1Y 6M6, Canada. (403)285-6844. E-mail: adventure@puzzlesbyshar.com. Website: www.puzzlesbyshar.com/adventur ebooks. Publishes digital books. **Publishes 30-50 titles/year. Receives 1,000 queries and 400 mss/year. 100% of books from first-time authors; 100% from unagented writers. Pays 20% royalty.** Publishes book 7 months after acceptance of ms. Accepts simultaneous submissions. Responds in 1 month to queries; 1 month to proposals; 5 months to mss. Book catalog online; ms guidelines provided by e-mail to invited authors.

Nonfiction: Biography, children's/juvenile, cookbook, how-to, humor, self-help. Subjects include Americana, animals, cooking/foods/nutrition, creative nonfiction, history, military/war, nature/environment. Query with synopsis via e-mail only. Reviews artwork/photos as part of ms package. Send GIF or JPEG images via e-mail.

Fiction: Adventure, historical, horror, humor, juvenile, mainstream/contemporary, military/war, mystery, romance, science fiction, short story collections, suspense, western, young adult. "Graphic sex/violence in excess is not necessary to tell a good or compelling story." Query with synopsis via e-mail only.

Recent Title(s): *Who! Me?*, by Sharon Kuntz (humor); *Star Ranger*, by Robert Blacketer (science fiction).

Tips: "We specialize in unpublished writers since they are the ones who need the most help and encouragement. As such, we do not encourage agency submissions. Manuscripts by invitation only. Materials sent via regular mail are returned only if adequate international postage is included (U.S. postage is not valid)."

THE ALTHOUSE PRESS, University of Western Ontario, Faculty of Education, 1137 Western Rd., London, Ontario N6G 1G7, Canada. (519)661-2096. Fax: (519)661-3833. E-mail: press@uwo.ca. Website: www.edu.uwo.ca/althousepre ss. Director: Dr. David Radcliffe. **Acquisitions:** Katherine Butson, editorial assistant. Publishes trade paperback originals and reprints. **Publishes 1-5 titles/year. Receives 30 queries and 19 mss/year. 50% of books from first-time authors; 100% from unagented writers. Pays 10% royalty. Offers $300 advance.** Publishes book 6 months after acceptance of ms. Accepts simultaneous submissions. Responds in 1 month to queries; 4 months to mss. Book catalog and ms guidelines free.

　　O⟶ "The Althouse Press publishes both scholarly research monographs in education, and professional books and materials for educators in elementary schools, secondary schools and faculties of education." De-emphasizing curricular or instructional materials intended for use by elementary or secondary school students.

Nonfiction: Subjects include education (scholarly). "Do not send incomplete manuscripts that are only marginally appropriate to our market and limited mandate." Reviews artwork/photos as part of ms package. Send photocopies.

Recent Title(s): *Hyper Texts*, by Ellen Rose; *For the Love of Teaching*, by Brent Kilbourn.

Tips: Audience is practising teachers and graduate education students.

ANNICK PRESS LTD., 15 Patricia Ave., Toronto, Ontario M2M 1H9, Canada. (416)221-4802. Fax: (416)221-8400. E-mail: annick@annickpress.com. Website: www.annickpress.com. **Acquisitions:** Rick Wilks, director (picturebooks, nonfiction, young adult fiction); Colleen MacMillan, associate publisher (YA, juvenile nonfiction). Publishes hardcover and trade paperback originals and mass market paperback reprints. **Publishes 25 titles/year. Receives 5,000 queries and 3,000 mss/year. 20% of books from first-time authors; 80-85% from unagented writers. Pays 10-12% royalty. Offers $2,000-4,000 advance.** Publishes book 2 years after acceptance of ms. Responds in 1 month to queries; 2 months to proposals; 3 months to mss. Book catalog free or online; ms guidelines free.

　　O⟶ Annick Press maintains "a commitment to high quality books that entertain and challenge. Our publications share fantasy and stimulate imagination, while encouraging children to trust their judgment and abilities."

Nonfiction: Children's/juvenile. Query with SASE. Reviews artwork/photos as part of ms package. Send photocopies.

Fiction: Juvenile, young adult. Query with SASE.

Recent Title(s): *Jungle Islands: My South Sea Adventure*, by Maria Coffey and Debora Pearson; *Leslie's Journal*, by Allan Stratton (young adult); *Night School*, by Loris Lesynski.

◼ ANVIL PRESS, 204-A 175 E. Broadway, Vancouver, British Columbia V5T 1W2, Canada. (604)876-8710. Fax: (604)879-2667. E-mail: subter@portal.ca. Website: www.anvilpress.com. **Acquisitions:** Brian Kaufman. Publishes trade paperback originals. **Publishes 6 titles/year. Receives 300 queries/year. 80% of books from first-time authors; 70% from unagented writers. Pays 15% royalty on net receipts. Offers advance.** Publishes book 8 months after acceptance of ms. Responds in 2 months to queries; 2 months to proposals; 6 months to mss. Book catalog for 9×12 SAE with 2 first-class stamps; ms guidelines for #10 SASE.

　　O⟶ "Anvil Press publishes contemporary adult fiction, poetry and drama, giving voice to up-and-coming Canadian writers, exploring all literary genres, discovering, nurturing and promoting new Canadian literary talent." Currently emphasizing urban/suburban themed fiction and poetry; de-emphasizing historical novels.

Fiction: Contemporary, modern literature—no formulaic or genre. Query with SASE.

Poetry: "Get our catalog, look at our poetry. We do very little poetry in book form—maybe 1-2 titles per year." Query or submit 12 sample poems.

Recent Title(s): *Snatch*, by Judy MacInnes Jr (poetry); *Touched*, by Jodi Lundgren (fiction).

Tips: Audience is young, informed, educated, aware, with an opinion, culturally active (films, books, the performing arts). "No U.S. authors, unless selected as the winner of our 3-Day Novel Contest. Research the appropriate publisher for your work."

N ◼ ARSENAL PULP PRESS, 103, 1014 Homer St., Vancouver, British Columbia V6B 2W9, Canada. (604)687-4233. Fax: (604)669-8250. E-mail: contact@arsenalpulp.com. Website: www.arsenalpulp.com. **Acquisitions:** Linda

Field, editor. Estab. 1980. Publishes hardcover and trade paperback originals and trade paperback reprints. **Publishes 16 titles/year. Receives 400 queries and 200 mss/year. 40% of books from first-time authors; 100% from unagented writers. Pays 15% royalty on wholesale price. Offers $500-1,000 advance.** Publishes book 1 year after acceptance of ms. Accepts simultaneous submissions. Responds in 1 month to queries; 4 months to proposals; 4 months to mss. Catalog for 9×12 SAE with 2 first-class stamps or online; ms guidelines for #10 SASE or online.
Nonfiction: Cookbook, humor, illustrated book, literary, cultural studies. Subjects include art/architecture, cooking/foods/nutrition, creative nonfiction, ethnic (Canadian, aboriginal issues), gay/lesbian, history (cultural), language/literature, multicultural, music/dance (popular), regional (British Columbia), sex, sociology, travel, women's issues/studies, film. Submit proposal package including outline, 2-3 sample chapter(s). Reviews artwork/photos as part of ms package.
Fiction: Erotica, ethnic, experimental, feminist, gay/lesbian, literary, multicultural, short story collections. Submit proposal package including 2-3 sample chapter(s), synopsis.
Recent Title(s): *How It All Vegan*, by Bernard & Kramer (nonfiction-cookbook); *Carnal Nation*, by Brooks & Grubisic (fiction anthology).

BEACH HOLME PUBLISHERS LTD., 226-2040 W. 12th Ave., Vancouver, British Columbia V6J 2G2, Canada. (604)733-4868. Fax: (604)733-4860. E-mail: bhp@beachholme.bc.ca. Website: www.beachholme.bc.ca. **Acquisitions:** Michael Carroll, publisher (adult and young adult fiction, poetry, creative nonfiction); Jen Hamilton, production manager. Estab. 1971. Publishes trade paperback originals. **Publishes 14 titles/year. Receives 1,000 submissions/year. 40% of books from first-time authors; 75% from unagented writers. Pays 10% royalty on retail price. Offers $500 average advance.** Publishes book 1 year after acceptance of ms. Responds in 4 months to queries. Manuscript guidelines free.
Imprints: Porcepic Books (literary); Sandcastle Books (children's/YA); Prospect Books (nonfiction)
  O— Beach Holme seeks "to publish excellent, emerging Canadian fiction, nonfiction and poetry and to contribute to Canadian materials for children with quality young adult historical novels."
Nonfiction: Subjects include creative nonfiction. Query with SASE or submit outline, 2 sample chapter(s).
Fiction: Experimental, literary, poetry, young adult. Interested in excellent quality, imaginative writing from writers published in Canadian literary magazines. Query with SASE or submit outline, 2 sample chapter(s).
Recent Title(s): *Ondine's Curse*, by Steven Manners; *What the Small Day Cannot Hold*, by Susan Musgrave.
Tips: "Make sure the manuscript is well written. We see so many that only the unique and excellent can't be put down. Prior publication is a must. This doesn't necessarily mean book-length manuscripts, but a writer should try to publish his or her short fiction."

BLIZZARD PUBLISHING, 73 Furby St., Winnipeg, Manitoba R3C 2A2, Canada. (204)775-2923. Fax: (204)775-2947. E-mail: info@blizzard.mb.ca. **Acquisitions:** Anna Synenko, managing editor (drama, theory and plays, nonfiction), David Fuller, co-ordinator (plays). Publishes trade paperback originals. **Publishes 9-10 titles/year. Receives 150 queries and 25 mss/year. 80% of books from first-time authors; 97% from unagented writers. Pays 18% royalty on retail price. Offers $500 advance.** Publishes book 1 year after acceptance of ms. Accepts simultaneous submissions. Responds in 6 months to mss. Book catalog for 10×12 SAE with $2 IRC; ms guidelines for #10 SAE and IRC.
Imprints: Bain & Cox (nonfiction)
Nonfiction: Drama, plays, dramatic theory, essays, criticism. Subjects include art/architecture, cooking/foods/nutrition. "Nonfiction tends to focus on the arts and deals with primarily Canadian issues although not exclusive. We publish some historical books—but they must have a unique angle and the focus is usually Canadian." Query with SASE.
Recent Title(s): *Cupboard Love: Dictionary of Culinary Curiosities*, by Mark Morton (cooking/etimology/reference); *Elizabeth Rex*, by Timothy Findley.

BOREALIS PRESS, LTD., 110 Bloomingdale St., Ottawa, Ontario K2C 4A4, Canada. (613)798-9299. Fax: (613)798-9747. E-mail: borealis@istar.ca. Frank Tierney, president. **Acquisitions:** Glenn Clever, senior editor. Estab. 1972. Publishes hardcover and paperback originals. **Publishes 10-20 titles/year. Receives 400-500 submissions/year. 80% of books from first-time authors; 95% from unagented writers. Pays 10% royalty on net receipts.** Publishes book 18 months after acceptance of ms. Responds in 2 months to queries. Book catalog for $3 and SASE.
Imprints: Tecumseh Press
  O— "Our mission is to publish work which will be of lasting interest in the Canadian book market." Currently emphasizing Canadian fiction, nonfiction, drama, poetry. De-emphasizing children's books.
Nonfiction: Biography, children's/juvenile, reference. Subjects include government/politics, history, language/literature, regional. "Only material Canadian in content." Looks for "style in tone and language, reader interest and maturity of outlook." Query with SASE or submit outline, 2 sample chapter(s). *No unsolicited mss.* Reviews artwork/photos as part of ms package.

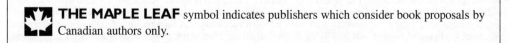

THE MAPLE LEAF symbol indicates publishers which consider book proposals by Canadian authors only.

Fiction: Adventure, ethnic, historical, literary, romance, short story collections, young adult. "Only material Canadian in content and dealing with significant aspects of the human situation." Query with SASE or submit 1-2 sample chapter(s), synopsis. *No unsolicited mss.*

Recent Title(s): *How Parliament Works: 5th ed*, by John Bejermi (nonfiction); *Irregular People*, by Janet Fehr (poetry); *Not in My Back Yard*, by Bryan Meadows (fiction).

THE BOSTON MILLS PRESS, 132 Main St., Erin, Ontario N0B 1T0, Canada. (519)833-2407. Fax: (519)833-2195. E-mail: books@bostonmillspress.com. Website: www.bostonmillspress.com. President: John Denison. **Acquisitions: Noel Hudson, managing editor. Estab. 1974. Publishes hardcover and trade paperback originals. Publishes 20 titles/year. Receives 100 submissions/year. 40% of books from first-time authors; 95% from unagented writers. Pays 8-15% royalty on retail price. Offers advance.** Publishes book 2 years after acceptance of ms. Accepts simultaneous submissions. Responds in 2 months to queries. Book catalog free.

○⊶ Boston Mills Press publishes specific market titles of Canadian and American interest including history, transportation and regional guidebooks. "We like very focused books aimed at the North American market."

Nonfiction: Coffee table book, gift book, illustrated book. Subjects include Americana, art/architecture, cooking/foods/nutrition, creative nonfiction, gardening, history, military/war, nature/environment, photography, recreation, regional, sports, travel, Canadiana. "We're interested in anything to do with Canadian or American history—especially transportation." No autobiographies. Query with SASE. Reviews artwork/photos as part of ms package. Send photocopies.

BRICK BOOKS, Box 20081, 431 Boler Rd., London, Ontario N6K 4G6, Canada. (519)657-8579. E-mail: brick.books@sympatico.ca. Website: www.brickbooks.ca. **Acquisitions:** Don McKay, editor (poetry), Stan Dragland, editor (poetry). Publishes trade paperback originals. **Publishes 6 titles/year. Receives 60 queries and 120 mss/year. 30% of books from first-time authors; 100% from unagented writers. Pays 10% royalty in books.** Publishes book 2 years after acceptance of ms. Responds in 1 month to queries; 3 months to proposals; 5 months to mss. Book catalog and ms guidelines free or online.

● Brick Books has a reading period of January 1-April 30. Manuscripts received outside that reading period will be returned.

Poetry: Writers must be Canadian citizens or landed immigrants. Query or submit 8-10 sample poems.

Recent Title(s): *Songs for Relinquishing the Earth*, Jan Zwicky; *Short Talks*, Anne Carson; *Rest on the Flight into Egypt*, A.F. Moritz.

Tips: "Writers without previous publications in literary journals or magazines are rarely considered by Brick Books for publication."

BROKEN JAW PRESS, Box 596, Station A, Fredericton, New Brunswick E3B 5A6, Canada. (506)454-5127. Fax: (506)454-5127. E-mail: jblades@nbnet.nb.ca. Website: www.brokenjaw.com. Publisher: Joe Blades. **Acquisitions:** R.M. Vaughan, editor (Canadian drama); Rob McLennan, editor (Canadian poetry, critical essays). Publishes Canadian-authored trade paperback originals and reprints. **Publishes 8-12 titles/year. 50% of books from first-time authors; 100% from unagented writers. Pays 10% royalty on retail price. Offers $0-100 advance.** Publishes book 18 months after acceptance of ms. Responds in 1 year to mss. Book catalog for 9×12 SAE with 2 first-class Canadian stamps in Canada; ms guidelines for #10 SASE.

Imprints: Book Rat, SpareTime Editions, Dead Sea Physh Products, Maritimes Arts Projects Productions

○⊶ "We are a small, mostly literary Canadian publishing house."

Nonfiction: Illustrated book, self-help. Subjects include creative nonfiction, gay/lesbian, history, language/literature, regional, women's issues/studies, contemporary culture. Reviews artwork/photos as part of ms package.

Fiction: Literary.

Recent Title(s): *What Was Always Hers*, by Uma Parameswaran (fiction); *Bagne, or, Criteria for Heaven*, by Rob McLennan (poetry).

Tips: "We don't want unsolicited manuscripts or queries, except in the context of the New Muse Award and the Poet's Corner Award."

THE BRUCEDALE PRESS, P.O. Box 2259, Port Elgin, Ontario N0H 2C0, Canada. (519)832-6025. Website: www.bmts.com/~brucedale. **Acquisitions:** Anne Duke Judd, editor-in-chief. Publishes hardcover and trade paperback originals. **Publishes 3 titles/year. Receives 50 queries and 30 mss/year. 75% of books from first-time authors; 100% from unagented writers. Pays royalty.** Publishes book 1 year after acceptance of ms. Accepts simultaneous submissions. Book catalog and ms guidelines for #10 SASE or online.

○⊶ The Brucedale Press publishes books and other materials of regional interest and merit as well as literary, historical and/or pictorial works.

Nonfiction: Biography, children's/juvenile, humor, illustrated book, reference. Subjects include history, humor, language/literature, memoirs, military/war, nature/environment, photography. "Invitations to submit are sent to writers and writers' groups on The Brucedale Press mailing list when projects are in progress. Send a #10 SASE to have your name added to the list. Unless responding to an invitation to submit, query first, with outline and sample chapter for book-length submissions. Submit full manuscript of work intended for children. A brief résumé of your writing efforts and successes is always of interest, and may bring future invitations, even if the present submission is not accepted for publication." Reviews artwork/photos as part of ms package.

Fiction: Fantasy, feminist, historical, humor, juvenile, literary, mainstream/contemporary, mystery, plays, poetry, romance, short story collections, young adult.
Recent Title(s): *Tales of the Unusual*, by Diane Madden (nonfiction); *Barricade Summer*, by Nancy-Lou Patterson (young adult); *Strong in My Skin*, by Jennifer Frankum (poetry).
Tips: "Our focus is very regional. In reading submissions, I look for quality writing with a strong connection to the Queen's Bush area of Ontario. Suggest all authors visit our website, get a catalogue and read our books before submitting."

CAITLIN PRESS, INC., P.O. Box 2387 Station B, Prince George, British Columbia V2N 2S6, Canada. (250)964-4953. Fax: (250)964-4970. E-mail: caitlin-press@telus.net. Website: caitlin_press.com. **Acquisitions:** Cynthia Wilson. Estab. 1977. Publishes trade paperback and soft cover originals. **Publishes 6-7 titles/year. Receives 105-120 queries and 50-100 mss/year. 100% from unagented writers. Pays 15% royalty on net sales.** Publishes book 18 months after acceptance of ms. Accepts simultaneous submissions. Responds in 6 months to queries.
    ○━ "We publish books about Canada's middle north—that region between the far north of the territories and the heavily populated southern corridor."
Nonfiction: Biography, cookbook. Subjects include cooking/foods/nutrition, history, photography, regional. Submit proposal package including outline. Reviews artwork/photos as part of ms package. Send photocopies.
Fiction: Adventure, historical, humor, mainstream/contemporary, short story collections, young adult. Query with SASE.
Poetry: Submit complete ms.
Recent Title(s): *Grizzly Bear Mountain*, by J. Boudreau (nonfiction); *Country Doctor*, by Ben Dlin (biography); *Better the devil you know*, by Betty Keller (fiction).
Tips: "Our area of interest is British Columbia and northern Canada. Submissions should reflect our interest area."

CANADIAN EDUCATORS' PRESS, 100 City Centre Dr., P.O. Box 2094, Mississauga, Ontario L5B 3C6, Canada. (905)826-0578. **Acquisitions:** S. Deonarine, manager. Publishes trade paperback originals. **Publishes 2 titles/year. Pays royalty.** Publishes book 1 year after acceptance of ms.
Nonfiction: Textbook. Subjects include education, government/politics, history, multicultural, philosophy, religion, sociology. Query with SASE. Reviews artwork/photos as part of ms package.
Recent Title(s): *Aboriginal Education in Canada*, by eds. K.P. Binda and Sharilyn Calliou; *21st Century Canadian Diversity*, Stephen E. Nancoo.

CANADIAN LIBRARY ASSOCIATION, 328 Frank St., Ottawa, Ontario K2P 0X8, Canada. (613)232-9625 ext. 322. Fax: (613)563-9895. E-mail: emorton@cla.ca. Website: www.cla.ca. Elizabeth Morton, editor, (Feliciter/Monographs). Publishes trade paperback originals. **Publishes 4 titles/year. Receives 10 queries and 5 mss/year. 50% of books from first-time authors; 100% from unagented writers. Pays 10% royalty on wholesale price.** Publishes book 6 months after acceptance of ms. Responds in 1 month to queries; 3 months to proposals; 3 months to mss. Book catalog and ms guidelines free.
    ○━ "CLA publishes practical/professional/academic materials with a Canadian focus or direct Canadian application as a service to CLA members and to contribute to the professional development of library staff."
Nonfiction: Reference, textbook. Subjects include history, language/literature, library science. Query with SASE or submit outline. Reviews artwork/photos as part of ms package. Send photocopies.
Recent Title(s): *Copyright Guide for Canadian Libraries*.
Tips: Audience is library and information scientists.

CANADIAN PLAINS RESEARCH CENTER, University of Regina, Regina, Saskatchewan S4S 0A2, Canada. (306)585-4795. Fax: (306)585-4699. E-mail: brian.mlazgar@uregina.ca. Website: www.cprc.uregina.ca. **Acquisitions:** Brian Mlazgar, coordinator. Estab. 1973. Publishes scholarly paperback originals and some casebound originals. **Publishes 8-10 titles/year. Receives 15-20 submissions/year. 35% of books from first-time authors. Offers advance.** Publishes book 2 years after acceptance of ms. Responds in 6 months to queries. Book catalog and ms guidelines free.
    ○━ Canadian Plains Research Center publishes scholarly research on the Canadian plains.
Nonfiction: Biography, illustrated book, technical, textbook. Subjects include business/economics, government/politics, history, nature/environment, regional, sociology. "The Canadian Plains Research Center publishes the results of research on topics relating to the Canadian Plains region, although manuscripts relating to the Great Plains region will be considered. Material *must* be scholarly. Do not submit health, self-help, hobbies, music, sports, psychology, recreation or cookbooks unless they have a scholarly approach. For example, we would be interested in acquiring a pioneer manuscript cookbook, with modern ingredient equivalents, if the material relates to the Canadian Plains/Great Plains region." Query with SASE or submit complete ms. Reviews artwork/photos as part of ms package.
Recent Title(s): *Discover Saskatchewan*, by Nilson (guide to historic sites and markers).
Tips: "Pay attention to manuscript preparation and accurate footnoting, according to *Chicago Manual of Style*."

CARSWELL THOMSON PROFESSIONAL PUBLISHING, One Corporate Plaza 2075 Kennedy Rd., Scarborough, Ontario M1T 3V4, Canada. (416)298-5024. Fax: (416)298-5094. E-mail: ROBERT.FREEMAN@carswell.com. Website: www.carswell.com. **Acquisitions:** Robert Freeman, vice president, legal, accounting and finance, and corporate groups. Publishes hardcover originals. **Publishes 150-200 titles/year. 30-50% of books from first-time authors. Pays 5-15% royalty on wholesale price. Offers $1,000-5,000 advance.** Publishes book 6 months after acceptance of ms. Accepts simultaneous submissions. Responds in 3 months to queries. Book catalog and ms guidelines free.

    O— Carswell Thomson is Canada's national resource of information and legal interpretations for law, accounting, tax and business professionals.

Nonfiction: Reference (legal, tax). "Canadian information of a regulatory nature is our mandate." Submit proposal package including outline, résumé.

Tips: Audience is Canada and persons interested in Canadian information; professionals in law, tax, accounting fields; business people interested in regulatory material.

CHA PRESS, 17 York St., Ottawa, Ontario K1N 9J6, Canada. (613)241-8005 ext. 264. Fax: (613)241-5055. E-mail: chapress@canadian-healthcare.org. Website: www.canadian-healthcare.org. **Acquisitions:** Eleanor Sawyer, director of publishing. **Publishes 6-8 titles/year. Receives 7 queries and 3 mss/year. 60% of books from first-time authors; 90% from unagented writers. Pays 10-17% royalty on retail price or makes outright purchase of $250-1,000. Offers $500-1,500 advance.** Responds in 3 months to queries. Book catalog and ms guidelines free.

    O— CHA Press strives to be Canada's health administration textbook publisher. "We serve readers in our broad continuum of care in regional health authorities, hospitals and health care facilities and agencies, which are governed by trustees." Currently emphasizing history of regionalization; accountability of boards/executives; executives and leadership. De-emphasizing hospital-based issues of any type.

Nonfiction: How-to, textbook, guides. Subjects include health/medicine, history. Query with SASE or submit outline.

Recent Title(s): *The Evolution of the Vancouver/Richmond Regional Health Board, 1992-98: A Case Study*, by Anne Cricton, PhD; *The Canadian Health Care Glossary: Terms and Abbreviations*, by Mark Edmonds.

Tips: Audience is healthcare facility managers (senior/middle); policy analysts/researchers; nurse practitioners and other healthcare professionals; trustees. "CHA Press is looking to expand its frontlist for 2001-2002 on issues specific to Canadian healthcare system reform; continuum of care issues; integrated health delivery. Don't underestimate amount of time it will take to write or mistake generic 'how-to' health for mass media as appropriate for CHA's specialty press."

CHARLTON PRESS, 2040 Yonge St., Suite 208, Toronto, Ontario M4S 1Z9, Canada. Fax: (416)488-4656. E-mail: chpress@charltonpress.com. Website: www.charltonpress.com. **Acquisitions:** Jean Dale, managing editor. Publishes trade paperback originals and reprints. **Publishes 15 titles/year. Receives 30 queries and 5 mss/year. 10% of books from first-time authors; 100% from unagented writers. Pays 10% royalty on wholesale price or makes variable outright purchase. Offers $1,000 advance.** Publishes book 6 months after acceptance of ms. Accepts simultaneous submissions. Responds in 1 month to queries; 1 month to proposals; 2 months to mss. Book catalog free.

Nonfiction: Reference (price guides on collectibles). Subjects include hobbies (numismatics, toys, military badges, ceramic collectibles, sports cards). Submit outline. Reviews artwork/photos as part of ms package. Send photocopies.

Recent Title(s): *Royal Doulton Figurines*, J. Dale (reference guide).

N CHEMTEC PUBLISHING, 38 Earswick Dr., Toronto-Scarborough, Ontario M1E 1C6, Canada. (416)265-2603. Fax: (416)265-1399. E-mail: info@chemtec.org. Website: www.chemtec.org/. **Acquisitions:** Anna Wypych, president. Publishes hardcover originals. **Publishes 5 titles/year. Receives 10 queries and 7 mss/year. 20% of books from first-time authors. Pays 5-15% royalty on retail price.** Publishes book 6 months after acceptance of ms. Accepts simultaneous submissions. Responds in 2 months to queries; 4 months to mss. Book catalog and ms guidelines free.

    O— Chemtec publishes books on polymer chemistry, physics and technology. "Special emphasis is given to process additives and books which treat subject in comprehensive manner."

Nonfiction: Technical, textbook. Subjects include science, environment, chemistry, polymers. Submit outline, sample chapter(s).

Recent Title(s): *Handbook of Fillers*, by George Wypych; *Handbook of Solvents*, by multiple authors.

Tips: Audience is industrial research and universities.

COACH HOUSE BOOKS, 401 Huron St. on bpNichol Lane, Toronto, Ontario M5S 2G5, Canada. (416)979-2217. Fax: (416)977-1158. E-mail: mail@chbooks.com. Website: www.chbooks.com. **Acquisitions:** Darren Wershler-Henry, editor. Publishes trade paperback originals. **Publishes 10 titles/year. 80% of books from first-time authors; 100% from unagented writers. Pays 10% royalty on retail price.** Publishes book 1 year after acceptance of ms. Responds in 6 months to queries. Book catalog and ms guidelines online.

Nonfiction: Artists' books. Query with SASE. *All unsolicited mss returned unopened.*

Fiction: Experimental, literary, plays. "Consult website for submissions policy." *All unsolicited mss returned unopened.*

Poetry: Consult website for guidelines. Query.

Recent Title(s): *Fidget*, by K. Goldsmith (poetry); *Inkblot Record*, by D. Farrell (poetry).

◪ CORMORANT BOOKS INC., 895 Don Mills Rd., 400-2 Park Centre, Toronto, Ontario M3C 1W3, Canada. (416)445-3333. Fax: (416)445-5967. Website: www.cormorantbooks.com. **Acquisitions:** Marc Côté, publisher. Publishes hardcover, trade paperback originals and reprints. **Publishes 10 titles/year. Receives 500 queries and 300 mss/ year. 50% of books from first-time authors; 50% from unagented writers. Pays 8-15% royalty on retail price. Offers $500-15,000 advance.** Publishes book 1-2 years after acceptance of ms. Accepts simultaneous submissions. Responds in 1 months to queries; 1 month to proposals; 3 months to mss. Book catalog and ms guidelines free or online.

O→ Cormorant publishes Canadian fiction and essay collections, occasional nonfiction titles, usually on literary themes. Currently emphasizing novels. De-emphasizing short stories.

Nonfiction: Biography. Subjects include creative nonfiction, history, memoirs, philosophy. Query with SASE.

Fiction: Cormorant is a highly literary company with hundreds of awards for literary excellence. Adventure, confession, ethnic, experimental, feminist, gay/lesbian, historical, humor, literary, mainstream/contemporary, multicultural, mystery, plays, poetry, regional, short story collections. Query with SASE or submit 3 sample chapter(s), synopsis or submit complete ms.

Recent Title(s): *Louder than the Sea*, by Wayne Bartlett (novel); *Invisible Among the Ruins*, by John Moss (nonfiction); *Flying in Silence*, by Gerry Turcotte (novel).

Tips: "Writers should determine, from a study of our list, whether their fiction or essay collection would be appropriate. *Canadian authors only.*"

COTEAU BOOKS, 2206 Dewdney Ave., Suite 401, Regina, Saskatchewan S4R 1H3, Canada. (306)777-0170. Fax: (306)522-5152. E-mail: coteau@coteaubooks.com. Website: www.coteaubooks.com. **Acquisitions:** Geoffrey Ursell, publisher. Estab. 1975. Publishes trade paperback originals and reprints. **Publishes 20 titles/year. Receives 200 queries and 200 mss/year. 50% of books from first-time authors; 100% from unagented writers. Pays 10% royalty on retail price.** Publishes book 1 year after acceptance of ms. Responds in 2 months to queries; 6 months to mss. Book catalog free; ms guidelines online.

O→ "Our mission is to publish the finest in Canadian fiction, nonfiction, poetry, drama and children's literature, with an emphasis on Saskatchewan and prairie writers." De-emphasizing science fiction, picture books.

Nonfiction: Coffee table book, reference. Subjects include creative nonfiction, ethnic, history, language/literature, memoirs, regional, sports, travel. Canadian authors only. Submit 3-4 sample chapter(s), author bio, SASE.

Fiction: Ethnic, fantasy, feminist, gay/lesbian, historical, humor, juvenile, literary, mainstream/contemporary, multicultural, multimedia, mystery, plays, poetry, regional, short story collections, spiritual, sports, young adult. Canadian authors only. Submit 3-4 sample chapter(s), author bio, SASE.

Poetry: Submit 20-25 sample poems or submit complete ms.

Recent Title(s): *Gold on Ice: The Story of the Sandra Schmirler Curling Team*, by Gary Scholz (nonfiction); *The Walnut Tree*, by Martha Blum (fiction); *The Long Landscape*, by Paul Wilson (poetry).

Tips: "Look at past publications to get an idea of our editorial program. We do not publish romance, horror or picture books, but are interested in juvenile and teen fiction from Canadian authors. Submissions may be made by e-mail (maximum 20 pages) with attachments."

CREATIVE BOUND INC., Box 424, 151 Tansley Dr., Carp, Ontario K0A 1L0, Canada. (613)831-3641. Fax: (613)831-3643. E-mail: info@creativebound.com. Website: www.creativebound.com. **Acquisitions:** Gail Baird, president. Publishes trade paperback originals. **Publishes 6-8 titles/year. Receives 250 queries and 80 mss/year. 30% of books from first-time authors; 100% from unagented writers. Pays 11-15% royalty on wholesale price.** Publishes book 5 months after acceptance of ms. Accepts simultaneous submissions. Responds in 1 month to queries; 3 months to proposals; 3 months to mss. Book catalog free.

O→ "We publish books that 'inspire, help and heal' in five categories: mind/body/spirit, personal growth, life balance, healing/recovery, parenting."

Nonfiction: Personal growth, life balance, stress management, mind/body/spirit, parenting, healing/recovery. Submit proposal package including outline, sample chapter(s). Reviews artwork/photos as part of ms package. Send photocopies.

Recent Title(s): *Vitamin C for Couples*, by Luke DeSadeleer; *It's Not About Time! Redefining Leisure in a Changing World*, by Joe Pavelka.

ECRITS DES FORGES, C.P. 335, 1497 Laviolette, Trois-Rivieres, Quebec G9A 5G4, Canada. (819)379-9813. Fax: (819)376-0774. E-mail: ecrits.desforges@aiqnet.com. **Acquisitions:** Gaston Bellemare, president. Publishes hardcover originals. **Publishes 40 titles/year. Receives 30 queries and 1,000 mss/year. 10% of books from first-time authors; 90% from unagented writers. Pays 10-30% royalty. Offers 50% advance.** Publishes book 9 months after acceptance of ms. Accepts simultaneous submissions. Responds in 9 months to queries. Book catalog free.

O→ Ecrits des Forges publishes only poetry written in French.

Poetry: Submit 20 sample poems.

Recent Title(s): *Ode au St-Laurent*, by Gatien Lapointe (poetry).

ECW PRESS, 2120 Queen St. E., Suite 200, Toronto, Ontario M4E 1E2, Canada. (416)694-3348. Fax: (416)698-9906. E-mail: ecw@sympatico.ca. Website: www.ecwpress.com. **Acquisitions:** Jack David, president (nonfiction); Michael Holmes, literary editor (fiction, poetry); Jennifer Hale, associate editor (pop culture, entertainment). Estab. 1979. Publishes hardcover and trade paperback originals. **Publishes 40 titles/year; imprint publishes 8 titles/year. Receives 500 queries and 300 mss/year. 30% of books from first-time authors. Pays 8-12% royalty on net receipts. Offers $300-5,000 advance.** Publishes book 18 months after acceptance of ms. Accepts simultaneous submissions. Responds in 1 month to queries; 2 months to proposals; 4 months to mss. Book catalog and ms guidelines free.

O→ ECW publishes nonfiction about people or subjects that have a substantial fan base. Currently emphasizing books about music, Wicca, gambling, TV and movie stars.

Nonfiction: Biography (popular), humor. Subjects include business/economics, creative nonfiction, gay/lesbian, general, government/politics, health/medicine, history, memoirs, money/finance, regional, sex, sports, women's issues/studies, contemporary culture, Wicca, gambling, TV and movie stars. Submit proposal package including outline, 4-5 sample chapter(s), SASE, IRC. Reviews artwork/photos as part of ms package. Send photocopies.
Fiction: "We publish literary fiction and poetry from Canadian authors exclusively. Literary, mystery, poetry, short story collections, suspense. Submit proposal package including 1-2 sample chapter(s), synopsis, SASE, IRC.
Poetry: "We publish Canadian poetry exclusively." Query or submit 4-5 sample poems.
Recent Title(s): *Too Close to the Falls*, by Catherine Gildiner; *Blakwidow: My First Year as a Professional Wrestler*, by Amanda Storm; *Burn*, by Paul Vermeersch (poetry).
Tips: "Visit our website *and* read a selection of our books."

EDGE SCIENCE FICTION AND FANTASY PUBLISHING, Box 1714, Calgary, Alberta T2P 2L7, Canada. (403)254-0160. Fax: (403)254-0456. E-mail: editor@edgewebsite.com. Website: www.edgewebsite.com. Editorial Manager: Matthew Pocock. **Acquisitions:** Jessie Tambay, Roxanne Bennett, Robyn Herrington, acquisitions editors. Publishes hardcover and trade paperback originals. **Publishes 2-4 titles/year. Receives 40 queries and 400 mss/year. 50% of books from first-time authors; 75% from unagented writers. Pays 10% royalty on wholesale price. Offers $300-1,000 advance.** Publishes book 18 months after acceptance of ms. Accepts simultaneous submissions. Responds in 4 months to queries; 4 months to proposals; 6 months to mss. Manuscript guidelines for #10 SASE.

O→ "Our goal is to publish quality science fiction and fantasy novels that attract a strong readership and generate interest within the industry."

Fiction: Fantasy, science fiction. "We are looking for all types of fantasy and science fiction, except juvenile/young adult." Query with SASE or submit 1 sample chapter(s), synopsis.
Recent Title(s): *The Black Chalice*, by Marie Jakober (historical fantasy); *Lyskarion: The Song of the Wind*, by Janice Cullum (fantasy).
Tips: "Audience is anyone who enjoys a well written science fiction or fantasy novel. Polish your manuscript before you submit it. Get your manuscript critiqued by others before you submit it."

ÉDITIONS DU NOROÎT, 6694, avenue Papineau, Montreal, Quebec H2G 2X2, Canada. (514)727-0005. Fax: (514)723-6660. E-mail: lenoroit@ca.inter.net. Website: www.logique.com. **Acquisitions:** Paul Belanger, director. Publishes trade paperback originals and reprints. **Publishes 27 titles/year. Receives 500 queries and 500 mss/year. 50% of books from first-time authors; 95% from unagented writers. Pays 10% royalty on retail price. Offers advance.** Publishes book 1 year after acceptance of ms. Accepts simultaneous submissions. Responds in 3 months to mss. Book catalog for #10 SASE.

O→ Éditions du Noiroît publishes poetry and essays on poetry.

Poetry: Submit 40 sample poems.
Recent Title(s): *Transfiguration*, by Jacques Brault/E.D. Blodgett; *Poemes*, by Jacques Brault; *Le cercle vicieux*, by Margaret Atwood.

[N] **ÉDITIONS LA LIBERTE INC.**, 3020 Chemin Ste-Foy, Ste-Foy, Quebec, G1X 3V6, Canada. (418)658-3763. Fax: (418)658-3763. **Acquisitions:** Nathalie Roy, director of operations. Publishes trade paperback originals. **Publishes 4-5 titles/year. Receives 125 queries and 100 mss/year. 75% of books from first-time authors; 90% from unagented writers. Pays 10% royalty on retail price.** Publishes book 4 months after acceptance of ms. Accepts simultaneous submissions. Book catalog free.

O→ Accepts only mss written in French. Specializes in history. De-emphasizing fiction and poetry.

Nonfiction: Biography, children's/juvenile. Subjects include Americana, animals, anthropology/archeology, child guidance/parenting, cooking/foods/nutrition, education, government/politics, history, hobbies, language/literature, music/dance, nature/environment, psychology, science, sociology. Submit proposal package including complete ms. *Writer's Market recommends sending a query with SASE first.*
Fiction: Historical, juvenile, literary, mainstream/contemporary, short story collections, young adult. Query with SASE.
Recent Title(s): *Au coeur de la Litterature D'enfance et de Jeunesse*, by Charlotte Guerette (nonfiction).

[N] **EMPYREAL PRESS**, P.O. Box 1746, Place Du Parc, Montreal, Quebec HZW 2R7, Canada. Publishes trade paperback originals. **Publishes 1-4 titles/year. 50% of books from first-time authors; 90% from unagented writers.-** Book catalog for #10 SASE.

O→ "Our mission is the publishing of Canadian and other literature which doesn't fit into any standard 'mold'—writing which is experimental yet grounded in discipline, imagination."

Fiction: Experimental, feminist, gay/lesbian, literary, short story collections. *No unsolicited mss.*
Recent Title(s): *Winter Spring Summer Fall*, by Robert Sandiford; *The Surface of Time*, by Louis Dudek.

FERNWOOD PUBLISHING LTD., P.O. Box 9409, Station A, Halifax, Nova Scotia B3K 5S3, Canada. (902)422-3302. E-mail: Fernwood@ISTAR.ca. Website: home.ISTAR.ca/~Fernwood. **Acquisitions:** Errol Sharpe, publisher (social science); Wayne Antony, editor (social science). Publishes trade paperback originals. **Publishes 12-15 titles/year. Receives 80 queries and 30 mss/year. 40% of books from first-time authors; 100% from unagented writers. Pays 7-10% royalty on wholesale price. Offers advance.** Publishes book 1 year after acceptance of ms. Accepts simultaneous submissions. Responds in 6 weeks to proposals. Book catalog and ms guidelines free.

O—¬ "Fernwood's objective is to publish critical works which challenge existing scholarship."

Nonfiction: Reference, textbook, scholarly. Subjects include agriculture/horticulture, anthropology/archeology, business/economics, education, ethnic, gay/lesbian, government/politics, health/medicine, history, language/literature, multicultural, nature/environment, philosophy, regional, sex, sociology, sports, translation, women's issues/studies, contemporary culture, world affairs. "Our main focus is in the social sciences and humanities, emphasizing labor studies, women's studies, gender studies, critical theory and research, political economy, cultural studies and social work—for use in college and university courses." Submit proposal package including outline, sample chapter(s). Reviews artwork/photos as part of ms package. Send photocopies.

Recent Title(s): *The Skin I'm In: Racism, Sports and Education*, by Christopher Spence.

GOOSE LANE EDITIONS, 469 King St., Fredericton, New Brunswick E3B 1E5, Canada. (506)450-4251. **Acquisitions:** Laurel Boone, editorial director. Estab. 1956. **Publishes 12-14 titles/year. Receives 500 submissions/ year. 20% of books from first-time authors; 75% from unagented writers. Pays royalty on retail price. Offers advance.** Responds in 6 months to queries. Manuscript guidelines for #10 SASE.

O—¬ Goose Lane publishes literary fiction and nonfiction from well-read and highly skilled authors.

Nonfiction: Biography, illustrated book. Subjects include art/architecture, history, language/literature, nature/environment, regional, women's issues/studies. Query with SASE.

Fiction: Literary (novels), short story collections. Our needs in fiction never change: Substantial, character-centered literary fiction. No children's, YA, mainstream, mass market, genre, mystery, thriller, confessional or sci-fi fiction. Query with SASE.

Recent Title(s): *16 Categories of Desire*, by Douglas Glover (fiction); *Joe Norris: Painted Visions of Nova Scotia*, by Bernard Riordon (nonfiction).

Tips: "Writers should send us outlines and samples of books that show a very well-read author who, in either fiction or nonfiction, has something of Canadian relevance to offer. We almost never publish books by non-Canadian authors, and we seldom consider submissions from Canadians living outside the country. If I were a writer trying to market a book today, I would contact the targeted publisher with a query letter and synopsis, and request manuscript guidelines. Purchase a recent book from the publisher in a relevant area, if possible. Always send an SASE with IRCs or suffient return postage in Canadian stamps for reply to your query and for any material you'd like returned should it not suit our needs."

GUERNICA EDITIONS, Box 117, Station P, Toronto, Ontario M5S 2S6, Canada. (416)658-9888. Fax: (416)657-8885. E-mail: guernicaeditions@cs.com. Website: www.guernicaeditions.com. **Acquisitions:** Antonio D'Alfonso, editor/publisher (poetry, nonfiction, novels); Ken Scambray, editor (US reprints). Estab. 1978. Publishes trade paperback originals, reprints and software. **Publishes 25 titles/year. Receives 1,000 submissions and 750 mss/year. 20% of books from first-time authors; 99% from unagented writers. Pays 8-10% royalty on retail price or makes outright purchase of $200-5,000. Offers $200-2,000 advance.** Publishes book 10 months after acceptance of ms. Responds in 1 month to queries; 6 months to proposals; 1 year to mss. Book catalog online.

O—¬ Guernica Editions is an independent press dedicated to the bridging of cultures. "We do original and translations of fine works. We are seeking essays on authors and translations with less emphasis on poetry."

Nonfiction: Biography. Subjects include art/architecture, creative nonfiction, ethnic, film/cinema/stage, gay/lesbian, government/politics, history, language/literature, memoirs, multicultural, music/dance, philosophy, psychology, regional, religion, sex, translation, women's issues/studies. Query with SASE. *All unsolicited mss returned unopened.* Reviews artwork/photos as part of ms package. Send photocopies.

Fiction: Erotica, feminist, gay/lesbian, literary, multicultural, plays, poetry, poetry in translation. "We wish to open up into the fiction world and focus less on poetry. We specialize in European, especially Italian, translations." Query with SASE. *All unsolicited mss returned unopened.*

Poetry: Feminist, gay/lesbian, literary, multicultural, poetry in translation. "We wish to have writers in translation. Any writer who has translated Italian poetry is welcomed. Full books only. Not single poems by different authors, unless modern, and used as an anthology. First books will have no place in the next couple of years." Query.

Recent Title(s): *Love Is Not Native to My Blood*, by Brian Day; *Us Fools Believing*, by Miriam Packer; *Doubly Suspect*, by Madeline Monette.

HARPERCOLLINS PUBLISHERS LTD., 55 Avenue Rd., Suite 2900, Toronto, Ontario M5R 3L2, Canada. (416)975-9334. Vice President/Publisher/Editor-in-Chief: Iris Tupholme. Publishes hardcover and trade paperback original and reprints, mass market paperback reprints. **Publishes 45 titles/year. Pays 8-15% royalty on retail price. Offers $1,500 to over six figures advance.** Publishes book 18 months after acceptance of ms.

Nonfiction: Biography, children's/juvenile, self-help. Subjects include business/economics, gardening, gay/lesbian, government/politics, health/medicine, history, language/literature, money/finance, nature/environment, religion, travel, women's issues/studies. Query first with SASE and appropriate Canadian postage or IRCs. *No unsolicited mss.*

Fiction: Ethnic, feminist, juvenile, literary, mainstream/contemporary, picture books, religious, short story collections, young adult. Query first with SASE and appropriate Canadian postage or IRCs. *No unsolicited mss.*

Recent Title(s): *The Geometry of Love—Space, Time, Mystery and Meaning in an Ordinary Church*, by Margaret Visser (nonfiction); *A Good House*, by Bonnie Burnard (fiction).

F.P. HENDRIKS PUBLISHING, 4806-53 St., Stettler, Alberta T0C 2L2, Canada. (403)742-6483. E-mail: editor@fphe ndriks.com. **Acquisitions:** Faye Boer, managing editor. **Publishes 2-5 titles/year. Receives 60 queries and 40 mss/ year. 80% of books from first-time authors; 90% from unagented writers. Pays 10% royalty. Offers $250-1,000 advance (to proven writers).** Publishes book 2 years after acceptance of ms. Accepts simultaneous submissions. Responds in 4 months to queries; 4 months to proposals; 6 months to mss. Book catalog free.

    O─ F.P. Hendriks' primary focus is teacher's resources in English/language arts and sciences including lessons and activities with solid theoretical background. Currently emphasizing sports/health/literacy fiction. De-emphasizing science.

Nonfiction: Self-help, textbook. Subjects include child guidance/parenting, education, health/medicine, language/literature, science, sports. Query with SASE or submit outline. Reviews artwork/photos as part of ms package. Send photocopies.

Fiction: Adventure, fantasy, humor, juvenile, mystery, science fiction, young adult. "Full length novels only. We plan to begin publishing young adult fiction in the above categories to commence 2001. Must include accompanying teacher resources or outline for same. Beware of lack of attention to intended audience; lack of attention to elements of plot." Query with SASE or submit synopsis.

Recent Title(s): *Hockey: Drill Solutions*, Dr. Randy Gregg.

Tips: "Primary audience is parents, sports coaches and teachers of elementary, middle school, junior high in English/ language arts and science."

HORSDAL & SCHUBART PUBLISHERS LTD., 618-425 Simcoe St., Victoria, British Columbia V8V 4T3, Canada. (250)360-0829. Fax: (250)360-0829. **Acquisitions:** Marlyn Horsdal, editor. Publishes hardcover originals and trade paperback originals and reprints. **Publishes 8-10 titles/year. 50% of books from first-time authors; 100% from unagented writers. Pays 15% royalty on wholesale price. Offers advance.** Publishes book 6 months after acceptance of ms. Accepts simultaneous submissions. Responds in 1 month to queries. Book catalog free.

Imprints: TouchWood Editions (creative nonfiction)

    O─ "We concentrate on Western and Northern Canada and nautical subjects and offer useful information, to give readers pause for thought, to encourage action to help heal the Earth." Currently emphasizing creative nonfiction. De-emphasizing regional histories.

Nonfiction: Biography. Subjects include anthropology/archeology, art/architecture, creative nonfiction, government/ politics, history, nature/environment, recreation, regional. Query with SASE or submit outline, 2-3 sample chapter(s). Reviews artwork/photos as part of ms package. Send photocopies.

Recent Title(s): *A Measure of Value*, by Chris Yorath (nonfiction); *Snow-Coming Moon*, by Stan Evans (fiction).

🔳 HOUSE OF ANANSI PRESS, 895 Don Mills Rd., 400-2 Park Centre, Toronto, Ontario M3C 1W3, Canada. (416)445-3333. Fax: (416)445-5967. E-mail: info@anansi.ca. Website: www.anansi.ca. **Acquisitions:** Martha Sharpe, publisher. Publishes hardcover and trade paperback originals. **Publishes 10-15 titles/year. Receives 750 queries/year. 5% of books from first-time authors; 99% from unagented writers. Pays 8-15% royalty on retail price. Offers $500-2,000 advance.** Publishes book 9 months after acceptance of ms. Accepts simultaneous submissions. Responds in 2 months to queries; 3 months to proposals; 4 months to mss.

    O─ "Our mission is to publish the best new literary writers in Canada and to continue to grow and adapt along with the Canadian literary community, while maintaining Anansi's rich history."

Nonfiction: Biography. Subjects include anthropology/archeology, gay/lesbian, government/politics, history, language/ literature, philosophy, science, sociology, women's issues/studies. "Our nonfiction list is literary, but not overly academic. Some writers submit academic work better suited for university presses or pop-psychology books, which we do not publish." Query with SASE or submit outline, 2 sample chapter(s). Reviews artwork/photos as part of ms package. Send photocopies.

Fiction: Experimental, feminist, gay/lesbian, literary, short story collections. "We publish literary fiction by Canadian authors. Authors must have been published in established literary magazines and/or journals. We only want to consider sample chapters." Query with SASE or submit 2 sample chapter(s), synopsis.

Poetry: "We only publish book-length works by Canadian authors. Poets must have a substantial résumé of published poems in literary magazines or journals. We only want samples from a ms." Submit 10-15 sample poems.

Recent Title(s): *The Rights Revolution*, by Michael Ignatieff (nonfiction); *This All Happened*, by Michael Winter (fiction); *A Pair of Scissors*, by Sharon Thesen (poetry).

Tips: "Submit often to magazines and journals. Read and buy other writers' work. Know and be a part of your writing community."

[N] 🔳 HUMANITAS, 990 Picard, Brossard, Quebec J4W 1S5, Canada. (514)466-9737. Fax: (514)466-9737. **Acquisitions: Constantin Stoiciu, president. Publishes hardcover originals. Publishes 14 titles/year. Receives 200 queries and 200 mss/year. 20% of books from first-time authors. Pays 10-12% royalty on wholesale price.** Publishes book 2 months after acceptance of ms. Accepts simultaneous submissions. Book catalog and ms guidelines free.

    O─ Humanitas is interested only in manuscripts written in French.

Nonfiction: Biography. Subjects include history, language/literature, philosophy, photography, science. Query. Reviews artwork/photos as part of ms package. Send photocopies.

Fiction: Fantasy, romance, short story collections. Query.

Poetry: Query.

Recent Title(s): *Enigmes de la Seduction Politique*, by Andrei Stoiciu (essay); *Cafe Prague*, by Serge Ouaknine (prose); *Burkina Blues*, by Angele Bassolé (poetry).

N INSOMNIAC PRESS, 192 Spadina Ave., Suite 403, Toronto, Ontario M5T 2C2, Canada. (416)504-6270. Fax: (416)504-9313. E-mail: mike@insomniacpress.com. Website: www.insomniacpress.com. Publishes trade paperback originals and reprints, mass market paperback originals and electronic originals and reprints. **Publishes 20 titles/year. Receives 250 queries and 1,000 mss/year. 50% of books from first-time authors; 80% from unagented writers. Pays 10-15% royalty on retail price. Offers $500-1,000 advance.** Publishes book 6 months after acceptance of ms. Responds in 1 week to queries; 2 months to proposals; 2 months to mss. Book catalog and ms guidelines online.

Nonfiction: Gift book, humor, self-help. Subjects include business/economics, creative nonfiction, gay/lesbian, government/politics, health/medicine, language/literature, money/finance, multicultural, religion, true crime. Very interested in areas such as true crime and generally in well-written and well-researched nonfiction on topics of wide interest. Query via e-mail, submit proposal package including outline, 2 sample chapter(s) or submit complete ms. Reviews artwork/photos as part of ms package. Send photocopies.

Fiction: Comic books, ethnic, experimental, gay/lesbian, humor, literary, mainstream/contemporary, multicultural, poetry, suspense. We publish a mix of commercial (mysteries) and literary fiction. Query via e-mail, submit proposal package including synopsis or submit complete ms.

Poetry: "Our poetry publishing is limited to 2-4 books per year and we are often booked up a year or two in advance." Submit complete ms.

Recent Title(s): *Landscape with Shipwreck: First Person Cinema and the Films of Phillip Hoffman*, edited by Karyn Sandlos and Mike Hoolboom (film studies); *Pedigree Girls*, by Sherwin Tija (humor/cartoon); *Ashes Are Bone and Dust*, by Jill Battson (poetry).

Tips: "We envision a mixed readership that appreciates up-and-coming literary fiction and poetry as well as solidly researched and provocative nonfiction. Peruse our website and familiarize yourself with what we've published in the past."

INSTITUTE OF PSYCHOLOGICAL RESEARCH, INC., 34 Fleury St. W., Montréal, Québec H3L 1S9, Canada. (514)382-3000. Fax: (514)382-3007. **Acquisitions:** Marie-Paule Chevrier, general director. Estab. 1958. Publishes hardcover and trade paperback originals and reprints. **Publishes 12 titles/year. Receives 15 submissions/year. 10% of books from first-time authors; 100% from unagented writers. Pays 10-12% royalty.** Publishes book 6 months after acceptance of ms. Responds in 2 months to queries.

○→ Institute of Psychological Research publishes psychological tests and science textbooks for a varied professional audience.

Nonfiction: Textbook. Subjects include philosophy, psychology, science, translation. "We are looking for psychological tests in French or English." Query with SASE or submit complete ms.

Recent Title(s): *épreuve individuelle d'habileté mentale*, by Jean-Marc Chevrier (intelligence test).

Tips: "Psychologists, guidance counselors, professionals, schools, school boards, hospitals, teachers, government agencies and industries comprise our audience."

ISER BOOKS, Faculty of Arts Publications, Memorial University of Newfoundland, FM 2006, St. John's, Newfoundland A1K 1A9, Canada. (709)737-8343. Fax: (709)737-7560. Website: www.mun.ca/iser/. **Acquisitions:** Al Potter, manager. Publishes trade paperback originals. **Publishes 3-4 titles/year. Receives 10-20 queries and 10 mss/year. 45% of books from first-time authors; 85% from unagented writers. Pays 6-10% royalty on wholesale price.** Publishes book 6 months after acceptance of ms. Responds in 1 month to queries; 2 months to proposals; 4 months to mss. Book catalog and ms guidelines free.

○→ Iser Books publishes research within such disciplines and in such parts of the world as are deemed of relevance to Newfoundland and Labrador.

Nonfiction: Biography, reference. Subjects include anthropology/archeology, ethnic, government/politics, history, multicultural, recreation, regional, sociology, translation, women's issues/studies. Query with SASE or submit proposal package including outline, 2-3 sample chapter(s).

Recent Title(s): *Finding Our Sea Legs*, by editors Barbara Neis and Lawrence Felt; *Place Names of the Northern Peninsula*, by editors Robert Hollett and William J. Kirwin.

KINDRED PRODUCTIONS, 4-169 Riverton Ave., Winnipeg, Manitoba R2L 2E5, Canada. (204)669-6575. Fax: (204)654-1865. E-mail: kindred@mbconf.ca. Website: www.mbconf.org/kindred.htm. **Acquisitions:** Marilyn Hudson, manager. Publishes trade paperback originals and reprints. **Publishes 3 titles/year. 1% of books from first-time authors; 100% from unagented writers. Pays 10-15% royalty on net receipts.** Publishes book 18 months after acceptance of ms. Accepts simultaneous submissions. Responds in 3 months to queries; 5 months to mss. Book catalog and ms guidelines free.

○→ "Kindred Productions publishes, promotes and markets print and nonprint resources that will shape our Christian faith and discipleship from a Mennonite Brethren perspective." Currently emphasizing inspirational with crossover potential. De-emphasizing personal experience, biographical. No children's books or fiction.

Nonfiction: Subjects include religion, inspirational. "Our books cater primarily to our Mennonite Brethren denomination readers." Query with SASE or submit outline, 2-3 sample chapter(s).

Recent Title(s): *Liberty in Confinement*, by Johannes Reimer.

Tips: "Most of our books are sold to churches, religious bookstores and schools. We are concentrating on devotional and inspirational books. We are accepting no children's manuscripts."

LAMBRECHT PUBLICATIONS, 1763 Maple Bay Rd., Duncan, British Columbia V9L 5N6, Canada. (250)748-8722. Fax: (250)748-8723. E-mail: helgal@cowichan.com. **Acquisitions:** Helga Lambrecht, publisher. Publishes hardcover, trade paperback originals and reprints. **Publishes 2 titles/year. Receives 6 queries/year. 50% of books from first-time authors. Pays 10% royalty on retail price. Offers advance.** Book catalog free.

○━ Lambrecht publishes local history books and cookbooks.
Nonfiction: Subjects include cooking/foods/nutrition, history, regional. *All unsolicited mss returned unopened.*

N: ☑ LOBSTER PRESS, 1620 Sherbrooke St. W, Suite C, Montreal, Quebec H3H 1C9, Canada. (514)904-1100. Fax: (514)904-1101. **Acquisitions:** Jane Pavanel, editor (fiction); Alison Fischer, editor (travel guides); Kim Bourgeois, editor (nonfiction and special projects). Publishes hardcover, trade paperback and mass market paperback originals. **Publishes 25 titles/year. Receives 200 queries and 1,500 mss/year. 90% of books from first-time authors; 75% from unagented writers. Pays 5-11% royalty on retail price. Offers $1,000-4,000 (Canadian) advance.** Publishes book 18 months after acceptance of ms. Accepts simultaneous submissions. Responds in 7 months to queries; 7 months to proposals; 10 months to mss. Book catalog free for #10 SASE (IRC or Canadian postage) or online; ms guidelines online.
Nonfiction: Children's/juvenile, illustrated book, self-help. Subjects include child guidance/parenting, creative nonfiction, history, sex, travel. Query with SASE (IRC or Canadian postage only) or submit complete ms. Reviews artwork/photos as part of ms package. Send photocopies.
Fiction: Adventure (for children), historical (for children), juvenile, picture books, young adult. Query with SASE (IRC or Canadian postage only) or submit complete ms.
Recent Title(s): *When I Grow Up, I Want to Be a Writer*, by Cynthia MacGregor (nonfiction); *Animal Sneezes*, by John Roy Bennetti, illus. by David Wysotski (picture book).

LONE PINE PUBLISHING, 10145 81st Ave., Edmonton, Alberta T6E 1W9, Canada. (403)433-9333. Fax: (403)433-9646. Website: www.lonepinepublishing.com. **Acquisitions:** Nancy Foulds, editorial director. Estab. 1980. Publishes trade paperback originals and reprints. **Publishes 12-40 titles/year. Receives 800 submissions/year. 75% of books from first-time authors; 95% from unagented writers. Pays royalty.** Responds in 3 months to queries. Book catalog free.
Imprints: Lone Pine, Home World, Pine Candle and Pine Cone
○━ Lone Pine publishes natural history and outdoor recreation—including gardening—titles, and some popular history and ghost story collections by region. " 'The World Outside Your Door' is our motto—helping people appreciate nature and their own special place." Currently emphasizing ghost stories by region, popular history.
Nonfiction: Subjects include animals, gardening, nature/environment, recreation, regional. The list is set for the next year and a half, but we are interested in seeing new material. Query with SASE or submit outline, sample chapter(s). Reviews artwork/photos as part of ms package.
Recent Title(s): *Annuals for Washington and Oregon*, by Alison Beck and Marianne Binetti; *Outlaws & Lawmen of the American West*, by M.A. Macpherson and Eli McLaren.
Tips: "Writers have their best chance with recreational or nature guidebooks. Most of our books are strongly regional in nature."

LYNX IMAGES, INC., 104 Scollard St., Toronto, Ontario M5R 1G2, Canada. (416)925-8422. Fax: (925)952-8352. E-mail: info@lynximages.com. Website: www.lynximages.com. **Acquisitions:** Russell Floren, president; Andrea Gutsche, director; Barbara Chesholm, producer. Publishes hardcover and trade paperback originals. **Publishes 6 titles/year. Receives 100 queries and 50 mss/year. 80% of books from first-time authors; 80% from unagented writers. Offers 40% advance.** Publishes book 1 year after acceptance of ms. Accepts simultaneous submissions.
○━ Lynx publishes historical tourism, travel, Canadian history, Great Lakes history. Currently emphasizing travel, history, nature. De-emphasizing boating, guides.
Nonfiction: Coffee table book, gift book, multimedia. Subjects include history, nature/environment, travel. Reviews artwork/photos as part of ms package.
Recent Title(s): *Disaster Canada*, by Janet Looker (book and video set); *Palaces of the Night*, by John Lindsay; *Northern Lights*, by David Baird.

N: ☑ McCLELLAND & STEWART LTD., 481 University Ave., Suite 900, Toronto, Ontario M5G 2E9, Canada. (416)598-1114. Publishes hardcover, trade paperback and mass market paperback originals and reprints. **Publishes 80 titles/year. Receives 1,000 queries/year. 10% of books from first-time authors; 30% from unagented writers. Pays 10-15% royalty on retail price (hardcover rates). Offers advance.** Publishes book 1 year after acceptance of ms. Responds in 3 months to proposals.
Imprints: McClelland & Stewart; New Canadian Library; Douglas Gibson Books; Emblem Editions
Nonfiction: "We publish books by Canadian authors or on Canadian subjects." Biography, coffee table book, how-to, humor, illustrated book, reference, self-help. Subjects include agriculture/horticulture, animals, art/architecture, business/economics, child guidance/parenting, cooking/foods/nutrition, education, gardening, gay/lesbian, government/politics,

health/medicine, history, hobbies, language/literature, military/war, money/finance, music/dance, nature/environment, philosophy, photography, psychology, recreation, religion, science, sociology, sports, translation, travel, women's issues/ studies, Canadiana. Submit outline. *All unsolicited mss returned unopened.*
Fiction: Experimental, historical, humor, literary, mainstream/contemporary, mystery, short story collections. "We publish quality fiction by prize-winning authors." Query. *All unsolicited mss returned unopened.*
Poetry: "Only Canadian poets should apply. We publish only four titles each year." Query. *No unsolicited mss.*
Recent Title(s): *The Blind Assassin*, by Margaret Atwood; *Anil's Ghost*, by Michael Ondaatje; *No Great Mischief*, by Alistair MacLeod.

McGRAW-HILL RYERSON LIMITED, 300 Water St., Whitby, Ontario L1N 9B6, Canada. (905)430-5116. Fax: (905)430-5044. E-mail: joanh@mcgrawhill.ca. Website: www.mcgrawhill.ca. **Acquisitions:** Joan Homewood, publisher. Publishes hardcover and trade paperback originals and revisions. **Publishes 20 titles/year. 10% of books from first-time authors; 60% from unagented writers. Pays 10% royalty on retail price. Offers $4,000 average advance.** Publishes book 1 year after acceptance of ms. Accepts simultaneous submissions. Responds in 6 months to queries.
○➤ McGraw-Hill Ryerson, Ltd., publishes books on Canadian business and personal finance for the Canadian market. Currently emphasizing business/management/financial planning/investing. De-emphasizing Canadian military history.
Nonfiction: Biography (business only), how-to, reference. Subjects include business/economics, history, money/finance. "No books and proposals that are American in focus. We publish primarily for the Canadian market, but work with McGraw-Hill U.S. to distribute business, management and training titles in U.S. and internationally." Query with SASE or submit proposal package including outline.
Recent Title(s): *Make Sure It's Deductible*, Evelyn Jacks; *The Relationship-Based Enterprise*, by Ray McKenzie.
Tips: "Writers have the best chance of selling us nonfiction business and personal finance books with a distinctly Canadian focus. Proposal guidelines are available. Thorough market research on competitive titles increases chances of your proposal getting serious consideration, as does endorsement by or references from relevant professionals."

MOOSE ENTERPRISE BOOK & THEATRE PLAY PUBLISHING, 684 Walls Side Rd., Sault Ste. Marie, Ontario P6A 5K6, Canada. (705)779-3331. Fax: (705)779-3331. **Acquisitions:** Richard Mousseau, owner/editor (fiction, history, general); Edmond Alcid, editor (poetry, children's, general). Publishes trade and mass market paperback originals. **Publishes 7-10 titles/year. Receives 10-15 queries and 10 mss/year. 60% of books from first-time authors; 100% from unagented writers. Pays 20-40% royalty on retail price.** Publishes book 6 months after acceptance of ms. Responds in 1 month to queries; 2 months to proposals; 2 months to mss. Book catalog and ms guidelines for #10 SASE.
Nonfiction: Biography, children's/juvenile. Subjects include history, memoirs, military/war. Query with SASE or submit proposal package including outline, 2 sample chapter(s), author bio. Reviews artwork/photos as part of ms package. Send photocopies.
Fiction: Adventure, historical, horror, humor, juvenile, military/war, mystery, picture books, plays, poetry, regional, science fiction, short story collections, western, young adult. Query with SASE or submit proposal package including 2 sample chapter(s), synopsis, author bio.
Poetry: Send author's bio and summary of project, typed, double spaced, one-sided. Query or submit 5 sample poems.
Recent Title(s): *A Long Exciting Trip to Peace*, by Angus Harnden (military/history); *Executor of Mercy*, by Edmond Alcid (adventure/novel); *Poems From My Heart*, by Gordon Hysen (poetry).
Tips: "Send only material that is of moral quality. Send bio of author."

NEW SOCIETY PUBLISHERS, P.O. Box 189, Gabriola, British Columbia V0R 1X0, Canada. (250)247-9737. Fax: (250)247-7471. E-mail: info@newsociety.com. Website: www.newsociety.com. **Acquisitions:** Chris Plant, editor. Publishes trade paperback originals and reprints and electronic originals. **Publishes 20 titles/year. Receives 300 queries and 200 mss/year. 50% of books from first-time authors; 80% from unagented writers. Pays 10-12% royalty on wholesale price. Offers $0-5,000 advance.** Publishes book 6 months after acceptance of ms. Accepts simultaneous submissions. Responds in 1 month to queries; 2 months to proposals. Book catalog and ms guidelines free or online.
Nonfiction: Biography, how-to, illustrated book, self-help. Subjects include business/economics, child guidance/parenting, creative nonfiction, education, government/politics, memoirs, nature/environment, philosophy, regional. Query with SASE or submit proposal package including outline, 2 sample chapter(s). Reviews artwork/photos as part of ms package. Send photocopies.
Recent Title(s): *Be the Difference: A Beginner's Guide to Changing the World*, by Danny Seo (activism).
Tips: Audience is activists, academics, progressive business people, managers. "Don't get an agent!"

NEWEST PUBLISHERS LTD., 201, 8540- 109 St., Edmonton, Alberta T6G 1E6, Canada. (403)432-9427. Fax: (403)433-3179. E-mail: info@newestpress.com. **Acquisitions:** Ruth Linka, general manager. Publishes trade paperback originals. **Publishes 13-16 titles/year. Receives 200 submissions/year. 40% of books from first-time authors; 90% from unagented writers.** Accepts simultaneous submissions. Responds in 6 months to queries. Book catalog for 9×12 SASE.
○➤ NeWest publishes Western Canadian fiction, nonfiction, poetry and drama.
Nonfiction: Literary/essays (Western Canadian authors). Subjects include ethnic, government/politics, history (Western Canada), Canadiana. Query.

Fiction: Literary. Submit complete ms.

Recent Title(s): *I'm Frankie Sturne*, by Dave Margoshes (fiction); *Watershed: Reflections in Water*, by Grant MacEwan (nonfiction); *Snake in Fridge*, by Brad Fraser (drama).

Tips: "Trend is towards more nonfiction submissions. Would like to see more full-length literary fiction."

N NORBRY PUBLISHING LIMITED, 520 Aberdeen Ave., Hamilton, Ontario L8P 2S2, Canada. (905)308-9877. Fax: (905)308-9869. E-mail: Norbry@norbry.com. Website: www.norbry.com. **Acquisitions:** Rebecca Pembry, president. Publishes mass market paperback originals. **Publishes 9 titles/year. 100% of books from unagented writers. Pays 10-20% royalty on retail price.** Publishes book 6 months after acceptance of ms. Accepts simultaneous submissions. Book catalog and ms guidelines free.

Nonfiction: Multimedia (CD-ROM and network), textbook, online courseware, testing systems, assessment tools and course management systems. Subjects include business/economics, computers/electronic, education, software, accounting. Query with SASE. Reviews artwork/photos as part of ms package. Send photocopies.

Recent Title(s): *Learning Simply Accounting 8.0 for Windows*, by Harvey Freedman and Joseph Toste; *ACCPAC 4.1 for Windows*, by John Stammers; *MYOB 9.0*, by Christine Heaney.

N NOVALIS, Bayard Presse. 49 Front St. E, Toronto, Ontario M5E 1B3, Canada. (416)363-3303. Fax: (416)363-9409. E-mail: novalis@interlog.com. Website: www.novalis.ca. **Acquisitions:** Kevin Burns, commissioning editor; Michael O'Hearn, publisher (theology, education); Anne Louise Mahoney, managing editor (self-help, parenting). Publishes hardcover and trade paperback originals and trade paperback reprints. **Publishes 25 titles/year. 25% of books from first-time authors; 50% from unagented writers. Pays 10-15% royalty on wholesale price. Offers $300-2,000 advance.** Publishes book 9 months after acceptance of ms. Responds in 2 months to queries; 1 month to proposals; 2 months to mss. Book catalog free or online; ms guidelines free.

    O→ "Novalis publishes for Roman Catholic, Christian and non-denominational readerships, but all of our books have a spiritual component or orientation, at the very least, where there is not an explicitly Christian viewpoint."

Nonfiction: Biography, children's/juvenile, gift book, humor, illustrated book, reference, self-help. Subjects include child guidance/parenting, education (Christian or Catholic), memoirs, multicultural, nature/environment, philosophy, religion, spirituality. Query with SASE.

Recent Title(s): *Women & Christianity: The First Thousand Years*, by Mary T. Malone (history, feminist studies); *How to Forgive: A Step-by-Step Guide*, by John Monbourquette (self-help).

N PACIFIC EDUCATIONAL PRESS, Faculty of Education. University of British Columbia, Vancouver, British Columbia V6T 1Z4, Canada. Fax: (604)822-6603. E-mail: cedwards@interchange.ubc.ca. **Acquisitions:** Catherine Edwards, director. Publishes trade paperback originals and cloth reference books. **Publishes 6-8 titles/year. Receives 200 submissions/year. 15% of books from first-time authors; 100% from unagented writers.** Accepts simultaneous submissions. Responds in 6 months to mss. Book catalog and ms guidelines for 9 × 12 SAE with IRCs.

    O→ Pacific Educational Press publishes books on the subject of education for an adult audience of teachers, scholars, librarians and parents. Currently emphasizing literature, education, social studies education, international issues and experiences in education.

Recent Title(s): *Teaching to Wonder: Responding to Poetry in the Secondary Classroom*, by Carl Leggo; *The Canadian Anthology of Social Studies*, by Roland Case and Penney Clark; *Shakespeare & Film*, by Neil Bechervaise.

N PEARSON PTR CANADA, (formerly Prentice Hall Canada and Addison Wesley Longman Canada), 26 Prince Andrew Place, Don Mills, Ontario M3C 2T8, Canada. (416)447-5101. Fax: (416)443-0948. Website: www.pearsonPTR. ca. **Acquisitions:** Andrea Crozier, editorial director. Estab. 1960. Publishes hardcover and trade paperback originals. **Publishes 50 titles/year. Receives 750-900 submissions/year. 15% of books from first-time authors; 50% from unagented writers. Pays royalty. Offers advance.** Publishes book up to 2 years after acceptance of ms. Responds in 3 months to queries. Manuscript guidelines for #10 SAE with 1 IRC.

Imprints: Prentice Hill Canada; ft.com; Prentice Hall/Financial Times

Nonfiction: Subjects include business/economics, computers/electronic, cooking/foods/nutrition, gardening, health/medicine, personal finance, personal growth, popular culture; all with Canadian and international interest.

Recent Title(s): *CommonSpace: Beyond Virtual Community*, by Darren Wershler-Henry and Mark Surman (computers/Internet/business/Internet marketing).

Tips: "Present a clear, concise thesis, well-argued with a thorough knowledge of existing competitive works. Take a look at submission guidelines on our website."

PENGUIN BOOKS CANADA LTD., The Penguin Group. 10 Alcorn Ave., Suite 300, Toronto, Ontario M4V 3B2, Canada. (416)925-0068. **Acquisitions:** Diane Turbide, editorial director (literary nonfiction, biography, social issues); Barbara Berson, senior editor (literary fiction and nonfiction; children's and young adult fiction; history/current events); Cynthia Good, president/publisher. **Offers advance.**

Nonfiction: Any Canadian subject by any Canadian authors. Query with SASE. *No unsolicited mss.*

Recent Title(s): *Titans*, by Peter C. Newman (business); *Home From the Vinyl Café*, by Stuart McLean (fiction); *Notes from the Hyena's Belly*, by Nega Mezlekia (memoir).

PICASSO PUBLICATIONS, INC., Picasso Entertainment Company. 10548-115 Street, Edmonton, Alberta T5H 3K6, Canada. (780)420-0417. Fax: (780)420-0475. E-mail: Randolph@picassopublications.com. Website: www.picasso publications.com. **Acquisitions:** Randolph Ross Sr., director (new business development); Luis Chacon Sr., director (operations director). Publishes hardcover and trade paperback originals, mass market paperback originals. **Publishes 35 titles/year; imprint publishes 5 titles/year. Receives 50,000 queries and 10,000 mss/year. 1% of books from first-time authors; 10% from unagented writers. Pays 10-12% royalty on retail price or makes outright purchase. Offers up to $1 million advance.** Publishes book 9 months after acceptance of ms. Accepts simultaneous submissions. Responds in 2 months to queries; 1 months to proposals; 3 months to mss. Book catalog and ms guidelines free online.
Imprints: Blink, Chronicle Fiction, Engima, Nebula, Mystic, Passion Enlightenment
○→ Picasso Publications publishes a wide variety of books for a mass market audience.
Nonfiction: Biography, children's/juvenile, coffee table book, cookbook, gift book, how-to, humor, illustrated book, multimedia, self-help. Subjects include Americana, animals, art/architecture, child guidance/parenting, cooking/foods/ nutrition, education, ethnic, gay/lesbian, government/politics, history, hobbies, humor, language/literature, military/war, money/finance, multicultural, recreation, religion, sex, sports, women's issues/studies. Query with SASE. Reviews artwork/photos as part of ms package. Send photocopies.
Fiction: Adventure, erotica, fantasy, feminist, gay/lesbian, gothic, historical, horror, humor, juvenile, literary, mainstream/contemporary, military/war, multicultural, multimedia, mystery, regional, religious, romance, science fiction, spiritual, sports, suspense, young adult. Query with SASE.
Recent Title(s): *Pain Behind the Smile*, by Leah Hulan (beauty queen memoir); *Shadowed Love*, by Martine Jardin (novel).

PLAYWRIGHTS CANADA PRESS, Playwrights Union of Canada. 54 Wolseley St., 2nd Floor, Toronto, Ontario M5T 1A5, Canada. (416)703-0201. Fax: (416)703-0059. E-mail: angela@puc.ca. Website: www.puc.ca. **Acquisitions:** Angela Rebeiro, publisher. Estab. 1972. Publishes paperback originals and reprints of plays. **Receives 40 submissions/ year. 50% of books from first-time authors; 50% from unagented writers. Pays 10% royalty on retail price.** Publishes book 1 year after acceptance of ms. Responds in 6 months to queries.
○→ Playwrights Canada Press publishes only drama by Canadian citizens or landed immigrants, which has received professional production.
Recent Title(s): *Belle*, by Florence Gibson; *Angelique*, by Lorena Gale; *It's All True*, by Jason Sherman.

PONDER PUBLISHING, INC., PO Box 23037, RPO McGillivray, Winnipeg, Manitoba R3T 5S3, Canada. (204)269-2985. Fax: (204)888-7159. E-mail: service@ponderpublishing. Website: www.ponderpublishing.com. **Acquisitions:** Mary Barton, senior editor; Pamela Walford, assistant editor. Publishes mass market paperback originals. Publishes 2-4 titles/year. Receives 25 queries and 300 submissions/year. 100% of books from first-time authors; 100% from unagented writers. Contracts vary and are negotiable but include signing bonuses (instead of advance) in addition to royalties.** Publishes book 1-2 years after acceptance of ms. Responds in 3 months to queries; 3 months to proposals; 3 months to mss. Book catalog and ms guidelines for #10 SASE or online.
Fiction: Romance. "Ponder Romance is the new voice in the genre. We are looking for contemporary romances that are relationship driven and offer an escape from the everyday through both exciting plot lines and fresh writing styles. Entertainment and humor are two key elements to the success of a Ponder Romance. We tell writers, forget what you know about writing romance, start with a dynamite story and weave the romance into it." Submit 3 sample chapter(s), synopsis.
Recent Title(s): *Oh Susannah*, by Selena Mindus; *Autumn's Eve*, by Jordanna Boston.
Tips: "Ponder Romance appeals to a wide spectrum of romance readers and has also won over many non-romance and even nonfiction readers. Read our books. Writers assume they know what we want simply because it's romance, but Ponder Romance is unique to the genre and our titles are unique to each other in a way that our writer's guidelines cannot fully convey. Ponder Romance forges a new path right down the middle between category and mainstream romance and combines the best elements of each."

PRESSES DE L'UNIVERSITÉ DE MONTREAL, 2910, boul Edouard-Montpetit, bureau 17, 3 etage, Montreal, Quebec H3T 1J7, Canada. (514)343-6933. Fax: (514)343-2232. E-mail: pum@umontreal.ca. Website: www.pum.umontr eal.ca. **Acquisitions:** Rene Bonenfant, editor-in-chief,. Publishes hardcover and trade paperback originals. **Publishes 40 titles/year. Pays 8-12% royalty on net receipts.** Publishes book 6 months after acceptance of ms. Responds in 1 month to queries; 1 month to proposals; 3 months to mss. Book catalog and ms guidelines free.
Nonfiction: Reference, textbook. Subjects include education, health/medicine, history, language/literature, philosophy, psychology, sociology, translation. Submit outline, 2 sample chapter(s).

PRODUCTIVE PUBLICATIONS, P.O. Box 7200 Station A, Toronto, Ontario M5W 1X8, Canada. (416)483-0634. Fax: (416)322-7434. **Acquisitions:** Iain Williamson, owner. Estab. 1985. Publishes trade paperback originals. **Publishes 24 titles/year. Receives 160 queries and 40 mss/year. 80% of books from first-time authors; 100% from unagented writers. Pays 10-15% royalty on wholesale price.** Publishes book 6 months after acceptance of ms. Accepts simultaneous submissions. Responds in 1 month to queries; 1 month to proposals; 3 months to mss. Book catalog free.
○→ "Productive Publications publishes books to help readers succeed and to help them meet the challenges of the

new information age and global marketplace." Interested in books on business, computer software, the Internet for business purposes, investment, stock market and mutual funds, etc. Currently emphasizing computers, software, personal finance. De-emphasizing jobs, how to get employment.

Nonfiction: How-to, reference, self-help, technical. Subjects include business/economics (small business and management), computers/electronic, hobbies, money/finance, software (business). "We are interested in small business/entrepreneurship/employment/self-help (business)/how-to—100 to 300 pages." Submit outline. Reviews artwork/photos as part of ms package. Send photocopies.

Recent Title(s): *How to Deliver Excellent Customer Service: A Step-by-Step Guide for Every Business*, by Julie Olley.

Tips: "We are looking for books written by *knowledgable, experienced experts* who can express their ideas *clearly* and *simply*."

PURICH PUBLISHING, Box 23032, Market Mall Post Office, Saskatoon, Saskatchewan S7J 5H3, Canada. (306)373-5311. Fax: (306)373-5315. E-mail: purich@sk.sympatico.ca. Website: www3.sk.sympatico.ca/purich. **Acquisitions:** Donald Purich, publisher (law, Aboriginal issues); Karen Bolstad, publisher (history). Publishes trade paperback originals. **Publishes 3-5 titles/year. 20% of books from first-time authors. Pays 8-12% royalty on retail price or makes outright purchase. Offers negotiable advance.** Publishes book within 4 months of completion of editorial work, after acceptance of ms. Accepts simultaneous submissions. Responds in 1 month to queries; 3 months to mss. Book catalog free.

   ⊶ Purich pubishes books on law, Aboriginal/Native American issues and Western Canadian history for the academic and professional trade reference market.

Nonfiction: Reference, technical, textbook. Subjects include agriculture/horticulture, ethnic, government/politics, history. "We are a specialized publisher and only consider work in our subject areas." Query with SASE.

Recent Title(s): *Protecting Indigenous Knowledge and Heritage*, by Dr. Marie Battiste and James (Sa'ke'j) Youngblood Henderson.

RAGWEED PRESS, 35 Alvin Ave., Toronto, Ontario M4T 2A7, Canada. (416)961-7700. Fax: (416)961-7808. E-mail: agosewich@balmur.com. **Acquisitions:** Sibyl Frei, managing editor. Publishes hardcover and trade paperback originals. **Publishes 3-5 titles/year; imprint publishes 3-5 titles/year. Pays 8-10% royalty on wholesale price or retail price. Offers advance.** Publishes book 1-2 years after acceptance of ms. Responds in 6 months to mss. Book catalog free; ms guidelines for #10 SASE.

Imprints: Ragweed

Nonfiction: Biography, children's/juvenile, gift book, illustrated book. Subjects include humor. "For nonfiction, we prefer to review agent-recommended proposals and, if accepted, work with the author or editor on developing the book from concept through to final manuscript." Query with SASE or submit proposal package. *No unsolicited mss.*

Fiction: Adventure, historical, juvenile, picture books, young adult. "Our children's, juvenile and young adult fiction features girl heroes (no rhyming stories for children). Again, prefer dealing through an agent." Query with SASE.

Recent Title(s): *Sweeping the Earth: Women Taking Action for a Healthy Planet*, edited by Miriam Wyman (feminist nonfiction anthology); *The Dog Wizarrd*, by Anne Louise MacDonald, illustrated by Brenda Jones (children's fiction for ages 5-8).

ROCKY MOUNTAIN BOOKS, #4 Spruce Centre SW, Calgary, Alberta T3C 3B3, Canada. (403)249-9490. Fax: (403)249-2968. E-mail: tonyd@rmbooks.com. Website: www.rmbooks.com. **Acquisitions:** Tony Daffern, publisher. Publishes trade paperback originals. **Publishes 5 titles/year. Receives 30 queries/year. 75% of books from first-time authors; 100% from unagented writers. Pays 10% royalty. Offers $1,000-2,000 advance.** Publishes book 1 year after acceptance of ms. Responds in 1 month to queries. Book catalog and ms guidelines free.

   ⊶ Rocky Mountain Books publishes on outdoor recreation, mountains and mountaineering in Western Canada.

Nonfiction: Biography, how-to. Subjects include nature/environment, recreation, regional, travel. "Our main area of publishing is outdoor recreation guides to Western and Northern Canada." Query with SASE.

Recent Title(s): *Pushing the Limits: The Story of Canadian Mountaineering*, by Chris Scott.

RONSDALE PRESS, 3350 W. 21st Ave., Vancouver, British Columbia V6S 1G7, Canada. Website: www.ronsdale press.com. **Acquisitions:** Ronald B. Hatch, director (fiction, poetry, social commentary); Veronica Hatch, managing director (children's literature). Publishes trade paperback originals. **Publishes 8 titles/year. Receives 100 queries and 200 mss/year. 60% of books from first-time authors; 95% from unagented writers. Pays 10% royalty on retail price.** Publishes book 1 year after acceptance of ms. Accepts simultaneous submissions. Responds in 1 week to queries; 1 month to proposals; 3 months to mss. Book catalog for #10 SASE.

   ⊶ Ronsdale publishes fiction, poetry, regional history, biography and autobiography, books of ideas about Canada, as well as children's books. Currently emphasizing YA historical fiction.

Nonfiction: Biography, children's/juvenile. Subjects include history, language/literature, nature/environment, regional.

Fiction: Short story collections, novels. Query with at least 80 pages.

Poetry: "Poets should have published some poems in magazines/journals and should be well-read in contemporary masters." Submit complete ms.

Recent Title(s): *Eyewitness*, by Maynard Thompson (YA historical fiction).

Tips: "Ronsdale Press is a literary publishing house, based in Vancouver, and dedicated to publishing books from across Canada, books that give Canadians new insights into themselves and their country. We aim to publish the best Canadian writers."

SAXON HOUSE CANADA, P.O. Box 6947, Station A, Toronto, Ontario M5W 1X6, Canada. (416)488-7171. Fax: (416)488-2989. **Acquisitions:** Dietrich Hummell, editor-in-chief (poetry, legends); W.H. Wallace, general manager (history, philosophy); Carla Saxon, CEO (printed music). Publishes hardcover originals and trade paperback reprints. **Publishes 4 titles/year. Receives 6 queries and 20 mss/year. 20% of books from first-time authors; 80% from unagented writers. Pays royalty on wholesale price or makes outright purchase. Offers advance.** Publishes book 15 months after acceptance of ms. Accepts simultaneous submissions. Responds in 4 months to mss.
Nonfiction: Illustrated book. Subjects include Americana, history, music/dance, philosophy, religion. Submit proposal package including 3 sample chapter(s), résumé. Reviews artwork/photos as part of ms package. Send photocopies.
Fiction: Historical, literary, poetry. Submit proposal package including 3 sample chapter(s), résumé.
Poetry: Submit 8 sample poems.
Recent Title(s): *The Journey to Canada*, by David Mills (history); *Voices From the Lake*, by E.M. Watts (illustrated ancient American Indian legend); *The Wine of Babylon*, by David Mills (epic poem).
Tips: "We want books with literary integrity. Historical accuracy and fresh narrative skills."

A **SCHOLASTIC CANADA LTD.**, 175 Hillmount Rd., Markham, Ontario L6C 1Z7, Canada. (905)887-7323. Fax: (905)887-1131. Website: www.scholastic.ca. Publishes hardcover and trade paperback originals. **Publishes 40 titles/year; imprint publishes 4 titles/year. 3% of books from first-time authors; 50% from unagented writers. Pays 5-10% royalty on retail price. Offers $1,000-5,000 (Canadian) advance.** Publishes book 1 year after acceptance of ms. Responds in 3 months to queries; 3 months to proposals. Book catalog for 8½ × 11 SAE with 2 first-class stamps (IRC or Canadian stamps only).
Imprints: North Winds Press; Les editions Scholastic
　　O→ Scholastic publishes books by Canadians and/or about Canada. Currently emphasizing junior nonfiction, Canadian interest, middle-grade fiction.
Nonfiction: Biography, children's/juvenile, how-to. Subjects include history, hobbies, nature/environment, recreation, science, sports. *Accepts agented submissions only. No unsolicited mss.*
Fiction: Juvenile (middle grade), young adult. *Accepts agented submissions only.*
Recent Title(s): *Up, Up, Down*, by Robert Munsch (picture book); *Money: Make It! Spend It! Save It!*, by J.E. Bogart (nonfiction); *In My Enemy's House*, by Carol Matas (fiction).

SHORELINE, 23 Ste-Anne, Ste-Anne-de-Bellevue, Quebec H9X 1L1, Canada. (514)457-5733. E-mail: bookline@total .net. Website: www.total.net/~bookline/. **Acquisitions:** Judy Isherwood, editor. Publishes trade paperback originals. **Publishes 4 titles/year. Pays 10% royalty on retail price.** Publishes book 1 year after acceptance of ms. Responds in 1 month to queries; 4 months to mss. Book catalog for 50¢.
　　O→ "Our mission is to support new authors by publishing works of considerable merit." Currently emphasizing biography, memoirs and local history. No fiction, war stories or pets.
Nonfiction: Biography, memoirs, local history. Subjects include Americana, art/architecture, education, ethnic, health/ medicine, history, humor, regional, religion, travel, women's issues/studies.
Recent Title(s): *Montreal Memories of the Century*, by John Collins (local history); *Return to Orrock*, by Wilhelmina Hays (memoir); *The Prophet of the Plains*, by Robert Tessier (poetry).
Tips: Query first.

SNOWAPPLE PRESS, Box 66024, Heritage Postal Outlet, Edmonton, Alberta T6J 6T4, Canada. **Acquisitions:** Vanna Tessier, editor. Publishes hardcover originals, trade paperback originals and reprints, mass market paperback originals and reprints. **Publishes 5-6 titles/year. Receives 300 queries/year. 50% of books from first-time authors; 100% from unagented writers. Pays 10-50% royalty on retail price or makes outright purchase or pays in contributor copies. Offers $100-200 advance.** Publishes book 2 years after acceptance of ms. Accepts simultaneous submissions. Responds in 1 month to queries; 3 months to proposals; 3 months to mss.
　　O→ "We focus on topics that are interesting, unusual and controversial." .
Fiction: Adventure, ethnic, experimental, fantasy, feminist, historical, literary, mainstream/contemporary, mystery, picture books, short story collections, young adult. Query with SASE. *No unsolicited mss.*
Poetry: Query.
Recent Title(s): *Thistle Creek*, by Vanna Tessier (fiction).
Tips: "We are a small press that will publish original, interesting and entertaining fiction and poetry."

SOUND AND VISION PUBLISHING LIMITED, 359 Riverdale Ave., Toronto, Ontario M4J 1A4, Canada. (416)465-2828. Fax: (416)465-0755. E-mail: musicbooks@soundandvision.com. Website: www.soundandvision.com. **Acquisitions:** Geoff Savage. Publishes trade paperback originals. **Publishes 3-5 titles/year. Receives 25 queries/year. 85% of books from first-time authors; 100% from unagented writers. Pays royalty on wholesale price. Offers $500-2,000 advance.** Responds in 1 month to queries.
　　O→ Sound and Vision specializes in books on musical humor and quotation books.
Nonfiction: Humor. Subjects include humor, music/dance. Query with SASE.

Recent Title(s): *The Thing I've Played with the Most*, by David E. Walden; *Opera Antics and Anecdotes*, by Stephen Tanner, cartoons by Umberto Taccola.

STELLER PRESS LTD., 13-4335 W. 10th Ave., Vancouver, British Columbia V6R 2H6, Canada. (604)222-2955. Fax: (604)222-2965. E-mail: harful@telus.net. **Acquisitions:** Guy Chadsey, publisher (outdoors/gardening). Publishes trade paperback originals. **Publishes 4 titles/year. 75% of books from first-time authors; 100% from unagented writers. Pays royalty on retail price. Offers $500-2,000 advance.** Accepts simultaneous submissions. Responds in 6 months to queries.

> ⚓ "All titles are specific to the Pacific Northwest." Currently emphasizing gardening, history, outdoors. De-emphasizing fiction, poetry.

Nonfiction: Subjects include gardening, history, nature/environment, regional, travel.

Recent Title(s): *Roses For the Pacific Northwest*, by Christine Allen; *Herbs For the Pacific Northwest*, by Moira Carlson.

N **TESSERACT BOOKS**, The Books Collective. 214-21 10405 Jasper Ave., Edmonton, Alberta T5J 3S2, Canada. (780)448-0590. Fax: (780)448-0640. E-mail: promo@bookscollective.com. Website: www.bookscollective.com. **Acquisitions:** Candas Jame Dorsey, editor. Publishes hardcover and trade paperback originals. **Publishes 6 titles/year. Receives 50 queries and 350 mss/year. 80% of books from first-time authors; 90% from unagented writers. Pays 8% royalty on retail price.** Publishes book 18 months after acceptance of ms. Accepts simultaneous submissions. Responds in 2 months to queries; 4 months to proposals; 6 months to mss. Book catalog for 9×12 SAE with 2 first-class stamps; ms guidelines online.

Imprints: River Books, Slipstream Books (Timothy J. Anderson, editor).

Nonfiction: Biography. Subjects include memoirs. "Our only nonfiction titles are striking, powerful memoirs." Query with SASE or submit outline, 3 sample chapter(s), SASE.

Fiction: Experimental, fantasy, poetry, science fiction, short story collections. Submit 3 sample chapter(s), synopsis, SASE.

Poetry: Query.

Recent Title(s): *The Edmonton Queen*, by Darrin Hagen (memoirs of a drag queen); *Stealing Magic*, by Tanya Huff (fantasy, short story collection); *Amelia's Aquarium*, by Zhaune Alexander (poetry).

Tips: "Audience is people interested in unusual stories, academics, people outside the mainstream. We only publish Canadian authors."

THOMPSON EDUCATIONAL PUBLISHING INC., 6 Ripley Ave., Suite 200, Toronto, Ontario M6S 3N9, Canada. (416)766-2763. Fax: (416)766-0398. E-mail: publisher@thompsonbooks.com. Website: www.thompsonbooks.com. **Acquisitions:** Keith Thompson, president. **Publishes 10 titles/year. Receives 15 queries and 10 mss/year. 80% of books from first-time authors; 100% from unagented writers. Pays 10% royalty on net receipts. Offers advance.** Publishes book 1 year after acceptance of ms. Responds in 1 month to queries. Book catalog free.

> ⚓ Thompson Educational specializes in high-quality educational texts in the social sciences and humanities.

Nonfiction: Textbook. Subjects include business/economics, education, ethnic, government/politics, multicultural, sociology, sports, women's issues/studies. Submit outline, 1 sample chapter(s), résumé.

Recent Title(s): *Sport Ethics*, by David Cruise Malloy and Saul Ross.

TRADEWIND BOOKS, 2216 Stephens St., Vancouver, British Columbia V6K 3W6, Canada. (604)730-0153. Fax: (604)730-0154. E-mail: tradewindbooks@yahoo.com. Website: www.tradewindbooks.com. **Acquisitions:** Michael Katz, publisher (picturebooks, young adult); Carol Frank, art director (picturebooks); Leslie Owen (acquisitions editor). Publishes hardcover and trade paperback originals. **Publishes 3-4 titles/year. Receives 1,000 submissions/year. 10% of books from first-time authors; 50% from unagented writers. Pays 8% royalty on retail price. Offers variable advance.** Publishes book 3 years after acceptance of ms. Accepts simultaneous submissions. Responds in 1 month to mss. Book catalog and ms guidelines online.

> ⚓ Tradewind Books publishes juvenile picturebooks, young adult novels and a nonfiction natural history series. Currently emphasizing nonfiction YA novels. Requires that submissions include evidence that author has had at least 3 titles published.

Fiction: Juvenile. Query with SASE or submit proposal package including 2 sample chapter(s), synopsis.

Recent Title(s): *The Girl Who Lost Her Smile*, by Karim Alrawi; *Wherever Bears Be*, Sue Ann Alderson (picturebook); *Mr. Belinsky's Bagels*, Ellen Schwartz (picturebook).

TRILOBYTE PRESS & MULTIMEDIA, (formerly Trilobyte Press) 1486 Willowdown Rd., Oakville, Ontario L6L 1X3, Canada. (905)847-7366. Fax: (905)847-3258. E-mail: mail@successatschool.com. Website: www.successatschool.com. **Acquisitions:** Danton H. O'Day, Ph.D., publisher. Publishes online electronic books for downloading via the Internet. **Publishes 3-4 titles/year. Receives 50 queries and 20 mss/year. 50% of books from first-time authors; 100% from unagented writers. Pays negotiable royalty.** Publishes book 2 months after acceptance of ms. Accepts simultaneous submissions. Responds in 1 month to queries; 2 months to proposals; 3 months to mss. Book catalog and ms guidelines online.

Nonfiction: How-to, reference, self-help, textbook. Subjects include education, health/medicine, science. "We are continually looking for guides to help students succeed in school and in their careers." Query with SASE or submit proposal package including outline, 2 sample chapter(s), résumé. Reviews artwork/photos as part of ms package.

Recent Title(s): *Write on Track—The Teaching Kit*, by Philip Dimitroff.

Tips: Audience is "people from high school through college age who want to do their best in school. Think about your submission—why us and why is your book worth publishing? Who will read it and why?"

TURNSTONE PRESS, 607-100 Arthur St., Winnipeg, Manitoba R3B 1H3, Canada. (204)947-1555. Fax: (204)942-1555. E-mail: editor@turnstonepress.mb.ca. Website: www.turnstonepress.com. **Acquisitions:** Manuela Dias, managing editor. Estab. 1976. Publishes trade paperback originals. **Publishes 10-12 titles/year. Receives 1,000 mss/year. 25% of books from first-time authors; 75% from unagented writers. Pays 10% royalty on retail price. Offers advance.** Publishes book 1 year after acceptance of ms. Responds in 4 months to queries. Book catalog for #10 SASE.

Imprints: Ravenstone (literary genre fiction)

O→ Turnstone Press is a literary press that publishes Canadian writers with an emphasis on writers from, and writing on, the Canadian West. "We are interested in publishing experimental/literary works that mainstream publishers may not be willing to work with." Currently emphasizing nonfiction-travel, memoir, eclectic novels. De-emphasizing formula or mainstream work.

Nonfiction: Subjects include memoirs, nature/environment, travel. Query with SASE.

Fiction: Adventure, ethnic, experimental, feminist, gothic, humor, literary, mainstream/contemporary, mystery, short story collections. Query with SASE.

Poetry: Submit complete ms.

Recent Title(s): *Marshwalker*, by John Weier (nonfiction); *In the Hands of the Living*, by Lillian Bouzane (fiction); *Waking Blood*, by Deborah Keahey (poetry).

Tips: "Writers are encouraged to view our list and check if submissions are appropriate. Would like to see more women's writing, travel, life-writing as well as eclectic novels. Would like to see 'non-formula' genre writing, especially *literary* mystery, gothic and noir for our new imprint."

THE UNIVERSITY OF ALBERTA PRESS, Ring House 2, Edmonton, Alberta T6G 2E1, Canada. (780)492-3662. Fax: (780)492-0719. E-mail: uap@gpu.srv.ualberta.ca. Website: www.ualberta.ca/~uap. **Acquisitions:** Leslie Vermeer, managing editor. Estab. 1969. Publishes trade paperback originals and trade paperback reprints. **Publishes 18-25 titles/year. Receives 400 submissions/year. 60% of books from first-time authors. Pays maximum 10% royalty on net price.** Publishes book within 2 years after acceptance of ms. Responds in 3 months to queries. Book catalog and ms guidelines free.

O→ The University of Alberta publishes books on the Canadian West, the North, multicultural studies, health sciences, the environment, earth sciences, native studies, Canadian history, natural science and Canadian prairie literature.

Nonfiction: Textbook. Subjects include art/architecture, government/politics, history, nature/environment, philosophy, regional, sociology. "Our interests include the Canadian West, the North, multicultural studies, health science and native studies." Submit outline, 1-2 sample chapter(s). Reviews artwork/photos as part of ms package. Send sample illustrations.

Recent Title(s): *The Alberta Elders' Cree Dictionary*, by Nancy LeClaire and George Cardinal, edited by Earle Waugh.

Tips: "Since 1969, the University of Alberta Press has earned recognition and awards from the Association of American University Presses, the Alcuin Society, the Book Publishers Association of Alberta and the Bibliographical Society of Canada, among others. Now we're growing—in the audiences we reach, the numbers of titles we publish, and our energy for new challenges. But we're still small enough to listen carefully, to work closely with our authors, to explore possibilities."

UNIVERSITY OF CALGARY PRESS, 2500 University Dr. NW, Calgary, Alberta T2N 1N4, Canada. (403)220-7578. Fax: (403)282-0085. E-mail: whildebr@ucalgary.ca. Website: www.ucalgary.ca/ucpress. **Acquisitions:** Walter Hildebrandt, acquisitions editor. Publishes hardcover and trade paperback originals and reprints. **Publishes 15-20 titles/year.** Publishes book 20 months after acceptance of ms. Responds in 1 month to queries; 2 months to proposals; 2 months to mss. Book catalog and ms guidelines free.

O→ "University of Calgary Press is committed to the advancement of scholarship through the publication of first-rate monographs and academic and scientific journals."

Nonfiction: Subjects include art/architecture, business/economics, health/medicine, philosophy, travel, women's issues/studies, world affairs. Canadian studies, post-modern studies, international relations. Submit outline, 2 sample chapter(s). SASE. Reviews artwork/photos as part of ms package. Send photocopies.

Recent Title(s): *Sights of Resistance: Approaches to Canadian Visual Culture*, by Robert J. Belton; *At Home Afloat: Women on the Waters of the Pacific Northwest*, by Nancy Pagh.

UPNEY EDITIONS, 19 Appalachian Crescent, Kitchener, Ontario N2E 1A3, Canada. **Acquisitions:** Gary Brannon, publisher. Publishes trade paperback originals. **Publishes 2-4 titles/year. Receives 200 queries and 100 mss/year. 33% of books from first-time authors; 100% from unagented writers. Pays 10% royalty on wholesale price. Offers advance.** Publishes book 9 months after acceptance of ms. Responds in 1 month to queries. Book catalog for #10 SASE.

O⊸ Upney Editions publishes non-mainstream, "niche" nonfiction. Currently emphasizing foreign travel and life-style, also cultural experiences. De-emphasizing biography and art/architecture.

Nonfiction: Biography, reference. Subjects include Americana, art/architecture, history, travel. "Remember that we are a Canadian small press, and our readers are mostly Canadians! We are specifically interested in popular history with cross-border U.S./Canada connection; also, popular travel literature (particularly Europe), but it must be witty and critically honest. No travel guides, cycling, hiking or driving tours! We prefer words to paint pictures rather than photographs, but line art will be considered. Queries or submissions that dictate publishing terms turn us right off. So do submissions with no SASE or submissions with return U.S. postage stamps. Enclose sufficient IRCs or we cannot return material. We prefer to see manuscripts well thought out chapter by chapter, not just a first chapter and a vague idea of the rest." Query with SASE or submit outline, 2 sample chapter(s). Reviews artwork/photos as part of ms package. Send photocopies.

Recent Title(s): *Looking for Momo in Tomo Domo*, by Nils Thompson.

Tips: "We will consider any nonfiction topic with the exception of religion, politics and finance. City/regional/destination specific travel material expertly illustrated with pen and ink sketches will catch our attention. Although our titles are directed to a general audience, our sales and marketing are focused on libraries (public, high school, college) 70% and 30% on bookstores. We are dismayed by the 'pushy' attitude of some submissions. We will not even look at 'finished package, ready-to-print' submissions, which seem to be growing in number. The authors of these instant books clearly need a printer and/or investor and not a publisher. Electronic submissions on disk are welcome—we are a Mac, QuarkX-Press environment."

VANWELL PUBLISHING LIMITED, 1 Northrup Crescent, P.O. Box 2131, St. Catharines, Ontario L2R 7S2, Canada. (905)937-3100. Fax: (905)937-1760. **Acquisitions:** Angela Dobler, general editor; Simon Kooter, military editor (collections, equipment, vehicles, uniforms, artifacts); Ben Kooter, publisher (general military). Estab. 1983. Publishes trade originals and reprints. **Publishes 7-9 titles/year. Receives 100 submissions/year. 85% of books from first-time authors; 100% from unagented writers. Pays 10% royalty on retail price. Offers $200 average advance.** Publishes book 1 year after acceptance of ms. Responds in 6 months to queries. Book catalog free.

O⊸ Vanwell is considered Canada's leading naval heritage publisher. Currently emphasizing military aviation, biography, WWI and WWII histories. Limited publishing in children's fiction and nonfiction, but not picture books. "We are seeing an increased demand for biographical nonfiction for ages 10-14."

Nonfiction: Biography, children's/juvenile, reference. Subjects include history, military/war, regional, women's issues/studies. Query with SASE. Reviews artwork/photos as part of ms package.

Recent Title(s): *In Search of Pegasus: The Canadian Airborne Experience*, by Bernd Horn/Michel Wyczynski; *The Canadian Submarine Service in Review*, by J. David Perkins.

Tips: "The writer has the best chance of selling a manuscript to our firm which is in keeping with our publishing program, well written and organized. Our audience: older male, history buff, war veteran; regional tourist; students. *Canadian* only military/aviation, naval, military/history and children's nonfiction have the best chance with us. We see more interest in collective or cataloguing forms of history, also in modeling and recreating military historical artifacts."

◼ **VÉHICULE PRESS**, Box 125, Place du Parc Station, Montreal, Quebec H2W 2M9, Canada. (514)844-6073. Fax: (514)844-7543. Website: www.vehiculepress.com. **Acquisitions:** Simon Dardick, president/publisher. Estab. 1973. Publishes trade paperback originals by Canadian authors only. **Publishes 15 titles/year. Receives 250 submissions/year. 20% of books from first-time authors; 95% from unagented writers. Pays 10-15% royalty on retail price. Offers $200-500 advance.** Publishes book 1 year after acceptance of ms. Responds in 4 months to queries. Book catalog for 9×12 SAE with IRCs.

Imprints: Signal Editions (poetry), Dossier Quebec (history, memoirs)

O⊸ "Montreal's Véhicule Press has published the best of Canadian and Quebec literature—fiction, poetry, essays, translations and social history."

Nonfiction: Biography. Subjects include government/politics, history, language/literature, memoirs, regional, sociology. Especially looking for Canadian social history. Query with SASE. Reviews artwork/photos as part of ms package.

Poetry: Contact: Carmine Starnino.

Recent Title(s): *The Water Gods: The Inside Story of a World Bank Project in Nepal*, by Anna Paskal (nonfiction); *Montreal of Yesterday: Jewish Life in Montreal 1900-1920*, by Israel Medres, translated from the Yiddish by Vivian Felsen (nonfiction); *White Stone: The Alice Poems*, by Stephanie Bolster (winner 1998 Governor General's Award for Poetry).

Tips: "We are interested only in Canadian authors."

WALL & EMERSON, INC., 6 O'Connor Dr., Toronto, Ontario M4K 2K1, Canada. (416)467-8685. Fax: (416)352-5368. E-mail: wall@wallbooks.com. Website: www.wallbooks.com. **Acquisitions:** Byron E. Wall, president (history of science, mathematics). Estab. 1987. Publishes hardcover originals and reprints. **Publishes 3 titles/year. Receives 10 queries and 8 mss/year. 50% of books from first-time authors; 100% from unagented writers. Pays 5-12% royalty on wholesale price.** Publishes book 1 year after acceptance of ms. Accepts simultaneous submissions. Responds in 1 month to queries; 1 month to proposals; 3 months to mss. Book catalog and ms guidelines free or online.

O⊸ "We are most interested in textbooks for college courses that meet well-defined needs and are targeted to their audiences." Currently emphasizing adult education, engineering. De-emphasizing social work.

Nonfiction: Reference, textbook. Subjects include education, health/medicine, philosophy, science. "We are looking for any undergraduate text that meets the needs of a well-defined course in colleges in the U.S. and Canada." Submit proposal package including outline, 2 sample chapter(s).

Recent Title(s): *Princinples of Engineering Economic Analysis; Voices Past and Present.*

Tips: "Our audience consists of college undergraduate students and college libraries. Our ideal writer is a college professor writing a text for a course he or she teaches regularly. If I were a writer trying to market a book today, I would identify the audience for the book and write directly to the audience throughout the book. I would then approach a publisher that publishes books specifically for that audience."

WHITECAP BOOKS LTD., 351 Lynn Ave., North Vancouver, British Columbia V7J 2C4, Canada. (604)980-9852. Fax: (604)980-8197. E-mail: whitecap@whitecap.ca. Website: www.whitecap.ca. **Acquisitions:** Leanne McDonald, rights and aquisitions associate. Publishes hardcover and trade paperback originals. **Publishes 24 titles/year. Receives 500 queries and 1,000 mss/year. 20% of books from first-time authors; 90% from unagented writers. Pays royalty. Offers negotiated advance.** Publishes book 18 months after acceptance of ms. Accepts simultaneous submissions. Responds in 2 months to proposals.

    O→ Whitecap Books publishes a wide range of nonfiction with a Canadian and international focus. Currently emphasizing children's nonfiction, natural history. De-emphasizing children's fiction.

Nonfiction: Children's/juvenile, coffee table book, cookbook. Subjects include animals, cooking/foods/nutrition, gardening, history, nature/environment, recreation, regional, travel. "We require an annotated outline. Writers should take the time to research our list. This is especially important for children's writers." Submit outline, 1 sample chapter(s), SASE. Reviews artwork/photos as part of ms package. Send photocopies.

Recent Title(s): *Seasons In the Rockies,* by Darwin Wiggett, Tom Till, Rebecca Gambo (nonfiction); *The Queen, The Bear and The Bumblebee,* by Dini Petty (fiction).

Tips: "We want well-written, well-researched material that presents a fresh approach to a particular topic."

YORK PRESS LTD., 152 Boardwalk Dr., Toronto, Ontario M4L 3X4, Canada. E-mail: yorkpress@sympatico.ca. Website: www3.sympatico.ca/yorkpress. **Acquisitions:** Dr. S. Elkhadem, general manager/editor. Estab. 1975. Publishes trade paperback originals. **Publishes 10 titles/year. Receives 50 submissions/year. 10% of books from first-time authors; 100% from unagented writers. Pays 10-20% royalty on wholesale price. Offers advance.** Publishes book 6 months after acceptance of ms. Responds in 2 weeks to queries.

    O→ "We publish scholarly books and creative writing of an experimental nature."

Nonfiction: Reference, textbook. Subjects include language/literature. Query with SASE.

Fiction: Experimental. Query with SASE.

Recent Title(s): *Herman Melville: Romantic & Prophet,* C.S. Durer (scholarly literary criticism); *The Moonhare,* Kirk Hampton (experimental novel).

Tips: "If I were a writer trying to market a book today, I would spend a considerable amount of time examining the needs of a publisher *before* sending my manuscript to him. The writer must adhere to our style manual and follow our guidelines exactly."

Book Producers

Book producers provide services for book publishers, ranging from hiring writers to editing and delivering finished books. Most book producers possess expertise in certain areas and will specialize in producing books related to those subjects. They provide books to publishers who don't have the time or expertise to produce the books themselves (many produced books are highly illustrated and require intensive design and color-separation work). Some work with on-staff writers, but most contract writers on a per-project basis.

Most often a book producer starts with a proposal; contacts writers, editors and illustrators; assembles the book; and sends it back to the publisher. The level of involvement and the amount of work to be done on a book by the producer is negotiated in individual cases. A book publisher may simply require the specialized skill of a particular writer or editor, or a producer could put together the entire book, depending on the terms of the agreement.

Writers have a similar working relationship with book producers. Their involvement depends on how much writing the producer has been asked to provide. Writers are typically paid by the hour, by the word, or in some manner other than on a royalty basis. Writers working for book producers usually earn flat fees. Writers may not receive credit (a byline in the book, for example) for their work, either. Most of the contracts require work for hire, and writers must realize they do not own the rights to writing published under this arrangement.

The opportunities are good, though, especially for writing-related work, such as fact checking, research and editing. Writers don't have to worry about good sales. Their pay is secured under contract. Finally, writing for a book producer is a good way to broaden experience in publishing. Every book to be produced is different, and the chance to work on a range of books in a number of capacities may be the most interesting aspect of all.

Book producers most often want to see a query detailing writing experience. They keep this information on file and occasionally even share it with other producers. When they are contracted to develop a book that requires a particular writer's experience, they contact the writer. There are well over 100 book producers, but most prefer to seek writers on their own. The book producers listed in this section have expressed interest in being contacted by writers. For a list of more producers, contact the American Book Producers Association, 160 Fifth Ave., Suite 625, New York NY 10010, or look in *Literary Market Place* (R.R. Bowker).

For a list of publishers according to their subjects of interest, see the nonfiction and fiction sections of the Book Publishers Subject Index. Information on book publishers and producers listed in the previous edition of *Writer's Market* but not included in this edition can be found in the General Index.

N **BOOK CREATIONS INC.**, Schillings Crossing Rd., Canaan NY 12029. (518)781-4171. Fax: (518)781-4170. **Acquisitions:** Elizabeth Tinsley, editorial director. Estab. 1973. Produces trade paperback and mass market paperback originals. **Publishes 10-15 titles/year. 75% from unagented writers. Pays royalty on net receipts or makes outright purchase. Offers variable advance.** Responds in 8 months to proposals.
Fiction: Primarily historical fiction. Adventure (contemporary action/adventure), historical, mystery, western (frontier). Submit proposal and 30 pages of the work in progress.
Recent Title(s): *Spirit Moon*, by William Sarabande; *The Horse Catchers Trilogy*, by Amanda Cockrell.

COURSE CRAFTERS, INC., 44 Merrimac St., Newburyport MA 01950. (978)465-2040. Fax: (978)465-5027. E-mail: lise@coursecrafters.com. Website: www.coursecrafters.com. **Acquisitions:** Lise B. Ragan, president. Produces textbooks and educational trade materials (Spanish/ESL). **Makes outright purchase.** Manuscript guidelines vary based upon project-specific requirements.

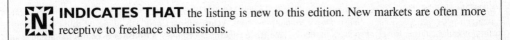

O─ "We package materials that teach language. We are particularly looking for innovative approaches and visually appealing presentations." Special focus is on language materials.

Nonfiction: Children's/juvenile, multimedia, reference, textbook (ESL, foreign language, reading/language arts). Subjects include education (preschool-adult), ethnic, language/literature, multicultural, translation. Submit résumé, publishing history, synopsis.

Tips: "Mail (or fax) résumé with list of projects related to specific experience with ESL, bilingual and/or foreign language textbook development. Also interested in storytellers and musicians for our new audio/game packages."

FARCOUNTRY PRESS, (formerly American & World Geographic Publishing), P.O. Box 5630, Helena MT 59604. (406)443-2842. Fax: (406)443-5480. E-mail: prodmgr@montanamagazine.com. Website: montanamagazine.com. **Acquisitions:** Kathy Springmeyer, production director; Merle Guy, sales director. Produces soft and hardcover books devoted to travel, tourism and outdoor recreation, with special emphasis on color photography. Mostly regional (northern Rockies, Pacific Northwest).

Nonfiction: Coffee table book, gift book, illustrated book. Subjects include recreation, regional, travel. Currently emphasizing Glacier and Yellowstone national parks, Lewis and Clark trail.

Recent Title(s): *Wild and Beautiful Glacier* (photo book); *Badlands of the High Plains* (photo book).

GLEASON GROUP, INC., 6 Old Kings Hwy., Norwalk CT 06850. (203)847-6658. **Acquisitions:** Gerald Gleason, president. **Publishes 10-15 titles/year. Work-for-hire**.

Nonfiction: Textbook. Subjects include computers; application software with CD-ROMs. Submit résumé. *No unsolicited mss.*

Recent Title(s): *Word 2000: A Professional Approach.*

Tips: "If writer is well versed in the most recent Microsoft Office software, and has written technical or software-related material before, he/she can send us their résumé."

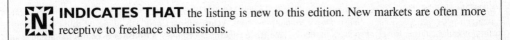 **THE HISTORY BANK INC.**, (formerly Laing Communications Inc.), P.O. Box 1568, Woodinville WA 98072. (425)481-8818. Fax: (425)402-7164 or tollfree (877)585-8818. E-mail: chris@thehistorybank.com. **Acquisitions:** Christine A. Laing, editorial director (all); Norman P. Bolotin, managing partner (sports history, Americana). Produces hardcover and trade paperback originals primarily for or in partnership with institutions and publishers. "We have expanded our services to museums throughout the U.S. and Canada, including e-publishing and book development and packaging." **Publishes 10-15 titles/year. 5% of books from first-time authors; 100% from unagented writers. Payment.** Responds in 1 month to queries; *Writer's Market recommends allowing 2 months for reply* to mss.

O─ Always seeking history and Americana. No longer producing software how-to books.

Nonfiction: Children's/juvenile, coffee table book, illustrated book, reference, technical, textbook. Subjects include Americana, health/medicine, history (US), military/war (Civil War), sports (baseball). Query with SASE. Reviews artwork/photos as part of ms package.

Recent Title(s): *Beyond the Mississippi: Early Westward Expansion of the United States* (Lodestar Books); *New England Furniture* (Wintertur Museum); *Arctic Visions* (University of Washington Press & McGill/Queens in Canada).

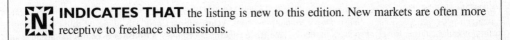 **LOUISE B. KETZ AGENCY**, 1485 First Ave., Suite 4B, New York NY 10021. (212)535-9259. **Acquisitions:** Louise B. Ketz, president. Produces and agents hardcover and paperback originals. **Publishes 3-5 titles/year. 90% from unagented writers. Pays flat fees and honoraria to writers.** Responds in 2 months to queries.

Nonfiction: Biography, reference. Subjects include Americana, business/economics, history, science, sports, women's issues/studies. Submit proposal package.

Recent Title(s): *Quantum Leaps in the Wrong Direction*; *The McFarland Baseball Quotations Dictionary*; *Concise Dictionary of Scientific Biography, 2nd Edition*.

Tips: "It is important for authors to list their credentials relevant to the book they are proposing (i.e., why they are qualified to write that nonfiction work). Also helps if author defines the market (who will buy the book and why)."

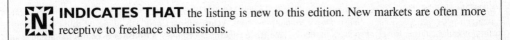 **GEORGE KURIAN REFERENCE BOOKS**, Box 519, Baldwin Place NY 10505. (914)962-3287. Fax: (914)962-3287. President: George Kurian. **Acquisitions:** Jeff Schultz, editor (general); Henry Sapinda, editor (religion, education, business). Produces hardcover originals. **Publishes 6 titles/year. 10% of books from first-time authors; 50% from unagented writers. Pays 10-15% royalty on net receipts.** Responds in 3 months to queries. Book catalog for 8½×11 SAE with 2 first-class stamps; ms guidelines for #10 SASE.

Imprints: International Encyclopedia Society; UN Studies Forum

O─ "Our goal is to publish innovative reference books for the library and trade market." Currently emphasizing history, politics, international relations, religion, children's and biography. No science, art or sports.

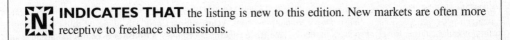 **INDICATES THAT** the listing is new to this edition. New markets are often more receptive to freelance submissions.

Nonfiction: Biography, illustrated book, reference, scholarly. Subjects include Americana, business/economics, education, ethnic, government/politics, history, language/literature, memoirs, military/war, multicultural, philosophy, photography, religion, travel, women's issues/studies, contemporary culture, world affairs. Query with SASE or submit proposal package.
Recent Title(s): *Datapedia of the United States.*
Tips: "We seek to provide accurate information on issues of global interest."

LAMPPOST PRESS INC., 710 Park Ave. #19-B, New York NY 10021-4944. (212)288-8474. **Acquisitions:** Roseann Hirsch, president. Estab. 1987. Produces hardcover, trade paperback and mass market paperback originals. **Publishes 25 titles/year. 50% of books from first-time authors; 85% from unagented writers. Pays 50% royalty or makes outright purchase.**
Nonfiction: Biography, children's/juvenile, cookbook, how-to, humor, illustrated book, self-help. Subjects include child guidance/parenting, cooking/foods/nutrition, gardening, health/medicine, money/finance, women's issues/studies. Query with SASE or submit proposal package. Reviews artwork/photos as part of ms package.

LAYLA PRODUCTIONS, INC., 370 E. 76th St., New York NY 10021. (212)879-6984. Fax: (212)639-9074. **Acquisitions:** Lori Stein, president. Publishes hardcover and trade paperback originals. **Publishes 6 titles/year. 50% of books from first-time authors; 50% from unagented writers. Pays 1-5% royalty or makes outright purchase, depending on contract with publisher. Offers $2,000-10,000 advance.** Does not return submissions, even those accompanied by SASE. Responds in 6 months to queries.
Nonfiction: Children's/juvenile, coffee table book, cookbook, how-to, humor, illustrated book. Subjects include Americana, cooking/foods/nutrition, gardening, history, photography, recreation. Does not return submissions, even those accompanied by a SASE. Query. Reviews artwork/photos as part of ms package.
Recent Title(s): *Spiritual Gardening* (Time-Life).

NEW ENGLAND PUBLISHING ASSOCIATES, INC., P.O. Box 5, Chester CT 06412. (860)345-READ. Fax: (860)345-3660. E-mail: nepa@nepa.com. Website: www.nepa.com. **Acquisitions:** Elizabeth Frost-Knappman, president; Edward W. Knappman, vice president/treasurer. Estab. 1983. Produces hardcover and trade paperback originals. **20% of books from first-time authors.** Responds in 6 weeks to queries.
  O—¬ NEPA develops adult and young adult reference and information titles and series for the domestic and international markets. "Our mission is to provide personalized service to a select list of mainly nonfiction clients." Currently emphasizing history, Asian affairs, biography, crime, science, literary criticism, current events, adventure, women's topics, gay topics, reference, business amd financial. De-emphasizing young adult, scholarly women's studies, scholarly reference.
Nonfiction: Biography, how-to, reference. Subjects include Americana, anthropology/archeology, business/economics, child guidance/parenting, ethnic, gay/lesbian, government/politics, health/medicine, history, language/literature, memoirs, military/war, money/finance, multicultural, nature/environment, philosophy, science, women's issues/studies, true crime, world affairs.
Recent Title(s): *Susan Sontag*, by Carl Rollyson and Lisa Paddock (Norton); *Dreams in the Key of Blue*, by John Philpin (Bantam).
Tips: "Revise, revise, revise and do not lose hope. We don't."

PUBLICOM, INC., 411 Massachusetts Ave., Acton MA 01720-3739. (978)263-5773. Fax: (978)263-7553. E-mail: info@publicom1.com. **Acquisitions:** Neil Sanders, vice president/textbook services. **Publishes 100-200 titles/year. Makes work-for-hire assignments for textbooks.**
Imprints: VanderWyk & Burnham
  O—¬ "We create and market leading-edge educational products and services."
Nonfiction: Textbook. Subjects include education, school disciplines K-college. Submit résumé, publishing history, synopsis.

SOMERVILLE HOUSE INC., (formerly Somerville House Books Limited), 24 Dinnick Crescent, Toronto, Ontario M4N 1C5, Canada. **Acquisitions:** Acquisition Department. Produces children's nonfiction. **Publishes 15 titles/year. 5% of books from first-time authors.** Responds in 4 months to queries. Manuscript guidelines for #10 SASE with postage (Canadian or IRC).
  O—¬ Currently emphasizing science and nature.
Nonfiction: Children's/juvenile. Subjects include cooking/foods/nutrition, education, hobbies, nature/environment, science, sports. Query with SASE.
Recent Title(s): *The Titanic Book and Submersible Model*; *Bakin Brownies*, by Susan Devins.
Tips: "We accept only children's nonfiction submissions."

VERNON PRESS, INC., 398 Columbus Ave., #355, Boston MA 02116-6008. (617)437-0388. Fax: (617)437-0894. E-mail: chris@vernonpress.com. Website: www.vernonpress.com. **Acquisitions:** Chris Dall, associate editor (art history, history, popular culture, travel). Produces hardcover and trade paperback originals. **Publishes 8-12 titles/year. 30% of books from first-time authors; 60% from unagented writers. Pays 50-60% royalty on net receipts or pays work-for-hire fee based on individual projects.** Responds in 6 weeks to queries.

O—¬ Vernon Press packages illustrated nonfiction titles for trade and academic presses. Currently emphasizing illustrated nonfiction for children/young adults.

Nonfiction: Children's/juvenile, coffee table book, gift book, illustrated book. Subjects include Americana, art/architecture, gardening, history, language/literature, music/dance, nature/environment, photography, regional, sports, translation, travel. Submit proposal package. Reviews artwork/photos as part of ms package. Send photocopies or duplicate transparencies.

Recent Title(s): *A Century of Boston Sports*, Richard Johnson (Northeastern University Press, 2000); *The Big Dig: Reshaping an American City*, Peter Vanderwarker (Little, Brown and Co., 2001).

THE WONDERLAND PRESS, 160 Fifth Ave., Suite 723, New York NY 10010. (212)989-2550. **Acquisitions:** John Campbell, president. Produces hardcover and trade paperback originals and mass market paperback originals. **Publishes 50 titles/year. 80% of books from first-time authors; 90% from unagented writers. Payment depends on the book: sometimes royalty with advance, sometimes work-for-hire.** Responds in 3 weeks to queries.

Nonfiction: Biography, coffee table book, how-to, humor, illustrated book, reference, self-help, TV scripts, screenplays. Subjects include art/architecture, business/economics, education, gardening, gay/lesbian, history, humor, money/finance, photography, psychology. Submit proposal package including sample chapter(s). Reviews artwork/photos as part of ms package.

Recent Title(s): *The Essential Jackson Pollock* (Abrams).

Tips: "Always submit in writing, never by telephone. Know your market intimately. Study the competition and decide whether there is a genuine need for your book, with a market base that will justify publication. Send us an enthused, authoritative, passionately written proposal that shows your mastery of the subject and that makes us say, 'Wow, we want that!'"

Consumer Magazines

Selling your writing to consumer magazines is as much an exercise of your marketing skills as it is of your writing abilities. Editors of consumer magazines are looking not simply for good writing, but for good writing which communicates pertinent information to a specific audience—their readers. Why are editors so particular about the readers they appeal to? Because it is only by establishing a core of faithful readers with identifiable and quantifiable traits that magazines attract advertisers. And with many magazines earning up to half their income from advertising, it is in their own best interests to know their readers' tastes and provide them with articles and features that will keep their readers coming back.

APPROACHING THE CONSUMER MAGAZINE MARKET

Marketing skills will help you successfully discern a magazine's editorial slant and write queries and articles that prove your knowledge of the magazine's readership to the editor. The one complaint we hear from magazine editors more than any other is that many writers don't take the time to become familiar with their magazine before sending a query or manuscript. Thus, editors' desks become cluttered with inappropriate submissions—ideas or articles that simply will not be of much interest to the magazine's readers.

You can gather clues about a magazine's readership—and thus establish your credibility with the magazine's editor—in a number of ways:

• Start with a careful reading of the magazine's listing in this section of *Writer's Market*. Most listings offer very straightforward information about their magazine's slant and audience.

• Study a magazine's writer's guidelines, if available. These are written by each particular magazine's editors and are usually quite specific about their needs and their readership.

• Check a magazine's website. Often writer's guidelines and a selection of articles are included in a publication's online version. A quick check of archived articles lets you know if ideas you want to propose have already been covered.

• Perhaps most important, read several current issues of the target magazine. Only in this way will you see firsthand the kind of stories the magazine actually buys.

• If possible, talk to an editor by phone. Many will not take phone queries, particularly those at the higher-profile magazines. But many editors of smaller publications will spend the time to help a writer over the phone.

Writers who can correctly and consistently discern a publication's audience and deliver stories that speak to that target readership will win out every time over writers who simply write what they write and send it where they will.

AREAS OF CURRENT INTEREST

Today's consumer magazines reflect societal trends and interests. As baby boomers age and the so-called "Generation X" comes along behind, magazines arise to address their concerns, covering topics of interest to various subsets of both of those wide-ranging demographic groups. Some areas of special interest now popular among consumer magazines include gardening, health & fitness, family leisure, computers, travel, fashion and cooking.

WHAT EDITORS WANT

In nonfiction, editors continue to look for short feature articles covering specialized topics. They want crisp writing and expertise. If you are not an expert in the area about which you are writing, make yourself one through research.

Always query before sending your manuscript. Don't e-mail or fax a query unless an editor specifically mentions an openness to this in the listing. Publishing, despite all the electronic advancements, is still a very paper-oriented industry. Once a piece has been accepted, however, many publishers now prefer to receive your submission via disk or modem so they can avoid re-keying the manuscript. Some magazines will even pay an additional amount for disk submission.

Fiction editors prefer to receive complete short story manuscripts. Writers must keep in mind that marketing fiction is competitive and editors receive far more material than they can publish. For this reason, they often do not respond to submissions unless they are interested in using the story. Before submitting material, check the market's listing for fiction requirements to ensure your story is appropriate for that market. More comprehensive information on fiction markets can be found in *Novel & Short Story Writer's Market* (Writer's Digest Books).

Many writers make their articles do double duty, selling first or one-time rights to one publisher and second serial or reprint rights to another noncompeting market. The heading, **Reprints**, offers details when a market indicates they accept previously published submissions, with submission form and payment information if available.

When considering magazine markets, be sure not to overlook opportunities with Canadian and international publications. Many such periodicals welcome submissions from U.S. writers and can offer writers an entirely new level of exposure for their work.

Regardless of the type of writing you do, keep current on trends and changes in the industry. Trade magazines such as *Writer's Digest*, *Folio:* and *Advertising Age* will keep you abreast of start-ups and shutdowns and other writing/business trends.

PAYMENT

Writers make their living by developing a good eye for detail. When it comes to marketing material, the one detail of interest to almost every writer is the question of payment. Most magazines listed here have indicated pay rates; some give very specific payment-per-word rates while others state a range. Any agreement you come to with a magazine, whether verbal or written, should specify the payment you are to receive and when you are to receive it. Some magazines pay writers only after the piece in question has been published. Others pay as soon as they have accepted a piece and are sure they are going to use it.

In *Writer's Market*, those magazines that pay on acceptance have been highlighted with the phrase **pays on acceptance** set in bold type. Payment from these markets should reach you faster than from markets who pay on publication. There is, however, some variance in the industry as to what constitutes payment "on acceptance"—some writers have told us of two- and three-month waits for checks from markets that supposedly pay on acceptance. It is never out of line to ask an editor when you might expect to receive payment for an accepted article.

So what is a good pay rate? There are no standards; the principle of supply and demand operates at full throttle in the business of writing and publishing. As long as there are more writers than opportunities for publication, wages for freelancers will never skyrocket. Rates vary widely from one market to the next, however, and the news is not entirely bleak. One magazine industry source puts the average pay rate for consumer magazine feature writing at $1.25 a word, with "stories that require extensive reporting . . . more likely to be priced at $2.50 a word." In our opinion, those estimates are on the high side of current pay standards. Smaller circulation magazines and some departments of the larger magazines will pay a lower rate.

Editors know that the listings in *Writer's Market* are read and used by writers with a wide range of experience, from those as-yet unpublished writers just starting out, to those with a successful, profitable freelance career. As a result, many magazines publicly report pay rates in the lower end of their actual pay ranges. Experienced writers will be able to successfully negotiate higher pay rates for their material. Newer writers should be encouraged that as your reputation grows (along with your clip file), you will be able to command higher rates. The article How Much Should I Charge? on page 70 gives you an idea of pay ranges for different freelance jobs.

WHAT'S NEW THIS YEAR?

We've added several features to make *Writer's Market* even more helpful in your search for the right magazine markets, features you won't find in any other writer's guide.

Many magazines are taking advantage of electronic media—and you should too. This year we've added information on whether a magazine accepts queries by e-mail or fax in addition to regular mail, and whether writers' guidelines are available online or by e-mail. We use a small computer icon to indicate that a magazine's website carries original online-only content and the online editor to address your query to.

Some areas of a magazine are more open to newer writers than others. Often writers unknown to the editor can break in with shorter features, columns or departments. This year we've added a key symbol (⚷) to identify the best ways to break in to *that* particular magazine.

Information at-a-glance

Last year we made some changes to help you access the information you need as efficiently as possible. Most immediately noticeable, we added a number of symbols at the beginning of each listing to quickly convey certain important information. In the Consumer Magazine section, symbols identify comparative payment rates (**$—$ $ $ $**); new listings (🅽); "opportunity" markets (⭐) that are at least 75% freelance written, appear quarterly or more frequently, and buy a high number of manuscripts; and magazines that do not accept freelance submissions (⊘). Different sections of *Writer's Market* include other symbols; check the front and back inside covers for an explanation of all the symbols used throughout the book.

We also highlighted important information in boldface, the "quick facts" you won't find in any other market book, but should know before you submit your work. To clearly identify the editorial "point person" at each magazine, the word "**Contact:**" identifies the appropriate person to query at each magazine. We also highlight what percentage of the magazine is freelance written, how many manuscripts a magazine buys per year of nonfiction, fiction, poetry and fillers and respective pay rates in each category.

Information on publications listed in the previous edition of *Writer's Market* but not included in this edition may be found in the General Index.

ANIMAL

The publications in this section deal with pets, racing and show horses, and other domestic animals and wildlife. Magazines about animals bred and raised for the market are classified in the Farm category of Trade, Technical & Professional Journals. Publications about horse racing can be found in the Sports section.

🅽 **$ $ AKC GAZETTE**, American Kennel Club, 260 Madison Ave., New York NY 10016. Fax: (212)696-8272. E-mail: gazette@akc.org. Website: www.akc.org/love/gazet.cfm. **Contact:** Erika Mansourrian. **85% freelance written.** Monthly magazine. "Geared to interests of fanciers of purebred dogs as opposed to commercial interests or pet owners. We require solid expertise from our contributors—we are *not* a pet magazine." Estab. 1889. Circ. 60,000. Pays on publication. Publishes ms an average of 6 months after acceptance. Byline given. Offers 10% kill fee. Buys first North American serial, electronic rights. Submit seasonal material 6 months in advance. Accepts queries by mail. Responds in 2 months to queries. Writer's guidelines for #10 SASE.
Nonfiction: General interest, how-to, humor, interview/profile, photo feature, travel, dog art, training and canine performance sports. No poetry, tributes to individual dogs or fiction. **Buys 30-40 mss/year.** Length: 1,000-3,000 words. **Pays $300-500.** Pays expenses of writers on assignment.
Photos: Photo contest guidelines for #10 SASE. State availability with submission. Reviews color transparencies, prints. Buys one-time rights. Pays $50-200/photo. Captions, identification of subjects, model releases required.
Fiction: Annual short fiction contest only. Guidelines for #10 SASE.
   ⬛ The online magazine carries original content not found in the print edition. Contact: Robert Keeley.
Tips: "Contributors should be involved in the dog fancy or expert in area they write about (veterinary, showing, field trialing, obedience training, dogs in legislation, dog art or history or literature). All submissions are welcome but author

must be a credible expert or be able to interview and quote the experts. Veterinary articles must be written by or with veterinarians. Humorous features or personal experiences relative to purebred dogs that have broader applications. For features generally, know the subject thoroughly and be conversant with jargon peculiar to the sport of dogs."

$ ⛏ ANIMALS, Massachusetts Society for the Prevention of Cruelty to Animals, 350 S. Huntington Ave., Boston MA 02130. (617)522-7400. Fax: (617)522-4885. **Contact:** Paula Abend, editor. **90% freelance written.** Bimonthly magazine covering "articles on wildlife (American and international), domestic animals, balanced treatments of controversies involving animals, conservation, animal welfare issues, pet health and pet care." Estab. 1868. Circ. 100,000. **Pays on acceptance.** Publishes ms an average of 5 months after acceptance. Byline given. Offers negotiable kill fee. Buys one-time rights, makes work-for-hire assignments. Submit seasonal material 6 months in advance. Responds in 6 weeks to queries. Sample copy for $2.95 and 9×12 SAE with 4 first-class stamps. Writer's guidelines for #10 SASE.
Nonfiction: Exposé, general interest, how-to, opinion, photo feature (animal and environmental issues and controversies), practical pet-care topics. "*Animals* does not publish breed-specific domestic pet articles or 'favorite pet' stories. Poetry and fiction are also not used." **Buys 50 mss/year.** Query with published clips. Length: 2,200 words maximum. Sometimes pays expenses of writers on assignment.
Photos: State availability with submission. Reviews contact sheets, 35 mm transparencies, 5×7 or 8×10 prints. Buys one-time rights. Payment depends on usage size and quality. Captions, identification of subjects, model releases required.
Columns/Departments: Books (reviews of books on animals and animal-related subjects), 300 words maximum; buys 18 mss/year. Profile (women and men who've gone to extraordinary lengths to aid animals), 800 words maximum; buys 6 mss/year. Query with published clips.
Tips: "Present a well-researched proposal. Be sure to include clips that demonstrate the quality of your writing. Stick to categories mentioned in *Animals'* editorial description. Combine well-researched facts with a lively, informative writing style. Feature stories are written almost exclusively by freelancers. We continue to seek proposals and articles that take a humane approach. Articles should concentrate on how issues affect animals, rather than humans."

$ $ APPALOOSA JOURNAL, Appaloosa Horse Club, 2720 West Pullman, Moscow ID 83843-0903. (208)882-5578. Fax: (208)882-8150. E-mail: journal@appaloosa.com. Website: www.appaloosajournal.com. **Contact:** Robin Hirzel, editor. **20-40% freelance written.** Monthly magazine covering Appaloosa horses. Estab. 1946. Circ. 25,000. Pays on publication. Publishes ms an average of 3 months after acceptance. Byline given. Buys first North American serial rights. Responds in 1 month to queries; 2 months to mss. Sample copy and writer's guidelines free.
• *Appaloosa Journal* no longer accepts material for columns.
Nonfiction: Historical/nostalgic, interview/profile, photo feature. **Buys 15-20 mss/year.** Query with or without published clips or send complete ms. Length: 800-2,000 words. **Pays $100-400.** Sometimes pays expenses of writers on assignment.
Photos: Send photos with submission. Payment varies. Captions, identification of subjects required.
■ The online magazine carries original content not found in the print edition. Contact: Michelle Barg, online editor.
Tips: "Articles by writers with horse knowledge, news sense and photography skills are in great demand. If it's a strong article about an Appaloosa, the writer has a pretty good chance of publication. A good understanding of the breed and the industry, breeders and owners is helpful. Make sure there's some substance and a unique twist."

$ $ ASPCA ANIMAL WATCH, The American Society for the Prevention of Cruelty to Animals, 315 E. 62nd St., New York NY 10021. (212)876-7700. Fax: (212)410-0087. E-mail: editor@aspca.org. Website: www.aspca.org. **Contact:** Marion Lane, editor. **40-50% freelance written.** Quarterly magazine covering animal welfare: companion animals, endangered species, farm animals, wildlife, animals in entertainment, laboratory animals and humane consumerism, i.e., fur, ivory, etc. "The ASPCA's mission is to alleviate pain, fear and suffering in all animals. As the voice of the ASPCA, *Animal Watch* is our primary means of communicating with and informing our membership. In addition to in-depth, timely coverage and original reporting on important humane issues, *Animal Watch* provides practical advice on companion animal care. The ASPCA promotes the adoption and responsible care of pets, and through the magazine we encourage excellent stewardship in areas such as nutrition, training, exercise and veterinary care." Estab. 1980. Circ. 330,000. **Pays on acceptance.** Publishes ms an average of 4 months after acceptance. Byline given. Buys first North American serial rights. Editorial lead time 6 months. Submit seasonal material 6 months in advance. Accepts queries by mail, e-mail, fax. Accepts simultaneous submissions. Responds in 3 months to queries. Sample copy for 10×13 SAE and 4 first-class stamps.
○┐ Break in with a submission to the Animals Abroad or Light Watch columns.
Nonfiction: Essays, exposé, historical/nostalgic, how-to, humor (respectful), interview/profile, photo feature, investigative, news, advocacy. No stories told from animals' point of view, religious stories, fiction or poetry, articles with strident animal rights messages or articles with graphic details. **Buys 25-30 mss/year.** Query with published clips. Length: 650-2,500 words. **Pays $750.** Sometimes pays expenses of writers on assignment.
Photos: State availability with submission. Reviews transparencies. Pays $75-300 or negotiates payment individually. Captions, identification of subjects, model releases required.
Columns/Departments: Light Watch (humor and light news), 150-300 words; Animals Abroad (first person by someone abroad), 650-700 words; Animals & the Law (balanced report on a legal or legislative subject), 650-700 words; Viewpoint (personal essay on humane subjects), 650-700 words. **Buys 10 mss/year.** Query with or without published clips. **Pays $75-225.**

insider report™

Writing for pet magazines: Focus on solid information

Moira Anderson Allen is a former editor of *Dog Fancy* magazine, and has been writing for pet magazines for more than 15 years. She has covered such diverse topics as the animal abuse/domestic violence connection, canine and feline cancer, and the folklore of cats. Allen is a member of the board of governors for the Cat Writers Association and a member of the Dog Writers Association of America; her book, *Coping with Sorrow on the Loss of Your Pet*, won a Dog Writers' "best book" award in 1988. Allen currently hosts the Writing-World.com website, and the Pet Loss Support Page (http://www.pet-loss.net).

Moira Anderson Allen

What special challenges set freelancing for the pet niche apart from other specialties?
Actually, I'd say that a better word would be "opportunities."
This market offers an excellent opportunity for less experienced writers to break in and build a collection of clips. The focus in this market is on solid information, and most pet-magazine editors are willing to deal with writers who haven't completely polished their style, if they can provide solid, worthwhile information.

For example, if you can interview someone who trains pets for commercials, or talk to a vet specializing in canine dentistry, or gather a selection of grooming tips for longhaired cats, you have a good chance of selling that article, even if your grammar isn't perfect. Editors of pet magazines can clean up punctuation problems, but don't have the time to go out and hunt up this kind of information—and it's the sort of information readers are hungry for.

What kind of pets and pet issues do you write about most often? Which are most popular with editors and consumers?
I generally write about care and how-to topics, such as how to take care of a new kitten. Editors are always in need of solid how-to information on the various "care" issues involving pets. This includes health care, general household care (e.g., how to build a doghouse, how to house-train your puppy), training, seasonal care, activities, grooming, feeding, special needs, etc. Anything that covers "taking better care of your pet" or "improving your pet's quality of life" (or improving the human/animal interaction) is popular with editors.

How would you break into this specialty if you were a beginning freelancer?
First, decide what type of pet you want to write about, and focus on that type. Second, determine what the basic [pet] owner needs to know, or wants to know. Third, submit a strong query that explains your topic. Fourth, find qualified experts to give you the information

you need to fill out that topic. (You should probably query first, of course, to get an assignment.) Do NOT try to quote books—most editors will discard an article immediately if it's simply built on book quotes. Finally, write the piece and send it in. If you are accepted, immediately follow up with a new proposal; pet editors like to find writers they can work with on a regular basis.

What is the general pay scale a freelancer can expect writing about pets?

The better publications pay around $300 to $500 for a feature article (around 2,000 words). Even some of the online publications pay close to that. Expect around $100 for filler-length material. Most publications also offer an additional fee for photos, or buy photos separately. Most likely, if you submit a text-photo package, you won't be paid the equivalent of the "text" rate and the rate for each individual photo if they'd been submitted separately, but you'll be paid a higher rate than for text alone.

What are the most common mistakes freelancers in this arena make (and can avoid)?

One thing pet writers need to remember is that consumers are *NOT* interested in stories of "your pet"—and neither are editors. This is the biggest mistake new writers make—sending in the story of their beloved pet. New writers tend to think the story is interesting because, after all, it's *THEIR* pet! But unless the story is truly unique, it will be rejected. Editors get these stories by the hundreds. Think about how to *HELP THE READER* and you'll be much more likely to make a sale. Another approach to avoid at all costs is the talking pet.

Have you had a favorite pet assignment? If so, what was it and why was it so memorable?

I'm not sure I'd call it "favorite," but my most memorable assignment was to examine the relationship between animal abuse and domestic violence. I talked to people who were researching this connection, including a woman who had set up a program through her humane society that enabled women to have a pet boarded so that they could seek help at a women's shelter. (Most women's shelters won't take pets, and many women won't leave an abusive situation if they have to leave a pet behind, as they know the pet is likely to be abused or even killed in their absence.) I found this article memorable because I felt I was doing more than just helping someone, say, groom their pet better—this is the sort of article that can make an important difference in people's lives.

Have you experienced the nightmare of all nightmare assignments? Describe it.

Oh, yeah! I won't name the publication, except to say that it was published by a humane organization. The editor kept changing her mind about what she wanted. She wanted profiles of various individuals, and gave me a list to choose from. Then she didn't like my choices, and wanted me to cover different people on the list. Then she kept changing the word-count. The terms of the project kept changing in midstream. I actually managed to get it done and get paid, and was rewarded in making contact with some very interesting people—but I swore never to work for that editor again. She did come back to me with another assignment, and I turned her down.

—*Kelly Milner Halls*

For interviews with the pros in more freelance niche markets, see Contemporary Culture, page 432; Entertainment, page 443; Games & Puzzles, page 462; Sports, page 708, Women's, page 782.

TOP TIP: "Write about things that have a genuine interest for you. If you just "go for the money," and write about things that you find personally boring, you'll lose the spark and enthusiasm that brought you into writing in the first place. You became a writer because, presumably, it was something you loved to do—so write about what you love, and you'll go on "loving" it. (Pet writing, by the way, is a great way to keep that spark alive, as it often combines two things that you love!)"

Tips: "The most important assets for an *Animal Watch* contributor are familiarity with the animal welfare movement in the U.S. and the ability to write lively, well-researched articles. We are always looking for positive stories about people and groups and businesses who are helping to protect animals in some way and may inspire others to do the same. We know the problems—share with us some solutions, some approaches that are working. Everything we publish includes 'How you can help....' We are as likely to assign a feature as a short piece for one of the departments."

$ $ THE BARK, The modern dog culture, The Bark, 2810 Eighth, Berkeley CA 94710. (510)704-0827. Fax: (510)704-0933. E-mail: editor@thebark.com. Website: www.thebark.com. **Contact:** Claudia Kawczynska, editor-in-chief. **50% freelance written.** Quarterly covering dogs in today's society. "*The Bark* brings a literate and entertaining approach to dog culture through essays, reviews, interviews and artwork. Our perspective is directed to the sophisticated reader. The point of view is topical, unsentimental and intelligent. We are smartly designed and stylish." Estab. 1997. Circ. 75,000. Pays on publication. Publishes ms an average of 6 months after acceptance. Byline given. Offers 20% kill fee. Buys first rights. Editorial lead time 3 months. Submit seasonal material 3 months in advance. Accepts queries by mail. Sample copy for $4.
Nonfiction: Book excerpts, essays, exposé, historical/nostalgic, how-to, humor, interview/profile, new product, opinion, personal experience, travel. Special issues: Upcoming special issues include dogs in the visual arts and dogs in literature. No "death of a dog" pieces. **Buys 10 mss/year.** Query with published clips. Length: 600-1,700 words. **Pays $50-400.**
Photos: State availability with submission. Reviews contact sheets.
Columns/Departments: Health (holistic), 1,000 words; Training (non-aversive), 1,000 words; Behavior, 800 words. **Pays $50-300.**
Fiction: Adventure, humorous, mystery, novel excerpts, slice-of-life vignettes. No religious. **Buys 4 mss/year.** Query. Length: 400-1,200 words.
Poetry: Avant-garde, free verse, haiku, light verse, traditional. **Buys 20 poems/year.**
Fillers: Lee Forgotson, senior editor. Anecdotes, facts, gags to be illustrated by cartoonist, newsbreaks, short humor. **Buys 20/year.** Length: 100-600 words. **Pays $25-150.**
Tips: "Have a true understanding of our editorial vision and have a true appreciation for dogs. Please become familiar with our magazine before submitting."

$ $ CAT FANCY, Cat Care for the Responsible Owner, Fancy Publications, Inc., P.O. Box 6050, Mission Viejo CA 92690. (949)855-8822. Website: www.catfancy.com. **Contact:** Keith Bush, managing editor. **90% freelance written.** Monthly magazine covering all aspects of responsible cat ownership. Estab. 1965. Pays on publication. Buys first North American serial rights. Editorial lead time 6 months. Responds in 3 months to queries. Writer's guidelines for #10 SASE.
Nonfiction: Engaging presentation of expert, up-to-date information. Must be cat oriented. Not reviewing fiction at this time. How-to, humor, photo feature, behavior, health, lifestyle. **Buys 70 mss/year.** Query with published clips. Length: 1,000-2,000 words. **Pays $50-450.**
Photos: Seeking photos of happy, healthy, well-groomed cats and kittens in studio or indoor settings. Buys one-time rights. Negotiates payment individually. Captions, identification of subjects, model releases required.
Columns/Departments: Most of our columns are written by regular contributors who are recognized experts in their fields.
Tips: "No fiction or poetry. Please read recent issues to learn the kind of articles we want. Then, show us in your query how you can contribute something new and unique."

$ $ CATS MAGAZINE, Primedia, 260 Madison Ave., 8th Floor, New York NY 10016. E-mail: info@catsmag.com. Website: www.catsmag.com. **Contact:** Beth Adelman, editor-in-chief. **80% freelance written.** Monthly magazine for owners and lovers of cats. Estab. 1945. Circ. 100,000. **Pays on acceptance.** Byline given. Buys exclusive print rights for 6 months, plus non-exclusive electronic rights. Editorial lead time 6 months. Submit seasonal material 6 months in advance. Accepts queries by mail.

Nonfiction: General interest (concerning cats), how-to (care, etc. for cats), personal experience, travel, nutrition, cats in art. Query. Length: 1,500-2,500 words. **Pays $50-500 for assigned articles.**

Photos: Photos are not required with articles. State availability with submission. Reviews 2¼×2¼ transparencies, color slides. Buys one-time rights. Identification of subjects required.

Columns/Departments: Cat Tales (true cat-theme short stories), 250-1,000 words. Send complete ms. **Pays $25.**

Tips: "Writer must show an affinity for cats. Extremely well-written, thoroughly researched, carefully thought-out articles have the best chance of being accepted. Innovative topics or a new twist on an old subject are always welcomed."

CATS USA, Guide to Buying and Caring for Purebred Kittens, Fancy Publications, P.O. Box 6050, Mission Viejo CA 92690. (949)855-8822. **Contact:** Keith Bush, editor. **90% freelance written.** Annual publication for purebred kitten buyers. Estab. 1993. Pays on publication. Buys first North American serial rights. Editorial lead time 6 months. Responds in 3 months to queries. Writer's guidelines for #10 SASE.

Nonfiction: Healthcare, training, breed information. **Buys 20 mss/year.** Query with published clips. Length: 1,000-2,000 words. **Pays $50-450.**

Photos: Looking for happy, healthy, well-groomed purebred cats and kittens in studio or indoor settings. Guidelines for #10 SASE. Buys one-time rights. Negotiates payment individually. Captions, identification of subjects, model releases required.

Tips: "No fiction or poetry. Please read a recent issue to learn the kind of articles we want. Then, show us in your query how you can contribute something new and unique."

$ $ THE CHRONICLE OF THE HORSE, P.O. Box 46, Middleburg VA 20118-0046. (540)687-6341. Fax: (540)687-3937. Website: www.chronofhorse.com. Editor: John Strassburger, Managing Editor: Nancy Comer. **Contact:** Beth Rasin, assistant editor. **80% freelance written.** Weekly magazine covering horses. "We cover English riding sports, including horse showing, grand prix jumping competitions, steeplechase racing, foxhunting, dressage, endurance riding, handicapped riding and combined training. We are the official publication for the national governing bodies of many of the above sports. We feature news, how-to articles on equitation and horse care and interviews with leaders in the various fields." Estab. 1937. Circ. 22,000. Pays for features on acceptance; news and other items on publication. Publishes ms an average of 4 months after acceptance. Byline given. Buys first North American serial rights, makes work-for-hire assignments. Submit seasonal material 3 months in advance. Accepts queries by mail, e-mail. Responds in 10 weeks to queries. Sample copy for $2 and 9×12 SAE. Writer's guidelines for #10 SASE or online.

☛ Break in by "clearing a small news assignment in your area ahead of time."

Nonfiction: General interest, historical/nostalgic (history of breeds, use of horses in other countries and times, art, etc.), how-to (trailer, train, design a course, save money, etc.), humor (centered on living with horses or horse people), interview/profile (of nationally known horsemen or the very unusual), technical (horse care, articles on feeding, injuries, care of foals, shoeing, etc.). Special issues: Steeplechase Racing (January); American Horse in Sport and Grand Prix Jumping (February); Horse Show (March); Intercollegiate (April); Kentucky 4-Star Preview (April); Junior and Pony (April); Dressage (June); Endurance issue (July); Combined Training (August); Hunt Roster (September); Vaulting and Handicapped (November); Stallion (December). No Q&A interviews, clinic reports, Western riding articles, personal experience or wild horses. **Buys 300 mss/year.** Query with or without published clips or send complete ms. Length: 6-7 pages. **Pays $150-250.**

Photos: State availability with submission. Reviews prints or color slides; accepts color for b&w reproduction. Buys one-time rights. Pays $25-30. Identification of subjects required.

Columns/Departments: Dressage, Combined Training, Horse Show, Horse Care, Racing over Fences, Young Entry (about young riders, geared for youth), Horses and Humanities, Hunting, Vaulting, Handicapped Riding, Trail Riding, 300-1,225 words; News of major competitions ("clear assignment with us first"), 1,500 words; Small local competitions, 800 words. Query with or without published clips or send complete ms. **Pays $25-200.**

Fillers: Anecdotes, newsbreaks, short humor, cartoons. **Buys 300/year.** Length: 50-175 words. **Pays $10-20.**

▣ The online magazine carries original content not found in the print edition and includes writer's guidelines. Contact: Melinda Goslin, online editor.

Tips: "Get our guidelines. Our readers are sophisticated, competitive horsemen. Articles need to go beyond common knowledge. Freelancers often attempt too broad or too basic a subject. We welcome well-written news stories on major events, but clear the assignment with us."

$ COONHOUND BLOODLINES, The complete magazine for the Houndsman and Coon Hunter, United Kennel Club, Inc., 100 E. Kilgore Rd., Kalamazoo MI 49002-5584. (616)343-9020. Fax: (616)343-7037. E-mail: vrand@ukcdogs.com. Website: www.ukcdogs.com. **Contact:** Vicki Rand, editor. **40% freelance written.** Monthly magazine covering all aspects of the 6 Coonhound dog breeds. "Writers must retain the 'slang' particular to dog people and to our readers—many of whom are from the South." Estab. 1925. Circ. 22,000. Pays on publication. Publishes ms an average of 6 months after acceptance. Byline given. Buys first North American serial rights, makes work-for-hire assignments. Editorial lead time 6 months. Submit seasonal material 6 months in advance. Accepts queries by mail, e-mail, fax, phone. Accepts simultaneous submissions. Responds in 6 weeks to queries. Sample copy for $3.

Nonfiction: General interest, historical/nostalgic, humor, interview/profile, new product, personal experience, photo feature, breed-specific. Special issues: Six of our 12 issues are each devoted to a specific breed of Coonhound. Treeing Walker (February); English (March); Black & Tan (April); Bluetick (May); Redbone (June); Plott Hound (July), 1,000-3,000 words and photos. **Buys 12-36 mss/year.** Query. Length: 1,000-5,000 words. **Pays $100.** Sometimes pays expenses of writers on assignment.
Photos: State availability with submission. Reviews contact sheets. Buys one-time rights. Negotiates payment individually. Captions, identification of subjects required.
Columns/Departments: Buys 6-12 mss/year. Pays $100.
Fiction: Must be about the Coonhound breeds or hunting with hounds. Adventure, historical, humorous, mystery. **Buys 3-6 mss/year.** Query. Length: 1,000-3,000 words. **Pays $100.**
Tips: "Hunting with hounds is a two-century old American tradition and an important part of the American heritage, especially east of the Mississippi. It covers a lifestyle as well as a wonderful segment of the American population, many of whom still live by honest, friendly values."

$ $⊠ DOG FANCY, Fancy Publications, Inc., P.O. Box 6050, Mission Viejo CA 92690-6050. Fax: (949)855-3045. E-mail: Sbiller@fancypubs.com. Website: www.dogfancy.com. **Contact:** Steven Biller, editor. **95% freelance written.** Monthly magazine for men and women of all ages interested in all phases of dog ownership. Estab. 1970. Circ. 286,000. Pays on publication. Publishes ms an average of 6 months after acceptance. Byline given. Offers $100 kill fee. Buys first North American serial rights. Submit seasonal material 6 months in advance. Accepts queries by mail. Accepts simultaneous submissions. Responds in 2 months to queries. Sample copy for $5.50. Writer's guidelines for #10 SASE.
Nonfiction: Book excerpts, general interest, how-to, humor, inspirational, interview/profile, new product, personal experience, photo feature, travel. "No stories written from a dog's point of view, poetry, anything that advocates irresponsible dog care, tributes to dogs that have died or beloved family pets." **Buys 100 mss/year.** Query. Length: 850-1,500 words. **Pays $200-500.**
Photos: State availability with submission. Reviews contact sheets, transparencies, prints. Buys electronic rights. Offers no additional payment for photos accepted with ms.
Columns/Departments: Dogs on the Go (travel with dogs), 600-700 words; Dogs That Make a Difference (heroic dogs), 800 words. **Buys 24 mss/year.** Query by mail only. **Pays $300-400.**
Fiction: Occasionally publishes novel excerpts.
   ▣ The online magazine carries original content not found in the print version. Contact: Stephanie Starr.
Tips: "We're looking for the unique experience that enhances the dog/owner relationship—with the dog as the focus of the story, not the owner. Medical articles are assigned to veterinarians. Note that we write for a lay audience (non-technical), but we do assume a certain level of intelligence. Read the magazine before making a pitch. Make sure your query is clear, concise and relevant."

$ $⊠ DOG WORLD, The Authority on Dog Care, Primedia Enthusiast Group, 500 N. Dearborn, Suite 1100, Chicago IL 60610. (312)396-0600. Fax: (312)467-7118. E-mail: dogworld3@aol.com. Website: www.dogworldmag.com. **Contact:** Donna Marcel, editor. **95% freelance written.** Monthly magazine covering dogs. "We write for the serious dog enthusiasts, breeders, veterinarians, groomers, etc., as well as a general audience interested in in-depth information about dogs." Estab. 1915. Circ. 61,000. **Pays on acceptance.** Byline given. Buys first North American serial rights. Editorial lead time 10 months. Submit seasonal material 4 months in advance. Accepts queries by mail. Responds in 6 months to queries. Writer's guidelines free.
Nonfiction: General interest (on dogs including health care, veterinary medicine, grooming, legislation, responsible ownership, show awards, obedience training, show schedules, kennel operations, dog sports, breed spotlights and histories), historical/nostalgic, new product, personal experience, technical, travel. Special issues: July (breed standards); February (puppy). No fluffy poems or pieces about dogs. **Buys approximately 80 mss/year.** Query by mail only with SASE. Length: 3,000-3,500 words. **Pay negotiable.** Sometimes pays expenses of writers on assignment.
Reprints: Send tearsheet, photocopy or typed ms with rights for sale noted and information about when and where the material previously appeared. Payment negotiated on individual basis.
Photos: State availability with submission. Buys one-time rights. Offers no additional payment for photos accepted with ms; occasionally negotiates payment individually for professional photos. Current rate for cover photo is $300; inside color photo $50-175; b&w $25-50, depending on size used. Payment on publication.
   ▣ The online magazine carries original content not found in the print edition. Contact: Peggy Moran.
Tips: "Get a copy of editorial calendar, stay away from 'fluffy' pieces—we run very few. Be able to translate technical/medical articles into what average readers can understand. Mention accompanying art—very important."

$⊠ EQUINE JOURNAL, 103 Roxbury St., Keene NH 03431-8801. (603)357-4271. Fax: (603)357-7851. E-mail: editorial@equinejournal.com. Website: www.equinejournal.com. **Contact:** Pat Payne, managing editor. **90% freelance written.** Monthly tabloid covering horses—all breeds, all disciplines. "To educate, entertain and enable amateurs and professionals alike to stay on top of new developments in the field. Covers horse-related activities from all corners of New England, New York, New Jersey, Pennsylvania and the Midwest." Estab. 1988. Circ. 26,000. Pays on publication. Byline given. Buys first North American serial, electronic rights. Editorial lead time 3 months. Submit seasonal material 4 months in advance. Accepts queries by mail, e-mail, fax, phone. Responds in 1 months to queries. Writer's guidelines for #10 SASE.

Nonfiction: General interest, how-to, interview/profile. **Buys 100 mss/year.** Query with published clips or send complete ms. Length: 1,500-3,000 words.

Photos: Send photos with submission. Reviews prints. Pays $10.

Columns/Departments: Horse Health (health-related topics), 1,200-1,500 words. **Buys 12 mss/year.** Query.

Fillers: Short humor. Length: 500-1,000 words. **Pays $40-75.**

$ $🔲 FIELD TRIAL MAGAZINE, Androscoggin Publishing, Inc., P.O. Box 98, Milan NH 03588-0098. (617)449-6767. Fax: (603)449-2462. E-mail: birddog@ncia.net. Website: www.fielddog.com/ftm. **Contact:** Craig Doherty, editor. **75% freelance written.** Quarterly magazine covering field trials for pointing dogs. "Our readers are knowledgeable sports men and women who want interesting and informative articles about their sport." Estab. 1997. Circ. 6,000. Pays on publication. Publishes ms an average of 6 months after acceptance. Byline given. Buys first North American serial rights. Editorial lead time 3 months. Submit seasonal material 6 months in advance. Accepts queries by mail, e-mail, fax. Accepts simultaneous submissions. Responds in 2 weeks to queries; 2 months to mss. Sample copy and writer's guidelines free or online.

Nonfiction: Book excerpts, essays, general interest, historical/nostalgic, how-to, interview/profile, opinion, personal experience. No hunting articles. **Buys 12-16 mss/year.** Query. Length: 1,000-3,000 words. **Pays $100-300.**

Photos: Send photos with submission. Buys one-time rights. Offers no additional payment for photos accepted with ms. Captions, identification of subjects required.

Fiction: Fiction that deals with bird dogs and field trials. **Buys 4 mss/year.** Send complete ms. Length: 1,000-2,500 words. **Pays $100-250.**

Tips: "Make sure you have correct and accurate information—we'll work with a writer who has good solid info even if the writing needs work."

Ⓝ $ $ THE GAITED HORSE, The One Magazine for all Gaited Horses, P.O. Box 3070, Deer Park WA 99006-3070. (509)276-4930. Fax: (509)276-4930. E-mail: editor@thegaitedhorse.com. Website: www.thegaitedhorse.com. **Contact:** Rhonda Hart-Poe, editor. Quarterly magazine. "Subject matter must relate in some way to gaited horses." Estab. 1998. Circ. 5,000. Pays on publication. Publishes ms an average of 2 months after acceptance. Byline given. Buys first North American serial rights, makes work-for-hire assignments. Editorial lead time 4 months. Submit seasonal material 4 months in advance. Accepts queries by mail, e-mail. Accepts simultaneous submissions. Responds in 6 weeks to queries; 1 month to mss. Sample copy for $3. Writer's guidelines free or online.

Nonfiction: Wants anything related to gaited horses, lifestyles, art, etc. Book excerpts, essays, exposé, general interest (gaited horses), historical/nostalgic, how-to, humor, interview/profile, new product, personal experience, photo feature, travel. "No 'My first horse' stories." **Buys 25 mss/year.** Query or send complete ms. Length: 1,000-2,500 words. **Pays $50-300.**

Photos: State availability of or send photos with submission. Reviews prints (3×5 or larger). Buys one-time rights. Negotiates payment individually. Captions, identification of subjects, model releases required.

Columns/Departments: Through the Legal Paces (equine owners rights & responsibilities); Horse Cents (financial advice for horse owners); Health Check (vet advice); Smoother Trails (trail riding), all 500-1,000 words. **Buys 24 mss/year.** Query. **Pays $100.**

Fillers: Anecdotes, newsbreaks, short humor. **Buys 20/year.** Length: 5-300 words. **Pays $10-50.**

Tips: "We are actively seeking to develop writers from within the various gaited breeds and equine disciplines. If you have a unique perspective on these horses, we would love to hear from you. Submit a query that targets any aspect of gaited horses and you'll have my attention."

$ THE GREYHOUND REVIEW, P.O. Box 543, Abilene KS 67410-0543. (785)263-4660. Fax: (785)263-4689. E-mail: nga@jc.net. Website: nga.jc.net. Editor: Gary Guccione. **Contact:** Tim Horan, managing editor. **20% freelance written.** Monthly magazine covering greyhound breeding, training and racing. Estab. 1911. Circ. 4,000. **Pays on acceptance.** Byline given. Buys first rights. Submit seasonal material 2 months in advance. Responds in 2 weeks to queries; 1 month to mss. Sample copy for $3. Writer's guidelines free.

Nonfiction: "Articles must be targeted at the greyhound industry: from hard news, special events at racetracks to the latest medical discoveries." How-to, interview/profile, personal experience. Do not submit gambling systems. **Buys 24 mss/year.** Query. Length: 1,000-10,000 words. **Pays $85-150.**

Reprints: Send photocopy. Pays 100% of amount paid for original article.

Photos: State availability with submission. Reviews 35mm transparencies, 8×10 prints. Buys one-time rights. Pays $10-50 photo. Identification of subjects required.

$ HORSE & COUNTRY CANADA, Equine Publications Inc., Box 1051, Smiths Falls, Ontario K7A 5A5, Canada. (613)275-1684. Fax: (613)275-1686. **Contact:** Judith H. McCartney, editor. **40% freelance written.** Magazine published 7 times/year covering equestrian issues. "A celebration of equestrian sport and the country way of life." Estab. 1994. Circ. 14,000. Pays on publication. Publishes ms an average of 3 months after acceptance. Byline sometimes given. Buys one-time rights. Accepts queries by mail.

Nonfiction: Book excerpts, historical/nostalgic, how-to, inspirational, new product, travel. Query with published clips. Length: 1,200-1,700 words. **Pays $25-150 for assigned articles; $25-100 for unsolicited articles.** Sometimes pays expenses of writers on assignment.

Photos: Send photos with submission. Reviews prints. Buys one-time rights. Pays $15-125/photo or negotiates payment individually. Captions required.

Columns/Departments: Back to Basics (care for horses); Ask the Experts (how to with horses); Nutrition (for horses), all 800 words. Query with published clips. **Pays $25-150.**

$ $ $ HORSE & RIDER, The Magazine of Western Riding, Primedia, P.O. Box 4101, 741 Corporate Circle, Suite A, Golden CO 80401. (720)836-1257. Fax: (720)836-1245. E-mail: hrsenrider@cowles.com. Website: www.equise arch.com. **Contact:** René E. Riley, executive editor. **10% freelance written.** Monthly magazine covering Western horse industry, competition, recreation. "*Horse & Rider*'s mission is to educate, inform and entertain both competitive and recreational riders with tightly focused training articles, practical stable management techniques, hands-on healthcare tips, safe trail-riding practices, well-researched consumer advice and a behind-the-scenes, you-are-there approach to major equine events." Estab. 1961. Circ. 164,000. **Pays on acceptance.** Publishes ms an average of 1 year after acceptance. Byline given. Offers $75 kill fee. Buys first North American serial rights. Editorial lead time 2 months. Submit seasonal material 6 months in advance. Accepts queries by mail. Responds in 3 months to queries; 3 months to mss. Sample copy and writer's guidelines free.

Nonfiction: Book excerpts, general interest, how-to (horse training, horsemanship), humor, interview/profile, new product, personal experience, photo feature, travel, horse health care, trail riding. **Buys 5-10 mss/year.** Send complete ms. Length: 1,000-3,000 words. **Pays $150-1,000.**

Photos: State availability of or send photos with submission. Buys rights on assignment or stock. Negotiates payment individually. Captions, identification of subjects, model releases required.

■ The online magazine carries original content not found in the print edition. Contact: René E. Riley.

Tips: Writers should have "patience, ability to accept critical editing and extensive knowledge of the Western horse industry."

$ $ HORSE ILLUSTRATED, The Magazine for Responsible Horse Owners, Fancy Publications, Inc., P.O. Box 6050, Mission Viejo CA 92690-6050. (949)855-8822. Fax: (949)855-3045. E-mail: horseillustrated@fancypubs.c om. Website: www.horseillustratedmagazine.com. Managing Editor: Karen Keb Acevedo. **Contact:** Moira Harris, editor. **90% freelance written.** Prefers to work with published/established writers but will work with new/unpublished writers. Monthly magazine covering all aspects of horse ownership. "Our readers are adults, mostly women, between the ages of 18 and 40; stories should be geared to that age group and reflect responsible horse care." Estab. 1976. Circ. 190,000. Pays on publication. Publishes ms an average of 8 months after acceptance. Byline given. Buys one-time rights, requires first North American rights among equine publications. Submit seasonal material 6 months in advance. Accepts queries by mail, e-mail. Responds in 3 months to queries. Writer's guidelines for #10 SASE.

Nonfiction: "We are looking for authoritative, in-depth features on trends and issues in the horse industry. Such articles must be queried first with a detailed outline of the article and clips. We rarely have a need for fiction." General interest, historical/nostalgic, how-to (horse care, training, veterinary care), inspirational, photo feature. No "little girl" horse stories, "cowboy and Indian" stories or anything not *directly* relating to horses. **Buys 20 mss/year.** Query or send complete ms. Length: 1,000-2,000 words. **Pays $100-400.**

Photos: Send photos with submission. Reviews 35mm and medium format transparencies, 4×6 prints.

Tips: "Freelancers can break in at this publication with feature articles on Western and English training methods; veterinary and general care how-to articles; and horse sports articles. We rarely use personal experience articles. Submit photos with training and how-to articles whenever possible. We have a very good record of developing new freelancers into regular contributors/columnists. We are always looking for fresh talent, but certainly enjoy working with established writers who 'know the ropes' as well. We are accepting less unsolicited freelance work—much is now assigned and contracted."

N $ $ HORSE SHOW, The Official Magazine of Equestrian Sport since 1937, American Horse Shows Association, 4047 Iron Works Parkway, Lexington KY 40511. (859)225-6923. Fax: (859)231-6662. E-mail: editor@ahsa. org. Website: www.ahsa.org. **Contact:** Christine E. Stafford, editor-in-chief. **10-30% freelance written.** Magazine published 10 times/year covering the equestrian sport. Estab. 1937. Circ. 75,000. Pays on publication. Byline given. Offers 50% kill fee. Buys first North American serial, first rights. Editorial lead time 1-5 months. Accepts queries by mail, e-mail, fax, phone. Sample copy and writer's guidelines free.

Nonfiction: Interview/profile, technical, all equestrian-related. **Buys 20-30 mss/year.** Query with published clips. Length: 500-3,500 words. **Pays $100-300.** Sometimes pays expenses of writers on assignment.

Photos: State availability with submission. Reviews contact sheets. Buys one-time rights. Offers $50-200/photo. Captions, identification of subjects, model releases required.

Columns/Departments: Horses of the Past (famous equines); Horse People (famous horsemen/women), both 500-1,000 words. **Buys 20-30 mss/year.** Query with published clips. **Pays $100.**

Tips: "Write via e-mail in first instance with samples, résumé, then mail original clips."

$ $ THE HORSE, Your Guide to Equine Health Care, P.O. Box 4680, Lexington KY 40544-4680. (859)276-6771. Fax: (859)276-4450. E-mail: kgraetz@thehorse.com. Website: www.thehorse.com. Managing Editor: Neil Cohen. **Contact:** Kimberly S. Graetz, editor. **75% freelance written.** Monthly magazine covering equine health and care. *The Horse* is an educational/news magazine geared toward the professional, hands-on horse owner. Estab. 1983. Circ. 40,000. **Pays on acceptance.** Publishes ms an average of 2 months after acceptance. Byline given. Buys Buys first world and electronic rights,. Accepts queries by mail. Responds in 2 months to queries. Sample copy for $2.95 or online. Writer's guidelines free.

⊶ Break in with short horse health news items.

Nonfiction: How-to, technical, topical interviews. "No first-person experiences not from professionals; this is a technical magazine to inform horse owners." **Buys 90 mss/year.** Query with published clips. Length: 500-5,000 words. **Pays $75-700 for assigned articles.**

Photos: Send photos with submission. Reviews transparencies. $35-350. Captions, identification of subjects required.

Columns/Departments: Up Front (news on horse health), 100-500 words; Equinomics (economics of horse ownership), Step by Step (feet and leg care), Nutrition, Back to Basics, all 1,800-2,500 words. **Buys 50 mss/year.** Query with published clips. **Pays $50-400.**

◼ The online magazine carries original content not found in the print edition, mostly news items.

Tips: "We publish reliable horse health information from top industry professionals around the world. Manuscript must be submitted electronically or on disk."

$ HORSES ALL, North Hill Publications, 278-19 St. NE, Calgary Alberta T2E 8P7, Canada. (403)248-9993. Fax: (403)248-8838. E-mail: horsesall@northhill.net. **Contact:** Editor. **40% freelance written.** Eager to work with new/unpublished writers. Monthly tabloid covering horse owners and the horse industry. Estab. 1977. Circ. 25,000. Pays on publication. Publishes ms an average of 3 months after acceptance. Byline given. Offers 30% kill fee. Buys first North American serial rights. Submit seasonal material 3 months in advance. Accepts queries by mail, e-mail, fax. Accepts simultaneous submissions. Sample copy and writer's guidelines for SAE.

Nonfiction: "We would prefer more general stories, no specific local events or shows." Book excerpts, essays, general interest, historical/nostalgic, how-to (training, horse care and maintenance), inspirational, interview/profile, personal experience, photo feature. **Buys 3 mss/year.** Query. Length: 800-1,400 words. **Pays $50-75 (Canadian).**

Photos: Send photos with submission. Reviews 3×5 or larger prints. Buys one-time rights. Captions, identification of subjects, model releases required.

Tips: "Our writers must be knowledgeable about horses and the horse industry, and be able to write features in a readable, conversational manner, but in third person only, please. While we do include coverage of major events in our publication, we generally require that these events take place in Canada. Any exceptions to this general rule are evaluated on a case-by-case basis."

$ ▧ I LOVE CATS, Hochman Associates, 900 Oak Tree Rd., Suite C, South Plainfield NJ 07080. (908)222-0990. Fax: (908)222-8228. E-mail: yankee@izzy.net. Website: www.iluvcats.com. **Contact:** Lisa Allmendinger, editor. **100% freelance written.** Bimonthly magazine. "*I Love Cats* is a general interest cat magazine for the entire family. It caters to cat lovers of all ages. The stories in the magazine include fiction, nonfiction, how-to, humorous and columns for the cat lover." Estab. 1989. Circ. 100,000. Pays on publication. Publishes ms an average of 1 year after acceptance. Byline given. Must sign copyright consent form. Buys all rights. Editorial lead time 6 months. Submit seasonal material 9 months in advance. Accepts queries by mail, e-mail, phone. Responds in 3 months to queries. Sample copy for $4. Writer's guidelines for #10 SASE, online or by e-mail.

Nonfiction: Essays, general interest, how-to, humor, inspirational, interview/profile, new product, opinion, personal experience, photo feature. No poetry. **Buys 100 mss/year.** Send complete ms. Length: 500-1,500 words. **Pays $50-150, contributor copies or other premiums if requested.** If requested. Sometimes pays expenses of writers on assignment.

Photos: (Please send copies; art will no longer be returned.). Send photos with submission. Buys all rights. Offers no additional payment for photos accepted with ms. Identification of subjects required.

Fiction: Adventure, fantasy, historical, humorous, mainstream, mystery, novel excerpts, slice-of-life vignettes, suspense. "This is a family magazine. No graphic violence, pornography or other inappropriate material. *I Love Cats* is strictly 'G-rated.' " **Buys 100 mss/year.** Send complete ms. Length: 500-1,500 words. **Pays $50-150.**

Fillers: Anecdotes, facts, short humor. **Buys 25/year. Pays $25.**

Tips: "Please keep stories short and concise. Send complete ms with photos, if possible. I buy lots of first-time authors. Nonfiction pieces with color photos are always in short supply. With the exception of the standing columns, the rest of the magazine is open to freelancers. Be witty, humorous or take a different approach to writing."

N KITTENS USA, Adopting and Caring for Your Kitten, Fancy Publications, P.O. Box 6050, Mission Viejo CA 92690. (949)855-8822. **Contact:** Keith Bush, editor. **90% freelance written.** Annual publication for kitten buyers. Estab. 1997. Pays on publication. Buys first North American serial rights. Editorial lead time 6 months. Responds in 3 months to queries. Writer's guidelines for #10 SASE.
Nonfiction: Healthcare, training, adoption. **Buys 20 mss/year.** Query with published clips. Length: 1,000-2,000 words. **Pays $50-450.**
Photos: Looking for happy, healthy, well-groomed cats and kittens in studio or indoor settings. Guidelines for #10 SASE. Buys one-time rights. Negotiates payment individually. Captions, identification of subjects, model releases required.
Tips: "No fiction or poetry. Please read recent issues to learn the kind of articles we want. Then, show us in your query how you can contribute something new and unique."

$ MINIATURE DONKEY TALK, Miniature Donkey Talk, Inc., 1338 Hughes Shop Rd., Westminster MD 21158-2911. (410)875-0118. Fax: (410)857-9145. E-mail: minidonk@qis.net. Website: www.qis.net/~minidonk/mdt.htm. Bonnie Gross, editor. **65% freelance written.** Bimonthly magazine covering miniature donkeys or donkeys, with articles on healthcare, promotion and management of donkeys for owners, breeders or donkey lovers. Estab. 1987. Circ. 4,925. **Pays on acceptance.** Publishes ms an average of 4 months after acceptance. Byline given. Buys first, second serial (reprint) rights. Editorial lead time 2 months. Submit seasonal material 3 months in advance. Accepts queries by mail, e-mail, fax. Responds in 1 week to queries; 1 month to mss. Sample copy for $5. Writer's guidelines free.
Nonfiction: Book excerpts, humor, interview/profile, personal experience. **Buys 6 mss/year.** Query with published clips. Length: 700-7,000 words. **Pays $25-100.**
Photos: State availability with submission. Reviews 3×5 prints. Buys one-time rights. Offers no additional payment for photos accepted with ms. Identification of subjects required.
Columns/Departments: Humor, 2,000 words; Healthcare 2,000-5,000 words; Management, 2,000 words. **Buys 50 mss/year.** Query. **Pays $25-100.**
Fiction: Humorous. **Buys 6 mss/year.** Query. Length: 3,000-7,000 words. **Pays $25-100.**
Fillers: Anecdotes, facts, gags to be illustrated by cartoonist, short humor. **Buys 12/year.** Length: 200-2,000 words. **Pays $15-35.**
Tips: "Simply send your manuscript. If on topic and appropriate, good possibility it will be published. We accept the following types of material: 1) Breeder profiles—either of yourself or another breeder. The full address and/or telephone number of the breeder will not appear in the article as this would constitute advertising; 2) Coverage of non-show events such as fairs, donkey gatherings, holiday events, etc. We do not pay for coverage of an event that you were involved in organizing; 3) Detailed or specific instructional or training material. We're always interested in people's training methods; 4) Relevant, informative equine health pieces. We much prefer they deal specifically with donkeys; however, we will consider articles specifically geared towards horses. If at all possible, substitute the word 'horse' for donkey. We reserve the right to edit, change, delete or add to health articles as we deem appropriate. Please be very careful in the accuracy of advice or treatment and review the material with a veterinarian; 5) Farm management articles; and 6) Fictional stories on donkeys."

$ $ MUSHING, Stellar Communications, Inc., P.O. Box 149, Ester AK 99725-0149. (907)479-0454. Fax: (907)479-3137. E-mail: editor@mushing.com. Website: www.mushing.com. Publisher: Todd Hoener. **Contact:** Erika Keiko Iseri, managing editor. Bimonthly magazine covering all aspects of the growing sports of dogsledding, skijoring, carting, dog packing and weight pulling. "*Mushing* promotes responsible dog care through feature articles and updates on working animal health care, safety, nutrition and training." Estab. 1987. Circ. 6,000. Pays within 60 days of publication. Publishes ms an average of 4 months after acceptance. Byline given. Buys first, second serial (reprint) rights. Submit seasonal material 4 months in advance. Accepts queries by mail, e-mail, fax, phone. Responds in 8 months to queries. Sample copy for $5, $6 US to Canada. Writer's guidelines free (call or e-mail for information) or online.
Nonfiction: "We consider articles on canine health and nutrition, sled dog behavior and training, musher profiles and interviews, equipment how-to's, trail tips, expedition and race accounts, innovations, sled dog history, current issues, personal experiences and humor." Historical/nostalgic, how-to, interview/profile. Special issues: Themes: Iditarod and long-distance racing (January/February); expeditions/peak of race season (March/April); health and nutrition (May/June); musher and dog profiles, summer activities (July/August); equipment, fall training (September/October); races and places (November/December). Query with or without published clips. Considers complete ms with SASE. Length: 1,000-2,500 words. **Pays $50-250.** Sometimes pays expenses of writers on assignment.
Photos: We look for good b&w and quality color for covers and specials. Send photos with submission. Reviews contact sheets, negatives, transparencies, prints. Buys one time and second reprint rights. Pays $20-165/photo. Captions, identification of subjects, model releases required.
Columns/Departments: Length: 500-1,000 words. Query with or without published clips or send complete ms.
Fiction: Considers short, well-written and relevant or timely fiction. Query with or without published clips or send complete ms. **Pay varies.**
Fillers: Anecdotes, facts, newsbreaks, short humor, cartoons, puzzles. Length: 100-250 words. **Pays $20-35.**

Tips: "Read our magazine. Know something about dog-driven, dog-powered sports."

[N] $ $ PAINT HORSE JOURNAL, American Paint Horse Association, P.O. Box 961023, Fort Worth TX 76161-0023. (817)834-2742. Fax: (817)222-8466. E-mail: tgantz@apha.com. Website: www.apha.com. **Contact:** Tracy Gantz, managing editor. **10% freelance written.** Works with a small number of new/unpublished writers/year. Monthly magazine for people who raise, breed and show Paint horses. Estab. 1966. Circ. 30,000. **Pays on acceptance.** Byline given. Offers negotiable kill fee. Buys first North American serial, reprint rights. Submit seasonal material 3 months in advance. Accepts queries by mail, e-mail, fax. Sample copy for $4. Writer's guidelines for #10 SASE.
Nonfiction: General interest (personality pieces on well-known owners of Paints), historical/nostalgic (Paint horses in the past—particular horses and the breed in general), how-to (train and show horses), photo feature (Paint horses), now seeking informative well-written articles on recreational riding. **Buys 4-5 mss/year.** Query. Length: 1,000-2,000 words. **Pays $35-450.**
Reprints: Send typed ms with rights for sale noted by e-mail preferrably. pays 30-50% of amount paid for an original article.
Photos: Photos must illustrate article and must include Paint horses. Send photos with submission. Reviews 35mm or larger transparencies, 3×5 or larger color glossy prints. Offers no additional payment for photos accepted with accompanying ms. Captions required.
Tips: "*PHJ* needs breeder-trainer articles, Paint horse marketing and timely articles from areas throughout the U.S. and Canada. We are looking for more recreational and how-to articles. We are beginning to cover equine activity such as trail riding, orienteering and other outdoor events. Photos with copy are almost always essential. Well-written first person articles are welcomed. Submit items that show a definite understanding of the horse business. Be sure you understand precisely what a Paint horse is as defined by the American Paint Horse Association. Use proper equine terminology."

[N] $ $ PET LIFE, Your Companion Animal Magazine, Magnolia Media Group, 3451 Boston Ave., Fort Worth TX 76116. (817)560-6100. Fax: (817)560-6196. E-mail: awilson@mmqweb.com. Website: www.petlifeweb.com. **Contact:** Alexis Wilson, editor. **85% freelance written.** Bimonthly magazine. "*PetLife* is America's premier companion animal magazine featuring stories that highlight the human-animal bond." Estab. 1995. **Pays on acceptance.** Publishes ms an average of 2 months after acceptance. Byline given. Buys all rights. Editorial lead time 3 months. Submit seasonal material 6 months in advance. Accepts queries by e-mail. Accepts simultaneous submissions. Responds in 1 month to queries. Sample copy for $3.95 or online. Writer's guidelines by e-mail.
Nonfiction: How-to, humor, inspirational, interview/profile, personal experience, photo feature, technical, book reviews. "We are apolitical—although we will occasionally publish stories on the prevention of animal abuse. We focus on the human-animal bond." **Buys 30 mss/year.** Query with published clips. Length: 200-1,500 words. **Pays $50-400.**
Photos: State availability with submission. Reviews transparencies. Buys all rights. Negotiates payment individually. Identification of subjects required.
Columns/Departments: Celebrity Interviews (well-known stars who are pet owners); DogLife/CatLife (info from the experts); Vet Perspective (info on specific health issues); Odd Pets (pets other than dogs and cats). **Buys 30 mss/ year.** Query. **Pays $100-300.**
Fillers: Anecdotes, facts, newsbreaks. **Buys 10/year. Pays $50.**
Tips: "Be familiar with the magazine. Be specific—what will the story say, who will you interview, suggest visuals. Be brief in your query. Always send a query—no unsolicited manuscripts accepted."

$ $ PETS MAGAZINE, Moorshead Magazines, Ltd., 505 Consumers Rd., Suite 500, Toronto Ontario M2J 4V8, Canada. (416)491-3699. Fax: (416)491-3996. E-mail: pets@moorshead.com. Website: www.pets-magazine.com. **Contact:** Edward Zapletal, editor. **40% freelance written.** Bimonthly magazine. For pet owners, primarily cat and dog owners, but we also cover rabbits, guinea pigs, hamsters, gerbils, birds and fish. Issues covered include: pet health care, nutrition, general interest, grooming, training humor, human-animal bond stories. Estab. 1983. Circ. 51,000. Pays within 30 days of publication. Publishes ms an average of 2 months after acceptance. Byline given. Offers 50% kill fee. Buys first North American serial rights. Editorial lead time 3 months. Submit seasonal material 2 months in advance. Accepts queries by e-mail. Sample copy for #10 SAE with IRCs. Writer's guidelines for 9½×4 SAE with IRCs or online.
• Please no U.S. postage on return envelope.
Nonfiction: General interest, humor, new product, personal experience, Vetrinary Medicine, Human Interest (i.e., working animal), Training, Obedience. No fiction. **Buys 10 mss/year.** Query. Length: 500-1,500 words. **Pays 12-18¢/ word (Canadian funds).**
Reprints: Accepts previously published submissions. **Pays 6-9¢/word.**
Photos: Prefers good color pictures or slides. Reviews photocopies. Buys one-time rights. Identification of subjects required.
Columns/Departments: Grooming Your Pet (mostly dogs and cats), 300-400 words. **Buys 6-12 mss/year.** Query.
Fillers: Facts. **Buys 5/year.** Length: 20-100 words. **Pays $10-20.**
Tips: "Always approach with a query letter first. E-mail is good if you've got it. We'll contact you if we like what we see. I like writing to be friendly, informative, well-balanced with pros and cons. Remember, we're catering to pet owners, and they are a discriminating audience."

$ $ THE QUARTER HORSE JOURNAL, P.O. Box 32470, Amarillo TX 79120. (806)376-4811. Fax: (806)349-6400. E-mail: aqhajrnl@aqha.org. Website: www.aqha.com. Editor-in-Chief: Jim Jennings. **Contact:** Jim Bret Campbell, editor. **20% freelance written.** Prefers to work with published/established writers. Monthly official publication of the american quarter horse association. Estab. 1948. Circ. 78,000. **Pays on acceptance.** Publishes ms an average of 6 months after acceptance. Byline given. Buys first North American serial rights. Submit seasonal material 6 months in advance. Accepts queries by mail, e-mail, fax. Responds in 2 months to queries.

    O⤸ Break in by "writing about topics tightly concentrated on the Quarter Horse industry while maintaining strong journalistic skills."

Nonfiction: Book excerpts, essays, how-to (fitting, grooming, showing, or anything that relates to owning, showing, or breeding), interview/profile (feature-type stories—must be about established horses or people who have made a contribution to the business), new product, opinion, personal experience, photo feature, technical (equine updates, new surgery procedures, etc.), travel, informational (educational clinics, current news). **Buys 20 mss/year.** Length: 800-1,800 words. **Pays $150-300.**

Photos: Reviews 2¼×2¼, 4×5 or 35mm transparencies, 4×5 glossy prints. Offers no additional payment for photos accepted with ms.

    ▣ The online magazine carries original content not found in the print edition. Contact: Jim Bret Campbell.

Tips: "Writers must have a knowledge of the horse business."

$ $▨ REPTILE & AMPHIBIAN HOBBYIST, T.F.H. Publications, One TFH Plaza, Neptune NJ 07753. (732)988-8400 ext. 243. Fax: (732)774-9224. Website: www.tfh.com. Editor-in-chief: Katherine J. Carlon. **Contact:** Tom Mazorlig, editor. **100% freelance written.** Monthly "Colorful, varied monthly covering reptiles and amphibians as pets aimed at beginning to intermediate hobbyists. Pet shop distribution. Writers must know their material, including scientific names, identification, general terrarium maintenance." Estab. 1995. Circ. 30,000. Pays 60 days after acceptance. Publishes ms an average of 6 months after acceptance. Byline given. Buys all rights. Editorial lead time 2 months. Responds in 1 month to queries; 2 months to mss. Sample copy for $4.50. Writer's guidelines free.

Nonfiction: General interest, interview/profile, personal experience, photo feature, technical, travel. **Buys 120 mss/year.** Query. Length: 1,500-2,000 words. **Pays $100-120.**

Photos: Send photos with submission. Reviews transparencies, prints. Buys non-exclusive rights. Offers $20/photo. Captions, identification of subjects, model releases required.

Columns/Departments: Herp People (profiles herp-related personalities); In Review (book reviews); Invertebrate Corner (terrarium invertebrates), all 1,500 words. **Buys 45 mss/year.** Query. **Pays $75-100.**

Tips: "Talk to the editor before sending anything. A short telephone conversation tells more about knowledge of subject matter than a simple query. I'll read anything, but it is very easy to detect an uninformed author. Very willing to polish articles from new writers."

Ⓝ $ ROCKY MOUNTAIN HORSE CONNECTION, Rocky Mountain Horse Connection, LLC, 313 Cantril St., Castle Rock CO 80104. (303)663-1300. Fax: (303)663-1331. E-mail: rmhc@horseconnection.com. Website: www.horseconnection.com. **Contact:** Christine DeHerrera, managing editor. **90% freelance written.** Magazine published 11 times/year covering horse owners and riders. "Our readers are horse owners and riders. They specialize in English riding. We primarily focus on show jumping and hunters, dressage, and three-day events, with additional coverage of driving, polo, and endurance." Estab. 1995. Circ. 25,000. Pays on publication. Publishes ms an average of 1 month after acceptance. Byline given. Buys first, second serial (reprint) rights. Editorial lead time 3 months. Submit seasonal material 3 months in advance. Accepts queries by mail, e-mail. Responds in 1 month to queries. Sample copy for $3.50 or online. Writer's guidelines for #10 SASE or online.

Nonfiction: Humor, interview/profile, personal experience, event reports. No general interest stories about horses. Nothing negative. No western, racing, or breed specific articles. No "my first pony" stories. **Buys 30-50 mss/year.** Query with published clips. Length: 500-1,000 words. **Pays $25 for assigned articles; $75 for unsolicited articles.** Sometimes pays expenses of writers on assignment.

Reprints: Accepts previously published submissions.

Photos: State availability with submission. Buys one-time rights. Negotiates payment individually.

Tips: "Please read the magazine. We are currently focused on the western states and we like stories about English riders from these states."

$▨ ROCKY MOUNTAIN RIDER MAGAZINE, Regional All-Breed Horse Monthly, P.O. Box 1011, Hamilton MT 59840. (406)363-4085. Fax: (406)363-1056. Website: www.rockymountainrider.com. **Contact:** Natalie Riehl, editor. **90% freelance written.** Monthly magazine "aiming to satisfy the interests of readers who enjoy horses." Estab. 1993. Circ. 14,000. Pays on publication. Publishes ms an average of 6 months after acceptance. Byline given. Buys one-time rights. Submit seasonal material 6 months in advance. Accepts simultaneous submissions. Responds in 1 month to queries; 2 months to mss. Sample copy free. Writer's guidelines for #10 SASE.

Nonfiction: Book excerpts, essays, general interest, historical/nostalgic, humor, interview/profile, new product, personal experience, photo feature, travel, cowboy poetry. **Buys 100 mss/year.** Send complete ms. Length: 500-2,000 words. **Pays $15-90.**

Photos: Send photos with submission. Buys one-time rights. Pays $5/photo. Captions, identification of subjects required.

Poetry: Light verse, traditional. **Buys 25 poems/year.** Submit maximum 10 poems. Length: 6-36 lines. **Pays $10.**

Fillers: Anecdotes, facts, gags to be illustrated by cartoonist, short humor. Length: 200-750 words. **Pays $15.**

Tips: "*RMR* is looking for positive, human interest stories that appeal to an audience of horsepeople. We accept profiles of unusual people or animals, history, humor, anecdotes, cowboy poetry, coverage of regional events and new products. We aren't looking for many 'how to' or training articles, and are not currently looking at any fiction."

[N] $ $ **TROPICAL FISH HOBBYIST MAGAZINE, The World's Most Widely Read Aquarium Monthly,** TFH Publications, Inc., One TFH Plaza, Neptune City NJ 07753. (732)988-8400. Fax: (732)988-9635. E-mail: editor@tfh.com. Managing Editor: Katherine Carlon. **Contact:** Mary Sweeney, editor. **90% freelance written.** Monthly magazine covering tropical fish. Estab. 1952. Circ. 50,000. **Pays on acceptance.** Byline given. Buys all rights. Editorial lead time 3 months. Submit seasonal material 6 months in advance. Accepts queries by e-mail. Responds immediately on electronic queries. Writer's guidelines by e-mail.
Nonfiction: "We cover any aspect of aquarium science, aquaculture, and the tropical fish hobby. Our readership is diverse—from neophytes to mini reef specialists. We require well-researched, well-written, and factually accurate copy, preferably with photos." **Buys 100-150 mss/year. Pays $100-250.**
Photos: State availability with submission. Reviews 2×2 transparencies. Buys multiple nonexclusive rights. Negotiates payment individually. Identification of subjects, model releases required.
Tips: "With few exceptions, all communication and submission must be electronic. We want factual, interesting and relevant articles about the aquarium hobby written by people who are obviously knowledgeable. We publish an enormous variety of article types. Review several past issues to get an idea of the scope."

ART & ARCHITECTURE

Listed here are publications about art, art history, specific art forms and architecture written for art patrons, architects, artists and art enthusiasts. Publications addressing the business and management side of the art industry are listed in the Art, Design & Collectibles category of the Trade section. Trade publications for architecture can be found in Building Interiors, and Construction & Contracting sections.

$ $ **THE AMERICAN ART JOURNAL,** Kennedy Galleries, Inc., 730 Fifth Ave., New York NY 10019. (212)541-9600. Fax: (212)977-3833. **Contact:** Jayne A. Kuchna, editor-in-chief. Prefers to work with published/established writers; works with a small number of new/unpublished writers each year. Annual magazine covering American art history of the 17th, 18th, 19th and 20th centuries, including painting, sculpture, architecture, photography, cultural history, etc., for people with a serious interest in American art, and who are already knowledgeable about the subject. Readers are scholars, curators, collectors, students of American art, or persons with a strong interest in Americana." Circ. 2,000. **Pays on acceptance.** Publishes ms an average of 6 months after acceptance. Byline given. Buys all rights, but will reassign rights to writers. Responds in 2 months to queries. Sample copy for $18.
Nonfiction: "All articles are about some phase or aspect of American art history. No how-to articles written in a casual or 'folksy' style. Writing style must be formal and serious." Historical. **Buys 10-15 mss/year.** Length: 2,500-8,000 words. **Pays $400-600.**
Photos: Reviews b&w only. Purchased with accompanying ms. Offers no additional payment for photos. Captions required.
Tips: "Articles must be scholarly, thoroughly documented, well-researched, well-written and illustrated. Whenever possible, all manuscripts must be accompanied by b&w photographs, which have been integrated into the text by the use of numbers."

[N] $ $ **AMERICAN INDIAN ART MAGAZINE,** American Indian Art, Inc., 7314 E. Osborn Dr., Scottsdale AZ 85251-6401. (602)994-5445. Fax: (602)945-9533. **Contact:** Roanne P. Goldfein, editorial director. **97% freelance written.** Works with many new/unpublished writers/year. Quarterly magazine covering Native American art, historic and contemporary, including new research on any aspect of Native American art north of the US-Mexico border. Estab. 1975. Circ. 30,000. Pays on publication. Publishes ms an average of 3 months after acceptance. Byline given. Buys first, one-time rights. Responds in 3 weeks to queries; 3 months to mss. Writer's guidelines for #10 SASE.
Nonfiction: New research on any aspect of Native American art. No previously published work or personal interviews with artists. **Buys 12-18 mss/year.** Query. Length: 1,000-2,500 words. **Pays $75-300.**
Photos: An article usually requires between 8 and 15 photographs. (Photos should be glossy 8×10 prints; color photos should be transparencies; 35mm slides are acceptable.). Buys one-time rights. Fee schedules and reimbursable expenses are decided upon by the magazine and the author.
Tips: "The magazine is devoted to all aspects of Native American art. Some of our readers are knowledgeable about the field and some know very little. We seek articles that offer something to both groups. Articles reflecting original research are preferred to those summarizing previously published information."

$ $ $ **AMERICANSTYLE MAGAZINE,** The Rosen Group, 3000 Chestnut Ave., Suite 304, Baltimore MD 21211. (410)889-3093. Fax: (410)243-7089. E-mail: hoped@rosengrp.com. Website: www.americanstyle.com. **Contact:** Hope Daniels, editor. **80% freelance written.** Quarterly magazine covering arts, crafts, travel and interior design. "*AmericanStyle* is a full-color lifestyle publication for people who love art. Our mandate is to nurture collectors with information that will increase their passion for contemporary art and craft and the artists who create it. *AmericanStyle*'s primary audience is contemporary craft collectors and enthusiasts. Readers are college-educated, age 35+, high-income earners with the financial means to collect art and craft, and to travel to national art and craft events in pursuit of their passions." Estab. 1994. Circ. 60,000. Pays on publication. Publishes ms an average of 6 months after acceptance. Buys first North American serial rights. Editorial lead time 9 months. Submit seasonal material 1 year in advance. Accepts queries by mail, e-mail, fax. Sample copy for $3. Writer's guidelines for #10 SASE.

- *AmericanStyle* is especially interested in freelance ideas about arts travel, profiles of contemporary craft collectors and established studio artists.

Nonfiction: Specialized arts/crafts interests. Length: 300-2,500 words. **Pays $500-800.** Sometimes pays expenses of writers on assignment.

Photos: Send photos with submission. Reviews oversized transparencies and 35mm slides. Negotiates payment individually. Captions required.

Columns/Departments: Portfolio (profiles of emerging artists); Arts Walk; Origins; One On One, all 800-1,200 words. Query with published clips. **Pays $500-700.**

Tips: "This is not a hobby-crafter magazine. Country crafts or home crafting is not our market. We focus on contemporary American craft art, such as ceramics, wood, fiber, glass, metal."

$ $ $ ⬛ **ART & ANTIQUES**, TransWorld Publishing, Inc., 2100 Powers Ferry Rd., Atlanta GA 30339. (770)955-5656. Fax: (770)952-0669. Editor: Barbara S. Tapp. **Contact:** Patti Verbanas, managing editor. **90% freelance written.** Magazine published 11 times/year covering fine art and antique collectibles and the people who collect them and/or create them. "*Art & Antiques* is the authoritative source for elegant, sophisticated coverage of the treasures collectors love, the places to discover them and the unique ways collectors use them to enrich their environments." Circ. 170,000. **Pays on acceptance.** Byline given. Offers 25% kill fee or $250. Buys all rights. Editorial lead time 8 months. Submit seasonal material 8 months in advance. Responds in 6 weeks to queries; 2 months to mss. Sample copy and writer's guidelines free.

Nonfiction: "We publish one 'interior design with art and antiques' focus feature a month." Essays, interview/profile (especially interested in profiles featuring collectors outside the Northwest and Northern California areas). Special issues: Designing with art & antiques (September and April); Asian art & antiques (October); Contemporary art (December). **Buys 200 mss/year.** Query with or without published clips. Length: 200-1,200 words. **Pays $200-1,200 for assigned articles.** Pays expenses of writers on assignment.

Photos: Scouting shots. Send photos with submission. Reviews contact sheets, transparencies, prints. Captions, identification of subjects required.

Columns/Departments: Art & Antiques Update (trend coverage and timely news of issues and personalities), 100-350 words; Review (thoughts and criticisms on a variety of worldwide art exhibitions throughout the year), 600-800 words; Value Judgements (experts highlight popular to undiscovered areas of collecting), 600-800 words; Emerging Artists (an artist on the cusp of discovery), 600-800 words; Collecting (profiles fascinating collectors, their collecting passions and the way they live with their treasures), 800-900 words; Discoveries (collections in lesser-known museums and homes open to the public), 800-900 words; Studio Session (peek into the studio of an artist who is currently hot or is a revered veteran allowing the reader to watch the artist in action), 800-900 words; Then & Now (the best reproductions being created today and the craftspeople behind the work), 800-900 words; World View (major art and antiques news worldwide; visuals preferred but not necessary), 600-800 words; Travelling Collector (hottest art and antiques destinations, dictated by those on editorial calendar; visuals preferred but not necessary), 800-900 words; Essay (first-person piece tackling a topic in a non-academic way; visuals preferred, but not necessary); Profile (profiles those who are noteworthy and describes their interests and passions; very character-driven and should reveal their personalities), 600-800 words. **Buys 200 mss/year.** Query by mail only with or without published clips. **Pays $200-800.**

Fillers: Facts, newsbreaks. **Buys 22/year.** Length: 150-300 words. **Pays $150-300.**

Tips: "Send scouting shots with your queries. We are a visual magazine and no idea will be considered without visuals. We are good about responding to writers in a timely fashion—excessive phone calls are not appreciated, but do check in if you haven't heard from us in two months. We like colorful, lively and creative writing. Have fun with your query. Multiple queries in a submission are allowed."

N̄ **$** ⬛ **ART CALENDAR MAGAZINE, The Business Magazine for Visual Artists**, P.O. Box 2675, Salisbury MD 21802. Fax: 410-572-5793. E-mail: roses@intercom.net. Website: www.artcalendar.com. **Contact:** Carolyn Proeber, publisher. **100% freelance written.** Monthly magazine. Estab. 1986. Circ. 7,700. Pays on publication. Sample copy for $5 prepaid.

- We welcome nuts-and-bolts, practical articles of interest to serious visual artists, emerging or professional. Examples: marketing how-to's, first-person stories on how an artist has built his career or an aspect of it, interviews with artists (business/career-building emphasis), and pieces on business practices and other topics of use to artists. The tone of our magazine is practical, can-do, and uplifting. Writers may use as many or as few words as necessary to tell the whole story.

Nonfiction: Essays (the psychology of creativity), how-to, interview/profile (successful artists with a focus on what made them successful — not necessarily rich and famous artists, but the guy-next-door who paints all day and makes a decent living doing it.), personal experience (artists making a difference (art teachers working with disabled students, bringing a community together, etc.), technical (new equipment, new media, computer software, Internet sites that are WAY cool that no one has heard of yet), Cartoons, art law, including pending legislation that affects artists (copyright law, Internet regulations, etc.). "We like nuts-and-bolts information about making a living as an artist. We do not run reviews or art historical pieces, nor do we like writing characterized by "critic-speak," philosophical hyperbole, psychological arrogance, politics, or New Age religion. Also, we do not condone a get-rich-quick attitude." Send complete ms. **Pays $100.** We can make other arrangements in lieu of pay, i.e. a subscription or copies of the magazine in which your article appears.

Reprints: Send photocopy or typed ms with information about when and where the material previously appeared. Pays $50.

Photos: Carolyn Proeber. Reviews b&w glossy or color prints. Pays $25.

Columns/Departments: Carolyn Proeber. If an artist or freelancer sends us good articles regularly, and based on results we feel that s/he is able to produce a column at least three times per year, we will invite him to be a Contributing Writer. If a gifted artist-writer can commit to producing an article on a monthly basis, we will offer him a regular column and the title Contributing Editor. Send complete ms.

[N] $ ART PAPERS, Atlanta Art Papers, Inc., P.O. Box 5748, Atlanta GA 31107-0748. (404)588-1837. Fax: (404)588-1836. E-mail: info@artpaper.org. **Contact:** Michael Pittari, editor. **95% freelance written.** Bimonthly magazine covering contemporary art and artists. "*Art Papers*, about regional and national contemporary art and artists, features a variety of perspectives on current art concerns. Each issue presents topical articles, interviews, reviews from across the US, and an extensive and informative artists' classified listings section. Our writers and the artists they cover represent the scope and diversity of the country's art scene." Estab. 1977. Circ. 12,000. Pays on publication. Publishes ms an average of 3 months after acceptance. Byline given. Not copyrighted. Buys all rights. Editorial lead time 2 months. Submit seasonal material 2 months in advance.

Nonfiction: Feature articles and reviews. **Buys 240 mss/year. Pays $40-100; unsolicited articles are on spec.**

Photos: Send photos with submission. Reviews color slides, b&w prints. Offers no additional payment for photos accepted with ms. Identification of subjects required.

Columns/Departments: Current art concerns and news. **Buys 8-10 mss/year.** Query. **Pays $30-100.**

$ $ ART SPIRIT!, Art Spirit! Inc., P.O. Box 460669, Fort Lauderdale FL 33346. (954)763-3338. Fax: (954)763-4481. E-mail: sfbiz@mindspring.com. **Contact:** Sherry Friedlander, editor. **90% freelance written.** Magazine published 3 times/year. "Art Spirit! covers music, art, drama, dance, special events." Estab. 1998. Circ. 20,000. Pays on publication. Publishes ms an average of 10 weeks after acceptance. Byline given. Buys first North American serial rights. Editorial lead time 3 months. Accepts queries by mail, e-mail, fax, phone. Responds in 2 weeks to queries. Sample copy by e-mail. Writer's guidelines free.

Nonfiction: "Must be about arts." Interview/profile, photo feature. Length: 650-1,500 words. **Pays $100-200.**

Photos: State availability of or send photos with submission.

Tips: "Information should interest the arts group."

[N] $ ARTICHOKE, Writings About the Visual Arts, Artichoke Publishing, 208-901 Jervis St., Vancouver, British Columbia V6E 2B6, Canada. Fax: (604)683-1941. E-mail: editor@artichoke.ca. Website: www.artichoke.ca. **Contact:** Paula Gustafson, editor. **90% freelance written.** Triannual magazine. "*Artichoke* is Western Canada's visual arts magazine. Writers must be familiar with Canadian art and artists." Estab. 1989. Circ. 1,500. **Pays on acceptance.** Publishes ms an average of 6 months after acceptance. Byline given. Offers 50% kill fee. Buys one-time rights. Editorial lead time 6 months. Accepts queries by mail, e-mail, fax. Accepts simultaneous submissions. Responds in 1 week to queries; 2 weeks to mss. Sample copy and writer's guidelines free.

Nonfiction: Essays, interview/profile, opinion, critical reviews about Canadian visual art. "*Artichoke* does not publish fiction, poetry or academic jargon." **Buys 100 mss/year.** Query with or without published clips or send complete ms. Length: 1,000-2,500 words. **Pays $125.**

Photos: State availability of or send photos with submission. Reviews transparencies, prints. Buys one-time rights. Offers no additional payment for photos accepted with ms. Captions, identification of subjects required.

$ $ THE ARTIST'S MAGAZINE, F&W Publications, Inc., 1507 Dana Ave., Cincinnati OH 45207-1005. (513)531-2690, ext. 467. Fax: (513)531-2902. E-mail: tamedit@fwpubs.com. Website: www.artistsmagazine.com. Editor: Sandra Carpenter. **Contact:** Senior Editor. **80% freelance written.** Works with a large number of new/unpublished writers each year. Monthly magazine covering primarily two-dimensional art instruction for working artists. "Ours is a highly visual approach to teaching the serious amateur artist techniques that will help him improve his skills and market his work. The style should be crisp and immediately engaging." Circ. 250,000. Pays on publication. Publishes ms an average of 6 months after acceptance. Binote given for feature material. Offers 25% kill fee. Buys first North American serial, second serial (reprint) rights. Responds in 3 months to queries. Sample copy for $4.50. Writer's guidelines for #10 SASE or online.

● Writers must have working knowledge of art techniques. This magazine's most consistent need is for instructional feature articles written in the artist's voice.

Nonfiction: "The emphasis must be on how the reader can learn some method of improving his artwork; or the marketing of it." Instructional only—how an artist uses a particular technique, how he handles a particular subject or medium, or how he markets his work. No unillustrated articles; no seasonal material; no travel articles; no profiles. **Buys 60 mss/year.** Length: 1,200-1,800 words. **Pays $200-350 and up.** Sometimes pays expenses of writers on assignment.

Photos: "Transparencies—in 4×5 or 35mm slide format—are required with every accepted article since these are essential for our instructional format. Full captions must accompany these." Buys one-time rights.

Tips: "Look at several current issues and read the author's guidelines carefully. Submissions must include artwork. Remember that our readers are fine artists and illustrators."

$ $ ARTNEWS, ABC, 48 W. 38th St., New York NY 10018. (212)398-1690. Fax: (212)768-4002. E-mail: goartnews@aol.com. Website: www.artnewsonline.com. **Contact:** Robin Cembalest, executive editor. Monthly "*Artnews* reports on art, personalities, issues, trends and events that shape the international art world. Investigative features focus on art ranging from old masters to contemporary, including painting, sculpture, prints and photography. Regular columns offer exhibition and book reviews, travel destinations, investment and appreciation advice, design insights and updates on major art world figures." Estab. 1902. Circ. 9,877. Accepts queries by mail, e-mail, fax, phone.

AZURE DESIGN, ARCHITECTURE AND ART, 20 Maud St., Suite 200, Toronto, Ontario M5V 2M5, Canada. (416)203-9674. Fax: (416)203-9842. E-mail: azure@interlog.com. Website: www.azureonline.com. **Contact:** Nelda Rodger, editor. **50% freelance written.** Magazine covering design and architecture. Estab. 1985. Circ. 20,000. Pays on publication. Publishes ms an average of 1 month after acceptance. Offers variable kill fee. Buys first rights. Editorial lead time up to 45 days. Responds in 6 weeks to queries.
Nonfiction: Buys 25-30 mss/year. Length: 350-2,000 words. **Payment varies.**
Columns/Departments: RearView (essay/photo on something from a building environment); and Forms & Functions (coming exhibitions, happenings in world of design), both 300-350 words. **Buys 30 mss/year.** Query. **Payment varies.**
Tips: "Try to understand what the magazine is about. Writers must be well-versed in the field of architecture and design. It's very unusual to get something from someone I haven't worked quite closely with and gotten a sense of who the writer is. The best way to introduce yourself is by sending clips or writing samples and describing what your background is in the field."

$ $ ✠ C, international contemporary art, C The Visual Arts Foundation, P.O. Box 5, Station B, Toronto, Ontario M5T 2T2, Canada. (416)539-9495. Fax: (416)539-9903. E-mail: cmag@istar.ca. Website: www.cmagazine.com. **Contact:** Joyce Mason, editor. **80% freelance written.** Quarterly magazine covering international contemporary art. "*C* provides a vital and vibrant forum for the presentation of contemporary art and the discussion of issues surrounding art in our culture, including feature articles, reviews and reports, as well as original artists' projects." Estab. 1983. Circ. 7,000. Pays on publication. Publishes ms an average of 4 months after acceptance. Byline given. Offers kill fee. Editorial lead time 3 months. Accepts queries by mail, e-mail, fax. Accepts simultaneous submissions. Responds in 6 weeks to queries; 4 months to mss. Sample copy for $10 (US). Writer's guidelines for #10 SASE.
Nonfiction: Essays, general interest, opinion, personal experience. **Buys 50 mss/year.** Length: 1,000-3,000 words. **Pays $150-500 (Canadian), $105-350 (US).**
Photos: State availability of or send photos with submission. Reviews 35mm transparencies or 8×10 prints. Buys one-time rights; shared copyright on reprints. Offers no additional payment for photos accepted with ms. Captions required.
Columns/Departments: Reviews (review of art exhibitions), 500 words. **Buys 30 mss/year.** Query. **Pays $125 (Canadian).**

N $ $ DIRECT ART MAGAZINE, Slow Art Productions, 870 Sixth Ave., New York NY 10001. (212)725-0999. E-mail: slowart@aol.com. Website: www.slowart.com. **Contact:** Paul Winslow, editor. **75% freelance written.** Semiannual fine art magazine covering alternative, anti-establishment, left-leaning fine art. Estab. 1998. Circ. 10,000. **Pays on acceptance.** Byline sometimes given. Offers 25% kill fee. Buys one-time, electronic rights. Editorial lead time 2 months. Submit seasonal material 3 months in advance. Accepts queries by mail, e-mail. Accepts simultaneous submissions. Responds in 2 weeks to queries; 1 month to mss. Sample copy for 9×12 SAE and 10 first-class stamps. Writer's guidelines for #10 SASE.
Nonfiction: Sylvi Alani, managing editor. Essays, exposé, historical/nostalgic, how-to, humor, inspirational, interview/profile, opinion, personal experience, photo feature, technical. **Buys 4-6 mss/year.** Query with published clips. Length: 1,000-3,000 words. **Pays $100-500.**
Reprints: Accepts previously published submissions.
Photos: State availability of or send photos with submission. Reviews 35mm slide transparencies. Buys one-time rights. Negotiates payment individually.
Columns/Departments: Query with published clips. **Pays $100-500.**

N $ ESPACE, Sculpture, Centre de Diffusion 3D, 4888 St. Denis, Montreal, Quebec H2J 2L6, Canada. (514)844-9858. Fax: (514)844-3661. E-mail: espace@espace-sculpture.com. Website: www.espace-sculpture.com. **Contact:** S. Fisette, editor. **95% freelance written.** Quarterly magazine covering sculpture events. "Canada's only sculpture publication, *Espace* represents a critical tool for the understanding of contemporary sculpture. Published 4 times a year, in English and French, *Espace* features interviews, in-depth articles and special issues related to various aspects of three dimensionality. Foreign contributors guarantee an international perspective and diffusion." Estab. 1987. Circ. 1,400. Pays on publication. Publishes ms an average of 3 months after acceptance. Byline given. Buys all rights. Editorial lead time 5 months. Submit seasonal material 3 months in advance. Accepts queries by mail. Accepts simultaneous submissions. Sample copy free.

Nonfiction: Essays, exposé. **Buys 60 mss/year.** Query. Length: 1,000-1,400 words. **Pays $50/page.**
Reprints: Accepts previously published submissions.
Photos: Send photos with submission. Reviews transparencies, prints. Offers no additional payment for photos accepted with ms.

$ $⊠ L.A. ARCHITECT, The Magazine of Design in Southern California, Balcony Press, 512 E. Wilson, Glendale CA 91206. (818)956-5313. Fax: (818)956-5904. E-mail: danette@balconypress.com. Website: www.laarch.com. **Contact:** Danette Riddle, editor. **80% freelance written.** Bimonthly magazine covering architecture, interiors, landscape and other design principles. "*L.A. Architect* is interested in architecture, interiors, product, graphics and landscape design as well as news about the arts. We encourage designers to keep us informed on projects, techniques, and products that are innovative, new, or nationally newsworthy. We are especially interested in new and renovated projects that illustrate a high degree of design integrity and unique answers to typical problems in the urban cultural and physical environment." Estab. 1999. Circ. 5,000. Pays on publication. Publishes ms an average of 3 months after acceptance. Byline given. Makes work-for-hire assignments. Editorial lead time 4 months. Submit seasonal material 4 months in advance. Accepts queries by mail, e-mail, fax. Responds in 1 month to queries; 1 month to mss. Sample copy for $3. Writer's guidelines for #10 SASE or online.
Nonfiction: Book excerpts, essays, historical/nostalgic, interview/profile, new product. "No technical; foo-foo interiors; non-Southern California subjects." **Buys 20 mss/year.** Length: 500-2,000 words. **Pay negotiable.**
Photos: State availability with submission. Buys one-time rights. Offers no additional payment for photos accepted with ms. Captions, identification of subjects, model releases required.
Tips: "Our magazine focuses on contemporary and cutting-edge work either happening in Southern California or designed by a Southern California designer. We like to find little-known talent which has not been widely published. We are not like *Architectural Digest* in flavor so avoid highly decorative subjects. Each project, product, or event should be accompanied by a story proposal or brief description and select images. Do not send original art without our written request; we make every effort to return materials we are unable to use, but this is sometimes difficult and we must make advance arrangements for original art."

$ $THE MAGAZINE ANTIQUES, Brant Publications, 575 Broadway, New York NY 10012. (212)941-2800. Fax: (212)941-2819. **Contact:** Allison Ledes, editor. **75% freelance written.** Monthly "Articles should present new information in a scholarly format (with footnotes) on the fine and decorative arts, architecture, historic preservation and landscape architecture." Estab. 1922. Circ. 65,835. Pays on publication. Publishes ms an average of 6 months after acceptance. Byline given. Buys all rights. Editorial lead time 6 months. Submit seasonal material 6 months in advance. Responds in 3 weeks to queries; 6 months to mss. Sample copy for $10.50.
Nonfiction: Historical/nostalgic, scholarly. **Buys 50 mss/year.** Length: 2,850-3,000 words. **Pays $250-500.** Sometimes pays expenses of writers on assignment.
Photos: State availability with submission. Reviews contact sheets, negatives, transparencies, prints. Buys one-time rights. Captions, identification of subjects required.

$ $ $ $⊠ METROPOLIS, The Magazine of Architecture and Design, Bellerophon Publications, 61 W. 23rd St., New York NY 10010. (212)627-9977. Fax: (212)627-9988. E-mail: edit@metropolismag.com. Website: www.metropolismag.com. Executive Editor: Martin Pedersen. **Contact:** Julien Devereux, managing editor. **80% freelance written.** Monthly magazine (combined issues February/March and August/September) for consumers interested in architecture and design. Estab. 1981. Circ. 45,000. Pays 60-90 days after acceptance. Publishes ms an average of 3 months after acceptance. Byline given. Makes work-for-hire assignments. Submit seasonal material 3 months in advance. Accepts queries by mail, e-mail, fax. Responds in 8 months to queries. Sample copy for $7.
Nonfiction: Martin Pedersen, executive editor. Essays (design, architecture, urban planning issues and ideas), interview/profile (of multi-disciplinary designers/architects). No profiles on individual architectural practices, information from public relations firms, or fine arts. **Buys 30 mss/year.** Length: 1,500-4,000 words. **Pays $1,500-4,000.**
Photos: Reviews contact sheets, 35mm or 4×5 transparencies or 8×10 b&w prints. Buys one-time rights. Payment offered for certain photos. Captions required.
Columns/Departments: The Metropolis Observed (architecture, design, and city planning news features), 100-1,200 words, **pays $100-1,200**; Perspective (opinion or personal observation of architecture and design), 1,200 words, **pays $1,200**; Enterprise (the business/development of architecture and design), 1,500 words, **pays $1,500**; In Review (architecture and book review essays), 1,500 words, **pays $1,500**. Direct queries to Julien Devereux, managing editor. **Buys 40 mss/year.** Query with published clips.
Tips: "Metropolis strives to tell the story of design to a lay person with an interest in the built environment, while keeping the professional designer engaged. The magazine examines the various design disciplines (architecture, interior design, product design, graphic design, planning, and preservation) and their social/cultural context. We're looking for the new, the obscure, or the wonderful. Also, be patient and don't expect an immediate answer after submission of query."

$ $MIX, independent art and culture magazine, Parallelogramme Artist-Run Culture and Publishing, Inc., 401 Richmond St. #446, Toronto, Ontario M5V 3A8, Canada. (416)506-1012. Fax: (416)506-0141. E-mail: mix @web.ca. Website: www.mixmagazine.com. **Contact:** Rosemary Heather, Sisi Penaloza, co-editors. **95% freelance written.** Quarterly magazine covering Artist-Run gallery activities. "Mix represents and investigates contemporary artistic practices and issues, especially in the progressive Canadian artist-run scene." Estab. 1973. Circ. 3,500. Pays on publication. Publishes ms an average of 6 months after acceptance. Byline given. Offers 40% kill fee. Buys first North American serial rights. Editorial lead time 6 months. Submit seasonal material 4 months in advance. Accepts queries by mail, e-mail, fax. Responds in 2 months to queries; 3 months to mss. Sample copy for $6.95, 8½ × 10¼ SAE and 6 first-class stamps. Writer's guidelines free or online.

Nonfiction: Essays, interview/profile. **Buys 12-20 mss/year.** Query with published clips. Length: 750-3,500 words. **Pays $100-450.**

Reprints: Send photocopy of article and information about when and where the article previously appeared.

Photos: State availability with submission. Buys one-time rights. Captions, identification of subjects required.

Columns/Departments: Features, 1,000-3,000 words; Art Reviews, 500 words. Query with published clips. **Pays $100-450.**

■ The online magazine carries original content not found in the print edition and includes writer's guidelines.

Tips: "Read the magazine and other contemporary art magazines. Understand the idea 'artist-run.' We're not interested in 'artsy-phartsy' editorial but rather pieces that are critical, dynamic and would be of interest to nonartists too."

$ $THE MODERNISM MAGAZINE, 333 N. Main St., Lambertville NJ 08530. (609)397-4104. Fax: (609)397-9377. E-mail: cgreenberg@ragoarts.com. Website: www.ragoarts.com/nj. Editor: David Rago. **Contact:** Cara Greenberg, managing editor. **80% freelance written.** Quarterly magazine covering 20th century art and design. "We are interested in objects and the people who created them. Our coverage begins in the 1920s with Art Deco and related movements, and ends with 1980s Post-Modernism, leaving contemporary design to other magazines. Our emphasis is on the decorative arts—furniture, pottery, glass, textiles, metalwork and so on—but we're moving toward more coverage of painting and sculpture." Estab. 1998. Circ. 20,000. Pays on publication. Publishes ms an average of 4 months after acceptance. Byline given. Offers 25% kill fee. Buys all rights. Editorial lead time 9 months. Submit seasonal material 9 months in advance. Accepts queries by mail, e-mail, fax. Accepts simultaneous submissions. Responds in 1 month to queries. Sample copy for $6.95. Writer's guidelines free.

Nonfiction: Book excerpts, essays, historical/nostalgic, interview/profile, new product, photo feature. "No first-person." **Buys 20 mss/year.** Query with published clips. Length: 2,000-2,500 words. **Pays $400 for assigned articles.**

Reprints: Accepts previously published submissions.

Photos: State availability of or send photos with submission. Reviews contact sheets, transparencies, prints. Buys one-time rights. Negotiates payment individually. Captions, identification of subjects required.

Tips: "Articles should be well-researched, carefully reported, and directed at a popular audience with a special interest in the Modernist movement. Please don't assume readers have prior familiarity with your subject; be sure to tell us the who, what, why, when and how of whatever you're discussing."

$ $NEW ART EXAMINER, Chicago New Art Association, 314 W. Institute Place, Chicago IL 60610. (312)649-9900. Fax: (312)649-9935. E-mail: examiner@newartexaminer.org. Website: www.newartexaminer.org. Editor: Kathryn Hixson. Managing Editor: Jan Estep. **Contact:** Kathy Rosenfeld, assistant editor. **95% freelance written.** Bimonthly magazine covering contemporary visual art. "*New Art Examiner* covers contemporary visual arts, with a special emphasis on art from the greater Midwest." Estab. 1971. Circ. 5,000. Publishes ms an average of 6 weeks after acceptance. Byline given. Buys all rights. Editorial lead time 10 months. Submit seasonal material 2 months in advance. Accepts queries by mail, e-mail. Sample copy for $6 plus shipping.

Nonfiction: Essays, interview/profile, criticism. **Buys 15 mss/year.** Query with published clips. Length: 100-5,000 words. **Pays $10-500.**

$ $SOUTHWEST ART, Sabot Publishing, 5444 Westheimer Rd., Suite 1440, Houston TX 77056. (713)296-7900. Fax: (713)850-1314. E-mail: southwestart@southwestart.com. Website: www.southwestart.com. **Contact:** Editors. **60% freelance written.** Monthly magazine "directed to art collectors interested in artists, market trends and art history of the American West." Estab. 1971. Circ. 60,000. **Pays on acceptance.** Publishes ms an average of 1 year after acceptance. Byline given. Offers $125 kill fee. Not copyrighted. Submit seasonal material 8 months in advance. Accepts queries by mail, e-mail, fax. Responds in 6 months to mss. Writer's guidelines free.

Nonfiction: Book excerpts, interview/profile. No fiction or poetry. **Buys 70 mss/year.** Query with published clips. Length: 1,400-1,600 words. **Pays $600 for assigned articles.**

Photos: Send photos with submission. Reviews 35mm, 2¼, 4×5 transparencies, 8×10 prints. Negotiates rights. Captions, identification of subjects required.

Tips: "Research the Southwest art market, send slides or transparencies with queries, send writing samples demonstrating knowledge of the art world."

$ $U.S. ART, MSP Communications, 220 S. Sixth St., Suite 500, Minneapolis MN 55402. (612)339-7571. Fax: (612)339-5806. E-mail: tmcormick@mspcommunications.com. Publisher: Frank Sisser. **Contact:** Tracy McCormick, managing editor. **40% freelance written.** Monthly magazine that reflects current events in the limited-edition-print market and educates collectors and the trade about the market's practices and trends. Departments/columns are staff-written. Distributed primarily through a network of 900 galleries as a free service to their customers. Circ. 50,000. **Pays on acceptance.** Publishes ms an average of 4 months after acceptance. Byline given. Offers 25% kill fee. Buys Buys all rights for a period of 60 days following publication of article. Editorial lead time 4 months. Accepts queries by mail, e-mail. Responds in 3 months to queries. Sample copy and writer's guidelines for #10 SASE.

Nonfiction: Two artist profiles per issue; an average of 6 features per issue including roundups of painters whose shared background of geographical region, heritage, or currently popular style illustrates a point; current events and exhibitions; educational topics on buying/selling practices and services available to help collectors purchase various print media. "Artists whose work is not available in print will not be considered for profiles." **Buys 4 mss/year.** Length: 1,000-2,000 words. **Pays $300-600 for features.**
Photos: Returns material after 2 months. Reviews color transparencies.
Tips: "We are open to writers whose backgrounds are not arts-specific. We generally do not look for art critics but prefer general-assignment reporters who can present factual material with flair in a magazine format. We also are open to opinion pieces from experts (gallery owners, publishers, consultants, show promoters) withing the industry."

$ WESTART, P.O. Box 6868, Auburn CA 95604. (530)885-0969. **Contact:** Martha Garcia, editor-in-chief. Semi-monthly 12-page tabloid emphasizing art for practicing artists and artists/craftsmen, students of art and art patrons. Estab. 1961. Circ. 4,000. Pays on publication. Byline given. Buys all rights. Sample copy and writer's guidelines free.
Nonfiction: Interview/profile, photo feature, informational. No hobbies. **Buys 6-8 mss/year.** Query or submit complete ms with SASE for reply or return. Phone queries OK. Length: 700-800 words. **Pays 50¢/column inch.**
Photos: Purchased with or without accompanying ms. Send b&w prints. Pays 50¢/column inch.
Tips: "We publish information which is current—that is, we will use a review of an exhibition only if exhibition is still open on the date of publication. Therefore, reviewer must be familiar with our printing and news deadlines."

[N] $ $ $ WILDLIFE ART, The Art Journal of the Natural World, Pothole Publications, Inc., 1428 E. Cliff Rd., Burnsville MN 55337. E-mail: pbarry@mail.winternet.com. Website: www.wildlifeartmag.com. Editor-in-Chief: Robert Koenke. **Contact:** Beth Mischek, editor. **80% freelance written.** Bimonthly magazine. "*Wildlife Art* is the world's largest wildlife art magazine. Features cover interviews on living artists as well as wildlife art masters, illustrators and conservation organizations. Special emphasis on landscape and plein-air paintings. Audience is publishers, collectors, galleries, museums, show promoters worldwide." Estab. 1982. Circ. 50,000. **Pays on acceptance.** Publishes ms an average of 6 months after acceptance. Byline given. Offers negotiable kill fee. Buys second serial (reprint) rights. Accepts queries by mail, phone. Responds in 6 months to queries. Sample copy for 9×12 SAE and 10 first-class stamps. Writer's guidelines for #10 SASE.
Nonfiction: General interest, historical/nostalgic, interview/profile. **Buys 40 mss/year.** Query with published clips, include artwork samples. Length: 800-5,000 words. **Pays $150-900.**
Columns/Departments: Buys 6 mss/year. Pays $100-300.
Tips: Best way to break in is to offer concrete story ideas; new talent; a new unique twist of artistic excellence.

ASSOCIATIONS

Association publications allow writers to write for national audiences while covering local stories. If your town has a Kiwanis, Lions or Rotary Club chapter, one of its projects might merit a story in the club's magazine. If you are a member of the organization, find out before you write an article if the publication pays members for stories; some associations do not. In addition, some association publications gather their own club information and rely on freelancers solely for outside features. Be sure to find out what these policies are before you submit a manuscript. Club-financed magazines that carry material not directly related to the group's activities are classified by their subject matter in the Consumer and Trade sections.

[N] $ AMERICA@WORK, AFL-CIO, 815 16th St. NW, Washington DC 20006. Fax: (202)508-6908. Website: www.afl-cio.org. **Contact:** Tula A. Connell, editor. **10% freelance written.** Monthly magazine covering issues of interest to working families/union members. Estab. 1996. Circ. 100,000. Pays on publication. Publishes ms an average of 3 months after acceptance. Byline given. Buys first North American serial rights. Editorial lead time 2 months. Submit seasonal material 3 months in advance. Accepts queries by mail, fax. Sample copy for $2.50.
Nonfiction: Essays, historical/nostalgic, how-to, interview/profile. **Buys 5-6 mss/year.** Query. Length: 600-2,000 words. **Pay varies depending on length.**
Photos: State availability with submission. Buys one-time rights. Identification of subjects, model releases required.

$ $ DAC NEWS, Official Publication of the Detroit Athletic Club, Detroit Athletic Club, 241 Madison Ave., Detroit MI 48226. (313)442-1034. Fax: (313)442-1047. E-mail: kenv@thedac.com. **Contact:** Kenneth Voyles, editor/publisher. **10% freelance written.** Magazine published 9 times/year. "DAC News is the magazine for Detroit Athletic Club members. It covers club news and events, plus general interest features." Estab. 1916. Circ. 4,500. Pays on publication. Publishes ms an average of 3 months after acceptance. Byline given. Buys one-time rights, makes work-for-hire assignments. Editorial lead time 3 months. Submit seasonal material 3 months in advance. Accepts queries by mail, phone. Responds in 1 month to queries. Sample copy free.

Nonfiction: General interest, historical/nostalgic, photo feature. "No politics or social issues—this is an entertainment magazine. We do not acccept unsolicited mss or queries for travel articles." **Buys 2-3 mss/year.** Length: 1,000-2,000 words. **Pays $100-500.** Sometimes pays expenses of writers on assignment.

Photos: Illustrations only. State availability with submission. Reviews transparencies, 4×6 prints. Buys one-time rights. Negotiates payment individually. Captions, identification of subjects, model releases required.

Tips: "Review our editorial calendar. It tends to repeat from year to year, so a freelancer with a fresh approach to one of these topics will get our attention quickly. It helps if articles have some connection with the DAC, but this is not absolutely necessary. We also welcome articles on Detroit history, Michigan history, or automotive history."

$ $ THE ELKS MAGAZINE, 425 W. Diversey, Chicago IL 60614-6196. (773)755-4740. E-mail: elksmag@elks.org. Website: www.elks.org/elksmag. Editor: Fred D. Oakes. **Contact:** Anna L. Idol, managing editor. **25% freelance written.** Magazine published 10 times/year with basic mission of being the "voice of the Elks." All material concerning the news of the Elks is written in-house. Estab. 1922. Circ. 1,200,000. **Pays on acceptance.** Buys first North American serial rights. Accepts queries by mail. Responds in 1 month to queries. Sample copy and writer's guidelines for 9×12 SAE with 4 first-class stamps or online.

Nonfiction: "We're really interested in seeing mss on business, technology, history, or just intriguing topics, ranging from sports to science." No fiction, politics, religion, controversial issues, travel, first-person, fillers, verse or queries. **Buys 20-30 mss/year.** Send complete ms. Length: 1,500-2,500 words. **Pays 20¢/word.**

Photos: If possible, please advise where photographs may be found. Photographs taken and submitted by the writer are paid for separately at $25 each.

Tips: "Check our website. Freelance articles are noted on the Table of Contents, but are not reproduced online, as we purchase only one-time rights. Please try us first. We'll get back to you soon."

N $ $ THE KEEPER'S LOG, U.S. Lighthouse Society, 244 Kearny St., San Francisco CA 94108. (415)362-7255. **Contact:** Wayne Wheeler, editor. **20% freelance written.** Quarterly magazine covering lighthouses, lightships and human interest relating to them. "Our audience is national (some foreign members). The magazine carries historical and contemporary information (articles) relating to technical, human interest, history, etc." Estab. 1984. Circ. 11,000. Pays on publication. Publishes ms an average of 6 months after acceptance. Byline given. Buys first rights. Editorial lead time 6 months. Accepts queries by mail. Responds in 1 week to queries. Sample copy for $5. Writer's guidelines for #10 SASE.

Nonfiction: Historical/nostalgic, personal experience, photo feature, technical. Ghost stories need not apply. **Buys 1 mss/year.** Query. Length: 2,500-5,000 words. **Pays $200-400.**

Photos: State availability with submission. Reviews 5×7 prints. Offers no additional payment for photos accepted with ms. Identification of subjects required.

$ $ $ KIWANIS, 3636 Woodview Trace, Indianapolis IN 46268-3196. (317)875-8755. Fax: (317)879-0204. E-mail: cjonak@kiwanis.org. Website: www.kiwanis.org. **Contact:** Chuck Jonak, managing editor. **50% freelance written.** Magazine published 10 times/year for business and professional persons and their families. Estab. 1917. Circ. 240,000. **Pays on acceptance.** Publishes ms an average of 3 months after acceptance. Byline given. Offers 40% kill fee. Buys first rights. Accepts queries by mail, e-mail, fax. Responds in 1 month to queries. Sample copy and writer's guidelines for 9×12 SAE with 5 first class stamps. Writer's guidelines online.

Nonfiction: Articles about social and civic betterment, small-business concerns, children, science, education, religion, family, health, recreation, etc. Emphasis on objectivity, intelligent analysis, and thorough research of contemporary issues. Positive tone preferred. Concise, lively writing, absence of clichés, and impartial presentation of controversy required. When applicable, include information and quotations from international sources. Avoid writing strictly to a US audience. "We have a continuing need for articles that concern helping youth, particularly prenatal through age five: day care, developmentally appropriate education, early intervention for at-risk children, parent education, safety and health. No fiction, personal essays, profiles, travel pieces, fillers, or verse of any kind. A light or humorous approach is welcomed where the subject is appropriate and all other requirements are observed." **Buys 40 mss/year.** Length: 1,500-2,500 words. **Pays $400-1,500.** Sometimes pays expenses of writers on assignment.

Photos: "We accept photos submitted with mss. Our rate for a ms with good photos is higher than for one without." Buys one-time rights. Identification of subjects, model releases required.

Tips: "We will work with any writer who presents a strong feature article idea applicable to our magazine's audience and who will prove he or she knows the craft of writing. First, obtain writer's guidelines and a sample copy. Study for general style and content. When querying, present detailed outline of proposed manuscript's focus and editorial intent. Indicate expert sources to be used, as well as article's tone and length. Present a well-researched, smoothly written ms that contains a 'human quality' with the use of anecdotes, practical examples, quotations, etc."

$ $ THE LION, 300 22nd St., Oak Brook IL 60523-8815. (630)571-5466. Fax: (630)571-8890. E-mail: rkleinfe@lionsclubs.org. Website: www.lionsclubs.org. **Contact:** Robert Kleinfelder, senior editor. **35% freelance written.** Works with a small number of new/unpublished writers each year. Monthly magazine covering service club organization for Lions Club members and their families. Estab. 1918. Circ. 540,000. **Pays on acceptance.** Publishes ms an average of 5 months after acceptance. Byline given. Buys all rights. Accepts queries by mail, fax, phone. Responds in 6 weeks to queries. Sample copy and writer's guidelines free.

Nonfiction: Welcomes humor, if sophisticated but clean; no sensationalism. Prefers anecdotes in articles. Photo feature (must be of a Lions Club service project), Informational (issues of interest to civic-minded individuals). No travel, biography or personal experiences. **Buys 4 mss/year.** Length: 500-2,200 words. **Pays $100-750.** Sometimes pays expenses of writers on assignment.

Photos: Purchased with or without accompanying ms or on assignment. "Photos should be at least 5×7 glossies; color prints are preferred. Be sure photos are clear and as candid as possible." Total purchase price for ms includes payment for photos accepted with ms. Captions required.

Tips: "Send detailed description of proposed article. Query first and request writer's guidelines and sample copy. Incomplete details on how the Lions involved actually carried out a project and poor quality photos are the most frequent mistakes made by writers in completing an article assignment for us. No gags, fillers, quizzes or poems are accepted. We are geared increasingly to an international audience. Writers who travel internationally could query for possible assignments, although only locally related expenses could be paid."

N $ THE OPTIMIST, Optimist International, 4494 Lindell Blvd., St. Louis MO 63108. (314)371-6000. Fax: (314)371-6006. E-mail: magazine@optimist.org. Website: www.optimist.org. **Contact:** Al Shon, managing editor. **5% freelance written.** Bimonthly magazine covering the work of Optimist clubs and members for members of the Optimist clubs in the US and Canada. Circ. 130,000. **Pays on acceptance.** Publishes ms an average of 4 months after acceptance. Buys first North American serial rights. Submit seasonal material 3 months in advance. Accepts queries by mail, e-mail, fax. Responds in 1 month to queries. Sample copy and writer's guidelines for 9×12 SAE with 4 first-class stamps.

Nonfiction: "We want articles about the activities of local Optimist clubs. These volunteer community-service clubs are constantly involved in projects, aimed primarily at helping young people. With over 4,000 Optimist clubs in the US and Canada, writers should have ample resources. Some large metropolitan areas boast several dozen clubs. We are also interested in feature articles on individual club members who have in some way distinguished themselves, either in their club work or their personal lives. Good photos for all articles are a plus and can mean a bigger check." How-to (self-improvement, philosophy or optimism). **Buys 1-2 mss/year.** Query. Length: 800-1,200 words. **Pays $100 and up.**

Reprints: Send photocopy. Pays 50% of amount paid for an original article.

Photos: "No mug shots or people lined up against the wall shaking hands." State availability with submission. Buys all rights. Payment negotiated. Captions required.

Tips: "Find out what the Optimist clubs in your area are doing, then find out if we'd be interested in an article on a specific club project. All of our clubs are eager to talk about what they're doing. Just ask them and you'll probably have an article idea. We would like to see short pieces on the positive effect an optimistic outlook on life can have on an individual. Examples of famous people who overcame adversity because of their positive attitude are welcome."

$ $ RECREATION NEWS, Official Publication of the ESM Association of the Capital Region, 7339 D Hanover Pkwy., Greenbelt MD 20770. (301)474-4600. Fax: (301)474-6283. E-mail: editor@recreationnews.com. Website: www.recreationnews.com. **Contact:** Francis X. Orphe, editor. **85% freelance written.** Monthly guide to leisure-time activities for federal and private industry workers covering outdoor recreation, travel, fitness and indoor pastimes. Estab. 1979. Circ. 104,000. Pays on publication. Publishes ms an average of 8 months after acceptance. Byline given. Buys first, second serial (reprint) rights. Submit seasonal material 10 months in advance. Accepts queries by mail, e-mail, fax, phone. Accepts simultaneous submissions. Responds in 2 months to queries. Sample copy and writer's guidelines for 9×12 SAE with $1.05 in postage.

Nonfiction: Articles Editor. Historical/nostalgic (Washington-related), personal experience (with recreation, life in Washington), travel (mid-Atlantic travel only), sports, hobbies. Special issues: skiing (December). **Buys 45 mss/year.** Query with published clips. Length: 800-2,000 words. **Pays $50-300.**

Reprints: Send tearsheet or typed ms with rights for sale noted and information on when and where the material previously appeared. Pays $50.

Photos: Photo Editor. State availability with submission. Pays $50-125 for transparency; $25. Captions, identification of subjects required.

Tips: "Our writers generally have a few years of professional writing experience and their work runs to the lively and conversational. We like more manuscripts in a wide range of recreational topics, including the off-beat. The areas of our publication most open to freelancers are general articles on travel and sports, both participational and spectator, also historic in the DC area. In general, stories on sites visited need to include info on nearby places of interest and places to stop for lunch, to shop, etc."

$ $ $ THE ROTARIAN, Rotary International, 1560 Sherman Ave., Evanston IL 60201-4818. (847)866-3000. Fax: (847)866-9732. E-mail: rotarian@rotaryintl.org. Website: www.rotary.org. **Contact:** Cary Silver, managing editor. **40% freelance written.** Monthly magazine for Rotarian business and professional men and women and their families, schools, libraries, hospitals, etc. "Articles should appeal to an international audience and in some way help Rotarians help other people. The organization's rationale is one of hope, encouragement and belief in the power of individuals talking and working together." Estab. 1911. Circ. 514,565. **Pays on acceptance.** Byline sometimes given. Kill fee negotiable. Buys one-time, all rights. Accepts queries by mail, e-mail. Sample copy for 9×12 SAE with 6 first-class stamps. Writer's guidelines for #10 SASE.

Nonfiction: General interest, humor, inspirational, photo feature, travel, sports, business, environmental. No fiction, religious or political articles. Query with published clips. Length: about 1,500 words. **Pays negotiable rate.**

Reprints: Send tearsheet, photocopy or typed ms with rights for sale noted and information about when and where the material previously appeared. Negotiates payment.

Photos: State availability with submission. Reviews contact sheets, transparencies. Buys one-time rights.

Columns/Departments: Manager's Memo (business), Database, Health Watch, Earth Diary, Travel Tips. 650 words. Query.

Tips: "The chief aim of *The Rotarian* is to report Rotary International news. Most of this information comes through Rotary channels and is staff written or edited. The best field for freelance articles is in the general interest category. These run the gamut from humor pieces and 'how-to' stories to articles about such significant concerns as business management, technology, world health and the environment."

$ $ $ SCOUTING, Boy Scouts of America, 1325 W. Walnut Hill Lane, P.O. Box 152079, Irving TX 75015-2079. (972)580-2367. Fax: (972)580-2367. E-mail: 103064.3363@compuserve.com. Website: www.scoutingmagazine.org. Executive Editor: Scott Daniels. **Contact:** Jon C. Halter, editor. **80% freelance written.** Magazine published 6 times/year covering Scouting activities for adult leaders of the Boy Scouts, Cub Scouts and Venturing. Estab. 1913. Circ. 1,000,000. **Pays on acceptance.** Publishes ms an average of 18 months after acceptance. Byline given. Offers 25% kill fee. Buys first North American serial rights. Editorial lead time 1 year. Submit seasonal material 1 year in advance. Accepts queries by mail, fax. Accepts simultaneous submissions. Responds in 1 month to queries; 2 months to mss. Sample copy for $2.50 and 9×12 SAE with 4 first-class stamps or online. Writer's guidelines for #10 SASE or online.

> ⊙━ Break in with "a profile of an outstanding Scout leader who has useful advice for new volunteer leaders (especially good if the situation involves urban Scouting or Scouts with disabilities or other extraordinary role)."

Nonfiction: Program activities; leadership techniques and styles; profiles; inspirational; occasional general interest for adults (humor, historical, nature, social issues, trends). Inspirational, interview/profile. **Buys 20-30 mss/year.** Query with published clips and SASE. Length: 600-1,200 words. **Pays $750-1,000 for major articles; $300-500 for shorter features.** Pays expenses of writers on assignment.

Reprints: Send photocopy of article and information about when and where the article previously appeared. "First-person accounts of meaningful scouting experiences (previously published in local newspapers, etc.) are a popular subject."

Photos: State availability with submission. Reviews transparencies, prints. Buys one-time rights. Identification of subjects required.

Columns/Departments: Way It Was (Scouting history), 1,000 words; Family Talk (family—raising kids, etc.), 600-750 words. **Buys 8-12 mss/year.** Query. **Pays $300-500.**

Fillers: "Limited to personal accounts of humorous or inspirational scouting experiences." Anecdotes, short humor. **Buys 15-25/year.** Length: 50-150 words. **Pays $25 on publication.**

▣ The online magazine carries original content not found in the print edition and includes writer's guidelines. Contact: Scott Daniels.

Tips: "*Scouting* magazine articles are mainly about successful program activities conducted by or for Cub Scout packs, Boy Scout troops, and Venturing crews. We also include features on winning leadership techniques and styles, profiles of outstanding individual leaders, and inspirational accounts (usually first person) or Scouting's impact on an individual, either as a youth or while serving as a volunteer adult leader. Because most volunteer Scout leaders are also parents of children of Scout age, *Scouting* is also considered a family magazine. We publish material we feel will help parents in strengthening their families. (Because they often deal with communicating and interacting with young people, many of these features are useful to a reader in both roles as parent and Scout leader)."

$ $ THE TOASTMASTER, Toastmasters International, 23182 Arroyo Vista, Rancho Santo, Margarita CA 92688. (949)858-8255. Fax: (949)858-1207. E-mail: sfrey@toastmasters.org. Website: www.toastmasters.org. **Contact:** Suzanne Frey, editor. **50% freelance written.** Monthly magazine on public speaking, leadership and club concerns. "This magazine is sent to members of Toastmasters International, a nonprofit educational association of men and women throughout the world who are interested in developing their communication and leadership skills. Members range from novice to professional speakers and from a wide variety of ethnic and cultural backgrounds, as Toastmasters is an international organization." Estab. 1932. Circ. 170,000. **Pays on acceptance.** Publishes ms an average of 10 months after acceptance. Byline given. Buys first, second serial (reprint), all rights. Submit seasonal material 3 months in advance. Accepts simultaneous submissions. Responds in 6 weeks to queries; 1 month to mss. Sample copy for 9×12 SAE with 4 first-class stamps. Writer's guidelines for #10 SASE or online.

Nonfiction: "Toastmasters members are requested to view their submissions as contributions to the organization. Sometimes asks for book excerpts and reprints without payment, but original contribution from individuals outside Toastmasters will be paid for at stated rates." How-to, humor, interview/profile (well-known speakers and leaders), communications, leadership, language use. **Buys 50 mss/year.** Query by mail only. Length: 1,000-2,500 words. **Pays $100-250.** Sometimes pays expenses of writers on assignment.

Reprints: Send typed ms with rights for sale noted and information about when and where the material previously appeared. Pays 50-70% of amount paid for an original article.

Photos: Reviews b&w prints. Buys all rights. No additional payment for photos accepted with ms. Captions required.

Tips: "We are looking primarily for 'how-to' articles on subjects from the broad fields of communications and leadership which can be directly applied by our readers in their self-improvement and club programming efforts. Concrete examples are useful. *Avoid sexist or nationalist language and 'Americanisms' such as baseball examples, etc.*"

N: **$** **TRAIL & TIMBERLINE**, The Colorado Mountain Club, 710 10th St., Suite 200, Golden CO 80401. (303)279-3080, ext. 105. Fax: (303)279-9690. E-mail: beckwt@cmc.org. Website: www.cmc.org. **Contact:** Tom Beckwith, editor. **80% freelance written.** Bimonthly official publication of the Colorado Mountain Club. "Articles in *Trail & Timberline* conform to the mission statement of the Colorado Mountain Club to unite the energy, interest and knowledge of lovers of the Colorado mountains, to collect and disseminate information, to stimulate public interest and to encourage preservation of the mountains of Colorado and the Rocky Mountain region." Estab. 1918. Circ. 10,500. Pays on publication. Publishes ms an average of 2 months after acceptance. Byline given. Buys all rights. Editorial lead time 6 months. Submit seasonal material 6 months in advance. Accepts queries by mail, e-mail. Responds in 1 week to queries; 1 month to mss. Sample copy for $5. Writer's guidelines free.

Nonfiction: Essays, humor, personal experience, photo feature, travel. **Buys 10-15 mss/year.** Query. Length: 500-2,000 words. **Pays $50.**

Photos: Send photos with submission. Reviews contact sheets, 35mm transparencies, 3×5 or larger prints, gif/jpeg files. Buys one-time rights. Offers no additional payment for photos accepted with ms. Captions, identification of subjects, model releases required.

Columns/Departments: Wild Colorado (conservation/public lands issues), 1,000 words; Education (mountain education/natural history), 500-1,000 words. **Buys 6-12 mss/year.** Query. **Pays $50.**

Poetry: Jared Smith, associate editor, poetry. Avant-garde, free verse, traditional. **Buys 6-12 poems/year.**

Tips: "Writers should be familiar with the purposes and ethos of the Colorado Mountain Club before querying. Writer's guidelines are available and should be consulted—particularly for poetry submissions. All submissions must conform to the mission statement of the Colorado Mountain Club."

$** **$ **VFW MAGAZINE**, Veterans of Foreign Wars of the United States, 406 W. 34th St., Kansas City MO 64111. (816)756-3390. Fax: (816)968-1169. E-mail: pbrown@vfw.org. Website: www.vfw.org. **Contact:** Rich Kolb, editor-in-chief. **40% freelance written.** Monthly magazine on veterans' affairs, military history, patriotism, defense and current events. "*VFW Magazine* goes to its members worldwide, all having served honorably in the armed forces overseas from World War II through Bosnia." Circ. 2,000,000. **Pays on acceptance.** Byline given. Offers 50% kill fee. Buys first rights. Submit seasonal material 6 months in advance. Accepts queries by mail, fax. Responds in 2 months to queries. Sample copy for 9×12 SAE with 5 first-class stamps.

O— Break in with "fresh and innovative angles on veterans' rights; stories on little-known exploits in U.S. military history. Will be particularly in the market for Korean War battle accounts during 2001-2003. Upbeat articles about severely disabled veterans who have overcome their disabilities; feel-good patriotism pieces; current events as they relate to defense policy; health and retirement pieces are always welcome."

Nonfiction: Veterans' and defense affairs, recognition of veterans and military service, current foreign policy, American armed forces abroad and international events affecting U.S. national security are in demand. **Buys 25-30 mss/year.** Query with 1-page outline, résumé and published clips. Length: 1,000 words. **Pays up to $500 maximum unless otherwise negotiated.**

Photos: Send photos with submission. Reviews contact sheets, negatives, color (2¼×2¼ preferred) transparencies, 5×7 or 8×10 b&w prints. Buys first North American rights. Captions, identification of subjects required.

Tips: "Absolute accuracy and quotes from relevant individuals are a must. Bibliographies useful if subject required extensive research and/or is open to dispute. Counsult *The Associated Press Stylebook* for correct grammar and punctuation. Please enclose a 3-sentence biography describing your military service and your military experience in the field in which you are writing. No phone queries."

ASTROLOGY, METAPHYSICAL & NEW AGE

Magazines in this section carry articles ranging from shamanism to extraterrestrial phenomena. With the coming millennium, there is increased interest in spirituality, angels, near death experiences, mind/body healing and other New Age concepts and figures. The following publications regard astrology, psychic phenomena, metaphysical experiences and related subjects as sciences or as objects of serious study. Each has an individual personality and approach to these phenomena. If you want to write for these publications, be sure to read them carefully before submitting.

$** **$ **FATE**, Llewellyn Worldwide, Ltd., P.O. Box 64383, St. Paul MN 55164-0383. Fax: (651)291-1908. E-mail: fate@llewellyn.com. Website: www.fatemag.com. **Contact:** Editor. **70% freelance written.** Estab. 1948. Circ. 65,000. Pays on publication. Byline given. Buys all rights. Responds in 3 months to queries. Sample copy and writer's guidelines for $3 and 9×12 SAE with 5 first-class stamps or online.

Nonfiction: Personal psychic and mystical experiences, 350-500 words. **Pays $25.** Articles on parapsychology, Fortean phenomena, cryptozoology, spiritual healing, flying saucers, new frontiers of science, and mystical aspects of ancient civilizations, 500-3,000 words. Must include complete authenticating details. Prefers interesting accounts of single events rather than roundups. "We very frequently accept manuscripts from new writers; the majority are individual's first-person accounts of their own psychic/mystical/spiritual experiences. We do need to have all details, where, when, why, who and what, included for complete documentation. We ask for a notarized statement attesting to truth of the article." Query. **Pays 10¢/word.**

Photos: Buys slides, prints, or digital photos/illustrations with ms. Pays $10.

Fillers: Fillers are especially welcomed and must be be fully authenticated also, and on similar topics. Length: 50-300 words.

Tips: "We would like more stories about *current* paranormal or unusual events."

MAGICAL BLEND MAGAZINE, A Primer for the 21st Century, P.O. Box 600, Chico CA 95927. (530)893-9037. Fax: (530)893-9076. E-mail: info@magicalblend.com. Website: www.magicalblend.com. **Contact:** Michael Peter Langevin, editor. **50% freelance written.** Bimonthly magazine covering social and mystical transformation. "*Magical Blend* endorses no one pathway to spiritual growth, but attempts to explore many alternative possibilities to help transform the planet." Estab. 1980. Circ. 100,000. Pays on publication. Publishes ms an average of 2 months after acceptance. Byline given. Accepts queries by mail, e-mail. Responds in 2 months to mss. Sample copy free. Writer's guidelines for #10 SASE.

  O─┐ Break in by "writing a great article that gives our readers something they can use in their daily lives or obtain 'name' interviews."

Nonfiction: "Articles must reflect our standards; see our magazine." Book excerpts, essays, general interest, inspirational, interview/profile, religious, travel. No poetry or fiction. **Buys 24 mss/year.** Send complete ms. Length: 1,000-5,000 words. **Pays $50-200.**

Photos: State availability with submission. Reviews transparencies. Buys all rights. Negotiates payment individually. Identification of subjects, model releases required.

Fillers: Newsbreaks. **Buys 12-20/year.** Length: 300-450 words. **Pay varies.**

$ $ $ ☒ NEW AGE, The Journal for Holistic Living, New Age Publishing, Inc., 42 Pleasant St., Watertown MA 02472. (617)926-0200. Website: www.newage.com. Editor-in-Chief: Jennifer Cook., Managing Editor: Elizabeth Phillips. **Contact:** Manuscript Editor. **90% freelance written.** Works with a small number of new/unpublished writers each year. Bimonthly magazine emphasizing "personal fulfillment and social change. The audience we reach is college-educated, social-service/hi-tech oriented, 25-55 years of age, concerned about social values, humanitarianism and balance in personal life." Estab. 1974. Circ. 225,000. **Pays on acceptance.** Publishes ms an average of 4 months after acceptance. Byline sometimes given. Offers 25% kill fee. Buys first North American serial, electronic rights. Editorial lead time 6 months. Submit seasonal material 6 months in advance. Accepts queries by mail. Accepts simultaneous submissions. Responds in 2 months to queries; 2 months to mss. Sample copy for $5 and 9×12 SAE. Writer's guidelines for #10 SASE.

  O─┐ No phone calls. The process of decision making takes time and involves more than one editor. An answer cannot be given over the phone.

Nonfiction: Book excerpts, essays, how-to (travel on business, select a computer, reclaim land, plant a garden), inspirational, interview/profile, new product, personal experience, religious, travel. Special issues: *Body & Soul: Holistic Living Guide; Body & Soul: Special Buyer's Guide; Body & Soul: Holistic Health Guide.* **Buys 100+ mss/year.** Query with published clips. Length: 100-2,500 words. **Pays 75¢-$1/word.** Pays expenses of writers on assignment.

Reprints: Send tearsheet or photocopy.

Photos: Send photos with submission. Reviews transparencies. Buys one-time rights. Negotiates payment individually. Captions, model releases required.

Columns/Departments: Holistic Health, Food/Nutrition, Spirit, Home, Community, Travel, Life Lessons. 600-1,300 words. **Buys 50 mss/year.** Query with published clips. **Pays 75¢-$1/word.**

Tips: "Submit short, specific news items to the Upfront department. Query first with clips. A query is one to two paragraphs—if you need more space than that to *present* the idea, then you don't have a clear grip on it. The next open area is columns: Reflections often takes first-time contributors. Read the magazine and get a sense of type of writing run in column. In particular we are interested in seeing inspirational, first-person pieces that highlight an engaging idea, experience or issue. We are also looking for new cutting-edge thinking. No e-mail or phone queries, please. Begin with a query, résumé and published clips — we will contact you for the manuscript."

$ ☒ NEW YORK SPIRIT MAGAZINE, (formerly *Free Spirit Magazine*), 107 Sterling Place, Brooklyn NY 11217. (718)638-3733. Fax: (718)230-3459. E-mail: office@nyspirit.com. Website: www.nyspirit.com. **Contact:** Paul English, editor. Bimonthly tabloid covering spirituality and personal growth and transformation. "We are a magazine that caters to the holistic health community in New York City." Circ. 50,000. **Pays on acceptance.** Publishes ms an average of 3 months after acceptance. Byline given. Buys first rights. Editorial lead time 1 month. Accepts simultaneous submissions. Responds in 1 month to queries. Sample copy for 8×10 SAE and 10 first-class stamps. Writer's guidelines free.

Nonfiction: Essays, how-to, humor, inspirational, interview/profile, photo feature. **Buys 30 mss/year.** Query with or without published clips. Length: 1,000-3,500 words. **Pays $150 maximum.**

Photos: State availability with submission. Model releases required.

Columns/Departments: Fitness (new ideas in staying fit), 1,500 words. **Pays $150.**

Fiction: Humorous, mainstream, inspirational. **Buys 5 mss/year.** Query with published clips. Length: 1,000-3,500 words. **Pays $150.**

Tips: "Be vivid and descriptive. We are *very* interested in hearing from new writers."

$ PANGAIA, Creating an Earth Wise Spirituality, Blessed Bee, Inc., Box 641, Point Arena CA 95468. (707)882-2052. Fax: (707)882-2793. E-mail: editor@pangaia.com. Website: www.pangaia.com. Editor-in-Chief: Anne Newkirk-Niven. **Contact:** Elizabeth Barrett, managing editor. **100% freelance written.** Quarterly journal of Earth spirituality covering Earth-based religions. "We publish articles pertinent to an Earth-loving readership. Mysticism, science, humor, tools all are described." Estab. 1997. Circ. 5,000. Pays on publication. Publishes ms an average of 6 months after acceptance. Byline given. Buys first North American serial rights. Editorial lead time 3 months. Submit seasonal material 3 months in advance. Accepts queries by mail, e-mail, fax. Responds in 1 month to queries; 1 month to mss. Sample copy for $5. Writer's guidelines for #10 SASE or online.
Nonfiction: Book excerpts, essays, historical/nostalgic, inspirational, interview/profile, personal experience, photo feature, religious, travel. No material on unrelated topics. **Buys 30 mss/year.** Send complete ms. Length: 1,000-3,500 words. **Pays $10-100.**
Photos: State availability with submission. Reviews prints. Buys one-time rights. Negotiates payment individually. Captions, identification of subjects required.
Fiction: Adventure, ethnic, fantasy, historical, humorous, religious, science fiction. No grim or abstract stories. **Buys 4 mss/year.** Send complete ms. Length: 1,500-4,000 words. **Pays $25-50.**
Poetry: Buys 2 poems/year. Submit maximum 4 poems. Length:100 lines.
Fillers: Short humor. **Buys 2/year.** Length: 500-700 words. **Pays $10.**
Tips: "Share a spiritual insight that can enlighten others. Back up your facts with citations where relevant, and make those facts sound like the neatest thing since self-lighting charcoal. Explain how to solve a problem; offer a new way to make the world a better place. We would also like to see serious scholarship on nature religion topics, material of interest to intermediate or advanced practicioners, which is both accurate and engaging."

$ SHAMAN'S DRUM, A Journal of Experiential Shamanism, Cross-Cultural Shamanism Network, P.O. Box 270, Williams OR 97544. (541)846-1313. Fax: (541)846-1204. **Contact:** Timothy White, editor. **75% freelance written.** Quarterly educational magazine of cross-cultural shamanism. "*Shaman's Drum* seeks contributions directed toward a general but well-informed audience. Our intent is to expand, challenge, and refine our readers' and our understanding of shamanism in practice. Topics include indigenous medicineway practices, contemporary shamanic healing practices, ecstatic spiritual practices, and contemporary shamanic psychotherapies. Our overall focus is cross-cultural, but our editorial approach is culture-specific—we prefer that authors focus on specific ethnic traditions or personal practices about which they have significant firsthand experience. We are looking for examples of not only how shamanism has transformed individual lives but also practical ways it can help ensure survival of life on the planet. We want material that captures the heart and feeling of shamanism and that can inspire people to direct action and participation, and to explore shamanism in greater depth." Estab. 1985. Circ. 14,000. Publishes ms an average of 6 months after acceptance. Byline given. Buys first North American serial, first rights. Editorial lead time 1 year. Responds in 3 months to queries. Sample copy for $5. Writer's guidelines for #10 SASE.
Nonfiction: Book excerpts, essays, interview/profile (please query), opinion, personal experience, photo feature. No fiction, poetry or fillers. **Buys 16 mss/year.** Send complete ms. Length: 5,000-8,000 words. **Pays 5-8¢/word, depending on how much we have to edit.**
Reprints: Send typed ms with rights for sale noted and information about when and where the material previously appeared. Pays 50% of amount paid for an original article.
Photos: Send photos with submission. Reviews contact sheets, transparencies, all size prints. Buys one-time rights. Offers $40-50/photo. Identification of subjects required.
Columns/Departments: Judy Wells, Earth Circles. Timothy White, Reviews. Earth Circles (news format, concerned with issues, events, organizations related to shamanism, indigenous peoples and caretaking Earth. Relevant clippings also sought. Reviews (in-depth reviews of books about shamanism or closely related subjects such as indigenous lifestyles, ethnobotany, transpersonal healing and ecstatic spirituality), 500-1,500 words. **Buys 8 mss/year.** Query. **Pays 5¢/word.**
Tips: "All articles must have a clear relationship to shamanism, but may be on topics which have not traditionally been defined as shamanic. We prefer original material that is based on, or illustrated with, first-hand knowledge and personal experience. Articles should be well documented with descriptive examples and pertinent background information. Photographs and illustrations of high quality are always welcome and can help sell articles."

$ WHOLE LIFE TIMES, P.O. Box 1187, Malibu CA 90265. (310)317-4200. Fax: (310)317-4206. E-mail: wholelifex @aol.com. Website: www.wholelifetimes.com. **Contact:** Kerri Hikida, associate editor. Monthly tabloid covering the holistic lifestyle. Estab. 1979. Circ. 58,000. Pays within 30-60 days after publication. Byline given. Buys first North American serial rights. Accepts queries by mail, e-mail, fax. Sample copy for $3. Writer's guidelines for #10 SASE.
Nonfiction: Book excerpts, exposé, how-to, inspirational, interview/profile, travel, health, healing, spiritual, food, leading-edge information, revelant celebrity profiles. Special issues: Healing Arts, Food & Nutrition, Spirituality, New Beginnings, Relationships, Longevity, Arts/Cultures Travel, Vitamins and Supplements, Women's Issues, Sexuality, Science & Metaphysics, Environment/Simple Living. **Buys 45 mss/year.** Query with published clips or send complete ms. **Pays 5-10¢/word for feature stories only.**
Reprints: Send typed ms with rights for sale noted and information about when and where the material previously appeared. Pays 50% of amount paid for an original article.

Columns/Departments: Healing, Parenting, Finance, Food, Personal Growth, Relationships, Humor, Travel, Politics, Sexuality, Spirituality and Psychology. Length: 750-1,200 words.
Tips: "Queries should show an awareness of current topics of interest in our subject area. We welcome investigative reporting and are happy to see queries that address topics in a political context. We are especially looking for articles on health and nutrition."

AUTOMOTIVE & MOTORCYCLE

Publications in this section detail the maintenance, operation, performance, racing and judging of automobiles and recreational vehicles. Publications that treat vehicles as means of shelter instead of as a hobby or sport are classified in the Travel, Camping & Trailer category. Journals for service station operators and auto and motorcycle dealers are located in the Trade Auto & Truck section.

$ $ AMERICAN IRON MAGAZINE, TAM Communications Inc., 1010 Summer St., Stamford CT 06905. (203)425-8777. Fax: (203)425-8775. **Contact:** Chris Maida, editor. **80% freelance written.** Family-oriented magazine publishing 13 issues/year covering Harley-Davidson and other US brands with a definite emphasis on Harleys. Circ. 80,000. Pays on publication. Not copyrighted. Publishes ms an average of 6 months after acceptance. Byline given. Responds in 3 months to queries. Sample copy for $5.
Nonfiction: "Clean and non-offensive. Stories include bike features, touring stories, how-to tech stories with step-by-step photos, historical pieces, profiles, events, opinion and various topics of interest to the people who ride Harley-Davidsons." No fiction. **Buys 60 mss/year. Pays $250 for touring articles with slides to first-time writers.**
Photos: Send SASE for return of photos. Reviews color slides or large transparencies.
Tips: "We're not looking for stories about the top ten biker bars or do-it-yourself tattoos. We're looking for articles about motorcycling, the people and the machines. If you understand the Harley mystique and can write well, you've got a good chance of being published."

N $ AMERICAN MOTORCYCLIST, American Motorcyclist Association, 13515 Yarmouth Dr., Pickerington OH 43147. (614)856-1900. Fax: (614)856-1920. E-mail: gharrison@ama-cycle.org. Website: www.ama-cycle.org. Managing Editor: Bill Wood. **Contact:** Greg Harrison, executive editor. **10% freelance written.** Monthly magazine for "enthusiastic motorcyclists, investing considerable time and money in the sport. We emphasize the motorcyclist, not the vehicle." Estab. 1947. Circ. 260,000. Pays on publication. Byline given. Buys first North American serial rights. Editorial lead time 3 months. Submit seasonal material 4 months in advance. Accepts queries by mail, e-mail. Responds in 5 weeks to queries; 6 weeks to mss. Sample copy for $1.25. Writer's guidelines free.
Nonfiction: Interview/profile (with interesting personalities in the world of motorcycling), personal experience, travel. **Buys 8 mss/year.** Query with or without published clips or send complete ms. Length: 1,000-2,500 words. **Pays minimum $8/published column inch.**
Photos: Send photos with submission. Reviews transparencies, prints. Buys one-time rights. Pays $50/photo minimum. Captions, identification of subjects required.
Tips: "Our major category of freelance stories concerns motorcycling trips to interesting North American destinations. Prefers stories of a timeless nature."

$ AMERICAN WOMAN ROAD & TRAVEL, 2424 Coolidge Rd., Suite 203, Troy MI 48084. (248)614-0017. Fax: (248)614-8929. E-mail: courtney@awroadandtravel.com. Website: www.awroadandtravel.com. **Contact:** Rachel L. Miller, associate editor. **80% freelance written.** Bimonthly magazine that is automotive/adventure lifestyle and service-oriented for women. Estab. 1988. Circ. online only. Pays on publication. Publishes ms an average of 3 months after acceptance. Byline given. Buys first, second serial (reprint) rights, makes work-for-hire assignments. Submit seasonal material 4 months in advance. Accepts queries by mail, e-mail. Responds in 3 months to queries. Writer's guidelines online.
Nonfiction: How-to, humor, inspirational, interview/profile, new product, photo feature, lifestyle; travel, auto and business content for upscale professional women. **Buys 30 mss/year.** Send complete ms. Length: 50-1,500 words. **Pay depends on quantity, quality and content. Byline-$100.**
Reprints: Send photocopy and information about when and where the material previously appeared.
Photos: Accepts photos via e-mail saved in jpg or gif formats saved in Word. Photos must be 3×5 or smaller. Send photos with submission. Reviews contact sheets, Kodachrome 64. Buys all rights. Captions, identification of subjects, model releases required.
Fillers: Anecdotes, facts, gags to be illustrated by cartoonist, newsbreaks, short humor. **Buys 12/year.** Length: 25-100 words. **Pays negotiable.**
Tips: "The AW Road & Travel reader is typically career and/or family oriented, independent, and adventurous. She demands literate, entertaining and useful information from a magazine enabling her to make educated buying decisions. It helps if the writer is into cars and trucks. We are a lifestyle type of publication more than a technical magazine. Positive attitudes wanted."

$ $ AUTO RESTORER, Fancy Publications, Inc., P.O. Box 6050, Mission Viejo CA 92690-6050. (949)855-8822, ext. 412. Fax: (949)855-3045. E-mail: tkade@fancypubs.com. **Contact:** Ted Kade, editor. **85% freelance written.** Monthly magazine covering auto restoration. "Our readers own old cars and they work on them. We help our readers by providing as much practical, how-to information as we can about restoration and old cars." Estab. 1989. Pays on publication. Publishes ms an average of 3 months after acceptance. Buys first North American serial, one-time rights. Submit seasonal material 4 months in advance. Accepts queries by mail, e-mail, fax. Responds in 2 months to queries. Sample copy for $5.50. Writer's guidelines free.

Nonfiction: How-to (auto restoration), new product, photo feature, technical, product evaluation. **Buys 60 mss/year.** Query with or without published clips. Length: 200-2,500 words. **Pays $150/published page, including photos and illustrations.**

Photos: Technical drawings that illustrate articles in black ink are welcome. Send photos with submission. Reviews contact sheets, transparencies, 5×7 prints. Offers no additional payment for photos accepted with ms.

Tips: "Query first. Interview the owner of a restored car. Present advice to others on how to do a similar restoration. Seek advice from experts. Go light on history and non-specific details. Make it something that the magazine regularly uses. Do automotive how-tos."

$ BACKROADS, The Local Source for Motorcycle Enthusiasts, Backroads Inc., P.O. Box 317, Branchville NJ 07826. (973)948-4176. Fax: (973)948-0823. E-mail: editor@backroadsusa.com. Website: www.backroadsusa.com. Managing Editor: Shira Kamil. **Contact:** Brian Rathjen, editor/publisher. **50% freelance written.** Monthly tabloid covering motorcycle touring. "*Backroads* is a motorcycle tour magazine geared toward getting motorcyclists on the road and traveling. We provide interesting destinations, unique roadside attractions and eateries plus Rip & Ride Route Sheets. We cater to all brands. If you really ride, you need *Backroads*." Estab. 1995. Circ. 40,000. Pays on publication. Publishes ms an average of 3 months after acceptance. Byline given. Buys one-time rights. Editorial lead time 1 month. Submit seasonal material 3 months in advance. Accepts queries by mail, e-mail, fax. Responds in 3 weeks to queries. Sample copy and writer's guidelines free.

Nonfiction: Shira Kamil, editor/publisher. Essays (motorcycle/touring), how-to, humor, new product, opinion, personal experience, technical, travel. "No long diatribes on 'how I got into motorcycles.' " **Buys 2-4 mss/year.** Query. Length: 500-3,000 words. **Pays 5¢/word minimum for assigned articles; 2¢/word minimum for unsolicited articles.** Pays writers contributor copies or other premiums for short pieces on event recaps.

Photos: Send photos with submission. Reviews contact sheets. Offers no additional payment for photos accepted with ms.

Columns/Departments: We're Outta Here (weekend destinations), 500-1,000 words; Great All American Diner Run (good eateries with great location), 300-800 words; Thoughts from the Road (personal opinion/insights), 250-500 words; Mysterious America (unique and obscure sights), 300-800 words; Big City Getaway (day trips), 500-1,000 words. **Buys 20-24 mss/year.** Query. **Pays 2¢/word-$50/article.**

Fiction: Adventure, humorous. **Buys 2-4 mss/year.** Query. Length: 500-1,500 words. **Pays 2-4¢/word.**

Fillers: Facts, newsbreaks. Length: 100-250 words. **Pays $0 for fillers.**

Tips: "We prefer destination-oriented articles in a light, layman's format, with photos (not transparencies). Stay away from any name-dropping and first-person references."

$ $ CANADIAN BIKER MAGAZINE, P.O. Box 4122, Victoria British Columbia V8X 3X4, Canada. (250)384-0333. Fax: (250)384-1832. E-mail: edit@canadianbiker.com. Website: canadianbiker.com. **Contact:** John Campbell, editor. **65% freelance written.** Magazine covering motorcycling. "A family-oriented motorcycle magazine whose purpose is to unite Canadian motorcyclists from coast to coast through the dissemination of information in a non-biased, open forum. The magazine reports on new product, events, touring, racing, vintage and custom motorcycling as well as new industry information." Estab. 1980. Circ. 20,000. Publishes ms an average of 1 year after acceptance. Byline given. Buys first rights. Editorial lead time 3 months. Accepts queries by mail, e-mail, fax, phone. Responds in 6 weeks to queries; 6 months to mss. Sample copy for $5 or online. Writer's guidelines free.

Nonfiction: All nonfiction must include photos and/or illustrations. General interest, historical/nostalgic, how-to, interview/profile (Canadian personalities preferred), new product, technical, travel. **Buys 12 mss/year.** Query with or without published clips or send complete ms. Length: 500-1,500 words. **Pays $100-200 for assigned articles; $80-150 for unsolicited articles.**

Photos: State availability of or send photos with submission. Reviews 4×4 transparencies, 3×5 prints. Buys one-time rights. Negotiates payment individually. Captions, identification of subjects, model releases required.

Tips: "We're looking for more racing features, rider profiles, custom sport bikes, quality touring stories, 'extreme' riding articles. Contact editor first before writing anything. Have original ideas, an ability to write from an authoritative point of view, and an ability to supply quality photos to accompany text. Writers should be involved in the motorcycle industry and be intimately familiar with some aspect of the industry which would be of interest to readers. Observations of the industry should be current, timely and informative."

N $ $ $ $ CAR STEREO REVIEW'S MOBILE ENTERTAINMENT, Technology In Motion, Hachette Filipacchi Magazines, 1633 Broadway, 45th Floor, New York NY 10019. (212)767-6000. Fax: (212)333-2434. E-mail: MobileEnt1@aol.com. **Contact:** Mike Mettler, editor-in-chief. **45% freelance written.** Published 6 times/year. "*Mobile Entertainment* is geared toward the mobile-electronics enthusiast, encompassing such things as mobile video, product test reports, installation techniques, new technologies such as MP3 and navigation, and music." Estab. 1987. Circ.

140,000. **Pays on acceptance.** Publishes ms an average of 3 months after acceptance. Byline given. Offers 25% kill fee. Buys first North American serial rights. Editorial lead time 4 months. Accepts queries by mail, e-mail, fax. Responds in 6 weeks to queries; 2 months to mss. Sample copy and writers guidelines free.

Nonfiction: "As we are a highly specialized publication, we won't look at anything non-specific to our audience's needs." How-to (installation techniques), interview/profile, new product, technical. **Buys 10-20 mss/year.** Query with published clips. Length: 200-3,000 words. **Pays $40-5,000 for assigned articles; $40-2,000 for unsolicited articles.** Sometimes pays expenses of writers on assignment.

Photos: State availability with submission. Reviews contact sheets, negatives, transparencies. Buys one-time rights. Negotiates payment individually. Identification of subjects, model releases required.

Columns/Departments: The Superhighway (mobile-electronics news and unique car-stereo applications—in a plane, boat, golf cart, tractor, etc.), 200 words. **Buys 6-10 mss/year.** Query with published clips. **Pays $75-100.**

Tips: "As we are experts in our field, and looked to as being the 'authority,' writers must have some knowledge of electronics, car stereo applications, and theory, especially in relation to the car environment. Our readers are not green-horns, and expect expert opinions. Be aware of the differences between mobile and portable electronics technology versus home entertainment."

$ $CC MOTORCYCLE NEWSMAGAZINE, Motomag Corp., P.O. Box 808, Nyack NY 10960. (845)353-MOTO. Fax: (845)353-5240. E-mail: info@motorcyclenewsmagazine.cc. Website: www.motorcyclenewsmagazine.cc. **Contact:** Mark Kalan, publisher/editor. **50% freelance written.** Monthly magazine featuring "positive coverage of motorcycling in America—riding, travel, racing and tech." Estab. 1989. Circ. 60,000. Pays on publication. Publishes ms an average of 2 months after acceptance. Byline given. Buys one-time rights. Editorial lead time 3 months. Submit seasonal material 3 months in advance. Accepts simultaneous submissions. Responds in 1 month to queries. Sample copy for $3. Writer's guidelines for #10 SASE.

Nonfiction: Essays, general interest, historical/nostalgic, how-to, humor, inspirational, interview/profile, new product, personal experience, photo feature, technical, travel. Special issues: Daytona Beach Blocktober Fest; Summer touring stories—travel. **Buys 12 mss/year.** Query with published clips. Length: 1,000-2,000 words. **Pays $50-250 for assigned articles; $25-125 for unsolicited articles.** Pays expenses of writers on assignment.

Reprints: Send tearsheet or photocopy. No payment.

Photos: State availability with submission. Reviews contact sheets, transparencies. Buys one-time rights. Negotiates payment individually. Captions, identification of subjects, model releases required.

Columns/Departments: Query with published clips.

Fiction: All fiction must be motorcycle related. Adventure, fantasy, historical, romance, slice-of-life vignettes. Query with published clips. Length: 1,500-2,500 words. **Pays $50-250.**

Poetry: Must be motorcycle related. Avant-garde, free verse, haiku, light verse, traditional. **Buys 6 poems/year.** Submit maximum 12 poems. Length: Length open. **Pays $10-50.**

Fillers: Anecdotes, cartoons. **Buys 12/year.** Length: 100-200 words. **Pays $10-50.**

Tips: "Ride a motorcycle and be able to construct a readable sentence!"

N $ $ CRUISING RIDER MAGAZINE, Running in Style, P.O. Box 1943, Sedona AZ 86336. (520)232-9293. E-mail: joshua@verdenet.com. **Contact:** Joshua Placa, editor. **50% freelance written.** Bimonthly coffee table magazine with national distribution for professional, affluent cruiser-style motorcycle enthusiasts. Crosses all brand lines in coverage. Query for events. Freestyle, technical, off-beat and humorous or travel (bike included) features. Estab. 1996. Circ. 200,000. Pays on publication. Publishes ms an average of 4 months after acceptance. Byline given. Buys all rights. Editorial lead time 2 months. Submit seasonal material 6 months in advance. Accepts simultaneous submissions. Responds as soon as possible to queries.

Nonfiction: General interest, how-to, humor, interview/profile, new product, personal experience, photo feature, technical, travel. **Buys 20-30 mss/year.** Query with published clips. Length: 500-2,500 words. **Pays $150-750.** Sometimes pays expenses of writers on assignment.

Photos: Send photos with submission. Buys all rights. Negotiates payment individually.

Columns/Departments: Street Scene (industry, insurance, government and legal news); Fashion (motor clothes/pictorial), 1,000 words; Cruise Control (riding safety), 1,000 words. **Buys some mss/year.** Query with published clips. **Pays $50-300.**

Fillers: Anecdotes, facts, news. Length: 50-200 words. **Pays $50-150.**

N $ $EASYRIDERS MAGAZINE, Paisano Publications, Inc., P.O. Box 3000, Agoura Hills CA 91301. (818)889-8740. Editor: Keith R. Ball, Managing Editor: Lisa Pedicini. **Contact:** Nancy Trier, executive assistant. **50% freelance written.** Monthly magazine covering motorcycle events and articles for Harley-Davidson type audience. Estab. 1971. Pays on publication. Byline given. Buys first rights. Editorial lead time 3 months. Submit seasonal material 3 month in advance. Writer's guidelines free.

Nonfiction: Book excerpts, essays, exposé, general interest, historical/nostalgic, how-to, humor, inspirational, interview/profile, new product, opinion, personal experience, photo feature, technical, travel. Query. Length: 1,000-3,000 words. **Pays 25¢/word.** Sometimes pays expenses of writers on assignment.

Photos: Send photos with submission. Buys all rights. Captions, identification of subjects, model releases required.

Fiction: Adventure, erotica, experimental, fantasy, historical, humorous, suspense, western, motorcycle stories.

N: $ $FOUR WHEELER MAGAZINE, 6420 Wilshire Blvd., 10th Floor, Los Angeles CA 90048-5502. (323)782-2380. Fax: (323)782-2494. Website: www.fourwheeler.com. **Contact:** Jon Thompson, editor. **20% freelance written.** Works with a small number of new/unpublished writers each year. Monthly magazine covering four-wheel-drive vehicles, back-country driving, competition and travel adventure. Estab. 1963. Circ. 355,466. Pays on publication. Publishes ms an average of 4 months after acceptance. Buys all rights. Submit seasonal material 4 months in advance. Accepts queries by mail.

Nonfiction: 4WD competition and travel/adventure articles, technical, how-tos, and vehicle features about unique four-wheel drives. "We like the adventure stories that bring four wheeling to life in word and photo: mud-running deserted logging roads, exploring remote, isolated trails or hunting/fishing where the 4x4 is a necessity for success." Query with photos. Length: 1,200-2,000 words; average 4-5 pages when published. **Pays $200-300/feature vehicles; $350-600/ travel and adventure; $100-800/technical articles.**

Photos: Requires professional quality color slides and b&w prints for every article. Prefers Kodachrome 64 or Fujichrome 50 in 35mm or 2¼ formats. "Action shots a must for all vehicle features and travel articles." Captions required.

Tips: "Show us you know how to use a camera as well as the written word. The easiest way for a new writer/ photographer to break into our magazine is to read several issues of the magazine, then query with a short vehicle feature that will show his or her potential as a creative writer/photographer."

N: $ $KIT CAR ILLUSTRATED, The leading magazine for component car enthusiasts, Primedia Ent. Group, 774 S. Placentia Ave., Placentia CA 92870. (714)937-2550. E-mail: mikeb@mcmullenargus.com. Website: www.gr8ride.com. **Contact:** Mike Blake, editor. **35% freelance written.** Bimonthly magazine covering kit cars and component street rods. Estab. 1984. Circ. 35,000. Pays on publication. Publishes ms an average of 4 months after acceptance. Byline given. Offers $100 kill fee. Buys electronic, all rights. Editorial lead time 4 months. Submit seasonal material 4 months in advance. Accepts queries by mail, e-mail, phone. Accepts simultaneous submissions. Responds in 3 weeks to queries; 1 month to mss.

Nonfiction: General interest, how-to, personal experience, kit car features with photos—mandatory; auto tech tips, build-ups and kit and component car construction pieces. No biographical pieces, company profiles, non-kit car oriented items. **Buys 25-30 mss/year.** Query. Length: 1,000-2,000 words. **Pays $250-750 for assigned articles; $100-500 for unsolicited articles.** Sometimes pays expenses of writers on assignment.

Photos: Send photos with submission. Reviews 35mm transparencies, 4×5 prints. Buys all rights. Offers no additional payment for photos accepted with ms. Captions, identification of subjects, model releases required.

Fillers: Facts. Length: 500-1,000 words. **Pays $100-150.**

Tips: "Submit great art, photos and illustrations, do the history on the car, the manufacturers, the power and aftermarket items and tie the owner and owner's personality into the article."

N: $ $ $MOTOR TREND, Petersen Publishing Co., 6420 Wilshire Blvd., Los Angeles CA 90048. (323)782-2220. Fax: (323)782-2355. E-mail: stonem@emapusa.com. Website: www.motortrend.com. **Contact:** C. Van Tune, editor. **5-10% freelance written.** Only works with published/established writers. Monthly magazine for automotive enthusiasts and general interest consumers. Circ. 1,250,000. Publishes ms an average of 3 months after acceptance. Buys all rights. Accepts queries by mail. Responds in 1 month to queries.

Nonfiction: "Automotive and related subjects that have national appeal. Emphasis on domestic and imported cars, road tests, driving impressions, auto classics, auto, travel, racing, and high-performance features for the enthusiast. Packed with facts. Freelancers should confine queries to photo-illustrated exotic drives and other feature material; road tests and related activity are handled inhouse. Fact-filled query suggested for all freelancers."

Photos: Buys photos of prototype cars and assorted automotive matter. Pays $25-500 for transparencies.

Columns/Departments: Car care (query Matt Stone, senior editor).

$ $MOTORCYCLE TOUR & CRUISER, TAM Communications, 1010 Summer St., Stamford CT 06905. (203)425-8777. Fax: (203)425-8775. E-mail: mtcmagazine@earthlink.net. **Contact:** Laura Brengelman, editor. **70% freelance written.** Monthly magazine covering motorcycling—tour and travel. Estab. 1993. Circ. 30,000. Pays on publication. Publishes ms an average of 6 months after acceptance. Byline given. Editorial lead time 4 months. Submit seasonal material 6 months in advance. Accepts queries by mail, fax. Accepts simultaneous submissions. Writer's guidelines free.

Nonfiction: How-to (motorcycle, travel, camping), interview/profile (motorcycle related), new product, photo feature (motorcycle events or gathering places with minimum of 1,000 words text), travel. No fiction. **Buys 100 mss/year.** Query with or without published clips or send complete ms. Length: 1,000-3,500 words. **Pays $150-350.**

Photos: Send photos with submission (slides preferred, prints accepted, b&w contact sheets for how-to). Buys one-time rights. Offers no additional payment for photos accepted with ms. Captions required.

Columns/Departments: Reviews (products, media, all motorcycle related), 300-750 words plus one or more photos. Query with published clips or send complete ms. **Pays $50-150.**

Fillers: Facts.

$ $OUTLAW BIKER, Outlaw Biker Enterprises, Inc., 5 Marine View Plaza, Suite 207, Hoboken NJ 07030. (201)653-2700. Fax: (201)653-7892. E-mail: editor@outlawbiker.com. Website: www.outlawbiker.com. **Contact:** Chris Miller, editor. **50% freelance written.** Magazine published 6 times/year covering bikers and their lifestyle. "All writers must be insiders of biker lifestyle. Features include coverage of biker events, profiles and humor." Estab. 1983. Circ.

150,000. Pays on publication. Publishes ms an average of 3 months after acceptance. Byline given. Buys first rights. Editorial lead time 3 months. Submit seasonal material 5 months in advance. Accepts queries by mail, e-mail, fax. Accepts simultaneous submissions. Responds in 2 weeks to queries; 2 months to mss. Sample copy for $5.98. Writer's guidelines for #10 SASE.

Nonfiction: Historical/nostalgic, humor, new product, personal experience, photo feature, travel. Special issues: Daytona Special, Sturgis Special (annual bike runs). No first time experiences—our readers already know. **Buys 10-12 mss/ year.** Send complete ms. Length: 100-1,000 words. **Pays $50-200.**

Photos: Send photos with submission. Reviews transparencies, prints. Buys one-time rights. Offers $0-10/photo. Captions, identification of subjects, model releases required.

Columns/Departments: Buys 10-12 mss/year. Send complete ms. **Pays $25-50.**

Fiction: Adventure, erotica, fantasy, historical,, humorous, romance, science fiction, slice-of-life vignettes, suspense. No racism. **Buys 10-12 mss/year.** Send complete ms. Length: 500-2,500 words. **Pays $50-200.**

Poetry: Avant-garde, free verse, haiku, light verse, traditional. **Buys 10-12 poems/year.** Submit maximum 12 poems. Length: 2-1,000 lines. **Pays $10-25.**

Fillers: Anecdotes, facts, gags to be illustrated by cartoonist, newsbreaks, short humor. **Buys 10-12/year.** Length: 500-2,000 words. **Pays $10-25.**

▣ The online magazine of *Outlaw Biker* carries original content not found in the print edition. Contact: Chris Miller.

Tips: "Writers must be insiders of the biker lifestyle. Manuscripts with accompanying photographs as art are given higher priority."

$ $ RIDER MAGAZINE, Ehlert Publishing Group, 2575 Vista Del Mar Dr., Ventura CA 93001. **Contact:** Mark Tuttle, editor. **60% freelance written.** Monthly magazine covering motorcycling. "*Rider* serves the all-brand motorcycle lifestyle/enthusiast with a slant toward travel and touring." Estab. 1974. Circ. 107,000. Pays on publication. Publishes ms an average of 6-12 months after acceptance. Byline given. Offers 25% kill fee. Buys first North American serial, electronic rights. Editorial lead time 4 months. Submit seasonal material 6 months in advance. Accepts queries by mail. Responds in 2 months to queries. Sample copy for $2.95. Writer's guidelines for #10 SASE.

〇┐ "The articles we do buy often share the following characteristics: 1. The writer queried us in advance by regular mail (not by telephone or e-mail) to see if we needed or wanted the story. 2. The story was well written and of proper length. 3. The story had sharp, uncluttered photos taken with the proper film—*Rider* does not buy stories without photos."

Nonfiction: General interest, historical/nostalgic, how-to (re: motorcycling), humor, interview/profile, personal experience, travel. Does not want to see "fiction or articles on 'How I Began Motorcycling.' " **Buys 40-50 mss/year.** Query. Length: 750-2,000 words. **Pays $150-750.**

Photos: Send photos with submission. Reviews contact sheets, transparencies, 5×7 (b&w only) prints. Buys one-time and electronic rights. Offers no additional payment for photos accepted with ms. Captions required.

Columns/Departments: Favorite Rides (short trip), 850-1,100 words. **Buys 12 mss/year.** Query. **Pays $150-750.**

Tips: "We rarely accept manuscripts without photos (slides or b&w prints). Query first. Follow guidelines available on request. We are most open to feature stories (must include excellent photography) and material for 'Rides, Rallies and Clubs.' Include information on routes, local attractions, restaurants and scenery in favorite ride submissions."

ℕ $ $ TRUCK TREND, The SUV & Pickup Authority, Emap USA, 6420 Wilshire Blvd., Los Angeles CA 90048-5515. (323)782-2220. Fax: (323)782-2355. E-mail: trucktrend@emapusa.com. Website: www.trucktrend.com. Managing Editor: Jacqueline Manfredi. **Contact:** Mark Williams, editor. **60% freelance written.** Bimonthly magazine covering trucks, SUVs, minivans, vans and travel. "*Truck Trend* readers want to know about what's new in the world of sport-utilities, pickups and vans. What to buy, how to fix up and where to go." Estab. 1998. Circ. 160,000. Pays on publication. Publishes ms an average of 3 months after acceptance. Byline given. Buys all rights. Editorial lead time 5 months. Submit seasonal material 6 months in advance. Accepts queries by mail. Sample copy for #10 SASE.

Nonfiction: How-to, travel. Special issues: Towing; Hot Rod Truck; ½ Ton Pickup; Diesel. No personal experience, humor or religious. **Buys 12 mss/year.** Query. Length: 500-1,800 words. **Pays $150-300/page.** Sometimes pays expenses of writers on assignment.

Photos: Send photos with submission. Reviews transparencies. Buys all rights. Offers no additional payment for photos accepted with ms. Captions, identification of subjects, model releases required.

▣ The online magazine carries original content not found in the print edition.

Tips: "Know the subject/audience. Start by using a previous story as a template. Call editor for advice after flushing story out. Understand the editor is looking to freelancers to make life easier."

ℕ $ $ $ VELOCITY MAGAZINE, Journal of the Honda Acura Club, Honda Acura Club International, 4324 Promenade Way, Suite 109, Marina Del Rey CA 90292. (310)822-6163. Fax: (310)822-5030. E-mail: staff@hondaclub.com. Website: www.hondaclub.com. Managing Editor: Suzanne Peauralto. **Contact:** Peter Frey, editor. **50% freelance written.** Quarterly magazine covering Honda and Acura autos and products for automotive general interest and enthusiasts. Estab. 1999. Circ. 50,000. Pays on publication. Publishes ms an average of 2 months after acceptance. Byline given. Offers 50% kill fee. Buys all rights. Editorial lead time 2 months. Submit seasonal material 2 months in advance. Accepts queries by mail, fax. Sample copy for $3. Writer's guidelines free.

Nonfiction: General interest, historical/nostalgic, new product, photo feature, automotive. **Buys 50 mss/year.** Query with published clips. Length: 400-1,000 words. **Pays 50¢/word.** Sometimes pays expenses of writers on assignment.
Reprints: Accepts previously published submissions.
Photos: Send photos with submission. Buys all rights. Negotiates payment individually. Captions, identification of subjects required.

AVIATION

Professional and private pilots and aviation enthusiasts read the publications in this section. Editors want material for audiences knowledgeable about commercial aviation. Magazines for passengers of commercial airlines are grouped in the Inflight category. Technical aviation and space journals and publications for airport operators, aircraft dealers and others in aviation businesses are listed under Aviation & Space in the Trade section.

N $ $ AIR LINE PILOT, The Magazine of Professional Flight Deck Crews, Air Line Pilots Association, 535 Herndon Parkway, P.O. Box 1169, Herndon VA 20172. (703)481-4460. Fax: (703)689-4370. E-mail: magazine@alpa .org. Website: www.alpa.org. **Contact:** Gary DiNunno, editor. **10% freelance written.** Prefers to work with published/ established writers; works with a small number of new/unpublished writers each year. Monthly magazine for airline pilots covering commercial aviation industry information—economics, avionics, equipment, systems, safety—that affects a pilot's life in professional sense. Also includes information about management/labor relations trends, contract negotiations, etc. Estab. 1931. Circ. 95,000. **Pays on acceptance.** Publishes ms an average of 6 months after acceptance. Offers 50% kill fee. Buys all rights except book rights. Submit seasonal material 6 months in advance. Responds in 2 months to queries. Sample copy for $2. Writer's guidelines for #10 SASE.
Nonfiction: Humor, inspirational, photo feature, technical. **Buys 20 mss/year.** Query with or without published clips or send complete ms and SASE. Length: 700-3,000 words. **Pays $100-600 for assigned articles; $50-600 for unsolicited articles.**
Reprints: Send photocopy of article or typed ms with rights for sale noted and information about when and where the material previously appeared. Pay varies.
Photos: "Our greatest need is for strikingly original cover photographs featuring ALPA flight deck crew members and their airlines in their operating environment." Send photos with submission. Reviews contact sheets, 35mm transparencies, 8×10 prints. Buys all rights for cover photos, one-time rights for inside color. Offers $10-35/b&w photo, $20-50 for color used inside and $400 for color used as cover. For cover photography, shoot vertical rather than horizontal. Identification of subjects required.
Tips: "For our feature section, we seek aviation industry information that affects the life of a professional airline pilot from a career standpoint. We also seek material that affects a pilot's life from a job security and work environment standpoint. Any airline pilot featured in an article must be an Air Line Pilot Association member in good standing. Our readers are very experienced and require a high level of technical accuracy in both written material and photographs."

$ [X] BALLOON LIFE, Balloon Life Magazine, Inc., 2336 47th Ave. SW, Seattle WA 98116-2331. (206)935-3649. Fax: (206)935-3326. E-mail: tom@balloonlife.com. Website: www.balloonlife.com. **Contact:** Tom Hamilton, editor-in-chief. **75% freelance written.** Monthly magazine covering sport of hot air ballooning. Estab. 1986. Circ. 4,000. Pays on publication. Byline given. Offers 50-100% kill fee. Buys non-exclusive all rights. Submit seasonal material 4 months in advance. Responds in 3 weeks to queries; 1 month to mss. Sample copy for 9×12 SAE with $2 postage. Writer's guidelines for #10 SASE.
Nonfiction: Book excerpts, general interest, how-to (flying hot air balloons, equipment techniques), interview/profile, new product, technical, events/rallies, safety seminars, balloon clubs/organizations, letters to the editor. **Buys 150 mss/ year.** Query with or without published clips or send complete ms. Length: 1,000-1,500 words. **Pays $50-75 for assigned articles; $25-50 for unsolicited articles.** Pays expenses of writers on assignment.
Reprints: Send tearsheet, photocopy or typed ms with rights for sale noted and information about when and where the material previously appeared. Pays 100% of amount paid for an original article or story.
Photos: Send photos with submission. Reviews transparencies, prints. Buys non-exclusive all rights. Offers $15/inside photos, $50/cover. Identification of subjects required.
Columns/Departments: Hangar Flying (real life flying experience that others can learn from), 800-1,500 words; Crew Quarters (devoted to some aspect of crewing), 900 words; Preflight (a news and information column), 100-500 words; pays $50. Logbook (recent balloon events—events that have taken place in last 3-4 months), 300-500 words; pays $20. **Buys 60 mss/year.** Send complete ms. **Pays $20-50.**
Fiction: Humorous. **Buys 3-5 mss/year.** Send complete ms. Length: 800-1,500 words. **Pays $50.**
Tips: "This magazine slants toward the technical side of ballooning. We are interested in articles that help to educate and provide safety information. Also stories with manufacturers, important individuals and/or of historic events and technological advances important to ballooning. The magazine attempts to present articles that show 'how-to' (fly, business opportunities, weather, equipment). Both our Feature Stories section and Logbook section are where most manuscripts are purchased."

$ CESSNA OWNER MAGAZINE, Jones Publishing, Inc., N7450 Aanstad Rd., P.O. Box 5000, Iola WI 54945. (715)445-5000. Fax: (715)445-4053. E-mail: editor@cessnaowner.org. Website: www.cessnaowner.org. **Contact:** John Kronschnabl, senior editor. **50% freelance written.** Monthly magazine covering Cessna single and twin-engine aircraft. "*Cessna Owner Magazine* is the official publication of the Cessna Owner Organization (C.O.O.). Therefore, our readers are Cessna aircraft owners, renters, pilots, and enthusiasts. Articles should deal with buying/selling, flying, maintaining, or modifying Cessnas. The purpose of our magazine is to promote safe, fun, and affordable flying." Estab. 1975. Circ. 6,000. Pays on publication. Publishes ms an average of 3 months after acceptance. Byline given. Buys first, one-time, second serial (reprint) rights, makes work-for-hire assignments. Editorial lead time 1 month. Submit seasonal material 3 months in advance. Accepts queries by mail, e-mail, fax, phone. Responds in 2 weeks to queries; 1 month to mss. Sample copy and writer's guidelines free or online.
Nonfiction: "We are always looking for articles about Cessna aircraft modifications. We also need articles on Cessna twin-engine aircraft. April, July, and October are always big issues for us, because we attend various airshows during these months and distribute free magazines. Feature articles on unusual, highly modified, or vintage Cessnas are especially welcome during these months. Good photos are also a must." Historical/nostalgic (of specific Cessna models), how-to (aircraft repairs and maintenance), new product, personal experience, photo feature, technical (aircraft engines and airframes). Special issues: Engines (maintenance, upgrades); Avionics (purchasing, new products). **Buys 24 mss/ year.** Query. Length: 1,500-3,500 words. **Pays 7-11¢/word.**
Reprints: Send typed ms with rights for sale noted and information about when and where the material previously appeared.
Photos: Send photos with submission. Reviews 3×5 and larger prints. Captions, identification of subjects required.
Tips: "Always submit a hard copy or ASCII formatted computer disk. Color photos mean a lot to us, and manuscripts stand a much better chance of being published when accompanied by photos. Freelancers can best get published by submitting articles on aircraft modifications, vintage planes, restorations, flight reports, twin-engine Cessnas, etc."

$ FLYER, N.W. Flyer, Inc., P.O. Box 39099, Lakewood WA 98439-0099. (253)471-9888. Fax: (253)471-9911. E-mail: kirk.gormley@flyer-online.com. Website: www.flyer-online.com. **Contact:** Kirk Gormley, editor. **30% freelance written.** Prefers to work with published/established writers. Biweekly tabloid covering general, regional, national and international aviation stories of interest to pilots, aircraft owners and aviation enthusiasts. Estab. 1949. Circ. 35,000. Pays 1 month after publication. Publishes ms an average of 3 months after acceptance. Byline given. Buys first North American serial, second serial (reprint) rights. Submit seasonal material 2 months in advance. Accepts queries by mail, e-mail, fax, phone. Responds in 2 months to queries. Sample copy for $3.50. Writer's guidelines for #10 SASE.
  O─ Break in by having "an aviation background, being up to date on current events, and being able to write. A 1,000-word story with good photos is the best way to see your name in print."
Nonfiction: "We stress news. A controversy over an airport, a first flight of a new design, storm or flood damage to an airport, a new business opening at your local airport—those are the sort of projects that may get a new writer onto our pages, if they arrive here soon after they happen. We are especially interested in reviews of aircraft." Personality pieces involving someone who is using his or her airplane in an unusual way, and stories about aviation safety are of interest. Query first on historical, nostalgic features and profiles/interviews. **Buys 100 mss/year.** Query with or without published clips or send complete ms. Length: 500-2,000 words. **Pays up to $10/printed column inch.** Sometimes pays expenses of writers on assignment.
Photos: Shoot clear, up-close photos, preferably color prints or slides. Send photos with submission. Pays $10/b&w photo and $50/cover photo 1 month after publication. Captions, identification of subjects required.
Tips: "The longer the story, the less likely it is to be accepted. If you are covering controversy, send us both sides of the story. Most of our features and news stories are assigned in response to a query."

$ $ PRIVATE PILOT, Y-Visionary, Inc., 265 S. Anita Dr., #120, Orange CA 92868. (714)939-9991 ext. 234. Fax: (714)939-9909. E-mail: bfedorko@earthlink.net. Website: www.privatepilotmag.com. **Contact:** Bill Fedorko, editoral director. **40% freelance written.** Monthly magazine covering general aviation. "*Private Pilot* is edited for owners and pilots of single and multi-engine aircraft." Estab. 1965. Circ. 85,000. Pays on publication. Publishes ms an average of 4 months after acceptance. Byline given. Offers 15% or $75 kill fee. Buys first North American serial rights. Editorial lead time 3 months. Submit seasonal material 6 months in advance. Accepts queries by mail, fax. Responds in 2 months to queries. Writer's guidelines for #10 SASE.
Nonfiction: General interest, historical/nostalgic, how-to, humor, inspirational, interview/profile, new product, opinion, personal experience, technical, travel, aircraft types. **Buys 12-15 mss/year.** Query. Length: 800-3,000 words. **Pays $350-650.** Sometimes pays expenses of writers on assignment.
Photos: State availability with submission. Reviews 35mm transparencies. Buys one-time rights. Negotiates payment individually. Captions, identification of subjects, model releases required.
Fiction: Adventure, historical, humorous, slice-of-life vignettes, All Aviation-Related. **Buys 12-15 mss/year.** Query. Length: 800-3,500 words. **Pays $300-600.**
  ▣ The online magazine carries original content not found in the print edition. Contact: Bill Fedorko, online editor.
Tips: "Send good queries. Readers are pilots who want to read about aircraft, places to go and ways to save money."

$ WOMAN PILOT, Aviatrix Publishing, Inc., P.O. Box 485, Arlington Heights IL 60006-0485. (847)797-0170. Fax: (847)797-0161. E-mail: womanpilot@womanpilot.com Website: www.womanpilot. **Contact:** Editor. **80% freelance written.** Bimonthly magazine covering women who fly all types of aircraft and careers in all areas of aviation. Personal profiles, historical articles and current aviation events. Estab. 1993. Circ. 6,000. Pays on publication. Publishes ms an average of 5 months after acceptance. Byline given. Buys first North American serial rights. Accepts queries by mail, e-mail, phone. Sample copy for $3. Writer's guidelines for #10 SASE or online.

O→ Break in with "interesting stories about women in aerospace with great photos."

Nonfiction: Book excerpts, historical/nostalgic, humor, interview/profile, new product, personal experience, photo feature. **Buys 35 mss/year.** Query with published clips or send complete ms. Length: 500-4,000 words. **Pays $20-55 for assigned articles; $20-40 for unsolicited articles.**

Reprints: Send tearsheet or typed ms with rights for sale noted and information about when and where the material previously appeared.

Photos: State availability of or send photos with submission. Buys one-time rights. Negotiates payment individually. Captions, identification of subjects, model releases required.

Fiction: Adventure, historical, humorous, slice-of-life vignettes. **Buys 4 mss/year.** Query with or without published clips. Length: 500-2,000 words. **Pays $20-35.**

Fillers: Cartoons. **Buys 6/year. Pays $10-20.**

■ The online magazine carries original content not found in the print edition and contains articles from back issues. Contact: Editor.

Tips: "If a writer is interested in writing articles from our leads, she/he should send writing samples and explanation of any aviation background. Include any writing background."

BUSINESS & FINANCE

Business publications give executives and consumers a range of information from local business news and trends to national overviews and laws that affect them. National and regional publications are listed below in separate categories. Magazines that have a technical slant are in the Trade section under Business Management, Finance or Management & Supervision categories.

National

$ $ $ BUSINESS ASSET, BUSINESS SENSE, SMART BUSINESS, YOUR BUSINESS, Baumer Financial Publishing, 820 W. Jackson Blvd., #450, Chicago IL 60607. (312)627-1020. Fax: (312)627-1105. E-mail: lterry@imagin epub.com. **Contact:** Lisa Terry, editor. **50% freelance written.** Quarterly magazine covering small business and entrepreneurs. Estab. 1998. Circ. *Business Asset* 25,000; *Business Sense* 85,000; *Smart Business* 60,000; *Your Business* 15,000. Pays on publication. Publishes ms an average of 4 months after acceptance. Byline given. Offers 33% kill fee. Buys first North American serial rights. Editorial lead time 6 months. Submit seasonal material 6 months in advance. Accepts queries by mail, e-mail, fax.

Nonfiction: How-to (finance, legal, technology, marketing, management, HR, insurance), small business profiles. No humor, personal experience, religious, opinion, book excerpts, travel. **Buys 10 mss/year.** Query with published clips. Length: 800-2,000 words. **Pays 50¢/word.**

Photos: State availability with submission. Buys one-time rights. Offers no additional payment for photos accepted with ms. Identification of subjects required.

Columns/Departments: Technology, Legal, Insurance, Marketing (for small business owners), 500-700 words. **Buys 5 mss/year.** Query with published clips. **Pays 50¢/word.**

$ $ $ $ BUSINESS 2.0 MAGAZINE, 5 Thomas Mellon Circle, Suite 305, San Francisco CA 94134. Fax: (415)656-8660. E-mail: jdaly@business2.com. Website: www.business2.com. Managing Editor: Judy Lewenthal. **Contact:** James Daly, editor-in-chief. Monthly magazine covering business in the Internet economy. Estab. 1998. Circ. 350,000. Pays on publication. Publishes ms an average of 3 months after acceptance. Byline given. Offers 20% kill fee. Buys all rights. Editorial lead time 2 months. Submit seasonal material 4 months in advance. Accepts queries by e-mail. Accepts simultaneous submissions. Sample copy free.

O→ Break in with fresh ideas on web-enabled business transformation—from the way companies are conceived and financed to how they develop markets and retain customers.

Nonfiction: Essays, exposé, new product, opinion, travel, new business ideas for the Internet. **Buys 40-50 mss/year.** Query with published clips. Length: 150-3,000 words. **Pays $1/word.** Pays expenses of writers on assignment.

■ The online magazine carries original content not found in the print edition. Contact: Ed Homicit, online editor.

⊠ $ $ DOLLARS AND SENSE, What's Left in Economics, Economic Affairs Bureau, 740 Cambridge St., Cambridge MA 02141-1401. (617)876-2434. Fax: (617)876-0008. E-mail: dollars@dollarsandsense.org. Website: www.dollarsandsense.org. **Contact:** Tami J. Friedman or Alejàndro Reuss, co-editors. **10% freelance written.** Bimonthly magazine covering economics, environmental and social justice. "We explain the workings of the U.S. and international economics, and provide leftist perspectives on current economic affairs. Our audience is a mix of activists, organizers, academics, liberals, unionists and other socially concerned people." Estab. 1974. Circ. 8,000. Pays on publication. Publishes ms an average of 4 months after acceptance. Byline given. Buys all rights. Editorial lead time 3 months. Submit seasonal material 2 months in advance. Accepts queries by mail, e-mail, fax, phone. Sample copy for $5 or online. Writer's guidelines online.

Nonfiction: Exposé, political economics. **Buys 6 mss/year.** Query with published clips. Length: 700-2,500 words. **Pays $0-200.** Sometimes pays expenses of writers on assignment.

Photos: State availability with submission. Buys one-time rights. Negotiates payment individually. Captions, identification of subjects required.

Tips: "Be familiar with our magazine and the types of communities interested in reading us. *Dollars and Sense* is a progressive economics magazine that explains in a popular way both the workings of the economy and struggles to change it. Articles may be on the environment, the World Bank, community organizing, urban conflict, inflation, unemployment, union reform, welfare, changes in government regulation—a broad range of topics that have an economic theme. Find samples of our latest issue on our homepage."

$ $ ENTREPRENEUR MAGAZINE, 2445 McCabe Way, Irvine CA 92614. (949)261-2325. Fax: (949)261-0234. E-mail: entmag@entrepreneur.com. Website: www.entrepreneur.com. **Contact:** Peggy Reeves Bennett, articles editor. **60% freelance written.** *Entrepreneur* readers already run their own businesses. They have been in business for several years and are seeking innovative methods and strategies to improve their business operations. They are also interested in new business ideas and opportunities, as well as current issues that affect their companies. **Pays on acceptance.** Publishes ms an average of 5 months after acceptance. Byline given. Buys first international rights. Submit seasonal material 6 months in advance. Accepts queries by mail, e-mail, fax. Responds in 3 months to queries. Sample copy for $7.20 from Order Department or online. Writer's guidelines for #10 SASE or by e-mail.

• *Entrepreneur* publishes the bimonthly *Entrepreneur International* which covers the latest in U.S. trends and franchising for an international audience. (This is not written for a U.S. audience.) They encourage writers with expertise in this area to please query with ideas. Sample copy $6.50 from Order Department.

Nonfiction: Columns not open to freelancers. How-to (information on running a business, dealing with the psychological aspects of running a business, profiles of unique entrprenuers), Current News/Trends (and their effect on small business). **Buys 10-20 mss/year.** Query with published clips. Length: 2000 words. **Payment varies.**

Photos: "We use color transparencies to illustrate articles. Please state availability with query." State availability with submission. Reviews standard color transparencies. Buys one-time rights.

Tips: "Read several issues of the magazine!Study the feature articles versus the columns. Probably 75 percent of our freelance rejections are for article ideas covered in one of our regular columns. Go beyond the typical, flat 'business magazine query'—how to write a press release, how to negotiate with vendors, etc.—and instead investigate a current trend and develop a story on how that trend affects small business. In your query, mention companies you'd like to use to illustrate examples and sources who will provide expertise on the topic."

$ $ ▣ ENTREPRENEUR'S BIZSTARTUPS.COM, Entrepreneur Media, Inc., 2445 McCabe Way, Irvine CA 92614. (949)261-2083. Fax: (949)755-0234. E-mail: bsumag@entrepreneur.com. Website: www.bizstartups.com. **Contact:** Karen E. Spaeder, managing editor. **10% freelance written.** Monthly online magazine for young entrepreneurs (age 23 to 35). We target tech-savvy, upscale and educated readers who are preparing to start a business within the next year or have started a business within the past 2 years. Articles cover ideas for hot businesses to start; how-to advice to help new entrepreneurs run and grow their businesses; cutting-edge technology, management and marketing trends; motivational topics and more. Estab. 1989. Circ. 250,000. **Pays on acceptance.** Byline given. Offers 20% kill fee. Buys first time international rights. Submit seasonal material 6 months in advance. Accepts queries by mail, e-mail. Responds in 3 months to queries. Writer's guidelines for #10 SASE.

O— Break in by "writing like you're 25, even if you're not."

Nonfiction: "Our readers don't necessarily have tons of money, but they make up for it in attitude, energy and determination. They're seeking ideas for hot businesses to start; how-to advice to help them run and grow their businesses; cutting-edge articles to keep them on top of the latest business trends; and motivational articles to get (and keep) them psyched up. No matter what your topic, articles should be packed with real-life examples of exciting young entrepreneurs doing things in new and different ways, plus plenty of pull-outs, sidebars and tips that can be presented in an eye-catching style. Types of features we are seeking include: Psychological (staying motivated, sparking creativity, handling stress, overcoming fear, etc.); profiles of successful young entrepreneurs with original, creative, outrageous ideas and strategies others can learn from; operating articles (how-to advice for running a business, such as finding financing, choosing a partner, marketing on a shoestring, etc.); issues (examination of how a current issue affects young entrepreneurs); industry round-ups (articles covering a particular industry and highlighting several young entrepreneurs in that industry, for example, gourmet food entrepreneurs, cigar entrepreneurs, specialty travel entrepreneurs); tech. We are always seeking people who can write interestingly and knowledgeably about technology." How-to, interview/profile, technical. Length: 1,200-1,800 words. **Pays $500 and up for features, $100 for briefs.**

Reprints: Send tearsheet and information about when and where the material previously appeared. Pay varies.

Photos: State availability with submission. Identification of subjects required.

Tips: "We are looking for irreverent, creative writers who can approach topics in new ways in terms of style, format and outlook. You must write in a way our audience can relate to. They want a lot of info, fast, with specifics on where to get more info and follow up. They're skeptical and don't believe everything they read. Tone should sound like a friend giving another friend the 'inside scoop'—not like a professor lecturing from an ivory tower. Humor helps a lot. How *not* to break in: Send a résumé without a query (I hate this—) or writing samples that are full of vague generalities."

$ $ $ INDIVIDUAL INVESTOR, Individual Investor Group, 125 Broad St., 14th Floor, New York NY 10004. (212)742-2277. Fax: (212)742-0747. Website: www.iionline.com. **Contact:** David Bumke, editor. **40% freelance written.** Monthly magazine covering stocks, mutual funds and personal finance. "Our readers range from novice to experienced investors. Our articles aim to be lively, informative, interesting, and to uncover 'undiscovered' investing opportunities." Circ. 500,000. **Pays on acceptance.** Publishes ms an average of 3 months after acceptance. Byline given. Buys all rights. Editorial lead time 2 months. Submit seasonal material 4 months in advance. Sample copy free.

Columns/Departments: David Bumke, editor. Educated Investor (investing basics and special topics), 1,500 words. **Buys 12 mss/year.** Query with published clips. **Pays up to $1/word.**

Tips: "Most ideas are generated inhouse and assigned to a stable of freelancers."

$ $ $ INDUSTRYWEEK, Leadership in Manufacturing, Penton Media, Inc., Penton Media Building, 1300 E. 9th St., Cleveland OH 44114. (216)696-7000. Fax: (216)696-7670. E-mail: tvinas@industryweek.com. Website: www.industryweek.com. Editor-in-Chief: Patricia Panchak. **Contact:** Tonya Vinas, managing editor. **30% freelance written.** Magazine published 18 times/year. *IndustryWeek* connects marketers and manufacturers and provides information that helps manufacturers drive continuous improvement throughout the enterprise. Every issue of *IndustryWeek* is edited for the management teams of today's most competitive manufacturing companies, as well as decision-makers in the service industries that support manufacturing growth and productivity." Estab. 1970. Circ. 233,000. **Pays on acceptance.** Publishes ms an average of 2 months after acceptance. Byline given. Offers 25% kill fee. Buys all rights. Accepts queries by mail, e-mail, fax, phone. Responds in 1 month to queries. Sample copy and writer's guidelines online.

Nonfiction: Book excerpts, exposé, interview/profile. "No first person articles." **Buys 25 mss/year.** Query with published clips. Length: 1,800-3,000 words. **Pays average of $1/word for all articles; reserves right to negotiate.** Sometimes pays expenses of writers on assignment.

Photos: Reviews contact sheets, negatives, transparencies, prints. Buys one-time rights. Negotiates payment individually. Captions, identification of subjects required.

Tips: "Pitch wonderful ideas targeted precisely at our audience. Read, re-read, and understand the writer's guidelines. *IndustryWeek* readers are primarily senior executives—people with the title of vice president, executive vice president, senior vice president, chief executive officer, chief financial officer, chief information officer, chairman, managing director, and president. *IW*'s executive readers oversee global corporations. While *IW*'s primary target audience is a senior executive in a U.S. firm, your story should provide information that any executive anywhere in the world can use. *IW*'s audience is primarily in companies in manufacturing and manufacturing-related industries."

[N] $ $ $ LATIN TRADE, Your Business Source for Latin America, Freedom Communications, Inc., 95 Merrick Way, Suite 600, Coral Gables FL 33134. (305)358-8373. Fax: (305)358-9166. Website: www.latintrade.com. **Contact:** Mike Zellner, editor. **55% freelance written.** Monthly magazine covering Latin American business. "*Latin Trade* covers cross-border business in Latin America for top executives doing business with the region." Estab. 1993. Circ. 105,000. Pays on publication. Publishes ms an average of 3 months after acceptance. Byline given. Offers 25% kill fee. Buys all rights, makes work-for-hire assignments. Editorial lead time 3 months. Submit seasonal material 6 months in advance. Accepts queries by mail, e-mail. Responds in 2 weeks to queries. Sample copy and writer's guidelines free.

Nonfiction: Exposé, historical/nostalgic, humor, interview/profile, travel, business news. No one-source stories or unsolicited stories. **Buys 50 mss/year.** Query with published clips. Length: 800-2,000 words. **Pays $200-1,000.** Sometimes pays expenses of writers on assignment.

Photos: State availability with submission. Reviews contact sheets. Buys one-time rights. Negotiates payment individually. Identification of subjects required.

[N] $ $ MYBUSINESS MAGAZINE, Hammock Publishing, 3322 W. End Ave., Suite 700, Nashville TN 37203. Fax: (615)386-9349. E-mail: lwaddle@hammock.com. Website: www.mybusinessmag.com. **Contact:** Lisa Waddle, editor. **75% freelance written.** Bimonthly magazine for small businesses. "We are a guide to small business success, however that is defined in the new small business economy. We explore the methods and minds behind the trends and celebrate the men and women leading the creation of the new small business economy." Estab. 1999. Circ. 600,000. **Pays on acceptance.** Publishes ms an average of 2 months after acceptance. Byline given. Offers 30% kill fee. Buys first North American serial, electronic rights. Editorial lead time 3 months. Submit seasonal material 3 months in advance. Accepts queries by mail, fax. Accepts simultaneous submissions. Responds in 2 weeks to queries. Sample copy and writer's guidelines free.

Nonfiction: Book excerpts, how-to (small business topics), humor, new product. **Buys 8 mss/year.** Query with published clips. Length: 200-1,800 words. **Pays $75-1,000.** Pays expenses of writers on assignment.

Fillers: Gags to be illustrated by cartoonist. **Buys 5/year.**

Tips: *MyBusiness* is sent bimonthly to the 600,000 members of the National Federation of Independent Business. "We're here to help small business owners by giving them a range of how-to pieces that evaluate, analyze and lead to solutions."

$ THE NETWORK JOURNAL, Black Professional and Small Business News, The Network Journal Communication, 139 Fulton St., Suite 407, New York, NY 10038. (212)962-3791. Fax: (212)962-3537. E-mail: tnj@obe1.com. Website: www.tnj.com. Editor: Njeru Waithaku. **Contact:** Aziz Adetimirn, publisher. **25% freelance written.** Monthly magazine covering business and career articles. *The Network Journal* caters to Black professionals and small-business owners, providing quality coverage on business, financial, technology and career news germane to the Black community. Estab. 1993. Circ. 11,000. Pays on publication. Byline given. Buys all rights. Editorial lead time 2 months. Submit seasonal material 3 months in advance. Accepts queries by mail, e-mail, fax, phone. Accepts simultaneous submissions. Sample copy for $1 or online. Writer's guidelines for SASE or online.

Nonfiction: How-to, interview/profile. Send complete ms. Length: 1,200-1,500 words. **Pays $75.** Sometimes pays expenses of writers on assignment.

Photos: Send photos with submission. Buys one-time rights. Offers $75/photo. Identification of subjects required.

Columns/Departments: Book reviews, 700-800 words; career management and small business development, 800 words. **Pays $75.**

■ The online magazine carries original content not found in the print version and includes writer's guidelines.

Tips: "We are looking for vigorous writing and reporting for our cover stories and feature articles. Pieces should have gripping leads, quotes that actually say something and that come from several sources. Unless it is a column, please do not submit a one-source story. Always remember that your article must contain a nutgraph—that's usually the third paragraph telling the reader what the story is about and why you are telling it now. Editorializing should be kept to a minimum. If you're writing a column, make sure your opinions are well-supported."

$ $ PERDIDO, Leadership with a Conscience, High Tide Press, 3650 W. 183rd St., Homewood IL 60430-2603. (708)206-2054. Fax: (708)206-2044. E-mail: managing.editor@hightidepress.com. Website: www.perdidomagazine.com. **Contact:** Diane J. Bell, editor. **60% freelance written.** Quarterly magazine covering leadership and management as they relate to mission-oriented organizations. "We are concerned with what's happening in organizations that are mission-oriented—as opposed to merely profit-oriented. *Perdido* is focused on helping conscientious leaders put innovative ideas into practice. We seek pragmatic articles on management techniques as well as esoteric essays on social issues. The readership of *Perdido* is comprised mainly of CEOs, executive directors, vice presidents, and program directors of nonprofit and for-profit organizations. We try to make the content of *Perdido* accessible to all decision-makers, whether in the nonprofit or for-profit world, government, or academia. *Perdido* actively pursues diverse opinions and authors from many different fields." Estab. 1994. Circ. 6,000. Pays on publication. Publishes ms an average of 3 months after acceptance. Byline given. Buys first North American serial, second serial (reprint) rights. Editorial lead time 4 months. Submit seasonal material 6 months in advance. Accepts queries by mail, e-mail, fax, phone. Accepts simultaneous submissions. Responds in 2 months to queries. Sample copy for 6×9 SAE with 2 first-class stamps or online. Writer's guidelines for #10 SASE or by e-mail.

Nonfiction: Book excerpts, essays, humor, inspirational, interview/profile. **Buys 12 mss/year.** Query with published clips. Length: 1,000-5,000 words. **Pays $70-350.**

Photos: State availability with submission. Reviews 5×7 prints. Buys one-time rights. Negotiates payment individually. Captions, identification of subjects, model releases required.

Columns/Departments: Book Review (new books on management/leadership), 800 words; Rewind, 750 words. **Buys 6 mss/year.** Send complete ms. **Pays $75.**

Tips: "Potential writers for *Perdido* should rely on the magazine's motto—Leadership with a Conscience—as a starting point for ideas. We're looking for thoughtful reflections or management that help people succeed. We're not asking for step-by-step recipes—'do this, do that.' In *Perdido*, we want readers to find thought-provoking, open-minded explorations of the moral dimensions of leadership from a socially aware, progressive perspective."

$ $ $ $ ⊡ PROFIT, The Magazine for Canadian Entrepreneurs, Rogers Media, 777 Bay St., 5th Floor, Toronto, Ontario M5W 1A7, Canada. (416)596-5016. Fax: (416)596-5111. E-mail: profit@profitmag.ca. Website: www.profitguide.com. **Contact:** Ian Portsmouth, managing editor. **80% freelance written.** Magazine published 8 times/year covering small and medium businesses. "We specialize in specific, useful information that helps our readers manage their businesses better. We want Canadian stories only." Estab. 1982. Circ. 110,000. **Pays on acceptance.** Publishes ms an average of 2 months after acceptance. Byline given. Offers variable kill fee. Buys first North American serial, electronic rights. Submit seasonal material 6 months in advance. Accepts queries by mail, e-mail, fax, phone. Responds in 1 month to queries; 6 weeks to mss. Sample copy for 9×12 SAE with 84¢ postage. Writer's guidelines free.

Nonfiction: How-to (business management tips), strategies and Canadian business profiles. **Buys 50 mss/year.** Query with published clips. Length: 800-2,000 words. **Pays $500-2,000.** Pays expenses of writers on assignment.

Columns/Departments: Finance (info on raising capital in Canada), 700 words; Marketing (marketing strategies for independent business), 700 words. **Buys 80 mss/year.** Query with published clips. **Pays $150-600.**

■ The online magazine carries original content not found in the print edition. Contact: Andrea Szego, online editor.

Tips: "We're wide open to freelancers with good ideas and some knowledge of business. Read the magazine and understand it before submitting your ideas—which should have a Canadian focus."

Ⓝ $ $ $ $ REPORT ON BUSINESS MAGAZINE, Globe and Mail, 444 Front St. W., Toronto, Ontario M5V 2S9, Canada. (416)585-5499. Fax: robmag@globeandmail.ca. Website: www.robmagnet.com. Editor: Patricia Best. **Contact:** Susan Macphail, managing editor. **50% freelance written.** Monthly business magazine "covering business like *Forbes* or *Fortune* which tries to capture major trends and personalities." Circ. 300,000. **Pays on acceptance.** Publishes ms an average of 4 months after acceptance. Byline given. Offers 50% kill fee. Buys first North American serial rights. Responds in 3 weeks to queries. Sample copy free.

Nonfiction: Book excerpts, exposé, interview/profile, new product, photo feature. Special issues: Quarterly technology report. **Buys 30 mss/year.** Query with published clips. Length: 2,000-4,000 words. **Pays $200-3,000.** Pays expenses of writers on assignment.
Tips: "For features send a one-page story proposal. We prefer to write about personalities involved in corporate events."

$ $ $ $ WORDS FOR SALE, 1149 Granada Ave., Salinas CA 93906. **Contact:** Lorna Gilbert, submission editor. Estab. 1968. **Pays on acceptance**.
Nonfiction: "Since 1968, we have sold almost every kind of written material to a wide variety of individual and corporate clients. We deal in both the written as well as the spoken word, from humorous one liners and nightclub acts, to informative medical brochures, political speeches, and almost everything in between. We are not agents. We are a company that provides original written material created especially for the specific needs of our current clients. Therefore, do not send us a sample of your work. As good as it may be, it is almost certainly unrelated to our current needs. Instead begin by finding out what our clients want and write it for them. What could be simpler? It gets even better: *We buy sentences—* That's right. Forget conceiving, composing, editing and polishing endless drafts of magazine articles or book manuscripts. Simply create the type of sentence or sentences we're looking for and we'll buy one or more of them. We respond promptly. We pay promptly." **Pays $1 and up/sentence.**
Tips: "The key to your selling something to us, is to *first* find out *exactly* what we are currently buying. To do this simply mail us a #10 SASE and we will send you a list of what we are anxious to buy at this time."

N $ $ WORKING MONEY, The Investors' Magazine, Technical Analysis, Inc., 4757 California Ave. SW, Seattle WA 98116-4499. (206)938-0570. Fax: (206)938-1307. E-mail: editor@traders.com. Website: www.working-money.com. Managing Editor: Elizabeth M.S. Flynn. **Contact:** Jayanthi Gopalakrishnan, editor. **20% freelance written.** Monthly (except january and july) magazine covering investing. "*Working Money* is the magazine for those who have earned their money and now want to learn how to invest it." Estab. 2000. Circ. 165,000. Pays on publication. Publishes ms an average of 6 months after acceptance. Byline given. Buys all rights. Editorial lead time 3 months. Submit seasonal material 6 months in advance. Accepts queries by mail, e-mail, fax. Responds in 2 weeks to queries; 1 month to mss. Sample copy for $5. Writer's guidelines for #10 SASE or online.
Nonfiction: "How-to articles are at the core of *Working Money*. Our readers want to know how to invest their money, not just where, but how to work with the paperwork, computer programs and institutions with which they'll need to work. How do you calculate the return on your investment? What are the dollars-and-cents implications of choosing a no-load vs. a load mutual fund. Show our readers." How-to, humor (occasional anecdotes about investing), new product (of note to investors), personal experience (focus on lessons learned and how they will help investors), technical (features of investment-related software and hardware, etc.), mutual funds, money management, financial planning. **Buys up to 150 mss/year.** Query with published clips. Length: 1,000-2,000 words. **Pays $50-360 for assigned articles; $50-300 for unsolicited articles.**
Photos: State availability with submission. Buys all rights. Offers $60-350/photo. Captions, identification of subjects, model releases required.
Columns/Departments: Mutual Funds (all aspects of mutual fund investing); Financial Planning (all aspects of financial planning); Money Management (as aspects of money management), all 1,000-2,000 words. **Buys 36 mss/year.** Query with published clips. **Pays $50-300.**
Tips: "We are not hypercritical of writing style, but accuracy is the key word. Completeness and accuracy are extremely important. Problems arising after publication will be directed to the author. Remember that *Working Money* is a how-to publication, so concentrate on instruction and elucidation."

Regional

$ $ ALASKA BUSINESS MONTHLY, Alaska Business Publishing, 501 W. Northern Lights Blvd., Suite 100, Anchorage AK 99503-2577. (907)276-4373. Fax: (907)279-2900. E-mail: info@akbizmag.com. Website: www.akbizmag.com. **Contact:** Debbie Cutler, editor. **80% freelance written.** Magazine covering Alaska-oriented business and industry. "Our audience is Alaska businessmen and women who rely on us for timely features and up-to-date information about doing business in Alaska." Estab. 1985. Circ. 10,000. Pays on publication. Publishes ms an average of 4 months after acceptance. Byline given. Offers $50 kill fee. Buys all rights. Editorial lead time 5 months. Submit seasonal material 5 months in advance. Accepts queries by mail, e-mail, fax. Responds in 1 month to queries. Sample copy for 9×12 SAE and 4 first-class stamps. Writer's guidelines free.
Nonfiction: General interest, how-to, interview/profile, new product (Alaska), opinion. No fiction, poetry or anything not pertinent to Alaska. **Buys approximately 130 mss/year.** Send complete ms. Length: 500-2,000 words. **Pays $150-300.** Sometimes pays expenses of writers on assignment.
Photos: State availability with submission.
Columns/Departments: Required Reading (business book reviews), Right Moves, Alaska this Month, Monthly Calendars (all Alaska related), all 500-1,200 words. **Buys 12 mss/year.** Send complete ms. **Pays $50-75.**
Tips: "Send a well-written manuscript on a subject of importance to Alaska businesses. We seek informative, entertaining articles on everything from entrepreneurs to heavy industry. We cover all Alaska industry to include mining,

tourism, timber, transportation, oil and gas, fisheries, finance, insurance, real estate, communications, medical services, technology and construction. We also cover Native and environmental issues, and occasionally feature Seattle and other communities in the Pacific Northwest."

N $ $ ATLANTIC BUSINESS MAGAZINE, Communications Ten Limited, 197 Water St., St. John's, Newfoundland A1C 6E7, Canada. (709)726-9300. Fax: (709)726-3013. E-mail: dchafe@atlanticbusinessmagazine.nf.ca. Website: www.atlanticbusinessmagazine.com. Managing Editor: Edwina Hutton. **Contact:** Dawn Chafe, editor. **60% freelance written.** Bimonthly magazine covering business in Atlantic Canada. "We discuss positive business developments, emphasizing that the four Atlantic provinces are a great place to do business." Estab. 1989. Circ. 30,000. Pays on publication. Publishes ms an average of 1 month after acceptance. Byline given. Buys one-time rights. Editorial lead time 2 months. Accepts queries by mail, e-mail, fax, phone. Sample copy and writer's guidelines free.
Nonfiction: Exposé, general interest, interview/profile, new product. "We don't want religious, technical or scholarly material. We are not an academic magazine." **Buys 36 mss/year.** Query with published clips. Length: 1,500-2,400 words. **Pays $300-750.** Sometimes pays expenses of writers on assignment.
Photos: Send photos with submission. Reviews contact sheets, transparencies, prints. Buys one-time rights. Negotiates payment individually. Captions, identification of subjects required.
Columns/Departments: Query with published clips.
Tips: "Writers should submit their areas of interest as well as samples of their work and if possible, suggested story ideas."

$ $ BIZLIFE MAGAZINE, (formerly Business Life Magazine), Business Life Magazine, Inc., 4101-A Piedmont Pkwy., Greensboro NC 27410-8110. (336)812-8801. Fax: (336)812-8832. E-mail: kmeekins@bizlife.com. Website: www.bizlife.com. **Contact:** Kay Meekins, editor-in-chief. **30% freelance written.** Monthly magazine. "*BizLife* is a monthly, full-color magazine profiling businesses and business people that have ties to the Piedmont Triad, are headquartered here, or have an impact on the lives of local business people." Estab. 1989. Circ. 14,000. Pays on the 15th of the month of publication. Publishes ms an average of 3 months after acceptance. Byline given. Offers kill fee. Buys first, second serial (reprint) rights. Editorial lead time 2 months. Submit seasonal material 5 months in advance. Accepts queries by mail, e-mail, fax. Accepts simultaneous submissions. Responds in 3 weeks to queries. Sample copy for 9 × 12 SASE and $3 postage. Writer's guidelines for #10 SASE.
Nonfiction: Book excerpts, general interest, interview/profile, travel. No articles without ties to NC or the Piedmont Triad region (except travel). **Buys 45 mss/year.** Query with published clips. Length: 1,500-2,000 words. **Pays $350.**
Photos: State availability with submission. Reviews 2 × 3 transparencies. Buys one-time rights. Negotiates payment individually. Captions, identification of subjects required.
   ■ The online magazine carries original content not found in the print edition. Contact: Kay Meekins, online editor.
Tips: "We are strictly a profile based magazine. All stories must be about local people, business people or businesses."

$ BOULDER COUNTY BUSINESS REPORT, 3180 Sterling Circle, Suite 201, Boulder CO 80301-2338. (303)440-4950. Fax: (303)440-8954. E-mail: jwlewis@bcbr.com. Website: www.bcbr.com. **Contact:** Jerry W. Lewis, editor. **50% freelance written.** Prefers to work with local published/established writers; works with a small number of new/unpublished writers each year. Biweekly newspaper covering Boulder County business issues. Offers "news tailored to a monthly theme and read primarily by Colorado businesspeople and by some investors nationwide. Philosophy: Descriptive, well-written articles that reach behind the scene to examine area's business activity." Estab. 1982. Circ. 10,000. Pays on publication. Publishes ms an average of 1 month after acceptance. Byline given. Buys one-time, second serial (reprint) rights. Responds in 1 month to queries; 2 weeks to mss. Sample copy for $1.44.
Nonfiction: All our issues are written around three or four monthly themes. No articles are accepted in which the subject has not been pursued in depth and both sides of an issue presented in a writing style with flair." Interview/profile, new product, explanation of competition in a particular line of business. **Buys 120 mss/year.** Query with published clips. Length: 750-1,200 words. **Pays $50-150.**
Photos: State availability with submission. Reviews b&w contact sheets. Buys one time and reprint rights. Pays $10/max for b&w contact sheet. Identification of subjects required.
Tips: "Must be able to localize a subject. In-depth articles are written by assignment. The freelancer located in the Colorado area has an excellent chance here."

BUSINESS JOURNAL OF CENTRAL NY, CNY Business Review, Inc., 231 Wallton St., Syracuse NY 13202-1230. (315)472-3104. Fax: (315)478-8166. E-mail: editor@cnybusinessjournal.com. Website: www.cnybusinessjournal.com. **Contact:** Charles McChesney, editor. **35% freelance written.** Weekly newspaper covering "business news in a 16-county area surrounding Syracuse. The audience consists of owners and managers of businesses." Estab. 1985. Circ. 8,000. Pays on publication. Publishes ms an average of 2 months after acceptance. Byline given. Offers kill fee. Buys first rights. Editorial lead time 1 month. Accepts queries by mail, e-mail, fax. Sample copy and writer's guidelines free.
Nonfiction: Humor, opinion. Query. Length: 750-2,000 words. **Pay varies.** Sometimes pays in contributor copies. Sometimes pays expenses of writers on assignment.
Photos: State availability with submission. Reviews contact sheets. Negotiates payment individually. Captions, identification of subjects, model releases required.
Columns/Departments: Query with published clips.
Fillers: Facts, newsbreaks, short humor. Length: 300-600 words. **Pays variable amount.**

▣ The online magazine carries original content not found in the print edition.
Tips: "The audience is comprised of owners and managers. Focus on their needs. Call or send associate editor story ideas: be sure to have a Central New York 'hook.' "

N **$ $ $**▨ **BUSINESS LONDON**, Bowes Publishers, 1174 Gainsburough Rd., London, Ontario N5Y 4X3, Canada. (519)472-7601. Fax: (519)473-7859. **Contact:** Gord Delamont, editor. **70% freelance written.** Monthly magazine covering London business. "Our audience is primarily small and medium businesses and entrepreneurs. Focus is on success stories and how to better operate your business." Estab. 1987. Circ. 14,000. Pays on publication. Publishes ms an average of 3 months after acceptance. Byline given. Offers 50% kill fee. Buys first rights. Editorial lead time 3 months. Responds in 3 months to mss. Sample copy for #10 SASE. Writer's guidelines free.
Nonfiction: How-to (business topics), humor, interview/profile, new product (local only), personal experience (must have a London connection). **Buys 30 mss/year.** Query with published clips. Length: 250-1,500 words. **Pays $125-500.**
Photos: Send photos with submission. Reviews contact sheets, transparencies. Buys one-time rights. Negotiates payment individually. Identification of subjects required.
Tips: "Phone with a great idea. The most valuable thing a writer owns is ideas. We'll take a chance on an unknown if the idea is good enough."

$ $BUSINESS NH MAGAZINE, 404 Chestnut St., Suite 201, Manchester NH 03101-1831. (603)626-6354. Fax: (603)626-6359. E-mail: bnhmag@aol.com. **Contact:** Matthew Mowry, editor. **50% freelance written.** Monthly magazine covering business, politics and people of New Hampshire. "Our audience consists of the owners and top managers of New Hampshire businesses." Estab. 1983. Circ. 13,000. Pays on publication. Publishes ms an average of 2 months after acceptance. Byline given. Accepts queries by e-mail, fax.
Nonfiction: How-to, interview/profile. "No unsolicited manuscripts; interested in New Hampshire writers only." **Buys 24 mss/year.** Query with published clips and résumé. Length: 750-2,500 words. **Pays $75-350.**
Photos: Both b&w and color photos used. Buys one-time rights. Pays $40-80.
Tips: "I *always* want clips and résumé with queries. Freelance stories are almost always assigned. Stories *must* be local to New Hampshire."

$CHARLESTON REGIONAL BUSINESS JOURNAL, Setcom, Inc., P.O. Box 446, Charleston SC 29402. (843)723-7702. Fax: (843)723-7060. E-mail: info@crbj.com. Website: www.crbj.com. Publisher: William Settlemyer. **Contact:** Andy Nelson, executive editor. **20% freelance written.** Biweekly newspaper covering local business. "We publish articles of interest to small business owners in the Charleston area, preferably with a local slant." Estab. 1995. Circ. 7,000. Pays on publication. Publishes ms an average of 1 month after acceptance. Byline given. Offers $40 kill fee. Editorial lead time 1 month. Submit seasonal material 2 months in advance. Accepts queries by mail, e-mail, fax. Accepts simultaneous submissions. Responds in 2 weeks to queries. Sample copy online.
Nonfiction: Interview/profile (business people), technical, other articles of interest to small business owners. No how-to's. **Buys 100 mss/year.** Query with published clips. Length: 400-800 words. **Pays $40-145.**
Photos: State availability with submission. Reviews e-mail photos (jpeg, 170 min resolution). Buys all rights. Offers $30/photo. Identification of subjects required.

N **$ $**▨ **COLORADO TECHNOLOGY, Denver edition**, Power Media Group, 13490 T1 Blvd., Suite 100, Dallas TX 75243. (972)690-6222 ext. 16. Fax: (972)690-6333. E-mail: editor@ttechnology.com or lkline@technology.com. Website: www.ttechnology.com. **Contact:** Laurie Kline, editor. **95% freelance written.** Monthly magazine covering technology in the Denver region. "*Colorado Technology* (and sibling publications *Texas Technology* and *Illinois Technology*) is a high-tech lifestyle magazine. We publish articles that discuss how technology affects our lives. Our audience is a mix of techies and mainstream consumers." Estab. 1997. Circ. 700,000. Pays on publication. Byline given. Offers $20 kill fee. Buys first North American serial, second serial (reprint), electronic rights, makes work-for-hire assignments. Editorial lead time 3 months. Submit seasonal material 3 months in advance. Accepts queries by mail, e-mail. Accepts simultaneous submissions. Responds in 3 weeks to queries; 2 months to mss. Sample copy and writer's guidelines free.
Nonfiction: Essays, exposé, general interest, historical/nostalgic, humor, interview/profile, new product, technical. "No computer hardware articles." **Buys 50 mss/year.** Query with published clips. Length: 1,200-3,500 words. **Pays $200-400.**
Photos: State availability with submission. Reviews contact sheets. Buys all rights. Negotiates payment individually. Captions, identification of subjects, model releases required.
Columns/Departments: Tech Law (technology law), 800-2,000 words; New Online (new stuff on the web/affecting the web), 800-2,000 words; Career Monthly (high-tech/information tech career issues), 800-3,000 words; High Speed Notes (info on Internet connectivity), 800-2,000 words. **Buys 30 mss/year.** Query with published clips. **Pays $75-200.**
Tips: "Review the types of topics we cover. We are more mainstream and hip and less nitty-gritty technical. Our articles are fresh and sometimes off-beat, but they always address how technology is affecting our lives. We publish articles ranging from online shopping to wireless technology."

N **$ $CRAIN'S DETROIT BUSINESS**, Crain Communications Inc., 1400 Woodbridge Ave., Detroit MI 48207-3187. (313)446-6000. Fax: (313)446-1687. E-mail: jmelton@crain.com. Website: www.crainsdetroit.com. Editor: Mary Kramer., Executive Editor: Cindy Goodaker. **Contact:** James Melton, special sections editor. **15% freelance**

written. Weekly tabloid covering business in the Detroit metropolitan area—specifically Wayne, Oakland, Macomb, Washtenaw and Livingston counties. Estab. 1985. Circ. 150,000. Pays on publication. Publishes ms an average of 1 month after acceptance. Byline given. Buys electronic, all rights. Accepts queries by mail, e-mail. Sample copy for $1.

• *Crain's Detroit Business* uses only area writers and local topics.

Nonfiction: New product, technical, business. **Buys 100 mss/year.** Query with published clips. Length: 30-40 words/column inch. **Pays $10/column inch.** Pays expenses of writers on assignment.

Photos: State availability with submission.

Tips: "Contact special sections editor in writing with background and, if possible, specific story ideas relating to our type of coverage and coverage area. We only use *local* writers."

N **$** **$** **ILLINOIS TECHNOLOGY, Chicago edition**, Power Media Group, 13490 T1 Blvd., Suite 100, Dallas TX 75243. (972)690-6222 ext. 16. Fax: (972)690-6333. E-mail: editor@ttechnology.com. Website: www.ttechnology.com. **Contact:** Laurie Kline, editor. **95% freelance written.** Monthly magazine covering technology in the Chicago region. "*Illinois Technology* (and its sibling publications *Texas Technology* and *Colorado Technology*)is a high-tech lifestyle magaizne. We publish articles that discuss how technology affects our lives. Our audience is a mix of techies and mainstream consumers." Estab. 1997. Circ. 700,000. Pays on publication. Byline given. Offers $20 kill fee. Buys first North American serial, second serial (reprint), electronic rights, makes work-for-hire assignments. Editorial lead time 3 months. Submit seasonal material 3 months in advance. Accepts queries by mail, e-mail. Accepts simultaneous submissions. Responds in 3 weeks to queries; 2 months to mss. Sample copy and writer's guidelines free.

Nonfiction: Essays, exposé, general interest, historical/nostalgic, humor, interview/profile, new product, technical. "No computer hardware articles." **Buys 50 mss/year.** Query with published clips. Length: 1,200-3,500 words. **Pays $200-400.**

Photos: State availability with submission. Reviews contact sheets. Buys all rights. Negotiates payment individually. Captions, identification of subjects, model releases required.

Columns/Departments: Tech Law (technology law), 800-2,000 words; New Online (new stuff on the web/affecting the web), 800-2,000 words; Career Monthly (high-tech/information tech career issues), 800-3,000 words; High Speed Notes (info on Internet connectivity), 800-2,000 words. **Buys 30 mss/year.** Query with published clips. **Pays $75-200.**

Tips: "Review the types of topics we cover. We are more mainstream and hip and less nitty-gritty technical. Our articles are fresh and sometimes off-beat, but they always address how technology is affecting our lives. We publish articles ranging from online shopping to wireless technology."

$ **IN BUSINESS WINDSOR**, Cornerstone Publications Inc., 1614 Lesperance Rd., Tecumseh, Ontario N8N 1Y3, Canada. (519)735-2080. Fax: (519)735-2082. E-mail: inbiz2@mnsi.net. Website: www.inbizwin.com. **Contact:** Gordon Hillman, publisher. **70% freelance written.** Monthly magazine covering business. "We focus on issues/ideas which are of interest to businesses in and around Windsor and Essex County (Ontario). Most stories deal with business and finance; occasionally we will cover health and sports issues that affect our readers." Estab. 1988. Circ. 10,000. **Pays on acceptance.** Byline given. Buys first rights. Editorial lead time 3 months. Submit seasonal material 3 months in advance. Accepts queries by mail, e-mail, fax, phone. Responds in 2 weeks to queries; 1 month to mss. Sample copy for $3.50.

Nonfiction: General interest, how-to, interview/profile. **Buys 25 mss/year.** Query with published clips. Length: 800-1,500 words. **Pays $70-150.** Sometimes pays expenses of writers on assignment.

$** **$ **INGRAM'S**, Show-Me Publishing, Inc., 306 E. 12th St., Suite 1014, Kansas City MO 64106. (816)842-9994. Fax: (816)474-1111. **Contact:** Editor. **50% freelance written.** Monthly magazine covering Kansas City business/executive lifestyle for "upscale, affluent business executives and professionals. Looking for sophisticated writing with style and humor when appropriate." Estab. 1975. Circ. 26,000. Pays 30 days after publication. Publishes ms an average of 2 months after acceptance. Byline given. Buys first, electronic rights. Editorial lead time 2 months. Submit seasonal material 3 months in advance. Accepts queries by mail, fax. Responds in 6 weeks to queries. Sample copy for $3.

Nonfiction: "All articles must have a Kansas City angle. We don't accept unsolicited mss except for opinion column." General interest, how-to (business and personal finance related), interview/profile (KC execs, politicians, celebrities), opinion, technical. **Buys 30 mss/year.** Query with published clips. Length: 500-3,000 words. **Pays $175-350.** Sometimes pays expenses of writers on assignment.

Columns/Departments: Say So (opinion), 1,500 words. **Buys 12 mss/year. Pays $175 max.**

Tips: "Writers must understand the publication and the audience—knowing what appeals to a business executive, entrepreneur, or professional in Kansas City."

N **$** **$** **JOHNSON COUNTY BUSINESS TIMES**, Sun Publications, Inc., 7373 W. 107th St., Overland Park KS 66212-2547. (913)649-8778. Fax: (913)381-9889. E-mail: placerte@sunpublications.com. **Contact:** Phil Placerte, editor. **5% freelance written.** Weekly magazine covering Johnson County business news. "Our magazine is written for local CEOs." Estab. 1994. Circ. 15,000. **Pays on acceptance.** Publishes ms an average of 1 month after acceptance. Byline given. Offers 25% kill fee. Buys first rights. Editorial lead time 1 month. Submit seasonal material 3 months in advance. Responds in 2 months to queries. Sample copy and writer's guidelines for $1.50 plus postage.

Nonfiction: How-to (business stories), interview/profile, business trend stories. **Buys 10 mss/year.** Query with published clips. Length: 600-3,000 words. **Pays $75-500.** Sometimes pays expenses of writers on assignment.

Photos: State availability with submission. Reviews negatives. Buys all rights. Negotiates payment individually. Identification of subjects required.

Columns/Departments: Query with published clips. **Pays $75-200.**

Tips: "Propose specific, well-though-out ideas that are a good fit for our audience. Stories must have a local angle."

$ $ THE LANE REPORT, Lane Communications Group, 201 E. Main St., 14th Floor, Lexington KY 40507. (859)244-3500. Fax: (859)244-3555. E-mail: editorial@lanereport.com. Website: www.kybiz.com. **Contact:** Claude Hammond, editorial director. **50% freelance written.** Monthly magazine covering statewide business. Estab. 1986. Circ. 14,000. Pays on publication. Byline given. Buys one-time rights. Editorial lead time 6 weeks. Submit seasonal material 3 months in advance. Accepts queries by mail, e-mail, fax. Accepts simultaneous submissions. Responds in 1 month to queries. Sample copy and writer's guidelines free.

Nonfiction: Essays, interview/profile, new product, photo feature. No fiction. **Buys 30-40 mss/year.** Query with published clips. Length: 500-2,000 words. **Pays $100-375.** Sometimes pays expenses of writers on assignment.

Photos: State availability with submission. Reviews contact sheets, negatives, transparencies, prints. Buys one-time rights. Negotiates payment individually. Identification of subjects required.

Columns/Departments: Small Business Advisor, Financial Advisor, Exploring Kentucky, Perspective, Spotlight on the Arts; all less than 1,000 words.

▣ The online magazine carries original content not found in the print edition. Contact: Claude Hammond, online editor.

Tips: "As Kentucky's only business and economics publication with a *statewide* focus, we look for features that incorporate perspectives from the Commonwealth's various regions and prominent industries—tying it all into the national picture when appropriate. We also look for insightful profiles and interviews of entrepreneurs and business leaders."

$ $ MASS HIGH TECH, Journal of New England Technology, American City Business Journals, 200 High St., Boston MA 02110. (617)478-0630. Fax: (617)478-0638. E-mail: editor@masshightech.com. Website: www.masshightech.com. Editor: Dyke Hendrickson. Associate Editor: Matt Kelly. **Contact:** Anne Taylor, special sections editor. **20% freelance written.** Weekly newspaper covering New England-based technology companies. "*Mass High Tech* is a weekly newspaper about the business deals and products of New England technology companies, read by technology executives, engineers, professors and high-tech workers." Estab. 1983. Circ. 23,000 per week. Pays on publication. Publishes ms an average of 1 month after acceptance. Byline given. Offers $50 kill fee. Buys all rights. Editorial lead time 3 months. Accepts queries by mail, e-mail, phone. Sample copy and writer's guidelines free.

Nonfiction: Opinion, technical. "No product reviews." Query. Length: 700-900 words. **Pays $125-165.**

Columns/Departments: E-commerce, Retailing, Stockwatch, Case Study, all 500 words. Query with published clips. **Pays 30¢/word.**

$ $ OKLAHOMA BUSINESS MONTHLY, (formerly Metro Journal), Langdon Publishing Co., 1603 S. Boulder, Tulsa OK 74119. (918)585-9924. Fax: (918)585-9926. E-mail: gretchen@langdonpublishing.com. Website: www.okbusinessmonthly.com. **Contact:** Gretchen Mullen, editor. **20% freelance written.** Monthly magazine covering all business topics and real estate. "*Oklahoma Business Monthly* is the only statewide business publication reaching the owner, president or CEO of virtually every Oklahoma business with annual revenue in excess of $1 million." Prefers Oklahoma based writers only. Estab. 1999. Circ. 10,000. Pays on publication. Byline given. Offers 50% kill fee. Editorial lead time 2 months. Submit seasonal material 3 months in advance. Accepts queries by mail, e-mail, fax. Accepts simultaneous submissions. Sample copy free. Writer's guidelines by e-mail.

Nonfiction: Exposé, how-to (business related), interview/profile, new product, personal experience, photo feature. Query with published clips. Length: 500-1,000 words. Pays expenses of writers on assignment.

Columns/Departments: E-commerce, Retailing, Stock Watch, Case Study; all 500 words. Query with published clips.

N $ $ PACIFIC BUSINESS NEWS, 1833 Kalakaua Ave., 7th Floor, Honolulu HI 96815-1512. (808)955-8100. Fax: (808)955-8031. E-mail: pbn@lava.net. Website: www.bizjournals.com/pacific. **Contact:** Bernie Silver, editor. **5% freelance written.** Weekly business newspaper. Estab. 1963. Circ. 14,500. Pays on publication. Byline given. Offers 50% kill fee. Buys all rights. Editorial lead time 1 month. Accepts queries by mail, e-mail, fax, phone. Responds in 2 weeks to queries. Sample copy free.

Nonfiction: Opinion, feature articles. Query with published clips. Length: 750-1,000 words. **Pays $150.**

Photos: State availability with submission. Reviews negatives. Buys all rights. Offers no additional payment for photos accepted with ms. Captions required.

N $ ROCHESTER BUSINESS JOURNAL, Rochester Business Journal, Inc., 55 St. Paul St., Rochester NY 14604. (716)546-8303. Fax: (716)546-3398. E-mail: rackley@rbj.net. Website: www.rbjdaily.com. Editor: Paul Ericson. Managing Editor: Mike Dickinson. **Contact:** Reid Ackley, associate editor. **10% freelance written.** Weekly tabloid covering local business. "The *Rochester Business Journal* is geared toward corporate executives and owners of small businesses, bringing them leading-edge business coverage and analysis first in the market." Estab. 1984. Circ. 10,000.

Pays on publication. Publishes ms an average of 1 month after acceptance. Byline given. Buys first, second serial (reprint), electronic rights. Editorial lead time 6 weeks. Accepts queries by mail, e-mail, fax. Responds in 1 week to queries. Sample copy free or by e-mail. Writer's guidelines for #10 SASE or by e-mail.

Nonfiction: How-to (business topics), news features, trend stories with local examples. Do not query about any topics that do not include several local examples—local companies, organizations, universities, etc. **Buys 110 mss/year.** Query with published clips. Length: 1,000-2,000 words. **Pays $100.**

Tips: "The *Rochester Business Journal* prefers queries from local published writers who can demonstrate the ability to write for a sophisticated audience of business readers. Story ideas should be about business trends illustrated with numerous examples of local companies participating in the change or movement."

N $ $ SACRAMENTO BUSINESS JOURNAL, American City Business Journals Inc., 1401 21st St., Suite 200, Sacramento CA 95814-5221. (916)447-7661. Fax: (916)447-2243. E-mail: bbuchanan@amcity.com. Website: www .sacramento.bcentral.com. Editor: Lee Wessman. **Contact:** Bill Buchanan, managing editor. **5% freelance written.** Weekly newspaper covering the Sacramento area's economy. "Our readers are decision makers. They own or manage companies, or are community leaders who want to know what's happening. They expect sophisticated, well-researched news. And they don't read fluff." Estab. 1984. Circ. 14,000. Pays on publication. Publishes ms an average of 1 month after acceptance. Byline sometimes given. Offers 50% kill fee. Buys all rights, makes work-for-hire assignments. Editorial lead time 2 months. Submit seasonal material 2 months in advance. Accepts queries by mail, e-mail, fax. Responds in 3 weeks to queries. Sample copy for $2 and SAE with 2 first-class stamps.

O— Break in by sending clips that demonstrate your ability to write a complete news story.

Nonfiction: Humor, interview/profile, new product, opinion, local business news and trends. "No public relations stories on behalf of specific companies or industries. No thinly sourced stories." **Buys 60 mss/year.** Query with published clips. Length: 500-1,500 words. **Pays $125-200.** Sometimes pays expenses of writers on assignment.

Photos: State availability with submission. Reviews contact sheets, prints. Buys one-time rights. Pays $25-50/photo. Captions, identification of subjects required.

Columns/Departments: Gary Chazen, associate editor. Small Biz (meaningful successes or failures), 750 words. **Buys 20 mss/year.** Query. **Pays $100-175.**

Tips: "Most of our freelance work is done on assignment with a three-week turnaround. We look for a regular stable of writers who can get an assignment, do the research and produce a well-focused story that reflects the drama of business and doesn't avoid controversy."

$ $ ▨ TEXAS TECHNOLOGY, Dallas, Austin, Houston and San Antonio editions, Power Media Group, 13490 TI Blvd., Suite 100, Dallas TX 75243. (972)690-6222 ext. 16. Fax: (972)690-6333. E-mail: editor@ttechnology. com or lkline@ttechnology.com. Website: www.ttechnology.com. **Contact:** Laurie Kline, editor. **95% freelance written.** Monthly magazine covering technology. "*Texas Technology* (and sibling magazines *Colorado Technology* and *Illinois Technology*) are high-tech lifestyle magazines. We publish articles that discuss how technology affects our lives. Our audience is a mix of techies and mainstream consumers." Estab. 1997. Circ. 700,000. Pays on publication. Byline given. Offers $20 kill fee. Buys first North American serial, second serial (reprint), electronic rights, makes work-for-hire assignments. Editorial lead time 3 months. Submit seasonal material 3 months in advance. Accepts queries by mail, e-mail. Accepts simultaneous submissions. Responds in 3 weeks to queries; 2 months to mss. Sample copy and writer's guidelines free.

Nonfiction: Essays, exposé, general interest, historical/nostalgic, humor, interview/profile, new product, technical. "No computer hardware articles." **Buys 50 mss/year.** Query with published clips. Length: 1,200-3,500 words. **Pays $200-400.**

Photos: State availability with submission. Reviews contact sheets. Buys all rights. Negotiates payment individually. Captions, identification of subjects, model releases required.

Columns/Departments: Tech Law (technology law), 800-2,000 words; New Online (new stuff on the Web/affecting the Web), 800-2,000 words; Career Monthly (high-tech/information tech career issues), 800-3,000 words; High Speed Notes (info on Internet connectivity), 800-2,000 words. **Buys 30 mss/year.** Query with published clips. **Pays $75-200.**

Tips: "Review the types of topics we cover. We are more mainstream and hip and less nitty-gritty technical. Our articles are fresh and sometimes off-beat, but they always address how technology is affecting our lives. We publish articles ranging from online shopping to wireless technology."

$ $ ▨ UTAH BUSINESS, The Magazine for Decision Makers, Olympus Publishing, 85 E. Fort Union Blvd., Midvale UT 84047-1531. (801)568-0114. E-mail: editor@utahbusiness.com. Website: www.utahbusiness.com. **Contact:** Gail Newbold, editor. **95% freelance written.** Monthly magazine. "*Utah Business* is a monthly magazine focusing on the people, practices, and principles that drive Utah's economy. Audience is business owners and executives." Estab. 1987. Circ. 35,000. Pays 2 weeks after publication. Byline given. Buys first, one-time, all rights, makes work-for-hire assignments. Editorial lead time 3 months. Submit seasonal material 5 months in advance. Accepts queries by mail, e-mail, fax. Accepts simultaneous submissions. Sample copy for $5, 8½×11 SAE and 8 first-class stamps. Writer's guidelines for #10 SASE.

O— Break in by "reviewing our editorial calendar, then querying us with an idea for a particular column or feature 4 months in advance."

Nonfiction: How-to (business), interview/profile (business), new product, technical (business/technical), business-related articles. "Everything we publish must have a Utah angle." **Buys 150-180 mss/year.** Length: 500-2,500 words. **Pays 20¢/word.** Sometimes pays expenses of writers on assignment.
Photos: State availability with submission. Reviews contact sheets, negatives, transparencies, prints. Buys one-time rights. Offers no additional payment for photos accepted with ms. Captions, identification of subjects, model releases required.
Columns/Departments: Query with published clips. **Pays 20¢/word.**
Tips: "Use common sense; tailor your queries and stories to this market. Use AP style and colorful leads. Read the magazine first!"

N **$ $ VERMONT BUSINESS MAGAZINE**, 2 Church St., Burlington VT 05401-4445. (802)863-8038. Fax: (802)863-8069. E-mail: vtbizmag@together.net. Website: www.vtbusinessmagazine.com. **Contact:** Timothy McQuiston, editor. **80% freelance written.** Monthly tabloid covering business in Vermont. Circ. 8,000. Pays on publication. Publishes ms an average of 1 month after acceptance. Byline given. Buys one-time rights. Responds in 2 months to queries. Sample copy for 11×14 SAE and 7 first-class stamps.
Nonfiction: Business trends and issues. **Buys 200 mss/year.** Query with published clips. Length: 800-1,800 words. **Pays $100-200.**
Reprints: Send tearsheet and information about when and where the material previously appeared.
Photos: Send photos with submission. Reviews contact sheets. Offers $10-35/photo. Identification of subjects required.
Tips: "Read daily papers and look for business angles for a follow-up article. We look for issue and trend articles rather than company or businessman profiles. Note: Magazine accepts Vermont-specific material only. The articles must be about Vermont."

CAREER, COLLEGE & ALUMNI

Three types of magazines are listed in this section: University publications written for students, alumni and friends of a specific institution; publications about college life for students; and publications on career and job opportunities. Literary magazines published by colleges and universities are listed in the Literary & "Little" section.

$ $ AMERICAN CAREERS, Career Communications, Inc., 6701 W. 64th St., Overland Park KS 66202. (913)362-7788. Fax: (913)362-4864. Website: www.carcom.com. **Contact:** Mary Pitchford, editor. **50% freelance written.** Quarterly high school and vocational school student publication covering careers, career statistics, skills needed to get jobs. "*American Careers* provides career, salary and education information to middle school and high school students. Self-tests help them relate their interests and abilities to future careers. Articles on résumés, interviews, etc., help them develop employability skills." Estab. 1989. Circ. 500,000. **Pays on acceptance.** Byline given. Buys all rights, makes work-for-hire assignments. Accepts simultaneous submissions. Responds in 1 month to queries. Sample copy for $3. Writer's guidelines for #10 SASE.
   O— Break in by "sending us query letters with samples and résumés. We want to 'meet' the writer before making an assignment."
Nonfiction: Career and education features related to 6 basic career paths: Arts and communication; business, management and related technology; health services; human services; industrial and engineering technology; and natural resources and agriculture. "No preachy advice to teens or articles that talk down to students." **Buys 20 mss/year.** Query by mail only with published clips. Length: 300-1,000 words. **Pays $100-450.** Pays expenses of writers on assignment.
Photos: State availability with submission. Reviews contact sheets, transparencies, prints. Buys all rights. Negotiates payment individually. Captions, identification of subjects, model releases required.
Tips: "Letters of introduction or query letters with samples and résumés are ways we get to know writers. Samples should include how-to articles and career-related articles. Articles written for teenagers also would make good samples. Short feature articles on careers, career-related how-to articles and self-assessment tools (10-20 point quizzes with scoring information) are primarily what we publish."

$ $ **THE BLACK COLLEGIAN, The Career & Self Development Magazine for African-American Students**, iMinorities.com, Inc., 909 Poydras St., 36th Floor, New Orleans LA 70112. (504)523-0154. Fax: (504)523-0271. E-mail: robert@black-collegiate.com. Website: www.black-collegian.com. **Contact:** Robert Miller, vice president/editor. **25% freelance written.** Semiannual magazine for African-American college students and recent graduates with an interest in career and job information, African-American cultural awareness, personalities, history, trends and current events. Estab. 1970. Circ. 118,000. Pays on publication. Byline given. Buys one-time rights. Submit seasonal material 2 months in advance. Accepts queries by mail, e-mail, fax. Responds in 6 months to queries. Sample copy for $4 and 9×12 SAE. Writer's guidelines for #10 SASE.
Nonfiction: Material on careers, sports, black history, news analysis. Articles on problems and opportunities confronting African-American college students and recent graduates. Book excerpts, exposé, general interest, historical/nostalgic, how-to (develop employability), inspirational, interview/profile, opinion, personal experience. Query. Length: 900-1,900 words. **Pays $100-500 for assigned articles.**

Photos: State availability of or send photos with submission. Reviews 8 × 10 prints. Captions, identification of subjects, model releases required.

> 🖳 The online magazine carries original content in addition to what's included in the print edition. Contact: Kathy De Joie, online editor.

Tips: Articles are published under primarily five broad categories: job hunting information, overviews of career opportunities and industry reports, self-development information, analyses and investigations of conditions and problems that affect African Americans, and celebrations of African-American success.

N̄ $ $ $ $ BROWN ALUMNI MAGAZINE, Brown University, Box 1854, Providence RI 02912-1854. (401)863-2873. Fax: (401)863-9599. E-mail: alumni_magazine@brown.edu. Website: www.brownalumnimagazine.com. Editor: Norman Boucher. **Contact:** Nadine Whealton, office manager. **50% freelance written.** Bimonthly magazine covering the world of Brown University and its alumni. "We are an editorially independent, general interest magazine covering the on-campus world of Brown University and the off-campus world of its alumni." Estab. 1900. Circ. 80,000. **Pays on acceptance.** Publishes ms an average of 3 months after acceptance. Byline given. Offers 30% kill fee. Buys first North American serial rights. Editorial lead time 3 months. Submit seasonal material 4 months in advance. Accepts queries by mail, e-mail, fax. Responds in 1 month to queries; 2 months to mss. Sample copy free.

Nonfiction: Book excerpts, essays, exposé, general interest, historical/nostalgic, humor, interview/profile, opinion, personal experience, photo feature, travel, profiles. No articles unconnected to Brown or its alumni. **Buys 50 mss/year.** Query with published clips. Length: 150-4,000 words. **Pays $200-2,000 for assigned articles; $100-1,500 for unsolicited articles.** Pays expenses of writers on assignment.

Photos: State availability with submission. Reviews contact sheets, transparencies. Buys one-time rights. Negotiates payment individually. Captions, identification of subjects required.

Columns/Departments: Under the Elms (news items about campus), 100-400 words; Arts & Culture (reviews of Brown authored works), 200-500 words; Alumni P.O.V. (essays by Brown alumni), 750 words; Sports (reports on Brown sports teams and athletes), 200-500 words. **Buys 30-40 mss/year.** Query with published clips. **Pays $100-500.**

Tips: "Be imaginative and be specific. A Brown connection is required for all stories in the magazine, but a Brown connection alone does not guarantee our interest. Ask yourself: Why should readers care about your proposed story? Also, we look for depth and objective reporting, not boosterism."

$ $🖾 CAREER FOCUS, For Today's Professional Lifestyles, Communications Publishing Group, Inc., 3100 Broadway, Suite 660, Kansas City MO 64111-2413. (816)960-1988. Fax: (816)960-1989. **Contact:** Associate Editor. **80% freelance written.** Bimonthly magazine "devoted to career and business-minded Blacks and Hispanics (ages 21-54)." Estab. 1988. Circ. 250,000. Pays on publication. Byline sometimes given. Buys first North American serial, one-time, second serial (reprint) rights. Submit seasonal material 6 months in advance. Accepts simultaneous submissions. Responds in 1 month to queries. Sample copy for 9 × 12 SAE and 4 first-class stamps. Writer's guidelines for #10 SASE.

> • The editor notes that if the writer can provide the manuscript on 3.25 disk, saved in generic ASCII, pay is $10 higher and chance of acceptance is greater.

Nonfiction: Looking for articles about changing careers as an adult, educational preparation for different careers, and up-and-coming professions. Book excerpts, general interest, how-to, humor, inspirational, interview/profile, personal experience, photo feature, technical, travel. Length: 750-2,000 words. **Pays $150-400 for assigned articles; 12¢/word for unsolicited articles.** Sometimes pays expenses of writers on assignment.

Reprints: Send tearsheet and information about when and where the material previously appeared. Pays 10¢/word.

Photos: State availability with submission. Reviews transparencies. Buys all rights. Pays $20-25/photo. Captions, identification of subjects, model releases required.

Columns/Departments: Profiles (successful Black and Hispanic young adult, ages 21-40). **Buys 30 mss/year.** Send complete ms. **Pays $50-250.**

Fiction: Adventure, ethnic, historical, humorous, mainstream, slice-of-life vignettes. **Buys 3 mss/year.** Send complete ms. Length: 500-2,000 words. **Pay varies.**

Fillers: Anecdotes, facts, gags to be illustrated by cartoonist, newsbreaks, short humor. **Buys 10/year.** Length: 25-250 words. **Pays $25-100.**

Tips: For new writers: Submit full ms that is double-spaced; clean copy only. If available, send clips of previously published works and résumé. Should state when available to write. Most open to freelancers are profiles of successful persons including photos. Profile must be of a Black or Hispanic adult living in the US. Include on first page of ms name, address, phone number, Social Security number and number of words in article.

$ $ CIRCLE K MAGAZINE, 3636 Woodview Trace, Indianapolis IN 46268-3196. (317)875-8755. Fax: (317)879-0204. E-mail: ckimagazine@kiwanis.org. Website: www.circlek.org. **Contact:** Shanna Mooney, executive editor. **60% freelance written.** Magazine published 5 times/year. "Our readership consists almost entirely of above-average college students interested in voluntary community service and leadership development. They are politically and socially aware and have a wide range of interests." Circ. 15,000. **Pays on acceptance.** Byline given. Buys first North American serial rights. Accepts queries by mail, e-mail, fax. Responds in 2 months to queries. Sample copy and writer's guidelines for large SAE with 3 first-class stamps or online.

> ⚬⚊ Break in by offering "fresh ideas for stories dealing with college students who are not only concerned with themselves. Our readers are concerned with making their communities better."

Nonfiction: Articles published in *Circle K* are of 2 types—serious and light nonfiction. "We are interested in general interest articles on topics concerning college students and their lifestyles, as well as articles dealing with careers, community concerns and leadership development." "No first person confessions, family histories or travel pieces." Query. Length: 1,500-2,000 words. **Pays $150-400.**

Photos: Purchased with accompanying ms; total price includes both photos and ms. Captions required.

Tips: "Query should indicate author's familiarity with the field and sources. Subject treatment must be objective and in-depth, and articles should include illustrative examples and quotes from persons involved in the subject or qualified to speak on it. We are open to working with new writers who present a good article idea and demonstrate that they've done their homework concerning the article subject itself, as well as concerning our magazine's style. We're interested in college-oriented trends, for example: entrepreneur schooling, high-tech classrooms, music, leisure and health issues."

$ ◪ COLLEGE BOUND, The Magazine for High School Students By College Students, Ramholtz Publishing Inc., 2071 Clove Rd., Suite 206, Staten Island NY 10304-1643. (718)273-5700. Fax: (718)273-2539. E-mail: editorial@collegebound.net. Website: www.collegebound.net. **Contact:** Gina LaGuardia, editor-in-chief. **85% freelance written.** Bimonthly magazine "written by college students for high school students and is designed to provide an inside view of college life." Estab. 1987. Circ. 95,000. Pays on publication. Publishes ms an average of 4 months after acceptance. Byline given. Buys first North American serial, second serial (reprint), electronic rights. Editorial lead time 4 months. Submit seasonal material 4 months in advance. Accepts queries by mail, e-mail. Responds in 5 weeks to queries. Sample copy and writer's guidelines for 9×12 SASE.

Nonfiction: How-to (apply for college, prepare for the interview, etc.), personal experience (college experiences). **Buys 30 mss/year.** Query with published clips. Length: 600-1,000 words. **Pays $70-100.**

Reprints: Send photocopy.

Photos: Send photos with submission. Reviews prints. Buys one-time rights. Offers no additional payment for photos accepted with ms.

Columns/Departments: Straight Up Strategies (think fun, service pieces: campus survival tips, admissions advice, etc.), 150-400 words; Cash Crunch (money-related tips, scholarship news, advice), 150-400 words; Personal Statement (first-person account of a college-related experience), 600-1,000 words; Debate Team (op-ed style views on college controversies), 500-600 words. **Buys 30 mss/year.** Query with published clips. **Pays $15-100.**

Fillers: Anecdotes, facts, newsbreaks, short humor. **Buys 10/year.** Length: 50-200 words. **Pays $15-25.**

◨ The online magazine carries original content not found in the print edition.

Tips: "College students from around the country (and those young at heart) are welcome to serve as correspondents to provide our teen readership with both personal accounts and cutting-edge, expert advice on the college admissions process and beyond. We're looking for well-researched articles packed with real-life student anecdotes and expert insight on everything from dealing with dorm life, choosing the right college, and joining a fraternity or sorority, to college dating, cool campus happenings, scholarship scoring strategies, and other college issues."

$ $ ◪ COLLEGE PREVIEW, A Guide for College-Bound Students, Communications Publishing Group, 3100 Broadway, Suite 660, Kansas City MO 64110. (816)960-1988. Fax: (816)960-1989. **Contact:** Editor. **80% freelance written.** Quarterly educational and career source guide. "Contemporary guide designed to inform and motivate Black and Hispanic young adults, ages 16-21 years old about college preparation, career planning and life survival skills." Estab. 1985. Circ. 600,000. Pays on publication. Buys first, second serial (reprint) rights, makes work-for-hire assignments. Submit seasonal material 6 months in advance. Accepts simultaneous submissions. Responds in 1 month to queries. Sample copy for 9×12 SAE and 4 first-class stamps. Writer's guidelines for #10 SASE.

● The editor notes that if the writer can provide the manuscript on 3.25 disk, saved in generic ASCII, pay is $10 higher and chance of acceptance is greater.

Nonfiction: Book excerpts (or reviews), general interest, how-to (dealing with careers or education), humor, inspirational, interview/profile (celebrity or), new product (as it relates to young adult market), personal experience, photo feature, technical, travel. Send complete ms. Length: 750-2,000 words. **Pays $150-400 for assigned articles; 12¢/word for unsolicited articles.** Sometimes pays expenses of writers on assignment.

Reprints: Send tearsheet, photocopy or typed ms with rights for sale noted and information about when and where the material previously appeared. Pays 10¢/word.

Photos: State availability with submission. Reviews transparencies. Offers $20-25/photo. Captions, identification of subjects, model releases required.

Columns/Departments: Profiles of Achievement (striving and successful minority young adults ages 16-35 in various careers), 500-1,500 words. **Buys 30 mss/year.** Send complete ms. **Pays 10¢/word.**

Fiction: Adventure, ethnic, historical, humorous, mainstream, slice-of-life vignettes. **Buys 3 mss/year.** Send complete ms. Length: 500-2,000 words. **Pay varies.**

Fillers: Anecdotes, facts, gags to be illustrated by cartoonist, newsbreaks, short humor. **Buys 10/year.** Length: 25-250 words. **Pays $25-100.**

Tips: For new writers—send complete ms that is double spaced; clean copy only. If available, send clips of previously published works and résumé. Should state when available to write. Include on first page of ms name, address, phone, Social Security number, word count and SASE.

$ $ ◪ COMMUNITY COLLEGE WEEK, CMA Publishing Inc., 10520 Warwick Ave., Suite B-8, Fairfax VA 22030. (703)385-2981. Fax: (703)385-1839. E-mail: scottc@cmabiccw.com. Website: www.ccweek.com. Assistant

Editor: Jamilah Evelyn. **Contact:** Scott Cech, editor. **80% freelance written.** Biweekly tabloid covering two-year colleges. "*Community College Week* is the nation's only independent newspaper covering news, features and trends at the country's 1,250 community, junior and technical colleges." Circ. 6,500. Pays on publication. Byline given. Offers $50 kill fee. Buys one-time rights. Editorial lead time 2 months. Submit seasonal material 2 months in advance. Accepts queries by e-mail. Responds in 2 weeks to queries. Sample copy free. Writer's guidelines by e-mail.

Nonfiction: Exposé, interview/profile, opinion, photo feature, book reviews. **Buys 260 mss/year.** Query with published clips. Length: 400-1,500 words. **Pays 25¢/word.** Sometimes pays expenses of writers on assignment.

Photos: State availability with submission. Buys one-time rights. Negotiates payment individually. Captions required.

Columns/Departments: Pays 35¢/word.

$ $⊠ DIRECT AIM, For Today's Career Strategies, Communications Publishing Group, 3100 Broadway, Pen Tower, Suite 660, Kansas City MO 64110. (816)960-1988. Fax: (816)960-1989. **Contact:** Editor. **80% freelance written.** Quarterly magazine providing an educational and career source guide for Black and Hispanic college students at traditional, non-traditional, vocational and technical institutions. "This magazine informs students about college survival skills and planning for a future in the professional world." Buys second serial (reprint) rights, makes work-for-hire assignments. Submit seasonal material 6 months in advance. Accepts simultaneous submissions. Responds in 1 month to queries. Sample copy for 9×12 SAE and 4 first-class stamps. Writer's guidelines for #10 SASE.

  • The editor notes that if the writer can provide the manuscript on 3.25 disk, saved in generic ASCII, pay is $10 higher and chance of acceptance is greater.

Nonfiction: Book excerpts (or reviews), general interest, how-to (dealing with careers or education), humor, inspirational, interview/profile (celebrity or), new product (as it relates to the young adult market), personal experience, photo feature, technical, travel. Query with or without published clips or send complete ms. Length: 750-2,000 words. **Pays $150-400 for assigned articles; 12¢/word for unsolicited articles.** Sometimes pays expenses of writers on assignment.

Reprints: Send photocopy with rights for sale noted and information about when and where the material previously appeared. Pays 10¢/word.

Photos: State availability with submission. Reviews transparencies. Offers $20-25/photo. Captions, identification of subjects, model releases required.

Columns/Departments: Profiles of Achievement (striving and successful minority young adult age 18-35 in various technical careers). **Buys 25 mss/year.** Send complete ms. **Pays $50-250.**

Fiction: Adventure, ethnic, historical, humorous, mainstream, slice-of-life vignettes. **Buys 3 mss/year.** Send complete ms. Length: 500-2,000 words. **Pay varies.**

Fillers: Anecdotes, facts, gags to be illustrated by cartoonist, newsbreaks, short humor. **Buys 30/year.** Length: 25-250 words. **Pays $25-100.**

Tips: For new writers—send complete ms that is double spaced; clean copy only. If available, send clips of previously published works and résumé. Should state when available to write. Include on first page of ms name, address, phone, Social Security number and word count. Photo availability is important.

$ $⊠ DIVERSITY, Career Opportunities & Insights, CASS Recruitment Media/CASS Communications, Inc., 1800 Sherman Ave., Suite 404, Evanston IL 60201-3769. (847)448-1019. Fax: (847)492-7373. E-mail: vicki.chung @casscom.com. Website: www.casscom.com. **Contact:** Vicki Chung, editor. **75% freelance written.** Quarterly magazine covering "career planning and job-hunting for minorities, women and people with disabilities, who are college or university seniors preparing to enter the workforce or graduate school. Readers will be interested in white-collar professional positions in a variety of industries." Estab. 1967. Circ. 21,000. **Pays on acceptance.** Publishes ms an average of 3 months after acceptance. Byline given. Buys first North American serial rights. Editorial lead time 3 months. Accepts queries by mail, e-mail. Responds in 3 weeks to queries; 1 month to mss. Sample copy for 10×12 SAE with 6 first-class stamps. Writer's guidelines for #10 SASE or by e-mail.

  ⚬┓ Break in with "a story targeted specifically to the concerns of women and minority college seniors who are getting ready to start their professional careers or go on to graduate school."

Nonfiction: "We would like to see more articles *by* minority/women/disabled college students or recent grads." How-to (job search and career management fundamentals), industry surveys and trends. Special issues: Top Career Opportunities for Minorities and Women (Winter 2002). **Buys 20-30 mss/year.** Query with published clips. Length: 1,500-2,000 words. **Pays $400-550 for assigned articles; $350 for unsolicited articles.** Pays phone expenses only of writers on assignment.

Photos: State availability with submission. Contact photo editor for guidelines. Identification of subjects required.

Columns/Departments: Columns are usually unpaid assignments.

Tips: "Remember our audience—college seniors who are minorities, women and persons with disabilities. Try to appeal to today's young, hip, Internet-savvy audience. Sources interviewed should reflect diversity."

$ $ EQUAL OPPORTUNITY, The Nation's Only Multi-Ethnic Recruitment Magazine for Black, Hispanic, Native American & Asian American College Grads, Equal Opportunity Publications, Inc., 1160 E. Jericho Turnpike, Suite 200, Huntington NY 11743-5405. (516)421-9469. Fax: (516)421-0359. E-mail: info@aol.com. Website: www.eop. com. **Contact:** James Schneider or Claudia Wheeler, editors. **70% freelance written.** Prefers to work with published/ established writers. Triannual magazine covering career guidance for minorities. "Our audience is 90% college juniors and seniors; 10% working graduates. An understanding of educational and career problems of minorities is essential." Estab. 1967. Circ. 15,000. Pays on publication. Publishes ms an average of 6 months after acceptance. Byline given.

Buys first rights. Editorial lead time 6 months. Submit seasonal material 6 months in advance. Accepts queries by mail, e-mail, fax, phone. Responds in 2 weeks to queries; 1 month to mss. Sample copy and writer's guidelines for 9×12 SAE with 5 first-class stamps.

• Distributed through college guidance and placement offices.

Nonfiction: Book excerpts, general interest (specific minority concerns), how-to (job hunting skills, personal finance, better living, coping with discrimination), humor (student or career related), interview/profile (minority role models), opinion (problems of minorities), personal experience (professional and student study experiences), technical (on career fields offering opportunities for minorites), travel (on overseas job opportunities), coverage of minority interests. **Buys 10 mss/year.** Query with or without published clips or send complete ms. Length: 1,000-2,000 words. **Pays 10¢/word.** Sometimes pays expenses of writers on assignment.

Reprints: Send information about when and where the material previously appeared. Pays 10¢/word.

Photos: Reviews 35mm color slides and b&w. Buys all rights. Pays $15/photo use. Captions, identification of subjects required.

Tips: "Articles must be geared toward questions and answers faced by minority and women students. We would like to see role-model profiles of professions."

N $ $ $ $ EXPERIENCE MAGAZINE, The magazine for building your career, experience.com inc., One Faneuil Hall Marketplace, Boston MA 02109. Fax: (617)305-7900. Website: www.experience.com. Editor: Danyel Barnard. **Contact:** Christopher Bordeau, associate editor. **50% freelance written.** Quarterly magazine on career development for young professionals. Estab. 1999. Circ. 1 million. Pays 45 days after acceptance. Publishes ms an average of 3 months after acceptance. Byline given. Offers 25% kill fee. Buys all rights. Editorial lead time 5 months. Accepts queries by mail, fax. Sample copy free. Writer's guidelines free or online.

Nonfiction: How-to, interview/profile, career-related. **Buys 20-30 mss/year.** Query with published clips. Length: 1,000-2,500 words. **Pays $500-2,500.** Sometimes pays expenses of writers on assignment.

$ $ ◪ FIRST OPPORTUNITY, Today's Career Options, Communications Publishing Group, 3100 Broadway, Suite 660, Kansas City MO 64111. (816)960-1988. Fax: (816)960-1989. **Contact:** Editor. **80% freelance written.** Resource publication focusing on advanced vocational/technical educational opportunities and career preparation for Black and Hispanic young adults, ages 16-21. Circ. 500,000. Pays on publication. Byline sometimes given. Buys first, one-time, second serial (reprint) rights, makes work-for-hire assignments. Submit seasonal material 6 months in advance. Accepts simultaneous submissions. Responds in 1 month to queries. Sample copy for 9×12 SAE and 4 first-class stamps. Writer's guidelines for #10 SASE.

• The editor notes that if the writer can provide the manuscript on 3.25 disk, saved in generic ASCII, pay is $10 higher and chance of acceptance is greater.

Nonfiction: Looking for articles about volunteering (how it can prepare young adults for a career), education preparation for different careers, and management skills for young adults. Book excerpts (or reviews), general interest, how-to (dealing with careers or education), humor, inspirational, interview/profile (celebrity or), new product (as it relates to young adult market), personal experience, photo feature, technical, travel. Length: 750-2,000 words. **Pays $150-400 for assigned articles; 12¢/word for unsolicited articles.** Sometimes pays expenses of writers on assignment.

Reprints: Send photocopy with rights for sale noted and information about when and where the material previously appeared. Pays 10¢/word.

Photos: State availability with submission. Reviews transparencies. Buys all rights. Offers $20-25/photo. Captions, identification of subjects, model releases required.

Columns/Departments: Profiles of Achievement (successful minority young adult, age 16-35 in various vocational or technical careers). **Buys 30 mss/year.** Send complete ms. **Pays $50-250.**

Fiction: Adventure, ethnic, historical, humorous, mainstream, slice-of-life vignettes. **Buys 3 mss/year.** Send complete ms. Length: 500-5,000 words. **Pay varies.**

Fillers: Anecdotes, facts, gags to be illustrated by cartoonist, newsbreaks, short humor. **Buys 10/year.** Length: 25-250 words. **Pays $25-100.**

Tips: For new writers—send complete ms that is double spaced; clean copy only. If available, send clips of previously published works and résumé. Should state when available to write. Include on first page of ms name, address, phone, Social Security number and word count. Photo availability is important.

N $ $ $ $ HARVARD MAGAZINE, Harvard Magazine Inc., 7 Ware St., Cambridge MA 02138. (617)495-5746. Fax: (617)495-0324. Website: www.harvardmagazine.com. **Contact:** John S. Rosenberg, editor. **35-50% freelance written.** Bimonthly magazine for Harvard University faculty, alumni and students. Estab. 1898. Circ. 225,000. Pays on publication. Publishes ms an average of 4 months after acceptance. Byline given. Buys one-time print and website rights. Editorial lead time 1 year. Accepts queries by mail, fax. Responds in 1 month. Sample copy online.

Nonfiction: Book excerpts, essays, interview/profile, journalism on Harvard-related intellectual subjects. **Buys 20-30 mss/year.** Query with published clips. Length: 800-10,000 words. **Pays $250-2,000.** Pays expenses of writers on assignment.

$ ◪ ▣ I LOVE MY JOB!, Herbelin Publishing, P.O. Box 74, Riverbank CA 95367. (209)869-6389. Fax: (209)869-6389. E-mail: herbelin@netfeed.com. Website: www.riverbankbooks.com. Managing Editor: Jocelyn Herbelin. **Contact:** Steve Herbelin, editor. **100% freelance written.** Biweekly online publication covering job- and workplace-related mini and short stories. Estab. 1997. Circ. 545. **Pays on acceptance.** Publishes ms an average of 1 month after acceptance. Byline given. Buys first North American serial, one-time rights. Editorial lead time 1 month. Submit seasonal material 1 month in advance. Accepts queries by mail, e-mail, fax. Accepts simultaneous submissions. Responds in 2 weeks to queries; 2 months to mss. Sample copy and writer's guidelines online or by e-mail.

Nonfiction: Humor, inspirational. **Buys 50 mss/year.** Send complete ms. Length: 25-4,000 words. **Pays $25-100.**

Fiction: Length: 2,000 words. **Pays $100.**

Tips: "Humorous, true anecdotes from the job and workplace are preferred."

$ $ KANSAS ALUMNI, Kansas Alumni Association, 1266 Oread Ave., Lawrence KS 66044-3169. (785)864-4760. Fax: (785)864-5397. E-mail: ksalumni@kualumni.org. Website: www.ukans.edu/~kualumni/. Editor: Jennifer Jackson Sanner. **Contact:** Chris Lazzarino, managing editor. **20% freelance written.** Bimonthly alumni association magazine covering the University of Kansas alumni and related subjects. "Our mission is to keep members of the Kansas Alumni Association connected with the University of Kansas. We cover KU in a straightforward manner, presenting all manner of news and features about KU." Estab. 1902. Circ. 40,000. **Pays on acceptance.** Publishes ms an average of 2 months after acceptance. Byline given. Offers 50% kill fee. Buys first North American serial, electronic rights. Editorial lead time 4 months. Submit seasonal material 6 months in advance. Accepts queries by mail. Responds in 1 month to queries; 2 months to mss. Sample copy and writer's guidelines free.

O── Break in with "alumni profiles—500-word pieces about interesting KU alumni around the world."

Nonfiction: Book excerpts, historical/nostalgic, humor, opinion, book reviews. **Buys 8-10 mss/year.** Query with published clips. Length: 500-2,000 words. **Pays $225-700.** Sometimes pays expenses of writers on assignment.

Photos: State availability with submission. Reviews contact sheets, transparencies. Buys one-time rights. Negotiates payment individually. Captions, identification of subjects, model releases required.

Columns/Departments: Alumni profiles (interesting KU alumni), 500 words. **Buys 15 mss/year.** Query with published clips. **Pays $250.**

Tips: "We prefer first contact by mail, though e-mail or phone calls can be used. We usually start new writers with alumni profiles. We rarely assign material to new writers; we prefer to have them submit profile and article ideas."

$ $ $ NOTRE DAME MAGAZINE, University of Notre Dame, 538 Grace Hall, Notre Dame IN 46556-5612. (219)631-5335. Fax: (219)631-6767. E-mail: ndmag.1@nd.edu. Website: www.nd.edu/~ndmag. Managing Editor: Carol Schaal. **Contact:** Kerry Temple, editor. **75% freelance written.** Quarterly magazine covering news of Notre Dame and education and issues affecting contemporary society. "We are a university magazine with a scope as broad as that found at a university, but we place our discussion in a moral, ethical, spiritual context reflecting our Catholic heritage." Estab. 1972. Circ. 142,000. **Pays on acceptance.** Publishes ms an average of 1 year after acceptance. Byline given. Buys first, electronic rights. Accepts queries by mail, e-mail, fax. Responds in 2 months to queries. Sample copy and writer's guidelines online.

Nonfiction: Opinion, personal experience, religious. **Buys 35 mss/year.** Query with published clips. Length: 600-3,000 words. **Pays $250-1,500.** Sometimes pays expenses of writers on assignment.

Photos: State availability with submission. Reviews b&w contact sheets, transparencies, 8×10 prints. Buys one-time and electronic rights. Identification of subjects, model releases required.

Columns/Departments: Perspectives (essays, often written in first-person, deal with a wide array of issues—some topical, some personal, some serious, some light). Query with or without published clips or send complete ms.

■ The online magazine carries original content not found in the print edition and includes writer's guidelines. Contact: Carol Schaal.

Tips: "The editors are always looking for new writers and fresh ideas. However, the caliber of the magazine and frequency of its publication dictate that the writing meet very high standards. The editors value articles strong in storytelling quality, journalistic technique, and substance. They do not encourage promotional or nostalgia pieces, stories on sports, or essays which are sentimentally religious."

$ $ OREGON QUARTERLY, The Magazine of the University of Oregon, 5228 University of Oregon Chapman Hall, Eugene OR 97403-5228. (541)346-5048. Fax: (541)346-5571. E-mail: quarterly@oregon.uoregon.edu. Website: www.uoregon.edu/~oq. Assistant Editor: Kathleen Holt. **Contact:** Guy Maynard. **50% freelance written.** Quarterly magazine covering people and ideas at the University of Oregon and the Northwest. Estab. 1919. Circ. 100,000. **Pays on acceptance.** Publishes ms an average of 3 months after acceptance. Byline given. Buys first North American serial rights. Accepts queries by mail, e-mail. Responds in 2 months to queries. Sample copy for 9×12 SAE with 4 first-class stamps or online.

O── Break in to the magazine with a profile (400 or 800 words) of a University of Oregon alumnus. Best to query first.

Nonfiction: Northwest issues and culture from the perspective of UO alumni and faculty. **Buys 30 mss/year.** Query with published clips. Length: 250-2,500 words. **Pays $100-750.** Sometimes pays expenses of writers on assignment.

Reprints: Send photocopy and information about when and where the material previously appeared. Pays 50% of amount paid for an original article.

Photos: State availability with submission. Reviews 8×10 prints. Buys one-time rights. Offers $10-25/photo. Identification of subjects required.

Fiction: Publishes novel excerpts.

Tips: "Query with strong, colorful lead; clips."

$ $ $ OREGON STATER, Oregon State University Alumni Association, 204 CH2M Hill Alumni Center, Corvallis OR 97331-6303. (503)737-0780. E-mail: george.edmonston@orst.edu. **Contact:** George Edmonston Jr., editor. **20% freelance written.** Tabloid covering news of Oregon State University and its alumni. Estab. 1915. Circ. 111,000. **Pays on acceptance.** Byline given. Buys one-time rights. Editorial lead time 4 months. Submit seasonal material 3 months in advance. Responds in 2 weeks to queries; 3 months to mss. Sample copy and writer's guidelines free.
Nonfiction: General interest, historical/nostalgic, humor, inspirational, interview/profile, personal experience, photo feature. **Buys 40 mss/year.** Query with or without published clips. Length: 2,000 words. **Pays $50-1,000.** Pays expenses of writers on assignment.
Photos: Send photos with submission. Buys one-time rights. Offers no additional payment for photos accepted with ms. Captions, identification of subjects, model releases required.

$ $ ⊠ THE PENN STATER, Penn State Alumni Association, Hintz Family Alumni Center, University Park PA 16802. (814)865-2709. Fax: (814)863-5690. E-mail: pennstater@psu.edu. Website: www.alumni.psu.edu. **Contact:** Tina Hay, editor. **75% freelance written.** Bimonthly magazine covering Penn State and Penn Staters. Estab. 1910. Circ. 123,000. **Pays on acceptance.** Publishes ms an average of 4 months after acceptance. Byline given. Offers 50% kill fee. Buys first North American serial, second serial (reprint) rights. Editorial lead time 3 months. Submit seasonal material 8 months in advance. Accepts queries by mail, e-mail, fax. Accepts simultaneous submissions. Responds in 3 months to queries. Sample copy and writer's guidelines free.
Nonfiction: Stories must have Penn State connection. Book excerpts (by Penn Staters), general interest, historical/nostalgic, interview/profile, personal experience, photo feature, book reviews, science/research. No unsolicited mss. **Buys 20 mss/year.** Query with published clips. Length: 200-3,000 words. **Pays competitive rates.** Pays expenses of writers on assignment.
Reprints: Send photocopy and information about when and where the material previously appeared. Payment varies.
Photos: Send photos with submission. Reviews transparencies, prints. Buys one-time rights. Negotiates payment individually. Captions required.
Tips: "We are especially interested in attracting writers who are savvy in creative nonfiction/literary journalism. Most stories must have a Penn State tie-in."

[N] $ $ PORTLAND MAGAZINE, The University of Portland Quarterly, 5000 N. Willamette Blvd., Portland OR 97203. **Contact:** Brian Doyle, editor. **70% freelance written.** Quarterly magazine covering University of Portland news, issues, concerns. Generally features are about spirituality (especially Catholicism), the Northwest, higher education, or the University itself. Estab. 1984. Circ. 28,000. Pays on publication. Publishes ms an average of 6 months after acceptance. Byline given. Buys first North American serial rights. Editorial lead time 8 months. Submit seasonal material 8 months in advance. Responds in 1 month to queries. Sample copy and writer's guidelines free.
Nonfiction: Book excerpts, essays, general interest, interview/profile, opinion, personal experience, religious. **Buys 6 mss/year.** Query with published clips or send complete ms. Length: 1,000-3,000 words. **Pays $100-500.** Sometimes pays expenses of writers on assignment.

$ $ THE PURDUE ALUMNUS, Purdue Alumni Association, Purdue Memorial Union 160, 101 N. Grant St., West Lafayette IN 47906-6212. (765)494-5182. Fax: (765)494-9179. E-mail: slmartin@purdue.edu. Website: www.purdue.edu/PAA. **Contact:** Sharon Martin, editor. **50% freelance written.** Prefers to work with published/established writers; works with small number of new/unpublished writers each year. Bimonthly magazine covering subjects of interest to Purdue University alumni. Estab. 1912. Circ. 65,000. Pays on publication. Publishes ms an average of 2 months after acceptance. Byline given. Buys first rights, makes work-for-hire assignments. Submit seasonal material 6 months in advance. Accepts queries by mail. Accepts simultaneous submissions. Responds in 3 weeks to queries. Sample copy for 9×12 SAE with 2 first-class stamps.
Nonfiction: Focus is on alumni, campus news, issues and opinions of interest to 65,000 members of the Alumni Association. Feature style, primarily university-oriented. Issues relevant to education. General interest, historical/nostalgic, humor, interview/profile, personal experience. **Buys 12-20 mss/year.** Length: 1,500-2,500 words. **Pays $250-500 for assigned articles.** Pays expenses of writers on assignment.
Photos: State availability with submission. Reviews b&w contact sheets and 5×7 prints.
Tips: "We have more than 300,000 living, breathing Purdue alumni. If you can find a good story about one of them, we're interested. We use local freelancers to do campus pieces."

[N] $ $ RIPON COLLEGE MAGAZINE, P.O. Box 248, Ripon WI 54971-0248. (920)748-8364. Fax: (920)748-9262. E-mail: booneL@ripon.edu. Website: www.ripon.edu. **Contact:** Loren J. Boone, editor. **15% freelance written.** Quarterly magazine that "contains information relating to Ripon College and is mailed to alumni and friends of the college." Estab. 1851. Circ. 14,000. Pays on publication. Publishes ms an average of 3 months after acceptance. Byline given. Makes work-for-hire assignments. Accepts queries by mail, e-mail, fax, phone. Responds in 2 weeks to queries.
Nonfiction: Historical/nostalgic, interview/profile. **Buys 4 mss/year.** Query with or without published clips or send complete ms. Length: 250-1,000 words. **Pays $25-350.**
Photos: State availability with submission. Reviews contact sheets. Buys one-time rights. Offers additional payment for photos accepted with ms. Captions, model releases required.
Tips: "Story ideas must have a direct connection to Ripon College."

N **$ $ $ $ RUTGERS MAGAZINE**, Rutgers University, Alexander Johnston Hall, New Brunswick NJ 08903. (732)932-7084, ext. 618. Fax: (732)932-8412. E-mail: lchambe@ur.rutgers.edu. **Contact:** Renee Olson, editor. **50% freelance written.** Quarterly university magazine of "general interest, but articles must have a Rutgers University or alumni tie-in." Circ. 110,000. **Pays on acceptance.** Publishes ms an average of 4 months after acceptance. Byline given. Offers 30-35% kill fee. Buys first North American serial rights. Submit seasonal material 8 months in advance. Accepts queries by mail, e-mail, fax. Responds in 1 month to queries. Sample copy for $3 and 9×12 SAE with 5 first-class stamps.

Nonfiction: Essays, general interest, historical/nostalgic, interview/profile, photo feature, science/research, humanities. No articles without a Rutgers connection. **Buys 15-20 mss/year.** Query with published clips. Length: 2,000-4,000 words. **Pays $1,800-2,200.** Pays expenses of writers on assignment.

Photos: State availability with submission. Buys one-time rights. Payment varies. Identification of subjects required.

Columns/Departments: Business; Opinion; Sports; Alumni Profiles (related to Rutgers), all 1,200-1,800 words. **Buys 6-8 mss/year.** Query with published clips. **Pays competitively.**

Fiction: Novel excerpts.

Tips: "Send an intriguing query backed by solid clips. We'll evaluate clips and topic for most appropriate use."

N **$ $ STEAMTUNNELS**, College Web Guide, 220 Boylston St., #302, Chestnut Hill MA 02467. Fax: (617)964-5065. E-mail: editor@steamtunnels.net. Website: www.steamtunnels.net. Editor: Robert Desmond. **Contact:** Keith Powers, managing editor. **30% freelance written.** Weekly magazine inserted in college newspapers. "We are a college-oriented service journalism magazine with an Internet flavor." Estab. 1999. Circ. 2 million. Pays on publication. Publishes ms an average of 2 months after acceptance. Byline given. Offers $50 kill fee. Buys all rights. Editorial lead time 2 months. Submit seasonal material 3 months in advance. Accepts queries by e-mail. Responds in 2 weeks to queries. Sample copy and writer's guidelines online.

Nonfiction: How-to, interview/profile, new product, technical. **Buys 100 mss/year.** Query. Length: 500-1,000 words. **Pays $100-500.** Sometimes pays expenses of writers on assignment.

Photos: State availability with submission. Negotiates payment individually. Captions, identification of subjects required.

Columns/Departments: Buys 5-10 mss/year. Query. **Pays $100-500.**

Tips: "Read about us online. Pitches should be short, one paragraph maximum, and e-mailed. If e-mail is unavailable, faxes may be sent. Be sure to include artwork suggestions, sources, and website links that support your article. Links should be relevant and take the information in the article 'one step further.' We're looking for articles on all topics as long as they appeal to college readers and have an Internet 'flavor.' "

$ **SUCCEED, The Magazine for Continuing Education**, Ramholtz Publishing Inc., 2071 Clove Rd., Suite 206, Staten Island NY 10304-1643. (718)273-5700. Fax: (718)273-2539. E-mail: editorial@collegebound.net. **Contact:** Gina LaGuardia, editor-in-chief. **85% freelance written.** Quarterly magazine. "*SUCCEED*'s readers are interested in continuing education, whether it be for changing careers or enhancing their current career." Estab. 1994. Circ. 155,000. Pays on publication. Publishes ms an average of 4 months after acceptance. Byline given. Buys first, second serial (reprint) rights. Editorial lead time 4 months. Submit seasonal material 4 months in advance. Accepts queries by mail, e-mail. Accepts simultaneous submissions. Responds in 5 weeks to queries. Sample copy for $1.50. Writer's guidelines for 9×12 SASE.

O— Break in with "an up-to-date, expert-driven article of interest to our audience with personal, real-life anecdotes as support—not basis—for exploration."

Nonfiction: Essays, exposé, general interest, how-to (change careers), interview/profile (interesting careers), new product, opinion, personal experience. **Buys 25 mss/year.** Query with published clips. Length: 1,000-1,500 words. **Pays $75-150.** Sometimes pays expenses of writers on assignment.

Reprints: Send photocopy.

Photos: Send photos with submission. Reviews negatives, prints. Buys one-time rights. Offers no additional payment for photos accepted with ms. Captions, identification of subjects required.

Columns/Departments: Tech Zone (new media/technology), 300-700 words; To Be... (personality/career profile), 600-800 words; Financial Fitness (finance, money management), 100-300 words; Memo Pad (short, newsworthy items that relate to today's changing job market and continuing education); Solo Success (how readers can "do it on their own," with recommended resources, books, and software). **Buys 10 mss/year.** Query with published clips. **Pays $50-75.**

Fillers: Facts, newsbreaks. **Buys 5/year.** Length: 50-200 words.

Tips: "Stay current and address issues of importance to our readers—lifelong learners and those in career transition. They're ambitious, hands-on and open to advice, new areas of opportunity, etc."

$ $ TOMORROW'S CHRISTIAN GRADUATE, WIN Press, P.O. Box 1357, Oak Park IL 60304. (708)524-5070. Fax: (708)524-5174. E-mail: WINPress7@aol.com. Website: www.christiangraduate.com. **Contact:** Phillip Huber, managing editor. **85% freelance written.** Annual magazine covering seminary and graduate school planning. "*Tomorrow's Christian Graduate* is a planning guide for adults pursuing a seminary or Christian graduate education and expresses the value of a seminary or Christian graduate education." Estab. 1998. Circ. 150,000. Pays on publication. Publishes ms an average of 4 months after acceptance. Byline given. Buys all rights. Editorial lead time 4 months. Accepts queries by mail, e-mail. Sample copy for $3. Writer's guidelines free.

O— Break in with "a well-written, researched piece that shows how readers can get into a Christian graduate school or seminary or explains some program available at such schools."

Nonfiction: First person and how-to features focus on all topics of interest to adults pursuing graduate studies. How-to, interview/profile, personal experience. No fiction or poetry. **Buys 10-15 mss/year.** Query with published clips. Length: 800-1,600 words. **Pays 8-15¢/word for assigned articles; 6-15¢/word for unsolicited articles.**

Photos: State availability with submission. Negotiates payment individually. Captions, identification of subjects, model releases required.

Tips: "We are open to working with new/unpublished authors, especially current graduate students, graduate professors, admissions personnel, career counselors, and financial aid officers."

N $ $ U.S. BLACK ENGINEER/HISPANIC ENGINEER, And Information Technology, Career Communications Group, Inc., 729 E. Pratt St., Suite 504, Baltimore MD 21202-3101. (410)244-7101. Fax: (410)752-1837. Website: www.blackfamily.net.net. **Contact:** Eric Addison, managing editor. **80% freelance written.** Quarterly magazine. "Both of our magazines are designed to bring technology issues home to people of color. We look at careers in technology and what affects career possibilities, including education. But we also look at how technology affects Black Americans and Latinos." Estab. 1976. Circ. 40,000. Pays on publication. Publishes ms an average of 1 month after acceptance. Byline given. Offers 50% kill fee. Makes work-for-hire assignments. Editorial lead time 2 months. Accepts queries by mail, e-mail, fax, phone. Responds in 2 months to queries. Sample copy for #10 SASE. Writer's guidelines for #10 SASE.

Nonfiction: How-to (plan a career, get a first job, get a good job), interview/profile, new product, technical (new technologies and people of color involved with them), Capitol Hill/federal reportage on technology and EEO issues. No opinion pieces, first-person articles, routine profiles with no news peg or grounding in science/technology issues. Length: 650-1,800 words. **Pays $250-600 for assigned articles.** Sometimes pays expenses of writers on assignment.

Photos: State availability with submission. Buys all rights. Negotiates payment individually. Captions, identification of subjects, model releases required.

Columns/Departments: Dot-Comets (rising new economy entrepreneurs); Color of Technology (Did you know that...?), 800 words; Pros on the Move (Black/Hispanic career moves), 500 words; My Greatest Challenge (up from the roots), 650 words; E-Commerce (websites of interest), 650 words; TechDollars (technology and finance), 650 words; Community News (related to science and technology), 650 words; Technology for Kids, 650 words; Technology Overseas, 650 words. **Buys 30 mss/year. Pays $250-300.**

Tips: "Call or come see me. Also contact us about covering our conferences, Black Engineer of the Year Awards and Women of Color Technology Awards."

$ WHAT MAKES PEOPLE SUCCESSFUL, The National Research Bureau, Inc., 320 Valley St., Burlington IA 52601. (319)752-5415. Fax: (319)752-3421. **Contact:** Nancy Heinzel, editor. **75% freelance written.** Quarterly magazine. Estab. 1948. Circ. 1,500. Pays on publication. Publishes ms an average of 1 year after acceptance. Byline given. Buys all rights. Submit seasonal material 8 months in advance. Accepts queries by mail, fax, phone. Sample copy and writer's guidelines for #10 SAE with 2 first-class stamps.

Nonfiction: General interest (personality, employee morale, guides to successful living, biographies of successful persons, etc.), how-to (be successful), opinion, personal experience. No material on health. **Buys 3-4 mss/year.** Query with outline. Length: 500-700 words. **Pays 4¢/word.**

Tips: Short articles (rather than major features) have a better chance of acceptance because all articles are short.

$ $ WPI JOURNAL, Worcester Polytechnic Institute, 100 Institute Rd., Worcester MA 01609-2280. Fax: (508)831-5820. E-mail: wpi-journal@wpi.edu. Website: www.wpi.edu/+Journal. **Contact:** Michael Dorsey, editor. **50% freelance written.** Quarterly alumni magazine covering science and engineering/education/business personalities for 25,000 alumni, primarily engineers, scientists, managers, national media. Estab. 1897. Circ. 28,000. Pays on publication. Publishes ms an average of 6 months after acceptance. Byline given. Buys one-time rights. Accepts queries by mail, e-mail, fax. Accepts simultaneous submissions. Responds in 1 month to queries. Sample copy online.

Nonfiction: Interview/profile (alumni in engineering, science, etc.), photo feature, features on people and programs at WPI. Query with published clips. Length: 500-4,000 words. **Pays negotiable rate.** Sometimes pays expenses of writers on assignment.

Photos: State availability with submission. Reviews contact sheets. Pays negotiable rate. Captions required.

■ The online magazine carries original content not found in the print edition.

Tips: "Submit outline of story, story idea or published work. Features are most open to freelancers. Keep in mind that this is an alumni magazine, so most articles focus on the college and its graduates."

CHILD CARE & PARENTAL GUIDANCE

Magazines in this section address the needs and interests of families with children. Some publications are national in scope, others are geographically specific. Some offer general advice for parents, while magazines such as *Catholic Parent* answer the concerns of smaller groups. Other markets that buy articles about child care and the family are included in the Religious and Women's sections and in the Trade Education and Counseling section. Publications for children can be found in the Juvenile and Teen & Young Adult sections.

ALL ABOUT KIDS MAGAZINE, Midwest Parenting Publications, 1077 Celestial St., #101, Cincinnati OH 45202. (513)684-0501. Fax: (513)684-0507. E-mail: editor@aak.com. Website: www.aak.com. **Contact:** Shelly Bucksot, editor. **100% freelance written.** Monthly magazine. *All About Kids* covers a myriad of parenting topics and pieces of information relative to families and children in greater Cincinnati. Estab. 1985. Circ. 60,000. Pays on publication. Publishes ms an average of 6 months after acceptance. Byline given. Buys first, electronic rights. Editorial lead time 3 months. Submit seasonal material 6 months in advance. Accepts queries by mail. Writer's guidelines free.

Nonfiction: Exposé, general interest, historical/nostalgic, how-to (family projects, crafts), humor, inspirational, interview/profile, opinion, photo feature, travel. Special issues: Maternity (January); Special Needs Children (May). No product or book reviews. **Buys 50 mss/year.** Send complete ms. Length: 750-3,000 words. **Pays $50-250 for assigned articles; $50-100 for unsolicited articles.**

Photos: State availability with submission.

Fillers: Anecdotes, facts, gags to be illustrated by cartoonist, short humor. **Buys 20/year.** Length: 350-800 words. **Pays $50-100.**

Tips: "Submit full-text articles with query letter. Keep in mind the location of the magazine and try to include relevant sidebars, sources, etc."

AT-HOME MOTHER, At-Home Mothers' Resource Center, 406 E. Buchanan Ave., Fairfield IA 52556-3810. E-mail: editor@athomemothers.com. Website: www.AtHomeMothers.com. **Contact:** Jeanette Lisefski, editor. **95% freelance written.** Quarterly magazine. "*At-Home Mother* provides support for at-home mothers and features up-beat articles that reinforce their choice to stay at home with their children, helping them to find maximum fulfillment in this most cherished profession. Through education and inspiration, we also help those mothers who want to stay at home find ways to make this goal a reality." Estab. 1997. Circ. 10,000. Pays on publication. Publishes ms an average of 3 months after acceptance. Byline given. Buys first North American serial, second serial (reprint), electronic rights. Editorial lead time 3 months. Accepts queries by mail, e-mail. Accepts simultaneous submissions. Responds in 2 months to queries; 4 months to mss. Sample copy for $4 or sample articles available online. Writer's guidelines for #10 SASE.

○➡ Break in with upbeat, positive articles containing experiences by other mothers in answers to mother's concerns relating to all aspects of at-home mothering.

Nonfiction: Essays, how-to (managing home, parenting, etc.), humor, inspirational, interview/profile, personal experience, photo feature. **Buys 60-100 mss/year.** Query. Length: 500-2,500 words. **Pays $25-150.**

Reprints: Send photocopy with rights for sale noted and information about when and where the material previously appeared. Pays 50% of amount paid for an original article.

Photos: State availability with submission. Reviews contact sheets, prints. Buys one-time rights. Offers $5-75/interior photo. Captions, identification of subjects, model releases required.

Columns/Departments: Choosing Home (making the choice for at-home mothering); Making Money at Home (home work and home business); Saving Money at Home (money saving ideas); Parenting (several topics and philosophy); Mother's Self Esteem & Happiness (self-care); Celebrating Motherhood (essay, poetry, personal experience); Managing at Home (home management); Teaching at Home (home schooling & children's activities); Learning at Home (home study), all 400-2,500 words. **Buys 60-100 mss/year.** Query. **Pays $10-150.**

Poetry: Avant-garde, free verse, haiku, light verse, traditional. **Buys 5-10 poems/year.** Length: 4-50 lines. **Pays $5-25.**

Fillers: Anecdotes, facts, short humor. **Buys 5-10/year.** Length: 20-500 words. **Pays $10-50.**

Tips: "Write specifically to at-home mothers. Articles must be uplifting and/or informative. Articles must show experience or insight into subject."

ATLANTA PARENT/ATLANTA BABY, 2346 Perimeter Park Dr., Suite 101, Atlanta GA 30346. (770)454-7599. Fax: (770)454-7699. E-mail: atlantaparent@atlantaparent.com. Website: www.atlantaparent.com. Editor: Liz White. **Contact:** Peggy Middendorf, managing editor. **50% freelance written.** Pays on publication. Publishes ms an average of 3 months after acceptance. Byline given. Buys one-time rights. Submit seasonal material 6 months in advance. Accepts queries by mail, e-mail. Responds in 4 months to queries. Sample copy for $3.

Nonfiction: General interest, how-to, humor, interview/profile, travel. Special issues: Private School (January); Camp (February); Health and Fitness (March); Birthday Parties (February and October); Maternity and Mothering (May);

MARKET CONDITIONS are constantly changing! If this is 2003 or later, buy the newest edition of *Writer's Market* at your favorite bookstore or order directly from Writer's Digest Books at (800)289-0963.

Childcare (July); Back-to-School (August); Teens (September); Holidays (November/December). No first-person accounts or philosophical discussions. **Buys 60 mss/year.** Query with or without published clips or send complete ms. Length: 800-2,100 words. **Pays $15-30.** Sometimes pays expenses of writers on assignment.

Reprints: Send tearsheet or photocopy with rights for sale noted and information about when and where the material previously appeared. **Pays $15-30.**

Photos: State availability of or send photos with submission. Reviews 3×5 photos. Buys one-time rights. Offers $10/photo.

Tips: "Articles should be geared to problems or situations of families and parents. Should include down-to-earth tips and be clearly written. No philosophical discussions or first-person narratives. We're also looking for well-written humor."

$ $ $ $ BABY TALK, The Parenting Group, 530 Fifth Ave., 4th Floor, New York NY 10036. (212)522-8989. Fax: (212)522-8750. Website: www.babytalk.com. **Contact:** Brittni Boyd, editorial assistant. **Mostly freelance written.** Magazine published 10 times/year. "*Baby Talk* is written primarily for women who are considering pregnancy or who are expecting a child, and parents of children from birth through 18 months, with the emphasis on pregnancy through first six months of life." Estab. 1935. Circ. 1,725,000. Byline given. Accepts queries by mail. Responds in 2 months to queries.

Nonfiction: Features cover pregnancy, the basics of baby care, infant/toddler health, growth and development, juvenile equipment and toys, work and day care, marriage and sex, "approached from a how-to, service perspective. The message—Here's what you need to know and why—is delivered with smart, crisp style. The tone is confident and reassuring (and, when appropriate, humorous and playful), with the backing of experts. In essence, *Baby Talk* is a training manual of parents facing the day-to-day dilemmas of new parenthood." No phone calls. Query with SASE. Length: 1,000-2,000 words. **Pays $500-2,000 depending on length, degree of difficulty and the writer's experience.**

Columns/Departments: 100-1,250 words. Several departments are written by regular contributors. Query with SASE. **Pays $100-1,000.**

Tips: "Please familiarize yourself with the magazine before submitting a query. Take the time to focus your story idea; scattershot queries are a waste of everyone's time."

$ ■ BIG APPLE PARENT/QUEENS PARENT/WESTCHESTER PARENT, Family Communications, Inc., 9 E. 38th St., 4th Floor, New York NY 10016. (212)889-6400. Fax: (212)689-4958. E-mail: hellonwheels@parentsknow.com. Website: www.parentsknow.com. **Contact:** Helen Freedman, executive editor. **90% freelance written.** Monthly tabloid covering New York City family life. "*BAP* readers live in high-rise Manhattan apartments; it is an educated, upscale audience. Often both parents are working full time in professional occupations. Child-care help tends to be one-on-one, in the home. Kids attend private schools for the most part. While not quite a suburban approach, some of our *QP* readers do have backyards (though most live in high-rise apartments). It is a more middle-class audience in Queens. More kids are in day care centers; majority of kids are in public schools. Our Westchester county edition is for suburban parents." Estab. 1985. Circ. 70,000, *Big Apple*; 65,000 *Queens Parent* and *Westchester Parent*. Pays 2 months after publication. Byline given. Offers 50% kill fee. Buys first New York area rights. Submit seasonal material 3 months in advance. Accepts queries by mail, e-mail, fax. Accepts simultaneous submissions. Responds immediately to queries. Sample copy and writer's guidelines free.

   O— Break in with "Commentary (op ed); newsy angles—but everything should be targeted to parents. We love journalistic pieces (as opposed to essays, which is what we mostly get.)"

Nonfiction: Book excerpts, essays, exposé, general interest, how-to, inspirational, interview/profile, opinion, personal experience, family health, education. "We're always looking for news and coverage of controversial issues." **Buys 150 mss/year.** Query with or without published clips or send complete ms. Length: 600-1,000 words. **Pays $35-50.** Sometimes pays expenses of writers on assignment.

Reprints: Send tearsheet or typed ms with rights for sale noted and information about when and where the material previously appeared. Pays same as article rate.

Photos: Reviews contact sheets, prints. Buys one-time rights. Offers $25/photo. Captions required.

Columns/Departments: Dads; Education; Family Finance. **Buys 50-60 mss/year.** Send complete ms.

Tips: "We have a very local focus; our aim is to present articles our readers cannot find in national publications. To that end, news stories and human interest pieces must focus on New York and New Yorkers. We are always looking for news and newsy pieces; we keep on top of current events, frequently giving issues that may relate to parenting a local focus so that the idea will work for us as well."

N $ $ $ BOISE FAMILY MAGAZINE, Magazine for Treasure Valley Parents, 13191 W. Scotfield St., Boise ID 83713-0899. (208)938-2119. Fax: (208)938-2117. E-mail: boisefamily@cs.com. Website: www.boisefamily.com. **Contact:** Liz Buckingham, editor. **90% freelance written.** Monthly magazine covering parenting, education, child development. "Geared to parents with children 14 years and younger. Focus on education, interest, activities for children. Positive parenting and healthy families." Estab. 1993. Circ. 19,000. Pays on publication. Publishes ms an average of 3 months after acceptance. Byline given. Offers 50% kill fee. Buys first North American serial rights. Editorial lead time 3 months. Submit seasonal material 3 months in advance. Accepts queries by mail, e-mail. Accepts simultaneous submissions. Responds in 2 months to queries. Sample copy for $1.50. Writer's guidelines for #10 SASE.

Nonfiction: Essays, how-to, interview/profile, new product. Special issues: Women's Health and Maternity (January); Birthday Party Fun; Family Choice Awards (February); Education; Home & Garden (March); Summer Camps (April);

Kids' Sports Guide (May); Summer, Family Travel; Fairs & Festivals (June/July); Back-to-School; the Arts (August/September); Fall Fun; Children's Health (October); Winter Family Travel; Holiday Ideas (November); Holiday Crafts and Traditions (December). No political or religious affiliation-oriented articles. **Buys 10 mss/year.** Query with published clips. Length: 900-1,300 words. **Pays $50-1,000.** Sometimes pays expenses of writers on assignment. Accepts previously published submissions.

Reprints: Accepts previously published submissions.

Photos: State availability with submission. Reviews 3×5 prints. Buys one-time rights. Negotiates payment individually. Captions required.

Columns/Departments: Crafts, travel, finance, parenting. Length: 700-900 words. Query with published clips. **Pays $50-100.**

N $ ☒ CATHOLIC PARENT, Our Sunday Visitor, 200 Noll Plaza, Huntington IN 46750-4310. (219)356-8400. Fax: (219)356-8472. E-mail: cparent@osv.com. Website: www.osv.com. **Contact:** Woodeene Koenig-Bricker, editor. **95% freelance written.** Bimonthly magazine. "We look for practical, realistic parenting articles written for a primarily Roman Catholic audience. The key is practical, not pious." Estab. 1993. Circ. 36,000. **Pays on acceptance.** Publishes ms an average of 6 months after acceptance. Byline given. Offers variable kill fee. Buys first North American serial rights. Editorial lead time 6 months. Submit seasonal material 6 months in advance. Accepts simultaneous submissions. Responds in 2 months to queries. Sample copy for $3.

● *Catholic Parent* is extremely receptive to first-person accounts of personal experiences dealing with parenting issues that are moving, emotionally engaging and uplifting for the reader. Bear in mind the magazine's mission to provide practical information for parents.

Nonfiction: Essays, how-to, humor, inspirational, personal experience, religious. **Buys 50 mss/year.** Send complete ms. Length: 850-1,200 words. **Pay varies.** Sometimes pays expenses of writers on assignment.

Photos: State availability with submission.

Columns/Departments: This Works (parenting tips), 200 words. **Buys 50 mss/year.** Send complete ms. **Pays $15-25.**

Tips: No poetry or fiction.

$ $ CHICAGO PARENT, Connecting with Families, Wednesday Journal, Inc., 141 S. Oak Park Ave., Oak Park IL 60302-2972. (708)386-5555. Fax: (708)524-8360. E-mail: chiparent@aol.com. Website: chicagoparent.com. Editor: Sharon Bloyd-Peshkin. **Contact:** Karen McCarthy, editorial assistant. **60% freelance written.** Monthly tabloid. "*Chicago Parent* has a distinctly local approach. We offer information, inspiration, perspective and empathy to Chicago-area parents. Our lively editorial mix has a 'we're all in this together' spirit, and articles are thoroughly researched and well written." Estab. 1988. Circ. 135,000 in three zones. Pays on publication. Publishes ms an average of 2 months after acceptance. Byline given. Offers 10-50% kill fee. Buys one-time, second serial (reprint), electronic rights. Editorial lead time 4 months. Submit seasonal material 4 months in advance. Accepts queries by mail. Responds in 6 weeks to queries. Sample copy for $3.95 and 11×17 SAE with $1.65 postage. Writer's guidelines for #10 SASE.

○─ Break in by "writing 'short stuff' items (front-of-the-book short items on local people, places and things of interest to families)."

Nonfiction: Essays, exposé, how-to (parent-related), humor, interview/profile, travel, local interest, investigative features. Special issues: include Chicago Baby and Healthy Child. "No pot-boiler parenting pieces, simultaneous submissions, previously published pieces or non-local writers (from outside the 6-county Chicago metropolitan area)." **Buys 40-50 mss/year.** Query with published clips. Length: 200-2,500 words. **Pays $25-300 for assigned articles; $25-100 for unsolicited articles.** Pays expenses of writers on assignment.

Photos: State availability with submission. Reviews contact sheets, negatives, prints. Buys one-time rights. Offers $0-40/photo; negotiates payment individually. Captions, identification of subjects required.

Columns/Departments: Healthy Child (kids' health issues), 850 words; Getaway (travel pieces), up to 1,200 words; other columns not open to freelancers. **Buys 30 mss/year.** Query with published clips or send complete ms. **Pays $100.**

Tips: "We don't like pot-boiler parenting topics and don't accept many personal essays unless they are truly compelling."

$ $ $ $ ☒ CHILD, Gruner + Jahr, 375 Lexington Ave., New York NY 10017-5514. (212)499-2000. Fax: (212)499-2038. E-mail: childmag@aol.com. Website: www.child.com. Editor-in-Chief: Miriam Arond., Managing Editor: Polly Chevalier. **Contact:** Submissions. **95% freelance written.** Monthly magazine covering parenting. Estab. 1986. Circ. 930,000. **Pays on acceptance.** Byline given. Offers 25% kill fee. Buys all rights. Editorial lead time 5 months. Submit seasonal material 6 months in advance. Accepts queries by mail. Responds in 2 months to queries. Sample copy for $3.95. Writer's guidelines for #10 SASE.

Nonfiction: Book excerpts, essays, interview/profile, personal experience, travel. No poetry. **Buys 50 feature, 20-30 short mss/year.** Query with published clips. Length: 650-2,500 words. **Pays $1/word for assigned articles.** Sometimes pays expenses of writers on assignment.

Photos: State availability with submission. Reviews transparencies. Buys one-time rights. Negotiates payment individually.

Columns/Departments: First Person (mother's or father's perspective). **Buys 100 mss/year.** Query with published clips. **Pays $1/word.**

■ The online magazine carries original content not found in the print edition. Contact: Miriam Arond.

Tips: "Stories should include opinions from experts as well as anecdotes from parents to illustrate the points being made. Lifestyle is key." *Child* receives too many inappropriate submissions. Please consider your work carefully before submitting.

$ $⊠ CHRISTIAN PARENTING TODAY, Christianity Today International, 465 Gundersen Dr., Carol Stream IL 60188-2489. (630)260-6200. Fax: (630)260-0114. E-mail: cpt@christianparenting.net. Website: www.christianparenting.net. Managing Editor: Carla Barnhill. Associate Editor: Jennifer Mangan. **Contact:** Lori Fedele, editorial coordintor. **90% freelance written.** Bimonthly magazine. "Strives to be a positive, practical magazine that targets real needs of today's family with authoritative articles based on real experience, fresh research and the timeless truths of the Bible. *CPT* provides parents information that spans birth to 14 years of age in the following areas of growth: Spiritual, social, emotional, physical, academic." Estab. 1988. Circ. 90,000. **Pays on acceptance.** Byline given. Buys first North American serial, second serial (reprint) rights. Submit seasonal material 8 months in advance. Responds in 2 months to mss. Sample copy for 9×12 SAE with $3 postage. Writer's guidelines for #10 SASE.
Nonfiction: Feature topics of greatest interest: practical guidance in spiritual/moral development and vaalues transfer; practical solutions to everyday parenting issues; tips on how to enrich readers' marriages; ideas for nurturing healthy family ties; family activities that focus on parent/child interaction; humorous pieces about everyday family life. Book excerpts, how-to, humor, inspirational, religious. **Buys 50 mss/year.** Length: 750-2,000 words. **Pays 12-20¢/word.**
Reprints: Send tearsheet, photocopy or typed ms with rights for sale noted and information about when and where the material previously appeared.
Photos: Do not submit photos without permission. State availability with submission. Reviews transparencies. Buys one-time rights. Model releases required.
Columns/Departments: Ideas That Work (family-tested parenting ideas from our readers), 25-100 words; Life In Our House (entertaining, true humorous stories about your family), 25-100 words; Growing Up (spiritual development topics from a Christian perspective), 420-520 words. **Pays $25-150.**
Tips: "Tell it like it is. Readers have a 'get real' attitude that demands a down-to-earth, pragmatic take on topics. Don't sugar-coat things. Give direction without waffling. If you've 'been there,' tell us. The first-person, used appropriately, is OK. Don't distance yourself from readers. They trust people who have walked in their shoes. Get reader friendly. Fill your article with nuts and bolts: developmental information, age-specific angles, multiple resources, sound-bite sidebars, real-life people and anecdotes and realistic, vividly explained suggestions."

🅽 $⊠ COUNTY KIDS, Journal Register Company, 250 Post Rd. E, Westport CT 06880. (203)227-2257. Fax: (203)227-8626. E-mail: countykids@ctcentral.com. Website: www.countykids.com. **Contact:** Molly Dorozenski, managing editor. **70% freelance written.** Monthly tabloid for Connecticut parents. "We publish articles that are well-researched and informative, yet written in a casual tone." Estab. 1988. Circ. 44,000. Pays on publication. Byline given. Buys first North American serial, second serial (reprint), electronic rights. Editorial lead time 2 months. Submit seasonal material 3 months in advance. Accepts queries by mail, e-mail, fax. Accepts simultaneous submissions. Responds in 2 months to queries. Sample copy and writer's guidelines free.
Nonfiction: Essays, exposé, general interest, how-to, humor, interview/profile, new product, opinion, personal experience, photo feature. Special issues: Camp; Daycare Options; Back-to-School; Divorce/Single Parenting. No fiction, poetry or cute kids stories. **Buys 40 mss/year.** Query with or without published clips or send complete ms. Length: 800-2,000 words. **Pays $35-100 for assigned articles; $25-75 for unsolicited articles.** Accepts previously published submissions.
Reprints: Accepts previously published submissions.
Photos: Send photos with submission. Reviews contact sheets, prints. Buys one-time rights. Offers no additional payment for photos accepted with ms. Identification of subjects required.
Columns/Departments: Mom's View/Dad's View (personal experience/humor), 800 words; Double Digits (tips on parenting teens), 800 words; Museum Moments (reviews of Connecticut museums), 800 words; Parentphernalia (fast facts, local news, parenting tips), 400 words. **Buys 25 mss/year.** Send complete ms. **Pays $25-35.**
Tips: "*County Kids* is looking for strong features with a Connecticut slant. We give preferences to local writers. Mom's View and Dad's View columns are a great way to get published in *County Kids*, as long as they're humorous and casual. Features sent with photos will be given priority, as will those with sidebars."

🅽 $ $⊠ EXPECTING, Family Communications, 37 Hanna Ave., Suite 1, Toronto, Ontario M6K 1W9, Canada. (416)537-2604. Fax: (416)538-1794. **Contact:** Tracy Hitchcock, editor. **100% freelance written.** Semiannual digest-sized magazine. Writers must be Canadian health professionals. Articles address all topics relevant to expectant parents. Estab. 1995. Circ. 100,000. **Pays on acceptance.** Publishes ms an average of 6 months after acceptance. Byline given. Buys all rights. Editorial lead time 6 months. Accepts queries by mail, fax. Responds in 2 months to queries.
Nonfiction: Medical. **Buys 6 mss/year.** Query with published clips. Length: 1,000-2,000 words. **Pays $300.** Sometimes pays expenses of writers on assignment.
Photos: State availability with submission. Buys all rights. Negotiates payment individually. Identification of subjects required.

$ $ FAITH & FAMILY, The Magazine of Catholic Living, (formerly *Catholic Faith & Family*), Circle Media, 33 Rossotto Dr., Hamden CT 06514. (203)288-5600. Fax: (203)288-5157. E-mail: editor@faithandfamily.com. **Contact:** Duncan Maxwell Anderson, editorial director. **70% freelance written.** Bimonthly magazine. "We publish practical and inspirational articles to help families build a Catholic civilization at home and evalgelize the world. Subjects include Catholic traditions, family psychology, crafts, recipes, beauty and fashion, good books and media, and spiritual journeys." Estab. 1966. Circ. 30,000. **Pays on acceptance.** Byline given. Buys first rights. Accepts queries by mail, e-mail, fax.

Nonfiction: Query. Length: 1,500-3,500 words.

Photos: Include duplicate prints or photocopies of any proposed photography subjects with query. For craft projects, include duplicate snapshot of finished project.

Columns/Departments: The Home Front; The Insider; Flair; The Season; Life Lessons; Faith & Folklore; Celebrations; Entertainment; The Where and How Guide; Spiritual Directions; Back Porch. Length: 600-1,200 words. Query or send complete ms. **Pays 50¢/published word.**

$ $ ⊠ **FAMILY DIGEST, The Black Mom's Best Friend!**, Family Digest Association, 696 San Ramon Valley Blvd., #349, Danville CA 94526. Fax: (925)838-4948. E-mail: editor@familydigest.com. **Contact:** Darryl Mobley, associate editor. **90% freelance written.** Quarterly magazine. "Our mission: Help black moms/female heads-of-household get more out of their roles as wife, mother, homemaker. Editorial coverage includes parenting, health, love and marriage, travel, family finances, and beauty and style. All designed to appeal to black moms." Estab. 1997. Circ. 2,100,000. Pays on publication. Publishes ms an average of 6 months after acceptance. Buys first North American serial, all rights. Editorial lead time 2 months. Submit seasonal material 3 months in advance. Accepts queries by e-mail. Accepts simultaneous submissions. Responds in 1 month to queries. Writer's guidelines by e-mail.

Nonfiction: "We are not political. We do not want articles that blame others. We do want articles that improve the lives of our readers." Book excerpts, general interest (dealing with relationships), historical/nostalgic, how-to, humor, inspirational, interview/profile, personal experience. Query with published clips. Length: 1,000-3,000 words. **Pays $100-500.** Sometimes pays expenses of writers on assignment.

Photos: Reviews negatives, transparencies, prints. Offers no additional payment for photos accepted with ms. Captions, identification of subjects, model releases required.

Columns/Departments: A Better You!(personal development), parenting, love and marriage, health, family finances, beauty and style. **Buys 100 mss/year.** Query with published clips. **Pays $100-500.**

Fiction: Erotica, ethnic, historical, humorous, novel excerpts, romance. Query with published clips.

Fillers: Anecdotes, facts, gags to be illustrated by cartoonist, short humor. **Buys 100 mss/year.** Length: 50-250 words.

$ ⊠ **THE FAMILY DIGEST**, P.O. Box 40137, Fort Wayne IN 46804. **Contact:** Corine B. Erlandson, editor. **95% freelance written.** Bimonthly magazine. *"The Family Digest* is dedicated to the joy and fulfillment of the Catholic family and its relationship to the Catholic parish." Estab. 1945. Circ. 150,000. Pays within 2 months of acceptance. Byline given. Buys first North American serial rights. Submit seasonal material 7 months in advance. Accepts queries by mail. Responds in 2 months to queries. Sample copy and writer's guidelines for 6×9 SAE with 2 first-class stamps.

Nonfiction: Family life, parish life, prayer life, Catholic traditions. Inspirational. **Buys 60 unsolicited mss/year.** Send complete ms. Length: 750-1,200 words. **Pays $40-60 for assigned articles.**

Reprints: Send typed ms with rights for sale noted and information about when and where the material previously appeared. **Pays 5¢/word.**

Fillers: Anecdotes, tasteful humor based on personal experience. **Buys 18/year.** Length: 25-100 words. **Pays $25.**

Tips: "Prospective freelance contributors should be familiar with the publication and the types of articles we accept and publish. We are especially looking for upbeat articles which affirm the simple ways in which the Catholic faith is expressed in daily life. Articles on family and parish life, including seasonal articles, how-to pieces, inspirational, prayer, spiritual life and Church traditions, will be gladly reviewed for possible acceptance and publication."

$ $ $ $ FAMILY LIFE, 530 Fifth Ave., New York NY 10036. (212)522-6240. Fax: (212)467-1248. E-mail: family_life@timeinc.com. Website: www.familylifemag.com. **Contact:** Jacqueline Leigh Ross, editorial assistant. **60% freelance written.** Magazine published 10 times/year for parents of children ages 5-12. Estab. 1993. Circ. 500,000. **Pays on acceptance.** Publishes ms an average of 4 months after acceptance. Byline given. Offers 25% kill fee. Buys first worldwide rights. Editorial lead time 6 months. Submit seasonal material 8 months in advance. Accepts queries by mail, e-mail, fax. Accepts simultaneous submissions. Responds in 2 months to queries. Sample copy for $3. Writer's guidelines for #10 SASE.

⊶ Break in through the Parent to Parent column ("We're always looking for new ideas here."), the Year by Year section, News & Views, or Fun Stuff (crafts that are original and a little bit wacky). "Short pieces for the front and back of the book are also good ways to break in."

Nonfiction: Book excerpts (on parenting), essays (on family topics), general interest, how-to (crafts, activities, recipes, computers), humor (essays), inspirational, new product, personal experience (essays), photo feature, travel (especially tips, 100-300 words long), health, child behavior, and essays on the above topics by experts who also have a good writing background. Does not want to see articles about children under 5, childbirth, or teenagers. Query with published clips. Length: 1,500-3,500 words. **Pays $1/word.** Pays expenses of writers on assignment.

Photos: State availability with submission. Reviews transparencies. Buys all rights. Negotiates payment individually.

Columns/Departments: Front- and back-of-the-book sections (newsy shorts on parenting topics, interesting travel destinations and tips and the latest health issues), 150-250 words; Year by Year section (stories on child development specific to ages 5-7, 7-9 and 9-12), 150-250 words, 400 maximum. Individual columns: Parent to Parent (story by a parent about life with his or her child that epitomizes one issue in child-rearing); Family Tech; Child Behavior; Health & Safety; Your Time. Length: 1,000-1,500 words. Query with published clips.

■ The online magazine carries original content not found in the print edition. Contact: Suelain Moy.

Tips: "Our readers are parents of children ages 5-12 who are interested in getting the most out of family life. Most are college educated and work hard at a full-time job. We want fresh articles dealing with the day-to-day issues that these families face, with personal insight, true anecdotes and professional opinion on how to handle them."

$ $ $ $ ☒ FAMILYFUN, Disney Magazine Publishing Inc., 244 Main St., Northampton MA 01060-3107. (413)585-0444. Fax: (413)586-5724. Website: www.familyfun.com. **Contact:** Jean Graham, editorial assistant. Magazine covering activities for families with kids ages 3-12. "*Family Fun* is about all the great things families can do together. Our writers are either parents or authorities in a covered field." Estab. 1991. Circ. 1,300,000. **Pays on acceptance.** Byline sometimes given. Offers 25% kill fee. Buys simultaneous rights, makes work-for-hire assignments. Editorial lead time 6 months. Submit seasonal material 6 months in advance. Accepts simultaneous submissions. Responds in 2 months to queries. Sample copy and writer's guidelines for $3 or online.

Nonfiction: Features Editor. Book excerpts, essays, general interest, how-to (crafts, cooking, educational activities), humor, interview/profile, personal experience, photo feature, travel. Special issues: Crafts, Holidays, Back to School, Summer Vacations. **Buys dozens mss/year.** Query with published clips. Length: 850-3,000 words. **Pays $1.25/word.** Pays expenses of writers on assignment.

Photos: State availability with submission. Reviews contact sheets, negatives, transparencies. Buys all rights. Offers $75-500/photo. Identification of subjects, model releases required.

Columns/Departments: Family Almanac, Cindy Littlefield, senior editor (simple, quick, practical, inexpensive ideas and projects—outings, crafts, games, nature activities, learning projects, and cooking with children), 200-400 words; query or send ms; **pays $100-$200/article or $75 for ideas.** Family Traveler, Jodi Butler, (brief, newsy items about family travel, what's new, what's great, and especially, what's a good deal), 100-125 words; send ms; **pays $100, also pays $50 for ideas.** Family Ties, Kathy Whittemore, senior editor (first-person column that spotlights some aspect of family life that is humorous, inspirational, or interesting); 1,300 words; send ms; **pays $1,300.** My Great Idea, Dawn Chipman, senior editor (explains fun and inventive ideas that have worked for writer's own family); 800-1,000 words; query or send ms; **pays $750 on acceptance;** also publishes best letters from writers and readers following column, send to My Great Ideas editor, 100-150 words, **pays $25 on publication. Buys 20-25 mss/year.**

Tips: "Many of our writers break into *FF* by writing for Family Almanac or Family Traveler (front-of-the-book departments)."

[N] $ GENESEE VALLEY PARENT MAGAZINE, 1 Grove St., Suite 204, Pittsford NY 14534. Fax: (716)264-0647. E-mail: GVParent@aol.com. **Contact:** Beth Pessin, editor. **80% freelance written.** Monthly magazine covering raising children ages infant-14. "*Genesee Valley Parent Magazine* is a publication that provides information and tips on issues related to raising young children and adolescents. We also have book reviews, a healthy family column, Teen Talk column and Growing Concerns, which addresses a range of developmental issues." Estab. 1994. Circ. 37,000. Pays on publication. Byline given. Buys one-time, second serial (reprint) rights, makes work-for-hire assignments. Editorial lead time 4 months. Submit seasonal material 4 months in advance. Accepts queries by mail, e-mail. Accepts simultaneous submissions. Responds in 3 months to queries; 3 months to mss. Sample copy for 8½×11 SAE and $1.21 postage. Writer's guidelines for #10 SASE or by e-mail.

Nonfiction: General interest, how-to, humor, opinion, personal experience. Special issues: Baby Guide (April), Family Finances (June), Teen issue (August). **Buys 50 mss/year.** Send complete ms. Length: 550-1,200 words. **Pays $100-130 for assigned articles; $30-45 for unsolicited articles.**

Photos: Send photos with submission. Buys one-time rights. Offers no additional payment for photos accepted with ms.

Columns/Departments: Parents Exchange (opinion/personal experience related to parenting); Healthy Family (anything related to keeping family members in good health); Teen Talk (issues related to raising teens), all 550-650 words. **Buys 20 mss/year.** Send complete ms. **Pays $35.**

Tips: "Well-written, well-researched articles on current topics/issues related to raising healthy, well-adjusted children is what we run. Look for new angles, fresh approaches to age-old problems and concerns, as well as topics/issues that are more cutting edge."

[N] $ GRAND RAPIDS PARENT MAGAZINE, Gemini Publications, 549 Ottawa Ave., NW, Grand Rapids MI 49503. (616)459-4545. Fax: (616)459-2004. **Contact:** Carole Valade, editor. Monthly magazine covering local parenting issues. "*Grand Rapids Parent Magazine* seeks to inform, instruct, amuse and entertain its readers and their families." Pays on publication. Byline given. Offers $25 kill fee. Buys first North American serial, simultaneous, all rights, makes work-for-hire assignments. Editorial lead time 3 months. Submit seasonal material 4 months in advance. Accepts simultaneous submissions. Responds in 2 months to queries; 6 months to mss. Writer's guidelines for #10 SASE.

Nonfiction: "The publication recognizes that parenting is a process that begins before conception/adoption and continues for a lifetime. The issues are diverse and ever changing. *Grand Rapids Parent* seeks to identify these issues and give them a local perspective, using local sources and resources." Query. **Pays $25-50.**

Photos: State availability with submission. Reviews contact sheets. Buys one-time or all rights. Offers $25/photo. Captions, identification of subjects, model releases required.

Columns/Departments: All local: law, finance, humor, opinion, mental health. **Pays $25.**

$ $ $ $ ◪ HEALTHY KIDS, Primedia, 249 W. 17th St., New York NY 10011-5300. (212)462-3300. Fax: (212)367-8332. Website: www.americanbaby.com. Editor: Laura Broadwell. **Contact:** Editorial assistant. **90% freelance written.** Bimonthly magazine addresses all elements that go into the raising of a healthy, happy child, from basic health-care information to an analysis of a child's growing mind and behavior patterns. Extends the wisdom of the pediatrician into the home, and informs parents of young children (ages birth to 10 years) about proper health care. The only magazine produced for parents in association with the American Academy of Pediatrics, the nonprofit organization of more than 55,000 pediatricians dedicated to the betterment of children's health. Estab. 1989. Circ. 1,550,000. **Pays on acceptance.** Byline given. Offers 33% kill fee. Submit seasonal material 9 months in advance. Responds in 2 months to queries. Writer's guidelines for #10 SASE.
● To ensure accuracy, all articles are reviewed by an Editorial Advisory Board comprised of distinguished pediatricians.
Nonfiction: How to help your child develop as a person, keep safe, keep healthy. Each issue also includes one comprehensive Health Report (2,500 words) that focuses on a health topic such as asthma, colds and flu, back care and posture, and brain development. Special issues: Good Eating——A complete guide to feeding your family (February/March); Summer Fun (June/July). No poetry or fiction. Query. Length: 2,000-2,500 words. **Pays $1,500-2,500.** Pays expenses of writers on assignment.
Columns/Departments: Let's Eat (advice on how to keep mealtimes fun and nutritious, along with some child-friendly recipes); Health Q&A (timely issues are addressed in a question and answer format); Behavior Basics (a helpful article on how to deal with some aspect of a child's behavior—from first friendships to temper tantrums). **Buys 20 mss/year.** Query. **Pays $1,200-1,500.**
◼ The online magazine carries original content not found in the print edition. Contact: Karen Bilich, online editor.
Tips: "A simple, clear approach is mandatory. Articles should speak with the voice of medical authority in children's health issues, while being helpful and encouraging, cautionary but not critical, and responsible but not preachy. All articles should include interviews with appropriate Academy-member pediatricians and other health care professionals."

$ ◪ HOME EDUCATION MAGAZINE, P.O. Box 1083, Tonasket WA 98855. (509)486-1351. E-mail: hem-editor@home-ed-magazine.com. Website: www.home-ed-magazine.com. **Contact:** Helen E. Hegener, managing editor. **80% freelance written.** Bimonthly magazine covering home-based education. We feature articles which address the concerns of parents who want to take a direct involvement in the education of their children—concerns such as socialization, how to find curriculums and materials, testing and evaluation, how to tell when your child is ready to begin reading, what to do when homeschooling is difficult, teaching advanced subjects, etc. Estab. 1983. Circ. 32,000. **Pays on acceptance.** Publishes ms an average of 4 months after acceptance. Byline given. Buys first North American serial, first, one-time, electronic rights. Submit seasonal material 6 months in advance. Accepts queries by mail, e-mail. Responds in 2 months to queries. Sample copy for $6.50. Writer's guidelines for #10 SASE or via e-mail.
○⇥ Break in by "reading our magazine, understanding how we communicate with our readers, having an understanding of homeschooling and being able to communicate that understanding clearly."
Nonfiction: Essays, how-to (related to home schooling), humor, interview/profile, personal experience, photo feature, technical. **Buys 40-50 mss/year.** Query with or without published clips or send complete ms. Length: 750-2,500 words. **Pays $50-100.** Sometimes pays expenses of writers on assignment.
Photos: Send photos with submission. Reviews enlargements, 35mm prints, b&w, cd-roms. Buys one-time rights. Pays $50/cover; $10/inside photos. Identification of subjects required.
Tips: "We would like to see how-to articles (that don't preach, just present options); articles on testing, accountability, working with the public schools, socialization, learning disabilities, resources, support groups, legislation and humor. We need answers to the questions that homeschoolers ask. Please, no teachers telling parents how to teach. Personal experience with homeschooling is most preferred approach."

$ ◪ HOMESCHOOLING TODAY, S Squared Productions Inc., P.O. Box 1608, Ft. Collins CO 80524. Fax: (970)224-1824. E-mail: publisher@homeschooltoday.com. Website: www.homeschooltoday.com. **Contact:** Maureen McCaffrey, editor. **75% freelance written.** Bimonthly magazine covering homeschooling. "We are a practical magazine for homeschoolers with a broadly Christian perspective." Estab. 1992. Circ. 25,000. Pays on publication. Publishes ms an average of 1 year after acceptance. Byline given. Offers $50 kill fee. Buys first rights. Editorial lead time 6 months. Submit seasonal material 1 year in advance. Accepts queries by mail, e-mail, fax. Accepts simultaneous submissions. Responds in 1 month to queries; 2 months to mss. Sample copy and writer's guidelines free.
Nonfiction: Book excerpts, how-to, inspirational, interview/profile, new product. No fiction or poetry. **Buys 30 mss/year.** Query. Length: 500-2,500 words. **Pays 8¢/word.**
Photos: State availability with submission. Buys one-time rights. Offers no additional payment for photos accepted with ms. Captions, identification of subjects required.

ℕ $ KIDS VT, Vermont's Favorite Parenting Newspaper, Kids VT, 10æ Alfred St., Burlington VT 05401. (802)865-0272. Fax: (802)865-0595. E-mail: kidsvt@mindspring.com. Website: www.kidsvt.com. **Contact:** Tracey Morehouse, editor. **80% freelance written.** Monthly newspaper covering parenting information. Articles "must be informative, current and pertinent to families/parents with kids birth to teen." Estab. 1994. Circ. 20,000. Pays on publication. Publishes ms an average of 2 months after acceptance. Buys local Vermont rights. Editorial lead time 2 months. Submit seasonal material 2 months in advance. Accepts queries by mail, e-mail, fax. Accepts simultaneous submissions. Writer's guidelines online or by e-mail.

Nonfiction: Parenting. **Buys 25-40 mss/year.** Query. Length: 400-2,000 words. **Pays $20-50.** Accepts previously published submissions.

Photos: State availability with submission. Buys one-time rights. Negotiates payment individually. Captions required.

$ $ ☒ METRO PARENT MAGAZINE, Metro Parent Publishing Group, 24567 Northwestern Hwy., Suite 150, Southfield MI 48075. (248)352-0990. Fax: (248)352-5066. E-mail: sdemaggio@metroparent.com. Website: www.metro parent.com. **Contact:** Susan DeMaggio, editor. **75% freelance written.** Monthly magazine covering parenting, women's health, education. "We are a local magazine on parenting topics and issues of interest to Detroit-area parents. Related issues: *Windsor, Ontario Parent; Ann Arbor Parent; African/American Parent; Metro Baby Magazine.*" Circ. 85,000. Pays on publication. Publishes ms an average of 3 months after acceptance. Byline given. Buys first rights. Editorial lead time 3 months. Submit seasonal material 3 months in advance. Accepts queries by mail, e-mail. Accepts simultaneous submissions. Responds in 2 weeks to queries; 3 months to mss. Sample copy for $2.50.

Nonfiction: Essays, humor, inspirational, personal experience. Special issues: Upcoming special issues will cover moms and dads working from home; working in general. "No run-of-the-mill first-person baby experiences!" **Buys 100 mss/year.** Send complete ms. Length: 1,500-2,500 words. **Pays $30-300 for assigned articles.**

Photos: State availability with submission. Buys one-time rights. Offers $100-200/photo or negotiates payment individually. Captions required.

Columns/Departments: Boredom Busters (kids crafts, things to do), 750 words; Women's Health (latest issues of 20-40 year olds), 750-900 words; Home on the Range (recipes, food topics), 750 words; Tweens 'N Teens (handling teen "issues"), 750-800 words. **Buys 50 mss/year.** Send complete ms. **Pays $75-150.**

$ $ NORTHWEST FAMILY MAGAZINE, MMB Publications, Inc., 2275 Lake Whatcom Blvd., Suite B-1, Bellingham WA 98226-2777. (360)734-3025. Fax: (360)734-1550. E-mail: nwfamilypub@earthlink.net. Website: www.nwfamily.com. **Contact:** Lisa Laskey, editor. **50% freelance written.** Monthly magazine providing information on parenting issues and helping local families to be in touch with resources, events and places in the Northwest and western Washington State. Estab. 1995. Circ. 50,000. Pays on publication. Publishes ms an average of 6 months after acceptance. Byline sometimes given. Buys one-time rights. Editorial lead time 3 months. Submit seasonal material 6 months in advance. Accepts queries by mail, e-mail. Accepts simultaneous submissions. Responds in 3 weeks to queries; 3 months to mss. Sample copy for $1.25. Writer's guidelines for #10 SASE.

Nonfiction: Essays, general interest, how-to (relating to children), humor, inspirational (non religious), interview/profile, new product, personal experience, photo feature, travel. **Buys 40-50 mss/year.** Send complete ms. Length: 300-1,400 words. **Pays $25-45.** Sometimes pays expenses of writers on assignment. Accepts previously published submissions.

Reprints: Accepts previously published submissions.

Photos: State availability with submission. Reviews negatives, prints (any size). Buys one-time rights. Negotiates payment individually. Model releases required.

Columns/Departments: School News (information about schools, especially local), 100-300 words; Community News (quick information for families in western Washington), 100-300 words; Reviews (videos/books/products for families), 100-300 words; Teen News (information of interest to parents of teens), 50-300 words. **Buys 8-10 mss/year.** Send complete ms. **Pays $10-20.**

Poetry: Lisa Laskey, editor. Avant-garde, free verse, haiku, light verse, traditional. "No heavy or negative content." **Buys 6 poems/year.** Submit maximum 5 poems. Length: 6-25 lines. **Pays $5-20.**

Tips: "Send entire article with word count. Topic should apply to parents (regional focus increases our need for your article) and be addressed in a positive manner—'How to' not 'How not to.'"

$ $ $ $ PARENTING MAGAZINE, 530 Fifth Ave., 4th Floor, New York NY 10036. (212)522-8989. Fax: (212)522-8699. Editor-in-Chief: Janet Chan., Executive Editor: Lisa Bain. **Contact:** Articles Editor. Published 10 times/year magazine "for parents of children from birth to six and older, and covering both the psychological and practical aspects of parenting." Estab. 1987. **Pays on acceptance.** Byline given. Offers 25% kill fee. Buys first rights. Sample copy for $2.95 and 9×12 SAE with 5 first-class stamps. Writer's guidelines for #10 SASE.

Nonfiction: Book excerpts, personal experience, child development/behavior/health, investigative reports. **Buys 20-30 mss/year.** Query with or without published clips. Length: 1,000-2,500 words. **Pays $1,000-3,000.** Pays expenses of writers on assignment.

Columns/Departments: Query to the specific departmental editor. Parent Reporter (news items relating to children/family), 100-400 words; Ages and Stages (child development and behavior), 100-400 words; Children's Health, 100-350 words. **Buys 50-60 mss/year.** Query. **Pays $50-400.**

Tips: "The best guide for writers is the magazine itself. Please familiarize yourself with it before submitting a query."

Ⓝ $ PARENTING WITH SPIRIT, Honoring the Spirituality of Children, The Institute for Spiritual Living, P.O. Box 1356, Taos NM 87571. E-mail: jfhaver@parentingwithspirit.com. Website: www.parentingwithspirit.com. Editor: Judith Costello. **Contact:** Jurgen F. Haver, managing editor. **65% freelance written.** Quarterly magazine. Estab. 1997. Circ. 1,100. **Pays on acceptance.** Publishes ms an average of 4 months after acceptance. Byline given. Buys first

North American serial rights. Editorial lead time 6 months. Submit seasonal material 6 months in advance. Accepts queries by mail, e-mail. Responds in 3 weeks to queries; 2 months to mss. Sample copy for $5. Writer's guidelines for #10 SASE.

Nonfiction: Book excerpts, how-to, inspirational, opinion, personal experience, spiritual. Nothing from a conservative religious viewpoint. **Buys 10-12 mss/year.** Query or send complete ms. Length: 300-1,200 words. **Pays $10-35.** Accepts previously published submissions.

Reprints: Accepts previously published submissions.

Photos: State availability with submission. Buys one-time rights. Offers no additional payment for photos accepted with ms.

☐ The online magazine carries original content not found in the print edition. Contact: Jurgen F. Haver, online editor.

Tips: "Our writers are committed to the holistic and spiritual perspective of *PWS*. Many have backgrounds in journalism (with good interviewing skills), education, spiritual counseling or psychotherapy. Ask for upcoming themes. Keep articles to 1,500 words or less."

$ $ PARENTS' PRESS, The Monthly Newspaper for Bay Area Parents, 1454 Sixth St., Berkeley CA 94710-1431. (510)524-1602. Fax: (510)524-0912. E-mail: parentsprs@aol.com. Website: www.parentspress.com. **Contact:** Dixie M. Jordan, editor. **25% freelance written.** Monthly tabloid for parents. Includes a special section for parents of teens and pre-teens. Estab. 1980. Circ. 75,000. Pays within 45 days of publication. Publishes ms an average of 4 months after acceptance. Buys all rights, including electronic, second serial (reprint) and almost always Northern California exclusive rights. Submit seasonal material 6 months in advance. Accepts queries by mail, e-mail. Accepts simultaneous submissions. Responds in 3 months to queries. Sample copy for $3. Writer's guidelines and editorial calendar for #10 SASE or online.

Nonfiction: "We require a strong Bay Area focus in almost all articles. Use quotes from experts and Bay Area parents. Please, no child-rearing tips or advice based on personal experience." Book excerpts, travel, well-researched articles on children's health, development, education, family activities. Special issues: Pregnancy, Birth & Baby, Family Travel, Back to School. **Buys 10-12 mss/year.** Send complete ms. Length: 300-1,500 words. **Pays $50-500 for assigned articles; $25-250 for unsolicited articles.**

Reprints: Send photocopy with rights for sale noted and information about when and where the material previously appeared. Pays up to $50.

Photos: State availability with submission. Reviews b&w prints (any size). Buys one-time rights. Offers $15/photo. Identification of subjects, model releases required.

Tips: "We're looking for more pieces with a Bay Area focus."

$ PEDIATRICS FOR PARENTS, Pediatrics for Parents, Inc., 747 53rd, #3, Philadelphia PA 19147-3321. Fax: (419)858-7221. E-mail: rich.sagall@pobox.com. **Contact:** Richard J. Sagall, editor. **10% freelance written.** Monthly newsletter covering children's health. "*Pediatrics For Parents* emphasizes an informed, common-sense approach to childhood health care. We stress preventative action, accident prevention, when to call the doctor and when and how to handle a situation at home. We are also looking for articles that describe general, medical and pediatric problems, advances, new treatments, etc. All articles must be medically accurate and useful to parents with children—prenatal to adolescence." Estab. 1981. Circ. 500. Pays on publication. Publishes ms an average of 4 months after acceptance. Byline given. Buys first North American serial, electronic rights. Accepts queries by mail, e-mail, fax. Accepts simultaneous submissions. Responds in 1 month to queries. Sample copy for $3. Writer's guidelines for #10 SASE or by e-mail.

Nonfiction: Medical. No first person or experience. **Buys 10 mss/year.** Query with or without published clips or send complete ms. Length: 200-1,000 words. **Pays $10-50.**

Reprints: Accepts previously published submissions.

$ ▨ SAN DIEGO FAMILY MAGAZINE, San Diego County's Leading Resource for Parents & Educators Who Care!, P.O. Box 23960, San Diego CA 92193-3960. (619)685-6970. Fax: (619)685-6978. E-mail: editor@sandiegofamily.com. Website: www.sandiegofamily.com. **Contact:** Sharon Bay, editor-in-chief. **75% freelance written.** Monthly magazine for parenting and family issues. "*SDFM* strives to provide informative, educational articles emphasizing positive parenting for our typical readership of educated mothers, ages 25-45, with an upper-level income. Most articles are factual and practical, a few are humor and personal experience. Editorial emphasis is uplifting and positive." Estab. 1982. Circ. 120,000. Pays on publication. Byline given. Buys first, one-time, second serial (reprint) rights. Editorial lead time 2 months. Submit seasonal material 3 months in advance. Responds in 2 months to queries; 3 months to mss. Sample copy and writer's guidelines for $3.50 with 9×12 SAE.

Nonfiction: How-to, interview/profile (influential or noted persons or experts included in parenting or the welfare of children), parenting, new baby help, enhancing education, family activities, articles of specific interest to San Diego. "No rambling, personal experience pieces." **Buys 75 mss/year.** Send complete ms. Length: 800 words maximum. **Pays $1.25/column inch.**

Reprints: Send typed ms with rights for sale noted and information about when and where the material previously appeared.

Photos: State availability with submission. Reviews contact sheets, 3½×5 or 5×7 prints. Buys one-time rights. Negotiates payment individually. Identification of subjects required.

Columns/Departments: Kids' Books (topical book reviews), 800 words. **Buys 12 mss/year.** Query. **Pays $1.25/ column inch.**

Fillers: Facts, newsbreaks (specific to family market). **Buys 10/year.** Length: 50-200 words. **Pays $1.25/column inch minimum.**

$ $⊠ SOUTH FLORIDA PARENTING, 5555 Nob Hill Rd., Sunrise FL 33351. (954)747-3050. Fax: (954)747-3055. E-mail: vmccash@tribune.com. Website: www.sfparenting.com. **Contact:** Vicki McCash Brennan, managing editor. **90% freelance written.** Monthly magazine covering parenting, family. "*South Florida Parenting* provides news, information and a calendar of events for readers in Southeast Florida. The focus is on positive parenting and things to do or information about raising children in South Florida." Estab. 1990. Circ. 110,000. Pays on publication. Byline given. Buys one-time, second serial (reprint), electronic rights, makes work-for-hire assignments. Editorial lead time 4 months. Submit seasonal material 5 months in advance. Accepts queries by mail, e-mail, fax. Accepts simultaneous submissions. Responds in 1 month to queries; 6 months to mss. Sample copy for 9×12 SAE with $2.95 postage. Writer's guidelines for #10 SASE.

    O➔ Best bet to break in: "Be a local South Florida resident (particular need for writers from the Miami-Dade area) and address contemporary parenting topics and concerns."

Nonfiction: How-to (parenting issues), humor (preferably not first-person humor about kids and parents), interview/ profile, personal experience, family and children's issues. Special issues: Education/Winter Health (January); Birthday Party (February); Summer Camp (March); Maternity (April); Florida/Vacation Guide (May); Kid Crown Awards (July); Back to School (August); Education (September); Holiday (December). **Buys 36-40 mss/year.** Query with or without published clips or send complete ms. Length: 500-2,000 words. **Pays $25-400.**

Reprints: Send photocopy or e-mail on spec. **Pays $25-50.**

Photos: State availability with submission. Reviews negatives, transparencies, prints. Buys one-time rights. Sometimes offers additional payment for photos accepted with ms.

Columns/Departments: Baby Basics (for parents of infants); Growing Concerns (child health); Preteen Power (for parents of preteens); Family Money (family finances), all 500-750 words. **Buys 30 mss/year.** Query with or without published clips or send complete ms. **Pays $40-150.**

Tips: "We want information targeted to the South Florida market. Multicultural and well-sourced is preferred. A unique approach to a universal parenting concern will be considered for publication. Profiles or interviews of courageous parents. Opinion pieces on child rearing should be supported by experts and research should be listed. First-person stories should be fresh and insightful. All writing should be clear and concise. Submissions can be typewritten, double-spaced, but the preferred format is on diskette or by e-mail."

$ $ $ SUCCESSFUL STUDENT, Imagination Publishing, 820 W. Jackson Blvd., Suite 450, Chicago IL 60607. (773)252-3200. Fax: (773)252-3290. E-mail: lterry@imaginepub.com. Website: www.imaginepub.com. **Contact:** Lisa Terry, editor. **30% freelance written.** Semiannual magazine for customers of Sylvan Learning Centers covering education. "We focus on education-related issues and study habits and tips. We frequently use expert writers and/or sources." Circ. 550,000. Pays on publication. Publishes ms an average of 5 months after acceptance. Byline given. Offers 33% kill fee. Buys first North American serial rights. Editorial lead time 6 months. Accepts queries by mail, e-mail, fax. Accepts simultaneous submissions.

    O➔ "Submit queries for how-to and trend articles that will help parents guide their child's education. No parenting stories."

Nonfiction: Book excerpts, essays, how-to (tips on studying, etc.), inspirational, interview/profile, new product, education trends, activities for families to learn together. No parenting stories. **Buys 2-4 mss/year.** Query with published clips. Length: 300-1,700 words. **Pays 50¢/word.** Pays expenses of writers on assignment.

Photos: State availability with submission. Buys one-time rights. Negotiates payment individually.

    ■ The online magazine carries original content not found in the print edition. Contact: Lisa Terry, online editor.

Tips: "We're looking for writers with strong voices and an understanding of our editorial categories, who have the ability to write clearly and concisely. Because many of our stories include expert sources, our writers have enough of an education background to recognize these people. We frequently ask writers to pull short facts or tips into sidebars to complement the main stories. Stories are carefully reviewed for accuracy and appropriateness by the editorial staff and an advisory board from Sylvan Learning Systems."

$ $ $ $ TODAY'S PARENT PREGNANCY & BIRTH, (formerly *Great Expectations*), 269 Richmond St. W, Toronto, Ontario M5V 1X1, Canada. (416)596-8680. Fax: (416)596-1991. Website: www.todaysparent.com. **Contact:** Editor. **100% freelance written.** Magazine published 3 times/year. "*P&B* helps, supports and encourages expectant and new parents with news and features related to pregnancy, birth, human sexuality and parenting." Estab. 1973. Circ. 200,000. **Pays on acceptance.** Publishes ms an average of 8 months after acceptance. Buys first North American serial rights. Editorial lead time 6 months. Responds in 6 weeks to queries. Sample copy and writer's guidelines for #10 SASE.

Nonfiction: Features about pregnancy, labor and delivery, post-partum issues. **Buys 12 mss/year.** Query with published clips. Length: 600-2,500 words. **Pays $350-2,000.** Sometimes pays expenses of writers on assignment.

Photos: State availability with submission. Rights negotiated individually. Pay negotiated individually.

Tips: "Our writers are professional freelance writers with specific knowledge in the childbirth field. *P&B* is written for a Canadian audience using Canadian research and sources."

$ $ TOLEDO AREA PARENT NEWS, Toledo Area Parent News, Inc., 1120 Adams St., Toledo OH 43624-1509. (419)244-9859. Fax: (419)244-9871. E-mail: meira@toledocitypaper.com. **Contact:** Meira Zucker, editor. **20% freelance written.** Monthly tabloid for Northwest Ohio/Southeast Michigan parents. Estab. 1992. Circ. 50,000. Pays on publication. Publishes ms an average of 1 month after acceptance. Byline given. Makes work-for-hire assignments. Editorial lead time 3 months. Accepts queries by mail, e-mail, fax. Responds in 1 month to queries. Sample copy for $1.50.

　　Oⁿ Break in with "local interest articles—Ohio/Michigan regional topics and examples preferred."

Nonfiction: "We use only local writers by assignment. We accept queries and opinion pieces only. Send cover letter to be considered for assignments." General interest, interview/profile, opinion. **Buys 10 mss/year.** Length: 1,000-2,500 words. **Pays $75-125.**

Photos: State availability with submission. Buys all rights. Negotiates payment individually. Identification of subjects required.

Tips: "We love humorous stories that deal with common parenting issues or features on cutting-edge issues."

$ WESTERN NEW YORK FAMILY, Western New York Family Inc., P.O. Box 265, 287 Parkside Ave., Buffalo NY 14215-0265. (716)836-3486. Fax: (716)836-3680. E-mail: wnyfamily@aol.com. Website: www.wnyfamilymagazine.com. **Contact:** Michele Miller, editor/publisher. **90% freelance written.** Monthly magazine covering parenting in Western NY. "Readership is largely composed of families with children ages newborn to 12 years. Although most subscriptions are in the name of the mother, 91% of fathers also read the publication. Strong emphasis is placed on how and where to find family-oriented events, as well as goods and services for children, in Western New York." Estab. 1984. Circ. 22,500. Pays on publication. Publishes ms an average of 18 months after acceptance. Byline given. Buys one-time, second serial (reprint), simultaneous rights. Editorial lead time 3 months. Submit seasonal material 3 months in advance. Accepts simultaneous submissions. Responds only if interested to queries. Sample copy for $2.50 and 9×12 SAE with 3 first-class stamps. Guidelines for #10 SASE or by e-mail.

　　Oⁿ Break in with either a "cutting edge" topic that is new and different in its relevance to current parenting challenges and trends or a "timeless" topic which is "evergreen" and can be kept on file to fill last minute holes.

Nonfiction: How-to (craft projects for kids, holiday, costume, etc.), humor (as related to parenting), personal experience (parenting related), travel (family destinations). Special issues: Birthday Celebrations (January); Cabin Fever (February); Having A Baby (March); Education & Enrichment (April); Mother's Day (May); Father's Day (June); Summer Fun (July and August); Back to School (September); Halloween Happenings (October); Family Issues (November); and Holiday Happenings (December). **Buys 50 mss/year.** Send complete ms by mail or e-mail. Unsolicited e-mail attachments are not accepted; paste text of article into body of e-mail. Length: 750-3,000 words. **Pays $50-125 for assigned articles; $20-50 for unsolicited articles.** Sometimes pays expenses of writers on assignment.

Reprints: Accepts previously published submissions.

Photos: State availability with submission. Reviews 3×5 prints. Buys one-time rights. Offers no additional payment for photos accepted with ms. Captions, identification of subjects, model releases required.

Fillers: Facts. **Buys 10/year.** Length: 450 words. **Pays $20.**

Tips: "We are interested in well-researched, nonfiction articles on surviving the newborn, preschool, school age and adolescent years. Our readers want practical information on places to go and things to do in the Buffalo area and nearby Canada. They enjoy humorous articles about the trials and tribulations of parenthood as well as 'how-to' articles (i.e., tips for finding a sitter, keeping your sanity while shopping with preschoolers, ideas for holidays and birthdays, etc.). Articles on making a working parent's life easier are of great interest as are articles written by fathers. We also need more material on pre-teen and young teen (13-15) issues. We prefer a warm, conversational style of writing."

$ $ $ $ WORKING MOTHER MAGAZINE, MacDonald Communications, 135 W. 50th St., 16th Floor, New York NY 10020-1201. (212)445-6100. Fax: (212)445-6174. E-mail: editors@workingmother.com. Website: www.workingmother.com. **Contact:** Articles Department. **90% freelance written.** Prefers to work with published/established writers; works with a small number of new/unpublished writers each year. Monthly magazine for women who balance a career with the concerns of parenting. Circ. 925,000. Publishes ms an average of 4 months after acceptance. Byline given. Offers kill fee. Buys all rights. Submit seasonal material 6 months in advance. Accepts queries by mail. Sample copy for $5; available by calling (800)925-0788. Writer's guidelines online.

Nonfiction: Service, humor, child development, material pertinent to the working mother's predicament. Humor, service, child development, material perinent to the working mother's predicament. **Buys 9-10 mss/year.** Query. Length: 1,500-2,000 words. Pays expenses of writers on assignment.

Tips: "We are looking for pieces that help the reader. In other words, we don't simply report on a trend without discussing how it specifically affects our readers' lives and how they can handle the effects. Where can they look for help if necessary?"

COMIC BOOKS

$ $ WIZARD: THE COMICS MAGAZINE, Wizard Entertainment, 151 Wells Ave., Congers NY 10920-2036. (845)268-2000. Fax: (845)268-0053. E-mail: aekardon@aol.com. Website: www.wizardworld.com. Editor: Brian Cunningham. Senior Editor: Joe Yanarella. **Contact:** Doug Goldstein, managing editor. **50% freelance written.** Monthly magazine covering comic books, science fiction and action figures. Estab. 1991. Circ. 209,000. Pays on publication. Publishes ms an average of 3 months after acceptance. Byline given. Offers 50% kill fee. Buys all rights. Editorial lead time 4 months. Accepts queries by mail, e-mail, fax. Responds in 6 weeks to queries. Sample copy and writer's guidelines free.

Nonfiction: Historical/nostalgic, how-to, humor, interview/profile, new product, personal experience, photo feature, First-person diary. No columns or opinion pieces. **Buys 100 mss/year.** Query with or without published clips. Length: 250-4,000 words. **Pays 15-20¢/word.** Sometimes pays expenses of writers on assignment.

Photos: State availability with submission. Buys all rights. Negotiates payment individually. Identification of subjects required.

Columns/Departments: Video Stuff (comic book, sci-fi and top-selling video games); Manga Mania (the latest news, anime, manga, toys, etc. from Japan); Coming Attractions (comic book-related movies and TV shows), 150-500 words. Query with published clips. **Pays $75-500.**

Tips: "Send plenty of samples showing the range of your writing styles. Have a good knowledge of comic books. Read a few issues to get the feel of the conversational 'Wizard Style.' "

CONSUMER SERVICE & BUSINESS OPPORTUNITY

Some of these magazines are geared to investing earnings or starting a new business; others show how to make economical purchases. Publications for business executives and consumers interested in business topics are listed under Business & Finance. Those on how to run specific businesses are classified by category in the Trade section.

N $ $ CONSUMER REPORTS, Consumers Union of US, Inc., 101 Truman Ave., Yonkers NY 10703-1057. (914)378-2000. Fax: (914)378-2904. Website: www.consumerreports.org. Managing Editor: David Heim. **Contact:** Margot Slade, editor. **5% freelance written.** Monthly magazine. "*Consumer Reports* is the leading product-testing and consumer-service magazine in the US. We buy very little freelance material, mostly from proven writers we have used before for finance and health columns." Estab. 1936. Circ. 4,100,000. **Pays on acceptance.** Publishes ms an average of 2 months after acceptance. Offers negotiable kill fee. Buys all rights. Editorial lead time 4 months. Submit seasonal material 6 months in advance. Accepts queries by mail.

Nonfiction: Technical, personal finance, personal health. **Buys 12 mss/year.** Query. Length: 1,000 words. **Pays variable rate.**

$ ECONOMIC FACTS, The National Research Bureau, Inc., 320 Valley St., Burlington IA 52601. (319)752-5415. Fax: (319)752-3421. **Contact:** Nancy Heinzel, editor. **75% freelance written.** Eager to work with new/unpublished writers; works with a small number of new/unpublished writers each year. Quarterly magazine. Estab. 1948. Pays on publication. Publishes ms an average of 1 year after acceptance. Byline given. Buys all rights. Sample copy and writer's guidelines for #10 SASE with 2 first-class stamps.

Nonfiction: General interest (private enterprise, government data, graphs, taxes, health care). **Buys 10 mss/year.** Query with outline of article. Length: 500-700 words. **Pays 4¢/word.**

$ $ HOME BUSINESS MAGAZINE, United Marketing & Research Company, Inc., 9582 Hamilton Ave. PMB 368, Huntington Beach CA 92646. Fax: (714)962-7722. E-mail: henderso@ix.netcom.com. Website: www.homebu sinessmag.com. **Contact:** Stacy Henderson, online editor. **75% freelance written.** "*Home Business Magazine* covers every angle of the home-based business market including: cutting edge editorial by well-known authorities on sales and marketing, business operations, the home office, franchising, business opportunities, network marketing, mail order and other subjects to help readers choose, manage and prosper in a home-based business; display advertising, classified ads and a directory of home-based businesses; technology, the Internet, computers and the future of home-based business; home-office editorial including management advice, office set-up, and product descriptions; business opportunities, franchising and work-from-home success stories." Estab. 1993. Circ. 95,000. Pays on publication. Publishes ms an average of 6 months after acceptance. Byline given. Makes work-for-hire assignments. Editorial lead time 4 months. Submit seasonal material 6 months in advance. Accepts queries by mail, e-mail, fax. Accepts simultaneous submissions. Sample copy for 9×12 SAE and 8 first-class stamps. Writer's guidelines for #10 SASE.

Nonfiction: Book excerpts, general interest, how-to (home business), inspirational, interview/profile, new product, personal experience, photo feature, technical, mail order, franchise, business management, internet, finance network marketing. No non-home business related topics. **Buys 40 mss/year.** Send complete ms. Length: 200-1,000 words. **Pays 20¢/word for assigned articles; $0-100 for unsolicited articles.**

Photos: Send photos with submission. Buys one-time rights. Offers no additional payment for photos accepted with ms. Identification of subjects required.

Columns/Departments: Marketing & Sales; Money Corner; Home Office; Management; Technology; Working Smarter; Franchising; Network Marketing, all 200-1,000 words. Send complete ms. **Pays $0-100.**

  The online magazine carries original content not found in the print edition. Contact: Herb Wetenkamp, online editor.

Tips: "Send complete information by mail as per our writer's guidelines and e-mail if possible. We encourage writers to submit Feature Articles (1-2 pages) and Departmental Articles (⅓-1½ pages). Please submit polished, well-written, organized material. It helps to provide subheadings within the article. Boxes, lists and bullets are encouraged because they make your article easier to read, use and reference by the reader. A primary problem in the past is that articles do not stick to the subject of the title. Please pay attention to the focus of your article and to your title. Please don't call to get the status of your submission. We will call if we're interested in publishing the submission."

$ $ $ $ KIPLINGER'S PERSONAL FINANCE, 1729 H St. NW, Washington DC 20006. (202)887-6400. Fax: (202)331-1206. Website: www.kiplinger.com. Editor: Fred W. Frailey. **Contact:** Dale Sanders. **10% freelance written.** Prefers to work with published/established writers. Monthly magazine for general, adult audience intersted in personal finance and consumer information. "*Kiplinger's* is a highly trustworthy source of information on saving and investing, taxes, credit, home ownership, paying for college, retirement planning, automobile buying and many other personal finance topics." Estab. 1947. Circ. 1,300,000. **Pays on acceptance.** Publishes ms an average of 2 months after acceptance. Buys all rights. Responds in 1 month to queries.
Nonfiction: "Most material is staff-written, but we accept some freelance. Thorough documentation is required for fact-checking." Query with published clips. Pays expenses of writers on assignment.
Tips: "We are looking for a heavy emphasis on personal finance topics."

$ $ LIVING SAFETY, A Canada Safety Council Publication for Safety in the Home, Traffic and Recreational Environments, 1020 Thomas Spratt Place, Ottawa, Ontario K1G 5L5, Canada. (613)739-1535. Fax: (613)739-1566. E-mail: jsmith@safety-council.org. Website: www.safety-council.org. **Contact:** Jack Smith, editor-in-chief. **65% freelance written.** Quarterly magazine covering off-the-job safety. "Off-the-job health and safety magazine covering topics in the home, traffic and recreational environments. Audience is the Canadian employee and his/her family." Estab. 1983. Circ. 100,000. **Pays on acceptance.** Publishes ms an average of 2 months after acceptance. Byline given. Buys all rights. Editorial lead time 4 months. Submit seasonal material 6 months in advance. Accepts queries by mail. Accepts simultaneous submissions. Responds in 1 month to queries. Sample copy and writer's guidelines free.
Nonfiction: General interest, how-to (safety tips, health tips), personal experience. **Buys 24 mss/year.** Query with published clips. Length: 1,000-2,500 words. **Pays $500 maximum.** Sometimes pays expenses of writers on assignment.
Reprints: Send tearsheet.
Photos: State availability with submission. Reviews contact sheets, negatives, transparencies, prints. Offers no additional payment for photos accepted with ms. Identification of subjects required.

$ MONEY SAVING IDEAS, The National Research Bureau, 320 Valley St., Burlington IA 52601. (319)752-5415. Fax: (319)752-3421. **Contact:** Nancy Heinzel, editor. **75% freelance written.** Quarterly magazine that features money saving strategies. "We are interested in money saving tips on various subjects (insurance, travel, heating/cooling, buying a house, ways to cut costs and balance checkbooks). Our audience is mainly industrial and office workers." Estab. 1948. Circ. 1,000. Pays on publication. Publishes ms an average of 1 year after acceptance. Byline given. Buys all rights. Sample copy and writer's guidelines for #10 SAE with 2 first-class stamps. Writer's guidelines for #10 SASE.
Nonfiction: How-to (save on grocery bills, heating/cooling bills, car expenses, insurance, travel). Query with or without published clips or send complete ms. Length: 500-700 words. **Pays 4¢/word.**
Tips: "Follow our guidelines. Keep articles to stated length, double-spaced, neatly typed. If writer wishes rejected manuscript returned include SASE. Name, address and word length should appear on first page."

$ $ ▧ SPARE TIME MAGAZINE, The Magazine of Money Making Opportunities, Kipen Publishing Corp., 2400 S. Commerce Dr., New Berlin WI 53151. (262)780-1070. Fax: (262)780-1071. E-mail: editor@spare-time.com. Website: www.sparetimemagazine.com. Bimonthly magazine covering affordable money-making opportunities. "We publish information the average person can use to begin and operate a spare-time business or extra income venture, with the possible goal of making it fulltime." Estab. 1955. Circ. 250,000. Pays on publication. Publishes ms an average of 3 months after acceptance. Byline given. Buys first North American serial rights. Editorial lead time 2 months. Submit seasonal material 3 months in advance. Accepts queries by mail, e-mail, fax, phone. Accepts simultaneous submissions. Responds in 1 month to queries; 2 months to mss. Sample copy for $2.50. Writer's guidelines and editorial calendar for #10 SASE or via e-mail.
Nonfiction: Book excerpts (and reviews, small business related), how-to (market, keep records, stay motivated, choose opportunity), interview/profile, personal experience (small business related). "No comparative or negative product reviews; political, philosophical or religious viewpoints; or controversial subjects." **Buys 22-33 mss/year.** Query. Length: 1,500-2,000 words. **Pays 15¢/word.**
Reprints: Send tearsheet, photocopy or typed ms and information about when and where the material previously appeared. Pays 50% of the original price.
Photos: State availability with submission. Reviews contact sheets, 3×5 or larger prints. Buys one-time rights. Pays $15/published photo. Captions, identification of subjects required.
Tips: "We look for articles that are unusual or unique; include examples of successful people whose experiences illustrate the points you're trying to make and inspire our readers with the hope that they, too, can succeed; quote experts rather than read like essays (if you're the expert, give some examples from your own experiences, but try to include comments from at least one other expert and one other person's real-life experience); add sidebars with check-off or

to-do lists, tips, examples or additional resources; and include art or photos—especially action photos—to 'dress up' your piece. It is always best to query. At all times keep in mind that the audience is the average person, not over-educated in terms of business techniques. The best pieces are written in lay language and relate to that type of person."

CONTEMPORARY CULTURE

These magazines often combine politics, current events and cultural elements such as art, litera-ture, film and music, to examine contemporary society. Their approach to institutions is typically irreverent and investigative. Some, like *Madison*, report on alternative culture and appeal to a young adult "Generation X" audience. Others treat mainstream culture for a baby boomer generation audience.

$ $ $ $ A&U, America's AIDS Magazine, Art & Understanding, Inc., 25 Monroe St., Albany NY 12210. (518)426-9010. Fax: (518)436-5354. E-mail: mailbox@aumag.org. Website: www.aumag.org. **Contact:** David Wag-goner, editor-in-chief. **50% freelance written.** Monthly magazine covering cultural responses to AIDS/HIV. Estab. 1991. Circ. 205,000. Pays on publication. Publishes ms an average of 3 months after acceptance. Byline given. Offers 20% kill fee. Buys first North American serial rights. Editorial lead time 6 months. Accepts queries by mail, e-mail. Accepts simultaneous submissions. Responds in 1 month to queries; 2 months to mss. Sample copy for $5. Writer's guidelines for #10 SASE.
Nonfiction: Book excerpts, essays, general interest, how-to, humor, interview/profile, new product, opinion, personal experience, photo feature, travel, reviews (film, theater, art exhibits, video, music, other media), Medical news. **Buys 120 mss/year.** Query with published clips. Length: 800-4,800 words. **Pays $250-2,500 for feature articles and cover stoires; $50-150 for reviews.** Sometimes pays expenses of writers on assignment.
Photos: State availability with submission. Reviews contact sheets, up to 4×5 transparencies, 5×7 to 8×10 prints. Buys one-time rights. Offers $50-500/photo. Captions, identification of subjects, model releases required.
Columns/Departments: The Culture of AIDS (reviews of books, music, film), 800 words; Viewpoint (personal opinion), 900-1,500 words; MediaWatch (mass media opinion), 800-1,200 words. **Buys 100 mss/year.** Send complete ms. **Pays $100-250.**
Fiction: Unpublished work only. Send complete ms. Length: 2,500-5,000 words. **Pays $150-750.**
Poetry: Any length/style (shorter works preferred). **Pays $75-150.**
Tips: "We're looking for more articles on youth and HIV/AIDS; more international coverage; more small-town America coverage."

N $ $ $ ADBUSTERS, Journal of the Mental Environment, The Media Foundation, 1243 W. 7th Ave., Vancouver, British Columbia V6J 2E7, Canada. (604)736-9401. Fax: (604)737-6021. Website: www.adbusters.org. Managing Editor: Dominique Ritter. **Contact:** Kalle Lasn, editor. **50% freelance written.** Bimonthly magazine. "We are an activist journal of the mental environment." Estab. 1989. Circ. 90,000. Pays 1 month after publication. Byline given. Offers 50% kill fee. Buys first rights. Accepts queries by mail, e-mail, fax. Accepts simultaneous submissions. Sample copy free. Writer's guidelines online.
Nonfiction: Essays, exposé, interview/profile, opinion. **Buys variable mss/year.** Query. Length: 250-3,000 words. **Pays $100/page for assigned articles; 50¢/word for unsolicited articles.**

$ $ AFTERIMAGE, The Journal of Media Arts & Cultural Criticism, Visual Studies Workshop, 31 Prince St., Rochester NY 14607. (716)442-8676. Fax: (716)442-1992. E-mail: afterimg@servtech.com. Website: www.v sw.org. **Contact:** Karen vanMeenen, editor. **75% freelance written.** Bimonthly tabloid covering photography, indepen-dent film and video, artists' books, related cultural studies. "We publish news briefs and reports as well as in-depth reviews and research-based scholarly feature articles on photography, video, independent film, artists' books, new technologies." Estab. 1972. Circ. 10,000. Pays 6 weeks after publication. Publishes ms an average of 4 months after acceptance. Byline given. Holds joint copyright with full permission for authors to reprint with appropriate publication citation line. Editorial lead time 6 months. Submit seasonal material 6 months in advance. Accepts queries by mail, e-mail, fax, phone. Responds in 2 weeks to queries; 1 month to mss. Sample copy and writer's guidelines free.
Nonfiction: Essays, historical/nostalgic, interview/profile, opinion, personal experience, scholarly features, film, books, festival, and exhibition reviews (especially from regions such as Florida, the Midwest and the desert Southwest). "No Hollywood film, no historical photo research unless new scholarship, and no queries about writing about your work or that of your organization/employer." **Buys 65-70 mss/year.** Query with published clips. Length: 1,000-10,000 words. **Pays 5¢/word up to maximum of $100 for news, reports, reviews; $150 for essays; $300 for features.**
Photos: State availability of or send photos with submission. Reviews transparencies, prints. Buys one-time rights. Offers no additional payment for photos accepted with ms. Captions, identification of subjects required.
Tips: "Query with specific idea and timeline by mail, as far in advance of event (for reports and reviews) as possible. Expect four-month turnaround time at longest. Expect two rounds of editorial input."

N $ THE AMERICAN DISSIDENT, ContraOstrich Press, 1837 Main St., Concord Massachusetts 01742. E-mail: enmarge@aol.com. Website: www.geocities.com/enmarge. **Contact:** G. Tod Slone, editor. **100% freelance written.**

insider report

Writing about books, authors: Background is essential

Though she started her freelance career writing for children's magazines, Spokane based freelancer Kelly Milner Halls now writes just as frequently about books and authors. Thanks to a flood of newspaper book sections, trade publications and consumer magazines dedicated to literature, she is offered more assignments than she has time to seriously consider. Her work regularly appears in dozens of publications including *Book, Booklist, VOYA, BookPage, Writer's Digest, The Book Report, The Chicago Tribune, The Denver Post, The Washington Post, The Atlanta Journal Constitution* and others.

What special challenges set freelancing for the publishing industry apart from other specialties?
Background is essential to writing about books and authors. If you decide to explore this niche, be prepared to read—a *LOT*. To write about an author's fourth book, it's helpful (and important) to know about the first three. I also find that the more I do, the more I am asked to do—for the same reasoning in reverse. If I've already interviewed Ridley Pearson or Catherine Ryan Hyde, I not only have far-reaching perspective on their work; they're also more likely to talk with me again.

What kind of books do you review or feature most often?
My personal favorites are upper-end young adult books and authors, sometimes referred to as "coming-of-age" stories. It's astounding to me that these amazing works are so often underappreciated and overlooked, because the work is really top-notch. Books by craftsmen like Chris Crutcher are as well-crafted as any mainstream book. But I write about almost any book assigned to me. I will *NOT* write about a book I out and out hate. It's just not in me to be mean.

How would you break into this specialty if you were a beginning freelancer?
As odd as it sounds, I'd start writing free reviews. There are *DOZENS* of websites and small publications that need reviews but can't pay for them. If I were trying to break in, I'd start there, writing professional quality reviews to build up my clip files. But remember, no matter who you write for, put in your best effort. You name is on that review. It will be noticed.

What is the general pay scale a freelancer can expect writing reviews and book features?
Like most freelance-friendly markets, the pay scale is *ALL* over the map. Expect anything from $25 to $150 for a 600-word review or feature for a newspaper book section, not bad considering they are normally weekly sections—four shots a month. Expect free clips or a percentage for most websites, though a few may offer a modest fee. Upscale glossy magazines like *People*

or *Book* pay well, but are flooded with queries. Trades like *Booklist, Five Owls* and *VOYA* don'tpay as well in terms of dollars, but carry with them a certain prestige.

What are the most common mistakes freelancers in this arena make (and can avoid)?

Submitting reviews too late for serious consideration. If you bought the book at the bookstore, it's probably too late to sell the review. Most publications want the reviews to come out *BEFORE* or exactly when the book hits the retail market. The other mistake I see is not reading the books you're supposed to review. If you commit to writing about a book or an author, commit to reading the book.

Have you had a favorite book assignment? If so, what was it and why was it so memorable?

Writing about "Whale Talk" author Chris Crutcher is always a treat because he's a true American hero. He's not only a gifted and critically acclaimed author, he's a family therapist who works with real kids. I also loved writing about Catherine Ryan Hyde because she was such a wonderful surprise. I hadn't discovered her work, so it was like Christmas with a new puppy.

Have you experienced the nightmare of all nightmare assignments? Describe it.

The toughest thing is to be all set to interview an author, then find they've forgotten at the last minute. I understand forgetting. But my editors don't forget. So that can leave me in a pretty significant bind if I don't plan ahead.

For interviews with the pros in more freelance niche markets, see Animals, page 368; Entertainment, page 443; Games & Puzzles, page 462; Sports, page 708, Women's, page 782.

⇒►◊◄⇐

TOP TIP: "Study the magic of the reslant. If you get an interview with Jerry Jenkins, why sell only *one* article about Jerry Jenkins? Why not sell one about the nature of Christian fiction to the *Denver Post*, one about his baseball passion to *Sports Illustrated*, one about his children's series to *Guidepost for Teens*, and one about his website to *Yahoo Life?* You get the idea. Think *reslant.*"

Semiannual magazine "offering hardcore criticism of all American icons and institutions in English, French or Spanish. Writers must be free of dogma, clear in mind, critical in outlook and courageous in behavior." Estab. 1998. Circ. 200. Pays on publication. Publishes ms an average of 6 months after acceptance. Byline given. Buys first North American serial, one-time rights. Editorial lead time 6 months. Accepts queries by mail. Responds in 3 weeks to queries; 3 months to mss. Sample copy for $7.

Nonfiction: Essays, interview/profile, opinion, personal experience. No typically pro-academic/literary industrial complex articles written by academics. **Buys 2-4 mss/year.** Query. Length: 250-900 words. **Pays $5 for assigned articles.** Pays in contributor's copies for poetry submissions and book reviews.

Photos: State availability with submission. Reviews prints. Buys one-time rights. Negotiates payment individually. Identification of subjects required.

Poetry: Free verse. Poetry with a message, not poetry for the sake of poetry, as in l'art pour l'art. Submit maximum 3-5 poems.

Tips: "*The American Dissident* publishes well-written dissident work (in English, French or Spanish) that expresses some sort of visceral indignation regarding the nation. Suggested areas of criticism include, though not exclusively: Corruption in academe, poet laureates paid for by the Library of Congress, sell-out beatniks and hippies, *artistes nonengagés,* politically controlled state and national cultural councils, media whores, Medicare-bilking doctors, justice-indifferent lawyers, autocratic judges, thug cops, other dubious careerists, the "happy" culture of extreme denial and aberrant rationalization, the democratic sham masking the plutocracy and, more generally, the human veil of charade placed upon the void of the universe."

N **$ $** **THE AMERICAN SCHOLAR**, Phi Beta Kappa, 1785 Massachusetts Ave. NW, 4th Floor, Washington DC 20036. (202)265-3808. Fax: (202)265-0083. E-mail: scholar@pbk.org. Editor: Anne Fadiman. **Contact:** Jean Stipicevic, managing editor . **100% freelance written.** Quarterly journal. "Our intent is to have articles written by scholars and experts but written in nontechnical language for an intelligent audience. Material covers a wide range in the arts, sciences, current affairs, history and literature." Estab. 1932. Circ. 25,000. Pays on publication. Publishes ms an average of 1 year after acceptance. Byline given. Offers 50% kill fee. Buys first rights. Editorial lead time 6 months. Submit seasonal material 6 months in advance. Accepts queries by mail, e-mail, fax. Responds in 2 weeks to queries; 2 months to mss. Sample copy for $8. Writer's guidelines for #10 SASE.
Nonfiction: Essays, historical/nostalgic, humor. **Buys 40 mss/year.** Query. Length: 3,000-5,000 words. **Pays $500 maximum.**
Poetry: "We have no special requirements of length, form or content for original poetry." Rob Farnsworth, poetry editor. **Buys 25 poems/year.** Submit maximum 3-4 poems. **Pays $50.**

N **$** **BOOK CLUB TODAY, Upbeat & Innovative Publication for Book Club Members**, Book Club Today, Inc., P.O Box 210165, Cleveland OH 44121-7165. Fax: (216)382-0644. E-mail: BookClubToday@aol.com. Website: www.BookClubToday.com. **Contact:** Bonnie Eaver, editor. **50% freelance written.** Bimonthly magazine covering information for reading groups. "We are looking for positive, upbeat articles to enhance book club and reading group meetings: Book reviews, discussion questions and author profiles. Books reviewed must stimulate lively discussions." Estab. 1999. Pays on publication. Publishes ms an average of 6 months after acceptance. Byline sometimes given. Buys first rights. Editorial lead time 4 months. Submit seasonal material 4 months in advance. Accepts queries by mail, e-mail, fax. Responds in 2 months to queries; 3 months to mss. Sample copy online.
Nonfiction: Interview/profile. No negative book reviews or satire. **Buys 60 mss/year.** Query or send complete ms. Length: 250-1,000 words. **Pays $15-50.** Sometimes pays expenses of writers on assignment.
Photos: State availability with submission.
Columns/Departments: Book Reviews (classics and new releases), 250-750 words, **pays $15-50**; Discussion Questions (for book club meetings), 10-15 questions/book, **pays $10-30**; Author Profiles (personal and professional information), 250-750 words, **pays $15-50**; Meeting of the Month (interview with book club member), 500-1,000 words, **pays $25-50**; Book Suggestion Column (interview author or librarian), 250-350 words, **pays $10-20**; Test Your Knowledge Literary Quiz (by assignment only), 10-15 questions and answers, **pays $25-50**; Biblio Basics (helpful hints for reading groups), 250-350 words, **pays $10-30**.
Tips: "Please review a sample issue first. Submit positive, upbeat, fun articles."

$ **BOOKPAGE**, Promotion, Inc., 2143 Belcourt Ave., Nashville TN 37212. (615)292-8926. Fax: (615)292-8249. E-mail: lynn@bookpage.com. Website: www.bookpage.com. **Contact:** Ms. Lynn L. Green, editor. **90% freelance written.** Monthly newspaper covering new book releases. "*BookPage* is a general interest consumer publication which covers a broad range of books. Bookstores and libraries buy *BookPage* in quantity to use as a way to communicate with their regular customers/patrons and keep them up to date on new releases. *BookPage* reviews almost every category of new books including popular and literary fiction, biography, memoir, history, science and travel. Many specialty genres (mystery, science fiction, business and finance, romance, cooking and audio books) are covered by regular columnists and are rarely assigned to other reviewers. We carry few, if any, reviews of backlist books, poetry, short story collections or scholarly books. *BookPage* editors assign all books to be reviewed, choosing from the hundreds of advance review copies we receive each month. We do not publish unsolicited reviews." Estab. 1988. Circ. 500,000. Byline given. Editorial lead time 3 months. Accepts queries by mail, e-mail, fax. Sample copy online. Writer's guidelines free.
Columns/Departments: Romance: Love, Exciting and New, 1,000 words; Business, 1,500 words; New and Good, 800 words; Mystery/Audio, 800-1,000 words. Query with published clips. **Pays $20/400-word review.**
Tips: "If you are interested in being added to our large roster of freelance reviewers, send an e-mail to the editor with a brief bio, a description of your reading interests, and samples of your writing particularly any book reviews you have written. We prefer experienced writers who can effectively communicate, with imagination and originality, what they liked about a particular book."

BOSTON REVIEW, E53-407, M.I.T., Cambridge MA 02139. (617)253-3642. E-mail: bostonreview@mit.edu. Website: bostonreview.mit.edu. Editor: Josh Cohen. **Contact:** Jefferson Decker, managing editor. **90% freelance written.** Bimonthly magazine of cultural and political analysis, reviews, fiction and poetry. "The editors are committed to a society and culture that foster human diversity and a democracy in which we seek common grounds of principle amidst our many differences. In the hope of advancing these ideals, the *Review* acts as a forum that seeks to enrich the language of public debate." Estab. 1975. Circ. 20,000. Publishes ms an average of 3 months after acceptance. Byline given. Buys first North American serial rights. Responds in 6 months to queries. Sample copy for $5 or online. Writer's guidelines for #10 SASE or online.
• The Boston Review also offers a poetry contest. See Contests & Awards/Poetry section.

Nonfiction: Critical essays and reviews. "We do not accept unsolicited book reviews: if you would like to be considered for review assignments, please send your résumé along with several published clips." **Buys 125 mss/year.** Query with published clips.

Fiction: Jodi Daynard, fiction editor. "I'm looking for stories that are emotionally and intellectually substantive and also interesting on the level of language. Things that are shocking, dark, lewd, comic, or even insane are fine so long as the fiction is *controlled* and purposeful in a masterly way. Subtlety, delicacy and lyricism are attractive too." **Buys 8 mss/year.** Length: 1,200-5,000 words.

Poetry: Mary Jo Bang and Timothy Donnelly, poetry editors.

N **$** **$** **BRUTARIAN, The Magazine That Dares To Be**, Box 25222, Arlington VA 22202-9222. E-mail: brutarian1@juno.com. **Contact:** Dominick Salemi, editor. **100% freelance written.** Quarterly magazine covering popular and unpopular culture. "A healthy knowledge of the great works of antiquity and an equally healthy contempt for most of what passes today as culture." Estab. 1991. Circ. 5,000. Pays on publication. Publishes ms an average of 3 months after acceptance. Byline given. Buys first, one-time rights. Editorial lead time 2 months. Submit seasonal material 3 months in advance. Accepts queries by mail. Responds in 1 week to queries; 2 months to mss. Sample copy for $6.

　　O➔ Break in with an interview with an up-and-coming rock band, film actor/actress or director or popular writer.

Nonfiction: Book excerpts, essays, exposé, general interest, historical/nostalgic, humor, interview/profile, opinion, photo feature, travel, reviews of books, film and music. **Buys 10-20 mss/year.** Send complete ms. Length: 1,000-10,000 words. **Pays $100-400.** Sometimes pays expenses of writers on assignment.

Reprints: Send typed ms with rights for sale noted and information about when and where the material previously appeared. Pays 50% of amount paid for an original article.

Photos: State availability with submission. Reviews contact sheets. Buys one-time rights. Offers no additional payment for photos accepted with ms. Captions, identification of subjects, model releases required.

Columns/Departments: Celluloid Void (critiques of cult and obscure films), 500-1,000 words; Brut Library (critiques of books), 500-1,000 words; Audio Depravation (short critiques of odd, R&B, jazz and R&R music), 50-100 words. **Buys 20-30 mss/year.** Send complete ms. **Pays $50 average.**

Fiction: Adventure, confessions, erotica, experimental, fantasy, horror, humorous, mystery, novel excerpts, suspense. **Buys 8-10 mss/year.** Send complete ms. Length: 1,000-10,000 words. **Pays $100-500, 10¢/word for established writers.**

Poetry: Avant-garde, free verse, traditional. **Buys 10-15 poems/year.** Submit maximum 3 poems. Length: 25-1,000 lines. **Pays $20-200.**

Tips: "Send resumé with completed manuscript. Avoid dry tone and excessive scholasticism. Do not cover topics or issues which have been done to death unless you have a fresh approach or new insights on the subject."

$ **CANADIAN DIMENSION**, Dimension Publications Inc., 91 Albert St., Room 2-B, Winnipeg, Manitoba, R3B 1G5, Canada. (204)957-1519. E-mail: info@canadiandimension.mb.ca. Website: www.canadiandimension.mb.ca. **Contact:** Ed Janzen. **80% freelance written.** Bimonthly magazine covering socialist perspective. "We bring a socialist perspective to bear on events across Canada and around the world. Our contributors provide in-depth coverage on popular movements, peace, labour, women, aboriginal justice, environment, third world and eastern Europe." Estab. 1963. Circ. 2,000. Pays on publication. Publishes ms an average of 6 months after acceptance. Accepts simultaneous submissions. Responds in 6 weeks to queries. Sample copy for $2. Writer's guidelines for #10 SASE.

Nonfiction: Interview/profile, opinion, reviews, political commentary and analysis, journalistic style. **Buys 8 mss/year.** Length: 500-2,000 words. **Pays $25-100.**

Reprints: Send typed ms with rights for sale noted and information about when and where the material previously appeared.

N **$** **COMMON GROUND**, Common Ground Publishing, 201-3091 W. Broadway, Vancouver, British Columbia V6K 2G9, Canada. (604)733-2215. Fax: (604)733-4415. E-mail: editor@commongroundmagazine.com. Senior Editor: Joseph Roberts. **Contact:** Robert Scheer, assistant editor. **90% freelance written.** Monthly tabloid covering health, environment, spirit, creativity and wellness. "We serve the cultural creative community." Estab. 1984. Circ. 70,000. Pays on publication. Publishes ms an average of 1 month after acceptance. Byline given. Buys one-time, second serial (reprint) rights. Editorial lead time 3 months. Submit seasonal material 3 months in advance. Accepts queries by e-mail. Accepts simultaneous submissions. Responds in 6 weeks to queries; 3 months to mss. Sample copy for $5. Writer's guidelines by e-mail.

Nonfiction: All topics must fit into "Body, Mind, Spirit" or environment themes. Book excerpts, how-to, inspirational, interview/profile, opinion, personal experience, religious, travel, call to action. **Buys 12 mss/year.** Send complete ms. Length: 500-2,500 words. **Pays 10¢/word (Canadian).**

Reprints: Accepts previously published submissions.

Photos: State availability with submission. Buys one-time rights. Offers no additional payment for photos accepted with ms. Captions required.

$** **$ **$** **FIRST THINGS**, Institute on Religion & Public Life, 156 Fifth Ave., Suite 400, New York NY 10010. (212)627-1985. Fax: (212)627-2184. E-mail: ft@firstthings.com. Website: www.firstthings.com. Editor-in-Chief: Richard John Neuhaus, Managing Editor: Matthew Berke, Associate Editor: Daniel Moloney. **Contact:** James Nuechterlein, editor. **70% freelance written.** "Intellectual journal published 10 times/year containing social and ethical commentary in broad sense, religious and ethical perspectives on society, culture, law, medicine, church and state, morality and mores." Estab. 1990. Circ. 32,000. Pays on publication. Publishes ms an average of 4 months after acceptance. Byline given. Buys all rights. Editorial lead time 2 months. Submit seasonal material 5 months in advance. Responds in 3 weeks to mss. Sample copy and writer's guidelines for #10 SASE.

Nonfiction: Essays, opinion. **Buys 60 mss/year.** Send complete ms. Length: 1,500-6,000 words. **Pays $300-800.** Sometimes pays expenses of writers on assignment.

Poetry: Traditional. **Buys 25-30 poems/year.** Length: 4-40 lines. **Pays $50.**

Tips: "We prefer complete manuscripts (hard copy, double-spaced) to queries, but will reply if unsure."

N $ $ $ ⊡ **FW MAGAZINE,** FW Omni Media Corp., 296 Richmond St. West, #302, Toronto, Ontario M5V 1X2, Canada. (416)591-6537. Fax: (416)591-2390. E-mail: angela@myfw.com. Website: www.myfw.com. Managing Editor: Angela Ryan. **Contact:** P.J. Tarasuk, editorial director. **80% freelance written.** Bimonthly magazine. "We are a lifestyle magazine that is geared to both males and females. Our readership is between 18-34 years old. We focus on the hottest new trends for our readers. We profile people in their 20s doing exciting ventures." Estab. 1993. Circ. 500,000. Pays on publication. Byline given. Offers 50% kill fee. Buys first, electronic rights. Editorial lead time 2 months. Submit seasonal material 3 months in advance. Accepts queries by fax, phone. Accepts simultaneous submissions. Responds in 1 month to queries; 2 months to mss. Sample copy free. Writer's guidelines by e-mail.

Nonfiction: Angela Ryan, senior editor. Exposé, general interest, how-to, interview/profile, new product, personal experience, photo feature, travel. **Buys 83 mss/year.** Query with published clips. Length: 500-3,000 words. **Pays $300-1,000.** Sometimes pays expenses of writers on assignment.

Photos: State availability with submission. Reviews contact sheets, negatives. Buys one-time rights. Negotiates payment individually. Captions, identification of subjects, model releases required.

Columns/Departments: Body (the newest trends in fitness); Travel (the new "hotspots" on a budget); Work (interesting jobs for people in their 20s); Fashion (profile new designers and trends); all 1,000 words. **Buys 50 mss/year.** Query. **Pays $300-1,000.**

⊡ The online magazine carries original content not found in the print edition. Contact: Angela Ryan, online editor.

Tips: "It is best to simply call P.J. Tarasuk at (416)591-6537 or Rose Cefalu at our L.A. office (323)931-3433."

$ $ $ $ ⊡ **MOTHER JONES,** Foundation for National Progress, 731 Market St., Suite 600, San Francisco CA 94103. (415)665-6637. Fax: (415)665-6696. E-mail: query@motherjones.com. Website: www.motherjones.com. Editor: Roger Cohn. **Contact:** Alastair Paulin, managing editor; Eric Bates, investigative editor; Roger Cohn, editor-in-chief; Monika Bauerlein, features editor; Tim Dickinson, associate editor. **80% freelance written.** Bimonthly magazine covering politics, investigative reporting, social issues and pop culture. "*Mother Jones* is a 'progressive' magazine—but the core of its editorial well is reporting (i.e., fact-based). No slant required. MotherJones.com is an online sister publication." Estab. 1976. Circ. 175,000. Pays on publication. Publishes ms an average of 4 months after acceptance. Byline given. Offers 33% kill fee. Buys first North American serial, first, one-time, electronic rights. Editorial lead time 4 months. Submit seasonal material 6 months in advance. Responds in 2 months to queries. Sample copy for $6 and 9×12 SAE. Writer's guidelines for #10 SASE and online.

Nonfiction: Book excerpts, essays, exposé, humor, interview/profile, opinion, personal experience, photo feature, current issues, policy. **Buys 70-100 mss/year.** Query with published clips. Length: 2,000-5,000 words. **Pays $1/word.** Sometimes pays expenses of writers on assignment.

Columns/Departments: query@motherjones.com. Outfront (short, newsy and/or outrageous and/or humorous items), 200-800 words; Profiles of "Hellraisers," 500 words. **Pays $1/word.**

Tips: "We're looking for hard-hitting, investigative reports exposing government cover-ups, corporate malfeasance, scientific myopia, institutional fraud or hypocrisy; thoughtful, provocative articles which challenge the conventional wisdom (on the right or the left) concerning issues of national importance; and timely, people-oriented stories on issues such as the environment, labor, the media, health care, consumer protection, and cultural trends. Send a great, short query and establish your credibility as a reporter. Explain what you plan to cover and how you will proceed with the reporting. The query should convey your approach, tone and style, and should answer the following: What are your specific qualifications to write on this topic? What 'ins' do you have with your sources? Can you provide full documentation so that your story can be fact-checked?"

N $ NEW HAVEN ADVOCATE, News & Arts Weekly, New Mass Media Inc., 1 Long Wharf Dr., New Haven CT 06511-5991. (203)789-0010. Fax: (203)787-1418. E-mail: editor@newhavenadvocate.com. Website: www.newhavenadvocate.com. **Contact:** Joshua Mamis, editor. **10% freelance written.** Weekly tabloid. "Alternative, investigative, cultural reporting with a strong voice. We like to shake things up." Estab. 1975. Circ. 55,000. Pays on publication. Byline given. Buys one-time rights, buys on speculation. Editorial lead time 1 month. Submit seasonal material 2 months in advance. Accepts simultaneous submissions. Responds in 1 month to queries.

Nonfiction: Book excerpts, essays, exposé, general interest, humor, interview/profile. **Buys 15-20 mss/year.** Query with published clips. Length: 750-2,000 words. **Pays $50-150.** Sometimes pays expenses of writers on assignment.

Photos: State availability with submission. Buys one-time rights. Captions, identification of subjects, model releases required.

Tips: "Strong local focus; strong literary voice, controversial, easy-reading, contemporary, etc."

$ $ PAPER MAGAZINE, Paper Publishing Co., Inc., 365 Broadway, 6th Floor, New York NY 10013. (212)226-4405. Fax: (212)226-5929. E-mail: davidh@papermag.com. **Contact:** David Hershkovits, editor/publisher. **30% freelance written.** Monthly magazine covering pop culture, fashion, entertainment. "The underground alternative for hip 18-35 year olds who like to know what's on the cutting edge now or tomorrow." Estab. 1984. Circ. 100,000. Pays on publication. Publishes ms an average of 2 months after acceptance. Byline given. Offers kill fee. Buys one-time rights. Editorial lead time 6 months. Submit seasonal material 6 weeks in advance. Accepts queries by mail, e-mail, fax. Writer's guidelines free.

Nonfiction: Book excerpts, exposé, general interest, interview/profile. Does not want to see ficiton. **Buys 60 mss/year.** Query with published clips. Length: 3,000 words. **Pays $5-500.** Sometimes pays expenses of writers on assignment.

Columns/Departments: Music, Stage, Film. Query with published clips. **Pays $5-500.**

Tips: "If you would like to write for us, please pitch you story idea in one or two paragraphs. We do not routinely assign stories to new writers. Send us two or three clips or writing samples. Briefly tell us why you're qualified to write the story you propose. We are not necessarily interested in work experience—*PAPER* prides itself on publishing stories by people with a unique perspective who are truly involved in their subject."

N $ READERS AND WRITERS MAGAZINE, The Source for Local Book News and Literary Events, Artichoke Publishing, P.O. Box 231023, Encinitas CA 92024. (760)632-9268. E-mail: editing@artichokepublishing.com. Co-Editor: Charles McStravick. **Contact:** Summer McStravick, co-editor. **80% freelance written.** Monthly magazine. "*Readers & Writers* is a monthly periodical for San Diego area residents that focuses on the pleasure of reading and the joys of writing. Besides book reviews, *Readers & Writers* contains a monthly feature article and several special sections, as well as an extensive local resources segment, a services directory, and an event calendar containing all local reading- and writing-related events." Estab. 2000. Circ. 20,000. **Pays on acceptance.** Publishes ms an average of 1 month after acceptance. Byline given. Buys first North American serial, first, second serial (reprint), electronic rights. Editorial lead time 2 months. Submit seasonal material 3 months in advance. Accepts queries by mail, e-mail. Accepts simultaneous submissions. Responds in 2 months to queries. Sample copy for $2. Writer's guidelines for #10 SASE.

Nonfiction: Book excerpts, essays, interview/profile, personal experience, photo feature, book reviews. "We do not print fiction or poetry." **Buys 24-48 mss/year.** Query with published clips or send complete ms. Length: 350-800 words/book reviews; 1,400-3,300 words/features. **Pays $18/book review; $50-75/article.**

Photos: State availability of or send photos with submission. Reviews send color copies or jpegs. Buys one-time rights. Negotiates payment individually. Identification of subjects required.

Tips: "When putting together our editorial calendar, we look for articles that will appeal to either readers, writers, or both. We strongly encourage queries for articles that have a local flavor or otherwise incorporate local, San Diego events."

N $ $ SHEPHERD EXPRESS, Alternative Publications, Inc., 413 N. Second St., Milwaukee WI 53203. (414)276-2222. Fax: (414)276-3312. Website: www.shepherd-express.com. **Contact:** Doug Hissou, metro editor or Dave Luhrssen, art and entertainment editor. **50% freelance written.** Weekly tabloid covering "news and arts with a progressive news edge and a hip entertainment perspective." Estab. 1982. Circ. 58,000. Pays on publication. Publishes ms an average of 2 weeks after acceptance. Submit seasonal material 1 month in advance. Accepts simultaneous submissions. Sample copy for $3.

Nonfiction: Book excerpts, essays, exposé, opinion. **Buys 200 mss/year.** Query with published clips or send complete ms. Length: 900-2,500 words. **Pays $35-300 for assigned articles; $10-200 for unsolicited articles.** Sometimes pays expenses of writers on assignment.

Photos: State availability with submission. Reviews prints. Buys one-time rights. Negotiates payment individually. Captions, identification of subjects, model releases required.

Columns/Departments: Opinions (social trends, politics, from progressive slant), 800-1,200 words; Books Reviewed (new books only: Social trends, environment, politics), 600-1,200 words. **Buys 10 mss/year.** Send complete ms.

Tips: "Include solid analysis with point of view in tight but lively writing. Nothing cute. Do not tell us that something is important, tell us why."

UTNE READER, 1624 Harmon Place, Suite 330, Minneapolis MN 55403. (612)338-5040. Fax: (612)338-6043. E-mail: editor@utne.com. Website: www.utne.com. **Contact:** Craig Cox, executive editor. Accepts queries by mail, e-mail, fax, phone.

• The *Utne Reader* has been a finalist three times for the National Magazine Award for general excellence.

○→ Break in with submissions for 'New Planet.'

Reprints: Send tearsheet or photocopy with rights for sale noted and information about when and where the material previously appeared.

Tips: "State the theme(s) clearly, let the narrative flow, and build the story around strong characters and a vivid sense of place. Give us rounded episodes, logically arranged."

N $ $ THE WOMEN'S REVIEW OF BOOKS, Wellesley College, 106 Central St., Wellesley MA 02481. Website: www.wellesley.edu/womensreview. **Contact:** Linda Gardiner, editor. **100% freelance written.** Monthly tabloid covering books by and about women. Offers "feminist review of recent books on the lives of women past and present."

Estab. 1983. Circ. 11,000. Pays on publication. Publishes ms an average of 1 month after acceptance. Byline given. Buys first North American serial rights. Accepts queries by mail, phone. Responds in 2 months to queries. Sample copy free.

Nonfiction: Book reviews. "We do not consider any unsolicited submissions. Queries only." **Buys 250 mss/year.** Query with published clips. **Pays $75-300.** Sometimes pays expenses of writers on assignment.

Tips: "We work only with experienced book reviewers."

N **$ $ $ $** YAPA, YAPA Inc., 310 E. 46th St., PHA, New York NY 10017. (212)557-2929. Fax: (212)557-6431. E-mail: dmj@yapa.com. Website: www.yapa.com. Web Editor: Torey Marcus. **Contact:** David Jamison, editor. **90% freelance written.** Quarterly online magazine covering career, lifestyle, education. "Career and lifestyle magazine is for 18-35-year-olds. Belief in creating balance between life, work, and spirit. Fun, authoritative, familiar tone, but not elitist or preachy." Estab. 2000. Circ. 500,000. **Pays on acceptance.** Publishes ms an average of 3 months after acceptance. Byline given. Offers 33% kill fee. Buys first North American serial, electronic rights. Editorial lead time 4 months. Submit seasonal material 5 months in advance. Accepts queries by mail, e-mail, fax. Accepts simultaneous submissions. Responds in 1 month to queries; 4 months to mss. Sample copy for 9×12 SAE and 9 first-class stamps. free or by e-mail.

Nonfiction: Essays, exposé, general interest, historical/nostalgic, how-to, humor, inspirational, interview/profile, new product, personal experience, photo feature, religious, technical, travel, money. No fiction. **Buys 20 mss/year.** Query with published clips. Length: 2,500-3,500 words. **Pays $1/word.** Pays expenses of writers on assignment.

Photos: State availability with submission. Reviews contact sheets. Buys all rights. Negotiates payment individually. Identification of subjects, model releases required.

Columns/Departments: Buys 130 mss/year. Query with published clips. **Pays $50-75.**

Tips: "Do not call with queries. Be patient; surf our website and familiarize yourself with us before submitting."

$ YES!, A Journal of Positive Futures, Positive Futures Network, P.O. Box 10818, Bainbridge Island WA 98110. (206)842-0216. Fax: (206)842-5208. E-mail: editors@futurenet.org. Website: www.futurenet.org. Editor: Sarah van Gelder. **Contact:** Carol Estes, associate editor. Quarterly magazine covering sustainability and community. "Interested in stories on building a positive future: sustainability, overcoming divisiveness, ethical business practices, etc." Estab. 1996. Circ. 14,000. Pays on publication. Byline given. Buys various rights. Editorial lead time 4 months. Accepts queries by mail. Accepts simultaneous submissions. Responds in 1 month to queries; 6 months to mss. Sample copy and writer's guidelines online.

   O—¬ Break in with book reviews.

Nonfiction: "Please check website for a detailed call for submission before each issue." Book excerpts, essays, how-to, humor, interview/profile, personal experience, photo feature, technical, environmental. Query with published clips. Length: 200-3,500 words. **Pays $20-50 for assigned articles.** Pays writers with 1-year subsciption and 2 contributor copies.

Reprints: Send photocopy or typed ms with rights for sale noted and information about when and where the material previously appeared. Pays 100% of amount paid for an original article.

Photos: State availability with submission. Reviews contact sheets, negatives, transparencies, prints. Buys one-time rights. Offers $20-75/photo. Identification of subjects required.

Columns/Departments: Query with published clips. **Pays $20-60.**

Tips: "Read and become familiar with the publication's purpose, tone and quality. We are about facilitating the creation of a better world. We are looking for writers who want to participate in that process. *Yes!* is less interested in bemoaning the state of our problems than in highlighting promising solutions. We are highly unlikely to accept submissions that simply state the author's opinion on what needs to be fixed and why. Our readers know *why* we need to move towards sustainability; they are interested in *how* to do so."

DETECTIVE & CRIME

Fans of detective stories want to read accounts of actual criminal cases, detective work and espionage. Markets specializing in crime fiction are listed under Mystery publications.

$ P. I. MAGAZINE, America's Private Investigation Journal, 755 Bronx, Toledo OH 43609. (419)382-0967. Fax: (419)382-0967. E-mail: pimag1@aol.com. Website: www.PIMAG.com. **Contact:** Bob Mackowiak, editor/publisher. **75% freelance written.** "Audience includes professional investigators, attorneys, paralegals and law enforcement personnel." Estab. 1988. Circ. 5,200. Pays on publication. Publishes ms an average of 3 months after acceptance. Byline given. Buys one-time rights. Submit seasonal material 3 months in advance. Accepts simultaneous submissions. Responds in 3 months to queries; 4 months to mss. Sample copy for $6.95.

Nonfiction: Interview/profile, personal experience, accounts of real cases. **Buys 4-10 mss/year.** Send complete ms. Length: 1,000 words and up. **Pays $75 minimum for unsolicited articles.**

Photos: Send photos with submission. Buys one-time rights. May offer additional payment for photos accepted with ms. Identification of subjects, model releases required.

Tips: "The best way to get published in *P. I.* is to write a detailed story about a professional P.I.'s true-life case. Absolutely no fiction. Unsolicited fiction manuscripts will not be returned."

DISABILITIES

These magazines are geared toward disabled persons and those who care for or teach them. A knowledge of disabilities and lifestyles is important for writers trying to break in to this field; editors regularly discard material that does not have a realistic focus. Some of these magazines will accept manuscripts only from disabled persons or those with a background in caring for disabled persons.

N **$** **$ ABILITIES, Canada's Lifestyle Magazine for People with Disabilities**, Canadian Abilities Foundation, #501-489 College St., Toronto, Ontario M6G 1A5, Canada. (416)923-1885. Fax: (416)923-9829. E-mail: able@abilities.ca. Website: www.abilities.ca. Editor: Raymond Cohen. **Contact:** Lisa Bendall, managing editor. **50% freelance written.** Quarterly magazine covering disability issues. *"Abilities* provides information, inspiration and opportunity to its readers with articles and resources covering health, travel, sports, products, technology, profiles, employment, recreation and more." Estab. 1987. Circ. 40,000. Pays on publication. Publishes ms an average of 3 months after acceptance. Byline given. Offers 50% kill fee. Buys first rights. Editorial lead time 3 months. Submit seasonal material 4 months in advance. Accepts queries by mail, e-mail, fax. Responds in 3 months to queries. Sample copy free. Writer's guidelines for #10 SASE, online or by e-mail.
Nonfiction: Book excerpts, general interest, how-to, humor, inspirational, interview/profile, new product, opinion, personal experience, photo feature, travel. Does not want "articles that 'preach to the converted'—contain info that people with disabilities likely already know, such as what it's like to have a disability." **Buys 30-40 mss/year.** Query or send complete ms. Length: 500-2,500 words. **Pays $50-400 (Canadian) for assigned articles; $50-300 (Canadian) for unsolicited articles.**
Reprints: Sometimes accepts previously published submissions (if stated as such).
Photos: State availability with submission.
Columns/Departments: The Lighter Side (humor), 600 words; Profile, 1,200 words.
Tips: "Do not contact by phone—send something in writing. Send a great idea that we haven't done before and make a case for why you'd be able to do a good job with it. Be sure to include a relevant writing sample."

$** **$ ACCENT ON LIVING, P.O. Box 700, Bloomington IL 61702-0700. (309)378-2961. Fax: (309)378-4420. E-mail: acntlvng@aol.com. Website: www.accentonliving.com. Betty Garee, editor. **75% freelance written.** Eager to work with new/unpublished writers. Quarterly magazine for physically disabled persons and rehabilitation professionals. Estab. 1956. Circ. 20,000. Pays on publication. Publishes ms an average of 6 months after acceptance. Byline given. Buys first, second serial (reprint) rights. Accepts queries by mail, e-mail, fax, phone. Responds in 1 month to queries. Sample copy and writer's guidelines for $3.50 and #10 SAE with 7 first-class stamps. Writer's guidelines for #10 SASE.
Nonfiction: Articles about new devices that would make a disabled person with limited physical mobility more independent; should include description, availability and photos. Medical breakthroughs for disabled people. Intelligent discussion articles on acceptance of physically disabled persons in normal living situations; topics may be architectural barriers, housing, transportation, educational or job opportunities, organizations, or other areas. How-to articles concerning everyday living, giving specific, helpful information so the reader can carry out the idea himself/herself. News articles about active disabled persons or groups. Good strong interviews. Vacations, accessible places to go, sports, organizations, humorous incidents, self-improvement and sexual or personal adjustment—all related to physically handicapped persons. "We are looking for upbeat material." **Buys 50-60 unsolicited mss/year.** Query. Length: 250-1,000 words. **Pays 10¢/word.**
Reprints: Send tearsheet and information about when and where the material previously appeared. **Pays 10¢/word.**
Photos: "We need good-quality color or b&w photos (or slides and transparencies)." Pays $10-50.
Tips: "Ask a friend who is disabled to read your article before sending it to *Accent*. Make sure that he/she understands your major points and the sequence or procedure."

$** **$ **$** **$ ARTHRITIS TODAY**, Arthritis Foundation., 1330 W. Peachtree St., Atlanta GA 30309. (404)872-7100. Fax: (404)872-9559. E-mail: atmail@arthritis.org. Website: www.arthritis.org. Editor: Cindy T. McDaniel. Managing Editor: Shannon Wilder., Executive Editor: Marcy O'Koon. **Contact:** Michele Taylor, assistant editor. **50% freelance written.** Bimonthly magazine covering living with arthritis; latest in research/treatment. *"Arthritis Today* is written for the more than 43 million Americans who have arthritis and for the millions of others whose lives are touched by an arthritis-related disease. The editorial content is designed to help the person with arthritis live a more productive, independent and painfree life. The articles are upbeat and provide practical advice, information and inspiration." Estab. 1987. Circ. 700,000. **Pays on acceptance.** Byline given. Offers kill fee. Buys first North American serial, second serial (reprint) rights. Editorial lead time 6 months. Submit seasonal material 6 months in advance. Accepts queries by mail, e-mail, fax. Accepts simultaneous submissions. Responds in 2 months to queries. Sample copy for 9x11 SAE with 4 first-class stamps. Writer's guidelines for #10 SASE.
Nonfiction: General interest, how-to (tips on any aspect of living with arthritis), inspirational, new product (arthritis-related), opinion, personal experience, photo feature, technical, travel (tips, news), service, nutrition, general health, lifestyle. **Buys 60-70 unsolicited mss/year.** Query with or without published clips or send complete ms. Length: 150-2,000 words. **Pays $150-2,000.** Pays expenses of writers on assignment.

Photos: Send photos with submission. Reviews prints. Buys one-time rights. Negotiates payment individually. Identification of subjects required.

Columns/Departments: Research Spotlight (research news about arthritis); LifeStyle (travel, leisure), 100-300 words; Well Being (arthritis-specific medical news), 100-300 words; Hero (personal profile of people with arthritis), 100-300 words. **Buys 10 mss/year.** Query with published clips. **Pays $150-300.**

Fillers: Facts, gags to be illustrated by cartoonist, short humor. **Buys 10/year.** Length: 40-100 words. **Pays $80-150.**

Tips: "Our readers are already well-informed. We need ideas and writers that give in-depth, fresh, interesting information that truly adds to their understanding of their condition and their quality of life. Quality writers are more important than good ideas. The staff generates many of our ideas but needs experienced, talented writers who are good reporters to execute them. Please provide published clips. In addition to articles specifically about living with arthritis, we look for articles to appeal to an older audience on subjects such as hobbies, general health, lifestyle, etc."

$ $ CAREERS & the disABLED, Equal Opportunity Publications, 1160 E. Jericho Turnpike, Suite 200, Huntington NY 11743. (516)421-9421. Fax: (516)421-0359. E-mail: info@aol.com. Website: www.eop.com. **Contact:** James Schneider, editor. **60% freelance written.** Quarterly magazine offering "role-model profiles and career guidance articles geared toward disabled college students and professionals and promotes personal and professional growth." Estab. 1967. Circ. 10,000. Pays on publication. Publishes ms an average of 6 months after acceptance. Byline given. Buys first North American serial rights. Editorial lead time 6 months. Submit seasonal material 6 months in advance. Accepts queries by mail, e-mail, fax, phone. Accepts simultaneous submissions. Responds in 3 weeks to queries. Sample copy for 9×12 SAE with 5 first-class stamps.

Nonfiction: Essays, general interest, how-to, interview/profile, new product, opinion, personal experience. **Buys 30 mss/year.** Query. Length: 1,000-2,500 words. **Pays 10¢/word, $350 maximum** Sometimes pays expenses of writers on assignment.

Reprints: Send information about when and where the material previously apeared.

Photos: Reviews transparencies, prints. Buys one-time rights. Offers $15-50/photo. Captions, identification of subjects, model releases required.

Tips: "Be as targeted as possible. Role-model profiles and specific career guidance strategies that offer advice to disabled college students are most needed."

[N] $ $ DIABETES INTERVIEW, Kings Publishing, 3715 Balboa St., San Francisco CA 94121. (415)387-4002. Fax: (415)387-3604. E-mail: daniel@diabetesinterview.com. Website: www.diabetesinterview.com. **Contact:** Daniel Trecroci, managing editor. **40% freelance written.** Monthly tabloid covering diabetes care. "*Diabetes Interview* covers the latest in diabetes care, medications and patient advocacy. Personal accounts are welcome as well as medical-oriented articles by MDs, RNs and CDEs (certified diabetes educators)." Estab. 1991. Circ. 40,000. Pays on publication. Publishes ms an average of 2 months after acceptance. Byline given. Buys all rights. Editorial lead time 2 months. Submit seasonal material 2 months in advance. Accepts queries by mail, e-mail, fax, phone. Sample copy online. Writer's guidelines free.

Nonfiction: Essays, how-to, humor, inspirational, interview/profile, new product, opinion, personal experience. **Buys 25 mss/year.** Query. **Pays 20¢/word.**

Reprints: Accepts previously published submissions.

Photos: State availability of or send photos with submission. Negotiates payment individually.

Tips: "Be actively involved in the diabetes community or have diabetes. However, writers need not have diabetes to write an article, but it must be diabetes-related."

$ $ DIABETES SELF-MANAGEMENT, R.A. Rapaport Publishing, Inc., 150 W. 22nd St., Suite 800, New York NY 10011-2421. (212)989-0200. Fax: (212)989-4786. E-mail: editor@diabetes-self-mgmt.com. Website: www.diabetes-self-mgmt.com. **Contact:** Ingrid Strauch, managing editor. **20% freelance written.** Bimonthly. "We publish how-to health care articles for motivated, intelligent readers who have diabetes and who are actively involved in their own health care management. All articles must have immediate application to their daily living." Estab. 1983. Circ. 480,000. Pays on publication. Publishes ms an average of 3 months after acceptance. Byline given. Offers 20% kill fee. Buys all rights. Submit seasonal material 6 months in advance. Accepts queries by mail, e-mail, fax, phone. Responds in 6 weeks to queries. Sample copy for $4 and 9×12 SAE with 6 first-class stamps or online. Writer's guidelines for #10 SASE.

   ● "We are extremely generous regarding permission to republish."

   O⌐ Break in by having extensive knowledge of diabetes.

Nonfiction: How-to (exercise, nutrition, diabetes self-care, product surveys), technical (reviews of products available, foods sold by brand name, pharmacology), travel (considerations and prep for people with diabetes). No personal experiences, personality profiles, exposés or research breakthroughs. **Buys 10-12 mss/year.** Query with published clips. Length: 1,500-2,500 words. **Pays $400-700 for assigned articles; $200-700 for unsolicited articles.**

Tips: "The rule of thumb for any article we publish is that it must be clear, concise, useful, and instructive, and it must have immediate application to the lives of our readers. If your query is accepted, expect heavy editorial supervision."

$ [image] DIALOGUE, Blindskills, Inc., P.O. Box 5181, Salem OR 97301-0181. (800)860-4224. Fax: (503)581-0178. E-mail: blindskl@teleport.com. Website: www.blindskills.com. **Contact:** Carol M. McCarl, editor. **70% freelance written.** Quarterly journal covering the visually impaired. Estab. 1961. Circ. 1,100. Pays on publication. Publishes ms an average of 8 months after acceptance. Byline given. Buys first rights. Editorial lead time 3 months. Submit seasonal material 3 months in advance. Accepts queries by mail, e-mail, fax. Sample copy for $6. One free sample on request. Available in Braille, 4-track audio cassette, large print and disk (for compatible IBM computer). Writer's guidelines for #10 SASE.

O→ Break in by "using accurate punctuation, grammar and structure, and writing about pertinent subject matter."

Nonfiction: Features material by visually impaired writers. Essays, general interest, historical/nostalgic, how-to (life skills methods used by visually impaired people), humor, interview/profile, new product, personal experience, sports, recreation, hobbies. No controversial, explicit sex, religious or political topics. **Buys 80 mss/year.** Send complete ms. Length: 500-1,200 words. **Pays $10-35 for assigned articles; $10-25 for unsolicited articles.**

Columns/Departments: All material should be relative to blind and visually impaired readers. Careers, 1,000 words; What Do You Do When? (dealing with sight loss), 1,000 words. **Buys 80 mss/year.** Send complete ms. **Pays $10-25.**

Fiction: Publishes material by visually impaired writers. Adventure, humorous, science fiction, slice-of-life vignettes, first person experiences. No controversial, explicit sex, religious or political topics. **Buys 6-8 mss/year.** Send complete ms. Length: 800-1,200 words. **Pays $15-25.**

$ $HEARING HEALTH, Voice International Publications, Inc., P.O. Drawer V, Ingleside TX 78362-0500. (361)776-7240. Fax: (361)776-3278. E-mail: ears2u@hearinghealthmag.com. Website: www.hearinghealthmag.com. **Contact:** Paula Bonillas, editor. **20% freelance written.** Quarterly magazine covering issues and concerns pertaining to hearing and hearing loss. Estab. 1984. Circ. 20,000. Pays on publication. Byline given. Buys one-time rights. Editorial lead time 2 months. Submit seasonal material 4 months in advance. Accepts queries by mail, fax. Accepts simultaneous submissions. Responds in 6 weeks to queries; 2 months to mss. Sample copy for $2 or online. Writer's guidelines for #10 SASE or online.

O→ "Break in with a fresh approach—positive, a splash of humor—or well-researched biographical or historical pieces about people with hearing loss."

Nonfiction: Book excerpts, essays, exposé, general interest, historical/nostalgic, humor, inspirational, interview/profile, new product, opinion, personal experience, photo feature, technical, travel. No self-pitying over loss of hearing. Query with published clips. Length: 500-2,000 words. **Pays $75-200.** Sometimes pays expenses of writers on assignment.

Reprints: Accepts previously published submissions.

Photos: State availability with submission. Reviews contact sheets. Buys one-time rights. Negotiates payment individually. Captions, identification of subjects, model releases required.

Columns/Departments: Kidink (written by kids with hearing loss), 300 words; People (shares stories of successful, everyday people who have loss of hearing), 300-400 words. **Buys 2 mss/year.** Query with published clips.

Fiction: Fantasy, historical, humorous, novel excerpts, science fiction. **Buys 2 mss/year.** Query with published clips. Length: 400-1,500 words.

Poetry: Avant-garde, free verse, light verse, traditional. **Buys 2 poems/year.** Submit maximum 2 poems. Length: 4-50 lines.

Fillers: Anecdotes, facts, gags to be illustrated by cartoonist, newsbreaks, short humor. **Buys 6/year.** Length: 25-1,500 words.

Tips: "We look for fresh stories, usually factual but occasionally fictitious, about coping with hearing loss. A positive attitude is a must for *Hearing Health*. Unless one has some experience with deafness or hearing loss—whether their own or a loved one's—it's very difficult to 'break in' to our publication. Experience brings about the empathy and understanding—the sensitivity—and the freedom to write humorously about any handicap or disability."

$ KALEIDOSCOPE, Exploring the Experience of Disability Through Literature and the Fine Arts, (formerly *Kaleidoscope: International Magazine of Literature, Fine Arts, and Disability*), Kaleidoscope Press, 701 S. Main St., Akron OH 44311-1019. (330)762-9755. Fax: (330)762-0912. E-mail: mshiplett@udsakron.org. Website: www.udsakron.org. **Contact:** Dr. Darshan Perusek, editor-in-chief; Gail Willmott, senior editor. **75% freelance written.** Eager to work with new/unpublished writers; appreciates work by established writers as well. Especially interested in work by writers with a disability, but features writers both with and without disabilities. Writers without a disability must limit themselves to our focus, while those with a disability may explore any topic (although we prefer original perspectives about experiences with disability). Semiannual. Subscribers include individuals, agencies and organizations that assist people with disabilities and many university and public libraries. Estab. 1979. Circ. 1,000. Byline given. Accepts queries by mail, fax. Responds in 3 weeks to queries. Sample copy for $5 prepaid. Writer's guidelines for #10 SASE.

● Rights return to author upon publication.

O→ Submit photocopies with SASE for return of work. Please type submissions (double spaced). All submissions should be accompanied by an autobiographical sketch. May include art or photos that enhance works, prefer b&w with high contrast.

Nonfiction: Articles related to disability. Book excerpts, essays, humor, interview/profile, personal experience, book reviews, articles related to disability. Special issues: Disability: Mythology/Folklore (July 2002, deadline March 2002); and Disability and the Road Less Traveled (January 2003, deadline August 2002). **Buys 8-15 mss/year.** Length: 5,000 words maximum. **Pays $25-125 plus 2 copies.**

Reprints: Send typed ms with rights for sale noted and information about when and where the material previously appeared.

Photos: Send photos with submission.

Fiction: Short stories, novel excerpts. Traditional and experimental styles. Works should explore experiences with disability. Use people-first language. Length: 5,000 words maximum.

Poetry: "Do not get caught up in rhyme scheme. High quality with strong imagery and evocative language." Reviews any style. **Buys 12-20 poems/year.** Submit maximum 5 poems.

Tips: "Articles and personal experiences should be creative rather than journalistic and with some depth. Writers should use more than just the simple facts and chronology of an experience with disability. Inquire about future themes of upcoming issues. Sample copy very helpful. Works should not use stereotyping, patronizing or offending language about disability. We seek fresh imagery and thought-provoking language."

ENTERTAINMENT

This category's publications cover live, filmed or videotaped entertainment, including home video, TV, dance, theater and adult entertainment. In addition to celebrity interviews, most publications want solid reporting on trends and upcoming productions. Magazines in the Contemporary Culture and General Interest sections also use articles on entertainment. For those publications with an emphasis on music and musicians, see the Music section.

$ CINEASTE, America's Leading Magazine on the Art and Politics of the Cinema, Cineaste Publishers, Inc., 200 Park Ave. S., #1601, New York NY 10003. (212)982-1241. Fax: (212)982-1241. E-mail: cineaste@cineaste.com. **Contact:** Gary Crowdus, editor-in-chief. **30% freelance written.** Quarterly magazine covering motion pictures with an emphasis on social and political perspective on cinema. Estab. 1967. Circ. 11,000. Pays on publication. Publishes ms an average of 4 months after acceptance. Byline given. Offers 50% kill fee. Buys first North American serial rights. Editorial lead time 3 months. Submit seasonal material 4 months in advance. Accepts queries by mail, e-mail, fax. Responds in 1 month to queries. Sample copy for $5. Writer's guidelines for #10 SASE.

O⇒ Break in by "being familiar with our unique editorial orientation—we are not just another film magazine."

Nonfiction: Book excerpts, essays, exposé, historical/nostalgic, humor, interview/profile, opinion. **Buys 20-30 mss/year.** Query with published clips. Length: 2,000-5,000 words. **Pays $30-100.**

Photos: State availability with submission. Reviews transparencies, 8×10 prints. Buys one-time rights. Offers no additional payment for photos accepted with ms. Identification of subjects required.

Columns/Departments: Homevideo (topics of general interest or a related group of films); A Second Look (new interpretation of a film classic or a reevaluation of an unjustly neglected release of more recent vintage); Lost and Found (film that may or may not be released or otherwise seen in the US but which is important enough to be brought to the attention of our readers); all 1,000-1,500 words. Query with published clips. **Pays $50 minimum.**

Tips: "We dislike academic jargon, obtuse Marxist teminology, film buff trivia, trendy 'buzz' phrases, and show biz references. We do not want our writers to speak of how they have 'read' or 'decoded' a film, but to view, analyze and interpret same. The author's processes and quirks should be secondary to the interests of the reader. Warning the reader of problems with specific films is more important to us than artificially 'puffing' a film because its producers or politics are agreeable. One article format we encourage is an omnibus review of several current films, preferably those not reviewed in a previous issue. Such an article would focus on films that perhaps share a certain political perspective, subject matter or generic concerns (e.g., films on suburban life, or urban violence, or revisionist Westerns). Like individual Film Reviews, these articles should incorporate a very brief synopsis of plots for those who haven't seen the films. The main focus, however, should be on the social issues manifested in each film and how it may reflect something about the current political/social/esthetic climate."

$ ⬡ DANCE INTERNATIONAL, 601 Cambie St., Suite 302, Vancouver, British Columbia V6B 2P1, Canada. (604)681-1525. Fax: (604)681-7732. E-mail: danceint@direct.ca. Website: www.danceinternational.org. **Contact:** Maureen Riches, editor. **100% freelance written.** Quarterly magazine covering dance arts. "Articles and reviews on current activities in world dance, with occasional historical essays; reviews of dance films, video and books." Estab. 1973. Circ. 4,500. Pays on publication. Publishes ms an average of 3 months after acceptance. Byline given. Offers 50% kill fee. Buys one-time rights. Editorial lead time 3 months. Submit seasonal material 6 weeks in advance. Accepts queries by mail, e-mail, fax, phone. Responds in 2 weeks to queries; 1 month to mss. Sample copy for $7. Writer's guidelines for #10 SASE.

Nonfiction: Book excerpts, essays, historical/nostalgic, interview/profile, personal experience, photo feature. **Buys 100 mss/year.** Query. Length: 1,200-2,200 words. **Pays $40-150.**

Photos: Send photos with submission. Reviews prints. Offers no additional payment for photos accepted with ms. Identification of subjects required.

Columns/Departments: Dance Bookshelf (recent books reviewed), 1,200 words; Regional Reports (events in each region), 1,200-2,000 words. **Buys 100 mss/year.** Query. **Pays $60-70.**

Tips: "Send résumé and samples of recent writings."

$ $ DANCE SPIRIT, Lifestyle Ventures, LLC, 250 W. 57th St., Suite 420, New York NY 10107. (212)265-8890. Fax: (212)265-8908. E-mail: editor@lifestyleventures.com. Website: www.dancespirit.com. Editorial Director: Julie Davis. **Contact:** Kimberly Gdula, executive editor. **50% freelance written.** Monthly magazine covering all dance

Writing about entertainment: Get your clips together

From drug-addicted actors to celebrity stalkers to Hollywood Scientologists, award-winning journalist and self-proclaimed "pit bull at heart," Mark Ebner has covered Los Angeles and the entertainment industry for almost two decades. Bylined in *Premier*, *Details*, *Spin*, the *News Times* and dozens of other publications, he's worked his way up the freelancing ranks. Ebner has also written for film, television and comic books; hosted his own nationally syndicated radio show, and recently co-authored his first nonfiction book with Internet movie sneak and freak, Harry Knowles of www.aint-it-cool-news.com.

Mark Ebner

What special challenges set freelancing for entertainment industry publications apart from other specialties?
"Entertainment journalism" is sort of an oxymoron in that most mainstream entertainment-oriented publications are practically vetted by movie studios and certainly beholden to the advertisers of the same ilk. I suppose the greatest challenge for the freelancer is the battle to see their honest, "warts and all" reportage make it to the published page. Brow-beating timid editors into submission is part of the game, as is the realization that 99 percent of what comes out of a celebrity publicist's mouth is a lie. Also, the thought of trying to pull a usable quote out of some spaced-out starlet makes a freelancer reach for the Pepto Bismol®. I don't know if entertainment journalism is all that different than other "specialty writing," but nowhere else will you find so much "spin," fear, greed, and so many egos.

What kind of topics do you write most often for entertainment magazines? Are there staples in the industry that "always" sell?
I'm the "down and dirty guy" who will spend months working on a Hollywood exposé that will more than likely get "killed" in favor of the publisher using the personality in question for an upcoming cover story. It's all politics, but there's a decent living to be made from "kill fees." I'm also the "go-to guy" when the publication is ready to hang a drug-addicted actor out to dry, or they need an exposé that every other career-conscious journalist is afraid to touch. The "staples" in the industry are "puff" celebrity profiles, lightweight stuff that any hack who can string quotes together is capable of. Which is not to say I'm above the occasional puff piece. They, too, pay the bills.

How would you break into this specialty if you were a beginning freelancer?
I hate to say it, but write for free. Find a glossy start-up magazine, or a local rag that features entertainment stuff, and get your clips together. Then find the mags that pay and start bugging

editors. Hint: A "senior editor" on any masthead is the person to start bugging first. Find a story, or snag an interview that you can claim an exclusive on. Make the editor *NEED* you. Keep bugging them until you bag an assignment. Remember: Part of their gig is to be bugged by neophyte freelancers, so don't be put off by their occasional moods.

What is the general pay scale a freelancer can expect writing about entertainment topics?

Entertainment writers' wages vary, and they don't necessarily adjust for inflation or cost-of-living increases. Low-end, believe it or not, is still around 25¢ a word. Mid-range is a buck-a-word, and a successful freelancer brings down between $1.50 and $2.50 a word. If you think you're hot, and want to sacrifice eventual ownership or copyright on your published stories, there are a handful of seldom-available "contract writer" positions out there. For instance, Dominick Dunne makes a comfortable high six-figure salary plus perks dishing the rich and famous at *Vanity Fair*. The key to making a decent living as a freelancer is to always have more assignments on your plate than you believe you can possibly handle, and never thinking that you're "above" an assignment. Never say "no."

What are the most common mistakes freelancers in this arena make (and can avoid)?

Not filing quarterly tax returns, and consistently missing deadlines are good ways to "write" your way out of a career. Try and get your copy in on time and remember—the taxman is not kind to work-for-hire types who invoice for untaxed editorial fees.

Have you had a favorite assignment? If so, what was it and why was it so memorable?

My favorite assignments are ones that ultimately impart some sort of honorable, useful message off the printed page. Also, a story that might effect worthwhile changes regarding the often-sordid subjects that I cover is a bonus. Going on location on an assignment can be fun. After years of complaining about never getting gigs in exotic locales, I finally got dispatched to Paris to interview Gabriel Byrne on a movie set. Our interview went great, and he arranged for me to meet Catherine Deneuve at a dinner party. Need I say more?

Have you experienced the nightmare of all nightmare assignments? Describe it.

I don't know . . . The nightmare assignments are usually the "for-the-money" jobs that I'm not enthused about in the first place. True investigative journalism is always an exciting challenge, puff-pieces are generally a headache. Unresponsive, self-important celebrities are always a nightmare. But then, one man's nightmare is another man's challenge.

—*Kelly Milner Halls*

For interviews with the pros in more freelance niche markets, see Animals, page 368; Contemporary Culture, page 432; Games & Puzzles, page 462; Sports, page 708, Women's, page 782.

TOP TIP: "Find a mentor. Someone who's been in the trenches long enough to realize that 'you've got to give it away to keep it.' I'm currently accepting pupils who are serious enough to have a sense of humor about the profession. I can be reached by e-mail at Ebner59@aol.com."

disciplines. *"Dance Spirit* is a special interest teen magazine for girls and guys who study and perform either through a studio or a school dance performance group." Estab. 1997. Circ. 130,000. Pays on publication. Publishes ms an average of 4 months after acceptance. Byline given. Offers 25% kill fee. Buys all rights. Editorial lead time 3 months. Submit seasonal material 6 months in advance. Accepts queries by mail, e-mail, fax. Responds in 3 months to queries; 4 months to mss. Sample copy for $4.95.

Nonfiction: Personal experience, photo feature, dance-related articles only. **Buys 100 mss/year.** Query with published clips. Length: 600-1,200 words. **Pays $100-500.** Sometimes pays expenses of writers on assignment.

Photos: Reviews transparencies. Buys all rights. Negotiates payment individually. Captions, identification of subjects, model releases required.

Columns/Departments: Ballet, jazz, tap, swing, hip hop, lyrical, pom, body, beauty, city focus, choreography, stars, nutrition.

■ The online magazine carries original content not found in the print edition. Contact: Kimberly Gdula.

Tips: "Reading the magazine can't be stressed enough. We look for writers with a dance background and experienced dancers/choreographers to contribute; succinct writing style, hip outlook."

$ $ DANCE SPIRITS IN MOTION, Lifestyle Ventures, LLC, 250 W. 57th St., Suite 420, New York NY 10107. (212)265-8890. Fax: (212)265-8908. E-mail: editor@dancespirit.com. **Contact:** Marisa Walker, managing editor. **50% freelance written.** Quarterly magazine covering dance teams, color guards and other performing groups. "Our audience is high school and college dance team and color guard members and their directors, coaches and choreographers." Circ. 50,000. **Pays on acceptance.** Publishes ms an average of 2 months after acceptance. Byline given. Offers 25% kill fee. Buys all rights. Editorial lead time 4 months. Submit seasonal material 6 months in advance. Accepts queries by mail, e-mail, fax. Accepts simultaneous submissions. Responds in 1 month to queries; 2 months to mss. Sample copy for cover price ($3.95 US, $4.95 Canada).

Nonfiction: Exposé, general interest (pertaining to the industry), historical/nostalgic, how-to (skill execution, preparation for camps and competitions), inspirational, interview/profile, personal experience. **Buys many mss/year.** Query. Length: 300-1,000 words. **Pays $0-200.** Sometimes pays expenses of writers on assignment.

Photos: Send photos with submission. Reviews transparencies, prints. Negotiates payment individually. Captions, identification of subjects, model releases required.

Columns/Departments: Team and individual profiles, skill how-to's, fundraising, costuming, makeup, health & fitness, industry news. Query. **Pays up to $200.**

Fillers: Anecdotes, facts, newsbreaks. **Buys many/year.** Length: 50-100 words. **Pays $25.**

■ The online magazine carries original content not found in the print edition.

Tips: "Have at least a working knowledge of dance and color guard industry—experience a plus. Keep queries brief. The writing style of the publication is casual, teen-oriented. Articles take a fun, yet educational approach on performing and training."

N $ $ DIRECTED BY, The Cinema Quarterly, Visionary Media, P.O. Box 1722, Glendora CA 91740-1722. Fax: (626)963-0235. E-mail: visionarycinema@yahoo.com. Website: www.directed-by.com. **Contact:** Carsten Dau, editor. **50% freelance written.** Quarterly magazine covering the craft of filmmaking. "Our articles are for readers particularly knowledgeable about the art and history of movies. Our purpose is to communicate our enthusiasm and interest in all levels of serious filmmaking." Estab. 1998. Circ. 12,000. Pays on publication. Publishes ms an average of 3 months after acceptance. Byline given. Offers 50% kill fee. Buys all rights. Editorial lead time 3 months. Submit seasonal material 3 months in advance. Accepts queries by mail, e-mail. Accepts simultaneous submissions. Responds in 6 weeks to queries. Sample copy for $5. Writer's guidelines free or by e-mail.

Nonfiction: Essays, historical/nostalgic, interview/profile, photo feature, on set reports. No gossip, celebrity-oriented material or movie reviews. **Buys 12 mss/year.** Query. Length: 500-7,500 words. **Pays $50-750.** Sometimes pays expenses of writers on assignment.

Photos: State availability with submission. Reviews contact sheets. Buys all rights. Offers no additional payment for photos accepted with ms. Captions, identification of subjects required.

Columns/Departments: Trends (overview/analysis of specific moviemaking movements/genres/subjects), 1,500-2,000 words; Focus (innovative take on the vision of a director), 1,500-2,000 words; Appreciation (overview of deceased/foreign director), 1,000-1,500 words; Final Cut (spotlight interview with contemporary director), 3,000 words; Perspectives (interviews/articles about film craftspeople other than directors), 1,500-2,000 words. **Buys 12 mss/year.** Query. **Pays $50-750.**

Tips: "If you are a movie buff, either have a unique perspective on an aspect of moviemaking in which you are well-informed or gain access to a director or relevant film craftsperson of artistic significance."

$ $ ◪ EAST END LIGHTS, The Quarterly Magazine for Elton John Fans, P.O. Box 621, Joplin MO 64802-0621. (417)437-1603. Fax: (417)206-2507. E-mail: submissions@eastendlights.com. **Contact:** Mark Norris, publisher. **90% freelance written.** Quarterly magazine covering Elton John. "In one way or another, a story must relate to Elton John, his activities or associates (past and present). We appeal to discriminating Elton fans. No gushing fanzine material. No current concert reviews." Estab. 1990. Circ. 1,700. Pays 3 weeks after publication. Publishes ms an average of 3 months after acceptance. Byline given. Offers 100% kill fee. Buys first, second serial (reprint) rights. Submit seasonal material 6 months in advance. Accepts queries by mail, e-mail, fax. Responds in 2 months to queries. Sample copy for $2.

Nonfiction: Book excerpts, essays, exposé, general interest, historical/nostalgic, humor, interview/profile. **Buys 20 mss/year.** Query with or without published clips or send complete ms. Length: 400-1,000 words. **Pays $75-250 for assigned articles; $75-150 for unsolicited articles.** Pays in contributor copies only when author requests it.

Reprints: Send tearsheet or photocopy with rights for sale noted and information about when and where the material previously appeared. Pays 50%.

Photos: State availability with submission. Reviews negatives and 5×7 prints. Buys one-time and all rights. Offers $40-75/photo.

Columns/Departments: Clippings (non-wire references to Elton John in other publications), maximum 200 words. **Buys 12 mss/year.** Send complete ms. **Pays $20-50.**

Tips: "Approach us with a well-thought-out story idea. We prefer interviews with Elton-related personalities—past or present; try to land an interview we haven't done. We are particularly interested in music/memorabilia collecting of Elton material."

ENTERTAINMENT TODAY, L.A.'s Entertainment Weekly Since 1967, Best Publishing Inc., 2325 W. Victory Blvd., Burbank CA 91506. Fax: (818)566-4030. E-mail: jsalazar@artnet.net. Website: www.entertainment-today.com. **Contact:** Brent Simon, managing editor. **40% freelance written.** Weekly print and online newspaper covering entertainment. Estab. 1967. Circ. 210,000. Pays on publication. Publishes ms an average of 3 months after acceptance. Byline given. Offers 25% kill fee. Buys one-time rights. Editorial lead time 2 months. Submit seasonal material 2 months in advance. Accepts queries by mail, e-mail, fax, phone. Accepts simultaneous submissions. Responds in 2 months to queries. Sample copy and writer's guidelines free.

Nonfiction: General interest, humor, interview/profile, opinion, photo feature, travel, any entertainment-related material. **Buys 6-12 mss/year.** Query with published clips. Length: 675-1,850 words.

Photos: State availability with submission. Offers no additional payment for photos accepted with ms. Identification of subjects required.

Columns/Departments: Book Report (book review, often entertainment-related), 415-500 words; Film Reviews, 300-600 words; Disc Domain (CD reviews), 250-400 words. **Buys 6-12 mss/year.** Query with published clips.

Fillers: Short humor.

▣ The online magazine carries original content not found in the print edition. Contact: Eric Layton.

$ $FANGORIA, Horror in Entertainment, Starlog Communications, Inc., 475 Park Ave. S., 8th Floor, New York NY 10016. (212)689-2830. Fax: (212)889-7933. Website: www.fangoria2000.com. **Contact:** Anthony Timpone, editor. **95% freelance written.** Works with a small number of new/unpublished writers each year. Magazine published 10 times/year covering horror films, TV projects, comics, videos and literature and those who create them. "We provide an assignment sheet (deadlines, info) to writers, thus authorizing queried stories that we're buying." Estab. 1979. Pays on publication. Publishes ms an average of 3 months after acceptance. Byline given. Buys all rights. Submit seasonal material 4 months in advance. Accepts queries by mail. Responds in 6 weeks to queries. Sample copy for $7 and 10×13 SAE with 4 first-class stamps. Writer's guidelines for #10 SASE.

◐ Break in by "reading the magazine regularly and exhibiting a professional view of the genre."

Nonfiction: Book excerpts; interview/profile of movie directors, makeup FX artists, screenwriters, producers, actors, noted horror/thriller novelists and others—with genre credits; special FX and special makeup FX how-it-was-dones (on filmmaking only). Occasional "think" pieces, opinion pieces, reviews, or sub-theme overviews by industry professionals. Avoids most articles on science fiction films—see listing for sister magazine *Starlog* in *Writer's Market* Science Fiction consumer magazine section. **Buys 100 mss/year.** Query with published clips. Length: 1,000-3,500 words. **Pays $100-250.** Pays expenses of writers on assignment.

Photos: State availability with submission. Reviews transparencies, prints (b&w, color). Captions, identification of subjects required.

Columns/Departments: Monster Invasion (exclusive, early information about new film productions; also mini-interviews with filmmakers and novelists). Query with published clips. **Pays $45-75.**

▣ The online magazine carries original content not found in the print edition.

Tips: "Other than recommending that you study one or several copies of *Fangoria*, we can only describe it as a horror film magazine consisting primarily of interviews with technicians and filmmakers in the field. Be sure to stress the interview subjects' words—not your own opinions as much. We're very interested in small, independent filmmakers working outside of Hollywood. These people are usually more accessible to writers, and more cooperative. *Fangoria* is also sort of a *de facto* bible for youngsters interested in movie makeup careers and for young filmmakers. We are devoted only to *reel* horrors—the fakery of films, the imagery of the horror fiction of a Stephen King or a Clive Barker—*we do not* want nor would we *ever* publish articles on real-life horrors, murders, etc. A writer must *like* and *enjoy* horror films and horror fiction to work for us. If the photos in *Fangoria* disgust you, if the sight of (*stage*) blood repels you, if you feel 'superior' to horror (and its fans), you aren't a writer for us and we certainly aren't the market for you. We love giving new writers their *first* chance to break into print in a national magazine. We are currently looking for Vancouver-, Arizona- and Las Vegas-based correspondents."

N $ $▨ FILM COMMENT, Film Society of Lincoln Center, 70 Lincoln Center Plaza, New York NY 10023. (212)875-5610. Fax: (212)875-5636. E-mail: filmcomment@filmline.com. Website: www.filmline.com. **Contact:** Mark Olsen, associate editor. **100% freelance written.** Bimonthly magazine covering film criticism and film history, "authoritative, personal writing (not journalism) reflecting experience of and involvement with film as an art form." Estab.

1962. Circ. 30,000. Pays on publication. Publishes ms an average of 2 months after acceptance. Byline given. Offers 50% kill fee (assigned articles only). Editorial lead time 6 weeks. Accepts queries by mail, e-mail, fax, phone. Accepts simultaneous submissions. Responds in 2 weeks to queries. Writer's guidelines free.

Nonfiction: Essays, historical/nostalgic, interview/profile, opinion. **Buys 100 mss/year.** Send complete ms. We respond to queries, but rarely assign a writer we don't know. Length: 800-8,000 words. **There is no fixed rate, but roughly based on 3 words/$1.**

Photos: State availability with submission. Buys one-time rights. No additional payment for photos accepted with ms.

Tips: "We are more or less impervious to 'hooks,' don't worry a whole lot about 'who's hot who's not,' or tying in with next fall's surefire big hit (we think people should write about films they've seen, not films that haven't even been finished). We appreciate good writing (writing, not journalism) on subjects in which the writer has some personal investment and about which he or she has something noteworthy to say. Demonstrate ability and inclination to write FC-worthy articles. We read and consider everything we get, and we do print unknowns and first-timers. Probably the writer with a shorter submission (1,000-2,000 words) has a better chance than with an epic article that would fill half the issue."

N: $5678 MAGAZINE, Champion Media, P.O. Box 5716, Derwood MD 20855. (301)216-0200. Fax: (301)869-7432. E-mail: durand5678@aol.com. Website: www.5678magazine.com. **Contact:** Barry Durand, editor. **50% freelance written.** Monthly magazine covering dance: Couples, line, country, swing. "All articles with a dance or dance music slant. Interviews, reviews, features—today's social dance." Estab. 1999. Circ. 10,000. Pays on publication. Publishes ms an average of 2 months after acceptance. Byline given. Buys first rights. Editorial lead time 2 months. Accepts queries by e-mail. Sample copy free. Writer's guidelines by e-mail.

Nonfiction: Historical/nostalgic, how-to, humor, interview/profile, photo feature. **Buys 60 mss/year.** Query. Length: 600-2,000 words. **Pays $35-100.** Sometimes pays expenses of writers on assignment.

Photos: Send photos with submission. Buys one-time rights. Negotiates payment individually. Captions, identification of subjects required.

Fiction: Humorous, slice-of-life vignettes. **Buys 10 mss/year.** Query. Length: 600-1,500 words. **Pays $35-100.**

$THE NEWFOUNDLAND HERALD, Sunday Herald Ltd., Box 2015, St. John's, Newfoundland A1C 5R7, Canada. (709)726-7060. Fax: (709)726-6971. E-mail: mdwyer@nfldherald.com. **Contact:** Mark Dwyer, assignment editor. **25% freelance written.** Weekly magazine. "We prefer Newfoundland and Labrador-related items." Estab. 1946. Circ. 30,000. Pays on publication. Publishes ms an average of 2 months after acceptance. Byline given. Buys all rights. Editorial lead time 2 months. Submit seasonal material 3 months in advance. Accepts queries by mail, e-mail, fax. Sample copy for $5. Guidelines free via fax or with SASE.

Nonfiction: General interest, how-to, interview/profile, investigative news. No opinion, humor, poetry, fiction, satire. **Buys 500 mss/year.** Query with published clips. Length: 350-1,700 words. **Pays $20 minimum.** Sometimes pays expenses of writers on assignment.

Reprints: Send typed ms with rights for sale noted (Mac disk or e-mail attachment of text preferred).

Photos: Send photos with submission. Buys one-time or all rights. Offers $7.50-25/photo. Captions required.

Columns/Departments: Music (current artists), Video/Movies (recent releases/themes), TV shows (Top 20); all 1,500-2,500 words. **Buys 500 mss/year.** Query with published clips.

Tips: "Know something about Newfoundlanders and Labradorians—for example, travel writers should know where we like to travel. Query first. No opinion pieces, satire, humor or poetry is purchased; fiction is not accepted. Original cartoons which focus on local politics will be considered. Photos should be submitted with all articles. Please use color 35mm print or slide film. No b&w photos unless otherwise requested. Please read several issues of the magazine before submitting any material to the *Herald.*"

$ $ $ PERFORMING ARTS MAGAZINE, Performing Arts Network, 10350 Santa Monica Blvd., #350, Los Angeles CA 90025. (310)551-1115. Fax: (310)551-2769. Website: www.performingartsmagazine.com. **Contact:** David Bowman, editor. **95% freelance written.** Monthly magazine covering arts and performing arts. "We cover performing arts events throughout the state of California only and articles should pertain to performances in California. Theatre-going audience." Estab. 1963. Circ. 570,000. Pays on publication. Byline given. Offers 50% kill fee. Buys all rights, makes work-for-hire assignments. Editorial lead time 3 months. Submit seasonal material 6 months in advance. Responds in 6 weeks to queries. Sample copy for 10×12 SAE with 5 first-class stamps.

Nonfiction: Interview/profile, new productions. "Do not send unsolicited mss." **Buys 75 mss/year.** Query with published clips. Length: 800-1,200 words. **Pays $500-1,000.** Sometimes pays expenses of writers on assignment.

Photos: State availability with submission. Buys all rights. Negotiates payment individually. Captions, identification of subjects required.

N: $ $ $ REQUEST MAGAZINE, Request Media, Inc., 10400 Yellow Circle Dr., Minnetonka MN 55343. (952)931-8740. Fax: (952)931-8490. E-mail: editors@requestmagazine.com. Website: www.requestmagazine.com. Editor: James Diers. **Contact:** Heidi Raschke, managing editor. **70% freelance written.** Bimonthly magazine. "*Request* offers sharp, enthusiastic coverage of the latest and best in music, movies, home video and all manner of entertainment." Part newsstand, part membership magazine for Musicland Group. Estab. 1989. Circ. 1.1 million. Pays as files go to press. Publishes ms an average of 2 months after acceptance. Byline given. Offers 50% kill fee. Buys first, electronic rights. Editorial lead time 4 months. Submit seasonal material 4 months in advance. Accepts queries by e-mail. Accepts simultaneous submissions. Sample copy for $2.95. Writer's guidelines by e-mail.

Nonfiction: Essays, general interest, humor, interview/profile, photo feature, reviews. **Buys 10-20 mss/year.** Query with published clips. Length: 150-2,500 words. **Pays $50-1,000.** Sometimes pays expenses of writers on assignment.

Photos: Send photos with submission. Reviews contact sheets. Photo rights negotiable. Negotiates payment individually. Identification of subjects required.

Columns/Departments: Jim Meyer, senior editor. Reviews (short, efficient CD and video reviews), 100-200 words. Query with published clips. **Pays $50-100.**

Tips: "We prefer enthusiastic pitches on noteworthy artists or releases, ideally with a pre-determined level of interview access or research. Our core audience consists of avid music and movie lovers aged 21 to 35."

Ⓝ $ $ RIGHT ON!, Sterling/McFadden, 233 Park Ave. S., 6th Floor, New York NY 10003. (212)780-3519. Fax: (212)780-3555. Website: www.rightonmag.com. **Contact:** Cynthia Horner, editorial director. **10% freelance written.** Monthly black entertainment magazine for teenagers and young adults. Circ. 250,000. Pays on publication. Publishes ms an average of 3 months after acceptance. Byline given. Buys all rights. Submit seasonal material 4 months in advance. Accepts queries by mail, fax. Responds in 1 month to queries.

Nonfiction: "We only publish entertainment-oriented stories or celebrity interviews." Interview/profile. **Buys 15-20 mss/year.** Query with or without published clips or send complete ms. Length: 500-4,000 words. **Pays $50-200.**

Photos: State availability with submission. Reviews transparencies, 8×10 b&w prints. Buys one-time or all rights. Offers no additional payment for photos accepted with ms. Identification of subjects required.

$ $Ⓧ SCI-FI ENTERTAINMENT, Sovereign Media, 11305 Sunset Hills Rd., Reston VA 20190. (703)471-1556. E-mail: sovmedia@erols.com. **Contact:** Dan Perez, editor. **100% freelance written.** Bimonthly magazine covering science fiction movies and television—old, new, upcoming sci-fi. Estab. 1994. Circ. 70,000. Pays 1-2 months after acceptance. Publishes ms an average of 1 month after acceptance. Byline given. Offers 10% kill fee. Buys first world rights. Editorial lead time 1 month. Submit seasonal material 3 months in advance. Accepts simultaneous submissions. Responds in 2 weeks to queries; 1 month to mss. Sample copy for $4.95. Writer's guidelines for #10 SASE.

Nonfiction: General interest, historical/nostalgic, interview/profile, new product (games), opinion, personal experience, photo feature. **Buys 100 mss/year.** Query. Length: 2,000-3,000 words. **Pays $200-500.** Sometimes pays expenses of writers on assignment.

Photos: State availability with submission. Buys one-time rights. Offers no additional payment for photos accepted with ms. Identification of subjects required.

Columns/Departments: Infinite Channels (games), 2,300 words; Video (video reviews), 2,400 words; Books (books on movies), 2,500 words. **Buys 6 mss/year.** Query with published clips.

$ $ SOAP OPERA UPDATE, Bauer Publishing, 270 Sylvan Ave., Englewood Cliffs NJ 07632. (201)569-6699. Fax: (201)569-2510. **Contact:** Sue Weiner, editor-in-chief. Biweekly "We cover daytime and prime time soap operas with preview information, in-depth interviews and exclusive photos, history, character sketches, events where soap stars are seen and participate." Mostly staff written; write for permission to query. Estab. 1988. Circ. 288,000. Buys all rights.

$ $ $ SOUND & VISION, (formerly *Stereo Review's Sound & Vision*), Hachette Filipacchi Magazines, Inc., 1633 Broadway, New York NY 10019. (212)767-6000. Fax: (212)767-5615. E-mail: soundandvision@hfmag.com. Website: www.soundandvisionmag.com. Editor-in-Chief: Bob Ankosko. Entertainment Editor: Ken Richardson. **Contact:** Michael Gaughn, features editor. **50% freelance written.** Published 10 times/year. Estab. 1958. Circ. 450,000. **Pays on acceptance.** Publishes ms an average of 4 months after acceptance. Byline given. Buys first North American serial, electronic rights. Accepts queries by mail, e-mail, fax. Sample copy for 9×12 SAE and 11 first-class stamps.

Nonfiction: Home theater, audio, video and multimedia equipment plus movie and music reviews, how-to-buy and how-to-use A/V gear, interview/profile. **Buys 25 mss/year.** Query with published clips. Length: 1,500-3,000 words. **Pays $1,000-1,500.**

Tips: "Send proposals or outlines, rather than complete articles, along with published clips to establish writing ability. Publisher assumes no responsibility for return or safety of unsolicited art, photos or manuscripts."

$ $Ⓧ STAGEBILL, Stagebill LLC, 823 United Plaza at 46th St., New York NY 10017. Fax: (212)949-0518. Website: www.stagebill.com. Editor: John Istel. **Contact:** Ben Mattison, managing editor. **80% freelance written.** Program distributed free to performing arts audiences covering dance, theater, opera, classical music, jazz and some film. "Our editorial is geared toward an educated and sophisticated arts audience. We suggest to writers that the closest analogous publication is the *New York Times'* Sunday Arts & Leisure section." Estab. 1924. Circ. 15,000,000/year. Pays on publication. Publishes ms an average of 2 months after acceptance. Byline given. Offers 50% kill fee. Buys 90 day exclusive rights, non-exclusive after that. Editorial lead time 2 months. Submit seasonal material 3 months in advance. Accepts queries by mail, e-mail. Responds in 2 weeks to queries; 1 month to mss. Sample copy online.

Nonfiction: Book excerpts, essays (on arts or cultural trends), humor, opinion. **Buys 200 mss/year.** Query with published clips. Length: 350-1,200 words. **Pays $250-400.** Sometimes pays expenses of writers on assignment.

Reprints: Accepts previously published submissions.

Photos: State availability with submission. Offers no additional payment for photos accepted with ms.

Columns/Departments: See/Hear (book/CD reviews), 200 words; By Design (art, design and fashion), 600-750 words; Critical Slant (opinions on culture), 350-400 words; Traveler (performing arts-oriented travel), 600-750 words; Deus Ex Machina (arts and technology), 600-750 words. **Buys 75 mss/year.** Query with published clips. **Pays $50-350.**

$ ▨ **TELE REVISTA, Su Mejor Amiga**, Teve Latino Publishing, Inc., P.O. Box 145179, Coral Gables FL 33114-5179. (305)445-1755. Fax: (305)445-3907. E-mail: telerevista@aol.com. Website: www.telerevista.com. **Contact:** Ana Pereiro, editor. **100% freelance written.** Monthly magazine covering Hispanic entertainment (US and Puerto Rico). "We feature interviews, gossip, breaking stories, behind-the-scenes happenings, etc." Estab. 1986. Pays on publication. Publishes ms an average of 3 months after acceptance. Byline sometimes given. Buys all rights. Editorial lead time 2 months. Submit seasonal material 3 months in advance. Accepts queries by mail, e-mail, fax. Sample copy free.
Nonfiction: Exposé, interview/profile, opinion, photo feature. **Buys 200 mss/year.** Query. **Pays $25-75.**
Photos: State availability of or send photos with submission. Buys all rights. Negotiates payment individually. Captions required.
Columns/Departments: Buys 60 mss/year. Query. **Pays $25-75.**
Fillers: Anecdotes, facts, gags to be illustrated by cartoonist, newsbreaks, short humor.

N: $ $ $XXL MAGAZINE, Harris Publications, 1115 Broadway, 8th Floor, New York NY 10010. (212)462-9500. E-mail: zenat@harris-pub.com. **Contact:** Zena Tsarfin, managing editor. **50% freelance written.** Bimonthly magazine "*XXL* is hip-hop on a higher level, an upscale urban lifestyle magazine." Estab. 1997. Circ. 175,000. Pays on publication. Byline given. Offers 25% kill fee. Buys all rights. Editorial lead time 4 months. Submit seasonal material 3 months in advance. Accepts queries by mail, e-mail.
Nonfiction: Interview/profile, music, entertainment, luxury materialism. Query with published clips. Length: 200-5,000 words. **Pays 50¢/word.** Pays expenses of writers on assignment.
Photos: State availability with submission. Reviews contact sheets, transparencies, prints. Buys "3 month no-see" rights. Captions, model releases required.
Tips: "Please send clips, query and cover letter by mail or e-mail."

ETHNIC & MINORITY

Ideas and concerns of interest to specific nationalities and religions are covered by publications in this category. General interest lifestyle magazines for these groups are also included. Many ethnic publications are locally oriented or highly specialized and do not wish to be listed in a national publication such as *Writer's Market*. Query the editor of an ethnic publication with which you're familiar before submitting a manuscript, but do not consider these markets closed because they are not listed in this section. Additional markets for writing with an ethnic orientation are located in the following sections: Career, College & Alumni; Juvenile; Literary & "Little"; Men's; Women's; and Teen & Young Adult.

$ $AFRICAN ACCESS MAGAZINE, Mainstreaming Africa, 44 Dalhurst Way NW, Calgary, Alberta T3A 1N7, Canada. (403)210-2726. Fax: (403)210-2484. E-mail: editor@africanaccess.com. Website: www.africanaccess.com. **Contact:** Chris Roberts, editor. **50% freelance written.** Quarterly magazine covering business, investment and travel in Africa. "AfriCan Access Magazine is Canada's guide to the African Renaissance. Our audience is internationally oriented: Business, investment and travel interest in Africa. Articles should have a North American-African connection." Estab. 1998. Circ. 5,000. Pays on publication. Publishes ms an average of 2 months after acceptance. Byline given. Offers 20% kill fee. Buys first North American serial, one-time, electronic rights. Editorial lead time 2 months. Accepts queries by mail, e-mail, fax, phone. Accepts simultaneous submissions. Responds in 2 weeks to queries; 1 month to mss. Sample copy for $5. Writer's guidelines online.
Nonfiction: "If Africa isn't part of the story, we aren't interested." Book excerpts (reviews), essays, exposé, general interest, how-to (do business, case studies, travel, invest), interview/profile, opinion, personal experience, photo feature, travel, investment/political analysis. **Buys 20 mss/year.** Query with published clips. Length: 600-2,000 words. **Pays $100-400 (Canadian) for assigned articles; $50-300 (Canadian) for unsolicited articles.** Pays sometimes in copies and/or advertising.
Reprints: Accepts previously published submissions.
Photos: State availability with submission. Buys one-time rights. Negotiates payment individually. Captions, identification of subjects required.
Columns/Departments: Recommended Reading: Reviews (book, film, TV, video, art reviews), 100-300 words; NGO Profile (work of an NGO active in Africa), 500-750 words; Travel Stories (humorous/adventure first person), 200-400 words; Business Profiles (detailed how-to look at SMEs active overseas), 400-750 words; Cyber Africa (Africa on the Internet, best sites), 200-350 words. **Buys 8-12 mss/year.** Query with published clips or send complete ms. **Pays $100.**
   ▣ The online magazine carries original content not found in the print edition.
Tips: "If a writer has first hand experience in Africa, has studied Africa, or is African, that helps! We want practical stories our readers can use."

N **$ AFRICAN VOICES**, African Voices Communications, Inc., 270 W. 96th St., New York NY 10025. (212)865-2982. Fax: (212)316-3335. E-mail: africanvoices@aol.com. Website: www.africanvoices.com. Managing Editor: Layding Kaliba. **Contact:** Carolyn A. Butts, editor. **85% freelance written.** Quarterly magazine covering art, film, culture. *"African Voices* is dedicated to highlighting the art, literature and history of people of color." Estab. 1992. Circ. 20,000. Pays on publication. Byline given. Buys first North American serial rights. Editorial lead time 3 months. Submit seasonal material 3 months in advance. Accepts queries by mail. Accepts simultaneous submissions. Responds in 3 months to queries. Sample copy for $5 or online. Writer's guidelines for #10 SASE.
Nonfiction: Book excerpts, essays, historical/nostalgic, humor, inspirational, interview/profile, photo feature, travel. Query with published clips. Length: 1,200-2,500 words. **Pays $25-100.**
Reprints: Accepts previously published submissions.
Photos: State availability with submission. Buys one-time rights. Negotiates payment individually.
Fiction: Kim Horne, fiction editor. Adventure, erotica, ethnic, experimental, fantasy, historical, horror, humorous, mainstream, mystery, novel excerpts, romance, science fiction, serialized novels, slice-of-life vignettes, suspense. **Buys 4 mss/year.** Send complete ms. Length: 500-2,500 words. **Pays $25-50.**
Poetry: Layding Kaliba, managing editor/poetry editor. Avant-garde, free verse, haiku, traditional. **Buys 10 poems/year.** Submit maximum 5 poems. Length: 5-100 lines. **Pays $10-20.**

$ **AIM MAGAZINE**, AIM Publishing Company, P.O. Box 1174, Maywood IL 60153. (708)344-4414. Fax: (206)543-2746. E-mail: ruthone@earthlink.net. Website: aimmagazine.org. **Contact:** Dr. Myron Apilado, editor. **75% freelance written.** Works with a small number of new/unpublished writers each year. Quarterly magazine on social betterment that promotes racial harmony and peace for high school, college and general audience. Estab. 1975. Circ. 10,000. Pays on publication. Publishes ms an average of 3 months after acceptance. Byline given. Offers 60% kill fee. Buys one-time rights. Submit seasonal material 6 months in advance. Accepts queries by mail, e-mail. Accepts simultaneous submissions. Responds in 2 months to queries. Sample copy and writer's guidelines for $4 and 9×12 SAE with $1.70 postage or online.
Nonfiction: Exposé (education), general interest (social significance), historical/nostalgic (Black or Indian), how-to (create a more equitable society), interview/profile (one who is making social contributions to community), book reviews, reviews of plays. No religious material. **Buys 16 mss/year.** Send complete ms. Length: 500-800 words. **Pays $25-35.**
Photos: Reviews b&w prints. Captions, identification of subjects required.
Fiction: "Fiction that teaches the brotherhood of man." Ethnic, historical, mainstream, suspense. **Buys 20 mss/year.** Send complete ms. Length: 1,000-1,500 words. **Pays $25-35.**
Poetry: Avant-garde, free verse, light verse. No "preachy" poetry. **Buys 20 poems/year.** Submit maximum 5 poems. Length: 15-30 lines. **Pays $3-5.**
Fillers: Anecdotes, newsbreaks, short humor. **Buys 30/year.** Length: 50-100 words. **Pays $5.**
Tips: "Interview anyone of any age who unselfishly is making an unusual contribution to the lives of less fortunate individuals. Include photo and background of person. We look at the nations of the world as part of one family. Short stories and historical pieces about Blacks and Indians are the areas most open to freelancers. Subject matter of submission is of paramount concern for us rather than writing style. Articles and stories showing the similarity in the lives of people with different racial backgrounds are desired."

$ $ AMBASSADOR MAGAZINE, National Italian American Foundation, 1860-19 St. NW, Washington DC 20009. (202)387-0600. Fax: (202)387-0800. E-mail: dona@niaf.org. Website: www.niaf.org. **Contact:** Dona De Sanctis, editor. **50% freelance written.** Magazine for Italian Americans covering Italian-American history and culture. "We publish nonfiction articles on little-known events in Italian-American history, and articles on Italian-American culture, traditions and personalities living and dead." Estab. 1989. Circ. 20,000. Pays on approval of final draft. Byline given. Offers 50% or $100 kill fee. Buys second serial (reprint) rights. Editorial lead time 3 months. Accepts queries by mail, e-mail, fax. Accepts simultaneous submissions. Responds in 1 month to queries. Sample copy and writer's guidelines free.
Nonfiction: Historical/nostalgic, interview/profile, personal experience, photo feature. **Buys 12 mss/year.** Send complete ms. Length: 1,500-2,500 words. **Pays $200.**
Photos: Send photos with submission. Reviews contact sheets, prints. Buys one-time rights. Offers no additional payment for photos accepted with ms. Captions, identification of subjects required.
Tips: "Good photos, clear prose and a good story-telling ability are all prerequisites."

N **$ AMERICAN JEWISH WORLD**, AJW Publishing Inc., 4509 Minnetonka Blvd., Minneapolis MN 55416. (952)259-5234. Fax: (952)920-6205. E-mail: amjewish@isd.net. **Contact:** Mordecai Specktor, managing editor. **10-20% freelance written.** Weekly newspaper covering local, national and international stories from a Jewish perspective. Estab. 1912. Circ. 6,500. Pays on publication. Byline given. Makes work-for-hire assignments. Submit seasonal material 3 months in advance. Accepts queries by mail, e-mail, fax. Accepts simultaneous submissions. Sample copy and editorial calendar free.
   ● *American Jewish World* is focusing more on Midwest and Minnesota angles.
Nonfiction: Essays, exposé, general interest, historical/nostalgic, humor, inspirational, interview/profile, opinion, personal experience, photo feature, religious, travel. **Buys 12-15 mss/year.** Query with or without published clips. Length: 750 words maximum. **Pays $25-75.**
Reprints: Send typed ms with rights for sale noted.

Photos: State availability with submission. Reviews prints. Buys one-time rights. Pays $25/photo. Identification of subjects required.

$ $ ◪ AMERICAN VISIONS, The Magazine of Afro-American Culture, 1101 Pennsylvania Ave. NW, Suite 820, Washington DC 20004. (202)347-3820. Fax: (202)347-4096. E-mail: editor@avs.americanvisions.com. Website: www.americanvisions.com. **Contact:** Joanne Harris, executive editor. **75% freelance written.** Bimonthly magazine. "Editorial is reportorial, current, objective, 'pop-scholarly.' Audience is ages 25-54, mostly black, college educated. The scope of the magazine includes the arts, history, literature, cuisine, genealogy and travel—all filtered through the prism of the African-American experience." Estab. 1986. Circ. 125,000. Pays 30 days after publication. Publishes ms an average of 2 months after acceptance. Byline given. Offers 25% kill fee. Buys second serial (reprint), all rights. Submit seasonal material 5 months in advance. Accepts queries by mail, e-mail. Accepts simultaneous submissions. Responds in 3 months to queries. Sample copy and writer's guidelines for #10 SASE.

Nonfiction: Publishes travel supplements—domestic, Africa, Europe, Canada, Mexico. Book excerpts, general interest, historical/nostalgic, interview/profile, photo feature, travel, literature. **Buys about 60-70 mss/year.** Query with or without published clips or send complete ms. Length: 500-2,500 words. **Pays $100-600 for assigned articles; $100-400 for unsolicited articles.** Pays expenses of writers on assignment.

Reprints: Send tearsheet or photocopy with rights for sale noted and information about when and where the material previously appeared. Pays $100.

Photos: State availability with submission. Reviews contact sheets, 3×5 transparencies. Buys one-time rights. Offers $15/minimum. Identification of subjects required.

Columns/Departments: Arts Scene, Books, Cuisine, Film, Music, Profile, Genealogy, Computers & Technology, Travel, 750-1,750 words. **Buys about 40 mss/year.** Send complete ms. **Pays $100-400.**

Tips: "Little-known but terribly interesting information about black history and culture is desired. Aim at an upscale audience. Send ms with credentials. Looking for writers who are enthusiastic about their topics."

Ⓝ $ $ ARMENIAN INTERNATIONAL MAGAZINE, 207 S. Brand Blvd., Suite 205, Glendale CA 91204. (818)246-7979. Fax: (818)246-0088. Website: www.AIMmagazine.com. **Contact:** Salpi H. Ghazarian, editor/publisher. **50% freelance written.** Monthly magazine about the Caucasus and the global Armenian diaspora. "Special reports and features about politics, business, education, culture, interviews and profiles. Each month, *AIM* is filled with essential news, situation analysis, and indepth articles with local and international coverage of events that affect Armenian life." Estab. 1989. Circ. 15,000. Pays on publication. Publishes ms an average of 3 months after acceptance. Byline given. Buys all rights. Accepts queries by mail, e-mail, fax. Responds in 2 weeks to queries; 6 weeks to mss.

Nonfiction: General interest, historical/nostalgic, interview/profile, photo feature, travel. Special issues: Armenian restaurants around the world. **Buys 60 mss/year.** Query with published clips. Length: 600-1,200 words. **Pays $50-400 for assigned articles; $50-200 for unsolicited articles.** Sometimes pays expenses of writers on assignment.

Reprints: Send photocopy.

Photos: State availability with submission. Reviews negatives, transparencies, prints. Offers $10-50/photo. Captions, identification of subjects required.

Fiction: Publishes novel excerpts upon approval.

Tips: "Have an interesting take on Armenian issues and their global significance or global issues and their significance for Armenia or Armenians."

$ ASIAN PAGES, Kita Associates, Inc., P.O. Box 11932, St. Paul MN 55111-1932. (952)884-3265. Fax: (952)888-9373. E-mail: asianpages@att.net. Website: www.asianpages.com. **Contact:** Cheryl Weiberg, editor-in-chief. **40% freelance written.** Biweekly newspaper covering the Asian community in the Midwest. "*Asian Pages* serves an audience of over twenty different Asian groups, including Cambodian, Chinese, Filipino, Hmong, Indian, Indonesian, Japanese, Korean, Laotian, Malaysian, Sri Lankan, Thai, Tibetan, and Vietnamese. In addition, *Asian Pages* has many non-Asian readers who, for many different reasons, have an interest in the vibrant Asian community. *Asian Pages* celebrates the achievements of the Asian community in the Midwest and promotes a cultural bridge among the many different Asian groups that the newspaper serves." Estab. 1990. Circ. 75,000. Pays on publication. Publishes ms an average of 8 months after acceptance. Byline given. Offers 50% kill fee. Buys first North American serial rights. Editorial lead time 4 months. Submit seasonal material 6 months in advance. Accepts queries by mail. Accepts simultaneous submissions. Responds in 1 month to queries; 2 months to mss. Sample copy for 9×12 SAE and 3 first-class stamps. Writer's guidelines for #10 SASE.

Nonfiction: "All articles must have an Asian slant. We're interested in articles on the Asian New Years, banking, business, finance, sports/leisure, home and garden, education and career planning. No culturally insensitive material." Essays, general interest, humor, inspirational, interview/profile, personal experience, travel. **Buys 50-60 mss/year.** Send complete ms. Length: 500-750 words. **Pays $40.**

Photos: State availability with submission. Reviews transparencies, prints. Buys one-time rights. Offers no additional payment for photos accepted with ms. Captions, identification of subjects required.

Columns/Departments: "Query with exceptional ideas for our market and provide 1-2 sample columns." **Buys 100 mss/year.** Query. **Pays $40.**

Fiction: Adventure, ethnic, humorous, stories based on personal experiences. No culturally insensitive material. Send complete ms. Length: 750-1,000 words. **Pays $40.**

Tips: "We look for articles that reflect a direct insight into Asian culture or being an Asian-American in today's society."

$ $⬚ THE B'NAI B'RITH INTERNATIONAL JEWISH MONTHLY, B'nai B'rith International, 1640 Rhode Island Ave. NW, Washington DC 20036. (202)857-2708. Fax: (202)296-1092. E-mail: ijm@bnaibrith.org. Website: bnaibrith.org. Editor: Eric Rozenman. **Contact:** Stacey Freed, managing editor. **90% freelance written.** Bimonthly magazine "specializing in social, political, historical, religious, cultural, 'lifestyle,' and service articles relating chiefly to the Jewish communities of North America and Israel. Write for the American Jewish audience, i.e., write about topics from a Jewish perspective." Estab. 1886. Circ. 110,000. Pays on publication. Publishes ms an average of 6 months after acceptance. Byline given. Offers 25% kill fee. Buys first rights. Editorial lead time 3 months. Submit seasonal material 5 months in advance. Accepts queries by mail, e-mail, fax. Accepts simultaneous submissions. Responds in 2 weeks to queries; 6 weeks to mss. Sample copy for $2. Writer's guidelines for #10 SASE or by e-mail.
Nonfiction: General interest pieces of relevance to the Jewish community of US and abroad. Interview/profile, photo feature, religious, travel. "No Holocaust memoirs, no first-person essays/memoirs." **Buys 18-20 mss/year.** Query with published clips. Length: 1,000-2,500 words. **Pays $300-750 for assigned articles; $300-600 for unsolicited articles.** Sometimes pays expenses of writers on assignment.
Photos: "Rarely assigned." Buys one-time rights.
Columns/Departments: Carla Lancit, assistant editor. Up Front (book, CD reviews; small/short items with Jewish interest), 150-200 words. **Buys 3 mss/year.** Query. **Pays $50.**
Tips: "Know what's going on in the Jewish world. Look at other Jewish publications also. Writers should submit clips with their queries. Read our guidelines carefully and present a good idea expressed well. Proofread your query letter."

$ CONGRESS MONTHLY, American Jewish Congress, 15 E. 84th St., New York NY 10028. (212)879-4500. **Contact:** Jack Fischel, managing editor. **90% freelance written.** Bimonthly magazine. "*Congress Monthly*'s readership is popular, but well-informed; the magazine covers political, social, economic and cultural issues of concern to the Jewish community in general and to the American Jewish Congress in particular." Estab. 1933. Circ. 35,000. Pays on publication. Publishes ms an average of 3 months after acceptance. Byline given. Buys one-time rights. Submit seasonal material 2 months in advance. Responds in 2 months to queries.
Nonfiction: General interest ("current topical issues geared toward our audience"). Travel, book, film and theater reviews. No technical material. Query. Length: 1,000-2,500 words. **Pays amount determined by article length and author experience.**
Photos: State availability with submission. Reviews b&w prints.

$ $ ESTYLO MAGAZINE, Latina Lifestyle, Mandalay Publishing, 3600 Wilshire Blvd., Suite 1903, Los Angeles CA 90010. (213)383-6300. Fax: (213)383-6499. E-mail: Estylo@aol.com. Editor: Linda Cauthen. **25% freelance written.** Magazine published 8 times/year covering fashion, beauty and entertainment for the affluent and mobile Latina. "It contains a variety of features and departments devoted to cuisine, fitness, beauty, fashion and entertainment topics." Estab. 1997. Circ. 90,000. Pays on publication. Publishes ms an average of 2 months after acceptance. Byline given. Buys first rights. Editorial lead time 3 months. Submit seasonal material 4 months in advance. Accepts queries by mail, e-mail. Accepts simultaneous submissions.
Reprints: Send photocopy.
Photos: State availability with submission. Reviews contact sheets. Buys all rights. Negotiates payment individually. Captions, identification of subjects, model releases required.

$ FILIPINAS, A Magazine for All Filipinos, Filipinas Publishing, Inc., 363 El Camino Real 1, Suite 100, South San Francisco CA 94080. (650)872-8650. Fax: (650)872-8651. E-mail: mail@filipinasmag.com. Website: www.filipinas mag.com. **Contact:** Mona Lisa Yuchengco, editor/publisher. Monthly magazine focused on Filipino American affairs. "*Filipinas* answers the lack of mainstream media coverage of Filipinos in America. It targets both Filipino immigrants and American-born Filipinos, gives in-depth coverage of political, social, cultural events in The Philippines and in the Filipino American community. Features role models, history, travel, food and leisure, issues and controversies." Estab. 1992. Circ. 40,000. Pays on publication. Publishes ms an average of 3 months after acceptance. Byline given. Offers $10 kill fee. Buys first, all rights. Editorial lead time 2 months. Submit seasonal material 4 months in advance. Accepts queries by mail, e-mail, fax. Responds in 5 weeks to queries; 18 months to mss. Sample copy for $5. Writer's guidelines for 9½×4 SASE or online.
  ⚬ₚ Break in with "a good idea outlined well in the query letter. Also, tenacity is key. If one idea is shot down, come up with another."
Nonfiction: Interested in seeing "more issue-oriented pieces, unusual topics regarding Filipino Americans and stories from the Midwest and other parts of the country other than the coasts." Exposé, general interest, historical/nostalgic, inspirational, interview/profile, opinion, personal experience, travel. No academic papers. **Buys 80-100 mss/year.** Query with published clips. Length: 800-1,500 words. **Pays $50-100; sometimes pays writers other than cash payment by agreement.**
Photos: State availability with submission. Reviews 2¼×2¼ and 4×5 transparencies. Buys one-time rights. Offers $15-35/photo. Captions, identification of subjects required.
Columns/Departments: Entree (reviews of Filipino restaurants), 1,200 words; Cultural Currents (Filipino traditions, beliefs), 1,500 words. Query with published clips. **Pays $50-75.**

$ $GERMAN LIFE, Zeitgeist Publishing Inc., 1068 National Hwy., LaVale MD 21502. (301)729-6012. Fax: (301)729-1720. E-mail: ccook@GermanLife.com. Website: www.GermanLife.com. **Contact:** Carolyn Cook, editor. **50% freelance written.** Bimonthly magazine covering German-speaking Europe. "*German Life* is for all interested in the diversity of German-speaking culture, past and present, and in the various ways that the United States (and North America in general) has been shaped by its German immigrants. The magazine is dedicated to solid reporting on cultural, historical, social and political events." Estab. 1994. Circ. 40,000. Pays on publication. Publishes ms an average of 6 months after acceptance. Byline given. Buys first North American serial rights. Editorial lead time 4 months. Submit seasonal material 6 months in advance. Accepts queries by mail, e-mail. Responds in 2 months to queries; 3 months to mss. Sample copy for $4.95 and SAE with 4 first-class stamps. Writer's guidelines free.

Nonfiction: General interest, historical/nostalgic, interview/profile, photo feature, travel. Special issues: Oktoberfest-related (October); seasonal relative to Germany, Switzerland or Austria (December); travel to German-speaking Europe (April). **Buys 50 mss/year.** Query with published clips. Length: 1,000-2,000 words. **Pays $200-500 for assigned articles; $200-350 for unsolicited articles.** Sometimes pays expenses of writers on assignment.

Photos: State availability with submission. Reviews color transparencies, 5×7 color or b&w prints. Buys one-time rights. Offers no additional payment for photos accepted with ms. Identification of subjects required.

Columns/Departments: German-Americana (regards specific German-American communities, organizations and/or events past or present), 1,200 words; Profile (portrays prominent Germans, Americans, or German-Americans), 1,000 words; At Home (cuisine, etc. relating to German-speaking Europe), 800 words; Library (reviews of books, videos, CDs, etc.), 300 words. **Buys 30 mss/year.** Query with published clips. **Pays $50-150.**

Fillers: Facts, newsbreaks. Length: 100-300 words. **Pays $50-150.**

Tips: "The best queries include several informative proposals. Writers should avoid overemphasizing autobiographical experiences/stories."

$ $HADAMAG MAGAZINE, (formerly *Hadassah*), 50 W. 58th St., New York NY 10019. (212)688-5217. Fax: (212)446-9521. E-mail: hadamag@aol.com. **Contact:** Leah Finkelshteyn, associate editor. **90% freelance written.** Monthly magazine (combined issues June-July and August-September). "*Hadamag* is a general interest Jewish feature and literary magazine. We speak to our readers on a vast array of subjects ranging from politics to parenting, to midlife crisis to Mideast crisis. Our readers want coverage on social and economic issues, Jewish women's (feminist) issues, the arts, travel and health." Circ. 300,000. Buys first rights. Sample copy and writer's guidelines for 9×12 SASE.

Nonfiction: Primarily concerned with Israel, Jewish communities around the world and American civic affairs as relates to the Jewish community. "We are also open to art stories that explore trends in Jewish art, literature, theater, etc. Will not assign/commission a story to a first-time writer for Hadamag." **Buys 10 unsolicited mss/year.** Query. Length: 1,500-2,000 words. Sometimes pays expenses of writers on assignment.

Photos: "We buy photos only to illustrate articles. Always interested in striking cover photos." Offers $50 for first photo, $35 for each additional photo.

Columns/Departments: "We have a family column and a travel column, but a query for topic or destination should be submitted first to make sure the area is of interest and the story follows our format."

Fiction: Short stories with strong plots and positive Jewish values. No personal memoirs, "schmaltzy" or shelter magazine fiction. Length: 1,500-2,000 words. **Pays $500 minimum.**

Tips: "We are interested in reading articles that offer an American perspective on Jewish affairs (1,500-2,000 words)."

N **$** **HORIZONS, The Jewish Family Journal**, Targum Press, 22700 W. Eleven Mile Rd., Southfield MI 48034. Fax: (888)298-9992. E-mail: horizons@netvision.net.il. Website: www.Targum.com. Managing Editor: Moshe Dombey. **Contact:** Miriam Zakon, chief editor. **100% freelance written.** Quarterly magazine covering the Orthodox Jewish family. "We include fiction and nonfiction, memoirs, essays, historical and informational articles, all of interest to the Orthodox Jew." Estab. 1994. Circ. 5,000. Pays 4-6 weeks after publication. Publishes ms an average of 6 months after acceptance. Byline given. Buys one-time rights. Editorial lead time 6 months. Submit seasonal material 8 months in advance. Accepts queries by mail, e-mail, fax. Accepts simultaneous submissions. Responds in 1 week to queries; 2 months to mss. Sample copy and writer's guidelines free.

Nonfiction: Essays, historical/nostalgic, humor, inspirational, interview/profile, opinion, personal experience, photo feature, travel. **Buys 150 mss/year.** Send complete ms. Length: 350-3,000 words. **Pays $5-150.**

Photos: State availability with submission. Buys one-time rights. Offers no additional payment for photos accepted with ms.

Fiction: Historical, humorous, mainstream, slice-of-life vignettes. Nothing not suitable to Orthodox Jewish values. **Buys 10-15 mss/year.** Send complete ms. Length: 800-3,000 words. **Pays $20-100.**

Poetry: Free verse, haiku, light verse, traditional. **Buys 30-35 poems/year.** Submit maximum 4 poems. Length: 3-28 lines. **Pays $5-10.**

Fillers: Anecdotes, short humor. **Buys 20/year.** Length: 50-120 words. **Pays $5.**

Tips: "*Horizons* publishes for the Orthodox Jewish market and therefore only accepts articles that are of interest to this market. We do not accept submissions dealing with political issues or Jewish legal issues. The tone is light and friendly and we therefore do not accept submissions that are of a scholarly nature. Our writers must be very familiar with our market. Anything that is not suitable for our readership doesn't stand a chance, no matter how high its literary merit."

N **$** INTERNATIONAL EXAMINER, 622 S. Washington, Seattle WA 98104. (206)624-3925. Fax: (206)624-3046. E-mail: tsojen@alumni.standford.org. Website: www.xaminer.com. **Contact:** Chong-Suk Han, managing editor. **75% freelance written.** Biweekly journal of Asian-American news, politics, and arts. "We write about Asian-American issues and theings of interest to Asian-Americans. We do not want stuff about Asian things (stories on your trip to China, Japanese Tea Ceremony, etc. will be rejected). Yes, we are in English." Estab. 1974. Circ. 12,000. Pays on publication. Publishes ms an average of 1 month after acceptance. Buys one-time rights. Editorial lead time 1 month. Submit seasonal material 2 months in advance. Accepts simultaneous submissions. Sample copy, writer's guidelines and editorial calendar for #10 SASE.

Nonfiction: Essays, exposé, general interest, historical/nostalgic, humor, interview/profile, opinion, personal experience, photo feature. **Buys 100 mss/year.** Query by mail, fax or e-mail with published clips. Length: 750-5,000 words, depending on subject. **Pays $25-100.** Sometimes pays expenses of writers on assignment.

Reprints: Accepts previously published submissions (as long as not published in same area). Send typed ms with rights for sale noted and information about when and where the material previously appeared. Pay negotiable.

Photos: State availability with submission. Reviews contact sheets. Buys one-time rights. Negotiates payment individually. Captions, identification of subjects required.

Fiction: Asian-American authored fiction. Holiday fiction issue; fiction by or about Asian-Americans. Holiday fiction contest submissions due by December 1. Novel excerpts. **Buys 1-2 mss/year.** Query.

Tips: "Write decent, suitable material on a subject of interest to Asian-American community. All submissions are reviewed; all good ones are contacted. It helps to call and run idea by editor before or after sending submissions."

$ $ JEWISH ACTION, Union of Orthodox Jewish Congregations of America, 11 Broadway, 14th Floor, New York NY 10004-1302. (212)613-8146. Fax: (212)613-0646. E-mail: chabbott@ou.org. Website: www.ou.org. Editor: Charlotte Friedland. **Contact:** Diane Chabbott, assistant editor. **80% freelance written.** Quarterly magazine covering a vibrant approach to Jewish issues, Orthodox lifestyle and values. Circ. 30,000. Pays 2 months after publication. Byline given. Not copyrighted. Submit seasonal material 4 months in advance. Accepts queries by mail, e-mail. Responds in 3 months to queries. Sample copy and guidelines for 9×12 SAE with 5 first-class stamps; sample articles available online.

O— Break in with a query for "Just Between Us" column.

Nonfiction: Current Jewish issues, history, biography, art, inspirational, humor, music and book reviews. "We are not looking for Holocaust or personal memoir." **Buys 30-40 mss/year.** Query with published clips. Length: 1,000-3,000 words. **Pays $100-400 for assigned articles; $75-150 for unsolicited articles.**

Photos: Send photos with submission. Identification of subjects required.

Columns/Departments: Just Between Us (personal opinion on current Jewish life and issues), 1,000 words. **Buys 4 mss/year.**

Fiction: Must have relevance to Orthodox reader. Length: 1,000-2,000 words.

Poetry: Buys limited number poems/year. Pays $25-75.

Tips: "Remember that your reader is well educated and has a strong commitment to Orthodox Judaism. Articles on the holidays, Israel and other common topics should offer a fresh insight. Because the magazine is a quarterly, we do not generally publish articles which concern specific timely events."

$ $ $ MOMENT, The Magazine of Jewish Culture, Politics and Religion, 4710 41st St. NW, Washington DC 20016. (202)364-3300. Fax: (202)364-2636. E-mail: editor@momentmag.com. Publisher/Editor: Hershel Shanks. **Contact:** Joshua Rolnick, managing editor. **90% freelance written.** Bimonthly magazine. "*Moment* is an independent Jewish bimonthly general interest magazine that specializes in cultural, political, historical, religious and 'lifestyle' articles relating chiefly to the North American Jewish community and Israel." Estab. 1975. Circ. 65,000. Pays on publication. Publishes ms an average of 6 months after acceptance. Byline given. Buys first North American serial rights. Editorial lead time 3 months. Submit seasonal material 6 months in advance. Accepts queries by mail, e-mail, fax. Accepts simultaneous submissions. Responds in 1 month to queries; 3 months to mss. Sample copy for $4.50 and SAE. Writer's guidelines online.

Nonfiction: "We look for meaty, colorful, thought-provoking features and essays on Jewish trends and Israel. We occasionally publish book excerpts, memoirs and profiles." **Buys 25-30 mss/year.** Query with published clips. Length: 2,500-4,000 words. **Pays $200-1,200 for assigned articles; $40-500 for unsolicited articles.**

Photos: State availability with submission. Buys one-time rights. Negotiates payment individually. Identification of subjects required.

Columns/Departments: 5761—snappy pieces of not more than 250 words about quirky events in Jewish communities, news and ideas to improve Jewish living; Olam (The Jewish World)—first-person pieces, humor and colorful reportage of 600-1,500 words; Book reviews (fiction and nonfiction) are accepted but generally assigned, 400-800 words. **Buys 30 mss/year.** Query with published clips. **Pays $50-250.**

Tips: "Stories for *Moment* are usually assigned, but unsolicited manuscripts are often selected for publication. Successful features offer readers an in-depth journalistic treatment of an issue, phenomenon, institution, or individual. The more the writer can follow the principle of 'show, don't tell,' the better. The majority of the submissions we receive are about The Holocaust and Israel. A writer has a better chance of having an idea accepted if it is not on these subjects."

$ $ NA'AMAT WOMAN, Magazine of NA'AMAT USA, the Women's Labor Zionist Organization of America, NA'AMAT USA, 350 Fifth Ave., Suite 4700, New York NY 10118. (212)563-5222. Fax: (212)563-5710.

Website: www.naamat.org. **Contact:** Judith A. Sokoloff, editor. **80% freelance written.** Magazine published 4 times/year covering Jewish themes and issues; Israel; women's issues; and social and political issues. Estab. 1926. Circ. 70,000. Pays on publication. Byline given. Not copyrighted. Buys first North American serial, first, one-time, second serial (reprint) rights, makes work-for-hire assignments. Accepts queries by mail, fax. Responds in 3 months to queries. Writer's guidelines for #10 SASE.

Nonfiction: "All articles must be of particular interest to the Jewish community." Exposé, general interest (Jewish), historical/nostalgic, interview/profile, opinion, personal experience, photo feature, travel, art, music, social and political issues, Israel. **Buys 20 mss/year.** Query with or without published clips or send complete ms. **Pays 10-15¢/word.**

Photos: State availability with submission. Buys one-time rights. Pays $25-45 for 4×5 or 5×7 prints. Captions, identification of subjects required.

Columns/Departments: Film and book reviews with Jewish themes. **Buys 20 mss/year.** Query with published clips or send complete ms. **Pays 10¢/word.**

Fiction: "Intelligent fiction with Jewish slant. No maudlin nostalgia or trite humor." Historical, humorous, novel excerpts, women-oriented. **Buys 3 mss/year.** Send complete ms. Length: 1,200-3,000 words. **Pays 10¢/word.**

$ $ NATIVE PEOPLES MAGAZINE, The Arts and Lifeways, 5333 N. Seventh St., Suite C-224, Phoenix AZ 85014-2804. (602)265-4855. Fax: (602)265-3113. E-mail: editorial@nativepeoples.com. Website: www.nativepeoples.com. **Contact:** Daniel Gibson, managing editor. Bimonthly magazine covering Native Americans. "High-quality reproduction with full color throughout. The primary purpose of this magazine is to offer a sensitive portrayal of the arts and lifeways of native peoples of the Americas." Estab. 1987. Circ. 50,000. Pays on publication. Byline given. Buys one-time rights. Accepts queries by mail, e-mail, fax. Responds in 2 months to queries. Writer's guidelines online.

Nonfiction: Pathways (travel section) most open to freelancers. Book excerpts (pre-publication only), historical/nostalgic, interview/profile (of interesting and leading natives from all walks of life, with an emphasis on arts), personal experience. **Buys 35 mss/year.** Query with published clips. Length: 1,000-2,500 words. **Pays 25¢/word.**

Photos: State availability with submission. Reviews all formats transparencies, prefers 35mm slides. Also accepts electronic photo images, inquire for details. Buys one-time rights. Offers $45-150/page rates, $250/cover photos. Identification of subjects required.

Tips: "We are focused upon authenticity and a positive portrayal of present-day Native American life and cultural practices. Our stories portray role models of native people, young and old, with a sense of pride in their heritage and culture. Therefore, it is important that the Native American point of view be incorporated in each story."

$ NJEMA MAGAZINE, Sesh Communications, 354 Hearne Ave., Cincinnati OH 45229. (513)961-3331. Fax: (513)961-0304. E-mail: sesh@fuse.net. **Contact:** Ronda M. Gooden. **25% freelance written.** Monthly magazine covering news of interest to African-Americans in Ohio, Indiana and Kentucky. Estab. 1955. Circ. 16,000. Pays on publication. Byline given. Buys all rights. Editorial lead time 2 months. Accepts queries by mail, e-mail, fax, phone.

Nonfiction: Book excerpts, essays, exposé, general interest, historical/nostalgic, how-to, humor, inspirational, interview/profile, new product, opinion, personal experience, photo feature, religious, technical, travel. **Buys 4 mss/year.** Query with published clips. Length: 500-1,000 words. **Pays $25-75.**

Photos: State availability with submission. Buys one-time rights. Offers no additional payment for photos accepted with ms. Captions, identification of subjects, model releases required.

$ $ ▣ RUSSIAN LIFE, RIS Publications, P.O. Box 567, Montpelier VT 05601. (802)223-4955. Fax: (802)223-4955. E-mail: ruslife@rispubs.com. Website: www.rispubs.com. Editor: Mikhail Ivanov. **Contact:** Paul Richardson, publisher. **40% freelance written.** Bimonthly magazine covering Russian culture, history, travel and business. "Our readers are informed Russophiles with an avid interest in all things Russian. But we do not publish personal travel journals or the like." Estab. 1956. Circ. 15,000. Pays on publication. Publishes ms an average of 2 months after acceptance. Byline given. Offers $25 kill fee. Buys first rights. Editorial lead time 2 months. Submit seasonal material 3 months in advance. Accepts queries by mail. Responds in 1 month to queries. Sample copy for 9×12 SAE and 6 first-class stamps. Writer's guidelines for #10 SASE or online.

O⌐ Break in with a "good travel essay piece covering remote regions of Russia."

Nonfiction: General interest, photo feature, travel. No personal stories, i.e., "How I came to love Russia." **Buys 15-20 mss/year.** Query. Length: 1,000-6,000 words. **Pays $100-300.**

Reprints: Accepts previously published submissions

Photos: Send photos with submission. Reviews contact sheets. Buys one-time rights. Negotiates payment individually. Captions required.

▣ The online magazine carries original content not found in the print edition.

Tips: "A straightforward query letter with writing sample or manuscript (not returnable) enclosed."

$ $ SCANDINAVIAN REVIEW, The American-Scandinavian Foundation, 58 Park Ave., New York NY 10016. (212)879-9779. Fax: (212)249-3444. Website: www.amscan.org. **Contact:** Adrienne Gyongy, editor. **75% freelance written.** triannual magazine. Triannual magazine for contemporary Scandinavia. Audience: Members, embassies, consulates, libraries. Slant: Popular coverage of contemporary affairs in Scandinavia. Estab. 1913. Circ. 4,000. Pays on publication. Publishes ms an average of 2 months after acceptance. Byline given. Buys first North American serial, second serial (reprint) rights. Editorial lead time 3 months. Submit seasonal material 3 months in advance. Responds in 6 weeks to queries. Sample copy online. Writer's guidelines free.

Nonfiction: General interest, interview/profile, photo feature, travel (must have Scandinavia as topic focus). Special issues: Scandinavian travel. No pornography. **Buys 30 mss/year.** Query with published clips. Length: 1,500-2,000 words. **Pays $300 maximum.**

Photos: Reviews 3×5 transparencies, prints. Buys one-time rights. Pays $25-50/photo; negotiates payment individually. Captions required.

N $ THE UKRAINIAN WEEKLY, Ukrainian National Association, 2200 Route 10, P.O. Box 280, Parsippany NJ 07054. (973)292-9800. Fax: (973)644-9510. E-mail: staff@ukrweekly.com. Website: www.ukrweekly.com. **Contact:** Roma Hadzewycz, editor-in-chief. **30% freelance written.** (mostly by a corps of regular contributors). Weekly tabloid covering news and issues of concern to Ukrainian community, primarily in North America but also around the world, and events in Ukraine. "We have a news bureau in Kyiv, capital of Ukraine." Estab. 1933. Circ. 7,000. Pays on publication. Publishes ms an average of 1 month after acceptance. Byline given. Buys first North American serial, second serial (reprint) rights, makes work-for-hire assignments. Submit seasonal material 1 month in advance. Accepts queries by mail, e-mail, fax. Responds in 1 month to mss. Sample copy for 9×12 SAE and 3 first-class stamps.

Nonfiction: Book excerpts, essays, exposé, general interest, historical/nostalgic, interview/profile, opinion, personal experience, photo feature, news events. Special issues: Easter, Christmas, anniversary of Ukraine's independence proclamation (August 24, 1991), student scholarships, anniversary of Chernobyl nuclear accident, summer events preview and year-end review of news. **Buys 80 mss/year.** Query with published clips. Length: 500-2,000 words. **Pays $45-100 for assigned articles; $25-100 for unsolicited articles.** Sometimes pays expenses of writers on assignment.

Reprints: Send typed ms with rights for sale noted and information about when and where the material previously appeared. Pays 25-50% of amount paid for an original article.

Photos: Send photos with submission. Reviews contact sheets, negatives, 3×5, 5×7 or 8×10 prints and slides. Offers no additional payment for photos accepted with ms.

Columns/Departments: News & Views (commentary on news events), 500-1,000 words. **Buys 10 mss/year.** Query. **Pays $25-50.**

Tips: "Become acquainted with the Ukrainian community in the US and Canada. The area of our publication most open to freelancers is community news—coverage of local events and personalities."

$ $ UPSCALE MAGAZINE, Exposure to the World's Finest, Upscale Communications, Inc., 600 Bronner Brothers Way SW, Atlanta GA 30310. (404)758-7467. Fax: (404)755-9892. E-mail: upscale8@mindspring.com. Website: www.upscalemagazine.com. **Contact:** Sheila Bronner, editor-in-chief. **75-80% freelance written.** Monthly magazine covering topics that inspire, inform, educate or relate to African-Americans. "*Upscale* is a general interest publication featuring a variety of topics—news, business, finance, technology, fine arts, beauty, health, fitness, travel, book and CD reviews, home, relationships, entertainment, parenting and spiritual issues among other issues—that affect the lives of African-Americans." Estab. 1989. Circ. 242,000. Byline given. Offers 25% kill fee. Buys all rights. Editorial lead time 5 months. Submit seasonal material 6 months in advance. Accepts queries by mail, e-mail, fax. Sample copy for $2. Writer's guidelines for free by written request.

Nonfiction: Book excerpts (reviews), general interest, historical/nostalgic, inspirational, interview/profile, personal experience, religious, travel. **Buys 135 mss/year.** Query. Length: Varies. **Pay varies according to article type, content and writer.**

Photos: State availability with submission. Reviews contact sheets, transparencies, prints. Buys one time or reprint rights. Negotiates payment individually. Captions, identification of subjects, model releases required.

Columns/Departments: Positively You (personal tragedies and triumphs); and Viewpoint (a fact-based view on current events). **Buys 6-10 mss/year.** Query.

Fiction: Publishes novel excerpts.

Tips: "Call to find out the name of the editor to address your query to. We do not accept unsolicited fiction, poetry or essays. Unsolicited nonfiction is accepted for our Positively You and Viewpoint sections only. Queries for exciting, innovative and informative nonfiction story ideas are welcome."

$ $ VISTA MAGAZINE, The Magazine for all Hispanics, Hispanic Publishing Corporation, 999 Ponce de Leon Blvd., Suite 600, Coral Gables FL 33134. (305)442-2462. Fax: (305)443-7650. E-mail: jlobaco@aol.com. Website: www.vistamagazine.com. **Contact:** Julia Bencomo Lobaco, editor. **50% freelance written.** Monthly magazine. "Monthly and Sunday supplement style magazine targeting Hispanic audience. Dual-language, Spanish/English, 50/50%. Stories appear in one language or another, not both. Topics of general interest, but with a Hispanic angle." Estab. 1985. Circ. 1,100,000. Pays on publication. Publishes ms an average of 2 months after acceptance. Byline given. Offers 25% kill fee. Buys all rights. Editorial lead time 2 months. Submit seasonal material 4 months in advance. Accepts queries by mail, e-mail, fax, phone. Sample copy free or online.

Nonfiction: Exposé, general interest, historical/nostalgic, how-to (home improvement), inspirational, interview/profile, new product, opinion, personal experience, photo feature, travel. "No creative writing, poems, etc." **Buys 40-50 mss/year.** Query with published clips. Length: 500-1,600 words. **Pays $250-450.** Sometimes pays expenses of writers on assignment.

Photos: State availability with submission.

Columns/Departments: In Touch (short profile of someone doing outstanding work in any area, i.e., education, business, health, etc.). **Pays $100.**

Tips: "Query by phone is usually best. Articles must be related to Hispanic, be of national interest, timely and, unless assigned by VISTA, should be 850-1,200 words—not longer."

[N] $ ⬥ WINDSPEAKER, Aboriginal Multi-Media Society of Alberta, 15001-112 Ave., Edmonton, Alberta T5M 2V6, Canada. (800)661-5469. Fax: (403)455-7639. E-mail: edwind@ammsa.com. Website: www.ammsa.com. **Contact:** Debora Lockyer, managing editor. **75% freelance written.** Monthly tabloid covering native issues. "Focus on events and issues that affect and interest native peoples, national or local." Estab. 1983. Circ. 18,000. Pays on publication. Publishes ms an average of 1 month after acceptance. Byline given. Offers $25 kill fee. Buys first rights. Editorial lead time 1 month. Submit seasonal material 2 months in advance. Accepts queries by mail, phone. Accepts simultaneous submissions. Sample copy and writer's guidelines free.
Nonfiction: Humor, interview/profile, opinion, personal experience, photo feature, travel, Reviews: books, music, movies. Special issues: Powwow (June); Travel supplement (May). **Buys 200 mss/year.** Query with published clips and SASE or by phone. Length: 500-800 words. **Pays $3-3.60/published inch.** Sometimes pays expenses of writers on assignment.
Photos: Send photos with submission. Reviews color negatives and prints. Buys one-time rights. Offers $15-50/photo. Will pay for film and processing. Identification of subjects required.
Columns/Departments: Arts reviews (Aboriginal artists), 300-500 words. **Buys 25 mss/year.** Query with published clips. **Pays $3-3.60/inch.**
Tips: "Knowledge of Aboriginal culture and political issues is a great asset."

FOOD & DRINK

Magazines appealing to gourmets, health-conscious consumers and vegetarians are classified here. Some publications emphasize "the art and craft" of cooking for food enthusiasts who enjoy developing these skills as a leisure activity. Another popular trend stresses healthy eating and food choices. Many magazines in the Health & Fitness category present a holistic approach to well-being through nutrition and fitness for healthful living. Magazines in General Interest and Women's categories also buy articles on food topics. Journals aimed at food processing, manufacturing and retailing are in the Trade section.

$ $ $ $ BON APPETIT, America's Food and Entertaining Magazine, Conde Nast Publications, Inc., 6300 Wilshire Blvd., Los Angeles CA 90048. (323)965-3600. Fax: (323)937-1206. Editor-in-Chief: William J. Garry. **Contact:** Victoria von Biel, executive editor. **90% freelance written.** Monthly magazine covering fine food, restaurants and home entertaining. "*Bon Appetit* readers are upscale food enthusiasts and sophisticated travelers. They eat out often and entertain four to six times a month." Estab. 1975. Circ. 1,331,853. **Pays on acceptance.** Byline given. Buys all rights. Submit seasonal material 1 year in advance. Responds in 6 weeks to queries. Writer's guidelines for #10 SASE.
  • *Bon Appetit* reports it is looking for food-related humor essays, profiles, etc. of less than 1,000 words. It is not interested in material about three-star dining in France or celebrity chefs.
Nonfiction: Travel (restaurant or food-related), food feature, dessert feature. "No cartoons, quizzes, poetry, historic food features or obscure food subjects." **Buys 80-120 mss/year.** Query with published clips. Length: 750-2,000 words. **Pays $500-1,800.** Pays expenses of writers on assignment.
Photos: Never send photos.
Tips: "We are not interested in receiving specific queries per se, but we are always looking for new good writers. They must have a good knowledge of the *Bon Appetit*-related topic (as shown in accompanying clips) and a light, lively style with humor. Nothing long and pedantic please."

$ $ ⬥ CHILE PEPPER, The Magazine of Spicy Foods, River Plaza 1701 River Run #702, Ft. Worth TX 76102. (817)877-1048. Fax: (817)877-8870. E-mail: editor@chilepepperhq.com. **Contact:** David K. Gibson, editor. **70-80% freelance written.** Bimonthly magazine on spicy foods. "The magazine is devoted to spicy foods, and most articles include recipes. We have a very devoted readership who love their food hot!" Estab. 1986. Circ. 85,000. Pays on publication. Buys first, second serial (reprint), electronic rights. Submit seasonal material 6 months in advance. Sample copy for 9×12 SAE and 5 first-class stamps. Writer's guidelines for #10 SASE.
Nonfiction: Book excerpts (cookbooks), how-to (cooking and gardening with spicy foods), humor (having to do with spicy foods), new product (hot products), travel (having to do with spicy foods). **Buys 50 mss/year.** Query by mail or e-mail only. Length: 1,000-3,000 words. **Pays $300 minimum for feature article.**
Reprints: Send tearsheet or photocopy and information about when and where the material previously appeared.
Photos: State availability with submission. Reviews contact sheets, negatives, transparencies, prints. Buys one-time rights. Offers $25/photo minimum. Captions, identification of subjects required.
Tips: "We're always interested in queries from *food* writers. Articles about spicy foods with six to eight recipes are just right. No fillers. Need location travel/food pieces from inside the U.S. and international."

$ $ $ $ COOKING LIGHT, The Magazine of Food and Fitness, Southern Progress Corp., P.O. Box 1748, Birmingham AL 35201-1681. (205)877-6000. Fax: (205)877-6600. Website: cookinglight.com. **Contact:** Jill Melton, senior food editor (food) or Donna Raskin, senior healthy living editor (fitness/healthy lifestyle). **75% freelance written.** Magazine published 11 times/year on healthy recipes and fitness information. "*Cooking Light* is a positive approach to a healthier lifestyle. It's written for healthy people on regular diets who are counting calories or trying to make calories count toward better nutrition. Moderation, balance and variety are emphasized. The writing style is fresh, upbeat and encouraging, emphasizing that eating a balanced, varied, lower-calorie diet and exercising regularly do not have to be boring." Estab. 1987. Circ. 1,600,000. **Pays on acceptance.** Publishes ms an average of 1 year after acceptance. Byline sometimes given. Offers 33% kill fee. Submit seasonal material 1 year in advance. Accepts queries by mail. Responds in 1 year to mss.

Nonfiction: Service approaches to nutrition, healthy recipes, fitness/exercise. Backup material a must. **Buys 150 mss/year.** Must query with résumé and published clips; no unsolicited mss. Response guaranteed with SASE. Length: 400-2,000 words. **Pays $250-2,000.** Pays expenses of writers on assignment.

☐ The online magazine carries original content not found in the print edition. Contact: Maelynn Cheung, managing editor, cookinglight.com.

Tips: "Emphasis should be on achieving a healthier lifestyle through food, nutrition, fitness, exercise information. In submitting queries, include information on professional background. Food writers should include examples of healthy recipes which meet the guidelines of *Cooking Light*."

N $ GOURMET FARE MAGAZINE, DRS Publishing Group, 1575 Old Alabama Rd., Suite 207-24, Roswell GA 30076. E-mail: info@gourmetfare.com. Website: www.gourmetfare.com. Editor: Diana R. Savastano. Managing Editor: Lisa D. Russo. **Contact:** Caroline North, associate editor. **50% freelance written.** Quarterly online food publication for food lovers including articles on travel, entertaining, health and more. Estab. 1993. Pays on publication. Byline given. Buys first rights. Editorial lead time 3 months. Submit seasonal material 3 months in advance. Accepts queries by e-mail. Accepts simultaneous submissions. Responds in 3 weeks to queries; 2 months to mss. Sample copy online.

Nonfiction: Humor, new product, travel. **Buys 20-50 mss/year.** Query. Length: 400-1,500 words. **Pays $45-150 for assigned articles; $35-75 for unsolicited articles.**

Reprints: Accepts previously published submissions.

Photos: State availability with submission.

Tips: "Review the publication for content and style. We are always looking for new and interesting articles about food, wine and food-related products. Query via e-mail."

$ $ HOME COOKING, House of White Birches, Publishers, 306 E. Parr Rd., Berne IN 46711. (219)589-4000 ext. 396. Fax: (219)589-8093. E-mail: homeuscooking@whitebirches.com. Website: www.whitebirches.com. Project Supervisor: Barb Sprunger. **Contact:** Shelly Vaughan James, editor. **60% freelance written.** Monthly "*Home Cooking* delivers dozens of kitchen-tested recipes from home cooks every month. Special monthly features offer recipes, tips for today's busy cooks, techniques for food preparation, nutritional hints and more. Departments cover topics to round out the cooking experience." Circ. 75,000. Pays within 45 days after acceptance. Publishes ms an average of 8 months after acceptance. Byline given. Buys Buys all or fist rights, occasionally one-time rights. Editorial lead time 6 months. Submit seasonal material 8 months in advance. Accepts queries by mail, e-mail. Accepts simultaneous submissions. Responds in 1 month to queries; 2 months to mss. Sample copy for 6×9 SAE and 3 first-class stamps.

○→ Break in with a submission or query to one of *Home Cooking*'s departments.

Nonfiction: How-to, humor, new product, personal experience, Recipes, book reviews, all in food/cooking area. No health/fitness or travel articles. **Buys 72 mss/year.** Query or send complete manuscript. Length: 250-750 words plus 6-8 recipes. **Pays $50-300 for assigned articles; $50-175 for unsolicited articles.** Sometimes pays expenses of writers on assignment.

Reprints: Accepts previously published submissions.

Photos: State availability with submission. Reviews prints. Negotiates payment individually. Model releases and identification of subjects required. Buys one-time rights.

Columns/Departments: Dinner Tonight (complete 30-minute meal with preparation guide), 500 words; Stirring Comments (book and product reviews), 100 words; Pinch of Sage (hints for the home cook), 200-500 words. **Buys 48 mss/year.** Query or send complete manuscript. **Pays $50-100.**

Fillers: Anecdotes, facts, newsbreaks, short humor. **Buys 15/year.** Length: 10-150 words. **Pays $15-25.**

Tips: "Departments are most open to new writers. All submissions should be written specifically for our publication. Be sure to check spelling, grammar and punctuation before mailing. If that means setting aside your manuscript for two weeks to regain your objectivity, do it. A sale two weeks later beats a rejection earlier. If you follow our style in your manuscript, we know you've read our magazine."

N $ $ $ HOMETOWN COOKING, Better Homes and Gardens, Meredith Corp., 1716 Locust St., Des Moines IA 50309. (515)284-3000. Website: www.hometowncook.com. **Contact:** Joy Taylor, editor. **50% freelance written.** Bimonthly magazine covering food, recipes and people. "*Hometown Cooking* provides home cooks with the very best recipes with an emphasis on those from community cookbooks." Estab. 1999. **Pays on acceptance.** Publishes ms an average of 6 months after acceptance. Byline sometimes given. Buys all rights, makes work-for-hire assignments. Editorial lead time 1 year. Submit seasonal material 18 months in advance. Accepts queries by mail. Responds in 1 month to queries; 2 months to mss. Sample copy online.

Nonfiction: Book excerpts, essays, general interest, historical/nostalgic, how-to, humor, inspirational, interview/profile. **Buys 30 mss/year.** Query with published clips. Length: 500-2,000 words. **Pays $300-1,000 for assigned articles.** Sometimes pays expenses of writers on assignment.
Poetry: Light verse. **Buys 6-12 poems/year.**
Fillers: Anecdotes, short humor. Length: 50-200 words. **Pays $50-100.**
Tips: "Have an appreciation for what kinds of foods mainstream families like, and are willing to prepare."

$ $KASHRUS MAGAZINE, The Bimonthly for the Kosher Consumer and the Trade, Yeshiva Birkas Reuven, P.O. Box 204, Parkville Station, Brooklyn NY 11204. (718)336-8544. **Contact:** Rabbi Yosef Wikler, editor. **25% freelance written.** Prefers to work with published/established writers, but will work with new/unpublished writers. Bimonthly magazine covering kosher food industry and food production. Estab. 1980. Circ. 10,000. Pays on publication. Publishes ms an average of 2 months after acceptance. Byline given. Offers 50% kill fee. Buys first, second serial (reprint) rights. Submit seasonal material 2 months in advance. Accepts queries by mail, phone. Accepts simultaneous submissions. Responds in 1 week to queries; 2 weeks to mss. Sample copy for $3.
Nonfiction: General interest, interview/profile, new product, personal experience, photo feature, religious, technical, travel. Special issues: International Kosher Travel (October); Passover (March). **Buys 8-12 mss/year.** Query with published clips. Length: 1,000-1,500 words. **Pays $100-250 for assigned articles; up to $100 for unsolicited articles.** Sometimes pays expenses of writers on assignment.
Reprints: Send tearsheet or photocopy and information about when and where the material previously appeared. Pays 25-50% of amount paid for an original article.
Photos: No guidelines; send samples or call. State availability with submission. Buys one-time rights. Offers no additional payment for photos accepted with ms.
Columns/Departments: Book Review (cook books, food technology, kosher food), 250-500 words; People in the News (interviews with kosher personalities), 1,000-1,500 words; Regional Kosher Supervision (report on kosher supervision in a city or community), 1,000-1,500 words; Food Technology (new technology or current technology with accompanying pictures), 1,000-1,500 words; Travel (international, national), must include Kosher information and Jewish communities, 1,000-1,500 words; Regional Kosher Cooking, 1,000-1,500 words. **Buys 8-12 mss/year.** Query with published clips. **Pays $50-250.**
Tips: "*Kashrus Magazine* will do more writing on general food technology, production, and merchandising as well as human interest travelogs and regional writing in 2002 than we have done in the past. Areas most open to freelancers are interviews, food technology, cooking and food preparation, dining, regional reporting and travel, but we also feature healthy eating and lifestyles, redecorating, catering, and hospitals and health care. We welcome stories on the availability and quality of Kosher foods and services in communities across the U.S. and throughout the world. Some of our best stories have been by non-Jewish writers about kosher observance in their region. We also enjoy humorous articles. Just send a query with clips and we'll try to find a storyline that's right for you, or better yet, call us to discuss a storyline."

$ $ RISTORANTE, Foley Publishing, P.O. Box 73, Liberty Corner NJ 07938. (908)766-6006. Fax: (908)766-6607. E-mail: barmag@aol.com. Website: www.bartender.com. **Contact:** Raymond Foley, publisher or Jaclyn Foley, editor. **75% freelance written.** Bimonthly magazine covering "Italian anything!" "*Ristorante—The magazine for the Italian Connoisseur.* For Italian restaurants and those who love Italian food, travel, wine and all things Italian!" Estab. 1994. Circ. 40,000. Pays on publication. Publishes ms an average of 3 months after acceptance. Byline sometimes given. Buys first North American serial, one-time rights. Editorial lead time 3 months. Submit seasonal material 3 months in advance. Responds in 1 month to queries; 2 months to mss. Sample copy and writer's guidelines for 9×12 SAE and 4 first-class stamps.
Nonfiction: Book excerpts, general interest, historical/nostalgic, how-to (prepare Italian foods), humor, new product, opinion, personal experience, travel. **Buys 25 mss/year.** Send complete ms. Length: 100-1,000 words. **Pays $100-350 for assigned articles; $75-300 for unsolicited articles.** Sometimes pays expenses of writers on assignment.
Reprints: Send tearsheet or photocopy and information about when and where the material previously appeared. Pays 25% of amount paid for an original article.
Photos: Send photos with submission. Reviews 3×5 prints. Buys one-time rights. Negotiates payment individually. Captions, model releases required.
Columns/Departments: Send complete ms. **Pays $50-200.**
Fillers: Anecdotes, facts, short humor. **Buys 10/year. Pays $10-50.**

N $ $ VEGGIE LIFE, Growing Green, Cooking Lean, Feeling Good, EGW Publishing, 1041 Shary Circle, Concord CA 94518. (510)671-9852. Fax: (510)671-0692. E-mail: smasters@egw.com. Website: www.veggielife.com. **Contact:** Shanna Masters, editor. **90% freelance written.** Biweekly magazine covering vegetarian cooking, natural health, herbal healing and organic gardening. Estab. 1992. Circ. 260,000. Pays half on acceptance, half on publication. Publishes ms an average of 4 months after acceptance. Byline given. Offers 25% kill fee. Buys all rights, makes work-for-hire assignments. Editorial lead time 6 months. Submit seasonal material 6 months in advance. Accepts queries by mail, e-mail. Responds in 4 months to queries. Writer's guidelines for #10 SASE.
Nonfiction: How-to (gardening), vegetarian cooking/recipes, natural health, herbal healing, nutrition, health/fitness. No animal rights issues/advocacy, religious/philosophical, personal opinion. **Buys 30-50 mss/year.** Query with published

clips. No phone calls, please. E-mail OK. Length: 1,500-2,000 words. **Pays 35¢/word**, more for credentialed professionals. Food features: 300-500 words plus 6-8 recipes. Recipes must be 30% or less in fat, no more than 10g per serving. **Pays 35¢/word plus $35/recipe.**

Photos: State availability with submission. Buys one-time rights or makes work-for-hire assignments. Negotiates payment individually. Captions, identification of subjects, model releases required.

Columns/Departments: Quick Cuisine, 100-150 words followed by 6-8 recipes prepared in 45 minutes or less each; Cooking with Soy, 150-200 word introduction followed by 4-5 eggless, dairy-free recipes made with a soy product. Remakes of old favorites encouraged. Query with published clips. **Pays 35¢/published word plus $35/published recipe.**

Tips: "Research back issues; be authoritative; no 'Why I Became a Vegetarian...' stories. Please state why you are qualified to write particular subject matter—a *must* on health/herbal mss. No article will be considered without sufficient fact verification information. Gender specific and age specific (i.e., children, adolescents, seniors) topics are encouraged. Photographs are a strong plus in considering gardening submissions."

N **$ $ WINE PRESS NORTHWEST**, Tri-City Herald, 107 N. Cascade St., Kennewick WA 99336. (509)582-1564. Fax: (509)582-1510. E-mail: editor@winepressnw.com. Website: www.winepressnw.com. Managing Editor: Eric Degerman. **Contact:** Andy Perdue, editor. **50% freelance written.** Quarterly magazine covering Pacific Northwest wine (Washington, Oregon, British Columbia, Idaho). "We focus narrowly on Pacific Northwest wine. If we write about travel, it's where to go to drink NW wine. If we write about food, it's what goes with NW wine. No beer, no spirits." Estab. 1998. Circ. 12,000. Pays on publication. Publishes ms an average of 3 months after acceptance. Byline given. Offers 20% kill fee. Buys first North American serial, electronic rights. Editorial lead time 3 months. Submit seasonal material 3 months in advance. Accepts queries by mail, e-mail, fax. Accepts simultaneous submissions. Responds in 1 month to queries. Sample copy free or online. Writer's guidelines free.

Nonfiction: General interest, historical/nostalgic, interview/profile, new product, photo feature, travel. No "beer, spirits, non-NW (California wine, etc.)" **Buys 30 mss/year.** Query with published clips. Length: 1,500-2,500 words. **Pays $250-300.** Sometimes pays expenses of writers on assignment.

Photos: State availability with submission. Reviews contact sheets. Buys one-time rights. Negotiates payment individually. Identification of subjects required.

■ The online magazine carries original content not found in the print edition. Contact: Andy Perdue, online editor.

Tips: "Writers must be familiar with *Wine Press Northwest* and should have a passion for the region, its wines and cuisine."

N **$ $ $ WINE SPECTATOR**, M. Shanken Communications, Inc., 387 Park Ave. S, New York NY 10016. (212)684-4224. Fax: (212)684-5424. E-mail: winespec@mshanken.com. Website: www.winespectator.com. **Contact:** Thomas Matthews, executive editor. **20% freelance written.** Prefers to work with published/established writers. Bi-weekly newsmagazine. Estab. 1976. Circ. 280,000. Pays within 30 days of publication. Publishes ms an average of 2 months after acceptance. Byline given. Buys all rights, makes work-for-hire assignments. Submit seasonal material 4 months in advance. Accepts queries by mail, fax. Responds in 3 months to queries. Sample copy for $5. Writer's guidelines for #10 SASE.

Nonfiction: General interest (news about wine or wine events), interview/profile (of wine, vintners, wineries), opinion, photo feature, travel, dining and other lifestyle pieces. No "winery promotional pieces or articles by writers who lack sufficient knowledge to write below just surface data." Query. Length: 100-2,000 words. **Pays $100-1,000.**

Photos: Send photos with submission. Buys all rights. Pays $75 minimum for color transparencies. Captions, identification of subjects, model releases required.

■ The online magazine carries original content not found in the print edition. Contact: Dana Nigro, online editor.

Tips: "A solid knowledge of wine is a must. Query letters essential, detailing the story idea. New, refreshing ideas which have not been covered before stand a good chance of acceptance. *Wine Spectator* is a consumer-oriented news magazine, but we are interested in some trade stories; brevity is essential."

$ $ WINE X MAGAZINE, Wine, Food and an Intelligent Slice of Vice, X Publishing, Inc., 880 Second St., Santa Rosa CA 95404-4611. (707)545-0992. Fax: (707)542-7062. E-mail: winex@winexwired.com. Website: www.wine xwired.com. **Contact:** Darryl Roberts, editor/publisher. **100% freelance written.** Bimonthly magazine covering wine and other beverages. "*Wine X* is a lifestyle magazine for young adults featuring wine, beer, spirits, music, movies, fashion, food, coffee, celebrity interviews, health/fitness." Estab. 1997. Circ. 35,000. Pays on publication. Publishes ms an average of 3 months after acceptance. Byline given. Not copyrighted. Buys first North American serial, electronic rights. Editorial lead time 3 months. Submit seasonal material 4 months in advance. Accepts queries by mail, e-mail, fax. Responds in 3 weeks to queries. Sample copy for $6. Writer's guidelines online.

Nonfiction: Essays, new product, personal experience, photo feature, travel. No restaurant reviews, wine collector profiles. **Buys 6 mss/year.** Query. Length: 500-1,500 words. **Pays $50-250 for assigned articles; $50-150 for unsolicited articles.** Sometimes pays expenses of writers on assignment.

Photos: Reviews transparencies. Buys one-time rights. Offers no additional payment for photos accepted with ms. Identification of subjects, model releases required.

Columns/Departments: Wine, Other Beverages, Lifestyle, all 1,000 words. **Buys 72 mss/year.** Query.

Fiction: Buys 6 mss/year. Query. Length: 1,000-1,500 words. **No pay for fiction.**

Poetry: Avant-garde, free verse, haiku, light verse, traditional. **Buys 2 poems/year.** Submit maximum 3 poems. Length: 10-1,500 lines.

Fillers: Short humor. **Buys 6/year.** Length: 100-500 words. **Pays $0-50.**
Tips: "See our website."

GAMES & PUZZLES

These publications are written by and for game enthusiasts interested in both traditional games and word puzzles and newer role-playing adventure, computer and video games. Other puzzle markets may be found in the Juvenile section.

$ THE BRIDGE BULLETIN, American Contract Bridge League, 2990 Airways Blvd., Memphis TN 38116-3847. (901)332-5586, ext. 291. Fax: (901)398-7754. E-mail: editor@acbl.org. Website: www.acbl.org. Managing Editor: Paul Linxwiler. **Contact:** Brent Manley, editor. **20% freelance written.** Monthly magazine covering duplicate (tournament) bridge. Estab. 1938. Circ. 155,000. Pays on publication. Publishes ms an average of 3 months after acceptance. Byline given. Buys first, second serial (reprint) rights. Editorial lead time 2 months. Accepts queries by mail, e-mail. Accepts simultaneous submissions.
   0-π Break in with a "humorous piece about bridge."
Nonfiction: Book excerpts, essays, how-to (play better bridge), humor, interview/profile, new product, personal experience, photo feature, technical, travel. **Buys 6 mss/year.** Query. Length: 500-2,000 words. **Pays $50/page.**
Photos: State availability with submission. Buys all rights. Negotiates payment individually. Identification of subjects required.
Tips: "Articles must relate to contract bridge in some way. Cartoons on bridge welcome."

N $ $ CHESS LIFE, United States Chess Federation, 3054 US Route 9W, New Windsor NY 12553-7698. (845)562-8350, ext. 154. Fax: (845)236-4852. E-mail: magazines@uschess.org. Website: www.uschess.org. **Contact:** Peter Kurzdorfer, editor. **15% freelance written.** Works with a small number of new/unpublished writers/year. Monthly magazine. *"Chess Life* is the official publication of the United States Chess Federation, covering news of most major chess events, both here and abroad, with special emphasis on the triumphs and exploits of American players." Estab. 1939. Circ. 70,000. Publishes ms an average of 8 months after acceptance. Byline given. Buys first or negotiable rights. Submit seasonal material 8 months in advance. Accepts queries by mail, e-mail, fax, phone. Accepts simultaneous submissions. Responds in 3 months to mss. Sample copy and writer's guidelines for 9×11 SAE with 5 first-class stamps.
Nonfiction: General interest, historical/nostalgic, humor, interview/profile (of a famous chess player or organizer), photo feature (chess centered), technical. All must have some relation to chess. No "stories about personal experiences with chess." **Buys 30-40 mss/year.** Query with samples if new to publication. Length: 3,000 words maximum. **Pays $100/page (800-1,000 words).** Sometimes pays expenses of writers on assignment.
Reprints: Send tearsheet, photocopy or typed ms with rights for sale noted and information about when and where the material previously appeared.
Photos: Reviews b&w contact sheets and prints and color prints and slides. Buys all or negotiable rights. Pays $25-35 inside; $100-300 for covers. Captions, identification of subjects, model releases required.
Columns/Departments: Chess Review (brief articles on unknown chess personalities) and "Chess in Everyday Life."
Fillers: Submit with samples and clips. Buys first or negotiable rights to cartoons and puzzles. **Pays $25 upon acceptance.**
Tips: "Articles must be written from an informed point of view—not from view of the curious amateur. Most of our writers are specialized in that they have sound credentials as chess players. Freelancers in major population areas (except New York and Los Angeles, which we already have covered) who are interested in short personality profiles and perhaps news reporting have the best opportunities. We're looking for more personality pieces on chess players around the country; not just the stars, but local masters, talented youths, and dedicated volunteers. Freelancers interested in such pieces might let us know of their interest and their range. Could be we know of an interesting story in their territory that needs covering. Examples of published articles include a locally produced chess television program, a meeting of chess set collectors from around the world, chess in our prisons, and chess in the works of several famous writers."

$ $ $ GAMES MAGAZINE, Games Publications, a division of Kappa Publishing Group, Inc., 7002 W. Butler Pike, Suite 210, Ambler PA 19002. (215)643-6385. Fax: (215)628-3571. E-mail: gamespub@voicenet.com. **Contact:** R. Wayne Schmittberger, editor-in-chief. **50% freelance written.** Magazine published 10 times/year covering puzzles and games. *"Games* is a magazine of puzzles, contests, and features pertaining to games and ingenuity. It is aimed primarily at adults and has an emphasis on pop culture." Estab. 1977. Circ. 80,000. Pays on publication. Publishes ms an average of 4 months after acceptance. Byline given. Offers 25% kill fee. Buys first North American serial, first, one-time, second serial (reprint), all rights, makes work-for-hire assignments. Editorial lead time 3 months. Submit seasonal material 6 months in advance. Accepts queries by mail, e-mail. Accepts simultaneous submissions. Responds in 6 weeks to queries; 3 months to mss. Sample copy for $5. Writer's guidelines for #10 SASE.
Nonfiction: Photo feature, puzzles, games. **Buys 100 puzzles/year and 3 mss/year.** Query. Length: 1,500-2,500 words. **Pays $750-1,200.** Sometimes pays expenses of writers on assignment.

insider report

Writing about games: Know your audience

Though he has a master's degree in creative writing, 30-year-old New York freelancer John Misak makes a substantial percentage of his yearly income writing about games—and has for the past four years. He splits his talents between print publications and paying Internet markets, and still finds time to write fiction (his first novel *Soft Case* was published in June of 2001). Like most freelancers, he believes geography has little impact on his success as a writer. His work has appeared in such industry staples as *PC Gamer* and *Bikini Magazine*, as well as on *PCGameworld* and *Gamespy*, two of the biggest websites dedicated to games.

© Credit

John Misak

What special challenges set freelancing for the gaming industry apart from other specialties?
The biggest challenge is the amount of free content on the Web related to gaming. With the fallout from the dot.com and advertising disasters, not many people are willing to pay for gaming content that is given away. On top of that, there are so many gamers looking to break into this field that it makes for some spirited competition, though that certainly isn't a bad thing.

What kind of games do you most often review or feature? Computer? Game System? Other? Which are most popular with magazines and consumers?
I do both computer and console game reviews. With the release of the Playstation 2 and the coming release of Microsoft's X-Box, console games have been getting the most attention, but because of the huge installed base of computers, computer games will always be popular, and reviews will always be in demand.

How would you break into this specialty if you were a beginning freelancer?
Breaking into the writing field can be harder than breaking into the Pentagon's computer (not that I would know, of course). Since gaming has been my hobby since I was nine, I figured I could use my experience in the field to help advance my writing career. It certainly paid off. In order to be a good writer, you have to constantly write, and I attribute getting my novel *Soft Case* published to my game reviewing that kept me at the top of my writing game.

The best way to break into game reviewing is to offer your reviews to a non-paying website to get exposure. That's how I started, and though you don't get paid, you get your games for free, often well before they are released for purchase. Once you get some experience, it will be easier to land a gig with a paying publisher.

What is the general pay scale a freelancer can expect writing about games?

It varies. Not so long ago, receiving $100 for a 500-word online review was common. Now it is about half that. Print publications generally pay about 10¢ a word, so they are about the same as their online counterparts.

What are the most common mistakes freelancers in this arena make (and can avoid)?

The biggest mistake is incorrectly perceiving the gaming audience. A wide variety of people play games, in all age groups, and more importantly, both sexes. This isn't a teenage, male-dominated audience anymore. That is a good thing.

Have you had a favorite game assignment? If so, what was it and why was it so memorable?

Without question, the assignment to cover the Electronic Entertainment Expo in California last year. Basically, it was a huge collection of every type of game imaginable, from every game publisher in the world. I was able to see things the average gamer never gets to see. It was a mind-boggling experience, and can best be described as gaming heaven.

Have you experienced the nightmare of all nightmare assignments? Describe it.

The same assignment. Though it was fun, the convention center was about the size of a large airport terminal, and every corner of it was filled. My feet hurt for a week afterwards, and I didn't get to see everything I wanted. It was a three-man job, really.

—*Kelly Milner Halls*

For interviews with the pros in more freelance niche markets, see Animals, page 368; Contemporary Culture, page 432; Entertainment, page 443; Sports, page 708; Women's, page 782.

TOP TIP: "I game myself—constantly. It occupies more of my time than anything else. Except maybe breathing, but I haven't really sat down and compared the numbers. So I'd say know your audience. And be patient. It takes a long time to really establish yourself as a freelancer, but if you stick with it, your hard work early on will be rewarded nicely."

Photos: State availability with submission. Reviews contact sheets, negatives, transparencies, prints. Buys one-time rights. Negotiates payment individually. Captions, identification of subjects, model releases required.
Columns/Departments: Gamebits (game/puzzle news), 250 words; Games & Books (product reviews), 350 words; Wild Cards (short text puzzles), 100 words. **Buys 50 mss/year.** Query. **Pays $25-250.**
Fiction: Adventure, mystery. **Buys 1-2 mss/year.** Query. Length: 1,500-2,500 words. **Pays $750-1,200.**
Tips: "Look for real-life people, places, or things that might in some way be the basis for a puzzle."

$ GIANT CROSSWORDS, Scrambl-Gram, Inc., Puzzle Buffs International, 41 Park Dr., Port Clinton OH 43452. (419)734-2600. **Contact:** S. Bowers, managing editor. **50% freelance written.** Eager to work with new/unpublished writers. Quarterly magazine with crossword puzzles and word games. Estab. 1970. **Pays on acceptance.** Publishes ms an average of 1 month after acceptance. Buys all rights. Responds in 1 month to queries.
Nonfiction: Crosswords and word games only. **Pays according to size of puzzle and/or clues.**
Tips: "We are expanding our syndication of original crosswords and our publishing schedule to include new titles and extra issues of current puzzle books."

N $ $ **INQUEST GAMER**, 151 Wells Ave., Congers NY 10920-2036. (845)268-2000. Fax: (845)268-0053. E-mail: TomS@inquestmag.com. Website: www.wizardworld.com. **Contact:** Tom Slizewski, managing editor. Monthly magazine covering all of adventure gaming, particularly collectible card games (i.e., Magic) but also roleplaying and fantasy, sci fi and board games. Pays on publication. Publishes ms an average of 2 months after acceptance. Byline given. Buys one-time, all rights. Accepts queries by mail, e-mail, fax, phone. Responds in 6 weeks to mss. Sample copy for $5. Writer's guidelines for #10 SASE.

O— Break in with short news pieces.

Nonfiction: Interview/profile (Q&As with big-name personalities in sci-fi and fantasy field, special access stories like set visits to popular TV shows or films). No advertorials or stories on older, non-current games. **Buys 60 mss/year.** Query with published clips. Length: 2,000-4,000 words. **Pays $350-1,000.**

Columns/Departments: On Deck (mini game reviews); technical columns on how to play currently popular games. **Buys 100 mss/year.** Query with published clips. **Pays $50-250.**

Tips: "*InQuest* is always looking for good freelance news and feature writers who are interested in card, roleplaying or electronic games. A love of fantasy or science fiction books, movies, or art is desirable. Experience is preferred; sense of humor a plus; a flair for writing mandatory. Above all you must be able to find interesting new angles to a story, work hard and meet deadlines."

N $ **SCHOOL MATES**, United States Chess Federation, 3054 US Route 9W, New Windsor NY 12553. (845)562-8350 ext. 154. Fax: (845)236-4852. E-mail: magazines@uschess.org. Website: www.uschess.org. Publication Director: Jay Hastings. **Contact:** Peter Kurzdorfer, editor. **10% freelance written.** Quarterly magazine of chess for the beginning (some intermediate) player. Includes instruction, player profiles, chess tournament coverage, listings. Estab. 1987. Circ. 30,000. Pays on publication. Publishes ms an average of 6 months after acceptance. Byline given. Buys first rights. Editorial lead time 2 months. Submit seasonal material 3 months in advance. Accepts queries by mail, e-mail, fax, phone. Accepts simultaneous submissions. Responds in 6 months to queries. Sample copy and writer's guidelines free.

Nonfiction: "We are not-for-profit; we try to make up for low $ rate with complimentary copies." Historical/nostalgic (of a famous scholastic chess personality or a scholastic chess event), how-to, humor, interview/profile (of a famous scholastic chess player or organizer), personal experience, photo feature, technical, travel, any other chess-related item. **Buys 10-20 mss/year.** Query. Length: 250-1,000 words. **Pays $50/1,000 words, $20 minimum.** Sometimes pays expenses of writers on assignment.

Reprints: Send tearsheet, photocopy or typed ms with rights for sale noted and information about when and where the material previously appeared. Pays 100% of amount paid for an original article.

Photos: Send photos with submission. Reviews prints. Buys one-time rights, pays $15 for subsequent use. Offers $25/ photo for first time rights. Captions, identification of subjects required.

Columns/Departments: Test Your Tactics/Winning Chess Tactics (explanation, with diagrams, of chess tactics; 8 diagrammed chess problems, e.g., "white to play and win in 2 moves"); Basic Chess (chess instruction for beginners). Query with published clips. **Pays $50/1,000 words ($20 minimum).**

Tips: "Know your subject; chess is a technical subject, and you can't fake it. Human interest stories on famous chess players or young chess players can be 'softer,' but always remember you are writing for children, and make it lively. We use the Frye readability scale (3rd-6th grade reading level), and items written on the appropriate reading level do stand out immediately! We are most open to human interest stories, puzzles, cartoons, photos. We are always looking for an unusual angle, e.g., (wild example) a kid who plays chess while surfing, or (more likely) a blind kid and how she plays chess with her specially-made chess pieces and board, etc."

GAY & LESBIAN INTEREST

The magazines listed here cover a wide range of politics, culture, news, art, literature and issues of general interest to gay and lesbian communities. Magazines of a strictly sexual content are listed in the Sex section.

$ **BAY WINDOWS, New England's Largest Gay and Lesbian Newspaper**, Bay Windows, Inc., 631 Tremont St., Boston MA 02118-2034. (617)266-6670. Fax: (617)266-5973. E-mail: news@baywindows.com. Website: www.bay windows.com. **Contact:** Peter Cassels, assistant editor or Rudy Kikel (arts), or Jeff Epperly (news). **30-40% freelance written.** Weekly newspaper of gay news and concerns. "*Bay Windows* covers predominantly news of New England, but will print non-local news and features depending on the newsworthiness of the story. We feature hard news, opinion, news analysis, arts reviews and interviews." Estab. 1983. Pays within 2 months of publication. Publishes ms an average of 2 months after acceptance. Byline given. Offers 50% kill fee. Buys varies rights, usually first serial rights. Submit seasonal material 3 months in advance. Accepts queries by mail, fax. Accepts simultaneous submissions. Responds in 3 months to queries. Sample copy for $5.

Nonfiction: General interest (with a gay slant), interview/profile, opinion, photo feature, hard news. **Buys 200 mss/ year.** Query with published clips or send complete ms. Length: 500-1,500 words. **Pays $25-100.**

Reprints: Send tearsheet or photocopy and information about when and where the material previously appeared. Pays 75% of amount paid for an original article.

Photos: Pays $25/published photo. Identification of subjects, model releases required.

Columns/Departments: Film, music, dance, books, art. Length: 500-1,500 words. Letters, opinion to Jeff Epperly, editor; news, features to Peter Cassels, assistant editor; arts, reviews to Rudy Kikel, arts editor. **Buys 200 mss/year. Pays $25-100.**
Poetry: Rudy Kikel. All varieties. **Buys 50 poems/year.** Length: 1-30 lines. **Pays in copies.**
Tips: "Too much gay-oriented writing is laden with the clichés and catch phrases of the movement. Writers must have intimate knowledge of gay community; however, this doesn't mean that standard English usage isn't required. We look for writers with new, even controversial perspectives on the lives of gay men and lesbians. While we assume gay is good, we'll print stories which examine problems within the community and movement. No pornography or erotica."

$ $CURVE MAGAZINE, Outspoken Enterprises, Inc., 1 Haight St., #B, San Francisco CA 94102. Fax: (415)863-1609. E-mail: editor@curvemag.com. Editor-in-Chief: Francis Stevens. **Contact:** Gretchen Lee, managing editor. **40% freelance written.** Magazine published 8 times/year covering lesbian general interest categories. "We want dynamic and provocative articles written by, about and for lesbians." Estab. 1991. Circ. 68,000. Pays on publication. Byline given. Offers 25% kill fee. Buys first North American serial rights. Editorial lead time 3 months. Submit seasonal material 3 months in advance. Accepts queries by mail, e-mail, fax. Sample copy for $3.95 with $2 postage. Writer's guidelines free.
Nonfiction: Book excerpts, exposé, general interest, interview/profile, photo feature, travel. Special issues: Pride issue (June); Music issue (July/August). No fiction or poetry. **Buys 25 mss/year.** Query. Length: 200-2,500 words. **Pays $40-300.** Sometimes pays expenses of writers on assignment.
Photos: Send photos with submission. Buys one-time rights. Offers $50-100/photo; negotiates payment individually. Captions, identification of subjects, model releases required.
Tips: "Feature articles generally fit into one of the following categories: Celebrity profiles (lesbian, bisexual or straight women who are icons for the lesbian community or actively involved in coalition-building with the lesbian community). Community segment profiles—e.g., lesbian firefighters, drag kings, sports teams (multiple interviews with a variety of women in different parts of the country representing a diversity of backgrounds). Non-celebrity profiles (activities of unknown or low-profile lesbian and bisexual activists/political leaders, athletes, filmmakers, dancers, writers, musicians, etc.). Controversial issues (spark a dialogue about issues that divide us as a community, and the ways in which lesbians of different backgrounds fail to understand and support one another. We are not interested in inflammatory articles that incite or enrage readers without offering a channel for action). Trends (community trends in a variety of areas, including sports, fashion, image, health, music, spirituality and identity). Visual essays (most of our fashion and travel pieces are developed and produced in-house. However, we welcome input from freelancers and from time to time publish outside work)."

$ $ $ $GENRE, Genre Publishing, 7080 Hollywood Blvd., #818, Hollywood CA 90028. (323)467-8300. Fax: (323)467-8365. E-mail: lfreeman@genremagazine.com. Website: www.genremagazine.com. Editor: Morris Weissinger. **Contact:** Leon Freeman, assistant editor. **60% freelance written.** Magazine published 11 times/year. "Genre, America's best-selling gay men's lifestyle magazine, covers entertainment, fashion, travel and relationships in a hip, upbeat, upscale voice." Estab. 1991. Circ. 50,000. Pays on publication. Publishes ms an average of 3 months after acceptance. Byline given. Offers 25% kill fee. Buys first North American serial, electronic rights. Editorial lead time 10 weeks. Submit seasonal material 10 weeks in advance. Accepts queries by mail, e-mail, fax. Sample copy for $6.95 ($5 plus $1.95 postage). Writer's guidelines for #10 SASE.
Nonfiction: Essays, exposé, general interest, historical/nostalgic, how-to, humor, inspirational, interview/profile, new product, opinion, personal experience, photo feature, religious, travel, relationships, fashion. Not interested in articles on 2 males negotiating a sexual situation or coming out stories. **Buys variable number mss/year.** Query with published clips. Length: 500-1,500 words. **Pays $150-1,600.**
Photos: State availability with submission. Reviews contact sheets, prints (3×5 or 5×7). Buys one-time rights. Negotiates payment individually. Model releases required.
Columns/Departments: Body (how to better the body); Mind (how to better the mind); Spirit (how to better the spirit), all 700 words; Reviews (books, movies, music, travel, etc.), 500 words. **Buys variable number of mss/year.** Query with published clips or send complete ms. **Pays $200 maximum.**
Fiction: Adventure, experimental,, humorous, mainstream, mystery, novel excerpts, religious, romance, science fiction, slice-of-life vignettes, suspense. **Buys 10 mss/year.** Send complete ms. Length: 2,000-4,000 words.
Tips: "Like you, we take our journalistic responsibilities and ethics very seriously, and we subscribe to the highest standards of the profession. We expect our writers to represent original work that is not libelous and does not infringe upon the copyright or violate the right of privacy of any other person, firm or corporation."

$ $GIRLFRIENDS MAGAZINE, Lesbian culture, politics, and entertainment, 3415 Cèsar Châvez, Suite 101, San Francisco CA 94110. (415)648-9464. Fax: (415)648-4705. E-mail: editorial@girlfriendsmag.com. Website: www.girlfriendsmag.com. **Contact:** Erin Blackwell, editor. Monthly lesbian magazine. "Girlfriends provides its readers with intelligent, entertaining and visually pleasing coverage of culture, politics, and entertainment—all from an informed and critical lesbian perspective." Estab. 1994. Circ. 75,000. Pays on publication. Publishes ms an average of 6 months after acceptance. Byline given. Offers 25% kill fee. Buys first rights, use for advertising/promoting Girlfriends. Editorial lead time 3 months. Submit seasonal material 6 months in advance. Accepts queries by mail, e-mail. Accepts simultaneous submissions. Responds in 3 weeks to queries; 2 months to mss. Sample copy for $4.95 plus $1.50 s/h or online. Writer's guidelines for #10 SASE or online.

● *Girlfriends* is not accepting fiction, poetry or fillers.

O→ Break in by sending a letter detailing interests and story ideas, plus résumé and published samples.

Nonfiction: Book excerpts, essays, exposé, historical/nostalgic, humor, interview/profile, new product, opinion, personal experience, photo feature, religious, technical, travel, investigative features. Special issues: Sex issue, gay pride issue, breast cancer issue. Special features: Best lesbian restaurants in the US; best places to live. **Buys 20-25 mss/year.** Query with published clips. Length: 1,000-3,500 words. **Pays 10-25¢/word.**

Reprints: Send photocopy or typed ms with rights for sale noted and information about when and where the material previously appeared. Negotiable payment.

Photos: Send photos with submission. Reviews contact sheets, 4×5 or 2¼×2¼ transparencies, prints. Buys one-time rights. Offers $30-250/photo. Captions, identification of subjects, model releases required.

Columns/Departments: Book reviews, 900 words; Music reviews, 600 words; Travel, 600 words; Opinion pieces, 1,000 words; Humor, 600 words. Query with published clips. **Pays 15¢/word.**

Tips: "Be unafraid of controversy—articles should focus on problems and debates raised in lesbian culture, politics, and sexuality. Avoid being 'politically correct.' We don't just want to know what's happening in the lesbian world, we want to know how what's happening in the world affects lesbians."

$ $ THE GUIDE, To Gay Travel, Entertainment, Politics and Sex, Fidelity Publishing, P.O. Box 990593, Boston MA 02199-0593. (617)266-8557. Fax: (617)266-1125. E-mail: theguide@guidemag.com. Website: www.guidem ag.com. **Contact:** French Wall, editor. **25% freelance written.** Monthly magazine on the gay and lesbian community. Estab. 1981. Circ. 30,000. **Pays on acceptance.** Publishes ms an average of 2 months after acceptance. Offers negotiable kill fee. Buys first rights. Submit seasonal material 2 months in advance. Accepts queries by mail, e-mail. Accepts simultaneous submissions. Responds in 3 months to queries. Sample copy for 9×12 SAE and 8 first-class stamps. Writer's guidelines for #10 SASE.

Nonfiction: Book excerpts (if yet unpublished), essays, exposé, general interest, historical/nostalgic, humor, interview/profile, opinion, personal experience, photo feature, religious. **Buys 24 mss/year.** Query with or without published clips or send complete ms. Length: 500-5,000 words. **Pays $85-240.**

Reprints: Occasionally buys previously published submissions. Pays 100% of amount paid for an original article.

Photos: Send photos with submission. Reviews contact sheets. Buys one-time rights. Pays $15 per image used. Captions, identification of subjects, model releases required.

Tips: "Brevity, humor and militancy appreciated. Writing on sex, political analysis and humor are particularly appreciated. We purchase very few freelance travel pieces; those that we do buy are usually on less commercial destinations."

$ $ HERO MAGAZINE, 451 N. La Cienega Blvd., Suite One, Los Angeles CA 90048. (310)360-8022. E-mail: editor@heromag.com. Website: www.heromag.com. **Contact:** Paul Horne, editorial director. **90% freelance written.** Monthly Award-winning general interest/service magazine for gay men. Estab. 1996. Circ. 100,000. Pays on publication. Publishes ms an average of 2 months after acceptance. Byline given. Buys one-time rights. Editorial lead time 2 months. Submit seasonal material 4 months in advance. Responds in 1 months to queries. Sample copy for $4.95. Writer's guidelines online.

Nonfiction: "*HERO* selects articles which challenge and broaden the current depiction of gay men in the media. Therefore, erotic material and overtly sexual submissions will likely be overlooked." Book excerpts, essays, general interest, how-to, humor, inspirational, interview/profile, opinion, personal experience, photo feature, technical, travel. **Buys 30 mss/year.** Query by mail with published clips. No queries by fax or e-mail. Length: 300-4,000 words. **Pays 10-50¢/word for print publication only, not for online publication.**

Reprints: Accepts previously published submissions.

Photos: Send photos with submission. Reviews contact sheets. Buys one-time rights. Offers no additional payment for photos accepted with ms. Model releases required.

Columns/Departments: Book (book features and reviews), 300-1,000 words. Family (profiles of gay fathers, children of gay parents), Youth (out gay kids making a difference); Boy Toys (technology, high-tech gadgets); Music and Theatre (interviews and reviews); Spirituality, all 500-1,000 words. **Buys 20 mss/year.** Query with published clips. **Pays 10-50¢/word.**

Tips: "*HERO* brings gay readers and a gay sensibility into the mainstream. We feature relationships and romance, spirituality, families, and health & fitness, in addition to fashion, entertainment, travel, and general how-to/better living articles. Successful freelancers will have read the magazine before querying. Please keep maximum one-page query letters brief and to the point."

N $ $ HX Magazine, Two Queens, Inc., 230 W. 17th St., Eighth Floor, New York NY 10011. (212)352-3535. Fax: (212)352-3596. E-mail: editor@hx.com. Website: www.hx.com. **Contact:** Trent Straube, editor. **25% freelance written.** Weekly magazine covering gay New York City nightlife and entertainment. "We publish a magazine for gay men who are interested in New York City nightlife and entertainment." Estab. 1991. Circ. 39,000. Pays on publication. Publishes ms an average of 1 month after acceptance. Byline given. Buys first North American serial, second serial (reprint), electronic rights. Editorial lead time 2 months. Submit seasonal material 2 months in advance. We must be exclusive East Coast publisher to accept. Only responds if interested to queries.

Nonfiction: General interest, arts and entertainment, celebrity profiles, reviews. **Buys 50 mss/year.** Query with published clips. Length: 500-2,000 words. **Pays $50-150; $25-100 for unsolicited articles.**

Reprints: Send tearsheet or photocopy with rights for sale noted and information about when and where the material previously appeared. Pays 50% of amount paid for an original article.

Photos: State availability with submission. Reviews contact sheets, negatives, 8×10 prints. Buys one-time, reprint and electronic reprint rights. Captions, identification of subjects, model releases required.

Columns/Departments: Buys 200 mss/year. Query with published clips. **Pays $25-125.**

$ IN STEP, In Step, Inc., 1661 N. Water St., #411, Milwaukee WI 53202. (414)278-7840. Fax: (414)278-5868. E-mail: editor@instepnews.com. Website: www.instepnews.com. Managing Editor: Jorge Cabal. **Contact:** William Attewell, editor. **30% freelance written.** Biweekly consumer tabloid for gay and lesbian readers. Estab. 1984. Circ. 15,000. Buys first North American serial, second serial (reprint) rights. Submit seasonal material 2 months in advance. Accepts queries by mail, e-mail. Accepts simultaneous submissions. Responds in 3 weeks to queries; 1 month to mss. Sample copy for $3. Writer's guidelines for #10 SASE.

Nonfiction: Book excerpts, exposé, historical/nostalgic, interview/profile, new product, opinion, religious, travel. Query. Length: 500-2,000 words. **Pays $15-100.**

Photos: State availability with submission. Reviews 5×7 prints. Buys one-time rights. Negotiates payment individually. Captions, identification of subjects, model releases required.

 ■ The online magazine carries original content not found in the print edition. Contact: William Attewell, online editor.

Tips: "E-mail flawless copy samples to get my attention. Be patient."

$ $ IN THE FAMILY, The Magazine for Queer People and Their Loved Ones, Family Magazine, Inc., P.O. Box 5387, Takoma Park MD 20913. (301)270-4771. Fax: (301)270-4660. E-mail: lmarkowitz@aol.com. Website: www.inthefamily.com. **Contact:** Laura Markowitz, editor. **20% freelance written.** Quarterly magazine covering lesbian, gay and bisexual family relationships. "Using the lens of psychotherapy, our magazine looks at the complexities of L/G/B family relationships as well as professional issues for L/G/B therapists." Estab. 1995. Circ. 3,000. Pays on publication. Publishes ms an average of 3 months after acceptance. Byline given. Offers 25% kill fee. Buys first rights. Editorial lead time 6 months. Submit seasonal material 4 months in advance. Responds in 1 month to queries; 3 months to mss. Sample copy for $5.50. Writers guidelines free or online.

Nonfiction: Essays, exposé, humor, opinion, personal experience, photo feature. "No autobiography or erotica." **Buys 4 mss/year.** Length: 2,500-4,000 words. **Pays $100-300 for assigned articles; $50-200 for unsolicited articles.** Sometimes pays expenses of writers on assignment.

Photos: State availability with submission. Reviews contact sheets. Buys one-time rights. Negotiates payment individually. Captions, identification of subjects, model releases required.

Columns/Departments: Karen Sundquist, senior editor. Family Album (aspects of a queer family life), 1,500 words; In the Therapy Room (clinical case presentations), 2,000 words; A Look at Research (relevant social science findings), 1,500 words; The Last Word (gentle humor), 800 words. **Buys 4 mss/year.** Send complete ms. **Pays $50-150.**

Fiction: Helena Lipstadt, fiction editor. Confessions, ethnic, slice-of-life vignettes, Family life theme for G/L/BS. No erotica, sci-fi, horror, romance, serialized novels or westerns. **Buys 4 mss/year.** Send complete ms. Length: 1,000-2,500 words. **Pays $50-100.**

Poetry: Helena Lipstadt, fiction editor. Avant-garde, free verse, haiku, light verse, traditional. **Buys 4 poems/year.** Submit maximum 6 poems. Length: 10-35 lines. **Pays $50-75.**

Tips: "*In the Family* takes an in-depth look at the complexities of lesbian, gay and bisexual family relationships, including couples and intimacy, money, sex, extended family, parenting and more. Readers include therapists of all sexual orientations as well as family members of lesbian, gay and bisexuals, and also queer people who are interested in what therapists have to say about such themes as how to recover from a gay bashing; how to navigate single life; how to have a good divorce; how to understand bisexuality; how to come out to children; how to understand fringe sexual practices; how to reconcile homosexuality and religion. Therapists read it to learn the latest research about working with queer families, to learn from the regular case studies and clinical advice columns. Family members appreciate the multiple viewpoints in the magazine. We look for writers who know something about these issues and who have an engaging, intelligent, narrative style. We are allergic to therapy jargon and political rhetoric."

$ $ $ METROSOURCE, MetroSource Publishing Inc., 180 Varick St., 5th Floor, New York NY 10014. (212)691-5127. Fax: (212)741-2978. E-mail: rwalsh@metrosource.com or eandersson@metrosource.com. Website: www.metrosource.com. **Contact:** Richard Walsh, editor-in-chief; Eric Andersson, assistant editor. **70% freelance written.** Quarterly magazine. "*MetroSource* is a celebration and exploration of urban gay and lesbian life. *MetroSource* is an upscale, glossy, four-color lifestyle magazine targeted to an urban, professional gay and lesbian readership." Estab. 1990. Circ. 85,000. Pays on publication. Publishes ms an average of 2 months after acceptance. Byline given. Editorial lead time 3 months. Submit seasonal material 4 months in advance. Accepts queries by mail, e-mail, fax, phone. Accepts simultaneous submissions. Sample copy for $5.

Nonfiction: Exposé, interview/profile, opinion, photo feature, travel. **Buys 20 mss/year.** Query with published clips. Length: 1,000-2,500 words. **Pays $100-900.**

Photos: State availability with submission. Negotiates payment individually. Captions, model releases required.

Columns/Departments: Book, film, television and stage reviews; health columns; and personal diary and opinion pieces. Word lengths vary. Query with published clips. **Pays $200.**

$ MOM GUESS WHAT NEWSPAPER, 1725 L St., Sacramento CA 95814. (916)441-6397. Fax: (916)441-6422. E-mail: info@mgwnews.com. Website: www.mgwnews.com. **Contact:** Linda Birner, editor. **80% freelance written.** Works with small number of new/unpublished writers each year. Biweekly tabloid covering gay rights and gay lifestyles. A newspaper for gay men, lesbians and their straight friends in the State Capitol and the Sacramento Valley area. First and oldest gay newspaper in Sacramento. Estab. 1977. Circ. 21,000. Publishes ms an average of 3 months after acceptance. Byline given. Buys all rights. Submit seasonal material 3 months in advance. Accepts queries by mail, e-mail. Responds in 2 months to queries. Sample copy for $1. Writer's guidelines for 10×13 SAE with 4 first-class stamps or online.

Nonfiction: Interview/profile and photo feature of international, national or local scope. **Buys 8 mss/year.** Query. Length: 200-1,500 words. **Payment depends on article.** Pays expenses of writers on assignment.

Reprints: Send tearsheet or photocopy and information about when and where the material previously appeared. Pay varies.

Photos: Send photos with submission. Reviews 5×7 prints. Buys one-time rights. Offers no additional payment for photos accepted with ms. Captions, identification of subjects required.

Columns/Departments: News, Restaurants, Political, Health, Film, Video, Book Reviews. **Buys 12 mss/year.** Query. **Payment depends on article.**

Tips: "*MGW* is published primarily from volunteers. With some freelancers payment is made. Put requirements in your cover letter. Byline appears with each published article; photos credited. Editors reserve right to edit, crop, touch up, revise, or otherwise alter manuscripts, and photos, but not to change theme or intent of the work. Enclose SASE postcard for acceptance or rejection. We will not assume responsibility for returning unsolicited material lacking sufficient return postage or lost in the mail."

[N] OUT, 110 Greene St., Suite 600, New York NY 10012. (212)242-8100. Fax: (212)242-8338. Website: www.out.com. Editor-in-Chief: Brendan Lemon. **Contact:** Department Editor. **80% freelance written.** Monthly national magazine covering gay and lesbian general-interest topics. "Our subjects range from current affairs to culture, from fitness to finance." Estab. 1992. Circ. 120,000. Pays on publication. Publishes ms an average of 3 months after acceptance. Byline given. Offers 25% kill fee. Buys first North American serial rights, second serial (reprint) rights for anthologies (additional fee paid) and 30-day reprint rights (additional fee paid if applicable). Editorial lead time 3 months. Submit seasonal material 5 months in advance. Accepts queries by mail. Accepts simultaneous submissions. Responds in 6 weeks to queries; 2 months to mss. Sample copy for $6. Writer's guidelines for #10 SASE.

Nonfiction: Book excerpts, essays, exposé, general interest, historical/nostalgic, humor, interview/profile, new product, opinion, personal experience, photo feature, travel, fashion/lifestyle. **Buys 200 mss/year.** Query with published clips and SASE. Length: 50-1,500 words. **Pays variable rate.** Sometimes pays expenses of writers on assignment.

Photos: State availability with submission. Reviews contact sheets, transparencies, prints. Buys one-time rights. Negotiates payment individually. Captions, identification of subjects, model releases required.

Tips: "*Out*'s contributors include editors and writers from the country's top consumer titles: Skilled reporters, columnists, and writers with distinctive voices and specific expertise in the fields they cover. But while published clips and relevant experience are a must, the magazine also seeks out fresh, young voices. The best guide to the kind of stories we publish is to review our recent issues—is there a place for the story you have in mind? Be aware of our long lead time. No phone queries, please."

$ OUTSMART, Up & Out Communications, 3406 Audubon Place, Houston TX 77006. (713)520-7237. Fax: (713)522-3275. E-mail: ann@outsmartmagazine.com. Website: www.outsmartmagazine.com. **Contact:** Ann Walton Sieber, editor. **70% freelance written.** Monthly magazine covering gay and lesbian issues. "*OutSmart* provides positive information to gay men, lesbians and their associates to enhance and improve the quality of our lives." Estab. 1994. Circ. 20,000. Pays on publication. Publishes ms an average of 2 months after acceptance. Byline given. Buys one-time, simultaneous rights, permission to publish online. Editorial lead time 2 months. Submit seasonal material 2 months in advance. Accepts queries by mail, e-mail, fax. Accepts simultaneous submissions. Responds in 6 weeks to queries; 2 months to mss. Sample copy and writer's guidelines online.

Nonfiction: Historical/nostalgic, interview/profile, opinion, personal experience, photo feature, travel, health/wellness, local/national news. **Buys 10 mss/year.** Send complete ms. Length: 450-2,300 words. **Pays $20-100.**

Reprints: Send photocopy.

Photos: State availability with submission. Reviews 4×6 prints. Buys one-time rights. Negotiates payment individually. Identification of subjects required.

■ The online magazine carries original content not found in the print edition and includes writer's guidelines.

Tips: "*OutSmart* is a mainstream publication that covers culture, politics, personalities, entertainment and health/wellness as well as local and national news and events. It is our goal to address the diversity of the lesbian and gay community, fostering understanding among all Houston's citizens."

[N] $ THE WASHINGTON BLADE, Washington Blade, Inc., 1408 U St., NW, Washington DC 20009-3916. (202)797-7000. Fax: (202)797-7040. E-mail: news@washblade.com. Website: www.washblade.com. **Contact:** Greg Varner, arts editor or Lyn Stoesen, opinion editor. **20% freelance written.** Nation's oldest and largest weekly news tabloid covering the gay/lesbian community. "Articles (subjects) should be written from or directed to a gay perspective."

Estab. 1969. Circ. 50,000. Publishes ms an average of 1 month after acceptance. Byline given. Buys first North American serial rights. Submit seasonal material 1 month in advance. Accepts queries by mail, e-mail, fax. Responds in 2 months to queries.

Nonfiction: Most news stories are staff-generated; writers with news or news feature ideas should query first.

Reprints: Send typed ms with rights for sale noted and information about when and where the material previously appeared.

Photos: "A photo or graphic with feature/lifestyle articles is particularly important. Photos with news stories are appreciated." Send photos by mail or e-mail. Pays $25 minimum. Photographers on assignment are paid mutually agreed upon fee plus expenses. Buys all rights. Captions required.

Columns/Departments: Arts (books, travel and profiles of gay figures in the arts); **pays 10-12¢/word**. Send submissions to Greg Varner, arts editor. Opinion column 1-2 times/week (reactions to political developments, cultural observations, and moving or funny personal stories), 900 words; **pays $25**. Send submissions to Lyn Stoesen, opinion editor. No sexually explicit material.

Tips: "We have a highly competent and professional staff of news reporters, and it is difficult to break in here as a freelancer covering news. Include a résumé, good examples of your writing, and know the paper before you send a manuscript for publication. We look for writers who are credible and professional, and for copy that is accurate, fair, timely, and objective in tone. We do not work with writers who play fast and loose with the facts. Before you send anything, become familiar with our publication. We get a lot of material that is completely inappropriate. Do not send sexually explicit material."

GENERAL INTEREST

General interest magazines need writers who can appeal to a broad audience—teens and senior citizens, wealthy readers and the unemployed. Each magazine still has a personality that suits its audience—one that a writer should study before sending material to an editor. Other markets for general interest material are in these Consumer categories: Contemporary Culture, Ethnic/Minority, Inflight, Men's, Regional and Women's.

$ AFRICAN AMERICAN MAGAZINE, Everyone Learns by Reading, Topaz Marketing & Distributing, 1014 Franklin SE, Grand Rapids MI 49507-1327. (616)243-4114, ext. 20. Fax: (616)243-6844. E-mail: wmathis@triton.net. Website: www.africanamericanmag.com. President & CEO: Patricia E. Mathis. **Contact:** Walter L. Mathis Sr., executive director. **50% freelance written.** Bimonthly magazine covering African Americans and other ethnic groups. "We are guided by the principles of fine press and are open to everyone regardless of their race, gender or religion." Estab. 1998. Circ. 15,000. Pays on publication. Editorial lead time 1 month. Submit seasonal material 1 month in advance. Accepts queries by mail, e-mail. Sample copy and writer's guidelines online.

Nonfiction: Book excerpts, essays, exposé, general interest, historical/nostalgic, how-to, humor, inspirational, interview/profile, new product, opinion, personal experience, photo feature, religious, technical, travel, book reviews (ethnic). **Pays negotiable rate.**

Photos: State availability of or send photos with submission. Reviews 3×5 prints. Buys one-time rights. Negotiates payment individually. Identification of subjects, model releases required.

Columns/Departments: Looking Within; Economic Focus; Positive Notes; Pastor's Perspective; Classified. **Buys 10 mss/year.** Query with published clips. **Pays negotiable rate.**

Fillers: Anecdotes, facts, newsbreaks. Length: 10-100 words.

Tips: "Dare to say what needs to be said, and to tell it like it is—whether it is 'popular' or not. Read a sample copy first and query if you have any further questions."

$ $ THE AMERICAN LEGION MAGAZINE, P.O. Box 1055, Indianapolis IN 46206-1055. (317)630-1200. Fax: (317)630-1280. E-mail: tal@legion.org. Website: www.legion.org. Editorial Administrator: Patricia Marschand. **Contact:** John Raughter, executive editor. **70% freelance written.** Prefers to work with published/established writers, but works with a small number of new/unpublished writers each year. Monthly magazine. "Working through 15,000 community-level posts, the honorably discharged wartime veterans of The American Legion dedicate themselves to God, country and traditional American values. They believe in a strong defense; adequate and compassionate care for veterans and their families; community service; and the wholesome development of our nation's youth. We publish articles that reflect these values. We inform our readers and their families of significant trends and issues affecting our nation, the world and the way we live. Our major features focus on the American flag, national security, foreign affairs, business trends, social issues, health, education, ethics and the arts. We also publish selected general feature articles, articles of special interest to veterans, and question-and-answer interviews with prominent national and world figures." Estab. 1919. Circ. 2,800,000. **Pays on acceptance.** Publishes ms an average of 6 months after acceptance. Byline given. Buys first North American serial rights. Accepts queries by mail, e-mail, fax. Responds in 2 months to queries. Sample copy for $3.50 and 9×12 SAE with 6 first-class stamps. Writer's guidelines for #10 SASE.

Nonfiction: Well-reported articles or expert commentaries cover issues/trends in world/national affairs, contemporary problems, general interest, sharply-focused feature subjects. Monthly Q&A with national figures/experts. General inter-

est, interview/profile. No regional topics or promotion of partisan political agendas. No personal experiences or war stories. **Buys 50-60 mss/year.** Query with SASE should explain the subject or issue, article's angle and organization, writer's qualifications and experts to be interviewed. Length: 300-2,000 words. **Pays 40¢/word and up.**
Photos: On assignment.
Tips: "Queries by new writers should include clips/background/expertise; no longer than 1½ pages. Submit suitable material showing you have read several issues. *The American Legion Magazine* considers itself 'the magazine for a strong America.' Reflect this theme (which includes economy, educational system, moral fiber, social issues, infrastructure, technology and national defense/security). We are a general interest, national magazine, not a strictly military magazine. We are widely read by members of the Washington establishment and other policy makers."

N **$** **$** 🔲 **AMERICAN PROFILE**, Publishing Group of America, 341 Cool Springs Blvd., Suite 400, Franklin TN 37067. (615)468-6000. Fax: (615)468-6100. E-mail: editorial@americanprofile.com. Website: www.americanprofile .com. Editor: Peter V. Fossel. **Contact:** Joyce Caruthers, associate editor. **95% freelance written.** Weekly magazine with national and regional editorial celebrating the people, places and experiences of hometowns across America. The four-color magazine is distributed through small to medium-size community newspapers. Estab. 2000. Circ. 3,000,000. **Pays on acceptance.** Byline given. Buys first, electronic, 6-month exclusive rights. Editorial lead time 3 months. Submit seasonal material 6 months in advance. Accepts queries by mail, e-mail, fax. Responds in 1 month. Writer's guidelines online.
Nonfiction: General interest, how-to, interview/profile, travel. No fiction, nostalgia, poetry, essays. **Buys 250 mss/ year.** Query with published clips. Length: 450-1,200 words. Pays expenses of writers on assignment.
Photos: State availability with submission. Reviews transparencies. Buys one-time rights, non-exclusive after 6 months. Negotiates payment individually. Captions, identification of subjects, model releases required.
Columns/Departments: Health, Family, Finances, Home, Gardening.
Tips: "We appreciate hard-copy submissions and one-paragraph queries for short manuscripts (less than 500 words) on food, gardening, nature, profiles, health and home projects for small-town audiences. **Must be out of the ordinary. Please visit the website to see our writing style."**

$ $ $ $ **THE ATLANTIC MONTHLY**, 77 N. Washington St., Boston MA 02114. Fax: (617)854-7877. Editor: Michael Kelly. Managing Editor: Cullen Murphy. **Contact:** C. Michael Curtis, senior editor. Monthly magazine of arts and public affairs. Circ. 500,000. **Pays on acceptance.** Byline given. Buys first North American serial rights. Accepts queries by mail, e-mail, fax. Response time to queries varies.
Nonfiction: Reportage preferred. Book excerpts, essays, general interest, humor, personal experience, religious, travel. Query with or without published clips or send complete ms. All unsolicited mss must be accompanied by SASE. Length: 1,000-6,000 words. **Payment varies**. Sometimes pays expenses of writers on assignment.
Fiction: "Seeks fiction that is clear, tightly written with strong sense of 'story' and well-defined characters." Literary and contemporary fiction. **Buys 12-15 mss/year.** Send complete ms. Length: 2,000-6,000 words. **Pays $3,000.**
Poetry: Peter Davison, poetry editor. **Buys 40-60 poems/year.**
   🔲 The online magazine carries original content not found in the print edition. Contact: Wen Stephenson, online editor.
Tips: Writers should be aware that this is not a market for beginner's work (nonfiction and fiction), nor is it truly for intermediate work. Study this magazine before sending only your best, most professional work. When making first contact, "cover letters are sometimes helpful, particularly if they cite prior publications or involvement in writing programs. Common mistakes: Melodrama, inconclusiveness, lack of development, unpersuasive characters and/or dialogue."

$ **BIBLIOPHILOS, A Journal of History, Literature, and the Liberal Arts**, The Bibliophile Publishing Co., Inc., 200 Security Building, Fairmont WV 26554. **Contact:** Dr. Gerald J. Bobango, editor. **65-70% freelance written.** Quarterly literary magazine concentrating on 19th century American and European history. "We see ourself as a forum for new and unpublished writers, historians, philosophers, literary critics and reviewers, and those who love animals. Audience is academic-oriented, college graduate, who believes in traditional Aristotelian-Thomistic thought and education, and has a fair streak of the Luddite in him/her. Our ideal reader owns no television, has never sent nor received e-mail, and avoids shopping malls at any cost. He loves books." Estab. 1981. Circ. 400. Pays on publication. Publishes ms an average of 4 months after acceptance. Byline given. Buys first North American serial rights. Editorial lead time 4 months. Submit seasonal material 4 months in advance. Accepts simultaneous submissions. Responds in 2 weeks to queries; 1 month to mss. Sample copy for $5.25., Writer's guidelines for 9½×4 SAE with 2 first-class stamps.
   ☞ Break in with "either prose or poetry which is illustrative of man triumphing over and doing without technology, pure Ludditism, if need be. Send material critical of the socialist welfare state, constantly expanding federal government (or government at all levels), or exposing the inequities of affirmative action, political correctness, and the mass media packaging of political candidates. We want to see a pre-1960 world view."
Nonfiction: Book excerpts, essays, general interest, historical/nostalgic, humor, interview/profile, opinion, personal experience, photo feature, travel, book review-essay, literary criticism. Special issues: Upcoming theme issues include an annual all book-review issue, containing 10-15 reviews and review-essays, or poetry about books and reading. Does not want to see "anything that Oprah would recommend, or that Erma Bombeck or Ann Landers would think humorous or interesting. No 'I found Jesus and it changed my life' material." **Buys 8-12 mss/year.** Query by mail only. Length: 1,500-3,000 words. **Pays $5-35.**

Photos: State availability with submission. Reviews 4×6 prints. Buys one-time rights. Negotiates payment individually. Identification of subjects required.

Columns/Departments: "Features" (fiction and nonfiction, short stories), 1,500-3,000 words; "Poetry" (batches of 5, preferably thematically related), 3-150 lines; "Reviews" (book reviews or review essays on new books or individual authors, current and past), 1,000-1,500 words; "Opinion" (man triumphing over technology and technocrats, the facade of modern education, computer fetishism), 1,000-1,500 words. **Buys 4 mss/year.** Query by mail only. **Pays $25-40.**

Fiction: Adventure, condensed novels, ethnic, experimental, historical, humorous, mainstream, mystery, novel excerpts, romance, slice-of-life vignettes, suspense, Utopian, Orwellian. "No 'I found Jesus and it turned my life around'; no 'I remember Mama, who was a saint and I miss her terribly'; no gay or lesbian topics; nothing harping on political correctness; nothing to do with healthy living, HMOs, medical programs, or the welfare state, unless it is against statism in these areas." **Buys 8-12 mss/year.** Length: 1,500-3,000 words. **Pays $25-40.**

Poetry: "Formal and rhymed verse gets read first." Free verse, light verse, traditional, political satire, doggerel. "No inspirational verse, or poems about grandchildren and the cute things they do." **Buys 50-75 poems/year.** Submit maximum 5 poems. Length: 3-150 lines. **Pays $5-25.**

Fillers: Anecdotes, short humor. **Buys 5-6/year.** Length: 25-100 words. **Pays $5-10.**

Tips: "Query first, and include a large SASE and $5.25 for sample issues and guidelines. Tell us of your academic expertise, what kinds of books you can review, and swear that you will follow Turabian's bibliographic form as set forth in the guidelines and no other. Do not call us, nor fax us, nor try e-mailing, which wouldn't work anyway. Avoid the cult of relevantism and contemporaneity. Send us perfect copy, no misspellings, no grammatical errors, no trendy, PC language."

$ $ CAPPER'S, Ogden Publications, Inc., 1503 SW 42nd St., Topeka KS 66609-1265. (913)274-4345. Fax: (913)274-4305. E-mail: cappers@cjnetworks.com. Website: www.cappers.com. Associate Editors: Cheryl Ptacek, Kandy Hopkins, Vicki Parks. Senior Editor: Jean Teller. **Contact:** Ann T. Crahan, editor. **25% freelance written.** Works with a small number of new/unpublished writers each year. Biweekly tabloid emphasizing home and family for readers who live in small towns and on farms. "*Capper's* is upbeat, focusing on the homey feelings people like to share, as well as hopes and dreams." Estab. 1879. Circ. 250,000. Pays for poetry and fiction on acceptance; articles on publication. Publishes ms an average of 8 months after acceptance. Byline given. Buys first North American serial, one-time rights. Editorial lead time 6 months. Submit seasonal material 3 months in advance. Accepts queries by mail. Responds in 6 weeks to queries; 6 months to mss. Sample copy for $1.95 or online. Writer's guidelines for #10 SASE or online.

Nonfiction: General interest, historical/nostalgic (local museums, etc.), inspirational, interview/profile, travel, people stories (accomplishments, collections, etc.). **Buys 50 mss/year.** Send complete ms. Length: 750 words maximum. **Pays $2.50/inch. Pays additional $5 if used online.**

Reprints: Accepts occasionally from noncompeting venues. Send typed ms with rights for sale noted and information about when and where the material previously appeared.

Photos: Send photos with submission. Buys one-time rights. Pays $5-20 for b&w glossy prints. Purchase price for ms includes payment for photos. Pays $10-30 for color prints, $40 for cover. Additional $5 if used online. Captions, identification of subjects required.

Columns/Departments: Heart of the Home (homemaker's letters, recipes, hints). Send complete ms. **Pays approximately $2 per printed inch.**

Fiction: "We buy very few fiction pieces—longer than short stories, shorter than novels." Adventure, historical, humorous, mainstream, mystery, romance, serialized novels, western. No explicit sex, violence or profanity. **Buys 4-5 mss/year.** Query. Length: 7,500-40,000 words. **Pays $75-300.**

Poetry: "The poems that appear in *Capper's* are not too difficult to read. They're easy to grasp. We're looking for everyday events and down-to-earth themes." Free verse, haiku, light verse, traditional, nature, inspiration. **Buys 150 poems/year.** Submit maximum 5 poems. Length: 4-16 lines. **Pays $10-15.**

Tips: "Study a few issues of our publication. Most rejections are for material that is too long, unsuitable or out of character for our magazine (too sexy, too much profanity, wrong kind of topic, etc.). On occasion, we must cut material to fit column space. No electronic submissions."

$ $ $ DIVERSION, 1790 Broadway, New York NY 10019. (212)969-7500. Fax: (212)969-7557. Website: www.diversionmag.com. **Contact:** Tom Passavant, editor-in-chief. Monthly magazine covering travel and lifestyle, edited for physicians. "*Diversion* offers an eclectic mix of interests beyond medicine. Regular features include stories on domestic and foreign travel destinations, discussions of food and wine, sports columns, guidance on gardening and photography, books, electronic gear, and information on investments and finance. The editorial reflects its readers' affluent lifestyles and diverse personal interests. Although *Diversion* doesn't cover health subjects, it does feature profiles of doctors who excel at nonmedical pursuits." Estab. 1973. Circ. 176,000. Pays 3 months after acceptance. Byline given. Offers 25% kill fee. Editorial lead time 4 months. Responds in 1 month to queries. Sample copy for $4.50. Guidelines available.

○┬ Break in by "querying with a brief proposal describing the focus of the story and why it would interest our readers. Include credentials and published clips."

Nonfiction: "We get loads of travel and food queries, but not enough in culture, the arts, sports, personal finance, etc." **Buys 70 mss/year.** Query with proposal, published clips, and author's credentials. Length: 1,800-2,000 words. **Pays $50-1,200.**

Columns/Departments: Travel, food & wine, photography, gardening, finance. Length: 1,200 words (columns) or 2,200 words (features). Query with proposal, published clips and author's credentials. **Pays $500-800.**

$ EDUCATION IN FOCUS, Books for All Times, Inc., P.O. Box 2, Alexandria VA 22313. (703)548-0457. E-mail: staff@bfat.com. Website: www.bfat.com. **Contact:** Joe David, editor. **80% freelance written.** Semiannual newsletter for public interested in education issues at all levels. "We are always looking for intelligent articles that provide educationally sound ideas that enhance the understanding of what is happening or what should be happening in our schools today. We are not looking for material that might be published by the Department of Education. Instead we want material from liberated and mature thinkers and writers, tamed by reason and humanitarianism." Estab. 1989. Circ. 1,000. **Pays on acceptance.** Publishes ms an average of 2 months after acceptance. Byline given. Buys first, one-time, second serial (reprint) rights; also book, newsletter and Internet rights. Editorial lead time 2 months. Accepts queries by mail, e-mail. Accepts simultaneous submissions. Responds in 1 month to queries. Sample copy for #10 SASE.

Nonfiction: "We prefer documented, intelligent articles that deeply inform. The best way to be quickly rejected is to send articles that defend the public school system as it is today, or was!" Book excerpts, exposé, general interest. **Buys 4-6 mss/year.** Query with published clips or send complete ms. Length: 3,000 words. Some longer articles can be broken into 2 articles - one for each issue. **Pays $25-75.**

Tips: "Maintain an honest voice and a clear focus on the subject."

$ $ $ FRIENDLY EXCHANGE, C-E Publishers: Publishers, Friendly Exchange Business Office, P.O. Box 2120, Warren MI 48090-2120. Publication Office: (810)753-8325. Fax: (248)447-7566. Website: www.friendlyexchange.com. **Contact:** Dan Grantham, editor. **80% freelance written.** Works with a small number of new/unpublished writers each year. Quarterly magazine for policyholders of Farmers Insurance Group of Companies exploring travel, lifestyle and leisure topics of interest to active families. "These are traditional families (median adult age 39) who live primarily in the area bounded by Ohio on the east and the Pacific Ocean on the west, along with Tennessee, Alabama, and Virginia." Estab. 1981. Circ. 6,200,000. **Pays on acceptance.** Publishes ms an average of 5 months after acceptance. Offers 25% kill fee. Buys all rights. Submit seasonal material 1 year in advance. Accepts simultaneous submissions. Responds in 2 months to queries. Sample copy for 9×12 SAE and 5 first-class stamps. Writer's guidelines for #10 SASE.

Nonfiction: "We provide readers with 'news they can use' through articles that help them make smart choices about lifestyle issues. We focus on home, auto, health, personal finance, travel and other lifestyle/consumer issues of interest to today's families. Readers should get a sense of the issues involved, and information that could help them make those decisions. Style is warm and colorful, making liberal use of anecdotes and quotes." **Buys 8 mss/year.** Query. Length: 200-1,200 words. **Pays $500-1,000, including expenses.**

Columns/Departments: Consumer issues, health and leisure are topics of regular columns.

Tips: "We concentrate on providing readers information relating to current trends. Don't focus on destination-based travel, but on travel trends. We prefer tightly targeted stories that provide new information to help readers make decisions about their lives. We don't take queries or manuscripts on first-person essays or humorous articles."

$ $ GRIT, American Life and Traditions, Ogden Publications, 1503 SW 42nd St., Topeka KS 66609-1265. (785)274-4300. Fax: (785)274-4305. E-mail: grit@cjnetworks.com. Website: www.grit.com. **Contact:** Donna Doyle, editor-in-chief. **90% freelance written.** Open to new writers. "*Grit* is Good News. As a wholesome, family-oriented magazine published for more than a century and distributed nationally, *Grit* features articles about family lifestyles, traditions, values and pastimes. *Grit* accents the best of American life and traditions—past and present. Our readers cherish family values and appreciate practical and innovative ideas. Many of them live in small towns and rural areas across the country; others live in cities but share many of the values typical of small-town America." Estab. 1882. Circ. 200,000. Pays on publication. Byline given. Buys first, all rights. Submit seasonal material 6 months in advance. Accepts queries by mail. Sample copy and writer's guidelines for $4 and 11×14 SAE with 4 first-class stamps. Sample articles online.

- *Grit* reports it is looking for articles about how soon-to-retire baby boomers are planning for retirement and how children are coping with aging parents.

- Break in through Departments such as Readers' True Stories, Pet Tales, Looking Back, Profile, Seasonal Readers Memories (Easter, Christmas, Mother's Day), Poetry.

Nonfiction: The best way to sell work is by reading each issue cover to cover. Humor, interview/profile, features (timely, newsworthy, touching but with a *Grit* angle), readers' true stories, outdoor hobbies, collectibles, gardening, crafts, hobbies, leisure pastimes. Special issues: Gardening (January-October); Health (twice a year); Travel (spring and fall); Collectibles; Pet issue; Canning Contest (essays and entries); Christmas. Query by mail only. Length: Main features run 1,200-1,500 words. Department features average 800-1,000 words. **Pays up to 22¢/word for features; pays flat rate for departments.**

Photos: Send photos with submission. Professional quality photos (b&w prints or color slides) increase acceptability of articles. Pays $25-200 each in features according to quality, placement and color/b&w. Payment for department photos included in flat rate.

Fiction: Short stories, 1,500-2,000 words; may also purchase accompanying art if of high quality and appropriate. Need serials (romance, westerns, mysteries) 3,500-10,000 words. Send ms with SASE to Fiction Dept.

Tips: "Articles should be directed to a national audience, mostly 40 years and older. Sources identified fully. Our readers are warm and loving. They want to read about others with heart. Tell us stories about someone unusual, an unsung hero, an artist of the backroads, an interesting trip with an emotional twist, a memory with a message, an ordinary person accomplishing extraordinary things. Tell us stories that will make us cry with joy." Send complete ms with photos for consideration.

$ $ $ $  HOPE MAGAZINE, How to be Part of the Solution, Hope Publishing, Inc., P.O. Box 160, Brooklin ME 04616. (207)359-4651. Fax: (207)359-8920. E-mail: info@hopemag.com. Website: www.hopemag.com. Editor-in-chief/Publisher: Jon Wilson. Editor: Kimberly Ridley. Associate Editor: Amy Rawe. Assistant Editor: Lane Fisher. **Contact:** Catherine Princell, editorial assistant. **90% freelance written.** Quarterly magazine covering humanity at its best and worst. "*Hope* is a solutions-oriented journal focused on people addressing personal and societal challenges with uncommon courage and integrity. A magazine free of religious, political, or New Age affiliation, *Hope* awakens the impulse we all have—however hidden or distant—to make our world more liveable, humane, and genuinely loving. We strive to evoke empathy among readers." Estab. 1996. Circ. 22,000. Pays on publication. Publishes ms an average of 6 months after acceptance. Byline given. Offers 20% kill fee. Buys first, one-time, second serial (reprint) rights. Editorial lead time 4 months. Submit seasonal material 6 months in advance. Accepts queries by mail. Accepts simultaneous submissions. Responds in 6 months to queries. Sample copy for $5. Writer's guidelines for #10 SASE.

Nonfiction: Book excerpts, essays, general interest, interview/profile, personal experience, photo feature. Nothing explicitly religious, political or New Age. **Buys 50-75 mss/year.** Query with published clips or writing samples and SASE. Length: 250-4,000 words. **Pays $50-2,000.** Sometimes pays expenses of writers on assignment.

Photos: "We are very interested in and committed to the photo essay form, and enthusiastically encourage photographers and photojournalists to query us with ideas, or to submit images for thematic photo essays." State availability of or send photos with submission. Reviews contact sheets, 5×7 prints. Buys one-time rights. Negotiates payment individually. Captions, identification of subjects required.

Columns/Departments: Departments Editor. Signs of Hope (inspiring dispatches/news), 250-500 words; Aspirations (reports on individuals or groups in their teens—or younger—who are engaged in works worthy of our recognition), 1,000-1,500 words; Arts of Hope (reviews and discussions of music, art, and literature related to hope), 1,000-2,000 words; Book Reviews (devoted primarily to nonfiction works in widely diverse subject areas related to struggle and triumph), 500-800 words. **Buys 50-60 mss/year.** Query with published clips or send complete ms and SASE. **Pays $50-150.**

Tips: "Write very personally, and very deeply. We're not looking for shallow 'feel-good' pieces. Approach uncommon subjects. Cover the ordinary in extraordinary ways. Go to the heart. Surprise us. Many stories we receive are too 'soft.' Absolutely no phone queries."

$  LIVING, For the Whole Family, Shalom Publishers, 13241 Port Republic Rd., Grottoes VA 24441. E-mail: tgether@aol.com. **Contact:** Melodie M. Davis, editor. **90% freelance written.** Quarterly newspaper. "*Living* is a quarterly 'good news' paper published to encourage and strengthen family life at all stages, directed to the general newspaper-reading public." Estab. 1992. Circ. 250,000. Pays on publication. Publishes ms an average of 9 months after acceptance. Byline given. Buys one-time, second serial (reprint) rights. Editorial lead time 6 months. Submit seasonal material 6 months in advance. Accepts simultaneous submissions. Responds in 2 months to queries; 6 months to mss. Sample copy for 9×12 SAE and 4 first-class stamps. Writer's guidelines for #10 SASE or by e-mail.

Nonfiction: General interest, humor, inspirational, personal experience. **Buys 40-50 mss/year.** Send complete ms. Length: 300-1,000 words. **Pays $35-50.**

Photos: State availability of or send photos with submission. Reviews 3×5 or larger prints. Buys one-time rights. Offers $25/photo. Identification of subjects required.

Tips: "This paper is for a general audience in the community, but written from a Christian-value perspective. It seems to be difficult for some writers to understand our niche—*Living* is not a 'religious' periodical but handles an array of general interest family topics and mentioning Christian values or truths as appropriate. Writing is extremely competitive and we attempt to publish only high quality writing."

$ $ $ $ NATIONAL GEOGRAPHIC MAGAZINE, 1145 17th St. NW, Washington DC 20036. (202)775-7868. Fax: (202)857-7252. Website: www.nationalgeographic.com. Editor: William Allen. **Contact:** Oliver Payne, senior assistant editor, manuscripts. **60% freelance written.** Prefers to work with published/established writers. Monthly magazine for members of the National Geographic Society. "Timely articles written in a compelling, 'eyewitness' style. Arresting photographs that speak to us of the beauty, mystery, and harsh realities of life on earth. Maps of unprecedented detail and accuracy. These are the hallmarks of *National Geographic* magazine. Since 1888, the *Geographic* has been educating readers about the world." Estab. 1888. Circ. 7,800,000.

    ⊶ Before querying, study recent issues and check a *Geographic Index* at a library since the magazine seldom returns to regions or subjects covered within the past 10 years.

Nonfiction: Senior Assistant Editor Oliver Payne. *National Geographic* publishes general interest, illustrated articles on science, natural history, exploration, cultures and geographical regions. Of the freelance writers assigned, a few are experts in their fields; the remainder are established professionals. Fewer than 1% of unsolicited queries result in assignments. Query (500 words with clips of published articles by mail to Senior Assitant Editor Oliver Payne. Do not send mss. Length: 2,000-8,000 words. Pays expenses of writers on assignment.

Photos: Query in care of the Photographic Division.

■ The online magazine carries original content not found in the print edition. Contact: Valerie May, online editor.

Tips: "State the theme(s) clearly, let the narrative flow, and build the story around strong characters and a vivid sense of place. Give us rounded episodes, logically arranged."

N̲ **$ $ $ THE NEW YORK TIMES**, 229 W. 43rd St., New York NY 10036. (212)556-1234. Fax: (212)556-3830. *The New York Times Magazine* appears in *The New York Times* on Sunday. The *Arts and Leisure* section appears during the week. The *Op Ed* page appears daily.

Nonfiction: *Lives*: "Most articles are assigned but some unsolicited material is published, especially in the "Lives" column, a weekly personal-essay feature. Views should be fresh, lively and provocative on national and international news developments, science, education, family life, social trends and problems, arts and entertainment, personalitieis, sports and the changing American scne." Length: 900 words. **Pays $1,000.** Address unsolicited essays with SASE to the "Lives" editor. *Arts & Leisure*: Wants "to encourage imaginativeness in terms of form and approach—stressing ideas, issues, trends, investigations, symbolic reporting and stories delving deeply into the creative achievements and processes of artists and entertainers—and seeks to break away from old-fashioned gushy, fan magazine stuff." Length: 1,500-2,000 words. **Pays $100-350**, depending on length. Address unsolicited articles with SASE to the Arts & Leisure Articles Editor. *Op Ed* page: "The Op Ed page is always looking for new material and publishes many people who have never been published before. We want material of universal relevance which people can talk about in a personal way. When writing for the Op Ed page, there is no formula, but the writing itself should have some polish. Don't make the mistake of pontificating on the news. We're not looking for more political columnists." Length: 750 words. **Pays $150**.

N̲ THE NEW YORKER, The New Yorker, Inc., 4 Times Square, New York NY 10036. (212) 286-5900. Editor: David Remnick. Weekly magazine. A quality magazine of interesting, well-written stories, articles, essays and poems for a literate audience. Estab. 1925. Circ. 750,000. **Pays on acceptance.** Responds in 10-12 weeks to mss.

● David Kahn was named publisher January 18, 2001.

Fiction: Publishes 1 ms/issue. **Payment varies.**

Poetry: Send poetry to "Poetry Department."

Tips: "Be lively, original, not overly literary. Write what you want to write, not what you think the editor would like."

$ $ $ NEWSWEEK, 251 W. 57th St., New York NY 10019. (212)445-4000. **Contact:** Pam Hamer. "*Newsweek* is edited to report the week's developments on the newsfront of the world and the nation through news, commentary and analysis." Accepts unsolicited mss for *My Turn*, a column of personal opinion. The 850-900 word essays for the column must be original, not published elsewhere and contain verifiable facts. **Payment is $1,000 on publication.** Circ. 3,180,000. Buys non-exclusive world-wide rights. Responds in 2 months only on submissions with SASE to mss.

N̲ **$ $ $ THE OLD FARMER'S ALMANAC**, Yankee Publishing Inc., Main St., Dublin NH 03444. **Contact:** Janice Stillman, editor. **95% freelance written.** Annual magazine covering weather, gardening, history, oddities, lore. "*The Old Farmer's Almanac* is the oldest continuously published periodical in North America. Since 1792, it has provided useful information for people in all walks of life: Tide tables for those who live near the ocean; sunrise tables and planting charts for those who live on the farm or simply enjoy gardening; recipes for those who like to cook; and forecasts for those who don't like the question of weather left up in the air. The words of the Almanac's founder, Robert B. Thomas, guide us still. 'Our main endeavor is to be useful, but with a pleasant degree of humour.'" Estab. 1792. Circ. 3,000,000. **Pays on acceptance.** Publishes ms an average of 9 months after acceptance. Byline given. Offers 33% kill fee. Buys first North American serial, electronic, all rights. Editorial lead time 6 months. Submit seasonal material 1 year in advance. Accepts queries by mail. Responds in 3 weeks to queries; 2 months to mss. Sample copy for $5 at bookstores or online. Writer's guidelines online.

Nonfiction: General interest, historical/nostalgic, how-to (garden, cook, save money), humor, weather, natural remedies, obscure facts, history, popular culture. No personal weather recollections/accounts, personal/family histories. Query with published clips. Length: 800-2,500 words. **Pays 65¢/word.** Sometimes pays expenses of writers on assignment.

Fillers: Anecdotes, short humor. **Buys 1-2/year.** Length: 100-200 words. **Pays 50¢/word.**

◤◢ OPEN SPACES, Open Spaces Publications, Inc., PMB 134, 6327-C SW Capitol Hwy., Portland OR 97201-1937. (503)227-5764. Fax: (503)227-3401. E-mail: info@open-spaces.com. Website: www.open-spaces.com. President: Penny Harrison. Managing Editor: James Bradley. **Contact:** Elizabeth Arthur, editor. **95% freelance written.** Quarterly general interest magazine. "*Open Spaces* is a forum for informed writing and intelligent thought. Articles are written by experts in various fields. Audience is varied (CEOs and rock climbers, politicos and university presidents, etc.) but is highly educated and loves to read good writing." Estab. 1997. Pays on publication. Publishes ms an average of 6 months after acceptance. Byline given. Offers 20% kill fee. Rights purchased vary with author and material. Editorial lead time 9 months. Accepts queries by mail, fax. Accepts simultaneous submissions. Sample copy for $10 or online. Writer's guidelines for #10 SASE or online.

Nonfiction: Essays, general interest, historical/nostalgic, how-to (if clever), humor, interview/profile, personal experience, travel. **Buys 35 mss/year.** Query with published clips. Length: 1,500-2,500 words; major articles: 2,500-6,000 words. **Pays variable amount.**

Photos: State availability with submission. Buys one-time rights. Captions, identification of subjects required.

Columns/Departments: David Williams, departments editor. Books (substantial topics such as the Booker Prize, The Newbery, etc.); Travel (must reveal insight); Sports (past subjects include rowing, swing dancing and ultimate); Unintended Consequences, 1,500-2,500 words. **Buys 20-25 mss/year.** Query with published clips or send complete ms. **Pay varies.**

Fiction: Ellen Teicher, fiction editor. "Quality is far more important than type. Read the magazine." **Buys 8 mss/year.** Length: 2,000-6,000 words. **Pay varies.**

Poetry: "Again, quality is far more important than type." Susan Juve-Hu, poetry editor. Submit maximum 3 poems with SASE.

Fillers: Anecdotes, short humor, cartoons, interesting of amusing Northwest facts, expressions, etc.

Tips: "*Open Spaces* reviews all manuscripts submitted in hopes of finding writing of the highest quality. We present a Northwest perspective as well as a national and international one. Best advice is read the magazine."

$ $ $ THE OXFORD AMERICAN, The Southern Magazine of Good Writing, The Oxford American, Inc., P.O. Box 1156, Oxford MS 38655. (662)236-1836. Fax: (662)236-3141. E-mail: oxam@watervalley.net. Website: www.oxfordamericanmag.com. Editor: Marc Smirnoff. **Contact:** Editorial Staff. **50-65% freelance written.** Bimonthly magazine covering the South. "*The Oxford American* is a general-interest literary magazine about the South." Estab. 1992. Circ. 30,000. Pays on publication. Publishes ms an average of 6 months after acceptance. Byline given. Offers 25% kill fee. Buys first North American serial, one-time rights. Editorial lead time 2 months. Submit seasonal material 4 months in advance. Accepts queries by mail. Responds in 3 weeks to queries; 3 months to mss. Sample copy for $6.50. Writer's guidelines for #10 SASE.

O→ Break in with "a brief, focused query highlighting the unusual, fresh aspects to your pitch, and clips. All pitches must have some Southern connection."

Nonfiction: Essays, general interest, humor, interview/profile, personal experience, Reporting, Memoirs concerning the South. **Buys 6 mss/year.** Query with published clips or send complete ms. **Pay varies.** Sometimes pays expenses of writers on assignment.

Photos: Buys one-time rights. Negotiates payment individually. Captions required.

Columns/Departments: Send complete ms. **Pay varies.**

Fiction: Novel Excerpts, Short Stories. **Buys 10 mss/year.** Send complete ms. **Pay varies.**

Tips: "Like other editors, I stress the importance of being familiar with the magazine. Those submitters who know the magazine always send in better work because they know what we're looking for. To those who don't bother to at least flip through the magazine, let me point out we only publish articles with some sort of Southern connection."

$ $ $ $ PARADE, The Sunday Magazine, Parade Publications, Inc., 711 Third Ave., New York NY 10017. (212)450-7000. Fax: (212)450-7284. Website: www.parade.com. Editor: Walter Anderson. Managing Editor: Larry Smith. **Contact:** Paula Silverman, articles editor. **95% freelance written.** Weekly magazine for a general interest audience. Estab. 1941. Circ. 81,000,000. **Pays on acceptance.** Publishes ms an average of 5 months after acceptance. Kill fee varies in amount. Buys one-time, all rights. Editorial lead time 1 month. Accepts queries by mail, fax. Accepts simultaneous submissions. Sample copy online. Writer's guidelines free.

Nonfiction: General interest (on health, trends, social issues or anything of interest to a broad general audience); interview/profile (of news figures, celebrities and people of national significance); and "provocative topical pieces of news value." Spot news events are not accepted, as *Parade* has a 1 month lead time. No fiction, fashion, travel, poetry, cartoons, nostalgia, regular columns, quizzes or fillers. Unsolicited queries concerning celebrities, politicians, sports figures, or technical are rarely assigned. **Buys 150 mss/year.** Query with published clips. Length: 1,000-1,200 words. **Pays $2,500 minimum.** Pays expenses of writers on assignment.

Tips: "Send a well-researched, well-written one-page proposal and enclose a SASE. Do not submit completed manuscripts."

$ ▨ RANDOM LENGTHS, Harbor Independent News, P.O. Box 731, San Pedro CA 90733-0731. (310)519-1016. Editor: James Elmendorf. **30% freelance written.** Biweekly tabloid covering alternative news/features. "*Random Lengths* follows Twain's dictum of printing news 'to make people mad enough to do something about it.' Our writers do exposés, scientific, environmental, political reporting and fun, goofy, insightful, arts and entertainment coverage, for a lefty, labor-oriented, youngish crowd." Estab. 1979. Circ. 30,000. Pays in 60 days. Byline given. Offers 50% kill fee. Buys all rights. Editorial lead time 1 month. Submit seasonal material 2 months in advance. Accepts simultaneous submissions. Responds in 6 weeks to queries. Sample copy for 9 × 13 SAE and 3 first-class stamps. Writer's guidelines free.

Nonfiction: Exposé, general interest, historical/nostalgic, interview/profile, opinion. Special issues: Labor Day, triannual book edition; women and black history months. **Buys 150 mss/year.** Query. Length: 300-2,000 words. **Pays 5¢/word.** Sometimes pays expenses of writers on assignment.

Photos: State availability with submission. Reviews prints. Buys all rights. Offers $10/photo. Captions, identification of subjects required.

Columns/Departments: Community News (local angle), 300-600 words; Commentary (national/world/opinion), 600-800 words; Feature (books/music/local events), 300-600 words. **Buys 75 mss/year.** Query. **Pays 5¢/word.**

Tips: "We use mostly local material and local writers, but we are open to current-event, boffo entertaining writing. Read other alternative weeklies for reference. We need local news most. Next, entertainment stuff with a local pitch."

$ $ $ $ READER'S DIGEST, Reader's Digest Rd., Pleasantville NY 10570-7000. Website: www.readersdigest. com. **Contact:** Editorial Correspondence. Monthly general interest magazine. "We are looking for contemporary stories of lasting interest that give the magazine variety, freshness and originality." Estab. 1922. Circ. 13,000,000. **Pays on acceptance.** Byline given. Buys exclusive world periodical and electronic rights, among others. Editorial lead time 3 months. Submit seasonal material 6 months in advance. Accepts queries by mail.

Nonfiction: Book excerpts, essays, exposé, general interest, historical/nostalgic, humor, inspirational, interview/profile, opinion, personal experience. Does not read or return unsolicited mss. **Buys 100 mss/year.** Query with published clips. Address article queries and tearsheets of published articles to the editors. Length: 1,000-2,500 words. **Original article rates generally begin at $5,000.**

Reprints: Send tearsheet or photocopy with rights for sale noted and information about when and where the material previously appeared. **Pays $1,200**/*Reader's Digest* page for World Digest rights (usually split 50/50 between original publisher and writer).

Columns/Departments: "Life's Like That contributions must be true, unpublished stories from one's own experience, revealing adult human nature, and providing appealing or humorous sidelights on the American scene. Length: 300 words maximum. **Pays $400** on publication. True, unpublished stories are also solicited for Humor in Uniform, Campus Comedy, Virtual Hilarity and All in a Day's Work. Length: 300 words maximum. **Pays $400** on publication. Towards More Picturesque Speech—the *first* contributor of each item used in this department is paid $50 for original material, $35 for reprints. For items used in Laughter, the Best Medicine, Personal Glimpses, Quotable Quotes, Notes From All Over, Points to Ponder and elsewhere in the magazine payment is as follows; to the *first* contributor of each from a published source, **$35 for original material, $30**/*Reader's Digest* two-column line." Original contributions become the property of *Reader's Digest* upon acceptance and payment. Previously published material must have source's name, date and page number. Contributions cannot be acknowledged or returned. Send complete anecdotes to *Reader's Digest*, Box 100, Pleasantville NY 10572-0100, fax to (914)238-6390 or e-mail laughlines@readersdigest.com.

Tips: "Roughly half the 20-odd articles we publish every month are reprinted from magazines, newspapers, books and other sources. The remaining 10 or so articles are original—most of them assigned, some submitted on speculation. While many of these are written by regular contributors, we're always looking for new talent and for offbeat subjects that help give our magazine variety, freshness and originality. Above all, in the writing we publish, *The Digest* demands accuracy—down to the smallest detail. Our worldwide team of 60 researchers scrutinizes every line of type, checking every fact and examining every opinion. For an average issue, they will check some 3500 facts with 1300 sources. So watch your accuracy. There's nothing worse than having an article fall apart in our research checking because an author was a little careless with his reporting. We make this commitment routinely, as it guarantees that the millions of readers who believe something simply because they saw it in *Reader's Digest* have not misplaced their trust."

$ $ $ $ READER'S DIGEST (CANADA), 1100 René-Lévesque Blvd. W., Montreal, Quebec H3B 5H5, Canada. (514)940-0751. Website: www.readersdigest.ca. Editor-in-Chief: Murray Lewis. **Contact:** Ron Starr, senior associate editor. **10-25% freelance written.** Monthly magazine of general interest articles and subjects. Estab. 1948. Circ. 1,300,000. **Pays on acceptance for original works.** Pays on publication for "pickups." Byline given. Offers $500 (Canadian) kill fee. Buys one-time rights (for reprints), all rights (for original articles). Submit seasonal material 5 months in advance. Accepts queries by mail, e-mail. Responds in 5 weeks to queries. Writer's guidelines for #10 SASE with Canadian postage or #10 SAE with 1 IRC.

Nonfiction: Senior Associate Editor: Ron Starr. "We're looking for true stories that depend on emotion and reveal the power of our relationships to help us overcome adversity; also for true first-person accounts of an event that changed a life for the better or led to new insight. No fiction, poetry or articles too specialized, technical or esoteric—read *Reader's Digest* to see what kind of articles we want." General interest, how-to (general interest), inspirational, personal experience. Query with published clips. Length: 3,000-5,000 words. **Pays minimum of $2,700.** Pays expenses of writers on assignment.

Reprints: Send previously published material to Peter Des Lauriers, senior associate editor. Payment is negotiable.

Photos: State availability with submission.

▣ The online magazine carries original content not found in the print edition. Contact: Peter Des Lauriers.

Tips: "*Reader's Digest* usually finds its freelance writers through other well-known publications in which they have previously been published. There are guidelines available and writers should read *Reader's Digest* to see what kind of stories we look for and how they are written. We do not accept unsolicited manuscripts."

$ READERS REVIEW, The National Research Bureau, Inc., 320 Valley St., Burlington IA 52601. (319)752-5415. Fax: (319)752-3421. **Contact:** Nancy Heinzel, editor. **75% freelance written.** The *Readers Review* works with a small number of new/unpublished writers each year, and is eager to work with new/unpublished writers. Quarterly magazine. Estab. 1948. Pays on publication. Publishes ms an average of 1 year after acceptance. Buys all rights. Submit seasonal material 7 months in advance. Sample copy and writer's guidelines for #10 SAE with 2 first-class stamps.

Nonfiction: General interest (steps to better health, attitudes on the job), how-to (perform better on the job, do home repairs, car maintenance), travel. **Buys 10-12 mss/year.** Query with outline or submit complete ms. Length: 500-700 words. **Pays 4¢/word.**

Tips: "Writers have a better chance of breaking in our publication with short articles."

$ ✠ REUNIONS MAGAZINE, P.O. Box 11727, Milwaukee WI 53211-0727. (414)263-4567. Fax: (414)263-6331. E-mail: reunions@execpc.com. Website: www.reunionsmag.com. **Contact:** Edith Wagner, editor. **75% freelance written.** Quarterly magazine covering reunions—all aspects, all types. "*Reunions Magazine* is primarily for people actively involved with family, class, military and other reunions. We want easy, practical ideas about organizing, planning, researching/searching, attending or promoting reunions." Estab. 1990. Circ. 18,000. Pays on publication. Publishes ms an average of 1 year after acceptance. Byline given. Buys one-time rights. Editorial lead time 6 months. Submit seasonal material 1 year in advance. Accepts queries by mail, e-mail, fax. Responds in 1 year. Sample copy free or online. Writer's guidelines for #10 SASE or online.

  O━ Break in "by providing an exciting, instructional article about reunions."

Nonfiction: "We can never get enough about activities at reunions, particularly family reunions with multigenerational activities. We would also like more reunion food-related material." Needs reviewers for books, videos, software (include your requirements). Historical/nostalgic, how-to, humor, interview/profile, new product, personal experience, photo feature, travel (all must be reunion-related). Special issues: Ethnic/African-American family reunions (Winter); food, kids stuff, theme parks, small venues (bed & breakfasts, dormitories, condos) (Summer); golf, travel and gaming features (Autumn); themes, cruises, ranch reunions and reunions in various sections of the US (Spring). **Buys 25 mss/year.** Query with published clips. Length: 500-2,500 words. **Pays $25.** Often rewards with generous copies.

Reprints: Send tearsheet, photocopy or typed ms with rights for sale noted and information about when and where the material previously appeared. **Usually pays $10.**

Photos: Always looking for vertical cover photos that scream: "Reunion!" State availability with submission. Reviews contact sheets, negatives, 35mm transparencies, prints. Buys one-time rights. Offers no additional payment for photos accepted with ms. Captions, identification of subjects, model releases required.

Fillers: Must be reunion-related. Anecdotes, facts, short humor. **Buys 20/year.** Length: 50-250 words. **Pays $5.**

  ▣ The online magazine carries original content not found in the print edition and includes writer's guidelines and articles. Contact: Edith Wagner, online editor.

Tips: "All copy must be reunion-related with strong reunion examples and experiences. Write a lively account of an interesting or unusual reunion, either upcoming or soon after while it's hot. Tell readers why reunion is special, what went into planning it and how attendees reacted. Our *Masterplan* section is a great place for a freelancer to start. Send us how-tos or tips on any aspect of reunion organizing. Open your minds to different types of reunions—they're all around!"

$ $ THE SATURDAY EVENING POST, The Saturday Evening Post Society, 1100 Waterway Blvd., Indianapolis IN 46202. (317)636-8881. Fax: (317)637-0126. E-mail: satevepst@aol.com. Website: www.satevepost.org. Travel Editor: Holly Miller. **Contact:** Patrick Perry, managing editor. **30% freelance written.** Bimonthly general interest, family-oriented magazine focusing on physical fitness, preventive medicine. "Ask almost any American if he or she has heard of *The Saturday Evening Post*, and you will find that many have fond recollections of the magazine from their childhood days. Many readers recall sitting with their families on Saturdays awaiting delivery of their *Post* subscription in the mail. *The Saturday Evening Post* has forged a tradition of 'forefront journalism.' *The Saturday Evening Post* continues to stand at the journalistic forefront with its coverage of health, nutrition, and preventive medicine." Estab. 1728. Circ. 400,000. Pays on publication. Publishes ms an average of 3 months after acceptance. Byline given. Buys second serial (reprint), all rights. Submit seasonal material 4 months in advance. Accepts queries by mail, fax. Accepts simultaneous submissions. Responds in 1 month to queries; 6 weeks to mss. Writer's guidelines for #10 SASE or online.

Nonfiction: Book excerpts, how-to (gardening, home improvement), humor, interview/profile, travel, medical, health, fitness. "No political articles or articles containing sexual innuendo or hypersophistication." **Buys 25 mss/year.** Query with or without published clips or send complete ms. Length: 750-2,500 words. **Pays $150 minumum, negotiable maximum.** Sometimes pays expenses of writers on assignment.

Photos: State availability with submission. Reviews negatives, transparencies. Buys one-time or all rights. Offers $50 minimum, negotiable maximum per photo. Identification of subjects, model releases required.

Columns/Departments: Travel (destinations); Post Scripts (well-known humorists); Post People (activities of celebrities). Length 750-1,500. **Buys 16 mss/year.** Query with published clips or send complete ms. **Pays $150 minimum, negotiable maximum.**

Poetry: Light verse.

Fillers: Post Scripts Editor: Steve Pettinga. Anecdotes, short humor. **Buys 200/year.** Length: 300 words. **Pays $15.**

Tips: "Areas most open to freelancers are Health, Fitness, Research Breakthroughs, Nutrition, Post Scripts and Travel. For travel we like text-photo packages, pragmatic tips, side bars and safe rather than exotic destinations. Query by mail, not phone. Send clips."

$ $ $ $ SMITHSONIAN MAGAZINE, MRC 951, Washington DC 20560-0951. (202)275-2000. E-mail: articles@simag.si.edu. Website: www.smithsonianmag.si.edu. **Contact:** Marlane A. Liddell, articles editor. **90% freelance written.** Monthly magazine for associate members of the Smithsonian Institution; 85% with college education. "*Smithsonian Magazine's* mission is to inspire fascination with all the world has to offer by featuring unexpected and entertaining editorial that explores different lifestyles, cultures and peoples, the arts, the wonders of nature and technology and much more. The highly educated, innovative readers of *Smithsonian* share a unique desire to celebrate life, seeking out the timely as well as timeless, the artistic as well as the academic and the thought-provoking as well as the humorous." Circ. 2,300,000. **Pays on acceptance.** Publishes ms an average of 6 months after acceptance. Offers 33% kill fee. Buys first North American serial rights. Editorial lead time 2 months. Submit seasonal material 3 months in advance. Responds in 2 months to queries. Sample copy for $5, c/o Judy Smith. Writer's guidelines for #10 SASE or online.

> ⊙━ "We consider focused subjects that fall within the general range of Smithsonian Institution interests, such as: cultural history, physical science, art and natural history. We are always looking for offbeat subjects and profiles. We do not consider fiction, poetry, political and news events, or previously published articles. We publish only twelve issues a year, so it is difficult to place an article in *Smithsonian*, but please be assured that all proposals are considered."

Nonfiction: "Our mandate from the Smithsonian Institution says we are to be interested in the same things which now interest or should interest the Institution: Cultural and fine arts, history, natural sciences, hard sciences, etc." **Buys 120-130 features (up to 5,000 words) and 12 short pieces (500-650 words)/year.** Query with published clips. **Pays various rates per feature, $1,500 per short piece.** Pays expenses of writers on assignment.

Photos: Purchased with or without ms and on assignment. "Illustrations are not the responsibility of authors, but if you do have photographs or illustration materials, please include a selection of them with your submission. In general, 35mm color transparencies or black-and-white prints are perfectly acceptable. Photographs published in the magazine are usually obtained through assignment, stock agencies, or specialized sources. No photo library is maintained and photographs should be submitted only to accompany a specific article proposal." Send photos with submission. Pays $400/full color page. Captions required.

Columns/Departments: Back Page humor, 500-650 words. Buys 12-15 department articles/year. Length: 1,000-2,000 words. **Pays $1,000.**

Tips: "We prefer a written proposal of one or two pages as a preliminary query. The proposal should convince us that we should cover the subject, offer descriptive information on how you, the writer, would treat the subject and offer us an opportunity to judge your writing ability. Background information and writing credentials and samples are helpful. All unsolicited proposals are sent to us on speculation and you should receive a reply within eight weeks. Please include a self-addressed stamped envelope. We also accept proposals via electronic mail at articles@simag.si.edu. If we decide to commission an article, the writer receives full payment on acceptance of the manuscript. If the article is found unsuitable, one-third of the payment serves as a kill fee."

$ $ $ ⊠ THE SUN, A Magazine of Ideas, The Sun Publishing Company, 107 N. Roberson St., Chapel Hill NC 27516. (919)942-5282. Website: www.thesunmagazine.org. **Contact:** Sy Safransky, editor. **90% freelance written.** Monthly magazine. "We are open to all kinds of writing, though we favor work of a personal nature." Estab. 1974. Circ. 50,000. Pays on publication. Publishes ms an average of 6 months after acceptance. Byline given. Buys first, one-time rights. Accepts queries by mail. Responds in 1 month to queries; 3 months to mss. Sample copy for $5. Writer's guidelines for SASE or online.

Nonfiction: Book excerpts, essays, general interest, interview/profile, opinion, personal experience, spiritual. **Buys 60 mss/year.** Send complete ms. Length: 7,000 words maximum. **Pays $300-1,000.** "Complimentary subscription is given in addition to payment (applies to payment for *all* works, not just nonfiction)."

Reprints: Send photocopy and information about when and where the material previously appeared. Pays 50% of amount paid for original article or story.

Photos: Send photos with submission. Reviews b&w prints. Buys one-time rights. Offers $50-200/photo. Model releases required.

Fiction: "We avoid stereotypical genre pieces like sci-fi, romance, western and horror. Read an issue before submitting." Literary. **Buys 24 mss/year.** Send complete ms. Length: 7,000 words maximum. **Pays $300-500.**

Poetry: Free verse, prose poems, short and long poems. **Buys 24 poems/year.** Submit maximum 6 poems. **Pays $50-200.**

TIME, Time Inc. Magazine, Time & Life Bldg., 1271 Avenue of the Americas, New York NY 10020. (212)522-1212. Fax: (212)522-0323. **Contact:** Jim Kelly, managing editor. Weekly magazine. "*Time* covers the full range of information that is important to people today—breaking news, national and world affairs, business news, societal and lifestyle issues, culture and entertainment news and reviews." Query before submitting. Estab. 1923. Circ. 4,150,000.

$ $ $ TOWN & COUNTRY, The Hearst Corp., 1700 Broadway, New York NY 10019. (212)903-5000. Fax: (212)262-7107. **Contact:** John Cantrell, deputy editor. **40% freelance written.** Monthly lifestyle magazine. "*Town & Country* is a lifestyle magazine for the affluent market. Features focus on fashion, beauty, travel, interior design, and the arts, as well as individuals' accomplishments and contributions to society." Estab. 1846. Circ. 488,000. **Pays on acceptance.** Byline given. Offers 25% kill fee. Buys first North American serial, electronic rights. Responds in 1 month to queries.

Nonfiction: "We're looking for engaging service articles for a high income, well-educated audience, in numerous categories: Travel, personalities, interior design, fashion, beauty, jewelry, health, city news, country life news, the arts, philanthropy." General interest, travel. **Buys 25 mss/year.** Query by mail only with clips before submitting. Length: Column items, 100-300 words; feature stories, 800-2,000 words. **Pays $2/word.**

Tips: "We have served the affluent market for over 150 years, and our writers need to be expert in the needs and interests of that market. Most of our freelance writers start by doing short pieces for our front-of-book columns, then progress from there."

$ $ $☒ TROIKA, Wit, Wisdom & Wherewithal, Lone Tout Publications, Inc., P.O. Box 1006, Weston CT 06883. (203)319-0873. Fax: (203)319-0755. E-mail: submit@troikamagazine.com. Website: www.troikamagazine.com. **Contact:** Celia Meadow, editor. **95% freelance written.** Quarterly magazine covering general interest, lifestyle. "A magazine for men and women seeking a balanced, three-dimensional lifestyle: Personal achievement, family commitment, community involvement. Readers are upscale, educated, 30-50 age bracket. The *Troika* generation is a mix of what is called the X generation and the baby boomers. We are that generation. We grew up with sex, drugs and rock 'n roll, but now it really is our turn to make a difference, if we so choose." Estab. 1993. Circ. 120,000. Pays 90 days from publication. Publishes ms an average of 6 months after acceptance. Byline given. Buys first North American serial rights, Internet rights. Editorial lead time 3 months. Submit seasonal material 6 months in advance. Accepts queries by mail, e-mail. Accepts simultaneous submissions. Responds in 2 months to mss. Sample copy for $5 or online. Writer's guidelines for #10 SASE or online.
Nonfiction: Essays, exposé, general interest, how-to (leisure activities, pro bono finance), humor, inspirational, interview/profile (music related), personal experience, international affairs, environment, parenting, cultural, celebrity profiles. **Buys 1,000 mss/year.** Query with or without published clips or send complete ms. Length: 800-3,000 words. **Pays $200-1,000 for assigned articles.**
Reprints: Send photocopy and information about when and where the material previously appeared.
Photos: State availability with submission. Reviews negatives, transparencies. Offers no additional payment for photos accepted with ms. Captions, identification of subjects, model releases required.
Columns/Departments: Literati; Pub Performances (literary, theater, arts, culture); Blueprints (architecture, interior design, fashion); Body of Facts (science); Hippocratic Horizons (health); Home Technology; Capital Commitments (personal finance); Athletics; Leisure; Mondiale (international affairs); all 750-1,200 words. **Buys 100 mss/year.** Query with or without published clips or send complete ms. **Pays $200 maximum.**
Fiction: Adventure,confessions, historical, mainstream, mystery, novel excerpts, slice-of-life vignettes, suspense, contemporary. **Buys 100 mss/year.** Send complete ms. Length: 3,000 words maximum. **Pays $200 maximum.**
   ◼ The online magazine carries original content not found in the print edition and includes writer's guidelines.

$ $☒ THE WORLD & I, The Magazine for Lifelong Learners, News World Communications, Inc., 3600 New York Ave. NE, Washington DC 20002. (202)635-4000. Fax: (202)269-9353. E-mail: editor@worldandimag.com. Website: www.worldandi.com. Editor: Morton A. Kaplan. Executive Editor: Michael Marshall. **Contact:** Gary Rowe, editorial office manager. **90% freelance written.** Monthly magazine. "A broad interest magazine for the thinking, educated person." Estab. 1986. Circ. 30,000. Pays on publication. Publishes ms an average of 6 months after acceptance. Byline given. Offers 20% kill fee. Submit seasonal material 5 months in advance. Accepts queries by mail. Responds in 6 weeks to queries; 10 weeks to mss. Sample copy for $5 and 9×12 SASE. Writer's guidelines for #10 SASE.
Nonfiction: "Description of Sections: Current Issues: Politics, economics and strategic trends covered in a variety of approaches, including special report, analysis, commentary and photo essay. The Arts: International coverage of music, dance, theater, film, television, craft, design, architecture, photography, poetry, painting and sculpture—through reviews, features, essays, opinion pieces and a 6-page Gallery of full-color reproductions. Life: Surveys all aspects of life in 22 rotating subsections which include: Travel and Adventure (first person reflections, preference given to authors who provide photographic images), Profile (people or organizations that are 'making a difference'), Food and Garden (must be accompanied by photos), Education, Humor, Hobby, Family, Consumer, Trends, and Health. Send SASE for complete list of subsections. Natural Science: Covers the latest in science and technology, relating it to the social and historical context, under these headings: At the Edge, Impacts, Nature Walk, Science and Spirit, Science and Values, Scientists: Past and Present, Crucibles of Science and Science Essay. Book World: Excerpts from important, timely books (followed by commentaries) and 10-12 scholarly reviews of significant new books each month, including untranslated works from abroad. Covers current affairs, intellectual issues, contemporary fiction, history, moral/religious issues and the social sciences. Currents in Modern Thought: Examines scholarly research and theoretical debate across the wide range of disciplines in the humanities and social sciences. Featured themes are explored by several contributors. Investigates theoretical issues raised by certain current events, and offers contemporary reflection on issues drawn from the whole history of human thought. Culture: Surveys the world's people in these subsections: Peoples (their unique characteristics and cultural symbols), Crossroads (changes brought by the meeting of cultures), Patterns (photo essay depicting the daily life of a distinct culture), Folk Wisdom (folklore and practical wisdom and their present forms), and Heritage (multicultural backgrounds of the American people and how they are bound to the whole). Photo Essay: Patterns, a 6- or 8-page photo essay, appears monthly in the Culture section. Emphasis is placed on comprehensive photographic coverage of a people or group, their private or public lifestyle, in a given situation or context. Accompanying word count: 300-500 words. Photos must be from existing stock, no travel subsidy. Life & Ideals, a 6- or 8-page photo essay, occasionally appears in the Life section. First priority is given to those focused on individuals or organizations that are 'making a difference.' Accompanying word count: 700-1,000 words." No *National Enquirer*-type articles. **Buys 1,200 mss/year.** Query with published clips. Length: 1,000-5,000 words. **Pays per article basis for assigned articles.** Seldom pays expenses of writers on assignment.
Reprints: Send typed ms with rights for sale noted and information about when and where the material previously appeared.

Photos: State availability with submission. Reviews contact sheets, transparencies, prints. Buys one-time rights. Payment negotiable. Identification of subjects, model releases required.
Fiction: Novel excerpts.
Poetry: Arts Editor. Avant-garde, free verse, haiku, light verse, traditional. **Buys 4-6 poems/year.** Submit maximum 5 poems. **Pays $30-75.**
Tips: "We accept articles from journalists, but also place special emphasis on scholarly contributions. It is our hope that the magazine will enable the best of contemporary thought, presented in accessible language, to reach a wider audience than would normally be possible through the academic journals appropriate to any given discipline."

HEALTH & FITNESS

The magazines listed here specialize in covering health and fitness topics for a general audience. Health and fitness magazines have experienced a real boom lately. Most emphasize developing healthy lifestyle choices in exercise, nutrition and general fitness. Many magazines offer alternative healing and therapies that are becoming more mainstream, such as medicinal herbs, health foods and a holistic mind/body approach to well-being. As wellness is a concern to all demographic groups, publishers have developed editorial geared to specific audiences: African-American women, older readers, men, women. Also see the Sports/Miscellaneous section where publications dealing with health and particular sports may be listed. For magazines that cover healthy eating, refer to the Food & Drink section. Many general interest publications are also potential markets for health or fitness articles. ring health topics from a medical perspective are listed in the Medical category of Trade.

$ $Ⅺ AMERICAN FITNESS, 15250 Ventura Blvd., Suite 200, Sherman Oaks CA 91403. (818)905-0040. Fax: (818)990-5468. Website: www.afaa.com. Publisher: Roscoe Fawcett. **Contact:** Ruzibel Guzman, senior editor. **75% freelance written.** Bimonthly magazine covering exercise and fitness, health and nutrition. "We need timely, in-depth, informative articles on health, fitness, aerobic exercise, sports nutrition, age-specific fitness and outdoor activity." Circ. 42,000. Pays 6 weeks after publication. Publishes ms an average of 6 months after acceptance. Byline given. Submit seasonal material 4 months in advance. Accepts queries by mail, fax. Accepts simultaneous submissions. Responds in 6 weeks to queries. Sample copy for $3 and SAE with 6 first-class stamps.
Nonfiction: Needs include health and fitness, including women's issues (pregnancey, family, pre- and post-natal, menopause and eating disorders); New research findings on exercise techniques and equipment; Aerobic exercise; Sports nutrition; Sports medicine; Innovations and trends in aerobic sports; Tips on teaching exercise and humorous accounts of fitness motivation; Physiology; Youth and senior fitness. Historical/nostalgic (history of various athletic events), inspirational, interview/profile (fitness figures), new product (plus equipment review), personal experience (successful fitness story), photo feature (on exercise, fitness, new sport), travel (activity adventures). No articles on unsound nutritional practices, popular trends or unsafe exercise gimmicks. **Buys 18-25 mss/year.** Query with published clips or send complete ms. Length: 800-1,200 words. **Pays $200 for features, $80 for news.** Sometimes pays expenses of writers on assignment.
Photos: Sports, action, fitness, aquatic aerobics competitions and exercise class. "We are especially interested in photos of high-adrenalin sports like rock climbing and mountain biking." Reviews transparencies, prints. Usually buys all rights; other rights purchased depend on use of photo. Pays $0 for b&w prints; $35 for transparencies. Captions, identification of subjects, model releases required.
Columns/Departments: Research (latest exercise and fitness findings); Alternative paths (non-mainstream approaches to health, wellness and fitness); Strength (latest breakthroughs in weight training); Clubscene (profiles and highlights of fitness club industry); Adventure (treks, trails and global challenges); Food (low-fat/non-fat, high-flavor dishes); Homescene (home workout alternatives); Clip 'n' Post (concise exercise research to post in health clubs, offices or on refrigerators). Length: 800-1,000 words. Query with published clips or send complete ms. **Pays $100-140.**
Tips: "Make sure to quote scientific literature or good research studies and several experts with good credentials to validate exercise trend, technique, or issue. Cover a unique aerobics or fitness angle, provide accurate and interesting findings, and write in a lively, intelligent manner. Please, no first person accouts of 'how I lost weight or discovered running.' *AF* is a good place for first-time authors or regularly published authors who want to sell spin-offs or reprints."

Ⓝ $ $ $AMERICAN HEALTH & FITNESS, CANUSA Publishing, 5775 McLaughlin Rd., Mississauga, Ontario L5R 3P7, Canada. Fax: (905)678-7311. Website: www.ahfmag.com. Publisher: Robert Kennedy. **Contact:** Kerrie-Lee Brown, editor. **85% freelance written.** Bimonthly magazine. "*American Health & Fitness* is designed to help male fitness buffs (18-39) to keep fit, strong, virile and healthy through sensible diet and exercise." Estab. 2000. Circ. 350,000. **Pays on acceptance.** Publishes ms an average of 4 months after acceptance. Byline given. Offers $500 kill fee. Buys all rights. Editorial lead time 4 months. Submit seasonal material 5 months in advance. Accepts queries by mail, fax. Responds in 1 month to queries; 6 months to mss. Sample copy for $5.

Nonfiction: Exposé, general interest, how-to, humor, inspirational, interview/profile, new product, personal experience, photo feature. **Buys 80-100 mss/year.** Send complete ms. Length: 1,400-2,000 words. **Pays $350-1,500 for assigned articles; $350-1,000 for unsolicited articles.** Sometimes pays expenses of writers on assignment.

Photos: Send photos with submission. Reviews 35mm transparencies. Buys all rights. Offers $50-1,000/photo. Captions, identification of subjects required.

Columns/Departments: Chiropractic; Personal Training; Strength & Conditioning; Dental; Longevity; Natural Health. **Buys 40 mss/year.** Send complete ms. **Pays $100-1,000.**

Fillers: Anecdotes, facts, gags to be illustrated by cartoonist, newsbreaks, short humor. **Buys 50-100/year.** Length: 100-200 words. **Pays $50-100.**

$ $ BETTER HEALTH, Better Health Magazine, 1450 Chapel St., New Haven CT 06511-4440. (203)789-3972. Fax: (203)789-4053. **Contact:** Cynthia Wolfe Boynton, editor/publishing director. **90% freelance written.** Prefers to work with published/established writers; will consider new/unpublished writers. Query first, do not send article. Bimonthly magazine devoted to health, wellness and medical issues. Estab. 1979. Circ. 500,000. **Pays on acceptance.** Byline given. Offers 20% kill fee. Buys first rights. Sample copy for $2.50. Writer's guidelines for #10 SASE.

Nonfiction: Wellness/prevention issues are of primary interest. New medical techniques or nonmainstream practices are not considered. No fillers, poems, quizzes, seasonal, heavy humor, inspirational or personal experience. Length: 1,500-3,000 words. **Pays $300-700.**

$ $ DELICIOUS LIVING!, Feel Good/Live Well, (formerly *Delicious!, Your Magazine of Natural Living*), New Hope Natural Media, 1401 Pearl St., Suite 200, Boulder CO 80302. E-mail: delicious@newhope.com. Website: www.healthwell.com. Editorial Director: Karen Raterman. **Contact:** Lara Evans, managing editor. **85% freelance written.** Monthly magazine covering natural products, nutrition, alternative medicines, herbal medicines. "*Delicious Living!* magazine empowers natural foods store shoppers to make health-conscious choices in their lives. Our goal is to improve consumers' perception of the value of natural methods in achieving health. To do this, we educate consumers on nutrition, disease prevention, botanical medicines and natural personal care products." Estab. 1985. Circ. 420,000. **Pays on acceptance.** Publishes ms an average of 6 months after acceptance. Byline given. Offers 20% kill fee. Editorial lead time 6 months. Submit seasonal material 8 months in advance. Accepts simultaneous submissions. Responds in 3 months to queries. Sample copy and writer's guidelines free.

Nonfiction: Book excerpts, how-to, interview/profile, personal experience (regarding natural or alternative health), health nutrition, herbal medicines, alternative medicine, environmental. **Buys 150 mss/year.** Query with published clips. Length: 500-2,000 words. **Pays $100-700 for assigned articles; $50-300 for unsolicited articles.**

Photos: State availability with submission. Reviews 3×5 prints. Buys one-time rights. Offers no additional payment for photos accepted with ms. Identification of subjects required.

Columns/Departments: Herbs (scientific evidence supporting herbal medicines), 1,500 words; Nutrition (new research on diet for good health), 1,200 words; Dietary Supplements (new research on vitamins/minerals, etc.), 1,200 words. Query with published clips. **Pays $100-500.**

■ The online magazine carries original content not found in the print edition. Contact: Kim Stewart, online editor.

Tips: "Highlight any previous health/nutrition/medical writing experience. Demonstrate a knowledge of natural medicine, nutrition, or natural products. Health practitioners who demonstrate writing ability are ideal freelancers."

$ $ FIT, Goodman Media Group, Inc., 1700 Broadway, 34th Floor, New York NY 10019. (212)541-7100. Fax: (212)245-1241. **Contact:** Rita Trieger, editor. **50% freelance written.** Works with a small number of new/unpublished writers each year. Bimonthly magazine covering fitness and health for active, young women. Circ. 125,000. Pays on publication. Publishes ms an average of 5 months after acceptance. Byline given. Offers 20% kill fee. Buys all rights. Submit seasonal material 6 months in advance. Accepts queries by mail, e-mail. Responds in 1 month if rejecting ms, longer if considering for publication.

O─ Break in by sending writing samples (preferably published) and a long list of queries/article ideas. The magazine reports it is looking for first-person accounts of new and interesting sports, adventures, etc.

Nonfiction: "We get many queries on how to treat/handle many physical and mental ailments—we wouldn't do an entire article on an illness that only 5% or less of the population suffers from." Health, Fitness, Sports, Beauty, Psychology, Relationships, Athletes, Nutrition. **Buys 20 mss/year.** Query with published clips. No phone queries. Length: 1,000-1,500 words.

Photos: Reviews contact sheets, transparencies, prints. Buys all rights. Identification of subjects, model releases required.

Columns/Departments: Finally Fit Contest. Readers can submit "before and after" success stories along with color slides or photos.

Tips: "We strive to provide the latest health and fitness news in an entertaining way—that means coverage of real people (athletes, regular women, etc.) and/or events (fitness shows, marathons, etc.), combined with factual information. First-person is okay. Looking for stories that are fun to read, revealing, motivational and informative."

$ $ $ $ FITNESS MAGAZINE, 375 Lexington Ave., New York NY 10017-5514. (212)499-2000. Fax: (212)499-1568. **Contact:** Liz Vaccariello, executive editor. Monthly magazine for women in their twenties and thirties who are interested in fitness and living a healthy life. "Do not call." **Pays on acceptance.** Byline given. Offers 20% kill fee. Buys first North American serial rights. Responds in 2 months to queries. Writer's guidelines for #10 SASE.

Nonfiction: "We need timely, well-written nonfiction articles on exercise and fitness, beauty, health, diet/nutrition, and psychology. We always include boxes and sidebars in our stories." **Buys 60-80 mss/year.** Query. Length: 1,500-2,500 words. **Pays $1,500-2,500.** Pays expenses of writers on assignment.
Reprints: Send photocopy. Negotiates fee.
Columns/Departments: Length:600-1,200 words. **Buys 30 mss/year.** Query. **Pays $800-1,500.**
Tips: "Our pieces must get inside the mind of the reader and address her needs, hopes, fears and desires. *Fitness* acknowledges that getting and staying fit is difficult in an era when we are all time-pressured."

$ $◨ ▣ FITNESSLINK, FitnessLink Inc., 53 Buttermilk Bridge Rd., Washington NJ 07882-4300. (908)689-8725. Fax: (908)689-8726. E-mail: shannon@fitnesslink.com. Website: www.fitnesslink.com. **Contact:** Shannon Entin, publisher and editor. **90% freelance written.** Daily consumer website covering fitness, sports, exercise and nutrition. "*FitnessLink* is an online fitness ezine, publishing the truth about fitness, sports training, and nutrition in our irreverent, 'tell it like it is' style. We dig beneath the sound bites to reveal the truth behind health and fitness fads." Estab. 1996. Circ. 800,000. Pays on publication. Publishes ms an average of 1 month after acceptance. Byline given. Buys first serial rights. Editorial lead time 1 month. Submit seasonal material 2 months in advance. Accepts queries by mail, e-mail, fax. Responds in 2 weeks to queries. Guidelines available at www.fitnesslink.com/info/guide.shtml.
  ● Fitnesslink is not accepting freelance submissions or queries at this time (Noted April 4, 2001)
Nonfiction: How-to (exercise, sports, nutrition), interview/profile, new product (reviews), personal experience (of extreme sport adventures or fitness makeovers), workout programs. **Buys 200 mss/year.** Length: 200-1,200 words. **Pays $40-400.**
Photos: State availability with submission. Reviews prints. Offers payment for photos in some cases. Identification of subjects required.
Tips: "We're looking for specific workouts for sports and 'adventure' activities. Since our publication is online, we archive all of our articles. It's important for writers to be aware of what we have already published and not duplicate the idea."

Ⓝ $ $ $ $INTOUCH, The Good Health Guide to Cancer Prevention and Treatment, PRR, Inc., 48 S. Service Rd., Suite 310, Melville NY 11747. Fax: (631)777-8700. E-mail: intouch@cancernetwork.com. Website: www.intouchlive.com. **Contact:** Randi Londer Gould, managing editor. **90% freelance written.** Bimonthly magazine focusing on cancer prevention and treatment. "*InTouch* offers comprehensive, authoritative, up-to-date information on cancer prevention and treatment. Written for the layman with an upbeat, positive tone." Estab. 1999. Circ. 150,000. **Pays on acceptance.** Publishes ms an average of 1 year after acceptance. Byline given. Offers 25% kill fee. Buys Purchases all rights for 6 months. Editorial lead time 6 months. Submit seasonal material 8 months in advance. Accepts queries by e-mail. Accepts simultaneous submissions. Responds in 6 weeks to queries. Sample copy and writer's guidelines free.
Nonfiction: Essays, interview/profile, health. Does not want personal stories of dealing with cancer unless it's a particularly good 600-word essay. **Buys 50 mss/year.** Query. Length: 1,000-3,000 words. **Pays $1/word.** Pays expenses of writers on assignment.
Photos: All photos are commissioned to professional photographers.
Columns/Departments: InSync (the mind/body connection. These stories usually focus on a type of complementary treatment such as biofeedback or meditation. Query. InSight (an essay page at the back of the book. We're looking for emotional stories that pull readers in and leave them with something to ponder.), 650 words, send complete ms. The InTouch Interview (a one-on-one, in-person interview with a prominent figure in the oncology community. No query required, but do contact us with your idea before interviewing the subject). An InTouch Report (a comprehensive treatment of a specific cancer).
Tips: "We look for lively, concise writing in the active voice. Look at our website to get a sense of topics we've covered. We welcome brief queries by e-mail. If it's a topic we'd like to assign, we ask for a longer query in the format described in our writer's guidelines."

$ $ $◨ LIFE EXTENSION MAGAZINE, 1100 West Commercial Blvd., Fort Lauderdale FL 33309. Fax: (954)202-7743. E-mail: lemagazine@lef.org. Website: www.lef.org. **Contact:** Rocio Paola Yaffar, editor-in-chief. **80% freelance written.** Monthly magazine covering "comprehensive medicine, health care, scientific findings, medical research and alternative therapies. *Life Extension* covers health and longevity, emphasizing scientific research backing novel therapies, medical findings and natural agents. Focus on current research-supported health briefs. Thoroughly researched medical articles complemented by interviews, book reviews, short health write-ups and profiles." Estab. 1994. Circ. 80,000. **Pays on acceptance.** Publishes ms an average of 6 months after acceptance. Byline given. Buys all rights. Editorial lead time 3 months. Accepts queries by e-mail. Sample copy free with e-mail request.
Nonfiction: Book excerpts, general interest, interview/profile, opinion, company profiles, case histories. Query via e-mail, mail published clips. Unsolicited mss will not be returned. Length: 2,000-4,000 words. **Pays 50¢/word.** Pays expenses of writers on assignment.
Reprints: Infrequently published reprints. Send article summary via e-mail with rights for sale noted and information on when and where the material appeared.
Photos: Most photography is by assignment. Photos supplied with assigned articles may be accepted. Unsolicited photos (including slides, electronic files, prints, etc.) will not be returned—do not send originals. Buys all rights. Negotiates payment individually. Identification of subjects required.

Columns/Departments: Point of view (opinion on comprehensive medicine/health care), 1,500-2,000 words. **Buys 12 mss/year.** Query via e-mail, mail published clips. **Pays 50¢/word.**

■ The online magazine carries original content not found in the print edition.

Tips: "A working knowledge of how to access medical research/abstracts essential. Must understand how latest research affects real people and influences medical progress as a whole."

$ $ $ $ MEN'S HEALTH, Rodale, 33 E. Minor St., Emmaus PA 18098. (610)967-5171. Fax: (610)967-7725. E-mail: TedSpiker@rodale.com. Website: www.menshealth.com. Editor-in-Chief: David Zinczenko, Editor: Greg Gutfeld, Executive Editor: Peter Moore. **Contact:** Ted Spiker, senior editor. **50% freelance written.** Magazine published 10 times/year covering men's health and fitness. *"Men's Health* is a lifestyle magazine showing men the practical and positive actions that make their lives better, with articles covering fitness, nutrition, relationships, travel, careers, grooming and health issues." Estab. 1986. Circ. 1,600,000. **Pays on acceptance.** Offers 25% kill fee. Buys all rights. Accepts queries by mail, fax. Responds in 3 weeks to queries. Writer's guidelines for #10 SASE.

○¬ Freelancers have the best chance with the front-of-the-book piece, Malegrams.

Nonfiction: "Authoritative information on all aspects of men's physical and emotional health. We rely on writers to seek out the right experts and to either tell a story from a first-person vantage or get good anecdotes." **Buys 30 features/year; 360 short mss/year.** Query with published clips. Length: 1,200-4,000 words for features, 100-300 words for short pieces. **Pays $1,000-5,000 for features; $100-500 for short pieces.**

Columns/Departments: Length: 750-1,500 words. **Buys 80 mss/year. Pays $750- 2,000.**

■ The online magazine carries original content not found in the print edition. Contact: Fred Zahradnick, online associate.

Tips: "We have a wide definition of health. We believe that being successful in every area of your life is being healthy. The magazine focuses on all aspects of health, from stress issues to nutrition to exercise to sex. It is 50% staff written, 50% from freelancers. The best way to break in is not by covering a particular subject, but by covering it within the magazine's style. There is a very particular tone and voice to the magazine. A writer has to be a good humor writer as well as a good service writer. Prefers mail queries. No phone calls, please."

$ $ $ MUSCLE & FITNESS, The Science of Living Super-Fit, Weider Health & Fitness, 21100 Erwin St., Woodland Hills, CA 91367. (818)884-6800. Fax: (818)595-0463. Website: www.muscle-fitness.com. **Contact:** Vincent Scalisi, editorial director; Bill Geiger, editor (training and other articles); Jo Ellen Krumm, managing editor (nutrition and food articles). **50% freelance written.** Monthly magazine covering bodybuilding and fitness for healthy, active men and women. It contains a wide range of features and monthly departments devoted to all areas of bodybuilding, health, fitness, injury prevention and treatment, and nutrition. Editorial fulfills two functions: information and entertainment. Special attention is devoted to how-to advice and accuracy. Estab. 1950. Circ. 500,000. Pays on publication. Publishes ms an average of 2 months after acceptance. Editorial lead time 5 months. Submit seasonal material 6 months in advance. Accepts queries by mail, fax. Responds in 1 month to queries.

Nonfiction: Bill Geiger, editor. "All features and departments are written on assignment." Book excerpts, how-to (training), humor, interview/profile, photo feature. **Buys 120 mss/year.** Query with published clips. Does not accept unsolicited mss. Length: 800-1,800 words. **Pays $250-800 for assigned articles.** Pays expenses of writers on assignment.

Reprints: Send photocopy with rights for sale noted and information about when and where the material previously appeared. Payment varies.

Photos: State availability with submission.

Tips: "Know bodybuilders and bodybuilding. Read our magazine regularly (or at least several issues), come up with new information or a new angle on our subject matter (bodybuilding training, psychology, nutrition, diets, fitness, etc.), then pitch us in terms of providing useful, unique, how-to information for our readers. Send a one-page query letter (as described in *Writer's Market*) to sell us on your idea and on you as the best writer for that article. Send a sample of your published work."

$ $ $ $ NATURAL HEALTH, Weider Publications, Inc., 70 Lincoln St., 5th Floor, Boston MA 02111. (617)753-8900. Fax: (617)457-0966. E-mail: naturalhealth@weiderpub.com. Website: www.naturalhealthmag.com. Editor: Rachel Streit. **Contact:** Maria Mandile, research editor. **50% freelance written.** Magazine published 8 times/year covering alternative health and natural living. "We are an authoritative guide to the best in natural self-care." Sample articles online. Estab. 1971. Circ. 300,000. **Pays on acceptance.** Publishes ms an average of 3 months after acceptance. Byline given. Offers 33% kill fee. Buys first, second serial (reprint) rights. Editorial lead time 6 months. Submit seasonal material 6 months in advance. Accepts simultaneous submissions.

○¬ Break in with a well-researched News & Notes piece.

Nonfiction: Book excerpts, exposé, how-to, inspirational, personal experience. No fiction, reprints from other publications or event coverage. **Buys 20 mss/year.** Query with published clips. Length: 150-3,000 words. **Pays $75-2,000.** Sometimes pays expenses of writers on assignment.

Photos: State availability with submission. Buys one-time rights.

Columns/Departments: My Story (personal account of illness or condition treated naturally), 1,500 words; News & Notes (health, fitness, body care news briefs), 125 words; Readers On (personal reflections on selected topics; see latest issue for topic), 100-500 words. **Buys 29 mss/year.** Query. **Pays $75-100.**

Tips: "Read the magazine. The recipes are always vegan. The products are non-chemical. Read books written by the advisory board members: Andrew Weil, James Gordon, Joseph Pizzorno, Jennifer Jacobs, etc."

N $ NEW LIVING, New Living Inc., 1212 Rt. 25A, Suite 1B, Stony Brook NY 11790. (631)751-8819. Fax: (631)751-8910. E-mail: newliving@aol.com. Website: www.newliving.com. **Contact:** Christine Lynn Harvey, editor. **10% freelance written.** Monthly newspaper. "Holistic health and fitness consumer news magazine covering herbal medicine, clinical nutrition, mind/body medicine, fitness, healthy recipes, product reviews, energy healing (reiki, chakra and sound) hypnosis, past life regression." Estab. 1991. Circ. 100,000. Pays on publication. Byline given. Makes work-for-hire assignments. Editorial lead time 2 months. Submit seasonal material 2 months in advance. Accepts queries by e-mail. Responds in 6 weeks to queries. Sample copy for 9×12 SAE with $1.21 postage. Writer's guidelines for #10 SASE.

Nonfiction: Needs only feature articles on holistic/natural health topics. Query. Length: 800-1,700 words. **Pays $25-100.**

Photos: State availability of or send photos with submission. Reviews contact sheets. Buys all rights. Offers $25-100/photo. Identification of subjects required.

Tips: "If you are going to send an article on herbal medicine please be an herbalist or author of a book on this topic; please see our website to see the kinds of articles we publish."

$ $ $ OXYGEN!, Serious Fitness for Serious Women, Muscle Mag International, 5775 McLaughlin Rd., Mississauga, Ontario L5R 3P7, Canada. (905)507-3545. Fax: (905)507-9935. **Contact:** Pamela Cottrell, editor-in-chief. **70% freelance written.** Bimonthly magazine covering women's health and fitness. "*Oxygen* encourages various exercise, good nutrition to shape and condition the body." Estab. 1997. Circ. 200,000. **Pays on acceptance.** Publishes ms an average of 4 months after acceptance. Byline given. Offers 25% kill fee. Buys all rights. Editorial lead time 3 months. Submit seasonal material 6 months in advance. Accepts queries by mail, fax. Responds in 5 weeks to queries; 2 months to mss. Sample copy for $5.

　○→ Break in with "a really strong query proving that it is well researched."

Nonfiction: Exposé, how-to (training and nutrition), humor, inspirational, interview/profile, new product, personal experience, photo feature. No "poorly researched articles that do not genuinely help the readers towards physical fitness, health and physique." **Buys 100 mss/year.** Send complete ms. Length: 1,400-1,800 words. **Pays $250-1,000.** Sometimes pays expenses of writers on assignment.

Reprints: Send tearsheet, photocopy or typed ms with rights for sale noted and information about when and where the material previously appeared. Pay varies.

Photos: State availability of or send photos with submission. Reviews contact sheets, 35mm transparencies, prints. Buys all rights. Offers $35-500. Identification of subjects required.

Columns/Departments: Nutrition (low-fat recipes), 1,700 words; Weight Training (routines and techniques), 1,800 words; Aerobics (how-tos), 1,700 words. **Buys 50 mss/year.** Send complete ms. **Pays $150-500.**

　▣ The online magazine carries original content not found in the print edition.

Tips: "Every editor of every magazine is looking, waiting, hoping and praying for the magic article. The beauty of the writing has to spring from the page; the edge imparted has to excite the reader because of its unbelievable information."

N $ $ $ POZ, POZ Publishing L.L.C., 349 W. 12th St., New York NY 10014. (212)242-2163. Fax: (212)675-8505. Website: www.poz.com. Managing Editor: Jennifer Hsu. **Contact:** Walter Armstrong, editor. **100% freelance written.** Monthly national magazine for people impacted by HIV and AIDS. "*POZ* is a trusted source of conventional and alternative treatment information, investigative features, survivor profiles, essays and cutting-edge news for people living with AIDS and their caregivers. *POZ* is a lifestyle magazine with both health and cultural content." Estab. 1994. Circ. 91,000. Pays 45 days after acceptance. Publishes ms an average of 3 months after acceptance. Byline given. Offers 20% kill fee. Buys first rights. Editorial lead time 4 months. Submit seasonal material 4 months in advance. Accepts simultaneous submissions. Sample copy and writer's guidelines free.

Nonfiction: Book excerpts, essays, exposé, historical/nostalgic, how-to, humor, inspirational, interview/profile, opinion, personal experience, photo feature. **Buys 180 mss/year.** Query with published clips. "We take unsolicited mss on speculation only." Length: 200-3,000 words. **Pays $50-1,000.** Sometimes pays expenses of writers on assignment.

Photos: Send photos with submission. Reviews contact sheets, negatives. Buys first rights. Negotiates payment individually. Identification of subjects required.

Columns/Departments: Life (personal experience); Back Page (humor); Data Dish (opinion/experience/information), all 600 words. **Buys 120 mss/year.** Query with published clips. **Pays $200-3,000.**

Fiction: Buys 10 mss/year. Send complete ms. Length: 700-2,000 words. **Payment negotiable.**

Poetry: Avant-garde, free verse, haiku, light verse, traditional. **Buys 12 poems/year.** Submit maximum 3 poems. Length: 10-40 lines. Payment negotiable.

Fillers: Anecdotes, facts, gags to be illustrated by cartoonist, newsbreaks, short humor. **Buys 90/year.** Length: 50-150 words. **Pays $50-75.**

$ $ $ SHAPE MAGAZINE, Weider Publications Inc., 21100 Erwin St., Woodland Hills CA 91367. (818)595-0593. Fax: (818)704-7620. Website: www.shapemag.com. Editor-in-Chief: Barbara Harris. **Contact:** Anne Russell, editorial director. **70% freelance written.** Prefers to work with published/established writers. Monthly magazine covering women's health and fitness. "*Shape* reaches women who are committed to the healthful, active lifestyles. Our readers are participating in a variety of sports and fitness related activities, in the gym, at home and outdoors, and they are also proactive about their health and are nutrition conscious." Estab. 1981. Circ. 900,000. **Pays on acceptance.** Offers 33% kill fee. Buys second serial (reprint), all rights. Submit seasonal material 8 months in advance. Responds in 2 months to queries. Sample copy for 9×12 SAE and 4 first-class stamps.

• Weider also publishes *Fit Pregnancy* (for pregnant and postpartum women); and *Jump* (for teenage girls).

Nonfiction: "We use some health and fitness articles written by professionals in their specific fields." Book excerpts, exposé (health, fitness, nutrition related), how-to (get fit), interview/profile (of fit women), health/fitness, recipes. Special issues: Every September is an anniversary issue. "No articles that haven't been queried first." **Buys 27 features/year and 36-54 short mss/year.** Query by mail only with published clips. Length: 3,000 words for features, 1,000 words for shorter pieces. **Pays $1/word.**

Photos: Submit slides or photos with photographer's name or institution to be credited. Captions, model releases required.

Tips: "Review a recent issue of the magazine. Provide source verification materials and sources for items readers may buy, including 800 numbers. Not responsible for unsolicited material. We reserve the right to edit any article."

$ $ ⊠ VIBRANT LIFE, A Magazine for Healthful Living, Review and Herald Publishing Assn., 55 W. Oak Ridge Dr., Hagerstown MD 21740-7390. (301)393-4019. Fax: (301)393-4055. E-mail: vibrantlife@rhpa.org. Website: www.vibrantlife.com. **Contact:** Larry Becker, editor. **80% freelance written.** Enjoys working with published/established writers; works with a small number of new/unpublished writers each year. Bimonthly magazine covering health articles (especially from a prevention angle and with a Christian slant). "The average length of time between acceptance of a freelance-written manuscript and publication of the material depends upon the topics: some immediately used; others up to 2 years." Estab. 1885. Circ. 50,000. **Pays on acceptance.** Byline given. Offers 50% kill fee. Submit seasonal material 9 months in advance. Accepts queries by mail, e-mail, fax. Responds in 1 month to queries. Sample copy for $1. Writer's guidelines for #10 SASE or online.

Nonfiction: "We seek practical articles promoting better health and a more fulfilled life. We especially like features on breakthroughs in medicine, and most aspects of health. We need articles on how to integrate a person's spiritual life with their health. We'd like more in the areas of exercise, nutrition, water, avoiding addictions of all types and rest—all done from a wellness perspective." Interview/profile (with personalities on health). **Buys 50-60 feature articles/year and 6-12 short mss/year.** Send complete ms. Length: 500-1,500 words for features, 25-250 words for short pieces. **Pays $75-300 for features, $50-75 for short pieces.**

Reprints: Send tearsheet and information about when and where the material previously appeared. Pays 50% of amount paid for an original article.

Photos: Not interested in b&w photos. Send photos with submission. Reviews 35mm transparencies.

Columns/Departments: Buys 12-18 department articles/year. Length: 500-650 words. **Pays $75-175.**

Tips: "*Vibrant Life* is published for baby boomers, particularly young professionals, age 40-55. Articles must be written in an interesting, easy-to-read style. Information must be reliable; no faddism. We are more conservative than other magazines in our field. Request a sample copy, and study the magazine and writer's guidelines."

$ $ VIM & VIGOR, America's Family Health Magazine, 1010 E. Missouri Ave., Phoenix AZ 85014-2601. (602)395-5850. Fax: (602)395-5853. E-mail: sallyc@mcmurry.com. Website: www.vigormagazine.com. **Contact:** Sally Clasen, associate publisher/editor. **75% freelance written.** Quarterly magazine covering health and healthcare. Estab. 1985. Circ. 1,100,000. **Pays on acceptance.** Publishes ms an average of 3 months after acceptance. Byline given. Buys all rights. Sample copy for 9×12 SAE with 8 first-class stamps or online. Writer's guidelines for #10 SASE.

Nonfiction: "Absolutely no complete manuscripts will be accepted/returned. All articles are assigned. Send published samples for assignment consideration. Any queries regarding story ideas will be placed on the following year's conference agenda and will be addressed on a topic-by-topic basis." Health, disease, medical breakthroughs, exercise/fitness trends, wellness, healthcare. **Buys 12 mss/year.** Send published clips by mail or e-mail. Length: 1,200 words. **Pays $500.** Pays expenses of writers on assignment.

Tips: "Writers must have consumer health care experience."

$ $ $ $ THE WALKING MAGAZINE, Walking Inc., 45 Bromfield St., Boston MA 02108. (617)574-0076. Fax: (617)338-7433. E-mail: letters@walkingmag.com. Website: www.walkingmag.com. **Contact:** Catherine Croteau, editorial assistant. **60% freelance written.** Bimonthly magazine covering health and fitness. "*The Walking Magazine* is written for healthy, active adults who are committed to fitness walking as an integral part of their lifestyle. Each issue offers advice on exercise techniques, diet, nutrition, personal care and contemporary health issues. It also covers information on gear and equipment, competition and travel, including foreign and domestic destinations for walkers." Estab. 1986. Circ. 650,000. **Pays on acceptance.** Byline given. Offers 25% kill fee. Editorial lead time 3 months. Accepts queries by mail, fax. Accepts simultaneous submissions. Responds in 2 months to queries. Sample copy for $3.95. Writer's guidelines for #10 SASE.

Nonfiction: Walks for travel and adventure, fitness, health, nutrition, fashion, equipment, famous walkers, other walking-related topics. **Buys 35-42 mss/year.** Query with published clips (no more than 3). Length: 1,500-2,500 words. **Pays $750-2,500.**

Columns/Departments: Walking Shorts, Take Charge, Health, Nutrition, Active Beauty, Weight Loss, Events, Shopping (gear and equipment), Escapes (travel), Ramblings (back page essay), 300-1,200 words. Query with published clips. **Pays $150-1,500.**

Tips: Needs "original insights and research relating to health, fitness, nutrition, or issues surrounding walking and walkers' needs."

$ $⊠ YOUR HEALTH & FITNESS, General Learning Communications, 900 Skokie Blvd., Northbrook IL 60062-1574. (847)205-3000. Fax: (847)564-8197. **Contact:** Debb Bastian, associate editorial director. **95% freelance written.** Prefers to work with published/established writers. Quarterly magazine. Needs "general, educational material on health, fitness and safety that can be read and understood easily by the layman." Estab. 1969. Circ. 1,000,000. Pays after publication. Publishes ms an average of 6 months after acceptance. No byline given (contributing editor status given in masthead). Buys all rights.

> O━ "All article topics assigned. No queries; if you're interested in writing for the magazine, send a cover letter, résumé, curriculum vitae and writing samples. All topics are determined a year in advance of publication by editors. No unsolicited manuscripts."

Nonfiction: All article topics assigned. General interest (health-related). **Buys approximately 65 mss/year.** No queries; if you're interested in writing for the magazine, send a cover letter, résumé, curriculum vitae and writing samples. All topics are determined a year in advance of publication by editors. No unsolicited mss. Length: 350-850 words. **Pay varies, commensurate with experience.**

Tips: "Write to a general audience with only a surface knowledge of health and fitness topics. Possible subjects include exercise and fitness, psychology, nutrition, safety, disease, drug data, and health concerns. No phone queries."

HISTORY

Listed here are magazines and other periodicals written for historical collectors, genealogy enthusiasts, historic preservationists and researchers. Editors of history magazines look for fresh accounts of past events in a readable style. Some publications cover an era, while others may cover a region or subject area, such as aviation history.

$ $⊠ AMERICA'S CIVIL WAR, Primedia History Group, 741 Miller Dr., SE, Suite D-2, Leesburg VA 20175-8920. (703)771-9400. Fax: (703)779-8345. E-mail: AmericasCivilWar@thehistorynet.com. Website: www.thehistorynet.com. Managing Editor: Carl Von Wodtke. **Contact:** Dana Shoaf, associate editor. **95% freelance written.** Bimonthly magazine covering "popular history and straight historical narrative for both the general reader and the Civil War buff covering strategy, tactics, personalities, arms and equipment." Estab. 1988. Circ. 80,000. Pays on publication. Publishes ms an average of 2 years after acceptance. Byline given. Buys all rights. Accepts queries by mail, e-mail, fax. Responds in 3 months to queries; 6 months to mss. Sample copy for $5. Writer's guidelines for #10 SASE or online.

Nonfiction: Historical/nostalgic, book notices, preservation news. No fiction or poetry. **Buys 24 mss/year.** Query. Length: 3,500-4,000 words and should include a 500-word sidebar. **Pays $300 and up.**

Photos: Send photos with submission or cite sources. "We'll order." Captions, identification of subjects required.

Columns/Departments: Personality (profiles of Civil War personalities); Men & Material (about weapons used); Commands (about units); Eyewitness to War (historical letters and diary excerpts). Length: 2,000 words. **Buys 24 mss/year.** Query. **Pays $150 and up.**

> ▣ The online magazine carries original content not found in the print edition and includes writer's guidelines. Contact: Roger Vance.

Tips: "All stories must be true. We do not publish fiction or poetry. Write an entertaining, well-researched, informative and unusual story that grabs the reader's attention and holds it. Include suggested readings in a standard format at the end of your piece. Manuscript must be typed, double-spaced on one side of standard white 8½×11, 16 to 30 pound paper—no onion skin paper or dot matrix printouts. All submissions are on speculation. Prefer subjects to be on disk (IBM- or Macintosh-compatible floppy disk) as well as a hard copy. Choose stories with strong art possibilities."

⊠ AMERICAN HERITAGE, 90 Fifth Ave., New York NY 10011. (212)367-3100. Fax: (212)367-3149. E-mail: mail@americanheritage.com. Website: www.americanheritage.com. **Contact:** Richard Snow, editor. **70% freelance written.** Magazine published 8 times/year. "*American Heritage* writes from a historical point of view on politics, business, art, current and international affairs, and our changing lifestyles. The articles are written with the intent to enrich the reader's appreciation of the sometimes nostalgic, sometimes funny, always stirring panorama of the American experience." Circ. 300,000. **Pays on acceptance.** Publishes ms an average of 6-12 months after acceptance. Byline given. Buys first North American serial, all rights. Submit seasonal material 1 year in advance. Responds in 2 months to queries. Writer's guidelines for #10 SASE.

> ● Before submitting material, "check our index to see whether we have already treated the subject."

Nonfiction: Wants "historical articles by scholars or journalists intended for intelligent lay readers rather than for professional historians." Emphasis is on authenticity, accuracy and verve. "Interesting documents, photographs and drawings are always welcome. Style should stress readability and accuracy." Historical/nostalgic. **Buys 30 unsolicited mss/year.** Query. Length: 1,500-6,000 words. **Pay varies.** Sometimes pays expenses of writers on assignment.

Tips: "We have over the years published quite a few 'firsts' from young writers whose historical knowledge, research methods and writing skills met our standards. The scope and ambition of a new writer tell us a lot about his or her future usefulness to us. A major article gives us a better idea of the writer's value. Everything depends on the quality of the material. We don't really care whether the author is 20 and unknown, or 80 and famous, or vice versa. No phone calls, please."

\$ \$ AMERICAN HISTORY, 6405 Flank Dr., Harrisburg PA 17112-2750. (717)657-9555. Website: www.thehistory net.com. **Contact:** Tom Huntington, editor. **60% freelance written.** Bimonthly magazine of cultural, social, military and political history published for a general audience. Estab. 1966. Circ. 100,000. **Pays on acceptance.** Byline given. Buys first rights. Responds in 10 weeks to queries. Sample copy and guidelines for \$5 (includes 3rd class postage) or \$4 and 9 × 12 SAE with 4 first-class stamps. Writer's guidelines for #10 SASE or online.
Nonfiction: Features events in the lives of noteworthy historical figures and accounts of important events in American history. Also includes pictorial features on artists, photographers and graphic subjects. "Material is presented on a popular rather than a scholarly level." **Buys 20 mss/year.** Query by mail only with published clips and SASE. Length: 2,000-4,000 words depending on type of article. **Pays \$500-700.**
Photos: Welcomes suggestions for illustrations.
   ◾ The online magazine occasionally carries original content not found in the print edition. Contact: Christine Techky, managing editor.
Tips: "Key prerequisites for publication are thorough research and accurate presentation, precise English usage and sound organization, a lively style, and a high level of human interest. Unsolicited manuscripts not considered. Inappropriate materials include: fiction, book reviews, travelogues, personal/family narratives not of national significance, articles about collectibles/antiques, living artists, local/individual historic buildings/landmarks and articles of a current editorial nature. Currently seeking articles on significant Civil War subjects. No phone, fax or e-mail queries, please."

\$ THE ARTILLERYMAN, Historical Publications, Inc., 234 Monarch Hill Rd., Tunbridge VT 05077. (802)889-3500. Fax: (802)889-5627. E-mail: mail@civilwarnews.com. **Contact:** Kathryn Jorgensen, editor. **60% freelance written.** Quarterly magazine covering antique artillery, fortifications and crew-served weapons 1750-1900 for competition shooters, collectors and living history reenactors using artillery. "Emphasis on Revolutionary War and Civil War but includes everyone interested in pre-1900 artillery and fortifications, preservation, construction of replicas, etc." Estab. 1979. Circ. 2,000. Pays on publication. Publishes ms an average of 6 months after acceptance. Byline given. Not copyrighted. Buys one-time rights. Accepts queries by mail, e-mail, fax. Accepts simultaneous submissions. Responds in 3 weeks to queries. Sample copy and writer's guidelines for 9 × 12 SAE with 4 first-class stamps.
   ⚬┐ Break in with an historical or travel piece featuring artillery—the types and history of guns and their use.
Nonfiction: Interested in "artillery *only*, for sophisticated readers. Not interested in other weapons, battles in general." Historical/nostalgic, how-to (reproduce ordnance equipment/sights/implements/tools/accessories, etc.), interview/profile, new product, opinion (must be accompanied by detailed background of writer and include references), personal experience, photo feature, technical (must have footnotes), travel (where to find interesting antique cannon). **Buys 24-30 mss/year.** Send complete ms. Length: 300 words minimum. **Pays \$20-60.** Sometimes pays expenses of writers on assignment.
Reprints: Send tearsheet or photocopy and information about when and where the material previously appeared. Pays 100% of amount paid for an original article.
Photos: Send photos with submission. Pays \$5 for 5 × 7 and larger b&w prints. Captions, identification of subjects required.
Tips: "We regularly use freelance contributions for Places-to-Visit, Cannon Safety, The Workshop and Unit Profiles departments. Also need pieces on unusual cannon or cannon with a known and unique history. To judge whether writing style and/or expertise will suit our needs, writers should ask themselves if they could knowledgeably talk *artillery* with an expert. Subject matter is of more concern than writer's background."

ℕ \$ \$ AVIATION HISTORY, Primedia History Group, 741 Miller Dr., SE, Suite D-2, Leesburg VA 20175-8920. (703)771-8400. Fax: (703)779-8345. E-mail: AviationHistory@thehistorynet.com. Website: www.thehistorynet.com. Managing Editor: Carl von Wodtke. **Contact:** Arthur Sanfelici, editor. **95% freelance written.** Bimonthly magazine covering military and civilian aviation from first flight to the jet age. It aims to make aeronautical history not only factually accurate and complete, but also enjoyable to varied subscriber and newsstand audience. Estab. 1990. Circ. 60,000. Pays on publication. Publishes ms an average of 2 years after acceptance. Byline given. Buys all rights. Editorial lead time 6 months. Submit seasonal material 1 year in advance. Accepts queries by mail, e-mail, fax. Accepts simultaneous submissions. Responds in 3 months to queries; 6 months to mss. Sample copy for \$5. Writer's guidelines for #10 SASE or online.
Nonfiction: Book excerpts, historical/nostalgic, interview/profile, personal experience, travel. **Buys 24 mss/year.** Query. Length: Feature articles should be 3,500-4,000 words, each with a 500-word sidebar, author's biography and book suggestions for further reading. **Pays \$300.**
Photos: State availability of art and photos with submissions, cite sources. "We'll order." Reviews contact sheets, negatives, transparencies. Buys one-time rights. Identification of subjects required.
Columns/Departments: People and Places; Enduring Heritage; Aerial Oddities; Art of Flight, all 2,000 words. **Pays \$150.** Book reviews, 300-750 words; **pays minimum \$30.**
   ◾ The online magazine carries original content not found in the print edition and includes writer's guidelines. Contact: Roger Vance.

Tips: "Choose stories with strong art possibilities. Include a hard copy as well as an IBM- or Macintosh-compatible floppy disk. Write an entertaining, informative and unusual story that grabs the reader's attention and holds it. All stories must be true. We do not publish fiction or poetry."

[N] $ CHRONICLE OF THE OLD WEST, P.O. Box 2859, Show Low AZ 85902. (520)532-2875. Fax: (520)532-5170. E-mail: OldPress@RavenHeart.com. Website: www.chronicleoftheoldwest.com. **Contact:** Dakota Livesay. **75% freelance written.** Monthly tabloid newspaper dedicated to Old West enthusiasts. Pays 30 days after publication. Publishes ms an average of 2 months after acceptance. Buys one-time rights. Accepts queries by mail, e-mail, fax, phone. Responds in 1 month to queries. Sample copy on request. Writer's guidelines for #10 SASE.
Nonfiction: Newspaper focuses on people and events of the 1800s. Book excerpts, opinion. No fiction. Query with or without published clips or send complete ms. Length: 500-2,000 words. **Pays 5-8¢/word.**
Photos: Photos are encouraged. Send photos with submission.
Columns/Departments: The Chuck Wagon (recipes of the Old West. It is necessary to include information on the history of the recipe); The Old West on Celluloid (how current and past western movies portray the Old West); The Old West Today (descriptions of places and events where people can experience the Old West through participation and observation. This needs to be submitted four months prior to the event). **Pays $10 for Chuck Wagon recipes; 5-8¢/word for other departments.**
Tips: "We are looking for the real flavor and atmosphere of the Old West, not technical or dry scholarly accounts. Articles should be written as if the author is a reporter for *Chronicle of the Old West* writing about a current event. We want to give the reader the feeling the event just took place, and the reader is at the time and location of the subject of the article."

$ $ [icon] CIVIL WAR TIMES ILLUSTRATED, 6405 Flank Dr., Harrisburg PA 17112. (717)657-9555. Fax: (717)657-9552. E-mail: cwt@cowles.com. Website: www.thehistorynet.com. Editor: Jim Kushlan. **Contact:** Carl Zebrowski. **90% freelance written.** Works with a small number of new/unpublished writers each year. Magazine published 7 times/year. "*Civil War Times* is the full-spectrum magazine of the Civil War. Specifically, we look for non-partisan coverage of battles, prominent military and civilian figures, the home front, politics, military technology, common soldier life, prisoners and escapes, period art and photography, the naval war, blockade-running, specific regiments and much more." Estab. 1962. Circ. 130,000. **Pays on acceptance.** Publishes ms an average of 18 months after acceptance. Buys all rights. Submit seasonal material 1 year in advance. Responds in 8 months to queries. Sample copy for $5.50. Writer's guidelines for #10 SASE.
Nonfiction: Interview/profile, photo feature, Civil War historical material. "Don't send us a comprehensive article on a well-known major battle. Instead, focus on some part or aspect of such a battle, or some group of soldiers in the battle. Similar advice applies to major historical figures like Lincoln and Lee. Positively no fiction or poetry." **Buys 20 freelance mss/year.** Query with clips and SASE. **Pays $75-600.**
Photos: Contact: Jeff King, art director.
Tips: "We're very open to new submissions. Send query after examining writer's guidelines and several recent issues. Include photocopies of photos that could feasibly accompany the article. Confederate soldiers' diaries and letters are welcome."

[N] $ $ [icon] COMMAND, Military History, Strategy & Analysis, XTR Corp., P.O. Box 4017, San Luis Obispo CA 93403. (805)546-9596. Fax: (805)546-0570. Managing Editor: Christopher Perello. **Contact:** Ty Bomba, editor-in-chief. **95% freelance written.** Bimonthly magazine. "*Command* is a magazine of popular—not scholarly—analytic military history." Estab. 1989. Circ. 35,000. Pays on publication. Publishes ms an average of 1 year after acceptance. Byline given. Buys first, all rights. Editorial lead time 2 months. Submit seasonal material 4 months in advance. Responds in 2 weeks to queries; 2 months to mss. Sample copy for $4.95. Writer's guidelines for #10 SASE.
Nonfiction: Book excerpts, essays, opinion, personal experience, photo feature, analytical-historical current military affairs. **Buys 36-48 mss/year.** Query. Length: 700-10,000 words. **Pays $35-500.**
Photos: Send photos with submission. Buys one-time or all rights. Negotiates payment individually. Captions required.
Tips: "Read guidelines and do what they say. Be broadly knowledgeable in military history, current affairs, etc."

$ $ GATEWAY HERITAGE, Missouri Historical Society, P.O. Box 11940, St. Louis MO 63112-0040. (314)746-4557. Fax: (314)746-4548. E-mail: jstevens@mohistory.org. Website: www.mohistory.org. **Contact:** Josh Stevens, assistant editor. **75% freelance written.** Quarterly magazine covering Missouri history. "*Gateway Heritage* is a popular history magazine which is sent to members of the Missouri Historical Society. Thus, we have a general audience with an interest in history." Estab. 1980. Circ. 6,200. Pays on publication. Publishes ms an average of 6 months after acceptance. Byline given. Offers $75 kill fee. Buys first North American serial rights. Editorial lead time 6 months. Submit seasonal material 1 year in advance. Accepts queries by mail, e-mail, fax. Responds in 2 weeks to queries; 2 months to mss. Sample copy for 9×12 SAE and 7 first-class stamps. Writer's guidelines for #10 SASE.
Nonfiction: Book excerpts, historical/nostalgic, interview/profile, personal experience, photo feature, scholarly essays, Missouri biographies, viewpoints on events, firsthand historical accounts, regional architectural history, literary history. No genealogies. **Buys 12-15 mss/year.** Query with published clips. Length: 3,500-5,000 words. **Pays $200 (average).**
Photos: State availability with submission.

Columns/Departments: Literary Landmarks (biographical sketches and interviews of famous Missouri literary figures) 1,500-2,500 words; Missouri Biographies (biographical sketches of famous and interesting Missourians)1,500-2,500 words; Gateway Album (excerpts from diaries and journals) 1,500-2,500 words. **Buys 6-8 mss/year.** Query with published clips. **Pays $250-500.**

Tips: "Ideas for our departments are a good way to break into *Gateway Heritage*."

$ ⬚ GOOD OLD DAYS, America's Premier Nostalgia Magazine, House of White Birches, 306 E. Parr Rd., Berne IN 46711. (219)589-4000. Website: www.GoodOldDays-magazine.com. **Contact:** Ken Tate, editor. **75% freelance written.** Monthly magazine of first person nostalgia, 1900-1955. "We look for strong narratives showing life as it was in the first half of this century. Our readership is comprised of nostalgia buffs, history enthusiasts and the people who actually lived and grew up in this era." Pays on publication. Publishes ms an average of 8 months after acceptance. Byline given. Prefers all rights, but will negotiate for First North American serial and one-time rights. Submit seasonal material 10 months in advance. Responds in 2 months to queries. Sample copy for $2. Writer's guidelines for #10 SASE.

Nonfiction: Regular features: Good Old Days on Wheels (transportation auto, plane, horse-drawn, tram, bicycle, trolley, etc.); Good Old Days In the Kitchen (favorite foods, appliances, ways of cooking, recipes); Home Remedies (herbs and poultices, hometown doctors, harrowing kitchen table operations). Historical/nostalgic, humor, interview/profile, personal experience, photo feature, favorite food/recipes, year-round seasonal material, biography, memorable events, fads, fashion, sports, music, literature, entertainment. No fiction accepted. **Buys 350 mss/year.** Query or send complete ms. Length: 500-1,500 words. **Pays $15-75, depending on quality and photos.**

Photos: Send photos with submission. Identification of subjects required.

Tips: "Most of our writers are not professionals. We prefer the author's individual voice, warmth, humor and honesty over technical ability."

N $ LIGHTHOUSE DIGEST, Lighthouse Digest, P.O. Box 1690, Wells ME 04090. (207)646-0515. Fax: (207)646-0516. E-mail: timh@lhdigest.com. Website: www.lighthousedigest.com. **Contact:** Tim Harrison, editor. **15% freelance written.** Monthly magazine covering. historical, fiction and news events about lighthouses and similar maritime stories. Estab. 1989. Circ. 24,000. Pays on publication. Publishes ms an average of 4 months after acceptance. Byline given. Buys one-time, electronic rights. Editorial lead time 3 months. Submit seasonal material 3 months in advance. Accepts queries by e-mail. Accepts simultaneous submissions. Responds in 6 weeks to queries. Sample copy free.

Nonfiction: Exposé, general interest, historical/nostalgic, humor, inspirational, personal experience, photo feature, religious, technical, travel. No historical data taken from books. **Buys 30 mss/year.** Send complete ms. Length: 2,500 words maximum. **Pays $75.**

Photos: Send photos with submission. Reviews prints. Buys all rights. Offers no additional payment for photos accepted with ms. Captions, identification of subjects required.

Fiction: Adventure, historical, humorous, mystery, religious, romance, suspense. **Buys 2 mss/year.** Send complete ms. Length: 2,500 words maximum. **Pays $75-150.**

Tips: "Read our publication and visit the website."

N $ $ $ $ MHQ, The Quarterly Journal of Military History, Primedia Enthusiast Publications, 741 Miller Dr. SE, Suite D-2, Leesburg VA 20175-8920. (703)771-9400. Fax: (703)779-8345. E-mail: mhq@thehistory.net.com. Website: www.thehistorynet.com. Editor: Rod Paschell. Managing Editor: Carl Von Wodtke. **Contact:** Christopher Anderson, senior editor. **100% freelance written.** Quarterly magazine covering military history. "*MHQ* offers readers in-depth articles on the history of warfare from ancient times into the 20th century. Authoritative features and departments cover military strategies, philosophies, campaigns, battles, personalities, weaponry, espionage and perspectives, all written in a lively and readable style. Articles are accompanied by classical works of art, contemporary illustrations, photographs and maps. Readers include serious students of military tactics, strategy, leaders and campaigns, as well as general world history enthusiasts. Many readers are currently in the military or retired officers." Estab. 1988. Circ. 30,000. Pays on publication. Byline given. Buys all rights. Editorial lead time 10 months. Submit seasonal material 1 year in advance. Accepts queries by mail, e-mail, fax. Accepts simultaneous submissions. Responds in 3 months to queries; 6 months to mss. Sample copy for $23 (hardcover), $13 (softcover); some articles online. Writer's guidelines for #10 SASE or online.

Nonfiction: Historical/nostalgic, personal experience, photo feature. No fiction or stories pertaining to collectibles or reenactments. **Buys 50 mss/year.** Query preferred; also accepts complete ms. Length: 1,000-5,000 words. **Pays $800-2,000 for assigned articles; $400-2,000 for unsolicited articles.**

Photos: Send photos with submission. Reviews transparencies, prints. Buys all rights. Negotiates payment individually. Identification of subjects required.

Columns/Departments: Artists on War (description of artwork of a military nature); Experience of War (first-person accounts of military incidents); Strategic View (discussion of military theory, strategy); Arms & Men (description of military hardware or unit), all up to 3,000 words. **Buys 20 mss/year.** Send complete ms. **Pays $400-800.**

▣ The online magazine carries original content not found in the print edition and includes writer's guidelines. Contact: Roger Vance.

Tips: "All stories must be true—we publish no fiction. Although we are always looking for variety, some subjects— World War II, the American Civil War, and military biography, for instance—are the focus of so many proposals that we are forced to judge them by relatively rigid criteria. We are always glad to consider articles on these subjects. However, less common ones—medieval, Asian, or South American military history, for example—are more likely to attract our attention. The likelihood that articles can be effectively illustrated often determines the ultimate fate of manuscripts. Many otherwise excellent articles have been rejected due to a lack of suitable art or photographs. Regular departments—columns on strategy, tactics, and weaponry, as well as book, film and video reviews—average 1,500 words. Our contributing editors provide most departments, but we often consider unsolicited proposals, especially for 'Experience of War,' which is personal reminiscence. These stories need not be combat experiences per se, but must be true first-person narratives. While the information we publish is scholarly and substantive, we prefer writing that is light, anecdotal, and above all, engaging, rather than didactic."

N **$ MILITARY HISTORY**, Primedia History Group, 741 Miller Dr., SE, Suite D-2, Leesburg VA 20175-8920. (703)771-9400. Fax: (703)779-8345. E-mail: MilitaryHistory@thehistorynet.com. Website: www.thehistorynet.com. Managing Editor: Carl von Wodtke. **Contact:** Jon Guttman, editor. **95% freelance written.** "We'll work with anyone, established or not, who can provide the goods and convince us as to its accuracy." Bimonthly magazine covering all military history of the world. "We strive to give the general reader accurate, highly readable, ofter narrative popular history, richly accompanied by period art." Circ. 115,000. Pays on publication. Publishes ms an average of 2 years after acceptance. Byline given. Buys all rights. Submit seasonal material 1 year in advance. Accepts queries by mail, e-mail, fax. Responds in 3 months to queries; 6 months to mss. Sample copy for $5. Writer's guidelines for #10 SASE or online.
Nonfiction: Historical/nostalgic, interview/profile (military figures of commanding interest), personal experience (only occasionally). **Buys 24 mss/year.** Query with published clips. "Submit a short, self-explanatory query summarizing the story proposed, its highlights and/or significance. State also your own expertise, access to sources or proposed means of developing the pertinent information." Length: 4,000 words with a 500-word sidebar. **Pays $400.**
Columns/Departments: Intrigue, Weaponry, Perspectives, Personality and review of books, video, CD-ROMs, software—all relating to military history. Length: 2,000 words. **Buys 24 mss/year.** Query with published clips. **Pays $200.**
   The online magazine carries original content not found in the print edition and includes writer's guidelines. Contact: Roger Vance.
Tips: "We would like journalistically 'pure' submissions that adhere to basics, such as full name at first reference, same with rank, and definition of prior or related events, issues cited as context or obscure military 'hardware.' Read the magazine, discover our style, and avoid subjects already covered. Pick stories with strong art possibilities (real art and photos), send photocopies, tell us where to order the art. Avoid historical overview; focus upon an event with appropriate and accurate context. Provide bibliography. Tell the story in popular but elegant style. Include a hard copy as well as an IBM- or Macintosh-compatible floppy disk."

$ $ PERSIMMON HILL, National Cowboy and Western Heritage Museum, 1700 NE 63rd St., Oklahoma City OK 73111. (405)478-6404. Fax: (405)478-4714. E-mail: editor@nationalcowboymuseum.org. Website: www.nationalco wboymuseum.org. **Contact:** M.J. Van Deventer, editor. **70% freelance written.** Prefers to work with published/established writers; works with a small number of new/unpublished writers each year. Quarterly magazine for an audience interested in Western art, Western history, ranching and rodeo, including historians, artists, ranchers, art galleries, schools, and libraries. Estab. 1970. Circ. 15,000. Pays on publication. Publishes ms an average of 2 years after acceptance. Byline given. Buys first rights. Responds in 3 months to queries. Sample copy for $10.50, including postage. Writer's guidelines for #10 SASE or online.
   ● The editor of *Persimmon Hill* reports: "We need more material on rodeo, both contemporary and historical. And we need more profiles on contemporary working ranches in the West."
Nonfiction: Historical and contemporary articles on famous Western figures connected with pioneering the American West, Western art, rodeo, cowboys, etc. (or biographies of such people), stories of Western flora and animal life and environmental subjects. "We want thoroughly researched and historically authentic material written in a popular style. May have a humorous approach to subject." "No broad, sweeping, superficial pieces; i.e., the California Gold Rush or rehashed pieces on Billy the Kid, etc." **Buys 35-50 mss/year.** Query by mail only with clips. Length: 1,500 words. Pays $150-250.
Photos: Purchased with ms or on assignment. Reviews color transparencies, glossy b&w prints. Pays according to quality and importance for b&w and color photos. Captions required.
Tips: "Send us a story that captures the spirit of adventure and indvidualism that typifies the Old West or reveals a facet of the Western lifestyle in comtemporary society. Excellent illustrations for articles are essential! We lean towards scholarly, historical, well-researched articles. We're less focused on Western celebrities than some of the other contemporary Western magazines."

$ $ $ $ PRESERVATION MAGAZINE, National Trust for Historic Preservation, 1785 Massachusetts Ave. NW, Washington DC 20036. (202)588-6388. **Contact:** Robert Wilson, editor. **75% freelance written.** Prefers to work with published/established writers. Bimonthly magazine covering preservation of historic buildings in the US. "We cover subjects related in some way to place. Most entries are features, department or opinion pieces." Circ. 250,000. Pays on publication. Publishes ms an average of 1 month after acceptance. Byline given. Offers variable kill fee. Buys one-time rights. Responds in 2 months to queries.
Nonfiction: Interview/profile, opinion, photo feature, travel, features, news. **Buys 30 mss/year.** Query with published clips. Length: 500-3,500 words. Sometimes pays expenses of writers on assignment, but not long-distance travel.

Tips: "Do not send or propose histories of buildings, descriptive accounts of cities or towns or long-winded treatises."

$ $ $ TIMELINE, Ohio Historical Society, 1982 Velma Ave., Columbus OH 43211-2497. (614)297-2360. Fax: (614)297-2367. E-mail: timeline@ohiohistory.org. **Contact:** Christopher S. Duckworth, editor. **90% freelance written.** Works with a small number of new/unpublished writers each year. Bimonthly magazine covering history, prehistory and the natural sciences, directed toward readers in the Midwest. Estab. 1885. Circ. 19,000. **Pays on acceptance.** Publishes ms an average of 1 year after acceptance. Byline given. Offers $75 minimum kill fee. Buys first North American serial, all rights. Submit seasonal material 6 months in advance. Accepts queries by mail, e-mail, fax. Responds in 3 weeks to queries; 6 weeks to mss. Sample copy for $6 and 9×12 SAE. Writer's guidelines for #10 SASE.
Nonfiction: Topics include the traditional fields of political, economic, military, and social history; biography; the history of science and technology; archaeology and anthropology; architecture; the fine and decorative arts; and the natural sciences including botany, geology, zoology, ecology, and paleontology. Book excerpts, essays, historical/nostalgic, interview/profile (of individuals), photo feature. **Buys 22 mss/year.** Query. Length: 1,500-6,000 words. Also vignettes of 500-1,000 words. **Pays $100-900.**
Photos: Submissions should include ideas for illustration. Send photos with submission. Reviews contact sheets, transparencies, 8×10 prints. Buys one-time rights. Captions, identification of subjects, model releases required.
Tips: "We want crisply written, authoritative narratives for the intelligent lay reader. An Ohio slant may strengthen a submission, but it is not indispensable. Contributors must know enough about their subject to explain it clearly and in an interesting fashion. We use high-quality illustration with all features. If appropriate illustration is unavailable, we can't use the feature. The writer who sends illustration ideas with a manuscript has an advantage, but an often-published illustration won't attract us."

$ $ TRACES OF INDIANA AND MIDWESTERN HISTORY, Indiana Historical Society, 450 W. Ohio St., Indianapolis IN 46202-3269. (317)232-1877. Fax: (317)233-0857. E-mail: rboomhower@indianahistory.org. Website: www.indianahistory.org/traces.htm. Executive Editor: Thomas A. Mason. **Contact:** Ray E. Boomhower, managing editor. **80% freelance written.** Quarterly magazine on Indiana and Midwestern history. "Conceived as a vehicle to bring to the public good narrative and analytical history about Indiana in its broader contexts of region and nation, *Traces* explores the lives of artists, writers, performers, soldiers, politicians, entrepreneurs, homemakers, reformers, and naturalists. It has traced the impact of Hoosiers on the nation and the world. In this vein, the editors seek nonfiction articles that are solidly researched, attractively written, and amenable to illustration, and they encourage scholars, journalists, and freelance writers to contribute to the magazine." Estab. 1989. Circ. 11,000. **Pays on acceptance.** Publishes ms an average of 6 months after acceptance. Byline given. Buys one-time rights. Submit seasonal material 1 year in advance. Responds in 3 months to mss. Sample copy and writer's guidelines for $5.25 (make checks payable to Indiana Historical Society) and 9×12 SAE with 7 first-class stamps or online. Writer's guidelines for #10 SASE.
Nonfiction: Book excerpts, historical essays, historical photographic features on topics of biography, literature, folklore, music, visual arts, politics, economics, industry, transportation and sports. **Buys 20 mss/year.** Send complete ms. Length: 2,000-4,000 words. **Pays $100-500.**
Photos: Send photos with submission. Reviews contact sheets, transparencies, photocopies, prints. Buys one-time rights. Pays "reasonable photographic expenses." Captions, identification of subjects, permissions required.
Tips: "Freelancers should be aware of prerequisites for writing history for a broad audience. Should have some awareness of this magazine and other magazines of this type published by Midwestern historical societies. Preference is given to subjects with an Indiana connection and authors who are familiar with *Traces*. Quality of potential illustration is also important."

$ TRUE WEST, True West Publishing, Inc., P.O. Box 8008, Cave Creek AZ 85327. (888)587-1881. Fax: (480)575-1903. E-mail: editor@truewestmagazine.com. Website: www.truewestmagazine.com. Executive Editor: Bob Boze Bell. **Contact:** Mare Rosenbaum, associate editor. **80% freelance written.** Works with a small number of new/unpublished writers each year. Monthly magazine covering Western American history from prehistory to 1930. "We want reliable research on significant historical topics written in lively prose for an informed general audience. More recent topics may be used if they have a historical angle or retain the Old West flavor of trail dust and saddle leather." Estab. 1953. Circ. 50,000. **Pays on acceptance.** Publishes ms an average of 6 months after acceptance. Byline given. Buys first North American serial rights. Editorial lead time 3 months. Submit seasonal material 6 months in advance. Accepts queries by mail, e-mail. Responds in 6 weeks to queries; 2 months to mss. Sample copy for $2 and 9×12 SAE. Writer's guidelines for #10 SASE.
  O— "We are looking for historically accurate stories on the Old West that make you go 'What happens next?' Think and write outside of the box. History should be fun. If you have a passion for the West and can write creatively, we will probably publish you."
Nonfiction: Book excerpts, historical/nostalgic, humor, interview/profile, travel. No fiction or unsupported, undocumented tales. **Buys 110 mss/year.** Query. Length: 1,200-5,000 words. **Pays $50-800.**
Photos: State availability with submission. Reviews contact sheets, negatives, 4×5 transparencies, 4×5 prints. Buys one-time rights. Offers $10-75/photo. Captions, identification of subjects, model releases required.
Columns/Departments: Bob Boze Bell, executive editor. True Reviews (book reviews), 300-800 words. **Buys 50 mss/year.** Query with published clips. **Pays $50-200.**
Fillers: Bob Boze Bell, executive editor. Anecdotes, facts, gags to be illustrated by cartoonist, newsbreaks, short humor. **Buys 30/year.** Length: 50-600 words. **Pays $30-250.**

Tips: "Do original research on fresh topics. Stay away from controversial subjects unless you are truly knowledgeable in the field. Read our magazines and follow our guidelines. A freelancer is most likely to break in with us by submitting thoroughly researched, lively prose on relatively obscure topics. First-person accounts rarely fill our needs. Historical accuracy and strict adherence to the facts are essential. We much prefer material based on primary sources (archives, court records, documents, contemporary newspapers and first-person accounts) to those that rely mainly on secondary sources (published books, magazines, and journals). Note: We are currently trying to take *True West* and *Old West* back to their 'roots' by publishing shorter pieces. Ideal length is between 1,500-3,000 words."

N $ $ VIETNAM, Primedia History Group, 741 Miller Dr., SE, #D-2, Leesburg VA 20175-8920. (703)779-9400. Fax: (703)779-8345. E-mail: Vietnam@thehistorynet.com. Website: www.thehistorynet.com. Managing Editor: Carl von Wodtke. **Contact:** David T. Zabecki, editor. **90% freelance written.** Bimonthly magazine providing in-depth and authoritative accounts of the many complexities that made the war in Vietnam unique, including the people, battles, strategies, perspectives, analysis and weaponry." Estab. 1988. Circ. 60,000. Pays on publication. Publishes ms an average of 2 years after acceptance. Byline given. Buys all rights. Accepts queries by mail, e-mail, fax. Responds in 3 months to queries; 6 months to mss. Sample copy for $5. Writer's guidelines for #10 SASE.
Nonfiction: Book excerpts (if original), historical/nostalgic (military), interview/profile, personal experience. "Absolutely no fiction or poetry; we want straight history, as much personal narrative as possible, but not the gung-ho, shoot-'em-up variety, either." **Buys 24 mss/year.** Query. Length: 4,000 words maximum; sidebars 500 words. **Pays $300 for features.**
Photos: Send photos with submission or state availability and cite sources. Identification of subjects required.
Columns/Departments: Arsenal (about weapons used, all sides); Personality (profiles of the players, all sides); Fighting Forces (various units or types of units: air, sea, rescue); Perspectives. Length: 2,000 words. Query. **Pays $150.**
   ■ The online magazine carries original content not found in the print edition and includes writer's guidelines. Contact: Roger Vance.
Tips: "Choose stories with strong art possibilities. Send hard copy plus an IBM- or Macintosh-compatible floppy disk. All stories must be true. We do not publish fiction or poetry. All stories should be carefully researched, third-person articles or firsthand accounts that give the reader a sense of experiencing historical events."

N $ $▨ WILD WEST, Primedia History Group, 741 Miller Dr., SE, Suite D-2, Leesburg VA 20175-8920. (703)771-9400. Fax: (703)779-8345. E-mail: gregl@cowles.com. Website: www.thehistorynet.com. Managing Editor: Carl Von Wodtke. **Contact:** Gregory Lalire, editor. **95% freelance written.** Bimonthly magazine covering the history of the American frontier, from its eastern beginnings to its western terminus. "*Wild West* covers the popular (narrative) history of the American West—events, trends, personalities, anything of general interest." Estab. 1988. Circ. 125,000. Pays on publication. Publishes ms an average of 2 years after acceptance. Byline given. Not copyrighted. Buys all rights. Editorial lead time 6 months. Submit seasonal material 1 year in advance. Accepts queries by mail, e-mail. Accepts simultaneous submissions. Responds in 3 months to queries; 6 months to mss. Sample copy for $5. Writer's guidelines for #10 SASE or online.
Nonfiction: Historical/nostalgic (Old West). No excerpts, travel, etc. Articles can be "adapted from" book. No fiction or poetry—nothing current. **Buys 36 mss/year.** Query. Length: 3,500 words with a 500-word sidebar. **Pays $300.**
Photos: State availability with submission. Reviews negatives, transparencies. Buys one-time rights. Offers no additional payment for photos accepted with ms. Captions, identification of subjects required.
Columns/Departments: Gunfighters & Lawmen, 2,000 words; Westerners, 2,000 words; Warriors & Chiefs; Western Lore, 2,000 words; Guns of the West, 1,500 words; Artist Week, 1,500 words; Books Reviews, 250 words. **Buys 36 mss/year.** Query. **Pays $150 for departments; book reviews paid by the word, minimum $40.**
   ■ The online magazine carries original content not found in the print edition. Contact: Roger Vance, online editor.
Tips: "Always query the editor with your story idea. Successful queries include a description of sources of information and suggestions for color and black-and-white photography or artwork. The best way to break into our magazine is to write an entertaining, informative and unusual story that grabs the reader's attention and holds it. We favor carefully researched, third-person articles that give the reader a sense of experiencing historical events. Include a hard copy as well as an IBM- or Macintosh-compatible floppy disk."

N $ $ WORLD WAR II, Primedia History Group, 741 Miller Dr., SE, Suite D-2, Leesburg VA 20175-8920. (703)771-9400. Fax: (703)779-8345. E-mail: WorldWarII@thehistorynet.com. Website: www.thehistorynet.com. Managing Editor: Carl Von Wodtke. **Contact:** Christopher Anderson, associate editor. **95% freelance written.** Prefers to work with published/established writers. Bimonthly magazine covering "military operations in World War II—events, personalities, strategy, national policy, etc." Estab. 1986. Circ. 160,000. Pays on publication. Publishes ms an average of 2 years after acceptance. Byline given. Buys all rights. Accepts queries by mail, e-mail, fax. Responds in 3 months to queries; 6 months to mss. Sample copy for $5. Writer's guidelines for #10 SASE or online.
Nonfiction: World War II military history. Submit anniversary related material 1 year in advance. No fiction. **Buys 24 mss/year.** Query. Length: Length: 4,000 words with a 500-word sidebar. **Pays $200 and up.**
Photos: For photos and other art, send photocopies and cite sources. "We'll order." State availability with submission. Captions, identification of subjects required.
Columns/Departments: Undercover (espionage, resistance, sabotage, intelligence gathering, behind the lines, etc.); Personality (WWII personalities of interest); Armaments (weapons, their use and development), all 2,000 words. Book reviews, 300-750 words. **Buys 18 (plus book reviews) mss/year.** Query. **Pays $100.**

■ The online magazine carries original content not found in the print edition and includes writer's guidelines. Contact: Roger Vance.

Tips: "List your sources and suggest further readings in standard format at the end of your piece—as a bibliography for our files in case of factual challenge or dispute. All submissions are on speculation. Include a hard copy as well as an IBM- or Macintosh-compatible floppy disk. All stories must be true. We do not publish fiction or poetry. Stories should be carefully researched."

HOBBY & CRAFT

Magazines in this category range from home video to cross-stitch. Craftspeople and hobbyists who read these magazines want new ideas while collectors need to know what is most valuable and why. Collectors, do-it-yourselfers and craftspeople look to these magazines for inspiration and information. Publications covering antiques and miniatures are also listed here. Publications covering the business side of antiques and collectibles are listed in the Trade Art, Design & Collectibles section.

$ THE AMERICAN MATCHCOVER COLLECTORS CLUB, The Retskin Report, P.O. Box 18481, Asheville NC 28814-0481. (828)254-4487. Fax: (828)254-1066. E-mail: bill@matchcovers.com. **Contact:** Bill Retskin, editor. **10% freelance written.** Quarterly newsletter for matchcover collectors and historical enthusiasts. Estab. 1986. Circ. 550. Pays on publication. Publishes ms an average of 3 months after acceptance. Byline given. Offers 20% kill fee. Buys first North American serial rights. Submit seasonal material 6 months in advance. Sample copy for 9 × 12 SAE and 2 first-class stamps. Writer's guidelines for #10 SASE.
Nonfiction: General interest, historical/nostalgic, how-to, humor, personal experience, photo feature. **Buys 2 mss/year.** Query with published clips. Length: 200-1,200 words. **Pays $25-50 for assigned articles; $10-25 for unsolicited articles.**
Photos: Send photos with submission. Reviews 5 × 7 prints and b&w contact sheets. Offers $2-5/photo. Captions, identification of subjects required.
Columns/Departments: Query with published clips.
Fiction: Historical. **Buys 2 mss/year.** Query with published clips. Length: 200-1,200 words. **Pays $25-50.**
Tips: "We are interested in clean, direct style with the collector audience in mind."

[N] $ ANTIQUE JOURNAL, Krause Publications/Antique Trader Publications, P.O. Box 1050, Dubuque IA 52004. (319)588-2073. Fax: (800)531-0880. E-mail: hillv@krause.com. Website: www.collect.com. **Contact:** Virginia Hill, managing editor. **15% freelance written.** Monthly newspaper covering antiques and collectibles. **Antique Journal** reaches antique collectors situated in California, Nevada, Oregon and Washington. Estab. 1991. Circ. 28,000. **Pays on acceptance.** Publishes ms an average of up to 1 year after acceptance. Byline given. Buys first, electronic rights. Editorial lead time 2 weeks. Accepts queries by mail, e-mail. Accepts simultaneous submissions. Sample copy and writer's guidelines free.
Photos: Send photos with submission. Reviews contact sheets. Buys all rights. Negotiates payment individually captions required.
Nonfiction: General interest, how-to, interview/profile, photo feature. **Buys 2 mss/year.** Query. Length: 500-1,200 words. **Pays $25-150.** Sometimes pays expenses of writers on assignment.
Tips: "Be knowledgable in antiques and collecting and have good photos."

$ $ ANTIQUE REVIEW, 1000 Bryant St., Dubuque IA 52003. (800)480-0130. E-mail: editor@antiquereview.net. Website: www.antiquereview.net. **Contact:** Charles Muller, editor. **60% freelance written.** Eager to work with new/unpublished writers. Monthly tabloid for an antique-oriented readership, "generally well-educated, interested in Early American furniture and decorative arts, as well as folk art." Estab. 1975. Circ. 10,000. Pays on publication. Publishes ms an average of 2 months after acceptance. Byline given. Buys first North American serial, second serial (reprint) rights. Accepts queries by mail, e-mail, phone. Responds in 3 months to queries. Sample copy for #10 SASE.
  • *Antique Review* has added a new section focusing on trends and collectibles.
Nonfiction: "The articles we desire concern history and production of furniture, pottery, china, and other quality Americana. In some cases, contemporary folk art items are acceptable. We are also interested in reporting on antiques shows and auctions with statements on conditions and prices." Query should show "author's familiarity with antiques, an interest in the historical development of artifacts relating to early America and an awareness of antiques market." **Buys 60-90 mss/year.** Query with published clips. Length: 200-2,000 words. **Pays $100-200.** Sometimes pays expenses of writers on assignment.
Reprints: Send tearsheet, photocopy or typed ms with rights for sale noted and information about when and where the material previously appeared. Pays 100% of amount paid for an original article.
Photos: Send photos with submission. Articles with photographs receive preference. Reviews 3 × 5 or larger glossy b&w or color prints. Payment included in ms price. Captions required.

Tips: "Give us a call and let us know of specific interests. We are more concerned with the background in antiques than in writing abilities. The writing can be edited, but the knowledge imparted is of primary interest. A frequent mistake is being too general, not becoming deeply involved in the topic and its research. We are interested in primary research into America's historic material culture."

N $ $ THE ANTIQUE TRADER WEEKLY, P.O. Box 1050, Dubuque IA 52004-1050. (319)588-2073, ext. 121. Fax: (800)531-0880. E-mail: traderpubs@aol.com. **Contact:** Kyle Husfloen, editor. **50% freelance written.** Works with a small number of new/unpublished writers each year. Weekly newspaper for collectors and dealers in antiques and collectibles. Estab. 1957. Circ. 60,000. Publishes ms an average of 1 year after acceptance. Buys all rights. Payment made at beginning of month following publication. Submit seasonal material 4 months in advance. Sample copy for $1 and #10 SASE. Writer's guidelines free.
Nonfiction: "We invite authoritative and well-researched articles on all types of antiques and collectors' items and in-depth stories on specific types of antiques and collectibles. No human interest stories. We do not pay for brief information on new shops opening or other material printed as a service to the antiques hobby." **Buys 60 mss/year.** Query or submit complete ms. Length: 1,000-2,000 words. **Pays $50-150 for features; $150-250 for feature cover stories.**
Photos: Submit a liberal number of good color photos to accompany articles. Uses 35mm slides for cover. Offers no additional payment for photos accepted with ms.
Tips: "Send concise, polite letter stating the topic to be covered in the story and the writer's qualifications. No 'cute' letters rambling on about some 'imaginative' story idea. Writers who have a concise yet readable style and know their topic are always appreciated. I am most interested in those who have personal collecting experience or can put together a knowledgeable and informative feature after interviewing a serious collector/authority."

N $ $ ANTIQUES & COLLECTING MAGAZINE, 1006 S. Michigan Ave., Chicago IL 60605. (312)939-4767. Fax: (312)939-0053. E-mail: lightnerpb@aol.com. **Contact:** Frances Graham, editor. **80% freelance written.** Monthly magazine covering antiques and collectibles. Estab. 1931. Circ. 20,000. Pays on publication. Publishes ms an average of 3 months after acceptance. Byline given. Buys first rights. Editorial lead time 2 months. Submit seasonal material 3 months in advance. Accepts queries by mail, e-mail, fax, phone. Responds in 3 weeks to queries; 2 months to mss. Sample copy free or by e-mail. Writer's guidelines free or by e-mail.
Nonfiction: Book excerpts, general interest, historical/nostalgic, how-to, interview/profile, opinion, personal experience, photo feature. **Buys 40-50 mss/year.** Query. Length: 1,000-1,600 words. **Pays $150-250 plus 4 copies.**
Photos: Send photos with submission. Reviews transparencies, prints. Buys one-time rights. Offers no additional payment for photos accepted with ms. Captions, identification of subjects required.
Fillers: Anecdotes, facts.

$ ⊠ AUTOGRAPH COLLECTOR, Odyssey Publications, 510-A South Corona Mall, Corona CA 92879-1420. (909)734-9636. Fax: (909)371-7139. E-mail: DBTOGI@aol.com. Website: www.AutographCollector.com. **Contact:** Ev Phillips, editor. **80% freelance written.** Monthly magazine covering the autograph collecting hobby. "The focus of *Autograph Collector* is on documents, photographs or any collectible item that has been signed by a famous person, whether a current celebrity or historical figure. Articles stress how and where to locate celebrities and autograph material, authenticity of signatures and what they are worth." Byline given. Offers negotiable kill fee. Buys all rights. Editorial lead time 2 months. Submit seasonal material 3 months in advance. Accepts queries by mail, e-mail, fax, phone. Responds in 2 weeks to queries. Sample copy and writer's guidelines free.
Nonfiction: "Articles must address subjects that appeal to autograph collectors and should answer six basic questions: Who is this celebrity/famous person? How do I go about collecting this person's autograph? Where can I find it? How scarce or available is it? How can I tell if it's real? What is it worth?" Historical/nostalgic, how-to, interview/profile, personal experience. **Buys 25-35 mss/year.** Query. Length: 1,600-2,000 words. **Pays 5¢/word.** Sometimes pays expenses of writers on assignment.
Photos: State availability with submission. Reviews transparencies, prints. Buys one-time rights. Offers $3/photo. Captions, identification of subjects required.
Columns/Departments: "*Autograph Collector* buys 8-10 columns per month written by regular contributors." **Buys 90-100 mss/year.** Query. **Pays $50 or as determined on a per case basis.**
Fillers: Anecdotes, facts. **Buys 20-25/year.** Length: 200-300 words. Pays $15.
Tips: "Ideally writers should be autograph collectors themselves and know their topics thoroughly. Articles must be well-researched and clearly written. Writers should remember that *Autograph Collector* is a celebrity-driven magazine and name recognition of the subject is important."

N $ BEAD & BUTTON, Kalmbach Publishing, 21027 Crossroads Circle, Waukesha WI 53186. (262)796-8776. E-mail: akorach@beadandbutton.com. Website: www.beadandbutton.com. Editor: Alice Korach. **Contact:** Lora Grosz-kiewicz, editorial assistant. **50% freelance written.** "*Bead & Button* is a bimonthly magazine devoted to techniques, projects, designs and materials relating to beads, buttons, and accessories. Our readership includes both professional and amateur bead and button makers, hobbyists, and enthusiasts who find satisfaction in making beautiful things." Estab. 1994. Circ. 80,000. **Pays on acceptance.** Publishes ms an average of 4 months after acceptance. Byline given. Offers $75 kill fee. Buys all rights. Accepts queries by mail, e-mail, fax. Writer's guidelines free, online or by e-mail.

Nonfiction: Historical/nostalgic (on beaded jewelry history), how-to (make beaded jewelry and accessories), humor (or inspirational—1 endpiece for each issue), interview/profile. **Buys 24-30 mss/year.** Send complete ms. Length: 750-3,000 words. **Pays $75-300.**

Photos: Send photos with submission. Offers no additional payment for photos accepted with ms. Identification of subjects required.

Columns/Departments: Chic & Easy (fashionable jewelry how-to); Beginner (easy-to-make jewelry how-to); Simply Earrings (fashionable earring how-to); Fun Fashion (trendy jewelry how-to), all 1,500 words. **Buys 12 mss/year.** Send complete ms. **Pays $75-150.**

Tips: "*Bead & Button* magazine primarily publishes how-to articles by the artists who have designed the piece. We publish one profile and one historical piece per issue. These would be the only applicable articles for non-artisan writers. Also our humorous and inspirational endpiece might apply."

$ $⚅ BLADE MAGAZINE, The World's #1 Knife Publication, Krause Publications, 700 E. State St., Iola WI 54990. (715)445-2214. Fax: (715)445-4087. E-mail: blade@krause.com. Website: www.krause.com. Managing Editor: Kathleen Smith. **Contact:** Joe Kertzman, managing editor. **60% freelance written.** Monthly magazine for knife enthusiasts who want to know as much as possible about quality knives and edged tools, hand-made and factory knife industries, antique knife collecting, etc. *Blade* is designed to highlight the romance and history of man's oldest tool, the knife. Our readers are into any and all knives used as tools/collectibles. Estab. 1973. Circ. 75,000. Pays on publication. Publishes ms an average of 1 year after acceptance. Byline given. Offers $20 kill fee. Buys all rights. Editorial lead time 4 months. Submit seasonal material 4 months in advance. Accepts queries by mail, e-mail, fax, phone. Responds in 3 months to queries. Sample copy for #10 SASE.

Nonfiction: "We would like to see articles on knives in adventuresome lifesaving situations." Book excerpts, exposé, general interest, historical/nostalgic (on knives), how-to, humor, new product, personal experience, photo feature, technical, travel, adventure (on a knife theme), celebrities who own knives, knives featured in movies with shots from the movie, etc. No articles on how to use knives as weapons. Np poetry. **Buys 50 mss/year.** Query. Length: 1,000-1,500 words. **Pays $125-300. "We will pay top dollar in the knife market."** Sometimes pays expenses of writers on assignment.

Photos: State availability of or send photos with submission. Offers no additional payment for photos accepted with ms. Captions, identification of subjects required.

Columns/Departments: Buys 60 mss/year. Query. **Pays $150-250.**

Fillers: Anecdotes, facts, newsbreaks. **Buys 1-2/year.** Length: 50-200 words. **Pays $25-50.**

Tips: "We are always willing to read submissions from anyone who has read a few copies and studied the market. The ideal article for us is a piece bringing out the romance, legend, and love of man's oldest tool—the knife. We like articles that place knives in peoples' hands—in life saving situations, adventure modes, etc. (Nothing gory or with the knife as the villain.) People and knives are good copy. We are getting more and better written articles from writers who are reading the publication beforehand. That makes for a harder sell for the quickie writer not willing to do his homework. Go to knife shows and talk to the makers and collectors. Visit knifemakers' shops and knife factories. Read anything and everything you can find on knives and knifemaking."

$ ⚅ BREW YOUR OWN, The How-to Homebrew Beer Magazine, Battenkill Communications, 5053 Main St., Suite A, Manchester Center VT 05255. (802)362-3981. Fax: (802)362-2377. E-mail: edit@byo.com. Website: www.byo.com. **Contact:** Kathleen Ring, editor. **85% freelance written.** Monthly magazine covering home brewing. "Our mission is to provide practical information in an entertaining format. We try to capture the spirit and challenge of brewing while helping our readers brew the best beer they can." Estab. 1995. Circ. 42,000. **Pays on acceptance.** Publishes ms an average of 4 months after acceptance. Byline given. Offers 25% kill fee. Buys all rights. Editorial lead time 3 months. Submit seasonal material 3 months in advance. Accepts queries by mail, e-mail, fax. Responds in 2 months to queries. Writer's guidelines for #10 SASE.

   Break in by "sending a detailed query in one of two key areas: how to brew a specific, interesting style of beer (with step-by-step recipes) or how to build your own specific piece of brewing equipment."

Nonfiction: Informational pieces on equipment, ingredients and brewing methods. Historical/nostalgic, how-to (home brewing), humor (related to home brewing), interview/profile (of professional brewers), personal experience, trends. **Buys 75 mss/year.** Query with published clips or description of brewing expertise. Length: 800-3,000 words. **Pays $50-150, depending on length, complexity of article and experience of writer.** Sometimes pays expenses of writers on assignment.

Photos: State availability with submission. Reviews contact sheets, transparencies, 5×7 prints, slides and electronic images. Buys all rights. Negotiates payment individually. Captions required.

Columns/Departments: News (humorous, unusual news about homebrewing), 50-250 words; Last Call (humorous stories about homebrewing), 700 words. **Buys 12 mss/year.** Query with or without published clips. **Pays $50.**

Tips: "*Brew Your Own* is for anyone who is interested in brewing beer, from beginners to advanced all-grain brewers. We seek articles that are straightforward and factual, not full of esoteric theories or complex calculations. Our readers tend to be intelligent, upscale, and literate."

$ $⚅ CLASSIC TOY TRAINS, Kalmbach Publishing Co., 21027 Crossroads Circle, Waukesha WI 53187. (262)796-8776. Fax: (262)796-1142. E-mail: editor@classtrain.com. Website: www.classtrain.com. **Contact:** Neil Besougloff, editor. **80% freelance written.** Magazine published 9 times/year covering collectible toy trains (O, S, Standard,

G scale, etc.) like Lionel, American Flyer, Marx, Dorfan, etc. "For the collector and operator of toy trains, *CTT* offers full-color photos of layouts and collections of toy trains, restoration tips, operating information, new product reviews and information, and insights into the history of toy trains." Estab. 1987. Circ. 72,000. **Pays on acceptance.** Publishes ms an average of 1 year after acceptance. Byline given. Buys all rights. Editorial lead time 3 months. Submit seasonal material 6 months in advance. Accepts queries by mail, e-mail. Responds in 3 weeks to queries; 1 month to mss. Sample copy for $4.95 plus s&h. Writer's guidelines for #10 SASE or online.

Nonfiction: General interest, historical/nostalgic, how-to (restore toy trains; design a layout; build accessories; fix broken toy trains), interview/profile, personal experience, photo feature, technical. **Buys 90 mss/year.** Query. Length: 500-5,000 words. **Pays $75-500.** Sometimes pays expenses of writers on assignment.

Photos: Send photos with submission. Reviews 4×5 transparencies, 5×7 prints preferred. Buys all rights. Offers no additional payment for photos accepted with ms or $15-75/photo. Captions required.

Fillers: Uses cartoons. **Buys 6/year. Pays $30.**

▣ The online magazine carries original content not found in the print edition and includes writer's guidelines. Contact: Mike Williams and Jim Schulz, online editors.

Tips: "It's important to have a thorough understanding of the toy train hobby; most of our freelancers are hobbyists themselves. One-half to two-thirds of *CTT*'s editorial space is devoted to photographs; superior photography is critical."

$ COLLECTIBLES CANADA, Canada's Guide to Contemporary Collectible Art, Trajan Publishing, 103 Lakeshore Rd., Suite 202, St. Catharines, Ontario L2N 2T6, Canada. (905)646-7744, ext. 229. Fax: (905)646-0995. E-mail: newsroom@collectiblescanada.net. Website: www.collectiblescanada.ca. Executive Editor: Gordon L. Bordewyk. **Contact:** Susan E. Pennell, editor. **90% freelance written.** Bimonthly magazine covering contemporary collectible art. "We provide news and profiles of limited edition collectible art from a positive perspective. We are an informational tool for collectors who want to read about the products they love." Circ. 50,000. Pays 1 month after publication. Publishes ms an average of 3 months after acceptance. Byline given. Buys first North American serial rights. Editorial lead time 6 months. Submit seasonal material 6 months in advance. Accepts queries by mail, e-mail, fax. Responds in 1 month to queries. Sample copy for $3.95 (Canadian) and $2.50 IRC. Writer's guidelines for #10 SASE.

Nonfiction: Historical/nostalgic (collectibles), interview/profile, new product, technical, collectible art such as figurines, dolls, bears, prints, etc. Special issues: "We publish both a Christmas issue and a nature issue (January-February)." No articles on antique related subjects (we cover contemporary collectibles). No articles about stamp, coin or sports collecting. **Buys 16 mss/year.** Query with published clips. Length: 500-1,200 words. **Pays $75-120 (Canadian).** Sometimes pays expenses of writers on assignment.

Photos: State availability with submission. Reviews negatives, transparencies, prints. Buys one-time rights. Negotiates payment individually. Identification of subjects required.

Columns/Departments: Book reviews (positive slant, primarily informational). Length: 500-800 words. **Buys 2 mss/year.** Query with published clips. **Pays $50-75** (Canadian).

Tips: "Read the magazine first. No odd collector profiles. I am very willing to work with beginning writers. Writers who can offer an article with a unique angle based on collectibles. Examples of past article ideas: 'The history of Fabergé,' 'Crossing the Lines: how collectibles go from art print to figurine, to plate to doll.' Send an e-mail with your idea and I'll evaluate it promptly."

$ $ COLLECTOR EDITIONS, Collector Communications Corp., 1107 Broadway, Suite 1210 N., New York NY 10010. (212)989-8700. Fax: (212)645-8976. Editor: Bonne Steffen. **Contact:** Joan Pursley, editor. **40% freelance written.** Works with a small number of new/unpublished writers each year. Magazine published 7 times/year covering collectible plates, figurines, cottages, prints, etc. "We specialize in contemporary (post-war ceramic, resin and glass) collectibles, including reproductions, but also publish articles about antiques, if they are being reproduced today and are generally available." "First assignments are always done on a speculative basis." Estab. 1973. Circ. 65,000. Pays within 30 days of acceptance. Publishes ms an average of 6 months after acceptance. Buys first North American serial rights. Responds in 2 months to queries. Sample copy for $2. Writer's guidelines for #10 SASE.

Nonfiction: "Short features about collecting, written in tight, newsy style. We specialize in contemporary (postwar) collectibles. Values for pieces being written about should be included." Historical/nostalgic, interview/profile, Informational. Special issues: Christmas Collectibles (December). **Buys 15-20 mss/year.** Query with samples. Length: 800-1,200 words. **Pays $250-400.** Sometimes pays expenses of writers on assignment.

Photos: "We want clear, distinct, full-frame images that say something." Reviews b&w and color photos. Offers no additional payment for photos accepted with ms. Captions required.

Tips: "Unfamiliarity with the field is the most frequent mistake made by writers in completing an article for us."

$ $ COLLECTOR'S MART, Contemporary Collectibles & Home Decor, Krause Publications, 700 E. State St., Iola WI 54990. (715)445-2214. Fax: (715)445-4087. E-mail: sieberm@krause.com. Website: www.collectorsmart.net. **Contact:** Mary L. Sieber, editor. **50% freelance written.** Bimonthly magazine covering contemporary collectibles, for collectors of all types. Estab. 1976. Circ. 170,000. Pays on publication. Publishes ms an average of 6 months after acceptance. Byline given. Buys perpetual non-exclusive rights. Editorial lead time 2 months. Submit seasonal material 4 months in advance. Accepts queries by mail, e-mail, fax. Responds in 1 month to mss. Writer's guidelines available.

○━ Break in with "exciting, interesting theme topics for collections, i.e., seaside, fun and functional, patio decor, etc."

Nonfiction: Inspirational (collectibles with religious themes), interview/profile (artists of collectibles), new product. **Buys 35-50 mss/year.** Send complete ms. Length: 1,000-2,000 words. **Pays $50-300.**

Photos: Send only color photos with submission. Reviews transparencies, prints, electronic images. Buys one-time rights. Offers no additional payment for photos accepted with ms. Captions required.

■ The online magazine carries original content not found in the print edition. Contact: Lisa Wilson.

Tips: "We're looking for more pieces on unique Christmas theme collectibles, i.e. tree toppers. Also includes giftware and home decor."

$ $ COLLECTORS NEWS, P.O. Box 306, Grundy Center IA 50638. (319)824-6981. Fax: (319)824-3414. E-mail: collectors@collectors-news.com. Website: collectors-news.com. **Contact:** Linda Kruger, managing editor. **20% freelance written.** Works with a small number of new/unpublished writers each year. Monthly magazine-size publication on newsprint, glossy cover, covering antiques, collectibles and nostalgic memorabilia. Estab. 1959. Circ. 9,500. Pays on publication. Publishes ms an average of 1 year after acceptance. Byline given. Buys first rights, makes work-for-hire assignments. Submit seasonal material 3 months in advance. Accepts queries by mail, e-mail, fax, phone. Responds in 2 weeks to queries; 6 weeks to mss. Sample copy for $4 and 9×12 SAE. Writer's guidelines free.

○━ Break in with articles on collecting online; history and values of collectibles and antiques; collectors with unique and/or extensive collections; using collectibles in the home decor; music collectibles; transportation collectibles; advertising collectibles; bottles; glass, china and silver; primitives; furniture; jewelry; lamps; western; textiles; toys; black memorabilia; political collectibles; movie memorabilia and any 20th century and timely subjects.

Nonfiction: General interest (any subject re: collectibles, antique to modern), historical/nostalgic (relating to collections or collectors), how-to (display your collection, care for, restore, appraise, locate, add to, etc.), interview/profile (covering individual collectors and their hobbies, unique or extensive; celebrity collectors, and limited edition artists), technical (in-depth analysis of a particular antique, collectible or collecting field), travel ("hot" antiquing places in the US). Special issues: 12-month listing of antique and collectible shows, flea markets and conventions, (January includes events January-December; June includes events June-May); Care & Display of Collectibles (September); holidays (October-December). **Buys 70 mss/year.** Query with sample of writing. Length: 800-1,000 words. **Pays $1.10/column inch.**

Photos: "Articles must be accompanied by photographs for illustration." A selection of 2-8 prints is suggested. "Articles are eligible for full-color front page consideration when accompanied by quality color prints, color slides, electronic images and/or color transparencies. Only one article is highlighted on the cover per month. Any article providing a color photo selected for front page use receives an additional $25." Reviews color or b&w prints. Buys first rights. Payment for photos included in payment for ms. Captions required.

Tips: "Present a professionally written article with quality illustrations—well-researched and documented information."

⃞N⃞ $ $ CQ AMATEUR RADIO, The Radio Amateur's Journal, CQ Communications, Inc., 25 Newbridge Rd., Hicksville NY 11801. Fax: (516)681-2926. E-mail: cq@cq-amateur-radio.com; query to w2vu@cq-amateur-radio.com. Website: www.cq-amateur-radio.com. Managing Editor: Gail Schieber. **Contact:** Richard Moseson, editor. **40% freelance written.** Monthly magazine covering amateur (ham) radio. "*CQ* is published for active ham radio operators and is read by radio amateurs in over 100 countries. All articles must deal with amateur radio. Our focus is on operating and on practical projects. A thorough knowledge of amateur radio is required." Estab. 1945. Circ. 60,000. Pays on publication. Publishes ms an average of 6 months after acceptance. Byline given. Buys first North American serial rights. Editorial lead time 4 months. Submit seasonal material 4 months in advance. Accepts queries by mail, e-mail, fax. Responds in 3 weeks to queries; 3 months to mss. Sample copy free. Writer's guidelines for #10 SASE, online or by e-mail.

Nonfiction: Historical/nostalgic, how-to, interview/profile, personal experience, technical, all related to amateur radio. **Buys 50-60 mss/year.** Query. Length: 2,000-4,000 words. **Pays $40/published page.**

Photos: State availability with submission. Reviews contact sheets, 4×6 prints, electronic photos also OK, tiff or jpeg files with 300 dpi resolution. Buys one-time rights. Offers no additional payment for photos accepted with ms. Captions, identification of subjects, model releases required.

Tips: "You must know and understand ham radio and ham radio operators. Most of our writers (95%) are licensed hams. Because our readers span a wide area of interests within amateur radio, don't assume they are already familiar with your topic. Explain. At the same time, don't write down to the readers. They are intelligent, well-educated people who will understand what you're saying when written and explained in plain English."

$ $ ⃞ CRITICAL CERAMICS, c/o Bennington College, Route 67A, Bennington VT 05201. E-mail: editor@criticalceramics.org. Website: www.criticalceramics.org. Editor: Thomas J. Wallace. **Contact:** Forrest Snyder, editor. **100% freelance written.** Online magazine covering contemporary ceramic art. Nonprofit. Estab. 1997. Circ. 5,000. Pays on publication. Publishes ms an average of 1 month after acceptance. Byline given. Buys non-exclusive electronic rights in perpetuity. Editorial lead time 1 month. Submit seasonal material 1 month in advance. Accepts queries by mail, e-mail. Accepts simultaneous submissions. Responds in 1 week to queries; 1 month to mss. Sample copy online. Writer's guidelines online or by e-mail.

Nonfiction: Book excerpts, essays, exposé, interview/profile, opinion, personal experience, photo feature, travel, cross-cultural dialog. **Buys 12-24 mss/year.** Query. Length: 750-1,500 words. **Pays $75-500 for assigned articles; $50-350 for unsolicited articles.** Sometimes pays expenses of writers on assignment.

Photos: State availability with submission. Reviews transparencies, 4×6 prints. Buys non-exclusive electronic rights in perpetuity. Negotiates payment individually. Captions, identification of subjects required.

Columns/Departments: Exhibition (reviews); Book Reviews; Video Reviews. **Buys 12-24 mss/year.** Query. **Pays $20-150.**

Tips: "Show enthusiasm for contemporary art with a unique view of subject area. This is a publication for professional contemporary ceramic artists."

$ $ CROCHET WORLD, House of White Birches, P.O. Box 776, Henniker NH 03242. Fax: (219)589-8093. Website: www.whitebirches.com. **Contact:** Susan Hankins, editor. **100% freelance written.** Bimonthly magazine covering crochet patterns. "*Crochet World* is a pattern magazine devoted to the art of crochet. We also feature a Q&A column, letters (swap shop) column and occasionally non-pattern manuscripts, but it must be devoted to crochet." Estab. 1978. Circ. 75,000. Pays on publication. Byline given. Buys all rights. Editorial lead time 4 months. Submit seasonal material 6 months in advance. Responds in 1 month to queries. Sample copy for $2. Writer's guidelines free.

Nonfiction: How-to (crochet). **Buys 0-2 mss/year.** Send complete ms. Length: 500-1,500 words. **Pays $50.**

Columns/Departments: Touch of Style (crocheted clothing); It's a Snap! (quick one-night simple patterns); Pattern of the Month, first and second prize each issue. **Buys dozens of mss/year.** Send complete pattern. **Pays $40-300.**

Poetry: Strictly crochet-related. **Buys 0-5 poems/year.** Submit maximum 2 poems. Length: 6-20 lines. **Pays $10-20.**

Fillers: Anecdotes, facts, short humor. **Buys 0-10/year.** Length: 25-200 words. **Pays $5-30.**

Tips: "Be aware that this is a pattern generated magazine for crochet designs. I prefer the actual item sent along with complete directions/graphs etc., over queries. In some cases a photo submission or good sketch will do. Crocheted designs must be well-made and original and directions must be complete. Write for Designer's Guidelines which detail how to submit designs. Non-crochet items, such as fillers, poetry *must* be crochet-related, not knit, not sewing, etc."

N $ DANCING USA, The Art of Ballroom Dance, Dancing USA LLC, 200 N. York Rd., Elmhurst IL 60126-2750. (630)782-1260. Fax: (630)617-9950. E-mail: ballroom@dancingusa.com. Website: www.dancingusa.com. **Contact:** Michael Fitzmaurice, editor. **60% freelance written.** Works with new writers. Biweekly magazine covering ballroom, swing and Latin dance: How-tos, technique, floor craft; source for dance videos, CDs, shoes, where to dance. Estab. 1983. Circ. 20,000. Pays on publication. Publishes ms an average of 6 months after acceptance. Byline given. Buys first North American serial rights. Editorial lead time 3 months. Submit seasonal material 4 months in advance. Accepts queries by mail, e-mail, fax. Responds in 2 months to queries; 2 months to mss. Sample copy for $4.50.

Nonfiction: Book excerpts, exposé, historical/nostalgic, how-to, humor, inspirational, interview/profile, new product, personal experience, photo feature, travel, commentary, all dance related. **Buys 30-40 mss/year.** Send complete ms. Length: 1,000-2,000 words. **Pays $25-75 for assigned articles; $10-50 for unsolicited articles.**

Photos: Send photos with submission. No additional payment.

Fiction: Looking for any type of fiction that includes a style of ballroom, Latin or swing dance, or the industry or enjoyment of ballroom dance as a main theme.

Tips: "Works with new writers. Hotstuff department features new dance-related products, books, and music. 4-8 features per issue from freelancers include dancer profiles, history of dancers, entertainers, expert dance advice, promoting dance. Each issue tries to include a city dance guide, a style of dance, dance functions, a major dance competition, and a celebrity profile. Example: Denver, Tango, Weddings, U.S. Championships, and Rita Moreno."

$ $ DECORATIVE ARTIST'S WORKBOOK, F&W Publications, Inc., 1507 Dana Ave., Cincinnati OH 45207-1005. (513)531-2690 ext. 461. Fax: (513)531-2902. E-mail: dawedit@fwpubs.com. Website: www.decorativeartist.com. **Contact:** Anne Hevener, editor. **75% freelance written.** Bimonthly magazine covering decorative painting projects and products of all sorts. Offers "straightforward, personal instruction in the techniques of decorative painting." Estab. 1987. Circ. 90,000. **Pays on acceptance.** Byline given. Offers 25% kill fee. Buys first North American serial rights. Submit seasonal material 8 months in advance. Accepts queries by mail, e-mail. Responds in 2 weeks to queries. Sample copy for $4.65 and 9×12 SAE with 5 first-class stamps.

Nonfiction: How-to (related to decorative painting projects), new product, technique. **Buys 30 mss/year.** Query with slides or photos. Length: 1,200-1,800 words. **Pays 15-25¢/word.**

🔲 The online magazine carries original content not found in the print edition. Contact: Anne Hevener, online editor.

Tips: "Create a design, surface or technique that is fresh and new to decorative painting. I'm looking for experts in the field who, through their own experience, can artfully describe the techniques involved. How-to articles are most open to freelancers. Be sure to query with photo/slides, and show that you understand the extensive graphic requirements for these pieces and can provide painted progressives—painted illustrations that show works in progress."

$ 🗹 DOLL WORLD, The Magazine for Doll Lovers, House of White Birches, 306 E. Parr Rd., Berne IN 46711. (219)589-4000. Fax: (219)589-8093. E-mail: doll_world@whitebirches.com. Website: www.dollworld-magazine.com. **Contact:** Vicki Steensma, editor. **90% freelance written.** Bimonthly magazine covering doll collecting, restoration. "Interested in informative articles about doll history, interviews with doll artists and collectors, and how-to articles." Estab. 1976. Circ. 65,000. Pays pre-publication. Byline given. Buys all rights. Submit seasonal material 9 months in advance. Accepts queries by e-mail, fax, phone. Responds in 2 months to queries. Writer's guidelines for #10 SASE.

Nonfiction: "Subjects with broad appeal to the 'boomer' generation." The editor reports an interest in seeing features on dolls of the 1930s-1960s. Historical/nostalgic (about dolls and collecting), how-to (about dolls—collecting, care, display, sell, buy), humor (about dolls), inspirational, interview/profile (those in the doll industry), new product, personal experience (dolls), photo feature (dolls), religious (dolls), technical (dolls), travel (dolls). **Buys 50 mss/year.** Send complete ms. **Pays $50 and up.**

Photos: Send top-quality photos or disk images (hi-res TIFF Mac format). Send photos with submission. Captions, identification of subjects required, written separate from ms text.

Tips: "Choose a specific manufacturer or artist and talk about his dolls or a specific doll—modern or antique—and explore its history and styles made. Be descriptive, but do not overuse adjectives. Use personal conversational tone. Be interested enough in the magazine to have looked at an issue of it."

$ $ DOLLHOUSE MINIATURES, Kalmbach Publishing Co., 21027 Crossroads Circle, Waukesha WI 53187-1612. (262)796-8776. Fax: (262)796-1383. E-mail: cstjacques@dhminiatures.com. Website: www.dhminiatures.com. Editor: Jane D. Lange. **Contact:** Candice St. Jacques, managing editor. **50% freelance written.** Monthly magazine covering dollhouse scale miniatures. "*Dollhouse Miniatures* is America's best-selling miniatures magazine and the definitive resource for artisans, collectors, and hobbyists. It promotes and supports the large national and international community of miniaturists through club columns, short reports, and by featuring reader projects and ideas." Estab. 1971. Circ. 45,000. **Pays on acceptance.** Byline given. Offers 10% kill fee. Buys all rights. Editorial lead time 6 months. Submit seasonal material 6 months in advance. Accepts queries by mail, e-mail. Responds in 1 month to queries; 2 months to mss. Sample copy free (one copy). Contact: Customer Service 800-446-5489. Writer's guidelines for #10 SASE or online.

Nonfiction: How-to (miniature projects of various scales in variety of media), interview/profile (artisans, collectors), photo feature (dollhouses, collections, museums). No articles on miniature shops or essays. **Buys 50-60 mss/year.** Query with or without published clips or send complete ms. Length: 500-1,500 words. **Pays $50-350 for assigned articles; $0-200 for unsolicited articles.** Pays expenses of writers on assignment.

Photos: "Photos are paid for with ms. Seldom buys individual photos." Send photos with submission. Reviews 35mm slides and larger, 3×5 prints. Buys all rights. Identification of subjects, captions preferred required.

Tips: "Familiarity with the miniatures hobby is very helpful. Accuracy to scale is extremely important to our readers. A complete package (manuscripts/photos) has a better chance of publication."

$ $ DOLLS, Collector Communications, 1107 Broadway, Suite 1210N, New York NY 10010. Fax: (212)645-8976. E-mail: nr@collector-online.com. Managing Editor: Bessie Nestoras. **Contact:** Nayda Rondon, editor. **75% freelance written.** Magazine published 10 times/year covering dolls, doll artists and related topics of interest to doll collectors and enthusiasts. "*Dolls* enhances the joy of collecting by introducing readers to the best new dolls from around the world, along with the artists and designers who create them. It keeps readers up-to-date on shows, sales and special events in the doll world. With beautiful color photography, *Dolls* offers an array of easy-to-read, informative articles that help our collectors select the best buys." Estab. 1982. Circ. 100,000. Pays on publication. Byline given. Buys first North American serial rights. Accepts queries by mail, e-mail, fax. Accepts simultaneous submissions. Responds in 1 month to queries.

Nonfiction: Historical/nostalgic, how-to, interview/profile, new product, photo feature. **Buys 55 mss/year.** Query with published clips or send complete ms. Length: 750-1,200 words. **Pays $100-400.** Sometimes pays expenses of writers on assignment.

Photos: Send photos with submission. Reviews transparencies. Buys one-time rights. Offers no additional payment for photos accepted with ms. Captions, identification of subjects, model releases required.

Tips: "Know the subject matter and artists. Having quality artwork and access to doll artists for interviews are big pluses. We need original ideas of interest to doll lovers."

$ $ $ FAMILY TREE MAGAZINE, Discover, Preserve & Celebrate Your Family's History, F&W Publications, 1507 Dana Ave., Cincinnati OH 45207. (513)531-2690. Fax: (513)531-2902. E-mail: ftmedit@fwpubs.com. Website: www.familytreemagazine.com. **Contact:** David A. Fryxell, editorial director. **75% freelance written.** Bimonthly magazine covering family history, heritage and genealogy. "*Family Tree Magazine* is a general-interest consumer magazine that helps readers discover, preserve and celebrate their family's history. We cover genealogy, ethnic heritage, personal history, genealogy websites and software, scrapbooking, photography and photo preservation, and other ways that families connect with their past." Estab. 1999. Circ. 73,000. **Pays on acceptance.** Publishes ms an average of 6 months after acceptance. Byline given. Offers 25% kill fee. Buys first, electronic rights. Editorial lead time 8 months. Submit seasonal material 8 months in advance. Accepts queries by mail, e-mail. Accepts simultaneous submissions. Responds in 1 month to queries. Sample copy for $6.25 or online. Writer's guidelines for #10 SASE or online.

O— Break in by suggesting a "useful, timely idea for our Toolkit section on a resource that our readers would love to discover."

Nonfiction: "Articles are geared to beginners but never talk down to the audience. We emphasize sidebars, tips and other reader-friendly 'packaging,' and each article aims to give the reader the resources necessary to take the next step in his or her quest for their personal past." Book excerpts, historical/nostalgic, how-to (genealogy), new product (photography, computer), technical (genealogy software, photography equipment), travel (with ethnic heritage slant). **Buys 60 mss/year.** Query with published clips. Length: 1,000-3,500 words. **Pays $250-800.** Sometimes pays expenses of writers on assignment.

Photos: State availability with submission. Reviews color transparencies. Buys one-time rights. Negotiates payment individually. Captions required.

■ The online magazine carries original content not found in the print edition and includes writer's guidelines. Contact: Susan Wenner, associate editor.

Tips: "We see too many broad, general stories on genealogy or records, and personal accounts of 'how I found great-aunt Sally' without how-to value."

$ $ FIBERARTS, The Magazine of Textiles, Altamont Press, 50 College St., Asheville NC 28801. (828)253-0467. Fax: (828)253-7952. E-mail: editor@fiberartsmagazine.com. Website: www.fiberartsmagazine.com. **Contact:** Sunita Patterson, editor. **90% freelance written.** Magazine published 5 times/year covering textiles as art and craft (contemporary trends in fiber sculpture, weaving, quilting, surface design, stitchery, papermaking, basketry, felting, wearable art, knitting, fashion, crochet, mixed textile techniques, ethnic dying, fashion, eccentric tidbits, etc.) for textile artists, craftspeople, hobbyists, teachers, museum and gallery staffs, collectors and enthusiasts. Estab. 1975. Circ. 23,745. Pays 30 days after publication. Publishes ms an average of 4 months after acceptance. Byline given. Buys first rights. Accepts queries by mail. Sample copy for $5. Writer's guidelines for #10 SAE with 2 first-class stamps.
Nonfiction: "Please be very specific about your proposal. Also, an important consideration in accepting an article is the kind of photos that you can provide as illustration. We like to see photos in advance." Essays, historical/nostalgic (ethnic), interview/profile (artist), opinion, personal experience, photo feature, technical, education, trends, exhibition reviews, textile news, book reviews. Query with brief outline, prose synopsis, SASE and visuals. No phone queries. Length: 250-2,000 words. **Pays $65-500.**
Photos: Color slides or b&w glossies must accompany every article. The more photos to choose from, the better. Please include a separate, number-keyed caption sheet. The names and addresses of those mentioned in the article or to whom the visuals are to be returned are necessary. Captions required.
Columns/Departments: Swatches (new ideas for fiber, unusual or offbeat subjects, work spaces, resources and marketing, techniques, materials, equipment, design and trends), 450 words and 2-4 photos; Profile (focuses on one artist), 450 words and 1 photo; Reviews (exhibits and shows; summarize quality, significance, focus and atmosphere, then evaluate selected pieces for aesthetic quality, content and technique—because we have an international readership, brief biographical notes or quotes might be pertinent for locally or regionally known artists), 500 words and 3-5 photos. (Do not cite works for which visuals are unavailable; you are not eligible to review a show in which you have participated as an artist, organizer, curator or juror.). **Pays $115-125.**
Tips: "Our writers are very familiar with the textile field, and this is what we look for in a new writer. Familiarity with textile techniques, history or events determines clarity of an article more than a particular style of writing. The writer should also be familiar with *Fiberarts* magazine. While the professional is essential to the editorial depth of *Fiberarts*, and must find timely information in the pages of the magazine, this is not our greatest audience. Our editorial philosophy is that the magazine must provide the non-professional textile enthusiast with the inspiration, support, useful information and direction to keep him or her excited, interested and committed. Although we address serious issues relating to the fiber arts as well as light, we're looking for an accessible rather than overly scholarly tone."

$ ⬛ FIBRE FOCUS, Magazine of the Ontario Handweavers and Spinners, P.O. Box 44009, Kitchener, Ontario N2N 3G7, Canada. E-mail: dburns@golden.net. Website: www.OHS.on.ca. **Contact:** Dianne Burns, editor. **90% freelance written.** Quarterly magazine covering handweaving, spinning, basketry, beading and other fibre arts. "Our readers are weavers and spinners. All articles deal with some aspect of these crafts." Estab. 1957. Circ. 1,000. Pays within 30 days after publication. Byline given. Buys one-time rights. Editorial lead time 6 months. Submit seasonal material 6 months in advance. Responds in 1 month to queries. Sample copy for $5 Canadian.
Nonfiction: How-to, interview/profile, new product, opinion, personal experience, technical, travel, book reviews. **Buys 40-60 mss/year.** Length: Varies. **Pays $25 Canadian per published page.**
Photos: Send photos with submission. Reviews 4×6 color prints. Buys one-time rights. Offers additional payment for photos accepted with ms. Captions, identification of subjects required.
Fiction: Humorous, slice-of-life vignettes. **Pays $25 Canadian per published page.**
Tips: "Submissions from men and women who love the fibre arts as much as we do are always welcome and stand a very good chance of being accepted. We need articles."

$ $ FINE TOOL JOURNAL, Antique & Collectible Tools, Inc., 27 Fickett Rd., Pownal ME 04069. (207)688-4962. Fax: (207)688-4831. E-mail: ceb@finetoolj.com. Website: www.finetoolj.com. **Contact:** Clarence Blanchard, president. **90% freelance written.** Quarterly magazine specializing in older or antique hand tools from all traditional trades. Readers are primarily interested in woodworking tools, but some subscribers have interests in such areas as leatherworking, wrenches, kitchen and machinist tools. Readers range from beginners just getting into the hobby to advanced collectors and organizations. Estab. 1970. Circ. 2,500. Pays on publication. Publishes ms an average of 6 months after acceptance. Byline given. Offers $50 kill fee. Buys first, second serial (reprint) rights. Editorial lead time 9 months. Submit seasonal material 6 months in advance. Accepts queries by mail. Responds in 2 months to queries; 3 months to mss. Sample copy for $5. Writer's guidelines for #10 SASE.
Nonfiction: "We're looking for articles about tools from all trades. Interests include collecting, preservation, history, values and price trends, traditional methods and uses, interviews with collectors/users/makers, etc. Most articles published will deal with vintage, pre-1950, hand tools. Also seeking articles on how to use specific tools or how a specific trade was carried out. However, how-to articles must be detailed and not just of general interest. We do on occasion

run articles on modern toolmakers who produce traditional hand tools." General interest, historical/nostalgic, how-to (make, use, fix and tune tools), interview/profile, personal experience, photo feature, technical. **Buys 24 mss/year.** Send complete ms. Length: 400-2,000 words. **Pays $50-200.** Pays expenses of writers on assignment.

Photos: Send photos with submission. Reviews 4×5 prints. Buys all rights. Negotiates payment individually. Identification of subjects, model releases required.

Columns/Departments: Stanley Tools (new finds and odd types), 300-400 words; Tips of the Trade (how to use tools), 100-200 words. **Buys 12 mss/year.** Send complete ms. **Pays $30-60.**

Tips: "The easiest way to get published in the *Journal* is to have personal experience or know someone who can supply the detailed information. We are seeking articles that go deeper than general interest and that knowledge requires experience and/or research. Short of personal experience, find a subject that fits our needs and that interests you. Spend some time learning the ins and outs of the subject and with hard work and a little luck you will earn the right to write about it."

$ $FINE WOODWORKING, The Taunton Press, P.O. Box 5506, Newtown CT 06470-5506. (203)426-8171. Fax: (203)270-6753. E-mail: fw@taunton.com. Website: www.taunton.com. Editor: Tim Schreiner. **Contact:** Anatole Burkin, executive editor. Bimonthly magazine on woodworking in the small shop. "All writers are also skilled woodworkers. It's more important that a contributor be a woodworker than a writer. Our editors (also woodworkers) will provide assistance." Estab. 1975. Circ. 270,000. **Pays on acceptance.** Byline given. Offers variable kill fee. Buys first rights, rights to republish in anthologies and use in promo pieces. Submit seasonal material 6 months in advance. Accepts simultaneous submissions. Responds in 2 months to queries. Writer's guidelines free and online.

> O→ "We're looking for good articles on almost all aspects of woodworking from the basics of tool use, stock preparation and joinery to specialized techniques and finishing. We're especially keen on articles about shop-built tools, jigs and fixtures or any stage of design, construction, finishing and installation of cabinetry and furniture. Whether the subject involves fundamental methods or advanced techniques, we look for high-quality workmanship, thoughtful designs, safe and proper procedures."

Nonfiction: How-to (woodworking). "No specs—our editors would rather see more than less." **Buys 120 mss/year.** Query with proposal letter. **Pays $150/magazine page for assigned articles.** Sometimes pays expenses of writers on assignment.

Photos: Send photos with submission. Reviews contact sheets, negatives, transparencies, prints. Buys one-time rights. Captions, identification of subjects, model releases required.

Columns/Departments: Notes & Comment (topics of interest to woodworkers); Question & Answer (woodworking Q&A); Methods of Work (shop tips); Tools & Materials (short reviews of new tools). **Buys 400 mss/year. Pays $10-150/published page.**

🔲 The online magazine carries original content not found in the print edition. Contact: Tim Sams, online editor.

Tips: "Send for authors guidelines and follow them. Stories about woodworking reported by non-woodworkers are *not* used. Our magazine is essentially reader-written by woodworkers."

$ $ FINESCALE MODELER, Kalmbach Publishing Co., 21027 Crossroads Circle, P.O. Box 1612, Waukesha WI 53187. (414)796-8776. Fax: (414)796-1383. E-mail: tthompson@finescale.com. Website: www.finescale.com. **Contact:** Paul Boyer. **80% freelance written.** Eager to work with new/unpublished writers. Magazine published 10 times/year "devoted to how-to-do-it modeling information for scale model builders who build non-operating aircraft, tanks, boats, automobiles, figures, dioramas, and science fiction and fantasy models." Circ. 60,000. **Pays on acceptance.** Publishes ms an average of 14 months after acceptance. Byline given. Buys all rights. Responds in 6 weeks to queries; 3 months to mss. Sample copy for 9×12 SAE and 3 first-class stamps.

• *Finescale Modeler* is especially looking for how-to articles for car modelers.

Nonfiction: How-to (build scale models), technical (research information for building models). Query or send complete ms. Length: 750-3,000 words. **Pays $55 published page minimum.**

Photos: Send photos with submission. Reviews transparencies, prints. Buys one-time rights. Pays $7.50 minimum for transparencies and $5 minimum for color prints. Captions, identification of subjects required.

Columns/Departments: *FSM* Showcase (photos plus description of model); *FSM* Tips and Techniques (model building hints and tips). **Buys 25-50 mss/year.** Send complete ms. **Pays $25-50.**

Tips: "A freelancer can best break in first through hints and tips, then through feature articles. Most people who write for *FSM* are modelers first, writers second. This is a specialty magazine for a special, quite expert audience. Essentially, 99% of our writers will come from that audience."

Ⓝ $ $FONS AND PORTER'S FOR THE LOVE OF QUILTING, (formerly *Sew Many Quilts*), Oxmoor House, 2100 Lakeshore Dr., Birmingham AL 35209. (205)877-6000. Fax: (205)877-6078. E-mail: kwiltz@aol.com. Website: www.fonsandporter.com. Editor: Susan Cleveland. Managing Editor: Rhonda Richards. **Contact:** Lauren Brooks, features editor. **50% freelance written.** Bimonthly magazine covering quilting. "*For the Love of Quilting* is published for beginning to intermediate quilters. We feature 8-10 projects per issue and one large feature related to quilting." Estab. 1996. Circ. 139,000. **Pays on acceptance.** Publishes ms an average of 1 year after acceptance. Byline given. Buys first, second serial (reprint) rights. Editorial lead time 1 year. Submit seasonal material 1 year in advance. Accepts queries by mail, fax. Accepts simultaneous submissions. Responds in 2 weeks to queries; 2 months to mss. Writer's guidelines for #10 SASE.

Nonfiction: Historical/nostalgic, how-to (quilting), humor, interview/profile, personal experience, photo feature. "No articles that cannot be supported with visuals." Nothing unrelated to quilting. **Buys 12 mss/year.** Query. Length: 1,000-3,000 words. **Pays $100-300.**

Photos: State availability of or send photos with submission. Reviews 4×5 transparencies, 4×6 prints. Buys all rights. Offers no additional payment for photos accepted with ms. Identification of subjects required.

Tips: "Be thoroughly knowledgeable and up-to-date in the craft of quilting and what today's quilters want."

$ $ GENEALOGICAL COMPUTING, Ancestry Inc., 360 West 4800 North, Provo UT 84604. (801)705-7000. Fax: (801)705-7001. E-mail: gceditor@ancestry.com. Website: www.ancestry.com. **Contact:** Elizabeth Kelly Kerstens, managing editor. **85% freelance written.** Quarterly magazine covering genealogy and computers. Estab. 1980. Circ. 32,000. Pays on publication. Publishes ms an average of 4 months after acceptance. Byline given. Buys all rights. Editorial lead time 4 months. Submit seasonal material 4 months in advance.

Nonfiction: How-to, interview/profile, new product, technical. **Buys 40 mss/year.** Query. Length: 1,500-2,500 words. **Pays $75-500.**

Reprints: Pays 75% of amount paid for an original article.

$ $ THE HOME SHOP MACHINIST, 2779 Aero Park Dr., P.O. Box 1810, Traverse City MI 49685. (616)946-3712. Fax: (616)946-3289. E-mail: jrice@villagepress.com. Website: www.villagepress.com. **Contact:** Joe D. Rice, editor. **95% freelance written.** Bimonthly magazine covering machining and metalworking for the hobbyist. Circ. 34,000. Pays on publication. Publishes ms an average of 2 years after acceptance. Byline given. Buys first North American serial rights. Responds in 2 months to queries. Sample copy free. Writer's guidelines for 9×12 SASE.

Nonfiction: How-to (projects designed to upgrade present shop equipment or hobby model projects that require machining), technical (should pertain to metalworking, machining, drafting, layout, welding or foundry work for the hobbyist). No fiction or "people" features. **Buys 40 mss/year.** Query with or without published clips or send complete ms. Length: open—"whatever it takes to do a thorough job." **Pays $40/published page, plus $9/published photo.**

Photos: Send photos with submission. Pays $9-40 for 5×7 b&w prints; $70/page for camera-ready art; $40 for b&w cover photo. Captions, identification of subjects required.

Columns/Departments: Book Reviews; New Product Reviews; Micro-Machining; Foundry. Length: 600-1,500 words. "Become familiar with our magazine before submitting." **Buys 25-30 mss/year.** Query. **Pays $40-70.**

Fillers: Machining tips/shortcuts. **Buys 12-15/year.** Length: 100-300 words. **Pays $30-48.**

Tips: "The writer should be experienced in the area of metalworking and machining; should be extremely thorough in explanations of methods, processes—always with an eye to safety; and should provide good quality b&w photos and/or clear dimensioned drawings to aid in description. Visuals are of increasing importance to our readers. Carefully planned photos, drawings and charts will carry a submission to our magazine much farther along the path to publication."

$ $ $ INTERNATIONAL WRISTWATCH MAGAZINE, International Wristwatch Magazine, Inc., 979 Summer St., Stamford CT 06905. (203)352-1817. Fax: (203)352-1820. E-mail: wristwatch@snet.net. Website: www.intlwrist watch.com. **Contact:** Gary Girdvainis, editor-in-chief. **50% freelance written.** Magazine covering wristwatches. "We're interested in all information about wristwatches—collecting, modern production, historical, etc." Estab. 1989. Circ. 30,000. Pays on publication. Publishes ms an average of 2 months after acceptance. Byline given. Offers 50% kill fee. Buys first rights. Editorial lead time 4 months. Accepts queries by mail, e-mail, fax, phone. Accepts simultaneous submissions.

Nonfiction: General interest, historical/nostalgic, interview/profile, new product, technical. No trade-related wristwatch matter. Query. Length: 500-3,000 words. **Pays 10¢-$1/word.** "Watch trade is possible option for payment."

Photos: State availability with submission. Reviews contact sheets. Buys one-time rights. Negotiates payment individually.

Columns/Departments: News (events sponsored by watch companies), 50 words; Market (new product section), 50-75 words; Auction (auction reports and analysis), 100-150 words; Collecting (collecting vintage watches), 1,000 words. Query. **Pays 10-50¢/word.**

$ $ KITPLANES, For designers, builders and pilots of experimental aircraft, A Primedia Publication, 8745 Aero Dr., Suite 105, San Diego CA 92123. (858)694-0491. Fax: (858)694-8147. E-mail: dave@kitplanes.com. Website: www.kitplanes.com. Managing Editor: Keith Beveridge. **Contact:** Dave Martin, editor. **70% freelance written.** Eager to work with new/unpublished writers. Monthly magazine covering self-construction of private aircraft for pilots and builders. Estab. 1984. Circ. 74,000. Pays on publication. Publishes ms an average of 3 months after acceptance. Byline given. Buys exclusive complete serial rights. Submit seasonal material 6 months in advance. Accepts queries by mail, e-mail. Responds in 2 weeks to queries; 6 weeks to mss. Sample copy for $5. Writer's guidelines free.

Nonfiction: "We are looking for articles on specific construction techniques, the use of tools, both hand and power, in aircraft building, the relative merits of various materials, conversions of engines from automobiles for aviation use, installation of instruments and electronics." General interest, how-to, interview/profile, new product, personal experience, photo feature, technical. No general-interest aviation articles, or "My First Solo" type of articles. **Buys 80 mss/year.** Query. Length: 500-3,000 words. **Pays $70-600 including story photos for assigned articles.**

Photos: State availability of or send photos with submission. Buys one-time rights. Pays $300 for cover photos. Captions, identification of subjects required.

Tips: "*Kitplanes* contains very specific information—a writer must be extremely knowledgeable in the field. Major features are entrusted only to known writers. I cannot emphasize enough that articles must be directed at the individual aircraft builder. We need more 'how-to' photo features in all areas of homebuilt aircraft."

N $ KNITTING DIGEST, House of White Birches, 306 E. Parr Rd., Berne IN 46711. (219)589-4000. Fax: (219)589-8093. E-mail: knitting_digest@whitebirches.com. Website: www.whitebirches.com. **Contact:** Jeanne Stauffer, editor. **100% freelance written.** Bimonthly magazine covering knitting designs and patterns. "We print only occasional articles, but are always open to knitting designs and proposals." Estab. 1993. Circ. 50,000. Pays within 2 months. Publishes ms an average of 6 months after acceptance. Byline given. Offers 100% kill fee. Buys all rights. Accepts queries by mail, e-mail. Accepts simultaneous submissions. Responds in 2 months to queries; 6 months to mss. Writer's guidelines for #10 SASE.
Nonfiction: How-to (knitting skills), technical (knitting field). **Buys 4-6 mss/year.** Send complete ms. Length: 500 words maximum. **Pays variable amount. Also pays in contributor copies.**
Tips: "Clear concise writing. Humor is appreciated in this field, as much as technical tips. The magazine is a digest, so space is limited. All submissions must be typed and double-spaced."

$ $ KNIVES ILLUSTRATED, The Premier Cutlery Magazine, 265 S. Anita Dr., Suite 120, Orange CA 92868-3310. (423)894-8319. Fax: (423)892-7254. E-mail: knivesillustrated@yahoo.com. Website: www.knivesillustrated.com. **Contact:** Bruce Voyles, editor. **40-50% freelance written.** Bimonthly magazine covering high-quality factory and custom knives. "We publish articles on different types of factory and custom knives, how-to make knives, technical articles, shop tours, articles on knife makers and artists. Must have knowledge about knives and the people who use and make them. We feature the full range of custom and high tech production knives, from miniatures to swords, leaving nothing untouched. We're also known for our outstanding how-to articles and technical features on equipment, materials and knife making supplies. We do not feature knife maker profiles as such, although we do spotlight some makers by featuring a variety of their knives and insight into their background and philosophy." Estab. 1987. Circ. 35,000. Pays on publication. Byline given. Editorial lead time 3 months. Accepts queries by mail, e-mail, fax. Responds in 2 weeks to queries. Sample copy available. Writer's guidelines for #10 SASE.
Nonfiction: General interest, historical/nostalgic, how-to, interview/profile, new product, photo feature, technical. **Buys 35-40 mss/year.** Query. Length: 400-2,000 words. **Pays $100-500.**
Photos: Send photos with submission. Reviews 35mm, 2¼×2¼, 4×5 transparencies, 5×7 prints, electronic images in tif, gip or jpg Mac format. Negotiates payment individually. Captions, identification of subjects, model releases required.
Tips: "Most of our contributors are involved with knives, either as collectors, makers, engravers, etc. To write about this subject requires knowledge. A 'good' writer can do OK if they study some recent issues. If you are interested in submitting work to *Knives Illustrated* magazine, it is suggested you analyze at least two or three different editions to get a feel for the magazine. It is also recommended that you call or mail in your query to determine if we are interested in the topic you have in mind. While verbal or written approval may be given, all articles are still received on a speculation basis. We cannot approve any article until we have it in hand, whereupon we will make a final decision as to its suitability for our use. Bear in mind we do not suggest you go to the trouble to write an article if there is doubt we can use it promptly."

N LAPIDARY JOURNAL, 60 Chestnut Ave., Suite 201, Devon PA 19333-1312. (610)964-6300. Fax: (610)293-0977. E-mail: LJEditorial@primediasi.com. Website: www.lapidaryjournal.com. Editor: Merle White. **Contact:** Hazel Wheaton, managing editor. **70% freelance written.** Monthly magazine covering gem, bead and jewelry arts. "Our audience is hobbyists who usually have some knowledge of and proficiency in the subject before they start reading. Our style is conversational and informative. There are how-to projects and profiles of artists and materials." Estab. 1947. Circ. 53,000. **Pays on acceptance.** Publishes ms an average of 4 months after acceptance. Byline given. Buys one-time and worldwide rights. Editorial lead time 3 months. Accepts queries by mail, e-mail. Sample copy online.
Nonfiction: Looks for conversational and lively narratives with quotes and anecdotes; Q&A's; interviews. How-to (jewelry/craft), interview/profile, new product, personal experience, technical, travel. Special issues: Bead Annual, Gemstone Annual, Jewelry Design issue. **Buys 100 mss/year.** Query. Length: 1,500-2,500 words preferred; 1,000-3,500 words acceptable; longer works occasionally published serially. Pays some expenses of writers on assignment.
Reprints: Send photocopy.
Tips: "Some knowledge of jewelry, gemstones and/or minerals is a definite asset. *Jewelry Journal* is a section within *Lapidary Journal* that offers illustrated, step-by-step instruction in gem cutting, jewelry making, and beading. Please request a copy of the *Jewelry Journal* guidelines for greater detail."

$ $ THE LEATHER CRAFTERS & SADDLERS JOURNAL, 331 Annette Court, Rhinelander WI 54501-2902. (715)362-5393. Fax: (715)362-5391. Managing Editor: Dorothea Reis. **Contact:** William R. Reis, publisher. **100% freelance written.** Bimonthly magazine. "A leather-working publication with how-to, step-by-step instructional articles using full-size patterns for leathercraft, leather art, custom saddle, boot and harness making, etc. A complete resource for leather, tools, machinery and allied materials plus leather industry news." Estab. 1990. Circ. 9,000. Pays on publication. Publishes ms an average of 2 months after acceptance. Byline given. Buys first North American serial, second serial (reprint) rights. Submit seasonal material 6 months in advance. Accepts queries by mail, fax, phone. Accepts simultaneous submissions. Responds in 1 month to mss. Sample copy for $5. Writer's guidelines for #10 SASE.

O-n Break in with a how-to, step-by-step leather item article from beginner through masters and saddlemaking.

Nonfiction: "I want only articles that include hands-on, step-by-step, how-to information." How-to (crafts and arts and any other projects using leather). **Buys 75 mss/year.** Send complete ms. Length: 500-2,500 words. **Pays $20-250 for assigned articles; $20-150 for unsolicited articles.**

Reprints: Send tearsheet or photocopy. Pays 50% of amount paid for an original article.

Photos: Send good contrast color print photos and full-size patterns and/or full-size photo-carve patterns with submission. Lack of these reduces payment amount. Captions required.

Columns/Departments: Beginners, Intermediate, Artists, Western Design, Saddlemakers, International Design and Letters (the open exchange of information between all peoples). Length: 500-2,500 words on all. **Buys 75 mss/year.** Send complete ms. **Pays 5¢/word.**

Fillers: Anecdotes, facts, gags to be illustrated by cartoonist, newsbreaks. Length: 25-200 words. **Pays $5-20.**

Tips: "We want to work with people who understand and know leathercraft and are interested in passing on their knowledge to others. We would prefer to interview people who have achieved a high level in leathercraft skill."

$ LINN'S STAMP NEWS, Amos Press, 911 Vandemark Rd., P.O. Box 29, Sidney OH 45365. (937)498-0801. Fax: (800)340-9501. E-mail: linns@linns.com. Website: www.linns.com. Editor: Michael Laurence. **Contact:** Michael Schreiber, managing editor. **50% freelance written.** Weekly tabloid on the stamp collecting hobby. All articles must be about philatelic collectibles. Our goal at *Linn's* is to create a weekly publication that is indispensable to stamp collectors. Estab. 1928. Circ. 55,000. Pays within one month of publication. Publishes ms an average of 1 month after acceptance. Byline given. Buys first rights, first worldwide serial rights. Submit seasonal material 2 months in advance. Responds in 6 weeks to queries. Sample copy free. Writer's guidelines for #10 SAE with 2 first-class stamps.

Nonfiction: General interest, historical/nostalgic, how-to, interview/profile, technical, club and show news, current issues, auction realization and recent discoveries. "No articles merely giving information on background of stamp subject. Must have philatelic information included." **Buys 300 mss/year.** Send complete ms. Length: 500 words maximum. **Pays $20-50.** Sometimes pays expenses of writers on assignment.

Photos: Good illustrations a must. Provide captions on a separate sheet of paper. Prefers crisp, sharp focus, high-contrast glossy b&w prints. Send photos with submission. Buys all rights. Offers no additional payment for photos accepted with ms. Captions required.

Tips: "Check and double check all facts. Footnotes and bibliographies are not appropriate to our newspaper style. Work citation into the text. Even though your subject might be specialized, write understandably. Explain terms. *Linn's* features are aimed at a broad audience of relatively novice collectors. Keep this audience in mind. Do not write down to the reader but provide information in such a way to make stamp collecting more interesting to more people. Embrace readers without condescending to them."

$ ⊡ LOST TREASURE, INC., P.O. Box 451589, Grove OK 74345. Fax: (918)786-2192. E-mail: managingeditor @losttreasure.com. Website: www.losttreasure.com. **Contact:** Patsy Beyerl, managing editor. **75% freelance written.** Monthly and annual magazines covering lost treasure. Estab. 1966. Circ. 55,000. Pays on publication. Byline given. Buys all rights. Accepts queries by mail, e-mail, fax. Responds in 1 month to queries; 2 months to mss. Sample copy for #10 SASE. Writer's guidelines for 10×13 SAE with $1.47 postage or online.

Nonfiction: *Lost Treasure*, a monthly, is composed of lost treasure stories, legends, folklore, how-to articles, treasure hunting club news, who's who in treasure hunting, tips. Length: 500-1,500 words. *Treasure Cache*, an annual, contains stories about documented treasure caches with a sidebar from the author telling the reader how to search for the cache highlighted in the story. **Buys 225 mss/year.** Query on *Treasure Cache* only. Length: 1,000-2,000 words. **Pays 4¢/word.**

Photos: Black & white or color prints, hand-drawn or copied maps, art with source credit with mss will help sell your story. We are always looking for cover photos with or without accompanying ms. Pays $100/published cover photo. Must be 35mm color slides, vertical. Pays $5/published photo. Captions required.

Tips: "We are only interested in treasures that can be found with metal detectors. Queries welcome but not required. If you write about famous treasures and lost mines, be sure we haven't used your selected topic recently and story must have a new slant or new information. Source documentation required. How-tos should cover some aspect of treasure hunting and how-to steps should be clearly defined. If you have a *Treasure Cache* story we will, if necessary, help the author with the sidebar telling how to search for the cache in the story. *Lost Treasure* articles should coordinate with theme issues when possible."

$ $ MEMORY MAKERS, The First Source for Scrapbooking Ideas, Satellite Press, 12365 Huron St., #500, Denver CO 80234. (303)452-1968. Fax: (303)452-2164. E-mail: editorial@memorymakersmagazine.com. Website: www w.memorymakersmagazine.com. **Contact:** Deborah Mock, editor. **25% freelance written.** Bimonthly magazine covering scrapbooking, hobbies and crafts. "*Memory Makers* is an international magazine that showcases ideas and stories of scrapbookers. It includes articles with information, instructions, and products that apply to men and women who make creative scrapbooks." Estab. 1996. Circ. 210,000. Pays on project completion. Publishes ms an average of 4 months after acceptance. Byline given. Buys all rights. Editorial lead time 6 months. Submit seasonal material 6 months in advance. Accepts queries by mail, e-mail. Accepts simultaneous submissions. Writer's guidelines for #10 SASE.

O-n Break in with articles on "unique craft techniques that can apply to scrapbooking and personal stories of how scrapbooking has impacted someone's life."

Nonfiction: Historical/nostalgic, how-to (scrapbooking), inspirational, interview/profile, new product, personal experience, photography. No "all-encompassing how-to scrapbook" articles. **Buys 6-10 mss/year.** Query with published clips. Length: 1,000-1,500 words. **Pays $100-750.**

Columns/Departments: Keeping It Safe (issues surrounding the safe preservation of scrapbooks), Scrapbooking 101 (how-to scrapbooking techniques for beginners), Photojournaling (new and useful ideas for improving scrapbook journaling), Modern Memories (computer and modern technology scrapbooking issues), all 500-700 words. Query with published clips. **Pays $150-300.**

N̲ $ $MILITARY TRADER, Antique Trader Publications/Krause Publications, 100 Bryant St., Dubuque IA 52001. (319)588-2073. Fax: (319)588-0888. E-mail: vonlannenb@krause.com. Website: www.collect.com. Managing Editor: Virginia Hill. **Contact:** Bill Van Lannen, editor. **90% freelance written.** Monthly magazine covering military collectibles. "For military collectors, *Military Trader* is the best monthly source of news, features, collecting advice, market info, shows, and events." Estab. 1994. Circ. 9,778. **Pays on acceptance.** Byline given. Buys first, one-time, electronic rights. Editorial lead time 1 month. Submit seasonal material 2 months in advance. Accepts queries by mail, e-mail, fax, phone. Accepts simultaneous submissions. Responds in 3 weeks to queries. Sample copy and writer's guidelines free.

Nonfiction: Book excerpts, essays, historical/nostalgic, interview/profile. Query. Length: 750-1,500 words. **Pays $50-300.** Sometimes pays expenses of writers on assignment.

Photos: Send photos with submission. Reviews contact sheets. Buys one-time rights. Negotiates payment individually. Captions required.

Columns/Departments: Pays $150-250.

Tips: "Be knowledgeable on military collectibles and/or military history. Plenty of good photos will make it easier to be published in our publication."

$MINIATURE QUILTS, Chitra Publications, 2 Public Ave., Montrose PA 18801. (570)278-1984. Fax: (570)278-2223. E-mail: chitraed@epix.net. Website: www.quilttownusa.com. **Contact:** Joyce Libal, senior editor. **40% freelance written.** Bimonthly magazine on miniature quilts. "We seek articles of an instructional nature (all techniques), profiles of talented quiltmakers and informational articles on all aspects of miniature quilts. Miniature is defined as quilts made up of blocks smaller than five inches." Estab. 1990. Circ. 70,000. Pays on publication. Publishes ms an average of 6 months after acceptance. Byline given. Buys second serial (reprint) rights. Submit seasonal material 8 months in advance. Accepts queries by mail, fax. Responds in 2 months to queries. Writer's guidelines for SASE or online.

    O─ "Best bet—a quilter writing about a new or unusual quilting technique."

Nonfiction: How-to, interview/profile (quilters who make small quilts), photo feature (about noteworthy miniature quilts or exhibits). Query. Length: 1,500 words maximum. **Pays $75/published page of text.**

Photos: Send photos with submission. Reviews 35mm slides and larger transparencies. Offers $20/photo. Captions, identification of subjects, model releases required.

Tips: "We're looking for articles (with slides or transparencies) on quilts in museum collections."

$ $MODEL RAILROADER, P.O. Box 1612, Waukesha WI 53187. Fax: (262)796-1142. E-mail: mrmag@mrmag.com. Website: www.trains.com. **Contact:** Jim Kelly, managing editor. Monthly magazine for hobbyists interested in scale model railroading. "We publish articles on all aspects of model-railroading and on prototype (real) railroading as a subject for modeling." Byline given. Buys exclusive rights. Accepts queries by mail, e-mail, fax. Responds in 2 months to queries.

    O─ "Study publication before submitting material." First-hand knowledge of subject almost always necessary for acceptable slant.

Nonfiction: Wants construction articles on specific model railroad projects (structures, cars, locomotives, scenery, benchwork, etc.). Also photo stories showing model railroads. Query. **Pays base rate of $90/page.**

Photos: Buys photos with detailed descriptive captions only. Pays $15 and up, depending on size and use. Pays double b&w rate for color; full color cover earns $200.

Tips: "Before you prepare and submit any article, you should write us a short letter of inquiry describing what you want to do. We can then tell you if it fits our needs and save you from working on something we don't want."

$ $MONITORING TIMES, Grove Enterprises Inc., P.O. Box 98, Brasstown NC 28902-0098. (828)837-9200. Fax: (828)837-2216. E-mail: mteditor@grove-ent.com. Website: www.grove-ent.com. Publisher: Robert Grove. **Contact:** Rachel Baughn, editor. **20% freelance written.** Monthly magazine for radio hobbyists. Estab. 1982. Circ. 30,000. Pays on publication. Publishes ms an average of 4 months after acceptance. Byline given. Buys first North American serial, second serial (reprint) rights. Submit seasonal material 4 months in advance. Accepts queries by mail, e-mail. Responds in 1 month to queries. Sample copy and writer's guidelines for 9 × 12 SAE and 9 first-class stamps.

    O─ Break in with a shortwave station profile or topic, or scanning topics of broad interest.

Nonfiction: General interest, how-to, humor, interview/profile, personal experience, photo feature, technical. **Buys 50 mss/year.** Query. Length: 1,500-3,000 words. **Pays average of $50/published page.**

Reprints: Send photocopy and information about when and where the material previously appeared. Pays 25% of amount paid for an original article.

Photos: Send photos with submission. Buys one-time rights. Captions required.

Columns/Departments: "Query managing editor."

Tips: "Need articles on radio communications systems and shortwave broadcasters. We are accepting more technical projects."

[N] $ THE NUMISMATIST, American Numismatic Association, 818 N. Cascade Ave., Colorado Springs CO 80903-3279. (719)632-2646. Fax: (719)634-4085. E-mail: anaedi@money.org. **Contact:** Barbara Gregory, editor/publisher. Monthly magazine covering numismatics (study of coins, tokens, medals and paper money). Estab. 1888. Circ. 28,500. Pays on publication. Publishes ms an average of 1 year after acceptance. Byline given. Buys first North American serial rights. Editorial lead time 2 months. Sample copy free.
Nonfiction: "Submitted material should present new information and/or constitute a contribution to numismatic education for the experienced collector and beginner alike." Book excerpts, essays, historical/nostalgic, opinion, technical. Special issues: First Strike, a supplement for young or new collectors, is published twice yearly, in December and June. **Buys 60 mss/year.** Query or send complete ms. Length: 3,500 words maximum. **Pays $2.75/column inch.** Sometimes pays expenses of writers on assignment.
Photos: Send photos with submission. Negotiates payment individually. Captions, identification of subjects required.
Columns/Departments: Send complete ms. **Pays $25-100.**

[icon] PACK-O-FUN, Projects For Kids & Families, Clapper Communications, 2400 Devon Ave., Des Plaines IL 60018-4618. (847)635-5800. Fax: (847)635-6311. Website: www.craftideas.com. Editor: Billie Ciancio. **Contact:** Irene Mueller, managing editor. **85% freelance written.** Bimonthly magazine covering crafts and activities for kids and those working with kids. Estab. 1951. Circ. 102,000. Pays 45 days after signed contract. Byline given. Buys all rights. Editorial lead time 6 months. Submit seasonal material 8 months in advance. Accepts queries by mail, fax. Accepts simultaneous submissions. Responds in 2 months to queries. Sample copy for $3.50 or online.
Nonfiction: "We request quick and easy, inexpensive crafts and activities. Projects must be original, and complete instructions are required upon acceptance." **Pay is negotiable.**
Reprints: Send tearsheet and information about when and where the material previously appeared.
Photos: Photos of project may be submitted in place of project at query stage.
Tips: "*Pack-O-Fun* is looking for original how-to projects for kids and those working with kids. Write simple instructions for crafts to be done by children ages 5-13 years. We're looking for recyclable ideas for throwaways. We seldom accept fiction unless accompanied by a craft or in skit form (appropriate for classrooms, scouts or Bible school groups). It would be helpful to check out our magazine before submitting."

$ $ [icon] PIECEWORK MAGAZINE, Interweave Press, Inc., 201 E. Fourth St., Loveland CO 80537-5655. (970)669-7672. Fax: (970)667-8317. E-mail: piecework@interweave.com. Website: www.interweave.com. Editor: Jeane Hutchins. **Contact:** Jake Rexus, assistant editor. **90% freelance written.** Bimonthly magazine covering needlework history. "*PieceWork* celebrates the rich tradition of needlework and the history of the people behind it. Stories and projects on embroidery, cross-stitch, knitting, crocheting and quilting, along with other textile arts, are featured in each issue." Estab. 1993. Circ. 60,000. Pays on publication. Byline given. Offers 30% kill fee. Buys first North American serial rights. Editorial lead time 6 months. Submit seasonal material 6 months in advance. Accepts queries by mail, e-mail, fax, phone. Responds in 6 months to queries. Sample copy and writer's guidelines free.
Nonfiction: Book excerpts, historical/nostalgic, how-to, interview/profile, new product. No contemporary needlework articles. **Buys 25-30 mss/year.** Send complete ms. Length: 1,000-2,000 words. **Pays $100/printed page.**
Photos: State availability of or send photos with submission. Reviews transparencies, prints. Buys one-time rights. Captions, identification of subjects, model releases required.
Tips: "Submit a well-researched article on a historical aspect of needlework complete with information on visuals and suggestion for accompanying project."

$ $ $ [icon] POPTRONIS, Gernsback Publications, Inc., 275-G Marcus Blvd., Hauppauge NY 11788. (631)592-6720. Fax: (631)592-6723. E-mail: clamorte@gernsback.com or popeditor@gernsback.com. Website: www.gernsback.com. **Contact:** Chris LaMorte, editor. **75% freelance written.** Monthly magazine on electronics technology and electronics construction, such as communications, computers, test equipment, components, video and audio. 92 year history in electronic publications. The new magazine *Poptronis* is a combination of 2 older publications, one of which began in 1929. Estab. 2000. Circ. 104,000. Publishes ms an average of 6 months after acceptance. Byline given. Buys all rights. Submit seasonal material 6 months in advance. Accepts queries by mail, e-mail. Responds in 2 months to queries; 4 months to mss. Sample copy and writer's guidelines free or online.
Nonfiction: How-to (electronic project construction), new product. **Buys 150-200 mss/year.** Send complete ms. Length: 1,000-10,000 words. **Pays $150-700 for assigned articles; $100-700 for unsolicited articles.**
Photos: Send photos with submission. Buys all rights. Offers no additional payment for photos accepted with ms. Captions, identification of subjects, model releases required.

$ POPULAR COMMUNICATIONS, CQ Communications, Inc., 25 Newbridge Rd., Hicksville NY 11801. (516)681-2922. Fax: (516)681-2926. E-mail: popularcom@aol.com. Website: www.popular-communications.com. **Contact:** Harold Ort, editor. **25% freelance written.** Monthly magazine covering the radio communications hobby. Estab. 1982. Circ. 40,000. Pays on publication. Publishes ms an average of 6 months after acceptance. Byline given. Buys first North American serial rights. Editorial lead time 3 months. Submit seasonal material 6 months in advance. Accepts queries by mail, e-mail. Responds in 1 month to queries; 2 months to mss. Sample copy free. Writer's guidelines for #10 SASE.

Nonfiction: General interest, how-to (antenna construction), humor, new product, photo feature, technical. **Buys 6-10 mss/year.** Query. Length: 1,800-3,000 words. **Pays $35/printed page.**

Photos: State availability with submission. Negotiates payment individually. Captions, identification of subjects, model releases required.

Tips: "Either be a radio enthusiast or know one who can help you before sending us an article."

$ $ $ $ POPULAR MECHANICS, Hearst Corp., 810 Seventh Ave., 6th Floor, New York NY 10019. (212)649-2000. Fax: (212)586-5562. E-mail: popularmechanics@hearst.com. Website: www.popularmechanics.com. **Contact:** Joe Oldham, editor-in-chief; Sarah Deem, managing editor. **up to 50% freelance written.** Monthly magazine on automotive, home improvement, science, boating, outdoors, electronics. "We are a men's service magazine that tries to address the diverse interests of today's male, providing him with information to improve the way he lives. We cover stories from do-it-yourself projects to technological advances in aerospace, military, automotive and so on." Estab. 1902. Circ. 1,400,000. **Pays on acceptance.** Publishes ms an average of 6 months after acceptance. Byline given. Offers 25% kill fee. Buys all rights. Submit seasonal material 6 months in advance. Responds in 3 weeks to queries; 1 month to mss. Writer's guidelines for SASE or online.

Nonfiction: General interest, how-to (shop projects, car fix-its), new product, technical. Special issues: Boating Guide (February); Home Improvement Guide (April); Consumer Electronics Guide (May); New Cars Guide (October); Woodworking Guide (November). No historical, editorial, or critique pieces. **Buys 2 mss/year.** Query with or without published clips or send complete ms. Length: 500-1,500 words. **Pays $500-1,500 for assigned articles; $300-1,000 for unsolicited articles.** Sometimes pays expenses of writers on assignment.

Photos: Usually assigns a photographer. "If you have photos, send with submission." Reviews slides. Buys all rights. Offers no additional payment for photos accepted with ms. Captions, identification of subjects, model releases required.

Columns/Departments: New Cars (latest and hottest cars out of Detroit and Europe), Car Care (Maintenance basics, How It Works, Fix-Its and New products: send to Don Chaikin. Electronics, Audio, Home Video, Computers, Photography: send to Tobey Grumet. Boating (new equipment, how-tos, fishing tips), Outdoors (gear, vehicles, outdoor adventures): send to Cliff Gromer. Home & Shop Journal: send to Steve Willson. Science (latest developments), Tech Update (breakthroughs) and Aviation (sport aviation, homebuilt aircraft, new commercial aircraft, civil aeronautics): send to Jim Wilson. All columns are about 800 words.

■ The online magazine carries original content not found in the print edition. Contact: Ken Juran, online editor.

$ $ POPULAR WOODWORKING, F&W Publications, 1507 Dana Ave., Cincinnati OH 45207. (513)531-2690, ext 407. Fax: (513)531-0919. E-mail: popwood@fwpubs.com. Website: www.popularwoodworking.com. Editor: Steve Shanesy. **Contact:** Christopher Schwarz, senior editor. **45% freelance written.** Magazine published 7 times/year. "*Popular Woodworking* invites woodworkers of all levels into a community of professionals who share their hard-won shop experience through in-depth projects and technique articles, which help the readers hone their existing skills and develop new ones. Related stories increase the readers' understanding and enjoyment of their craft. Any project submitted must be aesthetically pleasing, of sound construction and offer a challenge to readers. On the average, we use four freelance features per issue. Our primary needs are 'how-to' articles on woodworking. Our secondary need is for articles that will inspire discussion concerning woodworking. Tone of articles should be conversational and informal, as if the writer is speaking directly to the reader. Our readers are the woodworking hobbyist and small woodshop owner. Writers should have an extensive knowledge of woodworking, or be able to communicate information gained from woodworkers." Estab. 1981. Circ. 215,000. **Pays on acceptance.** Publishes ms an average of 10 months after acceptance. Byline given. Buys first rights. Submit seasonal material 6 months in advance. Accepts queries by mail, e-mail, fax, phone. Responds in 2 months to queries. Sample copy for $4.50 and 9×12 SAE with 6 first-class stamps or online.

○┅ "The project must be well designed, well constructed, well built and well finished. Technique pieces must have practical application."

Nonfiction: How-to (on woodworking projects, with plans), humor (woodworking anecdotes), technical (woodworking techniques). Special issues: Shop issue, Outdoor Projects issue, Tool issue, Holiday Projects issue. No tool reviews. **Buys 20 mss/year.** Query with or without published clips or send complete ms. **Pay starts at $150/published page.**

Reprints: Send photocopy with rights for sale noted and information about when and where the material previously appeared. Pays 25% of amount paid for an original article.

Photos: Photographic quality may affect acceptance. Need sharp close-up color photos of step-by-step construction process. Send photos with submission. Reviews color only, slides and transparencies, 3×5 glossies acceptable. Captions, identification of subjects required.

Columns/Departments: Tricks of the Trade (helpful techniques), Out of the Woodwork (thoughts on woodworking as a profession or hobby, can be humorous or serious), 500-1,500 words. **Buys 6 mss/year.** Query.

■ The online magazine carries original content not found in the print edition. Contact: Christopher Schwarz.

Tips: "Write an 'Out of the Woodwork' column for us and then follow up with photos of your projects. Submissions should include materials list, complete diagrams (blueprints not necessary), and discussion of the step-by-step process. We have become more selective on accepting only practical, attractive projects with quality construction. We are also looking for more original topics for our other articles."

N̄ $QUILT WORLD, House of White Birches, 306 E. Parr Rd., Berne IN 46711. (219)589-4000. Fax: (207)794-3290. E-mail: hatch@agate.net. **Contact:** Sandra L. Hatch, editor. **100% freelance written.** Works with a small number of new/unpublished writers each year. Bimonthly magazine covering quilting. "*Quilt World* is a general quilting publication. We accept articles about special quilters, techniques, coverage of unusual quilts at quilt shows, special interest quilts, human interest articles and patterns. We include 5-8 patterns in every issue. Reader is 30-70 years old, midwestern." Circ. 130,000. Pays 45 days after acceptance. Byline given. Buys first, one-time, all rights. Submit seasonal material 10 months in advance. Accepts queries by mail, e-mail. Responds in 3 months to queries. Writer's guidelines for #10 SASE.

Nonfiction: How-to, interview/profile (quilters), new product (quilt products), photo feature, technical. **Buys 18-24 mss/year.** Query or send complete ms. Length: Open. **Pays $50-100.**

Reprints: Send photocopy and information about when and where the material previously appeared.

Photos: Send photos with submission. Reviews transparencies, prints. Buys all or one-time rights. Offers $15/photo (except covers). Identification of subjects required.

Tips: "Read several recent issues for style and content."

$ $ THE QUILTER, (formerly *The Traditional Quilter*), All American Crafts, Inc., 243 Newton-Sparta Rd., Newton NJ 07860. (973)383-8080. Fax: (973)383-8133. E-mail: editors@thequiltermag.com. Website: www.thequiltermag.com. **Contact:** Laurette Koserowski, editor. **45% freelance written.** Bimonthly magazine on quilting. Estab. 1988. Pays on publication. Publishes ms an average of 6 months after acceptance. Byline given. Submit seasonal material 6 months in advance. Accepts queries by mail, phone. Responds in 2 months to queries. Sample copy for 9×12 SAE and 4 first-class stamps. Writer's guidelines for #10 SASE.

Nonfiction: Quilts and quilt patterns with instructions, quilt-related projects, interview/profile, photo feature—all quilt related. Query with published clips. Length: 350-1,000 words. **Pays 10-12¢/word.**

Photos: Send photos with submission. Reviews transparencies, prints. Buys one-time or all rights. Offers $10-15/photo. Captions, identification of subjects required.

Columns/Departments: Feature Teacher (qualified quilt teachers with teaching involved—with slides); Profile (award-winning and interesting quilters). Length: 1,000 words maximum. **Pays 10¢/word, $15/photo.**

$ $ ▧ QUILTING TODAY MAGAZINE, Chitra Publications, 2 Public Ave., Montrose PA 18801. (570)278-1984. Fax: (570)278-2223. E-mail: chitraed@epix.net. Website: www.quilttownusa.com. **Contact:** Joyce Libal, senior editor. **50% freelance written.** Bimonthly magazine on quilting, traditional and contemporary. "We seek articles that will cover one or two full pages (800 words each); informative to the general quilting public, present new ideas, interviews, instructional, etc." Estab. 1986. Circ. 70,000. Pays on publication. Publishes ms an average of 6 months after acceptance. Byline given. Buys second serial (reprint) rights. Submit seasonal material 8 months in advance. Accepts queries by mail, fax. Responds in 1 month to queries; 2 months to mss. Writer's guidelines for SASE or online.

O═ "Best bet—a quilter writing about a new or unusual quilting technique."

Nonfiction: Book excerpts, essays, how-to (for various quilting techniques), humor, interview/profile, new product, opinion, personal experience, photo feature. **Buys 20-30 mss/year.** Query or send complete ms. Length: 800-1,600 words. **Pays $75/full page of published text.**

Reprints: Send photocopy with rights for sale noted and information about when and where the material previously appeared. **Pays $75/published page**.

Photos: Send photos with submission. Reviews transparencies, 35mm slides. Offers $20/photo. Captions, identification of subjects required.

Tips: "Our publication appeals to traditional quilters. We're interested in articles (with slides or transparencies) on quilts in museum collections."

$ $ $RAILMODEL JOURNAL, Golden Bell Press, 2403 Champa St., Denver CO 80205. **Contact:** Robert Schleicher, editor. **80% freelance written.** Monthly magazine "for advanced model railroaders. 100% photojournalism. We use step-by-step how-to articles with photos of realistic and authentic models." Estab. 1989. Circ. 16,000. Pays on publication. Byline given. Offers 100% kill fee. Buys first, second serial (reprint) rights. Editorial lead time 6 months. Submit seasonal material 6 months in advance. Responds in 4 months to queries; 8 months to mss. Sample copy for $5.50. Writer's guidelines free.

Nonfiction: Historical/nostalgic, how-to, photo feature, technical. "No beginner articles or anything that could even be mistaken for a toy train." **Buys 70-100 mss/year.** Query. Length: 200-5,000 words. **Pays $60-800.** Sometimes pays expenses of writers on assignment.

Photos: Send photos with submission. Reviews contact sheets, 35mm transparencies, 5×7 prints. Buys one-time and reprint rights. Captions, identification of subjects, model releases required.

Tips: "Writers must understand dedicated model railroaders who recreate 100% of their model cars, locomotives, buildings and scenes from specific real-life prototypes. Close-up photos a must."

$ RENAISSANCE MAGAZINE, division of Queue, Inc., 338 Commerce Dr., Fairfield CT 06432. (800)232-2224. Fax: (800)775-2729. E-mail: sperrett@queueinc.com. Website: www.renaissancemagazine.com. **Contact:** Steven Perrett, managing editor. **90% freelance written.** Quarterly magazine covering the history of the Middle Ages and the Renaissance. "Our readers include historians, reenactors, roleplayers, medievalists and Renaissance Faire enthusiasts." Estab. 1996. Circ. 30,000. Pays on publication. Publishes ms an average of 1 year after acceptance. Byline given. Buys first North American serial rights. Editorial lead time 6 months. Submit seasonal material 4 months in advance. Accepts queries by mail, e-mail, fax, phone. Responds in 3 weeks to queries; 2 months to mss. Sample copy for $9. Writer's guidelines for #10 SASE or online.

- The editor reports an interest in seeing costuming "how-to" articles; and Renaissance Festival "insider" articles.

O— Break in by submitting short (500-1,000 word) articles as fillers or querying on upcoming theme issues.

Nonfiction: Essays, exposé, historical/nostalgic, how-to, interview/profile, new product, opinion, photo feature, religious, travel. **Buys 25 mss/year.** Query or send ms. Length: 1,000-5,000 words. **Pays 7¢/word.**

Photos: State availability with submission. Reviews contact sheets, negatives, transparencies, prints. Buys all rights. Offers no additional payment for photos accepted with ms or negotiates payment separately. Captions, identification of subjects, model releases required.

Columns/Departments: Book reviews, 500 words. Include original or good copy of book cover. "For interested reviewers, books can be supplied for review; query first." **Pays 5¢/word.**

Tips: "Send in all articles in the standard manuscript format with photos/slides or illustrations for suggested use. Writers *must* be open to critique and all historical articles should also include a recommended reading list. An SASE must be included to receive a response to any submission."

$ $▨ ROCK & GEM, The Earth's Treasures, Minerals and Jewelry, Miller Magazines, Inc., 4880 Market St., Ventura CA 93003-7783. (805)644-3824, ext. 29. Fax: (805)644-3875. E-mail: rockgemmag@aol.com. Website: www.rockngem.com. **Contact:** Lynn Varon, managing editor. **99% freelance written.** Monthly magazine covering rockhounding field trips, how-to lapidary projects, minerals, fossils, gold prospecting, mining, etc. "This is not a scientific journal. Its articles appeal to amateurs, beginners and experts, but its tone is conversational and casual, not stuffy. It's for hobbyists." Estab. 1971. Circ. 55,000. Pays on publication. Byline given. Buys first North American serial rights. Editorial lead time 4 months. Submit seasonal material 6 months in advance. Accepts queries by mail. Writer's guidelines for SASE or online.

Nonfiction: General interest, how-to, humor, personal experience, photo feature, travel. Does not want to see "The 25th Anniversary of the Pet Rock" or anything so scientific that it could be a thesis. **Buys 156-200 mss/year.** Send complete ms. Length: 1,575-3,000 words. **Pays $100-250.**

Photos: Send photos with submission. Reviews prints, slides or digital art on disk or CD only (provide thumbnails). Offers no additional payment for photos accepted with ms. Captions required.

Tips: "We're looking for more how-to articles and field trips with maps. Read writers guidelines very carefully and follow all instructions in them. Then be patient. Your manuscript may be published within a month or even three years from date of submission."

$ $ RUG HOOKING MAGAZINE, Stackpole Magazines, 1300 Market St., Suite 202, Lemoyne PA 17043-1420. (717)234-5091. Fax: (717)234-1359. E-mail: rughook@paonline.com. Website: www.rughookingonline.com. Editor: Patrice Crowley. **Contact:** Editorial Assistant. **75% freelance written.** Published 5 times/year magazine covering the craft of rug hooking. "This is the only magazine in the world devoted exclusively to rug hooking. Our readers are both novices and experts. They seek how-to pieces, features on fellow artisans and stories on beautiful rugs new and old." Estab. 1989. Circ. 10,000. **Pays on acceptance.** Publishes ms an average of 1 year after acceptance. Byline given. Buys all rights. Editorial lead time 6 months. Submit seasonal material 6 months in advance. Accepts queries by mail, e-mail, fax. Responds in 2 months to queries. Sample copy for $5.

Nonfiction: How-to (hook a rug or a specific aspect of hooking), personal experience. **Buys 30 mss/year.** Query with published clips. Length: 825-2,475 words. **Pays $74.25-222.75.** Sometimes pays expenses of writers on assignment.

Reprints: Send photocopy and information about when and where the material previously appeared.

Photos: Send photos with submission. Reviews 2×2 transparencies, 3×5 prints. Buys all rights. Negotiates payment individually. Identification of subjects required.

$ $▨ SCALE AUTO ENTHUSIAST, Kalmbach Publishing Co., 21027 Crossroads Circle, P.O. Box 1612, Waukesha WI 53187-1612. (262)796-8776. Fax: (262)796-1383. E-mail: kbell@kalmbach.com. Website: www.scaleautomag.com. **Contact:** Kirk Bell, editor. **70% freelance written.** Magazine published 8 times/year covering model car building. "We are looking for model builders, collectors and enthusiasts who feel their models and/or modeling techniques and experiences would be of interest and benefit to our readership." Estab. 1979. Circ. 75,000. Pays on publication. Publishes ms an average of 1 year after acceptance. Byline given. Buys all rights. Editorial lead time 4 months. Submit seasonal material 4 months in advance. Accepts queries by mail, e-mail, fax, phone. Responds in 2 months to queries; 3 months to mss. Sample copy and writer's guidelines free or online.

Nonfiction: Book excerpts, historical/nostalgic, how-to (build models, do different techniques), interview/profile, personal experience, photo feature, technical. Query or send complete ms. Length: 750-3,000 words. **Pays $75-100/ published page.**

Photos: When writing how-to articles be sure to take photos *during* the project. Send photos with submission. Reviews negatives, 35mm color transparencies, color glossy. Buys all rights. Negotiates payment individually. Captions, identification of subjects, model releases required.

Columns/Departments: Buys 50 mss/year. Query. **Pays $75-100.**

Tips: "First and foremost, our readers like how-to material: how-to paint, how-to scratchbuild, how-to chop a roof, etc. Basically, our readers want to know how to make their own models better. Therefore, any help or advice you can offer is what modelers want to read. Also, the more photos you send, taken from a variety of views, the better choice we have in putting together an outstanding article layout. Send us more photos than you would ever possibly imagine we could use. This permits us to pick and choose the best of the bunch."

N $ $ SEW NEWS, The Fashion Magazine for People Who Sew, Primedia Enthusiast Group, 741 Corporate Circle, Suite A, Golden CO 80401. (303)278-1010. Fax: (303)277-0370. E-mail: sewnews@sewnews.com. Website: www.sewnews.com. **Contact:** Linda Turner Griepentrog, editor. **90% freelance written.** Works with a small number of new/unpublished writers each year. Monthly magazine covering fashion-sewing. "Our magazine is for the beginning home sewer to the professional dressmaker. It expresses the fun, creativity and excitement of sewing." Estab. 1980. Circ. 175,000. **Pays on acceptance.** Publishes ms an average of 6 months after acceptance. Byline given. Buys all rights. Submit seasonal material 6 months in advance. Accepts queries by mail, e-mail, fax. Responds in 2 months to mss. Sample copy for $5.95. Writer's guidelines for #10 SAE with 2 first-class stamps or online.
- All stories submitted to *Sew News* must be on disk or by e-mail.

Nonfiction: How-to (sewing techniques), interview/profile (interesting personalities in home-sewing field). **Buys 200-240 mss/year.** Query with published clips if available. Length: 500-2,000 words. **Pays $25-500 for assigned articles.**
Photos: Prefers color photos or slides. Send photos with submission. Buys all rights. Payment included in ms price. Identification of subjects required.

    The online magazine carries some original content not found in the print edition and includes writer's guidelines. *Sew News* has a free online newsletter.

Tips: "Query first with writing sample and outline of proposed story. Areas most open to freelancers are how-to and sewing techniques; give explicit, step-by-step instructions plus rough art. We're using more home decorating content."

$ SHUTTLE SPINDLE & DYEPOT, Handweavers Guild of America, Inc., 3327 Duluth Highway, Two Executive Concourse, Suite 201, Duluth GA 30096. (770)495-7702. Fax: (770)495-7703. E-mail: weavespindye@compuserve.com. Website: www.weavespindye.org. Publications Manager: Pat King. **Contact:** Sandra Bowles, editor-in-chief. **60% freelance written.** Quarterly magazine. "Quarterly membership publication of the Handweavers Guild of America, Inc., *Shuttle Spindle & Dyepot* magazine seeks to encourage excellence in contemporary fiber arts and to support the preservation of techniques and traditions in fiber arts. It also provides inspiration for fiber artists of all levels and develops public awareness and appreciation of the fiber arts. *Shuttle Spindle & Dyepot* appeals to a highly educated, creative and very knowledgeable audience of fiber artists and craftsmen—weavers, spinners, dyers and basket makers." Estab. 1969. Circ. 30,000. Pays on publication. Publishes ms an average of 6 months after acceptance. Byline given. Buys first North American serial, second serial (reprint), electronic rights. Editorial lead time 8 months. Submit seasonal material 8 months in advance. Accepts queries by mail, e-mail, fax, phone. Sample copy for $7.50 plus shipping. Writer's guidelines online.

    Articles featuring up-and-coming artists, new techniques, cutting-edge ideas and designs, fascinating children's activities, and comprehensive fiber collections are a few examples of "best bet" topics.

Nonfiction: Inspirational, interview/profile, new product, personal experience, photo feature, technical, travel. "No self-promotional and no articles from those without knowledge of area/art/artists." **Buys 40 mss/year.** Query with published clips. Length: 1,000-2,000 words. **Pays $75-150.**
Photos: State availability with submission. Offers no additional payment for photos accepted with ms. Captions, identification of subjects, model releases required.
Columns/Departments: Books and Videos, News and Information, Calendar and Conference, Travel and Workshop, Guildview (all fiber/art related).
Tips: "Become knowledgeable about the fiber arts and artists. The writer should provide an article of importance to the weaving, spinning, dyeing and basket making community. Query by telephone (once familiar with publication) by appointment helps editor and writer.

$ SPORTS COLLECTORS DIGEST, Krause Publications, 700 E. State St., Iola WI 54990. (715)445-2214. Fax: (715)445-4087. E-mail: kpsports@aol.com. Website: www.krause.com. **Contact:** Tom Mortenson, editor. **25% freelance written.** Works with a small number of new/unpublished writers each year. Weekly magazine covering sports memorabilia. "We serve collectors of sports memorabilia—baseball cards, yearbooks, programs, autographs, jerseys, bats, balls, books, magazines, ticket stubs, etc." Estab. 1952. Circ. 38,000. Pays after publication. Publishes ms an average of 3 months after acceptance. Byline given. Buys first North American serial rights. Submit seasonal material 3 months in advance. Responds in 5 weeks to queries; 2 months to mss. Sample copy free. Writer's guidelines for #10 SASE.
Nonfiction: General interest (new card issues, research older sets), historical/nostalgic (old stadiums, old collectibles, etc.), how-to (buy cards, sell cards and other collectibles, display collectibles, ways to get autographs, jerseys and other memorabilia), interview/profile (well-known collectors, ball players—but must focus on collectibles), new product (new cards sets), personal experience (what I collect and why-type stories). No sports stories. "We are not competing with *The Sporting News, Sports Illustrated* or your daily paper. Sports collectibles only." **Buys 50-75 mss/year.** Query. Length: 300-3,000 words. **Pays $100-150.**
Reprints: Send tearsheet. Pays 100% of amount paid for an original article.
Photos: Unusual collectibles. Send photos with submission. Buys all rights. Pays $25-150 for b&w prints. Identification of subjects required.

Columns/Departments: Length: 500-1,500 words. "We have all the columnists we need but welcome ideas for new columns." **Buys 100-150 mss/year.** Query. **Pays $90-150.**

Tips: "If you are a collector, you know what collectors are interested in. Write about it. No shallow, puff pieces; our readers are too smart for that. Only well-researched articles about sports memorabilia and collecting. Some sports nostalgia pieces are OK. Write only about the areas you know about."

$ STAMP COLLECTOR, Krause Publications, 700 E. State St., Iola WI 54990-0001. (715)445-2214. Fax: (715)445-4612. E-mail: baumannf@krause.com. Website: www.stampcollector.net. **Contact:** Fred Baumann, associate editor. **10% freelance written.** Biweekly tabloid covering philately (stamp collecting). "For stamp collectors of all ages and experience levels." Estab. 1931. Circ. 17,941. Pays on publication. Publishes ms an average of 6 months after acceptance. Byline given. Buys first North American serial rights. Editorial lead time 1 month. Submit seasonal material 3 months in advance. Accepts queries by mail, e-mail. Accepts simultaneous submissions. Responds in 1 week to queries; 1 month to mss. Sample copy free.

Nonfiction: How-to (collecting stamps). Special issues: Upcoming specialty guides include world and US stamps, postal history, holiday gift guide, topical stamps, other specialty areas. Send complete ms. Length: 150-950 words. **Pays $25-100.** Sometimes pays writers with subscriptions and hobby books. Sometimes pays expenses of writers on assignment.

Photos: State availability with submission. Reviews prints. Buys one-time rights. Offers no additional payment for photos accepted with ms. Captions, identification of subjects required.

Columns/Departments: Postal History (a detailed look at how a particular stamp or cover played a role in moving the mail), 500-950 words. **Buys 6-10 mss/year.** Query. **Pays $25-75.**

Tips: "Submissions are pretty much limited to writers with stamp collecting experience and/or interest."

N $ SUNSHINE ARTIST, America's Premier Show & Festival Publication, Palm House Publishing Inc., 2600 Temple Dr., Winter Park FL 32789. (407)539-1399. Fax: (407)539-1499. E-mail: sunart@sunshineartists.com. Website: www.sunshineartist.com. Publisher: David Cook. **Contact:** Amy Detwiler, editor. Monthly magazine covering art shows in the US. "We are the premier-marketing/reference magazine for artists and crafts professionals who earn their living through art shows nationwide. We list more than 2,000 shows monthly, critique many of them and publish articles on marketing, selling and other issues of concern to professional show circuit artists." Estab. 1972. Circ. 12,000. Pays on publication. Publishes ms an average of 3 months after acceptance. Byline given. Buys first North American serial rights. Responds in 2 months to queries. Sample copy for $5.

Nonfiction: "We publish articles of interest to artists and crafts professionals who travel the art show circuit. Current topics include marketing, computers and RV living." No how-to. **Buys 5-10 freelance mss/year.** Query with or without published clips or send complete ms. Length: 1,000-2,000 words. **Pays $50-150.**

Reprints: Send photocopy and information about when and where the material previously appeared.

Photos: Send photos with submission. Offers no additional payment for photos accepted with ms. Captions, identification of subjects, model releases required.

$ $ TATTOO REVUE, Art & Ink Enterprises, Inc., 5 Marine View Plaza, Suite 207, Hoboken NJ 07030. (201)653-2700. Fax: (201)653-7892. E-mail: inked@skinartmag.com. Website: tattoorevue.com. Editor: Jean Chris Miller. **Contact:** Scot Rienecker, managing editor. **25% freelance written.** Interview and profile magazine published 10 times/year covering tattoo artists, their art and lifestyle. "All writers must have knowledge of tattoos." Features include interviews with tattoo artists and collectors." Estab. 1990. Circ. 100,000. Pays on publication. Publishes ms an average of 3 months after acceptance. Byline given. Buys one-time rights. Editorial lead time 3 months. Submit seasonal material 5 months in advance. Accepts queries by mail, e-mail, fax. Accepts simultaneous submissions. Responds in 2 weeks to queries. Sample copy for $5.98. Writer's guidelines for #10 SASE.

Nonfiction: Book excerpts, historical/nostalgic, humor, interview/profile, photo feature. Special issues: Publishes special convention issues—dates and locations provided upon request. "No first time experiences—our readers already know." **Buys 10-30 mss/year.** Query with published clips or send complete ms. Length: 500-2,500 words. **Pays $50-200.**

Photos: Send photos with submission. Reviews transparencies, prints. Buys one-time rights. Offers $0-10/photo. Captions, identification of subjects, model releases required.

Columns/Departments: **Buys 10-30 mss/year.** Query with or without published clips or send complete ms. **Pays $25-50.**

Fiction: Adventure, erotica, fantasy, historical, horror, humorous, science fiction, suspense. "No stories featuring someone's tattoo coming to life!" **Buys 10-30 mss/year.** Query with published clips or send complete ms. Length: 500-2,500 words. **Pays $50-100.**

Poetry: Avant-garde, free verse, haiku, light verse, traditional. **Buys 10-30 poems/year.** Submit maximum 12 poems. Length: 2-1,000 lines. **Pays $10-25.**

Fillers: Anecdotes, facts, gags to be illustrated by cartoonist, newsbreaks, short humor. **Buys 10-20/year.** Length: 50-2,000 words.

■ The online magazine carries original content not found in the print edition. Contact: Chris Miller.

Tips: "All writers must have knowledge of tattoos! Either giving or receiving."

$ $🖬 TEDDY BEAR REVIEW, Collector Communications Corp., 1107 Broadway, Suite 1210, New York NY 10010. (212)989-8700. E-mail: jp@collector-online.com. Website: www.teddybearreview.com. **Contact:** Joan Muyskens Pursley, editorial director. **65% freelance written.** Works with a small number of new/unpublished writers each year. Bimonthly magazine on teddy bears for collectors, enthusiasts and bearmakers. Estab. 1985. Pays 30 days after acceptance. Byline given. Buys first North American serial rights. Submit seasonal material 6 months in advance. Sample copy and writer's guidelines for $2 and 9×12 SAE.
Nonfiction: Book excerpts, historical/nostalgic, how-to, interview/profile. No nostalgia on childhood teddy bears. **Buys 30-40 mss/year.** Query with published clips. Length: 900-1,500 words. **Pays $100-350.** Sometimes pays expenses of writers on assignment.
Photos: Send photos with submission. Reviews transparencies, b&w prints. Buys one-time rights. Offers no additional payment for photos accepted with ms. Captions required.
Tips: "We are interested in good, professional writers around the country with a strong knowledge of teddy bears. Historical profile of bear companies, profiles of contemporary artists and knowledgeable reports on museum collections are of interest. We are looking for humorous, offbeat stories about teddy bears in general."

$ $THREADS, Taunton Press, 63 S. Main St., P.O. Box 5506, Newtown CT 06470. (203)426-8171. E-mail: threads@taunton.com. Website: www.threadsmagazine.com. **Contact:** Chris Timmons, editor. Bimonthly magazine covering sewing, garment construction, home decor and embellishments (quilting and embroidery). "We're seeking proposals from hands-on authors who first and foremost have a skill. Being an experienced writer is of secondary consideration." Estab. 1985. Circ. 165,000. Byline given. Offers $150 kill fee. Buys one-time, second serial (reprint) rights. Editorial lead time 4 months. Responds in 1-2 months to queries. Writer's guidelines for free or online.
Nonfiction: "We prefer first-person experience." **Pays $150/page.**
Columns/Departments: Product Reviews; Book Reviews; Tips; Closures (stories of a humorous nature). Query. **Pays $150/page.**
Tips: "Send us a proposal (outline) with photos of your own work (garments, samplers, etc.)."

$🖬 TOY CARS & MODELS, Krause Publications, 700 E. State St., Iola WI 54990-0001. (715)445-2214. Fax: (715)445-4087. E-mail: contacttoycars@krause.com. Website: www.toycarsmag.com. **Contact:** Merry Dudley, editor. **90% freelance written.** Monthly 4-color, glossy magazine covering toy vehicles/models. "We cover the hobby market for collectors of die-cast models, model kit builders and fans of all types of vehicle toys." Estab. 1998. Circ. 20,000. Pays on publication. Publishes ms an average of 1 year after acceptance. Byline given. Buys perpetual non-exclusive rights. Editorial lead time 4 months. Submit seasonal material 6 months in advance. Accepts queries by mail, e-mail, phone. Accepts simultaneous submissions. Responds in 2 weeks to queries; 2 months to mss. Sample copy for $4.50 or online. Writer's guidelines for SASE or online.
  Oⁿ Break in with "great color photos."
Nonfiction: Interested in seeing histories of obscure companies/toy lines/scale model/kits. General interest, historical/nostalgic, how-to (building or detailing models), interview/profile, new product, personal experience, photo feature, technical. No Hot Wheels history ("We would much rather see coverage of new Hot Wheels"). **Buys 25 mss/year.** Query with published clips. Length: 800-1,500 words. **Pays $30-100.** Sometimes pays expenses of writers on assignment.
Photos: Send photos with submission. Reviews negatives, 3×5 transparencies, 3×5 prints. Buys one-time rights. No additional payment for photos accepted with ms. Captions, identification of subjects, model releases required.
Columns/Departments: The Checkered Flag (nostalgic essays about favorite toys), 500-800 words; Helpful Hints (tips about model kit buildings, etc.), 25-35 words; Model Reviews (reviews of new die-cast and model kits), 100-350 words. **Buys 25 mss/year.** Query with published clips. **Pays $30-100.**
  🖳 The online magazine carries original content not found in the print version. Contact: Merry Dudley, online editor.
Tips: "Our magazine is for serious hobbyists looking for info about kit building, model quality, new product info and collectible value."

$ $TOY FARMER, Toy Farmer Publications, 7496 106 Ave. SE, LaMoure ND 58458-9404. (701)883-5206. Fax: (701)883-5209. E-mail: zekesez@aol.com. Website: www.toyfarmer.com. President: Claire D. Scheibe. Publisher: Cathy Scheibe. **Contact:** Cheryl Hegvik, editorial assistant. **65% freelance written.** Monthly magazine covering farm toys. Estab. 1978. Circ. 27,000. Pays on publication. Publishes ms an average of 1 month after acceptance. Byline given. Buys first North American serial rights. Editorial lead time 3 months. Submit seasonal material 3 months in advance. Accepts queries by mail, e-mail, fax, phone. Responds in 1 month to queries; 2 months to mss. Sample copy for $4. Writer's guidelines for #10 SASE.
  • Youth involvement is strongly encouraged.
Nonfiction: General interest, historical/nostalgic, humor, interview/profile, new product, personal experience, technical, book introductions. **Buys 100 mss/year.** Query with published clips. Length: 800-1,500 words. **Pays 10¢/word.** Sometimes pays expenses of writers on assignment.
Photos: State availability with submission. Reviews transparencies. Buys one-time rights. Offers no additional payment for photos accepted with ms.
Columns/Departments: Buys 36 mss/year. Query with published clips. **Pays 10¢/word.**

$ $⬚ TOY SHOP, Krause Publications, 700 E. State St., Iola WI 54990. (715)445-2214. Fax: (715)445-4087. E-mail: korbecks@krause.com. Website: www.toyshopmag.com. **Contact:** Sharon Korbeck, editorial director. **85-90% freelance written.** Biweekly tabloid covering toy collecting. "We cover primarily vintage collectible toys from the 1930s-present. Stories focus on historical toy companies, the collectibility of toys and features on prominent collections." Estab. 1988. Circ. 40,000. Pays on publication. Publishes ms an average of 8-30 months after acceptance. Byline given. Buys perpetual non-exclusive rights. Editorial lead time 6 months. Submit seasonal material 1 year in advance. Accepts queries by mail, e-mail. Accepts simultaneous submissions. Responds in 2 months to queries. Sample copy for $3.98. Writer's guidelines online.
Nonfiction: Historical/nostalgic (toys, toy companies), interview/profile (toy collectors), new product (toys), photo feature, features on old toys. No opinion, broad topics or poorly researched pieces. **Buys 100 mss/year.** Query. Length: 500-1,500 words. **Pays $50-200.** Contributor's copies included in payment. Sometimes pays expenses of writers on assignment.
Reprints: Send photocopy and information about when and where the material previously appeared.
Photos: State availability of or send photos with submission. Reviews negatives, transparencies, 3×5 prints and electronic photos. Rights purchased with ms rights. Negotiates payment individually. Captions, identification of subjects, model releases required.
Columns/Departments: Collector Profile (profile of toy collectors), 700-1,000 words. **Buys 25 mss/year.** Query. **Pays $50-150.**
Tips: "Articles must be specific. Include historical info, quotes, values of toys and photos with story. Talk with toy dealers and get to know the market."

$ $ TOY TRUCKER & CONTRACTOR, Toy Farmer Publications, 7496 106th Ave. SE, LaMoure ND 58458-9404. (701)883-5206. Fax: (701)883-5209. E-mail: zekesez@aol.com. Website: www.toytrucker.com. President: Claire D. Scheibe. Publisher: Cathy Scheibe. **Contact:** Cheryl Hegvik, editorial assistant. **75% freelance written.** Monthly magazine covering collectible toys. "We are a magazine on hobby and collectible toy trucks and construction pieces." Estab. 1990. Circ. 6,500. Pays on publication. Publishes ms an average of 3 months after acceptance. Byline given. Buys first North American serial rights. Editorial lead time 3 months. Submit seasonal material 3 months in advance. Accepts queries by mail, e-mail, fax, phone. Responds in 1 month to queries; 2 months to mss. Sample copy for $4. Writer's guidelines free.
Nonfiction: Historical/nostalgic, interview/profile, new product, personal experience, technical. **Buys 35 mss/year.** Query. Length: 800-2,400 words. **Pays 10¢/word.** Sometimes pays expenses of writers on assignment.
Photos: Send photos with submission. Offers no additional payment for photos accepted with ms. Captions, identification of subjects, model releases required.
Tips: "Send sample work that would apply to our magazine. Also, we need more articles on collectors or builders. We have regular columns, so a feature should not repeat what our columns do."

$ $ TRADITIONAL QUILTWORKS, The Pattern Magazine for Traditional Quilters, Chitra Publications, 2 Public Ave., Montrose PA 18801. (570)278-1984. Fax: (570)278-2223. E-mail: chitraed@epix.net. Website: www.quiltt ownusa.com. **Contact:** Joyce Libal, senior editor. **50% freelance written.** Bimonthly magazine on quilting. "We seek articles of an instructional nature, profiles of talented teachers, articles on the history of specific areas of quiltmaking (patterns, fiber, regional, etc.)." Estab. 1988. Circ. 70,000. Pays on publication. Publishes ms an average of 6 months after acceptance. Byline given. Buys second serial (reprint) rights. Submit seasonal material 8 months in advance. Accepts queries by mail, fax. Responds in 2 months to queries. Writer's guidelines for #10 SASE or online.
  O— "Best bet—a quilter writing about a new or unusual quilting technique."
Nonfiction: Historical, instructional, quilting education. **Buys 12-18 mss/year.** Query or send complete ms. Length: 1,500 words maximum. **Pays $75/published page of text.**
Reprints: Send photocopy and information about when and where the material previously appeared.
Photos: Send photos with submission. Reviews 35mm slides and larger transparencies (color). Offers $20/photo. Captions, identification of subjects, model releases required.
Tips: "Our publication appeals to traditional quilters."

$ TREASURE CHEST, The Information Source & Marketplace for Collectors and Dealers of Antiques and Collectibles, Treasure Chest Publishing Inc., 22 Parsonage St., #326, Providence RI 02903. (401)272-9444. **Contact:** David F. Donnelly, publisher. **100% freelance written.** Monthly newspaper on antiques and collectibles. Estab. 1988. Circ. 50,000. Pays on publication. Publishes ms an average of 3 months after acceptance. Byline given. Buys first, second serial (reprint) rights. Responds in 2 months to mss. Sample copy for 9×12 SAE with $2. Writer's guidelines for #10 SASE.
Nonfiction: Primarily interested in feature articles on a specific field of antiques or collectibles with reproducible photographs. **Buys 60-80 mss/year.** Send complete ms. Articles on disk or via e-mail preferred. Length: 750-1,000 words. **Pays $30-40 with photos.**
Reprints: Send tearsheet or photocopy and information about when and where the material previously appeared.
Tips: "Learn about your subject by interviewing experts—appraisers, curators, dealers."

$ $ WARMAN'S TODAY'S COLLECTOR, The Nation's Antiques and Collectibles Marketplace, (formerly *Today's Collector*), Krause Publications, 700 E. State St., Iola WI 54990-0001. (715)445-2214. Fax: (715)445-

4087. E-mail: korbeck@krause.com. Website: www.krause.com. **Contact:** Sharon Korbeck, editor. **90% freelance written.** Monthly magazine covering antiques and collectibles. *"Warman's Today's Collector* is for serious collectors of all types of antiques and collectibles." Estab. 1993. Circ. 40,000. Pays on publication. Publishes ms an average of 1 year after acceptance. Byline given. Offers 50% kill fee. Buys perpetual non-exclusive rights. Editorial lead time 2 months. Submit seasonal material 8 months in advance. Accepts queries by mail, e-mail, fax. Accepts simultaneous submissions. Responds in 3 weeks to queries; 3 months to mss. Sample copy for $3.95. Writer's guidelines free or online.

Nonfiction: How-to (antiques and collectibles), interview/profile, personal experience. No articles that are too general—specific collecting areas only. **Buys 60-80 mss/year.** Query or send complete ms. Length: 500-1,200 words. **Pays $50-200.** Sometimes pays expenses of writers on assignment.

Reprints: Send typed ms with rights for sale noted and information about when and where the material previously appeared. Pays 50% of amount paid for an original article.

Photos: State availability with submission. Reviews transparencies, prints. Buys one-time rights. Offers no additional payment for photos accepted with ms. Captions, identification of subjects required.

Columns/Departments: Collector profiles of prominent collections, auction/show highlights. Query. **Pays $50-200.**

Tips: "I want detailed articles about specific collecting areas—nothing too broad or general. Our articles need to inform readers of diverse collecting areas—from vintage to more 'modern' antiques and collectibles. I need lots of information about pricing and values, along with brief history and background."

N **$ $WEEKEND WOODCRAFTS,** EGW Publishing Inc., 1041 Shary Circle, Concord CA 94518. (925)671-9852. Fax: (925)671-0692. E-mail: rjoseph@egw.com. Website: www.weekendwoodcrafts.com. **Contact:** Robert Joseph, editor. Bimonthly magazine covering woodworking/crafts. "Projects that can be completed in one weekend." Estab. 1992. Circ. 91,000. Pays half on acceptance and half on publication. Publishes ms an average of 3 months after acceptance. Byline given. Buys first rights. Editorial lead time 2 months. Submit seasonal material 2 months in advance. Accepts queries by mail, e-mail. Accepts simultaneous submissions. Responds in 2 months to mss. Sample copy online. Writer's guidelines free.

Nonfiction: How-to (tips and tech), woodworking projects. **Buys 10 mss/year.** Send complete ms. Length: 400-1,500 words. **Pays $100-500.**

Photos: Send photos with submission. Reviews contact sheets, 4×6 prints. Buys all rights. Offers no additional payment for photos accepted with ms.

Tips: "Build simple and easy weekend projects, build one- to two-hour projects."

$ $WOODSHOP NEWS, Soundings Publications Inc., 35 Pratt St., Essex CT 06426-1185. (860)767-8227. Fax: (860)767-0645. E-mail: woodshopnews@att.net. Website: www.woodshopnews.com. Editor: Thomas K. Clark. **Contact:** A.J. Hamler, editor. **20% freelance written.** Monthly tabloid "covering woodworking for professionals and hobbyists. Solid business news and features about woodworking companies. Feature stories about interesting professional and amateur woodworkers. Some how-to articles." Estab. 1986. Circ. 100,000. Pays on publication. Publishes ms an average of 6 months after acceptance. Byline given. Offers 25% kill fee. Buys first North American serial rights. Submit seasonal material 4 months in advance. Accepts queries by mail, e-mail, fax. Responds in 1 month to queries. Sample copy online. Writer's guidelines free.

• *Woodshop News* needs writers in major cities in all regions except the Northeast. Also looking for more editorial opinion pieces.

Nonfiction: How-to (query first), interview/profile, new product, opinion, personal experience, photo feature. Key word is "newsworthy." No general interest profiles of "folksy" woodworkers. **Buys 15-25 mss/year.** Query with published clips or send complete ms. Length: 100-1,200 words. **Pays $50-500 for assigned articles; $40-250 for unsolicited articles.** Pays expenses of writers on assignment.

Photos: Send photos with submission. Reviews contact sheets, prints. Buys one-time rights. Offers $20-35/color photo; $250/color cover, usually with story. Captions, identification of subjects required.

Columns/Departments: Pro Shop (business advice, marketing, employee relations, taxes, etc. for the professional written by an established professional in the field), Finishing (how-to and techniques, materials, spraybooths, staining; written by experienced finishers), both 1,200-1,500 words. **Buys 18 mss/year.** Query. **Pays $200-300.**

Fillers: Small filler items, briefs, or news tips that are followed up by staff reporters. **Pays $10.**

Tips: "The best way to start is a profile of a business or hobbyist woodworker in your area. Find a unique angle about the person or business and stress this as the theme of your article. Avoid a broad, general-interest theme that would be more appropriate to a daily newspaper. Our readers are woodworkers who want more depth and more specifics than would a general readership. If you are profiling a business, we need standard business information such as gross annual earnings/sales, customer base, product line and prices, marketing strategy, etc. Color 35 mm photos are a must. We need more freelance writers from the Mid-Atlantic, Midwest and West Coast."

$ $WOODWORK, A Magazine For All Woodworkers, Ross Periodicals, P.O. Box 1529, Ross CA 94957-1529. (415)382-0580. Fax: (415)382-0587. E-mail: woodwrkmag@aol.com. Publisher: Tom Toldrian. **Contact:** John Lavine, editor. **90% freelance written.** Bimonthly magazine covering woodworking. "We are aiming at a broad audience of woodworkers, from the hobbyist to professional. Articles run the range from intermediate to complex. We cover such subjects as carving, turning, furniture, tools old and new, design, techniques, projects and more. We also feature profiles of woodworkers, with the emphasis being always on communicating woodworking methods, practices, theories and techniques. Suggestions for articles are always welcome." Estab. 1986. Circ. 80,000. Pays on publication. Byline given. Buys first North American serial, second serial (reprint) rights. Accepts queries by mail, e-mail, fax. Sample copy for $5 and 9×12 SAE with 6 first-class stamps. Writer's guidelines for #10 SASE.

Nonfiction: How-to (simple or complex, making attractive furniture), interview/profile (of established woodworkers that make attractive furniture), photo feature (of interest to woodworkers), technical (tools, techniques). "Do not send a how-to unless you are a woodworker." Query. Length: 1,500-2,000 words. **Pays $150/published page.**

Photos: Send photos with submission. Reviews 35mm slides. Buys one-time rights. Pays higher page rate for photos accepted with ms. Captions, identification of subjects required.

Columns/Departments: Tips and Techniques column, **pays $35-75.** Interview/profiles of established woodworkers; bring out woodworker's philosophy about the craft, opinions about what is happening currently. Good photos of attractive furniture a must. Section on how-to desirable. Query with published clips.

Tips: "Our main requirement is that each article must directly concern woodworking. If you are not a woodworker, the interview/profile is your best, really only chance. Good writing is essential as are good photos. The interview must be entertaining, but informative and pertinent to woodworkers' interests. Include sidebar written by the profile subject."

HOME & GARDEN

The baby boomers' turn inward, or "cocooning," has caused an explosion of publications in this category. Gardening magazines in particular have blossomed, as more people are developing leisure interests at home. Some magazines here concentrate on gardens; others on the how-to of interior design. Still others focus on homes and gardens in specific regions of the country. Be sure to read the publication to determine its focus before submitting a manuscript or query.

$ THE ALMANAC FOR FARMERS & CITY FOLK, Greentree Publishing, Inc., #319, 840 S. Rancho Dr., Suite 4, Las Vegas NV 89106. (702)387-6777. Website: www.thealmanac.com. **Contact:** Lucas McFadden, editor. **40% freelance written.** Annual almanac of "down-home, folksy material pertaining to farming, gardening, homemaking, animals, etc." Deadline: March 31. Estab. 1983. Circ. 800,000. Pays on publication. Publishes ms an average of 6 months after acceptance. Byline given. Buys first North American serial rights. Sample copy for $4.95.

　O— Break in with short, humorous, gardening, or how-to pieces.

Nonfiction: Essays, general interest, how-to, humor. No fiction or controversial topics. "Please, no first-person pieces!" **Buys 30 mss/year.** No queries please. Send complete ms by mail. Length: 350-1,400 words. **Pays $45/page.**

Poetry: Buys 1-4 poems/year. Pays $45 for full pages, otherwise proportionate share thereof.

Fillers: Anecdotes, facts, short humor, gardening hints. **Buys 60/year.** Length: 125 words maximum. **Pays $10-45.**

Tips: "Typed submissions essential as we scan in manuscript. Short, succinct material is preferred. Material should appeal to a wide range of people and should be on the 'folksy' side, preferably with a thread of humor woven in. No first-person pieces."

$ $ THE AMERICAN GARDENER, A Publication of the American Horticultural Society, 7931 E. Boulevard Dr., Alexandria VA 22308-1300. (703)768-5700. Fax: (703)768-7533. E-mail: editor@ahs.org. Website: www.ahs.org. Managing Editor: Mary Yee. **Contact:** David J. Ellis, editor. **75% freelance written.** Bimonthly magazine covering gardening and horticulture. "*The American Gardener* is the official publication of the American Horticultural Society (AHS), a national, nonprofit, membership organization for gardeners, founded in 1922. AHS is dedicated to educating and inspiring people of all ages to become successful, environmentally responsible gardeners by advancing the art and science of horticulture. Readers of *The American Gardener* are avid amateur gardeners; about 22% are professionals. Most prefer not to use synthetic pesticides." Estab. 1922. Circ. 26,000. Pays on publication. Publishes ms an average of 6 months after acceptance. Byline given. Offers 25% kill fee. Buys first North American serial rights and limited rights to run article on members-only website. Editorial lead time 4 months. Submit seasonal material at least 1 year in advance. Accepts queries by mail. Responds in 3 months to queries. Sample copy for $4. Writer's guidelines for #10 SASE.

Nonfiction: "Feature-length articles include in-depth profiles of individual plant groups, profiles of prominent American horticulturists and gardeners (living and dead), profiles of unusual public or private gardens, descriptions of historical developments in American gardening, descriptions of innovative landscape design projects (especially relating to use of regionally native plants or naturalistic gardening), and descriptions of important plant breeding and research programs tailored to a lay audience. We run a few how-to articles; these should address relatively complex or unusual topics that most other gardening magazines won't tackle—photography needs to be provided." **Pays $250-500 depending on length, complexity, author's horticultural background and publishing experience. Buys 30 mss/year.** Query with published clips. Length: 1,500-2,000 words.

Reprints: Rarely purchases second rights. Send photocopy of article with information on when and where it previously appeared. Pay varies.

Photos: Must be accompanied by postage-paid return mailer. State availability with submission. Reviews transparencies, prints. Buys one-time rights. Offers $50-200/photo. Identification of subjects required.

Columns/Departments: Natural Connections (explains a natural phenomenon—plant and pollinator relationships, plant and fungus relationships, parasites—that may be observed in nature or in the garden), 750-1,200 words; Habitat

Gardening (focuses on gardens designed to replicate regional plant communities and ecosystems, or landscape designers who specialize in such projects), 1,000-1,200 words; Urban Gardener (looks at a successful small space garden—indoor, patio, less than a quarter-acre; a program that successfully brings plants to city streets or public spaces; or a problem of particular concern to city dwellers), 750-1,200 words; Regional Happenings (events that directly affect gardeners only in 1 area, but are of interest to others: an expansion of a botanical garden, a serious new garden pest, the launching of a regional flower show, a hot new gardening trend), 250-300 words. **Buys 15 mss/year.** Query with published clips. **Pays $50-250.**

Tips: "Our readers are advanced, passionate amateur gardeners; about 20 percent are horticultural professionals. Our articles are intended to bring this knowledgeable group new information, ranging from the latest scientific findings that affect plants, to in-depth profiles of specific plant groups and the history of gardening and gardens in America."

$ $ ATLANTA HOMES AND LIFESTYLES, Weisner Publishing LLC, 1100 Johnson Ferry Rd., Suite 595, Atlanta GA 30342. (404)252-6670. Fax: (404)252-6673. Website: www.atlantahomesmag.com. **Contact:** Oma Blaise, editor. **65% freelance written.** Magazine published 8 times/year. "*Atlanta Homes and Lifestyles* is designed for the action-oriented, well-educated reader who enjoys his/her shelter, its design and construction, its environment, and living and entertaining in it." Estab. 1983. Circ. 33,091. Pays on publication. Publishes ms an average of 6 months after acceptance. Byline given. Buys all rights. Accepts queries by mail, fax. Responds in 3 months to queries. Sample copy for $3.95. Writer's guidelines online.

Nonfiction: Interview/profile, new product, photo feature, well-designed homes, gardens, local art, remodeling, food, preservation, entertaining. "We do not want articles outside respective market area, not written for magazine format, or that are excessively controversial, investigative or that cannot be appropriately illustrated with attractive photography." **Buys 35 mss/year.** Query with published clips. Length: 500-1,200 words. **Pays $400.** Sometimes pays expenses of writer on assignment.

Photos: Most photography is assigned. State availability with submission. Reviews transparencies. Buys one-time rights. Pays $40-50/photo. Captions, identification of subjects, model releases required.

Columns/Departments: Short Takes (newsy items on home and garden topics); Quick Fix (simple remodeling ideas); Cheap Chic (stylish decorating that is easy on the wallet); Digging In (outdoor solutions from Atlanta's gardeners); Big Fix (more extensive remodeling projects); Real Estate News. Length: 350-500 words. Query with published clips. **Pays $50-200.**

Tips: "Query with specific new story ideas rather than previously published material."

N $ $ AUSTIN HOME & LIVING, Publications & Communications Inc., 505 Cypress Creek,, Suite B, Cedar Park TX 78613. (512)926-4663. Fax: (512)331-3950. E-mail: bronas@pcinews.com. Website: www.AustinHomeAndLiving.com. **Contact:** Brona Stockton, associate publisher. **75% freelance written.** Bimonthly magazine. "*Austin Home & Living* showcases the homes found in Austin and provides tips on food, gardening and decorating." Estab. 1994. Circ. 20,000. Pays on publication. Publishes ms an average of 4 months after acceptance. Byline given. Offers 100% kill fee. Buys all rights. Editorial lead time 4 months. Submit seasonal material 6 months in advance. Accepts queries by mail, e-mail, fax. Responds in 1 month to queries; 2 months to mss. Sample copy and writer's guidelines free.

Nonfiction: How-to, interview/profile, new product, travel. **Buys 18 mss/year.** Query with published clips. Length: 500-2,000 words. **Pays $200 for assigned articles.** Pays expenses of writers on assignment.

Photos: State availability of or send photos with submission. Reviews negatives, transparencies, prints. Buys all rights. Offers no additional payment for photos accepted with ms. Captions required.

$ ✉ BACKHOME, Your Hands-On Guide to Sustainable Living, Wordsworth Communications, Inc., P.O. Box 70, Hendersonville NC 28793. (828)696-3838. Fax: (828)696-0700. E-mail: backhome@ioa.com. Website: www.BackHomemagazine.com. **Contact:** Lorna K. Loveless, editor. **80% freelance written.** Bimonthly magazine. *BackHome* encourages readers to take more control over their lives by doing more for themselves: productive organic gardening; building and repairing their homes; utilizing alternative energy systems; raising crops and livestock; building furniture; toys and games and other projects; creative cooking. *BackHome* promotes respect for family activities, community programs and the environment. Estab. 1990. Circ. 26,000. Pays on publication. Publishes ms an average of 1 year after acceptance. Byline given. Offers $25 kill fee at publisher's discretion. Buys first North American serial rights. Editorial lead time 3 months. Submit seasonal material 6 months in advance. Accepts queries by mail, e-mail, fax, phone. Responds in 6 weeks to queries; 2 months to mss. Sample copy $4 or online. Writer's guidelines for SASE or online.

● The editor reports an interest in seeing "more alternative energy experiences, *good* small houses, workshop projects (for handy persons, not experts) and community action others can copy."

○→ Break in by writing about personal experience (especially in overcoming challenges) in fields in which *Back-home* focuses.

Nonfiction: How-to (gardening, construction, energy, homebusiness), interview/profile, personal experience, technical, self-sufficiency. No essays or old-timey reminiscences. **Buys 80 mss/year.** Query. Length: 750-5,000 words. **Pays $25 (approximately)/printed page.**

Reprints: Send photocopy and information about when and where the material previously appeared. Pays $25/printed page.

Photos: Send photos with submission. Reviews 35mm slides and color prints. Buys one-time rights. Offers additional payment for photos published. Identification of subjects required.

Tips: "Very specific in relating personal experiences in the areas of gardening, energy, and homebuilding how-to. Third-person approaches to others' experiences are also acceptable but somewhat less desirable. Clear color photo prints, especially those in which people are prominent, help immensely when deciding upon what is accepted."

$ $ $ $ BETTER HOMES AND GARDENS, 1716 Locust St., Des Moines IA 50309-3023. (515)284-3044. Fax: (515)284-3763. Website: www.bhg.com. Editor-in-Chief: Karol DeWulf Nickell. **Contact:** Laura O'Neill, editor (Building); Nancy Byal, editor (Food & Nutrition); Mark Kane, editor (Garden/Outdoor Living); Catherine Hamrick, editor (Health); Richard Sowienski, editor (Education & Parenting); Lamont Olson, editor (Money Management, Automotive, Electronics); Becky Mollenkamp, editor (Features & Travel); Sandra Soria, editor (Interior Design). **10-15% freelance written.** Magazine "providing home service information for people who have a serious interest in their homes." "We read all freelance articles, but much prefer to see a letter of query rather than a finished manuscript." Estab. 1922. Circ. 7,605,000. **Pays on acceptance.** Buys all rights.
Nonfiction: Travel, Education, gardening, health, cars, home, entertainment. "We do not deal with political subjects or with areas not connected with the home, community, and family." No poetry or fiction. **Pay rates.**
Tips: Most stories published by this magazine go through a lengthy process of development involving both editor and writer. Some editors will consider *only* query letters, not unsolicited manuscripts. Direct queries to the department that best suits your story line.

N $ BIRDS & BLOOMS, Reiman Publications, 5925 Country Lane, Greendale WI 53129. E-mail: editors@birdsan dblooms.com. Website: www.birdsandblooms.com. **Contact:** Jeff Nowak, editor. **15% freelance written.** Bimonthly magazine focusing on the "beauty in your own backyard. *Birds & Blooms* is a sharing magazine that lets backyard enthusiasts chat with each other by exchanging personal experiences. This makes *Birds & Blooms* more like a conversation than a magazine, as readers share tips and tricks on producing beautiful blooms and attracting feathered friends to their backyards." Estab. 1995. Circ. 1,900,000. Pays on publication. Publishes ms an average of 7 months after acceptance. Byline given. Buys all rights. Editorial lead time 2 months. Submit seasonal material 4 months in advance. Accepts queries by mail, e-mail. Accepts simultaneous submissions. Responds in 2 months to queries; 2 months to mss. Sample copy for $2, 9×12 SAE and $1.95 postage. Writer's guidelines for #10 SASE.
Nonfiction: Essays, how-to, humor, inspirational, personal experience, photo feature, natural crafting and plan items for building backyard accents. No bird rescue or captive bird pieces. **Buys 12-20 mss/year.** Send complete ms. Length: 250-1,000 words. **Pays $100-400.**
Photos: Trudi Bellin, photo coordinator. Send photos with submission. Reviews transparencies, prints. Buys one-time rights. Identification of subjects required.
Columns/Departments: Backyard Banter (odds, ends and unique things); Bird Tales (backyard bird stories); Local Lookouts (community backyard happenings), all 200 words. **Buys 12-20 mss/year.** Send complete ms. **Pays $50-75.**
Fillers: Anecdotes, facts, gags to be illustrated by cartoonist. **Buys 25/year.** Length: 10-250 words. **Pays $10-75.**
Tips: "Focus on conversational writing—like you're chatting with a neighbor over your fence. Manuscripts full of tips and ideas that people can use in backyards across the country have the best chance of being used. Photos that illustrate these points also increase chances of being used."

N $ $ CALIFORNIA HOMES, The Magazine of Architecture, the Arts and Distinctive Design, McFadden-Bray Publishing Corp., P.O. Box 8655, Newport Beach CA 92658. (949)640-1484. Fax: (949)640-1665. E-mail: edit@calhomesmagazine.com. **Contact:** Susan McFadden, editor. **80% freelance written.** Bimonthly magazine covering California interiors, architecture, some food, travel, history, current events in the field. Estab. 1997. Circ. 40,000. Pays on publication. Publishes ms an average of 3 months after acceptance. Byline given. Offers 50% kill fee. Buys first North American serial rights. Editorial lead time 3 months. Submit seasonal material 6 months in advance. Accepts queries by mail, e-mail, fax. Responds in 1 month to queries; 2 months to mss. Sample copy for $3.95. Writer's guidelines for #10 SASE.
Nonfiction: Query. Length: 500-1,000 words. **Pays $250-500.** Sometimes pays expenses of writers on assignment.
Photos: State availability with submission. Buys one-time rights. Negotiates payment individually. Captions required.

$ $ $ CANADIAN HOME WORKSHOP, The Do-It-Yourself Magazine, Avid Media Inc., 340 Ferrier St., Suite 210, Markham, Ontario L3R 2Z5, Canada. (905)475-8440. Fax: (905)475-9246. E-mail: letters@canadianhome workshop.com. Website: www.canadianhomeworkshop.com. **Contact:** Douglas Thomson, editor. **90% freelance written.** Half of these are assigned. Magazine published 10 times/year covering the "do-it-yourself" market including woodworking projects, renovation, restoration and maintenance. Circ. 120,000. Pays 1 month after receipt. Byline given. Offers 50% kill fee. Rights are negotiated with author. Submit seasonal material 6 months in advance. Responds in 6 weeks to queries. Sample copy for 9×12 SAE. Writer's guidelines for #10 SASE.
Nonfiction: How-to (home maintenance, renovation, woodworking projects and features). **Buys 40-60 mss/year.** Query with published clips. Length: 1,500-2,500 words. **Pays $800-1,200.** Pays expenses of writers on assignment.
Photos: Send photos with submission. Payment for photos, transparencies negotiated with the author. Captions, identification of subjects, model releases required.
Tips: "Freelancers must be aware of our magazine format. Products used in how-to articles must be readily available across Canada. Deadlines for articles are four months in advance of cover date. How-tos should be detailed enough for the amateur but appealing to the experienced. Articles must have Canadian content: sources, locations, etc."

N **$ $CLASSIC AMERICAN HOME**, Hearst Magazines, 1790 Broadway, 14th Floor, New York NY 10019. Fax: (212)586-3455. E-mail: aspiezio@hearst.com. Editor: G. Jason Kontos. **Contact:** Amy Spiezio, chief copy editor. **20% freelance written.** Bimonthly magazine. "*Classic American Home* is a shelter book that celebrates historic and timeless design, architecture, decorative arts and decorating." Estab. 1975. Circ. 500,000. Pays on publication. Byline given. Buys all rights. Editorial lead time 5 months. Submit seasonal material 6 months in advance. Accepts queries by mail. Responds in 2 weeks to queries. Sample copy for #10 SASE. Writer's guidelines free.

Nonfiction: Contact individual department editors. General interest, historical/nostalgic, new product, travel. **Buys 2 mss/year.** Query with published clips. Length: 500-1,500 words. **Pays $500-750 for assigned articles.**

Photos: Send photos with submission. Buys all rights. Negotiates payment individually. Identification of subjects required.

Columns/Departments: Masterworks (craftsperson), 750 words. **Buys 2 mss/year.** Query. **Pays $500-700.**

Tips: "We accept few unsolicited story ideas, so the best way to propose an idea is with a detailed outline and snapshots."

N **$ $ $COASTAL LIVING**, Southern Progress Corp., 2100 Lakeshore Dr., Birmingham AL 35209. (205)877-6000. Fax: (205)877-6990. E-mail: lynn_carter@spc.com. Website: www.coastallivingmag.com. **Contact:** Lynn Carter, managing editor. Bimonthly magazine "for those who live or vacation along our nation's coasts. The magazine emphasizes home design and travel, but also covers a wide variety of other lifestyle topics and coastal concerns." Estab. 1997. Circ. 375,000. Responds in 2 months to queries.

Nonfiction: The magazine is roughly divided into 5 areas, with regular features, columns and departments for each area. **Currents** offers short, newsy features of 30-75 words on *New Products and Ideas* (fun accessories to upscale furnishings), *Happenings* (interesting events), and *Coastal Curiosities* (facts and statistics about the shore). **Travel** includes Getaways, Nature Travel and Sporting Life. **Homes** places the accent on casual living, with "warm, welcoming houses and rooms designed for living. Sections include *Building and Remodeling, Good Decisions* (featuring a particular construction component of building or remodeling, with installation or maintenance techniques), *New Communities* (profiles of environmentally sensitive coastal developments); and *Decorating*. **Food** is divided into *Entertaining* (recipes and tips) and *Seafood Primer* (basics of buying and preparing seafood). The **Lifestyle Service** section is a catch all of subjects to help readers live better and more comfortably: *The Good Life* (profiles of people who have moved to the coast), *Coastal Home* (original plans for the perfect coastal home), *So You Want to Live In...* (profiles of coastal communities), etc. Query with SASE.

Photos: State availability with submission.

■ The online magazine carries original content not found in the print edition. Contact: Susan Haynes, online editor.

Tips: "Query us with ideas that are very specifically targeted to the columns that are currently in the magazine."

N **$ $COLORADO HOMES & LIFESTYLES**, Wiesner Publishing, LLC, 7009 S. Potomac St., Englewood CO 80112-4029. (303)662-5204. Fax: (303)662-5307. E-mail: emcgraw@coloradohomesmag.com. Website: www.color adohomesmag.com. Managing Editor: Karen Blaschke. **Contact:** Evalyn McGraw, editor-in-chief. **75% freelance written.** Upscale shelter magazine published 9 times/year containing beautiful homes, gardens, travel articles, art and artists, food and wine, architecture, calendar, antiques, etc. All of Colorado is included. Geared toward home-related and lifestyle areas, personality profiles, etc. Estab. 1981. Circ. 35,000. **Pays on acceptance.** Publishes ms an average of 3 months after acceptance. Byline given. Offers 15% kill fee. Buys first North American serial rights. Editorial lead time 3 months. Submit seasonal material 1 year in advance. Accepts queries by mail, e-mail. Accepts simultaneous submissions. Responds in 2 months to queries. Sample copy and writer's guidelines for SASE.

● The editor reports that *Colorado Homes & Lifestyles* is doing many more lifestyle articles and needs more unusual and interesting worldwide travel stories.

Nonfiction: Fine homes and furnishings, regional interior design trends, interesting personalities and lifestyles, gardening and plants—all with a Colorado slant. Book excerpts, general interest, historical/nostalgic, new product, photo feature, travel. Special issues: Mountain Homes and Lifestyles (people, etc., January/February); Great Bathrooms (March/April); Home of the Year Contest (July/August); Great Kitchens (September/October). No personal essays, religious, humor, technical. **Buys 50-75 mss/year.** Query with published clips. Length: 1,200-1,500 words. **Pays $200-300.** Sometimes pays expenses of writers on assignment.

Reprints: Send photocopy or typed ms with rights for sale noted and information about when and where the material previously appeared. Pays 35-50% of amount paid for an original article.

Photos: Send photos with submission. Reviews 35mm, 4×5 and 2¼×2¼ color transparencies, b&w glossy prints. Identification of subjects, title and caption suggestions appreciated. Please include photographic credits required.

Columns/Departments: Gardening (informative); Artisans (profile of Colorado artisans/craftspeople and work); Travel (worldwide, personal experience preferred); Architecture (Colorado), all 1,100-1,300 words. **Buys 60-75 mss/year.** Query with published clips. **Pays $175-250.**

Fiction: Occasionally publishes novel excerpts.

■ The online magazine carries original content not found in the print edition. Contact: Danielle Fox, assistant editor.

Tips: "Send query, lead paragraph, clips (published and unpublished, if possible). Send ideas for story or stories. Include some photos, if applicable. The more interesting and unique the subject the better. A frequent mistake made by writers is failure to provide material with a style and slant appropriate for the magazine, due to poor understanding of the focus of the magazine."

$ $ $ COUNTRY HOME, Meredith Corp., 1716 Locust St., Des Moines IA 50309-3023. (515)284-2015. Fax: (515)284-2552. E-mail: countryh@mdp.com. Website: www.countryhomemagazine.com. Editor-in-Chief: Carol Sama Sheehan. **Contact:** Melissa Manning, assignments editor. Magazine published 8 times/year for people interested in the country way of life. "*Country Home* magazine is a lifestyle publication created for readers who share passions for American history, style, craftsmanship, tradition, and cuisine. These people, with a desire to find a simpler, more meaningful lifestyle, live their lives and design their living spaces in ways that reflect those passions." Estab. 1979. Circ. 1,000,000. Pays on completion of assignment. Publishes ms an average of 5 months after acceptance. Byline given. Submit seasonal material 6 months in advance. Accepts queries by mail. Responds in 6 weeks to queries. Sample copy for $4.95.

○── "We are not responsible for unsolicited manuscripts, and we do not encourage telephone queries."

Nonfiction: Architecture and Design, Families at Home, Travel, Food and Entertaining, Art and Antiques, Gardens and Outdoor Living, Personal Reflections. Query by mail only with writing samples and SASE. Length: 750-1,500 words. **Pays $500-1,500.**

Columns/Departments: Length: 500-750 words. Include SASE. Query with published clips. **Pays $300-500.**

■ The online magazine carries original content not found in the print edition. Contact: Lori Blackford, online editor.

$ $ $ COUNTRY LIVING, The Hearst Corp., 224 W. 57th St., New York NY 10019. (212)649-3509. **Contact:** Marjorie Gage, senior editor. Monthly magazine covering home design and interior decorating with an emphasis on country style. "A lifestyle magazine for readers who appreciate the warmth and traditions associated with American home and family life. Each monthly issue embraces American country decorating and includes features on furniture, antiques, gardening, home building, real estate, cooking, entertaining and travel." Estab. 1978. Circ. 1,600,000.

Nonfiction: Most open to freelancers: Antiques articles from authorities, personal essay. **Buys 20-30 mss/year.** Send complete ms and SASE. **Payment varies.**

Columns/Departments: Most open to freelancers: Readers Corner. Send complete ms and SASE. **Payment varies.**

Tips: "Know the magazine, know the market and know how to write a good story that will interest *our* readers."

N $ $ COUNTRY SAMPLER, Country Sampler, Inc., 707 Kautz Rd., St. Charles IL 60174. (630)377-8000. Fax: (630)377-8194. Website: www.sampler.com. Publisher: Margaret Borst. **Contact:** Paddy Kalahar Buratto, editor. Bimonthly magazine. "*Country Sampler* is a country decorating, antiques and collectibles magazine and a country product catalog." Estab. 1984. Circ. 462,263. Accepts queries by mail, fax.

Nonfiction: "Furniture, accessories and decorative accents created by artisans throughout the country are displayed and offered for purchase directly from the maker. Fully decorated room settings show the readers how to use the items in their homes to achieve the warmth and charm of the country look."

Tips: "Send photos and story idea for a country style house tour. Story should be regarding decorating tips and techniques."

N $ $ COUNTRY SAMPLER DECORATING IDEAS, Emmis Communications, 707 Kautz Rd., St, Charles IL 60174. Fax: (630)377-8194. E-mail: decideas@sampler.emmis.com. Website: www.decoratingideas.com. Managing Editor: Rita M. Woker. **Contact:** Mike Morris, editor. **60% freelance written.** Bimonthly magazine on home decor and home improvement. "This magazine is devoted to providing do-it-yourself decorating solutions for the average homeowner, through step-by-step projects, topical articles and real-life feature stories that inspire readers to create the country home of their dreams." **Pays on acceptance.** Publishes ms an average of 6 months after acceptance. Byline given. Makes work-for-hire assignments. Editorial lead time 4 months. Submit seasonal material 6 months in advance. Accepts queries by mail, e-mail, fax. Responds in 1 month to queries; 3 months to mss. Writer's guidelines free.

Nonfiction: Book excerpts, how-to (decorating projects), interview/profile, photo feature, house tours. Special issues: Decorate With Paint (February and July); Kitchen & Bath Ideas (May); Window & Wall Ideas (August); Re-Decorate (November). No opinion or fiction. **Buys 50 mss/year.** Query with published clips. Length: 500-1,500 words. **Pays $250-350.** Sometimes pays expenses of writers on assignment.

Photos: State availability with submission. Reviews transparencies, 3×5 prints. Buys negotiable rights. Negotiates payment individually. Captions, identification of subjects, model releases required.

Tips: "Query letters accompanied by published clips are your best bet. We do not accept unsolicited articles, but pay on acceptance for assigned articles. So it is best to sell us on an article concept and support that concept with similar published articles."

N $ $ $ DECORATING IDEAS, Woman's Day Special Interest Publications, Hachette-Filipacchi Magazines, 1633 Broadway, New York NY 10019. (212)767-6000. Fax: (212)767-5612. Editor: Carolyn Gatto. **Contact:** Amanda Rock, assistant managing editor. Magazine published 4 times/year covering home decorating. "This magazine aims to inspire and teach readers how to create a beautiful home." **Pays on acceptance.** Publishes ms an average of 3 months after acceptance. Byline given. Offers up to 25% kill fee. Buys first worldwide serial rights. Editorial lead time 6 months. Submit seasonal material 10 months in advance. Accepts queries by mail, fax. Responds in 2 months to mss. Writer's guidelines for #10 SASE.

Nonfiction: General interest, how-to (home decor projects for beginner/intermediate skill levels—sewing, woodworking, painting, etc.), interview/profile, new product, photo feature, technical, collectibles, hard to find services, unique stores. Query with published clips. Length: 250-1,000 words. **Payment varies based on length, writer, importance.** Sometimes pays expenses of writers on assignment.

Photos: Send representative photos with query. Buys one-time rights. Model releases required.

Columns/Departments: Step by Step (how-to instructions for 1 or 2 relevant projects that can be completed in a day or two), 400-800 words; Networking (Internet site reviews); Update; Discoveries. **Payment varies based on length, writer, and level/amount of research required.**

Tips: "Send a brief, clear query letter with relevant clips, and be patient. Before and after photos are very helpful, as are photos of ideas for Step by Step column. In addition to specific ideas and projects (for which how-to information is provided), we look at decorating trends, provide advice on how to get the most design for your money (with and without help from a professional), and highlight noteworthy new products and services." No phone queries please. Part of Woman's Day Special Interest Publications.

$ $ EARLY AMERICAN LIFE, (formerly *Early American Homes*), Celtic Moon Publishing, Inc., 207 House Ave., Suite 103, Camp Hill PA 17011. (717)730-6263. Fax: (717)730-6263. Website: www.earlyamericanlife.com. **Contact:** Virginia Stimmel, editor. **20% freelance written.** Bimonthly magazine for "people who are interested in capturing the warmth and beauty of the 1600 to 1840 period and using it in their homes and lives today. They are interested in antiques, traditional crafts, architecture, restoration and collecting." Estab. 1970. Circ. 130,000. **Pays on acceptance.** Publishes ms an average of 1 year after acceptance. Byline given. Buys worldwide rights. Accepts queries by mail, e-mail, fax. Responds in 3 months to queries. Sample copy and writer's guidelines for 9×12 SAE with 4 first-class stamps.

O→ Break in "by offering highly descriptive, entertaining, yet informational articles on social culture, decorative arts, antiques or well-restored and appropriately furnished homes that reflect middle-class American life prior to 1850."

Nonfiction: "Social history (the story of the people, not epic heroes and battles), travel to historic sites, antiques and reproductions, restoration, architecture and decorating. We try to entertain as we inform. We're always on the lookout for good pieces on any of our subjects. Would like to see more on how real people did something great to their homes." **Buys 40 mss/year.** Query with or without published clips or send complete ms. Length: 750-3,000 words. **Pays $100-600.** Pays expenses of writers on assignment.

Tips: "Our readers are eager for ideas on how to bring early America into their lives. Conceive a new approach to satisfy their related interests in arts, crafts, travel to historic sites, and especially in houses decorated in the Early American style. Write to entertain and inform at the same time. Be prepared to help us with sources for illustrations."

$ $ FLOWER AND GARDEN MAGAZINE, 51 Kings Highway W., Haddonfield NJ 08033-2114. (856)354-5034. Fax: (856)354-5147. E-mail: kcpublishing@earthlink.net. Website: http://flowerandgardenmag.com. **Contact:** Senior Editor. **80% freelance written.** Works with a small number of new/unpublished writers each year. Bimonthly picture magazine. "*Flower & Garden* focuses on ideas that can be applied to the home garden and outdoor environs; primarily how-to, but also historical and background articles are considered if a specific adaptation can be obviously related to home gardening." Estab. 1957. Circ. 300,000. **Pays on acceptance.** Publishes ms an average of 1 year after acceptance. Byline sometimes given. Buys first-time, nonexclusive, reprint rights. Accepts queries by mail, e-mail, fax. Responds in 2 months to queries. Sample copy for $3. Writer's guidelines for #10 SASE.

● The editor tells us good quality photos accompanying articles are more important than ever.

Nonfiction: Interested in illustrated articles on how to do certain types of gardening and descriptive articles about individual plants. Flower arranging, landscape design, house plants and patio gardening are other aspects covered. "The approach we stress is practical (how-to-do-it, what-to-do-it-with). We emphasize plain talk, clarity and economy of words. An article should be tailored for a national audience." **Buys 20-30 mss/year.** Query. Length: 500-1,000 words. **Pays variable rates depending on quality and kind of material and author's credentials, $200-500.**

Reprints: Send typed ms with rights for sale noted and information about when and where the material previously appeared.

Photos: Color slides and transparencies preferred, 35mm and larger but 35mm slides or prints not suitable for cover. Submit cover photos as 2¼×2¼ or larger transparencies. In plant or flower shots, indicate which end is up on each photo. Photos are paid for on publication, $60-175 inside, $300 for covers. An accurate packing list with appropriately labeled photographs and numbered slides with description sheet (including latin botanical and common names) is required.

Tips: "The prospective author needs good grounding in gardening practice and literature. Offer well-researched and well-written material appropriate to the experience level of our audience. Photographs help sell the story. Describe special qualifications for writing the particular proposed subject."

N $ $ GARDENING HOW-TO, North American Media Group, 12301 Whitewater Dr., Minnetonka MN 55343. (952)936-9333. Fax: (952)936-9755. E-mail: justin@gardeningclub.com. Website: www.gardeningclub.com. **Contact:** Justin W. Hancock, horticulture editor. **40% freelance written.** Bimonthly magazine covering gardening/horticulture. "*Gardening How-To* is the bimonthly publication of the National Home Gardening Club, headquartered in Minnetonka, Minnesota. As the primary benefit of membership in the Club, the magazine's aim is to provide timely, interesting, and inspiring editorial that will appeal to our audience of intermediate- to advanced-level home gardeners."

Estab. 1996. Circ. 600,000. **Pays on acceptance.** Publishes ms an average of 4 months after acceptance. Byline given. Offers 25% kill fee. Buys one-time rights. Editorial lead time 6 months. Submit seasonal material 6 months in advance. Accepts queries by mail, e-mail, fax. Sample copy for $3. Writer's guidelines for free or by e-mail.
Nonfiction: How-to (gardening/horticulture). **Buys 36 mss/year.** Query with published clips. Length: 1,000-2,000 words. **Pays $200-800.** Sometimes pays expenses of writers on assignment.
Photos: State availability with submission. Buys one-time rights. Negotiates payment individually.

$ $ THE HERB COMPANION, Herb Companion Press, 243 E. Fourth St., Loveland CO 80537. (970)663-0831. Fax: (970)663-0909. E-mail: HerbCompanion@HCPress.com. Website: www.discoverherbs.com. **Contact:** Dawna Duncan, editorial coordinator. **80% freelance written.** Bimonthly magazine about herbs: Culture, history, culinary, crafts and some medicinal use for both experienced and novice herb enthusiasts. Circ. 180,000. Pays on publication. Byline given. Buys all rights. Editorial lead time 4 months. Accepts queries by mail, e-mail, fax. Responds in 2 months to queries. Sample copy for $4. Writer's guidelines for #10 SASE.
Nonfiction: Practical horticultural, original recipes, historical, herbal crafts, helpful hints and book reviews. How-to, interview/profile. Submit by mail only detailed query or ms. Length: 4 pages or 1,000 words. **Pays 33¢/word.**
Photos: Returns photos and artwork. Send photos with submission. Prefers transparencies.
Tips: "New approaches to familiar topics are especially welcome. If you aren't already familiar with the content, style and tone of the magazine, we suggest you read a few issues. Technical accuracy is essential. Please use scientific as well as popular names for plants and cover the subject in depth while avoiding overly academic presentation. Information should be made accessible to the reader, and we find this is best accomplished by writing from direct personal experience where possible and always in an informal style."

N: $ $ HOME & CONDO, Southwest Florida's Resource for Home & Design Ideas, Gulfshore Communications, 9051 Tamiami Trail N, Suite 202, Naples FL 34108-2520. Fax: (941)643-5017. Managing Editor: Patti Pace. **Contact:** Nanci Theoret, editor. **90% freelance written.** Magazine published 6 times/year covering home design, interior design and gardening. "The writer is the expert, with information backed up by short, pertinent quotes from local professionals in the subject. Our readers are educated, affluent professionals, some with second or third homes in Naples, Florida. Go upscale!" Estab. 1980. Circ. 35,000. Pays on publication. Publishes ms an average of 5 months after acceptance. Byline given. Offers 40% kill fee. Buys first North American serial, electronic rights, makes work-for-hire assignments. Editorial lead time 4 months. Submit seasonal material 6 months in advance. Responds in 6 weeks to queries; 2 months to mss. Sample copy for 10×12 SAE and 6 first-class stamps. Writer's guidelines free.
Nonfiction: Home, interior design, architecture, gardening, outdoor life—all slanted for Southwest Florida homebuyer. **Buys 100 mss/year.** Query. Length: 1,000-2,000 words. **Pays $200-400.** Sometimes pays expenses of writers on assignment.
Photos: Send photos with submission. Reviews transparencies, 8×10 color prints. Buys one-time rights. Offers no additional payment for photos accepted with ms. Captions required.
Columns/Departments: By Design (interior or exterior home architecture), 850 words; Finishing Touches (post-construction elements), 800 words; Outdoor Living (landscaping, hardscapes, water features), 900 words. **Buys 50 mss/ year.** Send complete ms. **Pays $150-225.**
Tips: "Educate yourself on the topic and have Southwest Florida slant or relevance. This is a regional magazine (Ft. Myers-Marco Island) that reflects homes and grounds typical of the area with trends and choices as a highlight. *Home & Condo* is an upscale magazine and features only high-end treatments of its subjects."

$ HOME DIGEST, The Homeowner's Family Resource Guide, Home Digest International Inc., 268 Lakeshore Rd. E, Unit 604, Oakville, Ontario L6J 7S4, Canada. (905)844-3361. Fax: (905)849-4618. E-mail: homedigest@canada.c om. Website: www.home-digest.com. **Contact:** William Roebuck, editor. **25% freelance written.** Quarterly magazine covering house, home and life management for families in stand-alone houses in the greater Toronto region. "*Home Digest* has a strong service slant, combining useful how-to journalism with coverage of the trends and issues of home ownership and family life. In essence, our focus is on the concerns of families living in their own homes." Estab. 1995. Circ. 522,000. Pays on publication. Publishes ms an average of 3 months after acceptance. Byline given. Buys first North American serial rights. Editorial lead time 3 months. Submit seasonal material 5 months in advance. Accepts queries by mail, e-mail, fax. Accepts simultaneous submissions. Responds in 1 month to queries. Sample copy for 9×6 SAE and 2 Canadian first-class stamps. Writer's guidelines for #10 SASE or online.
Nonfiction: General interest, how-to (household hints, basic home renovation, decorating), humor (living in Toronto), inspirational. No opinion, fashion or beauty. **Buys 8 mss/year.** Query. Length: 350-700 words. **Pays $35-100 (Canadian).**
Photos: Send photos with submission. Reviews prints. Buys one-time rights. Pays $10-20/photo. Captions, identification of subjects, model releases required.
Columns/Departments: Household Hints (tested tips that work); Healthy Living (significant health/body/fitness news), both 300-350 words. **Buys 4-6 mss year.** Query. **Pays $40-50 (Canadian).**
Tips: "Base your ideas on practical experiences. We're looking for 'uncommon' advice that works."

$ $ HOMES & COTTAGES, The In-Home Show Ltd., 6557 Mississauga Rd., Suite D, Mississauga, Ontario L5N 1A6, Canada. (905)567-1440. Fax: (905)567-1442. E-mail: jadair@homesandcottages.com. Website: www.homesandcot tages.com. Editor: Janice Naisby. **Contact:** Jim Adair, editor-in-chief. **50% freelance written.** Magazine published 8 times/year covering building and renovating; "technically comprehensive articles." Estab. 1987. Circ. 64,000. Pays on publication. Publishes ms an average of 2 months after acceptance. Byline given. Offers 10% kill fee. Buys first North American serial rights. Editorial lead time 3 months. Submit seasonal material 3 months in advance. Accepts queries by mail. Sample copy for SAE. Writer's guidelines for #10 SASE.

Nonfiction: Looking for how-to projects and simple home improvement ideas. Humor (building and renovation related), new product, technical. **Buys 32 mss/year.** Query. Length: 1,000-2,000 words. **Pays $300-750.** Sometimes pays expenses of writers on assignment.

Photos: Send photos with submission. Reviews transparencies, prints. Buys one-time rights. Negotiates payment individually. Captions, identification of subjects required.

Tips: "Read our magazine before sending in a query. Remember that you are writing to a Canadian audience."

$ $ $ $ HOMESTYLE, (formerly *American Homestyle and Gardening Magazine*), Gruner + Jahr USA Publishing, 375 Lexington Ave., New York NY 10017. (212)499-2000. Fax: (212)499-1536. Editor-in-Chief: Kathleen Madden. **Contact:** Alison France, managing editor. Magazine published 10 times a year. "*Homestyle* is a guide to complete home design. It is edited for homeowners interested in decorating, building and remodeling products. It focuses on a blend of style, substance and service." Estab. 1986. Circ. 1,000,000. **Pays on acceptance.** Byline given. Offers 25% kill fee. Buys first North American serial rights. Writer's guidelines for #10 SASE.

Nonfiction: Writers with expertise in design, decorating, building or gardening. "Because stories begin with visual elements, queries without scouting photos rarely lead to assignments." Length: 600-2,000 words. **Pays $900-3,500.** Pays expenses of writers on assignment.

Tips: "Writers must have knowledge of interior design, remodeling or gardening."

$ $ $ HORTICULTURE, Gardening at Its Best, 98 N. Washington St., Boston MA 02114. (617) 742-5600. Fax: (617) 367-6364. E-mail: tfischer@primediasi.com. Website: www.hortmag.com. **Contact:** Thomas Fischer, executive editor. Magazine published 8 times/year. "*Horticulture*, the country's oldest gardening magazine, is designed for active amateur gardeners. Our goal is to offer a blend of text, photographs and illustrations that will both instruct and inspire readers." Circ. 250,000. Byline given. Offers kill fee. Buys first North American serial, one-time rights. Submit seasonal material 10 months in advance. Accepts queries by mail, e-mail, fax. Responds in 3 months to queries. Writer's guidelines for SASE or by e-mail.

Nonfiction: "We look for an encouraging personal experience, anecdote and opinion. At the same time, a thorough article should to some degree place its subject in the broader context of horticulture." Include disk where posisble. **Buys 15 mss/year.** Query with published clips, subject background material and SASE. Length: 1,000-2,000 words. **Pays $600-1,500.** Pays expenses of writers on assignment if previously arranged with editor.

Columns/Departments: Length: 100-1,500 words. Query with published clips, subject background material and SASE. Include disk where possible. **Pays $50-750.**

Tips: "We believe every article must offer ideas or illustrate principles that our readers might apply on their own gardens. No matter what the subject, we want our readers to become better, more creative gardeners."

N $ $ LAKESTYLE, Celebrating life on the water, Bayside Publications, Inc., P.O. Box 170, Excelsior MN 55331. (952)470-1380. Fax: (952)470-1389. E-mail: editor@lakestyle.com. Website: www.lakestyle.com. **Contact:** Nancy Jahnke, editor. **50% freelance written.** Quarterly magazine. "*Lakestyle* is committed to celebrating the lifestyle chosen by lake home and cabin owners." Estab. 2000. Circ. 40,000. Pays on publication. Publishes ms an average of 3 months after acceptance. Byline given. Offers 10% kill fee. Buys all rights. Editorial lead time 2 months. Submit seasonal material 3 months in advance. Accepts queries by mail, e-mail, fax, phone. Responds in 3 weeks to queries; 1 month to mss. Sample copy for $5. Writer's guidelines free.

Nonfiction: Essays, historical/nostalgic, how-to, humor, inspirational, interview/profile, new product, photo feature. No direct promotion of product. **Buys 15 mss/year.** Query with or without published clips or send complete ms. Length: 500-2,500 words. **Pays 25-50¢/word for assigned articles; 10-25¢/word for unsolicited articles.** Sometimes pays expenses of writers on assignment.

Photos: State availability of or send photos with submission. Rights purchased vary. Offers no additional payment for photos accepted with ms. Captions, identification of subjects, model releases required.

Columns/Departments: Lakestyle Entertaining (entertaining ideas); Lakestyle Gardening (gardening ideas); On the Water (boating/playing on the lake); Hidden Treasures (little known events); At the Cabin (cabin owner's information); all approximately 1,000 words. **Buys 10 mss/year.** Query with or without published clips or send complete ms. **Pays 10-25¢/word.**

Tips: "*Lakestyle* is interested in enhancing the lifestyle chosen by our readers, a thorough knowledge of cabin/lake home issues helps writers fulfill this goal."

N $ $ LOG HOME DESIGN IDEAS, Sabot Publishing, 1620 S. Lawe St., Suite 2, Appleton WI 54915. (920)830-1701. Fax: (920)830-1710. E-mail: editor@athenet.net. Website: www.lhdi.com. **Contact:** Teresa Hilgenberg, editor. **Less than 20% freelance written.** Bimonthly magazine covering log homes. "We are a full-color, slick publication devoted to log homes, their design and decoration, and the delight log home owners have for their lifestyle. Our readers are couples 30-35 years of age who either own a log home or dream of owning a modern manufactured or handcrafted log home." Estab. 1994. Circ. 200,000. Pays on publication. Publishes ms an average of 1 year after acceptance. Byline given. Buys first rights. Editorial lead time 9 months. Submit seasonal material 1 year in advance. Accepts queries by mail, e-mail, fax, phone. Responds in 6 months to queries.

O→ Break in by sending "attention-grabbing information packet about yourself including a cover letter, résumé, experience and written samples."

Nonfiction: Limited historical/nostalgic. Essays, how-to, interview/profile, personal experience, photo feature, technical. **Buys 2-6 mss/year.** Send complete ms. Length: 500-2,000 words. **Pays $100-500.** Sometimes pays expenses of writers on assignment.

Photos: Send photos with submission. Reviews contact sheets, negatives, 2½×2½ and 4×5 transparencies—color only. Buys one-time rights. Negotiates payment individually. Captions, identification of subjects, model releases required.

Columns/Departments: "We will consider well-written columns on interior decor, how-to/technical, 'folksy' essays. Show us what you can do, it may become a regular feature." Length: 250-600 words. **Buys 6 mss/year.** Send complete ms. **Pays $50-300.**

Tips: "Concentrate on satisfied log home owners and their experiences while planning, building and decorating their homes. We're also looking for new columns with a laid-back, folksy bent that will appeal to log home owners who have discovered the good life. The right columns could become regular features."

$ $ LOG HOME LIVING, Home Buyer Publications Inc., 4200-T Lafayette Center Dr., Chantilly VA 20151. (703)222-9411. Fax: (703)222-3209. E-mail: plobred@homebuyerpubs.com. Website: www.loghomeliving.com. **Contact:** Peter Lobred, editor. **50% freelance written.** Monthly magazine for enthusiasts who are dreaming of, planning for, or actively building a log home. Estab. 1989. Circ. 132,000. **Pays on acceptance.** Publishes ms an average of 6 months after acceptance. Byline given. Offers $100 kill fee. Buys first, second serial (reprint) rights. Editorial lead time 6 months. Submit seasonal material 6 months in advance. Accepts queries by mail. Responds in 6 weeks to queries. Sample copy for $4. Writer's guidelines for #10 SASE.

Nonfiction: Book excerpts, how-to (build or maintain log home), interview/profile (log home owners), personal experience, photo feature (log homes), technical (design/decor topics), travel. "We do not want historical/nostalgic material." **Buys 6 mss/year.** Query. Length: 1,000-2,000 words. **Pays $250-500.** Pays expenses of writers on assignment.

Reprints: Send tearsheet or photocopy and information about when and where the material previously appeared. Pays 50% of amount paid for an original article.

Photos: State availability with submission. Reviews contact sheets, 4×5 transparencies, 4×6 prints. Buys one-time rights. Negotiates payment individually.

Tips: "*Log Home Living* is devoted almost exclusively to modern manufactured and handcrafted kit log homes. Our interest in historical or nostalgic stories of very old log cabins, reconstructed log homes, or one-of-a-kind owner-built homes is secondary and should be queried first."

$ $ LOG HOMES ILLUSTRATED, Goodman Media Group, Inc., 419 Park Ave. South, New York NY 10016. (212)541-7100. Fax: (212)245-1241. Website: www.loghomeexpo.com or www.loghomesmag.com. Editor: Roland Sweet. **Contact:** Stacy Durr Albert, managing editor. **30-40% freelance written.** Bimonthly magazine. "*Log Homes Illustrated* presents full-color photo features and inspirational stories of people who have fulfilled their dream of living in a log home. We show readers how they can make it happen too." Estab. 1994. Circ. 126,000. Pays on publication. Publishes ms an average of 1 year after acceptance. Byline given. Buys first, second serial (reprint) rights. Editorial lead time 4 months. Submit seasonal material 6 months in advance. Accepts queries by mail, fax. Accepts simultaneous submissions. Sample copy for $3.99.

O→ To break in "include photos with queries if possible. Offer hands-on tips for our readers. Include sidebar ideas."

Nonfiction: Book excerpts, historical/nostalgic, how-to (gardening, building), new product, personal experience, photo feature, technical, travel, profile (architects). Special issues: Annual Buyer's Guide; PLANS issue. "We tend to stay away from articles that focus on just one craftsman, promotional pieces." **Buys 20-25 mss/year.** Query with published clips or send complete ms. Length: 1,200-3,000 words. **Pays $300-900.** Pays expenses of writers on assignment with limit agreed upon in advance.

Photos: Send photos with submission. Reviews 4×5 transparencies, slides or prints. Buys one-time rights. Negotiates payment individually. Captions required.

Columns/Departments: Diary (personal glimpses of log experience), 1,200-2,000 words; Going Places (visiting a log B&B, lodge, etc.), 1,200-2,000 words; Worth a Look (log churches, landmarks, etc.), 1,200-2,000 words; Gardening (rock gardens, water gardens, etc.), 2,000-3,000 words. **Buys 15 mss/year.** Query with published clips or send complete ms. **Pays $300-600.**

Tips: "Professional photos frequently make the difference between articles we accept and those we don't. Look for unique log structures in your travels, something we may not have seen before. We also consider carefully researched articles pertaining to insuring a log home, financing, contracting, etc."

MIDWEST HOME AND GARDEN, 10 S. Fifth St., Suite 1000, Minneapolis MN 55402. Fax: (612)371-5801. E-mail: editor@mnmo.com. Website: www.mnmo.com. **Contact:** Pamela Hill Nettleton, editor. **50% freelance written.** "*Midwest Home and Garden* is an upscale shelter magazine showcasing innovative architecture, interesting interior design, and beautiful gardens of the Midwest." Estab. 1997. Circ. 80,000. **Pays on acceptance.** Byline given. Accepts queries by mail, e-mail, fax. Writer's guidelines for #10 SASE.

Nonfiction: Profiles of regional designers, architects, craftspeople related to home and garden. Photo-driven articles on home decor and design, and gardens. Book excerpts, essays, how-to (garden and design), interview/profile (brief), new product, photo feature. Query with résumé, published clips, and SASE. Length: 300-1,000 words. **Payment negotiable.**
Columns/Departments: Back Home (essay on home/garden topics), 800 words; Design Directions (people and trends in home and garden), 300 words.
Tips: "We are always looking for great new interior design, architecture, and gardens—in Minnesota and in the Midwest."

$ $ MOUNTAIN LIVING, Wiesner Publishing, 7009 S. Potomac St., Englewood CO 80112. (303)397-7600. Fax: (303)397-7619. E-mail: irawlings@mountainliving.com. Website: www.mountainliving.com. **Contact:** Irene Rawlings, editor. **50% freelance written.** Bimonthly magazine covering "shelter and lifestyle issues for people who live in, visit or hope to live in the mountains." Estab. 1994. Circ. 35,000. **Pays on acceptance.** Publishes ms an average of 4 months after acceptance. Byline given. Offers 25% kill fee. Buys all rights. Editorial lead time 6 months. Submit seasonal material 6 months in advance. Accepts queries by mail, e-mail, phone. Accepts simultaneous submissions. Responds in 6 weeks to queries; 2 months to mss. Sample copy for $5 or online. Writer's guidelines for #10 SASE.
Nonfiction: Book excerpts, essays, historical/nostalgic, interview/profile, personal experience, photo feature, travel, home features. **Buys 30 mss/year.** Query with published clips. Length: 1,200-2,000 words. **Pays $250-500.** Sometimes pays expenses of writers on assignment.
Reprints: Send photocopy of article or typed ms with rights for sale noted. Payment varies.
Photos: State availability with submission. Buys one-time rights. Negotiates payment individually.
Columns/Departments: Architecture, Art, Sporting Life, Travel, Off the Beaten Path (out-of-the-way mountain areas in U.S.), History, Cuisine, Environment, Destinations (an art-driven department featuring a beautiful mountain destination in U.S.—must be accompanied by quality photograph), Trail's End (mountain-related essays). Length: 300-1,500 words. **Buys 35 mss/year.** Query with published clips. **Pays $50-500.**
Tips: "A deep understanding of and respect for the mountain environment is essential. Think out of the box. We love to be surprised. Write a brilliant, short query and always send clips."

$ $ ☐ NATIONAL NEIGHBORHOOD NEWS, Neighborhood America.com, 4380 Gulfshore Blvd. N., Suite 808, Naples FL 34103. (941)403-4305. Fax: (941)403-4835. E-mail: cmorrow@neighborhoodamerica.com. Website: www.nationalneighborhoodnews.com. **Contact:** Christina Morrow, content coordinator. **75% freelance written.** Online e-zine covering land use planning/environment/neighborhood. Pays on acceptance within 30 days of signed contract/edited article. Byline given. Not copyrighted. Buys electronic rights, archival rights. Editorial lead time 2 months. Accepts queries by e-mail. Accepts simultaneous submissions. Responds in 2 weeks to queries. Sample copy online. Writer's guidelines and sample contract free, online or by e-mail.
Nonfiction: General interest, interview/profile, news. No opinion/fiction. Query with bio or send complete ms. Length: 500-1,000 words. **Pays $300.**
Photos: Minimum of one photo required with accepted article. State availability of or send photos with submission. Offers no additional payment for photos accepted with ms.

Ⓝ $ $ $ $ ORGANIC GARDENING, Rodale, 33 E. Minor, Emmaus PA 18098. (610)967-8363. Fax: (610)967-7846. E-mail: Sandra.Weida@Rodale.com. Website: www.organicgardening.com. **Contact:** Sandra Weida, office coordinator. **75% freelance written.** Bimonthly magazine. "*Organic Gardening* is for gardeners who garden, who enjoy gardening as an integral part of a healthy lifestyle. Editorial shows readers how to grow anything they choose without chemicals. Editorial details how to grow flowers, edibles and herbs, as well as information on ecological landscaping. Also organic topics including soil building and pest control." Circ. 700,000. Pays between acceptance and publication. Byline given. Buys all rights. Accepts queries by mail, fax. Responds in 3 months to queries.
Nonfiction: "The natural approach to the whole home landscape." Query with published clips and outline. **Pays up to $1/word for experienced writers.**
☐ The online magazine carries original content not found in the print edition. Contact: Scott Meyer, online editor.
Tips: "If you have devised a specific technique that's worked in your garden, have insight into the needs and uses of a particular plant or small group of plants, or have designed whole gardens that integrate well with their environment, and, if you have the capacity to clearly describe what you've learned to other gardeners in a simple but engaging manner, please send us your article ideas. Read a recent issue of the magazine thoroughly before you submit your ideas. The scope and tone of our content has changed dramatically in the last year—be sure your ideas and your approach to presenting them jibe with the magazine as it is now. If you have an idea that you believe fits with our content, send us a one-page description of it that will grab our attention in the same manner you intend to entice readers into your article. Be sure to briefly explain why your idea is uniquely suited to our magazine. (We will not publish an article that has already appeared elsewhere. Also, please tell us if you are simultaneously submitting your idea to another magazine.) Tell us about the visual content of your idea—that is, what photographs or illustrations would you suggest be included with your article to get the ideas and information across to readers? If you have photographs, let us know. If you have never been published before, consider whether your idea fits into our Gardener to Gardener department. The shorter, narrowly focused articles in the department and its conversational tone make for a more accessible avenue into the magazine for inexperienced writers."

[N] PEOPLE, PLACES & PLANTS, P.O. Box 6131, Falmout ME 04105. (207)878-4953. Fax: (207)878-4957. E-mail: paul@ppplants.com. Website: www.ppplants.com. Paul Tukey, editor-in-chief. **50% freelance written.** Gardening magazine published 5 times/year focusing on New England. Circ. 52,000. **Pays on acceptance.** Publishes ms an average of 3 months after acceptance. Buys first rights. Responds in 1 month to queries. Sample copy by e-mail. Writer's guidelines by e-mail.

Nonfiction: Know the subject at hand; anecdotes help get readers interested in stories. Query. **Pays $50-500.**

Photos: Reviews slides. $50-500.

$ $ ROMANTIC HOMES, Y-Visionary Publishing, 265 Anita Dr., Suite 120, Orange CA 92868. (714)939-9991. Fax: (714)939-9909. Website: www.romantichomesmag.com. Editor: Ellen Paulin. **Contact:** Catherine Yarnovich, executive managing editor. **60% freelance written.** Monthly magazine covering home decor. "*Romantic Homes* is the magazine for women who want to create a warm, intimate, and casually elegant home—a haven that is both a gathering place for family and friends and a private refuge from the pressures of the outside world. The *Romantic Homes* reader is personally involved in the decor of her home. Features offer unique ideas and how-to advice on decorating, home furnishings, and gardening. Departments focus on floor and wall coverings, paint, textiles, refinishing, architectural elements, artwork, travel and entertaining. Every article responds to the reader's need to create a beautiful, attainable environment, providing her with the style ideas and resources to achieve her own romantic home." Estab. 1994. Circ. 140,000. **Pays on acceptance.** Publishes ms an average of 2 months after acceptance. Byline given. Buys all rights. Editorial lead time 5 months. Submit seasonal material 6 months in advance. Accepts queries by mail, fax. Accepts simultaneous submissions. Responds in 2 weeks to queries; 2 months to mss. Writer's guidelines for #10 SASE.

Nonfiction: "Not just for dreaming, *Romantic Homes* combines unique ideas and inspirations with practical how-to advice on decorating, home furnishings, remodeling and gardening for readers who are actively involved in improving their homes. Every article responds to the reader's need to know how to do it and where to find it." Essays, how-to, new product, travel. **Buys 150 mss/year.** Query with published clips. Length: 1,000-1,200 words. **Pays $500.**

Photos: State availability of or send photos with submission. Reviews transparencies. Buys all rights. Captions, identification of subjects, model releases required.

Columns/Departments: Departments cover antiques, collectibles, artwork, shopping, travel, refinishing, architectural elements, flower arranging, entertaining and decorating. Length: 400-600 words. **Pays $250.**

$ $ SAN DIEGO HOME/GARDEN LIFESTYLES, McKinnon Enterprises, Box 719001, San Diego CA 92171-9001. (619)571-1818. Fax: (619)571-6379. E-mail: sdhg@san.rr.com. Senior Editor: Phyllis Van Doren. **Contact:** Eva Ditler, managing editor. **50% freelance written.** Monthly magazine covering homes, gardens, food, intriguing people, real estate, art, culture, and local travel for residents of San Diego city and county. Estab. 1979. Circ. 50,000. Pays on publication. Publishes ms an average of 3 months after acceptance. Byline given. Buys first North American serial rights. Submit seasonal material 3 months in advance. Accepts queries by mail, e-mail, fax, phone. Responds in 3 months to queries. Sample copy for $4.

Nonfiction: Residential architecture and interior design (San Diego-area homes only), remodeling (must be well-designed—little do-it-yourself), residential landscape design, furniture, other features oriented towards upscale readers interested in living the cultured good life in San Diego. Articles must have a local angle. Query with published clips. Length: 700-2,000 words. **Pays $50-350 for assigned articles.**

Tips: "No out-of-town, out-of-state subject material. Most freelance work is accepted from local writers. Gear stories to the unique quality of San Diego. We try to offer only information unique to San Diego—people, places, shops, resources, etc. We plan more food and entertaining-at-home articles and more articles on garden products. We also need more in-depth reports on major architecture, environmental, and social aspects of life in San Diego and the border area."

$ $ SEATTLE HOMES AND LIFESTYLES, Wiesner Publishing LLC, 1221 East Pike St., Suite 204, Seattle WA 98122-3930. (206)322-6699. Fax: (206)322-2799. E-mail: falbert@seattlehomesmag.com. Website: www.seattleho mesmag.com. **Contact:** Fred Albert, editor. **60% freelance written.** Magazine published 7 times/year covering home design and lifestyles. "*Seattle Homes and Lifestyles* showcases the finest homes and gardens in the Northwest, and the personalities and lifestyles that make this region special. We try to help our readers take full advantage of the resources the region has to offer with in-depth coverage of events, travel, entertaining, shopping, food and wine. And we write about it with a warm, personal approach that underscores our local perspective." Estab. 1996. Circ. 30,000. **Pays on acceptance.** Publishes ms an average of 2 months after acceptance. Byline given. Offers 25% kill fee. Buys first, electronic rights. Editorial lead time 3 months. Submit seasonal material 4 months in advance. Accepts queries by mail. Accepts simultaneous submissions. Responds in 4 months to queries. Writer's guidelines for #10 SASE, online or by e-mail.

Nonfiction: General interest, how-to (decorating, cooking), interview/profile, photo feature, travel. "No essays, journal entries, sports coverage." **Buys 75 mss/year.** Query with published clips. Length: 300-1,500 words. **Pays $100-350.**

Photos: State availability with submission. Reviews contact sheets, transparencies, prints. Buys one-time rights. Negotiates payment individually. Captions, identification of subjects, model releases required.

Columns/Departments: Profiles (human interest/people making contribution to community), 300 words; Design Watch (consumer pieces related to home design), 1,200 words; Taking Off (travel to a region, not one sole destination), 1,500 words; Artisan's Touch (craftperson producing work for the home), 400 words. **Buys 50 mss/year.** Query with published clips. **Pays $100-250.**

Tips: "We're always looking for experienced journalists with clips that demonstrate a knack for writing engaging, informative features. We're also looking for writers knowledgeable about architecture and decorating who can communicate a home's flavor and spirit through the written word. Since all stories are assigned by the editor, please do not submit manuscripts. Send a résumé and three published samples of your work. Story pitches are not encouraged. Please mail all submissions—do not e-mail or fax. Please don't call—we'll call you if we have an assignment. Writers from the Northwest preferred."

$ $ $SOUTHERN ACCENTS, Southern Progress Corp., 2100 Lakeshore Dr., Birmingham AL 35209. (205)445-6000. Fax: (205)445-6990. Website: www.southernaccents.com. **Contact:** Frances MacDougall, managing editor. "*Southern Accents* celebrates the best of the South." Estab. 1977. Circ. 370,000. Accepts queries by mail. Responds in 2 months to queries.
Nonfiction: "Each issue features the finest homes and gardens along with a balance of features that reflect the affluent lifestyles of its readers, including architecture, antiques, entertaining, collecting and travel." Query by mail with SASE, clips, and photos.
　■ The online magazine carries original content not found in the print edition. Contact: Rex Perry, online editor.
Tips: "Query us only with specific ideas targeted to our current columns."

$ $TEXAS GARDENER, The Magazine for Texas Gardeners, by Texas Gardeners, Suntex Communications, Inc., P.O. Box 9005, Waco TX 76714-9005. (254)848-9393. Fax: (254)848-9779. E-mail: suntex@calpha.com. **Contact:** Chris Corby, editor. **80% freelance written.** Works with a small number of new/unpublished writers each year. Bimonthly magazine covering vegetable and fruit production, ornamentals and home landscape information for home gardeners in Texas. Estab. 1981. Circ. 30,000. Pays on publication. Publishes ms an average of 4 months after acceptance. Byline given. Buys first North American serial, all rights. Submit seasonal material 6 months in advance. Accepts queries by mail, e-mail, fax. Responds in 2 months to queries. Sample copy for $2.95 and SAE with 5 first-class stamps. Writer's guidelines for #10 SASE.
Nonfiction: "We use articles that relate to Texas gardeners. We also like personality profiles on hobby gardeners and professional horticulturists who are doing somehting unique." How-to, humor, interview/profile, photo feature. **Buys 50-60 mss/year.** Query with published clips. Length: 800-2,400 words. **Pays $50-200.**
Photos: "We prefer superb color and b&w photos; 90% of photos used are color." Send photos with submission. Reviews contact sheets, 2¼×2¼ or 35mm color transparencies, 8×10 b&w prints. Pays negotiable rates. Identification of subjects, model releases required.
Columns/Departments: Between Neighbors. **Pays $25.**
Tips: "First, be a Texan. Then come up with a good idea of interest to home gardeners in this state. Be specific. Stick to feature topics like 'How Alley Gardening Became a Texas Tradition.' Leave topics like 'How to Control Fire Blight' to the experts. High quality photos could make the difference. We would like to add several writers to our group of regular contributors and would make assignments on a regular basis. Fillers are easy to come up with in-house. We want good writers who can produce accurate and interesting copy. Frequent mistakes made by writers in completing an article assignment for us are that articles are not slanted toward Texas gardening, show inaccurate or too little gardening information or lack good writing style."

N $ $TIMBER FRAME HOMES, Home Buyer Publications, 4200-T Lafayette Center Dr., Chantilly VA 20151. Fax: (703)222-3209. E-mail: editor@timberframehomes.com. Website: www.timberframehomes.com. **Contact:** Tracy M. Ruff, editor. **50% freelance written.** Quarterly magazine for people who own or are planning to build contemporary timber frame homes. It is devoted exclusively to timber frame homes that have a freestanding frame and wooden joinery. Our interest in historical, reconstructed timber frames and one-of-a-kind owner-built homes is secondary and should be queried first. Estab. 1991. Circ. 92,500. **Pays on acceptance.** Publishes ms an average of 3 months after acceptance. Byline given. Offers $100 kill fee. Buys first rights. Accepts queries by mail, e-mail. Sample copy for $4. Writer's guidelines for #10 SASE.
Nonfiction: Book excerpts, general interest, how-to, interview/profile, new product, photo feature, technical. No historical articles. **Buys 15 mss/year.** Query with published clips. Length: 1,200-1,400 words. **Pays $300-500.** Sometimes pays expenses of writers on assignment.
Photos: State availability with submission. Reviews contact sheets, transparencies, prints. Buys one-time rights. Negotiates payment individually.
Columns/Departments: Constructive Advice (timber frame construction); Interior Elements (decorating); Drawing Board (design), all 1,200-1,400 words. **Buys 6 mss/year.** Query with published clips. **Pays $300-500.**

$ $ $TIMBER HOMES ILLUSTRATED, Goodman Media Group, Inc., 419 Park Ave. South, New York NY 10016. (212)541-7100. Fax: (212)245-1241. Website: www.goodmanmediagroup.com. Editor: Roland Sweet. **Contact:** Stacy Durr Albert, managing editor. **30% freelance written.** Magazine published 6 times/year. "*Timber Homes Illustrated* presents full-color photo features and stories about timber-frame, log, post-and-beam and other classic wood homes. We feature stories of homeowners who've achieved their dream and encouragement for those who dream of owning a timber home." Estab. 1996. Circ. 75,000. Pays on publication. Byline given. Buys first North American serial, second serial (reprint) rights. Editorial lead time 4 months. Submit seasonal material 6 months in advance. Accepts queries by mail, fax. Accepts simultaneous submissions. Sample copy for $4.99.

O— To break in "find a historical timber structure that we may not have discovered. Both U.S. and foreign examples will be considered. Try to provide photos."

Nonfiction: Book excerpts, historical/nostalgic, how-to (building), interview/profile (architects), personal experience, photo feature, travel. Special issues: Annual Buyer's Directory, Plans issue. No self-promotion pieces about furniture designers, etc. **Buys 15 mss/year.** Query with published clips or send complete ms. Length: 1,200-3,000 words. **Pays $300-900.** Pays expenses of writers on assignment with limit agreed upon in advance.

Photos: Send photos with submission. Reviews 4×5 transparencies, slides, prints. Buys one-time rights. Negotiates payment individually. Captions required.

Columns/Departments: Traditions (history of timber-framing), 1,200-3,000 words; Interior Motives (decorating timber homes), 1,200-2,200 words; Space & Place (decor ideas, timber-frame components), 1,200-2,000 words. **Buys 10 mss/year.** Query with published clips or send complete ms. **Pays $300-600.**

Tips: "We suggest including photos with your submission. Present a clear idea of where and how your story will fit into our magazine. We are always interested in seeing timber structures other than homes, such as wine vineyards or barns. Look for something unique—including unique homes."

N **$ $ UNIQUE HOMES MAGAZINE,** Network Communications, 327 Wall St., Princeton NJ 08540. Fax: (609)688-0201. E-mail: lkim@uniquehomes.com. Website: www.uniquehomes.com. Editor: Kathleen Carlin-Russell. **Contact:** Lauren Baier Kim, managing editor. **80% freelance written.** Bimonthly magazine covering luxury real estate for consumers and the high-end real estate industry. "Our focus is the luxury real estate market, i.e., trends and luxury homes (including luxury home architecture, interior design and landscaping)." Pays on publication. Publishes ms an average of 3 months after acceptance. Byline given. Makes work-for-hire assignments. Editorial lead time 3 months. Submit seasonal material 5 months in advance. Accepts queries by mail, e-mail, fax. Responds in 1 month to queries. Sample copy online.

Nonfiction: Looking for luxury interiors, architecture and landscaping, high-end luxury real estate profiles on cities and geographical regions. Special issues: Waterfront Properties; Golf issue; Ski issue. **Buys 32 mss/year.** Query with published clips and résumé. Length: 300-1,500 words. **Pays $150-550.** Sometimes pays expenses of writers on assignment.

Photos: State availability of or send photos with submission. Reviews transparencies, prints. Buys one-time rights. Negotiates payment individually. Captions required.

Columns/Departments: News and Reviews (timely shorts on real estate news and trends), 100 words; Creating Style (luxury interiors), 300-600 words; Creating Structure (luxury architecture), 300-600 words; Creating Scenery (luxury landscaping), 300-600 words. **Buys 18 mss/year.** Query with published clips and résumé. **Pays $150-550.**

Tips: "Always looking for creative and interesting story ideas on interior decorating, architecture and landscaping for the luxury home. For profiles on specific geographical areas, seeking writers with an in-depth personal knowledge of the luxury real estate trends in those locations."

$ $ VICTORIAN HOMES, Y-Visionary Publishing L.P., 265 S. Anita Dr., Suite 120, Orange CA 92868-3310. (714)939-9991 ext. 332. Fax: (714)939-9909. E-mail: ekotite@pacbell.net. Website: www.victorianhomesmag.com. Managing Editor: Cathy Yarnovich. **Contact:** Erika Kotite, editor. **90% freelance written.** Bimonthly magazine covering Victorian home restoration and decoration. "*Victorian Homes* is read by Victorian home owners, restorers, house museum management and others interested in the Victorian revival. Feature articles cover home architecture, interior design, furnishings and the home's history. Photography is *very* important to the feature." Estab. 1981. Circ. 100,000. Pays on acceptance. Publishes ms an average of 1 year after acceptance. Byline given. Offers $50 kill fee. Buys first North American serial, one-time rights. Editorial lead time 4 months. Submit seasonal material 1 year in advance. Accepts queries by mail, e-mail, fax. Accepts simultaneous submissions. Responds in 6 weeks to queries; 2 months to mss. Sample copy and writer's guidelines for SAE.

O— Break in with "access to good photography and reasonable knowledge of the Victorian era."

Nonfiction: "Article must deal with structures—no historical articles on Victorian people or lifestyles." How-to (create period style curtains, wall treatments, bathrooms, kitchens, etc.), photo feature. **Buys 30-35 mss/year.** Query. Length: 800-1,800 words. **Pays $300-500.** Sometimes pays expenses of writers on assignment.

Photos: State availability with submission. Reviews 2¼×2¼ transparencies. Buys one-time rights. Negotiates payment individually. Captions required.

HUMOR

Publications listed here specialize in gaglines or prose humor, some for readers and others for performers or speakers. Other publications that use humor can be found in nearly every category in this book. Some have special needs for major humor pieces; some use humor as fillers; many others are interested in material that meets their ordinary fiction or nonfiction requirements but also has a humorous slant. The majority of humor articles must be submitted as complete manuscripts or speculation because editors usually can't know from a query whether or not the piece will be right for them.

N $ COMEDY WRITERS ASSOCIATION NEWSLETTER, P.O. Box 605, Times Plaza Station, 542 Atlantic Ave., Brooklyn NY 11217-0605. (718)855-5057. **Contact:** Robert Makinson, editor. **10% freelance written.** Semiannual newsletter on comedy writing for association members. Estab. 1989. **Pays on acceptance.** Publishes ms an average of 3 months after acceptance. Byline given. Buys all rights. Accepts queries by mail. Responds in 2 weeks to queries; 1 month to mss. Sample copy for $5. Writer's guidelines for #10 SASE.
Nonfiction: "You may submit articles and byline will be given if used, but at present payment is only made for jokes. Emphasis should be on marketing, not general humor articles." How-to (articles about marketing, directories, Internet, new trends). Query. Length: 250-500 words.
Tips: "The easiest way to be mentioned in the publication is to submit short jokes. (Payment is $1-3 per joke). Jokes for professional speakers preferred. Include SASE when submitting jokes."

N $ FUNNY TIMES, A Monthly Humor Review, Funny Times, Inc., P.O. Box 18530, Cleveland Heights OH 44118. (216)371-8600. Fax: (216)371-8696. E-mail: ft@funnytimes.com. Website: www.funnytimes.com. **Contact:** Raymond Lesser, Susan Wolpert, editors. **10% freelance written.** Monthly tabloid for humor. "*Funny Times* is a monthly review of America's funniest cartoonists and writers. We are the *Reader's Digest* of modern American humor with a progressive/peace-oriented/environmental/politically activist slant." Estab. 1985. Circ. 58,000. Pays on publication. Publishes ms an average of 3 months after acceptance. Byline given. Buys one-time, second serial (reprint) rights. Editorial lead time 2 months. Accepts simultaneous submissions. Responds in 3 months to mss. Sample copy for $3 or 9×12 SAE with 4 first-class stamps. Writer's guidelines for #10 SASE.
Nonfiction: "We only publish humor or interviews with funny people (comedians, comic actors, cartoonists, etc.). Everything we publish is very funny. If your piece isn't extremely funny then don't bother to send it. Don't send us anything that's not outrageously funny. Don't send anything that other people haven't already read and told you they laughed so hard they peed their pants." Essays (funny), humor, interview/profile, opinion (humorous), personal experience (absolutely funny). **Buys 36 mss/year.** Send complete ms. Length: 500-700 words. **Pays $50 minimum.**
Reprints: Accepts previously published submissions.
Columns/Departments: Query with published clips.
Fiction: Humorous. **Buys 6 mss/year.** Query with published clips. Length: 500 words. **Pays $50-150.**
Fillers: Short humor. **Buys 6/year. Pays $20.**
Tips: "Send us a small packet (1-3 items) of only your very funniest stuff. If this makes us laugh we'll be glad to ask for more. We particularly welcome previously published material that has been well-received elsewhere."

$ $ MAD MAGAZINE, 1700 Broadway, New York NY 10019. (212)506-4850. Website: www.madmag.com. **Contact:** Editorial Dept. **100% freelance written.** Monthly magazine "always on the lookout for new ways to spoof and to poke fun at hot trends." Estab. 1952. **Pays on acceptance.** Publishes ms an average of 6 months after acceptance. Byline given. Buys all rights. Submit seasonal material 6 months in advance. Responds in 10 weeks to queries. Sample copy online. Writer's guidelines for #10 SASE.
Nonfiction: "Submit a premise with three of four examples of how you intend to carry it through, describing the action and visual content. Rough sketches desired but not necessary. One-page gags: two- to eight-panel cartoon continuities as minimum very funny, maximum hilarious!" Satire, parody. "We're *not* interested in formats we're already doing or have done to death like 'what they say and what they really mean.' *Don't* send previously published submissions, riddles, advice columns, TV or movie satires, book manuscripts, top ten lists, articles about Alfred E. Neuman, poetry, essays, short stories or other text pieces." **Buys 400 mss/year. Pays minimum of $400/**MAD page.
Tips: "Have fun! Remember to think visually! Surprise us! Freelancers can best break in with satirical nontopical material. Include SASE with each submission. Originality is prized. We like outrageous, silly and/or satirical humor."

$ $ $ $ WORDS FOR SALE, 1149 Granada Ave., Salinas CA 93906. **Contact:** Lorna Gilbert, submission editor. Estab. 1968. **Pays on acceptance**.
Nonfiction: "Since 1968, we have sold almost every kind of written material to a wide variety of individual and corporate clients. We deal in both the written as well as the spoken word, from humorous one liners and nightclub acts, to informative medical brochures, political speeches, and almost everything in between. We are not agents. We are a company that provides original written material created especially for the specific needs of our current clients. Therefore, do not send us a sample of your work. As good as it may be, it is almost certainly unrelated to our current needs. Instead begin by finding out what our clients want and write it for them. What could be simpler? It gets even better: *We buy sentences*— That's right. Forget conceiving, composing, editing and polishing endless drafts of magazine articles or book manuscripts. Simply create the type of sentence or sentences we're looking for and we'll buy one or more of them. We respond promptly. We pay promptly." **Pays $1 and up/sentence.**
Tips: "The key to your selling something to us, is to *first* find out *exactly* what we are currently buying. To do this simply mail us a #10 SASE and we will send you a list of what we are anxious to buy at this time."

INFLIGHT

Most major inflight magazines cater to business travelers and vacationers who will be reading, during the flight, about the airline's destinations and other items of general interest.

$ ABOARD PUBLISHING, 100 Almeria Ave., Suite 220, Coral Gables FL 33134. (305)441-9738. Fax: (305)441-9739. E-mail: sales@aboardpublishing.com. Website: www.aboardpublishing.com. **Contact:** Sarah Munoz, managing editor. **40% freelance written.** Bilingual inflight magazines designed to reach travelers to and from Latin America, carried on 7 major Latin-American airlines. Estab. 1976. Circ. 180,000. Pays on publication. Byline given. Buys one-time, simultaneous rights. Accepts queries by mail, fax. Accepts simultaneous submissions. Responds in 3 months.

Nonfiction: General interest, new product, photo feature, technical, travel, business, science, art, fashion. "No controversial or political material." **Buys 50 mss/year.** Query. Length: 750 words. **Pays $100-150.**

Reprints: Send photocopy with rights for sale noted and information about when and where the material previously appeared. Pays 0-50% of amount paid for an original article.

Photos: Send photos with submission. Reviews transparencies, 35mm slides. Buys one-time rights. Offers no additional payment for photos accepted with ms. Offers $20/photo minimum. Identification of subjects required.

Fillers: Facts. **Buys 6/year.** Length: 800-1,000 words. **Pays $100.**

Tips: "Send article with photos. We need travel material on Chile, Ecuador, Bolivia, El Salvador, Honduras, Guatemala, Uruguay, Nicaragua, Venezuela."

$ $ $ $ AMERICA WEST AIRLINES MAGAZINE, Skyword Marketing Inc., 4636 E. Elwood St., Suite 5, Phoenix AZ 85040-1963. (602)997-7200. **Contact:** Michael Derr, editor. **80% freelance written.** Monthly General interest magazine covering business, the arts, science, cuisine, travel, culture, lifestyle, sports. "We look for thoughtful writing, full of detail, and a writer's ability to create a sense of place." Estab. 1986. Circ. 135,000. Pays on publication. Publishes ms an average of 6 months after acceptance. Byline given. Offers 15% kill fee. Buys first North American serial rights. Editorial lead time 6 months. Submit seasonal material 6 months in advance. Accepts queries by mail. Accepts simultaneous submissions. Responds in 1 month to queries. Sample copy for $3. Writer's guidelines for #10 SASE.

Nonfiction: "Ours is not a traditional feature well, but a mix of short, medium and long articles, specialty subjects and special-format features, but all still with the graphic appeal of a traditional feature." Essays, general interest, historical/nostalgic, humor, interview/profile, personal experience, photo feature. No how-to, poetry or flying articles. Query with published clips. Length: 500-2,000 words. **Pays $150-2,000.** Sometimes pays expenses of writers on assignment.

Photos: State availability with submission. Reviews transparencies. Buys one-time rights. Offers $25-400/photo. Identification of subjects required.

Columns/Departments: This and That (a wide-ranging mix of timely, newsy and entertaining short articles), 150-600 words. Query with published clips.

Fiction: Adventure, historical, humorous, mainstream, mystery, slice-of-life vignettes. Nothing of a sexual or potentially controversial or offensive nature. **Buys 12 mss/year.** Send complete ms. Length: 200-3,000 words. **Pays $200-500.**

Tips: "In general, we prefer an informal yet polished style with personal, intimate storytelling. We especially appreciate visual, robust and passionate writing—a literary flair is never out of place. Be creative and capture a sense of the people and places you write about."

$ $ $ $ ATTACHÉ MAGAZINE, Pace Communications, 1301 Carolina St., Greensboro NC 27401. (336)378-6065. Fax: (336)378-8278. E-mail: AttacheAir@aol.com. Website: www.attachemag.com. Editor: Lance Elko. **Contact:** Abigail Seymour, managing editor. **75% freelance written.** Monthly magazine for travelers on U.S. Airways. "We focus on 'the best of the world' and use a humorous view." Estab. 1997. Circ. 441,000. **Pays on acceptance.** Publishes ms an average of 4 months after acceptance. Byline given. Offers kill fee. Editorial lead time 3 months. Accepts queries by mail, e-mail. Responds in 6 weeks to queries; 1 month to mss. Sample copy for $7.50 or online. Writer's guidelines for #10 SASE or online.

Nonfiction: Features are highly visual, focusing on some unusual or unique angle of travel, food, business, or other topic approved by an *Attaché* editor." Book excerpts, essays, general interest, personal experience, travel, food, lifestyle, sports. **Buys 50-75 mss/year.** Query with published clips. Length: 350-2,500 words. **Pays $350-2,500.** Sometimes pays expenses of writers on assignment.

Photos: State availability with submission. Reviews contact sheets, negatives, transparencies. Buys one-time rights. Negotiates payment individually. Identification of subjects, model releases required.

Columns/Departments: Passions includes several topics such as "Vices," "Food," "Golf," "Sporting," "Shelf Life," and "Things That Go"; Paragons features short lists of the best in a particular field or category, as well as 400-word pieces describing the best of something—for example, the best home tool, the best ice cream in Paris, and the best reading library. Each piece should lend itself to highly visual art. Informed Sources are departments of expertise and first-person accounts; they include "How It Works," "Home Front," "Improvement," and "Genius at Work." **Buys 50-75 mss/year.** Query. **Pays $500-2,000.**

Tips: "We look for cleverly written, entertaining articles with a unique angle, particularly pieces that focus on 'the best of' something. Study the magazine for content, style and tone. Queries for story ideas should be to the point and presented clearly. Any correspondence should include SASE."

$ $ CONNECTIONS, The Magazine of ASA, Graf/X Publishing, 3000 N. 2nd St., Minneapolis MN 55411. (612)520-2348. Fax: (612)520-2390. E-mail: m.quach@graf-x.net. **Contact:** Molly Quach, managing editor. Bimonthly Inflight magazine for ASA. "*Connections* covers travel, business, sports and celebrity profiles." Estab. 1995. Circ. 32,000. Pays 60 days after publication. Byline given. Buys first North American serial, second serial (reprint) rights, makes work-for-hire assignments. Editorial lead time 4 months. Submit seasonal material 4 months in advance. Accepts queries by mail, e-mail, fax. Accepts simultaneous submissions. Responds in 6 weeks to queries; 2 months to mss. Sample copy for 8×11 SAE and 3 first-class stamps. Writer's guidelines for #10 SASE.

Nonfiction: Book excerpts, general interest, how-to, humor, interview/profile, personal experience, travel. **Buys 10-20 mss/year.** Query with published clips. Length: 750-2,000 words. **Pays $50-500 for assigned articles.**

Tips: "Since this publication doubles as an airline marketing tool, the writers with the best chance are the ones who can write a piece with a positive slant, that is still informative and stylistic. Work published here needs to be ultimately positive but not sterile. Also, we need more e-commerce and business-related pieces."

$ $ $ ☒ **HEMISPHERES, Pace Communications for United Airlines**, 1301 Carolina St., Greensboro NC 27401. (336)378-6065. Website: www.hemispheresmagazine.com. **Contact:** Selby Bateman, senior editor (nonfiction) or Lisa Fann, articles editor (fiction). **95% freelance written.** Monthly magazine for the educated, sophisticated business and recreational frequent traveler on an airline that spans the globe. Estab. 1992. Circ. 500,000. **Pays on acceptance.** Publishes ms an average of 3 months after acceptance. Byline given. Offers 20% kill fee. Buys first world-wide rights. Editorial lead time 8 months. Submit seasonal material 8 months in advance. Accepts queries by mail. Responds in 2 months to queries; 4 months to mss. Sample copy for $7.50. Writer's guidelines for #10 SASE.

Nonfiction: "Keeping 'global' in mind, we look for topics that reflect a modern appreciation of the world's cultures and environment. No 'What I did (or am going to do) on a trip to...'" General interest, humor, personal experience. Query with published clips. Length: 500-3,000 words. **Pays 50¢/word and up.**

Photos: State availability with submission. Reviews transparencies "only when we request them." Buys one-time rights. Negotiates payment individually. Captions, identification of subjects, model releases required.

Columns/Departments: Making a Difference (Q&A format interview with world leaders, movers, and shakers. A 500-600 word introduction anchors the interview. We want to profile an international mix of men and women representing a variety of topics or issues, but all must truly be making a difference. No puffy celebrity profiles.); 15 Fascinating Facts (A snappy selection of one- or two-sentence obscure, intriguing, or travel-service-oriented items that the reader never knew about a city, state, country or destination.); Executive Secrets (Things that top executives know); Case Study (Business strategies of international companies or organizations. No lionizations of CEOs. Strategies should be the emphasis. "We want international candidates."); Weekend Breakaway (Takes us just outside a major city after a week of business for several activities for a physically active, action-packed weekend. This isn't a sedentary "getaway" at a "property."); Roving Gourmet (Insider's guide to interesting eating in major city, resort area, or region. The slant can be anything from ethnic to expensive; not just "best." The four featured eateries span a spectrum from "hole in the wall," to "expense account lunch" and on to "big deal dining."); Collecting (Occasional 800-word story on collections and collecting that can emphasize travel); Eye on Sports (Global look at anything of interest in sports); Vintage Traveler (Options for mature, experienced travelers); Savvy Shopper (Insider's tour of best places in the world to shop. Savvy Shopper steps beyond all those stories that just mention the great shopping at a particular destination. A shop-by-shop, gallery-by-gallery tour of the best places in the world.); Science and Technology (Substantive, insightful stories on how technology is changing our lives and the business world. Not just another column on audio components or software. No gift guides!); Aviation Journal (For those fascinated with aviation. Topics range widely.); Terminal Bliss (A great airports guide series); Grape And Grain (Wine and spirits with emphasis on education, not one-upmanship); Show Business (Films, music and entertainment); Musings (Humor or just curious musings); Quick Quiz (Tests to amuse and educate); Travel Trends (Brief, practical, invaluable, global, trend-oriented); Book Beat (Tackles topics like the Wodehouse Society, the birth of a book, the competition between local bookshops and national chains. Please, no review proposals.); What the World's Reading (residents explore how current best sellers tell us what their country is thinking). Length: 1,400 words. Query with published clips. **Pays 50¢/word and up.**

Fiction: Adventure, humorous, mainstream, Explorations of those issues common to all people but within the context of a particular culture. **Buys 14 mss/year.** Query. Length: 1,000-4,000 words. **Pays 50¢/word and up.**

Tips: "We increasingly require writers of 'destination' pieces or departments to 'live whereof they write.' Increasingly want to hear from U.S., U.K. or other English speaking/writing journalists (business & travel) who reside outside the U.S. in Europe, South America, Central America and the Pacific Rim—all areas that United flies. We're not looking for writers who aim at the inflight market. *Hemispheres* broke the fluffy mold of that tired domestic genre. Our monthly readers are a global mix on the cutting edge of the global economy and culture. They don't need to have the world filtered by US writers. We want a Hong Kong restaurant writer to speak for that city's eateries, so we need English speaking writers around the globe. That's the 'insider' story our readers respect. We use resident writers for departments such as Roving Gourmet, Savvy Shopper, On Location, 3 Perfect Days and Weekend Breakaway, but authoritative writers can roam in features. Sure we cover the US, but with a global view: No 'in this country' phraseology. 'Too American' is a frequent complaint for queries. We use UK English spellings in articles that speak from that tradition

---

⚡N⚡ INDICATES THAT the listing is new to this edition. New markets are often more receptive to freelance submissions.

and we specify costs in local currency first before US dollars. Basically, all of above serves the realization that today, 'global' begins with respect for 'local.' That approach permits a wealth of ways to present culture, travel and business for a wide readership. We anchor that with a reader service mission that grounds everything in 'how to do it.'"

$ $⊞ HORIZON AIR MAGAZINE, Paradigm Communications Group, 2701 First Ave., Suite 250, Seattle WA 98121. Fax: (206)448-6939. **Contact:** Michele Andrus Dill, editor. **90% freelance written.** Monthly Inflight magazine covering travel, business and leisure in the Pacific Northwest. *"Horizon Air Magazine* serves a sophisticated audience of business and leisure travelers. Stories must have a Northwest slant." Estab. 1990. Circ. 1,000,000. Pays on publication. Publishes ms an average of 1 year after acceptance. Byline given. Offers 33% kill fee. Buys first North American serial, electronic rights. Editorial lead time 6 months. Submit seasonal material 5 months in advance. Accepts queries by mail, fax. Sample copy for 10×12 SASE. Writer's guidelines for #10 SASE.
Nonfiction: Essays (personal), general interest, historical/nostalgic, how-to, humor, interview/profile, personal experience, photo feature, travel, Business. Special issues: include meeting planners' guide, golf, gift guide. No material unrelated to the Pacific Northwest. **Buys approximately 50 mss/year.** Query with published clips or send complete ms. Length: 1,500-3,000 words. **Pays $300-700.** Sometimes pays expenses of writers on assignment.
Photos: State availability with submission. Reviews transparencies, prints. Buys one-time rights. Negotiates payment individually. Captions, identification of subjects, model releases required.
Columns/Departments: Region (Northwest news/profiles), 200-400 words; Air Time (personal essays), 700 words. **Buys 15 mss/year.** Query with published clips. **Pays $100 (Region), $250 (Air Time).**

Ⓝ $ $ LATITUDES, 460 North Orlando Ave., Suite 200, Winter Park FL 32789. (407)571-4628. Fax: (407)571-4629. E-mail: latitudes@worldpub.net or natalia.decuba@worldpub.net. Editor: Natalia de Cuba Romero. **Contact:** Nicky Cirone, managing editor. **15% freelance written.** Bimonthly magazine covering American Eagle travel locations in Florida, the Caribbean and Bahamas. Estab. 1991. Circ. 85,000. Pays on publication. Publishes ms an average of 6-12 months after acceptance. Byline given. Buys first North American serial rights. Submit seasonal material 9 months in advance. Accepts queries by e-mail. Responds in 1 month to queries. Sample copy for 9×12 SAE and 5 first-class stamps. Writer's guidelines for #10 SASE.
  • *Latitudes* is published in English and Spanish.
  ☚ Break in by reading back issues, have novel ideas for departments, let us know where you have recently been or will be. No unsolicited mss, no phone queries. We use very little freelance material, perhaps 15%.
Nonfiction: Book excerpts (travel related), travel. Query with published clips. Length: 1,600 words. **Pays $250 minimum.** Sometimes pays expenses of writers on assignment.
Reprints: Send photocopy of article or typed ms with rights for sale noted. Pays 50% of amount paid for an original article.
Photos: State availability with submission. Reviews slides. Buys one-time rights. Offers $75-250/photo.
Columns/Departments: Tropical Pantry (food/dining in the Caribbean and Florida, i.e., St. Thomas Dining); Trends (i.e., Caribbean weddings, business meetings), both 700-800 words, **pays $150**; Taking Off (short destination pieces focusing on attractions/events), 350-500 words, **pays $75. Buys 1-2 mss/year.** Query.

Ⓝ $ $ MERIDIAN, Adventure Media, 650 S. Orcas St., Suite 103, Seattle WA 98108. Fax: (206)762-1886. E-mail: meridian@adventuremedia.com. Website: www.adventuremedia.com. **Contact:** Lisa Wogan, editor. **80% freelance written.** Monthly inflight magazine. "All queries must have a connection to the cities where Midway flies (mostly East Coast destinations). We're interested in things to see and do that are not on every tourism brochure: think off-the-beaten path. Also, we want to meet the people behind the story, whether it's a business short or a feature." Circ. 220,000. Pays 30 days after publication. Publishes ms an average of 3 months after acceptance. Byline given. Offers 25% kill fee. Buys first North American serial rights. Editorial lead time 3 months. Submit seasonal material 6 months in advance. Accepts queries by mail, e-mail. Accepts simultaneous submissions. Responds in 2 months to queries; 3 months to mss. Sample copy for $2. Writer's guidelines for #10 SASE or by e-mail.
Nonfiction: Essays, general interest, interview/profile, travel. No nostalgia, how-to or technical. Query with published clips. Length: 250-2,000 words. **Pays 25-35¢/word for assigned articles; 20-25¢/word for unsolicited articles.** Sometimes pays expenses of writers on assignment.
Photos: State availability with submission. Buys one-time rights. Negotiates payment individually. Identification of subjects, model releases required.
Columns/Departments: Departments include business, tech and dining.
Tips: "Start with front-of-the-book and back-of-the-book departments (business profiles, restaurant profiles, unusual event previews). If you can do a good job with a 300-word story, we'll feel more comfortable assigning longer pieces. Query by mail with one or two well-thought ideas, explaining why they'd work for our magazine."

$ ⊞ MIDWEST EXPRESS MAGAZINE, Paradigm Communications Group, 2701 First Ave., Suite 250, Seattle WA 98121. **Contact:** Steve Hansen, managing editor. **90% freelance written.** Bimonthly magazine for Midwest Express Airlines. "Positive depiction of the changing economy and culture of the US, plus travel and leisure features." Estab. 1993. Circ. 35,000. Pays on publication. Byline given. Buys first North American serial rights. Editorial lead time 9 months. Responds in 6 weeks to queries. Sample copy for 9×12 SASE. Writer's guidelines free.
  • *Midwest Express* continues to look for *sophisticated* travel and golf writing.

Nonfiction: Travel, business, sports and leisure. Special issues: "Need good ideas for golf articles in spring." No humor, how-to or fiction. **Buys 20-25 mss/year.** Query by mail only with published clips and résumé. Length: 250-3,000 words. **Pays $100 minimum.** Sometimes pays expenses of writers on assignment.

Columns/Departments: Preview (arts and events), 200-400 words; Portfolio (business), 200-500 words. **Buys 12-15 mss/year.** Query with published clips. **Pays $100-150.**

Tips: "Article ideas *must* encompass areas within the airline's route system. We buy quality writing from reliable writers. Editorial philosophy emphasizes innovation and positive outlook. Do not send manuscripts unless you have no clips."

$ $ $ $SOUTHWEST AIRLINES SPIRIT, 4333 Amon Carter Blvd., Fort Worth TX 76155-9616. (817)967-1804. Fax: (817)967-1571. E-mail: 102615.376@compuserve.com. Website: www.spiritmag.com. **Contact:** John Clark, editorial director. Monthly magazine for passengers on Southwest Airlines. Estab. 1992. Circ. 350,000. **Pays on acceptance.** Byline given. Buys first North American serial, electronic rights. Responds in 1 month to queries.

Nonfiction: "Seeking accessible, entertaining, relevant and timely glimpses of people, places, products and trends in the regions Southwest Airlines serves. Newsworthy/noteworthy topics; well-researched and multiple source only. Experienced magazine professionals only. Business, travel, technology, sports and lifestyle (food, fitness and culture) are some of the topics covered in *Spirit*." **Buys 40 mss/year.** Query by mail only with published clips. Length: 1,200-1,500 words. **Pays $1/word.** Pays expenses of writers on assignment.

Columns/Departments: Length: 800 to 1,000 words. **Buys 21 mss/year.** Query by mail only with published clips. **Pay varies.**

Fillers: Buys 12/year. Length: 250 words. **Pay varies.**

Tips: "*Southwest Airlines Spirit* magazine reaches nearly 1.6 million readers every month aboard Southwest Airlines. Our median reader is a college-educated, 44-year-old business person with a household income of nearly $100,000. Our stories tap the vitality of life through accessible, entertaining and oftentimes unconventional glimpses of people, places, products and trends in the regions that Southwest Airlines serves. Business, travel, technology, sports and lifestyle (food, fitness and culture) are some of the topics covered in *Spirit*."

$ $ SPIRIT OF ALOHA, The Inflight Magazine of Aloha Airlines and Island Air, Honolulu Publishing Co. Ltd., 36 Merchant St., Honolulu HI 96813. (808)524-7400. Fax: (808)531-2306. E-mail: jotaguro@honpub.com. Website: www.spiritofaloha.com. **Contact:** Janice Otaguro, editor. **50% freelance written.** Bimonthly magazine covering visitor activities/destinations and Hawaii culture and history. "Although we are an inflight magazine for an inter-island airline, we try to keep our editorial as fresh and lively for residents as much as for visitors." Estab. 1978. Circ. 60,000. **Pays on acceptance.** Publishes ms an average of 2 months after acceptance. Byline given. Buys first rights. Editorial lead time 2 months. Submit seasonal material 2 months in advance. Accepts queries by mail, e-mail. Responds in 2 months to queries. Sample copy and writer's guidelines free.

Nonfiction: All must be related to Hawaii. Book excerpts, general interest, historical/nostalgic, interview/profile, photo feature, travel. No poetry or "How I spent my vacation in Hawaii" type pieces. **Buys 24 mss/year.** Query with published clips. Length: 1,500-2,500 words. **Pays $500.** Sometimes pays expenses of writers on assignment.

Photos: State availability with submission. Reviews transparencies. Buys one-time rights. Negotiates payment individually. Captions, identification of subjects, model releases required.

[N] $ $ $[=] WASHINGTON FLYER MAGAZINE, 1707 L St., NW, Washington DC 20036. Fax: (202)331-2043. E-mail: readers@themagazinegroup.com. Website: www.fly2dc.com. Editor-in-Chief: Michael McCarthy. **Contact:** Stefanie Berry, senior editor. **60% freelance written.** Bimonthly magazine for business and pleasure travelers at Washington National and Washington Dulles International airports INSI. "Primarily affluent, well-educated audience that flies frequently in and out of Washington, DC." Estab. 1989. Circ. 182,000. **Pays on acceptance.** Byline given. Offers 25% kill fee. Buys first North American serial rights. Submit seasonal material 4 months in advance. Accepts queries by mail, e-mail, fax. Responds in 10 weeks to queries. Sample copy and writer's guidelines for 9 × 12 SAE with $2 postage.

O─ "First understand the magazine—from the nuances of its content to its tone. Best departments to get your foot in the door are 'Washington Insider' and 'Mini Escapes.' The former deals with new business, the arts, sports, etc. in Washington. The latter: getaways that are within four hours of Washington by car. Regarding travel, we're less apt to run stories on sedentary pursuits (e.g., inns, B&Bs, spas). Our readers want to get out and discover an area, whether it's DC or Barcelona. Action-oriented activities work best. Also, the best way to pitch is via e-mail."

Nonfiction: One international destination feature per issue, determined 6 months in advance. One feature per issue on aspect of life in Washington. General interest, interview/profile, travel, business. No personal experiences, poetry, opinion or inspirational. **Buys 20-30 mss/year.** Query with published clips. Length: 800-1,200 words. **Pays $500-900.**

Photos: State availability with submission. Reviews negatives, almost always color transparencies. Buys one-time rights. Considers additional payment for top-quality photos accepted with ms. Identification of subjects required.

Columns/Departments: Washington Insider, Travel, Hospitality, Airports and Airlines, Restaurants, Shopping, all 800-1,200 words. Query. **Pays $500-900.**

Tips: "Know the Washington market and issues relating to frequent business/pleasure travelers as we move toward a global economy. With a bimonthly publication schedule it's important that stories remain viable as possible during the magazine's two-month 'shelf life.' No telephone calls, please and understand that most assignments are made several months in advance. Queries are best sent via e-mail."

$ $ ZOOM! MAGAZINE, Valley Media, LLC, 503 W 2600 S, Bountiful UT 84010-7717. (801)693-7300. Fax: (801)693-7310. E-mail: mevans@murdocktravel.com. Mildred Evans, editor. **75% freelance written.** Bimonthly magazine covering general interest, places and events in cities on Vanguard Airlines' schedules. Estab. 1996. Circ. 15,000; issue readership 200,000. Pays on publication. Publishes ms an average of 6 months after acceptance. Byline given. Offers $50 kill fee. Buys one-time rights. Editorial lead time 3 months. Submit seasonal material 3 months in advance. Accepts queries by mail, e-mail. Responds in 1 month to queries; 3 months to mss. Sample copy for $2. Writer's guidelines free.
Nonfiction: General interest, historical/nostalgic, interview/profile, new product, travel. No articles on business, humor, Internet or health. **Buys 12 mss/year.** Query with or without published clips. Length: 1,000-2,500 words. **Pays $100-250.**
Tips: "Submit previously published clips with a specific idea."

JUVENILE

Just as children change and grow, so do juvenile magazines. Children's magazine editors stress that writers must read recent issues. A wide variety of issues are addressed in the numerous magazines for the baby boom echo. Respecting nature, developing girls' self-esteem and establishing good healthy habits all find an editorial niche. This section lists publications for children up to age 12. Magazines for young people 13-19 appear in the Teen and Young Adult category. Many of the following publications are produced by religious groups and, where possible, the specific denomination is given. A directory for juvenile markets, *Children's Writer's & Illustrator's Market*, is available from Writer's Digest Books.

N $ $ AMERICAN GIRL, Pleasant Company Publications, 8400 Fairway Place, Middleton WI 53562. (606)836-4848. Fax: (606)831-7089. E-mail: im_agmag_editor@pleasantco.com. Website: www.americangirl.com. Executive Editor: Kristi Thom. Managing Editor: Barbara Stretchberry. **Contact:** Magazine Department Assistant. **5% freelance written.** Bimonthly 4-color magazine covering hobbies, crafts, profiles and history of interest to girls ages 8-12. Estab. 1992. Circ. 750,000. **Pays on acceptance.** Byline given for larger features, not departments. Offers 50% kill fee. Buys first North American serial, all rights. Editorial lead time 6 months. Submit seasonal material 6 months in advance. Accepts queries by mail. Accepts simultaneous submissions. Responds in 3 months to queries. Sample copy for $3.95 check made out to American Girl and 9×12 SAE with $1.94 postage. Writer's guidelines for #10 SASE.
○⇥ Best opportunity for freelancers is the Girls Express section. "We're looking for short profiles of girls who are into sports, the arts, interesting hobbies, cultural activities, and other areas. A key: The girl must be the 'star' and the story must be from her point of view. Be sure to include the age of the girls you're pitching to us. If you have any photo leads, please send those, too. We also welcome how-to stories—how to send away for free things, hot ideas for a cool day, how to write the President and get a response. In addition, we're looking for easy crafts that can be explained in a few simple steps. Stories in Girls Express have to be told in no more than 175 words. We prefer to receive ideas in query form rather than finished manuscripts."
Nonfiction: Book excerpts, historical/nostalgic (the format of most historical pieces is not running text but copy blocks that work with photos; any photo research leads you can offer when you query will give us a better idea of story's feasibility), how-to, interview/profile, general contemporary interest. No historical profiles about obvious female heroines—Annie Oakley, Amelia Earhart; no romance or dating. **Buys 3-10 mss/year.** Query with published clips. Length: 100-800 words, depending on whether it's a feature or for a specific department. **Pays $300 minimum for feature articles.** Pays expenses of writers on assignment.
Photos: "We prefer to shoot." State availability with submission. Buys all rights.
Columns/Departments: Girls Express (short profiles of girls with unusual and interesting hobbies that other girls want to read about), 175 words; Giggle Gang (puzzles, games, etc—especially looking for seasonal). Query.
Fiction: Adventure, condensed novels, ethnic, historical, humorous, slice-of-life vignettes. No romance, science fiction, fantasy. **Buys 6 mss/year.** Query with published clips. Length: 2,300 words maximum. **Pays $500 minimum.**

N $ $ $ ARCHAEOLOGY'S DIG MAGAZINE, Archaeological Institute of America, 135 William St., New York NY 10038. (212)732-5154. Fax: (212)732-5707. E-mail: editor@dig.archaeology.org. Website: www.dig.archaeology.org. Editor: Stephen Hanks. **Contact:** Jarrett Lobell, associate editor. **50% freelance written.** Bimonthly magazine covering archaeology for kids ages 8-13. Estab. 1999. Circ. 50,000. Pays on publication. Publishes ms an average of 2 months after acceptance. Byline given. Offers 25% kill fee. Buys all rights. Editorial lead time 3 months. Submit seasonal material 3 months in advance. Accepts queries by mail, e-mail, fax. Responds in 1 week to queries; 1 month to mss. Writer's guidelines free.

Nonfiction: Personal experience, photo feature, travel, archaeological excavation reports. No fiction, paleontology stories. **Buys 12 mss/year.** Query with published clips. Length: 100-1,000 words. **Pays 50¢/word.**

Photos: State availability with submission. Buys one-time rights. Negotiates payment individually. Identification of subjects required.

Tips: "Please remember that this is a children's magazine for kids ages 8-13 so the tone is light-hearted, but scholarly, and as kid-friendly as possible."

$ BABYBUG, Carus Corporation, P.O. Box 300, Peru IL 61354. (815)224-6656. Editor-in-Chief: Marianne Carus. **Contact:** Paula Morrow, editor. **50% freelance written.** Board-book magazine published monthly except for combined may/june and july/august issues. "*Babybug* is 'the listening and looking magazine for infants and toddlers,' intended to be read aloud by a loving adult to foster a love of books and reading in young children ages 6 months-2 years." Estab. 1994. Circ. 45,000. Pays on publication. Publishes ms an average of 18 months after acceptance. Byline given. Buys first, second serial (reprint) rights. Editorial lead time 10 months. Submit seasonal material 1 year in advance. Accepts simultaneous submissions. Sample copy for $5. Writer's guidelines for #10 SASE.

Nonfiction: General interest. **Buys 5-10 mss/year.** Send complete ms. Length: 1-10 words. **Pays $25.**

Fiction: Anything for infants and toddlers. Adventure, humorous. **Buys 5-10 mss/year.** Send complete ms. Length: 2-8 short sentences. **Pays $25.**

Poetry: **Buys 8-10 poems/year.** Submit maximum 5 poems. Length: 2-8 lines. **Pays $25.**

Tips: "Imagine having to read your story or poem—out loud—fifty times or more! That's what parents will have to do. Babies and toddlers demand, 'Read it again'—Your material must hold up under repetition."

$ ✕ BOYS QUEST, Bluffton News Publishing, 103 N. Main, P.O. Box 227, Bluffton OH 45817. (419)358-4610. Website: www.boysquest.com. Editor: Marilyn Edwards. **Contact:** Virginia Edwards, associate editor. **70% freelance written.** Bimonthly magazine covering boys ages 6-12, with a mission to inspire boys to read, maintain traditional family values, and emphasize wholesome, innocent childhood interests. Estab. 1995. Circ. 10,000. Pays on publication. Byline given. Buys first North American serial rights. Editorial lead time 1 year. Submit seasonal material 1 year in advance. Accepts simultaneous submissions. Responds in 1 month to queries; 2 months to mss. Sample copy for $4. Writer's guidelines for #10 SASE.

Nonfiction: Include photos. General interest, historical/nostalgic, how-to (building), humor, interview/profile, personal experience. Send complete ms. Length: 300-700 words. **Pays 5¢/word.**

Reprints: Send photocopy or typed ms with rights for sale noted. Pays 5¢/word.

Photos: State availability of or send photos with submission. Buys one-time rights. Pays $5-10/photo. Model releases required.

Columns/Departments: Send complete ms. **Pays 5¢/word.**

Fiction: Adventure, historical, humorous. Send complete ms. Length: 300-700 words. **Pays 5¢/word.**

Poetry: Traditional. **Buys 25-30 poems/year.** Length: 10-30 lines. **Pays $10-15.**

Tips: "We are looking for lively writing, most of it from a young boy's point of view—with the boy or boys directly involved in an activity that is both wholesome and unusual. We need nonfiction with photos and fiction stories—around 500 words—puzzle, poems, cooking, carpentry projects, jokes and riddles. Nonfiction pieces that are accompanied by black and white photos are far more likely to be accepted than those that need illustrations."

$ $ $ ✕ BOYS' LIFE, Boy Scouts of America, P.O. Box 152079, Irving TX 75015-2079. Fax: (972)580-2079. Website: www.bsa.scouting.org. **Contact:** Michael Goldman, senior editor. **75% freelance written.** Prefers to work with published/established writers; works with small number of new/unpublished writers each year. Monthly magazine covering activities of interest to all boys ages 6-18. Most readers are Boy Scouts or Cub Scouts. Estab. 1911. Circ. 1,300,000. **Pays on acceptance.** Publishes ms an average of 1 year after acceptance. Buys one-time rights. Accepts queries by mail, fax. Responds in 2 months to queries. Sample copy for $3 and 9×12 SAE. Writer's guidelines for #10 SASE or online.

Nonfiction: Subject matter is broad, everything from professional sports to American history to how to pack a canoe. Look at a current list of the BSA's more than 100 merit badge pamphlets for an idea of the wide range of subjects possible. Uses strong photo features with about 500 words of text. Separate payment or assignment for photos. How-to, photo feature, Hobby and craft ideas. **Buys 60 mss/year.** Query with SASE. No phone queries. Length: Major articles run 500-1,500 words; preferred length is about 1,000 words including sidebars and boxes. **Pays $400-1,500.** Pays expenses of writers on assignment.

Columns/Departments: Rich Haddaway, associate editor. "Science, nature, earth, health, sports, space and aviation, cars, computers, entertainment, pets, history, music are some of the columns for which we use 300-750 words of text. This is a good place to show us what you can do." **Buys 75-80 mss/year.** Query. **Pays $250-300.**

Fiction: Fiction Editor. Include SASE. Adventure, humorous, mystery, science fiction. **Buys 12-15 mss/year.** Send complete ms. Length: 1,000-1,500 words. **Pays $750 minimum.**

Fillers: Freelance comics pages and scripts.

Tips: "We strongly recommend reading at least 12 issues of the magazine before you submit queries. We are a good market for any writer willing to do the necessary homework."

$ BREAD FOR GOD'S CHILDREN, Bread Ministries, Inc., P.O. Box 1017, Arcadia FL 34265. (863)494-6214. Fax: (863)993-0154. E-mail: bread@sunline.net. Editor: Judith M. Gibbs. **Contact:** Susan Callahan, editorial secretary.

10% freelance written. "An interdenominational Christian teaching publication published 8 times/year written to aid children and youth in leading a Christian life." Estab. 1972. Circ. 10,000. Pays on publication. Publishes ms an average of 6 months after acceptance. Byline given. Buys first rights. Accepts queries by mail. Accepts simultaneous submissions. Responds in 6 months to mss. Three sample copies for 9×12 SAE and 5 first-class stamps. Writer's guidelines for #10 SASE.

○→ Break in with a good story about a 6- 10-year-old gaining insight into a spiritual principle—without an adult preaching the message to him.

Reprints: Send tearsheet and information about when and where the material previously appeared.

Columns/Departments: Let's Chat (children's Christian values), 500-700 words; Teen Page (youth Christian values), 600-800 words; Idea Page (games, crafts, Bible drills). **Buys 5-8 mss/year.** Send complete ms. **Pays $30.**

Fiction: "We are looking for writers who have a solid knowledge of Biblical principles and are concerned for the youth of today living by those principles. Our stories must be well-written, with the story itself getting the message across—no preaching, moralizing or tag endings." No fantasy, science fiction, or non-Christian themes. **Buys 15-20 mss/year.** Send complete ms. Length: 600-800 words (young children), 900-1,500 words (older children). **Pays $40-50.**

Tips: "We're looking for more submissions on healing miracles and reconciliation/restoration. Follow usual guidelines for careful writing, editing, and proofreading. We get many manuscripts with misspellings, poor grammar, careless typing. Know your subject—writer should know the Lord to write about the Christian life. Study the publication and our guidelines."

$ $CALLIOPE, Exploring World History, Cobblestone Publishing Co., 30 Grove St., Suite C, Peterborough NH 03458-1454. (603)924-7209. Fax: (603)924-7380. E-mail: editorial@cobblestone.mv.com. Website: www.cobblestonepub.com. Editors: Rosalie and Charles Baker. **Contact:** Rosalie F. Baker, editor. **More than 50% freelance written.** Magazine published 9 times/year covering world history (East and West) through 1800 AD for 8- to 14-year-olds. Articles must relate to the issue's theme. Circ. 10,000. Pays on publication. Byline given. Buys all rights. Sample copy for $4.50 and 7½×10½ SASE with 4 first-class stamps or online. Writer's guidelines for SASE or online.

○→ Break in with a "well-written query on a topic that relates directly to an upcoming issue's theme, a writing sample that is well-researched and concise and a bibliography that includes new research."

Nonfiction: Articles must relate to the theme. Essays, general interest, historical/nostalgic, how-to (activities), humor, interview/profile, personal experience, photo feature, technical, travel, recipes. No religious, pornographic, biased or sophisticated submissions. **Buys 30-40 mss/year.** Query by mail only with published clips. Length: 700-800 words for feature articles; 300-600 words for supplemental nonfiction. **Pays 20-25¢/printed word.**

Photos: State availability with submission. Reviews contact sheets, color slides and b&w prints. Buys one-time rights. Pays $15-100 (color cover negotiated).

Columns/Departments: Activities (crafts, recipes, projects); up to 700 words. Query by mail only with published clips. **Pays on individual basis.**

Fiction: All fiction must be theme-related. **Buys 10 mss/year.** Query by mail only with published clips. Length: 1,000 words maximum. **Pays 20-25¢/word.**

Fillers: Puzzles and games (no word finds); crossword and other word puzzles using the vocabulary of the issue's theme; mazes and picture puzzles that relate to the theme. **Pays on individual basis.**

Tips: "A query must consist of all of the following to be considered (please use non-erasable paper): a brief cover letter stating the subject and word length of the proposed article; a detailed one-page outline explaining the information to be presented in the article; an extensive bibliography of materials the author intends to use in preparing the article; a self-addressed stamped envelope. (Authors are urged to use primary resources and up-to-date scholarly resources in their bibliography.) Writers new to *Calliope* should send a writing sample with the query. If you would like to know if your query has been received, please also include a stamped postcard that requests acknowledgement of receipt. In all correspondence, please include your complete address as well as a telephone number where you can be reached."

$CELEBRATE, WordAction Publishing Company, 6401 The Paseo, Kansas City MO 64131. (816)333-7000, ext. 2358. Fax: (816)333-4439. E-mail: mhammer@nazarene.org. Website: www.nazarene.org. Managing Editor: Jim Brightly. Editorial Director: Barbara Leonard. **Contact:** Melissa Hammer, early childhood curriculum editor. Weekly newspaper featuring a children's Sunday school theme. "*Celebrate* is a full-color story paper for three through six year olds which correlates directly with the WordAction Sunday school curriculum. It is designed to connect Sunday school learning with the daily living experiences and growth of the child." Circ. 12,000. Pays on publication. Publishes ms an average of 1 year after acceptance. Byline given. Buys multi-use rights. Editorial lead time 1 year. Submit seasonal material 1 year in advance. Accepts queries by mail, e-mail. Accepts simultaneous submissions. Responds in 2 weeks to queries; 1 month to mss. Writer's guidelines and theme list for #10 SASE.

MARKET CONDITIONS are constantly changing! If this is 2003 or later, buy the newest edition of *Writer's Market* at your favorite bookstore or order directly from Writer's Digest Books at (800)289-0963.

• This all-new story paper replaces *Together Time* and *Listen*, published by WordAction. Debut issue is September 2001.

Columns/Departments: Songs, Rhymes, Crafts, Fingerplays, Recipes, Simple (20 pt.) Dot-to-Dot picture ideas, simple puzzle or maze ideas. **Buys 30 mss/year.** Send complete ms. **Pays 25¢/line-$15.**

Poetry: "We prefer rhythmic, pattern poems, but will accept free-verse if thought and 'read aloud' effect flow smoothly. Include word pictures of subject matter relating to everyday experiences. Avoid portrayal of extremely precocious, abnormally mature children." **Buys 20 poems/year.** Submit maximum 5 poems. Length: 4-8 lines. **Pays 25¢/line; $2 minimum.**

Tips: "We're looking for activities and poems on specific Bible characters like Daniel, Ruth and Naomi, David, Samuel, Paul. We need activities and crafts based on our Bible themes. Write on a three- to six-year-old level of understanding. We are currently in need of recipes that children can do successfully with adult supervision. We specifically need freelance submissions focused at the kindergarten age level."

$ $CHICKADEE MAGAZINE, Discover a World of Fun, The Owl Group, Bayard Press Canada, 179 John St., Suite 500, Toronto, Ontario M5T 3G5, Canada. (416)340-2700. Fax: (416)340-9769. E-mail: owl@owlkids.com. Website: www.owlkids.com. **Contact:** Angela Keenlyside, managing editor. **25% freelance written.** Magazine published 9 times/year for 6- to 9-year-olds. "We aim to interest children in the world around them in an entertaining and lively way." Estab. 1979. Circ. 110,000 Canada and US. Pays on publication. Byline given. Buys all rights. Accepts queries by mail, e-mail, fax. Responds in 3 months to queries. Sample copy for $4 and SAE ($2 money order or IRCs). Writer's guidelines for SAE ($2 money order or IRCs).

Nonfiction: How-to (easy and unusual arts and crafts), personal experience (real children in real situations). No articles for older children; no religious or moralistic features.

Photos: Send photos with submission. Reviews 35mm transparencies. Identification of subjects required.

Fiction: Adventure, humorous. No talking animal stories or religious articles. **Pays $200 (US).**

Tips: "A frequent mistake made by writers is trying to teach too much—not enough entertainment and fun."

$ $⊠ CHILDREN'S PLAYMATE, Children's Better Health Institute, P.O. Box 567, Indianapolis IN 46206-0567. (317)636-8881 ext. 267. Fax: (317)684-8094. Website: www.cbhi.org/magazines/childrensplaymate/. **Contact:** (Ms.) Terry Harshman, editor. **40% freelance written.** Eager to work with new/unpublished writers. Magazine published 8 times/year for children ages 6-8. "We are looking for articles, poems, and activities with a health, fitness, or nutrition oriented theme. We try to present our material in a positive light, and we try to incorporate humor and a light approach wherever possible without minimizing the seriousness of what we are saying." Estab. 1929. Pays on publication. Byline given. Buys all rights. Submit seasonal material 8 months in advance. Responds in 3 months to queries. Sample copy for $1.75. Writer's guidelines for #10 SASE.

• May hold mss for up to 1 year before acceptance/publication.

O⊸ Include word count. Material will not be returned unless accompanied by a SASE.

Nonfiction: "A feature may be an interesting presentation on good health, exercise, proper nutrition and safety as well as science and historical breakthroughs in medicine." **Buys 25 mss/year.** Send complete ms. Length: 500 words maximum. **Pays up to 17¢/word.**

Fiction: Not buying much fiction right now except for rebus stories of 100-300 words and occasional poems. Vocabulary suitable for ages 6-8. Include word count. Send complete ms. **Pays minimum of 17¢/word.**

Fillers: Recipes, puzzles, dot-to-dots, color-ins, hidden pictures, mazes. Prefers camara-ready activities. Activity guidelines for #10 SASE. **Buys 25/year. Pay varies.**

Tips: "We need more historical nonfiction on medicine, medical breakthroughs (vaccines, etc.) and simple science articles with occasional experiments. We're especially interested in materials about health, nutrition, science, medicine, fitness, and fun."

$ $CLUBHOUSE MAGAZINE, Focus on the Family, 8605 Explorer Dr., Colorado Springs CO 80920. Fax: (719)531-3499. Website: www.clubhousemagazine.org. Editor: Jesse Florea. **Contact:** Suzanne Hadley, assistant editor. **25% freelance written.** Monthly magazine geared for Christian kids ages 8-12. Estab. 1987. Circ. 118,000. **Pays on acceptance.** Byline given. Buys one-time rights. Editorial lead time 5 months. Submit seasonal material 7 months in advance. Sample copy for $1.50 with 9×12 SASE. Writer's guidelines for #10 SASE.

O⊸ Break in by "being familiar with content and style. Well-written retellings of Bible stories with a different point of view are always a need."

Nonfiction: Essays, general interest, historical/nostalgic, how-to, inspirational, interview/profile, personal experience, photo feature, religious experience. **Buys 3 mss/year.** Send complete ms. Length: 800-1,200 words. **Pays 10-25¢/word.** Sometimes pays expenses of writers on assignment.

Photos: Send photos with submission. Reviews contact sheets. Negotiates payment individually. Captions, identification of subjects, model releases required.

Columns/Departments: Lookout (news/kids in community), 50 words. **Buys 5 mss/year.** Send complete ms. **Pays $75-150.**

Fiction: Fantasy, historical, humorous, mystery, religious, western, holiday, children's literature (Christian). Avoid contemporary, middle-class family settings (existing authors meet this need), poems (rarely printed), stories dealing with boy-girl relationships. **Buys 10 mss/year.** Send complete ms. Length: 400-1,600 words. **Pays $200-450.**

Fillers: Facts, newsbreaks. **Buys 2/year.** Length: 40-100 words. **Pays $50-150.**

N $ $ COBBLESTONE, Discover American History, Cobblestone Publishing, 30 Grove St., Suite C, Peterborough NH 03458-1457. (603)924-7209. Fax: (603)924-7380. Website: www.cobblestonepub.com. **Contact:** Meg Chorlian, editor. **100% freelance written.** (except letters and departments); approximately 1 issue/year is by assignment. Prefers to work with published/established writers. Monthly magazine (September-May) covering American history for children ages 8-14. "Each issues presents a particular theme, making it exciting as well as informative. Half of all subscriptions are for schools." All material must relate to monthly theme. Circ. 33,000. Pays on publication. Publishes ms an average of 4 months after acceptance. Byline given. Offers 50% kill fee. Buys all rights. Editorial lead time 8 months. Accepts simultaneous submissions. Responds in 4 months to queries. Sample copy for $4.95 and 7½×10½ SAE with 4 first-class stamps. Writer's guidelines and query deadlines with SASE.

Nonfiction: "Request a copy of the writer's guidelines to find out specific issue themes in upcoming months." Historical/nostalgic, interview/profile, personal experience, plays, biography, recipes, activities. No material that editorializes rather than reports. **Buys 80 mss/year.** Query by mail with published clips, outline and bibliography. Length: Feature articles 600-800 words; supplemental nonfiction 300-500 words. **Pays 20-25¢/printed word.**

Photos: Photos must relate to theme. State availability with submission. Reviews contact sheets, transparencies, prints. Buys one-time rights. Offers $15-50 for non-professional quality, up to $100 for professional quality. Captions, identification of subjects required.

Columns/Departments: Puzzles and Games (no word finds); crosswords and other word puzzles using the vocabulary of the issue's theme.

Fiction: Adventure, ethnic, historical, biographical fiction relating to them. Has to be very strong and accurate. **Buys 5 mss/year.** Query with published clips. Length: 500-800 words. **Pays 20-25¢/word.**

Poetry: Must relate to theme. Free verse, light verse, traditional. **Buys 5 poems/year.** Length: up to 50 lines.

$ $ CRICKET, Carus Publishing Co., P.O. Box 300, Peru IL 61354-0300. (815)224-6656. **Contact:** Marianne Carus, editor-in-chief. Monthly magazine for children ages 9-14. Estab. 1973. Circ. 73,000. Pays on publication. Byline given. Buys first publication rights in the English language. Submit seasonal material 1 year in advance. Responds in 3 months to mss. Sample copy for $5 and 9×12 SAE. Writer's guidelines for #10 SASE.

• *Cricket* is looking for more fiction and nonfiction for the older end of its 9-14 age range. It also seeks humorous stories and mysteries (*not* detective spoofs) fantasy and original fairy tales, stand-alone excerpts from unpublished novels and well-written/researched science articles.

Nonfiction: A short bibliography is required for all nonfiction articles. Travel, adventure, biography, foreign culture, geography, history, natural science, science, social science, sports, technology. Send complete ms. Length: 200-1,500 words. **Pays 25¢/word maximum.**

Reprints: Send typed ms with rights for sale noted and information about when and where the material previously appeared. Pays 50% of amount paid for an original article.

Fiction: Adventure, ethnic, fantasy, historical, humorous, mystery, novel excerpts, science fiction, suspense, western, fairy tales. No didactic, sex, religious or horror stories. **Buys 75-100 mss/year.** Send complete ms. Length: 200-2,000 words. **Pays 25¢/word maximum.**

Poetry: Buys 20-30 poems/year. Length: 25 lines maximum. **Pays $3/line maximum.**

$ CRUSADER MAGAZINE, P.O. Box 7259, Grand Rapids MI 49510-7259. Website: www.gospelcom.net/cadets/ . **Contact:** G. Richard Broene, editor. **40% freelance written.** Works with a small number of new/unpublished writers each year. Magazine published 7 times/year. "*Crusader Magazine* shows boys 9-14 how God is at work in their lives and in the world around them." Estab. 1958. Circ. 12,000. **Pays on acceptance.** Publishes ms an average of 8 months after acceptance. Byline given. Buys first North American serial, one-time, second serial (reprint), simultaneous rights. Rights purchased vary with author and material. Accepts queries by mail. Accepts simultaneous submissions. Responds in 2 months to queries. Sample copy for 9×12 SAE. Writer's guidelines for #10 SASE.

Nonfiction: Articles about young boys' interests: Sports (coaching tips, articles about athletes and developing Christian character through sports; b&w photos appreciated), outdoor activities (camping skills, nature study, survival exercises; practical 'how to do it' approach works best. 'God in nature' themes also appreciated if done without preachiness), science, crafts (made with easily accessible materials; must provide clear, accurate instructions), and problems. Emphasis is on a Christian perspective, but no simplistic moralisms. How-to, humor, inspirational, interview/profile, personal experience, informational. Special issues: Write for new themes list in February. **Buys 20-25 mss/year.** Send complete ms. Length: 500-1,500 words. **Pays 2-5¢/word.**

Reprints: Send typed ms with rights for sale noted. Pay varies.

Photos: Pays $4-25 for photos purchased with mss.

Columns/Departments: Project Page-uses simple projects boys 9-14 can do on their own.

Fiction: "Considerable fiction is used. Fast-moving stories that appeal to a boy's sense of adventure or sense of humor are welcome. Avoid preachiness. Avoid simplistic answers to complicated problems. Avoid long dialogue and little action." Length: 900-1,500 words. **Pays 2¢/word minimum.**

Fillers: Short humor, any type of puzzles.

Tips: "Best time to submit stories/articles is early in calendar year—in March or April. Also remember readers are boys ages 9-14. Stories must reflect or add to the theme of the issue."

N $ $⚒ CURRENT HEALTH I, The Beginning Guide to Health Education, General Learning Communications, 900 Skokie Blvd., Suite 200, Northbrook IL 60062-4028. (847)205-3141. Fax: (847)564-8197. E-mail: crubens tein@glcomm.com. **Contact:** Carole Rubenstein, senior editor. **95% freelance written.** An educational health periodical published monthly, September-April/May. "Our audience is 4th-7th grade health education students. Articles should be written at a 5th grade reading level. As a curriculum supplementary publication, info should be accurate, timely, accessible and highly readable." Estab. 1976. Circ. 152,000. Pays on publication. Publishes ms an average of 6 months after acceptance. Buys all rights.

Nonfiction: Health curriculum. **Buys 70 mss/year.** Query with introductory letter, résumé and clips. *No unsolicited mss. Articles are on assignment only.* Length: 950-2,000 words. **Pays $150-450**

Tips: "We are looking for good writers with preferably an education and/or health background, who can write for the age group in a scientifically accurate way. Ideally, the writer should be an expert in the area in which he or she is writing. All topics are open to freelancers: disease, drugs, fitness and exercise, psychology, nutrition, first aid and safety, relationships and personal health."

$ ⊠ DISCOVERIES, Word Action Publishing Co., 6401 The Paseo, Kansas City MO 64131. (816)333-7000, ext. 2728. Fax: (816)333-4439. Editor: Virginia Folsom. **Contact:** Katherine Hendrixson, editorial assistant. **75% freelance written.** Weekly Sunday school take-home paper. "Our audience is third and fourth graders. We require that the stories relate to the Sunday school lesson for that week." Circ. 5,000. Pays on publication. Publishes ms an average of 1 year after acceptance. Byline given. Buys multi-use rights. Accepts queries by mail, e-mail. Accepts simultaneous submissions. Responds in 6 weeks to queries; 2 months to mss. Sample copy and writer's guidelines for #10 SASE.

　○── "Follow theme list and guidelines. Make sure content is Biblically correct and relevant where necessary."

Reprints: Send typed ms with rights for sale noted and information about when and where the material previously appeared.

Fiction: Submit contemporary, true-to-life portrayals of 8- to 10-year-olds, written for a 3rd- to 4th-grade reading level. Religious themes. Must relate to our theme list. No fantasy, science fiction, abnormally mature or precocious children, personification of animals. **Buys 45 mss/year.** Send complete ms. Length: 400-500 words. **Pays 5¢/word.**

Fillers: Gags to be illustrated by cartoonist, puzzles, Bible trivia (need bibliography documentation). **Buys 100/year.** Length: 50-200 words. **Pays $15.**

Tips: "Follow our theme list, read the Bible verses that relate to the theme. September 2002 begins our new curriculum."

$ ⊠ DISCOVERY TRAILS, Gospel Publishing House, 1445 N. Boonville Ave., Springfield MO 65802-1894. (417)862-2781. Fax: (417)862-6059. E-mail: discoverytrails@gph.org. Website: www.radiantlife.org. **Contact:** Sinda S. Zinn, editor. **98% freelance written.** Weekly 4-page sunday school take-home paper. *Discovery Trails* is written for boys and girls 10-12 (slanted toward older group). Fiction, adventure stories showing children applying Christian principles in everyday living are used in the paper. **Pays on acceptance.** Publishes ms an average of 18 months after acceptance. Byline given. Buys one-time, second serial (reprint), simultaneous rights. Editorial lead time 18 months. Submit seasonal material 18 months in advance. Accepts simultaneous submissions. Responds in 1 month to ms. Sample copy and writer's guidelines for #10 SASE.

Nonfiction: Wants articles with reader appeal, emphasizing some phase of Christian living or historical, scientific or natural material which includes a spiritual lesson. Submissions should include a bibliography of facts. **Buys 15-20 mss/year.** Send complete ms. Length: 500 words maximum. **Pays 7-10¢/word.**

Reprints: Send typed ms with rights for sale noted and information about when and where the material previously appeared. Pays 7¢/word.

Fiction: Wants fiction that presents realistic characters working out their problems according to Bible principles, presenting Christianity in action without being preachy. Serial stories acceptable. Adventure, historical, humorous, mystery. No Bible fiction, "Halloween" or "Santa Claus" stories. **Buys 80-90 mss/year.** Send complete ms. Length: 1,000 words (except for serial stories). **Pays 7-10¢/word.**

Poetry: Light verse, traditional. **Buys 10 poems/year.** Submit maximum 2-3 poems. **Pays $5-15.**

Fillers: Bits & Bytes of quirky facts, puzzles, interactive activities, quizzes, word games, and fun activities that address social skills on a focused topic with accurate research, vivid writing, and spiritual emphasis. Crafts, how-to articles, recipes should be age appropriate, safe and cheap, express newness/originality and accuracy, a clear focus, and an opening that makes kids want to read and do it. **Buys 8-10/year.** Length: 300 words maximum.

Tips: "Follow the guidelines, remember the story should be interesting—carried by dialogue and action rather than narration—and appropriate for a Sunday school take-home paper. Don't send groups of stories in one submission."

Ⓝ $ $ ⊠ FACES, People, Places and Cultures, Cobblestone Publishing, 30 Grove St., Peterborough NH 03458. (603)924-7209. Fax: (603)924-7380. E-mail: faces@cobblestonepub.com. Website: www.cobblestonepub.com. **Contact:** Elizabeth Carpentiere, editor. **90-100% freelance written.** Monthly magazine published during school year. "*Faces* covers world culture for ages 9-14. It stands apart from other children's magazines by offering a solid look at one subject and stressing strong editorial content, color photographs throughout and original illustrations. *Faces* offers an equal balance of feature articles and activities, as well as folktales and legends." Estab. 1984. Circ. 15,000. Pays on publication. Publishes ms an average of 4 months after acceptance. Byline given. Offers 50% kill fee. Buys all rights. Editorial lead time 1 year. Accepts queries by mail, e-mail. Accepts simultaneous submissions. Sample copy for $4.95 and 7½× 10½ (or larger) SAE with $2 postage or online. Writer's guidelines for #10 SASE.

　● Cobblestone Publishing was acquired by Carus Publishing, publishers of *Ladybug* and *Cricket* magazines, among others.

O—¬ All material must relate to the theme of a specific upcoming issue in order to be considered. Writers new to *Faces* should send a writing sample with the query.

Nonfiction: Historical/nostalgic, humor, interview/profile, personal experience, photo feature, travel, recipes, activities, puzzles, mazes. All must relate to theme. **Buys 45-50 mss/year.** Query with published clips. Length: 800 words for feature articles; 300-600 for supplemental nonfiction; up to 700 words for activities. **Pays 20-25¢/word.**

Photos: State availability of photos with submission or send copies of related images for photo researcher. Reviews contact sheets, transparencies, prints. Buys one-time rights. Captions, identification of subjects, model releases required.

Fiction: Ethnic, historical, retold legends or folktales. Depends on theme. Query with published clips. Length: Up to 800 words. **Pays 20-25¢/word.**

Poetry: Avant-garde, free verse, haiku, light verse, traditional. Length: 100 words maximum.

Tips: "Freelancers should send for a sample copy of magazine and a list of upcoming themes and writer's guidelines. The magazine is based on a monthly theme (upcoming themes include the Ukraine, Bahamas, British Columbia and Canada). We appreciate professional queries that follow our detailed writer's guidelines."

$ $✕ THE FRIEND, 50 E. North Temple, Salt Lake City UT 84150-3226. Fax: (801)240-2270. **Contact:** Vivian Paulsen, managing editor. **50% freelance written.** Eager to work with new/unpublished writers as well as established writers. Monthly publication of The Church of Jesus Christ of Latter-Day Saints for children ages 3-11. Circ. 275,000. **Pays on acceptance.** Buys all rights. Submit seasonal material 8 months in advance. Responds in 2 months to mss. Sample copy and writer's guidelines for $1.50 and 9×12 SAE with 4 first-class stamps.

Nonfiction: Subjects of current interest, science, nature, pets, sports, foreign countries, things to make and do. "*The Friend* is particularly interested in stories based on true experiences." Special issues: Christmas, Easter. Submit complete ms with SASE. No queries please. Length: 1,000 words maximum. **Pays 10¢/word minimum.**

Fiction: Seasonal and holiday stories, stories about other countries and their children. Wholesome and optimistic; high motive, plot and action. Character-building stories preferred. Send complete ms. Length: 1,200 words maximum; stories for younger children should not exceed 250 words. **Pays 11¢/word minimum.**

Poetry: Serious, humorous, holiday. Any form with child appeal. **Pays $25 minimum.**

Tips: "Do you remember how it feels to be a child? Can you write stories that appeal to children ages 3-11 in today's world? We're interested in stories with an international flavor and those that focus on present-day problems. Send material of high literary quality slanted to our editorial requirements. Let the child solve the problem—not some helpful, all-wise adult. No overt moralizing. Nonfiction should be creatively presented—not an array of facts strung together. Beware of being cutesy."

$ $ $ GIRL'S LIFE, Monarch Publishing, 4517 Harford Rd., Baltimore MD 21214. Fax: (410)254-0991. Website: www.girlslife.com. Editor: Karen Bokram. **Contact:** Kelly A. White, executive editor. Bimonthly magazine covering girls ages 9-15. Estab. 1994. Circ. 2,000,000. Pays on publication. Publishes ms an average of 3 months after acceptance. Byline given. Buys first exclusive North American serial or all rights. Editorial lead time 4 months. Submit seasonal material 5 months in advance. Accepts queries by mail. Responds in 1 month to queries. Sample copy for $5 or online. Writer's guidelines for #10 SASE.

Nonfiction: Book excerpts, essays, general interest, how-to, humor, inspirational, interview/profile, new product, travel, beauty, relationship, sports. Special issues: Back to School (August/September); Fall, Halloween (October/November); Holidays, Winter (December/January); Valentine's Day, Crushes (February/March); Spring, Mother's Day (April/May); and Summer, Father's Day (June/July). **Buys 40 mss/year.** Query by mail with published clips. Submit complete mss on spec only. Length: 700-2,000 words. **Pays $150-800.**

Photos: State availability with submission. Reviews contact sheets, negatives, transparencies. Negotiates payment individually. Captions, identification of subjects, model releases required.

Columns/Departments: Sports; Try It! (new trends, celeb interviews); both 1,200 words. **Buys 20 mss/year.** Query with published clips. **Pays $150-450.**

Tips: Send queries with published writing samples and detailed résumé. "Have new ideas, a voice that speaks to our audience—not *down* to our audience—and supply artwork source (i.e. color slides)."

$✕ GUIDE, True Stories Pointing to Jesus, Review and Herald Publishing Association, 55 W. Oak Ridge Dr., Hagerstown MD 21740. (301)393-4038. Fax: (301)393-4055. E-mail: guide@rhpa.org. Website: www.guidemagazine.o rg. **Contact:** Randy Fishell, editor, or Helen Lee, assistant editor. **90% freelance written.** Weekly magazine featuring all-true stories showing God's involvement in 10- to 14-year-olds' lives. Estab. 1953. Circ. 33,000. **Pays on acceptance.** Publishes ms an average of 6 months after acceptance. Byline given. Buys first North American serial rights. Editorial lead time 8 months. Submit seasonal material 8 months in advance. Accepts queries by mail, e-mail, fax. Responds in 1 month to queries. Sample copy for SAE and 2 first-class stamps. Writer's guidelines for #10 SASE or online.

O—¬ Break in with "a true story that shows in a clear way that God is involved in a 10- to 14-year-old's life."

Nonfiction: Religious. "No fiction. Non-fiction should set forth a clearly evident spiritual application." **Buys 300 mss/year.** Send complete ms. Length: 750-1,500 words. **Pays $25-125.**

Reprints: Send photocopy. Pays 50% of usual rates.

Fillers: Games, puzzles, religious. **Buys 75/year. Pays $25-40.**

Tips: "The majority of 'misses' are due to the lack of a clearly evident (not 'preachy') spiritual application."

[N] $ $◨ GUIDEPOSTS FOR KIDS ON THE WEB, Guideposts, 1050 Broadway, Suite 6, Chesterton IN 46304. Fax: (219)926-3839. E-mail: gp4k@guideposts.org; send queries to rtolin@guideposts.org. Website: www.gp4k.c om. Editor: Mary Lou Carney. **Contact:** Rosanne Tolin, managing editor. **90% freelance written.** Online publication for kids 6-11. *"Guideposts for Kids on the Web* is an interactive, entertaining, and empowering place for kids to learn and play." Estab. 2001. Circ. 30,000 visitors/month. **Pays on acceptance.** Byline given. Buys electronic rights, non-exclusive print rights. Editorial lead time 2 months. Submit seasonal material 6 months in advance. Accepts queries by mail, e-mail, fax. Accepts simultaneous submissions. Responds in 6 weeks to queries; 2 months to mss. Sample copy online. Writer's guidelines for #10 SASE or online.
Nonfiction: General interest, historical/nostalgic, how-to, humor, inspirational, interview/profile. Does not want preachy stories that have really religious overtones. **Buys 60 mss/year.** Query with or without published clips or send complete ms. Length: 150-500 words. **Pays $100-500 for assigned articles; $50-400 for unsolicited articles.** Pays expenses of writers on assignment.
Photos: State availability of or send photos with submission. Buys all rights. Negotiates payment individually. Identification of subjects required.
Columns/Departments: Tips from the Top (tips from celebrity athletes who are good role models), 500 words; Cool Kids (profiles of kids 6-11 doing volunteer work), 200-500 words; Stories and poems (fiction), 300-1,000 words; Animals, Animals! (animal pieces), 100-400 words; God's Mysterious Ways (miraculous, true stories of God's power with a child as the protaganist), 150-300 words. **Buys 60 mss/year.** Query with or without published clips. **Pays $50-500.**
Fiction: Adventure, ethnic, fantasy, historical, humorous, mainstream, mystery, science fiction, serialized novels, suspense, From a child's perspective, avoid the adult voice. Does not want "stories about Bible-toting kids, stories where adults have all the answers." **Buys 12 mss/year.** Send complete ms. Length: 300-1,000 words. **Pays $200-600.**
Poetry: Avant-garde, free verse, haiku, light verse, traditional. **Buys 5-10 poems/year.** Submit maximum 6 poems. **Pays $25-50.**
Fillers: Facts, newsbreaks. **Buys 12-25/year. Pays $50-250.**
Tips: "Break in with our Cool Kids department or animal pieces. Make sure your kid voice is at work—don't be stiff in your approach when writing for gp4k.com. Think like a kid, use writing that will capture a child's attention. Keep copy tight and kid-friendly. Links to other great websites with more information on a particular subject are also essential."

$◪ HIGHLIGHTS FOR CHILDREN, 803 Church St., Honesdale PA 18431-1824. (570)253-1080. Managing Editor: Christine French Clark. **Contact:** Beth Troop, manuscript coordinator. **80% freelance written.** Monthly magazine for children ages 2-12. Estab. 1946. Circ. 3,000,000. **Pays on acceptance.** Buys all rights. Accepts queries by mail. Responds in 2 months to queries. Sample copy free. Writer's guidelines for #10 SASE.
Nonfiction: "We need articles on science, technology and nature written by persons with strong backgrounds in those fields. Contributions always welcomed from new writers, especially engineers, scientists, historians, teachers, etc., who can make useful, interesting facts accessible to children. Also writers who have lived abroad and can interpret the ways of life, especially of children, in other countries in ways that will foster world brotherhood. Sports material, biographies and articles of general interest to children. Direct, original approach, simple style, interesting content, not rewritten from encyclopedias. State background and qualifications for writing factual articles submitted. Include references or sources of information. Articles geared toward our younger readers (3-7) especially welcome, up to 400 words. Also buys original party plans for children ages 4-12, clearly described in 300-600 words, including drawings or samples of items to be illustrated. Also, novel but tested ideas in crafts, with clear directions and made-up models. Projects must require only free or inexpensive, easy-to-obtain materials. Especially desirable if easy enough for early primary grades. Also, fingerplays with lots of action, easy for very young children to grasp and to dramatize. Avoid wordiness. We need creative-thinking puzzles that can be illustrated, optical illusions, brain teasers, games of physical agility and other 'fun' activities." Query. Length: 900 words maximum. **Pays $50 for party plans; $25 for craft ideas; $25 for fingerplays.**
Photos: Reviews color 35mm slides, photos or art reference materials are helpful and sometimes crucial in evaluating mss.
Fiction: Unusual, meaningful stories appealing to both girls and boys, ages 2-12. "Vivid, full of action. Engaging plot, strong characterization, lively language." Prefers stories in which a child protagonist solves a dilemma through his or her own resources. Seeks stories that the child ages 8-12 will eagerly read, and the child ages 2-7 will begin to read and/or will like to hear when read aloud (400-900 words). "We publish stories in the suspense/adventure/mystery, fantasy and humor category, all requiring interesting plot and a number of illustration possiblities. Also need rebuses (picture stories 125 words or under), stories with urban settings, stories for beginning readers (100-400 words), sports and horse stories and retold folk tales. We also would like to see more material of 1-page length (300-500 words), both fiction and factual." "War, crime and violence are taboo." **Pays $100 minimum.**
Tips: "We are pleased that many authors of children's literature report that their first published work was in the pages of *Highlights*. It is not our policy to consider fiction on the strength of the reputation of the author. We judge each submission on its own merits. With factual material, however, we do prefer that writers be authorities in their field or people with first-hand experience. In this manner we can avoid the encyclopedic article that merely restates information readily available elsewhere. We don't make assignments. Query with simple letter to establish whether the nonfiction subject is likely to be of interest. A beginning writer should first become familiar with the type of material that *Highlights* publishes. Include special qualifications, if any, of author. Write for the child, not the editor. Write in a voice that children understand and relate to. Speak to today's kids, avoiding didactic, overt messages. Even though our general principles haven't changed over the years, we are contemporary in our approach to issues. Avoid worn themes."

$ 🖳 HOPSCOTCH, The Magazine For Girls, Bluffton News Publishing & Printing Co., P.O. Box 164, Bluffton OH 45817-0164. (419)358-4610. Website: www.hopscotchmagazine.com. Editor: Marilyn B. Edwards. **Contact:** Virginia Edwards, associate editor. **90% freelance written.** Bimonthly magazine covering basic subjects of interest to young girls. "*Hopscotch* is a digest-size magazine with a four-color cover and two-color format inside. It is designed for girls ages 6-12, with youngsters 8, 9 and 10 the specific target age; it features pets, crafts, hobbies, games, science, fiction, history, puzzles, careers, etc." Estab. 1989. Pays on publication. Byline given. Buys first, second serial (reprint) rights. Submit seasonal material 8 months in advance. Accepts simultaneous submissions. Responds in 3 weeks to queries; 2 months to mss. Sample copy for $4. Writer's guidelines, current theme list and needs for #10 SASE.

• *Hopscotch* has a sibling magazine, *Boys' Quest*, for ages 6-13, with the same old-fashioned values as *Hopscotch*.

Nonfiction: General interest, historical/nostalgic, how-to (crafts), humor, inspirational, interview/profile, personal experience, pets, games, fiction, careers, sports, cooking. "No fashion, hairstyles, sex or dating articles." **Buys 60 mss/ year.** Send complete ms. Length: 400-1,000 words. **Pays 5¢/word.**

Reprints: Send tearsheet, photocopy or typed ms with rights for sale noted. Pays 5¢/word.

Photos: Prefers b&w photos, but color photos accepted. Send photos with submission. Buys one-time rights. Pays $4-10/photo. Captions, identification of subjects, model releases required.

Columns/Departments: Science—nature, crafts, pets, cooking (basic), 400-700 words. Send complete ms. **Pays $10-35.**

Fiction: Adventure, historical, humorous, mainstream, mystery, suspense. **Buys 15 mss/year.** Send complete ms. Length: 600-900 words. **Pays 5¢/word.**

Poetry: Free verse, light verse, traditional. "No experimental or obscure poetry." Submit maximum 6 poems. **Pays $10-30.**

Tips: "Almost all sections are open to freelancers. Freelancers should remember that *Hopscotch* is a bit old-fashioned, appealing to *young* girls (6-12). We cherish nonfiction pieces that have a young girl or young girls directly involved in unusual and/or worthwhile activities. Any piece accompanied by decent photos stands an even better chance of being accepted. *Hopscotch* uses more nonfiction than fiction."

$ $HUMPTY DUMPTY'S MAGAZINE, Children's Better Health Institute, P.O. Box 567, Indianapolis IN 46206-0567. (317)636-8881. **Contact:** Nancy S. Axelrad, editor. **25% freelance written.** Magazine published 8 times/ year covering health, nutrition, hygiene, fitness and safety for children ages 4-6. "Our publication is designed to entertain and to educate young readers in healthy lifestyle habits. Fiction, poetry, pencil activities should have an element of good nutrition or fitness." Estab. 1948. Circ. 350,000. Pays on publication. Publishes ms an average of 8 months after acceptance. Byline given. Buys all rights. Editorial lead time 8 months. Submit seasonal material 10 months in advance. Accepts simultaneous submissions. Responds in 3 months to queries. Sample copy for $1.75. Writer's guidelines for #10 SASE.

Nonfiction: "Material must have a health theme—nutrition, safety, exercise, hygiene. We're looking for articles that encourage readers to develop better health habits without preaching. Very simple factual articles that creatively teach readers about their bodies. We use several puzzles and activities in each issue—dot-to-dot, hidden pictures and other activities that promote following instructions, developing finger dexterity and working with numbers and letters." Include word count. **Buys 3-4 mss/year.** Send complete ms. Length: 1,300 words maximum. **Pays 22¢/word.**

Photos: Send photos with submission. Buys all rights. Offers no additonal payment for photos accepted with ms.

Columns/Departments: Mix & Fix (no-cook recipes), 100 words. All ingredients must be nutritious—low fat, no sugar, etc.—and tasty. **Buys 8 mss/year.** Send complete ms. **Payment varies.**

Fiction: "We use some stories in rhyme and a few easy-to-read stories for the beginning reader. All stories should work well as read-alouds. Currently we need health/sports/fitness stories. We try to present our health material in a positive light, incorporating humor and a light approach wherever possible. Avoid stereotyping. Characters in contemporary stories should be realistic and reflect good, wholesome values." Include word count. **Buys 4-6 mss/year.** Send complete ms. Length: 350 words maximum. **Pays 22¢/word.**

Tips: "Get to know the magazine before submitting work—remember, we are only buying material with a health or fitness slant. Be creative about it."

$ $JACK AND JILL, Children's Better Health Institute, P.O. Box 567, Indianapolis IN 46206-0567. (317)636-8881. Fax: (317)684-8094. **Contact:** Daniel Lee, editor. **50% freelance written.** Magazine published 8 times/year for children ages 7-10. "Material will not be returned unless accompanied by SASE with sufficient postage." No queries. May hold material being seriously considered for up to 1 year. Estab. 1938. Circ. 200,000. Pays on publication. Publishes ms an average of 8 months after acceptance. Byline given. Buys all rights. Submit seasonal material 8 months in advance. Responds in 10 weeks to mss. Sample copy for $1.25. Writer's guidelines for #10 SASE.

Oᴙ Break in with nonfiction about ordinary kids with a news hook—something that ties in with current events, matters the kids are seeing on television and in mainstream news—i.e., space exploration, scientific advances, sports, etc.

Nonfiction: "Because we want to encourage youngsters to read for pleasure and for information, we are interested in material that will challenge a young child's intelligence *and* be enjoyable reading. Our emphasis is on good health, and we are in particular need of articles, stories, and activities with health, safety, exercise and nutrition themes. We try to present our health material in a positive light—incorporating humor and a light approach wherever possible without minimizing the seriousness of what we are saying. Straight factual articles are OK if they are short and interestingly written. We would rather see, however, more creative alternatives to the straight factual article. Items with a news hook will get extra attention. We'd like to see articles about interesting kids involved in out-of-the-ordinary activities. We're also interested in articles about people with unusual hobbies for our Hobby Shop department." **Buys 10-15 mss/year.** Send complete ms. Length: 500-800 words. **Pays 17¢/word minimum.**

Photos: When appropriate, photos should accompany ms. Reviews sharp, contrasting b&w glossy prints. Sometimes uses color slides, transparencies or good color prints. Buys one-time rights. Pays $15/photo.

Fiction: May include, but is not limited to, realistic stories, fantasy, adventure—set in past, present, or future. "All stories need a well-developed plot, action and incident. Humor is highly desirable. Stories that deal with a health theme need not have health as the primary subject." **Buys 20-25 mss/year.** Send complete ms. Length: 500-800 words. **Pays 15¢/word minimum.**

Fillers: Puzzles (including various kinds of word and crossword puzzles), poems, games, science projects, and creative craft projects. "We get a lot of these. To be selected, an item needs a little extra spark and originality. Instructions for activities should be clearly and simply written and accompanied by models or diagram sketches. We also have a need for recipes. Ingredients should be healthful; avoid sugar, salt, chocolate, red meat and fats as much as possible. In all material, avoid references to eating sugary foods, such as candy, cakes, cookies and soft drinks."

Tips: "We are constantly looking for new writers who can tell good stories with interesting slants—stories that are not full of out-dated and time-worn expressions. We like to see stories about kids who are smart and capable, but not sarcastic or smug. Problem-solving skills, personal responsibility and integrity are good topics for us. Obtain *current* issues of the magazine and *study* them to determine our present needs and editorial style."

$ $LADYBUG, The Magazine for Young Children, Carus Publishing Co., P.O. Box 300, Peru IL 61354-0300. (815)224-6656. Editor-in-Chief: Marianne Carus. **Contact:** Paula Morrow, editor. Monthly magazine for children ages 2-6. "We look for quality writing—quality literature, no matter the subject." Estab. 1990. Circ. 134,000. Pays on publication. Byline given. Buys first publication rights in the English language. Submit seasonal material 1 year in advance. Responds in 3 months to mss. Sample copy and guidelines for $5 and 9 × 12 SAE. Guidelines only for #10 SASE.

- *Ladybug* needs even more activities based on concepts (size, color, sequence, comparison, etc.) and interesting, appropriate nonfiction. Also needs articles and parent-child activities for its parents' section. See sample issues.

Nonfiction: Can You Do This?, 1-2 pages; The World Around You, 2-4 pages; activities based on concepts (size, color, sequence, comparison, etc.), 1-2 pages. "Most *Ladybug* nonfiction is in the form of illustration. We'd like more simple science, how-things-work and behind-the-scenes on a preschool level." **Buys 35 mss/year.** Send complete ms; no queries. Length: 250-300 words. **Pays up to 25¢/word.**

Fiction: Adventure, ethnic, fantasy, humorous, mainstream, mystery, folklore. **Buys 30 mss/year.** Send complete ms. Length: 850 words maximum. **Pays up to 25¢/word.**

Poetry: Light verse, traditional, humorous. **Buys 20 poems/year.** Submit maximum 5 poems. Length: 20 lines maximum. **Pays up to $3/line.**

Fillers: "We welcome interactive activities: rebuses, up to 100 words; *original* fingerplays and action rhymes (up to 8 lines)." Anecdotes, facts, short humor. **Buys 10/year.** Length: 250 words maximum. **Pays up to 25¢/word.**

Tips: "Reread manuscript *before* sending in. Keep within specified word limits. Study back issues before submitting to learn about the types of material we're looking for. Writing style is paramount. We look for rich, evocative language and a sense of joy or wonder. Remember that you're writing for preschoolers—be age-appropriate but not condescending. A story must hold enjoyment for both parent and child through repeated read-aloud sessions. Remember that people come in all colors, sizes, physical conditions and have special needs. Be inclusive!"

$ NATURE FRIEND, Carlisle Press, 2673 TR 421, Sugarcreek OH 44681. (330)852-1900. Fax: (330)852-3285. Managing Editor: Elaine Troyer. **Contact:** Marvin Wengerd, editor. **80% freelance written.** Monthly magazine covering nature. "*Nature Friend* includes stories, puzzles, science experiments, nature experiments—all submissions need to honor God as creator." Estab. 1983. Circ. 10,000. Pays on publication. Publishes ms an average of 10 months after acceptance. Byline given. Buys first, one-time rights. Editorial lead time 4 months. Submit seasonal material 2 months in advance. Accepts queries by mail, fax. Accepts simultaneous submissions. Responds in 4 weeks to queries; 4 months to mss. Sample copy for $2.50 postage paid. Writer's guidelines for $4 postage paid.

- Break in with a "conversational story about a nature subject that imparts knowledge and instills Christian values."

Nonfiction: How-to (nature, science experiments), photo feature, religious, Articles about interesting/unusual animals. No poetry, evolution, animals depicted in captivity. **Buys 50 mss/year.** Send complete ms. Length: 250-900 words. **Pays 5¢/word.**

Photos: Send photos with submission. Reviews prints. Buys one-time rights. Offers $35-50/photo. Captions, identification of subjects required.

Columns/Departments: Learning By Doing, Hands on! Hands on! Hands on! (anything about nature), 500-900 words. **Buys 20 mss/year.** Send complete ms.

Fillers: Facts, puzzles, short essays on something current in nature. **Buys 35/year.** Length: 150-250 words. **Pays 5¢/word.**

Tips: "We want to bring joy to children by opening the world of God's creation to them. We endeavor to educate with science experiments, stories, etc. We endeavor to create a sense of awe about nature's creator and a respect for His creation. I'd like to see more submissions on hands-on things to do with a nature theme (not collecting rocks or leaves—real stuff). Also looking for good stories that are accompanied by good photography."

$ $ NEW MOON, The Magazine for Girls & Their Dreams, New Moon Publishing, Inc., P.O. Box 3620, Duluth MN 55803-3620. (218)728-5507. Fax: (218)728-0314. E-mail: girl@newmoon.org. Website: www.newmoon.o rg. **Contact:** Deb Mylin, managing editor. **25% freelance written.** Bimonthly magazine covering girls ages 8-14, edited by girls ages 8-14. "In general, all material should be pro-girl and feature girls and women as the primary focus. *New Moon* is for every girl who wants her voice heard and her dreams taken seriously. *New Moon* celebrates girls, explores the passage from girl to woman and builds healthy resistance to gender inequities. The *New Moon* girl is true to herself and *New Moon* helps her as she pursues her unique path in life, moving confidently into the world." Estab. 1992. Circ. 30,000. Pays on publication. Publishes ms an average of 1 year after acceptance. Byline given. Buys all rights. Editorial lead time 6 months. Submit seasonal material 8 months in advance. Accepts queries by mail, e-mail, fax. Accepts simultaneous submissions. Responds in 8 months to mss. Sample copy for $6.50 or online. Writer's guidelines for SASE or online.

  ○▪ Adult writers can break in with "*Herstory* articles about less well-known women from all over the world, especially if it relates to one of our themes. Same as *Women's Work* articles. Girls can break in with essays and articles (non-fiction) that relate to a theme."

Nonfiction: Essays, general interest, humor, inspirational, interview/profile, opinion, personal experience (written by girls), photo feature, religious, travel, multicultural/girls from other countries. No fashion, beauty, or dating. **Buys 20 mss/year.** Query with or without published clips or send complete ms. Length: 600 words. **Pays 6-12¢/word.**

Reprints: Send typed ms with rights for sale noted and information about when and where the material previously appeared. Negotiates fee.

Photos: State availability with submission. Buys one-time rights. Negotiates payment individually. Captions, identification of subjects required.

Columns/Departments: Women's Work (profile of a woman and her job(s) relating the the theme), 600 words; Herstory (historical woman relating to theme), 600 words. **Buys 10 mss/year.** Query. **Pays 6-12¢/word.**

Fiction: Prefers girl-written material. All girl-centered. Adventure, fantasy, historical, humorous, slice-of-life vignettes. **Buys 6 mss/year.** Send complete ms. Length: 900-1,200 words. **Pays 6-12¢/word.**

Poetry: No poetry by adults.

Tips: "We'd like to see more girl-written feature articles that relate to a theme. These can be about anything the girl has done personally, or she can write about something she's studied. Please read *New Moon* before submitting to get a sense of our style. Writers and artists who comprehend our goals have the best chance of publication. We love creative articles—both nonfiction and fiction—that are not condescending to our readers. Keep articles to suggested word lengths; avoid stereotypes. Refer to our guidelines and upcoming themes."

$ ▣ ON THE LINE, Mennonite Publishing House, 616 Walnut Ave., Scottdale PA 15683-1999. (724)887-8500. Fax: (724)887-3111. E-mail: mary@mph.org. **Contact:** Mary Clemens Meyer, editor. **90% freelance written.** Works with a small number of new/unpublished writers each year. Monthly Christian magazine for children ages 9-14. "*On the Line* helps upper elementary and junior high children understand and appreciate God, the created world, themselves and others." Estab. 1908. Circ. 6,000. **Pays on acceptance.** Publishes ms an average of 1 year after acceptance. Byline given. Buys one-time rights. Submit seasonal material 6 months in advance. Accepts simultaneous submissions. Responds in 1 month to mss. Sample copy for 9×12 SAE and 2 first-class stamps.

Nonfiction: How-to (things to make with easy-to-get materials including food recipes), informational (300-500 word articles on wonders of nature, people who have made outstanding contributions). **Buys 95 mss/year.** Send complete ms. **Pays $15-35.**

Reprints: Send typed ms with rights for sale noted and information about when and where the material previously appeared. Pays 75% of amount paid for an original article.

Photos: Limited number of photos purchased with or without ms. Total purchase price for ms includes payment for photos. Pays $25-50 for 8×10 b&w photos.

Fiction: Adventure, humorous, religious, everyday problems. **Buys 50 mss/year.** Send complete ms. Length: 1,000-1,800 words. **Pays 3-5¢/word.**

Poetry: Light verse, religious. Length: 3-12 lines. **Pays $10-25.**

Fillers: Appropriate puzzles, cartoons and quizzes.

Tips: "Study the publication first. We need short well-written how-to and craft articles; also more puzzles. Don't send query; we prefer to see the complete manuscript."

$ $ OWL MAGAZINE, The Discovery Magazine for Children, Owl Group (owned by Bayard Press), 179 John St., Suite 500, Toronto, Ontario M5T 3G5, Canada. (416)340-2700. Fax: (416)340-9769. E-mail: owl@owl.on.ca. Website: www.owlkids.com. **Contact:** Mary Beth Leatherdale, editor. **25% freelance written.** Works with small number of new writers each year. Magazine published 9 times/year covering science and nature. Aims to interest children in their environment through accurate, factual information about the world presented in an easy, lively style. Estab. 1976. Circ. 75,000. Pays on publication. Byline given. Buys all rights. Submit seasonal material 1 year in advance. Accepts queries by mail, fax. Responds in 3 months to queries. Sample copy for $4.28. Writer's guidelines for SAE (large envelope if requesting sample copy) and money order for $1 postage (no stamps please).

Nonfiction: Book excerpts, general interest, how-to, humor, personal experience (real life children in real situations), photo feature (natural science, international wildlife and outdoor features), science, nature and environmental features. No problem stories with drugs, sex or moralistic views, or talking animal stories. **Buys 6 mss/year.** Query with published clips. Length: 500-1,500 words. **Pays $200-500 (Canadian).**

Photos: Send for photo package before submitting material. State availability with submission. Reviews 35mm transparencies. Identification of subjects required.

Tips: "Write for editorial guidelines first. Review back issues of the magazine for content and style. Know your topic and approach it from an unusual perspective. Our magazine never talks down to children. Our articles have a very light conversational tone and this must be reflected in any writing that we accept. We would like to see more articles about science and technology that aren't too academic."

$ $ POCKETS, The Upper Room, 1908 Grand Ave., P.O. Box 340004, Nashville TN 37203-0004. (615)340-7333. Fax: (615)340-7267. E-mail: pockets@upperroom.org. Website: www.upperroom.org. Editor: Janet R. Knight. **Contact:** Lynn Gilliam, associate editor. **60% freelance written.** Monthly (except february) magazine covering children's and families' spiritual formation. "We are a Christian, inter-denominational publication for children 6-11 years of age. Each issue reflects a specific theme." Estab. 1981. Circ. 94,000. **Pays on acceptance.** Byline given. Buys first North American serial rights. Submit seasonal material 1 year in advance. Responds in 6 weeks to mss. Sample copy for 7½×10½ or larger SAE and 4 first-class stamps. Writer's guidelines for #10 SASE or online.

● *Pockets* publishes fiction and poetry, as well as short, short stories (no more than 600 words) for children 4-7. They publish one of these stories per issue. Eager to work with new/unpublished writers.

Nonfiction: Each issue reflects a specific theme; themes available for #10 SASE. Interview/profile, personal experience, religious (retold scripture stories). No violence or romance. **Buys 5 mss/year.** Length: 400-1,000 words. **Pays 14¢/word.**

Reprints: Accepts one-time previously published submissions. Send typed ms with rights for sale noted and information about when and where the material previously appeared.

Photos: No photos unless they accompany an article. Send photos with submission. Reviews contact sheets, transparencies, prints. Buys one-time rights. Pays $25/photo.

Columns/Departments: Refrigerator Door (poetry and prayer related to themes), maximum 24 lines; Pocketsful of Love (family communications activities), 300 words; Peacemakers at Work (profiles of children working for peace, justice and ecological concerns), 300-800 words. **Pays 14¢/word.** Activities/Games (related to themes). **Pays $25 and up.** Kids Cook (simple recipes children can make alone or with minimal help from an adult). **Pays $25. Buys 20 mss/ year.**

Fiction: "Submissions do not need to be overtly religious. They should reflect daily living, lifestyle and problem-solving based on living as faithful disciples. They should help children experience the Christian life that is not always a neatly wrapped moral package but is open to the continuing revelation of God's will for their lives." Adventure, ethnic, slice-of-life vignettes. **Buys 44 mss/year.** Length: 600-1,400 words. **Pays 14¢/word.**

Poetry: Buys 22 poems/year. Length: 4-24 lines. **Pays $2/line, $25 minimum.**

    ▣ The online magazine carries original content not found in the print edition and includes writer's guidelines, themes and fiction-writing contest guidelines. Contact: Lynn Gilliam, associate editor.

Tips: "Theme stories, role models and retold scripture stories are most open to freelancers. We are also looking for nonfiction stories about children involved in peace/justice/ecology efforts. Poetry is also open. It is very helpful if writers send for themes. These are *not* the same as writer's guidelines. We have an annual Fiction Writing Contest. Contest guidelines available with #10 SASE or on our website."

$ SHINE, (formerly *Touch*), GEMS Girls' Clubs, P.O. Box 7259, Grand Rapids MI 49510. (616)241-5616. Fax: (616)241-5558. E-mail: sara@gemsgc.org. Website: www.gospelcom.net/gems. Editor: Jan Boone. **Contact:** Sara Lynn Hilton, managing editor. **80% freelance written.** Works with new and published/established writers. Monthly magazine "to show girls ages 9-14 how God is at work in their lives and in the world around them. Our readers are mainly girls from Christian homes who belong to GEMS Girls' Clubs, a relationship-building club program available through churches. The May/June issue annually features material written by our readers." Estab. 1971. Circ. 13,000. Pays on publication. Publishes ms an average of 1 year after acceptance. Byline given. Buys first North American serial, second serial (reprint) rights. Submit seasonal material 1 year in advance. Accepts simultaneous submissions. Responds in 2 months to queries. Sample copy for 9×12 SAE with 3 first class stamps and $1. Writer's guidelines for #10 SASE.

Nonfiction: "Because our magazine is published around a monthly theme, requesting the letter we send out twice a year to our established freelancers would be most helpful. We do not want easy solutions or quick character changes from good to bad. No pietistic characters. No 'new girl at school starting over after parents' divorce' stories. Constant mention of God is not necessary if the moral tone of the story is positive. We do not want stories that always have a happy ending." Needs include: Biographies and autobiographies of "heroes of the faith," informational (write for issue themes), multicultural materials. Humor (need much more), inspirational, interview/profile, personal experience (avoid the testimony approach), photo feature (query first), religious, travel. Special issues: School Skills Needed (September); Danger Ahead! Join the Rescue Squad (October); Lost and Found (November); Rescuing Christmas (December); Dial 9-1-1 (January); I'm Lonely...Rescue Me! (February); Danger...Beware! (March); Team Up With Mother Earth (April); You Want Me to Join What? (May/June). **Buys 10 unsolicited mss/year.** Send complete ms. Length: 200-800 words. **Pays $10-20 plus 2 copies.**

Reprints: Send typed ms with rights for sale noted and information about when and where the material previously appeared.

Photos: Purchased with or without ms. Reviews 5×7 or 8×10 clear glossy color prints. Appreciate multicultural subjects. Pays $25-50 on publication.

Columns/Departments: How-to (crafts); puzzles and jokes; quizzes. Length: 200-400 words. Send complete ms. **Pay varies.**

Fiction: Adventure (that girls could experience in their hometowns or places they might realistically visit), historical, humorous, mystery (believable only), religious (nothing preachy), romance (stories that deal with awakening awareness of boys are appreciated), slice-of-life vignettes, suspense (can be serialized). **Buys 20 mss/year.** Send complete ms. Length: 400-1,000 words. **Pays $20-50.**

Poetry: Free verse, haiku, light verse, traditional. **Buys 5 poems/year.** Length: 15 lines maximum. **Pays $5-15 minimum.**

Tips: "Prefers not to see anything on the adult level, secular material or violence. Writers frequently over-simplify the articles and often write with a Pollyanna attitude. An author should be able to see his/her writing style as exciting and appealing to girls ages 9-14. The style can be fun, but also teach a truth. Subjects should be current and important to *Touch* readers. Use our theme update as a guide. We would like to receive material with a multicultural slant."

$ $■ SPIDER, The Magazine for Children, Cricket Magazine Group, P.O. Box 300, Peru IL 61354. (815)224-6656. Fax: (815)224-6615. Editor: Thomas L. Bryant. **Contact:** Submissions Editor. **80% freelance written.** Monthly magazine covering literary, general interest. "*Spider* introduces 6- to 9-year-old children to the highest quality stories, poems, illustrations, articles and activities. It was created to foster in beginning readers a love of reading and discovery that will last a lifetime. We're looking for writers who respect children's intelligence." Estab. 1994. Circ. 87,000. Pays on publication. Publishes ms an average of 4 years after acceptance. Byline given. Buys first North American serial, second serial (reprint), all rights. Editorial lead time 9 months. Accepts simultaneous submissions. Responds in 4 months to mss. Sample copy for $5. Writer's guidelines for #10 SASE.

Nonfiction: A bibliography is required with all nonfiction submissions. Adventure, ethnic, fantasy, historical, humorous, mystery, science fiction, suspense, realisitc fiction, folk tales, fairy tales. **Buys 6-8 mss/year.** Send complete ms. Length: 300-800 words. **Pays $25.**

Reprints: Send photocopy with rights for sale noted and information about when and where the material previously appeared.

Photos: Send photos with submission. Reviews contact sheets, 35mm to 4×4 transparencies, 8×10 prints. Buys one-time rights. Offers $35-50/photo. Captions, identification of subjects, model releases required.

Fiction: Adventure, ethnic, fantasy, historical, humorous, mystery, science fiction, suspense, realistic fiction, folk tales, fairy tales. No romance, horror, religious. **Buys 15-20 mss/year.** Send complete ms. Length: 300-1,000 words. **Pays 25¢/word.**

Poetry: Free verse, traditional, nonsense, humorous, serious. No forced rhymes, didactic. **Buys 10-20 poems/year.** Submit maximum 5 poems. Length: 20 lines maximum. **Pays $3/line maximum.**

Fillers: Puzzles, mazes, games, brainteasers, math and word activities. **Buys 15-20/year. Payment depends on type of filler.**

Tips: "We'd like to see more of the following: Nonfiction, particularly photoessays, that focuses on an angle rather than providing an overview; fillers, puzzles, and 'takeout page' activities; folktales and humorous stories. Most importantly, do not write down to children."

$ STONE SOUP, The Magazine by Young Writers and Artists, Children's Art Foundation, P.O. Box 83, Santa Cruz CA 95063-0083. (831)426-5557. Fax: (831)426-1161. E-mail: editor@stonesoup.com. Website: www.stonesoup.com. Editor: Gilbert Sangari. **Contact:** Ms. Gerry Mandel, editor. **100% freelance written.** Bimonthly magazine of writing and art by children, including fiction, poetry, book reviews, and art by children through age 13. Audience is children, teachers, parents, writers, artists. "We have a preference for writing and art based on real-life experiences; no formula stories or poems." Estab. 1973. Pays on publication. Publishes ms an average of 3 months after acceptance. Buys all rights. Submit seasonal material 6 months in advance. Accepts queries by mail. Responds in 1 month to queries. Sample copy for $4 or online. Writer's guidelines for SASE or online.

Nonfiction: Historical/nostalgic, personal experience, book reviews. **Buys 12 mss/year.** Query with SASE. **Pays $25.**

Reprints: Send photocopy and information about when and where the material previously appeared. Pays 100% of amount paid for an original article.

Fiction: Adventure, ethnic, experimental, fantasy, historical, humorous, mystery, science fiction, slice-of-life vignettes, suspense. "We do not like assignments or formula stories of any kind." **Buys 60 mss/year.** Send complete ms. **Pays $25 for stories. Authors also receive 2 copies and discounts on additional copies and on subscriptions.**

Poetry: Avant-garde, free verse. **Buys 12 poems/year. Pays $25/poem.**

■ The online magazine carries original content not found in the print edition and includes writer's guidelines. Contact: Ms. Gerry Mandel, online editor.

Tips: "All writing we publish is by young people ages 13 and under. We do not publish any writing by adults. We can't emphasize enough how important it is to read a couple of issues of the magazine. We have a strong preference for writing on subjects that mean a lot to the author. If you feel strongly about something that happened to you or something you observed, use that feeling as the basis for your story or poem. Stories should have good descriptions, realistic dialogue and a point to make. In a poem, each word must be chosen carefully. Your poem should present a view of your subject and a way of using words that are special and all your own."

$ STORY FRIENDS, Mennonite Publishing House, 616 Walnut Ave., Scottdale PA 15683-1999. (724)887-3753. Fax: (724)887-3111. E-mail: rstutz@mph.org. **Contact:** Rose Mary Stutzman, editor. **80% freelance written.** Monthly magazine for children ages 4-9. "*Story Friends* is planned to nurture faith development in 4-9 year olds." Estab. 1905. Circ. 7,000. **Pays on acceptance.** Publishes ms an average of 1 year after acceptance. Byline given. Not copyrighted. Buys one-time, second serial (reprint) rights. Submit seasonal material 6 months in advance. Accepts simultaneous submissions. Responds in 2 months to queries. Sample copy for 9 × 12 SAE and 2 first-class stamps. Writer's guidelines for #10 SASE.

Nonfiction: How-to (craft ideas for young children), photo feature. **Buys 20 mss/year.** Length: 300-500 words. **Pays 3-5¢/word.**

Reprints: Send photocopy with rights for sale noted and information about when and where the material previously appeared. Pays 100% of amount paid for an original article.

Photos: Send photos with submission. Reviews 8½ × 11 b&w prints. Buys one-time rights. Offers $20-25/photo. Model releases required.

Fiction: Buys 50 mss/year. Send complete ms. Length: 300-800 words. **Pays 3-5¢/word.**

Poetry: Traditional. **Buys 20 poems/year.** Length: 4-16 lines. **Pays $10/poem.**

Tips: "Send stories that children from a variety of ethnic backgrounds can relate to; stories that deal with experiences similar to all children. Send stories with a humorous twist. We're also looking for well-planned puzzles that challenge and promote reading readiness."

$ $🖼 TURTLE MAGAZINE FOR PRESCHOOL KIDS, Children's Better Health Institute, P.O. Box 567, Indianapolis IN 46206-0567. (317)636-8881. Fax: (317)684-8094. Website: www.turtlemag.com. **Contact:** (Ms.) Terry Harshman, editor. **40% freelance written.** Bimonthly (monthly March, June, September, December) magazine. General interest, interactive magazine with the purpose of helping preschoolers develop healthy minds and bodies. Circ. 300,000. Pays on publication. Byline given. Buys all rights. Submit seasonal material 8 months in advance. Responds in 3 months to queries. Sample copy for $1.75. Writer's guidelines for #10 SASE.

● May hold mss for up to 1 year before acceptance/publication.

Nonfiction: "We use very simple science experiments. These should be pretested. We also publish simple, healthful recipes." **Buys 20 mss/year.** Length: 100-300 words. **Pays up to 22¢/word.**

Fiction: "Not buying much fiction right now except for rebus stories. All material should have a health or fitness slant. We no longer buy stories about 'generic' turtles because we now have PokeyToes, our own trade-marked turtle character. All should 'move along' and lend themselves well to illustration. Writing should be energetic, enthusiastic and creative—like preschoolers themselves. No queries, please." **Buys 20 mss/year.** Length: 150-300 words. **Pays up to 22¢/word.**

Poetry: "We're especially looking for action rhymes to foster creative movement in preschoolers. We also use short verse on our inside front cover and back cover."

Tips: "We are looking for more easy science experiments and simple, nonfiction health articles. We are trying to include more material for our youngest readers. Stories must be age-appropriate for two- to five-year-olds, entertaining and written from a healthy lifestyle perspective."

$ $ U.S. KIDS, A Weekly Reader Magazine, Children's Better Health Institute, P.O. Box 567, Indianapolis IN 46206-0567. (317)636-8881. **Contact:** Daniel Lee, editor. **50% freelance written.** Magazine published 8 times/year featuring "kids doing extraordinary things, especially activities related to health, sports, the arts, interesting hobbies, the environment, computers, etc." Estab. 1987. Circ. 230,000. Pays on publication. Publishes ms an average of 4 months after acceptance. Byline given. Buys all rights. Editorial lead time 6 months. Submit seasonal material 6 months in advance. Responds in 4 months to mss. Sample copy for $2.95 or online. Writer's guidelines for #10 SASE.

● *U.S. Kids* is being re-targeted for a younger audience.

Nonfiction: Especially interested in articles with a health/fitness angle. General interest, how-to, interview/profile, science, kids using computers, multicultural. **Buys 16-24 mss/year.** Send complete ms. Length: 400 words maximum. **Pays up to 25¢/word.**

Photos: State availability with submission. Reviews contact sheets, negatives, transparencies, color photocopies or prints. Buys one-time rights. Negotiates payment individually. Captions, identification of subjects, model releases required.

Columns/Departments: Real Kids (kids doing interesting things); Fit Kids (sports, healthy activities); Computer Zone. Length: 300-400 words. Send complete ms. **Pays up to 25¢/word.**

Fiction: Buys very little fictional material. **Buys 1-2 mss/year.** Send complete ms. Length: 400 words. **Pays up to 25¢/word.**

Poetry: Light verse, traditional, kid's humorous, health/fitness angle. **Buys 6-8 poems/year.** Submit maximum 6 poems. Length: 8-24 lines. **Pays $25-50.**

Fillers: Facts, newsbreaks, short humor, puzzles, games, activities. Length: 200-500 words. **Pays 25¢/word.**

Tips: "We are re-targeting magazine for first-, second-, and third-graders and looking for fun and informative articles on activities and hobbies of interest to younger kids. Special emphasis on fitness, sports and health. Availability of good photos a plus."

Ⓝ $ $🖼 WILD OUTDOOR WORLD (W.O.W.), Rocky Mountain Elk Foundation, P.O. Box 1329, Helena MT 59624. (406)449-1335. Fax: (406)449-9197. E-mail: wowgirl@qwest.net. **Contact:** Carolyn Zieg Cunningham, editorial director. **75% freelance written.** Magazine published 5 times/year covering North American wildlife for children ages 8-12. "*W.O.W.* emphasizes the conservation of North American wildlife and habitat. Articles reflect sound principles of ecology and environmental education. It stresses the 'web of life,' nature's balance and the importance of habitat." Estab. 1993. Circ. 150,000. **Pays on acceptance.** Publishes ms an average of 18 months after acceptance. Byline given. Buys first North American serial, electronic rights. Editorial lead time 4 months. Submit seasonal material 8 months in advance. Accepts queries by mail, e-mail, fax. Accepts simultaneous submissions. Responds in 2 months to queries. Sample copy for 9 × 12 SAE and 3 first-class stamps. Writer's guidelines for #10 SASE.

O➞ Break in with scientific accuracy, strong habitat focus; both educational and fun to read.

Nonfiction: Looking for life histories and habitat needs of wild animals. How-to (children's outdoor-related projects, camping, hiking, other healthy outdoor pursuits), interview/profile, personal experience. No anthropomorphism, no domestic animal stories. **Buys 24-30 mss/year.** Query. Length: 600-850 words. **Pays $100-300 maximum.**

Photos: *No unsolicited photos.* State availability with submission. Reviews 35mm transparencies. Buys one-time rights. Offers $50-250/photo. Captions, identification of subjects, model releases required.

Columns/Departments: Making a Difference (kids' projects that improve their environment and surrounding habitat), 500 words; Short Stuff (short items, puzzles, games, interesting facts about nature), 300 words. **Buys 25-30 mss/year.** Query. **Pays $50-100.**

Fillers: Facts. **Buys 15-20/year.** Length: 300 words maximum. **Pays $50-100.**

Tips: "Because our publisher is a nonprofit whose mission is to conserve habitat for wildlife, we look for a gentle conservation/habitat/outdoor ethics message. Stories should be scientifically accurate because the magazine is used in many classrooms. We also look for a hopeful, light-hearted, fun style."

$ ⚏ WONDER TIME, 6401 The Paseo Blvd., Kansas City MO 64131-1213. (816)333-7000. Fax: (816)333-4439. E-mail: psmits@nazarene.org. **Contact:** Pamela Smits. **50% freelance written.** Published by WordAction for children ages 6-8. Correlates to the weekly Sunday school lesson. Pays on publication. Publishes ms an average of 1 year after acceptance. Byline given. Buys all rights to reuse and for curriculum assignments rights. Accepts queries by mail, fax. Responds in 2 months to queries. Sample copy and writer's guidelines for 9 × 12 SAE with 2 first-class stamps.

Fiction: Uses true-to-life stories teaching honesty, truthfulness, kindness, helpfulness or other important spiritual truths; parent helps and growth tips (i.e., suggestions for family growth development based upon a theme), family activities. **Buys 40 mss/year.** Length: 100-200 words. **Pays $20 on publication.**

Tips: "Any stories that allude to church doctrine must be in keeping with Wesleyan beliefs. Avoid fantasy, precocious children or personification of animals. Write on a first to second grade readability level."

LITERARY & "LITTLE"

Fiction, poetry, essays, book reviews and scholarly criticism comprise the content of the magazines listed in this section. Some are published by colleges and universities, and many are regional in focus.

Everything about "little" literary magazines is different than other consumer magazines. Most carry few or no ads, and many do not seek them. Circulations under 1,000 are common. And sales often come more from the purchase of sample copies than from the newsstand.

The magazines listed in this section cannot compete with the pay rates and exposure of the high-circulation general interest magazines also publishing fiction and poetry. But most "little" literary magazines don't try. They are more apt to specialize in publishing certain kinds of fiction or poetry: traditional, experimental, works with a regional sensibility, or the fiction and poetry of new and younger writers. For that reason, and because fiction and poetry vary so widely in style, writers should *always* invest in the most recent copies of the magazines they aspire to publish in.

Many "little" literary magazines pay contributors only in copies of the issues in which their works appear. *Writer's Market* lists only those that pay their contributors in cash. However, *Novel & Short Story Writer's Market* includes nonpaying fiction markets, and has in-depth information about fiction techniques and markets. The same is true of *Poet's Market* for nonpaying poetry markets (both books are published by Writer's Digest Books). Many literary agents and book editors regularly read these magazines in search of literary voices not found in mainstream writing. There are also more literary opportunities listed in the Contests and Awards section.

$ AFRICAN AMERICAN REVIEW, Indiana State University, Department of English, Terre Haute IN 47809. (812)237-3267. Fax: (812)237-3156. E-mail: asdeco@isugw.indstate.edu. Website: web.indstate.edu/artsci/AAR. Managing Editor: Connie LeCompte. **Contact:** Joe Weixlmann, editor. **65% freelance written.** Quarterly magazine covering African-American literature and culture. "Essays on African-American literature, theater, film, art and culture generally; interviews; poetry and fiction by African-American authors; book reviews." Estab. 1967. Circ. 3,137. Pays on publication. Publishes ms an average of 1 year after acceptance. Byline given. Buys first North American serial rights. Editorial lead time 1 year. Responds in 1 month to queries; 3 months to mss. Sample copy for $7. Writer's guidelines for #10 SASE.

Nonfiction: Essays, interview/profile. **Buys 30 mss/year.** Query. Length: 3,500-6,000 words. **Pays $50-150.** Pays in contributors copies upon request.

Photos: State availability with submission. Offers no additional payment for photos accepted with ms. Captions required.

Fiction: Ethnic. **Buys 4 mss/year.** Send complete ms. Length: 2,500-5,000 words. **Pays $50-150.**

$ AGNI, Dept. WM, Boston University 236 Bay State Rd., Boston, MA 02215. (617)353-7135. Fax: (617)353-7134. E-mail: agni@bu.edu. Website: www.bu.edu/AGNI. **Contact:** Eric Grunwald, managing editor. Biannual magazine. "*AGNI* publishes poetry, fiction and essays. Also regularly publishes translations and is committed to featuring the work of emerging writers. We have published Derek Walcott, Joyce Carol Oates, Sharon Olds, John Updike, Ha Jin, John Keene, Jhumpa Lahiri, Robert Pinsky, and many others." Next reading period is November 1, 2001 to February 1, 2002. Estab. 1972. Circ. 2,000. Pays on publication. Publishes ms an average of 6 months after acceptance. Byline given. Buys first North American serial rights, rights to reprint in *AGNI* anthology (with author's consent). Editorial lead time 1 year. Accepts queries by mail. Accepts simultaneous submissions. Responds in 2 weeks to queries; 4 months to mss. Sample copy for $9 or online. Writer's guidelines for #10 SASE.

Fiction: Short stories. **Buys 6-12 mss/year.** Send complete ms with SASE. **Pays $20-150.**

Poetry: Buys more than 140 poems/year. Submit maximum 5 poems with SASE **Pays $20-150.**

The online magazine carries original content not found in the print edition. Contact: Askold Melnyczuk, online editor.

Tips: "We're looking for extraordinary translations from little-translated languages. It is important to look at a copy of *AGNI* before submitting, to see if your work might be compatible. Please write for guidelines or a sample."

$ $ ALASKA QUARTERLY REVIEW, ESB 208, University of Alaska-Anchorage 3211 Providence Dr., Anchorage AK 99508. (907)786-6916. E-mail: ayaqr@uaa.alaska.edu. Website: www.uaa.alaska.edu/aqr. **Contact:** Ronald Spatz, executive editor. **95% freelance written.** Semiannual magazine publishing fiction, poetry, literary nonfiction and short plays in traditional and experimental styles. Estab. 1982. Circ. 2,200. Honorariums on publication when funding permits. Publishes ms an average of 6 months after acceptance. Byline given. Buys first North American serial rights, upon request, rights will be transferred back to author after publication. Accepts queries by mail, e-mail. Responds in 4 months to queries; 4 months to mss. Sample copy for $6. Writer's guidelines for SASE or online.

● *Alaska Quarterly* reports they are always looking for freelance material and new writers.

Nonfiction: Literary nonfiction: essays and memoirs. **Buys 0-5 mss/year.** Query. Length: 1,000-20,000 words. **Pays $50-200 subject to funding.** Pays in contributor's copies and subscription when funding is limited.

Fiction: Experimental and traditional literary forms. No romance, children's or inspirational/religious. Publishes novel excerpts. **Buys 20-26 mss/year.** Also publishes drama: Experimental and traditional one-act plays. **Buys 0-2 mss/year.** Send complete ms. Length: up to 20,000 words. **Pays $50-200 subject to funding; pays in contributor's copies and subscriptions when funding is limited.**

Poetry: Avant-garde, free verse, traditional. No light verse. **Buys 10-30 poems/year.** Submit maximum 10 poems. **Pays $10-50 subject to availability of funds; pays in contributor's copies and subscriptions when funding is limited.**

The online magazine carries original content not found in the print edition and includes writer's guidelines.

Tips: "All sections are open to freelancers. We rely almost exclusively on unsolicited manuscripts. *AQR* is a nonprofit literary magazine and does not always have funds to pay authors."

$ AMELIA MAGAZINE, Amelia Press, 329 E St., Bakersfield CA 93304. (661)323-4064. Fax: (661)323-5326. E-mail: amelia@lightspeed.net. Website: www.ameliamagazine.net. **Contact:** Frederick A. Raborg, Jr. **100% freelance written.** Receptive to new writers. Eager to work with new/unpublished writers. Quarterly magazine. Publishes the finest poetry and fiction available, along with expert criticism and reviews intended for all interested in contemporary literature. *Amelia* also publishes two separate magazines each year: *Cicada* and *SPSM&H.* Estab. 1983. Circ. 1,750. **Pays on acceptance.** Publishes ms an average of 6 months after acceptance. Byline given. Offers 50% kill fee. Buys first North American serial rights. Submit seasonal material 2 months in advance. Responds in 3 months to mss. Sample copy for $10.95 (includes postage). Writer's guidelines for #10 SASE.

● An eclectic magazine, open to greater variety of styles—especially genre and mainstream stories unsuitable for other literary magazines.

Nonfiction: "Nothing overtly slick in approach. Criticism pieces must have depth; belles lettres must offer important insights into the human scene." Historical/nostalgic (in the form of belles lettres), humor (in fiction or belles lettres), interview/profile (poets and fiction writers), opinion (on poetry and fiction only), personal experience (as it pertains to poetry or fiction in the form of belles lettres), travel (in the form of belles lettres only), Criticism and book reviews of poetry and small press fiction titles. **Buys 8 mss/year.** Send complete ms with SASE. Length: 1,000-2,000 words. **Pays $25.** Sometimes pays expenses of writers on assignment.

Fiction: "We would consider slick fiction of the quality seen in *Esquire* or *Vanity Fair* and more excellent submissions in the genres—science fiction, wit, Gothic horror, traditional romance, stories with complex *raisons d'etre*; avant-garde ought to be truly avant-garde." Adventure, erotica, ethnic, experimental, fantasy, historical, horror, humorous, mainstream, mystery, novel excerpts, science fiction, suspense, western. No pornography ("good erotica is not the same thing"). **Buys 24-36 mss/year.** Send complete ms. Length: 1,000-5,000 words, sometimes longer. **Pays $35 or by arrangement for exceptional work.**

Poetry: "Shorter poems stand the best chance." Avant-garde, free verse, haiku, light verse, traditional. "No patently religious or stereotypical newspaper poetry." **Buys 100-240 poems/year.** Submit maximum 3 poems. Length: 3-100 lines. **Pays $2-25.**

Tips: "*Have something to say* and say it well. If you insist on waving flags or pushing your religion, then do it with subtlety and class. We enjoy a good cry from time to time, too, but sentimentality does not mean we want to see mush. Read our fiction carefully for depth of plot and characterization, then try very hard to improve on it. With the growth of quality in short fiction, we expect to find stories of lasting merit. I also hope to begin seeing more critical essays which, without sacrificing research, demonstrate a more entertaining obliqueness to the style sheets, more 'new journalism' than MLA. In poetry, we also often look for a good 'storyline' so to speak. Above all we want to feel a sense of honesty and value in every piece. No e-mail or fax manuscript submissions."

N $ ANTIETAM REVIEW, 41 S. Potomac, Hagerstown MD 21740-5512. (301)791-3132. Fax: (301)791-3132. E-mail: wcarts@intrepid.net. **Contact:** Cheryl Winger, managing editor. **100% freelance written.** Annual magazine covering fiction (short stories), poetry and b&w photography. Estab. 1982. Circ. 1,500. Pays on publication. Byline given. Accepts queries by mail, phone. Responds in 2 months to queries. Sample copy for $5.25 (back issue), $6.30 (current issue). Writer's guidelines for #10 SASE.

Fiction: Novel excerpts, short stories of a literary quality. No religious, romance, erotica, confession, horror or condensed novels. **Buys 9 mss/year.** Query with published clips or send complete ms. Length: 5,000 words. **Pays $50-100.**

Poetry: Paul Grant. Avant-garde, free verse, traditional. Does not want to see haiku, religious and most rhyme. **Buys 20-25 poems/year.** Submit maximum 5 poems. **Pays $15-25.**

Tips: "Spring annual issue will need fiction, poetry and b&w photography not previously published. Still seeking high quality work from both published and emerging writers. Writers must live in or be native of Maryland, Pennsylvania, Delaware, Virginia, West Virginia or District of Columbia. Also we now have a summer Literary Contest. We consider materials from September 1 through February 1. Offers cash prize and publication in *Antietam Review*."

$ THE ANTIGONISH REVIEW, St. Francis Xavier University, P.O. Box 5000, Antigonish, Nova Scotia B2G 2W5, Canada. (902)867-3962. Fax: (902)867-5563. E-mail: tar@stfx.ca. Managing Editor: Gertrude Sanderson. **Contact:** George Sanderson, editor. **100% freelance written.** Quarterly magazine. Estab. 1970. Circ. 850. Pays on publication. Publishes ms an average of 4 months after acceptance. Byline given. Offers variable kill fee. Rights retained by author. Editorial lead time 4 months. Submit seasonal material 4 months in advance. Accepts queries by mail, e-mail, fax. Responds in 1 month to queries; 4 months to mss. Sample copy for $4 or online. Writer's guidelines for #10 SASE or online.

Nonfiction: Essays, interview/profile, book reviews/articles. No academic pieces. **Buys 15-20 mss/year.** Query. Length: 1,500-5,000 words. **Pays $50-150.**

Fiction: Literary. No erotica. **Buys 35-40 mss/year.** Send complete ms. Length: 500-5,000 words.

Poetry: **Buys 100-125 poems/year.** Submit maximum 5 poems. **Pays in copies.**

Tips: "Send for guidelines and/or sample copy. Send ms with cover letter and SASE with submission."

$ ANTIOCH REVIEW, P.O. Box 148, Yellow Springs OH 45387-0148. **Contact:** Robert S. Fogarty, editor. Quarterly magazine for general, literary and academic audience. Estab. 1941. Circ. 5,100. Pays on publication. Publishes ms an average of 10 months after acceptance. Byline given. Rights revert to author upon publication. Responds in 3 months. Sample copy for $6. Writer's guidelines for #10 SASE.

Nonfiction: "Contemporary articles in the humanities and social sciences, politics, economics, literature and all areas of broad intellectual concern. Somewhat scholarly, but never pedantic in style, eschewing all professional jargon. Lively, distinctive prose insisted upon. We *do not* read simultaneous submissions." Length: 2,000-8,000 words. **Pays $10/ printed page.**

Fiction: "Quality fiction only, distinctive in style with fresh insights into the human condition." No science fiction, fantasy or confessions. **Pays $10/printed page.**

Poetry: "No light or inspirational verse. We do not read poetry May 1-September 1."

$ ARC, Canada's National Poetry Magazine, Arc Poetry Society, Box 7368, Ottawa, Ontario K1L 8E4, Canada. **Contact:** John Barton or Rita Donovan, co-editors. Semiannual magazine featuring poetry, poetry-related articles and criticism. "Our focus is poetry, and Canadian poetry in general, although we do publish writers from elsewhere. We are looking for the best poetry from new and established writers. We often have special issues. SASE for upcoming special issues and contests." Estab. 1978. Circ. 1,000. Pays on publication. Publishes ms an average of 6 months after acceptance. Byline given. Buys one-time rights. Responds in 4 months. Writer's guidelines for #10 SASE.

Nonfiction: Essays, interview/profile, book reviews. Query. Length: 1,000 words. **Pays $30/printed page (Canadian) and 2 copies.**

Photos: Send photos with submission. Buys one-time rights. Pays $300 for 10 photos.

Poetry: Avant-garde, free verse. **Buys 40 poems/year.** Submit maximum 6 poems. **Pays $30/printed page (Canadian).**

Tips: "Please include brief biographical note with submission."

N ✕ **B&A: NEW FICTION**, P.O. Box 702, Station P, Toronto, Ontario M5S 2Y4, Canada. (416)822-8708. E-mail: bloodaphorisms@hotmail.com. **Contact:** Sam Hiyate, publisher. **100% freelance written.** Quarterly magazine covering literary fiction. Estab. 1990. Circ. 2,000. Pays on publication. Publishes ms an average of 6 months after acceptance. Byline given. Buys first North American serial, anthology and electronic rights. Editorial lead time 2 months. Accepts simultaneous submissions. Sample copy for $6 (US). Writer's guidelines for #10 SASE with IRCs.
Fiction: Experimental, novel excerpts. No mystery, sci-fi, poetry. **Buys 20-30 mss/year.** Send complete ms. Length: 500-4,000 words. **Pays $35/printed page.**
Tips: See *B&A: New Fiction*'s annual fiction contest in the Contest and Awards section.

N $ **BELLINGHAM REVIEW**, Signpost Press, Mail Stop 9053, Western Washington University, Bellingham WA 98225. (360)650-4863. E-mail: bhreview@cc.wwu.edu. Website: www.wwu.edu/~bhreview. Editor: Brenda Miller. Managing Editor: Robin Parks. **Contact:** Poetry, Fiction or Creative Nonfiction editor. **100% freelance written.** Semiannual nonprofit magazine. *Bellingham Review* seeks literature of palpable quality; stories, essays and poems that nudge the limits of form, or execute traditional forms exquisitely. Estab. 1974. Circ. 1,500. Pays on publication. Publishes ms an average of 1 year after acceptance. Byline given. Buys first North American serial, one-time rights. Editorial lead time 1 year. Accepts queries by mail. Accepts simultaneous submissions. Responds in 2 months to mss. Sample copy for $7. Writer's guidelines free for #10 SASE or online.
Nonfiction: Nonfiction Editor. Essays, general interest, humor, interview/profile, personal experience. Does not want anything non-literary. **Buys 6 mss/year.** Send complete ms. Length: 9,000 words maximum. **Pays $20/published page, as funds allow. Also pays with contributor copies or other premiums.**
Fiction: Fiction Editor. No restrictions. Does not want anything non-literary. **Buys 6 mss/year.** Send complete ms. Length: 9,000 words maximum. **Pays $20/published page with a $50 minimum, as funds allow.**
Poetry: Poetry Editor. No restrictions. **Buys 30 poems/year.** Submit maximum 3 poems. Length: No restrictions. **Pays $20/published page with a $50 maximum.**
Tips: "Open submission period is from October 1 through February 1. Manuscripts arriving between February 2 and September 30 will be returned unread."

$ **BLACK WARRIOR REVIEW**, P.O. Box 862936, Tuscaloosa AL 35486-0027. (205)348-4518. Website: www.webdelsol.com/bwr. **90% freelance written.** Semiannual magazine of fiction, poetry, essays and reviews. Estab. 1974. Circ. 2,000. Pays on publication. Publishes ms an average of 6 months after acceptance. Byline given. Buys first rights. Responds in 2 weeks to queries; 3 months to mss. Sample copy for $8. Writer's guidelines for #10 SASE or online.
● Consistently excellent magazine. Placed stories and poems in recent *Best American Short Stories*, *Best American Poetry* and *Pushcart Prize* anthologies.
Nonfiction: Ander Monson, editor. Interview/profile, book reviews, literary/personal essays. **Buys 5 mss/year.** No queries; send complete ms. **Pays up to $100 and 2 contributor's copies.**
Fiction: Tommy Zurhellen, fiction editor. Publishes novel excerpts if under contract to be published. One story/chapter per envelope, please. **Buys 12 mss/year. Pays up to $150 and 2 contributor's copies.**
Poetry: Don Gilliland, poetry editor. **Buys 35 poems/year.** Submit maximum 3-6 poems. **Pays up to $75 and 2 contributor's copies.**
Tips: "Read the *BWR* before submitting; editors change each year. Send us your best work. Submissions of photos and/or artwork is encouraged. We sometimes choose unsolicited photos/artwork for the cover. Address all submissions to the appropriate genre editor."

$ $ ✕ **BOULEVARD**, Opojaz, Inc., 4579 Laclede Ave., #332, St. Louis MO 63108-2103. (314)361-2986. Fax: (314)361-5515. Website: www.richardburgin.com. **Contact:** Richard Burgin, editor. **100% freelance written.** Triannual magazine covering fiction, poetry and essays. "*Boulevard* is a diverse literary magazine presenting original creative work by well-known authors, as well as by writers of exciting promise." Estab. 1985. Circ. 3,500. Pays on publication. Publishes ms an average of 9 months after acceptance. Byline given. Offers no kill fee. Buys first North American serial rights. Accepts queries by mail, phone. Accepts simultaneous submissions. Responds in 2 weeks to queries; 2 months to mss. Sample copy for $7. Writer's guidelines for #10 SASE.
○➝ Break in with "a touching, intelligent and original story, poem or essay."
Nonfiction: Book excerpts, essays, interview/profile, opinion, photo feature. "No pornography, science fiction, children's stories or westerns." **Buys 10 mss/year.** Send complete ms. Length: 8,000 words. **Pays $50-250 (sometimes higher).**
Fiction: Confessions, experimental, mainstream, novel excerpts. "We do not want erotica, science fiction, romance, western or children's stories." **Buys 20 mss/year.** Send complete ms. Length: 8,000 words. **Pays $150-300.**
Poetry: Avant-garde, free verse, haiku, traditional. "Do not send us light verse." **Buys 80 poems/year.** Submit maximum 5 poems. Length: 200 lines. **$25-250 (sometimes higher).**
Tips: "Read the magazine first. The work *Boulevard* publishes is generally recognized as among the finest in the country. We continue to seek more good literary or cultural essays. Send only your best work."

N $ $ **BRICK, A Literary Journal**, Brick, Box 537, Station Q, Toronto, Ontario M4T 2M5, Canada. E-mail: info@brickmag.com. Website: www.brickmag.com. Editor: Linda Spalding. **Contact:** Michael Redhill, managing/contributing editor. **90% freelance written.** Semiannual magazine covering literature and the arts. "We publish literary nonfiction of a very high quality on a range of arts and culture subjects." Estab. 1975. Circ. 3,000. Pays on publication.

Publishes ms an average of 3 months after acceptance. Byline given. Buys first North American serial, one-time rights. Editorial lead time 5 months. Accepts queries by mail, e-mail. Responds in 6 weeks to queries; 4 months to mss. Sample copy for $10 or online. Writer's guidelines for free, online or by e-mail.

Nonfiction: Essays, historical/nostalgic, interview/profile, opinion, travel. No fiction, poetry, personal real-life experience or book reviews. **Buys 30-40 mss/year.** Send complete ms. Length: 250-6,000 words. **Pays $75-500 (Canadian).**

Photos: State availability with submission. Reviews transparencies, prints, gif/jpeg files. Buys one-time rights. Offers $25-50/photo.

Tips: "Brick is interested in polished work by writers who are widely read and in touch with contemporary culture. The magazine is serious, but not fusty. We like to feel the writer's personality in the piece, too."

$ $ THE CAPILANO REVIEW, The Capilano Press Society, 2055 Purcell Way, North Vancouver, British Columbia V7J 3H5, Canada. Fax: (604)990-7837. E-mail: tcr@capcollege.bc.ca. Website: www.capcollege.bc.ca/dept/TCR/tcr. **Contact:** Ryan Knighton, editor. **100% freelance written.** "Triannual visual and literary arts magazine that publishes only what the editors consider to be the very best fiction, poetry, drama or visual art being produced. *TCR* editors are interested in fresh, original work that stimulates and challenges readers. Over the years, the magazine has developed a reputation for pushing beyond the boundaries of traditional art and writing. We are interested in work that is new in concept and in execution." Estab. 1972. Circ. 900. Pays on publication. Byline given. Buys first North American serial rights. Accepts queries by mail. Responds in 1 month to queries; 5 months to mss. Sample copy for $9 or online. Writer's guidelines for #10 SASE with IRC or Canadian stamps or online.

Fiction: Novel excerpts (previously unpublished only), literary. Query by mail or send complete ms with SASE and Canadian postage or IRCs. **Buys 10-15 mss/year.** Length: 6,000 words. **Pays $50-200.**

Poetry: Avant-garde, free verse. **Buys 40 poems/year.** Submit maximum 5-10 poems with SASE. **Pays $50-200.**

$ THE CHARITON REVIEW, Truman State University, Kirksville MO 63501-9915. (660)785-4499. Fax: (660)785-7486. **Contact:** Jim Barnes, editor. **100% freelance written.** Semiannual (fall and spring) magazine covering contemporary fiction, poetry, translation and book reviews. Circ. 600. Pays on publication. Publishes ms an average of 6 months after acceptance. Byline given. Buys first North American serial rights. Accepts queries by mail. Responds in 1 week to queries; 1 month to mss. Sample copy for $5 and 7×10 SAE with 4 first-class stamps.

Nonfiction: Essays (essay reviews of books). **Buys 2-5 mss/year.** Send complete ms. Length: 1,000-5,000 words. **Pays $15.**

Fiction: Ethnic, experimental, mainstream, novel excerpts, traditional. "We are not interested in slick or sick material." **Buys 6-10 mss/year.** Send complete ms. Length: 1,000-6,000 words. **Pays $5/page (up to $50).**

Poetry: Avant-garde, traditional. **Buys 50-55 poems/year.** Submit maximum 5 poems. Length: Open. **Pays $5/page.**

Tips: "Read *Chariton*. Know the difference between good literature and bad. Know what magazine might be interested in your work. We are not a trendy magazine. We publish only the best. All sections are open to freelancers. Know your market or you are wasting your time—and mine. Do *not* write for guidelines; the only guideline is excellence."

N: $ THE CHATTAHOOCHEE REVIEW, Georgia Perimeter College, 2101 Womack Rd., Dunwoody GA 30338-4497. (770)551-3019. Website: www.gpc.peachnet.edu/~twadley/cr/index.htm. Editor: Lawrence Hetrick. **Contact:** Jo Ann Adkins, managing editor. Quarterly magazine. "We publish a number of Southern writers, but *Chattahoochee Review* is not by design a regional magazine. All themes, forms and styles are considered as long as they impact the whole person: heart, mind, intuition and imagination." Estab. 1980. Circ. 1,350. Pays on publication. Publishes ms an average of 3 months after acceptance. Byline sometimes given. Buys first rights. Accepts queries by mail, phone. Responds in 2 weeks to queries; 4 months to mss. Sample copy for $6. Writer's guidelines for #10 SASE.

Nonfiction: "We look for distinctive, honest personal essays and creative nonfiction of any kind, including the currently popular memoiristic narrative. We publish interviews with writers of all kinds: literary, academic, journalistic, and popular. We also review selected current offerings in fiction, poetry, and nonfiction, including works on photography and the visual arts, with an emphasis on important southern writers and artisits. We do not often, if ever, publish technical, critical, theoretical, or scholarly work about literature although we are interested in essays written for general readers about writers, their careers, and their work." Essays (interviews with authors, reviews). **Buys 10 mss/year.** Send complete ms. Length: 5,000 words maximum. **Pays $15/page for nonfiction and interviews; $50 for reviews; $100 for review essays.**

Photos: State availability with submission. Buys one-time rights. Offers $25. Negotiates payment individually. Identification of subjects required.

Fiction: Accepts all subject matter except science fiction and romance. **Buys 12 mss/year.** Send complete ms. Length: 6,000 words maximum. **Pays $20/page.**

Poetry: Avant-garde, free verse, haiku, light verse, traditional. **Buys 60 poems/year.** Submit maximum 5 poems. **Pays $50/poem.**

$ CHELSEA, Chelsea Associates, P.O. Box 773 Cooper Station, New York NY 10276. **Contact:** Richard Foerster, editor. **70% freelance written.** Semiannual magazine. "We stress style, variety, originality. No special biases or requirements. Flexible attitudes, eclectic material. We take an active interest, as always, in cross-cultural exchanges, superior translations, and are leaning toward cosmopolitan, interdisciplinary techniques, but maintain no strictures against traditional modes." Estab. 1958. Circ. 1,800. Pays on publication. Publishes ms an average of 6 months after acceptance. Byline given. Buys first North American serial rights. Accepts queries by mail. Responds in 6 months to mss. Sample copy for $6. Writer's guidelines for #10 SASE.

• *Chelsea* also sponsors fiction and poetry contests. Send SASE for guidelines.

Nonfiction: Essays, book reviews (query first with sample). **Buys 6 mss/year.** Send complete ms with SASE. Length: 6,000 words. **Pays $15/page.**

Fiction: Mainstream, novel excerpts, literary. **Buys 12 mss/year.** Send complete ms. Length: 5,000-6,000 words. **Pays $15/page.**

Poetry: Avant-garde, free verse, traditional. **Buys 60-75 poems/year. Pays $15/page.**

Tips: "We will begin reviewing unsolicited manuscripts after October 1, 2001. We only accept written correspondence. We are looking for more super translations, first-rate fiction and work by writers of color. No need to query; submit complete manuscript. We suggest writers look at a recent issue of *Chelsea*."

CHICKEN SOUP FOR THE SOUL, 101 Stories to Open the Heart and Rekindle the Spirit, Chicken Soup for the Soul Enterprises, Inc., P.O. Box 30880, Santa Barbara CA 93130. (805)682-6311. Fax: (805)563-2945. E-mail: nautio@chickensoup.com. Website: www.chickensoup.com. Managing Editor: Heather McNamara. **Contact:** Nancy Mitchell-Autio, acquisitions editor. **95% freelance written.** Paperback with 8-12 publications/year featuring inspirational, heartwarming, uplifting short stories. Estab. 1993. Circ. 37 titles; 52 million books in print. Pays on publication. Publishes ms an average of 8 months after acceptance. Byline given. Buys all rights. Accepts queries by mail, e-mail, fax. Accepts simultaneous submissions. Responds upon consideration to queries. Writer's guidelines online.

Nonfiction: Humor, inspirational, personal experience, religious. Special issues: Traveling, sisterhood, mother-daughter stories, Christian teen, Christmas stories, stories by and/or about men, on love, kindness, parenting, family, Nascar racing, athletes, teachers, fishing, adoption, volunteers. No sermons, essays, eulogies, term papers, journal entries, political or controversial issues. **Buys 1,000 mss/year.** Send complete ms. Length: 300-1,200 words. **Pays $300.**

Reprints: Accepts previously published submissions.

Poetry: Traditional. No controversial poetry. **Buys 50 poems/year.** Submit maximum 5 poems. **Pays $300.**

Fillers: Anecdotes, facts, gags to be illustrated by cartoonist, short humor. **Buys 50/year. Pays $300.**

Tips: "We prefer submissions to be sent via our website at www.chickensoup.com. Print submissions should be on 8½×11 paper in 12 point Times New Roman font. Type author's contact information appears on the first page of story. Stories are to be nonfiction. No anonymous or author unknown submissions are accepted. We do not return submissions."

$ CICADA, Amelia Magazine, 329 E St., Bakersfield CA 93304. (661)323-4064. E-mail: amelia@lightspeed.net. Website: www.ameliamagazine.net. **Contact:** Frederick A. Raborg, Jr., editor. **100% freelance written.** Quarterly magazine covering Oriental fiction and poetry (haiku, etc.). "Our readers expect the best haiku and related poetry forms we can find. Our readers circle the globe and know their subjects. We include fiction, book reviews and articles related to the forms or to the Orient." Estab. 1984. Circ. 800. Pays on publication. Publishes ms an average of 6 months after acceptance. Byline given. Offers 50% kill fee. Buys first North American serial rights. Editorial lead time 2 months. Submit seasonal material 3 months in advance. Accepts simultaneous submissions. Responds in 2 weeks to queries; 3 months to mss. Sample copy for $6. Writer's guidelines for #10 SASE.

Nonfiction: Essays, general interest, historical/nostalgic, humor, interview/profile, opinion, personal experience, travel. **Buys 1-3 mss/year.** Send complete ms. Length: 500-2,500 words. **Pays $10 for assigned articles.**

Photos: Send photos with submission. Reviews 5×7 or 8×10 b&w prints. Buys one-time rights. Offers $10-25/photo. Model releases required.

Fiction: Adventure, erotica, ethnic, experimental, fantasy, historical, horror, humorous, mainstream, mystery, romance, science fiction, slice-of-life vignettes, suspense. **Buys 4 mss/year.** Send complete ms. Length: 500-2,500 words. **Pays $10-20.**

Poetry: **Buys 400 poems/year.** Submit maximum 12 poems. Length: 1-50 lines. **Pays 3 best of issue poets $10.**

Fillers: Anecdotes, short humor. **Buys 1-4/year.** Length: 25-500 words. **Pays nothing for fillers.**

Tips: "Writers should understand the limitations of contemporary Japanese forms particularly. We also use poetry based on other Asian ethnicities and on the South Seas ethnicities. Don't be afraid to experiment within the forms. Be professional in approach and presentation."

$ CIMARRON REVIEW, Oklahoma State University, 205 Morrill Hall, OSU, Stillwater OK 74078-0135. (405)744-9476. E-mail: cimarronreview@hotmail.com. **Contact:** E.P. Walkiewicz, editor. **85% freelance written.** Quarterly magazine "We publish short fiction, poetry, and essays of serious literary quality by writers often published, seldom published and previously unpublished. We have no bias with respect to subject matter, form (traditional or experimental), or theme. Though we appeal to a general audience, many of our readers are writers themselves or members of a university community." Estab. 1967. Circ. 500. Pays on publication. Publishes ms an average of 1 year after acceptance. Byline given. Buys first North American serial rights. Accepts queries by mail. Responds in 3 months to mss. Sample copy for $5 and 7×10 SASE.

Nonfiction: Essays, general interest, historical/nostalgic, interview/profile, opinion, personal experience, travel, Literature and arts. "We are not interested in highly subjective personal reminiscences; obscure or arcane articles; or short, light 'human interest' pieces." **Buys 9-12 mss/year.** Send complete ms. Length: 1,000-7,500 words. **Pays $50 plus one-year subscription.**

Fiction: Mainstream, novel excerpts. No juvenile or genre fiction. **Buys 12-17 mss/year.** Send complete ms. Length: 1,250-7,000 words. **Pays $50.**

Poetry: Free verse, traditional. No haiku, light verse or religious poems. **Buys 55-70 poems/year.** Submit maximum 6 poems.

Tips: "For prose, submit legible, double-spaced typescript with name and address on manuscript. Enclose SASE and brief cover letter. For poetry, same standards apply, but single-spaced is conventional. Be familiar with high quality, contemporary writing. Evaluate your own work cafefully."

N $ COLORADO REVIEW, Center for Literary Publishing, Dept. of English, Colorado State University, Fort Collins CO 80523. (970)491-5449. E-mail: creview@colostate.edu. Website: www.coloradoreview.com. Managing Editor: Stephanie G'Schwind. **Contact:** David Milofsky, editor. Literary magazine published 3 times/year. Estab. 1972. Circ. 1,300. Pays on publication. Publishes ms an average of 1 year after acceptance. Byline given. Buys first North American serial rights. Editorial lead time 1 year. Accepts queries by mail. Responds in 2 months to mss. Sample copy for $10. Writer's guidelines for #10 SASE.

Nonfiction: Stephanie G'Schwind, managing editor. Personal essays. **Buys 3-5 mss/year.** Send complete ms. **Pays $5/page.**

Fiction: Short fiction. No genre fiction. **Buys 15-20 mss/year.** Send complete ms. **Pays $5/page.**

Poetry: Don Revell or Jorie Graham, poetry editors. Considers poetry of any style. **Buys 60-100 poems/year. Pays $5/page.**

Tips: Manuscripts are read from September 1 to April 30. Manuscripts recieved between May 1 and August 30 will be returned unread.

$ $ ☒ CONFRONTATION, A Literary Journal, Long Island University, Brookville NY 11548. (516)299-2720. Fax: (516)299-2735. E-mail: mtucker@liu.edu. Assistant to Editor: Michael Hartnett. **Contact:** Martin Tucker, editor-in-chief. **75% freelance written.** Semiannual magazine. "We are eclectic in our taste. Excellence of style is our dominant concern." Estab. 1968. Circ. 2,000. Pays on publication. Publishes ms an average of 1 year after acceptance. Byline given. Offers kill fee. Buys first North American serial, first, one-time, all rights. Accepts queries by mail, e-mail, phone. Accepts simultaneous submissions. Responds in 3 weeks to queries; 2 months to mss. Sample copy for $3.

Nonfiction: Essays, personal experience. **Buys 15 mss/year.** Send complete ms. Length: 1,500-5,000 words. **Pays $100-300 for assigned articles; $15-300 for unsolicited articles.**

Photos: State availability with submission. Buys one-time rights. Offers no additional payment for photos accepted with ms.

Fiction: Jonna Semeiks. "We judge on quality, so genre is open." Experimental, mainstream, novel excerpts, slice-of-life vignettes. **Buys 60-75 mss/year.** Send complete ms. Length: 6,000 words. **Pays $25-250.**

Poetry: Michael Hartnett. Avant-garde, free verse, haiku, light verse, traditional. **Buys 60-75 poems/year.** Submit maximum 6 poems. Length: Open. **Pays $10-100.**

Tips: "Most open to fiction and poetry. Study our magazine."

N $ THE CONNECTICUT POETRY REVIEW, The Connecticut Poetry Review Press, P.O. Box 818, Stonington CT 06378. Managing Editor: Harley More. **Contact:** J. Claire White. **60% freelance written.** Annual magazine covering poetry/literature. Estab. 1981. Circ. 500. **Pays on acceptance.** Byline sometimes given. Buys first rights. Editorial lead time 4 months. Submit seasonal material 4 months in advance. Accepts queries by mail. Responds in 1 month to queries; 3 months to mss. Sample copy for $3.50 and #10 SASE. Writer's guidelines for #10 SASE.

Nonfiction: Book excerpts, essays. **Buys 18 mss/year.**

Fiction: Experimental.

Poetry: Avant-garde, free verse, haiku, traditional. No light verse. **Buys 20-30 poems/year.** Submit maximum 4 poems. Length: 3-25 lines. **Pays $5-10.**

N $ CREATIVE NONFICTION, Creative Nonfiction Foundation, 5501 Walnut St., Suite 202, Pittsburgh PA 15232. (412)688-0304. Fax: (412)683-9173. E-mail: info@creativenonfiction.org. Website: www.creativenonfiction.org. Managing Editor: Leslie Aizenman. **Contact:** Lee Gutkind, editor. **100% freelance written.** Magazine published 3 times/year. "*Creative Nonfiction* is the first journal to focus exclusively upon the genre of creative nonfiction. It publishes personal essay, memoir and literary journalism on a broad range of subjects. Interviews with prominent writers and commentary about the genre also appear on its pages." Estab. 1993. Circ. 4,000. Pays on publication. Publishes ms an average of 1 year after acceptance. Byline given. Buys all rights. Editorial lead time 3 months. Accepts queries by mail, e-mail, fax, phone. Accepts simultaneous submissions. Responds in 3 weeks to queries; 6 months to mss. Sample copy for $10. Writer's guidelines online or by e-mail.

Nonfiction: Book excerpts, essays, interview/profile, personal experience, reviews of books. Does not want poetry, fiction, self-involved narratives that do not have larger meaning. **Buys 30 mss/year.** Send complete ms. Length: 5,000 words maximum. **Pays $10/page—more if grant money available for assigned articles.**

Tips: "Points to remember when submitting to *Creative Nonfiction:* strong reportage; well-written prose, attentive to language, rich with detail and distinctive voice; an informational quality or 'teaching element' offering the reader something to learn; a compelling, focused, sustained narrative that's well-structured, makes sense, and conveys a meaning. Manuscripts will not be accepted via fax."

N $ DESCANT, Descant Arts & Letters Foundation, P.O. Box 314, Station P, Toronto, Ontario M5S 2S8, Canada. (416)593-2557. E-mail: descant@web.net. Website: www.descant.on.ca. Editor: Karen Mulhallen. **Contact:** Nathan Whitlock, managing editor. Quarterly journal. Estab. 1970. Circ. 1,200. Pays on publication. Publishes ms an average of 16 months after acceptance. Editorial lead time 4 months. Accepts queries by mail, e-mail. Sample copy for $8. Writer's guidelines for #10 SASE.
Nonfiction: Book excerpts, essays, historical/nostalgic, interview/profile, personal experience, photo feature, travel. Query or send complete ms. **Pays $100 honorarium plus one-year subscription.**
Photos: State availability with submission. Reviews contact sheets, prints. Buys one-time rights. Offers no additional payment for photos accepted with ms. Send complete ms. **Pays $100.**
Poetry: Free verse, light verse, traditional. Submit maximum 10 poems.
Tips: "Familiarize yourself with our magazine before submitting."

$ $ $ DOUBLETAKE, 55 Davis Square, Somerville MA 02144. (617)591-9389. Fax: (617)625-6478. Website: www.doubletakemagazine.org. **Contact:** Fiction Editor. Pays on publication. Byline given. Buys first North American serial rights. Accepts simultaneous submissions. Responds in 3 months to mss. Sample copy for $12. Writer's guidelines for #10 SASE.
Fiction: "We accept realistic fiction in all of its variety. We look for stories with a strong, narrative voice and an urgency in the writing." **Buys 12 mss/year.** Send complete ms. Length: No preferred length. **Pays competitively.**
◨ The online magazine carries original content not found in the print edition and includes writer's guidelines.
Tips: "*Doubletake* looks for writing distinguished by economy, directness, authenticity and heart."

$ DREAMS & VISIONS, New Frontiers in Christian Fiction, Skysong Press, 35 Peter St. S., Orillia Ontario L3V 5A8, Canada. (705)329-1770. Fax: (705)329-1770. E-mail: skysong@bconnex.net. Website: www.bconnex.net/~skysong. **Contact:** Steve Stanton, editor. **100% freelance written.** Semiannual magazine. "Innovative literary fiction for adult Christian readers." Estab. 1988. Circ. 200. Pays on publication. Publishes ms an average of 1 year after acceptance. Byline given. Buys first North American serial, second serial (reprint) rights. Editorial lead time 1 year. Accepts queries by mail, e-mail. Accepts simultaneous submissions. Responds in 6 weeks to queries; 6 months to mss. Sample copy for $4.95. Writer's guidelines for #10 SASE or online.
Fiction: Experimental, fantasy, humorous, mainstream, mystery, novel excerpts, religious, science fiction, slice-of-life vignettes. "We do not publish stories that glorify violence or perversity." **Buys 10 mss/year.** Send complete ms. Length: 2,000-6,000 words. **Pays ½¢/word.**

$ DREAMS OF DECADENCE, P.O. Box 2988, Radford VA 24143-2988. (540)763-2925. Fax: (540)763-2924. E-mail: dreamsofdecadence@dnapublications.com. Website: www.dnapublications.com/dreams. **Contact:** Angela Kessler, editor. Quarterly magazine featuring vampire fiction and poetry. Pays on publication. Publishes ms an average of 6 months after acceptance. Buys first North American serial rights. Accepts simultaneous submissions. Responds in 1 month to queries; 1 month to mss. Sample copy for $5. Writer's guidelines for #10 SASE or online.
Fiction: "I like elegant prose with a Gothic feel. The emphasis is on dark fantasy rather than horror. No vampire feeds, vampire has sex, someone becomes a vampire pieces." **Buys 30-40 mss/year.** Send complete ms. Length: 1,000-15,000 words. **1-5¢/word.**
Poetry: "Looking for all forms; however, the less horrific and the more explicitly vampiric a poem is, the more likely it is to be accepted." **Pays $3/short poem; $5/long poem; $20/featured poet.**
Tips: "We look for atmospheric, well-written stories with original ideas, not rehashes."

$ ◨ 1812, A Magazine of New Writing & the Arts, New Writing, Box 1812, Amherst NY 14226-7812. E-mail: 1812@newwriting.com. Website: www.newwriting.com. Managing Editor: Richard Lynch. **Contact:** Sam Meade, co-editor. **98% freelance written.** Annual magazine. "*1812* is a magazine for new writers, new writing and new ways. Hopefully a war of sorts, a revolution and attempt to change the old guard." Estab. 1989. Pays on publication. Publishes ms an average of 6 months after acceptance. Byline given. Not copyrighted. Buys electronic rights. Editorial lead time 4 months. Accepts queries by mail, e-mail. Accepts simultaneous submissions. Responds in 1 month to queries; 4 months to mss. Sample copy and writer's guidelines free or online.
Nonfiction: Essays, how-to, interview/profile (unusual/philosophy writing associated). "No static prose." **Buys 1 mss/year.** Send complete ms. Length: 500 words. **Pays $50.**
Photos: State availability with submission. Reviews 35mm transparencies. Offers no additional payment for photos accepted with ms. Captions, identification of subjects, model releases required.
Fiction: Richard Lynch, co-editor. Experimental, mainstream, slice-of-life vignettes, contemporary, literary, new forms. "No death-from-cancer stories, I woke up stories, stories about cars and family trips, stories the writer never read over to edit." **Buys 5 mss/year.** Send complete ms. **Pays $50.**
Poetry: Avant-garde, free verse. "No light verse, love poems, kiss poems, musty poems, poems that rhyme so fluently that they don't mean anything." **Buys 5-10 poems/year.** Submit maximum 4 poems. Length: 3 lines. **Pays $25.**
Tips: "E-mail submissions are becoming popular and they are easy to respond to. Don't send attachments—cut and paste the text. We are looking for interesting writing, not a résumé or list of publications."

N $ EPOCH, Cornell University, 251 Goldwin Smith Hall, Cornell University, Ithaca NY 14853. (607)255-3385. Fax: (607)255-6661. Editor: Michael Koch. **Contact:** Joseph Martin, senior editor. **100% freelance written.** Magazine published 3 times/year. "Well-written literary fiction, poetry, personal essays. Newcomers always welcome. Open to mainstream and avant-garde writing." Estab. 1947. Circ. 1,000. Pays on publication. Byline given. Offers 100% kill fee. Buys first North American serial rights. Editorial lead time 6 months. Submit seasonal material 8 months in advance. Accepts queries by mail. Responds in 2 weeks to queries; 6 weeks to mss. Sample copy for $5. Writer's guidelines for #10 SASE.

Nonfiction: Send complete ms. Essays, interviews. No inspirational. **Buys 6-8 mss/year.** Send complete ms. Length: Open. **Pays $5-10/printed page.**

Photos: Send photos with submission. Reviews contact sheets, transparencies, any size prints. Buys one-time rights. Negotiates payment individually.

Fiction: Experimental, mainstream, novel excerpts, literary short stories. **Buys 25-30 mss/year.** Send complete ms. Length: open. **Pays $5 and up/printed page.**

Poetry: Nancy Vieira Couto. Avant-garde, free verse, haiku, light verse, traditional, all types. **Buys 30-75 poems/year.** Submit maximum 7 poems.

Tips: "Tell your story, speak your poem, straight from the heart. We are attracted to language and to good writing, but we are most interested in what the good writing leads us to, or where."

$ $ EVENT, Douglas College, P.O. Box 2503, New Westminster, British Columbia V3L 5B2, Canada. (604)527-5293. Fax: (604)527-5095. E-mail: event@douglas.bc.ca. Website: event.douglas.bc.ca. **Contact:** Ian Cockfield, managing editor. **100% freelance written.** Magazine published 3 times/year containing fiction, poetry, creative nonfiction and reviews. "We are eclectic and always open to content that invites involvement. Generally, we like strong narrative." Estab. 1971. Circ. 1,250. Pays on publication. Publishes ms an average of 8 months after acceptance. Byline given. Buys first North American serial rights. Accepts queries by mail, e-mail, fax, phone. Accepts simultaneous submissions. Responds in 1 month to queries; 4 months to mss. Sample copy for $5. Writer's guidelines for #10 SASE (Canadian postage/IRCs only).

• *Event* does not read manuscripts in July. No e-mail submissions. All submissions must include SASE (Canadian postage or international reply coupons only).

Fiction: Christine Dewar, fiction editor. "We look for readability, style and writing that invites involvement." Submit maximum 2 stories. **Buys 12-15 mss/year.** Send complete ms. Length: 5,000 words maximum. **Pays $22/page to $500.**

Poetry: Gillian Harding-Russell, poetry editor. "We tend to appreciate the narrative and sometimes the confessional modes." Free verse, prose. No light verse. **Buys 30-40 poems/year.** Submit maximum 10 poems. **Pays $25-500.**

Tips: "Write well and read some past issues of *Event*."

$ FIELD, Contemporary Poetry & Poetics, Oberlin College Press, 10 N. Professor St., Oberlin OH 44074-1095. (440)775-8408. Fax: (440)775-8124. E-mail: oc.press@oberlin.edu. Website: www.oberlin.edu/~ocpress. **Contact:** Linda Slocum, managing editor. **60% freelance written.** Semiannual magazine of poetry, poetry in translation, and essays on contemporary poetry by poets. No electronic submissions. Estab. 1969. Circ. 1,500. Pays on publication. Byline given. Buys first rights. Editorial lead time 4 months. Accepts queries by mail, e-mail, fax, phone. Responds in 6 weeks to mss. Sample copy for $7. Writer's guidelines online.

Poetry: Buys 100 poems/year. Submit maximum 10 poems with SASE. **Pays $15/page.**

Tips: "Submit 3-5 of your best poems with a cover letter. No simultaneous submissions and include a SASE. Keep trying! Submissions are read year-round."

$ FRANK, An International Journal of Contemporary Writing & Art, Association Frank, 32 rue Edouard Vaillant, Montreuil, France. (33)(1)48596658. Fax: (31)(1)48596668. E-mail: david@paris-anglo.com. Website: www.ReadFrank.com or www.frank.ly. **Contact:** David Applefield, editor. **80% freelance written.** Magazine covering contemporary writing of all genres. Bilingual. "Writing that takes risks and isn't ethnocentric is looked upon favorably." Estab. 1983. Circ. 4,000. Pays on publication. Publishes ms an average of 1 year after acceptance. Byline given. Buys one-time rights. Editorial lead time 6 months. Responds in 1 month to queries; 2 months to mss. Sample copy for $10. Writer's guidelines for #10 SASE or online.

Nonfiction: Interview/profile, travel. **Buys 2 mss/year.** Query. **Pays $100 for assigned articles.**

Photos: State availability with submission. Buys one-time rights. Negotiates payment individualy.

Fiction: Experimental, novel excerpts, international. **Buys 8 mss/year.** Send complete ms. Length: 1,000-3,000 words. **Pays $10/printed page.**

Poetry: Avant-garde, translations. **Buys 20 poems/year.** Submit maximum 10 poems. **Pays $20.**

Tips: "Suggest what you do or know best. Avoid query form letters—we won't read the ms. Looking for excellent literary/cultural interviews with leading American writers or cultural figures."

$ ▣ FUTURES MAGAZINE, 3039 38th Ave., Minneapolis MN 55406-2140. (612)724-4023. E-mail: babs@suspenseunlimited.net. Website: www.futuresforstorylovers.com. Editor: Barbara (Babs) Lakey. **Contact:** Babs Lakey, publisher. **98% freelance written.** Bimonthly print and online magazine. "We nourish writers and artists; attempt to throw out the net so they can fly without fear! The futures in commodities is a good analog for writers and artists. Their work, in many cases, is greatly undervalued. Their future market value will be higher than can be imagined. In the writing community there is a tremendous amount of energy; a rolling boil. It takes the form of many people with talent and motivation anxious to unleash their creative juices." Estab. 1998. Circ. 2,000. Pays on publication. Publishes ms an average of 8 months after acceptance. Byline given. Editorial lead time 8 months. Submit seasonal material 6 months in advance. Accepts queries by e-mail. Accepts simultaneous submissions. Responds in 1 week to queries; 2 months to mss. Sample copy for $5 includes shipping. Writer's guidelines online or by e-mail.

● The publisher reports that the print magazine now publishes fiction only.

O⇢ "Break in through the Starting Line column for new writers—tell us you are new!"

Nonfiction: Sally Carson, editor. Essays, exposé, general interest, historical/nostalgic, how-to, humor, inspirational, new product, opinion, personal experience, photo feature, technical, success stories with a point. "No political ranting or sappy memoirs." **Buys 50 mss/year.** Query. Length: 250-2,000 words. **No pay online yet; ad space given.**

Columns/Departments: Sally Carson, editor. Starting Line (fiction from first time publications, 1,000-4,000 words; Writer's Share (comments on life of a writer), 100 words. **Buys 60 mss/year.** Send complete ms. **No pay online yet; ad space given.**

Fiction: Brian Lawrence, editor. "We do serialized fiction too and love artists who are writers/writers who are artists. Illustrate your own work if you like." Adventure, ethnic, experimental, fantasy, historical, horror, humorous, mainstream, mystery, romance, science fiction, suspense, western. **Buys 120-150 mss/year.** Send complete ms. Length: 500-12,000 words. **Pays $5-25.**

Poetry: Scott Robison, editor. Avant-garde, free verse, light verse, traditional, narrative. **Buys 40-80 poems/year.** Submit maximum 5 poems. **Pays $2-5.**

Fillers: Illustrations with humor. **Pays $5-25.**

▣ The online magazine contains nonfiction, poetry, reviews and columns (the print version contains fiction only). Contact: Sally Carson (ealake1@aol.com) for nonfiction and columns, George Scott (futuresreviews@aol.com) for book and short story reviews, Scott Robison (poemfutures@hotmail.com) for poetry.

Tips: "Reading what we have published is still the best but we do love to see excitement and enthusiasm for the craft, and those who care enough to self-edit. Send SASE for anything you want returned and do not send mail that requires a signature on arrival. Give us a try. We want to see you succeed."

Ⓝ **$ $** THE GEORGIA REVIEW, The University of Georgia, 012 Gilbert Hall, University of Georgia, Athens GA 30602-9009. (706)542-3481. Fax: (706)542-0047. E-mail: bkeen@arches.uga.edu. Website: www.uga.edu/garev. Managing Editor: Annette Hatton. **Contact:** Stephen Corey, editor. **99% freelance written.** Quarterly journal. "Our readers are educated, inquisitive people who read a lot of work in the areas we feature, so they expect only the best in our pages. All work submitted should show evidence that the writer is at least as well-educated and well-read as our readers. Essays should be authoritative but accessible to a range of readers." Estab. 1947. Circ. 5,500. Pays on publication. Publishes ms an average of 6 months after acceptance. Byline given. Buys first North American serial rights. Accepts queries by mail. Responds in 2 weeks to queries; 3 months to mss. Sample copy for $7. Writer's guidelines for #10 SASE.

Nonfiction: Essays. "For the most part we are not interested in scholarly articles that are narrow in focus and/or overly burdened with footnotes. The ideal essay for *The Georgia Review* is a provocative, thesis-oriented work that can engage both the intelligent general reader and the specialist." **Buys 12-20 mss/year.** Send complete ms. **Pays $40/published page.**

Photos: Send photos with submission. Reviews 5×7 or larger prints. Buys one-time rights. Offers no additional payment for photos accepted with ms.

Fiction: "We seek original, excellent writing not bound by type. Ordinarily we do not publish novel excerpts or works translated into English and we strongly discourage authors from submitting these." **Buys 12-20 mss/year.** Send complete ms. **Pays $40/published page.**

Poetry: "We seek original, excellent poetry." **Buys 60-75 poems/year.** Submit maximum 5 poems. **Pays $3/line.**

Tips: "Unsolicited manuscripts will not be considered during the months of June, July, and August; all such submissions received during that period will be returned unread."

$ THE GETTYSBURG REVIEW, Gettysburg College, Gettysburg PA 17325. (717)337-6770. Fax: (717)337-6775. Website: www.gettysburgreview.com. Managing Editor: Cara Diaconoff. **Contact:** Peter Stitt, editor. Quarterly magazine. "Our concern is quality. Manuscripts submitted here should be extremely well-written." Reading period September-May. Estab. 1988. Circ. 4,000. Pays on publication. Byline given. Buys first North American serial rights. Editorial lead time 1 year. Submit seasonal material 9 months in advance. Accepts queries by mail, fax. Responds in 1 month to queries; 3 months to mss. Sample copy for $7. Writer's guidelines for #10 SASE.

Nonfiction: Essays. **Buys 20 mss/year.** Send complete ms. Length: 3,000-7,000 words. **Pays $25/page.**

Fiction: High quality, literary. Novel excerpts. **Buys 20 mss/year.** Send complete ms. Length: 2,000-7,000 words. **Pays $25/page.**

Poetry: **Buys 50 poems/year.** Submit maximum 3 poems. **Pays $2/line.**

$ $▣ GLIMMER TRAIN STORIES, Glimmer Train Press, Inc., 710 SW Madison St., #504, Portland OR 97205. (503)221-0836. E-mail: info@glimmertrain.com. Website: www.glimmertrain.com. **Contact:** Linda Swanson-Davies, co-editor. **90% freelance written.** Quarterly magazine covering short fiction. "We are interested in well-written, emotionally-moving short stories published by unknown, as well as known, writers." Estab. 1991. Circ. 16,000. **Pays on acceptance.** Byline given. Buys first rights. Accepts simultaneous submissions. Responds in 3 months to mss. Sample copy for $9.95 or online. Writer's guidelines for #10 SASE or online.

Fiction: "We are not restricted to any types." **Buys 32 mss/year.** Send complete ms. Length: 1,200-8,000 words. **Pays $500.**

Tips: "Manuscripts should be sent to us in the months of January, April, July and October. Be sure to include a sufficiently-stamped SASE. We are particularly interested in receiving work from new writers." See *Glimmer Train*'s contest listings in the Contest and Awards section.

$ GRAIN LITERARY MAGAZINE, Saskatchewan Writers Guild, P.O. Box 1154, Regina, Saskatchewan S4P 3B4, Canada. (306)244-2828. Fax: (306)244-0255. E-mail: grain.mag@sk.sympatico.ca. Website: www.skwriter.com. Business Administrator: Jennifer Still. **Contact:** Elizabeth Philips, editor. **100% freelance written.** Quarterly magazine covering poetry, fiction, creative nonfiction, drama. "*Grain* publishes writing of the highest quality, both traditional and innovative in nature. The *Grain* editors' aim: To publish work that challenges readers; to encourage promising new writers; and to produce a well-designed, visually interesting magazine." Estab. 1973. Circ. 1,500. Pays on publication. Publishes ms an average of 11 months after acceptance. Byline given. Buys first Canadian, serial rights. Editorial lead time 6 months. Accepts queries by mail, e-mail, fax, phone. Responds in 1 month to queries; 4 months to mss. Sample copy for $8 or online. Writer's guidelines for #10 SASE or online.

Nonfiction: Interested in creative nonfiction.

Photos: Submit 12-20 slides and b/w prints, short statement (200 words) and brief résumé. Reviews transparencies, prints. Pays $100 for front cover art, $30/photo.

Fiction: Literary fiction of all types. "No romance, confession, science fiction, vignettes, mystery." **Buys 40 mss/year. Pays $40-175.**

Poetry: "High quality, imaginative, well-crafted poetry." Submit maximum 10 poems and SASE with Canadian postage or IRC's. Avant-garde, free verse, haiku, traditional. No sentimental, end-line rhyme, mundane. **Buys 78 poems/year. Pays $40-175.**

Tips: "Sweat the small stuff. Pay attention to detail, credibility. Make sure you have researched your piece and that the literal and metaphorical support one another."

$ HAPPY, 240 E. 35th St., Suite 11A, New York NY 10016. E-mail: bayardx@aol.com. **Contact:** Bayard, editor. Pays on publication. Byline given. Buys one-time rights. Accepts queries by mail, e-mail. Accepts simultaneous submissions. Responds in 1 month to queries. Sample copy for $15. Writer's guidelines for #10 SASE.

Fiction: "We accept anything that's beautifully written. Genre isn't important. It just has to be incredible writing." Novel excerpts, short stories. **Buys 100-130 mss/year.** Send complete ms. Length: 6,000 words maximum. **Pays 1-5¢/ word.**

Tips: "Don't bore us with the mundane—blast us out of the water with the extreme!"

N $ HAYDEN'S FERRY REVIEW, Box 871502, Arizona State University, Tempe AZ 85287-1502. (480)965-1243. Fax: (480)965-2229. E-mail: hfr@asu.edu. Website: www.asu.edu/clas/english/HFR/main.html. **Contact:** Fiction, poetry or art editor. **85% freelance written.** Semiannual magazine. "*Hayden's Ferry Review* publishes best quality fiction, poetry and creative nonfiction from new, emerging and established writers." Estab. 1986. Circ. 1,300. Pays on publication. Publishes ms an average of 6 months after acceptance. Byline given. Buys first North American serial rights. Editorial lead time 3 months. Accepts queries by mail, e-mail. Accepts simultaneous submissions. Responds in 2 weeks to queries; 3 months to mss. Sample copy for $6. Writer's guidelines for #10 SASE.

Nonfiction: Essays, interview/profile, personal experience. **Buys 2 mss/year.** Send complete ms. Length: Open. **Pays $25-100.**

Photos: Send photos with submission. Reviews slides. Buys one-time rights. Offers $25/photo.

Fiction: Ethnic, experimental, humorous, novel excerpts, slice-of-life vignettes. **Buys 10 mss/year.** Send complete ms. Length: Open. **Pays $25-100.**

Poetry: Avant-garde, free verse, haiku, light verse, traditional. **Buys 60 poems/year.** Submit maximum 6 poems. Length: Open. **Pays $25-100.**

$ HIGH PLAINS LITERARY REVIEW, 180 Adams St., Suite 250, Denver CO 80206. (303)320-6828. Fax: (303)320-0463. Managing Editor: Phyllis A. Harwell. **Contact:** Robert O. Greer, Jr, editor-in-chief. **80% freelance written.** Triannual magazine. "The *High Plains Literary Review* publishes short stories, essays, poetry, reviews and interviews, bridging the gap between commercial quarterlies and academic reviews." Estab. 1986. Circ. 1,200. Pays on publication. Byline given. Buys first North American serial rights. Accepts simultaneous submissions. Responds in 3 months to queries; 3 months to mss. Sample copy for $4. Writer's guidelines for #10 SASE.

● Its unique editorial format—between commercial and academic—makes for lively reading. Could be good market for that "in between" story.

Nonfiction: Essays, reviews. **Buys 20 mss/year.** Send complete ms. Length: 10,000 words maximum. **Pays $5/page.**

Fiction: Ethnic, historical, humorous, mainstream. **Buys 12 mss/year.** Send complete ms. Length: 10,000 words maximum. **Pays $5/page.**

Poetry: **Buys 45 poems/year. Pays $10/page.**

N $ THE HOLLINS CRITIC, P.O. Box 9538, Hollins University, Roanoke VA 24020-1538. E-mail: acockrell@hollins.edu. Website: www.hollins.edu/academics/critic. Editor: R.H.W. Dillard. Managing Editor: Amanda Cockrell. **Contact:** Cathryn Hankla, poetry editor. **100% freelance written.** Magazine published 5 times/year. Estab. 1964. Circ. 400.

Pays on publication. Publishes ms an average of 2 years after acceptance. Byline given. Buys first North American serial rights. Accepts queries by mail. Accepts simultaneous submissions. Responds in 2 months to mss. Sample copy for $1.50. Writer's guidelines for #10 SASE.

Poetry: Avant-garde, free verse, traditional. **Buys 16-20 poems/year.** Submit maximum 5 poems. **Pays $25.**

Tips: "We accept unsolicited poetry submissions; all other content is by prearrangement."

N $ THE HUDSON REVIEW, A magazine of literature and the arts, The Hudson Review, Inc., 684 Park Ave., New York NY 10021. Fax: (212)774-1911. Managing Editor: Ronald Koury. **Contact:** Paula Deitz, editor. **100% freelance written.** Quarterly magazine publishing fiction, poetry, essays, book reviews; criticism of literature, art, theatre, dance, film and music; and articles on contemporary cultural developments. Estab. 1948. Circ. 5,000. Pays on publication. Publishes ms an average of 6 months after acceptance. Byline given. Only assigned reviews are copyrighted. Editorial lead time 3 months. Accepts queries by mail. Responds in 2 months to queries; 3 months to mss. Sample copy for $8. Writer's guidelines for #10 SASE.

Nonfiction: Paula Deitz. Essays, general interest, historical/nostalgic, opinion, personal experience, travel. **Buys 4-6 mss/year.** Send complete ms between January 1 and April 30 only; book reviews should be queried. Length: 3,500 words maximum. **Pays 2½¢/word.**

Fiction: Ronald Koury. **Buys 4 mss/year.** Send complete ms between June 1 and November 30 only. **Pays 2½¢/word.**

Poetry: Emily Montjoy, associate editor. **Buys 12-20 poems/year.** Submit maximum 8-10 poems between April 1 and July 31 only. **Pays 50¢/line.**

Tips: "We do not specialize in publishing any particular 'type' of writing; our sole criterion for accepting unsolicited work is literary quality. The best way for you to get an idea of the range of work we publish is to read a current issue. We do not consider simultaneous submissions. Unsolicted mss submitted outside of specified reading times will be returned unread."

$ INDIANA REVIEW, Indiana University, Ballantine Hall 465, 1020 E. Kirkwood, Bloomington IN 47405-7103. (812)855-4253. E-mail: inreview@indiana.edu. Website: www.indiana.edu/~inreview/ir.html. Associate Editor: David Daniels. **Contact:** Shannon Gibney, editor. **100% freelance written.** Biannual magazine. "*Indiana Review*, a non-profit organization run by IU graduate students, is a journal of previously unpublished poetry and fiction. Literary interviews and essays also considered. We publish innovative fiction and poetry. We're interested in energy, originality and careful attention to craft. While we publish many well-known writers, we also welcome new and emerging poets and fiction writers." Estab. 1976. Circ. 2,000. Pays on publication. Byline given. Buys first North American serial rights. Accepts queries by mail, e-mail, phone. Accepts simultaneous submissions. Responds in 2 weeks to queries; 3 months to mss. Sample copy for $8. Writer's guidelines for #10 SASE or online.

O— Break in with 500-1,000 word book reviews of fiction, poetry, nonfiction and literary criticism published within the last 2 years, "since this is the area in which there's the least amount of competition."

Nonfiction: "We are currently seeking submissions for an upcoming issue featuring the work of writers of color. Deadline: December 2001." Essays, interview/profile, creative nonfiction, reviews. No "coming of age/slice of life pieces." **Buys 5-7 mss/year.** Send complete ms. Length: 9,000 words maximum. **Pays $5/page plus 2 contributor's copies.**

Fiction: "We look for daring stories which integrate theme, language, character and form. We like polished writing, humor and fiction which has consequence beyond the world of its narrator." Ethnic, experimental, mainstream, novel excerpts, literary, short fictions, translations. No genre fiction. **Buys 14-18 mss/year.** Send complete ms. Length: 250-15,000 words. **Pays $5/page plus 2 contributor's copies.**

Poetry: Looks for inventive and skillful writing. Avant-garde, free verse. **Buys 80 poems/year.** Submit maximum 6 poems. Length: 5 lines minimum. **Pays $5/page plus 2 contributor's copies.**

Tips: "We're always looking for non-fiction essays that go beyond merely autobiographical revelation and utilize sophisticated organization and slightly radical narrative strategies. We want essays that are both lyrical and analytical where confession does not mean nostalgia. Read us before you submit. Often reading is slower in summer and holiday months. Only submit work to journals you would proudly subscribe to, then subscribe to a few. Take care to read the latest two issues and specifically mention work you identify with and why. Submit work that 'stacks up' with the work we've published."

$ INDIGENOUS FICTION, I.F. Publishing, P.O. Box 2078, Redmond WA 98073-2078. E-mail: deckr@earthlink.net. Website: home.earthlink.net/~deckr/if/intro.html. **Contact:** Sherry Decker, editor. **98% freelance written.** Triannual magazine covering short fiction, poetry and art. "We want literary—fantasy, dark fantasy, science fiction, horror, mystery and mainstream. We enjoy elements of the supernatural or the unexplained, odd, intriguing characters and beautiful writing. Most accepted stories will be between 2,500-4,500 words in length." Estab. 1998. Circ. 300. Pays on publication. Publishes ms an average of 6 months after acceptance. Byline given. Buys first North American serial, second serial (reprint) rights. Editorial lead time 6 months. Submit seasonal material 6 months in advance. Accepts queries by mail. Accepts simultaneous submissions. Responds in 2 weeks to queries; 1 month to mss. Sample copy for $6. Writer's guidelines for #10 SASE.

● At press time it was learned that Indigenous Fiction has been placed on temporary hiatus.

Fiction: Adventure, experimental, fantasy, horror, humorous, mainstream, mystery, science fiction, suspense, odd, bizarre, supernatural, unexplained. "No porn, abuse of children, gore; no it was all a dream, evil cat, unicorn or sweet nostalgic tales. No vignettes or slice-of-life (without beginning, middle and end)." **Buys 30 mss/year.** Send complete ms. Length: 500-8,000 words. **Pays $5-20, depending on length, and one contributor's copy.**

Poetry: Free verse, haiku, light verse, traditional. No poetry that neither tells a story nor evokes an image. **Buys 20 poems/year.** Submit maximum 5 poems. Length: 3-30 lines. **Pays $5.**

Fillers: Short humor. **Buys 6/year.** Length: 100-500 words. **Pays $5.**

Tips: "Proper manuscript format; no e-mail or fax submissions. No disks unless asked. We like beautiful, literary writing where something happens in the story. By literary we don't mean a long, rambling piece of beautiful writing for the sake of beauty—we mean characters and situations, fully developed, beautifully. Ghosts, time travel, parallel words, 'the bizarre'—fine! Vampires? Well, okay, but no cliches or media tie-ins. Vampire tales should be bone-chillingly dark, beautiful, erotic or humorous. Everything else has been done. Also, no deals with devil; revenge stories; gullible fool meets sexy vampire, ghost or disguised ghoul in a bar; gratuitous sex; traditional mysteries. Writers we admire: Joyce Carol Oates, Ray Bradbury, Pat Conroy, Dale Bailey, Tanith Lee."

$ **⊠** **THE IOWA REVIEW**, 308 EPB, The University of Iowa, Iowa City IA 52242. (319)335-0462. Fax: (319)335-2535. E-mail: iareview@blue.weeg.uiowa.edu. Website: www.uiowa.edu/~iareview/. **Contact:** David Hamilton, editor. Triannual magazine. Estab. 1970. Buys first North American serial rights, non-exclusive anthology, classroom, and online serial rights. Responds in 3 months. Sample copy for $6 and online. Writer's guidelines online.

• This magazine uses the help of colleagues and graduate assistants. Its reading period is September 1-January 31.

Tips: "We publish essays, reviews, novel excerpts, stories and poems and would like for our essays not always to be works of academic criticism. We have no set guidelines as to content or length." **Buys 65-80 unsolicited ms/year.** Submit complete ms with SASE. **Pays $1/line for verse; $10/page for prose.**

$ **JAPANOPHILE PRESS**, P.O. Box 7977, 415 N. Main St., Ann Arbor MI 48107. E-mail: japanophile@aol.com. Website: www.japanophile.com. **Contact:** Susan Aitken, editor. **80% freelance written.** Works with a small number of new/unpublished writers each year. Semiannual magazine for literate people interested in Japanese culture anywhere in the world. Estab. 1974. Pays on publication. Publishes ms an average of 3 months after acceptance. Byline given. Buys first North American serial rights. Accepts queries by mail, e-mail. Responds in 3 months to queries; 3 months to mss. Sample copy for $5, postpaid, or online. Writer's guidelines for #10 SASE or online.

○→ Break in with "nonfiction articles or short personal essays. We're also looking for nonfiction with photos, movie reviews, short short stories and Japan-related illustration."

Nonfiction: "We want material on Japanese culture in *North America or anywhere in the world*, even Japan. We want articles, preferably with photos, about persons engaged in arts of Japanese origin: A Virginia naturalist who is a haiku poet, a potter who learned raku in Japan, a vivid 'I was there' account of a Go tournament in California. We would like to hear more about what it's like to be a Japanese in the US. Our particular slant is a certain kind of culture wherever it is in the world: Canada, the US, Europe, Japan. The culture includes flower arranging, haiku, sports, religion, travel, art, photography, fiction, etc. It is important to study the magazine." Humor, interview/profile, opinion. **Buys 8 mss/year.** Query. Length: 1,800 words maximum. **Pays $8-25.**

Reprints: Send information about when and where the material previously appeared. Pays 100% of amount paid for original article.

Photos: Pays $10-50 for glossy prints. "We prefer b&w people pictures."

Columns/Departments: Regular columns and features are Tokyo Topics and Japan in North America. "We also need columns about Japanese culture in various American cities." Length: 1,000 words. Query. **Pays $1-25.**

Fiction: Themes should relate to Japan or Japanese culture. Annual contest pays $100 to best short story (contest reading fee $5). Should include 1 or more Japanese and non-Japanese characters in each story. Adventure, experimental, historical, humorous, mainstream, mystery, romance. Length: 1,000-4,000 words. **up to $25.**

Poetry: It must either relate to Japanese culture or be in a Japanese form such as haiku. Avant-garde, haiku, light verse, traditional. Length: 3-50 lines. **Pays $1-20.**

Fillers: Newsbreaks, short humor, clippings. Length: 200 words maximum. **Pays $1-5.**

Tips: "We want to see more articles about Japanese culture worldwide, including unexpected places, but especially US, Canada and Europe. Lack of convincing fact and detail is a frequent mistake." Publication deadlines are September 1 (winter issue) and March 1 (summer issue).

$ **THE JOURNAL**, The Ohio State University, 421 Denney Hall, 164 W. 17th Ave., Columbus OH 43210. (614)292-4076. Fax: (614)292-7816. E-mail: thejournal05@postbox.acs.ohio-state.edu. Website: www.cohums.ohio-state.edu/english/journals/the_journal/homepage.htm. **Contact:** Ellen Levy, associate editor. **100% freelance written.** Semiannual magazine. "We're open to all forms; we tend to favor work that gives evidence of a mature and sophisticated sense of the language." Estab. 1972. Circ. 1,500. Pays on publication. Byline given. Buys first North American serial rights. Accepts queries by mail. Accepts simultaneous submissions. Responds in 2 weeks to queries; 2 months to mss. Sample copy for $7 or online. Writer's guidelines for #10 SASE or online.

Nonfiction: Essays, interview/profile. **Buys 2 mss/year.** Query. Length: 2,000-4,000 words. **Pays $25 maximum.**

Columns/Departments: Reviews of contemporary poetry, 2,000-4,000 words. **Buys 2 mss/year.** Query. **Pays $25.**

Fiction: Novel excerpts, literary short stories. **Pays $25.**

Poetry: Avant-garde, free verse, traditional. **Buys 100 poems/year.** Submit maximum 5 poems. **Pays $25.**

Tips: No electronic submissions.

$ KALLIOPE, a journal of women's literature & art, Florida Community College at Jacksonville, 3939 Roosevelt Blvd., Jacksonville FL 32205. (904)381-3511. Website: www.fccj.org/kalliope. **Contact:** Mary Sue Koeppel, editor. **100% freelance written.** Triannual magazine. "*Kalliope* publishes poetry, short fiction, reviews, and b&w art, usually by women artists. We look for artistic excellence." Estab. 1978. Circ. 1,600. Pays on publication. Publishes ms an average of 3 months after acceptance. Byline given. Buys first rights. Accepts queries by mail, phone. Responds in 1 week to queries. Sample copy for $7 (recent issue) or $4 (back copy) or see sample issues online. Writer's guidelines for #10 SASE or online.
- *Kalliope's* reading period is September through May.
- Break in with a "finely crafted poem or short story or a Q&A with an established, well-published woman poet or literary novelist."

Nonfiction: Interview/profile (Q&A), reviews of new works of poetry and fiction. **Buys 6 mss/year.** Send complete ms. Length: 500-2,000 words. **Pays $10 honorarium if funds are available, otherwise 2 copies or subscription.**

Photos: "Visual art should be sent in groups of 4-10 works. We require b&w professional quality, glossy prints made from negatives. Please supply photo credits, model releases, date of work, title, medium, and size on the back of each photo submitted. include artist's résumé where applicable. we welcome an artist's statement of 50-75 words."

Fiction: Ethnic, experimental, novel excerpts, literary. **Buys 12 mss/year.** Send complete ms. Length: 100-2,000 words. **Pays $10 honorarium if funds are available, otherwise 2 copies or subscription.**

Poetry: Avant-garde, free verse, haiku, traditional. **Buys 75 poems/year.** Submit maximum 3-5 poems. Length: 2-120 lines. **Pays $10 honorarium if funds are available, otherwise 2 copies or subscription.**

Tips: "We publish the best of the material submitted to us each issue. (We don't build a huge backlog and then publish from that backlog for years.) Although we look for new writers and usually publish several with each issue alongside already established writers, we love it when established writers send us their work. We've recently published Tess Gallagher, Enid Shomer and one of the last poems by Denise Levertov. Send a bio with all submissions."

$ THE KENYON REVIEW, Kenyon College, Gambier OH 43022. (740)427-5208. Fax: (740)427-5417. E-mail: kenyonreview@kenyon.edu. Website: www.kenyonreview.org. **Contact:** David H. Lynn, editor. **100% freelance written.** Triannual magazine covering contemporary literature and criticism. An international journal of literature, culture and the arts dedicated to an inclusive representation of the best in new writing (fiction, poetry, essays, interviews, criticism) from established and emerging writers. Estab. 1939. Circ. 5,000. Pays on publication. Publishes ms an average of 1 year after acceptance. Byline given. Buys first rights. Editorial lead time 1 year. Submit seasonal material 1 year in advance. Accepts queries by mail. Responds in 4 months to queries. Sample copy for $9 or online. Writer's guidelines for 4×9 SASE or online.

$ THE KIT-CAT REVIEW, 244 Halstead Ave., Harrison NY 10528. (914)835-4833. **Contact:** Claudia Fletcher, editor. **100% freelance written.** Quarterly magazine. "*The Kit-Cat Review* is named after the 18th Century Kit-Cat Club, whose members included Addison, Steele, Congreve, Vanbrugh and Garth. Its purpose is to promote/discover excellence and originality. Some issues are part anthology." The autumn issue includes the winner of the annual Gavin Fletcher Memorial Prize for Poetry of $1,000. The winning poem is published shortly thereafter in a *Kit-Cat Review* ad in the *American Poetry Review*. Estab. 1998. Circ. 200. **Pays on acceptance.** Byline given. Buys one-time rights. Accepts queries by mail, phone. Responds in 1 week to queries; 1 month to mss. Sample copy for $7, payable to Claudia Fletcher.

Nonfiction: "Shorter pieces stand a better chance of publication." Book excerpts, essays, general interest, historical/nostalgic, humor, interview/profile, personal experience, travel. **Buys 2 mss/year.** Send complete ms with brief bio and SASE. Length: 5,000 words maximum. **Pays $25-100.**

Fiction: Experimental, novel excerpts, slice-of-life vignettes. No stories with "O. Henry-type formula endings. Shorter pieces stand a better chance of publication." **Buys 20 mss/year.** Send complete ms with brief bio and SASE. Length: 5,000 words maximum. **Pays $25-100.**

Poetry: Free verse, traditional. No excessively obscure poetry. **Buys 100 poems/year. Pays $10-100.**

Tips: "Obtaining a sample copy is strongly suggested. Include a short bio, SASE and word count for fiction and nonfiction submissions."

$ LEGIONS OF LIGHT, Box 874, Margaretville, NY 12455. (914)586-2759. Fax: (914)586-2759. E-mail: dancing_hawk@yahoo.com. **Contact:** Elizabeth Mami, editor. **100% freelance written.** Bimonthly magazine. "*Legions of Light* accepts all material except graphic violence or sex. All ages read the magazine, all subjects welcomed." Estab. 1990. Circ. 2,000. Pays on publication. Publishes ms an average of 2 years after acceptance. Byline sometimes given. Buys one-time rights. Editorial lead time 4 months. Submit seasonal material 6 months in advance. Accepts queries by mail, e-mail. Accepts simultaneous submissions. Responds in 6 weeks to queries. Sample copy for $3. Writer's guidelines for #10 SASE.

Nonfiction: Historical/nostalgic, humor, inspirational, interview/profile, personal experience, religious. No graphic violence or adult material. **Buys 10-20 mss/year.** Send complete ms. Length: 500-1,500 words. **Pays $5-10.**

Reprints: Send photocopy.

Photos: State availability with submission. Reviews 3×5 prints. Buys one-time rights. Offers no additional payment for photos accepted with ms. Identification of subjects required.

Fiction: Adventure, ethnic, experimental, fantasy, historical, horror, humorous, mainstream, mystery, novel excerpts, romance, science fiction, slice-of-life vignettes, suspense, western. No adult or graphic violence. **Buys 20-30 mss/year.** Send complete ms. Length: 1,500 words maximum. **Pays $5-10 or contributor copies**.

Poetry: Avant-garde, free verse, haiku, light verse, traditional. No erotica. **Buys 15-20 poems/year. Pays $5-10 or contributor copies.**

Fillers: Anecdotes, facts, newsbreaks, short humor. **Buys 5-15/year. Pays $5-10 or contributor copies.**

Tips: "*Legions of Light* caters to unpublished talent, especially children. Subscribers are used first, but subscribing is *not* a requirement to be accepted for publication. All are accepted, but due to overload, it does take time to actually get published. *All will though.* Calls and reminders are encouraged. I eventually get every one in."

N **$ LYNX EYE**, ScribbleFest Literary Group, 1880 Hill Dr., Los Angeles CA 90041-1244. (323)550-8522. Co-Editors Pam McCully, Kathryn Morrison. **Contact:** Pam McCully. **100% freelance written.** Quarterly journal. "Each issue of *Lynx Eye* offers thoughtful and thought-provoking reading." Estab. 1994. Circ. 500. **Pays on acceptance.** Publishes ms an average of 6 months after acceptance. Byline given. Offers 100% kill fee. Buys first North American serial rights. Editorial lead time 6 months. Submit seasonal material 6 months in advance. Accepts queries by mail. Accepts simultaneous submissions. Responds in 3 weeks to queries; 4 months to mss. Sample copy for $7.95. Writer's guidelines for #10 SASE.

Nonfiction: Essays. No memoirs. **Buys 6 mss/year.** Send complete ms. Length: 500-5,000 words. **Pays $10.**

Fiction: Ethnic, experimental, fantasy, historical,, humorous, mainstream, mystery, novel excerpts, romance, science fiction. **Buys 50 mss/year.** Send complete ms. Length: 500-5,000 words. **Pays $10.**

Poetry: Avant-garde, free verse, haiku, light verse, traditional. **Buys 50 poems/year.** Submit maximum 6 poems. Length: 30 lines maximum. **Pays $10.**

Tips: "Know your craft, including grammar, usage, active verbs, well-constructed sentences and paragraphs, and fully developed characters. We accept never-before-published work only"

$ $ THE MALAHAT REVIEW, The University of Victoria, P.O. Box 1700, STN CSC, Victoria British Columbia V8W 2Y2, Canada. (250)721-8524. E-mail: malahat@uvic.ca (for queries only). Website: web.uvic.ca/malahat. **Contact:** Marlene Cookshaw, editor. **100% freelance written.** Eager to work with new/unpublished writers. Quarterly magazine covering poetry, fiction and reviews. Estab. 1967. Circ. 1,000. **Pays on acceptance.** Publishes ms an average of 6 months after acceptance. Byline given. Offers 100% kill fee. Buys first world serial rights. Accepts queries by mail, e-mail. Responds in 2 weeks to queries; 3 months to mss. Sample copy for $10 (US). Writer's guidelines online.

Nonfiction: "Query first about review articles, critical essays, interviews and visual art which we generally solicit." Include SASE with Canadian postage or IRCs. **Pays $30/magazine page.**

Fiction: Buys 20 mss/year. Send complete ms. Length: 20 pages maximum. **Pays $30/magazine page.**

Poetry: Avant-garde, free verse, traditional. **Buys 100 poems/year.** Length: 5-10 pages. **Pays $30/magazine page.**

Tips: "Please do not send more than one manuscript (the one you consider your best) at a time. See the *Malahat Review's* long poem and novella contests in the Contest & Awards section."

$ $ MANOA, A Pacific Journal of International Writing, University of Hawaii Press, 1733 Donaghho Rd., Honolulu HI 96822. (808)956-3070. Fax: (808)956-7808. E-mail: fstewart@hawaii.edu. Website: www2.hawaii.edu/mjournal. Managing Editor: Patricia Matsueda. **Contact:** Frank Stewart, editor. Semiannual magazine. "High quality literary fiction, poetry, essays, personal narrative, reviews. About half of each issue devoted to U.S. writing, and half new work from Pacific and Asian nations. Our audience is primarily in the U.S., although expanding in Pacific countries. U.S. writing need not be confined to Pacific settings or subjects." Estab. 1989. Circ. 2,500. Pays on publication. Byline given. Buys first North American serial rights, non-exclusive, one-time print. Editorial lead time 6 months. Submit seasonal material 8 months in advance. Responds in 3 weeks to queries; 2 months to poetry mss; 4 months to fiction mss. Sample copy for $10 (US). Writer's guidelines for #10 SASE.

Nonfiction: Book excerpts, essays, interview/profile, creative nonfiction or personal narrative related to literature or nature; book reviews on recent books in arts, humanities and natural sciences, usually related to Asia, the Pacific or Hawaii or published in these places. No Pacific exotica. **Buys 3-4 (excluding reviews) mss/year.** Send complete ms. Length: 1,000-5,000 words. **Pays $25/printed page.**

Fiction: Ian MacMillan, fiction editor. "We're potentially open to anything of literary quality, though usually not genre fiction as such." No Pacific exotica. **Buys 12-18 in the US (excluding translation) mss/year.** Send complete ms. Length: 1,000-7,500 words. **Pays $100-500 normally ($25/printed page).**

Poetry: No light verse. **Buys 40-50 poems/year.** Submit maximum 5-6 poems. **Pays $25.**

Tips: "Although we are a Pacific journal, we are a general interest US literary journal, not limited to Pacific settings or subjects."

$ THE MASSACHUSETTS REVIEW, South College, University of Massachusetts, Amherst MA 01003-9934. (413)545-2689. Fax: (413)577-0740. E-mail: massrev@external.umass.edu. Website: www.massreview.org. **Contact:** Mary Heath, Jules Chametzky, Paul Jenkins, David Lenson, editors. Quarterly magazine. Estab. 1959. Pays on publication. Publishes ms an average of 18 months after acceptance. Buys first North American serial rights. Accepts queries by mail. Responds in 3 months to queries; 3 months to mss. Sample copy for $7 with 3 first-class stamps. Sample articles and writer's guidelines online.

• Does not return mss without SASE.

Nonfiction: Articles on literary criticism, women, public affairs, art, philosophy, music, and dance. No reviews of single books. Send complete ms or query with SASE. Length: 6,500 words maximum. **Pays $50.**

Fiction: Buys 2-3 mss/year. Length: 25-30 pages maximum. **Pays $50.**

Poetry: Submit maximum 6 poems. **Pays 35¢/line to $10 maximum.**

Tips: "No manuscripts are considered June-October. No fax or e-mail submissions."

$ $ MERLYN'S PEN, Fiction, Essays and Poems by America's Teens, Merlyn's Pen Inc., 4 King St., East Greenwich RI 02818. (401)885-5175. Fax: (401)885-5222. E-mail: merlynspen@aol.com. Website: www.merlynspen.com. **Contact:** R. James Stahl, editor. **100% freelance written.** Annual magazine. "We publish fiction, essays and poems by America's teen writers, age 11-19 exclusively." Estab. 1985. Circ. 5,000. Pays on publication. Publishes ms an average of 6 months after acceptance. Byline given. Buys all rights. Editorial lead time up to 10 months. Accepts queries by mail, e-mail, fax. Responds in 3 months to queries. Sample articles and writer's guidelines online.

Nonfiction: Essays, general interest, historical/nostalgic, humor, opinion, personal experience, travel. **Buys 10 mss/ year.** Send complete ms. Length: 100-5,000 words. **Pays $25-200.**

Fiction: Adventure, experimental, fantasy, historical,, humorous, mainstream, mystery, romance, science fiction, slice-of-life vignettes, suspense, one-act plays and dramatic monologues. **Buys 40 mss/year.** Send complete ms. Length: 100-5,000 words. **Pays $20-250.**

Poetry: Avant-garde, free verse, haiku, light verse, traditional. **Buys 25 poems/year.** Submit maximum 2 poems. Length: 3-250 lines. **Pays $20-250.**

■ The online magazine carries origianl content not found in the print edition and includes writer's guidelines. Contact: R. James Stahl, online editor.

Tips: "Contributors must be between ages 11-19. We select about 50 pieces out of 10,000 received and we do respond. Writers *must* use *our* cover sheet, which is on our website or free by calling (800)247-2027."

$ MICHIGAN QUARTERLY REVIEW, 3032 Rackham Bldg., 915 E. Washington, University of Michigan, Ann Arbor MI 48109-1070. (734)764-9265. E-mail: dorisk@umich.edu. Website: www.umich.edu/~mqr. **Contact:** Laurence Goldstein, editor. **75% freelance written.** Prefers to work with published/established writers. Quarterly magazine. Estab. 1962. Circ. 1,500. Pays on publication. Publishes ms an average of 1 year after acceptance. Byline given. Buys first serial rights. Accepts queries by mail. Responds in 2 months to queries; 2 months to mss. Sample copy for $2.50 with 2 first-class stamps.

● The Lawrence Foundation Prize is a $1,000 annual award to the best short story published in the *Michigan Quarterly Review* during the previous year.

Nonfiction: "*MQR* is open to general articles directed at an intellectual audience. Essays ought to have a personal voice and engage a significant subject. Scholarship must be present as a foundation, but we are not interested in specialized essays directed only at professionals in the field. We prefer ruminative essays, written in a fresh style and which reach interesting conclusions. We also like memoirs and interviews with significant historical or cultural resonance." **Buys 35 mss/year.** Query. Length: 2,000-5,000 words. **Pays $100-150.**

Fiction: No restrictions on subject matter or language. "We are very selective. We like stories which are unusual in tone and structure, and innovative in language." **Buys 10 mss/year.** Send complete ms. **Pays $10/published page.**

Poetry: Buys 10 poems/year. Pays $10/published page.

Tips: "Read the journal and assess the range of contents and the level of writing. We have no guidelines to offer or set expectations; every manuscript is judged on its unique qualities. On essays—query with a very thorough description of the argument and a copy of the first page. Watch for announcements of special issues which are usually expanded issues and draw upon a lot of freelance writing. Be aware that this is a university quarterly that publishes a limited amount of fiction and poetry; that it is directed at an educated audience, one that has done a great deal of reading in all types of literature."

N **$** MID-AMERICAN REVIEW, Dept. of English, Bowling Green State University, Bowling Green OH 43403. (419)372-2725. Fax: (419)372-6805. Website: www.bgsu.edu/midamericanreview. **Contact:** Michael Czyzniejewski, editor-in-chief. Willing to work with new/unpublished writers. Semiannual magazine of "the highest quality fiction, poetry and translations of contemporary poetry and fiction." Also publishes critical articles and book reviews of contemporary literature. Estab. 1981. Pays on publication when funding is available. Publishes ms an average of 6 months after acceptance. Byline given. Buys one-time rights. Accepts queries by mail, phone. Responds in 4 months to mss. Sample copy for $7 (current issue), $5 (back issue); $10 (rare back issues).

O— "Grab our attention with something original—even experimental—but most of all, well-written."

Nonfiction: Essays (articles focusing on contemporary authors and topics of current literary interest), Short book reviews (500-1,000 words). **Pays $10/page up to $50, pending funding.**

Fiction: Character-oriented, literary, experimental, short short. **Buys 12 mss/year.** Send complete ms; no queries. **Pays $10/page up to $50, pending funding.**

Poetry: Karen Craigo, poetry editor. Strong imagery and sense of vision. **Buys 60 poems/year. Pays $10/page up to $50, pending funding.**

Tips: "We are seeking translations of contemporary authors from all languages into English; submissions must include the original. We would also like to see more short shorts and essays."

$ miller's pond, H&H Press, RR 2, Box 241, Middlebury Center PA 16935. (570)376-3361. E-mail: cjhoughtaling@u sa.net. Website: millerspond.tripod.com. **Contact:** C.J. Houghtaling, editor. **100% freelance written.** Annual magazine featuring poetry with poetry book/chapbook reviews and interviews of poets. E-mail submissions must be on the form from the website millerspond.tripod.com. Estab. 1998. Circ. 200. Pays on publication. Publishes ms an average of 1 year after acceptance. Byline given. Buys one-time rights. Editorial lead time 1 year. Accepts queries by mail, e-mail. Accepts simultaneous submissions. Responds in 10 months to queries; 10 months to mss. Sample copy for $5 plus $3 p&h or online. Writer's guidelines for #10 SASE or online.

Nonfiction: Interview/profile, poetry chapbook reviews. **Buys 1-2 mss/year.** Query or send complete ms. Length: 100-500 words. **Pays $5.**

Poetry: Free verse. No religious, horror, vulgar, rhymed, preachy, lofty, trite, overly sentimental. **Buys 20-25 poems/year.** Submit maximum 3-5 poems. Length: 40 lines maximum. **Pays $2.**

▣ The online magazine carries original content not found in the print edition and includes writer's guidelines. Contact: Julie Damerell, online editor.

Tips: "View our website to see what we like. Study the contemporary masters: Billy Collins, Maxine Kumin, Colette Inez, Hayden Carruth. Always enclose SASE."

$ $ THE MISSOURI REVIEW, 1507 Hillcrest Hall, University of Missouri, Columbia MO 65211. (573)882-4474. Fax: (573)884-4671. E-mail: missouri_@missouri.edu. Website: www.missourireview.org. Associate Editor: Evelyn Somers. Poetry Editor: Marta Boswell. **Contact:** Speer Morgan, editor. **90% freelance written.** Triannual magazine. "We publish contemporary fiction, poetry, interviews, personal essays, cartoons, special features—such as 'History as Literature' series and 'Found Text' series—for the literary and the general reader interested in a wide range of subjects." Estab. 1978. Circ. 5,000. Offers signed contract. Byline given. Editorial lead time 6 months. Accepts queries by mail, e-mail, phone. Responds in 2 weeks to queries; 3 months to mss. Sample copy for $7 or online. Writer's guidelines for #10 SASE or online.

Nonfiction: Evelyn Somers, associate editor. Book excerpts, essays. No literary criticism. **Buys 10 mss/year.** Send complete ms. **Pays $30/printed page, up to $750.**

Fiction: Mainstream, novel excerpts, literary. No genre fiction. **Buys 25 mss/year.** Send complete ms. **Pays $30/printed page, up to $750.**

Poetry: Marta Boswell, poetry editor. Publishes 3-5 poetry features of 6-12 pages per issue. "Please familiarize yourself with the magazine before submitting poetry." **Buys 50 poems/year. Pays $125-250.**

▣ The online magazine carries original content not found in the print edition and includes writer's guidelines. Contact: Hoa Ngo, online editor.

Tips: "Send your best work."

N $ MODERN HAIKU, An Independent Journal of Haiku and Haiku Studies, P.O. Box 1752, Madison WI 53701-1752. (608)233-2738. Website: www.family-net.net/~brooksbooks/modernhaiku. **Contact:** Robert Spiess, editor. **85% freelance written.** Magazine published 3 times/year. "*Modern Haiku* published high quality material only. Haiku and related genres, articles on haiku, haiku book reviews and translations compose its contents. It has an international circulation and is widely subscribed to by university, school and public libraries." Estab. 1969. Circ. 575. Pays on acceptance for poetry; on publication for prose. Publishes ms an average of 3 months after acceptance. Byline given. Buys first North American serial rights. Editorial lead time 4 months. Accepts queries by mail, phone. Responds in 1 week to queries; 2 weeks to mss. Sample copy for $6.65. Writer's guidelines for #10 SASE.

Nonfiction: Essays (anything related to haiku). **Buys 40 mss/year.** Send complete ms. **Pays $5/page.**

Columns/Departments: Haiku & Senryu; Haibun; Articles (on haiku and related genres); book reviews (books of haiku or related genres), 4 pages maximum. **Buys 850 mss/year.** Send complete ms. **Pays $5/page.**

Poetry: Haiku, senryu. Does not want "general poetry, sentimental and pretty-pretty haiku or overtly pornographic." **Buys 800 poems/year.** Submit maximum 24 poems. **Pays $1.**

Tips: "Study the history of haiku, read books about haiku, learn the aesthetics of haiku and methods of composition. Write about your sense perceptions of the suchness of entities, avoid ego-centered interpretations."

$ NEW ENGLAND REVIEW, Middlebury College, Middlebury VT 05753. (802)443-5075. E-mail: nereview@mid dlebury.edu. Website: www.middlebury.edu/~nereview/. Editor: Stephen Donadio. Managing Editor: Jodee Stanley Rubins. **Contact:** On envelope: Poetry, Fiction, or Nonfiction Editor; on letter: Stephen Donadio. Quarterly magazine. Serious literary only. Reads September 1 to May 31 (postmark dates). Estab. 1978. Circ. 2,000. Pays on publication. Publishes ms an average of 6 months after acceptance. Byline given. Buys first North American serial rights. Accepts simultaneous submissions. Responds in 2 weeks to queries; 3 months to mss. Sample copy for $7. Writer's guidelines for #10 SASE.

Nonfiction: Serious literary only. Rarely accepts previously published submissions (out of print or previously published abroad only). **Buys 20-25 mss/year.** Send complete ms. Length: 7,500 words maximum, though exceptions may be made. **Pays $10/page ($20 minimum) and 2 copies.**

Fiction: Send 1 story at a time. Serious literary only, novel excerpts. **Buys 25 mss/year.** Send complete ms. **Pays $10/page ($20 minimum) and 2 copies.**

Poetry: **Buys 75-90 poems/year.** Submit maximum 6 poems. **Pays $10/page or $20 and 2 copies.**

Tips: "We consider short fiction, including shorts, short-shorts, novellas, and self-contained extracts from novels. We consider a variety of general and literary, but not narrowly scholarly, nonfiction; long and short poems; speculative, interpretive, and personal essays; book reviews; screenplays; graphics; translations; critical reassessments; statements by artists working in various media; interviews; testimonies; and letters from abroad. We are committed to exploration of all forms of contemporary cultural expression in the United States and abroad. With few exceptions, we print only work not published previously elsewhere."

$ NEW LETTERS, University of Missouri-Kansas City, University House, 5101 Rockhill Rd., Kansas City MO 64110-2499. (816)235-1168. Fax: (816)235-2611. E-mail: newletters@umkc.edu. Website: umkc.edu/newletters. Managing Editor: Robert Stewart. **Contact:** James McKinley, editor. **100% freelance written.** Quarterly magazine. "*New Letters* is intended for the general literate reader. We publish literary fiction, nonfiction, essays, poetry. We also publish art." Estab. 1934. Circ. 1,800. Pays on publication. Publishes ms an average of 5 months after acceptance. Byline given. Buys first North American serial rights. Editorial lead time 6 months. Submit seasonal material 6 months in advance. Accepts queries by mail, e-mail. Accepts simultaneous submissions. Responds in 1 month to queries; 3 months to mss. Sample copy for $5.50 (current issue) or sample articles online. Writer's guidelines for #10 SASE or on website.
  • Submissions are not read between May 15 and October 15.
Nonfiction: Essays. No self-help, how-to or non-literary work. **Buys 6-8 mss/year.** Send complete ms. Length: 5,000 words maximum. **Pays $40-100.**
Photos: Send photos with submission. Reviews contact sheets, 2×4 transparencies, prints. Buys one-time rights. Pays $10-40/photo.
Fiction: No genre fiction. **Buys 12 mss/year.** Send complete ms. Length: 5,000 words maximum. **Pays $30-75.**
Poetry: Avant-garde, free verse, haiku, traditional. No light verse. **Buys 40 poems/year.** Submit maximum 3 poems. Length: Open. **Pays $10-25.**
Tips: "We aren't interested in essays that are footnoted, essays usually described as scholarly or critical. Our preference is for creative nonfiction or personal essays. We prefer shorter stories and essays to longer ones (an average length is 3,500-4,000 words). We have no rigid preferences as to subject, style or genre, although commercial efforts tend to put us off. Even so, our only fixed requirement is on *good* writing."

[N] $ ⬛ THE NEW QUARTERLY, new directions in Canadian writing, St. Jerome's University, 200 University Ave. W, Waterloo, Ontario N2L 3G3, Canada. (519)884-8110. E-mail: newquart@watarts.uwaterloo.ca. Website: www.newquarterly.uwaterloo.ca. Editor: Kim Jernigan. **Contact:** Danielle Raymond, managing editor. **95% freelance written.** Quarterly book covering Canadian fiction and poetry. "Emphasis on emerging writers and genres, but we publish some traditional stuff as well if the language and narrative structure are fresh." Estab. 1980. Circ. 700. Pays on publication. Publishes ms an average of 4 months after acceptance. Byline given. Buys first Canadian rights. Editorial lead time 6 months. Accepts queries by mail, e-mail, phone. Accepts simultaneous submissions. Responds in 2 weeks to queries; 4 months to mss. Sample copy for $10 (cover price plus mailing). Writer's guidelines for #10 SASE or online.
Fiction: Kim Jernigan, fiction editor. Canadian work only. We are not interested in genre fiction. We are looking for innovative, beautifully crafted, deeply felt literary fiction. **Buys 20-25 mss/year.** Send complete ms. Length: 20 pages maximum. **Pays $150/story.**
Poetry: Randi Patterson, poetry editor. Avant-garde, free verse, traditional. Canadian work only. **Buys 60-80 poems/year.** Submit maximum 5 poems. Length: 4½ inches typeset. **Pays $25.**
Tips: "Reading us is the best way to get our measure. We don't have preconceived ideas about what we're looking for other than that it must be Canadian work (Canadian writers, not necessarily Canadian content). We want something that's fresh, something that will repay a second reading, something in which the language soars and the feeling is complexly rendered. Narrative innovation a plus."

[N] $ $ NEW YORK STORIES, LaGuardia/CUNY, 31-10 Thomson Ave., Long Island City NY 11101. (718)482-5673. E-mail: nystories@lagcc.cuny.edu. Website: www.newyorkstories.org. **Contact:** Daniel Caplice Lynch, editor-in-chief. **100% freelance written.** Magazine published 3 times/year. "Our purpose is to publish quality short fiction and New York centered nonfiction. We look for fresh approaches, artistic daring and story telling talent. We are especially interested in work that explores NYC's diversity—ethnic, social, sexual, psychological, economic and geographical." Circ. 1,500. Pays on publication. Publishes ms an average of 6 months after acceptance. Byline given. Buys first North American serial rights. Editorial lead time 6 months. Submit seasonal material 6 months in advance. Accepts queries by mail, e-mail. Accepts simultaneous submissions. Responds in 2 weeks to queries; 6 months to mss. Sample copy for $4. Writer's guidelines for #10 SASE, online or by e-mail.
Nonfiction: Essays, personal experience, all must be related to New York City. **Buys 25-30 mss/year.** Send complete ms. Length: 300-6,000 words. **Pays $100-750.**
Photos: Send photos with submission. Buys one-time rights. Negotiates payment individually. Model releases required.
Fiction: Seeks quality above all; also minority writers, New York City themes. Ethnic, experimental. **Buys 25 mss/year.** Send complete ms. Length: 300-6,000 words. **Pays $100-750.**
Tips: "Send your best work. Try briefer pieces, cultivate a fresh approach. For the NYC nonfiction pieces, look on your doorstep. Fresh angles of vision, dark humor and psychological complexity are the hallmarks of our short stories."

$ THE NORTH AMERICAN REVIEW, University of Northern Iowa, Cedar Falls IA 50614-0516. (319)273-6455. Website: webdelsol.com/NorthAmReview/NAR/. **Contact:** Vince Gotera, editor. **50% freelance written.** Bimonthly magazine. Circ. under 5,000. Pays on publication. Publishes ms an average of 9 months after acceptance. Byline given. Buys first rights. Accepts queries by mail, e-mail, fax, phone. Responds in 10 weeks. Sample copy for $5.

- This is one of the oldest and most prestigious literary magazines in the country. Also one of the most entertaining—and a tough market for the young writer.

O→ Break in with the "highest quality poetry, fiction and nonfiction on any topic but particularly interested in the environment, gender, race, ethnicity and class."

Nonfiction: No restrictions, but most nonfiction is commissioned. Query. **Pays $5/350 words; $20 minimum, $100 maximum.**

Fiction: No restrictions; highest quality only. Length: Open. **$5/350 words; $20 minimum, $100 maximum.**

Poetry: No restrictions; highest quality only. Length: Open. **Pays $1/line; $20 minimum, $100 maximum.**

Tips: "We like stories that start quickly and have a strong narrative arc. Poems that are passionate about subject, language, and image are welcome, whether they are traditional or experimental, whether in formal or free verse (closed or open form). Nonfiction should combine art and fact with the finest writing. We do not accept simultaneous submissions; these will be returned unread. We read poetry and nonfiction year-round; we read fiction only from January through March."

N $ $ NORTH CAROLINA LITERARY REVIEW, A Magazine of Literature, Culture, and History, English Dept., East Carolina University, Greenville NC 27858-4353. (252)328-1537. Fax: (252)328-4889. E-mail: Bauer M@mail.ecu.edu. Website: www.ecu.edu/english/journals/nclr. **Contact:** Margaret Bauer, editor. Annual magazine published in the fall covering North Carolina writers, literature, culture, history. "Articles should have a North Carolina slant. First consideration is always for quality of work. Although we treat academic and scholarly subjects, we do not wish to see jargon-laden prose; our readers, we hope, are found as often in bookstores and libraries as in academia. We seek to combine best elements of magazine for serious readers with best of scholarly journal." Estab. 1992. Circ. 750. Pays on publication. Publishes ms an average of 1 year after acceptance. Byline given. Buys first North American serial rights, rights returned to writer on request. Editorial lead time 6 months. Accepts queries by mail, e-mail. Responds in 1 month to queries; 6 months to mss. Sample copy for $10-15. Writer's guidelines for SASE or by e-mail.

O→ Break in with an article related to the special feature topic. Check the website for upcoming topics and deadlines.

Nonfiction: North Carolina-related material only. Book excerpts, essays, exposé, general interest, historical/nostalgic, humor, interview/profile, opinion, personal experience, photo feature, travel, reviews, short narratives, surveys of archives. "No jargon-laden academic articles." **Buys 25-35 mss/year.** Query with published clips. Length: 500-5,000 words. **Pays $50-300.**

Photos: State availability with submission. Reviews 5×7 or 8×10 prints; snapshot size or photocopy ok. Buys one-time rights. Negotiates payment individually. Captions and identification of subjects required; releases when appropriate required.

Columns/Departments: NC Writers (interviews, biographical/bibliographic essays); Reviews (essay reviews of North Carolina-related (fiction, creative nonfiction, poetry). Query with published clips. **Pays $50-300.**

Fiction: Must be North Carolina related—either by a NC-connected writer or set in NC. **Buys 3-4 mss/year.** Query. Length: 5,000 words maximum. **Pays $50-300.**

Poetry: NC poets only. **Buys 8-10 poems/year.** Length: 30-150 lines. **Pays $25-50.**

Fillers: Buys 2-10/year. Length: 50-300 words. **Pays $25-50.**

Tips: "By far the easiest way to break in is with special issue sections. We are especially interested in reports on conferences, readings, meetings that involve North Carolina writers, and personal essays or short narratives with strong sense of place. See back issues for other departments. These are the only areas in which we encourage unsolicited manuscripts; but we welcome queries and proposals for all others. Interviews are probably the other easiest place to break in; no discussions of poetics/theory, etc., except in reader-friendly (accessible) language; interviews should be personal, more like conversations, that explore connections between a writer's life and his/her work."

N $ NORTHWEST FLORIDA REVIEW, Okaloosa Island Press-The Gavis Corporation, P.O. Box 8122, Ft. Walton Beach FL 32548. Editor: Mario A. Petaccia. **Contact:** Dana Miller, fiction; Lola Haskins, poetry. **100% freelance written.** Semiannual magazine. "No special slant or philosophy. Just good writing in fiction, poetry and articles." Estab. 2001. Circ. 1,500. Pays on publication. Byline given. Buys first North American serial rights. Editorial lead time 3 months. Submit seasonal material 9 months in advance. Accepts queries by mail. Accepts simultaneous submissions. Responds in 1 month to queries; 3 months to mss. Sample copy for $5. Writer's guidelines for #10 SASE.

Nonfiction: Book excerpts, essays, humor, interview/profile. No religious, technical, travel, or how-to. **Buys 2 mss/year.** Send complete ms. Length: 1,000-3,000 words. **Pays $20.**

Photos: Buys one-time rights. Offers no additional payment for photos accepted with ms. Identification of subjects required.

Fiction: Experimental, humorous, mainstream, novel excerpts. **Buys 8 mss/year.** Send complete ms. Length: 1,500-5,000 words. **Pays $20.**

Poetry: Free verse. No haiku or light verse. **Buys 40-50 poems/year.** Submit maximum 3-5 poems. Length: 10-50 lines. **Pays $5.**

$ NOSTALGIA, A Sentimental State of Mind, Nostalgia Publications, P.O. Box 2224, Orangeburg SC 29116. Website: www.nospub.com. **Contact:** Connie L. Martin, editor. **100% freelance written.** Semiannual magazine for "true, personal experiences that relate faith, struggle, hope, success, failure and rising above problems common to all." Estab. 1986. Circ. 1,000. Pays on publication. Publishes ms an average of 1 year after acceptance. Byline given. Buys one-time rights. Submit seasonal material 6 months in advance. Responds in 6 weeks to queries. Sample copy for $5. Writer's guidelines for #10 SASE or online.

> O— The editor reports an interest in seeing "more humorous, funny experiences in life; need heartwarming more than sad. I would appreciate not receiving material all about Mom, Dad, Uncle, Aunt or siblings or pets. I need true personal experience."

Nonfiction: General interest, historical/nostalgic, humor, inspirational, opinion, personal experience, photo feature, religious, travel. Does not want to see anything with profanity or sexual references. **Buys 20 mss/year.** Send complete ms. Length: 1,500 words. **Payment varies.** Pays contributor's copies if preferred.

Reprints: Send tearsheet and information about when and where the material previously appeared. Payment varies.

Photos: State availability with submission. Offers no additional payment for photos accepted with ms.

Poetry: Free verse, haiku, light verse, traditional, modern prose. "No ballads; no profanity; no sexual references." Submit maximum 3 poems. Length: 45-50 lines maximum.

Tips: Write for guidelines before entering contests.

[N] $ ▣ NUKETOWN, 813 Porter St., Easton PA 18042. E-mail: editor@nuketown.com or fiction@nuketown.com. Website: www.Nuketown.com. Editor: Kenneth Newquist. **Contact:** Kirsten Lincoln, fiction editor. **80% freelance written.** Monthly online publication featuring genre fiction, role playing games, reviews. "*Nuketown*'s mission is to publish and promote heroic speculative fiction—with a pro-individual, pro-reason emphasis and on a professional basis—on the World Wide Web." Estab. 1996. Site averages 14,000 user sessions a month and 18,000 page views. Newsletter has 300 subscribers and is sent out on a weekly basis. Pays on publication. Byline given. Buys electronic rights and requires that the story not appear in another webzine for 3 months after its publication in *Nuketown*. Editorial lead time 2 months. Accepts queries by e-mail. Accepts simultaneous submissions. Responds in 2 weeks to queries; 1 month to mss. Sample copy and writer's guidelines online.

Reprints: Accepts previously published submissions, but only about stories that haven't appeared in print or on the web in the past year (though we don't mind if a story is archived on another site). Pays $10.

Fiction: Fantasy, horror, science fiction. "If the basic outlook of your story can be summed up as 'life's a bitch, then you die' or 'life's a bitch, you get eaten and *then* you die', or some other variation on that theme, then we're probably not going to be interested in your story. Please do not send us stories that are overloaded with scientific technobabble (like a bad episode of *Star Trek*) or paranormal gobbledygook (like a bad episode of *The X Files*). In short, don't let the special effects get in the way of your story. If you're not sure whether or not we'll like your story, send it in anyway—we'd like to read it. It might not be what we're looking for, but then again...We also do not want sex for the sake of sex, violence for the sake of violence, and profanity for the sake of—well, you get the idea. We don't ban these things from *Nuketown*, but we dislike stories (and movies for that matter) that throw in sex scenes for no apparent reason, while its characters spew profanity in a vain attempt to build depth." **Buys 34 mss/year.** Send complete ms. Length: 1,000-4,000 words. **Pays $20.**

Tips: "We want science fiction, fantasy and horror short stories with heroic overtones. This doesn't mean we're just looking for spandex-clad superheroes running around with shining teeth and ray guns (although we wouldn't mind some classic pulp fiction), but we do want stories with characters you can look up to. Aside from heroic stories, we're also looking for stories that have a positive outlook on the future and/or technology. We *are* interested in dark future stories with a strong hero—á la David Brin's *The Postman* or the movie *The Matrix*—but he/she needs to be heroic in the conventional sense of the word (no post-modern anti-heroes)."

[N] $ OASIS, A Literary Magazine, P.O. Box 626, Largo FL 33779-0626. (727)449-2186. E-mail: oasislit@aol.com. **Contact:** Neal Storrs, editor. **95% freelance written.** Quarterly magazine. "The only criterion is high literary quality of writing." Estab. 1992. Circ. 300. Pays on publication. Publishes ms an average of 4 months after acceptance. Byline given. Offers 100% kill fee. Buys first rights. Editorial lead time 4 months. Accepts queries by mail, e-mail, phone. Accepts simultaneous submissions. Responds in 1 day to queries; 1 day to mss. Sample copy for $7.50. Writer's guidelines for #10 SASE.

Fiction: Wants any well-written story. "The style should be powerfully original, and married to its subject. The style should seem to be the subject." **Buys 16 mss/year.** Send complete ms. Length: Open. **Pays $15.**

Poetry: "Prefer free verse with a distinct, subtle music. No superficial sentimentality or old-fashioned rhymes or rhythms. No limit to number of poems that may be submitted at one time." **Buys 16 poems/year.**

[N] $ $ THE PARIS REVIEW, 45-39 171st Place, Flushing NY 11358. (212)861-0016. Fax: (212)861-4504. Website: www.parisreview.com. **Contact:** George A. Plimpton, editor. Quarterly magazine. Pays on publication. Buys all rights. Accepts queries by mail. Response time varies. Sample copy for $11. Writer's guidelines for #10 SASE (from Flushing Office).

Fiction: Study the publication. Annual Aga Khan Fiction Contest award of $1,000. Query. Length: No length limit. **Pays $600.**

Poetry: Study the publication. Richard Howard, poetry editor.

Tips: Address submissions to proper department and mail to: 541 E. 72nd St., New York NY 10021.

$ $ PARNASSUS, Poetry in Review, Poetry in Review Foundation, 205 W. 89th St., #8-F, New York NY 10024. (212)362-3492. Fax: (212)875-0148. E-mail: parnew@aol.com. Managing Editor: Ben Downing. **Contact:** Herbert Leibowitz, editor. Semiannual magazine covering poetry and criticism. Estab. 1972. Circ. 1,500. Pays on publication. Publishes ms an average of 5 months after acceptance. Byline given. Buys one-time rights. Accepts queries by mail. Responds in 2 months. Sample copy for $15.

Nonfiction: Essays. **Buys 30 mss/year.** Query with published clips. Length: 1,500-7,500 words. **Pays $50-300.** Sometimes pays writers in contributor copies or other premiums rather than a cash payment upon request.

Poetry: Accepts most types of poetry. Avant-garde, free verse, traditional. **Buys 3-4 unsolicited poems/year.**

Tips: "Be certain you have read the magazine and are aware of the editor's taste. Blind submissions are a waste of everybody's time. We'd like to see more poems that display intellectual acumen and curiosity about history, science, music, etc. and fewer trivial lyrical poems about the self, or critical prose that's academic and dull. Prose should sing."

N $ PIG IRON SERIES, Pig Iron Press, P.O. Box 237, Youngstown OH 44501-0237. (330)747-6932. Fax: (330)747-0599. **Contact:** Jim Villani, publisher. **95% freelance written.** Annual magazine emphasizing literature/art for writers, artists and intelligent lay audience interested in popular culture. Circ. 1,000. Pays on publication. Publishes ms an average of 18 months after acceptance. Byline given. Buys one-time rights. Responds in 4 months to queries. Sample copy for $5. Writer's guidelines and current theme list for #10 SASE.

Nonfiction: General interest, opinion, criticism, new journalism and lifestyle. **Buys 6-12 mss/year.** Query. Length: 6,000 words maximum. **Pays $5/page minimum.**

Reprints: Send information about when and where the article previously appeared.

Photos: Send photos with submission. Buys one-time rights. Pays $5 minimum for 5×7 or 8×10 b&w glossy prints.

Fiction: Looking for narrative fiction, living history, novel excerpts, psychological fiction, environment, avant-garde, experimental, metafiction, satire, parody. **Buys 4-12 mss/year.** Send complete ms. Length: 6,000 words maximum. **Pays $5 minimum.**

Poetry: Avant-garde, free verse. **Buys 25-50 poems/year.** Submit maximum 5 or less poems. Length: Open. **Pays $5 minimum.**

Tips: "Looking for fiction and poetry that is sophisticated, elegant, mature and polished. Interested in literary works that are consistent with the fundamental characteristics of modern and contemporary literature, including magical realism, metafiction, new journalism, living history and populist."

$ PLEIADES, Pleiades Press, Dept. of English & Philosophy, Central Missouri State University, Warrensburg MO 64093. (660)543-4425. Fax: (660)543-8544. E-mail: kdp8106@cmsu2.cmsu.edu. **Contact:** R.M. Kinder, editor (fiction, essays); Kevin Prufer, editor (poetry, reviews); Susan Steinberg, editor; Eric Miles Williamson, editor. **100% freelance written.** Semiannual journal. "We publish contemporary fiction, poetry, interviews, literary essays, special-interest personal essays, reviews for a general and literary audience." (5½×8½ perfect bound). Estab. 1991. Circ. 3,000. Pays on publication. Publishes ms an average of 9 months after acceptance. Byline given. Buys first North American serial, second serial (reprint) rights, occasionally requests rights for TV, radio reading, website. Editorial lead time 9 months. Accepts queries by mail, e-mail, phone. Accepts simultaneous submissions. Responds in 2 months to queries; 2 months to mss. Sample copy for $5 (back issue), $6 (current issue). Writer's guidelines for #10 SASE.

  • "We also sponsor the Lena-Miles Wever Todd Poetry Series competition, a contest for the best book manuscript by an American or Canadian poet. The winner receives $1,000, publication by Pleiades Press and distribution by Louisiana State University Press. Deadline: Generally March 31, e-mail for firm deadline. Send SASE for guidelines."

Nonfiction: Book excerpts, essays, interview/profile, reviews. "Nothing pedantic, slick or shallow." **Buys 4-6 mss/ year.** Send complete ms. Length: 2,000-4,000 words. **Pays $10.**

Fiction: R.M. Kinder, editor. Ethnic, experimental, humorous, mainstream, novel excerpts, magic realism. No science fiction, fantasy, confession, erotica. **Buys 16-20 mss/year.** Send complete ms. Length: 2,000-6,000 words. **Pays $10.**

Poetry: Kevin Prufer, editor. Avant-garde, free verse, haiku, light verse, traditional. "Nothing didactic, pretentious, or overly sentimental." **Buys 40-50 poems/year.** Submit maximum 6 poems. **Pays $3/poem and contributor copies.**

Tips: "Show care for your material and your readers—submit quality work in a professional format. Include cover letter with brief bio and list of publications. Include SASE."

$ $ PLOUGHSHARES, Emerson College, Dept. M, 120 Boylston St., Boston MA 02116. Website: www.ploughshares.org. **Contact:** Don Lee, editor. Triquarterly magazine for "readers of serious contemporary literature." Circ. 6,000. Pays on publication. Publishes ms an average of 6 months after acceptance. Buys first North American serial rights. Accepts simultaneous submissions. Responds in 5 months. Sample copy for $9 (back issue). Writer's guidelines for #10 SASE.

  • A competitive and highly prestigious market. Rotating and guest editors make cracking the line-up even tougher, since it's difficult to know what is appropriate to send. The reading period is August 1 through March 31.

Nonfiction: Essays (personal and literary; accepted only occasionally). Length: 6,000 words maximum. **Pays $25/ printed page, $50-250.**
Fiction: Mainstream, literary. **Buys 25-35 mss/year.** Length: 300-6,000 words. **Pays $25/printed page, $50-250.**
Poetry: Avant-garde, free verse, traditional, blank verse. Length: Open. **Pays $25/printed page, $50-250.**
Tips: "We no longer structure issues around preconceived themes. If you believe your work is in keeping with our general standards of literary quality and value, submit at any time during our reading period."

N $POETRY, Modern Poetry Association, 60 W. Walton St., Chicago IL 60610. Fax: (312)255-3702. E-mail: poetry@poetrymagazine.org. Website: www.poetrymagazine.org. Editor: Joseph Parisi. Managing Editor: Helen Klaviter. **Contact:** Stephen Young, senior editor. **100% freelance written.** Monthly magazine. Estab. 1912. Circ. 10,000. Pays on publication. Publishes ms an average of 9 months after acceptance. Byline given. Buys all rights, copyright returned to author on request. Accepts queries by mail. Responds in 1 month to queries; 4 months to mss. Sample copy for $5 or online. Writer's guidelines for #10 SASE or online.
Nonfiction: Reviews (most are solicited). **Buys 14 mss/year.** Query. Length: 1,000-2,000 words. **Pays $2/page.**
Poetry: All styles and subject matter. **Buys 180-250 poems/year.** Submit maximum 4 poems. Length: Open. **Pays $2/ line.**

$POTTERSFIELD PORTFOLIO, Stork and Press, P.O. Box 40, Station A, Sydney, Nova Scotia B1P 6G9, Canada. Website: www.pportfolio.com. **Contact:** Douglas Arthur Brown, managing editor. Triannual magazine. "*Pottersfield Portfolio* is always looking for poetry and fiction that provides fresh insights and delivers the unexpected. The stories and poems that capture our attention will be the ones that most effectively blend an intriguing voice with imaginative language. Our readers expect to be challenged, enlightened and entertained." Estab. 1979. Circ. 2,000. Pays on publication. Publishes ms an average of 6 months after acceptance. Byline given. Buys first North American serial rights. Editorial lead time 3 months. Responds in 3 months to mss. Writer's guidelines for #10 SASE (Canadian postage or IRC only) or online.
Nonfiction: Book excerpts, essays, interview/profile, photo feature. **Buys 6 mss/year.** Query. Length: 500-5,000 words.
Fiction: Fiction editor. Experimental, novel excerpts, short fiction. No fantasy, horror, mystery, religious, romance, science fiction, western. **Buys 12-15 mss/year.** Send complete ms. Length: 500-5,000 words.
Poetry: Poetry editor. Avant-garde, free verse, traditional. **Buys 20-30 poems/year.** Submit maximum 10 poems.
Tips: Looking for creative nonfiction, essays.

$THE PRAIRIE JOURNAL OF CANADIAN LITERATURE, P.O. Box 61203, Brentwood Postal Services 217K-3630 Brentwood Rd., Calgary, Alberta T2L 2K6, Canada. E-mail: prairiejournal@iname.com. Website: www.geocities.com/prairiejournal. **Contact:** A. Burke, editor. **100% freelance written.** Semiannual magazine publishes quality poetry, short fiction, drama, literary criticism, reviews, bibliography, interviews, profiles and artwork. Estab. 1983. Circ. 600. Publication; "honorarium depends on grant." Byline given. Buys first North American serial rights. Accepts queries by mail, e-mail. Responds in 6 months to queries; 6 months to mss. Sample copy for $6 and IRC, Canadian stamps or 50¢ payment for postage. Writer's guidelines online.
Nonfiction: Essays, humor, interview/profile (Canadian authors), scholarly, literary, book reviews (Canadian authors). **Buys 5 mss/year.** Query; include IRC. **Pays $25-100.**
Photos: Send photocopies of photos with submission. Buys first North American rights. Offers additional payment for photos accepted with ms. Identification of subjects required.
Fiction: Literary. **Buys 10 mss/year.** Send complete ms. **Pays in contributor copies or honoraria for literary work.**
Poetry: Launching "Poem of the Month" feature online; guidelines online. Avant-garde, free verse. **Buys 10 poems/ year.** Submit maximum 6-10 poems.
Tips: "Commercial writers are advised to submit elsewhere. Art needed, black and white pen and ink drawings or good-quality photocopy. Do not send originals. We are strictly small press editors interested in highly talented, serious artists. We are oversupplied with fiction but seek more high-quality poetry, especially the contemporary long poem or sequences from longer works. We welcome freelancers."

$PRISM INTERNATIONAL, Department of Creative Writing, Buch E462-1866 Main Mall, University of British Columbia, Vancouver, British Columbia V6T 1Z1, Canada. (604)822-2514. Fax: (604)822-3616. E-mail: prism@interchange.ubc.ca. Website: www.arts.ubc.ca/prism. Executive Editor: Laisha Rosnau. **Contact:** Chris Labonté (fiction/nonfiction), Andrea MacPherson (poetry/drama), editors. **100% freelance written.** Eager to work with new/unpublished writers. Quarterly magazine emphasizing contemporary literature, including translations, for university and public libraries, and private subscribers. Estab. 1959. Circ. 1,200. Pays on publication. Publishes ms an average of 4 months after acceptance. Buys first North American serial rights. Accepts queries by mail, e-mail, fax, phone. Responds in 4 months to queries; 4 months to mss. Sample copy for $5 or online. Writer's guidelines for #10 SAE with 1 first-class Canadian stamp (Canadian entries) or 1 IRC (US entries) or online.
  O─ Break in by "sending unusual or experimental work (we get mostly traditional submissions) and playing with forms (e.g., nonfiction, prose poetry, etc.)"
Nonfiction: "*Creative* nonfiction that reads like fiction. Nonfiction pieces should be creative, exploratory, or experimental in tone rather than rhetorical, academic, or journalistic." No reviews, tracts or scholarly essays. **Pays $20/printed page.**

Fiction: For Drama: One acts preferred. Also interested in seeing dramatic monologues. **Buys 3-5 mss/year.** Send complete ms. Length: 25 pages maximum. **Pays $20/printed page.** For prose: Experimental, novel excerpts, traditional. **Buys 12-16 mss/year.** Send complete ms. Length: 25 pages maximum. **Pays $20/printed page and 1 year subscription.**
Poetry: Avant-garde, traditional. **Buys 20/issue poems/year.** Submit maximum 6 poems. **Pays $40/printed page and 1 year subscription.**
Tips: "We are looking for new and exciting fiction. Excellence is still our number one criterion. As well as poetry, imaginative nonfiction and fiction, we are especially open to translations of all kinds, very short fiction pieces and drama which work well on the page. Translations must come with a copy of the original language work. We pay an additional $10/printed page to selected authors whose work we place on our on-line version of *Prism*."

$ $ QUARTERLY WEST, University of Utah, 200 S. Central Campus Dr., Rm. 317, Salt Lake City UT 84112-9109. (801)581-3938. Website: chronicle.utah.edu/QW. **Contact:** Steve Tuttle, editor. Semiannual magazine. "We publish fiction, poetry, and nonfiction in long and short formats, and will consider experimental as well as traditional works." Estab. 1976. Circ. 1,900. Pays on publication. Publishes ms an average of 6 months after acceptance. Buys first North American serial, all rights. Accepts simultaneous submissions. Responds in 6 months to mss. Sample copy for $7.50 or online. Writer's guidelines for #10 SASE or online.
Nonfiction: Essays, interview/profile, Book reviews. **Buys 6-7 mss/year.** Send complete ms with SASE. Length: 10,000 words maximum. **Pays $25.**
Fiction: Lynn Kilpatrick. No preferred lengths; interested in longer, fuller short stories and short shorts. Ethnic, experimental, humorous, mainstream, novel excerpts, slice-of-life vignettes, short shorts, translations. **Buys 20-30 mss/year.** Send complete ms with SASE.
Poetry: David Hawkins. Avant-garde, free verse, traditional. **Buys 70-80 poems/year.** Submit maximum 5 poems. **Pays $15-100.**
Tips: "We publish a special section of short shorts every issue, and we also sponsor a biennial novella contest. We are open to experimental work—potential contributors should read the magazine! Don't send more than one story per submission, but submit as often as you like. Biennial novella competition guidelines available upon request with SASE."

$ $ QUEEN'S QUARTERLY, A Canadian Review, Queen's University, Kingston, Ontario K7L 3N6, Canada. (613)533-2667. Fax: (613)533-6822. E-mail: qquarter@post.queensu.ca. Website: info.queensu.ca/quarterly. **Contact:** Joan Harcourt, literary editor. **95% freelance written.** Quarterly magazine covering a wide variety of subjects, including science, humanities, arts and letters, politics and history for the educated reader. Estab. 1893. Circ. 3,000. Pays on publication. Publishes ms an average of 6 months after acceptance. Byline given. Buys first North American serial rights. Responds in 1 month. *Writer's Market* recommends allowing 2 months for reply to mss. Sample copy for $6.50 or online. Writer's guidelines online.
 • No reply/return without IRC
Fiction: Novel excerpts. **Buys 8-12 mss/year.** Send complete ms. Length: 2,000 words maximum. **Pays $150-250.**
Poetry: **Buys 25 poems/year.** Submit maximum 6 poems. Length: Open. **Offers 3 year subscription in lieu of payment.**
Tips: No multiple submissions. No more than six poems or two stories per submission.

$ RAIN CROW, Rain Crow Publishing, P.O. Box 11013, Chicago IL 60611. Fax: (503)214-6615. E-mail: msm@manley.org. Website: www.rain-crow.com/. **Contact:** Michael S. Manley, editor. Triannual magazine featuring well-crafted, original, entertaining fiction. "We publish new and established writers in many styles and genres. We are a publication for people passionate about the short story form." Estab. 1995. Circ. 1,000. Pays on publication. Publishes ms an average of 4 months after acceptance. Byline given. Buys one-time, electronic rights. Editorial lead time 4 months. Submit seasonal material 8 months in advance. Accepts queries by mail, e-mail. Accepts simultaneous submissions. Responds in 3 weeks to queries; 4 months to mss. Sample copy for $5. Writer's guidelines for #10 SASE, online or by e-mail.
Fiction: Erotica, experimental, mainstream, science fiction, literary. "No propaganda, pornography, juvenile, formulaic." **Buys 30 mss/year.** Send complete ms. Length: 250-8,000 words. **Pays $5-150.**
Tips: "Write to the best of your abilities, submit your best work. Present yourself and your work professionally. When we evaluate a submission, we ask, 'Is this something we would like to read again? Is this something we would give to someone else to read?' A good manuscript makes the reader forget they are reading a manuscript. We look for attention to craft: voice, language, character and plot working together to maximum effect. Unique yet credible settings and situations that entertain get the most attention."

$ RARITAN, A Quarterly Review, 31 Mine St., New Brunswick NJ 08903. (732)932-7887. Fax: (732)932-7855. Editor: Richard Poirier. **Contact:** Stephanie Volmer, managing editor. Quarterly magazine covering literature, general culture. Estab. 1981. Circ. 3,500. Pays on publication. Publishes ms an average of 1 year after acceptance. Byline given. Buys first North American serial rights. Editorial lead time 5 months. Accepts queries by mail. Accepts simultaneous submissions.
 • Raritan no longer accepts previously published submissions.
Nonfiction: Book excerpts, essays. **Buys 50 mss/year.** Send complete ms. Length: 15-30 pages.

$ RIVER STYX, Big River Association, 634 N. Grand Blvd., 12th Floor, St. Louis MO 63103. Website: www.riverstyx.org. Senior Editors: Quincy Troupe and Michael Castro. **Contact:** Richard Newman, editor. Triannual magazine.

"*River Styx* publishes the highest quality fiction, poetry, interviews, essays and visual art. We are an internationally distributed multicultural literary magazine." Manuscripts read May-November. Estab. 1975. Pays on publication. Publishes ms an average of 1 year after acceptance. Byline given. Buys one-time rights. Accepts queries by mail. Accepts simultaneous submissions. Responds in 4 months to mss. Sample copy for $7. Writer's guidelines for #10 SASE or online.

- River Styx has won several prizes, including Best American Poetry 1998; Pushcart Prize; and Stanley Hanks Prizes.

Nonfiction: Essays, interview/profile. **Buys 2-5 mss/year.** Send complete ms. **Pays 2 contributor copies, plus 1 year subscription; pays $8/page if funds are available.**
Photos: Send photos with submission. Reviews 5×7 or 8×10 b&w and color prints and slides. Buys one-time rights. Pays 2 contributor copies, plus 1 year subscription; $8/page if funds are available.
Fiction: Novel excerpts, short stories, literary. **Buys 6-9 mss/year.** Send complete ms. **Pays 2 contributor copies, plus 1 year subscription; $8/page if funds are available.**
Poetry: Avant-garde, free verse, formal. No religious. **Buys 40-50 poems/year.** Submit maximum 3-5 poems. **Pays 2 contributor copies plus a 1 year subscription; $8/page if funds are available.**

$ ROOM OF ONE'S OWN, A Canadian Quarterly of Women's Literature and Criticism, West Coast Feminist Literary Magazine Society, P.O. Box 46160, Station D, Vancouver, British Columbia V6J 5G5, Canada. Website: www.islandnet.com/Room/enter. **Contact:** Growing Room Collective. **100% freelance written.** Quarterly journal of feminist literature. Estab. 1975. Circ. 1,000. Pays on publication. Publishes ms within 1 year of acceptance. Byline given. Buys first North American serial rights. Editorial lead time 9 months. Responds in 3 months to queries; 6 months to mss. Sample copy for $7 or online. Writer's guidelines for #10 SAE with 2 IRCs (US postage not valid in Canada) or online.
Nonfiction: Reviews. **Buys 1-2 mss/year.** Send complete ms. Length: 1,000-2,500 words. **Pays $35 (Canadian) and 1 year subscription.**
Fiction: Feminist literature—short stories, creative nonfiction, essays by, for and about women. **Buys 40 mss/year.** Length: 2,000-5,000 words. **Pays $35 (Canadian) and 1 year subscription.**
Poetry: Avant-garde, free verse. "Nothing light, undeveloped." **Buys 40 poems/year.** Submit maximum 6 poems. Length: 3-80 lines. **Pays $35 (Canadian) and a 1 year subscription.**

$ $ ⬥ ROSEBUD, The Magazine For People Who Enjoy Good Writing, Rosebud, Inc., P.O. Box 459, Cambridge WI 53523. (608)423-4750. Website: www.rsbd.net. **Contact:** Rod Clark, editor. **100% freelance written.** Quarterly magazine "for people who love to read and write. Our readers like good storytelling, real emotion, a sense of place and authentic voice." Estab. 1993. Circ. 9,000. Pays on publication. Publishes ms an average of 2 months after acceptance. Byline given. Buys one-time, second serial (reprint) rights. Editorial lead time 3 months. Submit seasonal material 3 months in advance. Accepts simultaneous submissions. Sends acknowledgement postcard upon receipt of submission and responds in 5 months to queries. Sample copy for $6.95 or sample articles online. Writer's guidelines for SASE or online.

- Charges $1 reading fee.

Nonfiction: Book excerpts, essays, general interest, historical/nostalgic, humor, interview/profile, personal experience, travel, memoirs that have a literary sensibility. "No editorializing." Send complete ms. Length: 1,200-1,800 words. **Pays $45-195 and 3 contributor copies.**
Reprints: Send tearsheet or photocopy. Pays 100% of amount paid for an original article.
Photos: State availability with submission. Buys one-time rights. Offers no additional payment for photos accepted with ms. Captions, identification of subjects, model releases required.
Fiction: Ethnic, experimental, historical, humorous, mainstream, novel excerpts, slice-of-life vignettes, suspense. "No formula pieces." **Buys 80 mss/year.** Send complete ms. Length: 1,200-1,800 words. **Pays $15-50.**
Poetry: Avant-garde, free verse, traditional. No inspirational poetry. **Buys 36 poems/year.** Submit maximum 5 poems. Length: Open. **Pays $15-50 and 3 contributor copies.**
Tips: "Something has to 'happen' in the pieces we choose, but what happens inside characters is much more interesting to us than plot manipulation. We prefer to respond with an individualized letter (send SASE for this) and recycle submitted manuscripts. We will return your manuscript only if you send sufficient postage. As of June 2001, only manuscripts accompanied by a $1 fee will be read."

$ SHENANDOAH, The Washington and Lee University Review, Washington and Lee University, Troubadour Theater, 2nd Floor, Lexington VA 24450-0303. (540)463-8765. Website: www.w/u.edu/~shenando. Managing Editor: Lynn Leech. **Contact:** R.T. Smith, editor. Quarterly magazine. Estab. 1950. Circ. 2,000. Pays on publication. Publishes ms an average of 10 months after acceptance. Byline given. Buys first North American serial, one-time rights. Responds in 2 months to mss. Sample copy for $5. Writer's guidelines online.
Nonfiction: Book excerpts, essays. **Buys 6 mss/year.** Send complete ms. **Pays $25/page.**
Fiction: Mainstream, novel excerpts. No sloppy, hasty, slight fiction. **Buys 15 mss/year.** Send complete ms. **Pays $25/page.**
Poetry: No inspirational, confessional poetry. **Buys 70 poems/year.** Submit maximum 6 poems. Length: Open. **Pays $2.50/line.**

$ SHORT STUFF, for Grown-ups, Bowman Publications, 712 W. 10th St., Loveland CO 80537. (970)669-9139. E-mail: shortstf@oneimage.com. **Contact:** Donnalee Bowman, editor. **98% freelance written.** Bimonthly magazine. "We are perhaps an enigma in that we publish only clean stories in any genre. We'll tackle any subject, but don't allow obscene language or pornographic description. Our magazine is for grown-ups, *not* X-rated 'adult' fare." Estab. 1989. Circ. 10,400. Payment and contract upon publication. Byline given. Buys first North American serial rights. Editorial lead time 3 months. Submit seasonal material 3 months in advance. Responds in 6 months to mss. Sample copy for $1.50 and 9×12 SAE with 5 first-class stamps. Writer's guidelines for #10 SASE.

> **O—π** Break in with "a good, tight story. Cover letters stating what a great story is enclosed really turn me off, just a personal bit about the author is sufficient."

Nonfiction: Most nonfiction is staff written. Humor. Special issues: "We are holiday oriented and each issue reflects the appropriate holidays. **Buys 20 mss/year.** Send complete ms. Length: 500-1,500 words. **Pays $10-50.**

Photos: Send photos with submission. Buys one-time rights. Offers no additional payment for photos accepted with ms. Identification of subjects required.

Fiction: Adventure, historical, humorous, mainstream, mystery, romance, science fiction, suspense, western. **Buys 144 mss/year.** Send complete ms. Length: 500-1,500 words. **Pays $10-50.**

Fillers: Anecdotes, short humor. **Buys 200/year.** Length: 20-500 words. **Pays $1-5.**

Tips: "Don't send floppy disks or cartridges. Do include cover letter about the author, not a synopsis of the story. We are holiday oriented; mark on *outside* of envelope if story is for Easter, Mother's Day, etc. We receive 500 manuscripts each month. This is up about 200%. Because of this, I implore writers to send one manuscript at a time. I would not use stories from the same author more than once an issue and this means I might keep the others too long."

$ THE SOUTHERN REVIEW, 43 Allen Hall, Louisiana State University, Baton Rouge LA 70803-5001. (225)578-5108. Fax: (225)578-5098. E-mail: bmacon@lsu.edu. Website: www.LSU.edu/guests/wwwtsm. **Contact:** Michael Griffith, associate editor. **100% freelance written.** Works with a moderate number of new/unpublished writers each year. Quarterly magazine "with emphasis on contemporary literature in the United States and abroad, and with special interest in Southern culture and history." No queries. Reading period: September-May. Estab. 1935. Circ. 3,100. Pays on publication. Publishes ms an average of 6 months after acceptance. Byline given. Buys first North American serial rights. Accepts queries by mail. Responds in 2 months to mss. Sample copy for $8. Writer's guidelines for #10 SASE or online.

Nonfiction: Essays with careful attention to craftsmanship, technique and seriousness of subject matter. "Willing to publish experimental writing if it has a valid artistic purpose. Avoid extremism and sensationalism. Essays should exhibit thoughtful and sometimes severe awareness of the necessity of literary standards in our time." Emphasis on contemporary literature, especially Southern culture and history. No footnotes. **Buys 25 mss/year.** Length: 4,000-10,000 words. **Pays $12/page.**

Fiction: Short stories of lasting literary merit, with emphasis on style and technique; novel excerpts. Length: 4,000-8,000 words. **Pays $12/page.**

Poetry: Length: 1-4 pages. **Pays $20/page.**

N: $ THE SPIRIT THAT MOVES US, The Spirit That Moves Us Press, Inc., P.O. Box 720820WM, Jackson Heights NY 11372-0820. (718)426-8788. **Contact:** Morty Sklar, editor. Annual book of literary works. "We don't push any 'schools'; we're open to many styles and almost any subject matter. We favor work that expresses feeling, whether subtle or passionate. Irregularly we publish *Editor's Choice: Fiction, Poetry & Art from the U.S. Small Press*, which consists of selections from nominations made by other small literary publishers. When writers see our open call for nominations for this anthology, they should encourage their publishers to nominate their and other people's work." Estab. 1975. Pays on publication. Publishes ms an average of 3 months after acceptance. Byline given. Buys first North American serial, second serial (reprint) rights. Accepts queries by mail. Accepts simultaneous submissions. Responds in 2 weeks to queries; 3 months after deadline date on mss (nothing is accepted until everything is read). Sample copy for $5.75 for *15th Anniversary Issue*, $10.75 for *Editor's Choice* to readers of *Writer's Market*.

Nonfiction: Book excerpts, essays, interview/profile, personal experience. **Buys 20-30 mss/year for special issues.** Query for current theme. Length: 8,500 words maximum. **Pays $15-25 plus contributor's copy for assigned articles.** Pays in contributor copies if so requested by author. "Royalty set-up for single-author books, with a cash advance."

Reprints: Accepts previously published submissions (only for those collections that we specify). Send tearsheet or photocopy and information about when and where the material previously appeared. Pays 100% of amount paid for original article.

Photos: "Photos are considered for artistic merit, and not just illustrative function. All art that we use has to stand on its own." Reviews contact sheets, 8×10 prints. Buys one-time rights. Offers $15/photo; $100 for cover photos plus a free copy and 40% off additional copies.

Fiction: "Nothing slick or commercial." **Buys 15-30 mss/year.** Length: 8,500 words maximum. **Pays $15-25 plus a free copy and 40% off additional copies.**

Poetry: "Not interested in work that just tries to be smart, flashy, sensational; if it's technically skilled but conveys no feeling, we don't care about it for publication. We were the first U.S. publisher to bring out a collection by the Czech poet Nobel Laureate of 1984—and before he won the Nobel prize." **Buys 50-100 poems/year. Pays $15 (depending on length and funding/sales obtained) plus a free copy and 40% off additional copies.**

Tips: "Writers and visual artists should query first to see what we're working on if they haven't seen our latest call for manuscripts in *Poets & Writers* magazine or elsewhere. Send #10 SASE for themes and time frames."

[N] $ $ [■] THE SPOOK ONLINE MAGAZINE, Filmcity Productions, P.O. Box 281, Warrensburg NY 12885. E-mail: mhartman@thespook.com; for writer's guidelines write to editorial@thespook.com. Website: www.thespook.com. **Contact:** Michael Hartman. **10% freelance written.** Monthly online publication covering the literary horror genre. Publishes horror, mystery, science fiction. No sword and sorcery or dungeons and dragons. Estab. 2001. Circ. 100,000 visits/month. Pays on publication. Byline given. Offers 25% kill fee. Buys one-time rights. Editorial lead time 3 months. Submit seasonal material 3 months in advance. Accepts queries by e-mail. Accepts simultaneous submissions. Responds in 1 week to queries; 2 months to mss. Writer's guidelines by e-mail.
Nonfiction: Book excerpts, general interest, humor, interview/profile, new product, reviews of films, videos, books. **Buys 24 mss/year.** Query. Length: 1,000-5,000 words. **Pays $100-500 for assigned articles; $50-500 for unsolicited articles.** Sometimes pays expenses of writers on assignment.
Photos: State availability with submission. Reviews prints, gif, jpeg and tiff formats. Buys one-time rights. Negotiates payment individually. Identification of subjects, model releases required.
Fiction: Historical, horror, mystery, science fiction. **Buys 24 mss/year.** Query. Length: 1,000-5,000 words. **Pays $50-500.**
Tips: "The only real criterion for selecting fiction is how strongly it affects us when we read it. Manuscripts which stand out the most are those prepared and submitted properly."

$ SPORT LITERATE, Honest Reflections on Life's Leisurely Diversions, Pint-Size Publications, P.O. Box 577166, Chicago IL 60657-7166. Website: www.sportliterate.org. **Contact:** William Meiners, editor-in-chief. **95% freelance written.** Semiannual journal covering leisure/sport...life outside the daily grind of making a living. "*Sport Literate* publishes the highest quality creative nonfiction and poetry on themes of leisure and sport. Our writers use a leisure activity to explore a larger theme. This creative allegorical writing serves a broad audience." Estab. 1995. Circ. 1,500. Pays on publication. Publishes ms an average of 3 months after acceptance. Byline given. Buys first North American serial rights. Editorial lead time 3 months. Submit seasonal material 4 months in advance. Accepts queries by mail, e-mail (through website). Responds in 3 weeks to queries; 2 months to mss. Sample copy for $7.75. Writer's guidelines for #10 SASE or online.
Nonfiction: Essays, historical/nostalgic, humor, interview/profile, personal experience, travel, creative nonfiction. No book reviews, straight reporting on sports. **Buys 28 mss/year.** Send complete ms. Length: 250-5,000 words.
Photos: Steve Mend (contact through website). Accepts b&w photo essays "that tell a deeper story of folks passing their time."
Poetry: Frank Van Zant, poetry editor. Avant-garde, free verse, haiku, light verse, traditional. **Buys 25 poems/year.** Submit maximum 5 poems. Length: 30 lines maximum. **Pays $20 maximum.**
   [■] The online magazine carries original content not found in the print edition and includes writer's guidelines. Contact: Steve Mend, online editor.
Tips: "We like to explore all the avenues of the creative nonfiction form—personal essays, literary journalism, travel pieces, historical, humor and interviews—as they relate to our broad definition of sport. We don't publish fiction. Read any publication that you're submitting to. It can be a great time saver."

$ SPSM&H, *Amelia Magazine*, 329 E St., Bakersfield CA 93304. (661)323-4064. E-mail: amelia@lightspeed.net. Website: www.ameliamagazine.net. **Contact:** Frederick A. Raborg, Jr, editor. **100% freelance written.** Quarterly magazine featuring fiction and poetry with Romantic or Gothic theme. "*SPSM&H* (Shakespeare, Petrarch, Sidney, Milton and Hopkins) uses one short story in each issue and 20-36 sonnets, plus reviews of books and anthologies containing the sonnet form and occasional articles about the sonnet form or about some romantic or Gothic figure or movement. We look for contemporary aspects of the sonnet form." Estab. 1984. Circ. 600. Pays on publication. Publishes ms an average of 6 months after acceptance. Byline given. Offers 50% kill fee. Buys first North American serial rights. Editorial lead time 2 months. Submit seasonal material 3 months in advance. Accepts simultaneous submissions. Responds in 2 weeks to queries; 3 months to mss. Sample copy for $6. Writer's guidelines for #10 SASE.
Nonfiction: Anything related to sonnets or to romance. Essays, general interest, historical/nostalgic, humor, interview/profile, opinion. **Buys 1-4 mss/year.** Send complete ms. Length: 500-2,000 words. **Pays $10.**
Photos: Send photos with submission. Reviews 8×10 or 5×7 b&w prints. Buys one-time rights. Offers $10-25/photo. Model releases required.
Fiction: Confessions, erotica, experimental, fantasy, historical, humorous, mainstream, mystery, romance, slice-of-life vignettes, gay/lesbian. **Buys 4 mss/year.** Send complete ms. Length: 500-2,500 words. **Pays $10-20.**
Poetry: Sonnets, sonnet sequence. **Buys 140 poems/year.** Submit maximum 10 poems. Length: 14 lines. **Two best of issue poets receive $14.**
Fillers: Anecdotes, short humor. **Buys 2-4/year.** Length: 25-500 words. **No payment for fillers.**
Tips: "Read a copy certainly. Understand the limitations of the sonnet form and, in the case of fiction, the requirements of the romantic or Gothic genres. Be professional in presentation, and realize that neatness does count. Be contemporary and avoid Victorian verse forms and techniques. Avoid convolution and forced rhyme. Idiomatics ought to be contemporary. Don't be afraid to experiment. We consider John Updike's 'Love Sonnet' to be the extreme to which poets may experiment."

$ STAND MAGAZINE, Dept. of English, VCU, Richmond VA 23284-2005. (804)828-1331. E-mail: dlatane@vcu.edu. Website: saturn.vcu.edu/~dlatane/stand.html. Editors: Michael Hulse and John Kinsella. **Contact:** David Latané, U.S editor. **75% freelance written.** Quarterly magazine covering short fiction, poetry, criticism and reviews. "*Stand*

Magazine is concerned with what happens when cultures and literatures meet, with translation in its many guises, with the mechanics of language, with the processes by which the polity receives or disables its cultural makers. *Stand* promotes debate of issues that are of radical concern to the intellectual community worldwide." Estab. 1952. Circ. 3,000 worldwide. Pays on publication. Publishes ms an average of 10 months after acceptance. Byline given. Buys first world rights. Editorial lead time 2 months. Accepts queries by mail. Responds in 6 weeks to queries; 3 months to mss. Sample copy for $11. Writer's guidelines for #10 SASE with sufficient number of IRCs or online.

Nonfiction: "Reviews are commissioned from known freelancers." Reviews of poetry/fiction. **Buys 8 mss/year.** Query. Length: 200-5,000 words. **Pays $30/1,000 words.**

Fiction: Adventure, ethnic, experimental, historical, mainstream. "No genre fiction." **Buys 12-14 mss/year.** Send complete ms. Length: 8,000 words maximum. **Pays $37.50/1,000 words.**

Poetry: Avant-garde, free verse, traditional. **Buys 100-120 poems/year.** Submit maximum 6 poems. **Pays $37.50/ poem.**

Tips: "Poetry/fiction areas are most open to freelancers. *Stand* is published in England and reaches an international audience. North American writers should submit work to the U.S. address. While the topic or nature of submissions does not have to be 'international,' writers may do well to keep in mind the range of *Stand*'s audience."

$ THE STRAIN, Interactive Arts Magazine, 1307 Diablo, Houston TX 77532-3004. **Contact:** Norman Clark Stewart Jr., editor. **80% freelance written.** Monthly magazine. Estab. 1987. Pays on publication. Publishes ms an average of 3 years after acceptance. Byline given. Buys first, one-time, second serial (reprint) rights, makes work-for-hire assignments. Responds in 2 years.

Nonfiction: Alicia Alder, articles editor. Essays, exposé, how-to, humor, photo feature, technical. **Buys 2-20 mss/year.** Send complete ms. **Pays $5.**

Reprints: Send typed ms with rights for sale noted and information about when and where the material previously appeared.

Photos: Send photos with submission. Reviews transparencies, prints. Buys one-time rights. Identification of subjects, model releases required.

Columns/Departments: Charlie Mainze, editor. Multi-media performance art. Send complete ms. **Pays $5.**

Fiction: Michael Bond, editor. **Buys 1-35 mss/year.** Send complete ms. **Pays $5.**

Poetry: Annas Kinder, editor. Avant-garde, free verse, light verse, traditional. **Buys 100 poems/year.** Submit maximum 5 poems. **Pays $5.**

$ THE STRAND MAGAZINE, P.O. Box 1418, Birmingham MI 48012-1418. (800)300-6652. Fax: (248)874-1046. E-mail: strandmag@worldnet.att.net. **Contact:** A.F. Gulli, managing editor. Quarterly magazine covering mysteries, short stories, essays, book reviews. "Mysteries and short stories written in the classic tradition of this century's great authors." Estab. 1998. Pays on publication. Publishes ms an average of 4 months after acceptance. Byline given. Buys first North American serial rights. Responds in 1 month to queries; 4 months to mss. Writer's guidelines for #10 SASE.

Fiction: Mystery, suspense, tales of the unexpected, some horror and some humorous. Send complete ms. Length: 2,000-6,000 words. **Pays $50-175.**

Tips: "No gratuitous violence, sexual content or explicit language please."

N: $ TAMPA REVIEW, University of Tampa Press, 401 W. Kennedy Blvd., Tampa FL 33606. (813)253-6266. Website: tampareview.utampa.edu. **Contact:** Richard B. Mathews, director. Semiannual magazine published in hardback format. An international literary journal publishing art and literature from Florida and Tampa Bay as well as new work and translations from throughout the world. Estab. 1988. Circ. 500. Pays on publication. Publishes ms an average of 10 months after acceptance. Byline given. Buys first North American serial rights. Editorial lead time 18 months. Accepts queries by mail. Responds in 5 months to mss. Sample copy for $7. Writer's guidelines for #10 SASE.

Nonfiction: Elizabeth Winston, nonfiction editor. Book excerpts, general interest, interview/profile, personal experience. No "how-to" articles, fads, journalistic reprise, etc. **Buys 6 mss/year.** Send complete ms. Length: 250-7,500 words. **Pays $10/printed page.**

Photos: State availability with submission. Reviews contact sheets, negatives, transparencies, prints, digital files. Buys one-time rights. Offers $10/photo. Captions, identification of subjects required.

Fiction: Lisa Birnbaum and Kathleen Ochshorn, fiction editors. Literary. **Buys 6 mss/year.** Send complete ms. Length: 200-5,000 words. **Pays $10/printed page.**

Poetry: Don Morrill, poetry editor. Avant-garde, free verse, haiku, light verse, traditional, visual/experimental. No greeting card verse; hackneyed, sing-song, rhyme-for-the-sake-of-rhyme. **Buys 45 poems/year.** Submit maximum 10 poems. Length: 2-225 lines.

Tips: "Send a clear cover letter stating previous experience or background. Our editorial staff considers submissions between September and December for publication in the following year."

$ THEMA, Box 8747, Metairie LA 70011-8747. (504)887-1263. E-mail: thema@home.com. Website: www.litline. org/thema. **Contact:** Virginia Howard, editor. **100% freelance written.** Triannual magazine covering a different theme for each issue. Upcoming themes for SASE. "*Thema* is designed to stimulate creative thinking by challenging writers with unusual themes, such as 'laughter on the steps' and 'jogging on ice.' Appeals to writers, teachers of creative writing and general reading audience." Estab. 1988. Circ. 350. **Pays on acceptance.** Byline given. Buys one-time rights. Accepts queries by mail, e-mail. Responds in 5 months to mss. Sample copy for $8. Writer's guidelines for #10 SASE or online.

Reprints: Send typed ms with rights for sale noted and information about when and where the material previously appeared. Pays the same amount paid for original.

Fiction: Special Issues: The Power of Whim (November 1, 2001); Paper Tigers (March 1, 2002); Lost in Translation (July 1, 2002). Adventure, ethnic, experimental, fantasy, historical, humorous, mainstream, mystery, novel excerpts, religious, science fiction, slice-of-life vignettes, suspense, western. "No erotica." **Buys 30 mss/year. Pays $10-25.**

Poetry: Avant-garde, free verse, haiku, light verse, traditional. "No erotica." **Buys 27 poems/year.** Submit maximum 3 poems. Length: 4-50 lines. **Pays $10.**

Tips: "Be familiar with the themes. *Don't submit* unless you have an upcoming theme in mind. Specify the target theme on the first page of your manuscript or in a cover letter. Put your name on *first* page of manuscript only. (All submissions are judged in blind review after the deadline for a specified issue.) Most open to fiction and poetry. Don't be hasty when you consider a theme—mull it over and let it ferment in your mind. We appreciate interpretations that are carefully constructed, clever, subtle, well thought out."

$ $⊠ THE THREEPENNY REVIEW, P.O. Box 9131, Berkeley CA 94709. (510)849-4545. Website: www.thre epennyreview.com. **Contact:** Wendy Lesser, editor. **100% freelance written.** Works with small number of new/unpublished writers each year. Quarterly tabloid. "We are a general interest, national literary magazine with coverage of politics, the visual arts and the performing arts as well." Estab. 1980. Circ. 9,000. **Pays on acceptance.** Publishes ms an average of 1 year after acceptance. Byline given. Buys first North American serial rights. Responds in 1 month to queries; 2 months to mss. Sample copy for $10 or online. Writer's guidelines for SASE or online.

• Does not read mss in summer months.

Nonfiction: Essays, exposé, historical/nostalgic, personal experience, book, film, theater, dance, music, and art reviews. **Buys 40 mss/year.** Query with or without published clips or send complete ms. Length: 1,500-4,000 words. **Pays $200.**

Fiction: No fragmentary, sentimental fiction. **Buys 10 mss/year.** Send complete ms. Length: 800-4,000 words. **Pays $200.**

Poetry: Free verse, traditional. No poems "without capital letters or poems without a discernible subject." **Buys 30 poems/year.** Submit maximum 5 poems. **Pays $100.**

Tips: "Nonfiction (political articles, memoirs, reviews) is most open to freelancers."

$ TICKLED BY THUNDER, Helping Writers Get Published, Tickled by Thunder, 14076-86A Ave., Surrey, British Columbia V3W 0V9, Canada. (604)591-6095. E-mail: thunder@istar.ca. Website: www.home.istar.ca/~thunder. **Contact:** L. Lindner, publisher/editor. **100% freelance written.** Quarterly magazine on writing. "Our readers are generally writers hoping to improve their craft and gain writing experience/credits." Estab. 1990. Circ. 1,000. Pays on publication. Publishes ms an average of 4 months after acceptance. Byline given. Buys one-time rights. Editorial lead time 4 months. Submit seasonal material 6 months in advance. Accepts simultaneous submissions. Responds in 6 weeks to queries; 4 months to mss. Sample copy for $2.50 or sample articles online. Writer's guidelines for #10 SASE or online.

O→ Break in with "articles—more articles. Next best—write better than we can."

Nonfiction: Interview/profile, opinion, personal experience (must relate to writing). Does not want to see articles not slanted to writing. **Buys 4 mss/year.** Send complete ms. Length: 300-2,000 words. **Pays 5¢/line-$5.**

Photos: State availability with submission. Buys one-time rights. Identification of subjects, model releases required.

Fiction: Experimental, fantasy, humorous, mainstream, mystery, religious, science fiction, slice-of-life vignettes, suspense, western. No bad language—not even "damn" or "hell." **Buys 8-12 mss/year.** Send complete ms. Length: 300-2,000 words. **Pays 10¢/line-$5.**

Poetry: Avant-garde, free verse, haiku, light verse, traditional. "Nothing that requires a manual to understand." **Buys 12-20 poems/year.** Submit maximum 7 poems. Length: 50 lines. **Pays 2¢/line-$2.**

$ $ TIN HOUSE, McCormack Communications., Box 10500, Portland OR 97296. Website: www.tinhouse.com. Editor-in-Chief: Win McCormack. Managing Editor: Holly Macarthur. Editors: Rob Spillman, Elissa Schappell. **Contact:** Serena Crawford, assistant editor. **90% freelance written.** Quarterly magazine. "We are a general interest literary quarterly. Our watchword is quality. Our audience is people interested in literature in all its aspects, from the mundane to the exalted." Estab. 1998. Circ. 5,000. Pays on publication. Publishes ms an average of 1 year after acceptance. Byline given. Buys first North American serial rights, anthology rights. Editorial lead time 6 months. Submit seasonal material 6 months in advance. Accepts simultaneous submissions. Responds in 6 weeks to queries; 3 months to mss. Sample copy for $15. Writer's guidelines for #10 SASE.

Nonfiction: Book excerpts, essays, interview/profile, personal experience. Send complete ms. Length: 5,000 words maximum. **Pays $50-800 for assigned articles; $50-500 for unsolicited articles.** Sometimes pays expenses of writers on assignment.

Columns/Departments: Lost and Found (mini-reviews of forgotten or under appreciated books), up to 500 words; Readable Feasts (fiction or nonfiction literature with recipes), 2,000-3,000 words; Pilgrimage (journey to a personally significant place, especially literary), 2,000-3,000 words. **Buys 15-20 mss/year.** Send complete ms. **Pays $50-500.**

Fiction: Experimental, mainstream, novel excerpts, literary. **Buys 15-20 mss/year.** Send complete ms. Length: 5,000 words maximum. **Pays $200-800.**

Poetry: Amy Bartlett, poetry editor. Avant-garde, free verse, traditional. No prose masquerading as poetry. **Buys 20 poems/year.** Submit maximum 5 poems. **Pays $50-150.**

Tips: "Remember to send an SASE with your submission."

N ☐ **TRAGOS, Magazine of Consequence**, Tragos Publishing, 320 N. Stanley Ave., D, Los Angeles CA 90036. E-mail: submit@tragos.org. Website: http://tragos.org. **Contact:** Editor. **100% freelance written.** Bimonthly online publication. "*TRAGOS* is an American Magazine of Consequence publishing best-of-breed reportage, commentary, photography, fiction and words to songs." Estab. 2001. Circ. 10,000 visits/month. Pays on publication. Byline given. Offers 15% kill fee. Buys electronic rights. Accepts queries by mail, e-mail. Accepts simultaneous submissions. Responds in 2 months to mss. Writer's guidelines online at http://tragos.org/guidelines.html.
Nonfiction: Essays, exposé, general interest, humor, interview/profile, opinion, personal experience, photo feature, technical. **Buys 10 mss/year.** Send complete ms. Length: 250-5,000 words. **Pays $1.**
Photos: Send photos with submission. Reviews transparencies, jpeg format. Offers no additional payment for photos accepted with ms.

$ TRIQUARTERLY, 2020 Ridge Ave., Northwestern University, Evanston IL 60208-4302. (847)491-3490. Fax: (847)467-2096. **Contact:** Susan Firestone Hahn, editor. **70% freelance written.** Triannual magazine of fiction, poetry and essays, as well as artwork. Estab. 1964. Pays on publication. Publishes ms an average of 1 year after acceptance. Buys first North American serial rights, nonexclusive reprint rights. Responds in 3 months to queries; 3 months to mss. Sample copy for $5. Writer's guidelines for #10 SASE.
   • *TriQuarterly* has had several stories published in the *O. Henry Prize* anthology and *Best American Short Stories* as well as poetry in *Best American Poetry*. Eager to work with new/unpublished writers.
Nonfiction: Essays. No scholarly or critical essays except in special issues. Query.
Fiction: No prejudice against style or length of work; only seriousness and excellence are required. Does not accept or read mss between April 1 and September 30. **Buys 20-50 unsolicited mss/year. Payment varies depending on grant support.**
Poetry: Buys 20-50 poems/year. Payment varies depending on grant support.

N $ VIRGINIA ADVERSARIA, Empire Publishing, P.O. Box 2349, Poquoson VA 23662. E-mail: empirepub@hot mail.com. **Contact:** Bill Glose, editor. **90% freelance written.** Quarterly literary magazine. Estab. 2000. Circ. 1,500. Pays on publication. Publishes ms an average of 5 months after acceptance. Byline given. Buys one-time rights. Editorial lead time 3 months. Submit seasonal material 5 months in advance. Accepts queries by mail. Accepts simultaneous submissions. Responds in 5 weeks to queries; 2 months to mss. Sample copy for $4.50. Writer's guidelines for #10 SASE.
Nonfiction: Nonfiction articles must pertain to Virginia life or general topics. Nothing specialized outside our region. Book excerpts, essays, interview/profile, personal experience. **Buys 4-10 mss/year.** Query with published clips. Length: 500-3,000 words. **Pays $5-75.** Sometimes pays expenses of writers on assignment.
Photos: State availability with submission. Reviews prints. Buys one-time rights. Negotiates payment individually.
Columns/Departments: Exploring Virginia (events in Virginia coupled with background information), 2,000 words. **Buys 1-4 mss/year.** Query with published clips. **Pays $5-60.**
Fiction: Adventure, historical, humorous, mainstream, mystery, romance, slice-of-life vignettes, suspense, literary. **Buys 32 mss/year.** Send complete ms. Length: 6,000 words maximum. **Pays $60.**
Poetry: Nancy Powell, poetry editor. Free verse, light verse, traditional. No cute greeting card verse. **Buys 24 poems/year.** Submit maximum 6 poems. **Pays 1¢/word plus contributor's copy.**
Tips: "We prefer interviews with notable authors and have published interviews with bestsellers David Baldacci and Jan Karon in 2001. Fiction should be strong and well-crafted—if the piece excites you, send it in. Otherwise, revise and rework before submitting. Beginning writers are more successful sending short personal vignettes for use in the reflections column."

$ VIRGINIA QUARTERLY REVIEW, University of Virginia, One West Range, PO Box 400223, Charlottesville VA 22904-4223. (804)924-3124. Fax: (804)924-1397. Website: www.virginia.edu/vqr. **Contact:** Staige D. Blackford, editor. Quarterly magazine. "A national journal of literature and thought." Estab. 1925. Circ. 4,000. Pays on publication. Publishes ms an average of 1 year after acceptance. Byline given. Buys first rights. Editorial lead time 6 months. Submit seasonal material 6 months in advance. Responds in 2 weeks to queries; 2 months to mss. Sample copy for $5. Writer's guidelines for #10 SASE or online.
Nonfiction: Book excerpts, essays, general interest, historical/nostalgic, humor, inspirational, personal experience, travel. Send complete ms. Length: 2,000-4,000 words. **Pays $10/page maximum.**
Fiction: Adventure, ethnic, historical, humorous, mainstream, mystery, novel excerpts, romance. Send complete ms. Length: 2,000-4,000 words. **Pays $10/page maximum.**
Poetry: Gregory Orr, poetry editor. All types. Submit maximum 5 poems. **Pays $1/line.**

N $ VISIONS-INTERNATIONAL, Black Buzzard Press, 1007 Ficklen Rd., Fredericksburg VA 22405. (540)310-0730. **Contact:** B.R. Strahan, editor. **95% freelance written.** Magazine published 3 times/year featuring poetry, essays and reviews. Estab. 1979. Circ. 750. Pays on publication. Publishes ms an average of 6 months after acceptance. Byline given. Buys first North American serial rights. Editorial lead time 4 months. Accepts queries by mail. Responds in 3 weeks to queries; 2 months to mss. Sample copy for $4.50. Writer's guidelines for #10 SASE.
Nonfiction: Essays (by assignment after query), reviews. No sentimental, self-serving or religious submissions. Query. Length: 1 page maximum. **Pays $10 and complimentary copies.** Pays with contributor copies when grant money is unavailable.

Poetry: Avant-garde, free verse, traditional. No sentimental, religious, scurrilous, sexist, racist, amaturish, or over 3 pages. **Buys 140 poems/year.** Submit 3-6 poems Length: 2-120 lines.

Tips: "Know your craft. We are not a magazine for amateurs. We also are interested in translation from *modern* poets writing in any language into English."

N. WEST COAST LINE, A Journal of Contemporary Writing & Criticism, West Coast Review Publishing Society, 2027 EAA, Simon Fraser University, Burnaby British Columbia V5A 1S6, Canada. (604)291-4287. Fax: (604)291-5737. E-mail: wcl@sfu.ca. Website: www.sfu.ca/west-coast-line. **Contact:** Roger Farr, managing editor. Triannual magazine of contemporary literature and criticism. Estab. 1990. Circ. 500. Pays on publication. Buys one-time rights. Editorial lead time 4 months. Accepts queries by mail, e-mail. Responds in 2 weeks to queries; 3 months to mss. Sample copy for $10. Writer's guidelines for SASE (US must include IRC).

Nonfiction: Essays (literary/scholarly/critical), experimental prose. "No journalistic articles or articles dealing with nonliterary material." **Buys 8-10 mss/year.** Send complete ms. Length: 1,000-5,000 words. **Pays $8/page, 2 contributor's copies and a year's free subscription.**

Fiction: Experimental, novel excerpts. **Buys 3-6 mss/year.** Send complete ms. Length: 1,000-7,000 words. **Pays $8/page.**

Poetry: Avant-garde. "No light verse, traditional." **Buys 10-15 poems/year.** Submit maximum 5-6 pages maximum poems.

Tips: "Submissions must be either scholarly or formally innovative. Contributors should be familiar with current literary trends in Canada and the U.S. Scholars should be aware of current schools of theory. All submissions should be accompanied by a brief cover letter; essays should be formatted according to the MLA guide. The publication is not divided into departments. We accept innovative poetry, fiction, experimental prose and scholarly essays."

$ WESTERN HUMANITIES REVIEW, University of Utah, English Dept., 255 S. Central Campus Dr. Room 3500, Salt Lake City UT 84112-0494. (801)581-6070. Fax: (801)585-5167. E-mail: whr@mail.hum.utah.edu. Website: www.hum.utah.edu/whr. **Contact:** Samantha Ruckman, managing editor. Biannual magazine for educated readers. Estab. 1947. Circ. 1,000. Pays on publication. Publishes ms an average of 1 year after acceptance. Buys all rights. Accepts simultaneous submissions. Sample copy for $8.

Nonfiction: Barry Weller, editor-in-chief. Authoritative, readable articles on literature, art, philosophy, current events, history, religion and anything in the humanities. Interdisciplinary articles encouraged. Departments on films and books. **Buys 4-5 unsolicited mss/year.** Send complete ms. **Pays $5/published page.**

Fiction: Karen Brennan, fiction editor. Experimental. **Buys 8-12 mss/year.** Send complete ms. **Pays $5/published page.**

Poetry: Richard Howard, poetry editor.

Tips: "Because of changes in our editorial staff, we urge familiarity with *recent* issues of the magazine. Inappropriate material will be returned without comment. We do not publish writer's guidelines because we think that the magazine itself conveys an accurate picture of our requirements. Please, *no* e-mail submissions."

$ WHETSTONE, Barrington Area Arts Council, Box 1266, Barrington IL 60011. (847)382-5626. Fax: (847)382-3685. **Contact:** Dale Griffith, editor-in-chief; Chris Sweet, Lanny Ori, Charles White, associate editors. **100% freelance written.** Annual magazine featuring fiction, creative nonfiction and poetry. "We publish work by emerging and established authors for readers hungry for poetry and prose of substance." Estab. 1982. Circ. 800. Pays on publication. Publishes ms an average of 14 months after acceptance. Byline given. Not copyrighted. Buys first North American serial rights. Accepts simultaneous submissions. Responds in 5 months to mss. Sample copy and writer's guidelines for $5.

O— To break in, "send us your best work after it has rested long enough for you to forget it and therefore can look at it objectively to fine-tune before submitting."

Nonfiction: Essays (creative). "No articles." **Buys 0-3 mss/year.** Send complete ms. Length: 500-5,000 words. **Pays 2 copies and variable cash payment.**

Fiction: Novel excerpts (literary), short stories. **Buys 10-12 mss/year.** Send complete ms. Length: 500-5,000 words. **Pays 2 copies and variable cash payment.**

Poetry: Free verse, traditional. "No light verse, for children, political poems." **Buys 10-20 poems/year.** Submit maximum 7 poems. **Pays 2 copies and variable cash payment.**

Tips: "We look for fresh approaches to material. We appreciate careful work. Send us your best. We welcome unpublished authors. Though we pay in copies and small monetary amounts that depend on the generosity of our patrons and subscribers, we offer prizes for work published in *Whetstone*. These prizes totaled $1,000, and are given to three or more writers. The editors make their decisions at the time of publication. This is not a contest. In addition, we nominate authors for *Pushcart*; *Best American Short Stories*; *Poetry and Essays*; *O. Henry Awards*; *Best of the South*; Illinois Arts Council Awards; and other prizes and anthologies as they come to our attention. Though our press run is moderate, we work for our authors and offer a prestigious vehicle for their work."

$ WILLOW SPRINGS, 705 W. First Ave., Eastern Washington University, Spokane WA 99201. (509)623-4349. E-mail: cnhowell@mail.ewu.edu. **Contact:** Christopher Howell, editor. **100% freelance written.** Semiannual magazine.

"We publish quality contemporary poetry, fiction, nonfiction and works in translation." Estab. 1977. Circ. 1,500. Publishes ms an average of 4 months after acceptance. Byline given. Buys first rights. Editorial lead time 2 months. Responds in 2 months to queries; 2 months to mss. Sample copy for $5.50. Writer's guidelines for #10 SASE.
  • A magazine of growing reputation. Takes part in the AWP Intro Award program.
Nonfiction: Essays. **Buys 4 mss/year.** Send complete ms. **Pays 2 contributor copies.**
Fiction: Literary fiction only. "No genre fiction, please." **Buys 5-8 mss/year.** Send complete ms.
Poetry: Avant-garde, free verse. "No haiku, light verse or religious." **Buys 50-80 poems/year.** Submit maximum 6 poems. Length: 12 pages maximum.
Tips: "We do not read manuscripts in June, July and August."

$ WRITER'S BLOCK MAGAZINE, Canada's Leading Literary Digest, Box 32, 9944-33 Ave., Edmonton, Alberta T6N 1E8, Canada. **Contact:** Shaun Donnelly, publisher/editor. **100% freelance written.** Semiannual magazine covering genre fiction. We look for outstanding genre fiction and poetry (i.e., horror, mystery, romance, science fiction and western). Estab. 1994. Circ. 5,000. Pays on publication. Publishes ms an average of 6 months after acceptance. Byline given. Offers 50% kill fee. Buys first North American serial rights. Editorial lead time 6 months. Submit seasonal material 6 months in advance. Accepts simultaneous submissions. Responds in 2 weeks to queries; 3 months to mss. Sample copy for $5. Writer's guidelines for #10 SASE.
  O— "New writers have a better chance via the contest rather than regular submission because they aren't competing with writers like Koontz!"
Nonfiction: Humor, photo feature, Book reviews. **Buys 4-8 mss/year.** Send complete ms. Length: 250-5,000 words. **Pays Pays 2-5¢/word.**
Photos: Send photos with submission. Reviews prints. Buys one-time rights. Negotiates payment individualy.
Columns/Departments: Book reviews (genre fiction), 250-1,000 words. **Buys 2-4 mss/year.** Send complete ms. **Pays 2-5¢/word.**
Fiction: Adventure, fantasy,, humorous, mainstream, mystery, romance, science fiction, suspense, western. "No sex or profanity." **Buys 8-12 mss/year.** Send complete ms. Length: 500-5,000 words. **Pays 2-5¢/word.**
Poetry: Christine LeLacheur, associate editor. Avant-garde, free verse, haiku, light verse, traditional. **Buys 8-12 poems/year.** Submit maximum 5 poems. **Pays $5-25.**

$ $ THE YALE REVIEW, Yale University, P.O. Box 208243, New Haven CT 06520-8243. (203)432-0499. Managing Editor: Susan Bianconi. **Contact:** J.D. McClatchy, editor. **20% freelance written.** "No writer's guidelines available. Consult back issues." Estab. 1911. Pays prior to publication. Publishes ms an average of 1 year after acceptance. Buys one-time rights. Responds in 2 months to queries; 2 months to mss.
  • *The Yale Review* has published work chosen for the Pushcart anthology, *The Best American Poetry*, and the O. Henry Award.
Nonfiction: Authoritative discussions of politics, literature and the arts. No previously published submissions. Send complete ms with cover letter and SASE. Length: 3,000-5,000 words. **Pays $100-500.**
Fiction: Buys quality fiction. Length: 3,000-5,000 words. **Pays $100-500.**

$ $ $ ZOETROPE: ALL STORY, AZX Publications, 1350 Avenue of the Americas, 24th Floor, New York NY 10019-4801. (212)708-0400. Fax: (212)708-0475. E-mail: info@all-story.com. Website: www.all-story.com. **Contact:** Adrienne Brodeur, editor-in-chief. Quarterly magazine specializing in high caliber short fiction. "*Zoetrope: All Story* presents a new generation of classic stories. Inspired by the Coppola heritage of independence and creativity, the magazine is at once innovative and deeply traditional. *Zoetrope: All Story* explores the intersection of fiction and film and anticipates some of its stories becoming memorable films." Estab. 1997. Circ. 40,000. Publishes ms an average of 6 months after acceptance. Byline given. Buys first North American serial rights, 2 year film option. Accepts queries by mail. Accepts simultaneous submissions. Responds in 5 months to queries; 5 months to mss. Sample copy for $7.50. Writer's guidelines for SASE or online.
  • Does not accept submissions from June 1 through August 31. The winner of the 2001 National Magazine Award for Fiction.
Fiction: Literary short stories, one-act plays. No excerpts or reprints. **Buys 32-40 mss/year.** Send complete ms. **Pays $1,500.**
  ▣ The online magazine carries original content not found in the print edition and includes writer's guidelines. The website also features up-to-date information on news, events, contests, workshops, and more. In addition, the site links to Francis Ford Coppola's virtual studio, which is host to an online workshop for short story writers. Each month several virtual studio submissions are featured in the online supplement, All-Story Extra.
Tips: "We're always looking for tightly written stories that have a compelling narrative arc. Most of the stories that capture our attention have classic elements, such as strong characters and compelling themes, and illuminate the human condition with acute perception. *Zoetrope* considers unsolicited submissions of short stories no longer than 7,000 words. Excerpts from larger works, screenplays, treatments and poetry will be returned unread. We are unable to respond to submissions without an SASE."

$ ZYZZYVA, The Last Word: West Coast Writers & Artists, P.O. Box 590069, San Francisco CA 94159-0069. (415)752-4393. Fax: (415)752-4391. E-mail: editor@zyzzyva.org. Website: www.zyzzyva.org. **Contact:** Howard Junker, editor. **100% freelance written.** Works with a small number of new/unpublished writers each year. Magazine published in march, august and november. "We feature work by West Coast writers only. We are essentially a literary magazine, but of wide-ranging interests and a strong commitment to nonfiction." Estab. 1985. Circ. 4,000. **Pays on acceptance.** Publishes ms an average of 3 months after acceptance. Byline given. Buys First North American serial and one-time anthology rights. Accepts queries by mail, e-mail, fax, phone. Responds in 1 week to queries; 1 month to mss. Sample copy for $7 or online. Writer's guidelines online.

Nonfiction: Book excerpts, general interest, historical/nostalgic, humor, personal experience. **Buys 50 mss/year.** Query by mail or e-mail. Length: Open. **Pays $50.**

Photos: Reviews copies or slides only.

Fiction: Ethnic, experimental, humorous, mainstream. **Buys 20 mss/year.** Send complete ms. Length: Open. **Pays $50.**

Poetry: Buys 20 poems/year. Submit maximum 5 poems. Length: 3-200 lines. **Pays $50.**

Tips: "West Coast writers means those currently living in California, Alaska, Washington, Oregon or Hawaii."

MEN'S

Magazines in this section offer features on topics of general interest primarily to men. Magazines that also use material slanted toward men can be found in Business & Finance, Child Care & Parental Guidance, Ethnic/Minority, Gay & Lesbian Interest, General Interest, Health & Fitness, Military, Relationships and Sports sections. Magazines featuring pictorial layouts accompanied by stories and articles of a sexual nature, both gay and straight, appear in the Sex section.

$ $ $ CIGAR AFICIONADO, M. Shanken Communications, Inc., 387 Park Ave. S., New York NY 10016. (212)684-4224. Fax: (212)684-5424. Website: www.cigaraficionado.com. Editor: Marvin Shanken. **Contact:** Gordon Mott, executive editor. **75% freelance written.** Bimonthly magazine covering cigars and men's lifestyle. Estab. 1992. Circ. 400,000. **Pays on acceptance.** Publishes ms an average of 9 months after acceptance. Byline given. Offers 25% kill fee. Buys all rights. Editorial lead time 3 months. Submit seasonal material 3 months in advance. Accepts queries by mail, fax. Responds in 2 months to queries. Sample copy and writer's guidelines for SASE.

Nonfiction: Buys 80-100 mss/year. Query. Length: 2,000 words. **Pay varies.** Sometimes pays expenses of writers on assignment.

Columns/Departments: Length: 1,000 words. **Buys 20 mss/year. Payment varies.**

■ The online magazine carries original content not found in the print edition. Contact: Dave Savona, online editor.

$ $ $ $ ESQUIRE, 250 W. 55th St., New York NY 10019. (212)649-4020. Editor-in-Chief: David Granger. Senior Editor: A.J. Jacobs. Monthly magazine covering the ever-changing trends in American culture. Monthly magazine for smart, well-off men. General readership is college educated and sophisticated, between ages 30 and 45. Written mostly by contributing editors on contract. Rarely accepts unsolicited manuscripts. Estab. 1933. **Pays on acceptance.** Publishes ms an average of 2 months after acceptance. Offers 25% kill fee. Retains first worldwide periodical publication rights for 90 days from cover date. Editorial lead time 2 months.

Nonfiction: Focus is the ever-changing trends in American culture. Topics include current events and politics, social criticism, sports, celebrity profiles, the media, art and music, men's fashion. Queries must be sent by letter. **Buys 4 features and 12 shorter mss/year.** Length: Columns average 1,500 words; features average 5,000 words; short front of book pieces average 200-400 words. **Pays $1/word.**

Photos: Nancy Iacoi, photo editor. Uses mostly commissioned photography. Payment depends on size and number of photos.

Fiction: Adrienne Miller, literary editor. "Literary excellence is our only criterion." Accepts work chiefly from literary agencies. Novel excerpts, short stories, some poetry, memoirs, and plays.

Tips: "A writer has the best chance of breaking in at *Esquire* by querying with a specific idea that requires special contacts and expertise. Ideas must be timely and national in scope."

N $ GC MAGAZINE, LPI Publishing, P.O. Box 331775, Fort Worth TX 76136. (817)654-2334. Fax: (817)457-5298. E-mail: bellbrook@flash.net. Website: www.gc-magazine.com. Managing Editor: Thomas Foss. **Contact:** Jon Keeyes, editor. **80% freelance written.** Monthly magazine. "*GC Magazine* is a general entertainment magazine for men. We include entertainment celebrity interviews (movies, music, books) along with general interest articles for adult males." Estab. 1994. Circ. 53,000. Pays on publication. No byline given. Publishes ms an average of 3 months after acceptance. Buys one-time rights. Editorial lead time 3 months. Submit seasonal material 3 months in advance. Accepts queries by mail, e-mail, fax. Accepts simultaneous submissions. Responds in 1 month to queries. Sample copy for $1.50. Writer's guidelines for #10 SASE.

Nonfiction: Book excerpts, essays, exposé, general interest, historical/nostalgic, how-to, humor, interview/profile, opinion, personal experience, technical, travel, dating tips. No religious or "feel good" articles. **Buys 100 mss/year.** Query. Length: 1,000-4,000 words. **Pays 3-4¢/word for assigned articles; 2-3¢/word for unsolicited articles.** Sometimes pays expenses of writers on assignment.

Reprints: Accepts previously published submissions.

Photos: State availability with submission. Reviews 3×5 prints, gif/jpeg files. Buys one-time rights. Offers no additional payment for photos accepted with ms. Model releases required.

Columns/Departments: Actress feature (film actress interviews), 2,500 words; Author feature (book author interviews), 1,500 words; Music feature (singer or band interviews), 1,500 words. **Buys 50 mss/year.** Query. **Pays 2-3¢/ word.**

Fiction: Adventure, erotica, experimental, fantasy, historical, horror, humorous, mainstream, mystery, science fiction, suspense, western. No romance. **Buys 12 mss/year.** Send complete ms. Length: 1,000-3,000 words. **Pays 1¢/word plus contributor copies.**

Tips: "Submit material typed and free of errors. Writers should think of magazines like *Maxim* and *Details* when determining article ideas for our magazine. Our primary readership is adult males and we are seeking original and unique articles."

$ $ $HEARTLAND USA, UST Publishing, 100 W. Putnam Ave., Greenwich CT 06830-5316. (203)622-3456. Fax: (203)863-7296. E-mail: husaedit@ustnet.com. **Contact:** Brad Pearson, editor. **95% freelance written.** Bimonthly magazine for working men. "*HUSA* is a general interest lifestyle magazine for adult males—active outdoorsmen. The editorial mix includes hunting, fishing, sports, automotive, how-to, country music, human interest and wildlife." Estab. 1991. Circ. 901,000. **Pays on acceptance.** Byline given. Offers 20% kill fee. Buys first North American serial, second serial (reprint) rights. Submit seasonal material 1 year in advance. Accepts queries by mail, e-mail, fax. Accepts simultaneous submissions. Responds in 1 month to queries. Sample copy free. Writer's guidelines for #10 SASE.

Nonfiction: Book excerpts, general interest, historical/nostalgic, how-to, humor, inspirational, interview/profile, new product, personal experience, photo feature, technical, travel. "No fiction or dry expository pieces." **Buys 30 mss/year.** Query with or without published clips or send complete ms. Length: 350-1,200 words. **Pays 50-80¢/word for assigned articles; 25-80¢/word for unsolicited articles.** Sometimes pays expenses of writers on assignment.

Reprints: Send photocopy and information about when and where the material previously appeared. Pays 25% of amount paid for an original article.

Photos: Send photos with submission. Reviews transparencies. Buys one-time rights. Identification of subjects required.

Tips: "Features with the possibility of strong photographic support are open to freelancers, as are our departments. We look for a relaxed, jocular, easy-to-read style, and look favorably on the liberal use of anecdote or interesting quotations. Our average reader sees himself as hardworking, traditional, rugged, confident, uncompromising and daring."

$ $ $ $ THE INTERNATIONAL, The Magazine of Adventure and Pleasure for Men, Tomorrow Enterprises, 2228 E. 20th St., Oakland CA 94606. (510)532-6501. Fax: (510)536-5886. E-mail: tonyattomr@aol.com. **Contact:** Mr. Anthony L. Williams, managing editor. **70% freelance written.** Monthly magazine covering "bush and seaplane flying, seafaring, pleasure touring, etc. with adventure stories from all men who travel on sexual tours to Asia, Latin America, The Caribbean and the Pacific." Estab. 1997. Circ. 5,000. Pays on publication. Publishes ms an average of 2 months after acceptance. Buys first rights. Editorial lead time 2 months. Submit seasonal material 3 months in advance. Accepts queries by mail, e-mail. Accepts simultaneous submissions. Responds in 2 weeks to queries; 2 months to mss. Writer's guidelines free.

Nonfiction: Seafaring stories of all types published with photos. Military and veteran stories also sought as well as ex-pats living abroad. Especially interested in airplane flying stories with photos. Exposé, general interest, historical/ nostalgic, humor, interview/profile, opinion, personal experience, photo feature, travel. Special issues: No pornography, no family or "honeymoon" type travel. **Buys 40-50 mss/year.** Send complete ms. Length: 700 words maximum. **Pays $100-2,000 for assigned articles; $25-1,000 for unsolicited articles.** Sometimes pays expenses of writers on assignment.

Photos: Send photos with submission. Reviews negatives, 3×5 prints. Buys one-time or all rights. Offers no additional payment for photos accepted with ms. Identification of subjects required.

Columns/Departments: Asia/Pacific Beat; Latin America/Caribbean Beat (Nightlife, Adventure, Air & Sea), 450 words; Lifestyles Abroad (Expatriate Men's Doings Overseas), 600-1,000 words. **Buys 25 mss/year.** Send complete ms. **Pays $25-1,000.**

Fillers: Anecdotes, facts, gags to be illustrated by cartoonist, newsbreaks, short humor. **Buys 25/year.** Length: 200-600 words. **Pays $25-100.**

Tips: "If a single male lives in those parts of the world covered, and is either a pleasure tourist, pilot or seafarer, we are interested in his submissions. He can visit our upcoming website or contact us directly. Stories from female escorts or party girls are also welcomed."

$ $ $MEN'S JOURNAL, Wenner Media Inc., 1290 Avenue of the Americas, New York NY 10104-0298. (212)484-1616. Fax: (212)767-8213. Website: www.mensjournal.com. Editor: Sid Evans. **Contact:** Taylor A. Plimpton, editorial assistant. Magazine published 10 times/year covering general lifestyle for men, ages 25-49. "*Men's Journal* is for active men with an interest in participatory sports, travel, fitness and adventure. It provides practical, informative articles on how to spend quality leisure time." Estab. 1992. Circ. 550,000. Accepts queries by mail, fax.

   • *Men's Journal* won the National Magazine Award for Personal Science.

Nonfiction: Features and profiles 2,000-7,000 words; shorter features of 400-1,200 words; equipment and fitness stories, 400-1,800 words. Book excerpts, essays, exposé, general interest, historical/nostalgic, how-to, humor, new product, personal experience, photo feature, travel. Query with SASE. **Pay varies.**

$ SHARPMAN.COM, The Ultimate Guide's to Men's Living, SharpMan Media LLC, 11718 Barrington Court, No. 702, Los Angeles CA 90049-2930. (310)446-7915. Fax: (310)446-7965. E-mail: EMF@SharpMan.com.

Website: www.sharpman.com. Editor: Y.M. Reiss. **Contact:** Elizabeth Felicetti, managing editor. **50% freelance written.** Weekly online. "*SharpMan.com* is an online community for professional men, ages 18-35. The *SharpMan.com* magazine is designed to be 'the Ultimate Men's Guide to SharpLiving.' In articles on wardrobe, work, grooming, dating, health, toys and more, *SharpMan.com* attempts to provide meaningful instruction on where to go, what to do, how to dress, and what to buy." Estab. 1998. Circ. approximately 60,000. Pays on publication. Byline given. Buys all rights, exclusive rights to version posted (negotiable on excerpts from existing ms published for promotional purposes). Editorial lead time 2 months. Submit seasonal material 4 months in advance. Accepts queries by e-mail. Responds in 1 month to queries; 2 months to mss. Sample copy online. Writer's guidelines by e-mail.

Nonfiction: *Sharpman.com* frequently features writers who publish for the purpose of gaining professional recognition or promotion for published manuscripts and other services. Where a writer seeks to promote a product, remuneration is provided by way of a link to their desired URL, in lieu of cash. Men's interest: SharpDating, SharpWork, SharpTravel, SharpHealth, SharpGrooming, SharpToys (all in "how-to" form). Book excerpts, exposé, how-to, interview/profile, new product, technical, travel. **Buys 100 mss/year.** Query with published clips. Length: 600-2,000 words. **Pays $50.** Sometimes pays expenses of writers on assignment. Accepts submissions in a modified form with SharpMan Media, LLC retaining rights to modified product.

Photos: "Must be a 'legal' use of the photo provided." State availability with submission. Negotiates payment individually. Captions, identification of subjects, model releases required.

Columns/Departments: SharpTravel (for business and leisure travelers); SharpWork (oriented towards young professionals); and SharpDating (slanted towards men in their 20s-30s), all 600-2,000 words; SharpToys, 300-1,500 words; SharpHealth, 600-1,500 words; and SharpGrooming. We also publish a "Tip of the Week," generally 100-300 words. **Buys 100 mss/year.** Query with published clips. **Pays $50.**

Fillers: Facts. Length: 25-100 words. **Pays $5.**

Tips: "Familiarize yourself with our magazine's topics and tone. We write for a very specific audience. The Editorial Team prefers content written in the 'SharpMan Tone,' a fast, male-oriented tone that provides specific information on the subject at hand. Ideally, each article features 'top tips' or step-by-step 'how-to' language delivering specific information that can be easily and immediately implemented by the reader. *SharpMan.com* content is non-erotic in nature and articles may not include any inappropriate language."

$ $ $ SMOKE MAGAZINE, Life's Burning Desires, Lockwood Publications, 26 Broadway, Floor 9M, New York NY 10004. (212)391-2060. Fax: (212)827-0945. E-mail: editor@smokemag.com. Website: www.smokemag.com. Senior Editor: Michael Malone. **Contact:** Alyson Boxman, editor-in-chief. **75% freelance written.** Quarterly magazine covering cigars and men's lifestyle issues. "A large majority of *Smoke's* readers are affluent men, ages 28-40; active, educated and adventurous." Estab. 1995. Circ. 175,000. Pays 2 months after publication. Publishes ms an average of 3 months after acceptance. Byline given. Offers 25% kill fee. Buys first rights. Editorial lead time 2 months. Submit seasonal material 6 months in advance. Accepts queries by mail, e-mail. Accepts simultaneous submissions. Responds in 6 weeks to queries; 3 months to mss. Sample copy for $4.99.

O— Break in with "good nonfiction that interests guys—beer, cuisine, true-crime, sports, cigars, of course. Be original."

Nonfiction: Essays, exposé, general interest, historical/nostalgic, how-to, humor, interview/profile, opinion, personal experience, photo feature, technical, travel, true crime. **Buys 25 mss/year.** Query with published clips. Length: 1,500-3,000 words. **Pays $500-1,500.** Sometimes pays expenses of writers on assignment.

Photos: State availability with submission. Reviews 2¼ × 2¼ transparencies. Negotiates payment individually. Identification of subjects required.

Columns/Departments: Smoke Undercover, Smoke Slant (humor); What Lew Says (cigar industry news); Workin' Stiffs (world's best jobs), all 1,500 words. **Buys 20 mss/year.** Query with published clips. **Pays $500-1,500.**

Fillers: Anecdotes, facts, gags to be illustrated by cartoonist, newsbreaks, short humor. **Buys 12 fillers/year.** Length: 200-500 words. **Pays $200-500.**

■ The online magazine carries original content not found in the print edition.

Tips: "Send a short, clear query with clips. Go with your field of expertise: Cigars, sports, music, true crime, etc."

N $ $ $ UMM (URBAN MALE MAGAZINE), Canada's Only Lifestyle and Fashion Magazine for Men, UMM Publishing Inc., 6 Antares Dr., Phase 1, Unit 7, Nepean Ontario K2E 8A9, Canada. (613)723-6216. E-mail: editor@umm.ca. Website: www.umm.ca. Editor: Abbis Mahmoud. **Contact:** David Sachs, senior editor. **75% freelance written.** Bimonthly magazine covering men's interests. "Our audience is young men, aged 18-35. We focus on Canadian activities, interests, and lifestyle issues. Our magazine is fresh and energetic and we look for original ideas carried out with a spark of intelligence and/or humour (and you'd better spell humour with a 'u')." Estab. 1998. Circ. 80,000. Pays 1 month after publication. Publishes ms an average of 3 months after acceptance. Byline given. Buys first North American serial rights. Editorial lead time 3 months. Submit seasonal material 4 months in advance. Accepts queries by mail, e-mail. Accepts simultaneous submissions. Responds in 6 weeks to queries; 2 months to mss.

Nonfiction: Book excerpts, exposé, general interest, historical/nostalgic, how-to, humor, interview/profile, new product, personal experience, travel, adventure, cultural, sports, music. **Buys 80 mss/year.** Query with published clips. Length: 1,200-3,500 words. **Pays $100-400.** Sometimes pays expenses of writers on assignment.

Photos: State availability with submission. Reviews contact sheets, prints. Buys one-time rights. Negotiates payment individually.

Fillers: Anecdotes, facts, short humor. **Buys 35/year.** Length: 100-500 words. **Pays $50-150.**

Tips: "Be familiar with our magazine before querying. We deal with all subjects of interest to young men, especially those with Canadian themes. We are very open-minded. Original ideas and catchy writing are key."

MILITARY

These publications emphasize military or paramilitary subjects or other aspects of military life. Technical and semitechnical publications for military commanders, personnel and planners, as well as those for military families and civilians interested in Armed Forces activities are listed here. Publications covering military history can be found in the History section.

$ $ ARMY MAGAZINE, 2425 Wilson Blvd., Arlington VA 22201-3385. (703)841-4300. Fax: (703)841-3505. E-mail: armymag@ausa.org. Website: www.ausa.org/armyzine/. **Contact:** Mary Blake French, editor. **70% freelance written.** Prefers to work with published/established writers. Monthly magazine emphasizing military interests. Estab. 1904. Circ. 90,000. Pays on publication. Publishes ms an average of 5 months after acceptance. Byline given. Buys all rights. Submit seasonal material 3 months in advance. Accepts queries by mail. Sample copy for 9 × 12 SAE with $1 postage or online. Writer's guidelines for 9 × 12 SAE with $1 postage or online.
 • *Army Magazine* looks for shorter articles.
Nonfiction: "We would like to see more pieces about little-known episodes involving interesting military personalities. We especially want material lending itself to heavy, contributor-supplied photographic treatment. The first thing a contributor should recognize is that our readership is very savvy militarily. 'Gee-whiz' personal reminiscences get short shrift, unless they hold their own in a company in which long military service, heroism and unusual experiences are commonplace. At the same time, *Army* readers like a well-written story with a fresh slant, whether it is about an experience in a foxhole or the fortunes of a corps in battle." Historical/nostalgic (military and original), humor (military feature-length articles and anecdotes), interview/profile, new product, personal experience (dealing especially with the most recent conflicts in which the US Army has been involved: Desert Storm, Panama, Grenada), photo feature, technical. No rehashed history. No unsolicited book reviews. **Buys 8 mss/year.** Submit complete ms (hard copy and disk). Length: 1,000-1,500 words. **Pays 12-18¢/word.**
Photos: Send photos with submission. Reviews transparencies, prints, slides. Buys all rights. Pays $50-100 for 8 × 10 b&w glossy prints; $50-350 for 8 × 10 color glossy prints or 2¼ × 2¼ transparencies; will also accept 35mm. Captions required.
Columns/Departments: Military news, books, comment (*New Yorker*-type "Talk of the Town" items). **Pays $40-150.**

$ $ ARMY TIMES, Times News Group, Inc., 6883 Commercial Dr., Springfield VA 22159. (703)750-9000. Fax: (703)750-8622. E-mail: features@atpco.com. Website: www.armytimes.com. **Contact:** Chris Lawson, managing editor. Weekly for Army military personnel and their families containing career information such as pay raises, promotions, news of legislation affecting the military, housing, base activities and features of interest to military people. Estab. 1940. Circ. 230,000. **Pays on acceptance.** Byline given. Offers kill fee. Makes work-for-hire assignments. Accepts queries by mail, e-mail. Accepts simultaneous submissions. Responds in 1 month to queries. Sample copy and writer's guidelines for #10 SASE.
 ○→ Break in by "proposing specific feature stories that only you can write—things we wouldn't be able to get from 'generic' syndicated or wire material. The story must contain an element of mystery and/or surprise, and be entertaining as well as informative. Above all, your story must have a direct connection to military people's needs and interests."
Nonfiction: Features of interest to career military personnel and their families: food, relationships, parenting, education, retirement, shelter, health, and fitness, sports, personal appearance, community, recreation, personal finance, entertainment. No advice please. **Buys 150-175 mss/year.** Query. Length: 750-2,000 words. **Pays $100-500.**
Columns/Departments: Length: 500-900 words. **Buys 75 mss/year. Pays $75-125.**
 ▣ The online magazines carry original content not found in the print editions. Contact: Kent Miller, online editor.
Tips: Looking for "stories on active duty, reserve and retired military personnel; stories on military matters and localized military issues; stories on successful civilian careers after military service."

$ $ MILITARY TIMES, Times News Group, Inc. (subsidiary of Gannett Corp.), 6883 Commercial Dr., Springfield VA 22159. Fax: (703)750-8781. E-mail: features@atpco.com. Website: www.militarycity.com. Managing Editor: David Craig. **Contact:** G.E. Willis, features editor. **25% freelance written.** Weekly tabloid covering lifestyle topics for active, retired and reserve military members and their families. "Features need to have real military people in them, and appeal to readers in all the armed services. Our target audience is 90% male, young, fit and adventurous, mostly married and often with young children. They move frequently. Writer queries should approach ideas with those demographics and facts firmly in mind." Circ. 300,000. **Pays on acceptance.** Publishes ms an average of 2 months after acceptance. Byline given. Offers 25% kill fee. Buys first, electronic rights. Editorial lead time 2 months. Submit seasonal material 3 months in advance. Accepts queries by mail, e-mail, fax. Accepts simultaneous submissions. Responds in 6 weeks to queries. Sample copy for $2.25 or online. Writer's guidelines for SAE with 1 first-class stamp or by e-mail.

O— "Greatest need is in the adventure categories of sports, recreation, outdoor, personal fitness and running. Personal finance features are especially needed, but they must be specifically tailored to our military audience's needs and interests."

Nonfiction: Book excerpts, how-to, interview/profile, new product, photo feature, technical, travel, Sports, recreation, entertainment, health, personal fitness, self-image (fashion, trends), relationships, personal finance, food. "No poems, war memoirs or nostalgia, fiction, travel pieces that are too upscale (luxury cruises) or too focused on military monuments/museums." **Buys 110 mss/year.** Query with published clips. Length: 300-1,500 words. **Pays $100-500.** Sometimes pays expenses of writers on assignment.

Photos: State availability with submission. Reviews transparencies. Offers work-for-hire. Offers $75/photo. Captions, identification of subjects required.

Columns/Departments: Slices of Life (human-interest shorts), 300 words; Running (how-to for experienced runners, tips, techniques, problem-solving), 500 words; Personal Fitness (how-to, tips, techniques for working out, improving fitness), 500 words. **Buys 40 mss/year.** Query. **Pays $100-200.**

Tips: "Our *Lifelines* section appears every week with a variety of services, information and entertainment articles on topics that relate to readers' off-duty lives; or to personal dimensions of their on-duty lives. Topics include food, relationships, parenting, education, retirement, shelter, health and fitness, sports, personal appearances, community, recreation, personal finance and entertainment. We are looking for articles about military life, its problems and how to handle them, as well as interesting things people are doing, on the job and in their leisure. Keep in mind that our readers come from all of the military services. For instance, a story can focus on an Army family, but may need to include families or sources from other services as well. The editorial 'voice' of the section is familiar and conversational; good-humored without being flippant; sincere without being sentimental; savvy about military life but in a relevant and subtle way, never forgetting that our readers are individuals first, spouses or parents or children second, and service members third."

$ $NAVY TIMES, Army Times Publishing Co., 6883 Commercial Dr., Springfield VA 22159. (703)750-8636. Fax: (703)750-8767. E-mail: navylet@atpco.com. Website: www.navytimes.com. **Contact:** Alex Neil, editor. Weekly newspaper covering sea services. News and features of men and women in the Navy, Coast Guard and Marine Corps. Estab. 1950. Circ. 90,000. **Pays on acceptance.** Byline given. Buys first North American serial, second serial (reprint) rights. Submit seasonal material 2 months in advance. Writer's guidelines free.

Nonfiction: Historical/nostalgic, opinion. **Buys 100 mss/year.** Query. Length: 500-1,000 words. **Pays $50-500.** Sometimes pays expenses of writers on assignment.

Reprints: Send tearsheet.

Photos: Send photos with submission. Buys one-time rights. Offers $20-100/photo. Captions, identification of subjects required.

$ PARAMETERS, U.S. Army War College Quarterly, US Army War College, 122 Forbes Ave., Carlisle PA 17013-5238. (717)245-4943. E-mail: parameters@awc.carlisle.army.mil. Website: carlisle-www.army.mil/usawc/Parameters/. **Contact:** Col. Robert H. Taylor, USA Ret., editor. **100% freelance written.** Prefers to work with published/established writers or experts in the field. Readership consists of senior leaders of US defense establishment, both uniformed and civilian, plus members of the media, government, industry and academia. Subjects include national and international security affairs, military strategy, military leadership and management, art and science of warfare, and military history with contemporary relevance. Estab. 1971. Circ. 13,500. Pays on publication. Publishes ms an average of 6 months after acceptance. Byline given. Buys first North American serial rights. Accepts queries by mail, e-mail, phone. Responds in 6 weeks to queries. Sample copy and writer's guidelines free or online.

Nonfiction: Prefers articles that deal with current security issues, employ critical analysis and provide solutions or recommendations. Liveliness and verve, consistent with scholarly integrity, appreciated. Theses, studies and academic course papers should be adapted to article form prior to submission. Documentation in complete endnotes. Send complete ms. Length: 4,500 words average. **Pays $150 average (including visuals).**

Tips: "Make it short; keep it interesting; get criticism and revise accordingly. Write on a contemporary topic. Tackle a subject only if you are an authority. No fax submissions."

$ $⬛ PROCEEDINGS, U.S. Naval Institute, 291 Wood Rd., Annapolis MD 21402-5034. (410)268-6110. Fax: (410)295-1049. Website: www.usni.org. Editor: Fred H. Rainbow. **Contact:** Gordon Keiser, senior editor. **80% freelance written.** Monthly magazine covering Navy, Marine Corps, Coast Guard. Estab. 1873. Circ. 100,000. **Pays on acceptance.** Publishes ms an average of 9 months after acceptance. Byline given. Buys all rights. Editorial lead time 3 months. Responds in 2 months to queries. Sample copy for $3.95. Writer's guidelines free.

Nonfiction: Essays, historical/nostalgic, interview/profile, photo feature, technical. **Buys 100-125 mss/year.** Query with or without published clips or send complete ms. Length: 3,000 words. **Pays $60-150/printed page for unsolicited articles.**

Photos: State availability of or send photos with submission. Reviews transparencies, prints. Buys one-time rights. Offers $25/photo maximum.

Columns/Departments: Comment & Discussion (letters to editor), 750 words; Commentary (opinion), 1,000 words; Nobody Asked Me, But... (opinion), less than 1,000 words. **Buys 150-200 mss/year.** Query or send complete ms. **Pays $34-150.**

Fillers: Anecdotes. **Buys 20/year.** Length: 100 words. **Pays $25.**

$ $ $ $ THE RETIRED OFFICER MAGAZINE, 201 N. Washington St., Alexandria VA 22314-2539. (800)245-8762. Fax: (703)838-8179. E-mail: editor@troa.org. Website: www.troa.org. Editor: Col. Warren S. Lacy, USA-Ret. Managing Editor: Heather Lyons. **Contact:** Donna Budjenska. **60% freelance written.** Prefers to work with published/established writers. Monthly magazine for officers of the 7 uniformed services and their families. *"The Retired Officer Magazine* covers topics such as current military/political affairs, military history, travel, finance, hobbies, health and fitness, and military family and retirement lifestyles." Estab. 1945. Circ. 395,000. **Pays on acceptance.** Publishes ms an average of 1 year after acceptance. Byline given. Buys first North American serial rights. Accepts queries by mail, e-mail, fax. Responds in 3 months to queries. Sample copy and writer's guidelines for 9×12 SAE with 6 first-class stamps or online.

Nonfiction: Current military/political affairs, health and wellness, recent military history, travel, military family lifestyle. Emphasis now on current military and defense issues. "We rarely accept unsolicited manuscripts." **Buys 48 mss/year.** Query with résumé, sample clips and SASE. Length: 800-2,500 words. **Pays up to $1,700.**

Photos: Query with list of stock photo subjects. Original slides and transparencies must be suitable for color separation. Reviews transparencies. Pays $20 for each 8×10 b&w photo (normal halftone) used. Pays $75-200 for inside color; $300 for cover.

> ■ The online magazine carries original content not found in the print edition and includes writer's guidelines. Contact: Ronda Reid, online editor.

$ $ SELF RELIANCE JOURNAL, (formerly *American Survival Guide*), Y-Visionary Publishing, 265 S. Anita Dr., Suite 120, Orange CA 92868-3310. (714)939-9991 ext. 204. Fax: (714)939-9909. E-mail: jim4asg@aol.com. **Contact:** Jim Benson, editor. **60% freelance written.** Monthly magazine covering "self-reliance, defense, meeting day-to-day and possible future threats—survivalism for survivalists." Circ. 56,000. Pays on publication. Publishes ms an average of 1 year after acceptance. Byline given. Submit seasonal material 5 months in advance. Accepts queries by mail, e-mail, phone. Sample copy for $6. Writer's guidelines for #10 SASE.

> • *Self Reliance Journal* is always looking for more good material with quality artwork (photos). They want articles on recent events and new techniques, etc. giving the latest available information to their readers.

Nonfiction: How-to, interview/profile, personal experience (how I survived), photo feature (equipment and techniques related to survival in all possible situations), emergency medical, health and fitness, communications, transportation, food preservation, water purification, nutrition, tools, shelter, etc. "No general articles about how to survive. We want specifics and single subjects." **Buys 60-100 mss/year.** Query with or without published clips or send complete ms. Length: 1,500-3,000 words. **Pays $160-500.** Sometimes pays expenses of writers on assignment.

Photos: "One of the most frequent mistakes made by writers in completing an article assignment for us is sending photo submissions that are inadequate." Send photos with submission. Buys one-time rights. Captions, identification of subjects, model releases required.

Tips: "We need hard copy with computer disk and photos or other artwork. We only accept submissions that include both text and photos/illustrations. Prepare material of value to individuals who wish to sustain human life no matter what the circumstance. This magazine is a text and reference."

N $ $ $ $ SOLDIER OF FORTUNE, The Journal of Professional Adventurers, Omega Group, Ltd., P.O. Box 693, Boulder CO 80306-0693. (303)449-3750. Fax: (303)444-5617. E-mail: editor@sofmag.com. Website: www.sofmag.com. Managing Editor: Dwight Swift. Deputy Editor: Tom Reisinger. **Contact:** Marty Kufus, assistant editor. **50% freelance written.** Monthly magazine covering military, paramilitary, police, combat subjects and action/adventure. "We are an action-oriented magazine; we cover combat hot spots around the world. We also provide timely features on state-of-the-art weapons and equipment; elite military and police units; and historical military operations. Readership is primarily active-duty military, veterans and law enforcement." Estab. 1975. Circ. 175,000. Byline given. Offers 25% kill fee. Buys all rights; will negotiate. Submit seasonal material 5 months in advance. Responds in 3 weeks to queries; 1 month to mss. Sample copy for $5. Writer's guidelines for #10 SASE.

Nonfiction: Exposé, general interest, historical/nostalgic, how-to (on weapons and their skilled use), humor, interview/profile, new product, personal experience, photo feature (number one on our list), technical, travel, novel excerpts, combat reports, military unit reports and solid Vietnam and Operation Desert Storm articles. "No 'How I won the war' pieces; no op-ed pieces unless they are fully and factually backgrounded; no knife articles (staff assignments only). All submitted articles should have good art; art will sell us on an article." **Buys 75 mss/year.** Query with or without published clips or send complete ms. Send mss to articles editor; queries to managing editor. Length: 2,000-3,000 words. **Pays $150-250/page.** Sometimes pays expenses of writers on assignment.

Reprints: Send disk copy, photocopy of article and information about when and where the material previously appeared. Pays 25% of amount paid for an original article.

Photos: Send photos with submission. Reviews contact sheets, transparencies. Buys one-time rights. Pays $500 for cover photo. Captions, identification of subjects required.

Columns/Departments: Combat craft (how-to military and police survival skils); I Was There (first-person account of the arcane or unusual based in a combat or law-enforcement environment), both 600-800 words. **Buys 16 mss/year.** Send complete ms. **Pays $150.**

Fillers: Bulletin Board editor. Newsbreaks (military/paramilitary related has to be documented). Length: 100-250 words. **Pays $50.**

Tips: "Submit a professionally prepared, complete package. All artwork with cutlines, double-spaced typed manuscript with 5.25 or 3.5 IBM-compatible disk, if available, cover letter including synopsis of article, supporting documentation where applicable, etc. Manuscript must be factual; writers have to do their homework and get all their facts straight. One error means rejection. We will work with authors over the phone or by letter, tell them if their ideas have merit for an acceptable article, and help them fine-tune their work. I Was There is a good place for freelancers to start. Vietnam features, if carefully researched and art heavy, will always get a careful look. Combat reports, again, with good art, are number one in our book and stand the best chance of being accepted. Military unit reports from around the world are well received as are law-enforcement articles (units, police in action). If you write for us, be complete and factual; pros read *Soldier of Fortune*, and are very quick to let us know if we (and the author) err."

MUSIC

Music fans follow the latest industry news in these publications that range from opera to hip hop. Types of music and musicians or specific instruments are the sole focus of some magazines. Publications geared to the music industry and professionals can be found in the Trade Music section. Additional music and dance markets are found in the Contemporary Culture and Entertainment sections.

$ AMERICAN COUNTRY, Music Monthly, Publishing Services Inc., 820 Monroe NW, Suite 211A, Grand Rapids MI 49503. (616)458-1011. Fax: (616)458-2285. E-mail: brucep@gogrand.com. **Contact:** Bruce L. Parrott, editor. **50% freelance written.** Monthly tabloid covering country music. "*American Country* is a country music publication syndicated to radio stations around the country and featuring articles on country artists, album reviews, outdoor life, recipes, etc." Estab. 1992. Circ. 300,000. Pays on publication. Publishes ms an average of 2 months after acceptance. Byline given. Buys one-time rights, makes work-for-hire assignments. Editorial lead time 2 months. Accepts queries by mail, e-mail, fax, phone. Accepts simultaneous submissions. Responds in 1 week to queries. Sample copy and writer's guidelines free.
  ● The editor reports an interest in seeing articles about outdoor life—camping, hiking, hunting, fishing, etc.
Nonfiction: Interview/profile, new product (all pertaining to country music). No country music news. **Buys 40-50 mss/year.** Query with published clips. Length: 1,000-2,000 words. **Pays $10-50.**
Columns/Departments: CD Jukebox (album reviews), 50-100 words. **Buys 35-50 mss/year.** Query with published clips. **Pays $10.**
Tips: "Call and tell me the kind of stuff you're doing and send some copies. Have existing contacts within the Nashville music scene."

N $ $ AMERICAN RECORD GUIDE, Record Guide Productions, 4412 Braddock St., Cincinnati OH 45204. (513)941-1116. E-mail: rightstar@aol.com. **Contact:** Donald Vroon, editor. **90% freelance written.** Bimonthly 6×9 book covering classical music for music lovers and record collectors. Estab. 1935. Circ. 10,000. Pays on publication. Publishes ms an average of 2 months after acceptance. Byline given. Buys all rights. Editorial lead time 2 months. Accepts queries by mail, e-mail. Accepts simultaneous submissions. Sample copy for $7. Writer's guidelines free.
Nonfiction: Essays. **Buys 30-45 full-length mss and hundreds of reviews/year.** Query. **Pays $50-350 for assigned articles; $50-150 for unsolicited articles.**
Reprints: Send photocopy with rights for sale noted and information about when and where the material previously appeared.

$ AMERICAN SONGWRITER MAGAZINE, 1009 17th Ave. S., Nashville TN 37212-2201. (615)321-6096. Fax: (615)321-6097. E-mail: info@AmericanSongwriter.com. Website: www.AmericanSongwriter.com. Managing Editor: Lou Heffernan. **Contact:** Vernell Hackett, editor. **30% freelance written.** Bimonthly magazine about songwriters and the craft of songwriting for many types of music, including pop, country, rock, metal, jazz, gospel, and r&b. Estab. 1984. Circ. 5,000. Pays on publication. Publishes ms an average of 2 months after acceptance. Offers 25% kill fee. Buys first North American serial rights. Responds in 2 months to queries. Sample copy for $4. Writer's guidelines for #10 SASE.
Nonfiction: General interest, interview/profile, new product, technical, home demo studios, movie and TV scores, performance rights organizations. **Buys 20 mss/year.** Query with published clips. Length: 300-1,200 words. **Pays $25-60.**
Reprints: Send tearsheet or photocopy and information about when and where the material previously appeared. Pays same amount as paid for an original article.
Photos: Send photos with submission. Reviews 3×5 prints. Buys one-time rights. Offers no additional payment for photos accepted with ms. Identification of subjects required.
Tips: "*American Songwriter* strives to present articles which can be read a year or two after they were written and still be pertinent to the songwriter reading them."

N $ $ BASS PLAYER MAGAZINE, United Entertainment Media, 2800 Campus Dr., San Mateo CA 94403. (650)513-4400. Fax: (650)513-4642. E-mail: rjohnston@musicplayer.com. Website: www.bassplayer.com. **Contact:** Richard Johnston, editor. **50% freelance written.** Monthly online magazine covering "a wide variety of topics pertaining to bassists and their instruments, both electric and acoustic." Estab. 1989. Circ. 45,000. Pays on publication. Publishes ms an average of 4 months after acceptance. Byline given. Offers $100 kill fee. Buys all rights. Editorial lead time 4 months. Accepts queries by mail, e-mail. Writer's guidelines free.

Oᴦ Break in by "suggesting a shorter piece on a noteworthy but lesser-known player."

Nonfiction: "In addition to interviews with bass players in all styles of music, we look for practical pieces on 'in-the-trenches' aspects of playing, gigging, and recording; historical articles; how-to articles about music and equipment—in general, anything amateur or professional bass players would find useful and interesting. A story must appeal to dedicated musicians, but that's no excuse for dry writing." Historical/nostalgic, how-to, interview/profile. No unsolicited mss. **Buys 36 mss/year.** Query. Length: 500-1,200 words. **Pays $200.** Sometimes pays expenses of writers on assignment.

Photos: State availability with submission. Buys one-time rights.

Tips: "We prefer instructional material to be written by name players and teachers."

$ $BLUEGRASS UNLIMITED, Bluegrass Unlimited, Inc., P.O. Box 771, Warrenton VA 20188-0771. (540)349-8181 or (800)BLU-GRAS. Fax: (540)341-0011. E-mail: editor@bluegrassmusic.com. Website: www.bluegrassmusic.com. Editor: Peter V. Kuykendall. **Contact:** Sharon Watts, managing editor. **60% freelance written.** Prefers to work with published/established writers. Monthly magazine covering bluegrass, acoustic and old-time country music. Estab. 1966. Circ. 27,000. Pays on publication. Publishes ms an average of 4 months after acceptance. Byline given. Offers negotiated kill fee. Buys first North American serial, one-time, second serial (reprint), all rights. Submit seasonal material 4 months in advance. Accepts queries by mail, e-mail, fax. Responds in 2 weeks to queries; 2 months to mss. Sample copy free. Writer's guidelines for #10 SASE.

Nonfiction: General interest, historical/nostalgic, how-to, interview/profile, personal experience, photo feature, travel. No "fan"-style articles. **Buys 60-70 mss/year.** Query with or without published clips. Length: open. **Pays 8-10¢/word.**

Reprints: Send photocopy with rights for sale noted and information about when and where the material previously appeared. Payment is negotiable.

Photos: State availability of or send photos with submission. Reviews 35mm transparencies and 3×5, 5×7 and 8×10 b&w and color prints. Buys all rights. Pays $50-175 for transparencies, $25-60 for b&w prints, $50-250 for color prints. Identification of subjects required.

Fiction: Ethnic, humorous. **Buys 3-5 mss/year.** Query. Length: negotiable. **Pays 8-10¢/word.**

Tips: "We would prefer that articles be informational, based on personal experience or an interview with lots of quotes from subject, profile, humor, etc."

$ $CHAMBER MUSIC, Chamber Music America, 305 Seventh Ave., New York NY 10001-6008. (212)242-2022. Fax: (212)242-7955. E-mail: kkrenz@chamber-music.org. Website: www.chamber-music.org/magazine. **Contact:** Karissa Krenz, associate editor. Bimonthly magazine covering chamber music. Estab. 1977. Circ. 13,000. Pays on publication. Publishes ms an average of 5 months after acceptance. Byline given. Offers kill fee. Buys first rights. Editorial lead time 4 months. Accepts queries by mail, phone.

● Editor Johanna Keller left the publication December 4, 2000.

Nonfiction: Book excerpts, essays, humor, opinion, personal experience, issue-oriented stories of relevance to the chamber music fields written by top music journalists and critics, or music practitioners. No artist profiles, no stories about opera or symphonic work. **Buys 35 mss/year.** Query with published clips. Length: 2,500-3,500 words. **Pays $500 minimum.** Sometimes pays expenses of writers on assignment.

Photos: State availability with submission. Offers no payment for photos accepted with ms.

$ $ $ $ GUITAR ONE, The Magazine You Can Play, Cherry Lane Music, 6 E. 32nd St., 6th Floor, New York NY 10016. Fax: (212)251-0840. E-mail: editors@guitaronemag.com. Website: www.guitaronemag.com. **Contact:** Troy Nelson, editor. **75% freelance written.** Monthly magazine covering guitar news, artists, music, gear. Estab. 1996. Circ. 140,000. Pays on publication. Publishes ms an average of 1 month after acceptance. Byline given. Offers 50% kill fee. Buys one-time rights. Editorial lead time 3 months. Accepts queries by mail, e-mail, fax. Accepts simultaneous submissions. Sample copy online.

Nonfiction: Interview/profile (with guitarists). **Buys 15 mss/year.** Query with published clips. Length: 2,000-5,000 words. **Pays $300-1,200 for assigned articles; $150-800 for unsolicited articles.** Sometimes pays expenses of writers on assignment.

Photos: State availability of photos with submissions. Reviews negatives, transparencies, prints. Buys one-time rights. Negotiates payment individually.

Columns/Departments: Opening Axe (newsy items on artists), 450 words; Soundcheck (records review), 200 words; Gear Box (equipment reviews), 800 words.

Tips: "Find an interesting feature with a nice angle that pertains to guitar enthusiasts. Submit a well-written draft or samples of work."

Ⓝ $ $GUITAR PLAYER MAGAZINE, Miller Freeman, Inc., 411 Borel Ave., Suite 100, San Mateo CA 94402. (650)513-4300. Fax: (650)513-4646. E-mail: guitplyr@musicplayer.com. Website: www.guitarplayer.com. **Contact:** Michael Molenda, editor-in-chief. **50% freelance written.** Monthly magazine for persons "interested in guitars, guitarists, manufacturers, guitar builders, equipment, careers, etc." Circ. 150,000. **Pays on acceptance.** Publishes ms an average of 3 months after acceptance. Byline given. Buys first serial and all reprint rights. Responds in 6 weeks to queries. Writer's guidelines for #10 SASE.

Nonfiction: Publishes "wide variety of articles pertaining to guitars and guitarists: interviews, guitar craftsmen profiles, how-to features—anything amateur and professional guitarists would find fascinating and/or helpful. In interviews with 'name' performers, be as technical as possible regarding strings, guitars, techniques, etc. We're not a pop culture magazine, but a magazine for musicians. The essential question: What can the reader take away from a story to become a better player?" **Buys 30-40 mss/year.** Query. Length: Open. **Pays $250-450.** Sometimes pays expenses of writers on assignment.

Photos: Reviews b&w glossy prints, 35mm color transparencies. Buys one-time rights. Payment varies.

$ $ MODERN DRUMMER, 12 Old Bridge Rd., Cedar Grove NJ 07009. (201)239-4140. Fax: (201)239-7139. Editorial Director: William F. Miller. Senior Editor: Rick Van Horn. **Contact:** Ronald Spagnardi, editor-in-chief. **60% freelance written.** Monthly magazine for "student, semi-pro and professional drummers at all ages and levels of playing ability, with varied specialized interests within the field." Circ. 102,000. Pays on publication. Publishes ms an average of 3 months after acceptance. Buys all rights. Responds in 2 weeks to queries. Sample copy for $4.99. Writer's guidelines for #10 SASE.

Nonfiction: "All submissions must appeal to the specialized interests of drummers." How-to, interview/profile, new product, personal experience, technical, informational. **Buys 40-50 mss/year.** Query with published clips or send complete ms. Length: 5,000-8,000 words. **Pays $200-500.**

Reprints: Send photocopy with rights for sale noted and information about when and where the material previously appeared.

Photos: Reviews color transparencies, 8×10 b&w prints. Purchased with accompanying ms.

Columns/Departments: Jazz Drummers Workshop, Rock Perspectives, Rock 'N' Jazz Clinic, Driver's Seat (Big Band), In The Studio, Show Drummers Seminar, Teachers Forum, Drum Soloist, The Jobbing Drummer, Strictly Technique, Shop Talk, Latin Symposium. Book Reviews, Record Reviews, Video Reviews. Profile columns: Portraits, Up & Coming, From the Past. Length: 500-1,000 words. "Technical knowledge of area required for most columns." **Buys 40-50 mss/year.** Send complete ms. **Pays $50-150.**

Tips: "*MD* is looking for music journalists rather than music critics. Our aim is to provide information, not to make value judgments. Therefore, keep all articles as objective as possible. We are interested in how and why a drummer plays a certain way; the readers can make their own decisions about whether or not they like it."

N $ $ PROFILE, Vox Publishing, 3670 Central Pike, Suite J, Hermitage TN 37076. (615)872-8080, ext. 3312. Fax: (615)872-9786. E-mail: profile@profilemagazine.com. Website: www.profilemagazine.com. **Contact:** Chris Well, editor-in-chief. **70% freelance written.** Bimonthly magazine covering Christian books, music, art and more. "*Profile* is the only magazine of its kind, covering the spectrum of Christian products from books and music to children's resources and gifts. It reaches the core Christian retail customer—females between the ages of 21 and 50." Estab. 1998. Circ. 95,000. Pays within 30 days after publication. Publishes ms an average of 2 months after acceptance. Byline sometimes given. Buys first North American serial, electronic rights. Editorial lead time 6 months. Submit seasonal material 4 months in advance. Accepts queries by mail, e-mail, fax. Sample copy for $5.

Nonfiction: Interview/profile (artists), religious. No essays, inspirational pieces. **Buys 20-30 mss/year.** Query with published clips. Length: 500-2,500 words. **Pays 6-10¢/word for assigned articles.** Sometimes pays expenses of writers on assignment.

Photos: State availability with submission. Buys one-time rights. Offers no additional payment for photos accepted with ms. Identification of subjects required.

Columns/Departments: Noteworthy (brief profiles of Christian music artists), 400-600 words; Snapshots (brief profiles of people writing/making books), 400-600 words; Showcase (reviews of Christian books and music), 250 words. **Buys 30 mss/year.** Query with published clips. **Pays 6-10¢/word.**

Tips: "We're looking for people who can exhibit working knowledge of the authors, books and artists we cover. We also want to be convinced that they've read our magazine."

$ RELIX MAGAZINE, Music for the Mind, 180 Varick St., 5th Floor, New York NY 10014. (646)230-0100. E-mail: editor@relix.com. Website: www.relix.com. **Contact:** Aeve Baldwin, managing editor. **40% freelance written.** Eager to work with new writers. Bimonthly magazine focusing on new and independent bands, classic rock lifestyles and music alternatives such as roots, improvisational music, psychedelia and jambands. Estab. 1974. Circ. 90,000. Pays on publication. Publishes ms an average of 4 months after acceptance. Byline given. Buys all rights. Accepts queries by mail, e-mail. Responds in 6 months to queries. Sample copy for $5.

Nonfiction: Feature topics include jambands, reggae, Grateful Dead, bluegrass, jazz, country, rock, experimental, electronic and world music also deals with environmental, cultural and lifestyle issues. Historical/nostalgic, humor, interview/profile, new product, photo feature, technical, live reviews, new artists, hippy lifestyles, food, mixed media, books. Query by mail with published clips if available or send complete ms. Length: 300-1,500 words. **Pays $3/column inch.**

Photos: "Whenever possible, submit complete artwork with articles."

Columns/Departments: Query with published clips or send complete ms. **Pays variable rates.**

Tips: "The best part of working with freelance writers is discovering new music we might never have stumbled across."

SPIN, 205 Lexington Ave., 3rd Floor, New York NY 10016. (212)231-7400. Fax: (212)231-7312. President: John Rollins. **Contact:** Alan Light, editor-in-chief. Monthly magazine covering music and popular culture. "*Spin* covers progressive rock as well as investigative reporting on issues from politics to pop culture. Editorial includes reviews, essays, profiles and interviews on a wide range of music from rock to jazz. It also covers sports, movies, politics, humor, fashion and issues—from AIDS research to the environment. The editorial focuses on the progressive new music scene and young adult culture more from an 'alternative' perspective as opposed to mainstream pop music. The magazine discovers new bands as well as angles for the familiar stars." Estab. 1985. Circ. 525,000.

Nonfiction: Features are not assigned to writers who have not established a prior relationship with *Spin*. Cultural, political or social issues. New writers: submit complete ms with SASE. Established writers: query specific editor with published clips.

Columns/Departments: Most open to freelancers: Exposure (short articles on music and popular culture), 300-600 words, query Maureen Callahan, associate editor; Reviews (record reviews), 150 or 400 words, queries/mss to Jon Dolan, senior editor; Noise (music and new artists), query Tracey Pepper, senior associate editor. Query before submitting.

Tips: "The best way to break into the magazine is the Exposure and Reviews sections. We primarily work with seasoned, professional writers who have extensive national magazine experience and very rarely make assignments based on unsolicited queries."

$ $ SYMPHONY, American Symphony Orchestra League, 33 W. 60th St., Fifth Floor, New York NY 10023-7905. (212)262-5161, ext. 268. Fax: (212)262-5198. E-mail: editor@symphony.org. Website: www.symphony.org. **Contact:** Chester Lane, senior editor. **50% freelance written.** Bimonthly magazine for the orchestra industry and classical music enthusiasts covering classical music, orchestra industry, musicians. Writers should be knowledgeable about classical music and have critical or journalistic/repertorial approach. Circ. 18,500. **Pays on acceptance.** Publishes ms an average of 2 months after acceptance. Byline given. Buys first, one-time rights. Editorial lead time 6 months. Submit seasonal material 8 months in advance. Accepts queries by mail, e-mail, phone. Accepts simultaneous submissions. Writer's guidelines for #10 SASE.

Nonfiction: Book excerpts, essays, inspirational, interview/profile, opinion, personal experience (rare), photo feature (rare), issue features, trend pieces (by assignment only; pitches welcome). Does not want to see reviews, interviews. **Buys 30 mss/year.** Query with published clips. Length: 900-3,500 words. **Pays $150-600.** Sometimes pays expenses of writers on assignment.

Photos: State availability of or send photos with submission. Reviews contact sheets, negatives, prints, electronic photos. Buys one-time rights. Offers no additional payment for photos accepted with ms. Captions, identification of subjects required.

Columns/Departments: Repertoire (orchestral music—essays); Comment (personal views and opinions); Currents (electronic media developments); In Print (books); On Record (CD, DVD, video), all 1,000 words. **Buys 4 mss/year.** Query with published clips.

Tips: "We need writing samples before assigning pieces. We prefer to craft the angle with the writer, rather than adapt an existing piece. Pitches and queries should demonstrate a clear relevance to the American orchestra industry and should be timely."

[N] $ TRADITION, Nat. Trad. C.M.A., P.O. Box 492, Anita IA 50020. (712)762-4363. Fax: (712)762-4363. Editor: Bob Everhart. **20% freelance written.** Bimonthly magazine covering pioneer and old-time music. "Our 2,500 members are devoted fans of old-time, traditional mountain, country, bluegrass and folk music. Everything we print must be directed toward that audience." Estab. 1976. Circ. 2,500. Pays on publication. Publishes ms an average of 3 months after acceptance. Byline sometimes given. Buys one-time rights. Editorial lead time 3 months. Submit seasonal material 3 months in advance. Accepts simultaneous submissions. Responds in 3 months to queries. Sample copy and writer's guidelines for $4 and SASE.

Nonfiction: Book excerpts, essays, general interest, historical/nostalgic, personal experience, travel. **Buys 6-8 mss/year.** Query. **Pays $5-25.**

Photos: State availability with submission. Buys one-time rights. Offers no additional payment for photos accepted with ms. Identification of subjects required.

Poetry: Traditional.

Fillers: Anecdotes, facts, short humor.

[N] $ $ ULTIMATE AUDIO, En Garde Enterprises, Inc., 1710 First Ave., PMB #227, New York NY 10128. Fax: (718)796-2825. E-mail: edultimate@aol.com. Website: www.ultimateaudio.com. Editor: Tom O'Neil. Managing Editor: Kelli Shriver. **Contact:** Myles Astor, publisher. **100% freelance written.** Quarterly magazine. "Our magazine covers the finest in high-end audio equipment and music. Our writers use highly resolving audio systems to review and evaluate electronics, digital playback equipment, speakers and accessories. We cover all genres of music—on LP and CD—with an emphasis on the sound and performance." Estab. 1997. Circ. 12,000. Pays on publication (when subsequent issue is published). Publishes ms an average of 4 months after acceptance. Byline given. Buys first, second serial (reprint), electronic rights. Editorial lead time 4 months. Submit seasonal material 4 months in advance. Accepts queries by mail, e-mail, fax, phone. Responds in 2 weeks to queries. Sample copy for $4.

Nonfiction: General interest, how-to, interview/profile, new product, opinion, technical. **Buys 4 mss/year.** Length: 300-2,500 words. **Pays $100-500.** Sometimes pays expenses of writers on assignment.

Columns/Departments: Conversations With (interviews with women in audio), 2,500 words; Ultimate Vinyl Archivist (collectible records), 3,000 words; Websitings; High Res Dig. **Buys 1 mss/year.** Query. **Pays $150-500.**

$ $ $ $ VIBE, 215 Lexington Ave., 6th Floor, New York NY 10016. (212)448-7300. Fax: (212)448-7430. Website: www.vibe.com. Managing Editor: Jacklyn Monk. **Contact:** Individual editors as noted. Monthly magazine covering urban music and culture. "*Vibe* chronicles and celebrates urban music and the youth culture that inspires and consumes it." Estab. 1993. Circ. 800,000. Pays on publication. Buys first North American serial rights. Editorial lead time 4 months. Responds in 2 months to queries. Sample copy available on newsstands. Writer's guidelines for #10 SASE.
Nonfiction: Robert Simpson, deputy editor; Shani Saxon, music editor. Cultural, political or social issues. Query with published clips, résumé and SASE. Length: 800-3,000 words. **Pays $1/word.**
Columns/Departments: Start (introductory news-based section), 350-750 words. Send queries to Brett Johnson, senior editor. Revolutions (music reviews), 100-800 words. Send queries to Craig Seymour, associate music editor. Book reviews. Send queries to Robert Morales. Query with published clips, résumé and SASE. **Pays $1/word.**
Tips: "A writer's best chance to be published in *Vibe* is through the Start or Revolutions Sections. Keep in mind that *Vibe* is a national magazine, so ideas should have a national scope. People in Cali should care as much about the story as people in NYC. Also, *Vibe* has a four-month lead time. What we work on today will appear in the magazine four or more months later. Stories must be timely with respect to this fact."

MYSTERY

These magazines buy fictional accounts of crime, detective work, mystery and suspense. Skim through other sections to identify markets for fiction; some will consider mysteries. Markets for true crime accounts are listed under Detective & Crime.

$ HARDBOILED, Gryphon Publications, P.O. Box 209, Brooklyn NY 11228. Website: www.gryphonbooks.com. **Contact:** Gary Lovisi, editor. **100% freelance written.** Semiannual book covering crime/mystery fiction and nonfiction. "Hard-hitting crime fiction and private-eye stories—the newest and most cutting-edge work and classic reprints." Estab. 1988. Circ. 1,000. Pays on publication. Publishes ms an average of 18 months after acceptance. Byline given. Offers 100% kill fee. Buys one-time rights. Editorial lead time 1 year. Submit seasonal material 9 months in advance. Responds in 2 weeks to queries; 1 month to mss. Sample copy for $8 or double issue for $16 (add $1.50 book postage). Writer's guidelines for #10 SASE.
Nonfiction: Book excerpts, essays, exposé. **Buys 4-6 mss/year.** Query. Length: 500-3,000 words. **Pays 1 copy.**
Reprints: Query first.
Photos: State availability with submission.
Columns/Departments: Occasional review columns/articles on hardboiled writers. **Buys 2-4 mss/year.** Query.
Fiction: Mystery, hardboiled crime and private-eye stories, all on the cutting edge. **Buys 40 mss/year.** Send complete ms. Length: 500-3,000 words. **Pays $5-50.**

$ THE MYSTERY REVIEW, A Quarterly Publication for Mystery Readers, C. von Hessert & Associates, P.O. Box 233, Colborne, Ontario K0K 1S0, Canada. E-mail: mystrev@reach.net. Website: www.themysteryreview.com. **Contact:** Barbara Davey, editor. **80% freelance written.** Quarterly magazine covering mystery and suspense. "Our readers are interested in mystery and suspense books, films. All topics related to mystery—including real life unsolved mysteries." Estab. 1992. Circ. 5,000 (80% of distribution is in US). Pays on publication. Publishes ms an average of 6 months after acceptance. Byline given. Buys first North American serial rights. Editorial lead time 6 months. Submit seasonal material 6 months in advance. Accepts queries by mail, e-mail, fax. Responds in 6 weeks to queries; 1 month to mss. Sample copy for $5. Writer's guidelines for #10 SASE or online.
Nonfiction: Interview/profile, true life mysteries. Query. Length: 2,000-5,000 words. **Pays $30 maximum.**
Photos: Send photos with submission. Buys all rights. Offers no additional payment for photos accepted with ms. Identification of subjects, model releases required.
Columns/Departments: Book reviews (mystery/suspense titles only), 500 words; Truly Mysterious ("unsolved," less-generally-known, historical or contemporary cases; photos/illustrations required), 2,000-5,000 words; Book Shop Beat (bookstore profiles; questionnaire covering required information available from editor), 500 words. **Buys 50 mss/year.** Query with published clips. **Pays $10-30.**
Fillers: Puzzles, trivia, shorts (items related to mystery/suspense). **Buys 4/year.** Length: 100-500 words. **Pays $10-20.**

$ ⬛ ELLERY QUEEN'S MYSTERY MAGAZINE, Dell Magazines Fiction Group, 475 Park Ave. S., 11th Floor, New York NY 10016. (212)686-7188. Fax: (212)686-7414. E-mail: elleryqueen@dellmagazines.com. Website: www.mysterypages.com. **Contact:** Janet Hutchings, editor. **100% freelance written.** Magazine published 11 times/year featuring mystery fiction. Estab. 1941. Circ. 500,000 readers. **Pays on acceptance.** Publishes ms an average of 6 months after acceptance. Byline given. Buys first North American serial rights. Accepts simultaneous submissions. Responds in 3 months to mss. Sample copy for $5. Writer's guidelines for #10 SASE.
Fiction: "We publish every type of mystery: the suspense story, the psychological study, the private-eye story, the deductive puzzle—the gamut of crime and detection from the realistic (including stories of police procedure) to the more imaginative (including 'locked rooms' and 'impossible crimes'). We always need detective stories. Special consideration given to anything timely and original. No sex, sadism or sensationalism-for-the-sake-of-sensationalism, no gore

or horror. Seldom publishes parodies or pastiches." **Buys up to 120 mss/year.** Send complete ms. Length: most stories 3,000-10,000 words. Accepts longer and shorter submissions—including minute mysteries of 250 words and novellas of up to 20,000 words from established authors. **Pays 5-8¢/word, occasionally higher for established authors.**
Poetry: Short mystery verses, limericks. Length: 1 page, double spaced maximum.
Tips: "We have a Department of First Stories to encourage writers whose fiction has never before been in print. We publish an average of 11 first stories every year."

NATURE, CONSERVATION & ECOLOGY

These publications promote reader awareness of the natural environment, wildlife, nature preserves and ecosystems. Many of these "green magazines" also concentrate on recycling and related issues, and a few focus on environmentally-conscious sustainable living. They do not publish recreation or travel articles except as they relate to conservation or nature. Other markets for this kind of material can be found in the Regional; Sports (Hiking & Backpacking in particular); and Travel, Camping & Trailer categories, although magazines listed there require that nature or conservation articles be slanted to their specialized subject matter and audience. Some publications listed in Juvenile and Teen, such as *Wild Outdoor World* or *Owl*, focus on nature-related material for young audiences, while others occasionally purchase such material.

$ $ $ ⚄ AMC OUTDOORS, The Magazine of the Appalachian Mountain Club, Appalachian Mountain Club, 5 Joy St., Boston MA 02108. (617)523-0655. Fax: (617)523-0722. E-mail: meno@amcinfo.org. Website: www.out doors.org. **Contact:** Madeleine Eno, editor/publisher. **90% freelance written.** Monthly magazine covering outdoor recreation and conservation issues in the Northeast. Estab. 1907. Circ. 85,000. Pays on publication. Publishes ms an average of 3 months after acceptance. Byline given. Offers 25% kill fee. Buys all rights. Editorial lead time 3 months. Submit seasonal material 4 months in advance. Accepts queries by e-mail. Responds in 1 month to queries; 2 months to mss. Sample copy for 9 × 12 SASE. Writer's guidelines free or online.
Nonfiction: Looking for writing familiar to particularities of Northeast—landscape and conservation issues. Book excerpts, essays, exposé, general interest, historical/nostalgic, how-to, interview/profile, opinion, personal experience, photo feature, technical, travel. Special issues: Northern Forest Report (April) featuring the northern areas of New York, New Hampshire, Vermont, and Maine, and protection efforts for these areas. No "how hiking changed my life" or first-person outdoor adventure without a hook. **Buys 10 mss/year.** Query with or without published clips. Length: 500-3,000 words. Pays expenses of writers on assignment.
Photos: State availability with submission. Reviews contact sheets, transparencies, prints. Identification of subjects, model releases required.
Columns/Departments: Jane Roy Brown. News (environmental/outdoor recreation coverage of Northeast), 1,300 words. **Buys 40 mss/year.** Query. **Pays $250-1,200.**

$ $ $ AMERICAN FORESTS, American Forests, P.O. Box 2000, Washington DC 20013. (202)955-4500. Fax: (202)887-1075. E-mail: mrobbins@amfor.org. Website: www.americanforests.org. **Contact:** Michelle Robbins, editor. **75% freelance written.** (mostly assigned). Quarterly magazine "of trees and forests, published by a nonprofit citizens' organization that strives to help people plant and care for trees for ecosystem restoration and healthier communities." Estab. 1895. Circ. 25,000. **Pays on acceptance.** Publishes ms an average of 8 months after acceptance. Byline given. Buys one-time rights. Submit seasonal material 5 months in advance. Accepts queries by mail, e-mail. Responds in 2 months to queries. Sample copy for $2. Writer's guidelines for SASE or online.
    O— Break in with "stories that resonate with city dwellers who love trees, or small, forestland owners (private). This magazine is looking for more urban and suburban-oriented pieces.
Nonfiction: All articles should emphasize trees, forests, forestry and related issues. General interest, historical/nostalgic, how-to, humor, inspirational. **Buys 8-12 mss/year.** Query. Length: 1,200-2,000 words. **Pays $250-1,000.**
Reprints: Send tearsheet or typed ms with rights for sale noted and information about when and where the material previously appeared. Pays 50% of amount paid for original article.
Photos: Originals only. Send photos with submission. Reviews 35mm or larger transparencies, glossy color prints. Buys one-time rights. Offers no additional payment for photos accompanying ms. Captions required.
Tips: "We're looking for more good urban forestry stories, and stories that show cooperation among disparate elements to protect/restore an ecosystem. Query should have honesty and information on photo support. We *do not* accept fiction or poetry at this time."

$ $ $ ⚄ THE AMICUS JOURNAL, The Natural Resources Defense Council, 40 W. 20th St., New York NY 10011. Fax: (212)727-1773. E-mail: amicus@nrdc.org. Website: www.nrdc.org. **Contact:** Kathrin Day Lassila, editor. **75% freelance written.** Quarterly magazine covering national and international environmental issues. "*The Amicus Journal* is intended to provide the general public with a journal of thought and opinion on environmental affairs, particularly those relating to policies of national and international significance." Estab. 1979. Circ. 250,000. Pays on publication. Publishes ms an average of 6 months after acceptance. Byline given. Offers variable kill fee. Buys first North American serial, simultaneous, electronic rights. Submit seasonal material 6 months in advance. Accepts queries by mail, e-mail. Responds in 3 months to queries. Sample copy for $5. Writer's guidelines for #10 SASE.

Nonfiction: Environmental features. **Buys 12 mss/year.** Query with published clips. Length: 3,000. **Pays 50¢/word.** Sometimes pays expenses of writers on assignment.

Photos: State availability with submission. Reviews contact sheets, color transparencies, 8×10 b&w prints. Buys one-time rights. Negotiates payment individually. Captions, identification of subjects, model releases required.

Columns/Departments: News & Comment (summary reporting of environmental issues, tied to topical items), 700-2,000 words; International Notebook (new or unusual international environmental stories), 700-2,000 words; People, 2,000 words; Reviews (in-depth reporting on issues and personalities, well-informed essays on books of general interest to environmentalists interested in policy and history), 500-1,000 words. Query with published clips. **Pay negotiable.**

Poetry: Brian Swann, poetry editor. All poetry should be rooted in nature. Avant-garde, free verse, haiku, nature-based. **Buys 12 poems/year.** Length: 1 ms page. **Pays $75.**

Tips: "Please stay up to date on environmental issues, and review *The Amicus Journal* before submitting queries. Except for editorials all departments are open to freelance writers. Queries should precede manuscripts, and manuscripts should conform to the *Chicago Manual of Style*. *Amicus* needs interesting environmental stories—of local, regional or national import—from writers who can offer an on-the-ground perspective. Accuracy, high-quality writing, and thorough knowledge of the environmental subject are vital."

$ $ APPALACHIAN TRAILWAY NEWS, Appalachian Trail Conference, P.O. Box 807, Harpers Ferry WV 25425-0807. (304)535-6331. Fax: (304)535-2667. E-mail: editor@atconf.org. **Contact:** Robert A. Rubin, editor. **40% freelance written.** Bimonthly magazine. Estab. 1925. Circ. 35,000. **Pays on acceptance.** Byline given. Buys first North American serial, second serial (reprint) rights. Responds in 2 months to queries. Sample copy and writer's guidelines for $2.50. Writer's guidelines only for SASE.

• Articles must relate to Appalachian Trail.

Nonfiction: Publishes but does not pay for "hiking reflections." Essays, general interest, historical/nostalgic, how-to, humor, inspirational, interview/profile, photo feature, technical, travel. **Buys 15-20 mss/year.** Query with or without published clips, or send complete ms. Prefers e-mail queries. Length: 250-3,000 words. **Pays $25-300.** Pays expenses of writers on assignment.

Reprints: Send photocopy with rights for sale noted and information about when and where the material previously appeared.

Photos: State availability with submission. Reviews contact sheets, slides, 5×7 prints, digital images. Offers $25-125/photo; $300/cover. Identification of subjects required.

Tips: "Contributors should display a knowledge of or interest in the Appalachian Trail. Those who live in the vicinity of the Trail may opt for an assigned story and should present credentials and subject of interest to the editor."

$ $ THE ATLANTIC SALMON JOURNAL, The Atlantic Salmon Federation, P.O. Box 429, St. Andrews, New Brunswick E0G 2X0, Canada. Fax: (506)529-4985. E-mail: asfpub@nbnet.nb.ca. Website: www.asf.ca. **Contact:** Jim Gourlay, editor. **50-68% freelance written.** Quarterly magazine covering conservation efforts for the Atlantic salmon, catering to "affluent and responsive audience—the dedicated angler and conservationist." Circ. 10,000. Pays on publication. Publishes ms an average of 6 months after acceptance. Byline given. Buys first North American serial rights, one-time rights to photos. Submit seasonal material 3 months in advance. Accepts simultaneous submissions. Responds in 2 months to queries. Sample copy for 9×12 SAE with $1 (Canadian), or IRC. Writer's guidelines free.

Nonfiction: "We are seeking articles that are pertinent to the focus and purpose of our magazine, which is to inform and entertain our membership on all aspects of the Atlantic salmon and its environment, preservation and conservation." Exposé, historical/nostalgic, how-to, humor, interview/profile, new product, opinion, personal experience, photo feature, technical, travel, conservation, science, research and management. **Buys 15-20 mss/year.** Query with published clips. Length: 1,500-2,500 words. **Pays $200-400.** Sometimes pays expenses of writers on assignment.

Photos: State availability with submission. Pays $50 for 3×5 or 5×7 b&w prints; $50-100 for 2¼×3¼ or 35mm color slides. Captions, identification of subjects required.

Columns/Departments: Conservation issues and salmon research; the design, construction and success of specific flies (*Fit To Be Tied*); interesting characters in the sport; opinion pieces by knowledgeable writers, 900 words; *Casting Around* (short, informative, entertaining reports, book reviews and quotes from the world of Atlantic salmon angling and conservation). Query. **Pays $50-250.**

Tips: "Articles must reflect informed and up-to-date knowledge of Atlantic salmon. Writers need not be authorities, but research must be impeccable. Clear, concise writing is essential, and submissions must be typed. The odds are that a writer without a background in outdoor writing and wildlife reporting will not have the 'informed' angle I'm looking for. Our readership is well read and critical of simplification and generalization."

$ $ $ $ AUDUBON, The Magazine of the National Audubon Society, National Audubon Society, 700 Broadway, New York NY 10003-9501. Fax: (212)477-9069. E-mail: editor@audubon.org. Website: www.audubon.com. Editor-in-chief: David Seideman. **Contact:** Editor. **85% freelance written.** Bimonthly magazine "reflecting nature with joy and reverence and reporting the issues that affect and endanger the delicate balance and life on this planet." Estab. 1887. Circ. 460,000. **Pays on acceptance.** Byline given. Buys all rights. Accepts queries by mail, fax. Responds in 3 months to queries. Sample copy for $5 and postage or online. Writer's guidelines for #10 SASE or online.

● "No phone calls, please."

Nonfiction: "We are interested in nature/environmental articles with an emphasis on science and conservation." Essays, exposé, interview/profile, investigative. No humor, poetry or book excerpts. Query with published clips. Unsolicited mss will not be returned. Virtually all pieces are assigned; unsolicited story ideas rarely accepted. Length: 150-3,000 words. **Pays $100-3,000.** Pays expenses of writers on assignment.

Tips: "*Audubon* articles deal with the natural and human environment. They cover the remote as well as the familiar. What they all have in common, however, is that they have a story to tell, one that will not only interest *Audubon* readers, but that will interest everyone with a concern for the affairs of humans and nature. We want good solid journalism. We want stories of people and places, good news and bad: humans and nature in conflict, humans and nature working together, humans attempting to comprehend, restore and renew the natural world. We are looking for new voices and fresh ideas. Among the types of stories we seek: Profiles of individuals whose life and work illuminate some issues relating to natural history, the environment, conservation, etc.; balanced reporting on environmental issues and events here in North America; environmental education; advocacy; "citizen science"; analyses of events, policies, and issues from fresh points of view. We do not publish fiction or poetry. We're not seeking first-person meditations on 'nature,' accounts of wild animal rescue or taming, or birdwatching articles."

$ ⚡ THE BEAR DELUXE MAGAZINE, P.O. Box 10342, Portland OR 97296. (503)242-1047. Fax: (503)243-2645. E-mail: bear@teleport.com. Website: www.orlo.org/beardeluxe. **Contact:** Tom Webb, editor. **80% freelance written.** Quarterly magazine. "*The Bear Deluxe Magazine* provides a fresh voice amid often strident and polarized environmental discourse. Street level, solution-oriented and non-dogmatic, *The Bear Deluxe* presents lively creative discussion to a diverse readership." Estab. 1993. Circ. 17,000. Pays on publication. Publishes ms an average of 2 months after acceptance. Byline given. Offers 25% kill fee. Buys first rights. Editorial lead time 3 months. Submit seasonal material 4 months in advance. Accepts queries by mail, e-mail. Responds in 2 months to queries; 4 months to mss. Sample copy for $3. Writer's guidelines for #10 SASE or online.

Nonfiction: Book excerpts, essays, exposé, general interest, interview/profile, new product, opinion, personal experience, photo feature, travel, artist profiles. Special issues: publishes 1 theme/year. **Buys 40 mss/year.** Query with published clips. Length: 250-4,500 words. **Pays 5¢/word.** Sometimes pays expenses of writers on assignment.

Photos: State availability with submission. Reviews contact sheets, transparencies, 8 × 10 prints. Buys one-time rights. Offers $30/photo. Identification of subjects, model releases required.

Columns/Departments: Reviews (almost anything), 300 words; Hands-On (individuals or groups working on eco-issues, getting their hands dirty), 1,200 words; Talking Heads (creative first person), 500 words; News Bites (quirk of eco-news), 300 words; Portrait of an Artist (artist profiles), 1,200 words. **Buys 16 mss/year.** Query with published clips. **Pays 5¢/word, subscription and copies.**

Fiction: "Stories must have some environmental context." Adventure, condensed novels, historical, horror, humorous, mystery, novel excerpts, science fiction, western. **Buys 8 mss/year.** Send complete ms. Length: 750-4,500 words. **Pays 5¢/word.**

Poetry: Avant-garde, free verse, haiku, light verse, traditional. **Buys 16-20 poems/year.** Submit maximum 5 poems. Length: 50 lines maximum. **Pays $10, subscription and copies.**

Fillers: Facts, newsbreaks, short humor, "found writing." **Buys 10/year.** Length: 100-750 words. **Pays 5¢/word, subscription and copies.**

Tips: "Offer to be a stringer for future ideas. Get a copy of the magazine and guidelines, and query us with specific nonfiction ideas and clips. We're looking for original, magazine-style stories, not fluff or PR. Fiction, essay and poetry writers should know we have an open and blind review policy and should keep sending their best work even if rejected once. Be as specific as possible in queries."

$ $ BIRD WATCHER'S DIGEST, Pardson Corp., P.O. Box 110, Marietta OH 45750. (740)373-5285. E-mail: editor@birdwatchersdigest.com. Website: www.birdwatchersdigest.com. **Contact:** William H. Thompson III, editor. **60% freelance written.** Works with a small number of new/unpublished writers each year. Bimonthly magazine covering natural history—birds and bird watching. "*BWD* is a nontechnical magazine interpreting ornithological material for amateur observers, including the knowledgeable birder, the serious novice and the backyard bird watcher; we strive to provide good reading and good ornithology." Estab. 1978. Circ. 90,000. Pays on publication. Publishes ms an average of 2 years after acceptance. Byline given. Buys one-time, second serial (reprint) rights. Submit seasonal material 6 months in advance. Responds in 2 months to queries. Sample copy for $3.99 or online. Writer's guidelines for #10 SASE or online.

Nonfiction: "We are especially interested in fresh, lively accounts of closely observed bird behavior and displays and of bird-watching experiences and expeditions. We often need material on less common species or on unusual or previously unreported behavior of common species." Book excerpts, how-to (relating to birds, feeding and attracting, etc.), humor, personal experience, travel (limited, we get many). No articles on pet or caged birds; none on raising a baby bird. **Buys 75-90 mss/year.** Send complete ms. Length: 600-3,500 words. **Pays from $100.**

Photos: Send photos with submission. Reviews transparencies, prints. Buys one-time rights. Pays $75 minimum for transparencies, prints.

🔲 The online magazine carries content not found in the print edition and includes writer's guidelines.

Tips: "We are aimed at an audience ranging from the backyard bird watcher to the very knowledgeable birder; we include in each issue material that will appeal at various levels. We always strive for a good geographical spread, with material from every section of the country. We leave very technical matters to others, but we want facts and accuracy, depth and quality, directed at the veteran bird watcher and at the enthusiastic novice. We stress the joys and pleasures of bird watching, its environmental contribution, and its value for the individual and society."

$ $ $ CALIFORNIA WILD, Natural Science for Thinking Animals, California Academy of Sciences, Golden Gate Park, San Francisco CA 94118. (415)750-7117. Fax: (415)221-4853. E-mail: kkhowell@calacademy.org. Website: www.calacademy.org/calwild. **Contact:** Keith Howell, editor. **75% freelance written.** Quarterly magazine covering natural sciences and the environment. "Our readers' interests range widely from ecology to geology, from endangered species to anthropology, from field identification of plants and birds to armchair understanding of complex scientific issues." Estab. 1948. Circ. 32,000. Pays prior to publication. Publishes ms an average of 3 months after acceptance. Byline given. Offers 50% kill fee; maximum $200. Buys first North American serial, one-time rights. Editorial lead time 3 months. Submit seasonal material 6 months in advance. Accepts queries by mail, fax. Responds in 6 weeks to queries; 6 months to mss. Sample copy for 9×12 SASE or online. Writer's guidelines for #10 SASE or online.

Nonfiction: Personal experience, photo feature, biological and earth sciences. Special issues: Mostly California pieces, but also from Pacific Ocean countries. No travel pieces. **Buys 20 mss/year.** Query with published clips. Length: 1,000-3,000 words. **Pays $250-1,000 for assigned articles; $200-800 for unsolicited articles.** Sometimes pays expenses of writers on assignment.

Photos: State availability with submission. Reviews transparencies. Buys one-time rights. Offers $75-150/photo. Identification of subjects, model releases required.

Columns/Departments: Trail Less Traveled (unusual places); Wild Lives (description of unusual plant or animal); Science Track (innovative student, teacher, young scientist), all 1,000-1,500 words; Skywatcher (research in astronomy), 2,000-3,000 words. **Buys 12 mss/year.** Query with published clips. **Pays $200-400.**

Fillers: Facts. **Pays $25-50.**

Tips: "We are looking for unusual and/or timely stories about California environment or biodiversity."

N $ $ $ CANADIAN WILDLIFE, Tribute Publishing, 71 Barber Greene Rd., Don Mills Ontario M3C 2A2, Canada. (416)445-0544. Fax: (416)445-2894. E-mail: wild@tribute.ca. Editor: Kendra Toby. **Contact:** Gillian Girodat, assistant editor. **90% freelance written.** Magazine published 5 times/year covering wildlife conservation. Includes topics pertaining to wildlife, endangered species, conservation and natural history. When possible, it is beneficial if articles have a Canadian slant or the topic has global appeal. Estab. 1995. Circ. 25,000. **Pays on acceptance.** Publishes ms an average of 3 months after acceptance. Byline given. Offers 15% kill fee. Buys first North American serial rights. Editorial lead time 3 months. Submit seasonal material 4 months in advance. Accepts queries by mail, e-mail, fax. Responds in 3 weeks to queries; 2 months to mss. Sample copy for $3.25 (Canadian). Writer's guidelines free.

Nonfiction: Book excerpts, interview/profile, photo feature, science/nature. Special issues: Oceans issue (every June). No standard travel stories. **Buys 20 mss/year.** Query with published clips. Length: 800-2,500 words. **Pays $500-1,200 for assigned articles; $300-1,000 for unsolicited articles.** Sometimes pays expenses of writers on assignment.

Photos: Send photos with submission. Reviews transparencies. Buys one-time rights. Negotiates payment individually. Captions, identification of subjects, model releases required.

Columns/Departments: Vistas (science news), 200-500 words; Book Reviews, 100-150 words. **Buys 15 mss/year.** Query with published clips. **Pays $50-250.**

Tips: "*Canadian Wildlife* is a benefit of membership in the Canadian Wildlife Federation. Nearly 25,000 people currently receive the magazine. The majority of these men and women are already well-versed in topics concerning the environment and natural science; writers, however, should not make assumptions about the extent of a reader's knowledge of topics."

N $ CONSCIOUS CHOICE, The Journal of Ecology & Natural Living, Conscious Communications, Inc., 920 N. Franklin, Suite 202, Chicago IL 60610-3179. Fax: (312)751-3973. E-mail: james@consciouschoice.com. Website: www.consciouschoice.com. Editor: Sheri Reda. Managing Editor: Ross Thompson. **Contact:** James Faber, senior editor. **95% freelance written.** Monthly tabloid covering the environment, natural health and natural foods. Estab. 1988. Circ. 50,000. Pays on publication. Publishes ms an average of 6 months after acceptance. Byline given. Offers 50% kill fee. Buys first North American serial, electronic rights. Editorial lead time 6 months. Submit seasonal material 6 months in advance. Accepts queries by mail, e-mail. Accepts simultaneous submissions. Responds in 6 weeks to queries; 1 month to mss. Sample copy online. Writer's guidelines free, online or by e-mail.

Nonfiction: General interest, inspirational, interview/profile, new product, personal experience, technical. **Buys 5 mss/year.** Query with published clips. Length: 1,500 words. **Pays $75-150.** Sometimes pays expenses of writers on assignment.

$ $ 🖾 E THE ENVIRONMENTAL MAGAZINE, Earth Action Network, P.O. Box 5098, Westport CT 06881-5098. (203)854-5559. Fax: (203)866-0602. E-mail: info@emagazine.com. Website: www.emagazine.com. **Contact:** Jim Motavalli, editor. **60% freelance written.** Bimonthly magazine. "*E Magazine* was formed for the purpose of acting as a clearinghouse of information, news and commentary on environmental issues." Estab. 1990. Circ. 50,000. Pays on publication. Byline given. Buys first North American serial rights. Editorial lead time 3 months. Submit seasonal material 6 months in advance. Accepts queries by mail, e-mail, fax. Accepts simultaneous submissions. Sample copy for $5 or online. Writer's guidelines for #10 SASE.

• The editor reports an interest in seeing more investigative reporting.

Nonfiction: On spec or free contributions welcome. Exposé (environmental), how-to, feature (in-depth articles on key natural environmental issues), new product, book review. **Buys 100 mss/year.** Query with published clips. Length: 100-4,000 words. **Pays 20¢/word.**

Photos: State availability with submission. Reviews printed samples, e.g. magazine tearsheets, postcards, etc. to be kept on file. Buys one-time rights. Negotiates payment individually. Identification of subjects required.

Columns/Departments: In Brief/Currents (environmental news stories/trends), 400-1,000 words; Conversations (Q&As with environmental "movers and shakers"), 2,000 words; Tools For Green Living; Your Health; Eco-Travel; Eco-Home; Eating Right; Green Business; Consumer News (each 700-1,200 words). On spec or free contributions welcome. Query with published clips. **Pays 20¢/word.**

　　■ The online magazine carries original content not found in the print edition and includes writer's guidelines. Contact: Jim Motavalli, online editor.

Tips: "Contact us to obtain writer's guidelines and back issues of our magazine. Tailor your query according to the department/section you feel it would be best suited for. Articles must be lively, well-researched, balanced and relevant to a mainstream, national readership." On spec or free contributions welcome.

N $ $ ENVIRONMENT, Heldref Publications, 1319 18th St. NW, Washington DC 20036-1802. (202)296-6267. Fax: (202)296-5149. E-mail: env@heldref.org. Website: www.heldref.org. **Contact:** Barbara T. Richman, managing editor. **2% freelance written.** Magazine published 10 times/year for college students and teachers, scientists, business and government executives, citizens interested in environment or effects of technology and science in public affairs. Estab. 1958. Circ. 8,000. Pays on publication to professional writers. Publishes ms an average of 4 months after acceptance. Byline given. Buys all rights. Accepts queries by mail, fax. Responds in 3 months to queries. Writer's guidelines online.

Nonfiction: "All full-length articles must offer readers authoritative analyses of key environmental problems written in accessible language. Articles must be annotated (referenced), and all conclusions must follow logically from the facts and arguments presented." Prefers articles centering around policy-oriented, public decision-making, scientific and technological issues. Scientific and environmental material, effects of science on policymaking and vice versa. Query or submit 3 double-spaced copies of complete ms. Length: 2,500-4,000 words. **Pays $100-300.**

Photos: Send photos with submission. Captions, credits required.

Columns/Departments: Focus (education, energy, economics, public opinion, elucidating small portion of a larger problem), 1,000-1,700 words; Report on Reports (reviews of institutions and government reports), 1,500-2,000 words; Commentary, 750 words; Books of Note, 100-150 words.

Tips: "Address a large, global problem by looking at specific examples. Avoid overgeneralizations, one-sided arguments, and jargon."

$ $■ HIGH COUNTRY NEWS, High Country Foundation, P.O. Box 1090, Paonia CO 81428-1090. (303)527-4898. E-mail: betsym@HCN.org. Website: www.hcn.org. **Contact:** Betsy Marston, editor. **80% freelance written.** Weekly tabloid covering Rocky Mountain West, the Great Basin and Pacific Northwest environment, rural communities and natural resource issues in 10 western states for environmentalists, politicians, companies, college classes, government agencies, grass roots activists, public land managers, etc. Estab. 1970. Circ. 23,000. Pays on publication. Publishes ms an average of 2 months after acceptance. Byline given. Buys one-time rights. Accepts queries by mail. Responds in 1 month to queries. Sample copy and writer's guidelines for SAE or online.

Nonfiction: Exposé (government, corporate), interview/profile, personal experience, photo feature (centerspread), reporting (local issues with regional importance). **Buys 100 mss/year.** Query. Length: up to 3,000 words. **Pays 20¢/word minimum.** Sometimes pays expenses of writers on assignment.

Reprints: Send tearsheet and information about when and where the material previously appeared. Pays 15¢/word.

Photos: Send photos with submission. Reviews b&w prints. Captions, identification of subjects required.

Columns/Departments: Roundups (topical stories), 800 words; opinion pieces, 1,000 words.

Tips: "We use a lot of freelance material, though very little from outside the Rockies. Familiarity with the newspaper is a must. Start by writing a query letter. We define 'resources' broadly to include people, culture and aesthetic values, not just coal, oil and timber."

N $ $ HOOKED ON THE OUTDOORS, Adventure LLC, 524 E. Mendenhall, Bozeman MT 59715. (406)582-8173. Fax: (406)522-3744. E-mail: John@ruhooked.com. Website: www.ruhooked.com. Editor: John Byorth. Managing Editor: Nancy Coulter-Parker. **Contact:** Mark Miller, assistant editor. **60% freelance written.** "*Hooked on the Outdoors Magazine* is a bimonthly travel and gear guide for outdoorsy folk of all ages, shapes, sizes, religions, and mantras. No matter the background, all have the North American backyard in common. *Hooked* is the outdoor guide for readers who are multi-sport oriented and, just the same, people new to the outdoors, providing affordable, close to home destinations and gear alternative." Estab. 1998. Circ. 165,000. Pays within 30 days of publication. Publishes ms an average of 4 months after acceptance. Byline given. Offers 15% kill fee. Buys first North American serial rights. Editorial lead time 3 months. Submit seasonal material 6 months in advance. Accepts queries by mail, e-mail. Accepts simultaneous submissions. Responds in 6 weeks to queries; 2 months to mss. Sample copy for $5 and SAE with $1.75 postage. Writer's guidelines online.

Nonfiction: Book excerpts, essays, exposé, general interest, humor, interview/profile, new product, opinion, personal experience, photo feature, travel. Special issues: Travel Special (February 2002); Grassroots (conservation, clubs, outdoor schools, events; April 2002). **Buys 4 mss/year.** Query with published clips. Length: 350-1,800 words. **Pays 35-50¢/word.** Sometimes pays expenses of writers on assignment.

Photos: State availability with submission. Reviews contact sheets. Buys one-time rights. Offers $25-290. Captions, model releases required.

Columns/Departments: Nancy Coulter-Parker, executive editor. Outtakes/News & Issues (conservation, outdoor sports, etc), 300 words; Birds Bees Trees (essays on human relationships), 650 words. **Buys 30 mss/year.** Query with published clips. **Pays 35-50¢/word.**

Fillers: Anecdotes, facts, gags to be illustrated by cartoonist, newsbreaks, short humor. **Buys 50/year.** Length: 25-100 words. **Pays 25¢/word.**

Tips: "Send well thought out, complete queries reflective of research. Writers ought not query on topics already covered."

$ $ $ $ INTERNATIONAL WILDLIFE, National Wildlife Federation, 11100 Wildlife Center Dr., Reston VA 20190-5362. (703)438-6510. Fax: (703)438-6544. E-mail: pubs@nwf.org. Website: www.nwf.org/nwf. **Contact:** Jonathan Fisher, editor. **85% freelance written.** Prefers to work with published/established writers. Bimonthly magazine covering natural history and the environment in countries outside the US. "We are now assigning most articles but will consider detailed proposals for quality feature material of interest to a broad audience." Estab. 1971. Circ. 160,000. **Pays on acceptance.** Publishes ms an average of 4 months after acceptance. Buys exclusive first time worldwide rights and nonexclusive worldwide rights after publication. Accepts queries by mail, e-mail, fax. Responds in 6 weeks to queries. Writer's guidelines for #10 SASE.

○➔ Examine past issues for style and subject matter

Nonfiction: Focuses on world wildlife, environmental problems and peoples' relationship to the natural world as reflected in such issues as population growth, pollution, resource utilization, food production, etc. Stories deal with non-US subjects. Especially interested in articles on animal behavior and other natural history, first-person experiences by scientists in the field, well-reported coverage of wildlife-status case studies which also raise broader themes about international conservation and timely issues. Query. Length: 2,000 words. **Pays $2,000 minimum for long features.** Sometimes pays expenses of writers on assignment.

Photos: Purchases top-quality color photos; prefers packages of related photos and text, but single shots of exceptional interest and sequences also considered. Prefers Kodachrome or Fujichrome transparencies. Reviews transparencies. Buys one-time rights.

Tips: *"International Wildlife* readers include conservationists, biologists, wildlife managers and other wildlife professionals, but the majority are not wildlife professionals. In fact, *International Wildlife* caters to the unconverted—those people who may have only a passing interest in wildlife conservation. Consequently, our writers should avoid a common pitfall: talking only to an 'in group.' *International Wildlife* is in competition with television and hundreds of other periodicals for the limited time and attention of busy people. So our functions include attracting readers with engaging subjects, pictures and layouts; then holding them with interesting and entertaining, as well as instructional, text."

$ $ ▨ MOUNTAINFREAK, For Freaks Like Us, P.O. Box 4149 122½ N. Oak St., Telluride CO 81435. (970)728-9731. Fax: (970)728-9821. E-mail: freaks@mountainfreak.com. Website: www.mountainfreak.com. **Contact:** Lise Waring, managing editor. **90% freelance written.** Bimonthly magazine. Estab. 1996. Circ. 25,000. Pays 90 days after publication. Byline given. Offers 33% kill fee. Buys first North American serial, nonexclusive electronic rights. Editorial lead time up to 9 months. Accepts queries by mail. Sample copy for $7. Writer's guidelines for SASE or online.

Nonfiction: "Borrowing from the leaders of Bhutan, we hope to raise the level of Gross National Happiness in the world by providing a voice and an educational forum. We are for folks who think off the grid, a broad spectrum of doers, thinkers and dreamers whose love for the Earth's wild places defines their activities and attitudes. We embrace the world but bring a critical eye to it, too. We seek seasonally-appropriate, adrenaline-packed stories that included the cultural, political, personal and spiritual aspects of an adventure from any part of the world." Book excerpts, essays, exposé, general interest, how-to, humor, inspirational, personal experience, technical, travel, profile. **Buys 100 mss/year.** Query with published clips. Length: 100-3,000 words.

Photos: Send photos with submission. Offers $25-200/photo or negotiates indiviudally. Captions required.

Columns/Departments: Smoke Signals (environmental and political news), 100-1,000 words; Be Well (alternative health; because much of what used to be alternative has become mainstream, try to introduce us to something that is truly different), 700 words, **pays $250**; Get Lost (highlights destinations for travelers of all means, includes service sidebar), 1,350 words, **pays $300**; Cultural Vibrations (a perspective piece, this helps us see our culture from a new angle; topics range from appropriation of cultural traditions to the implications of technology), 1,000 words, **pays $200**; Good Biz (spotlights a company that not only creates quality products but combines production with conscientious business ethics), 380 words, **pays $100**; Bite This (discusses a healthy food ingredient, its merits and history; includes an original or attributed recipe), 1,100 words, **pays $250**; Hands On (a how-to section that goes beyond the basics; share the steps to build or do something useful or unusual; illustrative photos required as part of the story, but purchased separately), 700 words, **pays $150.** Query with published clips.

Fiction: "We seek literary stories. Outdoor fiction preferred." No "there I was," "tired but happy, etc." **Buys 6 mss/year.** Send complete ms. Length: 500-3,000 words. **Pays $150.**

Poetry: "We're not afraid of any topic or style, but prefer something with a connection to the earth." **Buys 6 poems/year.** Send complete ms. Length: 50 lines maximum. **Pays $25 plus 3 copies.**

▣ The online magazine carries original content not found in the print edition and includes writer's guidelines.

Tips: "Editorially, we stand on four legs: authentic adventure, soulful living, celebration, and activism. We think of ourselves as the nexus of altitude, attitude and culture. We're not about the newest gear, the hippest stuff, the latest adventure travel destination. We try to be insightful, adventurous, funny, activist, entertaining, beautiful, angry and celebratory about mountains and mountain life. We define mountains literally and metaphorically; mountainfreaks can be found in cities, underwater at coral atolls, in deserts. For nonfiction stories, please send us a tightly written query of not more than one page that begins with the lead you propose for the story. Hook us in, just as you would our readers. Understand our voice, let us hear yours, and tell us why they go together. We're not about peak bagging or first ascents; we're about worshipping the outdoors, the mountains, the air, the water. We'd like to hear from gentle travelers who are not out to conquer, but to understand. Read the magazine and guidelines before querying. If you have not published with us before, please also include no more than three clips of past work with your query. No e-mail queries unless you have published with us before. Most of our stories are written on assignment, but occasionally on spec. Only assigned and contracted pieces are eligible for kill fees (one-third the assigned fee). We require a two-to-three-sentence biography of yourself with your submission. Be whimsical. Tell us if your submission was simultaneously submitted to another magazine or published previously. We do not accept work from anyone who has a financial interest in a subject or product (in other words, if you work in PR, forget it)."

$ $ $ NATIONAL PARKS, 1300 19th St. NW, Suite 300, Washington DC 20036. (202)223-6722. Fax: (202)659-0650. E-mail: npmag@npca.org. Website: www.npca.org/. Editor-in-chief: Linda Rancourt. **Contact:** William Updike, asssitant editor. **60% freelance written.** Prefers to work with published/established writers. Bimonthly magazine for a largely unscientific but highly educated audience interested in preservation of National Park System units, natural areas and protection of wildlife habitat. Estab. 1919. Circ. 400,000. **Pays on acceptance.** Publishes ms an average of 2 months after acceptance. Offers 33% kill fee. Buys first North American serial rights. Responds in 5 months to queries. Sample copy for $3 and 9×12 SASE or online. Writer's guidelines for #10 SASE.

Nonfiction: All material must relate to U.S. national parks. Exposé (on threats, wildlife problems in national parks), descriptive articles about new or proposed national parks and wilderness parks, natural history pieces describing park geology, wildlife or plants, new trends in park use, legislative issues. No poetry, philosophical essays or first-person narratives. No unsolicited mss. Length: 2,000-2,500 words. **Pays $1,200 for full-length features; $500 for service articles.**

Photos: No color prints or negatives. Send for guidelines. Not responsible for unsolicited photos. Send photos with submission. Reviews color slides. Pays $150-350 inside; $525 for covers. Captions required.

Tips: "Articles should have an original slant or news hook and cover a limited subject, rather than attempt to treat a broad subject superficially. Specific examples, descriptive details and quotes are always preferable to generalized information. The writer must be able to document factual claims, and statements should be clearly substantiated with evidence within the article. *National Parks* does not publish fiction, poetry, personal essays or 'My trip to...' stories."

$ $ $ $ NATIONAL WILDLIFE, National Wildlife Federation, 11100 Wildlife Center Dr., Reston VA 20190. (703)438-6524. Fax: (703)438-6544. E-mail: pubs@nwf.org. Website: www.nwf.org/natlwild. **Contact:** Mark Wexler, editor. **75% freelance written.** Assigns almost all material based on staff ideas. Assigns few unsolicited queries. Bimonthly magazine. "Our purpose is to promote wise use of the nation's natural resources and to conserve and protect wildlife and its habitat. We reach a broad audience that is largely interested in wildlife conservation and nature photography." Estab. 1963. Circ. 660,000. **Pays on acceptance.** Publishes ms an average of 1 year after acceptance. Offers 25% kill fee. Buys all rights. Submit seasonal material 8 months in advance. Accepts queries by mail, e-mail, fax. Responds in 6 weeks to queries. Writer's guidelines for #10 SASE.

Nonfiction: General interest (2,500 word features on wildlife, new discoveries, behavior, or the environment), how-to (an outdoor or nature related activity), interview/profile (people who have gone beyond the call of duty to protect wildlife and its habitat, or to prevent environmental contamination and people who have been involved in the environment or conservation in interesting ways), personal experience (outdoor adventure), photo feature (wildlife), short 700-word features on an unusual individual or new scientific discovery relating to nature. "Avoid too much scientific detail. We prefer anecdotal, natural history material." **Buys 50 mss/year.** Query with or without published clips. Length: 750-2,500 words. **Pays $800-3,000.** Sometimes pays expenses of writers on assignment.

Photos: John Nuhn, photo editor. Send photos with submission. Reviews Kodachrome or Fujichrome transparencies. Buys one-time rights.

Tips: "Writers can break in with us more readily by proposing subjects (initially) that will take only one or two pages in the magazine (short features)."

$ $ $ $ NATURAL HISTORY, Natural History Magazine, Central Park W. at 79th St., New York NY 10024. (212)769-5500. Fax: (212)769-5511. E-mail: nhmag@amnh.org. **Contact:** Ellen Goldensohn, editor-in-chief. **15% freelance written.** Magazine published 10 times/year for well-educated audience: professional people, scientists and scholars. Circ. 300,000. **Pays on acceptance.** Publishes ms an average of 3 months after acceptance. Byline given. Buys first North American serial rights, becomes an agent for second serial (reprint) rights. Submit seasonal material 6 months in advance.

Nonfiction: "We are seeking new research on mammals, birds, invertebrates, reptiles, ocean life, anthropology, astronomy, preferably written by principal investigators in these fields. Our slant is toward unraveling problems in behavior, ecology, and evolution." **Buys 60 mss/year.** Query by mail or send complete ms. Length: 1,500-3,000 words. **Pays $500-2,500.**

Photos: Rarely uses 8×10 b&w glossy prints; pays $125/page maximum. Much color is used; pays $300 for inside and up to $600 for cover. Buys one-time rights.

Columns/Departments: Journal (reporting from the field); Findings (summary of new or ongoing research); Naturalist At Large; The Living Museum (relates to the American Museum of Natural History); Discovery (natural or cultural history of a specific place).

Tips: "We expect high standards of writing and research. We do not lobby for causes, environmental or other. The writer should have a deep knowledge of his subject, then submit original ideas either in query or by manuscript."

$ $ NATURE CANADA, Canadian Nature Federation, 1 Nicholas St., Suite 606, Ottawa, Ontario K1N 7B7, Canada. Fax: (613)562-3371. E-mail: cnf@cnf.ca. Website: www.cnf.ca. **Contact:** Barbara Stevenson, editor. Biannual magazine covering conservation, natural history and environmental/naturalist community. "*Nature Canada* is written for an audience interested in nature. Its content supports the Canadian Nature Federation's philosophy that all species have a right to exist regardless of their usefulness to humans. We promote the awareness, understanding and enjoyment of nature." Estab. 1971. Circ. 27,000. Pays on publication. Publishes ms an average of 3 months after acceptance. Byline given. Offers $100 kill fee. Buys all CNF rights (including electronic). Author retains resale rights elsewhere. Editorial lead time 3 months. Submit seasonal material 6 months in advance. Responds in 3 months to mss. Sample copy for $5. Writer's guidelines for SASE or online.

Nonfiction: Canadian environmental issues and natural history. **Buys 8 mss/year.** Query with published clips. Length: 2,000-4,000 words. **Pays 50¢/word (Canadian).**

Photos: State availability with submission. Buys one-time rights. Offers $40-100/photo (Canadian). Identification of subjects required.

Columns/Departments: The Green Gardener (naturalizing your backyard), 1,200 words; Small Wonder (on less well-known species such as invertebrates, nonvascular plants, etc.), 800-1,500 words; Connections (Canadians making a difference for the environment), 1,000-1,500 words; Pathways (about natural places to visit). **Buys 10 mss/year.** Query with published clips. **Pays 50¢/word (Canadian).**

Tips: "Our readers are knowledgeable about nature and the environment so contributors should have a good understanding of the subject. We also deal exclusively with Canadian issues and species."

$ $ $ OUTDOOR AMERICA, Izaak Walton League of America, 707 Conservation Lane, Gaithersburg MD 20878. (301)548-0150. Fax: (301)548-0146. E-mail: WLebzelter@iwla.org. Website: www.iwla.org. **Contact:** Will Lebzelter, editor. Quarterly magazine covering national conservation efforts/issues. "*Outdoor America*, one of the nation's most established conservation magazines, has been published by the Izaak Walton League, a national conservation organization, since 1922. A quarterly 4-color publication, *Outdoor America* is received by approximately 40,000 League members, as well as representatives of Congress and the media. Our audience, located predominantly in the midwestern and mid-Atlantic states, enjoys traditional recreational pursuits, such as fishing, hiking, hunting and boating. All have a keen interest in protecting the future of our natural resources and outdoor recreation heritage." Estab. 1922. Circ. 50,000. **Pays on acceptance.** Publishes ms an average of 2 months after acceptance. Accepts queries by mail, e-mail. Sample copy for $2.50. Writer's guidelines online.

Nonfiction: Conservation and natural resources; stories with national implications. Query or send ms for short items (500 words or less). Features are planned 6-12 months in advance. Length: 350-3,000 words. **Pays $150-1,000.**

N $ $ $ SEASONS, Ontario's Nature and Environment Magazine, Federation of Ontario Naturalists, 355 Lesmill Rd., Don Mills Ontario M3B 2W9, Canada. (416)444-8419. E-mail: seasons@ontarionature.org. Website: www.ontarionature.org. **Contact:** Nancy Clark, editor. **75% freelance written.** Quarterly magazine. "*Seasons* focuses on Ontario natural history, parks and environmental issues, with appeal for general readers as well as naturalists." Estab. 1963 (published as *Ontario Naturalist* 1963-1980. Circ. 13,000. **Pays on acceptance.** Publishes ms an average of 6 months after acceptance. Byline given. Offers 50% kill fee. Buys first Canadian serial rights. Editorial lead time 6 months. Submit seasonal material 1 year in advance. Accepts queries by mail, e-mail, fax. Responds in 3 months to mss. Sample copy for $7.50. Writer's guidelines for #10 SASE or online.

Nonfiction: Book excerpts, essays, general interest, how-to (identify species, be a better birder, etc.), humor, inspirational, interview/profile, opinion, personal experience, photo feature, travel. No cute articles about cute animals or biology articles cribbed from reference books. **Buys 16-20 mss/year.** Query with published clips. Length: 1,500-3,000 words. **Pays $350-1,000 (Canadian) for assigned articles.** Sometimes pays expenses of writers on assignment.

Photos: State availability with submission. Reviews 35mm transparencies. Buys one-time rights. Negotiates payment individually. Identification of subjects, model releases required.

Tips: "We are totally Ontario focused. We do not run articles on U.S. topics."

\$ \$ \$ \$ SIERRA, 85 Second St., 2nd Floor, San Francisco CA 94105-3441. (415)977-5656. Fax: (415)977-5794. E-mail: sierra.letters@sierraclub.org. Website: www.sierraclub.org. Editor-in-chief: Joan Hamilton. Senior Editors: Reed McManus, Paul Rauber. **Contact:** Robert Schildgen, managing editor. Works with a small number of new/unpublished writers each year. Bimonthly magazine emphasizing conservation and environmental politics for people who are well educated, activist, outdoor-oriented and politically well informed with a dedication to conservation. Estab. 1893. Circ. 575,000. **Pays on acceptance.** Publishes ms an average of 4 months after acceptance. Byline given. Offers negotiable kill fee. Buys first North American serial rights. Accepts queries by mail, fax. Responds in 2 months to queries. Sample copy for \$3 and SASE or online. Writer's guidelines online.

● The editor reports an interest in seeing pieces on environmental "heroes," thoughtful features on environmental issues in the Midwest and South (except Florida) and engaging stories about achievements of local activists.

Nonfiction: Exposé (well-documented articles on environmental issues of national importance such as energy, wilderness, forests, etc.), general interest (well-researched nontechnical pieces on areas of particular environmental concern), interview/profile, photo feature (photo essays on threatened or scenic areas), journalistic treatments of semi-technical topic (energy sources, wildlife management, land use, waste management, etc.). No "My trip to.." or "why we must save wildlife/nature" articles; no poetry or general superficial essays on environmentalism; no reporting on purely local environmental issues. **Buys 30-36 mss/year.** Query with published clips. Length: 800-3,000 words. **Pays \$450-4,000.**

Reprints: Send photocopy with rights for sale noted and information about when and where the material previously appeared. Reprints pay negotiable.

Photos: Tanuja Mehrotra, art and production manager. Send photos with submission. Buys one-time rights. Pays maximum \$300 for transparencies; more for cover photos.

Columns/Departments: Food for Thought (food's connection to environment); Good Going (adventure journey); Hearth & Home (advice for environmentally sound living); Body Politics (health and the environment); Way to Go (wilderness trips), 750 words. Lay of the Land (national/international concerns), 500-700 words. Mixed Media (book reviews), 200-300 words. **Pays \$50-500.**

◼ The online magazine carries original content not found in the print edition and includes writer's guidelines.

Tips: "Queries should include an outline of how the topic would be covered and a mention of the political appropriateness and timeliness of the article. Statements of the writer's qualifications should be included."

\$ SNOWY EGRET, The Fair Press, P.O. Box 9, Bowling Green IN 47833. (812)829-1910. Managing Editor: Ruth C. Acker. **Contact:** Editor. **95% freelance written.** Semiannual literary magazine featuring nature writing. "We publish works which celebrate the abundance and beauty of nature and examine the variety of ways in which human beings interact with landscapes and living things. Nature writing from literary, artistic, psychological, philosophical and historical perspectives." Estab. 1922. Circ. 400. Pays on publication. Publishes ms an average of 6 months after acceptance. Byline given. Buys first North American serial rights, one-time anthology rights or reprints rights. Editorial lead time 2 months. Accepts queries by mail. Accepts simultaneous submissions. Responds in 1 month to queries; 2 months to mss. Sample copy for 9 × 12 SASE and \$8. Writer's guidelines for #10 SASE.

○→ Break in with "an essay, story or short description based on a closely observed first-hand encounter with some aspect of the natural world."

Nonfiction: Essays, general interest, interview/profile, personal experience, travel. **Buys 10 mss/year.** Send complete ms. Length: 500-10,000 words. **Pays \$2/page.**

Columns/Departments: Jane Robertson, Woodnotes editor. Woodnotes (short descriptions of personal encounters with wildlife or natural settings), 200-2,000 words. **Buys 12 mss/year. Pays \$2/page.**

Fiction: Nature-oriented works (in which natural settings, wildlife or other organisms and/or characters who identify with the natural world are significant components. "No genre fiction, e.g., horror, western romance, etc." **Buys 4 mss/year.** Send complete ms. Length: 5,000-10,000 words. **Pays \$2/page.**

Poetry: Avant-garde, free verse, traditional. **Buys 30 poems/year.** Submit maximum 5 poems. **Pays \$4/poem or page.**

Tips: "The writers we publish invariably have a strong personal identification with the natural world, have examined their subjects thoroughly, and write about them sincerely. They know what they're talking about and show their subjects in detail, using, where appropriate, detailed description and dialogue."

\$ WHOLE EARTH, Point Foundation, 1408 Mission Ave., San Rafael CA 94901. (415)256-2800. Fax: (415)256-2808. E-mail: editor@wholeearthmag.com. Website: www.wholeearthmag.com. Editor: Peter Warshall, Managing Editor: Michael Stone. Assistant Editor: Emily Polk. **Contact:** Attn. Submissions. **70% freelance written.** "Quarterly periodical, descendent of the Whole Earth Catalog. Evaluates tools, ideas, and practices to sow the seeds for a long-term, viable planet." Estab. 1971. Circ. 30,000. Pays on publication. Publishes ms an average of 6 months after acceptance. Byline given. Buys one-time rights to articles; all rights for reviews. Editorial lead time 3 months. Accepts simultaneous submissions. Responds in 1 month (no promises) to mss. Sample copy online. Writer's guidelines for SASE or online.

Nonfiction: Essays, exposé, general interest, how-to, humor, interview/profile, new product, personal experience, photo feature, religious, travel, historical, book reviews. "No dull repeats of old ideas or material; no 'goddess' material, spiritual, New Age or 'Paths to . . .' " Send complete ms (queries are discouraged). Length: 500-3,000 words. **Pays negotiable rates for assigned articles.**

Photos: State availability with submission. Buys one-time rights. Negotiates payment individually.

Fiction: Rarely publishes fiction. **Buys 2-4 mss/year.**

Poetry: Avant-garde, free verse, haiku, light verse, traditional. No long works. **Buys 1-4 poems/year.** Length: 100 lines maximum. **Pay negotiable.**

Tips: "We like your personal voice: intimate, a lively conversation with an attentive friend. We like ideas, thoughts and events to appear to stand independent and clear of the narrator. Don't send a variation on an old idea. Show us you did your homework."

PERSONAL COMPUTERS

Personal computer magazines continue to evolve. The most successful have a strong focus on a particular family of computers or widely-used applications and carefully target a specific type of computer use, although as technology evolves, some computers and applications fall by the wayside. Be sure you see the most recent issue of a magazine before submitting material.

N $ $ $ COMPUTER BUYER'S GUIDE & HANDBOOK, Bedford Communications, 1410 Broadway, 21st Floor, New York NY 10018. E-mail: lsprimont@bedfordmags.com. Website: www.bedfordmags.com. **Contact:** Leigh Sprimont, editor-in-chief. **60% freelance written.** Monthly magazine covering computer hardware, software and peripherals; industry trends. "Publication is geared towards the computer buyer, with an emphasis on the small office." Estab. 1982. Pays on publication. Publishes ms an average of 3 months after acceptance. Byline given. Offers 25% kill fee. Buys all rights. Editorial lead time 4 months. Accepts queries by mail, e-mail. Responds in 1 month to queries. Sample copy online.

Nonfiction: How-to (e.g., install a CD-ROM drive), technical, hands-on reviews. No unsolicited mss. **Buys 80-100 mss/year.** Length: 600-5,500 words. Sometimes pays expenses of writers on assignment.

Tips: "Send résumé with feature-length clips (technology-related, if possible), to editorial offices. Unsolicited manuscripts are not accepted or returned."

$ $ COMPUTOREDGE, San Diego, Denver and Albuquerque's Computer Magazine, The Byte Buyer, Inc., P.O. Box 83086, San Diego CA 92138. (858)573-0315. Fax: (858)573-0205. E-mail: submissions@computoredge.com. Website: www.computoredge.com. Executive Editor: Leah Steward. **Contact:** Patricia Smith, senior editor. **90% freelance written.** "We are the nation's largest regional computer weekly, providing San Diego, Denver, and Albuquerque with entertaining articles on all aspects of computers. We cater to the novice/beginner/first-time computer buyer. Humor is welcome." Published as *Computer Edge* in San Diego and Denver; published as *Computer Scene* in Albuquerque. Estab. 1983. Circ. 175,000. Pays 30 days after publication. Byline given. Offers $15 kill fee. Buys first North American serial rights, one-week exclusive and 90-day non-exclusive web rights. Submit seasonal material 2 months in advance. Accepts queries by e-mail. Responds in 2 months to queries. Sample copy for SAE with 7 first-class stamps or online. Writer's guidelines online.

● Accepts electronic submissions only.

Nonfiction: General interest (computer), how-to, humor, personal experience. **Buys 80 mss/year.** Send complete ms. Length: 900-1,200 words. **Pays $100-200.**

Columns/Departments: Beyond Personal Computing (a reader's personal experience); Mac Madness (Macintosh-related); I Don't Do Windows (alternative operating systems). Length: 500-1,000 words. **Buys 80 mss/year.** Send complete ms. **Pays $50-145.**

Fiction: Confessions, fantasy, slice-of-life vignettes. **Buys 20 mss/year.** Send complete ms. Length: 900-1,200 words. **Pays $100-200.**

Tips: "Be relentless. Convey technical information in an understandable, interesting way. We like light material, but not fluff. Write as if you're speaking with a friend. Avoid the typical 'Love at First Byte' and the 'How My Grandmother Loves Her New Computer' article. We do not accept poetry. Avoid sexual innuendoes/metaphors. Reading a sample issue is advised."

$ $ $ $ MACADDICT, Imagine Media, 150 North Hill Dr., Suite 40, Brisbane CA 94005. (415)468-4684. Fax: (415)468-4686. E-mail: dreynolds@macaddict.com. Managing Editor: Jeff T. Herton. **Contact:** David Reynolds, editor-in-chief. **35% freelance written.** Monthly magazine covering Macintosh computers. "*MacAddict* is a magazine for Macintosh computer enthusiasts of all levels. Writers must know, love and own Macintosh computers." Estab. 1996. Circ. 200,000. Pays on publication. Publishes ms an average of 3 months after acceptance. Byline given. Buys all rights. Editorial lead time 3 months. Submit seasonal material 5 months in advance. Accepts queries by mail, e-mail. Responds in 1 month to queries.

Nonfiction: General interest, how-to, new product, photo feature, technical. No humor, case studies, personal experience, essays. **Buys 30 mss/year.** Query with or without published clips. Length: 250-5,000 words. **Pays $50-2,500.**

Photos: State availability with submission. Buys one-time rights. Negotiates payment individually. Captions, identification of subjects, model releases required.

Columns/Departments: Reviews (always assigned), 300-750 words; How-to's (detailed, step-by-step), 500-4,000 words; features, 1,000-4,000 words. **Buys 30 mss/year.** Query with or without published clips. **Pays $50-2,500.**

Fillers: Narasu Rebbapragada, editor. Get Info. **Buys 20/year.** Length: 50-500 words. **Pays $25-200.**

■ The online magazine carries original content not found in the print edition. Contact: Niko Coucouvanis, online editor.

Tips: "Send us an idea for a short one to two page how-to and/or send us a letter outlining your publishing experience and areas of Mac expertise so we can assign a review to you (reviews editor is Kris Fong). Your submission should have great practical hands-on benefit to a reader, be fun to read in the author's natural voice, and include lots of screenshot graphics. We require electronic submissions. Impress our reviews editor with well-written reviews of Mac products and then move up to bigger articles from there."

N: $ $ $ PC UPGRADE, Bedford Communications, 1410 Broadway, 21st Floor, New York NY 10018. E-mail: lsprimont@bedfordmags.com. Website: www.bedfordmags.com. **Contact:** Leigh Sprimont, editor-in-chief. **60% freelance written.** Bimonthly magazine covering computer hardware, software and peripherals; industry trends. "Publication is geared toward the computer buyer, with an emphasis on the small office." Estab. 1982. Pays on publication. Publishes ms an average of 3 months after acceptance. Byline given. Offers 25% kill fee. Buys all rights. Editorial lead time 4 months. Accepts queries by mail, e-mail. Responds in 1 month to queries. Sample copy online.

Nonfiction: How-to (e.g., how to install a CD-ROM drive), technical, hands-on reviews. **Buys 80-100 mss/year.** Query with published clips. "Will not accept unsolicited articles or manuscripts." Length: 600-5,500 words. Sometimes pays expenses of writers on assignment.

Tips: "Send résumé with feature-length (technology-related, if possible) clips to editorial offices. Unsolicited manuscripts are not accepted or returned."

$ $ $ ▨ WIRED MAGAZINE, Condé Nast Publications, 520 Third St., 3rd Floor, San Francisco CA 94107-1815. (415)276-5000. Fax: (415)276-5150. E-mail: submit@wired.com. Website: www.wired.com. Publisher: Dean Shutte. Editor-in-chief: Chris Anderson. **Contact:** Sonia Zjawinsky, editorial assistant. **95% freelance written.** Monthly magazine covering technology and digital culture. "We cover the digital revolution and related advances in computers, communications and lifestyles." Estab. 1993. Circ. 500,000. **Pays on acceptance.** Publishes ms an average of 3 months after acceptance. Byline given. Offers 25% kill fee. Buys all rights for items less than 1,000 words, first North American serial rights for pieces over 1,000 words. Editorial lead time 3 months. Responds in 3 weeks to queries. Sample copy for $4.95. Writer's guidelines for #10 SASE or e-mail guidelines@wired.com.

Nonfiction: Essays, interview/profile, opinion. "No poetry or trade articles." **Buys 85 features, 130 short pieces, 200 reviews, 36 essays, and 50 other mss/year.** Query. Pays expenses of writers on assignment.

Tips: "Send query letter with clips to Sonia Zjawinsky. Read the magazine. We get too many inappropriate queries. We need quality writers who understand our audience, and who understand how to query."

PHOTOGRAPHY

Readers of these magazines use their cameras as a hobby and for weekend assignments. To write for these publications, you should have expertise in photography. Magazines geared to the professional photographer can be found in the Professional Photography section.

$ NATURE PHOTOGRAPHER, Nature Photographer Publishing Co., Inc., P.O. Box 690518, Quincy MA 02269. (617)847-0091. Fax: (617)847-0952. E-mail: natureusphotographer@yahoo.com. Website: www.naturephotographerma g.com. **Contact:** Helen Longest-Saccone and Evamarie Mathaey, co-editors-in-chief/photo editors. **100% freelance written.** Written by field contributors and editors; write to above address to become a "Field Contributor." Quarterly magazine "emphasizing nature photography that uses low-impact and local less-known locations, techniques and ethics. Articles include how-to, travel to world-wide wilderness locations, and how nature photography can be used to benefit the environment and environmental education of the public." Estab. 1990. Circ. 25,000. Pays on publication. Buys one-time rights. Submit seasonal material 8 months in advance. Accepts queries by mail, e-mail. Accepts simultaneous submissions. Responds in 2 months to queries. Sample copy for 9×12 SAE and 6 first-class stamps. Writer's guidelines for #10 SASE or online.

Nonfiction: How-to (underwater, exposure, creative techniques, techniques to make photography easier, low-impact techniques, macro photography, large-format wildlife), photo feature, technical, travel. No articles about photographing in zoos or on game farms. **Buys 12-18 mss/year.** Query with published clips or writing samples. Length: 750-2,500 words. **Pays $75-150.**

Reprints: Send photocopy and information about when and where the material previously appeared. Pays 75% of amount *Nature Photographer* pays for an original article.

Photos: Send photos upon request. Do not send with submission. Reviews 35mm, 2¼×2¼ and 4×5 transparencies. Buys one-time rights. Offers no additional payment for photos accepted with ms. Identification of subjects required.

Tips: "Query with original, well-thought-out ideas and good writing samples. Make sure you send SASE. Areas most open are travel, how-to and conservation articles with dramatic slides to illustrate the articles. Must have good, solid research and knowledge of subject. Be sure to obtain guidelines by sending SASE with request before submitting query. If you have not requested guidelines within the last year, request an updated version, because *Nature Photographer* is now written by editors and field contributors and guidelines will outline how you can become a field contributor."

[N] $ $ PC PHOTO, Werner Publishing Corp., 12121 Wilshire Blvd., Suite 1200, Los Angeles CA 90025. Fax: (310)826-5008. Website: www.pcphotomag.com. Managing Editor: Chris Robinson. **Contact:** Rob Sheppard, editor. **60% freelance written.** Bimonthly magazine covering digital photography. "Our magazine is designed to help photographers better use digital technologies to improve their photography." Estab. 1997. Circ. 175,000. Pays on publication. Publishes ms an average of 4 months after acceptance. Byline given. Buys one-time rights. Editorial lead time 6 months. Submit seasonal material 6 months in advance. Accepts queries by mail. Responds in 1 month to queries. Sample copy for #10 SASE or online.

Nonfiction: How-to, personal experience, photo feature. **Buys 30 mss/year.** Query. Length: 1,200 words. **Pays $500 for assigned articles; $400 for unsolicited articles.**

Photos: Send photos with submission. Reviews contact sheets, inkjet prints. "We do not want to see original transparencies or negatives." Buys one-time rights. Offers $100/photo.

Tips: "Since *PCPHOTO* is a photography magazine, we must see photos before any decision can be made on an article, so phone queries are not appropriate. Ultimately, whether we can use a particular piece or not will depend greatly on the photographs and how they fit in with material already in our files. We take a fresh look at the modern photographic world by encouraging photography and the use of new technologies. Editorial is intended to demystify the use of modern equipment by emphasizing practical use of the camera and the computer, highlighting the technique rather than the technical."

$ $ PHOTO LIFE, Canada's Photography Magazine, Apex Publications Inc., One Dundas St. W, Suite 2500, P.O. Box 84, Toronto, Ontario M5G 1Z3, Canada. (800)905-7468. Fax: (800)664-2739. E-mail: editor@photolife.com. Website: www.photolife.com. **Contact:** Suzie Ketene, editor. **15% freelance written.** Bimonthly magazine. "*Photo Life* is geared to a Canadian and U.S. audience of advanced amateur photographers. *Photo Life* is not a technical magazine per se, but techniques should be explained in enough depth to make them clear." Estab. 1976. Circ. 73,500. Pays on publication. Publishes ms an average of 1 year after acceptance. Byline given. Buys one-time rights. Editorial lead time 4 months. Submit seasonal material 6 months in advance. Accepts queries by mail, e-mail. Accepts simultaneous submissions. Responds in 3 months to queries. Sample copy for $5.50. Writer's guidelines free via email.

Nonfiction: How-to (photo tips, technique), inspirational, photo feature, technical, travel. **Buys 10 mss/year.** Query with published clips or send complete ms. **Pays $100-600 (Canadian).**

Photos: Reviews transparencies, prints. Buys one-time rights. Negotiates payment individually. Captions, model releases required.

Tips: "We will review any relevant submissions that include a full text or a detailed outline of an article proposal. Accompanying photographs are necessary as the first decision of acceptance will be based upon images. Most of the space available in the magazine is devoted to our regular contributors. Therefore, we cannot guarantee publication of other articles within any particular period of time. Currently, we are overflowing with travel articles. You are still welcome to submit to this category, but the waiting period may be longer than expected (up to 1½ years). You may, however, use your travel photography to explain photo techniques. A short biography is optional."

$ $ $ PHOTO TECHNIQUES, Preston Publications, Inc., 6600 W. Touhy Ave., Niles IL 60714. (847)647-2900. Fax: (847)647-1155. E-mail: jwhite@phototechmag.com. Publisher: S. Tinsley Preston III. Managing Editor: Nancy Getz. **Contact:** Joe White. **50% freelance written.** Bimonthly publication covering photochemistry, lighting, optics, processing and printing, Zone system, special effects, sensitometry, etc. Aimed at advanced workers. Prefers to work with experienced photographer-writer; happy to work with excellent photographers whose writing skills are lacking. "Article conclusions often require experimental support." Estab. 1979. Circ. 35,000. Pays within 2 weeks of publication. Publishes ms an average of 8 months after acceptance. Byline given. Buys one-time rights. Sample copy for $5. Writer's guidelines for #10 SASE.

Nonfiction: How-to, photo feature, technical (product review), special interest articles within the above listed topics. Query or complete ms. Length: open, but most features run approximately 2,500 words or 3-4 magazine pages. **Pays $200-1,000 for well-researched technical articles.**

Photos: Photographers have a much better chance of having their photos published if the photos accompany a written article. Prefers 8×10 b&w and color prints. Buys one-time rights. Manuscript payment includes payment for photos. Captions, technical information required.

Tips: "Study the magazine! Virtually all writers we publish are readers of the magazine. We are now more receptive than ever to articles about photographers, history, aesthetics and informative backgrounders about specific areas of the photo industry or specific techniques. Successful writers for our magazine are doing what they write about."

[N] $ PICTURE MAGAZINE, 126 University Place, 5th Floor, New York NY 10003. (212)352-2700. Fax: (212)352-2155. E-mail: picmag@aol.com. Website: www.picturemagazine.com. **Contact:** Brock Wylan, editor. **100% freelance written.** Bimonthly magazine covering professional photography topics. Estab. 1995. Circ. 16,000. Pays on

---

FOR INFORMATION on setting your freelance fees, see How Much Should I Charge?

publication. Publishes ms an average of 2 months after acceptance. Byline given. Buys one-time rights. Editorial lead time 3 months. Submit seasonal material 3 months in advance. Accepts queries by e-mail only. Accepts simultaneous submissions. Sample copy and writer's guidelines free.

Nonfiction: General interest, how-to, interview/profile, new product, photo feature, technical. **Buys 5 mss/year.** Send complete ms. Length: 1,500-2,500 words. **Pays $150.** Pays expenses of writers on assignment.

Photos: State availability with submission. Buys one-time rights. Offers no additional payment for photos accepted with ms. Captions required.

$ TODAY'S PHOTOGRAPHER INTERNATIONAL, The Make Money With Your Camera Magazine, P.O. Box 777, Lewisville NC 27023. (336)945-9867. Fax: (336)945-3711. Website: www.aipress.com. Editor: Vonda H. Blackburn. **Contact:** Sarah Hinshaw, associate editor. **100% freelance written.** Bimonthly magazine addressing "how to make money—no matter where you live—with the equipment that you currently own." Editor's sweepstakes pays $500 for the best story in each issue. Estab. 1986. Circ. 78,000. Publishes ms an average of 6 months after acceptance. Byline given. Buys one-time rights. Editorial lead time 6 months. Submit seasonal material 6 months in advance. Accepts simultaneous submissions. Responds in 3 weeks to queries; 3 months to mss. Sample copy for $2, 9×12 SAE and 4 first-class stamps or for $3. Writer's guidelines free.

Nonfiction: How-to, opinion, personal experience, photo feature, technical, travel, new product. No "What I did on my summer vacation" stories.

Photos: State availability with submission. Reviews transparencies. Buys one-time rights. Offers no additional payment for photos accepted with ms. Captions, identification of subjects, model releases required.

Columns/Departments: Vonda Blackburn, editor. Books (how-to photography), 200-400 words; Sports (how-to photograph sports), 1,000 words. **Buys 40 mss/year.** Query. **Pays negotiable rate.**

Tips: Present a complete submission package containing: your manuscript, photos (with captions, model releases and technical data) and an inventory list of the submission package.

POLITICS & WORLD AFFAIRS

These publications cover politics for the reader interested in current events. Other publications that will consider articles about politics and world affairs are listed under Business & Finance, Contemporary Culture, Regional and General Interest. For listings of publications geared toward the professional, see Government & Public Service in the Trade section.

$ $ $ CALIFORNIA JOURNAL, 2101 K St., Sacramento CA 95816. (916)444-2840. Fax: (916)444-2339. E-mail: edit@statenet.com. Editor: Cindy Craft. **Contact:** Claudia Buck, managing editor. **20% freelance written.** Monthly magazine "with non-partisan coverage aimed at a literate, well-informed, well-educated readership with strong involvement in California issues, politics or government." Estab. 1970. Circ. 12,000. Pays on publication. Publishes ms an average of 3 months after acceptance. Byline given. Buys all rights. Accepts queries by mail, fax. Responds in 2 weeks to queries; 2 months to mss.

Nonfiction: Political analysis. Interview/profile (of state and local government officials), opinion (on politics and state government in California). No outright advocacy pieces, fiction, poetry, product pieces. **Buys 10 unsolicited mss/year.** Query. Length: 800-2,000 words. **Pays $300-1,000.** Sometimes pays expenses of writers on assignment.

Photos: State availability with submission. Reviews contact sheets. Buys all rights. Negotiates pay individually. Identification of subjects required.

Columns/Departments: Soapbox (opinion on current affairs), 800 words. **Does not pay.**

Tips: "Be well versed in political and environmental affairs as they relate to California."

$ $ CHURCH & STATE, Americans United for Separation of Church and State, 518 C St. NE, Washington DC 20002. (202)466-3234. Fax: (202)466-3353. E-mail: americansunited@au.org. Website: www.au.org. **Contact:** Joseph Conn, editor. **10% freelance written.** Monthly magazine emphasizing religious liberty and church/state relations matters. Strongly advocates separation of church and state. Readership is well-educated. Estab. 1947. Circ. 33,000. **Pays on acceptance.** Publishes ms an average of 2 months after acceptance. Buys all rights. Accepts queries by mail. Accepts simultaneous submissions. Responds in 2 months to queries. Sample copy and writer's guidelines for 9×12 SAE with 3 first-class stamps.

Nonfiction: Exposé, general interest, historical/nostalgic, interview/profile. **Buys 11 mss/year.** Query. Length: 800-1,600 words. **Pays $150-300 for assigned articles.** Sometimes pays expenses of writers on assignment.

Reprints: Send tearsheet, photocopy or typed ms with rights for sale noted and information about when and where the material previously appeared.

Photos: Send photos with submission. Buys one-time rights. Pays negotiable fee for b&w prints. Captions required.

Tips: "We're looking for feature articles on underreported local church-state controversies. We also consider 'viewpoint' essays that offer a unique or personal take on church-state issues. We are not a religious magazine. You need to see our magazine before you try to write for it."

$ COMMONWEAL, A Review of Public Affairs, Religion, Literature and the Arts, Commonweal Foundation, 475 Riverside Dr., Room 405, New York NY 10115. (212)662-4200. Fax: (212)662-4183. E-mail: commonweal@msn.com. Website: www.commonwealmagazine.org. Editor: Margaret O'Brien. **Contact:** Patrick Jordan, managing editor. Biweekly journal of opinion edited by Catholic lay people, dealing with topical issues of the day on public affairs, religion, literature and the arts. Estab. 1924. Circ. 20,000. **Pays on acceptance.** Byline given. Buys all rights. Submit seasonal material 2 months in advance. Responds in 2 months to queries. Sample copy free.

Nonfiction: Essays, general interest, interview/profile, personal experience, religious. **Buys 30 mss/year.** Query with published clips. Length: 2,000-2,500 words. **Pays $75-100.**

Columns/Departments: Upfronts (brief, newsy reportorials, giving facts, information and some interpretation behind the headlines of the day), 750-1,000 words; Last Word (usually of a personal nature, on some aspect of the human condition: spiritual, individual, political or social), 800 words.

Poetry: Rosemary Deen, poetry editor. Free verse, traditional. **Buys 20 poems/year. Pays 75¢/line.**

Tips: "Articles should be written for a general but well-educated audience. While religious articles are always topical, we are less interested in devotional and churchy pieces than in articles which examine the links between 'worldly' concerns and religious beliefs."

$ ▣ DISASTER NEWS NETWORK, Villagelife.org Inc., 7855 Rappahannock Ave., Suite 200, Jessup MD 20794. (443)755-9999. Fax: (443)755-9995. E-mail: susank@disasternews.net. Website: www.disasternews.net. **Contact:** Susan Kim, news editor. **100% freelance written.** Daily magazine. "The Disaster News Network is a comprehensive Internet site of timely news and information about U.S. disaster response and volunteer opportunities. DNN has been designed to be the primary first source of public information about U.S. disaster response efforts. Its news content is unusual because 100% of our content is original—DNN does not subscribe to any wire services or syndicates. The DNN news staff is located across the country, but meet regularly by telephone. All of the writers have previous daily news experience." Estab. 1998. Pays at end of the month. Publishes ms an average of 1 day after acceptance. Byline given. Buys all rights, makes work-for-hire assignments. Accepts queries by e-mail. Writer's guidelines free online or by e-mail.

Nonfiction: Religious, disaster response features. **Buys 600 mss/year.** Query with published clips. **Pays $85-100.** Pays expenses of writers on assignment.

Photos: Send photos with submission. Reviews prints. Buys all rights. Negotiates payment individually. Captions required.

Columns/Departments: Query. **Pays $85-100.**

Tips: "Daily news background/experience is helpful."

$ $ EMPIRE STATE REPORT, The Independent Magazine of Politics, Policy and the Business of Government, P.O. Box 9001, Mount Vernon NY 10552. (914)699-2020. Fax: (914)699-2025. E-mail: mdsa@cinn.com. Website: www.empirestatereport.com. Editor Director: Karen Raterman. **Contact:** Stephen Acunto, Jr., associate publisher/executive editor. Monthly magazine with "timely and independent information on politics, policy and governance for local and state officials throughout New York State." Estab. 1974. Circ. 16,000. Pays 2 months after publication. Byline given. Buys first North American serial rights. Accepts queries by mail, e-mail, fax, phone. Responds in 1 month to queries; 2 months to mss. Sample copy for $4.50 with 9 × 12 SASE or online. Writer's guidelines online.

○➔ Specifically looking for journalists with a working knowledge of legislative issues in New York State and how they affect businesses, municipalities, and all levels of government.

Nonfiction: Essays, exposé, interview/profile, opinion, analysis. Special issues: Editorial calendar available. **Buys 48 mss/year.** Query with published clips. Length: 500-4,500 words. **Pays $100-700.** Sometimes pays expenses of writers on assignment.

Photos: Send photos with submission. Reviews any size prints. Identification of subjects required.

Columns/Departments: Empire State Notebook (short news stories about state politics), 300-900 words; Perspective (opinion pieces), 900-950 words. Perspectives does not carry remuneration.

▣ The online magazine carries original content not found in the print edition and includes writer's guidelines. Contact: Stephen Acunto Jr.

Tips: "We are seeking journalists and non-journalists from throughout New York State who can bring a new perspective and/or forecast on politics, policy and the business of government."

$ $ EUROPE, Delegation of the European Commission, 2300 M St. NW, 3rd Floor, Washington DC 20037. (202)862-9555. Fax: (202)429-1766. Website: www.eurunion.org. Managing Editor: Peter Gwin. **Contact:** Robert Guttman, editor-in-chief. **50% freelance written.** Monthly magazine for anyone with a professional or personal interest in Europe and European/US relations. Estab. 1963. Circ. 75,000. Pays on publication. Publishes ms an average of 3 months after acceptance. Byline given. Offers 50% kill fee. Buys first, all rights. Editorial lead time 2 months. Submit seasonal material 4 months in advance. Accepts queries by mail, e-mail, fax, phone. Responds in 6 months to queries. Sample articles and writer's guidelines online.

Nonfiction: General interest, historical/nostalgic, interview/profile, interested in current affairs (with emphasis on economics, business and politics), the Single Market and Europe's relations with the rest of the world. Publishes monthly cultural travel pieces, with European angle. **Buys 20 mss/year.** Length: 600-1,500 words. **Pays $50-500 for assigned articles; $50-400 for unsolicited articles.**

Photos: Photos purchased with or without accompanying mss. Buys b&w and color. Pays $25-35 for b&w print, any size; $100 for inside use of transparencies; $450 for color used on cover; per job negotiable.
Columns/Departments: Art & Leisure (book, art, movie reviews, etc.), 200-800 words. **Pays $50-250.**
Tips: "We are always interested in stories that connect Europe to the U.S.—especially business stories. Company profiles, a U.S. company having success or vice versa, are a good bet. Also interested in articles on the 'euro' and good, new and different travel pieces."

N **$ THE LABOR PAPER, Serving Southern Wisconsin,** Union-Cooperative Publishing, 3030 39th Ave., Suite 110, Kenosha WI 53144. (262)657-6116. Fax: (262)657-6153. Website: www.laborpaper.homepage.com. **Contact:** Mark T. Onosko, editor. **30% freelance written.** Weekly tabloid covering union/labor news. Estab. 1935. Circ. 10,000. Pays on publication. Publishes ms an average of 2 months after acceptance. Byline given. Buys all rights. Editorial lead time 1 month. Submit seasonal material 1 month in advance. Accepts queries by mail, fax. Accepts simultaneous submissions. Sample copy and writer's guidelines free.
Nonfiction: Exposé, general interest, historical/nostalgic, humor, inspirational. **Buys 4 mss/year.** Query with published clips. Length: 300-1,000 words. **Pays $25.** Sometimes pays expenses of writers on assignment.
Photos: State availability with submission. Negotiates payment individually. Captions required.

$ $ THE NATION, 33 Irving Place, 8th Floor, New York NY 10003. (212)209-5400. Fax: (212)982-9000. E-mail: submissions@thenation.com. Website: www.thenation.com. Managing Editor: Laurie Grassi. Editor: Katrina Vanden Heuvel. **Contact:** Peggy Suttle, assistant to editor. **75% freelance written.** Works with a small number of new/unpublished writers each year. Weekly magazine "firmly committed to reporting on the issues of labor, national politics, business, consumer affairs, environmental politics, civil liberties, foreign affairs and the role and future of the Democratic Party." Estab. 1865. Pays on other. Buys first rights. Accepts queries by mail, e-mail, fax. Sample copy free. Writer's guidelines for 6×9 SASE.
• See the Contests & Awards section for the Discovery-*The Nation* poetry contest.
Nonfiction: "We welcome all articles dealing with the social scene, from an independent perspective." Queries encouraged. **Buys 100 mss/year. Pays $225-300.** Sometimes pays expenses of writers on assignment.
Columns/Departments: Editorial, 500-700 words. **Pays $75.**
Poetry: *The Nation* publishes poetry of outstanding aesthetic quality. Send poems with SASE. See the Contests & Awards section for the Discovery-*The Nation* poetry contest. Grace Shulman, poetry editor. **Pays $1/line.**
■ The online magazine carries original content not found in the print edition and includes writer's guidelines. Contact: Katrina Vanden Heuvel, editor.
Tips: "We are a journal of left/liberal political opinion covering national and international affairs. We are looking both for reporting and for fresh analysis. On the domestic front, we are particularly interested in civil liberties; civil rights; labor, economics, environmental and feminist issues and the role and future of the Democratic Party. Because we have readers all over the country, it's important that stories with a local focus have real national significance. In our foreign affairs coverage we prefer pieces on international political, economic and social developments. As the magazine which published Ralph Nader's first piece (and there is a long list of *Nation* "firsts"), we are seeking new writers."

$ $ POLICY REVIEW, The Heritage Foundation, 214 Massachusetts Ave. NE, Washington DC 20002. (202)546-4400. Fax: (202)608-6136. E-mail: polrev@heritage.org. Website: www.policyreview.com. **Contact:** Kelly Sullivan, editorial office manager. Bimonthly magazine. "We have been described as 'the most thoughtful, the most influential and the most provocative publication of the intellectual right.' *Policy Review* is a journal of essays and articles of general intellectual interest, with a particular emphasis on politics and social criticism." Estab. 1977. Circ. 20,000. Pays on publication. Byline given. Accepts queries by mail, e-mail, fax.
Nonfiction: Feature stories on various issues of public policy, conservative philosophy and theory, and citizenship. **Buys 4 mss/year.** Length: 2,000-6,000 words. **Pays average of $500.**

N **$ PROGRESSIVE POPULIST, Journal from America's Heartland,** P.O. Box 150517, Austin TX 78715-0517. (512)447-0455. Fax: (603)649-7871. E-mail: populist@usa.net. Website: www.populist.com. Managing Editor: Art Cullen. **Contact:** Jim Cullen, editor. **90% freelance written.** Biweekly tabloid covering politics and economics. "We cover issues of interest to workers, small businesses and family farmers and ranchers." Estab. 1995. Circ. 5,000. Pays on publication. Publishes ms an average of 1 month after acceptance. Byline given. Buys first North American serial, second serial (reprint) rights. Editorial lead time 3 weeks. Submit seasonal material 1 month in advance. Accepts queries by mail, e-mail, fax, phone. Accepts simultaneous submissions. Sample copy and writer's guidelines free.
Nonfiction: "We cover politics and economics. We are interested not so much in the dry reporting of campaigns and elections, or the stock markets and GNP, but in how big business is exerting more control over both the government and ordinary people's lives, and what people can do about it." Essays, exposé, general interest, historical/nostalgic, humor, interview/profile, opinion. "We are not much interested in 'sound-off' articles about state or national politics, although we accept letters to the editor. We prefer to see more 'journalistic' pieces, in which the writer does enough footwork to advance a story beyond the easy realm of opinion." **Buys 400 mss/year.** Query. Length: 600-2,500 words. **Pays $15-50.** Pays writers with contributor copies or other premiums if preferred by writer.
Reprints: Send photocopy with rights for sale noted and information about when and where the material previously appeared.

Photos: State availability with submission. Buys one-time rights. Negotiates payment individually. Identification of subjects required.

$ $ THE PROGRESSIVE, 409 E. Main St., Madison WI 53703-2899. (608)257-4626. Fax: (608)257-3373. E-mail: editorial@progressive.org. Website: www.progressive.org. **Contact:** Matthew Rothschild, editor. **75% freelance written.** Monthly. Estab. 1909. Pays on publication. Publishes ms an average of 6 weeks after acceptance. Byline given. Buys all rights. Accepts queries by mail. Responds in 1 month to queries. Sample copy for 9×12 SAE with 4 first-class stamps or sample articles online. Writer's guidelines for #10 SASE.
Nonfiction: Investigative reporting (exposé of corporate malfeasance and governmental wrongdoing), electoral coverage (a current electoral development that has national implications), social movement pieces (important or interesting event or trend in the labor movement, or the GLBT movement, or in the area of racial justice, disability rights, the environment, women's liberation), foreign policy pieces (a development of huge moral importance where the U.S. role may not be paramount), interviews (a long Q&A with a writer, activist, political figure, or musician who is widely known or doing especially worthwhile work), activism (highlights the work of activists and activist groups; increasingly, we are looking for good photographs of a dynamic or creative action, and we accompany the photos with a caption), book reviews (cover two or three current titles on a major issue of concern). Primarily interested in articles which interpret, from a progressive point of view, domestic and world affairs. Occasional lighter features. "*The Progressive* is a *political* publication. General interest is inappropriate. We do not want editorials, satire, historical pieces, philosophical peices or columns." Query. Length: 500-4,000 words. **Pays $250-500.**
Poetry: Publishes one original poem a month. "We prefer poems that connect up—in one fashion or another, however obliquely—with political concerns. **Pays $150.**
Tips: "Sought-after topics include electoral coverage, social movement, foreign policy, activism and book reviews."

$ $ TOWARD FREEDOM, A Progressive Perspective on World Events, Toward Freedom Inc., P.O. Box 468, Burlington VT 05422-0468. (802)654-8024. E-mail: info@towardfreedom.com. Website: www.towardfreedom.com. **Contact:** Greg Guma, editor. **75% freelance written.** Magazine published 8 times/year covering politics/culture, focus on Third World, Europe and global trends. "*Toward Freedom* is an internationalist journal with a progressive perspective on political, cultural, human rights and environmental issues around the world. Also covers the United Nations, the post-nationalist movements and U.S. foreign policy." Estab. 1952. Circ. 3,500. Pays on publication. Byline given. Buys first North American serial, one-time rights. Editorial lead time 1 month. Accepts queries by mail, e-mail. Responds in 3 months to queries. Sample copy for $3. Writer's guidelines for #10 SASE or online.
O→ Break in with "a clear, knowledgeable and brief query, either by e-mail or U.S. mail, along with the basis of your knowledge about the subject. We're also looking for a new hook for covering subjects we follow, as well as comparisons between the U.S. and other places. We're also eager to break stories that are being 'censored' in mainstream media."
Nonfiction: Essays, interview/profile, opinion, personal experience, travel, features, book reviews, foreign, political analysis. Special issues: Women's Visions (March); Global Media (December/January). **Buys 50-75 mss/year.** Query. Length: 700-2,500 words.
Photos: Send photos with submission. Reviews prints. Buys one-time rights. Offers $35 maximum/photo. Identification of subjects required.
Columns/Departments: *TF* Reports (from foreign correspondents), UN, Beyond Nationalism, Art and Book Reviews, all 800-1,200 words. **Buys 10-20 mss/year.** Query. **Pays up to 10¢/word.** Last Word (creative commentary), 900 words. **Buys 8 mss/year.** Query. **Pays $100.**
◼ The online magazine carries original content not found in the print edition and includes guidelines. Contact: Greg Guma.
Tips: "We're looking for articles linking politics and culture; effective first-person storytelling; proposals for global solutions with realistic basis and solid background; provocative viewpoints within the progressive tradition; political humor. We receive too many horror stories about human rights violations, lacking constructive suggestions and solutions; knee-jerk attacks on imperialism."

$ $ WASHINGTON MONTHLY, The Washington Monthly Company, 1611 Connecticut Ave. NW, Suite 4A, Washington DC 20009. (202)462-0128. Fax: (202)332-8413. E-mail: editors@washingtonmonthly.com. Website: www.washingtonmonthly.com. Editor: Charles Peters. **Contact:** Stephanie Mencimer, editor, or Nicholas Thompson, editor. **50% freelance written.** Monthly magazine covering politics, policy, media. "We are a neo-liberal publication with a long history and specific views—please read our magazine before submitting." Estab. 1969. Circ. 20,000. Pays on publication. Publishes ms an average of 2 months after acceptance. Byline given. Buys all rights. Editorial lead time 2 months. Submit seasonal material 4 months in advance. Accepts queries by mail, e-mail, fax, phone. Responds in 3 weeks to queries; 2 months to mss. Sample copy for 11×17 SAE with 5 first-class stamps or by e-mail. Writer's guidelines for #10 SASE, online or by e-mail.
Nonfiction: Book excerpts, essays, exposé, general interest, historical/nostalgic, interview/profile, opinion, personal experience, technical, 1st person political. "No humor, how-to or generalized articles." **Buys 10 mss/year.** Query with or without published clips or send complete ms. Length: 1,500-5,000 words. **Pays 10¢/word.**
Photos: State availability with submission. Reviews contact sheets, prints. Buys one-time rights. Negotiates payment individually.

Columns/Departments: Memo of the Month (memos); On Political Books, Booknotes (both reviews of current political books), 1,500-3,000 words. **Buys 10 mss/year.** Query with published clips or send complete ms. **Pays 10¢/word.**

Tips: "Call our editors to talk about ideas. Always pitch articles showing background research. We're particularly looking for first-hand accounts of working in government. We also like original work showing that the government is or is not doing something important. We have writer's guidelines, but do your research first."

N $ $ $ WORLD POLICY JOURNAL, World Policy Institute, 66 Fifth Ave., 9th Floor, New York NY 10011. (212)229-5808. Fax: (212)807-1294. E-mail: wrigleyl@newschool.edu. Website: www.worldpolicy.org. Editor: James Chace. **Contact:** Linda Wrigley, managing editor. **10% freelance written.** Quarterly journal covering international politics, economics, and security isssues, as well as historical and cultural essays, book reviews, profiles, and first-person reporting from regions not covered in the general media. "We are eager to work with new or unpublished writers as well as more established writers. We hope to bring principle and proportion, as well as a sense of reality and direction to America's discussion of its role in the world." Circ. 5,000. Pays on publication. Publishes ms an average of 3 months after acceptance. Byline given. Buys all rights. Accepts queries by mail, e-mail, fax. Responds in 3 months to queries. Sample copy for $7.95 and 9×12 SASE with 10 first-class stamps.

Nonfiction: Articles that "define policies that reflect the shared needs and interests of all nations of the world." Query. Length: 2,500-4,500 words. **Pays variable commission rate.**

PSYCHOLOGY & SELF-IMPROVEMENT

These publications focus on psychological topics, how and why readers can improve their own outlooks, and how to understand people in general. Many General Interest, Men's and Women's publications also publish articles in these areas. Magazines treating spiritual development appear in the Astrology, Metaphysical & New Age section, as well as in Religion, while markets for holistic mind/body healing strategies are listed in Health & Fitness.

$ $ PERSONAL JOURNALING MAGAZINE, F&W Publications, Inc., 1507 Dana Ave., Cincinnati OH 45207. Fax: (513)531-2902. E-mail: journaling@fwpubs.com. Website: www.journalingmagazine.com. **Contact:** Editor. **70% freelance written.** Bimonthly magazine covering journal writing. Estab. 1999. **Pays on acceptance.** Publishes ms an average of 3 months after acceptance. Byline given, contributors' page. Buys electronic rights. Editorial lead time 6 months. Sample copy online.

Nonfiction: *How-to*: short, easy-to-read how-to articles on keeping a journal that are original in style and fresh in content. *First person*: how has keeping a journal affected you personally and emotionally? Does your experience resonate with other journal-writers, yet it's a unique experience that no one else has gone through? If you can convey the experience clearly and compellingly, and within 2,000 words, send us your revised, polished first-person journal-writing essay. We'd be happy to take a look!" Book excerpts, essays, how-to, new product, personal experience, personal writing experience. **Buys 30 mss/year.** Query for features; send complete ms for first-person essays. Length: 1,500-2,000 words. **Pays 50¢/word.**

Columns/Departments: "Columns are not open to freelance submissions, but we're always looking for short, first-person pieces on journal writing for the beginnings department in our magazine. We also need helpful journal writing tips and advice, and suggestions on products you like to use for journaling and scrapbooking. For example, do you keep a family-recipe journal or a family-history journal? If so, what are some helpful lessons you've learned that you'd like to share?" **Buys 50 mss/year. Pays 30¢/word.**

Tips: "Please make sure your topic hasn't been covered in our magazine before and that the subject matter doesn't duplicate one of our columns. We're real picky about features and columns overlapping in subject matter."

N $ $ $ $ PSYCHOLOGY TODAY, Sussex Publishers, Inc., 49 E. 21st St., 11th Floor, New York NY 10010. (212)260-7210. Fax: (212)260-7445. E-mail: psychtoday@aol.com. Website: www.psychologytoday.com. **Contact:** Carin Gorrell, executive editor. Bimonthly magazine. "*Psychology Today* explores every aspect of human behavior, from the cultural trends that shape the way we think and feel to the intricacies of modern neuroscience. We're sort of a hybrid of a science magazine, a health magazine and a self-help magazine. While we're read by many psychologists, therapists and social workers, most of our readers are simply intelligent and curious people interested in the psyche and the self." Estab. 1967. Circ. 331,400. Pays on publication. Publishes ms an average of 3 months after acceptance. Byline given. Buys first North American serial rights. Editorial lead time 5 months. Accepts queries by mail. Responds in 1 month to queries. Sample copy for $3.50. Writer's guidelines for #10 SASE.

Nonfiction: "Nearly any subject related to psychology is fair game. We value originality, insight and good reporting; we're not interested in stories or topics that have already been covered *ad nauseum* by other magazines unless you can provide a fresh new twist and much more depth. We're not interested in simple-minded 'pop psychology.' " No fiction, poetry or first-person essays on "How I Conquered Mental Disorder X." **Buys 20-25 mss/year.** Query with published clips. Length: 1,500-4,000 words. **Pays $1,000-2,500.**

Columns/Departments: News Editor. News & Trends (short pieces, mostly written by staff, occasionally by freelancers), 150-300 words. Query with published clips. **Pays $150-300.**

$ ROSICRUCIAN DIGEST, Rosicrucian Order, AMORC, 1342 Naglee Ave., San Jose CA 95191-0001. (408)947-3600. Website: www.rosicrucian.org. **Contact:** Robin M. Thompson, editor-in-chief. Quarterly magazine (international) emphasizing mysticism, science, philosophy and the arts for educated men and women of all ages seeking alternative answers to life's questions. **Pays on acceptance.** Publishes ms an average of 6 months after acceptance. Byline given. Buys first, second serial (reprint) rights. Accepts queries by mail, phone. Responds in 3 months to queries. Sample copy free. Writer's guidelines for #10 SASE.

Nonfiction: How to deal with life—and all it brings us—in a positive and constructive way. Informational articles—new ideas and developments in science, the arts, philosophy and thought. Historical sketches, biographies, human interest, psychology, philosophical and inspirational articles. "We are always looking for good articles on the contributions of ancient civilizations to today's civilizations, the environment, ecology, inspirational (non-religious) subjects." No religious, astrological or political material or articles promoting a particular group or system of thought. Most articles are written by members or donated, but we're always open to freelance submissions. No book-length mss. Query. Length: 1,500-2,000 words. **Pays 6¢/word.**

Reprints: Prefers typed ms with rights for sale noted and information about when and where the article previously appeared, but tearsheet or photcopy acceptable. Pays 50% of amount paid for an original article; 100%.

Tips: "We're looking for more pieces on these subjects: our connection with the past—the important contributions of ancient civilizations to today's world and culture and the relevance of this wisdom to now; how to channel teenage energy/angst into positive, creative, constructive results (preferably written by teachers or others who work with young people—written for frustrated parents); and the vital necessity of raising our environmental consciousness if we are going to survive the coming millennium or even century."

$ SCIENCE OF MIND MAGAZINE, 3251 W. Sixth St., P.O. Box 75127, Los Angeles CA 90075-0127. (213)388-2181. Fax: (213)388-1926. E-mail: edit@scienceofmind.com. Website: www.scienceofmind.com. Editor-in-Chief: Kenneth Lind. **Contact:** Jim Shea, assistant editor. **30% freelance written.** Monthly magazine featuring articles on spirituality, self-help and inspiration. "Our publication centers on oneness of all life and spiritual empowerment through the application of Science of Mind principles." Pays on publication. Publishes ms an average of 5 months after acceptance. Byline given. Buys first North American serial rights. Submit seasonal material 6 months in advance. Accepts queries by mail. Responds to accepted articles only. Writer's guidelines for SASE or online.

Nonfiction: Book excerpts, essays, inspirational, interview/profile, personal experience (of Science of Mind), spiritual. **Buys 35-45 mss/year.** Length: 750-2,000 words. **Pays $25/printed page. Pays in copies for some features written by readers.**

Photos: Reviews 35mm transparencies, 5×7 or 8×10 b&w prints. Buys one-time rights.

Poetry: Inspirational, Science of Mind oriented. "We are not interested in poetry unrelated to Science of Mind Principles." **Buys 1-3 poems/year.** Submit maximum 3 poems. Length: 7-25 lines. **Pays $25.**

▣ The online magazine carries original content not found in the print edition. Contact: Randall Friesen.

Tips: "We are interested in first-person experiences of a spiritual nature having to do with the Science of Mind."

REGIONAL

Many regional publications rely on staff-written material, but others accept work from freelance writers who live in or know the region. The best regional publication to target with your submissions is usually the one in your hometown, whether it's a city or state magazine or a Sunday supplement in a newspaper. Since you are familiar with the region, it is easier to propose suitable story ideas.

Listed first are general interest magazines slanted toward residents of and visitors to a particular region. Next, regional publications are categorized alphabetically by state, followed by Canada. Publications that report on the business climate of a region are grouped in the regional division of the Business & Finance category. Recreation and travel publications specific to a geographical area are listed in the Travel, Camping & Trailer section. Keep in mind also that many regional publications specialize in specific areas, and are listed according to those sections. Regional publications are not listed if they only accept material from a select group of freelancers in their area or if they did not want to receive the number of queries and manuscripts a national listing would attract. If you know of a regional magazine that is not listed, approach it by asking for writer's guidelines before you send unsolicited material.

General

$ $▣ BLUE RIDGE COUNTRY, Leisure Publishing, P.O. Box 21535, Roanoke VA 24018-9900. (540)989-6138. Fax: (540)989-7603. E-mail: info@leisurepublishing.com. Website: www.blueridgecountry.com. **Contact:** Kurt

Rheinheimer, editor-in-chief. **75% freelance written.** Bimonthly magazine. "The magazine is designed to celebrate the history, heritage and beauty of the Blue Ridge region. It is aimed at adult, upscale readers who enjoy living or traveling in the mountain regions of Virginia, North Carolina, West Virginia, Maryland, Kentucky, Tennessee, South Carolina and Georgia." Estab. 1988. Circ. 75,000. Pays on publication. Publishes ms an average of 8 months after acceptance. Byline given. Offers $50 kill fee for commissioned pieces only. Buys first, second serial (reprint) rights. Submit seasonal material 6 months in advance. Accepts queries by mail, e-mail, fax. Responds in 2 months to queries; 2 months to mss. Sample copy for 9 × 12 SAE with 6 first-class stamps or online. Writer's guidelines for #10 SASE.

Nonfiction: "Looking for more backroads travel, history and legend/lore pieces." General interest, historical/nostalgic, personal experience, photo feature, travel. **Buys 25-30 mss/year.** Query with or without published clips or send complete ms. Length: 750-2,000 words. **Pays $50-250 for assigned articles; $25-250 for unsolicited articles.**

Photos: Send photos with submission. Reviews transparencies. Buys one-time rights. Pays $25-50/photo. Identification of subjects required.

Columns/Departments: Country Roads (shorts on people, events, travel, ecology, history, antiques, books); Mountain Inns (reviews of inns); Mountain Delicacies (cookbooks and recipes). **Buys 30-42 mss/year.** Query. **Pays $10-40.**

Tips: "Would like to see more pieces dealing with contemporary history (1940s-70s). Freelancers needed for regional departmental shorts and 'macro' issues affecting whole region. Need field reporters from all areas of Blue Ridge region. Also, we need updates on the Blue Ridge Parkway, Appalachian Trail, national forests, ecological issues, preservation movements."

$ CHRONOGRAM, Luminary Publishing, P.O. Box 459, New Paltz NY 12561. Fax: (914)256-0349. E-mail: info@c hronogram.com. Website: www.chronogram.com. **Contact:** Brian K. Mahoney, editor. **50% freelance written.** Monthly magazine covering regional arts and culture. "*Chronogram* features accomplished, literary writing on issues of cultural, spiritual and idea-oriented interest." Estab. 1994. Circ. 20,000. Pays on publication. Publishes ms an average of 3 months after acceptance. Byline given. Buys one-time rights. Editorial lead time 2 months. Submit seasonal material 3 months in advance. Accepts queries by mail, e-mail. Accepts simultaneous submissions. Responds in 2 weeks to queries; 1 month to mss. Sample copy and writer's guidelines online.

Nonfiction: Book excerpts, essays, exposé, general interest, historical/nostalgic, humor, interview/profile, opinion, personal experience, photo feature, religious, travel. "No health practitioners writing about their own healing modality." **Buys 24 mss/year.** Query with published clips. Length: 1,000-3,500 words. **Pays $75-150.**

Photos: State availability with submission. Reviews contact sheets. Buys one-time rights. Negotiates payment individually. Captions required.

Poetry: Lee Anne Albritton, poetry editor. Avant-garde, free verse, haiku, traditional.

Tips: "The editor's ears are always open for new voices and all story ideas are invited for pitching. *Chronogram* welcomes all voices and viewpoints as long as they are expressed well. We discriminate solely based on the quality of the writing, nothing else. Clear, thoughtful writing on any subject will be considered for publication in *Chronogram*. We publish a good deal of introspective first-person narratives and find that in the absence of objectivity, subjectivity at least is a quantifiable middle ground between ranting opinion and useless facts."

N $ $ $ $ COWBOYS & INDIANS MAGAZINE, The Premier Magazine of the West, Dusty Spur Publishing, 8214 Westchester Dr., Suite 800, Dallas TX 75225. (214)750-8222. Fax: (214)750-4522. E-mail: mail@cowb oysindians.com. Website: www.cowboysindians.com. Editor: Reid Slaughter. Managing Editor: Eric O'Keefe. **Contact:** Kelly Roberts, associate editor. **60% freelance written.** Magazine published 8 times/year covering people and places of the American West. "The Premier Magazine of the West, *Cowboys & Indians* captures the romance, drama and grandeur of the American frontier—both past and present—like no other publication. Undeniably exclusive, the magazine covers a broad range of lifestyle topics: art, home interiors, travel, fashion, Western film and Southwestern cuisine." Estab. 1993. Circ. 101,000. Pays on publication. Publishes ms an average of 2 months after acceptance. Byline given. Offers 20% kill fee. Buys first North American serial, electronic rights. Editorial lead time 4 months. Submit seasonal material 6 months in advance. Accepts queries by mail, e-mail, fax. Responds in 1 month to queries; 1 month to mss. Sample copy for $5. Writer's guidelines for free or by e-mail.

Nonfiction: Book excerpts, exposé, general interest, historical/nostalgic, interview/profile, photo feature, travel, art. No essays, humor or opinion. **Buys 60-75 mss/year.** Query. Length: 500-3,000 words. **Pays $250-5,000 for assigned articles; $250-1,000 for unsolicited articles.** Sometimes pays expenses of writers on assignment.

Photos: State availability with submission. Reviews contact sheets, 2¼ × 2¼ transparencies. Buys one-time rights. Negotiates payment individually. Captions, identification of subjects required.

Columns/Departments: Art, Travel, Music, Home Interiors, all 1,000 words. **Buys 50 mss/year.** Query. **Pays $250-1,500.**

Tips: "Our readers are educated, intelligent and well-read Western enthusiasts, many of whom collect Western Americana, read other Western publications, attend shows and have discerning tastes. Therefore, articles should assume a certain level of prior knowledge of Western subjects on the part of the reader. Articles should be readable and interesting to the novice and general interest reader as well. Please keep your style lively, above all things, and fast-moving, with snappy beginnings and endings. Wit and humor are always welcome."

$ $ GUESTLIFE, Monterey Bay/New Mexico/El Paso/St. Petersburg/Clearwater/Houston, Desert Publications, Inc., 303 N. Indian Canyon Dr., Palm Springs CA 92262. (760)325-2333. Fax: (760)325-7008. E-mail: edit@pal mspringslife.com. Website: www.guestlife.com. **Contact:** Jaime Cannon, managing editor. **95% freelance written.**

Annual prestige hotel room magazine covering history, highlights and activities of the area named (ex. *Monterey Bay GuestLife*). "*GuestLife* focuses on its respective area and is placed in hotel rooms in that area for the affluent vacationer." Estab. 1979. Pays on publication. Publishes ms an average of 9 months after acceptance. Byline given. Offers 25% kill fee. Buys electronic, all rights. Editorial lead time 4 months. Submit seasonal material 3 months in advance. Accepts queries by e-mail. Responds in 1 month to queries; 1 month to mss. Sample copy for $10.

Nonfiction: General interest (regional), historical/nostalgic, photo feature, travel. **Buys 3 mss/year.** Query with published clips. Length: 300-1,500 words. **Pays $100-500.**

Photos: State availability with submission. Reviews contact sheets. Buys all rights. Negotiates payment individually. Identification of subjects required.

Fillers: Facts. **Buys 3/year.** Length: 50-100 words. **Pays $50-100.**

$ $NOW AND THEN, The Appalachian Magazine, Center for Appalachian Studies and Services, P.O. Box 70556-ETSU, Johnson City TN 37614-0556. (423)439-6173. Fax: (423)439-6340. E-mail: woodsidj@etsu.edu. Website: cass.etsu.edu/n&t/guidelin.html. Managing Editor: Nancy Fischman. **Contact:** Jane Harris Woodside, editor-in-chief. **80% freelance written.** Triannual magazine covering Appalachian region from Southern New York to Northern Mississippi. "*Now & Then* accepts a variety of writing genres: fiction, poetry, nonfiction, essays, interviews, memoirs and book reviews. All submissions must relate to Appalachia and to the issue's specific theme. Our readership is educated and interested in the region." Estab. 1984. Circ. 1,000. Pays on publication. Publishes ms an average of 4 months after acceptance. Byline given. Buys all rights. Editorial lead time 6 months. Accepts queries by mail, e-mail, fax. Accepts simultaneous submissions. Responds in 5 months to queries; 5 months to mss. Sample copy for $7.50. Writer's guidelines for #10 SASE or online.

Nonfiction: Book excerpts, essays, general interest, historical/nostalgic, humor, interview/profile, opinion, personal experience, photo feature, book reviews from and about Appalachia. "We don't consider articles which have nothing to do with Appalachia; articles which blindly accept and employ regional stereotypes (dumb hillbillies, poor and down-trodden hillfolk and miners)." Query with published clips. Length: 1,000-2,500 words. **Pays $15-250 for assigned articles; $15-100 for unsolicited articles.** Sometimes pays expenses of writers on assignment.

Reprints: Send typed ms with rights for sale noted and information about when and where the material previously appeared. Pays 100% of amount paid for original article (typically $15-60).

Photos: State availability with submission. Buys one-time rights. Offers no additional payment for photos accepted with ms. Captions, identification of subjects required.

Fiction: "Fiction has to relate to Appalachia and to the issue's theme in some way." Adventure, ethnic, experimental, fantasy, historical, humorous, mainstream, slice-of-life vignettes. **Buys 3-4 mss/year.** Send complete ms. Length: 750-2,500 words. **Pays $15-100.**

Poetry: Free verse, haiku, light verse, traditional. "No stereotypical work about the region. I want to be surprised and embraced by the language, the ideas, even the form." **Buys 25-30 poems/year.** Submit maximum 5 poems. **Pays $10.**

Tips: "Get a copy of the magazine and read it. Then make sure your submission has a connection to Appalachia (check out www.arc.gov/aboutarc/region/regmap.htm) and fits in with an upcoming theme."

$ $ $ $SUNSET MAGAZINE, Sunset Publishing Corp., 80 Willow Rd., Menlo Park CA 94025-3691. (650)321-3600. Fax: (650)327-7537. E-mail: travelquery@sunset.com. Website: www.sunsetmagazine.com. Editor-in-Chief: Rosalie Muller Wright. **Contact:** Peter Fish, senior travel editor; Kathleen Brenzel, senior garden editor. Monthly magazine covering the lifestyle of the Western states. "*Sunset* is a Western lifestyle publication for educated, active consumers. Editorial provides localized information on gardening and travel, food and entertainment, home building and remodeling." Freelance articles should be timely and only about the 13 Western states. **Pays on acceptance.** Byline given. Garden section accepts queries by mail. Travel section prefers queries by e-mail. Guidelines for freelance travel items for #10 SASE addressed to Editorial Services.

Nonfiction: "Travel items account for the vast majority of *Sunset*'s freelance assignments, although we also contract out some short garden items. However *Sunset* is largely staff-written." Travel (in the West). **Buys 50-75 mss/year.** Query. Length: 550-750 words. **Pays $1/word.**

Columns/Departments: Building & Crafts, Food, Garden, Travel. Travel Guide length: 300-350 words. Direct queries to specific editorial department.

Tips: "Here are some subjects regularly treated in *Sunset*'s stories and Travel Guide items: Outdoor recreation (i.e., bike tours, bird-watching spots, walking or driving tours of historic districts); indoor adventures (i.e., new museums and displays, hands-on science programs at aquariums or planetariums, specialty shopping); special events (i.e., festivals that celebrate a region's unique social, cultural, or agricultural heritage). Also looking for great weekend getaways, backroad drives, urban adventures and culinary discoveries such as ethnic dining enclaves. Planning and assigning begins a year before publication date."

$ $ VILLAGE PROFILE, Community Maps, Guides and Directories, Progressive Publishing, Inc., 33 N. Geneva, Elgin IL 60120. (800)600-0134, ext. 221. E-mail: vp_editorial@ameritech.net. Website: www.villageprofile.com. **Contact:** David Gall, managing editor. **50% freelance written.** Annual local community guides covering 40 states. "We publish community guides and maps for (primarily) chambers of commerce across the U.S. Editorial takes on a factual, yet upbeat, positive view of communities. Writers need to be able to make facts and figures 'friendly,' to present information to be used by residents as well as businesses as guides are used for economic development."

Publishes 350 projects/year. Estab. 1988. **Pays on acceptance.** Publishes ms an average of 4 months after acceptance. Byline given. Buys electronic, all rights, makes work-for-hire assignments. Editorial lead time 2 months. Accepts queries by mail, e-mail. Sample copy for 9×12 SASE. Writer's guidelines free.
Nonfiction: Buys 100 mss/year. Query with published clips and geographic availability. Length: 1,000-4,000 words. **Pays $200-500 for assigned articles.** Sometimes pays expenses of writers on assignment.
Photos: State availability with submission. Negotiates payment individually. Identification of subjects required.
Tips: "Writers must meet deadlines, know how to present a positive image of a community without going overboard with adjectives and adverbs! Know how to find the info you need if our contact (typically a busy chamber executive) needs your help doing so. Availability to 'cover' a region/area is a plus."

$ $ $ YANKEE, Yankee Publishing Inc., P.O. Box 520, Dublin NH 03444-0520. (603)563-8111. Fax: (603)563-8252. E-mail: queries@yankeepub.com. Website: www.newengland.com. Editor: Jim Collins. **Contact:** (Ms.) Sam Darley, editorial assistant. **75% freelance written.** Monthly magazine covering New England. "Our mission is to express and perhaps, indirectly, preserve the New England culture—and to do so in an entertaining way. Our audience is national and has one thing in common—it loves New England." Estab. 1935. Circ. 500,000. Pays within 30 days of acceptance. Publishes ms an average of 10 months after acceptance. Byline given. Offers 33% kill fee. Buys first rights. Submit seasonal material 6 months in advance. Accepts queries by mail. Responds in 2 months to queries. Writer's guidelines for #10 SASE.
O─ Break in with a short item for the "Snippets" section.
Nonfiction: Essays, general interest, humor, interview/profile, personal experience. "No 'good old days' pieces, no dialect humor and nothing outside New England!" **Buys 30 mss/year.** Query with published clips and SASE. Length: 250-2,500 words. **Pays $100-1,500.** Pays expenses of writers on assignment.
Photos: Send photos with submission. Reviews contact sheets, transparencies. Buys one-time rights. Offers $50-150/photo. Identification of subjects required.
Columns/Departments: Snippets (short bits on interesting people, anecdotes, historical oddities), 100-400 words, **pays $50-200.** Great New England Cooks (profile recipes), 500 words, **pays $800.** Recipe with a History (family favorites that have a story behind them), 100-200 words plus recipe, **pays $50.** Travel, 25-200 words, query first, **pays $25-250. Buys 80 mss/year.** Query with published clips and SASE. **Pays $25-800.**
Fiction: Edie Clark, fiction editor. "We publish high-quality literary fiction that explores human issues and concerns in a specific place—New England." Novel excerpts. **Buys 4 mss/year.** Send complete ms. Length: 500-2,500 words. **Pays $1,000.**
Poetry: "We don't choose poetry by type. We look for the best." Jean Burden, poetry editor. "No inspirational, holiday-oriented, epic, limericks, etc." **Buys 40 poems/year.** Submit maximum 3 poems. Length: 2-20 lines. **Pays $50.**
■ The online magazine carries original content not found in the print edition. Contact: Erica Bollerud, online editor.
Tips: "Submit lots of ideas. Don't censor yourself—let *us* decide whether an idea is good or bad. We might surprise you. Remember we've been publishing for 65 years, so chances are we've already done every 'classic' New England subject. Try to surprise us—it isn't easy. These departments are most open to freelancers: Snippets and Recipe with a History. Study the ones we publish—the format should be apparent. It is to your advantage to read several issues of the magazine before sending us a query or a manuscript."

Alabama

$ $ MOBILE BAY MONTHLY, PMT Publishing, P.O. Box 66200, Mobile AL 36660. (334)473-6269. Fax: (334)479-8822. **Contact:** Chris McFadyen, editorial director. **25% freelance written.** *"Mobile Bay Monthly* is a monthly lifestyle magazine for the South Alabama/Gulf Coast region focusing on the people, ideas, issues, arts, homes, food, culture and businesses that make Mobile Bay an interesting place." Estab. 1990. Circ. 10,000. Pays on publication. Publishes ms an average of 4 months after acceptance. Byline given. Buys first rights. Editorial lead time 4 months. Submit seasonal material 6 months in advance. Sample copy for $2.
Nonfiction: Historical/nostalgic, interview/profile, personal experience, photo feature, travel. **Buys 10 mss/year.** Query with published clips. Length: 1,200-3,000 words. **Pays $100-300.**
Photos: State availability with submission. Buys one-time rights. Negotiates payment individually. Identification of subjects required.
Tips: "We use mostly local writers. Strong familiarity with the Mobile area is a must. No phone calls; please send query letters with writing samples."

Alaska

$ $ $ ▣ ALASKA, Exploring Life on the Last Frontier, 619 E. Ship Creek Ave., Suite 329, Anchorage AK 99501. (907)272-6070. Fax: (907)258-5360. Website: www.alaskamagazine.com. **Contact:** Donna Rae Thompson, editorial assistant. **70% freelance written.** Eager to work with new/unpublished writers. Monthly magazine covering topics "uniquely Alaskan." Estab. 1935. Circ. 205,000. Pays on publication. Publishes ms an average of 6 months after acceptance. Byline given. Buys first, one-time rights. Submit seasonal material 1 year in advance. Accepts queries by mail. Responds in 2 months to queries; 2 months to mss. Sample copy for $3 and 9×12 SAE with 7 first-class stamps. Writer's guidelines for #10 SASE.

O→ Break in by "doing your homework. Make sure a similar story has not appeared in the magazine within the last five years. It must be about Alaska."

Nonfiction: Historical/nostalgic, humor, interview/profile, personal experience, photo feature, travel, adventure, outdoor recreation (including hunting, fishing), Alaska destination stories. No fiction or poetry. **Buys 40 mss/year.** Query. Length: 100-2,500 words. **Pays $100-1,250.**

Photos: Send photos with submission. Reviews 35mm or larger transparencies. Captions, identification of subjects required.

Tips: "We're looking for top-notch writing—original, well-researched, lively. Subjects must be distinctly Alaskan. A story on a mall in Alaska, for example, won't work for us; every state has malls. If you've got a story about a Juneau mall run by someone who is also a bush pilot and part-time trapper, maybe we'd be interested. The point is *Alaska* stories need to be vivid, focused and unique. Alaska is like nowhere else—we need our stories to be the same way."

Arizona

$ $ ARIZONA FOOTHILLS MAGAZINE, Media That Deelivers, Inc., 8132 N. 87th Place, Scottsdale AZ 85258. (480)460-5203. Fax: (480)443-1517. E-mail: reneedee@azfoothillsmag.com. Website: www.azfoothillsmagazine.com. Editor: Renee Dee. **Contact:** Shannon Bartlett, departments editor. **50% freelance written.** Monthly magazine covering Arizona lifesyle. Estab. 1996. Circ. 50,000. Pays on publication. Publishes ms an average of 6 months after acceptance. Byline given. Editorial lead time 6 months. Submit seasonal material 4 months in advance. Accepts queries by mail, e-mail. Responds in 1 month to queries; 1 month to mss. Sample copy and writer's guidelines for #10 SASE.

O→ Break in by "submitting a story with a local angle and having several reader-service sidebars in mind."

Nonfiction: Renee Dee, publisher. General interest, how-to (decorate, paint, outdoor recreation), humor, inspirational, interview/profile, new product, personal experience, photo feature, travel, fashion, decor, arts. **Buys 30 mss/year.** Query with published clips. Length: 900-2,000 words. **Pays 15¢/word for assigned articles; 10¢/word for unsolicited articles.** Sometimes pays expenses of writers on assignment.

Photos: Send photos with submission. Reviews contact sheets, transparencies. Buys one-time rights. Negotiates payment individually. Captions, identification of subjects, model releases required.

Columns/Departments: Road-Tested Travel (in-state AZ travel); Great Escapes (outside AZ); Live Well (health and fitness). **Buys 21 mss/year.** Query with published clips. **Pays 10¢/word.**

Tips: "We prefer stories that appeal to my audience written with an upbeat, contemporary approach and reader service in mind."

$ $ $ ARIZONA HIGHWAYS, 2039 W. Lewis Ave., Phoenix AZ 85009-9988. (602)712-2024. Fax: (602)254-4505. Website: www.arizonahighways.com. **Contact:** Rebecca Mong, senior editor. **100% freelance written.** Magazine that is state-owned, designed to help attract tourists into and through Arizona. Estab. 1925. Circ. 425,000. **Pays on acceptance.** Buys first North American serial rights. Accepts queries by mail, e-mail, fax. Responds in 1 month to queries; 1 month to mss. Writer's guidelines for #10 SASE.

O→ Break in with "a concise query written with flair, backed by impressive clips that reflect the kind of writing that appears in *Arizona Highways*. The easiest way to break into the magazine for writers new to us is to propose short items for the Off-ramp section, contribute short humor anecdotes for the Humor page, or submit 650-word pieces for the Along the Way column."

Nonfiction: Feature subjects include narratives and exposition dealing with history, anthropology, nature, wildlife, armchair travel, out of the way places, small towns, Old West history, Indian arts and crafts, travel, etc. Travel articles are experience- based. All must be oriented toward Arizona. "We deal with professionals only, so include a list of current credits." **Buys 6 mss/year.** Query with a lead paragraph and brief outline of story. Length: 600-1,800 words. **Pays 35¢-$1/word.** Pays expenses of writers on assignment.

Photos: "We use transparencies of medium format, 4×5, and 35mm when appropriate to the subject matter, or they display exceptional quality or content. We prefer 35mm at 100 ISO or slower. Each transparency must be accompanied by information attached to each photograph: where, when, what. No photography will be reviewed by the editors unless the photographer's name appears on each and every transparency." Peter Ensenberger, photo editor. Buys one-time rights. Pays $100-600.

Columns/Departments: Focus on Nature (short feature in first or third person dealing with the unique aspects of a single species of wildlife), 800 words; Along the Way (short essay dealing with life in Arizona or a personal experience keyed to Arizona), 800 words; Back Road Adventure (personal back-road trips, preferably off the beaten path and outside major metro areas), 1,000 words; Weekend Getaways (focus on a town or area's tourist attractions and include insider tips on places to spend the night, eat, and shop), 1,200 words; Hike of the Month (personal experiences on trails anywhere in Arizona), 500 words; Arizona Humor (amusing short anecdotes about Arizona), 200 words maximum. **Pays $50-1,000, depending on department.**

■ The online magazine carries original content not found in the print edition. Contact: Rebecca Mong, senior editor.

Tips: "Writing must be of professional quality, warm, sincere, in-depth, well-peopled and accurate. Avoid themes that describe first trips to Arizona, the Grand Canyon, the desert, Colorado River running, etc. Emphasis is to be on Arizona adventure and romance as well as flora and fauna, when appropriate, and themes that can be photographed. Double check your manuscript for accuracy. Our typical reader is a 50-something person with the time, the inclination and the means to travel."

$ CAREFREE ENTERPRISE MAGAZINE, Arizona's Second-Oldest Magazine, Carefree Enterprise Magazine, Inc., P.O. Box 1145, Carefree AZ 85377. E-mail: staff@carefreeenterprise.com. Website: www.carefreeenterprise.com. Editor: Fran Barbano. **Contact:** Susan Smyth, assistant editor. **50% freelance written.** Magazine published 11 times/year. "*CEM* is a good news publication. We dwell on the positive, uplifting, and inspiring influences of life. We promote our areas and people. (We have readers across the country and overseas.)" Estab. 1963. Circ. 3,200. Pays within 3 months after publication. Publishes ms an average of 1 year after acceptance. Byline given. Buys first North American serial, first, one-time, second serial (reprint) rights. Editorial lead time up to 1 year. Submit seasonal material 6 months in advance. Accepts queries by mail, e-mail. Responds in 4 months to queries; 4 months to mss. Sample copy for $2 with 12×15 SAE with $1.93 postage or $4, includes postage. Writer's guidelines for #10 SASE.

Nonfiction: Book excerpts, general interest, historical/nostalgic, humor, inspirational, interview/profile, personal experience, photo feature, travel, health, alternative medicine. "Nothing negative or controversial." **Buys 50 mss/year.** Query with or without published clips or send complete ms. Length: 800-3,000 words. **Pays $50 for assigned articles; $5-50 for unsolicited articles.**

Photos: State availability with submission. Reviews transparencies, prints (up to 8×10). Buys one-time rights. Pays $5/photo. Captions, identification of subjects, model releases required.

Columns/Departments: Stephanie Bradley, assistant editor. Health, Golf (profile a course or pro), 300-500 words. **Buys 36 mss/year.** Query with or without published clips or send complete ms. **Pays $20-35.**

Fiction: Historical, humorous, general interest, inspirational. **Pays $50 maximum for features. Serial pays $50 maximum for each part.**

Poetry: Avant-garde, free verse, haiku, light verse, traditional. "Nothing negative, controversial or unacceptable to families." **Buys 4-12 poems/year.** Submit maximum 3 poems. **Pays $5-25.**

Fillers: Anecdotes, facts, short humor. **Buys 12-50/year.** Length: 100-500 words. **Pays $15-35.**

Tips: "We are particularly easy to work with. New and established writers should be familiar with our publication and audience (upscale, affluent, world-travelers, multiple home-owners). Our youngest columnist is a 16-year-old blind girl who writes from a teen's point of view and often touches on blindness, and how others interact with handicapped individuals. We are open and receptive to any/all good news, upbeat, family-oriented material. We could use more humor, inspiration, travel (regional and worldwide) and positive solutions to everyday challenges. We like to feature profiles of outstanding people (no politics) who are role model material. Be familiar with this publication."

$ $ CITY AZ, City AZ Publishing LLC, 2501 E. Camelback Rd., #120, Phoenix AZ 85016. (602)667-9798. Fax: (602)508-9454. E-mail: info@cityaz.com. Website: www.cityaz.com. **Contact:** Leigh Flayton, editor. **75% freelance written.** Bimonthly "lifestyle and culture magazine with an emphasis on modern design, culinary trends, cultural trends, fashion, great thinkers of our time and entertainment." Estab. 1997. Circ. 40,000. Pays 30 days after publication. Byline given. Offers 50% kill fee. Buys first, electronic rights. Editorial lead time 3 months. Submit seasonal material 3 months in advance. Accepts queries by mail, e-mail, fax, phone. Responds in 3 weeks to queries; 2 months to mss. Sample copy for e-mail request.

Nonfiction: General interest, interview/profile, new product, photo feature, travel, architecture. Query with published clips. Length: 300-2,000 words. **Pays $40-400.**

Photos: State availability with submission. Reviews contact sheets, negatives, transparencies, prints. Buys one-time or electronic rights. Negotiates payment individually. Identification of subjects, model releases required.

Columns/Departments: Design (articles on industrial/product design and firms, 2,000 words. **Buys 100 mss/year.** Query with published clips.

$ $ $ PHOENIX, Cities West Publishing, Inc., 4041 N. Central Ave., Suite 530, Phoenix AZ 85012. (602)234-0840. Fax: (602)604-0169. E-mail: phxmag@citieswestpub.com. **Contact:** Kathy Khoury, managing editor. **70% freelance written.** Monthly magazine covering regional issues, personalities, events, customs and history of the Southwest, state of Arizona and metro Phoenix. Estab. 1966. Circ. 60,000. Pays on publication. Publishes ms an average of 5 months after acceptance. Byline given. Buys first North American serial, one-time rights. Submit seasonal material 6 months in advance. Accepts queries by mail, e-mail. Responds in 2 months to queries; 2 months to mss. Sample copy for $3.50 and 9×12 SAE with 5 first-class stamps. Writer's guidelines for #10 SASE.

○➔ Break in with "short pieces of 150-300 words for the PHX-files highlighting local trends and personalities or with other short features of 750-1,000 words on same topics. Avoid the obvious. Look for the little-known, the funky and the offbeat."

Nonfiction: General interest, interview/profile, investigative, historical, service pieces (where to go and what to do around town). "No material dealing with travel outside the region or other subjects that don't have an effect on the area. No sports, politics, business, fiction or personal essays, please." **Buys 50 mss/year.** Query with published clips. Length: 150-2,000 words.

Tips: "Our audience consists of well-educated, affluent Phoenicians. Articles must have strong local connection, vivid, lively writing to put the reader in the story and present new information or a new way of looking at things."

SCOTTSDALE LIFE, The City Magazine, CitiesWest, 4041 N. Central, #A-100, Phoenix AZ 85012. (602)234-0840. Fax: (602)277-7857. E-mail: sdalelife@citieswestpub.com. **Contact:** Karlin McCarthy, editor. **50% freelance written.** Monthly magazine covering city and lifestyle, fashion, entertaining, people, business, society, dining. Estab. 1998. Circ. 40,000. **Pays on acceptance.** Byline given. Offers 10% kill fee. Buys electronic, all rights. Editorial lead time 2 months. Submit seasonal material 4 months in advance. Accepts queries by mail, e-mail. Responds in 1 month to queries. Sample copy free.

Nonfiction: All relating to the Arizona reader. Essays, exposé, general interest, historical/nostalgic, how-to, humor, inspirational, interview/profile, new product, personal experience, photo feature, travel. Special issues: Real Estate, Beauty & Health, Art, Golf, Lifestyle. **Buys 20 mss/year.** Query with published clips. Length: 1,000-2,000 words. **Payment varies.**

Photos: State availability with submission. Reviews transparencies, prints. Buys all rights. Negotiates payment individually. Captions, identification of subjects, model releases required.

Columns/Departments: City (briefs, mini-profiles); Artful Diversions (gallery reviews), both 300-500 words; Good Taste (dining reviews), 700 words. **Buys 50 mss/year.** Query with published clips. **Payment varies.**

Fiction: Adventure, historical, novel excerpts, slice-of-life vignettes, western. **Buys 2 mss/year.** Query with published clips. Length: 500-1,000 words. **Payment varies.**

Poetry: Cowboy poetry. **Buys 2-5 poems/year.**

Tips: "No idea is a bad idea. Do not fax or phone unless you have written first. Look for the local angle or a way to make the idea relevant to the Phoenix/Scottsdale reader. Suggest photo possibilities."

$ $ TUCSON LIFESTYLE, Conley Publishing Group, Ltd., Suite 12, 7000 E. Tanque Verde Rd., Tucson AZ 85715-5318. (520)721-2929. Fax: (520)733-6110. E-mail: tucsonlife@aol.com. **Contact:** Scott Barker, executive editor. **90% freelance written.** Prefers to work with published/established writers. Monthly magazine covering Tucson-related events and topics. Estab. 1982. Circ. 32,000. **Pays on acceptance.** Publishes ms an average of 6 months after acceptance. Byline given. Buys first North American serial rights. Submit seasonal material 1 year in advance. Accepts queries by mail, e-mail, fax. Responds in 2 months to queries; 3 months to mss. Sample copy for $2.95 plus $3 postage. Writer's guidelines free.

O— Features are not open to freelancers.

Nonfiction: All stories need a Tucson angle. "Avoid obvious tourist attractions and information that most residents of the Southwest are likely to know. No anecdotes masquerading as articles. Not interested in fish-out-of-water, Easterner-visiting-the-Old-West pieces." **Buys 20 mss/year. Pays $50-500.**

Photos: Query about electronic formats. Reviews contact sheets, 2¼×2¼ transparencies, 5×7 prints. Buys one-time rights. Pays $25-100/photo. Identification of subjects required.

Columns/Departments: In Business (articles on Tucson businesses and business people); Lifestylers (profiles of interesting Tucsonans). Query. **Pays $100-200.**

Tips: "Style is not of paramount importance; good, clean copy with an interesting lead is a must."

California

$ ANGELENO, The Toast of Los Angeles, 5670 Wilshire Blvd., Suite 700, Los Angeles CA 90036. (323)930-9400 ext. 2375. Fax: (323)930-9402. **Contact:** Alexandria Abramian. **50% freelance written.** Bimonthly magazine covering luxury lifestyle. "We cover the good things in life—fashion, fine dining, home design, the arts—from a sophisticated, cosmopolitan, well-to-do perspective." Estab. 1999. Circ. 50,000. Pays 2 months after receipt of invoice. Byline given. Offers 50% kill fee. Buys first, all rights. Editorial lead time 6 months. Submit seasonal material 6 months in advance. Responds in 1 month to queries; 1 month to mss. Sample copy for $7.15 for current issue; $8.20 for back issue. Writer's guidelines for #10 SASE.

Nonfiction: General interest, how-to (culinary, home design), interview/profile, photo feature (occasional), travel. No fiction; no unsolicited mss. Query with published clips. Length: 500-4,500 words. Pays expenses of writers on assignment.

Photos: State availability with submission. Reviews transparencies, prints. Buys one-time rights.

$ $ BRNTWD MAGAZINE, PTL Productions, 2118 Wilshire Blvd., #1060, Santa Monica CA 90403. (310)390-0251. Fax: (310)390-0261. E-mail: dylan@brntwdmagazine.com. Website: www.brntwdmagazine.com. **Contact:** Dylan Nugent, editor-in-chief. **100% freelance written.** Bimonthly magazine covering entertainment, business, lifestyles, reviews. "Wanting in-depth interviews with top entertainers, politicians and similar individuals. Also travel, sports, adventure." Estab. 1995. Circ. 70,000. Pays on publication. Byline given. Editorial lead time 3 months. Submit seasonal material 3 months in advance. Accepts queries by mail, e-mail, phone. Accepts simultaneous submissions. Sample copy for $5. Writer's guidelines available.

O— Break in with "strong editorial pitches on unique personalities, trends or travel destinations."

Nonfiction: Book excerpts, exposé, general interest, historical/nostalgic, humor, interview/profile, new product, opinion, personal experience, photo feature, travel. **Buys 80 mss/year.** Query with published clips. Length: 1,000-2,500 words. **Pays 10-15 ¢/word.**
Photos: State availability with submission. Reviews contact sheets, negatives, prints. Offers no additional payment for photos accepted with ms. Captions, identification of subjects required.
Columns/Departments: Reviews (film/books/theater/museum), 100-500 words; Sports (Southern California angle), 200-600 words. **Buys 20 mss/year.** Query with or without published clips or send complete ms. **Pays 15¢/word.**
Tips: "Los Angeles-based writers preferred for most articles."

N $ $ $ DIABLO MAGAZINE, The Magazine of the East Bay, Diablo Publications, 2520 Camino Diablo, Walnut Creek CA 94596. (925)943-1111. Fax: (925)943-1045. E-mail: d-mail@diablopubs.com. Website: www.diablomag.com. Editor: Susan Safipour. **Contact:** Robert Strohmeyer, managing editor. **50% freelance written.** Monthly magazine covering regional travel, food, homestyle and profiles in Contra Costa and southern Alameda counties and selected areas of Oakland and Berkeley. Estab. 1979. Circ. 45,000. **Pays on acceptance.** Publishes ms an average of 3 months after acceptance. Byline given. Offers 25% kill fee. Buys first rights. Editorial lead time 3 months. Submit seasonal material 5 months in advance. Accepts queries by mail, e-mail, fax. Accepts simultaneous submissions. Sample copy online. Writer's guidelines free.
Nonfiction: General interest, interview/profile, new product, photo feature, technical, travel. No restaurant profiles, out of country travel, non-local topics. **Buys 60 mss/year.** Query with published clips. Length: 600-3,000 words. **Pays $300-2,000.** Sometimes pays expenses of writers on assignment.
Photos: State availability with submission. Buys one-time rights. Negotiates payment individually.
Columns/Departments: Tech; Parenting; Homestyle; Food; Books; Health; Profiles; Local Politics, all 1,000 words. Query with published clips.
Tips: "We prefer San Francisco Bay area writers who are familiar with the area."

$ $ THE EAST BAY MONTHLY, The Berkeley Monthly, Inc., 1301 59th St., Emeryville CA 94608. (510)658-9811. Fax: (510)658-9902. E-mail: editorial@themonthly.com. **Contact:** Kira Halpern, editor. **95% freelance written.** Monthly tabloid. "We like stories about local people and issues, but we also accept ideas for articles about topics that range beyond the East Bay's borders or have little or nothing to do with the region." Estab. 1970. Circ. 75,000. Pays on publication. Byline given. Buys first, second serial (reprint) rights. Editorial lead time 2 months. Submit seasonal material 2 months in advance. Accepts queries by mail, phone. Accepts simultaneous submissions. Responds in 1 month to queries; 1 month to mss. Sample copy for $1. Writer's guidelines for #10 SASE.
Nonfiction: Essays, exposé, general interest, historical/nostalgic, humor, interview/profile, opinion, personal experience, photo feature, travel. **Buys 55 mss/year.** Query with published clips. Length: 1,500-3,000 words. **Pays $350-700.**
Reprints: Send tearsheet and information about when and where the material previously appeared.
Photos: State availability with submission. Reviews contact sheets, 4×5 transparencies, 8×10 prints. Buys one-time rights. Negotiates payment individually. Identification of subjects required.
Columns/Departments: Shopping Around (local retail news), 2,000 words; Food for Thought (local food news), 2,000 words; First Person, 2,000 words. **Buys 15 mss/year.** Query with published clips. **Pays 10¢/word.**
Fiction: Novel excerpts.

N $ $ GLUE, Style and Action in L.A., Glue Productions, Inc., P.O. Box 27067, Los Angeles CA 90027-0067. E-mail: gluemag@earthlink.net. Website: www.gluemag.com. **Contact:** Laurie Pike, editor/publisher. **75% freelance written.** Bimonthly magazine covering Los Angeles arts, entertainment, cutting-edge culture. Seeks "unique stories highlighting Los Angeles artists, trends and culture, with a progressive point of view." Estab. 1998. Circ. 75,000. Pays on publication. Publishes ms an average of 2 months after acceptance. Byline given. Offers 100% kill fee. Buys all rights. Editorial lead time 3 months. Submit seasonal material 3 months in advance. Accepts queries by e-mail. Responds in 2 weeks to queries. Sample copy for $5.50 (includes postage). Writer's guidelines by e-mail.
Nonfiction: Book excerpts, exposé, general interest, historical/nostalgic. No "first person essays, anything not related to LA and its current trends and culture." **Buys 10 mss/year.** Query with published clips. Length: 150-2,000 words. **Pays $500 maximum for assigned articles; $300 maximum for unsolicited articles.** Sometimes pays expenses of writers on assignment.
Photos: State availability with submission. Offers no additional payment for photos accepted with ms.
Tips: "Know the magazine—what we cover and our point of view. Have original ideas—stories that are not rehash."

$ $ L.A. WEEKLY, 6715 Sunset Blvd., Los Angeles CA 90020. (323)465-9909. Fax: (323)465-3220. Website: www.laweekly.com. Editor: Laurie Ochoa. Managing Editor: Kateri Butler. **Contact:** Janet Duckworth, features editor; Tom Christie, arts editor; Alan Mittelstaedt, news editor. **40% freelance written.** Weekly newspaper. "L.A. Weekly provides a fresh, alternative look at Los Angeles. We have arts coverage, news analysis and investigative reporting and a comprehensive calendar section." Estab. 1978. Circ. 225,000. Pays on publication. Byline given. Offers 33% kill fee. Buys first North American serial, electronic rights. Accepts queries by mail, e-mail, fax. Responds in 1 month to queries; 4 months to mss. Sample copy online.
Nonfiction: Essays, exposé, interview/profile. "No health, religion, fiction or poetry. We assign many articles to freelancers but accept very few unsolicited manuscripts." Query with published clips. No submissions through website. **Pays 34¢/word.**

Photos: State availability with submission.
Columns/Departments: Query with published clips. **Pays 34 ¢/word basic rate.**

$ $ $ $ LOS ANGELES MAGAZINE, Emmis Publishing, 5900 Wilshire Blvd., 10th Floor, Los Angeles CA 90036. (323)801-0100. Fax: (323)801-0105. Website: www.lamag.com. **Contact:** Kit Rachlis, editor-in-chief. **50% freelance written.** Monthly magazine about Southern California. "Our editorial mission is to provide an authentic, compelling voice that engages and entertains one of the most media-savvy audiences in the world. Showcasing the diversity and vitality of the city, *Los Angeles'* quest is to deliver a timely, vibrant, must-read magazine that is witty, funny, sophisticated and skeptical but not cynical—a book that has regional resonance and national import." Estab. 1963. Circ. 183,373. **Pays on acceptance.** Publishes ms an average of 4 months after acceptance. Byline given. Offers 30% kill fee. Buys first North American serial rights. Submit seasonal material 6 months in advance. Accepts queries by mail, fax. Responds in 3 months to queries; 3 months to mss. Sample copy for $6.50. Writer's guidelines for #10 SASE.

- *Los Angeles Magazine* continues to do stories with local angles, but it is expanding its coverage to include topics of interest on a national level.
- Break in with "a piece for the Buzz section. We're also looking for more breaking city (L.A. specific) stories on politics, lifestyle, business and education."

Nonfiction: "Coverage includes both high and low culture—people, places, politics, the Industry and lifestyle trends." Book excerpts (about L.A. or by famous L.A. author), essays, exposé (any local issue), general interest, historical/nostalgic (about L.A. or Hollywood), interview/profile (about L.A. person), photo feature. **Buys 100 mss/year.** Query with published clips. Length: 250-6,000 words. **Pays $50-6,000.** Sometimes pays expenses of writers on assignment.
Photos: Kathleen Clark, photo editor. Send photos with submission.
Columns/Departments: Length: 250-1,200 words. **Buys 170 mss/year.** Query with published clips. **Pays $100-2,000.**
Tips: "Please read the magazine before sending a query."

LOS ANGELES TIMES MAGAZINE, Los Angeles Times, 202 W. First St., Los Angeles CA 90012. (213)237-7811. Fax: (213)237-7386. **Contact:** Alice Short, editor. **50% freelance written.** Weekly magazine of regional general interest. Circ. 1,384,688. Payment schedule varies. Publishes ms an average of 2 months after acceptance. Byline given. Buys first North American serial rights. Submit seasonal material 3 months in advance. Accepts simultaneous submissions. Responds in 2 months to queries; 2 months to mss. Sample copy and writer's guidelines free.
Nonfiction: Covers California, the West, the nation and the world. Essays (reported), general interest, interview/profile, investigative and narrative journalism. Query with published clips. Length: 2,500-4,500 words.
Photos: Query first; prefers to assign photos. Reviews color transparencies, b&w prints. Buys one-time rights. Payment varies. Captions, identification of subjects, model releases required.
Tips: "Prospective contributors should know their subject well and be able to explain why a story merits publication. Previous national magazine writing experience preferred."

$ $ METRO SANTA CRUZ, Metro Newspapers, 115 Cooper St., Santa Cruz CA 95060. (831)457-9000. Fax: (831)457-5828. E-mail: mgant@metcruz.com. Website: www.metroactive.com. **Contact:** Michael Gant, editor. **20-30% freelance written.** Weekly newspaper. "*Metro* is for a sophisticated coastal university town audience—stories must be more in-depth with an unusual slant not covered in daily newspapers." Estab. 1994. Circ. 50,000. Pays on publication. Publishes ms an average of 2-5 weeks after acceptance. Byline given. Offers kill fee only with assignment memorandum signed by editor. Buys first North American serial, second serial (reprint) rights. Submit seasonal material 3 months in advance. Responds in 2 months to queries; 4 months to mss.
Nonfiction: Features include a cover story of 3,000-3,500 words and a hometown story of 1,000-1,200 words about an interesting character. Some local angle needed. Book excerpts, essays (personal), exposé, interview/profile (particularly entertainment oriented), music, personal essay. **Buys 75 mss/year.** Query with published clips. Length: 500-4,000 words. **Pays $50-500.**
Reprints: Send photocopy and information about when and where the material previously appeared. Pays $25-200.
Photos: Send photos with submission. Reviews contact sheets, negatives, any size transparencies, prints, digital (tiff 180dpi). Buys one-time rights. Pays $25-50/photo, more if used on cover. Captions, identification of subjects, model releases required.
Columns/Departments: MetroGuide (entertainment features, interviews), 500-3,000 words. Query with published clips. **Pays $25-200.**
Tips: "Seasonal features are most likely to be published, but we take only the best stuff. Local stories or national news events with a local angle will also be considered. Preferred submission format is by e-mail. We are enthusiastic about receiving freelance inquiries. What impresses us most is newsworthy writing, compellingly presented. We define news broadly and consider it to include new information about old subjects as well as a new interpretation of old information. We like stories which illustrate broad trends by focusing in detail on specific examples."

$ $ $ ORANGE COAST MAGAZINE, The Magazine of Orange County, Orange Coast Kommunications Inc., 3701 Birch St., Suite 100, Newport Beach CA 92660-2618. (949)862-1133. Fax: (949)862-0133. E-mail: ocmag@aol.com. Website: www.orangecoastmagazine.com. **Contact:** Anastacia Grenda, managing editor. **95% freelance written.** Monthly magazine "designed to inform and enlighten the educated, upscale residents of Orange County, California;

highly graphic and well researched." Estab. 1974. Circ. 50,000. **Pays on acceptance.** Publishes ms an average of 4 months after acceptance. Byline given. Offers 20% kill fee. Buys one-time rights. Submit seasonal material 6 months in advance. Accepts queries by mail. Accepts simultaneous submissions. Responds in 2 months to queries; 2 months to mss. Sample copy for $2.95 and 10×12 SAE with 8 first-class stamps. Writer's guidelines for #10 SASE.

O→ Break in with Short Cuts (topical briefs of about 100 words), pays $50; Escape (Pacific time zone travel pieces of about 600 words), pays $250.

Nonfiction: Absolutely no phone queries. Exposé (Orange County government, politics, business, crime), general interest (with Orange County focus), historical/nostalgic, interview/profile (prominent Orange County citizens), travel, guides to activities and services, local sports. Special issues: Health and Fitness (January); Dining and Entertainment (March); Home and Garden (June); Resort Guide (November); Holiday (December). **Buys 100 mss/year.** Query with published clips. Length: 2,000-3,000 words. **Pays $350-700 for assigned articles.**

Reprints: Send tearsheet, photocopy or typed ms with rights for sale noted and information about when and where the material previously appeared.

Columns/Departments: Most columns are not open to freelancers. Length: 1,000-2,000 words. **Buys 200 mss/year.** Query with or without published clips or send complete ms. **Pays $200 maximum.**

Fiction: Buys only under rare circumstances. Send complete ms. Length: 1,000-5,000 words. **Pays $250.**

◼ The online magazine carries original content not found in the print edition. Contact: Nancy Cheever, online editor.

Tips: "We're looking for more local personality profiles, analysis of current local issues, local takes on national issues. Most features are assigned to writers we've worked with before. Don't try to sell us 'generic' journalism. *Orange Coast* prefers articles with specific and unusual angles focused on Orange County. A lot of freelance writers ignore our Orange County focus. We get far too many generalized manuscripts."

$ $PALM SPRINGS LIFE, The California Prestige Magazine, Desert Publications, Inc., 303 N. Indian Canyon, Palm Springs CA 92262. (760)325-2333. Fax: (760)325-7008. Editor: Stewart Weiner. **Contact:** Sarah Hagerty, executive editor. **75% freelance written.** Monthly magazine covering "affluent resort/southern California/Palm Springs desert resorts. *Palm Springs Life* is a luxurious magazine aimed at the affluent market." Estab. 1958. Circ. 20,000. Pays on publication. Publishes ms an average of 3 months after acceptance. Byline given. Offers 25% kill fee. Buys all rights, negotiable. Submit seasonal material 6 months in advance. Responds in 3 weeks to queries. Sample copy for $3.95.

● Increased focus on desert region and business writing opportunities.

Nonfiction: Book excerpts, essays, interview/profile. Query with published clips. Length: 500-2,500 words. **Pays $50-750 for assigned articles; $25-500 for unsolicited articles.**

Photos: State availability with submission. Reviews contact sheets. Buys all rights. Pays $5-125/photo. Captions, identification of subjects, model releases required.

Columns/Departments: Around Town (local news), 50-250 words. **Buys 12 mss/year.** Query with or without published clips. **Pays $5-200.**

$ $SACRAMENTO MAGAZINE, 4471 D St., Sacramento CA 95819. (916)452-6200. Fax: (916)452-6061. Managing Editor: Darlena Belushin McKay. **Contact:** Krista Minard, editor. **100% freelance written.** Works with a small number of new/unpublished writers each year. Monthly magazine with a strong local angle on local issues, human interest and consumer items for readers in the middle to high income brackets. Estab. 1975. Circ. 29,000. Pays on publication. Publishes ms an average of 3 months after acceptance. Generally buys first North American serial rights and electronic rights, rarely second serial (reprint) rights. Accepts queries by mail. Responds in 2 months to queries; 2 months to mss. Sample copy for $4.50. Writer's guidelines for #10 SASE.

O→ Break in with submissions to City Lights.

Nonfiction: Local isues vital to Sacramento quality of life. "No e-mail, fax or phone queries will be answered." **Buys 5 unsolicited feature mss/year.** Query. Length: 1,500-3,000 words, depending on author, subject matter and treatment. **Pays $250 and up.** Sometimes pays expenses of writers on assignment.

Photos: Send photos with submission. Buys one-time rights. Payment varies depending on photographer, subject matter and treatment. Captions, identification of subjects, location, and date required.

Columns/Departments: Business, home and garden, first person essays, regional travel, gourmet, profile, sports, city arts (1,000-1,800 words); City Lights (250-300 words). **Pays $50-400.**

$ $SACRAMENTO NEWS & REVIEW, Chico Community Publishing, 1015 20th St., Sacramento CA 95814. (916)498-1234. Fax: (916)498-7920. E-mail: stevenj@newsreview.com or jacksong@newsreview.com. Website: www.newsreview.com. **Contact:** Steven T. Jones, news editor; Jackson Griffith, arts and lifestyle editor. **25% freelance written.** "We are an alternative news and entertainment weekly. We maintain a high literary standard for submissions; unique or alternative slant. Publication aimed at a young, intellectual audience; submissions should have an edge and strong voice." Estab. 1989. Circ. 95,000. Pays on publication. Publishes ms an average of 2 months after acceptance. Byline given. Offers 10% kill fee. Buys first, electronic rights. Editorial lead time 2 months. Submit seasonal material 2 months in advance. Accepts queries by mail, e-mail, fax, phone. Accepts simultaneous submissions. Responds in 1 month to queries; 2 months to mss. Sample copy for 50¢.

Nonfiction: Essays, exposé, general interest, humor, interview/profile, personal experience. Special issues: Publishes holiday gift guides (November/December). Does not want to see travel, product stories, business profile. **Buys 20-30 mss/year.** Query with published clips. Length: 750-5,000 words. **Pays $40-500.** Sometimes pays expenses of writers on assignment.
Photos: State availability with submission. Reviews 8 × 10 prints. Buys one-time rights. Negotiates payment individually. Identification of subjects required.
Columns/Departments: In the Mix (CD/TV/book reviews), 150-750 words. **Buys 10-15 mss/year.** Query with published clips. **Pays $10-300.**

$ $ SAN DIEGO MAGAZINE, San Diego Magazine Publishing Co., 401 W. A St., Suite 250, San Diego CA 92101. (619)230-9292. Fax: (619)230-9220. E-mail: rdonoho@sandiego-online.com. Editor: Tom Blair. **Contact:** Ron Donoho, managing editor. **30% freelance written.** Monthly magazine. "We produce informative and entertaining features about politics, community and neighborhood issues, sports, design and other facets of life in San Diego." Estab. 1948. Circ. 55,000. Pays on publication. Publishes ms an average of 2 months after acceptance. Byline given. Offers 25% kill fee. Buys first North American serial, second serial (reprint) rights. Editorial lead time 2 months. Submit seasonal material 4 months in advance. Accepts simultaneous submissions.
Nonfiction: Exposé, general interest, historical/nostalgic, how-to, interview/profile, travel. **Buys 12-24 mss/year.** Query with published clips or send complete ms. Length: 1,000-3,000 words. **Pays $250-750.** Sometimes pays expenses of writers on assignment.
Photos: State availability with submission. Buys one-time rights. Offers no additional payment for photos accepted with ms.

$ $ $ $ SAN FRANCISCO, Focus on the Bay Area, 243 Vallejo St., San Francisco CA 94111. (415)398-2800. Fax: (415)398-6777. E-mail: ltrottier@sanfran.com. Website: www.sanfran.com. **Contact:** Lisa Trottier, managing editor. **50% freelance written.** Monthly city/regional magazine. Estab. 1968. Circ. 180,000. Pays on publication. Publishes ms an average of 2 months after acceptance. Byline given. Offers 25% kill fee. Submit seasonal material 5 months in advance. Responds in 2 months to queries; 2 months to mss. Sample copy for $3.95.
Nonfiction: All stories should relate in some way to the San Francisco Bay Area (travel excepted). Exposé, interview/profile, travel, arts, politics, public issues, sports, consumer affairs. Query with published clips. Length: 200-4,000 words. **Pays $100-2,000 and some expenses.**

N: SAN FRANCISCO BAY GUARDIAN, 520 Hampshire St., San Francisco CA 94110-1417. (415)255-3100. Fax: (415)255-8762. E-mail: camille@sfbg.com. Website: www.sfbg.com. Editor/Publisher: Bruce Brugmann. **Contact:** Camille Taiara, editorial coordinator. **40% freelance written.** Works with a small number of new/unpublished writers each year. Weekly magazine specializing in investigative, consumer and lifestyle reporting for a sophisticated, urban audience. Estab. 1966. Circ. 140,000. Pays 2 weeks after publication. Publishes ms an average of 1 month after acceptance. Byline given. Buys first rights. Responds in 2 months to queries.
Nonfiction: City Editor (news), J.H. Tompkins (arts & entertainment), Annalee Newitz (culture). Publishes "incisive local news stories, investigative reports, features, analysis and interpretation, how-to, consumer and entertainment reviews. Most stories have a Bay Area angle." Freelance material should have a "public interest advocacy journalism approach." Query with 3 clips. Sometimes pays expenses of writers on assignment.
Reprints: Send tearsheet or photocopy and information about when and where the material previously appeared. Payment varies.
Photos: Victor Krumenacher, art director. Purchased with or without mss.
Tips: "Work with our volunteer intern projects in investigative, political and consumer reporting. We teach the techniques and send interns out to do investigative research. We like to talk to writers in our office before they begin doing a story."

$ $ $ SAN JOSE, The Magazine for Silicon Valley, Renaissance Publications, Inc., 4 N. Second St., Suite 550, San Jose CA 95113. (408)975-9300. Fax: (408)975-9900. E-mail: paul@sanjosemagazine.com. Website: www.sanjosemagazine.com. Publisher: Gilbert Sangari. **Contact:** Paul Lukes, managing editor. **10% freelance written.** Monthly magazine. "As the lifestyle magazine for those living at center of the technological revolution, we cover the people and places that make Silicon Valley the place to be for the new millennium. All stories must have a local angle, though they should be of national relevance." Estab. 1997. Circ. 60,000. Pays on publication. Publishes ms an average of 3 months after acceptance. Byline given. Offers 10% kill fee. Buys first North American serial rights, pays a flat $25 electronic rights fee. Editorial lead time 18 weeks. Submit seasonal material 6 months in advance. Accepts queries by mail, e-mail, fax. Accepts simultaneous submissions. Responds in 1 month to queries. Sample copy for $5. Writer's guidelines for #10 SASE.
> O→ "Get your feet wet by writing smaller pieces (200-500 words). Writers can get into my good graces by agreeing to write some of our unsigned pieces. What impresses the editor the most is meeting the assigned length and meeting deadlines."

Nonfiction: General interest, interview/profile, photo feature, travel. "No technical, trade or articles without a tie-in to Silicon Valley." **Buys 12 mss/year.** Query with published clips. Length: 1,000-2,000 words. **Pays 35¢/word.**
Photos: State availability with submission. Offers no additional payment for photos accepted with ms. Captions, identification of subjects, model releases required.

Columns/Departments: Fast Forward (a roundup of trends and personalities and news that has Silicon Valley buzzing; topics include health, history, politics, nonprofits, education, Q&As, business, technology, dining, wine and fashion). **Buys 5 mss/year.** Query. **Pays 35¢/word.**
Tips: "Study our magazine for style and content. Nothing is as exciting as reading a tightly written query and discovering a new writer."

Colorado

$ $ $ASPEN MAGAZINE, Ridge Publications, 720 E. Durant Ave., Suite E-8, Aspen CO 81612. (970)920-4040. Fax: (970)920-4044. E-mail: edit@aspenmagazine.com. Website: www.aspenmagazine.com. Editor: Janet C. O'Grady. **Contact:** Jamie Miller, managing editor. **30% freelance written.** Bimonthly magazine covering Aspen and the Roaring Fork Valley. "All things Aspen, written in a sophisticated, insider-oriented tone." Estab. 1974. Circ. 20,000. Within 30 days of publication. Byline sometimes given. Offers 10% kill fee. Buys first North American serial, electronic rights. Editorial lead time 2 months. Accepts queries by mail, e-mail, fax. Accepts simultaneous submissions. Responds in 2 months to queries; 6 months to mss. Sample copy for 9×12 SAE and 10 first-class stamps. Writer's guidelines for #10 SASE.
Nonfiction: Essays, new product, photo feature, historical, environmental and local issues, architecture and design, sports and outdoors, arts. "We do not publish general interest articles without a strong Aspen hook. We do not publish 'theme' (skiing in Aspen) or anniversary (40th year of Aspen Music Festival) articles, fiction, poetry or prewritten manuscripts." **Buys 30-60 mss/year.** Query with published clips. Length: 50-4,000 words. **Pays $50-1,000.** Sometimes pays expenses of writers on assignment.
Photos: State availability with submission. Reviews contact sheets, negatives, transparencies, prints. Identification of subjects, model releases required.

N $ $RELOCATING TO THE VAIL VALLEY, Showcase Publishing Inc., P.O. Box 8680, Prairie Village KS 66208. (913)648-5757. Fax: (913)648-5783. Editor: Dave Leathers. **Contact:** Liz Elliott, associate editor. Annual relocation guides, free for people moving to the area. Estab. 1986. Pays on publication. Publishes ms an average of 6 months after acceptance. Byline given. Buys one-time rights. Editorial lead time 4 months. Submit seasonal material 4 months in advance. Accepts queries by mail, fax. Accepts simultaneous submissions. Responds in 1 month to queries; 1 month to mss. Sample copy for $5 or online. Writer's guidelines online.
Nonfiction: Historical/nostalgic, travel, local issues. **Buys 8 mss/year.** Query with published clips. Length: 600-1,000 words. **Pays $60-350.** Sometimes pays expenses of writers on assignment.
Reprints: Accepts previously published submissions.
Photos: State availability of or send photos with submission. Reviews transparencies. Buys one-time rights. Offers no additional payment for photos accepted with ms. Identification of subjects required.
Tips: "Really read and understand our audience."

$ $STEAMBOAT MAGAZINE, Sundance Plaza, 1250 S. Lincoln Ave., P.O. Box 881659, Steamboat Springs CO 80488. (970)871-9413. Fax: (970)871-1922. E-mail: deb@steamboatmagazine.com. Website: www.steamboatmagaz ine.com. **Contact:** Deborah Olsen, editor. **80% freelance written.** Semiannual magazine "showcasing the history, people, lifestyles and interests of Northwest Colorado. Our readers are generally well-educated, well-traveled, upscale, active people visiting our region to ski in winter and recreate in summer. They come from all 50 states and many foreign countries. Writing should be fresh, entertaining and informative." Estab. 1978. Circ. 30,000. Pays 50% on acceptance, 50% on publication. Publishes ms an average of 6 months after acceptance. Byline given. Submit seasonal material 1 year in advance. Accepts queries by mail, e-mail, fax, phone. Responds in 3 months to queries. Sample copy for $3.95 and SAE with 10 first-class stamps. Writer's guidelines free.
Nonfiction: Book excerpts, essays, general interest, historical/nostalgic, humor, interview/profile, photo feature, travel. **Buys 10-15 mss/year.** Query with published clips. Length: 150-1,500 words. **Pays $50-300 for assigned articles.** Sometimes pays expenses of writers on assignment.
Photos: State availability with submission. Reviews transparencies. Buys one-time rights. Pays $50-250/photo. Captions, identification of subjects, model releases required.
Tips: "Western lifestyles, regional history, nature (including environmental subjects), sports and recreation are very popular topics for our readers. We're looking for new angles on ski/snowboard stories and activity-related stories. Please query first with ideas to make sure subjects are fresh and appropriate. We try to make subjects and treatments 'timeless' in nature because our magazine is a 'keeper' with a multi-year shelf life."

N $ $VAIL/BEAVER CREEK MAGAZINE, P.O. Box 1414, Vail CO 81658. (970)949-9170. Fax: (970)949-9176. E-mail: bergerd@vail.net. **Contact:** Don Berger, editor. **80% freelance written.** Semiannual magazine "showcasing the lifestyles and history of the Vail Valley. We are particularly interested in personality profiles, home and design features, the arts, winter and summer recreation and adventure stories, and environmental articles." Estab. 1975. Circ. 30,000. **Pays on acceptance.** Publishes ms an average of 6 months after acceptance. Byline given. Offers 100% kill fee. Buys one-time rights. Editorial lead time 1 year. Submit seasonal material 1 year in advance. Accepts queries by mail, e-mail. Accepts simultaneous submissions. Responds in 1 month to queries; 2 months to mss. Sample copy for $5.95 and SAE with 10 first-class stamps. Writer's guidelines free.

Nonfiction: Essays, general interest, historical/nostalgic, humor, interview/profile, personal experience, photo feature. **Buys 20-25 mss/year.** Query with published clips. Length: 500-3,000 words. **Pays 15-20¢/word.** Sometimes pays expenses of writers on assignment.

Reprints: Send typed ms with rights for sale noted and information about when and where the material previously appeared.

Photos: State availability with submission. Reviews transparencies. Buys one-time rights. Offers $50-250/photo. Captions, identification of subjects, model releases required.

Tips: "Be familiar with the Vail Valley and its 'personality.' Approach a story that will be relevant for several years to come. We produce a magazine that is a 'keeper.'"

Connecticut

$ $ $ CONNECTICUT MAGAZINE, Journal Register Company, 35 Nutmeg Dr., Trumbull CT 06611. (203)380-6600. Fax: (203)380-6610. E-mail: cmonagan@connecticutmag.com. Website: www.connecticutmag.com. Editor: Charles Monagan. **Contact:** Dale Salm, managing editor. **80% freelance written.** Prefers to work with published/ established writers who know the state and live/have lived here. Monthly magazine "for an affluent, sophisticated, suburban audience. We want only articles that pertain to living in Connecticut." Estab. 1971. Circ. 93,000. Pays on publication. Publishes ms an average of 4 months after acceptance. Byline given. Offers 20% kill fee. Buys first North American serial rights. Submit seasonal material 4 months in advance. Accepts queries by mail, e-mail, fax. Responds in 6 weeks to queries. Writer's guidelines for #10 SASE.

O→ Freelancers can best break in with "First" (short, trendy pieces with a strong Connecticut angle); find a story that is offbeat and write it in a lighthearted, interesting manner.

Nonfiction: Interested in seeing hard-hitting investigative pieces and strong business pieces (not advertorial). Book excerpts, exposé, general interest, interview/profile, topics of service to Connecticut readers. No personal essays. **Buys 50 mss/year.** Query with published clips. Length: 3,000 words maximum. **Pays $600-1,200.** Sometimes pays expenses of writers on assignment.

Photos: Send photos with submission. Reviews contact sheets, transparencies. Buys one-time rights. Pays $50 minimum/photo. Identification of subjects, model releases required.

Columns/Departments: Business, Health, Politics, Connecticut Calendar, Arts, Dining Out, Gardening, Environment, Education, People, Sports, Media. Length: 1,500-2,500 words. **Buys 50 mss/year.** Query with published clips. **Pays $400-700.**

Fillers: Short pieces about Connecticut trends, curiosities, interesting short subjects, etc. **Buys 50/year.** Length: 150-400 words. **Pays $75-150.**

▣ The online magazine carries original content not found in the print edition. Contact: Charles Monagan, online editor.

Tips: "Make certain your idea has not been covered to death by the local press and can withstand a time lag of a few months. Again, we don't want something that has already received a lot of press."

$ $ $ $ NORTHEAST MAGAZINE, The Hartford Courant, 285 Broad St., Hartford CT 06115-2510. (860)241-3700. Fax: (860)241-3853. E-mail: northeast@courant.com. Website: www.ctnow.com. Editor: Larry Bloom. **Contact:** Jane Bronfman, editorial assistant. **5% freelance written.** Weekly magazine for a Connecticut audience. Estab. 1982. Circ. 316,000. **Pays on acceptance.** Publishes ms an average of 5 months after acceptance. Byline given. Accepts queries by mail. Responds in 3 months to queries. Sample copy and writer's guidelines available.

Nonfiction: "We are primarily interested in hard-hitting nonfiction articles spun off the news and compelling personal stories, as well as humor, fashion, style and home. We have a strong emphasis on Connecticut subject matter." General interest (has to have a strong Connecticut tie-in), historical/nostalgic, In-depth investigations of stories behind the news (has to have strong Connecticut tie-in), Personal Essays (humorous or anecdotal). No poetry. **Buys 10 mss/year.** Query. Length: 750-2,500 words. **Pays $200-1,500.**

Photos: Most are assigned. "Do not send originals." State availability with submission.

Fiction: Confined to yearly fiction issue and "Word For Word" column (excerpts of soon-to-be published books by Connecticut authors or with Connecticut tie-ins). Length: 750-1,500 words.

Tips: "Less space available for all types of writing means our standards for acceptance will be much higher. It is to your advantage to read several issues of the magazine before submitting a manuscript or query. Virtually all our pieces are solicited and assigned by us, with about two percent of what we publish coming in 'over the transom.'"

Delaware

N $ $ DELAWARE TODAY, 3301 Lancaster Pike, Suite 5C, Wilmington DE 19805. (302)656-1809. Fax: (302)656-5834. E-mail: editors@delawaretoday.com. Website: www.delawaretoday.com. **Contact:** Marsha Mah, editor.

50% freelance written. Monthly magazine geared toward Delaware people, places and issues. "All stories must have Delaware slant. No pitches such as Delawareans will be interested in a national topic." Estab. 1962. Circ. 25,000. Pays on publication. Publishes ms an average of 4 months after acceptance. Byline given. Offers 50% kill fee. Buys all rights for 1 year. Editorial lead time 3 months. Submit seasonal material 6 months in advance. Responds in 2 months to queries. Sample copy for $2.95.

Nonfiction: Historical/nostalgic, interview/profile, photo feature, lifestyles, issues. Special issues: Newcomer's Guide to Delaware. **Buys 40 mss/year.** Query with published clips. Length: 100-3,000 words. **Pays $50-750 for assigned articles.** Sometimes pays expenses of writers on assignment.

Photos: State availability with submission. Buys one-time rights. Negotiates payment individually. Identification of subjects required.

Columns/Departments: Business, Health, History, People, all 1,500 words. **Buys 24 mss/year.** Query with published clips. **Pays $150-250.**

Fillers: Anecdotes, newsbreaks, short humor. **Buys 10/year.** Length: 100-200 words. **Pays $50-75.**

Tips: "No story ideas that we would know about, i.e., a profile of the governor. Best bets are profiles of quirky/unique Delawareans that we'd never know about or think of."

District of Columbia

$ $WASHINGTON CITY PAPER, 2390 Champlain St. NW, Washington DC 20009. (202)332-2100. Fax: (202)332-8500. E-mail: rbyrne@washcp.com. Website: www.washingtoncitypaper.com. Editor: Howard Witt. **Contact:** Richard Byrne, associate editor. **50% freelance written.** "Relentlessly local alternative weekly in nation's capital covering city and regional politics, media and arts. No national stories." Estab. 1981. Circ. 98,000. Pays on publication. Publishes ms an average of 6 weeks after acceptance. Byline given. Offers 10% kill fee for assigned stories. Buys first rights. Editorial lead time 7-10 days. Responds in 1 month to queries. Writer's guidelines for #10 SASE.

Nonfiction: Richard Byrne (District Line); Howard Witt (Covers). "Our biggest need for freelancers is in the District Line section of the newspaper: short, well-reported and local stories. These range from carefully-drawn profiles to sharp, hooky approaches to reporting on local institutions. We don't want op-ed articles, fiction, poetry, service journalism or play by play accounts of news conferences or events. We also purchase, but more infrequently, longer 'cover-length' stories that fit the criteria stated above. Full guide to freelance submissions can be found on website." **Buys 100 mss/ year.** Query with published clips or send complete ms. Length: District Line: 800-2,500 words; Covers: 4,000-10,000 words. **Pays 10-40¢/word.** Sometimes pays expenses of writers on assignment.

Photos: Make appointment to show portfolio to Jandos Rothstein, art director. Pays minimum of $75.

Columns/Departments: Leonard Roberge, arts editor. Music Writing (eclectic). **Buys 100 mss/year.** Query with published clips or send complete ms. **Pays 10-40¢/word.**

Tips: "Think local. Great ideas are a plus. We are willing to work with anyone who has a strong idea, regardless of vita."

$ $ $THE WASHINGTON POST, 1150 15th St. NW, Washington DC 20071. (202)334-7750. Fax: (202)334-1069. **Contact:** K.C. Summers, travel editor. **60% freelance written.** Prefers to work with published/established writers. Weekly newspaper travel section (Sunday). Pays on publication. Publishes ms an average of 6 months after acceptance. Byline given. Buys first North American serial rights. Usually responds in 1 month to queries; does not respond to unsolicited mss.

• "We are now emphasizing staff-written articles as well as quality writing from other sources. Stories are rarely assigned; all material comes in on speculation; there is no fixed kill fee." Travel must not be subsidized in any way.

Nonfiction: Emphasis is on travel writing with a strong sense of place, color, anecdote and history. Query with published clips. Length: 1,500-2,500 words, plus sidebar for practical information.

Photos: State availability with submission.

$ $ $THE WASHINGTONIAN, 1828 L St. NW, #200, Washington DC 20036. (202)296-3600. Fax: (202)862-3526. E-mail: editorial@washingtonian.com. Website: www.washingtonian.com. **Contact:** Courtney Martin, assistant editor. **20-25% freelance written.** Monthly magazine. "Writers should keep in mind that we are a general interest city-and-regional magazine. Nearly all our articles have a hard Washington connection. And, please, no political satire." Estab. 1965. Circ. 160,000. Pays on publication. Publishes ms an average of 3 months after acceptance. Byline given. Buys first North American serial rights, limited, non-exclusive electronic rights. Editorial lead time 10 weeks. Accepts queries by mail, fax. Writer's guidelines for #10 SASE.

Nonfiction: Book excerpts, exposé, general interest, historical/nostalgic (with specific Washington, D.C. focus), interview/profile, personal experience, photo feature, travel. **Buys 15-30 mss/year.** Query with published clips. **Pays 50¢/ word.** Sometimes pays expenses of writers on assignment.

Columns/Departments: Jack Limpert, editor. First Person (personal experience that somehow illuminates life in Washington area), 650-700 words. **Buys 9-12 mss/year.** Query. **Pays $325.**

The online magazine carries original content not found in the print edition. Contact: Cheryl Haser, online editor.

Tips: "The types of articles we publish include service pieces; profiles of people; investigative articles; rating pieces; institutional profiles; first-person articles; stories that cut across the grain of conventional thinking; articles that tell the reader how Washington got to be the way it is; light or satirical pieces (send the complete manuscript, not the idea, because in this case execution is everything); and fiction that tells readers how a part of Washington works or reveals something about the character or mood or people of Washington. Subjects of articles include the federal government, local government, dining out, sports, business, education, medicine, fashion, environment, how to make money, how to spend money, real estate, performing arts, visual arts, travel, health, nightlife, home and garden, self-improvement, places to go, things to do, and more. Again, we are interested in almost anything as long as it relates to the Washington area."

Florida

$ $ BOCA RATON MAGAZINE, JES Publishing, 6413 Congress Ave., Suite 100, Boca Raton FL 33487. (561)997-8683. Fax: (561)997-8909. E-mail: editor@bocamag.com. Website: www.bocamag.com. Associate Editor: Gail Friedman. **Contact:** Marie Speed, editor-in-chief. **70% freelance written.** Bimonthly lifestyle magazine "devoted to the residents of South Florida, featuring fashion, interior design, food, people, places and issues that shape the affluent South Florida market." Estab. 1981. Circ. 20,000. **Pays on acceptance.** Publishes ms an average of 3 months after acceptance. Byline given. Buys second serial (reprint) rights. Submit seasonal material 7 months in advance. Accepts simultaneous submissions. Responds in 1 month to queries. Sample copy for $4.95 and 10×13 SAE with 10 first-class stamps. Writer's guidelines for #10 SASE.
Nonfiction: General interest, historical/nostalgic, humor, interview/profile, photo feature, travel. Special issues: Interior Design (September-October); Beauty (January-February); Health (July-August). Query with published clips or send complete ms. Length: 800-2,500 words. **Pays $50-600 for assigned articles; $50-300 for unsolicited articles.**
Reprints: Send tearsheet. Payment varies.
Photos: Send photos with submission.
Columns/Departments: Body & Soul (health, fitness and beauty column, general interest), 1,000 words; Hitting Home (family and social interactions), 1,000 words. Query with published clips or send complete ms. **Pays $50-250.**
Tips: "We prefer shorter manuscripts, highly localized articles, excellent art/photography."

$ $ FLORIDA LIVING MAGAZINE, Florida Media, Inc., 102 Drennen Rd., Suite C-5, Orlando FL 32806. (407)816-9596. Fax: (407)816-9373. E-mail: editor@flaliving.com. Website: www.floridamagazine.com. Publisher: E. Douglas Cifers. **Contact:** Kristen Cifers. Monthly lifestyle magazine covering Florida travel, food and dining, heritage, homes and gardens and all aspects of Florida lifestyle. Full calendar of events each month. Estab. 1981. Circ. 201,000. Pays on publication. Publishes ms an average of 6 months after acceptance. Byline given. Buys first rights. Editorial lead time 3 months. Submit seasonal material 6 months in advance. Accepts queries by mail, e-mail, fax. Responds in 2 months to queries. Sample copy for $5. Writer's guidelines for #10 SASE.
• Interested in material on areas outside of the larger cities.
○⚡ Break in with stories specific to Florida showcasing the people, places, events and things that are examples of Florida's rich history and culture.
Nonfiction: Historical/nostalgic, interview/profile, travel, general Florida interest, out-of-the-way Florida places, dining, attractions, festivals, shopping, resorts, bed & breakfast reviews, retirement, real estate, business, finance, health, recreation, sports. **Buys 50-60 mss/year.** Query with published clips. Length: 500-2,500 words. **Pays $100-400 for assigned articles; $50-250 for unsolicited articles.**
Photos: Send photos with submission. Reviews 3×5 color prints and slides. Offers $6/photo. Captions required.
Columns/Departments: Golf, Homes & Gardenings, Heritage (all Florida-related); 750 words. **Buys 24 mss/year.** Query with published clips. **Pays $75-250.**

$ $ $ ▨ GULFSHORE LIFE, 9051 North Tamlami Trail N, Suite 202, Naples FL 34108. (941)594-9980. Fax: (941)594-9986. E-mail: editor@gulfshorelifemag.com. Website: www.gulfshorelifemag.com. **Contact:** Bob Morris, editor. **75% freelance written.** Magazine published 10 times/year for "southwest Florida, the workings of its natural systems, its history, personalities, culture and lifestyle." Estab. 1970. Circ. 35,000. Pays on publication. Publishes ms an average of 4 months after acceptance. Byline given. Buys first North American serial rights. Submit seasonal material 8 months in advance. Accepts queries by mail, e-mail, fax. Accepts simultaneous submissions. Sample copy for 9×12 SAE and 10 first-class stamps.
Nonfiction: All articles must be related to southwest Florida. Historical/nostalgic, interview/profile, issue/trend. **Buys 100 mss/year.** Query with published clips. Length: 500-3,000 words. **Pays $100-1,000.**
Photos: Send photos with submission. Reviews 35mm transparencies, 5×7 prints. Buys one-time rights. Pays $50-100. Identification of subjects, model releases required.
Tips: "We buy superbly written stories that illuminate southwest Florida personalities, places and issues. Surprise us!"

$ $ ▨ JACKSONVILLE, White Publishing Co., 1032 Hendricks Ave., Jacksonville FL 32207. (904)396-8666. Fax: (904)396-0926. **Contact:** Joseph White, editor. **50% freelance written.** Monthly magazine covering life and business in northeast Florida "for upwardly mobile residents of Jacksonville and the Beaches, Orange Park, St. Augustine and Amelia Island, Florida." Estab. 1985. Circ. 25,000. Pays on publication. Byline given. Offers 25-33% kill fee to writers on assignment. Buys first North American serial, second serial (reprint) rights. Editorial lead time 3 months. Submit seasonal material 4 months in advance. Responds in 6 weeks to queries; 1 month to mss. Sample copy for $5 (includes postage).

Nonfiction: All articles *must* have relevance to Jacksonville and Florida's First Coast (Duval, Clay, St. John's, Nassau, Baker counties). Book excerpts, exposé, general interest, historical/nostalgic, how-to (service articles), humor, interview/profile, personal experience, photo feature, travel, commentary, local business successes, trends, personalities, community issues, how institutions work. **Buys 50 mss/year.** Query with published clips. Length: 1,200-3,000 words. **Pays $50-500 for feature length pieces.** Sometimes pays expenses of writers on assignment.

Reprints: Send photocopy. Pay varies.

Photos: State availability with submission. Reviews contact sheets, transparencies. Buys one-time rights. Negotiates payment individually. Captions, model releases required.

Columns/Departments: Business (trends, success stories, personalities), 1,000-1,200 words; Health (trends, emphasis on people, hopeful outlooks), 1,000-1,200 words; Money (practical personal financial advice using local people, anecdotes and examples), 1,000-1,200 words; Real Estate/Home (service, trends, home photo features), 1,000-1,200 words; Travel (weekends; daytrips; excursions locally and regionally), 1,000-1,200 words; occasional departments and columns covering local history, sports, family issues, etc. **Buys 40 mss/year. Pays $150-250.**

Tips: "We are a writer's magazine and demand writing that tells a story with flair."

$ $ TALLAHASSEE MAGAZINE, Rowland Publishing Inc., 1932 Miccosokee Rd., P.O. Box 1837, Tallahassee FL 32308. (850)878-0554. Fax: (850)656-1871. E-mail: snoll@rolandinc.com. Website: www.rolandinc.com. **Contact:** Susan Noll, associate editor. **60-75% freelance written.** Bimonthly magazine covering Tallahassee area-North Florida and South Georgia. "*Tallahassee Magazine* is dedicated to reflecting the changing needs of a capital city challenged by growth and increasing economic, political and social diversity." Estab. 1979. Circ. 17,300. **Pays on acceptance.** Publishes ms an average of 3 months after acceptance. Byline given. Buys one-time rights. Editorial lead time 3 months. Submit seasonal material 4 months in advance. Accepts queries by mail, e-mail, fax. Accepts simultaneous submissions. Responds in 1 month to queries. Sample copy for $2.95 and #10 SAE with 4 first-class stamps; sample articles online. Writer's guidelines for #10 SASE.

Nonfiction: General interest, historical/nostalgic, how-to, humor, inspirational, interview/profile, personal experience, photo feature, travel, politics, sports, lifestyles. **Buys 10 mss/year.** Query or submit ms with SASE. Length: 1,000-1,500 words. **Pays $100-250.**

Reprints: Send typed ms with rights for sale noted and information about when and where the material previously appeared. Pays $100-350.

Photos: State availability with submission. Reviews 35mm transparencies, 3×5 prints. Buys one-time rights. Offers no additional payment for photos accepted with ms. Identification of subjects, model releases required.

Columns/Departments: Humor, Cooking, People and Social, all 850 words or less. **Buys 12-18 mss/year.** Query with published clips. **Pays $100.**

Tips: "Know the area we cover. This area is unusual in terms of the geography and the people. We are a Southern city, not a Florida city, in many ways. Know what we have published recently and don't try to sell us on an idea that we have published within three years of your query. Be lucid and concise and take enough time to get your facts straight. Make submissions on disk, either in Microsoft Word or Word Perfect."

Georgia

$ $ $ $ ATLANTA, 1330 Peachtree St., Suite 450, Atlanta GA 30309. (404)872-3100. Fax: (404)870-6219. E-mail: kdunnavant@atlantamag.emmis.com. Website: www.atlantamagazine.com. **Contact:** Keith Dunnavant, executive editor. Monthly magazine that explores people, pleasures, useful information, regional happenings, restaurants, shopping, etc., for a general adult audience in Atlanta, including subjects in government, sports, pop culture, urban affairs, arts and entertainment. "*Atlanta* magazine articulates the special nature of Atlanta and appeals to an audience that wants to understand and celebrate the uniqueness of the region. The magazine's mission is to serve as a tastemaker by virtue of in-depth information and authoritative, provocative explorations of issues, personalities and lifestyles." Circ. 69,000. **Pays on acceptance.** Byline given. Offers 25% kill fee. Buys first North American serial rights. Accepts queries by mail, e-mail, phone. Responds in 2 months to queries. Sample copy online.

Nonfiction: "*Atlanta* magazine articulates the special nature of Atlanta and appeals to an audience that wants to understand and celebrate the uniqueness of the region. The magazine's mission is to serve as a tastemaker by virtue of in-depth information and authoritative, provocative explorations of issues, personalities and lifestyles." General interest, interview/profile, travel. **Buys 36-40 mss/year.** Query with published clips. Length: 1,500-5,000 words. **Pays $300-2,000.** Pays expenses of writers on assignment.

Columns/Departments: Essay, travel. Length: 1,000-1,500 words. **Buys 30 mss/year.** Query with published clips. **Pays $500.**

Fiction: Accepts novel excerpts.

Fillers: Buys 80/year. Length: 75-175 words. **Pays $50-100.**

Tips: "Writers must know what makes their piece a story rather than just a subject."

$ $ATLANTA TRIBUNE: THE MAGAZINE, Black Atlanta's Business & Politics, L&L Communications, 875 Old Roswell Rd, Suite C-100, Roswell GA 30076. Fax: (770)642-6501. E-mail: rsherrell@atlantatribune.com. Website: www.atlantatribune.com. **Contact:** Rick Sherrell, editor. **90% freelance written.** Monthly magazine covering African-American business, careers, technology, wealth-building, politics and education. "The *Atlanta Tribune* is written for Atlanta's black executives, professionals and entrepreneurs with a primary focus of business, careers, technology, wealth-building, politics and education. Our publication serves as an advisor that offers helpful information and direction to the black entrepreneur." Estab. 1987. Circ. 30,000. **Pays on acceptance.** Byline given. Offers 10% kill fee. Buys electronic, all rights. Editorial lead time 4 months. Submit seasonal material 4 months in advance. Accepts queries by e-mail. Responds in 6 weeks to queries. Sample copy online or mail a request. Writer's guidelines online.

O─➤ Break in with "the ability to write feature stories that give insight into Black Atlanta's business community, technology, businesses and career and wealth-building opportunities. Also, stories with real social, political or economic impact."

Nonfiction: "Our special sections include Black History, Real Estate, Scholarship Roundup." Book excerpts, how-to (business, careers, technology), interview/profile, new product, opinion, technical. **Buys 100 mss/year.** Query with published clips. Length: 1,400-2,500 words. **Pays $250-600.** Sometimes pays expenses of writers on assignment.

Photos: State availability with submission. Reviews 2¼ x 2¼ transparencies. Buys one-time rights. Negotiates payment individually. Identification of subjects, model releases required.

Columns/Departments: Business, Careers, Technology, Wealth-Building, Politics and Education, all 400-600 words. **Buys 100 mss/year.** Query with published clips. **Pays $100-200.**

■ The online magazine carries original content not found in the print edition and includes writer's guidelines. Contact: Cherie S. White, online editor.

Tips: "Send a well-written, convincing query by e-mail that demonstrates that you have thoroughly read previous issues and reviewed our online writer's guidelines."

N $⬥ FLAGPOLE MAGAZINE, Flagpole, P.O. Box 1027, Athens GA 30603. (706)549-9523. Fax: (706)548-8981. E-mail: editor@flagpole.com. Website: www.flagpole.com. **Contact:** Pete McCommons, editor. **75% freelance written.** Local "alternative" weekly with a special emphasis on popular (and unpopular) music. "Will consider stories on national, international musicians, authors, politicians, etc., even if they don't have a local or regional news peg. However, those stories should be original, irreverent enough to justify inclusion. Of course, local/Southern news/feature stories are best. We like reporting, storytelling more than opinion pieces." Estab. 1987. Circ. 16,000. Pays on publication. Publishes ms an average of 1 month after acceptance. Byline given. Makes work-for-hire assignments. Editorial lead time 2 months. Submit seasonal material 2 months in advance. Responds in 2 weeks to queries; 1 month to mss. Sample copy online.

Nonfiction: Book excerpts, essays, exposé, interview/profile, new product, personal experience. **Buys 200 mss/year.** Query with published clips. Length: 600-3,500 words. Sometimes pays expenses of writers on assignment.

Reprints: Send tearsheet, photocopy or typed ms with rights for sale noted and information about when and where the material previously appeared.

Photos: State availability with submission. Reviews prints. Buys all rights. Negotiates payment individually. Captions required.

Columns/Departments: Lit. (book reviews), 800 words. **Buys 30 mss/year.** Send complete ms. **Pays $10.**

Tips: "Read our publication online before querying, but don't feel limited by what you see. We can't afford to pay much, so we're open to young/inexperienced writer-journalists looking for clips. Fresh, funny/insightful voices make us happiest, as does reportage over opinion. If you've ever succumbed to the temptation to call a pop record 'ethereal' we probably won't bother with your music journalism. No faxed submissions, please."

$ $ GEORGIA MAGAZINE, Georgia Electric Membership Corp., P.O. Box 1707, Tucker GA 30085. (770)270-6950. Fax: (770)270-6995. E-mail: ann.orowski@georgiaemc.com. Website: www.Georgiamagazine.org. **Contact:** Ann Orowski, editor. **50% freelance written.** "We are a monthly magazine for and about Georgians, with a friendly, conversational tone and human interest topics." Estab. 1945. Circ. 444,000. Pays on publication. Publishes ms an average of 4 months after acceptance. Byline given. Buys first North American serial, electronic rights. Editorial lead time 2 months. Submit seasonal material 6 months in advance. Accepts simultaneous submissions. Responds in 1 month to subjects of interest. Sample copy for $2. Writer's guidelines for #10 SASE.

Nonfiction: General interest (Georgia-focused), historical/nostalgic, how-to (in the home and garden), humor, inspirational, interview/profile, photo feature, travel. **Buys 24 mss/year.** Query with published clips. Length: 800-1,000 words; 500 words for smaller features and departments. **Pays $50-300.**

Photos: State availability with submission. Reviews contact sheets, transparencies, prints. Buys one-time rights. Negotiates payment individually. Identification of subjects, model releases required.

$ $ KNOW ATLANTA MAGAZINE, New South Publishing, 1303 Hightower Trail, Suite 101, Atlanta GA 30350. (770)650-1102. Fax: (770)650-2848. E-mail: editor1@knowatlanta.com. Website: www.knowatlanta.com. **Contact:** Geoff Kohl, editor. **80% freelance written.** Quarterly magazine covering the Atlanta area. "Our articles offer information on Atlanta that would be useful to newcomers—homes, schools, hospitals, fun things to do, anything that makes their move more comfortable." Estab. 1986. Circ. 192,000. Pays on publication. Byline given. Offers 100% kill fee. Buys first North American serial rights. Editorial lead time 2 months. Submit seasonal material 2 months in advance. Accepts queries by mail, e-mail, fax. Sample copy free.

O—┐ "Know the metro Atlanta area, especially hot trends in real estate. Writers who know about international relocation trends and commercial real estate topics are hot."

Nonfiction: General interest, how-to (relocate), interview/profile, personal experience, photo feature. No fiction. **Buys 20 mss/year.** Query with clips. Length: 1,000-2,000 words. **Pays $100-500 for assigned articles; $100-300 for unsolicited articles.** Sometimes pays expenses of writers on assignment.

Reprints: Accepts previously published submissions.

Photos: Send photos with submission. Reviews contact sheets. Buys one-time rights. Negotiates payment individually. Captions, identification of subjects required.

$ $ NORTH GEORGIA JOURNAL, Legacy Communications, Inc., P.O. Box 127, Roswell GA 30077. (770)642-5569. Fax: (770)642-1415. E-mail: sumail@mindspring.com. Website: mindspring.com/~north.ga.travel. **Contact:** Olin Jackson, publisher. **70% freelance written.** Quarterly magazine "for readers interested in travel, history, and mountain lifestyles of north Georgia." Estab. 1984. Circ. 18,861. Pays on publication. Publishes ms an average of 5 months after acceptance. Byline given. Offers 25% kill fee. Buys all rights. Editorial lead time 3 months. Submit seasonal material 6 months in advance. Accepts queries by mail, e-mail, fax. Sample copy for 9×12 SAE and 8 first-class stamps or online. Writer's guidelines for #10 SASE.

Nonfiction: Historical/nostalgic, how-to (survival techniques; mountain living; do-it-yourself home construction and repairs, etc.), interview/profile (celebrity), personal experience (anything unique or unusual pertaining to north Georgia mountains), photo feature (any subject of a historic nature which can be photographed in a seasonal context, i.e., old mill with brilliant yellow jonquils in foreground), travel (subjects highlighting travel opportunities in north Georgia). Query with published clips. **Pays $75-350.**

Photos: Send photos with submission. Reviews contact sheets, transparencies. Buys all rights. Negotiates payment individually. Captions, identification of subjects, model releases required.

Fiction: Accepts novel excerpts.

Tips: "Good photography is crucial to acceptance of all articles. Send written queries then *wait* for a response. *No telephone calls please.* The most useful material involves a first-person experience of an individual who has explored a historic site or scenic locale and *interviewed* a person or persons who were involved with or have first hand knowledge of a historic site/event. Interviews and quotations are crucial. Articles should be told in writer's own words."

Hawaii

$ $ HONOLULU, Honolulu Publishing Co., Ltd., 36 Merchant St., Honolulu HI 96813. (808)524-7400. Fax: (808)531-2306. E-mail: honmag@pixi.com. Publisher: John Alves. **Contact:** John Heckathorn, editor. **50% freelance written.** Prefers to work with published/established writers. Monthly magazine covering general interest topics relating to Hawaii residents. Estab. 1888. Circ. 30,000. **Pays on acceptance.** Publishes ms an average of 4 months after acceptance. Byline given. Buys first rights. Submit seasonal material 5 months in advance. Accepts queries by mail, e-mail. Accepts simultaneous submissions. Responds in 2 months to queries. Sample copy for $2 and 9×12 SAE with 8 first-class stamps. Writer's guidelines for #10 SASE.

Nonfiction: Exposé, general interest, historical/nostalgic, photo feature, all Hawaii-related. "We write for Hawaii residents, so travel articles about Hawaii are not appropriate." **Buys 30 mss/year.** Query with published clips if available. Length: 2,000-3,000 words. **Pays $100-700.** Sometimes pays expenses of writers on assignment.

Photos: Michael Le, art director. Send photos with submission. Buys one-time rights. Pays $75-175 for single image inside; $500 maximum for cover. Captions, identification of subjects, model releases required.

Columns/Departments: Calabash ("newsy," timely, humorous department on any Hawaii-related subject). **Buys 15 mss/year**, 50-750 words. **Pays $35-100.** First Person (personal experience or humor). **Buys 10 mss/year**, 1,500 words. **Pays $200-300.** Query with published clips or send complete ms.

Illinois

[N] $ BARFLY NEWSPAPER, A Guide to Chicago's Drinking Establishments, Barfly, Inc., P.O. Box 416580, Chicago IL 60641-6580. (773)489-6890. Fax: (773)489-7150. E-mail: tony@barflynews.com. Website: www.barflynews.com. **Contact:** Tony Gordon, managing editor. **40% freelance written.** Biweekly newspaper featuring "tavern tidbits, stories on beer, wine, spirits, events, live music, bar reviews. Readership is people who go to bars regularly." Estab. 1993. Circ. 24,000. Pays on publication. Publishes ms an average of 2 months after acceptance. Byline given. Buys all rights. Editorial lead time 2 months. Submit seasonal material 2 months in advance. Accepts queries by mail, e-mail, fax. Accepts simultaneous submissions. Responds in 2 weeks to queries; 1 month to mss. Sample copy for $2. Writer's guidelines free.

Nonfiction: Book excerpts, essays, exposé, general interest, historical/nostalgic, how-to, humor, inspirational, interview/profile, new product, opinion, personal experience, photo feature, technical, travel, bar reviews. No poetry. **Buys 100 mss/year.** Query with published clips. **Pays $25.**

Reprints: Accepts previously published submissions.

Photos: Send photos with submission. Reviews 5 × 7 prints. Buys all rights. Offers $12/photo. Identification of subjects required.

Tips: "Fax résumé and story ideas."

$ $ $ $ CHICAGO MAGAZINE, 500 N. Dearborn, Suite 1200, Chicago IL 60610-4901. Fax: (312)222-0699. E-mail: shane-tritsch@primediamags.com. Website: www.chicagomag.com. **Contact:** Shane Tritsch, managing editor. **50% freelance written.** Prefers to work with published/established writers. Monthly magazine for an audience which is "95% from Chicago area; 90% college educated; upper income, overriding interests in the arts, politics, dining, good life in the city and suburbs. Most are in 25-50 age bracket, well-read and articulate." Estab. 1968. Circ. 175,000. **Pays on acceptance.** Publishes ms an average of 3 months after acceptance. Buys first rights. Submit seasonal material 4 months in advance. Accepts queries by mail, e-mail. Responds in 1 month to queries. For sample copy, send $3 to Circulation Dept. Writer's guidelines for #10 SASE.

Nonfiction: "On themes relating to the quality of life in Chicago: Past, present, and future." Writers should have "a general awareness that the readers will be concerned, influential, longtime Chicagoans. We generally publish material too comprehensive for daily newspapers." Exposé, humor, personal experience, think pieces, profiles, spot news, historical articles. **Buys 100 mss/year.** Query; indicate specifics, knowledge of city and market, and demonstrable access to sources. Length: 200-6,000 words. **Pays $100-3,000 and up.** Pays expenses of writers on assignment.

Photos: Usually assigned separately, not acquired from writers. Reviews 35mm transparencies, color prints.

■ The online editor is Deborah Wilk.

Tips: "Submit detailed queries, be business-like and avoid clichéd ideas."

$ $ $ $ CHICAGO READER, Chicago's Free Weekly, Chicago Reader, Inc., 11 E. Illinois, Chicago IL 60611. (312)828-0350. Fax: (312)828-9926. E-mail: mail@chicagoreader.com. Website: www.chicagoreader.com. Editor: Alison True. **Contact:** Patrick Arden, managing editor. **50% freelance written.** Weekly Alternative tabloid for Chicago. Estab. 1971. Circ. 136,000. Pays on publication. Publishes ms an average of 3 months after acceptance. Byline given. No kill fee. Buys one-time rights. Editorial lead time up to 6 months. Accepts queries by mail, e-mail, fax. Accepts simultaneous submissions. Responds if interested to queries. Sample copy free. Writer's guidelines free or online.

Nonfiction: Book excerpts, essays, exposé, general interest, historical/nostalgic, humor, interview/profile, opinion, personal experience, photo feature. No celebrity interviews, national news or issues. **Buys 500 mss/year.** Send complete ms. Length: 4,000-50,000 words. **Pays $100-3,000.** Sometimes pays expenses of writers on assignment.

Reprints: Accepts previously published submissions.

Columns/Departments: Reading, First Person, Cityscape, Neighborhood News, all 1,500-2,500 words; arts and entertainment reviews, up to 1,200 words; calendar items, 400-1,000 words.

Tips: "Our greatest need is for full-length magazine-style feature stories on Chicago topics. We're *not* looking for: hard news (What the Mayor Said About the Schools Yesterday); commentary and opinion (What I Think About What the Mayor Said About the Schools Yesterday); poetry. We are not particularly interested in stories of national (as opposed to local) scope, or in celebrity for celebrity's sake (à la *Rolling Stone, Interview*, etc.). More than half the articles published in the *Reader* each week come from freelancers, and once or twice a month we publish one that's come in 'over the transom'—from a writer we've never heard of and may never hear from again. We think that keeping the *Reader* open to the greatest possible number of contributors makes a fresher, less predictable, more interesting paper. We not only publish unsolicited freelance writing, we depend on it. Our last issue in December is dedicated to original fiction."

$ $ $ CHICAGO SOCIAL, Chicago's Monthly Social Magazine, Prairie City Media, 727 N. Hudson Ave., #001, Chicago IL 60610. (312)787-4600. Fax: (312)787-4628. Publisher: Michael Blaise Kong. Editor-in-Chief: Royaa G. Silver. **Contact:** Gina Bozer, senior editor. **70% freelance written.** Monthly Luxury lifestyle magazine. "We cover the good things in life—fashion, fine dining, the arts, etc.—from a sophisticated, cosmopolitan, well-to-do perspective." Circ. 75,000. Pays 2 months after receipt of invoice. Byline given. Offers kill fee. Buys Buys first rights and all rights in this market. Editorial lead time 6 months. Submit seasonal material 6 months in advance. Responds in 1 month to queries. Sample copy for $7.15 for current issue; $8.20 for back issue. Writer's guidelines for #10 SASE.

Nonfiction: General interest, how-to (gardening, culinary, home design), interview/profile, photo feature (occasional), travel. No fiction. *No unsolicited mss.* Query with published clips only. Length: 500-4,500 words. **Pays $50-900.** Pays expenses of writers on assignment.

Photos: State availability with submission. Reviews transparencies, prints. Buys one-time rights. We pay for film and processing only.

Columns/Departments: Few Minutes With (Q&A), 800 words; City Art, Home Design, 2,000 words. Query with published clips only. **Pays $150-400.**

Tips: "Send résumé, clips and story ideas. Mention interest and expertise in cover letter. We need writers who are knowledgeable about home design, architecture, art, culinary arts, entertainment, fashion and retail."

N $ $ $ CITYTALK, Window To The World Communications, Inc., 5400 N. St. Louis Ave., Chicago IL 60625-4698. (773)583-5000. Fax: (773)509-5645. E-mail: citytalk@networkchicago.com. **Contact:** Robert S. Gallagher, editor. **60% freelance written.** Weekly newspaper mailed to members/supporters of WFMT and WTTW. Covers Chicago's arts, entertainment and culture. "We're looking for well-structured, sharply focused stories told with wit and a distinct point of view, with an emphasis on good writing." Estab. 2000. Circ. 183,000. Pays 2-3 weeks after receipt of invoice. Publishes ms an average of 1 month after acceptance. Byline given. Offers 50% kill fee. Buys first North American serial, electronic rights. Editorial lead time 5 weeks. Accepts queries by mail, e-mail, fax, phone. Responds in 2 weeks to queries. Sample copy free. Writer's guidelines for free or online.

Nonfiction: Book excerpts, essays, general interest, historical/nostalgic, humor, interview/profile, opinion, photo feature, travel. No hard news reports, crime stories or fiction. **Buys 700 mss/year.** Query with published clips. Length: 290-2,000 words. **Pays 50¢-$1/word.** Sometimes pays expenses of writers on assignment.

Reprints: Accepts previously published submissions.

Photos: State availability with submission. Reviews contact sheets, negatives, transparencies. Buys one-time rights. Negotiates payment individually. Captions, identification of subjects required.

$ ☒ ILLINOIS ENTERTAINER, Chicago's Music Monthly, Roberts Publishing, Inc., 124 W. Polk, #103, Chicago IL 60605. (312)922-9333. Fax: (312)922-9369. E-mail: ieeditors@aol.com. Website: www.illinoisentertainer.com. **Contact:** Michael C. Harris, editor. **80% freelance written.** Monthly free magazine covering "popular and alternative music, as well as other entertainment: film, theater, media." "We're more interested in new, unknown artists. Also, we cover lots of Chicago-area artists." Estab. 1974. Circ. 75,000. Pays on publication. Publishes ms an average of 2 months after acceptance. Byline given. Offers 50% kill fee. Buys first North American serial rights. Editorial lead time 2 months. Submit seasonal material 2 months in advance. Accepts queries by mail. Accepts simultaneous submissions. Responds in 2 months to queries. Sample copy for $5.

Nonfiction: Exposé, how-to, humor, interview/profile, new product, reviews. No personal, confessional, inspirational articles. **Buys 75 mss/year.** Query with published clips. Length: 600-2,600 words. **Pays $15-160.** Sometimes pays expenses of writers on assignment.

Reprints: Send typed ms with rights for sale noted and information about when and where the material previously appeared. Pays 100% of amount paid for an original article.

Photos: Send photos with submission. Reviews contact sheets, transparencies, 5×7 prints. Buys one-time rights. Offers $20-200/photo. Captions, identification of subjects, model releases required.

Columns/Departments: Spins (LP reviews), 250-300 words. **Buys 200-300 mss/year.** Query with published clips. **Pays $15.**

▨ The online magazine carries original content not found in the print edition. Contact: Michael C. Harris.

Tips: "Send clips, résumé, etc. and be patient. Also, sending queries that show you've seen our magazine and have a feel for it greatly increases your publication chances."

Ⓝ $ NEAR WEST GAZETTE, Near West Gazette Publishing Co., 1335 W. Harrison St., Suite 301, Chicago IL 60607. (312)243-4288. Editor: Mark J. Valentino. **Contact:** William S. Bike and Gail Mansfield, associate editors. **50% freelance written.** Works with new/unpublished writers. Monthly newspaper covering Near West Side of Chicago, West Loop and South Loop/Dearborn Park community. News and issues for residents, students and faculty of the neighborhood bordering the University of Illinois of Chicago. Estab. 1983. Circ. 10,000. Pays on publication. Publishes ms an average of 1 month after acceptance. Byline given. Buys one-time, simultaneous rights. Submit seasonal material 2 months in advance. Accepts simultaneous submissions. Responds in 5 weeks to queries. Sample copy for 11×14 SAE and 4 first-class stamps.

Nonfiction: Essays, exposé, general interest, historical/nostalgic, humor, inspirational, interview/profile, opinion, personal experience, religious, sports (must be related to Near West Side/West Loop/South Loop communities). Special issues: Christmas. No product promotions. **Buys 60 mss/year.** Length: 300-1,800 words. **Pays $60 for assigned articles.** Sometimes pays expenses of writers on assignment.

Reprints: Send photocopy and information about when and where the material previously appeared. Pays $60.

Photos: Send photos with submission. Reviews 5×7 prints. Buys one-time rights. Offers no additional payment for photos accepted with ms. Identification of subjects required.

Columns/Departments: Forum (opinion), 750 words; Streets (Near West Side/West Loop/South Loop history), 500 words. **Buys 12 mss/year.** Query. **Pays $60.**

Ⓝ $ $ NEWCITY, Chicago's News and Arts Weekly, New City Communications, Inc., 770 N. Halsted, Chicago IL 60622. (312)243-8786. Fax: (312)243-8802. E-mail: elaine@newcitynet.com. Website: www.newcitychicago.com. Editor: Brian Hieggelke. **Contact:** Elaine Richardson, managing editor. **50% freelance written.** Weekly magazine. Estab. 1986. Circ. 65,000. Pays 60 days after publication. Publishes ms an average of 1 month after acceptance. Byline given. Offers 20% kill fee in certain cases. Buys first rights and non-exclusive electronic rights. Editorial lead time 2 months. Submit seasonal material 2 months in advance. Accepts queries by e-mail. Responds in 1 month to mss. Sample copy for $3. Writer's guidelines for #10 SASE.

Nonfiction: Essays, exposé, general interest, interview/profile, personal experience, travel (related to traveling from Chicago and other issues particularly affecting travelers from this area), service. **Buys 100 mss/year.** Query by e-mail only. Length: 100-4,000 words. **Pays $15-450.** Rarely pays expenses of writers on assignment.

Photos: State availability with submission. Reviews contact sheets. Buys one-time rights. Captions, identification of subjects, model releases required.

Columns/Departments: Lit (literary supplement), 300-2,000 words; Music, Film, Arts (arts criticism), 150-800 words; Chow (food writing), 300-2,000 words. **Buys 50 mss/year.** Query by e-mail. **Pays $15-300.**

■ The online magazine carries original content not found in the print edition. Contact: Elaine Richardson, online editor.

Tips: "E-mail a solid, sharply written query that has something to do with what our magazine publishes."

Indiana

N **$** **$** EVANSVILLE LIVING, Tucker Publishing Group, 100 NW Second St., Suite 203, Evansville IN 47715-5725. (812)426-2115. Fax: (812)426-2134. E-mail: ktucker@evansvillelivingmagazine.com. Website: www.evansvilleli vingmagazine.com. **Contact:** Kristen Tucker, editor/publisher. **80-100% freelance written.** Bimonthly magazine covering Evansville, Indiana, and the greater area. "*Evansville Living* is the only full-color, glossy, 100+ page city magazine for the Evansville, Indiana, area. Regular departments include: Home Style, Garden Style, Day Tripping, Sporting Life, and Local Flavor (menus)." Estab. 2000. Circ. 50,000. **Pays on acceptance.** Publishes ms an average of 3 months after acceptance. Byline given. Buys all rights. Editorial lead time 6 months. Submit seasonal material 6 months in advance. Accepts queries by mail, e-mail, fax. Sample copy for $5 or online. Writer's guidelines for free or by e-mail.
Nonfiction: Essays, general interest, historical/nostalgic, photo feature, travel. **Buys 60-80 mss/year.** Query with published clips. Length: 200-600 words. **Pays $100-300.** Sometimes pays expenses of writers on assignment.
Reprints: Accepts previously published submissions.
Photos: State availability with submission. Reviews contact sheets, negatives, transparencies, prints. Buys all rights. Negotiates payment individually. Captions, identification of subjects required.
Columns/Departments: Home Style (home); Garden Style (garden); Sporting Life (sports); Local Flavor (menus), all 1,500 words. Query with published clips. **Pays $100-300.**

$** **$ INDIANAPOLIS MONTHLY, Emmis Publishing Corp., 40 Monument Circle, Suite 100, Indianapolis IN 46204. (317)237-9288. Fax: (317)684-2080. Website: www.indianapolismonthly.com. **Contact:** Rebecca Poynor Burns, editor. **30% freelance written.** Prefers to work with published/established writers. "*Indianapolis Monthly* attracts and enlightens its upscale, well-educated readership with bright, lively editorial on subjects ranging from personalities to social issues, fashion to food. Its diverse content and attention to service make it the ultimate source by which the Indianapolis area lives." Estab. 1977. Circ. 45,000. Pays on publication. Publishes ms an average of 2 months after acceptance. Byline given. Offers negotiable kill fee. Buys first North American serial, one-time rights. Editorial lead time 3 months. Submit seasonal material 3 months in advance. Accepts queries by mail, e-mail. Accepts simultaneous submissions. Responds in 3 weeks to queries. Sample copy for $6.10.
● This magazine is using more first-person essays, but they must have a strong Indianapolis or Indiana tie. It will consider nonfiction book excerpts of material relevant to its readers.
Nonfiction: Must have a strong Indianapolis or Indiana angle. Book excerpts (by Indiana authors or with strong Indiana ties), essays, exposé, general interest, interview/profile, photo feature. No poetry, fiction or domestic humor; no "How Indy Has Changed Since I Left Town," "An Outsider's View of the 500," or generic material with no or little tie to Indianapolis/Indiana. **Buys 35 mss/year.** Query by mail with published clips. Length: 200-3,000 words. **Pays $50-600.**
Reprints: Send typed ms with rights for sale noted and information about when and where the material previously appeared. *Accepts reprints only from non-competing markets.*
Photos: State availability with submission. Reviews upon request. Buys one-time rights. Negotiates payment individually. Captions, identification of subjects, model releases required.
Tips: "Our standards are simultaneously broad and narrow: broad in that we're a general interest magazine spanning a wide spectrum of topics, narrow in that we buy only stories with a heavy emphasis on Indianapolis (and, to a lesser extent, Indiana). Simply inserting an Indy-oriented paragraph into a generic national article won't get it: all stories must pertain primarily to things Hoosier. Once you've cleared that hurdle, however, it's a wide-open field. We've done features on national celebrities—Indianapolis native David Letterman and *Mir* astronaut David Wolf of Indianapolis, to name two—and we've published two-paragraph items on such quirky topics as an Indiana gardening supply house that sells insects by mail. Query with clips showing lively writing and solid reporting. No phone queries please."

Kansas

$** **$ KANSAS!, Kansas Department of Commerce and Housing, 700 SW Harrison St., Suite 1300, Topeka KS 66603-3712. (785)296-3479. Fax: (785)296-6988. E-mail: ksmagazine@kdoch.state.ks.us. **90% freelance written.** Quarterly magazine emphasizing Kansas travel attractions and events. Estab. 1945. Circ. 52,000. **Pays on acceptance.** Publishes ms an average of 1 year after acceptance. Byline given. Buys one-time rights. Submit seasonal material 8 months in advance. Accepts queries by mail. Responds in 2 months to queries. Sample copy and writer's guidelines available.
Nonfiction: "Material must be Kansas-oriented and have good potential for color photographs. The focus is on travel with articles about places and events that can be enjoyed by the general public. In other words, events must be open to the public, places also. Query letter should clearly outline story. We are especially interested in Kansas freelancers who can supply their own quality photos." General interest, photo feature, travel. Query by mail. Length: 750-1,250 words. **Pays $200-400.** Pays mileage and lodging of writers on assignment.

Photos: "We are a full-color photo/manuscript publication." Send photos (original transparencies only) with query. Pays $50-75 (generally included in ms rate) for 35mm or larger format transparencies. Captions required.

Tips: "History and nostalgia stories do not fit into our format because they can't be illustrated well with color photos. Submit a query letter describing one appropriate idea with outline for possible article and suggestions for photos."

Kentucky

$ BACK HOME IN KENTUCKY, Back Home in Kentucky Inc., P.O. Box 710, Clay City KY 40312-0710. (606)663-1011. Fax: (606)663-1808. E-mail: backhome@mis.net. **Contact:** Jerlene Rose, editor/publisher. **50% freelance written.** Bimonthly magazine "covering Kentucky heritage, people, places, events. We reach Kentuckians and 'displaced' Kentuckians living outside the state." Estab. 1977. Circ. 8,000. Pays on publication. Publishes ms an average of 6 months after acceptance. Byline given. Buys first North American serial rights. Submit seasonal material 6 months in advance. Responds in 2 months to queries. Sample copy for $3 and 9×12 SAE with $1.18 postage affixed. Writer's guidelines for #10 SASE.
  • Interested in profiles of Kentucky gardeners, cooks, craftspeople.

Nonfiction: Historical/nostalgic (Kentucky-related eras or profiles), photo feature (Kentucky places and events), travel (unusual/little known Kentucky places), profiles (Kentucky cooks, gardeners and craftspersons), memories (Kentucky related). No inspirational or religion. **Buys 25 mss/year.** Query with or without published clips or send complete ms. Length: 500-2,000 words. **Pays $50-150 for assigned articles; $25-75 for unsolicited articles.** "In addition to normal payment, writers receive 4 copies of issue containing their article."

Reprints: Send tearsheet and information about when and where the material previously appeared. Pays 50% of amount paid for an original article.

Photos: Send photos with submission. Reviews transparencies. Also looking for color transparencies for covers (inquire for specific topics). Vertical format. Pays $50-150. Photo credits given. Rights purchased depends on situation. Occasionally offers additional payment for photos accepted with ms. Identification of subjects, model releases required.

Columns/Departments: Travel, crafts, gardeners and cooks (all Kentucky), 500-750 words. **Buys 10-12 mss/year.** Query with published clips. **Pays $15-40.**

Tips: "We work mostly with unpublished writers who have a feel for Kentucky's people, places and events. Areas most open are little known places in Kentucky, unusual history and profiles of interesting Kentuckians, and Kentuckians with unusual hobbies or crafts."

$ $KENTUCKY LIVING, P.O. Box 32170, Louisville KY 40232-0170. (502)451-2430. Fax: (502)459-1611. **Contact:** Paul Wesslund, editor. Mostly freelance written. Prefers to work with published/established writers. Monthly feature magazine primarily for Kentucky residents. Estab. 1948. Circ. 450,000. **Pays on acceptance.** Publishes ms an average of 12 months after acceptance. Byline given. Buys first serial rights for Kentucky. Submit seasonal material at least 6 months in advance. Accepts simultaneous submissions. Responds in 1 month to queries. Sample copy for 9×12 SAE and 4 first-class stamps.

Nonfiction: Kentucky-related profiles (people, places or events), recreation, travel, leisure, lifestyle articles, book excerpts. **Buys 18-24 mss/year.** Query with or without published clips or send complete ms. **Pays $75-125 for "short" features (600-800 words); pays $150-350 for major articles (750-1,500 words).** Sometimes pays expenses of writers on assignment.

Photos: State availability of or send photos with submission. Reviews color slides and prints. Payment for photos included in payment for ms. Identification of subjects required.

Tips: "The quality of writing and reporting (factual, objective, thorough) is considered in setting payment price. We prefer general interest pieces filled with quotes and anecdotes. Avoid boosterism. Well-researched, well-written feature articles are preferred. All articles must have a strong Kentucky connection."

$ $KENTUCKY MONTHLY, Vested Interest Publications, 213 St. Clair St., Frankfort KY 40601. (502)227-0053. Fax: (502)227-5009. E-mail: membry@kentuckymonthly.com. Website: www.kentuckymonthly.com. Editor: Stephen M. Vest. **Contact:** Michael Embry, executive editor. **75% freelance written.** Monthly magazine. "We publish stories about Kentucky and Kentuckians, including those who live elsewhere." Estab. 1998. Circ. 30,000. Pays within 90 days of publication. Publishes ms an average of 3 months after acceptance. Byline given. Buys first North American serial rights. Editorial lead time 3 months. Submit seasonal material 4 months in advance. Accepts queries by mail, e-mail, fax. Accepts simultaneous submissions. Responds in 2 weeks to queries; 1 month to mss. Sample copy and writer's guidelines online.

Nonfiction: Book excerpts, general interest, historical/nostalgic, how-to, humor, interview/profile, photo feature, religious, travel, all with a Kentucky angle. **Buys 60 mss/year.** Query with or without published clips. Length: 300-2,000 words. **Pays $25-350 for assigned articles; $20-100 for unsolicited articles.**

Photos: State availability with submission. Reviews negatives. Buys all rights. Captions required.

Fiction: Adventure, historical, mainstream, novel excerpts, all Kentucky-related stories. **Buys 10 mss/year.** Query with published clips. Length: 1,000-5,000 words. **Pays $50-100.**

Tips: "We're looking for more fashion, home and garden, first-person experience, mystery. Please read the magazine to get the flavor of what we're publishing each month. We accept articles via e-mail, fax and mail."

$ $ LOUISVILLE MAGAZINE, 137 W. Muhammad Ali Blvd., Suite 101, Louisville KY 40202-1438. (502)625-0100. Fax: (502)625-0109. E-mail: loumag@loumag.com. Website: www.louisville.com. **Contact:** Bruce Allar, editor. **60% freelance written.** Monthly magazine "for and generally about people of the Louisville Metro area. Routinely covers arts, entertainment, business, sports, dining and fashion. Features range from news analysis/exposé to silly/funny commentary. We like lean, clean prose, crisp leads." Estab. 1950. Circ. 20,000. Publishes ms an average of 3 months after acceptance. Byline given. Offers 50% kill fee. Buys first North American serial rights. Editorial lead time 6 weeks. Submit seasonal material 6 months in advance. Accepts queries by mail, e-mail, fax. Responds in 3 months to queries. Sample copy for $2.95 or online.

Nonfiction: Essays, exposé, general interest, historical/nostalgic, interview/profile, photo feature. Special issues: City Guide (January); Kentucky Derby (April); EATS (September); Louisville Bride (December). **Buys 75 mss/year.** Query. Length: 500-3,500 words. **Pays $50-500 for assigned articles; $50-400 for unsolicited articles.**

Photos: State availability with submission. Reviews transparencies. Buys one-time rights. Offers $25-50/photo. Identification of subjects required.

Columns/Departments: End Insight (essays), 750 words. **Buys 10 mss/year.** Send complete ms. **Pays $100-150.**

Maine

[N] $ ISLESBORO ISLAND NEWS, P.O. Box 104, Islesboro ME 04848. (207)734-6921. Fax: (207)734-6519. E-mail: iinews@mint.net. **Contact:** Brenda Craig, publisher. **10% freelance written.** Monthly tabloid on the people and island of Islesboro. Estab. 1985. **Pays on acceptance.** Byline given. Buys one-time rights. Accepts queries by mail, fax. Sample copy for $4. Writer's guidelines for #10 SASE.

Nonfiction: Articles about contemporary issues on Islesboro, historical/nostalgic pieces, personality profiles, arts, lifestyles and businesses on Islesboro. Any story must have a definite Maine island connection. No travel pieces. Query or send complete ms. **Pays $20-50.**

Reprints: Send typed ms with rights for sale noted. Pay varies.

Photos: Send photos with submission.

Tips: "Writers must know the Penobscot Bay Islands. We are not interested in pieces of a generic island nature. We want things about Islesboro."

[N] $ $ MAINE TIMES, Maine Times Publishing Co., P.O. Box 2129, Bangor ME 04402. (207)947-4410. Fax: (207)947-4458. E-mail: mainetimes@mainetimes.com. Website: www.mainetimes.com. **Contact:** Jay Davis, editor. **50% freelance written.** Weekly tabloid covering the state of Maine. "*Maine Times* is a newspaper with stories long and short on the environment, politics, events, the arts, the Maine lifestyle. We look for good writing." Estab. 1968. Circ. 7,500. Pays on publication. Byline given. Offers negotiable kill fee. "For assigned stories we buy the material but follow a liberal reprint policy. For submitted pieces we pay for one-time rights." Submit seasonal material 2 months in advance. Accepts queries by mail, e-mail, fax. Sample copy free.

Nonfiction: Essays, opinion, personal experience, reviews. All articles must be queried in advance. **Buys 100 mss/year. Pays $50-800.**

Columns/Departments: Back of the Book (personal essays about Maine—high standard), 700-1,000 words; Other Voices (opinion pieces), 700-1,000 words; Reviews (books, plays, etc.), 400-600 words. **Buys 100 mss/year.** Query or send complete ms. **Pays $50-75.**

Poetry: Catherine Russell, features editor. Accepts all good poetry. **Buys 30 poems/year. Pays $50.**

Tips: "*Maine Times* is a lively, well-written weekly that explores Maine in its many forums. We love to publish fine personal essays and opinion pieces that inform our appreciation of Maine."

Maryland

$ $ $ $ BALTIMORE MAGAZINE, Inner Harbor East 1000 Lancaster St., Suite 400, Baltimore MD 21202. (410)752-4200. Fax: (410)625-0280. Website: www.baltimoremag.com. **Contact:** Ken Iglehart, managing editor. **50-60% freelance written.** Monthly "Pieces must address an educated, active, affluent reader and must have a very strong Baltimore angle." Estab. 1907. Circ. 57,000. Pays within 60 days of acceptance. Byline given. Buys first rights in all media. Submit seasonal material 4 months in advance. Accepts queries by mail, e-mail. Responds in 2 months to queries; 3 months to mss. Sample copy for $4.45. Writer's guidelines for #10 SASE.

> **O–** Break in through "Baltimore Inc., and B-Side—these are our shortest, newsiest sections and we depend heavily on tips and reporting from strangers. Please note that we are exclusively local. Submissions without a Baltimore angle may be ignored."

Nonfiction: Book excerpts (Baltimore subject or author), essays, exposé, general interest, historical/nostalgic, humor, interview/profile (with a Baltimorean), new product, personal experience, photo feature, travel (local and regional to Maryland *only*). "Nothing that lacks a strong Baltimore focus or angle." Query by mail with published clips or send complete ms. Length: 1,000-3,000 words. **Pays $25-2,500 for assigned articles; $25-500 for unsolicited articles.** Sometimes pays expenses of writers on assignment.

Columns/Departments: Hot Shot, Health, Education, Sports. Length: 1,000-5,000 words. "The shorter pieces are the best places to break into the magazine." Query with published clips.

■ The online magazine carries original content not found in the print edition. Contact: Mary-Rose Nelson, online editor.

Tips: "Writers who live in the Baltimore area can send résumé and published clips to be considered for first assignment. Must show an understanding of writing that is suitable to an educated magazine reader and show ability to write with authority, describe scenes, help reader experience the subject. Too many writers send us newspaper-style articles. We are seeking: 1) *Human interest features*—strong, even dramatic profiles of Baltimoreans of interest to our readers. 2) *First-person accounts* of experience in Baltimore, or experiences of a Baltimore resident. 3) *Consumer*—according to our editorial needs, and with Baltimore sources. Writers new to us have most success with small humorous stories and 1,000-word personal essays that exhibit risky, original thought."

Massachusetts

BOSTON GLOBE MAGAZINE, Boston Globe, P.O. Box 2378, Boston MA 02107. (617)929-2955. Website: www.gl obe.com/globe/magazine. Assistant Editors: Catherine Foster, Jan Freeman. **Contact:** Nick King, editor-in-chief. **50% freelance written.** Weekly magazine. Circ. 726,830. Pays on publication. Publishes ms an average of 2 months after acceptance. Buys non-exclusive electronic rights. Editorial lead time 2 months. Submit seasonal material 3 months in advance. Sample copy for 9×12 SAE and 2 first-class stamps.

Nonfiction: Book excerpts (first serial rights only), essays (variety of issues including political, economic, scientific, medical, and the arts), interview/profile (not Q&A). No travelogs, poetry, personal essays or fiction. **Buys up to 100 mss/year.** Query; SASE must be included with ms or queries for return. Length: 1,500-4,000 words. **Payment negotiable.**

Photos: Purchased with accompanying ms or on assignment. Reviews contact sheets. Pays standard rates according to size used. Captions required.

$ $ $ $ BOSTON MAGAZINE, 300 Massachusetts Ave., Boston MA 02115. (617)262-9700. Fax: (617)267-1774. Website: www.bostonmagazine.com. **Contact:** Jon Marcus, executive editor. **10% freelance written.** Monthly magazine covering the city of Boston. Estab. 1972. Circ. 125,000. Pays on publication. Publishes ms an average of 3 months after acceptance. Byline given. Offers 20% kill fee. Buys first North American serial rights. Editorial lead time 2 months. Submit seasonal material 4 months in advance. Accepts queries by mail, fax. Responds in 2 weeks to queries.

Nonfiction: Book excerpts, exposé, general interest, interview/profile, politics, crime, trends, fashion. **Buys 20 mss/ year.** Query. *No unsolicited mss.* Length: 1,200-12,000 words. Sometimes pays expenses of writers on assignment.

Photos: State availability with submission. Buys one-time rights. Negotiates payment individually.

Columns/Departments: Dining, Finance, City Life, Personal Style, Politics, Ivory Tower, Media, Wine, Boston Inc., Books, Theatre, Music. Query.

Tips: "Read *Boston*, and pay attention to the types of stories we use. Suggest which column/department your story might best fit, and keep your focus on the city and its environs. We like a strong narrative style, with a slightly 'edgy' feel—we rarely do 'remember when' stories. Think *city* magazine."

N: $ $ CAPE COD LIFE, including Martha's Vineyard and Nantucket, Cape Cod Life, Inc., P.O. Box 1385, Pocasset MA 02559-1385. (508)564-4466. Fax: (508)564-4470. E-mail: apetrucelli@capecodlife.com. Website: www.capecodlife.com. Editor: Brian F. Shortsleeve. **Contact:** Alan W. Petrucelli, managing editor. **80% freelance written.** Bimonthly magazine focusing on "area lifestyle, history and culture, people and places, business and industry, and issues and answers for year-round and summer residents of Cape Cod, Nantucket and Martha's Vineyard as well as non-residents who spend their leisure time here." Circ. 45,000. Pays 30 days after publication. Byline given. Offers 20% kill fee. Buys first North American serial rights, makes work-for-hire assignments. Submit seasonal material 6 months in advance. Accepts queries by mail, e-mail, fax. Responds in 3 months to queries; 3 months to mss. Sample copy for $5. Writer's guidelines for #10 SASE.

Nonfiction: Book excerpts, general interest, historical/nostalgic, interview/profile, new product, photo feature, travel, gardening, marine, nautical, nature, arts, antiques. **Buys 20 mss/year.** Query with or without published clips. Length: 1,000-3,000 words. **Pays $100-500.**

Photos: Photo guidelines for #10 SASE. first rights with right to reprint. Pays $25-225. Captions, identification of subjects required.

■ The online magazine carries original content not found in the print edition. Contact: Amy Berka, online editor.

Tips: "Freelancers submitting *quality* spec articles with a Cape Cod and Islands angle have a good chance at publication. We like to see a wide selection of writer's clips before giving assignments. We accept more spec work written about Cape Cod and Islands history than any other subject. We also publish *Cape Cod Home: Living and Gardening on the Cape and Islands* covering architecture, landscape design and interior design with a Cape and Islands focus."

$ $ PROVINCETOWN ARTS, Provincetown Arts, Inc., 650 Commercial St., Provincetown MA 02657. (508)487-3167. Fax: (508)487-8634. Website: www.capecodaccess.com. **Contact:** Christopher Busa, editor. **90% freelance written.** Annual magazine covering contemporary art and writing. "*Provincetown Arts* focuses broadly on the artists and writers who inhabit or visit the Lower Cape, and seeks to stimulate creative activity and enhance public awareness of the cultural life of the nation's oldest continuous art colony. Drawing upon a 75-year tradition rich in visual art, literature and theater, *Provincetown Arts* offers a unique blend of interviews, fiction, visual features, reviews, reporting and poetry." Estab. 1985. Circ. 8,000. Pays on publication. Publishes ms an average of 4 months after acceptance. Offers 50% kill fee. Buys one-time, second serial (reprint) rights. Editorial lead time 6 months. Submit seasonal material 6 months in advance. Responds in 3 weeks to queries; 2 months to mss. Sample copy for $10. Writer's guidelines for #10 SASE.

Nonfiction: Book excerpts, essays, humor, interview/profile. **Buys 40 mss/year.** Send complete ms. Length: 1,500-4,000 words. **Pays $150 minimum for assigned articles; $125 minimum for unsolicited articles.**

Photos: Send photos with submission. Reviews 8 × 10 prints. Buys one-time rights. Offers $20-$100/photo. Identification of subjects required.

Fiction: Mainstream, novel excerpts. **Buys 7 mss/year.** Send complete ms. Length: 500-5,000 words. **Pays $75-300.**

Poetry: **Buys 25 poems/year.** Submit maximum 3 poems. **Pays $25-150.**

$ $ WORCESTER MAGAZINE, 172 Shrewsbury St., Worcester MA 01604-4636. (508)755-8004. Fax: (508)755-4734. E-mail: editorial@worcestermag.com. Website: www.worcestermag.com. **Contact:** Marc Onigman, editor. **10% freelance written.** Weekly tabloid emphasizing the central Massachusetts region, especially the city of Worcester. Estab. 1976. Circ. 40,000. Pays on publication. Publishes ms an average of 3 weeks after acceptance. Byline given. Buys all rights. Submit seasonal material 2 months in advance. Accepts queries by mail, e-mail, fax. Does not respond to unsolicited material to mss.

  O—π Break in with "back of the book arts and entertainment articles."

Nonfiction: "We are interested in any piece with a local angle." Essays, exposé (area government, corporate), general interest, historical/nostalgic, humor, opinion (local), personal experience, photo feature, religious, interview (local). **Buys 75 mss/year.** Length: 500-1,500 words. **Pays 10¢/ word.**

Michigan

$ $ $ ANN ARBOR OBSERVER, Ann Arbor Observer Company, 201 E. Catherine, Ann Arbor MI 48104. Fax: (734)769-3375. E-mail: hilton@aaobserver.com. Website: www.arborweb.com. **Contact:** John Hilton, editor. **50% freelance written.** Monthly magazine. "We depend heavily on freelancers and we're always glad to talk to new ones. We look for the intelligence and judgment to fully explore complex people and situations, and the ability to convey what makes them interesting. We've found that professional writing experience is not a good predictor of success in writing for the *Observer*. So don't let lack of experience deter you. Writing for the *Observer* is, however, a demanding job. Our readers range from U-M faculty members to hourly workers at GT Products. That means articles have to be both accurate and accessible." Estab. 1976. Circ. 63,000. Pays on publication. Publishes ms an average of 2 months after acceptance. Byline given. Accepts queries by mail, e-mail, fax, phone. Responds in 3 weeks to queries; several months to mss. Sample copy for 12½ × 15 SAE with $3 postage. Writer's guidelines for #10 SASE.

Nonfiction: Historical, investigative features, profiles, brief vignettes. Must pertain to Ann Arbor. **Buys 75 mss/year.** Length: 100-7,000 words. **Pays up to $1,000.** Sometimes pays expenses of writers on assignment.

Columns/Departments: Inside Ann Arbor (short, interesting tidbits), 300-500 words. **Pays $125.** Around Town (unusual, compelling ancedotes), 750-1,500 words. **Pays $150-200.**

Tips: "If you have an idea for a story, write a 100-200-word description telling us why the story is interesting. We are open most to intelligent, insightful features of up to 5,000 words about interesting aspects of life in Ann Arbor."

[N] $ GRAND RAPIDS MAGAZINE, Gemini Corp., 549 Ottawa NW, Grand Rapids MI 49503. (616)549-4545. Fax: (616)459-4800. **Contact:** Carole Valade, editor. "*Grand Rapids* is a general interest magazine designed for those who live in the Grand Rapids metropolitan area or desire to maintain contact with the community." Estab. 1964. Pays on publication. Byline given. Editorial lead time 2 months. Submit seasonal material 2 months in advance. Sample copy for $2 and an SASE with $1.50 postage. Writer's guidelines for #10 SASE.

Nonfiction: "*Grand Rapids Magazine* is approximately 60 percent service articles—dining guide, calendar, travel, personal finance, humor and reader service sections—and 40 percent topical and issue-oriented editorial that centers on people, politics, problems and trends in the region." Query. **Pays $25-100.** Pays some expenses of writers on assignment.

$ HOUR DETROIT, Hour Media LLC, 117 W. Third St., Royal Oak MI 48067. (248)691-1800. Fax: (248)691-4531. E-mail: rbohy@hourdetroit.com. Managing Editor: George Bulanda. Senior Editor: Rebecca Powers. **Contact:** Ric Bohy, editor. **50% freelance written.** Monthly magazine. "General interest/lifestyle magazine aimed at a middle-to upper-income readership aged 17-70." Estab. 1996. Circ. 45,000. **Pays on acceptance.** Publishes ms an average of 2 months after acceptance. Byline given. Offers 30% kill fee. Buys first North American serial rights. Editorial lead time 1½ months. Submit seasonal material 12 months in advance. Accepts queries by mail, e-mail, fax. Sample copy for $6.

Nonfiction: Book excerpts, exposé, general interest, historical/nostalgic, interview/profile, new product, photo feature, technical, travel. **Buys 150 mss/year.** Query with published clips. Length: 300-2,500 words. Sometimes pays expenses of writers on assignment.

Photos: State availability with submission.

$ $ TRAVERSE, Northern Michigan's Magazine, Prism Publications, 148 E. Front St., Traverse City MI 49684. Fax: (231)941-8391. E-mail: traverse@traversemagazine.com. Website: www.traversemagazine.com. **Contact:** Jeff Smith, editor. **20% freelance written.** Monthly magazine covering northern Michigan life. "*Traverse* is a celebration of the life and environment of northern Michigan." Estab. 1981. Circ. 30,000. **Pays on acceptance.** Byline given. Offers 10% kill fee. Buys first North American serial rights. Editorial lead time 1 year. Submit seasonal material 1 year in advance. Accepts queries by mail, e-mail, fax, phone. Accepts simultaneous submissions. Responds in 2 months to queries. Sample copy for $3. Writer's guidelines for #10 SASE.
Nonfiction: Book excerpts, essays, general interest, historical/nostalgic, humor, interview/profile, personal experience, photo feature, travel. No fiction or poetry. **Buys 24 mss/year.** Query with published clips or send complete ms. Length: 1,000-3,200 words. **Pays $150-500.** Sometimes pays expenses of writers on assignment.
Photos: State availability with submission. Buys one-time rights. Negotiates payment individually.
Columns/Departments: Up in Michigan Reflection (essays about northern Michigan); Reflection on Home (essays about northern homes), both 700 words. **Buys 18 mss/year.** Query with published clips or send complete ms. **Pays $100-200.**
Tips: "When shaping an article for us, consider first that it must be strongly rooted in our region. The lack of this foundation element is one of the biggest reasons for our rejecting material. If you send us a piece about peaches, even if it does an admirable job of relaying the history of peaches, their medicinal qualities, their nutritional magnificence and so on, we are likely to reject if it doesn't include local farms as a reference point. We want sidebars and extended captions designed to bring in a reader not enticed by the main subject. Primarily we cover the Northwest Michigan counties of Antrim, Benzie, Charlevoix, Crawford, Emmet, Grand Traverse, Leelanau, Manistee, Otsego, Cheboygan and Mackinac. We have begun to venture beyond our traditional turf, however, and are periodically running pieces based in the eastern Lower Peninsula and the eastern Upper Peninsula. We are willing to look farther west in the Upper Peninsula if the topic has broad appeal. General categories of interest include nature and the environment, regional culture, personalities, the arts (visual, performing, literary), crafts, food & dining, homes, history and outdoor activities (e.g., fishing, golf, skiing, boating, biking, hiking, birding, gardening). We are keenly interested in environmental and land-use issues but seldom use material dealing with such issues as health care, education, social services, criminal justice and local politics. We use service pieces and a small number of how-to pieces, mostly focused on small projects for the home or yard. Also, we value research. We need articles built with information. Many of the pieces we reject use writing style to fill in for information voids. Style and voice are strongest when used as vehicles for sound research."

Minnesota

$ $ LAKE COUNTRY JOURNAL MAGAZINE, Evergreen Press of Brainerd, 1863 Design Dr., Baxter MN 56425. Fax: (218)825-7816. E-mail: jodi@lakecountryjournal.com. Website: www.lakecountryjournal.com. Contributing Editor: Linda Henry. **Contact:** Jodi Schwen, editor. **90% freelance written.** Bimonthly magazine covering central Minnesota's lake country. "We target a specific geographical niche in central Minnesota. The writer must be familiar with our area. We promote positive family values, foster a sense of community, increase appreciation for our natural and cultural environments, and provide ideas for enhancing the quality of our lives." Estab. 1996. Circ. 14,500. Pays on publication. Publishes ms an average of 6 months after acceptance. Byline given. Offers 25% kill fee. Buys first North American serial, second serial (reprint), electronic rights. Submit seasonal material 1 year in advance. Accepts queries by mail, e-mail. Responds in 2 months to queries; 3 months to mss. Sample copy for $5.
   O— Break in by "submitting department length first—they are not scheduled as far in advance as features. Always in need of original fillers."
Nonfiction: Essays, general interest, how-to, humor, interview/profile, personal experience, photo feature. "No articles that come from writers who are not familiar with our target geographical location." **Buys 30 mss/year.** Query with or without published clips. Length: 1,000-1,500 words. **Pays $100-175.** Sometimes pays expenses of writers on assignment.
Reprints: Accepts previously published submissions.
Photos: State availability with submission. Reviews transparencies. Buys one-time rights. Negotiates payment individually. Identification of subjects, model releases required.
Columns/Departments: Profile-People from Lake Country, 800 words; Essay, 800 words; Health (topics pertinent to central Minnesota living), 500 words; Family Fun, 500 words. **Buys 40 mss/year.** Query with published clips. **Pays $50-75.**
Fiction: Adventure, humorous, mainstream, slice-of-life vignettes, literary, also family fiction appropriate to Lake Country and seasonal fiction. **Buys 6 mss/year.** Send complete ms with SASE. Length: 1,500 words. **Pays $100-175.**
Poetry: Free verse. "Never use rhyming verse, avant-garde, experimental, etc." **Buys 20 poems/year.** Submit maximum 4 poems. Length: 8-32 lines. **Pays $25.**
Fillers: Anecdotes, short humor. **Buys 20/year.** Length: 100-500 words. **Pays $25.**
Tips: "Most of the people who will read your articles live in the north central Minnesota lakes area. All have some significant attachment to the area. We have readers of various ages, backgrounds, and lifestyles. After reading your article, we hope to have a deeper understanding of some aspect of our community, our environment, ourselves, or humanity in general. Tell us something new. Show us something we didn't see before. Help us grasp the significance

of your topic. Use analogies, allusions, and other literary techniques to add color to your writing. Add breadth by making the subject relevant to all readers—especially those who aren't already interested in your subject. Add depth by connecting your subject with timeless insights. If you can do this without getting sappy or didactic or wordy or dull, we're looking for you."

$ $ LAKE SUPERIOR MAGAZINE, Lake Superior Port Cities, Inc., P.O. Box 16417, Duluth MN 55816-0417. (218)722-5002. Fax: (218)722-4096. E-mail: edit@lakesuperior.com. Website: www.lakesuperior.com. Editor: Paul L. Hayden. **Contact:** Konnie LeMay, managing editor. **60% freelance written.** Works with a small number of new/unpublished writers each year. Please include phone number and address with e-mail queries. Bimonthly magazine covering contemporary and historic people, places and current events around Lake Superior. Estab. 1979. Circ. 20,000. Pays on publication. Publishes ms an average of 10 months after acceptance. Byline given. Buys first North American serial, second serial (reprint) rights. Submit seasonal material 1 year in advance. Accepts queries by mail, e-mail. Responds in 3 months to queries. Sample copy for $3.95 and 5 first-class stamps. Writer's guidelines for #10 SASE.
Nonfiction: Book excerpts, general interest, historical/nostalgic, humor, interview/profile (local), personal experience, photo feature (local), travel (local), city profiles, regional business, some investigative. **Buys 45 mss/year.** Query with published clips. Length: 300-2,200 words. **Pays $60-600.** Sometimes pays expenses of writers on assignment.
Photos: "Quality photography is our hallmark." Send photos with submission. Reviews contact sheets, 2x2 and larger transparencies, 4×5 prints. Offers $20 for b&w and $40 for color; $125 for covers. Captions, identification of subjects, model releases required.
Columns/Departments: Current events and things to do (for Events Calendar section), less than 300 words; Around The Circle (media reviews; short pieces on Lake Superior; Great Lakes environmental issues; themes, letters and short pieces on events and highlights of the Lake Superior Region); I Remember (nostalgic lake-specific pieces), up to 1,100 words; Life Lines (single personality profile with photography), up to 900 words. Other headings include Destinations, Nature, Wilderness Living, Heritage, Shipwreck, Chronicle, Lake Superior's Own, House for Sale. **Buys 20 mss/year.** Query with published clips. **Pays $60-90.**
Fiction: Ethnic, historic, humorous, mainstream, novel excerpts, slice-of-life vignettes, ghost stories. Must be targeted regionally. **Buys 2-3 mss/year.** Query with published clips. Length: 300-2,500 words. **Pays $1-125.**
   The online magazine carries original content not found in the print edition. Contact: Konnie Lemay, online editor.
Tips: "Well-researched queries are attended to. We actively seek queries from writers in Lake Superior communities. We prefer manuscripts to queries. Provide enough information on why the subject is important to the region and our readers, or why and how something is unique. We want details. The writer must have a thorough knowledge of the subject and how it relates to our region. We prefer a fresh, unused approach to the subject which provides the reader with an emotional involvement. Almost all of our articles feature quality photography, color or black and white. It is a prerequisite of all nonfiction. All submissions should include a *short* biography of author/photographer; mug shot sometimes used. Blanket submissions need not apply."

$ $ MINNESOTA MONTHLY, 10 S. Fifth St., Suite 1000, Minneapolis MN 55402. Fax: (612)371-5801. E-mail: phnettleton@mnmo.com. Website: www.mnmo.com. **Contact:** Pamela Hill Nettleton, editor. **50% freelance written.** "*Minnesota Monthly* is a regional lifestyle publication written for a sophisticated, well-educated audience living in the Twin Cities area and in greater Minnesota." Estab. 1967. Circ. 80,000. **Pays on acceptance.** Accepts queries by mail, e-mail. Writer's guidelines for #10 SASE.
Nonfiction: Regional issues, arts, services, places, people; essays (holiday, back page essays), book excerpts, exposé, general interest, historical/nostalgia, interview/profile, new product, photo feature, travel. "We want exciting, excellent, compelling writing with a strong Minnesota angle." Query with résumé, published clips and SASE. Length: 1,000-4,000 words. **Pay is negotiable.**
Columns/Departments: Portrait (photo-driven profile), 360 words; Just Asking (interview), 900 words; Midwest Traveler, 950-2,000 words; Postcards (chatty notes from Midwest towns), 300 words; Journey (diary/journal of a life-changing experience), 2,000 words. Query with résumé, published clips and SASE. **Pay negotiable.**
Fiction: Fiction in the June issue.
Tips: "Our readers are bright, artsy and involved in their communities. Writing should reflect that. Stories must all have a Minnesota angle. If you can write well, try us!"

Mississippi

$ $ MISSISSIPPI MAGAZINE, DownHome Publications, 5 Lakeland Circle, Jackson MS 39216. Fax: (601)982-8447. **Contact:** Jennifer Ellis, editor. **90% freelance written.** Bimonthly magazine covering Mississippi—the state and its lifestyles. "We are interested in positive stories reflecting Mississippi's rich traditions and heritage, and focusing on the contributions the state and its natives have made to the arts, literature and culture. In each issue we showcase homes and gardens, lifestyle issues, food, design, art and more." Estab. 1982. Circ. 30,000. Pays on publication. Publishes ms an average of 6 months after acceptance. Byline given. Offers 50% kill fee. Buys first North American serial rights. Editorial lead time 6 months. Submit seasonal material 1 year in advance. Accepts queries by mail, fax. Accepts simultaneous submissions. Responds in 3 months to queries. Sample copy and writer's guidelines for #10 SASE.

Nonfiction: General interest, historical/nostalgic, how-to (home decor), interview/profile, personal experience, travel. "No opinion, political, essay, book reviews, exposé." **Buys 15 mss/year.** Query. Length: 900-1,800 words. **Pays $150-350 for assigned articles; $75-200 for unsolicited articles.**

Photos: Send photos with query. Reviews transparencies, prints. Buys one-time rights. Negotiates payment individually. Captions, identification of subjects, model releases required.

Columns/Departments: Gardening (short informative article on a specific plant or gardening technique), 750-1,000 words; Culture Center (story about an event or person relating to Mississippi's art, music, theatre, or literature), 750-1,000 words; On Being Southern (personal essay about life in Mississippi. Only ms submissions accepted), 750 words. **Buys 6 mss/year.** Query. **Pays $150-225.**

Missouri

$ $FOCUS/KANSAS CITY, Communications Publishing Group, 3100 Broadway, #660, Kansas City MO 64111. (816)960-1988. Fax: (816)960-1989. **80% freelance written.** Quarterly magazine. "Positive how-to, motivational profiles." Estab. 1994. Circ. 30,000. Pays on publication. Publishes ms an average of 6 months after acceptance. Byline given. Buys first rights. Accepts simultaneous submissions. Responds in 1 month to queries. Sample copy for $3. Writer's guidelines for #10 SASE.

Nonfiction: Book excerpts, general interest, how-to, humor, inspirational, interview/profile, personal experience, photo feature, technical, travel. **Buys 15 mss/year.** Length: 750-2,000 words. **Pays $150-400 for assigned articles; 12¢/word for unsolicited articles.** Sometimes pays expenses of writers on assignment.

Photos: State availability with submission. Reviews transparencies. Buys all rights. Offers $20-25/photo. Captions, identification of subjects, model releases required.

Columns/Departments: Profiles of Achievement (regional Kansas Citians), 500-1,500 words. **Buys 30 mss/year. Pays 10¢/word.**

Fiction: Adventure, ethnic, historical, humorous, mainstream, slice-of-life vignettes. **Buys 3 mss/year.** Length: 25-250 words. **Pays $25-100.**

Fillers: Anecdotes, gags to be illustrated by cartoonist, newsbreaks, short humor. **Buys 10/year.** Length: 25-250 words. **Pays $25-100.**

Tips: "For new writers—send complete manuscript, double-spaced; clean copy only. If available, send clips of previously published work and résumé. Should state when available to write. Include on first page of manuscript: name, address, phone, social security number, word count and include SASE."

[N] $ $KANSAS CITY HOMES & GARDENS, Showcase Publishing Inc., P.O. Box 8680, Prairie Village KS 66208. (913)648-5757. Fax: (913)648-5783. E-mail: kchg@aol.com. Editor: Dave Leathers. **Contact:** Liz Elliott, associate editor. Bimonthly magazine. "Since 1986, Kansas City residents (mainly women) have embraced a local publication that speaks to them. Their home, lifestyle and family are featured with emphasis on high-quality, upscale decorating, building and living." Estab. 1986. Pays on publication. Byline given. Buys one-time rights. Editorial lead time 4 months. Submit seasonal material 4 months in advance. Accepts queries by mail, e-mail, fax. Accepts simultaneous submissions. Responds in 1 month to queries; 1 month to mss. Sample copy for $7.50 or online. Writer's guidelines online.

Nonfiction: Travel, home and garden. **Buys 8 mss/year.** Query with published clips. Length: 600-1,000 words. **Pays $60-350.** Sometimes pays expenses of writers on assignment.

Reprints: Accepts previously published submissions.

Photos: State availability of or send photos with submission. Reviews transparencies. Buys one-time rights. Offers no additional payment for photos accepted with ms. Identification of subjects required.

Columns/Departments: Time Away (places to take vacations to), 600 words. Query with published clips. **Pays $60-350.**

Tips: "Really read and understand our audience. Who are they and what do they want?"

$ $ $KANSAS CITY MAGAZINE, 118 Southwest Blvd., 3rd Floor, Kansas City MO 64108. (816)421-4111. Fax: (816)936-0509. Website: www.kcmag.com. **Contact:** Zim Loy, editor. **75% freelance written.** Magazine published 10 times a year. "Our mission is to celebrate living in Kansas City. We are a consumer lifestyle/general interest magazine focused on Kansas City, its people and places." Estab. 1994. Circ. 31,000. **Pays on acceptance.** Publishes ms an average of 3 months after acceptance. Byline given. Offers 10% kill fee. Buys first North American serial rights. Editorial lead time 4 months. Submit seasonal material 6 months in advance. Accepts queries by mail, e-mail, fax. Accepts simultaneous submissions. Sample copy for 8½×11 SAE or online.

Nonfiction: Exposé, general interest, interview/profile, photo feature. **Buys 15-20 mss/year.** Query with published clips. Length: 250-3,000 words.

Photos: Buys one-time rights. Negotiates payment individually.

Columns/Departments: Entertainment (Kansas City only), 1,000 words; Food (Kansas City food and restaurants only), 1,000 words. **Buys 10 mss/year.** Query with published clips.

[N] $ $MISSOURI LIFE, Missouri Life, Inc., P.O. Box 421, Fayette MO 65248-0421. Fax: (660)248-2310. E-mail: info@missourilife.com. Website: www.missourilife.com. Editor-in-Chief: Danita Allen Wood. **Contact:** Carol

Moczygemba, executive editor. **40% freelance written.** Bimonthly magazine covering the state of Missouri. "*Missouri Life*'s readers are mostly college-educated people with a wide range of travel and lifestyle interests. Our magazine discovers the people, places, and events—both past and present—that make Missouri a good place to live and/or visit." Estab. 1998. Circ. 50,000. **Pays on acceptance.** Byline sometimes given. Offers 50% kill fee. Buys one-time, all rights. Editorial lead time 3 months. Submit seasonal material 6 months in advance. Accepts queries by mail, fax. Responds in 1 month to queries; 2 months to mss. Sample copy online. Writer's guidelines for #10 SASE or online.

Nonfiction: General interest, historical/nostalgic, interview/profile, travel, all Missouri-related. **Buys 18 mss/year.** Query. Length: 300-2,000 words. **Pays $50-600.**

Photos: State availability with submission. Reviews transparencies. Buys all rights. Offers $50-150/photo. Captions, identification of subjects, model releases required.

Columns/Departments: Best of Missouri (people and places, past and present, written in an almanac style), 300 words maximum; Missouri Artist (features a Missouri artist), 500 words; Made in Missouri (products native to Missouri), 500 words; Missouri Memory (a personal memory of Missouri gone by), 500 words. **Pays $50-200.**

N $ $RELOCATING IN KANSAS CITY, Showcase Publishing Inc., P.O. Box 8680, Prairie Village KS 66208. (913)648-5757. Fax: (913)648-5783. Editor: Dave Leathers. **Contact:** Liz Elliott, associate editor. Annual relocation guides, free for people moving to the area. Estab. 1986. Pays on publication. Byline given. Buys one-time rights. Editorial lead time 4 months. Submit seasonal material 4 months in advance. Accepts queries by mail, fax. Accepts simultaneous submissions. Responds in 1 month to queries; 1 month to mss. Sample copy for $5 or online. Writer's guidelines online.

Nonfiction: Historical/nostalgic, travel, local issues. **Buys 8 mss/year.** Query with published clips. Length: 600-1,000 words. **Pays $60-350.** Sometimes pays expenses of writers on assignment.

Reprints: Accepts previously published submissions.

Photos: Reviews transparencies. Buys one-time rights. Offers no additional payment for photos accepted with ms. Identification of subjects required.

Tips: "Really read and understand our audience."

N $ $RELOCATING TO THE LAKE OF THE OZARKS, Showcase Publishing Inc, P.O. Box 8680, Prairie Village KS 66208. (913)648-5757. Fax: (913)648-5783. Editor: Dave Leathers. **Contact:** Liz Elliott, associate editor. Annual relocation guides, free for people moving to the area. Estab. 1986. Pays on publication. Publishes ms an average of 6 months after acceptance. Byline given. Buys one-time rights. Editorial lead time 4 months. Submit seasonal material 4 months in advance. Accepts queries by mail, fax. Accepts simultaneous submissions. Responds in 1 month to queries; 1 month to mss. Sample copy for $5 or online. Writer's guidelines online.

Nonfiction: Historical/nostalgic, travel, local issues. **Buys 8 mss/year.** Query with published clips. Length: 600-1,000 words. **Pays $60-350.** Sometimes pays expenses of writers on assignment.

Reprints: Accepts previously published submissions.

Photos: State availability of or send photos with submission. Reviews transparencies. Buys one-time rights. Offers no additional payment for photos accepted with ms. Identification of subjects required.

Tips: "Really read and understand our audience."

$ RIVER HILLS TRAVELER, Todd Publishing, Route 4, Box 4396, Piedmont MO 63957. (573)223-7143. Fax: (573)223-2117. E-mail: btodd@semo.net. Website: www.deepozarks.com. **Contact:** Bob Todd, online editor. **50% freelance written.** Monthly tabloid covering "outdoor sports and nature in the southeast quarter of Missouri, the east and central Ozarks. Topics like those in *Field & Stream* and *National Geographic*." Estab. 1973. Circ. 7,500. Pays on publication. Publishes ms an average of 2 months after acceptance. Byline given. Buys one-time rights. Editorial lead time 2 months. Submit seasonal material 1 year in advance. Accepts queries by e-mail. Accepts simultaneous submissions. Responds in 2 months to queries. Sample copy and writer's guidelines for SAE or online.

Nonfiction: Historical/nostalgic, how-to, humor, opinion, personal experience, photo feature, technical, travel. "No stories about other geographic areas." **Buys 80 mss/year.** Query with writing samples. Length: 1,500 word maximum. **Pays $15-50.** Sometimes pays expenses of writers on assignment.

Reprints: Send typed ms with rights for sale noted and information about when and where the material previously appeared.

Photos: Send photos with submission. Buys one-time rights. Negotiates payment individually. Pays $25 for covers.

  ■ The online magazine carries original content not found in the print edition and includes writer's guidelines. Contact: Bob Todd, online editor.

Tips: "We are a 'poor man's' *Field & Stream* and *National Geographic*—about the eastern Missouri Ozarks. We prefer stories that relate an adventure that causes a reader to relive an adventure of his own or consider embarking on a similar adventure. Think of an adventure in camping or cooking, not just fishing and hunting. How-to is great, but not simple instructions. We encourage good first-person reporting."

$ $SPRINGFIELD! MAGAZINE, Springfield Communications Inc., P.O. Box 4749, Springfield MO 65808-4749. (417)882-4917. **Contact:** Robert Glazier, editor. **85% freelance written.** Eager to work with a small number of new/unpublished writers each year. "This is an extremely local and provincial monthly magazine. No *general* interest articles." Estab. 1979. Circ. 10,000. Pays on publication. Publishes ms an average of 3-24 months after acceptance. Byline given. Buys first serial rights. Submit seasonal material 1 year in advance. Responds in 3 months to queries; 6 months to mss. Sample copy for $5.30 and 9½×12 ½ SAE.

Nonfiction: Local interest *only*; no material that could appeal to other magazines elsewhere. Book excerpts (Springfield authors only), exposé (local topics only), historical/nostalgic (top prority but must be local history), how-to, humor, interview/profile (needs more on females than males), personal experience, photo feature, travel (1 page/month). **Buys 150 mss/year.** Query with published clips by mail only or send complete ms with SASE. Length: 500-3,000 words. **Pays $35-250 for assigned articles.**

Photos: Send photos with query or ms. "Needs more phto features of a nostalgic bent." Reviews contact sheets, 4×6 color prints, 5×7 b&w prints. Buys one-time rights. Pays $5-35 for b&w, $10-50 for color. Captions, identification of subjects, model releases required.

Columns/Departments: Length varies, usually 500-2,500 words. **Buys 250 mss/year.** Query by mail or send complete ms.

Tips: "We prefer writers read eight or ten copies of our magazine prior to submitting any material for our consideration. The magazine's greatest need is for features which comment on these times in Springfield. We are overstocked with nostalgic pieces right now. We also need profiles about young women and men of distinction."

Montana

$ $MONTANA MAGAZINE, Lee Enterprises, P.O. Box 5630, Helena MT 59604-5630. (406)443-2842. Fax: (406)443-5480. E-mail: editor@montanamagazine.com. Website: www.montanamagazine.com. **Contact:** Beverly R. Magley, editor. **90% freelance written.** Bimonthly magazine. "Strictly Montana-oriented magazine that features community profiles, contemporary issues, wildlife and natural history, travel pieces." Estab. 1970. Circ. 40,000. Publishes ms an average of 1 year after acceptance. Byline given. on assigned stories only. Buys one-time rights. Submit seasonal material 1 year in advance. Accepts queries by mail, fax. Accepts simultaneous submissions. Responds in 6 months to queries. Sample copy for $5 or online. Writer's guidelines for #10 SASE or online.

Nonfiction: Query by September for summer material; March for winter material. Essays, general interest, interview/profile, photo feature, travel. Special issues: Special features on summer and winter destination points. No 'me and Joe' hiking and hunting tales; no blood-and-guts hunting stories; no poetry; no fiction; no sentimental essays. **Buys 30 mss/year.** Query with samples and SASE. Length: 300-3,000 words. **Pays 15¢/word.** Sometimes pays expenses of writers on assignment.

Reprints: Send photocopy of article with rights for sale noted and information about when and where the material previously appeared. Pays 50% of amount paid for an original article.

Photos: Send photos with submission. Reviews contact sheets, 35mm or larger format transparencies, 5×7 prints. Buys one-time rights. Offers additional payment for photos accepted with ms. Captions, identification of subjects, model releases required.

Columns/Departments: Memories (reminisces of early-day Montana life), 800-1,000 words; Outdoor Recreation, 1,500-2,000 words; Community Festivals, 500 words plus b&w or color photo; Humor, 800-1,000 words. Query with samples and SASE.

Tips: "We avoid commonly known topics so Montanans won't ho-hum through more of what they already know. If it's time to revisit a topic, we look for a unique slant."

Nevada

$ $NEVADA MAGAZINE, 401 N. Carson St., Carson City NV 89701-4291. (775)687-5416. Fax: (775)687-6159. E-mail: editor@nevadamagazine.com. Website: www.nevadamagazine.com. Editor: David Moore. **Contact:** Carolyn Graham, associate editor. **50% freelance written.** Works with a small number of new/unpublished writers each year. Bimonthly magazine published by the state of Nevada to promote tourism. Estab. 1936. Circ. 90,000. Pays on publication. Publishes ms an average of 8 months after acceptance. Byline given. Buys first North American serial rights. Submit seasonal material 6 months in advance. Accepts queries by mail, e-mail. Responds in 1 month to queries. Sample copy for $1. Writer's guidelines for #10 SASE.

　　O⌐ Break in with shorter departments, rather than trying to tackle a big feature. Good bets are Dining Out, Recreation, Casinoland, Side Trips, and Roadside Attractions.

Nonfiction: "We welcome stories and photos on speculation." Nevada topics only. Historical/nostalgic, humor, interview/profile, personal experience, photo feature, travel, recreational, think pieces. **Buys 40 unsolicited mss/year.** Send complete ms or query. Length: 500-1,800 words. **Pays $50-500.**

Photos: Send photo material with accompanying ms. Name, address and caption should appear on each photo or slide. Denise Barr, art director. Buys one-time rights. Pays $20-100 for color transparencies and glossy prints.

Tips: "Keep in mind the magazine's purpose is to promote Nevada tourism. Keys to higher payments are quality and editing effort (more than length). Send cover letter; no photocopies. We look for a light, enthusiastic tone of voice without being too cute; articles bolstered by facts and thorough research; and unique angles on Nevada subjects."

N **$ $**RELOCATING TO LAS VEGAS, Showcase Publishing Inc., P.O. Box 8680, Prairie Village KS 66208. (913)648-5757. Fax: (913)648-5783. Editor: Dave Leathers. **Contact:** Liz Elliott, associate editor. Annual relocation guides, free for people moving to the area. Estab. 1986. Pays on publication. Publishes ms an average of 6 months after acceptance. Byline given. Buys one-time rights. Editorial lead time 4 months. Submit seasonal material 4 months in advance. Accepts queries by mail, e-mail. Responds in 1 month to queries; 1 month to mss. Sample copy for $5 or online. Writer's guidelines online.
Nonfiction: Historical/nostalgic, travel, local issues. **Buys 8 mss/year.** Query with published clips. Length: 650-1,000 words. **Pays $60-350.** Sometimes pays expenses of writers on assignment.
Reprints: Accepts previously published submissions.
Photos: State availability with submission. Reviews transparencies. Buys one-time rights. Offers no additional payment for photos accepted with ms. Identification of subjects required.
Tips: "Really read and understand our audience."

New Hampshire

$ $NEW HAMPSHIRE MAGAZINE, Network Publications, Inc., 100 Main St., Nashua NH 03060. Fax: (603)889-5557. E-mail: editor@nhmagazine.com. Website: www.nhmagazine.com. **Contact:** Rick Broussard, editor. **50% freelance written.** Monthly magazine devoted to New Hampshire. "We want stories written for, by and about the people of New Hampshire with emphasis on qualities that set us apart from other states. We promote business and economic development." Estab. 1986. Circ. 24,000. Pays on publication. Byline given. Offers 25% kill fee. Buys all rights. Editorial lead time 3 months. Submit seasonal material 3 months in advance. Accepts queries by mail, e-mail, fax. Accepts simultaneous submissions. Responds in 2 months to queries; 3 months to mss.
Nonfiction: Essays, general interest, historical/nostalgic, photo feature, business. **Buys 30 mss/year.** Query with published clips. Length: 800-2,000 words. **Pays $25-175.** Sometimes pays expenses of writers on assignment.
Photos: State availability with submission. Rights purchased vary. Offers no additional payment for photos accepted with ms. Captions, identification of subjects, model releases required.
> ▣ The online magazine carries original content not found in the print edition. Contact: Rick Broussard, online editor.

Tips: Network Publications publishes 1 monthly magazine entitled *New Hampshire Magazine* and a "specialty" publication called *Destination New Hampshire.* "In general, our articles deal with the people of New Hampshire—their lifestyles and interests. We also present localized stories about national and international issues, ideas and trends. We will only use stories that show our readers how these issues have an impact on their daily lives. We cover a wide range of topics, including healthcare, politics, law, real-life dramas, regional history, medical issues, business, careers, environmental issues, the arts, the outdoors, education, food, recreation, etc. Many of our readers are what we call 'The New Traditionalists'—aging Baby Boomers who have embraced solid American values and contemporary New Hampshire lifestyles."

New Jersey

$ $ $ $NEW JERSEY MONTHLY, The Magazine of the Garden State, New Jersey Monthly LLC, 55 Park Place, P.O. Box 920, Morristown NJ 07963-0920. (973)539-8230. Fax: (973)538-2953. E-mail: editor@njmonthly.c om. Website: www.njmonthly.com. Editor: Nancy Nusser. **Contact:** Christopher Hann, senior editor. **75-80% freelance written.** Monthly magazine covering "just about anything to do with New Jersey, from news, politics and sports to decorating trends and lifestyle issues. Our readership is well-educated, affluent, and on average our readers have lived in New Jersey twenty years or more." Estab. 1976. Circ. 95,000. Pays on completion of fact-checking. Publishes ms an average of 3 months after acceptance. Byline given. Offers 20% kill fee. Buys first North American serial rights. Editorial lead time 3 months. Submit seasonal material 6 months in advance. Accepts queries by mail, e-mail, fax, phone. Accepts simultaneous submissions. Responds in 2 months to queries. Writer's guidelines for $2.95.
> ● This magazine continues to look for strong investigative reporters with novelistic style and solid knowledge of New Jersey issues.

Nonfiction: Book excerpts, essays, exposé, general interest, historical/nostalgic, humor, interview/profile, personal experience, photo feature, travel (within New Jersey). "No experience pieces from people who used to live in New Jersey or general pieces that have no New Jersey angle." **Buys 90-100 mss/year.** Query with published magazine clips and SASE. Length: 1,200-3,500 words. **Pays $750-2,000.** Pays reasonable expenses of writers on assignment with prior approval.
Photos: State availability with submission. Reviews transparencies, prints. Buys one-time rights. Payment negotiated. Identification of subjects, model releases required.
Columns/Departments: Exit Ramp (back page essay usually originating from personal experience but told in such a way that it tells a broader story of statewide interest), 1,400 words. **Buys 12 mss/year.** Query with published clips. **Pays $200-400.**
Fillers: Anecdotes. **Buys 12-15/year.** Length: 200-250 words. **Pays $100.**

Tips: "The best approach: Do your homework! Read the past year's issues to get an understanding of our well-written, well-researched articles that tell a tale from a well-established point of view."

N $ $ NEW JERSEY SAVVY LIVING, CTB, LLC, P.O. Box 607, Short Hills NJ 07078-0607. (973)379-7749. Fax: (973)379-4116. Website: www.njsavvyliving.com. **Contact:** Elaine Davis, editor. **90% freelance written.** Magazine published 5 times/year covering New Jersey residents with affluent lifestyles. "*Savvy* is a regional magazine for an upscale audience, ages 35-65. We focus on lifestyle topics such as decorating, fashion, people, travel and gardening." Estab. 1997. Circ. 60,000. Pays on publication. Publishes ms an average of 3 months after acceptance. Byline given. Offers $50 kill fee. Buys variable rights. Editorial lead time 3 months. Accepts queries by mail. Accepts simultaneous submissions. Response time varies. Sample copy for 9×12 SAE.
Nonfiction: General interest, historical/nostalgic, how-to, humor, inspirational, interview/profile, photo feature, travel, home/decorating. Special issues: Homes (March). No investigative, fiction, personal experience, and non-New Jersey topics (excluding travel). **Buys 50 mss/year.** Query with published clips. Length: 900-2,000 words. **Pays $250-500.**
Reprints: Accepts previously published submissions from non-conflicting markets only.
Photos: State availability with submission. Reviews contact sheets, negatives, transparencies, prints. Buys one-time rights. Offers no additional payment for photos accepted with ms. Captions, identification of subjects, model releases required.
Columns/Departments: Wine & Spirits (wine trends); Savvy Shoppers (inside scoop on buying); Intrepid Diner (restaurant review); Home Gourmet (from food to hostess gifts at home), all 900-1,000 words. **Buys 25 mss/year.** Query with published clips. **Pays $250.**
Fillers: Ann L. Light, assistant editor. Facts, newsbreaks. Length: 125-250 words. **Pays $25-50.**
Tips: "Offer ideas of interest to an upscale New Jersey readership. We love articles that utilize local sources and are well-focused. Trends are always a good bit, so come up with a hot idea and make us believe you can deliver."

$ $ THE SANDPAPER, Newsmagazine of the Jersey Shore, The SandPaper, Inc., 1816 Long Beach Blvd., Surf City NJ 08008-5461. (609)494-5900. Fax: (609)494-1437. E-mail: lbinews@hotmail.com. **Contact:** Jay Mann, managing editor. **10% freelance written.** Weekly tabloid covering subjects of interest to Jersey shore residents and visitors. "*The SandPaper* publishes two editions covering many of the Jersey Shore's finest resort communities including Long Beach Island and Ocean City, New Jersey. Each issue includes a mix of news, human interest features, opinion columns and entertainment/calendar listings." Estab. 1976. Circ. 60,000. Pays on publication. Publishes ms an average of 1 month after acceptance. Byline given. Offers 100% kill fee. Buys first, all rights. Submit seasonal material 3 months in advance. Accepts queries by mail, e-mail, fax, phone. Accepts simultaneous submissions. Responds in 1 month to queries. Sample copy for 9×12 SAE with 8 first-class stamps.
    O— "The opinion page and columns are most open to freelancers."
Nonfiction: Must pertain to New Jersey shore locale. Arts, entertaining news, reviews, essays, general interest, historical/nostalgic, humor, opinion, environmental submissons relating to the ocean, wetlands and pinelands. **Buys 10 mss/year.** Send complete ms. Length: 200-2,000 words. **Pays $25-200.** Sometimes pays expenses of writers on assignment.
Reprints: Send photocopy and information about when and where the material previously appeared. Pays 25-50% of amount paid for an original article.
Photos: Send photos with submission. Buys one-time or all rights. Offers $8-25/photo.
Columns/Departments: Speakeasy (opinion and slice-of-life, often humorous); Commentary (forum for social science perspectives); both 1,000-1,500 words, preferably with local or Jersey Shore angle. **Buys 50 mss/year.** Send complete ms. **Pays $30.**
Tips: "Anything of interest to sun worshippers, beach walkers, nature watchers and water sports lovers is of potential interest to us. There is an increasing coverage of environmental issues. We are steadily increasing the amount of entertainment-related material in our publication. Articles on history of the shore area are always in demand."

New Mexico

$ $ NEW MEXICO MAGAZINE, Lew Wallace Bldg., 495 Old Santa Fe Trail, Santa Fe NM 87501. (505)827-7447. Website: www.newmexico.com. Editor-in-Chief: Emily Drabanski. Associate Publisher: Jon Bowman. Senior Editor: Walter K. Lopez. Associate Editor/Photo Editor: Steve Larese. **Contact:** Any editor. Monthly magazine emphasizing New Mexico for a college-educated readership with above-average income and interest in the Southwest. Estab. 1923. Circ. 125,000. **Pays on acceptance.** Publishes ms an average of 8 months after acceptance. Buys first North American serial rights. Submit seasonal material 1 year in advance. Accepts queries by mail. Responds in 2 months to queries. Sample copy for $3.95. Writer's guidelines for SASE.
Nonfiction: New Mexico subjects of interest to travelers. Historical, cultural, informational articles. "We are looking for more short, light and bright stories for the 'Asi Es Nuevo Mexico' section. Also, we are buying 12 mss per year for our Makin Tracks series." **Buys 7-10 mss/issue.** General interest, historical/nostalgic, interview/profile, travel. "No columns, cartoons, poetry or non-New Mexico subjects." Query by mail with 3 published writing samples. No phone or fax queries. Length: 250-1,500 words. **Pays $100-600.**
Reprints: Rarely publishes reprints but sometimes publishes excerpts from novels and nonfiction books.

Photos: Purchased as portfolio or on assignment. "Photographers interested in photo assignments should send tearsheets to photo editor Steve Larese; slides or transparencies with complete caption information are accepted. Photographers name and telephone number should be affixed to the image mount." Buys one-time rights. Captions, model releases required.

Tips: "Your best bet is to write a fun, lively short feature (200-350 words) for our Asi Es Nuevo Mexico section that is a superb short manuscript on a little-known person, aspect of history or place to see in New Mexico. Faulty research will ruin a writer's chances for the future. Good style, good grammar. No generalized odes to the state or the Southwest. No sentimentalized, paternalistic views of Indians or Hispanics. No glib, gimmicky 'travel brochure' writing. No first-person vacation stories. We're always looking for well-researched pieces on unusual aspects of New Mexico and lively writing."

New York

$ $ ADIRONDACK LIFE, P.O. Box 410, Jay NY 12941-0410. (518)946-2191. Fax: (518)946-7461. E-mail: aledit @adirondacklife.com. Website: www.adirondacklife.com. **Contact:** Elizabeth Folwell, editor or Galen Crane, managing editor. **70% freelance written.** Prefers to work with published/established writers. Magazine published 8 issues/year, including special annual outdoor guide, emphasizes the Adirondack region and the North Country of New York State in articles covering outdoor activities, history and natural history directly related to the Adirondacks. Estab. 1970. Circ. 50,000. Pays 45 days after acceptance. Publishes ms an average of 6 months after acceptance. Byline given. Buys first North American serial rights. Submit seasonal material 1 year in advance. Accepts queries by mail, e-mail. Sample copy for $3 and 9×12 SAE. Writer's guidelines for #10 SASE or online.
   O— "For new writers, the best way to break into the magazine is through departments."
Nonfiction: "*Adirondack Life* attempts to capture the unique flavor and ethos of the Adirondack mountains and North Country region through feature articles directly pertaining to the qualities of the area." Special issues: Outdoors (May); Single-topic Collector's issue (September). **Buys 20-25 unsolicited mss/year.** Query with published clips. Length: 2,500-5,000 words. **Pays 25¢/word.** Sometimes pays expenses of writers on assignment.
Photos: All photos must have been taken in the Adirondacks. Each issue contains a photo feature. Purchased with or without ms on assignment. Send photos with submission. Reviews color transparencies, prints (b&w). Pays $125 for full page, b&w or color; $300 for cover (color only,vertical in format). Credit line given. All photos must be individually identified as to the subject or locale and must bear the photographer's name required.
Columns/Departments: Special Places (unique spots in the Adirondack Park); Watercraft; Barkeater (personal to political essays); Wilderness (environmental issues); Working (careers in the Adirondacks); Home; Yesteryears; Kitchen; Profile; Historic Preservation; Sporting Scene. Length: 1,200-2,400 words. Query with published clips. **Pays 25¢/word.**
Fiction: Considers first-serial novel excerpts in its subject matter and region.
Tips: "Do not send a personal essay about your meaningful moment in the mountains. We need factual pieces about regional history, sports, culture and business. We are looking for clear, concise, well-organized manuscripts that are strictly Adirondack in subject. Check back issues to be sure we haven't already covered your topic. Please do not send unsolicited manuscripts via e-mail. Check out our guidelines online."

$ $ $ AVENUE, 950 Third Ave., New York NY 10022. (212)758-9516. Fax: (212)758-7395. Editor-in-chief: Jill Brooke. **Contact:** Maileen Celis, managing editor. **25% freelance written.** Monthly magazine covering New York art, fashion, restaurants; business, design and travel. "As *Avenue* is intended for readers on Manhattan's Upper East Side our subject matter is generally high end, and most pieces focus on a New York personality." Estab. 1976. Circ. 80,000. Pays 60 days after publication. Publishes ms an average of 2 months after acceptance. Byline given. Offers 15% kill fee. Buys all rights. Editorial lead time 3 months. Submit seasonal material 3 months in advance. Accepts queries by mail, fax.
   O— Break in with memoir of life in New York or profiles of leading socialities.
Nonfiction: Essays, general interest, historical/nostalgic, interview/profile, personal experience, travel. **Buys 30 mss/ year.** Query with published clips. Length: 150-1,800 words. **Pays $150-1,500.** Pays expenses of writers on assignment.
Photos: State availability with submission. Reviews prints. Buys one-time rights. Negotiates payment individually. Identification of subjects, model releases required.
Tips: "Send submission by mail or fax after looking over a recent issue to familiarize yourself with our format."

$ BUFFALO SPREE MAGAZINE, David Laurence Publications, Inc., 5678 Main St., Buffalo NY 14221. (716)634-0820. Fax: (716)810-0075. E-mail: info@buffalospree.com. Website: www.buffalospree.com. **Contact:** Elizabeth Licata, editor. **90% freelance written.** Bimonthly city regional magazine. Estab. 1967. Circ. 25,000. Pays on publication. Publishes ms an average of 1 month after acceptance. Byline given. Buys first North American serial rights. Accepts queries by mail, e-mail, fax. Responds in 6 months to queries. Sample copy for $3.95 and 9×12 SAE with 9 first-class stamps.
Nonfiction: "Most articles are assigned not unsolicited." Interview/profile, travel, issue-oriented features, arts, living, food, regional. **Buys 5-10 mss/year.** Query with résumé and published clips. Length: 1,000-2,000 words. **Pays $125-250.**

Tips: "Send a well-written, compelling query or an interesting topic, and *great* clips. We no longer regularly publish fiction or poetry. Prefers material that is Western New York related."

$ $ CITY LIMITS, New York's Urban Affairs News Magazine, City Limits Community Information Service, 120 Wall St., 20th Floor, New York NY 10005. (212)479-3344. Fax: (212)344-6457. E-mail: citylimits@citylimits.org. Website: www.citylimits.org. **Contact:** Alyssa Katz, editor. **50% freelance written.** Monthly magazine covering urban politics and policy. "*City Limits* is a 25-year-old nonprofit magazine focusing on issues facing New York City and its neighborhoods, particularly low-income communities. The magazine is strongly committed to investigative journalism, in-depth policy analysis and hard-hitting profiles." Estab. 1976. Circ. 4,000. Pays on publication. Publishes ms an average of 3 months after acceptance. Byline given. Offers 50% kill fee. Buys first North American serial, second serial (reprint) rights. Editorial lead time 2 months. Accepts queries by mail, e-mail, fax. Accepts simultaneous submissions. Sample copy for $2.95. Writer's guidelines free.
Nonfiction: Book excerpts, exposé, humor, interview/profile, opinion, photo feature. No essays, polemics. **Buys 25 mss/year.** Query with published clips. Length: 400-3,500 words. **Pays $100-1,200 for assigned articles; $100-800 for unsolicited articles.** Pays expenses of writers on assignment.
Photos: State availability with submission. Reviews contact sheets, negatives, transparencies. Offers $50-100/photo.
Columns/Departments: Making Change (nonprofit business); Big Idea (policy news); Book Review, all 800 words; Urban Legend (profile); First Hand (Q&A), both 350 words. **Buys 15 mss/year.** Query with published clips. **Pays $100-200.**
Tips: "*City Limits'* specialty is covering low-income communities. We want to know how the news of the day is going to affect neighborhoods—at the grassroots. Among the issues we're looking for stories about housing, health care, criminal justice, child welfare, education, economic development, welfare reform, politics and government."

$ ⊠ NEW YORK NIGHTLIFE, MM&B Publishers, 990 Motor Pkwy., Central Islip NY 11722. (516)435-8890. Fax: (516)435-8925. E-mail: nynl@aol.com. **Contact:** Fran Petito, editor-in-chief. **75% freelance written.** Monthly magazine. "*Nightlife* features stories on topics concerning New Yorkers, from local events to new products. We also cover entertainment on both the local level and Hollywood." Estab. 1990. Circ. 56,000. Pays on publication. Publishes ms an average of 3 months after acceptance. Byline given. Buys first rights. Editorial lead time 2 months. Submit seasonal material 3 months in advance. Accepts queries by mail, e-mail, fax, phone. Responds in 2 weeks to queries. Sample copy for 11×14 SAE and 8 first-class stamps. Writer's guidelines for #10 SASE.
Nonfiction: General interest, how-to (home remodeling, decorating, etc.), humor, interview/profile, new product, travel. **Buys 100-120 mss/year.** Query with published clips. Length: 200-1,700 words. **Pays $50-125.**
Photos: State availability with submission. Reviews 3×5 transparencies, 5×7 prints. Buys one-time rights. Offers no additional payment for photos accepted with ms., Sometimes pays $15 per photo used.
Columns/Departments: Business (money matters, personal finance); Gourmet (recipes, new products); Health (medical news, exercise, etc.); all 600-750 words. Query with published clips. **Pays $50.**
Fiction: Humorous. **Buys 8-10 mss/year.** Query with published clips. Length: 600-750 words. **Pays $50.**
Tips: "We're looking for a flair for creative writing and an interest in celebrities, film, food and entertainment in general. No techies! Queries are happily reviewed and responded to. Feel free to follow up with a phone call 2-3 weeks later."

$ $ NEWSDAY, 235 Pinelawn Rd., Melville NY 11747-4250. (631)843-2900. Fax: (631)843-2375. Website: www.newsday.com. **Contact:** Noel Rubinton, viewpoints editor. Daily newspaper. Opinion section of daily newspaper. Estab. 1940. Circ. 555,203. Byline given.
Nonfiction: Seeks "opinion on current events, trends, issues—whether national or local, government or lifestyle. Must be timely, pertinent, articulate and opinionated. Preference for authors within the circulation area including New York City." Length: 700-800 words. **Pays $150.**
Tips: "It helps for prospective authors to be familiar with our paper and section."

$ $ SYRACUSE NEW TIMES, A. Zimmer, Ltd., 1415 W. Genesee St., Syracuse NY 13204. Fax: (315)422-1721. E-mail: editorial@syracusenewtimes.com. Website: www.newtimes.rway.com. **Contact:** Molly English, editor. **50% freelance written.** Weekly tabloid covering news, sports, arts and entertainment. "*Syracuse New Times* is an alternative weekly that can be topical, provocative, irreverent and intensely local." Estab. 1969. Circ. 46,000. Pays on publication. Publishes ms an average of 1 month after acceptance. Byline given. Buys one-time rights. Editorial lead time 3 months. Submit seasonal material 3 months in advance. Accepts simultaneous submissions. Responds in 2 weeks to queries; 1 month to mss. Sample copy for 9×11 SAE with 2 first-class stamps. Writer's guidelines for #10 SASE.
Nonfiction: Essays, general interest. **Buys 200 mss/year.** Query by mail with published clips. Length: 250-2,500 words. **Pays $25-200.**
Photos: State availability of or send photos with submission. Reviews 8×10 prints, color slides. Buys one-time rights. Offers $10-25/photo or negotiates payment individually. Identification of subjects required.
Tips: "Move to Syracuse and query with strong idea."

$ $ TIME OUT NEW YORK, Time Out New York Partners, LP, 627 Broadway, 7th Floor, New York NY 10012. (212)539-4444. Fax: (212)253-1174. E-mail: letters@timeoutny.com. Website: www.timeoutny.com. Editor-in-Chief: Cyndi Stivers. **Contact:** Sunny Lee, editorial assistant. **20% freelance written.** Weekly magazine covering entertainment in New York City. "Those who want to contribute to *Time Out New York* must be intimate with New York City and its environs." Estab. 1995. Circ. 102,000. Pays on publication. Publishes ms an average of 1 month after acceptance. Byline sometimes given. Offers 25% kill fee. Makes work-for-hire assignments. Accepts queries by mail, fax, phone. Responds in 2 months to queries.

    ○ᴖ Pitch ideas to the editor of the section to which you would like to contribute (i.e., film, music, dance, etc.). Be sure to include clips or writing samples with your query letter.

Nonfiction: Essays, general interest, how-to, humor, interview/profile, new product, travel (primarily within NYC area), reviews of various entertainment topics. No essays, articles about trends, unpegged articles. Query with published clips. Length: 250-1,500 words. **Pays 20¢/word for b&w features and $300/page for color features.**

Columns/Departments: Around Town (Billie Cohen); Art (Tim Griffin); Books & Poetry (Janet Steen); Technology (Adam Wisnieski); Cabaret (H. Scott Jolley); Check Out (Zoe Wolff); Clubs (Bruce Tantum); Comedy (Nikki Weinstein); Dance (Gia Kourlas); Eat Out (Salma Abdelnour); Film; Gay & Lesbian (Les Simpson); Kids (Barbara Aria); Music: Classical & Opera (Susan Jackson); Music: Rock, Jazz, etc. (Elisabeth Vincentelli); Radio (Ian Landau); Sports (Brett Martin); Television (Michael Freidson); Theater (Jason Zinoman); Video (Michael Freidson).

    ■ The online magazine carries original content not found in the print edition. Contact: Amy Brill, online editor.

Tips: "We're always looking for quirky, less-known news about what's going on in New York City."

North Carolina

$ $ AAA CAROLINAS GO MAGAZINE, 6600 AAA Dr., Charlotte NC 28212. Fax: (704)569-7815. Website: www.aaacarolinas.com. Managing Editor: Kristy Tolley. **Contact:** Tom Crosby, editor. **20% freelance written.** member publication for the american automobile association covering travel, auto-related issues. "We prefer stories that focus on travel and auto safety in North and South Carolina and surrounding states." Estab. 1922. Circ. 750,000. Pays on publication. Byline given. Buys all rights. Editorial lead time 2 months. Accepts queries by mail. Sample copy and writer's guidelines for #10 SASE.

Nonfiction: Travel (auto-related). Length: 750 words. **Pays 15¢/word.**

Photos: Send photos with submission. Reviews slides. Buys all rights. Offers no additional payment for photos accepted with ms. Identification of subjects required.

    ■ The online magazine carries original content not found in the print edition. Contact: Tom Crosby, editor.

Tips: "Submit regional stories relating to Carolinas travel."

$ $ $ CHARLOTTE MAGAZINE, Abarta Media, 127 W. Worthington Ave., Suite 208, Charlotte NC 28203. (704)335-7181. Fax: (704)335-3739. E-mail: editor@charlottemag.com. Website: www.charlottemag.com. **Contact:** Richard H. Thurmond, editorial director. **75% freelance written.** Monthly magazine covering Charlotte life. "This magazine tells its readers things they didn't know about Charlotte, in an interesting, entertaining and sometimes provocative style." Circ. 30,000. Pays within 30 days of acceptance. Publishes ms an average of 3 months after acceptance. Byline given. Offers 25% kill fee. Buys first North American serial rights. Editorial lead time 3 months. Submit seasonal material 6 months in advance. Accepts queries by mail, e-mail. Accepts simultaneous submissions. Responds in 6 months to mss. Sample copy for 8½×11 SAE and $2.09.

Nonfiction: Book excerpts, exposé, general interest, historical/nostalgic, interview/profile, photo feature, travel. **Buys 90-100 mss/year.** Query with published clips. Length: 200-3,000 words. **Pays 25-50¢/word.** Sometimes pays expenses of writers on assignment.

Photos: State availability with submission. Buys one-time rights. Negotiates payment individually. Identification of subjects required.

Columns/Departments: Buys 35-50 mss/year. Pays 25¢- 50¢/word.

Tips: "A story for *Charlotte* magazine could only appear in *Charlotte* magazine. That is, the story and its treatment are particularly germane to this area."

N $ $ CHARLOTTE PLACE MAGAZINE, Sandbar Communications, Inc., P.O. Box 22555, Charleston SC 29401. Fax: (843)856-7444. E-mail: RLMaggy@aol.com. **Contact:** Robin Maggy, editor-in-chief. Semiannual magazine covering Charlotte, North Carolina. Articles include interior design, art, profiles, opinions, gardening, money. Estab. 1995. Pays on publication. Publishes ms an average of 3 months after acceptance. Byline given. Buys first rights. Editorial lead time 6 months. Submit seasonal material 6 months in advance. Accepts queries by mail, e-mail, fax. Responds in 2 weeks to queries. Writer's guidelines by e-mail.

Nonfiction: How-to, interview/profile. **Buys 30 mss/year.** Query with published clips. Length: 1,200-3,500 words. **Pays 20¢/published word.** Sometimes pays expenses of writers on assignment.

Photos: State availability with submission. Reviews transparencies. Buys one-time rights. Negotiates payment individually. Captions, identification of subjects required.

Columns/Departments: Health & Wellness, In the Spotlight, Money Matters, Object Lesson, Past & Present, Talkback, Visual Arts, Weekend Gardener; all 1,200-3,500 words. **Pays 20¢/published word.**

Tips: "We are looking for articles that deviate from the traditional. As the writer, it is important to captivate the reader and make the reader feel, smell and taste the subject matter at hand."

$ $⊠ OUR STATE, Down Home in North Carolina, Mann Media, P.O. Box 4552, Greensboro NC 27404. (336)286-0600. Fax: (336)286-0100. E-mail: editorial@ourstate.com. Website: www.ourstate.com. **Contact:** Mary Ellis, editor. **95% freelance written.** Monthly magazine covering North Carolina. "*Our State* is dedicated to providing editorial about the history, destinations, out-of-the-way places and culture of North Carolina." Estab. 1933. Circ. 72,000. Pays on publication. Publishes ms an average of 6-24 months after acceptance. Byline given. Buys first North American serial rights. Editorial lead time 4 months. Submit seasonal material 4 months in advance. Accepts queries by mail, fax. Responds in 6 weeks to queries; 2 months to mss. Sample copy for $3.95. Writer's guidelines for #10 SASE.

Nonfiction: Book excerpts, historical/nostalgic, how-to, humor, personal experience, photo feature, travel. **Buys 60 mss/year.** Send complete ms. Length: 1,000-1,500 words. **Pays $125-300 for assigned articles; $50-125 for unsolicited articles.** Sometimes pays expenses of writers on assignment.

Photos: State availability with submission. Reviews 35mm or 4×6 transparencies. Buys one-time rights. Negotiates payment individually. Pays $15-350/photo, depending on size; $125-50 for photos assigned to accompany specific story; $500 maximum for cover photos. Identification of subjects required.

Columns/Departments: Tar Heel Memories (remembering something specific about NC), 1,200 words; Tar Heel Profile (profile of interesting North Carolinian), 1,500 words; Tar Heel Literature (review of books by NC writers and about NC), 300 words. **Buys 40 mss/year.** Send complete ms. **Pays $50-300.**

Tips: "We are developing a style for travel stories that is distinctly *Our State*. That style starts with outstanding photographs, which not only depict an area, but interpret it and thus become an integral part of the presentation. Our stories need not dwell on listings of what can be seen. Concentrate instead on the experience of being there, whether the destination is a hiking trail, a bed and breakfast, a forest or an urban area. What thoughts and feelings did the experience evoke? We want to know why you went there, what you experienced, and what impressions you came away with. With at least one travel story an issue, we run a short sidebar called "If you're going." It explains how to get to the destination; rates or admission costs if there are any; a schedule of when the attraction is open or list of relevant dates; and an address and phone number for readers to write or call for more information. This sidebar eliminates the need for general-service information in the story."

N $ $WILMINGTON MAGAZINE, City Publishing USA, Inc., 201 N. Front St., Wilmington NC 28401. E-mail: dbetz@wilmington.net. Managing Editor: Kristin Gibson. **Contact:** Don Betz, publisher. **100% freelance written.** Bimonthly magazine. "*Wilmington Magazine* appeals to residents, businesses and visitors alike. Our award-winning photography captures the faces and places of our community, complemented by articles that explore an indepth look at events and people." Estab. 1994. Circ. 8,000. Pays on publication. Publishes ms an average of 1 month after acceptance. Byline given. Buys first, one-time rights. Editorial lead time 6 weeks. Submit seasonal material 3 months in advance. Accepts simultaneous submissions. Responds in 1 month to queries.

Nonfiction: Essays, general interest, historical/nostalgic, humor, interview/profile, photo feature, travel. No negative exposés or self-promotion. **Buys 4 mss/year.** Query with published clips. Length: 900-2,000 words. **Pays 10-12½¢/ word.** Sometimes pays expenses of writers on assignment.

Photos: Send photos with submission. Reviews transparencies. Buys one-time rights. Offers $25-50/photo. Captions, identification of subjects, model releases required.

Columns/Departments: Arts & Entertainment, Restaurant Spotlight, both 1,500-1,800 words. **Buys 12 mss/year.** Query with published clips. **Pays 10-12½¢/word.**

Tips: "Be familiar with southeastern North Carolina."

North Dakota

$ $NORTH DAKOTA REC/RTC MAGAZINE, North Dakota Association of Rural Electric Cooperatives, 3201 Nygren Dr. NW, P.O. Box 727, Mandan ND 58554-0727. (701)663-6501. Fax: (701)663-3745. E-mail: kbrick@ndarec.c om. Website: www.ndarec.com. **Contact:** Kent Brick, editor. **40% freelance written.** Monthly magazine covering information of interest to memberships of electric cooperatives and telephone cooperatives. "We publish a general interest magazine for North Dakotans. We treat subjects pertaining to living and working in the northern Great Plains. We provide progress reporting on electric cooperatives and telephone cooperatives." Estab. 1954. Circ. 80,000. **Pays on acceptance.** Publishes ms an average of 6 months after acceptance. Byline given. Buys one-time rights, makes work-for-hire assignments. Editorial lead time 6 months. Submit seasonal material 6 months in advance. Accepts queries by mail, e-mail. Accepts simultaneous submissions.

Nonfiction: General interest, historical/nostalgic, how-to, humor, interview/profile, new product, travel. **Buys 20 mss/ year.** Query with published clips. Length: 1,500-2,000 words. **Pays $100-500 minimum for assigned articles; $300-600 for unsolicited articles.** Sometimes pays expenses of writers on assignment.

Photos: State availability with submission. Reviews contact sheets. Buys one-time rights. Negotiates payment individually. Identification of subjects required.

Columns/Departments: Energy use and financial planning, both 750 words. **Buys 6 mss/year.** Query with published clips. **Pays $100-300.**

Fiction: Historical, humorous, slice-of-life vignettes, western. **Buys 1 mss/year.** Query with published clips. Length: 1,000-2,500 words. **Pays $100-400.**

Tips: "Deal with what's real: Real data, real people, real experiences, real history, etc."

Ohio

$ 🖭 BEND OF THE RIVER MAGAZINE, P.O. Box 859, Maumee OH 43537. (419)893-0022. **Contact:** R. Lee Raizk, publisher. **90% freelance written.** This magazine reports that it is eager to work with new/unpublished writers. "We buy material that we like whether it is by an experienced writer or not." Monthly magazine for readers interested in northwestern Ohio history and nostalgia. Estab. 1972. Circ. 7,000. Pays on publication. Publishes ms an average of 6 months after acceptance. Byline given. Buys one-time rights. Submit seasonal material 2 months in advance. Responds in 1 month to queries. Sample copy for $1.25.
Nonfiction: "We deal heavily with Northwestern Ohio history and nostalgia. We are looking for old snapshots of the Toledo area to accompany articles, personal reflection, etc." Historical/nostalgic. Special issues: Deadline for holiday issue is November 1. **Buys 75 unsolicited mss/year.** Query with or without published clips or send complete ms. Length: 1,500 words. **Pays $10-75.**
Reprints: Send tearsheet and information about when and where the material previously appeared. Pays 100% of the amount paid for the original article.
Photos: Purchases b&w or color photos with accompanying ms. Pays $1 minimum. Captions required.
Tips: "Any Toledo area, well-researched nostalgia, local history will be put on top of the heap. If you send a picture with manuscript, it gets an A+! We pay a small amount but usually use our writers often and through the years. We're loyal."

🖹 THE CINCINNATI HERALD, Sesh Communications, 354 Hearne Ave., Cincinnati OH 45229. (513)961-3331. Fax: (513)961-0304. E-mail: sesh@fuse.net. Website: www.cincinnatiherald.com. **Contact:** Jan-Michele Kearney, editor. **25% freelance written.** Weekly newspaper for African Americans. Estab. 1955. Circ. 16,000. Pays on publication. Byline given. Buys all rights. Editorial lead time 2 months. Submit seasonal material 3 months in advance. Accepts queries by mail, e-mail, fax, phone. Accepts simultaneous submissions.
Nonfiction: Book excerpts, essays, exposé, general interest, historical/nostalgic, how-to, humor, inspirational, interview/profile, new product, opinion, personal experience, photo feature, religious, technical, travel. Query with published clips. Length: 300-700 words. **Pays $25-75.**
Photos: State availability with submission.

$ $ $ CINCINNATI MAGAZINE, One Centennial Plaza, 705 Central Ave., Suite 175, Cincinnati OH 45202. (513)421-4300. Fax: (513)562-2746. **Contact:** Kitty Morgan, editor. Monthly magazine emphasising Cincinnati living. Circ. 30,000. Pays on publication. Byline given. Buys first rights.
Nonfiction: Articles on personalities, business, sports, lifestyles, history relating to Cincinnati. Seeking to expand coverage of local authors. **Buys 12 mss/year.** Query. Length: 2,500-3,500 words. **Pays $500-1,000.**
Reprints: Send photocopy of article. Rarely accepts reprints of previously published submissions. Pays 50% of amount paid for orignial article.
Columns/Departments: Cincinnati dining, media, arts and entertainment, people, homes, politics, sports. Length: 1,000-1,500 words. **Buys 2-4 mss/year.** Query. **Pays $300-400.**
Tips: "Freelancers may find a market in At Home section (bimonthly), special advertising sections on varying topics from golf to cardiac care (query Special Projects Managing Editor Mary Beth Crocker). Always query in writing, with clips. All articles have a Cincinnati base. No generics, please. Also: no movie, book, theater reviews, poetry or fiction."

🖹 CLEVELAND MAGAZINE, City Magazines, Inc., 1422 Euclid Ave., #730Q, Cleveland OH 44115. (216)771-2833. Fax: (216)781-6318. E-mail: editorial@clevelandmagazine.com. Website: www.clevelandmagazine.com. **Contact:** Erin Hogan, editor. **60% freelance written.** Mostly by assignment. Monthly magazine with a strong Cleveland/northeast Ohio angle. Estab. 1972. Circ. 50,000. Pays on publication. Publishes ms an average of 3 months after acceptance. Byline given. Buys first, second serial (reprint), electronic rights. Editorial lead time 6 months. Submit seasonal material 8 months in advance. Accepts queries by mail, e-mail, fax. Accepts simultaneous submissions. Responds in 2 months to queries.
Nonfiction: Book excerpts, general interest, historical/nostalgic, home and garden, humor, interview/profile, travel. Query with published clips. Length: 800-5,000 words. **Pays $200-800.**
Columns/Departments: My Town (Cleveland first-person stories), 1,500 words. Query with published clips. **Pays $300.**

$ $ COLUMBUS MONTHLY, P.O. Box 29913, Columbus OH 43229-7513. (614)888-4567. Editor: Lenore E. Brown. **20-40% freelance written.** Prefers to work with published/established writers. Monthly magazine emphasizing subjects specifically related to Columbus and central Ohio. Pays on publication. Publishes ms an average of 2 months after acceptance. Byline given. Buys all rights. Responds in 1 month to queries. Sample copy for $4.89.
Nonfiction: "I like query letters that are well-written, indicate the author has some familiarity with *Columbus Monthly*, give me enough detail to make a decision and include at least a basic biography of the writer." No humor, essays or first person material. **Buys 4-5 unsolicited mss/year.** Query. Length: 400-4,500 words. **Pays 50-400.** Sometimes pays expenses of writers on assignment.
Photos: Send photos with submission. Pay varies for b&w or color prints. Model releases required.

Columns/Departments: Art, business, food and drink, politics, sports and theatre. Length: 1,000-2,000 words. **Buys 2-3 mss/year.** Query. **Pays $100-175.**
Tips: "It makes sense to start small—something for our City Journal section, perhaps. Stories for that section run between 400-1,000 words."

$ $ NORTHERN OHIO LIVE, LIVE Publishing Co.11320 Juniper Rd., Cleveland OH 44106. (216)721-1800. Fax: (216)721-2525. E-mail: bgleisser@livepub.com. **Contact:** Benjamin Gleisser, managing editor. **70% freelance written.** Monthly magazine covering Northern Ohio news, politics, business, arts, entertainment, education, and dining. "Reader demographic is mid-30s to 50s, though we're working to bring in the late 20s. Our readers are well educated, many with advanced degrees. They're interested in Northern Ohio's cultural scene and support it." Estab. 1980. Circ. 32,000. Pays on 20th of publication month. Publishes ms an average of 1 month after acceptance. Byline given. Offers 50% kill fee. Buys first North American serial rights. Editorial lead time 3 months. Submit seasonal material 4 months in advance. Responds in 3 weeks to queries; 2 months to mss. Sample copy for $3.
Nonfiction: All should have a Northern Ohio slant. Essays, exposé, general interest, humor, interview/profile, photo feature, travel. Special issues: Gourmet Guide (restaurants) (May). **Buys 100 mss/year.** Query with published clips. Length: 1,000-3,500 words. **Pays $100-1,000.** Sometimes pays expenses of writers on assignment.
Reprints: Send photocopy and information about when and where the material previously appeared.
Photos: State availability with submission. Reviews contact sheets, 4×5 transparencies, 3×5 prints. Buys one-time rights. Negotiates payment individually. Identification of subjects required.
Columns/Departments: News & Reviews (arts previews, personality profiles, general interest), 800-1,800 words. **Pays $200-300. Time & Place (essay), 400-450 words. Pays $100. Buys 60-70 mss/year.** Query with published clips.
Fiction: Novel excerpts.

$ $ $ OHIO MAGAZINE, Great Lakes Publishing Co., 62 E. Broad St., Columbus OH 43215-3522. (614)461-5083. Fax: (614)461-7648. E-mail: editorial@ohiomagazine.com. Website: www.ohiomagazine.com. **Contact:** Alyson Borgerding, managing editor. **70% freelance written.** Works with a small number of new/unpublished writers/year. Published 10 times a year magazine emphasizing Ohio-based travel, news and feature material that highlights what's special and unique about the state. Estab. 1978. Circ. 95,000. Pays on publication. Publishes ms an average of 6 months after acceptance. Byline given. Buys first North American serial, one-time, second serial (reprint), all rights, first serial rights. Submit seasonal material 6 months in advance. Accepts queries by mail, e-mail, fax. Responds in 3 months to queries; 3 months to mss. Sample copy for $3 and 9×12 SAE or online. Writer's guidelines for #10 SASE.
   o→ Break in by "knowing the magazine—read it thoroughly for several issues. Send good clips—that show your ability to write on topics we cover. We're looking for thoughtful stories on topics that are more contextual and less shallow. I want queries that show the writer has some passion for the subject."
Nonfiction: Length: 1,000-3,000 words. **Pays $800-1,800.** Sometimes pays expenses of writers on assignment.
Reprints: Send tearsheet or photocopy and information about when and where the material previously appeared. Pays 50% of amount paid for an original article.
Photos: Angie Packer, art director. Rate negotiable.
Columns/Departments: Length: 100-1,500 words. **Buys minimum 20 unsolicited mss/year. Pays $50-500.**
Tips: "Freelancers should send all queries in writing, not by telephone. Successful queries demonstrate an intimate knowledge of the publication. We are looking to increase our circle of writers who can write about the state in an informative and upbeat style. Strong reporting skills are highly valued."

$ $ OVER THE BACK FENCE, Southern and Northern Ohio's Own Magazine, Back Fence Publishing, Inc., P.O. Box 756, Chillicothe OH 45601. (740)772-2165. Fax: (740)773-7626. E-mail: backfenc@bright.net. Website: www.backfence.com. Sarah Williamson, managing editor. Quarterly magazine. "We are a regional magazine serving 20 counties in Southern Ohio and 10 counties in Northern Ohio. *Over The Back Fence* has a wholesome, neighborly style. It appeals to readers from young adults to seniors, showcasing art and travel opportunities in the area." Estab. 1994. Circ. 15,000. Pays on publication. Publishes ms an average of 2 years after acceptance. Byline given. Buys one-time North American serial rights or makes work-for-hire assignments. Editorial lead time 1 year. Submit seasonal material 1 year in advance. Accepts queries by mail. Accepts simultaneous submissions. Responds in 3 months to queries. Sample copy for $4 or on website. Writer's guidelines for #10 SASE or on website.
   o→ Break in with personality profiles (1,000 words), short features, columns (600 words); and features (1,000 words).
Nonfiction: General interest, historical/nostalgic, humor, inspirational, interview/profile, personal experience, photo feature, travel. **Buys 9-12 mss/year.** Query with or without published clips or send complete ms. Length: 750-1,000 words. **Pays 10¢/word minimum, negotiable depending on experience.**
Reprints: Send photocopy of article or short story and typed ms With rights for sale noted and information about when and where the material previously appeared. Negotiable.
Photos: "If sending photos as part of a text/photo package, please request our photo guidelines and submit color transparencies." Reviews color, 35mm or larger transparencies, prints 3.20×5. Buys one-time rights. $25-100/photo. Captions, identification of subjects, model releases required.
Columns/Departments: The Arts, 750-1,000 words; History (relevant to a designated county), 750-1,000 words; Inspirational (poetry or short story), 600-850 words; Profiles From Our Past, 300-600 words; Sport & Hobby, 750-1,000

words; Our Neighbors (i.e., people helping others), 750-1,000 words. All must be relevant to Southern or Northern Ohio. **Buys 24 mss/year.** Query with or without published clips or send complete ms. **Pays 10¢/word minimum, negotiable depending on experience.**

Fiction: Humorous. **Buys 4 mss/year.** Query with published clips. Length: 300-850 words. **Pays 10¢/word minimum, negotiable depending on experience.**

Poetry: Wholesome, traditional tree verse, light verse and rhyming. **Buys 4 poems/year.** Submit maximum 4 poems. Length: 4-32 lines. **Pays 10¢/word or $25 minimum.**

Tips: "Our approach can be equated to a friendly and informative conversation with a neighbor about interesting people, places and events in Southern Ohio (counties: Adams, Athens, Clinton, Fayette, Fairfield, Gallia, Greene, Highland, Hocking, Jackson, Lawrence, Meigs, Perry, Pickaway, Pike, Ross, Scioto, Vinton, Warren and Washington) and Northern Ohio (counties: Ashland, Erie, Western Cuyahoga, Huron, Lorain, Medina, Ottawa, Richland, Sandusky and Wayne)."

N $ $ PLAIN DEALER SUNDAY MAGAZINE, Plain Dealer Publishing Co., Plain Dealer Plaza, 1801 Superior Ave., Cleveland OH 44114. (216)999-4546. Fax: (216)515-2039. E-mail: eburbach@plaind.com. **Contact:** Ellen Stein Burbach, editor. **50% freelance written.** Weekly newspaper focusing on Cleveland and northeastern Ohio. Circ. 500,000. Pays on publication. Publishes ms an average of 3 months after acceptance. Byline given. Buys first, one-time rights, web rights. Submit seasonal material 3 months in advance. Accepts queries by mail, e-mail, fax. Responds in 1 month to queries; 2 months to mss. Sample copy for $1.

O— "Start small, with North by Northeast pieces."

Nonfiction: Must include focus on northeast Ohio people, places and issues. Book excerpts, essays, exposé, general interest, historical/nostalgic, humor, inspirational, interview/profile, new product, personal experience, photo feature, travel (only personal essays or local ties). **Buys 50-100 mss/year.** Query with published clips or send complete ms. Length: 800-4,000 words. **Pays $150-650 for assigned articles.**

Reprints: Send typed ms with rights for sale noted and information about when and where the material previously appeared.

Columns/Departments: North by Northeast (short upfront pieces), **pays $20-70**; Essays (personal perspective, memoir OK), **pays $150-200**, 900 words maximum; The Back Burner (food essays with recipe), **pays $200.**

Tips: "We're always looking for superior writers and great stories."

Oklahoma

$ $ OKLAHOMA TODAY, P.O. Box 53384, Oklahoma City OK 73152-9971. Fax: (405)522-4588. E-mail: mccune@oklahomatoday.com. Website: www.oklahomatoday.com. **Contact:** Louisa McCune, editor-in-chief. **80% freelance written.** Works with small number of new/unpublished writers each year. Bimonthly magazine covering people, places and things Oklahoman. "We are interested in showing off the best Oklahoma has to offer; we're pretty serious about our travel slant but regularly run history, nature and personality profiles." Estab. 1956. Circ. 50,000. Pays on publication. Publishes ms an average of 6 months after acceptance. Byline given. Buys first worldwide serial rights. Submit seasonal material 1 year in advance. Accepts queries by mail, e-mail. Responds in 4 months to queries. Sample copy for $3.95 and 9×12 SASE or online. Writer's guidelines for #10 SASE or online.

• *Oklahoma Today* has won Magazine of the Year, awarded by the International Regional Magazine Association, four out of the last eight years, and in 1999 won *Folio* magazine's Editorial Excellence Award for Best Regional Magazine. No phone queries.

O— "Start small. Look for possibilities for Across the Range. Even letters to the editor are good ways to 'get some ink.'"

Nonfiction: Book excerpts (on Oklahoma topics), historical/nostalgic (Oklahoma only), interview/profile (Oklahomans only), photo feature (in Oklahoma), travel (in Oklahoma). **Buys 20-40 mss/year.** Query with published clips. Length: 250-3,000 words. **Pays $25-750.**

Photos: "We are especially interested in developing contacts with photographers who live in Oklahoma or have shot here. Send samples and price range." Photo guidelines for SASE. Reviews 2¼×2¼ and 35mm color transparencies, high-quality transparencies, slides, and b&w prints. Buys one-time rights to use photos for promotional purposes. Pays $50-100 for b&w and $50-750 for color. Captions, identification of subjects, model releases required.

Fiction: Novel excerpts, occasionally short fiction.

Tips: "The best way to become a regular contributor to *Oklahoma Today* is to query us with one or more story ideas, each developed to give us an idea of your proposed slant. We're looking for *lively*, concise, well-researched and reported stories, stories that don't need to be heavily edited and are not newspaper style. We have a three-person full-time editorial staff, and freelancers who can write and have done their homework get called again and again."

Oregon

$ $🔲 CASCADES EAST, P.O. Box 5784, Bend OR 97708-5784. (541)382-0127. Fax: (541)382-7057. E-mail: sunpub@sun-pub.com. Website: www.sunpub.com. **Contact:** Geoff Hill, publisher/editor. **90% freelance written.**

Prefers to work with published/established writers. Quarterly magazine for "all ages as long as they are interested in outdoor recreation, history, people and arts and entertainment in Central Oregon: fishing, hunting, sight-seeing, golf, tennis, hiking, bicycling, mountain climbing, backpacking, rockhounding, skiing, snowmobiling, etc." Estab. 1972. Circ. 10,000 (distributed throughout area resorts and motels and to subscribers). Pays on publication. Publishes ms an average of 6 months after acceptance. Byline given. Buys all rights. Submit seasonal material 6 months in advance. Accepts queries by mail, e-mail, fax, phone. Responds in 3 months to queries. Sample copy for $5 and 9×12 SAE. Writer's guidelines for #10 SASE.

- *Cascades East* now accepts and prefers manuscripts along with a 3.5 disk. They can translate most word processing programs. You can also send electronic submissions.

Nonfiction: Art feature (on recognized Central Oregon artists of any medium, with color photos/transparencies and b&w photos); Homes & Living (unique custom/"dream" homes, architectual styles, alternative energy designs, interior designs, building locations, etc. in Central Oregon); 1,000-2,500 words with color photos/transparencies. General interest (first person experiences in outdoor central Oregon-with photos, can be dramatic, humorous or factual), historical/ nostalgic (for feature), personal experience (needed on outdoor subjects: dramatic, humorous or factual). "No articles that are too general, sight-seeing articles that come from a travel folder, or outdoor articles without the first-person approach." **Buys 20-30 unsolicited mss/year.** Query. Length: 1,000-2,000 words. **Pays 5-15¢/word.**

Reprints: Send photocopy and information about when and where the material previously appeared.

Photos: "Old photos will greatly enhance chances of selling a historical feature. First-person articles need b&w photos also." Buys one-time rights. $10-25 for b&w; $15-100 for transparencies. Captions required.

Columns/Departments: Short features on a successful Central Oregon businessperson making an impact on the community or excelling in the business market; local, national, or worldwide, with color/b&w photo. Length: 1,000-1,500 words. Query.

Tips: "Submit stories a year or so in advance of publication. We are seasonal and must plan editorials for summer 2002 in the spring of 2001, etc., in case seasonal photos are needed."

$ $OREGON COAST, 4969 Highway 101 N. #2, Florence OR 97439-0130. (541)997-8401 ext. 15 or (800)348-8401 ext. 15. Fax: (541)902-0400. E-mail: judy@ohwy.com. Website: www.ohwy.com. **Contact:** Judy Fleagle, managing editor. **65% freelance written.** Bimonthly magazine covering the Oregon Coast. Estab. 1982. Circ. 70,000. Pays after publication. Publishes ms an average of up to 1 year after acceptance. Byline given. Offers 33% kill fee. Buys first North American serial rights. Submit seasonal material 6 months in advance. Accepts queries by mail, e-mail. Responds in 3 months to queries. Sample copy for $4.50. Writer's guidelines for #10 SASE.

- This company also publishes *Northwest Travel* and *Oregon Outside*.

O→ Break in with "great photos with a story that has a great lead and no problems during fact-checking. Like stories that have a slightly different take on 'same-old' subjects and have good anecdotes and quotes. Stories should have satisfying endings. People who write like this is who we go back to again and again."

Nonfiction: "A true regional with general interest, historical/nostalgic, humor, interview/profile, personal experience, photo feature, travel and nature as pertains to Oregon Coast." **Buys 55 mss/year.** Query with published clips. Length: 500-1,500 words. **Pays $75-250 plus 2-5 contributor copies.**

Reprints: Send tearsheet or photocopy and information about when and where the material previously appeared. Pays an average of 60% of the amount paid for an original article.

Photos: Photo submissions with no ms or stand alone or cover photos. Send photos with submission. Reviews 35mm or larger transparencies. Buys one-time rights. Captions, identification of subjects, model releases (for cover), photo credits required.

Fillers: Newsbreaks (no-fee basis).

Tips: "Slant article for readers who do not live at the Oregon Coast. At least one historical article is used in each issue. Manuscript/photo packages are preferred over mss with no photos. List photo credits and captions for each historic print or color slide. Check all facts, proper names and numbers carefully in photo/ms packages. Need stories with great color photos—could be photo essays. Must pertain to Oregon Coast somehow."

$ $OREGON OUTSIDE, Educational Publications Foundation, 4969 Highway 101 N. #2, Florence OR 97439-0130. (800)348-8401. Fax: (541)902-0400. E-mail: judy@ohwy.com. Website: www.ohwy.com. **Contact:** Judy Fleagle, managing editor. **70% freelance written.** Quarterly magazine covering "outdoor activities for experts as well as for families and older folks, from easy hikes to extreme skiing. We like first person, lively accounts with lots of energy and quotes, anecdotes, compelling leads and satisfying endings. Nitty-gritty info can be in sidebars. Send a rough map if needed." Estab. 1993. Circ. 25,000. Publishes ms an average of 1 year after acceptance. Byline given. Offers 33% kill fee. Buys first North American serial (stories and story/photo packages) and one-time rights (stand alone photos, covers and calendars). Editorial lead time 8 months. Submit seasonal material 6 months in advance. Accepts queries by mail, e-mail. Responds in 3 months to queries. Sample copy for $4.50. Writer's guidelines for #10 SASE.

Nonfiction: Book excerpts, how-to, interview/profile, new product (if from Oregon), personal experience, photo feature. "Nothing overdone. We like understatement." Query with published clips. Length: 800-1,500 words. **Pays $75-250 plus 2-5 contributor copies.**

Reprints: Send photocopy and information about when and where the material previously appeared. Pays 60% of amount paid for an original article.

Photos: "We need more photos showing human involvement in the outdoors." Send photos with submission. Reviews 35mm up to 4×5 transparencies. Buys one-time rights. Pays $25-75 with story, $325/cover photo, $75/stand alone, $100/calendar. Captions, identification of subjects, model releases required.

Columns/Departments: Back Page (unusual outdoor photo with technical information), 80-100 words. Query with photo. **Pays $75.**

Fillers: Newsbreaks, events. **Buys 10/year.** Length: 200-400 words. **Does not pay for fillers.**

Tips: "A short piece with a couple super photos for a 1- or 2-page article" is a freelancer's best chance for publication. "Looking for more high energy articles and more photos with human involvement."

Pennsylvania

N $ $ BERKS COUNTY LIVING, West Lawn Graphic Communications, 801 Commerce St., P.O. Box 2195, Sinking Spring PA 19608. (610)678-2640. Fax: (610)678-2799. E-mail: treed@berkscountyliving.com. Website: www.berkscountyliving.com. **Contact:** Terry Scott Reed, managing editor. **90% freelance written.** Bimonthly magazine covering topics of interest to people living in Berks County PA. Estab. 2000. Circ. 15,000. Pays on publication. Publishes ms an average of 4 months after acceptance. Byline given. Offers 55-70% kill fee. Buys first North American serial rights. Editorial lead time 6 months. Submit seasonal material 4 months in advance. Accepts queries by mail, e-mail, fax. Accepts simultaneous submissions. Responds in 1 week to queries; 1 month to mss. Sample copy for 9×12 SAE and 2 first-class stamps. Writer's guidelines for #10 SASE or online.

Nonfiction: Exposé, general interest, historical/nostalgic, how-to, humor, inspirational, interview/profile, new product, photo feature, travel, food, health. **Buys 25 mss/year.** Query. Length: 1,600-2,800 words. **Pays $300-400.** Sometimes pays expenses of writers on assignment.

Reprints: Accepts previously published submissions.

Photos: State availability with submission. Reviews 35mm or greater transparencies, any size prints. Buys one-time rights. Negotiates payment individually. Captions, identification of subjects, model releases required.

$ $ CENTRAL PA, WITF, Inc., P.O. Box 2954, Harrisburg PA 17105-2954. (717)221-2800. Fax: (717)221-2630. E-mail: centralpa@centralpa.org. Website: www.centralpa.org. **Contact:** Steve Kennedy, senior editor. **90% freelance written.** Monthly magazine covering life in Central Pennsylvania. Estab. 1982. Circ. 42,000. Pays on publication. Publishes ms an average of 4 months after acceptance. Offers 20% kill fee. Buys first North American serial rights. Editorial lead time 3 months. Submit seasonal material 6 months in advance. Accepts queries by mail, e-mail, fax. Accepts simultaneous submissions. Responds in 6 weeks to queries. Sample copy for $3.50 and SASE. Writer's guidelines for #10 SASE.

O— Break in through Central Stories, Thinking Aloud, blurbs and accompanying events calendar.

Nonfiction: Essays, general interest, historical/nostalgic, how-to, humor, interview/profile, opinion, personal experience, photo feature, travel. Special issues: Dining/Food (January); Regional Insider's Guide (July); Best of Central PA (December). **Buys 50 mss/year.** Query with published clips or send complete ms. Length: 800-3,000 words. **Pays $200-750 for assigned articles; $50-500 for unsolicited articles.** Sometimes pays expenses of writers on assignment.

Photos: State availability with submission. Reviews contact sheets, transparencies, prints. Buys one-time rights. Negotiates payment individually. Identification of subjects required.

Columns/Departments: Central Stories (quirky, newsy, regional), 300 words; Thinking Aloud (essay), 1,200 words; Cameo (interview), 800 words. **Buys 90 mss/year.** Query with published clips or send complete ms. **Pays $50-100.**

Tips: "Wow us with something you wrote, either a clip or a manuscript on spec. If it's off target but shows you can write well and know the region, we'll ask for more. We're looking for creative nonfiction, with an emphasis on conveying valuable information through near literary-quality narrative."

$ $ PENNSYLVANIA, Pennsylvania Magazine Co., P.O. Box 755, Camp Hill PA 17001-0755. (717)697-4660. E-mail: pamag@aol.com. Publisher: Albert E. Holliday. **Contact:** Matt Holliday, editor. **90% freelance written.** Bimonthly magazine covering people, places, events and history in Pennsylvania. Estab. 1981. Circ. 33,000. Pays on acceptance except for articles (by authors unknown to us) sent on speculation. Publishes ms an average of 9 months after acceptance. Byline given. 25% kill fee for assigned articles. Buys first North American serial, one-time rights. Submit seasonal material 9 months in advance. Accepts queries by mail, e-mail. Responds in 1 month to queries. Sample copy for $2.95. Writer's guidelines for #10 SASE.

O— Break in with "a text/photo package—learn to take photos or hook up with a photographer who will shoot for our rates."

Nonfiction: Features include general interest, historical, photo feature, vacations and travel, people/family success stories, consumer-related inventions, serious statewide issues-all dealing with or related to Pennsylvania. Will not consider without illustrations; send photocopies of possible illustrations with query or mss. Include SASE. Nothing on Amish topics, hunting or skiing. **Buys 75-120 mss/year.** Query. Length: 750-2,500 words. **Pays 10-15¢/word.**

Reprints: Send photocopy with rights for sale noted and information about when and where the material previously appeared. Pays 5¢/word.

Photos: No original slides or transparencies. Americana Photo Journal includes 1-4 interesting photos and a 250-word caption; Photography Essay highlights annual photo essay contest entries. Reviews 35mm and $2\frac{1}{4} \times 2\frac{1}{4}$ color transparencies, 5×7 and 8×10 prints, color and b&w. Buys one-time rights. $15-25 for inside photos; up to $100 for covers. Captions required.

Columns/Departments: Panorama (short items about people, unusual events, family and individually owned consumer-related businesses), 250-900 words; Almanac (short historical items), 1,000-2,500 words; Museums, 400-500 words. All must be illustrated. Include SASE. Query. **10-15¢/word.**

Tips: "Our publication depends upon freelance work—send queries."

$ $ PENNSYLVANIA HERITAGE, Pennsylvania Historical and Museum Commission and the Pennsylvania Heritage Society, Commonwealth Keystone Building, Plaza Level, 400 North St., Harrisburg PA 17120-0053. (717)787-7522. Fax: (717)787-8312. E-mail: miomalley@state.pa.us. Website: www.paheritage.org. **Contact:** Michael J. O'Malley III, editor. **90% freelance written.** Prefers to work with published/established writers. Quarterly magazine. "*Pennsylvania Heritage* introduces readers to Pennsylvania's rich culture and historic legacy, educates and sensitizes them to the value of preserving that heritage and entertains and involves them in such a way as to ensure that Pennsylvania's past has a future. The magazine is intended for intelligent lay readers." Estab. 1974. Circ. 11,000. **Pays on acceptance.** Publishes ms an average of 1 year after acceptance. Byline given. Buys all rights. Accepts queries by mail, e-mail. Responds in 10 weeks to queries; 8 months to mss. Sample copy for $5 and 9×12 SAE or online. Writer's guidelines for #10 SASE or online.

• *Pennsylvania Heritage* is now considering freelance submissions that are shorter in length (2,000 to 3,000 words), pictorial/photographic essays, biographies of famous (and not-so-famous) Pennsylvanians and interviews with individuals who have helped shape, make, preserve the Keystone State's history and heritage.

Nonfiction: "Our format requires feature-length articles. Manuscripts with illustrations are especially sought for publication. We are now looking for shorter (2,000 words) manuscripts that are heavily illustrated with *publication-quality* photographs or artwork. We are eager to work with experienced travel writers for destination pieces on historical sites and museums that make up 'The Pennsylvania Trail of History.'" Art, science, biographies, industry, business, politics, transportation, military, historic preservation, archaeology, photography, etc. No articles which in no way relate to Pennsylvania history or culture. **Buys 20-24 mss/year.** Prefers to see mss with suggested illustrations. Length: 2,000-3,500 words. **Pays $100-500.**

Photos: State availability of or send photos with submission. Buys one-time rights. $25-200 for transparencies; $5-50 for b&w photos. Captions, identification of subjects required.

Tips: "We are looking for well-written, interesting material that pertains to any aspect of Pennsylvania history or culture. Potential contributors should realize that, although our articles are popularly styled, they are not light, puffy or breezy; in fact they demand strident documentation and substantiation (sans footnotes). The most frequent mistake made by writers in completing articles for us is making them either too scholarly or too sentimental or nostalgic. We want material which educates, but also entertains. Authors should make history readable and enjoyable. Our goal is to make the Keystone State's history come to life in a meaningful, memorable way."

$ $ PHILADELPHIA MAGAZINE, 1818 Market St., 36th Floor, Philadelphia PA 19103. (215) 564-7700. Fax: (215) 656-3500. Website: www.phillymag.com. President/Publisher: David R. Lipson. **Contact:** Mr. Loren Feldman, editor. Monthly magazine. "*Philadelphia* is edited for the area's community leaders and their families. It provides in-depth reports on crucial and controversial issues confronting the region—business trends, political analysis, metropolitan planning, sociological trends—plus critical reviews of the cultural, sports and entertainment scene." Estab. 1908. Circ. 133,083. Pays on other. Accepts queries by mail.

⚬┭ Break in by sending queries along with clips. "Remember that we are a general interest magazine that focuses exclusively on topics of interest in the Delaware Valley."

Nonfiction: "Articles range from law enforcement to fashion, voting trends to travel, transportation to theater, also includes the background studies of the area newsmakers." Query with clips and SASE.

Tips: "*Philadelphia Magazine* readers are an affluent, interested and influential group who can afford the best the region has to offer. They're the greater Philadelphia area residents who care about the city and its politics, lifestyles, business and culture."

$ $ $ PITTSBURGH MAGAZINE, WQED Pittsburgh, 4802 5th Ave., Pittsburgh PA 15213. (412)622-1360. Website: www.pittsburghmag.com. **Contact:** Michelle Pilecki, executive editor. **60% freelance written.** Monthly magazine. "*Pittsburgh* presents issues, analyzes problems and strives to encourage a better understanding of the community. Our region is western Pennsylvania, eastern Ohio, northern West Virginia and western Maryland." Estab. 1970. Circ. 75,000. Pays on publication. Publishes ms an average of 2 months after acceptance. Byline given. Offers kill fee. Buys first North American serial, second serial (reprint) rights. Submit seasonal material 6 months in advance. Accepts queries by mail. Responds in 2 months to queries. Sample copy for $2 (old back issues). Writer's guidelines online or via SASE.

• The editor reports a need for more hard news and stories targeting readers in their 30s and 40s, especially those with young families. Prefers to work with published/established writers. The monthly magazine is purchased on newsstands and by subscription, and is given to those who contribute $40 or more/year to public TV in western Pennsylvania.

Nonfiction: "Without exception—whether the topic is business, travel, the arts or lifestyle—each story is clearly oriented to Pittsburghers of today and to the greater Pittsburgh region of today." Must have greater Pittsburgh angle.

No fax, phone, or e-mail queries. No complete mss. Exposé, lifestyle, sports, informational, service, business, medical, profile. "We have minimal interest in historical articles and we do not publish fiction, poetry, advocacy or personal reminiscence pieces." Query in writing with outline and clips. Length: 3,500 words maximum. **Pays $300-1,500.**
Photos: Query. Pays pre-negotiated expenses of writer on assignment. Model releases required.
Columns/Departments: The Front (short, front-of-the-book items). Length: 300 words maximum. **Pays $50-150.**
Tips: "Best bet to break in is through hard news with a region-wide impact or service pieces or profiles with a regional interest. The point is that we want more stories that reflect our region, not just a tiny part. And we *never* consider any story without a strong regional focus."

$ $ WHERE & WHEN, Pennsylvania Travel Guide, The Barash Group, 403 S. Allen St., State College PA 16801. (800)326-9584. Fax: (814)238-3415. E-mail: arupe@barashgroup.com. Website: www.whereandwhen.com. **Contact:** Anissa Ruppert, editor. **75% freelance written.** Quarterly magazine covering travel and tourism in Pennsylvania. "*Where & When* presents things to see and do in Pennsylvania." Circ. 100,000. Pays on publication. Byline given. Offers 50% kill fee. Buys first North American serial rights. Editorial lead time 6 months. Submit seasonal material 6 months in advance. Responds in 1 month to queries. Sample copy and writer's guidelines free.
Nonfiction: Travel. **Buys 20-30 mss/year.** Query. Length: 800-2,500 words. **Pays $150-400.**
Photos: State availability with submission. Reviews transparencies, slides, prints. Buys one-time rights. Negotiates payment individually. Captions, identification of subjects required.
Columns/Departments: Bring the Kids (children's attractions); Heritage Traveler (state heritage parks); Small Town PA (villages and hamlets in Pennsylvania); On the Road Again (attractions along a particular road); all 800-1,200 words. **Buys 10 mss/year.** Query. **Pays $100-250.**

Rhode Island

$ $ $ RHODE ISLAND MONTHLY, The Providence Journal Company, 280 Kinsley Ave., Providence RI 02903. (401)421-2552. Fax: (401)277-8080. E-mail: paula_bodah@rimonthly.com. Website: www.rimonthly.com. Editor: Paula M. Bodah. **Contact:** Sarah Francis, managing editor. **80% freelance written.** Monthly magazine. "*Rhode Island Monthly* is a general interest consumer magazine with a strict Rhode Island focus." Estab. 1988. Circ. 41,000. **Pays on acceptance.** Publishes ms an average of 3 months after acceptance. Byline given. Offers 20% kill fee. Buys all rights for 90 days from date of publication. Editorial lead time 3 months. Submit seasonal material 6 months in advance. Accepts queries by mail, e-mail, fax. Responds in 6 weeks to queries; 1 month to mss. Sample copy online.
Nonfiction: Exposé, general interest, interview/profile, photo feature. **Buys 40 mss/year.** Query with published clips. Length: 1,800-3,000 words. **Pays $600-1,200.** Sometimes pays expenses of writers on assignment.

South Carolina

N $ $ CHARLESTON HOME DESIGN, Sandbar Communications, Inc., P.O. Box 22555, Charleston SC 29401. Fax: (843)856-7444. **Contact:** Robin Maggy, editor-in-chief. Semiannual magazine covering homes and interiors in Charleston, SC, and its surrounding areas. "Writer should be able to bring reader on tour of home, through strong quotes and descriptions." Estab. 1995. Pays on publication. Publishes ms an average of 3 months after acceptance. Byline given. Buys first rights. Editorial lead time 6 months. Submit seasonal material 6 months in advance. Accepts queries by mail, e-mail, fax. Responds in 2 weeks to queries. Writer's guidelines by e-mail.
Nonfiction: How-to, interview/profile. **Buys 30 mss/year.** Query with published clips. Length: 1,200-3,500 words. **Pays 20¢/published word.** Sometimes pays expenses of writers on assignment.
Photos: State availability with submission. Reviews transparencies. Buys one-time rights. Negotiates payment individually. Captions, identification of subjects required.
Columns/Departments: Architecture; Creative Minds; Attention to Detail; Collector's Closet; In the Garden; Projects; Personal Touches and Around the House, all 2,500 words. Query with published clips. **Pays 20¢/published word.**
Tips: "We are looking for articles that deviate from the traditional. As the writer, it is important to captivate the reader and make the reader feel, smell and taste the subject at hand."

$ $ HILTON HEAD MONTHLY, Voice of the Community, Frey Media, Inc., P.O. Box 5926, Hilton Head Island SC 29938. Fax: (843)842-5743. E-mail: hhmeditor@hargray.com. **Contact:** Rob Kaufman, editor. **75% freelance written.** Monthly magazine covering the business, people and lifestyle of Hilton Head, SC. "Our mission is to provide fresh, upbeat reading about the residents, lifestyle and community affairs of Hilton Head Island, an upscale, intensely pro-active resort community on the Eastern seaboard. We are not even remotely 'trendy,' but we like to see how national trends/issues play out on a local level. Especially interested in: home design and maintenance, entrepreneurship, nature, area history, golf/tennis/boating, volunteerism." Circ. 28,000. **Pays on acceptance.** Publishes ms an average of 6 months after acceptance. Byline given. Offers 50% kill fee. Buys first North American serial rights, makes work-for-hire assignments. Editorial lead time 3 months. Submit seasonal material 4 months in advance. Accepts queries by mail, e-mail, fax. Accepts simultaneous submissions. Responds in 1 week to queries; 4 months to mss. Sample copy for $3.

Nonfiction: Essays (short, personal), general interest, historical/nostalgic (history only), how-to (home related), humor, interview/profile (Hilton Head residents only), opinion (general humor or Hilton Head Island community affairs), personal experience, travel. No "exposé interviews with people who are not Hilton Head residents; profiles of people, events or businesses in Beaufort, SC, Savannah, GA, Charleston or other surrounding cities, unless it's within a travel piece." **Buys 225-250 mss/year.** Query with published clips. Length: 800-2,000 words. **Pays 10¢/word.**
Photos: State availability with submission. Reviews contact sheets, prints, slides; any size. Buys one-time rights. Negotiates payment individually.
Columns/Departments: Wellness (any general healthcare topic, especially for an older audience), 800-1,100 words; Focus (profile of Hilton Head Island personality/community leader), 1,000-1,300 words; Community (profile of Hilton Head Island volunteer organization), 800-1,100 words. Query with published clips. **Pays 10¢/word minimum.**
Tips: "Give us concise, bullet-style descriptions of what the article covers (in the query letter); choose upbeat, pro-active topics; delight us with your fresh (not trendy) description and word choice."

$ $ SANDLAPPER, The Magazine of South Carolina,, The Sandlapper Society, Inc., P.O. Box 1108, Lexington SC 29071-1108. (803)359-9941. Fax: (803)359-0629. E-mail: aida@sandlapper.org. Website: www.sandlapper.org. Editor: Robert P. Wilkins. **Contact:** Aida Rogers, managing editor. **35% freelance written.** Quarterly magazine focusing on the positive aspects of South Carolina. "*Sandlapper* is intended to be read at those times when people want to relax with an attractive, high-quality magazine that entertains and informs them about their state." Estab. 1989. Circ. 15,000 with a readership of 60,000. Pays during the dateline period. Publishes ms an average of 1 year after acceptance. Byline given. Buys first North American serial rights, right to reprint. Submit seasonal material 6 months in advance. Accepts queries by mail, e-mail, fax. Sample copy online. Writer's guidelines for #10 SASE.
Nonfiction: Feature articles and photo essays about South Carolina's interesting people, places, cuisine, things to do. Occasional history articles. Essays, general interest, humor, interview/profile, photo feature. Query with clips and SASE. Length: 800-3,000 words. **Pays $50-500.** Sometimes pays expenses of writers on assignment.
Photos: "*Sandlapper* buys black-and-white prints, color transparencies and art. Photographers should submit working cutlines for each photograph." Pays $25-75, $100 for cover or centerspread photo.
   ▣ The online magazine carries original content not found in the print edition. Contact: Dan Harmon.
Tips: "We're not interested in articles about topical issues, politics, crime or commercial ventures. Avoid first-person nostalgia and remembrances of places that no longer exist. We look for top-quality literature. Humor is encouraged. Good taste is a standard. Unique angles are critical for acceptance. Dare to be bold, but not too bold."

South Dakota

$ DAKOTA OUTDOORS, South Dakota,, Hipple Publishing Co., P.O. Box 669 333 W. Dakota Ave., Pierre SD 57501-0669. (605)224-7301. Fax: (605)224-9210. E-mail: office@capjournal.com. Editor: Kevin Hipple. **Contact:** Rachel Engbrecht, managing editor. **85% freelance written.** Monthly magazine on Dakota outdoor life, focusing on hunting and fishing. Estab. 1974. Circ. 7,000. Pays on publication. Publishes ms an average of 2 months after acceptance. Byline given. Submit seasonal material 3 months in advance. Accepts queries by mail, e-mail. Accepts simultaneous submissions. Responds in 3 months to queries. Sample copy for 9×12 SAE and 3 first-class stamps.
Nonfiction: "Topics should center on fishing and hunting experiences and advice. Other topics such as boating, camping, hiking, environmental concerns and general nature will be considered as well." General interest, how-to, humor, interview/profile, personal experience, technical (all on outdoor topics-prefer in the Dakotas). **Buys 120 mss/ year.** Send complete ms. Length: 500-2,000 words. **Pays $5-50.**
Reprints: Send typed ms with rights for sale noted and information about when and where the material previously appeared. 50% of amount paid for an original article.
Photos: Send photos with submission. Reviews 3×5 or 5×7 prints. Buys one-time rights. Offers no additonal payment for photos accepted with ms or negotiates payment individually. Identification of subjects required.
Columns/Departments: Kids Korner (outdoors column addressing kids 12-16 years of age). Length: 50-500 words. **Pays $5-15.**
Fiction: Adventure, humorous. **Buys 15 mss/year.** Send complete ms.
Fillers: Anecdotes, facts, gags to be illustrated by cartoonist, newsbreaks, short humor, line drawings of fish and game. Prefers 5×7 prints. **Buys 10/year.**
Tips: "Submit samples of manuscript or previous works for consideration; photos or illustrations with manuscript are helpful."

Tennessee

$ $ MEMPHIS, Contemporary Media, 460 Tennessee St., Memphis TN 38103. (901)521-9000. Fax: (901)521-0129. E-mail: memmag@memphismagazine.com. Website: www.memphismagazine.com. Editor: James Roper. Managing Editor: Frank Murtaugh. **Contact:** Michael Finger, senior editor. **30% freelance written.** Works with a small number of new/unpublished writers. Monthly magazine covering Memphis and the local region. "Our mission is to provide

Memphis with a colorful and informative look at the people, places, lifestyles and businesses that make the Bluff City unique." Estab. 1976. Circ. 24,000. Pays on publication. Publishes ms an average of 2 months after acceptance. Byline given. Offers 25% kill fee. Buys first North American serial rights. Editorial lead time 2 months. Submit seasonal material 3 months in advance. Accepts queries by mail, e-mail, fax. Accepts simultaneous submissions. Responds in 2 months to queries. Sample copy free or online. Writer's guidelines free.

Nonfiction: "Virtually all of our material has strong Memphis area connections." Essays, general interest, historical/nostalgic, interview/profile, photo feature, travel, interiors/exteriors. Special issues: Restaurant Guide and City Guide. **Buys 20 mss/year.** Query with published clips. Length: 500-3,000 words. **Pays 10-30¢/word.** Sometimes pays expenses of writers on assignment.

Photos: State availability with submission. Reviews contact sheets, transparencies. Buys one-time rights.

Columns/Departments: IntroSpective (personal experiences/relationships), 1,000-1,500 words; CityScape (local events/issues), 1,500-2,000 words; City Beat (peaople, places and things—some quirky), 200-400 words. **Buys 10 mss/year.** Query. **Pays 10-20¢/word.**

Fiction: Marilyn Sadler, associate editor. One story published annually as part of contest. Send complete ms. Length: 1,500-3,000 words.

Tips: "Send a query letter with specific ideas that apply to our short columns and departments. Good ideas that apply specifically to these sections will often get published."

Texas

$ $ $ HOUSTON PRESS, New Times, Inc., 1621 Milam, Houston TX 77002. (713)280-2400. Fax: (713)280-2496. Website: www.houstonpress.com. Editor: Margaret Downing. Managing Editor: Tim Carmen. Associate Editor: George Flynn. **Contact:** Kirsten Bubier, editorial administrator. **40% freelance written.** Weekly tabloid covering "news and arts stories of interest to a Houston audience. If the same story could run in Seattle, then it's not for us." Estab. 1989. Pays on publication. Publishes ms an average of 2 weeks after acceptance. Byline given. Buys first North American serial rights. Editorial lead time 2 months. Submit seasonal material 3 months in advance. Sample copy for $3.

Nonfiction: Tim Carman, managing editor. Exposé, general interest, interview/profile, arts reviews, music. Query with published clips. Length: 300-4,500 words. **Pays $10-1,000.** Sometimes pays expenses of writers on assignment.

Photos: State availability with submission. Buys all rights. Negotiates payment individually. Identification of subjects required.

N $ $ $ PAPERCITY, Dallas Edition, Urban Publishers, 3303 Lee Parkway, #340, Dallas TX 75219. (214)521-3439. Fax: (214)521-3178. E-mail: papercity2@aol.com. Editor-in-Chief: Holly Moore. **Contact:** Rebecca Sherman, Dallas editor. **10% freelance written.** Monthly magazine. "*Papercity* covers fashion, food, entertainment, home design and decoratives for urban Dallas and Houston. Our writing is lively, brash, sexy—it's where to read about the hottest restaurants, great chefs, where to shop, what's cool to buy, where to go and the chicest places to stay—from sexy, small hotels in New York, Los Angeles, London and Morocco, to where to buy the newest trends in Europe. We cover local parties with big photo spreads, and a hip nightlife column." Estab. 1994 (Houston); and 1998 (Dallas). Circ. 85,000 (Dallas). Pays on publication. Publishes ms an average of 1 month after acceptance. Byline given. Offers 10% kill fee. Buys first North American serial rights. Editorial lead time 2 months. Submit seasonal material 4 months in advance. Accepts queries by mail, e-mail, fax. Accepts simultaneous submissions. Responds in 3 weeks to queries; 1 month to mss. Sample copy for 9×12 SAE with $1.50 in first-class stamps. Writer's guidelines for #10 SASE or by e-mail.

Nonfiction: General interest, interview/profile, new product, travel, home decor, food. Special issues: Bridal (February); Travel (April); Restaurants (August). No straight profiles on anyone, especially celebrities. **Buys 10-12 mss/year.** Query with published clips. Length: 150-3,000 words. **Pays 35-50¢/word.**

Photos: State availability with submission. Reviews contact sheets, transparencies, prints. Buys one-time rights. Negotiates payment individually.

Tips: "Read similar publications such as *W, Tattler, Wallpaper, Martha Stewart Living* for new trends, style of writing, hip new restaurants. We try to be very 'of the moment' so give us something in Dallas, Houston, New York, Los Angeles, London, etc. that we haven't heard yet. Chances are if other hip magazines are writing about it so will we."

$ $ $ TEXAS HIGHWAYS, The Travel Magazine of Texas, Box 141009, Austin TX 78714-1009. (512)486-5858. Fax: (512)486-5879. E-mail: editors@texashighways.com. Website: www.texashighways.com. **Contact:** Jill Lawless, managing editor. **80% freelance written.** Monthly magazine "encourages travel within the state and tells the Texas story to readers around the world." Estab. 1974. Circ. 300,000. **Pays on acceptance.** Publishes ms an average of 1 year after acceptance. Buys first North American serial, electronic rights. Accepts queries by mail. Responds in 2 months to queries. Writer's guidelines for SASE or online.

Nonfiction: "Subjects should focus on things to do or places to see in Texas. Include historical, cultural and geographic aspects if appropriate. Text should be meticulously researched. Include anecdotes, historical references, quotations and, where relevant, geologic, botanical and zoological information." Query with description, published clips, additional background materials (charts, maps, etc.) and SASE. Length: 1,200-1,800 words. **Pays 40-50¢/word.**

Tips: "We like strong leads that draw in the reader immediately and clear, concise writing. Be specific and avoid superlatives. Avoid overused words. Don't forget the basics—who, what, where, why and how."

$ $ $✠ TEXAS PARKS & WILDLIFE, 3000 South I.H. 35, Suite 120, Austin TX 78704. (512)912-7000. Fax: (512)707-1913. Website: www.tpwmagazine.com. Managing Editor: Mary-Love Bigony. **Contact:** Executive Editor. **80% freelance written.** Monthly magazine featuring articles about Texas hunting, fishing, birding, outdoor recreation, game and nongame wildlife, state parks, environmental issues. All articles must be about Texas. Estab. 1942. Circ. 150,000. **Pays on acceptance.** Publishes ms an average of 6 months after acceptance. Byline given. Kill fee determined by contract, usually $200-250. Buys first rights. Submit seasonal material 6 months in advance. Accepts queries by mail. Responds in 1 month to queries; 3 months to mss. Sample copy and writer's guidelines online.
  • *Texas Parks & Wildlife* needs more hunting and fishing material.
Nonfiction: General interest (Texas only), how-to (outdoor activities), photo feature, travel (state parks). **Buys 60 mss/year.** Query with published clips. Length: 500-2,500 words.
Photos: Send photos to photo editor. Reviews transparencies. Buys one-time rights. Offers $65-350/photo. Captions, identification of subjects required.
Tips: "Read outdoor pages of statewide newspapers to keep abreast of news items that can lead to story ideas. Feel free to include more than one story idea in one query letter. All areas are open to freelancers. All articles must have a Texas focus."

Vermont

$ $✠ VERMONT LIFE MAGAZINE, 6 Baldwin St., Montpelier VT 05602-2109. (802)828-3241. Fax: (802)828-3366. E-mail: tslayton@life.state.vt.us. Website: www.vtlife.com. **Contact:** Thomas K. Slayton, editor-in-chief. **90% freelance written.** Prefers to work with published/established writers. Quarterly magazine. "*Vermont Life* is interested in any article, query, story idea, photograph or photo essay that has to do with Vermont. As the state magazine, we are most favorably impressed with pieces that present positive aspects of life within the state's borders." Estab. 1946. Circ. 85,000. Publishes ms an average of 9 months after acceptance. Byline given. Offers kill fee. Buys first North American serial rights. Submit seasonal material 1 year in advance. Accepts queries by mail, e-mail, fax. Responds in 1 month to queries. Writer's guidelines for #10 SASE.
  O─ Break in with "short humorous Vermont anecdotes for our 'Postboy' column."
Nonfiction: Wants articles on today's Vermont, those which portray a typical or, if possible, unique aspect of the state or its people. Style should be literate, clear and concise. Subtle humor favored. No "Vermont clichés"—maple syrup, town meetings or stereotyped natives. **Buys 60 mss/year.** Query by letter essential. Length: 1,500 words average. **Pays 25¢/word.**
Photos: Buys photos with mss; buys seasonal photographs alone. Prefers b&w contact sheets to look at first on assigned material. Color submissions must be 4×5 or 35mm transparencies. Gives assignments but only with experienced photographers. Query in writing. Buys one-time rights. Pays $75-200 inside color; $500 for cover. Captions, identification of subjects, model releases required.
  ▣ The online magazine carries original content not found in the print edition. Contact: Andrew Jackson.
Tips: "Writers who read our magazine are given more consideration because they understand that we want authentic articles about Vermont. If a writer has a genuine working knowledge of Vermont, his or her work usually shows it. Vermont is changing and there is much concern here about what this state will be like in years ahead. It is a beautiful, environmentally sound place now and the vast majority of residents want to keep it so. Articles reflecting such concerns in an intelligent, authoritative, non-hysterical way will be given very careful consideration. The growth of tourism makes us interested in intelligent articles about specific places in Vermont, their history and attractions to the traveling public."

Virginia

$ $ ALBEMARLE, Living in Jefferson's Virginia, Carden Jennings Publishing, 1224 W. Main St., Suite 200, Charlottesville VA 22903-2858. (804)817-2000. Fax: (804)817-2020. E-mail: albemarle@cjp.com. Website: www.cjp.com. **Contact:** Alison Dickie, associate publisher. **80% freelance written.** Bimonthly magazine. "Lifestyle magazine for central Virginia." Estab. 1987. Circ. 10,000. Pays on publication. Publishes ms an average of 4 months after acceptance. Byline given. Offers 30% kill fee. Buys first North American serial rights. Editorial lead time 6 months. Submit seasonal material 6 months in advance. Accepts queries by mail, e-mail, fax. Accepts simultaneous submissions. Responds in 1 month to queries; 2 months to mss. Sample copy for 10×12 SAE and 5 first-class stamps. Writer's guidelines for #10 SASE.
  O─ Break in with "a strong idea backed by good clips to prove abilities. Ideas should be targeted to central Virginia and lifestyle, which can be very broad—a renaissance man or woman approach to living."
Nonfiction: Essays, historical/nostalgic, interview/profile, photo feature, travel. "No fiction, poetry or anything without a direct tie to central Virginia." **Buys 30-35 mss/year.** Query with published clips. Length: 900-3,500 words. **Pays $75-225 for assigned articles; $75-175 for unsolicited articles.** Sometimes pays expenses of writers on assignment.

Photos: State availability with submission. Reviews transparencies. Buys one-time rights. Negotiates payment individually. Captions, identification of subjects, model releases required.

Columns/Departments: Etcetera (personal essay), 900-1,200 words; Flavors of Virginia (food), 900-1,100 words; Leisure (travel, sports), 3,000 words. **Buys 20 mss/year.** Query with published clips. **Pays $75-150.**

Tips: "Be familiar with the central Virginia area and lifestyle. We prefer a regional slant, which should include a focus on someone or something located in the region, or a focus on someone or something from the region making an impact in other parts of the world. Quality writing is a must. Story ideas that lend themselves to multiple sources will give you a leg up on the competition."

$ $ ◩ THE ROANOKER, Leisure Publishing Co., 3424 Brambleton Ave., P.O. Box 21535, Roanoke VA 24018-9900. (540)989-6138. Fax: (540)989-7603. E-mail: info@leisurepublishing.com. Website: www.theroanoker.com. **Contact:** Kurt Rheinheimer, editor. **75% freelance written.** Works with a small number of new/unpublished writers each year. Magazine published 6 times/year. *"The Roanoker* is a general interest city magazine for the people of Roanoke, Virginia and the surrounding area. Our readers are primarily upper-income, well-educated professionals between the ages of 35 and 60. Coverage ranges from hard news and consumer information to restaurant reviews and local history." Estab. 1974. Circ. 12,000. Pays on publication. Publishes ms an average of 4 months after acceptance. Byline given. Buys all rights, makes work-for-hire assignments. Submit seasonal material 4 months in advance. Accepts queries by mail, e-mail, fax. Responds in 2 months to queries. Sample copy for $2 and 9×12 SAE with 5 first-class stamps or online.

Nonfiction: "We're looking for more photo feature stories based in western Virginia. We place special emphasis on investigative and exposé articles." Exposé, historical/nostalgic, how-to (live better in western Virginia), interview/profile (of well-known area personalities), photo feature, travel (Virginia and surrounding states), periodic special sections on fashion, real estate, media, banking, investing. **Buys 30 mss/year.** Query with published clips or send complete ms. Length: 1,400 words maximum. **Pays $35-200.**

Reprints: Occasionally accepts previously published submissions. Send tearsheet. Pays 50% of amount paid for an original article.

Photos: Send photos with submission. Reviews color transparencies. Rights purchased vary. Pays $5-10 for 5×7 or 8×10 b&w prints; $10-50 for color transparencies. Captions, model releases required.

Columns/Departments: Skinny (shorts on people, Roanoke-related books, local issues, events, arts and culture).

Tips: "We're looking for more pieces on contemporary history (1930s-70s). It helps if freelancer lives in the area. The most frequent mistake made by writers in completing an article for us is not having enough Roanoke-area focus: use of area experts, sources, slants, etc."

Washington

Ⓝ $ $ METROPOLITAN LIVING, Prima Publishing, 400 Mercer St., Suite 408, Seattle WA 98109. (206)378-5888. Fax: (206)378-5855. E-mail: apeacock@metliving.com. Website: www.metliving.com. Assistant Editor: George Wolfe. **Contact:** Alison Peacock, editor. **90% freelance written.** Monthly magazine covering leisure and lifestyle in the Puget Sound area. *"Metropolitan Living* magazine values diversity and seeks stories about members of Seattle-area communities who may not otherwise be noticed for their extraordinary contributions." Estab. 1999. Circ. 42,000. Pays on publication. Publishes ms an average of 2 months after acceptance. Byline given. Offers 25% kill fee. Buys first North American serial rights, electronic rights for 45 days only. Editorial lead time 3 months. Submit seasonal material 4 months in advance. Accepts queries by mail, e-mail. Accepts simultaneous submissions. Responds in 6 months to queries. Sample copy for $2 or online. Writer's guidelines for free or by e-mail.

Nonfiction: Book excerpts, essays, exposé, general interest, historical/nostalgic, how-to, humor, inspirational, interview/profile, opinion, personal experience, photo feature, religious, travel. No "national rather than local slants, humor that is actually derisive to certain groups of people, PR pieces lauding products or people." **Buys 35-50 mss/year.** Query or send complete ms. Length: 500-3,000 words. **Pays $150-500 for assigned articles; $100-300 for unsolicited articles.** Sometimes pays expenses of writers on assignment.

Reprints: Accepts previously published submissions.

Photos: State availability with submission. Buys one-time rights. Identification of subjects required.

Columns/Departments: Fitness Finesse (mind and body health), 850 words; Intelligentsia (books and authors), 650 words plus short review); Food & Wine (restaurant reviews, food and wine pairings), reviews 500 words, wine 600 words; For Sport (local sports), 850 words; Sounding Off (anything opinionated), 850 words. **Buys 35-45 mss/year.** Query with published clips. **Pays $150-300.**

Tips: "Send a sample story that demonstrates skill at writing from the heart and profiling people and places well. E-mail is the best way to approach us. Queries that address little-known, not over-covered local people, places and things work well, too."

$ $ SEATTLE MAGAZINE, Tiger Oak Publications Inc., 423 Third Ave. W., Seattle WA 98119. (206)284-1750. Fax: (206)284-2550. E-mail: jkp@seattlemag.com. Website: www.seattlemag.com. Editor: Rachel Hart. **Contact:** J. Kingston Pierce, managing editor. Monthly magazine "serving the Seattle metropolitan area. Articles should be written with our readers in mind. They are interested in social issues, the arts, politics, homes and gardens, travel and maintaining the region's high quality of life." Estab. 1992. Circ. 45,000. Pays on or about 30 days after publication. Publishes ms an average of 3 months after acceptance. Byline given. Offers 25% kill fee. Buys first rights. Editorial lead time 6 months. Submit seasonal material 6 months in advance. Accepts queries by mail, e-mail, fax. Responds in 2 months to queries. Sample copy for #10 SASE. Writer's guidelines online.

O→ Break in by "suggesting short, newsier stories with a strong Seattle focus."

Nonfiction: Book excerpts (local), essays, exposé, general interest, humor, interview/profile, photo feature, travel, local/regional interest. Query with published clips. Length: 100-3,000 words. **Pays $50 minimum.** Sometimes pays expenses of writers on assignment.

Photos: State availability with submission. Buys one-time rights. Negotiates payment individually.

Columns/Departments: Scoop, Urban Safari, Voice, Trips, People, Environment, Hot Button, Fitness, Style, Eat and Drink. Query with published clips. **Pays $100-300.**

Tips: "The best queries include some idea of a lead and sources of information, plus compelling reasons why the article belongs specifically in *Seattle Magazine*. In addition, queries should demonstrate the writer's familiarity with the magazine. New writers are often assigned front- or back-of-the-book contents, rather than features. However, the editors do not discourage writers from querying for longer articles and are especially interested in receiving trend pieces, in-depth stories with a news hook and cultural criticism with a local angle."

Wisconsin

$ $ $ MILWAUKEE MAGAZINE, 417 E. Chicago St., Milwaukee WI 53202. (414)273-1101. Fax: (414)273-0016. E-mail: jfennell@qg.com. Website: www.milwaukeemagazine.com. **Contact:** John Fennell, editor. **40% freelance written.** Monthly magazine. "We publish stories about Milwaukee, of service to Milwaukee-area residents and exploring the area's changing lifestyle, business, arts, politics and dining." Circ. 40,000. Pays on publication. Publishes ms an average of 2 months after acceptance. Byline given. Offers 20% kill fee. Buys first rights. Submit seasonal material 6 months in advance. Accepts queries by mail, e-mail. Responds in 6 weeks to queries. Sample copy for $4.

Nonfiction: Essays, exposé, general interest, historical/nostalgic, interview/profile, photo feature, travel, Food and dining and other services. "No articles without a strong Milwaukee or Wisconsin angle." Length: 2,500-6000 words for full-length features; 800 words for two-page "breaker" features (short on copy, long on visuals). **Buys 30-50 mss/ year.** Query with published clips. **Pays $400-1,000 for full-length, $150-400 for breaker.** Sometimes pays expenses of writers on assignment.

Columns/Departments: Insider (inside information on Milwaukee, exposé, slice-of-life, unconventional angles on current scene), up to 500 words; Mini Reviews for Insider, 125 words; Endgame column (commentary), 850 words. Query with published clips. **Pays $50-250.**

Tips: "Pitch something for the Insider, or suggest a compelling profile we haven't already done. Submit clips that prove you can do the job. The department most open is Insider. Think short, lively, offbeat, fresh, people-oriented. We are actively seeking freelance writers who can deliver lively, readable copy that helps our readers make the most out of the Milwaukee area. Because we're only human, we'd like writers who can deliver copy on deadline that fits the specifications of our assignment. If you fit this description, we'd love to work with you."

$ $ WISCONSIN TRAILS, P.O. Box 317, Black Earth WI 53515-0317. (608)767-8000. Fax: (608)767-5444. E-mail: lkearney@wistrails.com. Website: www.wistrails.com. **Contact:** Laura Kearney, assistant editor. **40% freelance written.** Bimonthly magazine for readers interested in Wisconsin and its contemporary issues, personalities, recreation, history, natural beauty and arts. Estab. 1960. Circ. 55,000. Pays on publication. Publishes ms an average of 6 months after acceptance. Byline given. Buys first North American serial, one-time rights. Submit seasonal material 1 year in advance. Accepts queries by mail, e-mail, fax. Responds in 4 months to queries. Sample copy for $4.95. Writer's guidelines for #10 SASE.

O→ "We're looking for active articles about people, places, events and outdoor adventures in Wisconsin. We want to publish one in-depth article of state-wide interest or concern per issue, and several short (600-1,500 words) articles about short trips, recreational opportunities, personalities, restaurants, inns, history and cultural activities. We're looking for more articles about out-of-the-way Wisconsin places that are exceptional in some way and engaging pieces on Wisconsin's little-known and unique aspects."

Nonfiction: "Our articles focus on some aspect of Wisconsin life: an interesting town or event, a person or industry, history or the arts, and especially outdoor recreation. We do not use first-person essays or biographies about people who were born in Wisconsin but made their fortunes elsewhere. No poetry. No articles that are too local for our regional audience, or articles about obvious places to visit in Wisconsin. We need more articles about the new and little-known." **Buys 3 unsolicited mss/year.** Query or send outline. Length: 1,000-3,000 words. **Pays 25¢/word for assigned articles.** Sometimes pays expenses of writers on assignment.

Photos: Photographs purchased with or without mss or on assignment. Color photos usually illustrate an activity, event, region or striking scenery. Prefer photos with people in scenery. Black-and-white photos usually illustrate a given article. Reviews 35mm or larger transparencies. Pays $50 each for b&w on publication. Pays $50-75 for inside color; $100-200 for covers. Captions, labels with photographer's name required.

Tips: "When querying, submit well-thought-out ideas about stories specific to people, places, events, arts, outdoor adventures, etc. in Wisconsin. Include published clips with queries. Do some research—many queries we receive are pitching ideas for stories we recently have published. Know the tone, content and audience of the magazine. Refer to our writers' guidelines, or request them, if necessary."

Canadian/International

$ $ ABACO LIFE, Caribe Communications, P.O. Box 37487, Raleigh NC 27627. (919)859-6782. Fax: (919)859-6769. E-mail: jimkerr@mindspring.com. Website: www.abacolife.com. Managing Editor: Cathy Kerr. **Contact:** Jim Kerr, editor/publisher. **50% freelance written.** Quarterly magazine covering Abaco, an island group in the Northeast Bahamas. "*Abaco Life* editorial focuses entirely on activities, history, wildlife, resorts, people and other subjects pertaining to the Abacos. Readers include locals, vacationers, second home owners and other visitors whose interests range from real estate and resorts to scuba, sailing, fishing and beaches. The tone is upbeat, adventurous, humorous. No fluff writing for an audience already familiar with the area." Estab. 1979. Circ. 10,000. Pays on publication. Publishes ms an average of 2 months after acceptance. Byline given. Offers 40% kill fee. Buys one-time rights. Editorial lead time 2 months. Submit seasonal material 4 months in advance. Accepts queries by mail, e-mail. Accepts simultaneous submissions. Responds in 2 weeks to queries; 2 months to mss. Sample copy for $2. Writer's guidelines free.
Nonfiction: General interest, historical/nostalgic, how-to, interview/profile, personal experience, photo feature, travel. "No general first-time impressions. Articles must be specific, show knowledge and research of the subject and area—'Abaco's Sponge Industry'; 'Diving Abaco's Wrecks'; 'The Hurricane of '36.'" **Buys 8-10 mss/year.** Query or send complete ms. Length: 400-2,000 words. **Pays $150-350.**
Photos: State availability of or send photos with submission. Reviews transparencies, prints. Buys one-time rights. Offers $25-100/photo. Negotiates payment individually. Captions, identification of subjects, model releases required.
■ The online magazine carries original content not found in the print edition. Contact: Jim Kerr, online editor.
Tips: "Travel writers must look deeper than a usual destination piece, and the only real way to do that is spend time in Abaco. Beyond good writing, which is a must, we like submissions on Microsoft Word or Works, but that's optional. Color slides are also preferred over prints, and good ones go a long way in selling the story. Read the magazine to learn its style."

$ $ $ ALBERTAVIEWS, The Magazine About Alberta for Albertans, Local Perspectives Publishing, Inc., 520 23rd Ave. S.W., Calgary, Alberta T2S 0J5, Canada. (403)243-5334. Fax: (403)243-8599. E-mail: contactus@albertaviews.ab.ca. Website: www.albertaviews.ab.ca. Publisher/Editor: Jackie Flanagan. **Contact:** Marion Harrison, associate publisher. **50% freelance written.** Bimonthly magazine covering Alberta culture: politics, economy, social issues and art. "We are a regional magazine providing thoughtful commentary and background information on issues of concern to Albertans. Most of our writers are Albertans." Estab. 1997. Circ. 20,000. Pays on publication. Publishes ms an average of 3 months after acceptance. Byline given. Offers 50% kill fee. Buys first North American serial, electronic rights. Editorial lead time 3 months. Submit seasonal material 3 months in advance. Accepts queries by e-mail. Responds in 6 weeks to queries; 2 months to mss. Sample copy free. Writer's guidelines free, online, or by e-mail.
Nonfiction: Does not want anything not directly related to Alberta. Essays. **Buys 18 mss/year.** Query with published clips. Length: 3,000-5,000 words. **Pays $1,000-1,500 for assigned articles; $350-750 for unsolicited articles.** Sometimes pays expenses of writers on assignment.
Photos: State availability with submission. Buys one-time rights, web rights. Negotiates payment individually.
Fiction: Only fiction by Alberta writers. **Buys 6 mss/year.** Send complete ms. Length: 2,500-4,000 words. **Pays $1,000 maximum.**

$ ATLANTIC BOOKS TODAY, Atlantic Provinces Book Review Society, 1657 Barrington St., #502, Halifax, Nova Scotia B3J 2A1, Canada. (902)429-4454. E-mail: booksatl@istar.ca. **Contact:** Elizabeth Eve, managing editor. **50% freelance written.** Quarterly tabloid covering books and writers in Atlantic Canada. "We only accept written inquiries for stories pertaining to promoting interest in the culture of the Atlantic region." Estab. 1992. Circ. 20,000. Pays on publication. Byline given. Offers $25 kill fee. Buys one-time rights. Editorial lead time 6 months. Submit seasonal material 3 months in advance. Accepts queries by mail. Accepts simultaneous submissions. Responds in 1 month to queries. Sample copy and writer's guidelines for #10 SASE.
Nonfiction: Book excerpts, general interest. Query with published clips. Length: 1,000 words maximum. **Pays $120 maximum for assigned articles.** Sometimes pays expenses of writers on assignment.

N $ $ THE ATLANTIC CO-OPERATOR, Promoting Community Ownership, Atlantic Co-operative Publishers, 123 Halifax St., Moncton, New Brunswick E1C 8N5, Canada. Fax: (506)858-6615. E-mail: coop@nbnet.nb.ca. **Contact:** Cynthia Boudreau, editor. **95% freelance written.** Tabloid published 9 times/year covering co-operatives. "We publish articles of interest to the general public, with a special focus on community ownership and community economic development in Atlantic Canada." Estab. 1933. Pays on publication. Publishes ms an average of 2 months after acceptance. Byline given. Editorial lead time 2 months. Submit seasonal material 2 months in advance. Accepts queries by mail, e-mail, fax. Accepts simultaneous submissions. Responds in 3 weeks to queries.

Nonfiction: Exposé, general interest, historical/nostalgic, interview/profile. No political stories, economical stories, sports. **Buys 90 mss/year.** Query with published clips. Length: 500-2,000 words. **Pays 15¢/word.** Pays expenses of writers on assignment.

Reprints: Accepts previously published submissions.

Photos: State availability with submission. Reviews prints, gif/jpeg files. Buys one-time rights. Offers $25/photo. Identification of subjects required.

Columns/Departments: Health and Lifestyle (anything from recipes to travel), 800 words; International Page (cooperatives in developing countries, good ideas from around the world). **Buys 10 mss/year.** Query with published clips. **Pays 15¢/word.**

N **$ $ BEAUTIFUL BRITISH COLUMBIA**, 201-1669 W. 3rd Ave., Vancouver, British Columbia V6J 1K1, Canada. Fax: (604)738-4171. E-mail: ed@beautifulbc.ca. Website: www.beautifulbc.ca. Managing Editor: Anita Willis. **Contact:** Bryan McGill, editor. **80% freelance written.** Quarterly magazine covering British Columbia subjects. "A quarterly scenic geographic and travel magazine of British Columbia. Primary subjects: wildlife, parks and wilderness, travel, outdoor adventure, geography, history, eco-tourism, native culture, environment, heritage preservation." Estab. 1959. Circ. 170,000. **Pays on acceptance.** Publishes ms an average of 1 year after acceptance. Byline given. Offers 50% kill fee. Buys first worldwide rights. Editorial lead time 1 year. Submit seasonal material 1 year in advance. Accepts queries by mail. Responds in 1 month to queries; 1 month to mss. Sample copy for $5.95 (Canadian). Writer's guidelines for #10 SASE.

Nonfiction: "No poetry, fiction, people profiles; nothing unrelated to British Columbia." **Buys 20 mss/year.** Query with published clips. Length: 1,000-3,500 words. **Pays 50¢/word.** Sometimes pays expenses of writers on assignment.

Photos: Send photos with submission. Reviews transparencies. Buys one-time rights. Offers $100-500. Captions, identification of subjects, model releases required.

Columns/Departments: Columbiana (short British Columbia bits of history, environment, travel, news—illustrated with a single photo), 20-250 words. **Buys 20 mss/year.** Send complete ms. **Pays 50¢/word.**

Fillers: Facts, newsbreaks, short humor. **Buys 20/year.** Length: 10-250 words. **Pays 50¢/word.**

Tips: "We do not encourage submissions from contributors who live outside British Columbia. In our experience, only resident writers/photographers are able to provide the kind of in-depth, fresh, surprising perspectives on British Columbia that our readers demand."

$ $ $ THE BEAVER, Canada's History Magazine, Canada's National History Society, 478-167 Lombard Ave., Winnipeg, Manitoba R3B 0T6, Canada. (204)988-9300. Fax: (204)988-9309. E-mail: cnhs@historysociety.ca. Website: www.historysociety.ca. Associate Editor: Doug Whiteway. **Contact:** Annalee Greenberg, editor. **65% freelance written.** Bimonthly magazine covering Canadian history. Estab. 1920. Circ. 41,000. **Pays on acceptance.** Byline given. Offers $200 kill fee. Buys first North American serial, electronic rights. Editorial lead time 4 months. Submit seasonal material 8 months in advance. Accepts queries by mail. Accepts simultaneous submissions. Responds in 6 weeks to queries; 2 months to mss. Sample copy for 9×12 SAE and 2 first-class stamps. Writer's guidelines for #10 SASE or online.

O— Break in with a "new interpretation based on solid new research; entertaining magazine style."

Nonfiction: Photo feature (historical), historical (Canadian focus). Does not want anything unrelated to Canadian history. **Buys 30 mss/year.** Query with published clips. Length: 600-4,000 words. **Pays $400-1,000 for assigned articles; $300-600 for unsolicited articles.** Sometimes pays expenses of writers on assignment.

Photos: State availability with submission. Buys one-time rights. Offers no additional payment for photos accepted with ms. Identification of subjects, model releases required.

Columns/Departments: Book and other media reviews and Canadian history subjects, 600 words ("These are assigned to freelancers with particular areas of expertise, i.e., women's history, labour history, French regime, etc."). **Buys 15 mss/year. Pays $125.**

Tips: "*The Beaver* is directed toward a general audience of educated readers, as well as to historians and scholars. We are in the market for lively, well-written, well-researched, and informative articles about Canadian history that focus on all parts of the country and all areas of human activity. Subject matter covers the whole range of Canadian history, with particular emphasis on social history, politics, exploration, discovery and settlement, aboriginal peoples, business and trade, war, culture and sport. Articles are obtained through direct commission and by submission. Queries should be accompanied by a stamped, self-addressed envelope. *The Beaver* publishes articles of various lengths, including long features (from 1,500-4,000 words) that provide an in-depth look at an event, person or era; short, more narrowly focused features (from 600-1,500 words). Longer articles may be considered if their importance warrants publication. Articles should be written in an expository or interpretive style and present the principal themes of Canadian history in an original, interesting and informative way."

$ BRAZZIL, Brazzil, P.O. Box 50536, Los Angeles CA 90050. (323)255-8062. Fax: (323)257-3487. E-mail: brazzil@brazzil.com. Website: www.brazzil.com. **Contact:** Rodney Mello, editor. **60% freelance written.** Monthly magazine covering Brazilian culture. Estab. 1989. Circ. 12,000. Pays on publication. Publishes ms an average of 2 months after acceptance. Byline given. Offers 10% kill fee. Buys one-time rights. Editorial lead time 2 months. Submit seasonal material 2 months in advance. Accepts queries by mail, e-mail, fax, phone. Accepts simultaneous submissions. Responds in 2 weeks to queries. Sample copy free or online.

Nonfiction: "All subjects have to deal in some way with Brazil and its culture. We assume our readers know very little or nothing about Brazil, so we explain everything." Book excerpts, essays, exposé, general interest, historical/nostalgic, humor, interview/profile, opinion, personal experience, travel. **Buys 15 mss/year.** Query. Length: 800-5,000 words. **Pays $20-50.** Pays writers with contributor copies or other premiums by mutual agreement.

Reprints: Accepts previously published submissions. Send photocopy with rights for sale noted and information about when and where the material previously appeared. Pays 50% of amount paid for an original article.

Photos: State availability with submission. Reviews prints. Buys one-time rights. Offers no additional payment for photos accepted with ms. Identification of subjects required.

◼ The online version of *Brazzil* carries content not included in the print edition. Contact: Leda Mello, online editor.

Tips: "We are interested in anything related to Brazil: politics, economy, music, behavior, profiles. Please document material with interviews and statistical data if applicable. Controversial pieces are welcome."

$ $ $⚅ CANADIAN GEOGRAPHIC, 39 McArthur Ave., Ottawa, Ontario K1L 8L7, Canada. (613)745-4629. Fax: (613)744-0947. E-mail: editorial@cangeo.ca. Website: www.canadiangeographic.ca. **Contact:** Rick Boychuk, editor. **90% freelance written.** Works with a small number of new/unpublished writers each year. Bimonthly magazine. "*Canadian Geographic*'s colorful portraits of our ever-changing population show readers just how important the relationship between the people and the land really is." Estab. 1930. Circ. 240,000. **Pays on acceptance.** Publishes ms an average of 3 months after acceptance. Buys first Canadian rights. Accepts queries by mail, e-mail, fax. Responds in 1 month to queries. Sample copy for $5.95 Canadian and 9×12 SAE or online.

• *Canadian Geographic* reports a need for more articles on earth sciences.

Nonfiction: Buys authoritative geographical articles, in the broad geographical sense, written for the average person, not for a scientific audience. Predominantly Canadian subjects by Canadian authors. **Buys 30-45 mss/year.** Query. Length: 1,500-3,000 words. **Pays 80¢/word minimum.** Sometimes pays expenses of writers on assignment.

Photos: Pays $75-400 for color photos, depending on published size.

$ $ THE COTTAGE MAGAZINE, Country Living in Western Canada, Greenheart Publications, Ltd., 322 John St., Victoria, British Columbia V8T 1T3, Canada. (250)360-0709. Fax: (250)360-1709. E-mail: cottagemag@home.com. **Contact:** Caryl Worden, editor. **80% freelance written.** Bimonthly magazine covering recreational property in Western Canada. Estab. 1992. Circ. 10,000. Pays on publication. Publishes ms an average of 1 months after acceptance. Byline given. Offers 50% kill fee. Buys first North American serial rights. Editorial lead time 2 months. Submit seasonal material 6 months in advance. Accepts queries by e-mail, fax. Accepts simultaneous submissions. Responds in 1 month to queries; 2 months to mss. Sample copy for $2. Writer's guidelines for #10 SASE (Canadian stamps only).

⊶ Break in through practical "how-to" with good photos/diagrams on topics ranging from utilities (wells, septic, power, etc.) to building projects (sheds, docks, etc.) to recreational (boats, games, etc.); feature cottages from interior BC, Alberta and Saskatchewan.

Nonfiction: General interest, historical/nostalgic, how-to, humor, interview/profile, new product, personal experience, technical. **Buys 30 mss/year.** Query. Length: 200-2,000 words. **Pays $50-300.** Sometimes pays expenses of writers on assignment.

Photos: State availability with submission. Reviews contact sheets, transparencies, slides. Buys one-time rights. Offers no additional payment for photos accepted with ms. Cover photo, $100 (Canadian).

Columns/Departments: Utilities (solar and/or wind power), 650-700 words; Maintenance/Repairs; Getting Around (boats, bikes, etc.); Weekend Projects; Recycling. **Buys 10 mss/year.** Query. **Pays $100-200.**

Fillers: Anecdotes, facts, newsbreaks, seasonal tips. **Buys 12/year.** Length: 50-200 words. **Pays 20¢/word.**

Tips: "We're looking for practical info that allows readers to DIY or at least gives enough info to pursue topic further. Emphasis on alternative energy, water waste systems and innovative buildings/techniques/materials in Western Canada."

$ $⚅ OUTDOOR CANADA MAGAZINE, 340 Ferrier St., Suite 210, Markham, Ontario L3R 2Z5, Canada. (905)475-8440. Fax: (905)475-9560. E-mail: editorial@outdoorcanada.ca. Website: www.outdoorcanada.ca. **Contact:** Patrick Walsh, editor-in-chief. **90% freelance written.** Works with a small number of new/unpublished writers each year. Magazine published 8 times/year emphasizing noncompetitive outdoor recreation in Canada *only*. Estab. 1972. Circ. 95,000. Pays on publication. Publishes ms an average of 8 months after acceptance. Byline given. Buys first rights. Submit seasonal material 1 year in advance. Accepts queries by mail, e-mail. Responds in 1 month to queries. Mention *Writer's Market* in request for editorial guidelines.

Nonfiction: How-to, fishing, hunting, outdoor issues, outdoor destinations in Canada. **Buys 35-40 mss/year.** Query. Length: 2,500 words. **Pays $500 and up for assigned articles.**

Reprints: Send information about when and where the article previously appeared. Pay varies.

Photos: Emphasize people in the Canadian outdoors. Pays $100-250 for 35mm transparencies and $400/cover. Captions, model releases required.

ALWAYS CHECK the most recent copy of a magazine for the address and editor's name before you send in a query or manuscript.

Fillers: Short news pieces. **Buys 30-40/year.** Length: 100-500 words. **Pays $50 and up.**

■ The online magazine carries original content not found in the print edition. Contact: Aaron Kylie, online editor.

$ $ 🔲 THIS MAGAZINE, Red Maple Foundation, 401 Richmond St. W. #396, Toronto, Ontario M5V 3A8, Canada. (416)979-8400. Fax: (416)979-1143. E-mail: thismag@web.net. Website: www.thismag.org. **Contact:** Julie Crysler, editor. **80% freelance written.** Bimonthly magazine covering Canadian politics and culture. "*This* is Canada's leading alternative magazine. We publish stories on politics, culture and the arts that mainstream media won't touch." Estab. 1966. Circ. 6,000. Pays 1 month after publication. Publishes ms an average of 2 months after acceptance. Byline given. Buys first North American serial, electronic rights. Editorial lead time 6 weeks. Accepts queries by mail, e-mail, fax. Sample copy for $5 or online. Writer's guidelines for #10 SASE or by e-mail.

O→ "If unpublished or little-published, break in with shorter pieces tailored to the magazine's content. If published, pitch an unusual, under-reported idea."

Nonfiction: Essays (nonfiction/journalistic on cultural and political trends and social issues), how-to (with a political/activist bent), personal experience, provocative and well-argued manifestos, accessible arts/literary criticism. **Buys 60 mss/year.** Query with published clips. Length: 2,000-5,000 words. **Pays $250-500.**

Columns/Departments: Shorter essays, journalistic pieces; stylish interpretive front-section items; short capsule reviews of indie culture artifacts (zines, CDs, short films and videos) especially with a political edge. Length 200-2,000. **Pays $50-200.**

Tips: "We'd love to see more literary nonfiction with a strong voice and a political bent (no rants), strong cultural analysis that is au courant and suitable for a journalistic format, arts/literary criticism that is reasonably accessible."

$ $ $ 🔲 TORONTO LIFE, 59 Front St. E., Toronto, Ontario M5E 1B3, Canada. (416)364-3333. Fax: (416)959-4982. E-mail: editorial@torontolife.com. Website: www.tor-lifeline.com. **Contact:** John Macfarlane, editor. **95% freelance written.** Prefers to work with published/established writers. Monthly magazine emphasizing local issues and social trends, short humor/satire, and service features for upper income, well-educated and, for the most part, young Torontonians. Circ. 92,005. **Pays on acceptance.** Publishes ms an average of 4 months after acceptance. Byline given. Pays 50% kill fee for commissioned articles only. Buys first North American serial rights. Responds in 3 weeks to queries. Sample copy for $4.50 with SAE and IRCs.

Nonfiction: Uses most types of articles. **Buys 17 mss/issue.** Query with published clips and SASE. Length: 1,000-6,000 words. **Pays $500-5,000.**

Columns/Departments: "We run about five columns an issue. They are all freelanced, though most are from regular contributors. They are mostly local in concern and cover politics, business, performing arts, media, design and food." Length: 2,000 words. Query with SASE. **Pays $2,000.**

Tips: "Submissions should have strong Toronto orientation."

$ $ UP HERE, Life at the Top of the World, OUTCROP: The Northern Publishers, P.O. Box 1350, Yellowknife, Northwest Territories X1A 2N9, Canada. (867)920-4367. Fax: (867)873-2844. E-mail: cooper@uphere.ca. Website: www.uphere.ca. **Contact:** Cooper Langford, editor. **70% freelance written.** Magazine published 8 times/year covering general interest about Canada's North. "We publish features, columns and shorts about people, wildlife, native cultures, travel and adventure in Yukon, Northwest Territories and Nunavut, with an occasional swing into Alaska. Be informative, but entertaining." Estab. 1984. Circ. 35,000. Pays on publication. Byline given. Offers 50% kill fee. Buys first North American serial rights. Editorial lead time 6 months. Submit seasonal material 1 year in advance. Accepts queries by mail, e-mail, fax. Responds in 4 months to queries. Sample copy for $3.50 (Canadian) and 9×12 SASE with $1.45 Canadian postage. Writer's guidelines for legal-sized SASE and 45¢ Canadian postage.

O→ Break in with "precise queries with well-developed focuses for the proposed story."

Nonfiction: Essays, general interest, historical/nostalgic, how-to, humor, interview/profile, new product, personal experience, photo feature, technical, travel, lifestyle/culture. **Buys 25-30 mss/year.** Query. Length: 1,500-3,000 words. **Pays $250-750 or 15-25¢/word. Pays with advertising space where appropriate.**

Photos: "*Please* do not send unsolicited original photos, slides. Photocopies are sufficient." Send photos with submission. Reviews transparencies, prints. Buys one-time rights. Offers $25-350/photo (Canadian). Captions, identification of subjects required.

Columns/Departments: Write for updated guidelines, visit website or e-mail. **Buys 25-30 mss/year.** Query with published clips.

■ The online magazine carries original content not found in the print edition. Contact: Cooper Langford, online editor.

Tips: "We like well-researched, concrete adventure pieces, insights about Northern people and lifestyles, readable natural history. Features are most open to freelancers—travel, adventure and so on. We don't want a comprehensive 'How I spent my summer vacation' hour-by-hour account. We want stories with angles, articles that look at the North through a different set of glasses. Photos are important; you greatly increase your chances with top-notch images."

Ⓝ $ $ $ VANCOUVER MAGAZINE, Transcontinental Publications, Inc., 555 W. 12th Ave., Suite 300, East Tower, Vancouver, British Columbia V5Z 4L4, Canada. (604)877-7732. Fax: (604)877-4823. E-mail: mail@vanmag.com. Website: www.vanmag.com. **Contact:** Nick Rockel, editor. **70% freelance written.** Monthly magazine covering the city of Vancouver. Estab. 1967. Circ. 65,000. **Pays on acceptance.** Byline given. Offers negotiable kill fee. Buys first North American serial rights. Editorial lead time 2 months. Submit seasonal material 6 months in advance. Accepts queries by mail, e-mail, fax, phone. Accepts simultaneous submissions. Responds in 2 weeks to queries; 1 month to mss. Sample copy for $5. Writer's guidelines for #10 SASE or by e-mail.

Nonfiction: "We prefer to work with writers from a conceptual stage and have a six-week lead time. Most stories are under 1,500 words. Please be aware that we don't publish poetry and rarely publish fiction." Book excerpts, essays, historical/nostalgic, how-to, humor, interview/profile, new product, personal experience, photo feature, travel. **Buys 200 mss/year.** Query. Length: 200-3,000 words. **Pays 50¢/word.** Sometimes pays expenses of writers on assignment.

Photos: State availability with submission. Reviews contact sheets, negatives, transparencies, prints, gif/jpeg files. Buys negotiable rights. Negotiates payment individually. Captions, identification of subjects, model releases required.

Columns/Departments: Sport; Media; Bottomline (business); Cops, Robbers (crime); Civics (city issues), all 1,500 words. Query. **Pays 50¢/word.**

Tips: "Read back issues of the magazine. Almost all of our stories have a strong Vancouver angle. Submit queries by e-mail. Do not send complete stories."

$ $ $ WESTWORLD MAGAZINE, Canada Wide Magazines and Communications, 4180 Lougheed Hwy., 4th floor, Burnaby, British Columbia V5C 6A7, Canada. Fax: (604)299-9188. E-mail: acollette@canadawide.com. **Contact:** Ann Collette, editor. **80% freelance written.** Quarterly magazine distributed to members of The Canadian Automobile Association, with a focus on local (British Columbia), regional and international travel. Estab. 1983. Circ. 500,000. Pays on publication. Byline given. Offers 50% kill fee. Buys first North American serial, second serial (reprint) rights. Editorial lead time 6 months. Submit seasonal material 1 year in advance. Accepts simultaneous submissions. Writer's guidelines currently under revision.

• Editorial lineup for following year determined in June; queries held for consideration at that time. No phone calls.

Nonfiction: Travel (domestic and international). "No purple prose." **Buys 6 mss/year.** Query with published clips. Length: 800-1,500 words. **Pays 35-50¢/word.**

Reprints: Send photocopy and information about when and where the material previously appeared. Pays 50% of amount paid for an original article.

Photos: State availability of photos with submission, do not send photos until requested. Buys one-time rights. Offers $35-75/photo. Captions, identification of subjects, model releases required.

Columns/Departments: Query with published clips. **Pays 35-50¢/word.**

Tips: "Don't send gushy, travelogue articles. We prefer stories that are informative with practical, useful tips that are well written and researched. Approach an old topic/destination in a fresh/original way."

RELATIONSHIPS

These publications focus on lifestyles and relationships of single adults. Other markets for this type of material can be found in the Women's category. Magazines of a primarily sexual nature, gay or straight, are listed under the Sex category. Gay & Lesbian Interest contains general interest editorial targeted to that audience.

$ $ CONVERSELY, Conversely, Inc., PMB #121 3053 Fillmore St., San Francisco CA 94123-4009. E-mail: writers@conversely.com. Website: www.conversely.com. **Contact:** Alejandro Gutierrez, editor. **60-80% freelance written.** Monthly online literary magazine (some sections published weekly) covering relationships between women and men. "*Conversely* is dedicated to exploring relationships between women and men—every stage, every aspect—through different forms of writing: essays, memoirs, fiction. Our audience is both female and male, mostly in the 18-35 year age range. We look for writing that is intelligent, provocative and witty; we look for topics that are original and appealing to our readers." Estab. 2000. Pays on publication. Publishes ms an average of 3 months after acceptance. Byline given. Offers negotiable kill fee. Buys electronic rights (90 days exclusive; non-exclusive thereafter). Editorial lead time 3 months. Submit seasonal material 3 months in advance. Accepts queries by e-mail. Accepts simultaneous submissions. Responds in 2 weeks to queries; 2 months to mss. Sample copy and writer's guidelines online.

O-¬ Break in with "personal opinion essays for our 'Antidote' department."

Nonfiction: Essays, opinion, personal experience. "No how-to or anything that very overtly tries to teach or tell readers what to do or how to behave. No explicit sex." **Buys 30-36 mss/year.** Send complete ms. Length: 500-3,000 words. **Pays $50-150.** Sometimes pays expenses of writers on assignment.

Photos: State availability with submission. Negotiates payment individually.

Fiction: Mainstream. No erotica, science fiction, gothic, romance. **Buys 5-10 mss/year.** Send complete ms. Length: 500-3,000 words. **Pays $50-100.**

Tips: "We value writing that is original in its choice of subject and/or its approach to it. We prefer work that explores different and/or unconventional, yet engaging, aspects of relationships. We seek writing that achieves a balance between 'intelligent,' 'provocative' and 'witty.' Intelligent, as in complex and sophisticated. Provocative, as in it challenges the reader by presenting unexpected or non-traditional viewpoints. Witty, as in it uses clever humor, and the writing doesn't take itself too seriously. We turn down many otherwise fine submissions that discuss clichéd topics. We also turn down many well-written pieces in which the 'voice' is not right for us."

$ $ DIVORCE MAGAZINE, Segue Esprit Inc., 145 Front St., Suite 301, Toronto, Ontario M5A 1E3, Canada. E-mail: editors@divorcemag.com. Website: www.DivorceMagazine.com. **Contact:** Diana Shepherd, editor. **20% freelance written.** Quarterly magazine covering separation and divorce. "We have four quarterly editions: New York/New Jersey, Illinois, Southern California and Ontario. *Divorce Magazine* is designed to help people cope with the difficult transition of separation and divorce. Our mandate is to provide a unique, friendly resource of vital information and timely advice to help our readers survive—even thrive—during their divorce." Estab. 1996. Circ. 104,000. Pays on publication. Publishes ms an average of 6 months after acceptance. Byline given. Offers 25% kill fee. Buys all rights. Editorial lead time 3 months. Submit seasonal material 6 months in advance. Accepts queries by mail, e-mail, fax. Accepts simultaneous submissions. Responds in 6 months to queries. Sample copy for $3.95 with SASE (note to Americans: Must use International postage, not US postage). Writer's guidelines online at www.divorcemagazine.com/aboutus/writersubmit.

O→ Break in with "an article that will help people survive and thrive through separation and divorce."

Nonfiction: Book excerpts, how-to (see our website for previous examples), humor, family law. No first-person narrative stories (except for the humor column), poetry, fiction, celebrity gossip, "The Divorce From Hell" stories. **Buys 10-15 mss/year.** Query with published clips. Length: 1,000-3,000 words. **Pays 10-30¢/word.**

Columns/Departments: Last Word (humor). Length: 750 words. **Buys 4 mss/year.** Query with published clips. **Pays 10-20¢/word.**

■ The online magazine carries original content not found in the print edition. Contact: Diana Shepherd.

Tips: "We accept submissions in writing only. To get an idea of the types of articles we publish, visit our website."

N $ $ MARRIAGE PARTNERSHIP, Christianity Today International, 465 Gundersen Dr., Carol Stream IL 60188. Fax: (630)260-0114. E-mail: mp@marriagepartnership.com. Website: www.marriagepartnership.com. Executive Editor: Michael G. Maudlin. Managing Editor: Caryn D. Rivadeneira. **Contact:** Lori Fedele, editorial coordinator. **50% freelance written.** Quarterly magazine covering Christian marriages. "Our readers are married Christians. Writers must understand our readers." Estab. 1988. Circ. 55,000. **Pays on acceptance.** Publishes ms an average of 1 month after acceptance. Byline given. Offers 50% kill fee. Buys first North American serial rights. Editorial lead time 6 months. Submit seasonal material 1 year in advance. Accepts queries by mail, e-mail, fax. Responds in 10 weeks to queries; 2 months to mss. Sample copy for $5 or online. Writer's guidelines free.

Nonfiction: Book excerpts, essays, how-to, humor, inspirational, interview/profile, opinion, personal experience, religious. **Buys 20 mss/year.** Query with or without published clips. Length: 1,200-2,300 words. **Pays 15-30¢/word for assigned articles; 15¢/word for unsolicited articles.** Pays expenses of writers on assignment.

Columns/Departments: View Point (opinion), 1,000 words; Soul to Soul (inspirational), 1,500 words; Work It Out (problem-solving), 1,000 words. **Buys 10 mss/year.** Query with or without published clips. **Pays 15-30¢/word.**

Tips: "Think of topics with a fresh slant. Be ever mindful of our readers. Writers who can communicate with freshness, clarity and insight will receive serious consideration. We are looking for writers who are willing to candidly speak about their own marriages. We strongly urge writers who are interested in contributing to *Marriage Partnership* to read several issues to become thoroughly acquainted with our tone and slant."

RELIGIOUS

Religious magazines focus on a variety of subjects, styles and beliefs. Most are sectarian, but a number approach topics such as public policy, international affairs and contemporary society from a non-denominational perspective. Fewer religious publications are considering poems and personal experience articles, but many emphasize special ministries to singles, seniors or other special interest groups. Such diversity makes reading each magazine essential for the writer hoping to break in. Educational and inspirational material of interest to church members, workers and leaders within a denomination or religion is needed by the publications in this category. Religious magazines for children and teenagers can be found in the Juvenile and Teen & Young Adult classifications. Other religious publications can be found in the Contemporary Culture and Ethnic/Minority sections as well. Spiritual topics are also addressed in Astrology, Metaphysical and New Age as well as Health & Fitness. Publications intended to assist professional religious workers in teaching and managing church affairs are classified in Church Administration & Ministry in the Trade section.

$ AMERICA, 106 W. 56th St., New York NY 10019. (212)581-4640. Fax: (212)399-3596. E-mail: articles@americapress.org. Website: wwwamericapress.org. **Contact:** The Rev. Thomas J. Reese, editor. Published weekly for adult, educated, largely Roman Catholic audience. Estab. 1909. **Pays on acceptance.** Byline given. Buys all rights. Responds in 3 weeks to queries. Writer's guidelines free, by mail or online.

Nonfiction: "We publish a wide variety of material on religion, politics, economics, ecology and so forth. We are not a parochial publication, but almost all pieces make some moral or religious point." Articles on theology, spirituality, current political, social issues. "We are not interested in purely informational pieces or personal narratives which are self-contained and have no larger moral interest." Length: 1,500-2,000 words. **Pays $50-300.**

Poetry: Paul Mariani, poetry editor. Only 10-12 poems published a year, thousands turned down. **Buys 10-12 poems/ year.** Length: 15-30 lines.

$ $☒ ANGELS ON EARTH, Guideposts, 16 E. 34th St., New York NY 10016. (212)251-8100. E-mail: angelsed tr@guideposts.org. **Contact:** Colleen Hughes, editor-in-chief. **90% freelance written.** Bimonthly magazine. "*Angels on Earth* publishes true stories about God's messengers at work in today's world. We are interested in stories of heavenly angels and stories involving humans who have played angelic roles in daily life." Estab. 1995. Circ. 750,000. Pays on publication. Buys all rights. Editorial lead time 6 months. Submit seasonal material 6 months in advance. Accepts queries by mail. Responds in 3 months to queries.

Nonfiction: True, inspirational, personal experience (most stories are first-person experiences but can be ghost-written). Nothing that directly preaches, no how-to's. **Buys 80-100 mss/year.** Send complete ms with SASE. Length: 100-1,500 words. **Pays $25-500.**

Photos: State availability with submission. Buys one-time rights. Offers no additional payments for photos accepted with ms.

Columns/Departments: Catherine Scott, departments editor. Earning Their Wings (unusual stories of good deeds worth imitating); Only Human? (Is the angelic character a human being? The narrator is pleasantly unsure and so is the reader), both 500 words. **Pays $50-100.** Messages (brief, mysterious happenings, or letters describing how a specific article helped you). **Pays $25. Buys 20-30 mss/year.** Send complete ms with SASE.

$ THE ANNALS OF SAINT ANNE DE BEAUPRÉ, Redemptorist Fathers, P.O. Box 1000, St. Anne De Beaupré, Quebec G0A 3C0, Canada. (418)827-4538. Fax: (418)827-4530. Editor: Father Bernard Mercier, CSs.R. **Contact:** Father Roch Achard, managing editor. **80% freelance written.** Monthly Religious magazine. "Our mission statement includes dedication to Christian family values and devotion to St. Anne." Estab. 1885. Circ. 45,000. **Pays on acceptance.** Buys first North American serial rights. Editorial lead time 6 months. Submit seasonal material 6 months in advance. Responds in 1 month to queries. Sample copy and writer's guidelines for 8½×11 SAE and IRCs.

Nonfiction: Inspirational, religious. **Buys 350 mss/year.** Send complete ms. Length: 500-1,500 words. **Pays 3-4¢/ word plus 3 copies.**

Fiction: Religious, inspirational. "No senseless, mockery." **Buys 200 mss/year.** Send complete ms. Length: 500-1,500 words. **Pays 3-4¢/word.**

Tips: "Write something inspirational with spiritual thrust. Reporting rather than analysis is simply not remarkable. Each article must have a spiritual theme. Please only submit first North American rights mss with the rights clearly stated. We maintain an article bank and pick from it for each month's needs which loosely follows the religious themes for each month. Right now, our needs lean towards nonfiction of approximately 1,100 words."

Ⓝ $ THE ASSOCIATE REFORMED PRESBYTERIAN, Associate Reformed Presbyterian General Synod, 1 Cleveland St., Suite 110, Greenville SC 29601-3696. (864)232-8297, ext. 237. Fax: (864)271-3729. E-mail: arpmaged@a rpsynod.org. Website: www.arpsynod.org. **Contact:** Ben Johnston, editor. **5% freelance written.** Works with a small number of new/unpublished writers each year. Christian magazine serving a conservative, evangelical and Reformed denomination. Estab. 1976. Circ. 6,000. **Pays on acceptance.** Publishes ms an average of 4 months after acceptance. Byline given. Not copyrighted. Buys first, one-time, second serial (reprint) rights. Submit seasonal material 4 months in advance. Accepts queries by mail, e-mail, fax. Accepts simultaneous submissions. Responds in 1 month to queries. Sample copy for $1.50. Writer's guidelines for #10 SASE.

Nonfiction: Book excerpts, essays, inspirational, opinion, personal experience, religious. **Buys 10-15 mss/year.** Query. Length: 400-2,000 words. **Pays $70.**

Reprints: Send information about when and where the article previously appeared. Pays 100% of amount paid for an original article.

Photos: State availability with submission. Buys one-time rights. Offers $25 maximum/photo. Captions, identification of subjects required.

Fiction: Religious, children's. **"Currently overstocked." Pays $50 maximum.**

Tips: "Feature articles are the area of our publication most open to freelancers. Focus on a contemporary problem and offer Bible-based solutions to it. Provide information that would help a Christian struggling in his daily walk. Writers should understand that we are denominational, conservative, evangelical, Reformed and Presbyterian. A writer who appreciates these nuances would stand a much better chance of being published here than one who does not."

$ BIBLE ADVOCATE, Bible Advocate Press, Church of God (Seventh Day), P.O. Box 33677, Denver CO 80233. (303)452-7973. E-mail: BibleAdvocate@cog7.org/BA/. Website: www.cog7.org/BA/. Editor: Calvin Burrell. **Contact:** Sherri Langton, associate editor. **25% freelance written.** Religious magazine published 10 times/year. "Our purpose is to advocate the Bible and represent the Church of God (Seventh Day) to a Christian audience." Estab. 1863. Circ. 13,500. Pays on publication. Publishes ms an average of 9 months after acceptance. Byline given. Offers 50% kill fee.

Buys first, second serial (reprint), electronic rights. Editorial lead time 3 months. Submit seasonal material 6 months in advance. Accepts queries by mail, e-mail. Accepts simultaneous submissions. Responds in 2 months to queries. Sample copy for 9×12 SAE and 3 first-class stamps. Writer's guidelines for #SASE or online.

Nonfiction: Inspirational, opinion, personal experience, religious, Biblical studies. No articles on Christmas or Easter. **Buys 20-25 mss/year.** Send complete ms and SASE. Length: 1,500 words. **Pays $25-55.**

Reprints: Send typed ms with rights for sale noted.

Photos: Send photos with submission. Reviews prints. Offers payment for photos accepted with ms. Identification of subjects required.

Columns/Departments: Viewpoint (opinion), 600-700 words. **Buys 3 mss/year.** Send complete ms and SASE. **No payment for opinion pieces.**

Poetry: Free verse, traditional. No avant-garde. **Buys 10-12 poems/year.** Submit maximum 5 poems. Length: 5-20 lines. **Pays $20.**

Fillers: Anecdotes, facts. **Buys 5/year.** Length: 50-400 words. **Pays $10-20.**

Tips: "Be fresh, not preachy! We're trying to reach a younger audience now, so think how you can cover contemporary and biblical topics with this audience in mind. Articles must be in keeping with the doctrinal understanding of the Church of God (Seventh Day). Therefore, the writer should become familiar with what the Church generally accepts as truth as set forth in its doctrinal beliefs. We reserve the right to edit manuscripts to fit our space requirements, doctrinal stands and church terminology. Significant changes are referred to writers for approval. No fax or handwritten submissions, please."

$ $ CATHOLIC DIGEST, 2115 Summit Ave., St. Paul MN 55105-1081. (651)962-6739. Fax: (651)962-6758. E-mail: cdigest@stthomas.edu. Website: www.CatholicDigest.org. Editor: Richard J. Reece. **Contact:** Articles Editor. **15% freelance written.** Monthly magazine. "Publishes features and advice on topics ranging from health, psychology, humor, adventure and family, to ethics, spirituality and Catholics, from modern-day heroes to saints through the ages. Helpful and relevant reading culled from secular and religious periodicals." Estab. 1936. Circ. 509,385. Pays on acceptance for articles. Publishes ms an average of 4 months after acceptance. Byline given. Buys first, one-time, second serial (reprint) rights. Editorial lead time 4 months. Submit seasonal material 5 months in advance. Accepts queries by mail, e-mail, fax. Responds in 2 months to mss. Sample copy and writer's guidelines free.

Nonfiction: "Most articles we use are reprinted." Book excerpts, essays, general interest, historical/nostalgic, how-to, humor, inspirational, interview/profile, personal experience, religious, travel. **Buys 60 mss/year.** Send complete ms. Length: 1,000-3,000 words. **Pays $200-400.**

Reprints: Send tearsheet or typed ms with rights for sale noted and information about when and where the material previously appeared. Pays $100.

Photos: State availability with submission. Reviews contact sheets, transparencies, prints. Negotiates payment individually. Captions, identification of subjects, model releases required.

Columns/Departments: Buys 75 mss/year. Send complete ms. **Pays $4-50.**

Fillers: Filler Editor. Open Door (statements of true incidents through which people are brought into the Catholic faith, or recover the Catholic faith they had lost), 200-500 words; Signs of the Times (amusing or significant signs. Give exact source); In Our Parish (stories of parish life), 50-300 words; People Are Like That (original accounts of true incidents that illustrate the instinctive goodness of human nature), 200-500 words; Perfect Assist (original accounts of gracious or tactful remarks or actions), 200-500 words; Hearts Are Trumps (original accounts of true cases of unseeking kindness), 200-500 words; also publishes jokes, short anecdotes, quizzes and informational paragraphs, one-liners to 500 words. **Buys 200/year.** Length: 1 line minimum, 500 words maximum. **Pays $2/per published line upon publication.**

◨ The online magazine carries original content not found in the print edition and includes writer's guidelines. Contact: Kathleen Stauffer, managing editor.

Tips: "We're a lot more aggressive with inspirational/pop psychology/how-to articles these days. Spiritual and all other wellness self-help is a good bet for us. We would also like to see material with an innovative approach to traditional religion, articles that show new ways of looking at old ideas, problems."

$ $ CATHOLIC FORESTER, Catholic Order of Foresters, 355 Shuman Blvd., P.O. Box 3012, Naperville IL 60566-7012. Fax: (630)983-3384. E-mail: cofpr@aol.com. Website: www.catholicforester.com. Editor: Mary Ann File. **Contact:** Patricia Baron, associate editor. **20% freelance written.** Bimonthly magazine for members of the Catholic Order of Foresters, a fraternal insurance benefit society. *Catholic Forester* articles cover varied topics to create a balanced issue for the purpose of informing, educating and entertaining our readers. Circ. 100,000. **Pays on acceptance.** Buys first North American serial rights. Editorial lead time 6 months. Submit seasonal material 6 months in advance. Responds in 3 months to mss. Sample copy for 9×12 SAE and 4 first-class stamps. Writer's guidelines for #10 SASE.

Nonfiction: Inspirational, religious, travel, health, parenting, financial, money management, humor. **Buys 12-16 mss/ year.** Send complete ms by mail or fax. Rejected material will not be returned without accompanying SASE. Length: 500-1,500 words. **Pays 20¢/word.**

Photos: State availability with submission. Reviews transparencies. Buys one-time rights. Negotiates payment individually.

Fiction: Humorous, religious. **Buys 12-16 mss/year.** Length: 500-1,500 words. **Pays 20¢/word.**

Poetry: Light verse, traditional. **Buys 3 poems/year.** Length: 15 lines maximum. **Pays 20¢/word.**

Tips: "Our audience includes a broad age spectrum, ranging from youth to seniors. Nonfiction topics that appeal to our members include health and wellness, money management and budgeting, parenting and family life, interesting travels, insurance, nostalgia and humor. A good children's story with a positive lesson or message would rate high on our list."

$ $CATHOLIC NEAR EAST MAGAZINE, Catholic Near East Welfare Association, 1011 First Ave., New York NY 10022-4195. (212)826-1480. Fax: (212)826-8979. Website: www.cnewa.org. Executive Editor: Michael La Civita. **Contact:** Helen C. Packard, assistant editor. **50% freelance written.** Bimonthly magazine for a Catholic audience with interest in the Near East, particularly its current religious, cultural and political aspects. Estab. 1974. Circ. 100,000. Pays on publication. Publishes ms an average of 6 months after acceptance. Byline given. Buys all rights. Accepts queries by mail, fax. Responds in 2 months to queries. Sample copy and writer's guidelines for 7½ × 10½ SAE with 2 first-class stamps.
Nonfiction: "Cultural, devotional, political, historical material on the Near East, with an emphasis on the Eastern Christian churches. Style should be simple, factual, concise. Articles must stem from personal acquaintance with subject matter, or thorough up-to-date research." Length: 1,200-1,800 words. **Pays 20¢/edited word.**
Photos: "Photographs to accompany manuscript are welcome; they should illustrate the people, places, ceremonies, etc. which are described in the article. We prefer color transparencies but occasionally use b&w." Pay varies depending on use—scale from $50-300.
Tips: "We are interested in current events in the Near East as they affect the cultural, political and religious lives of the people."

$ $THE CHRISTIAN CENTURY, Christian Century Foundation, 104 S. Michigan Ave., Suite 700, Chicago IL 60605-1150. (312)263-7510. Fax: (312)263-7540. Website: www.christiancentury.org. **Contact:** David Heim, executive editor. **90% freelance written.** Eager to work with new/unpublished writers. Weekly magazine for ecumenically-minded, progressive Protestant church people, both clergy and lay. "Authors must have a critical and analytical perspective on the church and be familiar with contemporary theological discussion." Estab. 1884. Circ. 30,000. Pays on publication. Publishes ms an average of 3 months after acceptance. Byline given. Buys all rights. Editorial lead time 1 month. Submit seasonal material 4 months in advance. Accepts queries by mail, e-mail, fax, phone. Accepts simultaneous submissions. Responds in 1 week to queries; 2 months to mss. Sample copy for $3. Writer's guidelines online.
Nonfiction: "We use articles dealing with social problems, ethical dilemmas, political issues, international affairs and the arts, as well as with theological and ecclesiastical matters. We focus on issues of church and society, and church and culture." Essays, humor, interview/profile, opinion, religious. No inspirational. **Buys 150 mss/year.** Send complete ms; query appreciated, but not essential. Length: 1,000-3,000 words. **Pays $75-200 for assigned articles; $75-150 for unsolicited articles.**
Photos: State availability with submission. Reviews any size prints. Buys one-time rights. Offers $25-100/photo.
Fiction: Humorous, religious, slice-of-life vignettes. No moralistic, unrealistic fiction. **Buys 4 mss/year.** Send complete ms. Length: 1,000-3,000 words. **Pays $75-200.**
Poetry: Jill Pelaez Baumgaertner, poetry editor. Avant-garde, free verse, haiku, traditional. No sentimental or didactic poetry. **Buys 50/year poems/year.** Length: 20 lines. **Pays $50.**
Tips: "We seek manuscripts that articulate the public meaning of faith, bringing the resources of religious tradition to bear on such topics as poverty, human rights, economic justice, international relations, national priorities and popular culture. We are equally interested in articles that probe classical theological themes. We welcome articles that find fresh meaning in old traditions and which adapt or apply religious traditions to new circumstances. Authors should assume that readers are familiar with main themes in Christian history and theology; are unthreatened by the historical-critical study of the Bible; and are already engaged in relating faith to social and political issues. Many of our readers are ministers or teachers of religion at the college level."

$ CHRISTIAN COURIER, Reformed Faith Witness, 4-261 Martindale Rd., St. Catharines Ontario L2W 1A1, Canada. (905)682-8311. Fax: (905)682-8313. E-mail: cceditor@aol.com. **Contact:** Harry Der Nederlanden, editor. **20% freelance written.** Biweekly newspaper covering news of importance to Christians, comments and features. "We assume a Christian perspective which acknowledges that this world belongs to God and that human beings are invited to serve God in every area of society." Estab. 1945. Circ. 4,000. Pays 30 days after publication. Publishes ms an average of 2 months after acceptance. Byline given. Not copyrighted. Editorial lead time 1 month. Submit seasonal material 3 months in advance. Accepts simultaneous submissions. Responds only if material is accepted.
  O⊸ Break in by "addressing issues from a clearly biblical worldview without becoming moralistic, pietistic or didactic."
Nonfiction: Essays, historical/nostalgic, humor, inspirational, interview/profile, opinion, personal experience, religious, ideas, trends, developments in science and technology. **Buys 40 mss/year.** Send complete ms. Length: 500-1,500 words. **Pays $50-100 for assigned articles; $25-75 for unsolicited articles.**
Photos: State availability with submission. Pays $20/photo.

$ $CHRISTIAN HOME & SCHOOL, Christian Schools International, 3350 E. Paris Ave. SE, Grand Rapids MI 49512. (616)957-1070 ext. 239. Fax: (616)957-5022. E-mail: RogerS@CSIonline.org. Website: www.CSIonline.org/chs. Executive Editor: Gordon L. Bordewyk. **Contact:** Roger Schmurr, senior editor. **30% freelance written.** Works with a small number of new/unpublished writers each year. Bimonthly magazine covering family life and Christian education. "*Christian Home & School* is designed for parents in the United States and Canada who send their children to Christian schools and are concerned about the challenges facing Christian families today. These readers expect a mature, biblical perspective in the articles, not just a bible verse tacked onto the end." Estab. 1922. Circ. 65,000. Pays on publication. Publishes ms an average of 4 months after acceptance. Byline given. Buys first North American serial rights. Submit seasonal material 4 months in advance. Accepts queries by mail, e-mail. Responds in 1 month to queries. Sample copy and writer's guidelines for 9×12 SAE with 4 first-class stamps. Writer's guidelines only for #10 SAE or online.

• The editor reports an interest in seeing articles on how to raise polite kids in a rude world and good educational practices in Christian schools.

O— Break in by picking a contemporary parenting situation/problem, and writing to Christian parents.

Nonfiction: "We publish features on issues that affect the home and school and profiles on interesting individuals, providing that the profile appeals to our readers and is not a tribute or eulogy of that person." Book excerpts, interview/profile, opinion, personal experience, Articles on parenting and school life. **Buys 40 mss/year.** Send complete ms. Length: 1,000-2,000 words. **Pays $125-200.**

Photos: "If you have any color photos appropriate for your article, send them along."

Tips: "Features are the area most open to freelancers. We are publishing articles that deal with contemporary issues that affect parents. Use an informal easy-to-read style rather than a philosophical, academic tone. Try to incorporate vivid imagery and concrete, practical examples from real life. We look for manuscripts with a mature Christian perspective."

$ $ CHRISTIAN READER, Stories of Faith, Hope and God's Love, Christianity Today, 465 Gundersen Dr., Carol Stream IL 60188. (630)260-6200. Fax: (630)260-0114. E-mail: creditor@christianreader.net. Website: www.Christianreader.net. Editor: Bonne Steffen. **Contact:** Cynthia Thomas, editorial coordinator. **25% freelance written.** Bimonthly magazine for adult evangelical Christian audience. Estab. 1963. Circ. 185,000. Pays on acceptance; on publication for humor pieces. Byline given. Editorial lead time 5 months. Submit seasonal material 8 months in advance. Accepts queries by mail. Accepts simultaneous submissions. Responds in 1 month to queries. Sample copy for 5×8 SAE and 4 first-class stamps. Writer's guidelines for #10 SASE.

Nonfiction: Book excerpts, general interest, historical/nostalgic, humor, inspirational, interview/profile, personal experience, photo feature, religious. **Buys 100-125 mss/year.** Query with or without published clips or send complete ms. Length: 250-1,500 words. **Pays $125-600 depending on length.** Pays expenses of writers on assignment.

Reprints: Send tearsheet, photocopy or typed ms with rights for sale noted and information about when and where the material previously appeared. Pays 35-50% of amount paid for an original article.

Photos: Send photos with submission. Reviews transparencies, prints. Buys one-time rights. Negotiates payment individually. Identification of subjects required.

Columns/Departments: Lite Fare (adult church humor), 50-200 words; Kids of the Kingdom (kids say and do funny things), 50-200 words; Rolling Down the Aisle (humorous wedding tales), 50-200 words. **Buys 50-75 mss/year.** Send complete ms. **Pays $25-35.**

Fillers: Anecdotes, short fillers. **Buys 10-20/year.** Length: 100-250 words. **Pays $35.**

Tips: "Most of our articles are reprints or staff-written. Freelance competition is keen, so tailor submissions to meet our needs by observing the following: The *Christian Reader* audience is truly a general interest one, including men and women, urban professionals and rural homemakers, adults of every age and marital status, and Christians of every church affiliation. We seek to publish a magazine that people from the variety of ethnic groups in North America will find interesting and relevant."

$ $ CHRISTIAN SOCIAL ACTION, 100 Maryland Ave. NE, Washington DC 20002. (202)488-5631. Fax: (202)488-1617. E-mail: ealsgaard@umc-gbcs.org. **Contact:** Erik Alsgaard, editor. **10% freelance written.** Works with a small number of new/unpublished writers each year. Bimonthly magazine for "United Methodist clergy and lay people interested in in-depth analysis of social issues, with emphasis on the church's role or involvement in these issues." Circ. 50,000. Pays on publication. Publishes ms an average of 2 months after acceptance. Rights purchased vary with author and material. Accepts queries by mail, e-mail. Responds in 2 months to queries. Writer's guidelines for #10 SASE.

Nonfiction: "This is the social action publication of The United Methodist Church published by the denomination's General Board of Church and Society. Our publication tries to relate social issues to the church—what the church can do, is doing; why the church should be involved. We only accept articles relating to social issues, e.g., war, draft, peace, race relations, welfare, police/community relations, labor, population problems, drug and alcohol problems. No devotional, 'religious,' superficial material, highly technical articles, personal experience or poetry." **Buys 10-15 mss/year.** Query to show that you have expertise on a particular social issue, give credentials, and reflect a readable writing style. Length: 2,000 words maximum. **Pays $200-250.** Sometimes pays expenses of writers on assignment.

Reprints: Send tearsheet and information about when and where the material previously appeared. Payment negotiable.

Tips: "Write on social issues, but not superficially; we're more interested in finding an expert who can write (e.g., on human rights, alcohol problems, peace issues) than a writer who attempts to research a complex issue. Be clear, be brief, be understandable. No poetry."

$ $ CHRISTIANITY TODAY, 465 Gundersen Dr., Carol Stream IL 60188-2498. (630)260-6200. Fax: (630)260-8428. E-mail: CTEditor@ChristianityToday.com. Website: www.christianitytoday.com. **Contact:** Mark Galli, managing editor. **80% freelance written.** Works with a small number of new/unpublished writers each year. Biweekly magazine emphasizing orthodox, evangelical religion, "covers Christian doctrine, issues, trends and current events and news from a Christian perspective. It provides a forum for the expression of evangelical conviction in theology, evangelism, church life, cultural life, and society. Special features include issues of the day, books, films, missions, schools, music and services available to the Christian market." Estab. 1956. Circ. 154,000. Publishes ms an average of 6 months after acceptance. Buys first rights. Submit seasonal material at least 8 months in advance. Accepts queries by mail, e-mail, fax. Responds in 3 months to queries. Sample copy and writer's guidelines for 9×12 SAE with 3 first-class stamps.

Nonfiction: Book excerpts, essays, interview/profile, opinion, theological, ethical, historical, informational (not merely inspirational). **Buys 96 mss/year.** *Query only.* Unsolicited mss not accepted and not returned. Length: 1,000-4,000 words. **Pays negotiable rates.** Sometimes pays expenses of writers on assignment.

Reprints: Accepts previously published submissions. Pays 25% of amount paid for an original article.

Columns/Departments: The CT Review (books, the arts, and popular culture). Length: 900-1,000 words. **Buys 7 mss/year.** *Query only.*

　　■ The online magazine carries original content not found in the print edition. Contact: Ted Olsen, online editor.

Tips: "We are developing more of our own manuscripts and requiring a much more professional quality from others. Queries without SASE will not be answered and manuscripts not containing SASE will not be returned."

$ $ CHRYSALIS READER, R.R. 1, Box 4510, Dillwyn VA 23936. E-mail: chrysalis@hovac.com. Website: www.s wedenborg.com. Managing Editor: Susanna van Rensselaer. **Contact:** Richard Butterworth, editorial associate. **90% freelance written.** Biannual literary magazine on spiritually related topics. "*It is very important to send for writer's guidelines and sample copies before submitting.* Content of fiction, articles, reviews, poetry, etc., should be directly focused on that issue's theme and directed to the educated, intellectually curious reader." Estab. 1985. Circ. 3,000. Pays at page-proof stage. Publishes ms an average of 9 months after acceptance. Byline given. Buys first rights, makes work-for-hire assignments. Accepts queries by mail, e-mail. Responds in 1 month to queries; 4 months to mss. Sample copy for $10 and 8½×11 SAE. Writer's guidelines and copy deadlines for SASE or by e-mail.

　　● E-mail for themes and guidelines (no mss will be accepted by e-mail).

Nonfiction: Upcoming themes: Autumn (2001); Serendipity (2002). Essays, interview/profile. **Buys 20 mss/year.** Query. Length: 2,500-3,500 words. **Pays $50-250 for assigned articles; $50-150 for unsolicited articles.**

Photos: Send suggestions for illustrations with submission. Buys original artwork for cover and inside copy; b&w illustrations related to theme; pays $25-150. Buys one-time rights. Offers no additional payment for photos accepted with ms. Captions, identification of subjects required.

Fiction: Robert Tucker, fiction editor. Short fiction more likely to be published. Adventure, experimental, historical, mainstream, mystery, science fiction. **Buys 10 mss/year.** Query. Length: 2,500-3,500 words. **Pays $50-150.**

Poetry: Rob Lawson, senior editor. Avant-garde and traditional *but not religious.* **Buys 15 poems/year.** Submit maximum 6 poems. **Pays $25.**

$ $ COLUMBIA, 1 Columbus Plaza, New Haven CT 06510. (203)772-2130. Fax: (203)777-0114. E-mail: thickey @kofc-supreme.com. Website: www.kofc.org. **Contact:** Tim S. Hickey, editor. Monthly magazine for Catholic families. Caters primarily to members of the Knights of Columbus. Estab. 1921. Circ. 1,500,000. **Pays on acceptance.** Buys first North American serial rights. Accepts queries by mail, e-mail, fax. Sample copy and writer's guidelines free.

Nonfiction: Fact articles directed to the Catholic layman and his family dealing with current events, social problems, Catholic apostolic activities, education, ecumenism, rearing a family, literature, science, arts, sports and leisure. No reprints, poetry or cartoons. **Buys 20 mss/year.** Query with SASE. Length: 1,000-1,500 words. **Pays $300-600.**

　　■ The online magazine carries original content not found in the print edition. Contact: Tim S. Hickey, online editor.

Tips: "Few unsolicited manuscripts are accepted."

$ CONSCIENCE, A Newsjournal of Prochoice Catholic Opinion, Catholics for a Free Choice, 1436 U St. NW, Suite 301, Washington DC 20009-3997. (202)986-6093. E-mail: conscience@catholicsforchoice.org. Website: www.catholicsforchoice.org. **Contact:** Editor. **60% freelance written.** Sometimes works with new/unpublished writers. Quarterly newsjournal covering reproductive health and rights, including but not limited to abortion rights in the church, and church-state issues in US and worldwide. "A feminist, pro-choice perspective is a must, and knowledge of Christianity and specifically Catholicism is helpful." Estab. 1980. Circ. 12,000. Pays on publication. Publishes ms an average of 4 months after acceptance. Byline given. Buys first North American serial rights, makes work-for-hire assignments. Accepts queries by mail, e-mail. Responds in 4 months to queries. Sample copy for 9×12 SAE and 4 first-class stamps. Writer's guidelines for #10 SASE.

Nonfiction: Especially needs material that recognizes the complexity of reproductive issues and decisions, and offers original, honest insight. "Writers should be aware that we are a nonprofit organization." Book excerpts, interview/profile, opinion, personal experience (a small amount), issue analysis. **Buys 4-8 mss/year.** Query with published clips or send complete ms. Length: 1,500-3,500 words. **Pays $150-200.**

Reprints: Send typed ms with rights for sale noted and information about when and where the material previously appeared. Pays 20-30% of amount paid for an original article.

Photos: Prefers b&w prints. State availability with submission. Identification of subjects required.

Columns/Departments: Book reviews, 600-1,200 words. **Buys 4-8 mss/year. Pays $50-75.**

Tips: "Say something new on the issue of abortion, or sexuality, or the role of religion or the Catholic church, or women's status in the church. Thoughtful, well-researched and well-argued articles needed. The most frequent mistakes made by writers in submitting an article to us are lack of originality and wordiness."

$ $ CORNERSTONE, Cornerstone Communications, Inc., 939 W. Wilson, Chicago IL 60640-5718. (773)561-2450 ext. 2080. Fax: (773)989-2076. E-mail: fiction@cornerstonemag.com; poetry@cornerstonemag.com; nonfiction@cornerstonemag.com. Website: www.cornerstonemag.com. Editor: Jon Trott. **Contact:** Submissions Editor. **10% freelance written.** Eager to work with new/unpublished writers. Irregularly published magazine covering contemporary issues in the light of Evangelical Christianity. Estab. 1972. Pays after publication. Byline given. Buys first North American serial rights. Submit seasonal material 6 months in advance. Accepts simultaneous submissions. Does not return mss to mss. Sample copy and writer's guidelines for 8½×11 SAE with 5 first-class stamps.

● "We will contact you *only* if your work is accepted for possible publication. We *encourage* simultaneous submissions because we take so long to get back to people! E-mail all submissions to appropriate address (if e-mail is unavailable to you, we accept hard copies). Send no queries."

Nonfiction: Essays, personal experience, religious, well-researched articles on social issues. **Buys 1-2 mss/year.** E-mail complete ms. Length: 2,700 words maximum. **Pays 8-10¢/word.**

Reprints: E-mail ms with rights for sale noted and information about when and where the material previously appeared. Pays 8-10¢/word.

Columns/Departments: Music (interview with artists, mainly rock, focusing on artist's world view and value system as expressed in his/her music), Current Events, Personalities, Film and Book Reviews (focuses on meaning as compared and contrasted to biblical values). Length: 100-2,500 words (negotiable). **Buys 1-4 mss/year.** E-mail complete ms. **Pays 8-10¢/word.**

Fiction: "Articles may express Christian world view but should not be unrealistic or 'syrupy.' Other than porn, the sky's the limit. We want fiction as creative as the Creator." **Buys 1-4 mss/year.** Length: 250-2,500 words (negotiable). **Pays negotiable rate, 8-10¢/word.**

Poetry: "No limits *except* for epic poetry ("We've not the room!"). Avant-garde, free verse, haiku, light verse, traditional. **Buys 10-50 poems/year.** Submit maximum 5 poems. **Payment negotiated. 1-15 lines: $10; over 15 lines: $25.**

▣ The online magazine carries original content not found in the print edition. Contact: Jon Trott, online editor.

Tips: "A display of creativity which expresses a biblical world view without clichés or cheap shots at non-Christians is the ideal. We are known as one of the most avant-garde magazines in the Christian market, yet attempt to express orthodox beliefs in today's language. *Any* writer who does this well may be published by *Cornerstone*. Creative fiction is begging for more Christian participation. We anticipate such contributions gladly. Interviews where well-known personalities respond to the gospel are also strong publication possibilities."

$ $ DECISION, Billy Graham Evangelistic Association, 1300 Harmon Place, Minneapolis MN 55403-1988. (612)338-0500. Fax: (612)335-1299. E-mail: submissions@bgea.org. Website: www.decisionmag.org. Editor: Kersten Beckstrom. **Contact:** Bob Paulson, associate editor. **25-40% freelance written.** Works each year with small number of new/unpublished writers, as well as a solid stable of experienced writers. Monthly magazine with a mission "to set forth to every reader the Good News of salvation in Jesus Christ with such vividness and clarity that he or she will be drawn to make a commitment to Christ; to encourage, teach and strengthen Christians." Estab. 1960. Circ. 1,400,000. Pays on publication. Publishes ms an average of up to 18 months after acceptance. Byline given. Offers 50% kill fee. Buys first rights, assigns work-for-hire manuscripts, articles, projects. Editorial lead time 1 year. Submit seasonal material 10 months in advance. Responds in 3 months to mss. Sample copy for 9×12 SAE and 4 first-class stamps. Writer's guidelines for #10 SASE.

● Include telephone number with submission.

○─ "The best way to break into our publication is to submit an article with strong takeaway for the readers. Remember that your specific experience is not the point. The point is what you learned and applied that the readers could apply to their own experiences."

Nonfiction: How-to, inspirational, personal experience, religious, motivational. "No personality-centered articles or articles that are issue-oriented or critical of denominations." **Buys approximately 75 mss/year.** Send complete ms. Length: 400-1,500 words. **Pays $30-260.** Pays expenses of writers on assignment.

Photos: State availability with submission. Reviews prints. Buys one-time rights. Captions, identification of subjects, model releases required.

Columns/Departments: Where Are They Now? (people who have become Christians through Billy Graham Ministries), 500-600 words. **Buys 12 mss/year.** Send complete ms. **Pays $85.**

Poetry: Amanda Knoke, assistant editor. Free verse, light verse, traditional. **Buys 6 poems/year.** Submit maximum 7 poems. Length: 4-16 lines. **Pays 60¢/word.**

Fillers: Anecdotes. **Buys 50/year.** Length: 300-500 words. **Pays $25-75.**

Tips: "We are seeking personal conversion testimonies and personal experience articles that show how God intervened in a person's daily life and the way in which Scripture was applied in helping to solve the problem. The conversion testimonies describe in first person what author's life was like before becoming a Christian, how he/she committed his/her life to Christ and what difference Christ has made. We also look for vignettes on various aspects of personal evangelism. SASE required with submissions."

$ $▨ DISCIPLESHIP JOURNAL, NavPress, a division of The Navigators, P.O. Box 35004, Colorado Springs CO 80935-0004. (719)531-3514. Fax: (719)598-7128. E-mail: sue.kline@navpress.com. Website: www.discipleshipjournal.com. **Contact:** Sue Kline, editor. **90% freelance written.** Works with a small number of new/unpublished writers each year. Bimonthly magazine. "The mission of *Discipleship Journal* is to help believers develop a deeper relationship with Jesus Christ, and to provide practical help in understanding the scriptures and applying them to daily life and ministry. We prefer those who have not written for us before begin with non-theme articles about almost any aspect of Christian living. We'd like more articles that explain a Bible passage and show how to apply it to everyday life, as well as articles about developing a relationship with Jesus; reaching the world; growing in some aspect of Christian character; or specific issues related to leadership and helping other believers grow." Estab. 1981. Circ. 115,000. **Pays on acceptance.** Publishes ms an average of 6 months after acceptance. Byline given. Buys first North American serial, second serial (reprint), electronic rights. Submit seasonal material 6 months in advance. Accepts queries by mail, e-mail, fax. Responds in 6 weeks to queries. Sample copy and writer's guidelines for $2.56 and 9×12 SAE or online.

O→ Break in through departments (On the Home Front, Getting into God's Word, DJ Plus) and with non-theme feature articles.

Nonfiction: "We'd like to see more articles that encourage involvement in world missions; help readers in personal evangelism, follow-up, and Christian leadership; or show how to develop a real relationship with Jesus." Book excerpts (rarely), how-to (grow in Christian faith and disciplines; help others grow as Christians; serve people in need; understand and apply the Bible), inspirational, interpretation/application of the Bible. No personal testimony; humor; anything not directly related to Christian life and faith; politically partisan articles. **Buys 80 mss/year.** Query with published clips and SASE only. Length: 500-2,500 words. **Pays 25¢/word for first rights.** Sometimes pays expenses of writers on assignment.

Reprints: Send tearsheet and information about when and where the material previously appeared. Pays 5¢/word for reprints.

Tips: "Our articles are meaty, not fluffy. Study writer's guidelines and back issues and try to use similar approaches. Don't preach. Polish before submitting. About half of the articles in each issue are related to one theme. Freelancers should write to request theme list. We are looking for more practical articles on ministering to others and more articles on growing in Christian character. Be vulnerable. Show the reader that you have wrestled with the subject matter in your own life. We can no longer accept unsolicited manuscripts. Query first."

N $ $ THE DOOR, P.O. Box 1444, Waco TX 76703-1444. (214)827-2625. Fax: (254)752-4915. E-mail: rfd3@fl ash.net. Website: www.thedoormagazine.com. **Contact:** Robert Darden, senior editor. **90% freelance written.** Works with a large number of new/unpublished writers each year. Bimonthly magazine. "*The Door* is the world's only, oldest and largest religious humor and satire magazine." Estab. 1969. Circ. 14,000. Pays on publication. Publishes ms an average of 1 year after acceptance. Buys first rights. Accepts queries by mail. Responds in 3 months to mss. Sample copy for $5.98. Writer's guidelines for #10 SASE.

O→ Read several issues of the magazine first! Get the writer's guidelines.

Nonfiction: Looking for humorous/satirical articles on church renewal, Christianity and organized religion. Exposé, humor, interview/profile, religious. No book reviews or poetry. **Buys 30 mss/year.** Send complete ms. Length: 1,500 words maximum; 750-1,000 preferred. **Pays $60-200.** Sometimes pays expenses of writers on assignment.

Reprints: Send typed ms with rights for sale noted and information about when and where the material previously appeared. Pays 100% of amount paid for an original article.

■ The online magazine carries original content not found in the print edition. Contact: Robert Darden.

Tips: "We look for someone who is clever, on our wave length, and has some savvy about the evangelical church. We are very picky and highly selective. The writer has a better chance of breaking in with our publication with short articles since we are a bimonthly publication with numerous regular features and the magazine is only 52 pages. The most frequent mistake made by writers is that they do not understand satire. They see we are a humor magazine and consequently come off funny/cute (like *Reader's Digest*) rather than funny/satirical (like *National Lampoon*)."

$ DOVETAIL, A Journal By and For Jewish/Christian Families, Dovetail Institute for Interfaith Family Resources, 775 Simon Greenwell Ln., Boston KY 40107. (502)549-5499. Fax: (502)549-3543. E-mail: di-ifr@bardstown.c om. Website: www.dovetailpublishing.com. **Contact:** Mary Helene Rosenbaum, editor. **75% freelance written.** Bimonthly newsletter for interfaith families. "All articles must pertain to life in an interfaith (Jewish/Christian) family. We accept all kinds of opinions related to this topic." Estab. 1992. Circ. 1,500. Pays on publication. Publishes ms an average of 9 months after acceptance. Byline given. Buys first, one-time, second serial (reprint) rights. Editorial lead time 6 months. Submit seasonal material 6 months in advance. Accepts queries by mail, e-mail, fax, phone. Accepts simultaneous submissions. Responds in 3 months to queries. Sample copy for 9×12 SAE and 3 first-class stamps. Writer's guidelines free.

O→ Break in with "a fresh approach to standard interfaith marriage situations."

Nonfiction: Book reviews, 500 words. Pays $10 plus 2 copies. Book excerpts, interview/profile, opinion, personal experience. No fiction. **Buys 5-8 mss/year.** Send complete ms. Length: 800-1,000 words. **Pays $20 plus 2 copies.**

Photos: Send photos with submission. Reviews 5×7 prints. Buys one-time rights. Offers no additional payment for photos accepted with ms. Identification of subjects, model releases required.

Fillers: Anecdotes, short humor. **Buys 1-2/year.** Length: 25-100 words. **Pays $10.**

Tips: "Write on concrete, specific topics related to Jewish/Christian intermarriage: no proselytizing, sermonizing, or general religious commentary. Successful freelancers are part of an interfaith family themselves, or have done solid research/interviews with members of interfaith families. We look for honest, reflective personal experience. We're looking for more on alternative or nontraditional families, e.g., interfaith gay/lesbian, single parent raising child in departed partner's faith."

$ ▨ EVANGEL, Free Methodist Publishing House, P.O. Box 535002, Indianapolis IN 46253-5002. (317)244-3660. **Contact:** Julie Innes, editor. **100% freelance written.** Weekly take-home paper for adults. Estab. 1897. Circ. 20,000. Pays on publication. Publishes ms an average of 1 year after acceptance. Buys simultaneous, second serial (reprint) or one-time rights. Submit seasonal material 9 months in advance. Accepts queries by mail. Responds in 1 month to queries. Sample copy and writer's guidelines for #10 SASE.
Nonfiction: Interview (with ordinary person who is doing something extraordinary in his community, in service to others); profile (of missionary or one from similar service profession who is contributing significantly to society); personal experience (finding a solution to a problem common to young adults; coping with handicapped child, for instance, or with a neighborhood problem. Story of how God-given strength or insight saved a situation). Interview/ profile, personal experience. **Buys 125 mss/year.** Send complete ms. Length: 300-1,000 words. **Pays 4¢/word.**
Reprints: Send typed ms with rights for sale noted and information about when and where the material previously appeared.
Photos: Purchased with accompanying ms. Captions required.
Fiction: Religious themes dealing with contemporary issues dealt with from a Christian frame of reference. Story must "go somewhere." **Buys 50 mss/year.** Send complete ms.
Poetry: Free verse, light verse, traditional, religious. **Buys 20 poems/year.** Submit maximum 5 poems. Length: 4-24 lines. **Pays $10.**
Tips: "Seasonal material will get a second look. Write an attention-grabbing lead followed by an article that says something worthwhile. Relate the lead to some of the universal needs of the reader—promise in that lead to help the reader in some way. Lack of SASE brands author as a nonprofessional."

$ THE EVANGELICAL BAPTIST, Fellowship of Evangelical Baptist Churches in Canada, 18 Louvigny, Lorraine, Quebec J6Z 1T7, Canada. (450)621-3248. Fax: (450)621-0253. E-mail: eb@fellowship.ca. Website: www.fellowship.ca. **Contact:** Ginette Cotnoir, managing editor. **30% freelance written.** Magazine published 5 times/year covering religious, spiritual, Christian living, denominational and missionary news. "We exist to enhance the life and ministry of the church leaders of our association of churches—including pastors, elders, deacons and all the men and women doing the work of the ministry in local churches." Estab. 1953. Circ. 3,000. Pays on publication. Publishes ms an average of 6 months after acceptance. Byline given. Buys one-time, second serial (reprint) rights. Editorial lead time 4 months. Accepts queries by mail, e-mail. Accepts simultaneous submissions. Sample copy for 9 × 12 SAE with $1.50 in Canadian first-class stamps. Writer's guidelines for #10 SASE (Canadian stamps only).
O➜ Break in with items for "Church Life (how-to and how-we articles about church ministries, e.g., small groups, worship, missions) or Columns (Joy in the Journey, View from the Pew)."
Nonfiction: Religious. No poetry, fiction, puzzles. **Buys 12-15 mss/year.** Send complete ms. Length: 500-2,400 words. **Pays $25-50.**
Photos: State availability with submission. Reviews prints. Buys one-time rights. Offers no additional payment for photos accepted with ms. Captions required.
Columns/Departments: Church Life (practical articles about various church ministries, e.g., worship, Sunday school, missions, seniors, youth, discipleship); Joy in the Journey (devotional article re: a lesson learned from God in everyday life); View from the Pew (light, humorous piece with spiritual value on some aspect of Christian living), all 600-800 words. **Buys 10 mss/year.** Send complete ms. **Pays $25-50.**
Tips: "Columns and departments are the best places for freelancers. Especially looking for practical articles for Church Life from writers who are themselves involved in a church ministry. Looking for 'how-to' and 'how-we' approach."

$ EVANGELICAL MISSIONS QUARTERLY, A Professional Journal Serving the Missions Community, Billy Graham Center/Wheaton College, P.O. Box 794, Wheaton IL 60189. (630)752-7158. Fax: (630)752-7155. E-mail: emqjournal@aol.com. Website: www.wheaton.edu/bgc/emis. Editor: Gary Corwin. **Contact:** Managing Editor. **67% freelance written.** Quarterly magazine covering evangelical missions. "This is a professional journal for evangelical missionaries, agency executives and church members who support global missions ministries." Estab. 1964. Circ. 7,000. Pays on publication. Publishes ms an average of 18 months after acceptance. Byline given. Offers negotiable kill fee. Buys electronic, all rights. Editorial lead time 1 year. Accepts queries by mail, e-mail, fax, phone. Responds in 2 weeks to queries. Sample copy and writer's guidelines free.
Nonfiction: Essays, interview/profile, opinion, personal experience, religious. No sermons, poetry, straight news. **Buys 24 mss/year.** Query. Length: 800-3,000 words. **Pays $50-100.**
Photos: Send photos with submission. Buys first rights. Offers no additional payment for photos accepted with ms. Identification of subjects required.
Columns/Departments: In the Workshop (practical how to's), 800-2,000 words; Perspectives (opinion), 800 words. **Buys 8 mss/year.** Query. **Pays $50-100.**
▣ The online magazine carries original content not found in the print edition. Contact: Dona Diehl, online editor.

$ $EVANGELIZING TODAY'S CHILD, Child Evangelism Fellowship Inc., Box 348, Warrenton MO 63383-0348. (636)456-4321. Fax: (636)456-4321. E-mail: etceditor@cefinc.org. Website: www.cefinc.org/etcmag/. **Contact:** Elsie Lippy, editor. **50% freelance written.** Bimonthly magazine. "Our purpose is to equip Christians to win the world's children to Christ and disciple them. Our readership is Sunday school teachers, Christian education leaders and children's workers in every phase of Christian ministry to children up to 12 years old." Estab. 1942. Circ. 20,000. Pays within 90 days of acceptance. Publishes ms an average of 6 months after acceptance. Byline given. Offers kills fee. Buys first North American serial rights. Submit seasonal material 6 months in advance. Accepts queries by mail, e-mail, fax. Responds in 2 months to queries. Sample copy for $2. Writer's guidelines for #10 SASE.

Nonfiction: Unsolicited articles welcomed from writers with Christian education training or current experience in working with children. **Buys 35 mss/year.** Query. Length: 900 words. **Pays 10-14¢/word.**

Reprints: Send photocopy and information about when and where the material previously appeared. Pays 35% of amount paid for an original article.

N **$** **EXPRESSION, Christian Newspaper**, Sunshine Foundation International, Inc., P.O. Box 44148, Pittsburgh PA 15205-0348. (412)920-5547. Fax: (412)920-5549. E-mail: editor@expressionnews.org. Website: www.expressionne ws.org. **Contact:** Cathy Hickling, editor. **15% freelance written.** Monthly tabloid covering Christianity—non-denominational. "We believe that all Christians are one in Christ. To promote Christian unity, we publish articles concerning things that Christians have in common with one another. Also of interest are issues that tend to divide and cause strife. We publish the news about what Jesus is doing through the lives of people all over." Estab. 1981. Circ. 15,000. Pays on publication. Byline given. Buys one-time rights. Editorial lead time 1 month. Submit seasonal material 1 month in advance. Accepts queries by mail, e-mail. Accepts simultaneous submissions. Responds in 2 weeks to queries. Sample copy and writer's guidelines free.

Nonfiction: Inspirational, religious. No poetry. Query. Length: 400-1,600 words. **Pays $25-100 for assigned articles; $25-50 for unsolicited articles.**

Photos: Send photos with submission. Buys one-time rights. Offers no additional payment for photos accepted with ms. Captions, identification of subjects required.

Columns/Departments: Buys 2-4 mss/year. Query. **Pays $25-75.**

Fillers: Facts, newsbreaks. Length: 60-200 words. **Pays $25.**

Tips: "Stories should be written to be understood by the general public. Religious jargon and clichés should be avoided. If your story communicates effectively to the non-Christian, then anyone will be able to understand it. *Expression* needs and wants talented writers. If you have any ideas, do not hesitate to write and let us know. No idea is too outrageous. We desire originality and creativity."

$** **$ **FAITH TODAY, Informing Canadian Evangelicals On Thoughts, Trends, Issues and Events**, Evangelical Fellowship of Canada, MIP Box 3745, Markham, Ontario L3R 0Y4, Canada. (905)479-5885. Fax: (905)479-4742. E-mail: ft@efc-canada.com. Website: www.efc-canada.com. Managing Editor: Gail Reid. **Contact:** Bill Fledderus, senior editor. Bimonthly magazine. "*FT* is an interdenominational, evangelical news/feature magazine that informs Canadian Christians on issues facing church and society, and on events within the church community. It focuses on corporate faith interacting with society rather than on personal spiritual life. Writers should have a thorough understanding of the *Canadian evangelical* community." Estab. 1983. Circ. 18,000. Pays on publication. Publishes ms an average of 6 months after acceptance. Byline given. Offers 30-50% kill fee. Buys first rights. Editorial lead time 4 months. Accepts queries by mail, e-mail, fax. Responds in 6 weeks to queries. Sample copy for SASE in Canadian postage. Writer's guidelines for SASE in Canadian postage or by e-mail.

    O⚓ Break in by "researching the Canadian field and including in your query a list of the Canadian contacts (Christian or not) that you intend to interview."

Nonfiction: Book excerpts (Canadian authors only), essays (Canadian authors only), interview/profile (Canadian subjects only), opinion, religious, news feature. **Buys 75 mss/year.** Query. Length: 400-2,000 words. **Pays $100-500 Canadian, more for cover topic material.** Sometimes pays expenses of writers on assignment.

Reprints: Send photocopy. Rarely used. Pays 50% of amount paid for an original article.

Photos: State availability with submission. Reviews contact sheets. Buys one-time rights. Identification of subjects required.

Tips: "Query should include brief outline and names of the sources you plan to interview in your research. Use Canadian postage on SASE."

$ **THE FIVE STONES, Newsletter for Small Churches**, 69 Weymouth St., Providence RI 02906. (401)861-9405. E-mail: pappas@tabcom.org. **Contact:** Tony Pappas, editor. **33% freelance written.** Quarterly newsletter covering issues related to small church life. "*The Five Stones* is the only journal for the issues small congregations face. First-person articles and accounts of positive experiences best." Circ. 750. Pays on publication. Byline given. Not copyrighted. Editorial lead time 1 year. Submit seasonal material 1 year in advance. Accepts queries by mail, e-mail, fax, phone. Accepts simultaneous submissions. Responds in 1 month to queries; 4 months to mss. Sample copy for 9×12 SAE and 3 first-class stamps. Writer's guidelines for #10 SASE.

Nonfiction: Book excerpts, essays, general interest, historical/nostalgic, how-to, humor, inspirational, interview/profile, new product, personal experience, religious. **Buys 8-12 mss/year.** Send complete ms. Length: 1,500 words maximum. **Pays $5.**

Reprints: Accepts previously published submissions.

N **$** **FORWARD IN CHRIST, The Word from the WELS**, (formerly *Northwestern Lutheran*), WELS, 2929 N. Mayfair Rd., Milwaukee WI 53222-4398. (414)256-3888. Fax: (414)256-3899. E-mail: fic@sab.wels.net. Website: www.wels.net. **Contact:** Gary P. Baumler, editor. **5% freelance written.** Monthly magazine covering WELS news, topics, issues. The material usually must be written by or about WELS members. Estab. 1913. Circ. 56,000. Pays on publication. Publishes ms an average of 6 months after acceptance. Byline given. Buys one-time rights. Editorial lead time 3 months. Submit seasonal material 4 months in advance. Accepts queries by mail, e-mail, fax. Responds in 2 months to queries. Sample copy and writer's guidelines free.

Nonfiction: Julie Tessmer, senior communications assistant. Personal experience, religious. Query. Length: 550-1,200 words. **Pays $75/page, $12½ pages.** Sometimes pays expenses of writers on assignment.

Photos: State availability with submission. Reviews contact sheets. Buys one-time rights plus 1 month on Web. Negotiates payment individually. Captions, identification of subjects, model releases required.

Fillers: Gary Baumler, editor.

Tips: "Topics should be of interest to the majority of the members of the synod—the people in the pews. Articles should have a Christian viewpoint, but we don't want sermons. We suggest you carefully read at least five or six issues with close attention to the length, content and style of the features."

N $ ◪ GOD ALLOWS U-TURNS, Stories of Hope and Healing, #2 and #3, The God Allows U-Turns Project, P.O. Box 717, Faribault MN 55021-0717. Fax: (507)334-6464. E-mail: editor@godallowsuturns.com. Website: www.godallowsuturns.com. **Contact:** Allison Gappa Bottke, editor. **100% freelance written.** Christian inspirational book series. "Each anthology will contain over 100 uplifting, encouraging and inspirational true stories written by contributors from all over the world. Multiple volumes are planned." Published by Barbour Publishing under Promise Press imprint in association with Alive Communications, Inc. Estab. 2000. Pays on publication. Byline given. Accepts queries by mail, e-mail, fax. Accepts simultaneous submissions. Responds in 4 months to mss. Sample copy online. Writer's guidelines online or for #10 SASE.

Nonfiction: "Open to well-written personal inspirational pieces showing how faith in God can inspire, encourage and heal. True stories that must touch our emotions." Essays, historical/nostalgic, humor, inspirational, interview/profile, personal experience, religious. **Buys 100 mss/year. Pays $50-100 plus one copy of anthology.**

Tips: "See the website for a sample story. Keep it real. Ordinary people doing extraordinary things with God's help. These true stories must touch our emotions. Our contributors are a diverse group with no limits on age or denomination."

$ $ GROUP MAGAZINE, Group Publishing Inc., P.O. Box 481, Loveland CO 80539. (970)669-3836. Fax: (970)669-1994. E-mail: rlawrence@grouppublishing.com. Website: www.youthministry.com. Publisher: Tim Gilmour. Departments Editor: Kathy Dieterich. **Contact:** Rick Lawrence, editor. **60% freelance written.** Bimonthly magazine covering youth ministry. "Writers must be actively involved in youth ministry. Articles we accept are practical, not theoretical, and focused for local church youth workers." Estab. 1974. Circ. 57,000. **Pays on acceptance.** Publishes ms an average of 6 months after acceptance. Byline given. Offers $20 kill fee. Buys all rights. Submit seasonal material 7 months in advance. Responds in 2 months to queries. Sample copy for $2 and 9 × 12 SAE. Writer's guidelines for SASE or online.

Nonfiction: How-to (youth ministry issues). No personal testimony, theological or lecture-style articles. **Buys 50-60 mss/year.** Query. Length: 250-2,200 words. **Pays $40-250.** Sometimes pays expenses of writers on assignment.

Tips: "Submit a youth ministry idea to one of our mini-article sections—we look for tried-and-true ideas youth ministers have used with kids."

$ HOME TIMES, "A Good Little Newspaper for God & Country," Neighbor News, Inc., 3676 Collin Dr., #16, West Palm Beach FL 33406. (561)439-3509. Fax: (561)968-1758. E-mail: hometimes2@aol.com. Website: www.hometimes.org. **Contact:** Dennis Lombard, publisher/editor. **50% freelance written.** Monthly tabloid of conservative, pro-Christian news and views. "*Home Times* is a conservative newspaper written for the general public but with a Biblical worldview and family-values slant. It is not religious or preachy." Estab. 1988. Circ. 5,000. Pays on publication. Publishes ms an average of 3 months after acceptance. Byline given. Buys one-time rights. Editorial lead time 2 months. Submit seasonal material 2 months in advance. Accepts simultaneous submissions. Sample copy for $3. Writer's guidelines for #10 SASE.

Nonfiction: Essays, general interest, historical/nostalgic, how-to, humor, inspirational, interview/profile, opinion, personal experience, photo feature, religious, travel, current events. "Nothing preachy, moralistic or with churchy slant." **Buys 25 mss/year.** Send complete ms. Length: 500-900 words. **Pays $5 minimum for assigned articles.** Pays contributor's copies or subscriptions on mutual agreement.

Reprints: Send tearsheet or photocopy and information about when and where the material previously appeared. Pays $5-10.

Photos: Send photos with submission. Reviews any size prints. Buys one-time rights. Offers $5/photo used. Captions, identification of subjects, model releases required.

Columns/Departments: Buys 50 mss/year. Send complete ms. **Pays $5-15.**

Fiction: Historical, humorous, mainstream, religious, issue-oriented contemporary. "Nothing preachy, moralistic." **Buys 5 mss/year.** Send complete ms. Length: 500-700 words. **Pays $5-25.**

Poetry: Free verse, light verse, traditional. **Buys 12 poems/year.** Submit maximum 3 poems. Length: 2-24 lines. **Pays $5.**

Fillers: Anecdotes, facts, short humor, good quotes. **Buys 25/year.** Length: 100 word maximum. **Pays 3-6 issues on acceptance.**

Tips: "We encourage new writers. We are different from ordinary news or religious publications. We strongly suggest you read guidelines and sample issues. (Writer's subscription 12 issues for $12, regularly $16.) We are most open to material for new columns; journalists covering hard news in major news centers—with conservative slant. Also, lots of letters and short op-eds though we pay only in issues (3-6) for them. We're also looking for good creative nonfiction, especially historical, conservative and/or humorous."

$ $ INSIDE JOURNAL, The Hometown Newspaper of America's Prisoners, Prison Fellowship Ministries, P.O. Box 17429, Washington DC 20041-0429. (703)478-0100. Fax: (703)318-0235. E-mail: jpeck@pfm.org. Editor: Terry White. **Contact:** Jeff Peck, managing editor. **5% freelance written.** Bimonthly newspaper covering prisons, prison life, surviving prison. "*IJ* is a Christian newspaper written exclusively for prisoners. All content is passed through a Christian worldview to inspire hope and aid inmates in their present circumstances. Material must have direct influence on prison life with practical takeaway value for the readers." Estab. 1990. Circ. 400,000. Pays on publication. Publishes ms an average of 2 months after acceptance. Byline given. Buys first, second serial (reprint), simultaneous rights. Editorial lead time 2 months. Submit seasonal material 2 months in advance. Accepts queries by mail, e-mail. Accepts simultaneous submissions. Responds in 2 months to queries; 8 months to mss. Sample copy and writer's guidelines free.

Nonfiction: How-to (survive in prison, find a job, fight depression), humor, inspirational, interview/profile, religious. No fiction or Bible studies. **Buys 5 mss/year.** Send complete ms. Length: 500-1,500 words. **Pays $50-200.** Pays prisoners in contributor copies.

Photos: State availability of or send photos with submission. Reviews contact sheets, transparencies, prints. Buys one-time rights. Negotiates payment individually. Identification of subjects required.

Columns/Departments: Shortimer (preparing for release from prison); Especially for Women (how women cope with prison); Fatherly Advice (how to be a father in prison), all 750 words. **Buys 3 mss/year.** Send complete ms.

Tips: "Visit a prison, find out firsthand what inmates are dealing with. Or find an ex-prisoner who is making it on the outside. Interview person for 'How are you successful' tips. What are they doing differently to avoid returning to prison? Also, we need more celebrity interviews with people of Christian faith."

$ ◪ LIFEGLOW, Christian Record Services, P.O. Box 6097, Lincoln NE 68506. (402)488-0981. Fax: (402)488-7582. Gaylena Gibson, editor. **95% freelance written.** Large print Christian publication for sight-impaired over 25 covering health, handicapped people, uplifting articles. Estab. 1984. Circ. 32,700. **Pays on acceptance.** Publishes ms an average of 3 years after acceptance. Byline given. Buys one-time rights. Accepts queries by mail. Accepts simultaneous submissions. Responds in 5 weeks to queries; 4 months to mss. Sample copy for 7×10 SAE and 5 first-class stamps. Writer's guidelines for #10 SASE.

○━ "Write for an interdenominational Christian audience."

Nonfiction: Essays, general interest, historical/nostalgic, humor, inspirational, interview/profile, personal experience, travel, adventure, biography, careers, handicapped, health, hobbies, marriage, nature. **Buys 40 mss/year.** Send complete ms. Length: 200-1,400 words. **Pays 4-5¢/word and complimentary copies.**

Photos: Send photos with submission. Buys one-time rights. Negotiates payment individually.

Columns/Departments: Baffle U! (puzzle), 150 words, **pays $15-25/puzzle**; Vitality Plus (current health topics), length varies, **pays 4¢/word. Buys 10 mss/year.** Send complete ms.

Poetry: Light verse. **Buys very few poems/year.** Length: 12 lines. **Pays $10-20.**

Fillers: Anecdotes, facts, short humor. **Buys very few/year.** Length: 300 words maximum. **Pays 4¢/word.**

Tips: "Make sure manuscript has a strong ending that ties everything together and doesn't leave us dangling. Pretend someone else wrote it—would it hold your interest? Draw your readers into the story by being specific rather than abstract or general."

Ⓝ $ LIGHT AND LIFE MAGAZINE, Free Methodist Church of North America, P.O. Box 535002, Indianapolis IN 46253-5002. (317)244-3660. Fax: (317)248-9055. E-mail: llmauthors@fmcna.org. **Contact:** Doug Newton, editor. Works with a small number of new/unpublished writers each year. Bimonthly magazine emphasizing evangelical Christianity with Wesleyan slant for a cross section of adults. Also includes discipleship guidebook and national/international and denominational religion news. Estab. 1868. Circ. 19,000. Pays on publication. Byline given. Buys first North American serial rights. Accepts queries by mail. Sample copy for $4. Writer's guidelines for #10 SASE.

Nonfiction: Send complete ms. Length: varies. **Pays 4¢/word, 5¢/word if submitted on disk.**

Photos: Purchased without accompanying ms. Send photos with submission. Reviews slides. Pays $35 and higher for color or b&w photos.

$ $ LIGUORIAN, One Liguori Dr., Liguori MO 63057-9999. (636)464-2500. Fax: (636)464-8449. E-mail: aweinert@liguori.org. Website: www.liguori.org. Managing Editor: Cheryl Plass. **Contact:** Fr. Allan Weinert, CSSR, editor-in-chief. **25% freelance written.** Prefers to work with published/established writers. Magazine published 10 times/year for Catholics. "Our purpose is to lead our readers to a fuller Christian life by helping them better understand the teachings of the gospel and the church and by illustrating how these teachings apply to life and the problems confronting them as members of families, the church and society." Estab. 1913. Circ. 220,000. **Pays on acceptance.** Buys all rights but will reassign rights to author after publication upon written request. Submit seasonal material 8 months in advance. Accepts queries by mail, e-mail, fax, phone. Responds in 4 months to mss. Sample copy and writer's guidelines for 9×12 SAE with 3 first-class stamps or online.

Nonfiction: "Pastoral, practical and personal approach to the problems and challenges of people today." "No travelogue approach or unresearched ventures into controversial areas. Also, no material found in secular publications—fad subjects that already get enough press, pop psychology, negative or put-down articles." **Buys 60 unsolicited mss/year.** Length: 400-2,000 words. **Pays 10-12¢/word.** Sometimes pays expenses of writers on assignment.
Photos: Photographs on assignment only unless submitted with and specific to article.

$ ⬛ LIVE WIRE, Standard Publishing, 8121 Hamilton Ave., Cincinnati OH 45231. Fax: (513)931-0950. Website: www.standardpub.com. **Contact:** Margie Redford, editor. **100% freelance written.** Weekly newspaper. "A weekly Sunday school take-home newspaper geared to preteens (10-12-year-olds) who want to live a godly life and connect with Christ." Estab. 1997. Circ. 40,000. **Pays on acceptance.** Publishes ms an average of 1 year after acceptance. Byline given. Buys first, one-time, second serial (reprint), all rights. Editorial lead time 1 year. Submit seasonal material 1 year in advance. Accepts simultaneous submissions. Responds in 2 months to queries. Sample copy and writer's guidelines for #10 SASE.
Nonfiction: General interest, historical/nostalgic, interview/profile, personal experience, religious. **Buys 60-90 mss/ year.** Send complete ms. Length: 200-350 words. **Pays 3-7¢/word.**
Reprints: Accepts previously published submissions.
Photos: State availability with submission.

$ THE LIVING CHURCH, Living Church Foundation, 816 E. Juneau Ave., P.O. Box 514036, Milwaukee WI 53203. (414)276-5420. Fax: (414)276-7483. E-mail: tlc@livingchurch.org. Managing Editor: John Schuessler. **Contact:** David Kalvelage, editor. **50% freelance written.** Weekly magazine on the Episcopal church. News or articles of interest to members of the Episcopal church. Estab. 1878. Circ. 9,000. Does not pay unless article is requested. Publishes ms an average of 3 months after acceptance. Byline given. Buys one-time rights. Editorial lead time 3 weeks. Submit seasonal material 1 month in advance. Accepts queries by mail, e-mail, fax. Responds in 2 weeks to queries; 1 month to mss. Sample copy free. Writer's guidelines online.
Nonfiction: Opinion, personal experience, photo feature, religious. **Buys 10 mss/year.** Send complete ms. Length: 1,000 words. **Pays $25-100.** Sometimes pays expenses of writers on assignment.
Photos: Send photos with submission. Reviews any size prints. Buys one-time rights. Offers $15-50/photo.
Columns/Departments: Benediction (devotional), 250 words; Viewpoint (opinion), under 1,000 words. Send complete ms. **Pays $50 maximum.**
Poetry: Light verse, traditional.

$ LIVING LIGHT NEWS, Living Light Ministries, 5306 89th St., #200, Edmonton Alberta T6E 5P9, Canada. (780)468-6397. Fax: (780)468-6872. E-mail: shine@livinglightnews.org. Website: www.livinglightnews.org. **Contact:** Jeff Caporale, editor. **100% freelance written.** Bimonthly tabloid covering evangelical Christianity. "Our publication is a seeker-sensitive evangelical outreach oriented newspaper focusing on glorifying God and promoting a personal relationship with Him." Estab. 1985. Circ. 20,000. **Pays on publication.** Publishes ms an average of 2 months after acceptance. Byline sometimes given. Offers 100% kill fee. Buys first North American serial, first, one-time, second serial (reprint), simultaneous, all rights, makes work-for-hire assignments. Editorial lead time 2 months. Submit seasonal material 3 months in advance. Accepts queries by mail, e-mail, phone. Accepts simultaneous submissions. Responds in 2 months to queries; 2 months to mss. Sample copy for 10×13 SAE with $2.10 in IRCs. Writer's guidelines for #10 SASE with 1 IRC, online or by e-mail.
Oₙ Break in with "a story about a well-known Christian in sports or entertainment."
Nonfiction: General interest, humor, inspirational, interview/profile, religious, sports. Special issues: "We have a special Christmas issue focused on the traditional meaning of Christmas and a special Christian college supplement called New Horizons each spring." No issue-oriented, controversial stories. **Buys 50 mss/year.** Query with published clips. Length: 300-1,000 words. **Pays $30-100 for assigned articles; $10-100 for unsolicited articles.** Sometimes pays expenses of writers on assignment.
Reprints: Send tearsheet, photocopy or typed ms with rights for sale noted and information about when and where the material previously appeared. Pays 5¢/word.
Photos: State availability with submission. Reviews 3×5 prints, gif/jpeg files. Buys all rights. Offers $20/photo. Identification of subjects required.
Columns/Departments: Parenting (positive, helpful, punchy, humorous, Biblically based parenting pointers), 600 words; Humor (light-hearted anecdotes about God and the current culture in the world today), 600 words. **Buys 40 mss/ year.** Query with published clips. **Pays $10-25.**
Fiction: "We only want to see Christmas-related fiction." **Buys 10 mss/year.** Query with published clips. Length: 300-1,250 words. **Pays $10-100.**
Tips: "Please visit our website for a sample of our publication. All of our stories must be of interest to both Christians and non-Christians. We look for lively writing styles that are friendly, down-to-earth and engaging. We especially like celebrity profiles."

$ $ THE LOOKOUT, For Today's Growing Christian, Standard Publishing, 8121 Hamilton Ave., Cincinnati OH 45231-9981. (513)931-4050. Fax: (513)931-0950. E-mail: lookout@standardpub.com. Website: www.standardpub.com. Managing Editor: Alva Lee Hawley. **Contact:** Shawn McMullen, editor. **50% freelance written.** Weekly magazine for Christian adults, with emphasis on spiritual growth, family life, and topical issues. "Our purpose is to provide

Christian adults with practical, biblical teaching and current information that will help them mature as believers." Estab. 1894. Circ. 100,000. **Pays on acceptance.** Publishes ms an average of 1 year after acceptance. Byline given. Offers 33% kill fee. Buys first, one-time rights. Editorial lead time 6 months. Submit seasonal material 6 months in advance. Accepts queries by mail, e-mail, fax. Accepts simultaneous submissions. Responds in 3 weeks to queries; 2 months to mss. Sample copy and guidelines for 75¢. Writer's guidelines for #10 SASE.

• Audience is mainly conservative Christians.

Nonfiction: "Writers need to send for current theme list. We also use inspirational short pieces." Inspirational, interview/profile, opinion, personal experience, religious. No fiction or poetry. **Buys 100 mss/year.** Query with or without published clips or send complete ms. Length: 350-800 words. **Pays 5-12¢/word.** Sometimes pays expenses of writers on assignment.

Reprints: Accepts previously published submissions. Pays 60% of amount paid for original article.

Photos: State availability with submission. Buys one-time rights. Offers no additional payment for photos accepted with ms. Identification of subjects required.

Tips: "*The Lookout* publishes from a theologically conservative, nondenominational, and noncharismatic perspective. It is a member of the Evangelical Press Association. We have readers in every adult age group, but we aim primarily for those aged 35 to 55. Most readers are married and have older elementary to young adult children. But a large number come from other home situations as well. Our emphasis is on the needs of ordinary Christians who want to grow in their faith, rather than on trained theologians or church leaders. As a Christian general-interest magazine, we cover a wide variety of topics—from individual discipleship to family concerns to social involvement. We value well-informed articles that offer lively and clear writing as well as strong application. We often address tough issues and seek to explore fresh ideas or recent developments affecting today's Christians."

$ $ $ THE LUTHERAN, Magazine of the Evangelical Lutheran Church in America, 8765 W. Higgins Rd., Chicago IL 60631-4183. (773)380-2540. Fax: (773)380-2751. E-mail: lutheran@elca.org. Website: www.TheLutheran.org. Managing Editor: Sonia Solomonson. **Contact:** David L. Miller, editor. **15% freelance written.** Monthly magazine for "lay people in church. News and activities of the Evangelical Lutheran Church in America, news of the world of religion, ethical reflections on issues in society, personal Christian experience." Estab. 1988. Circ. 620,000. **Pays on acceptance.** Publishes ms an average of 6 months after acceptance. Byline given. Offers 50% kill fee. Buys first rights. Submit seasonal material 4 months in advance. Accepts queries by mail, e-mail. Responds in 6 weeks to queries. Sample copy and writer's guidelines free.

O-π Break in by checking out the theme list on the website and querying with ideas related to these themes.

Nonfiction: Inspirational, interview/profile, personal experience, photo feature, religious. "No articles unrelated to the world of religion." **Buys 40 mss/year.** Query with published clips. Length: 500-1,500 words. **Pays $400-700 for assigned articles; $100-500 for unsolicited articles.** Pays expenses of writers on assignment.

Photos: Send photos with submission. Reviews contact sheets, transparencies, prints. Buys one-time rights. Offers $50-175/photo. Captions, identification of subjects required.

Columns/Departments: Lite Side (humor—church, religious), In Focus, Living the Faith, Values & Society, In Our Churches, Our Church at Work, 25-100 words. Send complete ms. **Pays $10.**

▣ The online magazine carries original content not found in the print edition. Contact: Lorel Fox, online editor.

Tips: "Writers have the best chance selling us feature articles."

$ ✠ THE LUTHERAN DIGEST, The Lutheran Digest, Inc., P.O. Box 4250, Hopkins MN 55343. (952)933-2820. Fax: (952)933-5708. E-mail: tldi@lutherandigest.com. Website: www.lutherandigest.com. **Contact:** David L. Tank, editor. **95% freelance written.** Quarterly magazine covering Christianity from a Lutheran perspective. "Articles frequently reflect a Lutheran Christian perspective, but are not intended to be sermonettes. Popular stories show how God has intervened in a person's life to help solve a problem." Estab. 1953. Circ. 110,000. **Pays on acceptance.** Publishes ms an average of 6 months after acceptance. Byline given. Buys first, second serial (reprint) rights. Editorial lead time 9 months. Submit seasonal material 9 months in advance. Accepts queries by mail. Accepts simultaneous submissions. Responds in 1 month to queries; 4 months to mss. Sample copy for $3.50. Writer's guidelines free.

O-π Break in with "reprints from other publications that will fill less than three pages of *TLD*. Articles of one or two pages are even better. As a digest, we primarily look for previously published articles to reprint, however, we do publish about twenty to thirty percent original material. Articles from new writers are always welcomed and seriously considered."

Nonfiction: General interest, historical/nostalgic, how-to (personal or spiritual growth), humor, inspirational, personal experience, religious, nature, God's unique creatures. Does not want to see "personal tributes to deceased relatives or friends. They are seldom used unless the subject of the article is well-known. We also avoid articles about the moment a person finds Christ as his or her personal savior." **Buys 50-60 mss/year.** Send complete ms. Length: 1,500 words. **Pays $25-50.**

Reprints: Accepts previously published submissions. We prefer this as we are a digest and 70-80% of our articles are reprints. **Pays in contributor copies for some reprint permissions.**

Photos: State availability with submission. Buys one-time rights.

Tips: "An article that tugs on the 'heart strings' just a little and closes leaving the reader with a sense of hope is a writer's best bet to breaking into *The Lutheran Digest*."

$ THE LUTHERAN JOURNAL, 7317 Cahill Rd., Suite 201, Minneapolis MN 55439-2081. (952)562-1234. Fax: (952)941-3010. Publisher: Michael L. Beard. Editor: Rev. Armin U. Deye. **Contact:** Editorial Assistant. Magazine published 3 times/year for Lutheran Church members, middle age and older. Estab. 1938. Circ. 130,000. Pays on publication. Byline given. Buys one-time rights. Accepts simultaneous submissions. Responds in 4 months to queries. Sample copy for 9×12 SAE with 78¢ postage.

Nonfiction: Historical/nostalgic, how-to, humor, inspirational, interview/profile, personal experience, religious, interesting or unusual church projects, think articles. **Buys 25-30 mss/year.** Send complete ms. Length: 1,500 words maximum; occasionally 2,000 words. **Pays 1-4¢/word.**

Reprints: Send tearsheet, photocopy or typed ms with rights for sale noted and information about when and where the material previously appeared. Pays up to 50% of amount paid for an original article.

Photos: Send photocopies of b&w and color photos with accompanying ms. Please do not send original photos.

Poetry: Buys 2-3 poems/issue, as space allows. **Pays $5-30.**

Tips: "We strongly prefer a warm, personal style of writing that speaks directly to the reader. In general, writers should seek to convey information rather than express personal opinion, though the writer's own personality should be reflected in the article's style. Send submissions with SASE so we may respond."

$ LUTHERAN PARTNERS, Augsburg Fortress, Publishers, ELCA (DM), 8765 W. Higgins Rd., Chicago IL 60631-4195. (773)380-2875. Fax: (773)380-2829. E-mail: lpartmag@elca.org. Website: www.elca.org/dm/lp. Managing Editor: William A. Decker. **Contact:** Carl E. Linder, editor. **15-20% freelance written.** Bimonthly magazine covering issues of religious leadership. "We are a leadership magazine for the ordained and rostered lay ministers of the Evangelical Lutheran Church in America (ELCA), fostering an exchange of opinions on matters involving theology, leadership, mission and service to Jesus Christ. Know your audience: ELCA congregations and the various kinds of leaders who make up this church and their prevalent issues of leadership." Estab. 1979. Circ. 20,000. Pays on publication. Publishes ms an average of 6 months after acceptance. Byline given. Buys first, one-time, second serial (reprint), electronic rights. Editorial lead time 6 months. Submit seasonal material 6 months in advance. Accepts queries by mail, e-mail, fax, phone. Accepts simultaneous submissions. Responds in 1 month to queries; 6 months to mss. Sample copy for $2. Writer's guidelines free or online.

● The editor reports an interest in seeing articles on various facets of ministry from the perspectives of ethnic authors (Hispanic, African-American, Asian, Native American, Arab-American).

○┐ Break in through "Jottings" (practical how-to articles involving congregational ministry ideas; 500 words maximum)."

Nonfiction: Historical/nostalgic, how-to (leadership in faith communities), humor (religious cartoon), inspirational, opinion (religious leadership issues), religious, book reviews (query book review editor). "No exposés, no articles primarily promoting products/services; no anti-religion." **Buys 15-20 mss/year.** Query with published clips or send complete ms. Length: 500-2,000 words. **Pays $25-170.** Pays in copies for book reviews.

Photos: State availability with submission. Buys one-time rights. Generally offers no additional payment for photos accepted with ms. Captions, identification of subjects required.

Columns/Departments: Thelma Megill Cobbler, review editor. Partners Review (book reviews), 700 words. Query or submit ms. **Pays in copies.**

Fiction: Rarely accepts religious fiction. Query.

Poetry: Free verse, haiku, light verse, traditional, hymns. **Buys 6-10 poems/year.** Submit maximum 10 poems. **Pays $50-75.**

Fillers: Practical ministry (education, music, youth, social service, administration, worship, etc.) in congregation. **Buys 3-6/year.** Length: 500 words. **Pays $25.**

Tips: "Know congregational life, especially from the perspective of leadership, including both ordained pastor and lay staff. Think current and future leadership needs. It would be good to be familiar with ELCA rostered pastors, lay ministers, and congregations."

$ MENNONITE BRETHREN HERALD, 3-169 Riverton Ave., Winnipeg, Manitoba R2L 2E5, Canada. (204)669-6575. Fax: (204)654-1865. E-mail: mbherald@mbconf.ca. Website: www.mbherald.com. **Contact:** Jim Coggins, editor, Susan Brandt, managing editor. **25% freelance written.** Biweekly family publication "read mainly by people of the Mennonite faith, reaching a wide cross section of professional and occupational groups, including many homemakers. Readership includes people from both urban and rural communities. It is intended to inform members of events in the church and the world, serve personal and corporate spiritual needs, serve as a vehicle of communication within the church, serve conference agencies and reflect the history and theology of the Mennonite Brethren Church." Estab. 1962. Circ. 15,500. Pays on publication. Publishes ms an average of 6 months after acceptance. Byline given. Not copyrighted. Buys one-time rights. Accepts queries by e-mail, fax. Responds in 6 months to queries. Sample copy for $1 and 9×12 SAE with 2 IRCs.

● "Articles and manuscripts not accepted for publication will be returned if a SASE (Canadian stamps or IRCs) is provided by the writers."

Nonfiction: Articles with a Christian family orientation; youth directed, Christian faith and life, and current issues. Wants articles critiquing the values of a secular society, attempting to relate Christian living to the practical situations of daily living; showing how people have related their faith to their vocations. Send complete ms. Length: 250-1,500 words. **Pays $30-40.** Pays expenses of writers on assignment.

Reprints: Send tearsheet, photocopy or typed ms with rights for sale noted and information about when and where the material previously appeared. Pays 70% of amount paid for an original article.

Photos: Photos purchased with ms.

Columns/Departments: Viewpoint (Christian opinion on current topics), 850 words. Crosscurrent (Christian opinion on music, books, art, TV, movies), 350 words.

Poetry: Length: 25 lines maximum.

Tips: "We like simple style, contemporary language and fresh ideas. Writers should take care to avoid religious cliches."

$ $ MESSAGE MAGAZINE, Review and Herald Publishing, 55 West Oak Ridge Dr., Hagerstown MD 21740. (301)393-4099. Fax: (301)393-4103. E-mail: message@rhpa.org. Website: www.messagemagazine.org. Editor: Ron Smith. Associate Editor: Dwain Esmond. **Contact:** Pat Sparks Harris, administrative secretary. **10-20% freelance written.** Bimonthly magazine. "*Message* is the oldest religious journal addressing ethnic issues in the country. Our audience is predominantly black and Seventh-day Adventist; however, *Message* is an outreach magazine geared to the unchurched." Estab. 1898. Circ. 120,000. **Pays on acceptance.** Publishes ms an average of 12 months after acceptance. Byline given. Buys first North American serial rights. Editorial lead time 6 months. Submit seasonal material 6 months in advance. Responds in 9 months to queries. Sample copy and writer's guidelines free.

Nonfiction: General interest (to a Christian audience), how-to (overcome depression; overcome defeat; get closer to God; learn from failure, etc.), inspirational, interview/profile (profiles of famous African Americans), personal experience (testimonies), religious. **Buys 10 mss/year.** Send complete ms. Length: 800-1,300 words. **Pays $50-300.**

Photos: State availability with submission. Buys one-time rights. Identification of subjects required.

Columns/Departments: Voices in the Wind (community involvement/service/events/health info); Message, Jr. (stories for children with a moral, explain a biblical or moral principle); Recipes (no meat or dairy products—12-15 recipes and an intro); Healthspan (health issues); all 500 words. **Buys 12-15 mss/year.** Send complete ms. for Message, Jr. and Healthspan. Query editorial assistant with published clips for Voices in the Wind and Recipes. **Pays $50-300.**

Fiction: "We do not generally accept fiction, but when we do it's for Message, Jr. and/or has a religious theme. We buy about 3 (if that many) fiction manuscripts a year." **Buys 3 mss/year.** Send complete ms. Length: 500-700 words. **Pays $50-125.**

Fillers: Anecdotes, facts, newsbreaks. **Buys 1-5/year.** Length: 200-500 words. **Pays $50-125.**

▣ The online magazine carries original content not found in the print edition.

Tips: "Please look at the magazine before submitting manuscripts. *Message* publishes a variety of writing styles as long as the writing style is easy to read and flows—please avoid highly technical writing styles."

$ THE MESSENGER OF THE SACRED HEART, Apostleship of Prayer, 661 Greenwood Ave., Toronto, Ontario M4J 4B3, Canada. (416)466-1195. **Contact:** Rev. F.J. Power, S.J., editor. **20% freelance written.** Monthly magazine for "Canadian and U.S. Catholics interested in developing a life of prayer and spirituality; stresses the great value of our ordinary actions and lives." Estab. 1891. Circ. 15,000. **Pays on acceptance.** Byline given. Buys first rights. Submit seasonal material 5 months in advance. Responds in 1 month to queries. Sample copy for $1 and 7½×10½ SAE. Writer's guidelines for #10 SASE.

Fiction: Religious/inspirational; stories about people, adventure, heroism, humor, drama. **Buys 12 mss/year.** Send complete ms with SAE and IRCs (does not return ms without SASE). Length: 750-1,500 words. **Pays 6¢/word.**

Tips: "Develop a story that sustains interest to the end. Do not preach, but use plot and characters to convey the message or theme. Aim to move the heart as well as the mind. Before sending, cut out unnecessary or unrelated words or sentences. If you can, add a light touch or a sense of humor to the story. Your ending should have impact, leaving a moral or faith message for the reader."

$ $ MINNESOTA CHRISTIAN CHRONICLE, Beard Communications, 7317 Cahill Rd., Suite 201, Minneapolis MN 55439. (952)562-1234. Fax: (952)941-3010. E-mail: susan@mcchronicle.com. Website: www.mcchronicle.com. **Contact:** Doug Trouten, editor. **10% freelance written.** Biweekly newspaper covering Christian community in Minnesota. "Our readers tend to be conservative evangelicals with orthodox Christian beliefs and conservative social and political views." Estab. 1978. Circ. 21,000. Pays 1 month following publication. Publishes ms an average of 2 months after acceptance. Byline given. Buys one-time rights. Editorial lead time 1 month. Submit seasonal material 2 months in advance. Accepts queries by mail, e-mail. Accepts simultaneous submissions. Responds in 1 month to queries. Sample copy for $2. Writer's guidelines for #10 SASE.

Nonfiction: Exposé, general interest, historical/nostalgic, how-to, humor (Christian humor, satire, clean), inspirational, interview/profile, new product, personal experience, photo feature, religious. Special issues: Higher education guide, Christmas section, Christian school directory, Healthful Living, Life Resource Guide, Christian Ministries Directory. **Buys 36 mss/year.** Query. Length: 500-2,000 words. **Pays $20-200.**

Reprints: Send typed ms with rights for sale noted. Pays 50% of amount paid for an original article.

Photos: State availability with submission. Reviews contact sheets. Buys one-time rights. Negotiates payment individually. Captions required.

Tips: "Stories for the *Minnesota Christian Chronicle* must have a strong Minnesota connection and a clear hook for the Christian community. We do not publish general nonreligious stories or devotionals. We rarely buy from writers who are not in Minnesota."

$ THE MIRACULOUS MEDAL, 475 E. Chelten Ave., Philadelphia PA 19144-5785. (215)848-1010. **Contact:** Rev. William J. O'Brien, C.M., editor. **40% freelance written.** Quarterly magazine. Estab. 1915. **Pays on acceptance.** Publishes ms an average of 2 years after acceptance. Buys first North American serial rights. Accepts queries by mail. Responds in 3 months to queries. Sample copy for 6×9 SAE and 2 first-class stamps.

• Buys articles only on special assignment.

Fiction: Wants good general fiction—not necessarily religious, but if religion is basic to the story, the writer should be sure of his facts. Only restriction is that subject matter and treatment must not conflict with Catholic teaching and practice. Can use seasonal material, Christmas stories. Should not be pious or sermon-like. Length: 2,000 words maximum. Occasionally uses short-shorts from 1,000-1,250 words. **Pays 2¢/word minimum.**

Poetry: Preferably about the Virgin Mary or at least with a religious slant. Length: 20 lines maximum. **Pays 50¢/line minimum.**

$ $ MOODY MAGAZINE, Moody Bible Institute, 820 N. LaSalle Blvd., Chicago IL 60610. (312)329-2164. Fax: (312)329-2149. E-mail: moodyedit@moody.edu. Website: www.moody.edu. **Contact:** Andrew Scheer, managing editor. **62% freelance written.** Bimonthly magazine for evangelical Christianity. "Our readers are conservative, evangelical Christians highly active in their churches and concerned about applying their faith in daily living." Query first for all submissions by mail, but not by phone. Unsolicited mss will be returned unread. Estab. 1900. Circ. 112,000. **Pays on acceptance.** Publishes ms an average of 9 months after acceptance. Byline given. Buys first North American serial rights. Submit seasonal material 9 months in advance. Responds in 2 months to queries. Sample copy for 9×12 SAE with $2 first-class postage. Writer's guidelines for #10 SASE.

O— Break in with "non-cover, freestanding narrative articles."

Nonfiction: Personal narratives (on living the Christian life), a few reporting articles. "No biographies, historical articles, or studies of Bible figures." **Buys 55 mss/year.** Query. Length: 1,200-2,200 words. **Pays 15¢/word for queried articles; 20¢/word for assigned articles.** Sometimes pays expenses of writers on assignment.

Columns/Departments: First Person (the only article written for non-Christians; a personal conversion testimony written by the author [will accept "as told to's"]; the objective is to tell a person's testimony in such a way that the reader will understand the gospel and want to receive Christ as Savior), 800-900 words; News Focus (in-depth, researched account of current news or trend), 1,000-1,400 words. **Buys 12 mss/year.** May query by fax or e-mail for New Focus only. **Pays 15¢/word.**

Fiction: Will consider well-written contemporary stories that are directed toward spiritual application. Avoid cliched salvation accounts, biblical fiction, parables, and allegories. Length: 1,200-2,000 words. **Pays 15¢/word.**

Tips: "We want articles that cover a broad range of topics, but with one common goal: To foster application by a broad readership of specific biblical principles. *Moody* especially seeks narrative accounts showing one's realization and application of specific, scriptural principles in daily life. In generating ideas for such articles, we recommend a writer consider: what has God been 'working on' in your life in the past few years? How have you been learning to apply a new realization of what Scripture is commanding you to do? What difference has this made for you and those around you? By publishing accounts of people's spiritual struggles, growth and discipleship, our aim is to encourage readers in their own obedience to Christ. We're also looking for some pieces that use an anecdotal reporting approach."

$ $ MY DAILY VISITOR, Our Sunday Visitor, Inc., 200 Noll Plaza, Huntington IN 46750. (219)356-8400. E-mail: mdvisitor@osv.com. **Contact:** Catherine M. Odell, editor. **99% freelance written.** Bimonthly magazine of Scripture meditations based on the day's Catholic Mass readings. Circ. 30,000. **Pays on acceptance.** Publishes ms an average of 6 months after acceptance. Byline given. Not copyrighted. Buys one-time rights. Accepts queries by mail, e-mail. Responds in 2 months to queries. Sample copy and writer's guidelines for #10 SAE with 2 first-class stamps.

• "Guest editors write on assignment basis only."

Nonfiction: Inspirational, personal experience, religious. **Buys 12 mss/year.** Query with published clips. Length: 150-160 words times the number of days in month. **Pays $500 for 1 month (28-31) of meditations and 5 free copies.**

Tips: "Previous experience in writing Scripture-based meditations or essays is helpful."

$ $ NORTH AMERICAN VOICE OF FATIMA, Barnabite Fathers-North American Province, National Shrine Basilica of Our Lady of Fatima, 1023 Swann Rd., Youngstown NY 14174-0167. (716)754-7489. Fax: (716)754-9130. E-mail: pmccrsp@aol.com. Website: www.catholic-church.org/barnabites. **Contact:** Rev. Peter M. Calabrese, CRSP, editor. **90% freelance written.** Quarterly magazine covering Catholic spirituality. "The Barnabite Fathers wish to share the joy and challenge of the Gospel and to foster devotion to Our Lady, Mary, the Mother of the Redeemer and Mother of the Church who said at Cana: 'Do whatever He tells you.'" Estab. 1961. Circ. 1,200. Pays on publication. Publishes ms an average of 3 months after acceptance. Byline given. Buys first North American serial, one-time, second serial (reprint) rights, makes work-for-hire assignments. Editorial lead time 2 months. Submit seasonal material 2 months in advance. Accepts queries by mail, e-mail. Accepts simultaneous submissions. Responds in 3 weeks to queries; does not return unsolicited mss. Sample copy free. Writer's guidelines for #10 SASE.

Nonfiction: Inspirational, personal experience, religious. **Buys 32 mss/year.** Send complete ms. Length: 500-2,000 words. **Pays 5¢/word.**

Photos: Send photos with submission. Buys one-time rights. Offers no additional payment for photos accepted with ms. Identification of subjects required.

Columns/Departments: Book Reviews (religious), 500 words or less. Send complete ms. **Pays 5¢/word.**

Poetry: Free verse, traditional. **Buys 16-20 poems/year.** Length: 4 lines minimum. **Pays $10-25.**

Tips: "We are a Catholic spirituality magazine that publishes articles on faith-based themes—also inspirational or uplifting stories. While Catholic we also publish articles by non-Catholic Christians."

$ ▣ NOW WHAT?, (formerly *Bible Advocate Online*), Bible Advocate Press/Church of God (Seventh Day), P.O. Box 33677, Denver CO 80233. (303)452-7973. Fax: (303)452-0657. E-mail: BibleAdvocate@cog7.org. Website: nowwhat.cog7.org. Editor: Calvin Burrell. **Contact:** Sherri Langton, associate editor. **100% freelance written.** "Online religious publication covering social and religious topics; more inclusive of non-Christians." Estab. 1996. Pays on publication. Publishes ms an average of 3 months after acceptance. Byline given. Offers 50% kill fee. Buys first, second serial (reprint), electronic rights. Editorial lead time 3 months. Submit seasonal material 6 months in advance. Accepts queries by mail, e-mail. Accepts simultaneous submissions. Responds in 6 weeks to queries. Sample copy for 9×12 SAE and 2 first-class stamps. Writer's guidelines for #10 SASE and online.

    O→ "For the online magazine, write for the 'felt needs' of the reader and come up with creative ways for communicating to the unchurched."

Nonfiction: Inspirational, personal experience, religious. No Christmas or Easter pieces. **Buys 20-25 mss/year.** Send complete ms and SASE. Length: 1,500-1,800 words. **Pays $35-55.**

Reprints: Send typed ms with rights for sale noted and information about when and where the material previously appeared. Pays $15-35.

Photos: Send photos with submission. Buys one-time rights. Offers additional payment for photos accepted with ms. Identification of subjects required.

Fillers: Anecdotes, facts, resources. **Buys 6-10/year.** Length: 50-250 words. **Pays $10-20.**

Tips: "Be vulnerable in your personal experiences. Show, don't tell! Delete Christian jargon and write from perspective of a non-Christian. Significant changes are referred to writers for approval. No fax or handwritten submissions, please."

$ OBLATES, Missionary Association of Mary Immaculate, 9480 N. De Mazenod Dr., Belleville IL 62223-1160. (618)398-4848. Fax: (618)398-8788. Website: www.snows.org. Managing Editor: Christine Portell. **Contact:** Mary Mohrman, manuscripts editor. **15% freelance written.** Prefers to work with published writers. Bimonthly magazine. Inspirational magazine for Christians; audience mainly older Catholic adults. Circ. 500,000. **Pays on acceptance.** Publishes ms an average of 2 years after acceptance. Byline given. Buys first North American serial rights. Submit seasonal material 6 months in advance. Accepts queries by mail. Responds in 2 months to queries. Sample copy and writer's guidelines for 6×9 or larger SAE with 2 first-class stamps.

    ● "We no longer accept Christmas season material. Our November/December issue is all inhouse."

Nonfiction: Inspirational and personal experience with positive spiritual insights. No preachy, theological or research articles. Avoid current events and controversial topics. Send complete ms. Length: 500-600 words. **Pays $150.**

Poetry: "Emphasis should be on inspiration, insight and relationship with God." Light verse—reverent, well-written, perceptive, with traditional rhythm and rhyme. Submit maximum 2 poems. Length: 8-12 lines. **Pays $50.**

Tips: "Our readership is made up mostly of mature Americans who are looking for comfort, encouragement, and a positive sense of applicable Christian direction to their lives. Focus on sharing of personal insight to problem (i.e., death or change), but must be positive, uplifting. We have well-defined needs for an established market but are always on the lookout for exceptional work."

$ $ ON MISSION, North American Mission Board, SBC, 4200 North Point Pkwy., Alpharetta GA 30022-4176. (770)410-6284. Fax: (770)410-6105. E-mail: onmission@namb.net. Website: www.onmission.com. **Contact:** Carolyn Curtis, editor. **20% freelance written.** Bimonthly lifestyle magazine that popularizes evangelism and church planting. "*On Mission*'s primary purpose is to help readers and churches become more intentional about personal evangelism. *On Mission* equips Christians for leading people to Christ and encourages churches to reach new people through new congregations." Estab. 1997. Circ. 200,000. **Pays on acceptance.** Publishes ms an average of 6 months after acceptance. Byline given. Buys first North American serial, first, electronic rights. Editorial lead time 9 months. Submit seasonal material 9 months in advance. Accepts queries by mail, e-mail. Responds in 6 months to queries; 6 months to mss. Sample copy free or online. Writer's guidelines free, online or by e-mail.

    O→ Break in with a 600-word how-to article.

Nonfiction: How-to, humor, personal experience (stories of sharing your faith in Christ with a non-Christian). **Buys 30 mss/year.** Query with published clips. Length: 350-1,200 words. **Pays 25¢/word.** Pays expenses of writers on assignment.

Photos: State availability with submission. Reviews contact sheets, transparencies, prints. Buys one-time rights. Captions, identification of subjects required.

Columns/Departments: My Mission (personal evangelism), 700 words. **Buys 2 mss/year.** Query. **Pays 25¢/word.**

Tips: "Readers might be intimidated if those featured appear to be 'super Christians' who seem to live on a higher spiritual plane. Try to introduce subjects as three-dimensional, real people. Include anecdotes or examples of their fears and failures, including ways they overcame obstacles. In other words, take the reader inside the heart of the *On Mission* Christian and reveal the inevitable humanness that makes that person not only believable, but also approachable. We want the reader to feel encouraged to become *On Mission* by identifying with people like them who are featured in the magazine."

$ $ THE OTHER SIDE, 300 W. Apsley St., Philadelphia PA 19144-4285. (215)849-2178. Website: www.theothersi de.com. **Contact:** Dee Dee Risher, co-editor, Doug Davidson, co-editor. **80% freelance written.** Prefers to work with published/established writers. Bimonthly magazine emphasizing "spiritual nurture, prophetic reflection, forgotten voices and artistic visions from a progressive Christian perspective." Estab. 1965. Circ. 12,000. **Pays on acceptance.** Publishes ms an average of 6 months after acceptance. Byline given. Buys Buys all or first serial rights. Responds in 3 months to queries. Sample copy for $4.50. Writer's guidelines for #10 SASE or on website.

Nonfiction: Doug Davidson, co-editor. "Articles must be lively, vivid and down-to-earth, with a radical, faith-based Christian perspective." How-to, interview/profile, personal experience, Current social, political and economic issues in the US and around the world, Interpretative Essays, Spiritual Reflections, Biblical Interpretation. Length: 500-3,500 words. **Pays $25-300.**

Fiction: Monica Day, fiction editor. "Short stories, humor and satire conveying insights and situations that will be helpful to Christians with a radical commitment to peace and justice." Humorous. Length: 300-4,000 words. **Pays $25-250.**

Poetry: "Short, creative poetry that will be thought-provoking and appealing to radical Christians who have a strong commitment to spirituality, peace and justice." Jean Minahan, poetry editor. Submit maximum 4 poems. Length: 3-50 lines. **Pays $25.**

Tips: "We're looking for tightly written pieces (1,000-1,500 words) on interesting and unusual Christians (or Christian groups) who are putting their commitment to peace and social justice into action in creative and useful ways. We're also looking for provocative analytical and reflective pieces (1,000-4,000 words) dealing with contemporary social issues in the U.S. and abroad."

$ OUR FAMILY, Missionary Oblates of St. Mary's Province, P.O. Box 249, Battleford, Saskatchewan S0M 0E0, Canada. (306)937-7771. Fax: (306)937-7644. E-mail: editor@ourfamilymagazine.com. Website: www.ourfamilymagazine.com. **Contact:** Marie-Louise Ternier-Gommers, editor. **80% freelance written.** Prefers to work with published/established writers. Monthly magazine for Canadian Catholics. Estab. 1949. Circ. 7,000. **Pays on acceptance.** Publishes ms an average of 6 months after acceptance. Byline given. Offers 100% kill fee. Generally purchases first North American serial rights; also buys all, simultaneous, second serial (reprint) or one-time rights. Submit seasonal material 6 months in advance. Accepts queries by mail, e-mail. Accepts simultaneous submissions. Responds in 2 months to queries. Sample copy for 9×12 SAE with $3 Canadian postage or IRC only. Writer's guidelines, editorial policy and themes for upcoming issues on website.

Nonfiction: Faith dimension is essential for an article to be accepted. Humor (related to family life or husband/wife relations), inspirational, personal experience (with religious dimensions), photo feature (particularly in search of photo essays on human/religious themes and on persons whose lives are an inspiration to others). **We receive 50-70 submissions/month.** Length: 1,000-2,400 words. **Pays 7¢/word (Canadian); 5¢/word (US).**

Reprints: Send tearsheet, photocopy or typed ms with rights for sale noted and information about when and where the material previously appeared. Pays 5¢/word (Canadian); 3¢/word (US).

Photos: Photos purchased with or without accompanying ms. Pays $35 Canadian ($24 US) for 5×7 or larger b&w glossy prints and color photos (which are converted into b&w). Offers additional payment for photos accepted with ms (payment for these photos varies according to their quality). Free photo spec sheet for SAE with IRC.

Poetry: Must have a religious dimension. Avant-garde, free verse, haiku, light verse, traditional. **Buys 36-72 poems/year.** Length: 3-30 lines. **Pays 75¢/line (Canadian); 50¢/line (US).**

Fillers: Anecdotes, gags to be illustrated by cartoonist, short humor, jokes. **Buys 2-10/issue/year.**

Tips: "Writers should ask themselves whether this is the kind of an article, poem, etc. that a busy person would pick up and read in a few moments of leisure. We look for articles on the spirituality of marriage. We concentrate on recent movements and developments in the church to help make people aware of the new church of which they are a part. We invite reflections on ecumenical experiences."

OUR SUNDAY VISITOR, Our Sunday Visitor, Inc., 200 Noll Plaza, Huntington IN 46750. (219)356-8400. Fax: (219)356-8472. E-mail: oursunvis@osv.com. Website: www.osv.com. Managing Editor: Richard G. Beemer. **Contact:** Gerald Korson, editor. **10% freelance written.** (Mostly assigned). Weekly tabloid covering world events and culture from a Catholic perspective. Estab. 1912. Circ. 70,000. **Pays on acceptance.** Publishes ms an average of 1 month after acceptance. Byline given. Buys first rights. Accepts queries by mail, e-mail.

$ THE PENTECOSTAL MESSENGER, Messenger Publishing House, P.O. Box 850, Joplin MO 64802-0850. (417)624-7050. Fax: (417)624-7102. E-mail: johnm@pcg.org. Website: www.pcg.org. **Contact:** John Mallinak, editor. **10% freelance written.** Works with small number of new/unpublished writers each year. Monthly magazine covering Pentecostal Christianity. "*The Pentecostal Messenger* is the official organ of the Pentecostal Church of God. It goes to ministers and church members." Estab. 1919. Circ. 12,000. Pays on publication. Publishes ms an average of 6 months after acceptance. Byline given. Buys second serial (reprint), simultaneous rights. Submit seasonal material 4 months in advance. Accepts queries by mail, e-mail, phone. Accepts simultaneous submissions. Responds in 2 months to queries. Sample copy for 6×9 SAE and 2 first-class stamps. Writer's guidelines free.

Nonfiction: Spiritual solutions to life's problems, preferably through human experience, testimony, family-strengthening ideas, financial advice. Inspirational, religious. Send complete ms. Length: 400-1,200 words. **Pays 2¢/word.**

Reprints: Send tearsheet, photocopy or typed ms with rights for sale noted and information about when and where the material previously appeared. Pays 100% of amount paid for an original article.

Tips: "Articles need to be inspirational, informative, written from a positive viewpoint, and not extremely controversial. No blatant use of theology or sermonizing."

⊠ PIME WORLD, PIME Missionaries, 17330 Quincy St., Detroit MI 48221-2765. (313)342-4066. Fax: (313)342-6816. E-mail: pimeworld@pimeusa.org. Website: www.pimeusa.org. **Contact:** Christine Busque, managing editor. **10% freelance written.** Monthly (except July and August) magazine educating North American Catholics on the missionary nature of the Church and inviting them to realize their call to be missionaries. "The magazine also serves the purpose of making known the PIME Missionaries in North America by emphasizing the foreign missionary activities of the PIME Missionaries throughout the world. Our audience is largely high school educated, conservative in both religion and politics." Estab. 1954. Circ. 26,000. Pays on publication. Publishes ms an average of 5 months after acceptance. Byline given. Buys one-time rights. Editorial lead time 2 months. Submit seasonal material 2 months in advance. Accepts queries by mail, e-mail, fax, phone. Accepts simultaneous submissions. Responds in 2 weeks to queries; 2 months to mss. Sample copy free. Writer's guidelines for #10 SASE.

Nonfiction: Informational and inspirational foreign missionary activities of the Roman Catholic Church, Christian social commentary. Essays, inspirational, personal experience, photo feature, religious. **Buys 10 mss/year.** Query or send complete ms. Length: 800-1,200 words. **Pays $50-200.**

Reprints: Accepts previously published submissions.

Photos: State availability of or send photos with submission. Buys one-time rights. Pays $10/color photo. Identification of subjects required.

Tips: "Articles produced from a faith standpoint dealing with current issues of social justice, evagelization, witness, proclamation, pastoral work in the foreign missions, etc. Interviews of missionaries, both religious and lay, welcome. Good quality color photos greatly appreciated."

$ $⊠ THE PLAIN TRUTH, Renewing Faith & Values, Plain Truth Ministries, 300 W. Green St., Pasadena CA 91129. Fax: (626)304-8172. E-mail: Phyllis_Duke@ptm.org. Website: www.ptm.org. Editor: Greg Albrecht. **Contact:** Phyllis Duke, assistant editor. **90% freelance written.** Bimonthly magazine. "We seek to reignite the flame of shattered lives by illustrating the joy of a new life in Christ." Estab. 1935. Circ. 70,000. Pays on publication. Publishes ms an average of 8 months after acceptance. Byline given. Offers $50 kill fee. Buys all-language rights for *The Plain Truth* and its affiliated publications. Editorial lead time 6 months. Submit seasonal material 6 months in advance. Accepts queries by mail, e-mail. Accepts simultaneous submissions. Sample copy for 9×12 SAE and 4 first-class stamps. Writer's guidelines for #10 SASE or online.

Nonfiction: Inspirational, interview/profile, personal experience, religious. **Buys 48-50 mss/year.** Query with published clips and SASE. *No unsolicited mss.* Length: 750-2,500 words. **Pays 25¢/word.**

Reprints: Send tearsheet or photocopy of article or typed ms with rights for sale noted and information about when and where the article previously appeared with SASE for response. Pays 15¢/word.

Photos: State availability with submission. Reviews transparencies, prints. Buys one-time rights. Negotiates payment individually. Captions required.

Columns/Departments: Christian People (interviews with Christian leaders), 1,500 words. **Buys 6-12 mss/year.** Send complete ms. **Pays 15-25¢/word.**

Fillers: Anecdotes. **Buys 0-20/year.** Length: 25-200 words. **Pays 15-25¢/word.**

▣ The online magazine carries original content not found in the print edition and includes writer's guidelines.

Tips: "Material should offer biblical solutions to real-life problems. Both first-person and third-person illustrations are encouraged. Articles should take a unique twist on a subject. Material must be insightful and practical for the Christain reader. All articles must be well researched and biblically accurate without becoming overly scholastic. Use convincing arguments to support your Christian platform. Use vivid word pictures, simple and compelling language, and avoid stuffy academic jargon. Captivating anecdotes are vital."

$ PRESBYTERIAN RECORD, 50 Wynford Dr., North York Ontario M3C 1J7, Canada. (416)444-1111. Fax: (416)441-2825. E-mail: pcrecord@presbyterian.ca. Website: www.presbycan.ca/record. **Contact:** The Rev. John Congram, editor. **50% freelance written.** Eager to work with new/unpublished writers. Monthly magazine for a church-oriented, family audience. Circ. 55,000. Pays on publication. Publishes ms an average of 4 months after acceptance. Buys first North American serial, one-time, simultaneous rights. Submit seasonal material 3 months in advance. Accepts queries by mail, e-mail, fax. Responds in 2 months on accepted ms; returns rejected material in 3 months to mss. Sample copy and guidelines for 9×12 SAE with $1 Canadian postage or IRCs or online.

Nonfiction: Check a copy of the magazine for style. Inspirational, interview/profile, personal experience, religious. Special issues: Special upcoming themes: small groups in the church; conflict in the church; lay leadership. No material solely or mainly American in context. No sermons, accounts of ordinations, inductions, baptisms, receptions, church anniversaries or term papers. **Buys 15-20 unsolicited mss/year.** Query. Length: 600-1,500 words. **Pays $50 (Canadian).** Sometimes pays expenses of writers on assignment.

Reprints: Send tearsheet, photocopy or typed ms with rights for sale noted and information about when and where the material previously appeared.

Photos: When possible, photos should accompany manuscript; e.g., current events, historical events and biographies. Pays $15-20 for glossy photos. Uses positive transparencies for cover. Pays $50 plus. Captions required.

Columns/Departments: Vox Populi (items of contemporary and often controversial nature), 700 words; Mission Knocks (new ideas for congregational mission and service), 700 words.

▣ The online magazine carries original content not found in the print edition and includes writer's guidelines. Contact: Tom Dickey, online editor.

Tips: "There is a trend away from maudlin, first-person pieces redolent with tragedy and dripping with simplistic, pietistic conclusions. Writers often leave out those parts which would likely attract readers, such as anecdotes and direct quotes. Using active rather than passive verbs also helps most manuscripts."

$ $ PRESBYTERIANS TODAY, Presbyterian Church (U.S.A.), 100 Witherspoon St., Louisville KY 40202-1396. (502)569-5637. Fax: (502)569-8632. E-mail: today@pcusa.org. Website: www.pcusa.org/today. **Contact:** Eva Stimson, editor. **45% freelance written.** Prefers to work with published/established writers. Denominational magazine published 10 times/year covering religion, denominational activities and public issues for members of the Presbyterian Church (U.S.A.). "The magazine's purpose is to increase understanding and appreciation of what the church and its members are doing to live out their Christian faith." Estab. 1867. Circ. 70,000. **Pays on acceptance.** Publishes ms an average of 6 months after acceptance. Byline given. Offers 50% kill fee. Buys first North American serial rights. Editorial lead time 3 months. Submit seasonal material 3 months in advance. Accepts queries by mail, e-mail, fax, phone. Responds in 2 weeks to queries; 1 month to mss. Sample copy and writer's guidelines free.
    ○⊸ Break in with a "short feature for our 'Spotlight' department (300 words)."
Nonfiction: "Most articles have some direct relevance to a Presbyterian audience; however, *Presbyterians Today* also seeks well-informed articles written for a general audience that help readers deal with the stresses of daily living from a Christian perspective." How-to (everyday Christian living), inspirational, Presbyterian programs, issues, peoples. **Buys 20 mss/year.** Send complete ms. Length: 1,000-1,800 words. **Pays $300 maximum for assigned articles; $75-300 for unsolicited articles.**
Photos: State availability with submission. Reviews contact sheets, transparencies, b&w prints. Buys one-time rights. Negotiates payment individually. Identification of subjects required.

$ PRESERVING CHRISTIAN HOMES, General Youth Division, 8855 Dunn Rd., Hazelwood MO 63042. (314)837-7304. Fax: (314)837-4503. E-mail: youth@upci.org. Website: www.upci.org/youth. **Contact:** Todd Gaddy, editor and general youth director of promotions. **40% freelance written.** Bimonthly magazine covering Christian home and family. "All submissions must conform to Christian perspective." Estab. 1970. Circ. 4,500. Pays on publication. Publishes ms an average of 9 months after acceptance. Byline sometimes given. Buys one-time, simultaneous rights. Editorial lead time 6 months. Submit seasonal material 6 months in advance. Accepts queries by mail. Accepts simultaneous submissions. Responds in 2 weeks to queries; 2 months to mss. Sample copy for 10×13 SAE and 2 first-class stamps.
Nonfiction: General interest, humor, inspirational, personal experience, religious. Special issues: Mothers Day/Fathers Day. No "editorial or political." **Buys 15 mss/year.** Send complete ms. Length: 500-1,500 words. **Pays $30-40.**
Photos: State availability with submission. Buys all rights. Negotiates payment individually.
Fiction: Humorous, religious, slice-of-life vignettes. **Buys 6 mss/year.** Send complete ms. Length: 500-1,500 words. **Pays $30-40.**
Poetry: Free verse, light verse, traditional. **Buys 3 poems/year.** Submit maximum 5 poems. Length: 10-40 lines. **Pays $20-25.**
Fillers: Anecdotes, facts, short humor. **Buys 2/year.** Length: 50-200 words. **Pays $10-20.**
Tips: "Be relevant to today's Christian families!"

$ $ PRISM MAGAZINE, America's Alternative Evangelical Voice, Evangelicals for Social Action, 10 E. Lancaster Ave., Wynnewood PA 19096. (610)645-9391. Fax: (610)649-8090. E-mail: kristyn@esa-online.org. Website: www.esa-online.org. **Contact:** Kristyn Komarnicki, editor. **50% freelance written.** Bimonthly magazine covering Christianity and social justice. For holistic, biblical, socially-concerned, progressive Christians. Estab. 1993. Circ. 7,000. Pays on publication. Publishes ms an average of 3 months after acceptance. Byline given. Buys first North American serial rights. Editorial lead time 3 months. Submit seasonal material 4 months in advance. Accepts queries by mail, e-mail, fax, phone. Responds in 2 weeks to queries; 2 months to mss. Sample copy for $3. Writer's guidelines free.
    ● "We're a nonprofit, some writers are pro bono."
Nonfiction: Book excerpts (to coincide with book release date), essays, humor, inspirational, opinion, personal experience. **Buys 10-12 mss/year.** Send complete ms. Length: 500-3,000 words. **Pays $75-300 for assigned articles; $25-200 for unsolicited articles.**
Photos: Send photos with submission. Reviews prints. Buys one-time rights. Negotiates payment individually.
Tips: "We look closely at stories of holistic ministry. It's best to request a sample copy to get to know *PRISM*'s focus/style before submitting—we receive so many submissions that are not appropriate."

$ ⊠ PURPOSE, 616 Walnut Ave., Scottdale PA 15683-1999. (724)887-8500. Fax: (724)887-3111. E-mail: horsch@mph.org. Website: www.mph.org. **Contact:** James E. Horsch, editor. **95% freelance written.** Weekly magazine "for adults, young and old, general audience with varied interests. My readership is interested in seeing how Christianity works in difficult situations." Estab. 1968. Circ. 11,000. **Pays on acceptance.** Publishes ms an average of 8 months after acceptance. Buys one-time rights. Submit seasonal material 6 months in advance. Accepts simultaneous submissions. Responds in 3 months to queries. Sample copy and writer's guidelines for 6×9 SAE and 2 first-class stamps.
Nonfiction: Inspirational stories from a Christian perspective. "I want upbeat stories that deal with issues faced by believers in family, business, politics, religion, gender and any other areas—and show how the Christian faith resolves them. Purpose conveys truth through quality fiction or true life stories. Our magazine accents Christian discipleship. Christianity affects all of life, and we expect our material to demonstate this. I would like story-type articles about

individuals, groups and organizations who are intelligently and effectively working at such problems as hunger, poverty, international understanding, peace, justice, etc., because of their faith. Essays and how-to-do-it pieces must include a lot of anecdotal, life exposure examples." **Buys 130 mss/year.** Send complete ms. Length: 750 words. **Pays 5¢/word maximum. Buys one-time rights only.**

Reprints: Send tearsheet, photocopy or typed ms with rights for sale noted and information about when and where the material previously appeared.

Photos: Photos purchased with ms must be sharp enough for reproduction; requires prints in all cases. Pays $5-15 for b&w (less for color), depending on quality. Captions required.

Fiction: "Produce the story with specificity so that it appears to take place somewhere and with real people." Historical, humorous, religious.

Poetry: Free verse, light verse, traditional, blank verse. **Buys 130/year poems/year.** Length: 12 lines. **Pays $7.50-20/poem depending on length and quality. Buys one-time rights only.**

Fillers: Anecdotal items up to 599 words. **Pays 4¢/word maximum.**

Tips: "We are looking for articles which show the Christian faith working at issues where people hurt; stories need to be told and presented professionally. Good photographs help place material with us."

$ QUEEN OF ALL HEARTS, Montfort Missionaries, 26 S. Saxon Ave., Bay Shore NY 11706-8993. (631)665-0726. Fax: (631)665-4349. E-mail: pretre@worldnet.att.net. Website: www.montfortmissionaries.com. **Contact:** Roger Charest, S.M.M., managing editor. **50% freelance written.** Bimonthly magazine covering "Mary, Mother of Jesus, as seen in the sacred scriptures, tradition, history of the church, the early Christian writers, lives of the saints, poetry, art, music, spiritual writers, apparitions, shrines, ecumenism, etc." Estab. 1950. Circ. 2,000. **Pays on acceptance.** Publishes ms an average of 6 months after acceptance. Byline given. Not copyrighted. Submit seasonal material 6 months in advance. Accepts queries by mail, e-mail, fax, phone. Responds in 2 months to queries. Sample copy for $2.50.

Nonfiction: Essays, inspirational, interview/profile, personal experience, religious (Marialogical and devotional). **Buys 25 mss/year.** Send complete ms. Length: 750-2,500 words. **Pays $40-60.**

Photos: Send photos with submission. Reviews transparencies. Buys one-time rights. Pay varies.

Fiction: Religious. **Buys 6 mss/year.** Send complete ms. Length: 1,500-2,500 words. **Pays $40-60.**

Poetry: Joseph Tusiani, poetry editor. Free verse. **Buys approximately 10 poems/year.** Submit maximum 2 poems. **Pays in contributor copies.**

$ ◪ THE QUIET HOUR, Cook Communications Ministries, 4050 Lee Vance View, Colorado Springs CO 80918. (719)536-0100. Fax: (407)359-2850. E-mail: gwilde@mac.com. Managing Editor: Doug Schmidt. **Contact:** Gary Wilde, editor. **100% freelance written.** Devotional booklet published quarterly featuring daily devotions. "*The Quiet Hour* is the adult-level quarterly devotional booklet published by David C. Cook. The purpose of *The Quiet Hour* is to provide Bible-based devotional readings for Christians who are in the process of growing toward Christlikeness. Most often, *The Quiet Hour* is used at home, either in the morning or evening, as part of a devotional period. It may be used by individuals, couples or families. For those studying with our Bible-in-Life curriculum, it also helps them prepare for the upcoming Sunday school lesson." **Pays on acceptance.** Publishes ms an average of 14 months after acceptance. Byline given. Makes work-for-hire assignments. Editorial lead time 14 months. Responds in 3 months to queries. Writer's guidelines free.

Nonfiction: Daily devotionals. **Buys 52 mss/year.** Query by mail only with résumé and/or list of credits. **Pays $15-25 per devotional.**

Tips: "Send list of credits with query—especially other devotional writing. Do not send samples. We will assign the scripture passages to use."

$ $ REFORM JUDAISM, Union of American Hebrew Congregations, 633 3rd Ave., New York NY 10017-6778. (212)650-4240. Website: www.uahc.org/rjmag/. Editor: Aron Hirt-Manheimer. **Contact:** Joy Weinberg, managing editor. **30% freelance written.** Quarterly magazine of Reform Jewish issues. "*Reform Judaism* is the official voice of the Union of American Hebrew Congregations, linking the institutions and affiliates of Reform Judaism with every Reform Jew. *RJ* covers developments within the Movement while interpreting events and Jewish tradition from a Reform perspective." Pays on publication. Publishes ms an average of 3 months after acceptance. Byline given. Offers kill fee for commissioned articles. Buys first North American serial rights. Submit seasonal material 6 months in advance. Responds in 2 months to queries; 2 months to mss. Sample copy for $3.50. Writer's guidelines for SASE or online.

Nonfiction: Book excerpts, exposé, general interest, historical/nostalgic, inspirational, interview/profile, opinion, personal experience, photo feature, travel. **Buys 30 mss/year.** Submit complete ms with SASE. Length: Cover stories: 2,500-3,500 words; major feature: 1,800-2,500 words; secondary feature: 1,200-1,500 words; department (e.g., Travel): 1,200 words; letters: 200 words maximum; opinion: 525 words maximum. **Pays 30¢/word.** Sometimes pays expenses of writers on assignment.

Reprints: Send tearsheet, photocopy or typed ms with rights for sale noted and information about when and where the material previously appeared. Usually does not publish reprints.

Photos: Send photos with submission. Reviews 8×10/color or slides and b&w prints. Buys one-time rights. Pays $25-75. Identification of subjects required.

Fiction: Sophisticated, cutting-edge, superb writing. **Buys 4 mss/year.** Send complete ms. Length: 600-2,500 words. **Pays 30¢/word.**

◼ The online magazine carries original content not found in the print edition and includes writer's guidelines.

Tips: "We prefer a stamped postcard including the following information/checklist: _yes we are interested in publishing; _no, unfortunately the submission doesn't meet our needs; _maybe, we'd like to hold on to the article for now. Submissions sent this way will receive a faster response."

$ $ THE REPORTER, Women's American ORT, Inc., 315 Park Ave. S., 17th Floor, New York NY 10010. (800)51-WAORT, ext. 265. Fax: (212)674-3057. E-mail: mheller@waort.org. **Contact:** Marlene Heller, editor. **85% freelance written.** Quarterly Nonprofit journal published by Jewish women's organization covering Jewish women celebrities, issues of contemporary Jewish culture, Israel, anti-Semitism, women's rights, Jewish travel and the international Jewish community. Estab. 1966. Circ. 65,000. Payment time varies. Publishes ms an average of 1 year after acceptance. Byline given. Buys first North American serial rights. Submit seasonal material 6 months in advance. Accepts queries by mail, e-mail. Responds in 3 months to queries. Sample copy for 9 × 12 SAE and 3 first-class stamps. Writer's guidelines for #10 SASE.

O→ Break in with "a different look at a familiar topic, i.e., 'Jews without God' (Winter 2000). Won't consider handwritten or badly-typed queries. Unpublished writers are welcome. Others, include credits."

Nonfiction: Essays, exposé, humor, inspirational, opinion, personal experience, photo feature, religious, travel, Cover feature profiles a dynamic Jewish woman making a difference in Judaism, women's issues, education, entertainment, profiles, business, journalism, sports, arts. Query. Length: 1,800 words maximum. **Pays $200 and up.**

Photos: Send photos with submission. Identification of subjects required.

Columns/Departments: Education Horizon; Destination (Jewish sites/travel); Inside Out (Advocacy); Women's Business; Art Scene (interviews, books, films); Lasting Impression (uplifting/inspirational).

Fiction: Publishes novel excerpts and short stories as part of Lasting Impressions column. **Buys 4 mss/year.** Length: 800 words. **Pays $150-300.**

Tips: "Send query only by e-mail or postal mail. Show us a fresh look, not a rehash. Particularly interested in stories of interest to younger readers, ages 25-45."

$ REVIEW FOR RELIGIOUS, 3601 Lindell Blvd., Room 428, St. Louis MO 63108-3393. (314)977-7363. Fax: (314)977-7362. E-mail: review@slu.edu. Website: www.reviewforreligious.org. **Contact:** David L. Fleming, S.J., editor. **100% freelance written.** Bimonthly magazine for Roman Catholic priests, brothers and sisters. Estab. 1942. Pays on publication. Publishes ms an average of 9 months after acceptance. Byline given. Buys first North American serial rights, rarely buys second serial (reprint) rights. Accepts queries by mail, fax. Responds in 2 months to queries.

Nonfiction: Spiritual, liturgical, canonical matters only. Not for general audience. Length: 1,500-5,000 words. **Pays $6/page.**

Tips: "The writer must know about religious life in the Catholic Church and be familiar with prayer, vows, community life and ministry."

$ $ SHARING THE VICTORY, Fellowship of Christian Athletes, 8701 Leeds Rd., Kansas City MO 64129. (816)921-0909. Fax: (816)921-8755. E-mail: stv@fca.org. Website: www.fca.org. Editor: Allen Palmeri. **Contact:** David Smale, managing editor. **50% freelance written.** Prefers to work with published/established writers, but works with a growing number of new/unpublished writers each year. Published 9 times/year. "We seek to encourage and enable athletes and coaches at all levels to take their faith seriously on and off the 'field.' " Estab. 1959. Circ. 80,000. Pays on publication. Publishes ms an average of 4 months after acceptance. Byline given. Buys first rights. Submit seasonal material 3 months in advance. Responds in 3 months to queries; 3 months to mss. Sample copy for $1 and 9 × 12 SAE with 3 first-class stamps. Writer's guidelines for free for #10 SASE.

Nonfiction: Humor, inspirational, interview/profile (with name athletes and coaches solid in their faith), personal experience, photo feature. No "sappy articles on 'I became a Christian and now I'm a winner.' " **Buys 5-20 mss/year.** Query. Length: 500-1,000 words. **Pays $100-200 for unsolicited articles, more for the exceptional profile.**

Reprints: Send typed ms with rights for sale noted. Pays 50% of amount paid for an original article.

Photos: State availability with submission. Reviews contact sheets. Buys one-time rights. Pay depends on quality of photo but usually a minimum of $50. Model releases for required.

Poetry: Not accepting poetry in 2002.

Tips: "Profiles and interviews of particular interest to coed athlete, primarily high school and college age. Our graphics and editorial content appeal to youth. The area most open to freelancers is profiles on or interviews with well-known athletes or coaches (male, female, minorities) and offbeat but interscholastic team sports."

$ $ SIGNS OF THE TIMES, Pacific Press Publishing Association, P.O. Box 5353, Nampa ID 83653-5353. (208)465-2579. Fax: (208)465-2531. E-mail: mmoore@pacificpress.com. **Contact:** Marvin Moore, editor. **40% freelance written.** Works with a small number of new/unpublished writers each year. Monthly magazine. "We are a monthly Seventh-day Adventist magazine encouraging the general public to practice the principles of the Bible." Estab. 1874. Circ. 225,000. **Pays on acceptance.** Publishes ms an average of 6 months after acceptance. Byline given. Offers kill fee. Buys first North American serial, one-time, second serial (reprint) rights. Editorial lead time 1 year. Submit seasonal material 1 year in advance. Responds in 1 month to queries; 2 months to mss. Sample copy and writer's guidelines for 9 × 12 SAE with 3 first-class stamps. Writer's guidelines online.

Nonfiction: "We want writers with a desire to share the good news of reconciliation with God. Articles should be people-oriented, well-researched and should have a sharp focus. Gospel articles deal with salvation and how to experience it. While most of our gospel articles are assigned or picked up from reprints, we do occasionally accept unsolicited manuscripts in this area. Gospel articles should be 1,000 to 2,000 words. Christian lifestyle articles deal with the practical problems of everyday life from a biblical and Christian perspective. These are typically 1,000 to 1,200 words. We request that authors include sidebars that give additional information on the topic whenever possible. First-person stories must illuminate a spiritual or moral truth that the individual in the story learned. We especially like stories that hold the reader in suspense or that have an unusual twist at the end. First-person stories are typically 600 to 1,000 words long." General interest, how-to, humor, inspirational, interview/profile, personal experience, religious. **Buys 75 mss/ year.** Query by mail only with or without published clips or send complete ms. Length: 500-1,500 words. **Pays 10-20¢/ word.** Sometimes pays expenses of writers on assignment.

Reprints: Send tearsheet, photocopy or typed ms with rights for sale noted and information about when and where the material previously appeared. Pays 50% of amount paid for an original article.

Photos: Merwin Stewart, photo editor. Reviews b&w contact sheets, 35mm color transparencies, 5×7 or 8×10 b&w prints. Buys one-time rights. Pays $35-300 for transparencies; $20-50 for prints. Captions, identification of subjects, model releases required.

Columns/Departments: Send complete ms. **Pays $25-150.**

Fillers: "Short fillers can be inspirational/devotional, Christian lifestyle, stories, comments that illuminate a biblical text—in short, anything that might fit in a general Christian magazine." Length: 500-600 words.

Tips: "The audience for *Signs of the Times* includes both Christians and non-Christians of all ages. However, we recommend that our authors write with the non-Christian in mind, since most Christians can easily relate to articles that are written from a non-Christian perspective, whereas many non-Christians will have no interest in an article that is written from a Christian perspective. While *Signs* is published by Seventh-day Adventists, we mention even our own denominational name in the magazine rather infrequently. The purpose is not to hide who we are but to make the magazine as attractive to non-Christian readers as possible.We are especially interested in articles that respond to the questions of everyday life that people are asking and the problems they are facing. Since these questions and problems nearly always have a spiritual component, articles that provide a biblical and spiritual response are especially welcome. Any time you can provide us with one or more sidebars that add information to the topic of your article, you enhance your chance of getting our attention. Two kinds of sidebars seem to be especially popular with readers: Those that give information in lists, with each item in the list consisting of only a few words or at the most a sentence or two; and technical information or long explanations that in the main article might get the reader too bogged down in detail. Whatever their length, sidebars need to be part of the total word count of the article. We like the articles in *Signs of the Times* to have interest-grabbing introductions. One of the best ways to do this is with anecdotes, particularly those that have a bit of suspense or conflict."

$ SOCIAL JUSTICE REVIEW, 3835 Westminster Place, St. Louis MO 63108-3472. (314)371-1653. **Contact:** The Rev. John H. Miller, C.S.C., editor. **25% freelance written.** Works with a small number of new/unpublished writers each year. Bimonthly magazine. Estab. 1908. Publishes ms an average of 1 year after acceptance. Not copyrighted, however special articles within the magazine may be copyrighted, or an occasional special issue has been copyrighted due to author's request. Buys first North American serial rights. Sample copy for 9×12 SAE and 3 first-class stamps.

Nonfiction: Scholarly articles on society's economic, religious, social, intellectual, political problems with the aim of bringing Catholic social thinking to bear upon these problems. Query by mail only with SASE. Length: 2,500-3,000 words. **Pays about 2¢/word.**

Reprints: Send typed ms with rights for sale noted and information about when and where the material previously appeared. Pays about 2¢/word.

$ SPIRIT, Messenger Publishing House, P.O. Box 850, Joplin MO 64802-0850. (417)624-7050. Fax: (417)624-7102. E-mail: charlotteb@pcg.org. Website: www.pcg.org. **Contact:** Charlotte Beal, assistant editor. **80% freelance written.** Monthly magazine covering Pentecostal Christianity. "*Spirit* offers testimonials about the workings of the Holy Spirit in the lives of believers." Estab. 1919. Circ. 12,000. Pays on publication. Publishes ms an average of 6 months after acceptance. Byline given. Buys second serial (reprint), simultaneous rights. Submit seasonal material 4 months in advance. Accepts queries by mail, e-mail, phone. Accepts simultaneous submissions. Responds in 2 months to queries. Sample copy for 6×9 SAE SAE and 2 first-class stamps. Writer's guidelines free.

    ○⌐ Break in with good short inspirational material, particularly in the healing of relationships and marriages. Always need more personal testimonials of answered prayer.

Nonfiction: Spiritual solutions to life's problems, preferably through human experience, testimony, family-strengthening ideas and financial advice. Inspirational, religious. Send complete ms. Length: 400-1,200 words. **Pays 2¢/word.**

Reprints: Send tearsheet, photocopy or typed ms with rights for sale noted and information about when and where the material previously appeared. Pays 100% of amount paid for an original article.

Tips: "Articles need to be inspirational, informative, written from a positive viewpoint, and not extremely controversial. No blatant use of theology or sermonizing."

$ $ ST. ANTHONY MESSENGER, 1615 Republic St., Cincinnati OH 45210-1298. (513)241-5615. Fax: (513)241-0399. E-mail: stanthony@americancatholic.org. Website: www.AmericanCatholic.org. **Contact:** Father Jack Wintz, O.F.M., editor. **55% freelance written.** Monthly General interest magazine for a national readership of Catholic families, most of which have children or grandchildren in grade school, high school or college. Circ. 340,000. **Pays on**

acceptance. Publishes ms an average of 9 months after acceptance. Byline given. Buys electronic rights, first worldwide serial. Submit seasonal material 6 months in advance. Accepts queries by mail, e-mail, fax. Responds in 2 months to queries. Sample copy and writer's guidelines for 9×12 SAE with 4 first-class stamps.

Nonfiction: How-to (on psychological and spiritual growth, problems of parenting/better parenting, marriage problems/marriage enrichment), humor, inspirational, interview/profile, opinion (limited use; writer must have special qualifications for topic), personal experience (if pertinent to our purpose), photo feature, informational, social issues. **Buys 35-50 mss/year.** Query with published clips. Length: 1,500-2,500 words. **Pays 16¢/word.** Sometimes pays expenses of writers on assignment.

Fiction: Mainstream, religious. **Buys 12 mss/year.** Send complete ms. Length: 2,000-2,500 words. **Pays 16¢/word.**

Poetry: "Our poetry needs are very limited." Submit maximum 4-5 poems. Length: up to 20-25 lines; the shorter, the better. **Pays $2/line; $20 minimum.**

Tips: "The freelancer should consider why his or her proposed article would be appropriate for us, rather than for *Redbook* or *Saturday Review.* We treat human problems of all kinds, but from a religious perspective. Articles should reflect Catholic theology, spirituality and employ a Catholic terminology and vocabulary. We need more articles on prayer, scripture, Catholic worship. Get authoritative information (not merely library research); we want interviews with experts. Write in popular style; use lots of examples, stories and personal quotes. Word length is an important consideration."

$ STANDARD, Nazarene International Headquarters, 6401 The Paseo, Kansas City MO 64131. (816)333-7000. **Contact:** Everett Leadingham, editor. **100% freelance written.** Works with a small number of new/unpublished writers each year. Weekly inspirational paper with Christian reading for adults. Estab. 1936. Circ. 160,000. **Pays on acceptance.** Publishes ms an average of 18 months after acceptance. Byline given. Buys one-time, second serial (reprint) rights. Submit seasonal material 6 months in advance. Responds in 10 weeks to queries. Sample copy free. Writer's guidelines for SAE with 2 first-class stamps.

Reprints: Send tearsheet.

Fiction: Prefers fiction-type stories *showing* Christianity in action. Send complete ms. Length: 500-1,200 words. **Pays 31/2¢/word for first rights; 2¢/word for reprint rights.**

Poetry: Free verse, haiku, light verse, traditional. **Buys 50 poems/year.** Submit maximum 5 poems. Length: 50 lines. **Pays 25¢/line.**

Tips: "Stories should express Christian principles without being preachy. Setting, plot and characterization must be realistic."

N $ $ THE STANDARD, Magazine of the Baptist General Conference, Baptist General Conference, 2002 S. Arlington Heights Rd., Arlington Heights IL 60005. Fax: (847)228-5376. E-mail: jhanning@baptistgeneral.org. Website: www.bgcworld.org. **Contact:** Jodi Hanning, managing editor. **65% freelance written.** Non-profit, religious, evangelical Christian magazine published 10 times/year covering the Baptist General Conference. "*The Standard* is the official magazine of the Baptist General Conference (BGC). Articles related to the BGC, our churches, or by/about BGC people receive preference." Estab. early 1900. Circ. 9,000. Pays on publication. Byline given. Offers 50% kill fee. Buys first rights. Editorial lead time 6 months. Submit seasonal material 6 months in advance. Accepts queries by e-mail. Responds in 1 month to queries; 2 months to mss. Sample copy for #10 SASE. Writer's guidelines free.

Nonfiction: Book excerpts, general interest, how-to, inspirational, interview/profile, photo feature, religious, travel, sidebars related to theme. No sappy religious pieces, articles not intended for our audience. Ask for a sample instead of sending anything first. **Buys 20-30 mss/year.** Query with published clips. Length: 300-2,000 words. **Pays $50-240.** Sometimes pays expenses of writers on assignment.

Photos: State availability with submission. Reviews prints. Buys one-time rights. Offers $15/photo. Captions, identification of subjects, model releases required.

Columns/Departments: Bob Putman, associate editor. Around the BGC (blurbs of news happening in the BGC), 50-150 words. Send complete ms. **Pays $15-20.**

Tips: "Please study the magazine and the denomination. We will send sample copies to interested freelancers and give further information about our publication needs upon request. Freelancers who are interested in working an assignment are welcome to express their interest."

$ THESE DAYS, Presbyterian Publishing Corp., 100 Witherspoon St., Louisville KY 40202-1396. (502)569-5102. Fax: (502)569-5113. E-mail: kaysno@worldnet.att.net. **Contact:** Kay Snodgrass, editor. **95% freelance written.** Quarterly magazine covering religious devotionals. "*These Days* is published especially for the Cumberland Presbyterian Church, The Presbyterian Church in Canada, The Presbyterian Church (U.S.A.), The United Churches of Canada, and The United Church of Christ as a personal, family and group devotional guide." Estab. 1970. Circ. 200,000. **Pays on acceptance.** Publishes ms an average of 8 months after acceptance. Byline given. Buys all rights, makes work-for-hire assignments. Editorial lead time 10 months. Submit seasonal material 1 year in advance. Accepts queries by mail, e-mail. Responds in 6 months to queries; 10 months to mss. Sample copy for 6×9 SAE and 3 first-class stamps. Writer's guidelines for #10 SASE.

Nonfiction: "Use freelance in all issues. Only devotional material will be accepted. Send for application form and guidelines. Enclose #10 SASE." Devotions and devotional aids in our format. **Buys 365 mss/year; publishes very few unsolicited devotionals.** Query with or without published clips. Length: Devotionals, 250 words; These Moments, 500 words; These Times, 750 words. **Pays $14.25 for devotions; $30 for These Moments and $45 for These Times.**

Poetry: Buys 2-4 poems/year. Submit maximum 5 poems. Length: 3-20 lines. **Pays $15.**

Tips: "The best way to be considered is to send a one-page query that includes your religious affiliation and your religious, writing-related experience plus a sample devotion in our format and/or published clips of similar material. Read a current issue devotionally to get a feel for the magazine. We would also like to see more minority and Canadian writers."

$ ✖ TOGETHER, Shalom Publishers, Box 656, Route 2, Grottoes VA 24441. E-mail: tgether@aol.com. **Contact:** Melodie M. Davis, editor. **95% freelance written.** "*Together* is used quarterly by churches as an outreach paper to encourage readers to faith in Christ and God and participation in a local church. In addition to testimonies of spiritual conversion or journey, we publish general inspirational or family-related articles." Estab. 1986. Circ. 180,000. Pays on publication. Publishes ms an average of 9 months after acceptance. Byline given. Buys one-time, second serial (reprint) rights. Editorial lead time 6 months. Submit seasonal material 9 months in advance. Accepts simultaneous submissions. Responds in 2 months to queries; 6 months to mss. Sample copy for 9×12 SAE SAE and 4 first-class stamps. Writer's guidelines for #10 SASE or by e-mail.

Nonfiction: Inspirational, personal experience (testimony), religious. **Buys 22-24 mss/year.** Send complete ms. Length: 300-1,000 words. **Pays $35-50.**

Photos: State availability with submission. Reviews 3×5 prints. Buys one-time rights. Offers $25/photo. Identification of subjects required.

Tips: "We can use good contemporary conversion stories (to Christian faith) including as-told-to's. Read other stuff that is being published and then ask if your writing is up to the level of what is being published today."

$ $ ✖ U.S. CATHOLIC, Claretian Publications, 205 W. Monroe St., Chicago IL 60606. (312)236-7782. Fax: (312)236-8207. E-mail: editors@uscatholic.org. Website: www.uscatholic.org. Editor: Mark J. Brummel, CMF., Managing Editor: Meinrad Scherer-Emunds. **Contact:** Fran Hurst, editorial assistant. **100% freelance written.** Monthly magazine covering Roman Catholic spirituality. "*U.S. Catholic* is dedicated to the belief that it makes a difference whether you're Catholic. We invite and help our readers explore the wisdom of their faith tradition and apply their faith to the challenges of the 21st century." Estab. 1935. Circ. 50,000. **Pays on acceptance.** Publishes ms an average of 3 months after acceptance. Byline given. Buys first North American serial rights. Editorial lead time 8 months. Submit seasonal material 6 months in advance. Accepts queries by mail, e-mail, fax, phone. Responds in 1 month to queries; 2 months to mss. Sample copy for large SASE. Writer's guidelines for #10 SASE.

Nonfiction: Essays, inspirational, opinion, personal experience, religious. **Buys 100 mss/year.** Send complete ms. Length: 2,500-3,500 words. **Pays $250-600.** Sometimes pays expenses of writers on assignment.

Photos: State availability with submission.

Columns/Departments: Pays $250-600.

Fiction: Maureen Abood, literary editor. Mainstream, religious, slice-of-life vignettes. **Buys 4-6 mss/year.** Send complete ms. Length: 2,500-3,000 words. **Pays $300.**

Poetry: Maureen Abood, literary editor. Free verse. "No light verse." **Buys 12 poems/year.** Submit maximum 5 poems. Length: 50 lines. **Pays $75.**

THE UNITED CHURCH OBSERVER, 478 Huron St., Toronto Ontario M5R 2R3, Canada. (416)960-8500. Fax: (416)960-8477. E-mail: general@ucobserver.org. Website: www.ucobserver.org. **Contact:** Muriel Duncan, editor. **20% freelance written.** Prefers to work with published/established writers. Monthly Newsmagazine for people associated with The United Church of Canada. Deals primarily with events, trends and policies having religious significance. Most coverage is Canadian, but reports on international or world concerns will be considered. Pays on publication. Publishes ms an average of 4 months after acceptance. Byline usually given. Buys first serial rights and occasionally all rights. Accepts queries by mail, e-mail, fax.

Nonfiction: Occasional opinion features only. Extended coverage of major issues is usually assigned to known writers. Submissions should be written as news, no more than 1,200 words length, accurate and well-researched. No opinion pieces or poetry. Queries preferred. **Rates depend on subject, author and work involved.** Pays expenses of writers on assignment as negotiated.

Reprints: Send tearsheet or photocopy and information about when and where the material previously appeared. Payment negotiated.

Photos: Buys photographs with mss. Black & white should be 5×7 minimum; color 35mm or larger format. Payment varies.

Tips: "The writer has a better chance of breaking in at our publication with short articles; this also allows us to try more freelancers. Include samples of previous *news* writing with query. Indicate ability and willingness to do research, and to evaluate that research. The most frequent mistakes made by writers in completing an article for us are organizational problems, lack of polished style, short on research, and a lack of inclusive language."

$ ✖ THE UPPER ROOM, Daily Devotional Guide, P.O. Box 340004, Nashville TN 37203-0004. (615)340-7252. Fax: (615)340-7267. E-mail: TheUpperRoomMagazine@upperroom.org. Website: www.upperroom.org. Editor and Publisher: Stephen D. Bryant. **Contact:** Marilyn Beaty, editorial assistant. **95% freelance written.** Eager to work with new/unpublished writers. Bimonthly magazine "offering a daily inspirational message which includes a Bible reading, text, prayer, 'Thought for the Day,' and suggestion for further prayer. Each day's meditation is written by a different person and is usually a personal witness about discovering meaning and power for Christian living through scripture study which illuminates daily life." Circ. 2.2 million (US); 385,000 outside US. Pays on publication. Publishes ms an average of 1 year after acceptance. Byline given. Buys first North American serial rights, translation. Submit seasonal material 14 months in advance. Sample copy and writer's guidelines with a 4×6 SAE and 2 first-class stamps. Guidelines only for #10 SASE or online.

- "Manuscripts are not returned. If writers include a stamped, self-addressed postcard, we will notify them that their writing has reached us. This does not imply acceptance or interest in purchase. Does not respond unless material is accepted for publication."

Nonfiction: Inspirational, personal experience, Bible-study insights. Special issues: Lent and Easter 2001; Advent 2000. No poetry, lengthy "spiritual journey" stories. **Buys 365 unsolicited mss/year.** Send complete ms by mail or e-mail. Length:300 words. **Pays $25 per meditation.**

Tips: "The best way to break into our magazine is to send a well-written manuscript that looks at the Christian faith in a fresh way. Standard stories and sermon illustrations are immediately rejected. We very much want to find new writers and welcome good material. We are particularly interested in meditations based on Old Testament characters and stories. Good repeat meditations can lead to work on longer assignments for our other publications, which pay more. A writer who can deal concretely with everyday situations, relate them to the Bible and spiritual truths, and write clear, direct prose should be able to write for *The Upper Room*. We want material that provides for more interaction on the part of the reader—meditation suggestions, journaling suggestions, space to reflect and link personal experience with the meditation for the day. Meditations that are personal, authentic, exploratory and full of sensory detail make good devotional writing."

N **$ $ THE UU WORLD**, Unitarian Universalist Association, 25 Beacon St., Boston MA 02108-2800. (617)742-2100. Fax: (617)742-7025. E-mail: world@uua.org. Website: www.uuworld.org. Editor-in-Chief: Tom Stites. **Contact:** Robert Tarutis. **50% freelance written.** Bimonthly magazine "to promote and inspire denominational self-reflection; to inform readers about the wide range of Unitarian Universalist values, purposes, activities, aesthetics, and spiritual attitudes, and to educate readers about the history, personalities, and congregations that comprise UUism; to enhance its dual role of leadership and service to member congregations." Estab. 1987. Circ. 120,000. **Pays on acceptance.** Publishes ms an average of 1 year after acceptance. Byline given. Buys one-time rights. Editorial lead time 3 months. Submit seasonal material 3 months in advance. Accepts queries by mail, e-mail, fax. Responds in 2 months to queries; 3 months to mss. Sample copy and writer's guidelines for 9×12 SAE or online.

Nonfiction: All articles must have a clear UU angle. Essays, historical/nostalgic (Unitarian or Universalist focus), inspirational, interview/profile (with UU individual or congregation), photo feature (of UU congregation or project), religious. Special issues: "We are planning issues on family, spirituality and welfare reform." No unsolicited poetry or fiction. **Buys 5 mss/year.** Query with published clips. Length: 1,500-3,500 words. **Pays $400 minimum for assigned articles.** Sometimes pays expenses of writers on assignment.

Photos: State availability with submission. Reviews contact sheets. Buys one-time rights. Offers no additional payment for photos accepted with ms. Captions, identification of subjects, model releases required.

Columns/Departments: Living the Faith (profiles of UUs and UU congregations). **Pays $250-500 for assigned articles.**

$ $ THE WAR CRY, The Salvation Army, 615 Slaters Lane, Alexandria VA 22313. Fax: (703)684-5539. E-mail: warcry@usn.salvationarmy.org. Website: www.christianity.com/salvationarmyusa. Managing Editor: Jeff McDonald. **Contact:** Lt. Colonel Marlene Chase, editor-in-chief. **10% freelance written.** Biweekly magazine covering army news and Christian devotional writing. Estab. 1881. Circ. 400,000. **Pays on acceptance.** Publishes ms an average of 1 year after acceptance. Byline given. Buys one-time rights. Editorial lead time 6 weeks. Submit seasonal material 1 year in advance. Accepts queries by mail, e-mail. Responds in 1 month to queries. Sample copy and writer's guidelines free or online.

- "A best bet would be a well-written profile of an exemplary Christian or a recounting of a person's experiences that deepened the subject's faith and showed God in action. Most popular profiles are of Salvation Army programs and personnel."

Nonfiction: Humor, inspirational, interview/profile, personal experience, religious. No missionary stories, confessions. **Buys 40 mss/year.** Send complete ms. **Pays up to 20¢/word for assigned articles; 5-20¢/word for unsolicited articles.** Sometimes pays expenses of writers on assignment.

Reprints: Send typed ms with rights for sale noted and information about when and where the material previously appeared. Pays 12¢/word.

Photos: Buys one-time rights. Offers $35-200/photo. Identification of subjects required.

Fiction: Religious. **Buys 5-10 mss/year.** Send complete ms. Length: 1,200-1,500 words. **Pays up to 20¢/word.**

Poetry: Free verse. **Buys 10-20/year poems/year.** Submit maximum 5 poems. Length:16 lines. **Pays $20-50.**

Fillers: Anecdotes (inspirational). **Buys 10-20/year.** Length: 200-500 words. **Pays 15-20¢/word.**

- The online magazine carries original content not included in the print edition. Contact: Jeff McDonald, online editor.

Tips: "We are soliciting more short fiction, inspirational articles and poetry, interviews with Christian athletes, evangelical leaders and celebrities, and theme-focused articles."

$ THE WESLEYAN ADVOCATE, The Wesleyan Publishing House, P.O. Box 50434, Indianapolis IN 46250-0434. (317)570-5204. Fax: (317)570-5260. E-mail: communications@wesleyan.org. Executive Editor: Dr. Norman G.

Wilson. **Contact:** Jerry Brecheisen, managing editor. Monthly magazine of The Wesleyan Church. Estab. 1842. Circ. 20,000. Pays on publication. Byline given. Buys first rights or simultaneous rights (prefers first rights). Submit seasonal material 6 months in advance. Accepts simultaneous submissions. Responds in 2 weeks to queries. Sample copy for $2. Writer's guidelines for #10 SASE.

Nonfiction: Humor, inspirational, religious. Send complete ms. Length: 500-700 words. **Pays $25-150.**

Reprints: Send photocopy of article and typed ms with rights for sale noted and information about when and where the material previously appeared.

Tips: "Write for a guide."

$ THE WESLEYAN WOMAN, Wesleyan Publishing House, P.O. Box 50434, Indianapolis IN 46250. (317)570-5164. Fax: (317)570-5254. E-mail: wwi@wesleyan.org. Website: www.wesleyan.org. Editor: Nancy Heer. **Contact:** Martha Blackburn, managing editor. **60-70% freelance written.** "Quarterly instruction and inspiration magazine for women 20-80. It is read by believers mainly." Estab. 1980. Circ. 4,000. Pays on publication. Byline given. Buys one-time, second serial (reprint) rights. Editorial lead time 3 months. Submit seasonal material 6 months in advance. Accepts simultaneous submissions. Sample copy and writer's guidelines free or online.

Nonfiction: "We look for interesting, easy-to-read articles about the Christian life that capture the readers' interest. We look for uplifting articles that grab your attention; that inspire you to reach up to God with devotion, and out to those around us with unconditional love." General interest, how-to (ideas for service and ministry), humor, inspirational, personal experience, religious. "No 'preaching' articles that tell others what to do." **Buys 60 mss/year.** Query by mail only or send complete ms. Length: 200-700 words. **Pays 2-4¢/word.**

Reprints: Send tearsheet, photocopy or typed ms with rights for sale noted and information about when and where the material previously appeared. Pays 50-75% of amount paid for an original article.

Photos: Send photos with submission. Buys one-time rights. Offers $30/photo. Captions, identification of subjects required.

Fillers: Anecdotes, facts, newsbreaks, short humor. **Buys 20/year.** Length: 150-300 words. **Pays 2-4¢/word.**

Tips: "Send a complete article after seeing our guidelines. Articles that are of your personal journey are welcomed. We go for the nerve endings—touching the spots where women are hurting, perplexed or troubled. Every article must pass the text question. 'Why would today's busy, media-blitzed Christian woman want to read this article?' We seldom publish sermons and Bible studies. Our denomination has other magazines which do these."

$ $ ⊠ WHISPERS FROM HEAVEN, Publications International, Ltd., 7373 N. Cicero, Lincolnwood IL 60712. Fax: (847)329-5387. Editor: Julie Greene. Managing Editor: Becky Bell. **Contact:** Acquisitions Editor. **100% freelance written.** Bimonthly magazine covering inspirational human-interest. "We're looking for real-life experiences (personal and otherwise) that lift the human spirit and illuminate positive human traits and values: though many stories may deal with (the overcoming of) tragedy and/or difficult times, descriptions shouldn't be too visceral and the emphasis should be on adversity overcome with a positive result. *Whispers*, though inspiring, is not overtly religious." Estab. 1999. Circ. 50,000. **Pays on acceptance.** Publishes ms an average of 5 months after acceptance. Byline given. Buys all rights. Editorial lead time 5 months. Submit seasonal material 5 months in advance. Accepts queries by mail, fax. Accepts simultaneous submissions. Writer's guidelines free.

Nonfiction: General interest, inspirational, personal experience. "Nothing overtly religious or anything that explores negative human characteristics." **Buys 150 mss/year.** Query with or without published clips. Length: 1,000-1,200 words. **Pays $100-225.** Pays expenses of writers on assignment.

Tips: "We are particularly fond of stories (when they warrant it) that have a 'twist' at the end—an extra bit of surprising information that adds meaning and provides an emotional connecting point to the story itself."

$ WOMAN'S TOUCH, Assemblies of God Women's Ministries Department (GPH), 1445 Boonville Ave., Springfield MO 65802-1894. (417)862-2781. Fax: (417)862-0503. E-mail: womanstouch@ag.org. Website: www.ag.org/womanstouch. **Contact:** Darla Knoth, managing editor. **50% freelance written.** Willing to work with new/unpublished writers. Bimonthly inspirational magazine for women. "Articles and contents of the magazine should be compatible with Christian teachings as well as human interests. The audience is women of all walks of life." Estab. 1977. Circ. 15,000. Pays on publication. Publishes ms an average of 10 months after acceptance. Byline given. Buys first, second or one-time and electronic rights. Editorial lead time 10 months. Submit seasonal material 10 months in advance. Accepts queries by mail, e-mail, fax. Responds in 3 months to queries. Sample copy for 9½×11 SAE with 3 first-class stamps or online. Writer's guidelines for #10 SASE or online.

Nonfiction: Book excerpts, general interest, inspirational, personal experience, religious, Health. No fiction, poetry. **Buys 30 mss/year.** Send complete ms. Length: 200-600 words. **Pays $10-50 for assigned articles; $10-35 for unsolicited articles.**

Reprints: Send photocopy and information about when and where the material previously appeared. Pays 50-75% of amount paid for an original article.

Columns/Departments: A Final Touch (inspirational/human interest), 400 words; A Better You (health/wellness), 400 words; A Lighter Touch (true, unpublished anecdotes), 100 words.

◼ The online magazine carries original content not found in the print edition and includes writer's guidelines. Contact: Darla Knoth, online editor.

Tips: "Submit manuscripts on current issues of interest to women. Familiarize yourself with *Woman's Touch* by reading two issues before submitting an article."

$ ☒ WORLD CHRISTIAN, Global Activists for the Cause of Christ, WinPress, P.O. Box 1357, Oak Park IL 60304. (708)524-5070. Fax: (708)524-5174. E-mail: WINPress7@aol.com. **Contact:** Phillip Huber, managing editor. Quarterly magazine covering religious missions and evangelism. Estab. 1982. Circ. 30,000 (March, June, September), 150,000 (December). Pays on publication. Publishes ms an average of 6 months after acceptance. Byline given. Buys all rights. Editorial lead time 6 months. Accepts queries by mail, e-mail. Sample copy for $4. Writer's guidelines free.
   • The editor reports an interest in seeing good profiles of average Christians making a difference around the world.
   O—¬ Break in with well-written articles that show evidence of careful research from multiple sources, about interesting or unusual aspects of missions and evangelism.
Nonfiction: Book excerpts, essays, general interest, how-to, inspirational, interview/profile, opinion, personal experience, photo feature, religious, some sidebars. "No fiction, poetry or feel-good, warm, fuzzy stories about how God is important in a person's life." **Buys 50-60 mss/year.** Query with published clips. Length: 600-2,000 words. **Pays 6-15¢/word.** Sometimes pays expenses of writers on assignment.
Photos: State availability with submission. Negotiates payment individually. Captions, identification of subjects, model releases required.

$ ☒ WORLD PULSE, Billy Graham Center at Wheaton College, P.O. Box 794, Wheaton IL 60189. (630)752-7158. Fax: (630)752-7155. E-mail: pulsenews@aol.com. Website: www.wheaton.edu/bgc/emis. **Contact:** Editor. **50% freelance written.** Biweekly newsletter covering evangelical missions. "News and features on world evangelization written from an evangelical position." Estab. 1965. Circ. 5,000. Pays on publication. Byline given. Offers negotiable kill fee. Buys first North American serial rights. Accepts queries by mail, e-mail, fax. Responds in 2 weeks to queries; 1 month to mss. Sample copy and writer's guidelines free.
Nonfiction: Interview/profile, personal experience, photo feature, religious. No poetry, sermons or humor. **Buys 50 mss/year.** Query. Length: 500-1,000 words. **Pays $30-100.** Sometimes pays expenses of writers on assignment.
Photos: State availability with submission. Reviews prints. Buys one-time rights. Offers $25/photo. Identification of subjects required.
Columns/Departments: InterView (Q&A with newsmakers), 300-500 words. **Pays 10¢/word up to $50.**
Tips: "*Pulse* is not a daily newspaper. Don't write a vanilla news story (with just the 5 Ws and an H). Sprinkle human interest and memorable facts throughout the story. Try to inform *and* entertain."

RETIREMENT

January 1, 1996 the first baby boomer turned 50. With peak earning power and increased leisure time, this generation is able to pursue varied interests while maintaining active lives. More people are retiring in their 50s, while others are starting a business or traveling and pursuing hobbies. These publications give readers specialized information on health and fitness, medical research, finances and other topics of interest, as well as general articles on travel destinations and recreational activities.

$ ALIVE!, A Magazine for Christian Senior Adults, Christian Seniors Fellowship, P.O. Box 46464, Cincinnati OH 45246-0464. (513)825-3681. Editor: J. David Lang. **Contact:** A. June Lang, office editor. **60% freelance written.** Bimonthly magazine for senior adults 50 and older. "We need timely articles about Christian seniors in vital, productive lifestyles, travel or ministries." Estab. 1988. Pays on publication. Byline given. Buys first, second serial (reprint) rights. Submit seasonal material 6 months in advance. Accepts queries by mail. Responds in 2 months to queries. Sample copy for 9 × 12 SAE with 3 first-class stamps. Writer's guidelines for #10 SASE.
   • Membership $15/year. Organization membership may be deducted from payment at writer's request.
Nonfiction: General interest, humor, inspirational, interview/profile, photo feature, religious, travel. **Buys 25-50 mss/year.** Send complete ms and SASE. Length: 600-1,200 words. **Pays $18-75.**
Reprints: Send tearsheet, photocopy or typed ms with rights for sale noted and information about when and where the material previously appeared. Pays 60-75% of amount paid for an original article.
Photos: State availability with submission. Buys one-time rights. Offers $10-25. Identification of subjects, model releases required.
Columns/Departments: Heart Medicine (humorous personal anecdotes; prefer grandparent/granchild stories or anecdotes re: over-55 persons), 10-100 words. **Buys 50 mss/year.** Send complete ms and SASE. **Pays $2-25.**
Fiction: Adventure, humorous, religious, romance, slice-of-life vignettes, motivational, inspirational. **Buys 12 mss/year.** Send complete ms. Length: 600-1,200 words. **Pays $20-60.**
Fillers: Anecdotes, facts, gags to be illustrated by cartoonist, short humor. **Buys 15/year.** Length: 50-500 words. **Pays $2-15.**
Tips: "Include SASE and information regarding whether manuscript is to be returned or tossed."

$ $ $ $ MODERN MATURITY, American Association of Retired Persons, 601 E St., NW, Washington DC 20049. (202)434-6880. Website: www.aarp.org. **Contact:** Hugh Delehanty, editor. **50% freelance written.** Prefers to work with published/established writers. Bimonthly magazine. "*Modern Maturity* is devoted to the varied needs and active life interests of AARP members, age 50 and over, covering such topics as financial planning, travel, health, careers, retirement, relationships and social and cultural change. Its editorial content serves the mission of AARP seeking through education, advocacy and service to enhance the quality of life for all by promoting independence, dignity and purpose." Circ. 20,500,000. **Pays on acceptance.** Publishes ms an average of 6 months after acceptance. Byline given. Buys exclusive worldwide publication rights. Submit seasonal material 6 months in advance. Responds in 3 months to queries. Sample copy and writer's guidelines free.

Nonfiction: Careers, workplace, practical information in living, financial and legal matters, personal relationships, consumerism. Query first by mail only. *No unsolicited mss.* Length: up to 2,000 words. **Pays up to $3,000.** Sometimes pays expenses of writers on assignment.

Photos: Photos purchased with or without accompanying mss. Pays $250 and up for color; $150 and up for b&w.

Fiction: Very occasional short fiction.

Tips: "The most frequent mistake made by writers in completing an article for us is poor follow-through with basic research. The outline is often more interesting than the finished piece. We do not accept unsolicited manuscripts."

$ $ $ NEW CHOICES, The Magazine for Your Health, Money & Travel, Reader's Digest Publications, Inc., Reader's Digest Rd., Pleasantville NY 10570. Fax: (914)244-5888. E-mail: newchoices@readersdigest.com. **Contact:** Elaine Rubino, editorial administrative assistant. Magazine published 10 times/year. *"New Choices* is a lifestyle service magazine for adults 45 and over. Editorial focuses on health, money, food and travel." Estab. 1960. Circ. 600,000.

Nonfiction: Travel, planning for retirement, personal health and fitness, financial strategies, housing options, relationships, leisure pursuits. No phone calls. **Buys 60 mss/year.** Query with 2-3 published clips and SASE. No phone calls. Length: 500-2,000 words. **Pays $1/word, negotiable.**

Columns/Departments: Personal essays, online, bargains, taxes, cooking, travel, style. **Buys 84 mss/year.** Query with 2-3 published clips. No phone calls. **Pay varies.**

$ ☒ PLUS, (formerly *Senior Magazine*), 3565 S. Higuera St., San Luis Obispo CA 93401. (805)544-8711. Fax: (805)544-4450. E-mail: plusmag@fix.net. Publisher: Gary D. Suggs. **Contact:** George Brand, editor. **60% freelance written.** Monthly magazine covering seniors to inform and entertain the "over-50" but young-at-heart audience. Estab. 1981. Circ. 140,000. Pays on publication. Publishes ms an average of 2 months after acceptance. Byline given. Buys one-time rights. Editorial lead time 2 months. Submit seasonal material 2 months in advance. Accepts queries by mail. Accepts simultaneous submissions. Responds in 2 weeks to queries; 1 month to mss. Sample copy for 9×12 SAE with $1.50 postage.

Nonfiction: Historical/nostalgic, humor, interview/profile, personal experience, travel, book reviews, entertainment, health. Special issues: Second Careers; Going Back to School; Christmas (December); Travel (October, April). No finance, automotive, heavy humor, poetry or fiction. **Buys 60-70 mss/year.** Query with SASE or send complete ms. Length: 900-1,200 words. **Pays $1.50/inch.**

Photos: Send photos with submission. Reviews transparencies, 5×7 prints. Offers $5-15/photo.

Tips: "Request and read a sample copy before submitting."

$ SENIOR LIVING NEWSPAPERS, Metropolitan Radio Group, 318 E. Pershing St., Springfield MO 65806. (417)862-0852. Fax: (417)862-9079. E-mail: elefantwalk@msn.com. Website: www.seniorlivingnewspapers.com. Editor: Robert Smith. **Contact:** Joyce Yonker O'Neal, managing editor. **25-50% freelance written.** Monthly newspaper covering active seniors in retirement. "For people 55+. Positive and upbeat attitude on aging, prime-of-life times. Slant is directed to mid-life and retirement lifestyles. Readers are primarily well-educated and affluent retirees, homemakers and career professionals. *Senior Living* informs; health, fitness-entertains; essays, nostalgia, humor, etc." Estab. 1995. Circ. 40,000. Pays 30 days after publication. Publishes ms an average of 2 months after acceptance. Byline given. Buys first, second serial (reprint), electronic rights. Editorial lead time 3 months. Submit seasonal material 4 months in advance. Accepts queries by mail, e-mail. Responds in 2 weeks to queries; 1 month to mss. Sample copy for 9×12 SAE with 5 first-class stamps. Writer's guidelines for #10 SASE.

Nonfiction: Essays, general interest, historical/nostalgic, humor, inspirational, interview/profile, personal experience, photo feature, religious, travel, health-related. No youth-oriented, preachy, sugar-coated, technical articles. **Buys 65 mss/year.** Send complete ms. Length: 600-700 words. **Pays $20-35 for assigned articles; $5-35 for unsolicited articles.**

Photos: Send photos with submission. Buys one-time rights. Offers $5/photo. Captions, identification of subjects, model releases required.

Fillers: Anecdotes, facts, short humor. **Buys 15/year.** Length: 150-250 words. **Pays $5-10.**

Tips: "Beginning writers who are in need of byline clips stand a good chance if they indicate that they do not require payment for article. A query letter is not necessary, but a cover letter telling a bit about yourself is nice."

:N: $ VERMONT MATURITY MAGAZINE, P.O. Box 1158, Williston VT 05495. (802)878-0051. **Contact:** Marianne Apfelbaum, editor. **20-50% freelance written.** Monthly magazine covering adults age 50 and older. Designed to promote the ideas, interest and lifestyles of adults age 50 and older. Estab. 1993. Circ. 18,000. Pays on publication. Publishes ms an average of 2 months after acceptance. Byline given. Buys all rights. Editorial lead time 2 months. Submit seasonal material 3 months in advance. Accepts queries by mail. Sample copy for $1.

Nonfiction: Historical/nostalgic, interview/profile. Nothing that pertains to areas outside VT or adults under age 50. **Buys 5-10 mss/year.** Send complete ms. Length: 600-1,000 words. **Pays $50-100.** Sometimes pays expenses of writers on assignment.

Photos: Send photos with submission. Buys one-time rights. Offers no additional payment for photos accepted with ms. Identification of subjects required.

Columns/Departments: 50+ Fashion, 600-800 words with photo.

Tips: "Send a great sample article and photo. I like freelancers who can come up with their own story ideas! I am also desperately looking for a 50+ Fashion column."

ROMANCE & CONFESSION

Listed here are publications that need stories of romance ranging from ethnic and adventure to romantic intrigue and confession. Each magazine has a particular slant; some are written for young adults, others to family-oriented women. Some magazines also are interested in general interest nonfiction on related subjects.

N **$ AFFAIRE DE COEUR**, 3976 Oak Hill Rd., Oakland CA 94605. Fax: (510)632-8868. E-mail: sseven@msn.com. Website: www.affairedecoeur.com. **Contact:** Louise Snead, publisher. **56% freelance written.** Monthly magazine of book reviews, articles and information on publishing for romance readers and writers. Circ. 75,000. Pays on publication. Publishes ms an average of 1 year after acceptance. Byline given. Buys one-time rights. Sample copy for $5.

Nonfiction: Book excerpts, essays, general interest, historical/nostalgic, how-to, interview/profile, personal experience, photo feature. **Buys 2 mss/year.** Query. Length: 500-2,200 words. **Pays $25-35.** Sometimes pays writers with free ads.

Photos: State availability with submission. Reviews prints. Buys one-time rights. Identification of subjects required.

Columns/Departments: Reviews (book reviews), bios, articles, 2,000 words or less. "We do not accept freelance reviews."

Fiction: Fiction submissions accepted through our short story contest only, which runs from February to May 31 each year. Historical, mainstream, romance. **Pays $35.**

Fillers: Newsbreaks. **Buys 2/year.** Length: 50-100 words. **Does not pay.**

Tips: "Please send clean copy. Do not send material without SASE. Do not expect a return for 2-3 months. Type all information. Send some samples of your work."

$ THE BLACK ROMANCE GROUP, Black Confessions, Black Romance, Black Secrets, Bronze Thrills, Jive, True Black Experience, Sterling/McFadden Partnership, 233 Park Ave. S., 6th Floor, New York NY 10003. (212)780-3538. Fax: (212)780-3555. E-mail: tpowell@sterlingmacfadden.com. **Contact:** Takesha Powell, editor. **100% freelance written.** Eager to work with new/unpublished writers. Bimonthly magazine of romance and love. Pays on publication. Publishes ms an average of 2 months after acceptance. Byline given on special feature articles only but not short stories. Company maintains all property rights of stories. Accepts queries by mail, e-mail, fax, phone. Responds in 2 months to mss. Sample copy for 9×12 SAE with 5 first-class stamps. Writer's guidelines free.

Nonfiction: "We like our articles to have a down-to-earth flavor. They should be written in the spirit of sisterhood, fun and creativity. Come up with an original idea that our readers may not have thought of but will be dying to try out." How-to (relating to romance and love), feature articles on any aspect of relationships. Query with published clips. Length: 3-5 typed pages. **Pays $125.**

Fiction: Romance confessional stories told from an African-American female perspective. Stories should include two love scenes, alluding to sex. Include spicy, sexual topics of forbidden love, but not graphic detail. Stories must include a conflict between the heroine and her love interest. The age of characters can range from mid-teenage years through late thirties. Make stories exciting, passionate (uninhibited sexual fantasies) and romantic. Send complete ms. Length: 5,300-5,800 words. **Pays $100-125.**

Tips: "Follow our writer's guidelines and read a few sample copies before submitting your manuscript. Use a romance writer's phrase book as a guide when writing stories, especially love scenes. Submit stories with original, modern conflicts. Incorporate romance and sex in manuscripts, uninhibitedly—making the stories an exciting, passionate escape for readers to imagine fulfilling their secret desires."

$ ⊠ **TRUE ROMANCE**, Sterling/MacFadden Partnership, 233 Park Ave. S., New York NY 10003. (212)979-4800. Fax: (212)780-3555. E-mail: pvitucci@sterlingmacfadden.com. Website: www.truestory.com. **Contact:** Pat Vitucci, editor. **100% freelance written.** Monthly magazine for women, teens through retired, offering compelling confession stories based on true happenings, with reader identification and strong emotional tone. No third-person material. Estab. 1923. Circ. 225,000. Pays 1 month after publication. Buys all rights. Submit seasonal material 6 months in advance. Accepts queries by mail, e-mail, fax. Responds in 8 months to queries.

Nonfiction: Confessions, true love stories; mini-adventures: problems and solutions; dating and marital and child-rearing difficulties. Realistic yet unique stories dealing with current problems, everyday events; strong emotional appeal. **Buys 180 mss/year.** Submit ms. Length: 6,000-9,000 words. **Pays 3¢/word; slightly higher rates for short-shorts.**

Columns/Departments: That's My Child (photo and 50 words); Loving Pets (photo and 50 words), **both pay $50;** Cupid's Corner (photo and 500 words about you and spouse), **pays $100;** That Precious Moment (1,000 words about a unique experience), **pays $50.**
Poetry: Light romantic poetry. Length: 24 lines maximum. **Pays $10-30.**
Tips: "A timely, well-written story that is told by a sympathetic narrator who sees the central problem through to a satisfying resolution is *all* important to break into *True Romance*. We are always looking for interesting, emotional, identifiable stories."

RURAL

These publications draw readers interested in rural lifestyles. Surprisingly, many readers are from urban centers who dream of or plan to build a house in the country. Magazines featuring design, construction, log homes and "country" style interior decorating appear in Home & Garden.

$ $ THE COUNTRY CONNECTION, Ontario's Pro-Nature Magazine, Pinecone Publishing, P.O. Box 100,, Boulter Ontario K0L 1G0, Canada. (613)332-3651. Fax: (613)332-5183. E-mail: magazine@pinecone.on.ca. Website: www.pinecone.on.ca. **Contact:** Gus Zylstra, editor. **75% freelance written.** Semiannual magazine covering nature, heritage, the arts and 'green' tourism. "*The Country Connection* is a magazine for true nature lovers and the rural adventurer. Building on our commitment to heritage, cultural, artistic, and outdoor themes, we continually add new topics to illuminate the country experience of people living within nature. Our goal is to chronicle rural life in its many aspects, giving 'voice' to the countryside." Estab. 1989. Circ. 10,000. Pays on publication. Publishes ms an average of 6 months after acceptance. Byline given. Buys first rights. Editorial lead time 4 months. Submit seasonal material 4 months in advance. Accepts queries by mail, e-mail, phone. Sample copy for $4.55. Writer's guidelines for #10 SASE (in Canada) or SAE and IRC (in US) or online.
Nonfiction: General interest, historical/nostalgic, humor, opinion, personal experience, photo feature, travel, lifestyle, leisure, art and culture, vegan recipes. No hunting, fishing, animal husbandry or pet articles. **Buys 20 mss/year.** Send complete ms. Length: 500-2,000 words. **Pays 7-10¢/word.** Sometimes pays expenses of writers on assignment.
Photos: Send photos with submission. Reviews transparencies, prints. Buys one-time rights. Offers $10-50/photo. Captions required.
Columns/Departments: Pays 7-10¢/word.
Fiction: Adventure, fantasy, historical, humorous, slice-of-life vignettes, country living. **Buys 4 mss/year.** Send complete ms. Length: 500-1,500 words. **Pays 7-10¢/word.**
　□ The online magazine carries original content not found in the print edition. Contact: Gus Zylstra.
Tips: "Canadian content only. Send (original content) manuscript with appropriate support material such as photos, illustrations, maps, etc. Do not send American stamps. They have no value in Canada!"

$ COUNTRY FOLK, Salaki Publishing & Design, HC77, Box 608, Pittsburg MO 65724. (417)993-5944. Fax: (417)993-5944. E-mail: salaki@countryfolkmag.com. Website: www.countryfolkmag.com. **Contact:** Susan Salaki, editor. **100% freelance written.** Bimonthly magazine. "*Country Folk* publishes true stories and history of the Ozarks." Estab. 1994. Circ. 5,000. Pays on publication. Publishes ms an average of 3 months after acceptance. Byline given. Buys first rights. Editorial lead time 2 months. Submit seasonal material 3 months in advance. Accepts queries by mail, e-mail, fax, phone. Responds in 1 month to queries; 2 months to mss. Sample copy for $4. Writer's guidelines for #10 SASE.
　• *Country Folk* has increased from quarterly to bimonthly and doubled its circulation.
Nonfiction: Historical/nostalgic, how-to, humor, inspirational, personal experience, photo feature, true ghost stories of the Ozarks. **Buys 10 mss/year.** Prefers e-mail submissions. Length: 750-1,000 words. **Pays $5-20.** Pays writers with contributor copies or other premiums if we must do considerable editing to the work.
Photos: Send photos with submission. Buys one-time rights.
Fiction: Historical, humorous, mystery, novel excerpts. **Buys 10 mss/year.** Send complete ms. Length: 750-1,000 words. **Pays $5-50.**
Poetry: Haiku, light verse, traditional. **Buys 25 poems/year.** Submit maximum 3 poems. **Pays $1-5.**
Fillers: Anecdotes, facts, gags to be illustrated by cartoonist, newsbreaks, short humor. **Buys 25/year. Pays $1-5.**
Tips: "We want material from people who are born and raised in the country, especially the Ozark region. We accept submissions in any form, handwritten or typed. Many of the writers and poets whose work we publish are first-time submissions. Most of the work we publish is written by older men and women who have heard stories from their parents and grandparents about how the Ozark region was settled in the 1800s. Almost any writer who writes from the heart about a true experience from his or her youth will get published. Our staff edits for grammar and spelling errors. All the writer has to be concerned about is conveying the story."

$ $ FARM & RANCH LIVING, Reiman Publications, 5925 Country Lane, Greendale WI 53129. (414)423-0100. Fax: (414)423-8463. E-mail: editors@farmandranchliving.com. Website: www.farmandranchliving.com. **Contact:** Nick Pabst, editor. **30% freelance written.** Eager to work with new/unpublished writers. Bimonthly magazine aimed at families that farm or ranch full time. "*F&RL* is *not* a 'how-to' magazine—it focuses on people rather than products and profits." Estab. 1978. Circ. 480,000. Pays on publication. Publishes ms an average of 6 months after acceptance. Byline given. Buys first, one-time rights. Submit seasonal material 6 months in advance. Accepts queries by mail, e-mail, fax. Responds in 6 weeks to queries. Sample copy for $2. Writer's guidelines for #10 SASE.

○﹁ Break in with "photo-illustrated stories about present-day farmers and ranchers."

Nonfiction: Humor (rural only), inspirational, interview/profile, personal experience (farm/ranch related), photo feature, nostalgia, prettiest place in the country (photo/text tour of ranch or farm). No how-to articles or stories about "hobby farmers" (doctors or lawyers with weekend farms); no issue-oriented stories (pollution, animal rights, etc.). **Buys 30 mss/year.** Query with or without published clips or send complete ms. Length: 600-1,200 words. **Pays up to $200 for text/photo package. Payment for Prettiest Place negotiable.**

Reprints: Send photocopy with rights for sale noted. Payment negotiable.

Photos: Scenic. State availability with submission. Buys one-time rights. Pays $75-200 for 35mm color slides.

Fillers: Anecdotes, short humor (with farm or ranch slant), jokes. **Buys 50/year.** Length: 50-150 words. **Pays $10-25.**

Tips: "Our readers enjoy stories and features that are upbeat and positive. A freelancer must see *F&RL* to fully appreciate how different it is from other farm publications—ordering a sample is strongly advised (not available on newsstands). Photo features (about interesting farm or ranch families) and personality profiles are most open to freelancers."

$ FARM TIMES, 504 Sixth St., Rupert ID 83350. (208)436-1111. Fax: (208)436-9455. E-mail: farmtimeseditor@safe link.net. Website: www.farmtimes.com. **Contact:** Robyn Maxfield, managing editor. **50% freelance written.** Monthly tabloid for agriculture-farming/ranching. "*Farm Times* is dedicated to rural living in the Intermountain and Pacific Northwest. Stories related to farming and ranching in the states of Idaho, Montana, Nevada, Oregon, Utah, Washington and Wyoming are our mainstay, but farmers and ranchers do more than just work. Human interest articles that appeal to rural readers are used on occasion." Estab. 1987. Pays on publication. Byline given. Editorial lead time 1 month. Submit seasonal material 3 months in advance. Accepts queries by mail, e-mail. Responds in 2 months to queries. Sample copy for $2.50 or online. Writer's guidelines for #10 SASE.

• The editor reports an interest in seeing articles about global agriculture issues and trends that affect the Pacific Northwest and Intermountain West agriculture producer, rural health care and Western water issues.

○﹁ Break in by writing tight and including photos, charts or graphs if possible.

Nonfiction: Always runs one feature article of interest to women. Exposé, general interest, how-to, interview/profile, new product (few), opinion, farm or ranch issues, late breaking news. Special issues: Irrigation, Chemical/Fertilizer, Potato Production. No humor, essay, first person, personal experience or book excerpts. **Buys 200 mss/year.** Query with published clips or send complete ms. Length: 500-800 words. **Pays $1.50/column inch.**

Reprints: Send typed ms with rights for sale noted and information about when and where the material previously appeared. Pays 100% of amount paid for an original article.

Photos: Send photos with submission. Reviews contact sheets with negatives, 3×5 or larger prints, 300dpi tiff. Buys one-time rights. Offers $7/b&w inside, $35/color front page cover. Captions, identification of subjects, model releases required.

Columns/Departments: Horse (horse care/technical), 500-600 words; Rural Religion (interesting churches/missions/religious activities) 600-800 words; Dairy (articles of interest to dairy farmers) 600-800 words. **Buys 12 mss/year.** Query. **Pays $1.50/column inch.**

Tips: "Ag industry-related articles should have a Pacific Northwest and Intermountain West slant (crops, production techniques, etc.), or how they pertain to the global market. Write tight, observe desired word counts. Feature articles can vary between agriculture and rural living. Good quality photos included with manuscript increase publication chances. Articles should have farm/ranch/rural slant on various topics: health, travel (farmers vacation, too), financial, gardening/landscape, etc."

$ $ MOTHER EARTH NEWS, Ogden Publications, 1503 SW 42nd St., Topeka KS 66609-1265. (785)274-4300. E-mail: letters@motherearthnews.com. Website: www.motherearthnews.com. Managing Editor: K.C. Compton. **Contact:** Cheryl Long, editor. Mostly written by staff and team of established freelancers. Bimonthly magazine emphasizing country living, country skills, natural health and sustainable technologies for both long-time and would-be ruralites. "*Mother Earth News* is dedicated to presenting information that helps readers be more self-sufficient, financially independent, and environmentally aware." Circ. 350,000. Pays on publication. Byline given. Submit seasonal material 5 months in advance. Responds in 6 months to mss. Sample copy for $5. Writer's guidelines for #10 SASE.

• *Mother Earth News* was recently purchased by Ogden Publications, publishers of *Grit* and *Capper's*.

Nonfiction: How-to, alternative energy systems, gardening, home building, home retrofit and maintenance, energy-efficient structures, seasonal cooking, home business, nonfiction book excerpts. No fiction, please. **Buys 35-50 mss/**

ALWAYS ENCLOSE a self-addressed, stamped envelope (SASE) with all your queries and correspondence.

year. Query. "Sending a short, to-the-point paragraph is often enough. If it's a subject we don't need at all, we can answer it immediately. If it tickles our imagination, we'll ask to take a look at the whole piece. No phone queries, please." Length: 300-3,000 words. **Payment negotiated.**

Photos: "Although not essential, we very much encourage contributors to send good, usable photos with their mss." Reviews any size color transparencies, prints. Total purchase price for ms includes payment for photos. Captions, photo credits required. Include type of film, speed and lighting used.

Columns/Departments: Country Lore (down-home solutions to everyday problems); Bits & Pieces (snippets of news, events and silly happenings); Herbs & Remedies (home healing, natural medicine); Energy & Environment (ways to conserve energy while saving money; also alternative energy).

Tips: "Probably the best way to break in is to study our magazine, digest our writer's guidelines, and send us a concise article illustrated with color transparencies that we can't resist. When folks query and we give a go-ahead on speculation, we often offer some suggestions. Failure to follow those suggestions can lose the sale for the author. We want articles that tell what real people are doing to take charge of their own lives. Articles should be well-documented and tightly written treatments of topics we haven't already covered."

$ ⚡ RURAL HERITAGE, 281 Dean Ridge Lane, Gainesboro TN 38562-5039. (931)268-0655. E-mail: editor@rura lheritage.com. Website: www.ruralheritage.com. Publisher: Allan Damerow. **Contact:** Gail Damerow, editor. **98% free-lance written.** Willing to work with a small number of new/unpublished writers. Bimonthly magazine devoted to the training and care of draft animals and other traditional country skills. Estab. 1976. Circ. 4,500. Pays on publication. Publishes ms an average of 6 months after acceptance. Byline given. Buys first English language rights. Submit seasonal material 6 months in advance. Accepts queries by mail, e-mail. Responds in 3 months to queries. Sample copy for $7. Writer's guidelines for #10 SASE or online at www.ruralheritage.com/business_office/.

Nonfiction: How-to (crafting and farming), interview/profile (people using draft animals), photo feature. No articles on *mechanized* farming. **Buys 100 mss/year.** Query or send complete ms. Length: 1,200-1,500 words. **Pays 5¢/word.** Pays 100% of amount paid for an original article.

Photos: Six covers/year (color transparency or 5×7 horizontal print), animals in harness $75. Photo guidelines for #10 SASE or on website. Send photos with submission. Buys one-time rights. Pays $10. Captions, identification of subjects required.

Columns/Departments: Drafter's Features (draft animals used for farming, logging or pulling—their training and care), Crafting (horse-drawn implement designs and patterns), both 750-1,500 words; Humor, 750-900 words. **Pays 5¢/word.**

Poetry: Traditional. **Pays $5-25.**

Tips: "Thoroughly understand our subject: working draft animals in harness. We'd like more pieces on plans and instructions for constructing various horse-drawn implements and vehicles. Always welcome are: 1) Detailed descriptions and photos of horse-drawn implements, 2) Prices and other details of draft animal and implement auctions and sales."

$ $ RURALITE, P.O. Box 558, Forest Grove OR 97116-0558. (503)357-2105. Fax: (503)357-8615. E-mail: ruralite @ruralite.org. Website: www.ruralite.org. **Contact:** Curtis Condon, editor-in-chief. **80% freelance written.** Works with new, unpublished writers. Monthly magazine aimed at members of consumer-owned electric utilities throughout 10 western states, including Alaska. Publishes 48 regional editions. Estab. 1954. Circ. 325,000. **Pays on acceptance.** Byline given. Buys first rights. Accepts queries by mail. Responds in 1 month to queries. Sample copy and writer's guidelines for 10×13 SAE with 4 first-class stamps; guidelines also online.

Nonfiction: Looking for well-written nonfiction, dealing primarily with human interest topics. Must have strong Northwest perspective and be sensitive to Northwest issues and attitudes. Wide range of topics possible, from energy-related subjects to little-known travel destinations to interesting people living in areas served by consumer-owned electric utilities. Family-related issues, Northwest history (no encyclopedia rewrites), people and events, unusual tidbits that tell the Northwest experience are best chances for a sale. Special issues: Gardening (February 2001). **Buys 50-60 mss/year.** Query first; unsolicited manuscripts submitted without request rarely read by editors. Length: 300-2,000 words. **Pays $50-450.**

Reprints: Send typed ms with rights for sale noted and information about when and where the material previously appeared. Pays 50% of amount paid for an original article.

Photos: "Illustrated stories are the key to a sale. Stories without art rarely make it. Black-and-white prints, color slides, all formats accepted."

Tips: "Study recent issues. Follow directions when given an assignment. Be able to deliver a complete package (story and photos). We're looking for regular contributors to whom we can assign topics from our story list after they've proven their ability to deliver quality mss."

SCIENCE

These publications are published for laymen interested in technical and scientific developments and discoveries, applied science and technical or scientific hobbies. Publications of interest to the personal computer owner/user are listed in the Personal Computers section. Journals for scientists and engineers are listed in Trade in various sections.

$ $ AD ASTRA, The Magazine of the National Space Society, 600 Pennsylvania Ave. SE, Suite 201, Washington DC 20003-4316. (202)543-1900. Fax: (202)546-4189. E-mail: adastraed@aol.com. Website: www.nss.org/adastra. **Contact:** Frank Sietzen, Jr., editor-in-chief. **80% freelance written.** Bimonthly magazine covering the space program. "We publish non-technical, lively articles about all aspects of international space programs, from shuttle missions to planetary probes to plans for the future." Estab. 1989. Circ. 25,000. Pays on publication. Byline given. Buys first North American serial rights. Responds to queries when interested. Sample copy for 9 × 12 SASE. Writer's guidelines for #10 SASE.

Nonfiction: Book excerpts, essays, exposé, general interest, interview/profile, opinion, photo feature, technical. No science fiction or UFO stories. Query with published clips. Length: 1,500-3,000 words. **Pays $350-450 for features.**

Photos: State availability with submission. Reviews 3 × 5 color transparencies, 35mm slides. Buys one-time rights. Negotiates pay. Identification of subjects required.

Tips: "We require manuscripts to be accompanied by ASCII or Word or Word Perfect 7.0 floppy disk. Know the field of space technology, programs and policy. Know the players. Look for fresh angles. And, please, know how to write!"

$ $ $ AMERICAN ARCHAEOLOGY, The Archaeological Conservancy, 5301 Central Ave. NE, #402, Albuquerque NM 87108-1517. (505)266-9668. Fax: (505)266-0311. E-mail: archcons@nm.net. Website: www.americanarchaeology.org. Assistant Editor: Tamara Stewart. **Contact:** Michael Bawaya, editor. **60% freelance written.** Quarterly magazine. "We're a popular archaeology magazine. Our readers are very interested in this science. Our features cover important digs, prominent archaeologists and most any aspect of the science. We only cover North America." Estab. 1997. Circ. 35,000. **Pays on acceptance.** Publishes ms an average of 3 months after acceptance. Byline given. Offers 20% kill fee. Buys one-time, electronic rights. Editorial lead time 3 months. Accepts queries by mail, e-mail, fax. Responds in 3 weeks to queries; 1 month to mss.

Nonfiction: Archaeology. No fiction, poetry, humor. **Buys 12 mss/year.** Query with published clips. Length: 2,000-2,500 words. **Pays $700-1,000.** Sometimes pays expenses of writers on assignment.

Photos: State availability with submission. Reviews transparencies, prints. Buys one-time rights. Offers $300-1,000/photo. Negotiates payment individually. Identification of subjects required.

Tips: "Read the magazine. Features must have a considerable amount of archaeological detail."

$ $ ARCHAEOLOGY, Archaeological Institute of America, 135 William St., New York NY 10038. (212)732-5154. Fax: (212)732-5707. E-mail: peter@archaeology.org. Website: www.archaeology.org. **Contact:** Peter A. Young, editor-in-chief. **5% freelance written.** "*Archaeology* combines worldwide archaeological findings with photography, specially rendered maps, drawings, and charts. Articles cover current excavations, recent discoveries, and special studies of ancient cultures. Regular features: Newsbriefs, film and book reviews, current museum exhibits, Forum. We generally commission articles from professional archaeologists. The only magazine of its kind to bring worldwide archaeology to the attention of the general public." Estab. 1948. Circ. 200,000. **Pays on acceptance.** Byline given. Offers 25% kill fee. Buys first North American serial rights. Submit seasonal material 6 months in advance. Accepts queries by mail, e-mail, fax. Accepts simultaneous submissions. Sample copy and writer's guidelines free.

Nonfiction: Essays, general interest. **Buys 6 mss/year.** Query preferred. Length: 1,000-3,000 words. **Pays $750 maximum.** Sometimes pays expenses of writers on assignment.

Photos: Send photos with submission. Reviews 4 × 5 color transparencies, 35mm color slides. Identification of subjects, credits required.

■ The online magazine carries original content not found in the print edition. Contact: Mark Rose, online editor.

Tips: "We reach nonspecialist readers interested in art, science, history, and culture. Our reports, regional commentaries, and feature-length articles introduce readers to recent developments in archaeology worldwide."

$ $ THE ELECTRON, 1776 E. 17th St., Cleveland OH 44114-3679. (216)781-9400. Fax: (216)781-0331. Website: www.cie.wc.edu. Managing Editor: Michael Manning. **Contact:** Ted Sheroke, advertising manager. **80% freelance written.** Bimonthly tabloid on development and trends in electronics and high technology. Estab. 1934. Circ. 25,000. Pays on publication. Publishes ms an average of 2 months after acceptance. Byline given. Buys all rights. Responds as soon as possible to mss. Sample copy and writer's guidelines for 8½ × 11 SASE.

Nonfiction: All submissions must be electronics/technology related. Photo feature, technical (tutorial and how-to), technology news and feature, career and educational. Query with letter/proposal and published clips. Length: 800 words. **Pays $50-500.**

Reprints: Send photocopy of article or typed ms with rights for sale noted and information about when and where the material previously appeared. Does not pay for reprints.

Photos: State availability with submission. Reviews 8 × 10 and 5 × 7 b&w prints. Captions, identification of subjects required.

Tips: "We would like to receive educational electronics/technical articles. They must be written in a manner understandable to the beginning-intermediate electronics student. We are also seeking news/feature-type articles covering timely developments in high technology."

$ $ THE SCIENCES, 655 Madison Ave., 16th Floor, New York NY 10021. (212)838-6727. Fax: (212)355-3795. E-mail: sciences@nyas.org. Website: www.nyas.org. **Contact:** Peter Brown, editor-in-chief. **50% freelance written.**

Quarterly magazine. "*The Sciences* is the cultural magazine of science. This is the kind of magazine that scientists would come to after work, that they can talk about to a friend, a spouse, a colleague in another discipline." Pays on publication. Byline given. Accepts queries by mail, e-mail, fax.

    O–π Break in by offering an intimate knowledge of the scientific subject matter you want to write about. Though hard science is needed, a story must emerge from the hard science.

Nonfiction: Profiles, opinion, book or product reviews, features. Every piece must have "lots of science in it. It's important for writers to remember that many of our readers are members of the New York Academy of Science." Query with SASE. Length: 3,000 words. **Pays $500.**

$ $ $ $ SCIENTIFIC AMERICAN, 415 Madison Ave., New York NY 10017. (212)754-0550. Fax: (212)755-1976. E-mail: editors@sciam.com. Website: www.sciam.com. **Contact:** Philip Yam, news editor. Monthly magazine covering developments and topics of interest in the world of science. Query before submitting. "*Scientific American* brings its readers directly to the wellspring of exploration and technological innovation. The magazine specializes in first-hand accounts by the people who actually do the work. Their personal experience provides an authoritative perspective on future growth. Over 100 of our authors have won Nobel Prizes. Complementing those articles are regular departments written by *Scientific American*'s staff of professional journalists, all specialists in their fields. *Scientific American* is the authoritative source of advance information. Authors are the first to report on important breakthroughs, because they're the people who make them. It all goes back to *Scientific American*'s corporate mission: to link those who use knowledge with those who create it." Estab. 1845. Circ. 710,000.

Nonfiction: Freelance opportunities mostly in the news scan section; limited opportunity in feature well. **Pays $1/ word average.** Pays expenses of writers on assignment.

$ $ SKY & TELESCOPE, The Essential Magazine of Astronomy, Sky Publishing Corp., 49 Bay State Rd., Cambridge MA 02138. (617)864-7360. Fax: (617)576-0336. E-mail: skytel@skypub.com. Website: www.skypub.com. Editor: Leif J. Robinson. **Contact:** Bud Sadler, managing editor. **15% freelance written.** Monthly magazine covering astronomy. "*Sky & Telescope* is the magazine of record for astronomy. We cover amateur activities, research news, equipment, book and software reviews. Our audience is the amateur astronomer who wants to learn more about the night sky." Estab. 1941. Circ. 125,000. Pays on publication. Publishes ms an average of 6 months after acceptance. Byline given. Buys first rights. Editorial lead time 4 months. Submit seasonal material 1 year in advance. Accepts queries by mail, e-mail, fax. Responds in 3 weeks to queries; 1 month to mss. Sample copy for $3.99. Writer's Guidelines free by e-mail request to auguide@skypub.com, online or for #10 SASE.

Nonfiction: Essays, historical/nostalgic, how-to, opinion, personal experience, photo feature, technical. No poetry, crosswords, new age or alternative cosmologies. **Buys 10 mss/year.** Query. Length: 1,500-4,000 words. **Pays at least 20¢/word.** Sometimes pays expenses of writers on assignment.

Photos: Send photos with submission. Reviews contact sheets. Buys one-time rights. Negotiates payment individually. Identification of subjects required.

Columns/Departments: Focal Point (opinion), 1,000 words; Books & Beyond (reviews), 800 words; Amateur Astronomers (profiles), 1,500 words. **Buys 20 mss/year.** Query. **Pays 20¢/word.**

Tips: "Good artwork is key. Keep the text lively and provide captions."

$ $ $ STAR DATE, University of Texas McDonald Observatory, 2609 University Ave., #3.118, Austin TX 78712. Fax: (512)471-5060. E-mail: rjohnson@stardate.utexas.edu. Website: www.stardate.org. **Contact:** Rebecca Johnson, editor. **80% freelance written.** Bimonthly magazine covering astronomy. "*StarDate* is written for people with an interest in astronomy and what they see in the night sky, but no special astronomy training or background." Estab. 1975. Circ. 12,000. **Pays on acceptance.** Publishes ms an average of 4 months after acceptance. Byline given. Offers 25% kill fee. Buys first North American serial, electronic rights. Editorial lead time 6 months. Submit seasonal material 6 months in advance. Accepts queries by mail, e-mail, fax. Responds in 6 weeks to queries; 2 months to mss. Sample copy and writer's guidelines free.

    O–π "*StarDate* magazine covers a wide range of topics related to the science of astronomy, space exploration, skylore, and skywatching. Many of our readers rely on the magazine for most of their astronomy information, so articles may cover recent discoveries or serve as a primer on basic astronomy or astrophysics. We also introduce our readers to historical people and events in astronomy and space exploration, as well as look forward to what will make history next year or fifty years from now. *StarDate* topics should appeal to a wide audience, not just professional or amateur astronomers. Topics are not limited to hard-core science. When considering topics, look for undercovered subjects, or give a familiar topic a unique spin. Research findings don't have to make the front page of every newspaper in the country to be interesting. Also, if you'd like to write an historical piece, look for offbeat items and events; we've already covered Copernicus, Kepler, Tycho, Newton and the like pretty well."

Nonfiction: General interest, historical/nostalgic, interview/profile, photo feature, technical, travel, research in astronomy. "No first-person; first stargazing experiences; paranormal." **Buys 8 mss/year.** Query with published clips. Length: 1,500-3,000 words. **Pays $500-1,500.** Sometimes pays expenses of writers on assignment.

Photos: Send photos with submission. Reviews transparencies, prints. Buys one-time rights. Negotiates payment individually. Identification of subjects required.

Columns/Departments: Astro News (short astronomy news item), 250 words. **Buys 6 mss/year.** Query with published clips. **Pays $100-200.**

Tips: "Keep up to date with current astronomy news and space missions. No technical jargon."

$ $✉ **WEATHERWISE, The Magazine About the Weather**, Heldref Publications, 1319 18th St. NW, Washington DC 20036. (202)296-6267. Fax: (202)296-5149. E-mail: ww@heldref.org. Website: www.weatherwise.org. Associate Editor: Kimbra Cutlip. Editorial Assistant: Ellen Fast. **Contact:** Doyle Rice, managing editor. **75% freelance written.** Bimonthly magazine covering weather and meteorology. "*Weatherwise* is America's only magazine about the weather. Our readers range from professional weathercasters and scientists to basement-bound hobbyists, but all share a common craving for information about weather as it relates to technology, history, culture, society, art, etc." Estab. 1948. Circ. 32,000. Pays on publication. Publishes ms an average of 6 months after acceptance. Byline given. Offers 25% kill fee. Buys first North American serial, second serial (reprint), all rights. Editorial lead time 6 months. Submit seasonal material 6 months in advance. Accepts queries by mail, e-mail, fax, phone. Responds in 2 months to queries. Sample copy for $4 and 9×12 SAE with 10 first-class stamps. Writer's guidelines for #10 SASE or online.

> ⊶ "First, familiarize yourself with the magazine by taking a close look at the most recent six issues. (You can also visit our website, which features the full text of many recent articles.) This will give you an idea of the style of writing we prefer in *Weatherwise*. Then, read through our writer's guidelines (available from our office or on our website) which detail the process for submitting a query letter. As for the subject matter, keep your eyes and ears open for the latest research and/or current trends in meteorology and climatology that you feel would be appropriate for the general readership of *Weatherwise*. And always keep in mind weather's awesome power and beauty—its 'fun, fury, and fascination' that so many of our readers enjoy."

Nonfiction: Book excerpts, essays, general interest, historical/nostalgic, how-to, humor, interview/profile, new product, opinion, personal experience, photo feature, technical, travel. Special issues: Photo Contest (September/October deadline June 1). "No blow-by-blow accounts of the biggest storm to ever hit your backyard." **Buys 15-18 mss/year.** Query with published clips. Length: 1,500-2,500 words. **Pays $200-500 for assigned articles; $0-300 for unsolicited articles.** Sometimes pays expenses of writers on assignment.

Reprints: Send photocopy and information about when and where the material previously appeared. Pays 25% of amount paid for an original article.

Photos: Reviews contact sheets, negatives, prints, electronic files. Buys one-time rights. Negotiates pay individually. Captions, identification of subjects required.

Columns/Departments: Front & Center (news, trends, opinion), 300-400 words; Weather Talk (folklore and humor), 1,000 words; The Lee Word (humorous first-person accounts of adventures with weather), 1,000 words. **Buys 12-15 mss/year.** Query with published clips. **Pays $0-200.**

Tips: "Don't query us wanting to write about broad types like the Greenhouse Effect, the Ozone Hole, El Niño, etc. Although these are valid topics, you can bet you won't be able to cover it all in 2,000 words. With these topics and all others, find the story within the story. And whether you're writing about a historical storm or new technology, be sure to focus on the human element—the struggles, triumphs, and other anecdotes of individuals."

SCIENCE FICTION, FANTASY & HORROR

These publications often publish experimental fiction and many are open to new writers. More information on these markets can be found in the Contests & Awards section under the Fiction heading.

$ $✉ **ABORIGINAL SCIENCE FICTION**, The 2nd Renaissance Foundation Inc., P.O. Box 2449, Woburn MA 01888-0849. Website: www.aboriginalsf.com. Charles C. Ryan, editor. Fiction is 100% freelance written; articles generally assigned to regular columnists. Quarterly magazine. "We publish short, lively and entertaining science fiction short stories and poems, accompanied by b&w illustrations. We have a full-color cover and full-sized magazine format (8½×11 inches)." Estab. 1986. Circ. 6,000. Pays on publication. Publishes ms an average of 2 years after acceptance. Byline given. Buys first North American serial rights. Accepts queries by mail. Responds in 3 months to queries. Sample copy for $5.95 and 9×12 SAE with 4 first-class stamps. Writer's guidelines for #10 SASE or online.

Fiction: Science fiction of all types. "We do not use fantasy, horror, sword and sorcery or *Twighlight Zone*-type stories." **Buys 40-48 mss/year.** Send complete ms. Length: 2,000-6,500 words. **Pays $200.**

Poetry: Science and science fiction. **Buys 4-8 poems/year.** Length: 1-2 pages, typewritten.

Tips: "Read science fiction novels and all the science fiction magazines. Do not rely on science fiction movies or TV. We are open to new fiction writers who are making a sincere effort. We are now looking at short articles on cutting-edge science, 1,000-1,500 words. Pays $100 on publication."

N **$ $** **ANALOG SCIENCE FICTION & FACT**, Dell Magazine Fiction Group, 475 Park Ave. S, New York NY 10016. (212)686-7188. Fax: (212)686-7414. E-mail: analog@dellmagazines.com. Website: www.analogsf.com. **Contact:** Dr. Stanley Schmidt, editor. **100% freelance written.** Eager to work with new/unpublished writers. Monthly magazine for general future-minded audience. Accepts queries for serials and fact articles only; query by mail. Estab. 1930. **Pays on acceptance.** Publishes ms an average of 10 months after acceptance. Byline given. Buys first North American serial rights, nonexclusive foreign serial rights. Responds in 1 month to queries (send queries for serials and fact articles only). Sample copy for $5. Writer's guidelines for #10 SASE or online.

0— Break in by telling an "unforgettable story in which an original, thought-provoking, plausible idea plays an indispensible role."

Nonfiction: Looking for illustrated technical articles dealing with subjects of not only current but future interest, i.e., topics at the present frontiers of research whose likely future developments have implications of wide interest. **Buys 11 mss/year.** Query by mail only. Length: 5,000 words. **Pays 6¢/word.**

Fiction: "Basically, we publish science fiction stories. That is, stories in which some aspect of future science or technology is so integral to the plot that, if that aspect were removed, the story would collapse. The science can be physical, sociological or psychological. The technology can be anything from electronic engineering to biogenetic engineering. But the stories must be strong and realistic, with believable people doing believable things—no matter how fantastic the background might be." **Buys 60-100 unsolicited mss/year.** Send complete ms of short fiction; query about serials. Length: 2,000-80,000 words. **Pays 4¢/word for novels; 5-6¢/word for novelettes; 6-8¢/word for shorts under 7,500 words; $450-600 for intermediate lengths.**

Tips: "In query give clear indication of central ideas and themes and general nature of story line—and what is distinctive or unusual about it. We have no hard-and-fast editorial guidelines, because science fiction is such a broad field that I don't want to inhibit a new writer's thinking by imposing 'Thou Shalt Not's.' Besides, a really good story can make an editor swallow his preconceived taboos. I want the best work I can get, regardless of who wrote it—and I need new writers. So I work closely with new writers who show definite promise, but of course it's impossible to do this with every new writer. No occult or fantasy."

$ ☒ ▣ ANOTHEREALM, 287 Gano Ave., Orange Park FL 32073. (904)269-5429. E-mail: editor@anotherealm. com. Website: http://anotherealm.com. **Contact:** Jean Goldstrom, editor. **100% freelance written.** Quarterly magazine covering science fiction, fantasy and horror. "An e-zine of short (4,000 words and under) science fiction, fantasy and horror." Estab. 1998. Circ. 5,000/week. **Pays on acceptance.** Byline given. Buys first Internet rights. Editorial lead time 3 months. Submit seasonal material 3 months in advance. Accepts queries by e-mail. Responds in 2 weeks to queries; 2 months to mss. Sample copy and writer's guidelines online.

   • *Anotherealm* has gone to a quarterly frequency, decreasing the number of manuscripts published, and shortened the word length for submissions.

Fiction: Fantasy, horror, science fiction. No experimental, stream-of-consciousness, avante-garde or vampire stories. **Buys 12-15 mss/year.** Send complete ms. Length: 4,000 words. **Pays $10.**

Tips: "At least half of our writers made their first sale to *Anotherealm*."

$ ARTEMIS MAGAZINE, Science and Fiction for a Space-Faring Age, LRC Publications, Inc., 1380 E. 17th St., Suite 201, Brooklyn NY 11230-6011. E-mail: magazine@lrcpubs.com. Website: www.LRCPublications.com. **Contact:** Ian Randal Strock, editor. **90% freelance written.** Quarterly magazine covering the Artemis Project and manned space flight/colonization in general. "As part of the Artemis Project, we present lunar and space development in a positive light." Estab. 1999. **Pays on acceptance.** Publishes ms an average of 1 year after acceptance. Byline given. Buys first world English serial rights. Editorial lead time 3 months. Accepts queries by mail. Responds in 2 months to queries. Sample copy for $5. Writer's guidelines for #10 SASE or online.

Nonfiction: Essays, general interest, how-to (get to, build, or live in a lunar colony), humor, interview/profile, new product, opinion, technical, travel. **Buys 12-16 mss/year.** Send complete ms. Length: 5,000 words maximum. **Pays 3-5¢/word.**

Photos: State availability of or send photos with submission. Reviews transparencies, prints. Buys one-time rights. Negotiates payment individually. Captions, identification of subjects, model releases required.

Columns/Departments: News Notes (news of interest regarding the moon and manned space flight), under 300 words. **Buys 15-20 mss/year.** Send complete ms. **Pays 3-5¢/word.**

Fiction: Science fiction. "We publish near-term, new-Earth, hard sf. We don't want to see non-that." **Buys 12-16 mss/ year.** Send complete ms. Length: 15,000 words maximum (shorter is better). **Pays 3-5¢/word.**

Fillers: Newsbreaks, short humor, cartoons. **Buys 4-12/year.** Length: 100 words maximum. **Pays 3-5¢/word.**

Tips: "Know your material, and write me the best possible article/story you can. You want us to read your manuscript, so show us the courtesy of reading our magazine. Also, the Artemis Project website (wwww.asi.org) may be a good source of inspiration."

$ ASIMOV'S SCIENCE FICTION, Dell Magazine Fiction Group, 475 Park Avenue S, 11th Floor, New York NY 10016. (212)686-7188. Fax: (212)686-7414. E-mail: asimovs@dellmagazines.com. Executive Editor: Sheila Williams. **Contact:** Gardner Dozois, editor. **98% freelance written.** Works with a small number of new/unpublished writers each year. Magazine published 11 times a year, including 1 double issue. Estab. 1977. Circ. 50,000. **Pays on acceptance.** Buys first North American serial rights, nonexclusive foreign serial rights; reprint rights occasionally. Accepts queries by mail. Responds in 2 months to queries. Sample copy for $5 and 6½×9½ SAE or online. Writer's guidelines for #10 SASE or online.

Reprints: Send typed ms with rights for sale noted and information about when and where the material previously appeared.

Fiction: Science fiction primarily. Some fantasy and humor but no "Sword and Sorcery." No explicit sex or violence that isn't integral to the story. "It is best to read a great deal of material in the genre to avoid the use of some *very* old ideas." Buys 10mss/issue. Send complete ms and SASE with *all* submissions. Length: 750-15,000 words. **Pays 5-8¢/ word.**

Poetry: Length: 40 lines maximum. **Pays $1/line.**

Tips: "In general, we're looking for 'character-oriented' stories, those in which the characters, rather than the science, provide the main focus for the reader's interest. Serious, thoughtful, yet accessible fiction will constitute the majority of our purchases, but there's always room for the humorous as well. Borderline fantasy is fine, but no Sword & Sorcery, please. A good overview would be to consider that all fiction is written to examine or illuminate some aspect of human existence, but that in science fiction the backdrop you work against is the size of the Universe. Please do not send us submissions on disk. We've bought some of our best stories from people who have never sold a story before."

$ ✕ CHALLENGING DESTINY, New Fantasy & Science Fiction, Crystalline Sphere Publishing, RR #6, St. Marys, Ontario N4X 1C8, Canada. (519)584-7556. E-mail: csp@golden.net. Website: home.golden.net/~csp/. **Contact:** Dave Switzer and Bob Switzer, editors. **80% freelance written.** Quarterly magazine covering science fiction and fantasy. Estab. 1997. Circ. 200. Pays on publication. Publishes ms an average of 5 months after acceptance. Byline given. Buys first North American serial rights. Accepts queries by mail, e-mail. Accepts simultaneous submissions. Responds in 1 week to queries; 1 month to mss. Sample copy for $7.50 (Canadian), $6.50 (US). Writer's guidelines for #10 SASE or online.

Fiction: Fantasy, science fiction. **Buys 24 mss/year.** Send complete ms. Length: 2,000-10,000 words. **Pays 1¢/word (Canadian).**

Tips: "We're interested in stories where violence is rejected as a means for solving problems. We're also interested in stories with philosophical, political or religious themes. We're not interested in stories where the good guys kill the bad guys and then live happily ever after. Read an issue to see what kind of stories we publish. Many of the stories we publish are between 4,000 and 8,000 words and have interesting characters, ideas and plot."

$ $ THE CRYSTAL BALL, The Starwind Press, P.O. Box 98, Ripley OH 45167. (937)392-4549. E-mail: marlene@techgallery.com. **Contact:** Marlene Powell, editor. **90% freelance written.** Quarterly magazine covering science fiction and fantasy for young adult readers. "We are especially targeting readers of middle school age." Estab. 1997. **Pays on acceptance.** Publishes ms an average of 6 months after acceptance. Byline given. Offers 100% kill fee. Buys first, second serial (reprint) rights. Editorial lead time 4 months. Accepts queries by mail, e-mail, phone. Sample copy for 9×12 SASE and $3. Writer's guidelines for #10 SASE.

Nonfiction: How-to (science), interview/profile, personal experience, book reviews, science information. **Buys 4-6 mss/year.** Query. Length: 900-3,000 words. **Pays ¼¢/word.**

Reprints: Send typed ms with rights for sale noted and information about when and where the material previously appeared. Pays 100% of amount paid for an original article.

Photos: Send photos with submission. Negotiates payment individually. Captions, identification of subjects required.

Columns/Departments: Book Reviews (science fiction and fantasy), 100-200 words or less; museum reviews (science & technology, museums & centers, children's museums), 900 words. **Buys 10-15 mss/year.** Query. **Pays ¼¢/word.**

Fiction: Fantasy, science fiction. **Buys 10-12 mss/year.** Send complete ms. Length: 1,000-5,000 words. **Pays ¼¢/word.**

Tips: "Have a good feel for writing for kids. Don't 'write down' to your audience because they're kids. We look for articles of scientific and technological interest."

$ ▣ DEEP OUTSIDE SFFH, C&C Clocktower Books, PMB 260, 6549 Mission Gorge Rd., San Diego CA 92120. E-mail: outside@clocktowerfiction.com. Website: http://outside.clocktowerfiction.com. **Contact:** Brian Callahan and John Cullen, editors. **100% freelance written.** Online magazine. "*Deep Outside SFFH* is a paying professional magazine of science fiction and dark imaginative fiction, aimed at people who love to read well-plotted character-driven genre fiction." Estab. 1998. Pays within 90 days after acceptance. Publishes ms an average of 3 months after acceptance. Byline given. Buys first, electronic rights. Accepts queries by mail. Responds in 3 months to mss. Sample copy online. Writer's guidelines online.

O→ "Write the story we couldn't see coming. Get us excited about your characters and slammed by your unexpected but inevitable ending. Our favorite stories are original and exciting—they aren't rehashes of overdone monster movie themes. We love stories that take us to exotic locales."

Fiction: "We seek well-written, character-driven fiction that is tightly plotted, professionally executed, with attention to basics—grammar, punctuation, usage. No sword and sorcery, shared worlds, porno of any kind, excessive violence or gore beyond the legitimate needs of a story, no vulgarity unless it furthers the story (sparingly at that). No derivative works emulating TV shows or movies (e.g., *Star Trek*)." Horror, science fiction. **Buys 12 mss/year.** Send complete ms. Length: 1,500-5,000 words. **Pays 3¢/word.**

Tips: "Please read the tips and guidelines on the magazine's website for further and up-to-the-moment details. *Submissions by mail only.* Traditional format, #10 SASE minimum for reply. E-mail submissions will be deleted unread."

Ⓝ $ ▣ DRAGONS, KNIGHTS, AND ANGELS, The Magazine of Christian Fantasy and Science Fiction, Creative Mental Programming Ent. LLC, 5461 W. 4605 S., West Valley City, Utah 84120. E-mail: dkamagazine@quixnet.net. Website: www.dkamagazine.net. **Contact:** Rebecca Shelley, executive editor. **90% freelance written.** Quarterly online publication. *DKA Magazine* is a family friendly magazine of Christian fantasy and science fiction featuring short stories, poetry, art, and reader interaction. Estab. January 2000. Circ. 800 hits per issue. **Pays on acceptance.** Publishes ms an average of 6 months after acceptance. Byline sometimes given. Not copyrighted. Buys one-time, electronic rights. Editorial lead time 3 months. Submit seasonal material 3 months in advance. Accepts queries by mail, e-mail. Accepts simultaneous submissions. Responds in 3 weeks to queries (we prefer e-mail submissions); 3 months to mss. Sample copy and writer's guidelines online.

Columns/Departments: Interactive Arena is slanted toward interactive games, puzzles and activities. **Buys 4 mss/ year.** Query. **Pays $5-25.**

Fiction: "DKA Magazine is founded on the idea that the power of God is the greatest magic of all. While the stories we publish do not need to have an obvious moral, the protagonists must be motivated by moral values, or learn some moral value by the end of the story. This is a family magazine, so keep that in mind regarding language and content of the stories you submit." Fantasy, religious, science fiction. "We're getting too many mushy 'Not-Plots.' Remember, a short story needs a clear beginning, middle and end and must have conflict. The battle between good and evil is an integral part of fantasy. Don't be afraid to use it. Absolutely no erotica, gay/lesbian, excessive violence or foul language." **Buys 16 mss/year.** Send complete ms. Length: 500-2000 words. **Pays 1-1½¢/word.**

Poetry: Free verse, light verse, traditional. No erotic, dark, occult or gory poems. **Buys 12 poems/year.** Submit maximum 5 poems. Length: 4-500 lines. **Pays $10.**

Tips: "The editors of *DKA Magazine* found there was no market for fantasy and sci-fi in Christian magazines, and very little for light, feel-good, moral-teaching stories in sci-fi and fantasy magazines. Our mission is to bridge that gap. We try not to be heavy-handed on the Christian side and avoid stories that are preachy or are obviously a specific religion. On the other hand, we will not print dark, gruesome, sexually explicit or overly violent material. If you have a spell-binding story that leaves the reader feeling good at the end or pondering on important truths, that is what we want."

$ FLESH AND BLOOD, 121 Joseph St., Bayville NJ 08721. E-mail: HorrorJack@aol.com. Website: www.geocities. com/soho/lofts/3459/fnb.html. **Contact:** Jack Fisher, editor. **90% freelance written.** Triannual magazine covering horror/dark fantasy. Estab. 1997. Circ. 500. Pays within 3 months of acceptance. Publishes ms an average of 10 months after acceptance. Editorial lead time 1 month. Accepts queries by mail, e-mail. Responds in 2 weeks to queries; 2 months to mss. Sample copy for $4 (check payable to John Fisher). Writer's guidelines for #10 SASE or online.

  • The editor reports an interest in seeing powerful vignettes/stories with surrealism-avante-garde(ism) to them and original, unique ghost stories. The magazine recently won Best Magazine of the Year Award in the Jobs in Hell newsletter contest.

Fiction: Horror, slice-of-life vignettes, dark fantasy. "No garden-variety work, or work where the main character is a 'nut' killer, etc." **Buys 18-24 mss/year.** Length: 500-4,000 words. **½-2¢/word.**

Poetry: Avant-garde, free verse, horror/dark fantasy surreal, bizarre. "No rhyming, love pieces." **Buys 15-20 poems/ year.** Submit maximum 5 poems. Length: 3-25 lines. **Pays $5.**

Tips: "We like light horror over gore. Don't let the title deceive you. Surreal, bizarre, eccentric tales have a good chance. We especially like dark fantasy pieces and vignettes."

$ ⚑ THE MAGAZINE OF FANTASY & SCIENCE FICTION, Spilogale, Inc., P.O. Box 3447, Hoboken NJ 07030. (201)876-2551. Fax: (201)876-2551. E-mail: gordonfsf@aol.com. Website: www.fsfmag.com. **Contact:** Gordon Van Gelder, editor. **100% freelance written.** Monthly magazine covering fantasy fiction and science fiction. "*The Magazine of Fantasy and Science Fiction* publishes various types of science fiction and fantasy short stories and novellas, making up about 80% of each issue. The balance of each issue is devoted to articles about science fiction, a science column, book and film reviews, cartoons and competitions." Estab. 1949. Circ. 80,000. **Pays on acceptance.** Byline given. Buys first North American serial rights. Submit seasonal material 8 months in advance. Responds in 2 months to queries. Sample copy for $5. Writer's guidelines for #10 SASE or online.

Columns/Departments: Curiosities (forgotten books), 250 words. **Buys 11 mss/year. Pays $50.**

Fiction: Prefers character-oriented stories. Fantasy, horror, science fiction. No electronic submissions. **Buys 70-100 mss/year.** Send complete ms. Length: 2,000-25,000 words. **Pays 5-8¢/word.**

Tips: "We need more hard science fiction and humor."

$ ⚑ ON SPEC, The Copper Pig Writers Society, P.O. Box 4727, Edmonton Alberta T6E 5G6, Canada. E-mail: onspec@earthling.net. Website: www.icomm.ca/onspec/. General Editor: Jena Snyder; Fiction Editors: Barry Hammond, Susan MacGregor, Hazel Sangster, Jena Snyder, Diane L. Walton. **Contact:** Editorial Collective. **95% freelance written.** Quarterly magazine covering Canadian science fiction, fantasy and horror. Estab. 1989. Circ. 2,000. **Pays on acceptance.** Publishes ms an average of 1 year after acceptance. Byline given. Buys first North American serial rights. Editorial lead time 6 months. Accepts queries by mail, phone. Responds in 2 weeks to queries; 2 months after deadline to mss. Sample copy for $6. Writer's guidelines online.

Nonfiction: Commissioned only.

Fiction: Fantasy, horror, science fiction, magic realism. No media tie-in or shaggy-alien stories. **Buys 50 mss/year.** Length: 6,000 words maximum. **Pays $50-180 (Canadian).**

Poetry: "We rarely buy rhyming or religious material." Barry Hammond, poetry editor. Avant-garde, free verse. **Buys 6 poems/year.** Submit maximum 10 poems. Length: 4-100 lines. **Pays $20.**

Tips: "We want to see stories with plausible characters, a well-constructed, consistent, and vividly described setting, a strong plot and believable emotions; characters must show us (not tell us) their emotional responses to each other and to the situation and/or challenge they face. Also: don't send us stories written for television. We don't like media tie-ins, so don't watch TV for inspiration! Read, instead! Absolutely no e-mailed or faxed submissions. Strong preference given to submissions by Canadians."

$ THE SILVER WEB, A Magazine of the Surreal, Buzzcity Press, P.O. Box 38190, Tallahassee FL 32315. (850)385-8948. Fax: (850)385-4063. E-mail: buzzcity@yourvillage.com. **Contact:** Ann Kennedy, publisher/editor. **100% freelance written.** Semiannual magazine. "*The Silver Web* is a semi-annual publication featuring science fiction, dark fantasy and horror, fiction, poetry, art, and thought-provoking articles. The editor is looking for works ranging from speculative fiction to dark tales and all weirdness in between; specifically works of the surreal." Estab. 1988. Circ. 2,000. **Pays on acceptance.** Byline given. Offers 100% kill fee. Buys first North American serial, one-time, second serial (reprint) rights. Editorial lead time 2 months. Accepts queries by mail, e-mail. Accepts simultaneous submissions. Responds in 1 week to queries; 2 months to mss. Sample copy for $7.20; subscription: $12. Writer's guidelines for #10 SASE or via email.
Nonfiction: Book excerpts, essays, interview/profile, opinion. **Buys 6 mss/year.** Query. Length: 500-8,000 words. **Pays $20-250.**
Reprints: Send information before submitting ms about when and where the material previously appeared. Pays 100% of amount paid for an original article.
Photos: State availability with submission. Reviews prints. Buys one-time rights. Negotiates payment individually. Identification of subjects required.
Columns/Departments: Book Reviews, Movie Reviews, TV Reviews, all 3,000 words. **Buys 6 mss/year.** Send complete ms. **Pays $20-250.**
Fiction: Experimental, fantasy, horror, science fiction, surreal. "We do not want to see typical storylines, endings or predictable revenge stories." **Buys 20-25 mss/year.** Send complete ms. *Open to submissions January 1-August 31.* Length: 500-8,000 words. **Pays $10-320.**
Poetry: Avant-garde, free verse, haiku, light verse, traditional. **Buys 18-30 poems/year.** Submit maximum 5 poems. **Pays $10-50.**
Fillers: Art fillers. **Buys 10/year. Pays $5-10.**
Tips: "Give us an unusual unpredictable story with strong, believable characters we care about. Surprise us with something unique. We do look for interviews with people in the field (writers, artists, filmmakers)."

$ SPACE AND TIME, 138 W. 70th St., 4B, New York NY 10023-4468. Website: www.cith.org/space&time.html. Editor-in-Chief: Gordon Linzner. **Contact:** Gerard Houarner, fiction editor; Linda D. Addison, poetry editor. **99% freelance written.** Semiannual magazine of science fiction and fantasy. "We feature a mix of fiction and poetry in all aspects of the fantasy genre—science fiction, supernatural horror, sword & sorcery, mixed genre, unclassifiable. Its variety makes it stand out from more narrowly focused magazines. Our readers enjoy quality material that surprises and provokes." Estab. 1966. Circ. 2,000. **Pays on acceptance.** Publishes ms an average of 9 months after acceptance. Byline given. Buys first North American serial rights. Editorial lead time 1 year. Accepts queries by mail. Responds in 3 months to mss. Sample copy for $6.50. Writer's guidelines for #10 SASE or online.
Photos: Artwork (could include photos). Send nonreturnable photocopies. Reviews prints. Buys one-time rights. Pays $10 for interior illustration, $25 for cover, plus 2 contributor copies. Model releases required.
Fiction: Gerard Houarner, fiction editor. Fantasy, horror, science fiction, mixed genre (i.e. science-fiction-mystery, western-horror, etc.) and unclassifiable. "We do not want anything that falls outside of fantasy/science fiction (but that leaves a lot). No fiction set in a franchised universe, i.e., *Star Trek*." **Buys 20-24 mss/year.** Send complete ms. Length:10,000 words. **Pays 1¢/word plus 2 contributor copies; $5 minimum.**
Poetry: Linda D. Addison, poetry editor. "Do not send poetry without a solid connection to the genres we publish. Imaginative metaphors alone do not make fantasy." Avant-garde, free verse, haiku, light verse, traditional. **Buys 20 poems/year.** Submit maximum 5 poems. Length: no limits. **Pays 1¢/word ($5 minimum) plus 2 contributor copies.**
Tips: "Avoid clichés and standard plots unless you have something new to add."

$ $ STARLOG MAGAZINE, The Science Fiction Universe, Starlog Group, 475 Park Ave. S., 7th Floor, New York NY 10016-1689. Fax: (212)889-7933. E-mail: communications@starloggroup.com. Website: www.starlog2k.com. **Contact:** David McDonnell, editor. **90% freelance written.** Monthly magazine covering "the science fiction-fantasy genre: its films, TV, books, art and personalities." "We often provide writers with a list of additional questions for them to ask interviewees. Manuscripts *must* be submitted on computer disk or by e-mail. Printouts helpful." Estab. 1976. Pays on publication. Publishes ms an average of 4 months after acceptance. Byline given. Offers kill fee only to manuscripts. Buys all rights. Accepts queries by mail, e-mail, fax. Responds in 6 weeks to queries. Sample copy for $7. Writer's guidelines for #10 SASE.
- "We are somewhat hesitant to work with unpublished writers. We concentrate on interviews with actors, directors, writers, producers, special effects technicians and others. Be aware that 'sci-fi' and 'Trekkie' are seen as derogatory terms by our readers and by us."
- Break in by "doing something fresh, imaginative or innovative—or all three. Or by getting an interview we can't get. The writers who sell to us try *hard* and manage to meet one or both challenges."
Nonfiction: "We also sometimes cover science fiction/fantasy animation. We prefer article format as opposed to Q&A interviews." Book excerpts (having directly to do with SF films, TV or literature), interview/profile (actors, directors, screenwriters—who've done science fiction films—and science fiction novelists), movie/TV set visits. No personal

opinion think pieces/essays. *No* first person. Avoid articles on horror films/creators. Query first with published clips. Length: 500-3,000 words. **Pays $35 (500 words or less); $50-75 (sidebars); $150-275 (1,000-4,000 words).** Pays $50 for *each* reprint in each foreign edition or such.

Photos: "No separate payment for photos provided by film studios." State availability with submission. Buys all rights. Photo credit given. Pays $10-25 for color slide transparencies depending on quality. Captions, identification of subjects, credit line required.

Columns/Departments: Booklog (book reviews by assignment only). **Buys 150 reviews/year.** Book review, 125 words maximum. No kill fee. Query with published clips. **Pays $15 each.**

■ This online magazine carries original content not found in the print edition. Contact: David McDonnell, online editor.

Tips: "Absolutely *no fiction*. We do *not* publish it and we throw away fiction manuscripts from writers who *can't* be bothered to include SASE. Nonfiction only please! We are always looking for *fresh* angles on the various *Star Trek* shows, *The X-Files*, and *Star Wars*. Read the magazine more than once and don't just rely on this listing. Know something about science fiction films, TV and literature. Most full-length major assignments go to freelancers with whom we're already dealing. But if we like your clips and ideas, it's possible we'll give *you* a chance. No phone calls for *any* reason please—we *mean* that!"

N **$ STARSHIP EARTH**, Black Moon Publishing, P.O. Box 484, Bellaire OH 43906. E-mail: starshipearth@hotma il.com. Managing Editor: Kirin Lee. **Contact:** Silver Shadowhorse, fiction editor . 15% freelance nonfiction; 100% freelance fiction written. Bimonthly magazine featuring science fiction. "*Starship Earth* is geared toward science fiction fans of all ages. We do mostly nonfiction, but do print short stories. Our nonfiction focus: profiles of actors and industry people, conventions, behind the scenes articles on films and TV shows. We do cover action/adventure films and TV as well. Heavy *Star Trek* focus. We cover classic science fiction, too." Estab. 1996. Pays on publication. Publishes ms an average of 1 year after acceptance. Byline sometimes given. Buys first, one-time rights. Editorial lead time 1 year. Submit seasonal material 6 months in advance. Accepts queries by mail. Responds in 3 weeks to queries; 4 months to mss. Writer's guidelines for #10 SASE.

● *Starship Earth* is planning an anthology of short stories of up to 4,000 words. Stories submitted to *Starship Earth* will automatically be considered.

Nonfiction: General interest, how-to (relating to science fiction, writing, model building, crafts, etc.), interview/profile, new product (relating to sciece of science fiction), personal experience, photo feature, travel (relating to attending conventions), Behind the scenes of film/TV science fiction, Book reviews. **Buys variable number of mss/year.** Query. Length: up to 3,000 words. Please query for longer pieces. **Pays ½-3¢/word.** Pays in copies for book or film reviews. Sometimes pays expenses of writers on assignment.

Photos: State availability with submission. Reviews transparencies, prints. Buys one-time rights. Negotiates payment individually. Captions, identification of subjects, model releases required.

Columns/Departments: Jenna Dawson, assistant editor. Costumes, conventions/events, science fiction music, upcoming book, film, TV releases, film reviews, book reviews, new products, all up to 700 words. Query. **Does not pay for columns/departments pieces.**

Fiction: Ms. Silver Shadowhorse, editor. Fantasy, historical, science fiction. No erotic content, horror, "Sword & Sorcery," explicit violence, explicit language or religious material. "Short story needs are filled for the next year." **Buys variable number of mss/year.** Query. Length: 500-3,000 words. **Pays æ-3¢/word.**

Fillers: Jenna Dawson, assistant editor. Anecdotes, facts, newsbreaks, short humor. Length: 50-250 words. **Pays does not pay for fillers.**

Tips: "Follow guidelines and present a professional package. We are willing to work with new and unpublished writers in most areas. All manuscripts must be in standard format. We are always looking for new or unusual angles on old science fiction shows/films, conventions, costumes, fx and people in the business. Articles from interviews must have sparkle and be interesting to a variety of readers. Absolutely no gossip or fluff. Anyone sending a disposable manuscript can simply include their e-mail address instead of a SASE for reply."

$ THE URBANITE, Surreal & Lively & Bizarre, Urban Legend Press, P.O. Box 4737, Davenport IA 52808. Website: http://theurbanite.tripod.com/. **Contact:** Mark McLaughlin, editor. **95% freelance written.** Triannual magazine covering surreal fiction and poetry. "We look for quality fiction with a surrealistic tone. We prefer character-driven storylines. Our audience is urbane, culture-oriented, and hard to please!" Contributors to recent issues include Basil Copper, Jeffrey Osier, Alexa deMonterice, Rain Graves and Pamela Briggs. Estab. 1991. Circ. 1,000. **Pays on acceptance.** Publishes ms an average of 6 months after acceptance. Byline given. Buys first North American serial, second serial (reprint) rights. Editorial lead time 6 months. Accepts queries by mail. Responds in 1 month to queries; 2 months to mss. Sample copy for $5. Writer's guidelines for #10 SASE.

● Fiction from the magazine has been reprinted in *The Year's Best Fantasy and Horror* and England's *Best New Horror*, and a poem in *The Year's Best Fantastic Fiction*. The magazine has been nominated for the International Horror Guild Award.

Nonfiction: Each issue has a theme. Essays, humor, interview/profile. "We don't publish recipes, fishing tips or music/ CD reviews." **Buys up to 6 mss/year.** Query. Length: 500-3,000 words. **Pays $15-90 for assigned articles; $10-60 for unsolicited articles.**

Columns/Departments: "We haven't run any columns, but would like to. Unfortunately, we haven't seen any queries that really thrill us." **Pays $15-90.**

Fiction: Upcoming theme: No. 13: the All-Horror Issue. Send SASE for future themes. Experimental, fantasy, horror, humorous, science fiction, slipstream/cross genre, surrealism of all sorts. **Buys 54 mss/year.** Send complete ms. Length: 500-3,000. We do publish longer works, up to 10,000 words—but query first. **Pays $10-300 (2-3¢/word).**

Poetry: Each issue has a featured poet who receives 10 contributor copies. Avant-garde, free verse, traditional, Narrative Poetry. No haiku or light verse. **Buys 18 poems/year.** Submit maximum 3 poems. Length: Up to 2 ms pages. **Pays $10/poem.**

Tips: "Writers should familiarize themselves with surrealism in literature; too often, we receive stories filled with genre clichés. Also: We prefer character-driven stories. Don't just write because you want to see your name in print. Write because you have something to say."

SEX

Magazines featuring pictorial layouts accompanied by stories and articles of a sexual nature, both gay and straight, are listed in this section. Dating and single lifestyle magazines appear in the Relationships section. Other markets for articles relating to sex can be found in the Men's and Women's sections.

$✕ BUMP & GRIND, Hounds of Hell Publishing, P.O. Box 1319, Hudson, Quebec J0P 1H0, Canada. (450)458-1934. Fax: (450)458-2977. **Contact:** Gaetan Gavin Dumont, editor. **100% freelance written.** Monthly men's magazine covering "hard-core, anything goes (not an anal title), very dirty and lusty. All Hounds of Hell Publishing titles deal with hardcore sex." Estab. 1996. Circ. 40,000. Pays on 60 day terms. Publishes ms an average of 3 months after acceptance. Byline sometimes given. Buys all rights. Editorial lead time 3 months. Accepts queries by mail, e-mail, fax, phone. Accepts simultaneous submissions. Sample copy for $5 US per issue. Writer's guidelines for #10 SASE or by e-mail.

Fiction: "We will not accept anything to do with violence, children, non-consenting sex or degradation." **Buys 64 mss/year.** Send complete ms. Length: 1,300-2,000 words. **Pays $10-15/1,000 words.**

Tips: "Story length should not exceed 2,000 words. Cut the introduction—get straight to the sex. Stories of 800-1,200 words are needed. Open with a bang—is it interesting? Does it excite the reader? Be very descriptive and very graphic, but not violent. Be explicitly descriptive. We want to smell leather, taste the skin, and feel the action as it takes place. But the sex must be enjoyable for all participants; nobody does anything in these stories against their will."

$✕ BUTTIME STORIES, Hounds of Hell Publishing, P.O. Box 1319, Hudson, Quebec J0P 1H0, Canada. (450)458-1934. Fax: (450)458-2977. **Contact:** Gaetan Gavin Dumont, editor. **100% freelance written.** Monthly men's magazine covering anal adventure. "All Hounds of Hell Publishing titles deal with hardcore sex." Estab. 1996. Circ. 40,000. Pays on 60 day terms. Publishes ms an average of 3 months after acceptance. Byline sometimes given. Buys all rights. Editorial lead time 3 months. Accepts queries by mail, e-mail, fax, phone. Accepts simultaneous submissions. Sample copy for $5 US per issue. Writer's guidelines for #10 SASE or by e-mail.

Fiction: "We will not accept anything to do with violence, children, non-consenting sex or degradation." **Buys 64 mss/year.** Send complete ms. Length: 1,300-2,000 words. **Pays $10-15/1,000 words.**

Tips: "Story length should not exceed 2,000 words. Cut the introduction—get straight to the sex. Stories of 800-1,200 words are needed. Open with a bang—is it interesting? Does it excite the reader? Be very descriptive and very graphic, but not violent. Be explicitly descriptive. We want to smell leather, taste the skin, and feel the action as it takes place. But the sex must be enjoyable for all participants; nobody does anything in these stories against their will."

$✕ CHEATERS CLUB, Hounds of Hell Publishing, P.O. Box 1319, Hudson, Quebec J0P 1H0, Canada. (450)458-1934. Fax: (450)458-2977. **Contact:** Gaetan Gavin Dumont, editor. **100% freelance written.** Monthly men's magazine covering "swingers, lesbians, couples who invite others to join them; threesomes, foursomes and moresomes." "All Hounds of Hell Publishing titles deal with hardcore sex." Estab. 1996. Circ. 40,000. Pays on 60 day terms. Publishes ms an average of 3 months after acceptance. Byline sometimes given. Buys all rights. Editorial lead time 3 months. Accepts queries by mail, e-mail, fax, phone. Accepts simultaneous submissions. Sample copy for $5 US per issue. Writer's guidelines for #10 SASE or by e-mail.

Fiction: "We will not accept anything to do with violence, children, non-consenting sex or degradation." **Buys 64 mss/year.** Send complete ms. Length: 1,300-2,000 words. **Pays $10-15/1,000 words.**

Tips: "Story length should not exceed 2,000 words. Cut the introduction—get straight to the sex. Stories of 800-1,200 words are needed. Open with a bang—is it interesting? Does it excite the reader? Be very descriptive and very graphic, but not violent. Be explicitly descriptive. We want to smell leather, taste the skin, and feel the action as it takes place. But the sex must be enjoyable for all participants; nobody does anything in these stories against their will."

N $✕ FIRST HAND, Experiences For Loving Men, Firsthand, Ltd., 310 Cedar Lane, Teaneck NJ 07666. (201)836-9177. Fax: (201)836-5055. E-mail: firsthand3@aol.com. Publisher: Jackie Lewis. **Contact:** Don Dooley, editor. **75% freelance written.** Eager to work with new/unpublished writers. Magazine published 16 times/year covering homosexual erotica. Estab. 1980. Circ. 70,000. Pays on publication. Publishes ms an average of 8 months after acceptance. Byline given. Buys all rights (exceptions made) and second serial (reprint) rights. Submit seasonal material 10 months in advance. Responds in 4 months to mss. Sample copy for $5. Writer's guidelines for #10 SASE.

Reprints: Send photocopy. Pays 50% of amount paid for original articles.

Fiction: "We prefer fiction in the first person which is believable—stories based on the writer's actual experience have the best chance. We're not interested in stories which involve underage characters in sexual situations. Other taboos include bestiality, rape—except in prison stories, as rape is an unavoidable reality in prison—and heavy drug use. Writers with questions about what we can and cannot depict should write for our guidelines, which go into this in more detail. We print mostly self-contained stories; we will look at novel excerpts, but only if they stand on their own." Erotica. Length: Up to 5,000 words; average 2,000-3,000 words.

Tips: "*First Hand* is a very reader-oriented publication for gay men. Half of each issue is made up of letters from our readers describing their personal experiences, fantasies and feelings. Our readers are from all walks of life, all races and ethnic backgrounds, all classes, all religious and political affiliations, and so on. They are very diverse, and many live in far-flung rural areas or small towns; for some of them, our magazines are the primary source of contact with gay life, in some cases the only support for their gay identity. Our readers are very loyal and save every issue. We return that loyalty by trying to reflect their interests—for instance, by striving to avoid the exclusively big-city bias so common to national gay publications. So bear in mind the diversity of the audience when you write."

$ $ $ FOX MAGAZINE, Montcalm Publishing, 401 Park Ave. S., New York NY 10016-8802. (212)779-8900. Fax: (212)725-7215. Website: www.gallerymagazine.com. **Contact:** Harry Montana, senior editor. **50% freelance written.** Prefers to work with published/established writers. Monthly magazine "focusing on features of interest to the young American man." Estab. 1982. Circ. 300,000. Pays on publication. Byline given. Offers 25% kill fee. Buys first North American serial, non-exclusive, international, electronic serial rights or makes work-for-hire assignments. Submit seasonal material 6 months in advance. Responds in 1 month to queries; 2 months to mss. Sample copy for $8.95 (add $2 for Canadian and foreign orders). Writer's guidelines for #10 SASE.

Nonfiction: Investigative pieces of notable figures in adult entertainment, sex advice, porn star/stripper profiles, video reviews, on-the-set stories for adult movies, swinger convention news. **Buys 10-12 mss/year.** Query by mail only or send complete ms. Length: 1,500-2,500 words. **Pays $300-1,500. Special prices negotiated.** Sometimes pays expenses of writers on assignment.

Reprints: Send tearsheet, photocopy or typed ms with rights for sale noted and information about when and where the material previously appeared. Pays 25% of amount paid for an original article.

Photos: Send photos with submission. Reviews b&w or color contact sheets and negatives. Buys one-time rights. Pay varies. Captions preferred; model releases and photo IDs required.

Fiction: Erotic letters only (special guidelines available). **Buys 36-48 mss/year.** Send complete ms. Length: 250-1,500 words. **Pays $40/letter.**

$ $ $ $ GALLERY MAGAZINE, Montcalm Publishing Corp., 401 Park Ave. S., New York NY 10016-8802. (212)779-8900. Fax: (212)725-7215. E-mail: csobrien@gallerymagazine.com. Website: www.gallerymagazine.com. **Contact:** C.S. O'Brien, editorial director. **50% freelance written.** Prefers to work with published/established writers. Monthly magazine focusing on features of interest to the young American man. *Gallery* is a magazine aimed at entertaining and educating the contemporary man. *Gallery* covers political, cultural, and social trends on a national and global level through serious and provocative investigative reports, candid interviews, human-interest features, fiction, erotica, humor and photographic portfolios of beautiful women. Estab. 1972. Circ. 500,000. Pays on publication. Byline given. Offers 10-25% kill fee. Buys first North American serial, non-exclusive, international, electronic serial rights or makes work-for-hire assignments. Submit seasonal material 6 months in advance. Accepts queries by mail, e-mail, fax, phone. Responds in 1 month to queries; 2 months to mss. Back issue for $8.95 (add $2 for Canadian and foreign orders). Writer's guidelines for #10 SASE.

- *Gallery* works on Macintosh, so it accepts material on Mac or compatible disks if accompanied by hard copy.

O— Break in with "well-written, cutting-edge journalism, focusing on interesting subject matter (news, crime, sports, popular arts, etc.). No basic how-to's, introductory essays on tired subjects, or lame humor."

Nonfiction: General interest, interview/profile, new product, investigative pieces, sports, popular arts. **Buys 4-5 mss/ year.** Query with or without published clips or send complete ms. Length: 1,500-3,500 words. **Pays $1,500-2,500. Special prices negotiated.** Sometimes pays expenses of writers on assignment.

Reprints: Send tearsheet, photocopy or typed ms with rights for sale noted and information about when and where the material previously appeared. Pays 25% of amount paid for an original article or story.

Photos: Send photos with submission. Buys one-time rights. Pay varies for b&w or color contact sheets and negatives. Captions preferred; model release, photo ID required.

Fiction: Erotica only (special guidelines available). **Buys 12 mss/year.** Send complete ms. Length: 1,000-3,000 words. **Pays $350-500.**

Tips: "*Gallery* needs more up-to-the-moment celebrity interviews and is always interested in quirky, innovative writing, whether fiction or non-fiction."

$ $ GENESIS, Magna Publications, 210 Route 4 E., Suite 211, Paramus NJ 07652. (201)843-4004. Fax: (201)843-8636. E-mail: genesis@magnapublishing.com. Website: www.genesismagazine.com. Editor: Paul Gambino. **Contact:** Dan Davis, managing editor. **85% freelance written.** Monthly magazine. "Monthly men's sophisticate with celebrity interviews, erotic and non-erotic fiction, exposé, product and media reviews, lifestyle pieces." Estab. 1974. Circ. 450,000. Pays on publication. Publishes ms an average of 3 months after acceptance. Byline given. Offers 50% kill fee. Buys first, second serial (reprint) rights. Editorial lead time 4 months. Submit seasonal material 6 months in advance. Accepts simultaneous submissions. Responds in 1 month to queries; 2 months to mss. Sample copy for $6.99. Writer's guidelines for #10 SASE.

Nonfiction: Exposé, general interest, how-to, humor, interview/profile, new product, personal experience, photo feature, Film, music, book, etc., reviews, Lifestyle pieces. "No investigative articles not backed up by facts." **Buys 24 mss/ year.** Send complete ms. Length: 150-2,500 words. **Pays 22¢/word.** Sometimes pays expenses of writers on assignment.

Reprints: Send tearsheet, photocopy or typed ms with rights for sale noted and information about when and where the material previously appeared. Pays 50% of amount paid for an original article.

Photos: State availability with submission. Reviews 4×5 transparencies, 8×10 prints, slides. Buys first/exclusive rights. Negotiates payment individually. Captions, identification of subjects, model releases required.

Columns/Departments: Film/video/B movies (interviews, sidebars), music, books, consumer products, all 150-500 words. **Buys 30 mss/year.** Query with published clips or send complete ms. **Pays 22¢/word.**

Fiction: Adventure, horror, erotica, fantasy, humorous, mainstream, mystery, romance, science fiction, slice-of-life vignettes, suspense. **Buys 24 mss/year.** Query with or without published clips or send complete ms. Length: 2,500-3,500 words. **Pays $500.**

Fillers: Anecdotes, facts, newsbreaks, short humor. **Buys 24/year.** Length: 25-500 words. **Pays 22¢/word, $50 minimum.**

Tips: "Be patient, original and detail-oriented."

$ $ $ HUSTLER, HG Inc., 8484 Wilshire Blvd., Suite 900, Beverly Hills CA 90211. Fax: (213)651-2741. E-mail: dkapelovitz@lfp.com. Website: www.hustler.com. Editor: Allan MacDonell. **Contact:** Dan Kapelovitz, features editor. **60% freelance written.** Magazine published 13 times/year. "*Hustler* is the no-nonsense men's magazine, one that is willing to speak frankly about society's sacred cows and expose its hypocrites. The *Hustler* reader expects honest, unflinching looks at hard topics—sexual, social, political, personality profile, true crime." Estab. 1974. Circ. 750,000. Pays as boards ship to printer. Publishes ms an average of 3 months after acceptance. Byline given. Offers 20% kill fee. Buys all rights. Editorial lead time 4 months. Submit seasonal material 6 months in advance. Accepts queries by mail, e-mail, fax. Responds in 2 weeks to queries; 1 month to mss. Writer's guidelines for #10 SASE.

• *Hustler* is most interested in well-researched nonfiction reportage focused on sexual practices and subcultures.

Nonfiction: Book excerpts, exposé, general interest, how-to, interview/profile, personal experience, trends. **Buys 30 mss/year.** Query. Length: 3,500-4,000 words. **Pays $1,500.** Sometimes pays expenses of writers on assignment.

Columns/Departments: Sex play (some aspect of sex that can be encapsulated in a limited space), 2,500 words. **Buys 13 mss/year.** Send complete ms. **Pays $750.**

Fiction: "Difficult fiction market. While sex is a required element in *Hustler* fiction, we are not a market for traditional erotica—do not write a 'Hot Letter.' A successful fiction submission will both arouse the reader and take him into a world he may not be able to visit on his own. What an author is able to dream up in front of a computer is rarely as compelling as the product of first-hand experience and keen observation." **Buys 2 mss/year.** Send complete ms. Length: 3,000-3,500 words. **Pays $1,000.**

Fillers: Jokes and "Graffilthy," bathroom wall humor. **Pays $50-100.**

Tips: "Don't try and mimic the *Hustler* style. If a writer needs to be molded into our voice, we'll do a better job of it than he or she will. Avoid first- and second-person voice. The ideal manuscript is quote-rich, visual and is narratively driven by events and viewpoints that push one another forward."

$ HUSTLER BUSTY BEAUTIES, America's Breast Magazine, HG Publications, Inc., 8484 Wilshire Blvd., Suite 900, Beverly Hills CA 90211. (213)651-5400. Fax: (213)651-2741. E-mail: busty@lfp.com. Website: www.bustybeauty.com. **Contact:** N. Morgen Hagen, associate publisher. **40% freelance written.** Monthly men's sophisticate magazine. "*Hustler Busty Beauties* is an adult title that showcases attractive large-breasted women with accompanying erotic fiction, reader letters, humor." Estab. 1974. Circ. 180,000. Pays on publication. Publishes ms an average of 6 months after acceptance. Byline given. Buys all rights. Accepts queries by mail, e-mail, fax. Responds in 1 month to queries. Sample copy for $6 and 9×12 SAE. Writer's guidelines free.

Columns/Departments: LewDDD Letters (erotic experiences involving large-breasted women from first-person point-of-view), 500-1,000. **Buys 24-36 mss/year.** Send complete ms. **Pays $50-75.**

Fiction: Adventure, erotica, fantasy, humorous, mystery, science fiction, suspense. "No violent stories or stories without a bosomy female character." **Buys 13 mss/year.** Send complete ms. Length: 750-2,500 words. **Pays $250-500.**

Fillers: Jokes (appropriate for audience). **Pays $10-25.**

$ ⊠ IN TOUCH/INDULGE FOR MEN, In Touch International, Inc., 13122 Saticoy St., North Hollywood CA 91605-3402. (818)764-2288. Fax: (818)764-2307. E-mail: michael@intouchformen.com. Website: www.intouchformen. com. **Contact:** Michael W. Jimenez, editor. **80% freelance written.** Works with a small number of new/unpublished writers each year. Monthly magazine covering the gay male lifestyle, gay male humor and erotica. Estab. 1973. Circ. 70,000. Pays on publication. Byline given, pseudonym OK. Buys one-time rights. Accepts queries by mail, e-mail, fax. Accepts simultaneous submissions. Responds in 2 months to queries. Sample copy for $6.95. Writer's guidelines for #10 SASE or online.

○➔ Break in with "a clear, solid story that can be sent on disk or sent via e-mail."

Nonfiction: Rarely buys nonfiction. Send complete ms. Length: 3,000-3,500 words. **Pays $25-75.**

Photos: Send photos with submission. Reviews contact sheets, transparencies, prints. Buys one-time rights. Offers $25/photo. Captions, identification of subjects, model releases required.

Fiction: Gay male erotica. **Buys 82 mss/year.** Send complete ms. Length: 3,000-3,500 words. **Pays $75 maximum.**

Fillers: Short humor. **Buys 12/year.** Length: 1,500-2,500 words. **Pays $25-50.**

Tips: "Our publications feature male nude photos plus three fiction pieces, several articles, cartoons, humorous comments on items from the media, photo features. We try to present positive aspects of the gay lifestyle, with an emphasis on humor. Humorous pieces may be erotic in nature. We are open to all submissions that fit our gay male format; the emphasis, however, is on humor and the upbeat. We receive many fiction manuscripts but not nearly enough unique, innovative, or even experimental material."

$ KEY CLUB, Hounds of Hell Publishing, P.O. Box 1319, Hudson, Quebec J0P 1H0, Canada. (450)458-1934. Fax: (450)458-2977. **Contact:** Gaetan Gavin Dumont, editor. **100% freelance written.** Monthly men's magazine covering "first time anal virgins, new partners, new toys, new experiences. All Hounds of Hell Publishing titles deal with hardcore sex." Estab. 1996. Circ. 40,000. Pays on 60 day terms. Publishes ms an average of 3 months after acceptance. Byline sometimes given. Buys all rights. Editorial lead time 3 months. Accepts queries by mail, e-mail, fax, phone. Accepts simultaneous submissions. Sample copy for $5 US per issue. Writer's guidelines for #10 SASE.

Fiction: Erotica. "We will not accept anything to do with violence, children, non-consenting sex or degradation." **Buys 64 mss/year.** Send complete ms. Length: 1,300-2,000 words. **Pays $10-15/1,000 words.**

Tips: "Story length should not exceed 2,000 words. Cut the introduction—get straight to the sex. Stories of 800-1,200 words are needed. Open with a bang—is it interesting? Does it excite the reader? Be very descriptive and very graphic, but not violent. Be explicitly descriptive. We want to smell leather, taste the skin, and feel the action as it takes place. But the sex must be enjoyable for all participants; nobody does anything in these stories against their will."

$ $ NUGGET, Dugent Corp., 2201 W. Sample Rd., Building #9, Suite 4A, Pompano Beach FL 33073. Fax: (954)917-5821. E-mail: chris@dugent.com. Website: www.sexmags.com. **Contact:** Christopher James, editor-in-chief. **100% freelance written.** Monthly magazine covering fetish and kink. "*Nugget* is a one-of-a-kind publication which appeals to daring, open-minded adults who enjoy all forms of both kinky, alternative sex (S/M, B&D, golden showers, infantalism, amputeeism, catfighting, transvestism, fetishism, bisexuality, etc.) and conventional sex." Estab. 1960. Circ. 100,000. Pays on publication. Publishes ms an average of 1 year after acceptance. Byline given. Buys first North American serial rights. Editorial lead time 5 months. Submit seasonal material 1 year in advance. Accepts simultaneous submissions. Responds in 2 weeks to queries; 2 months to mss. Sample copy for $5. Writer's guidelines free.

Nonfiction: Interview/profile, Sexual matters/trends (fetish and kink angle). **Buys 8 mss/year.** Query. Length: 2,000-3,000 words. **Pays $200 minimum.**

Photos: Send photos with submission. Reviews transparencies. Buys one-time second rights. Offers no additional payment for photos accepted with ms. Model releases required.

Fiction: Erotica, fantasy. **Buys 20 mss/year.** Send complete ms. Length: 2,000-3,000 words. **Pays $200-250.**

Tips: Most open to fiction submissions. (Follow guidelines for suitable topics.)

N $ $ $ ⬚ PLAYGIRL, 801 Second Ave., New York NY 10017. (212)661-7878. Fax: (212)697-6343. Website: www.playgirlmag.com. Editor-in-Chief: Taseha Church. **Contact:** Ronnie Koenig, managing editor. **25% freelance written.** Prefers to work with published/established writers. Monthly magazine. "*PLAYGIRL* addresses the needs, interests and desires of women 18 years of age and older. We provide something no other American women's magazine can: An uninhibited approach to exploring sexuality and fantasy that empowers, enlightens and entertains. We publish features articles of all sorts: Interviews with top celebrities; essays and humor pieces on sexually related topics; first-person accounts of sensual adventures; articles on the latest trends in sex, love, romance and dating; and how-to stories that give readers sexy news they can use. We also publish erotic fiction and reader fantasies from a woman's perspective. The common thread—besides, of course, good, lively writing and scrupulous research—is a fresh, open-minded, inquisitive attitude." Circ. 500,000. Pays within 6 weeks of acceptance. Publishes ms an average of 5 months after acceptance. Byline given. Buys all rights. Submit seasonal material 6 months in advance. Accepts queries by mail. Responds in 3 months to mss. Writer's guidelines for #10 SASE.

Oᴙ Break in with pieces for Fantasy Forum. Send complete ms.

Nonfiction: Average issue: 3 articles; 1 celebrity interview. Essays, exposé (related to women's issues), general interest, interview/profile (Q&A format with major celebrities—pitch first), new product, articles on sexuality, medical breakthroughs, relationships, insightful, lively articles on current issues, investigative pieces particularly geared to *PLAYGIRL*'s focus on sex/dating/relationships. **Buys 6 mss/year.** Query with published clips. Length: 1,600-2,100 for fantasy forum; 1,500 for articles. **Pays $300-1,000 (varies); $25 for some fantasies, much more for celeb interviews.** Sometimes pays expenses of writers on assignment.

Tips: "Best bet for first-time writers: Fantasy Forum. No phone calls please."

$ STICKY BUNS, Hounds of Hell Publishing, P.O. Box 1319, Hudson, Quebec J0P 1H0, Canada. (450)458-1934. Fax: (450)458-2977. **Contact:** Gaetan Gavin Dumont, editor. **100% freelance written.** Monthly men's magazine covering "the anal fetish as well as S&M and bondage. All Hounds of Hell Publishing titles deal with hardcore sex." Estab.

1996. Circ. 40,000. Pays on 60 day terms. Publishes ms an average of 3 months after acceptance. Byline sometimes given. Buys all rights. Editorial lead time 3 months. Accepts queries by mail, e-mail, fax, phone. Accepts simultaneous submissions. Sample copy for $5 US per issue. Writer's guidelines for #10 SASE.

Fiction: Looking for "anal adventures; very sticky, lots of wet descriptions, oils, etc." "We will not accept anything to do with violence, children, non-consenting sex or degradation." **Buys 64 mss/year.** Send complete ms. Length: 1,300-2,000 words. **Pays $10-15/1,000 words.**

Tips: "Story length should not exceed 2,000 words. Cut the introduction—get straight to the sex. Stories of 800-1,200 words are needed. Open with a bang—is it interesting? Does it excite the reader? Be very descriptive and very graphic, but not violent. Be explicitly descriptive. We want to smell leather, taste the skin, and feel the action as it takes place. But the sex must be enjoyable for all participants; nobody does anything in these stories against their will."

$ $⊠ SWANK, Swank Publications, 210 Route 4 E., Suite 211, Paramus NJ 07652. (201)843-4004. Fax: (201)843-8636. E-mail: genesismag@aol.com. Website: www.swankmag.com. Editor: Paul Gambino. **Contact:** D.J., associate editor. **75% freelance written.** Works with new/unpublished writers. Monthly magazine on "sex and sensationalism, lurid. High quality adult erotic entertainment." Audience of men ages 18-38, high school and some college education, medium income, skilled blue-collar professionals, union men, some white-collar. Estab. 1954. Circ. 400,000. Pays on publication. Publishes ms an average of 4 months after acceptance. Byline given, pseudonym if wanted. Buys first North American serial rights. Submit seasonal material 6 months in advance. Accepts queries by mail. Responds in 3 weeks to queries; 1 month to mss. Sample copy for $6.95. Writer's guidelines for #10 SASE.

● *Swank* reports a need for more nonfiction, non-sex-related articles.

Nonfiction: Exposé (researched), adventure must be accompanied by color photographs. "We buy articles on sex-related topics, which don't need to be accompanied by photos." Interested in unusual lifestyle pieces. How-to, interviews with entertainment, sports and sex industry celebrities. Buys photo pieces on autos, action, adventure. "It is strongly recommended that a sample copy is reviewed before submitting material." **Buys 34 mss/year.** Query with or without published clips. **Pays $350-500.** Sometimes pays expenses of writers on assignment.

Reprints: Send tearsheet, photocopy or typed ms with rights for sale noted and information about when and where the material previously appeared. Pays 50% of amount paid for an original article.

Photos: "Articles have a much better chance of being purchased if you have accompanying photos." Alex Suarez, art director. Model releases required.

Fiction: "All of the fiction used by *Swank* is erotic in some sense—that is, both theme and content are sexual. New angles are always welcome. We will consider stories that are not strictly sexual in theme (humor, adventure, detective stories, etc.). However, these types of stories are much more likely to be considered if they portray some sexual element, or scene, within their context."

Tips: "All erotic fiction currently being used by *Swank* must follow certain legal guidelines."

$ $⊠ VARIATIONS, For Liberated Lovers, General Media Communications Inc., 11 Penn Plaza, 12th Floor, New York NY 10001. (212)702-6000. E-mail: variationsmag@generalmedia.com. Website: www.variations.com. **Contact:** Barbara Pizio, executive editor. **100% freelance written.** Monthly erotica magazine. "*Variations* offers readers a window into the sex lives of America's most exciting couples. Each issue is an elegantly erotic package of healthy sexual fact and fantasy reflecting the rich color in the rainbow of human delight." Estab. 1978. Circ. 300,000. **Pays on acceptance.** Publishes ms an average of 14 months after acceptance. Buys all rights. Editorial lead time 7 months. Submit seasonal material 10 months in advance. Responds in 1 month to queries; 2 months to mss. Sample copy from 888-312-BACK. Writer's guidelines for #10 SASE or by e-mail.

Nonfiction: Book excerpts, interview/profile, personal experience. "No humor, no poetry, no children, no one under 21, no relatives, no pets, no coercion." **Buys 50 mss/year.** Query by mail only or send complete ms. Length: 2,500-3,200 words. **Pays $400 maximum.**

Fiction: "Although *Variations* does not publish short stories or fiction style per se, we do run couple-oriented narrative pieces in which a person fully describes his or her favorite sex scenes squarely focused within one of our categories, in highly explicit erotic detail, using the best possible language." Erotica. Length: 2,800-3,200 words. **Pays $400 maximum.**

■ The online magazine carries original content not found in the print edition. Contact: Barbara Pizio, online editor.

Tips: "Read the magazine to familiarize yourself with our voice, style and categories. Write about what you're familiar with and the most comfortable discussing. We're looking for focused pieces which are carefully crafted by excellent writers. While we are seldom able to place pre-existing erotic fiction, we are always glad to work with newcomers who choose to go the distance to write successful pieces for us."

$⊠ WICKED FETISHES, Hounds of Hell Publishing, P.O. Box 1319, Hudson, Quebec J0P 1H0, Canada. (450)458-1934. Fax: (450)458-2977. **Contact:** Gaetan Gavin Dumont, editor. **100% freelance written.** Monthly "men's sophisticate" digest covering "fetish, domination/submission, feet, etc.—within the law. All Hounds of Hell Publishing titles deal with hardcore sex." Estab. 1996. Circ. 40,000. Pays on 60 day terms. Publishes ms an average of 3 months after acceptance. Byline sometimes given. Buys all rights. Editorial lead time 3 months. Accepts queries by mail, e-mail, fax, phone. Accepts simultaneous submissions. Sample copy for $5 US per issue. Writer's guidelines for #10 SASE.

Fiction: "We will not accept anything to do with violence, children, non-consenting sex or degradation." **Buys 64 mss/year.** Send complete ms. Length: 1,300-2,000 words. **Pays $10-15/1,000 words.**

Tips: "Story length should not exceed 2,000 words. Cut the introduction—get straight to the sex. Stories of 800-1,200 words are needed; send three of these stories to each one longer title. Open with a bang—is it interesting? Does it excite the reader? Be very descriptive and very graphic, but not violent. Be explicitly descriptive. We want to smell leather, taste the skin, and feel the action as it takes place. But the sex must be enjoyable for all participants; nobody does anything in these stories against their will."

SPORTS

A variety of sports magazines, from general interest to sports medicine, are covered in this section. For the convenience of writers who specialize in one or two areas of sport and outdoor writing, the publications are subcategorized by the sport or subject matter they emphasize. Publications in related categories (for example, Hunting & Fishing; Archery & Bowhunting) often buy similar material. Writers should read through this entire section to become familiar with the subcategories. Publications on horse breeding and hunting dogs are classified in the Animal section, while horse racing is listed here. Publications dealing with automobile or motorcycle racing can be found in the Automotive & Motorcycle category. Markets interested in articles on exercise and fitness are listed in the Health & Fitness section. Outdoor publications that promote the preservation of nature, placing only secondary emphasis on nature as a setting for sport, are in the Nature, Conservation & Ecology category. Regional magazines are frequently interested in sports material with a local angle. Camping publications are classified in the Travel, Camping & Trailer category.

Archery & Bowhunting

$ $⊠ BOW & ARROW HUNTING, Y-Visionary Publishing, LP, 265 S. Anita Dr., Suite 120, Orange CA 92868-3310. (714)939-9991. Fax: (714)939-9909. E-mail: editorial@bowandarrowhunting.com. Website: www.bowand arrowhunting.com. **Contact:** Joe Bell, editor. **70% freelance written.** Magazine published 9 times/year covering bowhunting. "Dedicated to serve the serious bowhunting enthusiast. Writers must be willing to share their secrets so our readers can become better bowhunters." Estab. 1962. Circ. 90,000. Pays on publication. Publishes ms an average of 2 months after acceptance. Byline given. Buys all rights. Submit seasonal material 6 months in advance. Accepts queries by mail. Accepts simultaneous submissions. Responds in 1 month to queries; 6 weeks to mss. Sample copy and writer's guidelines free.
Nonfiction: How-to, humor, interview/profile, opinion, personal experience, technical. **Buys 60 mss/year.** Send complete ms. Length: 1,700-3,000 words. **Pays $200-450.**
Photos: Send photos with submission. Reviews contact sheets, 35mm and 2¼×2¼ transparencies, 5×7 prints. Buys one-time or all rights. Offers no additional payment for photos accepted with ms. Captions required.
Fillers: Facts, newsbreaks. **Buys 12/year.** Length: 500 words. **Pays $20-100.**
Tips: "Inform readers how they can become better at the sport, but don't forget to keep it fun! Sidebars are recommended with every submission."

$ $ BOWHUNTER, The Number One Bowhunting Magazine, Primedia Enthusiast Publications, 6405 Flank Dr., Harrisburg PA 17112. (717)657-9555. Fax: (717)657-9552. E-mail: bowhunter@cowles.com. Website: www.bowhu nter.com. Founder/Editor-in-Chief: M.R. James. **Contact:** Jeff Waring, managing editor. **50% freelance written.** Bimonthly magazine covering hunting big and small game with bow and arrow. "We are a special-interest publication, produced by bowhunters for bowhunters, covering all aspects of the sport. Material included in each issue is designed to entertain and inform readers, making them better bowhunters." Estab. 1971. Circ. 181,455. **Pays on acceptance.** Publishes ms an average of 1 year after acceptance. Byline given. Buys first North American serial, one-time rights. Submit seasonal material 8 months in advance. Accepts queries by mail, e-mail. Responds in 1 month to queries; 5 weeks to mss. Sample copy for $2. Writer's guidelines free.
Nonfiction: "We publish a special 'Big Game' issue each Fall (September) but need all material by mid-March. Another annual publication, Whitetail Bowhunter, is staff written or by assignment only. Our latest special issue is the Gear Guide, which highlights the latest in equipment. We don't want articles that graphically deal with an animal's death. And, please, no articles written from the animal's viewpoint." General interest, how-to, interview/profile, opinion, personal experience, photo feature. **Buys 60 plus mss/year.** Query. Length: 250-2,000 words. **Pays $500 maximum for assigned articles; $100-400 for unsolicited articles.** Sometimes pays expenses of writers on assignment.
Photos: Send photos with submission. Reviews 35mm and 2¼×2¼ transparencies, 5×7 and 8×10 prints. Buys one-time rights. Offers $75-250/photo. Captions required.
Tips: "A writer must know bowhunting and be willing to share that knowledge. Writers should anticipate *all* questions a reader might ask, then answer them in the article itself or in an appropriate sidebar. Articles should be written with

the reader foremost in mind; we won't be impressed by writers seeking to prove how good they are—either as writers or bowhunters. We care about the reader and don't need writers with 'I' trouble. Features are a good bet because most of our material comes from freelancers. The best advice is: Be yourself. Tell your story the same as if sharing the experience around a campfire. Don't try to write like you think a writer writes.''

$ $ BOWHUNTING WORLD, Ehlert Publishing Group, 6420 Sycamore Lane N. #100, Maple Grove MN 55369. E-mail: mstrandlund@affinitygroup.com. **Contact:** Mike Strandlund, editor. **50% freelance written.** Bimonthly magazine with three additional issues for bowhunting and archery enthusiasts who participate in the sport year-round. Estab. 1952. Circ. 130,000. **Pays on acceptance.** Publishes ms an average of 5 months after acceptance. Byline given. Buys first, second serial (reprint) rights. Accepts queries by mail, e-mail. Responds in 3 weeks to queries; 6 weeks to mss. Sample copy for $3 and 9×12 SAE with 10 first-class stamps. Writer's guidelines for #10 SASE.
Nonfiction: How-to articles with creative slants on knowledgeable selection and use of bowhunting equipment and bowhunting methods. Articles must emphasize knowledgeable use of archery or hunting equipment, and/or specific bowhunting techniques. Straight hunting adventure narratives and other types of articles now appear only in special issues. Equipment-oriented aricles must demonstrate wise and insightful selection and use of archery equipment and other gear related to the archery sports. Some product-review, field-test, equipment how-to and technical pieces will be purchased. We are not interested in articles whose equipment focuses on random mentioning of brands. Technique-oriented aricles most sought are those that briefly cover fundamentals and delve into leading-edge bowhunting or recreational archery methods. Primarily focusing on retail archery and tournament coverage. **Buys 60 mss/year.** Query with or without published clips or send complete ms. Length: 1,500-3,000 words. **Pays $350-500.**
Photos: "We are seeking cover photos that depict specific behavioral traits of the more common big game animals (scraping whitetails, bugling elk, etc.) and well-equipped bowhunters in action. Must include return postage.''
Tips: "Writers are strongly advised to adhere to guidelines and become familiar with our format, as our needs are very specific. Writers are urged to query by e-mail. We prefer detailed outlines of six or so article ideas per query. Assignments are made for the next 18 months.''

$ $ PETERSEN'S BOWHUNTING, Petersen Publishing Company, L.L.C., 6420 Wilshire Blvd., Los Angeles CA 90048-5515. (323)782-2567. Fax: (323)782-2477. Editor: Jay Michael Strangis. **Contact:** David Dolhee, associate editor. **70% freelance written.** Magazine published 9 times/year covering bowhunting. "Very equipment oriented. Our readers are 'superenthusiasts,' therefore our writers must have an advanced knowledge of hunting archery." Circ. 196,000. **Pays on acceptance.** Byline given. Buys all rights. Editorial lead time 6 months. Submit seasonal material 6 months in advance. Accepts queries by mail. Responds in 1 month to queries. Writer's guidelines free.
Nonfiction: Emphasis is on how-to instead of personal. How-to, humor, interview/profile, new product, opinion, personal experience, photo feature. **Buys 50 mss/year.** Query. Length: 2,000 words. **Pays $300.**
Photos: Send photos with submission. Reviews contact sheets, 35mm transparencies, 5×7 prints. Buys one-time rights. Offers $35-250/photo. Captions, model releases required.
Columns/Departments: Query. **Pays $200-300.**
Fillers: Facts, newsbreaks. **Buys 12/year.** Length: 150-400 words. **Pays $25-75.**
Tips: Feature articles must be supplied in either 3.5 IBM (or compatible) or 3.5 Mac floppy disks.

Baseball

$ $ BASEBALL AMERICA, Baseball America Inc., P.O. Box 2089, Durham NC 27702. (919)682-9635. Fax: (919)682-2880. E-mail: willlingo@baseballamerica.com. Editor: Allan Simpson. Senior Editor: John Royster. **Contact:** Will Lingo, managing editor. **10% freelance written.** Biweekly tabloid covering baseball. *"Baseball America* is read by industry insiders and passionate, knowledgeable fans. Writing should go beyond routine baseball stories to include more depth or a unique angle." Estab. 1981. Circ. 80,000. Pays on publication. Publishes ms an average of 2 months after acceptance. Byline given. Buys one-time rights. Editorial lead time 1 month. Submit seasonal material 2 months in advance. Accepts simultaneous submissions. Sample copy for $3.25.
Nonfiction: Historical/nostalgic, interview/profile, theme or issue-oriented baseball features. "No major league player features that don't cover new ground; superficial treatments of baseball subjects." **Buys 10 mss/year.** Send complete ms. Length: 100-2,000 words. **Pays $10-500 for assigned articles; $10-250 for unsolicited articles.**
Photos: State availability with submission. Buys one-time rights. Negotiates payment individually. Identification of subjects required.
Tips: "We use little freelance material, in part because we have a large roster of excellent correspondents and because much of what we receive is too basic or superficial for our readership. Sometimes writers stray too far the other way and get too arcane. But we're always interested in great stories that baseball fans haven't heard yet.''

$ $ JUNIOR BASEBALL, America's Youth Baseball Magazine, America's Youth Baseball Magazine, 2D Publishing, P.O. Box 9099, Canoga Park CA 91309. (818)710-1234. E-mail: dave@juniorbaseball.com. Website: www.juniorbaseball.com. **Contact:** Dave Destler, editor. **25% freelance written.** Bimonthly magazine covering youth baseball. "Focused on youth baseball players ages 7-17 (including high school) and their parents/coaches. Edited to various reading levels, depending upon age/skill level of feature." Estab. 1996. Circ. 60,000. Pays on publication. Publishes

insider report

Writing about sports: Personality-driven pieces sell

Thirteen-year freelance veteran and former professional basketball star Fran Harris is also the author of four books, including
her latest, *SUMMER MADNESS: Inside the Wild, Wacky, Wonderful
World of the WNBA* (iUniverse, March 2001). Her syndicated column, *Raising Good Sports*, encourages healthy youth athletic experiences and was recently made into a television sports commentary segment. An ESPN broadcaster and filmmaker, Harris
resides in Texas. To learn more about her, please visit www.fran
harris.com.

Fran Harris

**What special challenges set freelancing for the sports
niche apart from other specialties?**
Sports news is often immediate . . . for instance, I can be writing
an article on the favorite of a championship series, the game changes and the underdog appears
to be about to win and my whole focus or angle will change. It's a very dynamic arena to write
in, which is one of the reasons I love sportswriting.

What kinds of sports features are most likely to be snapped up by editors?
Editors like features that are personality driven. Those that give some unique insight that the
average reader might not be aware of. Underdog, come-from-behind victories, comeback stories are all quite appealing to sports editors. And of course, controversy is always welcomed.

How would you break into this specialty if you were a beginning freelancer?
If I were looking to break into sportswriting I'd start at the lowest level of sports participation.
I'd become the beat writer for the town's little league sports teams. The stories may not be
as developed in terms of their careers but youth sports are great breeding ground for interesting and colorful storytelling and a great place to hone feature writing.

What is the general pay scale a freelancer can expect writing about sports?
The pay scale varies depending on the media outlet. I've written a 400-word feature for an
Internet site at $175 an article but my rate is typically $1-3 a word, so I've also been paid $750
for a 600-word sports feature or even $1,000 for a 500-word article. It just depends on the
terms of the negotiation . . . and there is always room for negotiating, no matter what those
editors tell you.

What are the most common mistake freelancers in this arena make (and can avoid)?
The most common mistake freelancers make in my opinion is not seeing the big picture.

While I don't recommend giving your writing away for the rest of your life, it's important to build your archives, build your name and establish yourself. It's OK to barter for your writing if you feel the byline is worth it. In other words, if *O* magazine were in a bind and they needed a sports feature and they offered me $2.75 instead of my asking price of $3 per word, I'd probably take it . . . after all, it is Oprah. So, be smart.

Have you had a favorite sports assignment? If so, what was it and why was it so memorable?
Actually my favorite sports assignment was writing my last book *SUMMER MADNESS: Inside the Wild, Wacky, Wonderful World of the WNBA*, because it allowed me to tackle so many different sports issues—broadcasting, salary inequities between women and men, dunking, and fan support to name only a few. But my most favorite freelance assignment was covering the WNBA's first-ever draft in April 2000. It was an historic event and to get to be an insider was truly amazing.

Have you experienced the nightmare of all nightmare assignments? Describe it.
Well, I've been pretty fortunate. I've not had a bad sports assignment but I did have a nightmare realize itself when I was writing a column for an Internet site a few months ago. For some reason I'd written the column in the body of an e-mail. Maybe I was pressed for time, I'm not sure. But just as I was finishing the column, my computer crashed. It shut down, restarted and my e-mail-written sports column had vanished like a bubble in thin air. I was devastated. And I learned a valuable lesson. *ALWAYS* write in a word processing program that recovers documents when your computer crashes, so that you won't have to cry on your keyboard all night as I did.
    —*Kelly Milner Halls*

For interviews with the pros in more freelance niche markets, see Animals, page 368; Contemporary Culture, page 432; Entertainment, page 443; Games & Puzzles, page 462; Women's, page 782.

———————⇒•◦•⇐———————

TOP TIP "My best advice is to always make each piece your best writing sample. Find ways to improve at your craft. For me, reading helps me to write better. Read award-winning pieces in your freelance field and try to figure out (if it's not obvious) why the writer is so highly regarded. Is it their storytelling skill? Their use of language, prose? Their wit or style? Or a combination of several variables? Never write crap. Make time to make your writing truly reflect the best you have to offer. It will eventually pay off big time, trust me."

ms an average of 4 months after acceptance. Byline given. Buys all rights. Editorial lead time 3 months. Submit seasonal material 3 months in advance. Accepts simultaneous submissions. Responds in 2 weeks to queries; 1 month to mss. Sample copy for $5 and online. Writer's guidelines for #10 SASE.
Nonfiction: How-to (skills, tips, features, how to play better baseball, etc.), interview/profile (with major league players; only on assignment), personal experience (from coaches' or parents' perspective). "No trite first-person articles about your kid." No fiction. **Buys 8-12 mss/year.** Query. Length: 500-1,000 words. **Pays $50-100.**
Photos: State availability with submission. Reviews 35mm transparencies, 3×5 prints. Offers $10-100/photo; negotiates payment individually. Captions, identification of subjects required.
Columns/Departments: When I Was a Kid (a current Major League Baseball player profile); Leagues, Tournaments (spotlighting a particular youth baseball league, organization, event, tournament); Industry (featuring businesses involved in baseball, e.g., how bats are made); Parents Feature (topics of interest to parents of youth ball players); all 1,000-

1,500 words. In the Spotlight (news, events, new products), 50-100 words; League Notebook (news, events, new ideas or tips geared to the parent or league volunteer, adult level), 250-500 words; Hot Prospect (written for the 14 and older competitive player. High school baseball is included, and the focus is on improving the finer points of the game to make the high school team, earn a college scholarship, or attract scouts, written to an adult level), 500-1,000 words. **Buys 8-12 mss/year. Pays $50-100.**

Tips: "Must be well-versed in baseball! Having a child who is very involved in the sport, or have extensive hands-on experience in coaching baseball, at the youth, high school or higher level. We can always use accurate, authoritative skills information and good photos to accompany is a big advantage! This magazine is read by experts."

Basketball

N $ $ $⊠ SLAM, Petersen Publications, 1115 Broadway, 8th Floor, New York NY 10010. E-mail: susan@harris-pub.com. Website: www.slamonline.com. **Contact:** Susan Price, managing editor. **70% freelance written.** Magazine published 10 times/year covering basketball; sports journalism with a hip-hop sensibility targeting ages 13-24. Estab. 1994. Circ. 200,000. Pays on publication. Publishes ms an average of 3 months after acceptance. Byline given. Offers 25% kill fee. Buys all rights. Accepts queries by mail, e-mail, fax. Writer's guidelines free.
Nonfiction: Interview/profile, team story. **Buys 150 mss/year.** Query with published clips. Length: 200-3,000 words. **Pays $100-1,000 for assigned articles.** Sometimes pays expenses of writers on assignment.
Photos: State availability with submission. Buys one-time rights. Negotiates payment individually.
  The online magazine carries original content not found in the print edition. Contact: Lang Whitaker, online editor.
Tips: "Pitch profiles of unknown players; send queries, not manuscripts; do not try to fake a hip-hop sensibility. Never contact the editor-in-chief. Story meetings are held every 6-7 weeks at which time all submissions are considered."

Bicycling

$ $ $⊠ ADVENTURE CYCLIST, Adventure Cycling Assn., Box 8308, Missoula MT 59807. (406)721-1776. Fax: (406)721-8754. E-mail: ddambrosio@adv-cycling.org. Website: www.adv-cycling.org. **Contact:** Daniel D'Ambrosio, editor. **75% freelance written.** Magazine published 9 times/year for Adventure Cycling Association members. Estab. 1975. Circ. 30,000. Pays on publication. Byline given. Buys first rights. Submit seasonal material 3 months in advance. Sample copy and guidelines for 9×12 SAE with 4 first-class stamps.
Nonfiction: How-to, humor, interview/profile, photo feature, technical, travel, U.S. or foreign tour accounts, special focus (on tour experience). **Buys 20-25 mss/year.** Query with or without published clips or send complete ms. Length: 800-2,500 words. **Pays $450-1,200.**
Reprints: Send photocopy.
Photos: Bicycle, scenery, portraits. State availability with submission. Reviews color transparencies. Identification of subjects, model releases required.

$ $ $ BICYCLING, Rodale Press, Inc., 135 N. 6th St., Emmaus PA 18098. (610)967-5171. Fax: (610)967-8960. E-mail: bicycling@rodale.com. Website: www.bicycling.com. Publisher: Nelson Pena. **Contact:** Doug Donaldson, associate editor. **25% freelance written.** Magazine published 11 times/year. "*Bicycling* features articles about fitness, training, nutrition, touring, racing, equipment, clothing, maintenance, new technology, industry developments, and other topics of interest to committed bicycle riders. Editorially, we advocate for the sport, industry, and the cycling consumer." Estab. 1961. Circ. 280,000. **Pays on acceptance.** Byline given. Buys all rights. Submit seasonal material 6 months in advance. Responds in 2 months to queries. Sample copy for $3.50. Writer's guidelines for #10 SASE.
Nonfiction: "We are strictly a bicycling magazine. We seek readable, clear, well-informed pieces. We sometimes run articles that are inspirational and inspiration might flavor even our most technical pieces. No fiction or poetry." How-to (on all phases of bicycle touring, repair, maintenance, commuting, new products, clothing, riding technique, nutrition for cyclists, conditioning), photo feature (on cycling events), technical (component review, query), travel (bicycling must be central here), fitness. **Buys 6 unsolicited mss/year.** Query. **Payment varies.** Sometimes pays expenses of writers on assignment.
Reprints: Send tearsheet or photocopy and information about when and where the material previously appeared.
Photos: State availability of or send photos with submission. Pays $15-250/photo. Captions, model releases required.
Fillers: Anecdotes.
Tips: "Our focus is narrowed to the how-to of cycling, how to be a better rider, and bicycling experiences."

$ $ BIKE MAGAZINE, EMAP USA, 33046 Calle Aviador, San Juan Capistrano CA 92675. (949)496-5922. Fax: (949)496-7849. **Contact:** Ron Ige, editor. **35% freelance written.** Magazine publishes 10 times/year covering mountain biking. Estab. 1993. Circ. 160,000. Pays on publication. Publishes ms an average of 2 months after acceptance. Byline given. Offers 25% kill fee. Buys first North American serial rights. Editorial lead time 4 months. Submit seasonal material 6 months in advance. Responds in 2 months to queries. Sample copy for $8. Writer's guidelines for #10 SASE.

O→ *Bike* receives many travel-related queries and is seeking more investigative journalism on matters that affect mountain bikers. Writers have a much better chance of publication if they tackle larger issues that affect mountain bikers, such as trail access or sport controversies (i.e., drugs in cycling). If you do submit a travel article, know that a great location is not a story in itself—there must also be a theme. Examine back issues before submitting a travel story; if *Bike* has covered your location before, they won't again (for at least 4-5 years).

Nonfiction: Writers should submit queries in March (April 1 deadline) for consideration for the following year's editions. All queries received by April 1 will be considered and editors will contact writers about stories they are interested in. Queries should include word count. Humor, interview/profile, personal experience, photo feature, travel. **Buys 20 mss/year.** Length: 1,000-2,500 words. **Pays 50¢/word.** Sometimes pays expenses of writers on assignment.

Photos: David Reddick, photo editor. Send photos with submission. Reviews color transparencies, b&w prints. Buys one-time rights. Negotiates payment individually. Captions, identification of subjects required.

Columns/Departments: Splatter (news), 300 words; Urb (details a great ride within 1 hour of a major metropolitan area), 600-700 words. Query year-round for Splatter and Urb. **Buys 20 mss/year. Pays 50¢/word.**

Tips: "Remember that we focus on hard core mountain biking, not beginners. We're looking for ideas that deliver the excitement and passion of the sport in ways that aren't common or predictable. Ideas should be vivid, unbiased, irreverent, probing, fun, humorous, funky, quirky, smart, good. Great feature ideas are always welcome, especially features on cultural matters or issues in the sport. However, you're much more likely to get published in *Bike* if you send us great ideas for short articles. In particular we need stories for our Splatter, a front-of-the-book section devoted to news, funny anecdotes, quotes, and odds and ends. These stories range from 50 to 300 words. We also need personality profiles of 600 words or so for our People Who Ride section. Racers are OK but we're more interested in grassroots people with interesting personalities—it doesn't matter if they're Mother Theresas or scumbags, so long as they make mountain biking a little more interesting. Short descriptions of great rides are very welcome for our Urb column; the length should be from 600-700 words."

N **$** **BIKE MIDWEST**, Columbus Sports Publications, 1350 W. Fifth Ave., #30, Columbus OH 43212. (614)486-2202. Fax: (614)486-3650. E-mail: bsb@buckeyesports.com. **Contact:** Nicole Weis, editor. **35% freelance written.** Monthly (april-october) tabloid covering bicycling. "We like articles to be in a more casual voice so our readers feel more like a friend than just a customer." Estab. 1986. Circ. 35,000. Pays on publication. Publishes ms an average of 1 month after acceptance. Byline given. Offers 100% or $75 kill fee. Buys all rights. Editorial lead time 1 month. Submit seasonal material 1 month in advance. Accepts queries by mail, e-mail, fax. Accepts simultaneous submissions. Responds in 2 months to queries; 2 months to mss. Sample copy and writer's guidelines free.

Nonfiction: Essays, general interest, historical/nostalgic, how-to (bicycle mechanics, i.e., how to change a flat tire, etc.), humor, inspirational, interview/profile, new product, opinion, personal experience, technical, travel. Special issues: April and October issues cover travel and tourism by bicycle. Nothing non-bike related. **Buys 14 mss/year.** Send complete ms. Length: 1,000-2,000 words. **Pays $35-75.**

Reprints: Accepts previously published submissions.

Photos: Send photos with submission. Reviews negatives, 3½×5 prints. Buys all rights. Offers $25-50/photo. Captions, identification of subjects, model releases required.

Columns/Departments: Metal Cowboy (experiences on a bicycle), 1,800 words; Bicycling News (experiences in bicycling), 1,200 words. **Buys 14 mss/year.** Send complete ms. **Pays $35-75.**

Tips: "Articles must be informative and/or engaging. Our readers like to be entertained. They also look for lots of information when articles are technical (product reviews, etc.)"

$ $ **CYCLE CALIFORNIA! MAGAZINE**, P.O. Box 189, Mountain View CA 94042. (650)961-2663. Fax: (650)968-9030. E-mail: cycleca@cyclecalifornia.com. Website: www.cyclecalifornia.com. **Contact:** Tracy L. Corral, editor/publisher. **75% freelance written.** Magazine published 11 times/year "covering Northern California bicycling events, races, people. Issues (topics) covered include bicycle commuting, bicycle politics, touring, racing, nostalgia, history, anything at all to do with riding a bike." Estab. 1995. Circ. 25,500. Pays on publication. Publishes ms an average of 3 months after acceptance. Byline given. Buys first North American serial rights. Editorial lead time 6 weeks. Submit seasonal material 6 weeks in advance. Accepts queries by mail, e-mail, phone. Accepts simultaneous submissions. Responds in 1 month to queries. Sample copy for 10×13 SAE with 3 first-class stamps. Writer's guidelines for #10 SASE.

Nonfiction: Historical/nostalgic, how-to, interview/profile, opinion, personal experience, technical, travel. Special issues: Bicycle Tour & Travel (January/February). No articles about any sport that doesn't relate to bicycling, no product reviews. **Buys 36 mss/year.** Query with or without published clips. Length: 500-1,500 words. **Pays 3-10¢/word.**

Photos: Send photos with submission. Reviews 3×5 prints. Buys one-time rights. Negotiates payment individually. Identification of subjects required.

Columns/Departments: Buys 2-3 mss/year. Query with published clips. **Pays 3-10¢/word.**

Tips: "E-mail or call editor with good ideas. While we don't exclude writers from other parts of the country, articles really should reflect a Northern California slant, or be of general interest to bicyclists. We prefer stories written by people who like and use their bikes."

N **FITNESS CYCLING**, Challenge Publications Inc., 8381 Canoga Ave., Canoga Park CA 91304-2605. (818)700-6868, ext. 104. Fax: (818)700-6282. E-mail: mail@challengeweb.com. Website: www.challengeweb.com. Managing

Editor: Rex Reese. **Contact:** Flint Burckart, executive editor. **30% freelance written.** Monthly magazine covering cycling, fitness, health and apparel. Dedicated to improving health and fitness level of individuals via cycling and related issues. Estab. 2000. Circ. 60,000. Pays on publication. Byline given. Offers no kill fee. Buys all rights. Editorial lead time 2 months. Submit seasonal material 2 months in advance. Accepts queries by mail, e-mail, fax. Accepts simultaneous submissions. Responds in 2 weeks to queries. Sample copy and writer's guidelines for #10 SASE.

Nonfiction: Book excerpts, general interest, how-to, inspirational, new product, personal experience, photo feature, technical, travel. No unrelated subjects or tech features without credentials and support. **Buys variable mss/year.** Query. Length: 500-1,000 words. **Pays variable amount.** Sometimes pays expenses of writers on assignment.

Photos: Send photos with submission. Reviews transparencies, 4×6 prints. Buys all rights. Offers no additional payment for photos accepted with ms. Captions, identification of subjects, model releases required.

Columns/Departments: New Products, 100-200 words; Destinations (travel/resorts/spas), 1,000-2,500 words. Query. **Pays variable amount.**

$USA CYCLING MAGAZINE, One Olympic Plaza, Colorado Springs CO 80909. (719)578-4581. Fax: (719)578-4596. E-mail: media@usacycling.org or joe@tpgsports.com. Website: www.usacycling.org or www.tpgsports.com. Editor: Patrice Quintero. **Contact:** Joseph Oberle, publications manager, (763)595-0808. **25% freelance written.** Bimonthly magazine covering reportage and commentary on American bicycle racing, personalities and sports physiology for USAC licensed cyclists. Estab. 1980. Circ. 52,000. Pays on publication. Publishes ms an average of 2 months after acceptance. Byline given. Accepts queries by mail, e-mail. Responds in 2 weeks to queries. Sample copy for 10×12 SAE and 2 first-class stamps.

Nonfiction: How-to (train, prepare for a bike race), inspirational, interview/profile, personal experience, photo feature. No comparative product evaluations. **Buys 15 mss/year.** Length: 800-1,200 words. **Pays $50-75.**

Reprints: Send photocopy.

Photos: State availability with submission. Buys one-time rights. Captions required.

The online magazine carries original content not found in the print edition. Contact: Patrice Quintero, online editor.

Tips: "We do not want race reports. We want features from 800-1,200 words on American Cycling activities. Our focus is on personalities, not opinions or competition."

$ $ VELONEWS, The Journal of Competitive Cycling, 1830 N. 55th St., Boulder CO 80301-2700. (303)440-0601. Fax: (303)444-6788. E-mail: vnedit@7dogs.com. Website: www.VeloNews.com. **Contact:** Kip Mickler, senior editor (ext. 185). **40% freelance written.** Monthly tabloid covering bicycle racing. Estab. 1972. Circ. 48,000. Pays on publication. Publishes ms an average of 1 month after acceptance. Byline given. Buys one-time worldwide rights. Responds in 3 weeks to queries.

Nonfiction: Freelance opportunities include race coverage, reviews (book and videos), health-and-fitness departments. **Buys 80 mss/year.** Query. Length: 300-1,200 words. **Pays $100-400.**

Reprints: Send typed ms with rights for sale noted and information about when and where the material previously appeared.

Photos: State availability with submission. Buys one-time rights. Pays $16.50 for b&w prints; $200 for color used on cover. Captions, identification of subjects required.

Boating

$ $ $ BASS & WALLEYE BOATS, The Magazine of Performance Fishing Boats, Poole Publications, Inc., 20700 Belshaw Ave., Carson CA 90746. (310)537-6322. Fax: (310)537-8735. E-mail: editorbwb@aol.com. Editor: Doug Thompson. **Contact:** Mark Halvorsen, managing editor. **50% freelance written.** Magazine published 9 times/year. "*Bass & Walleye Boats* is published 9 times/year for the bass and walleye fisherman/boater. Directed to give priority to the boats, the tech, the how-to, the after-market add-ons and the devices that help anglers enjoy their boating experience." Estab. 1994. Circ. 65,000. **Pays on acceptance.** Byline given. Offers 25% kill fee. Buys first North American serial rights. Editorial lead time 2 months. Submit seasonal material 3 months in advance. Accepts queries by mail, e-mail, fax. Responds ASAP to queries. Sample copy for $3.95 and 9×12 SAE with 7 first-class stamps. Writer's guidelines free.

Break in by writing as an expert on using, modifying and tuning bass and walleye boats/engines for performance fishing use. Writer must be knowledgeable and able to back up document articles with hard sources. Also, your photography skills need to be honed for a marine environment.

Nonfiction: General interest, how-to, interview/profile, photo feature, technical. Special issues: Annual towing guide and new boats. No fiction. **Buys about 120 mss/year.** Query. Length: 1,000-3,000 words. **Pays $300-1,000.** Sometimes pays expenses of writers on assignment.

Photos: State availability with submission. Reviews 2¼×2¼ transparencies, 35mm slides. Buys one-time rights. Negotiates payment individually. Captions, identification of subjects required.

Tips: "Write from and for the bass and walleye boaters' perspective."

$ $⊡ CANOE & KAYAK MAGAZINE, Canoe America Associates, 10526 NE 68th St., Suite 3, Kirkland WA 98033. (425)827-6363. Fax: (425)827-1893. E-mail: editor@canoekayak.com. Website: www.canoekayak.com. Editor: Tim Jackson. **Contact:** Robin Stanton, managing editor. **75% freelance written.** Bimonthly magazine. "*Canoe & Kayak Magazine* is North America's #1 paddlesports resource. Our readers include flatwater and whitewater canoeists and kayakers of all skill levels. We provide comprehensive information on destinations, technique and equipment. Beyond that, we cover canoe and kayak camping, safety, the environment, and the history of boats and sport." Estab. 1972. Circ. 70,000. Pays on publication. Publishes ms an average of 6 months after acceptance. Byline given. Buys first international rights, which includes electronic and anthology rights. Editorial lead time 4 months. Submit seasonal material 6 months in advance. Accepts queries by mail, e-mail. Responds in 2 months to queries. Sample copy and writer's guidelines for 9×12 SAE with 7 first-class stamps.

> **O→** Break in with good destination or Put-In (news) pieces with excellent photos. "Take a good look at the types of articles we publish before sending us any sort of query."

Nonfiction: Historical/nostalgic, how-to (canoe, kayak camp; load boats; paddle whitewater, etc.), personal experience, photo feature, technical, travel. Special issues: Whitewater Paddling; Beginner's Guide; Kayak Touring; Canoe Journal. "No cartoons, poems, stories in which bad judgement is portrayed or 'Me and Molly' articles." **Buys 25 mss/year.** Query with or without published clips or send complete ms. Length: 400-2,500 words. **Pays $25-800 for assigned articles; $25-450 for unsolicited articles.**

Photos: "Some activities we cover are canoeing, kayaking, canoe fishing, camping, canoe sailing or poling, backpacking (when compatible with the main activity) and occasionally inflatable boats. We are not interested in groups of people in rafts, photos showing disregard for the environment, gasoline-powered, multi-horsepower engines unless appropriate to the discussion, or unskilled persons taking extraordinary risks." State availability with submission. Reviews 35mm transparencies, 4×6 prints. Buys one-time rights. Offers $25-500/photo. Captions, identification of subjects, model releases required.

Columns/Departments: Put In (environment, conservation, events), 650 words; Destinations (canoe and kayak destinations in US, Canada), 1,500 words; Traditions (essays: traditional paddling), 750 words. **Buys 40 mss/year.** Send complete ms. **Pays $100-350.**

Fillers: Anecdotes, facts, newsbreaks. **Buys 20/year.** Length: 200-500 words. **Pays $25-50.**

Tips: "Start with Put-In articles (short featurettes) or short, unique equipment reviews. Or give us the best, most exciting article we've ever seen—with great photos. Read the magazine before submitting."

$ $ $ CHESAPEAKE BAY MAGAZINE, Boating at Its Best, Chesapeake Bay Communications, 1819 Bay Ridge Ave., Annapolis MD 21403. (410)263-2662. Fax: (410)267-6924. E-mail: editor@cbmmag.net. Managing Editor: Jane Meneely. **Contact:** Wendy Mitman Clarke, executive editor. **60% freelance written.** Monthly magazine covering boating and the Chesapeake Bay. "Our readers are boaters. Our writers should know boats and boating. Read the magazine before submitting." Estab. 1972. Circ. 46,000. Pays within 60 days after acceptance. Publishes ms an average of 1 year after acceptance. Byline given. Buys first North American serial rights. Editorial lead time 1 year. Submit seasonal material 1 year in advance. Accepts queries by mail, e-mail, fax, phone. Accepts simultaneous submissions. Responds in 2 months to queries; 3 months to mss. Sample copy for $5.19 prepaid.

> **O→** "Read our Channel 9 column and give us some new ideas. These are short news items, profiles and updates: 200-800 words."

Nonfiction: Destinations, boating adventures, how-to, marina reviews, history, nature, environment, lifestyles, personal and institutional profiles, boat-type profiles, boatbuilding, boat restoration, boating anecdotes, boating news. **Buys 30 mss/year.** Query with published clips. Length: 300-3,000 words. **Pays $100-1,000.** Pays expenses of writers on assignment.

Photos: Buys one-time rights. Offers $45-150/photo, $350/day rate for assignment photography. Captions, identification of subjects required.

Tips: "Send us unedited writing samples (not clips) that show the writer can write, not just string words together. We look for well-organized, lucid, lively, intelligent writing."

N̄ $ $ $ CRUISING WORLD, The Sailing Company, 5 John Clarke Rd., Newport RI 02840-0992. (401)845-5100. Fax: (401)845-5180. Website: www.cruisingworld.com. Editor: Herb McCormick. Managing Editor: Elaine Lembo. **Contact:** Tim Murphy, executive editor. **90% freelance written.** Monthly magazine covering sailing, cruising/adventuring; do-it-yourself boat improvements. "*Cruising World* is a publication by and for small sailboat owners who spend time in home waters as well as voyaging the world. Its readership is extremely loyal, savvy and driven by independent thinking." Estab. 1974. Circ. 150,000. **Pays on acceptance for articles;** on publication for photography. Publishes ms 2 years after acceptance. Byline given. Buys 6-month, all-world, first-time rights (amendable). Editorial lead time 6 months. Submit seasonal material 1 year in advance. Accepts queries by mail. Accepts simultaneous submissions. Responds in 1 month to queries; 4 months to mss. Sample copy free. Writer's guidelines online.

Nonfiction: Book excerpts, essays, exposé, general interest, historical/nostalgic, how-to, humor, interview/profile, new product, opinion, personal experience, photo feature, technical, travel. No travel articles that have nothing to do with cruising aboard sailboats from 20-50 feet in length. **Buys hundreds of mss/year.** Send complete ms. **Pays $50-1,500 for assigned articles; $50-1,000 for unsolicited articles.** Sometimes pays expenses of writers on assignment.

Photos: Send photos with submission. Reviews negatives, transparencies, color slides preferred. Buys one-time rights. Negotiates payment individually. Also buys stand alone photos. Captions required.

Columns/Departments: Shoreline (sailing news, people and short features; contact Nim Marsh), 500 words maximum; Hands-on Sailor (refit, voyaging, seamanship, how-to; contact Darrell Nicholson), 1,000-1,500 words. **Buys hundreds of mss/year.** Query with or without published clips or send complete ms. **Pays $100-700.**
Tips: "*Cruising World*'s readers know exactly what they want to read, so our best advice to freelancers is to carefully read the magazine and envision which exact section or department would be the appropriate place for proposed submissions."

$ $ GO BOATING MAGAZINE, America's Family Boating Magazine, Duncan McIntosh Co., 17782 Cowan, Suite C, Irvine CA 92614. (949)660-6150. Fax: (949)660-6172. E-mail: editorial@goboatingamerica.com. Website: http://goboatingamerica.com. **Contact:** Mary Pivovaroff, managing editor. **60% freelance written.** Magazine published 6 times/year covering family power boating. Typical reader "owns a power boat between 14-32 feet long and has for 3-9 years. Boat reports that appear in *Go Boating* are designed to give readers a quick look at a new model. They must be lively, entertaining and interesting to our savvy boat-owning readership." Estab. 1997. Circ. 125,000. Pays on publication. Publishes ms an average of 6 months after acceptance. Byline given. Buys first North American serial rights. Editorial lead time 3 months. Submit seasonal material 6 months in advance. Accepts simultaneous submissions (if noted as such). Responds in 3 months to queries. Sample copy free. Writer's guidelines for #10 SASE.
Nonfiction: General interest, how-to, humor, new product, personal experience, travel. **Buys 10-15 mss/year.** Query. Length: 1,000-1,200 words. **Pays $150-400.** Sometimes pays expenses of writers on assignment.
Photos: State availability with submission. Reviews transparencies, prints. Buys one-time rights. Offers $50-250/photo. Identification of subjects, model releases required.
Fillers: Anecdotes, facts, newsbreaks. Length: 250-500 words. **Pays $50-100.**
Tips: "Every vessel has something about it that makes it stand apart from all the others. Tell us what makes this boat different from all the rest on the market today. Include specifications and builder's address and phone number. See past issues for format."

$ $ HEARTLAND BOATING, The Waterways Journal, Inc., 319 N. Fourth St., Suite 650, St. Louis MO 63102. (314)241-4310 or (800)366-9630. Fax: (314)241-4207. E-mail: info@heartlandboating.com. Website: www.heart landboating.com. **Contact:** H. Nelson Spencer, editor/publisher. **70% freelance written.** Magazine published 9 times/year covering recreational boating on the inland waterways of mid-America, from the Great Lakes south to the Gulf of Mexico and over to the east. "Our writers must have experience with and a great interest in boating, particularly in the area described above. *Heartland Boating*'s content is both informative and humorous—describing boating life as the heartland boater knows it. We are boaters and enjoy the outdoor, water-oriented way of life. The content reflects the challenge, joy and excitement of our way of life afloat. We are devoted to both power and sailboating enthusiasts throughout middle America; houseboats are included. The focus is on the freshwater inland rivers and lakes of the heartland, primarily the waters of the Tennessee, Cumberland, Ohio, Missouri and Mississippi rivers, the Tennessee-Tombigbee Waterway and the lakes along these rivers." Estab. 1989. Circ. 16,000. Pays on publication. Publishes ms an average of 3 months after acceptance. Byline given. Buys first North American serial, first, electronic rights. Editorial lead time 3 months. Submit seasonal material 6 months in advance. Accepts queries by mail, e-mail, fax, phone. Responds in 1 month to queries. Sample copy and writer's guidelines free.
Nonfiction: How-to (articles about navigation information and making time spent aboard easier and more comfortable), humor, personal experience (sharing experiences aboard and on cruises in our coverage area), technical (boat upkeep and maintenance), travel (along the rivers and on the lakes in our coverage area and on-land stops along the way). Special issues: Annual Boat Show/New Products issue in December looks at what is coming out on the market for the coming year. **Buys 110 mss/year.** Query with published clips or send complete ms. Length: 850-1,500 words. **Pays $100-300.**
Reprints: Send tearsheet, photocopy or typed ms and information about when and where the material previously appeared. Pays 50% of amount paid for original article.
Photos: Send photos with submission. Reviews transparencies, prints. Buys one-time rights. Offers no additional payment for photos accepted with ms.
Columns/Departments: Food Afloat (recipes easy to make when aboard), Books Aboard (book reviews), Handy Hints (small boat improvement projects), Waterways History (on-water history tidbits), all 850 words. **Buys 45 mss/ year.** Query with published clips or send complete ms. **Pays $75-150.**
Tips: "We usually plan an editorial schedule for the coming year in August. Submitting material between May and July will be most helpful for the planning process, although we accept submissions year-round."

$ $ HOT BOAT, LFP Publishing, 8484 Wilshire Blvd., Suite 900, Beverly Hills CA 90211. (323)651-5400. Fax: (323)951-0384. **Contact:** Brett Bayne, executive editor. **50% freelance written.** Monthly magazine on performance boating (16-35 feet), water skiing and water sports in general. "We're looking for concise, technically oriented 'how-to' articles on performance modifications; personality features on interesting boating-oriented personalities, and occasional event coverage." Circ. 30,000. Pays on publication. Publishes ms an average of 3 months after acceptance. Byline given. Buys second serial (reprint), all rights. Submit seasonal material 3 months in advance. Responds in 3 weeks to queries; 1 month to mss. Sample copy for $3 and 9 × 12 SAE with $1.35 postage.
Nonfiction: How-to (increase horsepower, perform simple boat-related maintenance), humor, interview/profile (racers and manufacturers), new product, personal experience, photo feature, technical. "Absolutely no sailing—we deal strictly in powerboating." **Buys 30 mss/year.** Query with published clips. Length: 500-2,000 words. **Pays $75-450.** Sometimes pays expenses of writers on assignment.

Reprints: Pays $150-200/printed page.
Photos: Send photos with submission. Reviews transparencies. Buys all rights. Captions, identification of subjects, model releases required.
Tips: "We're always open to new writers. If you query with published clips and we like your writing, we can keep you on file even if we reject the particular query. It may be more important to simply establish contact. Once we work together there will be much more work to follow."

N **$ $ HOUSEBOAT MAGAZINE, The Family Magazine for the American Houseboater**, Harris Publishing, Inc., 360 B St., Idaho Falls ID 83402. Fax: (208)522-5241. E-mail: hbeditor@houseboatmagazine.com. Website: www.houseboatmagazine.com. **Contact:** Jeff Hunter, editor. **40% freelance written.** Monthly magazine for houseboaters, who enjoy reading everything that reflects the unique houseboating lifestyle. If it is not a houseboat-specific article, please do not query. Estab. 1990. Circ. 25,000. Pays on publication. Publishes ms an average of 3 months after acceptance. Byline given. Offers 25% kill fee. Buys first North American serial, electronic rights. Editorial lead time 6 months. Submit seasonal material 6 months in advance. Accepts queries by mail, e-mail, fax. Accepts simultaneous submissions. Responds in 1 month to queries; 2 months to mss. Sample copy for $5. Writer's guidelines free.
Nonfiction: How-to, interview/profile, new product, personal experience, travel. **Buys 36 mss/year.** Query. Length: 1,000-1,200 words. **Pays $150-300.**
Photos: State availability with submission. Reviews negatives, transparencies. Buys one-time rights. Offers no additional payment for photos accepted with ms. Captions, model releases required.
Columns/Departments: Pays $50-175.
Tips: "As a general rule, how-to articles are always in demand. So are stories on unique houseboats or houseboaters. You are less likely to break in with a travel piece, of which we are flooded."

N **$ LAKELAND BOATING, The Magazine for Great Lakes Boaters**, O'Meara-Brown Publications, 500 Davis St., Suite 1000, Evanston IL 60201-4802. (847)869-5400. Fax: (847)869-5989. E-mail: LB@omeara-brown.com. Associate Editor: Dave Mull. **Contact:** Matthew Wright, editor. **50% freelance written.** Magazine covering Great Lakes boating. Estab. 1946. Circ. 60,000. Pays on publication. Byline given. Buys first North American serial rights. Responds in 4 months to queries. Sample copy for $5.50 and 9×12 SAE with 6 first-class stamps. Writer's guidelines free.
Nonfiction: Book excerpts, historical/nostalgic, how-to, interview/profile, personal experience, photo feature, technical, travel, must relate to boating in Great Lakes. No inspirational, religious, exposé or poetry. **Buys 20-30 mss/year.** Length: 800-3,00 words. **Pays $100-600.**
Photos: State availability with submission. Reviews prefers 35mm transparencies. Buys one-time rights. Captions required.
Columns/Departments: Bosun's Locker (technical or how-to pieces on boating), 100-1,000 words. **Buys 40 mss/year.** Query. **Pays $30-100.**

N **$ NOR'WESTING**, Nor'westing Publications, 513 Bay St., #7, Port Orchard WA 98366. (360)874-1992. Fax: (360)874-1987. Website: www.norwesting.com. **Contact:** Chuck Gould, editor. **75% freelance written.** Monthly magazine. "We want to pack our pages with cruising articles, special Northwest destinations, local boating personalities, practical boat maintenance tips." Estab. 1965. Circ. 19,000. Pays 1 month after publication. Publishes ms an average of 2 months after acceptance. Byline given. Buys first North American serial rights. Editorial lead time 3 months. Submit seasonal material 3 months in advance. Accepts queries by mail, e-mail. Accepts simultaneous submissions (note where it's being submitted). Responds in 2 months to queries. Sample copy and writer's guidelines for large SASE.
Nonfiction: Historical/nostalgic, how-to (boat outfitting, electronics, fish, galley), interview/profile (boater personalities), new product, personal experience (cruising), photo feature, technical, travel (local destination). **Buys 35-40 mss/year.** Query or send complete ms. Length: 1,500-3,000 words. **Pays $100-500.**
Reprints: Send tearsheet with rights for sale noted and information about when and where the material previously appeared. Payment varies.
Photos: Send photos with submission. Reviews transparencies, 3×5 prints. Buys one-time rights. Negotiates payment individually. Identification of subjects required.
Columns/Departments: Trailerboating (small craft boating—tech/destination), 700-900 words; Galley Ideas (cooking afloat—recipes/ideas), 700-900 words; Hardwired (boating electronics), 1,000 words; Cruising Fisherman (fishing tips, destinations), 700-900 words. **Buys 36-40 mss/year.** Query with published clips. **Pays $50-75.**
Fiction: Novel excerpts.
Tips: "Include specifics on destinations—how many moorage buoys, cost for showers, best time to visit. Any hazards to watch for while approaching? Why bother going if excitement for area/boating doesn't shine through?"

$ NORTHERN BREEZES, SAILING MAGAZINE, Northern Breezes, Inc., 3949 Winnetka Ave. N, Minneapolis MN 55427. (612)542-9707. Fax: (612)542-8998. E-mail: thomnbreez@aol.com. Website: www.sailingbreezes.com. Managing Editor: Thom Burns. **Contact:** Gloria Peck, editor. **70% freelance written.** Monthly magazine for the Upper Midwest sailing community. Estab. 1989. Circ. 22,300. Pays on publication. Byline given. Buys first North American serial rights. Editorial lead time 1 months. Submit seasonal material 3 months in advance. Accepts queries by mail, e-mail, fax, phone. Responds in 1 month to queries; 2 months to mss. Sample copy free. Writer's guidelines online.

Nonfiction: Book excerpts, how-to (sailing topics), humor, inspirational, interview/profile, new product, personal experience, photo feature, technical, travel. No boating reviews. **Buys 24 mss/year.** Query with published clips. Length: 300-2,000 words.

Reprints: Accepts previously published submissions.

Photos: Send photos with submission. Reviews negatives, 35mm slides, 3×5 or 4×6 prints. Buys one-time rights. Offers no additional payment for photos accepted with ms. Captions required.

Columns/Departments: This Old Boat (sailboat), 500-1,000 words; Surveyor's Notebook, 500-800 words. **Buys 8 mss/year.** Query with published clips. **Pays $50-150.**

■ The online magazine carries original content not found in the print edition and includes writer's guidelines. Contact: Thom Burns, online editor.

Tips: "Query with a regional connection already in mind."

$ $▨ OFFSHORE, Northeast Boating at its Best, Offshore Communications, Inc., 220 Reservoir St., Suite 9, Needham MA 02494. (781)449-6204. Fax: (781)449-9702. E-mail: editors@offshoremag.net. Website: www.offshore mag.net. **Contact:** Lisa Fabian, production editor. **80% freelance written.** Monthly magazine covering power and sailboating on the coast from Maine to New Jersey. Estab. 1976. Circ. 35,000. **Pays on acceptance.** Publishes ms an average of 5 months after acceptance. Byline given. Offers 50% kill fee. Buys first North American serial rights. Submit seasonal material 6 months in advance. Accepts queries by mail. Accepts simultaneous submissions. Writer's guidelines for #10 SASE.

Nonfiction: Articles on boats, boating, New York, New Jersey and New England coastal places and people, Northeast coastal history. **Buys 90 mss/year.** Query with or without published clips or send complete ms. Length: 1,200-2,500 words. **Pays $350-500 for features, depending on length.**

Photos: Reviews 35mm slides. Buys one-time rights. Pays $150-300. Identification of subjects required.

Tips: "Writers must demonstrate a familiarity with boats and with the Northeast coast. Specifically we are looking for articles on boating destinations, boating events (such as races, rendezvous and boat parades), on-the-water boating adventures, boating culture, maritime museums, maritime history, boating issues (such as safety and the environment), seamanship, fishing, how-to stories and essays. Note: Since *Offshore* is a regional magazine, all stories must focus on the area from New Jersey to Maine. We are always open to new people, the best of whom may gradually work their way into regular writing assignments. Important to ask for (and follow) our writer's guidelines if you're not familiar with our magazine."

$ $▨ PACIFIC YACHTING, Western Canada's Premier Boating Magazine, OP Publishing Ltd., 780 Beatty St., Suite 300, Vancouver, British Columbia V6B 2M1, Canada. (604)606-4644. Fax: (604)687-1925. E-mail: editor@pacificyachting.net. Website: www.pacificyachting.net. **Contact:** Simon Hill, editor. **90% freelance written.** Monthly magazine covering all aspects of recreational boating on British Columbia's coast. "The bulk of our writers and photographers not only come from the local boating community, many of them were long-time *PY* readers before coming aboard as a contributor. The *PY* reader buys the magazine to read about new destinations or changes to old haunts on the B.C. coast and to learn the latest about boats and gear." Circ. 19,000. Pays on publication. Publishes ms an average of 6 months after acceptance. Byline given. Buys first North American serial, simultaneous rights. Editorial lead time 4 months. Submit seasonal material 6 months in advance. Accepts queries by mail, e-mail, fax. Sample copy for $4.95 plus postage charged to VISA credit card. Writer's guidelines free.

Nonfiction: Historical/nostalgic (BC coast only), how-to, humor, interview/profile, personal experience, technical (boating related), travel, cruising and destination on the B.C. coast. "No articles from writers who are obviously not boaters!" Query. Length: 1,500-2,000 words. **Pays $150-500.** Pays expenses of writers on assignment.

Photos: Send photos with submission. Reviews transparencies, 4×6 prints and slides. Buys one-time rights. Offers no additional payment for photos accepted with ms. Offers $25-300 for photos accepted alone. Identification of subjects required.

Columns/Departments: Currents (current events, trade and people news, boat gatherings and festivities), 50-250 words. Reflections, Cruising, 800-1,000 words. Query. **Pay varies.**

Tips: "We strongly encourage queries before submission (written with SAE and IRCs, or by phone or e-mail). While precise nautical information is important, colorful anecdotes bring your cruise to life. Both are important. In other words, our reader wants you to balance important navigation details with first-person observations, blending the practical with the romantic. Write tight, write short, write with the reader in mind, write to inform, write to entertain. Be specific, accurate and historic."

$ $ PONTOON & DECK BOAT, Harris Publishing, Inc., 520 Park Ave., Idaho Falls ID 83402. (208)524-7000. Fax: (208)522-5241. E-mail: brady@pdbmagazine.com. Website: www.pdbmagazine.com. **Contact:** Brady L. Kay, editor. **15% freelance written.** Magazine published 8 times/year. "We are a boating niche publication geared towards the pontoon and deck boating lifestyle and consumer market. Our audience is comprised of people who utilize these boats for varied family activities and fishing. Our magazine is promotional of the PDB industry and its major players. We seek to give the reader a two-fold reason to read our publication: To celebrate the lifestyle and to do it aboard a first-class craft." Estab. 1995. Circ. 84,000. Pays on publication. Byline given. Buys one-time rights. Editorial lead time 2 months. Submit seasonal material 3 months in advance. Accepts simultaneous submissions. Responds in 6 weeks to queries; 3 months to mss. Sample copy and writer's guidelines free.

Nonfiction: How-to, personal experience, technical, remodeling, rebuilding. "We are saturated with travel pieces, no general boating, no humor, no fiction, poetry." **Buys 15 mss/year.** Query with or without published clips or send complete ms. Length: 600-2,000 words. **Pays $50-300.** Sometimes pays expenses of writers on assignment.

Photos: State availability with submission. Reviews transparencies. Rights negotiable. Captions, model releases required.

Columns/Departments: No Wake Zone (short, fun quips); Better Boater (how-to). **Buys 6-12 mss/year.** Query with published clips. **Pays $50-150.**

Tips: "Be specific to pontoon and deck boats. Any general boating material goes to the slush pile. The more you can tie together the lifestyle, attitudes and the PDB industry, the more interest we'll take in what you send us."

$ $ $ POWER & MOTORYACHT, Primedia, 260 Madison Ave., 8th Floor, New York NY 10016. (917)256-2200. Fax: (917)256-2282. E-mail: dbyrne@primediasi.com. Editor: Richard Thiel. Managing Editor: Jeanine Detz. **Contact:** Diane M. Byrne, executive editor. **20% freelance written.** Monthly magazine covering powerboating. "*Power & Motoryacht* is devoted exclusively to the high-end powerboat market, those boats 24 feet or larger. Every reader owns at least one powerboat in this size range. Our magazine reaches virtually every U.S. owner of a 40-foot or larger powerboat—the only publication that does so. For our readers, boating is not a hobby, it's a lifestyle." Estab. 1985. Circ. 157,000. **Pays on acceptance.** Publishes ms an average of 6 months after acceptance. Byline given. Offers 33% kill fee. Buys first North American serial and permanent electronic rights. Editorial lead time 1 year. Submit seasonal material 6 months in advance. Accepts queries by mail, e-mail, fax. Accepts simultaneous submissions. Responds in 1 month to queries. Sample copy for 10×12 SASE. Writer's guidelines for #10 SASE.

○⊸ Break in by "knowing the boat business—know which manufacturers specialize in cruising boats vs. sportfishing boats, for example, and know the difference between production-built and semi-custom vessels. Be an authority on the subject you're pitching—our readers can spot uninformed writers!"

Nonfiction: How-to (how to fix things, install things, shop for boats and accessories smarter, etc.), humor, interview/profile, personal experience, technical, travel. **Buys 10-15 mss/year.** Query with published clips. Length: 800-1,400 words. **Pays $500-1,200.** Sometimes pays expenses of writers on assignment.

Photos: State availability with submission; unsolicited images will not be returned. Reviews 4×5 transparencies. Buys one-time rights. Offers no additional payment for photos accepted with ms. Captions, identification of subjects required.

Tips: "Writers must be authorities on the subject matter they write about—our readers have an average of 31 years' experience on the water, so they want experts to provide advice and information. Some of our regular feature themes are seamanship (rules of the road and boating protocol techniques); cruising (places readers can take their own boats for a few days' enjoyment); maintenance (tips on upkeep and repair); engines (innovations that improve efficiency and/or lessen environmental impact)."

$ $ POWER BOATING CANADA, 1020 Brevik Place, Suites 4 & 5, Mississauga, Ontario L4W 4N7, Canada. (905)624-8218. Fax: (905)624-6764. **Contact:** Steve Fennell, editor. **70% freelance written.** Bimonthly magazine covering recreational power boating. "*Power Boating Canada* offers boating destinations, how-to features, boat tests (usually staff written), lifestyle pieces—with a Canadian slant—and appeal to recreational power boaters across the country." Estab. 1984. Circ. 50,000. Pays on publication. Publishes ms an average of 3 months after acceptance. Byline given. Buys first North American serial rights. Editorial lead time 2 months. Submit seasonal material 3 months in advance. Responds in 1 month to queries; 2 months to mss. Sample copy free.

Nonfiction: "Any articles related to the sport of power boating, especially boat tests." Historical/nostalgic, how-to, interview/profile, personal experience, travel (boating destinations). No general boating articles or personal anecdotes. **Buys 40-50 mss/year.** Query. Length: 1,200-2,500 words. **Pays $150-300.** Sometimes pays expenses of writers on assignment.

Reprints: Send photocopy with rights for sale noted and information about when and where the material previously appeared.

Photos: Send photos with submission. Reviews contact sheets, negatives, transparencies, prints. Buys one-time rights. Pay varies; no additional payment for photos accepted with ms. Captions, identification of subjects required.

N: $ $ $ POWERBOAT, Nordskog Publishing Inc., 1691 Spinnaker Dr., #206, Ventura CA 93001. (805)639-2222. Fax: (805)639-2220. E-mail: edit-dpt@powerboatmag.com. Website: www.powerboatmag.com. Managing Editor: Brett Becker. **Contact:** Jo Stich, editor. **25% freelance written.** Magazine published 11 times/year covering performance boating. Estab. 1973. Circ. 41,000. Pays on publication. Publishes ms an average of 3 months after acceptance. Byline given. Offers negotiable kill fee. Buys first North American serial, electronic rights. Editorial lead time 3 months. Submit seasonal material 4 months in advance. Accepts queries by mail, e-mail, fax. Sample copy online.

Nonfiction: Interview/profile, new product, photo feature. No general interest boating stories. **Buys numerous mss/year.** Query. Length: 300-2,000 words. **Pays $125-1,200.** Sometimes pays expenses of writers on assignment.

Photos: State availability with submission. Reviews negatives. Buys one-time rights. Captions required.

$ $ $ SAIL, 84 State St., Boston MA 02109-2262. (617)720-8600. Fax: (617)723-0912. E-mail: sailmail@primediasi.com. Website: www.sailmag.com or www.sailbuyersguide.com. Editor: Patience Wales. **Contact:** Amy Ullrich, managing editor. **50% freelance written.** Monthly magazine "written and edited for everyone who sails—aboard a coastal or bluewater cruiser, trailerable, one-design or offshore racer, or daysailer. How-to and technical articles concentrate on techniques of sailing and aspects of design and construction, boat systems, and gear; the feature section emphasizes the fun and rewards of sailing in a practical and instructive way." Estab. 1970. Circ. 180,000. **Pays on acceptance.** Publishes ms an average of 10 months after acceptance. Byline given. Buys first North American serial rights. Accepts queries by mail, e-mail, fax. Responds in 10 weeks to queries. Writer's guidelines for SASE or online.

Nonfiction: How-to, personal experience, technical, Distance cruising, Destinations. Special issues: "Cruising, chartering, fitting-out, special race (e.g., America's Cup), boat show." **Buys 100 mss/year.** Query. Length: 1,500-3,000 words. **Pays $200-800.** Sometimes pays expenses of writers on assignment.

Photos: Reviews ASA transparencies. Pay varies, up to $600 if photo used on cover. Captions, identification of subjects, credits required.

Columns/Departments: Sailing Memories (short essay); Sailing News (cruising, racing, legal, political, environmental); Under Sail (human interest). Query. **Pays $25-400.**

　　■ The online magazine carries original content not found in the print edition and includes writer's guidelines. Contact: Kimball Livingston, online editor.

Tips: "Request an articles specification sheet. We look for unique ways of viewing sailing. Skim old issues of *Sail* for ideas about the types of articles we publish. Always remember that *Sail* is a sailing magazine. Stay away from gloomy articles detailing all the things that went wrong on your boat. Think constructively and write about how to avoid certain problems. You should focus on a theme or choose some aspect of sailing and discuss a personal attitude or new philosophical approach to the subject. Notice that we have certain issues devoted to special themes—for example, chartering, electronics, commissioning, and the like. Stay away from pieces that chronicle your journey in the day-by-day style of a logbook. These are generally dull and uninteresting. Select specific actions or events (preferably sailing events, not shorebound activities), and build your articles around them. Emphasize the sailing."

$ $ $ SAILING MAGAZINE, 125 E. Main St., Port Washington WI 53074-0249. (262)284-3494. Fax: (262)284-7764. E-mail: sailing@execpc.com. Website: www.sailingonline.com. Publisher: William F. Schanen. **Contact:** Gregory O. Jones, editor. Monthly magazine for the experienced sailor. Estab. 1966. Circ. 52,000. Pays on publication. Buys one-time rights. Accepts queries by mail, e-mail. Responds in 2 months to queries.

　　○╌ "Let us get to know your writing with short newsy, sailing-oriented pieces with good slides for our Splashes section. Query for upcoming theme issues; read the magazine; writing must show the writer loves sailing as much as our readers. We are always looking for fresh stories on new destinations with vibrant writing and top-notch photography. Always looking for short (100-1,500 word) articles or newsy items."

Nonfiction: "Experiences of sailing, cruising and racing or cruising to interesting locations, whether a small lake near you or islands in the Southern Ocean, with first-hand knowledge and tips for our readers. Top-notch photos with maps, charts, cruising information complete the package. No regatta sports unless there is a story involved." Book excerpts, how-to (tech pieces on boats and gear), interview/profile, personal experience, travel (by sail). **Buys 15-20 mss/year.** Length: 750-2,500 words. **Pays $100-800.**

Photos: Reviews color transparencies. Pays $50-400. Captions required.

Tips: Prefers text in Word on disk for Mac or to e-mail address. "No attached files, please."

$ $⊠ SEA KAYAKER, Sea Kayaker, Inc., P.O. Box 17029, Seattle WA 98107-0729. (206)789-1326. Fax: (206)781-1141. E-mail: karin@seakayakermag.com. Website: www.seakayakermag.com. Editor: Christopher Cunningham. **Contact:** Karin Redmond, executive editor. **95% freelance written.** Bimonthly publication. "*Sea Kayaker* is a bimonthly publication with a worldwide readership that covers all aspects of kayak touring. It is well-known as an important source of continuing education by the most experienced paddlers." Estab. 1984. Circ. 28,000. Pays on publication. Publishes ms an average of 6 months after acceptance. Byline given. Offers 10% kill fee. Buys first North American serial rights. Editorial lead time 4 months. Submit seasonal material 4 months in advance. Accepts queries by mail, e-mail, fax, phone. Responds in 2 months to queries. Sample copy for $5.75. Writer's guidelines for SASE.

Nonfiction: Essays, historical/nostalgic, how-to (on making equipment), humor, interview/profile, new product, opinion, personal experience, technical, travel. **Buys 50 mss/year.** Query with or without published clips or send complete ms. Length: 1,500-5,000 words. **Pays 18-20¢/word for assigned articles; 12-15¢/word for unsolicited articles.**

Photos: Send photos with submission. Reviews transparencies, prints. Buys one-time rights. Offers $15-400. Captions, identification of subjects required.

Columns/Departments: Technique, Equipment, Do-It-Yourself, Food, Safety, Health, Environment, Book Reviews; 1,000-2,500 words. **Buys 40-45 mss/year.** Query. **Pays 12-20¢/word.**

Tips: "We consider unsolicited manuscripts that include a SASE, but we give greater priority to brief descriptions (several paragraphs) of proposed articles accompanied by at least two samples—published or unpublished—of your writing. Enclose a statement as to why you're qualified to write the piece and indicate whether photographs or illustrations are available to accompany the piece."

SEA MAGAZINE, America's Western Boating Magazine, Duncan McIntosh Co., 17782 Cowan, Suite C, Irvine CA 92614. (949)660-6150. Fax: (949)660-6172. Website: www.goboatingamerica.com. **Contact:** Eston Ellis, managing editor. Monthly magazine covering West Coast power boating. Estab. 1908. Circ. 50,000. Pays on publication. Publishes ms an average of 3 months after acceptance. Byline given. Buys first North American serial rights. Editorial lead time 3 months. Submit seasonal material 6 months in advance. Accepts simultaneous submissions. Responds in 3 months to queries.

Nonfiction: "News you can use" is kind of our motto. All articles should aim to help boat owners make the most of their boating experience. How-to, new product, personal experience, technical, travel. **Buys 36 mss/year.** Query with or without published clips or send complete ms. Length: 1,000-1,500 words. **Pay varies.** Sometimes pays expenses of writers on assignment.

Photos: State availability with submission. Reviews transparencies. Buys one-time rights. Offers $50-250/photo. Captions, identification of subjects, model releases required.

\$ \$ SOUTHERN BOATING MAGAZINE, The South's Largest Boating Magazine, Southern Boating & Yachting Inc., 330 N. Andrews Ave., Ft. Lauderdale FL 33301. (954)522-5515. Fax: (954)522-2260. E-mail: sboating@s outhernboating.com. Editor: Skip Allen. **Contact:** David Strickland. **50% freelance written.** Monthly magazine. "Upscale monthly yachting magazine focusing on SE U.S., Bahamas, Caribbean and Gulf of Mexico." Estab. 1972. Circ. 40,000. Pays on publication. Publishes ms an average of 2 months after acceptance. Byline given. Buys one-time rights. Editorial lead time 6 weeks. Submit seasonal material 2 months in advance. Accepts queries by mail, e-mail, fax, phone. Sample copy free.

 O→ Break in with destination, how-to and technical articles.

Nonfiction: How-to (boat maintenance), travel (boating related, destination pieces). **Buys 100 mss/year.** Query. Length: 600-3,000 words. **Pays $200.**

Photos: State availability of or send photos with submission. Reviews transparencies, prints. Buys one-time rights. Offers $50/photo max. Captions, identification of subjects, model releases required.

Columns/Departments: Weekend Workshop (how to/maintenance), 600 words; What's New in Electronics (electronics), 1,000 words; Engine Room (new developments), 1,000 words. **Buys 24 mss/year.** Query. **Pays $150.**

\$ WAVELENGTH PADDLING MAGAZINE, Wave-Length Communications, Inc., 2735 North Rd., Site 41, C39, Gabriola Island, British Columbia V0R 1X0, Canada. (250)247-9789. Fax: (250)247-9789. E-mail: wavenet@island.net. Website: www.wavelengthmagazine.com. **Contact:** Alan Wilson, editor. **75% freelance written.** Bimonthly magazine covering sea kayaking. "We promote safe paddling, guide paddlers to useful products and services and explore coastal environmental issues." Estab. 1991. Circ. 50,000 plus Internet readers. Pays on publication. Publishes ms an average of 4 months after acceptance. Byline given. Offers 10% kill fee. Buys first North American serial, electronic rights. Editorial lead time 4 months. Submit seasonal material 4 months in advance. Accepts queries by mail, e-mail, phone. Responds in 2 months to queries. Sample copy for $2 or online. Writer's guidelines free or online.

 O→ "Sea kayaking content, even if from a beginner's perspective, is essential. We like a light approach to personal experiences and humor is appreciated. Good detail (with maps and pics) for destinations material. Write to our feature focus."

Nonfiction: Book excerpts, how-to (paddle, travel), humor, interview/profile, new product, opinion, personal experience, technical, travel, trips, advice. **Buys 25 mss/year.** Query. Length: 1,000-2,000 words. **Pays $50-75.** Pays businesses with advertising.

Photos: State availability with submission. Reviews 4×6 prints. Buys first and electronic rights. Offers $25-50/photo. Captions, identification of subjects required.

Fillers: Anecdotes, facts, gags to be illustrated by cartoonist, newsbreaks, short humor. **Buys 8-10/year.** Length: 25-250 words. **Pays $10-25.**

Tips: "You must know paddling—although novice paddlers are welcome. A strong environmental or wilderness appreciation component is advisable. We are willing to help refine work with flexible people. E-mail queries preferred. Check out our Editorial Calendar for our upcoming features."

\$ \$ WOODENBOAT MAGAZINE, The Magazine for Wooden Boat Owners, Builders, and Designers, WoodenBoat Publications, Inc., P.O. Box 78, Brooklin ME 04616. (207)359-4651. Fax: (207)359-8920. Website: www.w oodenboat.com. Editor-in-Chief: Jonathan A. Wilson. Senior Editor: Mike O'Brien. Associate Editor: Tom Jackson. **Contact:** Matthew P. Murphy, editor. **50% freelance written.** Bimonthly magazine for wooden boat owners, builders and designers. "We are devoted exclusively to the design, building, care, preservation, and use of wooden boats, both commercial and pleasure, old and new, sail and power. We work to convey quality, integrity and involvement in the creation and care of these craft, to entertain, inform, inspire, and to provide our varied readers with access to individuals who are deeply experienced in the world of wooden boats." Estab. 1974. Circ. 106,000. Pays on publication. Publishes ms an average of 1 year after acceptance. Byline given. Offers variable kill fee. Buys first North American serial rights. Accepts simultaneous submissions. Responds in 3 weeks to queries; 2 months to mss. Sample copy for $4.50. Writer's guidelines for #10 SASE.

Nonfiction: Technical (repair, restoration, maintenance, use, design and building wooden boats). No poetry, fiction. **Buys 50 mss/year.** Query with published clips. Length: 1,500-5,000 words. **Pays $200-250/1,000 words.** Sometimes pays expenses of writers on assignment.

Reprints: Send tearsheet or typed ms with rights for sale noted and information about when and where the material previously appeared.

Photos: Send photos with submission. Reviews negatives. Buys one-time rights. Pays $15-75 b&w, $25-350 color. Identification of subjects required.

Columns/Departments: On the Waterfront pays for information on wooden boat-related events, projects, boatshop activities, etc. Uses same columnists for each issue. Length: 250-1,000 words. Send complete information. **Pays $5-50.**

Tips: "We appreciate a detailed, articulate query letter, accompanied by photos, that will give us a clear idea of what the author is proposing. We appreciate samples of previously published work. It is important for a prospective author to become familiar with our magazine first. It is extremely rare for us to make an assignment with a writer with whom we have not worked before. Most work is submitted on speculation. The most common failure is not exploring the subject material in enough depth."

$ $ $ YACHTING, AOL/Time Warner, 20 E. Elm St., Greenwich CT 06830. (203)625-4480. Fax: (203)625-4481. Website: www.yachtingmagazine.com. Publisher: Peter Beckenbach. Editor-in-Chief: Kenny Wooton. **30% freelance written.** Monthly magazine. "Monthly magazine written and edited for experienced, knowledgeable yachtsmen." Estab. 1907. Circ. 132,000. **Pays on acceptance.** Byline given. Buys first North American serial, electronic rights. Editorial lead time 2 months. Submit seasonal material 6 months in advance. Accepts queries by mail, e-mail, fax. Responds in 1 month to queries; 3 months to mss. Sample copy free. Writer's guidelines online.
Nonfiction: Personal experience, technical. **Buys 50 mss/year.** Query with published clips. Length: 750-800 words. **Pays $150-1,500.** Pays expenses of writers on assignment.
Photos: Send photos with submission. Reviews transparencies. Negotiates payment individually. Captions, identification of subjects, model releases required.
Tips: "We require considerable expertise in our writing because our audience is experienced and knowledgeable. Vivid descriptions of quaint anchorages and quainter natives are fine, but our readers want to know how the yachtsmen got there, too. They also want to know how their boats work. *Yachting* is edited for experienced, affluent boatowners—power and sail—who don't have the time or the inclination to read sub-standard stories. They love carefully crafted stories about places they've never been or a different spin on places they have, meticulously reported pieces on issues that affect their yachting lives, personal accounts of yachting experiences from which they can learn, engaging profiles of people who share their passion for boats, insightful essays that evoke the history and traditions of the sport and compelling photographs of others enjoying the game as much as they do. They love to know what to buy and how things work. They love to be surprised. They don't mind getting their hands dirty or saving a buck here and there, but they're not interested in learning how to make a masthead light out of a mayonnaise jar. If you love what they love and can communicate like a pro (that means meeting deadlines, writing tight, being obsessively accurate and never misspelling a proper name), we'd love to hear from you."

Bowling

[N] $ $ BOWLING, Dept. WM, 675 N. Brookfield Rd., Brookfield WI 53045. (262)641-2003. Fax: (262)641-2005. **Contact:** Bill Vint, editor. **15% freelance written.** Bimonthly magazine. Official publication of the American Bowling Congress. Estab. 1934. Circ. 100,000. **Pays on acceptance.** Publishes ms an average of 2 months after acceptance. Byline given. Buys variable rights, usually all rights. Responds in 1 month to mss. Sample copy for $2.50.
Nonfiction: "This is a specialized field and the average writer attempting the subject of bowling should be well-informed. However, anyone is free to submit material for approval." Wants articles about unusual ABC sanctioned leagues and tournaments, personalities, etc., featuring male bowlers. Nostalgia articles also considered. No first-person articles or material on history of bowling. No poems, songs or fiction. Length: 500-1,200 words. **Pays $100-300 for assigned articles.**
Photos: Pays $25-50/photo.
Tips: "Submit feature material on bowlers, generally amateurs competing in local leagues, or special events involving the game of bowling. Should have connection with ABC membership. Queries should be as detailed as possible so that we may get a clear idea of what the proposed story would be all about. It saves us time and the writer time. Samples of previously published material in the bowling or general sports field would help. Once we find a talented writer in a given area, we're likely to go back to him in the future. We're looking for good writers who can handle assignments professionally and promptly."

Football

[N] $ TIGER INSIDER, Upstate Publishing, Inc., PMB 125, 1027 S. Pendleton St., Suite B, Easley SC 29673. Fax: (305)675-0365. E-mail: thood2@hotmail.com. Website: www.Thetigernet.com. **Contact:** Tommy Hood, managing editor. **100% freelance written.** Bimonthly magazine covering Clemson football. "*Tiger Insider* covers Clemson football and everything that surrounds it—the players, coaches, recruits. Anything remotely associated with Clemson football is considered for publication in the magazine. National issues that are relevant to Clemson football are also considered for inclusion in the magazine." Estab. 1999. Circ. 1,000. Pays on publication. Byline given. Offers 50% kill fee. Buys one-time rights. Editorial lead time 2 months. Submit seasonal material 2 months in advance. Accepts queries by mail, e-mail, fax. Accepts simultaneous submissions. Sample copy online. Writer's guidelines by e-mail.
Nonfiction: Book excerpts, interview/profile, college football. **Buys 30 mss/year.** Query with published clips. Length: 800-2,500 words. **Pays $50-100.**
Reprints: Accepts previously published submissions.

Photos: State availability with submission. Reviews gif/jpeg files. Buys one-time rights. Negotiates payment individually. Identification of subjects required.

Tips: "E-mail with query and clips. Our readers are diehard Clemson football fans and consider anything remotely associated with Clemson football important: Where are they now? Features on recruits. Features on the schools that Clemson recruits against are all appropriate as well as features on current Clemson players and coaches."

Gambling

N BLACKJACK FORUM, RGE Publishing, 414 Santa Clara Ave., Oakland CA 94610. (510)465-6452. Fax: (510)652-4330. E-mail: asnyder@rge21.com; orders@rge21.com for queries. Website: www.rge21.com. **Contact:** Arnold Snyder, editor. **40% freelance written.** Quarterly magazine covering casino blackjack. "For sophisticated and knowledgeable casino gamblers interested in legal issues, mathematical analyses, computer simulations, techniques. This is not a get-rich-quick type mag." Estab. 1981. Circ. 2,500. Pays on publication. Publishes ms an average of 6 months after acceptance. Byline given. Buys first, second serial (reprint) rights. Editorial lead time 6 months. Submit seasonal material 6 months in advance. Accepts queries by e-mail. Responds in 4 months to queries. Sample copy for $12.50.

Nonfiction: Exposé, how-to, personal experience, technical, travel. **Buys 10-12 mss/year.** Query with clips or send complete ms. Length: 200-3,000 words. **Pays $35/page for assigned articles.** Sometimes pays expenses of writers on assignment.

Reprints: Send tearsheet or photocopy with rights for sale noted and information about when and where the material previously appeared. Pay negotiable.

Photos: State availability of or send photos with submission. Reviews contact sheets, prints. Buys one-time rights. Negotiates payment individually.

Columns/Departments: Around the States (reports on blackjack conditions in US casinos); Around The World (ditto for foreign casinos), both 200-1,500 words. **Buys 25 mss/year.** Query or send complete ms. **Pays in contributor's copies—$35/published page.**

Tips: "Be very knowledgeable about casino blackjack, especially familiar with all noted authors—Thorp, Revere, Uston, Wong, Griffin, Carlson, etc."

$ $ CHANCE MAGAZINE, The Best of Gaming, ARC Publishing, LLC, 16 E. 41st St., 2nd Floor, New York NY 10017. Fax: (212)889-3630. E-mail: bphillips@chancemag.com. Website: www.chancemag.com. **Contact:** Buster Phillips, managing editor. **50% freelance written.** Bimonthly magazine covering gambling lifestyle, upscale resorts, food, wine, spas, etc. "*Chance* is an upscale magazine for readers interested in getting the most out of a gambling vacation. From travel, resorts and spas, to tips and advice on gaming, *Chance* is a smartly written and fun guide for the gaming connoisseur." Circ. 190,000. Pays on publication. Publishes ms an average of 3 months after acceptance. Byline given. Offers 25% kill fee. Buys first North American serial rights. Editorial lead time 6 months. Submit seasonal material 6 months in advance. Accepts queries by mail, e-mail, fax. Sample copy online.

Nonfiction: General interest, how-to, interview/profile, personal experience, photo feature, anything gambling related. No systems or self-promotion. **Buys 50 mss/year.** Query with published clips or send complete ms. Length: 1,200-3,500 words. **Pays $150-600 for assigned articles.** Sometimes pays expenses of writers on assignment.

Photos: State availability with submission. Payment negotiated individually.

Columns/Departments: The Intelligent Player (advanced advice for the serious gambler), 2,000 words; Ante (short, quick upfront pieces), 300-600 words. **Buys 12 mss/year.** Send complete ms. **Pays $150-500.**

Tips: "Either be a gambling fan with specific knowledge or be familiar with the life of a high roller—luxuries that somehow tie in to casinos and gaming. Above all, be a good writer with experience."

N $ $ PLAYERS' GUIDE TO LAS VEGAS SPORTS BOOKS WITH OFF SHORE BETTING GUIDE, Players Guide, 11000 S. Eastern Ave., #1618, Henderson NV 89052-2965. (702)361-4602. Fax: (702)361-4605. E-mail: buzzdaly@aol.com. Website: www.buzzdaly.com. **Contact:** Buzz Daly, editor. **20-50% freelance written.** Annual magazine, weekly tabloid and website covering sports wagering and online gaming. "We address the needs and interests of people who bet on sports. We focus on legal activities in Las Vegas and off shore, and do features on bookmakers, oddsmakers, professional bettors, etc. Although many readers are casual/recreationally, we do not 'dumb down' our coverage. Our readers are regular bettors who do not apologize for this activity." Estab. 1994. Circ. 75,000. **Pays on acceptance.** Byline given. Offers 10% or 100% kill fee. Buys first, electronic rights. Editorial lead time 2 months. Accepts queries by mail, e-mail. Responds in 2 weeks to queries; 1 week to mss. Sample copy for $3.95.

Nonfiction: "Our magazine is an annual. Our period for obtaining stories is from mid March to early June. But our website uses material all year long." Book excerpts, interview/profile, new product. No exposés, handicapping tips, stories about losing, getting stiffed, etc. We have no interest in stories based on trite material or clichés." **Buys variable mss/year.** Query with published clips. Length: 300-1,500 words. **Pays $50-400.** Sometimes pays expenses of writers on assignment.

Photos: Send photos with submission. Reviews contact sheets, prints. Buys one-time rights. Offers no additional payment for photos accepted with ms. Identification of subjects, model releases required.

Tips: "A writer must be a bettor to be considered as a contributor. He does not need to state it, we can tell by the material. We look for fresh insight and original story ideas. However, an old idea presented imaginatively and with sophistication will be considered. For instance, the ups and downs of being or dealing with a local bookmaker, with revealing anecdotes falls within our parameters. We have no interest in hard luck stories, bad bets, etc."

General Interest

$ $ ROCKY MOUNTAIN SPORTS MAGAZINE, Rocky Mountain Sports, Inc., 1521 Central St., Suite 1C, Denver CO 80211. (303)477-9770. Fax: (303)477-9747. E-mail: rheaton@rockymountainsports.com. Website: www.roc kymountainsports.com. Publisher: Mary Thorne. **Contact:** Rebecca Heaton, editor. **50% freelance written.** Monthly magazine covering sports in Colorado. "*Rocky* is a magazine for sports-related lifestyles and activities. Our mission is to reflect and inspire the active lifestyle of Rocky Mountain residents." Estab. 1986. Circ. 80,000. Pays on publication. Publishes ms an average of 2 months after acceptance. Byline given. Buys second serial (reprint) rights. Editorial lead time 3 months. Submit seasonal material 2 months in advance. Accepts queries by mail, e-mail, fax. Responds in 3 weeks to queries; 2 months to mss. Sample copy and writer's guidelines for #10 SASE.
- The editor says she wants to see mountain outdoor sports writing *only*. No ball sports, hunting or fishing.
- Break in with "Rocky Mountain angle—off the beaten path."

Nonfiction: Book excerpts, essays, exposé, how-to, humor, inspirational, interview/profile, new product, opinion, personal experience, photo feature, travel. Special issues: Snowboarding (December); Alpine and Nordic (January and February); Running (March); Adventure Travel (April), Triathlon (May), Paddling and Climbing (July), Mountain Biking (June), Women's Sports (September). No articles on football, baseball, basketball or other sports covered in depth by newspapers. **Buys 24 mss/year.** Query with published clips. Length: 2,500 words maximum. **Pays $150 minimum.** Sometimes pays expenses of writers on assignment.

Reprints: Send photocopy and information about when and where the material previously appeared. Pays 20-25% of amount paid for original article.

Photos: State availability with submission. Reviews transparencies, prints. Buys one-time rights. Captions, identification of subjects required.

Columns/Departments: Starting Lines (short newsy items); Running, Cycling, Fitness, Nutrition, Sports Medicine, Off the Beaten Path (sports we don't usually cover). **Buys 20 mss/year.** Query. **Pays $25-300.**

Tips: "Have a Colorado angle to the story, a catchy cover letter, good clips and demonstrate that you've read and understand our magazine and its readers."

$ SILENT SPORTS, Waupaca Publishing Co., P.O. Box 152, Waupaca WI 54981-9990. (715)258-5546. Fax: (715)258-8162. E-mail: info@silentsports.net. Website: www.silentsports.net. **Contact:** Greg Marr, editor. **75% freelance written.** Monthly magazine covering running, cycling, cross-country skiing, canoeing, kayaking, snowshoeing, in-line skating, camping, backpacking and hiking aimed at people in Wisconsin, Minnesota, northern Illinois and portions of Michigan and Iowa. "Not a coffee table magazine. Our readers are participants from rank amateur weekend athletes to highly competitive racers." Estab. 1984. Circ. 10,000. Pays on publication. Publishes ms an average of 3 months after acceptance. Byline given. Offers 20% kill fee. Buys one-time rights. Submit seasonal material 4 months in advance. Accepts queries by mail, e-mail, fax. Responds in 3 months to queries. Sample copy and writer's guidelines for 10×13 SAE with 7 first-class stamps.
- The editor needs local angles on in-line skating, recreation bicycling and snowshoeing.

Nonfiction: All stories/articles must focus on the Upper Midwest. General interest, how-to, interview/profile, opinion, technical, travel. **Buys 25 mss/year.** Query. Length: 2,500 words maximum. **Pays $15-100.** Sometimes pays expenses of writers on assignment.

Reprints: Send typed ms with rights for sale noted and information about when and where the material previously appeared. Pays 50% of amount paid for an original article.

Photos: State availability with submission. Reviews transparencies. Buys one-time rights. Pays $5-15 for b&w story photos; $50-100 for color covers.

Tips: "Where-to-go and personality profiles are areas most open to freelancers. Writers should keep in mind that this is a regional, Midwest-based publication. We want only stories/articles with a focus on our region."

$ $ $ SPIKE, The Magazine from Finish Line, Emmis Publishing, One Emmis Plaza, 40 Monument Circle, Suite 100, Indianapolis IN 46204. E-mail: jbt@indymonthly.emmis.com. **Contact:** John Thomas, special projects editor. **100% freelance written.** Quarterly magazine. "*Spike* goes to customers of Finish Line, a chain of more than 300 athletic shoe and apparel stores. Most readers are young males with an interest in sports and pop culture. Writing should be bright, hip and tight." Estab. 1997. Circ. 1 million. Pays on publication. Publishes ms an average of 3 months after acceptance. Byline given. Buys first North American serial, one-time rights. Editorial lead time 4 months. Submit seasonal material 6 months in advance. Accepts queries by mail, e-mail. Sample copy for 9×12 SAE and 5 first-class stamps.

Nonfiction: General interest, how-to (fitness), interview/profile, new product. No first-person essays. No unsolicited mss. **Buys 12-15 mss/year.** Query with published clips. Length: 750-2,000 words. **Pays $250-1,000.** Sometimes pays expenses of writers on assignment.

Columns/Departments: Fitness (for ages 15-20); Music (hot new groups); High Tech (games, web pages, etc. that are sports related), all 500-750 words. **Buys 12 mss/year.** Query with published clips. **Pays $50-500.**
Tips: "Demonstrated access to and ability to work with top athletes and pop-culture figures is a plus."

$ SPORTS ETC, The Northwest's Outdoor Magazine, Sports Etc, 11715 Greenwood Ave. N, Seattle WA 98133. (206)418-0747. Fax: (206)418-0746. E-mail: staff@sportsetc.com. Website: www.sportsetc.com. **Contact:** Carolyn Price, editor. **80% freelance written.** Monthly magazine covering outdoor recreation in the Pacific Northwest. "Writers must have a solid knowledge of the sport they are writing about. They must be doers." Estab. 1988. Circ. 40,000. Pays on publication. Publishes ms an average of 3 months after acceptance. Byline given. Buys first rights. Editorial lead time 2 months. Submit seasonal material 4 months in advance. Accepts queries by mail, e-mail, fax. Accepts simultaneous submissions. Sample copy and writer's guidelines for $3.
Nonfiction: Interview/profile, new product, travel. Query with published clips. Length: 750-1,500 words. **Pays $10-50.** Sometimes pays expenses of writers on assignment.
Photos: Send photos with submission. Reviews negatives, transparencies. Buys all rights. Captions, identification of subjects, model releases required.
Columns/Departments: Your Health (health and wellness), 750 words. **Buys 10-12 mss/year.** Query with published clips. **Pays $40-50.**
Tips: "*Sports Etc* is written for the serious Pacific Northwest outdoor recreationalist. The magazine's look, style and editorial content actively engage the reader, delivering insightful perspectives on the sports it has come to be known for—alpine skiing, bicycling, hiking, in-line skating, kayaking, marathons, mountain climbing, Nordic skiing, running and snowboarding. *Sports Etc* magazine wants vivid writing, telling images and original perspectives to produce its smart, entertaining monthly."

$ $ $ $ SPORTS ILLUSTRATED, Time Inc. Magazine Co., Sports Illustrated Building, 135 W. 50th St., New York NY 10020. (212)522-1212. **Contact:** Myra Gelband, senior editor. Weekly magazine. "*Sports Illustrated* reports and interprets the world of sport, recreation and active leisure. It previews, analyzes and comments upon major games and events, as well as those noteworthy for character and spirit alone. It features individuals connected to sport and evaluates trends concerning the part sport plays in contemporary life. In addition, the magazine has articles on such subjects as fashion, physical fitness and conservation. Special departments deal with sports equipment, books and statistics." Estab. 1954. Circ. 3,339,000. Accepts queries by mail.

Golf

$ $ ARIZONA, THE STATE OF GOLF, TPG Sports Inc., 1710 Douglas Dr. N., Golden Valley MN 55422. (763)595-0808. Fax: (763)595-0016. E-mail: joe@tpgsports.com or rchrist@azgolf.org. Website: www.tpgsports.com or www.azgolf.org. **Contact:** Joseph Oberle, publications manager. **50% freelance written.** Bimonthly magazine covering golf in Arizona, the official publication of the Arizona Golf Association. Estab. 1999. Circ. 45,000. **Pays on acceptance.** Byline given. Buys all rights. Editorial lead time 6 months. Submit seasonal material 3 months in advance. Accepts queries by mail. Accepts simultaneous submissions. Sample copy and writer's guidelines free.
Nonfiction: Book excerpts, essays, historical/nostalgic, how-to (golf), humor, inspirational, interview/profile, new product, opinion, personal experience, photo feature. **Buys 20-30 mss/year.** Query with or without published clips. Length: 500-2,000 words. **Pays $50-500.** Sometimes pays expenses of writers on assignment.
Reprints: Accepts previously published submissions.
Photos: State availability with submission. Reviews contact sheets. Rights purchased varies. Negotiates payment individually. Captions, identification of subjects required.
Columns/Departments: Short Strokes (golf news and notes), Improving Your Game (golf tips), Out of Bounds (guest editorial—800 words). Query.

$ $ CHICAGO DISTRICT GOLFER, TPG Sports Inc., 1710 Douglas Dr. N., Golden Valley MN 55422. (763)595-0808. Fax: (763)595-0016. E-mail: joe@tpgsports.com. Website: www.tpgsports.com or www.cdga.org. **Contact:** Joseph Oberle, publications manager. **9% freelance written.** Bimonthly magazine covering golf in Illinois, the official publication of the Chicago District Golf Association and Golf Association of Illinois. Estab. 1922. Circ. 71,000. Pays on acceptance or publication. Byline given. Buys all rights. Editorial lead time 2 months. Submit seasonal material 3 months in advance. Accepts queries by mail, e-mail. Accepts simultaneous submissions. Sample copy and writer's guidelines free.
Nonfiction: Book excerpts, general interest, historical/nostalgic, how-to (golf), humor, interview/profile, new product, opinion, personal experience, photo feature, technical, travel. **Buys 25-35 mss/year.** Query with or without published clips. Length: 500-5,000 words. **Pays $50-500.** Sometimes pays expenses of writers on assignment.
Reprints: Accepts previously published submissions.
Photos: State availability with submission. Reviews contact sheets. Negotiates payment individually. Captions, identification of subjects required.
Columns/Departments: CDGA/GAI Update (news and notes), Club Profile, The Rules of Golf (golf rules explanations and discussions); and Turfgrass Update (course maintenance issues). Query.

N **$ $ $** GOLF & TRAVEL, Turnstile Publishing Co., 49 W. 45th St., 6th Floor, New York NY 10036. (212)536-9812. Fax: (212)536-9888. E-mail: rjberler@aol.com. Website: www.travelgolf.com. **Contact:** Ron Berler, managing editor. **50% freelance written.** Magazine published 7 times/year. *Golf & Travel* wants "solid travel writing with a critical eye. No fluff. No common tourist stops unless you've got a unique angle. Destination stories with golf as one of the elements, but not the only element." Estab. 1997. Circ. 225,000. **Pays on acceptance.** Publishes ms an average of 3 months after acceptance. Byline given. Buys first, all rights. Editorial lead time 2 months. Submit seasonal material 18 months in advance. Accepts queries by mail. Responds only if interested to queries. Sample copy for $3.95 plus postage; (800)678-9717. Writer's guidelines for #10 SASE.

Nonfiction: Humor, interview/profile, travel. "No articles about golf courses only; no articles on common golf destinations; no articles written in 'fluff' language." **Buys 30 mss/year.** Query with published clips. Responds only if interested. Length: 100-3,500 words. **Pays $50-5,000.** Pays expenses of writers on assignment.

Columns/Departments: Starter (golf packages, golf events, golf destination news), 100-150 words; Road & Driver, (great road trips with golf along the way) 1,000 words; Main Course (golf/golf destinations and food/wine), 250 words; Fairway Living (destination or issue-related stories about places to live that offer good golf environment), 1,300-1,750 words; Suite Spot (lesser known golf resort), 250 words. Query with published clips. **Pays $50-2,500.**

Fiction: Novel excerpts.

Tips: "Must be established travel writer with great destination stories in their clips file. Clips must demonstrate unusual angles—off the beaten path. Knowledge of golf extremely helpful. Straight golf writers are not encouraged to query. We do not cover golf instruction, golf equipment or golf teaching aids. We are interested in writers who can combine the two subjects of golf and travel with a third element that is not easily named but has to do with a sophisticated tone, an intelligent attitude, a sensitive eye and, where appropriate, a sense of humor or irony. Magazines whose editorial voice we like include *Town & Country, Men's Journal, Departures, Saveur* and *Smart Money.*"

$ $ $ GOLF CANADA, Official Magazine of the Royal Canadian Golf Association, RCGA/Relevant Communications, 1333 Dorval Dr., Oakville, Ontario L6J 4Z3, Canada. (905)849-9700. Fax: (905)845-7040. E-mail: golfcanada@rcga.org. Website: www.rcga.org. Managing Editor: Chad Schella. **Contact:** John Tenpenny, editor. **80% freelance written.** Magazine published 4 times/year covering Canadian golf. "*Golf Canada* is the official magazine of the Royal Canadian Golf Association, published to entertain and enlighten members about RCGA-related activities and to generally support and promote amateur golf in Canada." Estab. 1994. Circ. 135,000. **Pays on acceptance.** Byline given. Offers 100% kill fee. Buys first translation, electronic rights. Editorial lead time 3 months. Submit seasonal material 6 months in advance. Accepts queries by mail, e-mail, fax, phone. Sample copy free.

Nonfiction: Historical/nostalgic, interview/profile, new product, opinion, photo feature, travel. No professional golf-related articles. **Buys 42 mss/year.** Query with published clips. Length: 750-3,000 words. **Pays 60¢/word including electronic rights.** Sometimes pays expenses of writers on assignment.

Photos: State availability with submission. Reviews contact sheets, negatives, transparencies, prints. Buys all rights. Negotiates payment individually. Captions required.

Columns/Departments: Guest Column (focus on issues surrounding the Canadian golf community), 700 words. Query. **Pays 60¢/word including electronic rights.**

Tips: "Keep story ideas focused on Canadian competitive golf."

$ $ $ $ GOLF DIGEST WOMAN, The New York Times Company Magazine Group, Inc., 1120 Avenue of the Americas, New York NY 10036. (212)789-3000. Fax: (212)789-3112. E-mail: gdwoman@golfdigest.com. Website: www.gdwoman.com. Managing Editor: John Stoltenberg. **Contact:** Rona Cherry, editor-in-chief. **70% freelance written.** Quarterly magazine covering golf lifestyle. "Our magazine celebrates the game, sense of style, way of life enjoyed by sophisticated boomer women with a passion for golf." Circ. 250,000. **Pays on acceptance.** Byline given. Offers 20% kill fee. Buys all rights. Accepts queries by mail, e-mail, fax. Responds in 3 weeks to queries; 1 month to mss.

Nonfiction: Book excerpts, essays, general interest, historical/nostalgic, how-to (golf related), humor, inspirational, interview/profile, new product, personal experience, photo feature, travel. **Buys 75 mss/year.** Query. Length: 250-2,500 words. **Pays $1/word.** Sometimes pays expenses of writers on assignment.

Photos: State availability with submission. Buys one-time rights. Negotiates payment individually. Model releases required.

Columns/Departments: Playing Through (first person/inspirational piece related to golf experiences); Body/Health (staying healthy—mid life active woman health issues), both 600 words; and At the Turn (humor/games). **Pays $1-2/word.**

$ GOLF NEWS MAGAZINE, Premier Golf Magazine Since 1984, Golf News Magazine, 73-280 El Paseo, Suite 6, Palm Desert CA 92260. (760)836-3700. Fax: (760)836-3703. E-mail: golfnews@aol.com. Website: www.golfnewsmag.com. **Contact:** Dan Poppers, editor/publisher. **70% freelance written.** Monthly magazine covering golf. "Our publication specializes in the creative treatment of the sport of golf, offering a variety of themes and slants as related to golf. If it's good writing and relates to golf, we're interested." Estab. 1984. Circ. 18,000. **Pays on acceptance.** Publishes ms an average of 2 months after acceptance. Byline given. Offers negotiable kill fee. Buys first rights, makes work-for-hire assignments. Editorial lead time 2 months. Submit seasonal material 2 months in advance. Accepts queries by mail, e-mail, fax. Accepts simultaneous submissions. Responds in 1 month to queries; 2 months to mss. Sample copy for $2 and 9×12 SAE with 4 first-class stamps.

Nonfiction: "We will consider any topic related to golf that is written well with high standards." Book excerpts, essays, exposé, general interest, historical/nostalgic, how-to, humor, inspirational, interview/profile, opinion, personal experience, photo feature, technical, travel, real estate. **Buys 20 mss/year.** Query with published clips. **Pays $25-125.**
Photos: State availability with submission. Buys one-time rights. Negotiates payment individually. Identification of subjects required.
Columns/Departments: Submit ideas. **Buys 10 mss/year.** Query with published clips. **Pays $25-100.**
■ The online magazine carries original content not found in the print edition.
Tips: "Solid, creative, good, professional writing. Stay away from clichés and the hackneyed. Only good writers need apply. We are a national award-winning magazine looking for the most creative writers we can find."

$ $ $ GOLF TIPS, The Game's Most In-Depth Instruction & Equipment Magazine, Werner Publishing Corp., 12121 Wilshire Blvd., Suite 1200, Los Angeles CA 90025. (310)820-1500. Fax: (310)826-5008. E-mail: editors@ golftipsmag.com. Website: www.golftipsmag.com. Senior Editor: Mike Chwasky. Editor at Large: Tom Ferrell. **Contact:** David DeNunzio, editor. **95% freelance written.** Magazine published 9 times/year covering golf instruction and equipment. "We provide mostly concise, very clear golf instruction pieces for the serious golfer." Estab. 1986. Pays on publication. Publishes ms an average of 2 months after acceptance. Byline given. Offers 33% kill fee. Buys first, second serial (reprint) rights. Editorial lead time 3 months. Submit seasonal material 4 months in advance. Responds in 1 month to queries. Sample copy and writer's guidelines free.
Nonfiction: Book excerpts, how-to, interview/profile, new product, photo feature, technical, travel, all golf related. "Generally golf essays rarely make it." **Buys 125 mss/year.** Send complete ms. Length: 250-2,000 words. **Pays $300-1,000 for assigned articles; $300-800 for unsolicited articles.** Occassionally negotiates other forms of payment. Sometimes pays expenses of writers on assignment.
Photos: State availability with submission. Reviews 2×2 transparencies. Buys all rights. Negotiates payment individually. Captions, identification of subjects required.
Columns/Departments: Stroke Saver (very clear, concise instruction), 350 words; Lesson Library (book excerpts—usually in a series), 1,000 words; Travel Tips (formatted golf travel), 2,500 words. **Buys 40 mss/year.** Query with or without published clips or send complete ms. **Pays $300-850.**
■ The online magazine carries original content not found in the print edition. Contact: Tom Ferrell, online editor.
Tips: "Contact a respected PGA Professional and find out if they're interested in being published. A good writer can turn an interview into a decent instruction piece."

$ $ ▧ GOLF TRAVELER, Official Publication of Golf Card International, Affinity Group, Inc., 2575 Vista del Mar, Ventura CA 93001. Fax: (805)667-4217. Website: www.golfcard.com. **Contact:** Valerie Law, editorial director. **50% freelance written.** Bimonthly magazine "is the membership magazine for the Golf Card, an organization that offers its members reduced or waived greens fees at 3,500 affiliated golf courses in North America." Estab. 1976. Circ. 100,000. **Pays on acceptance.** Byline given. Offers 33% kill fee. Buys first North American serial, electronic rights. Editorial lead time 3 months. Submit seasonal material 5 months in advance. Accepts simultaneous submissions. Responds in 1 month to queries. Sample copy for $2.50 plus 9×12 SASE.
Nonfiction: Book excerpts, essays, how-to, interview/profile, new product, personal experience, photo feature, technical. No poetry or cartoons. **Buys 12 mss/year.** Query with published clips or send complete ms. Length: 500-2,500 words. **Pays $75-500.**
Reprints: Accepts previously published submissions.
Photos: Send photos with submission. Reviews transparencies. Buys one-time rights. Negotiates payment individually. Identification of subjects, model releases required.

$ $ THE GOLFER, Heather & Pine Publishing, 21 E. 40th St., New York NY 10016. (212)696-2484. Fax: (212)696-1678. E-mail: thegolfer@walrus.com. Editor: H.K. Pickens. **Contact:** Paul Rogers, senior editor. **40% freelance written.** Bimonthly magazine covering golf. "A sophisticated, controversational tone for a lifestyle-oriented magazine." Estab. 1994. Circ. 253,000. Pays on publication. Publishes ms an average of 2 months after acceptance. Byline given. Offers negotiable kill fee. Buys all rights. Editorial lead time 2 months. Submit seasonal material 4 months in advance. Accepts queries by mail, e-mail, fax. Accepts simultaneous submissions. Sample copy free.
Nonfiction: Book excerpts, essays, general interest, historical/nostalgic, how-to, humor, inspirational, interview/profile, new product, opinion, personal experience, photo feature, technical, travel. Send complete ms. Length: 300-2,000 words. **Pays $150-600.**
Reprints: Accepts previously published submissions.
Photos: Send photos with submission. Reviews any size transparencies. Buys one-time rights.

Ⓝ $ $ $ $ LUXURY GOLF HOMES & RESORTS, Luxury Media Corp., One Acton Place, Acton MA 01720. (978)795-3000. Fax: (978)795-3266. Website: www.theluxurysource.com. **Contact:** James Y. Bartlett, editor. **80% freelance written.** Bimonthly lifestyle magazine for avid, upscale golfers. Estab. 1999. Circ. 100,000. Pays on publication. Publishes ms an average of 3 months after acceptance. Byline given. Offers 50% kill fee. Buys first North American serial, electronic rights. Editorial lead time 3 months. Submit seasonal material 3 months in advance. Accepts queries by mail, e-mail. Accepts simultaneous submissions. Responds in 3 weeks to queries. Sample copy and writer's guidelines free.

Nonfiction: General interest, historical/nostalgic, interview/profile, travel. **Buys 20-25 mss/year.** Query. Length: 200-2,500 words. **Pays $100-2,000.** Sometimes pays expenses of writers on assignment.

Photos: State availability with submission. Reviews transparencies. Buys one-time rights. Negotiates payment individually.

Tips: "Writers must know the game of golf. This is a magazine for knowledgeable, sophisticated golfers who live and appreciate the upscale golf lifestyle."

$ $ MICHIGAN LINKS, TPG Sports Inc., 1710 Douglas Dr. N., Golden Valley MN 55422. (763)595-0808. Fax: (763)595-0016. E-mail: joe@tpgsports.com or tbranch@gam.org. Website: www.tpgsports.com or www.gam.org. Managing Editor: Tonia Branch. **Contact:** Joseph Oberle, publications manager. **80% freelance written.** Bimonthly magazine covering golf in Michigan, the official publication of the Golf Association of Michigan. Estab. 1997. Circ. 40,000. Pays on acceptance or publication. Byline sometimes given. Buys all rights. Editorial lead time 6 months. Submit seasonal material 3 months in advance. Accepts queries by mail, e-mail. Accepts simultaneous submissions. Sample copy and writer's guidelines free.

Nonfiction: Book excerpts, essays, historical/nostalgic, how-to (golf), humor, inspirational, interview/profile, new product, opinion, personal experience, photo feature, technical (golf equipment). **Buys 30-40 mss/year.** Query with or without published clips or send complete ms. Length: 500-5,000 words. **Pays $50-500.** Sometimes pays expenses of writers on assignment.

Reprints: Accepts previously published submissions on a case-by-case basis.

Photos: State availability with submission. Reviews contact sheets. Rights purchased varies. Negotiates payment individually. Captions, identification of subjects required.

Columns/Departments: Forecaddie (news and notes); Playing by the Rules (golf rules explanations and discussion); Turf Talk (course maintenance issues). Query.

$ $ MINNESOTA GOLFER, 6550 York Ave. S, Suite 211, Edina MN 55435. (952)927-4643. Fax: (952)927-9642. E-mail: editor@mngolf.org. Website: www.mngolf.org. **Contact:** W.P. Ryan, editor. **75% freelance written.** Bimonthly magazine covering golf in Minnesota, the official publication of the Minnesota Golf Association. Estab. 1975. Circ. 72,500. Pays on acceptance or publication. Byline given. Buys all rights. Editorial lead time 6 months. Submit seasonal material 3 months in advance. Accepts queries by mail, fax. Accepts simultaneous submissions.

Nonfiction: Book excerpts, essays, historical/nostalgic, how-to (golf), humor, inspirational, interview/profile, new product, opinion, personal experience, photo feature. **Buys 18-20 mss/year.** Query with published clips. Length: 500-2,500 words. **Pays $50-500.** Sometimes pays expenses of writers on assignment.

Photos: State availability with submission. Reviews contact sheets, transparencies. Rights purchased varies. Negotiates payment individually. Captions, identification of subjects required.

Columns/Departments: Punch shots (golf news and notes). Magazine features rotating departments on the following: Women's Page; Golf Business News; Rules, etiquette and news for beginning golfers; New Equipment; Travel; Opinion; Golf players and personalities with links to Minnesota. Query.

N $ $ PACIFIC GOLF, Canada Wide Magazines & Communications Ltd., 4180 Lougheed Hwy., 4th Floor, Burnaby, British Columbia V5C 6A7, Canada. (604)299-7311. Fax: (604)299-9188. E-mail: acollette@canadawide.com. **Contact:** Ann Collette, editor. **80% freelance written.** Quarterly magazine. "Pacific Golf appeals to B.C.'s golfers and reflects the west coast golf experience. We concentrate on the new, the influential, Canadian golfers and subject matter based in British Columbia." Circ. 20,000. Pays on publication. Publishes ms an average of 2 months after acceptance. Byline given. Offers variable kill fee. Buys first Canadian rights. Editorial lead time 4 months. Submit seasonal material 4 months in advance. Responds in 6 weeks to mss.

Nonfiction: Query with published clips. Length: 500-1,800 words. **Pays 40-50¢/word.** Sometimes pays expenses of writers on assignment.

Photos: State availability with submission.

$ $ $ $ SCORE GOLF MAGAZINE, Canadian Controlled Media Communications, 5397 Eglinton Ave. W, Toronto, Ontario M9C 5K6, Canada. (416)928-2909. Fax: (416)928-1357. E-mail: weeksy@idirect.com. Website: www.scoregolf.com. Publisher: (Mr.) Kim Locke. **Contact:** Robert Weeks, managing editor. **70% freelance written.** Works with a small number of new/unpublished writers each year. Magazine published 6 times/year covering golf. "*Score Golf Magazine* provides seasonal coverage of the Canadian golf scene, professional, amateur, senior and junior golf for men and women golfers in Canada, the US and Europe through profiles, history, travel, editorial comment and instruction." Estab. 1980. Circ. 150,000 audited. **Pays on acceptance.** Byline given. Offers negotiable kill fee. Buys second serial (reprint), all rights. Submit seasonal material 8 months in advance. Responds in 8 months to queries. Sample copy for $3.50 and 9×12 SAE with IRCs. Writer's guidelines for #10 SASE.

Nonfiction: Book excerpts (golf), historical/nostalgic (golf and golf characters), interview/profile (prominent golf professionals), photo feature (golf), travel (golf destinations only). No personal experience, technical, opinion or general interest material. Most articles are by assignment only. **Buys 25-30 mss/year.** Query with published clips. Length: 700-3,500 words. **Pays $200-1,500.**

Photos: Send photos with query or ms. Buys all rights. Pays $50-100 for 35mm transparencies (postives) or $30 for 8×10 or 5×7 b&w prints. Captions, identification of subjects, model releases required.

Columns/Departments: Profile (historical or current golf personalities or characters); Great Moments ("Great Moments in Canadian Golf"—description of great single moments, usually game triumphs); New Equipment (Canadian availability only); Travel (golf destinations, including "hard" information such as greens fees, hotel accommodations, etc.); Instruction (by special assignment only; usually from teaching golf professionals); The Mental Game (psychology of the game, by special assignment only); History (golf equipment collections and collectors, developments of the game, legendary figures and events), all 700-1,700 words. **Buys 17-20 mss/year.** Query with published clips or send complete ms. **Pays $140-400.**

Tips: "Only writers with an extensive knowledge of golf and familiarity with the Canadian golf scene should query or submit in-depth work to *Score Golf*. Many of our features are written by professional people who play the game for a living or work in the industry. All areas mentioned under Columns/Departments are open to freelancers. Most of our *major* features are done on assignment only."

$ $ TEXAS GOLFER MAGAZINE, Golfer Magazines, Inc., 10301 Northwest Freeway, Suite 418, Houston TX 77092. (713)680-1680. Fax: (713)680-0138. Editor: Bob Gray. **Contact:** David Widener, managing editor. **10% freelance written.** Monthly tabloid covering golf in Texas. Estab. 1984. Circ. 50,000. Pays on publication. Publishes ms an average of 2 months after acceptance. Byline given. Buys first, one-time, second serial (reprint) rights. Editorial lead time 2 months. Submit seasonal material 3 months in advance. Responds in 2 weeks to queries; 1 month to mss. Sample copy free. Prefers direct phone discussion for writer's guidelines.
- *Texas Golfer Magazine* was created by the merger of two publications: *Gulf Coast Golfer* and *North Texas Golfer*.
Nonfiction: Book excerpts, humor, personal experience, all golf-related. No stories about golf outside of Texas. **Buys 20 mss/year.** Query. **Pays $50-425.**
Photos: State availability with submission. Reviews contact sheets, prints. Buys one-time rights. No additional payment for photos accepted with ms, but pays $125 for cover photo. Captions, identification of subjects required.
Tips: "Most of our purchases are in how-to area, so writers must know golf quite well and play the game."

$ $ VIRGINIA GOLFER, TPG Sports Inc., 1710 Douglas Dr. N., Golden Valley MN 55422. (763)595-0808. Fax: (763)595-0016. E-mail: joe@tpgsports.com. Editor: Harold Pearson. **Contact:** Joseph Oberle, publications manager. **65% freelance written.** Bimonthly magazine covering golf in Virginia, the official publication of the Virginia Golf Association. Estab. 1983. Circ. 33,000. Pays on publication. Byline given. Buys all rights. Editorial lead time 6 months. Submit seasonal material 3 months in advance. Accepts queries by mail, e-mail. Accepts simultaneous submissions. Sample copy and writer's guidelines free.
Nonfiction: Book excerpts, essays, historical/nostalgic, how-to (golf), humor, inspirational, interview/profile, personal experience, photo feature, technical (golf equipment), where to play, golf business. **Buys 30-40 mss/year.** Query with or without published clips or send complete ms. Length: 500-2,500 words. **Pays $50-500.** Sometimes pays expenses of writers on assignment.
Reprints: Accepts previously published submissions.
Photos: State availability with submission. Reviews contact sheets. Rights purchased varies. Negotiates payment individually. Captions, identification of subjects required.
Columns/Departments: Chip ins & Three Putts (news notes), Rules Corner (golf rules explanations and discussion), Pro Tips, Golf Travel (where to play), Golf Business (what's happening?). Query.

Guns

N $ $ THE ACCURATE RIFLE, Precision Shooting Inc., 222 McKee St., Manchester CT 06040-4800. (860)645-8776. Fax: (860)643-8215. Website: www.theaccuraterifle.com. **Contact:** Dave Brennan, editor. **30-35% freelance written.** Monthly magazine covering "the specialized field of 'extreme rifle accuracy' excluding rifle competition disciplines." Estab. 2000. Circ. 8,000. Pays on publication. Publishes ms an average of 3 months after acceptance. Byline given. Buys first North American serial rights. Editorial lead time 2 months. Submit seasonal material 3 months in advance. Accepts queries by mail, fax. Responds in 2 weeks to queries; 1 month to mss. Sample copy free.
Nonfiction: General interest, historical/nostalgic, how-to, humor, interview/profile, personal experience. "Nothing common to newsstand firearms publications. This has a very sophisticated and knowledgable readership." **Buys 36 mss/year.** Query. Length: 1,800-3,000 words. **Pays $200-500.**
Photos: Send photos with submission. Reviews 4×6 prints. Buys one-time rights. Offers no additional payment for photos accepted with ms. Captions required.
Tips: "Call the editor first and tell him what topic you propose to write about. Could save time and effort."

$ $ GUN DIGEST, DBI Books, Inc., Division of Krause Publications, 700 E. State St., Iola WI 54990. (888)457-2873. Fax: (715)445-4087. **Contact:** Ken Ramage, editor-in-chief. **50% freelance written.** Prefers to work with published/established writers but works with a small number of new/unpublished writers each year. Annual journal covering guns and shooting. Estab. 1944. **Pays on acceptance.** Publishes ms an average of 20 months after acceptance. Byline given. Buys all rights. Responds as time allows.
Nonfiction: Buys 25 mss/year. Query. Length: 500-5,000 words. **Pays $100-600 for text/art package.**

Photos: State availability with submission. Reviews 8×10 b&w prints. Payment for photos included in payment for ms. Captions required.

Tips: Award of $1,000 to author of best article (juried) in each issue.

$ $ GUNS MAGAZINE, Suite 200, 591 Camino de la Reina, San Diego CA 92108. (619)297-5352. Fax: (619)297-5353. **Contact:** Scott Ferrell, editor. **25% freelance written.** Monthly magazine for firearms enthusiasts covering firearms, reviews, tactics and related products. Circ. 200,000. Pays on publication. Publishes ms an average of 6 months after acceptance. Offers $50 kill fee. Buys all world rights. Responds in 1 month to queries. Writer's guidelines for #10 SASE.

Nonfiction: Test reports on new firearms; round-up articles on firearms types; guns for specific purposes (hunting, target shooting, self-defense); custom gunmakers; and history of modern guns. **Buys 10 mss/year.** Query. Length: 1,000-2,500 words. **Pays $300-500.**

Photos: Major emphasis on quality photography. Additional payment of $50-200 for color, 2¼×2¼ and 4×5 transparencies preferred.

$ $ MUZZLE BLASTS, National Muzzle Loading Rifle Association, P.O. Box 67, Friendship IN 47021. (812)667-5131. Fax: (812)667-5137. E-mail: nmlra@nmlra.org. Website: www.nmlra.org. Editor: Eric A. Bye. **Contact:** Terri Trowbridge, director of publications. **65% freelance written.** Monthly magazine. "Articles must relate to muzzleloading or the muzzleloading era of American history." Estab. 1939. Circ. 25,000. Pays on publication. Publishes ms an average of 6 months after acceptance. Byline given. Offers $50 kill fee. Buys first North American serial, one-time, second serial (reprint) rights. Editorial lead time 4 months. Submit seasonal material 6 months in advance. Responds in 1 month to mss. Sample copy and writer's guidelines free.

Nonfiction: Book excerpts, general interest, historical/nostalgic, how-to, humor, interview/profile, new product, personal experience, photo feature, technical, travel. "No subjects that do not pertain to muzzleloading." **Buys 80 mss/year.** Query. Length: 2,500 words. **Pays $150 minimum for assigned articles; $50 minimum for unsolicited articles.**

Photos: Send photos with submission. Reviews 5×7 prints. Buys one-time rights. Negotiates payment individually. Captions, model releases required.

Columns/Departments: Buys 96 mss/year. Query. **Pays $50-200.**

Fiction: Must pertain to muzzleloading. Adventure, historical, humorous. **Buys 6 mss/year.** Query. Length: 2,500 words. **Pays $50-300.**

Fillers: Facts. **Pays $50.**

The online magazine carries original content not found in the print edition.

N $ $ PRECISION SHOOTING, Precision Shooting Inc., 222 McKee St., Manchester CT 06040-4800. (860)645-8776. Fax: (860)643-8215. Website: www.precisionshooting.com. **Contact:** Dave Brennan, editor. **30-35% freelance written.** Monthly magazine covering "the specialized field of 'extreme rifle accuracy' including rifle competition disciplines." Estab. 1956. Circ. 17,500. Pays on publication. Publishes ms an average of 3 months after acceptance. Byline given. Buys first North American serial rights. Editorial lead time 2 months. Submit seasonal material 3 months in advance. Accepts queries by mail, fax. Responds in 2 weeks to queries; 1 month to mss. Sample copy free.

Nonfiction: General interest, historical/nostalgic, how-to, humor, interview/profile, personal experience. "Nothing common to newsstand firearms publications. This has a very sophisticated and knowledgeable readership." **Buys 36 mss/year.** Query. Length: 1,800-3,000 words. **Pays $200-500.**

Photos: Send photos with submission. Reviews 4×6 prints. Buys one-time rights. Offers no additional payment for photos accepted with ms. Captions required.

Tips: "Call the editor first and tell him what topic you propose to write about. Could save time and effort."

N $ $ SHOTGUN NEWS, Primedia, Box 1790, Peoria IL 61656. (309)679-5408. Fax: (309)679-5476. E-mail: sgnews@primediasi.com. Website: www.shotgunnews.com. **Contact:** Robert W. Hunnicutt, general manager/editor. **95% freelance written.** Tabloid published every 10 days covering firearms, accessories, ammunition and militaria. "The nation's oldest and largest gun sales publication. Provides up-to-date market information for gun trade and consumers." Estab. 1946. Circ. 100,000. **Pays on acceptance.** Publishes ms an average of 3 months after acceptance. Byline given. Buys first North American serial rights. Editorial lead time 1 month. Submit seasonal material 3 months in advance. Responds in 1 month to queries. Sample copy free.

Nonfiction: Historical/nostalgic, how-to, technical. No political pieces, fiction or poetry. **Buys 50 mss/year.** Query. Length: 1,000-3,000 words. **Pays $200-500 for assigned articles.** Sometimes pays expenses of writers on assignment.

Photos: Send photos with submission. Reviews prints. Buys one-time rights. Offers no additional payment for photos accepted with ms. Captions required.

Hiking/Backpacking

$ $ $ BACKPACKER, Rodale, 33 E. Minor St., Emmaus PA 18098-0099. (610)967-8296. Fax: (610)967-8181. E-mail: bpeditor@backpacker.com. Website: www.backpacker.com. **Contact:** Jon Dorn, managing editor. **50%**

freelance written. Magazine published 9 times/year covering wilderness travel for backpackers. Estab. 1973. Circ. 280,000. **Pays on acceptance.** Byline given. Buys one-time, all rights. Accepts queries by mail, e-mail, fax. Responds in 1 month to queries. Writer's guidelines for #10 SASE or online.

Nonfiction: "What we want are features that let us and the readers 'feel' the place, and experience your wonderment, excitement, disappointment or other emotions encountered 'out there.' If we feel like we've been there after reading your story, you've succeeded." Essays, exposé, historical/nostalgic, how-to (expedition planner), humor, inspirational, interview/profile, new product, opinion, personal experience, technical, travel. No step-by-step accounts of what you did on your summer vacation—stories that chronicle every rest stop and gulp of water. Query with published clips. Length: 750-2,000 words. **Pays $400-2,000.**

Photos: State availability with submission. Buys one-time rights. Pay varies.

Columns/Departments: Signpost, "News From All Over" (adventure, environment, wildlife, trails, techniques, organizations, special interests—well-written, entertaining, short, newsy item), 50-500 words; Body Language (in-the-field health column), 750-1,200 words; Moveable Feast (food-related aspects of wilderness: nutrition, cooking techniques, recipes, products and gear), 500-750 words; Weekend Wilderness (brief but detailed guides to wilderness areas, providing thorough trip-planning information, only enough anecdote to give a hint, then the where/when/hows), 500-750 words; Know How (ranging from beginner to expert focus, written by people with solid expertise, details ways to improve performance, how-to-do-it instructions, information on equipment manufacturers and places readers can go), 300-1,000 words; and Backcountry (personal perspectives, quirky and idiosyncratic, humorous critiques, manifestos and misadventures, interesting angle, lesson, revelation or moral), 750-1,200 words. **Buys 50-75 mss/year.** Query with published clips. No phone calls regarding story ideas. Written or e-mail queries only. **Pays $200-1,000.**

◼ The online magazine carries original content not found in the print edition.

Tips: "Our best advice is to read the publication—most freelancers don't know the magazine at all. The best way to break in is with an article for the Backcountry, Weekend Wilderness or Signpost Department."

$ $ $ $▨ OUTSIDE, Mariah Media Inc., Outside Plaza, 400 Market St., Santa Fe NM 87501. (505)989-7100. Website: www.outsidemag.com. Editor: Hal Espen. **Contact:** Assistant to the Editor. **90% freelance written.** Monthly magazine. "*Outside* is a monthly national magazine for active, educated, upscale adults who love the outdoors and are concerned about its preservation." Estab. 1977. Circ. 550,000. Pays after acceptance. Publishes ms an average of 3 months after acceptance. Byline given. Offers 25% kill fee. Buys first North American serial rights. Submit seasonal material 5 months in advance. Writer's guidelines for #10 SASE.

Nonfiction: Book excerpts, essays, general interest, how-to, interview/profile (major figures associated with sports, travel, environment, outdoor), photo feature (outdoor photography), technical (reviews of equipment, how-to), travel (adventure, sports-oriented travel). Do not want to see articles about sports that we don't cover (basketball, tennis, golf, etc.). **Buys 40 mss/year.** Query with published clips. Length: 1,500-4,000 words. **Pays $1/word.** Pays expenses of writers on assignment.

Photos: "Do not send photos; if we decide to use a story, we may ask to see the writer's photos." Reviews transparencies. Buys one-time rights. Captions, identification of subjects required.

Columns/Departments: Dispatches (news, events, short profiles relevant to outdoors), 200-1,000 words; Destinations (places to explore, news, and tips for adventure travelers), 250-400 words; Review (evaluations of products), 200-1,500 words. **Buys 180 mss/year.** Query with published clips.

◼ The online magazine carries original content not found in the print edition. Contact: Amy Marr, online editor.

Tips: "Prospective writers should study the magazine before querying. Look at the magazine for our style, subject matter and standards." The departments are the best areas for freelancers to break in.

Hockey

$ $ $ AMERICAN HOCKEY INC., Official Publication of USA Hockey, c/o TPG Sports, Inc., 1710 Douglas Dr. N., #201, Golden Valley MN 55422. (763)595-0808. Fax: (763)595-0016. E-mail: joe@tpgsports.com. Editor: Harry Thompson. **Contact:** Joseph Oberle, publications manager. **60% freelance written.** Magazine published 10 times/year covering amateur hockey in the US. "The world's largest hockey magazine, *AHM* is the official magazine of USA Hockey, Inc., the national governing body of hockey." Estab. 1980. Circ. 422,000. Pays on acceptance or publication. Byline given. Buys all rights. Editorial lead time 6 months. Submit seasonal material 4 months in advance. Accepts simultaneous submissions. Sample copy and writer's guidelines free.

Nonfiction: Essays, general interest, historical/nostalgic, how-to (play hockey), humor, inspirational, interview/profile, new product, opinion, personal experience, photo feature, travel, hockey camps, pro hockey, juniors, college, NCAA hockey championships, Olympics, youth, etc. **Buys 20-30 mss/year.** Query. Length: 500-5,000 words. **Pays $50-1,000.** Pays expenses of writers on assignment.

Reprints: Accepts previously published submissions.

Photos: State availability with submission. Reviews contact sheets. Rights purchased varies. Negotiates payment individually. Captions, identification of subjects required.

Columns/Departments: Short Cuts (news and notes), Coaches' Corner (teaching tips), USA Hockey, Inline Notebook (news and notes). **Pays $150-250.**

Fiction: Adventure, humorous, slice-of-life vignettes. **Buys 10-20 mss/year. Pays $150-1,000.**

Fillers: Anecdotes, facts, gags to be illustrated by cartoonist, newsbreaks, short humor. **Buys 20-30/year.** Length: 10-100 words. **Pays $25-250.**

Tips: Writers must have a general knowledge and enthusiasm for hockey, including ice, inline, street and other. The primary audience is youth players in the US.

$ $ MINNESOTA HOCKEY JOURNAL, Official Publication of Minnesota Hockey, Inc., c/o TPG Sports, Inc., 1710 Douglas Dr. N., Golden Valley MN 55422. (763)595-0808. Fax: (763)595-0016. E-mail: joe@tpgsports.com. Website: www.tpgsports.com. Editor: Ross Bernstein. **Contact:** Joseph Oberle, publications manager. **50% freelance written.** Journal published 4 times/year. Estab. 2000. Circ. 40,000. Pays on acceptance or publication. Byline given. Buys all rights. Editorial lead time 6 months. Submit seasonal material 4 months in advance. Accepts simultaneous submissions. Sample copy and writer's guidelines free.

Nonfiction: Essays, general interest, historical/nostalgic, how-to (play hockey), humor, inspirational, interview/profile, new product, opinion, personal experience, photo feature, travel, hockey camps, pro hockey, juniors, college, Olympics, youth, etc. **Buys 5-10 mss/year.** Query. Length: 500-5,000 words. **Pays $100-500.** Sometimes pays expenses of writers on assignment.

Reprints: Accepts previously published submissions.

Photos: State availability with submission. Reviews contact sheets. Rights purchased vary. Negotiates payment individually. Captions, identification of subjects required.

Columns/Departments: Hot Shots (news and notes), Open Ice (opinion). **Pays $50-250.**

Fillers: Anecdotes, facts, gags to be illustrated by cartoonist, newsbreaks, short humor, game page with puzzles. **Buys 5-10 mss/year.** Length: 10-100 words. **Pays $25-250.**

Horse Racing

$ $ AMERICAN TURF MONTHLY, Star Sports Corp., 306 Broadway, Lynbrook NY 11563. (516)599-2121. Fax: (516)599-0451. E-mail: editor@americanturf.com. Website: www.americanturf.com. **Contact:** James Corbett, editor-in-chief. **90% freelance written.** Monthly magazine covering Thoroughbred racing, handicapping and wagering. "Squarely focused on Thoroughbred handicapping and wagering. *ATM* is a magazine for horseplayers, not owners, breeders or 12-year-old girls enthralled with ponies." Estab. 1946. Circ. 28,000. Pays on publication. Publishes ms an average of 4 months after acceptance. Byline given. Makes work-for-hire assignments. Editorial lead time 2 months. Submit seasonal material 2 months in advance. Accepts queries by mail, e-mail. Responds in 1 month to queries. Sample copy and writer's guidelines free.

Nonfiction: Handicapping and wagering features. Special issues: Triple Crown/Kentucky Derby (May); Saratoga/Del Mar (August); Breeder's Cup (November). No historical essays, bilious 'guest editorials,' saccharine poetry, fiction. **Buys 50 mss/year.** Query. Length: 800-2,000 words. **Pays $75-300 for assigned articles; $100-500 for unsolicited articles.**

Photos: Send photos with submission. Reviews 3×5 transparencies, prints. Buys one-time rights. Offers $25 interior b&w; $150 for cover. Identification of subjects required.

Fillers: Newsbreaks, short humor. **Buys 5/year.** Length: 400 words. **Pays $25.**

◼ The online magazine carries original content not found in the print version. Contact: Scott Romick, online editor.

Tips: "Send a good query letter specifically targeted at explaining how this contribution will help our readers to cash a bet at the track!"

$ $ THE QUARTER RACING JOURNAL, American Quarter Horse Association, P.O. Box 32470, Amarillo TX 79120. (806)376-4888. Fax: (806)349-6400. E-mail: richc@aqha.org. Website: www.aqha.com/racing. Executive Editor: Jim Jennings. **Contact:** Richard Chamberlain, editor. **10% freelance written.** Monthly magazine. "The official racing publication of the American Quarter Horse Association. We promote quarter horse racing. Articles include training, breeding, nutrition, sports medicine, health, history, etc." Estab. 1988. Circ. 9,000. **Pays on acceptance.** Publishes ms an average of 3 months after acceptance. Buys first North American serial rights. Submit seasonal material 3 months in advance. Accepts queries by mail, e-mail. Responds in 1 month to queries. Sample copy and writer's guidelines free.

Nonfiction: Historical/nostalgic (must be on quarter horses or people associated with them), how-to (training), opinion, nutrition, health, breeding. Special issues: Yearlings (August), subject to negotiation, Stallions (December). Query. Length: 700-1,500 words. **Pays $150-300.**

Reprints: Send photocopy and information about when and where the material previously appeared.

Photos: Send photos with submission. Additional payment for photos accepted with ms might be offered. Captions, identification of subjects required.

Fiction: Novel excerpts.

◼ The online magazine carries original content not found in the print edition. Contact: Richard Chamberlain, online editor.

Tips: "Query first—must be familiar with quarter horse racing and be knowledgeable of the sport. The *Journal* directs its articles to those who own, train and breed racing quarter horses, as well as fans and handicappers. Most open to features covering training, nutrition, health care. Use a knowledgeable source with credentials."

Hunting & Fishing

$ $⊠ ALABAMA GAME & FISH, Game & Fish, P.O. Box 741, Marietta GA 30061. **Contact:** Jimmy Jacobs, editor. See *Game & Fish*.

$ $ AMERICAN HUNTER, 11250 Waples Mill Rd., Fairfax VA 22030-9400. (703)267-1335. Fax: (703)267-3971. E-mail: publications@nrahq.org. Website: www.nra.org. Editor: John Zent. **Contact:** Scott Olmsted, associate editor. Monthly magazine for hunters who are members of the National Rifle Association. "*American Hunter* contains articles dealing with various sport hunting and related activities both at home and abroad. With the encouragment of the sport as a prime game management tool, emphasis is on technique, sportsmanship and safety. In each issue hunting equipment and firearms are evaluated, legislative happenings affecting the sport are reported, lore and legend are retold and the business of the Association is recorded in the Official Journal section." Circ. 1,000,000. **Pays on acceptance.** Byline given. Buys first North American serial, second serial (reprint) rights. Accepts queries by mail, e-mail. Responds in 3 months to queries. Writer's guidelines for #10 SASE.
Nonfiction: Factual material on all phases of hunting: Expository how-to, where-to, and general interest pieces; humor: personal narratives; and semi-technical articles on firearms, wildlife management or hunting. Features fall into five categories: Deer, upland birds, waterfowl, big game and varmints/small game. Special issues: Pheasants, whitetail tactics, black bear feed areas, mule deer, duck hunters' transport by land and sea, tech topics to be decided; rut strategies, muzzleloader moose and elk, fall turkeys, staying warm, goose talk, long-range muzzleloading. Not interested in material on fishing, camping, or firearms knowledge. Query. Length: 1,800-2,000 words. **Pays up to $800.**
Reprints: Send typed ms with rights for sale noted and information about when and where the material previously appeared.
Photos: No additional payment made for photos used with ms; others offered from $75-600.
Columns/Departments: Hunting Guns, Hunting Loads and Public Hunting Grounds. Study back issues for appropriate subject matter and style. Length: 1,200-1,500 words. **Pays $300-450.**
Tips: "Although unsolicited manuscripts are welcomed, detailed query letters outlining the proposed topic and approach are appreciated and will save both writers and editors a considerable amount of time. If we like your story idea, you will be contacted by mail or phone and given direction on how we'd like the topic covered. NRA Publications accept all manuscripts and photographs for consideration on a specualtion basis only. Story angles should be narrow, but coverage must have depth. How-to articles are popular with readers and might range from methods for hunting to techniques on making gear used on successful hunts. Where-to articles should contain contacts and information needed to arrange a similar hunt. All submissions are judged on three criteria: Story angle (it should be fresh, interesting, and informative); quality of writing (clear and lively—capable of holding the readers' attention throughout); and quality and quantity of accompanying photos (sharpness, reproduceability, and connection to text are most important.)"

$ $⊠ ARKANSAS SPORTSMAN, Game & Fish, P.O. Box 741, Marietta GA 30061. (770)953-9222. **Contact:** Ken Duke. See *Game & Fish*.

$ $⊠ BASSMASTER MAGAZINE, B.A.S.S. Publications, 5845 Carmichael Pkwy., Montgomery AL 36117. (334)272-9530. Fax: (334)396-8230. E-mail: editorial@bassmaster.com. Website: www.bassmaster.com. **Contact:** Dave Precht, editor. **80% freelance written.** Magazine published 10 times/year about largemouth, smallmouth and spotted bass, offering "how-to" articles for dedicated beginning and advanced bass fishermen, including destinations and new product reviews. Estab. 1968. Circ. 600,000. **Pays on acceptance.** Publishes ms an average of 1 year after acceptance. Byline given. Buys electronic rights. Editorial lead time 2 months. Submit seasonal material 6 months in advance. Accepts queries by mail, e-mail. Responds in 2 months to queries. Sample copy for $2. Writer's guidelines for #10 SASE.
 • Needs destination stories (how to fish a certain area) for the Northwest and Northeast.
Nonfiction: Historical/nostalgic, how-to (patterns, lures, etc.), interview/profile (of knowledgeable people in the sport), new product (reels, rods and bass boats), travel (where to go fish for bass), Conservation related to bass fishing. "No first person, personal experience type articles." **Buys 100 mss/year.** Query. Length: 500-2,500 words. **Pays $100-500.**
Photos: Send photos with submission. Reviews transparencies. Buys all rights. Offers no additional payment for photos accepted with ms, but pays $700 for color cover transparencies. Captions, model releases required.
Columns/Departments: Short Cast/News/Views/Notes/Briefs (upfront regular feature covering news-related events such as new state bass records, unusual bass fishing happenings, conservation, new products and editorial viewpoints). Length: 250-400 words. **Pays $100-3,000.**
Fillers: Anecdotes, newsbreaks. **Buys 4-5/year.** Length: 250-500 words. **Pays $50-100.**
Tips: "Editorial direction continues in the short, more direct how-to article. Compact, easy-to-read information is our objective. Shorter articles with good graphics, such as how-to diagrams, step-by-step instruction, etc., will enhance a writer's articles submitted to *Bassmaster Magazine*. The most frequent mistakes made by writers in completing an article for us are poor grammar, poor writing, poor organization and superficial research. Send in detailed queries outlining specific objectives of article, obtain writer's guidelines. Be as concise as possible."

$ $⊠ BC OUTDOORS, OP Publishing, 780 Beatty St., Suite 300, Vancouver, British Columbia V6B 2M1, Canada. (604)606-4644. Fax: (604)687-1925. **Contact:** Roegan Lloydd.

● As of June 2001, *BC Outdoors* split into two publications: The bimonthly *BC Outdoors Sport Fishing* and the quarterly *BC Outdoors Hunting & Shooting*.

N **$** **$** ⊠ **BC OUTDOORS HUNTING & SHOOTING**, OP Publishing, 780 Beatty St., Suite 300, Vancouver, British Columbia V6B 2M1, Canada. (604)606-4644. Fax: (604)687-1925. E-mail: outdoorsgroupeditorial@oppublishing.com. Website: www.oppublishing.com. Editor: George Gruenfeld. **Contact:** Roegan Lloyd, managing editor. **80% freelance written.** Quarterly magazine covering hunting, shooting, camping and backroads. Pays on publication. Publishes ms an average of 3 months after acceptance. Byline given. Offers negotiable kill fee. Buys first North American serial rights. Sample copy and writer's guidelines for 8×10 SAE with 7 Canadian first-class stamps or IRC.

● As of June 2001, *BC Outdoors* magazine split into two publications: The bimonthly *BC Outdoors Sport Fishing* and the quarterly *BC Outdoors Hunting & Shooting*.

Nonfiction: "We would like to receive how-to, where-to features dealing with hunting in British Columbia." How-to (new or innovative articles on hunting subjects), personal experience (outdoor adventure), outdoor topics specific to British Columbia. **Buys 50 mss/year.** Query. Length: 1,700-2,000 words. **Pays $300-500.**

Photos: State availability with submission. Buys one-time rights; buys other rights for cover photo. Pays $25-75 on publication for 5×7 b&w prints; $35-150 for color 35mm transparencies. Captions, identification of subjects required.

Tips: "Wants in-depth information, professional writing only. Emphasis on environmental issues. Those pieces with a conservation component have a better chance of being published. Subject must be specific to British Columbia. We receive many manuscripts written by people who obviously do not know the magazine or market. The writer has a better chance of breaking in with short, lesser-paying articles and fillers, because we have a stable of regular writers who produce most main features."

N **$** **$** ⊠ **BC OUTDOORS SPORT FISHING**, OP Publishing, 780 Beatty St., Suite 300, Vancouver, British Columbia V6B 2M1, Canada. (604)606-4644. Fax: (604)687-1925. E-mail: outdoorsgroupeditorial@oppublishing.com. Website: www.oppublishing.com. Editor: George Gruenfeld. **Contact:** Roegan Lloyd, managing editor. **80% freelance written.** Magazine published 6 times/year covering fresh and saltwater fishing, camping and backroads. Pays on publication. Publishes ms an average of 3 months after acceptance. Byline given. Offers negotiable kill fee. Buys first North American serial rights. Sample copy and writer's guidelines for 8×10 SAE with 7 Canadian first-class stamps or IRC.

● As of June 2001, *BC Outdoors* magazine split into two publications: The bimonthly *BC Outdoors Sport Fishing* and the quarterly *BC Outdoors Hunting & Shooting*.

Nonfiction: "We would like to receive how-to, where-to features dealing with fishing in British Columbia." How-to (new or innovative articles on fishing subjects), personal experience (outdoor adventure), outdoor topics specific to British Columbia. **Buys 60 mss/year.** Query. Length: 1,700-2,000 words. **Pays $300-500.**

Photos: State availability with submission. Buys one-time rights; buys other rights for cover photo. Pays $25-75 on publication for 5×7 b&w prints; $35-150 for color 35mm transparencies. Captions, identification of subjects required.

Tips: "Wants in-depth information, professional writing only. Emphasis on environmental issues. Those pieces with a conservation component have a better chance of being published. Subject must be specific to British Columbia. We receive many manuscripts written by people who obviously do not know the magazine or market. The writer has a better chance of breaking in with short, lesser-paying articles and fillers, because we have a stable of regular writers who produce most main features."

N **$** **$** **THE BIG GAME FISHING JOURNAL**, Offshore Informational Publications, 1800 Bay Ave., Point Pleasant NJ 08742. (732)840-4900. Fax: (732)223-2449. E-mail: captlen@aol.com. Website: www.bgf-journal.com. Senior Publisher: Leonard Belcaro. **Contact:** Chris Bohlman, managing editor. **90% freelance written.** Bimonthly magazine covering big game fishing. "We require highly instructional articles prepared by qualified writers/fishermen." Estab. 1994. Circ. 45,000. Pays on publication. Byline given. Offers 50% kill fee. Buys first North American serial rights. Editorial lead time 3 months. Submit seasonal material 3 months in advance. Accepts queries by mail, e-mail. Accepts simultaneous submissions. Responds in 2 weeks to queries; 1 month to mss. Writer's guidelines free.

Nonfiction: How-to, interview/profile, technical. **Buys 50-70 mss/year.** Send complete ms. Length: 2,000-3,000 words. **Pays $200-400.** Sometimes pays expenses of writers on assignment.

Photos: Send photos with submission. Reviews transparencies. Buys one-time rights. Offers no additional payment for photos accepted with ms. Captions required.

Tips: "Our format is considerably different than most publications. We prefer to receive articles from qualified anglers on their expertise—if the author is an accomplished writer, all the better. We require highly-instructional articles that teach both novice and expert readers."

$** **$ **BUGLE, Elk Country and the Hunt**, Rocky Mountain Elk Foundation, 2291 W. Broadway, Missoula MT 59808. (406)523-4570. Fax: (406)523-4550. E-mail: bugle@rmef.org. Website: www.rmef.org. Editor: Dan Crockett. **Contact:** Lee Cromrich, assistant editor. **50% freelance written.** Bimonthly magazine covering elk conservation and elk hunting. "*Bugle* is the membership publication of the Rocky Mountain Elk Foundation, a nonprofit wildlife conservation group; it also sells on newsstands. Our readers are predominantly hunters, many of them conservationists who care deeply about protecting wildlife habitat. Hunting stories and essays should celebrate the hunting experience, demonstrating respect for wildlife, the land and the hunt. Articles on elk behavior or elk habitat should include personal observations and entertain as well as educate." Estab. 1984. Circ. 195,000. **Pays on acceptance.** Publishes ms an average of 9 months after acceptance. Byline given. Offers variable kill fee. Buys one-time rights. Editorial lead time 6 months. Submit seasonal material 6 months in advance. Accepts queries by mail, e-mail, fax, phone. Responds in 1 month to queries; 3 months to mss. Sample copy for $5. Writer's guidelines for #10 SASE.

O→ Preparation: "read as many issues of *Bugle* as possible to know what the Elk Foundation and magazine are about. Then write a strong query with those things in mind. Send it with clips of other published or unpublished pieces representative of story being proposed."

Nonfiction: Book excerpts, essays, general interest (elk related), historical/nostalgic, humor, interview/profile, opinion, personal experience, photo feature. No how-to, where-to. **Buys 20 mss/year.** Query with or without published clips or send complete ms. Length: 1,500-4,500 words. **Pays 20¢/word and 3 contributor copies; more issues at cost.**

Reprints: Send typed ms with rights for sale noted and information about when and where the material previously appeared. Pays 75% of amount paid for original article.

Columns/Departments: Situation Ethics, 1,000-2,000 words; Thoughts & Theories, 1,500-4,000 words; Women in the Outdoors, 1,000-2,500 words. **Buys 13 mss/year.** Query with or without published clips or send complete ms. **Pays 20¢/word.**

Fiction: Adventure, historical, humorous, novel excerpts, slice-of-life vignettes, western. No fiction that doesn't pertain to elk or elk hunting. **Buys 4 mss/year.** Query with or without published clips or send complete ms. Length: 1,500-4,500 words. **Pays 20¢/word.**

Poetry: Free verse, haiku, light verse, traditional. **Buys 6 poems/year.** Submit maximum 6 poems.

Tips: "Creative queries (250-500 words) that showcase your concept and your style remain the most effective approach. We're hungry for submissions for three specific columns: Situation Ethics, Thoughts & Theories, and Women in the Outdoors. Send a SASE for guidelines. We also welcome strong, well-reasoned opinion pieces on topics pertinent to hunting and wildlife conservation, and humorous pieces about elk behavior or encounters with elk (hunting or otherwise). We'd also like to see more humor; more natural history pertaining to elk and elk country; more good, thoughtful writing from women."

$ $⊠ CALIFORNIA GAME & FISH, Game & Fish, Box 741, Marietta GA 30061. **Contact:** Burt Carey, editor. See *Game & Fish*.

$ $⊠ DEER & DEER HUNTING, Krause Publications, 700 E. State St., Iola WI 54990-0001. Fax: (715)445-4087. **Contact:** Dan Schmidt, managing editor. **95% freelance written.** Magazine published 9 times/year covering white-tailed deer and deer hunting. "Readers include a cross section of the deer hunting population—individuals who hunt with bow, gun or camera. The editorial content of the magazine focuses on white-tailed deer biology and behavior, management principle and practices, habitat requirements, natural history of deer, hunting techniques, and hunting ethics. We also publish a wide range of 'how-to' articles designed to help hunters locate and get close to deer at all times of the year. The majority of our readership consists of two-season hunters (bow and gun) and approximately one-third camera hunt." Estab. 1977. Circ. 140,000. **Pays on acceptance.** Byline given. Editorial lead time 6 months. Submit seasonal material 6 months in advance. Accepts queries by mail. Responds in 3 months to queries. Sample copy for 9×12 SASE. Writer's guidelines free.

Nonfiction: General interest, historical/nostalgic, how-to, inspirational, photo feature. No "Joe and me" articles. **Buys 30-50 mss/year.** Query. Length: 750-3,000 words. **Pays $150-525 for assigned articles; $150-325 for unsolicited articles.** Sometimes pays expenses of writers on assignment.

Photos: Send photos with submission. Reviews transparencies. Negotiates payment individually. Captions, identification of subjects, model releases required.

Fiction: "Mood" deer hunting pieces. **Buys 9 mss/year.** Send complete ms.

Fillers: Facts, newsbreaks. **Buys 40-50/year.** Length: 100-500 words. **Pays $15-150.**

Tips: "Feature articles dealing with deer biology or behavior should be documented by scientific research (the author's or that of others) as opposed to a limited number of personal observations."

$ $ DISCOVERING AND EXPLORING NEW JERSEY'S FISHING STREAMS AND THE DELAWARE RIVER, New Jersey Sportsmen's Guides, P.O. Box 100, Somerdale NJ 08083. Fax: (856)665-8656. Website: www.njsportsmensguides.com. **Contact:** Steve Perrone, editor. **60-70% freelance written.** Annual magazine covering freshwater stream and river fishing. Estab. 1993. Circ. 2,500. **Pays on acceptance.** Publishes ms an average of 6 months after acceptance. Byline given. Buys first rights, makes work-for-hire assignments. Editorial lead time 6 months. Accepts queries by mail. Sample copy for $14.50 postage paid.

Nonfiction: How-to fishing and freshwater fishing. **Buys 6-8 mss/year.** Query with published clips. Length: 500-2,000 words. **Pays $75-250.**

Photos: State availability with submission. Reviews 4×5 transparencies, prints. Buys one-time rights. Negotiates payment individually. Captions, identification of subjects, model releases required.

Tips: "We want queries with published clips of articles describing fishing expectations on New Jersey streams and the Delaware River."

$ $ THE DRAKE MAGAZINE, For People Who Fish, Paddlesport Publishing, P.O. Box 5450, Steamboat Springs CO 80477-5450. (970)879-1450. Fax: (970)870-1404. E-mail: bieline@paddlermagazine.com. Website: www.drakemag.com. **Contact:** Tom Bie, managing editor. **70% freelance written.** Annual magazine for people who love fishing. Pays 30 days after publication. Publishes ms an average of 1 year after acceptance. Byline given. Buys first North American serial rights. Editorial lead time 1 year. Submit seasonal material 1 year in advance. Accepts queries by mail. Responds in 6 months to mss.

O➡ To break in "Tippets is the best bet: Short, 200-600 word essays on any aspect of the fishing world. Rodholders is another good area (profiles of people who fish)."

Nonfiction: Book excerpts, essays, general interest, historical/nostalgic, humor, interview/profile, opinion, personal experience, photo feature, travel (fishing related). **Buys 8 mss/year.** Query. Length: 250-3,000 words. **Pays 10-20¢/ word "depending on the amount of work we have to put into the piece."**

Photos: State availability with submission. Reviews contact sheets, negatives, transparencies. Buys one-time rights. Offers $25-250/photo.

▣ The online magazine carries original content not found in the print version. Contact: Tom Bie, online editor.

$ $ $ $ FIELD & STREAM, 2 Park Ave., New York NY 10016-5695. Editor: Slaton White. **Contact:** David E. Petzal, executive editor. **50% freelance written.** Monthly magazine. "Broad-based service magazine for the hunter and fisherman. Editorial content ranges from very basic how-to stories detailing a useful technique or a device that sportsmen can make, to articles of penetrating depth about national hunting, fishing, and related activities. Also humor and personal essays, nostalgia and 'mood pieces' on the hunting or fishing experience and profiles on outdoor people." Estab. 1895. Circ. 1,790,400. **Pays on acceptance.** Byline given. Buys first rights. Accepts queries by mail. Responds in 2 weeks to queries. Writer's guidelines for #10 SASE.

Nonfiction: Length: 1,500 words for features. Payment varies depending on the quality of work, importance of the article. Pays $800 and up to $1,000 and more on a sliding scale for major features. *Field & Stream* also publishes regional sections with feature articles on hunting and fishing in specific areas of the country. The sections are geographically divided East, Midwest, West and South, and appear 12 months/year. Query by mail only: regional articles and ideas by mail to Regionals Editor. Query. Length: 100-600 words. **Pays $100-400.**

Photos: Send photos with submission. Reviews slides (prefers color). Buys first rights. When purchased separately, pays $450 minimum for color.

Columns/Departments: Personal essays suitable for the "Finally..." department, 750-800 words.

Fillers: Buys short "how it's done" fillers, 75-150 words, on unusual or helpful subjects. Also buys short (up to 500 words) pieces on tactics or techniques for specific hunting or fishing situations; short "Field Guide" pieces on natural phenomena as related to hunting and fishing; "Myths and Misconceptions," short pieces debunking a commonly held belief about hunting and fishing; short "Outdoor Basics"; and short pieces for the "Up Front" section that run the gamut from natural history to conservation news, anecdotal humor, short tips, and carefully crafted opinion pieces (word length: 25-400).

Tips: "Writers are encouraged to submit queries on article ideas. These should be no more than a paragraph or two, and should include a summary of the idea, including the angle you will hang the story on, and a sense of what makes this piece different from all others on the same or a similar subject. Many queries are turned down because we have no idea what the writer is getting at. Be sure that your letter is absolutely clear. We've found that if you can't sum up the point of the article in a sentence or two, the article doesn't have a point. Pieces that depend on writing style, such as humor, mood, and nostalgia or essays often can't be queried and may be submitted in manuscript form. The same is true of short tips. All submissions to *Field & Stream* are on an on-spec basis. Before submitting anything, however, we encourage you to *study*, not simply read, the magazine. Many pieces are rejected because they do not fit the tone or style of the magazine, or fail to match the subject of the article with the overall subject matter of *Field & Stream*. Above all, study the magazine before submitting anything."

$ $ ▨ THE FISHERMAN, LIF Publishing Corp., 14 Ramsey Rd., Shirley NY 11967-4704. (631)345-5200. Fax: (631)345-5304. E-mail: melfish@aol.com. Publisher: Fred Golofaro. Associate Publisher: Pete Barrett. Senior Editor: Tim Coleman. **Contact:** Tom Melton, managing editor. **75% freelance written.** Weekly magazine covering fishing with an emphasis on saltwater. Circ. 110,000. Pays on publication. Byline given. Offers variable kill fee. Submit seasonal material 2 months in advance. Accepts queries by mail, e-mail. Responds in 6 weeks to queries. Sample copy and writer's guidelines free.

Nonfiction: General interest, historical/nostalgic, how-to, interview/profile, personal experience, photo feature, technical, travel. Special issues: Boat & Motor Buyer's Guide and Winter Workbench (January); Tackle, Trout (March); Inshore Fishing (April); Saltwater Fly, Party Boat, Black Bass (May); Offshore Fishing (June); Surf Fishing (August); Striped Bass (October); Travel (December). "No 'Me and Joe' tales. We stress how, when, where and why." **Buys 300 mss/year.** Length: 1,000-1,500 words. **Pays $110-150.**

Photos: Send photos with submission. Offers no additional payment for photos accepted with ms, but offers $50-100 for single color cover photos. Identification of subjects required.

Tips: "Focus on specific how-to and where-to subjects within each region."

$ $ ▨ FLORIDA GAME & FISH, Game & Fish, Box 741, Marietta GA 30061. (770)953-9222. **Contact:** Jimmy Jacobs, editor. See *Game & Fish*.

$ $ FLORIDA SPORTSMAN, Wickstrom Communications Division of PRIMEDIA Special Interest Publications, 2700 S. Kanner Hwy., Stuart FL 34994. (561)219-7400. Fax: (561)219-6900. E-mail: editor@floridasportsman.com. Website: www.floridasportsman.com. **Contact:** Jeff Weakley, editor. **30% freelance written.** Monthly magazine cover-

ing fishing, boating and related sports—Florida and Caribbean only. "*Florida Sportsman* is edited for the boatowner and offshore, coastal and fresh water fisherman. It provides a how, when and where approach in its articles, which also includes occasional camping, diving and hunting stories—plus ecology; in-depth articles and editorials attempting to protect Florida's wilderness, wetlands and natural beauty." Circ. 115,000. **Pays on acceptance.** Publishes ms an average of 6 months after acceptance. Byline given. Buys all rights. Submit seasonal material 6 months in advance. Accepts queries by mail. Responds in 2 months to queries; 1 month to mss. Sample copy free. Writer's guidelines for #10 SASE.
Nonfiction: "We use reader service pieces almost entirely—how-to, where-to, etc. One or two environmental pieces per issue as well. Writers must be Florida based, or have lengthy experience in Florida outdoors. All articles must have strong Florida emphasis. We do not want to see general how-to-fish-or-boat pieces which might well appear in a national or wide-regional magazine." Essays (environment or nature), how-to (fishing, hunting, boating), humor (outdoors angle), personal experience (in fishing, etc.), technical (boats, tackle, etc., as particularly suitable for Florida specialities). **Buys 40-60 mss/year.** Query. Length: 1,500-2,500 words. **Pays $450.**
Photos: Send photos with submission. Reviews 35mm transparencies, 4×5 and larger prints. Buys all rights. Offers no additional payment for photos accepted with ms. Pays up to $1,000 for cover photos.
Tips: "Feature articles are most open to freelancers; however there is little chance of acceptance unless contributor is an accomplished and avid outdoorsman *and* a competent writer-photographer with considerable experience in Florida."

$ $⚡ **FLY FISHING IN SALT WATERS**, World Publications, Inc., 460 N. Orlando Ave., Suite 200, Winter Park FL 32789-7061. (407)628-4802. Fax: (407)628-7061. E-mail: editor@flyfishinsalt.com. Website: www.flyfishinsalt .com. **Contact:** David Ritchie, editor. **90% freelance written.** Bimonthly magazine covering fly fishing in salt waters anywhere in the world. Estab. 1994. Circ. 44,000. Pays on publication. Publishes ms an average of 1 year after acceptance. Byline given. Buys first North American serial, electronic rights. Editorial lead time 3 months. Submit seasonal material 2 months in advance. Accepts queries by mail, e-mail. Responds in 1 month to queries; 2 months to mss. Sample copy for $3, plus $1 S&H. Writer's guidelines for #10 SASE.
   O→ Break in with "well written original material that is oriented toward teaching a new idea, concept, location, technique, etc."
Nonfiction: Book excerpts, essays, historical/nostalgic, how-to, interview/profile, new product, personal experience, photo feature, technical, travel, resource issues (conservation). **Buys 40-50 mss/year.** Query with or without published clips. Length: 1,500-2,500 words. **Pays $400-500.**
Photos: Send photos with submission. Reviews 35mm color transparencies. Buys one-time rights. Offers no additional payment for photos accepted with ms; pays $80-300/photo if purchased separately. Captions, identification of subjects required.
Columns/Departments: Legends/Reminiscences (history-profiles-nostalgia), 2,000-2,500 words; Resource (conservation issues), 1,000-1,500 words; Fly Tier's Bench (how to tie saltwater flies), 1,000-1,500 words, photos or illustrations critical; Boating (technical how-to), 2,000-2,500 words; Saltwater 101 (for beginners, tackle tips and techniques), 1,000-2,000 words. **Buys 25-30 mss/year.** Query. **Pays $400-500.**
Fiction: Adventure, humorous, mainstream, all dealing with fly fishing. **Buys 2-3 mss/year.** Send complete ms. Length: 2,000-3,000 words. **Pays $500.**
Fillers: Most fillers are staff written.
   ◾ The online magazine carries original content not found in the print edition. Contact: David Ritchie, online editor.
Tips: "Follow up on your inquiry with a phone call."

$ $FLYFISHING & TYING JOURNAL, A Compendium for the Complete Fly Fisher, Frank Amato Publications, P.O. Box 82112, Portland OR 97282. (503)653-8108. Fax: (503)653-2766. E-mail: kim@amatobooks.com. Website: www.amatobooks.com. **Contact:** Kim Koch, editor. **70% freelance written.** Quarterly magazine covering flyfishing and fly tying for both new and veteran anglers. Every issue is seasonally focused: Spring, summer, fall and winter. Estab. 1980. Circ. 60,000. Pays on publication. Byline given. Buys first rights. Editorial lead time up to 1 year. Submit seasonal material up to 1 year in advance. Accepts queries by mail. Responds in 1 month to queries; 2 months to mss. Writer's guidelines for #10 SASE. Attn: Kim Koch.
Nonfiction: How-to, personal experience. **Buys 55-60 mss/year.** Query. Length: 1,000-2,000 words. **Pays $200-600.**
Photos: State availability with submission. Reviews transparencies. Buys one-time rights. Offers no additional payment for photos accepted with ms. Captions, identification of subjects, model releases required.

$ FUR-FISH-GAME, 2878 E. Main, Columbus OH 43209-9947. **Contact:** Mitch Cox, editor. **65% freelance written.** Monthly magazine for outdoorsmen of all ages who are interested in hunting, fishing, trapping, dogs, camping, conservation and related topics. Estab. 1900. Circ. 111,000. **Pays on acceptance.** Publishes ms an average of 7 months after acceptance. Byline given. Buys first, all rights. Responds in 2 months to queries. Sample copy for $1 and 9×12 SAE. Writer's guidelines for #10 SASE.
Nonfiction: "We are looking for informative, down-to-earth stories about hunting, fishing, trapping, dogs, camping, boating, conservation and related subjects. Nostalgic articles are also used. Many of our stories are 'how-to' and should appeal to small-town and rural readers who are true outdoorsmen. Some recents articles have told how to train a gun dog, catch big-water catfish, outfit a bowhunter and trap late-season muskrat. We also use personal experience stories and an occasion profile, such as an article about an old-time trapper. 'Where-to' stories are used occasionally if they have broad appeal." Query. Length: 500-3,000 words. **Pays $50-150 or more for features depending upon quality, photo support and importance to magazine.**

Photos: Send photos with submission. Reviews transparencies, color prints (5×7 or 8×10). Pays $25 for separate freelance photos. Captions, credits required.

Tips: "We are always looking for quality how-to articles about fish, game animals or birds that are popular with everyday outdoorsmen but often overlooked in other publications, such as catfish, bluegill, crappie, squirrel, rabbit, crows, etc. We also use articles on standard seasonal subjects such as deer and pheasant, but like to see a fresh approach or new technique. Instructional trapping articles are useful all year. Articles on gun dogs, ginseng and do-it-yourself projects are also popular with our readers. An assortment of photos and/or sketches greatly enhances any manuscript, and sidebars, where applicable, can also help. No phone queries, please."

$ $⚡ **GAME & FISH**, 2250 Newmarket Pkwy., Suite 110, Marietta GA 30067. (770)953-9222. Fax: (770)933-9510. **Contact:** Ken Dunwoody, editorial director. **90% freelance written.** Publishes 30 different monthly outdoor magazines, each one covering the fishing and hunting opportunities in a particular state or region (see individual titles and editors). Estab. 1975. Circ. 575,000. Pays 60 days prior to cover date of issue. Publishes ms an average of 7 months after acceptance. Byline given. Offers negotiable kill fee. Buys first North American serial rights. Submit seasonal material 8 months in advance. Responds in 3 months to queries. Sample copy for $3.50 and 9×12 SASE. Writer's guidelines for #10 SASE.

Nonfiction: Prefers queries over unsolicited mss. Length: 1,500-2,400 words. **Pays $125-300; additional payment made for electronic rights.**

Photos: Reviews transparencies, b&w prints. Buys one-time rights. Cover photos $250, inside color $75 and b&w $25. Captions, identification of subjects required.

Fiction: Adventure, humorous, nostalgia pertaining to hunting and fishing. Length: 1,100-2,500 words. **Pays $125-250; additional payment made for electronic rights.**

Tips: "Our readers are experienced anglers and hunters, and we try to provide them with useful, specific articles about where, when and how to enjoy the best hunting and fishing in their state or region. We also cover topics concerning game and fish management. Most articles should be tightly focused and aimed at outdoorsmen in one particular state. After familiarizing themselves with our magazine(s), writers should query the appropriate state editor (see individual listings) or send to Ken Dunwoody."

$ $⚡ **GEORGIA SPORTSMAN**, Game & Fish, Box 741, Marietta GA 30061. (770)953-9222. **Contact:** Jimmy Jacobs, editor. See *Game & Fish*.

$ $⚡ **GREAT PLAINS GAME & FISH**, Game & Fish, Box 741, Marietta GA 30061. (770)953-9222. **Contact:** Nick Gilmore, editor. See *Game & Fish*.

$ $⚡ **ILLINOIS GAME & FISH**, Game & Fish, Box 741, Marietta GA 30061. (770)953-9222. **Contact:** Dennis Schmidt, editor. See *Game & Fish*.

$ $⚡ **INDIANA GAME & FISH**, Game & Fish, Box 741, Marietta GA 30061. (770)953-9222. **Contact:** Ken Freel, editor. See *Game & Fish*.

$ $⚡ **IOWA GAME & FISH**, Game & Fish, Box 741, Marietta GA 30061. (770)953-9222. **Contact:** Nick Gilmore, editor. See *Game & Fish*.

$ $⚡ **KENTUCKY GAME & FISH**, Game & Fish, Box 741, Marietta GA 30061. (770)953-9222. **Contact:** Ken Freel, editor. See *Game & Fish*.

$ $⚡ **LOUISIANA GAME & FISH**, Game & Fish, Box 741, Marietta GA 30061. (770)953-9222. **Contact:** Ken Duke. See *Game & Fish*.

$ $⚡ **THE MAINE SPORTSMAN**, P.O. Box 365, Augusta ME 04330. (207)626-3315. E-mail: ursushpv@mint. net. Website: www.mainesportsman.com. **Contact:** Harry Vanderweide, editor. **80% freelance written.** Monthly tabloid. "Eager to work with new/unpublished writers, but because we run over 30 regular columns, it's hard to get into *The Maine Sportsman* as a beginner." Estab. 1972. Circ. 30,000. Pays during month of publication. Publishes ms an average of 3 months after acceptance. Byline given. Buys first rights. Accepts queries by mail, e-mail. Responds in 2 weeks to queries.

Nonfiction: "We publish only articles about Maine hunting and fishing activities. Any well-written, researched, knowledgeable article about that subject area is likely to be accepted by us." **Buys 25-40 mss/year.** Send complete ms. Length: 200-2,000 words. **Pays $20-300.** Sometimes pays expenses of writers on assignment.

Reprints: Send typed ms with rights for sale noted. Pays 100% of amount paid for an original article.

Photos: "We can have illustrations drawn, but prefer 1-3 b&w photos." Send photos with submission. Pays $5-50 for b&w print.

Tips: "We publish numerous special sections each year and are eager to buy Maine-oriented articles on snowmobiling, ice fishing, boating, salt water and deer hunting. Send articles or queries. You can e-mail us at ursushpv@mint.net."

\$ \$ ☒ **MARLIN, The International Sportfishing Magazine**, Marlin Magazine, a division of World Publications, Inc., P.O. Box 2456, Winter Park FL 32790. (407)628-4802. Fax: (407)628-7061. E-mail: marlin@worldzine.com. **Contact:** David Ritchie, editor. **90% freelance written.** Bimonthly magazine. "*Marlin* covers the sport of big game fishing (billfish, tuna, dorado and wahoo). Our readers are sophisticated, affluent and serious about their sport—they expect a high-class, well-written magazine that provides information and practical advice." Estab. 1982. Circ. 40,000. **Pays on acceptance.** Publishes ms an average of 3 months after acceptance. Byline given. Buys first North American serial rights. Submit seasonal material 3 months in advance. Sample copy and writer's guidelines for \$3.20 and SAE.
Nonfiction: General interest, how-to (bait-rigging, tackle maintenance, etc.), new product, personal experience, photo feature, technical, travel. "No freshwater fishing stories. No 'me & Joe went fishing' stories." **Buys 30-50 mss/year.** Query with published clips. Length: 800-3,000 words. **Pays \$250-500.**
Reprints: Send photocopy and information about when and where the material previously appeared. Pays 50-75% of amount paid for original article.
Photos: State availability with submission. Reviews original slides, please. Buys one-time rights. Offers \$50-300 for inside use, \$1,000 for a cover.
Columns/Departments: Tournament Reports (reports on winners of major big game fishing tournaments), 200-400 words; Blue Water Currents (news features), 100-400 words. **Buys 25 mss/year.** Query. **Pays \$75-250.**
Tips: "Tournament reports are a good way to break in to *Marlin*. Make them short but accurate, and provide photos of fishing action or winners' award shots (*not* dead fish hanging up at the docks!). We always need how-tos and news items. Our destination pieces (travel stories) emphasize where and when to fish, but include information on where to stay also. For features: crisp, high action stories with emphasis on exotic nature, adventure, personality, etc.—nothing flowery or academic. Technical/how-to: concise and informational—specific details. News: Again, concise with good details—watch for legislation affecting big game fishing, outstanding catches, new clubs and organizations, new trends and conservation issues."

\$ **MICHIGAN OUT-OF-DOORS**, P.O. Box 30235, Lansing MI 48909. (517)371-1041. Fax: (517)371-1505. E-mail: dknick@mucc.org. Website: www.mucc.org. **Contact:** Dennis C. Knickerbocker, editor. **75% freelance written.** Monthly magazine emphasizing Michigan outdoor recreation, especially hunting and fishing, conservation, nature and environmental affairs. Estab. 1947. Circ. 100,000. **Pays on acceptance.** Publishes ms an average of 6 months after acceptance. Byline given. Buys first North American serial rights. Submit seasonal material 6 months in advance. Accepts queries by mail, phone. Responds in 1 month to queries. Sample copy for \$3.50. Writer's guidelines free or online.
　　O—¬ Break in by "writing interestingly about an *unusual* aspect of Michigan natural resources and/or outdoor recreation.
Nonfiction: "Stories must have a Michigan slant unless they treat a subject of universal interest to our readers." Exposé, historical/nostalgic, how-to, interview/profile, opinion, personal experience, photo feature. Special issues: Archery Deer Hunting (October); Firearm Deer Hunting (November); Cross-country Skiing and Early-ice Lake Fishing (December or January). No humor or poetry. **Buys 96 mss/year.** Send complete ms. Length: 1,000-2,000 words. **Pays \$90 minimum for feature stories.**
Photos: Buys one-time rights. Offers no additional payment for photos accepted with ms; others \$20-175. Captions required.
Tips: "Top priority is placed on true accounts of personal adventures in the out-of-doors—well-written tales of very unusual incidents encountered while hunting, fishing, camping, hiking, etc."

\$ \$ ☒ **MICHIGAN SPORTSMAN**, Game & Fish, Box 741, Marietta GA 30061. (770)953-9222. **Contact:** Dennis Schmidt, editor. See *Game & Fish.*

\$ ☒ **MID WEST OUTDOORS**, Mid West Outdoors, Ltd., 111 Shore Drive, Hinsdale (Burr Ridge) IL 60521-5885. (630)887-7722. Fax: (630)887-1958. E-mail: glaulunen@midwestoutdoors.com. Website: www.MidWestOutdoors.com. **Contact:** Gene Laulunen, editor. **100% freelance written.** Monthly tabloid emphasizing fishing, hunting, camping and boating. Estab. 1967. Circ. 45,000. Pays on publication. Publishes ms an average of 3 months after acceptance. Byline given. Buys simultaneous rights. Submit seasonal material 2 months in advance. Accepts simultaneous submissions. Responds in 3 weeks to queries. Sample copy for \$1 or online. Writer's guidelines for #10 SASE or online.
Nonfiction: How-to (fishing, hunting, camping in the Midwest), where-to-go (fishing, hunting, camping within 500 miles of Chicago). "We do not want to see any articles on 'my first fishing, hunting or camping experiences,' 'cleaning my tackle box,' 'tackle tune-up,' or 'catch and release.'" **Buys 1,800 unsolicited mss/year.** Send complete ms. Length: 1,000-1,500 words. **Pays \$15-30.**
Reprints: Send tearsheet.
Photos: Reviews slides and b&w prints. Buys all rights. Offers no additional payment for photos accompanying ms. Captions required.

MARKETS THAT WERE listed in the 2001 edition of *Writer's Market* but do not appear this year are listed in the General Index with a notation explaining why they were omitted.

Columns/Departments: Fishing, Hunting. Send complete ms. **Pays $30.**

Tips: "Break in with a great unknown fishing hole or new technique within 500 miles of Chicago. Where, how, when and why. Know the type of publication you are sending material to."

$ $ ◩ **MID-ATLANTIC GAME & FISH**, Game & Fish, Box 741, Marietta GA 30061. (770)953-9222. **Contact:** Ken Freel, editor. See *Game & Fish*.

$ $ ◩ **MINNESOTA SPORTSMAN**, Game & Fish, Box 741, Marietta GA 30061. (770)953-9222. **Contact:** Dennis Schmidt, editor. See *Game & Fish*.

$ $ ◩ **MISSISSIPPI GAME & FISH**, Game & Fish, Box 741, Marietta GA 30061. (770)953-9222. **Contact:** Ken Duke, editor. See *Game & Fish*.

$ $ ◩ **MISSOURI GAME & FISH**, Game & Fish, Box 741, Marietta GA 30061. (770)953-9222. **Contact:** Ken Duke. See *Game & Fish*.

$ $ ◩ **MUSKY HUNTER MAGAZINE**, P.O. Box 340, St. Germain WI 54558. (715)477-2178. Fax: (715)477-8858. Editor: Jim Saric. **Contact:** Steve Heiting. **90% freelance written.** Bimonthly magazine on musky fishing. "Serves the vertical market of musky fishing enthusiasts. We're interested in how-to where-to articles." Estab. 1988. Circ. 34,000. Pays on publication. Publishes ms an average of 4 months after acceptance. Byline given. Buys first, one-time rights. Submit seasonal material 4 months in advance. Responds in 2 months to queries. Sample copy for 9×12 SAE with $1.93 postage. Writer's guidelines for #10 SASE.

Nonfiction: Historical/nostalgic (related only to musky fishing), how-to (modify lures, boats and tackle for musky fishing), personal experience (must be musky fishing experience), technical (fishing equipment), travel (to lakes and areas for musky fishing). **Buys 50 mss/year.** Send complete ms. Length: 1,000-2,500 words. **Pays $100-300 for assigned articles; $50-300 for unsolicited articles.** Payment of contributor copies or other premiums negotiable.

Photos: Send photos with submission. Reviews 35mm transparencies, 3×5 prints. Buys one-time rights. Offers no additional payment for photos accepted with ms. Identification of subjects required.

$ $ ◩ **NEW ENGLAND GAME & FISH**, Game & Fish, Box 741, Marietta GA 30061. (770)953-9222. **Contact:** Steve Carpenteri, editor. See *Game & Fish*.

$ $ **NEW JERSEY LAKE SURVEY FISHING MAPS GUIDE**, New Jersey Sportsmen's Guides, P.O. Box 100, Somerdale NJ 08083. (856)783-1271. Fax: (856)665-8656. Website: www.njsportsmensguides.com. **Contact:** Steve Perrone, editor. **40% freelance written.** Annual magazine covering freshwater lake fishing. "*New Jersey Lake Survey Fishing Maps Guide* is edited for freshwater fishing for trout, bass, perch, catfish and other species. It contains 140 pages and approximately 100 full-page maps of the surveyed lakes that illustrate contours, depths, bottom characteristics, shorelines and vegetation present at each location. The guide includes a 10-page chart which describes over 250 fishing lakes in New Jersey. It also includes more than 125 fishing tips and 'Bass'n Notes.'" Estab. 1989. Circ. 3,500. **Pays on acceptance.** Publishes ms an average of 6 months after acceptance. Byline given. Buys first rights, makes work-for-hire assignments. Editorial lead time 6 months. Accepts queries by mail, fax. Sample copy for $14.50 postage paid.

Nonfiction: How to fishing, freshwater fishing. Length: 500-2,000 words. **Pays $75-250.**

Photos: State availability with submission. Reviews transparencies, 4×5 slides or 4×6 prints. Buys one-time rights. Captions, identification of subjects, model releases required.

Tips: "We want queries with published clips of articles describing fishing experiences on New Jersey lakes and ponds."

$ $ ◩ **NEW YORK GAME & FISH**, Game & Fish, Box 741, Marietta GA 30061. (770)953-9222. **Contact:** Steve Carpenteri, editor. See *Game & Fish*.

$ $ **NORTH AMERICAN WHITETAIL, The Magazine Devoted to the Serious Trophy Deer Hunter**, Game & Fish Publications, 2250 Newmarket Pkwy., Suite 110, Marietta GA 30067. (770)953-9222. Fax: (770)933-9510. **Contact:** Gordon Whittington, editor. **70% freelance written.** Magazine published 8 times/year about hunting trophy-class white-tailed deer in North America, primarily the US. "We provide the serious hunter with highly sophisticated information about trophy-class whitetails and how, when and where to hunt them. We are not a general hunting magazine or a magazine for the very occasional deer hunter." Estab. 1982. Circ. 130,000. Pays 65 days prior to cover date of issue. Publishes ms an average of 6 months after acceptance. Byline given. Offers negotiable kill fee. Buys first North American serial rights. Submit seasonal material 10 months in advance. Accepts queries by mail, fax, phone. Responds in 3 months to mss. Sample copy for $3.50 and 9×12 SAE with 7 first-class stamps. Writer's guidelines for #10 SASE.

Nonfiction: How-to, interview/profile. **Buys 50 mss/year.** Query. Length: 1,000-3,000 words. **Pays $150-400.**

Photos: Send photos with submission. Reviews 35mm transparencies, 8×10 prints. Buys one-time rights. Offers no additional payment for photos accepted with ms. Captions, identification of subjects required.

Columns/Departments: Trails and Tails (nostalgic, humorous or other entertaining styles of deer-hunting material, fictional or nonfictional), 1,200 words. **Buys 8 mss/year.** Send complete ms. **Pays $150.**

Tips: "Our articles are written by persons who are deer hunters first, writers second. Our hard-core hunting audience can see through material produced by non-hunters or those with only marginal deer-hunting expertise. We have a continual need for expert profiles/interviews. Study the magazine to see what type of hunting expert it takes to qualify for our use, and look at how those articles have been directed by the writers. Good photography of the interviewee and his hunting results must accompany such pieces."

$ $ ⬛ NORTH CAROLINA GAME & FISH, Game & Fish, Box 741, Marietta GA 30061. (770)953-9222. Fax: (770)933-9510. **Contact:** David Johnson, editor. See *Game & Fish*.

$ $ ⬛ OHIO GAME & FISH, Game & Fish, Box 741, Marietta GA 30061. (770)953-9222. **Contact:** Steve Carpenteri, editor. See *Game & Fish*.

$ $ ⬛ OKLAHOMA GAME & FISH, Game & Fish, Box 741, Marietta GA 30061. (770)953-9222. Fax: (770)933-9510. **Contact:** Nick Gilmore, editor. See *Game & Fish*.

$ $ ⬛ ONTARIO OUT OF DOORS, Rogeis Media, 777 Bay St., 28th Floor, Toronto, Ontario M5W 1A7, Canada. (416)596-5815. Fax: (416)596-2517. E-mail: jkerr@rmpublishing.com. Website: www.fishontario.com. Editor: Burt Myers. **Contact:** John Kerr, managing editor. **90% freelance written.** Magazine published 10 times/year covering the outdoors (hunting, fishing, camping). Estab. 1968. Circ. 93,865. **Pays on acceptance.** Publishes ms an average of 6 months after acceptance. Byline given. Offers 100% kill fee. Buys first, electronic rights. Editorial lead time 6 months. Submit seasonal material 6 months in advance. Accepts queries by mail, e-mail, fax. Responds in 3 months to queries. Sample copy and writer's guidelines free.
Nonfiction: Book excerpts, essays, exposé, how-to (fishing and hunting), humor, inspirational, interview/profile, new product, opinion, personal experience, photo feature, technical, travel (where-to), wildlife management, environmental concerns. Special issues: Travel (March); Trout (April). "No 'Me and Joe' features or articles written from a women's point of view on how to catch a bass." **Buys 100 mss/year.** Length: 500-2,500 words. **Pays $750 maximum for assigned articles; $700 maximum for unsolicited articles.** Sometimes pays expenses of writers on assignment.
Photos: Send photos with submission. Reviews transparencies. Buys one time and electronic rights. Pays $450-750 for covers. Captions required.
Columns/Departments: Trips & Tips (travel pieces), 50-150 words; Short News, 50-500 words. **Buys 30-40 mss/year.** Query. **Pays $50-250.**
Fiction: Humorous, novel excerpts. **Buys 6 mss/year.** Send complete ms. Length: 1,000 words. **Pays $500 maximum.**
Fillers: Facts, newsbreaks. **Buys 40/year.** Length: 25-100 words. **Pays $15-50.**
Tips: "With the exception of short news stories, it is suggested that writers query prior to submission."

$ $ $ OUTDOOR LIFE, The Sportsman's Authority Since 1898, Times Mirror Magazines, 2 Park Ave., New York NY 10016. (212)779-5000. Fax: (212)779-5366. E-mail: olmagazine@aol.com. Website: www.outdoorlife.com. Editor: Todd W. Smith. Managing Editor: Camille Cozzone Rankin. **Contact:** Colin Moore, executive editor. **60% freelance written.** Magazine published 10 times/year covering hunting and fishing in North America. "*Outdoor Life* is a major national source of information for American and Canadian hunters and anglers. It offers news, regional reports, adventure stories, how-to, regular advice from experts, profiles and equipment tests." Estab. 1898. Circ. 1,350,000. **Pays on acceptance.** Publishes ms an average of 6 months after acceptance. Byline given. Buys first North American serial, electronic rights. Editorial lead time 4 months. Submit seasonal material 5 months in advance. Accepts queries by mail, e-mail, fax. Responds in 1 month to queries; 2 months to mss. Sample copy for 9×12 SAE plus proper postage. Writer's guidelines for #10 SASE.
Nonfiction: All articles must pertain to hunting and fishing pursuits. Essays, exposé, how-to, interview/profile, personal experience, travel, Interesting/weird news stories. Query with published clips. Length: 100-2,000 words. **Pays $500-3,000.** Sometimes pays expenses of writers on assignment.
Photos: Do not send photos until requested.
Columns/Departments: Frank Minter, senior associate editor; Scott Bowen, associate editor; Colin Moore, executive editor. Regionals, 150-300 words; Compass, 250-500 words; Snap Shots, 150 words; Private Lessons, 500-700 words. **Buys 500 mss/year.** Query with published clips. **Pays $75-500.**
Fillers: Scott Bowen, Compass editor. Facts, newsbreaks. **Buys 40-50/year.** Length: 150 words. **Pays $75.**
Tips: "If someone catches a record fish or takes a record game animal, or has a great adventure/survival story, they may try to submit a full-sized feature, but the story must be exceptional."

Ⓝ $ THE OUTDOORS MAGAZINE, For the Better Hunter, Angler & Trapper, Elk Publishing, Inc., 1 King St., Burlington VT 05401. (802)860-0003. Fax: (802)860-0003. E-mail: OutdoorMagazine@aol.com. Website: www.vermontoutdoors.com. **Contact:** James Ehlers, editor. **80% freelance written.** Monthly magazine covering wildlife conservation. "New England hunting, fishing and trapping magazine with a focus on environmental and conservation issues." Estab. 1996. Circ. 9,500. Pays on publication. Publishes ms an average of 1 year after acceptance. Byline given. Offers 10% kill fee. Buys first North American serial rights. Editorial lead time 1 year. Submit seasonal material 6 months in advance. Accepts queries by mail. Responds in 1 month to queries; 3 months to mss. Sample copy online or by e-mail. Writer's guidelines free.

Nonfiction: Book excerpts, essays, exposé, general interest, historical/nostalgic, how-to, interview/profile, new product, opinion, personal experience, technical. **Buys 200 mss/year.** Query with published clips. Length: 750-2,500 words. **Pays $20-150 for assigned articles.**

Photos: State availability with submission. Reviews contact sheets. Buys one-time rights. Pays $15-75/photo. Identification of subjects required.

Columns/Departments: Buys 100 mss/year. Query with published clips. **Pays $20-60.**

Fillers: Anecdotes, facts.

Tips: "*Know* the publication, not just read it, so you understand the audience. Patience and thoroughness will go a long way."

$ $ ⚃ PENNSYLVANIA ANGLER & BOATER, Pennsylvania Fish and Boat Commission, P.O. Box 67000, Harrisburg PA 17106-7000. (717)705-7844. E-mail: amichaels@state.pa.us. Website: www.fish.state.pa.us. **Contact:** Art Michaels, editor. **80% freelance written.** Bimonthly magazine covering fishing, boating and related conservation topics in Pennsylvannia. Circ. 30,000. Pays 2 months after acceptance. Publishes ms an average of 8 months after acceptance. Byline given. Buys varying rights. Submit seasonal material 8 months in advance. Responds in 1 month to queries; 2 months to mss. Sample copy for 9×12 SAE with 9 first-class stamps. Writer's guidelines for #10 SASE.
Nonfiction: How-to (and where-to), technical. No saltwater or hunting material. **Buys 100 mss/year.** Query. Length: 500-2,500 words. **Pays $25-300.**
Photos: Send photos with submission. Reviews 35mm and larger transparencies. Rights purchased vary. Offers no additional payment for photos accompanying mss. Captions, identification of subjects, model releases required.

$ $ ⚃ PENNSYLVANIA GAME & FISH, Game & Fish, Box 741, Marietta GA 30061. (770)953-9222. **Contact:** Steve Carpenteri, editor. See *Game & Fish.*

$ $ PETERSEN'S HUNTING, Petersen Publishing Co., 6420 Wilshire Blvd., Los Angeles CA 90048. (323)782-2743. Fax: (323)782-2477. **Contact:** J. Scott Rupp, editor. **30% freelance written.** Monthly magazine covering sport hunting. "We are a 'how-to' magazine devoted to all facets of sport hunting, with the intent to make our readers more knowledgeable, more successful and safer hunters." Circ. 380,000. Pays on scheduling. Publishes ms an average of 9 months after acceptance. Byline given. Buys all rights. Responds in 1 month to queries. Writer's guidelines on request.
Nonfiction: General interest, historical/nostalgic, how-to (on hunting techniques), travel. Special issues: Hunting Annual (August). **Buys 30 mss/year.** Query. Length: 2,400 words. **Pays $350 minimum.**
Photos: Send photos with submission. Reviews 35mm transparencies. Buys one-time rights. Captions, identification of subjects, model releases required.

Ⓝ $ $ RACK MAGAZINE, Adventures in Trophy Hunting, Buckmasters Ltd., P.O. Box 244022, Montgomery AL 36124-4022. (800)240-3337. Fax: (334)215-3535. E-mail: mhandley@buckmasters.com. Website: www.rackmag.rivals.com. **Contact:** Mike Handley, editor. **10-15% freelance written.** Hunting magazine published monthly (August-January). "*Rack Magazine* caters to deer hunters and chasers of other big game animals who prefer short stories detailing the harvests of exceptional specimens. There are no how-to, destination or human interest stories; only pieces describing particular hunts." Estab. 1999. Circ. 100,000. Pays on publication. Publishes ms an average of 11 months after acceptance. Byline given. Buys first North American serial, second serial (reprint) rights. Editorial lead time 9 months. Accepts queries by e-mail, phone. Accepts simultaneous submissions. Responds in 1 month to queries. Sample copy free. Writer's guidelines by e-mail.
Nonfiction: Interview/profile, personal experience. *Rack Magazine* does not use how-to, destination, humor, general interest or hunter profiles. **Buys 35-40 mss/year.** Query. Length: 500-1,500 words. **Pays $250.**
Reprints: Accepts previously published submissions.
Photos: Send photos with submission. Reviews transparencies. Offers no additional payment. "We pay $500 for first time use as a cover." Captions, identification of subjects required.
Tips: "We're only interested in stories about record book animals (those scoring high enough to qualify for BTR, B&C, P&Y, SCI or Longhunter). Whitetails must be scored by a certified BTR/Buckmasters measurer and their antlers must register at least 160 inches on the BTR system. Deer scoring 190 or better on the B&C or P&Y scales would be candidates, but the hunter would have to have his or her buck scored by a BTR measurer."

$ $ ⚃ ROCKY MOUNTAIN GAME & FISH, Game & Fish, Box 741, Marietta GA 30061. Fax: (770)933-9510. **Contact:** Burt Carey, editor. See *Game & Fish.*

$ $ ⚃ SAFARI MAGAZINE, The Journal of Big Game Hunting, Safari Club International, 4800 W. Gates Pass Rd., Tucson AZ 85745. (520)620-1220. Fax: (520)618-3555. E-mail: sskinner@safariclub.org. Website: www.safariclub.org. Director of Publications/Editor: Steve Comus. **Contact:** Stan Skinner, managing editor. **90% freelance written.** Bimonthly journal covering international big game hunting and wildlife conservation. Circ. 40,000. Pays on publication. Publishes ms an average of 18 months after acceptance. Byline given. Buys all rights. Submit seasonal material 1 year in advance. Accepts queries by mail, e-mail. Responds in 2 weeks to queries; 6 weeks to mss. Sample copy for $4. Writer's guidelines for #10 SASE.

☛ Break in with "engaging, suspenseful, first-person stories of big-game hunts that involve unique circumstances or unusual regions and animals. Conservation stories should include reputable, known sources in the field, plenty of facts and be supported by scientific data."

Nonfiction: Photo feature (wildlife), travel (firearms, hunting techniques, etc.). **Buys 72 mss/year.** Query with or without published clips or send complete ms. Length: 2,000 words. **Pays $300 for professional writers, less if not professional.**

Photos: State availability of or send photos with submission. Buys first rights. Payment depends on size in magazine. Pays up to $45 for b&w; $100 color. Captions, identification of subjects, model releases required.

Tips: "Study the magazine. Send complete manuscript and photo package. Make it appeal to knowledgeable, world-traveled big game hunters. Features on conservation contributions from big game hunters around the world are open to freelancers. We have enough stories on first-time African safaris. We need North and South American, European and Asian hunting stories, plus stories dealing with wildlife conservation, especially as it applies to our organization and members."

$ $🖪 SALT WATER SPORTSMAN MAGAZINE, 263 Summer St., Boston MA 02210. (617)303-3660. Fax: (617)303-3661. E-mail: editor@saltwatersportsman.com. Website: www.saltwatersportsman.com. **Contact:** Barry Gibson, editor. **85% freelance written.** Monthly magazine. "*Salt Water Sportsman* is edited for serious marine sport fishermen whose lifestyle includes the pursuit of game fish in US waters and around the world. It provides information on fishing trends, techniques and destinations, both local and international. Each issue reviews offshore and inshore fishing boats, high-tech electronics, innovative tackle, engines and other new products. Coverage also focuses on sound fisheries management and conservation." Circ. 165,000. **Pays on acceptance.** Publishes ms an average of 5 months after acceptance. Byline given. Offers 100% kill fee. Buys first North American serial rights. Submit seasonal material 8 months in advance. Accepts queries by mail, e-mail, fax. Responds in 1 month to queries. Sample copy and writer's guidelines for #10 SASE.

Nonfiction: "Readers want solid how-to, where-to information written in an enjoyable, easy-to-read style. Personal anecdotes help the reader identify with the writer." How-to, personal experience, technical, travel (to fishing areas). **Buys 100 mss/year.** Query. Length: 1,200-2,000 words. **Pays $300-750.**

Reprints: Send tearsheet. Pays up to 50% of amount paid for original article.

Photos: Reviews color slides. Pays $1,000 minimum for 35mm, 2¼×2¼ or 8×10 transparencies for cover. Offers additional payment for photos accepted with ms. Captions required.

Columns/Departments: Sportsman's Tips (short, how-to tips and techniques on salt water fishing, emphasis is on building, repairing, or reconditioning specific items or gear). Send complete ms.

Tips: "There are a lot of knowledgeable fishermen/budding writers out there who could be valuable to us with a little coaching. Many don't think they can write a story for us, but they'd be surprised. We work with writers. Shorter articles that get to the point which are accompanied by good, sharp photos are hard for us to turn down. Having to delete unnecessary wordage—conversation, cliches, etc.—that writers feel is mandatory is annoying. Often they don't devote enough attention to specific fishing information."

$ $🖪 SHOTGUN SPORTS MAGAZINE, America's leading shotgun magazine, Shotgun Sports, Inc., P.O. Box 6810, Auburn CA 95604. (530)889-2220. Fax: (530)889-9106. E-mail: shotgun@shotgunsportsmagazine.com. Website: www.shotgunsportsmagazine.com. **Contact:** Frank Kodl, editorial director. **100% freelance written.** Magazine published 11 times/year covering shotgun sports and shotgun hunting. "We cover any and all activities performed with a shotgun—sporting clays, trapshooting, skeet, hunting, gunsmithing, shotshell patterning, shotshell reloading, mental exercises to improve performance, equipment tests—anything that has a shotgun approach to the subject." Estab. 1978. Circ. 120,000. Pays on publication. Publishes ms an average of 6 months after acceptance. Byline given. Buys first North American serial, all rights. Editorial lead time 4 months. Submit seasonal material 5 months in advance. Accepts queries by mail, e-mail, fax, phone. Responds in 3 weeks to queries; 3 months to mss. Sample copy and writer's guidelines free.

Nonfiction: Book excerpts, exposé, general interest, historical/nostalgic, how-to, humor, interview/profile, opinion, personal experience, photo feature, technical. "No stories that invite going to a specific club or sponsored hunting trip that appear to be payback pieces." **Buys 50-75 mss/year.** Query with or without published clips or send complete ms. Length: 1,000-5,000 words. **Pays $50-200.** Sometimes pays expenses of writers on assignment.

Photos: State availability with submission. Reviews contact sheets, transparencies, prints. Buys all rights. Offers no additional payment for photos accepted with ms. Captions, identification of subjects required.

Fillers: Anecdotes, facts, newsbreaks, short humor. **Buys 10/year.** Length: 100-1,000 words. **Pays $15-50.**

Tips: "Take a fresh approach. Writers for *Shotgun Sports* should have firsthand knowledge of hunting, trapshooting, skeet or sporting clays or be knowledgeable in other areas of shotgunning such as collecting, repairing or reloading. Current issues of *Shotgun Sports* are the best guide to our style. Try to create a professional, yet friendly article. Quality is the key. I would rather see 1,000 well-written words than 5,000 which have to be edited and rewritten before they become readable. Photographs of high quality are almost always required with any submission. In some cases, we can provide additional photographs from our files."

$ $🖪 SOUTH CAROLINA GAME & FISH, Game & Fish, Box 741, Marietta GA 30061. (770)953-9222. **Contact:** David Johnson, editor. See *Game & Fish.*

$ $⊠ SOUTH CAROLINA WILDLIFE, P.O. Box 167, Rembert Dennis Bldg., Columbia SC 29202-0167. (803)734-3972. E-mail: scwmed@scdnr.state.sc.us. Editor: John Davis. **Contact:** Linda Renshaw, managing editor. **75% freelance written.** Bimonthly magazine for South Carolinians interested in wildlife and outdoor activities. Estab. 1954. Circ. 60,000. **Pays on acceptance.** Publishes ms an average of 6 months after acceptance. Byline given. Buys first rights. Responds in 2 months to queries. Sample copy free.
Nonfiction: "Realize that the topic must be of interest to South Carolinans and that we must be able to justify using it in a publication published by the state department of natural resources—so if it isn't directly about outdoor recreation, a certain plant or animal, it must be somehow related to the environment and conservation. Readers prefer a broad mix of outdoor related topics (articles that illustrate the beauty of South Carolina's outdoors and those that help the reader get more for his/her time, effort, and money spent in outdoor recreation). These two general areas are the ones we most need. Subjects vary a great deal in topic, area and style, but must all have a common ground in the outdoor resources and heritage of South Carolina. Review back issues and query with a one-page outline citing sources, giving ideas for photographs, explaining justification and giving an example of the first two paragraphs." Does not need any column material. Generally does not seek photographs. The publisher assumes no responsibility for unsolicited material. **Buys 25-30 mss/year.** Query. Length: 1,000-3,000 words. **Pays $200-400.**
Tips: "We need more writers in the outdoor field who take pride in the craft of writing and put a real effort toward originality and preciseness in their work. Query on a topic we haven't recently done. Frequent mistakes made by writers in completing an article are failure to check details and go in-depth on a subject."

$ $ $ SPORT FISHING, The Magazine of Saltwater Fishing, 460 N Orlando Ave., Suite 200, Winter Park FL 32789-7061. (407)571-4574. Fax: (407)571-4576. E-mail: jason.cannon@worldpub.net. **Contact:** Jason Cannon, managing editor. **50% freelance written.** Magazine covering saltwater sports fishing. Estab. 1986. Circ. 150,000. Pays within 6 weeks of acceptance. Byline given. Offers $100 kill fee. Buys first North American serial, one-time rights. Submit seasonal material 5 months in advance. Accepts queries by mail, e-mail, fax. Responds in 2 weeks to queries. Sample copy for #10 SASE. Writer's guidelines for #10 SASE or by e-mail.
   O— Break in with freelance pieces for the *Tips & Techniques News* and *Fish Tales* departments.
Nonfiction: How-to (rigging & techniques tips), technical, Conservation, Where-to (all on sport fishing). **Buys 32-40 mss/year.** Query. Length: 2,000-3,000 words. **Pays $800-1,500.**
Photos: Send photos with submission. Reviews transparencies and returns within 1 week. Buys one-time rights. Pays $75-300 inside; $1,000 cover.
Columns/Departments: Fish Tales (humorous sport fishing anecdotes); Rigging (how-to rigging for sport fishing); Technique (how-to technique for sport fishing), 800-1,200 words. **Buys 8-24 mss/year.** Send complete ms. **Pays $250.**
Tips: "Don't query unless you are familiar with the magazine; note—*salt water only*. Find a fresh idea or angle to an old idea. We welcome the chance to work with new/unestablished writers who know their stuff—and how to say it."

$ $⊠ TENNESSEE SPORTSMAN, Game & Fish, Box 741, Marietta GA 30061. (770)953-9222. **Contact:** David Johnson, editor. See *Game & Fish*.

$ $⊠ TEXAS SPORTSMAN, Game & Fish, Box 741, Marietta GA 30061. (770)953-9222. **Contact:** Nick Gilmore, editor. See *Game & Fish*.

$ $ TIDE MAGAZINE, Coastal Conservation Association, 220W, 4801 Woodway, Houston TX 77056. (713)626-4222. Fax: (713)961-3801. E-mail: tide@joincca.org. **Contact:** Doug Pike, editor. Bimonthly magazine on saltwater fishing and conservation of marine resources. Estab. 1977. Circ. 60,000. Pays on publication. Byline given. Buys one-time rights. Submit seasonal material 6 months in advance. Responds in 1 month to queries.
Nonfiction: Essays, exposé, general interest, historical/nostalgic, humor, opinion, personal experience, travel, Related to saltwater fishing and Gulf/Atlantic coastal habitats. **Buys 30 mss/year.** Query with published clips. Length: 1,200-1,500 words. **Pays $250-350 for ms/photo package.**
Photos: Reviews negatives, 35mm transparencies, color negatives/prints. Buys one-time rights. Pays $50-100. Captions required.

$ $⊠ TRAPPER & PREDATOR CALLER, Krause Publications Inc., 700 E. State St., Iola WI 54990. (715)445-2214. Fax: (715)445-4087. E-mail: waitp@krause.com. Website: www.trapperpredatorcaller.com. **Contact:** Paul Wait, editor. **90% freelance written.** Monthly tabloid covering trapping, predator calling and muzzleloading. "Our editorial goal is to entertain and educate our readers with national and regional articles that promote trapping and predator calling." Estab. 1975. Circ. 41,000. Pays on publication. Buys first North American serial rights. Submit seasonal material 6 months in advance. Sample copy and writer's guidelines free.
Nonfiction: How-to, humor, interview/profile, new product, opinion, personal experience. **Buys 100 mss/year.** Query with or without published clips or send complete ms. Length: 1,200-2,500 words. **Pays $80-250 for assigned articles; $40-200 for unsolicited articles.**
Photos: Send photos with submission. Reviews prints. Buys one-time rights. Offers no additional payment for photos accepted with ms. Captions, identification of subjects required.
   ▣ The online magazine carries original content not found in the print edition. Contact: Paul Wait.
Tips: "Detailed how-to articles receive strongest consideration."

$ $✕ TURKEY & TURKEY HUNTING, Krause Publications, 700 E. State St., Iola WI 54990-0001. (715)445-2214 ext. 484. Fax: (715)445-4087. E-mail: lovettb@krause.com. Website: www.turkeyandturkeyhunting.com. **Contact:** Brian Lovett, editor. **90% freelance written.** Bimonthly magazine covering turkey hunting and turkey biology. "*Turkey & Turkey Hunting* is for serious, experienced turkey hunters." Estab. 1983. Circ. 28,000. **Pays on acceptance.** Publishes ms an average of 1 year after acceptance. Byline given. Offers 50% kill fee. Buys first North American serial rights. Editorial lead time 1 year. Submit seasonal material 1 year in advance. Accepts queries by mail. Sample copy and writer's guidelines free.

Nonfiction: How-to, personal experience. **Buys 45 mss/year.** Query with published clips. Length: 2,000 words. **Pays $275-300.** Pays expenses of writers on assignment.

Photos: Send photos with submission. Reviews transparencies. Buys one-time rights. Offers $75-300/photo, depending on size. Pays on publication for photos.

Tips: "Have a thorough knowledge of turkey hunting and the hunting industry. Send fresh, informative queries, and indicate topics you'd feel comfortable covering on assignment."

$ $ TURKEY CALL, Wild Turkey Center, P.O. Box 530, Edgefield SC 29824-0530. (803)637-3106. Fax: (803)637-0034. E-mail: scrowder@nwtf.net or dhowlett@nwtf.net. Editor: Jay Langston. **Contact:** Stephanie Crowder, publishing assistant; Doug Howlett, managing editor. **50-60% freelance written.** Eager to work with new/unpublished writers and photographers. Bimonthly Educational magazine for members of the National Wild Turkey Federation. Estab. 1973. Circ. 145,000. Pays on acceptance for assigned articles, on publication for unsolicited articles. Publishes ms an average of 6 months after acceptance. Byline given. Buys one-time rights. Accepts queries by mail, e-mail. Responds in 1 month., Queries required to queries Submit complete package if article is assigned., Wants original mss only to mss. Sample copy for $3 and 9×12 SAE. Writer's guidelines for #10 SASE or online.

    O➔ Break in with a knowledgeable, fresh point of view. Articles must be tightly written.

Nonfiction: Feature articles dealing with the hunting and management of the American wild turkey. Must be accurate information and must appeal to national readership of turkey hunters and wildlife management experts. May use some fiction that educates or entertains in a special way. No poetry or first-person accounts of remarkable hunting trips. Length: up to 2,500 words. **Pays $100 for short fillers of 600-700 words, $200-500 for features.**

Reprints: Send photocopy and information about when and where the material previously appeared. Pays 50% of amount paid for the original article.

Photos: "We want quality photos submitted with features." Art illustrations also acceptable. "We are using more and more inside color illustrations." No typical hunter-holding-dead-turkey photos or setups using mounted birds or domestic turkeys. Photos with how-to stories must make the techniques clear (example: how to make a turkey call; how to sculpt or carve a bird in wood). Reviews transparencies. Buys one-time rights. Pays $35 minimum for b&w photos and simple art illustrations; up to $100 for inside color, reproduced any size; $200-400 for covers.

Tips: "The writer should simply keep in mind that the audience is 'expert' on wild turkey management, hunting, life history and restoration/conservation history. He/she *must know the subject*. We are buying more third-person, more fiction, more humor—in an attempt to avoid the 'predictability trap' of a single subject magazine."

$ $✕ VIRGINIA GAME & FISH, Game & Fish, Box 741, Marietta GA 30061. (770)953-9222. **Contact:** David Johnson, editor. See *Game & Fish*.

$ $✕ WASHINGTON-OREGON GAME & FISH, Game & Fish, Box 741, Marietta GA 30061. **Contact:** Burt Carey, editor. See *Game & Fish*.

$ $✕ WEST VIRGINIA GAME & FISH, Game & Fish, Box 741, Marietta GA 30061. (770)953-9222. **Contact:** Ken Freel, editor. See *Game & Fish*.

$ $ WESTERN OUTDOORS, 3197-E Airport Loop, Costa Mesa CA 92626. (714)546-4370. Fax: (714)662-3486. E-mail: woutdoors@aol.com. **Contact:** Lew Carpenter, editor. **60% freelance written.** Magazine emphasizing fishing, boating for California, Oregon, Washington, Baja California, and Alaska. "We are the West's leading authority on fishing techniques, tackle and destinations, and all reports present the latest and most reliable information." Estab. 1961. Circ. 100,000. **Pays on acceptance.** Publishes ms an average of 6 months after acceptance. Buys first North American serial rights. Submit seasonal material 6 months in advance. Accepts queries by mail, e-mail, fax. Responds in 6 weeks to queries. Sample copy free. Writer's guidelines for #10 SASE.

Nonfiction: Where-to (catch more fish, improve equipment, etc.), how-to informational, photo feature. "We do not accept poetry or fiction." **Buys 36-40 assigned mss/year.** Query. Length: 1,500-2,000 words. **Pays $450-600.**

Photos: Reviews 35mm slides. Offers no additional payment for photos accepted with ms; pays $350-500 for covers. Captions required.

Tips: "Provide a complete package of photos, map, trip facts and manuscript written according to our news feature format. Excellence of color photo selections make a sale more likely. Include sketches of fishing patterns and techniques to guide our illustrators. Graphics are important. The most frequent mistake made by writers in completing an article for us is that they don't follow our style. Our guidelines are quite clear. One query at a time via mail, e-mail, fax. No phone calls. You can become a regular *Western Outdoors* byliner by submitting professional quality packages of fine writing accompanied by excellent photography. Pros anticipate what is needed, and immediately provide whatever else we request. Furthermore, they meet deadlines!"

N $ $⊠ WESTERN SPORTSMAN, 780 Beatty St., Suite 300, Vancouver British Columbia V6B 2M1, Canada. (604)606-4644. Fax: (604)687-1925. E-mail: oppubl@istar.ca. **Contact:** George Gruenefeld, editor. **90% freelance written.** Bimonthly magazine for fishermen, hunters, campers and others interested in outdoor recreation. "Note that our coverage area is British Columbia, Alberta, Saskatchewan, Manitoba, Yukon and Northwest Territory. We try to include as much information as possible on all subjects in each edition. Therefore, we often publish fishing articles in our winter issues along with a variety of winter stories." Estab. 1968. Circ. 29,000. Pays on publication. Byline given. Rights purchased vary with author and material. Usually buys first North American serial or second serial (reprint) rights. Accepts queries by mail, e-mail, fax. Responds in 1 month to queries. Sample copy for $4 and 9×12 SAE with 4 IRCs (US). Writer's guidelines for free with SAE and IRC (US).

Nonfiction: "It is necessary that all articles can identify with our coverage area. We are interested in manuscripts from writers who have had an interesting fishing or hunting experience. We also publish other informational pieces as long as they relate to our coverage area. We are most interested in articles which tell about the average guy living on beans, guiding his own boat, stalking his game and generally doing his own thing in our part of Western Canada than a story describing a well-to-do outdoorsmen traveling by motorhome, staying at an expensive lodge with guides doing everything for him except catching the fish or shooting the big game animal. The articles that are submitted to us need to be prepared in a knowledgeable way and include more information than the actual fish catch or animal or bird kill. Discuss the terrain, the people involved on the trip, the water or weather conditions, the costs, the planning that went into the trip, the equipment and other data closely associated with the particular event. We're always looking for new writers." **Buys 60 mss/year.** Submit complete ms and SASE or IRCs. Length: 1,800-2,000 words. **Payment negotiable.**
Reprints: Send typed ms with rights for sale noted and information about when and where the material previously appeared.
Photos: Photos purchased with ms with no additional payment. Also purchased without ms. Pays $150 for 35mm or larger transparency for front cover.

$ $⊠ WISCONSIN OUTDOOR JOURNAL, Krause Publications, 700 E. State St., Iola WI 54990-0001. (715)445-2214. Fax: (715)445-4087. Website: www.wisoutdoorjournal.com. **Contact:** Brian Lovett, editor. **95% freelance written.** Magazine published 8 times/year covering Wisconsin hunting, fishing, trapping and wildlife. "*Wisconsin Outdoor Journal* is more than a straight hook-and-bullet magazine. Though *WOJ* carries how-to and where-to information, it also prints narratives, nature features and state history pieces to give our readers a better appreciation of Wisconsin's outdoors." Estab. 1987. Circ. 48,000. **Pays on acceptance.** Publishes ms an average of 1 year after acceptance. Byline given. Buys first North American serial rights. Editorial lead time 1 year. Submit seasonal material 1 year in advance. Accepts queries by mail. Responds in 2 months to queries. Sample copy and writer's guidelines for #10 SASE. Writer's guidelines for #10 SASE.
Nonfiction: Book excerpts, essays, historical/nostalgic, how-to, interview/profile, personal experience, photo feature. No stories focusing on out-of-state topics; no general recreation (hiking, biking, skiing) features. **Buys 65 mss/year.** Query with published clips. Length: 1,600-2,000 words. **Pays $150-250.** Pays expenses of writers on assignment.
Photos: Send photos with submission. Reviews transparencies. Buys one-time rights. Offers $75-275/photo.
Columns/Departments: Wisconsin Field Notes (anecdotes, outdoor news items not extensively covered by newspapers, interesting outdoor occurrences, all relevant to Wisconsin; may include photos), 50-750 words. **Pays $5-75 on publication.**
Fiction: Adventure, historical, nostalgic. "No eulogies of a good hunting dog." **Buys 10 mss/year.** Send complete ms. Length: 1,500-2,000 words. **Pays $100-250.**
Tips: "Don't submit personal hunting and fishing stories. Seek fresh, new topics, such as an analysis of long-term outdoor issues. Writers need to know Wisconsin intimately—stories that appear as regionals in other magazines probably won't be printed within *WOJ*'s pages."

$ $⊠ WISCONSIN SPORTSMAN, Game & Fish, Box 741, Marietta GA 30061. (770)953-9222. **Contact:** Dennis Schmidt, editor. See *Game & Fish*.

Martial Arts

$ $⊠ INSIDE KUNG-FU, The Ultimate In Martial Arts Coverage!, CFW Enterprises, 4201 Vanowen Place, Burbank CA 91505. (818)845-2656. Fax: (818)845-7761. E-mail: davecater@cfwenterprises.com. **Contact:** Dave Cater, editor. **90% freelance written.** Monthly magazine for those with "traditional, modern, athletic and intellectual tastes. The magazine slants toward little-known martial arts, and little-known aspects of established martial arts." Estab. 1973. Circ. 125,000. Pays on publication date on magazine cover. Publishes ms an average of 6 months after acceptance. Byline given. Offers 20% kill fee. Buys first North American serial rights. Editorial lead time 6 months. Submit seasonal material 6 months in advance. Accepts simultaneous submissions. Responds in 1 month to queries; 2 months to mss. Sample copy for $2.95 and 9×12 SAE with 5 first class stamps. Writer's guidelines for #10 SASE.
Nonfiction: "Articles must be technically or historically accurate." *Inside Kung-Fu* is looking for external type articles (fighting, weapons, multiple hackers). Book excerpts, essays, exposé (topics relating to martial arts), general interest, historical/nostalgic, how-to (primarily technical materials), inspirational, interview/profile, new product, personal experi-

ence, photo feature, technical, travel, cultural/philosophical. No "sports coverage, first-person articles or articles which constitute personal aggrandizement." **Buys 120 mss/year.** Query or send complete ms. Length: 1,500-3,000 words (8-10 pages, typewritten and double-spaced). **Pays $125-175.**

Reprints: Send tearsheet or typed ms with rights for sale noted and information about when and where the material previously appeared. No payment.

Photos: State availability of or send photos with submission. Reviews contact sheets, negatives, 5×7 or 8×10 color prints. Buys all rights. No additional payment for photos. Captions, identification of subjects, model releases required.

Fiction: "Fiction must be short (1,000-2,000 words) and relate to the martial arts. We buy very few fiction pieces." Adventure, historical, humorous, mystery, novel excerpts, suspense. **Buys 2-3 mss/year.**

Tips: "See what interests the writer. May have a better chance of breaking in at our publication with short articles and fillers since smaller pieces allow us to gauge individual ability, but we're flexible—quality writers get published, period. The most frequent mistakes made by writers in completing an article for us are ignoring photo requirements and model releases (always number one—and who knows why? All requirements are spelled out in writer's guidelines)."

N $KUNGFU QIGONG, Wisdom for Body and Mind, TC Media, 40748 Encyclopedia Circle, Fremont CA 94538. (510)656-5100. Fax: (510)656-8844. E-mail: info@kungfumagazine.com. Website: www.kungfumagazine.com. **Contact:** Martha Burr, editor. **70% freelance written.** Bimonthly magazine covering Chinese martial arts and culture. "*Kungfu Qigong* covers the full range of Kungfu culture, including healing, philosophy, meditation, yoga, Fengshui, Buddhism, Taoism, history and the latest events in art and culture, plus insightful features on the martial arts." Circ. 50,000. Pays on publication. Byline given. Buys first North American serial, electronic rights. Editorial lead time 4 months. Submit seasonal material 4 months in advance. Accepts queries by mail, e-mail, fax, phone. Responds in 2 months to queries; 3 months to mss. Sample copy for $3.99 or online. Writer's guidelines free or online.

Nonfiction: Book excerpts, exposé, general interest, historical/nostalgic, how-to, interview/profile, personal experience, photo feature, religious, technical, travel, cultural perspectives. No poetry or fiction. **Buys 100 mss/year.** Query. Length: 500-2,500 words. **Pays $35-125.**

Photos: Send photos with submission. Reviews 5×7 prints, gif/jpeg files. Buys one-time rights. Offers no additional payment for photos accepted with ms. Captions, identification of subjects required.

Tips: "Check out our website and get an idea of past articles."

$ $ T'AI CHI, Leading International Magazine of T'ai Chi Ch'uan, Wayfarer Publications, P.O. Box 39938, Los Angeles CA 90039. (323)665-7773. Fax: (323)665-1627. E-mail: taichi@tai-chi.com. Website: www.tai-chi.com. **Contact:** Marvin Smalheiser, editor. **90% freelance written.** Bimonthly magazine covering T'ai Chi Ch'uan as a martial art and for health and fitness. "Covers T'ai Chi Ch'uan and other internal martial arts, plus qigong and Chinese health, nutrition and philosophical disciplines. Readers are practitioners or laymen interested in developing skills and insight for self-defense, health and self-improvement." Estab. 1977. Circ. 30,000. Pays on publication. Publishes ms an average of 3 months after acceptance. Byline given. Buys first North American serial rights. Editorial lead time 3 months. Submit seasonal material 6 months in advance. Accepts queries by mail, e-mail, fax. Responds in 3 weeks to queries; 3 months to mss. Sample copy for $3.95. Writer's guidelines for #10 SASE or online.

O— Break in by "understanding the problems our readers have to deal with learning and practicing T'ai Chi, and developing an article that deals with one or more of those problems."

Nonfiction: Book excerpts, essays, how-to (on T'ai Chi Ch'uan, qigong and related Chinese disciplines), interview/profile, personal experience. "Do not want articles promoting an individual, system or school." **Buys 50-60 mss/year.** Query with or without published clips or send complete ms. Length: 1,200-4,500 words. **Pays $75-500.** Sometimes pays expenses of writers on assignment.

Photos: Send photos with submission. Reviews color transparencies, color or b&w 4×6 or 5×7 prints. Buys one-time and reprint rights. Offers no additional payment for photos accepted with ms, but overall payment takes into consideration the number and quality of photos. Captions, identification of subjects, model releases required.

Tips: "Think and write for practitioners and laymen who want information and insight and who are trying to work through problems to improve skills and their health. No promotional material."

Miscellaneous

$CANADIAN RODEO NEWS, Canadian Rodeo News, Ltd., #223, 2116 27th Ave. NE, Calgary, Alberta T2E 7A6, Canada. (403)250-7292. Fax: (403)250-6926. E-mail: crn@rodeocanada.com. Website: www.rodeocanada.com. **Contact:** Lisa Cannady, editor. **60% freelance written.** Monthly tabloid covering "Canada's professional rodeo (CPRA) personalities and livestock. Read by rodeo participants and fans." Estab. 1964. Circ. 4,800. Pays on publication. Publishes ms an average of 1 month after acceptance. Byline given. Buys first, second serial (reprint) rights. Editorial lead time 1 month. Submit seasonal material 1 month in advance. Accepts queries by mail, e-mail, fax. Accepts simultaneous submissions. Responds in 1 month to queries; 2 months to mss. Sample copy and writer's guidelines free.

Nonfiction: General interest, historical/nostalgic, interview/profile. **Buys 70-80 mss/year.** Query. Length: 500-1,200 words. **Pays $30-60.**

Reprints: Send photocopy of article or typed ms with rights for sale noted and information about when and where the material previously appeared. Pays 100% of amount paid for an original article.

Photos: Send photos with submission. Reviews 4×6 prints. Buys one-time rights. Offers $15-25/cover photo.

Tips: "Best to call first with the story idea to inquire if it is suitable for publication. Readers are very knowledgeable of the sport, so writers need to be as well."

$ ⊠ FENCERS QUARTERLY MAGAZINE, 6751 CR 3850, Peace Valley MO 65788. (417)256-0432. E-mail: evangel@atlascomm.net or ale@townsqr.com. Editor-in-Chief: Nick Evangelista. **Contact:** Anita Evangelista, managing editor. **60% freelance written.** Quarterly magazine covering fencing, fencers, history of sword/fencing/dueling, modern techniques and systems, controversies, personalities of fencing, personal experience. "This is a publication for all fencers and those interested in fencing; we favor the grassroots level rather than the highly-promoted elite. Readers will have a grasp of terminology of the sword and refined fencing skills—writers must be familiar with fencing and current changes and controversies. We are happy to air any point of view on any fencing subject, but the material must be well-researched and logically presented." Estab. 1996. Circ. 5,000. Pays prior to or at publication. Publishes ms an average of 6 months after acceptance. Byline given. Offers 25% kill fee. Buys first North American serial, second serial (reprint), electronic rights, makes work-for-hire assignments. Editorial lead time 3 months. Submit seasonal material 6 months in advance. Accepts queries by mail, e-mail. Accepts simultaneous submissions. Responds in 1 week or less for e-mail; 1 month for snail mail if SASE; no reply if no SASE and material not usable. Sample copy for $2 and 8×10 SAE with 2 first-class stamps. Writer's guidelines for #10 SASE or by e-mail.

Nonfiction: "All article types acceptable—however, we have seldom used fiction or poetry (though will consider if has special relationship to fencing)." How-to should reflect some aspect of fencing or gear. Personal experience welcome. No articles "that lack logical progression of thought, articles that rant, 'my weapon is better than your weapon' emotionalism, puff pieces, or public relations stuff." **Buys 100 mss/year.** Query with or without published clips or send complete ms. Length: 100-4,000 words. **Pays $100-200 (rarely) for assigned articles; $10-60 for unsolicited articles.**

Photos: Send photos by mail or as e-mail attachment. Prefers prints, all sizes. Buys all rights. Negotiates payment individually. Captions, identification of subjects, model releases required.

Columns/Departments: Cutting-edge news (sword or fencing related), 100 words; reviews of books/films, 300 words; fencing generations (profile), 200-300 words; tournament results (veteran events only please), 200 words. **Buys 40 mss/year.** Send complete ms. **Pays $10-20.**

Fiction: Will consider all as long as strong fencing/sword slant is major element. No erotica. Query with or without published clips or send complete ms. Length: 1,500 words maximum. **Pays $25-100.**

Poetry: Will consider all which have distinct fencing/sword element as central. No erotica. Submit maximum 10 poems. Length: Up to 100 lines. **Pays $10.**

Fillers: Anecdotes, facts, gags to be illustrated by cartoonist, newsbreaks. **Buys 30/year.** Length: 100 words maximum. **Pays $5.**

Tips: "We love new writers! Professionally presented work impresses us. We prefer complete submissions, and e-mail or disk (Win 3.x/MS Works 3.0/ASCII) are our favorites. Ask for our writer's guidelines. Always aim your writing to knowledgeable fencers who are fascinated by this subject, take their fencing seriously, and want to know more about its history, current events and controversies. Action photos should show proper form—no flailing or tangled-up images, please. We want to know what the "real" fencer is up to these days, not just what the Olympic contenders are doing. If we don't use your piece, we'll tell you why not."

$ $ POLO PLAYERS' EDITION, Rizzo Management Corp., 3500 Fairlane Farms Rd., Suite 9, Wellington FL 33414. (561)793-9524. Fax: (561)793-9576. E-mail: info@poloplayersedition.com. Website: www.poloplayersedition.com. **Contact:** Gwen Rizzo, editor. Monthly magazine on polo—the sport and lifestyle. "Our readers are affluent, well-educated, well-read and highly sophisticated." Circ. 6,150. **Pays on acceptance.** Publishes ms an average of 2 months after acceptance. Kill fee varies. Buys first North American serial rights, makes work-for-hire assignments. Submit seasonal material 3 months in advance. Accepts queries by mail, e-mail, fax, phone. Accepts simultaneous submissions. Responds in 3 months to queries. Writer's guidelines for #10 SAE with 2 stamps.

Nonfiction: Historical/nostalgic, interview/profile, personal experience, photo feature, technical, travel. Special issues: Annual Art Issue/Gift Buying Guide; Winter Preview/Florida Supplement. **Buys 20 mss/year.** Query with published clips or send complete ms. Length: 800-3,000 words. **Pays $150-400 for assigned articles; $100-300 for unsolicited articles.** Sometimes pays expenses of writers on assignment.

Reprints: Send tearsheet or typed ms with rights for sale noted and information about when and where the material previously appeared. Pays 50% of amount paid for an original article.

Photos: State availability of or send photos with submission. Reviews contact sheets, transparencies, prints. Buys one-time rights. Offers $20-150/photo. Captions required.

Columns/Departments: Yesteryears (historical pieces), 500 words; Profiles (clubs and players), 800-1,000 words. **Buys 15 mss/year.** Query with published clips. **Pays $100-300.**

Fiction:

Tips: "Query us on a personality or club profile or historic piece or, if you know the game, state availability to cover a tournament. Keep in mind that ours is a sophisticated, well-educated audience."

$ PRIME TIME SPORTS & FITNESS, GND Prime Time Publishing, P.O. Box 6097, Evanston IL 60204. (847)784-1194. Fax: (847)784-1194. E-mail: dadorner@aol.com. Website: www.bowldtalk.com. Managing Editor: Steven Ury. **Contact:** Dennis A. Dorner, editor. **80% freelance written.** Monthly magazine covering seasonal pro sports, health club sports and fitness. Estab. 1974. Circ. 35,000. Pays on publication. Publishes ms an average of 6 months after acceptance. Byline given. Buys all rights; will assign back to author in 85% of cases. Submit seasonal material 6 months in advance. Accepts queries by mail, e-mail. Accepts simultaneous submissions. Responds in 6 months to queries. Sample copy on request. Writer's guidelines online.

O⟶ Break in with a 400-600-word fiction piece or a 400-word instructional article.

Nonfiction: "We love short articles that get to the point. Nationally oriented big events and national championships." Book excerpts (fitness and health), exposé (in tennis, fitness, racquetball, health clubs, diets), general interest, historical/nostalgic, how-to (expert instructional pieces on any area of coverage), humor (large market for funny pieces on health clubs and fitness), inspirational, interview/profile, new product, opinion (only from recognized sources who know what they are talking about), personal experience (definitely humorous), photo feature (on related subjects), technical (on exercise and sport), travel (related to fitness, tennis camps, etc.), adult (slightly risque and racy fitness), news reports (on racquetball, handball, tennis, running events). Special issues: Swimwear (March); Baseball Preview (April); Summer Fashion (July); Pro Football Preview (August); Aerobic Wear (September); Fall Fashion (October); Ski Issue (November); Workout and Diet Routines (December/January). "No articles on local only tennis and racquetball tournaments without national appeal." **Buys 150 mss/year.** Length: 2,000 words maximum. **Pays $50-200.** Sometimes pays expenses of writers on assignment.

Reprints: Send tearsheet, photocopy or typed ms with rights for sale noted and information about when and where the material previously appeared. Pays 20% of amount paid for an original article or story.

Photos: Nancy Thomas, photo editor. Specifically looking for fashion photo features. Send photos with submission. Buys all rights,. Pays $20-75 for b&w prints. Captions, identification of subjects, model releases required.

Columns/Departments: George Thomas, column/department editor. New Products; Fitness Newsletter; Handball Newsletter; Racquetball Newsletter; Tennis Newsletter; News & Capsule Summaries; Fashion Spot (photos of new fitness and bathing suits and ski equipment). Length: 50-250 words ("more if author has good handle to cover complete columns"). "We want more articles with photos and we are searching for one woman columnist, Diet and Nutrition." **Buys 100 mss/year.** Send complete ms. **Pays $25-50.**

Fiction: Judy Johnson, fiction editor. "Upbeat stories are needed." Erotica, fantasy, humorous, novel excerpts, religious, romance. **Buys 20 mss/year.** Send complete ms. Length: 500-2,500 words maximum. **Pays $100-250.**

Poetry: Free verse, haiku, light verse, traditional, *on related subjects only*. Length: Up to 150 words. **Pays $25-50.**

▣ The online magazine carries original content not found in the print edition and includes writer's guidelines. Contact: Bob Eres, online editor.

Tips: "Send us articles dealing with court club sports, exercise and nutrition that exemplify an upbeat 'you can do it' attitude. Pro sports previews 3-4 months ahead of their seasons are also needed. Good short fiction or humorous articles can break in. Expert knowledge of any related subject can bring assignments; any area is open. We consider everything as a potential article, but are turned off by credits, past work and degrees. We have a constant demand for well-written articles on instruction, health and trends in both. Other articles needed are professional sports training techniques, fad diets, tennis and fitness resorts, photo features with aerobic routines. A frequent mistake made by writers is in length—articles are too long. When we assign an article, we want it newsy if it's news and opinion if opinion."

$ PRORODEO SPORTS NEWS, Professional Rodeo Cowboys Association, 101 ProRodeo Dr., Colorado Springs CO 80919. (719)593-8840. Fax: (719)548-4889. E-mail: mblackwell@prorodeo.com. Website: www.prorodeo.com. **Contact:** Mike Blackwell, editor. **10% freelance written.** Biweekly magazine covering professional rodeo. "Our readers are extremely knowledgeable about the sport of rodeo, and anyone who writes for us should have that same in-depth knowledge." Estab. 1952. Circ. 40,000. Pays on publication. Publishes ms an average of 1 month after acceptance. Byline given. Buys first, one-time rights, makes work-for-hire assignments. Editorial lead time 2 months. Submit seasonal material 2 months in advance. Responds in 2 weeks to queries. Sample copy for #10 SASE. Writer's guidelines free.

Nonfiction: Historical/nostalgic, how-to, humor, interview/profile, photo feature, technical. **Buys 20 mss/year.** Query with published clips. Length: 300-1,000 words. **Pays $50-100.** Sometimes pays expenses of writers on assignment.

Photos: State availability with submission. Reviews 8 × 10 prints. Buys one-time rights. Offers $15-85/photo. Identification of subjects required.

$ SKYDIVING, 1725 N. Lexington Ave., DeLand FL 32724. (904)736-4793. Fax: (904)736-9786. E-mail: editor@skydivingmagazine.com. **Contact:** Sue Clifton, editor. **25% freelance written.** Monthly tabloid featuring skydiving for sport parachutists, worldwide dealers and equipment manufacturers. "*Skydiving* is a news magazine. Its purpose is to deliver timely, useful and interesting information about the equipment, techniques, events, people and places of parachuting. Our scope is national. *Skydiving*'s audience spans the entire spectrum of jumpers, from first-jump students to veterans with thousands of skydives. Some readers are riggers with a keen interest in the technical aspects of parachutes, while others are weekend 'fun' jumpers who want information to help them make travel plans and equipment purchases." Circ. 14,200. Pays on publication. Publishes ms an average of 3 months after acceptance. Byline given. Buys one-time rights. Accepts simultaneous submissions. Responds in 1 month to queries. Sample copy for $2. Writer's guidelines for 9 × 12 SAE with 4 first-class stamps.

Nonfiction: Average issue includes 3 feature articles and 3 columns of technical information. "Send us news and information on how-to, where-to, equipment, techniques, events and outstanding personalities who skydive. We want articles written by people who have a solid knowledge of parachuting." No personal experience or human interest articles. Query. Length: 500-1,000 words. **Pays $25-100.** Sometimes pays expenses of writers on assignment.

Photos: State availability with submission. Reviews 5×7 and larger b&w glossy prints. Offers no additional payment for photos accepted with ms. Captions required.

Fillers: Newsbreaks. Length: 100-200 words. **Pays $25 minimum.**

Tips: "The most frequent mistake made by writers in completing articles for us is that the writer isn't knowledgeable about the sport of parachuting. Articles about events are especially time-sensitive so yours must be submitted quickly. We welcome contributions about equipment. Even short, 'quick look' articles about new products are appropriate for *Skydiving*. If you know of a drop zone or other place that jumpers would like to visit, write an article describing its features and tell them why you liked it and what they can expect to find if they visit it. Avoid first-person articles."

N **$ $** **WINDY CITY SPORTS**, Windy City Publishing, 1450 W. Randolph St., Chicago IL 60607. (312)421-1551. Fax: (312)421-1454. E-mail: jason@windycitysportsmag.com. Website: www.windycitysports.com. **Contact:** Jason Effmann, managing editor. **25% freelance written.** Monthly tabloid covering amateur sports. "Writers must have knowledge of the sport they've been hired to cover. In most cases, these an endurance sports, such as running, cycling, triathlon or adventure racing." Circ. 110,000. Pays on publication. Publishes ms an average of 1 month after acceptance. Byline given. Buys one-time rights. Editorial lead time 2 months. Accepts queries by mail, e-mail. Sample copy and writer's guidelines free.

Nonfiction: Essays, general interest, how-to, humor, interview/profile, opinion, personal experience, photo feature, technical. **Buys up to 35 mss/year.** Query with published clips. Length: 700-1,500 words. **Pays $150-400 for assigned articles; $100-300 for unsolicited articles.** Sometimes pays expenses of writers on assignment.

Photos: Send photos with submission. Reviews prints. Buys one-time rights. Negotiates payment individually. Captions, identification of subjects required.

Columns/Departments: Cool Down (humorous, personal experience), 800-1,000 words; Nutrition (advice and information on diet), 500-800 words; Health/Wellness (advice and information on general health), 500-800 words. Query with published clips. **Pays $150-300.**

Tips: "You should try to make it fun. We like to see anecdotes, great quotes and vivid descriptions. Quote Chicago area people as often as possible. If that's not possible, try to stick to the Midwest or people with Chicago connections."

Motor Sports

$ $ **AUTO RACING DIGEST**, Century Publishing, 990 Grove St., Evanston IL 60207-4370. (847)491-6440. Fax: (847)491-6203. Editor: William Wagner. **Contact:** Scott Plagenhoef, associate editor. **100% freelance written.** Bimonthly digest. "focusing on American stock-car racing. Occasionally features F1, Indy car style." Estab. 1974. Circ. 50,000. Pays on publication. Publishes ms an average of 1 month after acceptance. Byline given. Offers 50% kill fee. Buys all rights. Editorial lead time 6 weeks. Submit seasonal material 6 weeks in advance. Accepts simultaneous submissions. Responds in 1 month to queries. Sample copy for $5.

Nonfiction: Essays, exposé, general interest, opinion, technical. No "remember when" pieces. No personal experience unless extraordinary. **Buys 70 mss/year.** Query. Length: 1,200-2,000 words. **Pays $50-200.** Sometimes pays expenses of writers on assignment.

Photos: State availability with submission. Reviews negatives, 35mm, 4×6 transparencies, 8×10 prints. Buys one-time rights. Offers $10-30/photo; $100 for cover. Identification of subjects required.

Columns/Departments: Circuit To Circuit (racing roundup), 1,000 words; Biz (business), 500-1,000 words; Notes & Quotes (racing filler), 1,000 words. **Buys 25 mss/year.** Query. **Pays $50-150.**

Tips: "Query by mail. Clips should reflect subject matter you're trying to sell me."

$ $ **DRAG RACING USA**, McMullen/Argus Publishing, 774 S. Placentia Ave., Placentia CA 92870. (714)939-2544. Website: www.dragracingusaweb.com. Managing Editor: Debra Wentz. **Contact:** Randy Fish, editor/editorial director. Monthly magazine covering bracket cars and drag racing. Estab. 1989. Circ. 45,000. Pays on publication. Publishes ms an average of 6 months after acceptance. Byline given. Buys first North American serial rights. Accepts queries by mail.

Nonfiction: Automotive how-to and technical. **Buys 35 mss/year.** Query by mail only. Length: 500-4,000 words. **Pays $150/page.**

Photos: Send photos with submission.

Tips: "Contact by mail first."

N **$** **THE HOOK MAGAZINE, The Magazine for Antique & Classic Tractor Pullers**, Greer Town, Inc., 209 S. Marshall, Box 16, Marshfield MO 65706. (417)468-7000. Fax: (603)590-1743. E-mail: thehook@pcis.net. Website: pcis.net/thehook. Managing Editor: Sherry Linville. **Contact:** Dana Greer Marlin, owner/president. **80% freelance written.** Bimonthly magazine covering tractor pulling. Estab. 1992. Circ. 6,000. Pays on publication. Byline given. Buys one-time, electronic rights. Editorial lead time 6 months. Submit seasonal material 6 months in advance. Accepts queries by mail, e-mail, fax. Accepts simultaneous submissions. Responds in 3 weeks to queries; 2 months to mss. Sample copy for 8½×11 SAE with 4 first-class stamps or online. Writer's guidelines for #10 SASE.

   ○→ "Our magazine is easy to break into. Puller profiles are your best bet. Features on individuals and their tractors, how they got into the sport, what they want from competing."

Nonfiction: How-to, interview/profile, new product, personal experience, photo feature, technical, event coverage. **Buys 25 mss/year.** Send complete ms. Length: 500-1,500 words. **Pays $70 for technical articles; $35 for others.**
Photos: Send photos with submission. Reviews 3×5 prints. Buys one-time and online rights. Negotiates payment individually. Captions, identification of subjects, model releases required.
Fillers: Anecdotes, short humor. **Buys 6/year.** Length: 100 words.
Tips: "Write 'real'; our readers don't respond well to scholarly tomes. Use your everyday voice in all submissions and your chances will go up radically."

$ $ SAND SPORTS MAGAZINE, Wright Publishing Co. Inc., P.O. Box 2260, Costa Mesa CA 92628. (714)979-2560 ext. 107. Fax: (714)979-3998. Website: www.sandsports.net. **Contact:** Michael Sommer, editor. **20% freelance written.** Bimonthly magazine covering vehicles for off-road and sand dunes. Estab. 1995. Circ. 25,000. Pays on publication. Byline given. Buys first, one-time rights. Editorial lead time 3 months. Submit seasonal material 6 months in advance. Accepts queries by mail. Sample copy and writer's guidelines free.
Nonfiction: How-to (technical-mechanical), photo feature, technical. **Buys 20 mss/year.** Query. Length: 1,500 words minimum. **Pays $125-175/page.** Sometimes pays expenses of writers on assignment.
Photos: Send photos with submission. Reviews contact sheets, transparencies, 5×7 prints. Buys one-time rights. Negotiates payment individually. Captions, identification of subjects, model releases required.

$ $ ▨ SPEEDWAY ILLUSTRATED, Performance Media, LLC, 107 Elm St., Salisbury MA 01952. (978)465-9099. Fax: (978)465-9033. E-mail: rsneddon@speedwayillustrated.com. Website: www.speedwayillustrated.com. Executive Editor: Dick Berggren. **Contact:** Rob Sneddon, editor. **80% freelance written.** Monthly magazine covering stock car racing. Estab. 2000. Circ. 125,000. Pays on publication. Byline given. Buys first rights. Editorial lead time 6 weeks. Accepts queries by mail, fax. Responds in 2 weeks to queries. Sample copy and writer's guidelines free.
Nonfiction: Interview/profile, opinion, personal experience, photo feature, technical. **Buys 300 mss/year.** Query. **Pays variable rate.**
Photos: Send photos with submission. Reviews transparencies. Buys all rights. Offers $40-250/photo. Captions, identification of subjects, model releases required.
Columns/Departments: We seek short items with photos. **Buys 100 mss/year. Pays $25-200.**
Tips: "We pay for everything that is published and aggressively seek short, high-interest value pieces that are accompanied by strong photography."

Running

$ INSIDE TEXAS RUNNING, 9514 Bristlebrook Dr., Houston TX 77083. (281)498-3208. Fax: (281)879-9980. E-mail: insideTx@aol.com. Website: www.InsideTexasRunning.com. **Contact:** Joanne Schmidt, editor. **70% freelance written.** Monthly (except june and august) tabloid covering running and running-related events. "Our audience is made up of Texas runners who may also be interested in cross training." Estab. 1977. Circ. 10,000. **Pays on acceptance.** Publishes ms an average of 2 months after acceptance. Byline given. Submit seasonal material 2 months in advance. Responds in 1 month to mss. Sample copy for $1.50. Writer's guidelines for #10 SASE.
    ○➤ "The best way to break in to our publication is to submit brief (2 or 3 paragraphs) fillers for our 'Texas Roundup' section."
Nonfiction: Various topics of interest to runners: Profiles of newsworthy Texas runners of all abilities; unusual events; training interviews. Special issues: Fall Race Review (September); Marathon Focus (October); Shoe Review (March); Resource Guide (December). **Buys 20 mss/year.** Send complete ms. Length: 500-1,500 words. **Pays $100 maximum for assigned articles; $50 maximum for unsolicited articles.**
Reprints: Send tearsheet, photocopy or typed ms with rights for sale noted and information about when and where the material previously appeared.
Photos: Send photos with submission. Buys one-time rights. Offers $25 maximum/photo. Captions required.
    ▣ The online magazine carries original content not found in the print edition.
Tips: "Writers should be familiar with the sport and the publication."

$ $ NEW YORK RUNNER, New York Road Runners Club, 9 E. 89th St., New York NY 10128. (212)423-2260. Fax: (212)423-0879. E-mail: newyorkrun@nyrrc.org. Website: www.nyrrc.org. **Contact:** Lisa Schwartz, associate editor. Bimonthly Regional sports magazine covering running, racewalking, nutrition and fitness. Estab. 1958. Circ. 45,000. Pays on publication. Byline given. Offers 33% kill fee. Buys first North American serial rights. Submit seasonal material 4 months in advance. Accepts queries by mail, e-mail, fax. Accepts simultaneous submissions. Responds in 2 months to queries. Sample copy for $3. Writer's guidelines for #10 SASE.
    ● Material should be of interest to members of the New York Road Runners Club.
    ○➤ Break in through departments *Runner Diary* (essay); *Footnote* (humor); or *On the Roads* (interesting places to run).
Nonfiction: Running and marathon articles. Interview/profile (of runners). Special issues: N.Y.C. Marathon (submissions in by August 1). No non-running stories. **Buys 25 mss/year.** Query. Length: 750-1,000 words. **Pays $50-250.**

Reprints: Send photocopy and information about when and where the material previously appeared. Pays 25-50% of amount paid for an original article.

Photos: Send photos with submission. Reviews 8×10 b&w prints. Buys one-time rights. Offers $35-300/photo. Captions, identification of subjects, model releases required.

Columns/Departments: Runner Diary (role of running in one's day, routine or life, usually first-person), 1,000 words; On the Road (running routes in the New York City metropolitan region which offer unique scenery, have interesting history or landmarks or are little known), 1,000 words; Crosstraining (areas of fitness that will enhance running performance), 1,000-1,200 words; Running Briefs (anything noteworthy in the running world, such as new products and volunteer opportunities), 250-500 words. Query.

Tips: "Be knowledgeable about the sport of running. Write like a runner."

$ $ $ $ RUNNER'S WORLD, Rodale, 33 E. Minor St., Emmaus PA 18098. (610)967-5171. Deputy Editor: Bob Wischnia. **Contact:** Adam Bean, managing editor. **5% freelance written.** Monthly magazine on running, mainly long-distance running. "The magazine for and about distance running, training, health and fitness, nutrition, motivation, injury prevention, race coverage, personalities of the sport." Estab. 1966. Circ. 500,000. Pays on publication. Publishes ms an average of 6 months after acceptance. Byline given. Buys all rights. Submit seasonal material 6 months in advance. Accepts queries by mail. Responds in 2 months to queries. Writer's guidelines for #10 SASE.

   O━ Break in through columns *Women's Running*, *Human Race* and *Finish Line*. Also *Warmups*, which mixes international running news with human interest stories. If you can send us a unique human interest story from your region, we will give it serious consideration.

Nonfiction: How-to (train, prevent injuries), interview/profile, personal experience. No "my first marathon" stories. No poetry. **Buys 5-7 mss/year.** Query. **Pays $1,500-2,000.** Pays expenses of writers on assignment.

Photos: State availability with submission. Buys one-time rights. Identification of subjects required.

Columns/Departments: Finish Line (back-of-the-magazine essay, personal experience—humor); Women's Running (essay page written by and for women). **Buys 24 mss/year.** Send complete ms. **Pays $300.**

   ▣ The online magazine carries original content not found in the print edition. Contact: Marty Post.

Tips: "We are always looking for 'Adventure Runs' from readers—runs in wild, remote, beautiful and interesting places. These are rarely race stories but more like backtracking/running adventures. Great color slides are crucial, 2,000 words maximum."

[N] $ $ RUNNING TIMES, The Runner's Best Resource, Fitness Publishing, Inc., 213 Danbury Rd., Wilton CT 06897. (203)761-1113. Fax: (203)761-9933. E-mail: editor@runningtimes.com. Website: www.runningtimes.com. Managing Editor: Marc Chalufour. **Contact:** Jonathan Beverly, editor. **40% freelance written.** Magazine published 10 times/year covering distance running and racing. "*Running Times* is the national magazine for the experienced running participant and fan. Our audience is knowledgeable about the sport and active in running and racing. All editorial relates specifically to running: improving performance, enhancing enjoyment, or exploring events, places, and people in the sport." Estab. 1977. Circ. 70,000. Pays on publication. Publishes ms an average of 3 months after acceptance. Byline given. Buys first North American serial, second serial (reprint), electronic rights. Editorial lead time 3 months. Submit seasonal material 6 months in advance. Accepts queries by mail, e-mail. Responds in 3 weeks to queries; 2 months to mss. Sample copy for $5. Writer's guidelines for #10 SASE.

Nonfiction: Book excerpts, essays, historical/nostalgic, how-to (training), humor, inspirational, interview/profile, new product, opinion, personal experience (with theme, purpose, evidence of additional research and/or special expertise), photo feature, travel, news, reports. No basic, beginner how-to, generic fitness/nutrition, or generic first-person accounts. **Buys 25 mss/year.** Query. Length: 1,500-3,000 words. **Pays $200-500 for assigned articles; $100-300 for unsolicited articles.** Sometimes pays expenses of writers on assignment.

Photos: State availability with submission. Buys one-time rights. Negotiates payment individually. Identification of subjects required.

Columns/Departments: Training (short topics related to enhancing performance), 1,000 words; Sports-Med (application of medical knowledge to running), 1,000 words; Nutrition (application of nutritional principles to running performance), 1,000 words; Cool Down (lighter toned essay on an aspect of the running life), 400 words. **Buys 30 mss/year.** Query. **Pays $50-200.**

Fiction: Any genre, with running-related theme or characters. **Buys 1-2 mss/year.** Send complete ms. Length: 1,500-3,000 words. **Pays $100-500.**

Tips: "Thoroughly get to know runners and the running culture, both at the participant level and the professional, elite level."

$ $ TRAIL RUNNER, The Magazine of Running Adventure, North South Publications, 5455 Spine Rd., Mezz. A, Boulder CO 80301. (303)499-8410. Fax: (303)530-3729. E-mail: editor@trailrunnermag.com. Website: www.trailrunnermag.com. **Contact:** Brian Metzler, editor. **65% freelance written.** Bimonthly magazine covering all aspects of off-road running. "The only nationally circulated four-color glossy magazine dedicated to covering trail running." Estab. 1999. Circ. 40,000. Pays on publication. Publishes ms an average of 2 months after acceptance. Byline given. Offers $50 kill fee. Buys first North American serial, electronic rights. Editorial lead time 3 months. Submit seasonal material 5 months in advance. Accepts queries by mail, e-mail. Accepts simultaneous submissions. Responds in 3 weeks to queries; 2 months to mss. Sample copy for $3. Writer's guidelines free, online or by e-mail.

Nonfiction: Essays, exposé, general interest, historical/nostalgic, how-to, humor, inspirational, interview/profile, new product, opinion, personal experience, photo feature, technical, travel, racing. No gear reviews, race results. **Buys 30-40 mss/year.** Query with published clips. Length: 800-2,000 words. **Pays 30-40¢/word.** Sometimes pays expenses of writers on assignment.

Photos: Send photos with submission. Reviews 35mm transparencies, prints. Buys one-time rights. Offers $50-250/photo. Identification of subjects, model releases required.

Columns/Departments: Monique Cole, senior editor. Training (race training, altitude training, etc.), 800 words; Adventure (off-beat aspects of trail running), 600-800 words; Wanderings (personal essay on any topic related to trail running), 600 words; Urban Escapes (urban trails accessible in and around major US sites), 800 words; Personalities (profile of a trail running personality), 1,000 words. **Buys 5-10 mss/year.** Query with published clips. **Pays 30-40¢/word.**

Fiction: Adventure, fantasy, slice-of-life vignettes. **Buys 1-2 mss/year.** Query with published clips. Length: 1,000-1,500 words. **Pays 25-35¢/word.**

Fillers: Anecdotes, facts, gags to be illustrated by cartoonist, newsbreaks, short humor. **Buys 50-60/year.** Length: 75-400 words. **Pays 25-35¢/word.**

◼ The online magazine carries original content not found in the print edition. Contact: Phil Mislinski.

Tips: "Best way to break in is with interesting and unique trail running news, notes and nonsense from around the world. Also, check the website for more info."

$ $ TRIATHLETE MAGAZINE, The World's Largest Triathlon Magazine, Triathlon Group of North America, 2037 San Elijo, Cardiff CA 92007. (760)634-4100. Fax: (760)634-4110. E-mail: cgandolfo@triathletemag.com. Website: www.triathletemag.com. **Contact:** Christina Gandolfo, editor. **50% freelance written.** Monthly magazine. "In general, articles should appeal to seasoned triathletes, as well as eager newcomers to the sport. Our audience includes everyone from competitive athletes to people considering their first event." Estab. 1983. Circ. 50,000. Pays on publication. Byline given. Buys second serial (reprint), all rights. Editorial lead time 3 months. Submit seasonal material 6 months in advance. Accepts queries by mail, e-mail. Accepts simultaneous submissions. Sample copy for $5.

Nonfiction: How-to, interview/profile, new product, photo feature, technical. "No first-person pieces about your experience in triathlon or my-first-triathlon stories." **Buys 36 mss/year.** Query with published clips. Length: 1,000-3,000 words. **Pays $200-600.** Sometimes pays expenses of writers on assignment.

Photos: State availability with submission. Reviews transparencies. Buys first North American rights. Offers $50-300/photo.

Tips: "Writers should know the sport and be familiar with the nuances and history. Training-specific articles that focus on new, but scientifically based, methods are good, as are seasonal training pieces."

Skiing & Snow Sports

$ $ AMERICAN SNOWMOBILER, The Enthusiast Magazine, Recreational Publications, Inc., 2715 Upper Afton Rd., Suite 100, St. Paul MN 55119-4774. (651)738-1953. Fax: (651)738-2302. E-mail: editor@amsnow.com. Website: www.amsnow.com. **Contact:** Anna Boisjoli, assistant editor. **30% freelance written.** Magazine published 6 times seasonally covering snowmobiling. Estab. 1985. Circ. 90,000. **Pays on acceptance.** Publishes ms an average of 4 months after acceptance. Byline given. Buys all rights. Editorial lead time 4 months. Submit seasonal material 6 months in advance. Accepts queries by mail, e-mail, fax. Responds in 1 month to queries; 2 months to mss. Writer's guidelines for #10 SASE.

○─ Break in with "a packet complete with résumé, published clips and photos (or color copies of available photos) and a complete query with a few paragraphs to get me interested and to give an idea of the angle the writer will be taking. When sending an e-mail, do not attach anything."

Nonfiction: Seeking race coverage for online version. General interest, historical/nostalgic, how-to, interview/profile, new product, personal experience, photo feature, travel. **Buys 10 mss/year.** Query with published clips. Length: 1,000-2,000 words. **Pay varies for assigned articles; $100 minimum for unsolicited articles.**

Photos: State availability with submission. Buys all rights. Offers no additional payment for photos accepted with ms. Captions, identification of subjects, model releases required.

◼ The online magazine carries original content not found in the print edition. Contact: Anna Boisjoli or Wade West.

$ $ POWDER, The Skier's Magazine, Emap USA, P.O. Box 1028, Dana Point CA 92629. (949)496-5922. Fax: (949)496-7849. E-mail: powdermag@emapUSA.com. **Contact:** Keith Carlson, editor. **40% freelance written.** Magazine published 7 times/year covering skiing for expert skiers. Estab. 1972. Circ. 110,000. **Pays on acceptance.** Byline given. Buys first North American serial rights. Editorial lead time 3 months. Submit seasonal material 3 months in advance. Accepts queries by mail, e-mail, fax. Responds in 2 months to queries. Sample copy for $8. Writer's guidelines free.

Photos: Send photos with submission if available. Reviews 35mm transparencies. Buys one-time rights. Negotiates payment individually. Identification of subjects required.

$ SKATING, United States Figure Skating Association, 20 First St., Colorado Springs CO 80906-3697. (719)635-5200. Fax: (719)635-9548. E-mail: lfawcett@usfsa.org. **Contact:** Laura Fawcett, editor. Official publication of the USFSA published 10 times/year. "*Skating* magazine is the official publication of U.S. Figure Skating and thus we cover skating at both the championship and grass roots level." Estab. 1923. Circ. 48,000. Pays on publication. Publishes ms an average of 3 months after acceptance. Byline given. Buys first rights. Accepts queries by mail, e-mail, fax.

> ○┐ The best way for a writer to break in is through the "Ice Time with—..." department, which features USFSA members (skaters, coaches, volunteers, etc.) who have unique or interesting stories to tell. This is a feature that highlights members and their accomplishments and stories on and off the ice (800-1,500 words).

Nonfiction: General interest, historical/nostalgic, how-to, interview/profile (background and interests of skaters, coaches, volunteers or other USFSA members), photo feature, technical and competition reports, figure skating issues and trends, sports medicine. **Buys 10 mss/year.** Query. Length: 500-2,500 words. **Pay varies.**

Photos: Photos purchased with or without accompanying ms. Query. Pays $15 for 8×10 or 5×7 b&w glossy prints and $35 for color prints or transparencies.

Columns/Departments: Ice Breaker (news briefs), Foreign Competition Reports, Ice Time With... (features on USFSA members), Sports Medicine, In Synch (synchronized skating news); On the Lookout (up and coming athletes). Length: 500-2,000 words.

Tips: "We want writing by experienced persons knowledgeable in the technical and artistic aspects of figure skating with a new outlook on the development of the sport. Knowledge and background in technical aspects of figure skating is helpful, but not necessary to the quality of writing expected. We would like to see articles and short features on USFSA volunteers, skaters and other USFSA members who normally wouldn't get recognized, as opposed to features on championship-level athletes, which are usually assigned to regular contributors. Good quality color photos are a must with submissions. Also would be interested in seeing figure skating "issues and trends" articles, instead of just profiles. No professional skater material. Synchronized skating and adult skating are the two fastest growing aspects of the USFSA. We would like to see more stories dealing with these unique athletes."

$ $ $ SKI MAGAZINE, Times Mirror Magazines, 929 Pearl St., Suite 200, Boulder CO 80302. (303)448-7600. Fax: (303)448-7638. Website: www.skinet.com. Editor-in-Chief: Andy Bigford. **Contact:** Maureen Drummey, assistant editor. **15% freelance written.** Monthly magazine. "*Ski* is a ski-lifestyle publication written and edited for recreational skiers. Its content is intended to help them ski better (technique), buy better (equipment and skiwear), and introduce them to new experiences, people and adventures." Estab. 1936. Circ. 430,000. **Pays on acceptance.** Publishes ms an average of 3 months after acceptance. Byline given. Offers 15% kill fee. Buys first North American serial rights. Submit seasonal material 8 months in advance. Responds in 1 month to queries. Sample copy for 9×12 SAE and 5 first-class stamps.

Nonfiction: Essays, historical/nostalgic, how-to, humor, interview/profile, personal experience. **Buys 5-10 mss/year.** Send complete ms. Length: 1,000-3,500 words. **Pays $500-1,000 for assigned articles; $300-700 for unsolicited articles.** Pays expenses of writers on assignment.

Photos: Send photos with submission. Buys one-time rights. Offers $75-300/photo. Captions, identification of subjects, model releases required.

Columns/Departments: Ski Life (interesting people, events, oddities in skiing), 150-300 words; Going Places (items on new or unique places, deals or services available to skiers); and Take It From Us (special products or services available to skiers that are real values or out of the ordinary), 25-50 words.

Fillers: Facts, short humor. **Buys 10/year.** Length: 60-75 words. **Pays $50-75.**

Tips: "Writers must have an extensive familiarity with the sport and know what concerns, interests and amuses skiers. Columns are most open to freelancers."

$ $ $ $ SKIING, Times Mirror Magazines, Inc., 929 Pearl St., Suite 200, Boulder CO 80302. (303)448-7600. Fax: (303)448-7676. E-mail: helen.olsson@tmm.com. Website: www.skiingmag.com. Editor-in-Chief: Rick Kahl. **Contact:** Helen Olsson, executive editor. Magazine published 7 times/year for skiers who deeply love winter, who live for travel, adventure, instruction, gear and news. "*Skiing* is the user's guide to winter adventure. It is equal parts jaw-dropping inspiration and practical information, action and utility, attitude and advice. It relates the lifestyles of dedicated skiers and captures their spirit of daring and exploration. Dramatic photography transports readers to spine-tingling mountains with breathtaking immediacy. Reading *Skiing* is almost as much fun as being there." Estab. 1948. Circ. 400,000. Byline given. Offers 40% kill fee.

Nonfiction: **Buys 10-15 features (1,500-2,000 words) and 12-24 short pieces (100-500 words).** Query. **Pays $1,000-2,500/feature; $100-500/short piece.**

Columns/Departments: Length: 200-1,000 words. **Buys 2-3 mss/year.** Query. **Pays $150-1,000.**

> ▣ The online magazine carries original content not found in the print edition. Contact: Adam Hirshfield, online editor.

Tips: "Consider less obvious subjects: smaller ski areas, specific local ski cultures, unknown aspects of popular resorts. Be expressive, not merely descriptive! We want readers to feel the adventure in your writing—to tingle with the excitement of skiing steep powder, of meeting intriguing people, of reaching new goals or achieving dramatic new insights. We want readers to have fun, to see the humor in and the lighter side of skiing and their fellow skiers."

$ $ SNOW GOER, Ehlert Publishing Group, 6420 Sycamore Lane, Maple Grove MN 55369. Fax: (763)383-4499. E-mail: jprusak@affinitygroup.com. Website: www.snowmobilenews.com. **Contact:** John T. Prusak, editor. **5%**

freelance written. Magazine published 6 times/year covering snowmobiling. "*Snow Goer* is a hard-hitting, tell-it-like-it-is magazine designed for the ultra-active snowmobile enthusiast. It is fun, exciting, innovative and on the cutting edge of technology and trends." Estab. 1967. Circ. 76,000. Pays on publication. Publishes ms an average of 5 months after acceptance. Byline given. Buys first, one-time rights. Editorial lead time 5 months. Submit seasonal material 6 months in advance. Accepts queries by mail, e-mail, fax. Accepts simultaneous submissions. Responds in 3 months to queries. Sample copy for 8 × 10 SAE and 4 first-class stamps.
Nonfiction: General interest, how-to, interview/profile, new product, personal experience, photo feature, technical, travel. **Buys 6 mss/year.** Query. Length: 500-4,000 words. **Pays $50-500.** Sometimes pays expenses of writers on assignment.
Photos: State availability with submission. Reviews contact sheets, negatives, prints. Buys one-time rights or all rights. Negotiates payment individually. Captions, identification of subjects required.

$ $ SNOW WEEK, The Snowmobile Racing Authority, Ehlert Publishing Group, 6420 Sycamore Lane N., Maple Grove MN 55369. (763)383-4400. Fax: (763)383-4499. E-mail: eskogman@affinitygroup.com. Website: www.snowmobilenews.com. **Contact:** Eric Skogman, managing editor. **15% freelance written.** Magazine published 18 times/year covering snowmobile racing. "We cover snowmobile racing from coast to coast for hard core fans. We get in the pits, inside the race trailers and pepper our race coverage with behind the scenes details." Estab. 1973. Circ. 26,000. Pays on publication. Publishes ms an average of 2 months after acceptance. Byline given. Buys first, one-time, simultaneous rights. Editorial lead time 2 weeks. Accepts queries by mail, e-mail, fax, phone. Sample copy for 8 × 11 SAE and 4 first-class stamps.
Nonfiction: Technical, race coverage. **Buys 20 mss/year.** Query. Length: 500-4,000 words. **Pays $50-450.** Sometimes pays expenses of writers on assignment.
Photos: State availability with submission. Reviews contact sheets, prints. Buys one-time rights. Offers no additional payment for photos accepted with ms. Captions, identification of subjects required.
Tips: "Writers should also be fans of the sport, know how to write and photograph races."

$ $ SNOWEST MAGAZINE, Harris Publishing, 360 B St., Idaho Falls ID 83402. (208)524-7000. Fax: (208)522-5241. E-mail: lindstrm@snowest.com. Publisher: Steve Janes. **Contact:** Lane Lindstrom, editor. **10-25% freelance written.** Monthly magazine. "*SnoWest* covers the sport of snowmobiling, products and personalities in the western states. This includes mountain riding, deep powder and trail riding as well as destination pieces, tech tips and new model reviews." Estab. 1972. Circ. 160,000. Pays on publication. Publishes ms an average of 2 months after acceptance. Byline given. Buys first North American serial rights. Editorial lead time 6 months. Submit seasonal material 3 months in advance. Sample copy and writer's guidelines free.
Nonfiction: How-to (fix a snowmobile, make it high performance), new product, technical, travel. **Buys 3-5 mss/year.** Query with published clips. Length: 500-1,500 words. **Pays $150-300.**
Photos: Send photos with submission. Buys one-time rights. Negotiates payment individually. Captions, identification of subjects required.

Soccer

$ $⊠ SOCCER DIGEST, Century Publishing, 990 Grove St., Evanston IL 60207-4370. (847)491-6440. Fax: (847)491-6203. **Contact:** Scott Plagenhoef, associate editor. **80% freelance written.** "Bimonthly digest featuring investigative reportage on national and international soccer. Writers must be well-established and previously published." Estab. 1977. Circ. 45,000. Pays on publication. Publishes ms an average of 1 month after acceptance. Byline given. Offers 50% kill fee. Buys all rights. Editorial lead time 6 weeks. Submit seasonal material 2 months in advance. Accepts queries by mail, e-mail. Accepts simultaneous submissions. Responds in 1 month to queries. Sample copy for $5. Writer's guidelines free.
Nonfiction: Essays, exposé, general interest, interview/profile, opinion. No how-to, nostalgic, humor, personal experience. **Buys 40 mss/year.** Query. Length: 1,200-2,000 words. **Pays $75-500.** Sometimes pays expenses of writers on assignment.
Photos: State availability with submission. Reviews negatives, 35mm transparencies, 8 × 10 prints, jpeg or tiff files. Buys one-time rights. Offers $10-50/photo, $100 for cover. Captions required.
Columns/Departments: Touch Line (opinion), 1,000-2,000 words; Biz (business-related), 500-1,000 words. **Buys 12 mss/year.** Query. **Pays $75-200.**
Tips: "Send query by mail or e-mail. Include related clips—do not deluge us with cooking clips (for example) if you're trying to sell me a sports story!"

$ $ SOCCER JR., Scholastic Inc., 27 Unquowa Rd., Fairfield CT 06430-5015. (203)259-5766. Fax: (203)256-1119. E-mail: jschoff@soccerjr.com. Website: www.soccerjr.com. **Contact:** Jill Schoff, associate editor. Magazine covering soccer as it relates to children. "The editorial focus of *Soccer Jr.* is on the fun and challenge of soccer, and is aimed at boys and girls, ages 8-14, who live in the U.S. and love soccer." Estab. 1992. Circ. 150,000. **Pays on acceptance.** Not copyrighted. Byline given. Accepts queries by mail, e-mail. Accepts simultaneous submissions. Responds in 6 weeks to queries. Sample copy for $4; $8 (US) for non-US residents.

Nonfiction: Coverage of major soccer events and personalities, also games and puzzles. Special issues: Publishes coach's edition (once a year); soccer parents edition (twice a year). **Buys 10-20 mss/year.** Length: 500-1,200 words. **Pays $50-600.**

Reprints: Accepts previously published submissions.

Fiction: Short fiction stories with a soccer focus. **Pays $50-600.**

$ $ SOCCER NOW, Official Publication of the American Youth Soccer Organization, American Youth Soccer Organization, 12501 S. Isis Ave., Hawthorne CA 90250. (800)USA-AYSO or (310)643-6455. Fax: (310)643-5310. E-mail: soccernow@ayso.org. Website: www.soccer.org. **Contact:** David Brown, editor. Quarterly magazine covering soccer (AYSO and professional). "For AYSO members, both players (age 5-18) and their parents. Human interest about AYSO players and adult volunteers, or professional players (especially if they played in AYSO as kids)." Estab. 1976. Circ. 470,000. Pays on publication. Publishes ms an average of 3 months after acceptance. Byline given. Makes work-for-hire assignments. Editorial lead time 3 months. Accepts queries by mail, e-mail, fax. Responds in 1 month to queries. Sample copy free on request.

Nonfiction: General interest (soccer), historical/nostalgic, how-to (playing tips subject to approval by Director of Coaching), interview/profile, personal experience, photo feature. Query. Length: 400-1,000 words. **Pays $50-200.** Sometimes pays expenses of writers on assignment.

Photos: Send photos with submission. Reviews contact sheets, transparencies, prints. Buys one-time rights. Offers $0-50/photo. Identification of subjects required.

Columns/Departments: Headlines (news); Team Tips (instructional); Game Zone (games for kids—e.g., soccer-related word puzzles). Query. **Pays $0-50.**

Tennis

$ $ TENNIS WEEK, Tennis News, Inc., 341 Madison Ave., 6th Floor, New York NY 10017. (212)808-4750. Fax: (212)983-6302. **Contact:** Heather H. Holland, managing editor. **10% freelance written.** Biweekly magazine covering tennis. "For readers who are either tennis fanatics or involved in the business of tennis." Estab. 1974. Circ. 80,000. Pays on publication. Byline given. Buys all rights. Editorial lead time 1 month. Submit seasonal material 1 month in advance. Responds in 1 month to queries. Sample copy for $3.

Nonfiction: **Buys 15 mss/year.** Query with or without published clips. Length: 1,000-2,000 words. **Pays $300.**

Water Sports

$ $ DIVER, Seagraphic Publications, Ltd., Box 1312, Station A, Delta British Columbia V4M 3Y8, Canada. (604)948-9937. Fax: (604)948-9985. E-mail: divermag@axion.net. Website: www.divermag.com. Publisher: Peter Vassilopoulos. **Contact:** Stephanie Bold, editor. Magazine published 9 times/year emphasizing scuba diving, ocean science and technology for a well-educated, outdoor-oriented readership. Circ. 17,500. Payment follows publication. Publishes ms an average of up to 1 year after acceptance. Byline given. Buys first North American serial rights. Accepts queries by mail, e-mail, fax, phone. Responds in up to 3 months to queries.

● "Articles are subject to being accepted for use in supplement issues on tabloid." Travel features considered only August through October for use following year.

Nonfiction: Buys 6 freelance travel items/year. General interest (underwater oriented), historical/nostalgic (shipwrecks, treasure artifacts, archeological), how-to (underwater activities such as photography), humor, interview/profile (underwater personalities in all spheres—military, sports, scientific or commercial), personal experience (related to diving), photo feature (marine life), technical (related to oceanography, commercial/military diving, etc.), travel (dive resorts). No subjective product reports. **Buys 25 mss/year; 6 freelance travel items/year.** Submit complete ms with SAE and IRCs. Length: 800-1,000 words. **Pays $2.50/column inch.**

Photos: "Features are mostly those describing dive sites, experiences, etc. Photo features are reserved more as specials, while almost all articles must be well illustrated with color or b&w prints supplemented by color transparencies." Submit original photo material with accompanying ms. Buys one-time rights. Pays $15 minimum for 5×7 or 8×10 b&w glossy prints; $20 minimum for 35mm color transparencies. Captions, model releases required.

Columns/Departments: Book reviews. Length: 200 words maximum. Send complete ms. **No payment.**

Fillers: Anecdotes, newsbreaks, short humor. **Buys 8-10/year.** Length: 50-150 words. **No payment for news items.**

Tips: "No phone calls about status of manuscript. Write if no response within reasonable time. Only brief, to-the-point correspondence will be answered. Lengthy communications will probably result in return of work unused. Publisher assumes no liability to use material even after lengthy waiting period. Acceptances subject to final and actual use."

$ $ IMMERSED MAGAZINE, The International Technical Diving Magazine, Immersed LLC, FDR Station, P.O. Box 947, New York NY 10150-0947. (201)792-1331. Fax: (212)259-9310. E-mail: bsterner@prodigy.net or bob@i mmersed.com. Website: www.immersed.com. **Contact:** Bob Sterner, publisher/editor. **60% freelance written.** Quarterly magazine covering scuba diving. "Advances on the frontier of scuba diving are covered in theme-oriented issues that

examine archeology, biology, history, gear and sciences related to diving. We emphasize training, education and safety."
Estab. 1996. Circ. 25,000. Pays on publication. Byline given. Offers kill fee. Buys one-time, electronic rights. Editorial
lead time 6 months. Accepts queries by mail, e-mail, fax, phone. Sample copy online. Writer's guidelines for #10 SASE.

O➤ Break in with "how-to equipment rigging stories or travel stories on unusual but accessible destinations."

Nonfiction: Historical/nostalgic, how-to, interview/profile, new product, personal experience, photo feature, technical,
travel. No poetry, opinion diatribes, axe-grinding exposés. **Buys 30 mss/year.** Query. Length: 500-2,000 words. **Pays
$150-250.** Sometimes pays expenses of writers on assignment.

Photos: Send photos with submission. Reviews transparencies, prints. Buys one-time and promotional website rights.
Offers no additional payment for photos accepted with ms. Captions required.

Columns/Departments: Technically Destined (travel), 1,200 words; Rigging For Success (how-to, few words/heavily
illustrated); Explorer (personality profile), 2,000 words; Tech Spec (product descriptions), 1,000 words; New Products
(product press releases), 200 words; Book Review (book review), 800 words. **Buys 12 mss/year.** Query. **Pays $150-
250.**

Fillers: Newsbreaks. **Pays 35¢/word.**

Tips: "Query first with a short, punchy paragraph that describes your story and why it would be of interest to our
readers. There's bonus points for citing which feature or department would be most appropriate for your story."

$ $ PADDLER MAGAZINE, World's No. 1 Canoeing, Kayaking and Rafting Magazine, Paddlesport Publishing, P.O. Box 5450, Steamboat Springs CO 80477-5450. (970)879-1450. Fax: (970)870-1404. E-mail: bieline@paddl
ermagazine.com. Website: www.paddlermagazine.com. Editor: Eugene Buchanan. **Contact:** Tom Bie, managing editor.
70% freelance written. Bimonthly magazine covering paddle sports. "*Paddler* magazine is written by and for those
knowledgeable about river running, flatwater canoeing and sea kayaking. Our core audience is the intermediate to
advanced paddler, yet we strive to cover the entire range from beginners to experts. Our editorial coverage is divided
between whitewater rafting, whitewater kayaking, canoeing and sea kayaking. We strive for balance between the Eastern
and Western U.S. paddling scenes and regularly cover international expeditions. We also try to integrate the Canadian
paddling community into each publication." Estab. 1991. Circ. 80,000. Pays on publication. Publishes ms an average
of 6 months after acceptance. Byline given. Buys first North American serial rights, one-time electronic rights. Editorial
lead time 3 months. Submit seasonal material 6 months in advance. Accepts queries by mail, e-mail. Responds in 6
months to queries. Sample copy for $3 with 8½×11 SASE. Writer's guidelines for #10 SASE.

O➤ Break in through "The Hotline section at the front of the magazine."

Nonfiction: Book excerpts, essays, general interest, historical/nostalgic, how-to, humor, inspirational, interview/profile,
new product, opinion, personal experience, photo feature, technical, travel (must be paddlesport related). **Buys 75 mss/
year.** Query. Length: 100-3,000 words. **Pays 10-25¢/word (more for established writers) for assigned articles; 10-
20¢/word for unsolicited articles.** Sometimes pays expenses of writers on assignment.

Photos: Submissions should include photos or other art. State availability with submission. Reviews contact sheets,
negatives, transparencies. Buys one-time rights. Offers $25-200/photo.

Columns/Departments: Hotline (timely news and exciting developments relating to the paddling community. Stories
should be lively and newsworthy), 150-750 words; Paddle People (unique people involved in the sport and industry
leaders), 600-800 words; Destinations (informs paddlers of unique places to paddle—we often follow regional themes
and cover all paddling disciplines; submissions should include map and photo, 800 words); Marketplace (gear reviews,
gadgets and new products, and is about equipment paddlers use, from boats and paddles to collapsible chairs, bivy sacks
and other accessories), 250-800 words; Paddle Tales (short, humorous anecdotes), 75-300 words; Skills (a "How-to"
forum for experts to share tricks of the trade, from playboating techniques to cooking in the backcountry), 250-1,000
words. Query. **Pays 20-25¢/word.**

Tips: "We prefer queries, but will look at manuscripts on speculation. No phone queries please. Be familiar with the
magazine and offer us unique, exciting ideas. Most positive responses to queries are on spec, but we will occasionally
make assignments."

$ $ ☒ SPORT DIVER, World Publications, 460 N. Orlando Ave., Suite 200, Winter Park FL 32789-2988.
(407)571-4584. Fax: (407)571-4585. E-mail: kirk.brown@worldpub.net. Website: www.sportdiver.com. Kirk Brown,
managing editor. **75% freelance written.** Bimonthly magazine covering scuba diving. "We portray the adventure and
fun of diving—the reasons we all started diving in the first place." Estab. 1993. Circ. 175,000. Pays on publication,
sometimes on acceptance. Byline given. Offers 50% kill fee. Buys first North American serial rights. Editorial lead time
3 months. Submit seasonal material 4 months in advance. Accepts queries by e-mail. Responds in 2 weeks to queries;
3 months to mss. Writer's guidelines for #10 SASE.

Nonfiction: Personal experience, travel, diving. No non-diving related articles. **Buys 150 mss/year.** Query with SASE.
Length: 800-2,000 words. **Pays $300-500.**

Photos: State availability with submission. Reviews transparencies. Buys one-time rights. Offers $50-200/photo; $1,000
for covers. Captions required.

Columns/Departments: Divebriefs (shorts), 150-450 words. Query. **Pays $50-250.**

▪ The online magazine carries original content not found in the print edition. Contact: Matt Keleman, online
editor.

Tips: "Know diving, and even more importantly, know how to write. It's getting much more difficult to break into the
market due to a recent series of takeovers."

$ $ SWIM MAGAZINE, The Official Magazine of U.S. Masters Swimming, Sports Publications, Inc., 90 Bell Rock Plaza, Suite 200, Sedona AZ 86351. (520)284-4005. Fax: (520)284-2477. E-mail: swimworld@aol.com. Website: www.swimworld.com. **Contact:** Dr. Phillip Whitten, editor. **50% freelance written.** Bimonthly magazine for adults interested in swimming for fun, fitness and competition. Readers are fitness-oriented adults from varied social and professional backgrounds who share swimming as part of their lifestyle. Readers are well-educated, affluent and range in age from 20-100 with most in the 30-49 age group; about 50% female, 50% male." Estab. 1984. Circ. 46,000. Pays 1 month after publication. Publishes ms an average of 3 months after acceptance. Byline given. Buys all rights. Editorial lead time 3 months. Submit seasonal material 3 months in advance. Accepts simultaneous submissions. Responds in 1 month to queries; 4 months to mss. Sample copy for $5 (prepaid) and 9×12 SAE with 4 first-class stamps. Writer's guidelines for #10 SASE.

Nonfiction: "Articles need to be informative as well as interesting. In addition to fitness and health articles, we are interested in exploring fascinating topics dealing with swimming for the adult reader." Book excerpts, essays, exposé, general interest, historical/nostalgic, how-to (training plans and techniques), humor, inspirational, interview/profile (people associated with fitness and competitive swimming), new product (articles describing new products for fitness and competitive training), personal experience, photo feature, technical, travel, general health. **Buys 12-18 mss/year.** Query with or without published clips. Length: 250-2,500 words. **Pays 12¢/word minimum.**

Photos: Send photos with submission. Negotiates payment individually. Captions, identification of subjects, model releases required.

Tips: "*Always* query first. Writers should be familiar with or an expert in adult fitness and/or adult swimming. Our how-to and profile articles best typify *Swim Magazine*'s style for fitness and competitive swimmers. *Swim Magazine* accepts medical guidelines and exercise physiology articles primarily by M.D.s and Ph.Ds."

$ $ SWIMMING TECHNIQUE, Sports Publications, Inc., 90 Bell Rock Plaza, Suite 200, Sedona AZ 86351. (520)284-4005. Fax: (520)284-2477. E-mail: swimworld@aol.com. Website: www.swiminfo.com. Managing Editor: Mr. Bob Engram. **Contact:** Dr. Phillip Whitten, editor. **75% freelance written.** Quarterly magazine for professional swim coaches, covering swimming techniques. "Covers all aspects of swimming technique and training." Estab. 1963. Circ. 9,000. Pays on publication. Publishes ms an average of 4 months after acceptance. Byline given. Buys first, all rights. Editorial lead time 4 months. Submit seasonal material 4 months in advance. Accepts queries by mail, e-mail, fax, phone. Responds in 1 month to queries. Sample copy for $5. Writer's guidelines free.

Nonfiction: Book excerpts, essays, how-to (swim & technique), interview/profile, opinion, personal experience, technical. **Buys 16-20 mss/year.** Query with published clips. Length: 500-4,000 words. **Pays 12-15¢/word.** Sometimes pays expenses of writers on assignment.

Photos: Send photos with submission. Buys all rights. Negotiates payment individually. Captions, identification of subjects required.

$ $ SWIMMING WORLD, Sports Publications, Inc., 90 Bell Rock Plaza, Suite 200, Sedona AZ 86351. (520)284-4005. Fax: (520)284-2477. E-mail: swimworld@aol.com. Website: www.swiminfo.com. Managing Editor: Bob Ingram. **Contact:** Dr. Phillip Whitten, editor-in-chief. **25-50% freelance written.** Monthly magazine. "*Swimming World* is recognized as the authoritative source in the sport of swimming. It publishes articles about all aspects of competitive swimming." Estab. 1959. Circ. 39,700. Pays on publication. Byline given. Kill fee negotiated. Buys all rights. Editorial lead time 2 months. Submit seasonal material 3 months in advance. Accepts queries by mail, e-mail, fax, phone. Accepts simultaneous submissions. Responds in 1 month to queries. Sample copy for $5 and SAE with 4 first-class stamps. Writer's guidelines free.

Nonfiction: Book excerpts, essays, exposé, general interest, historical/nostalgic, how-to, humor, inspirational, interview/profile, new product, opinion, personal experience, photo feature, technical, travel. **Buys 30 mss/year.** Query. Length: 300-3,000 words. **Pays $75-400.** Sometimes pays expenses of writers on assignment.

Photos: State availability with submission. Reviews prints. Buys negotiable rights. Negotiates payment individually. Captions, identification of subjects, model releases required.

Columns/Departments: Buys 18 mss/year. Query with published clips. **Pays $75-200.**

🖳 The online magazine carries original content not found in the print edition.

N $ $ WAKE BOARDING MAGAZINE, World Publications, Inc., P.O. Box 2456, Winter Park FL 32790. Fax: (407)628-7061. E-mail: editor@wakeboardingmag.com. Website: www.wakeboardingmag.com. Editor: Jeff Barton. **Contact:** Kevin Michael, managing editor. **10% freelance written.** Magazine published 9 times/year covering wakeboarding. "*Wake Boarding Magazine* is the leading publication for wakeboarding in the world. Articles must focus on good riding, first and foremost, then good fun and good times. Covers competition, travel, instruction, personalities and humor." Estab. 1994. Circ. 65,000. Pays on publication. Publishes ms an average of 3 months after acceptance. Byline given. Buys all rights. Editorial lead time 4 months. Submit seasonal material 4 months in advance. Accepts queries by mail, e-mail. Accepts simultaneous submissions. Responds in 1 week to queries; 1 month to mss. Sample copy and writer's guidelines free.

Nonfiction: General interest, how-to (wakeboarding instruction), humor, interview/profile, new product, photo feature, travel. "No Weekend Wallys having fun on the lake. Serious riders only. Nothing to do with water skiing or barefooting." **Buys 6-8 mss/year.** Send complete ms. Length: 1,000-2,500 words. **Pays $200-500.**

Photos: Send photos with submission. Reviews slide transparencies. Buys all rights. Negotiates payment individually. Captions, identification of subjects required.

Columns/Departments: Random Notes (events, travel stories), 600-750 words. **Buys 6-8 mss/year.** Send complete ms. **Pays $50-200.**

Tips: "Contact us first before presuming article is worthy. What may be cool to you might not fit our readership. Remember, *WBM*'s readership is made up of a lot of teenagers, so buck authority every chance you get."

$ THE WATER SKIER, USA Water Ski, 1251 Holy Cow Rd., Polk City FL 33868-8200. (863)324-4341. Fax: (863)325-8259. E-mail: satkinson@usawaterski.org. Website: www.usawaterski.org. Scott Atkinson, editor. **10-20% freelance written.** Magazine published 9 times/year. "*The Water Skier* is the membership magazine of USA Water Ski, the national governing body for organized water skiing in the United States. The magazine has a controlled circulation and is available only to USA Water Ski's membership, which is made up of 20,000 active competitive water skiers and 10,000 members who are supporting the sport. These supporting members may participate in the sport but they don't compete. The editorial content of the magazine features distinctive and informative writing about the sport of water skiing only." Estab. 1951. Circ. 30,000. Pays on other. Byline given. Offers 30% kill fee. Editorial lead time 4 months. Submit seasonal material 6 months in advance. Responds in 2 weeks to queries. Sample copy for $3.50. Writer's guidelines for #10 SASE.

O₄ Most open to material for feature articles (query editor with your idea).

Nonfiction: Historical/nostalgic (has to pertain to water skiing), interview/profile (call for assignment), new product (boating and water ski equipment), travel (water ski vacation destinations). **Buys 10-15 mss/year.** Query. Length: 1,500-3,000 words. **Pays $100-150.**

Reprints: Send photocopy. Pay negotiable.

Photos: State availability with submission. Reviews contact sheets. Buys all rights. Negotiates payment individually. Captions, identification of subjects required.

Columns/Departments: The Water Skier News (small news items about people and events in the sport), 400-500 words. Other topics include safety, training (3-event, barefoot, disabled, show ski, ski race, kneeboard and wakeboard); champions on their way; new products. Query. **Pays $50-100.**

▣ The online magazine carries original content not found in the print edition. Contact: Scott Atkinson, online editor.

Tips: "Contact the editor through a query letter (please no phone calls) with an idea. Avoid instruction, these articles are written by professionals. Concentrate on articles about the people of the sport. We are always looking for interesting stories about people in the sport. Also, short news features which will make a reader say to himself, 'Hey, I didn't know that.' Keep in mind that the publication is highly specialized about the sport of water skiing."

N $ $ WATERSKI MAGAZINE, The World's Leading Water Skiing Magazine, World Publications, 330 W. Canton Ave., Winter Park FL 32789. (407)628-4802. Fax: (407)628-7061. E-mail: waterski@worldzine.com. **Contact:** Todd Rosticelli, editor. **25% freelance written.** Magazine published 9 times/year for water skiing and related watersports. "*WaterSki* instructs, advises, enlightens, informs and creates an open forum for skiers around the world. It provides definitive information on instruction, products, people and travel destinations." Estab. 1978. Circ. 105,000. **Pays on acceptance.** Publishes ms an average of 4 months after acceptance. Offers 25% kill fee. Buys first North American serial, second serial (reprint) rights. Editorial lead time 2 months. Submit seasonal material 2 months in advance. Responds in 1 month to queries; 2 months to mss. Sample copy for 8½×11 SAE and 4 first-class stamps. Writer's guidelines for #10 SASE.

Nonfiction: General interest, historical/nostalgic, how-to (water ski instruction boating-related), interview/profile, new product, photo feature, technical, travel. Nothing unrelated to water skiing. **Buys 10 mss/year.** Query with published clips. Length: 800-2,000 words. **Pays negotiable amount.** Sometimes pays expenses of writers on assignment.

Photos: Send photos with submission. Reviews 2¼×2¼ transparencies, all slides. Buys one-time rights on color, all rights on b&w. Negotiates payment individually. Identification of subjects required.

Columns/Departments: Shortline (interesting news of the sport), 300 words. **Buys 10 mss/year.** Query with published clips. **Pays $75-125.**

Fillers: Anecdotes, facts, gags to be illustrated by cartoonist, newsbreaks, short humor. **Buys 15/year.** Length: 200-500 words. **Pays $75-125.**

Tips: "I recommend a query call to see if there are any immediate openings in the calendar. Follow-up with a published submission (if applicable). Writers should have some interest in the sport, and understand its people, products and lifestyle. The features sections offer the most opportunity for freelancers. One requirement: It must have a positive, strong water skiing slant, whether it be personality, human interest or travel."

Wrestling

$ ⬚ WRESTLING WORLD, Sterling/MacFadden, 233 Park Ave. S., New York NY 10003. (212)780-3500. Fax: (212)780-3555. E-mail: sterlingsports@yahoo.com. **Contact:** Mike Greenblatt, editor. **100% freelance written.** Monthly magazine for professional wrestling fans. "We run profiles of top wrestlers and managers and articles on current topics of interest on the mat scene." Circ. 100,000. **Pays on acceptance.** Byline given. Buys first North American serial rights. Responds in 2 weeks to queries. Sample copy for $4 and SAE with 3 first-class stamps.

Nonfiction: Interview/profile, photo feature. "No general think pieces." **Buys 100 mss/year.** Query with or without published clips or send complete ms. Length: 1,500-2,500 words. **Pays $75-125.**
Photos: State availability with submission. Reviews 35mm transparencies, prints. Buys one-time rights. Offers $25-50/photo package. Pays $50-150 for transparencies. Identification of subjects required.
Tips: "Anything topical has the best chance of acceptance. Articles on those hard-to-reach wrestlers stand an excellent chance of acceptance."

TEEN & YOUNG ADULT

Publications in this category are for teens (13-19). Publications for college students are in Career, College & Alumni. Those for younger children are in Juvenile.

$ $ CAMPUS LIFE, Christianity Today, Inc., 465 Gundersen Dr., Carol Stream IL 60188. (630)260-6200. Fax: (630)260-0114. E-mail: clmag@campuslife.com. Website: www.campuslife.net. **Contact:** Amber Penney, assistant editor. **35% freelance written.** Magazine published 9 times/year for the Christian life as it relates to today's teen. "*Campus Life* is a magazine for high-school and early college-age teenagers. Our editorial slant is not overtly religious. The indirect style is intended to create a safety zone with our readers and to reflect our philosophy that God is interested in all of life. Therefore, we publish 'message stories' side by side with general interest, humor, etc." Estab. 1942. Circ. 100,000. **Pays on acceptance.** Publishes ms an average of 5 months after acceptance. Byline given. Offers 50% kill fee. Buys first, one-time rights. Editorial lead time 4 months. Accepts queries by mail, fax. Responds in 5 weeks to queries. Sample copy for $3 and 8 × 10 SAE with 3 first-class stamps. Writer's guidelines for #10 SASE or online.
Nonfiction: Humor, personal experience, photo feature. **Buys 15-20 mss/year.** Query with published clips. Length: 750-1,500 words. **Pays 15-20¢/word minimum.**
Reprints: Send tearsheet, photocopy or typed ms with rights for sale noted and information about when and where the material previously appeared. Pays $50.
Photos: State availability with submission. Buys one-time rights. Negotiates payment individually. Model releases required.
Fiction: Buys 1-5 mss/year. Query. Length: 1,000-2,000 words. **Pays 15-20¢/word.**
Tips: "The best way to break in to *Campus Life* is through writing first-person or as-told-to first-person stories. We want stories that capture a teen's everyday 'life lesson' experience. A first-person story must be highly descriptive and incorporate fictional technique. While avoiding simplistic religious answers, the story should demonstrate that Christian values or beliefs brought about a change in the young person's life. But query first with theme information telling the way this story would work for our audience."

$ THE CONQUEROR, United Pentecostal Church International, 8855 Dunn Rd., Hazelwood MO 63042-2299. (314)837-7300. Fax: (314)837-4503. E-mail: youth@upci.org. Website: www.upci.org/youth. **Contact:** Travis Miller, editor. **80% freelance written.** Bimonthly magazine covering Christian youth. "*The Conqueror* addresses the social, intellectual and spiritual concerns of youth aged 12-21 years from a Christian viewpoint." Estab. 1957. Circ. 6,000. Pays on publication. Publishes ms an average of 4 months after acceptance. Buys one-time rights. Editorial lead time 4 months. Submit seasonal material 4 months in advance. Accepts queries by mail, e-mail, fax. Accepts simultaneous submissions. Responds in 2 months to mss. Sample copy for 9 × 12 SAE with 3 first-class stamps. Writer's guidelines free.
Nonfiction: Essays, general interest, historical/nostalgic, inspirational, personal experience, religious. **Buys 18 mss/year.** Send complete ms. Length: 250-1,250 words. **Pays $15-30.**
Reprints: Accepts previously published submissions.
Photos: State availability with submission. Offers no additional payment for photos accepted with ms.
Columns/Departments: Time Out for Truth (applying Biblical truth to everyday living), 750 words. **Buys 6-10 mss/year.** Send complete ms. **Pays $30 maximum.**
Fiction: Adventure, ethnic, historical, humorous, mainstream, religious, slice-of-life vignettes. Send complete ms. Length: 250-1,250 words. **Pays $15-30.**
Poetry: Traditional. **Buys 2-4 poems/year.** Submit maximum 5 poems. **Pays $15.**
Fillers: Anecdotes, gags to be illustrated by cartoonist, short humor. **Buys 4/year.** Length: 100 words. **Pays $15.**
Tips: "Choose subjects relevant to single youth. Most subjects *are* relevant if properly handled. Today's youth are interested in more than clothes, fashion, careers and dating. Remember our primary objective: Inspiration—to portray happy, victorious living through faith in God."

$ ENCOUNTER, Standard Publishing, 8121 Hamilton Ave., Cincinnati OH 45231-2323. (513)931-4050. Fax: (513)931-0950. Website: www.standardpub.com. **Contact:** Kelly Carr, editor. **90% freelance written.** Weekly magazine for "teens, age 13-19, from Christian backgrounds who generally receive this publication in their Sunday School classes or through subscriptions." "We use freelance material in every issue. Our theme list is available on a quarterly basis. Writers need only give us their name and address in order to be added to our mailing list." **Pays on acceptance.** Publishes ms an average of 1 year after acceptance. Byline given. Buys first, second serial (reprint) rights. Submit seasonal material 1 year in advance. Accepts queries by mail. Responds in 2 months to queries. Sample copy and writer's guidelines for 9 × 12 SAE with 2 first-class stamps.

Nonfiction: "We want articles that promote Christian values and ideals." No puzzles. General interest (school, church, family, dating, sports, part-time jobs), humor, inspirational, personal experience, religious. Submit complete ms. Include Social Security number on ms. Length: 800-1,100 words. **Pays 6-8¢/word.**

Reprints: Send typed ms with rights for sale noted. Pays 5¢/word.

Fiction: "All fiction should have some message for the modern Christian teen. Fiction should deal with all subjects in a forthright manner, without being preachy and without talking down to teens. No tasteless manuscripts that promote anything adverse to the Bible's teachings." Adventure, humorous, religious, suspense. Send complete ms. Length: 900-1,100 words. **Pays 6-8¢/word.**

Tips: "Don't be trite. Use unusual settings or problems. Use a lot of illustrations, a good balance of conversation, narration, and action. Style must be clear, fresh—no sermonettes or sickly-sweet fiction. Take a realistic approach to problems. Be willing to submit to editorial policies on doctrine; knowledge of the *Bible* a must. Also, be aware of teens today, and what they do. Language, clothing, and activities included in manuscripts should be contemporary. We are also looking for articles about real teens who are making a difference in their school, community or church. Articles for this feature should be approx. 900 words in length. We would also like a picture of the teen or group of teens to run with the article."

$ $✍ GUIDEPOSTS FOR TEENS, Guideposts, P.O. Box 638, Chesterton IN 46304. (219)929-4429. Fax: (219)926-3839. E-mail: gp4t@guideposts.org. Website: www.gp4teens.com. Editor-in-Chief: Mary Lou Carney. **Contact:** Betsy Kohn, editor. **90% freelance written.** Bimonthly magazine serving as an inspiration for teens. "*Guideposts for Teens* is a 48-page, 4-color, value-centered magazine that offers teens ages 12-18 true, first-person stories packed with adventure and inspiration. Our mission is to empower teens through lively, positive, thought-provoking content: Music reviews, how-tos, advice, volunteer opportunities, news, quizzes, profiles of positive role models—both celebrity and ordinary teens. *Guideposts for Teens* helps our readers discover sound values that will enable them to lead successful, hope-filled lives." Estab. 1998. Circ. 200,000. **Pays on acceptance.** Byline sometimes given. Offers 25% kill fee. Buys all rights. Editorial lead time 6 months. Submit seasonal material 6 months in advance. Accepts queries by mail, e-mail. Accepts simultaneous submissions. Responds in 1 month to queries; 2 months to mss. Sample copy for $4.50. Writer's guidelines for #10 SASE.

Nonfiction: Nothing written from an adult point of view. How-to, humor, inspirational, interview/profile, personal experience, religious. **Buys 80 mss/year.** Query. Length: 700-2,000 words. **Pays $175-500 for assigned articles; $150-400 for unsolicited articles.** Pays expenses of writers on assignment.

Photos: State availability with submission. Buys one-time rights. Negotiates payment individually. Identification of subjects required.

Columns/Departments: Quiz (teen-relevant topics, teen language), 1,000 words; How-to (strong teen voice/quotes, teen topics), 750-1,000 words; Profiles (teens who initiate change/develop service projects), 300-500 words; Humor (essays teens can relate to), 750 words. **Buys 40 mss/year.** Query with published clips. **Pays $175-400.**

Fillers: Short humor (cartoons, jokes, short humor, quotes). **Buys 20/year.** Length: 100-300 words. **Pays $25-100.**

　　▪ The online magazine carries original content not found in the print edition. Contact: Chris Lyon, managing editor.

Tips: "We are eagerly looking for a number of things: teen how-to pieces, quizzes, humor. Most of all, though, we are about TRUE STORIES in the *Guideposts* tradition. Teens in dangerous, inspiring, miraculous situations. These first-person (ghostwritten) true narratives are the backbone of *GP4T*—and what sets us apart from other publications."

$✍ INSIGHT, A Spiritual Lift for Teens, The Review and Herald Publishing Association, 55 W. Oak Ridge Dr., Hagerstown MD 21740. E-mail: insight@rhpa.org. Website: www.insightmagazine.org. **Contact:** Lori Peckham, editor. **80% freelance written.** Weekly magazine covering spiritual life of teenagers. "*Insight* publishes true dramatic stories, interviews, and community and mission service features that relate directly to the lives of Christian teenagers, particularly those with a Seventh-day Adventist background." Estab. 1970. Circ. 20,000. Pays on publication. Publishes ms an average of 4 months after acceptance. Byline given. Buys first, second serial (reprint) rights. Editorial lead time 6 months. Submit seasonal material 6 months in advance. Accepts queries by mail, e-mail, fax. Responds in 1 month to mss. Sample copy for $2 and #10 SASE. Writer's guidelines for #10 SASE or online.

　　● "*Big Deal*" appears in *Insight* often, covering a topic of importance to teens. Each feature contains: An opening story involving real teens (can be written in first-person), "Scripture Picture" (a sidebar that discusses what the Bible says about the topic) and another sidebar (optional) that adds more perspective and help.

Nonfiction: How-to (teen relationships and experiences), humor, interview/profile, personal experience, photo feature, religious. **Buys 120 mss/year.** Send complete ms. Length: 500-2,000 words. **Pays $25-150 for assigned articles; $25-125 for unsolicited articles.**

Reprints: Send typed ms with rights for sale noted and information about when and where the material previously appeared. Pays $50.

Photos: State availability with submission. Reviews contact sheets, negatives, transparencies, prints. Buys one-time rights. Negotiates payment individually. Model releases required.

Columns/Departments: Big Deal (topic of importance to teens) 1,200-1,700 words; Interviews (Christian culture figures, especially musicians), 2,000 words; It Happened to Me (first-person teen experiences containing spiritual insights), 1,000 words; On the Edge (dramatic true stories about Christians), 2,000 words; So I Said...(true short stories in the first person of common, everyday events and experiences that taught the writer something), 300-500 words. Send complete ms. **Pays $25-125.**

Tips: "Skim two months of *Insight*. Write about your teen experiences. Use informed, contemporary style and vocabulary. Become a Christian if you haven't already."

$ $ KEYNOTER, Key Club International, 3636 Woodview Trace, Indianapolis IN 46268-3196. E-mail: Keynoter@ Kiwanis.org. Website: www.Keyclub.org. **Contact:** Amy L. Wiser, executive editor. **65% freelance written.** Monthly magazine for youth (December/January combined issue), distributed to members of Key Club International, a high school service organization for young men and women. Estab. 1946. Circ. 171,000. **Pays on acceptance.** Publishes ms an average of 5 months after acceptance. Byline given. Buys first North American serial rights. Submit seasonal material 7 months in advance. Accepts queries by mail, e-mail. Accepts simultaneous submissions. Responds in 2 months to queries. Sample copy for 65¢ and 8½×11 SAE. Writer's guidelines for SASE.
Nonfiction: "We would like to receive self-help and school-related nonfiction on leadership, community service, and teen issues." Book excerpts (included in articles), general interest (for intelligent teen audience), historical/nostalgic (generally not accepted), how-to (advice on how teens can enhance the quality of lives or communities), humor (accepted if adds to story), interview/profile (rarely purchased), new product (affecting teens), photo feature (if subject is right), technical (understandable and interesting to teen audience), travel (must apply to club travel schedule), academic, self-help, subjects that entertain and inform teens on topics that relate directly to their lives. *"Please, no first-person confessions, fiction or articles that are written down to our teen readers. No filler, or book, movie or music reviews."*. **Buys 10-15 mss/year.** Query with SASE. Length: 1,200-1,500 words. Sometimes pays expenses of writers on assignment.
Reprints: Send tearsheet or photocopy and information about when and where the material previously appeared.
Photos: State availability with submission. Reviews negatives, color contact sheets. Buys one-time rights. Payment for photos included in payment for manuscript. Identification of subjects required.
Tips: "We want to see articles written with attention to style and detail that will enrich the world of teens. Articles must be thoroughly researched and must draw on interviews with nationally and internationally respected sources. Our readers are 13-18, mature and dedicated to community service. We are very committed to working with good writers, and if we see something we like in a well-written query, we'll try to work it through to publication."

N $ $ $ $ LATINGIRL MAGAZINE, The Hispanic Teen Magazine, Nosotras LLC, 70 Hudson St., 5th Floor, Hoboken NJ 07030. (201)876-9600. Fax: (201)876-9640. E-mail: editor@latingirlmag.com. Website: www.latingirlmag.com. Editor: Lu Herrara. **Contact:** Jeanette Del Valle, senior editor. **75% freelance written.** Bimonthly magazine covering Hispanic entertainment, culture and beauty. *"Latingirl* is made for smart, savvy girls, who care about their family, friends, and cultural background; their appearance; their education; and being heard! The magazine combines Hispanic cultures with U.S. teen culture to provide current information that entertains, enlightens, and empowers readers. Each issue contains the latest fashion and beauty trends, celebrity stories, insightful peer stories, horoscopes, helpful resources, advice on dating, health, family life, school, and careers, as well as reviews on music, books, and the Internet. Through these features and columns, the magazine shares the readers' joys, hopes, and aspirations, as well as their celebration of being bicultural." Estab. 1998. Circ. 125,000. Pays on publication. Publishes ms an average of 4 months after acceptance. Byline sometimes given. Offers 25% kill fee. Buys first North American serial rights. Editorial lead time 8 months. Submit seasonal material 8 months in advance. Accepts queries by mail, e-mail, fax. Responds in 4 months to queries; 4 months to mss. Writer's guidelines free.
Nonfiction: Exposé, general interest, how-to (beauty tips, fashion and exercise), interview/profile, new product, photo feature. Special issues: Relationship issue (February/March); Spring Fashion/Prom issue (April/May); Summer Fun/ Music issue (June/July); Back to School issue (August/September); Hispanic Heritage (October/November); Holiday issue (December/January). **Buys 300 mss/year.** Query with published clips. Length: 500-2,000 words. **Pays $1/word.** Sometimes pays expenses of writers on assignment.
Photos: Send photos with submission. Buys one-time rights. Negotiates payment individually. Identification of subjects, model releases required.
Columns/Departments: Hermosura (beauty stories, how-tos, Q&As, tips for hair, makeup and skin care), 50-150 words; Body & Soul (health articles, exercise tips, teen interviews), 400 words; In The Zone (entertainment stories on music, movies and TV, new products, book reviews, CD reviews, website reviews, celebrity interviews), 50-500 words; Mi Barrio (Hispanic culture, profiles, teen stories/interviews), 400-1,000 words. **Buys 300 mss/year.** Query with published clips. **Pays $1/word.**
Fillers: Gabriella Leff, associate editor. Facts. **Buys 10-20/year.** Length: 50-100 words. **Pays $1/word.**
Tips: "The best queries we receive target a specific department. For example, one writer I recently assigned submitted a great back-to-school pitch, complete with article outline, a list of teens she'd interview and some very good questions she had about how I wanted the story angle to go."

$ LISTEN MAGAZINE, The Health Connection, 55 W. Oak Ridge Dr., Hagerstown MD 21740. (301)393-4019. Fax: (301)393-4055. E-mail: listen@healthconnection.org. Editor: Lincoln Steed. **Contact:** Anita Jacobs, associate editor. **50% freelance written.** Monthly magazine specializing in tobacco, drug and alcohol prevention, presenting positive alternatives to various tobacco, drug and alcohol dependencies. *"Listen* is used in many high school classes and by professionals: Medical personnel, counselors, law enforcement officers, educators, youth workers, etc." Circ. 40,000. **Pays on acceptance.** Publishes ms an average of 6 months after acceptance. Byline given. Buys first rights for use in *Listen*, reprints, and associated material. Accepts queries by mail, e-mail, fax. Accepts simultaneous submissions. Responds in 2 months to queries. Sample copy for $1 and 9×12 SASE. Writer's guidelines for SASE.

○━ Break in with "a fresh approach with a surprise ending."

Nonfiction: Seeks articles that deal with causes of drug use such as poor self-concept, family relations, social skills, peer pressure. Especially interested in youth-slanted articles or personality interviews encouraging non-alcoholic and non-drug ways of life and showing positive alternatives. Also interested in good activity articles of interest to teens; an activity that teens would want to do instead of taking abusive substances because they're bored. Teenage point of view is essential. Also seeks narratives which portray teens dealing with youth conflicts, especially those related to the use of or temptation to use harmful substances. Growth of the main character should be shown. "Submit an article with an ending that catches you by surprise. We don't want typical alcoholic story/skid-row bum, or AA stories. We are also being inundated with drunk-driving accident stories. Unless yours is unique, consider another topic." **Buys 30-50 unsolicited mss/year.** Query. Length: 1,000-1,200 words. **Pays 5-10¢/word.** Sometimes pays expenses of writers on assignment.

Reprints: Send photocopy of article or typed manuscript with rights for sale noted and information about when and where the material previously appeared. Pays their regular rates.

Photos: Color photos preferred, but b&w acceptable. Purchased with accompanying manuscript. Captions required.

Fillers: Word square/general puzzles are also considered. **Pays $15.**

Tips: "True stories are good, especially if they have a unique angle. Other authoritative articles need a fresh approach. In query, briefly summarize article idea and logic of why you feel it's good. Make sure you've read the magazine to understand our approach."

$ ⊠ LIVE, A Weekly Journal of Practical Christian Living, Gospel Publishing House, 1445 N. Boonville Ave., Springfield MO 65802-1894. (417)862-2781. Fax: (417)862-6059. E-mail: rl-live@gph.org. Website: www.radiant life.org. **Contact:** Paul W. Smith, senior editor, adult resources. **100% freelance written.** Quarterly magazine for weekly distribution covering practical Christian living. "*LIVE* is a take-home paper distributed weekly in young adult and adult Sunday school classes. We seek to encourage Christians in living for God through fiction and true stories which apply biblical principles to everyday problems." Estab. 1928. Circ. 125,000. **Pays on acceptance.** Publishes ms an average of 18 months after acceptance. Byline given. Buys first, second serial (reprint) rights. Editorial lead time 12 months. Submit seasonal material 18 months in advance. Accepts queries by mail, e-mail, fax, phone. Accepts simultaneous submissions. Responds in 2 weeks to queries; 2 months to mss. Sample copy and writer's guidelines for #10 SASE or writer's guidelines *only* online.

○━ Break in with "true stories that demonstrate how the principles in the Bible work in every day circumstances as well as crises."

Nonfiction: Inspirational, religious. No preachy articles or stories that refer to religious myths (e.g. Santa Claus, Easter Bunny, etc.). **Buys 50-100 mss/year.** Send complete ms. Length: 400-1,500 words. **Pays 7-10¢/word.**

Reprints: Send tearsheet, photocopy or typed ms with rights for sale noted and information about when and where the material previously appeared. Pays 7¢/word.

Photos: Send photos with submission. Reviews 35mm transparencies and 3×4 prints or larger. Buys one-time rights. Offers $35-60/photo. Identification of subjects required.

Fiction: Religious, inspirational. No preachy fiction, fiction about Bible characters or stories that refer to religious myths (e.g. Santa Claus, Easter Bunny, etc.). No science or Bible fiction. **Buys 50 mss/year.** Send complete ms. Length: 800-1,600 words. **Pays 7-10¢/word.**

Poetry: Free verse, haiku, light verse, traditional. **Buys 15-24 poems/year.** Submit maximum 3 poems. Length: 12-25 lines. **Pays $35-60.**

Fillers: Anecdotes, short humor. **Buys 12-36/year.** Length: 300-600 words. **Pays 7-10¢/word.**

Tips: "Don't moralize or be preachy. Provide human interest articles with Biblical life application. Stories should consist of action, not just thought-life; interaction, not just insight. Heroes and heroines should rise above failures, take risks for God, prove that scriptural principles meet their needs. Conflict and suspense should increase to a climax! Avoid pious conclusions. Characters should be interesting, believable and realistic. Avoid stereotypes. Characters should be active, not just pawns to move the plot along. They should confront conflict and change in believable ways. Describe the character's looks and reveal his personality through his actions to such an extent that the reader feels he has met that person. Readers should care about the character enough to finish the story. Feature racial, ethnic and regional characters in rural and urban settings."

$ $ $ $ MH-18, Fitness, Sports, Girls, Gear, Life, Rodale Inc., 400 S. 10th St., Emmaus PA 18049. Fax: (610)967-7725. Website: www.mh-18.com. Editor: Jeff Csatari. Senior Editor: Stan Zukowski. **Contact:** Jenny Everett, assistant editor. **80% freelance written.** Quarterly magazine covering sports, fitness, girls, gear, life. "*Men's Health* for teenage boys, ages 13-18." Estab. 2000. **Pays on acceptance.** Byline sometimes given. Offers 25% kill fee. Buys all rights. Editorial lead time 4 months. Submit seasonal material 5 months in advance. Accepts queries by mail. Responds in 1 month to queries.

Nonfiction: General interest, how-to, humor, interview/profile, new product. No fiction. **Buys 150 mss/year.** Query with published clips. Length: 100-2,000 words. **Pays $1/word.** Pays expenses of writers on assignment.

Photos: State availability with submission.

Columns/Departments: Stan Zukowski, senior editor/web editor. Playbook (fitness, sports, gear, girls), 100 words. **Buys 500 mss/year.** Query with published clips. **Pays 50¢-$1/word.**

Fillers: Anecdotes, facts, newsbreaks, short humor. **Buys 100/year.** Length: 10-300 words. **Pays 50¢-$1/word.**

$ $ THE NEW ERA, 50 E. North Temple, Salt Lake City UT 84150. (801)240-2951. Fax: (801)240-2270. E-mail: cur-editorial-newera@ldschurch.org. **Contact:** Larry A. Hiller, managing editor. **20% freelance written.** Monthly magazine for young people (ages 12-18) of the Church of Jesus Christ of Latter-day Saints (Mormon), their church leaders and teachers. Estab. 1971. Circ. 230,000. **Pays on acceptance.** Publishes ms an average of 1 year after acceptance. Byline given. Buys all rights. Submit seasonal material 1 year in advance. Accepts queries by mail, e-mail, fax. Responds in 2 months to queries. Sample copy for $1.50 and 9×12 SAE with 2 first-class stamps. Writer's guidelines for SASE.
Nonfiction: Material that shows how the Church of Jesus Christ of Latter-day Saints is relevant in the lives of young people today. Must capture the excitement of being a young Latter-day Saint. Special interest in the experiences of young Mormons in other countries. No general library research or formula pieces without the *New Era* slant and feel. How-to, humor, inspirational, interview/profile, personal experience, informational. Query. Length: 150-1,200 words. **Pays 3-12¢/word.** Pays expenses of writers on assignment.
Photos: Uses b&w photos and transparencies with manuscripts. Individual photos used for *Photo of the Month*. Payment depends on use, $10-125 per photo.
Columns/Departments: Of All Things (news of young Mormons around the world); How I Know; Scripture Lifeline. **Pays 3-12¢/word.**
Fiction: Must relate to young Mormon audience. Adventure, humorous, relationships. **Pays 3¢/word minimum.**
Poetry: Must relate to editorial viewpoint. Free verse, light verse, traditional, blank verse, all other forms. **Pays 25¢/line minimum.**
Tips: "The writer must be able to write from a Mormon point of view. We're especially looking for stories about successful family relationships and personal growth. We anticipate using more staff-produced material. This means freelance quality will have to improve. Try breaking in with a department piece for 'How I Know' or 'Scripture Lifeline.' Well-written, personal experiences are always in demand."

$ $ $ $ SEVENTEEN, 850 Third Ave., New York NY 10022. (212)407-9700. Fax: (212)407-9899. Website: www.seventeen.com. Editor-in-Chief: Patrice G. Aderoft. **Contact:** Tamara Glenny, deputy editor; Darcy Jacobs, senior editor. **50% freelance written.** Monthly magazine. "*Seventeen* is a young woman's first fashion and beauty magazine. Tailored for young women in their teens and early twenties, *Seventeen* covers fashion, beauty, health, fitness, food, college, entertainment, fiction, plus crucial personal and global issues." Circ. 2,400,000. **Pays on acceptance.** Publishes ms an average of 6 months after acceptance. Byline given. Offers 25% kill fee. Buys one-time rights. Accepts queries by mail, fax. Responds in 3 months to queries. Writer's guidelines available.
O— Break in with the Who Knew section, which contains shorter items, or *Quiz.*
Nonfiction: Articles and features of general interest to young women who are concerned with intimate relationships and how to realize their potential in the world; strong emphasis on topicality and service. Send brief outline and query, including typical lead paragraph, summing up basic idea of article with clips of previously published works. Articles are commissioned after outlines are submitted and approved. Length: 1,200-2,500 words. **Pays $1/word, occasionally more for assigned articles.** Pays expenses of writers on assignment.
Photos: Sara Shaoul, photo editor. Photos usually by assignment only.
Fiction: Darcy Jacobs, fiction editor. Thoughtful, well-written stories on subjects of interest to girls between the ages of 12 and 21. Avoid formula stories—"She's blonde and pretty; I'm not,"—no heavy moralizing or condescension of any sort. We also have an annual fiction contest. Length: 1,000-3,000 words. **Pays $500-2,000.**
  ▣ The online magazine carries original content not found in the print edition. Contact: Katherine Raymond, online editor.
Tips: "Writers have to ask themselves whether or not they feel they can find the right tone for a *Seventeen* article—a tone which is empathetic yet never patronizing; lively yet not superficial. Not all writers feel comfortable with, understand or like teenagers. If you don't like them, *Seventeen* is the wrong market for you. An excellent way to break in to the magazine is by contributing ideas for quizzes or the Voice (personal essay) column."

$ $ SPIRIT, Lectionary-based Weekly for Catholic Teens, Good Ground Press, 1884 Randolph Ave., St. Paul MN 55105-1700. (651)690-7010. Fax: (651)690-7039. E-mail: jmcsj9@aol.com. Managing Editor: Therese Sherlock, CSJ. **Contact:** Joan Mitchell, CSJ, editor. **50% freelance written.** Weekly newsletter for religious education of Catholic high schoolers. "We want realistic fiction and nonfiction that raises current ethical and religious questions and that deals with conflicts that teens face in multi-racial contexts. The fact we are a religious publication does *not* mean we want pious, moralistic fiction." Estab. 1981. Circ. 26,000. Pays on publication. Publishes ms an average of 6 months after acceptance. Byline given. Buys all rights. Editorial lead time 6 months. Submit seasonal material 6 months in advance. Accepts queries by mail, e-mail, fax. Accepts simultaneous submissions. Responds in 1 month to queries. Sample copy and writer's guidelines free.
Nonfiction: "No Christian confessional, born-again pieces." Interview/profile, personal experience, religious, Roman Catholic leaders, human interest features, social justice leaders, projects, humanitarians. **Buys 4 mss/year.** Query with published clips or send complete ms. Length: 1,000-1,200 words. **Pays $200-225 for assigned articles; $150 for unsolicited articles.**
Photos: State availability with submission. Reviews 8×10 prints. Buys one-time rights. Offers $85-125/photo. Identification of subjects required.
Fiction: "We want realistic pieces for and about teens—non-pedantic, non-pious. We need good Christmas stories that show spirit of the season, and stories about teen relationship conflicts (boy/girl, parent/teen)." Conflict vignettes. **Buys 10 mss/year.** Query with published clips or send complete ms. Length: 1,000-1,200 words. **Pays $150-200.**

Tips: "Writers must be able to write from and for teen point of view rather than adult or moralistic point of view. In nonfiction, interviewed teens must speak for themselves. Query to receive call for stories, spec sheet, sample issues."

$ TODAY'S CHRISTIAN TEEN, Marketing Partners, Inc., P.O. Box 100, Morgantown PA 19543. (610)913-0796. Fax: (610)913-0797. E-mail: tcpubs@mkpt.com. Editor: Jerry Thacker. **Contact:** Elaine Williams, assistant editor. **75% freelance written.** Quarterly magazine covering teen issues from a Biblical perspective. *"Today's Christian Teen* is designed to deal with issues in the life of Christian teenagers from a conservative perspective." Estab. 1990. Circ. 100,000. Pays on publication. Publishes ms an average of 1 year after acceptance. Byline sometimes given. Buys simultaneous rights. Editorial lead time 1 year. Submit seasonal material 1 year in advance. Accepts queries by mail, e-mail, fax. Accepts simultaneous submissions. Responds in 1 month to queries; 3 months to mss. Sample copy for 9×12 SAE with 4 first-class stamps. Writer's guidelines for #10 SASE.

    O⟶ "Make your article practical, using principles from KJV Bible."

Nonfiction: Inspirational, personal experience, religious. **Buys 10 mss/year.** Send complete ms. Length: 800-1,200 words. **Pays $150.**

Reprints: Accepts previously published submissions.

Photos: Offers no additional payment for photos accepted with ms.

$ $ $ $ TWIST, Bauer Publishing, 270 Sylvan Ave., Englewood Cliffs NJ 07632. Fax: (201)569-4458. E-mail: twistmail@aol.com. Website: www.twistmagazine.com. Editor: Richard Spencer. **Contact:** Kristin McKeon, deputy editor. **5% freelance written.** Monthly entertainment magazine targeting 14- to 19-year-old girls. Estab. 1997. Circ. 700,000. **Pays on acceptance.** Publishes ms an average of 3 months after acceptance. Byline given. Offers 20% kill fee. Buys first North American serial rights. Editorial lead time 3 months. Submit seasonal material 4 months in advance. Accepts queries by mail. Accepts simultaneous submissions. Responds in 1 month to queries.

Nonfiction: "No articles written from an adult point of view about teens—i.e., a mother's or teacher's personal account." Personal experience (real teens' experiences, preferably in first person). **Pays minimum $50 for short item; up to $1/word for longer pieces.** Pays expenses of writers on assignment.

Photos: State availability with submission. Negotiates payment individually. Identification of subjects, model releases required.

    ▣ The online magazine carries original content not found in the print edition. Contact: Kristin McKeon, online editor.

Tips: "Tone must be conversational, neither condescending to teens nor trying to be too slangy. If possible, send clips that show an ability to write for the teen market. We are in search of real-life stories, and writers who can find teens with compelling real-life experiences (who are willing to use their full names and photographs in the magazine). Please refer to a current issue to see examples of tone and content. No e-mail queries or submissions, please."

$ $ WHAT MAGAZINE, What! Publishers Inc., 108-93 Lombard Ave., Winnipeg, Manitoba R3B 3B1, Canada. (204)985-8160. Fax: (204)957-5638. E-mail: l.malkin@m2ci.mb.ca. **Contact:** Leslie Malkin, editor. **40% freelance written.** Magazine published 5 times during the school year covering teen issues and pop culture. *"What* magazine is distributed to high school students across Canada. We produce a mag that is empowering, interactive and entertaining. We respect the reader—today's teens are smart and creative (and critical)." Estab. 1987. Circ. 250,000. Pays 30 days after publication. Publishes ms an average of 3 months after acceptance. Byline given. Offers negotiable kill fee. Buys first North American serial rights. Editorial lead time 5 months. Submit seasonal material 5 months in advance. Accepts queries by mail, e-mail, fax. Responds in 2 months to queries; 1 month to mss. Sample copy for 9×12 SAE with Canadian postage. Writer's guidelines for #10 SAE with Canadian postage.

Nonfiction: General interest, interview/profile, Issue-Oriented Features. No cliché teen material. **Buys 6-10 mss/year.** Query with published clips. Length: 700-1,900 words. **Pays $100-300 (Canadian).** Sometimes pays expenses of writers on assignment.

Photos: Send photos with submission. Reviews transparencies, 4×6 prints. Negotiates payment individually. Identification of subjects required.

Tips: "We're looking for more coverage of issues that affect Canadian teens in particular. Because *What* magazine is distributed through schools (with the consent of school officials), it's important that each issue find the delicate balance between very cool and very responsible. We target very motivated young women and men. Pitches should stray from cliche and stories should challenge readers with depth, insight and color. All stories must be meaningful to a Canadian readership."

$ WITH, The Magazine for Radical Christian Youth, Faith and Life Press, 722 Main St., P.O. Box 347, Newton KS 67114-0347. (316)283-5100. Fax: (316)283-0454. E-mail: deliag@gcmc.org. Website: www.withonline.org. **Contact:** Carol Duerksen, editor. **60% freelance written.** Magazine published 8 times/year for teenagers. "We are the magazine for Mennonite, Brethren, and Mennonite Brethren youth. Our purpose is to disciple youth within congregations." Circ. 6,100. **Pays on acceptance.** Byline given. Buys one-time rights. Submit seasonal material 6 months in advance. Accepts queries by mail, fax. Accepts simultaneous submissions. Responds in 1 month to queries; 2 months to mss. Sample copy for 9×12 SAE with 4 first-class stamps. Writer's guidelines and theme list for #10 SASE. Additional detailed guidelines for first-person stories, how-to articles and/or fiction available for #10 SASE.

    O⟶ Break in with "well-written true stories from teen's standpoint."

Nonfiction: How-to, humor, personal experience, religious, Youth. **Buys 15 mss/year.** Send complete ms. Length: 400-1,800 words. **Pays 5¢/word for simultaneous rights; higher rates for articles written on assignment; 3¢/word for reprint rights and for unsolicited articles.** Sometimes pays expenses of writers on assignment.

Reprints: Send typed ms with rights for sale noted and information about when and where the material previously appeared. Pays 60% of amount paid for an original article.

Photos: Send photos with submission. Reviews 8×10 b&w prints. Buys one-time rights. Offers $10-50/photo. Identification of subjects required.

Fiction: Humorous, religious, youth, parables. **Buys 15 mss/year.** Send complete ms. Length: 500-2,000 words. **Payment same as nonfiction.**

Poetry: Avant-garde, free verse, haiku, light verse, traditional. **Buys 0-2 poems/year. Pays $10-25.**

Tips: "We're looking for more wholesome humor, not necessarily religious—fiction, nonfiction, cartoons, light verse. Christmas and Easter material has a good chance with us because we receive so little of it."

$ ☒ YOUNG & ALIVE, Christian Record Services, P.O. Box 6097, Lincoln NE 68506. Website: www.christianreco rd.org. **Contact:** Gaylena Gibson, editor. **95% freelance written.** Large-print Christian material for sight-impaired people age 12-25 (also in braille), covering health, handicapped people, uplifting articles. "Write for an interdenominational Christian audience—we also like to portray handicapped individuals living normal lives or their positive impact on those around them." Submit seasonal material anytime. Estab. 1976. Circ. 25,000 large print; 3,000 braille. **Pays on acceptance.** Publishes ms an average of 3 years after acceptance. Byline given. Buys one-time rights. Accepts queries by mail. Accepts simultaneous submissions. Responds in 5 weeks to queries; 4 months to mss. Sample copy for 7×10 SAE with 5 first-class stamps. Writer's guidelines for #10 SASE or included with sample copy.

Nonfiction: Essays, general interest, historical/nostalgic, humor, inspirational, personal experience, travel, adventure (true), biography, camping, careers, handicapped, health, hobbies, holidays, nature, sports. **Buys 40 mss/year.** Send complete ms. Length: 200-1,400 words. **Pays 4-5¢/word. "We do provide complimentary copies in addition to payment."**

Photos: Send photos with submission. Reviews 3×5 to 10×12 prints. Buys one-time rights. Negotiates payment individually. Model releases required.

Fillers: Anecdotes, facts, short humor. Length: 300 words maximum. **Pays 4¢/word.**

Tips: "Make sure article has a strong ending that ties everything together. Pretend someone else wrote it—would it hold your interest? Draw your readers into the story by being specific rather than abstract or general."

$ $ ☒ YOUTH UPDATE, St. Anthony Messenger Press, 1615 Republic St., Cincinnati OH 45210-1298. (513)241-5615. Fax: (513)241-0399. E-mail: CarolAnn@americancatholic.org. Website: www.AmericanCatholic.org. **Contact:** Carol Ann Morrow, editor. **90% freelance written.** Monthly newsletter of faith life for teenagers. *Youth Update* is "designed to attract, instruct, guide and challenge Catholics of high school age by applying the Gospel to modern problems/situations." Circ. 24,000. **Pays on acceptance.** Publishes ms an average of 6 months after acceptance. Byline given. Responds in 3 months to queries. Sample copy and writer's guidelines for #10 SASE.

Nonfiction: Inspirational, practical self help, spiritual. **Buys 12 mss/year.** Query or send outline. **Pays $375-400.**

    🖥 The online magazine mirrors the print edition. Contact: Carol Ann Morrow.

Tips: "Write for a 15-year-old with a C+ average."

TRAVEL, CAMPING & TRAILER

Travel magazines give travelers in-depth information about destinations, detailing the best places to go, attractions in the area and sites to see—but they also keep them up to date about potential negative aspects of these destinations. Publications in this category tell tourists and campers the where-tos and how-tos of travel. This category is extremely competitive, demanding quality writing, background information and professional photography. Each publication has its own slant. Sample copies should be studied carefully before sending submissions.

$ AAA GOING PLACES, Magazine for Today's Traveler, AAA Auto Club South, 1515 N. Westshore Blvd., Tampa FL 33607. (813)289-5923. Fax: (813)289-6245. Phyllis Zeno, editor-in-chief. **50% freelance written.** Bimonthly magazine on auto news, driving tips, cruise travel, tours. Estab. 1982. Circ. 2,300,000. Pays on publication. Publishes ms an average of 6 months after acceptance. Byline given. Buys one-time rights. Submit seasonal material 9 months in advance. Accepts simultaneous submissions. Responds in 2 months. Writer's guidelines for SAE.

Nonfiction: Travel stories feature domestic and international destinations with practical information and where to stay, dine and shop, as well as personal anecdotes and historical background; they generally relate to tours currently offered by AAA Travel Agency. Historical/nostalgic, how-to, humor, interview/profile, personal experience, photo feature, travel. Special issues: Cruise Guide and Europe Issue. **Buys 15 mss/year.** Send complete ms. Length: 500-1,500 words. **Pays $50/printed page.**

Photos: State availability with submission. Reviews 2×2 transparencies. Offers no additional payment for photos accepted with ms. Captions required.

Columns/Departments: AAAway We Go (local attractions in Florida, Georgia or Tennessee).

Tips: "We prefer lively, upbeat stories that appeal to a well-traveled, sophisticated audience, bearing in mind that AAA is a conservative company."

$ $ AAA TODAY, 1515 N. Westshore Blvd., Tampa FL 33607. (813)289-1391. Fax: (813)288-7935. E-mail: sklim@aaasouth.com. Sandy Klim, editor. **25% freelance written.** Bimonthly magazine covering travel destinations. Estab. 1960. Circ. 4,000,000. Pays on publication. Publishes ms an average of 6 months after acceptance. Byline given. Editorial lead time 1 year. Submit seasonal material 1 year in advance. Accepts queries by mail. Sample copy and writer's guidelines free.

Nonfiction: Travel. **Buys 18 mss/year.** Query with published clips. Length: 500-1,500 words. **Pays $250.**

Photos: State availability with submission.

$ $ AAA MIDWEST TRAVELER, AAA Auto Club of Missouri, 12901 N. 40 Dr., St. Louis MO 63141. (314)523-7350 ext. 6301. Fax: (314)523-6982. E-mail: dreinhardt@aaamissouri.com. Website: www.aaamissouri.com/travelermagazines. Editor: Michael J. Right. **Contact:** Deborah Reinhardt, managing editor. **80% freelance written.** Bimonthly magazine covering travel and automotive safety. "We provide members with useful information on travel, auto safety and related topics." Estab. 1901. Circ. 440,000. **Pays on acceptance.** Byline given. Offers $50 kill fee. Not copyrighted. Buys first North American serial, second serial (reprint), electronic rights. Editorial lead time 1 year. Submit seasonal material 6 months in advance. Accepts queries by mail, e-mail, fax. Accepts simultaneous submissions. Responds in 1 month to queries; 1 month to mss. Sample copy for 10 × 13 SAE and 4 first-class stamps. Writer's guidelines for #10 SASE.

Nonfiction: Travel. No humor, fiction, poetry or cartoons. **Buys 20-30 mss/year.** Query; query with published clips the first time. Length: 800-1,200 words. **Pays $250-350.**

Photos: State availability with submission. Reviews transparencies, prints. Buys one-time and electronic rights. Offers no additional payment for photos accepted with ms. Captions required.

Tips: "Send queries between December and February, as we plan our calendar for the following year. Request a copy. Serious writers ask for media kit to help them target their piece. Travel destinations and tips are most open to freelancers; all departments and auto-related news handled by staff. We see too many 'Here's a recount of our family vacation' manuscripts. Go easy on first-person accounts."

$ $ ARUBA NIGHTS, Nights Publications Inc., 1831 Rene Levesque Blvd. W., Montreal, Quebec H3H 1R4, Canada. (514)931-1987. Fax: (514)931-6273. E-mail: editor@nightspublications.com. Website: www.nightspublications.com. Managing Editor: Zelly Zuskin. **Contact:** Stephen Trotter, editor. **90% freelance written.** Annual magazine covering the Aruban vacation lifestyle experience with an upscale, upbeat touch. Estab. 1988. Circ. 225,000. **Pays on acceptance.** Publishes ms an average of 9 months after acceptance. Byline given. Buys first North American serial, first Caribbean rights. Editorial lead time 1 month. Accepts queries by mail, e-mail, fax. Responds in 2 weeks to queries; 1 month to mss. Sample copy for $5 (make checks payable to Nights Publications Inc.). Writer's guidelines by e-mail.

   O— *Aruba Nights* is looking for more articles on nightlife experiences.

Nonfiction: General interest, historical/nostalgic, how-to (relative to Aruba vacationers), humor, inspirational, interview/profile, opinion, personal experience, photo feature, travel, Eco-tourism, Aruban culture, art, activities, entertainment, topics relative to vacationers in Aruba. "No negative pieces or stale rewrites." **Buys 5-10 mss/year.** Send complete ms, include SAE with Canadian postage or IRC. Length: 250-750 words. **Pays $100-250.**

Photos: State availability with submission. Reviews transparencies. Buys one-time rights. Pays $50/photo. Captions, identification of subjects, model releases required.

Tips: "Demonstrate your voice in your query letter. Be descriptive, employ vivid metaphors. Stories should immerse the reader in a sensory adventure. Focus on individual aspects of the Aruban lifestyle and vacation experience (e.g., art, music, culture, a colorful local character, a personal experience, etc.), rather than generalized overviews. Provide an angle that will be entertaining to vacationers who are already there. E-mail submissions accepted."

$ $ ASU TRAVEL GUIDE, ASU Travel Guide, Inc., 1525 Francisco Blvd. E., San Rafael CA 94901. (415)459-0300. Fax: (415)459-0494. E-mail: chris@asuguide.com. Website: www.asutravelguide.com. Editor: Cindy T. McDaniel. Executive Editor: Marcy O'Koon. **Contact:** Christopher Gil, managing editor. **80% freelance written.** Quarterly guidebook covering international travel features and travel discounts for well-traveled airline employees. Estab. 1970. Circ. 50,000. **Pays on acceptance.** Publishes ms an average of 4 months after acceptance. Byline given. Buys first North American serial, first, second serial (reprint) rights. Submit seasonal material 6 months in advance. Accepts simultaneous submissions. Responds in 1 year. Sample copy for 6 × 9 SAE and 5 first-class stamps. Writer's guidelines for #10 SASE.

Nonfiction: International travel articles "similar to those run in consumer magazines. Not interested in amateur efforts from inexperienced travelers or personal experience articles that don't give useful information to other travelers." Destination pieces only; no "Tips on Luggage" articles. Unsolicited mss or queries without SASE will not be acknowledged. No telephone queries. Travel (international). **Buys 16 mss/year.** Length: 1,800 words. **Pays $200.**

Reprints: Send tearsheet and information about when and where the material previously appeared. Pays 100% of amount paid for an original article.

Photos: "Interested in clear, high-contrast photos." Reviews 5 × 7 and 8 × 10 b&w or color prints. Payment for photos is included in article price; photos from tourist offices are acceptable.

Tips: "Query with samples of travel writing and a list of places you've recently visited. We appreciate clean and simple style. Keep verbs in the active tense and involve the reader in what you write. Avoid 'cute' writing, coined words and stale cliches. The most frequent mistakes made by writers in completing an article for us are: 1) Lazy writing—using words to describe a place that could describe any destination such as 'there is so much to do in (fill in destination) that whole guidebooks have been written about it'; 2) Including fare and tour package information—our readers make arrangements through their own airline."

$ BIG WORLD, Big World Publishing, P.O. Box 8743-G, Lancaster PA 17604. E-mail: subs@bigworld.com. Website: www.bigworld.com. **Contact:** Jim Fortney, editor. **85% freelance written.** Quarterly magazine covering independent travel. "Big World is a magazine for people who like their travel on the cheap and down-to-earth. And not necessarily because they have to—but because they want to. It's for people who prefer to spend their travelling time responsibly discovering, exploring, and learning, in touch with local people and their traditions, and in harmony with the environment. We're looking for casual, first-person narratives that take into account the cultural/sociological/political side of travel." Estab. 1995. Circ. 12,000. Pays on publication. Publishes ms an average of 3 months after acceptance. Byline given. Buys one-time rights. Editorial lead time 2 months. Submit seasonal material 4 months in advance. Accepts queries by mail, e-mail. Responds in 1 month to queries; 2 months to mss. Sample copy for $4. Writer's guidelines for #10 SASE or online.
Nonfiction: How-to, new product, opinion, personal experience, photo feature, travel, tips on transportation bargains and adventuring, Overseas work study advice. **Buys 32-40 mss/year.** Query. Length: 500-4,000 words. **Pay varies; sometimes pays with subscriptions.**
Reprints: Send photocopy. Pays 50% of amount paid for an original article.
Photos: Reviews prints. Buys one-time rights. Negotiates payment individually. Captions required.
Columns/Departments: Readers Writes (book reviews by subscribers), 400-500 words; Dispatches (slice-of-life pieces), 200-800 words; Hostel Intentions, My Town, Bike World, Better Adventuring. **Pay varies.**
Tips: "Take a look at the glossy, fluffy travel mags in the bookstore. They're *not* what we're about. We're *not* looking for romantic getaway pieces or lap-of-luxury bits. Our readers are decidedly downbeat and are looking for similarly minded on-the-cheap and down-to-earth, first-person articles. Be breezy. Be yourself. First-time writers especially encouraged. You can submit your story to us on paper or 3.5 disc."

$ $ BONAIRE NIGHTS, Nights Publications Inc., 1831 René Levesque Blvd. W., Montreal, Quebec H3H 1R4, Canada. (514)931-1987. Fax: (514)931-6273. E-mail: editor@nightspublications.com. **Contact:** Stephen Trotter, editor. **90% freelance written.** Annual magazine covering Bonaire vacation experience. "Upbeat entertaining lifestyle articles: Colorful profiles of locals, eco-tourism; lively features on culture, activities (particularly scuba and snorkeling), special events, historical attractions, how-to features. Audience is North American tourists." Estab. 1993. Circ. 60,000. **Pays on acceptance.** Publishes ms an average of 9 months after acceptance. Byline given. Buys first North American serial rights, first Caribbean rights. Editorial lead time 1 month. Accepts queries by mail, e-mail, fax. Responds in 2 weeks to queries; 1 month to mss. Sample copy for $5 (make check payable to Night Publications, Inc). Writer's guidelines by e-mail.
Nonfiction: General interest, historical/nostalgic, how-to, humor, inspirational, interview/profile, opinion, personal experience, photo feature, travel, lifestyle, local culture, art, activities, scuba diving, snorkling, eco-tourism. **Buys 6-9 mss/year.** Query. Length: 250-750 words. **Pays $100-250.**
Photos: State availability with submission. Reviews transparencies. Pays $50/slide. Captions, identification of subjects, model releases required.
Tips: "Demonstrate your voice in your query letter. Focus on the Bonaire lifestyle, what sets it apart from other islands. We want personal experience, not generalized overviews. Be positive and provide an angle that will appeal to vacationers who are already there. Our style is upbeat, friendly, fluid and descriptive."

N $ CAMPERS MONTHLY, Mid Atlantic Edition—New York to Virginia; Northeast Edition—Maine to New York, P.O. Box 260, Quakertown PA 18951. (215)536-6420. Fax: (215)536-6509. E-mail: werv2@aol.com. **Contact:** Paula Finkbeiner, editor. **50% freelance written.** Monthly (except December) tabloid. "With the above emphasis, we want to encourage our readers to explore all forms of outdoor recreation using a tent or recreational vehicle as a 'home away from home.' Travel—places to go, things to do and see." Estab. 1991 (Mid-Atlantic), 1993 (Northeast). Circ. 35,000 (Mid-Atlantic), 25,000 (Northeast). Pays on publication. Publishes ms an average of 2 months after acceptance. Byline given. Buys simultaneous rights. Editorial lead time 2 months. Submit seasonal material 4 months in advance. Accepts queries by mail, e-mail. Accepts simultaneous submissions. Responds in 2 months to mss. Sample copy and writer's guidelines for 10×13 SASE.
O─ Break in by finding a "little-known" destination in either of the regions covered.
Nonfiction: Historical/nostalgic (tied into a camping trip), how-to (selection, care, maintenance of RV's, tents, accessories, etc.), humor, personal experience, technical, travel (camping in the Mid-Atlantic or Northeast region). Special issues: Snowbird Issue (October)—geared towards campers heading South; Christmas Gift Ideas (November). "This is generally the only time we accept articles on areas outside our coverage area." **Buys 20-40 mss/year.** Send complete ms. Length: 800-2,000 words. **Pays $90-150 for assigned articles; $50 or more for unsolicited articles.** Sometimes pays expenses of writers on assignment.
Reprints: Send photocopy with rights for sale noted and information about when and where the material previously appeared. Pays 50% of amount paid for an original article.

Photos: Send photos with submission. Reviews 5×7 or 8×10 glossy b&w and color prints. Offers $3-5/photo. Don't send snapshots or polaroids.

Columns/Departments: Campground Cook (ideas for cooking in RV's, tents and over campfires; include recipes), 500-1,000 words; Tales From the Road (humorous stories of "on-the-road" travel), 350-800 words; Tech Tips (technical pieces on maintenance and enhanced usage of RV-related equipment), 350-1,800 words; Cybersite (websites of interest to RVer's), 500-1,000 words. **Buys 10-15 mss/year.** Send complete ms. **Pays $40-60.**

Fiction: Humorous, slice-of-life vignettes. **Buys 10 mss/year.** Query. Length: 300-1,000 words. **Pays $60-75.**

Fillers: Facts, short humor (must be RV-oriented). **Buys 8/year.** Length: 30-350 words. **Pays $20-35.**

Tips: Most open to freelancers are "destination pieces focusing on a single attraction or activity or closely clustered attractions are always needed. General interest material, technical or safety ideas (for RVs) is an area we're always looking for pieces on. Off-the-beaten track destinations always get priority. We're always looking for submissions for destination pieces for our Mid-Atlantic edition."

CAMPERWAYS, CAMP-ORAMA, CAROLINA RV TRAVELER, FLORIDA RV TRAVELER, NORTH-EAST OUTDOORS, SOUTHERN RV & TEXAS RV, Woodall Publications Corp., P.O. Box 8686, Ventura CA 93002. (800)323-9076. Fax: (805)667-4122. E-mail: editor@woodallpub.com. Website: www.woodalls.com. **Contact:** Melinda Baccanari, senior managing editor. **75% freelance written.** Monthly tabloid covering RV lifestyle. "We're looking for articles of interest to RVers. Lifestyle articles, destinations, technical tips, interesting events and the like make up the bulk of our publications. We also look for region-specific travel and special interest articles." Circ. 30,000. **Pays on acceptance.** Byline given. Offers 50% kill fee. Buys first North American serial rights. Submit seasonal material 4 months in advance. Accepts queries by mail, e-mail. Responds in 3 weeks to queries; 1 month to mss. Sample copy free. Writer's guidelines for #10 SASE.

Nonfiction: How-to, humor, inspirational, interview/profile, new product, opinion, personal experience, technical, travel. No "Camping From Hell" articles. **Buys 1,000 mss/year.** Query with published clips. Length: 500-2,000 words. **Payment varies.**

Photos: State availability with submission. Prefers slides. Reviews negatives, 4×5 transparencies, 4×5 prints. Buys first North American serial rights. Pays $5/photo. Captions, identification of subjects required.

Columns/Departments: Gadgets & Gears (new product reviews), 600 words; RV Renovations (how-to building/renovations project), 1,000 words; Stopping Points (campground reviews), 1,000 words. **Buys 100 mss/year.** Query with published clips. **Payment negotiable.**

Tips: "Be an expert in RVing. Make your work readable to a wide variety of readers, from novices to full-timers."

$ $ CAMPING CANADA'S RV LIFESTYLES, 1020 Brevik Place, Mississauga, Ontario L4W 4N7, Canada. (905)624-8218. Fax: (905)624-6764. Website: www.rvlifemag.com. **Contact:** Darryl Simmons, editorial director. **50% freelance written.** Magazine published 7 times/year (monthly January-June and November). "*Camping Canada's RV Lifestyles* is geared to readers who enjoy travel/camping. Upbeat pieces only. Readers vary from owners of towable trailers or motorhomes to young families and entry-level campers (no tenting)." Estab. 1971. Circ. 51,000. Pays on publication. Byline given. Buys first North American serial rights. Editorial lead time 2 months. Responds in 1 month to queries; 2 months to mss. Sample copy free.

Nonfiction: How-to, personal experience, technical, travel. No inexperienced, unresearched or too general pieces. **Buys 20-30 mss/year.** Query. Length: 1,200-2,000 words. **Pay varies.** Sometimes pays expenses of writers on assignment.

Reprints: Send photocopy with rights for sale noted and information about when and where the material previously appeared.

Photos: Send photos with submission. Buys one-time rights. Offers no additional payment for photos accepted with ms.

Tips: "Pieces should be slanted toward RV living. All articles must have an RV slant. Canadian content regulations require 95% Canadian writers."

$ $ $ $ CARIBBEAN TRAVEL AND LIFE, 460 N. Orlando Ave., Suite 200, Winter Park FL 32789. (407)628-4802. Fax: (407)628-7061. E-mail: editor@caribbeantravelmag.com. Website: www.caribbeantravelmag.com. Executive Editor: Bob Friel. **Contact:** Jessica Chapman, managing editor. **80% freelance written.** Prefers to work with published/established writers. Magazine published 9 times/year covering travel to the Caribbean, Bahamas and Bermuda for sophisticated, upscale audience. Estab. 1985. Circ. 135,000. **Pays on acceptance.** Publishes ms an average of 2 months after acceptance. Byline given. Offers 25% kill fee. Buys first North American serial rights. Submit seasonal material 4 months in advance. Accepts queries by mail, e-mail. Responds in 2 months to queries; 2 months to mss. Sample copy for 9×12 SAE and 9 first-class stamps. Writer's guidelines for #10 SASE.

Om Break in through columns and departments. "We are in the process of redesigning and editorially restructuring the magazine, so read recent issues and know where we have visited. Be prepared to contribute short items for departments before getting a feature assignment."

Nonfiction: General interest, how-to, interview/profile, personal experience, travel, culture. No guidebook rehashing, superficial destination pieces or critical exposés. **Buys 50-60 mss/year.** Query. Length: 300-2,500 words. **Pays $200-2,000 for assigned articles.**

Photos: State availability with submission. Reviews 35mm transparencies, prints. Buys one-time rights. Pays $100-1,000/photo. Captions, identification of subjects required.

Columns/Departments: Travel (hotels, destinations); Day Trip (excursions); Caribbean Life (people, arts, culture, music); Caribbean Kitchen (restaurants, chefs, food). Length: 500-1,250 words. Buys one-time rights. Query with published clips and SASE. **Pays $250-500.**

▣ The online magazine carries original content not found in the print edition. Contact: Stephen Hammel-Smith.

Tips: "We're always looking for new takes on the oft-visited places we must return to again and again—Virgin Islands, Bahamas, etc. Our only requirements are that the writing be superb, the subject be something unique and interesting, and the writer must know his/her subject. We are NOT interested in stories about the well-known, over-publicized and commonly visited places of the Caribbean. Our readers have likely already 'been there, done that.' We want to guide them to the new, the unusual and the interesting. Please do not call and do not send a complete manuscript unless requested by an editor. E-mail queries OK from writers we know. Newcomers should send writing samples by snail mail."

$ $ CHICAGO TRIBUNE, Travel Section, 435 N. Michigan Ave., Chicago IL 60611. (312)222-3999. Fax: (312)222-0234. E-mail: rcurwen@tribune.com. **Contact:** Randy Curwen, editor. Weekly newspaper Sunday 22-page travel section aimed at vacation travelers. Circ. 1,100,000. Pays on publication. Publishes ms an average of 6 weeks after acceptance. Byline given. Buys one-time rights, microfilm, online and cd/rom useage. Submit seasonal material 2 months in advance. Accepts simultaneous submissions. Responds in 1 month to mss. Sample copy for large SAE and $1.50 postage. Writer's guidelines for #10 SASE.
Nonfiction: Essays, general interest, historical/nostalgic, how-to (travel, pack), humor, opinion, personal experience, photo feature, travel. Special issues: "There will be 16 special issues in the next 18 months." **Buys 150 mss/year.** Send complete ms. Length: 500-2,000 words. **Pays $150-500.**
Photos: State availability with submission. Reviews 35mm transparencies, 8×10 or 5×7 prints. Buys one-time rights. Pays $100/color photo; $25/b&w; $100 for cover. Captions required.
Tips: "Be professional. Use a word processor. Make the reader want to go to the area being written about. Only 1% of manuscripts make it."

$ ▨ CLUBMEX, 3450 Bonita Rd., Suite 103, Chula Vista CA 91910-5200. (619)422-3022. Fax: (619)422-2671. **Contact:** Chuck Stein, publisher/editor. **75% freelance written.** Bimonthly newsletter. "Our readers are travelers to Baja California and Mexico, and are interested in retirement, RV news, fishing and tours. They are knowledgeable but are always looking for new places to see." Estab. 1975. Circ. 5,000. Pays on publication. Publishes ms an average of 2 months after acceptance. Byline given. Buys first North American serial rights. Submit seasonal material 3 months in advance. Responds in 1 month to queries; 1 month to mss. Sample copy and writer's guidelines for 9×12 SAE with 2 first-class stamps.
  ● *Clubmex* accepts articles dealing with all of Mexico. They want upbeat, positive articles about Mexico which motivate readers to travel there by car.
Nonfiction: Historical/nostalgic, humor, interview/profile, personal experience, travel. **Buys 36-50 mss/year.** Send complete ms. Length: 900-1,500 words. **Pays $65 for the cover story; $50 for other articles used; $25 for informative short pieces.**
Reprints: Send tearsheet, photocopy or typed ms with rights for sale noted and information about when and where the material previously appeared. Pays 100% of amount paid for original article.
Photos: State availability with submission. Reviews 3×5 prints. Buys one-time rights. Offers no additional payment for photos accepted with ms. Captions required.

$ $ ▨ COAST TO COAST MAGAZINE, Affinity Group, Inc., 2575 Vista Del Mar Dr., Ventura CA 93001-3920. Fax: (805)667-4217. Website: www.rv.net. **Contact:** Valerie Law, editorial director. **80% freelance written.** Magazine published 8 times/year for members of Coast to Coast Resorts. "*Coast to Coast* focuses on travel, recreation and good times, with most stories targeted to recreational vehicle owners." Estab. 1982. Circ. 200,000. **Pays on acceptance.** Publishes ms an average of 5 months after acceptance. Byline given. Offers 33% kill fee. Buys first North American serial, electronic rights. Submit seasonal material 5 months in advance. Responds in 1 month to queries; 2 months to mss. Sample copy for $4 and 9×12 SASE. Writer's guidelines available.
Nonfiction: Book excerpts, essays, general interest, historical/nostalgic, how-to, humor, inspirational, interview/profile, new product, opinion, personal experience, photo feature, technical, travel. No poetry, cartoons. **Buys 50 mss/year.** Query with published clips. Length: 500-2,500 words. **Pays $75-600.**
Reprints: Send photocopy and information about when and where the material previously appeared. Pays approximately 50% of amount paid for original article.
Photos: Send photos with submission. Reviews transparencies. Buys one-time rights. Pays $50-600/photo. Identification of subjects required.
Tips: "Send clips or other writing samples with queries, or story ideas will not be considered."

$ $ ▨ CURACAO NIGHTS, Nights Publications Inc., 1831 Rene Levesque Blvd. West, Montreal, Quebec H3H 1R4, Canada. (514)931-1987. Fax: (514)931-6273. E-mail: editor@nightspublications.com. Managing Editor: Zelly Zuskin. **Contact:** Stephen Trotter, editor. **90% freelance written.** Annual magazine covering the Curacao vacation experience. "We are seeking upbeat, entertaining lifestyle articles; colorful profiles of locals; lively features on culture, activities, night-life, eco-tourism, special events, gambling; how-to features; humor. Our audience is North American vacationers." Estab. 1989. Circ. 155,000. **Pays on acceptance.** Publishes ms an average of 9 months after acceptance.

Byline given. Buys first North American serial rights. Editorial lead time 1 month. Accepts queries by mail, e-mail, fax. Responds in 2 weeks to queries; 1 month to mss. Sample copy for $5 (check payable to Nights Publications Inc.). Writer's guidelines by e-mail.

Nonfiction: General interest, historical/nostalgic, how-to (help a vacationer get the most from their vacation), humor, inspirational, interview/profile, opinion, personal experience, photo feature, travel, eco-tourism, lifestyle, local culture, art, activities, night life, topics relative to vacationers in Curacao. "No negative pieces, generic copy, or stale rewrites." **Buys 5-10 mss/year.** Query with published clips, include SASE and either Canadian postage or IRC. Length: 250-750 words. **Pays $100-250.**

Photos: State availability with submission. Reviews transparencies. Buys one-time rights. Pays $50/photo. Captions, identification of subjects, model releases required.

Tips: "Demonstrate your voice in your query letter. Focus on individual aspects of the island lifestyle and vacation experience (e.g., art, music, culture, a colorful local character, a personal experience, etc.), rather than a generalized overview. Provide an angle that will be entertaining to vacationers who are already on the island. Our style is upbeat, friendly, fluid, and descriptive."

$ $ $ ENDLESS VACATION MAGAZINE, Endless Vacation, 9998 N. Michigan Rd., Carmel IN 46032-9640. (317)805-8120. Fax: (317)805-9507. **Contact:** Julie Woodard, senior editor. Prefers to work with published/established writers. Bimonthly magazine. "*Endless Vacation* is the vacation-idea magazine edited for people who love to travel. Each issue offers articles for America's dedicated and frequent leisure travelers—time-share owners. Articles and features explore the world through a variety of vacation opportunities and options for travelers who average 4 weeks of leisure travel each year." Estab. 1974. Circ. 1,219,393. **Pays on acceptance.** Publishes ms an average of 6 months after acceptance. Byline given. Buys first North American serial rights. Accepts simultaneous submissions. Responds in 2 months. Sample copy for $5 and 9 × 12 SAE with 5 first-class stamps. Writer's guidelines for #10 SASE.

Nonfiction: Senior Editor. Most articles are from established writers already published in *Endless Vacation*. *Accepts very few unsolicited pieces.* **Buys 24 mss/year.** Query with published clips via mail (no phone calls). Length: 1,500-2,000 words. **Pays $500-1,000 for assigned articles; $250-800 for unsolicited articles.** Sometimes pays expenses of writers on assignment.

Photos: Reviews transparencies, 35mm slides. Buys one-time rights. Pays $300-1,300/photo. Identification of subjects required.

Columns/Departments: Weekender (on domestic weekend vacation travel); Healthy Traveler; Family Vacationing; Taste (on food-related travel topics), 800-1,000 words. Also news items for Facts, Fads and Fun Stuff column on travel news, products and the useful and unique in travel, 100-200 words. Query with published clips via mail (no phone calls). **Pays $100/item.**

Tips: "We will continue to focus on travel trends and timeshare resort destinations. Articles must be packed with pertinent facts and applicable how-tos. Information—addresses, phone numbers, dates of events, costs—must be current and accurate. We like to see a variety of stylistic approaches, but in all cases the lead must be strong. A writer should realize that we require first-hand knowledge of the subject and plenty of practical information. For further understanding of *Endless Vacation*'s direction, the writer should study the magazine and guidelines for writers."

$ $ FAMILY MOTOR COACHING, Official Publication of the Family Motor Coach Association, 8291 Clough Pike, Cincinnati OH 45244-2796. (513)474-3622. Fax: (513)388-5286. E-mail: magazine@fmca.com. Website: www.fmca.com. Director of Communications: Pamela Wisby Kay. **Contact:** Robbin Gould, editor. **80% freelance written.** Monthly magazine emphasizing travel by motorhome, motorhome mechanics, maintenance and other technical information. "We prefer that writers be experienced RVers. *Family Motor Coaching* magazine is edited for the members and prospective members of the Family Motor Coach Association who own or are about to purchase self-contained, motorized recreational vehicles known as motorhomes. Featured are articles on travel and recreation, association news and activities, plus articles on new products and motorhome maintenance and repair. Approximately ⅓ of editorial content is devoted to travel and entertainment, ⅓ to association news, and ⅓ to new products, industry news and motorhome maintenance." Estab. 1963. Circ. 130,000. **Pays on acceptance.** Publishes ms an average of 8 months after acceptance. Byline given. Buys first North American serial rights. Submit seasonal material 4 months in advance. Accepts queries by mail, e-mail, fax. Responds in 3 months. Sample copy for $3.99. Writer's guidelines for #10 SASE.

Nonfiction: How-to (do-it-yourself motor home projects and modifications), humor, interview/profile, new product, technical, motorhome travel (various areas of country accessible by motorhome), bus conversions, nostalgia. **Buys 90-100 mss/year.** Query with published clips. Length: 1,000-2,000 words. **Pays $100-500.**

Photos: State availability with submission. Prefers North American serial rights but will consider one-time rights on photos only. Offers no additional payment for b&w contact sheets, 35mm or 2¼ × 2¼ color transparencies. Captions, model releases, photo credits required.

Tips: "The greatest number of contributions we receive are travel; therefore, that area is the most competitive. However, it also represents the easiest way to break in to our publication. Articles should be written for those traveling by self-contained motorhome. The destinations must be accessible to motorhome travelers and any peculiar road conditions should be mentioned."

$ $ FRONTIER MAGAZINE, Adventure Media, 650 S. Orcas St., Suite 103, Seattle WA 98108. (206)762-1922. Fax: (206)762-1886. E-mail: swilson@adventuremedia.com. Website: adventuremedia.com. **Contact:** M. Susan Wilson, managing editor. **60% freelance written.** Monthly magazine covering travel, with special emphasis on the Rocky

Mountain states. "*Frontier Magazine* is a sophisticated yet fun-to-read magazine that celebrates the Rocky Mountain lifestyle. It celebrates those attitudes, traditions and issues that define the modern west." Estab. 1998. Circ. 250,000. Pays on publication. Publishes ms an average of 4 months after acceptance. Byline given. Offers 25% kill fee. Buys first North American serial rights. Editorial lead time 4 months. Submit seasonal material 4 months in advance. Accepts queries by mail, e-mail. Responds in 2 months to queries; 2 months to mss. Sample copy for $2 (shipping and handling). Writer's guidelines for #10 SASE.

Nonfiction: Essays, general interest, historical/nostalgic, humor (essays), interview/profile, photo feature, travel. Special issues: Golf guide (October); and Ski guide (November). "We do not accept fiction, religious or how-to articles." **Buys 15 mss/year.** Query with published clips. Length: 350-1,500 words. **Pays 25-50¢/word.**

Photos: State availability with submission. Reviews duplicate slides only. Buys one-time rights. Negotiates payment individually. Identification of subjects required.

Columns/Departments: Nancy Alton, senior editor. Local Color (tourist-oriented events around the route system), 50-500 words; Creature Comforts (hotel/restaurant reviews), 700 words; Local Flavor (restaurants, chefs or specialty cuisine along the Frontier Airline route system). **Buys 30 mss/year.** Query with published clips. **Pays $50-150.**

Tips: "Know the airline's route system—we accept stories only from/about these areas. Submit clips with all queries."

[N] $ $ GO MAGAZINE, AAA Carolinas, P.O. Box 29600, Charlotte NC 28229-9600. (704)569-7733. Fax: (704)569-7815. E-mail: trcrosby@aaaga.com. Website: www.aaacarolinas.com. **Contact:** Jacquie Hughett, assistant editor. **10% freelance written.** Bimonthly newspaper covering travel, automotive, safety (traffic) and insurance. "Consumer-oriented membership publication providing information on complex or expensive subjects—car buying, vacations, traffic safety problems, etc." Estab. 1928. Circ. 750,000. Pays on publication. Publishes ms an average of 2 months after acceptance. Buys second serial (reprint), simultaneous rights, makes work-for-hire assignments. Editorial lead time 6 weeks. Submit seasonal material 6 weeks in advance. Accepts queries by mail, fax. Responds in 2 weeks to queries; 2 months to mss. Sample copy for SAE with 4 first-class stamps. Writer's guidelines for #10 SASE.

Nonfiction: How-to (fix auto, travel safety, etc.), travel, Automotive insurance, traffic safety. **Buys 12-14 mss/year.** Query with published clips. Length: 600-900 words. **Pays 15¢/published word.**

Photos: Send photos with submission. Buys one-time rights. Offers no additional payment for photos accepted with ms.

$ [▨] HEALING RETREATS & SPAS, 24 E. Cota St., Santa Barbara CA 93101. (805)962-7107. Fax: (805)962-1337. E-mail: editorial@healingretreats.com. Website: www.healingretreats.com. Editor: Anthony Carroccio. **Contact:** Eden Marriott Kennedy, managing editor. **90% freelance written.** Bimonthly magazine covering retreats, spas, health and lifestyle issues. "We try to present healing and nurturing *alternatives* for the global community, and provide a bridge between travel, health, and New Age magazine material." Estab. 1996. Circ. 45,000. Pays on publication. Publishes ms an average of 1 year after acceptance. Byline given. Buys one-time rights. Editorial lead time 6 months. Submit seasonal material 6 months in advance. Accepts queries by mail, e-mail, fax. Responds in 6 months to queries; 6 months to mss. Sample copy for $6.95. Writer's guidelines for #10 SASE.

Nonfiction: Book excerpts, general interest, how-to (at-home therapies), interview/profile, new product, photo feature, travel (spas and retreats only), health alternatives. **Buys 50 mss/year.** Query with published clips. Length: 700-3,000 words. Pays in contributor copies if writer wants 20 or more copies for self-promotion.

Photos: Send photos with submission. Reviews transparencies. Buys one-time rights. Offers no additional payment for photos accepted with ms. Captions required.

Columns/Departments: Buys 40 mss/year. Send complete ms. **Pays $25-50.**

Tips: "Writers can break in with well-written, first-hand knowledge of an alternative health issue or therapy. Even our travel pieces require this type of knowledge. Once a writer proves capable, other assignments can follow. We're particularly looking for stories on religious retreats—ashrams, monasteries, zen centers. Please, no more 'I was stressed out from my life, I went to a spa, now I feel great, the end.'"

$ $ HIGHROADS MAGAZINE, AAA Arizona, 3144 N. 7th Ave., Phoenix AZ 85013. (602)274-1116 ext. 2239. Fax: (602)277-1194. E-mail: highroads@arizona.aaa.com. **Contact:** Rebecca Antiocco, editor. **25% freelance written.** Bimonthly magazine covering travel. "*Highroads* is sent to AAA members in Arizona, and provides information about local, national and international travel destinations. It also provides membership-related information." Estab. 1931. Circ. 360,000. Pays on publication. Publishes ms an average of 3 months after acceptance. Byline given. Buys one-time rights, makes work-for-hire assignments. Editorial lead time 3 months. Submit seasonal material 3 months in advance. Accepts queries by mail, e-mail, fax. Accepts simultaneous submissions. Sample copy and writer's guidelines free.

Nonfiction: Interview/profile (local), personal experience (travel related), photo feature (travel related), travel. **Buys 15 mss/year.** Query with published clips. Length: 1,000-1,500 words. **Pays 25-40¢/word for assigned articles; 25-35¢/word for unsolicited articles.**

Photos: State availability with submission. Reviews transparencies. Buys one-time rights. Pays $50-500/photo. Identification of subjects required.

Columns/Departments: En Route Arizona (Arizona destinations); Calendar (Arizona), both 500 words. **Buys 5-10 mss/year.** Query with or without published clips. **Pays 25-35¢/word.**

Tips: "We encourage writers to submit concise queries, not more than one page, outlining one story idea. We prefer stories that have a well-defined, third-person voice. Articles should convey the magic and wonder of a destination. Facts must be fully researched and accurate."

$ $HIGHWAYS, The Official Publication of the Good Sam Club, TL Enterprises Inc., 2575 Vista Del Mar, Ventura CA 93001. (805)667-4100. Fax: (805)667-4454. E-mail: goodsam@goodsamclub.com. Website: www.goodsam club.com/highways. **Contact:** Ronald H. Epstein, associate publisher. **40% freelance written.** Monthly magazine (November/December issues combined) covering recreational vehicle lifestyle. "All of our readers—since we're a membership publication—own or have a motorhome, trailer, camper or van conversion. Thus, our stories include road-travel conditions and terms and information about campgrounds and locations." Estab. 1966. Circ. 950,000. **Pays on acceptance.** Publishes ms an average of 6 months after acceptance. Byline given. Offers 50% kill fee. Buys first North American serial, electronic rights. Editorial lead time 15 weeks. Submit seasonal material 5 months in advance. Accepts queries by mail, e-mail, fax. Responds in 3 weeks to queries; 2 months to mss. Sample copy and writer's guidelines free or online.

Nonfiction: How-to (repair/replace something on an RV), humor, technical, travel (all RV related). **Buys 15-25 mss/year.** Query. Length: 1,500-2,500 words.

Photos: Send photos with submission. Reviews contact sheets, negatives, transparencies, prints. Buys one-time rights. No additional payment for photos accepted with ms. Captions, identification of subjects, model releases required.

Columns/Departments: Beginners (people buying an RV for the first time), 1,200 words; View Points (issue-related), 750 words. Query. **Pays $200-250.**

Tips: "Understand RVs and RVing. It's a unique lifestyle and different than typical traveling. Aside from that, we welcome good writers!"

$ $INTERLINE ADVENTURES, Grand Adventures Tour and Travel Publishing Corp., 211 E. 7th St., Suite 1100, Austin TX 78701. (512)391-2050. Fax: (512)391-2092. E-mail: ckosta@perx.com. Website: www.perx.com. Editor: Mr. In Churl Yo. **Contact:** Christina Kosta, senior editor. **75% freelance written.** Bimonthly magazine covering airline employee travel. "This bimonthly publication features destinations worldwide. In-depth features explore a destination's sights, cost, shopping, cuisine and nightlife for well-traveled airline employees." Circ. 100,000. Pays on publication. Publishes ms an average of 2 months after acceptance. Byline given. Buys one-time, second serial (reprint) rights, makes work-for-hire assignments. Editorial lead time 4 months. Accepts queries by mail, e-mail, fax. Accepts simultaneous submissions. Responds in 1 month to queries; 1 month to mss. Sample copy and writer's guidelines free.

Nonfiction: Interview/profile, new product, travel. No fiction. **Buys 60 mss/year.** Query. Length: 800-2,500 words. **Pays $350-600 for assigned articles; $150-450 for unsolicited articles.** Sometimes pays expenses of writers on assignment.

Photos: State availability with submission. Buys one-time rights. Pays $30-150/photo. Identification of subjects required.

Columns/Departments: Weekender (domestic weekend destinations); Cuisine (different types/recipes); Great Outdoors (sports or outdoors); all 900 words. Query.

Tips: "Stories must appeal to active and retired airline employees predominantly from the US, but from other parts of the world as well. We like solidly researched, fun and informative feature articles on all types of destinations and cruise vacations."

N $ $INTERNATIONAL LIVING, Agora Ireland Ltd., 5 Catherine St., Waterford Ireland. 353-51-304-557. Fax: 353-51-304-561. E-mail: lgalvin@InternationalLiving.com. Website: www.InternationalLiving.com. Managing Editor: Robin Finlay. **Contact:** Len Galvin, assistant editor. **50% freelance written.** Monthly newsletter covering retirement, travel, investment and real estate overseas. "We do not want descriptions of how beautiful places are. We want specifics, recommendations, contacts, prices, names, addresses, phone numbers, etc. We want offbeat locations and off-the-beaten-track spots." Estab. 1981. Circ. 500,000. Pays on publication. Publishes ms an average of 3 months after acceptance. Byline given. Offers 25-50% kill fee. Buys all rights. Editorial lead time 2 months. Submit seasonal material 3 months in advance. Accepts queries by mail, e-mail, fax. Accepts simultaneous submissions. Responds in 2 months to mss. Sample copy for #10 SASE. Writer's guidelines free.

⊶ Break in by writing about something real. If you find it a chore to write the piece you're sending us, then chances are, we don't want it.

Nonfiction: How-to (get a job, buy real estate, get cheap airfares overseas, start a business, etc.), interview/profile (entrepreneur abroad), new product (travel), personal experience, travel, shopping, cruises. Special issues: "We produce special issues each year focusing on Asia, Eastern Europe and Latin America." No descriptive, run-of-the-mill travel articles. **Buys 100 mss/year.** Send complete ms. Length: 500-2,000 words. **Pays $200-500 for assigned articles; $100-400 for unsolicited articles.**

Photos: State availability with submission. Reviews contact sheets, negatives, transparencies, prints. Buys all rights. Offers $50/photo. Identification of subjects required.

Fillers: Facts. **Buys 20/year.** Length: 50-250 words. **Pays $25-100.**

▣ The online magazine carries original content not found in the print version. Contact: Len Galvin, online editor.

Tips: "Make recommendations in your articles. We want first-hand accounts. Tell us how to do things: how to catch a cab, order a meal, buy a souvenir, buy property, start a business, etc. *International Living*'s philosophy is that the world is full of opportunities to do whatever you want, whenever you want. We will show you how."

$ ✪ THE INTERNATIONAL RAILWAY TRAVELER, Hardy Publishing Co., Inc., P.O. Box 3747, San Diego CA 92163. (619)260-1332. Fax: (619)296-4220. E-mail: irt.trs@aol.com. Website: www.irtsociety.com. **Contact:** Gena Holle, editor. **100% freelance written.** Monthly newsletter covering rail travel. Estab. 1983. Circ. 3,500. Pays within 1 month of the publication date. Byline given. Offers 25% kill fee. Buys first North American serial, one-time, electronic rights. Editorial lead time 4 months. Submit seasonal material 6 months in advance. Responds in 1 month to queries; 2 months to mss. Sample copy for $6. Writer's guidelines for #10 SASE.

Nonfiction: General interest, how-to, interview/profile, new product, opinion, personal experience, travel, book reviews. **Buys 24-30 mss/year.** Query with published clips or send complete ms. Length: 800-1,200 words. **Pays 3¢/word.**

Photos: Include SASE for return of photos. Send photos with submission. Reviews contact sheets, negatives, transparencies, prints (8×10 preferred; will accept 5×7). Buys first North American serial, electronic rights. Offers $10 b&w; $20 cover photo. Costs of converting slides and negatives to prints are deducted from payment. Captions, identification of subjects required.

Tips: "We want factual articles concerning world rail travel which would not appear in the mass-market travel magazines. *IRT* readers and editors love stories and photos on off-beat train trips as well as more conventional train trips covered in unconventional ways. With *IRT*, the focus is on the train travel experience, not a blow-by-blow description of the view from the train window. Be sure to include details (prices, passes, schedule info, etc.) for readers who might want to take the trip."

Ⓝ $ $ INTERVAL WORLD, 6262 Sunset Dr., Miami FL 33143. E-mail: intervaleditors@interval-intl.com. Website: www.intervalworld.com. Editor: Elizabeth Willard. **Contact:** Amy Drew Teitler, managing editor. **34% freelance written.** Quarterly magazine covering travel. *Interval World* magazine is distributed to Interval International members in the US, Canada and Caribbean. Estab. 1980. Circ. 800,000. **Pays on acceptance.** Publishes ms an average of 3 months after acceptance. Byline given. Editorial lead time 6 months. Accepts queries by mail, e-mail.

Nonfiction: How-to, new product, photo feature, travel, health, pastimes, adventure travel. **Buys 20-25 mss/year. Pays 25¢/word.**

Photos: State availability with submission. Reviews transparencies. Buys print and electronic rights. Negotiates payment individually. Captions, identification of subjects, model releases required.

Tips: "Send résumé, cover letter and several clips (preferably travel). Do not send unsolicited submissions/articles."

$ $ $ $ ✪ ISLANDS, An International Magazine, Islands Media Corp., P.O. Box 4728, Santa Barbara CA 93140-4728. (805)745-7100. Fax: (805)745-7102. E-mail: editorial@islands.com. Website: www.islands.com. **Contact:** Joan Tapper, editor. **95% freelance written.** Magazine published 8 times/year covering "accessible and once-in-a-lifetime islands from many different perspectives: Travel, culture, lifestyle. We ask our authors to give us the essence of the island and do it with literary flair." Estab. 1981. Circ. 220,000. **Pays on acceptance.** Publishes ms an average of 8 months after acceptance. Byline given. Offers 25% kill fee. Buys all rights. Accepts queries by mail, e-mail, fax. Responds in 2 months to queries; 6 weeks to mss. Sample copy for $6. Writer's guidelines for #10 SASE or online.

Nonfiction: "Each issue contains 4-5 feature articles and numerous departments. Any authors who wish to be commissioned should send a detailed proposal for an article, an estimate of costs (if applicable) and samples of previously published work. The majority of our feature manuscripts are commissioned." Book excerpts, essays, general interest, interview/profile, personal experience, photo feature, travel, island-related material. No service stories. **Buys 25 feature mss/year.** Query with published clips or send complete ms. Length: 2,000-4,000 words. **Pays $1,000-4,000.** Sometimes pays expenses of writers on assignment.

Photos: "Fine color photography is a special attraction of *Islands*, and we look for superb composition, technical quality and editorial applicability." Label slides with name and address, include captions, and submit in protective plastic sleeves. Reviews 35mm transparencies. Buys one-time rights. Pays $75-300 for 35mm transparencies. Identification of subjects required.

Columns/Departments: Horizons section and Art Beat (all island related), 200-600 words; Crossroads (columns and experiences that highlight island life), 500-1,500 words; Island Wise (travel experiences, classic island hotel, classic island eatery, great enrichment experience), 700-1,000 words; Insiders (list 10 things to do in well-visited islands), 800 words. **Buys 50 mss/year.** Query with published clips. **Pays $25-1,000.**

Tips: "A freelancer can best break in to our publication with front- or back-of-the-book stories. Stay away from general, sweeping articles. We will be using big name writers for major features; will continue to use newcomers and regulars for columns and departments."

$ ▣ KAFENIO, Where Europe Is Only a Mouseclick Away, Meier & Jacobson, Box 142, Karpathos 85700, Greece. (+30)245 31716. Fax: (+30)245 31716. E-mail: editor@kafeniocom.com. Website: www.kafeniocom.com. Publisher: Alf B. Meier. **Contact:** Roberta Beach Jacobson, editor. **60-65% freelance written.** Monthly magazine covering European life and culture. "*Kafenio*, focusing on European life and culture, has adult readers in North America, Europe, Africa and Australia." Estab. 2000. Circ. 25,300. **Pays on acceptance.** Publishes ms an average of 2 months after acceptance. Byline given. Buys electronic rights. Editorial lead time 2 months. Submit seasonal material 2 months in advance. Accepts queries by e-mail. Responds in 3 days to queries; 3 days to mss.

Nonfiction: essay@kafeniocom.com. Nonfiction for Speakers Table department only. Essays, humor, inspirational, opinion, personal experience, travel (all first-person only). Send complete ms. Length: 600 words maximum. **Pays $100.**

Reprints: Accepts previously published submissions.

Tips: "Know something about Europe. Have a little fun with your writing. If you don't enjoy it, others won't either. Remember, our readers either live in or travel to Europe."

$ $MICHIGAN LIVING, AAA Michigan, 2865 Waterloo, Troy MI 48084. (248)816-9265. Fax: (248)816-2251. E-mail: michliving@aol.com. **Contact:** Ron Garbinski, editor. **50% freelance written.** Monthly magazine. "*Michigan Living* is edited for the residents of Michigan and contains information about travel and lifestyle activities in Michigan, the U.S. and around the world. Articles also cover automotive developments, highway safety. Regular features include a car care column, a calendar of coming events, restaurant and overnight accomodations reviews and news of special interest to Auto Club members." Estab. 1922. Circ. 1,099,000. Pays on publication. Publishes ms an average of 6 months after acceptance. Byline given. Offers 20% kill fee. Buys first North American serial rights. Submit seasonal material 9 months in advance. Accepts queries by e-mail. Responds in 6 weeks to queries; 6 weeks to mss.
Nonfiction: Travel articles on US and Canadian topics. **Buys few unsolicited mss/year.** Query. Length: 200-1,000 words. **Pays $75-600 for assigned articles.**
Photos: Photos purchased with accompanying ms. Reviews transparencies. Pays $450 for cover photos; $50-400 for color transparencies. Captions required.
Tips: "In addition to descriptions of things to see and do, articles should contain accurate, current information on costs the traveler would encounter on his trip. Items such as lodging, meal and entertainment expenses should be included, not in the form of a balance sheet but as an integral part of the piece. We want the sounds, sights, tastes, smells of a place or experience so one will feel he has been there and knows if he wants to go back. Requires travel-related queries via e-mail."

$ $MOTORHOME, TL Enterprises, 2575 Vista Del Mar Dr., Ventura CA 93001. (805)667-4100. Fax: (805)667-4484. Website: www.motorhomemagazine.com. Editorial Director: Barbara Leonard. **Contact:** Sherry McBride, senior managing editor. **60% freelance written.** Monthly magazine. "*MotorHome* is a magazine for owners and prospective buyers of self-propelled recreational vehicles who are active outdoorsmen and wide-ranging travelers. We cover all aspects of the RV lifestyle; editorial material is both technical and nontechnical in nature. Regular features include tests and descriptions of various models of motorhomes, travel adventures and hobbies pursued in such vehicles, objective analysis of equipment and supplies for such vehicles and do-it-yourself articles. Guides within the magazine provide listings of manufacturers, rentals and other sources of equipment and accessories of interest to enthusiasts. Articles must have an RV slant and excellent transparencies accompanying text." Estab. 1968. Circ. 144,000. **Pays on acceptance.** Publishes ms an average of within 1 year of acceptance. Byline given. Offers 30% kill fee. Buys first North American serial, electronic rights. Editorial lead time 4 months. Submit seasonal material 6 months in advance. Accepts queries by mail, fax, phone. Responds in 1 month to queries; 2 months to mss. Sample copy free. Writer's guidelines for #10 SASE.
   O➤ Break in with *Crossroads* items.
Nonfiction: General interest, historical/nostalgic, how-to, humor, interview/profile, new product, personal experience, photo feature, technical, travel, celebrity profiles, recreation, lifestyle, legislation, all RV-related. No diaries of RV trips or negative RV experiences. **Buys 120 mss/year.** Query with or without published clips. Length: 250-2,500 words. **Pays $300-600.**
Photos: Send photos with submission. Reviews 35mm slides. Buys one-time rights. Offers no additional payment for art accepted with ms. Pays $500+ for covers. Captions, identification of subjects, model releases required.
Columns/Departments: Crossroads (offbeat briefs of people, places and events of interest to travelers), 100-200 words; Keepers (tips, resources). Query with or without published clips or send complete ms. **Pays $100.**
   ■ The online magazine carries original content not found in the print version. Contact: Sherry McBride, online editor.
Tips: "If a freelancer has an idea for a good article, it's best to send a query and include possible photo locations to illustrate the article. We prefer to assign articles and work with the author in developing a piece suitable to our audience. We are in a specialized field with very enthusiastic readers who appreciate articles by authors who actually enjoy motorhomes. The following areas are most open: Crossroads—brief descriptions of places to see or special events, with one photo/slide, 100-200 words; travel—places to go with a motorhome, where to stay, what to see, etc.; we prefer not to use travel articles where the motorhome is secondary; and how-to—personal projects on author's motorhomes to make travel easier, unique projects, accessories. Also articles on unique personalities, motorhomes, humorous experiences. Be sure to submit appropriate photography (35mm slides) with at least one good motorhome shot to illustrate travel articles. No phone queries, please."

$NATURALLY, Nude Recreation Travel, Events Unlimited Publishing Co., P.O. Box 317, Newfoundland NJ 07435-0317. (973)697-3552. Fax: (973)697-8313. Website: www.internaturally.com. **Contact:** Bernard Loibl, editor. **90% freelance written.** Quarterly magazine covering wholesome family nude recreation and travel locations. "*Naturally* nude recreation looks at why millions of people believe that removing clothes in public is a good idea, and at places specifically created for that purpose—with good humor, but also in earnest. *Naturally* nude recreation takes you to places where your personal freedom is the only agenda, and to places where textile-free living is a serious commitment." Estab. 1981. Circ. 35,000. Pays on publication. Byline given. Buys first, one-time rights. Editorial lead time 4 months. Submit seasonal material 4 months in advance. Accepts queries by mail, e-mail, fax. Accepts simultaneous submissions. Sample copy for $9. Writer's guidelines free.

Nonfiction: Frequent contributors and regular columnists, who develop a following through *Naturally*, are paid from the Frequent Contributors Budget. Payments increase on the basis of frequency of participation. General interest, interview/profile, personal experience, photo feature, travel. **Buys 12 mss/year.** Send complete ms. Length: 2 pages. **Pays $70/published page including photos.**

Reprints: Accepts previously published submissions.

Photos: Send photos with submission. Reviews contact sheets, negatives, transparencies, prints. Buys one-time rights. Payment for photos included in payment forms.

Fillers: Cheryl Hanenberg, associate editor. Anecdotes, facts, gags to be illustrated by cartoonist, newsbreaks, short humor.

Tips: "*Naturally* nude recreation invokes the philosophies of naturism and nudism, but also activities and beliefs in the mainstream that express themselves, barely: Spiritual awareness, New Age customs, pagan and religious rites, alternative and fringe lifestyle beliefs, artistic expressions and many individual nude interests. Our higher purpose is simply to help restore our sense of self. Although the term 'nude recreation' may, for some, conjure up visions of sexual frivolities inappropriate for youngsters—because that can also be technically true—these topics are outside the scope of *Naturally* magazine. Here the emphasis is on the many varieties of human beings, of all ages and backgrounds, recreating in their most natural state, at extraordinary places, their reasons for doing so, and the benefits they derive."

N $ $ NEWSDAY, 235 Pinelawn Rd., Melville NY 11747. (631)843-2980. Fax: (631)843-2375. E-mail: travel@newsday.com. **Contact:** Marjorie Robins, travel editor. **30% freelance written.** General readership of Sunday newspaper travel section. Estab. 1940. Circ. 650,000. Pays on publication. Buys all rights for New York area only. Simultaneous submissions considered if outside of New York area.

Nonfiction: No assignments to freelancers. No query letters. Complete typewritten mss only accepted on spec. All trips must be paid for in full be writer; proof required. Service stories preferred. Destination pieces must be for the current year. Length: 1,200 words maximum.

Photos: Color slides and b&w photos accepted; pays $50-250, depending on size of photo used.

$ $ NORTHWEST TRAVEL, Northwest Regional Magazines, P.O. Box 18000, Florence OR 97439. (541)997-8401or (800)348-8401. Fax: (541)902-0400. E-mail: judy@ohwy.com. Website: www.ohwy.com. Co-editor: Jim Forst. **Contact:** Judy Fleagle, managing editor. **60% freelance written.** Bimonthly magazine. "We like energetic writing about popular activities and destinations in the Pacific Northwest. *Northwest Travel* aims to give readers practical ideas on where to go in the region. Magazine covers Oregon, Washington, Idaho and British Columbia; occasionally Alaska and Western Montana." Estab. 1991. Circ. 50,000. Pays after publication. Publishes ms an average of 8 months after acceptance. Buys first North American serial rights. Submit seasonal material 6 months in advance. Accepts queries by mail, e-mail. Responds in 3 months. Sample copy for $4.50. Writer's guidelines for #10 SASE.

   0→ Have good slides to go with a story that is lively with compelling leads, quotes, anecdotes, and no grammar problems.

Nonfiction: Book excerpts, general interest, historical/nostalgic, interview/profile (rarely), photo feature, travel (only in Northwest region). "No cliché-ridden pieces on places that everyone covers." **Buys 40 mss/year.** Query with or without published clips. Length: 1,250-2,000 words. **Pays $100-350 for feature articles and 2-5 contributor copies.**

Reprints: Send photocopy and information about when and where the material previously appeared. Pays 50% of amount paid for original article.

Photos: "Put who to credit and model releases needed on cover photos—will pay extra for those needing and having model releases." State availability with submission. Reviews transparencies, prefers dupes. Buys one-time rights. Captions, identification of subjects required.

Columns/Departments: Restaurant Features, 1,000 words. **Pays $125.** Worth a Stop (brief items describing places "worth a stop"), 300-350 words. **Pays $50.** Back Page (photo and text package on a specific activity, season or festival with some technical photo info), 80 words and 1 slide. **Pays $75. Buys 25-30 mss/year.** Send complete ms. **Pays $50-125.**

Tips: "Write fresh, lively copy (avoid clichés) and cover exciting travel topics in the region that haven't been covered in other magazines. A story with stunning photos will get serious consideration. The department most open to freelancers is the Worth a Stop department. Take us to fascinating and interesting places we might not otherwise discover."

$ PATHFINDERS, Travel Information for People of Color, 6424 N. 13th St., Philadelphia PA 19126. (215)927-9950. Fax: (215)927-3359. E-mail: blaktravel@aol.com. Website: www.Pathfinderstravel.com. **Contact:** Joseph P. Blake, managing editor. **75% freelance written.** Quarterly magazine covering travel for people of color, primarily African-Americans. "We look for lively, original, well-written stories that provide a good sense of place, with useful information and fresh ideas about travel and the travel industry. Our main audience is African-Americans, though we do look for articles relating to other persons of color: Native Americans, Hispanics and Asians." Estab. 1997. Circ. 50,000. Pays on publication. Byline given. Buys first North American serial, electronic rights. Accepts queries by mail, e-mail. Responds in 2 months to queries; 2 months to mss. Sample copy at bookstores (Barnes & Noble, Borders, Waldenbooks). Writer's guidelines online.

   0→ Break in through *Looking Back*, 600-word essay on travel from personal experience that provides a historical perspective and US travel with cultural perspective.

Nonfiction: Interested in seeing more Native American stories, places that our readers can visit and rodeos (be sure to tie-in African-American cowboys). Essays, historical/nostalgic, how-to, personal experience, photo feature, travel (all vacation travel oriented). "No more pitches on Jamaica." **Buys 16-20 mss/year.** Send complete ms. Length: 1,200-1,400 words for cover stories; 1,000-1,200 words for features. **Pays $100.**

Photos: State availability with submission.

Columns/Departments: Chef's Table, Post Cards from Home, 500-600 words. Send complete ms. **Pays $100.**

Tips: "We prefer seeing finished articles rather than queries. All articles are submitted on spec. Articles should be saved in either WordPerfect of Microsoft Word, double-spaced and saved as a text-only file. Include a hard copy. E-mail articles are accepted only by request of the editor."

N $ $ PILOT GETAWAYS MAGAZINE, Airventure Publishing LLC, P.O. Box 550, Glendale CA 91209-0550. (818)241-1890. Fax: (818)241-1895. E-mail: editor@pilotgetaways.com. Website: www.pilotgetaways.com. **Contact:** John Kounis, editor. **90% freelance written.** Quarterly magazine covering aviation travel for private pilots. "*Pilot Getaways* is a travel magazine for private pilots. Our articles cover destinations that are easily accessible by private aircraft, including details such as airport transportation, convenient hotels and attractions. Other regular features include Fly-in dining, Flying Tips and Bush Flying." Estab. 1998. Circ. 20,000. Pays on publication. Byline given. Buys first North American serial, electronic rights. Editorial lead time 4 months. Submit seasonal material 9 months in advance. Accepts queries by mail, e-mail, fax, phone. Accepts simultaneous submissions. Responds in 2 weeks to queries; 2 months to mss. Sample copy and writer's guidelines free.

Nonfiction: Travel (specifically travel guide articles). "We rarely publish articles about events that have already occurred, such as travel logs about trips the authors have taken or air show reports." **Buys 30 mss/year.** Query. Length: 1,000-3,500 words. **Pays $100-500.**

Reprints: Accepts previously published submissions.

Photos: State availability with submission. Reviews contact sheets, negatives, 35mm transparencies, prints, gif/jpeg files. Buys one-time rights. Negotiates payment individually. Captions, identification of subjects required.

Columns/Departments: Weekend Getaways (short fly-in getaways), 2,000 words; Fly-in Dining (reviews of airport restaurants), 1,200 words; Flying Tips (tips & pointers on flying technique), 1,000 words; Bush Flying (getaways to unpaved destinations), 1,500 words. **Buys 20 mss/year.** Query. **Pays $100-500.**

Tips: "*Pilot Getaways* follows a specific format, which is factual and informative. We rarely publish travel logs that chronicle a particular journey. Rather, we prefer travel guides with phone numbers, addresses, prices, etc., so that our readers can plan their own trips. The exact format is described in our writer's guidelines."

$ $ $ PORTHOLE CRUISE MAGAZINE, Panoff Publishing, 4517 NW 31st Ave., Wingate Commons, Ft. Lauderdale FL 33309-3403. (954)377-7777. Fax: (954)377-7000. E-mail: jrush@ppigroup.com. Website: www.porth ole.com. Editorial Director: Dale Rim. **Contact:** Jill Rush, managing editor. **90% freelance written.** Bimonthly magazine covering the cruise industry. "*Porthole Cruise Magazine* entices its readers into taking a cruise vacation by delivering information that is timely, accurate, colorful and entertaining." Estab. 1992. Circ. 35,000. Pays on publication. Publishes ms an average of 6 months after acceptance. Byline given. Offers 35% kill fee. Buys second serial (reprint), electronic rights. Editorial lead time 8 months. Submit seasonal material 5 months in advance. Accepts queries by mail, e-mail, fax. Accepts simultaneous submissions. Responds in 2 months to queries; 6 months to mss. Sample copy for 8×11 SAE and $3 postage. Writer's guidelines for #10 SASE.

Nonfiction: Book excerpts, essays (your cruise experience), exposé, general interest (cruise-related), historical/nostalgic, how-to (pick a cruise, not get seasick, travel tips), humor, interview/profile (crew on board or industry executives), new product, personal experience, photo feature, travel (off-the-beaten path, adventure, ports, destinations, cruises), onboard fashion, spa articles, duty-free shopping port shopping, ship reviews. Special issues: Cuba, Europe. No articles on destinations that can't be reached by ship. "Please, please do not send us accounts of your lovely, spectacular, or breathtaking family cruise vacations from the point of embarkation to debarkation. Concentrate on vivid details, personal experiences and go beyond the normal, 'We cruised to...' Include out-of-the-ordinary subject matter. Try to transport the reader from the pages to the places you traveled rather than simply giving a laundry list of what you saw. Please don't write asking for a cruise so that you can do an article! You must be an experienced cruise writer to do a ship review." **Buys 75 mss/year.** Query with published clips or send complete ms. Length: 1,000-3,000 words. **Pays $400-1,200 for assigned articles; $250-1,000 for unsolicited articles.** Pays expenses of writers on assignment.

Reprints: Send photocopy of article or typed ms with rights for sale noted and information about when and where the material previously appeared. Negotiates payment.

Photos: Linda Douthat, creative director. State availability with submission. Reviews transparencies, prints. Buys one-time rights. Negotiates payment individually. Captions, identification of subjects, model releases required.

Columns/Departments: Deckadence (luxury); Ombudsman (investigative), "My" Port City (personal accounts of experiences in certain destination), both 1,200 words; Beautiful Thing (spa service on board), 700 words; Brass Tacks (consumer-oriented travel tips, short bits); Personality Plus (intriguing travel-oriented profiles); Fashion File (onboard fashion), all 400 words. Also humor, cruise cuisine, shopping, photo essays. **Buys 50 mss/year.** Query with published clips or send complete ms. **Pays $400-1,200.**

Fillers: Facts, gags to be illustrated by cartoonist, newsbreaks, short humor. **Buys 30/year.** Length: 25-200 words. **Pays 25¢/word.**

The online magazine carries original content not found in the print edition and includes writer's guidelines.

Tips: "We prefer to be queried via e-mail. Submit an outline showing how you will incorporate anecdotes and dialogue. Clips are not necessary. Offbeat, original travel stories are preferred. Tie-ins to celebrity culture, pop culture, arts/ entertainment, politics, cuisine, architecture, are highly regarded."

N $ $ $ $ SPA, Healthy Living, Travel & Renewal, Islands Media, 6309 Carpinteria Ave., Carpinteria CA 93013. (805)745-7100. Fax: (805)745-7102. Website: www.spamagazine.com. **Contact:** Maryann Hammers, editor-in-chief. Bimonthly magazine covering health spas: treatments, travel, cuisine, fitness, beauty. "Approachable and accessible, yet authoritative and full of advice, *Spa* is the place to turn for information and tips on nutrition, spa cuisine/recipes, beauty, health, skin care, travel (to spas), fitness, wellness, and renewal. Sometimes humorous and light, sometimes thoughtful and introspective, *Spa* is always helpful, insightful and personal." Pays within 30 days upon acceptance. Byline given. Offers 25% kill fee. Buys first North American serial, all rights. Editorial lead time 3 months. Submit seasonal material 8 months in advance. Accepts queries by mail, e-mail. Sample copy for $6. Writer's guidelines for #10 SASE or by e-mail.
Nonfiction: Essays, how-to (beauty), humor, interview/profile (celebrities only), personal experience, travel. Does not want "a general article on a spa you have visited." **Buys 30 mss/year.** Query with published clips. Length: 1,500-3,000 words. **Pays $1,125-2,500.** Sometimes pays expenses of writers on assignment.
Columns/Departments: New & Newsworthy (profiles of new or newsworthy spas), 500 words; Life in Balance (pros offer advice), 750-1,000 words; Mind & Body (feeling good and being well inside and out), 750-1,500 words; Looking Good (beauty column), 750-1,500 words; My Space (essay about a particular spa experience), 750-1,000 words; Daybreak (brief profiles of several spas in a city), 300-500 words; Spa Selections (book, video, music reviews), 150-200 words. **Buys 60 mss/year.** Query with published clips. **Pays $400-750.**
Tips: "When you pitch a story, have a story idea, angle or something special in mind. We don't accept 'general' spa stories. Send query with samples of previously published work. Enclose an SASE and allow at least 2 months for a response."

$ $ ✉ ST. MAARTEN NIGHTS, Nights Publications Inc., 1831 Rene Levesque Blvd. W., Montreal, Quebec H3H 1R4, Canada. (514)931-1987. Fax: (514)931-6273. E-mail: editor@nightspublications.com. Website: www.nightspublications.com. Managing Editor: Zelly Zuskin. **Contact:** Stephen Trotter, editor. **90% freelance written.** Annual magazine covering the St. Maarten/St. Martin vacation experience seeking "upbeat entertaining lifestyle articles." "Our audience is the North American vacationer." Estab. 1981. Circ. 225,000. **Pays on acceptance.** Publishes ms an average of 9 months after acceptance. Byline given. Buys first North American serial rights, first Caribbean rights. Editorial lead time 1 month. Accepts queries by mail, e-mail, fax, phone. Responds in 2 weeks to queries; 1 month to mss. Sample copy for $5 (make checks payable to Nights Publications Inc.). Writer's guidelines by e-mail.
○→ "Let the reader experience the story; utilize the senses; be descriptive."
Nonfiction: Lifestyle with a lively, upscale touch. Include SASE with Canadian postage or IRC. General interest, historical/nostalgic, how-to (gamble), humor, inspirational, interview/profile, opinion, personal experience, photo feature, travel, colorful profiles of islanders, sailing, ecological, eco-tourism, local culture, art, activities, entertainment, night life, special events, topics relative to vacationers in St. Maarten/St. Martin. "No negative pieces or stale rewrites or cliché copy." **Buys 8-10 mss/year.** Query with published clips. Length: 250-750 words. **Pays $100-250.**
Photos: State availability with submission. Reviews transparencies. Buys one-time rights. Pays $50/photo. Captions, identification of subjects, model releases required.
Tips: "Our style is upbeat, friendly, fluid and descriptive. Our magazines cater to tourists who are already at the destination, so ensure your story is of interest to this particular audience. We welcome stories that offer fresh angles to familiar tourist-related topics."

$ $ ✉ TIMES OF THE ISLANDS, The International Magazine of the Turks & Caicos Islands, Times Publications Ltd., P.O. Box 234, Caribbean Place, Providenciales Turks & Caicos Islands, British West Indies. (649)946-4788. Fax: (649)941-3402. E-mail: timespub@tciway.tc. Website: www.timespub.tc. **Contact:** Kathy Borsuk, editor. **60% freelance written.** Quarterly magazine covering The Turks & Caicos Islands. "*Times of the Islands* is used by the public and private sector to inform visitors and potential investors/developers about the Islands. It goes beyond a superficial overview of tourist attractions with in-depth articles about natural history, island heritage, local personalities, new development, offshore finance, sporting activities, visitors' experiences and Caribbean fiction." Estab. 1988. Circ. 6,000-9,000. Pays on publication. Publishes ms an average of 6 months after acceptance. Byline given. Buys second serial (reprint) rights, publication rights for 6 months with respect to other publications distributed in Caribbean. Editorial lead time 4 months. Submit seasonal material at least 4 months in advance. Accepts queries by mail, fax. Accepts simultaneous submissions. Responds in 6 weeks to queries; 2 months to mss. Sample copy for $6. Writer's guidelines for #10 SASE or online.

Nonfiction: Book excerpts, essays, general interest (Caribbean art, culture, cooking, crafts), historical/nostalgic, humor, interview/profile (locals), personal experience (trips to the Islands), photo feature, technical (island businesses), travel, Book reviews, nature, ecology, business (offshore finance), watersports. **Buys 20 mss/year.** Query. Length: 500-3,000 words. **Pays $200-600.**

Reprints: Send photocopy and information about when and where the material previously appeared. Payment varies.

Photos: Send photos with submission. Reviews slides, prints, digital photos. Offers no additional payment for photos accepted with ms. Pays $15-100/photo. Identification of subjects required.

Columns/Departments: On Holiday (unique experiences of visitors to Turks & Caicos), 500-1,500 words. **Buys 4 mss/year.** Query. **Pays $200.**

Fiction: Adventure, ethnic, historical, humorous, mystery, novel excerpts. **Buys 2-3 mss/year.** Query. Length: 1,000-3,000 words. **Pays $250-400.**

Tips: "Make sure that the query/article specifically relates to the Turks and Caicos Islands. The theme can be general (ecotourism, for instance), but the manuscript should contain specific and current references to the Islands. We're a high-quality magazine, with a small budget and staff and are very open-minded to ideas (and manuscripts). Writers who have visited the Islands at least once would probably have a better perspective from which to write."

$ $ TRAILER LIFE, America's No. 1 RV Magazine, Affinity Group, Inc., 2575 Vista Del Mar Dr., Ventura CA 93001. (805)667-4100. Fax: (805)667-4184. E-mail: bleonard@affinitygroup.com. Website: www.trailerlife.com. Associate Editor: Millie Evans. **Contact:** Barbara Leonard, editorial director. **40% freelance written.** Monthly magazine. *"Trailer Life* magazine is written specifically for active people whose overall lifestyle is based on travel and recreation in their RV. Every issue includes product tests, travel articles, and other features—ranging from lifestyle to vehicle maintenance." Estab. 1941. Circ. 280,000. **Pays on acceptance.** Publishes ms an average of 6 months after acceptance. Byline given. Offers 30% kill fee for assigned articles that are not acceptable. Buys first North American serial, electronic rights. Editorial lead time 4 months. Submit seasonal material 6 months in advance. Accepts queries by mail. Responds in 2 months to queries; 2 months to mss. Sample copy free. Writer's guidelines for #10 SASE.

　　O— Break in with a "small piece for the Campground Spotlight or Etc. section; a short article on an interesting RV trip."

Nonfiction: Historical/nostalgic, how-to (technical), humor, new product, opinion, personal experience, travel. No vehicle tests, product evaluations or road tests; tech material is strictly assigned. No diaries or trip logs, no non-RV trips; nothing without an RV-hook. **Buys 75 mss/year.** Query with or without published clips. Length: 250-2,500 words. **Pays $125-700.** Sometimes pays expenses of writers on assignment.

Photos: Send photos with submission. Reviews transparencies, b&w contact sheets. Buys one-time and occasionally electronic rights. Offers no additional payment for photos accepted with ms, does pay for supplemental photos. Identification of subjects, model releases required.

Columns/Departments: Campground Spotlight (report with 1 photo of campground recommended for RVers), 250 words; Bulletin Board (news, trends of interest to RVers), 100 words; Etcetera (useful tips and information affecting RVers), 240 words. **Buys 70 mss/year.** Query or send complete ms. **Pays $75-250.**

　　■ The online magazine carries original content not found in the print edition. Contact: Barbara Leonard.

Tips: "Prerequisite: Must have RV focus. Photos must be magazine quality. These are the two biggest reasons why manuscripts are rejected. Our readers are travel enthusiasts who own all types of RVs (travel trailers, truck campers, van conversions, motorhomes, tent trailers, fifth-wheels) in which they explore North America and beyond, embrace the great outdoors in national, state and private parks. They're very active and very adventurous."

$ ▧ TRANSITIONS ABROAD, P.O. Box 1300, Amherst MA 01004-1300. (413)256-3414. Fax: (413)256-0373. E-mail: editor@transitionsabroad.com. Website: www.TransitionsAbroad.com. Editor/Publisher: Clay Hubbs. **Contact:** Max Hartshorne, managing editor. **80-90% freelance written.** Bimonthly magazine resource for low-budget international travel, often with an educational or work component. Focus is on the alternatives to mass tourism. Estab. 1977. Circ. 20,000. Pays on publication. Byline given. Buys first, second serial (reprint) rights. Accepts queries by mail, e-mail. Responds in 1 month. Sample copy for $6.45. Writer's guidelines for #10 SASE or online.

　　O— Break in by sending "a fascinating article (1,000 words) with very updated pratical information and color slides or prints with people in them, or an article on a job you got overseas and how someone else could do it."

Nonfiction: Lead articles (up to 1,500 words) provide first-hand practical information on independent travel to featured country or region (see topics schedule). **Pays $75-150.** Also, how to find educational and specialty travel opportunities, practical information (evaluation of courses, special interest and study tours, economy travel), travel (new learning and cultural travel ideas). Foreign travel only. Few destination ("tourist") pieces or first-person narratives. *Transitions Abroad* is a resource magazine for independent, educated, and adventurous travelers, not for armchair travelers or those addicted to packaged tours or cruises. Emphasis on information—which must be usable by readers—and on interaction with people in host country. **Buys 20 unsolicited mss/year.** Query with credentials and SASE. Include author's bio and e-mail with submissions. Length: 500-1,500 words. **Pays $25-150.**

Photos: Photos increase likelihood of acceptance. Send photos with submission. Buys one-time rights. Pays $10-45 for color prints or color slides, $150 for covers (color slides only). Captions, identification of subjects required.

Columns/Departments: Worldwide Travel Bargains (destinations, activities and accomodations for budget travelers—featured in every issue); Tour and Program Notes (new courses or travel programs); Travel Resources (new information and ideas for independent travel); Working Traveler (how to find jobs and what to expect); Activity Vacations (travel opportunities that involve action and learning, usually by direct involvement in host culture); Responsible Travel (information on community-organized tours). Length: 1,000 words maximum. **Buys 60 mss/year.** Send complete ms. **Pays $20-50.**

Fillers: Info Exchange (information, preferably first-hand—having to do with travel, particularly offbeat educational travel and work or study abroad). **Buys 10/year.** Length: 750 words maximum. **Pays complimentary 1 year subscription.**

☐ The online magazine carries original content not found in the print edition and includes writer's guidelines.

Tips: "We like nuts and bolts stuff, practical information, especially on how to work, live, and cut costs abroad. Our readers want usable information on planning a travel itinerary. Be specific: Names, addresses, current costs. We are very interested in educational and long-stay travel and study abroad for adults and senior citizens. *Overseas Travel Planner* published each year in July provides best information sources on work, study, and independent travel abroad. Each bimonthly issue contains a worldwide directory of educational and specialty travel programs."

$ $ $ $ ☒ TRAVEL + LEISURE, American Express Publishing Corp., 1120 Avenue of the Americas, New York NY 10036. (212)382-5600. E-mail: tlquery@amexpub.com. Website: www.travelandleisure.com. Editor-in-Chief: Nancy Novogrod. Executive Editor: Barbara Peck. **Contact:** Mark Orwoll, managing editor. **80% freelance written.** Monthly magazine. "*Travel + Leisure* is a monthly magazine edited for affluent travelers. It explores the latest resorts, hotels, fashions, foods and drinks." Circ. 1,000,000. **Pays on acceptance.** Byline given. Offers 25% kill fee. Buys first world rights. Accepts queries by mail, e-mail. Responds in 6 weeks to queries; 6 weeks to mss. Sample copy for $5.50 from (800)888-8728 or P.O. Box 2094, Harlan, IA 51537-4094. Writer's guidelines for #10 SASE.

    O➔ There is no single editorial contact for *Travel + Leisure*. It is best to find the name of the editor of each section, as appropriate for your submission.

Nonfiction: Buys 40-50 features (3,000-5,000 words) and 200 short pieces (125-500 words). Query (e-mail preferred). Travel. **Pays $4,000-6,000/feature; $100-500/short piece.** Pays expenses of writers on assignment.

Photos: Discourages submission of unsolicited transparencies. Buys one-time rights. Payment varies. Captions required.

Columns/Departments: Length: 1,200-2,500 words. **Buys 125-150 mss/year. Pays $1,000-2,500.**

Tips: "Read the magazine. There are two regional editions: East and West. Short-takes sections (e.g., "*T+L* Reports" and "Smart Going") are best places to start."

$ $ ☒ TRAVEL AMERICA, The U.S. Vacation Magazine, World Publishing Co., 990 Grove St., Evanston IL 60201-4370. (847)491-6440. Editor-in-Chief/Associate Publisher: Bob Meyers. **Contact:** Randy Mink, managing editor. **80% freelance written.** Bimonthly magazine covering US vacation travel. Estab. 1985. Circ. 300,000. Byline given. Buys first North American serial rights. Submit seasonal material 6 months in advance. Responds in 1 month to queries; 6 weeks to mss. Sample copy for $5 and 9×12 SASE with $1.60 postage.

Nonfiction: Primarily destination-oriented travel articles and resort/hotel profiles and roundups, but will consider essays, how-to, humor, nostalgia, Americana. "U.S. destination travel features must have personality and strong sense of place, developed through personal experiences, quotes, humor, human interest, local color. We prefer people-oriented writing, not dry guidebook accounts and brochure-style fluff. Always in the market for nationwide roundup stories— past roundups have included US Gambling Meccas and Top 10 Amusement Parks. Also short slices of Americana focusing on nostalgia, collectibles and crafts, ethnic communities and celebrations, special events. It is best to study current contents and query by mail only first." **Buys 60 mss/year.** Length: 1,000 words. **Pays $150-300.**

Reprints: Send typed ms with rights for sale noted. Payment varies.

Photos: Top-quality original color slides preferred. Prefers photo feature package (ms plus slides), but will purchase slides only to support a work in progress. Buys one-time rights. Captions required.

Tips: "Because we are heavily photo-oriented, superb slides are our foremost concern. The most successful approach is to send 2-3 sheets of slides with the query or complete ms. Include a list of other subjects you can provide as a photo feature package."

$ TRAVEL IMPULSE, Sun Tracker Enterprises Ltd., 9336 117th St., Delta, British Columbia V4C 6B8, Canada. (604)951-3238. Fax: (604)951-8732. E-mail: editor@suntrackercafe.com. Website: www.suntrackercafe.com. **Contact:** Susan M. Boyce, editor/publisher. **95% freelance written.** Quarterly magazine. "We work with at least one new writer each issue and are always looking for new voices. *Travel Impulse* is a quarterly magazine for people who love to travel— in fact, they find travel irresistible. Appeal to their sense of adventure and the playfulness of travel. Many of our readers like to 'pick up and go' at short notice and are looking for inexpensive, unique ways to accomplish that." Estab. 1984. Circ. 1,000. Pays 2 weeks after publication. Publishes ms an average of 8 months after acceptance. Byline given. Buys first North American serial, second serial (reprint) rights. Editorial lead time 8 months. Submit seasonal material 8 months in advance. Accepts queries by mail. Responds in 2 months to queries; 4 months to mss. Sample copy for $6. Writer's guidelines for #10 SASE or online.

    O➔ "Write in first person and tell me about *your* experience. I'm not looking for another advertisement—I want stories about real places and real people."

Nonfiction: Include Canadian postage or IRC. Humor, interview/profile, new product (travel gadgets and gear), personal experience, photo feature. No political commentary. **Buys 20-25 mss/year.** Query by mail only or send complete ms. Length: 800-1,000 words. **Pays $20-30 for features.**

Photos: No originals until requested, but photos greatly enhance your chances of acceptance. State availability with submission. Reviews prints (4×6 preferred). Buys rights with ms. Offers no additional payment for photos accepted with ms. Captions, identification of subjects, model releases required.

Tips: "Our readers find travel irresistible. Entice them with unusual destinations and unique ways to travel inexpensively. Show us the playful side of travel."

$ $ $⊡ **trips, a travel journal**, 155 Filbert St., Suite 245, Oakland CA 94607. (510)834-3433. Fax: (510)834-2663. E-mail: office@tripsmag.com. Website: www.tripsmag.com. **Contact:** Tony Stucker, editor-in-chief. **90% freelance written.** Bimonthly magazine. "*trips* magazine is the travel journal for active travelers looking for travel information in an unusual, offbeat, irreverent voice. We are looking for travel articles that would not, or could not, appear anywhere else. We want the exotic, unusual destinations, but we are also looking for traditional sites viewed in unconventional ways. All editorial should be as interesting and entertaining to someone whether they're planning on visiting a destination, have just returned from the destination or never plan on going there. It should educate and inform, but also entertain. Travel is fun—travel writing should be as well." Estab. 1997. Circ. 100,000. Pays on publication. Publishes ms an average of 3 months after acceptance. Byline given. Buys first North American serial rights. Editorial lead time 6 months. Submit seasonal material 6 months in advance. Accepts queries by mail, e-mail. Accepts simultaneous submissions. Responds in 6 weeks to queries; 6 weeks to mss. Sample copy for 10×13 SAE and 7 first-class stamps. Writer's guidelines for #10 SASE.

O–¬ Break in through well-developed, informative or offbeat pieces for our smaller sections, i.e., "Tips," "A Travel Journal," "Lessons In" and "Vice."

Nonfiction: Especially looking for "how-to" tips and advice, reader service pieces and funny/goofy filler for "Customs" section. Book excerpts, essays, exposé, general interest, how-to, humor, interview/profile, new product, personal experience, photo feature, travel. No "run-of-the-mill travel stories that would appear in Sunday travel sections." **Buys 40 mss/year.** Query with published clips. Length: 450-6,000 words. **Pays $100-1,500.** Sometimes pays expenses of writers on assignment.

Reprints: Send photocopy and information about when and where the material previously appeared.

Photos: State availability with submission. Reviews contact sheets, negatives. Buys one-time rights. Negotiates payment individually. Identification of subjects required.

Columns/Departments: "Lessons In..." (travel reader service); "Vice" (unusual vices from around the world); "A Travel Journal" (first person essays), all 800-1,000 words. **Buys 30 mss/year.** Query. **Pays $100-500.**

Tips: "We want to develop relationships with writers around the world. If you don't have a piece that works now, perhaps a future trip will yield something that's right. E-mail queries encouraged."

$ $ $VOYAGEUR, The Magazine of Carlson Hospitality Worldwide, Pace Communications, 1301 Carolina St., Greensboro NC 27401. (336)378-6065. Fax: (336)378-8272. Editor: Jaci H. Ponzoni. **Contact:** Sarah Lindsay, senior editor. **90% freelance written.** Quarterly magazine in-room magazine for Radisson hotels and affiliates. "*Voyageur* is an international magazine published quarterly for Carlson Hospitality Worldwide and distributed in the rooms of Radisson Hotels & Resorts, Radisson Seven Sea Cruises, and Country Inns & Suites By Carlson throughout North and South America, Europe, Australia, Africa, Asia and the Middle East. All travel-related stories must be in destinations where Radisson or Country Inns & Suites have hotels." Estab. 1992. Circ. 160,000. Pays on publication. Publishes ms an average of 2 months after acceptance. Offers 25% kill fee. Buys first North American serial rights. Editorial lead time 4 months. Submit seasonal material 6 months in advance. Accepts queries by mail. Responds in 2 months to queries; 2 months to mss. Sample copy for $5. Writer's guidelines for #10 SASE.

O–¬ Break in with a "well-thought-out, well-written, well-researched query on a city or area the writer lives in or knows well—one where Carlson has a presence (Radisson or Country Inns)."

Nonfiction: The Cover Story is an authoritative yet personal profile of a destination where Radisson has a major presence, featuring a mix of standard and off-the-beaten-path activities and sites including sightseeing, recreation, restaurants, shopping and cultural attractions. Length: 1,200 words plus At a Glance, a roundup of useful and intriguing facts for travelers. The Cultural Feature brings to life some aspect of a country's or region's arts and culture, including performing, culinary, visual and folk arts. The successful article combines a timely sample of activities for travelers with a sense of the destination's unique spirit or personality as reflected in the arts. Must be a region where Radisson has a major presence. Length: 900 words. Query with published clips. **Pays $800-1,200.** Sometimes pays expenses of writers on assignment.

Photos: State availability with submission. Reviews contact sheets, transparencies, prints. Buys one-time rights. Negotiates payment individually. Identification of subjects, model releases required.

Columns/Departments: A place-specific shopping story with cultural context and upscale attitude, 250 words and 50-word mini-sidebar; an action-oriented, first-person story focusing on travel involving sports such as biking, kayaking, scuba diving, hiking or sailing, 250 words plus 50-word mini-sidebar; Agenda (insights into conducting business and traveling for business internationally), 250 words with 50-word mini-sidebar; Au Revoir (an evocative, first-person book back at an appealing Carlson destination), 350 words. **Buys 24 mss/year.** Query with published clips. **Pays $300-400.**

Tips: "We look for authoritative, energetic and vivid writing to inform and entertain business and leisure travelers, and we are actively seeking writers with an authentic European, Asian, Latin American, African or Australian perspective. Travel stories should be authoritative yet personal."

$ WESTERN RV NEWS, 64470 Sylvan Loop, Bend OR 97701. (541)318-8089. Fax: (541)318-0849. E-mail: editor@westernrvnews.com. Website: www.westernrvnews.com. **Contact:** Terie Snyder, editor. **75% freelance written.** Monthly magazine for owners of recreational vehicles and those interested in the RV lifestyle. Estab. 1966. Pays on publication. Publishes ms an average of 6 months after acceptance. Byline given. Buys first, second serial (reprint) rights. Accepts queries by mail, e-mail, fax. Accepts simultaneous submissions. Responds in 2 months to queries; 2 months to mss. Sample copy for 9×12 SAE and 5 first-class stamps. Writer's guidelines for #10 SASE.

Nonfiction: How-to (RV oriented, purchasing considerations, maintenance), humor (RV experiences), new product (with ancillary interest to RV lifestyle), personal experience (varying or unique RV lifestyles), technical (RV systems or hardware), travel. "No articles without an RV slant." **Buys 100 mss/year.** Submit complete ms on paper or diskette. Length: 250-1,200 words. **Pays $20-100.**

Reprints: Photocopy of article or typed ms with rights for sale noted and information about when and where the material previously appeared. Pays 60% of *Western RV News* first rights.

Photos: Send photos with submission. Reviews b&w or color slides or photos. Can submit on 3.5" IBM-compatible disk. Buys one-time rights. Pays $5/photo. Captions, identification of subjects, model releases required.

Fillers: Encourage anecdotes, RV related tips and short humor. Length: 50-250 words. **Pays $5-25.**

Tips: "Highlight the RV lifestyle! Western travel articles should include information about the availability of RV sites, dump stations, RV parking and accessibility. Thorough research and a pleasant, informative writing style are paramount. Technical, how-to, and new product writing is also of great interest. Photos enhance the possibility of article acceptance."

WOMEN'S

Women have an incredible variety of publications available to them. A number of titles in this area have been redesigned to compete in the crowded marketplace. Many have stopped publishing fiction and are focusing more on short, human interest nonfiction articles. Magazines that also use material slanted to women's interests can also be found in the following categories: Business and Finance; Child Care and Parental Guidance; Contemporary Culture; Food & Drink; Gay & Lesbian Interest; Health & Fitness; Hobby & Craft; Home & Garden; Relationships; Religious; Romance & Confession; and Sports.

$ $ BBW, Real Women, Real Beauty, Aeon Publishing Group, Inc., P.O. Box 1297, Elk Grove CA 95759-1297. Fax: (916)684-7628. E-mail: sesmith@bbwmagazine.com. Website: www.bbwmagazine.com. **Contact:** Sally E. Smith, editor-in-chief. **50% freelance written.** Bimonthly magazine covering fashion and lifestyle for women size 16+. "*BBW* strives to inspire women all sizes of large to celebrate their beauty and enrich their lives by providing them with affirming information and resources in the areas of fashion and beauty, health and well-being, entertainment and romance, and work and leisure." Estab. 1979. Circ. 100,000. Pays on publication. Publishes ms an average of 2 months after acceptance. Byline given. Offers 20% kill fee. Buys all rights. Editorial lead time 4 months. Accepts queries by mail, e-mail, fax. Responds in 1 month. Sample copy for $5. Writer's guidelines for #10 SASE, online, or by e-mail.

Nonfiction: Book excerpts, essays, exposé, general interest, how-to (beauty/style), humor, new product, opinion, photo feature, travel. "No first-person narratives, poetry, fiction." **Buys 18 mss/year.** Query with published clips. Length: 800-2,500 words. **Pays $125-500.**

Photos: State availability with submission. Reviews contact sheets, negatives, 2¼×2¼ transparencies, slides. Buys all rights. Offers no additional payment for photos accepted with ms. Captions, model releases required.

Columns/Departments: Personal Best (improve well-being), 1,200 words; Careers (tools to manage/enhance careers), 1,500 words; Finance (increase financial security), 1,200 words; Perspectives (male perspective), 800 words; Last Word (humorous end page), 700 words; Destinations (travel within US), 1,200 words; Entertaining, 1,000 words. **Buys 30 mss/year.** Query with published clips. **Pays $125-250.**

Fillers: Anecdotes, facts (products, trends, style, fashion, reviews). **Buys 12/year.** Length: 100-200 words. **Pays $25.**

Tips: "Pitch specific articles/topics—2-3 sentences summarizing your proposed topic, and communicating how the piece will be written, i.e., interviews, sidebars, etc."

$ $ $ BRIDAL GUIDE, R.F.P., LLC, 3 E. 54th St., 15th Floor, New York NY 10022. (212)838-7733. Fax: (212)308-7165. Website: www.bridalguidemag.com. Editor-in-Chief: Diane Forden. **Contact:** Denise Schipani, executive editor; Laurie Bain Wilson, travel editor for travel features. **50% freelance written.** Bimonthly magazine covering relationships, sexuality, fitness, wedding planning, psychology, finance, travel. Prefers to work with experienced/published writers. **Pays on acceptance.** Accepts queries by mail. Responds in 3 months to queries; 3 months to mss. Sample copy for $5 and SAE with 4 first-class stamps. Writer's guidelines available.

Nonfiction: "Please do not send queries concerning beauty and fashion, since we produce them in-house. We do not accept personal wedding essays, fiction, or poetry. Address travel queries to travel editor." All correspondence accompanied by an SASE will be answered. **Buys 100 mss/year.** Query with published clips. Length: 1,000-2,000 words. **Pays 50¢/word.**

Photos: Photography and illustration submissions should be sent to the art department. Robin Zachary, art director; Catherine Diaz, associate art director.

Columns/Departments: The only columns written by freelancers cover finance and wedding-planning issues. Welcome queries from men who are engaged or married for Groom with a View essay.

◾ The online magazine carries original content not found in the print version. Contact: Karla Vermeulen, online editor.

Tips: "We are looking for service-oriented, well-researched pieces that are journalistically written. Writers we work with use at least three expert sources, such as physicians, book authors, and business people in the appropriate field. Our tone is conversational yet authoritative. Features are also generally filled with real-life anecdotes. We also do features that are completely real-person based—such as roundtables of bridesmaids discussing their experiences, or grooms-to-be talking about their feelings about getting married. In queries, we are looking for a well thought-out idea, the specific angle of focus the writer intends to take, and the sources he or she intends to use. Queries should be brief and snappy—and titles should be supplied to give the editor an even better idea of the direction the writer is going in."

$ $ BRIDE AGAIN, The Only Magazine Designed for Second Time Brides, 1240 N. Jefferson Ave., Suite G, Anaheim CA 92807. (714)632-7000. Fax: (714)632-5405. E-mail: editor@brideagain.com. Website: www.brideagain. com. **Contact:** Beth Ramirez, editor. Quarterly magazine for the encore bride. "*Bride Again* is targeted primarily to women ages 35-45 and secondarily to those 45 and over. They have been married at least once before, and most likely have children from a previous marriage or will be marrying someone with children. They have a career and income of over $45,000 per year, and are more mature and sophisticated than the 26-year-old first-time bride." Estab. 1997. Circ. 125,000. Pays on publication. Byline given. Writer's guidelines for #10 SASE.

Nonfiction: "Topics can be on, but not limited to: Remarriage, blending families, becoming a stepmother, combining households, dealing with children in the wedding party, children—his, mine and ours, joint custody, dealing with difficult ex-spouses, real dresses for real women, legal aspects of remarriage, pre- and post-nuptial agreements, alternatives to the wedding veil, unusual wedding and/or honeymoon locations." Interfaith marriages; handling extended step families; having another child together. How-to, humor, inspirational, interview/profile, personal experience. No queries please. Send complete ms. Length: 1,000 words. **Pays 35¢/word.**

Photos: Does not purchase photos.

Columns/Departments: Finances, Blending Families, Religion, Groom's Viewpoint, Unusual Honeymoon Locations, Beauty for Ages 30+/40+/50+, Remarriage, Fashion; all 800-1,000 words. Book reviews (on the feature topics listed above), 250 words. Send complete ms. **Pays 35¢/word.**

Tips: "All articles must be specific to encore brides."

$ $ $ $ CHATELAINE, 777 Bay St., #800, Toronto, Ontario M5W 1A7, Canada. (416)596-5000. Fax: (416)596-5516. E-mail: editors@chatelaine.com. Website: www.chatelaine.com. **Contact:** Caroline Connell, managing editor. Monthly magazine. "*Chatelaine* is edited for Canadian women ages 25-49, their changing attitudes and lifestyles. Key editorial ingredients include health, finance, social issues and trends, high profile personalities and politics, as well as fashion, beauty, food and home decor. Regular departments include Health pages, Entertainment, Humour, How-to." **Pays on acceptance.** Byline given. Offers 25-100% kill fee. Buys first, electronic rights. Accepts queries by mail. Writer's guidelines for #10 SASE with postage.

○→ Break in with one-page, 800-word service columns.

Nonfiction: Seeks "agenda-setting reports on national issues and trends as well as pieces on health, careers, personal finance and other facts of Canadian life." **Buys 50 mss/year.** Query with published clips and SASE. Length: 1,000-2,500 words. **Pays $1,000-2,500.** Pays expenses of writers on assignment.

Columns/Departments: Length: 500-1,000 words. Query with published clips and SASE. **Pays $500-750.**

◾ The online magazine carries original content not found in the print edition. Contact: Trish Snyder, online editor.

$ ▨ CINCINNATI WOMAN MAGAZINE, Niche Publishing and Media L.L.C., P.O. Box 8170, West Chester OH 45069-8170. (513)851-8916. Fax: (513)851-8916. E-mail: cincinnatiwoman@cinci.rr.com. Editor: Cathy Habes. **Contact:** Alicia Wiehe, publisher. **90% freelance written.** Monthly magazine covering women's issues and needs. "Dedicated exclusively to capturing the spirit of Cincinnati-area women, we are committed to providing our readers with information as well as inspiration." Estab. 1998. Circ. 35,000. Pays on publication. Publishes ms an average of 4 months after acceptance. Byline given. Buys one-time rights. Editorial lead time 2 months. Submit seasonal material 3 months in advance. Accepts queries by mail, e-mail. Accepts simultaneous submissions. Responds in 2 weeks to queries. Sample copy for 8×10 SAE and 3 first-class stamps. Writer's guidelines for #10 SASE.

Nonfiction: Book excerpts, essays, general interest, how-to, humor, inspirational, interview/profile, new product, opinion, personal experience, photo feature, travel, health/beauty. **Buys 50 mss/year.** Query with published clips or send complete ms. Length: 500-1,000 words. **Pays $80 maximum for assigned articles; $30 maximum for unsolicited articles.**

Reprints: Send photocopy of article or typed ms with rights for sale noted and information about when and where the material previously appeared.

Photos: State availability with submission. Reviews transparencies, 4×6 prints. Buys one-time rights. Offers no additonal payment for photos accepted with ms. Captions, identification of subjects required.

Columns/Departments: Body Shop (health/beauty nuggets), 700 words; *CWM* Cooks (entertaining and recipes), 700 words; *CWM* Style (women's fashion), 700 words; *CWM* Travel, 700 words. **Buys 30 mss/year.** Query with published clips or send complete ms. **Pays $30.**

insider report

Writing for women's magazines: Write from the heart

After a tough divorce and a stint at the Census Bureau, 39-year-old single mother Deanna Pease was ready for a job that would pay the bills and keep her available for her two children. Thanks to a mentor at *Woman's World*, freelance writing became her niche. "Since I was given my first assignment as a freelance writer in June of 1999," Pease says, "I have written more than 150 features." In addition to *Woman's World*, *Parade* and *First for Women* have answered her gender-specific query calls.

Deanna Pease

What special challenges set freelancing for women's magazines apart from other specialties?
You have to write from the heart. The women's markets want a lot of emotion, not just dry facts and statistics. You write scenes (show, not tell) and you must be able to weave the facts in while making the reader feel the heartbreaks and joys of the subject.

What kind of topics do you write most often for women's magazines? Are there staples in the industry that "always" sell?
I write "Real-Life Stories" for *WW*, and my work for *First* appeared in the "Women Like You" section.

How would you break into this specialty if you were a beginning freelancer?
First, study your market. Read several issues, cover-to-cover, even the ads. The ads tell you a lot about the target market you want to write for. Pampers or Depends? Mercedes or Chevy? Disneyland vacations or retirement condos? Then study back issues for a prevailing style. This was especially important for me, as the Real-Life Stories in *Woman's World* all embody the same very specific style. Once you identify such a common thread, practice writing that style until you are comfortable with it. Next, you start hunting for stories that are perfect for your target market. The Internet is an unlimited research tool, and newspapers or TV are good. Remember, every lead must have adequate contact information.

What are the most common mistakes freelancers in this arena make (and can avoid)?
The assigning editor at *WW* told me that the most common mistake would-be first-timers make is being unavailable. When she gets an approved lead in her hands, she wants to get it out to a writer as quickly as possible. Sometimes the assignment is a "super rush" and she needs it completed in three days. Every hour can be crucial. I learned that lesson the hard way

when I returned home from grocery shopping one day with two messages on my voicemail. The first message, a $750 assignment, mine for the taking. The second, 45 minutes later, "Sorry, had to give it to another writer . . ." Now, I carry a beeper!

Have you had a favorite assignment? If so, what was it and why was it so memorable?
I would have to say I have a favorite category. The *Saved!* features are rescue stories and are different from the other categories I write; the action of the stories take place over a much shorter time span, a day or a few hours, as opposed to the months or years that would be covered in most stories. It's a more dramatic, fast-paced kind of writing, making it more like fiction writing.

Have you experienced the nightmare of all nightmare assignments? Describe it.
I'm very fortunate in that I love my job and writing is usually not difficult for me. But since I had Valley Fever a few years ago, every cold brings on bouts of chronic fatigue. During those (fortunately rare) periods, every keystroke is like lifting a 20-pound weight with a finger. But it's a job, with a boss at the other end with expectations that must be met. So at times like those, you have to just sit down and do it. Missing a deadline, especially on a rush job, could easily be career suicide.
—*Kelly Milner Halls*

For interviews with the pros in more freelance niche markets, see Animals, page 368; Contemporary Culture, page 432; Entertainment, page 443; Games & Puzzles, page 462; Sports, page 708.

TOP TIP: "To get that very first assignment, you must learn to write query letters that will convince an editor in one page that you can do the job you're asking for. The query should read like a shorter version of the assignment you hope to write. It should conform to the style and format of the magazine you want to write for. It should have a beginning, a middle, and an end, not just be a jumble of facts. Still, that darned editor may throw away your first try. (Editors are often reluctant to take a chance on unproven writers.) So you send her another one the next week, and another the week after that. Don't give up easily, persistence pays in this business!"

Fiction: Adventure, confession, horror, humorous, mainstream, mystery, religious, romance, slice-of-life vignettes. **Buys 20 mss/year.** Query with published clips or send complete ms. Length: 700-1,200 words. **Pays $30.**
Poetry: Avant-garde, free verse, light verse, traditional. **Buys 5 poems/year.** Submit maximum 3 poems. Length: 5-60 lines. **Pays $20.**
Fillers: Anecdotes, facts, newsbreaks, short humor. **Buys 5/year.** Length: 50-100 words. **Pays $15.**
Tips: "We're looking for material on 20-something, dating, fashion, first-time mom experiences, holistic health, cooking, short personal essays."

$ $ COMPLETE WOMAN, For All The Women You Are, Associated Publications, Inc., 875 N. Michigan Ave., Suite 3434, Chicago IL 60611-1901. (312)266-8680. Editor: Bonnie L. Krueger. **Contact:** Lora Wintz, executive editor. **90% freelance written.** Bimonthly magazine. "Manuscripts should be written for today's busy women, in a concise, clear format with useful information. Our readers want to know about the important things: Sex, love, relationships, career and self-discovery. Examples of true-life anecdotes incorporated into articles work well for our readers, who are always interested in how other women are dealing with life's ups and downs." Estab. 1980. Circ. 350,000. Pays 45 days after acceptance. Publishes ms an average of 6 months after acceptance. Byline given. Buys first North American serial, second serial (reprint), simultaneous rights. Editorial lead time 6 months. Submit seasonal material 5 months in advance. Accepts queries by mail. Accepts simultaneous submissions. Responds in 2 months to queries; 2 months to mss. Writer's guidelines for #10 SASE.

O— "Break in with writing samples that relate to the magazine. Also, the editor reports a need for more relationship stories."

Nonfiction: "We want self-help articles written for today's woman. Articles that address dating, romance, sexuality and relationships are an integral part of our editorial mix, as well as inspirational and motivational pieces." Book excerpts, exposé (of interest to women), general interest, how-to (beauty/diet-related), humor, inspirational, interview/ profile (celebrities), new product, personal experience, photo feature, Sex, love, relationship advice. **Buys 60-100 mss/ year.** Query with published clips or send complete ms. Length: 800-2,000 words. **Pays $160-400.** Sometimes pays expenses of writers on assignment.

Reprints: Send tearsheet, photocopy or typed ms with rights for sale noted and information about when and where the material previously appeared.

Photos: Photo features with little or no copy should be sent to Gail Mitchell. Send photos with submission. Reviews 2¼ or 35mm transparencies, 5×7 prints. Buys one-time rights. Pays $35-100/photo. Captions, identification of subjects, model releases required.

Tips: "Freelance writers should review publication, review writer's guidelines, then submit their articles for review. We're looking for new ways to explore the usual topics, written in a format that will be easy for our readers (24-40+ women) to understand. We also like sidebar information that readers can review quickly before or after reading the article. Our focus is relationship-driven, with an editorial blend of beauty, health and career."

$ $ $ $ CONDÉ NAST BRIDE'S, Condé Nast, 4 Times Square, 6th Floor, New York NY 10036. Fax: (212)286-8331. Website: www.brides.com. Editor-in-Chief: Millie Bratten. **Contact:** Sally Kilbridge, managing editor. **75% freelance written.** Bimonthly magazine covering all things related to the bride—engagement, the wedding and marriage. All articles are written for the engaged woman planning her wedding. Estab. 1934. Circ. 500,000. **Pays on acceptance.** Publishes ms an average of 6 months after acceptance. Byline given. Offers 15% kill fee. Buys all rights. Editorial lead time 6 months. Submit seasonal material 1 year in advance. Accepts queries by mail. Responds in 3 months to queries. Writer's guidelines for #10 SASE.

Nonfiction: Topic (1) Personal essays on wedding planning, aspects of weddings or marriage. Length: 800 words. Written by brides, grooms, attendants, family members, friends in the first person. The writer's unique experience qualifies them to tell this story. (2) Articles on specific relationship and lifestyle issues. Length: 800 words. Select a specialized topic in the areas of relationships, religion, in-laws, second marriage, finances, careers, health, fitness, nutrition, sex, decorating, or entertaining. Written either by experts (attorneys, doctors, financial planners, marriage counselors, etc) or freelancers who interview and quote experts and real couples. (3) In-depth explorations of relationship and lifestyle issues. Length: 2,000-3,000 words. Well-researched articles on finances, health, sex, wedding and marriage trends. Should include statistics, quotes from experts and real couples, a resolution of the issues raised by each couple. Book excerpts, essays, how-to, personal experience. No humor. **Buys 36 mss/year.** Query with published clips. Length: 800-2,000 words. **Pays 75¢-$1/word for assigned articles.** Pays expenses of writers on assignment.

Photos: State availability with submission. Negotiates payment individually.

Columns/Departments: Length: 750 words. Query with published clips. **Pays 75¢-$1/word.**

Tips: "We look for good, helpful relationship pieces that will help a newlywed couple adjust to marriage. Wedding planning articles are usually written by experts or depend on a lot of interviews with experts. Writers must have a good idea of what we would and would not do: Read the 3 or 4 most recent issues. What separates us from the competition is quality-writing, photographs, amount of information. All articles are assigned with some consumer slant, with the exception of personal essays."

N $ $ $ $ COSMOPOLITAN, The Hearst Corp., 224 W. 57th St., New York NY 10019. (212)649-2000. **Contact:** Michele Promaulayko, executive editor. **25% freelance written.** Monthly magazine for 18- to 35-year-old single, married, divorced women—all working. "*Cosmopolitan* is edited for young women for whom beauty, fashion, fitness, career, relationships and personal growth are top priorities. Nutrition, personal finance, home/lifestyle and celebrities are other interests reflected in the editorial lineup." Estab. 1886. Circ. 2,300,100. **Pays on acceptance.** Byline given. Offers 10-15% kill fee. Buys all magazine rights and occasionally negotiates first North American rights. Submit seasonal material 6 months in advance. Responds in 1 week to queries; 3 weeks to mss. Sample copy for $2.95. Writer's guidelines for #10 SASE.

• *Cosmopolitan* also has *Cosmogirl* for teens. Send SASE for guidelines.

Nonfiction: Book excerpts, how-to, humor, opinion, personal experience, anything of interest to young women. **Buys 350 mss/year.** Query with published clips or send complete ms. Length: 500-3,500 words. **Pays $2,000-3,500 for features; $1,000-1,500 for short pieces.** Pays expenses of writers on assignment.

Reprints: Accepts previously published submissions appearing in minor publications. Send tearsheet of article or typed ms with rights for sale noted and information about when and where the material previously appeared. Pays 100% of amount paid for an original article.

Tips: "Combine information with entertainment value, humor and relatability." Needs "information- and emotion- and fun-packed relationship and sex service stories; first-person stories that deal with women's issues; essays from both men and women on topics that more women either relate to or are curious about." This editorial team headed American *Marie Claire* until September 1996.

$ COUNTRY WOMAN, Reiman Publications, 5400 South 60th Street, Greendale WI 53129. (414)423-0100. **Contact:** Kathleen Anderson, managing editor. **75-85% freelance written.** Bimonthly magazine. "*Country Woman* is for contemporary rural women of all ages and backgrounds and from all over the U.S. and Canada. It includes a sampling of the diversity that makes up rural women's lives—love of home, family, farm, ranch, community, hobbies, enduring values, humor, attaining new skills and appreciating present, past and future all within the context of the lifestyle that surrounds country living." Estab. 1970. **Pays on acceptance.** Byline given. Buys first North American serial, one-time, second serial (reprint) rights. Submit seasonal material 5 months in advance. Accepts queries by mail. Responds in 2 months to queries; 3 months to mss. Sample copy for $2. Writer's guidelines for #10 SASE.

○→ Break in with "fiction, nostalgia and inspirational pieces. Study the magazine carefully before submitting."

Nonfiction: Articles must be written in a positive, light and entertaining manner. General interest, historical/nostalgic, how-to (crafts, community projects, decorative, antiquing, etc.), humor, inspirational, interview/profile, personal experience, photo feature (packages profiling interesting country women-all pertaining to rural women's interests). Query. Length: 1,000 words maximum. **Pays $35-150.**

Reprints: Send typed ms with rights for sale noted and information about when and where the material previously appeared. Payment varies.

Photos: Uses only excellent quality color photos. No b&w. "We pay for photo/feature packages." State availability of or send photos with submission. Reviews 35mm or 2.25 transparencies, excellent-quality color prints. Buys one-time rights. Captions, identification of subjects, model releases required.

Columns/Departments: Why Farm Wives Age Fast (humor), I Remember When (nostalgia) and Country Decorating. Length: 500-1,000 words. **Buys 10-12 mss/year.** Query or send ms. **Pays $50-125.**

Fiction: Main character *must* be a country woman. All fiction must have a country setting. Fiction must have a positive, upbeat message. Includes fiction in every issue. Would buy more fiction if stories suitable for our audience were sent our way. Send complete ms. Length: 750-1,000 words. **Pays $90-125.**

Poetry: Light verse, traditional. "Poetry must have rhythm and rhyme! It must be country-related, positive and upbeat. Always looking for seasonal poetry." **Buys 6-12 poems/year.** Submit maximum 6 poems. Length: 4-24 lines. **Pays $10-25.**

Tips: "We have broadened our focus to include 'country' women, not just women on farms and ranches but also women who live in a small town or country home and/or simply have an interest in country-oriented topics. This allows freelancers a wider scope in material. Write as clearly and with as much zest and enthusiasm as possible. We love good quotes, supporting materials (names, places, etc.) and strong leads and closings. Readers relate strongly to where they live and the lifestyle they've chosen. They want to be informed and entertained, and that's just exactly why they subscribe. Readers are busy—not too busy to read—but when they do sit down, they want good writing, reliable information and something that feels like a reward. How-to, humor, personal experience and nostalgia are areas most open to freelancers. Profiles, to a certain degree, are also open. Be accurate and fresh in approach."

$ $ $ $ FAMILY CIRCLE MAGAZINE, Gruner & Jahr, 375 Lexington Ave., New York NY 10017-5514. (212)499-2000. Fax: (212)499-1987. E-mail: nclark@familycircle.com. Website: www.familycircle.com. Editor-in-Chief: Susan Ungaro. **Contact:** Nancy Clark, deputy editor. **80% freelance written.** Magazine published every 3 weeks. "We are a national women's service magazine which covers many stages of a woman's life, along with her everyday concerns about social, family and health issues." Estab. 1932. Circ. 5,000,000. Byline given. Offers 20% kill fee. Buys one-time, all rights. Editorial lead time 4 months. Submit seasonal material 4 months in advance. Responds in 2 months to queries; 2 months to mss. Writer's guidelines for #10 SASE.

○→ Break in with "Women Who Make A Difference." Send queries to Marilyn Balamaci, senior editor.

Nonfiction: "We look for well-written, well-reported stories told through interesting anecdotes and insightful writing. We want well-researched service journalism on all subjects." Essays, humor, opinion, personal experience, women's interest subjects such as family and personal relationships, children, physical and mental health, nutrition and self-improvement. No fiction or poetry. **Buys 200 mss/year.** Query with SASE. Length: 1,000-2,500 words. **Pays $1/word.** Pays expenses of writers on assignment.

Columns/Departments: Women Who Make a Difference (profiles of volunteers who have made a significant impact on their community), 1,500 words; Profiles in Courage/Love (dramatic narratives about women and families overcoming adversity), 2,000 words; Full Circle (opinion/point of view on current issue/topic of general interest to our readers), 750 words; Humor, 750 words. **Buys 200 mss/year.** Query with published clips and SASE. **Pays $1/word.**

Tips: "Query letters should be concise and to the point. Also, writers should keep close tabs on *Family Circle* and other women's magazines to avoid submitting recently run subject matter."

$ $ $ $ HARPER'S BAZAAR, The Hearst Corp., 1700 Broadway, New York, NY 10019. (212)903-5000. Publisher: Cynthia Lewis. **Contact:** Mary Dunenwald, executive editor. "*Harper's Bazaar* is a monthly specialist magazine for women who love fashion and beauty. It is edited for sophisticated women with exceptional taste. *Bazaar* offers ideas in fashion and beauty, and reports on issues and interests relevant to the lives of modern women." Estab. 1867. Circ. 711,000. Pays on publication. Byline given. Offers 25% kill fee. Buys worldwide rights. Responds in 2 months to queries.

Nonfiction: Buys 36 mss/year. Query with published clips. Length: 2,000-3,000 words. **Payment negotiable.**

Columns/Departments: Length: 500-700 words. **Payment negotiable.**

N $ I DO FOR BRIDES, Pinnacle Publishing Company, 4798 Long Island Dr. NW, Atlanta GA 30342. (404)255-1234. Fax: (404)255-2575. E-mail: editorial.ppc@mindspring.com. Website: www.idoforbrides.com. **Contact:** Lissa Poirot, publisher/editor. **60% freelance written.** Quarterly magazine covering the bridal industry. The magazine includes

hints for wedding preparation, bridal attire, honeymoon and wedding destinations. Publishes 3 regional versions: Alabama; Tennessee; and Washington, DC, Maryland and Virginia. Estab. 1996. Circ. 100,000. Publishes ms an average of 8 months after acceptance. Byline sometimes given. Buys all rights. Editorial lead time 8 months. Submit seasonal material 8 months in advance. Accepts queries by mail, e-mail. Accepts simultaneous submissions.
Nonfiction: Book excerpts, essays, general interest, historical/nostalgic, how-to (bridal-related), humor, inspirational, interview/profile, new product, opinion, personal experience, photo feature, religious, travel. **Buys 8 mss/year.** Query. Length: 300-1,000 words. **Pays variable rate.**

$ THE LINK & VISITOR, Baptist Women's Missionary Society of Ontario and Quebec, 414-195 The West Mall, Etobicoke, Ontario M9C 5K1, Canada. (416)491-2750. Fax: (416)491-2541. **Contact:** Editor. **50% freelance written.** Magazine published 6 times/ year "designed to help Baptist women grow their world, faith, relationships, creativity, and mission vision-evangelical, egalitarian, Canadian." Estab. 1878. Circ. 4,300. Pays on publication. Publishes ms an average of 6 months after acceptance. Byline given. Buys one-time, second serial (reprint), simultaneous rights, makes work-for-hire assignments. Editorial lead time 2 months. Submit seasonal material 3 months in advance. Accepts simultaneous submissions. Sample copy for 9×12 SAE with 2 first-class Canadian stamps. Writer's guidelines free.
Nonfiction: "Articles must be biblically literate. No easy answers, American mindset or U.S. focus, retelling of Bible stories, sermons." Inspirational, interview/profile, religious. **Buys 30-35 mss/year.** Send complete ms. Length: 750-2,000 words. **Pays 5-10¢/word (Canadian).** Sometimes pays expenses of writers on assignment.
Photos: State availability with submission. Reviews any prints. Buys one-time rights. Offers no additional payment for photos accepted with ms. Captions required.
Tips: "Canadian women writers preferred."

N LONG ISLAND WOMAN, Maraj, Inc., P.O. Box 309, Island Park NY 11558. Fax: (516)889-6983. E-mail: editor@liwomanonline.com. Website: www.liwomanonline.com. Managing Editor: Andrew Elias. **Contact:** Pat Simms-Elias, editorial director. **75-80% freelance written.** Monthly magazine covering issues of importance to women—health, family, finance, arts, entertainment, travel, home. Estab. 2001. Circ. 32,000. Pays on publication. Publishes ms an average of 3 months after acceptance. Byline given. Offers 50% kill fee. Buys one-time rights. Editorial lead time 3 months. Submit seasonal material 3 months in advance. Accepts queries by mail, e-mail, fax. Accepts simultaneous submissions. Responds in 6 weeks to queries; 3 months to mss. Sample copy for $3. Writer's guidelines for free, online or by e-mail.
Nonfiction: Book excerpts, essays, general interest, how-to, humor, interview/profile, new product, opinion, personal experience, travel, reviews. **Buys 75-100 mss/year.** Query with published clips or send complete ms. Length: 300-1,500 words. **Pays $50-150 for assigned articles; $35-120 for unsolicited articles.** Sometimes pays expenses of writers on assignment.
Reprints: Accepts previously published submissions.
Photos: State availability of or send photos with submission. Reviews 5×7 prints. Buys one-time rights. Offers $10-25/photo. Captions, identification of subjects, model releases required.
Columns/Departments: Humor, Health Issues, Family Issues, Financial and Business Issues, Book Reviews and Books, Arts and Entertainment, Travel and Leisure, Home and Garden, all 500-1,000 words. **Buys 75-100 mss/year.** Query with published clips or send complete ms. **Pays $50-100.**
Fiction: Humorous. **Buys 10 mss/year.** Query with published clips or send complete ms. Length: 500-1,000 words. **Pays $50-100.**

$ $ $ MODERN BRIDE, Primedia, 249 W. 17th St., New York NY 10011. (212)462-3472. Fax: (212)367-8342. Website: www.modernbride.com. Editor-in-Chief: Antonia van der Meer. **Contact:** Christina Cush, executive editor. "*Modern Bride* is designed as the bride-to-be's guide to planning her wedding, honeymoon, and first home or apartment. Issues cover: (1) bridal fashion (including grooms, attendants, and mothers-of-the-bride), travel trousseau and lingerie; (2) home furnishings (tableware, furniture, linens, appliances, housewares, accessories, etc.); (3) honeymoon travel (covering the honeymoon hotspots around the world). Additional regular features include beauty, sex, health and fitness; wedding gifts; wedding planning tips; relationships; financial advice; and shopping information." Estab. 1949. Circ. 400,000. **Pays on acceptance.** Byline given. Offers 25% kill fee. Editorial lead time 6 months. Accepts queries by mail. Responds in 6 weeks to queries.
Nonfiction: Personal experience, relationship/sex articles, planning articles. **Buys 10 unsolicited mss/year.** Query with published clips. Length: 500-2,000 words. **Pays according to experience of writer and difficulty/length of assignment.** Sometimes pays expenses of writers on assignment.
Reprints: Send tearsheet of article or short story. Pays 50% of amount paid for original article.
Columns/Departments: Voices and On His Mind (personal experiences of bride and groom).
■ The online magazine carries original content not found in the print edition. Contact: Christine Ford, online content editor.

$ $ MORE MAGAZINE, Meredith Corp., 125 Park Ave., New York NY 10017. Fax: (212)455-1433. Website: www.lhj.com/more/. Editor-in-Chief: Myrna Blyth. **Contact:** Stephanie Woodard, articles editor. **90% freelance written.** Bimonthly magazine covering smart, sophisticated 40- to 60-year-old women. Estab. 1998. Circ. 700,000. **Pays on acceptance.** Publishes ms an average of 3 months after acceptance. Byline given. Offers 25% kill fee. Buys first North American serial, first, all rights. Editorial lead time 4 months. Submit seasonal material 6 months in advance. Accepts queries by mail, fax. Responds in 3 months. Writer's guidelines for #10 SASE.

Nonfiction: Essays, exposé, general interest, interview/profile, personal experience, travel, crime, food. **Buys 50 mss/year.** Query with published clips. Length: 300-2,500 words. **Pays variable rate depending on writer/story length.** Pays expenses of writers on assignment.

Photos: State availability with submission. Negotiates payment individually. Captions, identification of subjects, model releases required.

Columns/Departments: Buys 20 mss/year. Query with published clips. **Pays $300.**

$ 🔀 MOXIE MAGAZINE, For the Woman Who Dares, 1230 Glen Ave., Berkeley CA 94708. (510)540-5510. E-mail: emily@moxiemag.com. Website: www.moxiemag.com. **Contact:** Emily Hancock, editor-in-chief. **95% freelance written.** Quarterly magazine covering women who are putting together lives that work. "*Moxie* is filled with positive, upbeat, first-person accounts aimed at women who do not need a quiz to figure out what to do in bed. *Moxie* provides vibrant, often feisty examples of real women doing real things in the real world." Estab. 1998. Circ. 10,000. Pays on publication. Publishes ms an average of 3 months after acceptance. Byline given. Buys one-time, second serial (reprint) rights. Editorial lead time 3 months. Accepts queries by e-mail. Accepts simultaneous submissions. Responds in 2 months to queries; 2 months to mss. Sample copy for $5. Writer's guidelines for #10 SASE, online or by e-mail.

○➔ Break in with "offbeat stories for the woman who dares. Send complete ms (no queries, please) via e-mail only."

Nonfiction: Interested in seeing feminist theory woven into first-person stories. Book excerpts, essays, historical/nostalgic, humor, interview/profile, opinion, personal experience, photo feature. No " 'confessional,' whining or poor-me articles." **Buys 50-75 mss/year.** Send complete ms by e-mail only. Length: 800-4,000 words. **Pays $10-25.**

Photos: State availability with submission. Reviews contact sheets, prints. Rights belong to photographer. Offers no additional payment for photos accepted with ms. Offers $25-50/photo. Negotiates payment individually. Identification of subjects, model releases required.

Columns/Departments: News Flash (news items of pressing interest to women); Maverick Women (women who stand out—historical and contemporary). **Buys 4-6 mss/year.** Query. **Pays $10-25.**

Fiction: Adventure, ethnic, humorous, slice-of-life vignettes. No erotic, fantasy, confessional, mystery, horror, sci-fi, suspense. **Buys 8-12 mss/year.** Send complete ms by e-mail only. Length: 800-4,000 words. **Pays $10-25.**

Poetry: Avant-garde, free verse, haiku, light verse. **Buys 6-10 poems/year.** Submit maximum 4 poems. Length: 10-100 lines. **Pays $10-25.**

Fillers: Anecdotes, facts, newsbreaks, short humor. **Buys 12/year.** Length: 15-100 words.

■ The online magazine carries original content not found in the print edition and includes writer's guidelines. Contact: Emily Hancock, online editor.

Tips: "E-mail submissions please."

$ $ $ $ 🔀 MS. MAGAZINE, Liberty Media for Women, UC, 20 Exchange Place, 22nd Floor, New York NY 10005. (212)509-2092. Fax: (212)509-2407. E-mail: info@msmagazine.com. Website: www.msmagazine.com. Editor-in-Chief: Marcia Gillespie. Editor: Gloria Jacobs. **Contact:** Manuscripts Editor. **30% freelance written.** Bimonthly magazine on women's issues and news. Estab. 1972. Circ. 150,000. Byline given. Offers 30% kill fee. Buys first North American serial rights. Responds in 2 months. Sample copy for $9. Writer's guidelines for #10 SASE.

Nonfiction: International and national (US) news, the arts, books, popular culture, feminist theory and scholarship, ecofeminism, women's health, spirituality, political and economic affairs. Photo essays. **Buys 4-5 features (3,500 words) and 4-5 short pieces (500 words)/year.** Query with published clips. Length: 300-3,500 words. **Pays $1/word.** Pays expenses of writers on assignment.

Reprints: Send tearsheet or typed ms with rights for sale noted and information about when and where the material previously appeared. Pays 50% of amount paid for original article.

Photos: State availability with submission. Buys one-time rights. Identification of subjects, model releases required.

Columns/Departments: Length: 3,000 words maximum. **Buys 4-5 mss/year.** Length: 3,000 words maximum. **Pays $1/word.**

Tips: Needs "international and national women's news, investigative reporting, personal narratives, humor, world-class fiction and poetry, and prize-winning journalists and feminist thinkers."

$ $ 🔀 GRACE ORMONDE WEDDING STYLE, Elegant Publishing Inc., P.O. Box 89, Barrington RI 02806. (401)245-9726. Fax: (401)245-5371. E-mail: yanni@WeddingStyleMagazine.com. Website: www.WeddingStyleMagazine.com. Editor: Grace Ormonde. **Contact:** Yannis Tzoumas, editorial director/publisher. **90% freelance written.** Annual magazine covering wedding and special event planning resource. "*Grace Ormonde Wedding Style* is a wedding and special event planning magazine with editorial covering home and home decorating, women's health issues, cooking, beauty and travel." Estab. 1997. Circ. 65,000. Pays on publication. Publishes ms an average of 4 months after acceptance. Accepts queries by mail, e-mail, fax.

Nonfiction: General interest, how-to, interview/profile, personal experience, travel. **Buys 35 mss/year.** Query. Length: 300-3,500 words. **Pays $100-300.** Sometimes pays expenses of writers on assignment.

Photos: State availability with submission. Reviews transparencies. Negotiates payment individually.

Columns/Departments: Wedding related (flowers, beauty, etc.), 450 words, **buys 25 mss/year**; Women's Health, 3,000 words, **buys 1 ms/year**; Home Decorating/Cooking, 400 words, **buys 5 mss/year**; Travel, 350 words, **buys 3 mss/year**. Query. **Pays $100-300.**

Poetry: Avant-garde, free verse, light verse, traditional. **Buys 10 poems/year.** Length: 4-28 lines. **Pays $50-100.**

Fillers: Anecdotes, facts.

Tips: "Be well informed about the wedding planning industry. Most editorial is a 'how-to.' In a constantly changing industry with new styles, techniques, etc. it is important for the writer to keep up to date with trends, ideas, etc."

$ $ $ REDBOOK MAGAZINE, 224 W. 57th St., New York NY 10019. **90% freelance written.** Monthly magazine. "*Redbook* addresses young married women between the ages of 25 and 44. Most of our readers are married with children 12 and under; over 60 percent work outside the home. The articles entertain, educate and inspire our readers to confront challenging issues. Each article must be timely and relevant to *Redbook* readers' lives." Estab. 1903. Circ. 3,200,000. **Pays on acceptance.** Publishes ms an average of 6 months after acceptance. Rights purchased vary with author and material. Responds in 3 months. Writer's guidelines for #10 SASE.

○ᴚ "Please review at least the past six issues of *Redbook* to better understand subject matter and treatment."

Nonfiction: Articles Department. Subjects of interest: Social issues, parenting, sex, marriage, news profiles, true crime, dramatic narratives, money, psychology, health. Query with published clips and SASE. Length: Articles: 2,500-3,000 words; short articles, 1,000-1,500 words.

▣ The online magazine carries original content not found in the print edition. Contact: Jennifer Woodhouse, online editor.

Tips: "Most *Redbook* articles require solid research, well-developed anecdotes from on-the-record sources, and fresh, insightful quotes from established experts in a field that pass our 'reality check' test."

$ $ $ $ ◩ ROSIE, (formerly *McCall's*), Gruner + Jahr, 375 Lexington Ave., New York NY 10017-5514. (212)499-2000. Fax: (212)499-1778. **Contact:** Cathy Cavender, editor-in-chief. **90% freelance written.** Monthly magazine. Circ. 4,200,000. **Pays on acceptance.** Publishes ms an average of 6 months after acceptance. Byline given. Offers 20% kill fee. Buys first North American serial rights. Accepts queries by mail. Responds in 2 months to queries; 2 months to mss.

Nonfiction: The editors are seeking meaningful stories of personal experience and well-researched action-oriented articles and narratives dealing with social problems concerning readers. Topics must have broad appeal, but they must be approached in a fresh, new, you-haven't-read-this-elsewhere way. **Pays $1/word.** Looking for articles on subjects of interest to women: health, personal narratives, celebrity biographies and autobiographies, etc. Almost all features on food, fashion, beauty and decorating are staff-written. **Buys 200-300 mss/year.** Query. Length: 1,500-2,000 words. **Pays $1/word.** Sometimes pays expenses of writers on assignment.

◪ $ $ TODAY'S BRIDE, Family Communications, 37 Hanna Ave., Suite #1, Toronto, Ontario M6K 1W9, Canada. (416)537-2604. Fax: (416)538-1794. Website: www.todaysbride.com. Editor: Bettie Bradley. **Contact:** Tracy Hitchcock, assistant editor. **10% freelance written.** Less than 10%. Semiannual magazine "geared to engaged couples looking for bridal fashion and wedding planning tips. All standard planning pieces and travel are written in-house; freelance articles we purchase look at something unique or different." Estab. 1980. Circ. 108,000. **Pays on acceptance.** Byline given. Buys all rights. Editorial lead time 6 months. Accepts queries by mail, e-mail, fax. Accepts simultaneous submissions. Responds in 1 month to queries.

Nonfiction: Humor, opinion, personal experience. No travel and standard planning pieces (i.e., choosing flowers, music, etc.). Query with or without published clips or send complete ms. Length: 800-1,400 words. **Pays $250-300.**

Reprints: Send tearsheet, photocopy or typed ms with rights for sale noted and information about when and where the material previously appeared. Pays $250-300 (Canadian).

Photos: Send photos with submission. Reviews transparencies, prints. Rights purchased negotiated on individual basis. Negotiates payment individually. Identification of subjects required.

Tips: "Send us tight writing about topics relevant to all brides and grooms (easy on the personal anecdotes). Pieces about exceptionally unique weddings are occasionally accepted. We'd also like to see more articles written by men, especially articles for grooms."

$ $ TODAY'S CHRISTIAN WOMAN, 465 Gundersen Dr., Carol Stream IL 60188-2498. (630)260-6200. Fax: (630)260-0114. E-mail: tcwedit@christianitytoday.com. Website: www.todayschristianwoman.net. Managing Editor: Jane Johnson Struck. Associate Editor: Camerin Courtney. **Contact:** Ginger Kolbaba, associate editor. **50% freelance written.** Bimonthly magazine for Christian women of all ages, single and married, homemakers and career women. "*Today's Christian Woman* seeks to help women deal with the contemporary issues and hot topics that impact their lives, as well as provide depth, balance, and a biblical perspective to the relationships they grapple with daily in the following arenas: Family, friendship, faith, marriage, single life, self, work, and health." Estab. 1979. Circ. 330,000. **Pays on acceptance.** Publishes ms an average of 6 months after acceptance. Byline given. Buys first rights. Submit seasonal material 9 months in advance. Accepts queries by mail, e-mail, fax. Responds in 2 months to queries; 2 months to mss. Sample copy for $5. Writer's guidelines for #10 SASE or online.

Nonfiction: How-to, narrative, inspirational. *Practical* spiritual living articles, 1,500-1,800 words. Humor (light, first-person pieces that include some spiritual distinctive), 1,000-1,500 words. Issues (first-person, true-life stories that give a personal perspective on a current hot topic), 1,500-1,800 words. "The query should include article summary, purpose and reader value, author's qualifications, suggested length, date to send and SASE for reply." How-to, inspirational. Query. *No unsolicited mss.* **Pays 20-25¢/word.**

Columns/Departments: Faith @ Work (recent true story of how you shared your faith with someone on the job), 100-200 words; **pays $25.** My Favorite Web Site (a short description of a web site you've found particularly helpful or interesting), 100 words; **pays $25.** Readers' Picks (a short review of your current favorite CD or book, and why), 200 words; **pays $25.** My Story (1st person, true-life dramatic story of how you solved a problem or overcame a difficult situation), 1,500-1,800 words; **pays $300.** Small Talk (true humorous or inspirational anecdotes about children), 50-100 words; **pays $25.** Does not return or acknowledge submissions to these departments.

Tips: "Articles should be practical and contain a distinct evangelical Christian perspective. While *TCW* adheres strictly to this underlying perspective in all its editorial content, articles should refrain from using language that assumes a reader's familiarity with Christian or church-oriented terminology. Bible quotes and references should be used selectively. All Bible quotes should be taken from the New International Version if possible. All articles should be highly anecdotal, personal in tone, and universal in appeal."

N: $ $ WEDDINGBELLS, WEDDINGBELLS, Inc., 50 Wellington St. E., Suite 200, Toronto, Ontario M5E 1C8, Canada. (416)862-8479. Fax: (416)862-2184. E-mail: info@weddingbells.com. Website: www.weddingbells.com. Editor: Crys Stewart. **Contact:** Michael Killingsworth, managing editor. **10% freelance written.** Semiannual magazine covering bridal, wedding, setting up home. Estab. 1985. Circ. 107,000 (Canada), 325,000 (USA). Pays on completion of assignment. Publishes ms an average of 6 months after acceptance. Byline sometimes given. Offers 25% kill fee. Buys first North American serial, second serial (reprint), electronic rights. Accepts queries by mail, fax. Responds in 2 months to queries; 2 months to mss.

Nonfiction: Book excerpts, bridal service pieces. **Buys 22 mss/year.** Query with published clips. **Pays variable rates for assigned articles.** Sometimes pays expenses of writers on assignment.

N: $ $ $ $ WOMAN'S DAY, 1633 Broadway, 42nd Floor, New York NY 10019. (212)767-6000. Fax: (212)767-5610. Website: www.womansday.com. **Contact:** Jane Chesnutt, editor-in-chief. **75% freelance written.** Magazine published 17 times/year. "*Woman's Day* is written and edited for the contemporary woman. *Woman's Day* editorial package covers the various issues that are important to women today: Food & Nutrition, Health & Fitness, Beauty & Fashion, as well as the traditional values of Home, Family and Children. The changing needs of women are also addressed with articles and more in-depth *WD* Reports that focus on Religion, Money Management, At-Home Business, Law and Relationships." Circ. 6,000,000. **Pays on acceptance.** Byline given. Offers 25% kill fee. Responds in 1 month to queries.

Nonfiction: Uses articles on all subjects of interest to women—family life, childrearing, education, homemaking, money management, careers, family health, work and leisure activities. Also interested in fresh, dramatic narratives of women's lives and concerns. "These must be lively to read with a high emotional content." **Payment varies** depending on length, type, writer, and whether it's for regional or national use, but rates are high. Pays a bonus fee in addition to regular rate for articles based on writer's ideas (as opposed to assigned story.) Bonus fee is an additional 20% of fee (up to $500). "We no longer accept unsolicited manuscripts except for backtalk essays of 750 words—and cannot return or be responsible for those that are sent to us." Length: 500-1,500 depending on material. Pays expenses of writers on assignment.

Columns/Departments: "We welcome short (750 words), thought-provoking spirited essays on controversial topics for Back Talk page. We prefer to cover significant issues that concern a large number of women and families rather than the slight or trivial or those that affect only a few. Essays are usually based on personal experience and always written in the first person, but they must have reader identification." Submit completed essays only, no queries, with SASE. **Pays $2,000.**

Fillers: Neighbors columns **pay $75/each** for brief practical suggestions on homemaking, childrearing and relationships. Address to the editor of the section.

Tips: "Our primary need is for ideas with broad appeal that can be featured on the cover. These include diet stories, organizing tips and money saving information. We're buying more short pieces. Submissions must be double spaced and must include a SASE and clips. Faxes and e-mails will not be read."

$ $ WOMEN IN BUSINESS, American Business Women's Association (The ABWA Company Inc.), 9100 Ward Pkwy., P.O. Box 8728, Kansas City MO 64114-0728. (816)361-6621. Fax: (816)361-4991. E-mail: abwa@abwahq.org. Website: www.abwa.org. **Contact:** Rachel Warbington, editor. **30% freelance written.** Bimonthly magazine covering issues affecting working women. "How-to features for career women on business trends, small-business ownership, self-improvement and retirement issues. Profiles of ABWA members only." Estab. 1949. Circ. 90,000. **Pays on acceptance.** Publishes ms an average of 3 months after acceptance. Byline given. Buys first North American serial rights. Editorial lead time 3 months. Accepts queries by mail, e-mail, fax. Accepts simultaneous submissions. Responds in 3 weeks to queries; 2 months to mss. Sample copy for 9×12 SAE and 4 first-class stamps. Writer's guidelines for #10 SASE.

O→ Break in by "having knowledge of the business world and how women fit into it."

Nonfiction: How-to, interview/profile (ABWA members only), computer/Internet. No fiction or poetry. **Buys 3% of submitted mss/year.** Query. Length: 1,000-1,500 words. **Pays variable rates.**

Photos: State availability with submission. Reviews 3×5 prints. Buys all rights. Offers no additional payment for photos accepted with ms. Identification of subjects required.

Columns/Departments: Life After Business (concerns of retired business women); It's Your Business (entrepreneurial advice for business owners); Career Smarts (career advice for every woman). Length: 315-700 words. Query. **Payment varies.**

Tips: "All articles must feature ABWA members as sources."

Trade, Technical & Professional Journals

Many writers who pick up a *Writer's Market* for the first time do so with the hope of selling an article or story to one of the popular, high-profile consumer magazines found on newsstands and in bookstores. Many of those writers are surprised to find an entire world of magazine publishing that exists outside the realm of commercial magazines and that they may have never known about—trade journals. Writers who *have* discovered trade journals have found a market that offers the chance to publish regularly in subject areas they find interesting, editors who are typically more accessible than their commercial counterparts and pay rates that rival those of the big-name magazines.

Trade journal is the general term for any publication focusing on a particular occupation or industry. Other terms used to describe the different types of trade publications are business, technical and professional journals. They are read by truck drivers, brick layers, farmers, fishermen, heart surgeons—let's not forget butchers, bakers, and candlestick makers—and just about everyone else working in a trade or profession. Trade periodicals are sharply angled to the specifics of the professions they report on. They offer business-related news, features and service articles that will foster their readers' professional development. A beautician reads *American Salon* to keep up with developments in hair care and cosmetics as well as business management. Readers of *Wine Business Monthly* find the latest news and information about viticulture.

Trade magazine editors tell us their readers are a knowledgeable and highly interested audience. Writers for trade magazines have to either possess knowledge about the field in question or be able to report it accurately from interviews with those who do. Writers who have or can develop a good grasp of a specialized body of knowledge will find trade magazine editors who are eager to hear from them. And since good writers with specialized knowledge are a somewhat rare commodity, trade editors tend, more than typical consumer magazine editors, to cultivate ongoing relationships with writers. If you can prove yourself as a writer who "delivers," you will be paid back with frequent assignments and regular paychecks.

An ideal way to begin your foray into trade journals is to write for those that report on your present profession. Whether you've been teaching dance, farming or working as a paralegal, begin by familiarizing yourself with the magazines that serve your occupation. After you've read enough issues to have a feel for the kinds of pieces they run, approach the editors with your own article ideas. If you don't have experience in a profession but can demonstrate an ability to understand (and write about) the intricacies and issues of a particular trade that interests you, editors will still be willing to hear from you.

Photographs help increase the value of most stories for trade journals. If you can provide photos, mention that in your query or send copies. Since selling photos with a story usually means a bigger paycheck, it is worth any freelancer's time to develop basic camera skills.

Query a trade journal as you would a consumer magazine. Most trade editors like to discuss an article with a writer first and will sometimes offer names of helpful sources. Mention any direct experience you may have in the industry in your cover letter. Send a resume and clips if they show you have some background or related experience in the subject area. Read each listing carefully for additional submission guidelines.

To stay abreast of new trade magazines starting up, watch for news in *Folio:* and *Advertising Age* magazines. Another source for information about trade publications is the *Business Publica-*

tion Advertising Source, published by Standard Rate and Data Service (SRDS) and available in most libraries. Designed primarily for people who buy ad space, the volume provides names and addresses of thousands of trade journals, listed by subject matter.

Information on trade publications listed in the previous edition of *Writer's Market* but not included in this edition can be found in the General Index.

ADVERTISING, MARKETING & PR

Trade journals for advertising executives, copywriters and marketing and public relations professionals are listed in this category. Those whose main focus is the advertising and marketing of specific products, such as home furnishings, are classified under individual product categories. Journals for sales personnel and general merchandisers can be found in the Selling & Merchandising category.

$ $ $ BRAND PACKAGING, Independent Publishing Co., 210 S. Fifth St., St. Charles IL 60174. (630)377-0100. Fax: (630)377-1688. E-mail: jpeters@brandpackaging.com. Website: www.brandpackaging.com. Managing Editor: Lisa Joerin. **Contact:** James W. Peters, editor. **15% freelance written.** Bimonthly magazine covering how packaging can be a marketing tool. "We publish strategies and tactics to make products stand out on the shelf. Our market is brand managers who are marketers but need to know something about packaging." Estab. 1997. Circ. 35,000. **Pays on acceptance.** Publishes ms an average of 2 months after acceptance. Byline given. Makes work-for-hire assignments. Editorial lead time 3 months. Submit seasonal material 3 months in advance. Accepts queries by mail, fax. Sample copy and writer's guidelines free.
Nonfiction: How-to, interview/profile, new product. **Buys 30 mss/year.** Send complete ms. Length: 600-2,400 words. **Pays $150-1,200.**
Photos: State availability with submission. Reviews contact sheets, 35mm transparencies, 4×5 prints. Buys one-time rights. Negotiates payment individually. Identification of subjects required.
Columns/Departments: Whatever happened to... (packaging failures); New Technology (new packaging technology), both 600 words. **Buys 20 mss/year.** Query. **Pays $150-400.**
■ The online magazine carries original content not found in the print edition.
Tips: "Be knowledgeable on marketing techniques and be able to grasp packaging techniques. Be sure you focus on packaging as a marketing tool. Use concrete examples. We are not seeking case histories at this time."

$ DECA DIMENSIONS, 1908 Association Dr., Reston VA 20191. (703)860-5000. Fax: (703)860-4013. E-mail: carol_lund@deca.org. Website: www.DECA.org. **Contact:** Cindy Sweeney, editor. **30% freelance written.** Bimonthly magazine covering professional development, business, career training. "*Deca Dimensions* is the membership magazine for the Association of Marketing Students—primarily ages 16-20 in all 50 states and Canada. The magazine is delivered through the classroom. Students are interested in developing professional, leadership and career skills." Estab. 1947. Circ. 160,000. Pays on publication. Byline given. Buys first, second serial (reprint) rights. Editorial lead time 3 months. Submit seasonal material 4 months in advance. Accepts queries by mail, e-mail, fax, phone. Accepts simultaneous submissions. Sample copy free.
Nonfiction: "Interested in seeing trends/forecast information of interest to audience (how do you forecast? why? what are the trends for the next 5 years in fashion or retail?)." Essays, general interest, how-to (get jobs, start business, plan for college, etc.), interview/profile (business leads), personal experience (working), leadership development. **Buys 10 mss/year.** Send complete ms. Length: 800-1,000 words. **Pays $125 for assigned articles; $100 for unsolicited articles.**
Reprints: Send photocopy and information about when and where the material previously appeared. Pays 85% of amount paid for an original article.
Photos: State availability with submission. Reviews negatives, transparencies, prints. Buys one-time rights. Offers $15-25/photo. Captions required.
Columns/Departments: Professional development, leadership, 350-500 words. **Buys 6 mss/year.** Send complete ms. **Pays $75-100.**
Fillers: Anecdotes, facts, short humor. Length: 50-200 words. **Pays $25-50.**

MEDIA INC., Pacific Northwest Media, Marketing and Creative Services News, P.O. Box 24365, Seattle WA 98124-0365. (206)382-9220. Fax: (206)382-9437. E-mail: media@media-inc.com. Website: www.media-inc.com. Publisher: James Baker. **Contact:** Elizabeth Bye, editor. **30% freelance written.** Quarterly magazine covering Northwest US media, advertising, marketing and creative-service industries. Audience is Northwest ad agencies, marketing professionals, media and creative-service professionals. Estab. 1987. Circ. 10,000. Byline given. Responds in 1 month to queries. Sample copy for 9×12 SAE and 6 first-class stamps.
Tips: "It is best if writers live in the Pacific Northwest and can report on local news and events in Media Inc.'s areas of business coverage."

$ $ SIGNCRAFT, The Magazine for Today's Sign Maker, SignCraft Publishing Co., Inc., P.O. Box 60031, Fort Myers FL 33906. (941)939-4644. Fax: (941)939-0607. E-mail: signcraft@signcraft.com. Website: www.signcraft.com. **Contact:** Tom McIltrot, editor. **10% freelance written.** Bimonthly magazine covering the sign industry. "Like any trade magazine, we need material of direct benefit to our readers. We can't afford space for material of marginal interest." Estab. 1980. Circ. 16,000. Pays on publication. Publishes ms an average of 6 months after acceptance. Byline given. Offers negotiable kill fee. Buys first North American serial, all rights. Accepts queries by mail, e-mail, fax. Responds in 1 month to queries. Sample copy and writer's guidelines for $3.
Nonfiction: "All articles should be directly related to quality commercial signs. If you are familiar with the sign trade, we'd like to hear from you." Interview/profile. **Buys 10 mss/year.** Query with or without published clips. Length: 500-2,000 words. **Pays up to $350.**
Reprints: Accepts previously published submissions.

$ $ SIGNS OF THE TIMES, The Industry Journal Since 1906, ST Publications, Dept. WM, 407 Gilbert Ave., Cincinnati OH 45202-2285. (513)421-2050. Fax: (513)421-5144. E-mail: sconner@stpubs.com. Website: www.signweb.com. **Contact:** Susan Conner, senior editor. **15-30% freelance written.** Monthly magazine covering the sign and outdoor advertising industries. Estab. 1906. Circ. 17,000. Pays on publication. Publishes ms an average of 3 months after acceptance. Byline given. Buys variable rights. Accepts queries by mail, e-mail, fax, phone. Responds in 3 months to queries. Sample copy and writer's guidelines for $9×12$ SAE with 10 first-class stamps.
Nonfiction: Historical/nostalgic (regarding the sign industry), how-to (carved signs, goldleaf, etc.), interview/profile (focusing on either a signshop or a specific project), photo feature (query first), technical (sign engineering, etc.). Nothing "nonspecific on signs, an example being a photo essay on 'signs I've seen.' We are a trade journal with specific audience interests." **Buys 15-20 mss/year.** Query with published clips. **Pays $150-500.**
Reprints: Send tearsheet or typed ms with rights for sale noted and information about when and where the material previously appeared. Payment is negotiated.
Photos: "Sign industry-related photos only. We sometimes accept photos with funny twists or misspellings." Send photos with submission.
Fillers: Open to queries; request rates.
　　■ The online magazine carries original content not found in the print edition.
Tips: "Be thoroughly familiar with the sign industry, especially in the CAS-related area. Have an insider's knowledge plus an insider's contacts."

ART, DESIGN & COLLECTIBLES

The businesses of art, art administration, architecture, environmental/package design and antiques/collectibles are covered in these listings. Art-related topics for the general public are located in the Consumer Art & Architecture category. Antiques and collectibles magazines for enthusiasts are listed in Consumer Hobby & Craft. (Listings of markets looking for freelance artists to do artwork can be found in *Artist's and Graphic Designer's Market*, Writer's Digest Books.)

$ AIRBRUSH ACTION MAGAZINE, Airbrush Action, Inc., 1985 Swarthmore Ave., Lakewood NJ 08701. (732)364-2111. Fax: (732)367-5908. E-mail: cstieglitz@monmouth.com. Website: www.airbrushaction.com. **Contact:** Kate Priest, editor. **80% freelance written.** Bimonthly magazine covering the spectrum of airbrush applications: Illustration, t-shirt airbrushing, fine art, automotive and sign painting, hobby/craft applications, wall murals, fingernails, body airbrushing, artist profiles, reviews and more. Estab. 1985. Circ. 60,000. Pays in 30 days. Publishes ms an average of 6 months after acceptance. Byline given. Offers 50% kill fee. Buys all rights. Editorial lead time 6 months. Submit seasonal material 6 months in advance. Accepts queries by mail, e-mail, fax, phone. Accepts simultaneous submissions. Sample copy and writer's guidelines free.
Nonfiction: How-to, humor, inspirational, interview/profile, new product, personal experience, technical. Nothing unrelated to airbrush. Query with published clips. **Pays 10¢/word.** Sometimes pays expenses of writers on assignment.
Photos: Send photos with submission. Buys all rights. Negotiates payment individually. Captions, identification of subjects, model releases required.
Columns/Departments: Query with published clips.
　　■ The online magazine carries original content not found in the print edition. Contact: Cliff Stieglitz.
Tips: "Send bio and writing samples. Send well-written technical information pertaining to airbrush art. We publish a lot of artist profiles—they all sound the same. Looking for new pizzazz!"

[N] $ THE APPRAISERS STANDARD, New England Appraisers Association, 5 Gill Terrace, Ludlow VT 05149-1003. (802)228-7444. E-mail: llt44@ludl.tds.net. **Contact:** Linda L. Tucker, publisher/editor. **50% freelance written.** Works with a small number of new/unpublished writers each year. Quarterly magazine covering the appraisals of antiques, art, collectibles, jewelry, coins, stamps and real estate. "The writer should be extremely knowledgeable on the subject, and the article should be written with appraisers in mind, with prices quoted for objects, good pictures and descriptions of articles being written about.'. Estab. 1980. Circ. 1,300. Pays on publication. Publishes ms an average of

1 year after acceptance. Short bio and byline given. Buys first and simultaneous rights. Submit seasonal material 2 months in advance. Accepts queries by mail, e-mail. Accepts simultaneous submissions. Responds in 1 month to queries; 2 months to mss. Sample copy for 9×12 SAE with 78¢ postage. Writer's guidelines for #10 SASE.

Nonfiction: "All geared toward professional appraisers." Interview/profile, personal experience, technical, travel. Query with or without published clips or send complete ms. Length: 700 words. **Pays $50.**

Reprints: Send typed ms with rights for sale noted and information about when and where the material previously appeared.

Photos: Send photos with submission. Reviews negatives, prints. Buys one-time rights. Offers no additional payment for photos accepted with ms. Identification of subjects required.

Tips: "Interviewing members of the association for articles, reviewing, shows and large auctions are all ways for writers who are not in the field to write articles for us. Articles should be geared to provide information which will help the appraisers with ascertaining value, detecting forgeries or reproductions, or simply providing advice on appraising the articles.

N $ $ $ $ ARCHITECTURAL RECORD, McGraw-Hill, 2 Penn Plaza, 9th Floor, New York NY 10121. (212)904-2594. Fax: (212)904-4256. Website: www.architecturalrecord.com. Editor: Robert Ivy, FAIA, Managing Editor: Ingrid Whitehead. **Contact:** Linda Ransey. **50% freelance written.** Monthly magazine covering architecture and design. "Our readers are architects, designers and related professionals." Estab. 1891. Circ. 102,000. Pays on publication. Publishes ms an average of 2 months after acceptance. Byline given. Offers 25% kill fee. Buys all rights. Editorial lead time 2 months. Submit seasonal material 2 months in advance. Accepts queries by mail. Responds in 2 weeks to queries; 2 months to mss. Sample copy and writer's guidelines online.

$ $ $ HOW, Design Ideas at Work, F&W Publications, Inc., 1507 Dana Ave., Cincinnati OH 45207-1005. (513)531-2222. Fax: (513)531-2902. E-mail: editorial@howdesign.com. Website: www.howdesign.com. **Contact:** Bryn Mooth, editor. **75% freelance written.** Bimonthly magazine covering graphic design and illustration business. "*HOW: Design Ideas at Work* strives to serve the business, technological and creative needs of graphic-design professionals. The magazine provides a practical mix of essential business information, up-to-date technological tips, the creative whys and hows behind noteworthy projects, and profiles of professionals who are impacting design. The ultimate goal of *HOW* is to help designers, whether they work for a design firm or for an inhouse design department, run successful, creative, profitable studios." Estab. 1985. Circ. 38,000. **Pays on acceptance.** Byline given. Buys first North American serial rights. Responds in 6 weeks to queries. Sample copy for cover price plus $1.50 (cover price varies per issue). Writer's guidelines for #10 SASE.

Nonfiction: Interview/profile, new product, business tips, environmental graphics, digital design, hot design markets. Special issues: Self-Promotion Annual (September/October); Business Annual (November/December); International Annual of Design (March/April); Creativity/Paper/Stock Photography (May/June); Digital Design Annual (July/August). No how-to articles for beginning artists or fine-art-oriented articles. **Buys 40 mss/year.** Query with published clips and samples of subject's work, artwork or design. Length: 1,500-2,000 words. **Pays $700-900.** Sometimes pays expenses of writers on assignment.

Photos: State availability with submission. Reviews information updated and verified. Buys one-time rights. Captions required.

Columns/Departments: Design Disciplines (focuses on lucrative fields for designers/illustrators); Production (ins, outs and tips on production); Interactivity (behind the scenes of electronically produced design projects); Software Review and Workspace (takes an inside look at the design of creatives' studios). Other columns include Tech FAQ (answers to readers questions) and Biz Tips (business issues that impact design studios), 1,200-1,500 words. **Buys 35 mss/year.** Query with published clips. **Pays $250-400.**

Tips: "We look for writers who can recognize graphic designers on the cutting-edge of their industry, both creatively and business-wise. Writers must have an eye for detail, and be able to relay *HOW*'s step-by-step approach in an interesting, concise manner—without omitting any details. Showing you've done your homework on a subject—and that you can go beyond asking 'those same old questions'—will give you a big advantage."

$ $ LETTER ARTS REVIEW, 1302 Greenbriar Dr., Norman OK 73072. Fax: (405)364-8914. E-mail: lar@wavelin x.net. Website: www.letterarts.com. **Contact:** Karyn L. Gilman, editor. **98% freelance written.** Quarterly magazine covering lettering and related book arts, both historical and contemporary in nature. Eager to work with new/unpublished writers with calligraphic expertise and language skills. Estab. 1982. Circ. 5,500. Pays on publication. Publishes ms an average of 9 months after acceptance. Byline given. Offers 20% kill fee. Buys first rights. Accepts queries by mail, e-mail, fax. Responds in 3 months to queries. Sample copy for 9×12 SAE and 8 first-class stamps. Writer's guidelines for #10 SASE.

Nonfiction: Historical/nostalgic, interview/profile, opinion, contemporary. **Buys 50 mss/year.** Query with or without published clips or send complete ms. Length: 1,000-2,000 words. **Pays $50-250 for assigned articles; $25-200 for unsolicited articles.** Sometimes pays expenses of writers on assignment.

Photos: State availability with submission. Reviews contact sheets, negatives, transparencies, prints. Buys one-time rights. Pays agreed upon cost. Captions, identification of subjects required.

Columns/Departments: Book Reviews, Viewpoint (critical), 500-1,500 words; Ms. (discussion of manuscripts in collections), 1,000-2,000 words; Profile (contemporary calligraphic figure), 1,000-2,000 words; exhibition reviews; font reviews. Query. **Pays $50-200.**

Tips: "*Letter Arts Review*'s primary objective is to encourage the exchange of ideas on calligraphy and the lettering arts—its past and present as well as trends for the future. Historical research, typography, graphic design, fine press and artists' books, and other related aspects of the lettering arts are welcomed. Third person is preferred, however first person will be considered if appropriate. Writer should realize that this is a specialized audience."

N: $ $TEXAS ARCHITECT, Texas Society of Architects, 816 Congress Ave., Suite 970, Austini TX 78701. (512)478-7386. Fax: (512)478-0528. E-mail: xssharpe@texasarchitect.org. Website: www.texasarchitect.org. Publisher: Canan Yetmen. **Contact:** Stephen Sharpe, editor. **30% freelance written.** Mostly written by unpaid members of the professional society. Bimonthly journal covering architecture and architects of Texas. "*Texas Architect* is a highly visually-oriented look at Texas architecture, design and urban planning. Articles cover varied subtopics within architecture. Readers are mostly architects and related building professionals." Estab. 1951. Circ. 12,000. Pays on publication. Publishes ms an average of 3 months after acceptance. Byline given. Buys one-time, all rights, makes work-for-hire assignments. Submit seasonal material 4 months in advance. Accepts queries by mail, e-mail. Responds in 6 weeks to queries. Sample copy and writer's guidelines free or online.
Nonfiction: Interview/profile, photo feature, technical, Book reviews. Query with published clips. Length: 100-2,000 words. **Pays $50-100 for assigned articles.**
Photos: Send photos with submission. Reviews contact sheets, 35mm or 4×5 transparencies, 4×5 prints. Buys one-time rights. Offers no additional payment for photos accepted with ms. Identification of subjects required.
Columns/Departments: News (timely reports on architectural issues, projects and people), 100-500 words. **Buys 10 mss/year.** Query with published clips. **Pays $50-100.**

AUTO & TRUCK

These publications are geared to automobile, motorcycle and truck dealers; professional truck drivers; service department personnel; or fleet operators. Publications for highway planners and traffic control experts are listed in the Government & Public Service category.

$ $AUTO RENTAL NEWS, Bobit Publishing Co., 21061 S. Western Ave., Torrance CA 90501. (310)533-2470. Fax: (310)533-2503. E-mail: cathy.stephens@bobit.com. Website: www.autorentalnews.com. **Contact:** Cathy Stephens, executive editor. **33% freelance written.** Bimonthly magazine covering auto rental. Estab. 1986. Circ. 17,000. Pays on publication. Publishes ms an average of 4 months after acceptance. Byline given. Buys first, electronic rights. Editorial lead time 2 months. Submit seasonal material 1 month in advance. Accepts queries by mail, e-mail, fax. Sample copy and writer's guidelines free.
Nonfiction: How-to, new product, travel. **Buys 10 mss/year.** Query with published clips. Length: 1,800-2,500 words. **Pays $100-400.** Sometimes pays expenses of writers on assignment.
Photos: Send photos with submission. Reviews prints. Buys one time rights. Offers no additional payment for photos accepted with ms. Identification of subjects required.

N: $ $AUTOINC., Automotive Service Association, 1901 Airport Freeway, Bedford TX 76021. (817)283-6205. Fax: (817)685-0225. E-mail: editor@asashop.org. Website: www.autoinc.org. Managing Editor: Levy Joffrion. **Contact:** Angie Wilson, editor. **25% freelance written.** Monthly magazine covering independent automotive repair. "The mission of *AutoInc.*, ASA's official publication, is to be the informational authority for ASA and industry members nationwide. Its purpose is to enhance the professionalism of these members through management, technical and legislative articles, researched and written with the highest regard for accuracy, quality and integrity." Estab. 1952. Circ. 16,000. Pays on publication. Publishes ms an average of 2 months after acceptance. Byline given. Buys all rights. Editorial lead time 2 months. Accepts queries by mail, e-mail, fax. Accepts simultaneous submissions. Responds in 6 weeks to queries; 2 months to mss. Sample copy for $5 or online. Writer's guidelines online or by e-mail.
Nonfiction: How-to (automotive repair), technical. No book reviews, product or company-oriented material. **Buys 10 mss/year.** Query with published clips. Length: 1,200-1,700 words. **Pays $250-500.** Sometimes pays expenses of writers on assignment.
Photos: State availability of or send photos with submission. Reviews 2×3 transparencies, 3×5 prints. Buys one-time and electronic rights. Negotiates payment individually. Captions, identification of subjects, model releases required.
Tips: "Learn about the automotive repair industry, specifically the independent shop segment. Understand the high-tech requirements needed to succeed today."

$ $BUSINESS FLEET, Managing 10-50 Company Vehicles, Bobit Publishing, 21061 S. Western Ave., Torrance CA 90501-1711. (310)533-2592. Fax: (310)533-2503. E-mail: steve.elliott@bobit.com. Website: www.businessfleet.com. **Contact:** Steve Elliott, executive editor. **30% freelance written.** Bimonthly magazine covering businesses which operate 10-50 company vehicles. "While it's a trade publication aimed at a business audience, *Business Fleet* has a lively, conversational style. The best way to get a feel for our 'slant' is to read the magazine." Estab. 2000. Circ. 100,000. **Pays on acceptance.** Publishes ms an average of 2 months after acceptance. Byline given. Offers 25% kill

fee. Buys first, second serial (reprint), electronic rights. Editorial lead time 2 months. Submit seasonal material 2 months in advance. Accepts queries by mail, e-mail, fax. Responds in 2 weeks to queries; 2 months to mss. Sample copy and writer's guidelines free.
Nonfiction: How-to, interview/profile, new product, personal experience, photo feature, technical. **Buys 16 mss/year.** Query with published clips. Length: 500-2,000 words. **Pays $50-400.** Pays with contributor copies or other premiums by prior arrangement. Sometimes pays expenses of writers on assignment.
Photos: State availability with submission. Reviews 3×5 prints. Buys one-time, reprint and electronic rights. Negotiates payment individually. Captions required.
 The online magazine carries original content not found in the print edition. Contact: Steve Elliott, online editor.
Tips: "Our mission is to educate our target audience on more economical and efficient ways of operating small fleets, and to inform the audience of the latest vehicles, products, and services available to small commercial companies. Be knowledgeable about automotive and fleet-oriented subjects."

CALTRUX, Moving the Industry That Moves California, California Trucking Association, 3251 Beacon Blvd., West Sacramento CA 95691. (916)373-3500. Fax: (916)373-3664. E-mail: whoemann@caltrux.org. Website: www.caltrux.org. **Contact:** Warren Hoemann, editor. **10% freelance written.** Monthly magazine covering the trucking industry in California. "We feature news and information impacting the second-largest industry in the state, which provides jobs for one in twelve working Californians. Readership: 2,500 association member companies, state legislature, highway patrol, regulatory agencies." Estab. 1949. Circ. 4,400. Pays on publication. Publishes ms an average of 3 months after acceptance. Byline given. Buys first North American serial rights, negotiable. Editorial lead time 3 months. Submit seasonal material 6 months in advance. Accepts queries by mail, e-mail, fax. Accepts simultaneous submissions. Sample copy for 9×12 SAE and 2 first-class stamps. Writer's guidelines for #10 SASE.
Nonfiction: "We look for feature material of high interest to the decision-makers of California's trucking industry." Interview/profile, photo feature, technical. **Buys 10-15 mss/year.** Query with published clips. Length: 500-1,500 words. **Sometimes pays writers in endorsements.**
Photos: State availability of or send photos with submission. Reviews contact sheets. Buys negotiable rights. Negotiates payment individually. Captions, identification of subjects, model releases required.
Columns/Departments: Query with published clips.
Tips: "Material must be of immediate importance to the California trucking company decision-maker, or of long-term interest."

$ $ FLEET EXECUTIVE, The Magazine of Vehicle Management, The National Association of Fleet Administrators, Inc., 100 Wood Ave. S, Suite 310, Iselin NJ 08830-2716. (732)494-8100. Fax: (732)494-6789. E-mail: publications@nafa.org. Website: www.nafa.org. **Contact:** Jessica Sypniewski, managing editor. **50% freelance written.** Monthly magazine covering automotive fleet management. "*NAFA Fleet Executive* focuses on car, van and light-duty truck management in U.S. and Canadian corporations, government agencies and utilities. Editorial emphasis is on general automotive issues; improving jobs skills, productivity and professionalism; legislation and regulation; alternative fuels; safety; interviews with prominent industry personalities; technology; Association news; public service fleet management; and light-duty truck fleet management." Estab. 1957. Circ. 4,000. Pays on publication. Publishes ms an average of 4 months after acceptance. Buys all rights. Editorial lead time 2 months. Accepts queries by mail, e-mail, fax. Accepts simultaneous submissions. Responds in 1 month to queries. Sample copy online. Writer's guidelines free.
Nonfiction: "NAFA hosts its Fleet Management Institute, an educational conference and trade show, which is held in a different city in the U.S. and Canada each year. *Fleet Executive* would consider articles on regional attractions, particularly those that might be of interest to those in the automotive industry, for use in a conference preview issue of the magazine. The preview issue is published one month prior to the conference. Information about the conference, its host city, and conference dates in a give year may be found on NAFA's Web site, www.nafa.org, or by calling the association at (732)494-8100." Interview/profile, technical. **Buys 12 mss/year.** Query with published clips. Length: 500-3,000 words. **Pays $500 maximum.**
Photos: State availability with submission. Reviews electronic images.
Tips: "The sample articles online at www.nafa.org/admenu.htm should help writers get a feel of the journalistic style we require."

$ $ GLASS DIGEST, Ashlee Publishing, 18 E. 41st St., New York NY 10017. (212)376-7722. Fax: (212)376-7723. E-mail: shannon@ashlee.com. Website: www.ashlee.com. **Contact:** Shannon Scharkey, editor. **15% freelance written.** Monthly magazine covering flat glass, glazing, auto glass. Estab. 1921. Pays on publication. Publishes ms an average of 2 months after acceptance. Byline given. Buys first, all rights, makes work-for-hire assignments. Editorial lead time 3 months. Accepts queries by mail, e-mail, fax. Accepts simultaneous submissions.
Nonfiction: Photo feature, technical. "No reports on stained glass hobbyists or art glass." **Buys 16-20 mss/year.** Query. Length: 1,000-2,000 words. **Pays $100-400.** Sometimes pays expenses of writers on assignment.
Photos: State availability with submission. Negotiates payment individually. Identification of subjects required.
Tips: "Architecturally interesting projects with good photography make excellent features for *Glass Digest*."

N $ $ NEW ENGLAND MECHANIC, P.O. Box M, Franklin MA 02038. (508)528-6211. **Contact:** M. Zingraff, managing editor. **40% freelance written.** Bimonthly newspaper covering automotive repair, testing, maintenance. "Our slant on technical information is both for advanced technician and apprentice. We cover news on laws and regulations, some management information and profiles of shops and wholesales." Estab. 1996. Circ. 5,000. **Pays on acceptance.** Byline given. Offers 50% kill fee on assignments only. Buys one-time, second serial (reprint) rights. Editorial lead time 1 month. Responds in 2 months to queries. Writer's guidelines for #10 SASE.

Nonfiction: General interest, how-to, interview/profile, technical. **Buys 18 mss/year.** Query with published clips. Length: 500-1,500 words. **Pays $100-200 for assigned articles; $35-100 for unsolicited articles.**

Photos: State availability with submission. Reviews contact sheets, 3×5 or larger prints. Buys one-time rights. Pays $25 for first photo, $10 each additional photos in series. Captions, identification of subjects required.

Columns/Departments: Query.

Fillers: Facts. **Buys 6/year.** Length: 150 words. **Pays $25-50.**

$ $ OVERDRIVE, The Voice of the American Trucker, Randall Publishing Co./Overdrive, Inc., 3200 Rice Mine Rd., Tuscaloosa AL 35406. (205)349-2990. Fax: (205)750-8070. E-mail: mheine@randallpub.com. Website: www. etrucker.net. Editorial Director: Linda Longton. **Contact:** Max Heine, senior editor. **10% freelance written.** Monthly magazine for independent truckers. Estab. 1961. Circ. 140,000. Pays on publication. Publishes ms an average of 2 months after acceptance. Byline given. Offers 10% kill fee. Buys all North American rights, including electronic rights. Responds in 2 months to queries. Sample copy and writer's guidelines for 9×12 SASE.

Nonfiction: All must be related to independent trucker interest. Essays, exposé, how-to (truck maintenance and operation), interview/profile (successful independent truckers), personal experience, photo feature, technical. Query with or without published clips or send complete ms. Length: 500-2,000 words. **Pays $200-1,000 for assigned articles.**

Photos: Send photos with submission. Reviews transparencies, prints and slides. Buys all rights. Offers $25-150/photo.

Tips: "Talk to independent truckers. Develop a good knowledge of their concerns as small-business owners, truck drivers and individuals. We prefer articles that quote experts, people in the industry and truckers to first-person expositions on a subject. Get straight facts. Look for good material on truck safety, on effects of government regulations, and on rates and business relationships between independent truckers, brokers, carriers and shippers."

$ PML, The Market Letter for Porsche Automobiles, PML Consulting, P.O. Box 6010, Oceanside CA 92058. (760)940-9170. Fax: (760)940-9170. E-mail: pat@pmletter.com. Website: www.pmletter.com. **Contact:** Pat Van Buskirk, owner. **100% freelance written.** Monthly magazine covering technical tips, personality profiles and race coverage of Porsche automobiles. Estab. 1981. Circ. 1,500. Pays on publication. Publishes ms an average of 2 months after acceptance. Byline given. Buys one-time rights. Editorial lead time 2 months. Submit seasonal material 2 months in advance. Accepts queries by mail, e-mail, fax, phone. Accepts simultaneous submissions. Responds in 2 weeks to queries; 1 month to mss. Sample copy for $5. Writer's guidelines for #10 SASE.

Nonfiction: General interest, historical/nostalgic, how-to, humor, interview/profile, new product, personal experience, photo feature, technical, travel, race results. **Buys 30-40 mss/year.** Query with published clips. Length: 500-2,000 words. **Pays $30-50 and up, depending on length and topic.** Sometimes pays expenses of writers on assignment.

Photos: Send photos with submission. Reviews 8×10 b&w prints. Buys one-time rights. Negotiates payment individually. Captions, identification of subjects, model releases required.

Fillers: Anecdotes, facts, gags to be illustrated by cartoonist, newsbreaks, short humor. **Pays negotiable amount.**

Tips: "Check any auto-related magazine for types, styles of articles. We are looking for people doing anything unusual or interesting in the Porsche world. Submit well-prepared, thoroughly-edited articles with photos."

$ $ ROAD KING MAGAZINE, For the Professional Driver, Hammock Publishing, Inc., 3322 West End Ave. #700, Nashville TN 37203. (615)385-9745. Fax: (615)386-9349. E-mail: roadking@hammock.com. Website: www.road king.com. Editor: Tom Berg. **Contact:** Bill Hudgins, editor-in-chief. **80% freelance written.** Bimonthly magazine. "*Road King* is published bimonthly for long-haul truckers. It celebrates the lifestyle and work and profiles interesting and/or successful drivers. It also reports on subjects of interest to our audience, including outdoors, vehicles, music and trade issues." Estab. 1963. Circ. 229,900. **Pays on acceptance.** Publishes ms an average of 4 months after acceptance. Byline given. Offers negotiable kill fee. Buys first North American serial, electronic rights. Editorial lead time 3 months. Submit seasonal material 4 months in advance. Accepts queries by mail, e-mail. Responds in 2 months to queries. Sample copy for 9×12 SAE and 5 first-class stamps. Writer's guidelines for #10 SASE.

Nonfiction: How-to (trucking-related), humor, interview/profile, new product, personal experience, photo feature, technical, travel. Special issues: RoadRunner Tools (the latest tools, techniques and industry developments to help them run a smarter, more efficient trucking business; Haul of Fame (salutes drivers whose work or type of rig makes them unique); At Home on the Road ("creature comfort" products, services and information for the road life, including what's new, useful, interesting or fun for cyber-trucking drivers); Fleet Focus (asks fleet management about what their companies offer, and drivers about why they like it there); Weekend Wheels (from Harleys to Hondas, most drivers have a passion for their "other" set of wheels. This section looks at this aspect of drivers' lives). "No fiction, poetry." **Buys 20 mss/year.** Query with published clips. Length: 850-2,000 words. **Pay negotiable.** Sometimes pays expenses of writers on assignment.

Photos: State availability with submission. Reviews contact sheets. Buys negotiable rights. Negotiates payment individually. Identification of subjects, model releases required.

Columns/Departments: Lead Driver (profile of outstanding trucker), 250-500 words; Roadrunner (new products, services suited to the business of trucking or to truckers' lifestyles), 100-250 words. **Buys 6-10 mss/year.** Query. **Pay negotiable.**

Fillers: Anecdotes, facts, gags to be illustrated by cartoonist, short humor. Length: 100-250 words. **Pays $50.**

⬛ The online magazine of *Road King* carries original content not found in the print edition. Contact: Bill Hudgins.

$ $ **RV TRADE DIGEST, Your Source for Management, Marketing and Production Information**, Cygnus Business Media Inc., 1233 Janeville Ave., Fort Atkinson WI 53538. (800)547-7377 ext. 349. Fax: (920)563-1702. **Contact:** Greg Gerber, editor. **25% freelance written.** Monthly magazine. "RV Trade Digest seeks to help RV dealers become more profitable and efficient. We don't want fluff and theory. We want tested and proven ideas other dealers can apply to their own businesses. We believe sharing best practices helps everyone in the industry stay strong." Estab. 1980. Circ. 17,000. Pays 30 days after publication. Publishes ms an average of 3 months after acceptance. Byline given. Buys first North American serial rights. Editorial lead time 3 months. Submit seasonal material 4 months in advance. Accepts simultaneous submissions. Responds in 2 months to queries. Sample copy and writer's guidelines free.
Nonfiction: How-to (install, service parts, accessories), interview/profile (of industry leaders or successful RV dealers), new product (with emphasis on how to best sell and market the product), technical, business subjects, mobile electronics. Does not want articles about RV travel experience. **Buys 8-12 mss/year.** Length: 1,000-2,000 words. **Pays $300-500.** Pays expenses of writers on assignment.
Photos: Send photos with submission. Reviews transparencies, prints. Buys one-time rights. Negotiates payment individually. Model releases required.
Columns/Departments: Dealer Pro-File, Profit Central, Modern Manager, Shop Talk, Industry Insider.
Tips: "Send complete manuscript. Queries must include background/experience and published clips."

$ $ **SPORT TRUCK & SUV ACCESSORY BUSINESS, Covering the Light Truck-Van-SUV Aftermarket**, Cygnus Business Media, 1233 Janesville Ave., Ft. Atkinson WI 53533. (920)563-6388. Fax: (920)563-1702. E-mail: peter.hubbard@cygnuspub.com. **Contact:** Peter A. Hubbard, editor. **25% freelance written.** "*Sport Truck & SUV Accessory Business* is a bimonthly trade magazine designed to provide light truck accessory dealers and installers with advice on improving their retail business practices, plus timely information about industry trends and events. Each issue's editorial package includes a dealer profile, plus features aimed at meeting the distinct needs of store owners, managers and counter sales people. The magazine also provides aftermarket, OEM and trade association news, three separate new product sections, plus an analysis of light truck sales." Estab. 1996. Circ. 15,000. Pays 30 days after publication. Publishes ms an average of 3 months after acceptance. Byline given. Buys first North American serial rights. Editorial lead time 3 months. Submit seasonal material 4 months in advance. Accepts simultaneous submissions. Responds in 1 month to queries. Sample copy and writer's guidelines free.
　O⇥ Break in with "a feature on a top truck or SUV retailer in your area."
Nonfiction: General interest, interview/profile, new product, technical, Considers cartoons. No travel, installation how-to's. **Buys 20-30 mss/year.** Query. Length: 1,000-2,000 words. **Pays $300-500.**
Photos: Send photos with submission. Reviews transparencies, prints. Buys one-time rights. Negotiates payment individually. Model releases required.
Tips: "Send query with or without completed manuscripts. Background/experience and published clips are required."

$ $ **TODAY'S TRUCKING**, New Communications Group, 130 Belfield Rd., Toronto, Ontario M9W 1G1, Canada. (416)614-2200. Fax: (416)614-8861. E-mail: editors@todaystrucking.com. Website: www.todaystrucking.com. Editor: Stephen Petit. **Contact:** Rolf Lockwood. **15% freelance written.** Monthly magazine covering the trucking industry in Canada. "We reach nearly 30,000 fleet owners, managers, owner-operators, shop supervisors, equipment dealers, and parts distributors across Canada. Our magazine has a strong service slant, combining useful how-to journalism with analysis of news, business issues, and heavy-duty equipment trends. Before you sit down to write, please take time to become familiar with *Today's Trucking*. Read a few recent issues." Estab. 1987. Circ. 30,000. **Pays on acceptance.** Byline given. Buys first North American serial, second serial (reprint) rights. Editorial lead time 2 months. Submit seasonal material 3 months in advance. Accepts queries by mail, e-mail, fax. Sample copy and writer's guidelines free.
Nonfiction: How-to, interview/profile, technical. **Buys 20 mss/year.** Query with published clips. Length: 500-2,000 words. **Pays 40¢/word.** Sometimes pays expenses of writers on assignment.
Photos: State availability with submission.
Columns/Departments: Pays 40¢/word.

$ **TOWING & RECOVERY PHOOTNOTES**, Trader Publishing Co., 100 W. Plume St., Norfolk VA 23510. (877)219-7734. Fax: (757)314-2508. E-mail: pnotes@ix.netcom.com or thornton@traderonline.com. **Contact:** Shirley Thornton, general manager. **100% freelance written.** Monthly tabloid newspaper covering the towing business. "*Phootnotes*' mission is, increasing profits through education and knowledge." Estab. 1991. Circ. 46,000. Pays on publication. Publishes ms an average of 2 months after acceptance. Byline given. Buys industry rights. Editorial lead time 1 month. Submit seasonal material 2 months in advance. Accepts queries by mail, e-mail, fax. Sample copy free.
　O⇥ Break in by "sending us first-hand experiences in the towing and recovery field with practical advice for the towing business operator or color photos of unusual recoveries or tow trucks."
Nonfiction: Technical, business management. Query. Length: 800-1,200 words. **Pays $50-100.**
Reprints: Accepts previously published submission not in the same industry.
Columns/Departments: Business Management (related to towing industry), 500-800 words. **Buys 12-18 mss/year.** Query. **Pays $50-100.**

AVIATION & SPACE

In this section are journals for aviation business executives, airport operators and aviation technicians. Publications for professional and private pilots are in the Consumer Aviation section.

N̄ $ $ AIRCRAFT MAINTENANCE TECHNOLOGY, Cygnus Business Media, 1233 Janesville Ave., Fort Atkinson WI 53538. (920)563-6388. Fax: (920)563-1699. E-mail: editor@amtonline.com. Website: www.amtonline.c om. Senior Technical Editor: Joe Escobar. **Contact:** Michelle Garetson, editor. **10% freelance written.** Magazine published 10 times/year covering aircraft maintenance. *"Aircraft Maintenance Technology* provides aircraft maintenance professionals world-wide with a curriculum of technical, professional, and managerial development information that enables them to more efficiently and effectively perform their jobs. Estab. 1989. Circ. 44,000 worldwide. Pays on publication. Publishes ms an average of 2 months after acceptance. Byline given. Offers $50 kill fee. Buys all rights, makes work-for-hire assignments. Editorial lead time 3 months. Submit seasonal material 6 months in advance. Accepts queries by mail, e-mail, fax. Accepts simultaneous submissions. Responds in 2 weeks to queries; 1 month to mss. Sample copy free. Writer's guidelines for #10 SASE or by e-mail.
Nonfiction: How-to, technical, safety, human factors. Special issues: Aviation career issue (August). No travel/pilot-oriented pieces. **Buys 10-12 mss/year.** Query with published clips. Length: 600-1,500 words, technical articles 2,000 words. **Pays $200.**
Photos: State availability with submission. Buys one-time rights. Offers no additional payment for photos accepted with ms. Captions, identification of subjects, model releases required.
Columns/Departments: Professionalism, 1,000-1,500 words; Safety Matters, 600-1,000 words; Human Factors, 600-1,000 words. **Buys 10-12 mss/year.** Query with published clips. **Pays $200.**
Tips: "This is a technical magazine, which is approved by the FAA and Transport Canada for recurrency training for technicians. Freelancers should have a strong background in aviation, particularly maintenance, to be considered for technical articles. Columns/Departments: freelancers still should have a strong knowledge of aviation to slant professionalism, safety and human factors pieces to that audience."

$ $ AVIATION INTERNATIONAL NEWS, The Newsmagazine of Corporate, Business and Regional Aviation, The Convention News Co., P.O. Box 277, 214 Franklin Ave., Midland Park NJ 07432. (201)444-5075. Fax: (201)444-4647. E-mail: editor@ainonline.com. Website: www.ainonline.com. Managing Editor: Nigel Moll. **Contact:** R. Randall Padfield, editor-in-chief. **30-40% freelance written.** Monthly magazine (with onsite issues published at three conventions and two air shows each year) covering business and commercial aviation with news features, special reports, aircraft evaluations and surveys on business aviation worldwide, written for business pilots. "While the heartbeat of *AIN* is driven by the news it carries, the human touch is not neglected. We pride ourselves on our people stories about the industry's 'movers and shakers' and others in aviation who make a difference." Estab. 1972. Circ. 35,000. **Pays on acceptance** or upon receipt of writer's invoice. Publishes ms an average of 2 months after acceptance. Byline given. Offers variable kill fee. Buys first North American serial and second serial (reprint) rights and makes work-for-hire assignments. Editorial lead time 2 months. Submit seasonal material 3 months in advance. Accepts queries by mail, e-mail, fax. Responds in 6 weeks to queries; 2 months to mss. Sample copy for $10. Writer's guidelines for 9×12 SAE with 3 first-class stamps or online.
   O— Break in with "local news stories relating to business, commercial and regional airline aviation—think turbine-powered aircraft (no stories about national airlines, military aircraft, recreational aviation or history."
Nonfiction: "We hire freelancers to work on our staff at three aviation conventions and two international airshows each year. Must have strong reporting and writing skills and knowledge of aviation." How-to (aviation), interview/profile, new product, opinion, personal experience, photo feature, technical. No puff pieces. "Our readers expect serious, real news." **Buys 150-200 mss/year.** Query with published clips. Length: 200-3,000 words. **Pays 30¢/word.** Pays expenses of writers on assignment.
Photos: Send photos with submission. Reviews contact sheets, transparencies, prints. Buys one-time rights. Negotiates payment individually. Captions required.
   ▣ The online weekly newsletter carries original content not found in the print version. This subscription-based newsletter requires 45-50 news items of about 100 words each week. Contact: Steve Pope, spope@ainonline.com.
Tips: "Our core freelancers are professional pilots with good writing skills, good journalists and reporters with an interest in aviation (some with pilot licenses) or technical experts in the aviation industry. The ideal *AIN* writer has an intense interest in and strong knowledge of aviation, a talent for writing news stories and journalistic cussedness. Hit me with a strong news story relating to business avaiation that takes me by surprise—something from your local area or area of expertise. Make it readable, fact-filled and in the inverted-pyramid style. Double-check facts and names. Interview the right people. Send me good, clear photos and illustrations. Send me well-written, logically ordered copy. Do this for me consistently and we may take you along on our staff to one of the conventions in the U.S. or an airshow in Paris, Singapore, London or Dubai."

N̄ $ $ AVIATION MAINTENANCE, Phillips Business Information, LLC, 1201 Seven Locks Rd., Suite 300, Potomac MD 20854. (301)340-7788, ext. 2265. Fax: (301)762-4196. E-mail: am@phillips.com. Website: www.aviation mx.com. Managing Editor: Lee Ann Tegtmeier. **Contact:** Matt Thurber, editor. **60% freelance written.** Monthly magazine covering aircraft maintenance from small to large aircraft. Aviation Maintenance delivers news and information about the aircraft maintenance business for mechanics and management at maintenance shops, airlines, and corporate flights departments. Estab. 1982. Circ. 38,000. **Pays on acceptance.** Publishes ms an average of 2 months after acceptance. Byline given. Kill fee varies. Buys all rights. Editorial lead time 3 months. Submit seasonal material 3 months in advance. Accepts queries by mail, e-mail, fax, phone. Responds in 1 week to queries; 1 month to mss. Sample copy online. Writer's guidelines free.

Nonfiction: Exposé, interview/profile, technical. Special issues: April-Career Supplement aimed at Junior and High School students. No fiction, technical how-to or poetry. **Buys 50 mss/year.** Query with or without published clips. Length: 700-1,500 words. **Pays 35¢/word.** Pays expenses of writers on assignment.

Photos: State availability with submission. Buys all rights. Negotiates payment individually. Captions, identification of subjects required.

Columns/Departments: Intelligence (news), 200-500 words; Postflight (profile of aircraft mechanic), 800 words plus photo. **Buys 12 mss/year.** Query with or without published clips. **Pays $200-250.**

Tips: "Writer must be intimately familiar with or involved in aviation, either as a pilot or preferably a mechanic or a professional aviation writer. Best place to break in is in the Intelligence News section or with a Postflight profile of an interesting mechanic."

$ $ GSE TODAY, 1135 Commerce Dr., Las Cruces NM 88011. (505)521-1172. Fax: (505)521-1164. E-mail: richard@gsetoday.com. Website: www.gsetoday.com. **Contact:** Richard Rowe, editor. **50% freelance written.** Magazine published 8 times/year. "Our readers are those aviation professionals who are involved in ground support—the equipment manufacturers, the suppliers, the ramp operators, ground handlers, airport and airline managers. We cover issues of interest to this community—deicing, ramp safety, equipment technology, pollution, etc." Estab. 1993. Circ. 15,000. Pays on publication. Publishes ms an average of 2 months after acceptance. Buys all rights. Editorial lead time 2 months. Accepts queries by mail, e-mail, fax. Responds in 3 weeks to queries; 3 months to mss. Sample copy for 9×11 SAE and 5 first-class stamps.

Nonfiction: How-to (use or maintain certain equipment), humor, interview/profile, new product, opinion, photo feature, technical aspects of ground support and issues, industry events, meetings, new rules and regulations. **Buys 12-20 mss/ year.** Send complete ms. Length: 400-3,000 words. **Pays 25¢/published word.**

Reprints: Send photocopy or typed ms with rights for sale noted and information about when and where the article previously appeared. Pays 50% of the amount paid for an original article.

Photos: Send photos with submission. Reviews 5×7 prints. Buys all rights. Offers no additional payment for photos accepted with ms. Identification of subjects required.

Tips: "Write about subjects that relate to ground services. Write in clear and simple terms—personal experience is always welcome. If you have an aviation background or ground support experience, let us know."

BEAUTY & SALON

N $ $ AMERICAN SALON, Advanstar, One Park Ave., LBBY 2, New York NY 10016. (212)951-6600. Fax: (212)951-6624. Website: www.advanstar.com. Editor: Robbin McClain. **Contact:** Tina Lee, associate editor. **5% freelance written.** Monthly magazine covering "business stories of interest to salon owners and stylists, distributors and manufacturers of professional beauty products." Estab. 1878. Circ. 132,000. **Pays on acceptance.** Publishes ms an average of 3 months after acceptance. Byline given. Buys first North American serial, first rights. Editorial lead time 3 months. Accepts queries by mail. Sample copy and writer's guidelines free.

    O→ Break in with "extensive experience (in writing and the beauty industry); topic of article must be relevant. Very hard to get into our mag."

$ $ BEAUTY STORE BUSINESS, Serving Open-Line and Professional-Only Stores and Distributors, Creative Age Communications, 7628 Densmore Ave., Van Nuys CA 91406-2042. (818)782-7328. Fax: (818)782-7450. E-mail: mbirenbaum@creativeage.com. **Contact:** Marc Birenbaum, editor. **60% freelance written.** Magazine published 7 times/year covering beauty store business management. "The publication is read by beauty store owners and managers—professional-only stores of salon industry distributors, open-to-the public stores, salon stores and ethnic stores." Estab. 1994. Circ. 15,000. **Pays on acceptance.** Publishes ms an average of 3 months after acceptance. Byline given. Offers negotiable kill fee. Buys all rights. Editorial lead time 3 months. Submit seasonal material 4 months in advance. Accepts queries by mail, e-mail, fax. Responds in 1 week to queries; 2 weeks to mss. Sample copy free.

Nonfiction: How-to (business management, merchandising, retailing), interview/profile (industry leaders). "No business articles available in general-circulation publications." **Buys 6-8 mss/year.** Query. Length: 1,500-2,500 words. **Pays $250-525 for assigned articles.** Sometimes pays expenses of writers on assignment.

Photos: Do not send computer art electronically. State availability with submission. Reviews transparencies, computer art. Buys all rights. Negotiates payment individually. Captions, identification of subjects required.

$ $ COSMETICS, Canada's Business Magazine for the Cosmetics, Fragrance, Toiletry and Personal Care Industry, Rogers Media, 777 Bay St., Suite 405, Toronto, Ontario M5W 1A7, Canada. (416)596-5817. Fax: (416)596-5179. E-mail: rwood@rmpublishing.com. Website: www.cosmeticsmag.com. **Contact:** Ronald A. Wood, editor. **35% freelance written.** Bimonthly magazine. "Our main reader segment is the retail trade—department stores, drugstores, salons, estheticians—owners and cosmeticians/beauty advisors; plus manufacturers, distributors, agents and suppliers to the industry." Estab. 1972. Circ. 13,000. **Pays on acceptance.** Publishes ms an average of 3 months after acceptance. Byline given. Offers 50% kill fee. Buys all rights. Editorial lead time 4 months. Submit seasonal material 4 months in advance. Accepts queries by mail. Responds in 1 month to queries. Sample copy for $6 (Canadian) and 8% GST.

Nonfiction: General interest, interview/profile, photo feature. **Buys 60 mss/year.** Query. Length: 250-1,200 words. **Pays 25¢/word.** Sometimes pays expenses of writers on assignment.

Photos: Send photos with submission. Reviews 2½ up to 8×10 transparencies, prints 4×6 up to 8×10. Buys all rights. Offers no additional payment for photos accepted with ms. Captions, identification of subjects, model releases required.

Columns/Departments: Behind the Scenes (brief profile of person directly involved with the Canadian industry), 300 words and portrait photo. "All articles assigned on a regular basis from correspondents and columnists that we know personally from the industry." **Buys 28 mss/year. Pays 25¢/word.**

🖵 The online magazine carries original content not found in the print edition. Contact: Ronald A. Wood, online editor.

Tips: "Must have broad knowledge of the Canadian cosmetics, fragrance and toiletries industry and retail business. 99.9% of freelance articles are assigned by the editor to writers involved with the Canadian cosmetics business."

$ $ DAYSPA, For the Salon of the Future, Creative Age Publications, 7628 Densmore Ave., Van Nuys CA 91406. (818)782-7328. Fax: (818)782-7450. E-mail: dayspamag@aol.com. Website: wwwdayspamagazine.com. Managing Editor: Linda Kossoff. **Contact:** Linda Lewis, executive editor. **60% freelance written.** Bimonthly magazine covering the business of day spas, skincare salons, wellness centers. "*Dayspa* includes only well targeted business articles directed at the owners and managers of high-end, multi-service salons, day spas, resort spas and destination spas." Estab. 1996. Circ. 31,000. **Pays on acceptance.** Publishes ms an average of 4 months after acceptance. Byline given. Buys first, one-time rights. Editorial lead time 4 months. Submit seasonal material 4 months in advance. Accepts queries by mail, e-mail, fax, phone. Responds in 2 months to queries. Sample copy for $5.

Nonfiction: Book excerpts, how-to, interview/profile, photo feature. **Buys 40 mss/year.** Query. Length: 1,200-3,000 words. **Pays $150-500.**

Photos: Send photos with submission. Buys one-time rights. Negotiates payment individually. Identification of subjects, model releases required.

Columns/Departments: Legal Pad (legal issues affecting salons/spas); Money Matters (financial issues), both 1,200-1,500 words. **Buys 20 mss/year.** Query. **Pays $150-300.**

$ $ DERMASCOPE MAGAZINE, The Encyclopedia of Aesthetics & Spa Therapy, Geneva Corporation, 2611 N. Belt Line Rd., Suite 140, Sunnyvale TX 75182. (972)226-2309. Fax: (972)226-2339. E-mail: dermascope@aol.com. Website: www.dermascope.com. **Contact:** Saundra Wallens, editor-in-chief. Monthly magazine Covering aesthetics (skin care) and body and spa therapy. "Our magazine is a source of practical advice and continuing education for skin care, body and spa therapy professionals. Our main readers are salon, day spa and destination spa owners, managers or technicians." Estab. 1976. Circ. 15,000. Pays on publication. Publishes ms an average of 6 months after acceptance. Byline given. Buys all rights. Editorial lead time 3 months. Submit seasonal material 6 months in advance. Accepts queries by mail, fax. Responds in 1 month to queries; 6 months to mss. Sample copy online.

Nonfiction: Interested in seeing non-product specific how-to articles with photographs. Book excerpts, general interest, historical/nostalgic, how-to, inspirational, personal experience, photo feature, technical. **Buys 6 mss/year.** Query with published clips. Length: 1,500-2,500 words. **Pays $50-250.**

Photos: State availability with submission. Reviews 4×5 prints. Buys all rights. Offers no additional payment for photos accepted by ms. Captions, identification of subjects, model releases required.

Tips: "Write from the practitioner's point of view. Step-by-step how to's that show the skin care and body and spa therapist practical methodology are a plus. Would like more business and finance ideas, applicable to the industry."

N $ $ DERMATOLOGY INSIGHTS, A Patient's Guide to Healthy Skin, Hair and Nails, American Academy of Dermatology, 930 N. Meacham Rd., Schaumburg IL 60173. (847)330-0230. E-mail: dmonti@aad.org. Website: www.aad.org. Managing Editor: Lara Lowery. **Contact:** Dean Monti, editor. **60% freelance written.** Semiannual magazine covering dermatology. *Dermatology Insights* contains "educational and informative articles for consumers about dermatological subjects." Estab. 2000. **Pays on acceptance.** Publishes ms an average of 4 months after acceptance.

Byline given. Buys all rights, makes work-for-hire assignments. Editorial lead time 4 months. Submit seasonal material 4 months in advance. Accepts queries by mail, e-mail. Responds in 3 weeks to queries; 1 month to mss. Sample copy free.

Nonfiction: General interest, how-to, interview/profile, new product, personal experience, photo feature, technical. **Buys 10-15 mss/year.** Query. Length: 750 words maximum. **Pays flat rate of $40/hour.** Sometimes pays expenses of writers on assignment.

Photos: State availability with submission. Buys all rights. Negotiates payment individually. Identification of subjects required.

Columns/Departments: Patient Perspective (patient's first hand account). **Buys 2-3 mss/year.** Query. **Pays flat rate of $40/hour.**

MASSAGE & BODYWORK, Associated Bodywork & Massage Professionals, 1271 Sugarbush Dr., Evergreen CO 80439-9766. (303)674-8478. Fax: (303)674-0859. E-mail: editor@abmp.com. Website: www.abmp.com. **Contact:** Karrie Mowen, editor. **85% freelance written.** Bimonthly magazine covering therapeutic massage/bodywork. "A trade publication for the massage therapist, bodyworker and esthetician. An all-inclusive publication encompassing everything from traditional Swedish massage to energy work to other complementary therapies (i.e.-homeopathy, herbs, aromatherapy, etc.)." **Pays on acceptance.** Publishes ms an average of 6 months after acceptance. Buys first North American serial, one-time, electronic rights. Editorial lead time 6 months. Submit seasonal material 6 months in advance. Accepts queries by mail, e-mail, fax, phone. Responds in 1 month to queries; 5 months to mss. Writer's guidelines free.

Nonfiction: Essays, exposé, how-to (technique/modality), interview/profile, opinion, personal experience, technical, travel. No fiction. **Buys 60-75 mss/year.** Query with published clips. Length: 1,000-3,000 words.

Reprints: Accepts previously published submissions.

Photos: State availability with submission. Reviews contact sheets. Buys one-time rights. Negotiates payment individually. Captions, identification of subjects, model releases required.

Columns/Departments: Buys 20 mss/year.

Tips: "Know your topic. Offer suggestions for art to accompany your submission. *Massage & Bodywork* looks for interesting, tightly-focused stories concerning a particular modality or technique of massage, bodywork, somatic and esthetic therapies. The editorial staff welcomes the opportunity to review manuscripts which may be relevant to the field of massage, bodywork and esthetic practices, in addition to more general pieces pertaining to complementary and alternative medicine. This would include the widely varying modalities of massage and bodywork, (from Swedish massage to Polarity therapy), specific technique articles and ancillary therapies, including such topics as biomagnetics, aromatherapy and facial rejuvenation. Reference lists relating to technical articles should include the author, title, publisher and publication date of works cited. Word count: 1,500 to 4,000 words; longer articles negotiable."

$ $ MASSAGE MAGAZINE, Keeping Those Who Touch—In Touch, 1636 W. First Ave., Suite 100, Spokane WA 99204-0620. (831)477-1176. E-mail: edit@massagemag.com. Website: www.massagemag.com. **Contact:** Karen Menehan, editor. **40% freelance written.** Bimonthly magazine covering massage-bodywork and related healing arts. Estab. 1985. Circ. 80,000. **Pays on acceptance.** Publishes ms an average of 1 year after acceptance. Byline given. Buys first North American serial rights. Accepts queries by mail, e-mail. Responds in 2 months to queries; 3 months to mss. Sample copy and writer's guidelines free.

Nonfiction: Book excerpts, essays, general interest, how-to, inspirational, interview/profile, personal experience, photo feature, technical, experiential. Length: 600-2,000 words. **Pays $50-300 for assigned articles.**

Reprints: Send tearsheet of article and typed ms with rights for sale noted and information about when and where the material previously appeared. Pays 50-75% of amount paid for an original article.

Photos: Send photos with submission. Buys one-time rights. Offers $10-25/photo. Identification of subjects, identification of photographer required.

Columns/Departments: Profiles; Table Talk (news briefs); Practice Building (business); Technique; Body/mind. Length: 800-1,200 words. **Pays $100-400.**

Fillers: Facts, newsbreaks. Length: 100-800 words. **Pays $125 maximum.**

Tips: "In-depth feature articles that detail the benefits of massage are a high priority. Study a few back issues so you know what topics and tone we're looking for."

$ $ SKIN INC. MAGAZINE, The Complete Business Guide for Face & Body Care, Allured Publishing Corp., 362 S. Schmale Rd., Carol Stream IL 60188. (630)653-2155. Fax: (630)653-2192. E-mail: taschetta-millane@allured.com. Website: www.skininc.com. Publisher: Marian Raney. **Contact:** Melinda Taschetta-Millane, editor. **30% freelance written.** Magazine published 12 times/year. "Manuscripts considered for publication that contain original and new information in the general fields of skin care and makeup, dermatological and esthetician-assisted surgical techniques. The subject may cover the science of skin, the business of skin care and makeup, and plastic surgeons on healthy (i.e., non-diseased) skin. Subjects may also deal with raw materials, formulations and regulations concerning claims for products and equipment." Estab. 1988. Circ. 16,000. Pays on publication. Publishes ms an average of 6 months after acceptance. Byline given. Buys all rights. Editorial lead time 6 months. Submit seasonal material 1 year in advance. Accepts queries by mail, e-mail, fax, phone. Responds in 2 weeks to queries; 1 month to mss. Sample copy and writer's guidelines free.

Nonfiction: General interest, how-to, interview/profile, personal experience, technical. **Buys 6 mss/year.** Query with published clips. Length: 2,000 words. **Pays $100-300 for assigned articles; $50-200 for unsolicited articles.**

Photos: State availability with submission. Reviews 3×5 prints. Buys one-time rights. Offers no additional payment for photos accepted with ms. Captions, identification of subjects, model releases required.

Columns/Departments: Finance (tips and solutions for managing money), 2,000-2,500 words; Personnel (managing personnel), 2,000-2,500 words; Marketing (marketing tips for salon owners), 2,000-2,500 words; Retail (retailing products and services in the salon environment), 2,000-2,500 words. Query with published clips. **Pays $50-200.**

Fillers: Facts, newsbreaks. **Buys 6/year.** Length: 250-500 words. **Pays $50-100.**

Tips: "Have an understanding of the skin care industry."

BEVERAGES & BOTTLING

Manufacturers, distributors and retailers of soft drinks and alcoholic beverages read these publications. Publications for bar and tavern operators and managers of restaurants are classified in the Hotels, Motels, Clubs, Resorts & Restaurants category.

N BAR & BEVERAGE BUSINESS MAGAZINE, Mercury Publications Ltd., 1839 Inkster Blvd., Winnipeg, Manitoba R2X 1R3, Canada. (204)954-2085. Fax: (204)954-2057. E-mail: mp@mercury.mb.ca. Website: www.mercury.mb .ca/. Editor: Kelly Gray. **Contact:** Kristi Balon, editorial coordinator. **33% freelance written.** Bimonthly magazine providing information on the latest trends, happenings, buying-selling of beverages and product merchandising. Estab. 1998. Circ. 16,077. Pays 30-45 days from receipt of invoice. Byline given. Offers 33% kill fee. Buys first rights. Submit seasonal material 3 months in advance. Accepts queries by mail, e-mail, fax. Accepts simultaneous submissions. Responds in 2 weeks to queries. Sample copy and writer's guidelines free or by e-mail.

Nonfiction: How-to (making a good drink, training staff, etc.), interview/profile. No industry reports, profiles on companies. Query with published clips. Length: 500-9,000 words. **Pays 25-35¢/word.** Sometimes pays expenses of writers on assignment.

Photos: State availability with submission. Reviews negatives, transparencies, 3×5 prints, jpeg, eps or tiff files. Buys all rights. Negotiates payment individually. Captions required.

Columns/Departments: Out There (bar & bev news in various parts of the country), 100-500 words. Query. **Pays $0-100.**

Tips: "Send an e-mailed, faxed or mailed query outlining their experience, interests and pay expectations. A requirement also is clippings."

$ $ THE BEVERAGE JOURNAL, Michigan Edition, MI Licensed Beverage Association, 920 N. Fairview Ave., Lansing MI 48912. (518)374-9611. Fax: (517)374-1165. E-mail: ktuinstra@mlba.org. Website: www.mlba.org. Editor: Richard Allen. **Contact:** Amy Shock, assistant editor. **40-50% freelance written.** Monthly magazine covering hospitality industry. "A monthly trade magazine devoted to the beer, wine and spirits industry in Michigan. It is dedicated to serving those who make their living serving the public and the state through the orderly and responsible sale of beverages." Estab. 1983. Circ. 4,200. Pays on publication. Buys one-time, second serial (reprint) rights, makes work-for-hire assignments. Editorial lead time 3 months. Submit seasonal material 3 months in advance. Accepts queries by mail, e-mail. Responds in 2 weeks to queries; 1 month to mss. Sample copy for $5 or online.

Nonfiction: Essays, general interest, historical/nostalgic, how-to (make a drink, human resources, tips, etc.), humor, interview/profile, new product, opinion, personal experience, photo feature, technical. **Buys 24 mss/year.** Send complete ms. Length:1,000 words. **Pays $20-200.**

Reprints: Accepts previously published submissions.

Columns/Departments: Interviews (legislators, others), 750-1,000 words; Personal experience (waitstaff, customer, bartenders), 500 words. "Open to essay content ideas." **Buys 12 mss/year.** Send complete ms. **Pays $25-100.**

Tips: "We are particularly interested in nonfiction concerning responsible consumption/serving of alcohol. We are looking for reviews, company profiles, personal experiences that would benefit our audience. Our audience is a busy group of business owners and hospitality professionals striving to obtain pertinent information that is not too wordy."

N $ $ BEVERAGE MEDIA, Beverage Media Group, 116 John St., 21st Floor, New York NY 10038. (212)571-3232. Fax: (917)344-4973. E-mail: kwolfe@bevaccess.com. Website: www.bevaccess.com. Managing Editor: Kristen Wolfe. **Contact:** Perry Luntz, national editor. **25-30% freelance written.** Monthly magazine covering retail selling of beverage alcohol products, responsible drinking, changing demographics, product usage. Estab. 1936. Circ. 140,000. Pays on publication. Publishes ms an average of 3 months after acceptance. Byline given. Buys first, electronic rights. Editorial lead time 2 months. Submit seasonal material 2 months in advance. Accepts queries by e-mail. Sample copy free.

Nonfiction: Historical/nostalgic, how-to (retailing), interview/profile, new product. No "anti-drinking or use of derogatory words (i.e., booze)." **Buys 12-15 mss/year.** Query with published clips. Length: 300-1,500 words. **Pays $200.** Sometimes pays expenses of writers on assignment.

Photos: State availability with submission. Buys one-time rights. Negotiates payment individually. Identification of subjects required.

$ $ VINEYARD & WINERY MANAGEMENT, 3535 Industrial Dr., Suite A3, Santa Rosa CA 95403. (707)566-3810. Fax: (707)566-3815. E-mail: gparnell@vwm-online.com. Website: www.vwm-online.com. **Contact:** Graham Parnell, managing editor. **80% freelance written.** Bimonthly magazine of professional importance to grape growers, winemakers and winery sales and business people. Estab. 1975. Circ. 4,500. Pays on publication. Byline given. Buys first North American serial, simultaneous rights. Accepts queries by e-mail. Responds in 3 weeks to queries; 1 month to mss. Sample copy free. Writer's guidelines for #10 SASE.

Nonfiction: Subjects are technical in nature and explore the various methods people in these career paths use to succeed, and also the equipment and techniques they use successfully. Business articles and management topics are also featured. The audience is national with western dominance. How-to, interview/profile, new product, technical. **Buys 30 mss/year.** Query. Length: 300-5,000 words. **Pays $30-1,000.** Sometimes pays expenses of writers on assignment.

Photos: State availability with submission. Reviews contact sheets, negatives, transparencies. Black and white often purchased for $20 each to accompany story material; 35mm and/or 4×5 transparencies for $50 and up; 6/year of vineyard and/or winery scene related to story. Identification of subjects required.

Tips: "We're looking for long-term relationships with authors who know the business and write well. Electronic submissions required; query for formats."

BOOK & BOOKSTORE

Publications for book trade professionals from publishers to bookstore operators are found in this section. Journals for professional writers are classified in the Journalism & Writing category.

$ BLOOMSBURY REVIEW, A Book Magazine, Dept. WM, Owaissa Communications Co., Inc., P.O. Box 8928, Denver CO 80201. (303)455-3123. Fax: (303)455-7039. E-mail: bloomsb@aol.com. **Contact:** Marilyn Auer, editor. **75% freelance written.** Bimonthly tabloid covering books and book-related matters. "We publish book reviews, interviews with writers and poets, literary essays and original poetry. Our audience consists of educated, literate, *non-specialized* readers." Estab. 1980. Circ. 50,000. Pays on publication. Publishes ms an average of 4 months after acceptance. Byline given. Buys first, one-time rights. Accepts queries by mail. Responds in 4 months to queries. Sample copy for $4 and 9×12 SASE. Writer's guidelines for #10 SASE.

Nonfiction: "Summer issue features reviews, etc., about the American West. *We do not publish fiction.*" Essays, interview/profile, book reviews. **Buys 60 mss/year.** Query with published clips or send complete ms. Length: 800-1,500 words. **Pays $10-20. Sometimes pays writers with contributor copies or other premiums "if writer agrees."**

Reprints: Considered but not encouraged. Send photocopy of article and information about when and where the article previously appeared. Pays 100% of amount paid for an original article.

Photos: State availability with submission. Reviews prints. Buys one-time rights. Offers no additional payment for photos accepted with ms.

Columns/Departments: Book reviews and essays, 500-1,500 words. **Buys 6 mss/year.** Query with published clips or send complete ms. **Pays $10-20.**

Poetry: Ray Gonzalez, poetry editor. Avant-garde, free verse, haiku, light verse, traditional. **Buys 20 poems/year.** Submit maximum 5 poems. **Pays $5-10.**

Tips: "We appreciate receiving published clips and/or completed manuscripts. Please—no rough drafts. Book reviews should be of new books (within 6 months of publication)."

$ $ FOREWORD MAGAZINE, ForeWord Magazine Inc., 129 E. Front St., Traverse City MI 49684. (231)933-3699. Fax: (231)933-3899. E-mail: mlink@forewordmagazine.com. Website: www.forewordmagazine.com. **Contact:** Mardi Link, editor-in-chief. **35% freelance written.** Monthly magazine covering independent and university presses for booksellers and librarians with articles, news, book reviews. Estab. 1998. Circ. 15,000. Pays on publication. Publishes ms an average of 1 month after acceptance. Byline given. Buys all rights. Editorial lead time 3 months. Submit seasonal material 5 months in advance. Accepts queries by mail, e-mail, fax. Responds in 2 weeks to queries; 1 month to mss. Sample copy for 8×10 SASE.

Nonfiction: Book excerpts, essays, exposé, interview/profile, opinion. **Buys 20 mss/year.** Query with published clips or send complete ms. Length: 600-4,000 words. **Pays $45-400 for assigned articles; $45-250 for unsolicited articles.** Pays phone expenses only of writers on assignment.

Photos: State availability with submission. Reviews prints. Buys all rights. Offers no additional payment for photos accepted with ms. Captions required.

Columns/Departments: Pays $45-400.

Tips: "Be knowledgeable about the needs of booksellers and librarians—remember we are an industry trade journal, not a how-to or consumer publication. We review books prior to publication, so book reviews are always assigned—but send us a note telling subjects you wish to review in as well as a résumé."

$ 🖳 INDEPENDENT PUBLISHER, The Jenkins Group, 400 W. Front St., #4A, Traverse City MI 49684. (231)933-0445. Fax: (231)933-0448. E-mail: jimb@bookpublishing.com. Website: www.independentpublisher.com. **Contact:** Jim Barnes, managing editor. **25% freelance written.** Monthly magazine. "*Independent Publisher* is a monthly online trade journal for small and independent publishing companies. We focus on marketing, promoting and producing books and how independent publishers can compete in this competitive industry. We also run profiles of successful publishers, an awards section and new title listings." Estab. 1983. Circ. 10,000. Pays on publication. Publishes ms an average of 1 month after acceptance. Byline given. Editorial lead time 2 months. Submit seasonal material 4 months in advance. Accepts queries by e-mail. Accepts simultaneous submissions. Responds in 3 weeks to queries; 1 month to mss. Sample copy and writer's guidelines free.

Nonfiction: Book excerpts, essays, exposé, how-to, interview/profile, opinion. "No consumer-oriented stories. We are a trade magazine for publishers." **Buys 12 mss/year.** Query with published clips. Length: 1,000-4,000 words.

Photos: State availability with submission. Reviews transparencies, prints. Buys one-time rights. Offers no additional payment for photos accepted with ms. Identification of subjects required.

Columns/Departments: Book Biz; Industry Update; Calendar of Events; Passageways to Profit (distribution strategies); PublishItRight.com (how-to); Inklings (writing for books, film and stage); For Love of Books (book arts), all 1,200-1,600 words. **Buys 6 mss/year.** Query with published clips. **Pays $50-100.**

Tips: "We're looking for in-depth profiles of publishers who find new ways to market their books."

BRICK, GLASS & CERAMICS

These publications are read by manufacturers, dealers and managers of brick, glass and ceramic retail businesses. Other publications related to glass and ceramics are listed in the Consumer Art & Architecture and Consumer Hobby & Craft sections.

N $ $ GLASS MAGAZINE, For the Architectural Glass Industry, National Glass Association, 8200 Greensboro Dr., McLean VA 22102-. (703)442-4890. Fax: (703)442-0630. E-mail: charles@glass.org. Website: www.glass.org. **Contact:** Charles Cumpston, editor. **25% freelance written.** Prefers to work with published/established writers. Monthly magazine covering the architectural glass industry. Circ. 23,291. **Pays on acceptance.** Publishes ms an average of 6 months after acceptance. Byline given. Kill fee varies. Buys first rights. Accepts queries by mail, e-mail, fax. Responds in 2 months to mss. Sample copy for $5 and 9×12 SAE with 10 first-class stamps.

Nonfiction: Interview/profile (of various glass businesses; profiles of industry people or glass business owners), new product, technical (about glazing processes). **Buys 10 mss/year.** Query with published clips. Length: 1,000 words minimum. **Pays $150-300 for assigned articles.**

Photos: State availability with submission.

Tips: *Glass Magazine* is doing more inhouse writing; freelance cut by half. "Do *not* send in general glass use stories. Research the industry first, then query."

$ STAINED GLASS, Stained Glass Association of America, 6 S.W. Second St., #107, Lee's Summit MO 64063. (800)438-9581. Fax: (816)524-9405. E-mail: sgmagaz@kcnet.com. Website: www.stainedglass.org. **Contact:** Richard Gross, editor. **70% freelance written.** Quarterly magazine. "Since 1906, *Stained Glass* has been the official voice of the Stained Glass Association of America. As the oldest, most respected stained glass publication in North America, *Stained Glass* preserves the techniques of the past as well as illustrates the trends of the future. This vital information, of significant value to the professional stained glass studio, is also of interest to those for whom stained glass is an avocation or hobby." Estab. 1906. Circ. 5,000. Pays on publication. Publishes ms an average of 6 months after acceptance. Byline given. Buys one-time rights. Editorial lead time 3 months. Submit seasonal material 6 months in advance. Accepts queries by mail, e-mail, fax. Responds in 3 months to queries. Sample copy and writer's guideline free.

O— Break in with "excellent photography and in-depth stained glass architectural knowledge."

Nonfiction: Strong need for technical and how to create architectural type stained glass. Glass etching, use of etched glass in stained glass compositions, framing. How-to, humor, interview/profile, new product, opinion, photo feature, technical. **Buys 9 mss/year.** Query or send complete ms but must include photos or slides—very heavy on photos. **Pays $125/illustrated article; $75/non-illustrated.**

Reprints: Accepts previously published submissions from non-stained glass publications only. Send tearsheet of article. Payment negotiable.

Photos: Send photos with submission. Reviews 4×5 transparencies, send slides with submission. Buys one-time rights. Pays $75 for non-illustrated. Pays $125 plus 3 copies for line art or photography. Identification of subjects required.

Columns/Departments: Teknixs (technical, how-to, stained and glass art), word length varies by subject. "Columns must be illustrated." **Buys 4 mss/year.** Query or send complete ms, but must be illustrated.

Tips: "We need more technical articles. Writers should be extremely well versed in the glass arts. Photographs are extremely important and must be of very high quality. Submissions without photographs or illustrations are seldom considered unless something special and writer states that photos are available. However, prefer to see with submission."

$ $ US GLASS, METAL & GLAZING, Key Communications Inc., P.O. Box 569, Garrisonville VA 22463. (540)720-5584. Fax: (540)720-5687. E-mail: egiard@glass.com. Website: www.uglassmag.com. **Contact:** Ellen Giard, editor. **25% freelance written.** Monthly magazine for companies involved in the auto glass and flat glass trades. Estab. 1966. Circ. 23,000. Pays on publication. Publishes ms an average of 3 months after acceptance. Byline given. Buys all rights. Editorial lead time 3 months. Submit seasonal material 2 months in advance. Accepts queries by mail, e-mail, fax. Accepts simultaneous submissions. Responds in 1 month to queries; 2 months to mss. Sample copy and writer's guidelines online.

Nonfiction: Buys 12 mss/year. Query with published clips. **Pays $300-600 for assigned articles.** Sometimes pays expenses of writers on assignment.

Photos: State availability with submission. Reviews contact sheets. Buys first North American rights. Offers no additional payment for photos accepted with ms. Captions, identification of subjects required.

■ The online magazine carries original content not found in the print edition. Contact: Holly Carter or Ellen Giard.

BUILDING INTERIORS

Owners, managers and sales personnel of floor covering, wall covering and remodeling businesses read the journals listed in this category. Interior design and architecture publications may be found in the Consumer Art, Design & Collectibles category. For journals aimed at other construction trades see the Construction & Contracting section.

$ $PWC, Painting & Wallcovering Contractor, Finan Publishing Co. Inc., 107 W. Pacific Ave., St. Louis MO 63119-2323. (314)961-6644. Fax: (314)961-4809. E-mail: jbeckner@finan.com. Website: www.paintstore.com. **Contact:** Jeffery Beckner, editor. **90% freelance written.** Bimonthly magazine. "*PWC* provides news you can use: Information helpful to the painting and wallcovering contractor in the here and now." Estab. 1928. Circ. 30,000. Pays 30 days after acceptance. Publishes ms an average of 1 month after acceptance. Byline given. Offers variable kill fee. Buys first North American serial rights. Editorial lead time 2 months. Submit seasonal material 2 months in advance. Accepts simultaneous submissions. Responds in 2 weeks to queries. Sample copy free.

Nonfiction: Essays, exposé, how-to (painting and wallcovering), interview/profile, new product, opinion, personal experience. **Buys 40 mss/year.** Query with published clips. Length: 1,500-2,500 words. **Pays $300 minimum.** Pays expenses of writers on assignment.

Reprints: Send photocopy and information about when and where the material previously appeared. Negotiates payment.

Photos: State availability of or send photos with submission. Reviews contact sheets, negatives, transparencies, digital prints. Buys all rights. Offers no additional payment for photos accepted with ms. Identification of subjects required.

Columns/Departments: Anything of interest to the small businessman, 1,250 words. **Buys 2 mss/year.** Query with published clips. **Pays $50-100.**

Tips: "We almost always buy on an assignment basis. The way to break in is to send good clips, and I'll try and give you work."

N $ $REMODELING, Hanley-Wood, LLC, One Thomas Circle NW, Suite 600, Washington DC 20005. (202)452-0800. Fax: (202)785-1974. E-mail: cfishburn@hanley-wood.com. Website: www.remodelingmagazine.com. Editor-in-Chief: Paul Deffenbaugh. **Contact:** Christine Fishburn, managing editor. **10% freelance written.** Monthly magazine covering residential and light commercial remodeling. "We cover the best new ideas in remodeling design, business, construction and products." Estab. 1985. Circ. 80,000. Pays on publication. Publishes ms an average of 3 months after acceptance. Byline given. Offers 5¢/word kill fee. Buys first North American serial rights. Accepts queries by mail, e-mail, fax. Responds in 1 month to queries. Sample copy and writer's guidelines free.

Nonfiction: Interview/profile, new product, technical, small business trends. **Buys 6 mss/year.** Query with published clips. Length: 250-1,000 words. **Pays 50¢/word.** Sometimes pays expenses of writers on assignment.

Photos: State availability with submission. Reviews 4×5 transparencies, slides, 8×10 prints. Buys one-time rights for print and electronic format. Offers $25-125/photo. Captions, identification of subjects, model releases required.

■ The online magazine carries original content not found in the print edition. Contact: John Butterfield, online editor.

Tips: "We specialize in service journalism for remodeling contractors. Knowledge of the industry is essential."

N $ $WALLS & CEILINGS, Dept. SMM, 755 W. Big Beaver Rd., Troy MI 48084. (248)244-1735. Fax: (248)362-5103. E-mail: mazures@bnp.com. Website: www.wconline.com. **Contact:** Sarah Mazure, editor. **20% freelance written.** Monthly magazine for contractors involved in lathing and plastering, drywall, acoustics, fireproofing, curtain walls, movable partitions together with manufacturers, dealers, and architects. Estab. 1938. Circ. 30,000. Pays on publication. Publishes ms an average of 6 months after acceptance. Byline given. Buys all rights. Submit seasonal material 4 months in advance. Accepts queries by mail, e-mail, phone. Accepts simultaneous submissions. Responds in 6 months to queries. Sample copy for 9×12 SAE with $2 postage. Writer's guidelines for #10 SASE.

○─ Break in with technical expertise in drywall, plaster, stucco.

Nonfiction: How-to (drywall and plaster construction and business management), technical. **Buys 20 mss/year.** Query or send complete ms. Length: 1,000-1,500 words. **Pays $50-500.** Sometimes pays expenses of writers on assignment.

Reprints: Send tearsheet or photocopy with rights for sale noted and information about when and where the material previously appeared. Pays 50% of the amount paid for an original article.

Photos: Send photos with submission. Reviews contact sheets, negatives, transparencies, prints. Buys one-time rights. Captions, identification of subjects required.

■ The online magazine carries original content not found in the print edition.

BUSINESS MANAGEMENT

These publications cover trends, general theory and management practices for business owners and top-level business executives. Publications that use similar material but have a less technical slant are listed in the Consumer Business & Finance section. Journals for middle management, including supervisors and office managers, appear in the Management & Supervision section. Those for industrial plant managers are listed under Industrial Operations and under sections for specific industries, such as Machinery & Metal. Publications for office supply store operators are included in the Office Environment & Equipment section.

$ $ ACCOUNTING TODAY, Faulkner & Gray, 11 Penn Plaza, New York NY 10001. (212)967-7000. **Contact:** Rick Telberg, editor. Biweekly newspaper. "*Accounting Today* is the newspaper of record for the accounting industry." Estab. 1987. Circ. 35,000. Pays on publication. Publishes ms an average of 1 month after acceptance. Byline given. Buys all rights. Editorial lead time 2 weeks. Responds in 1 month to queries. Sample copy for $5.
Nonfiction: Book excerpts, essays, exposé, how-to, interview/profile, new product, travel. **Buys 35 mss/year.** Query with published clips. Length: 500-1,500 words. **Pays 25-50¢/word for assigned articles.** Pays expenses of writers on assignment.
Photos: State availability with submission. Negotiates payment individually.

$ $ $ ACROSS THE BOARD, The Conference Board Magazine, The Conference Board, 845 Third Ave., New York NY 10022-6679. (212)759-0900. Fax: (212)339-0214. E-mail: atb@conference-board.org. Website: www.conference-board.org. Managing Editor: Al Vogl, Managing Editor: Matthew Budman. **Contact:** Vadim Liberman, assistant to editor. **60% freelance written.** Bimonthly magazine covering business—focuses on higher management. "*Across the Board* is a nonprofit magazine of ideas and opinions for leaders in business, goverment and other organizations. The editors present business perspectives on timely issues, including management practices, foreign policy, social issues, and science and technology. *Across the Board* is neither an academic business journal not a 'popular' manual. That means we aren't interested in highly technical articles about business strategy. It also means we don't publish oversimple 'how-to' articles. We are an idea magazine, but the ideas should have practical overtones. We let *Forbes, Fortune* and *Business Week* do most of the straight reporting, while we do some of the critical thinking; that is, we let writers explore the implications of the news in depth. *Across the Board* tries to provide different angles on important topics, and to bring to its readers' attention issues that they might otherwise not devote much thought to." Circ. 30,000. Pays on publication. Publishes ms an average of 4 months after acceptance. Byline given. Offers 20% kill fee. Buys first rights. Editorial lead time 6 months. Submit seasonal material 6 months in advance. Accepts queries by mail, e-mail, fax, phone. Accepts simultaneous submissions. Responds in 3 weeks to queries. Sample copy free. Writer's guidelines for #10 SASE or online.
Nonfiction: Book excerpts, essays, humor, opinion, personal experience. No new product information. **Buys 50 mss/year.** Query with published clips or send complete ms. Length: 500-4,000 words. **Pays $50-2,500.** Sometimes pays expenses of writers on assignment.
Photos: State availability with submission. Reviews contact sheets. Buys one-time or all rights. Negotiates payment individually. Captions, identification of subjects required.
Tips: "We let *Forbes, Fortune* and *Business Week* do most of the straight reporting, while we do some of the critical thinking; that is, we let writers explore the implications of the news in depth. *Across the Board* tries to provide different angles on important topics, and to bring to its readers' attention issues that they might otherwise not devote much thought to. We emphasize the human side of organizational life at all levels. We're as concerned with helping managers who are 'lonely at the top' as with motivating workers and enhancing job satisfaction."

$ $ AMERICAN DRYCLEANER/COIN-OP/CLEAN CAR/AMERICAN LAUNDRY NEWS, American Trade Magazines/Crain Communications Inc., 500 N. Dearborn, Chicago IL 60610. (312)337-7700. Fax: (312)337-8654. E-mail: atmpub@aol.com. **Contact:** Ian Murphy, managing editor. **20% freelance written.** Monthly tabloid covering drycleaning, coin laundry, coin car cleaning, institutional laundry. Estab. 1934. Circ. 25,000. Pays on publication. Publishes ms an average of 1 month after acceptance. Byline given. Offers 10% kill fee. Buys first, second serial (reprint), all rights. Editorial lead time 2 months. Submit seasonal material 2 months in advance. Accepts queries by mail, e-mail, fax, phone. Accepts simultaneous submissions. Responds in 1 month to queries; 4 months to mss. Sample copy for 6×9 SAE and 2 first-class stamps.
Nonfiction: Ian P. Murphy, managing editor. How-to (general biz, industry-specific), interview/profile, new product, personal experience, technical. No inspirational, consumer-geared. **Buys 12-15 mss/year.** Query. Length: 600-2,000 words. **Pays $50-500 for assigned articles; $25-250 for unsolicited articles.** Sometimes pays expenses of writers on assignment.
Photos: State availability with submission. Reviews contact sheets, negatives, 4×5 or slide transparencies, 3×5-5×7 prints. Buys one-time rights. Negotiates payment individually. Identification of subjects required.
Columns/Departments: Ian P. Murphy, managing editor. General Business, 1,200 words. **Buys 72 mss/year.** Send complete ms. **Pays $50-150.**

Tips: "Each magazine is geared toward small-business owners in these specific industries. Writers will find professional experience in the industry is a plus; general small-business articles are often used, but tailored to each magazine's audience."

$ $ BEDTIMES, The Business Journal for the Sleep Products Industry, International Sleep Products Association, 501 Wythe St., Alexandria VA 22304-1917. (703)683-8371. Fax: (703)683-4503. E-mail: kburns@sleepproducts.org. Website: www.sleepproducts.org. Managing Editor: Kathleen Smith. **Contact:** Kathleen Burns, editor. **20-40% freelance written.** Monthly magazine covering the mattress manufacturing industry. "Our news and features are straight forward—we are not a lobbying vehicle for our association. No special slant or philosophy." Estab. 1917. Circ. 4,000. **Pays on acceptance.** Publishes ms an average of 4 months after acceptance. Byline sometimes given. Buys first North American serial rights. Editorial lead time 2 months. Accepts queries by e-mail, fax. Accepts simultaneous submissions. Responds in 1 month to queries. Sample copy for $4. Writer's guidelines for #10 SASE or by e-mail.

   O-n Break in with "Headlines"—short news stories. We also use freelancers for our monthly columns on "New Products," "Newsmakers," and "Snoozebriefs." Query first.

Nonfiction: Interview/profile, photo feature. Special issues: Philanthropy in the workplace (November). "No pieces that do not relate to business in general or mattress industry in particular." **Buys 15-25 mss/year.** Query with published clips. Length: 500-3,500 words. **Pays 35-50¢/word.**

Photos: State availability with submission. Buys one-time rights. Negotiates payment individually. Identification of subjects required.

Columns/Departments: Millennium Milestones (companies marking anniversaries from 25 to 150 years), 1,000 words. **Buys 10-12 mss/year.** Query with 3 published clips. **Pays $250-350 depending on length and degree of difficulty in getting the story.**

Tips: "Cover stories are a major outlet for freelance submissions. Once a story is written and accepted, the author is encouraged to submit suggestions to the graphic designer of the magazine regarding ideas for the cover illustration as well as possible photos/graphs/charts, etc. to be used with the story itself. Topics have included annual industry forecast; physical expansion of industry facilities; e-commerce; flammability and home furnishings; the risks and rewards of marketing overseas; the evolving family business; the shifting workplace environment; and what do consumers really want?"

[N] $ CA MAGAZINE, Canadian Institute of Chartered Accountants, 277 Wellington St. W, Toronto, Ontario M5V 3H2, Canada. (416)977-3222. Fax: (416)204-3409. E-mail: camagazine@cica.ca. Website: www.camagazine.com. **Contact:** Christian Bellavance, editor-in-chief. **30% freelance written.** Magazine published 10 times/year covering accounting. "CA Magazine is the leading accounting publication in Canada and the preferred information source for chartered accountants and financial executives. It provides a forum for discussion and debate on professional, financial and other business issues." Estab. 1911. Circ. 74,834. **Pays on acceptance.** Publishes ms an average of 3 months after acceptance. Byline given. Offers 30% kill fee. Buys all rights. Editorial lead time 4 months. Accepts queries by e-mail. Responds in 1 month to queries. Sample copy and writer's guidelines online.

Nonfiction: Book excerpts, financial/accounting business. **Buys 30 mss/year.** Query. Length: 2,500-3,500 words. **Pays honorarium for chartered accountants; freelance rate varies.**

$ $ CBA MARKETPLACE, CBA Service Corp., P.O. Box 62000, Colorado Springs CO 80962. E-mail: publications@cbaonline.org. Website: www.cbaonline.org. **Contact:** Lora Riley, managing editor. **20% freelance written.** Monthly magazine covering the Christian retail industry. "Writers must have knowledge of and direct experience in the Christian retail industry. Subject matter must specifically pertain to the Christian retail audience." Estab. 1968. **Pays on acceptance.** Publishes ms an average of 3 months after acceptance. Byline given. Buys all rights. Editorial lead time 3 months. Submit seasonal material 6 months in advance. Accepts queries by mail, e-mail. Responds in 2 months to queries. Sample copy for $9.50 or online.

Nonfiction: Christian retail. **Buys 24 mss/year.** Query. Length: 750-1,500 words. **Pays 15-25¢/word.**

Fillers: Cartoons. **Buys 12/year. Pays $150.**

Tips: "Only experts on Christian retail industry, completely familiar with retail audience and their needs and considerations, should submit a query. Do not submit articles unless requested."

$ $ $ $ CONQUEST, (formerly *Global Technology Business*), 1931 Old Middlefield Way, Suite Z, Mountain View CA 94043-2559. (650)934-2301. Fax: (650)321-5597. E-mail: almiller@dasar.com. Website: www.conquestmagazine.com. **Contact:** Amy Miller, managing editor. Monthly magazine covering global IT and e-business for high-tech executives. "*Conquest* focuses on information technology from a global perspective. In the US, over 60,000 executives in the high-tech industry rely on *Conquest* to follow the global integration of technologies and the strategies, products and alliances of global IT provides." Estab. 1998. Circ. 60,000. Pays on billing cycle. Publishes ms an average of 4 months after acceptance. Byline sometimes given. Buys all rights. Accepts queries by e-mail, phone. Sample copy online.

Nonfiction: Book excerpts, exposé, general interest, how-to, global business team, hard-hitting perspective. **Buys 50 mss/year.** Length: 500-3,000 words. **Pays $500-2,500.**

Columns/Departments: Pays $500-2,500.

$ $ CONTINGENCY PLANNING & MANAGEMENT, Witter Publishing, 84 Park Ave., Flemington NJ 08822. (908)788-0343. Fax: (908)788-3782. E-mail: cpmmagazine@witterpublishing.com. Website: ContingencyPlan ning.com. Managing Editor: Michelle Simonelli. **Contact:** Andy Hagg, editor. Monthly magazine covering business continuity/contingency planning. "*Contingency Planning & Management* magazine is the comprehensive information source for business continuity. We go out to decision-makers for the Fortune 1000 interested in risk management, contingency planning and disaster recovery." Estab. 1996. Circ. 35,000 qualified. Pays on publication. Publishes ms an average of 2 months after acceptance. Byline given. Buys all rights. Editorial lead time 3 months. Accepts queries by mail, e-mail, fax, phone. Responds in 1 week to queries. Sample copy and writer's guidelines free.
Nonfiction: How-to, interview/profile, technical. "No personal material." **Buys 2 mss/year.** Query with published clips. Length: 1,500-3,500 words. **Pays up to $200.**
Photos: State availability with submission. Reviews negatives, transparencies, prints. Buys all rights. Negotiates payment individually. Captions, identification of subjects, model releases required.

N $ $ CONTRACT MANAGEMENT, National Contract Management Association, 1912 Woodford Rd, Vienna VA 22182. Fax: (703)448-0939. E-mail: cm@ncmahq.org. Website: www.ncmahq.org. **Contact:** Misty Mealey, editor-in-chief. **15% freelance written.** Monthly magazine covering contract and business management. "Most of the articles published in *Contract Management (CM)* are written by members, although one does not have to be an NCMA member to be published in the magazine. Articles should concern some aspect of the contract management profession, whether at the level of a beginner or that of the advanced practitioner." Estab. 1960. Circ. 23,000. Pays on publication. Publishes ms an average of 3 months after acceptance. Byline given. Buys one-time rights. Editorial lead time 10 weeks. Submit seasonal material 3 months in advance. Accepts queries by mail, e-mail, fax, phone. Accepts simultaneous submissions. Responds in 2 weeks to queries; 1 month to mss. Sample copy and writer's guidelines free.
Nonfiction: Essays, general interest, how-to, humor, inspirational, new product, opinion, technical. No company or CEO profiles—please read a copy of publication before submitting. **Buys 6-10 mss/year.** Query with published clips. Length: 1,000-2,500 words. **Pays $300; association members paid in 3 copies.**
Reprints: Accepts previously published submissions. Buys one-time rights.
Photos: Offers no additional payment for photos accepted with ms. Captions, identification of subjects required.
Columns/Departments: Professional Development (self-improvement in business), 1,000-1,500 words; Back to Basics (basic how-tos and discussions), 1,500-2,000 words. **Buys 2 mss/year.** Query with published clips. **Pays $300.**
Tips: "Query and read at least one issue. Visit website to better understand our audience."

$ $ CONTRACTING PROFITS, Trade Press Publishing, 2100 W. Florist Ave., Milwaukee WI 53209. (414)228-7701. E-mail: dianna.b@tradepress.com. Website: www.cleanlink.com/cp. **Contact:** Dianna Bisswurm, editor. **40% freelance written.** Magazine published 9 times/year covering "building service contracting, business management advice." "We are the pocket MBA for this industry—focusing not only on cleaning-specific topics, but also discussing how to run businesses better and increase profits through a variety of management articles." Estab. 1995. Circ. 32,000. Pays within 30 days of submission. Byline given. Buys all rights. Editorial lead time 2 months. Submit seasonal material 3 months in advance. Accepts queries by mail, e-mail. Sample copy online. Writer's guidelines free.
Nonfiction: Exposé, how-to, interview/profile, technical. "No product-related reviews or testimonials." **Buys 30 mss/year.** Query with published clips. Length: 1,200-3,000 words. **Pays $100-500.** Sometimes pays expenses of writers on assignment.
Columns/Departments: Query with published clips.
Tips: "Read back issues on our website and be able to understand some of those topics prior to calling."

$ CONVENTION SOUTH, Covey Communications Corp., 2001 W. First St., P.O. Box 2267, Gulf Shores AL 36547-2267. (334)968-5300. Fax: (334)968-4532. E-mail: info@conventionsouth.com. Website: www.conventionsouth.com. Editor: J. Talty O'Connor. **Contact:** Kristen McIntosh, executive editor. **50% freelance written.** Monthly tabloid for meeting planners who plan events in the South. Topics relate to the meetings industry—how-to articles, industry news, destination spotlights. Estab. 1983. Circ. 11,800. Pays on publication. Publishes ms an average of 2 months after acceptance. Byline given. Buys first, second serial (reprint) rights. Editorial lead time 3 months. Submit seasonal material 4 months in advance. Accepts queries by mail, e-mail, fax. Accepts simultaneous submissions. Responds in 2 months to queries. Sample copy free. Writer's guidelines for #10 SASE.
Nonfiction: How-to (relative to meeting planning/travel), interview/profile, photo feature, technical, travel. **Buys 50 mss/year.** Query. Length: 1,250-3,000 words. **Pays $75-150.** Pays in contributor copies or other premiums if arranged in advance. Sometimes pays expenses of writers on assignment.
Reprints: Send photocopy and information about when and where the material previously appeared. Pay negotiable.
Photos: Send photos with submission. Reviews 5×7 prints. Buys one-time rights. Offers no additional payment for photos accepted with ms. Captions, identification of subjects required.
Columns/Departments: How-to (related to meetings), 700 words. **Buys 12 mss/year.** Query with published clips. **Payment negotiable.**
Tips: "Know who our audience is and make sure articles are appropriate for them."

N $ $ EXPANSION MANAGEMENT MAGAZINE, Growth Strategies for Companies On the Move, Penton Media, Inc., 9500 Nall, Suite 400, Overland Park KS 66207. (913)381-4800. Fax: (913)381-8858. Editor: Bill King. **Contact:** Lance Yoder, managing editor. **75% freelance written.** Monthly magazine covering economic development. Estab. 1986. Circ. 45,000. **Pays on acceptance.** Publishes ms an average of 1 month after acceptance. Byline given. Buys all rights, makes work-for-hire assignments. Editorial lead time 2 months. Sample copy for $7. Writer's guidelines free.

Nonfiction: "*Expansion Management* presents articles and industry reports examining relocation trends, strategic planning, work force hiring, economic development agencies, relocation consultants and state, province and county reviews and profiles to help readers select future expansions and relocation sites." **Buys 120 mss/year.** Query with published clips. Length: 1,000-1,500 words. **Pays $200-400 for assigned articles.** Sometimes pays expenses of writers on assignment.

Photos: Send photos with submission. Buys one-time rights. Offers no additional payment for photos accepted with ms. Captions required.

Tips: "Send clips first, then call me."

$ $ $ EXPO, Atwood Publishing LLC, 11600 College Blvd., Overland Park KS 66210. (913)469-1185. Fax: (913)469-0806. E-mail: dvasos@expoweb.com. Website: www.expoweb.com. Managing Editor: Janine Taylor. **Contact:** Danica Vasos, editor-in-chief. **80% freelance written.** Magazine covering expositions. "*EXPO* is the information and education resource for the exposition industry. It is the only magazine dedicated exclusively to the people with direct responsibility for planning, promoting and operating trade and consumer shows. Our readers are show managers and their staff, association executives, independent show producers and industry suppliers. Every issue of *EXPO* contains in-depth, how-to features and departments that focus on the practical aspects of exposition management, including administration, promotion and operations." Pays on publication. Byline given. Offers 50% kill fee. Buys first North American serial rights. Editorial lead time 3 months. Accepts queries by mail, e-mail, fax. Responds in 3 weeks to queries. Sample copy free. Writer's guidelines free or online.

Nonfiction: How-to, interview/profile. Query with published clips. Length: 600-2,400 words. **Pays 50¢/word.** Pays expenses of writers on assignment.

Photos: State availability with submission.

Columns/Departments: Profile (personality profile), 650 words; Exhibitor Matters (exhibitor issues) and EXPOTech (technology), both 600-1,300 words. **Buys 10 mss/year.** Query with published clips.

Tips: "*EXPO* now offers shorter features and departments, while continuing to offer in-depth reporting. Editorial is more concise, using synopsis, bullets and tidbits whenever possible. Every article needs sidebars, call-outs, graphs, charts, etc., to create entry points for readers. Headlines and leads are more provocative. And writers should elevate the level of shop talk, demonstrating that *EXPO* is the leader in the industry. We plan our editorial calendar about one year in advance, but we are always open to new ideas. Please query before submitting a story to *EXPO*—tell us about your idea and what our readers would learn. Include your qualifications to write about the subject and the sources you plan to contact."

N: $ $ IN TENTS, The Magazine for the Tent Rental and Special-Event Industries, Industrial Fabrics Association International, 1801 County Rd. B W, Roseville MN 55113-4061. (612)225-6970. Fax: (612)225-6966. E-mail: intents@ifai.com. Website: www.ifai.com. **Contact:** John Gehner, editor. **50% freelance written.** Quarterly magazine covering tent-rental and special-event industries. Estab. 1994. Circ. 15,000. **Pays on acceptance.** Publishes ms an average of 2 months after acceptance. Byline given. Buys all rights. Editorial lead time 3 months. Accepts queries by mail, e-mail, fax. Sample copy and writer's guidelines free.

 O→ Break in with familiarity of tent rental, special events, tent manufacturing and fabric structures industries. Or lively, intelligent writing on technical subjects.

Nonfiction: How-to, interview/profile, new product, photo feature, technical. **Buys 10-12 mss/year.** Query. Length: 800-4,000 words. **Pays $100-450.** Sometimes pays expenses of writers on assignment.

Photos: State availability with submission. Reviews contact sheets, negatives, transparencies, prints. Buys one-time rights. Negotiates payment individually. Captions, identification of subjects, model releases required.

Tips: "We look for lively, intelligent writing that makes technical subjects come alive."

$ $ MEETINGS MEDIA, (formerly *Meetings in the West*), Stamats Communications, 550 Montgomery St., #750, San Francisco CA 94111. (415)788-2005. Fax: (415)788-0301. E-mail: leesa.witty@meetings4U.com. Website: www.meetings4U.com. Managing Editor: Leesa Witty. **Contact:** Tyler Davidson, editor. **75% freelance written.** Monthly tabloid covering meeting, event and conference planning. Estab. 1986. Circ. 25,000. Pays 1 month after publication. Publishes ms an average of 1 month after acceptance. Byline given. Buys first North American serial, electronic rights. Editorial lead time 3 months. Submit seasonal material 3 months in advance. Accepts queries by mail, e-mail, fax. Responds in 3 weeks to queries. Sample copy for 9×13 SAE and 5 first-class stamps. Writer's guidelines for #10 SASE or online.

 O→ "Break in with travel experience and destination knowledge, strong clips, meetings and event planning knowledge and experience. Our magazine is heavy on travel destinations. We are always looking for area experts."

Nonfiction: How-to (save money, theme party ideas, plan interesting meetings, etc.), travel (as it pertains to meetings and conventions, what to do after the convention, etc.). "No first-person fluff. We are a business magazine." **Buys 30 mss/year.** Query with published clips. Length: 1,200-2,000 words. **Pays 20¢/word.**

Photos: State availability with submission. Buys one-time rights. Offers no additional payment for photos accepted with ms. Identification of subjects required.

Tips: "We're looking for more technology feature and economy articles (1,200 words) regarding meeting planning."

\$ \$ MINORITY BUSINESS ENTREPRENEUR (MBE), 3528 Torrance Blvd., Suite 101, Torrance CA 90503. (310)540-9398. Fax: (310)792-8263. E-mail: mbewbe@mbemag.com. Website: www.mbemag.com. **Contact:** Angela Cranon, editor-in-chief. **50% freelance written.** Bimonthly magazine covering minority and women business ownership and development. "*MBE* magazine examines programs in the public and private sectors designed to develop minority and women owned businesses into viable enterprises. *MBE* magazine covers a broad range of industries, from construction and banking to telecommunications and high tech." Estab. 1984. Circ. 40,000. Pays on publication. Byline given. Buys first North American serial rights. Editorial lead time 3 months. Accepts queries by mail, e-mail. Responds in 3 weeks to queries. Sample copy for 9½×12½ SAE and 7 first-class stamps. Writer's guidelines free.
Nonfiction: Interview/profile. Nothing unrelated to minority or women's business. **Buys 4-6 mss/year.** Query with published clips. Length: 750-1,000 words. **Pays $0-300.** Sometimes pays expenses of writers on assignment.
Tips: Every issue features a Cover Story (spotlighting the achievements of an individual entrepreneur); Corporate View (highlighting corporate minority and women supplier programs); and Different Drummers (profiling innovators, risk takers, visionaries).

\$ \$ NORTHEAST EXPORT, A Magazine for New England Companies Engaged in International Trade, Commerce Publishing Company, Inc., P.O. Box 254, Northborough MA 01532. (508)351-2925. Fax: (508)351-6905. E-mail: editor@northeast-export.com. Website: www.northeast-export.com. **Contact:** Carlos Cunha, editor. **30% freelance written.** Bimonthly Business-to-business magazine. "*Northeast Export* is the only publication directly targeted at New England's international trade community. All stories relate to issues affecting New England companies and feature only New England-based profiles and examples. Estab. 1997. Circ. 13,500. **Pays on acceptance.** Byline given. Offers 10% kill fee. Buys all rights. Editorial lead time 2 months. Accepts queries by mail, e-mail, fax. Sample copy free.
Nonfiction: How-to, interview/profile, travel, industry trends/analysis. "We will not take unsolicited articles. Query first with clips." **Buys 10-12 mss/year.** Query with published clips and SASE. No unsolicited material. Length: 800-2,000 words. **Pay varies.**
Photos: State availability of or send photos with submission. Reviews 2¼ transparencies, 5×7 prints. Buys one-time rights. Negotiates payment individually. Captions, identification of subjects, model releases required.
Tips: "We're looking for writers with availability; the ability to write clearly about tough, sometimes very technical subjects; the fortitude to slog through industry jargon to get the story straight; a knowledge of international trade issues and/or New England transportation infrastructure. We're interested in freelancers with business writing and magazine experience, especially those with contacts in the New England manufacturing, finance and transportation communities."

\$ \$ PORTABLE RESTROOM OPERATOR, Rangoon Moon Inc., P.O. Box 904, Dahlonega GA 30533. (706)864-6838. Fax: (706)864-9851. E-mail: sesails@yahoo.com. Website: www.1promag.com. Managing Editor: M.A. Watson. **Contact:** Kevin Gralton, editor. **50% freelance written.** Magazine published 9 times/year covering portable sanitation. Estab. 1998. **Pays on acceptance.** Publishes ms an average of 2 months after acceptance. Byline given. Editorial lead time 1 month. Submit seasonal material 2 months in advance. Accepts queries by mail, e-mail, fax.
Nonfiction: Quality articles that will be of interest to our readers. Studies on governmental changes, OSHA regulations, and sanitation articles that deal with portable restrooms are of strong interest. Exposé (government relations, OSHA, EPS associated, trends, public attitudes, etc.), general interest (state portable restroom associations, conventions, etc.), historical/nostalgic, humor, inspirational, new product, personal experience, technical. Query or send complete ms. Length: Length is not important. **Pays 15¢/word.**
Photos: No negatives. "We need good contrast." Send photos with submission. Buys one-time rights. Pays $15 for b&w and color prints that are used. Captions, model releases required.
Tips: "Material must pertain to portable sanitation industry."

\$ \$ \$ \$ PROFESSIONAL COLLECTOR, Pohly & Partners, 27 Melcher St., 2nd Floor, Boston MA 02210-1516. (617)451-1700. Fax: (617)338-7767. E-mail: procollector@pohlypartners.com. Website: www.pohlypartners.com. **Contact:** Karen English, editor. **90% freelance written.** Quarterly magazine published for Western Union's Financial Services Inc.'s Quick Collect Service, covering debt collection business/lifestyle issues. "We gear our articles directly to the debt collectors and their managers. Each issue offers features covering the trends and players, the latest technology, and other issues affecting the collections industry. It's all designed to help collectors be more productive and improve their performance." Estab. 1993. Circ. 161,000. Pays on publication. Byline given. Buys first North American serial rights. Editorial lead time 9 months. Submit seasonal material 9 months in advance. Accepts queries by mail, e-mail, fax. Sample copy and writer's guidelines free.
Nonfiction: General interest, how-to (tips on good collecting), humor, interview/profile, new product, book reviews. **Buys 10-15 mss/year.** Query with published clips. Length: 400-2,000 words. **Pay negotiable for assigned articles.** Sometimes pays expenses of writers on assignment.
Photos: State availability with submission. Reviews contact sheets, 3×5 prints. Buys one-time rights. Negotiates payment individually. Captions, identification of subjects, model releases required.
Columns/Departments: Industry Roundup (issues within industry), 500-1,000 words; Tips, 750-1,000 words; Q&A (questions & answers for collectors), 1,500 words. **Buys 15-20 mss/year.** Query with published clips. **Pay negotiable.**
Tips: "Writers should be aware that *Professional Collector* is a promotional publication, and that its content must support the overall marketing goals of Western Union. It helps to have extensive insider knowledge about the debt collection industry."

$ $ PROGRESSIVE RENTALS, The Voice of the Rental-Purchase Industry, Association of Progressive Rental Organizations, 1504 Robin Hood Trail, Austin TX 78703. (800)204-2776. Fax: (512)794-0097. E-mail: jsherrier @apro-rto.com. Website: www.apro-rto.com. **Contact:** Julie Stephen Sherrier, editor. **50% freelance written.** Bimonthly magazine covering the rent-to-own industry. *"Progressive Rentals* is the only publication representing the rent-to-own industry and members of APRO. The magazine covers timely news and features affecting the industry, association activities and member profiles. Awarded best 4-color magazine by the American Society of Association Executives in 1999." Estab. 1980. Circ. 5,500. **Pays on acceptance.** Publishes ms an average of 2 months after acceptance. Byline given. Offers 25% kill fee. Buys first North American serial rights. Editorial lead time 2 months. Submit seasonal material 4 months in advance. Accepts queries by mail, e-mail, fax, phone. Accepts simultaneous submissions. Responds in 1 month to queries; 2 months to mss. Sample copy free.
Nonfiction: Exposé, general interest, how-to, inspirational, interview/profile, technical, industry features. **Buys 12 mss/year.** Query with published clips. Length: 1,200-2,500 words. **Pays $150-700.** Sometimes pays expenses of writers on assignment.

$ $ RENTAL MANAGEMENT, American Rental Association, 1900 19th St., Moline IL 61265. (309)764-2475. Fax: (309)764-1533. E-mail: brian.alm@ararental.org. Website: www.rentalmanagementmag.com. Managing Editor: Tamera Dawson. **Contact:** Brian R. Alm, editor. **30% freelance written.** Monthly magazine for the equipment rental industry worldwide (*not* property, real estate, appliances, furniture or cars), emphasizing management topics in particular but also marketing, merchandising, technology, etc. Estab. 1970. Circ. 17,700. **Pays on acceptance.** Publishes ms an average of 3 months after acceptance. Byline sometimes given. Buys first North American serial rights. Editorial lead time 2 months. Submit seasonal material 3 months in advance. Accepts queries by mail, e-mail, fax.
Nonfiction: Business management and marketing. **Buys 20-25 mss/year.** Query with published clips. Does not respond to unsolicited work unless being considered for publication. Length: 600-1,500 words. **Pay is negotiated.** Sometimes pays expenses of writers on assignment.
Reprints: Send tearsheet or typed ms with rights for sale noted and information about when and where the material previously appeared.
Photos: State availability with submission. Reviews contact sheets, negatives, 35mm or 2¼ transparencies, any size prints. Buys one-time rights. Negotiates payment individually. Identification of subjects required.
Columns/Departments: "We are adequately served by existing columnists and have a long waiting list of others to use pending need." **Buys 20 mss/year.** Query with published clips. **Pay is negotiated.**
Tips: "Show me you can write maturely, cogently and fluently on management matters of direct and compelling interest to the small-business owner or manager in a larger operation; no sloppiness, no unexamined thoughts, no stiffness or affectation—genuine, direct and worthwhile English. Knowledge of the equipment rental industry is a distinct plus."

N $ $ SBN MAGAZINE, Small Business News Inc., 14725 Detroit Ave., #200, Cleveland OH 44107. (216)228-6397. Fax: (216)529-8924. Website: www.sbnonline.com. **Contact:** Dustin S. Klein, editor. **5% freelance written.** Monthly business magazine with an audience made up of business owners and top decision makers. *"SBN* is smart ideas for growing companies. Best practices, winning strategies. The pain—and joy—of running a business. Every issue delves into the minds of the most innovative executives in Northeast Ohio and across the nation to report on how market leaders got to the top and what strategies they use to stay there." Estab. 1989. Pays on publication. Publishes ms an average of 2 months after acceptance. Byline given. Offers 50% kill fee. Buys first North American serial, second serial (reprint), electronic rights. Editorial lead time 3 months. Submit seasonal material 3 months in advance. Accepts queries by mail, e-mail, phone. Accepts previously published submissions. Responds in 2 weeks to queries; 1 month to mss. Sample copy online. Writer's guidelines by e-mail.
Nonfiction: How-to, interview/profile. No breaking news or straight personality profiles. **Buys 2-5 mss/year.** Query with published clips. Length: 450-1,500 words. **Pays $200-500.** Sometimes pays expenses of writers on assignment.
Photos: State availability with submission. Reviews negatives, prints. Buys one-time, reprint or web rights. Offers no additional payment for photos accepted with ms. Identification of subjects required.
Columns/Departments: Another View (business management related), 500-700 words. **Buys 6-8 mss/year.** Query.
Tips: "The best way to submit to *SBN* is to read us—either online or in print. Remember, our audience is made up of top level business executives and owners."

$ THE STATE JOURNAL, The State Journal Corp., 904 Virginia St. E., Charleston WV 25301. (304)344-1630. Fax: (304)345-2721. E-mail: sjeditor@aol.com. Website: www.statejournal.com. **Contact:** Jack Bailey, editor. **30% freelance written.** Weekly "We are a weekly journal dedicated to providing stories of interest to the business community in West Virginia." Estab. 1984. Circ. 12,000. Pays on publication. Publishes ms an average of 2 months after acceptance. Byline given. Buys first rights. Editorial lead time 2 months. Submit seasonal material 4 months in advance. Accepts queries by mail, e-mail, fax. Responds in 3 weeks to queries; 2 months to mss. Sample copy and writer's guidelines for #10 SASE.
Nonfiction: General interest, interview/profile, new product, opinion, (All business related). **Buys 150 mss/year.** Query. Length: 250-1,500 words. **Pays $50.** Sometimes pays expenses of writers on assignment.
Photos: State availability with submission. Reviews contact sheets. Buys one-time rights. Offers $15/photo. Captions required.
Columns/Departments: Business related, especially slanted toward WV. **Buys 25 mss/year.** Query. **Pays $50.**
Tips: "Localize your work—mention West Virginia specifically in the article; or talk to business people in West Virginia.

$ $UDM, Upholstery Design & Management, Chartwell Communications, 380 E. Northwest Hwy., Suite 300, Des Plaines IL 60016-2208. (847)390-6700. Fax: (847)390-7100. E-mail: mchazin@chartcomm.com. Website: www.udmonline.com. **Contact:** Michael Chazin, editor/associate publisher. **10-20% freelance written.** Monthly Business-to-business magazine covering upholstered furniture/industry management. "*UDM* targets suppliers, manufacturers and retailers/resellers of upholstered furniture for the home, office, institution. Because we are highly specialized, we need writers with a knowledge of the furniture industry and familiarity and ability to identify new style trends." Estab. 1989. Circ. 9,500. Pays on publication. Publishes ms an average of 2 months after acceptance. Byline usually given. Buys first North American serial rights. Accepts queries by mail, e-mail. Responds in 2 weeks to queries; 2 months to mss. Sample copy free.

Nonfiction: Interview/profile. **Buys 15 mss/year.** Query. Length: 500-2,500 words. **Pays $250-700.** Sometimes pays expenses of writers on assignment.

Photos: Reviews transparencies, prints. Offers no additional payment for photos accepted with ms. Captions, identification of subjects required.

Columns/Departments: "Open to suggestions." **Buys 15 mss/year. Pays $250-500.**

Tips: "Writers must have inside knowledge of furniture/upholstery or be privy to knowledge. We try to stay on the leading edge of color and style trends—12-18 months before they hit retail stores."

CHURCH ADMINISTRATION & MINISTRY

Publications in this section are written for clergy members, church leaders and teachers. Magazines for lay members and the general public are listed in the Consumer Religious section.

$ THE AFRICAN AMERICAN PULPIT, Judson Press, 588 N. Gulph Rd., King of Prussia PA 19406. (610)768-2128. Fax: (610)768-2441. E-mail: Victoria.McGoey@abc-usa.org. Website: www.judsonpress.com/TAAP. Editors: Martha Simmons, Frank A. Thomas. **Contact:** Victoria McGoey, managing editor. **100% freelance written.** Quarterly magazine covering African American preaching. "*The African American Pulpit* is a quarterly journal that serves as a repository for the very best of African American preaching and provides practical and creative resources for persons in ministry." Estab. 1997. Circ. 2,000. Pays on publication. Publishes ms an average of 6 months after acceptance. Byline always given. Buys first rights. Editorial lead time 9 months. Submit seasonal material 1 year in advance. Accepts queries by mail, e-mail, fax, phone. Accepts simultaneous submissions. Writer's guidelines online or by e-mail.

Nonfiction: Sermons/articles relating to African American preaching and the African American Church. Book excerpts, essays, how-to (craft a sermon), inspirational, interview/profile, opinion, religious. **Buys 60 mss/year.** Send complete ms. Length: 1,500-3,000 words.

$ 🖻 CE CONNECTION COMMUNIQUE, Creative Christian Ministries, P.O. Box 12624, Roanoke VA 24027. Fax: (540)342-7511. E-mail: ccmbbr@juno.com. **Contact:** Betty Robertson, editor. **25% freelance written.** Monthly e-newsletter, "a vehicle of communication for pastors, local church Christian education leaders and volunteer teachers." Estab. 1995. **Pays on acceptance.** Publishes ms an average of 6 months after acceptance. Byline given. Buys one-time rights. Editorial lead time 6 months. Submit seasonal material 6 months in advance. Accepts simultaneous submissions. Responds in 6 months to queries. Writer's guidelines for #10 SASE.

Nonfiction: How-to, new product. **Buys 12 mss/year.** Send complete ms. Length: 100-600 words. **Pays $5-10.**

$ 🔣 CHURCH EDUCATOR, Educational Ministries, Inc., 165 Plaza Dr., Prescott AZ 86303. (520)771-8601. Fax: (520)771-8621. E-mail: edmin2@aol.com. **Contact:** Linda Davidson, editor. **95% freelance written.** Monthly magazine covering resources for Christian educators. "*Church Educator* has programming ideas for the Christian educator in the mainline Protestant church. We are *not* on the conservative, fundamental side theologically, so slant articles to the liberal side. Programs should offer lots of questions and not give pat answers." Estab. 1978. Circ. 4,500. Pays 60 days after publication. Publishes ms an average of 2 months after acceptance. Byline given. Buys first rights. Editorial lead time 3 months. Submit seasonal material 7 months in advance. Accepts queries by mail, e-mail, fax, phone. Accepts simultaneous submissions. Responds in 2 weeks to queries; 4 months to mss. Sample copy for 9×12 SAE and 4 first-class stamps. Writer's guidelines free.

Nonfiction: How-to, religious. Special issues: How to recruit volunteers; Nurturing faith development of children. No testimonials. **Buys 200 mss/year.** Send complete ms. Length: 500-2,000 words. **Pays 3¢/word.**

Fiction: Religious. "No 'How God Saved My Life' or 'How God Answers Prayers.' " **Buys 10 mss/year.** Send complete ms. Length: 500-1,500 words. **Pays 3¢/word.**

Tips: "We are always looking for material on the seasons of the church year: Advent, Lent, Pentecost, Epiphany. Write up a program for one of those seasons directed toward children, youth, adults or intergenerational."

$ CREATOR MAGAZINE, Bimonthly Magazine of Balanced Music Ministries, 451 Hudson, Healdsburg CA 95448. (707)473-9836. E-mail: creator@creatormagazine.com. **Contact:** Rod Ellis, editor. **35% freelance written.** Bimonthly magazine. "Most readers are church music directors and worship leaders. Content focuses on the spectrum of worship styles from praise and worship to traditional to liturgical. All denominations subscribe. Articles on worship, choir rehearsal, handbells, children's/youth choirs, technique, relationships, etc." Estab. 1978. Circ. 6,000. Pays on publication. Publishes ms an average of 3 months after acceptance. Byline given. Buys first, one-time, second serial (reprint) rights, occasionally buys no rights. Editorial lead time 3 months. Submit seasonal material 4 months in advance. Accepts queries by mail. Accepts simultaneous submissions. Sample copy for 9×12 SAE and 5 first-class stamps. Writer's guidelines free.

Nonfiction: Essays, how-to (be a better church musician, choir director, rehearsal technician, etc.), humor (short personal perspectives), inspirational, interview/profile (call first), new product (call first), opinion, personal experience, photo feature, religious, technical (choral technique). Special issues: July/August is directed toward adult choir members, rather than directors. **Buys 20 mss/year.** Query or send complete ms. Length: 1,000-10,000 words. **Pays $30-75 for assigned articles; $30-60 for unsolicited articles.** Pays expenses of writers on assignment.

Photos: State availability of or send photos with submission. Reviews negatives, 8×10 prints. Buys one-time rights. Offers no additional payment for photos accepted with ms. Captions required.

Columns/Departments: Hints & Humor (music ministry short ideas, anecdotes [cute] ministry experience), 75-250 words; Inspiration (motivational ministry stories), 200-500 words; Children/Youth (articles about specific choirs), 1,000-5,000 words. **Buys 15 mss/year.** Query or send complete ms. **Pays $20-60.**

▣ The online magazine carries original content not found in the print edition.

Tips: "Request guidelines and stick to them. If theme is relevant and guidelines are followed, we'll probably publish."

$ CROSS & QUILL, The Christian Writers Newsletter, Christian Writers Fellowship International, 1624 Jefferson Davis Rd., Clinton SC 29325-6401. (864)697-6035. E-mail: cwfi@cwfi-online.org. Website: www.cwfi-online. org. **Contact:** Sandy Brooks, editor/publisher. **75% freelance written.** Bimonthly journal featuring information and encouragement for writers. "We serve Christian writers and others in Christian publishing. We like informational and how-to articles." Estab. 1976. Circ. 1,000. Pays on publication. Publishes ms an average of 6 months after acceptance. Byline given. Buys first, second serial (reprint) rights. Editorial lead time 6 months. Submit seasonal material 6 months in advance. Accepts queries by mail. Responds in 2 weeks to queries; 2 months to mss. Sample copy for $2 with 9×11 SAE and 2 first-class stamps. Writer's guidelines for #10 SASE.

    0→ Break in by writing "good informational, substantive how-to articles. Right now we're particularly looking for articles on juvenile writing and owning and operating writers groups—successes and learning experiences; also organizing and operating writers workshops and conferences."

Nonfiction: How-to, humor, inspirational, interview/profile, new product, technical. **Buys 25 mss/year.** Send complete ms. Length: 300-800 words. **Pays $10-25.** Sometimes pays in contributor copies or other premiums for fillers, poetry.

Photos: State availability with submission.

Poetry: Free verse, haiku, light verse, traditional. **Buys 6 poems/year.** Submit maximum 3 poems. Length: 12 lines. **Pays $5.**

Tips: "Study guidelines and follow them. No philosophical, personal reflection or personal experiences."

$ $ GROUP MAGAZINE, Group Publishing, Inc., 1515 Cascade Ave., Loveland CO 80538. (970)669-3836. Fax: (970)679-4372. E-mail: greditor@grouppublishing.com. Website: www.youthministry.com. Editor: Rick Lawrence. **Contact:** Kathy Dieterich, assistant editor. **50% freelance written.** Bimonthly magazine for Christian youth workers. "*Group* is the interdenominational magazine for leaders of Christian youth groups. *Group*'s purpose is to supply ideas, practical help, inspiration and training for youth leaders." Estab. 1974. Circ. 55,000. **Pays on acceptance.** Byline sometimes given. Buys all rights. Editorial lead time 4 months. Submit seasonal material 5 months in advance. Accepts queries by mail, e-mail, fax. Responds in 6 weeks to queries; 2 months to mss. Sample copy for $2 plus 10×12 SAE and 3 first-class stamps. Writer's guidelines for #10 SASE.

Nonfiction: Inspirational, personal experience, religious. No fiction. **Buys 30 mss/year.** Query. Length: 175-2,000 words. **Pays $125-225 for assigned articles; $35-125 for unsolicited articles.** Sometimes pays expenses of writers on assignment.

Columns/Departments: Try This One (short ideas for group use), 300 words; Hands-On-Help (tips for youth leaders), 175 words; Strange But True (profiles remarkable youth ministry experience), 500 words. **Pays $35-40.**

$ $ THE JOURNAL OF ADVENTIST EDUCATION, General Conference of SDA, 12501 Old Columbia Pike, Silver Spring MD 20904-6600. (301)680-5075. Fax: (301)622-9627. E-mail: 74617.1231@compuserve.com. **Contact:** Beverly J. Rumble, editor. Bimonthly (except skips issue in summer) professional journal covering teachers and administrators in Seventh Day Adventist school systems. Estab. 1939. Circ. 7,500. Pays on publication. Publishes ms an average of 1 year after acceptance. Byline given. Buys first rights. Editorial lead time 1 year. Accepts queries by mail, e-mail, fax, phone. Responds in 6 weeks to queries; 4 months to mss. Sample copy for 10×12 SAE and 5 first-class stamps. Writer's guidelines free.

Nonfiction: Theme issues have assigned authors. Book excerpts, essays, how-to (education-related), personal experience, photo feature, religious, education. "No brief first-person stories about Sunday Schools." Query. Length: 1,000-1,500 words. **Pays $25-300.**

ALWAYS ENCLOSE a self-addressed, stamped envelope (SASE) with all your queries and correspondence.

Reprints: Send tearsheet or photocopy and information about when and where the material previously appeared.
Photos: State availability of or send photos with submission. Reviews prints. Buys one-time rights. Negotiates payment individually. Captions required.
Tips: "Articles may deal with educational theory or practice, although the *Journal* seeks to emphasize the practical. Articles dealing with the creative and effective use of methods to enhance teaching skills or learning in the classroom are especially welcome. Whether theoretical or practical, such essays should demonstrate the skillful integration of Seventh-day Adventist faith/values and learning."

$ ⚡ KIDS' MINISTRY IDEAS, Review and Herald Publishing Association, 55 W. Oak Ridge Dr., Hagerstown MD 21740. (301)393-4115. Fax: (301)393-4055. E-mail: kidsmin@rhpa.org. Managing Editor: Tamara Michelenko Terry. **Contact:** Patricia Fritz, editor. **95% freelance written.** "A quarterly resource for those leading children to Jesus, *Kids' Ministry Ideas* provides affirmation, pertinent and informative articles, program ideas, resource suggestions, and answers to questions from a Seventh-day Adventist Christian perspective." Estab. 1991. Circ. 5,000. **Pays on acceptance.** Publishes ms an average of 3 months after acceptance. Byline given. Offers variable kill fee. Buys first North American serial, electronic rights. Editorial lead time 3 months. Submit seasonal material 3 months in advance. Accepts queries by mail, e-mail, fax. Responds in 3 weeks to queries; 3 months to mss. Sample copy and writer's guidelines free.
Nonfiction: Inspirational, new product (related to children's ministry), articles fitting the mission of *Kids' Ministry Ideas.* **Buys 40-60 mss/year.** Send complete ms. Length: 500-1,500 words. **Pays $120 for assigned articles; $80 for unsolicited articles.**
Photos: State availability with submission. Buys one-time rights. Captions required.
Columns/Departments: Buys 20-30 mss/year. Query. **Pays $60-120.**
Tips: "Request writers' guidelines and a sample issue."

$ $ ⚡ LEADERSHIP, A Practical Journal for Church Leaders, Christianity Today International, 465 Gundersen Dr., Carol Stream IL 60188. (630)260-6200. Fax: (630)260-0114. E-mail: ljeditor@leadershipjournal.net. Website: www.LeadershipJournal.net. Editor: Marshall Shelley. Associate Editor: Eric Reed. **Contact:** Dawn Zemke, editorial coordinator. **75% freelance written.** Works with a small number of new/unpublished writers each year. Quarterly magazine. Writers must have a "knowledge of and sympathy for the unique expectations placed on pastors and local church leaders. Each article must support points by illustrating from real life experiences in local churches." Estab. 1980. Circ. 65,000. **Pays on acceptance.** Publishes ms an average of 6 months after acceptance. Byline given. Offers 33% kill fee. Buys first, electronic rights. Editorial lead time 6 months. Submit seasonal material 6 months in advance. Accepts queries by mail, e-mail, fax. Responds in 3 weeks to queries; 2 months to mss. Sample copy for $5 or online. Writer's guidelines free with SASE or online.
Nonfiction: How-to, humor, interview/profile, personal experience, Sermon Illustrations. "No articles from writers who have never read our journal." **Buys 60 mss/year.** Query. Length: 300-3,000 words. **Pays $35-400.** Sometimes pays expenses of writers on assignment.
Photos: Send photos with submission. Reviews contact sheets. Buys one-time rights. Offers $25-250/photo. Captions, identification of subjects, model releases required.
Columns/Departments: Eric Reed, managing editor. Growing Edge (book/software reviews); Ministry Staff (stories from church staffers), both 500 words. **Buys 8 mss/year.** Query. **Pays $100-200.**
Tips: "Every article in *Leadership* must provide practical help for problems that church leaders face. *Leadership* articles are not essays expounding a topic or editorials arguing a position or homilies explaining biblical principles. They are how-to articles, based on first-person accounts of real-life experiences in ministry. They allow our readers to see 'over the shoulder' of a colleague in ministry who then reflects on those experiences and identifies the lessons learned. As you know, a magazine's slant is a specific personality that readers expect (and it's what they've sent us their subscription money to provide). Our style is that of friendly conversation rather than directive discourse—what I learned about local church ministry rather than what you need to do."

$ PASTORAL LIFE, Society of St. Paul, P.O. Box 595, Canfield OH 44406-0595. (330)533-5503. Fax: (330)533-1076. E-mail: bro_joshua@hotmail.com. Website: www.albahouse.org. **Contact:** Rev. Matthew Roehrig, editor. **66% freelance written.** Works with new/unpublished writers. "Monthly magazine designed to focus on the current problems, needs, issues and all important activities related to all phases of Catholic pastoral work and life." Estab. 1953. Circ. 2,000. Pays on publication. Publishes ms an average of 4 months after acceptance. Byline given. Buys first rights. Accepts queries by mail, e-mail, fax, phone. Responds in 1 month to queries. Sample copy and writer's guidelines for 6×9 SAE and 4 first-class stamps.
Nonfiction: "*Pastoral Life* is a professional review, principally designed to focus attention on current problems, needs, issues and important activities related to all phases of pastoral work and life." **Buys 30 unsolicited mss/year.** Query with outline before submitting ms. Length: 3,000-3,500 words. **Pays 4¢/word minimum.**
Tips: "Articles should have application for priests and Christian leadership to help them in their ministries and lives."

Ⓝ $ $ THE PRIEST, Our Sunday Visitor, Inc., 200 Noll Plaza, Huntington IN 46750-4304. (219)356-8472. Fax: (219)356-8472. E-mail: tpriest@osv.com. Website: www.osv.com. Editor: Msg. Owen F. Campion. **Contact:** Murray Hubley, associate editor. **80% freelance written.** Monthly magazine. "We run articles that will aid priests in their day-to-day ministry. Includes items on spirituality, counseling, administration, theology, personalities, the saints, etc." **Pays**

on acceptance. Byline given. Buys first North American serial rights. Editorial lead time 3 months. Submit seasonal material 4 months in advance. Accepts queries by mail, e-mail, fax, phone. Responds in 5 weeks to queries; 3 months to mss. Sample copy and writer's guidelines free.

Nonfiction: Essays, historical/nostalgic, humor, inspirational, interview/profile, opinion, personal experience, photo feature, religious. **Buys 96 mss/year.** Send complete ms. Length: 1,500-5,000 words. **Pays $200 minimum for assigned articles; $50 minimum for unsolicited articles.**

Photos: Send photos with submission. Reviews transparencies, prints. Buys one-time rights. Negotiates payment individually. Captions, identification of subjects required.

Columns/Departments: Viewpoint (whatever applies to priests and the Church), 1,000 words. **Buys 36 mss/year.** Send complete ms. **Pays $50-100.**

Tips: "Say what you have to say in an interesting and informative manner and stop. Freelancers are most often published in 'Viewpoints.' Please do not stray from the magisterium of the Catholic Church."

$ $REV., Group Publishing, Inc., 1515 Cascade Ave., Loveland CO 80538-8681. (970)669-3836. Fax: (970)679-4392. E-mail: rector@Rev-magazine.com. Website: www.onlinerev.com. Editor: Paul Allen. **Contact:** Kristi Rector, associate editor. **25% freelance written.** Bimonthly magazine for pastors. "We offer practical solutions to revolutionize and revitalize ministry." Estab. 1997. Circ. 25,000. **Pays on acceptance.** Publishes ms an average of 6 months after acceptance. Byline given. Makes work-for-hire assignments. Editorial lead time 6 months. Submit seasonal material 8 months in advance. Accepts queries by mail, e-mail. Responds in 2 months to queries. Writer's guidelines for #10 SASE or online.

○┐ Break in with short, practical department pieces.

Nonfiction: Ministry, leadership and personal articles with practical application. "No devotions, articles for church members, theological pieces." **Buys 18-24 mss/year.** Query or send complete ms. Length: 1,800-2,000 words. **Pays $300-400.**

Columns/Departments: Preaching & Teaching (preparation & techniques); Worship (all aspects of the worship service); Personal Growth (personal or spiritual growth); Team Work (working with staff and volunteer leaders); Family Ministry (helping families including singles and elderly); Outreach (local and missions); Discipleship (small groups and one-on-one); Current Trends (trends that affect the church), Home Front (pastor's family), Church Biz (leadership and administration), all 250-300 words. **Buys 25 mss/year.** Send complete ms. **Pays $35-50.**

Fillers: Cartoons. **Buys 12/year. Pays $50.**

Tips: "We're most open to submissions for our departments. Remember that we focus on practical articles with an edgy tone."

$ $TEAM NYI MAGAZINE, Resourcing Nazarene Youth Workers, Nazarene Publishing House, 6401 The Paseo, Kansas City MO 64131. Fax: (816)333-4315. E-mail: TeamNYI@nazarene.org. Website: www.nazarene.org/nyi. **Contact:** Jeff Edmondson, editor. **85% freelance written.** Quarterly magazine covering youth ministry. "Published as a resource for the youth pastor or lay youth worker on the business and philosophical work of youth ministry." Estab. 1997. Circ. 10,000. **Pays on acceptance.** Publishes ms an average of 9 months after acceptance. Byline given. Buys first, second serial (reprint) rights. Editorial lead time 6 months. Submit seasonal material 6 months in advance. Accepts queries by mail, e-mail, fax. Responds in 1 month to queries; 6 months to mss. Sample copy for 9×12 SASE and 4 first-class stamps.

Nonfiction: Essays, how-to, humor, inspirational, interview/profile, opinion, personal experience, religious, technical. "Please do not send fiction, poetry, historical or exposé." **Buys 15 mss/year.** Query, send complete ms. Length: 1,000-1,500 words. **Pays $25-100.**

Photos: State availability with submission. Offers no additional payment for photos accepted with ms.

Columns/Departments: Query, send complete ms.

Fillers: Anecdotes, facts, short humor. Length: 50-100 words. **Pays nothing for fillers.**

Tips: "E-mail query is the fastest way to get our attention. Cover letter with an attached article is fine too. Make sure your ideas are timely. No ministry ideas that worked in the '70s and '80s. Teens in the 21st century are a whole different animal."

$ $TODAY'S CATHOLIC TEACHER, The Voice of Catholic Education, Peter Li Education Group, 330 Progress Rd., Dayton OH 45449. (937)847-5900. Fax: (937)847-5910. E-mail: mnoschang@peterli.com. Website: www. catholicteacher.com. **Contact:** Mary C. Noschang, editor. **60% freelance written.** Magazine published 6 times/year during school year covering Catholic education for grades K-12. "We look for topics of interest and practical help to teachers in Catholic elementary schools in all curriculum areas including religion technology, discipline, motivation." Estab. 1972. Circ. 50,000. Pays on publication. Publishes ms an average of 2 months after acceptance. Byline given. Buys first and all rights and makes work-for-hire assignments. Editorial lead time 3 months. Submit seasonal material 6 months in advance. Accepts queries by mail, e-mail, fax. Accepts simultaneous submissions. Responds in 1 month to queries; 3 months to mss. Sample copy for $3 or online. Writer's guidelines online.

Nonfiction: Interested in articles detailing ways to incorporate Catholic values into academic subjects other than religion class. Essays, how-to, humor, interview/profile, personal experience. "No articles pertaining to public education." **Buys 15 mss/year.** Query or send complete ms. Length: 1,500-3,000 words. **Pays $150-300.** Sometimes pays expenses of writers on assignment.

Photos: State availability with submission. Reviews transparencies, prints. Buys one-time rights. Offers $20-50/photo. Captions, identification of subjects, model releases required.

Tips: "Although our readership is primarily classroom teachers, *Today's Catholic Teacher* is read also by principals, supervisors, superintendents, boards of education, pastors, and parents. *Today's Catholic Teacher* aims to be for Catholic educators a source of information not available elsewhere. The focus of articles should span the interests of teachers from early childhood through junior high. Articles may be directed to just one age group yet have wider implications. Preference is given to material directed to teachers in grades four through eight. The desired magazine style is direct, concise, informative and accurate. Writing should be enjoyable to read, informal rather than scholarly, lively, and free of educational jargon."

N $ TODAY'S CHRISTIAN PREACHER, Marketing Partners, Inc., 3 Park Plaza, Reading PA 19610-1399. (610)913-0796. Fax: (610)913-0797. E-mail: tcpubs@mktpt.com. Editor: Jerry Thacker. **Contact:** Elaine Williams, assistant editor. **10% freelance written.** Quarterly magazine offering articles for pastors. *"Today's Christian Preacher* is designed to meet the personal needs of the man of God." Estab. 1992. Circ. 25,000. Pays on publication. Publishes ms an average of 1 year after acceptance. Buys simultaneous rights. Editorial lead time 1 year. Submit seasonal material 1 year in advance. Accepts queries by mail, e-mail, fax. Accepts simultaneous submissions. Responds in 1 month to queries; 3 months to mss. Sample copy for 9 × 12 SAE and 4 first-class stamps. Writer's guidelines for #10 SASE.

○→ Break in with "concise, practical information for the pastor in his personal life, not sermons or church issues."

Nonfiction: Inspirational, religious. **Buys 5 mss/year.** Send complete ms. Length: 800-1,000 words. **Pays $150 for assigned articles.**

Photos: Offers no additional payment for photos accepted with ms.

$ WORLD PULSE, (formerly *Pulse*), Evangelism and Missions Information Service/Wheaton College, P.O. Box 794, Wheaton IL 60189. (630)752-7158. Fax: (630)752-7155. E-mail: pulsenews@aol.com. **Contact:** Managing Editor. **60% freelance written.** Semimonthly newsletter covering mission news and trends. "We provide current information about evangelical Christian missions and churches around the world. Most articles are news-oriented, although we do publish some features and interviews." Estab. 1965. Circ. 5,000. Pays on publication. Publishes ms an average of 2 months after acceptance. Byline given. Offers 50% kill fee. Buys first, all rights. Editorial lead time 2 months. Accepts queries by mail, e-mail, fax, phone. Responds in 2 weeks to queries; 1 month to mss. Sample copy and writer's guidelines free.

○→ Break in with "coverage of the subjects requested, bringing to the task both the topic's essential components, but with a dash of style, as well."

Nonfiction: Interview/profile, photo feature, religious, technical. Does not want anything that does not cover the world of evangelical missions. **Buys 50-60 mss/year.** Query with published clips. Length: 300-1,000 words. **Pays $25-100.** Sometimes pays expenses of writers on assignment.

Photos: Send photos with submission. Reviews contact sheets. Buys all rights. Negotiates payment individually. Identification of subjects required.

Tips: "Have a knowledge of and appreciation for the evangelical missions community, as well as for cross-cultural issues. Writing must be economical, with a judicious use of quotes and examples."

$ $ WORSHIP LEADER MAGAZINE, CCM Communications, 104 Woodmont Blvd., 3rd Floor, Nashville TN 37205-2245. (615)386-3011. Fax: (615)385-4112. E-mail: ddisabatino@ccmcom.com. Website: www.worshipleader.org. Executive Editor: Chuck Fromm. **Contact:** David Di Sabatino, managing editor. **80% freelance written.** Bimonthly magazine covering all aspects of Christian worship. *"Worship Leader Magazine* exists to challenge, serve, equip and train those involved in leading the 21st century Church in worship. The intended readership is the worship team (all those who plan and lead) of the local church." Estab. 1992. Circ. 50,000. Pays on publication. Byline given. Offers 50% kill fee. Buys first North American serial, all rights. Editorial lead time 3 months. Submit seasonal material 6 months in advance. Responds in 6 weeks to queries; 3 months to mss. Sample copy for $5. Writer's guidelines for #10 SASE.

Nonfiction: General interest, how-to (related to purpose/audience), inspirational, interview/profile, opinion. **Buys 15-30 mss/year.** Query with published clips. Length: 1,200-2,000 words. **Pays $200-800 for assigned articles; $200-500 for unsolicited articles.** Sometimes pays expenses of writers on assignment.

Photos: State availability with submission. Buys one-time rights. Negotiate payment individually. Identification of subjects required.

Tips: "Our goal has been and is to provide the tools and information pastors, worship leaders, and ministers of music, youth, and the arts need to facilitate and enhance worship in their churches. In achieving this goal, we strive to maintain high journalistic standards, biblical soundness, and theological neutrality. Our intent is to present the philosophical, scholarly insight on worship, as well as the day-to-day, 'putting it all together' side of worship, while celebrating our unity and diversity."

$ $ YOUR CHURCH, Helping You With the Business of Ministry, Christianity Today, Inc., 465 Gundersen Dr., Carol Stream IL 60188. (630)260-6200. Fax: (630)260-0114. E-mail: yceditor@yourchurch.net. Website: www.your church.net. Editor: Phyllis Ten Eishof. **Contact:** Randy Bishop, associate editor. **70% freelance written.** Bimonthly magazine. "Articles pertain to the business aspects of ministry pastors are called upon to perform: administration, purchasing, management, technology, building, etc." Estab. 1955. Circ. 150,000. **Pays on acceptance.** Publishes ms an

average of 4 months after acceptance. Byline given. Buys one-time rights. Submit seasonal material 5 months in advance. Accepts queries by mail, e-mail, fax, phone. Accepts simultaneous submissions. Responds in 1 month to queries; 2 months to mss. Sample copy for 9×12 SAE and 5 first-class stamps. Writer's guidelines for 9×12 SAE with 5 first-class stamps.
Nonfiction: How-to, new product, technical. Special issues: Church Management, Construction. **Buys 25 mss/year.** Send complete ms. Length: 900-1,500 words. **Pays about 15¢/word.**
Reprints: Send photocopy and information about when and where the material previously appeared. Pays 30% of the amount paid for an original article.
Photos: State availability with submission. Reviews 4×5 transparencies, 5×7 or 8×10 prints. Buys one-time rights. Offers no additional payment for photos accepted with ms. Captions, identification of subjects, model releases required.
Tips: "The editorial is generally geared toward brief and helpful articles dealing with some form of church business. Concise, bulleted points from experts in the field are typical for our articles."

$ YOUTH AND CHRISTIAN EDUCATION LEADERSHIP, Pathway Press, 1080 Montgomery Ave., P.O. Box 2250, Cleveland TN 37320-2250. (423)478-7599. Fax: (423)478-7616. E-mail: Ann.Steely@PathwayPress.org. Editor: Tony P. Lane. **Contact:** Ann Steely, editorial assistant. **25% freelance written.** Quarterly magazine covering Christian education. "*Youth and Christian Education Leadership* is written for teachers, youth pastors, children's pastors, and other local Christian education workers." Estab. 1976. Circ. 10,000. **Pays on acceptance.** Publishes ms an average of 6 months after acceptance. Buys one-time rights. Editorial lead time 6 months. Submit seasonal material 6 months in advance. Accepts queries by mail, e-mail. Accepts simultaneous submissions. Responds in 3 months to mss. Sample copy for $1 and 9×12 SASE. Writer's guidelines free.
Nonfiction: How-to, humor (in-class experience), inspirational, interview/profile, motivational; seasonal short skits. **Buys 16 mss/year.** Send complete ms; include SSN. Send SASE for return of ms. Length: 400-1,200 words. **$25-45.**
Reprints: Send typed, double-spaced ms with rights for sale noted and information about when and where the material previously appeared. Pays 80% of amount paid for an original article.
Photos: State availability with submission. Reviews contact sheets, transparencies. Buys one-time rights. Negotiates payment individually.
Columns/Departments: Sunday School Leadership, Reaching Out (creative evangelism), The Pastor and Christian Education, Preschool, Elementary, Teen, Adult, Drawing Closer, Kids Church; all 500 words. Send complete ms with SASE. **Pays $25-45.**
Tips: "Become familiar with the publication's content and submit appropriate material. We are continually looking for 'fresh ideas' that have proven to be successful."

CLOTHING

N $ $ EMB-EMBROIDERY/MONOGRAM BUSINESS, Bill Communications, 1199 S. Belt Line, Suite 100, Cappell TX 75019. (972)906-6500. Fax: (972)906-6701. E-mail: lhowle@mfi.com. Website: www.embmag.com. **Contact:** Lola Howle, editor. **30% freelance written.** Monthly magazine covering computerized embroidery and digitizing design. "Readable, practical business and/or technical articles that show our readers how to succeed in their profession." Estab. 1994. Circ. 26,000. **Pays on acceptance.** Publishes ms an average of 3 months after acceptance. Byline given. Buys all rights. Editorial lead time 3 months. Submit seasonal material 6 months in advance. Accepts queries by mail, e-mail. Accepts simultaneous submissions. Sample copy for $7.
Nonfiction: How-to (embroidery, sales, marketing, design, general business info), interview/profile, new product, photo feature, technical (computerized embroidery). **Buys 4-6 mss/year.** Query. Length: 800-2,000 words. **Pays $200 and up for assigned articles.**
Photos: Send photos with submission. Reviews transparencies, prints. Negotiates payment individually.
Tips: "Show us you have specified knowledge, experience or contacts in the embroidery industry or a related field."

$ $ MADE TO MEASURE, Halper Publishing Company, 600 Central Ave., Suite 226, Highland Park IL 60035. (847)433-1114. Fax: (847)433-6602. E-mail: mtm@halper.com. Website: www.halper.com. **Contact:** Rick Levine, editor/publisher. **10% freelance written.** Semiannual magazine covering uniforms and career apparel. "A semi-annual magazine/buyers' reference containing leading sources of supply, equipment and services of every description related to the Uniform, Career Apparel, Tailoring and allied trades, throughout the entire U.S." Estab. 1930. Circ. 25,000. **Pays on acceptance.** Publishes ms an average of 2 months after acceptance. Byline given. Buys first North American serial rights. Editorial lead time 4 months. Submit seasonal material 4 months in advance. Accepts queries by mail, e-mail. Accepts simultaneous submissions. Responds in 3 weeks to queries. Sample copy free or online.
Nonfiction: "Please only consider sending queries related to stories to companies that wear or make uniforms, career apparel or identifying apparel." Historical/nostalgic, interview/profile, new product, personal experience, photo feature, technical. **Buys 5 mss/year.** Query with published clips. Length: 1,000-3,000 words. **Pays $300-600.** Sometimes pays expenses of writers on assignment.
Photos: State availability with submission. Reviews contact sheets, any prints. Buys one-time rights. Negotiates payment individually.

Tips: "We look for features about large and small companies who wear uniforms (restaurants, hotels, industrial, medical, public safety, etc.)."

N $ $ $ TEXTILE RENTAL, Uniform and Linen Service Management Trends, Textile Rental Services Assoc. of America, 1130 E. Hallandale Beach Blvd., Suite B, Hallandale Beach FL 33009. (954)457-7555. Fax: (954)457-3890. E-mail: jadams@trsa.org. Website: www.trsa.org. **Contact:** John D. Adams, managing editor. **30% freelance written.** Monthly magazine covering management and trends for uniform and linen rental executives. "*Textile Rental* covers government, environment, labor, workplace safety, regulatory compliance, technology, the economy, plant operations, strategic management, marketing, sales and service." **Pays on acceptance.** Publishes ms an average of 1 month after acceptance. Byline given. Offers negotiable kill fee. Buys first North American serial, electronic rights. Editorial lead time 3 months. Submit seasonal material 4 months in advance. Accepts queries by mail, e-mail. Accepts simultaneous submissions. Responds in 1 months to queries; 3 months to mss. Sample copy free or online. Writer's guidelines for #10 SASE.
Nonfiction: Historical/nostalgic, how-to, humor, inspirational, interview/profile, new product, personal experience, photo feature, technical, travel. **Buys 12-15 mss/year.** Query with published clips. Length: 1,000-5,000 words. **Pays $350-1,000.** Pays in contributor copies at writer's request. Sometimes pays expenses of writers on assignment.
Reprints: Send typed ms with rights for sale noted and information about when and where the material previously appeared. negotiable.
Photos: Send photos with submission. Reviews contact sheets, negatives, transparencies. Buys all rights. Negotiates payment individually. Captions, identification of subjects required.
Columns/Departments: Query. **Pays $50-350.**
Fillers: Anecdotes, facts, gags to be illustrated by cartoonist, newsbreaks, short humor. **Buys 25-30/year.** Length: 150-500 words. **Pays $50-300.**
Tips: "The content of what you write is more important than your prose. As a professional working in the textile rental industry, you have valuable insight into industry concerns. Your association magazine is an excellent forum for exchanging perspectives with your peers about issues such as new technology, experiences with workers' compensation, consolidation in the industry, and new market opportunities."

CONFECTIONERY & SNACK FOODS

These publications focus on the bakery, snack and candy industries. Journals for grocers, wholesalers and other food industry personnel are listed in Groceries & Food Products.

$ $ PACIFIC BAKERS NEWS, 3155 Lynde St., Oakland CA 94601. (510)532-5513. **Contact:** C.W. Soward, publisher. **30% freelance written.** Eager to work with new/unpublished writers. Monthly newsletter for commercial bakeries in the western states. Estab. 1961. Pays on publication. No byline given; uses only 1-paragraph news items.
Nonfiction: Uses bakery business reports and news about bakers. Buys only brief "boiled-down news items about bakers and bakeries operating only in Alaska, Hawaii, Pacific Coast and Rocky Mountain states. We welcome clippings. We need monthly news reports and clippings about the baking industry and the donut business." No pictures, jokes, poetry or cartoons. Length: 10-200 words. **Pays 10¢/word for news and 6¢/word for clips.**

CONSTRUCTION & CONTRACTING

Builders, architects and contractors learn the latest industry news in these publications. Journals targeted to architects are also included in the Consumer Art & Architecture category. Those for specialists in the interior aspects of construction are listed under Building Interiors.

N $ $ ADVANCED MATERIALS & COMPOSITES NEWS AND COMPOSITES eNEWS, International Business & Technology Intelligence on High Performance M&P, Composites Worldwide Inc., 991C Lomas Santa Fe Dr., MC469, Solana Beach CA 92075-2125. (858)755-1372. Fax: (858)755-5271. E-mail: info@compositesnews.com. Website: www.compositesnews.com. Managing Editor: Susan Loud. **Contact:** Steve Loud, editor. **5% freelance written.** Bimonthly newsletter covering advanced materials and fiber-reinforced composites. *Advanced Materials and Composites News* "covers markets, materials, processes and organization for all sectors of the global hi-tech materials world. Audience is management, academics, government, suppliers and fabricators. Focus on news about growth opportunities." Estab. 1978. Circ. 10,000. Pays on publication. Publishes ms an average of 1 months after acceptance. Byline sometimes given. Buys all rights. Editorial lead time 2 weeks. Submit seasonal material 3 months in advance. Accepts queries by e-mail. Responds in 1 month to queries; 1 month to mss. Sample copy for #10 SASE.
Nonfiction: New product, technical. **Buys 4-6 mss/year.** Query. Length: 100-700 words. **Pays $100-400.**
Photos: State availability with submission. Reviews 4×5 transparencies. Buys all rights. Offers no additional payment for photos accepted with ms. Captions, identification of subjects, model releases required.

$ $AUTOMATED BUILDER, CMN Associates, Inc., 1445 Donlon St., Suite 16, Ventura CA 93003. (805)642-9735. Fax: (805)642-8820. E-mail: info@automatedbuilder.com. Website: www.automatedbuilder.com. Editor-in-Chief: Don Carlson. **Contact:** Bob Mendel. **10% freelance written.** Monthly magazine specializing in management for industrialized (manufactured) housing and volume home builders. "Our material is technical in content, and concerned with new technologies or improved methods for in-plant building and components related to building. Online content is uploaded from the monthly print material." Estab. 1964. Circ. 25,000. **Pays on acceptance.** Publishes ms an average of 3 months after acceptance. Byline given. Buys first North American serial rights. Editorial lead time 2 months. Submit seasonal material 2 months in advance. Accepts queries by mail, e-mail, fax. Responds in 2 weeks to queries. Sample copy free.

Nonfiction: Case history articles on successful home building companies which may be 1) production (big volume) home builders; 2) mobile home manufacturers; 3) modular home manufacturers; 4) prefabricated (panelized) home manufacturers; 5) house component manufacturers; or 6) special unit (in-plant commercial building) manufacturers. Also uses interviews, photo features and technical articles. "No architect or plan 'dreams'. Housing projects must be built or under construction." **Buys 6-8 mss/year.** Query. Phone queries OK. Length: 250-500 words. **Pays $300.**

Photos: State availability with submission. Reviews 35mm or larger—35mm preferred transparencies, wants 4×5, 5×7 or 8×10 glossies. No additional payment. Captions, identification of subjects required.

Tips: "Stories often are too long, too loose; we prefer 500 to 750 words. We prefer a phone query on feature articles. If accepted on query, article usually will not be rejected later."

$ $CAM MAGAZINE, Construction Association of Michigan, 43636 S. Woodward, Bloomfield Hills MI 48302-3204. (248)972-1000. Fax: (248)972-1001. E-mail: cammagazine@cam-online.com. Website: www.cam-online.com. **Contact:** Phyllis L. Brooks, editor. **5% freelance written.** Monthly magazine covering all facets of the construction industry. "*CAM Magazine* is devoted to the growth and progress of individuals and companies serving and servicing the industry. It provides a forum on new construction-related technology, products and services, plus publishes information on industry personnel changes and advancements." Estab. 1978. Circ. 5,000. Pays on publication. Byline given. Buys all rights. Editorial lead time 2 months. Submit seasonal material 3 months in advance. Accepts queries by mail, e-mail, fax, phone. Sample copy and editorial subject calendar with query and SASE.

Nonfiction: Construction-related only. **Buys 3 mss/year.** Query with published clips. Length: Length: features 1,000-2,000 words; will also review short pieces. **Pays $250-500.**

Photos: Send photos with submission. Reviews contact sheets, negatives, transparencies, color or b&w prints. Buys one-time rights. Offers no additional payment for photos accepted with ms.

Tips: "Anyone having *current* knowledge or expertise on trends and innovations related to construction is welcome to submit articles. Our readers are construction experts."

$ $CONCRETE CONSTRUCTION, (formerly *Aberdeen's Concrete Construction*), Hanley-Wood, LLC., 426 S. Westgate St., Addison IL 60101. (630)543-0870. Fax: (630)543-5399. E-mail: cceditor@wocnet.com. Website: www.worldofconcrete.com. Editor: Ward Malisch. **Contact:** Pat Reband, managing editor. **20% freelance written.** Monthly magazine for concrete contractors, engineers, architects, specifiers and others who design and build residential, commercial, industrial and public works, cast-in-place concrete structures. It also covers job stories and new equipment in the industry. Estab. 1956. Circ. 80,000. **Pays on acceptance.** Publishes ms an average of 4 months after acceptance. Byline given. Editorial lead time 4 months. Submit seasonal material 4 months in advance. Accepts queries by mail, e-mail, fax. Responds in 2 weeks to queries; 1 month to mss. Sample copy and writer's guidelines free.

Nonfiction: How-to, new product, personal experience, photo feature, technical, job stories. **Buys 7-10 mss/year.** Query with published clips. Length: 2,000 words maximum. **Pays $250 or more for assigned articles; $200 minimum for unsolicited articles.** Pays expenses of writers on assignment.

Photos: Send photos with submission. Reviews contact sheets, negatives, transparencies, prints. Buys one-time rights. Offers no additional payment for photos accepted with ms. Captions required.

Tips: "Have a good understanding of the concrete construction industry. How-to stories only accepted from industry experts. Job stories must cover procedures, materials, and equipment used as well as the project's scope."

[N] $ $CONCRETE HOMES, Publications and Communications Inc., 505 Cypress Creek Rd., Suite B, Cedar Park TX 78613. (512)926-4663. Fax: (512)331-3950. E-mail: homes@pci.news.com. Editor: Chantal Rice. **Contact:** Brona Stockton, associate publisher . **50% freelance written.** Quarterly magazine covering concrete construction. "*Concrete Homes* reaches builders and home buyers. It covers new homes being built with concrete, the advantages of concrete and building techniques." Estab. 1998. Circ. 20,000. Pays on publication. Publishes ms an average of 4 months after acceptance. Byline given. Offers 100% kill fee. Buys all rights. Editorial lead time 4 months. Submit seasonal material 6 months in advance. Accepts queries by mail. Responds in 1 month to queries; 2 months to mss. Sample copy and writer's guidelines free.

Nonfiction: How-to, new product, technical. **Buys 6 mss/year.** Query with published clips. Length: 500-2,000 words. **Pays $200 for assigned articles.** Pays expenses of writers on assignment.

Photos: State availability with submission. Reviews negatives, transparencies, prints. Buys all rights. Offers no additional payment for photos accepted with ms. Captions required.

$ $ $THE CONCRETE PRODUCER, The Aberdeen Group, 426 S. Westgate St., Addison IL 60101. (630)705-2623. Fax: (630)543-3112. E-mail: dtalend@wocnet.com. Website: www.worldofconcrete.com. **Contact:** Rick Yelton, editor. **30% freelance written.** Monthly magazine covering concrete production. "Our audience consists of producers who have succeeded in making concrete the preferred building material through management, operating, quality control, use of the latest technology, or use of superior materials." Estab. 1982. Circ. 18,000. Pays on publication. Publishes ms an average of 2 months after acceptance. Byline given. Buys second serial (reprint) rights. Editorial lead time 4 months. Accepts queries by mail, e-mail, fax, phone. Responds in 1 week to queries; 2 months to mss. Sample copy for $4. Writer's guidelines free.

Nonfiction: How-to (promote concrete), new product, technical. **Buys 10 mss/year.** Send complete ms. Length: 500-2,000 words. **Pays $200-1,000.** Sometimes pays expenses of writers on assignment.

Photos: State availability with submission. Reviews 2×2 transparencies, 3×5 prints. Offers no additional payment for photos accepted with ms. Captions, identification of subjects required.

$CONSTRUCTION EQUIPMENT GUIDE, 470 Maryland St., Ft. Washington PA 19034. (800)523-2200 or (215)885-2900. Fax: (215)885-2910. E-mail: editorial@constructionequipguide.com. **Contact:** Melissa Buchanan, editor-in-chief. **30% freelance written.** Biweekly newspaper. "We are looked at as the primary source of information in the construction industry by equipment manufacturers, sellers and users. We cover the Midwest, Northeast, Southwest and Southeast states with our 4 editions published biweekly. We give the latest news on current construction projects, legislative actions, political issues, mergers and acquisitions, new unique applications of equipment and in-depth features." Estab. 1957. Circ. 120,000. Pays on publication. Publishes ms an average of 1 month after acceptance. Byline given. Buys all rights. Accepts queries by mail, e-mail, fax, phone. Sample copy and writer's guidelines free.

Nonfiction: General interest, historical/nostalgic, how-to (winterizing construction equipment, new methods of construction applications), interview/profile, new product, personal experience, photo feature, technical. **Buys 200-600 mss/year.** Query with published clips. Length: 150-1,200 words. **Negotiates payment individually.**

Photos: Send photos with submission. Negotiates payment individually. Captions, identification of subjects required.

Tips: "Keep an eye out for commercial construction in your area. Take note of the name of the contractors on site. Then give us a call to see if you should follow up with a full story and photos. Pay attention to large and small jobs right around you. Read articles in *Construction Equipment Guide* to learn what information is important to our readers, who are equipment users, sellers and makers."

[N] $ $CONSTRUCTION SPECIFIER, 99 Canal Center Plaza, Suite 300, Alexandria VA 22314-1588. (703)684-0300. Fax: (703)684-0465. E-mail: ksears@csinet.org. **Contact:** Katie Sears, editor. **50% freelance written.** Works with a small number of new/unpublished writers each year. Monthly magazine for architects, engineers, specification writers and project managers. Estab. 1949. Circ. 19,000. Pays on publication. Publishes ms an average of 3 months after acceptance. Buys Buys world serial rights. Editorial lead time 3 months. Sample copy for 9×12 SAE and 6 first-class stamps. Writer's guidelines for #10 SASE.

Nonfiction: Looking for articles on selection and specification of products, materials, practices and methods used in non-residential construction projects, specifications as related to construction design, plus legal and management subjects. Query. Length: 2,500-3,500 words. **Pays up to 15¢/published word (negotiable), plus art.** Pays minor expenses of writers on assignment, to an agreed upon limit.

Reprints: Send information about when and where the article appeared. Does not pay for reprints.

Photos: Photos desirable in consideration for publication; line art, sketches, diagrams, charts and graphs also desired. Full color transparencies may be used; 8×10 glossies, 3¼ slides preferred. Payment negotiable.

Tips: "Make sure articles are technical and nonproprietary."

$ $EQUIPMENT JOURNAL, Canada's National Equipment Newspaper, 5160 Explorer Dr., Unit 6, Mississauga, Ontario L4W 4T7, Canada. (800)667-8541. Fax: (905)629-7988. E-mail: equipmentjournal@globalserve.net. Website: www.equipmentjournal.com. **Contact:** Michael Anderson, editor. **10% freelance written.** Journal published 17 times/year covering heavy equipment used in construction, mining and forestry industries. Estab. 1966. Circ. 25,000. Pays on publication. Byline given. Makes work-for-hire assignments. Editorial lead time 1 month. Submit seasonal material 1 month in advance. Accepts queries by mail, e-mail, fax, phone. Accepts simultaneous submissions. Sample copy free.

Nonfiction: Interview/profile, new product, technical. "No material that falls outside of *EJ*'s mandate—the Canadian equipment industry." **Buys 10 mss/year.** Query. Length: 500-1,000 words. **Pays $100-200.** Sometimes pays expenses of writers on assignment.

Photos: State availability with submission. Reviews 4×6 prints. Buys all rights. Negotiates payment individually. Identification of subjects required.

Tips: "Provide an idea for a story that is uniquely Canadian."

$ $ $HARD HAT NEWS, Lee Publications, Inc., 6113 State Highway 5, Palatine Bridge NY 13428. (518)673-3237. Fax: (518)673-2381. E-mail: ffanning@LeePub.com. Website: www.LeePub.com. **Contact:** Fred Fanning, editor. **80% freelance written.** Biweekly tabloid covering heavy construction, equipment, road and bridge work. "Our readers are contractors and heavy construction workers involved in excavation, highways, bridges, utility construction and underground construction." Estab. 1980. Circ. 24,000. Byline given. Editorial lead time 2 weeks. Submit seasonal material 2 weeks in advance. Accepts queries by mail, e-mail, fax, phone. Sample copy and writer's guidelines free.

　　O─ "We especially need writers with some knowledge of heavy construction, although anyone with good composition and interviewing skills is welcome. Focus on major construction in progress in your area."

Nonfiction: Also 'Job Stories,' (a brief overall description of the project, the names and addresses of the companies and contractors involved, and a description of the equipment used, including manufacturers' names and model numbers. Quotes from the people in charge, as well as photos, are important, as are the names of the dealers providing the equipment). Interview/profile, new product, opinion, photo feature, technical. Send complete ms. Length: 50-1,400 words. **Pays $2.50/inch.** Sometimes pays expenses of writers on assignment.
Photos: Send photos with submission. Reviews prints, slides. Offers $5/photo. Captions, identification of subjects required.
Columns/Departments: New Products; Association News; Parts and Repairs; Attachments; Trucks and Trailers; People on the Move.
Fillers: Cartoons. **Pays $10/cartoon.**
Tips: "Every issue has a focus—see our editorial calender. Special consideration is given to a story that coincides with the focus. A color photo is necessary for the front page. Vertical shots work best. We need more writers in Maryland, Delaware and the Washington, DC area. Also, we are expanding our distribution into the Mid-Atlantic states and need writers in Virginia, Tennessee, North Carolina and South Carolina."

$ $HEAVY EQUIPMENT NEWS, Vulcan Publications, 33 Inverness Center Parkway, Suite 300, Birmingham AL 35243. Fax: (205)380-1384. E-mail: aboatright@vulcanpub.com. Website: www.heavyequipmentnews.com. **Contact:** Ashley Boatright, senior editor. **40-50% freelance written.** Monthly magazine covering construction equipment and construction industry. "*Heavy Equipment News* is an editorial-driven publication for the construction contractor, focusing on job sites, asphalt-road building, concrete, business management, equipment selection and material handling." Estab. 1995. Circ. 70,000. **Pays on acceptance.** Publishes ms an average of 3 months after acceptance. Byline given. Offers 10% kill fee. Buys first North American serial, second serial (reprint), electronic rights. Editorial lead time 6 months. Submit seasonal material 6 months in advance. Accepts queries by mail, e-mail, fax. Responds in 2 weeks to queries; 1 month to mss. Sample copy for #10 SASE. Writer's guidelines free.
Nonfiction: How-to, interview/profile, new product, personal experience, technical. **Buys 24 mss/year.** Query with published clips. Length: 1,200-1,500 words. **Pays $500.**
Photos: Reviews transparencies, prints. Buys all rights. Offers no additional payment for photos accepted with ms. Captions, identification of subjects required.
Columns/Departments: Asphalt Road, Concrete Batch, Material Handling Advances, Truck Stop. Query with published clips. **Pays $300.**

$ $MC MAGAZINE, The Voice of the Manufactured Concrete Products Industry, National Precast Concrete Association, 10333 N. Meridian St., Suite 272, Indianapolis IN 46290. (317)571-9500. Fax: (317)571-0041. E-mail: pmanning@precast.org. Website: www.precast.org. **Contact:** John Minnick, executive editor. **75% freelance written.** Quarterly magazine covering manufactured concrete products. "*MC Magazine* is a publication for owners and managers of factories that produce concrete materials used in construction. We publish business articles, technical articles, company profiles, safety articles and project profiles with the intent of educating our readers in order to increase the quality and use of precast concrete." Estab. 1995. Circ. 8,500. **Pays on acceptance.** Publishes ms an average of 6 months after acceptance. Byline given. Buys first North American serial, second serial (reprint), all rights. Editorial lead time 3 months. Accepts queries by mail, e-mail, fax. Accepts simultaneous submissions. Responds in 1 month to queries; 2 months to mss. Sample copy for 9×12 SAE and 8 first-class stamps or online. Writer's guidelines for #10 SASE, online or by e-mail.
Nonfiction: How-to (business), interview/profile, technical (concrete manufacturing). "No humor, essays, fiction or fillers." **Buys 16-20 mss/year.** Query or send complete ms. Length: 2,000-3,500 words. **Pays $250-700.** Sometimes pays expenses of writers on assignment.
Photos: State availability with submission. Buys all rights. Offers no additional payment for photos accepted with ms. Captions required.
Tips: "Understand the audience and the purpose of the magazine. We have an ongoing need for business-related articles that would be pertinent to small- to mid-sized manufacturers. Understanding audience interests and needs is important and expressing a willingness to tailor a subject to get the right slant is critical. Our primary freelance needs are about general business or technology topics. Of course, if you are an engineer or a writer specializing in industry, construction or manufacturing technology, other possibilities would certainly exist. Writing style should be concise, yet lively and entertaining. Avoid cliches. We require a third-person perspective, encourage a positive tone and active voice, and welcome a humorous tone where appropriate. For stylistic matters, follow the *Chicago Manual of Style*."

MICHIGAN CONTRACTOR & BUILDER, CMD Group, 40000 Grand River, Suite 404, Novi MI 48375-2147. (248)471-5811. Fax: (248)471-6103. E-mail: akalousdian@cahners.com. **Contact:** Aram Kalousdian. **25% freelance written.** Weekly magazine covering the commercial construction industry in Michigan (no home building). "*Michigan Contractor & Builder's* audience is contractors, equipment suppliers, engineers and architects. The magazine reports on construction projects in Michigan. It does not cover homebuilding. Stories should focus on news or innovative techniques or materials in construction." Estab. 1907. Circ. 3,700. Pays 30 days after publication. Byline given. Buys all rights. Accepts queries by mail, e-mail, fax, phone. Sample copy free.
Nonfiction: Michigan construction projects. **Buys 52 mss/year.** Query with published clips. Length: 1,500 words with 5-7 photos. **Pay is negotiable.**

Photos: Send photos with submission. Reviews original prints. Buys all rights. Offers no additional payment for photos accepted with ms. Captions required.

N̄ $ $ NW BUILDER MAGAZINE, Pacific NW Sales & Marketing, Inc., 16200 SW Pacific Hwy., PMB #182, Tigard OR 97224. (503)624-7077. Fax: (503)624-9198. E-mail: mgreditor@nwbuildermagazine.com. Website: www.nwbuildermagazine.com. **Contact:** Patrick Sherman. **10-50% freelance written.** Monthly journal covering NW residential and commercial building. "Articles must address pressing topics for builders in our region with a special emphasis on the business aspects of construction." Estab. 1996. Circ. 25,000. Pays on acceptance of revised ms. Publishes ms an average of 1 month after acceptance. Byline given. Buys first North American serial, electronic rights. Editorial lead time 2 months. Submit seasonal material 3 months in advance. Accepts queries by mail, e-mail, fax. Responds in 1 week to queries; 1 month to mss. Sample copy free or online. Writer's guidelines free.
Nonfiction: How-to, interview/profile, new product, technical. No personal bios unless they teach a valuable lesson to those in the building industry. **Buys 40 mss/year.** Query. Length: 500-1,500 words. **Pays $50-300.** Sometimes pays expenses of writers on assignment.
Photos: State availability with submission. Buys first North American serial and electronic rights. Offers no additional payment for photos accepted with ms. Captions, identification of subjects, model releases required.
Columns/Departments: Engineering; Construction; Architecture & Design; Tools & Materials; Heavy Equipment; Business & Economics; Legal Matters; E-build; Building Green, all 750-1,000 words. Query.
Tips: Writers should "email an intro as to why he/she should write for us. A thorough knowledge of our publication is crucial. Also, must be a Northwest slant."

N̄ $ $ PENNSYLVANIA BUILDER, Pennsylvania Builders Association, 600 N. 12th St., Lemoyne PA 17043. (717)730-4380. Fax: (717)730-4396. E-mail: scornbower@pahomes.org. Website: www.pahomes.org. **Contact:** Susan H. Cornbower, director of publications. **10% freelance written.** "Quarterly trade publication for builders, remodelers, subcontractors and other affiliates of the home building industry in Pennsylvania." Estab. 1988. Circ. 12,200. Pays on publication. Publishes ms an average of 1 year after acceptance. Byline given. Buys one-time rights. Editorial lead time 3 months. Submit seasonal material 9 months in advance. Accepts queries by mail, e-mail. Accepts simultaneous submissions. Responds in 2 weeks to queries; 3 months to mss. Sample copy free. Writer's guidelines by e-mail.
Nonfiction: General interest, how-to, new product, technical. No personnel or company profiles. **Buys 1-2 mss/year.** Send complete ms. Length: 800-1,200 words. **Pays $250.** Sometimes pays expenses of writers on assignment.
Reprints: Accepts previously published submissions.
Photos: Send photos with submission. Reviews negatives, transparencies, prints. Buys one-time rights. Negotiates payment individually. Captions, identification of subjects required.

$ $ PERMANENT BUILDINGS & FOUNDATIONS (PBF), R.W. Nielsen Co., 350 E. Center St., Suite 201, Provo UT 84606-3276. (801)373-0013. E-mail: rnielsen@pbf.org. Website: www.pbf.org. Managing Editor: Carolyn R. Nielsen. **Contact:** Roger W. Nielsen, editor. **15% freelance written.** Magazine published 8 times/year. "*PBF* readers are contractors who build residential, commercial and industrial buildings. Editorial focus is on materials that last: Concrete and new technologies to build solid, energy efficient structures, insulated concrete and tilt-up, waterproofing, underpinning, roofing and the business of contracting and construction." Estab. 1989. Circ. 30,000. Pays on publication. Byline given. Buys first North American serial rights. Editorial lead time 1 month. Submit seasonal material 2 months in advance. Accepts queries by mail, e-mail, phone. Responds in 2 weeks to queries; 1 month to mss. Sample copy for 9×12 SASE or online. Writer's guidelines free or online.
Nonfiction: How-to (construction methods, management techniques), humor, interview/profile, new product, technical, book reviews, tool reviews. Special issues: Water proofing February, Insulated Concrete Forming supplement April. Special issues: Water proofing (February); Insulated Concrete Forming supplement (April). **Buys 15 mss/year.** Query. Length: 500-1,500 words. **Pays $150-750 for assigned articles; $50-500 for unsolicited articles.** Sometimes pays expenses of writers on assignment.
Photos: State availability with submission. Reviews contact sheets. Buys one-time rights. Offers no additional payment for photos accepted with ms. Captions, identification of subjects required.
Columns/Departments: Marketing Tips, 250-500 words; Q&A (solutions to contractor problems), 200-500 words. Query. **Pays $50-500.**
■ The online magazine carries original content not found in the print edition. Contact: Roger Nielsen.

N̄ $ $ REEVES JOURNAL, Business News Publishing Co., 23211 South Pointe Dr., Suite 101, Laguna Hills CA 92653. Fax: (949)859-7845. E-mail: reevesjrnl@aol.com. Website: www.reevesjournal.com. **Contact:** Scott Marshutz, editor. **25% freelance written.** Monthly magazine covering building subcontractors—plumbers, HVAC contractors. Estab. 1920. Circ. 15,000. Pays on publication. Byline given. Buys first North American serial, electronic rights. Editorial lead time 3 months. Accepts queries by mail, e-mail, fax. Responds in 1 month to queries; 2 months to mss. Sample copy free. Writer's guidelines for #10 SASE.
● "Knowledge of building construction, water science, engineering is extremely helpful. Even better—former plumbing, HVAC experience, and a great command of the English language."
Nonfiction: "Only articles applicable to plumbing/HVAC subcontracting trade in the western US." How-to, interview/profile, new product, technical. Query with published clips. Length: 500-11,500 words. **Pays $50-350.** Pays phone expenses.

Photos: State availability with submission. Buys all rights. Negotiates payment individually. Captions, identification of subjects required.

▣ The online magazine carries original content not found in the print edition. Contact: Scott Marshutz.

Tips: "Know the market—we're not just another builder publication. Our target audience is the plumbing, HVAC contractor—new construction, mechanical, and service and repair. We cover the western U.S. (plus Texas)."

N $ $ UNDERGROUND CONSTRUCTION, Oildom Publishing Co. of Texas, Inc., P.O. Box 219368, Houston TX 77218-9368. (281)558-6930. Fax: (281)558-7029. E-mail: rcarpen@undergroundinfo.com. Website: www.undergroundinfo.com. **Contact:** Robert Carpenter, editorial director. **35% freelance written.** Monthly magazine covering underground oil and gas pipeline, water and sewer pipeline, cable construction for contractors and owning companies. Circ. 34,500. Publishes ms an average of 6 months after acceptance. Buys first North American serial rights. Accepts queries by mail, e-mail, fax, phone. Responds in 1 month to mss.

Nonfiction: How-to, job stories. Query with published clips. Length: 1,000-2,000 words. **Pays $3-500.** Sometimes pays expenses of writers on assignment.

Photos: Send photos with submission. Reviews color prints and slides. Buys one-time rights. Captions required.

Tips: "We supply guidelines outlining information we need." The most frequent mistake made by writers in completing articles is unfamiliarity with the field.

DRUGS, HEALTHCARE & MEDICAL PRODUCTS

CANADIAN PHARMACEUTICAL JOURNAL, 1785 Alta Vista Dr., Suite 105, Ottawa Ontario K1G 3X6, Canada. (613)739-2879. Fax: (613)739-7765. E-mail: cpj@cyberus.ca. Website: www.keithhealthcare.com. **Contact:** Andrew Reinboldt, editor. Works with a small number of new/unpublished writers each year. Monthly journal for pharmacists. Estab. 1868. Circ. 13,038. Pays after editing. Publishes ms an average of 6 months after acceptance. Buys first rights. Accepts queries by mail, e-mail, fax. Responds in 2 months to queries. Sample copy and writer's guidelines free.

Nonfiction: Relevant to Canadian pharmacy. Publishes continuing education, pharmacy practice, education and legislation. Length: 200-400 words (for news notices); 800-1,500 words (for articles). Historical/nostalgic, how-to, interview/profile, personal experience. Query. **Payment varies.** Sometimes pays expenses of writers on assignment.

Photos: Reviews color and b&w glossies purchased with mss. Captions, model releases required.

Tips: "Query with complete description of proposed article, including topic, sources (in general), length, payment requested, suggested submission date, and whether photographs will be included. It is helpful if the writer has read a *recent* copy of the journal; we are glad to send one if required. References should be included where appropriate (this is vital where medical and scientific information is included). Send three copies of each manuscript. Author's degree and affiliations (if any) and writing background should be listed."

$ $ $ HOME CARE MAGAZINE, For Business Leaders in Home Health Care, Intertec Publishing Corp., 23815 Stuart Ranch Rd., Malibu CA 90265-8987. Fax: (310)317-0264. E-mail: marie_blakey@intertec.com. Website: www.homecaremag.com. Managing Editor: Susanne Hopkins. **Contact:** Marie Blakey, editor. **20% freelance written.** Monthly journal covering the needs of home medical equipment retailers. "We provide product and business advice and market analysis to small family-held companies that offer medical equipment and related services to patients in a home setting." Estab. 1979. Circ. 17,000. Pays on publication. Publishes ms an average of 3 months after acceptance. Byline given. Buys first, second serial (reprint) rights. Editorial lead time 3 months. Accepts queries by mail, e-mail, fax. Accepts simultaneous submissions. Responds in 6 weeks to queries; 3 weeks to mss. Sample copy online.

Nonfiction: How-to (by assignment). **Buys multiple mss/year.** Query with published clips. Length: 500-2,500 words. **Pays 50¢/word.** Sometimes pays expenses of writers on assignment.

Photos: State availability with submission. Buys all rights. Captions, identification of subjects, model releases required.

Tips: "Contributors should have knowledge of health industry."

$ $ SUNWEAR VISION, (formerly *Sunwear*), Frames Data, 16269 Laguna Canyon Rd., Ste 100, Irvine CA 92618. (949)788-0150. Fax: (949)788-0130. E-mail: cwalker@framesdata.com. Website: www.framesdata.com. **Contact:** Christie Walker, editor. **20% freelance written.** Magazine published 3 times/year for the eye wear industry. "*Sunwear Vision* brings readers current information on all the latest designs and innovations available in the field of fashion and sports sunwear." Estab. 1970. Circ. 30,000. Pays 1 month prior to publication. Publishes ms an average of 3 months after acceptance. Byline given. Buys first North American serial rights. Editorial lead time 3 months. Submit seasonal material 3 months in advance. Accepts simultaneous submissions. Responds in 1 week to queries. Sample copy for 8×10 SAE and 2 first-class stamps.

Nonfiction: How-to, new product. **Buys 10 mss/year.** Query with published clips. Length: 800-1,600 words. **Pays $300-500.** Sometimes pays expenses of writers on assignment.

Photos: Send photos with submission. Buys one-time rights. Offers no additional payment for photos accepted with ms. Captions, identification of subjects required.

Tips: "Write for the doctor. How can doctors make more money selling sunwear?"

$ $ TECHNOLOGY VISION, (formerly *FramesData.com*), Frames Data, 16269 Laguna Canyon Rd., Suite 100, Irvine CA 92618. (949)788-0150. Fax: (949)788-0130. E-mail: cwalker@framesdata.com. Website: www.framesdata.com. **Contact:** Christie Walker, editor. **20% freelance written.** Magazine for the eyewear industry. "*Technology Vision*, published five times a year, features articles for eyecare professionals who are looking for the newest and best means to improve their practices and increase profits through technology." Estab. 1970. Circ. 18,000. Pays 1 month after acceptance. Publishes ms an average of 3 months after acceptance. Byline given. Buys first North American serial rights. Editorial lead time 3 months. Submit seasonal material 3 months in advance. Accepts queries by mail, e-mail. Accepts simultaneous submissions. Responds in 2 weeks to queries; 1 month to mss. Sample copy for 8×10 SAE and 2 first-class stamps.
Nonfiction: How-to, new product. **Buys 10 mss/year.** Query with published clips. Length: 800-1,600 words. **Pays $300-500.** Sometimes pays expenses of writers on assignment.
Photos: Send photos with submission. Buys one-time rights. Offers no additional payment for photos accepted with ms. Captions, identification of subjects required.
Tips: "Write on how technology can help optometrists to sell more product."

$ $ $ VALIDATION TIMES, Washington Information Source Co., 6506 Old Stage Rd., Suite 100, Rockville MD 20852-4326. (301)770-5553. Fax: (301)468-0475. E-mail: wis@fdainfo.com. Website: www.fdainfo.com. **Contact:** Kenneth Reid, publisher. Monthly newsletter covering regulation of pharmaceutical and medical devices. "We write to executives who have to keep up on changing FDA policies and regulations, and on what their competitors are doing at the agency." Estab. 1992. Pays on publication. Publishes ms an average of 1 month after acceptance. Byline given. Makes work-for-hire assignments. Editorial lead time 1 month. Submit seasonal material 1 month in advance. Accepts queries by mail. Responds in 1 month to queries. Sample copy and writer's guidelines free.
Nonfiction: How-to, technical, regulatory. No lay interest pieces. **Buys 50-100 mss/year.** Query. Length: 600-1,500 words. **Pays $100/half day; $200 full day "to cover meetings and same rate for writing."** Sometimes pays expenses of writers on assignment.
Tips: "If you're covering a conference for non-competing publications, call me with a drug or device regulatory angle."

EDUCATION & COUNSELING

Professional educators, teachers, coaches and counselors—as well as other people involved in training and education—read the journals classified here. Many journals for educators are non-profit forums for professional advancement; writers contribute articles in return for a byline and contributor's copies. *Writer's Market* includes only educational journals that pay freelancers for articles. Education-related publications for students are included in the Consumer Career, College & Alumni; and Teen & Young Adult sections. Listings in the Childcare & Parental Guidance and Psychology & Self-Improvement sections of Consumer Magazines may also be of interest.

$ $ ARTS & ACTIVITIES, Publishers' Development Corporation, Dept. WM, 591 Camino de la Reina, Suite 200, San Diego CA 92108-3104. (619)819-4530. Fax: (619)297-5353. Website: www.artsandactivities.com. **Contact:** Maryellen Bridge, editor-in-chief. **95% freelance written.** Eager to work with new/unpublished writers. Monthly (except July and August) magazine covering art education at levels from preschool through college for educators and therapists engaged in arts and crafts education and training. Estab. 1932. Circ. 20,000. Pays on publication. Publishes ms an average of 1 year after acceptance. Byline given. Buys first North American serial rights. Submit seasonal material 6 months in advance. Accepts queries by mail. Responds in 3 months to queries. Sample copy for 9×12 SAE and 8 first-class stamps. Writer's guidelines for #10 SASE.
  ● Editors here are seeking more materials for upper elementary and secondary levels on printmaking, ceramics, 3-dimensional design, weaving, fiber arts (stitchery, tie-dye, batik, etc.), crafts, painting and multicultural art.
Nonfiction: Historical/nostalgic (arts, activities, history), how-to (classroom art experiences, artists' techniques), interview/profile (of artists), opinion (on arts activities curriculum, ideas of how to do things better, philosophy of art education), personal experience (this ties in with the how-to, we like it to be personal, no recipe style), articles of exceptional art programs. **Buys 80-100 mss/year.** Length: 200-2,000 words. **Pays $35-150.**
Tips: "Frequently in unsolicited manuscripts, writers obviously have not studied the magazine to see what style of articles we publish. Send for a sample copy to familiarize yourself with our style and needs. The best way to find out if his/her writing style suits our needs is for the author to submit a manuscript on speculation. We prefer an anecdotal style of writing, so that readers will feel as though they are there in the art room as the lesson/project is taking place. Also, good quality photographs of student artwork are important. We are a *visual* art magazine!"

$ THE ATA MAGAZINE, The Alberta Teachers' Association, 11010 142nd St., Edmonton, Alberta T5N 2R1, Canada. (780)447-9400. Fax: (780)455-6481. E-mail: postmaster@teachers.ab.ca. Website: www.teachers.ab.ca. Editor: Tim Johnston. **Contact:** Raymond Gariepy, associate editor. Quarterly magazine covering education. Estab. 1920. Circ. 39,500. Pays on publication. Publishes ms an average of 4 months after acceptance. Byline given. Offers $25 kill fee.

Buys one-time rights. Editorial lead time 2 months. Submit seasonal material 2 months in advance. Accepts queries by mail, e-mail, fax, phone. Accepts simultaneous submissions. Responds in 2 months to queries. Sample copy and writer's guidelines free.

Nonfiction: Education-related topics. Query with published clips. Length: 500-1,250 words. **Pays $75 Canadian.**

Photos: Send photos with submission. Reviews 4×6 prints. Negotiates rights. Negotiates payment individually. Captions required.

N $ $ ATHLETIC MANAGEMENT, Momentum Media Sports Publishing, 2488 N. Triphammer Rd., Ithaca NY 14850. (607)257-6970, ext. 18. Fax: (607)257-7328. E-mail: ef@momentummedia.com. Website: www.athleticsearch.com. **Contact:** Eleanor Frankel, editor. **20% freelance written.** Bimonthly magazine covering management of high school and college athletics. "The magazine is written for athletic directors. Articles are how-to and must be well-organized." Estab. 1988. Circ. 30,000. Pays on publication. Publishes ms an average of 2 months after acceptance. Byline given. Buys first North American serial, first, second serial (reprint), electronic, all rights, makes work-for-hire assignments. Editorial lead time 3 months. Accepts queries by mail, e-mail, fax. Responds in 2 weeks to queries. Sample copy for #10 SASE.

Nonfiction: How-to. Query with published clips. Length: 1,500-3,000 words. **Pays $400-800.** Sometimes pays expenses of writers on assignment.

Tips: "Provide writing samples that show you can write a well-organized, how-to article."

N $ $ $ CHILDREN'S VOICE, Child Welfare League of America, 440 First St. NW, 3rd Floor, Washington DC 20001-2085. (202)638-2952. Fax: (202)638-4004. E-mail: voice@cwla.org. Website: www.cwla.org/pubs. **Contact:** Steve Boehm, editor. **10% freelance written.** Bimonthly magazine covering "issues of importance for children and families, professionals who work with children and families at risk, and advocates and policymakers who work in their behalf. Sample topics include fostercare and adoption, child abuse and neglect, juvenile justice, pregnant and parenting teens, childcare and early child and early childhood development, troubled youth, homeless youth, etc." Estab. 1991. Circ. 20,000. Pays on publication. Publishes ms an average of 6 months after acceptance. Byline given. Buys all rights. Editorial lead time 6 months. Submit seasonal material 6 months in advance. Accepts queries by mail, e-mail, fax. Responds in 2 weeks to queries; 2 months to mss. Sample copy for 9×12 SAE and 3 first-class stamps. Writer's guidelines online.

Nonfiction: Essays, general interest, interview/profile, opinion, personal experience, successful programs. No poetry, advertisements for products or services disguised as feature articles. **Buys 6-10 mss/year.** Query. Length: 1,800-2,800 words. **Pays 25-50¢/word. Generally does not pay cash for professionals in the field of child welfare.** Sometimes pays expenses of writers on assignment.

Photos: State availability with submission. Reviews contact sheets. Buys all rights. Negotiates payment individually. Captions, identification of subjects, model releases required.

Tips: "Writers must know the field of child welfare or have intimate knowledge of an aspect that is unique, insightful, studied and authoritative. Material that promotes a product or service is not suitable."

$ THE CHRISTIAN CLASSROOM, Great River Publishing Company, Inc., 2026 Exeter Rd., Suite 2, Germantown TN 38138. (901)624-5911. Fax: (901)624-5910. E-mail: tcc@grtriver.com. Website: www.grtriver.com. **Contact:** Sherry Campbell, editor. **25% freelance written.** "*The Christian Classroom* is the only national magazine devoted exclusively to the interests and issues of concern to teachers in Christian schools." Estab. 1997. Circ. 20,000. Pays on publication. Publishes ms an average of 6 months after acceptance. Byline given. Offers negotiable kill fee. Buys all rights. Editorial lead time 3 months. Submit seasonal material 3 months in advance. Accepts queries by mail, e-mail, fax. Responds in 2 weeks to queries; 3 months to mss. Sample copy and writer's guidelines free.

Nonfiction: Book excerpts, essays, how-to (get students involved as well as parents, etc.), inspirational, interview/profile, new product, personal experience, religious. "No articles that preach rather than give practical advice." **Buys 20 mss/year.** Query. Length: 300-1,500 words. **Pay negotiable.**

Photos: State availability with submission. Reviews prints up to 8×10. Buys one-time rights. Offers no additional payment for photos accepted with ms. Model releases required.

Tips: "Submit articles of current interest to Christian school teachers."

$ THE CHRISTIAN SCHOOL ADMINISTRATOR, Great River Publishing Company, Inc., 2026 Exeter Rd., Suite 2, Germantown TN 38138. (901)624-5911. Fax: (901)624-5910. E-mail: csa@grtriver.com. Website: www.grtriver.com. **Contact:** Sherry Campbell, editor. **35% freelance written.** Bimonthly "*The Christian School Administrator* provides Christian school administrators with news and information on such topics as legal issues, school financial management, parent and school relations, curriculum and educational materials, student recruitment, new technologies and school improvements. These administrators all face the same issues of budgeting, setting tuition rates, attracting new students, buying new equipment, fund raising and setting strong academic standards in a Christian environment." Estab. 1993. Circ. 13,000. Pays on publication. Publishes ms an average of 6 months after acceptance. Byline given. Offers negotiable kill fee. Buys all rights. Editorial lead time 3 months. Submit seasonal material 3 months in advance. Accepts queries by mail, e-mail, fax, phone. Responds in 2 weeks to queries; 3 months to mss. Sample copy and writer's guidelines free.

Nonfiction: Book excerpts, essays, historical/nostalgic, how-to, inspirational, interview/profile, personal experience, photo feature, religious. "No articles that preach rather than give advice or relate experiences." **Buys 20-30 mss/year.** Query. Length: 300-1,500 words. **Pay negotiable.**

Photos: State availability with submission. Reviews up to 8×10 prints. Buys one-time rights. Offers no additional payment for photos accepted with ms. Model releases required.

Tips: "Writers should be familiar with private Christian schools, their practices, problems and issues of interest and concern to them."

$CLASS ACT, Class Act, Inc., P.O. Box 802, Henderson KY 42419. E-mail: classact@henderson.net. Website: www.henderson.net/~classact. **Contact:** Susan Thurman, editor. **50% freelance written.** Newsletter published 9 times/ year covering English/language arts education. "Our writers must know English as a classroom subject and should be familiar with writing for teens. If you can't make your manuscript interesting to teenagers, we're not interested." Estab. 1993. Circ. 300. **Pays on acceptance.** Publishes ms an average of 6 months after acceptance. Byline given. Offers 100% kill fee. Buys all rights. Editorial lead time 2 months. Submit seasonal material 3 months in advance. Accepts queries by mail, e-mail. Accepts simultaneous submissions. Responds in 1 month to queries. Sample copy for $3. Writer's guidelines for #10 SASE or online.

   O→ Break in with "an original, ready-for-classroom-use article that provides tips for writing (but geared to a teenage audience)."

Nonfiction: How-to (games, puzzles, assignments relating to English education). "No Masters theses; no esoteric articles; no poetry; no educational theory or jargon." **Buys 12 mss/year.** Send complete ms. Length: 100-2,000 words. **Pays $10-40.**

Columns/Departments: Writing assignments (innovative, thought-provoking for teens), 500-1,500 words; puzzles, games (English education oriented), 200 words; teacher tips (bulletin boards, time-saving devices), 100 words. "E-mailed manuscripts (not attachments) are encouraged. Articles on disk (MS Word or Works) also are encouraged." Send complete ms. **Pays $10-40.**

Fillers: Teacher tips. **Pays $10.**

Tips: "Please know the kind of language used by junior/senior high students. Don't speak above them. Also, it helps to know what these students *don't* know, in order to explain or emphasize the concepts. Clip art is sometimes used but is not paid extra for. We like material that's slightly humorous while still being educational. We are especially open to innovative writing assignments, educational puzzles and games, and instructions on basics. Again, be familiar with this age group. Remember we are geared for English teachers."

$ $HISPANIC OUTLOOK IN HIGHER EDUCATION, 210 Rt 4 East, Ste 310, Paramus NJ 07652. (201)587-8800, ext 100. Fax: (201)587-9105. E-mail: sloutlook@aol.com. Website: www.hispanicoutlook.com. Editor: Adalyn Hixson. **Contact:** Sue Lopez-Isa, managing editor. **50% freelance written.** Biweekly magazine. "We're looking for higher education story articles, with a focus on Hispanics and the advancements made by and for Hispanics in higher education." Circ. 28,000. Pays on publication. Publishes ms an average of 2 months after acceptance. Byline given. Editorial lead time 2 months. Submit seasonal material 3 months in advance. Accepts queries by mail, e-mail, fax. Accepts simultaneous submissions. Sample copy free.

   O→ Break with "issues articles such as new laws in higher education."

Nonfiction: Historical/nostalgic, interview/profile (of academic or scholar), opinion (on higher education), personal experience, all regarding higher education only. **Buys 20-25 mss/year.** Query with published clips. Length: 1,750-2,000 words. **Pays $400 minimum for assigned articles.** Pays expenses of writers on assignment.

Photos: Send photos with submission. Reviews b&w or color prints. Offers no additional payment for photos accepted with ms.

Tips: "Articles explore the Hispanic experience in higher education. Special theme issues address sports, law, health, corporations, heritage, women, and a wide range of similar issues; however, articles need not fall under those umbrellas."

$ $ $ $PREVENTION UPDATE, A Publication Devoted to Preventing the Exploitation of Children, Committee for Children, 2203 Airport Way S, Suite 500, Seattle WA 98134-2035. (800)634-4449. Fax: (206)343-1445. E-mail: lwalls@cfchildren.org. Website: www.cfchildren.org. **Contact:** Lisa Walls, editor. **30% freelance written.** Quarterly newsletter covering education and counseling. "Committee for Children is a not-for-profit organization whose mission is to promote the safety, well-being, and social development of children by creating quality educational programs for educators, families and communities. *Prevention Update* is Committee for Children's newsletter, mailed quarterly to our clients (those who've purchased our curricula—primarily school teachers and administrators and staff at youth organizations such as the Boys and Girls Clubs)." Estab. 1985. Circ. 17,000. Pays on publication. Publishes ms an average of 5 months after acceptance. Byline given. Buys first, second serial (reprint) rights. Editorial lead time 8 months. Accepts queries by mail, e-mail. Accepts simultaneous submissions. Responds in 1 month to queries; 3 months to mss. Sample copy and writer's guidelines free.

   ● Please read the magazine's description carefully and obtain a sample copy before submitting. *Prevention Update* is a trade journal for educators and school administrators. Query first.

Nonfiction: Interview/profile, technical. "Nothing that does not deal with child sexual abuse prevention, violence prevention, or social and emotional skills education." No poetry or fiction. **Buys varying number of mss/year.** Query with published clips. Length: 500-2,000 words. **Pays $250-1,125.**

Photos: Send photos with submission. Reviews 8×10 prints. Buys all rights. Offers no additional payment for photos accepted with ms. Identification of subjects, model releases required.

Columns/Departments: Notes From the Field (volunteer experiences, classroom work), 500-1,000 words. **Buys 2 mss/year.** Query with published clips. **Payment varies.**

Tips: "Stories should strive to educate clients; convey practical information for use in the classroom; build relationships between CFC and its clients; assist clients in their work; and help clients convince their constituents of the programs' benefits."

N $ $ $ PTO TODAY, The Magazine for Parent Group Leaders, PTO Today, Inc., 2 Celinda Dr., Franklin MA 02038. (508)541-9130. Fax: (508)541-6129. E-mail: publisher@ptotoday.com. Website: www.ptotoday.com. **Contact:** Tim Sullivan, publisher. **40% freelance written.** Bimonthly magazine covering the work of school parent-teacher groups. "We celebrate the work of school parent volunteers and provide resources to help them do that work more effectively." Estab. 1999. Circ. 80,000. Pays on publication. Publishes ms an average of 2 months after acceptance. Byline given. Offers 40% kill fee. Buys first North American serial, electronic, all rights. Editorial lead time 4 months. Submit seasonal material 4 months in advance. Accepts queries by e-mail. Sample copy online.

Nonfiction: Exposé, general interest, historical/nostalgic, how-to (anything related to PTO/PTA), interview/profile, new product, personal experience. **Buys 14 mss/year.** Query. Length: 800-3,000 words. **Pays 30¢-$1/word for assigned articles; $100-500 for unsolicited articles.** Sometimes pays expenses of writers on assignment.

Photos: State availability with submission. Buys one-time rights. Negotiates payment individually. Identification of subjects required.

Tips: "It's difficult for us to find talented writers with strong experience with parent groups. This experience is a big plus."

$ SCHOOL ARTS MAGAZINE, 50 Portland St., Worcester MA 01608-9959. Fax: (610)683-8229. Website: www.davis-art.com. **Contact:** Eldon Katter, editor. **85% freelance written.** Monthly magazine (September-May), serving arts and craft education profession, K-12, higher education and museum education programs written by and for art teachers. Estab. 1901. Pays on publication. Publishes ms an average of 3 months after acceptance. Buys all rights. Accepts queries by mail, phone. Responds in 3 months to queries. Sample copy and writer's guidelines free.

   O→ Break in with "professional quality photography to illustrate art lessons."

Nonfiction: Articles on art and craft activities in schools. Should include description and photos of activity in progress, as well as examples of finished artwork. Query or send complete ms and SASE. Length: 600-1,400 words. **Pays $30-150.**

   ■ The online magazine carries original content not found in the print edition.

Tips: "We prefer articles on actual art projects or techniques done by students in actual classroom situations. Philosophical and theoretical aspects of art and art education are usually handled by our contributing editors. Our articles are reviewed and accepted on merit and each is tailored to meet our needs. Keep in mind that art teachers want practical tips, above all—more hands-on information than academic theory. Write your article with the accompanying photographs in hand." The most frequent mistakes made by writers are "bad visual material (photographs, drawings) submitted with articles, or a lack of complete descriptions of art processes; and no rationale behind programs or activities. Familiarity with the field of art education is essential. Review recent issues of *School Arts*."

N $ $ $ TEACHER MAGAZINE, Editorial Projects in Education, 6935 Arlington Rd., Bethesda MD 20814. Fax: (301)280-3150. E-mail: info@teachermagazine.org. Website: www.teachermagazine.org. Managing Editor: Samantha Stainburn. **Contact:** Rich Shea, executive editor. **40% freelance written.** Magazine published 8 times/year covering the teaching profession. "One of the major thrusts of the current school reform movement is to make teaching a true profession. *Teacher Magazine* plays a central role in that effort. It is a national communications network that provides teachers with the information they need to be better practitioners and effective leaders." Estab. 1989. Circ. 120,000. Pays on publication. Publishes ms an average of 1 month after acceptance. Byline given. Offers 25% kill fee. Buys first North American serial, electronic rights. Editorial lead time 3 months. Submit seasonal material 4 months in advance. Accepts queries by mail, e-mail, fax. Responds in 2 months to queries. Sample copy online. Writer's guidelines free.

Nonfiction: Book excerpts, essays, interview/profile, personal experience, photo feature, investigative. No "how-to" articles. **Buys 56 mss/year.** Query with published clips. Length: 1,000-5,000 words. **Pays 50¢/word.** Sometimes pays expenses of writers on assignment.

Photos: State availability with submission. Reviews contact sheets, transparencies, prints. Buys one-time rights. Negotiates payment individually. Identification of subjects, model releases required.

Columns/Departments: Current events, forum. Query with published clips. **Pays 50¢/word.**

Tips: "Sending us a well-researched query letter accompanied by clips that demonstrate you can tell a good story is the best way to break into *Teacher Magazine*. Describe the characters in your proposed article. What scenes do you hope to include in the piece?"

$ TEACHERS OF VISION, (formerly *Vision*), Christian Educators Association, P.O. Box 41300, Pasadena CA 91114. (626)798-1124. Fax: (626)798-2346. E-mail: vision@ceai.org. Website: www.ceai.org. Editor: Forrest L. Turpen. **Contact:** Judy Turpen, contributing editor. **30% freelance written.** Newsletter published 9 times/year for Christian teachers in public education. "*Teachers of Vision*'s articles inspire, inform and equip teachers and administrators in the educational arena. Readers look for organizational news and general interest education articles. Topics include prayer in public schools, union activities, religious expression and activity in public schools and legal rights of Christian educators. Our audience is primarily public school educators. Other readers include teachers in private schools, university professors, school administrators, parents and school board members." Estab. 1953. Circ. 10,000. **Pays on publication.** Publishes ms an average of 6 months after acceptance. Byline given. Buys first North American serial, second serial (reprint) rights. Editorial lead time 6 months. Submit seasonal material 4 months in advance. Accepts queries by mail, e-mail, fax, phone. Accepts simultaneous submissions. Responds in 1 month to queries; 6 months to mss. Sample copy for 9×12 SAE and 4 first-class stamps. Writer's guidelines for #10 SASE or online.

Nonfiction: How-to, humor, inspirational, interview/profile, opinion, personal experience, religious. "Nothing preachy." **Buys 15-20 mss/year.** Query or send complete ms if 2,000 words or less. Length: 600-2,500 words. **Pays $30-40.**

Reprints: Accepts previously published submissions. Pays $30.

Photos: State availability with submission. Buys one-time and reprint rights. Offers no additional payment for photos accepted with ms.

Columns/Departments: Query. **Pays $30-40.**

Fillers: Send with SASE—must relate to public education.

Tips: "We are looking for material on living out one's faith in appropriate, legal ways in the public school setting."

$ $ TEACHING THEATRE, Educational Theatre Association, 2343 Auburn Ave., Cincinnati OH 45219-2819. (513)421-3900. Fax: (513)421-7077. E-mail: jpalmarini@etassoc.org. Website: www.etassoc.org. **Contact:** James Palmarini, editor. **65% freelance written.** Quarterly magazine covering education theater K-12, primary emphasis on secondary level education. "*Teaching Theatre* emphasizes the teaching, theory, philosophy issues that are of concern to teachers at the elementary, secondary, and—as they relate to teaching K-12 theater—college levels. We publish work that explains specific approaches to teaching (directing, acting, curriculum development and management, etc.); advocates curriculum reform; or offers theories of theater education." Estab. 1989. Circ. 3,500. **Pays on acceptance.** Publishes ms an average of 3 months after acceptance. Byline given. Buys one-time rights. Editorial lead time 2 months. Submit seasonal material 3 months in advance. Accepts simultaneous submissions. Responds in 1 month to queries; 3 months to mss. Sample copy for $2. Writer's guidelines for #10 SASE.

Nonfiction: "*Teaching Theatre*'s audience is well-educated and most have considerable experience in their field; *generalist* articles are discouraged; readers already *possess* basic skills." Book excerpts, essays, how-to, interview/profile, opinion, technical theater. **Buys 20 mss/year.** Query. **Pays $100-300.**

Photos: State availability with submission. Reviews contact sheets, 5×7 and 8×10 transparencies, prints. Offers no additional payment for photos accepted with ms.

Tips: Wants articles that address the needs of the busy but experienced high school theater educators. "Fundamental pieces, on the value of theater education are *not* of value to us—our readers already know that."

$ $ $ $ TEACHING TOLERANCE, The Southern Poverty Law Center, 400 Washington Ave., Montgomery AL 36104. (334)264-0286. Fax: (334)264-3121. Website: www.teachingtolerance.org. **Contact:** Elsie Williams, managing editor. **65% freelance written.** Semiannual magazine. "*Teaching Tolerance* is dedicated to helping K-12 teachers promote tolerance and understanding between widely diverse groups of students. Includes articles, teaching ideas, and reviews of other resources available to educators." Estab. 1991. Circ. 600,000. **Pays on acceptance.** Byline given. Buys all rights. Editorial lead time 6 months. Submit seasonal material 6 months in advance. Accepts queries by mail, fax. Sample copy and writer's guidelines free or online.

Nonfiction: Essays, how-to (classroom techniques), personal experience (classroom), photo feature. "No jargon, rhetoric or academic analysis. No theoretical discussions on the pros/cons of multicultural education." **Buys 6-8 mss/year.** Query with published clips. Length: 1,000-3,000 words. **Pays $500-3,000 for assigned articles.** Pays expenses of writers on assignment.

Photos: State availability with submission. Reviews contact sheets, transparencies. Buys one-time rights. Captions, identification of subjects required.

Columns/Departments: Essays (personal reflection, how-to, school program), 400-800 words; Idea Exchange (special projects, successful anti-bias activities), 250-500 words; Student Writings (short essays dealing with diversity, tolerance & justice), 300-500 words. **Buys 8-12 mss/year.** Query with published clips. **Pays $50-1,000.**

◼ The online magazine carries original content not found in the print edition and includes writer's guidelines. Contact: Tim Walker, online editor.

Tips: "We want lively, simple, concise writing. The writing style should be descriptive and reflective, showing the strength of programs dealing successfully with diversity by employing clear descriptions of real scenes and interactions, and by using quotes from teachers and students. We ask that prospective writers study previous issues of the magazine and writer's guidelines before sending a query with ideas. Most open to articles that have a strong classroom focus. We are interested in approaches to teaching tolerance and promoting understanding that really work—approaches we might not have heard of. We want to inform our readers; we also want to inspire and encourage them. We know what's happening nationally; we want to know what's happening in your neighborhood classroom."

FOR INFORMATION on setting your freelance fees, see How Much Should I Charge?

$ TECH DIRECTIONS, Prakken Publications, Inc., P.O. Box 8623, Ann Arbor MI 48107-8623. (734)975-2800. Fax: (734)975-2787. E-mail: tom@techdirections.com. Website: www.techdirections.com. **Contact:** Tom Bowden, managing editor. **100% freelance written.** Eager to work with new/unpublished writers. Monthly magazine (except June and July) covering issues, trends and activities of interest to industrial, vocational, technical and technology educators at the elementary through post-secondary school levels. Estab. 1934. Circ. 43,000. Pays on publication. Publishes ms an average of 1 year after acceptance. Byline given. Buys all rights. Responds in 1 month to queries. Sample copy for $5. Writer's guidelines for #10 SASE or online.

Nonfiction: Uses articles pertinent to the various teaching areas in industrial and technology education (woodwork, electronics, drafting, machine shop, graphic arts, computer training, etc.). Prefers authors who have direct connection with the field of industrial and/or technical education. "The outlook should be on innovation in educational programs, processes or projects that directly apply to the industrial/technical education area." Main focus: Technical career and education. General interest, how-to, opinion, personal experience, technical, think pieces, interviews and coverage of new products. **Buys 135 unsolicited mss/year.** Length: 2,000-3,000 words. **Pays $50-150.**

Photos: Send photos with submission. Reviews color prints. Payment for photos included in payment for ms. Will accept electronic art as well.

Columns/Departments: Direct from Washington (education news from Washington DC); Technology Today (new products under development); Technologies Past (profiles the inventors of last century); Mastering Computers, Technology Concepts (project orientation).

Tips: "We are most interested in articles written by industrial, vocational and technical educators about their class projects and their ideas about the field. We need more and more technology-related articles, especially written for the community college level."

ELECTRONICS & COMMUNICATION

These publications are edited for broadcast and telecommunications technicians and engineers, electrical engineers and electrical contractors. Included are journals for electronic equipment designers and operators who maintain electronic and telecommunication systems. Publications for appliance dealers can be found in Home Furnishings & Household Goods.

$ THE ACUTA JOURNAL OF TELECOMMUNICATIONS IN HIGHER EDUCATION, ACUTA, 152 W. Zandale Dr., Suite 200, Lexington KY 40503-2486. (859)278-3338. Fax: (859)278-3268. E-mail: pscott@acuta.org. Website: www.acuta.org. **Contact:** Patricia Scott, communications manager. **20% freelance written.** Quarterly professional association journal covering telecommunications in higher education. "Our audience includes, primarily, middle to upper management in the telecommunications department on college/university campuses. They are highly skilled, technology-oriented professionals who provide data, voice and video communications services for residential and academic purposes." Estab. 1997. Circ. 2,200. Pays on publication. Publishes ms an average of 6 months after acceptance. Byline given. Buys first rights. Editorial lead time 6 months. Accepts queries by mail, e-mail, fax, phone. Responds in 1 month to queries; 2 months to mss. Sample copy for 9×12 SAE and 6 first-class stamps. Writer's guidelines free.

   O─¬ Break in with a campus study or case profile. "Contact me with your idea for a story. Convince me that you can handle the level of technical depth required."

Nonfiction: "Each issue has a focus. Available with writer's guidelines. We are only interested in articles described in article types." How-to (telecom), technical (telecom), case study, college/university application of technology. **Buys 6-8 mss/year.** Query. Length: 1,200-4,000 words. **Pays 8-10¢/word.** Sometimes pays expenses of writers on assignment.

Photos: State availability with submission. Reviews prints. Offers no additional payment for photos accepted with ms. Captions, model releases required.

Tips: "Our audience expects every article to be relevant to telecommunications on the college/university campus, whether it is related to technology, facilities, or management. Writers must read back issues to understand this focus and the level of technicality we expect."

N $ $ $ COMMUNICATIONS NEWS, Nelson Publishing, 2504 N. Tamiami Trail, Nokomis FL 34275. (941)966-9521. Fax: (941)966-2590. E-mail: kena@comnews.com. Website: www.comnews.com. **Contact:** Ken Anderberg, editor. **10% freelance written.** Monthly magazine covering communications networks with "controlled circulation for data and voice communications, specifically network managers. Solutions-oriented for end users of networking software and equipment at medium-sized to large organizations." Estab. 1966. Circ. 90,000. Pays on publication. Publishes ms an average of 2 months after acceptance. Byline given. Offers 25% kill fee. Buys first rights and web reprint rights. Editorial lead time 4 months. Accepts queries by mail, e-mail. Responds in 2 weeks to queries.

Nonfiction: Interview/profile, new product, networking solutions. **Buys 20 mss/year.** Query with published clips. Length: 800-1,500 words. **Pays $100-1,200.** Pays expenses of writers on assignment.

Photos: Send photos with submission. Reviews transparencies. Buys one-time and web reprint rights. Negotiates payment individually. Identification of subjects required.

Tips: "All submissions and initial contacts should be written and submitted by e-mail. We advise checking our website for latest editorial calendar and guidelines."

$ $ DIGITAL OUTPUT, The Business Guide for Electronic Publishers, The Doyle Group, 13000 Sawgrass Village Center, Suite 18, Ponte Vedra Beach FL 32082. (904)285-6020. Fax: (904)285-9944. E-mail: gsharpless@digitalo utput.net. Website: www.digitaloutput.net. Senior Editor: Shannon Powers-Jones, Assistant Editor: Criston G. Schellenger. **Contact:** Gregory Sharpless, editor-in-chief/associate publisher. **50% freelance written.** Monthly magazine covering electronic publishing and digital imaging, with articles ranging from digital capture and design to electronic prepress and digital printing. "*Digital Output* is a national business publication for electronic publishers and digital imagers, providing monthly articles which examine the latest technologies and digital methods and discuss how to profit from them. Our readers include service bureaus, prepress and reprographic houses, designers, printers, ad agencies, corporate communications and others." Estab. 1994. Circ. 30,000. Pays on publication. Publishes ms an average of 2 months after acceptance. Byline given. Offers 10-20% kill fee. Buys one-time rights including electronic rights for archival posting. Editorial lead time 3 months. Submit seasonal material 3 months in advance. Accepts queries by mail, e-mail, fax. Responds in 3 weeks to queries; 1 month to mss. Sample copy for $4.50 or online. Writer's guidelines for #10 SASE.

Nonfiction: How-to, interview/profile, technical, case studies. **Buys 36 mss/year.** Query with published clips. Length: 1,500-4,000 words. **Pays $250-600.**

Photos: State availability with submission.

Tips: "We're a business publication for professional digital imagers, so the writer should always keeps in mind that our readers want the business angle in every story—profits and economics, management tips and so on. Find a high-profile project and work the story 'backward' to find the digital angle (e.g., the electronic prepress story behind the most recent Harry Potter book)."

N $ $ ELECTRONIC SERVICING & TECHNOLOGY, The Professional Magazine for Electronics and Computer Servicing, P.O. Box 12487, Overland Park KS 66282-2487. (913)492-4857. E-mail: cpersedit@aol.com. **Contact:** Conrad Persson, editor. **80% freelance written.** Monthly magazine for service technicians, field service personnel, and avid servicing enthusiasts, who service audio, video, and computer equipment. Estab. 1950. Circ. 30,000. Pays on publication. Publishes ms an average of 4 months after acceptance. Byline given. Buys one-time rights. Editorial lead time 2 months. Accepts queries by mail, e-mail, fax, phone. Accepts simultaneous submissions. Responds in 1 month to queries; 2 months to mss. Sample copy and writer's guidelines free.

○→ Break in by knowing how to service consumer electronics products and being able to explain it in writing in good English.

Nonfiction: Book excerpts, how-to (service consumer electronics), new product, technical. **Buys 40 mss/year.** Query or send complete ms. **Pays $50/page.**

Reprints: Send typed ms with rights for sale noted and information about when and where the material previously appeared.

Photos: Send photos with submission. Buys one-time rights. Offers no additional payment for photos accepted with ms.

Columns/Departments: Business Corner (business tips); Computer Corner (computer servicing tips); Video Corner (understanding/servicing TV and video), all 1,000-2,000 words. **Buys 30 mss/year.** Query or send complete ms. **Pays $100-300.**

Tips: "Writers should have a strong background in electronics, especially consumer electronics servicing. Understand the information needs of consumer electronics service technicians, and be able to write articles that address specific areas of those needs."

$ $ $ GLOBAL WIRELESS, The international newspaper for the wireless communications industry, Crain Communications, Inc., 777 E. Speer Blvd., Denver CO 80203. (303)733-2500. Fax: (303)733-9941. E-mail: swendelk@crain.com. Website: www.globalwirelessnews.com. **Contact:** Sandra Wendelken, editor. **80% freelance written.** Magazine published 7 times/year covering international wireless telecommunications. Estab. 1998. Circ. 14,000. Pays on publication. Buys first, second serial (reprint) rights, makes work-for-hire assignments. Editorial lead time 3 months. Accepts queries by mail, e-mail, fax. Responds in 2 weeks to queries. Sample copy for $7.

Nonfiction: Interview/profile, technical, News/News analysis. "No articles that are too general. You can't write for this publication unless you are very experienced in reporting on telecommunications and can write detailed, topical, analysis-oriented articles." **Buys 70-90 mss/year.** Query with published clips. Length: 200-1,400 words. **Pays 50-70¢/word.** Pays expenses of writers on assignment.

Photos: State availability with submission. Reviews contact sheets, 4×6 prints. Buys one-time rights. Negotiates payment individually. Captions, identification of subjects required.

ENERGY & UTILITIES

People who supply power to homes, businesses and industry read the publications in this section. This category includes journals covering the electric power, natural gas, petroleum, solar and alternative energy industries.

$ $ELECTRICAL APPARATUS, The Magazine of Electromechanical & Electronic Application & Maintenance, Barks Publications, Inc., 400 N. Michigan Ave., Chicago IL 60611-4198. (312)321-9440. Fax: (312)321-1288. Senior Editor: Keith N. Jones. **Contact:** Elsie Dickson, editorial director. Monthly magazine for persons working in electrical and electronic maintenance, chiefly in industrial plants, who install and service electrical motors, transformers, generators, controls and related equipment. Estab. 1967. Circ. 17,000. **Pays on acceptance.** Publishes ms an average of 3 months after acceptance. Byline given. Buys Buys all rights unless other arrangements made. Accepts queries by mail, fax. Responds in 1 week to queries; 1 month to mss. Sample copy for $4.

Nonfiction: Technical. Length: 1,500-2,500 words. **Pays $250-500 for assigned articles.**

Tips: "All feature articles are assigned to staff and contributing editors and correspondents. Professionals interested in appointments as contributing editors and correspondents should submit résumé and article outlines, including illustration suggestions. Writers should be competent with a camera, which should be described in résumé. Technical expertise is absolutely necessary, preferably an E.E. degree, or practical experience. We are also book publishers and some of the material in *EA* is now in book form, bringing the authors royalties. Also publishes an annual directory, subtitled *ElectroMechanical Bench Reference*."

$ $ELECTRICAL WORLD MAGAZINE, McGraw-Hill, 20140 Scholar Dr., Suite 212, Hagerstown MD 21742. (301)745-5742. Fax: (301)745-8815. E-mail: editorew@aol.com. Website: www.electricalworld.com. **Contact:** Patricia Irwin, editor-in-chief. **80% freelance written.** Bimonthly magazine covering electrical transmission and distribution. "Our audience consists mainly of electric utility engineers, substation and line personnel. Articles cover all angles of T&D work." Estab. 1875. Circ. 41,000. Pays on publication. Byline given. Buys all rights, makes work-for-hire assignments. Editorial lead time 4 months. Accepts queries by mail, e-mail, fax, phone. Responds in 3 weeks to queries; 1 month to mss. Sample copy online. Writer's guidelines by e-mail.

Nonfiction: Technical. "No articles that only mention one manufacturer or consultant and no long advertisements that look like articles." **Buys 60 mss/year.** Query. Length: 800-2,500 words. **Pays $300-1,500 for assigned articles.** Sometimes pays expenses of writers on assignment.

Photos: State availability with submission. Reviews contact sheets, negatives, transparencies, prints. Buys one-time rights. Offers no additional payment for photos accepted with ms. Captions required.

Columns/Departments: Automation (utility automation), 300-800 words; Power Puzzles (brain teasers), 300-800 words; Engineer's Notebook (technical explanation), 800 words. **Buys 20 mss/year.** Query. **Pays $50-300.**

Tips: "If you have experience in the T&D field and are willing to work hard on improving your writing, query me. Article angles most likely to succeed: Info that is immediately useful to readers; how others solve their T&D problems; critical industry developments. No editorials."

N $ $NATIONAL PETROLEUM NEWS, 250 S. Wacker Dr., Suite 1150, Chicago IL 60606. (312)977-0999. Fax: (312)980-3135. E-mail: dwight@mail.aip.com. Website: www.npn-net.com. **Contact:** Darren Wight, editor. **3% freelance written.** Prefers to work with published/established writers. Monthly magazine for decision-makers in the oil marketing and convenience store industry. Estab. 1909. Circ. 11,000. Pays on acceptance if done on assignment. Publishes ms an average of 2 months after acceptance. Rights vary with author and material; usually buys all rights. Accepts queries by mail, e-mail, fax.

• This magazine is particularly interested in articles on international industry-related material.

Nonfiction: Material related directly to developments and issues in the oil marketing and convenience store industry and "how-to" and "what-with" case studies. "No unsolicited copy, especially with limited attribution regarding information in story." **Buys 3-4 mss/year.** Length: 2,000 words maximum. **Pays $50-150/printed page.** Sometimes pays expenses of writers on assignment.

Reprints: Send typed ms on disk with rights for sale noted and information about when and where the article previously appeared

Photos: Pays $150/printed page. Payment for b&w photos "depends upon advance understanding."

■ The online magazine carries original content not found in the print edition. Contact: Darren Wight, online editor.

$ $PUBLIC POWER, Dept. WM, 2301 M St. NW, Washington DC 20037-1484. (202)467-2948. Fax: (202)467-2910. E-mail: jlabella@appanet.org. Website: www.appanet.org. **Contact:** Jeanne LaBella, editor. **60% freelance written.** Prefers to work with published/established writers. Bimonthly trade journal. Estab. 1942. **Pays on acceptance.** Publishes ms an average of 3 months after acceptance. Byline given. Accepts queries by mail, e-mail, fax. Responds in 6 months to queries. Sample copy and writer's guidelines free.

Nonfiction: Features on municipal and other local publicly owned electric utilities. **Pays $400 and up.**

Photos: Reviews transparencies, slides and prints.

Tips: "We look for writers who are familiar with energy policy issues."

N $ $ $PUBLIC UTILITIES FORTNIGHTLY, Public Utilities Reports, 8229 Boone Blvd., Suite 401, Vienna VA 22182. Fax: (703)847-0683. E-mail: radford@pur.com. Website: www.pur.com. Editor: Bruce Radford. **Contact:** Regina R. Johnson, managing editor. **65% freelance written.** Biweekly (monthly during August and December) magazine covering the electric, natural gas and telecommunications markets. "We are rooted in regulation. That is our history. However, to be competitive we need to anticipate issues 6-12 months out. Writing for our readers requires 'forward thinking.'" Estab. 1928. Circ. 6,627. **Pays on acceptance.** Publishes ms an average of 3 months after acceptance. Byline given. Offers $250 kill fee. Buys all rights. Editorial lead time 2 months. Accepts queries by e-mail. Accepts simultaneous submissions. Responds in 1 month to queries; 2 months to mss. Sample copy for 10×13 SAE and 5 first-class stamps. Writer's guidelines online.

Nonfiction: Technical (features). No interview/profiles, essays, opinion pieces, nuts-and-bolts articles. **Buys 8 mss/ year.** Query with published clips. Length: 2,500-3,000 words. **Pay varies.** Pays writers with contributor copies or other premiums for assigned pieces by experts in the field. Sometimes pays expenses of writers on assignment.

Photos: State availability with submission. Reviews transparencies. Buys one-time rights. Negotiates payment individually. Captions, identification of subjects, model releases required.

Tips: "Know the business. Know the publication, and that's hard, as we're a $129/year subscription-based publication. Libraries and university libraries subscribe, and our website is somewhat informative. We are a trade publication, but we like stories that quote sources around all sides of an issue. We like issues that spring from regulation but that haven't yet blipped on the radar. We're looking for well-rounded features, proposed in queries that surprise us."

$ $ $ TEXAS CO-OP POWER, Texas Electric Cooperatives, Inc., Box 9589, Austin TX 78766. (512)454-0311. Website: www.texas-ec.org/tcp/tcp.html. Deputy Editor: Lisa Germany. **Contact:** Christopher Cook, editor. **50% freelance written.** Monthly magazine covering rural Texas life, people and places. "*Texas Co-op Power* provides 800,000 households and businesses educational and technical information about electric cooperatives in a high-quality and entertaining format to promote the general welfare of cooperatives, their member-owners and the areas in which they serve." Estab. 1948. Circ. 800,000. **Pays on acceptance.** Publishes ms an average of 6 months after acceptance. Byline given. Offers $100 kill fee. Buys first, electronic rights. Editorial lead time 3 months. Submit seasonal material 6 months in advance. Accepts queries by mail, e-mail, fax. Accepts simultaneous submissions. Responds in 1 month to queries; 2 months to mss. Sample copy free or online. Writer's guidelines for #10 SASE.

Nonfiction: General interest, historical/nostalgic, interview/profile, photo feature, travel. **Buys 40 mss/year.** Query with published clips. Length: 1,000-2,000 words. **Pays $400-1,000.** Sometimes pays expenses of writers on assignment.

Photos: State availability with submission. Reviews transparencies, prints. Buys one-time rights. Negotiates payment individually. Identification of subjects, model releases required.

Columns/Departments: Garden Patch (for amateur gardeners), 650 words. **Buys 10 mss/year.** Query with published clips. **Pays $250-300.**

Tips: "We're looking for Texas-related, rural-based articles, often first-person, always lively and interesting."

$ $ $ UTILITY BUSINESS, Intertec/PRIMEDIA, 9800 Metcalf, Overland Park KS 66212. Website: utilitybusiness.com or telecomclick.com. Editor: Martin Rosenberg. **Contact:** Dawn Hightower, managing editor. Monthly magazine covering electric, natural gas, telephone and water utilities for executives and managers. Estab. 1998. Circ. 50,000. Pays on publication. Publishes ms an average of 2 months after acceptance. Byline given. Buys all rights. Editorial lead time 3 months. Submit seasonal material 2 months in advance. Accepts queries by mail, e-mail, fax. Responds in 2 weeks to queries. Sample copy for 11×14 SAE.

Nonfiction: General interest, interview/profile, technical. **Buys 24 mss/year.** Query with published clips. Length: 1,500-2,500 words. **Pays 50¢/word.** Sometimes pays expenses of writers on assignment.

Photos: Send photos with submission. Buys one-time rights. Negotiates payment individually.

ENGINEERING & TECHNOLOGY

Engineers and professionals with various specialties read the publications in this section. Publications for electrical, electronics and telecommunications engineers are classified separately under Electronics & Communication. Magazines for computer professionals are in the Information Systems section.

$ $ CABLING SYSTEMS, Southam Inc., 1450 Don Mills Rd., Don Mills Ontario M3B 2X7, Canada. (416)442-2124. Fax: (416)442-2214. E-mail: jstrom@corporate.southam.ca. Website: www.cablingsystems.com. **Contact:** Janine Strom, editor. **50% freelance written.** Published 8 times/year magazine covering structured cabling/telecommunications industry. "*Cabling Systems* is written for engineers, designers, contractors, and end users who design, specify, purchase, install, test and maintain structured cabling and telecommunications products and systems." Estab. 1998. Circ. 11,000. Pays on publication. Publishes ms an average of 1 month after acceptance. Byline given. Buys all rights. Editorial lead time 3 months. Submit seasonal material 1 month in advance. Accepts queries by mail, e-mail, phone. Accepts simultaneous submissions. Sample copy online. Writer's guidelines free.

Nonfiction: Technical (case studies, features). "No reprints or previously written articles. All articles are assigned by editor based on query or need of publication." **Buys 20 mss/year.** Query with published clips. Length: 1,500-2,500 words. **Pays 40-50¢/word.** Sometimes pays expenses of writers on assignment.

Photos: State availability with submission. Reviews contact sheets, prints. Negotiates payment individually. Captions, identification of subjects required.

Columns/Departments: Focus on Engineering/Design, Focus on Installation, Focus on Maintenance/Testing, all 1,500 words. **Buys 7 mss/year.** Query with published clips. **Pays 40-50¢/word.**

Tips: "Visit our website to see back issues, and visit links on our website for background."

N: $ $ CEE NEWS, 9800 Metcalf Ave., Overland Park KS 66212. (913)967-1806. Website: www.ceenews.com. **Contact:** Mike Harrington, managing editor. **30% freelance written.** Monthly magazine covering news, products and business important to electrical professionals. Readership includes engineers, contractors and facility managers. Circ. 95,000. Pays on publication. Publishes ms an average of 2 months after acceptance. Rights purchased vary by article. Sample copy and writer's guidelines for phone request to Mike Harrington.
Nonfiction: Seeking news on maintenance and electrical construction. Query. Length: 500-2,000 words. **Pays $40¢/ word.**

$ $ FLOW CONTROL, The Magazine of Fluid Handling Systems, Witter Publishing Corp., 84 Park Ave., Flemington NJ 08822. (908)788-0343 ext. 141. Fax: (908)788-8416. E-mail: flowcontrol@witterpublishing.com. Website: www.flowcontrolnetwork.com. Managing Editor: Mary Beth Schwartz. **Contact:** Ron Piechota, editor. **90% freelance written.** Monthly magazine covering fluid handling systems. "*Flow Control* is the technology resource for the fluid handling industry's critical disciplines of control, containment and measurement. *Flow Control* provides solutions for system design, operational and maintenance challenges in all process and OEM applications." Estab. 1995. Circ. 40,000. Pays on publication. Publishes ms an average of 1 month after acceptance. Byline given. Buys all rights. Accepts queries by mail, e-mail, fax, phone.
Nonfiction: How-to (design or maintenance), technical. No glorified product releases. **Buys 18 mss/year.** Query with published clips or send complete ms. Length: 1,000-2,500 words. **Pays $250-350.** Sometimes pays writers with contributor copies or other premiums.
Photos: Offers no additional payment for photos accepted with ms. Captions, identification of subjects required.
Columns/Departments: Query with published clips or send complete ms. **Pays $250.**
Tips: "Anyone involved in flow control technology and/or applications may submit a manuscript for publication. Articles should be informative and analytical, containing sufficient technical data to support statements and material presented. Articles should not promote any individual product, service, or company. Case history features, describing the use of flow control technologies in specific applications, are welcomed."

N: $ $ HIGH TECHNOLOGY CAREERS, c/o Writers Connection, P.O. Box 24770, San Jose CA 95154-4770. (408)264-1045. E-mail: meeral@aol.com. **Contact:** Meera Lester, managing editor. **100% freelance written.** Magazine published every 6 weeks. "We buy three full-length feature articles (1,200 words) that examine cutting-edge or futuristic developments of high technology and their effects on life as we know it. These articles may include up to three sidebars. All material must provide a nonacademic and lively treatment of developments in computers, science, the Internet, aerospace, biotechnology, etc." Circ. 348,000. Pays on publication. Publishes ms an average of 3 months after acceptance. Byline given. Offers 25% kill fee. Buys all rights. Accepts queries by mail, e-mail. Responds in 2 months to mss. Sample copy for 9 × 12 SAE with $4 in postage. Writer's guidelines for #10 SASE.
Nonfiction: "We buy three full-length feature articles (1,200 words) that examine cutting-edge or futuristic developments of high technology and their effects on life as we know it. These articles may include up to three sidebars. All material must provide a nonacademic and lively treatment of developments in computers, science, the Internet, aerospace, biotechnology, etc." General interest (with high-tech tie-in), technical. **Buys 60-75 mss/year. Pays 25¢/word.** Sometimes pays expenses of writers on assignment.
Photos: State availability with submission.
Columns/Departments: Publishes 12 750-word (career-oriented) columns aimed at high-tech professionals: How-To, On-the-Job Strategies, The Next Step, Ethics, Health & Fitness, Innovations, Lifestyle, Manager's Corner, Online Job-Search Strategies, Small Business Entrepreneur, High-Tech News in Brief and Valley News (staff written). **Buys 60-75 mss/year.** Query with published clips. **Pays 17½¢/2word.**

$ $ LIGHTING DESIGN & APPLICATION, Illuminating Engineering Society of North America, 120 Wall St., 17th Floor, New York NY 10005-4001. (212)248-5000. Fax: (212)248-5018. E-mail: ldanewman@aol.com. **Contact:** Chris Palermo, editor. **40% freelance written.** Monthly magazine. "*LD&A* is geared to professionals in lighting design and the lighting field in architecture, retail, entertainment, etc. From designers to educators to sales reps, *LD&A* has a very unique, dedicated and well-educated audience." Estab. 1971. Circ. 10,000. **Pays on acceptance.** Publishes ms an average of 4 months after acceptance. Byline given. Buys first rights. Editorial lead time 4 months. Submit seasonal material 6 months in advance. Accepts queries by mail, e-mail, fax, phone. Accepts simultaneous submissions. Responds in 2 weeks to queries. Sample copy free.
Nonfiction: "Every year we have entertainment, outdoor, retail and arts and exhibits issues. Historical/nostalgic, how-to, opinion, personal experience, photo feature, technical. "No articles blatantly promoting a product, company or individual." **Buys 6-10 mss/year.** Query. Length: 1,500-2,200 words. **Pays $300-400 for assigned articles.**
Photos: Send photos with submission. Reviews 4 × 5 transparencies. Offers no additional payment for photos accepted with ms. Captions required.
Columns/Departments: Essay by Invitation (industry trends), 1,200 words. Query. **Does not pay for columns.**
Tips: "Most of our features detail the ins and outs of a specific lighting project. From Ricky Martin at the Grammys to the Getty Museum, *LD&A* gives its readers an in-depth look at how the designer(s) reached their goals."

$ $ $ MINNESOTA TECHNOLOGY, Inside Technology and Manufacturing Business, Minnesota Technology, Inc., 111 Third Ave. S., Minneapolis MN 55401. (612)672-3412. Fax: (612)339-5214. E-mail: lball@mntech.org.

Website: mntechnologymag.com. **Contact:** Linda Ball, editor. **75% freelance written.** Bimonthly magazine. "*Minnesota Technology* is read bimonthly by owners and top management of Minnesota's technology and manufacturing companies. The magazine covers technology trends and issues, global trade, management techniques and finance. We profile new and growing companies, new products and the innovators and entrepreneurs of Minnesota's technology sector." Estab. 1991. Circ. 20,000. **Pays on acceptance.** Publishes ms an average of 5 months after acceptance. Byline given. Offers 25% kill fee. Buys first North American serial rights. Editorial lead time 6 months. Submit seasonal material 1 year in advance. Accepts queries by mail, e-mail, fax. Responds in 1 month to queries. Sample copy for 9 × 12 SAE and 5 first-class stamps. Writer's guidelines for #10 SASE.

Nonfiction: General interest, how-to, interview/profile. **Buys 60 mss/year.** Query with published clips. Length: 500-2,000 words. **Pays $175-800.** Pays expenses of writers on assignment.

Columns/Departments: Viewpoint (Q&A format, provocative ideas from busines and industry leaders), 700 words; Tech Watch (cutting edge, gee whiz technology), 250-500 words. **Buys 10 mss/year.** Query with published clips. **Pays $150-300.**

■ The online magazine carries original content not found in the print edition and includes writers guidelines. Contact: Linda Ball, online editor.

Tips: "Query with ideas for short profiles of fascinating Minnesota technology people and business written to interest even the most nontechnical person."

$ $ MINORITY ENGINEER, An Equal Opportunity Career Publication for Professional and Graduating Minority Engineers, Equal Opportunity Publications, Inc., 1160 E. Jericho Turnpike, Suite 200, Huntington NY 11743. (516)421-9421. Fax: (516)421-0359. E-mail: info@aol.com. Website: www.eop.com. **Contact:** James Schneider, editor. **60% freelance written.** Prefers to work with published/established writers. Triannual magazine covering career guidance for minority engineering students and minority professional engineers. Estab. 1969. Circ. 15,000. Pays on publication. Publishes ms an average of 6 months after acceptance. Byline given. Buys first rights. Accepts queries by mail, e-mail, fax, phone. Accepts simultaneous submissions. Sample copy and writer's guidelines for 9 × 12 SAE with 5 first-class stamps.

Nonfiction: "We're interested in articles dealing with career guidance and job opportunities for minority engineers." Book excerpts, general interest (on specific minority engineering concerns), how-to (land a job, keep a job, etc.), interview/profile (minority engineer role models), new product (new career opportunities), opinion (problems of ethnic minorities), personal experience (student and career experiences), technical (on career fields offering opportunities for minority engineers), articles on job search techniques, role models. No career-guidance strategies or role-model profiles. Query. Length: 1,000-2,000 words. **Pays 10¢/word.** Sometimes pays expenses of writers on assignment.

Reprints: Send typed ms with rights for sale noted and information about when and where the material previously appeared. Pays 100% of amount paid for an original article.

Photos: State availability with submission. Reviews transparencies, prints. Buys all rights. Pays $15. Captions required.

Tips: "Articles should focus on career guidance, role model and industry prospects for minority engineers. Prefer articles related to careers, not politically or socially sensitive."

$ $ ▣ PROGRESSIVE ENGINEER, Buck Mountain Publishing Co., RR 3, Box 356, Lewisburg PA 17837. (570)568-8444. E-mail: progress@idweb.com. Website: www.progressiveengineer.com. **Contact:** Tom Gibson, editor. **75% freelance written.** Bimonthly online magazine. "*Progressive Engineer* is written for all disciplines of engineers in the Mid-Atlantic and northeast regions (VA, NC, MD, WV, DE, DC, PA, NJ, CT, RI, MA, VT, NH, ME). We take a less technical slant than most engineering magazines and cover the engineers behind the technology as well as the technology itself. Promotes the profession of engineering by writing about engineers, projects and related activities." Estab. 1997. Pays on publication. Publishes ms an average of 4 months after acceptance. Byline given. Offers $25 kill fee. Buys first North American serial, second serial (reprint) rights. Editorial lead time 6 months. Accepts queries by mail, e-mail. Accepts simultaneous submissions. Responds in 3 weeks to queries; 1 month to mss. Writer's guidelines on request.

Nonfiction: The editor reports a need for more profiles of engineers. Exposé, general interest, historical/nostalgic, interview/profile, technical, travel. **Buys 30 mss/year.** Query with published clips. Length: 800-2,000 words. **Pays $150-300.** Sometimes pays expenses of writers on assignment.

Reprints: Send tearsheet, photocopy or typed ms with rights for sale noted and information about when and where the material previously appeared. Pays 50% of amount paid for original article.

Photos: State availability with submission. Reviews contact sheets, transparencies, prints, digital images. Buys one-time rights. Offers $25. Captions, identification of subjects required.

Columns/Departments: Profiles (individual engineers), 1,000 words; Business/Career Topics (affecting engineers), 1,000 words; Travel, Places to Visit (see technology in action), 1,000 words. Query with published clips. **Pays $150.**

Tips: "If you know of an engineer doing something interesting or unique in your area, we'd like to hear about it."

$ $ WOMAN ENGINEER, An Equal Opportunity Career Publication for Graduating Women and Experienced Professionals, Equal Opportunity Publications, Inc., 1160 E. Jericho Turnpike, Suite 200, Huntington NY 11743. (516)421-9478. Fax: (516)421-0359. E-mail: claudia@eop.com. Website: www.eop.com. **Contact:** Claudia Wheeler, editor. **60% freelance written.** Works with a small number of new/unpublished writers each year. Triannual magazine covering career guidance for women engineering students and professional women engineers. Estab. 1968.

Circ. 16,000. Pays on publication. Publishes ms an average of 1 year after acceptance. Byline given. Buys first North American serial rights. Accepts queries by e-mail. Responds in 3 months to queries. Sample copy and writer's guidelines free.

Nonfiction: "Interested in articles dealing with career guidance and job opportunities for women engineers. Looking for manuscripts showing how to land an engineering position and advance professionally. We want features on job-search techniques, engineering disciplines offering career opportunities to women; companies with career advancement opportunities for women; problems facing women engineers and how to cope with such problems; and role-model profiles of successful women engineers, especially in major U.S. corporations." Query. Length: 1,000-2,500 words. **Pays 10¢/word.**

Photos: Reviews color slides but will accept b&w. Buys all rights. Pays $15. Captions, identification of subjects required.

Tips: "We are looking for 800-1,000 word first-person 'As I See It, personal perspectives.'"

ENTERTAINMENT & THE ARTS

The business of the entertainment/amusement industry in arts, film, dance, theater, etc. is covered by these publications. Journals that focus on the people and equipment of various music special-ties are listed in the Music section, while art and design business publications can be found in Art, Design & Collectibles. Entertainment publications for the general public can be found in the Consumer Entertainment section.

$ $ BOXOFFICE MAGAZINE, RLD Publishing Co., 155 S. El Molino Ave., Suite 100, Pasadena CA 91101. (626)396-0250. Fax: (626)396-0248. E-mail: boxoffice@earthlink.net. Website: www.boxoffice.com. Editor-in-chief: Kim Williamson. **Contact:** Christine James, managing editor. **15% freelance written.** Monthly magazine about the motion picture industry for members of the film industry: theater owners, film producers, directors, financiers and allied industries. Estab. 1920. Circ. 8,000. Pays on publication. Publishes ms an average of 4 months after acceptance. Byline given. Buys all rights, including electronic publishing. Submit seasonal material 4 months in advance. Accepts queries by mail, e-mail, fax. Sample copy for $10.

O─ "*Boxoffice* magazine is particularly interested in freelance writers who can write business articles on the exhibition industry or technical writers who are familiar with projection/sound equipment and new technologies such as digital cinema."

Nonfiction: "We are a general news magazine about the motion picture industry and are looking for stories about trends, developments, problems or opportunities facing the industry. Almost any story will be considered, including corporate profiles, but we don't want gossip or celebrity coverage." Book excerpts, essays, historical/nostalgic, interview/profile, new product, personal experience, photo feature, technical, investigative "all regarding movie theater business." Query with published clips. Length: 800-2,500 words. **Pays 10¢/word or set price.**

Photos: State availability with submission. Pays $10 maximum for 8×10 b&w prints. Captions required.

■ The online magazine carries original content not found in the print edition. Contact: Kim Williamson.

Tips: "Request a sample copy, indicating you read about *Boxoffice* in *Writer's Market.* Write a clear, comprehensive outline of the proposed story and enclose a résumé and clip samples."

N $ $ $ $ CABLE WORLD, Primedia, 5680 Greenwood Plaza, Greenwood Village CO 80111. (720)489-3186. Fax: (720)489-3218. E-mail: andy_grossman@intertec.com. Website: www.cableworld.com. Editor: Andy Gross-man. **Contact:** Jon Lafayette, managing editor. **50% freelance written.** Weekly magazine covering cable television. "We market toward operators of cable TV systems." Estab. 1987. Circ. 22,000. Pays on publication. Publishes ms an average of 1 month after acceptance. Offers 50% kill fee. Buys all rights. Editorial lead time 2 weeks. Accepts queries by mail, e-mail, fax, phone. Accepts simultaneous submissions. Responds in 1 week to queries. Sample copy and writer's guidelines free.

Nonfiction: Book excerpts, interview/profile, opinion, technical. No investigative reports or stories critical of advertis-ers. **Buys 100 mss/year.** Query. Length: 1,000-2,500 words. **Pays $1/word.** Pays expenses of writers on assignment.

Photos: State availability with submission. Reviews gif/jpeg files. Buys all rights. Negotiates payment individually. Identification of subjects required.

Columns/Departments: Broadband Technology (TV tech), 750 words; Programming (TV shows), 750 words; Be-tween the Lines (personal shorts), 350 words; People (personal shorts), 100 words. **Buys 50 mss/year. Pays $1/word.**

Poetry: Light verse, traditional. No dirty poetry. **Buys 10 poems/year.** Submit maximum 5 poems. Length: 20-50 lines. **Pays $1/word.**

Tips: "Keep trying—we may not bite the first time. Be sure to attribute submissions."

$ CALLBOARD, Monthly Theatre Trade Magazine, Theatre Bay Area, 870 Market St., #375, San Francisco CA 94102-3002. (415)430-1140. Fax: (415)430-1145. E-mail: tba@theatrebayarea.org. Website: www.theatrebayarea.org. **Contact:** Karen McKevitt, editor. **50% freelance written.** Monthly magazine for local theater in the SF Bay area. "We publish news, views, essays and features on the Northern California theater industry. We also include listings, audition notices and job resources." Estab. 1976. Circ. 5,000. Pays on publication. Publishes ms an average of 4 months after acceptance. Byline given. Offers 50% kill fee. Buys first rights. Editorial lead time 6 weeks. Submit seasonal material 2 months in advance. Accepts queries by mail, e-mail, phone. Accepts simultaneous submissions. Responds in 1 month to queries. Sample copy for $6.

Nonfiction: Book excerpts, essays, opinion, personal experience, technical (theater topics only), features. No reviews or profiles of actors. **Buys 12-15 mss/year.** Query with published clips. Length: 800-2,000 words. **Pays $100-200 for assigned articles; $35-75 for department articles.** Pays expenses of writers on assignment.

Reprints: Send tearsheet or typed ms with rights for sale noted and information about when and where the material previously appeared. Pays 25% of amount paid for an original article.

Photos: State availability with submission. Reviews contact sheets, 5×7 prints. Buys one-time rights. Offers no additional payment for photos accepted with ms. Identification of subjects required.

$ CAMPUS ACTIVITIES, Cameo Publishing Group, P.O. Box 509, Prosperity SC 29127. (800)728-2950. Fax: (803)321-2049. E-mail: cameopub@aol.com or campusactivities.org. Website: www.cameopub.com. Editor: Laura Moore, Managing Editor: Robin Hellman. **Contact:** WC Kirby, publisher. **75% freelance written.** Magazine published 8 times/year covering entertainment on college campuses. *Campus Activities* goes to entertainment buyers on every campus in the US. Features stories on artists (national and regional), speakers and the programs at individual schools. Estab. 1991. Circ. 5,200. Pays on publication. Publishes ms an average of 2 months after acceptance. Byline given. Offers 15% kill fee if accepted and not run. Buys first, second serial (reprint), electronic rights. Editorial lead time 2 months. Submit seasonal material 2 months in advance. Accepts queries by mail, e-mail, fax. Accepts simultaneous submissions. Responds in 1 month to queries; 2 months to mss. Sample copy for $3.50. Writer's guidelines free.

Nonfiction: Interview/profile, photo feature. Accepts no unsolicited articles. **Buys 40 mss/year.** Query. Length: 1,400-3,000 words. **Pays $250.** Sometimes pays expenses of writers on assignment.

Photos: State availability with submission. Reviews contact sheets, negatives, 3×5 transparencies. Buys one-time rights. Negotiates payment individually. Identification of subjects required.

Tips: "Writers who have ideas, proposals and special project requests should contact the publisher prior to any commitment to work on such a story. The publisher welcomes innovative and creative ideas for stories and works with writers on such proposals which have significant impact on our readers."

N $ $ DANCE TEACHER, The Practical Magazine of Dance, Lifestyle Ventures, 250 57th St., Suite 420, New York NY 10107. (212)265-8890, ext. 20. Fax: (212)265-8908. E-mail: samoruso@lifestyleventures.com. Website: www.dance-teacher.com. **Contact:** Susan Amoruso, managing editor. **80% freelance written.** Magazine published 10 times/year. "Our readers are professional dance educators, business persons and related professionals in all forms of dance." Estab. 1979. Circ. 8,000. Pays on publication. Publishes ms an average of 3 months after acceptance. Byline given. Buys Negotiates rights and permission to reprint on request. Submit seasonal material 6 months in advance. Accepts queries by mail, e-mail, fax, phone. Responds in 3 months to mss. Sample copy for 9×12 SAE and 6 first-class stamps. Writer's guidelines free by mail or online.

Nonfiction: How-to (teach, business), interview/profile, new product, personal experience, photo feature. Special issues: Auditions (January); Summer Programs (February); Music & More (July/August); Costumes and Production Preview (November); College/Training Schools (December). No PR or puff pieces. All articles must be well researched. **Buys 50 mss/year.** Query. Length: 700-2,000 words. **Pays $100-250.**

Photos: Send photos with submission. Reviews contact sheets, negatives, transparencies, prints. Limited photo budget.

■ The online magazine carries original content not found in the print edition. Contact: Susan Amoruso.

Tips: "Read several issues—particularly seasonal. Stay within writer's guidelines."

$ $ DRAMATICS MAGAZINE, Educational Theatre Association, 2343 Auburn Ave., Cincinnati OH 45219-2815. (513)421-3900. Fax: (513)421-7077. E-mail: dcorathers@etassoc.org. Website: www.etassoc.org. **Contact:** Donald Corathers, editor-in-chief. **70% freelance written.** Monthly magazine for theater arts students, teachers and others interested in theater arts education. "*Dramatics* is designed to provide serious, committed young theatre students and their teachers with the skills and knowledge they need to make better theatre; to be a resource that will help high school juniors and seniors make an informed decision about whether to pursue a career in theatre, and about how to do so; and to prepare high school students to be knowledgeable, appreciative audience members for the rest of their lives." Estab. 1929. Circ. 37,000. **Pays on acceptance.** Publishes ms an average of 3 months after acceptance. Byline given. Buys first North American serial rights. Submit seasonal material 3 months in advance. Accepts queries by mail, e-mail, fax. Accepts simultaneous submissions. Responds in 3 months to queries longer than 3 months on unsolicited mss to mss. Sample copy for 9×12 SAE with 5 first-class stamps. Writer's guidelines free.

O⊸ "The best way to break in is to know our audience—drama students, teachers and others interested in theater—and to write for them."

Nonfiction: How-to (technical theater, directing, acting, etc.), humor, inspirational, interview/profile, photo feature, technical. **Buys 30 mss/year.** Send complete ms. Length: 750-3,000 words. **Pays $50-400.** Sometimes pays expenses of writers on assignment.

Reprints: Send tearsheet, photocopy or typed ms with rights for sale noted and information about when and where the material previously appeared. Pays up to 75% of amount paid for original.

Photos: Query. Purchased with accompanying ms. Reviews transparencies. Total price for ms usually includes payment for photos.

Fiction: Drama (one-act and full-length plays). Prefers unpublished scripts that have been produced at least once. "No plays for children, Christmas plays or plays written with no attention paid to the conventions of theater." **Buys 5-9 mss/ year.** Send complete ms. **Pays $100-400.**

Tips: "Writers who have some practical experience in theater, especially in technical areas, have a leg-up here, but we'll work with anybody who has a good idea. Some freelancers have become regular contributors. Others ignore style suggestions included in our writer's guidelines."

$ $ $ EMMY MAGAZINE, Academy of Television Arts & Sciences, 5220 Lankershim Blvd., North Hollywood CA 91601-3109. (818)754-2800. Fax: (818)761-8524. E-mail: emmymag@emmys.org. Website: www.emmys.org. **Contact:** Gail Polevoi, editor. **90% freelance written.** Prefers to work with published/established writers. Bimonthly magazine on television for TV professionals. Circ. 14,000. Pays on publication or within 6 months. Publishes ms an average of 4 months after acceptance. Byline given. Offers 25% kill fee. Buys first North American serial rights. Accepts queries by mail, e-mail, fax. Responds in 1 month to queries. Sample copy for 9×12 SAE and 6 first-class stamps. Writer's guidelines online.

Nonfiction: Articles on contemporary issues, trends, and VIPs (especially those behind the scenes) in broadcast and cable TV; programming and new technology. "Looking for profiles of fascinating people who work 'below the line' in television. Also, always looking for new writers who understand technology and new media and can writer about it in an engaging manner. We require TV industry expertise and clear, lively writing." Query with published clips. Length: 1,700 words. **Pays $900-1,000.**

Columns/Departments: Most written by regular contributors, but newcomers can break into Labors of Love. Length: 500-1,500 words, depending on department. Query with published clips. **Pays $250-750.**

Tips: "Please review recent issues before querying us. Query with published, television-related clips. No fanzine, academic or nostalgic approaches, please. Demonstrate experience in covering the business of television and your ability to write in a lively and compelling manner about programming trends and new technology. Identify fascinating people behind the scenes, not just in the executive suites but in all ranks of the industry."

$ $ RELEASE PRINT, The Magazine of Film Arts Foundation, Film Arts Foundation, 346 9th St., 2nd Floor, San Francisco CA 94103. (415)552-8760. Fax: (415)552-0882. Website: www.filmarts.org. **Contact:** Thomas J. Powers, editor. **80% freelance written.** Monthly magazine covering U.S. independent filmmaking. "We have a knowledgeable readership of film and videomakers. They are interested in the financing, production, exhibition and distribution of independent films and videos. They are interested in practical and technical issues and, to a lesser extent, aesthetic ones." Estab. 1977. Circ. 5,000. Pays on publication. Publishes ms an average of 3 months after acceptance. Byline given. Buys all rights for commissioned works. For works submitted on spec, buys first rights and requests acknowledgement of Release Print in any subsequent publication. Editorial lead time 3 months. Accepts queries by mail. Responds in 3 weeks to queries; 2 months to mss. Writer's guidelines for 9×12 SASE with $1.47 postage.

O─► Break in with a proposal for an article or interview of an American experimental, documentary or very low budget feature film/video maker with ties to the San Francisco Bay area (or an upcoming screening in this area). Submit at least 3 months prior to publication date.

Nonfiction: Interview/profile, personal experience, technical, Book Reviews. No film criticism or reviews. **Buys 30-35 mss/year.** Query. Length: 300-2,000 words. **Pays 10¢/word.** Sometimes pays expenses of writers on assignment.

Photos: Send photos with submission. Reviews prints. Buys one-time rights. Offers no additional payment for photos accepted with ms. Identification of subjects required.

Columns/Departments: Book Reviews (independent film & video), 800-1,000 words. **Buys 4 mss/year.** Query. **Pays 10¢/word.**

N: $ SOUTHERN THEATRE, Southeastern Theatre Conference, P.O. Box 9868, Greensboro NC 27429-0868. E-mail: publications@setc.org. Website: www.setc.org/pubs.html. **Contact:** Deanna Thompson, editor. **100% freelance written.** Quarterly magazine covering theatre. "*Southern Theatre* is *the* magazine covering all aspects of theatre in the Southeast, from innovative theatre companies to important trends to people making a difference in the region. All stories must be written in a popular magazine style but with subject matter appropriate for theatre professionals (not the general public). The audience includes members of the Southeastern Theatre Conference, founded in 1949 and the nation's largest regional theatre organization. These members include individuals involved in professional, community, college/ university, children's and secondary school theatre. The magazine also is purchased by more than 100 libraries." Estab. 1962. Circ. 3,600. **Pays on acceptance.** Publishes ms an average of 3 months after acceptance. Byline given. Buys first North American serial, first, one-time, second serial (reprint), electronic rights. Editorial lead time 3 months. Submit seasonal material 6 months in advance. Accepts queries by mail, e-mail. Responds in 6 weeks to queries; 3 months to mss. Sample copy for $6. Writer's guidelines free, online or by e-mail.

Nonfiction: Looking for stories on design/technology, playwriting, acting, directing, all with a Southeastern connection. General interest (innovative theatres and theatre programs; trend stories), interview/profile (people making a difference in Southeastern theatre). Special issues: Playwriting (fall issue, all stories submitted by January 1). No scholarly articles. **Buys 15-20 mss/year.** Query with or without published clips or send complete ms. Length: 1,000-3,000 words. **Pays $25.** Pays in contributor copies for book reviews, sidebars and other short stories. Sometimes pays expenses of writers on assignment.

Photos: State availability of or send photos with submission. Reviews transparencies, prints. Buys one-time, electronic rights. Offers no additional payment for photos accepted with ms. Captions, identification of subjects, model releases required.

Columns/Departments: Outside the Box (innovative solutions to problems faced by designers and technicians), 800-1,000 words; Words, words, words (reviews of books on theatre), 400-550 words. **Buys 2-4 mss/year.** Query or send complete ms. **Pays $25.**

Tips: "Look for a theatre or theatre person in your area that is doing something different or innovative that would be of interest to others in the profession, then write about that theatre or person in a compelling way. We also are looking for well-written trend stories (talk to theatres in your area about trends that are affecting them), and we especially like stories that help our readers do their jobs more effectively. Send an e-mail detailing a well-developed story idea, and ask if we're interested."

FARM

The successful farm writer focuses on the business side of farming. For technical articles, editors feel writers should have a farm background or agricultural training, but there are opportunities for the general freelancer too. The following farm publications are divided into seven categories, each specializing in a different aspect of farming: equipment; crops & soil management; dairy farming; livestock; management; miscellaneous; and regional.

Agricultural Equipment

$ $ IMPLEMENT & TRACTOR, Freiberg Publishing, 2302 W. First St., Cedar Falls IA 50613. (319)277-3599. Fax: (319)277-3783. E-mail: mshepherd@cfu.net. Website: www.ag-implement.com. **Contact:** Mary Shepherd, editor. **15% freelance written.** Bimonthly magazine covering farm equipment, light construction, commercial turf and lawn and garden equipment. "*Implement & Tractor* offers technical and business news for equipment dealers, manufacturers, consultants and others involved as suppliers to the industry. Writers must know US and global machinery and the industry trends." Estab. 1895. Circ. 8,500. **Pays on acceptance.** Publishes ms an average of 6 months after acceptance. Byline given. Buys all rights. Editorial lead time 4 months. Accepts queries by mail, e-mail, fax. Responds in 2 months to queries. Sample copy for $6.

Nonfiction: Interview/profile (dealer or manufacturer), new product, photo feature, technical. No lightweight technical articles, general farm machinery articles or farmer profiles articles. Query with published clips. Length: 200-600 words. **Pays $100-250.** Sometimes pays expenses of writers on assignment.

Photos: State availability with submission. Reviews contact sheets. Buys one-time rights. Offers no additional payment for photos accepted with ms. Captions, identification of subjects required.

Tips: "Know the equipment industry, have an engineer's outlook for analyzing machinery and a writer's skills to communicate that information. Technical background is helpful, as is mechanical aptitude."

Crops & Soil Management

$ $ AMERICAN FRUIT GROWER, Meister Publishing, 37733 Euclid Ave., Willoughby OH 44094. (440)942-2000. Fax: (440)942-0662. E-mail: afg_edit@meisternet.com. **Contact:** Laurie Sanders, managing editor. **30% freelance written.** Annual magazine covering commercial fruit growing. "How-to" articles are best. Estab. 1880. Circ. 50,000. Pays on publication. Publishes ms an average of 4 months after acceptance. Byline given. Buys first rights. Editorial lead time 2 months. Submit seasonal material 4 months in advance. Accepts queries by mail, e-mail, fax, phone. Responds in 2 weeks to queries; 2 months to mss. Sample copy and writer's guidelines free.

Nonfiction: How-to (better grow fruit crops). **Buys 6-10 mss/year.** Query with published clips or send complete ms. Length: 800-1,200 words. **Pays $200-250.** Sometimes pays expenses of writers on assignment.

Photos: Send photos with submission. Reviews prints, slides. Buys one-time rights. Negotiates payment individually.

$ $ COTTON GROWER MAGAZINE, Meister Publishing Co., 65 Germantown Court, #220, Cordova TN 38018. (901)756-8822. Fax: (901)756-8879. Editor: Bill Spencer. **Contact:** Al Fava, senior editor. **15% freelance written.** Monthly magazine covering cotton production, cotton markets and related subjects. Readers are mostly cotton producers who seek information on production practices, equipment and products related to cotton. Estab. 1901. Circ. 50,000. **Pays on acceptance.** Publishes ms an average of 2 months after acceptance. Byline given. Buys first rights. Editorial lead time 2 months. Submit seasonal material 2 months in advance. Accepts queries by mail, e-mail, fax, phone. Accepts simultaneous submissions. Sample copy free.

Nonfiction: Interview/profile, new product, photo feature, technical. No fiction or humorous pieces. **Buys 5-10 mss/year.** Query with published clips. Length: 500-800 words. **Pays $200-400.** Pays expenses of writers on assignment.

Photos: State availability with submission. Reviews transparencies. Buys all rights. Offers no additional payment for photos accepted with ms. Captions, identification of subjects required.

N **$ $ $ CPM, Crop Production Magazine**, Media Products Inc./United Agri Products, P.O. Box 1-B, Eugene OR 97440. (541)687-2315 or (800)874-3276. Fax: (541)686-0248. E-mail: editor@CPMmagazine.com. Website: www. CPMmagazine.com. **Contact:** Denise Wendt, editor. **80% freelance written.** Magazine published 6 times/year covering agriculture and crop production. *"CPM provides practical information on crop production strategies and tools. We publish how-to, solution-oriented information for large, commercial farmers. We have expanded our editorial scope to include timely, national issues of interest to farmers. Our goal is to provide information that will help farmers produce a better crop, save money or improve their bottom line."* Estab. 1987. Circ. 190,000. **Pays on acceptance.** Publishes ms an average of 6 months after acceptance. Byline given. Buys all rights. Submit seasonal material 8 months in advance. Accepts queries by mail, e-mail, fax, phone. Sample copy and writer's guidelines available on request.

Nonfiction: How-to (crop production/farm management), interview/profile, new product, technical (sprayer technology, equipment updates), success stories. Query with published clips. Length: 500-1,500 words. **Pays $500-1,000.**

Photos: Send slides with submission. Articles without photos will be returned. Buys all rights. Offers no additional payment for photos accepted with manuscript. Captions, identification of subjects, model releases required.

Columns/Departments: From the Field, Market News, New Products and Label Updates.

Tips: "We're looking for stories that provide farmers with practical information they can take to the field. We need established ag writers with a good understanding of issues important to farmers. Flexibility in working with editors to shape stories is important."

$ $ THE FRUIT GROWERS NEWS, Great American Publishing, P.O. Box 128, Sparta MI 49345. (616)887-9008. Fax: (616)887-2666. E-mail: gentry@iserv.net. Website: www.fruitgrowersnews.com. Editor: Matt McCollum. **Contact:** Karen Gentry, associate editor. **25% freelance written.** Monthly tabloid covering agriculture. "Our objective is to provide commercial fruit growers of all sizes information to help them succeed." Estab. 1970. Circ. 28,000. Pays on publication. Publishes ms an average of 2 months after acceptance. Makes work-for-hire assignments. Editorial lead time 1 month. Submit seasonal material 1 month in advance. Accepts queries by mail, e-mail, fax, phone. Accepts simultaneous submissions. Responds in 2 weeks to queries; 1 month to mss. Sample copy free.

Nonfiction: Essays, general interest, how-to, interview/profile, new product, opinion, technical. No advertorials, other "puff pieces." **Buys 72 mss/year.** Query with published clips. Length: 800-1,100 words. **Pays $100-200.** Sometimes pays expenses of writers on assignment.

Photos: Send photos with submission. Reviews prints. Buys one-time rights. Offers $10-20/photo. Captions required.

$ GRAINEWS, Farm Business Communications (division of United Grain Growers), P.O. Box 6600, Winnipeg, Manitoba R3C 3A7, Canada. (204)944-5587. Fax: (204)944-5416. E-mail: asirski@fbc.unitedgrain.ca. **Contact:** Andy Sirski, editor-in-chief or David Bedard, managing editor (dbedard@fbc.unitedgr). **80% freelance written.** Newspaper published 18 times/year covering agriculture/agribusiness. **Pays on acceptance.** Publishes ms an average of 1 month after acceptance. Byline given. Buys first rights. Editorial lead time 1 month. Submit seasonal material 1 month in advance. Accepts queries by mail, e-mail, fax, phone. Responds in 2 weeks to queries. Sample copy free.

Nonfiction: Indepth how-to articles on various aspects of farming. "Every article should be written from the farmer's perspective." General interest, historical/nostalgic, humor, new product, opinion, personal experience, technical. Query. **Pays $150 for assigned articles; $25 for unsolicited articles.** Sometimes pays expenses of writers on assignment.

Photos: State availability with submission. Buys one-time rights. Offers no additional payment for photos accepted with ms. Captions, identification of subjects required.

Poetry: Andy Sirski, editor. Traditional. **Pays $25.**

Tips: "We want writers who are farmers. We love 'how-to' articles on farm-related repairs, etc. Ask yourself how your story will help or entertain other farmers, and if it doesn't, don't send it."

$ $ GRAPE GROWER MAGAZINE, Western Ag Publishing Co., 4969 E. Clinton Way #104, Fresno CA 93727. (559)252-7000. Fax: (559)252-7387. E-mail: editorial@westagpubco.com. **Contact:** Randy Bailey, editor; Robert Fujimoto, assistant editor. **20% freelance written.** Monthly magazine covering viticulture and winerys. Estab. 1968. Circ. 12,000. Pays on publication. Publishes ms an average of 4 months after acceptance. Byline sometimes given. Buys all rights, makes work-for-hire assignments. Editorial lead time 2 months. Submit seasonal material 3 months in advance. Accepts queries by mail, e-mail, fax, phone. Accepts simultaneous submissions. Responds in 2 weeks to queries; 1 month to mss. Sample copy free by e-mail.

Nonfiction: How-to, interview/profile, new product, personal experience. Query or send complete ms. Length: 900-1,500 words. Sometimes pays expenses of writers on assignment.

Photos: Send photos with submission. Reviews transparencies, prints. Buys all rights.

$ ONION WORLD, Columbia Publishing, P.O. Box 9036, Yakima WA 98909-0036. (509)248-2452, ext. 152. Fax: (509)248-4056. E-mail: brent@freshcut.com. Website: www.onionworld.net. **Contact:** Brent Clement, managing editor. **50% freelance written.** Monthly magazine covering the world of onion production and marketing for onion growers and shippers. Estab. 1985. Circ. 5,500. Pays on publication. Publishes ms an average of 1 month after acceptance.

Byline given. Not copyrighted. Buys first North American serial rights. Submit seasonal material 1 month in advance. Accepts queries by mail, e-mail, fax, phone. Accepts simultaneous submissions. Responds in 1 month to queries. Sample copy for 9×12 SAE and 5 first-class stamps.

• Columbia Publishing also produces *Fresh Cut, The Tomato Magazine, Potato Country and Carrot Country.*

Nonfiction: General interest, historical/nostalgic, interview/profile. **Buys 60 mss/year.** Query. Length: 1,200-1,500 words. **Pays 5¢/word for assigned articles.**

Reprints: Send photocopy and information about when and where the material previously appeared. Pays 50% of amount paid for an original article.

Photos: Send photos with submission. Buys all rights. Offers no additional payment for photos accepted with ms unless it's a cover shot. Captions, identification of subjects required.

Tips: "Writers should be familiar with growing and marketing onions. We use a lot of feature stories on growers, shippers and others in the onion trade—what they are doing, their problems, solutions, marketing plans, etc."

$ $ RICE JOURNAL, SpecCom International, Inc., 3000 Highwoods Blvd., Raleigh NC 27604-1029. (919)872-5040. Fax: (919)876-6531. E-mail: editor@ricejournal.com. Website: www.ricejournal.com. Editor: Mary Evans. **Contact:** Mary Ann Rood, managing editor. **5% freelance written.** Monthly (January-June) magazine covering rice farming. "Articles must discuss rice production practices. Readers are rice farmers. Include on-farm interview with one or more farmers who use the featured agronomic practice. Must include photo of the farmer involved in a farming activity." Estab. 1897. Circ. 10,000. Pays on publication. Byline given. Buys first rights. Editorial lead time 2 months. Accepts queries by mail, e-mail, fax. Responds in 2 weeks to queries; 2 months to mss. Sample copy online. Writer's guidelines for #10 SASE.

Nonfiction: Book excerpts, how-to, personal experience, photo feature, technical, farmer production tips. Special issues: January: land preparation; February: water management; March: weed control; April: rice diseases and management; May: insect control, tracked vehicles; June: harvest, curing. No recipes, cooking. **Buys 2 mss/year.** Query. Length: 600-2,000 words. **Pays $50-400.**

Photos: State availability with submission. Buys one-time rights. Offers no additional payment for photos accepted with ms. Captions, identification of subjects required.

$ $ SEED TRADE NEWS, Ball Publishing, 335 N. River St., Batavia IL 60510. (630)208-9080. Fax: (630)208-9350. E-mail: sbruhn@seedtradenews.com. Website: www.seedtradenews.com. **Contact:** Sherri Bruhn, editor. **15% freelance written.** Monthly magazine covering seed breeding. Estab. 1923. Circ. 6,809. Pays on publication. Publishes ms an average of 4 months after acceptance. Byline given. Offers 25% kill fee. Buys first North American serial rights. Editorial lead time 4 months. Submit seasonal material 4 months in advance. Accepts queries by mail, e-mail, fax, phone. Accepts simultaneous submissions.

Nonfiction: Interview/profile, technical. **Buys 10 mss/year.** Query with published clips. Length: 300-1,800 words. **Pays $125-800.** Sometimes pays expenses of writers on assignment.

Photos: Send photos with submission. Reviews slides. Buys one-time rights. Negotiates payment individually. Captions, identification of subjects required.

Columns/Departments: Industry Watch (industry, company, association news); Seed Strategies (business tips, market trends); Genetic Edge (agricultural biotechnology news, patents); Ground Work (agronomics, turf, vegetable, ornamentals), all 350 words. **Buys 10 mss/year.** Send complete ms. **Pays $100-400.**

   ■ The online magazine carries original content not found in the print edition. Contact: Amit Patel, online editor.

$ $ THE VEGETABLE GROWERS NEWS, Great American Publishing, P.O. Box 128, Sparta MI 49345. (616)887-9008. Fax: (616)887-2666. E-mail: gentry@iserv.net. Website: www.vegetablegrowersnews.com. Editor: Matt McCollum. **Contact:** Karen Gentry, associate editor. **25% freelance written.** Monthly tabloid covering agriculture. "Our objective is to provide commercial vegetable growers of all sizes information to help them succeed." Estab. 1970. Circ. 28,000. Pays on publication. Publishes ms an average of 2 months after acceptance. Makes work-for-hire assignments. Editorial lead time 1 month. Submit seasonal material 1 month in advance. Accepts queries by mail, e-mail, fax, phone. Accepts simultaneous submissions. Responds in 2 weeks to queries; 1 month to mss. Sample copy free.

Nonfiction: Essays, general interest, how-to, interview/profile, new product, opinion, technical. No advertorials, other "puff pieces." **Buys 72 mss/year.** Query with published clips. Length: 800-1,100 words. **Pays $100-200.** Sometimes pays expenses of writers on assignment.

Photos: Send photos with submission. Reviews prints. Buys one-time rights. Offers $10-20/photo. Captions required.

MARKETS THAT WERE listed in the 2001 edition of *Writer's Market* but do not appear this year are listed in the General Index with a notation explaining why they were omitted.

Dairy Farming

$ DAIRY GOAT JOURNAL, P.O. Box 10, 128 E. Lake St., Lake Mills WI 53551. (920)648-8285. Fax: (920)648-3770. **Contact:** Dave Thompson, editor. **45% freelance written.** Monthly journal. "We are looking for clear and accurate articles about dairy goat owners, their herds, cheesemaking, and other ways of marketing products. Some readers own two goats; others own 1,500 and are large commercial operations." Estab. 1917. Circ. 8,000, including copies to more than 70 foreign countries. Pays on publication. Byline given.
Nonfiction: Information on personalities and on public issues affecting dairy goats and their owners. How-to articles with plenty of practical information. Health and husbandry articles should be written with appropriate experience or academic credentials. **Buys 100 mss/year.** Query with published clips. Length: 750-2,500 words. **Pays $50-150.** Pays expenses of writers on assignment.
Photos: Color or b&w. Vertical or horizontal for cover. Goats and/or people. Pays $100 maximum for 35mm slides for covers; $20-70 for inside use or for b&w. Identification of subjects required.
Tips: "We love good articles about dairy goats and will work with beginners, if you are cooperative."

[N] $ $ WESTERN DAIRYBUSINESS, Dept. WM, Heritage Complex, 4500 S. Laspina, Tulare CA 93274. (559)687-3160. Fax: (559)687-3166. Website: www.dairybusiness.com. **Contact:** Todd Fitchette, editor (tfitchette@dairybusiness.com), Shana Davis, managing editor (sdavis@dairybusiness.com). **10% freelance written.** Prefers to work with published/established writers. Monthly magazine dealing with large herd commercial dairy industry. Rarely publishes information about non-Western producers or daily groups and events. Estab. 1922. Circ. 17,000. Pays on acceptance or publication. Publishes ms an average of 3 months after acceptance. Byline given. Buys first North American serial rights. Submit seasonal material 3 months in advance. Accepts queries by mail, e-mail. Responds in 1 month to queries. Sample copy for 9×12 SAE and 4 first-class stamps.
Nonfiction: Special emphasis on: Environmental stewardship, herd management systems, business management, facilities/equipment, forage/cropping. Interview/profile, new product, opinion, industry analysis. "No religion, nostalgia, politics or 'mom and pop' dairies." Query or send complete ms. Length: 300-1,500 words. **Pays $25-400 for assigned articles.**
Reprints: Seldom accepts previously published submissions. Send information about when and where the article previously appeared. Pays 50% of amount paid for an original article.
Photos: Photos are a critical part of story packages. Send photos with submission. Reviews contact sheets, 35mm or 2¼×2¼ transparencies. Buys one-time rights. Pays $25 for b&w; $50-100 for color. Captions, identification of subjects required.
Tips: "Know the market and the industry, be well-versed in large-herd dairy management and business."

Livestock

$ $ ANGUS BEEF BULLETIN, Angus Productions, Inc., 3201 Frederick Ave., St. Joseph MO 64506. (816)383-5200. Fax: (816)233-6575. E-mail: shermel@angus.org. Website: www.angusebeefbulletin.com. **Contact:** Shauna Hermel, editor. **45% freelance written.** Tabloid published 4 times/year covering commercial cattle industry. "The *Bulletin* is mailed free to commercial cattlemen who have purchased an Angus bull, and had the registration transferred to them within the last 3 years." Estab. 1985. Circ. 63,000. Pays on publication. Publishes ms an average of 3 months after acceptance. Byline given. Buys first, electronic rights. Editorial lead time 3 months. Submit seasonal material 3 months in advance. Accepts queries by mail, e-mail. Accepts simultaneous submissions. Responds in 3 weeks to queries; 3 months to mss. Sample copy for $5. Writer's guidelines for #10 SASE.
Nonfiction: How-to (cattle production), interview/profile, technical (cattle production). **Buys 10 mss/year.** Query with published clips. Length: 800-2,500 words. **Pays $50-600.** Pays expenses of writers on assignment.
Photos: Send photos with submission. Reviews 5×7 transparencies, 5×7 glossy prints. Buys all rights. Offers $25/photo. Identification of subjects required.
Tips: "Read the publication *Angus Journal* and have a firm grasp of the commercial cattle industry and how the Angus breeds fit in that industry."

$ $ $ ANGUS JOURNAL, Angus Productions Inc., 3201 Frederick Ave., St. Joseph MO 64506-2997. (816)383-5200. Fax: (816)233-6575. E-mail: shermel@angusjournal.com. Website: www.angusjournal.com. **Contact:** Shauna Hermel, editor. **40% freelance written.** Monthly magazine covering Angus cattle. "The *Angus Journal* is the official magazine of the American Angus Association. Its primary function as such is to report to the membership association activities and information pertinent to raising Angus cattle." Estab. 1919. Circ. 23,500. Pays on publication. Publishes ms an average of 3 months after acceptance. Byline given. Buys first, electronic rights. Editorial lead time 2 months. Submit seasonal material 3 months in advance. Accepts queries by mail, e-mail, fax. Accepts simultaneous submissions. Responds in 3 weeks to queries; 2 months to mss. Sample copy for $5. Writer's guidelines for #10 SASE.
Nonfiction: How-to (cattle production), interview/profile, technical (related to cattle). **Buys 20-30 mss/year.** Query with published clips. Length: 800-3,500 words. **Pays $50-1,000.** Pays expenses of writers on assignment.
Photos: Send photos with submission. Buys all rights. Offers $25-400/photo. Identification of subjects required.

■ The online magazine carries original content not found in the print edition. Contact: Shauna Hermel, online editor.

Tips: "Read the magazine and have a firm grasp of the cattle industry."

$ $ THE BRAHMAN JOURNAL, Sagebrush Publishing Co., Inc., P.O. Box 220, Eddy TX 76524-0220. (254)859-5451. Fax: (254)859-5451. **Contact:** Joe Ed Brockett, editor. **10% freelance written.** Monthly magazine covering Brahman cattle. Estab. 1971. Circ. 4,000. Pays on publication. Publishes ms an average of 2 months after acceptance. Byline given. Not copyrighted. Buys first North American serial, one-time, second serial (reprint) rights, makes work-for-hire assignments. Submit seasonal material 3 months in advance. Sample copy for 9×12 SAE and 5 first-class stamps.

Nonfiction: General interest, historical/nostalgic, interview/profile. Special issues: Herd Bull (July); Texas (October). **Buys 3-4 mss/year.** Query with published clips. Length: 1,200-3,000 words. **Pays $100-250 for assigned articles.**

Reprints: Send typed ms with rights for sale noted. Pays 50% of amount paid for an original article.

Photos: Photos needed for article purchase. Send photos with submission. Reviews 4×5 prints. Buys one-time rights. Offers no additional payment for photos accepted with ms. Captions required.

$ $ FEED LOT MAGAZINE, Feed Lot Inc., P.O. Box 850, Dighton KS 67839. (316)397-2838. Fax: (316)397-2839. Website: www.feedlotmagazine.com. **Contact:** Robert A. Strong, editor. **40% freelance written.** Bimonthly magazine. "The editorial information content fits a dual role: large feedlots and their related cow/calf, operations, and large 500pl cow/calf, stocker operations. The information covers all phases of production from breeding, genetics, animal health, nutrition, equipment design, research through finishing fat cattle. *Feed Lot* publishes a mix of new information and timely articles which directly effect the cattle industry." Estab. 1993. Circ. 12,000. Pays on publication. Publishes ms an average of 2 months after acceptance. Byline given. Offers 50% kill fee. Buys all rights. Editorial lead time 2 months. Submit seasonal material 6 months in advance. Accepts queries by mail. Responds in 1 month to queries. Sample copy and writer's guidelines for $1.50.

Nonfiction: Interview/profile, new product (cattle-related), photo feature. Send complete ms. Length: 100-400 words. **Pays 10¢/word.**

Reprints: Send tearsheet or typed ms with rights for sale noted and information about when and where the material previously appeared. Pays 50% of amount paid for an original article.

Photos: State availability of or send photos with submission. Reviews contact sheets. Buys all rights. Negotiates payment individually. Captions, model releases required.

Tips: "Know what you are writing about—have a good knowledge of the subject."

$ SHEEP! MAGAZINE, P.O. Box 10, 128 E. Lake St., Lake Mills WI 53551. (920)648-8285. Fax: (920)648-3770. **Contact:** Dave Thompson, editor. **35% freelance written.** Prefers to work with published/established writers. Monthly magazine. "We're looking for clear, concise, useful information for sheep raisers who have a few sheep to a 1,000 ewe flock." Estab. 1980. Circ. 15,000. Pays on publication. Byline given. Offers $30 kill fee. Buys Buys all rights or makes work-for-hire assignments. Submit seasonal material 3 months in advance.

Nonfiction: Information (on personalities and/or political, legal or environmental issues affecting the sheep industry). Health and husbandry articles should be written be someone with extensive experience or appropriate credentials (i.e., a veterinarian or animal scientist); features (on small businesses that promote woold products and stories about local and regional sheep producers' groups and their activities); first-person narratives. Book excerpts, how-to (on innovative lamb and wool marketing and promotion techniques, efficient record-keeping systems or specific aspects of health and husbandry), interview/profile (on experienced sheep producers who detail the economics and management of their operation), new product (of value to sheep producers; should be written by someone who has used them), technical (on genetics health and nutrition). **Buys 80 mss/year.** Query with published clips or send complete ms. Length: 750-2,500 words. **Pays $45-150.** Pays expenses of writers on assignment.

Reprints: Send tearsheet or photocopy. Pays 40% of amount paid for an original article.

Photos: Color—vertical compositions of sheep and/or people—for cover. Use only b&w inside magazine. Black and white, 35mm photos or other visuals improve chances of a sale. Buys all rights. Pays $100 maximum for 35mm color transparencies; $20-50 for 5×7 b&w prints. Identification of subjects required.

Tips: "Send us your best ideas and photos! We love good writing!"

N. WESTERN LIVESTOCK REPORTER, Western Livestock Reporter, Inc., P.O. Box 30758, Billings MT 59107. (406)259-4589. Fax: (406)259-6888. E-mail: wlrpubs@imt.net. Website: www.cattleplus.com. **Contact:** Chuck Rightmire, editor. Weekly newspaper. "Our audience is professional cattle and sheep producers. Material must speak to people who have been in the business for years. We print stories on livestock news, industry news, health issues in cattle, and others intended for our readers." Estab. 1940. Circ. 13,000. Pays on publication. Publishes ms an average of 1 month after acceptance. Byline given. Buys first, one-time, second serial (reprint) rights. Editorial lead time 1 week. Submit seasonal material 2 months in advance. Accepts queries by mail, e-mail. Accepts simultaneous submissions. Sample copy online.

Nonfiction: How-to, humor, interview/profile. Special issues: Performance issues last 2 weeks in March. Does not want those which are new accounts of issues the industry has been working on for years. **Buys 52 mss/year.** Send complete ms. Length: 750 words. **Pays $35-150.** Sometimes pays expenses of writers on assignment.

Photos: Send photos with submission. Reviews prints. Buys one-time rights. Offers $7.50/photo. Captions, identification of subjects required.
Poetry: Cowboy poetry. **Buys 3-4 poems/year.** Submit maximum 4 poems. Length: 36.

Management

N $ AG JOURNAL, Arkansas Valley Publishing, P.O. Box 500, La Junta CO 81050-0500. (800)748-1997. Fax: (719)384-2867. E-mail: journal@ria.net. Website: www.agjournalonline.com. **Contact:** Jeanette Larson, managing editor. **20% freelance written.** Weekly journal covering agriculture. "The Ag Journal covers people, issues and events relevant to ag producers in our seven state region (Colorado, Kansas, Oklahoma, Texas, Wyoming, Nebraska, New Mexico)." Estab. 1949. Circ. 11,000. Pays on publication. Publishes ms an average of 2 weeks after acceptance. Byline given. Buys first, one-time rights, makes work-for-hire assignments. Editorial lead time 1 month. Submit seasonal material 1 month in advance. Accepts queries by e-mail. Responds in 2 weeks to queries. Sample copy and writer's guidelines free.
Nonfiction: How-to, interview/profile, new product, opinion, photo feature, technical. Query by e-mail only. **Pays $1-1.50/printed column inch for assigned articles.** Sometimes pays expenses of writers on assignment.
Photos: State availability with submission. Buys one-time rights. Offers $4.50-25/photo. Captions, identification of subjects required.
Tips: "Query by e-mail."

N $ AGVENTURES, Schatz Publishing Group, 11950 W. Highland Ave., Blackwell OK 74631-9511. (580)628-4551. Fax: (580)628-2011. E-mail: agventures@aol.com. Website: www.agventures.com. **Contact:** Sheree Lewis, manager. **95% freelance written.** Bimonthly business-to-business magazine covering agricultural business opportunities. Estab. 1997. Circ. 5,000. Pays on publication. Publishes ms an average of 3 months after acceptance. Byline sometimes given. Offers 50% kill fee. Buys all rights. Editorial lead time 3 months. Submit seasonal material 3 months in advance. Accepts queries by mail, e-mail, fax, phone. Accepts simultaneous submissions. Responds in 2 weeks to queries; 1 month to mss. Sample copy for $4. Writer's guidelines free.
Nonfiction: Interview/profile (research). "No personal experience (nothing in the first person)." **Buys 30-40 mss/ year.** Send complete ms. Length: 2,000-3,000 words. **Pays $75-150.**
Photos: Send photos with submission. Reviews 4×6 prints. Buys all rights. Pays $20/photo. Captions, model releases required.
Tips: "We want ideas on how people are making money on their small acreage and articles that tell how they do it. The best way to get accepted is to imitate the format of existing articles."

$ $ NEW HOLLAND NEWS, P.O. Box 1895, New Holland PA 17557-0903. Website: www.newholland.com/na. **Contact:** Gary Martin, editor. **60% freelance written.** Works with a small number of new/unpublished writers each year. Magazine published 8 times/year covering agriculture; designed to entertain and inform farm families. Estab. 1960. **Pays on acceptance.** Publishes ms an average of 10 months after acceptance. Byline given. Offers negotiable kill fee. Buys first North American serial rights. Submit seasonal material 6 months in advance. Accepts queries by mail. Responds in 2 months to queries. Sample copy and writer's guidelines for 9×12 SAE with 2 first-class stamps.
O→ Break in with an "agricultural 'economic' success story with all the management details."
Nonfiction: "We need strong photo support for articles of 1,200-1,700 words on farm management and farm human interest." Inspirational, photo feature. **Buys 40 mss/year.** Query. **Pays $700-900.** Pays expenses of writers on assignment.
Photos: Send photos with submission. Reviews color transparencies. Buys one-time rights. Pays $50-300, $500 for cover shot. Captions, identification of subjects, model releases required.
Tips: "The writer must have an emotional understanding of agriculture and the farm family and must demonstrate in the article an understanding of the unique economics that affect farming in North America. We want to know about the exceptional farm managers, those leading the way in agriculture. Use anecdotes freely."

Miscellaneous

N $ $ BEE CULTURE, P.O. Box 706, Medina OH 44256-0706. Fax: (330)725-5624. E-mail: kim@airoot.com. Website: www.airoot.com. **Contact:** (Mr.) Kim Flottum, editor. **50% freelance written.** Monthly magazine for beekeepers and those interested in the natural science of honey bees, with environmentally-oriented articles relating to honey bees or pollination. Estab. 1873. Pays on both publication and acceptance. Publishes ms an average of 4 months after acceptance. Buys first North American serial rights. Accepts queries by mail, e-mail, fax, phone. Responds in 1 month to mss. Sample copy for 9×12 SAE and 5 first-class stamps. Writer's guidelines for SASE or by e-mail.
O→ Break in with marketing strategies, interviews of successful beekeepers or beekeeping science, making management of bees easier or less expensive.

Nonfiction: Interested in articles giving new ideas on managing bees. Also looking for articles on honey bee/environment connections or relationships. Also uses success stories about commercial beekeepers. Interview/profile, personal experience, photo feature. No "how I began beekeeping" articles. No highly advanced, technical and scientific abstracts or impractical advice. Length: 2,000 words average. **Pays $40-60/published page and up.**
Reprints: Send photocopy and information about when and where the material previously appeared. Pays 50% of amount paid for an original article, on negotiation.
Photos: "B&W or color prints, 5×7 standard, but 3×5 are OK. 35mm slides, mid-format transparencies are excellent. Electronic images accepted and encouraged." Pays $7-10 each, $50 for cover photos.
Tips: "Do an interview story on commercial beekeepers who are cooperative enough to furnish accurate, factual information on their operations. Frequent mistakes made by writers in completing articles are that they are too general in nature and lack management knowledge."

Regional

N **$** **AGRI-TIMES NORTHWEST**, Sterling Ag LLC, 124 S. Main, P.O. Box 1626, Pendleton OR 97801. (541)276-6202. Fax: (541)278-4778. **Contact:** Sterling Allen, publisher. **50% freelance written.** Biweekly newspaper covering agriculture in western Idaho, eastern Oregon and eastern Washington. "News, features about regional farmers/ agribusiness only." Estab. 1983. Circ. 4,000. Pays on 15th of month after publication. Publishes ms an average of 1 month after acceptance. Byline given. Buys one-time rights. Submit seasonal material 1 months in advance. Accepts simultaneous submissions. Responds in 1 month to queries. Sample copy for 50¢ and 8×10 SAE with 4 first-class stamps. Writer's guidelines for #10 SASE.
Nonfiction: How-to (regional farming and ranching), humor (regional farming and ranching), interview/profile (regional farmers/ranchers), photo feature (regional agriculture), technical (regional farming and ranching). **Buys 25 mss/ year.** Query with or without published clips or send complete ms. Length: 750 words maximum. **Pays 75¢/col. in.**
Reprints: Send typed ms with rights for sale noted and information about when and where the material previously appeared.
Photos: Send photos with submission. Reviews contact sheets, negatives, prints. Buys one-time rights. Offers $5-10/ photo. Captions, identification of subjects required.
Tips: "Focus on our region's agriculture. Be accurate."

N **$ $** **AMERICAN AGRICULTURIST**, Farm Progress Companies, P.O. Box 4475, Gettysburg PA 17325. (717)334-4300. Fax: (717)334-3129. E-mail: jvogel@farmprogress.com. Website: www.farmprogress.com. **Contact:** John Vogel, editor. **12% freelance written.** Monthly magazine covering New York farming. "We publish cutting-edge technology with ready on-farm application." Estab. 1842. Circ. 11,535. Pays on publication. Publishes ms an average of 3 months after acceptance. Byline given. Buys first rights. Editorial lead time 3 months. Submit seasonal material 3 months in advance. Accepts queries by mail, e-mail, fax, phone. Accepts simultaneous submissions. Responds in 2 weeks to queries; 1 month to mss. Sample copy for 9×12 SAE and 6 first-class stamps. Writer's guidelines for #10 SASE.
Nonfiction: Essays, exposé, general interest, historical/nostalgic, how-to, humor, inspirational, interview/profile, new product, opinion, personal experience, photo feature, religious, technical, all related to New York farming. **Buys 4 mss/ year.** Query. Length: 500-1,000 words. **Pays $150-300.** Sometimes pays expenses of writers on assignment.
Photos: Send photos with submission. Reviews transparencies, prints, gif/jpeg files. Buys one-time rights. Offers $75-200/photo. Captions, identification of subjects, model releases required.
Columns/Departments: Kathleen O'Connor, editorial assistant. Country Air (humor, nostalgia, inspirational), 300-400 words; Family Favorites, 100 words. **Buys 36 mss/year.** Send complete ms. **Pays $15-50.**
Poetry: Kathleen O'Connor, editorial assistant. All poetry must have a link to New York farming. Free verse, light verse, traditional. **Buys 2 poems/year.** Length: 12-40 lines. **Pays $50.**

$ $ **FLORIDA GROWER, The Oldest Spokesman For Florida Agriculture**, Meister Publishing Co., 1555 Howell Branch Rd., Suite C-204, Winter Park FL 32789. (407)539-6552. E-mail: michael-allen@meisternet.com. Editor: Michael Allen. **Contact:** Michael Allen. **10% freelance written.** Monthly magazine "edited for the Florida farmer with commercial production interest primarily in citrus, vegetables, and other ag endeavors." "Our goal is to provide articles which update and inform on such areas as production, ag financing, farm labor relations, technology, safety, education and regulation." Estab. 1907. Circ. 14,500. Pays on publication. Byline given. Buys all rights. Editorial lead time 2 months. Submit seasonal material 3 months in advance. Accepts queries by mail, e-mail, fax, phone. Responds in 1 month to queries. Sample copy for 9×12 SAE and 5 first-class stamps. Writer's guidelines free.
Nonfiction: Interview/profile, photo feature, technical. Query with published clips. Length: 750-1,000 words. **Pays $150-250.**
Photos: Send photos with submission.

$ $ **MAINE ORGANIC FARMER & GARDENER**, Maine Organic Farmers & Gardeners Association, RR 2, Box 594, Lincolnville ME 04849. (207)763-3043. E-mail: jenglish@midcoast.com. Website: www.mofga.org. **Contact:** Jean English, editor. **40% freelance written.** Prefers to work with published/established local writers. Quarterly magazine. "*MOF&G* promotes and encourages sustainable agriculture and environmentally sound living. Our primary focus is organic farming, gardening and forestry, but we also deal with local, national and international agriculture, food and environmental issues." Estab. 1976. Circ. 10,000. Pays on publication. Publishes ms an average of 8 months after acceptance. Byline and bio offered. Buys first North American serial, first, one-time, second serial (reprint) rights. Submit seasonal material 1 year in advance. Accepts queries by mail, e-mail. Accepts simultaneous submissions. Responds in 2 months to queries. Sample copy for $2 and SAE with 7 first-class stamps. Writer's guidelines free.

Nonfiction: Book reviews; how-to based on personal experience, research reports, interviews. Profiles of farmers, gardeners, plants. Information on renewable energy, recycling, nutrition, health, non-toxic pest control, organic farm management and marketing. "We use profiles of New England organic farmers and gardeners and news reports (500-1,000 words) dealing with US/international sustainable ag research and development, rural development, recycling projects, environmental and agricultural problems and solutions, organic farms with broad impact, cooperatives and community projects." **Buys 30 mss/year.** Query with published clips or send complete ms. Length: 250-3,000 words. **Pays $20-200.**

Reprints: Send typed ms with rights for sale noted and information about when and where the material previously appeared. Pays 50% of amount paid for an original article.

Photos: State availability of b&w photos with query; send 3×5 b&w photos with ms. State availability with submission. Buys one-time rights. Captions, identification of subjects, model releases required.

Tips: "We are a nonprofit organization. Our publication's primary mission is to inform and educate, but we also want readers to enjoy the articles."

[N] $ $ MARYLAND FARMER, Farm Progress Companies, P.O. Box 4475, Gettysburg PA 17325. (717)334-4300. Fax: (717)334-3129. E-mail: jvogel@farmprogress.com. Website: www.farmprogress.com. **Contact:** John Vogel, editor. **12% freelance written.** Monthly magazine covering mid-Atlantic Region farming. "We publish cutting-edge technology with ready on-farm application." Estab. 1975. Circ. 4,778. Pays on publication. Publishes ms an average of 3 months after acceptance. Byline given. Buys first rights. Editorial lead time 3 months. Submit seasonal material 3 months in advance. Accepts queries by mail, e-mail, fax, phone. Accepts simultaneous submissions. Responds in 2 weeks to queries; 1 month to mss. Sample copy for 9×12 SAE and 6 first-class stamps. Writer's guidelines for #10 SASE.

Nonfiction: Essays, exposé, general interest, historical/nostalgic, how-to, humor, inspirational, interview/profile, new product, opinion, personal experience, photo feature, religious, technical, all related to mid-Atlantic farming. **Buys 4 mss/year.** Query. Length: 500-1,000 words. **Pays $150-300.** Sometimes pays expenses of writers on assignment.

Photos: Send photos with submission. Reviews transparencies, prints, gif/jpeg files. Buys one-time rights. Offers $75-200/photo. Captions, identification of subjects, model releases required.

Columns/Departments: Kathleen O'Connor, editorial assistant. Country Air (humor, nostalgia, inspirational), 300-400 words; Family Favorites, 100 words. **Buys 36 mss/year.** Send complete ms. **Pays $15-50.**

Poetry: All poems must have a link to farming. Kathleen O'Connor, editorial assistant. Free verse, light verse, traditional. **Buys 2 poems/year.** Length: 12-40 lines. **Pays $50.**

[N] $ $ NEW ENGLAND FARMER, Farm Progress Companies, P.O. Box 4475, Gettysburg PA 17325. (717)334-4300. Fax: (717)334-3129. E-mail: jvogel@farmprogress.com. Website: www.farmprogress.com. **Contact:** John Vogel, editor. **12% freelance written.** Monthly magazine covering New England farming. "We publish cutting-edge technology with ready on-farm application." Estab. 1822. Circ. 7,089. Pays on publication. Publishes ms an average of 3 months after acceptance. Byline given. Buys first rights. Editorial lead time 3 months. Submit seasonal material 3 months in advance. Accepts queries by mail, e-mail, fax, phone. Responds in 2 weeks to queries; 1 month to mss. Sample copy for 9×12 SAE and 6 first-class stamps. Writer's guidelines for #10 SASE.

Nonfiction: Essays, exposé, general interest, historical/nostalgic, how-to, humor, inspirational, interview/profile, new product, opinion, personal experience, photo feature, religious, technical, all related to New England farming. **Buys 4 mss/year.** Query. Length: 500-1,000 words. **Pays $150-300.** Sometimes pays expenses of writers on assignment.

Photos: Send photos with submission. Reviews transparencies, prints, gif/jpeg files. Buys one-time rights. Offers $75-200/photo. Captions, identification of subjects, model releases required.

Columns/Departments: Kathleen O'Connor, editorial assistant. Country Air (humor, nostalgia, inspirational), 100-400 words; Family Favorites, 100 words. **Buys 36 mss/year.** Send complete ms. **Pays $15-50.**

Poetry: All poetry must be related to New England farming. Kathleen O'Connor, editorial assistant. Free verse, light verse, traditional. **Buys 2 poems/year.** Length: 12-40 lines. **Pays $50.**

[N] $ PENNSYLVANIA FARMER, Farm Progress Publications Northeast Group, P.O. Box 4475, Gettysburg PA 17325. (717)334-4300. Fax: (717)334-3129. E-mail: jvogel@farmprogress.com. Website: www.farmprogress.com. **Contact:** John Vogel, editor. **20% freelance written.** Monthly magazine covering cutting-edge technology and news to help farmers improve their operations. Estab. 1877. Circ. 16,569. Pays on publication. Publishes ms an average of 3 months after acceptance. Buys first rights. Editorial lead time 3 months. Submit seasonal material 3 months in advance. Accepts queries by mail, e-mail, fax, phone. Accepts simultaneous submissions. Responds in 2 weeks to queries; 1 month to mss. Sample copy for 9×12 SAE and 6 first-class stamps. Writer's guidelines for #10 SASE.

O⟶ Break in with "cutting-edge technology with ready on-farm application; and appropriate seasonal articles, short stories, poetry about living on a farm; and farm traditional recipes."

Nonfiction: Essays, exposé, historical/nostalgic, how-to, humor, inspirational, interview/profile, new product, opinion, personal experience, photo feature, religious, technical. No stories without a strong tie to Mid-Atlantic farming. **Buys 40 mss/year.** Query. Length: 500-1,000 words. **Pays $150-300.** Sometimes pays expenses of writers on assignment.
Photos: Send photos with submission. Reviews 35mm transparencies, prints. Pays $75-200 for each color photo accepted with ms. Captions, identification of subjects required.
Columns/Departments: Kathleen O'Connor, editorial assistant. Country Air (humor, nostalgia, inspirational), 300-400 words; Family Favorites, 100 words. **Buys 36 mss/year.** Send complete ms. **Pays $15-50.**
Poetry: All poetry must have a link to farming. Kathleen O'Connor, editorial assistant. Free verse, light verse, traditional. **Buys 2 poems/year.** Length: 12-40 lines. **Pays $50.**

FINANCE

These magazines deal with banking, investment and financial management. Publications that use similar material but have a less technical slant are listed under the Consumer Business & Finance section.

N **$ $** AMERICA'S COMMUNITY BANKER, 900 19th St. NW, Suite 400, Washington DC 20006. (202)857-3100. Fax: (202)857-5581. E-mail: ktause@acbankers.org. Website: www.acbankers.org. **Contact:** Kathryn Tause, editor. **25% freelance written.** Monthly magazine. "*America's Community Banker* is written for senior managers and executives of community financial institutions. The magazine covers all aspects of financial institution management, with an emphasis on strategic business issues and trends. Recent features have included check imaging, fair lending, trends in mortgage finance and developing an investor regulations program." Circ. 14,000. **Pays on acceptance.** Publishes ms an average of 2 months after acceptance. Byline given. Offers 20% kill fee. Buys first North American serial rights. Editorial lead time 3 months. Submit seasonal material 6 months in advance. Responds in 1 month to queries. Sample copy and writer's guidelines free.
Nonfiction: "Articles must be well-researched and backed up by a variety of sources, preferably senior managers of financial institution or experts associated with the banking industry." How-to (articles on various aspects of a financial institution's operations). **Buys 6 mss/year.** Query with published clips. Length: 1,000-2,700 words. **Pays 50¢/word.**
Photos: Send photos with submission. Reviews contact sheets, negatives, prints. Buys one-time rights. Identification of subjects required.
Columns/Departments: Nationwide News (news items on banking and finance), 100-500 words; Technology Report (news on techology for community bankers); and Surveys and Trends (information on the banking business and business in general). **Buys 25 mss/year.** Query with published clips.
Tips: "The best way to develop a relationship with *America's Community Banker* is through our two departments, Nationwide News and Technology Report. If writers can prove themselves reliable there first, major feature assignments may follow."

$ $ BANK DIRECTOR, Board Member, Inc., 2 Maryland Farms, Suite 123, Brentwood TN 37027. (615)309-3200. Fax: (615)371-0899. E-mail: bankdirector@boardmember.com. Editor: Deborah Scally. **Contact:** Chantel DeDominicis, assistant editor. **75% freelance written.** Quarterly magazine. "*Bank Director* is the only magazine written for directors of financial companies. Each quarterly issue focuses on the information directors need, from mergers and acquisitions to retail strategies, compensation and technology." Estab. 1990. Circ. 42,000. Pays on publication. Publishes ms an average of 2 months after acceptance. Byline given. Offers negotiable (20% average) kill fee. Buys all rights. Editorial lead time 3 months. Submit seasonal material 3 months in advance. Accepts queries by mail, fax, phone. Responds in 3 weeks to queries; 2 months to mss. Sample copy free.
Nonfiction: Financial/banking. **Buys 16-20 mss/year.** Query with published clips. Length: 2,000-5,000 words. **Pays 30-75¢/word.** Sometimes pays expenses of writers on assignment.
Photos: State availability with submission. Buys one-time rights. Negotiates payment individually. Identification of subjects required.
Columns/Departments: For You Review, 250-500 words; Boardroom Basics, 2,000-3,000 words; Perspective (opinion), 2,000-3,000 words. **Buys 10 mss/year.** Query with published clips. **Pays 30-50¢/word.**
Tips: "Call or write with a story idea relevant to our audience—bank directors."

$ $ $ $ BANKING STRATEGIES, Bank Administration Institute (BAI), 1544 Bishop Hollow Run, Dunwoody GA 30338. E-mail: kcline@bai.org. Website: www.bai.org/bankingstrategies. **Contact:** Kenneth Cline, senior editor. **70% freelance written.** Magazine covering banking and financial services. "Magazine covers banking from a strategic and managerial perspective for its senior financial executive audience. Each issue includes in-depth trend articles and interviews with influential executives." Offers variable kill fee. Buys all rights. Accepts queries by mail, e-mail. Responds almost immediately to queries.
Nonfiction: How-to (articles that help institutions be more effective and competitive in the marketplace), interview/profile (executive interviews). "No topic queries, we assign stories to freelancers. I'm looking for qualifications as opposed to topic queries. I need experienced writers/reporters." **Buys 30 mss/year.** E-queries preferred. **Pays $1.20/word for assigned articles.**

Tips: "Demonstrate ability and financial services expertise. I'm looking for freelancers who can write according to our standards, which are quite high."

$ $ $ $ BLOOMBERG WEALTH MANAGER, Bloomberg L.P., P.O. Box 888, Princeton NJ 08542-0888. (609)279-3000. Fax: (609)279-7150. E-mail: wealthmanager@bloomberg.net. Website: www.wealth.bloomberg.com. Editor: Robert Casey. **Contact:** Mary Ann McGuigan, managing editor. **90% freelance written.** Magazine published 10 times/year for financial advisors. "Stories should provide insight and information for the financial adviser. Put yourself on the adviser's side of the table and cover the issues thoroughly from his/her perspective. The piece should delve beneath the surface. We need specific examples, professional caveats, advice from professionals." Estab. 1999. Circ. 45,000. **Pays on acceptance.** Publishes ms an average of 3 months after acceptance. Byline given. Offers 30% kill fee. Buys first North American serial rights. Editorial lead time 2 months. Submit seasonal material 2 months in advance. Accepts queries by mail, e-mail, fax, phone. Responds in 1 month to queries.

Nonfiction: Book excerpts, interview/profile, technical. Do not submit anything that does not deal with financial planning issues or the financial markets. **Buys 30-40 mss/year.** Query with published clips. Length: 1,500-3,000 words. **Pays $1.50-2/word for assigned articles.** Sometimes pays expenses of writers on assignment.

Columns/Departments: Expertly Speaking, Tax Strategies, Retirement, Executive Compensation (all financial planning), all 1,900 words. **Buys 10-15 mss/year.** Query with published clips. **Pays $1.50-2/word.**

◼ The online magazine carries original content not found in the print edition. Contact: Matt Stichnoth.

Tips: "*Wealth Manager* is a trade magazine. All pieces should be written from the perspective of a financial adviser who has wealthy clients."

N̄ $ $ $ $ BUSINESS CREDIT MAGAZINE, The Publication for Credit and Financial Professionals, The National Association of Credit Management, 8840 Columbia, 100 Parkway, Columbia MD 21045. (410)423-1842. Fax: (410)740-5574. E-mail: normat@nacm.org. Website: www.nacm.org. **Contact:** Norma J. Templin, managing editor. **95% freelance written.** Magazine published 10 times/year covering business credit. Membership consists of 52 US affiliated associations and an international arm: Finance, Credit, and International Business that operates in Europe and throughout the world, and consists of 800 multinational firms in the US and 30 countries. Articles are directed at the interchange of credit information, practices and methods as well as articles concerning bankruptcy cases and laws. Estab. 1898. Circ. 35,000. Pays on publication. Publishes ms an average of 6 months after acceptance. Byline given. Offers 100% kill fee. Buys one-time rights, makes work-for-hire assignments. Accepts queries by mail, e-mail, fax, phone. Responds in 2 weeks to queries; 2 months to mss. Sample copy for $7. Writer's guidelines by e-mail or fax.

Nonfiction: "We have numerous conferences all over the globe throughout the year. We try to find local writers and photographers to cover them." Interview/profile, technical. **Buys 36 mss/year.** Send complete ms. Length: 1,500-3,000 words. **Pays $1/word-$2,500.** Sometimes pays expenses of writers on assignment.

Photos: Offers no additional payment for photos accepted with ms unless by prior arrangement.

Columns/Departments: Professional at Work (business/office/credit), 1,500 words. Personnel Matters (personnel/collections), 1,500 words. Business Law (retention/forfeiting/bankruptcy), 2000 words. **Buys 3-4/issue mss/year.** Send complete ms. **"We run 3-4 columns/issue. Virtually all are submitted by freelancers who are not paid, but are bylined."**

Fillers: Gags to be illustrated by cartoonist. **Pays $350 maximum.**

Tips: "Read the magazine. If you are qualified to writer for *BC* in terms of content, submit articles by fax, e-mail, or mail. Content more important than writer's ability: we clean up all manuscripts to greater or lesser degree."

$ $ $ COLLECTIONS & CREDIT RISK, The Monthly Magazine for Collections and Credit Policy Professionals, Faulkner & Gray Inc., 300 S. Wacker Dr., Suite 1800, Chicago IL 60606. (312)913-1334. Fax: (312)913-1365. E-mail: Darren.Waggoner@tfn.com. Website: www.collectionsworld.com. Editor: David E. Whiteside. **Contact:** Darren Waggoner, executive editor. **33% freelance written.** Monthly journal covering debt collections and credit risk management. "Collections & Credit Risk reports and analyzes events and trends affecting consumer and commercial credit practices and debt collections. The entire credit cycle is covered from setting credit policy and making loan decisions to debt recovery, collections, bankruptcy and debt sales." Estab. 1996. Circ. 22,000. **Pays on acceptance.** Publishes ms an average of 3 months after acceptance. Byline given. Kill fee determined case by case. Buys one-time, all rights. Editorial lead time 3 months. Accepts queries by mail, e-mail, fax. to queries. Sample copy free or online.

O→ Break in with a "a query with clips of business trend stories using 8-10 sources and demonstrating strong analysis."

Nonfiction: Interview/profile, technical, business news and analysis. "No unsolicited submissions accepted—freelancers work on assignment only." **Buys 30-40 mss/year.** Query with published clips. Length: 1,800-3,000 words. **Pays $800-1,000.** Sometimes pays expenses of writers on assignment.

Photos: Send photos with submission. Buys one-time rights. Negotiates payment individually. Identification of subjects required.

◼ The online magazine carries original content not found in the print edition.

Tips: "This is a business news and analysis magazine focused on events and trends affecting the credit-risk management and collections industry. Our editorial approach is modeled after *Business Week, Forbes, Fortune, Wall Street Journal.* No fluff accepted."

[N] $ $ CREDIT UNION MANAGEMENT, Credit Union Executives Society, 6410 Enterprise Lane, Madison WI 53719-1143. (608)271-2664. Fax: (608)271-2303. E-mail: mary@cues.org. Website: www.cumanagement.org. **Contact:** Mary Arnold or Theresa Sweeney, editors. **44% freelance written.** Monthly magazine covering credit union, banking trends management, HR, marketing issues. "Our philosophy mirrors the credit union industry of cooperative financial services." Estab. 1978. Circ. 7,413. **Pays on acceptance.** Publishes ms an average of 2 months after acceptance. Editorial lead time 3 months. Submit seasonal material 4 months in advance. Accepts queries by mail, e-mail, fax, phone. Accepts simultaneous submissions. Responds in 2 weeks to queries; 1 month to mss. Sample copy and writer's guidelines free.

Nonfiction: Book excerpts, how-to (be a good mentor/leader, recruit, etc.), interview/profile, technical. **Buys 74 mss/year.** Query with published clips. Length: 700-2,400 words. **Pays $250-350.** Pays phone expenses only of writers on assignment.

Columns/Departments: Management Network (book/web reviews, briefs), 300 words; Trends (marketing trends), 700 words; Point of Law, 700 words; Plugged In (new technology/operations trends), 700 words. Query with published clips. **Pays $250-350.**

Tips: "The best way is to e-mail an editor; include résumé. Follow up with mailing cover letter and clips. Knowledge of financial services is very helpful."

$ $ EQUITIES MAGAZINE LLC, 160 Madison Ave., 3rd Floor, New York NY 10016. (212)213-1300. Fax: (212)213-5872. Website: www.equitiesmagazine.com. **Contact:** Robert J. Flaherty, editor. **50% freelance written.** "We are a seven-issues-a-year financial magazine covering the fastest-growing public companies in the world. We study the management of companies and act as critics reviewing their performances. We aspire to be 'The Shareholder's Friend.' We want to be a bridge between quality public companies and sophisticated investors." Estab. 1951. Circ. 18,000. Pays on publication. Publishes ms an average of 2 months after acceptance. Byline given. Buys all rights. Accepts queries by mail. Sample copy for 9×12 SAE and 5 first-class stamps.

Nonfiction: "We must know the writer first as we are careful about whom we publish. A letter of introduction with résumé and clips is the best way to introduce yourself. Financial writing requires specialized knowledge and a feel for people as well, which can be a tough combination to find." Carries guest columns by famous money managers who are not writing for cash payments, but to showcase their ideas and approach. Exposé, new product, technical. **Buys 30 mss/year.** Query with published clips. Length: 300-1,500 words. **Pays $250-750 for assigned articles, more for very difficult or investigative pieces.** Pays expenses of writers on assignment.

Photos: Send color photos with submission. Reviews contact sheets, negatives, transparencies, prints. Offers no additional payment for photos accepted with ms. Identification of subjects required.

Columns/Departments: Pays $25-75 for assigned items only.

Tips: "Give us an idea for a story on a specific publically-owned company, whose stock is traded on NASDAQ, the NYSE, or American Stock Exchange. Anyone who enjoys analyzing a business and telling the story of the people who started it, or run it today, is a potential *Equities* contributor. But to protect our readers and ourselves, we are careful about who writes for us. We do not want writers who are trading the stocks of the companies they profile. Business writing is an exciting area and our stories reflect that. If a writer relies on numbers and percentages to tell his story, rather than the individuals involved, the result will be numbingly dull."

$ $ $ THE FEDERAL CREDIT UNION, National Association of Federal Credit Unions, P.O. Box 3769, Washington DC 20007-0269. (703)522-4770. Fax: (703)524-1082. E-mail: tfcu@nafcunet.org. Website: www.nafcunet.org. Executive Editor: Patrick M. Keefe. **Contact:** Robin Johnston, publisher/managing editor. **25% freelance written.** "Looking for writers with financial, banking or credit union experience, but will work with inexperienced (unpublished) writers based on writing skill. Published bimonthly, *The Federal Credit Union* is the official publication of the National Association of Federal Credit Unions. The magazine is dedicated to providing credit union management, staff and volunteers with in-depth information they can use to fulfill their duties and better serve their members. The editorial focus includes coverage of management issues, operations, technology as well as volunteer-related issues." Estab. 1967. Circ. 11,136. Pays on publication. Publishes ms an average of 3 months after acceptance. Byline given. Buys first North American serial rights. Submit seasonal material 5 months in advance. Accepts queries by mail, e-mail, fax. Accepts simultaneous submissions. Responds in 2 months to queries. Sample copy for 10×13 SAE and 5 first-class stamps. Writer's guidelines for #10 SASE.

Break in with "pithy, informative, thought-provoking items for our 'Briefs' section (for free or a small fee of $50-100)."

Nonfiction: Humor, inspirational, interview/profile. Query with published clips and SASE. Length: 1,200-2,000 words. **Pays $400-800.**

Photos: Send photos with submission. Reviews 35mm transparencies, 5×7 prints. Buys all rights. Offers no additional payment for photos accepted with ms. Pays $50-500. Identification of subjects, model releases required.

The online magazine carries original content not found in the print edition. Contact: Robin Johnston.

Tips: "We would like more articles on how credit unions are using technology to serve their members and more articles on leading-edge technologies they can use in their operations. If you can write on current trends in technology, human resources, or strategic planning, you stand a better chance of being published than if you wrote on other topics."

$ $ $ FINANCIAL PLANNING, Thomson Financial, 40 W. 57th St., 11th Fl., New York NY 10019. (212)765-5311. Fax: (212)765-8189. E-mail: thomas.johnson@tfn.com. Website: www.financial-planning.com. Editor: Evan Simonoff. **Contact:** Thomas W. Johnson, editor-in-chief. **30-40% freelance written.** Monthly magazine covering stocks, bonds, mutual funds, retirement and estate planning insurance. Estab. 1971. Circ. 100,000. Pays on publication. Publishes ms an average of 3 months after acceptance. Byline given. Offers 15% kill fee. Buys all rights. Editorial lead time 3 months. Submit seasonal material 4 months in advance. Accepts queries by mail, e-mail. Responds in 3 weeks to queries; 1 month to mss. Sample copy for $10. Writer's guidelines free.

Nonfiction: Book excerpts, how-to, interview/profile, new product, opinion, technical. No product endorsements. **Buys 25-30 mss/year.** Query (e-mail preferred). Length: 1,800-2,500 words. **Pays 50¢/word.** Sometimes pays expenses of writers on assignment.

Photos: State availability with submission. Reviews contact sheets, any size prints. Offers no additional payment for photos accepted with ms. Identification of subjects required.

▣ The online magazine carries original content not found in the print edition. Contact: Jennifer Reed, online editor.

Tips: "Avoid articles that are too general—ours is a professional readership who require thoughtful, in-depth analysis of financial issues. A submission that includes charts, graphs and statistical data is much more likely to pique our interest than overviews of investing."

ℕ ILLINOIS BANKER, Illinois Bankers Association, 133 S. Fourth St., Suite 300, Springfield IL 62701. (217)789-9340. Fax: (217)789-5410. **Contact:** Debbie Jemison, editor. "Our audience is approximately 3,000 bankers and vendors related to the banking industry. The purpose of the publication is to educate and inform readers on major public policy issues affecting banking today, as well as provide new ideas that can be applied to day-to-day operations and management. Writers may not sell or promote a product or service." Estab. 1891. Circ. 2,500. Publishes ms an average of 3 months after acceptance. Byline given. Buys first North American serial rights. Editorial lead time 2 months. Accepts simultaneous submissions. Responds in 3 months to queries. Sample copy and writer's guidelines free.

Nonfiction: "It is *IBA* policy that writers do not sell or promote a particular product, service or organization within the content of an article written for publication." Essays, historical/nostalgic, interview/profile, new product, opinion, personal experience. Query. Length: 1,000-1,500 words.

Photos: State availability with submission. Reviews contact sheets, negatives, transparencies, prints. Captions, identification of subjects required.

Tips: "Articles published in *Illinois Banker* address current issues of key importance to the banking industry in Illinois. Our intention is to keep readers informed of the latest industry news, developments and trends, as well as provide necessary technical information. We publish articles on any topic that affects the banking industry, provided the content is in agreement with Association policy and position. Because we are a trade association, most articles need to be reviewed by an advisory committee before publication; therefore, the earlier they are submitted the better. Some recent topics include: agriculture, bank architecture, commercial and consumer credit, marketing, operations/cost control, security and technology. In addition, articles are also considered on the topics of economic development and business/banking trends in Illinois and the Midwest region."

$ $ $ $ MORTGAGE BANKING, The Magazine of Real Estate Finance, Mortgage Bankers Association of America, 1919 Pennsylvania Ave., NW, Washington DC 20006. (202)557-2853. Fax: (202)721-0245. E-mail: janet_he witt@mbaa.org. Website: www.mbaa.org. Associate Editor: Lesley Hall. **Contact:** Janet Reilley Hewitt, editor-in-chief. Monthly magazine covering real estate finance. "Timely examinations of major news and trends in the business of mortgage lending for both commercial and residential real estate." Estab. 1939. Circ. 10,000. **Pays on acceptance.** Publishes ms an average of 2 months after acceptance. Byline given. Negotiates kill fee. Buys one-time rights, makes work-for-hire assignments. Editorial lead time 2 months. Submit seasonal material 3 months in advance. Accepts queries by mail, e-mail, fax. Accepts simultaneous submissions. Responds in 1 month to queries; 4 months to mss. Sample copy and writer's guidelines free.

Nonfiction: Book excerpts, essays, interview/profile, opinion. Special issues: Commercial real estate special supplemental issue (February); Internet guide supplemental issue (September). **Buys 30 mss/year.** Query. Length: 3,000-4,000 words. **Pays $1,000-3,000.** Sometimes pays expenses of writers on assignment.

Photos: State availability with submission. Reviews prints. Buys one-time rights. Negotiates payment individually. Identification of subjects, model releases required.

Columns/Departments: Book reviews (current, relevant material), 300 words; executive essay (industry executive's personal views on relevant topic), 750-1,000 words. **Buys 2 mss/year.** Query. **Pay negotiated.**

Tips: "Trends in technology, current and upcoming legislation that will affect the mortgage industry are good focus."

$ $ SERVICING MANAGEMENT, The Magazine for Loan Servicing Professionals, LDJ Corp., P.O. Box 2180, Waterbury CT 06722-2180. (800)325-6745 ext. 241. Fax: (203)755-3480. E-mail: fabrini@sm-online.com. Website: www.sm-online.com. **Contact:** Julius Fabrini, editor. **15% freelance written.** Monthly magazine covering residential mortgage servicing. Estab. 1989. Circ. 22,000. **Pays on acceptance.** Publishes ms an average of 2 months after acceptance. Byline given. Buys all rights. Accepts queries by mail, e-mail, fax. Responds in 2 weeks to queries. Sample copy and writer's guidelines free.

⊶ Break in by "submitting a query for Servicing Reports, a monthly department featuring news and information about mortgage servicing and the industry. It should be informative, topical and include comments by industry professionals."

Nonfiction: How-to, interview/profile, new product, technical. **Buys 10 mss/year.** Query. Length: 1,500-2,500 words. Will pay industry experts with contributor copies or other premiums rather than a cash payment.

Photos: State availability with submission. Reviews contact sheets. Buys all rights. Offers no additional payment for photos accepted with ms. Identification of subjects required.
Columns/Departments: Buys 5 mss/year. Query. **Pays $200.**

N̲ $ $ $ TRADERS MAGAZINE, Securities Data Publishing, 40 W. 57th St., New York NY 10019. (212)803-8847. Fax: (212)747-0965. E-mail: byrnej@tfn.com. **Contact:** John Aidan Byrne, editor. **35% freelance written.** Monthly magazine plus 2 specials covering equity trading and technology. "Understanding how retail and institutional trades are done on NASDAQ and The New York Stock Exchange and appreciation of trading as a unique and demanding job." Circ. 6,000 (controlled). Pays on publication. Publishes ms an average of 2 months after acceptance. Byline given. Buys all rights. Editorial lead time 2 months. Submit seasonal material 3 months in advance. Accepts queries by mail, e-mail, phone. Sample copy free to writers on assignment.
　　O— Needs more "buy-side" stories (on mutual fund, pension fund traders, etc.)
Nonfiction: Book excerpts, exposé, general interest, historical/nostalgic, how-to, humor, interview/profile, new product, opinion, personal experience, religious, technical. Special issues: Correspondent clearing (every market) and market making survey of broker deadlines. No stories that are related to fixed income and other non-equity topics. **Buys 12-20 mss/year.** Query with published clips or send complete ms. Length: 750-2,800 words. **Pays 50¢-$1/word.**
Columns/Departments: Special Features (market regulation and human interest), 1600 words; Trading & Technology, 1,600 words; Washington Watch (market regulation), 750 words. Query with published clips. **Pays 50¢-$1/word.**
Fiction: Ethnic, historical, humorous, mystery, science fiction, slice-of-life vignettes. No erotica. **Buys 1 mss/year.** Query with or without published clips or send complete ms. Length: 2,100-2,800 words. **Pays 50¢-$2/word.**
Tips: "Boil it all down and don't bore the hell out of readers. Advice from a distinguished scribe which we pass along. Learn to explain equity market making and institutional trading in a simple, direct manner. Don't waffle. Have a trader explain the business to you if necessary."

FISHING

$ $ PACIFIC FISHING, Salmon Bay Communications, 4209 21st Ave., #402, Seattle WA 98199. (206)216-0111. Fax: (206)216-0222. E-mail: Brad@pfmag.com. Website: www.pfmag.com. **Contact:** Brad Warren, editor. **75% freelance written.** Works with some new/unpublished writers. Monthly magazine for commercial fishermen and others in the West Coast commercial fishing industry. "*Pacific Fishing* views the fisherman as a small businessman and covers all aspects of the industry, including harvesting, processing and marketing." Estab. 1979. Circ. 11,000. Pays on publication. Publishes ms an average of 2 months after acceptance. Byline given. Offers 10-15% kill fee on assigned articles deemed unsuitable. Buys one-time rights. Accepts queries by mail, e-mail, fax, phone. Responds in 3 weeks to queries. Sample copy and writer's guidelines for 9 × 12 SAE with 10 first-class stamps.
Nonfiction: "Articles must be concerned specifically with commercial fishing. We view fishermen as small business-men and professionals who are innovative and success-oriented. To appeal to this reader, *Pacific Fishing* offers 4 basic features: Technical, how-to articles that give fishermen hands-on tips that will make their operation more efficient and profitable; practical, well-researched business articles discussing the dollars and cents of fishing, processing and market-ing; profiles of a fisherman, processor or company with emphasis on practical business and technical areas; and in-depth analysis of political, social, fisheries management and resource issues that have a direct bearing on West Coast commercial fishermen." Editors here are putting more focus on local and international seafood marketing, technical coverage of gear and vessels. Interview/profile, technical (usually with a business book or slant). **Buys 20 mss/year.** Query noting whether photos are available, and enclosing samples of previous work and SASE. Length: varies, one-paragraph news items to 3,000-word features. **Pays 10-15¢/word for most assignments.** Sometimes pays expenses of writers on assignment.
Reprints: Send photocopy and information about when and where the material previously appeared. Pays 100% of the amount paid for an original article.
Photos: "We need good, high-quality photography, especially color, of West Coast commercial fishing. We prefer 35mm color slides." Our rates are $200 for cover; $50-100 for inside color; $25-75 for b&w and $10 for table of contents.

FLORISTS, NURSERIES & LANDSCAPERS

Readers of these publications are involved in growing, selling or caring for plants, flowers and trees. Magazines geared to consumers interested in gardening are listed in the Consumer Home & Garden section.

N̲ $ $ DIGGER, Oregon Association of Nurserymen, 2780 S.E. Harrison, Suite 102, Milwaukie OR 97222. (503)653-8733. Fax: (503)653-3956. E-mail: csivesind@oan.org. Website: www.nurseryguide.com. **Contact:** Cam Sivesind, manager of publications and communications. **50% freelance written.** Monthly magazine covering nursery and greenhouse industry. "Our readers are mainly nursery and greenhouse operators and owners who propagate nursery stock/crops, so we write with them in mind." Circ. 5,000. Pays on receipt of copy. Publishes ms an average of 2 months after acceptance. Byline given. Offers 100% kill fee. Buys first North American serial rights. Editorial lead time 6 weeks. Submit seasonal material 2 months in advance. Accepts queries by mail, e-mail, fax, phone. Sample copy and writer's guidelines free.

Nonfiction: General interest, how-to (propagation techniques, other crop-growing tips), interview/profile, personal experience, technical. Special issues: Farwest Magazine (August)—this is a triple-size issues that runs in tandem with our annual Trade Show (11,500 circulation for this issue). "No articles not related or pertinent to nursery and greenhouse industry." **Buys 20-30 mss/year.** Query. Length: 800-2,000 words. **Pays $125-400 for assigned articles; $100-300 for unsolicited articles.** Sometimes pays expenses of writers on assignment.

Photos: State availability with submission. Reviews negatives, slides, 5×7 prints. Buys one-time rights. Offers $25-150/photo. Captions, identification of subjects required.

Tips: "Our best freelancers are familiar with or have experience in the horticultural industry. Some 'green' knowledge is a definite advantage."

N $ $ THE FLORIST, The Leading Magazine for Professional Florists, (formerly *Florist*), The FTD Association, 33031 Schoolcraft Rd., Livonia MI 48150-1618. (800)383-4383. Fax: (734)466-8978. E-mail: bgillis@ftdassociation.org. Website: www.ftdassociation.org. Editor-in-Chief: Sallyann Roberts Moore. **Contact:** Barbara Gillis, managing editor. **5% freelance written.** Monthly magazine for retail flower shop owners, managers and floral designers. Other readers include floriculture growers, wholesalers, researchers and teachers. Circ. 22,000. **Pays on acceptance.** Publishes ms an average of 2 months after acceptance. Pays 10-25% kill fee. Buys one-time rights. Accepts queries by mail. Responds in 1 month to queries.

Oₙ Break in with articles that "source unique FTD Association Shops for profiles. Provide 'shorts' on unique uses for flowers and the florists who created them. Report on unique uses of technology in flower shops."

Nonfiction: Articles should pertain to marketing, merchandising, financial management or personnel management in a retail flower shop. Also, giftware, floral and interior design trends. No general interest, fiction or personal experience. **Buys 5 unsolicited mss/year.** Query with published clips. Length: 1,200-1,500 words. **Pays $200-400.**

Photos: State availability. Buys one-time rights. Pays $10-25 for 5×7 b&w photos or color transparencies.

🔲 The online magazine carries original content not found in the print edition. Contact: Barbara Gillis, online editor.

Tips: "We're looking for strong business management stories specifically for retail florists, who are manufacturers (of floral designs) as well as retailers. Also articles on consumer purchasing trends/behaviors, and how to create attractive window displays. Business management articles must deal specifically with retail flower shops and their unique merchandise and concerns. Gear your writing to flower shops specifically and exhibit an understanding of the industry's wire service idiosyncracies and loyalties. Send samples of published work with query. Suggest several ideas in query letter. No consumer-oriented flower story queries."

$ GROWERTALKS, Ball Publishing, 335 N. River St., P.O. Box 9, Batavia IL 60510. (630)208-9080. Fax: (630)208-9350. E-mail: beytes@growertalks.com. Website: www.growertalks.com. **Contact:** Chris Beytes, editor. **50% freelance written.** Monthly magazine. "*GrowerTalks* serves the commercial greenhouse grower. Editorial emphasis is on floricultural crops: bedding plants, potted floral crops, foliage and fresh cut flowers. Our readers are growers, managers and owners. We're looking for writers who've had experience in the greenhouse industry." Estab. 1937. Circ. 9,500. Pays on publication. Publishes ms an average of 3 months after acceptance. Byline given. Buys first North American serial rights. Editorial lead time 4 months. Submit seasonal material 3 months in advance. Accepts queries by mail, e-mail, fax. Responds in 1 month to queries. Sample copy and writer's guidelines free.

Nonfiction: How-to (time- or money-saving projects for professional flower/plant growers), interview/profile (ornamental horticulture growers), personal experience (of a grower), technical (about growing process in greenhouse setting). "No articles that promote only one product." **Buys 36 mss/year.** Query. Length: 1,200-1,600 words. **Pays $125 minimum for assigned articles; $75 minimum for unsolicited articles.**

Photos: State availability with submission. Reviews 2½×2½ slides and 3×5 prints. Buys one-time rights. Negotiates payment individually. Captions, identification of subjects, model releases required.

🔲 The online magazine carries original content not found in the print edition. Contact: Chris Beytes, online editor.

Tips: "Discuss magazine with ornamental horticulture growers to find out what topics that have or haven't appeared in the magazine interest them."

$ $ THE GROWING EDGE, New Moon Publishing, Inc., 341 SW Second St., Corvallis OR 97333. (541)757-2511. Fax: (541)757-0028. E-mail: Doug@growingedge.com. Website: www.growingedge.com. **Contact:** Doug Peckenpaugh, editor. **85% freelance written.** Bimonthly magazine covering indoor and outdoor high-tech gardening techniques and tips. Estab. 1980. Circ. 20,000. Pays on publication. Publishes ms an average of 3 months after acceptance. Byline given. Buys first serial and reprint rights. Submit seasonal material 6 months in advance. Accepts queries by mail, e-mail. Responds in 3 months to queries. Sample copy for $3. Writer's guidelines by #10 SASE or online.

Oₙ Break in with "a detailed, knowledgeable e-mail story pitch."

Nonfiction: How-to, interview/profile, personal experience (must be technical), book reviews, general horticulture and agriculture. Query. Length: 500-3,500 words. **Pays 20¢/word (10¢ for first rights, 5¢ for non-exclusive reprint and non-exclusive electronic rights).**

Reprints: Send tearsheet, photocopy or typed ms with rights for sale noted and information about when and where the material previously appeared. Payment negotiable.

Photos: Buys first and reprint rights. Pays $25-175. Pays on publication. Credit line given.

Tips: Looking for more hydroponics articles and information that will give the reader/gardener/farmer the "growing edge" in high-tech gardening and farming on topics such as high intensity grow lights, water conservation, drip irrigation, advanced organic fertilizers, new seed varieties and greenhouse cultivation.

$ $LANDSCAPE TRADES, Landscape Ontario, 7856 Fifth Line S, RR4, Milton, Ontario L9T 2X8, Canada. (905)875-1805. Fax: (905)875-0183. E-mail: lo@hort-trades.com. Website: www.hort-trades.com. **Contact:** Linda Erskine, editor. Magazine published 9 times/year for the horticultural industry. "*Landscape Trades* is written for landscape contractors, grounds maintenance, growers and retail garden centers." Estab. 1979. Circ. 8,275. Pays on publication. Publishes ms an average of 2 months after acceptance. Byline given. Buys all rights. Editorial lead time 2 months. Submit seasonal material 3 months in advance. Accepts queries by mail, e-mail, fax, phone. Sample copy and writer's guidelines free.
Nonfiction: How-to, interview/profile, technical. "No consumer-based articles." **Buys 10 mss/year.** Query with published clips. Length: 1,000-2,500 words. **Pays 15-25¢/word for assigned articles; 15¢/word for unsolicited articles.** Sometimes pays expenses of writers on assignment.
Photos: Send photos with submission. Reviews negatives, transparencies, prints. Buys all rights. Negotiates payment individually. Captions, identification of subjects required.
Columns/Departments: Grower's Six Pack, 700 words; CompuFacts (computer tech), 1,000 words. **Buys 5 mss/year.** Send complete ms. **Pays 15-25¢/word.**
Tips: "Submit query and article outline first."

$ $ORNAMENTAL OUTLOOK, Your Connection To The South's Horticulture Industry, Meister Publishing Co., 1555 Howell Branch Rd., Suite C204, Winter Park FL 32789. (407)539-6552. Fax: (407)539-6544. E-mail: oo_edit@meisterpubl.com. **Contact:** Michael Allen, managing editor. **50% freelance written.** Monthly magazine. "*Ornamental Outlook* is written for commercial growers of ornamental plants in the Southeast U.S. Our goal is to provide interesting and informative articles on such topics as production, legislation, safety, technology, pest control, water management and new varieties as they apply to Southeast growers." Estab. 1991. Circ. 12,500. Pays 30 days after publication. Publishes ms an average of 4 months after acceptance. Byline given. Buys all rights. Editorial lead time 2 months. Submit seasonal material 3 months in advance. Accepts queries by mail, e-mail, fax, phone. Responds in 3 months to queries. Sample copy for 9 × 12 SAE and 5 first-class stamps. Writer's guidelines free.
Nonfiction: Interview/profile, photo feature, technical. "No first-person articles. No word-for-word meeting transcripts or all-quote articles." Query with published clips. Length: 750-1,000 words. **Pays $250/article including photos.**
Photos: Send photos with submission. Reviews contact sheets, transparencies, prints. Buys one-time rights. Captions, identification of subjects required.
Tips: "I am most impressed by written queries that address specific subjects of interest to our audience, which is the *Southeast* grower of *commercial* horticulture. Our biggest demand is for features, about 1,000 words, that follow subjects listed on our editorial calendar (which is sent with guidelines). Please do not send articles of national or consumer interest."

$ $TREE CARE INDUSTRY MAGAZINE, National Arborist Association, 3 Perimeter Rd. Unit 1, Manchester NH 03103-3341. (800)733-2622 or (603)314-5380. E-mail: garvin@natlarb.com. Website: www.natlarb.com. Mark Garvin, editor. **50% freelance written.** Monthly magazine covering tree care and landscape maintenance. Estab. 1990. Circ. 28,500. Pays within 30 days of publication. Publishes ms an average of 3 months after acceptance. Byline given. Buys first North American serial rights. Editorial lead time 10 weeks. Submit seasonal material 3 months in advance. Accepts queries by mail, e-mail, fax, phone. Responds in 2 weeks to queries; 2 months to mss. Sample copy for 9 × 12 SAE and 6 first-class stamps. Writer's guidelines free.
Nonfiction: Book excerpts, historical/nostalgic, interview/profile, new product, technical. **Buys 40 mss/year.** Query with published clips. Length: 900-3,500 words. **Pays negotiable rate.**
Photos: Send photos with submission. Reviews prints. Buys one-time and web rights. Negotiate payment individually. Captions, identification of subjects required.
Columns/Departments: Management Exchange (business management-related); 1,200-1,800 words; Industry Innovations (inventions), 1,200 words; From The Field (OP/ED from practitioners), 1,200 words. **Buys 40 mss/year.** Send complete ms. **Pays $100 and up.**
Tips: "Preference is given to writers with background and knowledge of the tree care industry; our focus is relatively narrow. Preference is also given to photojournalists willing to work on speculation."

GOVERNMENT & PUBLIC SERVICE

Listed here are journals for people who provide governmental services at the local, state or federal level or for those who work in franchised utilities. Journals for city managers, politicians, bureaucratic decision makers, civil servants, firefighters, police officers, public administrators, urban transit managers and utilities managers are listed in this section.

$ AMERICAN FIRE JOURNAL, Fire Publications, Inc., 9072 Artesia Blvd., Bellflower CA 90706. (562)866-1664. Fax: (562)867-6434. E-mail: afjm@accessl.net. Editor: Carol Carlsen Brooks. **Contact:** John Ackenman, publisher. **90% freelance written.** Monthly magazine covering fire service. "Written by firefighters for firefighters." Estab. 1940s. Circ. 6,000. Pays on publication. Publishes ms an average of 6 months after acceptance. Byline given. Buys first rights. Editorial lead time 3 months. Submit seasonal material 3 months in advance. Accepts queries by mail, e-mail, fax, phone. Responds in 2 weeks to queries; 2 months to mss. Sample copy for $3.50. Writer's guidelines free.

Nonfiction: Historical/nostalgic, how-to, new product, opinion, photo feature, technical. **Buys 50 mss/year.** Send complete ms. Any length. **Pays $150 maximum.**

Photos: Send photos with submission. Reviews contact sheets, negatives, transparencies, prints (any size). Buys one-time rights. Offers $5-50/photo. Captions required.

Columns/Departments: Hot Flashes (news/current events), 100-300 words; Innovations (new firefighting tricks and techniques), 300-1,000 words. **Buys 2-4 mss/year.** Send complete ms. **Pays $10 maximum.**

Fillers: Anecdotes, facts, newsbreaks. **Buys 2-4/year.** Length: 300-1,000 words. **Pays $25 maximum.**

Tips: "Content of articles is generally technical, tactical, educational or related to fire service legislation, current events or recent emergency incidents. We do not publish fiction or people profiles. We do, however, accept manuscripts for a monthly column of fire-service-related humor. Your punctuation, grammar and spelling are not our primary concerns. We have editors to correct these. We are more interested in your expertise, knowledge and experience in fire service subjects. However, it is important to spell names, places and organizations correctly, as our editors may not be familiar with them. Do not include opinions (unless you are submitting a Guest Editorial), unsubstantiated statements or untested tactics in your article. Accuracy is essential. Be sure of your facts, and always attribute information and identify sources."

$ CHIEF OF POLICE MAGAZINE, National Association of Chiefs of Police, 3801 Biscayne Blvd., Miami FL 33137. (305)573-0070. Fax: (305)573-9819. E-mail: policeinfo@aphf.org. Website: www.aphf.org. **Contact:** Jim Gordon, executive editor. Bimonthly journal for law enforcement commanders (command ranks). Circ. 13,500. **Pays on acceptance.** Publishes ms an average of 6 months after acceptance. Byline given. Buys first rights. Submit seasonal material 6 months in advance. Accepts queries by mail, e-mail, fax. Accepts simultaneous submissions. Responds in 2 weeks to queries. Sample copy for $3 and 9×12 SAE with 5 first-class stamps. Writer's guidelines for #10 SASE.

O→ Break in with "a story concerning command officers or police family survivors."

Nonfiction: "We want stories about interesting police cases and stories on any law enforcement subject or program that is positive in nature." General interest, historical/nostalgic, how-to, humor, inspirational, interview/profile, new product, personal experience, photo feature, religious, technical. "No exposé types or anti-police." **Buys 50 mss/year.** Send complete ms. Length: 600-2,500 words. **Pays $25-75 for assigned articles; $25-100 for unsolicited articles.** Sometimes pays expenses of writers on assignment.

Photos: Send photos with submission. Reviews 5×6 prints. Buys one-time rights. Pays $5-10 for b&w; $10-25 for color. Captions required.

Columns/Departments: New Police (police equipment shown and tests), 200-600 words. **Buys 6 mss/year.** Send complete ms. **Pays $5-25.**

Fillers: Anecdotes, short humor, law-oriented cartoons. **Buys 100/year.** Length: 100-1,600 words. **Pays $5-25.**

Tips: "Writers need only contact law enforcement officers right in their own areas and we would be delighted. We want to recognize good commanding officers from sergeant and above who are involved with the community. Pictures of the subject or the department are essential and can be snapshots. We are looking for interviews with police chiefs and sheriffs on command level with photos."

$ $ CORRECTIONS TECHNOLOGY & MANAGEMENT, Hendon Publishing, Inc., 1000 Skokie Blvd, Suite 500, Wilmette IL 60091. (847)256-8555. Fax: (847)256-8574. E-mail: tim@hendonpub.com. Website: www.ctmmag.com. **Contact:** Tim Burke, editor-in-chief. **40% freelance written.** Magazine covering correctional facility management. "We focus on positive stories of corrections professionals doing their job. For stories...lots of quotes, dramatic photos. Make it real. Make it useful." Estab. 1997. Circ. 15,000. Pays 30 days after publication. Publishes ms an average of 3 months after acceptance. Byline given. Buys first North American serial rights. Editorial lead time 4 months. Submit seasonal material 6 months in advance. Responds in 1 month to mss. Sample copy for 9×12 SAE and 6 first-class stamps.

Nonfiction: Facility design; technology; management; health care; food services; safety; trainings; interview/profile; photo features. "Nothing 'general market.' Must be corrections-specific." **Buys 30 mss/year.** Query with published clips. Length: 2,000-2,500 words.

Photos: Send photos with submission. Reviews transparencies, 8×10 prints. Buys all rights. Negotiates payment individually. Captions, identification of subjects, model releases required.

Columns/Departments: Corrections Profile (spotlight on one facility), 2,000 words; Tactical Profile (products in corrections tactics), 1,000 words. **Buys 3 mss/year.** Query with published clips. **Pays 10-15¢/word.**

[N] $ $ COUNTY, Texas Association of Counties, P.O. Box 2131, Austin TX 78768. (512)478-8753. Fax: (512)477-1324. E-mail: jiml@county.org. Website: www.county.org. **Contact:** Jim Lewis, editor. **15% freelance written.** Bimonthly magazine covering county and state government in Texas. "We provide elected and appointed county officials with insights and information that helps them do their jobs and enhances communications among the independent office-holders in the courthouse." Estab. 1988. Circ. 5,500. **Pays on acceptance.** Publishes ms an average of 2 months after acceptance. Byline given. Makes work-for-hire assignments. Editorial lead time 2 months. Submit seasonal material 4 months in advance. Accepts queries by mail, e-mail, phone. Responds in 2 weeks to queries; 1 month to mss. Sample copy and writer's guidelines for 8×10 SAE with 3 first-class stamps.

Nonfiction: Historical/nostalgic, photo feature, government innovations. **Buys 5 mss/year.** Query with published clips. Length: 1,000-3,000 words. **Pays $300-500.** Sometimes pays expenses of writers on assignment.

Photos: State availability with submission. Buys all rights. Negotiates payment individually. Captions, identification of subjects, model releases required.

Columns/Departments: Safety; Human Resources; Risk Management (all directed toward education of Texas county officials), maximum length 1,000 words. **Buys 2 mss/year.** Query with published clips. **Pays $300.**

Tips: "Identify innovative practices or developing trends that affect Texas county officials and have the basic journalism skills to write a multi-sourced, informative feature."

$ $ FIRE CHIEF, Intertec Publishing Corp., 35 E. Wacker Dr., Suite 700, Chicago IL 60601. (312)726-7277. Fax: (312)726-0241. E-mail: scott_baltic@intertec.com. Website: www.firechief.com. **Contact:** Scott Baltic, editor. **90% freelance written.** Monthly magazine. "*Fire Chief* is the management magazine of the fire service, addressing the administrative, personnel, training, prevention/education, professional development and operational issues faced by chiefs and other fire officers, whether in paid, volunteer or combination departments. We're potentially interested in any article that can help them do their jobs better, whether that's as incident commanders, financial managers, supervisors, leaders, trainers, planners, or ambassadors to municipal officials or the public." Estab. 1956. Circ. 50,000. Pays on publication. Publishes ms an average of 6 months after acceptance. Byline given. Kill fee negotiable. Buys first, one-time, second serial (reprint), all rights. Editorial lead time 2 months. Submit seasonal material 4 months in advance. Accepts queries by mail, e-mail, fax. Responds in 1 month to queries; 2 months to mss. Sample copy and writer's guidelines free or online.

Nonfiction: "If your department has made some changes in its structure, budget, mission or organizational culture (or really did reinvent itself in a serious way), an account of that process, including the mistakes made and lessons learned, could be a winner. Similarly, if you've observed certain things that fire departments typically could do a lot better and you think you have the solution, let us know." How-to, technical. **Buys 50-60 mss/year.** Query with published clips. Length: 1,500-8,000 words. **Pays $50-400.** Sometimes pays expenses of writers on assignment.

Photos: State availability with submission. Reviews transparencies, prints. Buys one-time or reprint rights. Captions, identification of subjects required.

Columns/Departments: Training Perspectives, EMS Viewpoints, Sound Off, 1,000-1,800 words.

Tips: "Writers who are unfamiliar with the fire service are very unlikely to place anything with us. Many pieces that we reject are either too unfocused or too abstract. We want articles that help keep fire chiefs well informed and effective at their jobs."

$ $ FIREHOUSE MAGAZINE, Cygnus Business Media, 445 Broad Hollow Rd., Suite 21, Melville NY 11747. (631)845-2700. Fax: (631)845-7109. E-mail: peter@firehouse.com. Website: www.firehouse.com. Editor-in-Chief: Harvey Eisner. **Contact:** Peter Matthews, assistant editor. **85% freelance written.** Works with a small number of new/unpublished writers each year. Monthly magazine. "*Firehouse* covers major fires nationwide, controversial issues and trends in the fire service, the latest firefighting equipment and methods of firefighting, historical fires, firefighting history and memorabilia. Fire-related books, fire safety education, hazardous materials incidents and the emergency medical services are also covered." Estab. 1976. Circ. 127,000. Pays on publication. Byline given. Accepts queries by mail, e-mail, fax. Sample copy for 9×12 SAE and 8 first-class stamps. Writer's guidelines free or online.

Nonfiction: Book excerpts (of recent books on fire, EMS and hazardous materials), historical/nostalgic (great fires in history, fire collectibles, the fire service of yesteryear), how-to (fight certain kinds of fires, buy and maintain equipment, run a fire department), technical (on almost any phase of firefighting, techniques, equipment, training, administration), trends in the fire service. No profiles of people or departments that are not unusual or innovative, reports of nonmajor fires, articles not slanted toward firefighters' interests. No poetry. **Buys 100 mss/year.** Query with or without published clips. Length: 500-3,000 words. **Pays $50-400 for assigned articles.**

Photos: Send photos with submission. Pays $25-200 for transparencies and color prints. Cannot accept negatives. Captions, identification of subjects required.

Columns/Departments: Training (effective methods); Book Reviews; Fire Safety (how departments teach fire safety to the public); Communicating (PR, dispatching); Arson (efforts to combat it). Length: 750-1,000. **Buys 50 mss/year.** Query or send complete ms. **Pays $100-300.**

Tips: "Have excellent fire service credentials and be able to offer our readers new information. Read the magazine to get a full understanding of the subject matter, the writing style and the readers before sending a query or manuscript. Send photos with manuscript or indicate sources for photos. Be sure to focus articles on firefighters."

$ FOREIGN SERVICE JOURNAL, 2101 E St. NW, Washington DC 20037-2990. (202)944-5511. Fax: (202)338-8244. E-mail: journal@afsa.org. Website: www.afsa.org. **Contact:** Bob Guldin, editor. **75% freelance written.** Monthly magazine for Foreign Service personnel and others interested in foreign affairs and related subjects. Estab. 1924. Pays on publication. Publishes ms an average of 3 months after acceptance. Byline given. Buys first North American serial rights. Accepts queries by mail, e-mail, fax. Responds in 1 month to queries. Sample copy for $3.50 and 10×12 SAE with 6 first-class stamps. Writer's guidelines for #10 SASE.

O─ Break in through "Postcard from Abroad—short items (600 words) on life abroad."

Nonfiction: Uses articles on "diplomacy, professional concerns of the State Department and Foreign Service, diplomatic history and articles on Foreign Service experiences. Much of our material is contributed by those working in the profession. Informed outside contributions are welcomed, however." Essays, exposé, humor, opinion, personal experience. **Buys 15-20 unsolicited mss/year.** Query. Length: 1,000-4,000 words. **Offers honoraria.**
Fiction: Publishes short stories about foreign service life in the annual August fiction issue.
Tips: "We're more likely to want your article if it has something to do with diplomacy or U.S. foreign policy."

\$ \$THE JOURNAL OF SAFE MANAGEMENT OF DISRUPTIVE AND ASSAULTIVE BEHAVIOR, Crisis Prevention Institute, Inc., 3315-K N. 124th S, Brookfield WI 53005. Fax: (262)783-5906. E-mail: info@crisispreve ntion.com. Website: www.crisisprevention.com. **Contact:** Diana B. Kohn, editor/advertising manager. **20% freelance written.** Quarterly journal covering safe management of disruptive and assaultive behavior. "Our audience is human service and business professionals concerned about workplace violence issues. *CPI* is the world leader in violence prevention training." Estab. 1980. Circ. 12,000. Pays on publication. Publishes ms an average of 6 months after acceptance. Byline given. Offers 50% kill fee. Buys one-time, second serial (reprint) rights. Editorial lead time 6 months. Submit seasonal material 3 months in advance. Responds in 1 month to queries. Sample copy and writer's guidelines free.
Nonfiction: "Each quarterly issue is specifically devoted to one topic. Inquire about topics by e-mail." Interview/ profile, new product, opinion, personal experience, research. Inquire for editorial calendar. **Buys 5-10 mss/year.** Query. Length: 1,500-3,000 words. **Pays \$50-300 for assigned articles; \$50-100 for unsolicited articles.**
Tips: "For more information on CPI, please refer to our website."

\$ LAW AND ORDER, Hendon Co., 1000 Skokie Blvd., Wilmette IL 60091. (847)444-3300. Fax: (847)444-3333. E-mail: esanow@hendonpub.com. Website: www.lawandordermag.com. **Contact:** Ed Sanow, editor-in-chief. **90% freelance written.** Prefers to work with published/established writers. Monthly magazine covering the administration and operation of law enforcement agencies, directed to police chiefs and supervisors. Estab. 1952. Circ. 38,000. Pays on publication. Publishes ms an average of 6 months after acceptance. Byline given. Buys first North American serial rights. Submit seasonal material 3 months in advance. Accepts queries by mail, e-mail, fax, phone. Responds in 1 month to queries. Sample copy for 9×12 SAE. Writer's guidelines free.
Nonfiction: General police interest. How-to (do specific police assignments), new product (how applied in police operation), technical (specific police operation). Special issues: Communications (January); Buyers Guide (February); International (March); Community Relations (April); Administration (May); Science & Technology (June); Mobile Patrol (July); Uniforms & Equipment (August); Weapons (September); Investigations (November); Training (December). No articles dealing with courts (legal field) or convicted prisoners. No nostalgic, financial, travel or recreational material. **Buys 150 mss/year.** Query; no simultaneous queries. Length: 2,000-3,000 words. **Pays 10-25¢/word.**
Photos: Send photos with submission. Reviews transparencies, prints. Buys all rights. Pays \$25-40/photo. Identification of subjects required.
Tips: "*L&O* is a respected magazine that provides up-to-date information that police chiefs can use. Writers must know their subject as it applies to this field. Case histories are well received. We are upgrading editorial quality—stories *must* show some understanding of the law enforcement field. A frequent mistake is not getting photographs to accompany article."

\$ \$NATIONAL FIRE & RESCUE, SpecComm International, Inc., 3000 Highwoods Blvd., Suite 300, Raleigh NC 27604. (919)872-5040. Fax: (919)876-6531. E-mail: editor@nfrmag.com. Website: www.nfrmag.com. **Contact:** Phil Powell, managing editor. **80% freelance written.** Bimonthly magazine. "*National Fire & Rescue* is a bimonthly magazine devoted to informing the nation's fire and rescue services, with special emphasis on fire departments serving communities of less than 25,000. It is the *Popular Science* for fire and rescue with easy-to-understand information on science, technology and training." Estab. 1980. Circ. 35,000. Pays on publication. Publishes ms an average of 5 months after acceptance. Byline given. Offers 50% kill fee. Buys first North American serial rights. Editorial lead time 2 months. Submit seasonal material 3 months in advance. Accepts simultaneous submissions. Responds in 1 month to queries. Call for writer's guidelines.
Nonfiction: Book excerpts, how-to, humor, inspirational, interview/profile, new product, personal experience, photo feature. No pieces marketing specific products or services. **Buys 40 mss/year.** Query with published clips. Length: 600-2,000 words. **Pays \$100-350 for assigned articles; \$100-200 for unsolicited articles.** Pays expenses of writers on assignment.
Photos: State availability with submission. Buys one-time rights. Offers \$35-150/photo. Identification of subjects required.
Columns/Departments: Leadership (management); Training; Special Operations, all 800 words. **Buys 16 mss/year.** Send complete ms. **Pays \$100-150.**

ALWAYS CHECK the most recent copy of a magazine for the address and editor's name before you send in a query or manuscript.

Tips: "Discuss your story ideas with the editor."

$ $ $ $NFPA JOURNAL, National Fire Protection Association, P.O. Box 9101, Quincy MA 02269-9101. (617)984-7562. Fax: (617)984-7090. E-mail: nfpajournal@nfpa.org. Website: www.nfpa.org. Publisher: Kathie Robinson. **Contact:** Denise Laitinen, managing editor. **50% freelance written.** Bimonthly magazine covering fire safety, fire science, fire engineering. "The *NFPA Journal*, the official journal of the NFPA, reaches all of the association's various fire safety professionals. Covering major topics in fire protection and suppression, the bimonthly *Journal* carries investigation reports; special NFPA statistical studies on large-loss and multiple-death fires, fire fighter deaths and injuries, and other annual reports; articles on fire protection advances and public education; and information of interest to NFPA members. Fire fighting techniques and fire department management are also covered." Estab. 1969. Circ. 74,000. **Pays on acceptance.** Publishes ms an average of 1 year after acceptance. Byline given. Buys all rights. Editorial lead time 6 months. Accepts queries by e-mail, fax. Responds in 2 weeks to queries. Sample copy and writer's guidelines free.
Nonfiction: Technical. No fiction, product pieces or human interest. **Buys 10 mss/year.** Query. Length: 2,000-5,000 words. **Pays $1,200-2,200 for assigned articles.** Sometimes pays expenses of writers on assignment.
Photos: State availability with submission. Buys one-time rights. Negotiates payment individually. Captions, identification of subjects, model releases required.
Tips: "Query or call. Be familiar with our publication and audience. We happily send out sample issues and guidelines. Because we are a peer-reviewed journal, we can not endorse or promote particular products—no infomercials please! We appreciate and value quality writers who can provide well-written material on technical subjects related to fine and life safety."

$ $ 9-1-1 MAGAZINE, Official Publications, Inc., 18201 Weston Place, Tustin CA 92780-2251. (714)544-7776. Fax: (714)838-9233. E-mail: publisher@9-1-1magazine.com. Website: www.9-1-1magazine.com. **Contact:** Randall Larson, editor. **85% freelance written.** Bimonthly magazine for knowledgeable emergency communications professionals and those associated with this respectful profession. "*9-1-1 Magazine* is published to provide information valuable to all those interested in this exciting and rewarding profession." Estab. 1989. Circ. 13,000. Pays on publication. Publishes ms an average of 2 months after acceptance. Byline given. Offers 20% kill fee. Buys one-time, second serial (reprint) rights. Accepts queries by mail, e-mail, fax. Responds in 2 months to queries; 3 months to mss. Sample copy for 9×12 SAE and 5 first-class stamps. Writer's guidelines for #10 SASE.
Nonfiction: New product, photo feature, technical, Incident report. **Buys 20-30 mss/year.** Query with SASE. We prefer queries, but will look at manuscripts on speculation. Most positive responses to queries are considered on spec, but occasionally we will make assignments. Length: 1,000-2,500 words. **Pays 10¢/word.**
Photos: Send photos with submission. Reviews color transparencies, prints. Buys one-time rights. Offers $50-100/interior, $300/cover. Captions, identification of subjects required.
Fillers: Cartoons. **Buys 10/year. Pays $25.**
   ☐ The online magazine carries original content not found in the print edition.
Tips: "What we don't need are 'my first call' articles, or photography of a less-than-excellent quality. We seldom use poetry or fiction. *9-1-1 Magazine* is published for a knowledgeable professional in this industry. Our primary considerations in selecting material are: quality, appropriateness of material, brevity, knowledge of our readership, accuracy, accompanying photography, originality, wit and humor, a clear direction and vision, and proper use of the language."

$ $ $PLANNING, American Planning Association, 122 S. Michigan Ave., Suite 1600, Chicago IL 60603. (312)431-9100. Fax: (312)431-9985. E-mail: slewis@planning.org. Website: www.planning.org. **Contact:** Sylvia Lewis, editor. **25% freelance written.** Monthly magazine emphasizing urban planning for adult, college-educated readers who are regional and urban planners in city, state or federal agencies or in private business or university faculty or students. Estab. 1972. Circ. 30,000. Pays on publication. Publishes ms an average of 2 months after acceptance. Byline given. Buys all rights. Accepts queries by mail, e-mail, fax. Responds in 2 months to queries. Sample copy and writer's guidelines for 9×12 SAE with 5 first-class stamps.
Nonfiction: "It's best to query with a fairly detailed, one-page letter. We'll consider any article that's well written and relevant to our audience. Articles have a better chance if they are timely and related to planning and land use and if they appeal to a national audience. All articles should be written in magazine feature style." Exposé (on government or business, but topics related to planning, housing, land use, zoning), general interest (trend stories on cities, land use, government), how-to (successful government or citizen efforts in planning, innovations, concepts that have been applied), technical (detailed articles on the nitty-gritty of planning, zoning, transportation but no footnotes or mathematical models). Also needs news stories up to 500 words. **Buys 2 features and 1 news story/year.** Length: 500-2,000 words. **Pays $150-1,000.**
Photos: "We prefer that authors supply their own photos, but we sometimes take our own or arrange for them in other ways." State availability with submission. Buys one-time rights. Pays $100 minimum for photos used on inside pages and $300 for cover photos. Captions required.

$ $ POLICE AND SECURITY NEWS, DAYS Communications, Inc., 1208 Juniper St., Quakertown PA 18951-1520. (215)538-1240. Fax: (215)538-1208. E-mail: jdevery@policeandsecuritynews.com. **Contact:** James Devery, editor. **40% freelance written.** Bimonthly tabloid on public law enforcement and private security. "Our publication is designed to provide educational and entertaining information directed toward management level. Technical information written for the expert in a manner that the non-expert can understand." Estab. 1984. Circ. 21,000. Pays on publication.

Publishes ms an average of 2 months after acceptance. Byline given. Buys first North American serial rights. Accepts queries by mail, e-mail, fax, phone. Accepts simultaneous submissions. Sample copy and writer's guidelines for 9×12 SAE with $1.93 postage.

Nonfiction: Al Menear, articles editor. Exposé, historical/nostalgic, how-to, humor, interview/profile, opinion, personal experience, photo feature, technical. **Buys 12 mss/year.** Query. Length: 200-4,000 words. **Pays 10¢/word. Sometimes pays in trade-out of services.**

Reprints: Send tearsheet, photocopy or typed ms with rights for sale noted and information about when and where the material previously appeared.

Photos: State availability with submission. Reviews 3×5 prints. Buys one-time rights. Offers $10-50/photo.

Fillers: Facts, newsbreaks, short humor. **Buys 6/year.** Length: 200-2,000 words. **Pays 10¢/word.**

$ POLICE TIMES, American Federation of Police & Concerned Citizens, Inc., 3801 Biscayne Blvd., Miami FL 33137. (305)573-0070. Fax: (305)573-9819. **Contact:** Jim Gordon, executive editor. **80% freelance written.** Eager to work with new/unpublished writers. Quarterly magazine covering "law enforcement (general topics) for men and women engaged in law enforcement and private security, and citizens who are law and order concerned." Circ. 55,000. **Pays on acceptance.** Publishes ms an average of 6 months after acceptance. Byline given. Buys second serial (reprint) rights. Submit seasonal material 4 months in advance. Accepts queries by mail, fax. Accepts simultaneous submissions. Sample copy for $2.50 and 9×12 SAE with 3 first-class stamps. Writer's guidelines for #10 SASE.

Nonfiction: Book excerpts, essays (on police science), exposé (police corruption), general interest, historical/nostalgic, how-to, humor, interview/profile, new product, personal experience (with police), photo feature, technical (all police related). Special issues: "We produce a special edition on police killed in the line of duty. It is mailed May 15 so copy must arrive six months in advance. Photos required." No anti-police materials. **Buys 50 mss/year.** Send complete ms. Length: 200-4,000 words. **Pays $25-100. Payment includes right to publish on organization's website.**

Photos: Send photos with submission. Reviews 5×6 prints. Buys all rights. Offers $5-25/photo. Identification of subjects required.

Columns/Departments: Legal Cases (lawsuits involving police actions); New Products (new items related to police services); Awards (police heroism acts). Length: 200-1,000. **Buys variable number of mss/year.** Send complete ms. **Pays $25-75.**

Fillers: Fillers are usually humorous stories about police officer and citizen situations. Special stories on police cases, public corruptions, etc., are most open to freelancers. Anecdotes, facts, newsbreaks, short humor, cartoons. **Buys 100/year.** Length: 50-100 words. **Pays $5-10.**

TRANSACTION/SOCIETY, Bldg. 4051, Rutgers University, New Brunswick NJ 08903. (732)445-2280 ext. 83. Fax: (732)445-3138. E-mail: ihorowitz@transactionpub.com. Website: www.transactionpub.com. Publisher: Jonathan B. Imber. **Contact:** Irving Louis Horowitz, editor. **10% freelance written.** Prefers to work with published/established writers. Bimonthly magazine for social scientists (policymakers with training in sociology, political issues and economics). Estab. 1962. Circ. 45,000. Pays on publication. Publishes ms an average of 6 months after acceptance. Byline given. Buys all rights. Responds in 3 months to queries. Sample copy and writer's guidelines for 9×12 SAE with 5 first-class stamps.

Nonfiction: Andrew McIntosh, managing editor. "Articles of wide interest in areas of specific interest to the social science community. Must have an awareness of problems and issues in education, population and urbanization that are not widely reported. Articles on overpopulation, terrorism, international organizations." Book excerpts, essays, interview/profile, photo feature. No general think pieces. Query. **Pays for assigned articles only.**

Photos: Douglas Harper, photo editor. Pays $200 for photographic essays done on assignment or upon publication.

Tips: "Submit an article on a thoroughly unique subject, written with good literary quality. Present new ideas and research findings in a readable and useful manner. A frequent mistake is writing to satisfy a journal, rather than the intrinsic requirements of the story itself. Avoid posturing and editorializing."

[N] $ $ YOUR VIRGINIA STATE TROOPER MAGAZINE, Virginia State Police Association, 6944 Forest Hill Ave., Richmond VA 23225. E-mail: vspa@aol.com. **Contact:** Tammy Poole, editor. **65% freelance written.** Triannual magazine covering police topics for troopers and special agents (state police), related employees and legislators. Estab. 1974. Circ. 4,000. **Pays on acceptance.** Publishes ms an average of 3 months after acceptance. Byline given. Buys Buys first North American serial, one-time rights and all rights on assignments. Submit seasonal material 4 months in advance. Accepts queries by mail. Accepts simultaneous submissions. Responds in 2 months to queries.

Nonfiction: Book excerpts (law enforcement related), exposé (consumer or police-related), general interest, historical/nostalgic, how-to, humor, interview/profile (notable police figures), technical (radar), travel (VA sites), fitness/health. **Buys 30-40 mss/year.** Query with published clips or send complete ms. Length: 2,500 words. **Pays $250 maximum/article (10¢/word).** Sometimes pays expenses of writers on assignment.

Photos: Send photos with submission. Buys one-time rights. Pays $50 maximum for prints to accompany ms. Captions required.

Fillers: Cartoons. Send copies. Buys one-time rights. **Buys 20 cartoons/year. Pays $20.**

Tips: "In addition to items of interest to the VA State Police, general interest is sometimes featured."

GROCERIES & FOOD PRODUCTS

In this section are publications for grocers, food wholesalers, processors, warehouse owners, caterers, institutional managers and suppliers of grocery store equipment. See the section on Confectionery & Snack Foods for bakery and candy industry magazines.

$ $ $ **DISTRIBUTION CHANNELS, AWMA's Magazine for Candy, Tobacco, Grocery and General Merchandise Marketers,** American Wholesale Marketers Association, 1128 16th St. NW, Washington DC 20036. (202)463-2124. Fax: (202)467-0559. E-mail: jillk@awmanet.org. Website: www.distributionchannels.org. **Contact:** Jill Kosko, editor-in-chief. **75% freelance written.** Magazine published 10 times/year. "We cover trends in candy, tobacco, groceries, beverages, snacks and other product categories found in convenience stores, grocery stores and drugstores, plus distribution topics. Contributors should have prior experience writing about the food, retail and/or distribution industries. Editorial includes a mix of columns, departments and features (2-6 pages). We also cover AWMA programs." Estab. 1948. Circ. 10,000. **Pays on acceptance.** Publishes ms an average of 2 months after acceptance. Byline given. Editorial lead time 4 months. Accepts queries by mail, e-mail, fax.
Nonfiction: How-to, technical, Industry trends; also profiles of distribution firms. No comics, jokes, poems or other fillers. **Buys 80 mss/year.** Query with published clips. Length: 1,200-3,600 words. **Pays $200-1,200 generally.** Sometimes pays industry members who author articles. Pays expenses of writers on assignment.
Photos: Authors must provide artwork (with captions) with articles.
Tips: "We're looking for reliable, accurate freelancers with whom we can establish a long-term working relationship. We need writers who understand this industry. We accept very few articles on speculation. Most are assigned. To consider a new writer for an assignment, we must first receive his or her résumé, at least two writing samples and references. We only work with full-time freelancers."

$ $ **FRESH CUT MAGAZINE, The Magazine for Value-added Produce,** Columbia Publishing, P.O. Box 9036, Yakima WA 98909-0036. (509)248-2452. Fax: (509)248-4056. E-mail: ken@freshcut.com. **Contact:** Ken Hodge, editor. **40% freelance written.** Monthly magazine covering minimally processed fresh fruits and vegetables, packaged salads, etc. "We want informative articles about processing produce. We also want stories about how these products are sold at retail, in restaurants, etc." Estab. 1993. Circ. 18,464. Pays on publication. Publishes ms an average of 2 months after acceptance. Byline given. Buys all rights. Editorial lead time 2 months. Submit seasonal material 3 months in advance. Accepts queries by mail, e-mail, fax, phone. Responds in 1 month to queries; 2 months to mss. Sample copy for 9×12 SAE. Writer's guidelines for #10 SASE.
Nonfiction: Historical/nostalgic, new product, opinion, technical. Special issues: Retail (May); Foodservice (February); Packaging Technology (December). **Buys 2-4 mss/year.** Query with published clips. **Pays $5/column inch for assigned articles; $75-125 for unsolicited articles.**
Reprints: Send tearsheet with rights for sale noted and information about when and where the material previously appeared. Pays 50% of amount paid for an original article.
Photos: Send photos with submission. Reviews transparencies. Buys one-time rights. Offers no additional payment for photos accepted with ms. Identification of subjects required.
Columns/Departments: Packaging; Food Safety; Processing/Engineering. **Buys 20 mss/year.** Query. **Pays $125-200.**
Fillers: Facts. Length: 300 words maximum. **Pays $25-50.**

$ $ **HEALTH PRODUCTS BUSINESS,** CYGNUS Business Media Inc., 445 Broad Hollow Rd., Suite 21, Melville NY 11747. (631)845-2700. Fax: (631)845-2723. Website: www.healthproductsbusiness.com. **Contact:** Michael Schiavetta, associate editor. **70% freelance written.** Monthly magazine covering natural health products. "The business magazine for natural products retailers." Estab. 1954. Circ. 16,000. Pays on publication. Publishes ms an average of 3 months after acceptance. Byline given. Buys first North American serial rights. Editorial lead time 4 months. Submit seasonal material 3 months in advance. Accepts queries by mail, fax. Sample copy for $3. Writer's guidelines free.
Nonfiction: Store profile. Query. **Pays $200-250.**
Photos: State availability with submission.
   ■ The online magazine carries original content not found in the print edition. Contact: Michael Schiavetta, online editor.
Tips: "We are always looking for well-written store profiles with a lot of detailed information, but new writers should always query first to receive writer's guidelines and other necessary information. We prefer writers with industry experience/interest."

$ $ **PRODUCE MERCHANDISING,** Vance Publishing Corp., 10901 W. 84th Terrace, Lenexa KS 66214. (913)438-8700. Fax: (913)438-0691. E-mail: jkresin@producemerchandising.com. Website: www.producemerchandising.com. Editor: Elaine Symanski. **Contact:** Janice M. Kresin, editor. **33% freelance written.** Monthly magazine. "The magazine's editorial purpose is to provide information about promotions, merchandising and operations in the form of ideas and examples. *Produce Merchandising* is the only monthly journal on the market that is dedicated solely to produce merchandising information for retailers." Circ. 12,000. **Pays on acceptance.** Publishes ms an average of 3 months after acceptance. Byline given. Buys all rights. Editorial lead time 3 months. Accepts queries by mail. Responds in 2 weeks to queries. Sample copy free.

Nonfiction: How-to, interview/profile, new product, photo feature, technical (contact the managing editor for a specific assignment). **Buys 48 mss/year.** Query with published clips. Length: 1,000-1,500 words. **Pays $200-600.** Pays expenses of writers on assignment.

Photos: State availability of or send photos with submission. Reviews color slides and 3×5 or larger prints. Buys all rights. Offers no additional payment for photos accepted with ms. Captions, identification of subjects, model releases required.

Columns/Departments: Contact editor for a specific assignment. **Buys 30 mss/year.** Query with published clips. **Pays $200-450.**

Tips: "Send in clips and contact the editor with specific story ideas. Story topics are typically outlined up to a year in advance."

$ $ THE SERVER FOODSERVICE NEWS, Business Communications, Inc., 157 S. 26th St., Pittsburgh PA 15203. (412)381-5029. Fax: (412)381-5205. E-mail: editorial@theservernews.com. Website: www.theservernews.com. **Contact:** Lori Monahan, executive editor. **10-15% freelance written.** Monthly tabloid covering food service, restaurant industry, C-stores, supermarket chains. "*The Server Foodservice News* is edited for the food service industry. It is edited for restaurant personnel, liquor licenses, chain operation, personnel, etc. *The Server* provides pertinent data about new products, trends and other vital information. *The Server Foodservice News* is a national publication with a regional focus and a local flair. Michigan, Ohio, West Virginia, Maryland, Delaware, New Jersey, New York, and Pennsylvania are states that are covered with editorial features, current events and the people who make them happen in the foodservice industry." Estab. 1979. Circ. 25,000. Pays on publication. Byline given. Buys all rights. Accepts queries by mail, e-mail, fax. Sample copy for $3.95. Writer's guidelines free.

Nonfiction: General interest, historical/nostalgic, interview/profile, new product. No restaurant reviews. Query. Length: 400-800 words. **Pays 10-15¢/word.**

Photos: Send photos with submission. Reviews contact sheets. Buys all rights. Offers $5/photo. Captions, identification of subjects, model releases required.

■ The online magazine carries original content not found in the print edition. Contact: Lori Monahan.

N WESTERN GROCER MAGAZINE, Mercury Publications Ltd., 1839 Inkster Blvd., Winnipeg, Manitoba R2X 1R3, Canada. (204)954-2085. Fax: (204)954-2057. E-mail: mp@mercury.mb.ca. Website: www.mercury.mb.ca/. Editor: Frank Yeo. **Contact:** Kristi Balon, editorial coordinator. **75% freelance written.** Bimonthly magazine covering the grocery industry. Reports profiles on independent food stores, supermarkets, manufacturers and food processors, brokers, distributors and wholesalers. Estab. 1916. Circ. 15,500. Pays 30-45 days from receipt of invoice. Byline given. Offers 33% kill fee. Buys first rights. Submit seasonal material 3 months in advance. Accepts queries by mail, e-mail, fax. Accepts simultaneous submissions. Responds in 2 weeks to queries. Sample copy and writer's guidelines free or by e-mail.

Nonfiction: How-to, interview/profile. No industry reports or profiles on companies. Query with published clips. Length: 500-9,000 words. **Pays 25-35¢/word.** Sometimes pays expenses of writers on assignment.

Photos: State availability with submission. Reviews negatives, transparencies, 3×5 prints, jpeg, eps or tif files. Buys all rights. Negotiates payment individually. Captions required.

Fillers: Facts. Length: 100 words.

Tips: "Send an e-mailed, faxed or mailed query outlining your experience, interests and pay expectations. A requirement also is clippings."

WHOLE FOODS, Informing and Educating Natural Product Retailers, WFC, Inc., 3000 Hadley Rd., South Plainfield NJ 07080-1117. Fax: (908)769-1171. E-mail: user886276@aol.com. Website: www.wfcinc.com. Assistant Editor: Caroline Krastek. **Contact:** Alan Richman, editor. Infrequent user of freelance. Monthly magazine covering the natural products industry. "Virtually all stories should in some way enable retailers of natural products (i.e., health foods, vitamins, herbs, etc.) to do their work more easily or more effectively." Estab. 1978. Circ. 14,000. Pays on publication. Publishes ms an average of 9 months after acceptance. Byline given. Buys all rights. Editorial lead time 3 months. Submit seasonal material 1 year in advance. Responds in 3 weeks to queries; 2 months to mss. Sample copy for $10.

Nonfiction: All must relate to natural products industry. Book excerpts, essays, how-to, interview/profile. **Buys 2-5 mss/year.** Query with published clips. Length: 1,000-3,000 words. **Pay varies.**

Photos: State availability with submission. Buys all rights. Offers no additional payment for photos accepted with ms. Captions, identification of subjects, model releases, photo credits are available when requested required.

HARDWARE

Journals for general and specialized hardware wholesalers and retailers are listed in this section. Journals specializing in hardware for a certain trade, such as plumbing or automotive supplies, are classified with other publications for that trade.

$ $ $ FASTENING, McGuire Fasteners, Inc., 293 Hopewell Dr., Powell OH 43065-9350. (614)848-3232. Fax: (614)848-5045. E-mail: mmcguire@mail.fastening.com. Website: www.fastening.com. **Contact:** Mike McGuire, editor/publisher. **50% freelance written.** Quarterly "Quarterly magazine seeking to advance fastener design and application engineering. Readership is made up of OEM design/application engineers and PAS." Estab. 1995. Circ. 28,000. Pays 30 days after publication. Publishes ms an average of 1 month after acceptance. Byline given. Buys all rights. Editorial lead time 2 months. Submit seasonal material 2 months in advance. Accepts simultaneous submissions. Sample copy and writer's guidelines free.

Nonfiction: How-to (fastening), new product. "No company profiles that are ads." **Buys 10-12 mss/year.** Query with published clips. Length: 500-2,000 words. **Pays $200-800.** Pays expenses of writers on assignment.

Photos: Send photos with submission. Reviews negatives. Buys all rights. Offers no additional payment for photos accepted with ms. Captions, identification of subjects, model releases required.

Columns/Departments: Case Study (history of applications), 800-1,000 words; Company Profile, 1,800-2,000 words with photos. **Buys 8-10 mss/year.** Query with published clips. **Pays $200-800.**

Fillers: Anecdotes. **Buys 2-3/year.** Length: 200-600 words. **Pays $50-100.**

Tips: *Fastening* seeks technical articles in regards to fasteners and applications.

HOME FURNISHINGS & HOUSEHOLD GOODS

Readers rely on these publications to learn more about new products and trends in the home furnishings and appliance trade. Magazines for consumers interested in home furnishings are listed in the Consumer Home & Garden section.

[N] $ FINE FURNISHINGS INTERNATIONAL, G&W McNamara Publishing, 4215 White Bear Publishing, Suite 100, St. Paul MN 55110. Fax: (651)653-4308. E-mail: ffiedit@gwmcnamara.com. Website: www.ffimagazine.com. **Contact:** Jolene Turner, managing editor. Bimonthly magazine covering the high-end furniture industry. Estab. 1997. Circ. 22,400. Pays on publication. Publishes ms an average of 3 months after acceptance. Byline given. Offers $150-250 kill fee. Buys all rights. Editorial lead time 2 months. Submit seasonal material 3 months in advance. Accepts queries by mail, e-mail. Sample copy for $6. Writer's guidelines free.

Nonfiction: Historical/nostalgic, how-to, interview/profile, technical. Query. **Pays $150.** Sometimes pays expenses of writers on assignment.

Tips: "The most helpful experience is if a writer has knowledge of interior design or, specifically, fine furniture. We already have a pool of journalists, although we welcome clips from writers who would like to be considered for assignments. Our style is professional business writing—no flowery prose. Articles tend to be to the point as our readers are busy professionals who read for information, not for leisure."

[N] $ $ $ HOME FURNISHINGS RETAILER, (formerly *Home Furnishings Executive*), National Home Furnishings Association (NHFA), P.O. Box 2396, High Point NC 27261. (336)801-6152. Fax: (336)883-1195. E-mail: lcasinger@nhfa.org. **Contact:** Lisa G. Casinger, editor. **75% freelance written.** Monthly magazine published by NHFA covering the home furnishings industry. "We hope that home furnishings retailers view our magazine as a profitability tool. We want each issue to help them make money or save money." Estab. 1927. Circ. 17,000. **Pays on acceptance.** Publishes ms an average of 6 weeks after acceptance. Byline given. Buys first North American serial rights. Editorial lead time 3 months. Accepts queries by mail, e-mail. Responds in 1 month to queries. Sample copy available with proper postage. Writer's guidelines for #10 SASE.

⊶ Break in by "e-mailing queries that pertain to our market - furniture retailers. We publish articles that give our readers tangible ways to improve their business."

Nonfiction: Query with published clips. Length: Features: 3,000-5,000 words. **Pays $350-500 for assigned articles.**

Photos: State availability with submission. Reviews transparencies. Buys one-time rights. Negotiates payment individually. Identification of subjects required.

Columns/Departments: Columns cover business and product trends that shape the home furnishings industry; Advertising and Marketing; Finance; Technology; Training; Creative Leadership; Law; Style and Operations. Length: 1,200-1,500 words. Query with published clips.

Tips: "Our readership includes owners of small 'ma and pa' furniture stores, executives of medium-sized chains (two to ten stores), and executives of big chains. Articles should be relevant to retailers and provide them with tangible information, ideas, and products to better their business."

[N] $ THE WALL PAPER, G&W McNamara Publishing, 4215 White Bear Parkway, Suite 100, St. Paul MN 55110-7635. Fax: (651)653-4308. E-mail: twpedit@gwmcnamara.com. Website: www.thewallpaper.com. **Contact:** Jolene Turner, managing editor. Tabloid published 10 times/year on the wall coverings industry. Estab. 1979. Circ. 16,700. Pays on publication. Byline given. Offers $150-250 kill fee. Buys all rights. Editorial lead time 2 months. Submit seasonal material 3 months in advance. Accepts queries by mail, e-mail. Responds in 2 months to queries. Sample copy for $4. Writer's guidelines free.

Nonfiction: Historical/nostalgic, how-to, interview/profile. Query with published clips. **Pays $150.** Sometimes pays expenses of writers on assignment.

Photos: State availability with submission. Reviews 4×6 or larger transparencies, 4×6 or 8×10 prints. Buys all rights. Offers no additional payment for photos accepted with ms. Captions required.
Tips: "Most of all we need creative ideas and approaches to topics in the field of furniture and interior design. A writer needs to be knowledgeable in the field because our readers would know if information was inaccurate. We are looking mostly for features on specific topics or on installation or design."

N $ $ WINDOW FASHIONS, G&W McNamara Publishing, Inc., 4215 White Bear Pkwy., Suite 100, St. Paul MN 55110. Fax: (651)653-4308. E-mail: wf@gwmcnamara.com. Website: www.window-fashions.com. **Contact:** Jolene Turner, assistant editor. **30% freelance written.** Monthly magazine "dedicated to the advancement of the window fashions industry, *Window Fashions* magazine provides comprehensive information on design and business principles, window fashion aesthetics and product applications. The magazine serves the window treatment industry, including designers, retailers, dealers, specialty stores, workrooms, manufacturers, fabricators and others associated with the field of interior design. Writers should be thoroughly knowledgable on the subject and submittals need to be comprehensive." Estab. 1981. Circ. 27,500. Pays on publication. Publishes ms an average of 3 months after acceptance. Byline given. Offers $150-250 kill fee. Buys all rights. Editorial lead time 3 months. Submit seasonal material 4 months in advance. Accepts queries by mail, e-mail. Accepts simultaneous submissions. Sample copy for $5. Writer's guidelines free.
Nonfiction: How-to (window fashion installation), interview/profile (of designers), personal experience. "No broad topics not specific to the window fashions industry." **Buys 24 mss/year.** Query or send complete ms. Length: 800-1,500 words. **Pays $150.**
Tips: "The most helpful experience is if a writer has knowledge of interior design or, specifically, window treatments. We already have a pool of generalists, although we welcome clips from writers who would like to be considered for assignments. Our style is professional business writing—no flowery prose. Articles tend to be to the point, as our readers are busy professionals who read for information, not for leisure. Most of all we need creative ideas and approaches to topics in the field of window treatments and interior design. A writer needs to be knowledgeable in the field because our readers would know if information were inaccurate."

HOSPITALS, NURSING & NURSING HOMES

In this section are journals for medical and nonmedical nursing home personnel, clinical and hospital staffs and medical laboratory technicians and managers. Journals publishing technical material on medical research and information for physicians in private practice are listed in the Medical category.

AMERICAN JOURNAL OF NURSING, 345 Hudson St., 16th Floor, New York NY 10014. (212)886-1200. Fax: (212)886-1206. E-mail: ajn@lww.com. Website: www.nursingcenter.com. **Contact:** Diana Mason, editor-in-chief. Monthly magazine covering nursing and health care. Estab. 1900. Circ. 342,000. Pays on publication. Publishes ms an average of 6 months after acceptance. Byline given. Accepts queries by mail. Responds in 2 weeks to queries; 10 weeks to mss. Sample copy and writer's guidelines free.
Nonfiction: Practical, hands-on clinical articles of inrerest to hospital and staff nurses; professional issues; personal experience. Now accepting poetry, short stories and personal essays. Nurse-authors only accepted fo publication. Opinion, personal experience.
Photos: Now accepting paintings, drawings, photos of sculpture and other artwork. Reviews b&w and color transparencies, prints. Identification of subjects, model releases required.
Tips: "*American Journal of Nursing* is particularly interested in articles dealing with women's health issues and implications for nursing care. Send an outline with query letter."

$ JOURNAL OF CHRISTIAN NURSING, Nurses Christian Fellowship, InterVarsity Christian Fellowship, P.O. Box 7895, Madison WI 53707-7895. (602)274-4823, ext. 401. E-mail: jcn@ivcf.org. Website: www.ncf-jcn.org. Editor: Judith Allen Shelly. **Contact:** Melodee Yohe, managing editor. **30% freelance written.** Quarterly magazine covering spiritual care, ethics, crosscultural issues, etc. "Our target audience is Christian nurses in the U.S., and we are nondenominational in character. We are prolife in position. We strive to help Christian nurses view nursing practice through the eyes of faith. Articles must be relevant to Christian nursing and consistent with our statement of faith." Estab. 1984. Circ. 10,000. **Pays on acceptance.** Publishes ms an average of 1-2 years after acceptance. Byline given unless subject matter requires pseudonym. Offers 50% kill fee. Buys first, second serial (reprint) rights, rarely; all rights, only multiple-authored case studies. Editorial lead time up to 2 years. Submit seasonal material 1 year in advance. Accepts queries by mail, e-mail, fax. Responds in 1 month to queries; 2 months to mss. Sample copy for $5 and SAE with 4 first-class stamps. Writer's guidelines for #10 SASE or online.
Nonfiction: How-to, humor, inspirational, interview/profile, opinion, personal experience, photo feature, religious, all must be appropriate for Christian nurses. Poetry not accepted. No purely academic articles, subjects not appropriate for Christian nurses, devotionals, Bible study. **Buys 20-30 mss/year.** Send complete ms. Length: 6-12 pages (typed, double spaced). **Pays $25-80 and up to 8 complimentary copies.**
Reprints: Send tearsheet or photocopy and information about when and where the material previously appeared.

Photos: State availability of or send photos with submission. No rights purchased; all photos returned. Offers no additional payment for photos accepted with ms. Identification of subjects, model releases required.

Columns/Departments: Book Reviews (Resources). **No payment for Book Reviews.**

Tips: "Unless an author is a nurse, it will be unlikely that he/she will have an article accepted—unless it's a very interesting story about a nurse who is involved in creative ministry with a strong faith dimension."

$ $ $NURSING SPECTRUM, Florida Edition, Nursing Spectrum, 1001 W. Cypress Creek Rd., Ste. 300, Ft. Lauderdale FL 33309. (954)776-1455. Fax: (954)776-1456. E-mail: pclass@nursingspectrum.com. Website: www.nursin gspectrum.com. **Contact:** Phyllis Class, RN, editorial director. **80% freelance written.** Biweekly magazine covering registered nursing. "We support and recognize registered nurses. All articles must have at least one RN in byline. We prefer articles that feature nurses in our region, but articles of interest to all nurses are welcome, too. We look for substantive, yet readable articles. Our bottom line—timely, relevant, and compelling articles that support nurses and help them excel in their clinical and professional careers." Estab. 1991. Circ. 53,928. Pays on publication. Byline given. Buys all rights. Editorial lead time 3 months. Submit seasonal material 4 months in advance. Accepts queries by mail, e-mail, fax, phone. Responds in 1 month to queries; 4 months to mss. Sample copy and writer's guidelines free.

> O→ "Having an original idea is paramount and the first step in writing an article. We are looking for success stories, nurses to be proud of, and progress that is helping patients. If you and your colleagues have dealt with and learned from a thorny issue, tell us how. What is new in your field? Consider your audience: all RNs, well-educated, and of various specialties. Will they relate, be inspired, learn something? The best articles are both interesting and informative."

Nonfiction: General interest, how-to (career management), humor, interview/profile, personal experience, photo feature. Special issues: Critical Care, nursing management. "No articles that do not have at least one RN on the byline." **Buys 125 plus mss/year.** Length: 700-1,200 words. **Pays $50-800 for assigned articles.** Sometimes pays expenses of writers on assignment.

Photos: Buys one-time rights. Negotiates payment individually. Captions, identification of subjects, model releases required.

Columns/Departments: Perspectives in Leadership (nurse managers); Advanced Practice (advanced practice nurses); Humor Infusion (cartoon, amusing anecdotes); Career Fitness (career tips, types of careers). **Buys 75 mss/year.** Query with published clips. **Pays $50-120.**

Tips: "Write in 'magazine' style—as if talking to another RN. Use to-the-point, active language. Narrow your focus. Topics such as 'The Future of Nursing' or 'Dealing With Change' are too broad and non-specific. Use informative but catchy titles and subheads (we can help with this). If quoting others be sure quotes are meaningful and add substance to the piece. To add vitality, you may use statistics and up-to-date references. Try to paint a complete picture, using pros and cons. Be both positive and realistic."

$ $ $NURSING SPECTRUM, New England edition, Nursing Spectrum, 1050 Waltham St., Suite 510, Waltham MA 02421. (781)863-2300. Fax: (781)863-6277. E-mail: jborgatti@nursingspectrum.com. Website: www.nursi ngspectrum.com. **Contact:** Joan Borgatti, RN, editor. **80% freelance written.** Biweekly magazine covering registered nursing. "We support and recognize registered nurses. All articles must have at least one RN in byline. We prefer articles that feature nurses in our region, but articles of interest to all nurses are welcome, too. We look for substantive, yet readable articles. Our bottom line—timely, relevant, and compelling articles that support nurses and help them excel in their clinical and professional careers." Estab. 1997. Circ. 114,555. Byline given. Accepts queries by mail, e-mail, fax, phone.

> ● See *Nursing Spectrum, Florida Edition* for article needs.

> ▣ The online magazine carries original content not found in the print edition. Contact: Cynthia Saver, RN, editor.

$ $ $NURSING SPECTRUM, Washington, DC/Baltimore edition, Nursing Spectrum, 803 W. Broad St., Ste. 500, Falls Church VA 22046. (703)237-6515. Fax: (703)237-6299. E-mail: csaver@nursingspectrum.com. Website: www.nursingspectrum.com. **Contact:** Cindy Saver, RN, editor. **80% freelance written.** Biweekly journal covering registered nursing. "We support and recognize registered nurses. All articles must have at least one RN in byline. We prefer articles that feature nurses in our region, but articles of interest to all nurses are welcome, too. We look for substantive, yet readable articles. Our bottom line—timely, relevant, and compelling articles that support nurses and help them excel in their clinical and professional careers." Estab. 1990. Circ. 55,000.

> ● See *Nursing Spectrum, Florida Edition* for article needs.

Ⓝ $ $NURSEZONE.COM, AMN Healthcare Inc., 12235 El Camino Real, Suite 200, San Diego CA 92130. (858)720-6227. Fax: (866)510-1905. E-mail: Carol.Burke@NurseZone.com. Website: www.nursezone.com. **Contact:** Carol Burke, editorial director. **50% freelance written.** Daily online publication covering the professional and personal lives of nurses. Estab. 2000. Circ. 10,000 visits/month. Pays on publication. Byline given. Offers variable kill fee. Buys second serial (reprint), electronic, all rights, makes work-for-hire assignments. Editorial lead time up to 1 month. Submit seasonal material 1 month in advance. Accepts queries by mail, e-mail. Responds in 1 month to queries. Writer's guidelines for #10 SASE.

Nonfiction: Book excerpts, exposé, general interest, historical/nostalgic, humor, inspirational, interview/profile, new product, personal experience, photo feature, technical, travel, career-related for nurses, finance, news by specialty, medical news, holistic approaches to medicine. No consumer-related health articles. **Buys variable mss/year.** Query with published clips. Length: 500-2,000 words. **Pays $100-300.** Sometimes pays expenses of writers on assignment.

Photos: State availability with submission. Reviews contact sheets, 5×7 prints, gif/jpeg/tiff formats. Buys all and electronic rights. Negotiates payment individually. Captions, identification of subjects, model releases required.

Columns/Departments: Medical News (medical news relevant to working nurses); News by Specialty; Holistic Approaches (information on holistic techniques and therapies, herbs and interactions); Devices and Technology (latest news affecting working nurses); Career Advice (unique stories about involving nurses, information for career nurses); Travel Stories (how this might relate to nurses); Travel Tips (suggestions for travelers); Nursing Conferences (coverage of news), all 300-800 words; Real Stories (stories about nurses working in today's industry), 200-2,000 words; Your Finances (financial news, information, tips relevant to today's nurses), 300-1,000 words. Query. **Pays $100-300.**

Fiction: Nancy Fagan, content manager. Condensed Novels, historical, humorous, novel excerpts, romance, slice-of-life vignettes, anything related to nurses or written by nurses. **Buys variable number of mss/year.** Query with published clips. Length: 500-2,500 words. **Pays $100-300.**

Tips: "Find an angle unique to nurses; personal stories by or about nurses are always welcome; try to have a nurse in the byline."

HOTELS, MOTELS, CLUBS, RESORTS & RESTAURANTS

These publications offer trade tips and advice to hotel, club, resort and restaurant managers, owners and operators. Journals for manufacturers and distributors of bar and beverage supplies are listed in the Beverages & Bottling section.

$ $ BARTENDER MAGAZINE, Foley Publishing, P.O. Box 158, Liberty Corner NJ 07938. (908)766-6006. Fax: (908)766-6607. E-mail: barmag@aol.com. Website: www.bartender.com. Editor: Jaclyn M. Wilson. **Contact:** Jackie Foley, publisher. **100% freelance written.** Prefers to work with published/established writers; eager to work with new/unpublished writers. Quarterly magazine emphasizing liquor and bartending for bartenders, tavern owners and owners of restaurants with full-service liquor licenses. Circ. 147,000. Pays on publication. Publishes ms an average of 3 months after acceptance. Byline given. Buys first North American serial, first, one-time, second serial (reprint), simultaneous, all rights. Submit seasonal material 3 months in advance. Accepts simultaneous submissions. Responds in 2 months to mss. Sample copy for 9×12 SAE and 4 first-class stamps.

Nonfiction: General interest, historical/nostalgic, how-to, humor, interview/profile (with famous bartenders or ex-bartenders), new product, opinion, personal experience, photo feature, travel, Nostalgia, Unique bars, New techniques, New drinking trends, Bar sports, Bar magic tricks. Special issues: Annual Calendar and Daily Cocktail Recipe Guide. Send complete ms and SASE. Length: 100-1,000 words.

Reprints: Send tearsheet and information about when and where the material previously appeared. Pays 25% of amount paid for an original article.

Photos: Send photos with submission. Pays $7.50-50 for 8×10 b&w glossy prints; $10-75 for 8×10 color glossy prints. Captions, model releases required.

Columns/Departments: Bar of the Month; Bartender of the Month; Drink of the Month; Creative Cocktails; Bar Sports; Quiz; Bar Art; Wine Cellar; Tips from the Top (from prominent figures in the liquor industry); One For the Road (travel); Collectors (bar or liquor-related items); Photo Essays., Length: 200-1,000 words. Query by mail only with SASE. **Pays $50-200.**

Fillers: Anecdotes, newsbreaks, short humor, Clippings, Jokes, Gags. Length: 25-100 words. **Pays $5-25.**

Tips: "To break in, absolutely make sure that your work will be of interest to all bartenders across the country. Your style of writing should reflect the audience you are addressing. The most frequent mistake made by writers in completing an article for us is using the wrong subject."

CHEF, The Food Magazine for Professionals, Talcott Communications Corp., 20 N. Wacker Dr., Suite 1865, Chicago IL 60606. (312)849-2220. Fax: (312)849-2174. E-mail: chef@talcott.com. Website: www.chefmagazine.com. Managing Editor: Kate Harrigan. **Contact:** Brent T. Frei, editor-in-chief. **40% freelance written.** Monthly magazine covering chefs in all food-service segments. "*Chef* is the one magazine that communicates food production to a commercial, professional audience in a meaningful way." Circ. 50,000. **Pays on acceptance.** Byline given. Offers 10% kill fee. Buys first North American serial, second serial (reprint) rights. Editorial lead time 2 months. Submit seasonal material 4 months in advance. Accepts queries by mail, e-mail, fax. Responds in 3 weeks to queries; 2 months to mss. Sample copy and writer's guidelines free.

Nonfiction: Book excerpts, essays, exposé, general interest, historical/nostalgic, how-to (create a dish or perform a technique), humor, inspirational, interview/profile, new product, opinion, personal experience, photo feature, technical. **Buys 24-36 mss/year.** Query. Length: 750-1,500 words. **Pays $250-500.** Sometimes pays expenses of writers on assignment.

Reprints: Accepts previously published submissions.

Photos: State availability with submission. Reviews transparencies. Buys one-time rights. Negotiates payment individually. Captions, identification of subjects required.

Columns/Departments: Taste (modern versions of classic dishes), 1,000-1,200 words; Dish (professional chef profiles), 1,000-1,200 words; Savor (themed recipes), 1,000-1,500 words; Spin (menu trends), 750-1,250 words. **Buys 12-18 mss/year.** Query. **Pays $250-400.**

Tips: "Know food and apply it to the business of chefs. Always query first, *after* you've read our magazine. Tell us how your idea can be used by our readers to enhance their businesses in some way."

$ $ CHRISTIAN CAMP & CONFERENCE JOURNAL, Christian Camping International U.S.A., P.O. Box 62189, Colorado Springs CO 80962-2189. (719)260-9400. Fax: (719)260-6398. E-mail: editor@cciusa.org. Website: www.cciusa.org. **Contact:** Natalee Roth, editor. **75% freelance written.** Prefers to work with published/established writers. Bimonthly magazine emphasizing the broad scope of organized camping with emphasis on Christian camping. "All who work in youth camps and adult conferences read our magazine for inspiration and to get practical help in ways to serve in their operations." Estab. 1963. Circ. 7,500. Pays on publication. Publishes ms an average of 4 months after acceptance. Byline given. Buys negotiable rights. Submit seasonal material 6 months in advance. Accepts queries by mail, e-mail. Responds in 1 month to queries. Sample copy for $2.25 plus 9×12 SASE. Writer's guidelines for #10 SASE.

Nonfiction: General interest (trends in organized camping in general, Christiam camping in particular), how-to (anything involved with organized camping from motivating staff, to programming, to record keeping, to camper follow-up), inspirational, interview/profile (with movers and shakers in Christian camping; submit a list of basic questions first), opinion (letter to the editor). **Buys 20-30 mss/year.** Query required. Length: 500-3,000 words. **Pays 12¢/word.**

Reprints: Send photocopy and information about when and where the material previously appeared. Pays 50% of amount paid for an original article.

Photos: Price negotiable for 35mm color transparencies.

The online magazine carries original content not found in the print edition. Contact: Natalee Roth, online editor.

Tips: "The most frequent mistake made by writers is that they send articles unrelated to our readers. Ask for our publication guidelines first. Profiles/interviews are the best bet for freelancers."

CLUB MANAGEMENT, The Resource for Successful Club Operations, Finan Publishing Company, 107 W. Pacific Ave., St. Louis MO 63119-2323. (314)961-6644. Fax: (314)961-4809. E-mail: avincent@finan.com. Website: www.club-mgmt.com. **Contact:** Anne Marie Vincent, editor. Bimonthly magazine covering club management, private club market, hospitality industry. Estab. 1925. Circ. 16,702. Pays on publication. Publishes ms an average of 2 months after acceptance. Buys first North American serial, electronic rights. Accepts queries by mail, e-mail, fax.

Nonfiction: General interest, historical/nostalgic, how-to, interview/profile, personal experience, photo feature, technical, travel. **Buys 100 mss/year.** Query with published clips. Length: 1,500-2,500 words.

Photos: State availability with submission.

Columns/Departments: Sports (private club sports: golf, tennis, yachting, fitness, etc.).

Tips: "We don't accept blind submissions. Please submit a résumé and clips of writer's work."

N $ $ EL RESTAURANTE MEXICANO, P.O. Box 2249, Oak Park IL 60303-2249. (708)445-9454. Fax: (708)445-9477. E-mail: brendar@enteract.com. **Contact:** Kathleen Furore, editor. Quarterly magazine covering Mexican restaurants. "*El Restaurante Mexicano* offers features and business-related articles that are geared specifically to owners and operators of Mexican, Tex-Mex and Southwestern cuisine restaurants." Estab. 1997. Circ. 25,000. Pays on publication. Publishes ms an average of 3 months after acceptance. Byline given. Buys first North American serial rights. Responds in 2 months to queries. Sample copy free.

Nonfiction: Looking for stories about unique Mexican restaurants and about business issues that affect Mexican restaurant owners. "No specific knowledge of food or restaurants is needed; the key qualification is to be a good reporter who knows how to slant a story toward the Mexican restaurant operator." **Buys 2-4 mss/year.** Query with published clips. Length: 1,200-1,800 words. **Pays $225.** Pays expenses of writers on assignment.

Tips: "Query with a story idea and tell how it pertains to Mexican restaurants."

$ $ HOSPITALITY TECHNOLOGY, Edgell Communications, 4 Middlebury Blvd., Randolph NJ 07869. (973)252-0100. Fax: (973)252-9020. E-mail: jskorupa@edgellmail.com. Website: www.htmagazine.com. **Contact:** Joe Skorupa, senior editor. **85% freelance written.** Magazine published 9 times/year. "We cover the technology used in foodservice and lodging. Our readers are the end-users, who have varying degrees of technical knowledge." Estab. 1996. Circ. 16,000. **Pays on acceptance.** Publishes ms an average of 1 month after acceptance. Byline given. Offers 100% kill fee. Makes work-for-hire assignments. Editorial lead time 2 months. Submit seasonal material 3 months in advance. Accepts queries by mail, e-mail, fax, phone. Responds in 2 weeks to queries. Sample copy and writer's guidelines free.

Nonfiction: How-to, interview/profile, new product, technical. Special issues: "Our Buyers Guide includes editorial material on market overviews. Published in November of each year. We also publish two studies each year, the Restaurant Industry Technology Study and the Lodging Industry Technology Study." No unsolicited mss. **Buys 30 mss/year.** Query with published clips. Length: 1,000-1,200 words. **Pays $600.** Sometimes pays expenses of writers on assignment.

Photos: State availability of or send photos with submission. Reviews contact sheets, negatives, 5×7 transparencies, 5×7 prints. Buys all rights. Offers no additional payment for photos accepted with ms or offers $100-200/photo, or negotiates payment individually. Captions, identification of subjects, model releases required.

N **$ $ HOTELIER**, Kostuch Publications, 23 Lesmill Rd., Don Mills Ontario M3B 3P6, Canada. (416)447-0888. Fax: (416)447-5333. E-mail: rcaira@foodservice.ca. Website: www.foodserviceworld.com. Associate Editor: Carol Neshevich. **Contact:** Rosanna Caira, editor. **40% freelance written.** Bimonthly magazine covering the Canadian hotel industry. Estab. 1989. Circ. 8,000. Pays on publication. Byline given. Buys first North American serial rights. Editorial lead time 3 months. Submit seasonal material 2 months in advance. Accepts queries by mail, fax. Sample copy and writer's guidelines free.
Nonfiction: How-to, new product. No case studies. **Buys 30-50 mss/year.** Query with or without published clips. Length: 700-1,500 words. **Pays $35 for assigned articles.** Sometimes pays expenses of writers on assignment.
Photos: Send photos with submission. Offers $30-75/photo.

N **$ $ $ PIZZA TODAY, The Monthly Professional Guide to Pizza Profits**, Macfadden Protech, LLC, P.O. Box 1347, New Albany IN 47151. (812)949-0909. Fax: (812)941-9711. E-mail: scoomes@pizzatoday.com. Website: www.PizzaToday.com. **Contact:** Steve Coomes, editor-in-chief. **30% freelance written.** Works only with publishes/established writers. Monthly magazine for the pizza industry, covering trends, features of successful pizza operators, business and management advice, etc. Estab. 1983. Circ. 40,000. **Pays on acceptance.** Publishes ms an average of 2 months after acceptance. Byline given. Offers 10-30% kill fee. Buys all rights. Submit seasonal material 3 months in advance. Accepts queries by mail, e-mail, fax. Responds in 2 months to queries; 3 weeks to mss. Sample copy for 10×13 SAE and 6 first-class stamps. Writer's guidelines for #10 SASE.
Nonfiction: Interview/profile, entrepreneurial slants, pizza production and delivery, employee training, hiring, marketing and business management. No fillers, humor or poetry. **Buys 50 mss/year.** Length: 1,000-1,500 words. **Pays 50¢/word, occasionally more.** Sometimes pays expenses of writers on assignment.
Photos: Reviews contact sheets, negatives, transparencies, color slides, 5×7 prints. Captions required.
Tips: "Writers should have a strong pizza business and foodservice background."

$ $ RESORT MANAGEMENT & OPERATIONS, The Resort Resource, Finan Publishing Company, 107 W. Pacific Ave., St. Louis MO 63119-2323. (314)961-6644. Fax: (314)961-4809. E-mail: dmarshal@finan.com. Website: www.resort-mgmt.com. **Contact:** Dan Marshall, editor. Bimonthly magazine covering resort management and operations, hospitality industry. Estab. 1998. Circ. 15,116. **Pays on acceptance.** Buys first North American serial, electronic rights. Accepts queries by mail, e-mail, fax.
Nonfiction: "Do not send blind submissions. We assign pieces based on queries and clips only." **Buys 100 mss/year.** Query with published clips. Length: 1,500-2,500 words.
Tips: "Plese submit résumé and clips of writer's work."

N **RESTAURANTS USA**, National Restaurant Association, 1200 17th St. NW, Washington DC 20036. (800)424-5156. Fax: (202)973-3959. E-mail: jbatty@dileart.org. Website: www.restaurant.org. Managing Editor: Sarah Smith Hamaker. **Contact:** Jennifer Batty, editor. **40% freelance written.** Monthly magazine covering restaurant industry. "*Restaurants USA* is a how-to magazine for owners, operators, caterers, fast-food franchises, mom-and-pop operators and corporate executives." Estab. 1980. Circ. 44,000. **Pays on acceptance.** Publishes ms an average of 3 months after acceptance. Byline given. Buys all rights. Editorial lead time 3 months. Submit seasonal material 6 months in advance. Accepts queries by mail, e-mail, fax. Accepts simultaneous submissions. Responds in 6 weeks to queries; 2 months to mss. Sample copy and writer's guidelines free.
Nonfiction: How-to, business and management topics, technology as it relates to the restaurant industry. No humor, personal experience. **Buys 20-30 mss/year.** Query. Length: 1,500-2,500 words. **Pay varies.**
Photos: Send photos with submission. Reviews negatives, transparencies, prints. Buys one-time rights. Offers no additional payment for photos accepted with ms. Identification of subjects required.
Tips: "Any article written for *Restaurants USA* should help readers conduct their businesses more effectively, suggest new ideas or highlight trends with an emphasis on facts within the how-to framework. If a particular article does not lend itself to the how-to treatment—such as an article that explains a trend—then it should be accompanied by a sidebar, which contains related tips or practical information."

N **$ $ WESTERN HOTELIER MAGAZINE**, Mercury Publications Ltd., 1839 Inkster Blvd., Winnipeg, Manitoba R2X 1R3, Canada. (204)954-2085. Fax: (204)954-2057. E-mail: mp@mercury.mb.ca. Website: www.mercury.mb.ca/. Editor: Kelly Gray. **Contact:** Kristi Balon, editorial coordinator. **45% freelance written.** Quarterly magazine covering the hotel industry. Circ. 4,342. Pays 30-45 days from receipt of invoice. Byline given. Offers 33% kill fee. Buys first rights. Submit seasonal material 3 months in advance. Accepts queries by mail, e-mail, fax. Accepts simultaneous submissions. Responds in 2 weeks to queries. Sample copy and writer's guidelines free or by e-mail.
Nonfiction: How-to (train staff), interview/profile. No industry reports or profiles on companies. Query with published clips. Length: 500-9,000 words. **Pays 25-35¢/word.** Sometimes pays expenses of writers on assignment.
Photos: State availability with submission. Reviews negatives, transparencies, 3×5 prints, jpeg, eps or tif files. Buys all rights. Negotiates payment individually. Captions required.

Columns/Departments: Across the West (hotel news from various parts of Western Canada), 100-500 words. Query. **Pays $0-100.**

Fillers: Facts. Length: 100 words.

Tips: "Send an e-mailed, faxed or mailed query outlining your experience, interests and pay expectations. A requirement also is clippings."

N $ $ WESTERN RESTAURANT NEWS, Mercury Publications Ltd., 1839 Inkster Blvd., Winnipeg, Manitoba R2X 1R3, Canada. (204)954-2085. Fax: (204)954-2057. E-mail: mp@mercury.mb.ca. Website: www.mercury.mb .ca/. Editor: Kelly Gray. **Contact:** Kristi Balon, editorial coordinator. **33% freelance written.** Bimonthly magazine covering the restaurant trade. Reports profiles and industry reports on associations, regional business developments etc. Estab. 1994. Circ. 14,532. Pays 30-45 days from receipt of invoice. Byline given. Offers 33% kill fee. Buys first rights. Submit seasonal material 3 months in advance. Accepts queries by mail, e-mail, fax. Accepts simultaneous submissions. Sample copy and writer's guidelines free or by e-mail.

Nonfiction: How-to, interview/profile. No industry reports or profiles on companies. Query with published clips. Length: 500-9,000 words. **Pays 25-35¢/word.** Sometimes pays expenses of writers on assignment.

Photos: State availability with submission. Reviews negatives, transparencies, 3×5 prints, jpeg, eps or tif files. Buys all rights. Negotiates payment individually. Captions required.

Columns/Departments: Across the West (restaurant news from Western Canada), 100-500 words. Query. **Payment varies.**

Fillers: Facts. Length: 100 words.

Tips: "Send an e-mailed, faxed or mailed query outlining your experience, interests and pay expectations. A requirement also is clippings."

INDUSTRIAL OPERATIONS

Industrial plant managers, executives, distributors and buyers read these journals. Some industrial management journals are also listed under the names of specific industries. Publications for industrial supervisors are listed in Management & Supervision.

$ $ CANADIAN PLASTICS, Southam Publishing Magazine Group, 1450 Don Mills Rd, Don Mills, Ontario M3B 2X7, Canada. (416)442-2290. Fax: (416)442-2213. E-mail: mlegault@corporate.southam.com. Associate Editor: Cindy Macdonald. **Contact:** Michael LeGault, editor. **20% freelance written.** Monthly magazine covering plastics. "*Canadian Plastics Magazine* reports on and interprets development in plastics markets and technologies for plastics processors and end-users based in Canada." Estab. 1942. Circ. 11,000. Pays on publication. Publishes ms an average of 3 months after acceptance. Byline sometimes given. Offers 25% kill fee. Editorial lead time 2 months. Submit seasonal material 4 months in advance. Responds in 2 weeks to queries; 1 month to mss. Sample copy free.

Nonfiction: Technical, industry news (Canada only). **Buys 6 mss/year.** Query with published clips. Length: 400-1,600 words. **Pays $120-350.** Sometimes pays expenses of writers on assignment.

Photos: State availability with submission.

Columns/Departments: Pays $100-300.

Tips: "Give the editor a call."

N $ $ COMMERCE & INDUSTRY, Mercury Publications Ltd., 1839 Inkster Blvd., Winnipeg, Manitoba R2X 1R3, Canada. (204)954-2085. Fax: (204)954-2057. E-mail: mp@mercury.mb.ca. Website: www.mercury.mb.ca/. Editor: Frank Yeo. **Contact:** Kristi Balon, editorial coordinator. **75% freelance written.** Bimonthly magazine covering the business and industrial sectors. Industry reports and company profiles provide readers with an indepth insight into key areas of interest in their profession. Estab. 1947. Circ. 18,876. Pays 30-45 days from receipt of invoice. Byline given. Offers 33% kill fee. Buys first rights. Submit seasonal material 3 months in advance. Accepts queries by mail, e-mail, fax. Accepts simultaneous submissions. Responds in 2 weeks to queries. Sample copy and writer's guidelines free or by e-mail.

Nonfiction: How-to, interview/profile. No industry reports or profiles on companies. Query with published clips. Length: 500-9,000 words. **Pays 25-35¢/word.** Sometimes pays expenses of writers on assignment.

Photos: State availability with submission. Reviews negatives, transparencies, 3×5 prints, jpeg, eps or tif files. Buys all rights. Negotiates payment individually. Captions required.

Tips: "Send an e-mailed, faxed or mailed query outlining your experience, interests and pay expectations. A requirement also is clippings."

INDUSTRIAL FABRIC PRODUCTS REVIEW, Industrial Fabrics Association International, 1801 County Rd. B W, Roseville MN 55113-4061. (651)222-2508. Fax: (651)225-6966. E-mail: gdnordstrom@ifai.com. Website: www.ifai. com. **Contact:** Galynn Nordstrom, editorial director. **50% freelance written.** staff- and industry-written. Monthly magazine covering industrial textiles and products made from them for company owners, salespeople and researchers in a variety of industrial textile areas. Estab. 1915. Circ. 11,000. Pays on publication. Publishes ms an average of 2 months after acceptance. Byline given. Buys all rights. Accepts queries by mail, e-mail, phone. Responds in 1 month to queries.

O→ Break in by "researching the industry/magazine audience and editorial calendar. The editorial calendar is available on our website at ifai.com. We rarely buy material not directed specifically at our markets."

Nonfiction: Technical, marketing and other topics related to any aspect of industrial fabric industry from fiber to finished fabric product. Special issues: new products, new fabrics and equipment. No historical or apparel-oriented articles. **Buys 8-10 mss/year.** Query with phone number. Length: 1,200-3,000 words.

Tips: "We encourage freelancers to learn our industry and make regular, solicited contributions to the magazine. We do not buy photography."

[N] $ $ $ PEM PLANT ENGINEERING & MAINTENANCE, Clifford/Elliot Ltd., 3228 S. Service Rd., 2nd Floor, West Wing, Burlington Ontario L7N 3H8, Canada. (905)634-2100. Fax: (905)634-2238. E-mail: editor@industrial sourcebook.com. Website: www.industrialsourcebook.com. **Contact:** Paul Challen, editor. **30% freelance written.** Bimonthly magazine looking for "informative articles on issues that affect plant floor operations and maintenance." Circ. 18,500. Pays on publication. Publishes ms an average of 3 months after acceptance. Byline given. Buys one-time rights. Editorial lead time 4 months. Submit seasonal material 4 months in advance. Accepts simultaneous submissions. Responds in 3 weeks to queries; 1 month to mss. Sample copy and writer's guidelines free.

Nonfiction: How-to (how-to keep production downtime to a minimum, how-to better operate an industrial operation), new product, technical. **Buys 6 mss/year.** Query with published clips. Length: 750-4,000 words. **Pays $500-1,400 (Canadian).** Sometimes pays expenses of writers on assignment.

Photos: State availability with submission. Reviews transparencies, prints. Buys one-time rights. Negotiates payment individually. Captions required.

Tips: "Information can be found at our website. Call us for sample issues, ideas, etc."

[N] $ $ QUALITY DIGEST, 40 Declaration Dr., Suite 100, Chico CA 95973. (530)893-4095. Fax: (530)893-0395. E-mail: editorial@qualitydigest.com. Website: www.qualitydigest.com. **Contact:** Scott M. Paton, editor-in-chief. **75% freelance written.** Monthly magazine covering quality improvement. Estab. 1981. Circ. 75,000. **Pays on acceptance.** Byline given. Buys all rights. Submit seasonal material 4 months in advance. Accepts queries by mail, e-mail, fax. Accepts simultaneous submissions. Responds in 3 months to mss. Sample copy and writer's guidelines free.

Nonfiction: Book excerpts, how-to (implement quality programs and solve problems for benefits, etc.), interview/profile, opinion, personal experience, technical. **Buys 2-5 mss/year.** Query with or without published clips or send complete ms. Length: 800-3,000 words. **Pays $200-600 for assigned articles.** Pays in contributor copies for unsolicited mss. Sometimes pays expenses of writers on assignment.

Reprints: Send tearsheet and information about when and where the material previously appeared.

Photos: Send photos with submission. Reviews any size prints. Buys one-time rights. Offers no additional payment for photos accepted with ms. Captions, identification of subjects, model releases required.

■ The online magazine carries original content not found in the print edition and includes writer's guidelines. Contact: Dirk Dusharme.

Tips: "Please be specific in your articles. Explain what the problem was, how it was solved and what the benefits are. Tell the reader how the technique described will benefit him or her. We feature shorter, tighter, more focused articles than in the past. This means we have more articles in each issue. We're striving to present our readers with concise, how-to, easy-to-read information that makes their job easier."

$ $ WEIGHING & MEASUREMENT, WAM Publishing Co., P.O. Box 270, Roscoe IL 61073-0270. (815)636-7739. Fax: (815)636-7741. E-mail: dwam34@inwave.com. Website: www.weighingandmeasurement.com. **Contact:** David M. Mathieu, editor. Bimonthly magazine for users of industrial scales. Estab. 1914. Circ. 13,900. **Pays on acceptance.** Byline given. Offers 20% kill fee. Buys all rights. Accepts queries by mail, e-mail, fax, phone. Responds in 2 weeks to queries. Sample copy for $2.

Nonfiction: Interview/profile (with presidents of companies), personal experience (guest editorials on government involvement in business, etc.), technical, Profile (about users of weighing and measurement equipment), Product reviews. **Buys 15 mss/year.** Query on technical articles; submit complete ms for general interest material. Length: 1,000-2,500 words. **Pays $175-300.**

INFORMATION SYSTEMS

These publications give computer professionals more data about their field. Consumer computer publications are listed under Personal Computers.

$ $ $ CARD TECHNOLOGY, Tracking the future of card systems and applications, Faulkner & Gray, 3005 Wacker Dr., 18th Floor, Chicago IL 60606. Fax: (312)913-1340. E-mail: don.davis@tfn.com. Website: www.cardte chnology.com. Managing Editor: Dan Balaban. **Contact:** Don Davis, editor. **20% freelance written.** Monthly magazine covering smart cards. "*Card Technology* covers all uses of smart cards worldwide, as well as other advanced plastic card technologies. Aimed at senior management, not technical staff. Our readership is global, as is our focus." Estab.

1996. Circ. 28,000. **Pays on acceptance.** Byline given. Offers negotiable kill fee. Buys all rights. Editorial lead time 1 month. Submit seasonal material 2 months in advance. Accepts queries by e-mail. Responds in 1 week to queries; 1 month to mss. Sample copy free.

Nonfiction: Interview/profile, opinion. **Buys 15 mss/year.** Query with published clips. Length: 2,000-4,000 words. **Pays $500-1,500.** Sometimes pays expenses of writers on assignment.

Photos: State availability with submission. Reviews contact sheets, negatives, transparencies, prints. Rights negotiable. Negotiates payment individually. Identification of subjects required.

◼ The online magazine carries original content not found in the print edition. Contact: Don Davis.

Tips: "We are especially interested in finding freelancers outside of North America who have experience writing about technology issues for business publications."

N $ $ $ CHANNEL BUSINESS, The News Magazine for Value-Added Reselling, Maclean Hunter, 777 Bay St., 4th Floor, Toronto Ontario M5W 1A7, Canada. (416)596-5000. Fax: (416)593-3166. **Contact:** Alison Eastwood, editor. **70% freelance written.** A biweekly Canadian business publication for companies selling computer hardware, software and services, emphasizing strategies for adding value to IT. Topics include high tech trends, business management sales and marketing strategies. Estab. 1988. Circ. 16,183. **Pays on acceptance.** Publishes ms an average of 1 month after acceptance. Byline given. Buys negotiable rights. Editorial lead time 2 months. Sample copy free.

Nonfiction: Interview/profile, new product, technical. **Buys 21 mss/year.** Query with published clips. Length: 800-3,000 words. **Pays $400-800 for assigned articles.**

Photos: State availability with submission. Reviews slides or 4×6 prints. prefers color. Buys negotiable rights. Negotiates payment individually. Identification of subjects required.

Columns/Departments: Small Business (tips for small resellers and system integratory profiles of successful small businesses), 800 words. **Buys 6 mss/year.** Query with published clips. **Pays $400.**

Tips: "Writers need familiarity with technology, specifically with issues that relate to resellers and system integrators. Call before submitting any stories."

$ $ $ DESKTOP ENGINEERING, Complete Computing Resource for Engineers, Helmers Publishing, P.O. Box 874, Peterborough NH 03458. (603)924-9631. Fax: (603)924-4004. E-mail: de-editors@helmers.com. Website: www.deskeng.com. **Contact:** Jennifer M. Runyon, managing editor. **90% freelance written.** Monthly magazine covering microcomputer hardware/software for hands-on design and mechanical engineers and engineering management. Estab. 1995. Circ. 62,000. Pays on publication. Publishes ms an average of 4 months after acceptance. Byline given. Buys all rights. Editorial lead time 3 months. Accepts queries by mail, e-mail, fax, phone. Responds in 6 weeks to queries; 6 months to mss. Sample copy free; editorial calendar online.

Nonfiction: How-to, new product, technical, reviews. "No fluff." **Buys 120 mss/year.** Query. Length: 750-3,000 words. **Pays 60¢/word for assigned articles; negotiable for unsolicited articles.** Sometimes pays expenses of writers on assignment.

Photos: Send photos with submission. Negotiates payment individually. Captions required.

Columns/Departments: Product Briefs (new products), 50-100 words; Reviews (software, hardware, books), 500-1,500 words. **Buys 30 mss/year.** Query. **Payment varies.**

◼ The online magazine carries original content not found in the print edition. Contact: Jennifer M. Runyon.

Tips: "Call the editors or e-mail them for submission tips."

$ $ $ $ GOVERNMENT COMPUTER NEWS, 8601 Georgia Ave., Suite 300, Silver Spring MD 20910. (301)650-2100. Fax: (301)650-2111. E-mail: editor@gen.com. Website: www.gcn.com. **Contact:** Thomas Temin, editorial director. Biweekly for government information technology managers. **Pays on acceptance.** Byline given. Offers variable kill fee. Buys all rights. Responds in 1 month to queries. Sample copy free. Writer's guidelines for #10 SASE.

Nonfiction: **Buys 30 mss/year.** Query. Length: 700-1,200 words. **Pays $800-2,000.** Pays expenses of writers on assignment.

Columns/Departments: Length: 400-600 words. No freelance columns accepted. **Buys 75 mss/year.** Query. **Pays $250-400.**

Fillers: Buys 10/year. Length: 300-500 words. **Pays $250-450.**

Tips: Needs "technical case histories of applications of computers to governmental missions and trends in information technology."

$ $ $ INFORMATION WEEK, 600 Community Dr., Manhasset NY 11030. (516)562-5000. Fax: (516)562-5036. E-mail: speterso@cmp.com. Website: www.informationweek.com. Editor-in-Chief: Bob Evans. **Contact:** Helen Somerset, editorial assistant. **20% freelance written.** Weekly magazine for information systems managers. Estab. 1985. Circ. 440,000. **Pays on acceptance.** Publishes ms an average of 1 month after acceptance. Byline given. Offers 25% kill fee. Buys first rights, non-exclusive serial rights. Accepts simultaneous submissions. Responds in 1 month to mss. Sample copy free. Writer's guidelines for #10 SASE.

Nonfiction: Book excerpts, how-to, interview/profile, new product, technical, News analysis, company profiles. **Buys 30 mss/year.** Query with published clips. Length: 1,500-4,000 words. **Pays $1.10/word minimum.** Pays expenses of writers on assignment.

Reprints: Considers prviously published submissions.

Tips: Needs "feature articles on technology trends—all with a business angle. We look at implementations by users, new products, management issues, intranets, the Internet, web, networks, PCs, objects, workstations, sewers, etc. Our competitors are tabloids—we're better written, more selective, and more analytical."

$ $ ITrecruitermag.com, Employment opportunities and career news for information technology professionals, Quantum Communications Group, Inc., 1493 Chain Bridge Rd., #100, McLean VA 22101. (703)714-9462. Fax: (708)714-9482. E-mail: articles@itrecruitermag.com. Website: itrecruitermag.com. Editor: Loretta W. Prencipe, Senior Editor: Rima Assaker. **Contact:** (by e-mail) articles@itrecruitermag.com. **50% freelance written.** Bimonthly magazine covering information technology recruitment. "*ITrecruitermag.com* is the multimedia source for IT career news and opportunities. Every article must help the IT professional gain an insight into IT work force, career advancement or industry trends." Pays on publication. Publishes ms an average of 2 months after acceptance. Byline given. Offers negotiable kill fee. Buys all rights. Editorial lead time 3 months. Submit seasonal material 4 months in advance. Accepts queries by mail, e-mail, fax. Accepts simultaneous submissions. Sample copy and writer's guidelines free.

Nonfiction: Our sections include: Community; Tech Training; Money; Management 101; and Trends. Book excerpts, how-to, interview/profile, opinion, technical. No "rehashing of the fact that there is an IT labor shortage. Our readers know that." **Buys approximately 60 mss/year.** Query with published clips. Length: 700-2,100 words. **Pays 30¢/word.** Sometimes pays expenses of writers on assignment.

Reprints: Accepts previously published submissions.

Photos: Send photos with submission. Offers no additional payment for photos accepted with ms. Captions, identification of subjects required.

Columns/Departments: Recruiters' Corner (how-to and advice for technical recruiters and hiring managers). Query.

Tips: All articles should include quotes from IT professionals—our readers' colleagues. Writing should be clear, crisp, simple, informal and direct. Use active verbs. Each article should answer at least two of the following questions. Does this piece: Assist the IT professional in managing his career, assist the IT professional in managing his staff, or convey cutting-edge IT workforce issues?

$ JOURNAL OF INFORMATION ETHICS, McFarland & Co., Inc., Publishers, 720 Fourth Ave. S, St. Cloud State University, St. Cloud MN 56301. (320)255-4822. Fax: (320)255-4778. E-mail: hauptman@stcloudstate.edu. **Contact:** Robert Hauptman, LRTS, editor. **90% freelance written.** Semiannual scholarly journal. "Addresses ethical issues in all of the information sciences with a deliberately interdisciplinary approach. Topics range from electronic mail monitoring to library acquisition of controversial material. The journal's aim is to present thoughtful considerations of ethical dilemmas that arise in a rapidly evolving system of information exchange and dissemination." Estab. 1992. Circ. 500. Pays on publication. Publishes ms an average of 9 months after acceptance. Byline given. Buys all rights. Submit seasonal material 8 months in advance. Accepts queries by mail, e-mail, fax, phone. Sample copy for $21. Writer's guidelines free.

Nonfiction: Essays, opinion, book reviews. **Buys 10 mss/year.** Send complete ms. Length: 500-3,500 words. **Pays $25-50 depending on length.**

Tips: "Familiarize yourself with the many areas subsumed under the rubric of information ethics, e.g., privacy, scholarly communication, errors, peer review, confidentiality, e-mail, etc. Present a well-rounded discussion of any fresh, current or evolving ethical topic within the information sciences, or involving real-world information collection/exchange."

$ $ NEWS/400, Duke Communications International, 221 E. 29th St., Loveland CO 80538. (970)663-4700. Fax: (970)663-3285. E-mail: editors@as400network.com. Website: www.news400.com. **Contact:** Gina Schlagel, assistant acquisitions editor. **40% freelance written.** Magazine published 14 times/year. "Programming, networking, IS management, technology for users of IBM AS/400 platform." Estab. 1982. Circ. 30,000 (international). Pays on publication. Publishes ms an average of 3 months after acceptance. Byline given. Offers 50% kill fee. Buys first, second serial (reprint), all rights. Editorial lead time 4 months. Submit seasonal material 4 months in advance. Accepts queries by mail, e-mail, fax, phone. Responds in 3 weeks to queries; 5 weeks to mss. Writer's guidelines online.

Nonfiction: Book excerpts, opinion, technical. **Buys 70 mss/year.** Query. Length: 1,500-2,500 words. **Pays 17-50¢/ word for assigned articles.** Pays in contributor copies upon request of the author. Sometimes pays expenses of writers on assignment.

Reprints: Send photocopy. Payment negotiable.

Photos: State availability with submission. Offers no additional payment for photos accepted with ms.

Columns/Departments: Dialog Box (computer industry opinion), 1,500 words; Load'n'go (complete utility). **Buys 24 mss/year.** Query. **Pays $250-1,000.**

■ The online magazine carries original content not found in the print edition and includes writer's guidelines. Contact: Gina Schlagel.

Tips: "Be familiar with IBM AS/400 computer platform."

$ $ $ ▣ PLANET IT, News, Technology, Advice, Community, CMP Media, 600 Community Dr., Manhasset NY 11030. E-mail: pkrass@cmp.com. Website: www.PlanetIT.com. Managing Editor: Joy Blake. **Contact:** Peter Krass, editor. **25% freelance written.** Website covering information technology. "Our audience consists of information technology professionals in business, government, education and healthcare." Estab. 1998. Circ. 250,000. **Pays on acceptance.** Byline given. Offers 25% kill fee. Buys first, electronic rights. Editorial lead time 1 month. Accepts queries by e-mail. Responds in 2 weeks to queries; 1 month to mss. Sample copy online.

Nonfiction: How-to, new product, opinion, technical. No poetry, fiction, essays. Query with published clips. Length: 1,500 words. **Pays 75¢-$1.** Pays expenses of writers on assignment.

[N] PUBLISH, Internet Communication for the New Economy, 462 Boston St., Topsfield MA 01983. (978)887-7900. Fax: (978)887-6117. E-mail: edit@publish.com. Website: www.publish.com. Editor-in-Chief: Renee LeWinter. **Contact:** M. Reyen. **80% freelance written.** Monthly magazine for Internet communication professionals. "*Publish* focuses on the critical issues facing senior-level professionals who are leading their companies into the Internet Communication Age while managing the content and marketing strategies, and overall site operations. Designed to bridge the gap between communications strategy and marketing technology, editorial provides communication strategists guidance and insightful analysis along with the latest news and features impacting today's Internet, communications and e-commerce strategies." Estab. 1986. Circ. 97,000. Pays on publication. Publishes ms an average of 5 months after acceptance. Byline given. Buys all rights.

Nonfiction: Analysis, feature stories, news, trends. **Buys 120 mss/year.** Query with published clips. No unsolicited mss. Length: 400-2,300 words.

Photos: Send photos with submission. Captions, identification of subjects required.

Tips: "We prefer to be contacted by e-mail or mail."

SYS ADMIN, CMP Media, Inc., 1601 W. 23rd St., Suite 200, Lawrence KS 66046. (785)838-7555. Fax: (785)841-2047. E-mail: REndsley@MFI.com. Website: www.sysadminmag.com. Editor: Ralph Barker. **Contact:** Rikki Endsley, associate managing editor. **90% freelance written.** Monthly magazine. "*Sys Admin* is written for UNIX systems administrators. Articles are practical and technical. Our authors are practicing UNIX systems administrators." Estab. 1992. Circ. 60,000. Pays on publication. Publishes ms an average of 6 months after acceptance. Byline given. Offers $150 kill fee. Buys all rights. Editorial lead time 4 months. Accepts queries by mail, e-mail, fax, phone. Accepts simultaneous submissions. Responds in 1 month to queries. Sample copy free.

Nonfiction: Technical. **Buys 40-60 mss/year.** Query. Length: 1,000 words. **Payment varies.**

INSURANCE

$ $ $ BUSINESS & HEALTH, Keys to Workforce Productivity, Medical Economics Publishing Co., 5 Paragon Dr., Montvale NJ 07645-1742. (201)358-7276. Fax: (201)772-2686. E-mail: rick.service@medec.com. Website: www.businessandhealth.com. **Contact:** Richard Service, editor. **60% freelance written.** Published 10 times/year. "*B&H* carries articles about how employers can cut their health care costs and improve the quality of care they provide to workers. We also write about health care policy at the federal, state and local levels." Estab. 1983. Circ. 45,000. **Pays on acceptance.** Publishes ms an average of 2 months after acceptance. Byline given. Offers 20% kill fee. Buys all rights. Editorial lead time 2 months. Submit seasonal material 4 months in advance. Accepts queries by mail, e-mail, fax. Responds in 3 months to mss. Writer's guidelines for #10 SASE.

Nonfiction: How-to (cut health care benefits costs, provide better care), Case studies (of successful employer-led efforts); trend piece on broad issues such as 24-hour coverage or benefits for retirees. **Buys approximately 50 mss/year.** Query with published clips and SASE. Length: 2,000-3,500 words. **Pays $1,000-1,700 for features.** Pays expenses of writers on assignment.

Columns/Departments: Primarily staff written but will consider queries.

Tips: "Please be familiar with *B&H* and follow writer's guidelines. Articles should combine a business angle with a human interest approach and address both cost-containment and quality of care. Include cost-benefit analysis data and material for charts or graphs whenever possible."

$ FLORIDA UNDERWRITER, National Underwriter Co., 9887 Fourth St., N., Suite 230, St. Petersburg FL 33702-2488. (727)576-1101. Fax: (727)577-4002. Editorial Director: Ian Mackenzie. **Contact:** James E. Seymour, editor. **20% freelance written.** Monthly magazine. "*Florida Underwriter* covers insurance for Florida insurance professionals: producers, executives, risk managers, employee benefit administrators. We want material about any insurance line, Life & Health or Property & Casualty, but *must* have a Florida tag—Florida authors preferred." Estab. 1984. Circ. 10,000. Pays on publication. Publishes ms an average of 3 months after acceptance. Byline given. Buys all rights. Submit seasonal material 3 months in advance. Accepts queries by mail, fax. Accepts simultaneous submissions. Responds in 1 month to mss. Sample copy and writer's guidelines free.

Nonfiction: "Industry experts contribute in return for exposure." Essays, exposé, historical/nostalgic, how-to, interview/profile, new product, opinion, technical. "We don't want articles that aren't about insurance for insurance people or those that lack Florida angle. No puff pieces. Note: Most non-inhouse pieces are contributed gratis by industry experts." **Buys 6 mss/year.** Query with or without published clips or send complete ms. Length: 500-1,500 words. **Pays $50-150 for assigned articles; $25-100 for unsolicited articles.** Sometimes pays expenses of writers on assignment.

Reprints: Send tearsheet, photocopy or typed ms with rights for sale noted and information about when and where the material previously appeared. Pays 40% of amount paid for an original article.

Photos: State availability of or send photos with submission. Reviews 5×7 prints. Offers no additional payment for photos accepted with ms. Identification of subjects required.

$ $ GEICO DIRECT, K.L. Publications, 2001 Killebrew Dr., Suite 105, Bloomington MN 55425-1879. (952)854-0155. Fax: (952)854-9440. E-mail: klpub@aol.com. **Contact:** Jan Brenny, editor. **60% freelance written.** Semiannual magazine published for the government Employees Insurance Company (GEICO) policyholders. Estab. 1988. Circ. 4,000,000. **Pays on acceptance.** Byline given. Buys first North American serial rights. Accepts queries by mail. Responds in 3 months to queries. Writer's guidelines for #10 SASE.

    O—**⚡** Break in by "submitting an idea (or editorial approach) for auto/home safety or themed regional travel—one theme with several destinations around the country—that is unique, along with proof of research and writing ability."

Nonfiction: Americana, home and auto safety, car care, financial, lifestyle. General interest (for 50 plus audience), how-to (auto/home related only), technical (auto), travel. Query with published clips. Length: 1,000-2,200 words. **Pays $300-650.**

Photos: Reviews 35mm transparencies. Payment varies.

Columns/Departments: Moneywise, 50+, Your Car. Length: 500-600 words. Query with published clips. **Pays $175-350.**

Tips: "We prefer work from published/established writers, especially those with specialized knowledge of the insurance industry, safety issues and automotive topics."

JEWELRY

$ $ AJM: THE AUTHORITY ON JEWELRY MANUFACTURING, (formerly *American Jewelry Manufacturers*), Manufacturing Jewelers and Suppliers of America, 45 Royal Little Dr., Providence RI 02904. (401)274-3840. Fax: (401)274-0265. E-mail: ajm@ajm-magazine.com. Website: www.ajm-magazine.com. **Contact:** Rich Youmans, editor/associate publisher. **75% freelance written.** Monthly magazine. "*AJM* is a monthly magazine providing technical, marketing and business information for finished jewelry manufacturers and supporting industries." Estab. 1956. **Pays on acceptance.** Publishes ms an average of 6 months after acceptance. Byline given. Buys all rights for limited period of 18 months. Editorial lead time 1 year. Submit seasonal material 6 months in advance. Accepts queries by mail, e-mail, fax. Responds in 2 months to mss. Sample copy and writer's guidelines free.

Nonfiction: All articles should focus on jewelry manufacturing techniques, especially how-to and technical articles. How-to, new product, technical. "No generic articles for a wide variety of industries, articles for hobbyists, or articles written for a consumer audience. Our focus is professional jewelry manufacturers and designers, and articles for AJM should be carefully targeted for this audience." **Buys 40 mss/year.** Query. Length: 2,500-3,000 words. **Pays $300-500 for assigned articles.** Sometimes pays expenses of writers on assignment.

Reprints: Occasionally accepts previously published submissions. Query.

Photos: State availability with submission. Buys one-time rights. Negotiates payment individually. Captions required.

Tips: "Because our editorial content is highly focused and specific, we assign most article topics rather than relying on outside queries. We are, as a result, always seeking new writers comfortable with business and technical topics who will work with us long term and whom we can develop into 'experts' in jewelry manufacturing. We invite writers to send an introductory letter and clips highlighting business and technical writing skills if they would like to be considered for a specific assignment."

$ THE DIAMOND REGISTRY BULLETIN, 580 Fifth Ave., #806, New York NY 10036. (212)575-0444. Fax: (212)575-0722. E-mail: diamond58@aol.com. Website: www.diamondregistry.com. **Contact:** Joseph Schlussel, editor-in-chief. **50% freelance written.** Monthly newsletter. Estab. 1969. Pays on publication. Buys all rights. Submit seasonal material 1 month in advance. Accepts queries by mail, e-mail. Accepts simultaneous submissions. Responds in 3 weeks to mss. Sample copy for $5.

Nonfiction: How-to (ways to increase sales in diamonds, improve security, etc.), interview/profile (of interest to diamond dealers or jewelers), Prevention advice (on crimes against jewelers). Send complete ms. Length: 50-500 words. **Pays $75-150.**

Tips: "We seek ideas to increase sales of diamonds."

$ $ FASHION ACCESSORIES, S.C.M. Publications, Inc., P.O. Box 859, Mahwah NJ 07430-0859. (201)684-9222. Fax: (201)684-9228. **Contact:** Samuel Mendelson, publisher. Monthly newspaper covering costume or fashion jewelry. Published for executives in the manufacturing, wholesaling and retail buying of fashion jewelry and accessories. Estab. 1951. Circ. 9,500. **Pays on acceptance.** Byline given. Not copyrighted. Buys first rights. Submit seasonal material 3 months in advance. Sample copy for $2 and 9×12 SAE with 4 first-class stamps.

Nonfiction: Essays, general interest, historical/nostalgic, interview/profile, new product. **Buys 20 mss/year.** Query with published clips. Length: 1,000-2,000 words. **Pays $100-300.**

Photos: Send photos with submission. Reviews 4×5 prints. Buys one-time rights. Offers no additional payment for photos accepted with ms.

Columns/Departments: Fashion Report (interviews and reports of fashion news), 1,000-2,000 words.

Tips: "We are interested in anything that will be of interest to costume jewelry buyers."

$ $LUSTRE, The Jeweler's Magazine on Design & Style, Cygnus Publishing Company, 24 Mountain Ridge Dr., Cedar Grove NJ 07009. (631)845-2700. Fax: (631)845-7109. E-mail: loraine. depasque@cygnuspub.com. Website: www.lustremag.com. Managing Editor: Matthew Kramer. **Contact:** Lorraine DePasque, editor-in-chief. Bimonthly trade magazine covering fine jewelry and related accessories. "*LUSTRE* is dedicated to helping the retail jeweler stock, merchandise, sell and profit from upscale, high-quality brand name and designer jewelry. Many stories are how-to. We also offer sophisticated graphics to showcase new products." Estab. 1997. Circ. 12,200. Pays on publication. Publishes ms an average of 4 months after acceptance. Byline given. Offers 50% kill fee. Buys all rights. Editorial lead time 4 months. Submit seasonal material 4 months in advance. Accepts queries by mail. Responds in 4 weeks to queries. Sample copy free.

Nonfiction: How-to, new product. **Buys 18 mss/year.** Query with published clips. Length: 1,000-2,500 words. **Pays $500.** Sometimes pays expenses of writers on assignment.

Photos: State availability with submission. Buys one-time rights plus usage for one year after publication date (but not exclusive usage). Offers no additional payment for photos accepted with ms. Captions, identification of subjects required.

Columns/Departments: Celebrity Link (tie in designer jewelry with celebrity), 500 words; Details (news about designer jewelry), 500 words; International Eye, 500 words. **Buys 8 mss/year.** Query. **Pays $500.**

Tips: "Step 1: Request an issue sent to them; call (212) 921-1091; ask for assistant. Step 2: Write a letter to Lorraine with clips. Step 3: Lorraine will call back. Background in jewelry is helpful."

N $ $MODERN JEWELER, Cygnus Business Media, 19 W. 44th St., Suite 1405, New York NY 10036-5902. (212)921-1091. Fax: (212)921-5539. Website: www.modernjeweler.com. Managing Editor: Matthew Kramer. **Contact:** Barbara Moss, editor. **20% freelance written.** Monthly magazine covering fine jewelry and watches. Estab. 1901. Circ. 33,000. **Pays on acceptance.** Publishes ms an average of 2 months after acceptance. Byline given. Buys all rights. Editorial lead time 2 months. Submit seasonal material 2 months in advance. Accepts queries by mail, fax. Responds in 3 weeks to queries; 3 months to mss. Sample copy for SAE.

Nonfiction: Technical. **Buys 7-10 mss/year.** Query with published clips. **Pays $350 for assigned articles; $100 for unsolicited articles.** Sometimes pays expenses of writers on assignment.

Photos: State availability with submission. Reviews transparencies, prints. Buys one-time or all rights.

Tips: "Requires knowledge of retail business, experience in dealing with retail and manufacturing executives and analytical writing style."

JOURNALISM & WRITING

Journalism and writing magazines cover both the business and creative sides of writing. Writing publications offer inspiration and support for professional and beginning writers. Although there are many valuable writing publications that do not pay, we list those that pay for articles.

N $ $ $ $AMERICAN JOURNALISM REVIEW, 1117 Journalism Bldg., University of Maryland, College Park MD 20742. (301)405-8803. Fax: (301)405-8323. E-mail: editor@ajr.org. Website: www.ajr.org. Editor: Rem Rieder. **Contact:** Valarie Basheda, managing editor. **80% freelance written.** Monthly magazine covering print, broadcast and online journalism. "Mostly journalists subscribe. We cover ethical issues, trends in the industry, coverage that falls short." Circ. 27,000. Pays within 30 days after publication. Publishes ms an average of 2 months after acceptance. Byline given. Offers 50% kill fee. Buys first North American serial, electronic rights. Editorial lead time 1 month. Accepts queries by mail, e-mail, fax. Responds in 3 weeks to queries. Sample copy for $4.95 pre-paid or online. Writer's guidelines free or online.

Nonfiction: Exposé, humor, interview/profile, personal experience, ethical issues. **Buys many mss/year.** Query with published clips or send complete ms. Length: 500-4,000 words. **Pays $250-2,000.** Pays expenses of writers on assignment.

Fillers: Lori Robertson, assistant managing editor. Anecdotes, facts, short humor. Length: 150-500 words. **Pays $100-250.**

Tips: "Write a short story for the front-of-the-book section. We prefer queries to completed articles. Include in a page what you'd like to write about, who you'll interview, why it's important and why you should write it."

$AUTHORSHIP, National Writers Association, 3140 S. Peoria, #295, Aurora CO 80014. (303)841-0246. E-mail: sandywrter@aol.com. Editor: Sandy Whelchel. **Contact:** Kathe Gustafson. Quarterly magazine covering writing articles only. "Association magazine targeted to beginning and professional writers. Covers how-to, humor, marketing issues." Disk and e-mail submissions given preference. Estab. 1950s. Circ. 4,000. **Pays on acceptance.** Byline given. Buys first North American serial, second serial (reprint) rights. Editorial lead time 3 months. Submit seasonal material 6 months in advance. Accepts simultaneous submissions. Responds in 2 months to queries. Sample copy for #10 SASE.

Nonfiction: Writing only. Poetry (January/February). **Buys 25 mss/year.** Query or send complete ms. Length: 900 words. **Pays $10 or discount on memberships and copies.**

Photos: State availability with submission. Reviews 5×7 prints. Buys one-time rights. Offers no additional payment for photos accepted with ms. Identification of subjects, model releases required.
Tips: "Members of National Writers Association are given preference."

$ BOOK DEALERS WORLD, North American Bookdealers Exchange, P.O. Box 606, Cottage Grove OR 97424. (541)258-2625. Fax: (541)258-2625. Website: www.bookmarketingprofits.com. **Contact:** Al Galasso, editorial director. **50% freelance written.** Quarterly magazine covering writing, self-publishing and marketing books by mail. Circ. 20,000. Pays on publication. Publishes ms an average of 3 months after acceptance. Byline given. Buys first North American serial, second serial (reprint) rights. Accepts simultaneous submissions. Responds in 1 month to queries. Sample copy for $3.
Nonfiction: Book excerpts (writing, mail order, direct mail, publishing), how-to (home business by mail, advertising), interview/profile (of successful self-publishers), positive articles on self-publishing, New Writing Angles, Marketing. **Buys 10 mss/year.** Send complete ms. Length: 1,000-1,500 words. **Pays $25-50.**
Reprints: Send typed ms with rights for sale noted and information about when and where the material previously appeared. Pays 80% of amount paid for an original article.
Columns/Departments: Print Perspective (about new magazines and newsletters); Self-Publisher (on successful self-publishers and their marketing strategy). Length: 250-1,000 words. **Buys 20 mss/year.** Send complete ms. **Pays $5-20.**
Fillers: Fillers concerning writing, publishing or books. **Buys 6/year.** Length: 100-250 words. **Pays $3-10.**
Tips: "Query first. Get a sample copy of the magazine."

[N] $ BRIDGES ROMANCE MAGAZINE, Bridges Romance Magazine, P.O. Box 1738, Aztec NM 87410. Fax: (505)564-3705. E-mail: editor@bridges.mag.com. Website: www.bridgesmag.com. Managing Editor: Sherri Buerkle. **Contact:** Nicke Martinez, editor-in-chief. **65% freelance written.** Bimonthly magazine covering women's fiction reading and writing. "We are printed in a flip-format. One half of the magazine is geared toward readers of women's fiction (book reviews, author profiles, etc.) while the other half is geared toward authors. We need writing how-to's, editor/publisher profiles, researching articles, etc." Estab. 2000. Pays on publication. Publishes ms an average of 2 months after acceptance. Byline given. Buys first North American serial, one-time, second serial (reprint) rights. Editorial lead time 3 months. Submit seasonal material 4 months in advance. Accepts queries by e-mail. Accepts simultaneous submissions. Responds in 6 weeks to queries; 3 months to mss. Sample copy for 9×12 SAE and 4 first-class stamps. Writer's guidelines for #10 SASE or by e-mail.
Nonfiction: How-to (writing technique), interview/profile, opinion. "All special projects are assigned. We don't accept freelance submissions for this purpose." Book reviews are done inhouse. **Buys 50 mss/year.** Query. Length: 500-2,000 words. **Pays 1-10¢/word for assigned articles; 1-5¢/word for unsolicited articles.**
Photos: State availability with submission. Buys one-time rights. Offers no additional payment for photos accepted with ms.
Tips: "Please make sure your topic is well researched and your ideas are clearly conveyed. Our readers don't just want to know why you think something is important, but also how your experience or expertise can benefit them. Target authors—our reader's portion is almost completely done by *Bridges* staff."

$ BYLINE, P.O. Box 130596, Edmond OK 73013-0001. (405)348-5591. E-mail: mpreston@bylinemag.com. Website: www.bylinemag.com. **Contact:** Marcia Preston, editor/publisher. **80% freelance written.** Eager to work with new/unpublished writers. Magazine published 9 times/year for writers and poets. Estab. 1981. **Pays on acceptance.** Publishes ms an average of 3 months after acceptance. Byline given. Buys first North American serial rights. Editorial lead time 3 months. Submit seasonal material 6 months in advance. Accepts queries by mail, e-mail. Accepts simultaneous submissions. Responds in 2 months or less to queries. Sample copy for $4 postpaid. Writer's guidelines for #10 SASE or online.
➤ "First $ale is probably the easiest way to break in."
Nonfiction: "We're always searching for appropriate, well-written features on topics we haven't covered for a couple of years." Needs articles of 1,500-1,800 words connected with writing and selling. No profiles of writers. **Buys approximately 75 mss/year.** Prefers queries; will read complete mss. Send SASE. Length: 1,500-1,800 words. **Pays $75.**
Columns/Departments: End Piece (humorous, philosophical or motivational personal essay related to writing), 700 words, pays $35; First Sale (account of a writer's first sale), 200-300 words, pays $20; Only When I Laugh (writing-related humor), 50-600 words; pays $15-25; Great American Bookstores (unique, independent bookstores), 500-600 words. Send complete ms. **Pays $30-40.**
Fiction: Mainstream, genre, literary. No science fiction, erotica or extreme violence. **Buys 11 mss/year.** Send complete ms. Length: 2,000-4,000 words. **Pays $100.**
Poetry: "All poetry should connect in some way with the theme or writing or writers." Sandra Soli, poetry editor. Free verse, haiku, light verse, traditional. **Buys 100 poems/year.** Submit maximum 3 poems. Length: Under 30 lines. **Pays $10 plus free issue.**
Tips: "We're open to freelance submissions in all categories. We're always looking for clear, concise feature articles on topics that will help writers write better, market smarter, and be more successful. Strangely, we get many more short stories than we do features, but we buy more features. If you can write a friendly, clear and helpful feature on some aspect of writing better or selling more work, we'd love to hear from you."

$ CANADIAN WRITER'S JOURNAL, P.O. Box 5180, New Liskeard, Ontario P0J 1P0, Canada. (705)647-5424. Fax: (705)647-8366. E-mail: cwj@ntl.sympatico.ca. Website: www.nt.net/~cwj/index.htm. **Contact:** Carole Roy, managing editor. **75% freelance written.** Bimonthly magazine for writers. Accepts well-written articles by inexperienced writers. Estab. 1982. Circ. 350. Pays on publication. Publishes ms an average of 9 months after acceptance. Byline given. Buys one-time rights. Accepts queries by mail, e-mail, fax, phone. Responds in 2 months to queries. Sample copy for $4 and $1 postage. Writer's guidelines for #10 SAE and IRC or online.

Nonfiction: Looking for articles on how to break into niche markets. How-to (articles for writers). **Buys 50-55 mss/year.** Query optional. **Pays $5/published magazine page (approx. 450 words).**

Reprints: Send typed ms with rights for sale noted and information about when and where the material previously appeared.

Fiction: Requirements currently being met by annual contest. Send SASE for rules, or see guidelines on website.

Poetry: Short poems or extracts used as part of articles on the writing of poetry.

Tips: "We prefer short, tightly written, informative how-to articles. U.S. writers note that U.S. postage cannot be used to mail from Canada. Obtain Canadian stamps, use IRCs or send small amounts in cash."

[N] $ E CONTENT MAGAZINE, Digital Content Strategies & Resources, Online Inc., 213 Danbury Rd., Wilton CT 06897. Fax: (203)761-1444. E-mail: info@onlineinc.com. Website: www.econtentmag.com. **Contact:** Bill Mickey, editor. **90% freelance written.** Monthly magazine covering digital content trends, strategies, etc. "E Content is a business publication. Readers need to stay on top of industry trends and developments." Estab. 1979. Circ. 12,000. Pays within 60 days of receipt of ms. Byline given. Offers 20-50% kill fee. Buys all rights. Editorial lead time 5 months. Accepts queries by e-mail. Responds in 3 weeks to queries; 1 month to mss. Sample copy and writer's guidelines online.

Nonfiction: Book excerpts, exposé, how-to, interview/profile, new product, opinion, technical, news features. No academic or straight Q&A. **Buys 48 mss/year.** Query with published clips. Length: 1,000-2,000 words. **Pays $1.** Sometimes pays expenses of writers on assignment.

Photos: State availability with submission. Buys one-time rights. Negotiates payment individually. Captions required.

Columns/Departments: Profiles (short profile of unique company, person or product), 1,100 words; New Features (breaking news of content-related topics), 500 words maximum. **Buys 40 mss/year.** Query with published clips. **Pays $1.**

Tips: "Take a look at the website. Most of the time, an e-mail query with specific article ideas works well. A general outline of talking points is good, too. State prior experience."

[N] $ FELLOW SCRIPT, InScribe Christian Writers' Fellowship, 333 Hunter's Run, Edmonton Alberta T6R 2N9, Canada. (780)988-5622. Fax: (780)430-0139. E-mail: submissions@inscribe.org. Website: www.inscribe.org. **Contact:** Elsie Montgomery, editor. **100% freelance written.** Published 5 times annually writers' newsletter featuring Christian writing. "Our readers are Christians with a commitment to writing. Among our readership are best-selling authors and unpublished beginning writers. Submissions to us should include practical information, something the reader can put into practice the same day she reads it." Estab. 1980. Circ. 250. Pays on publication. Publishes ms an average of 2 months after acceptance. Byline given. Offers 50% kill fee. Buys one-time rights. Editorial lead time 3 months. Submit seasonal material 4 months in advance. Accepts queries by mail, e-mail, fax, phone. Accepts simultaneous submissions. Responds in 1 month to queries; 2 months to mss. Sample copy for 9×12 SAE and 2 first-class stamps. Writer's guidelines for #10 SASE.

    0→ "The best bet to break in at FellowScript is to write something very specific that will be useful to writers. We receive far too many 'general' submissions which try to cover too much territory in one article. Choose your topic and keep a narrow focus."

Nonfiction: Essays, exposé, how-to (for writers), inspirational, interview/profile, new product, personal experience, photo feature, religious. "Does not want poetry, fiction or think piece, commentary articles." **Buys 15-25 mss/year.** Send complete ms. Length: 250-900 words. **Pays $30-50 for assigned articles; $15-30 for unsolicited articles.**

Photos: State availability with submission. Reviews 4×6 prints. Buys one-time rights. Negotiates payment individually. Captions, identification of subjects required.

Columns/Departments: Book reviews, 150-300 words; market updates and profiles, 50-300 words (both for writers). **Buys 5 mss/year.** Send complete ms. **Pays 1 copy or $5.**

Fillers: Facts, newsbreaks. **Buys 5-10/year.** Length: 25-75 words. **Pays 1 copy or $5.**

Tips: "Send your complete manuscript by post or e-mail. If you send it by post, offer it by e-mail as well. Tell us a bit about yourself. Write in a casual, first-person, anecdotal style. Be sure your article is full of practical material, something that can be applied. Most of our accepted freelance submissions fall into the 'how to' category, and involve tasks, crafts or procedures common to writers, as our magazine is solely devoted to instructing and encouraging writers. Please do not swamp us with inspirational articles (e.g., 'How I sold My First Story'), as we receive too many of these already."

$ $ FREELANCE WRITER'S REPORT, CNW Publishing, Inc., Main St., P.O. Box A, North Stratford NH 03590-0167. (603)922-8338. Fax: (603)922-8339. E-mail: danakcnw@ncia.net. Website: www.writers-editors.com. **Contact:** Dana K. Cassell, editor. **25% freelance written.** Monthly magazine. "*FWR* covers the marketing and business/office management aspects of running a freelance writing business. Articles must be of value to the established freelancer; nothing basic." Estab. 1982. Pays on publication. Publishes ms an average of 6 months after acceptance. Byline given.

Buys one-time rights. Editorial lead time 2 months. Submit seasonal material 2 months in advance. Accepts queries by mail, e-mail. Accepts simultaneous submissions. Responds in 1 week to queries; 1 month to mss. Sample copy for 6×9 SAE with 2 first-class stamps (for back copy); $4 for current copy. Writer's guidelines online.
Nonfiction: Book excerpts, how-to (market, increase income or profits). No articles about the basics of freelancing. **Buys 50 mss/year.** Send complete ms. Length: 500-900 words. **Pays 10¢/word.**
Reprints: Accepts previously published submissions.
 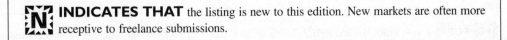 The online magazine carries original content not found in the print edition and includes writer's guidelines.
Tips: "Write in a terse, newsletter style."

N $ ▣ INSCRIPTIONS MAGAZINE, 500 Seventh Ave., 8th Floor, New York NY 10018. E-mail: Editor@inscriptionsmagazine.com. Website: www.inscriptionsmagazine.com. **Contact:** Jade Walker, editor. **100% freelance written.** Weekly e-zine covering writing, editing, publishing. "*Inscriptions* is the weekly e-zine for professional writers. Our focus is to help working writers and editors find work, paying markets and contests offering cash prizes." Estab. 1998. Pays on publication. Publishes ms an average of 2 months after acceptance. Byline given. Buys one-time, electronic rights. Editorial lead time 3 months. Submit seasonal material 3 months in advance. Accepts queries by e-mail. Responds in 2 weeks to queries. Sample copy free. Writer's guidelines online or by e-mail.
Nonfiction: "Authors can opt for advertising in lieu of payments." Book excerpts, how-to, humor, interview/profile. **Buys 150 mss/year.** Query. Length: 500-1,500 words. **Pays $5-40.**
Fillers: Buys 50/year. Length: 25-300 words. **Pays nothing for fillers.**
Tips: "Articles must focus on writing or publishing-related issues (including interviews, how to's, troubleshooting, etc.). Inscriptions does not publish fiction, poetry or other nonfiction articles, unless the submissions have won our sponsored monthly contest. Interviews should be conducted with working writers, authors, writing teachers, editors, agents or publishers. All interviews must be approved in advance. Inscriptions accepts reprints of writing-related articles. The publication where the article originally appeared will be credited. However, you must hold the copyright to the article, in order to submit it to us."

$ MAINE IN PRINT, Maine Writers and Publishers Alliance, 14 Maine St., Suite 416, Brunswick ME 04011. (207)729-8808. Fax: (207)725-1014. Website: www.mainewriters.org. Editor: John Cole. Bimonthly newsletter for writers, editors, teachers, librarians, etc., focusing on Maine literature and the craft of writing. Estab. 1975. Circ. 3,000. Pays on publication. Publishes ms an average of 2 months after acceptance. Byline given. Buys one-time rights. Editorial lead time 2 months. Accepts queries by mail. Accepts simultaneous submissions. Sample copy and writer's guidelines free.
Nonfiction: Essays, how-to (writing), interview/profile, technical. No creative writing, fiction or poetry. **Buys 20 mss/ year.** Query with published clips. Length: 400-1,500 words. **Pays $25-75 for assigned articles.**
Reprints: Send tearsheet and information about when and where the material previously appeared. Pays $25.
Photos: State availability with submission. Offers no additional payment for photos accepted with ms.
Columns/Departments: Front-page articles (writing related), 500-1,500 words. **Buys 20 mss/year.** Query. **Pays $25 minimum.**
Tips: "Become a member of Maine Writers & Publishers Alliance. Become familiar with Maine literary scene."

N $ $ $ MASTHEAD, The Magazine About Magazines, North Island Publishing, 1606 Sedlescomb Dr., Unit 8, Mississauga, Ontario L4X 1M6, Canada. (905)625-7070. Fax: (905)625-4856. E-mail: wshields@masthead.ca. Website: www.mastheadonline.com. **Contact:** William Shields, editor. **40% freelance written.** Journal published 10 times/year covering the Canadian magazine industry. "With its lively mix of in-depth features, news stories, service pieces, surveys, tallies and spirited commentary, this independent journal provides detailed coverage and analysis of the events, issues, personalities and technologies shaping Canada's magazine industry." Estab. 1987. Circ. 4,200. Pays on publication. Publishes ms an average of 2 months after acceptance. Byline given. Offers 50% kill fee. Buys first North American serial rights. Editorial lead time 1 month. Accepts queries by mail. Accepts simultaneous submissions. Responds in 2 weeks to queries; 1 month to mss. Sample copy free. Writer's guidelines free or by e-mail.
Nonfiction: "We generally pay $600-850 for a cover story running 2,000-2,500 words, depending on the amount of research, etc. required. For the most part, *Masthead* generates feature ideas in-house and then assigns the stories to regular contributors. When space permits, we sometimes run shorter features or service pieces (1,000-1,500 words) for a flat rate of $350." Book excerpts, essays, exposé, historical/nostalgic, how-to, humor, interview/profile, new product, opinion, personal experience, technical. No articles that have nothing to do with Canadian magazines. Length: 100-3,000 words. **Pays Pays $30-850 (Canadian).** Sometimes pays expenses of writers on assignment.
Photos: State availability with submission. Negotiates payment individually. Identification of subjects required.

N INDICATES THAT the listing is new to this edition. New markets are often more receptive to freelance submissions.

Columns/Departments: Back of the Book, the guest column pays freelancers a flat rate of $350 and runs approximately 950 words. Back of the Book columns examine and/or comment on issues or developments relating to any department: editorial, art, production, circulation, publishing, advertising, etc. **Buys 10 mss/year.** Query with published clips. **Pays $350 (Canadian).**

Fiction: Novel excerpts. No excerpts that have nothing to do with Canadian magazines. Query with published clips.

☐ The online magazine carries original content not found in the print edition. Contact: William Shields.

Tips: "Have a solid understanding of the Canadian magazine industry. A good way to introduce yourself is to propose small articles on new magazines."

$ ☒ NEW WRITER'S MAGAZINE, Sarasota Bay Publishing, P.O. Box 5976, Sarasota FL 34277-5976. (941)953-7903. E-mail: newriters@aol.com. Website: www.newriters.com. **Contact:** George J. Haborak, editor. **95% freelance written.** Bimonthly magazine. "*New Writer's Magazine* believes that *all* writers are *new* writers in that each of us can learn from one another. So, we reach pro and non-pro alike." Estab. 1986. Circ. 5,000. Pays on publication. Byline given. Buys first rights. Accepts queries by mail. Responds in 3 weeks to queries; 1 month to mss. Sample copy for $3. Writer's guidelines for #10 SASE.

Nonfiction: General interest, how-to (for new writers), humor, interview/profile, opinion, personal experience (with pro writer). **Buys 50 mss/year.** Send complete ms. Length: 700-1,000 words. **Pays $10-50.**

Photos: Send photos with submission. Reviews 5×7 prints. Offers no additional payment for photos accepted with ms. Captions required.

Fiction: "We offer a special fiction contest held each year with cash prizes." Experimental, historical, humorous, mainstream, slice-of-life vignettes. "Again we do *not* want anything that does not have a tie-in with the writing life or writers in general." **Buys 2-6 mss/year.** Send complete ms. Length: 700-800 words. **Pays $20-40.**

Poetry: Free verse, light verse, traditional. Does not want anything *not* for writers. **Buys 10-20 poems/year.** Submit maximum 3 poems. Length: 8-20 lines. **Pays $5 minimum.**

Fillers: For cartoons, writing lifestyle slant. **Buys 20-30/year. Pays $10 maximum.** Anecdotes, facts, newsbreaks, short humor. **Buys 5-15/year.** Length: 20-100 words. **Pays $5 maximum.**

Tips: "Any article *with photos* has a good chance, especially an *up close and personal* interview with an established professional writer offering advice, etc. Short profile pieces on new authors also receive attention."

$ OHIO WRITER, Poets League of Greater Cleveland, P.O. Box 91801, Cleveland OH 44101. **Contact:** Stephen and Gail Bellamy, editors. **75% freelance written.** Bimonthly magazine covering writing and Ohio writers. Estab. 1987. Pays on publication. Publishes ms an average of 4 months after acceptance. Byline given. Buys one-time, second serial (reprint) rights. Editorial lead time 4 months. Submit seasonal material 4 months in advance. Accepts queries by mail. Responds in 6 weeks to mss. Sample copy for $2.50. Writer's guidelines for #10 SASE.

Nonfiction: "All articles must related to the writing life or Ohio writers, or Ohio publishing scene." Essays, how-to, humor, inspirational, interview/profile, opinion, personal experience. **Buys 24 mss/year.** Send complete ms and SASE. Length: 2,000-2,500 words. **Pays $25 minimum, up to $50 for lead article, other payment under arrangement with writer.**

Reprints: Send typed ms with rights for sale noted and information about when and where the material previously appeared. Pays 50% of amount paid for an original article.

Columns/Departments: Subjectively Yours (opinions, controversial stance on writing life), 1,500 words; Reveiws (Ohio writers, publishers or publishig), 400-600 words; Focus on (Ohio publishing scene, how to write/publish certain kind of writing, e.g., travel), 1,500 words. **Buys 6 mss/year.** Send complete ms. **Pays $25-50; $5/book review.**

Tips: "We look for articles about writers and writing, with a special emphasis on activities in our state. However, we publish articles by writers throughout the country that offer something helpful about the writing life. Profiles and interviews of writers who live in Ohio are always needed. *Ohio Writer* is read by both beginning and experienced writers and hopes to create a sense of community among writers of different genres, abilities and backgrounds. We want to hear a personal voice, one that engages the reader. We're looking for intelligent, literate prose that isn't stuffy."

$ $ ONLINE PUBLISHERS DIGEST, Digest Publications, 29 Fostertown Rd., Medford NJ 08055. (606)953-4900. Fax: (609)953-4905. Website: www.limodigest.com. **Contact:** Don Truax, editor. Trade journal covering internet publishing. Pays on publication. Publishes ms an average of 2 months after acceptance. Byline given. Makes work-for-hire assignments. Editorial lead time 1 year. Submit seasonal material 2 months in advance. Accepts queries by mail, e-mail, fax. Accepts simultaneous submissions. Responds in 2 weeks to queries.

Nonfiction: Historical/nostalgic, how-to (start company marketing), humor, inspirational, interview/profile, new product, personal experience, photo feature, technical. **Buys 1-2 mss/year.** Length: 700-1,900 words. **Pays 7-22¢/word.** Sometimes pays writers with advertising trade-outs.

Reprints: Accepts previously published submissions.

Photos: Send photos with submission. Reviews negatives. Buys all rights. Negotiates payment individually. Captions, identification of subjects, model releases required.

Columns/Departments: Pays 7-22¢/word.

Fillers: Facts, gags to be illustrated by cartoonist, newsbreaks. **Buys 24/year.** Length: 25-100 words. **Pays 7-22¢/word.**

$ $ POETS & WRITERS MAGAZINE, 72 Spring St., New York NY 10012. Fax: (212)226-3963. E-mail: editor@pw.org. Website: www.pw.org. **Contact:** Therese Eiben, editor. **100% freelance written.** Bimonthly professional trade journal for poets and fiction writers and creative nonfiction writers. Estab. 1973. Circ. 70,000. Pays on acceptance of finished draft. Publishes ms an average of 4 months after acceptance. Byline given. Offers 20% kill fee. Buys first North American serial rights. Submit seasonal material 4 months in advance. Accepts queries by mail. Responds in 6 weeks to mss. Sample copy for $4.95 to Sample Copy Dept. Writer's guidelines for #10 SASE.

• No poetry or fiction.

Nonfiction: How-to (craft of poetry or fiction writing), interview/profile (with poets or fiction writers). "We do not accept submissions by fax or e-mail." **Buys 35 mss/year.** Query with published clips or send complete ms. Length: 500-2,500 depending on topic words.

Photos: State availability with submission. Reviews b&w prints. Offers no additional payment for photos accepted with ms.

Columns/Departments: Literary and publishing news, 500-1,000 words; profiles of emerging and established poets and fiction writers, 2,000-3,000 words; regional reports (literary activity in US), 1,000-2,00 words. Query with published clips or send complete ms. **Pays $150-300.**

$ SCAVENGER'S NEWSLETTER, 833 Main, Osage City KS 66523-1241. (913)528-3538. E-mail: foxscav1@jc.net or foxscav1@hotmail.com. Website: www.jlgiftsshop.com/scav/index.html. **Contact:** Janet Fox, editor. **10% freelance written.** Eager to work with new/unpublished writers. Monthly newsletter covering markets for science fiction/fantasy/horror/mystery materials especially with regard to the small press. Estab. 1984. Circ. 550. **Pays on acceptance.** Publishes ms an average of 8 months after acceptance. Byline given. Buys one-time rights. Accepts queries by e-mail. Accepts simultaneous submissions. Responds in 1 month to mss if SASE included. Sample copy for $2.50. Writer's guidelines for #10 SASE.

Nonfiction: Essays, general interest, how-to (write, sell, publish science fiction/fantasy/horror/mystery), humor, interview/profile (writers, artists in the field), opinion. **Buys 12-15 mss/year.** Send complete ms. Length: 1,000 words. **Pays $5.**

Reprints: Send information about when and where the material previously appeared. Pays 100% of amount paid for an original article.

Fiction: "Seeking a few (4-6) outstanding pieces of flash fiction to 1,200 words in the genre of SF/fantasy/horror/mystery. Looking for work that uses poetry techniques to make a short piece seem like a complete story." **Pays $5.**

Poetry: All related to science fiction/fantasy/horror/mystery genres. Avant-garde, free verse, haiku, traditional. **Buys 24 poems/year.** Submit maximum 3 poems. Length: 10 lines maximum. **Pays $3.**

Tips: "Because this is a small publication, it has occasional overstocks. We're especially looking for articles."

$ $ WRITER'S DIGEST, 1507 Dana Ave., Cincinnati OH 45207. (513)531-2690 ext. 483. E-mail: wd submissions @fwpubs.com. Website: www.writersdigest.com. **Contact:** Katie DuMont, associate editor. **70% freelance written.** Monthly magazine about writing and publishing. "Our readers write fiction, nonfiction, plays and scripts. They're interested in improving writing skills and the ability to sell their work and find new outlets for their talents." Estab. 1920. Circ. 175,000. **Pays on acceptance.** Publishes ms an average of 6 months after acceptance. Byline given. Offers 20% kill fee. Buys first world serial rights for one-time editorial use, possible electronic posting, microfilm/microfiche use and magazine promotional use. Pays 25% reprint fee and 10% for electronic use in fee-charging mediums. Submit seasonal material 8 months in advance. Accepts queries by mail, e-mail. Responds in 1 month to mss. Guidelines and editorial calendar available online.

○┭ "Break in through Markets Spotlight, or with a 500-1,000 word 'how-to' article."

Nonfiction: "What we need is the how-to article: How to write compelling leads and conclusions, how to improve your character descriptions, how to become more efficient and productive. We like plenty of examples, anecdotes and details in our articles—so other writers can actually see what's been done successfully by the author of a particular piece. On how-to technique articles, we prefer to work with writers with a proven track record of success. For example, don't pitch us an article on creating effective dialog if you've never had a work of fiction published. Don't query about setting up a book tour if you've never done one. We like our articles to speak directly to the reader through the use of the first-person voice. We are seldom interested in author interviews and 'evergreen' topics are not accepted unless they are timely and address industry trends. For example, we'd only accept an article on query letters if it addressed concerns about the changing marketplace. We're looking for timely articles dealing with publishing as a dynamic, changing business." Must have fax to receive galleys. "Don't send articles today that would have fit in WD five years ago. No articles titled 'So You Want to Be a Writer,' and no first-person pieces without something readers can learn from in the sharing of the story. Avoid the 'and then I wrote' article that is a promotional vehicle for you without tips on how others can put your experience to work." **Buys 60 mss/year.** We only accept electronic final manuscripts. Length: 500-1,800 words. **Pays 25-40¢/word.** Sometimes pays expenses of writers on assignment.

Tips: "Two-thirds of assignments are based on staff-generated ideas. Only about 25 unsolicited queries for features are assigned per year. Note that our standing columns and departments are not open to freelance submissions. Further, we buy at most five interviews/profiles per year; nearly all that we publish are staff-written. Candidates for First Success interviews (all of which are conducted in-house) should send galleys and information about themselves at least five months before their book's pubilcation date to Kelly Nickell at the address above."

$ WRITER'S FORUM, Writer's Digest School, 1507 Dana Ave., Cincinnati OH 45207. (513)531-2690, ext. 343. Fax: (513)531-0798. E-mail: wdsforum@fwpubs.com. Website: www.writersdigestschool.com. **Contact:** Maria Altevers, editor. **100% freelance written.** Tri-annual newsletter covering writing techniques, marketing and inspiration for students enrolled in fiction and nonfiction writing courses offered by Writer's Digest School. Estab. 1970. Circ. 10,000. **Pays on acceptance.** Publishes ms an average of 6 months after acceptance. Byline given. Buys first, second serial (reprint) rights. Accepts queries by mail, e-mail. Accepts simultaneous submissions. Sample copy free.

O→ Break in with something "how-to" oriented that is geared toward beginning writers and/or writers just breaking into print.

Nonfiction: How-to (write or market short stories, or articles, novels and nonficiton books). **Buys 12 mss/year.** Prefers complete mss to queries. Length: 500-1,000 words. **Pays $25.**

N **$** **WRITER'S GUIDELINES & NEWS, The Who, What, When, and Where Magazine for Writers**, P.O. Box 310647, Jamaica NY 11431-0647. (718)380-0080. E-mail: WGandNews@aol.com. **Contact:** Christopher L. Buono, editor-in-chief. **70% freelance written.** Quarterly magazine covering writing. "We consider ourselves 'the friend of the writer,' so we are very flexible. We will consider anything, well-written, with a writing slant for beginning as well as professional writers." Estab. 1988. Circ. 2,500. Pays on publication. Publishes ms an average of 6 months after acceptance. Byline given. Buys first North American serial rights. Editorial lead time 4 months. Submit seasonal material 4 months in advance. Accepts queries by mail, e-mail. Responds in 1 month to queries; 4 months to mss. Sample copy for $5. Writer's guidelines for #10 SASE.

O→ Break in with "short articles with photos and 'newsy' items about writers or the writing profession have the best chance of acceptance. Inform and entertain. Write for writers."

Nonfiction: All submissions must include a SASE for reply and/or return. Essays, general interest, how-to (on writing), humor, inspirational, interview/profile, opinion, personal experience. "No articles without a writing slant." **Buys 60 mss/year.** Send complete ms. Length: 750-1,500 words. **Pays $5-25.**

Photos: Send photos with submission. Reviews 5×7 prints. Buys one-time rights. Offers no additional payment for photos accepted with ms. Captions required.

$ **WRITERS INFORMATION NETWORK, The Professional Association for Christian Writers**, P.O. Box 11337, Bainbridge Island WA 98110. (206)842-9103. Fax: (206)842-0536. E-mail: writersinfonetwork@juno.com. Website: www.bluejaypub.com/win. **Contact:** Elaine Wright Colvin, editor. **33 1/3% freelance written.** Bimonthly magazine covering religious publishing industry. Estab. 1983. Circ. 1,000. **Pays on acceptance.** Publishes ms an average of 1-4 months after acceptance. Byline given. Buys first North American serial rights. Editorial lead time 2 months. Submit seasonal material 2 months in advance. Accepts queries by e-mail. Responds in 1 month to mss. Sample copy for $5, 9×12 SAE with 4 first-class stamps. Writer's guidelines for #10 SASE.

O→ Break in by "getting involved in the Christian publishing (CBA) industry; interview CBA published authors, CBA editors or CBA bookstore managers."

Nonfiction: How-to (writing), humor, inspirational, interview/profile, new product, opinion, personal experience (for advanced/professional writers only), religious, technical. No beginners basics material used. Send complete ms. Length: 50-800 words. **Pays $5-50, sometimes pays other than cash.** Sometimes pays expenses of writers on assignment.

Columns/Departments: Industry News, Market News, Changes in the Industry, Watch on the World, Poetry News, Speakers Microphone, Conference Schedule, Look Over My Shoulder, new books reviewed or announced, Bulletin Board, Computer Corner. Send complete ms in body of e-mail or as an e-mail attachment.

$ **WRITERS' JOURNAL, The Complete Writer's Magazine**, Val-Tech Media, P.O. Box 394, Perham MN 56573-0394. (218)346-7921. Fax: (218)346-7924. E-mail: writersjournal@wadena.net. Website: www.writersjournal.c om. Managing Editor: John Ogroske. **Contact:** Leon Ogroske, editor. **90% freelance written.** Bimonthly trade magazine covering writing. "*Writers' Journal* is read by thousands of aspiring writers whose love of writing has taken them to the next step: Writing for money. We are an instructional manual giving writers the tools and information necessary to get their work published. We also print works by authors who have won our writing contests." Estab. 1980. Circ. 26,000. Pays on publication. Publishes ms an average of 10 months after acceptance. Byline given. Buys one-time rights. Editorial lead time 8 months. Submit seasonal material 8 months in advance. Accepts queries by mail, e-mail, fax, phone. Accepts simultaneous submissions. Responds in 6 weeks to queries; 3 months to mss. Sample copy for $5.

Nonfiction: Looking for articles on fiction writing (plot development, story composition, character development, etc.) and writing "how-to." Book excerpts, essays, exposé, general interest (to writers), humor, inspirational, interview/profile, new product, opinion, personal experience, photo feature, technical. No erotica. **Buys 45 mss/year.** Send complete ms. Length: 800-2,500 words. **Pays $12-40 for assigned articles.** Pays in contributor copies or other premiums if author agrees.

Photos: State availability with submission. Reviews contact sheets, prints. Buys one-time rights. Negotiates payment individually. Model releases required.

Columns/Departments: Book and Software Reviews, 200 words; For Beginners Only (helpful advice to beginners), 800-2,500 words. **Buys 30 mss/year.** Send complete ms. **Pays $12-40.**

Fiction: "We only publish winners of our fiction contests—16 contests/year."

Poetry: Esther Leiper-Jefferson, poetry editor. No erotica. **Buys 25 poems/year.** Submit maximum 4 poems. Length: 25 lines. **Pays $5.**

Fillers: Anecdotes, facts, gags to be illustrated by cartoonist, short humor. **Buys 20/year.** Length: 200 words. **Pays $10.**

Tips: "Appearance must be professional with no grammatical or spelling errors submitted on white paper, double spaced with easy-to-read font. We want articles that will help writers improve technique in writing, style, editing, publishing, and story construction. We are interested in how writers use new and fresh angles to break into the writing markets."

$ WRITERS' POTPOURRI, Mea Productions, 55 Binks Hill Rd., Plymouth NH 03264. Fax: (603)536-4851. E-mail: me.allen@juno.com. Website: homepage.fcgnetworks.net/jetent/mea. **Contact:** Mary Emma Allen, editor. **25% freelance written.** Newsletter for writers covering writing and publishing. "This is a self-help, how-to publication for and by writers on writing and publishing in print and on the Internet." Estab. 1996. Circ. 100. **Pays on acceptance.** Publishes ms an average of 6 months after acceptance. Byline given. Editorial lead time 6 months. Accepts queries by mail, e-mail, fax. Accepts simultaneous submissions. Prefer complete ms to queries; responds in 2 months to mss. Sample copy for $1 and #10 SAE. Writer's guidelines for #10 SASE, online, by e-mail.

Nonfiction: How-to, personal experience. **Buys 6-8 mss/year.** Length: 250-500 words. **Pays $5-10 plus 2 copies.**

Columns/Departments: Book Nook (reviews of writing books), 150 words. **Buys 4 mss/year. Pays $5.**

Fillers: Newsbreaks. Length: 25-100 words. **Pays nothing because these are announcements of the writer's work.**

Tips: "The articles need to be within the word limitation and you'll have more success with the 250-word articles. I seldom use long articles. The articles must be how-to tips and information for writers on writing, selling manuscripts, self-publishing, teaching workshops, giving author visits, promotion, book signings,etc."

N $ WRITING THAT WORKS, The Business Communications Report, 7481 Huntsman Blvd., #720, Springfield VA 22153-1648. E-mail: inq@writingthatworks.com. Website: www.writingthatworks.com/wtw.htm. **Contact:** John De Lellis, editor/publisher. Monthly newsletter on business writing and communications. "Our readers are company writers, editors, communicators and executives. They need specific, practical advice on how to write well as part of their job." Estab. 1983. Pays within 45 days of acceptance. Publishes ms an average of 3 months after acceptance. Byline sometimes given. Buys all rights. Editorial lead time 2 months. Accepts queries by mail, e-mail. Responds in 1 month to queries. Sample copy and writer's guidelines online.

Nonfiction: Practical, short, how-to articles and quick tips on business writing techniques geared to company writers, editors, publication staff and communicators. "We're always looking for shorts—how-to tips on business writing." How-to. **Buys 120 mss/year.** Accepts electronic final mss. Length: 100-500 words. **Pays $35-150.**

Columns/Departments: Writing Techniques (how-to business writing advice); Style Matters (grammar, usage and editing); Online Publishing (writing, editing and publishing for the Web); Managing Publications; PR & Marketing (writing).

Fillers: Short tips on writing or editing. Mini-reviews of communications websites for business writers, editors and communicators. Length: 100-150 words. **Pays $35.**

Tips: "We do not use material on how to get published or how to conduct a freelancing business. Format your copy to follow *Writing That Works* style. Include postal and e-mail addresses, phone numbers and website URLs and prices for products/services mentioned in articles."

$ $ $ $ WRITTEN BY, The Magazine of the Writers Guild of America, West, 7000 W. Third St., Los Angeles CA 90048. (323)782-4699. Fax: (323)782-4699. E-mail: writtenby@wga.org. **Contact:** Richard Stayton, editor. **40% freelance written.** Monthly magazine. "*Written By* is the premier monthly magazine written by and for America's screen and TV writers. We focus on the craft of screenwriting and cover all aspects of the entertainment industry from the perspective of the writer. We are read by all screenwriters and most entertainment executives." Estab. 1987. Circ. 17,000. **Pays on acceptance.** Publishes ms an average of 2 months after acceptance. Byline given. Offers 10% kill fee. Buys first North American serial, electronic rights. Editorial lead time 4 months. Submit seasonal material 4 months in advance. Accepts queries by mail, e-mail, fax, phone. Writer's guidelines for #10 SASE.

○⊸ Break in with "an exclusive profile or Q&A with a major TV or screenwriter."

Nonfiction: Book excerpts, essays, historical/nostalgic, humor, interview/profile, opinion, personal experience, photo feature, technical (software). No "how to break into Hollywood," "how to write scripts"-type beginner pieces. **Buys 20 mss/year.** Query with published clips. Length: 500-3,500 words. **Pays $500-2,500 for assigned articles.** Sometimes pays expenses of writers on assignment.

Photos: State availability with submission. Reviews transparencies. Buys one-time rights. Offers no additional payment for photos accepted with ms. Captions, identification of subjects, model releases required.

Columns/Departments: Pays $1,000 maximum.

▣ The online magazine carries original content not found in the print edition. Contact: Scott Roeben.

Tips: "We are looking for more theoretical essays on screewriting past and/or present. Also the writer must *always* keep in mind that our audience is made up primarily of working writers who are inside the business, therefore all articles need to have an 'insider' feel and not be written for those who are still trying to break in to Hollywood. We prefer submissions on diskette or e-mail."

LAW

While all of these publications deal with topics of interest to attorneys, each has a particular slant. Be sure that your subject is geared to a specific market—lawyers in a single region, law students, paralegals, etc. Publications for law enforcement personnel are listed under Government & Public Service.

$ $ $ $ ABA JOURNAL, The Lawyer's Magazine, American Bar Association, 750 N. Lake Shore Dr., Chicago IL 60611. (312)988-6018. E-mail: abajournal@abanet.org. Website: www.abanet.org/journal/home.html. Editor: Gary Hengstler. **Contact:** Debra Cassens, managing editor. **10% freelance written.** Monthly magazine covering law. "The *ABA Journal* is an independent, thoughtful and inquiring observer of the law and the legal profession. The magazine is edited for members of the American Bar Association." Circ. 389,000. **Pays on acceptance.** Byline given. Makes work-for-hire assignments. Accepts queries by mail, e-mail. Sample copy and writer's guidelines free.
Nonfiction: Legal features. "We don't want anything that does not have a legal theme. No poetry or fiction." **Buys 5 mss/year.** Query with published clips. Length: 1,400-3,500 words. **Pays $800-2,000 for assigned articles.**
Columns/Departments: Law Beat (reports on legal news and trends), 750-1,500 words; Solo Network (advice for solo practitioners), 1,000 words; In the Office (life on the job for lawyers), 750-1,500 words; In re Technology (technology for lawyers), 750-1,500 words; Lawyer Lifestyles (life outside work for lawyers), 400-2,000 words. **Buys 50 mss/year.** Query with published clips. **Pays $350-1,200.**

$ $ $ $ CALIFORNIA LAWYER, Daily Journal Corporation, 1145 Market St., 8th Floor, San Francisco CA 94103. (415)252-0500. Fax: (415)252-2482. E-mail: peter_allen@dailyjournal.com. Website: www.dailyjournal.com. Managing Editor: Tema Goodwin. **Contact:** Peter Allen, editor. **85% freelance written.** Monthly magazine of law-related articles and general-interest subjects of appeal to lawyers and judges. "Our primary mission is to cover the news of the world as it affects the law and lawyers, helping our readers better comprehend the issues of the day and to cover changes and trends in the legal profession. Our readers are all 140,000 California lawyers, plus judges, legislators and corporate executives. Although we focus on California and the West, we have subscribers in every state. *California Lawyer* is a general interest magazine for people interested in law. Our writers are journalists." Estab. 1981. Circ. 140,000. **Pays on acceptance.** Publishes ms an average of 3 months after acceptance. Byline given. Offers 25% kill fee. Buys first North American serial, electronic rights. Editorial lead time 3 months. Accepts queries by mail, e-mail, fax. Sample copy and writer's guidelines for #10 SASE.
　○⊸ Break in by "showing us clips—we usually start people out on short news stories."
Nonfiction: Essays, general interest, interview/profile, News and feature articles on law-related topics. "We are interested in concise, well-written and well-researched articles on issues of current concern, as well as well-told feature narratives with a legal focus. We would like to see a description or outline of your proposed idea, including a list of possible sources." **Buys 36 mss/year.** Query with or without published clips or send complete ms. Length: 500-5,000 words. **Pays $250-2,000.** Pays expenses of writers on assignment.
Photos: Louise Kollenbaum, art director. State availability with submission. Reviews prints. Identification of subjects, model releases required.
Columns/Departments: California Esq. (current legal trends). 300 words. **Buys 30 mss/year.** Query with or without published clips. **Pays $50-250.**

COLORADO JOURNAL, A Daily Journal Corp. Publication, Daily Journal Corp., 717 17th St., Suite 2710, Denver CO 80202. (303)222-3202. Fax: (303)292-5821. E-mail: Ethel_Bennett@dailyjournal.com. Website: www.dailyjournal.com. Editor: Katrina Dewey. **Contact:** Ethel Bennett, executive editor. **20-30% freelance written.** Weekly tabloid covering legal issues. Estab. 1996. Circ. 2,000. Pays on publication. Byline given. Buys all rights. Editorial lead time 1 month. Submit seasonal material 1 month in advance. Accepts queries by mail, e-mail, fax, phone. Responds in 1 month to queries. Sample copy and writer's guidelines free.
Nonfiction: Exposé, general interest, how-to, interview/profile, photo feature, technical. Query. Length: 1,200-2,000 words. Sometimes pays expenses of writers on assignment.
Photos: State availability with submission. Reviews contact sheets. Buys all rights. Negotiates payment individually. Identification of subjects required.
Columns/Departments: Ethel Bennett, legal editor. Query.

N: $ $ $ $ CORPORATE LEGAL TIMES, 656 W. Randolph St., #500-E, Chicago IL 60661-2114. (312)654-3500. E-mail: jking@cltmag.com. Website: www.corporatelegaltimes.com. **Contact:** Jennifer E. King, managing editor. **50% freelance written.** Monthly tabloid. "*Corporate Legal Times* is a monthly national magazine that gives general counsel and inhouse attorneys information on legal and business issues to help them better manage corporate law departments. It routinely addresses changes and trends in law departments, litigation management, legal technology, corporate governance and inhouse careers. Law areas covered monthly include: Intellectual property, international, technology, project finance, e-commerce and litigation. All articles need to be geared toward the inhouse attorney's perspective." Estab. 1991. Circ. 45,000. Pays on publication. Publishes ms an average of 3 months after acceptance. Byline given. Buys all rights. Editorial lead time 3 months. Submit seasonal material 3 months in advance. Accepts queries by mail, e-mail. Responds in 3 weeks to queries. Sample copy for $17. Writer's guidelines for #10 SASE.

Nonfiction: Interview/profile, news about legal aspects of business issues and events. **Buys 12-25 mss/year.** Query with published clips. Length: 500-3,000 words. **Pays $500-2,000.**

Photos: State availability with submission. Reviews color transparencies, b&w prints. Buys all rights. Offers $25-150/ photo. Identification of subjects required.

Tips: "Our publication targets general counsel and inhouse lawyers. All articles need to speak to them—not to the general attorney population. Query with clips and a list of potential inhouse sources. Non-paid, contributed articles from law firm attorneys are accepted only if there is an inhouse attorney co-author."

$ $ $ JOURNAL OF COURT REPORTING, National Court Reporters Association, 8224 Old Courthouse Rd., Vienna VA 22182. (703)556-6272. Fax: (703)556-6291. E-mail: pwacht@ncrahq.org. **Contact:** Peter Wacht, editor. **20% freelance written.** Monthly (bimonthly july/august and november/december) magazine. "The *Journal of Court Reporting* has two complementary purposes: to communicate the activities, goals and mission of its publisher, the National Court Reporters Association; and, simultaneously, to seek out and publish diverse information and views on matters significantly related to the information/court reporting profession." Estab. 1905. Circ. 34,000. **Pays on acceptance.** Publishes ms an average of 3 months after acceptance. Byline given. Buys one-time rights, makes work-for-hire assignments. Editorial lead time 3 months. Accepts simultaneous submissions. Sample copy for $5. Writer's guidelines free.

Nonfiction: Essays, historical/nostalgic, how-to, interview/profile, new product, technical. **Buys 10 mss/year.** Query. Length: 1,200 words. words. **Pays $55-1,000.** Sometimes pays expenses of writers on assignment.

Photos: State availability with submission. Buys one-time rights. Offers no additional payment for photos accepted with ms. Captions, identification of subjects, model releases required.

$ $ $ LAW OFFICE COMPUTING, James Publishing, 3505 Cadillac Ave., Suite H, Costa Mesa CA 92626. (714)755-5469. Fax: (714)751-5508. E-mail: editorloc@jamespublishing.com. Website: www.lawofficecomputing.com. **Contact:** Amanda Clifford, managing editor. **90% freelance written.** Bimonthly magazine covering legal technology industry. "*Law Office Computing* is a magazine written for attorneys and other legal professionals. It covers the legal technology field and features software reviews, profiles of prominent figures in the industry and 'how to' type articles." Estab. 1991. Circ. 8,000. Pays on publication. Publishes ms an average of 2 months after acceptance. Byline given. Buys first North American serial rights. Editorial lead time 4 months. Submit seasonal material 4 months in advance. Accepts queries by mail, e-mail, fax. Sample copy free. Writer's guidelines online.

Nonfiction: How-to, humor, interview/profile, new product, technical, Looking for Macintosh and Linux articles. **Buys 30 mss/year.** Query. Length: 2,000-4,000 words. **Pays on a case-by-case basis.** Sometimes pays expenses of writers on assignment.

Photos: State availability with submission.

Columns/Departments: Tech profile (profile firm using technology), 1,200 words; My Solution, 1,500 words; Software reviews: Short reviews (a single product), 400-800 words; Software Shootouts (two or three products going head-to-head), 1,000-1,500 words; Round-Ups/Buyer's Guides (8 to 15 products), 300-500 words per product. Each type of software review article has its own specific guidelines. Request the appropriate guidelines from your editor. **Buys 6 mss/year.** Query. **Pays on a case-by-case basis.**

Tips: "If you are a practicing attorney, legal MIS or computer consultant, try the first-person My Solution column or a short review. If a professional freelance writer, technology profiles or a news story regarding legal technology are best; since most of our other copy is written by legal technology professionals."

N $ $ THE LEGAL INTELLIGENCER, American Lawyer Media, 1617 JFK Blvd., Suite 1750, Philadelphia PA 19103. (215)557-2300. E-mail: zanh@palawnet.com. Website: www.palawnet.com. **Contact:** Zan Hale, editor-in-chief. **5% freelance written.** Daily newspaper with a weekly surburban edition. "*The Legal Intelligencer* covers the Philadelphia courts and legal community. We are a daily newspaper, not a legal journal, and articles should be written accordingly." Estab. 1843. Circ. 10,000. Pays on publication. Byline given. Buys all rights. Editorial lead time 1 month. Accepts queries by mail, e-mail, fax. Responds in 2 weeks to queries. Sample copy for $5. Writer's guidelines for #10 SASE.

Nonfiction: Interview/profile, technical (law). Special issues: Business of law, business law, real estate, litigation, special section (see editorial calendar). Vendors and attorneys write for the marketing value. Query. Length: 800-2,000 words. **Pays $60-250.**

Photos: State availability with submission. Offers no additonal payment for photos accepted with ms.

N $ $ THE NATIONAL JURIST, Crittenden Magazines, 2035 N. Lincoln St., Arlington VA 22207. (703)294-5500. Fax: (703)294-5512. **Contact:** Tom Stabile, editor. **10% freelance written.** Bimonthly magazine covering law literature. Estab. 1991. Circ. 100,000. Pays on publication. Offers 20% kill fee. Buys all rights. Accepts queries by mail, e-mail, fax, phone.

Nonfiction: General interest, how-to, humor, interview/profile. **Buys 4 mss/year.** Query. Length: 750-3,000 words. **Pays $100-500 for assigned articles.**

Photos: State availability with submission. Reviews contact sheets. Negotiates payment individually.

Columns/Departments: Pays $100-500.

$ $ THE PENNSYLVANIA LAWYER, Pennsylvania Bar Association, P.O. Box 186, 100 South St., Harrisburg PA 17108-0186. E-mail: editor@pabar.org. Executive Editor: Marcy Carey Mallory; Editor: Geoff Yuda. **Contact:** Donald C. Sarvey, editorial director. **25% freelance written.** Prefers to work with published/established writers. Bimonthly magazine published as a service to the legal profession and the members of the Pennsylvania Bar Association. Estab. 1979. Circ. 30,000. **Pays on acceptance.** Publishes ms an average of 6 months after acceptance. Byline given. Buys first, one-time rights. Submit seasonal material 6 months in advance. Accepts queries by mail, e-mail. Responds in 2 months to queries; 2 months to mss. Sample copy for $2. Writer's guidelines for #10 SASE.
Nonfiction: All features must relate in some way to Pennsylvania lawyers or the practice of law in Pennsylvania. How-to, interview/profile, law-practice management, technology. **Buys 8-10 mss/year.** Query. Length: 1,200-2,000 words. **Pays $50 for book reviews; $75-400 for assigned articles; $150 for unsolicited articles.** Sometimes pays expenses of writers on assignment.
Photos: State availability with submission. Reviews contact sheets. Buys one-time rights. Negotiates payment individually. Identification of subjects required.

$ $ STUDENT LAWYER, The Magazine of the Law Student Division, American Bar Association, 750 N. Lake Shore Dr., Chicago IL 60611. (312)988-6048. Fax: (312)988-6081. E-mail: abastulawyer@abanet.org. Website: www.abanet.org/lsd. **Contact:** Ira Pilchen, editor. **85% freelance written.** Works with a small number of new writers each year. Monthly magazine. "*Student Lawyer* is a legal-affairs features magazine that competes for a share of law students' limited spare time, so the articles we publish must be informative, lively, well-researched good reads." Estab. 1972. Circ. 35,000. **Pays on acceptance.** Publishes ms an average of 3 months after acceptance. Byline given. Buys first rights. Editorial lead time 5 months. Submit seasonal material 6 months in advance. Accepts queries by mail, e-mail, phone. Writer's guidelines online.
Nonfiction: Essays (on legal affairs), interview/profile (prominent person in law-related fields), opinion (on matters of current legal interest). No fiction, please. **Buys 25 mss/year.** Query with published clips. Length: 2,500-4,000 words. **$500-1,200 for features.** Sometimes pays expenses of writers on assignment.
Columns/Departments: Profile (profiles out-of-the-ordinary lawyers), 1,200 words; Coping (dealing with law school), 1,200 words; Online (Internet and the law), 1,200 words; Leagal-ease (language and legal writing), 1,200 words; Jobs (marketing to legal employers), 1,200 words; Opinion (opinion on legal issue), 800 words. **Buys 45 mss/year.** Query with published clips. **Pays $200-500.**
Tips: "*Student Lawyer* actively seeks good new reporters and writers eager to prove themselves. Legal training definitely not essential; writing talent is. The writer should not think we are a law review; we are a features magazine with the law (in the broadest sense) as the common denominator. Find issues of national scope and interest to write about; be aware of subjects the magazine—and other media—have already covered and propose something new. Write clearly and well. Expect to work with editor to polish manuscripts to perfection. We do not make assignments to writers with whose work we are not familiar. If you're interested in writing for us, send a detailed, thought-out query with three previously published clips. We are always willing to look at material on spec. Sorry, we don't return manuscripts."

LUMBER

N $ $ BUILDING MATERIAL DEALER, National Lumber & Building Material Dealers Association, 1405 Lilac Dr. N, Minneapolis MN 55422. Fax: (763)582-3024. Website: www.dealer.org. **Contact:** Carla Waldenman, editor. **10% freelance written.** Monthly magazine covering the lumber and building center industry. Estab. 1985. Circ. 30,000. Pays on publication. Publishes ms an average of 2 months after acceptance. Byline given. Buys one-time rights. Editorial lead time 3 months. Submit seasonal material 3 months in advance. Accepts queries by mail, fax. Accepts simultaneous submissions. Responds in 2 months to queries; 1 month to mss. Sample copy for $5.
Nonfiction: New product, technical. No general business, interviews/profiles. **Buys 24 mss/year.** Query with published clips. Length: 600-2,500 words. **Pays $100-300.** Sometimes pays expenses of writers on assignment.
Reprints: Accepts previously published submissions.
Photos: State availability with submission. Buys one-time rights. Offers no additional payment for photos accepted with ms. Identification of subjects required.

$ $ SOUTHERN LUMBERMAN, Hatton-Brown Publishers, P.O. Box 681629, Franklin TN 37068-1629. (615)791-1961. Fax: (615)591-1035. E-mail: ngregg@southernlumberman.com. Website: www.southernlumberman.com. **Contact:** Nanci P. Gregg, editor. **20% freelance written.** Works with a small number of new/unpublished writers each year. Monthly journal for the sawmill industry. Estab. 1881. Circ. 15,000. Pays on publication. Publishes ms an average of 3 months after acceptance. Byline given. Buys first North American serial rights. Submit seasonal material 6 months in advance. Responds in 1 month to queries; 2 months to mss. Sample copy for $3 and 9×12 SAE with 5 first-class stamps. Writer's guidelines for #10 SASE.
Nonfiction: How-to (sawmill better), technical, equipment analysis, sawmill features. **Buys 10-15 mss/year.** Query with or without published clips or send complete ms. Length: 500-2,000 words. **Pays $150-350 for assigned articles; $100-250 for unsolicited articles.** Sometimes pays expenses of writers on assignment.
Reprints: Send tearsheet or photocopy of article and information about when and where the article previously appeared. Pays 25-50% of amount paid for an original article.

Photos: Always looking for news feature types of photos featuring forest products, industry materials or people. Send photos with submission. Reviews transparencies, 4×5 color prints. Pays $10-25/photo. Captions, identification of subjects required.

Tips: "Like most, we appreciate a clearly-worded query listing merits of suggested story—what it will tell our readers they need/want to know. We want quotes, we want opinions to make others discuss the article. Best hint? Find an interesting sawmill operation owner and start asking questions—I bet a story idea develops. We need color photos too. Find a sawmill operator and ask questions—what's he doing bigger, better, different. We're interested in new facilities, better marketing, improved production."

N̲ $ $TIMBERWEST, Timber/West Publications, LLC, P.O. Box 610, Edmonds WA 98020-0160. Fax: (425)771-3623. E-mail: timberwest@forestnet.com. Website: www.forestnet.com. **Contact:** Diane Mettler, managing editor. **75% freelance written.** Monthly magazine covering logging and lumber segment of the forestry industry in the northwest. "We publish primarily profiles on loggers and their operations, with an emphasis on the machinery, in Washington, Oregon, Idaho, Montana, Northern California and Alaska. Some timber issues are highly controversial and although we will report on the issues, this is a pro-logging publication. We don't publish articles with a negative slant on the timber industry." Estab. 1975. Circ. 10,000. **Pays on acceptance.** Byline given. Not copyrighted. Buys first North American serial, second serial (reprint) rights. Editorial lead time 3 months. Accepts queries by mail, fax. Responds in 3 weeks to queries. Sample copy for $2. Writer's guidelines for #10 SASE.

Nonfiction: Historical/nostalgic, interview/profile, new product. No articles that put the timber industry in a bad light—such as environmental articles against logging. **Buys 50 mss/year.** Query with published clips. Length: 1,100-1,500 words. **Pays $350.** Pays expenses of writers on assignment.

Photos: Send photos with submission. Reviews contact sheets, transparencies, prints, gif/jpeg files. Buys all rights. Offers no additional payment for photos accepted with ms. Captions, identification of subjects required.

Fillers: Facts, newsbreaks. **Buys 10/year.** Length: 400-800 words. **Pays $100-250.**

Tips: "We are always interested in profiles of loggers and their operations in Alaska, Oregon, Washington, Montana and Northern California. Also articles pertaining to current industry topics, such as fire abatement, sustainable forests or new technology. Read an issue to get a clear idea of the type of material TimberWest publishes. The audience is primarily loggers and topics that focus on an 'evolving' timber industry versus a 'dying' industry will find a place in the magazine. When querying, a clear overview of the article will enhance acceptance."

MACHINERY & METAL

$ANVIL MAGAZINE, Voice of the Farrier & Blacksmith, P.O. Box 1810, 2770 Sourdough Flat, Georgetown CA 95634. (530)333-2142. Fax: (530)333-2906. E-mail: anvil@anvilmag.com. Website: www.anvilmag.com. Editor: Andy Juell; Publisher: Ron Edwards. **Contact:** Mimi Clark, senior editor. **40% freelance written.** Monthly magazine covering "how-to articles on hoof care and horseshoeing and blacksmithing, tips on running your own farrier or blacksmith business and general articles on those subjects." Estab. 1978. Circ. 4,000. Pays on publication. Publishes ms an average of 1 year after acceptance. Byline sometimes given. Buys first North American serial rights. Editorial lead time 3 months. Submit seasonal material 6 months in advance. Accepts queries by mail, e-mail, fax. Accepts simultaneous submissions. Sample copy for $6. Writer's guidelines free.

Nonfiction: Material has to be specific to the subjects of horseshoeing, hoof care, farrier interests, blacksmithing interest. General interest, historical/nostalgic, how-to, humor, interview/profile, new product, opinion, photo feature, technical, Book reviews of farrier/blacksmithing publications. **Buys 8-10 mss/year.** Send complete ms. Length: 1,200-1,600 words. **Pays $25-200.** Sometimes pays expenses of writers on assignment.

Photos: Send photos with submission. Reviews transparencies. Buys one-time rights. Offers $25 additional payment for photos accepted with ms. Negotiates payment individually if photos only, such as for a how-to article. Identification of subjects required.

Poetry: Traditional on blacksmithing and farriery subjects only. No cowboy poetry. **Buys 5-6 poems/year.** Submit maximum 1-2 poems. Length: 20-40 lines lines. **Pays $25.**

Tips: "Write clearly and concisely. Our readers are professionals. Stay away from generic topics or general horsemanship. Our most popular features are "how to's" and interviews. For interviews, don't be bashful—ask the tough questions."

$ $ $CUTTING TOOL ENGINEERING, CTE Publications, 400 Skokie Blvd., Suite 395, Northbrook IL 60062-7903.. (847)498-9100. Fax: (847)559-4444. Website: www.ctemag.com. **Contact:** Don Nelson, editor. **50% freelance written.** Monthly magazine covering industrial metal cutting tools and metal cutting operations. "*Cutting Tool Engineering* serves owners, managers and engineers who work in manufacturing, specifically manufacturing that involves cutting or grinding metal or other materials. Writing should be geared toward improving manufacturing processes." Circ. 35,000. 1 week before publication. Publishes ms an average of 2 months after acceptance. Byline given. Offers 50% kill fee. Buys all rights. Editorial lead time 2 months. Accepts queries by mail, fax. Accepts simultaneous submissions. Responds in 2 months to mss. Sample copy and writer's guidelines free.

Nonfiction: How-to, interview/profile, opinion, personal experience, technical. "No fiction, articles that don't relate to manufacturing." **Buys 30 mss/year.** Length: 1,500-3,000 words. **Pays $450-1,000.** Pays expenses of writers on assignment.
Photos: State availability with submission. Reviews transparencies. Buys all rights. Negotiates payment individually. Captions required.
Columns/Departments: Talking Points (interview with industry subject), 600 words; Cutting Remarks (opinion piece), 900 words; Manager's Desk (shop owner), 700 words; Back To Basics (tool review), 500 words. **Buys 28 mss/ year.** Query with published clips. **Pays $150-300.**
Tips: "For queries, write two clear paragraphs about how the proposed article will play out. Include sources that would be in the article."

N $ $ $ THE FABRICATOR, The Croydon Group, Ltd., 833 Featherstone Rd., Rockford IL 61107. (815)399-8700. Fax: (815)484-7700. Website: www.thefabricator.com. **Contact:** Mike Dorcey, managing editor. **15% freelance written.** Monthly magazine covering metal forming and fabricating. Our purpose is to disseminate information about modern metal forming and fabricating techniques, machinery, tooling and management concepts for the metal fabricator. Estab. 1971. Circ. 55,000. Pays on publication. Byline given. Buys all rights. Editorial lead time 6 months. Accepts queries by mail, e-mail. Responds in 2 weeks to queries; 2 months to mss. Sample copy and writer's guidelines free.
Nonfiction: How-to, technical, company profile. Special issues: Forecast issue (January). No unsolicited case studies. Query with published clips. Length: 800-1,200 words. **Pays 40-80¢/word.** Sometimes pays expenses of writers on assignment.
Photos: State availability with submission. Reviews contact sheets. Rights purchased depends on photographer requirements. Negotiates payment individually. Captions, identification of subjects required.
Columns/Departments: Eye on Europe (metal fabricating in Europe); Asia Chronicle (metal fabricating in Asia), both 800 words. **Buys 1 mss/year.** Query. **Pays 40-80¢/word.**

N $ $ $ MANUFACTURING SYSTEMS, Cahners Business Information, 2000 Clearwater Dr., Oak Brook IL 60523-8809. (630)320-7041. Fax: (630)320-7088. E-mail: rmichel@cahners.com. Website: www.manufacturingsyste ms.com. **Contact:** Editor: Kevin Parker. Monthly magazine. "*Manufacturing Systems* is about the use of information technology to improve productivity in discrete manufacturing and process industries." Estab. 1984. Circ. 105,000. Pays on publication. Publishes ms an average of 3 months after acceptance. Byline sometimes given. Buys first North American serial rights. Editorial lead time 3 months. Submit seasonal material 4 months in advance. Accepts queries by e-mail. Sample copy free.
Nonfiction: Interview/profile, new product, technical. **Buys 9 mss/year.** Send complete ms. Length: 1,200-2,000 words. Pays expenses of writers on assignment.
Photos: Send photos with submission. No additional payment for photos. Captions required.

N $ MATERIAL HANDLING WHOLESALER, Specialty Publications International, Inc., P.O. Box 725, Dubuque IA 52004-0725. (319)557-4495. Fax: (319)557-4499. E-mail: dmillius@mhwmag.com. Website: www.mhwmag.c om. **Contact:** Hilary Hawley, editor. **100% freelance written.** Monthly magazine covering material handling industry. MHW is published monthly for new and used equipment dealers, equipment manufacturers, manufacturer reps, parts suppliers and service facilities serving the material handling industry. Estab. 1979. Circ. 13,000. Pays on publication. Publishes ms an average of 2 months after acceptance. Byline given. Buys first rights. Editorial lead time 1 month. Submit seasonal material 2 months in advance. Accepts queries by mail, e-mail, fax. Accepts simultaneous submissions. Sample copy for $29 annually-3rd class. Writer's guidelines free.
Nonfiction: General interest, how-to, inspirational, new product, opinion, personal experience, photo feature, technical, material handling news.
Photos: Send photos with submission. Reviews 3×5 prints. Buys all rights. Offers no additional payment for photos accepted with ms.
Columns/Departments: Aftermarket (aftermarket parts and service); Battery Tech (batteries for lifts-MH equipment; Marketing Matters (sales trends in MH industry); Internet at Work (internet trends), all 1,200 words. **Buys 3 mss/year.** Query. **Pays $0-50.**
   ◾ The online magazine carries original content not found in the print edition. Contact: Jan Day, online editor.

N $ $ NEW STEEL MAGAZINE, Voice of Today's Global Industry, Cahners Business Information, 2000 Clearwater Dr., Oak Brook IL 60523. (630)320-7053. Fax: (630)320-7105. E-mail: aritt@cahners.com. Website: www.ne wsteel.com. **Contact:** Adam Ritt, executive editor. **15% freelance written.** Monthly magazine covering the steel industry. "*Iron Age/New Steel* serves the ferrous and non-ferrous metal producing industries. Also included are others allied to the field including engineering and architectural services, as well as miscellaneous business services. Qualified recipients are corporate management, operating management, maintenance, engineering, metallurgical and chemical, purchasing, and research and development, managers and engineers in the above industries." Estab. 1855. Circ. 19,000. **Pays on acceptance.** Publishes ms an average of 1 month after acceptance. Byline given. Buys first, all rights. Editorial lead time 1 month. Responds in 2 weeks to queries. Sample copy free.
Nonfiction: Does not want to see applications at work or any public-relations copy. Does not publish unsolicited articles. Query with published clips. Do not send ms without prior approval. Length: 750-10,000 words. Pays expenses of writers on assignment.

Photos: Send photos with submission. Reviews contact sheets, transparencies. Buys all rights. Negotiates payment individually. Captions, identification of subjects required.

■ The online magazine carries original content not found in the print edition. Contact: Adam Ritt.

Tips: "Write stories specifically about the steel industry using sources from within the industry."

$ $ ORNAMENTAL AND MISCELLANEOUS METAL FABRICATOR, National Ornamental And Miscellaneous Metals Association, 532 Forest Pkwy., Suite A, Forest Park GA 30297. Fax: (404)363-2857. E-mail: nomma2@aol.com. **Contact:** Todd Daniel, editor. **20% freelance written.** Bimonthly magazine "to inform, educate and inspire members of the ornamental and miscellaneous metalworking industry." Estab. 1959. Circ. 10,000. Pays when article is actually received. Byline given. Buys one-time rights. Editorial lead time 2 months. Submit seasonal material 2 months in advance. Accepts queries by mail, e-mail, fax. Responds in 1 month to queries. Sample copy for 9 × 12 SAE and 6 first-class stamps. Writer's guidelines for $1.

Nonfiction: Book excerpts, essays, exposé, general interest, historical/nostalgic, how-to, humor, inspirational, interview/profile, new product, opinion, personal experience, photo feature, technical. **Buys 5-7 mss/year.** Query. Length: 1,200-2,000 words. **Pays $250-275 for assigned articles; $50 for unsolicited articles.** Pays expenses of writers on assignment.

Reprints: Send tearsheet, photocopy or typed ms with rights for sale noted and information about when and where the material previously appeared. Pays 100% of amount paid for an original article.

Photos: State availability with submission. Reviews contact sheets, negatives, transparencies, prints. May offer additonal payment for photos accepted with ms. Model releases required.

Tips: "Make article relevant to our industry. Don't write in passive voice."

N̲ $ $ $ PRACTICAL WELDING TODAY, The Croydon Group, Ltd., 833 Featherstone Rd., Rockford IL 61107-6302. (815)227-8282. Fax: (815)484-7715. E-mail: stephaniev@thefabricator.com. Website: www.thefabricator.com. Managing Editor: Mike Dorcey. **Contact:** Stephanie Vaughan, associate editor. **15% freelance written.** Bimonthly magazine covering welding. "We generally publish how-to, educational articles that teach people about a process or how to do something better." Estab. 1997. Circ. 40,000. Pays on publication. Byline given. Buys all rights. Editorial lead time 6 months. Accepts queries by mail, e-mail. Responds in 2 weeks to queries; 2 months to mss. Sample copy and writer's guidelines free.

Nonfiction: How-to, technical, company profiles. Special issues: Forecast issue on trends in welding (January/February). No promotional, one-sided, persuasive articles, unsolicited case studies. **Buys 5 mss/year.** Query with published clips. Length: 800-1,200 words. **Pays 40-80¢/word.** Sometimes pays expenses of writers on assignment.

Photos: State availability with submission. Reviews contact sheets. Rights purchased depends on photographer requirements. Negotiates payment individually. Captions, identification of subjects required.

Columns/Departments: Inspection Connection (inspecting welds), 700 words. **Buys 1-2 mss/year.** Query with published clips. **Pays 40-80¢/word.**

Tips: "Follow our author guidelines and editorial policies to write a how-to piece from which our readers can benefit."

N̲ $ $ SPRINGS, The Magazine of Spring Technology, Spring Manufacturing Institute, 2001 Midwest Rd., Suite 106, Oak Brook IL 60523-1335. (630)495-8588. Fax: (630)495-8595. **Contact:** Rita Schauer, editor. **10% freelance written.** Bimonthly magazine covering precision mechanical spring manufacture. Articles should be aimed at spring manufacturers." Estab. 1962. Circ. 8,900. Pays on publication. Publishes ms an average of 6 months after acceptance. Byline given. Buys first rights. Editorial lead time 4 months. Accepts simultaneous submissions. Sample copy and writer's guidelines free.

Nonfiction: General interest, how-to, interview/profile, opinion, personal experience, technical. **Buys 4-6 mss/year.** Length: 2,000-10,000 words. **Pays $100-600 for assigned articles; $50-300 for unsolicited articles.**

Photos: State availability with submission. Reviews transparencies, prints. Buys one-time rights. Offers no additional payment for photos accepted with ms. Captions required.

Fillers: Facts, newsbreaks. **Buys 4/year.** Length: 200-1,000 words. **Pays $25-50.**

Tips: "Call the editor. Contact springmakers and spring industry suppliers and ask about what interests them. Include interviews/quotes from people in the spring industry in the article. The editor can supply contacts."

N̲ $ $ STAMPING JOURNAL, The Croydon Group, Ltd., 833 Featherstone Rd., Rockford IL 61107. (815)399-8700. Fax: (815)484-7700. Website: www.thefabricator.com. Managing Editor: Mike Dorcey. **Contact:** Kara Pipitone, associate editor. **15% freelance written.** Bimonthly magazine covering metal stamping. "We look for how-to, educational articles—non-promotional." Estab. 1989. Circ. 35,000. Pays on publication. Byline given. Buys all rights. Editorial lead time 6 months. Accepts queries by mail, e-mail, fax, phone. Responds in 2 weeks to queries; 2 months to mss. Sample copy and writer's guidelines free.

Nonfiction: How-to, technical, company profile. Special issues: Forecast issue (January). No unsolicited case studies. **Buys 5 mss/year.** Query with published clips. Length: 1,000 words. **Pays 40-80¢/word.** Sometimes pays expenses of writers on assignment.

Photos: State availability with submission. Reviews contact sheets. Rights purchased depends on photographer requirements. Negotiates payment individually. Captions, identification of subjects required.

■ The online magazine carries original content not found in the print edition. Contact: Lincoln Brunner, online editor.

Tips: "Articles should be impartial and should not describe the benefits of certain products available from certain companies. They should not be biased toward the author's or against a competitor's products or technologies. The publisher may refuse any article that does not conform to this guideline."

N̄ $ $ $ 33 METALPRODUCING, Penton Media, Inc., 1300 E. Ninth St., Cleveland OH 44114. (216)696-7000. Fax: (216)931-9524. E-mail: whuskonen@penton.com. Website: www.33metalproducing.com. **Contact:** Wallace D. Huskonen, editor. **50% freelance written.** Monthly magazine covering producing metal mill products from ore/scrap. "The mission of *33 Metalproducing* is to provide timely, authoritative and useful information on domestic and global trends in the metalproducing industry (SIC 33) for operating management engineers, and other management personnel." Estab. 1962. Circ. 18,000. Pays on publication. Publishes ms an average of 1 month after acceptance. Byline given. Editorial lead time 2 months. Accepts queries by mail, e-mail, fax, phone. Responds in 2 weeks to queries; 1 month to mss. Sample copy and writer's guidelines free.
Nonfiction: Book excerpts, interview/profile, technical. **Buys 20 mss/year.** Query with published clips. Length: 750-3,000 words. **Pays $100-1,000.**
Photos: State availability with submission. Reviews contact sheets, negatives, transparencies, prints. Buys all rights. Offers no additional payment for photos accepted with ms. Captions, identification of subjects required.
　　■ The online magazine carries original content not found in the print edition. Contact: Wallace D. Huskonen.
Tips: "A freelance writer should demonstrate ability to use the language of metalproducing in producing features for *33MP.*"

N̄ $ $ $ TPJ—THE TUBE & PIPE JOURNAL, The Croydon Group, Ltd., 833 Featherstone Rd., Rockford IL 61107. (815)227-8262. Fax: (815)484-7713. E-mail: ericl@thefabricator.com. Website: www.thefabricator.com. Managing Editor: Michael Dorcey. **Contact:** Eric Lundin, associate editor. **15% freelance written.** Magazine published 8 times/year covering metal tube and pipe. Educational perspective—emphasis is on "how-to" articles to accomplish a particular task or how to improve on a process. New trends and technologies are also important topics. Estab. 1990. Circ. 30,000. Pays on publication. Byline given. Buys all rights. Editorial lead time 6 months. Accepts queries by mail, e-mail. Responds in 2 weeks to queries; 2 months to mss. Sample copy and writer's guidelines free.
Nonfiction: Any new or improved tube production or fabrication process—includes manufacturing, bending and forming tube (metal tube only). How-to, technical, company profile. Special issues: Forecast issue (January). No unsolicited case studies. **Buys 5 mss/year.** Query with published clips. Length: 800-1,200 words. **Pays 40-80¢/word.** Sometimes pays expenses of writers on assignment.
Photos: State availability with submission. Reviews contact sheets. Rights purchased depends on photographer requirements. Negotiates payment individually. Captions, identification of subjects required.
Columns/Departments: Manager's Notebook (management tips, information news), 1,000 words. **Pays 40¢/word.**
Tips: "Submit a detailed proposal, including an article outline, to the editor."

$ $ WIRE ROPE NEWS & SLING TECHNOLOGY, VS Enterprises, P.O. Box 871, Clark NJ 07066. (908)486-3221. Fax: (732)396-4215. E-mail: vsent@aol.com. Website: www.wireropenews.com. Editor: Barbara McGrath, Managing Editor: Conrad Miller. **Contact:** Edward J. Bluvias, publisher. **100% freelance written.** Bimonthly magazine "published for manufacturers and distributors of wire rope, chain, cordage, related hardware, and sling fabricators. Content includes technical articles, news and reports describing the manufacturing and use of wire rope and related products in marine, construction, mining, aircraft and offshore drilling operations." Estab. 1979. Circ. 3,400. **Pays on acceptance.** Publishes ms an average of 6 months after acceptance. Byline sometimes given. Buys all rights. Editorial lead time 2 months. Submit seasonal material 2 months in advance. Accepts queries by mail, fax. Accepts simultaneous submissions.
Nonfiction: General interest, historical/nostalgic, interview/profile, photo feature, technical. **Buys 30 mss/year.** Send complete ms. Length: 2,500-5,000 words. **Pays $300-500.**
Photos: Send photos with submission. Reviews contact sheets, 5×7 prints. Buys all rights. Offers no additional payment for photos accepted with ms. Identification of subjects required.

MAINTENANCE & SAFETY

N̄ $ BREATHING AIR DIGEST, Sub-Aquatics, Inc., Publications Division, 8855 E. Broad St., Reynoldsburg OH 43068. (614)864-1235. Fax: (614)864-0071. Website: www.breathingair.com. Editor: Richard Lauer. **Contact:** William McBride, managing editor. **25% freelance written.** Semiannual magazine. "Our audience is primarily those involved with the production, handling, and use of high-pressure pure breathing air, particularly fire and safety departments, dive stores, etc. We are interested in articles of 500-1,500 words related to tips, experiences, technology and applications." Estab. 1989. Circ. 12,000. Pays on publication. Publishes ms an average of 1 year after acceptance. Byline given. Buys first, one-time rights. Editorial lead time 1 year. Accepts queries by mail. Accepts simultaneous submissions. Responds in 6 weeks to queries; 2 months to mss. Sample copy for 9×12 SAE and 4 first-class stamps.
Nonfiction: How-to, new product, personal experience, photo feature, technical. "We are not interested in brand-specific promotional material." **Buys 3-6 mss/year.** Send complete ms. Length: 500-1,500 words. **Pays $50-70.**

Photos: Send photos with submission. Reviews negatives, transparencies, prints. Buys one-time rights. Offers no additional payment for photos accepted with ms.

Columns/Departments: Send complete ms. **Pays $50-70.**

Tips: "We most want articles that will be of use to others in this field. Often, the relating of 'bad' experiences can be helpful."

$ $ $ CANADIAN OCCUPATIONAL SAFETY, Clifford/Elliot Ltd., 3228 S. Service Rd., Suite 209, Burlington, Ontario L7N 3H8, Canada. (905)634-2100 ext. 35. Fax: (905)634-2238. E-mail: mgault@cos-mag.com. Website: www.cos-mag.com. **Contact:** Michelle Gault, editor. **40% freelance written.** Bimonthly magazine. "We want informative articles dealing with issues that relate to occupational health and safety." Estab. 1989. Circ. 14,000. Pays on publication. Publishes ms an average of 3 months after acceptance. Byline given. Buys one-time rights. Editorial lead time 4 months. Submit seasonal material 4 months in advance. Accepts queries by mail, e-mail, fax, phone. Responds in 3 weeks to queries; 1 month to mss. Sample copy and writer's guidelines free.

Nonfiction: How-to, interview/profile. **Buys 30 mss/year.** Query with published clips. Length: 750-2,000 words. **Payment varies.** Sometimes pays expenses of writers on assignment.

Photos: State availability with submission. Reviews transparencies. Buys one-time rights. Negotiates payment individually. Captions required.

Tips: "Present us with an idea for an article that will interest workplace health and safety professionals, with cross-Canada appeal."

$ CLEANING BUSINESS, P.O. Box 1273, Seattle WA 98111. (206)622-4241. Fax: (206)622-6876. E-mail: ccs@cleaningconsultants.com. Website: www.cleaningconsultants.com. William R. Griffin, Publisher. **Contact:** Jim Saunders, associate editor. **80% freelance written.** Quarterly magazine. "We cater to those who are self-employed in any facet of the cleaning and maintenance industry and seek to be top professionals in their field. *Cleaning Business* is published for self-employed cleaning professionals, specifically carpet, upholstery and drapery cleaners; janitorial and maid services; window washers; odor, water and fire damage restoration contractors. Our readership is small but select. We seek concise, factual articles, realistic but definitely upbeat." Circ. 6,000. Pays 1 month after publication. Publishes ms an average of 3 months after acceptance. Byline given. Buys first North American serial, second serial (reprint), all rights, makes work-for-hire assignments. Submit seasonal material 6 months in advance. Responds in 3 months to mss. Sample copy for $3 and 8×10 SAE with 3 first-class stamps. Writer's guidelines for #10 SASE.

Nonfiction: Exposé (safety/health business practices), how-to (on cleaning, maintenance, small business management), humor (clean jokes, cartoons), interview/profile, new product (must be unusual to rate full article—mostly obtained from manufacturers), opinion, personal experience, technical. Special issues: "What's New?" (February). No "wordy articles written off the top of the head, obviously without research, and needing more editing time than was spent on writing." **Buys 40 mss/year.** Query with or without published clips. Length: 500-3,000 words.

Photos: "Magazine size is 8½×11—photos need to be proportionate. Also seeks full-color photos of relevant subjects for cover." State availability with submission. Buys one-time rights. Pays $5-25 for "smallish" b&w prints. Captions, identification of subjects, model releases required.

Columns/Departments: "Ten regular columnists now sell four columns per year to us. We are interested in adding Safety & Health and Fire Restoration columns (related to cleaning and maintenance industry). We are also open to other suggestions—send query." **Buys 36 mss/year.** Query with or without published clips. **Pays $15-85.**

Fillers: Anecdotes, gags to be illustrated by cartoonist, newsbreaks, short humor, Jokes, Gags. **Buys 40/year.** Length: 3-200 words. **Pays $1-20.**

Tips: "We are constantly seeking quality freelancers from all parts of the country. A freelancer can best break in to our publication with fairly technical articles on how to do specific cleaning/maintenance jobs; interviews with top professionals covering this and how they manage their business; and personal experience. Our readers demand concise, accurate information. Don't ramble. Write only about what you know and/or have researched. Editors don't have time to rewrite your rough draft. Organize and polish before submitting."

[N] $ $ EXECUTIVE HOUSEKEEPING TODAY, The International Executive Housekeepers Association, 1001 Eastwind Dr., Suite 301, Westerville OH 43081. (614)895-7166. Fax: (614)895-1248. E-mail: avance@ieha.org. Website: www.ieha.org. **Contact:** Andi Vance, editor. **95% freelance written.** Monthly magazine for "nearly 8,000 decision makers responsible for housekeeping management (cleaning, grounds maintenance, laundry, linen, pest control, waste management, regulatory compliance, training) for a variety of institutions: hospitality, healthcare, education, retail, government." Estab. 1930. Circ. 5,500. **Pays on acceptance.** Publishes ms an average of 6 months after acceptance. Byline given. Buys first North American serial rights. Editorial lead time 2 months. Submit seasonal material 3 months in advance. Accepts queries by mail, e-mail, fax, phone. Sample copy and writer's guidelines free.

Nonfiction: General interest, interview/profile, new product (related to magazine's scope), personal experience (in housekeeping profession), technical. **Buys 30 mss/year.** Query with published clips. Length: 500-1,500 words. **Pays $150-250.**

Photos: State availability with submission. Reviews negatives. Buys one-time rights. Offers no additional payment for photos accepted with ms. Identification of subjects required.

Columns/Departments: Federal Report (OSHA/EPA requirements), 1,000 words; Industry News; Management Perspectives (industry specific), 500-1,500 words. Query with published clips. **Pays $150-250.**

Tips: "Have a background in the industry or personal experience with any aspect of it."

N̄ **$ $PEST CONTROL MAGAZINE**, 7500 Old Oak Blvd., Cleveland OH 44130. (440)243-8100. Fax: (440)891-2683. Website: www.pestcontrolmag.com. **Contact:** Lisa Shaheen, editor. Monthly magazine for professional pest management professionals and sanitarians. Estab. 1933. Circ. 20,000. Pays on publication. Buys all rights. Submit seasonal material 2 months in advance. Accepts queries by mail, e-mail, phone. Responds in 1 month to mss.

　　O┓ Break in with "information directly relating to the field—citing sources that are either industry experts (university or otherwise) or direct quotes from pest/management professionals."

Nonfiction: How-to, humor, inspirational, interview/profile, new product, personal experience (stories about pest management operations and their problems). Must have trade or business orientation. No general information type of articles desired. **Buys 3 mss/year.** Query or send complete ms. Length: 1,000 words. **Pays $150-500 minimum.**
Photos: State availability with submission. Pays $50-500 for 8×10 color or transparencies for front cover graphics. No additional payment for photos used with ms.
Columns/Departments: Regular columns use material oriented to this profession. Length: 750 words.

　　■ The online magazine carries original content not found in the print edition. Contact: Heather Gooch.

MANAGEMENT & SUPERVISION

This category includes trade journals for middle management business and industrial managers, including supervisors and office managers. Journals for business executives and owners are classified under Business Management. Those for industrial plant managers are listed in Industrial Operations.

$ $HR MAGAZINE, On Human Resource Management, Society for Human Resource Management, 1800 Duke St., Alexandria VA 22314-3499. (703)548-3440. Fax: (703)548-9140. E-mail: hrmag@shrm.org. Website: www.shrm.org. Editor: Leon Rubis. **Contact:** Karen Caldwell, editorial assistant. **70% freelance written.** Monthly magazine covering human resource management professions with special focus on business news that affects the workplace including compensation, benefits, recruiting, training and development, management trends, court decisions, legislative actions and government regulations. Estab. 1948. Circ. 150,000. **Pays on acceptance.** Publishes ms an average of 2 months after acceptance. Byline given. Buys all rights. Editorial lead time 4 months. Accepts queries by mail, e-mail, fax. Responds in 1 month to queries. Sample copy free.

　　O┓ Break in by having "relevant writing experience and a sharp, narrowly-focused article idea on something new or not well-covered elsewhere."

Nonfiction: Technical, expert advice and analysis, news features. **Buys 50 mss/year.** Query. Length: 1,800-2,500 words. Pays expenses of writers on assignment.
Photos: State availability with submission. Buys one-time rights. Identification of subjects, model releases required.
Tips: "Readers are members of the Society for Human Resource Management (SHRM), mostly HR managers with private employers."

N̄ **$ $INCENTIVE**, Bill Communications, Dept. WM, 770 Broadway, New York NY 10003. (646)654-7644. Fax: (646)654-7650. E-mail: valonzo@incentivemag.com. Website: www.incentivemag.com. **Contact:** Vincent Alonzo, editor. Monthly magazine covering sales promotion and employee motivation: managing and marketing through motivation. Estab. 1905. Circ. 41,000. **Pays on acceptance.** Publishes ms an average of 3 months after acceptance. Byline given. Buys all rights. Accepts queries by mail, e-mail, fax. Responds in 1 month to queries; 2 months to mss. Sample copy for 9×12 SAE.
Nonfiction: General interest (motivation, demographics), how-to (types of sales promotion, buying product categories, using destinations), interview/profile (sales promotion executives), travel (incentive-oriented), Corporate case studies. **Buys 48 mss/year.** Query with published clips. Length: 1,000-2,000 words. **Pays $250-700 for assigned articles; does not pay for unsolicited articles.** Pays expenses of writers on assignment.
Reprints: Send tearsheet and information about when and where the material previously appeared. Pays 50% of the amount paid for an original article.
Photos: Send photos with submission. Reviews contact sheets, transparencies. Offers some additional payment for photos accepted with ms. Identification of subjects required.
Tips: "Read the publication, then query."

$MANAGE, 2210 Arbor Blvd., Dayton OH 45439. (937)294-0421. Fax: (937)294-2374. E-mail: doug@nma1.org. Website: www.nma1.org. **Contact:** Douglas E. Shaw, editor-in-chief. **60% freelance written.** Works with a small number of new/unpublished writers each year. Quarterly magazine for first-line and middle management and scientific/

technical managers. Estab. 1925. Circ. 30,000. **Pays on acceptance.** Publishes ms an average of 6 months after acceptance. Buys first North American serial rights, reprint privileges; book rights remain with the author. Responds in 3 months to queries. Sample copy and writer's guidelines for 9×12 SAE and 3 first-class stamps.

Nonfiction: "All material published by *Manage* is in some way management-oriented. Most articles concern one or more of the following categories: Communications, executive abilities, human relations, job status, leadership, motivation and productivity and professionalism. Articles should be specific and tell the manager how to apply the information to his job immediateely. Be sure to include pertinent examples, and back up statements with facts." "*Manage* does not want essays or academic reports, but interesting, well-written and practical articles for and about management." Length: 600-1,000 words. **Pays 5¢/word.**

Reprints: Send photocopy. Pays 100% of amount paid for an original article.

Tips: "Keep current on management subjects; submit timely work. Include word count on first page of manuscript."

$ SUPERVISION, 320 Valley, Burlington IA 52601. Fax: (319)752-3421. Publisher: Michael S. Darnall. **Contact:** Teresa Levinson, editor. **95% freelance written.** Monthly magazine for first-line foremen, supervisors and office managers. "*Supervision*'s objective is to provide informative articles which develop the attitudes, skills, personal and professional qualities of supervisory staff, enabling them to use more of their potential to maximize productivity, minimize costs, and achieve company and personal goals." Estab. 1939. Circ. 2,620. Pays on publication. Publishes ms an average of 6 months after acceptance. Buys all rights. Accepts queries by mail, fax, phone. Responds in 1 month to mss. Sample copy and writer's guidelines for 9×12 SAE with 4 first-class stamps; mention *Writer's Market* in request.

Nonfiction: How-to (cope with supervisory problems, discipline, absenteeism, safety, productivity, goal setting, et.), personal experience (unusual success story of foreman or supervisor). No sexist material written from only a male viewpoint. **Buys 12 mss/year.** Include biography and/or byline with ms submissions. Author photos requested. Length: 1,500-1,800 words. **Pays 4¢/word.**

Tips: "Following AP stylebook would be helpful." Uses no advertising. Send correspondence to Editor.

N $ $ $ WORKFORCE MAGAZINE, ACC Communications, Inc., 245 Fischer Ave., B-2, Costa Mesa CA 92626. (714)751-1883. Fax: (714)751-4106. E-mail: mailroom@workforce.com. Website: www.workforce.com. Managing Editor: Carroll Lachnit. **Contact:** Ronda Lathion, editorial administrator. **90% freelance written.** Monthly magazine for human resource professionals. "*Workforce* readers are the new breed of HR professionals. They are actively working to make their businesses better. They are college educated and have been in the HR field an average of 12 years. Readers work in all industries, and they work in organizations of all sizes." Estab. 1922. Circ. 40,000. **Pays on acceptance.** Publishes ms an average of 1 month after acceptance. Byline given. Offers 50% kill fee. Buys first North American serial, electronic rights. Editorial lead time 3 months. Accepts queries by mail, e-mail, fax, phone. Sample copy and writer's guidelines free or online.

Nonfiction: Book excerpts, general interest, how-to, humor, inspirational, interview/profile, new product, opinion, personal experience, case studies. **Buys 20 mss/year.** Query. Length: 500-2,500 words. **Pays negotiable amount, usually $1/word.** Sometimes pays expenses of writers on assignment.

Photos: State availability with submission. Buys one-time rights. Offers no additional payment for photos accepted with ms.

Tips: "Get samples of the magazine. Check out our website."

MARINE & MARITIME INDUSTRIES

$ $ PROFESSIONAL MARINER, Journal of the Maritime Industry, Navigator Publishing, 18 Danforth St., Portland ME 04101. (207)772-2466. Fax: (207)772-2879. E-mail: editors@professionalmariner.com. **Contact:** Evan True, editor. **50% freelance written.** Bimonthly magazine covering professional seamanship and maritime industry news. Estab. 1993. Circ. 29,000. Pays on publication. Byline given. Buys all rights. Editorial lead time 3 months. Accepts queries by mail, e-mail, fax, phone. Accepts simultaneous submissions.

Nonfiction: For professional mariners on vessels and ashore. Seeks submissions on industry news, regulations, towing, piloting, technology, engineering, business, maritime casualties and feature stories about the maritime industry. Does accept "sea stories" and personal professional experiences as correspondence pieces. **Buys 15 mss/year.** Query. Length: Varies; short clips to long profiles/features. **Pays 15¢/word.** Sometimes pays expenses of writers on assignment.

Photos: Send photos with submission. Reviews slides, prints. Buys one-time rights. Negotiates payment individually. Captions, identification of subjects required.

Tips: "Remember that our audience is professional mariners and other marine professionals. Stories must be written at a level that will benefit this group."

MEDICAL

Through these journals physicians, therapists and mental health professionals learn how other professionals help their patients and manage their medical practices. Publications for nurses, laboratory technicians and other medical personnel are listed in the Hospitals, Nursing and

Nursing Home section. Publications for drug store managers and drug wholesalers and retailers, as well as hospital equipment suppliers, are listed with Drugs, Health Care and Medical Products. Publications for consumers that report trends in the medical field are found in the Consumer Health and Fitness categories.

$ $ $ AMA ALLIANCE TODAY, American Medical Association Alliance, Inc., 515 N. State St., Chicago IL 60610. (312)464-4470. Fax: (312)464-5020. E-mail: amaa@ama-assn.org. Website: www.ama-assn.org/alliance. **Contact:** Catherine Potts, MSJ, editor. **25% freelance written.** Quarterly magazine for physicians' spouses. Works with both established and new writers. Estab. 1965. Circ. 60,000. **Pays on acceptance.** Publishes ms an average of 6 months after acceptance. Buys first rights. Accepts queries by mail, e-mail, fax. Accepts simultaneous submissions. Sample copy for 9×12 SAE and 2 first-class stamps.
> O→ Break in with a "solid understanding of issues affecting physicians and their families with a special emphasis on the perspective of the physician's spouse or child."

Nonfiction: All articles must be related to the experiences of physicians' spouses. Current health issues; financial topics, physicians' family circumstances, business management and volunteer leadership how-to's. Query with clear outline of article—what points will be made, what conclusions drawn, what sources will be used. Length: 1,000 words. **Pays $300-800.**
Photos: Uses all color visuals. State availability with submission.
Tips: "Emphasize trends in healthcare as they affect the spouses and children of physicians."

N $ $ $ AMERICA'S PHARMACIST, National Community Pharmacists Association, 205 Daingerfield Rd., Alexandria VA 22314. (703)683-8200. Fax: (703)683-3619. E-mail: Robert.Malone@ncpanet.com. Website: www.ncpanet.org. **Contact:** Robert A. Malone, editor. **10% freelance written.** Monthly magazine. "*America's Pharmacist* publishes business and management information and personal profiles of independent community pharmacists, the magazine's principal readers." Estab. 1904. Circ. 25,000. Pays on publication. Publishes ms an average of 3 months after acceptance. Byline given. Offers 20% kill fee. Buys all rights. Editorial lead time 3 months. Submit seasonal material 3 months in advance. Accepts queries by mail, e-mail, fax. Accepts simultaneous submissions. Responds in 1 week to queries; 2 weeks to mss. Sample copy and writer's guidelines free.
Nonfiction: Interview/profile, business information. **Buys 3 mss/year.** Query. Length: 1,500-2,500 words. **Pays $500-1,000.** Sometimes pays expenses of writers on assignment.
Photos: State availability with submission. Reviews contact sheets. Buys one-time rights. Negotiates payment individually. Captions, identification of subjects, model releases required.

N EVERY SECOND COUNTS, The Emergency Response Magazine, National Safety Council, 1121 Spring Lake Dr., Itasca IL 60143-3201. Fax: (630)775-2285. E-mail: parkerj@nsc.org. Website: www.nsc.org. Editor: Jennifer Grow. **Contact:** James Parker, associate editor. **100% freelance written.** Bimonthly magazine about EMTs, firefighters, paramedics and first-aid instructors. Estab. 1999. Circ. 48,000. **Pays on acceptance.** Publishes ms an average of 1 month after acceptance. Byline given. Buys all rights. Submit seasonal material 6 months in advance. Accepts queries by mail, e-mail, fax. Responds in 4 months to queries; 4 months to mss. Sample copy for 8×10 SAE and 2 first-class stamps. Writer's guidelines for #10 SASE.
Nonfiction: Exposé, general interest, historical/nostalgic, how-to, interview/profile, new product, opinion, personal experience, photo feature. **Buys 40 mss/year.** Query with published clips. Length: 2,000-3,000 words. **Payment determined on a per assignment basis.**
Photos: Send photos with submission. Reviews contact sheets, transparencies, prints, gif/jpeg files. Buys one-time rights. Offers $50/photo. Identification of subjects, model releases required.
Columns/Departments: Play It Safe (sport safety and sport emergencies), 1,500 words. **Buys 6 mss/year.** Query with published clips. **Payment decided on a per assignment basis.**

N $ $ FIRE-RESCUE MAGAZINE, Jems Communications, P.O. Box 2789, Carlsbad CA 92018-2789. (760)804-6692. Fax: (760)930-9567. E-mail: noble.sprayberry@jems.com. Website: www.jems.com. **Contact:** Michelle Garrido, deputy editor. **75% freelance written.** Monthly magazine covering technical aspects of being a firefighter/rescuer. Estab. 1988. Circ. 50,000. y. Buys first North American serial, one-time rights. Submit seasonal material 6 months in advance. Accepts queries by mail, e-mail. Responds in 3 weeks to queries; 2 months to mss. Sample copy and writer's guidelines for 9×12 SAE with 5 first-class stamps or online.
Nonfiction: How-to, new product, photo feature, technical, Incident review/report. Special issues: Fire suppression, incident command, vehicle extrication, rescue training, mass-casualty incidents, water rescue/major issues facing the fire service. **Buys 15-20 mss/year.** Query with published clips or send complete ms. Length: 1,000-3,000 words. **Pays $125-250.** Sometimes pays expenses of writers on assignment.
Photos: Send photos with submission. Reviews contact sheets, negatives, 2×2 and 35mm transparencies, 5×7 prints. Buys one-time rights. Offers $20-200.
> ■ The online magazine carries original content not found in the print edition.

Tips: "Read our magazine, spend some time with a fire department. We focus on all aspects of fire and rescue. Emphasis on techniques and new technology, with color photos as support."

N̄ $ $ $HEALTHPLAN, American Association of Health Plans, 1129 20th St. NW, Suite 600, Washington DC 20036. (202)778-3246. Fax: (202)331-7487. E-mail: gfauntleroy@aahp.org. Website: www.aahp.org. Editor: Louise Kertesz. **Contact:** Glenda Fauntleroy, managing editor. **75% freelance written.** Bimonthly magazine. "*Healthplan* is geared toward administrators in HMOs, PPOs, and similar health plans. Articles must ask 'why' and 'how' and answer with examples. Articles should inform and generate interest and discussion about topics on anything from patient care to regulatory issues." Estab. 1990. Circ. 7,000. Pays within 30 days of acceptance of article in final form. Publishes ms an average of 2 months after acceptance. Byline given. Offers 30% kill fee. Buys all rights. Editorial lead time 2 months. Submit seasonal material 4 months in advance. Accepts queries by mail, e-mail, fax, phone. Accepts simultaneous submissions. Sample copy and writer's guidelines free.

Nonfiction: Book excerpts, how-to (how industry professionals can better operate their health plans), opinion. "We do not accept stories that promote products." **Buys 20 mss/year.** Query with published clips or send complete ms. Length: 1,800-2,500 words. **Pays 65¢/word minimum for assigned articles.** Pays phone expenses of writers on assignment.

Photos: State availability with submission. Reviews contact sheets. Buys all rights. Offers no additional payment for photos accepted with ms.

Columns/Departments: Information Technology (case study or how-to); Chronic Care (case studies), 1,800 words; Preventive Care (case study or discussion of public health); The Market (market niches for HMOs—with examples), all 1,800 words. **Buys 6 mss/year.** Query with published clips or send complete ms. **Pays 65¢/word minimum.**

Tips: "Follow the current health care debate. Look for health plan success stories in your community; we like to include case studies on a variety of topics—including patient care, provider relations, regulatory issues—so that our readers can learn from their colleagues. Our readers are members of our trade association and look for advice and news. Topics relating to the quality of health plans are the ones more frequently assigned to writers, whether a feature or department. We also welcome story ideas. Just send us a letter with the details."

$ $🔲 JEMS, The Journal of Emergency Medical Services, Jems Communications, 1947 Camino Vida Roble, Suite 200, Carlsbad CA 92008-2789. (760)431-9797. Fax: (760)930-9567. Website: www.jems.com. **Contact:** A.J. Heightman, editor. **95% freelance written.** Monthly magazine directed to personnel who serve the pre-hospital emergency medicine industry: Paramedics, EMTs, emergency physicians and nurses, administrators, EMS consultants, etc. Estab. 1980. Circ. 45,000. Pays on publication. Publishes ms an average of 6 months after acceptance. Byline given. Buys all North American serial rights. Submit seasonal material 6 months in advance. Accepts queries by mail, e-mail, fax. Responds in 6 weeks to queries. Sample copy and writer's guidelines free.

Nonfiction: Essays, exposé, general interest, how-to, humor, interview/profile, new product, opinion, personal experience, photo feature, technical, continuing education. **Buys 50 mss/year.** Query. **Pays $200-400.**

Photos: State availability with submission. Reviews 4×6 prints. Buys one-time rights. Offers $25 minimum per photo. Identification of subjects, model releases required.

Columns/Departments: Length: 850 words maximum. "Columns and departments are staff-written with the exception of commentary on EMS issues and practices." Query with or without published clips. **Pays $50-250.**

Tips: "Please submit a one-page query letter before you send a manuscript. Your query should answer these questions: 1) What specifically are you going to tell *JEMS* readers? 2) Why do *JEMS* readers need to know this? 3) How will you make your case (i.e., literature review, original research, interviews, personal experience, observation)? Your query should explain your qualifications, as well as include previous writing samples."

$ $MANAGED CARE, 275 Phillips Blvd., Trenton NJ 08618-1426. (609)671-2100. Fax: (609)882-3213. E-mail: editors@managedcaremag.com. Website: www.managedcaremag.com. **Contact:** John Marcille, editor. **50% freelance written.** Monthly magazine. "We emphasize practical, usable information that helps the physician or HMO administrator cope with the options, challenges and hazards in the rapidly changing health care industry. Our regular readers understand that 'health care reform' isn't a piece of legislation; it's an evolutionary process that's already well under way. But we hope to help our readers also keep the faith that led them to medicine in the first place." Estab. 1992. Circ. 60,000. **Pays on acceptance.** Publishes ms an average of 1 month after acceptance. Byline given. Offers 20% kill fee. Buys all rights. Editorial lead time 3 months. Submit seasonal material 4 months in advance. Accepts queries by mail, e-mail, fax. Responds in 3 weeks to queries; 2 months to mss. Sample copy free.

Nonfiction: Book excerpts, general interest (trends in health-care delivery and financing, quality of care, and employee concerns), how-to (deal with requisites of managed care, such as contracts with health plans, affiliation arrangements, accreditation, computer needs, etc.), original research and review articles that examine the relationship between health care delivery and financing. Also considered occasionally are personal experience, opinion, interview/profile and humor pieces, but these must have a strong managed care angle and draw upon the insights of (if they are not written by) a knowledgeable MD or managed care professional. **Buys 40 mss/year.** Query with published clips. Length: 1,000-3,000 words. **Pays 50-60¢/word.** Pays expenses of writers on assignment.

Photos: State availability with submission. Reviews contact sheets, negatives, transparencies, prints. Buys first-time rights. Negotiates payment individually.

Columns/Departments: Michael Dalzell, senior editor. News/Commentary (usually staff-written, but factual anecdotes involving managed care's effect on providers are welcome), 100-300 words; Employer Update (focuses on practical advice for purchasers of healthcare), 800-1,000 words; State Initiatives (looks at state-level trends in managed care with national implications). **Pays $100-600.**

🖥 The online magazine carries original content not found in the print edition. Contact: John Marcille.

Tips: "Know our audience (physicians and health plan executives) and their needs. Study our website to see what we cover. We work with many first-time contributors."

$ $ $ $ MEDICAL ECONOMICS, 5 Paragon Dr., Montvale NJ 07645-1742. (201)358-7367. Fax: (201)722-2688. E-mail: helen.mckenna@medec.com. Website: www.memag.com. **Contact:** Helen A. McKenna, outside copy editor. **10% freelance written.** Semimonthly magazine (24 times/year). "*Medical Economics* is a national business magazine read by M.D.s and D.O.s in office-based practice. Our purpose is to be informative and useful to practicing physicians in the professional and financial management of their practices. We look for contributions from writers who know—or will make the effort to learn—the non-clinical concerns of today's physician. These writers must be able to address those concerns in feature articles that are clearly written and that convey authoritative information and advice. Our articles focus very narrowly on a subject, and explore it in depth." Circ. 162,000. **Pays on acceptance.** Offers 25% kill fee. Buys first world publication rights. Accepts queries by mail, e-mail, fax. Sample copy free.
Nonfiction: Articles about private physicians in innovative, pioneering and/or controversial situations affecting medical care delivery, patient relations or malpractice prevention/litigation; personal finance topics. "We do not want overviews or pieces that only skim the surface of a general topic. We address physician readers in a conversational, yet no-nonsense tone, quoting recognized experts on office management, personal finance, patient relations and medical-legal issues." **Buys 40-50 mss/year.** Query with published clips. Length: 1,500-2,500 words. **Pays $1,200-2,500 for assigned articles.** Pays expenses of writers on assignment.
Photos: Will negotiate an additional fee for photos accepted for publication.
Tips: "We look for articles about physicians who run high-quality, innovative practices suited to the age of managed care. We also look for how-to service articles—on practice-management and personal-finance topics—which must contain anecdotal examples to support the advice. Read the magazine carefully, noting its style and content. Then send detailed proposals or outlines on subjects that would interest our mainly primary-care physician readers."

N $ $ MEDICAL IMAGING, 295 Promenade St., Suite 2, Providence RI 02908. (401)455-0555. Fax: (401)455-1551. E-mail: mtierney@mwc.com. Website: www.medicalimagingmag.com. **Contact:** Mary Tierney, editor. **60% freelance written.** Monthly magazine covering diagnostic imaging equipment. Estab. 1986. Circ. 20,000. Pays on publication. Publishes ms an average of 2 months after acceptance. Byline given. Buys all rights. Editorial lead time 2 months. Responds to query letters to queries. Sample copy for $10 prepaid.
Nonfiction: Interview/profile, technical. "No general interest/human interest stories about healthcare. Articles *must* deal with our industry, diagnostic imaging." **Buys 6 mss/year.** Query with published clips. Length: 1,500-2,500 words. Sometimes pays expenses of writers on assignment.
Photos: State availability with submission. Reviews negatives. Buys all rights. Offers no additional payment for photos accepted with ms. Identification of subjects, model releases required.
Tips: "Send a letter with an interesting story idea that is applicable to our industry, diagnostic imaging. Then follow up with a phone call. Areas most open to freelancers are features and technology profiles. You don't have to be an engineer or doctor but you have to know how to talk and listen to them."

$ $ MODERN PHYSICIAN, Essential Business News for the Executive Physician, Crain Communications, 740 N. Rush St., Chicago IL 60611-2590. (312)649-5324. Fax: (312)649-5393. Website: www.modernphysician.com. **Contact:** Karen Petitte, editor. **40% freelance written.** Biweekly magazine covering business and management news for doctors. "*Modern Physician* offers timely topical news features with lots of business information—revenues, earnings, financial data." Estab. 1997. Circ. 31,000. **Pays on acceptance.** Publishes ms an average of 2 months after acceptance. Byline given. Buys all rights. Editorial lead time 2 months. Accepts queries by mail, e-mail, fax, phone. Responds in 6 weeks to queries. Sample copy free. Writer's guidelines sent after query.
　　○⊸ Break in with a regional story involving business or physicians.
Nonfiction: Length: 1,000-2,000 words. **Pays 40-50¢/word.**

N $ $ THE NEW PHYSICIAN, 1902 Association Dr., Reston VA 20191. **Contact:** Rebecca Sernett, editor. **50% freelance written.** Magazine published 9 times/year for medical students, interns, residents and educators. Circ. 30,000. **Pays on acceptance.** Publishes ms an average of 2 months after acceptance. Accepts simultaneous submissions. Responds in 2 months to mss. Sample copy for 10×13 SAE and 5 first-class stamps. Writer's guidelines for #10 SASE.
Nonfiction: Articles on social, political, economic issues in medical education/health care. **Buys 14 mss/year.** Query or send complete ms. Length: 800-3,000 words. **Pays 25-50¢/word; higher fees for selected pieces.** Sometimes pays expenses of writers on assignment.
Reprints: Send photocopy and information about when and where the material previously appeared. Pay varies.
Tips: "Although we are published by an association (the American Medical Student Association), we are not a 'house organ.' We are a professional magazine for readers with a progressive view on health care issues and a particular interest in improving medical education and the health care system. Our readers demand sophistication on the issues we cover. Freelancers should be willing to look deeply into the issues in question and not be satisfied with a cursory review of those issues."

$ $ PHYSICIAN, Focus on the Family, 8605 Explorer Dr., Colorado Springs CO 80920. (719)531-3400. Fax: (719)531-3499. E-mail: physician@macmail.fotf.org. Website: www.family.org. Managing Editor: Charles Johnson. **Contact:** Susan Stevens, editor. **20% freelance written.** Bimonthly magazine. "The goal of our magazine is to encourage physicians in their faith, family and medical practice. Writers should understand the medical lifestyle." Estab. 1989. Circ. 87,000. **Pays on acceptance.** Publishes ms an average of 6 months after acceptance. Byline given. Buys first North American serial rights. Editorial lead time 1 year. Accepts queries by mail, e-mail, fax. Responds in 2 months to queries. Sample copy for SASE.

Nonfiction: General interest, interview/profile, personal experience, religious, technical. "No patient's opinions of their doctor." **Buys 20-30 mss/year.** Query. Length: 900-2,400 words. **Pays $100-500 for assigned articles.** Sometimes pays expenses of writers on assignment. Accepts previously published submissions.

Photos: State availability with submission. Reviews transparencies. Buys one-time rights. Negotiates payment individually.

Tips: "Most writers are M.D.'s."

$ $ PODIATRY MANAGEMENT, Kane Communications, Inc., P.O. Box 750129, Forest Hills NY 11375. (718)897-9700. Fax: (718)896-5747. E-mail: bblock@prodigy.net. Website: www.podiatrymgt.com. Publisher: Scott C. Borowsky. **Contact:** Barry Block, editor. Magazine published 9 times/year for practicing podiatrists. "Aims to help the doctor of podiatric medicine to build a bigger, more successful practice, to conserve and invest his money, to keep him posted on the economic, legal and sociological changes that affect him." Estab. 1982. Circ. 13,000. Pays on publication. Byline given. Buys first North American serial, second serial (reprint) rights. Submit seasonal material 4 months in advance. Accepts queries by e-mail. Accepts simultaneous submissions. Responds in 2 weeks to queries. Sample copy for $3 and 9×12 SAE. Writer's guidelines for #10 SASE.

Nonfiction: Book excerpts, general interest (taxes, investments, estate, estate planning, recreation, hobbies), how-to (establish and collect fees, practice management, , organize office routines, supervise office assistants, handle patient relations), interview/profile (about interesting or well-known podiatrists), personal experience, "These subjects are the mainstay of the magazine, but offbeat articles and humore are always welcome." **Buys 25 mss/year.** Send tax and financial articles to Martin Kruth, 5 Wagon Hill Lane, Avon CT 06001. Length: 1,000-2,500 words. **Pays $150-600.**

Reprints: Send photocopy. Pays 33% of amount paid for an original article.

Photos: State availability with submission. Buys one-time rights. Pays $15 for b&w contact sheet.

Tips: "We are looking for articles on minorities in podiatry."

N: $ $ STITCHES, The Journal of Medical Humour, Stitches Publishing Inc., 16787 Warden Ave., R.R. #3, Newmarket, Ontario L3Y 4W1, Canada. (905)853-1884. Fax: (905)853-6565. **Contact:** Simon Hally, editor. **90% freelance written.** Monthly magazine covering humor for physicians. "*Stitches* is read primarily by physicians in Canada. Stories with a medical slant are particularly welcome, but we also run a lot of non-medical material. It must be funny and, of course, brevity is the soul of wit." Estab. 1990. Circ. 37,500. Pays on publication. Publishes ms an average of 2 months after acceptance. Byline given. Buys first North American serial, electronic rights. Editorial lead time 1 month. Submit seasonal material 4 months in advance. Responds in 6 weeks to queries; 2 months to mss. Sample copy and writer's guidelines free.

Nonfiction: Humor, personal experience. **Buys 30 mss/year.** Send complete ms. Length: 200-2,000 words. **Pays 35¢/ word (Canadian).**

Fiction: Humorous. **Buys 40 mss/year.** Send complete ms. Length: 200-2,000 words. **Pays 35¢/word (Canadian).**

Poetry: Humorous. **Buys 2 poems/year.** Submit maximum 5 poems. Length: 2-30 lines.

Fillers: Gags to be illustrated by cartoonist, short humor. **Pays negotiable rate.**

Tips: "Due to the nature of humorous writing, we have to see a completed manuscript, rather than a query, to determine if it is suitable for us. Along with a short cover letter, that's all we require."

$ $ STRATEGIC HEALTH CARE MARKETING, Health Care Communications, 11 Heritage Lane, P.O. Box 594, Rye NY 10580. (914)967-6741. Fax: (914)967-3054. E-mail: healthcomm@aol.com. Website: www.strategich ealthcare.com. **Contact:** Michele von Dambrowski, editor. **90% freelance written.** Monthly newsletter covering health care marketing and management in a wide range of settings including hospitals, medical group practices, home health services, and managed care organizations. Emphasis is on strategies and techniques employed within the health care field and relevant applications from other service industries. Works with published/established writers only. Estab. 1984. Pays on publication. Publishes ms an average of 2 months after acceptance. Byline given. Offers 25% kill fee. Buys first North American serial rights. Accepts queries by mail, e-mail. Responds in 1 month to queries. Sample copy for 9×12 SAE and 3 first-class stamps. Guidelines sent with sample copy only.

• *Strategic Health Care Marketing* is specifically seeking writers with expertise/contacts in managed care, patient satisfaction and demand management.

Nonfiction: "Preferred format for feature articles is the case history approach to solving marketing problems. Crisp, almost telegraphic style." How-to, interview/profile, new product, technical. **Buys 50 mss/year.** *No unsolicited mss.* Length: 700-3,000 words. **Pays $100-400.** Sometimes pays expenses of writers on assignment with prior authorization.

Photos: Photos, unless necessary for subject explanation, are rarely used. State availability with submission. Reviews contact sheets. Buys one-time rights. Offers $10-30/photo. Captions, model releases required.

■ The online magazine carries original content not found in the print edition. Contact: Mark Gothberg.

Tips: "Writers with prior experience on business beat for newspaper or newsletter will do well. We require a sophisticated, in-depth knowledge of health care and business. This is not a consumer publication—the writer with knowledge of both health care and marketing will excel. Absolutely no unsolicited manuscripts; any received will be returned or discarded unread."

$ $ $ $ UNIQUE OPPORTUNITIES, The Physician's Resource, U O Inc., 455 S. Fourth Ave., Suite 1236, Louisville KY 40202. Fax: (502)587-0848. E-mail: bett@uoworks.com. Website: www.uoworks.com. Editor: Mollie Vento Hudson. **Contact:** Bett Coffman, associate editor. **45% freelance written.** Bimonthly magazine covering physician relocation and career development. "Published for physicians interested in a new career opportunity. It offers physicians useful information and first-hand experiences to guide them in making informed decisions concerning their first or next career opportunity. It provides regular features and columns about specific aspects of the search process." Estab. 1991. Circ. 80,000. Pays 30 days after acceptance. Publishes ms an average of 2 months after acceptance. Byline given. Offers 15-33% kill fee. Buys first North American serial, electronic rights. Editorial lead time 3 months. Submit seasonal material 6 months in advance. Responds in 2 months to queries. Sample copy for 9 × 12 SAE and 6 first-class stamps. Writer's guidelines for #10 SASE.
Nonfiction: Practice options and information of interest to physicians in career transition. **Buys 14 mss/year.** Query with published clips. Length: 1,500-3,500 words. **Pays $750-2,000.** Sometimes pays expenses of writers on assignment.
Photos: State availability with submission. electronic rights. Negotiates payment individually. Identification of subjects, model releases required.
Columns/Departments: Remarks (opinion from physicians and industry experts on physician career issues), 500-1,000 words; Technology (technical articles relating to medicine or medical practice and business) 1,000-1,500 words. Query with published clips. **Payment negotiated individually.**
   ■ The online magazine carries original content not found in the print edition.
Tips: "Submit queries via letter or e-mail with ideas for articles that directly pertain to physician career issues, such as specific or unusual practice opportunities, relocation or practice establishment subjects, etc. Feature articles are most open to freelancers. Physician sources are most important, with tips and advice from both the physicians and business experts. Physicians like to know what other physicians think and do and appreciate suggestions from other business people."

MUSIC

Publications for musicians and for the recording industry are listed in this section. Other professional performing arts publications are classified under Entertainment & the Arts. Magazines featuring music industry news for the general public are listed in the Consumer Entertainment and Music sections. (Markets for songwriters can be found in *Songwriter's Market*, Writer's Digest Books.)

$ $ CLASSICAL SINGER MAGAZINE, (formerly *The New York Opera Newsletter*), P.O. Box 278, Maplewood NJ 07040. (973)348-9549. Fax: (973)378-2372. E-mail: freemang@classicalsinger.com. Website: www.classicalsinger.com. **Contact:** Freeman Gunter, managing editor. Monthly magazine covering classical singers. Estab. 1988. Circ. 5,000. Pays on publication. Publishes ms an average of 3 months after acceptance. Byline given. Offers 35% kill fee. Buys one-time, second serial (reprint) rights. Editorial lead time 3 months. Submit seasonal material 3 months in advance. Accepts queries by mail, e-mail, fax. Responds in 1 month to queries. Sample copy and writer's guidelines free.
   O─┐ Break in with a well-written review of a performance—written in a helpful tone with attention paid to all singers.
Nonfiction: Editorial calendar available on request. "Looking for material about unions, novel ways to make money as a singer and getting applause." Book excerpts, exposé (carefully done), how-to, humor, interview/profile, new product, personal experience, photo feature, religious, technical, travel. No advertorial, agenda-tainted, complaints. Query with published clips. Length: 1,000-2,500 words. **Pays 20¢/word.** Sometimes pays expenses of writers on assignment.
Photos: Send photos with submission. Buys one-time rights. Negotiates payment individually. Captions required.
   ■ The online magazine carries original content not found in the print edition.
Tips: "*Classical Singer Magazine*, is a 36+ page monthly magazine for singers and about singers. Our purpose is to increase respect for the profession and to connect the classical singer to opportunities, information, and support. Non-singers are welcome to submit queries but will need singers as their source."

$ CLAVIER MAGAZINE, The Instrumentalist Publishing Co., 200 Northfield Rd., Northfield IL 60093. (847)446-5000. Fax: (847)446-6263. **Contact:** Judy Nelson, editor. **1% freelance written.** Magazine published 10 times/year. featuring practical information on teaching subjects that are of value to studio piano teachers and interviews with major artists. Estab. 1937. Circ. 16,000. Pays on publication. Publishes ms an average of 18 months after acceptance. Byline given. Buys all rights. Submit seasonal material 6 months in advance. Accepts queries by mail, fax, phone. Responds in 6 weeks to queries. Sample copy and writer's guidelines free.
Nonfiction: "Artists should be of interest and direct practical value to concert pianists, harpsichordists and organists who are teachers of piano, organ, harpsichord and electronic keyboards. Topics may include pedagogy, technique, performance, ensemble playing and accompanying." Historical/nostalgic, how-to, interview/profile, photo feature. Length: 10-12 double-spaced pages. **Pays small honorarium.**
Reprints: Occasionally we will reprint a chapter in a book.
Photos: Send photos with submission. Reviews negatives, 2¼ × 2¼ transparencies, 3 × 5 prints. Buys all rights. Offers no additional payment for photos accepted with ms. Identification of subjects required.

\$ \$ MIX MAGAZINE, Intertec Publishing, 6400 Hollis St., Suite 12, Emeryville CA 94608. Fax: (510)693-5143. E-mail: 74673.3872@compuserve.com. Website: www.mixmag.com. Editor: George Petersen. **Contact:** Blair Jackson, executive editor. **50% freelance written.** Monthly magazine covering pro audio. *"Mix* is a trade publication geared toward professionals in the music/sound production recording and post-production industries. We include stories about music production, sound for picture, live sound, etc. We prefer in-depth technical pieces that are applications-oriented." Estab. 1977. Circ. 50,000. Pays on publication. Publishes ms an average of 3 months after acceptance. Byline given. Offers 50% kill fee. Buys first North American serial rights. Editorial lead time 10 weeks. Submit seasonal material 3 months in advance. Responds in 2 weeks to queries; 1 month to mss. Sample copy for $6. Writer's guidelines free.
Nonfiction: How-to, interview/profile, new product, technical, Project/Studio Spotlights. Special issues: Sound for picture supplement (April, September), Design issue. **Buys 60 mss/year.** Query. Length: 500-2,000 words. **Pays $300-800 for assigned articles; $300-400 for unsolicited articles.**
Photos: State availability with submission. Reviews 4×5 transparencies, prints. Buys one-time rights. Negotiates payment individually. Captions, identification of subjects required.
Tips: "Send Blair Jackson a letter outlining the article, including a description of the topic, information sources, what qualifies writers for the story, and mention of available graphics. A writing sample is also helpful."

N \$ \$ \$ OPERA NEWS, Metropolitan Opera Guild, Inc., 70 Lincoln Center Plaza, New York NY 10023-6593. (212)769-7080. Fax: (212)769-7007. Website: www.operanews.com. Editor/Publisher: Rudolph S. Rauch. Executive Editor: F. Paul Driscoll. **Contact:** Kitty March, editor. **75% freelance written.** Monthly magazine for people interested in opera; the opera professional as well as the opera audience. Estab. 1936. Circ. 120,000. Pays on publication. Publishes ms an average of 4 months after acceptance. Byline given. Buys first serial rights only. Editorial lead time 4 months. Sample copy for $4.
○┐ Break in by "showing incisive knowledge of opera and the opera scene. We look for knowledgeable and informed writers who are capable of discussing opera in detailed musical terms—but in an engaging way."
Nonfiction: Most articles are commissioned in advance. Monthly issues feature articles on various aspects of opera worldwide. Emphasis is on high quality writing and an intellectual interest to the opera-oriented public. Historical/nostalgic, interview/profile, opinion, personal experience, informational, think pieces, opera reviews. Query. Length: 1,500-2,800 words. **Pays $450-1,200.** Sometimes pays expenses of writers on assignment.
Photos: State availability with submission. Buys one-time rights.
Columns/Departments: Buys 24 mss/year.

\$ SONGWRITER'S MONTHLY, The Stories Behind Today's Songs, 332 Eastwood Ave., Feasterville PA 19053. (215)953-0952. Fax: (215)953-0952. E-mail: a1foster@aol.com. Website: www.lafay.com/sm. **Contact:** Allen Foster, editor. **40% freelance written.** Monthly magazine covering songwriting. Estab. 1992. Circ. 2,500. **Pays on acceptance.** Publishes ms an average of 6 months after acceptance. Byline given. Offers 100% kill fee. Buys first, one-time rights. Editorial lead time 3 months. Submit seasonal material 6 months in advance. Accepts queries by mail, e-mail, fax. Responds in 2 weeks to queries; 1 month to mss. Sample copy and writer's guidelines free.
○┐ Break in with "a great how-to article."
Nonfiction: How-to (write better songs, get a deal, etc.), technical. No interviews or reviews. **Buys 48 mss/year.** Query. Length: 300-800 words. **Pays $15.**
Reprints: Send information about when and were the article previously appeared. Pays $15.
Photos: State availability with submission. Reviews prints. Offers no additional payment for photos accepted with ms. Identification of subjects required.
Fillers: Anecdotes, facts, newsbreaks, short humor. **Buys 60/year.** Length: 25-300 words. **Pays $0-5.**
Tips: *"Songwriter's Monthly* needs 500-word articles which deal with one very specific aspect of songwriting or the music business. We've been around for 10 years and are only interested in truly fresh ideas. No general 'How to write a hit' articles, please."

OFFICE ENVIRONMENT & EQUIPMENT

\$ \$ OFFICE DEALER, Updating the Office Products Industry, P.O. Box 1028, Mt. Airy NC 27030. (336)783-0000. Fax: (336)783-0045. E-mail: lbouchey@advi.net. Website: www.os-od.com. **Contact:** Lisa M. Bouchey, editor. **80% freelance written.** Bimonthly magazine covering the office product industry. *"Office Dealer* is an industry publication serving subscribers involved in the reselling of office supplies, furniture and equipment." Estab. 1987. Circ. 17,000. Pays on publication. Byline given. Buys first North American serial rights. Editorial lead time 4 months. Submit seasonal material 6 months in advance. Accepts queries by mail, e-mail, fax. Accepts simultaneous submissions. Responds in 1 month to queries; 2 months to mss. Sample copy and writer's guidelines free.
Nonfiction: Book excerpts, interview/profile, new product, technical. "We do not publish a great deal of computer-related information—although that will continue to change as the digital age evolves." **Buys 30 mss/year.** Length: 1,500-2,200 words. **Pays $400-650.** Sometimes pays expenses of writers on assignment.
Photos: State availability with submission. Reviews contact sheets, prints. Buys one-time rights. Negotiates payment individually. Captions, identification of subjects, model releases required.

Columns/Departments: Selling Power (sales tips/techniques), 800-1,000 words. **Buys 6 mss/year.** Query. **Pays $150-300.**

Tips: "Feature articles for the year are outlined in an editorial calendar published each fall. Although changes can occur, we make every effort to adhere to the published calendar. Feature articles are written by our staff or by freelance writers. We do not accept corporate 'byline' articles. We seek publishable stories written to an agreed-upon length, with text for agreed-upon components—such as sidebars. Stories should be as generic as possible, free of jargon, vague statements, unconfirmed facts and figures, and corporate superlatives. Each query should include the primary focus of the proposed article, the main points of discussion, and a list of any sources to be described or interviewed in the story. Samples of a writer's past work and clips concerning the proposed story are helpful."

$ $ OFFICE SOLUTIONS, The Magazine for Office Professionals, Quality Publishing, P.O. Box 1028, Mt. Airy NC 27030. (336)783-0000. Fax: (336)783-0045. E-mail: lbouchey@advi.net. Website: www.os-od.com. **Contact:** Lisa M. Bouchey, editor. **80% freelance written.** Monthly magazine covering the office environment. "*Office Solutions* subscribers are responsible for the management of their office environments." Estab. 1984. Circ. 107,000. Pays on publication. Publishes ms an average of 2 months after acceptance. Byline given. Buys first North American serial rights. Editorial lead time 3 months. Submit seasonal material 4 months in advance. Accepts queries by mail, e-mail, fax. Accepts simultaneous submissions. Responds in 3 weeks to queries; 2 months to mss. Sample copy and writer's guidelines free.

Nonfiction: "Our audience is responsible for general management of an office environment, so articles should be broad in scope and not too technical in nature." Book excerpts, interview/profile, new product, technical. **Buys 75 mss/year.** Query. Length: 1,500-2,200 words. **Pays $400-650.** Sometimes pays expenses of writers on assignment.

Photos: State availability with submission. Reviews contact sheets, prints. Buys one-time rights. Negotiates payment individually. Captions, identification of subjects, model releases required.

Columns/Departments: Cyberspeak (computer terminology), 800-1,000 words; Do It Yourself ('how to run' the office better), 1,000-2,000 words; Wireless World (wireless technology development), 1,000-1,200 words. **Buys 20 mss/year.** Query. **Pays $150-400.**

Fillers: Facts, short humor. **Buys 10-15 issue/year.** Length: 500-800 words. **Pays $150-250.**

Tips: "Feature articles for the year are outlined in an editorial calendar published each fall. Although changes can occur, we make every effort to adhere to the published calendar. Feature articles are written by our staff or by freelance writers. We seek publishable stories written to an agreed-upon length, with text for agreed-upon components—such as sidebars. Stories should be as generic as possible, free of jargon, vague statements, unconfirmed facts and figures, and corporate superlatives. Each query should include the primary focus of the proposed article, the main points of discussion, and a list of any sources to be described or interviewed in the story. Queries should be a single page or less and include a SASE for reply. Samples of a writer's past work and clips concerning the proposed story are helpful."

PAPER

N $ $ BOXBOARD CONTAINERS, Intertec Publishing Co., Dept. WM, 29 N. Wacker Dr., Chicago IL 60606-3298. (312)726-2802. Fax: (312)726-2574. E-mail: diana_shkolink@intertec.com. Website: www.boxboard.com. Editor: Matt Coleman. **Contact:** Cristen Bolan, managing editor. Monthly magazine covering box and carton manufacturing for corrugated box, folding carton, setup box manufacturers internationally emphasizing technology and management. Circ. 15,000. Pays on publication. Byline given. Buys first North American serial rights. Submit seasonal material 2 months in advance. Accepts queries by mail, fax. Responds in 1 month to mss. Sample copy free.

Nonfiction: How-to, interview/profile, new product, opinion, personal experience, photo feature, technical. **Buys 10 mss/year.** Query. Length: 2,000-6,000 words. **Pays $75-350 for assigned articles; $75-250 for unsolicited articles.** Sometimes pays expenses of writers on assignment.

Photos: Send photos with submission. Reviews 35mm, 4×5, 6×6 transparencies, 8×10 prints. Buys one-time rights. Offers no additional payment for photos accepted with ms. Captions, identification of subjects, model releases required.

　　■ The online magazine carries original content not found in the print edition. Contact: Troy Burkholder, online editor.

Tips: Features are most open to freelancers.

$ $ THE PAPER STOCK REPORT, News and Trends of the Paper Recycling Markets, McEntee Media Corp., 9815 Hazelwood Ave., Cleveland OH 44149. (440)238-6603. Fax: (440)238-6712. E-mail: psr@recycle.cc. Website: www.recycle.cc. **Contact:** Ken McEntee, editor. Biweekly newsletter covering market trends, news in the paper recycling industry. "Audience is interested in new innovative markets, applications for recovered scrap paper as well as new laws and regulations impacting recycling." Estab. 1990. Circ. 2,000. Pays on publication. Publishes ms an average of 1 month after acceptance. Byline given. Buys first, all rights. Editorial lead time 2 months. Submit seasonal material 2 months in advance. Accepts queries by mail, e-mail, fax, phone. Accepts simultaneous submissions. Responds in 1 month to queries. Sample copy for #10 SAE with 55¢ postage.

Nonfiction: Book excerpts, essays, exposé, general interest, historical/nostalgic, interview/profile, new product, opinion, photo feature, technical, All related to paper recycling. **Buys 0-13 mss/year.** Send complete ms. Length: 250-1,000 words. **Pays $50-250 for assigned articles; $25-250 for unsolicited articles.** Pays expenses of writers on assignment.

Photos: State availability with submission. Reviews contact sheets. Negotiates payment individually. Identification of subjects required.

◼ The online magazine carries original content not found in the print edition. Contact: Ken McEntee, online editor.

Tips: "Article must be valuable to readers in terms of presenting new market opportunities or cost-saving measures."

$ $ RECYCLED PAPER NEWS, Independent Coverage of Environmental Issues in the Paper Industry, McEntee Media Corporation, 9815 Hazelwood Ave., Cleveland OH 44149. (440)238-6603. Fax: (440)238-6712. E-mail: rpn@recycle.cc. Website: www.recycle.cc. **Contact:** Ken McEntee, president. **10% freelance written.** Monthly newsletter. "We are interested in any news impacting the paper recycling industry as well as other environmental issues in the paper industry, i.e., water/air pollution, chlorine-free paper, forest conservation, etc., with special emphasis on new laws and regulations." Estab. 1990. Pays on publication. Publishes ms an average of 2 months after acceptance. Buys first, all rights. Editorial lead time 1 month. Submit seasonal material 1 month in advance. Accepts queries by mail, e-mail, fax, phone. Accepts simultaneous submissions. Responds in 2 months to queries. Sample copy for 9×12 SAE and 55¢ postage. Writer's guidelines for #10 SASE.

Nonfiction: Book excerpts, essays, how-to, interview/profile, new product, opinion, personal experience, photo feature, technical, new business, legislation, regulation, business expansion. **Buys 0-5 mss/year.** Query with published clips. **Pays $10-500.** Pays writers with contributor copies or other premiums by prior agreement.

Reprints: Accepts previously published submissions.

Columns/Departments: Query with published clips. **Pays $10-500.**

Tips: "We appreciate leads on local news regarding recycling or composting, i.e., new facilities or businesses, new laws and regulations, unique programs, situations that impact supply and demand for recyclables, etc. International developments are also of interest."

PETS

Listed here are publications for professionals in the pet industry—pet product wholesalers, manufacturers, suppliers, and retailers, and owners of pet specialty stores, grooming businesses, aquarium retailers and those interested in the pet fish industry. Publications for pet owners are listed in the Consumer Animal section.

$ $ GROOM & BOARD, H.H. Backer Associates Inc., 200 S. Michigan Ave., Suite 840, Chicago IL 60604-2404. (312)663-4040. Fax: (312)663-5676. E-mail: groomboard@aol.com. Editor: Karen Long MacLeod. **Contact:** Cathy Foster. **90% freelance written.** Published 9 times /year. magazine. "Groom & Board is the only national trade publication for pet-care professionals, including pet groomers, boarding kennel operators and service-oriented veterinarians. Features emphasize professional development, including progressive business management, animal handling procedures, emerging business opportunities and profiles of successful pet-care operations." Estab. 1980. Circ. 14,186. **Pays on acceptance.** Publishes ms an average of 3 months after acceptance. Byline given. Buys first North American serial, one-time, exclusive industry rights. Sample copy available.

Nonfiction: How-to (groom specific breeds of pets, run business, etc.), interview/profile (successful grooming and/or kennel operations), technical. No consumer-oriented articles or stories about a single animal (animal heroes, grief, etc.). **Buys 40 mss/year.** Query by phone after 3 pm CST. **Pays $100-400 for assigned articles; $70-125 for unsolicited articles.** Sometimes pays expenses of writers on assignment.

Photos: Reviews transparencies, 5×7 glossy prints. Buys one-time rights. Captions, identification of subjects required.

$ $ PET AGE, H.H. Backer Associates, Inc., 200 S. Michigan Ave., Suite 840, Chicago IL 60604-2383-2404. (312)663-4040. Fax: (312)663-5676. E-mail: petage@aol.com. Editor Karen Long MacLeod. **Contact:** Cathy Foster. **90% freelance written.** Monthly magazine for pet/pet supplies retailers, covering the complete pet industry. Prefers to work with published/established writers. Estab. 1971. Circ. 23,022. **Pays on acceptance.** Publishes ms an average of 6 months after acceptance. Byline given. Buys first North American serial, one-time rights, exclusive industry rights. Submit seasonal material 6 months in advance. Sample copy available.

Nonfiction: How-to, interview/profile (of a successful, well-run pet retail operation), technical, business management—all trade related. No general retailing articles or consumer-oriented pet articles. **Buys 120 mss/year.** Query by phone after 3 pm CST. Query with the name and location of a pet operation you wish to profile and why it would make a good feature. **Pays $500 for assigned articles.** Sometimes pays expenses of writers on assignment.

Photos: Reviews transparencies, slides and 5×7 glossy prints. Buys one-time rights. Captions, identification of subjects required.

Tips: "This is a business publication for busy people, and must be very informative in easy-to-read, concise style. Articles about animal care or business practices should have the pet-retail angle or cover issues specific to this industry."

N $ $ PET PRODUCT NEWS, Fancy Publications, P.O. Box 6050, Mission Viejo CA 92690. (949)855-8822. Fax: (949)855-3045. **Contact:** Scott Andresen, managing editor. **70% freelance written.** Monthly magazine. "*Pet Product News* covers business/legal and economic issues of importance to pet product retailers, suppliers and distributors, as well as product information and animal care issues. We're looking for straightforward articles on the proper care of dogs, cats, birds, fish and exotics (reptiles, hamsters, etc.) as information the retailers can pass on to new pet owners." Estab. 1947. Circ. 30,000. Pays on publication. Byline given. Offers $50 kill fee. Buys first North American serial rights. Editorial lead time 3 months. Submit seasonal material 4 months in advance. Accepts queries by mail, fax. Responds in 2 weeks to queries. Sample copy for $5.50. Writer's guidelines for #10 SASE.

Nonfiction: General interest, interview/profile, new product, photo feature, technical. "No cute animal stories or those directed at the pet owner." **Buys 150 mss/year.** Query. Length: 500-1,500 words. **Pays $175-350.**

Columns/Departments: "The Pet Dealer" (timely news stories about business issues affecting pet retailers), 800-1,000 words; "Industry News" (news articles representing coverage of pet product suppliers, manufacturers, distributors and associations), 800-1,000 words; Dog & Cat (products and care of), 1,000-1,500 words; Fish & Bird (products and care of), 1,000-1,500 words; Small Mammals (products and care of), 1,000-1,500 words; Pond/Water Garden (products and care of), 1,000-1,500 words. **Buys 120 mss/year.** Query. **Pays $150-300.**

Tips: "Be more than just an animal lover. You have to know about health, nutrition and care. Product and business articles are told in both an informative and entertaining style. Talk to pet store owners and see what they need to know to be better business people in general, who have to deal with everything from balancing the books and free trade agreements to animal rights activists. All sections are open, but you have to be knowledgeable on the topic, be it taxes, management, profit building, products, nutrition, animal care or marketing."

PLUMBING, HEATING, AIR CONDITIONING & REFRIGERATION

$ $ HEATING PLUMBING AIR CONDITIONING, 777 Bay St., Toronto, Ontario M5W 1A7, Canada. (416)596-5000. Fax: (416)596-5536. **Contact:** Kerry Turner, editor. **20% freelance written.** Monthly magazine. For a prompt reply, "enclose a sheet on which is typed a statement either approving or rejecting the suggested article which can either be checked off, or a quick answer written in and signed and returned." Estab. 1923. Circ. 16,500. Pays on publication. Publishes ms an average of 3 months after acceptance. Accepts queries by mail, e-mail, fax, phone. Responds in 2 months to queries. Sample copy free.

➙ Break in with technical, "how-to," Canadian-specific applications/stories.

Nonfiction: News, business management articles that will inform, educate, motivate and help readers to be more efficient and profitable who design, manufacture, install, sell, service maintain or supply all mechanical components and systems in residential, commercial, institutional and industrial installations across Canada. How-to, technical. Length: 1,000-1,500 words. **Pays 25¢/word.** Sometimes pays expenses of writers on assignment.

Reprints: Send tearsheet or photocopy with rights for sale noted and information about when and where the material previously appeared.

Photos: Prefers 4×5 or 5×7 glossies. Photos purchased with ms.

Tips: "Topics must relate directly to the day-to-day activities of *HPAC* readers in Canada. Must be detailed, with specific examples, quotes from specific people or authorities—show depth. We specifically want material from other parts of Canada besides southern Ontario. Not really interested in material from US unless specifically related to Canadian readers' concerns. We primarily want articles that show *HPAC* readers how they can increase their sales and business step-by-step based on specific examples of what others have done."

N $ INDOOR COMFORT NEWS, Institute of Heating & Air Conditioning Industries, Inc., 454 W. Broadway, Glendale CA 91204. (818)551-1555. Fax: (818)551-1115. E-mail: s.fitzpatrick@ihaci.org. Website: www.ihaci.org. **Contact:** Shawn Fitzpatrick, editor. **10% freelance written.** Monthly tabloid. "We cover the heating, cooling, ventilating and refrigeration industries in Washington, Oregon, California, Nevada, Arizona and Texas. Our audience is made up of contractors, engineers and service technicians." Estab. 1955. Circ. 20,000. Pays on publication. Publishes ms an average of 3 months after acceptance. Byline given. Buys one-time rights. Editorial lead time 1 month. Submit seasonal material 3 months in advance. Accepts queries by mail, fax. Responds in 2 weeks to queries; 1 month to mss. Sample copy for 8×10 SAE and $1.25 postage.

Nonfiction: Book excerpts, essays, historical/nostalgic, how-to (equipment, sales, etc.), humor, interview/profile, new product, personal experience, technical. **Buys 10-15 mss/year.** Query with published clips. Length: 700-1,500 words. **Pays $75-150.** Sometimes pays expenses of writers on assignment.

Photos: Send photos with submission. Reviews 3×5 prints. Buys one-time rights. Offers no additional payment for photos accepted with ms. Captions, identification of subjects required.

Tips: "We're looking for specific coverage of industry events and people in the geographic areas we cover. Know the industry. Send a query rather than making original contact via phone."

N $ SNIPS MAGAZINE, 755 W. Big Beaver Rd., Troy MI 48084-4900. (248)244-6467. Fax: (248)362-0317. E-mail: base@bnp.com. Website: www.bnp.com/snips. **Contact:** Ed Bas, editor. **2% freelance written.** Monthly magazine for sheet metal, warm air heating, ventilating, air conditioning and roofing contractors. Estab. 1932. Publishes ms an average of 3 months after acceptance. Buys all rights. Accepts queries by mail, e-mail, fax, phone.

➙ Break in with a "profile of a local contractor in our industries."

Nonfiction: Material should deal with information about contractors who do sheet metal, warm air heating, airconditioning, ventilation and metal roofing work; also about successful advertising campaigns conducted by these contractors and the results. Length: Under 1,000 words unless on special assignment. **Pays $200.**

Photos: Negotiable.

$ $WESTERN HVACR NEWS, Trade, News International, 4444 Riverside Dr., #202, Burbank CA 91505-4048. Fax: (818)848-1306. E-mail: News@hvacrnews.com. Website: www.hvacrnews.com. **Contact:** Gary McCarty. Monthly tabloid covering heating, ventilation, air conditioning and refrigeration. "We are a trade publication writing about news and trends for those in the trade." Estab. 1981. Circ. 31,000. Pays on publication. Byline sometimes given. Buys first North American serial rights. Editorial lead time 2 months. Submit seasonal material 2 months in advance. Accepts queries by mail, e-mail. Responds in 1 month to queries. Sample copy online. Writer's guidelines by e-mail.
Nonfiction: General interest, how-to, interview/profile, photo feature, technical. **Buys 25 mss/year.** Query with published clips. Length: 250-1,000 words. **Pays 25¢/word.** Sometimes pays expenses of writers on assignment.
Photos: Send photos with submission. Buys one-time rights. Offers $10 minimum. Negotiates payment individually. Identification of subjects required.
Columns/Departments: Technical only. **Buys 24 mss/year. Pays 20¢/word.**
Tips: "Writers must be knowledgeable about the HVACR industry."

PRINTING

$ $IN-PLANT GRAPHICS, North American Publishing Co., 401 N. Broad St., Philadelphia PA 19108. Fax: (215)238-5457. E-mail: editor.ipg@napco.com. Website: www.ipgonline.com. **Contact:** Bob Neubauer, editor. **10% freelance written.** *"In-Plant Graphics* features articles designed to help in-house printing departments increase productivity, save money and stay competitive. *IPG* features advances in graphic arts technology and shows in-plants how to put this technology to use. Our audience consists of print shop managers working for (non-print related) corporations (i.e., hospitals, insurance companies, publishers, non-profits), universities and government departments. They often oversee graphic design, prepress, printing, bindery and mailing departments." Estab. 1951. Circ. 24,600. Pays on publication. Publishes ms an average of 5 months after acceptance. Byline given. Buys first North American serial rights. Editorial lead time 2 months. Submit seasonal material 3 months in advance. Accepts queries by mail, e-mail, fax. Writer's guidelines online.
Nonfiction: "Stories include profiles of successful in-house printing operations (not commercial or quick printers); updates on graphic arts technology (new features, uses); reviews of major graphic arts and printing conferences (seminar and new equipment reviews)." New product (graphic arts), technical (graphic arts/printing/prepress). No articles on desktop publishing software or design software. No Internet publishing articles. **Buys 5 mss/year.** Query with published clips. Length: 800-1,500 words. **Pays $250-350.** Pays writers with contributor copies or other premiums for consultants who agree to write just for exposure.
Photos: State availability with submission. Reviews transparencies, prints. Buys one-time rights. Negotiates payment individually. Captions, identification of subjects required.
■ The online magazine carries original content not found in the print edition. Contact: Bob Neubauer.
Tips: "To get published in *IPG*, writers must contact the editor with an idea in the form of a query letter that includes published writing samples. Writers who have covered the graphic arts in the past may be assigned stories for an agreed-upon fee. We don't want stories that tout only one vendor's products and serve as glorified commercials. All profiles must be well-balanced, covering a variety of issues. If you can tell us about an in-house printing operation that is doing innovative things, we will be interested."

$ $PRINT & GRAPHICS PRINTING JOURNAL; SOUTHERN GRAPHICS; PRINTING VIEWS, 1818 Pot Spring Rd., #102, Timonium MD 21093. (410)628-7826. Fax: (410)628-7829. E-mail: david.lindsay@cygnuspub.com. Website: www.printandgraphicsmag.com. Publisher: Kaj Spencer. **Contact:** David Lindsay, editor. **50% freelance written.** Monthly tabloid of the commercial printing industry for owners and executives of graphic arts firms. Eager to work with new/unpublished writers. Circ. 20,000. Pays on publication. Publishes ms an average of 2 months after acceptance. Byline given. Offers kill fee. Buys one-time rights. Accepts queries by mail. Accepts simultaneous submissions. Responds in 2 months to queries. Sample copy for $2.
Nonfiction: "All articles should relate to graphic arts management or production." Book excerpts, historical/nostalgic, how-to, interview/profile, new product, opinion, personal experience, photo feature, technical. **Buys 200 mss/year.** Query with published clips. Length: 750-1,500 words. **Pays $250-350.**
Reprints: Send photocopy and information about when and where the material previously appeared. Pays $150 flat fee. Publishes trade book excerpts.
Photos: State availability with submission. Captions, identification of subjects required.

PROFESSIONAL PHOTOGRAPHY

Journals for professional photographers are listed in this section. Magazines for the general public interested in photography techniques are in the Consumer Photography section. (For listings of markets for freelance photography use *Photographer's Market*, Writer's Digest Books.)

N $ $ NEWS PHOTOGRAPHER, National Press Photographers, Inc., 1446 Conneaut Ave., Bowling Green OH 43402. (419)352-8175. Fax: (419)354-5435. E-mail: magazine@nppa.org. Website: www.nppa.org. **Contact:** James R. Gordon, editor. Published 12 times/year. "*News Photographer* magazine is dedicated to the advancement of still and television news photography. The magazine presents articles, interviews, profiles, history, new products, electronic imaging and news related to the practice of photojournalism." Estab. 1946. Circ. 11,000. **Pays on acceptance.** Publishes ms an average of 4 months after acceptance. Byline given. Offers 100% kill fee. Buys one-time rights. Editorial lead time 2 months. Submit seasonal material 2 months in advance. Accepts queries by mail, e-mail, fax, phone. Accepts simultaneous submissions. Responds in 1 month to queries. Sample copy for 9×12 SAE and 3 first-class stamps. Writer's guidelines free.
Nonfiction: Historical/nostalgic, how-to, interview/profile, new product, opinion, personal experience, photo feature, technical. **Buys 10 mss/year.** Query. Length: 1,500 words. **Pays $300.** Pays expenses of writers on assignment.
Photos: State availability with submission. Reviews negatives, 35mm transparencies, 8×10 prints. Buys one-time rights. Negotiates payment individually. Captions, identification of subjects required.
Columns/Departments: Query.

$ $ THE PHOTO REVIEW, 140 E. Richardson Ave., Suite 301, Langhorne PA 19047. (215)891-0214. Fax: (215)891-9258. E-mail: info@photoreview.org. Website: www.photoreview.org. Managing Editor: Nancy Brokaw. **Contact:** Stephen Perloff, chief editor. **50% freelance written.** Quarterly magazine covering art photography and criticism. "*The Photo Review* publishes critical reviews of photography exhibitions and books, critical essays, and interviews. We do not publish how-to or technical articles." Estab. 1980. Circ. 2,000. Pays on publication. Publishes ms an average of 9-12 months after acceptance. Byline given. Buys first rights. Editorial lead time 3 months. Submit seasonal material 6 months in advance. Accepts queries by mail. Accepts simultaneous submissions. Responds in 2 months to queries; 3 months to mss. Sample copy for $7. Writer's guidelines for #10 SASE.
Nonfiction: Interview/profile, photography essay, critical review. No how-to articles. **Buys 20 mss/year.** Send complete ms. Length: 15-20 typed pages. **Pays $10-250.**
Reprints: Send tearsheet, photocopy or typed ms with rights for sale noted and information about when and where the material previously appeared. Payment varies.
Photos: Send photos with submission. Reviews contact sheets, transparencies, prints. Buys all rights. Offers no additional payment for photos accepted with ms. Captions required.

$ $ PHOTOGRAPHIC PROCESSING, Cygnus Publishing, 445 Broad Hollow Rd., Melville NY 11747. Fax: (631)845-2797. E-mail: bill.schiffner@cygnuspub.com. Website: www.labsonline.com. **Contact:** Bill Schiffner, editor. **30% freelance written.** Monthly magazine covering photographic (commercial/minilab) and electronic processing markets. Estab. 1965. Circ. 23,000. Pays on publication. Publishes ms an average of 4 months after acceptance. Byline given. Offers $75 kill fee. Editorial lead time 3 months. Submit seasonal material 3 months in advance. Accepts simultaneous submissions. Sample copy and writer's guidelines free.
Nonfiction: How-to, interview/profile, new product, photo processing/digital imaging features. **Buys 30-40 mss/year.** Query with published clips. Length: 1,500-2,200 words. **Pays $275-350 for assigned articles; $250-300 for unsolicited articles.**
Photos: Looking for digitally manipulated covers. Send photos with submission. Reviews 4×5 transparencies, 4×6 prints. Buys one-time rights. Offers no additional payment for photos accepted with ms. Captions required.
Columns/Departments: Surviving in 2000 (business articles offering tips to labs on how to make their businesses run better), 1,500-1,800 words; Business Side (getting more productivity out of your lab). **Buys 10 mss/year.** Query with published clips. **Pays $150-250.**

N $ $ SHUTTERBUG/eDIGITALPHOTO.COM, Primedia, 5211 S. Washington Ave., Titusville FL 32780. E-mail: editor@shutterbug.net. Website: www.shutterbug.net. Managing Editor: Bonnie Paulk. **Contact:** George Schaub, editor. **90% freelance written.** Monthly tabloid covering photography and digital imaging. "Written for the avid amateur, part-time and fulltime professional photographers. Covers equipment techniques, profiles, technology and news in both silver-halide and digital imaging." Estab. 1972. Circ. 90,000. Pays on publication. Publishes ms an average of 90 days after acceptance. Byline given. Offers 50% kill fee. Buys first North American serial, second serial (reprint), electronic rights. Editorial lead time 3 months. Submit seasonal material 6 months in advance. Accepts queries by mail. Responds in 1 month to queries; 1 month to mss. Writer's guidelines for #10 SASE.
Nonfiction: How-to, interview/profile, new product, photo feature, technical, travel. **Buys 100 mss/year.** Query with or without published clips. Length: 1,000-2,000 words. **Payment rate depends on published length.** Sometimes pays expenses of writers on assignment.
Photos: Send photos with submission. Reviews contact sheets, transparencies, cd-roms. Buys one-time rights. Offers no additional payment for photos accepted with ms. Captions, model releases required.

$ $ TODAY'S PHOTOGRAPHER INTERNATIONAL, American Image Press Inc., P.O. Box 777, Lewisville NC 27023. (336)945-9867. Fax: (336)945-3711. Website: www.aipress.com. **Contact:** Vonda H. Blackburn, editor. **100% freelance written.** Bimonthly "The make money with your camera magazine." Estab. 1984. Circ. 93,000. Pays on publication. Publishes ms an average of 4 months after acceptance. Byline given. Buys simultaneous rights. Editorial lead time 4 months. Submit seasonal material 8 months in advance. Accepts simultaneous submissions. Responds in 1 month to queries; 2 months to mss. Sample copy for $3. Writer's guidelines free.

Nonfiction: How freelance photographers make money. How-to (make money with your camera). Nothing outside making money with a camera. Query. Length: 800-2,000 words. **Pays $50-200.**
Photos: State availability with submission. Reviews contact sheets, transparencies, prints. Buys one-time rights. Offers no additional payment for photos accepted with ms. Captions, identification of subjects, model releases required.
Columns/Departments: Query with published clips.

REAL ESTATE

$ $ AREA DEVELOPMENT MAGAZINE, Sites and Facility Planning, Halcyon Business Publications, Inc., 400 Post Ave., Westbury NY 11590. (516)338-0900, ext. 211. Fax: (516)338-0100. E-mail: gerri@area-development.com. Website: www.area-development.com. Managing Editor: Pam Karr. **Contact:** Geraldine Gambale, editor. **80% freelance written.** Prefers to work with published/established writers. Monthly magazine covering corporate facility planning and site selection for industrial chief executives worldwide. Estab. 1965. Circ. 45,000. Pays on publication. Publishes ms an average of 2 months after acceptance. Byline given. Buys all rights. Accepts queries by mail, fax. Responds in 3 months to queries. Sample copy free. Writer's guidelines for #10 SASE.
Nonfiction: Related areas of site selection and facility planning such as taxes, labor, government, energy, architecture and finance. Historical/nostalgic (if it deals with corporate facility planning), how-to (experiences in site selection and all other aspects of corporate facility planning), interview/profile (corporate executives and industrial developers). **Buys 75 mss/year.** Query. Length: 1,500-2,000 words. **Pays 30¢/word.** Sometimes pays expenses of writers on assignment.
Photos: State availability with submission. Reviews transparencies. Negotiates payment individually. Captions, identification of subjects required.
  ■ The online magazine carries original content not found in the print edition. Contact: Geraldine Gambale, online editor.

N $ $ CANADIAN PROPERTY MANAGEMENT, Mediaedge Communications Inc., 5255 Yonge St., Suite 1000, North York, Ontario M2N 6P4, Canada. (416)512-8186. Fax: (416)512-8344. E-mail: robert@mediaedge.com. Website: www.mediaedge.ca. **Contact:** Robert Colman, editor. **10% freelance written.** Magazine published 8 times/ year covering Canadian commercial, industrial, institutional (medical and educational), residential properties. "*Canadian Property Management* magazine is a trade journal supplying building owners and property managers with Canadian industry news, case law reviews, technical updates for building operations and events listings. Feature building and professional profile articles are regular features." Estab. 1985. Circ. 14,500. Pays on publication. Publishes ms an average of 3 months after acceptance. Byline given. Buys all rights. Editorial lead time 2 months. Submit seasonal material 2 months in advance. Accepts queries by mail, e-mail, fax, phone. Accepts simultaneous submissions. Responds in 3 weeks to queries; 2 months to mss. Sample copy for $5, subject to availability. Writer's guidelines free.
Nonfiction: Interview/profile, technical. "No promotional articles (e.g., marketing a product or service geared to this industry)!" Query with published clips. Length: 700-1,200 words. **Pays 35¢/word.**
Photos: State availability with submission. Reviews transparencies. Offers no additional payment for photos accepted with ms. Captions, identification of subjects, model releases required.
Tips: "We do not accept promotional articles serving companies or their products. Freelance articles that are strong, information-based pieces that serve the interests and needs of property managers and building owners stand a better chance of being published. Proposals and inquiries with article ideas are appreciated the most. A good understanding of the real estate industry (management structure) is also helpful for the writer."

$ $ $ $ COMMERCIAL INVESTMENT REAL ESTATE, CCIM, 430 N. Michigan Ave., Suite 800, Chicago IL 60611-4092. (312)321-4460. Fax: (312)321-4530. E-mail: magazine@ccim.com. Website: www.ccim.com/magazine. **Contact:** Barbara Stevenson, editor. **10% freelance written.** Bimonthly magazine. "*CIRE* offers practical articles on current trends and business development ideas for commercial investment real estate practitioners." Estab. 1982. Circ. 12,500. **Pays on acceptance.** Publishes ms an average of 4 months after acceptance. Byline given. Buys all rights. Editorial lead time 4 months. Submit seasonal material 4 months in advance. Accepts queries by mail, e-mail, fax. Responds in 2 weeks to queries; 1 month to mss. Sample copy for 9×12 SAE with 5 first-class stamps or online. Writers guidelines for #10 SASE or online.
  ☞ Break in by sending résumé and feature-length clips, "including commercial real estate-related clips if available. We keep writers' materials on file for assigning articles."
Nonfiction: How-to, technical, Business strategies. **Buys 6-8 mss/year.** Query with published clips. Length: 2,000-3,500 words. **Pays $1,000-1,600.**
Photos: May ask writers to have sources. Send images to editors.
Tips: "Always query first with a detailed outline and published clips. Authors should have a background in writing on business or real estate subjects."

$ $ THE COOPERATOR, The Co-op and Condo Monthly, Yale Robbins, LLC, 31 E. 28th St., 12th Floor, New York NY 10016. (212)683-5700. Fax: (212)696-1268. E-mail: judy@cooperator.com. Website: www.cooperator.com. **Contact:** Judith C. Grover, managing editor. **20% freelance written.** Monthly tabloid covering real estate. "*The Cooperator* covers condominium and cooperative issues in New York and beyond. It is read by unit owners and shareholders, board members and managing agents. We have just become a national publication and are interested in receiving articles from states outside of New York." Estab. 1980. Circ. 60,000. Pays on publication. Publishes ms an average of 3 months after acceptance. Byline given. Buys all rights, makes work-for-hire assignments. Submit seasonal material 3 months in advance. Accepts queries by mail, e-mail, fax. Responds in 2 weeks to queries. Sample copy free.

Nonfiction: All articles related to co-op and condo ownership. Interview/profile, new product, personal experience. No submissions without queries. **Buys 20 mss/year.** Query with published clips. Length: 1,000-2,000 words. **Pays $150-250.** Sometimes pays expenses of writers on assignment.

Photos: State availability with submission. Reviews contact sheets, negatives, transparencies. Rights purchased vary. Negotiates payment individually. Captions, identification of subjects required.

Columns/Departments: Management Profile (profile of prominent management company); Building Finance (investment and financing issues); Buying and Selling (market issues, etc.), all 1,500 words. **Buys 20 mss/year.** Query with published clips. **Pays $150-250.**

Tips: "You must have experience doing journalistic reporting, especially real estate, business, legal or financial. Must have published clips to send in with résumé and query."

$ $ FLORIDA REALTOR MAGAZINE, Florida Association of Realtors, 7025 Augusta National Dr., Orlando FL 32822-5017. (407)438-1400. Fax: (407)438-1411. E-mail: FLRealtor@Fl.realtorUSA.com. Website: Floridarealtormagazine.com. Assistant Editor: Jamie Floer. **Contact:** Tracey Lawton, editor-in-chief. **30% freelance written.** Journal published 11 times/year covering Florida real estate. "As the official publication of the Florida Association of Realtors, we provide helpful articles for our 67,000 members. We try to stay up on the trends and issues that affect business in Florida's real estate market." Estab. 1925. Circ. 67,000. Pays on publication. Publishes ms an average of 1 month after acceptance. Byline given. Editorial lead time 2 months. Accepts queries by mail, e-mail, fax, phone. Accepts simultaneous submissions. Sample copy online.

Nonfiction: Book excerpts, how-to, inspirational, interview/profile, new product, all with real estate angle—Florida-specific is good. "No fiction, poetry." **Buys varying number of mss/year.** Query with published clips. Length: 800-1,500 words. **Pays $200-400.** Sometimes pays expenses of writers on assignment. Accepts previously published submissions.

Photos: State availability with submission. Buys one-time rights. Negotiates payment individually. Captions, identification of subjects, model releases required.

Columns/Departments: "Rarely used." Occasionally publishes: Promotional Strategies, 900 words; Technology & You, 1,000 words; Realtor Advantage, 1,500 words. **Buys varying number of mss/year. Pay varies.**

Fillers: Short humor. **Buys varying number/year.**

Tips: "Build a solid reputation for specializing in real estate-specific writing in state/national publications."

$ $ $ MULTIFAMILY EXECUTIVE, MGI Publications, 301 Oxford Valley Rd., Suite 804, Yardley PA 19067. (215)321-5112. Fax: (215)321-5122. E-mail: ibromberg@mgipublications.com. Website: www.multifamilyexecutive.com. Editor: Edward J. McNeill, Jr. **Contact:** Miriam Lupkin. **35% freelance written.** Magazine published 12 times/year. "We target senior level executives in the multifamily housing industry—builders, developers, owners and managers." Circ. 25,000. Pays on publication. Publishes ms an average of 2 months after acceptance. Byline given. Buys first North American serial rights. Editorial lead time 3 months. Submit seasonal material 4 months in advance. Accepts queries by mail, e-mail, fax, phone. Responds in 2 months to queries. Sample copy for 9×12 SAE and 8 first-class stamps. Writer's guidelines free.

Nonfiction: Book excerpts, how-to, interview/profile, new product, opinion. **Buys 15-20 mss/year.** Query with published clips. Length: 750-1,500 words. **Pays $100-1,000 for assigned articles; $100-500 for unsolicited articles.** Sometimes pays expenses of writers on assignment.

Photos: State availability with submission. Reviews transparencies. Buys all rights. Negotiates pay individually. Identification of subjects, model releases required.

Columns/Departments: Financial, Legal, Senior Housing, Affordable Housing (all written to an advanced level of multifamily executives); all 750-850 words. **Buys 8 mss/year.** Query with published clips. **Pays $100-400.**

$ $ $ NATIONAL RELOCATION & REAL ESTATE, RIS Publishing Inc., 50 Water St., Norwalk CT 06854. (203)855-1234. Fax: (203)852-7208. E-mail: erin@rismedia.com. Website: rismedia.com. Editor: Frank Sziros. **Contact:** Erin Harrison, managing editor. **30-50% freelance written.** Monthly magazine covering residential real estate and corporate relocation. "Our readers are professionals within the relocation and real estate industries; therefore, we require our writers to have sufficient knowledge of the workings of these industries in order to ensure depth and accuracy

---

MARKET CONDITIONS are constantly changing! If this is 2003 or later, buy the newest edition of *Writer's Market* at your favorite bookstore or order directly from Writer's Digest Books at (800)289-0963.

in reporting." Estab. 1980. Circ. 35,000. Pays on publication. Byline sometimes given. Offers 20-50% kill fee. Buys all rights. Editorial lead time 4 months. Accepts queries by mail, e-mail. Responds in 2 weeks to queries. Sample copy free.

Nonfiction: Exposé, how-to (use the Internet to sell real estate, etc.), interview/profile, new product, opinion, technical. Query with published clips. Length: 250-1,500 words. Pays unsolicited article writers with contributor copies upon use. Sometimes pays expenses of writers on assignment.

Photos: Send photos with submission. Reviews transparencies. Offers no additional payment for photos accepted with ms. Captions required.

Columns/Departments: Query with published clips.

■ The online magazine carries original content not found in the print edition. Website features daily news service, written submissions and other information on publication. Contact: Mike Patrick.

Tips: "All queries must be done in writing. Phone queries are unacceptable. Any clips or materials sent should indicate knowledge of the real estate and relocation industries. In general, we are open to all knowledgeable contributors."

$ $ PROPERTIES MAGAZINE, Properties Magazine, Inc., P.O. Box 112127, Cleveland OH 44111. (216)251-0035. Fax: (216)251-0064. E-mail: kkrych@bright.net. Editor: Kenneth C. Krych. **25% freelance written.** Monthly magazine covering real estate, residential, commerical construction. "*Properties Magazine* is published for executives in the real estate, building, banking, design, architectural, property management, tax and law community—busy people who need the facts presented in an interesting and informative format." Estab. 1946. Circ. over 6,000. Pays on publication. Publishes ms an average of 2 months after acceptance. Byline given. Buys first rights. Editorial lead time 2 months. Submit seasonal material 2 months in advance. Accepts queries by mail, fax. Responds in 3 weeks to queries. Sample copy for $2.50.

Nonfiction: General interest, how-to, humor, new product. Special issues: Upcoming theme issues: Environmental issues (September); Security/fire protection (October); Tax issues (November); Computers in real estate (December). **Buys 30 mss/year.** Send complete ms. Length: 500-2,000 words. **Pays 50¢/column line.** Sometimes pays expenses of writers on assignment.

Photos: Send photos with submission. Reviews prints. Buys one-time rights. Offers no additional payment for photos accepted with ms. Negotiates payment individually. Captions required.

Columns/Departments: Buys 25 mss/year. Query or send complete ms. **Pays 50¢/column line.**

$ $ RETIREMENT COMMUNITY BUSINESS, Great River Publishing Company, Inc., 2026 Exeter Rd., Suite 2, Germantown TN 38138. (901)624-5911. Fax: (901)624-5910. E-mail: rcb@grtriver.com. Website: www.grtriver.com. **Contact:** Sherry Campbell, editor. **25% freelance written.** Quarterly magazine covering management of retirement and assisted living communities. Estab. 1992. Circ. 15,000. Pays on publication. Publishes ms an average of 6 months after acceptance. Byline given. Offers negotiable kill fee. Buys all rights. Editorial lead time 3 months. Submit seasonal material 3 months in advance. Accepts queries by mail, e-mail, fax, phone. Responds in 2 weeks to queries; 3 months to mss. Sample copy and writer's guidelines free.

Nonfiction: Only articles specific to industry. General interest, how-to (management and operational issues of seniors housing), interview/profile, new product, personal experience, photo feature, travel. **Buys 20-30 mss/year.** Query with published clips. Length: 300-1,500 words. **Pay is negotiated.**

Photos: State availability with submission. Buys all rights. Offers no additional payment for photos accepted with ms. Model releases required.

Tips: "Writers should have basic knowledge of the industry sufficient to understand some management issues. Writer should understand what a retirement or assisted living community is and isn't."

RESOURCES & WASTE REDUCTION

$ $ COMPOSTING NEWS, The Latest News in Composting and Scrap Wood Management, McEntee Media Corporation, 9815 Hazelwood Ave., Cleveland OH 44149. (440)238-6603. Fax: (440)238-6712. E-mail: cn@recycle.cc. **Contact:** Ken McEntee, editor. **5% freelance written.** Monthly newsletter. "We are interested in any news impacting the composting industry including new laws, regulations, new facilities/programs, end-uses, research, etc." Estab. 1992. Circ. 1,000. Pays on publication. Publishes ms an average of 1 month after acceptance. Buys first, all rights. Editorial lead time 1 month. Submit seasonal material 1 month in advance. Accepts queries by mail, e-mail, fax, phone. Accepts simultaneous submissions. Responds in 2 months to queries. Sample copy for 9×12 SAE and 55¢ postage. Writer's guidelines for #10 SASE.

Nonfiction: Book excerpts, essays, general interest, how-to, interview/profile, new product, opinion, personal experience, photo feature, technical, new business, legislation, regulation, business expansion. **Buys 0-5 mss/year.** Query with published clips. Length: 100-5,000 words. **Pays $10-500.** Pays writers with contributor copies or other premiums by prior agreement.

Columns/Departments: Query with published clips. **Pays $10-500.**

■ The online magazine carries original content not found in the print edition. Contact: Ken McEntee.

Tips: "We appreciate leads on local news regarding composting, i.e., new facilities or business, new laws and regulations, unique programs, situations that impact supply and demand for composting. International developments are also of interest."

$ $ $ EROSION CONTROL, The Journal for Erosion and Sediment Control Professionals, Forester Communications, Inc., 5638 Hollister Ave., Suite 301, Santa Barbara CA 93101. (805)681-1300. Fax: (805)681-1311. E-mail: eceditor@forester.net. Website: www.erosioncontrol.com. **Contact:** Janice Kaspersen, editor. **60% freelance written.** Magazine published 9 times/year covering all aspects of erosion prevention and sediment control. "*Erosion Control* is a practical, hands-on, 'how-to' professional journal. Our readers are civil engineers, landscape architects, builders, developers, public works officials, road and highway construction officials and engineers, soils specialists, farmers, landscape contractors and others involved with any activity that disturbs significant areas of surface vegetation." Estab. 1994. Circ. 20,000. Pays 30 days after acceptance. Publishes ms an average of 3 months after acceptance. Byline given. Buys all rights. Editorial lead time 4 months. Submit seasonal material 4 months in advance. Accepts queries by mail, e-mail, fax, phone. Accepts simultaneous submissions. Responds in 3 weeks to queries. Sample copy and writer's guidelines free.
Nonfiction: Photo feature, technical. **Buys 15 mss/year.** Query with published clips. Length: 3,000-4,000 words. **Pays $700-850.** Sometimes pays expenses of writers on assignment.
Photos: Send photos with submission. Reviews transparencies, prints. Buys all rights. Offers no additional payment for photos accepted with ms. Captions, identification of subjects, model releases required.
Tips: "Writers should have a good grasp of technology involved, good writing and communication skills, unbounded curiosity and no hidden agenda. Most of our freelanced articles include extensive interviews with engineers, contractors, developers, or project owners, and we often provide contact names for articles we assign."

$ $ MSW MANAGEMENT, The Journal for Municipal Solid Waste Professionals, Forester Communications, Inc., 5638 Hollister Ave., Suite 301, Santa Barbara CA 93117. (805)681-1300. Fax: (805)681-1311. E-mail: editor@forester.net. Website: www.mswmanagement.net. **Contact:** John Trotti, editor. **70% freelance written.** Bimonthly magazine. "*MSW Management* is written for *public sector* solid waste professionals—the people working for the local counties, cities, towns, boroughs and provinces. They run the landfills, recycling programs, composting, incineration. They are responsible for all aspects of garbage collection and disposal; buying and maintaining the associated equipment; and designing, engineering and building the waste processing facilities, transfer stations and landfills." Estab. 1991. Circ. 25,000. Pays on publication. Byline given. Buys all rights. Editorial lead time 4 months. Submit seasonal material 4 months in advance. Accepts queries by mail, e-mail, fax, phone. Accepts simultaneous submissions. Responds in 6 weeks to queries; 2 months to mss. Sample copy and writer's guidelines free.
Nonfiction: Photo feature, technical. "No rudimentary, basic articles written for the average person on the street. our readers are experienced professionals with years of practical, in-the-field experience. Any material submitted that we judge as too fundamental will be rejected." **Buys 15 mss/year.** Query. Length: 3,000-4,000 words. **Pays $350-650.** Sometimes pays expenses of writers on assignment.
Photos: Send photos with submission. Reviews transparencies, prints. Buys all rights. Offers no additional payment for photos accepted with ms. Captions, identification of subjects, model releases required.
  ▣ The online magazine carries original content not found in the print edition. Contact: John Trotti.
Tips: "We're a small company, easy to reach. We're open to any and all ideas as to possible editorial topics. We endeavor to provide the reader with usable material, and present it in full color with graphic embellishment whenever possible. Dry, highly technical material is edited to make it more palatable and concise. Most of our feature articles come from freelancers. Interviews and quotes should be from public sector solid waste managers and engineers—*not* PR people, *not* manufacturers. Strive to write material that is 'over the heads' of our readers. If anything, attempt to make them 'reach.' Anything submitted that is too basic, elementary, fundamental, rudimentary, etc. cannot be accepted for publication."

N $ $ $ STORMWATER, The Journal for Surface Water Quality Professionals, Forester Communications, Inc., 5638 Hollister Ave., Suite 301, Santa Barbara CA 93117. (805)681-1300. Fax: (805)681-1311. E-mail: sweditor@forester.net. Website: www.stormh2o.com. **Contact:** Janice Kaspersen, editor. **25% freelance written.** "*Stormwater* is a practical business journal for professionals involved with surface water quality issues, protection, projects, and programs. Our readers are municipal employees, regulators, engineers, and consultants concerned with stormwater management." Estab. 2000. Circ. 20,000. Publishes ms an average of 3 months after acceptance. Byline given. Editorial lead time 4 months. Submit seasonal material 4 months in advance. Accepts queries by mail, e-mail. Accepts simultaneous submissions. Responds in 3 weeks to queries. Writer's guidelines free.
Nonfiction: Technical. **Buys 10 mss/year.** Query with published clips. Length: 3,000-4,000 words. **Pays $700-850.** Sometimes pays expenses of writers on assignment.
Photos: Send photos with submission. Buys all rights. Offers no additional payment for photos accepted with ms. Captions, identification of subjects, model releases required.
Tips: "Writers should have a good grasp of the technology and regulations involved in stormwater management and good interviewing skills. Our freelanced articles include extensive interviews with engineers, stormwater managers, and project owners, and we often provide contact names for articles we assign. See past editorial content online."

$ $ WATER WELL JOURNAL, National Ground Water Association, 601 Dempsey Rd., Westerville OH 43081. Fax: (614)898-7786. E-mail: jross@ngwa.org. Website: www.ngwa.org. **Contact:** Jill Ross, director of publications. **25% freelance written.** Monthly magazine covering the ground water industry; well drilling. "Each month the *Water Well Journal* covers the topics of drilling, rigs and heavy equipment, pumping systems, water quality, business management, water supply, on-site waste water treatment, and diversification opportunities, including geoexchange installations, environmental remediation, irrigation, dewatering and foundation installation. It also offers updates on regulatory issues that impact the ground water industry." Estab. 1948. Circ. 30,000. Pays on publication. Publishes ms an average of 3 months after acceptance. Byline given. Buys all rights. Editorial lead time 2 months. Submit seasonal material 3 months in advance. Accepts queries by mail, e-mail, fax, phone. Responds in 2 weeks to queries; 1 month to mss. Sample copy for 9 × 12 SAE and 2 first-class stamps. Writer's guidelines free.
Nonfiction: Essays (sometimes), historical/nostalgic (sometimes), how-to (recent examples include how to chlorinate a well; how to buy a used rig; how to do bill collections), interview/profile, new product, personal experience, photo feature, technical, business managment. No company profiles; extended product releases. **Buys up to 20 mss/year.** Query with published clips. Length: 1,000-4,000 words. **Pays $100-600.**
Photos: State availability with submission. Offers $50-250/photo. Captions, identification of subjects required.
Tips: "Some previous experience or knowledge in groundwater/drilling/construction industry helpful. Published clips a must."

SELLING & MERCHANDISING

Sales personnel and merchandisers interested in how to sell and market products successfully consult these journals. Publications in nearly every category of Trade also buy sales-related materials if they are slanted to the product or industry with which they deal.

N $ $ BALLOONS AND PARTIES MAGAZINE, Partilife Publications, 65 Sussex St., Hackensack NJ 07601. (201)441-4224. Fax: (201)342-8118. E-mail: mark@balloonsandparties.com. Website: www.balloonsandparties.com. **Contact:** Mark Zettler, publisher. **10% freelance written.** International trade journal for professional party decorators and for gift delivery businesses published 6 times/year. Estab. 1986. Circ. 7,000. Pays on publication. Publishes ms an average of 3 months after acceptance. Byline given. Buys all rights. Submit seasonal material 6 months in advance. Accepts queries by mail, e-mail, fax, phone. Responds in 6 weeks to queries. Sample copy for 9 × 12 SAE.
Nonfiction: Essays, how-to, interview/profile, new product, personal experience, photo feature, technical, craft. **Buys 12 mss/year.** Query with or without published clips or send complete ms. Length: 500-1,500 words. **Pays $100-300 for assigned articles; $50-200 for unsolicited articles.** Sometimes pays expenses of writers on assignment.
Reprints: Send typed ms with rights for sale noted and information about when and where the material previously appeared Length: up to 2,500 words. Pays 10¢/word.
Photos: Send photos with submission. Reviews 2 × 2 transparencies, 3 × 5 prints. Buys all rights. Captions, identification of subjects, model releases required.
Columns/Departments: Problem Solver (small business issues); Recipes That Cook (centerpiece ideas with detailed how-to), 400-1,000 words. Send complete ms with photos.
Tips: "Show unusual, lavish, and outstanding examples of balloon sculpture, design and decorating and other craft projects. Offer specific how-to information. Be positive and motivational in style."

N $ $ COLLEGE STORE, National Association of College Stores, 500 E. Lorain, Oberlin OH 44074. (216)775-7777. Fax: (216)775-4769. E-mail: thecollegestore@nacs.org. Website: www.nacs.org. **Contact:** Keith Galestock, editor. **50% freelance written.** Bimonthly magazine. "*College Store* is the journal of record for the National Association of College Stores and serves its members by publishing information and expert opinion on all phases of college store retailing." Estab. 1923. Circ. 7,200. **Pays on acceptance.** Byline given. Buys all rights. Editorial lead time 3 months. Submit seasonal material 6 months in advance. Accepts queries by mail, e-mail, fax. Responds in 1 month to queries. Sample copy free.
Nonfiction: "Articles must have clearly defined connection to college stores and collegiate retailing." How-to, interview/profile, personal experience, technical (unique attributes of collete stores/personnel). **Buys 4-6 unsolicited mss/ year.** Query with published clips. Length: 1,500-3,000 words. **Pays $400 minimum for assigned articles; $200 minimum for unsolicited articles.** Sometimes pays expenses of writers on assignment.
Reprints: Send tearsheet or photocopy with rights for sale noted. Pay negotiable.
Photos: Send photos with submission. Reviews 2¼ × 2¼ transparencies, 5 × 7 prints. Buys varying rights. Negotiates payment individually. Captions, identification of subjects required.
Tips: "It's best if writers work (or have worked) in a college store. Articles on specific retailing successes are most open to freelancers—they should include information on how well an approach worked and the reasons for it, whether they are specific to a campus or region, etc."

$ $ CONVENIENCE STORE DECISIONS, Donohue-Meehan Publishing, Two Greenwood Square, Suite 410, Bensalem PA 19020. (215)245-4555. Fax: (215)245-4060. E-mail: jgordon@penton.com. **Contact:** Jay Gordon, editor. **40% freelance written.** Monthly magazine. "*CSD* is read by executives of convenience store companies and seeks to be the 'idea store' by reporting on all facets of these specialized retail businesses, such as the marketing and merchandising of gasoline, food and merchandise." Estab. 1990. Circ. 42,000. Pays on publication. Byline given. Makes work-for-hire assignments. Editorial lead time 2 months. Submit seasonal material 4 months in advance. Accepts queries by mail, e-mail, fax. Sample copy free.

> O→ Break in with a "demonstrated knowledge of finance and business, with special emphasis on retail. Keen powers of observation and attention to detail are also prized."

Nonfiction: How-to, interview/profile, new product, technical. **Buys 24 mss/year.** Query with published clips. Length: 500-2,500 words. **Pays $400-600.** Pays expenses of writers on assignment.

Photos: State availability with submission. Negotiates payment individually.

Columns/Departments: Sensible Ideas. Query. **Pays $100-200.**

Tips: "Writers with strong retail/business writing experience should write or call Bill Donahue, managing editor. We will work to find an acceptable 'trial' assignment (for pay) to assess the writer's abilities. Do not send boiler plate features on finance and human resource topics that are customized for our market by adding the words convenience store. Don't waste our time!"

$ EVENTS BUSINESS NEWS, S.E.N. Inc., 523 Route 38, Suite 207, Cherry Hill NJ 08002. (856)488-5255. Fax: (856)488-8324. **Contact:** Norman Zelnick, assistant to the editor. **20% freelance written.** Bimonthly magazine covering special events across North America, including fesivals fairs, auto shows, home shows, trade shows, etc. Covers 15 categories of shows/events. Byline given. Buys first rights. Submit seasonal material 3 months in advance. Accepts queries by mail. Sample copy and writer's guidelines free.

Nonfiction: How-to, interview/profile, new product, event review. Special issues: Annual special event directory, covering over 38,000 events. No submissions unrelated to selling at events. Query. Length: 400-750 words. **Pays $2.50/ column inch.**

Reprints: Send photocopy of article and information about when and where the article previously appeared.

Photos: Send photos with submission. Reviews contact sheets. Buys one-time rights. Offers $20/photo. Captions required.

Columns/Departments: Five columns monthly (dealing with background of event, vendors or unique facets of industry in North America). Length: 400-700 words. Query with published clips. **Pays $3/column inch.**

N $ $ $ GIFTWARE BUSINESS, Bill Communications, 1 Penn Plaza, 10th Floor, New York NY 10119. Fax: (212)279-3960. E-mail: mmorgenthal@billcom.com. Website: www.giftline.com. Editor: Chris Gigley. **Contact:** Michael Morgenthal, managing editor. **10% freelance written.** Monthly magazine, newsletter and online product. "The magazine is for the serious gift retailer." Estab. 1943. Circ. 30,000. Pays on publication. Publishes ms an average of 3 months after acceptance. Byline given. Buys all rights. Editorial lead time 2 months. Submit seasonal material 6 months in advance. Accepts queries by mail, e-mail, fax. Sample copy free.

Nonfiction: How-to, interview/profile, new product, personal experience. Query with published clips. Length: 500-2,000 words. **Pays 50-75¢/word.** Sometimes pays expenses of writers on assignment.

Photos: Send photos with submission. Reviews 4×6 transparencies, 5×7 prints. Buys all rights. Offers no additional payment for photos accepted with ms. Captions required.

Columns/Departments: Pays 50¢/word.

$ $ GIFTWARE NEWS, Talcott Corp., 20 N. Walker Dr., Suite 1865, Chicago IL 60606. (312)849-2220. Fax: (312)849-2174. **Contact:** John Saxtan, editor. **55% freelance written.** Monthly magazine covering gifts, collectibles, and tabletops for giftware retailers. Estab. 1976. Circ. 35,000. Pays on publication. Publishes ms an average of 2 months after acceptance. Byline given. Buys all rights. Submit seasonal material 4 months in advance. Responds in 2 months to mss. Sample copy for $5.

Nonfiction: How-to (sell, display), new product. **Buys 50 mss/year.** Query with published clips or send complete ms. Length: 1,500-2,500 words. **Pays $200-350 for assigned articles; $150-250 for unsolicited articles.**

Photos: Send photos with submission. Reviews 4×5 transparencies, 5×7 prints. Offers no additional payment for photos accepted with ms. Identification of subjects required.

Columns/Departments: Stationery, giftbaskets, collectibles, holiday, merchandise, tabletop, wedding market and display—all for the gift retailer. Length: 1,500-2,500 words. **Buys 36 mss/year.** Send complete ms. **Pays $100-250.**

Tips: "We are not looking so much for general journalists but rather experts in particular fields who can also write."

$ $ NEW AGE RETAILER, Continuity Publishing, 1300 N. State St., #105, Bellingham WA 98225. (800)463-9243. Fax: (360)676-0932. E-mail: molly@newageretailer.com. Website: www.newage.retailer.com. **Contact:** Molly Trimble, editor. **90% freelance written.** Bimonthly magazine for retailers of New Age books, music and merchandise. "The goal of the articles in *New Age Retailer* is usefulness—we strive to give store owners and managers practical, in-depth information they can begin using immediately. We have three categories of articles: retail business methods that give solid information about the various aspects of running an independent store; inventory articles that discuss a particular New Age subject or trend and include lists of books, music, and products suitable for store inventory; and education articles that help storeowners and managers gain knowledge and stay current in New Age subjects." Estab. 1987. Circ. 6,000. Pays on publication. Publishes ms an average of 4 months after acceptance. Byline given. Offers

10% kill fee. Buys first North American serial, second serial (reprint), simultaneous, electronic rights. Editorial lead time 4 months. Submit seasonal material 4 months in advance. Accepts queries by mail, e-mail, fax, phone. Accepts simultaneous submissions. Responds in 1 month to queries; 2 months to mss. Sample copy for $5.

Nonfiction: Book excerpts, how-to, interview/profile, new product, opinion, personal experience, religious, technical, Business principles. No self-promotion for writer's company or product. Writer must understand independent retailing and New Age subjects. **Buys 50 mss/year.** Query with published clips. Length: 1,500-5,000 words. **Pays $150-300 for assigned articles; $75-250 for unsolicited articles.** Sometimes pays with advertisement space in magazine. Sometimes pays expenses of writers on assignment.

Photos: State availability of or send photos with submission. Reviews 2×3 prints (minimum size). Buys one-time rights. Negotiates payment individually. Captions required.

Columns/Departments: Mara Applebaum, associate editor. The Inspired Enterprise (New Age business tips for independent retailers), 2,500 words. **Buys 5-7 mss/year.** Query with published clips. **Pays $200-300.**

Tips: "E-mail Molly Trimble (molly@newageretailer.com), or phone her at (800)463-9243, ext. 3014. Describe your expertise in the New Age market and independent retailing. Have an idea for an article ready to pitch. Promise only what you can deliver."

$ $ NICHE, The Magazine For Progressive Retailers, The Rosen Group, 3000 Chestnut Ave., Suite 304, Baltimore MD 21211. (410)889-3093. Fax: (410)243-7089. E-mail: hoped@rosengrp.com. **Contact:** Hope Daniels, editor. **75% freelance written.** Quarterly business-to-business magazine for the progressive craft gallery retailer. Each issue includes retail gallery profiles, store design trends, management techniques and merchandising strategies for small business owners. Estab. 1988. Circ. 20,000. Pays on publication. Publishes ms an average of 6 months after acceptance. Byline given. Buys first North American serial rights. Editorial lead time 4 months. Submit seasonal material 9 months in advance. Accepts queries by mail, e-mail, fax. Responds in 6 weeks to queries; 1 month to mss. Sample copy for $3.

Nonfiction: *Niche* is looking for in-depth articles on store security, innovative merchandising/display or marketing and promotion. Stories of interest to independent retailers, such as gallery owners, may be submitted. Interview/profile, photo feature, articles targeted to independent retailers and small business owners. **Buys 20-28 mss/year.** Query with published clips. **Pays $300-700.** Sometimes pays expenses of writers on assignment.

Photos: Send photos with submission. Reviews 4×5 transparencies, slides. Negotiates payment individually. Captions required.

Columns/Departments: Retail Details (general retail information); Artist Profiles (biographies of American Craft Artists); Resources (book/video/seminar reviews pertaining to retailers). Query with published clips. **Pays $25-300.**

$ $ $ $ OPERATIONS & FULFILLMENT, Primedia/Intertec Publishing, 11 Riverbend Dr. S., P.O. Box 4949, Stamford CT 06907-2524. (203)358-3124, ext. 764. E-mail: david_pluviose@intertec.com. Website: www.opsandfulfill ment.com. **Contact:** David Pluviose, assistant editor. **25% freelance written.** Monthly magazine covering catalog/ direct mail operations. "*Operations & Fulfillment (O&F)* is a monthly publication that offers practical solutions for catalog online, and direct response operations management. The magazine covers such critical areas as material handling, bar coding, facility planning, transportation, call centers, warehouse management, information systems, online fulfillment and human resources." Estab. 1993. Circ. 17,600. Pays on publication. Publishes ms an average of 2 months after acceptance. Buys first North American serial rights. Editorial lead time 2 months. Accepts queries by mail, e-mail, phone. Responds in 1 week to queries. Sample copy and writer's guidelines free.

Nonfiction: Book excerpts, how-to, interview/profile, new product, technical. **Buys 4-6 mss/year.** Query with published clips. Length: 2,500-3,000 words. **Pays $1,000-1,800.**

Photos: "In addition to the main article, you must include at least one sidebar of about 400 words that contains a detailed example or case study of how a direct-to-customer catalog company implements or benefits from the process you're writing about; a check list or set of practical guidelines (e.g., "Twelve Ways to Ship Smarter") that describe how to implement what you suggest in the article; supporting materials such as flow charts, graphs, diagrams, illustrations and photographs (these must be clearly labeled and footnoted); and an author biography of no more than 75 words." Send photos with submission. Captions, identification of subjects required.

Tips: "Writers need some knowledge of the direct-to-customer industry. They should be able to deal clearly with highly technical material; provide attention to detail and painstaking research."

$ $ PARTY & PAPER RETAILER, 107 Mill Plain Rd., Suite 204, Danbury CT 06811-6100. (203)730-4090. Fax: (203)730-4094. E-mail: editor@partypaper.com. Website: www.partypaper.com. **Contact:** Jacqueline Shanley, editor-in-chief. **90% freelance written.** Monthly magazine covering "every aspect of how to do business better for owners of party and fine stationery shops. Tips and how-tos on display, marketing, success stories, merchandising, operating costs, e-commerce, retail technology, etc." Estab. 1986. Circ. 20,000. Pays on publication. Offers 15% kill fee. Buys first North American serial rights. Editorial lead time 6 months. Submit seasonal material 6 months in advance. Accepts queries by mail, e-mail, fax. Responds in 2 months to queries. Sample copy for $6.

    O⊷ Especially interested in news items on party retail industry for our Press Pages. Also, new column on Internet retailing ("Cyberlink") which covers all www-related topics.

Nonfiction: Book excerpts, how-to ((retailing related)), new product. No articles written in first person. **Buys 100 mss/year.** Query with published clips. Length: 800-1,800 words. Pays phone expenses only of writers on assignment.

Reprints: Send tearsheet or photocopy of article and information about when and where the article previously appeared.

Photos: State availability with submission. Reviews transparencies. Buys one-time rights. Negotiates payment individually. Captions, identification of subjects required.

Columns/Departments: Shop Talk (successful party/stationery store profile), 1,800 words; Storekeepint (selling, employees, market, running store), 800 words; Cash Flow (anything finance related), 800 words; On Display (display ideas and how-to). **Buys 30 mss/year.** Query with published clips. **Payment varies.**

■ The online magazine carries original content not found in the print edition.

$ $ TRAVEL GOODS SHOWCASE, The source for luggage, business cases and accessories, (formerly *Showcase International*), Travel Goods Association, 350 Fifth Ave, Suite 2624, New York NY 10118. (212)695-2340. Fax: (212)643-8021. E-mail: john@travel-goods.org. Website: www.travel-goods.org. Editor: Michele M. Pittenger. **Contact:** John Misiano, senior editor. **5-10% freelance written.** Bimonthly magazine covering travel goods, accessories, trends and new products. *"Travel Goods Showcase* contains articles for retailers, dealers, manufacturers and suppliers, about luggage, business cases, personal leather goods, handbags and accessories. Special articles report on trends in fashion promotions, selling and marketing techniques, industry statistics and other educational and promotional improvements and advancement." Estab. 1975. Circ. 14,500. **Pays on acceptance.** Publishes ms an average of 2 months after acceptance. Byline given. Offers $50 kill fee. Editorial lead time 3 months. Submit seasonal material 2 months in advance. Accepts queries by mail, e-mail. Responds in 2 weeks to queries; 1 month to mss. Sample copy and writer's guidelines free.

Nonfiction: Interview/profile, new product, technical, travel, retailer profiles with photos. "No manufacturer profiles." **Buys 3 mss/year.** Query with published clips. Length: 1,200-1,600 words. **Pays $200-500.**

SPORT TRADE

Retailers and wholesalers of sports equipment and operators of recreation programs read these journals. Magazines about general and specific sports are classified in the Consumer Sports section.

$ $ ARROWTRADE MAGAZINE, A Magazine for Retailers, Distributors & Manufacturers of Bowhunting Equipment, Arrow Trade Publishing Corporation, 2295 E. Newman Rd., Lake City MI 49651. (231)328-3006. Fax: (231)328-3060. E-mail: atrade@freeway.net. **Contact:** Tim Dehn, editor. **25% freelance written.** Bimonthly magazine covering the archery industry. "Our readers are interested in articles that help them operate their business better. They are primarily owners or managers of sporting goods stores and archery pro shops." Estab. 1996. Circ. 10,000. **Pays on acceptance.** Publishes ms an average of 2 months after acceptance. Byline given. Buys first North American serial rights. Editorial lead time 2 months. Accepts queries by mail, e-mail, fax. Responds in 2 weeks to queries; 2 weeks to mss. Sample copy for 9×12 SAE and 10 first-class stamps. Writer's guidelines for #10 SASE.

○━ *ArrowTrade Magazine* needs queries from veterans interested in writing for our industry audience. Our readers are primarily retailers of bowhunting equipment. "Find an unusual business combination, like someone selling archery plus cowboy boots, motorcycles, taxidermy—and submit it, 1,100-1,400 words for 'Archery Plus.' "

Nonfiction: Interview/profile, new product. "Generic business articles won't work for our highly specialized audience." **Buys 15 mss/year.** Query with published clips. Length: 1,800-2,800 words. **Pays $350-550.**

Photos: Send photos with submission. Reviews contact sheets, negatives, 35mm transparencies, 4×6 prints. Offers no additional payment for photos accepted with ms. Captions required.

Columns/Departments: Dealer Workbench (repair and tuning bows), 1,600 words; Bow Report (tests and evaluations of current models), 2,400 words; Archery Plus (short profiles of retailers who combine archery with other product lines.). **Buys 12 mss/year.** Query with published clips. **Pays $250-475.**

Tips: "Our readers are hungry for articles that help them decide what to stock and how to do a better job selling or servicing it. Articles needed typically fall into one of these categories: business profiles on outstanding retailers, manufacturers or distributors; equipment articles that cover categories of gear, citing trends in the market and detailing why products have been designed a certain way and what type of use they're best suited for; basic business articles that help dealers do a better job of promoting their business, managing their inventory, training their staff, etc. Good interviewing skills are a must, as especially in the equipment articles we like to see a minimum of six sources."

$ $ $ CASINO EXECUTIVE MAGAZINE, G.E.M. Communications, 1771 E. Flamingo Rd., Suite 207A, Las Vegas NV 89119. (702)735-0446. Fax: (702)735-0344. E-mail: dmckee@gemcomm.com. Website: www.casino-executive.com. Editor: Doug Puppel. **Contact:** David McKee, managing editor. Monthly magazine covering the US gaming industry. *"Casino Executive* is a business magazine covering the gaming industry in the U.S. Contributors should be knowledgeable about the workings of the gaming industry, its companies and personalities." Estab. 1995. Circ. 20,000. Pays on publication. Publishes ms an average of 3 months after acceptance. Byline given. Buys first rights. Editorial lead time 2 months. Submit seasonal material 4 months in advance. Accepts queries by mail, e-mail, fax, phone. Responds in 1 month to queries. Sample copy and writer's guidelines free.

Nonfiction: General interest, how-to, interview/profile, new product, technical ((relating to gaming industry)). **Buys 10-20 mss/year.** Query with published clips. Length: 800-2,500 words. **Pays $100-1,000.**

Photos: State availability with submission. Reviews transparencies. Buys negotiable rights. Negotiates payment individually.

Columns/Departments: Gaming Law; Marketing (casino marketing); Compensation (industry salaries); Corporate Cultures (company environment); Food and Beverage (management of); Managing the Casino Hotel; Retail & Entertainment (management-casino), all 800 words. **Buys 20-30 mss/year. Pays $200.**

Tips: "Writers should be familiar with Casino Executive Magazine and the gaming industry. We are a business magazine, and queries and submissions should reflect that. Most of the content is assigned so writers should query the editor with ideas rather than submit material."

$ $ FITNESS MANAGEMENT, Issues and Solutions in Fitness Services, Leisure Publications, Inc., 215 S. Highway 101, Suite 110, P.O. Box 1198, Solana Beach CA 92075-0910. (858)481-4155. Fax: (858)481-4228. E-mail: edit@fitnessmanagement.com. Website: www.fitnessworld.com. Co-publisher: Edward H. Pitts. **Contact:** Ronale Tucker, editor. **50% freelance written.** Monthly magazine. "Readers are owners, managers and program directors of physical fitness facilities. *FM* helps them run their enterprises safely, efficiently and profitably. Ethical and professional positions in health, nutrition, sports medicine, management, etc., are consistent with those of established national bodies." Estab. 1985. Circ. 26,000. Pays on publication. Publishes ms an average of 5 months after acceptance. Byline given. Offers 50% kill fee. Buys all rights (all articles published in FM are also published and archived on its website). Submit seasonal material 6 months in advance. Accepts queries by mail, e-mail, fax. Responds in 3 months to queries. Sample copy for $5. Writer's guidelines for #10 SASE.

Nonfiction: Book excerpts (prepublication), how-to (manage fitness center and program), new product (no pay), photo feature (facilities/programs), technical, News of fitness research and major happenings in fitness industry. No exercise instructions or general ideas without examples of fitness businesses that have used them successfully. **Buys 50 mss/ year.** Query. Length: 750-2,000 words. **Pays $60-300 for assigned articles.** Pays expenses of writers on assignment.

Photos: Send photos with submission. Reviews contact sheets, 2×2 and 4×5 transparencies, prefers glossy prints, 5×7 to 8×10. Captions, model releases required.

■ The online magazine carries original content not found in the print edition. Contact: Ronale Tucker.

Tips: "We seek writers who are expert in a business or science field related to the fitness-service industry or who are experienced in the industry. Be current with the state of the art/science in business and fitness and communicate it in human terms (avoid intimidating academic language; tell the story of how this was learned and/or cite examples or quotes of people who have applied the knowledge successfully)."

N $ $ GOLF COURSE MANAGEMENT, Golf Course Superintendents Association of America, 1421 Research Park Dr., Lawrence KS 66049. (785)842-2456. Fax: (785)932-3665. E-mail: shollister@gcsaa.org. Website: www.gcsaa.org. **Contact:** Scott Hollister, editor. **85% freelance written.** Monthly magazine covering the golf course superintendent. "*GCM* helps the golf course superintendent become more efficient in all aspects of their job." Estab. 1924. Circ. 40,000. **Pays on acceptance.** Publishes ms an average of 6 months after acceptance. Byline given. Buys Buys first North American serial rights, web rights and makes work-for-hire assignments. Editorial lead time 6 months. Submit seasonal material 6 months in advance. Accepts simultaneous submissions. Responds in 3 weeks to queries; 1 month to mss. Sample copy and writer's guidelines free.

Nonfiction: How-to, interview/profile. No articles about playing golf. **Buys 40 mss/year.** Query. Length: 1,500-2,500 words. **Pays $300-450 for assigned articles.** Sometimes pays expenses of writers on assignment.

Photos: Send photos with submission. Buys all rights. Offers no additional payment for photos accepted with ms. Identification of subjects required.

Tips: "Writers should have prior knowledge of the golf course superintendent profession."

$ $ GOLF COURSE NEWS, The Newspaper for the Golf Course Industry, United Publications Inc., P.O. Box 997, 102 Lafayette St., Yarmouth ME 04096. (207)846-0600. Fax: (207)846-0657. E-mail: aoverbeck@golfcoursenews.com. Website: www.golfcoursenews.com. Managing Editor: Peter Blais. **Contact:** Andrew Overbeck, managing editor. **15% freelance written.** Monthly tabloid "written with the golf course superintendent in mind. Our readers are superintendents, course architects and builders, owners and general managers." Estab. 1989. Circ. 25,000. **Pays on acceptance.** Publishes ms an average of 2 months after acceptance. Byline given. Buys first North American serial rights. Editorial lead time 1 month. Submit seasonal material 2 months in advance. Accepts queries by mail, e-mail, fax, phone. Responds in 2 months to queries; 2 months to mss. Sample copy and writer's guidelines free.

Nonfiction: Book excerpts, general interest, interview/profile, new product, opinion, photo feature. "No how-to articles." **Buys 24 mss/year.** Query with published clips. Length: 500-1,000 words. **Pays $200.** Sometimes pays expenses of writers on assignment.

Photos: Send photos with submission. Reviews negatives, transparencies, prints. Buys one-time rights. Offers no additional payment for photos accepted with ms. Identification of subjects required.

Columns/Departments: On the Green (innovative ideas on the golf course), 500-800 words; Shop Talk (in the maintenance facility). **Buys 4 mss/year.** Query with published clips. **Pays $200-500.**

■ The online magazine carries original content not found in the print edition. Contact: Andrew Overbeck, online editor.

Tips: "Keep your eye out for news affecting the golf industry. Then contact us with your story ideas. We are a national paper and accept both national and regional interest articles. We are interested in receiving features on development of golf projects. We also have an international edition—aptly called *Golf Course News International*—published four times per year."

$ $ NSGA RETAIL FOCUS, National Sporting Goods Association, 1601 Feehanville Dr., Suite 300, Mt. Prospect IL 60056-6035. (847)296-6742. Fax: (847)391-9823. E-mail: info@nsga.org. Website: www.nsga.org. **Contact:** Larry N. Weindruch, editor/publisher. **25% freelance written.** Works with a small number of new/unpublished writers each year. Bimonthly magazine. "*NSGA Retail Focus* serves as a bimonthly trade journal for presidents, CEOs and owners of more than 22,000 retail sporting goods firms." Estab. 1948. Circ. 3,000. Pays on publication. Publishes ms an average of 1 month after acceptance. Byline given. Offers kill fee. Buys first, second serial (reprint), electronic rights. Submit seasonal material 6 months in advance. Accepts queries by mail, e-mail. Sample copy for 9×12 SAE and 5 first-class stamps.
Nonfiction: Interview/profile, photo feature. "No articles written without sporting goods retail businesspeople in mind as the audience. In other words, no generic articles sent to several industries." **Buys 12 mss/year.** Query with published clips. **Pays $75-500.** Sometimes pays expenses of writers on assignment.
Photos: State availability with submission. Reviews contact sheets, negatives, transparencies, 5×7 prints. Buys one-time rights. Payment negotiable.
Columns/Departments: Personnel Management (succinct tips on hiring, motivating, firing, etc.); Sales Management (in-depth tips to improve sales force performance); Retail Management (detailed explanation of merchandising/inventory control); Advertising (case histories of successful ad campaigns/ad critiques); Legal Advisor; Computers; Store Design; Visual Merchandising; all 1,500 words. **Buys 12 mss/year.** Query. **Pays $75-300.**

N $ $ $ ON-SITE FITNESS, On-Site Fitness, 7801 N. Lamar, #D97, Austin TX 78752. (512)236-0236. Fax: (512)236-0473. E-mail: osf@onsitefitness.com. Website: www.onsitefitness.com. **Contact:** Shannon McIntire, managing editor. **50% freelance written.** Bimonthly online magazine covering on-site fitness centers in corporate wellness, hospitality fitness, multi-family fitness and university recreation markets. Estab. 1998. Circ. 20,000. Pays 30 days after article due date. Publishes ms an average of 2 months after acceptance. Byline given. Buys second serial (reprint), electronic rights. Editorial lead time 2 months. Submit seasonal material 2 months in advance. Accepts queries by e-mail. Responds in 3 weeks to queries; 1 month to mss. Sample copy online. Writer's guidelines by e-mail.
Nonfiction: How-to, interview/profile, new product, photo feature. We are not a health and fitness publication. Our editorial is targeted to the fitness center managers, not the exercisers. **Buys 50 mss/year.** Length: 300-1,500 words. **Pays 50-75¢/word.** Sometimes pays expenses of writers on assignment.
Photos: State availability with submission. Buys one-time rights. Negotiates payment individually. Model releases required.
Columns/Departments: Legally Speaking (safety and liability issues), 500 words; Consider This (fresh ideas for fitness centers), 300 words; Marketing Matters (use marketing effectively to promote fitness facility), 500 words; Purchasing Power (how to make smart purchasing decisions), 500 words. **Buys 30 mss/year. Pays 50-75¢/word.**
Tips: "I want a query that takes a different angle to subject, but still is pertinent to market."

$ $ POOL & SPA NEWS, Leisure Publications, 4160 Wilshire Blvd., Los Angeles CA 90010. (323)964-4800. Fax: (323)964-4842. E-mail: psn@poolspanews.com. Website: poolspanews.com. **Contact:** Pervin Lakdawalla, editor. **15% freelance written.** Bimonthly magazine covering the swimming pool and spa industry for builders, retail stores and service firms. Estab. 1960. Circ. 16,300. Pays on publication. Publishes ms an average of 2 months after acceptance. Buys all rights. Accepts queries by mail. Responds in 2 weeks to queries. Sample copy for $5 and 9×12 SAE and 11 first-class stamps.
Nonfiction: Interview/profile, technical. Send résumé with published clips. Length: 500-2,000 words. **Pays $150-600.** Pays expenses of writers on assignment.
Reprints: Send typed ms with rights for sale noted and information about when and where the material previously appeared. Payment varies.
Photos: Payment varies.
Columns/Departments: Pay varies.
   ■ The online magazine carries original content not found in the print edition. Contact: Pervin Lakdawalla, online editor.

$ $ SKI AREA MANAGEMENT, Beardsley Publications, P.O. Box 644, 45 Main St. N, Woodbury CT 06798. (203)263-0888. Fax: (203)266-0452. E-mail: sam@saminfo.com. Website: www.saminfo.com. Editor: Jennifer Rowan. **Contact:** Jonathan Gourlay, managing editor. **85% freelance written.** Bimonthly magazine covering everything involving the management and development of ski resorts. "We are the publication of record for the North American ski industry. We report on new ideas, developments, marketing and regulations with regard to ski and snowboard resorts. Everyone from the CEO to the lift operator of winter resorts reads our magazine to stay informed about the people and procedures that make ski areas successful." Estab. 1962. Circ. 4,500. Pays on publication. Byline given. Offers kill fee. Buys all rights. Editorial lead time 2 months. Submit seasonal material 3 months in advance. Accepts queries by mail, e-mail. Responds in 2 weeks to queries. Sample copy for 9×12 SAE with $3 postage or online. Writer's guidelines for #10 SASE.

Nonfiction: Historical/nostalgic, how-to, interview/profile, new product, opinion, personal experience, technical. "We don't want anything that does not specifically pertain to resort operations, management or financing." **Buys 25-40 mss/ year.** Query. Length: 500-2,500 words. **Pays $50-400.**
Reprints: Accepts previously published submissions.
Photos: Send photos with submission. Reviews transparencies, prints. Buys one-time rights or all rights. Offers no additional payment for photos accepted with ms. Identification of subjects required.

■ The online magazine carries original content not found in the print edition. Contact: Olivia Rowan.
Tips: "Know what you are writing about. We are read by people dedicated to skiing and snowboarding and to making the resort experience the best possible for their customers."

N **$ $ THOROUGHBRED TIMES**, Thoroughbred Times Company, Inc., 496 Southland Dr., P.O. Box 8237, Lexington KY 40533. (859)260-9800. **Contact:** Mark Simon, editor. **10% freelance written.** Weekly tabloid "written for professionals who breed and/or race thoroughbreds at tracks in the U.S. Articles must help owners and breeders understand racing to help them realize a profit." Estab. 1985. Circ. 23,000. Pays on publication. Publishes ms an average of 1 month after acceptance. Byline given. Offers 50% kill fee. Buys all rights. Submit seasonal material 2 months in advance. Responds in 2 weeks to mss.
Nonfiction: General interest, historical/nostalgic, interview/profile, technical. **Buys 52 mss/year.** Query. Length: 500-2,500 words. **Pays 10-20¢/word.** Sometimes pays expenses of writers on assignment.
Photos: State availability with submission. Reviews prints. Buys one-time rights. Offers $25/photo. Identification of subjects required.
Columns/Departments: Vet Topics; Business of Horses; Pedigree Profiles; Bloodstock Topics; Tax Matters; Viewpoints; Guest Commentary.
Tips: "We are looking for farm stories and profiles of owners, breeders, jockeys and trainers."

$ $ WHITETAIL BUSINESS, Krause Publications, Inc., 700 E. State St., Iola WI 54990. (715)445-2214 ext. 425. Fax: (715)445-4087. Website: www.whitetailbusiness.com. Associate Editors: Jennifer Pillath and Dan Schmidt. **Contact:** Pat Durkin, editor. Annual magazine. "*Whitetail Business* targets the hunting industry's driving force, the white-tailed deer hunting market. Archery, modern firearm and muzzleloader retail dealers make their largest profit from whitetail hunters, and *Whitetail Business* devotes itself to this largest profit category." Estab. 1997. Circ. 11,000. Pays on acceptance. Byline given. Offers $50 kill fee. Buys first North American serial rights. Editorial lead time 1 year. Submit seasonal material 1 year in advance. Accepts queries by mail. Sample copy and writer's guidelines free.
Nonfiction: Personal experience, technical, retail management and topics relating to trade shows and the outdoor industry. No humor. Query with or without published clips. Length: 400-1,500 words. **Pays $200-350.**
Photos: State availability with submission. Reviews transparencies. Buys one-time rights. Offers $25-300/photo. Identification of subjects required.
Columns/Departments: Archery, Firearms/Muzzleloaders, Marketing (all dealing with white-tailed deer hunting); all 400 words. Query with published clips. **Pays $250 maximum.**
Fillers: Anecdotes. Length: 100 words maximum. **Pays $25 maximum.**
Tips: "Keep it short."

STONE, QUARRY & MINING

$ $ CANADIAN MINING JOURNAL, Southam Magazine Group Limited, 1450 Don Mills Rd., Don Mills, Ontario M3B 2X7, Canada. (416)510-6742. Fax: (416)442-2175. E-mail: jwerniuk@corporate.southam.ca. **Contact:** Jane Werniuk, editor. **5% freelance written.** Bimonthly magazine covering mining and mineral exploration by Canadian companies. "*Canadian Mining Journal* provides articles and information of practical use to those who work in the technical, administrative and supervisory aspects of exploration, mining and processing in the Canadian mineral exploration and mining industry." Estab. 1879. Circ. 10,000. Pays on publication. Publishes ms an average of 3 months after acceptance. Byline given. Buys one-time, electronic rights, makes work-for-hire assignments. Submit seasonal material 3 months in advance. Accepts queries by mail, e-mail, fax, phone. Responds in 1 week to queries; 1 month to mss.
Nonfiction: Opinion, technical, operation descriptions. **Buys 6 mss/year.** Query with published clips. Length: 500-1,400 words. **Pays $100-600.** Pays expenses of writers on assignment.
Photos: State availability with submission. Reviews 4×6 prints or high resolution files. Buys one-time rights. Negotiates payment individually. Captions, identification of subjects required.
Columns/Departments: Guest editorial (opinion on controversial subject related to mining industry), 600 words. **Buys 3 mss/year.** Query with published clips. **Pays $150.**
Tips: "I need articles about mine sites that it would be expensive/difficult for me to reach. I also need to know that the writer is competent to understand and describe the technology in an interesting way."

N **$ COAL PEOPLE MAGAZINE**, Al Skinner Inc., Dept. WM, 629 Virginia St. W, P.O. Box 6247, Charleston WV 25362. (304)342-4129. Fax: (304)343-3124. Editor/Publisher: Al Skinner. **Contact:** Christina Karawan, president. **50% freelance written.** Monthly magazine. "Most stories are about people or historical—either narrative or biographical on all levels of coal people, past and present—from coal execs down to grass roots miners. Most stories are upbeat—

showing warmth of family or success from underground up!" Estab. 1976. Circ. 11,000. Pays on publication. Publishes ms an average of 3 months after acceptance. Byline given. Buys first, second serial (reprint) rights, makes work-for-hire assignments. Submit seasonal material 2 months in advance. Responds in 3 months to mss. Sample copy for 9×12 SAE and 10 first-class stamps.

Nonfiction: Book excerpts (and film if related to coal), historical/nostalgic (coal towns, people, lifestyles), humor (including anecdotes and cartoons), interview/profile (for coal personalities), personal experience (as relates to coal mining), photo feature (on old coal towns, people, past and present). Special issues: calendar issue for more than 300 annual coal shows, association meetings, etc. (January); surface mining/reclamation award (July); Christmas in Coal Country (December). No poetry, fiction or environmental attacks on the coal industry. **Buys 32 mss/year.** Query with published clips. Length: 5,000 words. **Pays $75 for assigned articles.**

Reprints: Send tearsheet and information about when and where the material previously appeared. Pays 50% of amount paid for an original article.

Photos: Send photos with submission. Reviews contact sheets, transparencies, 5×7 prints. Buys one-time reprint rights. Captions, identification of subjects required.

Columns/Departments: Editorials—anything to do with current coal issues (non-paid); Mine'ing Our Business (bull pen column—gossip—humorous anecdotes); Coal Show Coverage (freelance photojournalist coverage of any coal function across the US). Length: 300-500 words. **Buys 10 mss/year.** Query. **Pays $15.**

Fillers: Anecdotes. **Buys 10/year.** Length: 300 words. **Pays $15.**

Tips: "We are looking for good feature articles on coal people, towns, companies—past and present, color slides (for possible cover use) and b&w photos to complement stories. Could also use a few news writers to take photos and do journalistic coverage on coal events across the country. Slant stories more toward people and less on historical. More faces and names than old town, company store photos. Include more quotes from people who lived these moments!" The following geographical areas are covered: Eastern Canada; Mexico; Europe; China; Russia; Poland; Australia; as well as U.S. states: Alabama, Tennessee, Virginia, Washington, Oregon, North and South Dakota, Arizona, Colorado, Alaska and Wyoming.

$ $ COLORED STONE, Lapidary Journal/Primedia Inc., 60 Chestnut Ave., Suite 201, Devon PA 19333-1312. (610)964-6300. Fax: (610)293-0977. E-mail: CSeditorial@primediasi.com. Website: www.colored-stone.com. **Contact:** Morgan Beard, editor-in-chief. **50% freelance written.** Bimonthly magazine covering the colored gemstone industry. "*Colored Stone* covers all aspects of the colored gemstone (i.e., no diamonds) trade. Our readers are manufacturing jewelers and jewelry designers, gemstone dealers, miners, retail jewelers and gemologists." Estab. 1987. Circ. 11,000. **Pays on acceptance.** Publishes ms an average of 2 months after acceptance. Byline given. Buys one-time, all rights. Editorial lead time 2 months. Submit seasonal material 4 months in advance. Accepts queries by mail, e-mail, fax. Accepts simultaneous submissions. Responds in 1 month to queries; 2 months to mss. Sample copy and writer's guidelines free.

Nonfiction: Exposé, interview/profile, new product, technical. "No articles intended for the general public." **Buys 35-45 mss/year.** Query with published clips. Length: 400-2,200 words. **Pays $200-600.**

Photos: State availability with submission. Reviews any size transparencies, 4×6 prints and up. Buys one-time rights. Offers $15-50/photo. Captions, identification of subjects, model releases required.

Tips: "Demonstrating a background in the industry or willingness to learn is helpful. So is attention to detail, i.e., if you've read that we're a trade magazine, don't send us a consumer-oriented 'puff' piece."

[N] $ $ CONTEMPORARY STONE & TILE DESIGN, Business News Publishing Co., 299 Market St., Suite 320, Saddle Brook NJ 07663. (201)291-9001. Fax: (201)291-9002. E-mail: info@stoneworld.com. Website: www.stoneworld.com. Publisher: Alex Bachrach. **Contact:** Michael Reis, editorial director, or Jennifer Adams, editor. Quarterly magazine covering the full range of stone and tile design and architecture—from classic and historic spaces to current projects. Estab. 1995. Circ. 14,000. Pays on publication. Publishes ms an average of 3 months after acceptance. Byline given. Buys first rights. Submit seasonal material 6 months in advance. Responds in 3 weeks to queries. Sample copy for $10.

Nonfiction: Overall features on a certain aspect of stone design/tile work, or specific articles on individual architectural projects. Interview/profile (prominent architect/designer or firm), photo feature, technical, architectural design. **Buys 8 mss/year.** Query with published clips. Length: 1,500-3,000 words. **Pays $6/column inch.** Pays expenses of writers on assignment.

Photos: State availability with submission. Reviews transparencies, prints. Buys one-time rights. Pays $10/photo accepted with ms. Captions, identification of subjects required.

Columns/Departments: Upcoming Events (for the architecture and design community); Stone Classics (featuring historic architecture); question and answer session with a prominent architect or designer. Length: 1,500-2,000 words. **Pays $6/inch.**

Tips: "The visual aspect of the magazine is key, so architectural photography is a must for any story. Cover the entire project, but focus on the stonework or tile work and how it relates to the rest of the space. Architects are very helpful in describing their work and often provide excellent quotes. As a relatively new magazine, we are looking for freelance submissions and are open to new feature topics. This is a narrow subject, however, so it's a good idea to speak with an editor before submitting anything."

$ $ $ MINING VOICE, National Mining Association, 1130 17th St., NW, Washington DC 20036-4677. (202)463-2625. Fax: (202)857-0135. E-mail: miningvoice@nma.org. Website: www.nma.org. **Contact:** Jeanne Chircop, editor. **60% freelance written.** Bimonthly magazine. *"Mining Voice* magazine is intended to serve as the 'voice' of America's hardrock and coal mining industries, informing and educating readers about business issues impacting mining companies. Stories should be written to appeal to those both inside and outside the industry." Estab. 1995. Circ. 8,500. **Pays on acceptance.** Publishes ms an average of 3 months after acceptance. Byline given. Offers $50 kill fee. Buys all rights. Editorial lead time 3 months. Submit seasonal material 3 months in advance. Accepts queries by mail, e-mail, fax. Responds in 2 months to queries. Sample copy and writer's guidelines free.

Nonfiction: General interest, interview/profile, business interest. No promotional articles, satire, anti-mining, religious, technical. **Buys 50 mss/year.** Query with published clips. Length: 250-3,000 words. **Pays $50-1,200.** Sometimes pays expenses of writers on assignment.

Photos: State availability with submission. Reviews prints. Buys one-time rights. Negotiates payment individually. Identification of subjects required.

Columns/Departments: Mineral Focus (the use of minerals in everyday life), 750 words; Personalities (mining industry employees with interesting outside accomplishments), 750 words; Briefings (soft news items pertaining to mining), 250-350 words. **Buys 25 mss/year.** Query with published clips. **Pays $50-300.**

Tips: "Writers should familiarize themselves with business, political and social trends affecting American business in general and mining in particular. Each issue is theme-based, so obtain a copy of our editorial calendar (available on our website) and guidelines before querying."

$ $ PIT & QUARRY, Advanstar Communications, 7500 Old Oak Blvd., Cleveland OH 44130. (440)891-2607. Fax: (440)891-2675. E-mail: pitquar@en.com. Website: www.pitandquarry.com. Managing Editor: Darren Constantino. **Contact:** Mark S. Kuhar, editor. **20-30% freelance written.** Monthly magazine covering nonmetallic minerals, mining and crushed stone. Audience has "knowledge of construction-related markets, mining, minerals processing, etc." Estab. 1916. Circ. 25,000. **Pays on acceptance.** Publishes ms an average of 6 months after acceptance. Byline given. Buys first North American serial rights. Editorial lead time 6 months. Accepts queries by mail, e-mail, fax, phone. Accepts simultaneous submissions. Responds in 1 month to queries; 4 months to mss. Sample copy for 9×12 SAE and 4 first-class stamps.

Nonfiction: How-to, interview/profile, new product, technical. No humor or inspirational articles. **Buys 12-15 mss/year.** Query. Length: 1,200-2,500 words. **Pays $250-700 for assigned articles; $250-500 for unsolicited articles.** Pays writers with contributor copies or other premiums for simple news items, etc. Sometimes pays expenses of writers on assignment.

Photos: State availability with submission. Buys one-time rights. Offers no additional payment for photos accepted with ms. Identification of subjects, model releases required.

Columns/Departments: Environmental, economics, safety, law, community relations. Length: 700 words. **Buys 5-10 mss/year.** Query. **Pays $250-300.**

■ The online magazine sometimes carries original content not found in the print edition.

Tips: "Be familiar with quarry operations (crushed stone or sand and gravel), not coal or metallic minerals mining. Know construction markets. We need more West Coast-focused stories."

Nː $ $ STONE WORLD, Business News Publishing Company, 299 Market St., Third Floor, Saddle Brook NJ 07663. (201)291-9001. Fax: (201)291-9002. E-mail: info@stoneworld.com. Website: www.stoneworld.com. **Contact:** Michael Reis, editor, or Jennifer Adams, managing editor. Monthly magazine on natural building stone for producers and users of granite, marble, limestone, slate, sandstone, onyx and other natural stone products. Estab. 1984. Circ. 18,000. Pays on publication. Publishes ms an average of 6 months after acceptance. Byline given. Buys first North American serial, second serial (reprint) rights. Submit seasonal material 6 months in advance. Responds in 2 months to queries. Sample copy for $10.

Nonfiction: How-to (fabricate and/or install natural building stone), interview/profile, photo feature, technical, architectural design, artistic stone uses, statistics, factory profile, equipment profile, trade show review. **Buys 10 mss/year.** Query with or without published clips or send complete ms. Length: 600-3,000 words. **Pays $6/column inch.** Pays expenses of writers on assignment.

Reprints: Send photocopy with rights for sale noted and information about when and where the material previously appeared. Pays 50% of amount paid for an original article.

Photos: State availability with submission. Reviews transparencies, prints. Buys one-time rights. Pays $10/photo accepted with ms. Captions, identification of subjects required.

Columns/Departments: News (pertaining to stone or design community); New Literature (brochures, catalogs, books, videos, etc., about stone); New Products (stone products); New Equipment (equipment and machinery for working with stone); Calendar (dates and locations of events in stone and design communities). Query or send complete ms. Length 300-600 words. **Pays $6/inch.**

Tips: "Articles about architectural stone design accompanied by professional color photographs and quotes from designing firms are often published, especially when one unique aspect of the stone selection or installation is highlighted. We are also interested in articles about new techniques of quarrying and/or fabricating natural building stone."

TOY, NOVELTY AND HOBBY

N $ $ MODEL RETAILER, Resources for Successful Hobby Retailing, Kalmbach Publishing Co., 21027 Crossroads Circle, Waukesha WI 53187-1612. (262)796-8776. Fax: (262)796-1383. E-mail: staff@modelretailer.com. Website: www.modelretailer.com. **Contact:** Mark Savage, editor. **15% freelance written.** Monthly magazine. "*Model Retailer* covers the business of hobbies, from financial and shop management issues to industry trends and the latest product releases. Our goal is to provide hobby shop entrepreneurs with the tools and information they need to be successful retailers." Estab. 1987. Circ. 6,000 (controlled circulation). **Pays on acceptance.** Publishes ms an average of 3 months after acceptance. Byline given. Buys first rights. Editorial lead time 3 months. Submit seasonal material 6 months in advance. Accepts queries by mail, e-mail, fax. Sample copy and writer's guidelines free.
Nonfiction: How-to (business), new product. "No articles that do not have a strong hobby or small retail component." **Buys 6-12 mss/year.** Query with published clips. Length: 750-2,000 words. **Pays $250-500 for assigned articles; $100-250 for unsolicited articles.** Sometimes pays expenses of writers on assignment.
Photos: State availability with submission. Reviews 4×6 prints. Buys one-time rights. Negotiates payment individually. Captions, identification of subjects required.
Columns/Departments: Shop Management, Sales Marketing, Technology Advice, 500-750 words; Industry Trends. **Buys 20 mss/year.** Query with published clips. **Pays $100-200.**

TRANSPORTATION

These publications are for professional movers and people involved in transportation of goods. For magazines focusing on trucking see also Auto & Truck.

$ $ ITS WORLD, Technology and Applications for Intelligent Transportation Systems, Scranton Gillette Communications, 380 E. Northwest Highway, Suite 200, Des Plaines IL 60016. (847)391-1000. Fax: (847)390-0408. E-mail: itseditor@sgcmail.com. Website: www.itsworld.com. **Contact:** Tim Gregorski, managing editor. **50% freelance written.** Bimonthly tabloid covering intelligent transportation systems (the application of communications and computer technologies to surface transportation). "We focus on ITS based global projects, and the logistics of these projects." Estab. 1996. Circ. 25,000. Pays on publication. Publishes ms an average of 2 months after acceptance. Byline given. Buys all rights. Editorial lead time 2 months. Submit seasonal material 2 months in advance. Accepts queries by e-mail, fax, phone. Accepts simultaneous submissions. Responds in 6 weeks to queries; 1 month to mss. Sample copy and writer's guidelines free.
Photos: Send photos with submission. Reviews negatives, 2×7 transparencies, prints. Offers no additional payment for photos accepted with ms. Captions, identification of subjects required.
Columns/Departments: World Watch (trends, activities and market opportunities in intelligent transportation systems in a country or region outside the U.S.); Washington Watch (ITS issues/Washington D.C. perspective); editorials (ITS issues/opinions), all 1,500 words. Query.
Tips: "Expertise in surface transportation and/or the application of advanced technologies (telecommunications, computers, etc.) to surface transportation is a must. Writers who demonstrate this through published works and other background information will be given highest consideration."

N $ $ METRO MAGAZINE, Bobit Publishing Co., 21061 S. Western Ave., Torrance CA 90501. E-mail: metrom ag@bobit.com. Website: www.transit-center.com. Editor: Cliff Henke. **Contact:** Leslie Davis, managing editor. **10% freelance written.** Magazine published 9 times/year covering public transportation. "*Metro Magazine* delivers business, government policy and technology developments that are *industry specific* to public transportation." Estab. 1904. Circ. 20,500. **Pays on acceptance.** Publishes ms an average of 2 months after acceptance. Byline given. Offers 80% kill fee. Buys all rights. Editorial lead time 3 months. Submit seasonal material 3 months in advance. Accepts queries by e-mail. Responds in 2 weeks to queries; 1 month to mss. Sample copy for $8. Writer's guidelines by e-mail.
Nonfiction: How-to, interview/profile (of industry figures), new product (related to transit—bus and rail—private bus), technical. **Buys 6-10 mss/year.** Query. Length: 400-1,500 words. **Pays $80-400.**
Photos: State availability with submission. Buys all rights. Negotiates payment individually. Captions, identification of subjects, model releases required.
Columns/Departments: Query. **Pays $20¢/word.**
   ■ The online magazine carries original content not found in the print edition. Contact: Leslie Davis.

TRAVEL

Travel professionals read these publications to keep up with trends, tours and changes in transportation. Magazines about vacations and travel for the general public are listed in the Consumer Travel section.

N **$** **$** **LEISURE GROUP TRAVEL**, Premier Tourism Marketing, P.O. Box 609, Palos Heights IL 60463-0609. (708)923-1284. Fax: (708)923-1694. E-mail: info@leisuregrouptravel.com. Website: www.leisuregrouptravel.com. **Contact:** Jeff Gayduk, editor. **15% freelance written.** Quarterly magazine covering group travel. We cover destinations and editorial relevant to the group travel market. Estab. 1994. Circ. 13,789. Pays on publication. Byline sometimes given. Buys first rights. Editorial lead time 6 months. Submit seasonal material 6 months in advance. Accepts queries by mail, e-mail.
Nonfiction: Travel. **Buys 6-12 mss/year.** Query with published clips. Length: 1,200-3,000 words. **Pays $0-500.**
Tips: "Experience in writing for 50+ travel marketplace a bonus."

$** **$ **$** **RV BUSINESS**, Affinity Group, Inc., 2575 Vista del Mar Dr., Ventura CA 93001. (800)765-1912. Fax: (805)667-4484. E-mail: rvb@tl.com. **Contact:** John Sullaway, editor. **50% freelance written.** Monthly magazine. "*RV Business* caters to a specific audience of people who manufacture, sell, market, insure, finance, service and supply, components for recreational vehicles." Estab. 1972. Circ. 21,000. **Pays on acceptance.** Publishes ms an average of 2 months after acceptance. Byline given. Offers kill fee. Buys first North American serial rights. Editorial lead time 3 months. Accepts queries by mail, e-mail. Sample copy free.
Nonfiction: New product, photo feature, industry news and features. "No general articles without specific application to our market." **Buys 300 mss/year.** Query with published clips. Length: 125-2,200 words. **Pays $35-1,500.** Sometimes pays expenses of writers on assignment.
Photos: Send photos with submission. Reviews 35mm transparencies. Buys one-time rights. Offers $25-400/photo. Captions, identification of subjects required.
Columns/Departments: Top of the News (RV industry news), 75-400 words; Business Profiles, 400-500 words; Features (indepth industry features), 800-2,000 words. **Buys 300 mss/year.** Query. **Pays $35-1,500.**
Tips: "Query. Send one or several ideas and a few lines letting us know how you plan to treat it/them. We are always looking for good authors knowledgeable in the RV industry or related industries. We need more articles that are brief, factual, hard hitting and business oriented. Review other publications in the field, including enthusiast magazines."

$** **$ **SPECIALTY TRAVEL INDEX**, Alpine Hansen, 305 San Anselmo Ave., #313, San Anselmo CA 94960. (415)455-1643. Fax: (415)459-4974. E-mail: info@specialtytravel.com. Website: www.specialtytravel.com. Editor: C. Steen Hansen. **Contact:** Susan Kostrzewa, managing editor. **90% freelance written.** Semiannual magazine covering adventure and special interest travel. Estab. 1980. Circ. 45,000. Pays on receipt and acceptance of all materials. Byline given. Buys one-time rights. Editorial lead time 3 month. Submit seasonal material 3 months in advance. Accepts queries by mail, e-mail. Writer's guidelines on request.
Nonfiction: How-to, personal experience, photo feature, travel. **Buys 15 mss/year.** Query. Length: 1,250 words. **Pays $200 minimum.**
Reprints: Send tearsheet. Pays 100% of amount paid for an original article.
Photos: State availability with submission. Reviews 35mm transparencies, 5×7 prints. Negotiates payment individually. Captions, identification of subjects required.
Tips: "Write about group travel and be both creative and factual. The articles should relate to both the travel agent booking the tour and the client who is traveling."

$ **STAR SERVICE**, Reed Travel Group, 500 Plaza Dr., Secaucus NJ 07090. (201)902-2000. Fax: (201)319-1797. E-mail: sgordon@starserviceonline.com. Website: www.starserviceonline.com. **Contact:** Steven R. Gordon, editor-in-chief. "Eager to work with new/unpublished writers as well as those working from a home base abroad, planning trips that would allow time for hotel reporting, or living in major ports for cruise ships." Worldwide guide to accommodations and cruise ships sold to travel professionals on subscription basis. Estab. 1960. Pays 15 days after publication. Buys all rights. Accepts queries by mail, e-mail, fax. Responds in 1 month to queries. Writer's guidelines and list of available assignments for #10 SASE.
   Break in by "being willing to inspect hotels in remote parts of the world."
Nonfiction: Objective, critical evauations of hotels and cruise ships suitable for international travelers, based on personal inspections. Freelance correspondents ordinarily are assigned to update an entire state or country. "Assignment involves on-site inspections of all hotels and cruise ships we review; revising and updating published reports; and reviewing new properties. Qualities needed are thoroughness, precision, perserverance and keen judgment. Solid research skills and powers of observation are crucial. Travel writing experience is highly desirable. Reviews must be colorful, clear, and documented with hotel's brochure, rate sheet, etc. We accept no advertising or payment for listings, so reviews should dispense praise and criticism where deserved." Now accepting queries for destination assignments with deadlines in June 2002. Query should include details on writer's experience in travel and writing, clips, specific forthcoming travel plans, and how much time would be available for hotel or ship inspections. Sponsored trips are acceptable. **Buys 5,000 mss/year. Pays $25/report used.**
   The online magazine carries original content not found in the print edition. Contact: Steven R. Gordon.
Tips: "We may require sample hotel or cruise reports on facilities near freelancer's hometown before giving the first assignment. No byline because of sensitive nature of reviews."

$** **$ **VACATION INDUSTRY REVIEW**, Interval International, 6262 Sunset Dr., P.O. Box 431920, South Miami FL 33243-1920. (305)666-1861 ext. 7022. Fax: (305)668-3408. E-mail: gleposky@interval-intl.com. Website: www.resortdeveloper.com. **Contact:** George Leposky, editor. **30% freelance written.** Bimonthly magazine covering leisure lodgings (timeshare resorts, fractionals, and other types of vacation-ownership properties). "The readership of *VIR* consists of people who develop, finance, market, sell, and manage timeshare resorts and mixed-use projects such as hotels, resorts, and second-home communities with a vacation-ownership component; and suppliers of products and services to the vacation-ownership industry." Prefers to work with published/established writers. Estab. 1982. Circ. 19,000. Pays on publication. Publishes ms an average of 6 months after acceptance. Byline given. Buys all rights or makes work-for-hire assignments. Submit seasonal material 6 months in advance. Accepts queries by mail, e-mail, fax, phone. Responds in 1 month to queries. Sample copy for 9 × 12 SAE and 3 first-class stamps or online. Writer's guidelines for #10 SASE or by e-mail.

> O— Break in by writing a letter to tell us about yourself, and enclosing two or three (non-returnable) samples of published work that show you can meet our specialized needs.

Nonfiction: Essays, how-to, interview/profile, new product, opinion, personal experience, technical, travel. No consumer travel, hotel, or non-vacation real-estate material. **Buys 6-8 mss/year.** Query with published clips. Length: 1,000-1,500 words. **Pays 30¢/word.** Sometimes pays expenses of writers on assignment.

Photos: Send photos with submission. Reviews 35mm transparencies, electronic images. Buys one-time rights. Generally offers no additional payment for photos accepted with ms. Captions, identification of subjects required.

Tips: "We *do not* want consumer-oriented destination travel articles. We want articles about the business aspects of the vacation-ownership industry: entrepreneurship, project financing, design and construction, sales and marketing, operations, management—anything that will help our readers plan, build, sell and run a quality vacation-ownership property that satisfies the owners/guests and earns a profit for the developer and marketer. We're also interested in owner associations at vacation-ownership resorts (not residential condos). Requires electronic submissions. Query for details."

VETERINARY

$ $ VETERINARY ECONOMICS, Business Solutions for Practicing Veterinarians, Veterinary Healthcare Communications, 8033 Flint, Lenexa KS 66214. (913)492-4300. Fax: (913)492-4157. E-mail: ve@vetmedpub.com. Website: www.vetmedpub.com. Managing Editor: Elizabeth Brown. **Contact:** Marnette Falley, editor. **20% freelance written.** Monthly magazine covering veterinary medicine. "We address the business concerns and management needs of practicing veterinarians." Estab. 1960. Circ. 52,000. Pays on publication. Publishes ms an average of 3 months after acceptance. Byline given. Buys first rights. Editorial lead time 3 months. Submit seasonal material 3 months in advance. Accepts queries by mail, e-mail, fax. Accepts simultaneous submissions. Responds in 3 months to queries. Sample copy and writer's guidelines free.

Nonfiction: How-to, interview/profile, new product, personal experience. **Buys 24 mss/year.** Query with or without published clips or send complete ms. Length: 1,000-2,000 words. **Pays $50-400.**

Photos: Send photos with submission. Reviews transparencies, prints. Buys one-time rights. Offers no additional payment for photos accepted with ms. Captions, identification of subjects required.

Columns/Departments: Practice Tips (easy, unique business tips), 200-300 words. Send complete ms. **Pays $35.**

Tips: "Among the topics we cover: Veterinary hospital design, client relations, contractual and legal matters, investments, day-to-day management, marketing, personal finances, practice finances, personnel, collections, and taxes. We also cover news and issues within the veterinary profession; for example, articles might cover the effectiveness of Yellow Pages advertising, the growing number of women veterinarians, restrictive-covenant cases, and so on. Freelance writers are encouraged to submit proposals or outlines for articles on these topics. Most articles involve interviews with a nationwide sampling of veterinarians; we will provide the names and phone numbers if necessary. We accept only a small number of unsolicited manuscripts each year; however, we do assign many articles to freelance writers. All material submitted by first-time contributors is read on speculation, and the review process usually takes 12 to 16 weeks. Our style is concise yet conversational, and all manuscripts go through a fairly rigorous editing process. We encourage writers to provide specific examples to illustrate points made throughout their articles."

Scriptwriting

Everyone has a story to tell, something to say. In telling that story as a play, movie, TV show or educational video you have selected that form over other possibilities. Scriptwriting makes some particular demands, but one thing remains the same for authors of novels, nonfiction books and scripts: you'll learn to write by rewriting. Draft after draft your skills improve until, hopefully, someone likes your work enough to hire you.

Whether you are writing a video to train doctors in a new surgical technique, alternative theater for an Off-Broadway company or you want to see your name on the credits of the next Harrison Ford movie, you must perfect both writing and marketing skills. A successful scriptwriter is a talented artist and a savvy business person. But marketing must always be secondary to writing. A mediocre pitch for a great script will still get you farther than a brilliant pitch for a mediocre script. The art and craft of scriptwriting lies in successfully executing inspiration.

Writing a script is a private act. Polishing it may involve more people as you ask friends and fellow writers to take a look at it. Marketing takes your script public in an effort to find the person willing to give the most of what you want, whether it's money, exposure or control, in return for your work.

There are accepted ground rules to presenting and marketing scripts. Following those guidelines will maximize your chances of getting your work before an audience.

Presenting your script professionally earns a serious consideration of its content. Certain scripts have a definite format and structure. An educational video written in a one-column format, a feature film much longer than 120 pages or an hour-long TV show that peaks during the first 20 minutes indicates an amateur writer. There are several sources for correct formats, including *Formatting & Submitting Your Manuscript*, by Jack and Glenda Neff and Don Prues (Writer's Digest Books) and *The Complete Guide to Standard Script Formats*, by Cole and Haig.

Submission guidelines are similar to those for other types of writing. The initial contact is a one-page query letter, with a brief synopsis and a few lines as to your credits or experience relevant to the subject of your script. Never send a complete manuscript until it is requested. Almost every script sent to a producer, studio, or agent must be accompanied by a release form. Ask the producer or agent for this form when invited to submit the complete script. Always include a self-addressed stamped envelope if you want your work returned; a self-addressed stamped postcard will do for acknowledgement or reply if you do not need your script returned.

Most writers break in with spec scripts, written "for free," which serve as calling cards to show what they can do. These scripts plant the seeds of your professional reputation by making the rounds of influential people looking to hire writers, from advertising executives to movie moguls. Good writing is more important than a specific plot. Make sure you are sending out your best work; a first draft is not a finished product. Have several spec scripts completed, as a producer will often decide that a story is not right for him, or a similar work is already in production, but will want to know what else you have. Be ready for that invitation.

Writing a script is a matter of learning how to refine your writing so that the work reads as a journey, not a technical manual. The best scripts have concise, visceral scenes that demand to be presented in a specific order and accomplish definite goals.

Educational videos have a message that must be expressed economically and directly, engaging the audience in an entertaining way while maintaining interest in the topic. Theatrical plays are driven by character and dialogue that expose a thematic core and engender enthusiasm or involvement in the conflict. Cinematic screenplays, while more visually-oriented, are a series of discontinuous scenes stacked to illuminate the characters, the obstacles confronting them and the resolution they reach.

A script is a difficult medium—written words that sound natural when spoken, characters that are original yet resonate with the audience, believable conflicts and obstacles in tune with the end result. One theater added to their listing the following tip: "Don't write plays. Write novels, short stories, anything but plays. But if you *must* write plays. . . ." If you are compelled to present your story visually, be aware of the intense competition. Hone it, refine it, keep working on it until it can be no better, then look for the best home you can find. That's success.

BUSINESS & EDUCATIONAL WRITING

"It's no longer the plankton of the filmmaking food chain," says Kirby Timmons, creative director of the video production company CRM Films. Scripts for corporate training, business management and education videos have become as sophisticated as those designed for TV and film, and they carry the additional requirement of conveying specific content. With an audience that is increasingly media literate, anything that looks and feels like a "training film" will be dead in the water. The trick is to produce a script that engages, compels *and* informs about the topic, whether it's customer relations, listening skills or effective employee management, while staying on a tight budget.

This can create its own challenges, but is an excellent way to increase your skills and exercise your craft. Good scriptwriters are in demand in this field. There is a strong emphasis on producing a polished complete script before filming begins, and a writer's involvement doesn't end until the film is "in the can."

A remarkably diverse industry, educational and corporate video is a $18-25 billion business, compared to theatrical films and TV, estimated at $5 billion. And there is the added advantage that opportunities are widespread, from large local corporations to small video production houses in your area. Larger companies often have inhouse video production companies, but others rely on freelance writers. Your best bet would be to find work with companies that specialize in making educational and corporate video while at the same time making yourself known to the creative directors of in-house video staffs in large corporations. Advertising agencies are also a good source of work, as they often are asked by their clients for help in creating films and use freelance writers and producers.

Business and educational video is a market-driven industry, with material created either in response to a general need or a specific demand. The production company usually identifies a subject and finds the writer. As such, there is a perception that a spec script will not work in this media. While it is true that, as in TV and theatrical films, a writer's spec script is rarely produced, it is a good résumé of qualifications and sample of skills. It can get you other work even though it isn't produced. Your spec script should demonstrate a knowledge of this industry's specific format. For the most part video scripts are written in two-columns, video on the left, audio on the right. A variety of references cover the basics of video script format. Computer software is available to format the action and dialogue.

Aside from the original script, another opportunity for the writer is the user's guide that often accompanies a video. If you are hired to create the auxiliary material you'll receive a copy of the finished video and write a concurrent text for the teacher or implementor to use.

Networking is very important. There is no substitute for calling companies and finding out what is in your area. Contact local training and development companies and find out who they serve and what they need. It pays to join professional organizations such as the Association of Visual Communicators and the Association for Training and Development, which offer seminars and conventions. Making the rounds at a business convention of video producers with your business card could earn you a few calls and invitations to submit writing samples.

Budgets are tighter for educational or corporate videos than for theatrical films. You'll want to work closely with the producer to make sure your ideas can be realized within the budget. Your fee will vary with each job, but generally a script written for a production house in a subject area with broad marketability will pay $5,000-7,000. A custom-produced video for a specific company will usually pay less. The pay does not increase exponentially with your experience; large increases come if you choose to direct and produce as well as write.

With the expansion of cable TV-based home shopping opportunities, direct response TV (informercials) is an area with increasing need for writers to create the scripts that sell the products. Production companies are located across the country, and more are popping up as the business grows. Pay can range from $5,000-18,000, depending on the type, length and success of the program.

The future of business and educational video lies in interactive media or multimedia. Interactive media combines computer and video technology to create a product that doesn't have to progress along a linear path. Videos that offer the viewer the opportunity to direct the course of events hold exciting possibilities for corporate training and educational applications. Writers will be in high demand as stories offer dozens of choices in storylines. Interactive video will literally eat up pages of script as quickly as a good writer produces them. A training session may last only 20 minutes, but the potential untapped story lines could add up to hours worth of script that must be written, realized and made available. From training salespeople to doctors, or teaching traffic rules to issues in urbanization, corporate and educational video is about to undergo a tremendous revolution.

Information on business and educational script markets listed in the previous edition of *Writer's Market* but not included in this edition can be found in the General Index.

ABS ENTERPRISES, P.O. Box 5127, Evanston IL 60204-5127. (847)982-1414. Fax: (847)982-1418. E-mail: absenterprises@mindspring.com. **Contact:** Alan Soell, owner. "We produce material for all levels of corporate, medical, cable and educational institutions for the purposes of training and development, marketing and meeting presentations. We also are developing programming for the broadcast areas." **75% freelance written.** Buys all rights. Accepts previously produced material. Query with synopsis, résumé. Responds in 2 weeks to queries. **Pays by contractual agreement.**
Needs: Videotapes, multimedia kits, tapes and cassettes, Internet audio, television shows/series. Currently interested in "sports instructional series that could be produced for the consumer market on tennis, gymnastics, bowling, golf, aerobics, health and fitness, cross-country skiing and cycling. Also motivational and self-improvement type videos and film ideas to be produced. These could cover all ages '6-60' and from professional to blue collar jobs. These two areas should be 30 minutes and be timeless in approach for long shelf life. Sports audience, age 25-45; home improvement 25-65. Cable TV needs include the two groups of programming detailed here. We are also looking for documentary work on current isssues, nuclear power, solar power, urban development, senior citizens"but with a new approach."
Tips: "Send a listing of past experience, plus project ideas and expertise. I am looking for innovative approaches to old problems that just don't go away. The approach should be simple and direct so there is immediate audience identification with the presentation. I also like to see a sense of humor used. Trends in the media field include interactive video with disk—for training purposes."

A/V CONCEPTS CORP., 30 Montauk Blvd., Oakdale NY 11769-1399. (631)567-7227. Fax: (631)567-8745. E-mail: editor@edconpublishing.com. Website: www.edconpublishing.com. **Contact:** Laura Solimene, editor. Estab. 1971. Produces supplementary materials for elementary-high school students, either on grade level or in remedial situations. **100% freelance written.** "All scripts/titles are by assignment only. Do not send manscripts." Employs video, book and personal computer media. Buys all rights. Writing samples returned with 9×12 SAE with 5 first-class stamps. Responds in 1 month to outline, 6 weeks on final scripts. **Pays $300 and up.**
Needs: Main concentration in language arts, mathematics and reading. "Manuscripts must be written using our lists of vocabulary words and meet our readability formula requirements. Specific guidelines are devised for each level. Student activities required. Length of manuscript and subjects will vary according to grade level for which material is prepared. Basically, we want material that will motivate people to read."
Tips: "Writers must be highly creative and disciplined. We are interested in high interest/low readability materials. Send writing samples, published or unpublished."

SAM BLATE ASSOCIATES, LLC, 10331 Watkins Mill Dr., Montgomery Village MD 20886-3950. (301)840-2248. Fax: (301)990-0707. E-mail: info@writephotopro.com. Website: www.writephotopro.com. **Contact:** Sam Blate, presi-

dent. "Produces educational and multimedia including IBM-PC material for business, education, institutions and state and federal governments. **We work with 2 local writers/year on a per-project basis—it varies as to business conditions and demand."** Buys first rights when possible. Query with writing samples and SASE for return. Responds in 1 month to queries. **Payment "depends on type of contract with principal client." Pays some expenses of writers on assignment.**
Needs: Scripts on technical, business and outdoor subjects.
Tips: "Writers must have a strong track record of technical and aesthetic excellence. Clarity and accuracy are not next to divinity—they are above it."

HAYES SCHOOL PUBLISHING CO., INC., 321 Pennwood Ave., Wilkinsburg PA 15221-3398. (412)371-2373. Fax: (412)371-6408. E-mail: chayes@hayespub.com. Website: www.hayespub.com. **Contact:** Clair N. Hayes III, president. Estab. 1940. Produces material for school teachers and principals, elementary through high school. Also produces charts, workbooks, teacher's handbooks, posters, bulletin board material and reproducible blackline masters (grades K-12). **25% freelance written.** Prefers to work with published/established writers. **Buys 5-10 scripts/year from unpublished/unproduced writers. 100% of scripts produced are unagented submissions.** Buys all rights. Catalog for 9 × 12 SAE with 3 first-class stamps. Query. Responds in 3 months to scripts. **Pays $25 minimum.**
Needs: Educational materials only. Particularly interested in foreign language material and educational material for elementary school level.

JIST PUBLISHING, 8902 Otis Ave., Indianapolis IN 46216. (317)613-4200. Fax: (317)613-4309. E-mail: info@jist.com. Website: www.jist.com. **Contact:** Kelli Lawrence, video production manager. Estab. 1981. Produces career counseling, motivational materials (youth to adult) that encourage good planning and decision making for a successful future. **Buys 4-5 script(s)/year. Works with 3-4 writer(s)/year.** Buys all rights. Accepts previously produced material. Free catalog. Query with synopsis. Responds in 3 months to queries.
Needs: Videotapes, multimedia kits. 15-30 minute video VHS tapes on job search materials and related markets.
Tips: "We need writers for long formats, such as scripts and instructor's guides, as well as short formats for catalogs, press releases, etc. We pay a royalty on finished video productions. We repackage, market, duplicate and take care of all other expenses when we acquire existing programs. Average sell price is $149. Producer gets a percentage of this and is not charged for any costs. Contact us, in writing, for details."

PALARDO PRODUCTIONS, 1807 Taft Ave., Suite 4, Hollywood CA 90028. (323)469-8991. Fax: (323)469-8991. E-mail: palardopro@aol.com. Website: www.palardo.com. **Contact:** Paul Ardolino, director. Estab. 1971. Produces material for youth ages 13-35. **Buys 3-4 script(s)/year.** Buys all rights. Query with synopsis, résumé. Responds in 2 weeks to queries; 1 month to scripts. **Pays in accordance with WGA standards.**
Needs: Videotapes, multimedia kits, tapes and cassettes. "We are seeking comedy feature scripts involving technology and coming of age; techno-shortform projects."
Tips: "Do not send a complete script—only synopsis of four pages or less *first*."

N CHARLES RAPP ENTERPRISES, INC., 1650 Broadway, New York NY 10019. (212)247-6646. **Contact:** Howard Rapp, president. Estab. 1954. Produces materials for firms and buyers. **Works with 5 writers/year.** Accepts previously produced material. Submit résumé or sample of writing. Responds in 1 month to queries; 2 months to scripts. **Pays in accordance with WGA standards.**
Needs: Videotapes, treatments, scripts.

N PETER SCHLEGER COMPANY, 200 Central Park S., 27-B, New York NY 10019-1415. (212)245-4973. E-mail: pschleger@yahoo.com. Website: www.schleger.com. **Contact:** Peter Schleger, president. Produces material primarily for employee populations in corporations and non-profit organizations. "Typical programs are customized workshops or specific individual programs from subjects such as listening and presentation skills to medical benefits communication. No program is longer than 10 minutes. If they need to be, they become shorter modules." Buys all rights. Accepts previously produced material. Submit completed script, résumé. Responds in 1 month to scripts. **Makes outright purchase.**
Needs: Produces sound filmstrips, video and printed manuals and leader's guides.
Tips: "We are looking to receive and keep on file a résumé and short, completed script sample of a program not longer than 10 minutes. The shorter the better to get a sense of writing style and the ability to structure a piece. We would also like to know the fees the writer expects for his/her work. Either per-diem, by project budget or by finished script page. We want communications professionals with a training background or who have written training programs, modules and the like. We want to know of people who have written print material, as well. We do not want to see scripts that have been written and are looking for a producer/director. We will look at queries for possible workshops or new approaches for training, but these must be submitted as longshots only; it is not our primary business. As we also produce video and audio media, we will work with writers who have clients needing these services."

SPENCER PRODUCTIONS, INC., P.O. Box 2247, Westport CT 06880. (212)865-8829. **Contact:** Bruce Spencer, general manager; Alan Abel, creative director. Produces material for high school students, college students and adults. Occasionally uses freelance writers with considerable talent. Query. Responds in 1 month to queries. **Pay negotiable.**
Needs: Tapes and cassettes. Satirical material only.

Tips: "For a comprehensive view of our humor requirements, we suggest viewing our feature film production, *Is There Sex After Death* (Rated R), starring Buck Henry. It is available at video stores. Or read *Don't Get Mad.. Get Even* and *How to Thrive on Rejection* by Alan Abel (published by W.W. Norton), both available from Barnes & Noble or Amazon." Also Books-on-Tape. "Send brief synopsis (one page) and outline (2-4 pages)."

TALCO PRODUCTIONS, 279 E. 44th St., New York NY 10017-4354. (212)697-4015. Fax: (212)697-4827. **Contact:** Alan Lawrence, president; Marty Holberton, vice president. Estab. 1968. Produces variety of material for TV, radio, business, trade associations, nonprofit organizations, public relations (chiefly political and current events), etc. Audiences range from young children to senior citizens. **20-40% freelance written. Buys scripts from published/ produced writers only.** Buys all rights. No previously produced material. Submit résumé, production history. Responds in 3 weeks to queries. **Makes outright purchase. Pays in accordance with WGA standards. Sometimes pays the expenses of writers on assignment.**
Needs: Films, videotapes, tapes and cassettes, CDs. "We maintain a file of writers and call on those with experience in the same general category as the project in production. *We do not accept unsolicited manuscripts.* We prefer to receive a writer's résumé listing credits. If his/her background merits, we will be in touch when a project seems right." Talco reports that it is doing more public relations-oriented work: Print, videotape and radio.
Tips: "Concentration is now in TV productions. Production budgets will be tighter."

N. **ED TAR ASSOCIATES, INC.**, 230 Venice Way, Venice CA 90291. (310)306-2195. Fax: (310)306-0654. **Contact:** Ed Tar, president. Estab. 1972. Audience is dealers, salespeople, public. Buys all rights. No previously produced material. Submit résumé, writing samples. **Makes outright purchase.**
Needs: Films (16, 35mm), videotapes, tapes and cassettes, slides, business theater, live shows, TV infomercials. "We are constantly looking for *experienced* writers of corporate, product and live show scripts."

PLAYWRITING

TV and movies are visual media where the words are often less important than the images. Writing plays uses different muscles, different techniques. Plays are built on character and dialogue—words put together to explore and examine characters.

The written word is respected in the theater by producer, cast, director and even audience, to a degree unparalleled in other formats. While any work involving so many people to reach its final form is in essence a collaboration, it is presided over by the playwright and changes can be made only with her approval, a power many screenwriters can only envy. If a play is worth producing, it will be produced "as is."

Counterbalancing the greater freedom of expression are the physical limitations inherent in live performance: a single stage, smaller cast, limited sets and lighting and, most importantly, a strict, smaller budget. These conditions affect not only what but also how you write.

Start writing your play by reading. Your local library has play anthologies. Check the listings in this section for play publishers such as Baker's Plays and Samuel French. Reading gives you a feel for how characters are built, layer by layer, word by word, how each interaction presents another facet of a character. Exposition must mean something to the character, and the story must be worth telling for a play to be successful.

There are plenty of books, seminars and workshops to help you with the writing of your play. The development of character, setting, dialogue and plot are skills that will improve with each draft. The specific play format is demonstrated in *Formatting & Submitting Your Manuscript*, by Jack and Glenda Neff and Don Prues (Writer's Digest Books) and *The Complete Book of Standard Script Formats*, by Cole and Haig.

Once your play is finished you begin marketing it, which can take as long (or longer) than writing it. Before you begin you must have your script bound (three brads and a cover are fine) and copyrighted at the Copyright Office of the Library of Congress or registered with the Writers Guild of America. Write either agency and ask for information and an application.

Your first goal will be to get at least a reading of your play. You might be lucky and get a small production. Community theaters or smaller regional houses are good places to start. Volunteer at a local theater. As prop mistress or spotlight operator you will get a sense of how a theater operates, the various elements of presenting a play and what can and cannot be done, physically as well as dramatically. Personal contacts are important. Get to know the literary manager or artistic director of local theaters, which is the best way to get your script considered for production. Find out about any playwrights' groups in your area through local theaters or the drama departments of nearby colleges and universities. Use your creativity to connect with people that might be able to push your work higher.

Contests can be a good way to get noticed. Many playwriting contests offer as a prize at least a staged reading and often a full production. Once you've had a reading or workshop production, set your sights on a small production. Use this as a learning experience. Seeing your play on stage can help you view it more objectively and give you the chance to correct any flaws or inconsistencies. Incorporate any comments and ideas from the actors, director or even audience that you feel are on the mark into revisions of your script.

Use a small production also as a marketing tool. Keep track of all the press reviews, any interviews with you, members of the cast or production and put together a "press kit" for your play that can make the rounds with the script.

After you've been produced you have several directions to take your play. You can aim for a larger commercial production; you can try to get it published; you can seek artistic grants. After you have successfully pursued at least one of those avenues you can look for an agent. Choosing one direction does not rule out pursuing others at the same time. *The Dramatists Sourcebook*, published annually by Theatre Communications Group (355 Lexington Ave., New York NY 10017) lists opportunities in all these areas. The Dramatists Guild (1501 Broadway, Suite 701, New York NY 10036-5601) has three helpful publications: a bimonthly newsletter with articles, news and up-to-date information and opportunities; a quarterly journal; and an annual directory, a resource book for playwrights listing theaters, agents, workshops, grants, contests, etc.

Good reviews in a smaller production can get you noticed by larger theaters paying higher royalties and doing more ambitious productions. To submit your play to larger theaters you'll put together a submission package. This will include a one-page query letter to the literary manager or dramaturg briefly describing the play. Mention any reviews and give the number of cast members and sets. You will also send a two to three-page synopsis, a ten-page sample of the most interesting section of your play, your résumé and the press kit you've assembled. Do not send your complete manuscript until it is requested.

You can also explore publishing your play. *Writer's Market* lists many play publishers. When your script is published your play will make money while someone else does the marketing. You'll be listed in a catalog that is sent out to hundreds or thousands of potential performance spaces—high schools, experimental companies, regional and community theaters—for possible production. You'll receive royalty checks for both performance fees and book sales. In contacting publishers you'll want to send your query letter with the synopsis and reviews.

There are several sources for grants. Some are federal or state, but don't overlook sources closer to home. The category "Arts Councils and Foundations" in Contests and Awards in this book lists a number of sources. On the national level contact the NEA Theater Program Fellowship for Playwrights (1100 Pennsylvania Ave. NW, Washington DC 20506). State arts commissions are another possible source, and also offer opportunities for involvement in programs where you can meet fellow playwrights. Some cities have arts and cultural commissions that offer grants for local artists. PEN publishes a comprehensive annual book, *Grants and Awards Available to American Writers* that also includes a section for Canadian writers. The latest edition is available from the PEN American Center (568 Broadway, New York NY 10012).

Once you have been produced on a commercial level, your play has been published or you have won an important grant, you can start pursuing an agent. This is not always easy. Fewer agents represent playwrights alone—there's more money in movies and TV. No agent will represent an unknown playwright. Having an agent does *not* mean you can sit back and enjoy the ride. You will still need to get out and network, establishing ties with theaters, directors, literary managers, other writers, producers, state art agencies and publishers, trying to get your work noticed. You will have some help, though. A good agent will have personal contacts that can place your work for consideration at a higher level than your efforts alone might.

There is always the possibility of moving from plays to TV and movies. There is a certain cachet in Hollywood surrounding successful playwrights. The writing style will be different—more visually oriented, less dependent on your words. The money is better, but you will have less command over the work once you've sold that copyright. It seems to be easier for a playwright to cross over to movies than for a screenwriter to cross over to plays.

Writing can make you feel isolated, even when your characters are so real to you they seem to be in the room as you write. Sometimes the experience and companionship of other playwrights is what you need to get you over a particular hurdle in your play. Membership and service organizations such as The Dramatists Guild, The International Women's Writing Guild and local groups such as the Playwright's Center in Minneapolis and the Northwest Playwright's Guild in Seattle can help you feel still a part of this world as you are off creating your own.

Information on playwriting markets listed in the previous edition of *Writer's Market* but not included in this edition can be found in the General Index.

A.S.K. THEATER PROJECTS, 11845 W. Olympic Blvd., Suite 1250W, Los Angeles CA 90064. (310)478-3200. Fax: (310)478-5300. E-mail: info@askplay.org. Website: www.askplay.org. **Contact:** Mead Hunter, director of literary programs. Estab. 1989. "A.S.K. offers an energetic, year-round slate of developmental programs, each one designed to address new work for the stage at a different level of its evolution. Please consult our web site for more detailed information and submission deadlines." Query with synopsis and sample pages. Responds in 4 months. Obtains no rights. **Pays $150 for staged readings; $1,000 for workshop productions.**
   • A.S.K. publishes a biannual magazine, *Parabasis*, which focuses on news and issues surrounding the art, business and craft of contemporary playwriting. Playwrights are asked to query about proposed articles.
Needs: "We are always looking for adventurous new work by highly original voices. Because our focus is on development opportunities rather than production, we favor works in progress that can still benefit from one of our developmental programs."
Tips: "We are a nonprofit organization dedicated to new plays and playwrights. We do not produce plays for commercial runs, nor do we request any future commitment from the playwright should their play find a production through our reading or workshop programs."

N ABINGDON THEATRE CO., 432 W. 42nd St., New York NY 10036. (212)736-6604. Fax: (212)736-6608. **Contact:** Jann Buttram or Pamela Paul, artistic directors. Estab. 1993. **Produces 2 main stage/3 workshop plays/year.** Professional productions for a general audience. Submit complete script. Responds in 4 months. Buys variable rights. **Pay is negotiated.** Include SASE for return of manuscript.
Needs: All scripts should be suitable for small stages. No musicals where the story line is not very well-developed and the driving force of the piece.

ACTORS & PLAYWRIGHTS' INITIATIVE, 359 South Burdick St., Suite 205, Kalamazoo MI 49007. (616)343-8090. Fax: (616)343-8450. E-mail: theaterapi@aol.com. **Contact:** Tucker Rafferty, literary manager. Estab. 1989. Professional theatre with resident company. Member of Theatre Communications Group. **Produces 7 main stage selections with 3 'Late Night' experimentals per year. Season: September to July.** Audience is primarily 25-45 liberal professionals and academics. Must write for submission guidelines. *No unsolicited scripts.*
Needs: Character driven, social/political and adaptations. *No musicals.* API is a 120-seat "black box" theatre with flexible staging in a new multi-purpose arts center in downtown Kalamazoo. Cast limit 10; emphasis on character and lighting, not sets.
Tips: "Study the greats—from Sophocles to Mamet."

ACTORS THEATRE OF LOUISVILLE, 316 W. Main St., Louisville KY 40202-4218. (502)584-1265. Fax: (502)561-3300. E-mail: tpalmer@actorstheatre.org. Website: www.actorstheatre.org. **Contact:** Tanya Palmer, literary manager. Estab. 1964. **Produces approximately 30 new plays of varying lengths/year.** Professional productions are performed for subscription audience from diverse backgrounds. Agented submissions only for full-length plays; open submissions to National Ten-Minute Play Contest (plays 10 pages or less). Responds in 9 months to submissions, mostly in the fall. Buys variable rights. **Offers variable royalty.**
Needs: "We are interested in full-length, one-act and ten-minute plays and in plays of ideas, language, humor, experiment and passion."

ALABAMA SHAKESPEARE FESTIVAL, 1 Festival Dr., Montgomery AL 36117-4605. Fax: (334)271-5348. Website: www.asf.net. Artistic Director: Kent Thompson. **Contact:** Gwen Orel, literary manager. **Produces 14 plays/year.** Inhouse productions for general and children's audience. Unsolicited scripts accepted for the Southern Writers' Project only. Responds in 1 year. **Pays royalty.**
Needs: "Through the Southern Writers' Project, ASF develops works by Southern writers, works that deal with the South and/or African-American themes, and works that deal with Southern and/or African-American history."

ALLEYWAY THEATRE, 1 Curtain Up Alley, Buffalo NY 14202-1911. (716)852-2600. Fax: (716)852-2266. E-mail: email@alleyway.com. Website: alleyway.com. **Contact:** Joanna Brown, dramaturg. Estab. 1990. **Produces 4 full-length, 10-15 short plays/year.** Submit complete script; include tape for musicals. Responds in 6 months. Buys first production, credit rights. **Pays 7% royalty plus travel and accommodations for opening.**
   • Alleyway Theatre also sponsors the Maxim Mazumdar New Play Competition. See the Contest & Awards section for more information.
Needs: "Theatrical" work as opposed to mainstream TV.
Tips: Sees a trend toward social issue-oriented works. Also interested in "non-traditional" children's pieces. "Plays on social issues should put action of play ahead of political message. Not interested in adapted screen plays. Theatricality and setting are central."

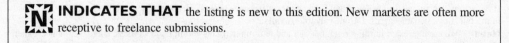 **ALLIANCE THEATRE COMPANY**, 1280 Peachtree St. NE, Atlanta GA 30309. (404)733-4650. Fax: (404)733-4625. E-mail: ATCLiterary@woodruffcenter.org. Website: www.alliancetheatre.org. **Contact:** Freddie Ashley, literary assistant. Estab. 1969. **Produces 11 plays/year.** Professional production for local audience. Query with synopsis or submit through agent. Enclose SASE. Responds in 9 months.
Needs: Full-length scripts and scripts for young audiences (max. length 60 minutes).
Tips: "The Alliance is committed to producing works that speak especially to a culturally diverse community; chief among these are plays with compelling stories or engaging characters told in adventurous or stylish ways. Please submit via mail, e-mail or fax."

ALLIED THEATRE GROUP, 3055 South University Drive, Fort Worth TX 76109-5608. (817)784-9378. Fax: (817)924-9454. E-mail: atg@flash.net. Website: www.alliedtheatre.org. Artistic Director: Jim Covault. **Contact:** Natalie Gaupp, literary associate. Estab. 1979. **Produces 8 plays/year.** 6 plays are performed in our 200-seat regional theatre, in Fort Worth's Stage West. 2 plays are performed as Shakespeare in the Park, in Fort Worth's Trinity Park. Audience varies. Query with synopsis; please submit sample pages in lieu of complete script. Responds in 6 months. Buys negotiable rights. **Pay is negotiated.**
Needs: A variety of plays, including new works as well as classics. No children's theatre contributions, please.
Tips: *Please* submit sample pages rather than the entire script.

AMELIA MAGAZINE, 329 E St., Bakersfield CA 93304. (805)323-5826. Fax: (805)323-5826. E-mail: amelia@lightspeed.net. **Contact:** Frederick A. Raborg, Jr., editor. Estab. 1983. **Publishes 1 play/year.** Submit complete script. Responds in 2 months. Buys first North American serial rights only. **Pays $150 plus publication as winner of annual Frank McClure One-Act Play Award (for the contest, deadline is May 15 annually with an entry fee of $15). No fee for normal submissions and consideration.**
Needs: "Plays with virtually any theme or concept. We look for excellence within the one-act, 45-minute running time format. We welcome the avant-garde and experimental. We do not object to the erotic, though not pornographic. Fewer plays are being produced on Broadway, but the regionals seem to be picking up the slack. That means fewer equity stages and more equity waivers."

AMERICAN CONSERVATORY THEATER, 30 Grant Ave., San Francisco CA 94108-5800. (415)439-2445. Website: www.act-sfbay.org. Artistic Director: Carey Perloff. **Contact:** Paul Walsh, dramaturg. Estab. 1965. **Produces 8 plays/year.** Plays are performed in Geary Theater, a 1,000-seat classic proscenium. No unsolicited scripts or queries.

AMERICAN RENEGADE THEATRE CO., 11136 Magnolia Blvd., North Hollywood CA 91601. (818)763-1834. Fax: (818)763-8082. Website: www.americanrenegade.com. Artistic Director: David A. Cox. **Contact:** Barry Thompson, dramaturg. Estab. 1991. **Produces 6-8 plays/year.** Plays will be performed in an Equity 99 seat plan for adult audiences; 99 seat theater and 45 seat theater in the heart of thriving Noho Arts District. Query with synopsis and SASE. **Pays 6% royalty.**
Needs: "Predominantly naturalistic, contemporary full length, but also one-acts and more experimental material on smaller stage. Mostly American authors and subject matter." No one-person plays.

N INDICATES THAT the listing is new to this edition. New markets are often more receptive to freelance submissions.

APPLE TREE THEATRE, 595 Elm Pl., Suite 210, Highland Park IL 60035. (847)432-8223. Fax: (847)432-5214. Website: www.appletreetheatre.com. Artistic Director: Eileen Boevers. **Contact:** Kristy Henry, administrative assistant. Estab. 1983. **Produces 5 plays/year.** "Professional productions intended for an adult audience mix of subscriber base and single-ticket holders. Our subscriber base is extremely theater-savvy and intellectual." Submit query and synopsis, along with tapes for musicals. Rights obtained vary. **Pays variable royalty.** Return SASE submissions only if requested.
Needs: "We produce a mixture of musicals, dramas, classical, contemporary and comedies. Length: 90 minutes-2 ½ hours. Small space, unit set required. No fly space, 3¼ thrust stage. Maximum actors 15.
Tips: "No farces or large-scale musicals. Theater needs small shows with one-unit sets due to financial concerns. Also note the desire for non-linear pieces that break new ground. *Please do not submit unsolicited manuscripts—send letter and description*; if we want more, we will request it."

ARENA PLAYERS REPERTORY COMPANY, 296 Route 109, East Farmingdale NY 11735. (516)293-0674. Fax: (516)777-8688. Producer/Director: Frederic De Feis. **Contact:** Audrey Perry, literary manager. Estab. 1954. **Produces 19 plays/year (at least 1 new play).** Professional production on either Arena Players' Main Stage or Second Stage Theatres. Intended for a conventional, middle-class audience. Query with synopsis or submit complete ms. Responds in 1 year. **Pays flat fee of $400-600.**
Needs: Main Stage season consists of Neil Simon-type comedies, Christie-esque mysteries and contemporary dramas. Prefers single set plays with a minimal cast (2 to 8 people). Only full-length plays will be considered.
Tips: No one-acts and musicals.

ARIZONA THEATRE COMPANY, P.O. Box 1631, Tucson AZ 85702. (520)884-8210. Fax: (520)628-9129. E-mail: swyer@aztheatreco.org. Website: www.aztheatreco.org. **Contact:** Samantha K. Wyer, associate artistic director. Estab. 1966. **Produces 6 plays/year.** Arizona Theatre Company is the State Theatre of Arizona and plans the season with the population of the state in mind. Agented submissions only, though Arizona writers may submit unsolicited scripts. Responds in 6 months. **Pay negotiated.**
Needs: Full length plays of a variety of genres and topics and full length musicals. No one-acts.
Tips: "Please include in the cover letter a bit about your current situation and goals. It helps in responding to plays."

ARKANSAS REPERTORY THEATRE, P.O. Box 110, Little Rock AR 72203-0110. (501)378-0445. Fax: (501)378-0012. E-mail: therep@alltel.net. Website: www.therep.org. Producing Director: Robert Hupp. **Contact:** Brady Mooy, literary manager. Estab. 1976. **Produces 8-10 plays/year.** "Professional productions for adult audiences. No kids' shows please." Query with synopsis. Responds in 6 months. Keeps 5% rights for 5 years. **Payment varies on the script, number of performances, if it was commissioned, which stage it's produced on.**
Needs: "We produce plays for a general adult audience. We do everything from intense dramas to farce. Only full-length plays." "We look for shows with less than 10 characters, but we have done epics as well. Smaller casts are preferred."
Tips: No one-acts or children's shows. Playwrights are invited to enter the Arkansas Repertory Theatre Competition for New American Comedy. See the Contests & Awards section for details.

ART STATION THEATRE, 5384 Manor Dr., P.O. Box 1998, Stone Mountain GA 30086. (770)469-1105. Fax: (770)469-0355. E-mail: info@artstation.org. Website: www.artstation.org. **Contact:** Jon Goldstein, literary manager. Estab. 1986. **Produces 5 plays/year.** "ART Station Theatre is a professional theater located in a contemporary arts center in Stone Mountain, which is part of Metro Atlanta." Audience consists of middle-aged to senior, suburban patrons. Query with synopsis or submit complete ms. Responds in 6 months. **Pays 5-7% royalty.**
Needs: Full length comedy, drama and musicals, preferably relating to the human condition in the contemporary South. Cast size no greater than 6.

ARTISTS REPERTORY THEATRE, 1516 S.W. Alder St., Portland OR 97205. E-mail: allen@artistsrep.org. Website: www.artistsrep.org. **Contact:** Allen Nause, artistic director. Estab. 1982. **Produces 6 plays/year.** Plays performed in professional theater with a subscriber-based audience. Send synopsis, sample and résumé. No unsolicited mss accepted. Responds in 6 months. **Pays royalty.**
Needs: "Full-length, hard-hitting, emotional, intimate, actor-oriented shows with small casts (rarely exceeds 10-13, usually 2-7). Language and subject matter are not a problem." No one-acts or children's scripts.

ASOLO THEATRE COMPANY, 5555 N. Tamiami Trail, Sarasota FL 34234. (941)351-9010. Fax: (941)351-5796. E-mail: bruce_rodgers@asolo.org. Website: www.asolo.org. **Contact:** Bruce E. Rodgers, associate artistic director. Estab. 1960. **Produces 7-8 plays/year.** A LORT theater with 2 intimate performing spaces. No unsolicited scripts. Send a letter with 1-page synopsis, 1 page of dialogue and SAE. Responds in 8 months. **Negotiates rights and payment.**
Needs: Play must be full length. "We operate with a resident company in rotating repertory. We have a special interest in adaptations of great literary works."

BAILIWICK REPERTORY, Bailiwick Arts Center, 1229 W. Belmont Ave., Chicago IL 60657-3205. (773)883-1090. Fax: (773)885-2017. E-mail: bailiwickr@aol.com. Website: www.bailiwick.org. **Contact:** David Zak, artistic director. Estab. 1982. **Produces 5 mainstage plays (classic and newly commissioned) each year; 50 1-acts in annual Directors**

Festival. Pride Performance Series (gay and lesbian), includes one acts, poetry, workshops, and staged adaptations of prose. Submit year-round. One-act play fest runs July-August. Responds in 9 months for full-length only. **Pays 6% royalty.**
Needs: "We need daring scripts that break the mold. Large cast or musicals are OK. Creative staging solutions are a must."
Tips: "Know the rules, then break them creatively and *boldly*! Please send SASE for manuscript submission guidelines *before you submit* or get manuscript guidelines at our website."

BAKER'S PLAYS PUBLISHING CO., P.O. Box 699222, Boston MA 02269-9222. (617)745-0805. Fax: (617)745-9891. E-mail: info@bakersplays.com. Website: www.bakersplays.com. **Contact:** John B. Welch, chief editor. Estab. 1845. **Publishes 20-30 straight plays and musicals. Works with 2-3 unpublished/unproduced writers annually. 80% freelance written.** Plays performed by amateur groups, high schools, children's theater, churches and community theater groups. **75% of scripts unagented submissions.** Submit complete script with news clippings, résumé. Submit complete cassette of music with musical submissions. Responds in 4 months. **Pay varies; negotiated royalty split of production fees; 10% book royalty.**
Needs: "We are finding strong support in our new division—plays from young authors featuring contemporary pieces for high school production."
Tips: "We are particularly interested in adaptation of lesser-known folk tales from around the world. Also of interest are plays which feature a multicultural cast and theme. Collections of one-act plays for children and young adults tend to do very well. Also, high school students: Write for guidelines for our High School Playwriting Contest."

N BARTER THEATRE, P.O. Box 867, Abingdon VA 24212-0867. (540)628-2281. Fax: (540)628-4551. E-mail: barter@naxs.com. Website: www.bartertheatre.com. **Contact:** Tom Celli, associate artistic director. Estab. 1933. **Produces 14 plays/year.** Plays performed in residency at 2 facilities, a 500-seat proscenium theater and a smaller 150-seat flexible theater. "Our plays are intended for diversified audiences of all ages." Submit synopsis and dialogue sample only with SASE. Responds in 9 months. **Pays negotiable royalty.**
● Barter Theatre often premieres new works.
Needs: "We are looking for good plays, comedies and dramas, that entertain and are relevant; plays that comment on the times and mankind; plays that are universal. We prefer casts of 4-12, single or unit set. Hard language can be a factor."
Tips: "Looking for material that can appeal to a diverse audience and have a strong family audience."

N BLOOMSBURG THEATRE ENSEMBLE, Box 66, Bloomsburg PA 17815. (570)784-5530. Fax: (570)784-4912. Ensemble Director: James Goode. **Contact:** Play Section Chair. Estab. 1979. **Produces 6 plays/year.** Professional productions for a non-urban audience. Query with synopsis. Responds in 9 months. Buys negotiable rights **Pays 6-9% royalty. Pays $50-70 per performance.** "Because of our non-urban location, we strive to expose our audience to a broad range of theatre—both classical and contemporary. We are drawn to language and ideas and to plays that resonate in our community. We are most in need of articulate comedies and cast sizes under 6."
Tips: "Because of our non-urban setting we are less interested in plays that focus on dilemmas of city life in particular. Most of the comedies we read are cynical. Many plays we read would make better film scripts; static/relationship-heavy scripts that do not use the 'theatricality' of the theatre to an advantage."

N BOARSHEAD THEATER, 425 S. Grand Ave., Lansing MI 48933. Website: www.boarshead.org. **Contact:** John Peakes, art director. Estab. 1966. **Produces 8 plays/year (6 mainstage, 2 Young People's Theater productions in-house), 4 or 5 staged readings**. Mainstage Actors' Equity Association company; also Youth Theater—touring to schools by our intern company. Query with one-page synopsis, cast list (with descriptions), 5-10 pages of representative dialogue, description of setting and self-addressed postcard for our response. Responds in 1 month to queries and synopsis. Full scripts (if requested) in 8 months. **Pays royalty for mainstage productions, transport/per diem for staged readings.**
Needs: Thrust stage. Cast usually 8 or less; occasionally up to 20. Prefer staging which depends on theatricality rather than multiple sets. "No musicals considered. Send full length plays (only) to John Peakes, art director; no one-acts. For Young People's Theater, send one-act plays (only)."
Tips: Plays should not have multiple sets—too many scripts read like film scripts. Focus on intelligence, theatricality, crisp, engaging dialogue.

CELEBRATION THEATRE, 7985 Santa Monica Blvd., Suite 109-1, West Hollywood CA 90046. (323)957-1884. E-mail: tjacobson@LACMA.ORG. Artistic Director: Derek Charles Livingston. **Contact:** Tom Jacobson, literary manager. Estab. 1983. **Produces 4 plays/year.** "We are a 64-seat professional community-based theater which celebrates gay and lesbian culture and provides a forum for professional and emerging writers, directors, designers and performers." Query with synopsis. Responds in 1 year. **Pays variable royalty.**
Needs: Gay and lesbian stage plays including full-lengths, one-acts, musicals, solo shows, performance pieces and experimental works. Celebration Theater has a thrust stage 16 feet wide and 20 feet deep with a 12-foot ceiling.
Tips: "Although Celebration accepts unsolicited ms, we prefer a letter of inquiry with a brief description of the play and SASE. Plays are accepted year-round. We do consider second productions, but prefer premiering work by Southern California lesbian and gay writers."

N CENTRE STAGE—SOUTH CAROLINA!, P.O. Box 8451, Greenville SC 29604-8451. (864)233-6733. Fax: (864)233-3901. E-mail: information@centrestage.org. Website: www.centrestage.org. **Contact:** Martha Rasche, Play Reading Committee chair. Estab. 1983. **Produces 10 plays/year.** "We are a TCG professional theater. Our youth theater targets ages 10-18, and our mainstage tragets all ages." Query with synopsis or send complete ms. Reports in 2 months; written acknowledgement sent on receipt. **Pays negotiable royalty.**
Needs: "Our productions include all types musicals, comedies, dramas. We produce for entertainment, education and issue themes." Seeking full-length plays that have not had prior production; can be one-act if the material is fully developed, i.e. "How I Learned to Drive" or "Wit." Cast size 1-25. Staging: Single set or revolve. Props: Some limitation, particularly with extra large prop requirements.
Tips: No restrictions on material. Sees "a shift in what attracts today's audiences, and what competes for their time. The more entertainment value a production has, the larger the audience that is attracted to it."

CHARLOTTE REPERTORY THEATRE, 129 W. Trade St., Charlotte NC 28202. (704)333-8587. Fax: (704)333-0224. E-mail: info@charlotterep.org. Website: www.charlotterep.org. Literary Manager: Claudia Carter Covington. **Contact:** Carol Bellamy, literary associate. Estab. 1976. "We are a not-for-profit regional theater." Submit complete script with SASE. Responds in 3 months. **Writers receive free plane fare and housing for festival, stipend.**
Needs: Need full-length scripts not previously produced professionally. Seeking plays for staged readings at the Festival of New American Plays, not for full productions. No limitations in cast, props, stage, etc. No musicals, children's theater.

CHILDREN'S STORY SCRIPTS, Baymax Productions, 2219 W. Olive Ave., PMB 130, Burbank CA 91506-2648. (818)787-5584. E-mail: baymax@earthlink.net. **Contact:** Deedra Bebout, editor. Estab. 1990. "Our audience consists of children, grades K-8 (5-13-year-olds)." Send complete script with SASE. Responds in 1 month. Licenses all rights to story; author retains copyright. **Pays graduated royalty based on sales.**
Needs: "We add new titles as we find appropriate stories. We look for stories which are fun for kids to read, involve a number of readers throughout, and dovetail with school subjects. This is a must! Not life lessons...school subjects."
Tips: "The scripts are not like theatrical scripts. They combine dialogue and prose narration, á la Readers Theatre. If a writer shows promise, we'll work with him. Our most important goal is to benefit children. We want stories that bring alive subjects studied in classrooms. Facts must be worked unobtrusively into the story—the story has to be fun for the kids to read. Send #10 SASE for guidelines with samples. We do not respond to submissions without SASE."

CHILDSPLAY, INC., P.O. Box 517, Tempe AZ 85280. (480)858-2127. Fax: (480)350-8584. E-mail: childsplay_az@hotmail.com. Website: www.tempe.gov/childsplay. **Contact:** Graham Whitehead, associate artistic director. Estab. 1978. **Produces 5-6 plays/year.** "Professional touring and in-house productions for youth and family audiences." Submit synopsis, character descriptions and 7- 10-page dialogue sample. Responds in 6 months. **Pays royalty of $20-35/performance (touring) or pays $3,000-8,000 commission. Holds a small percentage of royalties on commissioned work for 3-5 years.**
Needs: Seeking *theatrical* plays on a wide range of contemporary topics. "Our biggest market is K-6. We need intelligent theatrical pieces for this age group that meet touring requirements and have the flexibility for in-house staging. The company has a reputation, built up over 25 years, of maintaining a strong aesthetic. We need scripts that respect the audience's intelligence and support their rights to dream and to have their concerns explored. Innovative, theatrical and *small* is a constant need." Touring shows limited to 5-6 actors; in-house shows limited to 6-10 actors.
Tips: No traditionally-handled fairy tales. "Theater for young people is growing up and is able to speak to youth and adults. The material *must* respect the artistry of the theater and the intelligence of our audience. Our most important goal is to benefit children. If you wish your materials returned send SASE."

CIRCUIT PLAYHOUSE/PLAYHOUSE ON THE SQUARE, 51 S. Cooper, Memphis TN 38104. (901)725-0776. **Contact:** Jackie Nichols, artistic director. **Produces 16 plays/year. 100% of scripts unagented submissions. Works with 1 unpublished/unproduced writer/year.** Professional plays performed for the Memphis/Mid-South area. Member of the Theatre Communications Group. Contest held each fall. Submit complete script. Responds in 6 months. Buys percentage of royalty rights for 2 years. **Pays $500.**
Needs: All types; limited to single or unit sets. Casts of 20 or fewer.
Tips: "Each play is read by three readers through the extended length of time a script is kept. Preference is given to scripts for the southeastern region of the U.S."

CITY THEATRE COMPANY, 57 S. 13th St., Pittsburgh PA 15203. E-mail: caquiline@citytheatre-pgh.org. Website: www.citytheatre-pgh.org. **Contact:** Carlyn Ann Aquiline, resident dramaturg/literary manager. **Produces 8 plays/year.** "City Theatre is a LORT D company, whose mission is to provide an artistic home for the development and production of contemporary plays of substance and ideas that engage and challenge diverse audiences. We seek, commission and develop new, innovative or offbeat theatrical plays that engage the intellect as well as the emotions; works of unconventional form, content and/or language; and plays by underrepresented voices (e.g. women, writers of color, disabled). Our facilities include a 270-seat Mainstage theatre and the 99-seat Hamburg Studio Theatre." Also produces a young playwrights festival. Submit through agent or query with synopsis and character breakdown, 15-20 page dialogue sample, résumé and development/production history. No unsolicited or e-mail submissions. Responds in 10 months. Obtains no rights. **Pays commission and/or royalty.**

Needs: Normal cast limit 8. We are not presently considering one-acts or children's plays. No unsolicited or e-mail submissions. No phone calls.

I.E. CLARK PUBLICATIONS, P.O. Box 246, Schulenburg TX 78956-0246. Website: www.ieclark.com. **Contact:** Donna Cozzaglio, general manager. Estab. 1956. Publishes 10-15 plays/year for educational theater, children's theater, religious theater, regional professional theater and community theater. Publishes unagented submissions. Catalog for $3. Writer's guidelines for #10 SASE. Submit complete script, 1 at a time with SASE. Responds in 6 months. Buys all available rights; "We serve as an agency as well as a publisher." **Pays standard book and performance royalty, amount and percentages dependent upon type and marketability of play.**
- "One of our specialties is "Young Adult Awareness Drama"—plays for ages 13 to 25 dealing with sex, drugs, popularity, juvenile, crime, and other problems of young adults. We also need plays for children's theatre, especially dramatizations of children's classic literature.

Needs: "We are interested in plays of all types—short or long. Audiotapes of music or videotapes of a performance are requested with submissions of musicals. We require that a play has been produced (directed by someone other than the author); photos, videos and reviews of the production are helpful. No limitations in cast, props, staging, etc. Plays with only one or two characters are difficult to sell. We insist on literary quality. We like plays that give new interpretations and understanding of human nature. Correct spelling, punctuation and grammar (befitting the characters, of course) impress our editors."

Tips: Publishes plays only. "Entertainment value and a sense of moral responsibility seem to be returning as essential qualities of a good play script. The era of glorifying the negative elements of society seems to be fading rapidly. Literary quality, entertainment value and good craftsmanship rank in that order as the characteristics of a good script in our opinion. 'Literary quality' means that the play must—in beautiful, distinctive, and un-trite language—say something; preferably something new and important concerning man's relations with his fellow man or God; and these 'lessons in living' must be presented in an intelligent, believable and creative manner. Plays for children's theater are tending more toward realism and childhood problems, but fantasy and dramatization of fairy tales are also needed."

N A CLEVELAND PLAY HOUSE, 8500 Euclid Ave., Cleveland OH 44106. (216)795-7000. Artistic Director: Peter Hackett. **Contact:** Seth Gordon, director of new play development. Estab. 1915. **Produces 10 plays/year.** "We have five theatres, 100-550 seats." Query with synopsis; agented submissions only. Responds in 3 months. **Pay is negotiable.**
Needs: All styles and topics of new plays.

CLEVELAND PUBLIC THEATRE, 6415 Detroit Ave., Cleveland OH 44102. (216)631-2727. Fax: (216)631-2575. E-mail: cpt@en.com. Website: www.clevelandartists.net/cpt. **Contact:** Literary Manager. Estab. 1982. **Produces 6-8 full productions/year.** Also sponsors Festival of New Plays. 150-seat "Main Stage" and 700-seat Gordon Square Theatre. "Our audience believes that art touches your heart and your nerve endings." Query with synopsis and dialogue sample for full season. Rights negotiable. **Pays $15-100 per performance.**
Needs: Poetic, experimental, avant-garde, political, multicultural works that need a stage (not a camera); interdisciplinary cutting-edge work (dance/performance art/music/visual); works that stretch the imagination and conventional boundaries. CPT presents performed work that addresses the issues and challenges of modern life. Particular focus is given to alternative, experimental, poetic, political works, with particular attention to those created by women, people of color, gays/lesbians.
Tips: "No conventional comedies, musicals, adaptations, children's plays—if you think Samuel French would love it, we probably won't. No TV sitcoms or soaps masquerading as theater. Theater is *not* TV or films. Learn the impact of what live bodies do to an audience in the same room. We are particularly interested in artists from our region who can grow with us on a longterm basis."

COLONY THEATRE COMPANY, (formerly Colony Studio Theatre), 555 N. Third St., Burbank CA 91502-1103. Website: www.colonytheatre.org. **Contact:** Wayne Liebman, literary manager. **Produces 6 plays/year.** Professional 276-seat theater with thrust stage. Casts from resident company of professional actors. Send SASE for query guidelines or check online. Responds only if interested. Negotiated rights. **Pays royalty for each performance.**
Needs: Full length (90-120 minutes) with a cast of 4-12. No musicals or experimental works.
Tips: "We seek works of theatrical imagination and emotional resonance on universal themes."

N CONFRONTATION, A Literary Journal, C.W. Post of Long Island University, Brookville NY 11548-1300. (516)299-2720. Fax: (516)299-2735. **Contact:** Martin Tucker, editor. Estab. 1968. **Publishes 2 plays/year.** Submit complete script. Responds in 2 months. Obtains all rights, but releases first serial rights on request of author. **Pays up to $50.**
Needs: "We have an annual one-act play contest, open to all forms and styles."

CONTEMPORARY DRAMA SERVICE, Meriwether Publishing Ltd., P.O. Box 7710, Colorado Springs CO 80933. Fax: (719)594-9916. E-mail: merpcds@aol.com. Website: www.contemporarydrama.com. Editor: Arthur Zapel. **Contact:** Theodore Zapel, associate editor. Estab. 1969. **Publishes 50-60 plays/year.** "We are specialists in theater arts books and plays for middle grades, high schools and colleges. We publish textbooks for drama courses of all types. We also publish for mainline liturgical churches—drama activities for church holidays, youth activities and fundraising entertainments. These may be plays, musicals or drama-related books." Query with synopsis or submit complete script. Responds in 6 weeks. Obtains either amateur or all rights. **Pays 10% royalty or negotiates purchase.**

• Contemporary Drama Service is now looking for play or musical adaptations of classic stories by famous authors and playwrights. Also looking for parodies of famous movies or historical and/or fictional characters, i.e. Robin Hood, Rip Van Winkle, Buffalo Bill, Huckleberry Finn.

Needs: "Most of the plays we publish are one acts, 15-45 minutes in length. We also publish full-length two-act musicals or three-act plays 90 minutes in length. We prefer comedies. Musical plays must have name appeal either by prestige author or prestige title adaptation. Musical shows should have large casts for 20 to 25 performers. Comedy sketches, monologues and plays are welcomed. We prefer simple staging appropriate to middle school, high school, college or church performance. We like playwrights who see the world with a sense of humor. Offbeat themes and treatments are accepted if the playwright can sustain a light touch. In documentary or religious plays we look for good research and authenticity. We are publishing many scenebooks for actors (which can be anthologies of great works excerpts), scenebooks on special themes and speech and theatrical arts textbooks. We also publish many books of monologs for young performers. We are especially interested in authority-books on a variety of theater-related subjects."

Tips: Contemporary Drama Service is looking for creative books on comedy, monologs, staging amateur theatricals and Christian youth activities. "Our writers are usually highly experienced in theatre as teachers or performers. We welcome books that reflect their experience and special knowledge. Any good comedy writer of monologs and short scenes will find a home with us."

DALLAS CHILDREN'S THEATER, 2215 Cedar Springs, Dallas TX 75201. E-mail: family@dct.org. Website: www.dct.org. **Contact:** Robyn Flatt, executive director. Estab. 1984. **Produces 11 plays/year.** Professional theater for family and student audiences. Query with synopsis, number of actors required, any material regarding previous productions of the work, and a demo tape or lead sheets (for musicals). Responds in 8 months. Rights negotiable. **Pays negotiable royalty.** No materials will be returned without a SASE included.

Needs: Substantive material appropriate for youth and family audiences. Most consideration given to full-length, non-musical works, especially classic and contemporary adaptations of literature. Also interested in social, topical issue-oriented material. Very interested in scripts which enlighten diverse cultural experiences, particularly Hispanic and African-American experiences. Prefers scripts with no more than 15 cast members; 6-12 is ideal.

Tips: No adult experience material. "We are a family theater." Not interested in material intended for performance by children or in a classroom. Productions are performed by professional adults. Children are cast in child-appropriate roles. "We receive far too much light musical material that plays down to children and totally lacks any substance. Be patient. We receive an enormous amount of submissions. Most of the material we have historically produced has had previous production. We are not against perusing non-produced material, but it has rarely gone into our season unless we have been involved in its development."

DETROIT REPERTORY THEATRE, 13103 Woodrow Wilson, Detroit MI 48238-3686. (313)868-1347. Fax: (313)868-1705. **Contact:** Barbara Busby, literary manager. Estab. 1957. **Produces 4 plays/year.** Professional theater, 194 seats operating on A.E.A. SPT contract Detroit metropolitan area. Submit complete ms in bound folder, cast list and description with SASE. Responds in 6 months. **Pays royalty.**

Needs: Wants issue-oriented works. Cast limited to no more than 7 characters. No musicals or one-act plays.

DIVERSIONARY THEATRE, 4545 Park Blvd., San Diego CA 92116. (619)220-6830. **Contact:** Chuck Zito, executive director. Estab. 1985. **Produces 6 (usually 1 new) plays/year.** Non-professional productions for primarily gay, lesbian, bisexual and transgender audiences. Query with synopsis. Responds in 3 months. Buys first performance rights. **Pays 6% royalty.**

Needs: Previously unproduced works. Full-length with gay, lesbian or transgender themes. Prefer unit setting.

Tips: "We've seen a lot of sitcoms—show us something different from a bunch of white guys sitting around having wacky relationship problems."

DIXON PLACE, 309 E. 26th St., New York NY 10010-1902. (212)532-1546. Fax: (212)532-1094. Website: www.dixonplace.org. **Contact:** Ellie Covan, artistic director/founder. Estab. 1986. **Produces 12 plays/year.** "We present play readings at our downtown, off-off Broadway performance venue." Audience is usually made up of supporters of the writer, and other artists. Submit 10-page script sample with synopsis. Responds in 6 months. **Pays flat fee.**

Needs: Musicals, one-acts, full-length plays, not already read or workshopped in New York. Particularly interested in non-traditional, either in character, content, structure and/or themes. "We almost never produce kitchen sink, soap opera-style plays about AIDS, coming out, unhappy love affairs, getting sober or lesbian parenting. We regularly present new works, plays with innovative structure, multi-ethnic content, non-naturalistic dialogue, irreverent musicals and the elegantly bizarre. We are an established performance venue with a very diverse audience. We have a reputation for bringing our audience the unexpected."

DORSET THEATRE FESTIVAL, Box 510, Dorset VT 05251-0510. (802)867-2223. Fax: (802)867-0144. E-mail: theatre@sover.net. Website: www.theatredirectories.com. **Contact:** Jill Charles, artistic director. Estab. 1976.

Produces 5 plays/year, 1 a new work. "Our plays will be performed in our Equity summer stock theatre and are intended for a sophisticated community." Agented submissions only. Responds in 6 months. **Rights and compensation negotiated.**
Needs: "Looking for full-length contemporary American comedy or drama." Limited to a cast of 6.
Tips: "Language and subject matter appropriate to general audience."

DRAMATIC PUBLISHING, 311 Washington St., Woodstock IL 60098. (815)338-7170. Fax: (815)338-8981. E-mail: plays@dramaticpublishing.com. Website: www.dramaticpublishing.com. **Contact:** Linda Habjan, editor. Publishes paperback acting editions of original plays, musicals, adaptations and translations. **Publishes 50-70 titles/year. Receives 250-500 queries and 600 mss/year. Catalog and ms guidelines free. Pays 10% royalty on scripts; performance royalty varies.**
● Dramatic Publishing is seeking more material for the high school market and community theater.
Needs: Interested in playscripts appropriate for children, middle and high schools, colleges, community, stock and professional theaters. Send full ms.
Tips: "We publish all kinds of plays for the professional stock and amateur market: full lengths, one acts, children's plays, musicals, adaptations."

DRAMATICS MAGAZINE, 2343 Auburn Ave., Cincinnati OH 45219. (513)421-3900. Fax: (513)421-7077. E-mail: dcorathers@etassoc.org. Website: www.etassoc.org. **Contact:** Don Corathers, editor. Estab. 1929. **Publishes 7 plays/year.** For high school theater students and teachers. Submit complete script. Responds in 3 months. Buys first North American serial rights only.
Needs: "We are seeking one-acts to full-lengths that can be produced in an educational theater setting." No musicals.
Tips: "No melodrama, farce, children's theater, or cheap knock-offs of TV sitcoms or movies. Fewer writers are taking the time to learn the conventions of theater—what makes a piece work on stage, as opposed to film and television—and their scripts show it. We're always looking for good interviews with working theatre professionals."

THE EAST VILLAGE EXPERIMENTAL THEATRE COMPANY, 3711 President St., Philadelphia PA 19114. E-mail: info@EastVillageETC.org. Website: www.EastVillageETC.org. **Contact:** Randy Lee Hartwig, executive director. Estab. 2000. **Publishes 12-15 plays/year.** Performs for a variety of artists at a variety of venues - school to performance art. Query with synopsis, résumé, writing samples and production history. Responds in 2 months. "We develop new projects of performance from radio and video to film and theatre. Once the project has reached production we are publishing manuscripts, videotapes, films, audio tapes, scores. etc." **Pays lease per performance.** Include SASE for return of materials.
Needs: "We are looking for interdisciplinary and multimedia projects in film, video, radio, theatre, performance art, dance, music and site-specific events."
Tips: "The performing arts audiences are seeking exciting and honest works that are less linear and narrative and more visual and associative. We are seeking to combine visual, media and performing arts in formats and venues that are suitable to the work and content of the project."

EAST WEST PLAYERS, 244 S. San Pedro St., Suite 301, Los Angeles CA 980012-3832. (213)625-7000, ext. 27. Fax: (213)625-7111. E-mail: info@eastwestplayers.org. Website: www.eastwestplayers.org. Artistic Director: Tim Dang. **Contact:** Ken Narasaki, literary manager. Estab. 1965. **Produces 5 plays/year.** Professional theater performing under Equity 99-seat contract, presenting plays which explore the Asian-Pacific or Asian-American experience. Query with synopsis. Responds in 3 months. **Pays royalty against percentage of box office.**
Needs: "Whether dramas, comedies, performance art, or musicals, all plays must either address the Asian-American experience or have a special resonance when cast with Asian-American actors."

EL PORTAL CENTER FOR THE ARTS, 5269 Lankershim Blvd., North Hollywood CA 91601. (818)508-4234. Fax: (818)508-5113. **Contact:** Jim Brochu, artistic director. Estab. 1999. **Produces 8 plays/year.** Equity LORT D (370 seats) and Equity Waiver (99 seats). *Agented submissions only.* Responds in 6 months. **Pays royalty.** Include SASE for return of submission.
Needs: "We are looking for established plays by well-known playwrights. We don't produce new work." Limited to small shows; 8 characters maximum.

ELDRIDGE PUBLISHING CO., P.O. Box 1595, Venice FL 34284. (941)496-4679. Fax: (941)493-9680. E-mail: info@histage.com. Website: www.histage.com. Editor: Susan Shore. **Contact:** Chris Angermann, acquisitions editor. Estab. 1906. Publishes 100-110 new plays/year for junior high, senior high, church and community audience. Query with synopsis (acceptable) or submit complete ms (preferred). Please send cassette tapes with any musicals. Responds in 2 months. Buys all rights. **Pays 50% royalties and 10% copy sales in general market. Makes outright purchase of $200-600 in religious market.**
Needs: "We are most interested in full-length plays and musicals for our school and community theater market. Nothing lower than junior high level, please. We always love comedies but also look for serious, high caliber plays reflective of today's sophisticated students. We also need one-acts and plays for children's theater. In addition, in our religious market we're always searching for holiday or any time plays."

Tips: "Submissions are welcomed at any time. Authors are paid royalties twice a year. They receive complimentary copies of their published plays, the annual catalog and 50% discount if buying additional copies."

A **THE EMPTY SPACE THEATRE**, 3509 Fremont Ave. N, Seattle WA 98103. (206)547-7633. Fax: (206)547-7635. E-mail: emptyspace@speakeasy.org. Website: www.emptyspace.org. **Contact:** Adam Greenfield, literary manager. Estab. 1970. Produces 5 plays/year between October and July. Professional productions. *Agented submissions only, unless a writer is from the Northwest.* Reponds to queries in 2 months, mss in 4 months. **Typically, we ask for something close to 5% of the author's royalties for 5 years. Pays 6-10% royalty or $2,500-10,000 playwright commission.**
Needs: Full-length plays, full-length musicals, solo pieces, translations, adaptations. "The Empty Space strives to make theatre an event—bold, provocative, celebratory—brings audience and artists to a common ground through an uncommon experience." Prefers small casts.
Tips: "The Empty Space produces work that specifically supports our artistic vision—generally rough and bold plays that seek to engage audiences on a visceral level; highly theatrical works."

ENCORE PERFORMANCE PUBLISHING, P.O. Box 692, Orem UT 84059-0692. (801)376-6199. Fax: (801)796-3965. E-mail: encoreplay@aol.com. Website: www.encoreplay.com. **Contact:** Michael C. Perry, editor. Estab. 1979. **Produces 40 plays/year.** "Our audience consists of all ages with emphasis on the family; educational institutions from elementary through college/university, community theaters and professional theaters." No unsolicited mss. Query with synopsis, production history and SASE. Responds in 1 month to queries; 3 months to scripts. Submit from May-August. **Pays 50% performance royalty; 10% book royalty.**
Needs: "We are looking for plays with strong message about or for families, plays with young actors among cast, any length, all genres. We prefer scripts with at least close or equal male/female roles, could lean to more female roles." Plays must have had at least 2 fully staged productions. Unproduced plays can be read with letter of recommendation accompanying the query.
Tips: "No performance art pieces or plays with overtly sexual themes or language. Looking for adaptations of Twain and other American authors."

N **THE ENSEMBLE STUDIO THEATRE**, 549 W. 52nd St., New York NY 10019. (212)247-4982. Fax: (212)664-0041. Website: www.ensemblestudiotheatre.org. Artistic Director: Curt Dempster. **Contact:** Tom Rowan, literary manager. Estab. 1971. Produces 250 projects/year for off-off Broadway developmental theater in a 100-seat house, 60-seat workshop space. Do not fax mss or résumés. Submit complete ms. Responds in 6 months. **Standard production contract: mini contract with Actors' Equity Association or letter of agreement. Pays $80-1,000.**
Needs: Full-length plays with strong dramatic actions and situations and solid one-acts, humorous and dramatic, which can stand on their own. Musicals also accepted; send tape of music. Special programs include Going to the River Series, which workshops new plays by African-American women, and the Sloan Project, which commissions new works on the topics of science and technology. Seeks "original plays with strong dramatic action, believable characters and dynamic ideas. We are interested in writers who respect the power of language." No verse-dramas or elaborate costume dramas.
Tips: Deadline for one-act play marathon submissions is December 1. Full-length plays accepted year-round. "We are dedicated to developing new American plays."

ENSEMBLE THEATRE OF CINCINNATI, 1127 Vine St., Cincinnati OH 45248. (513)421-3555. Fax: (513)421-8002. E-mail: etcin@aol.com. Website: cincyetc.com. **Contact:** D. Lynn Meyers, producing artistic director. Estab. 1987. **Produces 9 plays/year.** Professional year-round theater. Query with synopsis, submit complete ms or submit through agent. Responds in 6 months. **Pays 5-10% royalty.**
Needs: Dedicated to good writing, any style for a contemporary, small cast. Small technical needs, big ideas.

N **THE ESSENTIAL THEATRE**, 995 Greenwood Ave. #6, Atlanta GA 30306. (404)876-8471. **Contact:** Peter Hardy, artistic director. Estab. 1987. **Produces 3 plays/year.** "Professional theatre on a small budget, for adventurous theatregoers interested in new plays." Submit complete script. Responds in 2 years. **Pays $20 per performance.** Include SASE for return of submission.
Needs: "We are interested in new full-length plays by American writers. No topic, genre or style limitations."

FIRST STAGE, P.O. Box 38280, Los Angeles CA 90038. (323)850-6271. Fax: (323)850-6295. E-mail: firststge@aol.com. Website: www.firststagela.org. **Contact:** Dennis Safren, literary manager. Estab. 1983. **Produces 50 plays/year.** First Stage is a non-profit organization dedicated to bringing together writers, actors and directors in the development of new material for stage and screen. Submit complete script. Responds in 6 months.
Needs: Original non-produced plays in any genre. Correct play format. No longer than two hours.
Tips: No TV sitcoms. "We are a development organization."

A **FLORIDA STAGE**, 262 S. Ocean Blvd., Manalapan FL 33462. (561)585-3404. Fax: (561)588-4708. Website: www.floridastage.org. **Contact:** Des Gallant, literary manager. Estab. 1985. **Produces 5 plays/year.** Professional equity productions; 250 seat thrust; looking for edgy work that deals with issues and ideas; stylistically innovative. *Agented submissions only.* Responds in 1 year. Buys production rights only. **Pays royalty.** Include SASE for return of script.

Needs: "We need drama and comedy; issue-oriented plays, innovative in their use of language, structure and style." No more than 8 actors.

Tips: No kitchen sink; no Neil Simon type comedy; no TV sitcom type material. "We see a propensity for writing scripts that forget the art of the theater and that are overly influenced by TV and film. Theater's most important asset is language. It is truly refreshing to come across writers who understand this. Eric Overmyer is a great example."

FLORIDA STUDIO THEATRE, 1241 N. Palm Ave., Sarasota FL 34236. (941)366-9017. Fax: (941)955-4137. E-mail: james@fst2000.org. **Contact:** James Ashford, casting and literary coordinator. **Produces 7 established and 9 new plays/year.** FST is a professional, not-for-profit theater. Plays are produced in 173-seat mainstage and 109-seat cabaret theater for subscription audiences. FST operates under a small professional theater contract of Actor's Equity. No unsolicited scripts. Send synopsis and 10 pages of dialogue. Responds in 1 month. **Pays $200 for workshop production of new script.**

Needs: Contemporary plays, musicals, musical revues. Prefers casts of no more than 8 and single sets on mainstage, 3-4 in cabaret.

Tips: "We are looking for material for our Cabaret Theatre—musical revues, one-two character musicals. All should be in two acts and run no longer than 90 minutes, including a 15 minute intermission. Also seeking dramas and comedies for the mainstage."

THE FOOTHILL THEATRE COMPANY, P.O. Box 1812, Nevada City CA 95959. (530)265-9320. Fax: (530)265-9325. E-mail: ftc@foothilltheatre.org. Website: www.foothilltheatre.org. **Contact:** Gary Wright, associate artist. Estab. 1977. **Produces 6-9 plays/year.** "We are a professional theater company operating under an Actors' Equity Association contract for part of the year, and performing in the historic 246-seat Nevada Theatre (built in 1865) and at an outdoor amphitheatre on the north shore of Lake Tahoe. We also produce a new play development program called New Voices of the Wild West that endeavors to tell the stories of the non-urban Western United States." The audience is a mix of locals and tourists. Query with synopsis or submit complete script. Responds in 1 year. Buys negotiable rights. **Pay varies.**

Needs: "We are most interested in plays which speak to the region and its history, as well as to its current concerns." "No melodramas. Theatrical, above all."

Tips: "At present, we're especially interested in unproduced plays that speak to the rural and semi-rural American West for possible inclusion in our new play reading and development program, New Voices of the Wild West. History plays are okay, as long as they don't sound like you wrote them with an encyclopedia open in your lap. The best way to get our attention is to write something we haven't seen before, and write it well."

FOUNTAIN THEATRE, 5060 Fountain Ave., Los Angeles CA 90029. (323)663-2235. Fax: (323)663-1629. E-mail: ftheatre@aol.com. Website: fountaintheatre.com. Artistic Directors: Deborah Lawlor, Stephen Sachs. **Contact:** Simon Levy, dramaturg. Estab. 1990. Produces both a theater and dance season. Produced at Fountain Theatre (99-seat equity plan). *Query through agent or recommendation of theater professional.* Query with synopsis to Simon Levy, producing director/dramaturg. Responds in 6 months. Rights acquired vary. **Pays royalty.**

Needs: Original plays, adaptations of American literature, "material that incorporates dance or language into text with unique use and vision."

THE FREELANCE PRESS, P.O. Box 548, Dover MA 02030-2207. (508)785-8250. Fax: (508)785-8291. **Contact:** Narcissa Campion, managing director. Estab. 1984. **Publishes 4 plays/year for children/young adults.** Submit complete ms with SASE. Responds in 4 months. **Pays 70% of performance royalties to authors. Pays 10% script and score royalty.**

Needs: "We publish original musical theater to be performed by young people, dealing with issues of importance to them. Also adapt 'classics' into musicals for 8- to 16-year-old age groups to perform." Large cast, flexible.

SAMUEL FRENCH, INC., 45 W. 25th St., New York NY 10010. (212)206-8990. Fax: (212)206-1429. E-mail: samuelfrench@earthlink.net. Website: www.samuelfrench.com. **Contact:** Lawrence Harbison, senior editor. Estab. 1830. Publishes paperback acting editions of plays. **Publishes 30-40 titles/year. Receives 1,500 submissions/year, mostly from unagented playwrights. 10% of publications are from first-time authors; 20% from unagented writers. Pays 10% royalty on retail price, plus amateur and stock royalties on productions.**

Needs: Comedies, mysteries, children's plays, high school plays.

Tips: "Broadway and Off-Broadway hit plays, light comedies and mysteries have the best chance of selling to our firm. Our market is comprised of theater producers—both professional and amateur—actors and students. Read as many plays as possible of recent vintage to keep apprised of today's market; write plays with good female roles; and be one hundred percent professional in approaching publishers and producers. We recommend (not require) that submissions be in the format used by professional playwrights in the U.S., as illustrated in our playlet *Guidelines*, which sells for $4 post-paid. No plays with all-male casts, radio plays or verse plays."

GENERIC PLAYS, P.O. Box 81, Bristol TN 37621-0081. **Contact:** Cody Miller, publisher. Estab. 1999. **Publishes 20 plays/year.** Audience is professional, college and community groups. Submit complete ms. Include score and tape/CD for musicals. Responds in 9 months. **Pays 75% royalty plus 25% script/book royalty.** Enclose SASE for return of materials and/or #10 SASE for notification.

Needs: "We are very interested in musicals, adaptations and translations. Also, plays by or dealing with minorities."
Tips: No one acts which are not part of a series or would constitute a full evening. Any musicals submitted without a score will not be considered. Plays must have been previously produced and accompanied by a program and reviews (does not apply to musicals).

[N] [A] THE GENESIUS GUILD INC., P.O. Box 2213, New York NY 10108-2213. (212)946-5625. Website: www.genesiusguild.org. **Contact:** Thomas Morrissey, artistic director. Estab. 1995. **Produces 5-7 plays/year.** New York Off-Broadway showcase and workshops. Query with synopsis; agented submissions only. Responds in 1 year. **Pays negotiable royalty.** Include SASE for return of submission.
Needs: Varies. See website for further information.

GEORGE STREET PLAYHOUSE, 9 Livingston Ave., New Brunswick NJ 08901. (732)246-7717. Website: www.geo rgestplayhouse.org. Artistic Director: David Saint. **Contact:** George Ryan, literary manager. **Produces 6 plays/year.** Professional regional theater (LORT C). *No unsolicited scripts. Agent or professional recommendation only.* Query with synopsis, character breakdown and up to 10 sample pages. Responds in 10 months to scripts.
Needs: Full-length dramas, comedies and musicals with a fresh perspective on society. Prefers cast size under 9; "ideal" cast size is 5-7 characters, one unit set. Also presents 40-minute social-issue plays appropriate for touring to school-age children; cast size limited to 4-5 actors.
Tips: "We produce up to four new plays and one new musical each season. It is our firm belief that theater reaches the mind via the heart and the funny bone. Our work tells a compelling, personal, human story that entertains, challenges and stretches the imagination."

GEVA THEATRE, 75 Woodbury Blvd., Rochester NY 14607. (716)232-1366. **Contact:** Marge Betley, literary manager. **Produces 7-10 plays/year.** Professional and regional theater, modified thrust, 552 seats; second stage, 180 seats. Subscription and single-ticket sales. Query with sample pages and synopsis. Responds in 2 months.
Needs: Full-length plays, translations and adaptations.

[A] GRETNA THEATRE, P.O. Box 578, Mt. Gretna PA 17064. Fax: (717)964-2189. E-mail: gretnatheatre@paonline. com. Website: www.mtgretna.com/theatre. **Contact:** Pat Julian, producing director. Estab. 1923. "Plays are performed at a professional equity theater during summer." *Agented submissions only.* **Pays negotiable royalty (6-12%).**
Needs: "We produce full-length plays for a summer audience—subject, language and content are important." Prefer "Package" or vehicles which have "Star" role.
Tips: "No one-acts. No 'Romantic Comedy.' "

[N] THE HARBOR THEATRE, 160 W. 71st St., 20A, New York NY 10023. (212)787-1945. Website: www.harborthe atre.org. **Contact:** Stuart Warmflash, artistic director. Estab. 1993. **Produces 1-2 plays/year.** Off-off Broadway showcase. Query and synopsis. Responds in 10 weeks. **Makes outright purchase of $500.** Include SASE for return of submission.
Needs: Full-length and one-act festival. *"We only accept plays developed in our workshop."*

[N] [A] HARTFORD STAGE COMPANY, 50 Church St., Hartford CT 06103. (203)525-5601. Website: www.hartfo rdstage.org. **Contact:** Chris Baker, literary director. Estab. 1963. **Produces 6 plays/year.** Regional theater productions with a wide range in audience.
Needs: Classics, new plays, musicals. *Agented submissions only.* No queries or synopses.

HEUER PUBLISHING CO., 210 2nd St., Suite 301, Cedar Rapids IA 52406-0248. (319)364-6311. Fax: (319)364-1771. E-mail: editor@hitplays.com. Website: www.hitplays.com. Owner/Editor: C. Emmett McMullen. **Contact:** Geri Albrecht, associate editor. Estab. 1928. Publishes plays, musicals and theatre texts for junior and senior high schools and community theatres. Query with synopsis or submit complete script. Responds in 2 months. Purchases amateur rights only. **Pays royalty or makes outright purchase.**
Needs: "One-, two- and three-act plays and musicals suitable for middle, junior and senior high school productions. Preferably comedy or mystery/comedy with a large number of characters and minimal set requirements. Please avoid controversial or offensive subject matter."

[N] HONOLULU THEATRE FOR YOUTH, 2846 Ualena St., Honolulu HI 96819-1910. (808)839-9885. Fax: (808)839-7018. Website: www.htyweb.org. **Contact:** Mark Lutwak, artistic director. Estab. 1955. **Produces 8 plays/ year.** Professional company performing for young people and families throughout the state of Hawaii. Query and synopsis. **Pays 6-7½% royalty.** Include SASE for return of submission.
Needs: Plays that will speak to the children of Hawaii about their culture(s), history, and the world. Plays are targeted to narrow age ranges: Lower and upper elementary, middle school, high school and preschool. Six actors maximum; 75 minutes maximum. No large cast musicals.
Tips: "Avoid too many omniscient narrators and talking down at children."

HORIZON THEATRE COMPANY, P.O. Box 5376, Atlanta GA 31107. (404)523-1477. E-mail: horizonco@mindspri ng.com. Website: www.horizontheatre.com. **Contact:** Jennifer Hebblethwaite, literary manager. Artistic Director: Lisa Adler. Estab. 1983. **Produces 5 plays/year.** Professional productions. Query with synopsis and résumé. Responds in 2 years. Buys rights to produce in Atlanta area. **Pays 6-8% royalty or $50-75/performance.**
Needs: "We produce contemporary plays with realistic base, but which utilize heightened visual or language elements. Interested in comedy, satire, plays that are entertaining and topical, but also thought provoking. Also particular interest in plays by women or with Southern themes." No more than 10 in cast.
Tips: "No plays about being in theater or film; no plays without hope; no plays that include playwrights as leading characters; no all-male casts; no plays with all older (50 plus) characters. Southern theme plays considered for New South for the New Century new play festival."

N: ILLINOIS THEATRE CENTRE, 317 Artists' Walk, P.O. Box 397, Park Forest IL 60466. (708)481-3510. Fax: (708)481-3693. E-mail: ilthctr@bigplanet.com. Website: www.ilthctr.org. Artistic Director: Etel Billig. **Contact:** Alex-andra Murdoch, literary manager. Estab. 1976. **Produces 8 plays/year.** Professional Resident Theatre Company in our own space for a subscription-based audience. Query with synopsis or agented submission. Responds in 2 months. Buys casting and directing and designer selection rights. **Pays 7-10% royalty.**
Needs: All types of 2-act plays, musicals, dramas. Prefers cast size of 6-10.
Tips: Always looking for mysteries and comedies. "Make sure your play arrives between November and January when play selections are made."

INDIANA REPERTORY THEATRE, 140 W. Washington St., Indianapolis IN 46204-3465. (317)635-5277. Fax: (317)236-0767. Artistic Director: Janet Allen. **Contact:** Literary Manager. Estab. 1972. **Produces 9 plays/year.** Plays are produced and performed at the Indiana Repertory Theatre, the state's only professional, nonprofit resident theatre. Audiences range from child to adult, depending on show. Query with synopsis. Responds in 2 months to synopsis; 6 months to ms. Rights and payment negotiated individually.
Needs: Full-length plays; adaptations of well-known literary works; plays about Indiana and the Midwest; African-American plays; Native American plays; contemporary comedies; plays with compelling characters, situations, language and theatrical appeal. Prefer casts of 8 or fewer.
Tips: No musicals or plays that would do as well in film and on TV.

N: INTERACT THEATRE COMPANY, The Adrienne, 2030 Sansom St., Philadelphia PA 19103. (215)568-8077. Fax: (215)568-8095. E-mail: interact@interacttheatre.org or loebell@interacttheatre.org. Website: www.interacttheatre.o rg. **Contact:** Larry Loebell, literary manager. Estab. 1988. **Produces 3 plays/year.** Produces professional productions for adult audience. Query with synopsis and bio. No unsolicited scripts. Responds in 4 months. **Pays 2-8% royalty or $25-100/performance.**
Needs: Contemporary dramas and comedies that explore issues of political, social, cultural or historical significance. "Virtually all of our productions have political content in the foregound of the drama." Prefer plays that raise interesting questions without giving easy, predictable answers. We are interested in new plays. Special program: Showcase of New Plays each January. Staged readings of new plays by Philadelphia area playwrights. Deadline June 1. Send SASE after April 1 for information. Limit cast to 9 or 10. No romantic comedies, no family dramas, no agit prop.

JEWEL BOX THEATRE, 3700 N. Walker, Oklahoma City OK 73118-7099. (405)521-1786. Fax: (405)525-6562. **Contact:** Charles Tweed, production director. Estab. 1956. **Produces 6 plays/year.** Amateur productions. 3,000 season subscribers and general public. Submit complete script. Responds in 4 months. **Pays $500 contest prize.**
Needs: Send SASE for entry form during September-October. "We produce dramas and comedies. Only full-length plays can be accepted. Our theater is in-the-round, so we adapt plays accordingly." Deadline: mid-January.

N: JEWISH ENSEMBLE THEATRE, 6600 W. Maple Rd., West Bloomfield MI 48322. (248)788-2900. Fax: (248)788-5160. **Contact:** Evelyn Orbach, artistic director. Estab. 1989. **Produces 5 plays/year.** Professional productions at the Aaron DeRoy theatre (season) and Millennium Centre (schools), as well as tours to schools. Submit complete script. Responds in 1 year. Obtains rights for our season productions and staged readings for festival. **Pays 6-10% royalty or honorarium for staged reading—$100/full-length play.**
Needs: "We do few children's plays except original commissions; we rarely do musicals." Cast limited to a maximum of 8 actors.

N: JUNETEENTH LEGACY THEATRE, P.O. Box 3463, Louisville KY 40201-3463. Fax: (502)589-9902. **Contact:** Lorna Littleway, producing director. Estab. 1999. **Produces 15 plays/year.** Professional productions for mainstage, readers theatre tour and a festival of staged readings. General and youth audiences. Submit complete script. Responds in "several" months. **Pays 50%/performance for mainstage; 15%/performance for full-length; 10%/performance for one-act for readers theatre tour. No royalty for festival of staged readings.** Include SASE for return of script.
Needs: Any genre or length is acceptable, but plays must address one of five themes: African American 19th-century experience; pre and Harlem Renaissance; Caribbean/Native American influence on African Americans; contemporary issues and African American youth; and new images of women.
Tips: "There is a $10 script processing fee. Make checks payable to Juneteenth Legacy Theatre."

N KITCHEN DOG THEATER, 3120 McKinney Ave., Dallas TX 75204. (214)953-2258. Fax: (214)953-1873. **Contact:** Dan Day, artistic director. Estab. 1990. **Produces 8 plays/year.** Kitchen Dog has two performance spaces: a 100-seat black box and a 200-seat thrust. Submit complete manuscript with SASE. Each year the deadline for submissions is March 15. Writers are notified by May 15. Buys rights to full production or staged reading. **Pays $40-75 per performance; $500-1,000 for winner of New Works Festival.**
Needs: "We are interested in experimental plays, literary adaptations, historical plays, political theater, gay and lesbian work, culturally diverse work, and small musicals. Ideally, cast size would be 1-5, or more if doubling roles is a possibility." No romantic/light comedies or material that is more suited for television than the theater.
Tips: "We are interested in plays that are theatrical and that challenge the imagination—plays that are for the theater, rather than T.V. or film."

KUMU KAHUA, 46 Merchant St., Honolulu HI 96813. (808)536-4222. Fax: (808)536-4226. **Contact:** Harry Wong, artistic director. Estab. 1971. **Produces 5 productions, 3-4 public readings/year.** "Plays performed at new Kumu Kahua Theatre, flexible 120-seat theater, for community audiences." Submit complete script. Responds in 4 months. **Pays royalty of $50/performance; usually 12 performances of each production.**
Needs: "Plays must have some interest for local Hawai'i audiences, preferably by being set in Hawai'i or dealing with some aspect of the Hawaiian experience." Prefer small cast, with simple staging demands.
Tips: "We need time to evaluate scripts (our response time is four months)."

LARK THEATRE COMPANY/PLAYWRIGHTS WEEK, 939 Eighth Ave., New York NY 10019. (212)246-2676. Fax: (212)246-2609. E-mail: submissions@larktheatre.org. Website: www.larktheatre.org. **Contact:** Miles Lott, literary manager; John C. Eisner, producing director. Estab. 1994. **Produces 5 plays/year, 8 during Playwrights Week.** "Our mission is to 'ready new plays for production.' Hence, we are a play development organization. We offer readings and developmental workshops, sometimes in limited runs off-Broadway." Submit complete script. Responds in 8 months. No rights purchased at outset for Playwrights Week. Usually an off-Broadway option at next level of developmental production. **Pay varies. Sometimes pays travel per diem for Playwrights Week.**
Needs: "We focus on the language of live theatre. Although we have no specific restrictions, we like to see creative use of language and theatrical innovation. Our taste is for simple staging and resonant, truthful language."
Tips: No television scripts or screenplays. "It is time to hear new voices for the theater. The focus should be on storytelling. We seek long-term developmental relationships with playwrights. Sometimes we choose a play because we are interested in the writer's voice as much as the work in question."

LILLENAS PUBLISHING CO., P.O. Box 419527, Kansas City MO 64141-6527. (816)931-1900. Fax: (816)412-8390. E-mail: drama@lillenas.com. Website: www.lillenas.com/drama. **Contact:** Kim Messer, product manager. Estab. 1926. "We publish on two levels: (1) Program Builders—seasonal and topical collections of recitations, sketches, dialogues and short plays; (2) Drama Resources which assume more than one format: (a) full-length scripts, (b) one-acts, shorter plays and sketches all by one author, (c) collection short plays and sketches by various authors. All program and play resources are produced with local church and Christian school in mind. Therefore there are taboos." Queries are encouraged, but synopsis and complete scripts are read. Responds in 3 months. "First rights are purchased for Program Builder scripts. For Drama Resources, we purchase all print rights." **Drama Resources are paid on a 10% royalty, whether full-length scripts, one-acts, or sketches. No advance.**
  ● This publisher is more interested in one-act and full-length scripts—both religious and secular. Monologues are of lesser interest than previously. There is more interest in Readers' Theatre.
Needs: 98% of Program Builder materials are freelance written. Scripts selected for these publications are outright purchases; verse is minimum of 25¢/line, prose (play scripts) are minimum of $5/double-spaced page. "Lillenas Drama Resources is a line of play scripts that are, for the most part, written by professionals with experience in productions as well as writing. However, while we do read unsolicited scripts, more than half of what we publish is written by experienced authors whom we have already published."
Tips: "All plays need to be presented in standard play script format. We welcome a summary statement of each play. Purpose statements are always desirable. Approximate playing time, cast and prop lists, etc. are important to include. We are interested in fully scripted traditional plays, reader's theater scripts, choral speaking pieces. Contemporary settings generally have it over Biblical settings. Christmas and Easter scripts must have a bit of a twist. Secular approaches to these seasons (Santas, Easter bunnies, and so on), are not considered. We sell our product in 10,000 Christian bookstores and by catalog. We are probably in the forefront as a publisher of religious drama resources." Request a copy of our newsletter and/or catalog."

N LIVE BAIT THEATER, 3914 N. Clark St., Chicago IL 60613. (773)871-1212. Fax: (773)871-3191. **Contact:** Sharon Evans, artistic director. Estab. 1987. **Produces 2-4 plays/year.** "Professional, non-Equity productions here at our space in Chicago, for sophisticated local audiences." Query with synopsis or submit complete script. Responds in 6 months. Buys first production rights and residuals. **Pays 3-6% royalty.** Include SASE for return of submitted materials.
Needs: "We produce only new works by local playwrights (Chicago area). We produce both original plays and adaptations of literature to the stage. We seek properties that put a heavy emphasis on the visual element, use rich and compelling language, and explore unconventional subject matter." Prefers plays with smaller casts, suitable for an intimate 50-70 seat space.

Ⓐ LONG WHARF THEATRE, 222 Sargent Dr., New Haven CT 06511. (203)787-4284. Fax: (203)776-2287. Website: www.longwharf.org. **Contact:** Stefan Lanfer, literary associate. Estab. 1965. **Produces 8 plays/year.** Professional regional theatre. Query with synopsis, sample dialogue (first 10 pages) and SASE. *Agented submissions only.* Responds in 1 month to queries.
Needs: Full-length plays, translations, adaptations. Special interest: Dramatic plays and comedies about human relationships, social concerns, ethical and moral dilemmas.

MAGIC THEATRE, INC., Bldg. D, Fort Mason, San Francisco CA 94123. (415)441-8001. Fax: (415)771-5505. E-mail: magicthtre@aol.com. Website: www.magictheatre.org. Artistic Director: Larry Eilenberg. **Contact:** Laura Hope Owen, literary manager and festival director. Estab. 1967. **Produces 6 mainstage plays/year, plus monthly reading series and several festivals each year which contain both staged readings and workshop productions.** Regional theater. Query with synopsis and dialogue sample (10 pages). Responds in 6 months. **Pays royalty or per performance fee.**
Needs: "Plays that are innovative in theme and/or craft, cutting-edge political concerns, intelligent comedy. Full-length only, strong commitment to multicultural work."
Tips: "Not interested in classics, conventional approaches and cannot produce large-cast plays. Send query to Laura Hope Owen, literary manager."

MANHATTAN THEATRE CLUB, 311 W. 43rd St., 8th Floor, New York NY 10036. (212)399-3000. Fax: (212)399-4329. E-mail: lit@mtc-nyc.org. Website: www.manhattantheatreclub.com. Director of Artistic Development: Clifford Lee Johnson III. **Contact:** Christian Parker, literary manager. **Produces 8 plays/year.** Two-theater performing arts complex classified as off-Broadway, using professional actors. Solicited and agent submissions only. No queries. Responds in 6 months.
Needs: "We present a wide range of new work, from this country and abroad, to a subscription audience. We want plays about contemporary concerns and people. All genres are welcome. Multiple set shows are discouraged. Average cast is eight. MTC also maintains an extensive play development program."

Ⓐ McCARTER THEATRE, 91 University Place, Princeton NJ 08540. Website: www.mccarter.org. **Contact:** Charles McNulty, literary manager. **Produces 5 plays/year; 1 second stage play/year.** Produces professional productions for a 1,077-seat theater. Query with synopsis; *agented submissions only.* Responds in 1 month; agent submissions 3 months. **Pays negotiable royalty.**
Needs: Full length plays, musicals, translations.

MERIWETHER PUBLISHING LTD., 885 Elkton Dr., Colorado Springs CO 80907-3557. Fax: (719)594-9916. E-mail: Merpcds@aol.com. Website: meriwetherPublishing.com. President: Mark Zapel. Editor: Arthur L. Zapel. **Contact:** Ted Zapel, associate editor. Estab. 1969. "Our Contemporary Drama Service division **publishes 60-70 plays/year."** **80% written by unpublished writers. Buys 40-60 scripts/year from unpublished/unproduced writers. 90% of scripts are unagented submissions.** "We publish how-to materials in book and video formats. We are interested in materials for middle school, high school and college level students only. Query with synopsis/outline, résumé of credits, sample of style and SASE. Catalog available for $2 postage. Responds in 1 month to queries; 2 months to full-length mss. **Offers 10% royalty or makes outright purchase.**
Needs: Musicals for a large cast of performers. 1-act or 2-act comedy plays with large casts. Book mss on theatrical arts subjects, especially books of short scenes for amateur and professional actors. "We are now looking for scenebooks with special themes: 'scenes for young women,' 'comedy scenes for two actors,' etc. These need not be original, provided the compiler can get letters of permission from the original copyright owner. We are interested in all textbook candidates for theater arts subjects. Christian children's activity book mss also accepted. We will consider elementary level religious materials and plays, but no elementary level children's secular plays."
Tips: "We publish a wide variety of speech contest materials for high-school students. We are publishing more full length play scripts and musicals based on classic literature or popular TV shows, provided the writer includes letter of clearance from the copyright owner. Our educational books are sold to teachers and students at college and high-school levels. Our religious books are sold to youth activity directors, pastors and choir directors. Another group of buyers is the professional theater, radio and TV category. We will be especially interested in full length (two- or three-act) plays with name recognition, either the playwright or the adaptation source."

METROSTAGE, 1201 N. Royal St., Alexandria VA 22314. (703)548-9044. Fax: (703)548-9089. Website: www.metrost age.org. **Contact:** Carolyn Griffin, producing artistic director. Estab. 1984. **Produces 4-5 plays/year.** Professional productions for 150-seat theatre, general audience. Query with synopsis, 10 page dialogue sample, play production history. Responds in 3 months. **Payment negotiable, sometimes royalty percentage, sometimes per performance.**

WRITERSMARKET.COM at http://www.WritersMarket.com features streamlined searches, personalized market information as well as new markets, daily updates and more.

Needs: Contemporary themes, small cast (up to 6 actors), unit set.
Tips: "Plays should have *already* had readings and workshops before being sent for our review. Do not send plays that have never had a staged reading."

MILL MOUNTAIN THEATRE, Market Square, Center in Square, Roanoke VA 24011-1437. (540)342-5749. Fax: (540)342-5745. E-mail: outreach@millmountain.org. Website: www.millmountain.org. Executive Director: Jere Lee Hodgin. **Contact:** Maryke Huyding, literary coordinator. **Produces 8 established plays, 10 new one-acts and 2 new full-length plays/year.** Mill Mountain Theatre, 400 seats, flexible proscenium stage; Theatre B, 125 seats, flexible stage. "Some of the professional productions will be on the main stage and some in our smaller Waldron stage." Accepts unsolicited one-acts only. Send query, synopsis and 10-page dialogue sample for all other submissions. Include cassette for musicals. Responds to queries in 6 weeks; responds to scripts in 8 months.
Needs: Full-length plays, one-acts, musicals, solo pieces. Interested in plays with racially mixed casts. Accepts submissions for 'Centerpieces' (monthly lunchtime staged readings of unpublished 25-35 minute one-acts by emerging playwrights). Cast limit of 15 for plays, 24 for musicals. Prefers unit set.
Tips: "Subject matter and character variations are open, but gratuitous language and acts are not acceptable unless they are artistically supported. A play based on large amounts of topical reference or humor has a very short life. Be sure you have written a play and not a film script." Mill Mountain Theatre sponsors an annual new play competition. See the Contests & Awards section for details.

MOVING ARTS, 514 South Spring St., Los Angeles CA 90013-2304. (213)622-8906. Fax: (213)622-8946. E-mail: treynichols@movingarts.org. Website: www.movingarts.org. Artistic Directors: Lee Wochner and Julie Briggs. **Contact:** Trey Nichols, literary director. Estab. 1992. **Produces 10 plays/year.** Professional productions produced under Actors Equity Association 99-Seat Plan. "Our audiences are eclectic, literate, diverse adults." Query with synopsis, 10-20 page dialogue sample, bio, cover letter. Responds in 9 months. Obtains 5% of future income for 5-year period. **Pays 6% of box office gross.** Include SASE for return of submissions.
Needs: Full-length and one-act plays. (One-act plays accepted *only* for our Premiere One-Act Competition. $10 entry fee, $200 1st prize. Submission period is November 1-February 28. Send SASE or e-mail for full guidelines.) "Original drama or comedy that is bold, challenging, and edgy; plays that speak to the human condition in a fresh and startling way. We are not limited to any particular style or genre; we are confined only by the inherent truth of the material." Cast limit of 8. Theatre is a 60-seat black box. Limited backstage space, no fly space, limited wing space. "No plays that are like sitcoms or showcases, or too 'well-made.' We don't do plays for children (although we welcome young audiences) and tend to stay away from period pieces, heavy dramas, and performance art. Los Angeles has a very exciting theatre scene today. The most exhilarating work is in the smaller theatres (Circle X, Evidence Room, Zoo District, Bottom's Dream, and Actors Gang, to name a few). The BCT (Big Cheap Theatre) ethic, its spirit and grace and sense of wonder, is the blood that pumps life into this recent shift in the American theatre aesthetic, and writers— *especially* writers—need to know what this is about."
Tips: "If you're a Southern California playwright, come see our play readings and shows. Party with us! Get to know us, our spirit and our work. If not, control the controllable. You can't control our reaction to your work, but you can keep your cover letter brief, polite and to the point. If you've been referred by a writer or director we've worked with, mention it. If you've seen prior productions, we appreciate it. When we read your work, we respond to the writing, but professionalism (or lack thereof) affects our evaluation in terms of potential artistic relationship, 3-hole punch script, 2-3 fasteners, SASE, clean copy, it all matters. Be patient with our process. Don't pester with follow-up queries. We love playwrights, so trust that your work will recieve as much time and attention as our limited but committed resources allow."

NEW AMERICAN THEATER, 118 N. Main St., Rockford IL 61101. (815)963-9454. Fax: (815)963-7215. Website: www.newamericantheater.com. **Contact:** Richard Raether, artistic director. Estab. 1972. The New American Theater is a professional equity theater company performing on two stages: A thrust stage with 280-seat house and a 90-seat second stage. Submit synopsis with SASE—send full scripts only when requested.
Needs: New works for "New Voices in the Heartland," an annual play festival of staged readings. The works may have been workshopped, but not previously produced. Event is in September. 2002 festival queries accepted until December 2001.
Tips: "We look for new work that addresses contemporary issues; we do not look for work of any one genre or production style."

NEW JERSEY REPERTORY COMPANY, Lumia Theatre, 179 Broadway, Long Branch NJ 07740. (732)229-3166. Fax: (732)229-3167. Estab. 1997. **Produces 6 plays/year.** Professional productions year round. Submit complete script. Responds in 1 year. Rights negotiable. **Makes outright purchase.**
Needs: Prefers small cast and unit or simple set.

NEW PLAYS INCORPORATED, P.O. Box 5074, Charlottesville VA 22905. (804)979-2777. Fax: (804)984-2230. E-mail: patwhitton@aol.com. Website: www.newplaysforchildren.com. **Contact:** Patricia Whitton Forrest, publisher. Estab. 1964. **Publishes 3-6 plays/year.** Publishes for children's or youth theaters. Submit complete script. Responds in 2 months. Buys all semi-professional and amateur rights in U.S. and Canada. **Pays 50% royalty on productions, 10% on sale of books.**

Needs: "I have eclectic taste—plays must have quality and originality in whatever genres, topics, styles or lengths the playwright chooses."

Tips: "No adaptations of stuff that has already been adapted a million times, e.g., *Tom Sawyer, A Christmas Carol*, or plays that sound like they've been written by the guidance counselor. There will be more interest in youth theater productions with moderate to large casts (15 people). Plays must have been produced, directed by someone other than the author or author's spouse. People keep sending us material suitable for adults—this is not our market. Read our online catalog."

NEW REPERTORY THEATRE, P.O. Box 610418, Newton Highlands MA 02161-0418. (617)332-7058. Fax: (617)527-5217. E-mail: ricknewrep@aol.com. Website: www.newrep.org. **Contact:** Rick Lombardo, producing artistic director. Estab. 1984. **Produces 5 plays/year.** Professional theater, general audience. Query with synopsis and dialogue sample. Buys production and subsidiary rights. **Pays 5-10% royalty.**

Needs: Idea laden, all styles, full-length only. Small cast, unit set.

Tips: No sit-coms like comedies. Incorporating and exploring styles other than naturalism.

N. NEW THEATRE, 4120 Laguna St., Coral Gables FL 33155. (305)443-5373. Fax: (305)443-1642. E-mail: admin@new-theatre.com. Website: www.new-theatre.com. **Contact:** Rafael De Acha, artistic director. Estab. 1986. **Produces 7 plays/year.** Professional productions. Query and synopsis. Responds in 2 months. Rights subject to negotiation. **Pay negotiable.**

Needs: Full-length. Interested in non-realistic, language plays. No musicals; no large casts.

Tips: "No kitchen sink realism. Send a simple query with synopsis. Be mindful of social issues."

NEW TUNERS THEATRE, 1225 W. Belmont Ave., Chicago IL 60657. (773)929-7367 ext. 22. Fax: (773)327-1404. E-mail: tbtuners@aol.com. Website: adamczyk.com/newtuners. **Contact:** John Sparks, artistic director. **Produces mostly readings of new works, 4 skeletal productions**, and the "Stages Festival of New Works" each year in July. "Mostly developed in our New Tuners workshop. Some scripts produced are unagented submissions. Plays performed in 3 small off-Loop theaters are seating 148 for a general theater audience, urban/suburban mix." Submit synopsis, sample scene, CD or cassette tape and piano/vocal score of three songs, and author bios. Responds in 3 months.

Needs: Musicals *only*. "We're interested in all forms of musical theater including more innovative styles. Our production capabilities are limited by the lack of space, but we're very creative and authors should submit anyway. The smaller the cast, the better. We are especially interested in scripts using a younger (35 and under) ensemble of actors. We mostly look for authors who are interested in developing their scripts through workshops, readings and production." No casts over 12. No one-man shows or 'single author' pieces."

Tips: "We would like to see the musical theater articulating something about the world around us, as well as diverting an audience's attention from that world." Offers Script Consultancy—a new program designed to assist authors and composers in developing new musicals through private feedback sessions with professional dramaturgs and musical directors. For further info contact (773)929-7367, ext. 22.

N. NEW YORK STATE THEATRE INSTITUTE, 37 First St., Troy NY 12180. (518)274-3485. Fax: (518)274-3815. E-mail: nysti@capital.net. Website: www.nysti.org. **Contact:** Ed. Lange, associate artistic director. **Produces 5 plays/year.** Professional regional productions for adult and family audiences. Query with synopsis. Responds in 1 month. **Pay varies.**

Needs: "We are not interested in material for 'mature' audiences. Submissions must be scripts of substance and intelligence geared to family audiences."

Tips: Do not submit complete script unless invited after review of synopsis.

N. NEW YORK THEATRE WORKSHOP, 83 E. Fourth St., New York NY 10003. Fax: (212)460-8996. Artistic Director: James C. Nicola. **Contact:** Kate Spencer, literary manager. Estab. 1979. **Produces 4-6 full productions and approximately 50 readings/year.** Plays are performed off-Broadway, Equity off-Broadway contract. Audience is New York theater-going audience and theater professionals. Query with synopsis, 10-page sample scene and tape/CD/video (if appropriate). Responds in 5 months. Buys option to produce commercially; percentage of box office gross from commercial and percentage of author's net subsidiary rights within specified time limit from our original production. **Pays fee because of limited run, with additional royalty payments for extensions; $1,500-2,000 fee range.**

• The New York Theatre Workshop offers Van Lier Playwriting Fellowships for emerging writers of color based in New York City. Address inquiries to Chiori Miyagawa, artistic associate.

Needs: Full-length plays, one-acts, translations/adaptions, musical theater pieces; proposals for performance projects. Socially relevant issues, innovative form and language. Plays utilizing more than 8 actors usually require outside funding.

Tips: "No overtly commercial and conventional musicals or plays."

NORTH SHORE MUSIC THEATRE, 62 Dunham Rd., Beverly MA 01915. (978)232-7203. Fax: (978)921-0793. E-mail: jlarock@nsmt.org. Website: www.nsmt.org. **Contact:** John La Rock, associate producer. Estab. 1955. **Produces 8 plays/year.** Plays are performed at Arena theater for 22,000 subscribers. Submit letter of interest, synopsis, production details, SASE. Responds in 4 months. Rights negotiable. **Pay negotiable.**

Needs: Musicals only (adult and children's), with cast size under 15.

Tips: No straight plays, opera.

NORTHLIGHT THEATRE, 9501 Skokie Blvd., Skokie IL 60077. (847)679-9501. Fax: (847)679-1879. Website: www.northlight.org. **Contact:** Gavin Witt, literary manager. Estab. 1975. **Produces 5 plays/year.** "We are a professional, Equity theater, LORT D. We have a subscription base of over 8,000, and have a significant number of single ticket buyers." Query with synopsis. No unsolicited manuscripts accepted. Responds in 3 months. Buys production rights plus royalty on future mountings. **Pays royalty.**
Needs: "Full-length plays, translations, adaptations, musicals. Interested in plays of 'ideas'; plays that are passionate and/or hilarious; plays of occasional intelligence and complexity. Generally looking for cast size of 6 or fewer, but there are exceptions made for the right play."
Tips: "Please, do not try to do what television and film do better; preferably, avoid sending domestic realism."

THE O'NEILL PLAYWRIGHTS CONFERENCE, (formerly The National Playwrights Conference/New Drama for Media Project at the Eugene O'Neill Theater Center), 534 W. 42 St., New York NY 10036. (212)244-7008. Fax: (212)967-2957. Artistic Director: James Houghton. **Contact:** Beth Whitaker, artistic associate. Estab. 1965. **Produces 12-15 plays/year.** The O'Neill Center theater is located in Waterford, Connecticut, and operates under an Equity LORT contract. There are three theaters: Barn—250 seats, Ampitheater—300 seats, Edith Oliver Theater—150 seats. Please send #10 SASE for guidelines in the fall. *Do not send full scripts.* Decision by late April. We accept submissions September 15-November 1 of each year. Conference takes place during June/July each summer. Playwrights selected are in residence for one month and receive a four-day workshop and two script-in-hand readings with professional actors and directors. **Pays stipend plus room, board and transportation.**

N: OLDCASTLE THEATRE COMPANY, Box 1555, Bennington VT 05201-1555. (802)447-0564. Fax: (802)442-3704. **Contact:** Eric Peterson, artistic director. **Produces 6 plays/year.** A not-for-profit theater company. Plays are performed in the new Bennington Center for the Arts, by a professional Equity theater company (in a May-October season) for general audiences, including residents of a three-state area and tourists during the vacation season. Submit complete script. Responds in 6 months. **Pay negotiable**
Needs: Produces classics, musicals, comedy, drama, most frequently American works. Usual performance time is 2 hours.

OMAHA THEATER COMPANY FOR YOUNG PEOPLE, 2001 Farnam St., Omaha NE 68102. (402)345-4852. **Contact:** James Larson, artistic director. **Produces 6 plays/year.** "Our target audience is children, preschool-high school and their parents." Query with synopsis. Responds in 9 months. **Pays royalty.**
Needs: "Plays must be geared to children and parents (PG rating). Titles recognized by the general public have a stronger chance of being produced." Cast limit: 25 (8-10 adults). No adult scripts.
Tips: "Unproduced plays may be accepted only after a letter of inquiry (familiar titles only!)."

THE OPEN EYE THEATER, P.O. Box 959, Margaretville NY 12455. (845)586-1660. Fax: (845)586-1660. E-mail: openeye@catskill.net. Website: www.theopeneye.org. **Contact:** Amie Brockway, producing artistic director. The Open Eye is a not-for-profit professional theater company working in New York City since 1972, in the rural villages of Delaware County, NY since 1991, and on tour. The theater specializes in the development of new plays for multi-generational audiences (children ages 8 and up, and adults of all ages). Ensemble plays with music and dance, culturally diverse and historical material, myth, folklore, and stories with universal themes are of interest. Program includes readings, developmental workshops, and fully staged productions.
Tips: Send one-page letter with one-paragraph plot synopsis, cast breakdown and setting, résumé and SAE. "We will provide the stamp and contact you *if we want to see the script.*"

OREGON SHAKESPEARE FESTIVAL, P.O. Box 158, Ashland OR 97520. (541)482-2111. Fax: (541)482-0446. Website: www.osfashland.org. **Contact:** Stephany Smith-Pearson, literary assistant. Estab. 1935. **Produces 11 plays/year.** The Angus Bowmer Theater has a thrust stage and seats 600. The Black Swan is an experimental space and seats 140. The Elizabethan Outdoor Theatre seats 1,200 (stages almost exclusively Shakespearean productions there, mid-June-September). Professional recommendation only. Responds in 6 months. Negotiates individually for rights with the playwright's agent. **Pays royalty.**
Needs: "A broad range of classic and contemporary scripts. One or two fairly new scripts/season. Also a play readings series which focuses on new work. Plays must fit into our ten-month rotating repertory season. Black Swan shows usually limited to seven actors." Small musicals OK. Submissions from women and minority writers are strongly encouraged. No one-acts.
Tips: "We're always looking for a good comedy which has scope. We tend to prefer plays with a literary quality. We want plays to explore the human condition with language, metaphor and theatricality. We encourage translations of foreign plays as well as adaptations of non-dramatic material."

PEGASUS THEATRE, 3916 Main St., Dallas TX 75226-1228. (214)821-6005. Fax: (214)826-1671. E-mail: comedy@pegasustheatre.org. Website: www.pegasustheatre.com. **Contact:** Steve Erwin, new plays manager. Estab. 1985. **Produces 3 plays/year.** Produces plays under an Umbrella Agreement with AEA. "Our productions are presented for the general public to attend." Query with synopsis, 10 sample pages. Responds in 6 months. **Pays 5-8% royalty.**
Needs: New and original comedies with a satiric slant. Limit cast size to under 10, single set.

Tips: "No murder-mysteries, please. We'd rather not look at one-acts that don't have companion pieces or at plays that read and play like extended-length sitcoms. Neatness and proper formatting always make a better impression—even with the best of scripts."

N A PHILADELPHIA THEATRE COMPANY, 230 S. 15th St., 4th Floor, Philadelphia PA 19102. (215)985-1400. Fax: (215)985-5800. Website: www.phillytheatreco.com. **Contact:** Michele Volansky, dramaturg. Estab. 1974. **Produces 4 plays/year.** Agented submissions only.
Needs: Philadelphia Theatre Company produces contemporary American plays. No musicals or children's plays.
Tips: "Our work is challenging and risky—look to our history for guidance."

PIONEER DRAMA SERVICE, INC., P.O. Box 4267, Englewood CO 80155-4267. (303)779-4035. Fax: (303)779-4315. E-mail: playwrights@pioneerdrama.com. Website: www.pioneerdrama.com. Publisher: Steven Fendrich. **Contact:** Beth Somers, submissions editor. Estab. 1963. **Publishes 30 plays/year.** Plays are performed by schools, colleges, community theaters, recreation programs, churches and professional children's theaters for audiences of all ages. Query preferred. Responds in 2 weeks. Retains all rights. Buys All rights. **Pays royalty.**
• All submissions automatically entered in Shubert Fendrich Memorial Playwriting Contest.
Needs: "Musicals, comedies, mysteries, dramas, melodramas and children's theater. Two-acts up to 90 minutes; children's theater, 1 hour. Prefers many female roles, simple sets. Plays need to be appropriate for amateur groups." Prefers secular plays.
Tips: Interested in adaptations of classics of public domain works appropriate for children and teens. Also plays that deal with social issues for teens and preteens. "Check out the website to see what we carry and if your material would be appropriate. Make sure to include query letter, proof of productions and an SASE."

N PITTSBURGH PUBLIC THEATER, 621 Penn Ave., Pittsburgh PA 15222. (412)316-8200. Artistic Director: Ted Pappas. **Contact:** Becky Rickard. Estab. 1975. **Produces 7 plays/year.** O'Reilly Theater, 650 seats, thrust seating. Query with synopsis or agented submissions between February and April. Responds in 4 months.
Needs: Full-length plays, adaptations and musicals.

□ PLAYERS PRESS, INC., P.O. Box 1132, Studio City CA 91614-0132. **Contact:** Robert W. Gordon, editorial vice president. **Publishes 20-30 plays/year.** "We deal in all entertainment areas and handle publishable works for film and television as well as theater. Performing arts books, plays and musicals. All plays must be in stage format for publication." Also produces scripts for video and material for cable television. Query with #10 SASE, reviews and proof of production. Responds in 1 month. Buys negotiable rights. "We prefer all rights." **Pays 10-75% royalty. Makes outright purchase of $100-25,000. Pays $5,000 per performance. Pays per performance royalties.**
Needs: "We prefer comedies, musicals and children's theater, but are open to all genres. We will rework the script after acceptance. We are interested in the quality, not the format. Performing Arts Books that deal with theater how-to are of strong interest."
Tips: "Send only material requested. Do not telephone."

N PLAYSCRIPTS.COM, P.O. Box 380996, Cambridge MA 02238-0996. E-mail: info@playscripts.com. Website: www.playscripts.com. **Contact:** Douglas Rand, editor. Estab. 1999. Audience is professional, community, college, high school and children's theaters worldwide. Send complete ms, preferably via e-mail; see website for guidelines. Responds in 8 months. Buys exclusive publication and performance licensing rights. **Pays negotiated book and production royalties.**
Needs: "Playscripts.com publishes one-act and full-length plays for professional, community, college, high school and children's theaters. We are open to a wide diversity of writing styles and content."
Tips: "Playscripts.com is a play publishing company that emphasizes secure and innovative use of the Internet. We provide all of the same licensing and book production services as a traditional play publisher, along with unique online features that maximize the exposure of each dramatic work."

PLAYWRIGHTS HORIZONS, 416 W. 42nd St., New York NY 10036. (212)564-1235. Fax: (212)594-0296. Website: www.playwrightshorizons.org. Artistic Director: Tim Sanford. **Contact:** Sonya Sobieski, literary manager (plays); send musicals Attn: Musical Theatre Program. Estab. 1971. **Produces 6 plays/year.** Plays performed off-Broadway for a literate, urban, subscription audience. Submit complete ms with author bio; include tape for musicals. Responds in 6 months. Negotiates for future rights. **Pays royalty. Makes outright purchase.**
Needs: "We are looking for new, full-length plays and musicals by American authors."
Tips: "No adaptations, children's theater, biographical or historical plays. We look for plays with a strong sense of language and a clear dramatic action that truly use the resources of the theater."

PLAYWRIGHTS THEATRE OF NEW JERSEY, 33 Green Village Rd., Madison NJ 07940. (973)514-1787. Fax: (973)514-2060. E-mail: playNJ@aol.com. Website: www.PTNJ.org. Artistic Director: John Pietrowski. **Contact:** Peter Hays, literary manager. Estab. 1986. **Produces 3 plays/year.** "We operate under a Small Professional Theatre Contract (SPT), a development theatre contract with Actors Equity Association. Readings are held under a staged reading code." Submit synopsis, first 10 pages, short bio, and production history with SASE. Responds in 1 year. "For productions we ask the playwright to sign an agreement that gives us exclusive rights to the play for the production period and for 30 days following. After the 30 days we give the rights back with no strings attached, except for commercial productions. We ask that our developmental work be acknowledged in any other professional productions." **Makes outright purchase of $750.**

● Scripts are accepted September 1 through April 30 only. Write for guidelines before submitting.
Needs: Any style or length; full length, one acts, musicals.
Tips: "We are looking for American plays in the early stages of development—plays of substance, passion, and light (comedies and dramas) that raise challenging questions about ourselves and our communities. We prefer plays *that can work only on the stage* in the most theatrical way possible—plays that are not necessarily 'straight-on' realistic, but rather ones that use imagery, metaphor, poetry and musicality in new and interesting ways. Plays go through a three-step development process: A roundtable (inhouse reading), a public concert reading and then a workshop production."

N: PLAYWRIGHTS' PLATFORM, 164 Brayton Rd., Boston MA 02135. (617)630-9704. **Contact:** George Sauer, producing director. Estab. 1974. **Produces 50-80 readings/year.** Plays are read in staged readings at Massachusetts College of Art (Boston). Query with synopsis. Responds in 2 months. Include SASE for return of submission.
Needs: Any types of plays. No racist or sexist material.

A: PLOWSHARES THEATRE CO., 2870 E. Grand Blvd., Suite 600, Detroit MI 48202-3146. (313)872-0279. Fax: (313)872-0067. **Contact:** Gary Anderson, producing artistic director. Estab. 1989. **Produces 5 plays/year.** Professional productions intended for African-American audience and those who appreciate African-American culture. Query with synopsis; agented submissions only. Responds in 8 months.

POLARIS NORTH, c/o Martella, 1265 Broadway #803, New York NY 10001. (212)684-1985. **Contact:** Diane Martella, treasurer. Estab. 1974. **Produces 15-20 plays/year.** "We have a studio workshop with professional actors and directors and mixed general-theater and professional audiences." Submit complete manuscript. Must include #10 SASE for response or ms SASE for script return. Responds in 2 months.
● "Workshops are to assist writers—no charge to audience. **No payment.**"
Needs: "We workshop one-act plays only. (Less than 30 minutes, not previously produced or workshopped. No musicals; no monologues; no situational skits; good writing and characters more important than genre or topic)."
Tips: No sexually oriented plays, no stage nudity. "The mission of our One Acts in Performance Project is to encourage and develop new playwrights by giving them an opportunity to see their work done (and be involved in the creative process) and to get audience feedback on their work."

PORTLAND STAGE COMPANY, P.O. Box 1458, Portland ME 04104. (207)774-1043. Fax: (207)774-0576. E-mail: portstage@aol.com. Artistic Director: Anita Stewart. **Contact:** Lisa DiFranza, literary manager. Estab. 1973. **Produces 7 plays/year.** Professional productions at the Portland Performing Arts Center. Send first 10 pages with synopsis. Responds in 3 months. Buys 3- or 4-week run in Maine. **Pays royalty.**
Needs: Developmental Staged Readings: Little Festival of the Unexpected.
Tips: "Work developed in Little Festival generally will be more strongly considered for future production."

PRIMARY STAGES COMPANY, INC., 131 W. 45 St., 2nd fl., New York NY 10036. (212)840-9705. Fax: (212)840-9725. **Contact:** Tyler Marchant, associate artistic director. Estab. 1983. **Produces 4 plays/year.** All plays are produced professionally off-Broadway at Primary Stages Theatre, 99 seat proscenium stage; Phil Bosakowski Theatre, 65 seat proscenium stage. Agented submissions or synopsis, 10 sample pages, résumé, SASE; cassette or CD for musicals. Responds in 6 months. **Pays flat fee.** Guidelines for SASE.
Needs: Full-length plays, small cast (6 or fewer) musicals. New York City or American Premiers only, written by American playwrights. Small cast (2-8), unit set or simple changes, no fly or wing space.
Tips: Best submission time: September-June. Chances: Over 2,000 scripts read, 4-5 produced. Women and minorities encouraged to submit. Submission policy on website.

N: PRINCE MUSIC THEATER, (formerly American Music Theatre Festival), 100 S. Broad St., Suite 650, Philadelphia PA 19110. (215)972-1000. Fax: (215)972-1020. Website: www.princemusictheater.org. **Contact:** Ben Levit, artistic director. Estab. 1983. **Produces 4 plays/year.** Professional musical productions. Send synopsis and sample audio tape with no more than 4 songs. Responds in 6 months. **Pays royalty.**
Needs: Song-driven music theater/opera pieces, varied musical styles. Nine in orchestra, 10-14 cast, 36×60 stage.
Tips: Innovative topics and use of media, music, technology a plus. Sees trends of arts in technology (interactive theater, virtual reality, sound design); works are shorter in length (1-1½ hours with no intermissions or two hours with intermission).

N: PUERTO RICAN TRAVELING THEATRE, 141 W. 94th St., New York NY 10036. (212)354-1293. Fax: (212)307-6769. **Contact:** Miriam Colon Valle, founder/artistic director. Estab. 1967. **Produces 3 plays/year.** Two plays performed in our theater, one during the summer in the streets, parks, playgrounds. Professional Theatre, Actors Equity LOA contract. Query with synopsis. Retain some subsidiary rights. Fee negotiable, but we are a small theater. **Pay negotiable.**
Needs: Primarily plays by Latinos or Spaniards. Prefer strong story lines. Limit 8 characters. No fly space, little wing space. The stage is 19×21. No sitcoms or revues.

Tips: "Make certain the play is for the stage, not for TV or films. That means larger than life characters, heightened language."

ℕ ROUND HOUSE THEATRE, 12210 Bushey Dr. #101, Silver Spring MD 20902. (301)933-9530. Fax: (301)933-2321. Artistic Director: Jerry Whiddon. **Contact:** Danisha Crosby, production manager. **Produces 5-7 pays/year.** Also produces New Voices, a play reading series of *local* playwrights (8/year). Professional AEA Theatre. Query with synopsis; send complete scripts for New Voices. Responds in 6 months. **Pays negotiated percentage for productions; no payment for New Voices readings.** Include SASE for return of submission.
Needs: Full-length, multiple genres and styles. Limited to casts of 12 and under.

SALTWORKS THEATRE COMPANY, 2553 Brandt School Rd., Wexford PA 15090-7931. (724)934-2820. Fax: (724)934-2815. Website: www.saltworks.org. **Contact:** Scott Kirk, artistic director. Estab. 1981. **Produces 8-10 plays/year.** Educational tour: 200+ performances in PA, OH, WV, MD, NJ; mainstage; local amateur productions. Query with synopsis. Responds in 2 months. Obtains regional performance rights for educational grants. **Pays $25 per performance.**
Needs: Social issues addressing violence prevention, sexual responsibility, peer pressures, tobacco use, bullying, racial issues/diversity, drug and alcohol abuse (grades 1-12). Limited to 5 member cast, 2 men/3 women.

ℕ SHAW FESTIVAL THEATRE, P.O. Box 774, Niagara-on-the-Lake, Ontario L0S 1J0, Canada. (905)468-2153. Fax: (905)468-5438. Website: shawfest.sympatico.ca. **Contact:** Christopher Newton, artistic director. Estab. 1962. **Produces 10 plays/year.** "Professional summer festival operating three theaters (Festival: 861 seats; Court House: 324 seats; Royal George: 328 seats). We also host some music and some winter rentals. Shaw Festival presents the work of George Bernard Shaw and his contemporaries written during his lifetime (1856-1950) and in 2000 we expanded the mandate to include works written about the period of his lifetime." Query with SASE or SAE and IRC's, depending on country of origin. We prefer to hold rights for Canada and northestern US, also potential to tour. **Pays 5-10% royalty.**
Needs: "We operate an acting ensemble of up to 75 actors; this includes 14 actors/singers and we have sophisticated production facilities. During the summer season (April-October) the Academy of the Shaw Festival sometimes organizes workshops of new plays."
Tips: "We are a large acting company specializing in plays written between 1856-1950 (during Shaw's lifetime) and in plays about that period."

SOUTH COAST REPERTORY, P.O. Box 2197, Costa Mesa CA 92628-1197. (714)708-5500. Fax: (714)545-0391. Website: www.scr.org. Dramaturg: Jerry Patch. **Contact:** Jennifer Kiger, literary manager. Estab. 1964. **Produces 11 plays/year.** Professional nonprofit theater; a member of LORT and TCG. "We operate in our own facility which houses 507-seat mainstage theater and 161-seat second stage theater. We have a combined subscription audience of 21,000." Query with synopsis and 10 sample pages of dialogue. Scripts considered with agent. Responds in 4 months. Acquires negotiable rights. **Pays royalty.**
Needs: "We produce full lengths. We prefer plays that address contemporary concerns and are dramaturgically innovative. A play whose cast is larger than 15-20 will need to be extremely compelling, and its cast size must be justifiable."
Tips: "We don't look for a writer to write for us—he or she should write for him or herself. We look for honesty and a fresh voice. We're not likely to be interested in writers who are mindful of *any* trends. Originality and craftsmanship are the most important qualities we look for."

SOUTH COAST REPERTORY'S HISPANIC PLAYWRIGHT'S PROJECT, P.O. Box 2197, Costa Mesa CA 92628-2797. (714)708-5500, ext. 5405. Fax: (714)545-0391. E-mail: juliette@scr.org. Website: www.scr.org. **Contact:** Juliette Carrillo, director of HPP. Estab. 1985. **Produces 3 workshops/readings/year.** "The Hispanic Playwrights Project is a workshop for the development of new plays by Latina/Latino writers. While focusing on the developmental process, the Project also serves to increase the visibility of work by emerging and established Hispanic-American playwrights and to encourage production of that work in the nation's resident theatres. In the past 15 years, more than half of the plays developed have gone on to productions at theatres across the U.S. Playwrights chosen for HPP will be brought to Costa Mesa to participate in a workshop with a director, dramaturg, and cast of professional actors. Together, they will work on the script, preparing it for a presentation before a public audience." Submit complete script with a synopsis and biography by January 15, 2002. Early submissions are highly encouraged. Include SASE if script is to be returned. Responds in 2 months. Holds rights to do production for 30 days after reading. **Pays per diem, travel and lodging for workshop.**
Needs: Writers must be of Latino heritage. No plays entirely in Spanish (must be mostly English). No musicals or solo pieces. New and unproduced plays are preferred, but previously produced plays that would benefit from further development may also be considered. Selected playwrights will be notified by April 1, 2002.

STAGE ONE: The Louisville Children's Theatre, 501 W. Main St., Louisville KY 40202-3300. (502)589-5946. Fax: (502)588-5910. E-mail: stageone@kca.org. Website: www.stageone.org. **Contact:** Moses Goldberg, producing director. Estab. 1946. **Produces 6-7 plays/year.** Plays performed by an Equity company for young audiences ages 4-18; usually does different plays for different age groups within that range. Submit complete script. Responds in 4 months. **Pays negotiable royalty.**

Needs: "Good plays for young audiences of all types: Adventure, fantasy, realism, serious problem plays about growing up or family entertainment. Ideally, cast at twelve or less. Honesty, visual potentiality, worthwhile story and characters are necessary. An awareness of children and their schooling is a plus. No campy material or anything condescending to children. Musicals accepted if they are fairly limited in orchestration."

STAGES REPERTORY THEATRE, 3201 Allen Parkway, Houston TX 77091. (713)527-0220. Fax: (713)527-8669. Website: www.stagestheatre.com. **Contact:** Rob Bundy, artistic director. Estab. 1975. **Produces 12-14 plays/year.** Query with synopsis. Responds in 8 months. **Pays 3-10% royalty.** Enclose SASE.
Needs: Full-length, theatrical, non-realistic work. 6-8 characters maximum. "Unit set with multiple locations is preferable." No "kitchen sink" dramas. Plays also accepted October 1-February 14 for submission into the Southwest Festival of New Plays, held every June. Categories include Women's Playwrights' Division, Texas Playwrights' Division, Children's Theatre Playwrights' Division and Latino Playwrights' Division. More information can be found on website.

N A STAMFORD THEATRE WORKS, 95 Atlantic St., Stamford CT 06901. (203)359-4414. Fax: (203)356-1846. E-mail: STWCT@aol.com. Website: www.stamfordtheatreworks.org. **Contact:** Steve Karp, producing director. Estab. 1988. **Produces 4-6 plays/year.** Professional productions for an adult audience. Agented submissions or queries with a professional recommendation. Responds in 3 months. **Pays 5-8% royalty.** Include SASE for return of submission.
Needs: Plays of social relevance; contemporary work. Limited to unit sets; maximum cast of about 8.

STATE THEATER COMPANY, 719 Congress Ave., Austin TX 78701. (512)472-5143. Fax: (512)472-7199. E-mail: admin@statetheatercompany.com. **Contact:** John Walch, artistic associate. Estab. 1982. **Produces 6 plays/year.** "Strong commitment to and a history of producing new work." Responds in late summer. **Pays royalty.**
Needs: Full length, translations, adaptations.
Tips: Also sponsors annual new play awards. Submit first 15 pages of plays, brief synopsis, and résumé.

A STEPPENWOLF THEATRE COMPANY, 758 W. North Ave., Chicago IL 60610. (312)335-1888. Fax: (312)335-0808. Website: www.steppenwolf.org. Artistic Director: Martha Lavey. **Contact:** Edward Sobel, literary manager. Estab. 1976. **Produces 9 plays/year.** 500 and 300 seat subscriber audience. Many plays produced at Steppenwolf have gone to Broadway. "We currently have 20,000 savvy subscribers." Query with synopsis, 10 pages sample dialogue and a short résumé or bio; agented submissions only. Responds in 6 months. Buys commercial, film and television in addition to production rights. **Pays 6-8% royalty.**
Needs: "Actor-driven works are crucial to us, plays that explore the human condition in our time. We max at around ten characters."
Tips: No musicals or romantic/light comedies. Plays get produced at STC based on ensemble member interest.

N A STUDIO ARENA THEATRE, 710 Main St., Buffalo NY 14202. (716)856-8025. Website: www.studioarena.org. **Contact:** Mark Hogan, assistant to the artistic director. Estab. 1965. **Produces 6-8 plays/year.** Professional productions. *Agented submissions only.*
Needs: Full-length plays. No fly space.
Tips: "Do not fax or send submissions via the Internet. Submissions should appeal to a diverse audience. We do not generally produce musicals."

TADA!, 120 W. 28th St., New York NY 10001. (212)627-1732. Fax: (212)243-6736. E-mail: tada@tadatheater.com. Website: www.tadatheater.com. **Contact:** Janine Nina Trevens, artistic director. Estab. 1984. **Produces 2-4 plays/year.** "TADA! produces original musicals and plays performed by children at our 95-seat theater. Productions are for family audiences." Submit complete script and tape, if musical. Responds in 6 months. **Pays 5% royalty. Commission fee.**
 • TADA! also sponsors a one-act play competition for their Spring Staged Reading Series. Works must be original, unproduced and unpublished one-acts. Plays may be geared toward teen audiences. Call for deadlines.
Needs: "Generally pieces run from 45-70 minutes. Must be enjoyed by children and adults and performed by a cast of children ages 8-17."
Tips: "No redone fairy tales or pieces where children are expected to play adults. Be careful not to condescend when writing for children's theater."

THE TEN-MINUTE MUSICALS PROJECT, P.O. Box 461194, West Hollywood CA 90046. (323)651-4899. **Contact:** Michael Koppy, producer. Estab. 1987. **Produces 1-10 plays/year.** "Plays performed in Equity regional theaters in the US and Canada." Deadline August 31; notification by December 15. Submit complete script, lead sheets and cassette. Buys performance rights. **Pays $250 royalty advance upon selection, against equal share of performance royalties when produced.**
Needs: Looking for complete short stage musicals playing between 7-14 minutes. Limit cast to 10 (5 women, 5 men).

TENNESSEE STAGE COMPANY AND ACTOR'S CO-OP, P.O. Box 1186, Knoxville TN 37901. (865)546-4280. **Contact:** Tom Parkhill, artistic director. Estab. 1989 Tennessee Stage Company; 1997 Actor's Co-op. **Produces 13 plays/year.** "Venue is a 100 seat black box theater. They are professional productions (non-Equity) for a general audience in the Knoxville area." Submit complete script. Responds in 3 months. **Pays small royalty.**

Needs: The Tennessee Stage Company runs toward comedy, and prefers a play with a subtle approach and feel if there is a message intended. The Actor's Co-op is a broader based company producing mainstream work, off-beat material and experimental work. Any material will be considered. "Generally our productions run toward a simple staging. While heavily technical plays will be considered a more simple piece will have a stronger chance of getting an opportunity here."
Tips: "Write a good light comedy with a smallish cast and a simple setting."

[N] THEATER AT LIME KILN, 14 S. Randolph St., Lexington VA 24450. (540)463-7088. Fax: (540)463-1082. **Contact:** John Healey, artistic director. Estab. 1984. **Produces 3 (1 new) plays/year.** Outdoor summer theater. Query with synopsis. Responds in 3 months. Buys performance rights. **Pays $25-75 per performance.**
Needs: Plays that explore the history and heritage of the Appalachian region. Minimum set required.

THEATER BY THE BLIND, 306 W. 18th St., New York NY 10011. (212)243-4337. Fax: (212)243-4337. E-mail: ashiotis@panix.com. Website: www.tbtb.org. **Contact:** Ike Schambelan, artistic director. Estab. 1979. **Produces 2 plays/year.** "Off-off Broadway, Theater Row, general audiences, seniors, students, disabled. If play transfers, we'd like a piece." Submit complete script. Responds in 3 months. **Pays $250-500 per production.**
Needs: Genres about blindness.

THE THEATER OF NECESSITY, 11702 Webercrest, Houston TX 77048. (713)733-6042. Estab. 1981. **Produces 8 plays/year.** "We usually keep script on file unless we are certain we will never use it." Plays are produced in a small professional theater. Submit complete script. Responds in 2 years. Buys performance rights. **Pays standard royalties (average $500/run).**
Needs: "Any play in a recognizable genre must be superlative in form and intensity. Experimental plays are given an easier read. We move to larger venue if the play warrants the expense."

[N] THEATER OF THE FIRST AMENDMENT, George Mason University, MS 3E6, Fairfax VA 22030. **Contact:** Kristin Johnsen-Neshati, dramaturg. Estab. 1990. **Produces 3 plays/year.** Professional productions performed in an Equity LOA 150-seat theater. Query and synopsis. Responds in 3 months. **Pays combination of percentage of box office gross against a guaranteed minimum royalty.**

[N] THEATRE & COMPANY, 27 King St. W, P.O. Box 876, Kitchener, Ontario N2G 4C5, Canada. (519)571-7080. Fax: (519)571-9051. Website: www.theatreandcompany.org. Artistic Director: Stuart Scadron-Wattles. **Contact:** Henry Bakker, literary manager. Estab. 1988. **Produces 6 plays/year.** Professional (non-equity) productions for a general audience. Query with synopsis, 10 pages of sample dialogue and SAE with IRCs. Responds in 1 year. **Pays $50-100 per performance.**
  ● Theatre & Company is particularly interested in work by Canadians.
Needs: Full-length; comedy or drama. Looking for small cast (less than 8) ensemble comedies. "Our emphasis is on regional writers familiar with our work. There is no 'best bet.' We want good stage writing that hits hard on a number of levels: Heart, head, gut and funnybone." No cast above 10; prefers unit staging.
Tips: Looks for "innovative writing for an audience which loves the theater. Avoid current trends toward shorter scenes. Playwrights should be aware that they are writing for the stage, not television."

THEATRE THREE, P.O. Box 512, 412 Main St., Port Jefferson NY 11777-0512. (631)928-9202. Fax: (631)928-9120. Website: www.theatrethree.org. **Contact:** Jeffrey Sanzel, artistic director. Estab. 1969. **"We produce an Annual Festival of One-Act Plays on our Second Stage."** Deadline for submission is September 30. Send SASE for festival guidelines. Responds in 6 months. "We ask for exclusive rights up to and through the festival." **Pays $70 for the run of the festival.**
Needs: One-act plays. Maximum length: 40 minutes. "Any style, topic, etc. We require simple, suggested sets and a maximum cast of six. No adaptations, musicals or children's works."
Tips: "Too many plays are monologue-dominant. Please—reveal your characters through action and dialogue."

[A] THEATRE THREE, 2800 Routh St., Dallas TX 75201. (214)871-2933. Fax: (214)871-3139. E-mail: theatre3@air mail.com. Website: www.vline.net/theatre3. **Contact:** Jac Alder, executive producer-director. Estab. 1961. **Produces 7 plays/year.** Professional regional theatre, in-the-round. Audience is college age to senior citizens. Query with synopsis; *agented submissions only.* Responds in 6 months. **Contractual agreements vary.**
Needs: Musicals, dramas, comedies, bills of related one-acts. Modest production requirement; prefer casts no larger than 10.
Tips: No parodies or political commentary/comedy. Most produced playwrights at Theatre Three (to show "taste" of producer) are Moliere, Sondheim, Ayckbourne, Miller, Stoppard, Durong (moralists and irony-masters).

THEATRE WEST, 3333 Cahuenga W., Los Angeles CA 90068-1365. (323)851-4839. Fax: (323)851-5286. E-mail: theatrewest@theatrewest.org. Website: www.theatrewest.org. **Contact:** Chris DiGiovanni and Doug Haverty, moderators of the Writers Workshop. Estab. 1962. "99-seat waiver productions in our theater. Audiences are primarily young urban professionals." Submit script, résumé and letter requesting membership. Responds in 4 months. Contracts a percentage of writer's share to other media if produced on MainStage by Theatre West. **Pays royalty based on gross box office,**

Needs: Full-length plays only, no one-acts. Uses minimalistic scenery, no fly space.

Tips: "Theatre West is a dues-paying membership company. Only members can submit plays for production. So you must first seek membership to the Writers Workshop. We accept all styles of theater writing, but theater only—no screenplays, novels, short stories or poetry will be considered for membership."

THEATRE WEST VIRGINIA, P.O. Box 1205, Beckley WV 25802-1205. (304)256-6800. Fax: (304)256-6807. E-mail: twv@cwv.net. Website: wvweb.com/www/TWV. **Contact:** Marina Dolinger, artistic director. Estab. 1955. **Produces 6 plays/year.** Professional educational touring theatre—K-6 and 7-12 grade levels. Outdoor drama, musicals. Query and synopsis. Responds in 3 months. **Pays 3-6% royalty.**

Needs: Appropriate material for K through 12. Cast limited to 6 actors/van and truck tour.

Tips: Material needs to be educational, yet entertaining.

THEATREWORKS/USA, 151 W. 26th St., 7th Floor, New York NY 10001. (212)647-1100. Fax: (212)924-5377. E-mail: malltop@theatreworksusa.org. Website: www.theatreworksusa.org. **Contact:** Michael Alltop, assistant artistic director. Estab. 1961. **Produces 3-6 plays/year.** Professional Equity productions for young audiences. Weekend series at Equitable Towers, NYC. Also, national and regional tours of each show. Query with synopsis. Responds in 6 months. Obtains performing rights. **Pays 6% royalty.**

Needs: "One-hour musicals or plays with music written for K-3rd or 3rd-7th grade age groups. Subjects: Historical, biography, classic literature, fairy tales with specific point of view, contemporary literature. Also, adaptations of classic literature for high school, up to all actors." Limited to 5-6 actors and a portable set. Do not rely on lighting or special effects.

Tips: "No campy, 'fractured' fairy tales, shows specifically written to teach or preach, shows relying heavily on narrators or 'kiddy theater' filled with pratfalls, bad jokes and audience participation. Write smart. Kids see a lot these days, and they are sophisticated. Don't write down to them. They deserve a good, well-told story. Seeing one of our shows will provide the best description. We commission almost all of our own work, so most submissions will not have a chance of being produced by us. We read submissions to gauge a playwright's style and appropriateness for possible future projects."

TROUPE AMERICA INC., 528 Hennepin Ave., Suite 206, Minneapolis MN 55403. (612)333-3302. Fax: (612)333-4337. E-mail: cwollan@mninter.net. Website: www.troupeamerica.com. **Contact:** Curt Wollan, president/executive director. Estab. 1987. **Produces 10-12 plays/year.** Professional production in Minneapolis or on the road. Intended for general and family audiences as well as community arts series and University Arts Series audiences. Query with sample of script, synopsis and CD or cassette tape of music. Responds in 1 year. Buys the right to perform and license the production for 10 years. **Pays 2½-5% royalty.**

Needs: Family holiday musicals—2 hours with intermission and small cast musicals. Biographic musicals—2 hours with intermission. Musical adaptations of famous works—2 hours with intermission. Smaller contained musicals get attention and single set scripts do as well.

Tips: No heavy dramas, political plays (unless satirical) and any play dealing with sex, drugs or violence. The size of the cast is important. The smaller the size, the more likely it will get produced. Economics is a priority. If possible, send an invitation to other productions of the script.

UNICORN THEATRE, 3828 Main St., Kansas City MO 64111. (816)531-7529 ext. 18. Fax: (816)531-0421. Website: www.unicorntheatre.org. Producing Artistic Director: Cynthia Levin. **Contact:** Herman Wilson, literary assistant. **Produces 6-8 plays/year.** "We are a professional Equity Theatre. Typically, we produce plays dealing with contemporary issues." Send complete script (to Herman Wilson) with brief synopsis, cover letter, bio, character breakdown and SASE if script is to be returned. Include SASP if acknowledgement of receipt is desired. Responds in 8 months.

Needs: Prefers contemporary (post-1950) scripts. Does not accept musicals, one-acts, or historical plays. A royalty/prize of $1,000 will be awarded the playwright of any play selected through this process, The National Playwright Award. This script receives production as part of the Unicorn's regular season.

URBAN STAGES, 17 E. 47th St., New York NY 10017. (212)421-1380. Fax: (212)421-1387. E-mail: UrbanStage@aol.com. Website: www.urbanstages.com. Artistic Director: Frances Hill. Literary Manager: David Sheppard. **Contact:** T.L. Reilly, producing director. Estab. 1986. **Produces 2-4 plays/year.** Professional productions off or off off Broadway"-throughout the year. General audience. Submit complete script. Responds in 4 months. If produced, option for 6 months. **Pays royalty**

Needs: Both one-act and full-length; generally 1 set or styled playing dual. Good imaginative, creative writing. Cast limited to 3-7.

Tips: "We tend to reject 'living-room' plays. We look for imaginative settings. Be creative and interesting with intellectual content. All submissions should be bound. Send SASE. We are looking for plays with ethnic backgrounds."

WALNUT STREET THEATRE, Ninth and Walnut Streets, Philadelphia PA 19107. (215)574-3550. Fax: (215)574-3598. Producing Artistic Director: Bernard Havard. **Contact:** Beverly Elliott, literary manager. Estab. 1809. **Produces 10 plays/year.** "Our plays are performed in our own space. WST has 3 theaters—a proscenium (mainstage), 1,052

seats; 2 studios, 79-99 seats. We have a subscription audience, largest in the nation." Writers must be members of the Dramatists' Guild. Query with synopsis, 10-20 pages of dialogue, character breakdown and bio. Responds in 5 months. Rights negotiated per project. **Pays negotiable royalty or makes outright purchase.**
Needs: "Full-length dramas and comedies, musicals, translations, adaptations and revues. The studio plays must have a cast of no more than four and use simple sets."
Tips: "Bear in mind that on the mainstage we look for plays with mass appeal, Broadway-style. The studio spaces are our off-Broadway. No children's plays. Our mainstage audience goes for work that is entertaining and light. Our studio season is where we look for plays that have bite and are more provocative." Include SASE for return of materials.

WATERLOO COMMUNITY PLAYHOUSE, P.O. Box 433, Waterloo IA 50704-0433. (319)235-0367. Fax: (319)235-7489. E-mail: wcpbhct@cedarnet.org. **Contact:** Charles Stilwill, managing artistic director. Estab. 1917. **Produces 11 plays/year.** Plays performed by Waterloo Community Playhouse with a volunteer cast. "We are one of the few theaters with a committment to new scripts. We do at least one and have done as many as four a year. We have 4,300 season members. Average attendance is 3,300. We do a wide variety of plays. Our public isn't going to accept nudity, too much sex, too much strong language. We don't have enough Black actors to do all-Black shows. Theater has done plays with as few as 2 characters and as many as 98. We also produce children's theater. Please, no loose pages." Submit complete script. Responds in 1 year. **Makes outright purchase of $400-500.**
Needs: "For our Children's Theater and our Adult Annual Holiday (Christmas) show, we are looking for good adaptations of name stories. Most recently: *Miracle on 34th Street, Best Christmas Pageant Ever*, and *It's A Wonderful Life*."

WEST COAST ENSEMBLE, P.O. Box 38728, Los Angeles CA 90038. (323)876-9337. Fax: (323)876-8916. Website: wcensemble.org. **Contact:** Les Hanson, artistic director. Estab. 1982. **Produces 6 plays/year.** Plays performed at a theater in Hollywood. Submit complete script. Responds in 9 months. Obtains exclusive rights in southern California to present the play for the period specified. Ownership and rights remain with the playwright. **Pays $25-45 per performance.**
Needs: Prefers a cast of 6-12.
Tips: "Submit the script in acceptable dramatic script format."

N. WESTBETH THEATRE CENTER INC., 151 Bank St., New York NY 10014. (212)691-2272. Fax: (212)924-7185. E-mail: wbethzach@aol.com. Website: www.westbeththeatre.com. **Contact:** Zachary Morris, curator, Westbeth New Works Program. Estab. 1977. Professional off-Broadway theater. Five performance spaces, including a Music Hall and a Café Theatre. Audience consists of artists, NY professionals, and downtown theatergoers. Send résumé, one page project proposal—or one page synopsis with cast and production requirements for scripted plays—any relevant audio/visual material, and an SASE. **Pay varies.**
• The New Works Program has expanded its focus to include performance proposals from a range of various disciplines including dancers, playwrights, musicians, and other performance artists. Recent productions include The Umbilical Brothers in *THWAK*, Eddie Izzard's *Dressed to Kill* and *Circle*, and *Lypsinka, the Boxed Set*.
Needs: Proposals should be sharp, urban, and contemporary—period pieces or plays set in rural/regional locales will not be considered.
Tips: "Artists must reside in NYC or surrounding areas and be desirous of extensive development and intense collaboration."

N. THE WESTERN STAGE, 156 Homestead Ave., Salinas CA 93901. (831)755-6929. Fax: (831)755-6954. Artistic Director: Tom Humphrey. **Contact:** Jeffrey Heyer, literary manager. Estab. 1974. **Produces 8 plays/year.** "The Western Stage program is an innovative combination of the best of educational and professional regional theater. Our productions serve an ethnically diverse community." Query with synopsis. Responds in 6 weeks to queries; 3 months to requested scripts. **Pays 6-12% royalty.** Include SASE for return of submission.
Needs: Full-length plays, adaptations, plays for young audiences, musicals, cabaret/revues. Special interests: Adaptations of works of literary significance, large-cast plays.

N. WILLOWS THEATRE COMPANY, 1975 Diamond Blvd., B-230, Concord CA 94520. (925)798-1300. Fax: (925)676-5726. E-mail: willowsth@aol.com. Website: www.willowstheatre.org. Artistic Director: Richard Elliott. **Produces 6 plays/year.** "Professional productions for a suburban audience." Accepts new manuscripts in April and May only; accepts queries year-round. Responds in 2 weeks to queries; 6 months to scripts. **Pays standard royalty.**
Needs: "Commercially viable, small-medium size musicals or comedies that are popular, rarely produced or new. Certain stylized plays or musicals with a contemporary edge to them (e.g., *Les Liasons Dangereuses, La Bete, Candide*)." No more than 15 actors. Unit or simple sets with no fly space, no more than 7 pieces. "We are not interested in one-character pieces."
Tips: "Our audiences want light entertainment, comedies and musicals."

N. A THE WILMA THEATER, 265 S. Broad St., Philadelphia PA 19107. (215)893-9456. Fax: (215)893-0895. E-mail: info@wilmatheater.org. Website: www.wilmatheater.org. **Contact:** Carrie Ryan, literary manager/dramaturg. Estab. 1980. **Produces 4 plays/year.** LORT-C 300 seat theater, 7,500 subscribers. *Agented submissions only* or full ms recommended by a literary manager, dramaturg or other theater professional. Responds in 6 months.

Needs: Full-length plays, translations, adaptations and musicals from an international repertoire with emphasis on innovative, bold staging; world premieres; ensemble works; works with poetric dimension; plays with music; multimedia works; social issues. Prefer cast limit of 12. Stage 44'x46'.

Tips: "Before submitting any material to The Wilma Theater, please research our production history. Considering the types of plays we have produced in the past, honestly assess whether or not your play would suit us. In general, I believe researching the various theaters to which you send your play is important in the long and short run. Different theaters have different missions and therefore seek out material corresponding with those goals. In other words, think through what is the true potential of your play and this theater, and if it is a compatible relationship."

THE WOMEN'S PROJECT AND PRODUCTIONS, 55 West End Ave., New York NY 10023. (212)765-1706. Fax: (212)765-2024. Website: www.womensproject.org. **Contact:** Karen Keagle, literary manager. Estab. 1978. **Produces 3 plays/year.** Professional Off-Broadway productions. Query with synopsis and 10 sample pages of dialogue. Responds in 8 months.

Needs: "We are looking for full-length plays, written by women."

N A WOOLLY MAMMOTH THEATRE COMPANY, 917 M St. NW, Washington DC 20001-4303. (202)289-2443, ext. 513. E-mail: woollymamm@aol.com. Artistic Director: Howard Shalwitz. **Contact:** Mary Resing, literary manager. Estab. 1980. **Produces 4 plays/year.** Produces professional productions for the general public. *Agented submissions only.* Responds in 6 months to scripts; very interesting scripts often take much longer. Buys first- and second-class production rights. **Pays variable royalty.**

Needs: "We look for plays with a distinctive authorial voice. Our work is word- and actor-driven. One-acts and issue-driven plays are not used." Cast limit of 5.

SCREENWRITING

Practically everyone you meet in Los Angeles, from your airport cabbie on, is writing a script. It might be a feature film, movie of the week, TV series or documentary, but the sheer amount of competition can seem overwhelming. Some will never make a sale, while others make a decent living on sales and options without ever having any of their work produced. But there are those writers who make a living doing what they love and see their names roll by on the credits. How do they get there? How do *you* get there?

First, work on your writing. You'll improve with each script, so there is no way of getting around the need to write and write some more. It's a good idea to read as many scripts as you can get your hands on. Check your local bookstores and libraries. Script City (8033 Sunset Blvd., Suite 1500, Hollywood CA 90046, (800)676-2522) carries thousands of movie and TV scripts, classics to current releases, as well as books, audio/video seminars and software in their $2 catalog. Book City (6631 Hollywood Blvd., Hollywood CA 90028, (800)4-CINEMA) has film and TV scripts in all genres and a large selection of movie books in their $2.50 catalog.

There are lots of books that will give you the "rules" of format and structure for writing for TV or film. Samuel French (7623 Sunset Blvd., Hollywood CA 90046 (213)876-0570) carries a number of how-to books and reference materials on these subjects. The correct format marks your script as a professional submission. Most successful scriptwriters will tell you to learn the correct structure, internalize those rules—and then throw them away and write intuitively.

Writing for TV

To break into TV you must have spec scripts—work written for free that serves as a calling card and gets you in the door. A spec script showcases your writing abilities and gets your name in front of influential people. Whether a network has invited you in to pitch some ideas, or a movie producer has contacted you to write a first draft for a feature film, the quality of writing in your spec script got their attention and that may get you the job.

It's a good idea to have several spec scripts, perhaps one each for three of the top five shows in the format you prefer to work in, whether it's sitcom (half-hour comedies), episodic (one hour series) or movie of the week (two hour dramatic movies). Perhaps you want to showcase the breadth of your writing ability; your portfolio could include a few prime time sitcoms (i.e., *Friends, Everybody Loves Raymond, Will & Grace, Drew Carey*), and one or two episodics in a particular genre (i.e., *The Sopranos, Law and Order, NYPD Blue* or *Dawson's Creek, Felicity,*

Buffy the Vampire Slayer). These are all "hot" shows for writers and can demonstrate your abilities to create believable dialogue for characters already familiar to your intended readers. For TV and cable movies you should have completed original scripts (not sequels to existing movies) and you might also have a few for episodic TV shows.

In choosing the shows you write spec scripts for you must remember one thing: don't write a script for a show you want to work on. If you want to write for *Will & Grace*, for example, you'll send a *Dharma & Greg* script and vice versa. It may seem contradictory, but it is standard practice. It reduces the chances of lawsuits, and writers and producers can feel very proprietary about their show and their stories. They may not be objective enough to fairly evaluate your writing. In submitting another similar type of show you'll avoid those problems while demonstrating comparable skills.

In writing your TV script you must get *inside* the show and understand the characters' internal motivations. You must immerse yourself in how the characters speak, think and interact. Don't introduce new characters in a spec script for an existing show—write believable dialogue for the characters as they are portrayed. Be sure to choose a show that you like—you'll be better able to demonstrate your writing ability through characters you respond to.

You must also understand the external factors. How the show is filmed bears on how you write. Most sitcoms are shot on videotape with three cameras, on a sound stage with a studio audience. Episodics are often shot on film with one camera and include on-location shots. *Dharma and Greg* has a flat, evenly-lit look and takes place in a limited number of locations. *NYPD Blue* has a gritty realism with varying lighting and a variety of settings.

Another important external influence in writing for TV is the timing of commercials in conjunction with the act structure. There are lots of sources detailing the suggested content and length of acts, but generally a sitcom has a teaser (short opening scene), two acts and a tag (short closing scene), and an episodic has a teaser, four acts and a tag. Each act closes with a turning point. Watching TV analytically and keeping a log of events will reveal some elements of basic structure. *Successful Scriptwriting*, by Wolff & Cox (Writer's Digest Books), offers detailed discussions of various types of shows.

Writing for the movies

With feature films you may feel at once more liberated and more bound by structure. An original movie script contains characters you have created, with storylines you design, allowing you more freedom than you have in TV. However, your writing must still convey believable dialogue and realistic characters, with a plausible plot and high-quality writing carried through the roughly 120 pages. The characters must have a problem that involves the audience. When you go to a movie you don't want to spend time watching the *second* worst night of a character's life. You're looking for the big issue that crystallizes a character, that portrays a journey with important consequences.

At the same time you are creating, you should also be constructing. Be aware of the basic three act structure for feature films. Scenes can be of varying lengths, but are usually no longer than three to three and a half pages. Some writers list scenes that must occur, then flesh them out from beginning to end, writing with the structure of events in mind. The beginning and climactic scenes are the easiest; it's how they get there from here that's difficult.

Many novice screenwriters tend to write too many visual cues and camera directions into their scripts. Your goal should be to write something readable, like a "compressed novella." Write succinct resonant scenes and leave the camera technique to the director and producer. In action/adventure movies, however, there needs to be a balance since the script demands more visual direction.

It seems to be easier for TV writers to cross over to movies. Cable movies bridge the two, and are generally less derivative and more willing to take chances with a higher quality show designed to attract an audience not interested in network offerings. Cable is also less susceptible to advertiser pullout, which means it can tackle more controversial topics.

Feature films and TV are very different and writers occupy different positions. TV is a medium for writers and producers; directors work for them. Many TV writers are also producers. In feature films the writers and producers work for the director and often have little or no say about what happens to the work once the script has been sold. For TV the writer pitches the idea; for feature films generally the producer pitches the idea and then finds a writer.

Marketing your scripts

If you intend to make writing your profession you must act professionally. Accepted submission practices should become second nature.

- The initial pitch is made through a query letter, which is no longer than one page with a one paragraph synopsis and brief summary of your credits if they are relevant to the subject of your script.
- Never send a complete manuscript until it is requested.
- Almost every script sent to a producer, studio or agent must be accompanied by a release form. Ask for that company's form when you receive an invitation to submit the whole script. Mark your envelope "release form enclosed" to prevent it being returned unread.
- Always include a self-addressed stamped envelope (SASE) if you want your work returned; a disposable copy may be accompanied by a self-addressed stamped postcard for reply.
- Allow four to six weeks from receipt of your manuscript before writing a follow-up letter.

When your script is requested, be sure it's written in the appropriate format. Unusual binding, fancy covers or illustrations mark an amateur. Three brass brads with a plain or black cover indicate a pro.

There are a limited number of ideas in the world, so it's inevitable that similar ideas occur to more than one person. Hollywood is a buyer's market and a release form states that pretty clearly. An idea is not copyrightable, so be careful about sharing premises. The written expression of that idea, however, can be protected and it's a good idea to do so. The Writers Guild of America can register scripts for television and theatrical motion pictures, series formats, storylines and step outlines. You need not be a member of the WGA to use this service. Copyrighting your work with the Copyright Office of the Library of Congress also protects your work from infringement. Contact either agency for more information and an application form.

If you are a writer, you should write—all the time. When you're not writing, read. There are numerous books on the art, craft and business of screenwriting. See the Publications of Interest at the end of *Writer's Market* for a few or check the catalogs of companies previously mentioned. The different industry trade papers such as *Daily Variety* and *Hollywood Reporter* can keep you in touch with the day to day news and upcoming events. Specialty newsletters such as *Hollywood Scriptwriter* (P.O. Box 10277, Burbank CA 91510, (818)845-5525, http://www.hollywoodscript writer.com) offer tips from successful scriptwriters and agents. The *Hollywood Creative Directory* is an extensive list of production companies, studios and networks that also lists companies and talent with studio deals.

Computer services have various bulletin boards and chat hours for scriptwriters that provide contact with other writers and a chance to share information and encouragement.

It may take years of work before you come up with a script someone is willing to take a chance on. Those years need to be spent learning your craft and understanding the business. Polishing scripts, writing new material, keeping current with the industry and networking constantly will keep you busy. When you do get that call you'll be confident in your abilities and know that your hard work is beginning to pay off.

Information on screenwriting markets listed in the previous edition of *Writer's Market* but not included in this edition can be found in the the the General Index.

ALEXANDER/ENRIGHT AND ASSOCIATES, 201 Wilshire Blvd., 3rd Floor, Santa Monica CA 90401. **Contact:** Sarah Koepple, development associate. Produces for a general television audience. **Buys 3 script(s)/year. Works with many writer(s)/year.** Buys TV and film rights only. Accepts previously produced material. Query with synopsis. Responds in 1 month to queries; 6 weeks to scripts.
Needs: Women-driven dramas, but will accept others. Also, reality-based stories as well as 1 hour documentary ideas. No unsolicited mss. No extreme violence, horror or stalkers.

☐ ALLIED ARTISTS, INC., 859 N. Hollywood Way, Suite 377, Burbank CA 91505. (818)594-4089. **Contact:** John Nichols, vice president, development. Estab. 1990. Produces material for broadcast and cable television, home video and film. **Buys 3-5 script(s)/year. Works with 10-20 writer(s)/year.** Buys first or all rights. Accepts previously produced material. Submit synopsis, outline. Responds in 2 months to queries; 3 months to scripts. **Pays in accordance with WGA standards.**
Needs: Films, videotapes. Social issue TV special (30-60 minutes); special interest home video topics; instruction and entertainment; positive values feature screenplays.
Tips: "We are looking for positive, up-lifting dramatic stories involving real people situations. Future trend is for more reality-based programming, as well as interactive television programs for viewer participation. Please do not call. Send written queries or email to mac@alliedartistsonline.com."

☒ THE AMERICAN MOVING PICTURE COMPANY INC., 838 N. Doheny Dr., #904, Los Angeles CA 90069. (310)276-0750. E-mail: mm2k@earthlink.net. **Contact:** Isabel Casper, vice president/creative affairs. Estab. 1979. Theatrical motion picture audience. Produced 4 theatrical motion pictures. Buys screenplay rights and ancillaries. Does not return submissions. Query with synopsis. Responds in 1 month to queries. **Pays in accordance with WGA standards.**
Needs: Films (35mm), commercial. "We want commercial and unique material."

☒ ☐ AMERICAN WORLD PICTURES INC., 21700 Oxnard St., Suite 660, Woodland Hills CA 91367. (818)715-1480. Fax: (818)715-1081. E-mail: awpics@earthlink.net. **Contact:** Brian Etting or Terese Linden Kohn, development/acquisitions. Video/television market—adults. **Buys 4 script(s)/year. Works with 5 writer(s)/year.** Buys all rights. Accepts previously produced material. Query. Responds in 2 months to queries; 3 months to scripts.
Needs: Films (35mm). Action, suspense, thriller, horror genres only.
Tips: Strong characters, strong dialogue.

ANGEL FILMS, 967 Highway 40, New Franklin MO 65274-9778. (573)698-3900. Fax: (573)698-3900. E-mail: angelfilm@aol.com. **Contact:** Matthew Eastman, vice president of production. Estab. 1980. Produces material for feature films, television. **Buys 10 script(s)/year. Works with 20 writer(s)/year.** Buys all rights. Accepts previously produced material. Query with synopsis. Responds in 1 month to queries; 2 months to scripts. **Makes outright purchase.**
Needs: Films (35mm), videotapes. "We are looking for projects that can be used to produce feature film and television feature film and series work. These would be in the areas of action adventure, comedy, horror, thriller, science fiction, animation for children." Also looking for direct to video materials.
Tips: "Don't copy others. Try to be original. Don't overwork your idea. As far as trends are concerned, don't pay attention to what is 'in.' By the time it gets to us it will most likely be on the way 'out.' And if you can't let your own grandmother read it, don't send it. Slow down on western submissions. They are not selling. If you wish material returned, enclose proper postage with all submissions. Send SASE for response to queries and return of scripts."

ANGEL'S TOUCH PRODUCTIONS, 4872 Topanga Canyon Blvd., Suite 344, Woodland Hills CA 91364. **Contact:** Phil Nemy, director of development. Estab. 1986. Professional screenplays and teleplays. Rights negotiated. Submit synopsis. Responds in 8 months to queries. **Payment negotiated.**
Needs: Films. All types, all genres, only full-length teleplays and screenplays—no one-acts.
Tips: "We only seek feature film screenplays, television screenplays, and episodic teleplays. No phone calls!"

AVALANCHE ENTERTAINMENT, 11041 Santa Monica Blvd., Suite 511, Los Angeles CA 90025. **Contact:** Richard Hull. Estab. 1993. All audiences. **Buys 2 script(s)/year. Works with 10-15 writer(s)/year.** Buys all rights. Accepts previously produced material. Query with synopsis or résumé. Responds in 1 month to queries; 3 months to scripts.

FOR EXPLANATIONS OF THESE SYMBOLS,
SEE THE INSIDE FRONT AND BACK COVERS OF THIS BOOK.

Needs: Films (35 mm), videotapes. High concept, excellent dialogue, screenplays, especially youth-oriented (age 35 and under) "feel-good" movies, music-oriented movies.

N: THE BADHAM COMPANY, 8447 Wilshire Blvd., Suite 212, Beverly Hills CA 90211. (818)990-9495. Fax: (818)981-9163. Website: www.badhamcompany.com. **Contact:** Cammie Crier-Herbert, co-producer/head of development. Estab. 1991. Theatrical audience. **Buys 1 script(s)/year. Works with 2 writer(s)/year.** Buys first rights. Accepts previously produced material. Query with synopsis. Responds in 1 month to queries.
Needs: Films (35 mm).
Tips: "It's too easy to write action and ignore characters."

BAUMGARTEN-MERIMS ENTERTAINMENT, (formerly Baumgarten-Prophet Entertainment), 1640 S. Sepulveda Blvd., Suite 218, Los Angeles CA 90025. (310)996-1885. Fax: (310)996-1892. E-mail: baumgartenmerims@yahoo.com. **Contact:** Adam Merims, producer, or Eric Morris, creative executive. Estab. 1994. Audience is motion picture and television viewers. **Buys 35 script(s)/year. Works with 100 writer(s)/year.** Buys motion picture and television rights. Accepts previously produced material. Query with synopsis. Responds in 1 month to queries. **Pays in accordance with WGA standards.**
Needs: Films (35 mm), videotapes. "We have feature projects in development at Disney, Sony, Fox, Warner Brothers and Bel Air. We have TV projects with Showtime, HBO, TNT and A&E. We are always looking for good material."
Tips: Interested in original motion picture, television and cable material. Movies and dramatic series

BEYOND: VON GARNIER-MCCORKINDALE ENTERTAINMENT, (formerly VM Butterfly). Fax: (323)954-8222. **Contact:** Laura McCorkindale, producer; Katja von Garnier, director. Estab. 1991. **Buys 5 script(s)/year.** Buys all rights. Query with synopsis. "Fax one page of completed screenplay with genre type and 1-2 sentence logline at the top to the attention of Trevor Harbert." Responds in 1 month if interested. **Payment negotiated.**
Needs: Feature film screenplays. Our films range from medium budget intelligent, artistic independent films to big budget, commercial studio films. All genres accepted (favorites: Magical realism, dramas, sophisticated romantic comedies, drama-comedies, true stories, metaphysical/spiritual).
Tips: "Take time writing your synopsis and be detailed! Synopsis should be as well written as your screenplay and not more than one page. Although we are looking for all types of screenplays, we are especially drawn to innovative, magical and inspirational stories that enlighten and instill humanity. We do not accept unsolicited phone calls, so please correspond only via fax."

BIG EVENT PICTURES, 11288 Ventura Blvd., #909, Studio City CA 91604. E-mail: bigevent1@hotmail.com. **Contact:** Michael Cargile, president. Produces feature films for theaters, cable TV and home video. PG, R, and G-rated films. Query by e-mail. Respond to queries in 1 month. Producers will respond if interested.
Needs: Films. All genres. Looking for good material from writers who have taken the time to learn the unique and difficult craft of scriptwriting.
Tips: "Interesting query letters intrigue us—and tell us something about the writer. Query letter should include a short 'log line' or 'pitch' encapsulating 'what this story is about' and should be no more than 1 page in length. We look for unique stories with strong characters and would like to see more action and science fiction submissions. We make movies that we would want to see. Producers are known for encouraging new (e.g. unproduced) screenwriters and giving real consideration to their scripts."

A: BIG STAR MOTION PICTURES LTD., 13025 Yonge St., #201, Richmond Hill Ontario L4E 1Z5, Canada. (416)720-9825. Fax: (905)773-3153. E-mail: bigstar@pathcom.com. **Contact:** Frank A. Deluca. Estab. 1991. **Buys 1-2 script(s)/year. Works with 5-10 writer(s)/year.** Query with synopsis. Script should be submitted by agent or lawyer. Responds in 3 months to queries; 3 months to scripts.
Needs: Films (35 mm). "We are active in all medias, but are primarily looking for television projects, cable, network, etc. Family films are of special interest."

CANVAS HOUSE FILMS, 3671 Bear St., #E, Santa Ana CA 92704. **Contact:** Mitch Teemley, producer. Estab. 1994. General audience. **Buys 2-3 script(s)/year. Works with 10-15 writer(s)/year.** Buys first rights, all rights. Accepts previously produced material. Query with synopsis, résumé, production history. Responds in 1 month to queries; 4 months to scripts. **Pays in accordance with WGA standards.**
Needs: Films (35 mm). "Quality feature-length filmscripts—all types, but no lurid, 'hard-R'-rated material."
Tips: "Know proper formatting and story structure. There is a need for 'family' material that can appeal to *grown-ups*."

N: CLARK FILM PRODUCTIONS, INC., P.O. Box 773, Balboa CA 92661. E-mail: howieccc@prodigy.net. **Contact:** Mr. Steven Clark, president. Estab. 1987. General audience. **Buys 1 script(s)/year. Works with 4 writer(s)/year.** Buys first rights. Accepts previously produced material. Query with synopsis and outline. Responds in 6 months to queries. **Pays in accordance with WGA standards.**
Needs: Family-oriented, general audience materials, with universal appeal.

COBBLESTONE FILMS, 1484 Reeves St., Suite 203, Los Angeles CA 90035. E-mail: cstonefilms@aol.com. **Contact:** Jacqui Adler, producer. Estab. 1997. TV and film. Accepts previously produced material. Query with synopsis. Responds in 1 month to queries. **Pays in accordance with WGA standards.**
Needs: Films (35 mm). Looking for completed screenplays only for the following genres: Drama, horror, suspense-thrillers.
Tips: "Please send 1-page query letters."

CPC ENTERTAINMENT, 840 N. Larrabee St., #2322, Los Angeles CA 90069. (310)652-8194. Fax: (310)652-4998. E-mail: chane@compuserve.com. **Contact:** Peggy Chene, producer/director; Sylvie de la Riviere, vice president creative affairs; Clayton W. Herzog, development associate. Feature and TV. **Buys 15 script(s)/year. Works with 24 writer(s)/year.** Buys all rights. Submit resumé, 1 sentence premise, and 3 sentence synopsis. Prefers e-mail queries. Responds in 2 weeks to queries; 3 months to scripts. **Makes outright purchase. Pays in accordance with WGA standards.**
Needs: Needs feature and TV movie screenplays: Small independent, or any budget for thrillers, true stories, action/adventure, character driven stories of any genre.

EAST EL LAY FILMS, 12041 Hoffman St., Studio City CA 91604. (818)769-4565. Fax: (818)769-1917. **Contact:** Daniel Kuhn, president, Co-President: Susan Coppola (director). Estab. 1992. Low-budget feature films for television markets. Buys first rights and options for at least 1 year with refusal rights. Query with synopsis, résumé. **Pays royalty, makes outright purchase, option fee.**
Needs: Films (35 mm), videotapes. Produces and directs own features and documentaries.

ENTERTAINMENT PRODUCTIONS, INC., 2118 Wilshire Blvd., #744, Santa Monica CA 90403. (310)456-3143. Fax: (310)456-8950. **Contact:** M.E. Lee, story editor; Edward Coe, producer. Estab. 1971. Produces theatrical and television productions. Query with synopsis and a Writer Submission Release. Responds to queries in 1 month only if SASE is included. **Purchases rights by negotiations.**
Needs: Scripts having the power to attract audiences worldwide. Will consider participation, co-production.
Tips: "Submit your one strongest writing."

FEURY/GRANT ENTERTAINMENT, (formerly Joseph Feury Entertainment), 441 West End Ave. #10A, New York NY 10024-5328. (212)724-9290. Fax: (212)724-9233. **Contact:** Joseph Feury, executive producer. Estab. 1982. Buys all rights. Accepts previously produced material. Query with synopsis. **Pays negotiated option.**
Needs: Films.

FILMSAAVY ENTERTAINMENT, 16931 Dearborn St., Northridge CA 91343. E-mail: filmsaavy@aol.com. Website: www.FilmSaavy.Saavedra.com. **Contact:** Michael Eastin, story editor. Estab. 1995. **Buys 2-5 script(s)/year. Works with 5 writer(s)/year.** Buys all rights. Accepts previously produced material. Query with synopsis. Responds in 2 months to queries; 3 months to scripts. **Pays in accordance with WGA standards.**
Needs: Films (35 mm). Feature length motion-picture screenplays based on original ideas. Any genre accepted, but prefer comedies, dramas and historical biographies.
Tips: "Literate stories with strong, original characters, fresh ideas and life-affirming themes get our attention. We're a production company that primarily seeks product for director Craig Saavedra, and therefore material with a director already attached is less appealing to us."

FOUNTAIN PRODUCTIONS, 500 S. Buena Vista, Burbank CA 91521-0180. **Contact:** Peter M. Green, president. Estab. 1999. Audience is kids, teens, family. **Buys 10 script(s)/year. Works with 20 writer(s)/year.** Buys first rights or all rights. Industry referrals only. Responds in 1 month to queries. **Pays in accordance with WGA standards.**
Needs: Films (35 mm).

N **GRADE A ENTERTAINMENT**, 368 N. La Cienega Blvd., Los Angeles CA 90048-1925. E-mail: GradeAProd@aol.com. **Contact:** Andy Cohen. Estab. 1996. All audiences. **Buys 5-10 script(s)/year. Works with 25 writer(s)/year.** Buys all rights. Accepts previously produced material. Query with synopsis via e-mail only. Responds in 1 month to queries. **Pays in accordance with WGA standards.**
Needs: Films (35mm). Looking for well-written, well-developed, completed feature film scripts only.

N **STEPHAN GRAY**, 205 S. Beverly Dr., Suite 212, Los Angeles CA 90212. (310)888-0090. E-mail: Bhlit@cs.com. Website: www.beverlyhillslit.com. **Contact:** Stephan Gray, CEO. **Works with 4-8 writer(s)/year.** Options scripts. Accepts previously produced material. Query with synopsis.
Needs: Films (35mm). "Most writers should review my website at www.beverlyhillslit.com."

N **GREEN GRASS BLUE SKY COMPANY**, 10000 Riverside Dr., Suites 15-17, Toluca Lake CA 91602. E-mail: ggbscompany@hotmail.com. **Contact:** Frank Catalano, president. Estab. 1997. General audience. Buys all rights. Accepts previously produced material. Query only (no scripts). Responds in 2 months to queries. **Pay varies depending upon project.**
Needs: Films.
Tips: "Seeks projects with poetry and spirit. No shoot-em ups."

BETH GROSSBARD PRODUCTIONS, 5168 Otis Ave., Tarzana CA 91356. Fax: (818)705-7366 or (310)841-5934. **Contact:** K. Jacobs, development associate; Beth Grossbard, producer. Estab. 1994. **Buys 6 script(s)/year. Works with 20+ writer(s)/year.** Buys first rights and true-life story rights. Query with synopsis, treatment/outline. Responds in 2 months to queries; 3 months to scripts. **Pays in accordance with WGA standards.**
Needs: Films (35 mm).
Tips: "Develops material for television, cable and feature film markets. Areas of interest include: True stories, family dramas, social issues, young adult themed and children's stories, historical/biographical accounts. Will also consider plays, book proposals, small press books, or concept pages for film development."

A **HBO FILMS**, 2049 Century Park E., Suite 3600, Los Angeles CA 90067. Fax: (310)201-9552. Website: www.hbo.com. **Contact:** Bettina Moss, story editor. Query with synopsis (1 page or shorter) **through agent or lawyer only**. No unrepresented writers. Do *not* email your query. Responds in 1 month to queries. **Payment varies.**
Needs: Features for TV. Looks at all genres except family films with children as main protagonists. Focus on socially relevant material and true stories. "HBO looks for true stories, known people, controversy, politics, etc. *Not* looking for standard movie-of-the-week fare."
Tips: "Make sure industry standards are adhered to. Not interested in looking at work that is unprofessionally presented. Only submit synopsis if you have a true story or fiction completed script or book. Not interested in partially completed projects."

N **IFM FILM ASSOCIATES INC.**, 1328 E. Palmer Ave., Glendale CA 91205-3738. (818)243-4976. Fax: (818)550-9728. E-mail: ifmfilm@aol.com or ifmfilm@reelplay.com. **Contact:** Brad Benjamin, executive assistant. Estab. 1994. Film and television all media world wide. **Buys 10 script(s)/year. Works with 30 writer(s)/year.** Buys all rights. No previously produced material. Catalog for SAE with $3. Query with synopsis. Responds in 1 month to queries; 3 months to scripts. **Pays in accordance with WGA standards.**
Needs: Films (35mm). Thrillers, family, action.

INTERNATIONAL HOME ENTERTAINMENT, 1440 Veteran Ave., Suite 650, Los Angeles CA 90024. (323)663-6940. **Contact:** Jed Leland, Jr., assistant to the president. Estab. 1976. Buys first rights. Query. Responds in 2 months to queries. **Pays in accordance with WGA standards.**
    ⊶ Looking for material that is international in scope.
Tips: "Our response time is faster on average now (3-6 weeks), but no replies without a SASE. No unsolicited mss. We do not respond to unsolicited phone calls."

JOADA PRODUCTIONS, INC., (formerly The Sheldon/Post Company), 1437 Rising Glen Rd., Los Angeles CA 90069. **Contact:** David Sheldon, producer. Estab. 1980. Produces feature films as well as movies and series for television. Buys all rights. Query with synopsis, writing samples, SASE. Responds in 2 months to queries. **Pays in accordance with WGA standards.**
Needs: "We look for all types of material, including comedy, family stories, suspense dramas, horror, sci-fi, thrillers, action-adventure." True stories should include news articles or other documentation.
Tips: "A synopsis should tell the entire story with the entire plot—including a beginning, a middle and an end. The producers have been in the business with 20th Century Fox, Orion/MGM, Columbia Pictures and currently have contracts with Montel Williams, Baltimore Spring Creek Productions and Paramount Pictures."

MARTY KATZ PRODUCTIONS, 1250 6th St., Suite 205, Santa Monica CA 90401. (310)260-8501. Fax: (310)260-8502. Website: www.hollywood-101.com. **Contact:** Frederick Levy, vice president, development. Estab. 1992. Produces material for all audiences. Buys first, all and film rights. Accepts previously produced material. Query. Responds in 1 month to queries.
Needs: Films (35 mm).

THE KAUFMAN COMPANY, 12400 Wilshire Blvd, 12th Floor, Los Angeles CA 90025. Website: www.thekaufmancompany.com. **Contact:** Gregg Tilson, director of development or Courtney Morrison, story editor. Estab. 1990. Intended for all audiences. **Buys 5-10 script(s)/year. Works with 10 writer(s)/year.** Buys all rights. Query with synopsis. Responds in 3 weeks to queries; 3 months to scripts. **Pays in accordance with WGA standards.**
Needs: We option screenplays and mss for television, cable and film. "Must be a truly engaging story—no personal slice-of-life melodramas."

LANCASTER GATE ENTERTAINMENT, 16001 Ventura Blvd., #110, Encino CA 91436. (818)995-6000. E-mail: LichtMueller@hotmail.com. **Contact:** Brian K. Schlichter, vice president, development and production. Estab. 1989. Theatrical and television. **Works with dozens of writer(s)/year.** Rights purchased negotiable. Query. Responds in 1 month to queries. **Pays in accordance with WGA standards.**
Needs: Films (35-70 mm). Feature and television scripts, pitches.

N **DAVID LANCASTER PRODUCTIONS**, 3356 Bennett Dr., Los Angeles CA 90068-1704. (323)874-1415. Fax: (323)874-7749. E-mail: brnolan023@netzero.net. **Contact:** Barry R. Nolan, director of development. Estab. 1985. **Buys 8-10 script(s)/year. Works with 18-25 writer(s)/year.** Buys film and TV rights. Query with synopsis and pitch.

Needs: Looking for strong character pieces in the thriller, noir, action and true to life genres. High-concept indedependent features with a budget of $2-4 million.
Tips: "Submissions must be solicited by the company. Open to pitches via fax or e-mail. Writer does not need to have representation. All submissions should be professional in nature (i.e., proper format, proper binding, free from mistakes, etc." Accepts pitches/synopses by e-mail or fax. No phone pitches.

ARNOLD LEIBOVIT ENTERTAINMENT, (formerly Talking Rings Entertainment), P.O. Box 80141, Las Vegas NV 89180. E-mail: director@scifistation.com. Website: www.scifistation.com. **Contact:** Barbara Schimpf, vice president, production; Arnold Leibovit, director/producer. Estab. 1988. Produces material for motion pictures and television. **Works with 1 writer(s)/year.** Query with synopsis. A submission release must be included with all queries. Responds in 2 months to queries. **Pays in accordance with WGA standards.**
Needs: Films (35mm), videotapes. "Prefers high concept, mixed genres, comedy, adventure, sci-fi/fantasy, as well as unusual, visually rich, character-driven smaller works with unusual twists, comic sensibility, pathos and always the unexpected."
Tips: "New policy: Submission of logline and synopsis for evaluation first. Do not send scripts until we ask for them. An Arnold Leibovit Entertainment release form must be completed and returned with material. Accepting loglines via e-mail at director@scifistation.com."

N: LEO FILMS, 6249 Langdon Ave., Van Nuys CA 91411. (323)666-7140. Fax: (323)666-7414. E-mail: steve@leofilms.com. Website: www.leofilms.com. **Contact:** Steve Lustgarten, president. Estab. 1989. Feature/film. **Buys 2 script(s)/year. Works with 2 writer(s)/year.** Buys all rights. Accepts previously produced material. Query with synopsis. Responds in 1 month to queries; 2 months to scripts. **Pay varies—options and sales.**
Needs: Films (35 mm). "Looking for good stories-honor, urban, action."
Tips: E-mail first if available. "Will also consider novels, short stories and treatments that have true movie potential."

LICHT/MUELLER FILM CORP., E-mail: LichtMueller@hotmail.com. Website: www.licht-mueller.com. **Contact:** Doug Hammond. Estab. 1983. Produces material for all audiences. Accepts previously produced material. Query with synopsis. Responds in 1 month to queries; 3 months to scripts.
Needs: Films (35 mm). "Scripts for feature films."
Tips: "We tend to focus on comedy, but are open to most other genres. Visit website for submission policy."

LOCKWOOD FILMS (LONDON) INC., 12569 Boston Dr., RR #41, London Ontario N6H 5L2, Canada. (519)657-3994. Fax: (519)657-3994. E-mail: nancycjohnson@hotmail.com. **Contact:** Nancy Johnson, president. Estab. 1974. Entertainment and general broadcast for kids 9-12 and family viewing. **Works with 5-6 writer(s)/year.** Query with synopsis, résumé, writing samples. Submissions will not be considered without a signed proposal agreement; we will send one upon receiving submissions. **Pays negotiated fee.**
Needs: Family entertainment: Series, seasonal specials, mini-series, and MOW. Also feature films, documentaries.
Tips: "Potential contributors should have a fax machine and should be prepared to sign a 'proposal submission agreement.' We are in development with national broadcaster on live-action family drama series. Looking for international co-production opportunities. Writers from the US sending proposals with a SASE with American postage should understand we can not mail those envelopes in Canada. If they send a Union Postale Universelle (International Response Coupon) we can respond."

N: LOIS LUGER PRODUCTIONS, 10542 Whipple St., Los Angeles CA 91602. (818)487-6750. **Contact:** Wendy Arthur, vice president current affairs. Estab. 1986. **Buys 6 script(s)/year. Works with 20 writer(s)/year.** Buys all rights, excluding book publishing rights. Accepts previously produced material. Query with synopsis. Responds in 1 month to queries; 3 months to scripts. **Pays in accordance with WGA standards.**
Needs: Films.

▢ MEDIACOM DEVELOPMENT CORP., P.O. Box 6331, Burbank CA 91510-6331. (818)594-4089. **Contact:** Felix Girard, director/program development. Estab. 1978. **Buys 8-12 script(s)/year.** Buys all rights or first rights. Query with writing samples. Responds in 1 month to queries. **Negotiates payment depending on project.**
Needs: Films, videotapes, multimedia kits, tapes and cassettes. Publishes software ("programmed instruction training courses"). Looking for new ideas for CD-ROM titles.
Tips: "Send short samples of work. Especially interested in flexibility to meet clients' demands, creativity in treatment of precise subject matter. We are looking for good, fresh projects (both special and series) for cable and pay television markets. A trend in the audiovisual field that freelance writers should be aware of is the move toward more interactive video disc/computer CRT delivery of training materials for corporate markets."

MICHAEL MELTZER PRODUCTIONS, 8530 Holloway Dr., #327, Los Angeles CA 90069. (310)289-0702. E-mail: melmax@aol.com. **Contact:** Michael Meltzer, producer. Query with synopsis. Responds in 1 month to queries; 2 months to scripts.
Needs: Films (35 mm).

MINDSTORM LLC, 1434 Sixth St., Suite 1, Santa Monica CA 91401. Fax: (310)393-6622. **Contact:** Karina Duffy, president. Estab. 1998. Audience is mid-20s-30s. **Buys 6 script(s)/year. Works with 8 writer(s)/year.** Buys all rights. Query with synopsis, résumé, writing samples, production history. Query by fax only. Responds in 1 month to queries. **Pays in accordance with WGA standards.**
Needs: Videotapes.
Tips: "Create a script that is unique, has good character development and a solid point to it. Looking for talented young up and coming directors with shorts. Also looking for female-driven scripts, mostly drama or romantic comedy."

MONAREX HOLLYWOOD CORPORATION, 9421½ W. Pico Blvd., Los Angeles CA 90035. **Contact:** Chris D. Nebe, president. Estab. 1978. All audiences. **Buys 3-4 script(s)/year. Works with 5-10 writer(s)/year.** Buys all rights. Query with synopsis. Responds in 1 month to queries. **Pays in accordance with WGA standards.**
Needs: Films (35mm), videotapes. Needs dramatic material with strong visuals, action, horror, dance, romantic comedies, anything commercially viable. We are only interested in screenplays.

NHO ENTERTAINMENT, 550 Euclid St., Santa Monica CA 90402. E-mail: nho-ent@hotmail.com. Website: www.nhoentertainment.com. **Contact:** Mark Costa, partner. Estab. 1999. All audiences. **Buys 5-10 script(s)/year. Works with 10-15 writer(s)/year.** Buys all rights. Accepts previously produced material. Catalog for #10 SASE. Query with synopsis, résumé, writing samples, production history. Responds in 1 month to queries. **Pays in accordance with WGA standards.**
Needs: Films, videotapes, multimedia kits, tapes and cassettes. "We are currently accepting all forms of submissions and encourage all writers with material to send query letters."

ORBIT PICTURES, 714 N. LaBrea Ave., Hollywood CA 90038. (213)525-2626. E-mail: orbit@orbitEG.com. **Contact:** Kevin Moreton, vice president, production. Estab. 1987. Feature film; theatrical audience. **Buys 5 script(s)/year. Works with 15 writer(s)/year.** Buys all rights. Accepts previously produced material. Query with synopsis. Responds in 1 month to queries. **Buys option and writing fees against a purchase price.**
Needs: Films (35mm).
Tips: "Looking for well-written, distinctive stories in script form, or suitable for adaptation to script form, to serve as the basis for our feature film projects: Drama, comedy, sci-fi, thrillers and horror."

POP/ART FILM FACTORY, 513 Wilshire Blvd., #215, Santa Monica CA 90401. E-mail: dzpff@earthlink.net. Website: www.home.earthlink.net/~dzpff. **Contact:** Daniel Zirilli, CEO/director. Estab. 1990. Produces material for "all audiences/feature films." Query with synopsis. **Pays on per project basis.**
Needs: Films (35mm), multimedia kits, documentaries. "Looking for interesting productions of all kinds. We're producing 3 feature films/year, and 15-20 music-oriented projects. Also exercise and other special interest videos."
Tips: "Send a query/pitch letter and let me know if you are willing to write on spec (for the first job only; you will be paid if the project is produced). Be original. Do not play it safe. If you don't receive a response from anyone you have ever sent your ideas to, or you continually get rejected, don't give up if you believe in yourself. Good luck and keep writing!" Will look at "reels" (¾ or VHS).

🎬 **PROMARK ENTERTAINMENT GROUP**, 3599 Cahuenga Blvd. W., Los Angeles CA 90026. (323)878-0404. Fax: (323)878-0486. E-mail: gwishnick@promarkgroup.com. **Contact:** Gil Wishnick, vice president development. Promark is a foreign sales company, producing theatrical films for the foreign market. **Buys 8-10 script(s)/year. Works with 8-10 writer(s)/year.** Buys all rights. Query with synopsis (shorter is better). Responds in 1 month to queries; 2 months to scripts. **Makes outright purchase.**
    ○➤ Promark is concentrating on action-thrillers in the vein of *The Net* or *Marathon Man*. They are not looking for science fiction and are concentrating on suspense/action stories.
Needs: Films (35mm). "We are looking for screenplays in the action thriller genre. Our aim is to produce lower budget films that have a solid, novel premise—a smart but smaller scale independent film (like a low budget *The Fugitive*). Our films are male-oriented, urban in setting with a strong male lead. We try to find projects with a fresh premise, a clever hook and strong characters. We are not interested in comedies, dramas or horror films, ever. Among the recent films we've produced are: *Contaminated Man*, a medical thriller, starring William Hurt and Peter Weller; *Pilgrim* with Ray Liotta, which follows an amnesiac's search for himself and a fortune he has stolen; *The Stick Up* with James Spader."

THE PUPPETOON STUDIOS, P.O. Box 80141, Las Vegas NV 89180. E-mail: director@scifistation.com. Website: www.scifistation.com. **Contact:** Arnold Leibovit, director. Estab. 1987. "Broad audience." **Works with 1 writer(s)/year.** Query with synopsis. Submission release required with all queries. Do not send script unless requested. Responds in 2 month to queries. **Pays in accordance with WGA standards.**
Needs: Films (35mm). "We are seeking animation properties including presentation drawings and character designs. The more detailed drawings with animation scripts the better. Always looking for fresh broad audience material." No novels, plays, poems, treatments; no submissions on disk.

◘ RANDWELL PRODUCTIONS, INC., 11111 Santa Monica Blvd., Suite 525, Los Angeles CA 90025-3339. **Contact:** Tom Kageff, vice president. Estab. 1997. TV and features audience. **Buys 3-4 script(s)/year. Works with 2-3 writer(s)/year.** Buys all rights. Query with synopsis. Responds in 2 weeks to queries; 3 months to scripts. **Pays in accordance with WGA standards.**
Needs: Films (35mm). Good character pieces with a strong plot and/or strong concepts. No sci-fi, no westerns.
Tips: "Please keep synopsis to no more than one page. We hardly if ever request a copy of unsolicited material so don't be surprised if we pass."

RED HOTS ENTERTAINMENT, 3105 Amigos Dr., Burbank CA 91504-1806. (818)954-0092. **Contact:** Dan Pomeroy, senior vice president/development; Chip Miller, producer/director. Estab. 1990. **Buys 1 script(s)/year. Works with 1-2 writer(s)/year.** Buys first and all rights. No previously produced material. Query with synopsis, release form, personal bio, SASE. Responds in 5 months to queries; 6 months to scripts. **Pays in accordance with WGA standards, negotiable on writer's previous credits, etc.**
Needs: Films (16 and 35mm), videotapes. "We are a feature film and television and music video production company and have no audiovisual material needs."
Tips: "Best advice possible: Originality, uniqueness, write from your instincts and don't follow trends. Screenplays and T.V. scripts should be mailed to our Burbank, CA production office with a proper industry release form, a 1-page synopsis, and SASE, please. No hi-tech stories, fatal disease things. Looking for youth-driven material and solid literate material with unique premise and characters with substance. No period themes."

◘ REEL LIFE WOMEN, 10158 Hollow Glen Circle, Bel Air CA 90077. (310)271-4722. Fax: (310)274-0503. E-mail: feigenparrentlit@aol.com. **Contact:** Joanne Parrent, co-president. Estab. 1996. Mass audiences. **Buys 3-4 script(s)/year.** Accepts previously produced material. Query with synopsis, résumé. SASE. Responds in 2 months to queries. **Pays in accordance with WGA standards.**
Needs: Films. Looking for full-length scripts for feature films or television movies only. Must be professionally formatted and under 130 pages. All genres considered particularly drama, comedy, action, suspense. No series or episode TV scripts.
Tips: "Must be professional screenwriters. We are not interested in writers who don't know their craft well. That said, we are looking for interesting, unique stories, which have good roles for actresses. We are not interested in women in stereotypical roles, as the male hero's sidekick, as passive helpmates, etc."

TIM REID PRODUCTIONS, One New Millennium Dr., Petersburg VA 23805. (804)957-4200. **Contact:** Jarene Fleming, development executive. Estab. 1996. MOW's for network TV. Query with synopsis. Responds in 1 month to queries.
Needs: Multicultural TV movies with positive black images, also series and documentary.
Tips: Does not want to see stereotypical urban dysfunctional premises

Ⓝ SHORELINE ENTERTAINMENT, INC., (formerly Shoreline Pictures), 1875 Century Park E., Suite 600, Los Angeles CA 90067. (310)551-2060. Fax: (310)201-0729. E-mail: jfranco@shorelineentertainment.com. Website: www.shorelineentertainment.com. **Contact:** Joel Franco, director of development. Estab. 1993. Mass audience. **Buys 8 script(s)/year. Works with 8 writer(s)/year.** Buys all rights. Query. Responds in 2 weeks to queries.
Needs: Films (35, 70mm). Looking for commercial, exciting films. Thrillers (suspense/action) and big budget action fare. Completed screenplays only. Principal of our company co-produced *Glengarry Glen Ross; The Visit; Price of Glory; and Flight of Fancy.*"
Tips: "Looking for character driven films that are commercial as well as independent. Completed screenplays only. Especially looking for big-budget action, thrillers. We accept submissions by mail, e-mail or fax. No unsolicited screenplays, please."

Ⓝ SILVER LION FILMS, 701 Santa Monica Blvd., Suite 240, Santa Monica CA 90401. (310)393-9177. Fax: (310)458-9372. E-mail: dkzfilms@earthlink.net. **Contact:** David Kohner Zuckerman, director of development. Estab. 1988. General audience. Query. Responds in 3 months to queries; 6 months to scripts. **Pays percentage of budget.**
Needs: Films (35mm).

◘ SKYLARK FILMS, 1123 Pacific St., Santa Monica CA 90405. (310)396-5753. Fax: (310)396-5753. E-mail: skylarkdev@aol.com. **Contact:** Jason Pogni, director of development. Estab. 1990. **Buys 6 script(s)/year.** Buys first or all rights. Accepts previously produced material. Query with synopsis. Responds in 1 month to queries; 2 months to scripts. **Pays in accordance with WGA standards.**
   O➝ Skylark Films is now seeking action, suspense and thrillers.
Needs: Films (TV, cable, feature).
Tips: "True stories of romance or tragedy/redemption stories and contemporary issues for TV MOW's and cable. High concept, high stakes, action or romantic comedy for feature film."

⊠ SKYLINE PARTNERS, 10550 Wilshire Blvd., #304, Los Angeles CA 90024. (310)470-3363. Fax: (310)470-0060. E-mail: fkuehnert@earthlink.com. **Contact:** Fred Kuehuert. Estab. 1990. Produces material for theatrical, television, video audiences. **Buys 3 script(s)/year.** Buys all rights. Query with synopsis. Responds to query/synopsis within 2 weeks and if script is requested will respond within 1 month. **Pay negotiable.**
Needs: Films (35mm).
Tips: "First, send a treatment so a determination can be made if the genre is something we're looking for. Secondly, we will contact writer if there is preliminary interest. Thirdly, send complete script plus release form."

☐ ALAN SMITHEE FILMS, 7510 Sunset Blvd., #525, Hollywood CA 90046. Website: www.smithee.com/films. **Contact:** Cinjun Sinclair, story analyst; Fred Smythe, director. Estab. 1990. Mass, cable television and theatrical releases. **Buys 1 script(s)/year. Works with 5 writer(s)/year.** Buys first or all rights, or options short-term. No previously produced material. Query with synopsis. Responds in 2 months to queries. **Pays in accordance with WGA standards.**
Needs: Films (35mm), videotapes. Wants internationally marketable material. No specific needs, varies constantly with market.
Tips: "There is no 'best bet.' It's a competitive market. Our needs are slave to the ups and downs of the industry."

SOUTH FORK PRODUCTIONS, P.O. Box 1935, Santa Monica CA 90406-1935. Fax: (310)829-5029. E-mail: soforkprods@ireland.com. **Contact:** Jim Sullivan, producer. Estab. 1980. Produces material for TV and film. **Buys 2 script(s)/year. Works with 4 writer(s)/year.** Buys all rights. Query with synopsis, résumé, SASE. **Pays in accordance with WGA standards.**
　　○┐ South Fork is currently looking for Irish-based scripts.
Needs: Films (16, 35mm), videotapes.
Tips: "Follow established formats for treatments. SASE for return."

SPIRIT DANCE ENTERTAINMENT, 1023 North Orange Dr., Los Angeles CA 90038-2317. (323)512-7988. E-mail: meridian39301@earthlink.net. **Contact:** Robert Wheaton, story editor. Estab. 1997. A general film audience of all ages. Particularly interested in reaching young, college-educated adults. **Buys 1-5 script(s)/year. Works with 1-5 writer(s)/year.** Buys all rights. Accepts previously produced material. Query. Responds in 2 months to queries. **Pays in accordance with WGA standards.**
Needs: Films (35mm). "Well-crafted feature length (approximately 90-120 pages) scripts with a strong emotional core and well-developed characters. We will consider contemporary material of almost any genre which is broad in scope and appeal. With more intimate stories and period pieces, the writing must be exceptional. We are always interested in female driven stories and material that explores people of different cultures. Youth-oriented scripts (including children's stories) that are fresh and original are also of interest to us."
Tips: "Material should demonstrate writer's passion for the material and not simply be written for the market. Due to the enormous volume of submissions, we are unable to respond to every query. If you have received no response after 2 months, assume that the company has passed on your submission. If there is interest in seeing the complete work, it must be submitted through a WGA signatory agent, entertainment attorney or a bona fide production company. As a policy, we do not accept material by unrepresented writers (this includes writers who sign release forms)."

⊠ STARLIGHT PICTURES, 1725 S. Rainbow Blvd., #2-186, Las Vegas NV 89102. E-mail: ideamaster@aol.com. **Contact:** Brian McNeal, development executive. Estab. 1989. Audience is world-wide movie-going public. **Buys 3 script(s)/year. Works with 3 writer(s)/year.** Buys all rights. Accepts previously produced material. Query with synopsis. Responds in 3 months to queries; 4 months to scripts. **Pays in accordance with WGA standards or sometimes an option against larger purchase amounts.**
Needs: Films (35 mm). "Not necessarily looking at this time, but 'good' scripts will always get our attention. Prefer well-written dramatic scripts set in *any* genre."
Tips: "It is sad to say that Hollywood is inundated with scripts by writers that possess 7th grade writing skills. This makes it harder for the 'good' scripts by real writers to get noticed. Please learn your craft before submitting material."

STUDIO MERRYWOOD, a division of EduMedia, 1199 Whitney Ave., Apt. G7, Hamden CT 06517-2804. (203)777-6957. Fax: (203)777-6265. E-mail: rdsetc@att.net. Website: www.bardsworld.com. **Contact:** Raúl daSilva, CEO/creative director. Estab. 1984. Produces feature films, documentaries. "We are not seeking any externally written screenplays for features but will engage produced screenwriters as consultants if they have been further recognized in the industry through leadership or international competitive festival prizes."
Needs: "Currently, no external material is sought. This may change. Thus, seasoned, professional writers may e-mail us for a status on needs. As in Tips, below, please lead your e-mail letter with a paragraph on your qualifications."
Tips: "This is not a market for novice writers. We are a small, creative shop and cannot train neophyte, unpublished or unproduced writers who would best try larger markets and media facilities. We cannot return or even acknowledge any unsolicited material and will discard such material. Those qualified please contact us first by e-mail with your qualifications and your offerings."

SUMMERS ENTERTAINMENT, 5230 Linwood Dr., Los Angeles CA 90027. (323)665-5400. E-mail: csent@pacbell.net. **Contact:** Cathleen Summers, producer. Buys motion picture/TV rights and Internet rights. Accepts previously produced material. Query with synopsis. Responds in 1 month to queries. **Pays in accordance with WGA standards.**

O→ "If writer has good project that requires guidance or rewrite in order to be sold, will discuss possibility. Or if film financed by independent, but, to date, all move to WGA." Looking for interesting "Commercial" stories designed for the visual medium of filmic storytelling.
Tips: "Please tell us enough so we understand the concept. Genre or total generalization is too vague to consider. You do not need to reveal all but enough for us to know why you are so enthusiastic."

VANGUARD PRODUCTIONS, 12111 Beatrice St., Culver City CA 90230. **Contact:** Terence M. O'Keefe, president. Estab. 1985. **Buys 1 script(s)/year.** Buys all rights. Accepts previously produced material. Query with synopsis, résumé. Responds in 3 months to queries; 6 months to scripts. **Pays in accordance with WGA standards, negotiated option.**
Needs: Films (35mm), videotapes.

[N] [symbol] WOODBERRY PRODUCTIONS, 3410 Descanso Dr., Suite 4, Los Angeles CA 90026. (323)668-9170. E-mail: lindagrae@aol.com. **Contact:** Linda Graeme, producer. Estab. 1994. Drama producer—film and TV. **Works with 2-3 writer(s)/year.** Options film & TV rights only. Query with synopsis, writing samples. Responds in 1 month to queries; 3 months to scripts. **Pays in accordance with WGA standards.**
Needs: Drama production for film and TV. Looking for character-driven dramatic material. Usual 2-hour. No big-budget, high-action studio fare.
Tips: Break in with a "letter/email with short and concise description of project, plus brief rundown of writing history."

THE WOOFENILL WORKS, INC., 516 E. 81st St., Suite #3, New York NY 10028-2530. (212)734-2578. Fax: (212)734-3186. E-mail: woofenill@earthlink.net. Website: home.earthlink.net/~woofenill/. **Contact:** Kathy Winthrop, creative executive. Estab. 1990. Theatrical audience. **Buys 4-7 script(s)/year. Works with 10 writer(s)/year.** Buys all rights. Query with synopsis. Responds in 2 months to queries; 4 months to scripts. **Acquires option, then payment on production.**
Needs: Films (35mm).
Tips: "We suggest that interested writers first review the company's website and in particular, the section General Business Parameters."

[symbol] ZACHARY ENTERTAINMENT, 273 S. Swall Dr., Beverly Hills CA 90211-2612. Fax: (310)289-9788. E-mail: zacharyent@aol.com. **Contact:** David O. Miller, development associate. Estab. 1981. Audience is film goers of all ages, television viewers. **Buys 5-10 script(s)/year. Works with 30 writer(s)/year.** Rights purchased vary. Query with synopsis. Responds in 2 weeks to queries; 3 months to scripts. **Payment varies.**
Needs: Films for theatrical, cable and network television release.
Tips: "Submit logline (one line description) and a short synopsis of storyline. Short biographical profile, focus on professional background. SASE required for all mailed inquiries. If submissions are sent via e-mail, subject must include specific information or else run the risk of being deleted as junk mail. All genres accepted but ideas must be commercially viable, high concept, original and marketable."

MARKETS THAT WERE listed in the 2001 edition of *Writer's Market* but do not appear this year are listed in the General Index with a notation explaining why they were omitted.

Syndicates

Newspaper syndicates distribute columns, cartoons and other written material to newspapers around the country—and sometimes around the world. Competition for syndication slots is stiff. The number and readership of newspapers are dropping. With paper costs high, there are fewer pages and less money to spend in filling them. Coveted spots in general interest, humor and political commentary are held by big-name columnists such as Ellen Goodman, Bob Herbert and Cal Thomas. And multitudes of aspiring writers wait in the wings, hoping one of these heavy hitters will move on to something else and leave the spotlight open.

Although this may seem discouraging, there are in fact many areas in which less-known writers are syndicated. Syndicates are not looking for general interest or essay columns. What they are looking for are fresh voices that will attract readers. As consumer interests and lifestyles change, new doors are being opened for innovative writers capable of covering emerging trends.

Most syndicates distribute a variety of columns, cartoons and features. Although the larger ones are usually only interested in running ongoing material, smaller ones often accept short features and one-shots in addition to continuous columns. Specialized syndicates—those that deal with a single area such as business—often sell to magazines, trade journals and other business publications as well as to newspapers.

THE WINNING COMBINATION

In presenting yourself and your work, note that most syndicated columnists start out writing for local newspapers. Many begin as staff writers, develop a following in a particular area, and are then picked up by a syndicate. Before approaching a syndicate, write for a paper in your area. Develop a good collection of clips that you feel is representative of your best writing.

New ideas are paramount to syndication. Sure, you'll want to study the popular columnists to see how their pieces are structured (most are short—from 500-750 words—and really pack a punch), but don't make the mistake of imitating a well-known columnist. Syndicates are looking for original material that is timely, saleable and original. Do not submit a column to a syndicate on a subject it already covers. The more unique the topic, the greater your chances. Most importantly, be sure to choose a topic that interests you and one you know well.

APPROACHING MARKETS

Request a copy of a syndicate's writer's guidelines. It will give you information on current needs, submission standards and response times. Most syndicates prefer a query letter and about six sample columns or writing samples and a SASE. You may also want to include a client list and business card if available. If you have a particular area of expertise pertinent to your submission, mention this in your letter and back it up by sending related material. For highly specialized or technical matter, provide credentials to show you are qualified to handle the topic.

In essence, syndicates act as agents or brokers for the material they handle. Writing material is usually sold as a package. The syndicate will promote and market the work to newspapers (and sometimes to magazines) and keep careful records of sales. Writers receive 40-60 percent of gross receipts. Some syndicates may also pay a small salary or flat fee for one-shot items.

Syndicates usually acquire all rights to accepted material, although a few are now offering writers and artists the option of retaining ownership. In selling all rights, writers give up ownership and future use of their creations. Consequently, sale of all rights is not the best deal for writers, and has been the reason many choose to work with syndicates that buy less restrictive rights. Before signing a contract with a syndicate, you may want to go over the terms with an attorney or with an agent who has a background in law. The best contracts will usually offer the writer a percentage of gross receipts (as opposed to net receipts) and will not bind the writer for longer than five years.

THE SELF-SYNDICATION OPTION

Many writers choose to self-syndicate. This route allows you to retain all rights, and gives you the freedom of a business owner. But as a self-syndicated writer, you must also act as your own manager, marketing team and sales force. You must develop mailing lists, and a pricing, billing and collections structure.

Payment is usually negotiated on a case-by-case basis. Small newspapers may offer only $10-20 per column, but larger papers may pay much more (for more information on pay rates, see How Much Should I Charge? on page 70). The number of papers you deal with is only limited by your marketing budget and your tenacity.

If you self-syndicate, be aware that some newspapers are not copyrighted, so you should copyright your own material. It's less expensive to copyright columns as a collection than individually. For more information on copyright procedures, see Copyrighting Your Writing in the Business of Writing section.

FOR MORE INFORMATION . . .

A complete listing of syndicates with contact names and the features they represent can be found in the *Editor & Publisher Syndicate Directory* (770 Broadway, New York NY 10003-9595). The weekly magazine, *Editor & Publisher*, also has news articles about syndicates and can provide you with information about changes and events in the industry.

Information on syndicates listed in the previous edition of *Writer's Market* but not included in this edition can be found in the General Index.

N **AMERICAS BEST AUTO**, 6708 Auburn Ave. W., Bradenton FL 34207. (941)758-5039. E-mail: brucehubbard@ earthlink.net. **Contact:** Bruce Hubbard. Estab. 1990. **50% freelance written on contract. Buys 50 feature(s)/year.** Syndicates to magazines, newspapers, Internet. Query with or without published clips. Responds in 1 week. Buys second serial (reprint) rights. **Pays often on acceptance.**
Needs: Newspaper columns. Buys single (one shot) features, articles series. **Pays $100 minimum. Pays $25-700 for photos.** *Americas Best Auto, 100 Best Hotels,* and *One Tank Test Drive.*

ARTISTMARKET.COM, 35336 Spring Hill, Farmington Hills MI 48331-2044. (248)661-8585. Fax: (248)788-1022. E-mail: editor@artistmarket.com. Website: www.artistmarket.com. **Contact:** David Kahn, editor. Estab. 1996. Syndicates to magazines, newspapers, Internet. Submit written features in 250 words or less via e-mail, postal mail or disk (PC format).
Needs: Fillers, short humor features, all written works for publication in magazines, newspapers, etc. Send samples. **Pays 50% author's percentage.** Currently syndicates cartoonists, comic strips, puzzles, fillers, etc. Publishes "www. artistmarket.com" website directed to newspaper, magazine editors and website publishers.

AUTO DIGEST SYNDICATE, P.O. Box 459, Prineville OR 97754-0459. (541)923-4688. Fax: (815)346-9002. E-mail: adigest@iname.com. **Contact:** Bill Schaffer, co-owner. Estab. 1992. **17% freelance written on contract. Buys 50 feature(s)/year. Works with 3-4 writer(s)/year.** Syndicates to newspapers, Internet. Query. Responds in 2 months. Buys first North American serial rights. **Pays when paid by publication.**
Needs: Newspaper columns, news items. **All writers equally split fee after expenses.** Currently syndicates: *New Car Reviews,* by Bill and Barbara Schaffer (800-1,000 words plus photo); *Auto Update* and *Car Quiz,* by Bill and Barbara Schaffer (400-500 words); *Auto Forum,* by Chip Keen (400-500 words).

BLACK PRESS SERVICE, INC., 166 Madison Ave., New York NY 10016. (212)686-6850. Fax: (212)686-7308. **Contact:** Roy Thompson, editor. Estab. 1966. **10% freelance written on contract; 10% freelance written on one-time basis. Buys hundreds of feature(s)/year. Works with hundreds of writer(s)/year.** Syndicates to magazines, newspapers, radio. Send complete ms. Responds in 2 months. Buys all rights.

Needs: Magazine columns, magazine features, newspaper columns, newspaper features, news items, radio broadcast material. Buys single (one shot) features, articles series, current events oriented article series. **Pays variable flat rate.** Currently syndicates *Bimonthly Report*, by staff (roundup of minority-oriented news).

CONTINENTAL FEATURES/CONTINENTAL NEWS SERVICE, 501 W. Broadway, P.M.B #265 Plaza A, San Diego CA 92101-3802. (858)492-8696. E-mail: continentalnewstime@lycos.com. Website: pages.hotbot.com/current/ newstime. **Contact:** Gary P. Salamone, editor-in-chief. Estab. 1981. **100% freelance written on contract.** "Writers who offer the kind and quality of writing we seek stand an equal chance regardless of experience." Syndicates to magazines, newspapers. Query. Responds in 1 month. Writer's guidelines for #10 SASE.
Needs: Magazine features, newspaper features. "Feature material should fit the equivalent of one-quarter to one-half standard newspaper page, and Continental News considers an ultra-liberal or ultra-conservative slant inappropriate." **Pays 70% author's percentage.** Currently syndicates *News and Comment*, by Charles Hampton Savage (general news commentary/analysis); *Portfolio*, (cartoon/caricature art); *Sports and Families*, by former American League Pitcher David Frost; *Traveler's Checks*, by Ann Hattes; and *OnVideo*, by Harley Lond; over 50 features in all.
Tips: "CF/CNS is working to develop a feature package of greater interest and value to an English-speaking international audience. That is, those writers who can accompany their economic-social-political analyses (of foreign countries) with photo(s) of the key public figure(s) involved are particularly in demand. Official photos (8×10 down to 3×5) of key government leaders available from the information ministry/press office/embassy will be acceptable. CF/CNS emphasizes analytical/explanatory articles, but muckraking articles (where official-photo requests are inopportune) are also encouraged."

COPLEY NEWS SERVICE, P.O. Box 120190, San Diego CA 92112. (619)293-1818. E-mail: infofax@copleynews.c om. Website: www.copleynews.com. **Contact:** Glenda Winders, editorial director. **15% freelance written on one-time basis.** Most stories produced by news bureaus or picked up from Copley newspapers. **Offers 200 features/week.** Syndicates to newspapers, Internet. Query with published clips. Responds in 6 months. Buys first rights.
Needs: Comic strips, travel stories, columns on technology, new ideas. **Pays $100/story or negotiated monthly salary.**
Tips: "Writer needs to have a sense of competition for space in newspapers and offer features of broad, timely appeal. Competition is keen, but we are always on the lookout for good writers and fresh ideas."

CRICKET COMMUNICATIONS, INC., P.O. Box 527, Ardmore PA 19003-0527. (610)789-2480 or (610)924-9158. Fax: (610)924-9159. E-mail: crcktinc@aol.com. **Contact:** E. A. Stern, senior editor. Estab. 1975. **10% freelance written on contract; 10% freelance written on one-time basis. Works with 2-3 new previously unpublished writer(s)/year.** Syndicates to newspapers, trade magazines. Query with published clips. Responds in 1 month. Buys all rights.
Needs: Magazine columns, magazine features, newspaper columns, newspaper features, news items. All tax and financial-oriented (700-1,500 words); also newspaper columns, features and news items directed to small business. **Pays $50-500.** Currently syndicates *Hobby/Business*, by Mark E. Battersby (tax and financial); *Farm Taxes*, by various authors; and *Small Business Taxes*, by Mark E. Battersby.

N CROSSWORD.ORG, P.O. Box 1503, New York NY 10021. (212)535-6811. **Contact:** Alfred Neumann, editor. Estab. 1998. **60% freelance written on contract; 40% freelance written on one-time basis.** Syndicates to magazines, newspapers. Responds in 1 month. Buys all rights.
Needs: Crossword puzzles. **Pays $350 for Sunday puzzle; $150 for daily puzzle.** Currently publishes online with PuzzleAmerica.com.

DANY NEWS SERVICE, 22 Lesley Dr., Syosset NY 11791. (516)921-4611. **Contact:** David Nydick, president and editor. **5% freelance written on one-time basis. Buys 10-12 feature(s)/year. Works with 5-10 writer(s)/year.** Syndicates to newspapers. Send complete ms. Responds in 2 weeks. Buys all rights. **Pays on acceptance.**
Needs: Newspaper features. **Pays $100-500 and up flat rate.** Currently syndicates *You, Your Child and School*; *You, Your Child and Entertainment*; *You, Your Child and Sports*.

DEMKO'S AGEVENTURE SYNDICATED NEWS SERVICE, 21946 Pine Trace, Boca Raton FL 33428-3057. (561)482-6271. E-mail: ageventure@demko.com. Website: Website: www.demko.com. Estab. 1983. **25% freelance written on contract; 25% freelance written on one-time basis. Buys 52 feature(s)/year. Works with 27 writer(s)/ year.** Syndicates to magazines, radio, newspapers, Internet. Query via e-mail. Responds in 1 month. **Pays on acceptance.**
Needs: News items. Buys single (one shot) features, articles series. Currently syndicates *Senior Living* (500-750 words) lifestyle feature columns—staff writer; *Sonic Boomers* (150-200 words and photo) personal profiles (ages 40-50); *Aging America* (50-75 words) mature market news items.
Tips: "Stick with what you know in order to avoid superficial content. Query via e-mail with 2-3 work samples. Be assertive and upfront—specify your product and costs/prices in advance."

N DORSEY COMMUNICATIONS, 9239 Donery Rd., Los Angeles CA 90069. (310)273-2245. **Contact:** Helen Dorsey, CEO. Estab. 1980. **25% freelance written on one-time basis. Buys 5-10 feature(s)/year. Works with 2-3 writer(s)/year.** Syndicates to magazines, newspapers. Query only, no guidelines. Buys all rights.
Needs: Newspaper columns, newspaper features, news items, fillers. Buys article series. **Pays 25% author's percentage. Additional payment for photos.** Currently syndicates *Celebrity Cookbook*, by Johna Blinn (foodstyle); *Up Close and Personal*, by Helen Dorsey (celebrity interviews).

EDITORIAL CONSULTANT SERVICE, P.O. Box 524, West Hempstead NY 11552-1206. Fax: (516)481-5487. E-mail: Alongo42033.com. **Contact:** Arthur A. Ingoglia, editorial director. Estab. 1964. **40% freelance written on contract; 25% freelance written on one-time basis.** Adds about 10 new columnists/year. **Works with 75 writer(s)/year.** Syndicates to magazines, radio, newspapers, automotive trade and consumer publications. Query. Responds in 2 months. Buys all rights. Writer's guidelines for #10 SASE.
Needs: Magazine columns, magazine features, newspaper columns, newspaper features, news items, radio broadcast material. Prefers carefully documented material with automotive slant. Also considers automotive trade features. Will consider article series. Submit 2-3 columns. No horoscope, child care, lovelorn or pet care. **Pays varies, usually averages 50% author's percentage. Additional payment for 8×10 b&w and color photos accepted with ms.**
Tips: "Emphasis is placed on articles and columns with an automotive slant. We prefer consumer-oriented features, how to save money on your car, what every woman should know about her car, how to get more miles per gallon, etc."

[N] ENVIRONMENT NEWS SERVICE (ENS), 322 Seventh Ave., 3rd Floor, New York NY 10001. (212)279-4350. E-mail: new@ens-news.com. Website: www.ens-news.com. **Contact:** Jim Crabtree. Estab. 1990. **30% freelance written on contract. Works with 125 writer(s)/year. Works with 10-15 new previously unpublished writer(s)/year.** Syndicates to Internet. Does not return submissions; accepts queries only. Query only. Responds in 1 week. Buys first North American serial rights. **Pays on acceptance.** Free writer's guidelines.
Needs: News items. Buys single (one shot) features, articles series, Late-breaking news only. **Pays flat rate. Additional payment for photos.**
Tips: "ENS uses only late-breaking environmental news. No features. Writers do best in regions where a great deal of legislation or events occur."

HISPANIC LINK NEWS SERVICE, 1420 N St. NW, Washington DC 20005. (202)234-0280. Fax: (202)234-4090. E-mail: editor@hispaniclink.org. **Contact:** Patricia Guadalupe, editor; Charles A. Ericksen, publisher. Estab. 1980. **50% freelance written on contract; 50% freelance written on one-time basis.** Syndicates to 60 newspapers and magazines with circulations from 5,000 to 300,000. **Buys 156 feature(s)/year. Works with 50 writer(s)/year. Works with 5 new previously unpublished writer(s)/year.** Query or send complete ms. For reprints, send photocopy of article. Responds in 1 month. Buys second serial (reprint) rights, negotiable rights. Free writer's guidelines.
Needs: Newspaper columns, newspaper features. "We prefer 650-700 word op/ed, analysis or news features geared to a general national audience, but focus on issue or subject of particular interest to Hispanics. Some longer pieces accepted occasionally." **Pays $25-100. Pays $25 for guest columns.** Currently syndicates *Hispanic Link*, by various authors (opinion and/or feature columns). Syndicated through Los Angeles Times Syndicate.
  ○━ "We're always looking for strong news features or personal stories relating to holidays—Christmas, Mother's/Father's Day, Valentines, Easter, etc."
Tips: "We would especially like to get topical material and vignettes relating to Hispanic presence and progress in the U.S. and Puerto Rico. Provide insights on Hispanic experience geared to a general audience. Of the columns we accept, 85-90% are authored by Hispanics; the Link presents Hispanic viewpoints and showcases Hispanic writing talent through its subscribing newspapers and magazines. Copy can be submitted in English or Spanish. We syndicate both languages."

HOLLYWOOD INSIDE SYNDICATE, P.O. Box 49957, Los Angeles CA 90049-0957. (818)509-7840. Fax: (818)509-7840. E-mail: hollywood@ez2.net. Website: www.ez2.net/hollywood. **Contact:** John Austin, editor. Estab. 1968. **10% freelance written on contract; 40% freelance written on one-time basis.** Purchases entertainment-oriented mss for syndication to newspapers in San Francisco, Philadelphia, Detroit, Montreal, London, Sydney, Manila, South Africa, etc. Accepts previously published submissions, only if published in the US or Canada. Responds in 3 months. Response time depends on timeliness of material.
Needs: News items (column items concerning entertainment—motion pictures—personalities and jet setters for syndicated column; 250-300 words). Also considers series of 1,500-word articles. "Query first. Also off-beat travel pieces but not on areas covered extensively in the Sunday supplements; not luxury cruise liners but lower cost cruises. We also syndicate nonfiction book subjects—sex, travel, etc., to overseas markets. Also require 1,500-word celebrity profiles on internationally-recognized celebrities. We stress *internationally*." Currently syndicates *Books of the Week* column and *Celebri-Quotes, Movie Trivia Quiz, Hollywood Inside, Hollywood Star Features.*
  ○━ Writing for the Hollywood Inside Syndicate should be geared for the worldwide web and the international consumer, concise and to the point, without "flowery" sentences. "Anything on world wide celebrities will be welcome but not in the first person. No: 'I asked him/her...' etc. We concentrate on film 'stars,' not TV."
Tips: "Study the entertainment pages of Sunday (and daily) newspapers to see the type of specialized material we deal in. Perhaps we are different from other syndicates, but we deal with celebrities. No 'I' journalism such as 'when I spoke to Cloris Leachman.' Many freelancers submit material from the 'dinner theater' and summer stock circuit of 'gossip type' items from what they have observed about the 'stars' or featured players in these productions—how they act off stage, who they romance, etc. We use this material."

INTERPRESS OF LONDON AND NEW YORK, 90 Riverside Drive, New York NY 10026. (212)873-0772. **Contact:** Jeffrey Blyth, editor-in-chief. Estab. 1971. **10% freelance written on one-time basis. Buys 10-12 feature(s)/year.** Syndicates to radio, newspapers. Query. Responds in 1 week. Buys all rights. Writer's guidelines for #10 SASE.

Needs: Magazine features, newspaper features, off-beat feature stories. Buys single (one shot) features. **Pays 60% author's percentage. Additional payment for photos.** Currently syndicates *Destination America*, by various writers (travel series); *Book World*, by Myrna Grier (book news/reviews); *Dateline NY*, by various writers (show biz news/features); *Music World* (news about new CDs and recordings). Also columns on media and medical news.

LOS ANGELES TIMES SYNICATE INTERNATIONAL, 202 W. First St., Los Angeles CA 90053. (213)237-6354. E-mail: constance.pollock@latsi.com. Website: www.lats.com. Syndicates to the global market, exclusive of the U.S. Column proposals should be sent to Associate Editor Constance Pollock. Responds in 2 months. Buys varying rights.
Needs: Material ranges from 800-2,000 words. LATSI editors also buy entertainment, health and fitness, food, travel and environmental articles for inclusion in weekly packages. Currently syndicates Dr. Henry Kissinger, Alvin Toffler, Shimon Peres, Carlos Fuentes, William Pfaff and Alvaro Vargas Llosa.

MEGALO MEDIA, P.O. Box 1503, New York NY 10021. Website: www.puzzleamerica.com. **Contact:** J. Baxter Newgate, president. Estab. 1972. **50% freelance written on contract; 50% freelance written on one-time basis. Works with 5 new previously unpublished writer(s)/year.** Syndicates to magazines, newspapers. Query. Responds in 1 month. Buys all rights. Writer's guidelines for #10 SASE.
Needs: Crossword puzzles. Buys single (one shot) features. **Pays flat rate of $150 for Sunday puzzle.** Currently syndicates *National Challenge*, by J. Baxter Newgate (crossword puzzle); *Crossword Puzzle* by J. Baxter Newgate.

MOTOR NEWS MEDIA CORPORATION, 7177 Hickman Rd. Suite 11-D, Urbandale IA 50322. (515)270-6782. Fax: (515)270-8752. E-mail: mnmedia@uswest.net. Website: www.motornewsmedia.com. Estab. 1995. **90% freelance written on contract; 10% freelance written on one-time basis. Buys 132-150 feature(s)/year. Works with 10-12 writer(s)/year. Works with 2-4 new previously unpublished writer(s)/year.** Syndicates to newspapers, Internet. Query. Responds in 6 weeks. Buys first North American serial rights, second serial (reprint) rights. **Pays within 45 days of publication.**
Needs: Newspaper features. Buys single (one shot) features, articles series, automotive series. Currently syndicates *Roadworthy*, by Ken Chester, Jr.; *Credit & Coverage*, by Tom Brownell; *Hard Bargains*, by Neal White; *Dateline: Detroit!*, by Kailoni Yates; *Street Talk*, by Mike Fornataro; *Neal's Garage* by Neal White; *High & Mighty*, by Robin Bailey; *Ask Mr. Fix-It*, by Andy Mikonis; *Ask Dr. Gizmo*, by Phil Arendt; *Motocycling*, by Jim Kelly; *Timeless Nostalgia*, by Bill Vance; *Car Concerns*, by Susan Frissell; and *RV Traveling*, by Bill and Jan Moeller.
Tips: "We look for unique automotive content to round out our current offerings. Not interested in new vehicle reviews."

THE NATIONAL FINANCIAL NEWS SERVICES, 331 W. Boot Rd., West Chester PA 19380. (610)344-7380. Fax: (610)696-1184. E-mail: brucenfns@aol.com. Website: www.nfns.com. **Contact:** Bruce Meyers. Estab. 1985. **2% freelance written on contract. Buys 52 feature(s)/year. Works with 1 new previously unpublished writer(s)/year.** Syndicates to newspapers. Query. Buys all rights. **Pays on acceptance.**
Needs: Currently syndicates *Mortgages This Week*, by Al Bowman.

NATIONAL NEWS BUREAU, P.O. Box 43039, Philidelphia PA 19129-0628. (215)849-9016. Fax: (610)696-1184. **Contact:** Harry Jay Katz, editor. **20% freelance written on contract; 35-40% freelance written on one-time basis. Buys 100 feature(s)/year. Works with 200 writer(s)/year. Works with 50% new new previously unpublished writer(s)/year.** Syndicates to magazines, newspapers. Query with published clips. Responds in 2 weeks. Buys all rights. **Pays on publication.** Writer's guidelines for 9×12 SAE with 3 first-class stamps.
Needs: Magazine features, newspaper columns, newspaper features. "We do many reviews and celebrity interviews. Only original, assigned material." Buys single (one shot) features, articles series, film reviews, etc. **Pays $5-200 flat rate or 50% author's percentage. Offers $5-200 additional payment for photos accompanying ms.**

NEWS USA, 7777 Leesburg Pike, #307, Falls Church VA 22305. (703)734-6300. Website: www.newsusa.com. **Contact:** Katherine Egan, editorial director. Estab. 1988. **90% freelance written on contract. Buys 200 feature(s)/ year. Works with 20 writer(s)/year.** Syndicates to radio, newspapers, Internet. Query. Responds in 2 months. Buys all rights. **Pays on acceptance.** Writer's guidelines for #10 SASE.
Needs: Newspaper features. "I only buy articles I commission from freelancers." **Pays $50 flat rate.**

PRESS ASSOCIATES, INC., 815 15th St. NW, Washington DC 20005. (202)638-0444. Fax: (202)638-0955. E-mail: painews@bellatlantic.net. Website: www.pressassociates.com. **Contact:** Mark Gruenberg, president/editor. Estab. 1957. **5% freelance written on contract. Buys 100 feature(s)/year. Works with 2 writer(s)/year.** Union newspapers and publications. Query. Responds in 2 months. Buys first North American serial rights. **Pays on publication.** Free writer's guidelines.
Needs: News items. Buys single (one shot) features. **Pays 25¢/published word; maximum of $25. Additional payment for photos.** "One-paragraph proposals with SASE only. Must be news—no opinion pieces—and pro-worker."
Tips: "We are *labor*-oriented. We do not syndicate outside of our subscribing readers."

SCRAMBL-GRAM INC., 41 Park Dr., Port Clinton OH 43452. (419)734-2600. Website: www.puzzlebuffs.com. **Contact:** S. Bowers, managing editor. Estab. 1978. **50% freelance written on one-time basis. Buys 300 feature(s)/**

year. Works with 20-30 writer(s)/year. Works with 3-5 new previously unpublished writer(s)/year. Syndicates to magazines, newspapers, Internet. Responds in 1 month. Buys all rights. **Pays on acceptance.** Writer's guidelines for #10 SASE.

Needs: "We accept only crossword puzzles. Submit one or two examples of your work and if interested, we will send you information and materials to produce puzzles for us." **Rates are based on the size of the crossword, pays $25-60 per puzzle.**

Tips: "Our crosswords appear weekly in *STAR Magazine, National Enquirer, Country Weekly,* and numerous other magazines and newspapers. Crosswords should be edited to remove obscure and archaic words. Foreign words should be kept to a minimum. The puzzle should be fun and challenging but achievable."

N SENIOR WIRE, 2377 Elm St., Denver CO 80207. (303)355-3882. E-mail: clearmountain@qwest.net. Website: www.newmaturity.com. **Contact:** Allison St. Claire, editor/publisher. Estab. 1988. Monthly news, information and feature syndication service to various senior publications, and companies interested in senior market. Circulation nation-wide, in Canada and India, varies per article depending on which articles are bought for publication. Submit seasonal/holiday material 3 months in advance. Prefers mss; queries only with SASE. Responds in 3 months. **Pays 50% of fee for each use of ms ($15-50). Pays on publication.** Writer's guidelines for $1 with SASE.

Needs: Does not want "anything aimed at less than age 55-plus market; anything patronizing or condescending to seniors." Seasonal features, especially those with a nostalgic angle (750-800 words); personal travel experiences as a mature traveler (700-1,000 words); personal essays and commentary (500-750 words). The following topics currently are covered by assigned columnists and similar material has little chance of immediate acceptance: National legislation; financial and legal advice; golf; Internet; automotive; fitness; food; collectibles; Q&A on relationships; and beauty tips after 50. **Accepts 12 mss in each category/year.**

Tips: "That quintessential sweet little old lady in the rocking chair, Whistler's mother, was just 50 years old when she posed for that painting. Today, the average age of the Rolling Stones in 55. Most of our client papers like to emphasize active, thoughtful, concerned seniors and are currently picking up material that shows seniors living in the 'real,' i.e., contemporary, world. For example, do you have your own personal fax yet; how has a computer changed your life; what kind of new cars are you looking at? What adventures have you been involved in? What impact are you/seniors having on the world around them—and vice versa? Currently overloaded with humor. Seeking regular columnists in following: Senior sexuality, psychology, grandparenting and alternative health."

THE SPORTS NETWORK, 95 James Way, Southhampton PA 18966. (215)942-7890. Fax: (215)942-7647. E-mail: psokol@sportsnetwork.com. Website: www.sportsnetwork.com. Estab. 1980. **30% freelance written on contract; 10-15% freelance written on one-time basis. Buys 200-250 feature(s)/year. Works with 50-60 writer(s)/year. Works with 10-15 new previously unpublished writer(s)/year.** Syndicates to magazines, radio, newspapers, has the added benefit of being an international sports wire service with established awareness globally furnishing exposure world-wide for its writers/clients. Query with published clips. Responds immediately. Buys all rights. Free writer's guidelines.

Needs: Magazine columns, magazine features, newspaper columns, newspaper features, news items, fillers, radio and broadcast material. Looking for single features (timely sports pieces, from 700-1,000 words). Seeking ongoing coverage pieces of teams (professional), leagues (professional), conferences (college) and sports, 1-2 times weekly. **Payments variable.** Currently syndicates *The Sandlot Shrink,* by Dennis LePore; *Infosport,* by Julie Lanzillo; *The Women's Basketball Journal, Bball Stats,* by Robert Chaikin.

Tips: "The competition for sports is fast and furious, so right time and place, with a pinch of luck, are ingredients that complement talent. Making inroads to one syndicate for even one feature is an amazing door opener. Focus on the needs of that syndicate or wire service (as in the case with TSN) and use that as a springboard to establish a proven track record with quality work that suits specific needs. Don't give up and don't abandon the day job. This takes commitment, desire, knowledge of the topic, and willingness to work at it while being able to handle rejection. No one who reads submissions really 'knows' and the history of great rejections would fill volumes, from *Gone with the Wind* to Snoopy and Garfield. We are different in that we are looking for specific items and not a magical cartoon (although sports cartoons will work), feature or story. Give us your best in sports and make certain that is is in tune with what is happening right now or is able to stand the test of time, be an evergreen and everlasting if it is a special feature."

TEENAGE CORNER, INC., 70-540 Gardenia Ct., Rancho Mirage CA 92270. **Contact:** Mrs. David J. Lavin. **Buys 122 feature(s)/year.** Syndicates to newspapers. Send complete ms. Responds in 1 week.

Needs: Newspaper features (500 words). **Pays $25, material is not copyrighted.**

■ TV DATA, 333 Glen St., Glens Falls NY 12801. (518)792-9914. Fax: (800)660-7185. E-mail: mskotnicki@tvdata.com. Website: www.tvdata.com. **Contact:** Monique Skotnicki, features managing editor. **70% freelance written on contract; 30% freelance written on one-time basis. Buys 100 feature(s)/year. Works with 20 writer(s)/year.** Syndicates to newspapers, Internet. Query with published clips. Responds in 1 month. Buys all rights. **Pays on publication.**

Needs: Newspaper columns, newspaper features, fillers.

   ○→ Submissions must be: TV-related; no more than 1,000 words; written according to AP style; sent as a Quark or Microsoft Word attachment.

Tips: "Submissions should be television-related features about trends, stars, sports, movies, the Internet, etc. They should be approximately 1,000 words and written according to AP style."

Greeting Cards & Gift Ideas

How many greeting cards did you buy last year? Americans bought nearly six billion cards last year. That's according to figures published by The Greeting Card Association, a national trade organization representing the multi-billion dollar greeting card industry.

In fact, nearly 50 percent of all first class mail now consists of greeting cards. And, of course, card manufacturers rely on writers to supply them with enough skillfully crafted sentiments to meet the demand. The perfect greeting card verse is one that will appeal to a large audience, yet will make each buyer feel that the card was written exclusively for him or her.

Two greeting card companies dominate this industry; together, Hallmark and American Greetings supply 85 percent of all cards sold. The other 15 percent are published by nearly 2,000 companies who have found success mainly by not competing head to head with the big two but by choosing instead to pursue niche markets—regional and special-interest markets that the big two either cannot or do not supply.

A PROFESSIONAL APPROACH TO MARKETS

As markets become more focused, it's important to keep current on specific company needs. Familiarize yourself with the differences among lines of cards by visiting card racks. Ask retailers which lines are selling best. You may also find it helpful to read trade magazines such as *Gifts and Decorative Accessories* and *Party and Paper Retailer* (www.partypaper.com). These publications will keep you apprised of changes and events within the field, including seminars and trade shows.

Once you find a card line that appeals to you, write to the company and request its market list, catalog or submission guidelines (usually available for a SASE or a small fee). This information will help you determine whether or not your ideas are appropriate for that market.

Submission procedures vary among greeting card publishers, depending on the size and nature of the company. Keep in mind that many companies (especially the large ones) will not review your writing samples until you've signed and returned their disclosure contract or submission agreement, assuring them that your material is original and has not been submitted elsewhere.

Some editors prefer to see individual card ideas on 3×5 cards, while others prefer to receive a number of complete ideas on $8\frac{1}{2} \times 11$ bond paper. Be sure to put your best pieces at the top of the stack. Most editors do not want to see artwork unless it is professional, but they do appreciate conceptual suggestions for design elements. If your verse depends on an illustration to make its point or if you have an idea for a unique card shape or foldout, include a dummy card with your writing samples.

The usual submission includes from 5 to 15 card ideas and an accompanying cover letter, plus mechanical dummy cards, if necessary. Some editors also like to receive a résumé, client list and business card. Some do not. Be sure to check the listings and the company's writer's guidelines for such specifications before submitting material.

Payment for greeting card verse varies, but most firms pay per card or per idea; a handful pay small royalties. Some companies prefer to test a card first and will pay a small fee for a test card idea. In some instances, a company may even purchase an idea and never use it.

Greeting card companies will also buy ideas for gift products and may use card material for a number of subsequent items. Licensing—the sale of rights to a particular character for a variety of products from mugs to T-shirts—is a growing part of the industry. Because of this, however, note that most card companies buy all rights. We now include in this section markets for licensed product lines such as mugs, bumper stickers, buttons, posters and the like.

Information of interest to writers wishing to know more about working with the greeting card industry is available from the Greeting Card Association (1200 G Street NW, Suite 760, Washington, DC 20005).

MANAGING YOUR SUBMISSIONS

Because you will be sending out many samples, you may want to label each sample. Establish a master card for each verse idea and record where and when each was sent and whether it was rejected or purchased. Keep all cards sent to one company in a batch and give each batch a number. Write this number on the back of your return SASE to help you match up your verses as they are returned.

Information on greeting card companies listed in the previous edition of *Writer's Market* but not included in this edition can be found in the General Index.

N. THE CALLIGRAPHY COLLECTION INC., 2604 NW 74th Place, Gainesville FL 32653. (352)375-8530. Fax: (352)374-9957. Email: artistkaty@aol.com. **Acquisitions:** Katy Fischer, owner. Responds in 6 months. Buys all rights. Pays on publication.
Needs: Conventional, humorous, inspirational, sensitivity, soft line. "A line of framed prints of watercolors with calligraphy." Prefers unrhymed verse, but will consider rhymed. Submit 3 ideas/batch. **Pays $75-200/framed print idea.**
Other Product Lines: Gift books, plaques, musical picture frames.
Tips: "We are looking for sentimental and inspirational sayings such as can be given to friends or family, or used as a wedding or graduation gift, but that do not mention specific occasions as such. For example, Mother saying that could be given all year as well as on Mother's Day. Our main markets are women 20 to 50 years of age. We are looking for verses that tell someone significant how much they mean to you, how important their friendship is or what is special about knowing them. All that in 35 words or less. We are looking for sayings to incorporate into items that caring people would like to give as lasting gifts."

CARDMAKERS, PO Box 236, 66 High Bridge Rd., Lyme NH 03768. (603)795-4422. Fax: (603)795-4222. Email: info@cardmakers.com. Website: www.cardmakers.com. **Acquisitions:** Peter D. Diebold, owner. Estab. 1978. **Receives hundreds of submissions/year.** Submit seasonal/holiday material 10 months in advance. Responds in 3 months. Buys greeting card rights. **Pays on acceptance.** Writer's guidelines/market list for #10 SASE.
Needs: Humorous, Holiday (mostly) and everyday. "We like upbeat humor, skip sick or raunchy. Our customers use our cards to greet their customers. So a positive approach/result is desirable." Prefers unrhymed verse ideas.
Tips: "We are primarily a direct marketer of business-to-business greetings targeted to specific interest groups—i.e., stockbrokers, boaters, etc. We also publish everyday cards for those same specific interests. So far, all our ideas and captions have been generated internally. We work with many freelancers on design and have recently decided to solicit ideas from writers. Please don't call or e-mail. To get our attention, make a card that reflects your most clever idea. Mail it to us with a return postcard (postage paid of course) and give us check-off options with degree of interest from 0-10. We'll know if you have what we need and you'll hear from us quicker."

COLORS BY DESIGN, 7723 Densmore Ave., Van Nuys CA 91436. (818)376-1226. Fax: (818)376-1669. Website: www.cbdcards.com. **Acquisitions:** Angie Novak, vice president. Estab. 1985. **20% freelance written. Receives 500 submissions/year; bought 200 freelance ideas last year.** Does not return submissions not accompanied by SASE. Buys all rights. Pays on publication. Writer's guidelines/market list for #10 SASE with Attn: Writers Guidelines.
Needs: Birthday, anniversary, friendship, holiday. No humor or poetry. Submit 3×5 cards with name and address on each. Process can take 4-6 months.
Tips: "We are interested in soft, heartfelt sentiments of no longer than three lines."

N. COMSTOCK CARDS, 600 S. Rock, Suite 15, Reno NV 89502-4115. (775)856-9400. Fax: (775)856-9406. Email: cindyt@intercomm.com. Website: www.comstockcards.com. **Acquisitions:** Cindy Thomas, production manager. Estab. 1986. **35% freelance written. Receives 2,000 submissions/year; bought 150 freelance ideas last year.** Submit seasonal/holiday material 12 months in advance. Responds in 5 weeks. Buys all rights. **Pays on acceptance.** Writer's guidelines/market list for #10 SASE. Market list issued one time only.
Needs: Humorous, informal, invitations. "Puns, put-downs, put-ons, outrageous humor aimed at a sophisticated, adult female audience. Also risqué cartoon cards." No conventional, soft line or sensitivity hearts and flowers, etc. **Pays $50-75/card idea. Cartoons negotiable.**
Other Product Lines: Notepads, cartoon cards, invitations.

Tips: "Always keep holiday occasions in mind and personal me-to-you expressions that relate to today's occurrences. Ideas must be simple and concisely delivered. A combination of strong image and strong gag line make a successful greeting card. Consumers relate to themes of work, sex and friendship combined with current social, political and economic issues."

EPHEMERA, INC., P.O. Box 490, Phoenix OR 97535. Email: mail@ephemera-inc.com. Website: www.ephemera-inc.com. **Acquisitions:** Editor. Estab. 1979. **95% freelance written. Receives 1,050 submissions/year. Bought 200 slogans for novelty buttons, stickers and magnets last year.** Responds in 3 months. Buys all rights. **Pays on acceptance.** Writer's guidelines/market list for #10 SASE. Complete full color catalog for $4.
Needs: Humorous. "Make us laugh out loud. We want provocative, irreverent and outrageously funny slogans. Topics include women's issues, the President, job attitudes, current events, pop culture, advertising satire, religion, pets, coffee, booze, pot, drugs, sexual come-ons and put-downs, aging, slacker angst, gays and lesbians, etc. We sell these high impact gems of wit to trendy card and gift shops, bookstores, record shops, fashion boutiques, head shops, sex shops, gay, feminist and political stores, etc. For over 20 years we have been known as *the* place for intelligent, in-your-face humor." **Pays $40/slogan.**

KATE HARPER DESIGNS,. Email: kateharp@aol.com Subject: Guidelines. Website: hometown.aol.com/kateharp/myhomepage/index.html. **Acquisitions:** via e-mail or website. Estab. 1993. **100% freelance written.** Submit seasonal/holiday material 12 months in advance. Pays flat fee for usage, not exclusive, plus author's name credit. **Pays on acceptance.**
   O→ Kate Harper Designs offers guidelines and tips on its website. For freelance writer's guidelines see http://hometown.aol.com/kateharp/myhomepage/personal.html. For writing tips for greeting cards see http://hometown.aol.com/kateharp/myhomepage/profile.html. For the Kid Quotes contest see http://hometown.aol.com/kateharp/myhomepage/index.html. To request guidelines by e-mail send to kateharp@aol.com (with guidelines request in the subject line.).
Needs: Humorous, informal, inspirational, sensitivity, everyday. "We are looking for birthday, Valentine and love, thanks, humor." Prefers unrhymed verse ideas. Submit 10 ideas/batch.
   ● Ms. Harper notes she wants to see more quotes by children.
Tips: "Quotes needed about work, family, love, kids, career, technology and marriage with a twist of humor. Something a working mom would laugh at and/or tips on how to have it all and still live to tell about it. Be adventurous and say what you really think in first person. What is ironic about this world we live in? What is the message you want to put out in the world? Don't be afraid to take risks and push beyond greeting card stereotypes. Nothing cute or sweet. Avoid quotes about women and weight, PMS, chocolate, diet, sex. Write as if you were talking to your best friend at the kitchen table. Be personal, and speak with an 'I' voice, like you've been there. We seek out new and unknown writers with a zing. Avoid traditional ideas of card quotes. Serious quotes also considered. Quotes must be 20 words or less. For front of the card only. Do not send quotes for inside of card."

INSPIRATIONS UNLIMITED, P.O. Box 9097, Cedar Pines Park CA 92322. Estab. 1984. **Bought 50 freelance ideas last year.** Submit seasonal/holiday material 6 months in advance. Responds in 1 month. Pays on publication.
Needs: Conventional, informal, inspirational, sensitivity. Submit 10 ideas/batch on numbered 3×5 cards. Prefers unrhymed verse ideas.
Tips: "Send heart to heart messages—something that tugs at the heart."

J-MAR BY UNIVERSAL DESIGN, P.O. Box 23149, Waco TX 76702. (254)751-0100. Fax: (254)751-0054. Email: abrown@j-mar-gifts.com. Website: www.j-mar-gifts.com. **Acquisitions:** Amy Brown, product marketing manager. Estab. 1984. **25% freelance written. Receives 200 submissions/year; bought 25 freelance ideas last year.** All submissions filed. Responds in 6 weeks. Buys all rights. **Pays on acceptance.**
   ● TandyCrafts, Inc., parent company of J-Mar, has sold the company to Florida-based Universal Designs, Inc.
Needs: Humorous, inspirational. Our most focused attention will be on proposals for new topics/themes and/or product lines. Looking for friendship, motivational, family, encouragement, christenings, pastor/church thank you. Submit each piece on a separate page, and include name, address, phone number, date and sample title on each page; include SASE. Accepts rhymed or unrhymed verse.
Tips: "J-Mar's target audience is the Christian market. J-Mar appreciates submissions focused on core inspirational Christian values, verses and themes. Keep a very positive, inspirational tone. Submissions can include biblical references or verses, poems and/or text."

Ⓝ NOVO CARD PUBLISHERS, INC., 3630 W. Pratt Ave., Lincolnwood IL 60712. (847)763-0077. Fax: (847)763-0020. Email: art@novocard.com. Website: www.novocard.com. Estab. 1926. **80% freelance written. Receives 500 submissions/year; bought 200 freelance ideas last year.** Submit seasonal/holiday material 8 months in advance. Responds in 2 months. Buys worldwide greeting card rights. **Pays on acceptance.** Writer's guidelines/market list for #10 SASE. Market list available to writer on mailing list basis.
Needs: Announcements, conventional, humorous, informal, inspirational, invitations, juvenile, sensitivity, soft line, studio.

OATMEAL STUDIOS, P.O. Box 138W3, Rochester VT 05767. (802)767-3171. **Acquisitions:** Helene Lehrer, creative director. Estab. 1979. **85% freelance written. Bought 200-300 freelance ideas last year.** Responds in 6 weeks. **Pays on acceptance.** Current market list for #10 SASE
   ● "Humor, conversational in tone and format, sells best for us."

Needs: Humorous, birthday, friendship, anniversary, get well cards, etc. Also Christmas, Hanukkah, Mother's Day, Father's Day, Easter, Valentine's Day, etc. Will review concepts. Humorous material (clever and very funny) year-round. Prefers unrhymed verse ideas. **Current pay schedule available with guidelines.**

Other Product Lines: Notepads, stick-on notes.

Tips: "The greeting card market has become more competitive with a greater need for creative and original ideas. We are looking for writers who can communicate situations, thoughts, and relationships in a funny way and apply them to a birthday, get well, etc., greeting and we are willing to work with them in targeting our style. We will be looking for material that says something funny about life in a new way."

P.S. GREETINGS, 5731 North Tripp Ave., Chicago IL 60646. (773)267-6069. Fax: (773)267-6150. **Acquisitions:** Art Director. **100% freelance written. Bought 200-300 freelance ideas last year.** Submit seasonal/holiday material 6 months in advance. Responds in 1 month. **Pays on acceptance.** Writer's guidelines/market list for #10 SASE or check them out on the website.

Needs: Conventional, humorous, inspirational, invitations, juvenile, sensitivity, soft line, studio. Accepts rhymed or unrhymed verse. Submit 10 ideas/batch. **Pays one-time flat fee.**

PLUM GRAPHICS INC., P.O. Box 136, Prince Station, New York NY 10012. (212)337-0999. Fax: (212)633-9910. Email: plumgraphi@aol.com. **Acquisitions:** Michelle Reynoso, operations manager. Estab. 1983. **100% freelance written. Receives 500-1,000 submissions/year; bought 30-40 freelance ideas last year.** Responds in 4 months. Buys greeting card and stationery rights. Pays on publication. Guidelines for SASE, sent 2 times/year with the development of new cards.

    ○⇥ "We don't want general submissions. We want them to relate to our next line."

Needs: Humorous. Fun copy to appeal to a wide range of ages. Prefers unrhymed verse ideas.

Tips: "Humor is always appreciated. We want short, to-the-point lines."

PORTAL PUBLICATIONS, 201 Almeda Del Prado, Novato CA 94941. (800)227-1720. Fax: (415) 382-3377. Email: peters@portalpub.com. Website: www.portalpub.com. **Acquisitions:** Editorial Department. Estab. 1954. **25% freelance written. Receives 200 submissions/year; bought 50 freelance ideas last year.** Responds in 3 months. Pays on publication.

Needs: Inspirational, humorous (cute and alternative). Also copy for humorous and inspirational posters. "Please send 10-15 samples of your work so that we may keep it on file. If in the future, we have need for writers for our greeting cards or other products we will contact you."

Other Product Lines: Calendars, posters.

Tips: "Upscale, cute, soft, alternative, humorous cards for bookstores, card stores, chain stores and college bookstores."

ROCKSHOTS, INC., 20 Van Dam St., New York NY 10013. (212)243-9661. Fax: (212)604-9060. Website: www.rock shots.com. **Acquisitions:** Bob Vesce, editor. Estab. 1979. **Bought 75 greeting card verse (or gag) freelance ideas last year.** Responds in 1 month. Buys greeting card rights. Writer's guidelines/market list for #10 SASE

    ● Rockshots has moved to a new address.

Needs: Humorous, soft line. Looking for a combination of sexy and humorous come-on type greeting ("sentimental is not our style"); and insult cards ("looking for cute insults"). "Card gag can adopt a sentimental style, then take an ironic twist and end on an off-beat note." No Sentimental or conventional material. Prefers gag lines on 8x11 paper with name, address, and phone and social security numbers in right corner, or individually on 3×5 cards. Submit 10 ideas/batch. **Pays $50/gag line.**

Tips: "Rockshots is an outrageous, witty, adult, and sometimes shocking card company. Our range of style starts at cute and whimsical and runs the gamut all the way to totally outrageous and unbelievable. Rockshot cards definitely stand out from all the 'mainstream' products on the market today. Some of the images we are famous for inclue 'sexy' photos of 500 to 600 pound female models, smart-talking grannies, copulating animals, and of course, incredibly sexy shots of nude and semi-nude men and women. Some of our best-selling cards are photos with captions that start out leading the reader in one direction, and then zings them with a punch line totally out of left field, but also hysterically apropos. As you can guess, we do not shy away from much. Be creative, be imaginative, be funny, but most of all, be different. Do not hold back because of society's imposed standards, but let it all pour out. It's always good to mix sex and humor, as sex always sells. Remember that 70% to 80% of our audience is women, so get in touch with your 'feminine' side, your bitchy feminine side. Your gag line will be illustrated by a Rockshots photograph or drawing, so try and think visually. It's always a good idea to preview our cards at your local store if this is possible to give you a feeling of our style."

⌷N⌷ SCHURMAN FINE PAPERS, 101 New Montgomery St., 6th Floor, San Francisco CA 94105. Fax: (707) 428-0641. **Acquisitions:** Text Editor. Estab. 1950. **10% freelance written. Receives 500 submissions/year; bought 25 freelance ideas last year.** Responds in 2 months. **Pays on acceptance.** Writer's guidelines/market list for #10 SASE.

Needs: Inspirational. Sentimental, contemporary, romance, friendship, seasonal and everyday categories. Send humor ideas to: Laffs by Marcel at address above. Prefers unrhymed verse, but on juvenile cards rhyme is OK. Submit 10-15 ideas/batch.

Tips: "Offer clever, sophisticated, fresh text concepts. Avoid 'bathroom humor' and other off-color text directions. Sentimental text works best if it is short and elegant (not long, maudlin or syrupy). We do not use poetry as card text. Historically, our nostalgic and art museum cards sell best. However, we are moving toward more contemporary cards and humor. Target market: upscale, professional, well-educated; average age 40; more female. Be original."

N̳ SILVER VISIONS, P.O. Box 610415, Newton Highlands MA 02461. (617)244-9504. **Acquisitions:** B. Kaufman, editor. Estab. 1981. Submit seasonal/holiday material 1 year in advance. Responds in 6 months. Pays on publication. Writer's guidelines/market list for #10 SASE.
Needs: Humorous. humorous Jewish, contemporary occasion for photography line. "Copy must work with a photograph; in other words, submit copy that can be illustrated photographically." Submit 10-16 ideas/batch.

SNAFU DESIGNS, Box 16643, St. Paul MN 55116. Fax: (651)698-8661. Email: cardinfo@snafucards.com. **Acquisitions:** Scott F. Austin, editor. Estab. 1985. Responds in 6 weeks. Buys all rights. **Pays on acceptance.** Writer's guidelines/market list for #10 SASE.
Needs: Humorous, informal. Specifically seeking birthday, friendship, thank you, anniversary, congratulations, get well, new baby, Christmas, Valentine's Day. Submit no more than 10 ideas/batch. **Pays $100/idea.**
Tips: "We use clever ideas that are simple and concisely delivered and are aimed at a sophisticated adult audience. Off-the-wall humor that pokes fun at the human condition. Please do not submit anything cute."

SPS STUDIOS INC., Publishers of Blue Mountain Arts®, Dept. WM, P.O. Box 1007, Boulder CO 80306-1007. Fax: (303)447-0939. Email: editorial@spsstudios.com. **Acquisitions:** Editorial Department. Estab. 1971. **Bought 100 freelance ideas last year.** Submit seasonal/holiday material 4 months in advance. Responds in 4-6 months. Buys worldwide, exclusive rights, anthology rights. Pays on publication. Writer's guidelines/market list for #10 SASE
   O─ "We like to receive original, sensitive poetry and prose on love, friendship, family, philosophies, and any other topic that one person might want to communicate or share with another person. Writings on special occasions (birthday, anniversary, graduation, etc.) as well as the challenges, difficulties, and aspirations of life are also considered. Important note: Because of the large volume of poetry we receive written to mothers, sons, and daughters, we are only accepting highly original and creative poetry that expresses new thoughts and sentiments on these themes."
Needs: Announcements, sensitivity. "We are interested in reviewing poetry and writings that would be appropriate for greeting cards, which means that they should reflect a message, feeling, or sentiment that one person would want to share with another. We'd like to receive sensitive, original submissions about love relationships, family members, friendships, philosophies, and any other aspect of life. Poems and writings for specific holidays (Christmas, Valentine's Day, etc.) and special occasions, such as graduation, birthdays, anniversary, and get well are also considered." **Pays $200/poem for each of first two works chosen for publication on a card (payment scale escalates after that); $25 for anthology rights.**
Other Product Lines: Calendars, gift books, prints, mugs.
Tips: "We strongly suggest that you familiarize yourself with our products before submitting material, although we caution you not to study them too hard. We do not need more poems that sound like something we've already published. We're looking for poetry that expresses real emotions and feelings, so we suggest that you have someone specific in mind (a friend, relative, etc.) as you write. The majority of the poetry we publish does not rhyme. We do not wish to receive books, unless you are interested in having portions excerpted for greeting cards; nor do we wish to receive artwork or photography. We prefer that submissions be typewritten, one poem per page, with name and address on every page. Only a small portion of the freelance material we receive is selected each year, either for publication on a notecard or in a gift anthology, and the review process can also be lengthy, but please be assured that every manuscript is given serious consideration."

N̳ UNIQUE GREETINGS, INC., P.O. Box 5783, Manchester NH 03108. Estab. 1988. **10% freelance written. Receives 15 submissions/year.** Submit seasonal/holiday material 1 year in advance. Responds in 6 months. Buys all rights. Writer's guidelines/market list for SASE. Market list regularly revised.
Needs: Watercolors, cute animals, flower scenes, etc. Prefers unrhymed verse ideas. Submit 12 ideas/batch.
Tips: "General and Happy Birthday sell the best."

N̳ WARNER PRESS, PUBLISHERS, 1200 E. Fifth St., P.O. Box 2499, Anderson IN 46018-9988. Email: krhodes@ warnerpress.org. **Acquisitions:** Karen Rhodes, product/marketing editor. **10% freelance written.** Responds in 2 months. Buys all rights for bulletin use only. **Pays on acceptance.**
   O─ "Presentation is important. Image isn't everything but handwritten submissions do not make a positive impression. Neatly typed or computer-generated pieces are much easier to read. Your ability to communicate clearly and professionally will receive a more favorable response."
Needs: Inspirational. Religious themes; sensitive prose and inspirational verse for Sunday bulletins. Write for guidelines, then submit 10 pieces of writing appropriate to their needs, 1-5 poems and 5 devotionals, or 10 of one category.
Other Product Lines: Also accepts ideas for coloring and activity books. Warner Press is now accepting material for boxed cards.
Tips: "We receive large numbers of submissions for Christmas and Easter—writing for less popular holidays heightens the chance of your work being published. Communion may seem to be a less interesting topic, but we need more submissions for that topic because we design a variety of bulletins with the communion theme. Submit material that relates to a wide audience, not just material that is meaningful to you personally. We receive a number of submissions dealing with the death of family members and other personal experiences that are beautiful and touching, but that do not relate to a larger audience."

Contests & Awards

The contests and awards listed in this section are arranged by subject. Nonfiction writers can turn immediately to nonfiction awards listed alphabetically by the name of the contest or award. The same is true for fiction writers, poets, playwrights and screenwriters, journalists, children's writers and translators. You'll also find general book awards, fellowships offered by arts councils and foundations, and multiple category contests.

New contests and awards are announced in various writer's publications nearly every day. However, many lose their funding or fold—and sponsoring magazines go out of business just as often. We have contacted the organizations whose contests and awards are listed here with the understanding that they are valid through 2000-2001. If you are using this section in 2002 or later, keep in mind that much of the contest information listed here will not be current. Requirements such as entry fees change, as do deadlines, addresses and contact names.

To make sure you have all the information you need about a particular contest, always send a self-addressed, stamped, business-sized envelope (#10 SASE) to the contact person in the listing before entering a contest. The listings in this section are brief, and many contests have lengthy, specific rules and requirements that we could not include in our limited space. Often a specific entry form must accompany your submission. A response with rules and guidelines will not only provide specific instructions, it will also confirm that the award is still being offered.

When you receive a set of guidelines, you will see that some contests are not for some writers. The writer's age, previous publication, geographic location and the length of the work are common matters of eligibility. Read the requirements carefully to ensure you don't enter a contest for which you are not qualified. You should also be aware that every year, more and more contests, especially those sponsored by "little" literary magazines, are charging entry fees.

Contest and award competition is very strong. While a literary magazine may publish ten short stories in an issue, only one will win the prize in a contest. Give yourself the best chance of winning by sending only your best work. There is always a percentage of manuscripts cast off immediately as unpolished, amateurish or wholly unsuitable for the competition.

To avoid first-round rejection, make certain that you and your work qualify in every way for the award. Some contests are more specific than others. There are many contests and awards for a "best poem," but some award only the best lyric poem, sonnet or haiku.

Winning a contest or award can launch a successful writing career. Take a professional approach by doing a little extra research. Find out who the previous winner of the award was by investing in a sample copy of the magazine in which the prize-winning article, poem or short story appeared. Attend the staged reading of an award-winning play. Your extra effort will be to your advantage in competing with writers who simply submit blindly.

If a contest or award requires nomination by your publisher, ask your publisher to nominate you. Many welcome the opportunity to promote a work (beyond their own, conventional means). Just be sure the publisher has plenty of time before the deadline to nominate your work.

Further information on funding for writers is available at most large public libraries. See the *Annual Register of Grant Support* (National Register Publishing Co., a division of Reed-Elsevier, *Foundations and Grants to Individuals* (Foundation Center, 79 Fifth Ave., New York NY 10003) and *Grants and Awards Available to American Writers* (PEN American Center, 568 Broadway, New York NY 10012). For more listings of contests and awards for fiction writers, see *Novel & Short Story Writer's Market* (Writer's Digest Books). *Poet's Market* (Writer's Digest Books) lists contests and awards available to poets. *Children's Writer's & Illustrator's Market* (Writer's

Digest Books) has a section of contests and awards, as well. Two more good sources for literary contests are *Poets & Writers* (72 Spring St., New York NY 10012), and the *Associated Writing Programs Newsletter* (Old Dominion University, Norfolk VA 23529). Journalists should look into the annual Journalism Awards Issue of *Editor & Publisher* magazine (11 W. 19th St., New York NY 10011), published in the last week of December. Playwrights should be aware of the newsletter put out by The Dramatists Guild, (234 W. 44th St., New York NY 10036).

Information on contests and awards listed in the previous edition of *Writer's Market* but not included in this edition can be found in the General Index.

General

THE ANISFIELD-WOLF BOOK AWARDS, The Cleveland Foundation, 1422 Euclid Ave., Suite 1400, Cleveland OH 44115. (216)861-3810. Fax: (216)861-1729. E-mail: asktcf@clevefdn.org. Website: www.anisfield-wolf.org. **Contact:** Marcia Bryant. "The Anisfield-Wolf Book Award annually honors books which contribute to our understanding of racism or our appreciation of the diversity of human culture published during the year of the award." Judged by five-member panel chaired by Dr. Henry Louis Gates of Harvard University and including Joyce Carol Oates, Rita Dove, Stephen Jay Gould and Simon Schama. Any work addressing issues of racial bias or human diversity may qualify. Deadline: January 31. Guidelines for SASE. Prize: $20,000.

ARTSLINK PROJECTS AWARD, CEC International Partners, 12 W. 31st St., New York NY 10001. (212)643-1985 ext. 22. Fax: (212)643-1996. E-mail: artslink@cecip.org. Website: www.cecip.org. **Contact:** Jennifer Gullace, ArtsLink coordinator. Offered annually to enable artists of all media to work in Central and Eastern Europe with colleagues there on collaborative projects. Check website for deadline and other information. Prize: Up to $10,000.

BANTA AWARD, Wisconsin Library Association, co Literary Awards Comm., 5250 E. Terrace Dr., Suite A-1, Madison WI 53718-8345. (608)245-3640. Website: www.wla.lib.wi.us. **Contact:** Chair, Literary Award Committee. Offered annually for books published during the year preceding the award. The Literary Awards Committee reviews all works by Wisconsin authors that are not edited, revised editions, textbooks or written in foreign languages. Review copies or notification of books, along with verification of the author's ties to Wisconsin, may be submitted to the Committee, by the publisher or author. Only open to writers born, raised or currently living in Wisconsin. Deadline: March of calendar year following publication. Prize: $500, a trophy given by the Banta Corporation Foundation, and presentation at the Annual Conference of the Wisconsin Library Association between late October and early November.

N THE BOARDMAN TASKER AWARD FOR MOUNTAIN LITERATURE, The Boardman Tasker Charitable Trust, 40 Wingate Rd., London W6 0UR, United Kingdom. 0208 743 4845. E-mail: pippa@pippasouthward.demon.co.uk. **Contact:** Pippa Southward. Offered annually for books published for the first time in the UK between November 1 of previous year and October 31 of year of the prize. This award recognizes "a book which has made an outstanding contribution to mountain literature in book format and not the format of a magazine or other periodical. It must be written or have been translated into the English language." Writers may obtain information but entry is by publishers only. "No restriction of nationality, but work must be published or distributed in the U.K." Deadline: August 1. Guidelines for SASE. Prize: 2,000 and attendant publicity.

N COLUMBUS BOOK DISCOVERY AWARD, Hollywood Network Inc., 433 N. Camden Dr. #600, Beverly Hills CA 90210. (310)288-1881. Fax: (310)475-0193. E-mail: awards@screenwriters.com. Website: www.screenwriters.com. **Contact:** Carlos de Abreu. Offered annually for unpublished material. Deadline: November 1. Guidelines for SASE. Charges $75 fee. Prize: Option rights up to $10,000. Winner will be offered an option for film rights.

N EDITORS' BOOK AWARD, Pushcart Press, P.O. Box 380, Wainscott NY 11975. (516)324-9300. **Contact:** Bill Henderson, president. Unpublished books. "All manuscripts must be nominated by an editor in a publishing house." Open to any writer. Deadline: October 15. Guidelines for SASE.

N THE MARIAN ENGEL AWARD, The Writers' Trust of Canada, 40 Wellington St. E, Suite 300, Toronto, Ontario M5E 1C7, Canada. (416)504-8222. Fax: (416)504-9090. E-mail: info@writerstrust.com. Website: www.writerstrust.com. **Contact:** Candice Cartier. The Engel Award is presented annually at the Great Literary Dinner Party to a female Canadian writer for a body of work in hope of continued contribution to the richness of Canadian literature. Prize: $10,000.

N **FRONTIERS IN WRITING**, Panhandle Professional Writers, PO Box 19303, Amarillo TX 79114. E-mail: pcs@arn.net. Website: users.arn.net/~ppw. Offered annually for unpublished work to encourage new writers and to bring them to the attention of the publishing industry. Deadline: March 1. Guidelines for SASE. Charges varying fee. Prize: Varies, see guidelines.

N **CORETTA SCOTT KING AWARDS**, American Library Association, 50 E. Huron St., Chicago IL 60611. (312)280-4294. Fax: (312)280-3256. E-mail: olos@ala.org. Website: www.ala.org/srrt/csking. **Contact:** Tanga Morris, administrative assistant. Offered annually to an African-American author and illustrator to promote understanding and appreciation of culture and contributions of all people. Guidelines for SASE. Prize: $1,000 and set of encyclopedias from World Book & Encyclopedia Britannica.

N **DOROTHEA LANGE—PAUL TAYLOR PRIZE**, Center for Documentary Studies at Duke University, 1317 W. Pettigrew St., Durham NC 27705. (919)660-3663. Fax: (919)681-7600. E-mail: alexad@duke.edu. Website: cds.aas.d uke/l-t/. **Contact:** Alexa Dilworth. Offered annually to "promote the collaboration between a writer and a photographer in the formative or fieldwork stages of a documentary project. Collaborative submissions on any subject are welcome." Guidelines for SASE or on website. Deadline: January 31. Submissions accepted during January only. Prize: $10,000.

STANLEY MARCUS AWARD FOR BEST BOOK DESIGN, Texas Institute of Letters, Southwest Texas State University, San Marcos TX 78666. (512)245-2428. Fax: (512)245-7462. E-mail: mb13@swt.edu. Website: www.English. swt.edu/css/TIL/rules.htm. **Contact:** Mark Busby. Offered annually for work published January 1-December 31. Open to Texas residents or those who have lived in Texas for two consecutive years. Deadline: First working day of new year. Guidelines for SASE. Prize: $750.

MATURE WOMAN GRANTS, The National League of American Pen Women, 1300 17th St. N.W., Washington DC 20036. Fax: (202)452-6868. E-mail: nlapw1@juno.com. Website: members.aol.com/penwomen/pen.htm. **Contact:** Mary Jane Hillery, national scholarship chair, 66 Willow Rd., Sudbury MA 01776-2663. Offered every 2 years to further the 35+ age woman and her creative purposes in art, music and letters. Open to US citizens. Award announced by March 1, even-numbered years. Send letter stating age, background and purpose for the monetary award. Send SASE for information. Deadline: October 1, odd-numbered years. Charges $8 fee with entry. Prize: $1,000 each in art, letters and music.

MISSISSIPPI REVIEW PRIZE, Mississippi Review, U.S.M. Box 5144, Hattiesburg MS 39406. (601)266-4321. Fax: (601)266-5757. E-mail: rief@netdoor.com. Website: orca.otr.usm.edu/mrw. **Contact:** Rie Fortenberry, contest director. Offered annually for unpublished fiction and poetry. Guidelines available online or with SASE. Charges $15 fee. Prize: $1,000 each for fiction and poetry winners.

N **THE W.O. MITCHELL LITERARY PRIZE**, The Writers' Trust of Canada, 40 Wellington St. E, Suite 300, Toronto, Ontario M5E 1C7, Canada. (416)504-8222. Fax: (416)504-9090. E-mail: info@writerstrust.com. Website: www.writerstrust.com. **Contact:** Candice Cartier. Offered annually for a writer who has produced an outstanding body of work and has acted during his/her career as a "caring mentor" for other writers. They must also have published a work of fiction or had a new stage play produced during the 3-year period for each competition. Every third year the W.O. Mitchell Literary Prize will be awarded to a writer who works in French. Prize: $15,000.

N **NATIONAL OUTDOOR BOOK AWARD**, Box 8128, Idaho State University, Pocatello ID 83209. (202)282-3912. E-mail: wattron@isu.edu. Website: www.isu.edu/outdoor/bookpol.htm. **Contact:** Ron Watters. Offered annually for books published June 1, 2001-September 1, 2002. Eight categories: History/biography, outdoor literature, instructional texts, outdoor adventure guides, nature guides, children's books, design/artistic merit and nature and the environment. Additionally, a special award, the Outdoor Classic Award, is given annually to books which, over a period of time, have proven to be exceptionally valuable works in the outdoor field. Application forms and eligibilty requirements are available online. Deadline: September 1. Charges $55 fee. Prize: Winning books will have the National Outdoor Book Award medallion used on their book jackets.

OHIOANA WALTER RUMSEY MARVIN GRANT, Ohioana Library Association, 274 E. First Ave., Columbus OH 43201. (614)466-3831. Fax: (614)728-6974. E-mail: ohioana@sloma.state.oh.us. Website: www.oplin.lib.oh.us/OHIOANA. **Contact:** Linda Hengst. Offered annually to encourage young writers; open to writers under age 30 who have not published a book. Entrants must have been born in Ohio or have lived in Ohio for at least 5 years. Enter 6 pieces of prose totaling 10-60 pages. Deadline: January 31. Prize: $1,000.

PEN CENTER WEST LITERARY AWARDS, PEN Center West, 672 S. Lafayette Park Place, #41, Los Angeles CA 90057. (213)365-8500. Fax: (213)365-9616. E-mail: pen@pen-usa-west.org. Website: www.pen-usa-west.org. **Contact:** Christina L. Apeles, awards coordinator. Estab. 1952. Offered for work published or produced in the previous calendar year. Open to writers living west of the Mississippi River. Award categories: Drama, screenplay, teleplay, journalism. Deadline: 4 copies must be received by January 31. Prize: $1,000 and awards.

N PULITZER PRIZES, The Pulitzer Prize Board, 709 Journalism, Columbia University, New York NY 10027. (212)854-3841. Website: www.pulitzer.org. **Contact:** Seymour Topping, administrator. Estab. 1917. Journalism in US newspapers (published daily or weekly), and in letters, drama and music by Americans. Deadline: February 1 (journalism); March 1 (music and drama); July 1 and November 1 (letters).

N DAVID RAFFELOCK AWARD FOR PUBLISHING EXCELLENCE, National Writers Association, 3140 S. Peoria #295, Aurora CO 80014. (303)841-0246. Fax: (303)841-2607. E-mail: sandywrter@aol.com. Website: www.nationalwriters.com. **Contact:** Sandy Whelchel. Contest is offered annually for books published the previous year. The purpose of this contest is to assist published authors in marketing their works and to reward outstanding published works. Deadline: May 1. Guidelines for SASE. Charges $100 fee. Prize: Publicity tour, including airfare, valued at $5,000.

N ROCKY MOUNTAIN ARTISTS' BOOK COMPETITION, Hemingway Western Studies Center, Boise State University, 1910 University Dr., Boise ID 83725. (208)426-1999. Fax: (208)426-4373. E-mail: ttrusky@boisestate.edu. Website: www.boisestate.edu/hemingway/. **Contact:** Tom Trusky. Offered annually "to publish multiple edition artists' books of special interest to Rocky Mountain readers. Topics must be public issues (race, gender, environment, etc.). Authors may hail from Topeka or Ulan Bator, but their books must initially have regional appeal." Acquires first rights. Open to any writer. Deadline: September 1-December 1. Guidelines for SASE. Prize: $500, publication, standard royalties.

N BYRON CALDWELL SMITH AWARD, Hall Center for the Humanities, 1540 Sunflower Rd., Lawrence KS 66045-7618. (785)864-4798. Offered in odd years to an individual who lives or is employed in Kansas, and who has authored an outstanding book published in the previous 2 calendar years. Translations are eligible. Deadline: March 1. Guidelines for SASE. Prize: $2,000.

TORONTO MUNICIPAL CHAPTER IODE BOOK AWARD, Toronto Municipal Chapter IODE, 40 St. Clair Ave. E., Toronto, Ontario M4T 1M9, Canada. (416)925-5078. Fax: (416)925-5127. **Contact:** IODE Education Committee. Offered annually for childrens' books published by a Canadian publisher. Author and illustrator must be Canadian citizens residing in or around Toronto. Deadline: Early November. Prize: $1,000.

TOWSON UNIVERSITY PRIZE FOR LITERATURE, College of Liberal Arts, Towson University, Towson MD 21252. (410)704-2128. **Contact:** Dean, College of Liberal Arts. Estab. 1979. Book or book-length manuscript that has been accepted for publication, written by a Maryland author of no more than 40 years of age. Deadline: June 15. Guidelines for SASE. Prize: $2,000.

N ROBERT TROUP PAINE PRIZE, Harvard University Press, 79 Garden St., Cambridge MA 02138. Website: www.hup.harvard.edu. **Contact:** Michael Fisher. Offered every 4 years for writing on science and the practical arts (subject changes every 4 years). Deadline: See website for deadlines. Guidelines for SASE. Prize: $3,000.

FRED WHITEHEAD AWARD, Texas Institute of Letters, Southwest Texas State University, San Marcos TX 78666. (512)245-2428. Fax: (512)245-7462. E-mail: mb13@swt.edu. Website: www.English.swt.edu/css/TIL/rules.htm. **Contact:** Mark Busby. Offered annually for the best design for a trade book. Open to Texas residents or those who have lived in Texas for 2 consecutive years. Deadline: January 3. Guidelines for SASE. Prize: $750.

N WHITING WRITERS' AWARDS, Mrs. Giles Whiting Foundation, 1133 Avenue of the Americas, 22nd Floor, New York NY 10036. **Contact:** Barbara K. Bristol, director. "The Foundation gives annually $35,000 each to up to ten writers of poetry, fiction, nonfiction and plays. The awards place special emphasis on exceptionally promising emerging talent." Direct applications and informal nominations are not accepted by the Foundation.

N L.L. WINSHIP/PEN NEW ENGLAND AWARD, PEN New England, P.O. Box 400725, Cambridge MA 02140. (617)499-9550. E-mail: awards@pen-ne.org. Website: www.pen-ne.org. **Contact:** Mary Sullivan, coordinator. Offered annually for work published in the previous calendar year. This annual prize is offered for the best book by a New England author or with a New England topic or setting. Open to fiction, nonfiction and poetry. Deadline: December 1. Guidelines for SASE.

WORLD FANTASY AWARDS ASSOCIATION, P.O. Box 43, Mukilted WA 98275-0043. Website: www.worldfantasy.org. **Contact:** Peter Dennis Pautz. Estab. 1975. Offered annually for previously published work recommended by previous convention attendees in several categories, including life achievement, novel, novella, short story, anthology, collection, artist, special award-pro and special award non-pro. Works are recommended by attendees of current and previous two years' conventions, and a panel of judges. Deadline: July 1.

N WRITERS' LEAGUE OF TEXAS MANUSCRIPT CONTEST, Writers' League of Texas, 1501 W. Fifth St., #E-2, Austin TX 78703. (512)499-8914. Fax: (512)499-0441. E-mail: awl@writersleague.org. Website: www.writersleague.org. **Contact:** Jim Bob McMillan. Offered annually for unpublished work. "The contest is open to all writers in five categories: Mainstream, mystery/suspense/action-adventure, romance, science fiction/fantasy/horror, and western. Deadline: May 1. Guidelines for SASE. Charges $20 fee. Prize: Recognition at Agents & Editors Conference, cash prize, and meeting with an agent or editor who selected winner.

Nonfiction

AMWA MEDICAL BOOK AWARDS COMPETITION, American Medical Writers Association, 40 W. Gude Dr., Rockville MD 20850-1192. (301)294-5303. E-mail: amwa@amwa.org. Website: www.amwa.org. **Contact:** Book Awards Committee. Offered annually to honor the best medical book published in the previous year in each of three categories: Books for Physicians, Books for Allied Health Professionals, and Trade Books. Deadline: March 1. Charges $20 fee.

[N] ANTHEM ESSAY CONTEST, The Ayn Rand Institute, P.O. Box 6099, Department DB, Inglewood CA 90312. (310)306-9232. Fax: (310)306-4925. E-mail: essay@aynrand.org. Website: www.aynrand.org/contests. **Contact:** Sean Saulsbury. Estab. 1992. Offered annually to encourage analytical thinking and excellence in writing, and to expose students to the philosophic ideas of Ayn Rand. "For information contact your English teacher or guidance counselor or visit our website." Annualy. Deadline: April 1. Prize: 1st-$2,000; 10 2nd-$500; 20 3rd-$200; 45 Finalist-$50; 175 Semifinalist-$30.

[N] ATLAS SHRUGGED ESSAY COMPETITION, Ayn Rand Institute, 4640 Admiralty Way, Suite 406, Marina del Rey CA 90292. (310)306-9232. Fax: (310)306-4925. E-mail: seans@aynrand.org. Website: www.aynrand.org/contests. **Contact:** Sean Saulsbury. Offered annually to encourage analytical thinking and excellence in writing, and to expose students to the philosophic ideas of Ayn Rand. Essays are judged both on style and content. Essay length: 1,000-1,200 words. Guidelines on website. Open to students enrolled full-time in an undergraduate program. Deadline: March 31. Prize: 1st-$5,000; 2nd(3 awards)-$1,000; 3rd(5 awards)-$400.

[N] BANCROFT PRIZE, Columbia University-Office of University Ceremonies, 202A Law Library, New York NY 10027. (212)854-2825. Fax: (212)854-6466. E-mail: jrb60@columbia.edu. Website: www.columbia.edu. **Contact:** Jennifer Brogan. Offered annually for work published previously. Winning submissions will be chosen in either or both of the following categories: American history (including biography) and diplomacy. Deadline: November 1. Guidelines for SASE. Prize: $4,000 for the winning entry in each category.

[N] RAY ALLEN BILLINGTON PRIZE, Organization of American Historians, 112 N. Bryan Ave., Bloomington IN 47408-4199. (812)855-9852. Fax: (812)855-0696. E-mail: awards@oah.org. Website: www.oah.org. **Contact:** Kara Hamm. Offered in even years for the best book in American frontier history, defined broadly so as to include the pioneer periods of all geographical areas and comparison between American frontiers and others. Deadline: October 1. Guidelines for SASE. Prize: $1,000, a certificate and a medal.

BIRKS FAMILY FOUNDATION AWARD FOR BIOGRAPHY, Canadian Author's Association, Box 419, 320 S. Shores Rd., Campbellford, Ontario K0L 1L0, Canada. (705)653-0323. Fax: (705)653-0593. E-mail: canauth@redden.on.ca. Website: www.canauthors.org. **Contact:** Alec McEachern. Offered annually for a previously published biography about a Canadian. Deadline: December 15. Guidelines for SASE. Charges $20 (Canadian) entry fee. Prize: $2,500 and a silver medal.

BOWLING WRITING COMPETITION, American Bowling Congress Publications, 5301 S. 76th St., Greendale WI 53129-1127. Fax: (414)421-3013. E-mail: mmille@bowlinginc.com. Website: www.bowl.com. **Contact:** Mark Miller, contributing editor. Estab. 1935. Offered for feature, editorial and news all relating to the sport of bowling. Deadline: December 15. Prize: 1st-place in each division: $300. In addition, News and Editorial-$225, $200, $175, $150, $75 and $50; Feature-$225, $200, $175, $150, $125, $100, $75, $50 and $50; with five honorable mention certificates awarded in each category.

BRITISH COUNCIL PRIZE, North American Conference on British Studies Dept., Austin TX 78712-1163. (512)475-7204. Fax: (512)475-7222. E-mail: levack@mailiutexas.edu. **Contact:** Brian P. Levack, executive secretary. Offered annually for best book by a North American scholar published in previous year in any field of British Studies after 1800. Open to American or Canadian citizens or permanent residents. Deadline: April 1. Guidelines for SASE. Prize: $1,000.

THE BROSS PRIZE, The Bross Foundation, Lake Forest College 555 N. Sheridan, Lake Forest IL 60045. (847)735-5175. Fax: (847)735-6192. E-mail: rmiller@lfc.edu. **Contact:** Professor Ron Miller. Offered every 10 years for unpublished work "to award the best book or treatise on the relation between any discipline or topic of investigation and the Christian religion." Next contest in 2010. Manuscripts awarded prizes become property of the college. Open to any writer. Deadline: September 1 of contest year. Guidelines for SASE. Prize: Award varies depending on interest earned.

JOHN BULLEN PRIZE, Canadian Historical Association, 395 Wellington, Ottawa, Ontario K1A 0N3, Canada. (613)233-7885. Fax: (613)567-3110. E-mail: cha-shc@archives.ca. Website: www.cha-shc.ca. **Contact:** Joanne Mineault. Offered annually for an outstanding historical dissertation for a doctoral degree at a Canadian university. Open only to Canadian citizens or landed immigrants. Deadline: November 30. Guidelines for SASE. Prize: $500.

CANADIAN AUTHORS ASSOCIATION LELA COMMON AWARD FOR CANADIAN HISTORY, Box 419, 320 S. Shores Rd., Campbellford, Ontario K0L 1L0, Canada. (705)653-0323. Fax: (705)653-0593. E-mail: canauth@redden.on.ca. Website: www.canauthors.org. **Contact:** Alec McEachern. Offered annually for a work of historical nonfiction on a Canadian topic by a Canadian author. Deadline: December 15. Guidelines for SASE. Charges $20 entry fee (Canadian). Prize: $2,500 and a silver medal.

CANADIAN LIBRARY ASSOCIATION STUDENT ARTICLE CONTEST, Canadian Library Association, 328 Frank St., Ottawa, Ontario K2P 0X8, Canada. (613)232-9625 ext. 318. Fax: (613)563-9895. Website: www.cla.ca. **Contact:** Brenda Shields. Offered annually to "unpublished articles discussing, analyzing or evaluating timely issues in librarianship or information science." Open to all students registered in or recently graduated from a Canadian library school, a library techniques program or faculty of education library program. Submissions may be in English or French. Deadline: March 15. Guidelines for SASE. Prize: 1st-$150, publication and trip to CLA's annual conference; 1st runner-up-$150 and $75 in CLA publications; 3rd runner-up-$75 and $75 in CLA publications.

THE DOROTHY CHURCHILL CAPPON CREATIVE NONFICTION AWARD, *New Letters*, 5101 Rockhill Road, Kansas City MO 64110. (816)235-1168. Fax: (816)235-2611. E-mail: newletters@umkc.edu. Website: www.umkc.edu/newletters. **Contact:** Aleatha Ezra or Mary Ellen Buck. Contest is offered annually for unpublished work to discover and reward new and upcoming authors. Acquires first North American serial rights. Open to any writer. Deadline: Third week of May. Guidelines for SASE. Charges $10 fee. Prize: 1st-$1,000 and publication in a volume of *New Letters*; two runners-up will receive a year's subscription and will be considered for publication.

MORTON N. COHEN AWARD, Modern Language Association, 26 Broadway, Third Floor, New York NY 10004-1789. (646)576-5141. Fax: (646)458-0030. E-mail: awards@mla.org. Website: www.mla.org. **Contact:** Coordinator of Book Prizes. Estab. 1989. Awarded in odd-numbered years for a previously published distinguished edition of letters. At least 1 volume of the edition must have been published during the previous 2 years. Editors need not be members of the MLA. Deadline: May 1. Guidelines for SASE. Prize: $1,000 and a certificate.

CARR P. COLLINS AWARD, The Texas Institute of Letters, Southwest Texas State University, San Marcos TX 78666. (512)245-2428. Fax: (512)245-7462. E-mail: mb13@swt.edu. Website: www.English.swt.ecu/css/TIL/rules.htm. **Contact:** Mark Busby. Offered annually for work published January 1-December 31 of the previous year to recognize the best nonfiction book by a writer who was born in Texas or who has lived in the state for at least 2 consecutive years at one point or a writer whose work has some notable connection with Texas. Deadline: January 3. Guidelines for SASE. Prize: $5,000.

COMPETITION FOR WRITERS OF B.C. (BRITISH COLUMBIA) HISTORY, B.C. Historical Federation, #306-225 Belleville St., Victoria, British Columbia V8V 4T9, Canada. (250)382-0288. **Contact:** Shirley Cuthbertson, chairman. Offered annually to nonfiction books published during contest year "to promote the history of British Columbia." Book must contain any facet of B.C. history. Submit 2 copies to the contest and they become the property of B.C. Historical Federation. Open to any writer. Deadline: December 31. Guidelines for SASE. Prize: 1st-The Lieutenant Governor's Medal for Historical Writing and $300; 2nd-$200; 3rd-$100.

AVERY O. CRAVEN AWARD, Organization of American Historians, 112 N. Bryan Ave., Bloomington IN 47408-4199. (812)855-9852. Fax: (812)855-0696. E-mail: awards@oah.org. Website: www.oah.org. **Contact:** Kara Hamm. Offered annually for the most original book on the coming of the Civil War, the Civil War years or the Era of Reconstruction, with the exception of works of purely military history. Deadline: October 1. Guidelines for SASE. Prize: $500 and a certificate.

CREATIVE NON-FICTION COMPETITION, No Noun-Sense, 147-2211 No. 4 Road, Richmond British Columbia V6X 3X1, Canada. (604)825-8861. Fax: (604)214-1306. E-mail: editor@webprospects.com. Website: www.nonounsense.com. **Contact:** Erin Berringer. Offered annually for unpublished work to promote the art of creative nonfiction. Guidelines on website. Open to any writer. Deadline: April 21. Charges $10. Prize: 1st-$200; 2nd-$50; 3rd-$25. Winner and four honourable mentions up will be published on the No Noun-Sense website.

CREATIVE NON-FICTION CONTEST, Event, P.O. Box 2503, New Westminster, British Columbia V3L 5B2, Canada. (604)527-5293. Fax: (604)527-5095. E-mail: event@douglas.bc.ca. Website: event.douglas.bc.ca. **Contact:** Ian Cockfield, managing editor. Offered annually for unpublished creative nonfiction. Guidelines for SASE (Canadian postage/IRCs only). Acquires first North American serial rights for the three winning entries. Open to any writer, except Douglas College employees. Deadline: April 15. Charges $25 entry fee, which includes 1-year subscription; US residents, pay in US funds. Prize: Three winners will each receive $500 plus payment for publication.

THE CREATIVE NON-FICTION CONTEST, sub-TERRAIN Magazine & Anvil Press Publishers, #204-A 175 E. Broadway, Vancouver, British Columbia V5T 1W2, Canada. (604)876-8710. Fax: (604)879-2667. E-mail: subter@portal .ca. **Contact:** Brian Kaufman. Offered annually for creative nonfiction, not limited to any specific topic or subject. Length: 2,000-4,000 words. Submissions to be accompanied by a SASE and a typed 8½×11 paper, double spaced (no disks or e-mail submissions, please). Deadline: August 1. Charges $15/story. Prize: $250 cash prize plus publication in the fall issue of *sub-TERRAIN* magazine. All entrants receive a one-year subscription to *sub-TERRAIN*.

N; MERLE CURTI AWARD, Organization of American Historians, 112 N. Bryan Ave., Bloomington IN 47408-4199. (812)855-9852. Fax: (812)855-0696. E-mail: awards@oah.org. Website: www.oah.org. **Contact:** Kara Hamm. Offered annually for books in the field of American social history (even-numbered years) and intellectual history (odd-numbered years). Deadline: October 1. Guidelines for SASE. Prize: $1,000, a certificate and a medal.

ANNIE DILLARD AWARD IN CREATIVE NONFICTION (formerly Annie Dillard Award in Nonfiction), Bellingham Review, Mail Stop 9053, Western Washington University, Bellingham WA 98225. (360)650-4863. E-mail: bhreview@cc.wwu.edu. Website: www.wwu.edu/~bhreview. **Contact:** Brenda Miller. Offered annually for unpublished essays on any subject and in any style. Deadline: January 5-March 5. Guidelines for SASE. Prize: 1st-$1,000; 2nd-$300; 3rd-$200, plus publication and copies.

GORDON W. DILLON/RICHARD C. PETERSON MEMORIAL ESSAY PRIZE, American Orchid Society, Inc., 16700 AOS Ln., Delray Beach FL 33446-4351. (561)404-2043. Fax: (561)404-2045. E-mail: jmengel@aos.org. Website: www.orchidweb.org. **Contact:** Jane Mengel. Estab. 1985. "An annual contest open to all writers. The theme is announced each May in the *Orchids* magazine. All themes deal with an aspect of orchids, such as repotting, growing, hybridizing, etc. Unpublished submissions only." Themes in past years have included Orchid Culture, Orchids in Nature and Orchids in Use. Buys one-time rights. Deadline: November 30. Prize: Cash award and certificate. Winning entry usually published in the May issue of *Orchids* magazine.

N; 💷 THE DONNER PRIZE, The Award for Best Book on Canadian Public Policy, The Donner Canadian Foundation, C/O 112 Braemore Gardens, Toronto, Ontario M6G 2C8, Canada. (416)652-7179. Fax: (416)658-5205. E-mail: meisner@interlog.com. Website: www.donnerbookprize.com. **Contact:** Meisner Publicity, prize manager, Joanna Kotsopoulos or Susan Meisner. Offered annually for nonfiction published January 1-December 31, 2001 that highlights the importance of public policy and to reward excellent work in this field. Entries must be published in either English or French. Open to Canadian citizens. Deadline: November 30. Guidelines for SASE. Prize: 1st-$25,000, two runners-up-$10,000 each.

N; THE FREDERICK DOUGLASS BOOK PRIZE, Gilder Lehrman Center for the Study of Slavery, Resistance & Abolition of Yale University, P.O. Box 208206, New Haven CT 06520-8206. (203)432-3339. Fax: (203)432-6943. E-mail: gilder.lehrman.center@yale.edu. Website: www.yale.edu/glc/. **Contact:** Robert P. Forbes, associate director. Offered annually for books published the previous year. "The annual prize of $25,000 for the most outstanding book published on the subject of slavery, resistance, and/or abolition, is awarded to scholars whose distinguished work makes a contribution to the history of slavery and abolition and promotes understanding of a subject matter critical to the U.S. and to the entire human community." Deadline: April 1. Guidelines for SASE. Prize: $25,000 and a bronze medallion.

N; 💷 THE DRAINIE-TAYLOR BIOGRAPHY PRIZE, The Writers' Trust of Canada, 40 Wellington St. E, Suite 300, Toronto, Ontario M5E 1C7, Canada. (416)504-8222. Fax: (416)504-9090. E-mail: info@writerstrust.com. Website: www.writerstrust.com. **Contact:** Candice Cartier. Awarded annually to a Canadian author for a significant work of biography, autobiography or personal memoir. Prize: $10,000.

EDUCATOR'S AWARD, The Delta Kappa Gamma Society International P.O. B, Austin TX 78767-1589. (512)478-5748. Fax: (512)478-3961. E-mail: ebarron@deltakappagamma.org. Website: www.deltakappagamma.org. **Contact:** Evelyn Barron, executive coordinator. Offered annually for quality research and nonfiction published January-December of previous year. This award recognizes educational research and writings of women authors whose book may influence the direction of thought and action necessary to meet the needs to today's complex society. The book must be written by one or two women who are citizens of any country in which The Delta Kappa Gamma Society International is organized: Canada, Costa Rica, El Salvador, Finland, Germany, Great Britain, Guatemala, Iceland, Mexico, The Netherlands, Norway, Puerto Rico, Sweden, U.S. Guideslines (required) for SASE. Deadline: February 1. Prize: $1,500.

EVERETT E. EDWARDS MEMORIAL AWARD (formerly the Everett E. Edwards Award), Agricultural History Society, 618 Ross Hall, Iowa University, Ames IA 50011-1202. (515)294-5620. Fax: (515)294-6390. E-mail: aghist@iastate.edu. Website: www.iastate.edu/~history_info/ahahs/awards.htm. **Contact:** R. Douglas Hurt. Offered annually for best graduate paper written during the calendar year on any aspect of agricultural and rural studies, broadly interpreted, submitted by a graduate student. Open to submission by any graduate student. Send mss directly to R. Douglas Hurt. Deadline: December 31. Prize: $200 and publication of the paper in the scholarly journal, *Agricultural History*.

THE CHARLES C. ELDREDGE PRIZE OF THE SMITHSONIAN AMERICAN ART MUSEUM, Smithsonian American Art Museum, Washington DC 20560. E-mail: lynaghp@saam.si.edu. Website: AmericanArt.si.edu. **Contact:** Pat Lynagh. Offered annually for previously published outstanding scholarship in the field of American art in the previous 3 years. It seeks to recognize originality and thoroughness of research, excellence of writing, clarity of method, and significance for professional or public audiences. "Nominations cannot be accepted from the author or publisher of any nominated book." Deadline: December 1. Guidelines for SASE. Prize: $2,000.

DAVID W. AND BEATRICE C. EVANS BIOGRAPHY & HANDCART AWARDS, Mountain West Center for Regional Studies, Utah State University, Logan UT 84322-0735. (435)797-3630. Fax: (435)797-3899. E-mail: mwc@usu .edu. Website: www.usu.edu/~pioneers/mwc.html. **Contact:** Glenda Nesbit, office manager. Estab. 1983. Offered to encourage the writing of biography about people who have played a role in Mormon Country. (Not the religion, the country: Intermountain West with parts of Southwestern Canada and Northwestern Mexico.) Publishers or authors may nominate books. Criteria for consideration: Work must be a biography or autobiography on "Mormon Country"; must be submitted for consideration for publication year's award; new editions or reprints are not eligible; manuscripts are not accepted. Submit 4 copies. Deadline: December 1. Guidelines for SASE. Prize: $10,000 and $1,000.

WALLACE K. FERGUSON PRIZE, Canadian Historical Association, 395 Wellington, Ottawa, Ontario K1A 0N3, Canada. (613)233-7885. Fax: (615)567-3110. E-mail: cha-shc@archives.ca. Website: www.cha-shc.ca. **Contact:** Joanne Mineault. Offered to a Canadian who has published the outstanding scholarly book in a field of history other than Canadian history. Deadline: December 1. Guidelines for SASE. Prize: $1,000.

GILBERT C. FITE DISSERTATION AWARD, Agricultural History Society, 618 Ross Hall, Ames IA 50011-1202. (515)294-5620. Fax: (515)294-6390. E-mail: aghist@iastate.edu. Website: www.iastate.edu/~history_info/ahahs/awards.htm. **Contact:** R. Douglas Hart. Award is presented to the author of the best dissertation on agricultural history, broadly construed, completed during the calendar year. Deadline: December 31. Guidelines for SASE. Prize: $300 honorararium.

THE FOUNTAINHEAD ESSAY CONTEST, The Ayn Rand Institute, P.O. Box 6099, Dept. DB, Inglewood CA 90312. (310)306-9232. Fax: (310)306-4925. E-mail: essay@aynrand.org. Website: www.aynrand.org/contests/. Estab. 1985, Offered annually to encourage analytical thinking and excellence in writing, and to expose students to the philosophic ideas of Ayn Rand. "For information contact your English teacher or guidance counselor, or visit our website." Length: 800-1,600 words. Deadline: April 15. Prize: 1st-$10,000; 5 2nd-$2,000; 10 3rd-$1,000; 35 Finalist-$100; 200 Semifinalist-$50.

GEORGE FREEDLEY MEMORIAL AWARD, Theatre Library Association, Benjamin Rosenthal Library, Queens College, C.U.N.Y., 65-30 Kissena Blvd., Flushing NY 11367. (718)997-3672. Fax: (718)997-3753. E-mail: rlw$lib@qc1. qc.edu. Website: http://tla.library.unt.edu. **Contact:** Richard Wall, Book Awards Committee chair. Estab. 1968. Offered for a book published in the US during the previous calendar year on a subject related to live theatrical performance (including cabaret, circus, pantomime, puppetry, vaudeville, etc.). Eligible books may include biography, history, theory, criticism, reference or related fields. Prize: $250 and certificate to the winner; $100 and certificate for Honorable Mention.

GEILFUSS, HUNTER & SMITH FELLOWSHIPS, State Historical Society of Wisconsin, 816 State St., Madison WI 53706-1482. (608)264-6464. Fax: (608)264-6486. E-mail: mestevens@mail.shsw.wisc.edu. Website: www. shsw.wisc.edu. **Contact:** Michael Stevens. Offered quarterly for unpublished writing on Wisconsin history. Guidelines for SASE or on website at: www.shsw.wisc.edu/research/fellowships.html. Rights acquired if award is accepted. Prize: $500-3,000.

LIONEL GELBER PRIZE, Lionel Gelber Foundation, 112 Braemore Gardens, Toronto, Ontario M6G 2C8, Canada. (416)652-1947 or (416)656-3722. Fax: (416)658-5205. E-mail: meisner@interlog.com. **Contact:** Sherry Naylor, prize manager. Offered annually for the year's most outstanding work of nonfiction in the field of international relations. Books must be published in English or English translation September 1, 2000-August 31, 2001. Guidelines for SASE. However, the publisher must submit the title on behalf of the author. Deadline: May 31. Guidelines for SASE. Prize: $50,000 (Canadian funds).

GOVERNOR GENERAL'S LITERARY AWARD FOR LITERARY NONFICTION, Canada Council for the Arts, 350 Albert St., P.O. Box 1047, Ottawa, Ontario K1P 5V8, Canada. (613)566-4414 ext. 5576. Fax: (613)566-4410. E-mail: joanne.larocque-poirier@canadacouncil.ca. Website: www.canadacouncil.ca. **Contact:** Joanne Larocque-Poirier. Offered for work published Sept. 1, 2001, to Sept. 30, 2002. Given annually to the best English language and the best French language work of literary nonfiction by a Canadian. Publishers submit titles for consideration. Deadline: April or August 2002, depending on the book's publication date. Prize: $15,000.

JAMES T. GRADY—JAMES H. STACK AWARD FOR INTERPRETING CHEMISTRY FOR THE PUBLIC, American Chemical Society, 1155 16th St. NW, Washington DC 20036-4800. (202)452-2109. Fax: (202)776-8211. E-mail: awards@acs.org. Website: www.acs.org/awards/grady-stack.html. **Contact:** Michael Shea. Offered annually for previously published work to recognize, encourage and stimulate outstanding reporting directly to the public, which materially increases the public's knowledge and understanding of chemistry, chemical engineering and related fields. Guidelines online at website. Rules of eligibility: A nominee must have made noteworthy presentations through a medium of public communication to increase the American public's understanding of chemistry and chemical progress. This information shall have been disseminated through the press, radio, television, films, the lecture platform, books, or pamphlets for the lay public. Deadline: February 1. Prize: $3,000, gold medal with a presentation box and certificate; plus travel expenses to the meeting at which the award will be presented.

GUIDEPOSTS YOUNG WRITERS CONTEST, Guideposts, 16 E. 34th St., New York NY 10016. (212)251-8100. **Contact:** James McDermont. Offered annually for unpublished high school juniors and seniors. Stories "needn't be about a highly dramatic situation, but it should record an experience that affected you and deeply changed you. Remember, Guideposts stories are true, not fiction, and they show how faith in God has made a specific difference in a person's life." "We accept submissions after announcement is placed in the October issue each year. If the manuscript is placed, we require all rights to the story in that version." Open only to high school juniors or seniors. Deadline: November 26, 2001. Prize: 1st-$10,000, 2nd-$8,000, 3rd-$6,000; 4th-$4,000; 5th-$3,000; 6th through 10th-$1,000; 11th through 20th-$250 gift certificate for college supplies.

N: JOHN GUYON NONFICTION PRIZE, Crab Orchard Review, English Dept., Southern Illinois University Carbondale, Carbondale IL 62901-4503. (618)453-6833. Fax: (618)453-8224. Website: www.siu.edu/~crborchd. **Contact:** Jon C. Tribble, managing editor. Offered annually for unpublished work. This competition seeks to reward excellence in the writing of creative nonfiction. This is not a prize for academic essays. Crab Orchard Review acquires first North American serial rights to submitted works. Deadline: February 1-March 15. Guidelines for SASE. Charges $10, which includes a year's subscription to *Crab Orchard Review*. Prize: $1,000 and publication.

ALBERT J. HARRIS AWARD, International Reading Association, Division of Research and Policy, 800 Barksdale Rd., Newark DE 19714-8139. (302)731-1600 ext. 423. Fax: (302)731-1057. E-mail: research@reading.org. **Contact:** Marcella Moore. Offered annually to recognize outstanding published works on the topics of reading disabilities and the prevention, assessment or instruction of learners experiencing difficulty learning to read. Open to any writer. Deadline: September 15. Guidelines for SASE. Prize: monetary award and recognition at the International Reading Association's annual convention.

N: ELLIS W. HAWLEY PRIZE, Organization of American Historians, 112 N. Bryan Ave., Bloomington IN 47408-4199. (812)855-9852. Fax: (812)855-0696. E-mail: awards@oah.org. Website: www.oah.org. **Contact:** Kara Hamm. Offered annually for the best book-length historical study of the political economy, politics or institutions of the US, in its domestic or international affairs, from the Civil War to the present. Books must be written in English. Deadline: October 1. Guidelines for SASE. Prize: $500.

N: HENDRICKS MANUSCRIPT AWARD, New Netherland Project, New York State Library, CEC, Eighth Floor, Albany New York 12220-0536. (518)474-6067. Fax: (518)473-0472. E-mail: cgehring@mail.nysed.gov. Website: www.nnp.org. **Contact:** Charles Gehring. Offered annually for the best published or unpublished manuscript focusing on any aspect of the Dutch colonial experience in North America. Deadline: February 15. Guidelines for SASE. Prize: $1,500.

HIGHSMITH LIBRARY LITERATURE AWARD, (formerly G.K. Hall Award for Library Literature), American Library Association, 50 E. Huron St., Chicago IL 60611. (312)280-3247. Fax: (312)280-3257. E-mail: awards@ala.org. Offered annually to previously published books that make an outstanding contribution to library literature. Guidelines for SASE or by e-mail. Deadline: December 1. Prize: $500 and framed citation.

THE KIRIYAMA PACIFIC RIM BOOK PRIZE, Kiriyama Pacific Rim Institute, 2130 Fulton St., San Francisco CA 94117-1080. (415)422-5984. Fax: (415)422-5933. E-mail: admin@pacificrimvoices.org. Website: www.pacificrimvoices.org. **Contact:** Jeannine Cuevas, project coordinator. Offered for work published October 1-September 30 of the award year to promote books that will contribute to better understanding and increased cooperation throughout all areas of the Pacific Rim. Guidelines and entry form on request. Books must be submitted for entry by the publisher. Proper entry forms must be submitted. Contact the administrators of the prize for complete rules and entry forms. *Editor's note: The mailing address for this contest will change as of November, 2001, to: 650 Delancey St., Suite 201, San Francisco CA 94107.* Deadline: July 2, 2002. Prize: $30,000 to be divided equally between the author of one fiction and of one nonfiction book.

KATHERINE SINGER KOVACS PRIZE, Modern Language Association, 26 Broadway, Third Floor, New York NY 10004-1789. (646)576-5141. Fax: (646)458-0030. E-mail: awards@mla.org. Website: www.mla.org. **Contact:** Coordinator of Book Prizes. Estab. 1990. Offered annually for a book published during the previous year in English in the field of Latin American and Spanish literatures and cultures. Books should be broadly interpretive works that enhance understanding of the interrelations among literature, the other arts, and society. Author need not be a member of the MLA. Deadline: May 1. Guidelines for SASE. Prize: $1,000 and a certificate.

N LERNER-SCOTT PRIZE, Organization of American Historians, 112 N. Bryan Ave., Bloomington IN 47408-4199. (812)855-9852. Fax: (812)855-0696. E-mail: awards@oah.org. Website: www.oah.org. **Contact:** Kara Hamm. Offered annually for the best doctoral dissertation in US women's history. Deadline: November 1 for a dissertation completed in the previous academic year (July 1-June 30). Guidelines for SASE. Prize: $1,000 and a certificate.

N LINCOLN PRIZE AT GETTYSBURG COLLEGE, Gettysburg College and Lincoln & Soldiers Institute, 233 N. Washington St., Gettysburg PA 17325. (717)337-6590. Fax: (717)337-6596. E-mail: civilwar@gettysburg.edu. Website: www.gettysburg.edu/lincoln_prize. **Contact:** Rosemary Connelly. Offered annually for the finest scholarly work in English on the era of the American Civil War. The award will usually go to a book published in the previous year, however articles, essays and works of fiction may be submitted. Guidelines for SASE or on website. Deadline: November 1. Prize: $50,000.

N THE LOFT CREATIVE NONFICTION PROGRAM, The Loft Literary Center, 1011 Washington Ave. S., Suite 200, Open Book, Minneapolis MN 55415. (612)215-2575. Fax: (612)215-2576. E-mail: loft@loft.org. Website: www.loft.org. **Contact:** Jerod Santek. Offered annually "to provide emerging nonfiction writers with an opportunity to work intensively with nationally noted authors of nonfiction." Eligibility: Entrants must not have published a book of creative nonfiction, must reside in Minnesota, and must not have previously participated in The Loft's creative nonfiction program. Deadline: March 15. Guidelines for SASE. Charges $10 fee. Prize: Two week-long residencies with the writers at The Loft and a stipend to defray costs.

WALTER D. LOVE PRIZE, North American Conference on British Studies, History Department, University of Texas, Austin TX 78712. (512)475-7204. Fax: (512)475-7222. E-mail: levack@mail.utexas.edu. **Contact:** Brian P. Levack, executive secretary. Offered annually for best article in any field of British Studies. Open to American or Canadian writers. Deadline: April 1. Guidelines for SASE. Prize: $150.

JAMES RUSSELL LOWELL PRIZE, Modern Language Association, 26 Broadway, Third Floor, New York NY 10004-1789. (646)576-5141. Fax: (646)458-0030. E-mail: awards@mla.org. Website: www.mla.org. **Contact:** Coordinator of Book Prizes. Offered annually for literary or linguistic study, or critical edition or biography published in previous year. Open to MLA members only. Deadline: March 1. Guidelines for SASE. Prize: $1,000 and a certificate.

N SIR JOHN A. MACDONALD PRIZE, Canadian Historical Association, 395 Wellington, Ottawa, Ontario K1A 0N3, Canada. (613)233-7885. Fax: (613)567-3110. E-mail: cha-shc@archives.ca. Website: www.cha-shc.ca. **Contact:** Joanne Mineault. Offered annually to award a previously published nonfiction work of Canadian history "judged to have made the most significant contribution to an understanding of the Canadian past." Open to Canadian citizens only. Deadline: December 1. Guidelines for SASE. Prize: $1,000.

MACLEAN HUNTER ENDOWMENT LITERARY NON-FICTION PRIZE, PRISM international, Buch E462 - 1866 Main Mall, Vancouver, British Columbia V6T 1Z1, Canada. (604)822-2514. Fax: (604)822-3616. E-mail: prism@interchange.ubc.ca. Website: www.arts.ubc.ca/prism. **Contact:** Belinda Bruce, executive editor. Offered annually for published and unpublished writers to promote and reward excellence in literary nonfiction writing. PRISM buys North American serial rights upon publication; "we also buy limited web rights for pieces selected for website." Open to anyone except students and faculty of the Creative Writing Program at UBC. Deadline: September 30. Guidelines for SASE. Charges $20 fee. Prize: $1,500 for the winning entry plus $20/page for the publication of the winner in *PRISM*'s winter issue.

HOWARD R. MARRARO PRIZE, Modern Language Association, 26 Broadway, Third Floor, New York NY 10004-1789. (646)576-5141. Fax: (646)458-0030. E-mail: awards@mla.org. Website: www.mla.org. **Contact:** Coordinator of Book Prizes. Offered in even-numbered years for a scholarly book or essay on any phase of Italian literature or comparative literature involving Italian, published in previous 2 years. Authors must be members of the MLA. Deadline: May 1, 2000. Guidelines for SASE. Prize: $1,000 and a certificate.

MID-LIST PRESS FIRST SERIES AWARD FOR CREATIVE NONFICTION, Mid-List Press, 4324 12th Ave. S, Minneapolis MN 55407-3218. Fax: (612)823-8387. E-mail: guide@midlist.org. Website: www.midlist.org. **Contact:** Lane Stiles, senior editor. Open to any writer who has never published a book of creative nonfiction. Submit either a collection of essays or a single book-length work; minimum length 50,000 words. Accepts simultaneous submissions. Guidelines and entry form for SASE or on website. Deadline: March 31-July 1. Charges $20 fee. Prize: Awards include publication and an advance against royalties.

KENNETH W. MILDENBERGER PRIZE, Modern Language Association, 26 Broadway, Third Floor, New York NY 10004-1789. (646)576-5141. Fax: (646)458-0030. E-mail: awards@mla.org. Website: www.mla.org. **Contact:** Coordinator of Book Prizes. Offered annually for a research publication (articles in odd-numbered years and books in even-numbered years) from the previous biennium in the field of teaching foreign languages and literatures. In 2002 the award will be given to book published in 2000 or 2001. Author need not be a member. Deadline: May 1. Guidelines for SASE. Prize: $500 for articles and $1,000 for books, a certificate and a year's membership in the MLA.

MLA PRIZE FOR A DISTINGUISHED BIBLIOGRAPHY, Modern Language Association, 26 Broadway, Third Floor, New York NY 10004-1789. (646)576-5141. Fax: (646)458-0030. E-mail: awards@mla.org. Website: www.mla.o rg. **Contact:** Coordinator of Book Prizes. Offered even-numbered years for enumerative and descriptive bibliographies published in monographic, book or electronic format in the previous biennium. Open to any writer or publisher. Deadline: May 1, 2000. Guidelines for SASE. Prize: $1,000 and a certificate.

MLA PRIZE FOR A DISTINGUISHED SCHOLARLY EDITION, Modern Language Association, 26 Broadway, Third Floor, New York NY 10004-1789. (646)576-5141. Fax: (646)458-0030. E-mail: awards@mla.org. Website: www. mla.org. **Contact:** Coordinator of Book Prizes. Offered in odd-numbered years. Work published between 2001 and 2002 qualifies for the 2003 competition. To qualify for the award, an edition should be based on an examination of all available relevant textual sources; the source texts and the edited text's deviations from them should be fully described; the edition should employ editorial principles appropriate to the materials edited, and those principles should be clearly articulated in the volume; the text should be accompanied by appropriate textual and other historical contextual information; the edition should exhibit the highest standards of accuracy in the presentation of its text and apparatus; and the text and apparatus should be presented as accessibly and elegantly as possible. Editor need not be a member of the MLA. Deadline: May 1. Guidelines for SASE. Prize: $1,000 and a certificate.

MLA PRIZE FOR A FIRST BOOK, Modern Language Association, 26 Broadway, Third Floor, New York NY 10004-1789. (646)576-5141. Fax: (646)458-0030. E-mail: awards@mla.org. Website: www.mla.org. **Contact:** Coordinator of Book Prizes. Offered annually for the first book-length scholarly publication by a current member of the association. To qualify, a book must be a literary or linguistic study, a critical edition of an important work, or a critical biography. Studies dealing with literary theory, media, cultural history and interdisciplinary topics are eligible; books that are primarily translations will not be considered. Deadline: April 1. Guidelines for SASE. Prize: $1,000 and a certificate.

MLA PRIZE FOR INDEPENDENT SCHOLARS, Modern Language Association, 26 Broadway, Third Floor, New York NY 10004-1789. (646)576-5141. Fax: (646)458-0030. E-mail: awards@mla.org. Website: www.mla.org. **Contact:** Coordinator of Book Prizes. Offered annually for a book in the field of English or another modern language or literature published in previous year. Authors who are enrolled in a program leading to an academic degree or who hold tenured or tenure-track positions in higher education are not eligible. Authors need not be members of MLA. Guidelines and application form for SASE. Deadline: May 1. Prize: $1,000, a certificate and a year's membership in the MLA.

N **GEORGE JEAN NATHAN AWARD FOR DRAMATIC CRITICISM**, Cornell University, Department of English, Goldwin Smith Hall, Ithaca NY 14853. (607)255-6801. Fax: (607)255-6661. E-mail: english_chair@cornell.e du. **Contact:** Chair, Dept. of English. Offered annually to the American "who has written the best piece of drama criticism during the theatrical year (July 1-June 30), whether it is an article, an essay, treatise or book." Only published work may be submitted; author must be an American citizen. Guidelines for SASE. Prize: $10,000 and a trophy.

N **NATIONAL BUSINESS BOOK AWARD**, PricewaterhouseCoopers and Bank of Montreal, 77 King St. W, Toronto, Ontario M5K 1G8, Canada. (416)941-8344. Fax: (416)941-8345. E-mail: maf@idirect.com. Website: www.pwc global.com. **Contact:** Faye Mattachione. Offered annually for books published January 1-December 31 to recognize excellence in business writing in Canada. Publishers nominate books. Deadline: December 31. Prize: $10,000.

NATIONAL WRITERS ASSOCIATION NONFICTION CONTEST, The National Writers Association, 3140 S. Peoria, #295, Aurora CO 80014. (303)841-0246. Fax: (303)841-2607. E-mail: sandywrter@aol.com. **Contact:** Sandy Whelchel, director. Annual contest "to encourage writers in this creative form and to recognize those who excel in nonfiction writing. Deadline: December 31. Guidelines for SASE. Charges $18 fee. Prize: 1st-$200; 2nd-$100; 3rd-$50.

THE FREDERIC W. NESS BOOK AWARD, Association of American Colleges and Universities, 1818 R St. NW, Washington DC 20009. (202)387-3760. Fax: (202)265-9532. E-mail: info@aacu.nw.dc.us. Website: www.aacu-edu.org. **Contact:** Linda Beach. Offered annually for work previously published July 1-June 30 of the year in which it is being considered. "Each year the Frederic W. Ness Book Award Committee of the Association of American Colleges and Universities recognizes books which contribute to the understanding and improvement of liberal education." Guidelines for SASE and on website. "Writers may nominate their own work; however, we send letters of invitation to publishers to nominate qualified books." Deadline: August 15. Prize: $2,000 and presentation at the association's annual meeting; transportation and one night hotel for meeting are also provided.

N **NORTH AMERICAN INDIAN PROSE AWARD**, University of Nebraska Press, 233 N. Eighth St., Lincoln NE 68588-0255. Fax: (402)472-0308. E-mail: gdunham1@unl.edu. **Contact:** Gary H. Dunham, editor, Native American studies. Offered for the best new nonfiction work by an American Indian writer. Deadline: July 1. Prize: Publication by the University of Nebraska Press with $1,000 advance.

OUTSTANDING DISSERTATION OF THE YEAR AWARD, International Reading Association, 800 Barksdale Rd., P.O. Box 8139, Newark DE 19714-8139. (302)731-1600 ext. 423. Fax: (302)731-1057. E-mail: research@reading.o rg. **Contact:** Marcella Moore. Offered annually to recognize dissertations in the field of reading and literacy. Deadline: October 1. Guidelines for SASE. Prize: $1,000.

THE PEARSON WRITERS' TRUST NON-FICTION PRIZE (formerly the Viacom Canada Writers' Trust Nonfiction Prize), The Writers' Trust of Canada, 40 Wellington St. E, Suite 300, Toronto, Ontario M5E 1C7, Canada. (416)504-8222. Fax: (416)504-9090. E-mail: info@writerstrust.com. Offered annually for a work of nonfiction published in the previous year. Applications for SASE. Deadline: Late July or mid November, depending on publication date. Prize: $10,000 (Canadian), and up to 4 runner-up prizes of $1,000 (Canadian).

LOUIS PELZER MEMORIAL AWARD, Organization of American Historians, Journal of American History, 1215 E. Atwater, Indiana University, Bloomington IN 47401. (812)855-9852. Fax: (812)855-0696. E-mail: awards@oah. org. Website: www.oah.org. **Contact:** Kara Hamm. Offered annually for the best essay in American history by a graduate student. The essay may be about any period or topic in the history of the US, and the author must be enrolled in a graduate program at any level, in any field. Length: 7,000 words maximum. Deadline: November 30. Guidelines for SASE. Prize: $500, a medal, a certificate and publication of the essay in the *Journal of American History*.

PEN/ARCHITECTURAL DIGEST AWARD FOR LITERARY WRITING ON THE VISUAL ARTS, PEN American Center, 568 Broadway, New York NY 10012. Fax: (212)334-2181. E-mail: jm@pen.org. Website: www.pen.o rg. **Contact:** John Morrone, literary awards manager. Offered annually for an outstanding book, published in the US the previous year, of criticism or commentary on one or more of the visual arts, which may include architecture, interior design, landscape studies, painting, photography and sculpture. Send 3 copies of each eligible book. Eligible books must have been published in the current calendar year. Open to US writers. Deadline: December 15; earlier submissions recommeded. Prize: $10,000.

PEN/JERARD FUND, PEN American Center, 568 Broadway, New York NY 10012. (212)334-1660. Fax: (212)334-2181. E-mail: jm@pen.org. **Contact:** John Morrone. Estab. 1986. Biennial grant offered in odd-numbered years for an American woman writer of nonfiction for a booklength work in progress. Deadline: Next Award: January 2, 2003. Prize: $5,500 grant.

PEN/MARTHA ALBRAND AWARD FOR FIRST NONFICTION, PEN American Center, 568 Broadway, New York NY 10012. (212)334-1660. Fax: (212)334-2181. E-mail: jm@pen.org. **Contact:** John Morrone, coordinator. Offered annually for a first published book of general nonfiction distinguished by qualities of literary and stylistic excellence. Eligible books must have been published in the calendar year under consideration. Authors must be American citizens or permanent residents. Although there are no restrictions on the subject matter of titles submitted, non-literary books will not be considered. Books should be of adult nonfiction for the general or academic reader. Publishers, agents and authors themselves must submit 3 copies of each eligible title. Deadline: December 15. Prize: $1,000.

PEN/MARTHA ALBRAND AWARD FOR THE ART OF THE MEMOIR, Pen American Center, 568 Broadway, New York NY 10012. (212)334-1660. Fax: (212)334-2181. E-mail: jm@pen.org. **Contact:** John Morrone. Offered annually to an American author for his/her memoir published in the current calendar year, distinguished by qualities of literary and stylistic excellence. Send 3 copies of each eligible book. Open to American writers. Deadline: December 15. Prize: $1,000.

PEN/SPIELVOGEL-DIAMONSTEIN AWARD, PEN American Center, 568 Broadway, New York NY 10012. (212)334-1660. Fax: (212)334-2181. E-mail: jm@pen.org. **Contact:** John Morrone. Offered for the best previously unpublished collection of essays on any subject by an American writer. "The $5,000 prize is awarded to preserve the dignity and esteem that the essay form imparts to literature." The essays included in books submitted may have been previously published in magazines, journals or anthologies, but must not have collectively appeared before in book form. Books will be judged on literary character and distinction of the writing. Publishers, agents, or the authors must submit 4 copies of each eligible title. Deadline: December 15. Prize: $5,000.

JAMES A. RAWLEY PRIZE, Organization of American Historians, (812)855-9852. Fax: (812)855-0696. E-mail: awards@oah.org. Website: www.oah.org. **Contact:** Award and Prize Committee Coordinator. Offered annually for a book dealing with the history of race relations in the US. Books must have been published in the current calendar year. Before submitting a nomination, a listing of current committee members and details about individual prizes must be obtained by sending SASE to: Award and Prize Committee Coordinator, Organization of American Historians, 112 N. Bryan Ave., Bloomington IN 47408-4199. Deadline: October 1; books to be published after Oct. 1 of the calendar year may be submitted as page proofs. Prize: $1,000 and a certificate.

PHILLIP D. REED MEMORIAL AWARD FOR OUTSTANDING WRITING ON THE SOUTHERN ENVI-RONMENT, Southern Environmental Law Center, 201 W. Main St., Charlottesville VA 22902. (804)977-4090. Fax: (804)977-1483. E-mail: selcva@selcva.org. Website: www.SouthernEnvironment.org. **Contact:** Cathryn McCue, award director. Offered annually for pieces published in the previous calendar year "to encourage and promote writing about natural resources in the South." Two categories: Journalistic non-fiction (newspaper and magazine articles) and Literary non-fiction (essays and books). Minimum length: 3,000 words. Deadline: March. Guidelines for SASE. Prize: $1,000 in each category.

EVELYN RICHARDSON MEMORIAL LITERARY AWARD, Writers' Federation of Nova Scotia, 1113 Marginal Rd., Halifax, Nova Scotia B3H 4P7, Canada. (902)423-8116. Fax: (902)422-0881. E-mail: talk@writers.ns.ca. Website: www.writers.ns.ca. **Contact:** Jane Buss, executive director. Contest is offered annually for best nonfiction book by Nova Scotian published during the previous calendar year. Send four copies with letter. Open to writers who were born and have spent a considerable portion of their lives, or have lived for the past two years in Nova Scotia. Deadline: December 1. Prize: Cash award and prize ceremony.

THE CORNELIUS RYAN AWARD, The Overseas Press Club of America, 40 W. 45th St., New York NY 10036. (212)626-9220. Fax: (212)626-9210. **Contact:** Sonya Fry, executive director. Offered annually for excellence in a nonfiction book on foreign affairs. Generally publishers nominate the work, but writers may also submit in their own name. The work must be published and on the subject of foreign affairs. Deadline: January 31. Charges $100 fee. Prize: Certificate and $1,000.

THEODORE SALOUTOS AWARD, Agricultural History Society, Iowa State University, Ames IA 50011-1202. (515)294-1596. Fax: (515)294-6390. E-mail: rdhurt@iastate.edu. Website: www.iastate.edu/~istory-info/aghistry.htm. **Contact:** R. Douglas Hurt. Offered annually for best book on US agricultural history broadly interpreted. Open nominations. Deadline: December 31. Prize: $500.

SASKATCHEWAN NONFICTION AWARD, Saskatchewan Book Awards Inc., Box 1921, Regina, Saskatchewan S4P 3E1, Canada. (306)569-1585. Fax: (306)569-4187. E-mail: sk.bookawards@dlcwest.com. Website: www .bookawards.sk.ca. **Contact:** Joyce Wells, executive director. Offered annually for work published October 1, 2001, to September 14, 2002. This award is presented to a Saskatchewan author for the best book of nonfiction, judged on the quality of writing. Deadline: First deadline: July 31; Final deadline: Sept. 14. Guidelines for SASE. Charges $15 (Canadian). Prize: $1,500.

SASKATCHEWAN SCHOLARLY WRITING AWARD, Saskatchewan Book Awards Inc., Box 1921, Regina, Saskatchewan S4P 3E1, Canada. (306)569-1585. Fax: (306)569-4187. E-mail: sk.bookawards@dlcwest.com. Website: www.bookawards.sk.ca. **Contact:** Joyce Wells, executive director. Offered annually for work published October 1, 2001, to September 14, 2002. This award is presented to a Saskatchewan author for the best contribution to scholarship. The work must recognize or draw on specific theoretical work within a community of scholars, and participate in the creation and transmission of knowledge. Deadline: First deadline: July 31; final deadline: September 14. Guidelines for SASE. Charges $15 (Canadian). Prize: $1,500.

THE BARBARA SAVAGE 'MILES FROM NOWHERE' MEMORIAL AWARD, The Mountaineers Books, 1001 SW Klickitat Way, Suite 201, Seattle WA 98134. (206)223-6303. Fax: (206)223-6306. E-mail: mbooks@mountaineers.o rg. Website: www.mountaineers.org. **Contact:** Cassandra Conyers. Offered in even-numbered years for previously unpublished book-length nonfiction personal adventure narrative. Narrative must be based on an outdoor adventure involving hiking, mountain climbing, bicycling, paddle sports, skiing, snowshoeing, nature, conservation, ecology, or adventure travel not dependent upon motorized transport. Subjects *not* acceptable include hunting, fishing, or motorized or competitive sports. Deadline: May 1, 2003. Guidelines for SASE. Prize: $3,000 cash award, a $12,000 guaranteed advance against royalties and publication by The Mountaineers.

ALDO AND JEANNE SCAGLIONE PRIZE FOR ITALIAN STUDIES, Modern Language Association, 26 Broadway, Third Floor, New York NY 10004-1789. (646)576-5141. Fax: (646)458-0030. E-mail: awards@mla.org. Website: www.mla.org. **Contact:** Coordinator of Book Prizes. Offered in odd-numbered years for a scholarly book on any phase of Italian literature or culture or comparative literature involving Italian, including works on literary or cultural theory, science, history, art, music, society, politics, cinema and linguistics, preferably but not necessarily relating other disciplines to literature. Books must have been published in year prior to competition. Authors must be members of the MLA. Deadline: May 1. Guidelines for SASE. Prize: $2,000 and a certificate.

ALDO AND JEANNE SCAGLIONE PRIZE FOR STUDIES IN GERMANIC LANGUAGES, Modern Language Association, 26 Broadway, Third Floor, New York NY 10004-1789. (646)576-5141. Fax: (646)458-0030. E-mail: awards@mla.org. Website: www.mla.org. **Contact:** Coordinator of Book Prizes. Offered in even-numbered years for outstanding scholarly work appearing in print in the previous two years and written by a member of the MLA, on the linguistics or literatures of the Germanic languages. Works of literary history, literary criticism, and literary theory are eligible; books that are primarily translations are not. Deadline: May 1. Guidelines for SASE. Prize: $2,000 and a certificate.

ALDO AND JEANNE SCAGLIONE PRIZE FOR STUDIES IN SLAVIC LANGUAGES AND LITERATURES, Modern Language Association, 26 Broadway, Third Floor, New York NY 10004-1789. (646)576-5141. Fax: (646)458-0030. E-mail: awards@mla.org. Website: www.mla.org. **Contact:** Coordinator of Book Prizes. Offered each odd-numbered year for books published in the previous 2 years. Books published in 2001 or 2002 are eligible for the 2003 award. Membership in the MLA is not required. Works of literary history, literary criticism, philology and literary theory are eligible; books that are primarily translations are not. Deadline: May 1. Guidelines for SASE. Prize: $2,000 and a certificate.

ALDO AND JEANNE SCAGLIONE PRIZE IN COMPARATIVE LITERARY STUDIES, Modern Language Association, 26 Broadway, Third Floor, New York NY 10004-1789. (646)576-5141. Fax: (646)458-0030. E-mail: awards @mla.org. Website: www.mla.org. **Contact:** Coordinator of Book Prizes. Offered annually for outstanding scholarly work published in the preceding year in the field of comparative literary studies involving at least 2 literatures. Author must be a member of the MLA. Works of scholarship, literary history, literary criticism and literary theory are eligible; books that are primarily translations are not. Deadline: May 1. Guidelines for SASE. Prize: $2,000 and a certificate.

ALDO AND JEANNE SCAGLIONE PRIZE IN FRENCH AND FRANCOPHONE STUDIES, Modern Language Association, 26 Broadway, Third Floor, New York NY 10004-1789. (646)576-5141. Fax: (646)458-0030. E-mail: awards@mla.org. Website: www.mla.org. **Contact:** Coordinator of Book Prizes. Offered annually for work published in the preceding year that is an outstanding scholarly work in the field of French or francophone linguistic or literary studies. Author must be a member of the MLA. Works of scholarship, literary history, literary criticism and literary theory are eligible; books that are primarily translations are not. Deadline: May 1. Guidelines for SASE. Prize: $2,000 and a certificate.

ALDO AND JEANNE SCAGLIONE PUBLICATION AWARD FOR A MANUSCRIPT IN ITALIAN LITERARY STUDIES, Modern Language Association, 26 Broadway, Third Floor, New York NY 10004-1789. (646)576-5141. Fax: (646)458-0030. E-mail: awards@mla.org. Website: www.mla.org. **Contact:** Coordinator of Book Prizes. Awarded annually to an author of a manuscript dealing with any aspect of the languages and literatures of Italy, including medieval Latin and comparative studies or intellectual history if main thrust is clearly related to the humanities. Materials from ancient Rome are eligible if related to postclassical developments. Also translations of classical works of prose and poetry produced in Italy prior to 1900 in any language (e.g., neo-Latin, Greek) or in a dialect of Italian (e.g., Neapolitan, Roman, Sicilian). Work can be in English or Italian. Manuscript must have been favorably evaluated by a not-for-profit press that is a member of the Association of American University Presses. Authors must be members of the MLA and currently reside in the United States or Canada. Deadline: August 1. Guidelines for SASE. Prize: Subvention to press for publication of manuscript and a certificate to author.

🅽 ⬚ SCIENCE IN SOCIETY BOOK AWARDS, Canadian Science Writers' Association, P.O. Box 75, Station A, Toronto, Ontario M5W 1A2, Canada. (416)408-4566. Fax: (416)408-1044. E-mail: cswa@interlog.com. Website: www.interlog.com/~cswa. **Contact:** Andy F. Visser-deVries. Offered annually for a first edition work published in Canada from January 1-December 31 of that year. Two awards: Children's Book Award and General Science Book Award, available for and to the general public with value in promoting greater understanding of science. Works entered become property of CSWA. Open to Canadia citizens only. Deadline: December 15. Guidelines for SASE. Prize: $1,000 and a plaque. Acquires Works entered become property of CSWA.

SCIENCE WRITING AWARDS IN PHYSICS AND ASTRONOMY, American Institute of Physics, 1 Physics Ellipse, College Park MD 20740-3843. (301)209-3090. Fax: (301)209-0846. E-mail: pubinfo@aip.org. Website: www.aip.org/aip/writing. **Contact:** Flory Gonzalez. Offered for previously published articles, booklets or books "that improve public understanding of physics and astronomy." Four categories: Articles or books intended for children, preschool-15 years old; broadcast media involving radio or television; journalism, written by a professional journalist; and science, written by physicists, astronomers or members of AIP or affiliated societies. Guidelines by phone, e-mail or website. Deadline: March 1. Prize: $3,000, engraved Windsor chair and certificate awarded in each category.

MINA P. SHAUGHNESSY PRIZE, Modern Language Association, 26 Broadway, Third Floor, New York NY 10004-1789. (646)576-5141. Fax: (646)458-0030. E-mail: awards@mla.org. Website: www.mla.org. **Contact:** Coordinator of Book Prizes. Offered annually for research publication (book) in the field of teaching English language, literature, rhetoric and composition published during preceding year. Authors need not be members of the MLA. Deadline: May 1. Guidelines for SASE. Prize: $1,000, a certificate and a year's membership in the MLA.

🅽 AMAURY TALBOT PRIZE FUND FOR AFRICAN ANTHROPOLOGY, Barclays Bank Trust Limited, E&T Centre, P.O. Box 15, Osborne Court, Gadbrook Park, Rudheath Northwich Cheshire CW9 7UE, England. Annual award for previously published nonfiction on anthropological research relating to Africa. Only works published the previous calendar year are eligible. Preference given to those relating to Nigeria and then West Africa. All applications, together with 2 copies of the book, article or work in question, should be sent by January 31 to: Amaury Talbot Prize coordinator, Royal Anthropological Institute, 50 Fitzroy St., London W1P 5HS England. Open to any writer. Guidelines for SASE. Prize: The Institute undertakes the administration of the Prize on behalf of the Trustees, Barclays Bank Trust Company Limited. Entries will *not* be returned.

THE THEATRE LIBRARY ASSOCIATION AWARD, Theatre Library Association, Benjamin Rosenthal Library, Queens College, C.U.N.Y., 65-30 Kissena Blvd., Flushing NY 11367. (718)997-3672. Fax: (718)997-3753. E-mail:

rlw$lib@qc1.qc.edu. Website: http://tla.library.unt.edu. **Contact:** Richard Wall, Book Awards Committee chair. Estab. 1973. Offered for a book published in the US within the previous calendar year on a subject related to recorded or broadcast performance (including motion pictures, television and radio). Eligible books may include biography, history, theory, criticism, reference or related fields. Deadline: February 15 of year following eligibility. Prize: $250 and certificate to the winner; $100 and certificate for Honorable Mention.

HARRY S. TRUMAN BOOK AWARD, Harry S. Truman Library Institute for National & International Affairs, 500 West U.S. Hwy. 24, Independence MO 64050-1798. (816)833-0425. Fax: (816)833-2715. E-mail: library@truman.nara.g ov. Website: www.trumanlibrary.org. **Contact:** Book Award Administrator. Offered in even-numbered years for a book published January 1, 2000-December 31, 2001, dealing "primarily and substantially with some aspect of the history of the United States between April 12, 1945 and January 20, 1953, or with the public career of Harry S. Truman. Deadline: January 20, 2002. Guidelines for SASE. Prize: $1,000.

FREDERICK JACKSON TURNER AWARD, Organization of American Historians, (812)855-9852. Fax: (812)855-0696. E-mail: awards@oah.org. Website: www.oah.org. **Contact:** Award and Prize Committee Coordinator. Offered annually for an author's first book on some significant phase of American history and also to the press that submits and publishes it. The entry must comply with the following rules: 1) the work must be the first book-length study of history published by the author; 2) if the author has a Ph.D., he/she must have received it no earlier than seven years prior to submission of the manuscript for publication; 3) the work must be published in the calendar year before the award is given; 4) the work must deal with some significant phase of American history. Before submitting a nomination, a listing of current committee members and details about individual prizes must be obtained by sending SASE to: Award and Prize Committee Coordinator, Organization of American Historians, 112 N. Bryan Ave., Bloomington IN 47408-4199. Deadline: October 1. Prize: $1,000, certificate and medal.

L. KEMPER AND LEILA WILLIAMS PRIZE, The Historic New Orleans Collection and Louisiana Historical Association, 533 Royal St., New Orleans LA 70130-2179. Fax: (504)598-7108. Website: www.hnoc.org. **Contact:** Chair, Williams Prize Committee. Director: John H. Lawrence. Offered annually for the best published work on Louisiana history. Deadline: January 15. Prize: $1,500 and a plaque.

WRITERS' JOURNAL ANNUAL TRAVEL WRITING CONTEST, Val-Tech Media, P.O. Box 394, Perham MN 56573. (218)346-7921. Fax: (218)346-7924. E-mail: writersjournal@wadena.net. Website: www.writersjournal.com. **Contact:** Leon Ogroske. Offered annually for unpublished work. Buys one-time rights. Open to any writer. Deadline: November 30. Guidelines for SASE. Charges $5 fee. Prize: 1st-$50, 2nd-$25, 3rd-$15 plus honorable mentions. Prize-winning stories and selected honorable mentions will be published in *Writer's Journal* magazine.

N **THE WRITERS' TRUST OF CANADA'S SHAUGHNESSY COHEN AWARD FOR POLITICAL WRITING**, The Writers' Trust of Canada, 40 Wellington St. E, Suite 300, Toronto, Ontario M5E 1C7, Canada. (416)504-8222. Fax: (416)504-9090. E-mail: info@writerstrust.com. Website: www.writerstrust.com. **Contact:** Candice Cartier. Offered annually for "a nonfiction book of outstanding literary merit that enlarges our understanding of contemporary Canadian political and social issues." Prize: $10,000.

N **LAMAR YORK PRIZE FOR NONFICTION CONTEST**, *The Chattahoochee Review*, Georgia Perimeter College, 2101 Womack Road, Dunwoody GA 30338-4497. (770)551-3019. Website: www.gpc.peachnet.edu/~twadley/cr/index.htm. **Contact:** JoAnn Adkins, managing editor. Offered annually for unpublished creative nonfiction and non-scholarly essays. *The Chattahoochee Review* buys first rights only for winning essay/manscript for the purpose of publication in the summer issue. Deadline: January 15. Guidelines for SASE. Charges $10 fee per entry. Prize: $1,000 and publication in the summer issue.

Fiction

EDWARD ABBEY SHORT FICTION AWARD, The Bear Deluxe Magazine, P.O. Box 10342, Portland OR 97296. (503)242-1047. Fax: (503)243-2645. E-mail: bear@teleport.com. Website: www.orlo.org/beardeluxe. **Contact:** Thomas L. Webb. Offered annually for unpublished short fiction to recognize new environmental writing in the spirit of Edward Abbey. New forms, styles and humor welcome. Guidelines for SASE. Acquires first North American serial rights. Open to any writer. Deadline: December 31 (postmark). Charges $5 fee. Prize: $500 and publication; publication to Honorable Mention winners.

AIM MAGAZINE SHORT STORY CONTEST, P.O. Box 1174, Maywood IL 60153-8174. (708)344-4414. Website: www.AIMMagazine.org. **Contact:** Myron Apilado, editor. Estab. 1974. Offered for unpublished short stories (4,000 words maximum) "promoting brotherhood among people and cultures. Deadline: August 15.

THE AMETHYST REVIEW ANNUAL WRITING CONTEST, The Amethyst Review/Marcasite Press, 23 Riverside Ave., Truro, Nova Scotia B2N 4G2, Canada. (902)895-1345. E-mail: amethyst@col.auracom.com (for information only). Website: www.col.auracom.com/~amethyst. **Contact:** Penny Ferguson, editor. Offered annually for unpublished (and not simultaneously submitted) fiction to encourage excellence in writing and to reward the writer. Guidelines for SASE (include IRCs for SASEs from outside of Canada). Acquires first North American serial rights for published works. After publication, rights revert to author. Open to any writer. Deadline: January 31. Charges $14 Canadian, $16 US. Prize: $100 for each category and publication.

N: ANNUAL OPEN SHORT STORY COMPETITION, No Noun-Sense, 147-2211 No. 4 Road, Richmond, British Columbia V6X 3X1, Canada. (604)825-8865. Fax: (604)214-1306. E-mail: editor@webprospects.com. Website: www.nonounsense.com. **Contact:** Erin Berringer. Offered annually for unpublished work to promote and nurture the talents of writers. Guidelines on website. Open to any writer. Deadline: August 21. Charges $10. Prize: 1st-$200; 2nd-$50; 3rd-$25. Winner and four honourable mentions will be published on the No Noun-Sense website, along with their bios.

ANVIL PRESS INTERNATIONAL 3-DAY NOVEL WRITING CONTEST, Anvil Press, 204-A 175 E. Broadway, Vancouver, British Columbia V5T 1W2, Canada. (604)876-8710. Fax: (604)879-2667. E-mail: subter@portal.ca. Website: www.anvilpress.com. **Contact:** Brian Kaufman. Estab. 1988. Offered annually for the best novel written in three days (Labor Day weekend). Entrants return finished novels to Anvil Press for judging. To register, send SASE (IRC if from the US) for details. Deadline: Friday before Labor Day weekend. Charges $25 fee.

ARIADNE PRIZE, Ariadne Press, 4817 Tallahassee Ave., Rockville MD 20853. (301)949-2514. Fax: (301)949-2514. **Contact:** Carol Hoover. Offered annually dependent on financing to encourage and promote the publication of novels by emerging writers. No rights are acquired by contest entry. Open to "non-established" writers. Deadline: January 15-June 1. Guidelines for SASE. Charges $50 fee (includes brief critique). Prize: $500 plus publication by Ariadne Press.

N: ART COOP FICTION FELLOWSHIP, Cottonwood Art Co-operative, 725 Ashland, Houston TX 77007-1424. E-mail: art_coop@yahoo.com. Website: www.geocities.com/art_coop. **Contact:** Victor Gonzalez. For most recent information, please visit website or write for guidelines with SASE. Submit with cover sheet, bio, and publications list. Open to any writer. Deadline: May 1. Charges $15 for 3-50 page portfolio. For additional flat fee of $15 and SASE, feedback provided on fiction. Prize: Cash award to be determined, not less than $250, and publication to support serious, aspiring authors.

AUTHORS IN THE PARK SHORT STORY CONTEST, Authors in the Park, P.O. Box 85, Winter Park FL 32790-0085. (407)658-4520. E-mail: foley@magicnet.net. **Contact:** David or Jennifer Foley. Estab. 1985. Offered annually to help exposé fiction writers to literary journals. Length: 5,000 words maximum. Guidelines for SASE or by e-mail. Open to any writer. Deadline: April 30. Charges $12 fee. Prize: 1st-$1,000, 2nd-$500, 3rd-$250.

N: B&A FICTION CONTEST, P.O. Box 702, Station P, Toronto, Ontario M5S 2Y4, Canada. (416)535-1233. E-mail: bloodaphorisms@hotmail.com. **Contact:** Sam Hiyate, publisher. Purpose is "to discover new writers and generate more excitement for their work in the literary community." Annual competition for short stories from any genre. Guidelines for SASE or IRC. Open to any writer. Charges $20 (Canadian). Prize: Cash prizes to be determined; each entrant receives a 1-year subscription to *B&A*.

N: BEST PRIVATE EYE NOVEL CONTEST, Private Eye Writers of America and St. Martin's Press, 175 Fifth Ave., New York NY 11215. (212)674-5151. Fax: (212)254-4553. Offered annually for unpublished, book-length manuscripts in the "private-eye" genre. Open to authors who have not published a "private-eye" novel. Deadline: August 1. Guidelines for SASE. Prize: Advance against future royalties of $10,000 and publication by St. Martin's Press.

BONOMO MEMORIAL LITERATURE PRIZE, Italian Americana, URI/CCE, 80 Washington St., Providence RI 02903. (401)277-5306. Fax: (401)277-5100. **Contact:** Carol Bonomo Albright. Offered annually for the best fiction, essay, or memoir that is published annually by an Italian American. Acquires first North American serial rights. Guidelines for SASE. Prize: $250.

BOSTON REVIEW SHORT STORY CONTEST, Boston Review, E-53-407 MIT, Cambridge MA 02139. (617)494-0708. Website: http:bostonreview.mit.edu. Stories should not exceed 4,000 words and must be previously unpublished. Deadline: September 1. Charges $15 fee, payable to *Boston Review*, check or money order. Prize: $1,000 and publication in the December/January issue of *Boston Review*.

BOULEVARD SHORT FICTION CONTEST FOR EMERGING WRITERS, Boulevard Magazine, 4579 Laclede Ave., #332, St. Louis MO 63108-2103. (314)361-2986. Fax: (314)361-5515. Website: www.richardburgin.com. **Contact:** Richard Burgin. Offered annually for unpublished short fiction to award a writer who has not yet published a book of fiction, poetry or creation nonfiction with a nationally distributed press. "We hold first North American rights on anything not previously published." Open to any writer with no previous publication by a nationally known press. Deadline: December 15. Guidelines for SASE. Charges $15 fee per story. Prize: $1,500 and publication in one of the next year's issues.

[N] RAY BRADBURY SHORT STORY FELLOWSHIP, New Century Writer Awards, 32 Alfred St., Suite B, New Haven CT 06512-3927. (203)469-8824. Fax: (203)468-0333. E-mail: newcenturywriter@yahoo.com. Website: www.newcenturywriter.org. **Contact:** Jason Marchi, executive director. Open to all writers, both non-published and those with limited publication history, who enter at least one short story into the annual New Century Writers Award Competition (see listing for complete details). The fellowship is awarded to one short story writer each year. The winner attends the highly touted week-long Zoetrope Short Story Writer's Workshop at Francis Ford Coppola's Blancaneaux Lodge in Belize, Central America, during the first week of July. Special note: The Ray Bradbury Short Story Fellowship winner is considered to be the Grand Prize Winner of the fiction portion of the New Century Writer Awards, and is not awarded to any of the Top 10 cash winners. See website for details on the Zoetrope Workshop and a list of past instructors. Guidelines/entry forms for #10 SASE. Deadline: February 15. Charges $30 fee. Prize: The fellowship is worth approximately $4,500-5,000, and includes aifrare, workshop fees, first class accomodations and all meals at Blancaneaux Lodge (excluding alcoholic beverages), and $500 spending money.

BRAZOS BOOKSTORE SHORT STORY AWARD, The Texas Institute of Letters, Southwest Texas State University, San Marcos TX 78666. (512)245-2428. Fax: (512)245-7462. E-mail: mb13@swt.edu. Website: www.English.swt.ecu/css/TIL/rules.htm. **Contact:** Mark Busby. Offered annually for work published January 1-December 31 of previous year to recognize the best short story. The story submitted must have appeared in print for the first time to be eligible. Writers must have been born in Texas, must have lived in Texas for at least two consecutive years or the subject matter of the work must be associated with Texas. Deadline: January 3. Guidelines for SASE. Prize: $750.

[#] CANADIAN AUTHORS ASSOCIATION AWARD FOR FICTION, Box 419, 320 South Shores Rd., Campbellford, Ontario K0L 1L0, Canada. (705)653-0323. Fax: (705)653-0593. E-mail: canauth@redden.on.ca. Website: www.canauthors.org. **Contact:** Alec McEachern. Offered annually for a full-length novel by a Canadian citizen. Deadline: December 15. Guidelines for SASE. Charges $20 fee (Canadian). Prize: $2,500 and a silver medal.

[#] CANADIAN AUTHORS ASSOCIATION JUBILEE AWARD FOR SHORT STORIES, P.O. Box 419, 320 S. Shores Rd., Campbellford, Ontario K0L 1L0, Canada. (705)653-0323. Fax: (705)653-0593. E-mail: canauth@redden.on.ca. Website: www.canauthors.org. **Contact:** Alec McEachern. Offered annually for a collection of short stories by a Canadian author. Deadline: December 15. Guidelines for SASE. Charges $20 fee (Canadian). Prize: $2,500 and a medal.

[N] THE ALEXANDER PATTERSON CAPPON FICTION AWARD, *New Letters*, 5101 Rockhill Rd., Kansas City MO 64110. (816)235-1168. Fax: (816)235-2611. E-mail: newletters@umkc.edu. Website: www.umkc.edu/newletters. **Contact:** Aleatha Ezra or Mary Ellen Buck. Offered annually for unpublished work to discover and reward new and upcoming writers. Buys first North American serial rights. Open to any writer. Deadline: Third week in May. Guidelines for SASE. Charges $10. Prize: 1st-$1,000 and publication in a volume of *New Letters*; two runners-up will receive a year's subscription and will be considered for publication.

DARK OAK MYSTERY CONTEST, Oak Tree Press, 915 W. Foothill Blvd., Suite 411, Claremont CA 91711-3356. (909)625-8400. Fax: (909)624-3930. E-mail: oaktreepub@aol.com. Website: www.oaktreebooks.com. **Contact:** Billie Johnson. Offered annually for an unpublished mystery manuscript (up to 85,000 words) of any sort from police procedurals to amateur sleuth novels. Acquires first North American, audio and film rights to winning entry. Open to authors not published in the past 3 years. Deadline: June 30. Guidelines for SASE. Charges $25 fee. Prize: 1st-publishing contract from Oak Tree Press; 2nd-ms analysis; 3rd-selection of Oak Tree books.

[N] DISCOVER GREAT NEW WRITERS AWARD, Barnes & Noble Inc., 122 Fifth Ave., New York NY 10011. (212)633-3511. Fax: (212)352-3602. E-mail: jlamar@bn.com. Website: www.bn.com. **Contact:** Jill Lamar. Offered annually for the most promising American first novelist published each year. Publishers submit titles for consideration; self-published titles not accepted. Prize: $10,000, crystal award, and over $75,000 in marketing support.

[N] DAVID DORNSTEIN MEMORIAL CREATIVE WRITING CONTEST FOR YOUNG ADULT WRITERS, The Coalition for the Advancement of Jewish Education, 261 W. 35th St., Floor 12A, New York NY 10001. Fax: (212)268-4214. E-mail: cajeny@caje.org. Website: www.caje.org. **Contact:** Lauren Sims, operations manager. Contest offered annually for unpublished short story based on a Jewish theme or topic. Writer must prove age of 18-35 years old. Submit only 1 story each year. Deadline: December 31. Guidelines for SASE. Prize: 1st-$700; 2nd-$200; 3rd-$100, and publication in the *Jewish Education News*.

[N] JACK DYER FICTION PRIZE, Crab Orchard Review, Dept. of English, Southern Illinois University Carbondale, Carbondale IL 62901-4503. (618)453-6833. Fax: (618)453-8224. Website: www.siu.edu/~crborchd. **Contact:** Jon C. Tribble, managing editor. Offered annually for unpublished short fiction. Crab Orchard Review acquires first North American serial rights to all submitted work. Open to any writer. Deadline: February 1-March 15. Guidelines for SASE. Charges $10, which includes a year's subscription to *Crab Orchard Review*. Prize: $1,000 and publication.

THE WILLIAM FAULKNER CREATIVE WRITING COMPETITION, The Pirate's Alley Faulkner Society, 624 Pirate's Alley, New Orleans LA 70116-3254. (504)586-1609. E-mail: faulkhouse@aol.com. Website: www.wordsandmu

sic.org. **Contact:** Rosemary James, director. Offered annually for unpublished mss to encourage publisher interest in a promising writer's novel, novella, novel-in-progress, short story, personal essay, poem, or short story by a high school student. The Society retains the right to publish excerpts of longer fiction; short stories in toto. Open to all authors working in English. Additional information on the competition and the festival is on the website. Deadline: April 1. Charges entry fee: Novel-$35; novella-$30; novel-in-progress, $30; short story, personal essay and individual poem-$25; high school short story-$10 (paid by school). Prize: Novel-$7,500; novella-$2,500; novel-in-progress-$2,000; short story-$1,500; personal essay-$1,000; individual poem-$750; high school-$750 for student and $250 for sponsoring teacher. The Society also awards gold medals in William Faulkner's likeness; air fare and hotel expenses for winners to attend Words & Music: A Literary Feast in New Orleans, encompassing a major national writers' conference and Happy Birthday, Mr. Faulkner!, the Faulkner Society's gala annual meeting, at which winners are presented by their judges. Note: For foreign residents the Society pays airfare only from selected US points of entry.

FICTION OPEN, Glimmer Train Press, 710 SW Madison St. #504, Portland OR 97205. (503)221-0836. E-mail: info@glimmertrain.com. Website: www.glimmertrain.com. **Contact:** Linda Swanson-Davies. Offered annually for un-published stories as "a platform for all themes, all lengths, all writers." Open to any writer. Include SASE for results. Deadline: June 30. Charges $15 fee per story. Prize: 1st-$2,000 and publication in *Glimmer Train Stories*; 2nd-$1,000 and possible publication; 3rd-$600 and possible publication.

N: FICTIONLINE, Fictionline Press Inc., E-mail: support@fictionline.com. Website: www.fictionline.com. **Contact:** Scott Southwick, managing editor. Always open—one of every 500 submissions is selected. Open to unpublished literary short fiction. Guidelines on website; all inquiries and entries must be submitted electronically. Open to any fiction writer with web access and a credit card (the $2.36 reading fee is collected online, by secure server). Charges $2.36 fee, which (excluding credit card processing fee) goes toward prizes. Prize: $1,000 and publication at fictionline.com.

N: F. SCOTT FITZGERALD SHORT STORY CONTEST, F. Scott Fitzgerald Literary Conference Inc., 111 Maryland Ave., Rockville MD 20850. (301)309-9461. Fax: (301)294-8073. **Contact:** Marily Mullan. Offered annually for unpublished short stories. Deadline: July 15. Guidelines for SASE. Charges $25 fee; no entry fee for students. Prize: Adults: 1st-$1,000; 2nd-4th-$200 each. Students: 1st-$250; 2nd-4th-$100 each.

H.E. FRANCIS SHORT STORY AWARD, University of Alabama in Huntsville & Ruth Hindman Foundation, 301 Sparkman Dr. N.W., Huntsville AL 35805. E-mail: MaryH71997@aol.com. Website: www.uah.edu. **Contact:** Mary Hindman, editor. Offered annually for unpublished work. Acquires first time publication rights. Deadline: December 31. Guidelines for SASE. Charges $15 reading fee. Prize: $1,000.

N: DANUTA GLEED LITERARY AWARD FOR FIRST BOOK OF SHORT FICTION, The Writers' Union of Canada, 40 Wellington St. E., Third Floor, Toronto, Ontario M5E 1C7, Canada. (416)703-8982. Fax: (416)504-7656. E-mail: twuc@the-wire.com. Website: www.writersunion.ca. **Contact:** Caroline Sin. Offered annually to Canadian writers for the best first collection of published short stories in the English language. Must have been published in the previous calendar year. Submit 4 copies. Deadline: January 15. Guidelines for SASE. Prize: 1st-$5,000; $500 to each of 2 runners-up.

GLIMMER TRAIN'S FALL SHORT-STORY AWARD FOR NEW WRITERS, Glimmer Train Press, Inc., 710 SW Madison St., Suite 504, Portland OR 97205-2900. (503)221-0836. E-mail: info@glimmertrain.com. Website: www.glimmertrain.com. **Contact:** Linda Swanson-Davies. Offered for any writer whose fiction hasn't appeared in a nationally-distributed publication with a circulation over 5,000. "Send original, unpublished short (1,200-8,000 words) story with $12 reader fee for each story entered. Title page to include name, address, phone; Short Story Award for New Writers must be written on outside of envelope. No need for SASE as materials will not be returned." Notification on January 2. Deadline: August 1-September 30 (postmark). Charges $12 fee per story. Prize: Winner receives $1,200, publication in *Glimmer Train Stories* and 20 copies of that issue. First/second runners-up receive $500/$300, respectively, and consideration for publication. All applicants receive the issue of *Glimmer Train Stories* containing the winning story.

GLIMMER TRAIN'S SPRING SHORT-STORY AWARD FOR NEW WRITERS, Glimmer Train Press, Inc., 710 SW Madison St., Suite 504, Portland OR 97205-2900. (503)221-0836. E-mail: info@glimmertrain.com. Website: www.glimmertrain.com. **Contact:** Linda Swanson-Davies. Offered for any writer whose fiction hasn't appeared in a nationally-distributed publication with a circulation over 5,000. "Send original, unpublished short (1,200-8,000 words) story with $12 reader fee for each story entered. Title page to include name, address, phone; Short Story Award for New Writers must be written on outside of envelope. No need for SASE as materials will not be returned." Notification on July 1. Deadline: February 1-March 31 (postmark). Charges $12 fee per story. Prize: Winner receives $1,200, publication in *Glimmer Train Stories* and 20 copies of that issue. First/second runners-up receive $500/$300, respectively, and consideration for publication. All applicants receive the issue of *Glimmer Train Stories* containing the winning story.

N: GOVERNOR GENERAL'S LITERARY AWARD FOR FICTION, Canada Council for the Arts, 350 Albert St., P.O. Box 1047, Ottawa, Ontario K1P 5V8, Canada. (613)566-4414 ext. 5576. Fax: (613)566-4410. E-mail: joanne.larocque-poirier@canadacouncil.ca. Website: www.canadacouncil.ca. **Contact:** Joanne Larocque-Poirier.

Offered annually for the best English-language and the best French-language work of fiction by a Canadian published September 1, 2001, to Sept. 30, 2002. Publishers submit titles for consideration. Deadline: April or August 2002, depending on the book's publication date. Prize: $15,000.

N: THE RICHARD HALL MEMORIAL GAY MEN'S SHORT FICTION CONTEST, The James White Review, P.O. Box 73910, Washington DC 20056-3910. (202)462-7924. E-mail: merlapatrick@aol.com. Website: www.lambdalit. org. **Contact:** Paul Willis, executive director. Offered annually for unpublished short stories to recognize emerging gay writers. Subject must be gay men. Open to writers not previously published in a magazine with circulation of 10,000 or over. Deadline: September 1. Guidelines for SASE. Charges $15 fee. Prize: $1,000 and publication.

DRUE HEINZ LITERATURE PRIZE, University of Pittsburgh Press 3347 Forbes Ave., Pittsburgh PA 15261. Website: www.pitt.edu/Œpress. **Contact:** Melanie Shrawder, assistant to the director. Estab. 1981. Collection of short fiction. Offered annually to writers who have published a book-length collection of fiction or a minimum of 3 short stories or novellas in commercial magazines or literary journals of national distribution. Does not return manuscripts. Deadline: Submit in May and June only. Guidelines for SASE. Prize: $10,000.

ERNEST HEMINGWAY FOUNDATION PEN AWARD FOR FIRST FICTION, PEN New England P.O. Box 400725, North Cambridge MA 02140. (617)499-9550. Fax: (617)353-7134. E-mail: mary@pen-ne.org. Website: www. pen-ne.org. **Contact:** Mary Louise Sullivan. Offered for first-published novel or short story collection by an American author. Guidelines and entry form for SASE. Deadline: December 15.

LORIAN HEMINGWAY SHORT STORY COMPETITION, Hemingway Days Festival, P.O. Box 993, Key West FL 33041-0993. (305)294-0320. Fax: (305)292-3653. E-mail: calico2419@aol.com. Website: www.shortstorycompetitio n.com. **Contact:** Carol Shaughnessy, co-coordinator. Estab. 1981. Fax and e-mail for guideline requests only. Offered annually for unpublished short stories up to 3,000 words. Deadline: June 15. Guidelines for SASE. Charges $10/story postmarked by June 1, $15/story postmarked by June 15; no stories accepted after June 15. Prize: 1st-$1,000; 2nd and 3rd-$500; runner-up awards; honorable mentions will also be awarded.

L. RON HUBBARD'S WRITERS OF THE FUTURE CONTEST, P.O. Box 1630, Los Angeles CA 90078. (323)466-3310. Website: www.writersofthefuture.com. **Contact:** Algis Budrys, director. Offered for unpublished work "to find, reward and publicize new speculative fiction writers so they may more easily attain to professonal writing careers." Open to new and amateur writers who have not professionally published a novel or short novel, more than one novelette or more than 3 short stories. Eligible entries are short stories or novelettes (under 17,000 words) of science fiction or fantasy. Guidelines for SASE or on website. Deadline: December 31, March 31, June 30, September 30. Prize: Awards quarterly 1st place-$1,000; 2nd place-$750; and 3rd place-$500. Annual Grand Prize: $4,000.

N: HWYL AWARD FOR UNDERGRADUATE FICTION, Diversity Incorporated/Furrow: Literary Arts Review, P.O. Box 8573, Madison WI 53708. (608)345-2363. E-mail: hwyl@diversityincorporated.com. Website: www.diversityi ncorporated.com. **Contact:** Benjamin LeRoy. Offered annually for unpublished work to celebrate quality fiction written by undergraduates. Entrants must be undergraduate students as of the semester ending before the deadline. Deadline: December 31. Guidelines for SASE. Prize: 1st-$250; 2nd-$100; 3rd-$50; top 10 stories published online.

N: INDIANA REVIEW FICTION CONTEST, *Indiana Review*, BH 465/Indiana University, Bloomington IN 47405-7103. (812)855-3439. Fax: (812)855-4253. E-mail: inreview@indiana.edu. Website: www.indiana.edu/~inrev iew/ir.html. **Contact:** Shannon Gibney. Offered annually for unpublished work. All entries considered for publication. Judged by guest judges; Brett Lott judged the 2000 contest. Maxiumum story length is 15,000 words (no minimum). Open to any writer. Deadline: Late October. Guidelines for SASE. Charges $12 fee (includes prize issue). Prize: $1,000.

INTERNATIONAL IMITATION HEMINGWAY COMPETITION, PEN Center West, 672 S. La Fayette Park Place, Suite 41, Los Angeles CA 90057. (213)365-8500. Fax: (213)365-9616. Website: www.pen-usa-west.org. **Contact:** Bill Kraines, executive director. Offered annually for unpublished one-page (500 words) parody of Hemingway. Must mention Harry's Bar and must be funny. Uncertain if will run in 2001. Write or call PEN for deadline or access. Prize: Winner receives round trip transportation for two to Florence, Italy and dinner at Harry's Bar & American Grill in Florence.

JAPANOPHILE ANNUAL SHORT STORY CONTEST, Japanophile, P.O. Box 7977, 415 N. Main St., Ann Arbor MI 48107-7977. (734)930-1553. Fax: (734)930-9968. E-mail: jpnhand@japanophile.com. Website: www.japanophile.c om. **Contact:** Susan Aitken, director; Jason Bredle, associate editor. Offered annually for unpublished work to encourage good fiction-writing that contributes to understanding of Japan and Japanese culture. Deadline: December 31. Guidelines for SASE. Charges $5 fee. Prize: $100, certificate, and usually publication.

JESSE H. JONES AWARD, The Texas Institute of Letters, Southwest Texas State University, San Marcos TX 78666. (512)245-2428. Fax: (512)245-7462. E-mail: mb13@swt.edu. Website: www.English.swt.ecu/css/TIL/rules.htm. **Contact:** Mark Busby. Offered annually for work published January 1-December 31 of year before award is given to recognize the writer of the best book of fiction entered in the competition. Writers must have been born in Texas, or have lived in the state for at least two consecutive years at some time, or the subject matter of the work should be associated with the state. Deadline: January 3. Guidelines for SASE. Prize: $6,000.

JAMES JONES FIRST NOVEL FELLOWSHIP, Wilkes University, English Department, Kirby Hall, Wilkes-Barre PA 18766. (570)408-4530. Fax: (570)408-7829. E-mail: english@wilkes.edu. Website: wilkes1.wilkes.edu/~english/jones.html. **Contact:** Darin Fields, humanities chairman. Offered annually for unpublished novels, novellas and closely-linked short stories (all works-in-progress). "The award is intended to honor the spirit of unblinking honesty, determination and insight into modern culture exemplified by the late James Jones." The competition is open to all American writers who have not previously published novels. Deadline: March 1. Charges $15 fee. Prize: $5,000.

LAURIE, Smoky Mountain Romance Writers, P.O. Box 70802, Knoxville TN 37938. (865)947-4595. E-mail: smrw@yahoo.com. Website: www.smrw.org. **Contact:** Leanne Hinkle. Offered annually to honor excellence in unpublished romance fiction. Guidelines and entry forms for SASE or on website. Participants must furnish a valid Romance Writers of America membership number to enter. Deadline: February 8. Charges $25 fee. Prize: Finalists have their entry read by an acquiring editor or agent. 1st-place wins a Laurie Pendant and finalist and winners receive certificates.

N THE LAWRENCE FOUNDATION AWARD, *Prairie Schooner*, 201 Andrews Hall, P.O. Box 880334, Lincoln NE 68588-0334. (402)472-0911. Fax: (402)472-9771. E-mail: eflanagan2@unl.edu. Website: www.unl.edu/schooner/psmain.htm. **Contact:** Hilda Raz. Offered annually for the best short story published in *Prairie Schooner* in the previous year. Prize: $1,000.

URSULA K. LEGUIN PRIZE FOR IMAGINATIVE FICTION, Rosebud, P.O. Box 459, Cambridge WI 53523. Website: www.rsbd.net. **Contact:** J. Rod Clark, editor. Annual contest for unpublished stories. Acquires first rights. Open to any writer. Deadline: December 31. Charges $10/story fee. Prize: $1,000 plus publication in *Rosebud*.

N LITERAL LATTÉ FICTION AWARD, Literal Latté, 61 E. Eighth St., Suite 240, New York NY 10003. (212)260-5532. E-mail: LitLatte@aol.com. Website: www.literal-latte.com. **Contact:** Jenine Bockman. Offered annually for unpublished fiction. Guidelines for SASE or on website. Open to any writer. Deadline: January 15. Charges $10/story fee or $15/story including subscription. Prize: $1,000 and publication in *Literal Latté* .

LONG FICTION CONTEST, White Eagle Coffee Store Press, P.O. Box 383, Fox River Grove IL 60021. (847)639-9200. E-mail: wecspress@aol.com. Website: http://members.aol.com/wecspress. **Contact:** Frank E. Smith, publisher. Offered annually since 1993 for unpublished work to recognize and promote long short stories of 8,000-14,000 words (about 30-50 pages). Sample of previous winner: $5.95, including postage. Open to any writer, no restrictions on materials. Deadline: December 15. Guidelines for SASE. Charges $15 fee, $5 for second story in same envelope. Prize: $500 and publication plus 25 copies of chapbook.

THE MALAHAT REVIEW NOVELLA PRIZE, The Malahat Review, Box 1700 STN CSC, Victoria, British Columbia V8W 2Y2, Canada. (250)721-8524. E-mail: malahat@uvic.ca. Website: web.uvic.ca/malahat. **Contact:** Marlene Cookshaw, editor. Offered every 2 years (even years) to promote unpublished novellas. Obtains first world rights. After publication rights revert to the author. Open to any writer. Deadline: March 1. Guidelines for SASE. Charges $30 fee (includes a one-year subscription to *Malahat*, published quarterly). Prize: $500, plus payment for publication ($30/page).

N MALICE DOMESTIC GRANTS FOR UNPUBLISHED WRITERS, Malice Domestic, P.O. Box 31137, Bethesda MD 20284-1137. Website: www.erols.com/malice. **Contact:** Grants chair. Offered annually for unpublished work. Malice awards two grants to unpublished writers in the Malice Domestic genre at its annual convention in May. The competition is designed to help the next generation of Malice authors get their first work published and to foster quality Malice literature. Writers who have been published previously in the mystery field, including publication of a mystery novel, short story or nonfiction work, are ineligible to apply. Members of the Malice Domestic Board of Directors and their families are ineligible to apply. Malice encourages applications from minority candidates. Guidelines for SASE or on website. Deadline: December 15. Prize: $500.

N MAYHAVEN AWARDS FOR FICTION, Mayhaven Publishing, 803 Buckthorn Circle, P.O. Box 557, Mahomet IL 61853. (217)586-4493. Fax: (217)586-6330. E-mail: ibfipone@aol.com. Website: www.mayhavenpublishing.com. **Contact:** Doris Replogle Wenzel. Offered annually for unpublished work "to provide additional opportunities for authors. We give awards in both adult and children's fiction." All entrants will be notified of the contest winners. Deadline: December 31. Guidelines for SASE. Charges $45 fee. Prize: 1st-place winners receive publication of work and royalties on sales.

MARY MCCARTHY PRIZE IN SHORT FICTION, Sarabande Books, P.O. Box 4456, Louisville KY 40204. (502)458-4028. Fax: (502)458-4065. E-mail: sarabandeb@aol.com. Website: www.SarabandeBooks.org. **Contact:**

Kirby Gann, managing editor. Offered annually to publish an outstanding collection of stories, novellas or short novel (less than 250 pages). All finalists considered for publication. Deadline: January 1-February 15. Guidelines for SASE. Charges $20 fee. Prize: $2,000 and publication, standard royalty contract.

MID-LIST PRESS FIRST SERIES AWARD FOR SHORT FICTION, Mid-List Press 4324 12th Ave. S., Minneapolis MN 55407-3218. (612)822-3733. Fax: (612)823-8387. E-mail: guide@midlist.org. Website: www.midlist.org. **Contact:** Lane Stiles, senior editor. Open to any writer who has never published a book-length collection of short fiction (short stories, novellas); minimum 50,000 words. Accepts simultaneous submissions. Enclose SAS postcard for acknowledgment of receipt of manuscript. Guidelines and entry form for SASE or on website. Deadline: March 31-July 1. Charges $20 fee. Prize: Awards include publication and an advance against royalties.

MID-LIST PRESS FIRST SERIES AWARD FOR THE NOVEL, Mid-List Press, 4324-12th Ave. S., Minneapolis MN 55407-3218. (612)822-3733. Fax: (612)823-8387. E-mail: guide@midlist.org. Website: www.midlist.org. **Contact:** Lane Stiles, senior editor. Offered annually for unpublished novels to locate and publish quality manuscripts by first-time writers, particularly those mid-list titles that major publishers may be rejecting. Guidelines for SASE or on website. Open to any writer who has never published a novel. Deadline: February 1. Charges $20 fee. Prize: Advance against royalties, plus publication.

MILKWEED NATIONAL FICTION PRIZE, Milkweed Editions, 1011 Washington Ave. S., Suite 300, Minneapolis MN 55415. (612)332-3192. Fax: (612)215-2550. **Contact:** Elisabeth Fitz, first reader. Estab. 1986. Annual award for unpublished works. "Milkweed is looking for a novel, novella, or a collection of short stories. Manuscripts should be of high literary quality and must be double-spaced and between 150-400 pages in length." "SAS mailer large enough to hold your manuscript must accompany submission for manuscript to be returned. If no SAS mailer is sent along, manuscript will be recycled." Winner will be chosen from the manuscripts Milkweed accepts for publication each year. All manuscripts submitted to Milkweed will automatically be considered for the prize. Submission directly to the contest is no longer necessary. "Must be written in English. Writers should have previously published a book of fiction or three short stories (or novellas) in magazines/journals with national distribution." Catalog available on request for $1.50. Deadline: Open. Guidelines for SASE. Prize: Publication by Milkweed Editions and a cash advance of $7,500 against royalties agreed upon in the contractual arrangement negotiated at the time of acceptance.

C. WRIGHT MILLS AWARD, The Society for the Study of Social Problems, 906 McClung Tower, University of Tennessee, Knoxville TN 37996-0490. (865)974-3620. Fax: (865)974-7013. E-mail: mkoontz3@utk.edu. Website: www.it.utk.edu/sssp. **Contact:** Michele Koontz, admistrative officer. Offered annually for fiction published the previous year to recognize fiction that critically addresses an issue of contemporary public importance. Deadline: January 15. Prize: $500 stipend.

N: KATHLEEN MITCHELL AWARD, Arts Management Pty. Ltd., Station House L. 4, 790 George St., Sydney NSW 2000, Australia. 61-2-92125066. Fax: 61-2-92117762. E-mail: claudia@artsmanagement.com.au. **Contact:** Claudia Crosariol. Offered in even years for novels published in the previous two years. Author must have been under age 30 when the novel was published. Entrants must be Australian or British born or naturalized Australian citizens, and have resided in Australia for the last year. The award is for a novel of the highest literary merit. Deadline: March 31. Guidelines for SASE. Prize: $5,000 (Australian).

N: MOONLIGHT & MAGNOLIA FICTION WRITING CONTEST, P.O. Box 180489, Richmond MS 39218-0489. (601)932-6670. E-mail: Hoover59@aol.com. **Contact:** K. Mark Hoover. Offered annually for unpublished work to recognize and encourage new and unpublished writers throughout the South while rewarding excellence in genre writing. "Southern writers are encouraged to participate, but the contest is world-wide. Regional contestants will not be given any preference during judging." Open to works of science fiction, fantasy and horror. Length: 10,000 words maximum. Open to writers who have not published more than 2 stories in a nationally-distributed magazine with a circulation over 5,000. Judge changes annually and is always a professional genre writer/editor who knows what it takes to write/market/publish a good story. 2001 final judge is James Van Pelt. Deadline: October 31. Guidelines for SASE. Charges $7.50, $2.50 each additional story; maximum 3 stories/contestant. Prize: 1st-$250; 2nd-$100; 3rd-$50. Top 10 finalists receive certificates suitable for framing. Winners announced January 31.

MYSTERY NOVEL AWARD, Salvo Press, P.O. Box 9095, Bend OR 97708. E-mail: publisher@salvopress.com. Website: www.salvopress.com. **Contact:** Scott Schmidt, publisher. Offered annually for the best unpublished mystery, suspense, thriller or espionage novel. Guidelines for SASE or on website. Deadline: July 15. Charges $25 fee. Prize: Publication under a standard royalty contract by Salvo Press.

N: MYSTERY WRITER'S CONTEST, No Noun-Sense, 147-2211 No. 4 Road, Richmond, British Columbia V6X 3X1, Canada. (604)825-8861. Fax: (614)214-1306. E-mail: editor@webprospects.com. Website: www.nonounsense.com. **Contact:** Erin Berringer. Offered annually for unpublished work to promote and nurture mystery writers. Guidelines on website. Open to any writer. Deadline: September 21. Charges $8. Prize: 1st-$100; 2nd-$50; 3rd-$25. Winner and four honourable mentions will be published on the No Noun-Sense website, along with their bios.

NATIONAL WRITERS ASSOCIATION NOVEL WRITING CONTEST, The National Writers Association, 3140 S. Peoria, #295, Aurora CO 80014. (303)841-0246. Fax: (303)841-2607. **Contact:** Sandy Whelchel, director. Annual contest "to help develop creative skills, to recognize and reward outstanding ability and to increase the opportunity for the marketing and subsequent publication of novel manuscripts. Deadline: April 1. Charges $35 fee. Prize: 1st-$500; 2nd-$300; 3rd-$200.

NATIONAL WRITERS ASSOCIATION SHORT STORY CONTEST, The National Writers Association, 3140 S. Peoria, #295, Aurora CO 80014. (303)841-0246. Fax: (303)841-2607. **Contact:** Sandy Whelchel, director. Annual contest "to encourage writers in this creative form and to recognize those who excel in fiction writing. Deadline: July 1. Guidelines for SASE. Charges $15 fee. Prize: 1st-$200; 2nd-$100; 3rd-$50.

NEW CENTURY WRITER AWARDS (FICTION), 32 Alfred St., Suite B, New Haven CT 06512-3927. (203)469-8824. Fax: (203)468-0333. E-mail: newcenturywriter@yahoo.com. Website: www.newcenturywriter.org. **Contact:** Jason J. Marchi, executive director. Offered annually to discover emerging writers of short stories and novels. No poetry or children's picture books. Guidelines/entry forms for #10 SAE. All entrants receive 1-year subscription to *The Anvil*, an educational newsletter for writers. Open to all writers, both non-published and those with limited publication history. Call if you doubt your eligibility. Also provides the annual Ray Bradbury Short Story Fellowship for a short fiction writer to attend the Zoetrope Short Story Writers' Workshop at Francis Ford Coppola's Blancaneaux Lodge in Belize, Central America (see Ray Bradbury Short Story Fellowship listing for complete details). Fellowship winner is considered the Grand Prize Winner of the fiction portion of the New Century Writer Awards and the fellowship is *not* awarded to any of the Top 10 cash winners. Also provides other fellowships and tuition assistance to select writers' workshops and programs. Tips: "We seek to encourage writers with cash awards and to connect writers to our numerous alliance companies in the film production and publishing industries. We also produce a popular reading series in New York City of works selected from annual finalists. Please call for application package—all submission details are included." Deadline: February 15. Charges $30 entry fee. Prize: 1st-$3,000; 2nd-$1,000; 3rd-$500; 4th-10th-$100.

NEW MUSE AWARD, Broken Jaw Press, Box 596 Station A, Fredericton, New Brunswick E3B 5A6, Canada. E-mail: jblades@nbnet.nb.ca. Website: www.brokenjaw.com. **Contact:** Joe Blades. Offered annually for unpublished fiction manuscripts of 80-120 pages to encourage development of book-length manuscripts by Canadian writers without a first fiction book published. Guidelines for SASE (with Canadian postage). Deadline: January 31. Charges $20 fee (all entrants receive copy of winning book upon publication). Prize: Book publication on trade terms.

NEW YORK STORIES SHORT FICTION CONTEST, New York Stories, LaGuardia/CUNY E103, 31-10 Thomson Ave., Long Island City NY 11101. (718)482-5673. E-mail: nystories@lagcc.cuny.edu. Website: www.newyorkstories.org. **Contact:** Daniel Caplice Lynch. Offered annually for unpublished work to showcase new, quality short fiction. Stories must not exceed 6,000 words. Open to any writer. Deadline: August 31. Guidelines for SASE. Charges $15 fee. Prize: 1st-$750 and publication; 2nd-$250.

FRANK O'CONNOR AWARD FOR SHORT FICTION, *descant*, Texas Christian University's literary journal, TCU Box 297270, Fort Worth TX 76129. (817)257-6537. Fax: (817)257-6239. E-mail: descant@tcu.edu. **Contact:** Dave Kuhne, editor. Offered annually for unpublished short stories. Publication retains copyright but will transfer it to the author upon request. Deadline: September-April. Guidelines for SASE. Prize: $500.

THE FLANNERY O'CONNOR AWARD FOR SHORT FICTION, The University of Georgia Press, 330 Research Dr., Athens GA 30602-4901. (706)369-6135. Fax: (706)369-6131. E-mail: mnunnell@ugapress.uga.edu. Website: www.uga.edu/ugapress. **Contact:** Margaret Nunnelley, competition coordinator. Estab. 1981. Does not return manuscripts. Manuscripts must be 200-275 pages long. Authors do not have to be previously published. Deadline: April 1-May 31. Guidelines for SASE. Charges $15 fee. Prize: $1,000 and publication under standard book contract.

CHRIS O'MALLEY PRIZE IN FICTION, *The Madison Review*, Dept. of English, 600 N. Park St., Madison WI 53706. (608)263-0566. E-mail: madreview@mail.studentorg.wisc.edu. Website: mendota.english.wisc.edu/~MadRev. **Contact:** Fiction Editor. Offered annually for previously unpublished work. Chosen from a field of about 500 stories submitted Sept. 1-30 each year. "We want to encourage interest and excellence in the short story genre." Submissions must be 25 pages or less. All contest entries are considered as submissions to *The Madison Review* and cannot be returned. Guidelines for SASE, by e-mail or on website. No e-mail submissions. Deadline: September 1-30. Charges $5 fee. Prize: $500 and publication in the spring issue of *The Madison Review*.

THE OMAHA PRIZE, The Backwaters Press, 3502 N. 52nd St., Omaha NE 68104-3506. (402)451-4052. Fax: (402)421-4052. E-mail: gkosm62735@aol.com. Website: www.thebackwaterspress.homestead.com. **Contact:** Greg Kosmicki. Offered annually for unpublished novels, though parts of the submitted novels may have been previously published in magazines. Guidelines for SASE, by e-mail or on website. Deadline: December 4 (postmark). Charges $20. Prize: $1,000 and publication in an edition of at least 750 copies under standard book contract.

OTTAWA PUBLIC LIBRARY ANNUAL SHORT STORY CONTEST, Ottawa Public Library, 101 Centrepointe Dr., Ottawa, Ontario K2G 5K7, Canada. (613)727-6646. E-mail: patricia.chuba@library.ottawa.on.ca.

Website: www.library.ottawa.on.ca. **Contact:** Patricia Chuba, contest director. Offered annually for unpublished short stories (written in French or English) to encourage writing in the community. Open to residents of Ottawa, Ontario, age 18 or older. Deadline: March 1, 2002. Guidelines for SASE. Charges $5/story fee. Prize: 1st-$500; 2nd-$250; 3rd-$100.

PATERSON FICTION PRIZE, One College Blvd., Paterson NJ 07505-1179. (973)684-6555. Fax: (973)684-5843. E-mail: mgillan@pccc.cc.nj.us. Website: www.pccc.cc.nj.us/poetry. **Contact:** Maria Mazziotti Gillan, director. Offered annually for a novel or collection of short fiction published the previous calendar year. Deadline: April 1. Guidelines for SASE. Prize: $1,000.

WILLIAM PEDEN PRIZE IN FICTION, *The Missouri Review*, 1507 Hillcrest Hall, Columbia MO 65211. (573)882-4474. Fax: (573)884-4671. Website: www.missourireview.org. **Contact:** Hoa Ngo, managing editor. Offered annually "for the best story published in the past volume year of the magazine. All stories published in *MR* are automatically considered." Prize: $1,000 and reading/reception.

PEN/FAULKNER AWARDS FOR FICTION, PEN/Faulkner Foundation, 201 E. Capitol St., Washington DC 20003. (202)675-0345. Fax: (202)608-1719. E-mail: delaney@folger.edu. Website: www.penfaulkner.org. **Contact:** Janice F. Delaney, executive director. Offered annually for best book-length work of fiction by an American citizen published in a calendar year. Deadline: October 31. Prize: $15,000 (one winner), 5,000 (4 nominees).

PEREGRINE FICTION PRIZE (formerly The Peregrine Prize), *Peregrine*, the Literary Journal of Amherst Writers & Artists, P.O. Box 1076, Amherst MA 01004-1076. (413)253-3307. Fax: (413)253-7764. E-mail: awapress@aol.com. Website: www.amherstwriters.com. **Contact:** Nancy Rose. Offered annually for unpublished fiction. Open to any writer. Deadline: April 1. Guidelines for SASE. Charges $10 fee. Prize: $500, plus publication in *Peregrine*. Entrants who reside in Western Massachusetts are also eligible for The "Best of the Nest" Prize.

POCKETS FICTION-WRITING CONTEST, The Upper Room, 1908 Grand Ave., P.O. Box 340004, Nashville TN 37203-0004. (615)340-7333. E-mail: pockets@upperroom.org. Website: www.upperroom.org. **Contact:** Lynn W. Gilliam. Offered annually for unpublished work to discover new writers. Deadline: March 1-August 15. Guidelines for SASE. Prize: $1,000 and publications in *Pockets*.

PREMIO AZTLAN, University of New Mexico, Alburquerque NM 87131. (505)277-0582. **Contact:** Teresa Marquez. Offered annually for work published Jan. 1-Dec. 31, 2001, to encourage and reward emerging chicano/a writers at the beginning of their careers. Deadline: December 1, 2001. Guidelines for SASE. Prize: $1,000 and an invitation to a reading at the University of New Mexico.

PRISM INTERNATIONAL ANNUAL SHORT FICTION CONTEST, Prism International, Creative Writing Program, UBC, Buch E462, 1866 Main Mall, Vancouver, British Columbia V6T 1Z1, Canada. (604)822-2514. Fax: (604)822-3616. E-mail: prism@interchange.ubc.ca. Website: www.arts.ubc.ca/prism. **Contact:** Fiction Contest Manager. Offered annually for unpublished work to award the best in contemporary fiction. Works of translation are eligible. Guidelines for SASE, by e-mail or on website. Acquires first North American serial rights upon publication and limited web rights for pieces selected for website. Open to any writer. Deadline: December 31. Charges $22/story, $5 each additional story (outside Canada pay US currency); includes subscription. Prize: 1st-$2,000; runners-up(5)-$200 each; winner and runners-up published.

THOMAS H. RADDALL ATLANTIC FICTION PRIZE, Writers' Federation of Nova Scotia, 1113 Marginal Rd., Halifax, Nova Scotia B3H 4P7, Canada. (902)423-8116. Fax: (902)422-0881. E-mail: talk@writers.ns.ca. Website: www.writers.ns.ca. **Contact:** Jane Buss. Offered annually to fiction published during the year preceding the competition. The Prize "honors the best fiction writing by an Atlantic born (Nova Scotia, New Brunswick, Newfoundland, Prince Edward Island) or resident (2 years) writer." Forward 4 copies of published book of fiction to the Writers' Federation of Nova Scotia. Deadline: December 1. Prize: $5,000 (Canadian funds) and prize ceremony.

HAROLD U. RIBALOW AWARD, Hadassah WZOA, 50 W. 58th St., New York NY 10019. (212)688-0227. Fax: (212)446-9521. **Contact:** Dorothy Silfen. Editor: Alan Tigay. Offered annually for English-language books of fiction (novel or short stories) on a Jewish theme published the previous calendar year. Books should be submitted by the publisher. Deadline: April. Prize: $1,000.

RIVER CITY WRITING AWARDS IN FICTION, The University of Memphis/Hohenberg Foundation, Dept. of English, Memphis TN 38152. (901)678-4591. Fax: (901)678-2226. Website: www.people.memphis.edu/~rivercity. **Con-**

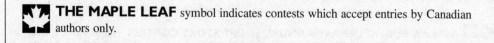

THE MAPLE LEAF symbol indicates contests which accept entries by Canadian authors only.

tact: Thomas Russell. Offered annually for unpublished short stories of 7,500 words maximum. Guidelines for SASE or visit our website. Open to any writer. Deadline: March 1. Charges $10, which is put toward a one year subscription for *River City*. Prize: 1st-$2,000; 2nd-$500; 3rd-$300.

[N] ☙ THE ROGERS WRITERS' TRUST FICTION PRIZE, The Writers' Trust of Canada, 40 Wellington St. E, Suite 300, Toronto, Ontario M5E 1C7, Canada. (416)504-8222. Fax: (416)504-9090. E-mail: info@writerstrust.com. Website: www.writerstrust.com. **Contact:** Candice Cartier. Awarded annually for a distinguished work of fiction, either a novel or short story collection, published within the previous year. Prize: $10,000.

[N] ROMANCE AND BEYOND CONTEST, Romance and Beyond/Briada Press Inc., PMB 9, 3527 Ambassador Caffery Parkway, Lafayette LA 70503-5130. E-mail: RBeyond@aol.com. Website: www.RomanceandBeyond.com. Offered annually for unpublished work in 3 categories: Paranormal/supernatural; science fiction/futuristic; and fantasy/fairy tale. "Most (or all) of the internal conflict must be created - then resolved - by the emotional/spiritual/physical attraction between the hero and heroine. Tone can be very dark to humorous, but the story must be a romance with a happy ending. Sources of external conflict are left to your imagination, the more original the better." Entry form for SASE or on website. Deadline: March 1. Charges $15 fee. Prize: Grand-$100; 1st (in each category)-$50; 2nd (in each category)-$25; 3rd (in each category)-no cash prize. Winners also receive a non-cash prize and certificate. Grand and 1st-place winners will receive an offer of publication in *Romance and Beyond*.

[N] ROMANCE WRITER'S CONTEST, No Noun-Sense, 147-2211 No. 4 Road, Richmond British Columbia V6X 3X1, Canada. (604)825-8861. Fax: (604)214-1306. E-mail: editor@webprospects.com. Website: www.nonounsense.com. **Contact:** Erin Berringer. Offered annually for unpublished work to promote and nurture romance writers. Guidelines on website. Open to any writer. Deadline: January 21. Charges $10. Prize: 1st-$200; 2nd-$50; 3rd-$25. The winner and four honourable mentions will be published on the No Noun-Sense website, along with their bios.

THE SANDSTONE PRIZE IN SHORT FICTION, The Ohio State University Press and the MFA Program in Creative Writing at The Ohio State University, 1070 Carmack Rd., Columbus OH 43210-1002. (614)292-1462. Fax: (614)292-2065. E-mail: ohiostatepress@osu.edu. Website: ohiostatepress.org. **Contact:** Bill Roorbach, fiction editor. Offered annually to published and unpublished writers. Submissions may include short stories, novellas or a combination of both. Manuscripts must be 150-300 typed pages; novellas must not exceed 125 pages. No employee or student of The Ohio State University is eligible. Deadline: Accepts in January only. Charges $20 fee. Prize: $1,500, publication under a standard book contract, an invitation to The Ohio State University to give a public reading and give a master class in creative writing.

[N] ☙ SASKATCHEWAN FICTION AWARD, Saskatchewan Book Awards Inc., Box 1921, Regina, Saskatchewan S4P 3E1, Canada. (306)569-1585. Fax: (306)569-4187. E-mail: sk.bookawards@dlcwest.com. Website: www.bookawards.sk.ca. **Contact:** Joyce Wells, executive director. Offered annually for work published October 1, 2001, to September 14, 2002. This award is presented to a Saskatchewan author for the best book of fiction (novel or short fiction), judged on the quality of writing. Deadline: First deadline: July 31; final deadline: September 14. Guidelines for SASE. Charges $15 (Canadian). Prize: $1,500.

MICHAEL SHAARA AWARD FOR EXCELLENCE IN CIVIL WAR FICTION, US Civil War Center, LSU, Raphael Semmes Dr., Baton Rouge LA 70803. (225)578-3151. Fax: (225)578-4876. E-mail: lwood@lsu.edu. Website: www.cwc.lsu.edu. **Contact:** Leah Jewett, director. Offered annually for fiction published January 1-December 31 ""to encourage examination of the Civil War from unique perspectives or by taking an unusual approach." All Civil War fiction, except children's books, is eligible. Nominations should be made by publishers, but authors and critics can nominate as well. Deadline: December 31. Guidelines for SASE. Prize: $1,000.

JOHN SIMMONS SHORT FICTION AWARD and IOWA SHORT FICTION AWARDS, Iowa Writers' Workshop, 102 Dey House, 507 N. Clinton St., Iowa City IA 52242-1000. Offered annually for a collection of short stories. Anyone who has not published a book of prose fiction is eligible to apply. Deadline: August 1-September 30. Prize: Publication by the University of Iowa Press.

[N] ELIZABETH SIMPSON SMITH AWARD, Charlotte Writers Club, P.O. Box 220954, Charlotte NC 28222-0954. E-mail: lorinorman@CETLink.net. **Contact:** Lori Norman, 2002 ESS Award Chairperson. Offered annually for unpublished short stories by North Carolina and South Carolina residents. Deadline: April 30. Guidelines for SASE. Charges $10 fee. Prize: $500 and a plaque.

KAY SNOW WRITING AWARDS, Willamette Writers, 9045 SW Barbur Blvd., Suite 5A, Portland OR 97219. (503)452-1592. Fax: (503)452-0372. E-mail: wilwrite@teleport.com. Website: www.willamettewriters.com. **Contact:** Elizabeth Shannon. Contest offered annually to "offer encouragement and recognition to writers with unpublished submissions." Acquires right to publish excerpts from winning pieces one time in their newsletter. Deadline: May 14. Guidelines for SASE. Charges $15 fee; no fee for student writers. Prize: 1st-$300, 2nd-$150, 3rd-$50; excerpts published in Willamette Writers newsletter and winners acknowledged at banquet during writing conference. Student writers win $50 in categories for grades 1-5, 6-8 and 9-12. $500 Liam Callen Memorial Award goes to best overall entry.

SOUTH CAROLINA FICTION PROJECT, South Carolina Arts Commission, 1800 Gervais St., Columbia SC 29201. (803)734-8696. Fax: (803)734-8526. Website: www.state.sc.us/arts. **Contact:** Sara June Goldstein, contest director. Offered annually for unpublished short stories of 2,500 words or less. *The Post and Courier* newspaper (Charleston SC) purchases first publication rights. Open to any writer who is a legal resident of South Carolina and 18 years of age or older. 12 stories are selected for monthly publication. Deadline: January 16. Guidelines for SASE. Prize: $500.

THE SOUTHERN REVIEW/LOUISIANA STATE UNIVERSITY SHORT FICTION AWARD, Louisiana State University, 43 Allen Hall, Baton Rouge LA 70803. (225)578-5108. Fax: (225)578-5098. E-mail: bmacon@LSU.edu or mgriffi@unix1.sncc.LSU.edu. Offered for first collections of short stories by Americans published in the US during the previous year. Publisher or author may enter by mailing 2 copies of the collection. Deadline: January 31.

N STRICTLY FICTION CONTEST, No Noun-Sense, 147-2211 No. 4 Road, Richmond British Columbia V6X 3X1, Canada. (604)825-8861. Fax: (604)214-1306. E-mail: editor@webprospects.com. Website: www.nonounsense.com. **Contact:** Erin Berringer. Offered annually for unpublished work to promote the talents of writers. Guidelines on website. Open to any writer. Deadline: March 21. Charges $35. Prize: 1st-$500; 2nd-$250; 3rd-$100. First-place and four runners-up will be published on the No Noun-Sense website, along with their bios.

sub-TERRAIN SHORT STORY CONTEST, sub-TERRAIN Magazine, P.O. Box 3008 MPO, Vancouver, British Columbia V6B 3X5, Canada. (604)876-8710. Fax: (604)879-2667. E-mail: subter@portal.ca. **Contact:** Brian Kaufman. Offered annually to foster new and upcoming writers. 2,000 word limit. Deadline: January 1-May 15. Guidelines for SASE. Charges $15 fee for first story, $5 for additional entries. Prize: $500 (Canadian), publication in summer issue and 1-year subscription to *sub-TERRAIN*.

TAMARACK AWARD, Minnesota Monthly, 10 S. Fifth St., #1000, Minneapolis MN 55402. (612)371-5842. Fax: (612)371-5801. E-mail: stieck@mnmo.com. Website: www.minnesotamonthly.com. **Contact:** Sarah Tieck, assistant editor. Offered annually for unpublished fiction. Buys one-time publication rights. Open to residents of MN, ND, SD, IA, WI and MI. Deadline: May. Guidelines for SASE. Prize: $400 and publication.

N SYDNEY TAYLOR MANUSCRIPT COMPETITION, Association of Jewish Libraries, 315 Maitland Ave., Teaneck NJ 07666. (201)862-0312. Fax: (201)862-0362. E-mail: rkglasser@aol.com. Website: www.jewishlibraries.org. **Contact:** Rachel Glasser, coordinator. Offered annually for unpublished authors of books only. "Material should be a work of fiction in English, with universal appeal of Jewish content for readers aged 8-11 years. It should deepen the understanding of Judaism for all children, Jewish and non-Jewish, and reveal positive aspects of Jewish life. No short stories or plays. Length: 64-200 pages." Judged by 5 AJL member librarians. Guidelines for SASE or on website. Open to any writer. Deadline: January 15. Prize: $1,000.

N THE PETER TAYLOR PRIZE FOR THE NOVEL, Knoxville Writers' Guild and University of Tennessee Press, P.O. Box 2565, Knoxville TN 37901-2565. Website: www.knoxvillewritersguild.org. **Contact:** Brian Griffin. Offered annually for unpublished work to discover and publish novels of high literary quality. Guidelines for SASE or on website. Open to U.S. residents writing in English. Members of the Knoxville Writers' Guild do the initial screening. A widely published novelist chooses the winner from a pool of finalists. 2000 judge: George Garrett. 2001 judge: Doris Betts. Deadline: February 1-April 30. Charges $20 fee. Prize: $1,000 publication by University of Tennessee Press under a standard royalty contract.

N THOROUGHBRED TIMES FICTION CONTEST, *Thoroughbred Times Magazine*, 496 Southland Dr., Lexington KY 40503. (859)260-9800. Fax: (859)260-9812. E-mail: copy@thoroughbredtimes.com. Website: www.thoroughbredtimes.com. **Contact:** Mary Simon. Offered every two years for unpublished work to recocgnize outstanding fiction written about the Thoroughbred racing industry. Maximum length: 5,000 words. *Thoroughbred Times* receives first North American serial rights and reserves the right to publish any and all entries in the magazine. Deadline: December 31, 2001. Prize: 1st-$800 and publication in *Thoroughbred Times* in March 2002; 2nd-$400 and publication; 3rd-$250 and publication.

N THREE OAKS PRIZE FOR FICTION, Story Line Press, P.O. Box 1240, Ashland OR 97520-0055. (541)512-8792. Fax: (541)512-8793. E-mail: mail@storylinepress.com. Website: www.storylinepress.com. Offered annually to find and publish the best work of fiction. Open to any writer. Deadline: April 30. Guidelines for SASE. Charges $25. Prize: $1,500 cash award and book publication.

STEVEN TURNER AWARD, The Texas Institute of Letters, Southwest Texas State University, San Marcos TX 78666. (512)245-2428. Fax: (512)245-7462. E-mail: mb13@swt.edu. Website: www.English.swt.ecu/css/TIL/rules.htm. **Contact:** Mark Busby. Offered annually for work published January 1-December 31 for the best first book of fiction. Writers must have been born in Texas, or have lived in the state for at least two consecutive years at some time, or the subject matter of the work should be associated with the state. Deadline: January 3. Guidelines for SASE. Prize: $1,000.

VERY SHORT FICTION AWARD, Glimmer Train Press, Inc., 710 SW Madison St., Suite 504, Portland OR 97205-2900. (503)221-0836. E-mail: info@glimmertrain.com. Website: glimmertrain.com. **Contact:** Linda Swanson-Davies.

Offered twice yearly to encourage the art of the very short story. "Send your unpublished very short story with $10 reading fee/story. Word count: 2,000 max. Must be postmarked April 1-July 31 (summer contest) or November 1-January 31 (winter contest). Cover letter optional. First page of story to include name, address, phone, word count. 'VSF' must be written on the outside of the envelope. Winners will be called by November 1 (for summer contest) or May 1 (for winter contest). Include SASE for results." Deadline: April 1-July 31 or November 1-January 31. Charges $10 fee per story. Prize: 1st-$1,200, publication in *Glimmer Train Stories* (circulation 13,000), and 20 copies of that issue. Runners-up-$500, $300, respectively and consideration for publication.

N WAASMODE FICTION CONTEST, *Passages North*, Dept. of English, Northern Michigan University, 1401 Presque Isle Ave., Marquette MI 49855. (906)227-1203. Fax: (906)227-1096. E-mail: passages@nmu.edu. Website: vm.nmu.edu/passages/http/home.html. **Contact:** Miriam Moeller. Offered every two years to publish new voices in literary fiction. Deadline: Submit September 15-January 15. Guidelines for SASE. Charges $8 reading fee per story. Prize: $1,000 and publication for winner; 2 honorable mentions also published; all entrants receive a copy of *Passages North*.

PAUL A. WITTY SHORT STORY AWARD, Executive Office, International Reading Association, P.O. Box 8139, Newark DE 19714-8139. (302)731-1600 ext. 293. Fax: (302)731-1057. Website: www.reading.org. **Contact:** Janet Butler, public information associate. Offered to reward author of an original short story published in a children's periodical which serves as a literary standard that encourages young readers to read periodicals. Write for deadlines and guidelines. Prize: $1,000.

THOMAS WOLFE FICTION PRIZE, North Carolina Writers' Network, 3501 Hwy. 54 W., Studio C, Chapel Hill NC 27516. (919)967-9540. Fax: (919)929-0535. E-mail: mail@ncwriters.org. Website: www.ncwriters.org. **Contact:** Whitney Vaughan, program coordinator. Offered annually for unpublished work "to recognize a notable work of fiction—either short story or novel excerpt—while honoring one of North Carolina's best writers—Thomas Wolfe." Past judges have included Anne Tyler, Barbara Kingsolver, C. Michael Curtis and Randall Kenan. Deadline: August 31. Guidelines for SASE. Charges $7 fee. Prize: $1,000 and potential publication.

TOBIAS WOLFF AWARD IN FICTION, *Bellingham Review*, Mail Stop 9053, Western Washington University, Bellingham WA 98225. (360)650-4863. E-mail: bhreview@cc.wwu.edu. Website: www.wwu.edu/~bhreview/. **Contact:** Brenda Miller. Offered annually for unpublished short stories. Deadline: January 5-March 5. Guidelines for SASE. Prize: 1st-$1,000; 2nd-$300; 3rd-$200; plus publication and subscription.

N WORLD'S BEST SHORT SHORT STORY FICTION CONTEST, English Dept., Writing Program, Florida State University, Tallahassee FL 32306. (850)644-2640. E-mail: sundog@english.fsu.edu. Website: www.english.fsu.edu/sundog. **Contact:** Jarret Keene, editor, *SUNDOG: The Southeast Review*. Estab. 1986. Annual award for unpublished short short stories (no more than 300 words). Deadline: April 15. Charges $2 fee per story. Prize: $300 and a box of Florida oranges.

WRITERS' JOURNAL ANNUAL FICTION CONTEST, Val-Tech Media, P.O. Box 394, Perham MN 56573. (218)346-7921. Fax: (218)346-7924. E-mail: writersjournal@wadena.net. Website: www.writersjournal.com. **Contact:** Leon Ogroske. Offered annually for previously unpublished fiction. Buys one-time rights. Open to any writer. Deadline: January 30. Guidelines for SASE. Charges $5 reading fee. Prize: 1st-$50, 2nd-$25, 3rd-$15, plus honorable mentions. Prize-winning stories and selected honorable mentions published in *Writers' Journal* magazine.

WRITERS' JOURNAL ANNUAL HORROR/GHOST CONTEST, Val-Tech Media, P.O. Box 394, Perham MN 56573. (218)346-7921. Fax: (218)346-7924. E-mail: writersjournal@wadena.net. Website: www.writersjournal.com. **Contact:** Leon Ogroske. Offered annually for previously unpublished works. Buys one-time rights. Open to any writer. Deadline: March 30. Guidelines for SASE. Charges $5 fee. Prize: 1st-$50, 2nd-$25, 3rd-$15, plus honorable mentions. Prize-winning stories and selected honorable mentions published in *Writers' Journal* magazine.

WRITERS' JOURNAL ANNUAL ROMANCE CONTEST, Val-Tech Media, P.O. Box 394, Perham MN 56573. (218)346-7921. Fax: (218)346-7924. E-mail: writersjournal@wadena.net. Website: www.writersjournal.com. **Contact:** Leon Ogroske. Offered annually for previously unpublished works. Buys one-time rights. Open to any writer. Deadline: July 30. Guidelines for SASE. Charges $5 fee. Prize: 1st-$50, 2nd-$25, 3rd-$15, plus honorable mentions. Prize-winning stories and selected honorable mentions published in *Writers' Journal* magazine.

WRITERS' JOURNAL ANNUAL SHORT STORY CONTEST, Val-Tech Media, P.O. Box 394, Perham MN 56573. (218)346-7921. Fax: (218)346-7924. E-mail: writersjournal@wadena.net. Website: www.writersjournal.com. **Contact:** Leon Ogroske. Offered annually for previously unpublished short stories. Buys one-time rights. Open to any writer. Deadline: May 30. Guidelines for SASE. Charges $7 reading fee. Prize: 1st-$250, 2nd-$100, 3rd-$50, plus honorable mentions. Prize-winning stories and selected honorable mentions published in *Writers' Journal* magazine.

ZOETROPE SHORT STORY CONTEST, Zoetrope: All-Story, 1350 Avenue of the Americas, 24th Floor, New York NY 10019. (212)708-0400. Fax: (212)708-0475. Website: www.all-story.com. **Contact:** Gheña Glijansky, assistant editor. Annual contest for unpublished short stories. Open to any writer. Deadline: October 1. Guidelines for SASE or online. Charges $15 fee. Prize: 1st-$1,000, 2nd-$500, 3rd-$250; plus 10 honorable mentions.

Poetry

THE MILTON ACORN PRIZE FOR POETRY, Poetry Forever, P.O. Box 68018, Hamilton, Ontario L8M 3M7, Canada. (905)312-1779. Fax: (905)312-8285. Offered annually for poems up to 30 lines. Deadline: May 15. Charges $3 fee. Prize: 3 prizes of up to $100 and broadsheet publication.

THE ACORN-RUKEYSER CHAPBOOK CONTEST, Mekler & Deahl, Publishers, 237 Prospect St., S., Hamilton, Ontario L8M 2Z6, Canada. (905)312-1779. Fax: (905)312-8285. E-mail: james@meklerdeahl.com. Website: www.mekl erdeahl.com. Offered annually for published or unpublished poetry manuscripts up to 30 pages. Deadline: September 30. Charges $10 fee (US). Prize: 1st—$100 and 50 copies of the chapbook; runner-up—$100.

AKRON POETRY PRIZE, University of Akron Press, 374B Bierce Library, Akron OH 44325-1703. (330)972-5342. Fax: (330)972-8364. E-mail: uapress@uakron.edu. Website: www.uakron.edu/uapress/poetry.html. **Contact:** Elton Glaser, poetry editor. Annual book contest for unpublished poetry. "The Akron Poetry Prize brings to the public writers with original and compelling voices. Books must exhibit three essential qualities: Mastery of language, maturity of feeling, and complexity of thought." Guidelines available online or for SASE. The final selection will be made by a nationally prominent poet. The University of Akron Press has the right to publish the winning manuscript, inherent with winning the Poetry Prize. Open to all poets writing in English. Deadline: May 15-June 30. Charges $25 fee. Prize: Winning poet receives $1,000 and publication of book.

ANAMNESIS PRESS POETRY CHAPBOOK AWARD COMPETITION, Anamnesis Press, P.O. Box 95, Ridgecrest CA 93556. (760)375-8555. Fax: (760)375-8559. E-mail: anamnesispress@cs.com. Website: www.anamnesispress.c om. **Contact:** Keith Allen Daniels. Offered annually to preserve and promote outstanding imaginative poetry. Acquires one-time right to publish chapbook in a limited edition of 200-300 copies. Open to all writers. Recommends that poets purchase a sample chapbook for $6 (postpaid) before submitting their work. Deadline: March 15. Guidelines for SASE. Charges $15 fee. Prize: $1,000, certificate, 20 copies of winning chapbook.

ANHINGA PRIZE FOR POETRY, Anhinga Press, P.O. Box 10595, Tallahassee FL 32302. (850)521-9920. Fax: (850)442-6363. E-mail: info@anhinga.org. Website: www.anhinga.org. **Contact:** Rick Campbell. Offered annually for a book-length collection of poetry by an author who has not published more than one book of poetry. Guidelines for SASE or on website. Open to any writer writing in English. Deadline: February 15-May 1. Charges $20 fee. Prize: $2,000 and publication.

ANNUAL POETRY CONTEST, National Federation of State Poetry Societies, 1220 W. Koradine Dr., South Jordan UT 84095. E-mail: irvkimber@Lgcy.com. **Contact:** Patricia A. Kimber. Estab. 1959. Previously unpublished poetry. "Fifty categories. Flier lists them all." Guidelines for SASE. Must have guidelines to enter. Deadline: March 15. Prize: All awards are announced in June. Top awards only (not honorable mentions) published the following June.

Ṅ THE ANNUAL PRAIRIE SCHOONER STROUSSE AWARD, Prairie Schooner, 201 Andrews Hall, P.O. Box 880334, Lincoln NE 68588-0334. (402)472-0911. Fax: (402)472-9771. E-mail: eflanagan2@unl.edu. Website: www.unl.edu/schooner/psmain.htm. **Contact:** Hilda Raz. Offered annually for the best poem or group of poems published in *Prairie Schooner* in the previous year. Prize: $500.

Ṅ ART COOP POETRY FELLOWSHIP, Cottonwood Art Co-operative, 725 Ashland, Houston TX 77007-1424. E-mail: art_coop@yahoo.com. Website: www.geocities.com/art_coop. **Contact:** Victor Gonzalez. For most recent information, please visit website or write for guidelines with SASE. Submit with cover sheet, bio, and publications list. Open to any writer. Deadline: May 1. Charges $15 for up to 3 poems, $2 each thereafter. For additional flat $15 fee and SASE, feedback provided on poems. Prize: Cash award to be determined, not less than $250, and publication to support serious, aspiring poets. Open to any writer.

Ṅ THE BACKWATERS PRIZE, The Backwaters Press, 3502 N. 52nd St., Omaha NE 68104-3506. (402)451-4052. Fax: (402)451-4052. E-mail: gkosm62735@aol.com. Website: www.thebackwaterspress.homestead.com. **Contact:** Greg Kosmicki. Offered annually to find the best collection of poems, or single long poem, to publish and help further the poet's career. Collections must be unpublished, however parts of the manuscript may have been published as a chapbook, or individual poems may have been previously published in magazines. Deadline: June 4. Charges $20 fee. Prize: $1,000 and publication of the winning manuscript in an edition of at least 750 copies in perfect bound format.

THE HERB BARRETT AWARD, for Short Poetry in the Haiku Tradition, Mekler & Deahl, Publishers, 237 Prospect St. S., Hamilton, Ontario L8M 2Z6, Canada. (905)312-1779. Fax: (905)312-8285. E-mail: james@meklerdeahl.com.

Website: www.meklerdeahl.com. Offered annually for short poems in the haiku tradition. Writers retain all rights. Open to any writer. Deadline: November 30. Charges $10 fee (US); maximum 10 entries. Prize: 1st-$200 (US); 2nd-$150 (US); 3rd-$100 (US); all entrants receive a copy of the published anthology, entrants with poetry in the anthology receive 2 copies.

BLUESTEM POETRY AWARD, Department of English, Emporia State University 1200, Emporia KS 66801. (316)341-5216. Fax: (316)341-5547. E-mail: bluestem@emporia.edu. Website: www.emporia.edu/bluestem/index.htm. **Contact:** Philip Heldrich, award director. Offered annually "to recognize outstanding poetry." Full-length, single-author collections, at least 48 pages long. Deadline: March 1. Charges $18 fee. Prize: $1,000 and a published book.

THE FREDERICK BOCK PRIZE, *Poetry*, 60 W. Walton St., Chicago IL 60610. (312)255-3703. E-mail: poetry@poetr ymagazine.org. Website: www.poetrymagazine.org. **Contact:** Joseph Parisi, editor. Offered annually for poems published in *Poetry* during the preceding year (October through September). *Poetry* buys all rights to the poems published in the magazine. Copyrights are returned to the authors on request. Any writer may submit poems to *Poetry*. Guidelines for SASE. Prize: $300.

THE BORDIGHERA BILINGUAL ITALIAN-AMERICAN POETRY PRIZE, Sonia Raiziss-Giop Foundation, 57 Montague St. #8G, Brooklyn NY 11201-3356. E-mail: daniela@garden.net. Website: www.ItalianAmericanWriters.com. **Contact:** Daniela Gioseffi. Offered annually for an unpublished collection of poetry "to find the best manuscripts of poetry in English, by an American of Italian descent, to be translated into quality Italian and published bilingually. Deadline: May 31. Guidelines for SASE. Prize: $2,000 and bilingual book publication to be divided between poet and translator.

BOSTON REVIEW POETRY CONTEST, Boston Review, E-53-407 MIT, Cambridge MA 02139. (617)494-0708. Submit up to 5 unpublished poems, no more than 10 pages total. Deadline: June 1. Charges $15 fee, payable to *Boston Review*, check or money order. Prize: $1,000 and publication in the October/November issue of *Boston Review*.

bp NICHOL CHAPBOOK AWARD, Phoenix Community Works Foundation, 316 Dupont St., Toronto Ontario M5R 1V9, Canada. (416)964-7919. Fax: (416)964-6941. E-mail: pcwf@web.net. Website: www.pcwf.on.ca. **Contact:** Philip McKenna, award director. Offered annually to a chapbook (10-48 pp) of poetry in English, published in Canada in the previous year. Deadline: March 30. Guidelines for SASE. Prize: $1,000 (Canadian).

BARBARA BRADLEY AWARD, New England Poetry Club, 11 Puritan Rd., Arlington MA 02476-7710. **Contact:** Virginia Thayer. Offered annually for a lyric poem under 21 lines, written by a woman. Deadline: June 30. Guidelines for SASE. Charges $10 entry fee for nonmembers (up to 3 poems). Prize: $200.

BRITTINGHAM PRIZE IN POETRY/FELIX POLLAK PRIZE IN POETRY, University of Wisconsin Press, Dept. of English, 600 N. Park St., University of Wisconsin, Madison WI 53706. **Contact:** Ronald Wallace, contest director. Estab. 1985. Offered for unpublished book-length manuscripts of original poetry. Submissions must be *received* by the press *during* the month of September, accompanied by a SASE for contest results. Does *not* return manuscripts. One entry fee covers both prizes. Guidelines for SASE. Charges $20 fee, payable to University of Wisconsin Press. Prize: $1,000 and publication of the 2 winning manuscripts.

THE DOROTHY BRUNSMAN POETRY PRIZE, Bear Star Press, 185 Hollow Oak Dr., Cohasset CA 95973. (530)891-0360. E-mail: bgumbo@aol.com. Website: www.bearstarpress.com. **Contact:** Beth Spencer. Offered annually to support the publication of one volume of poetry. Guidelines for SASE or on website. Open to poets living in western US (those in Mountain and Pacific time zones, and Alaska and Hawaii). Deadline: November 30. Charges $16 fee. Prize: $1,000 and publication.

GERALD CABLE BOOK AWARD, Silverfish Review Press, P.O. Box 3541, Eugene OR 97403-0541. (503)344-5060. E-mail: sfrpress@aol.com. **Contact:** Rodger Moody, series editor. Purpose is to publish a poetry book by a deserving author who has yet to publish a full-length book. Open to any writer. Deadline: November 15. Guidelines for SASE. Charges $20 reading fee. Prize: $1,000.

CANADIAN AUTHORS ASSOCIATION AWARD FOR POETRY, Box 419, 320 S. Shores Rd., Campbellford, Ontario K0L 1L0, Canada. (705)653-0323. Fax: (705)653-0593. E-mail: canauth@redden.on.ca. Website: www.can authors.org. **Contact:** Alec McEachern. Offered annually for a volume of poetry by a Canadian citizen. Deadline: December 15. Guidelines for SASE. Charges $20 fee (Canadian). Prize: $2,500 and a silver medal.

HAYDEN CARRUTH AWARD, Copper Canyon Press, P.O. Box 271, Port Townsend WA 98368. (360)385-4925. Fax: (360)385-4985. E-mail: poetry@coppercanyonpress.org. Website: www.coppercanyonpress.org. **Contact:** Joseph Bednarik. Offered annually for unpublished work. Contest is for new and emerging poets who have published no more than 2 full-length books of poetry. Chapbooks of 32 pages or less are not considered to be full-length, and books published in other genres do not count toward the 2-book limit. Deadline: November 30. Guidelines for SASE. Charges $20 fee. Prize: $1,000 advance and book publication by Copper Canyon Press.

[N] JOHN CIARDI POETRY AWARD FOR LIFETIME ACHIEVEMENT, Italian Americana, URI/CCE, 80 Washington St., Providence RI 02903-1803. Fax: (401)277-5100. Website: www.uri.edu/prov/italian/italian.html. **Contact:** Carol Bonomo Albright, editor. Offered annually for *lifetime* achievement in all aspects of poetry: Creative, critical, etc. Applicants should have at least 2 books published. Open to Italian Americans only. Guidelines for SASE. Prize: $1,000.

CLEVELAND STATE UNIVERSITY POETRY CENTER PRIZE, Cleveland State University Poetry Center, 1983 E. 24 St., Cleveland OH 44115-2440. (216)687-3986. Fax: (216)687-6943. E-mail: poetrycenter@csuohio.edu. Website: www.ims.csuohio.edu/poetry/poetrycenter.html. **Contact:** Rita Grabowski, poetry center coordinator. Estab. 1962. Offered annually to identify, reward and publish the best unpublished book-length poetry manuscript submitted (40 pages of poetry, minimum). "Submission implies willingness to sign standard royalty contract for publication if manuscript wins." One or more of the other finalist manuscripts may also be published for standard royalty (no prize). Does not return manuscripts. Deadline: Submissions accepted November-January only (postmark deadline is February 1). Guidelines for SASE. Charges $20 fee. Prize: $1,000 and publication.

THE COLORADO PRIZE FOR POETRY, Colorado Review/Center for Literary Publishing, Department of English, Colorado State University, Ft. Collins CO 80523. (970)491-5449. E-mail: creview@colostate.edu. Website: www.colorad oreview.com. **Contact:** Stephanie G'Schwind, managing editor. Offered annually to an unpublished collection of poetry. Deadline: January 14, 2002. Charges $25 fee. Prize: $2,000 and publication of book.

[N] BETSY COLQUITT AWARD FOR POETRY, *descant*, Texas Christian Univesity's literary journal, TCU Box 297270, Fort Worth TX 76129. (817)257-6537. Fax: (817)257-6239. E-mail: descant@tcu.edu. **Contact:** Dave Kuhne, editor. Offered annually for unpublished poems or series of poems. Publication retains copywright but will transfer it to the author upon request. Deadline: September-April. Guidelines for SASE. Prize: $500.

CONTEMPORARY POETRY SERIES, University of Georgia Press, 330 Research Dr., Suite B100, Athens GA 30602-4901. (706)369-6135. Fax: (706)369-6131. E-mail: mnunnell@ugapress.uga.edu. Website: www.uga.edu/ugapre ss. **Contact:** Margaret Nunnelley. Offered 2 times/year. Two awards: One for poets who have not had a full-length book of poems published (deadline in September), and one for poets with at least one full-length publication (deadline in January). Guidelines for SASE. Charges $15 fee.

CRAB ORCHARD AWARD SERIES IN POETRY, Crab Orchard Review and Southern Illinois University Press, Department of English, Carbondale IL 62901-4503. (618)453-6833. Website: www.siu.edu/~crborchd. **Contact:** Jon C. Tribble, series editor. Offered annually for collections of unpublished poetry. Visit website for current deadlines. Charges $20 fee. Prize: 1st-$3,000 and publication; 2nd-$1,000 and publication.

[N] ALICE FAY DI CASTAGNOLA AWARD, Poetry Society of America, 15 Gramercy Park S., New York NY 10003. (212)254-9628. Fax: (212)673-2352. Website: www.poetrysociety.org. **Contact:** Brett Lauer, programs associate. Offered annually for a manuscript-in-progress of poetry or verse-drama. Guidelines for SASE or on website. Deadline: December 21. Prize: $1,000.

EMILY DICKINSON AWARD IN POETRY, Universities West Press, P.O. Box 788, Flagstaff AZ 86004-0788. (520)774-9574. E-mail: glenn@usa.net. Website: popularpicks.com. **Contact:** Glenn Reed. Offered annually for unpublished poetry in any form or style, and on any subject. Winner grants UWP one-time rights to publish the award-winning poem in its anthology. "A submission should include 1-3 poems, total entry not to exceed 6 pages, short biographical statement, reading fee of $10, and a SASE or e-mail address for results. Award is open to all writers. (Current students and employees of Northern Arizona University may not enter.)" Deadline: August 31. Guidelines for SASE. Charges $10 fee. Prize: $1,000 and publication in an anthology of poems published by Universities West Press. All finalists and winners will be published.

DISCOVERY/THE NATION, The Joan Leiman Jacobson Poetry Prizes, The Unterberg Poetry Center of the 92nd Street YM-YWHA, 1395 Lexington Ave., New York NY 10128. (212)415-5759. Website: www.92ndsty.org. **Contact:** Jennifer Cayer, assistant to the director. Open to poets who have not published a book of poems (chapbooks, self-published books included). Must have guidelines; send SASE, call or see website. Open to any writer. Deadline: January. Charges $5 fee.

MILTON DORFMAN POETRY PRIZE, Rome Art & Community Center, 308 W. Bloomfield St., Rome NY 13440. (315)336-1040. Fax: (315)336-1090. **Contact:** Deborah O'Shea, director. Estab. 1990. "The purpose of the Milton Dorfman Poetry Prize is to offer poets an outlet for their craft. All submissions must be previously unpublished. Deadline: July 1-November 1. Guidelines for SASE. Charges $5 fee per poem. Prize: 1st-$500; 2nd-$200; 3rd-$100.

EDITORS' PRIZE, Spoon River Poetry Review, Campus Box 4241, English Dept., Illinois State University, Normal IL 61790-4241. (309)438-7906. Website: www.litline.org/spoon. **Contact:** Lucia Cordell Getsi, editor. Offered annually for unpublished poetry "to identify and reward excellence." Guidelines for SASE or on website. Open to all writers. Deadline: April 15. Charges fee of $16 per 3 poems (entitles entrant to a year's subscription valued at $15). Prize: 1st-$1,000, two $100 runner-up prizes; publication of first place, runners-up, and selected honorable mentions.

T.S. ELIOT PRIZE FOR POETRY, Truman State University Press, New Odyssey Series, 100 E. Normal St., Kirksville MO 63501-4221. (660)785-7199. Fax: (660)785-4480. E-mail: tsup@truman.edu. Website: www2.truman.edu/tsup. **Contact:** Nancy Reschly. Offered annually for unpublished English-language poetry. Deadline: October 31. Guidelines for SASE. Charges $25 fee. Prize: $2,000 and publication.

N: MAURICE ENGLISH POETRY AWARD, 2222 Rittenhouse Square, Philadelphia PA 19103-5505. Fax: (215)732-1382. **Contact:** Helen W. Drutt English. Offered annually for a distinguished book of poems published in the previous calendar year. Poets must be over 50 years of age to enter the contest. Deadline: February 15. Prize: $3,000, plus a public reading in Philadelphia.

ROBERT G. ENGLISH/POETRY IN PRINT, P.O. Box 30981, Albuquerque NM 87190-0981. (505)888-3937. Fax: (505)888-3937. Website: www.poets.com/RobertEnglish.html. **Contact:** Robert G. English. Offered annually "to help a poetry writer accomplish their own personal endeavors. Hopefully the prize amount of the Poetry in Print award will grow to a higher significance." "The contest is open to any writer of any age. Hopefully to prepare writers other than just journalists with a stronger desire to always tell the truth." No limit to number of entries; 30-line limit per poem. Deadline: August 1. Charges $5/poem. Prize: $500.

N: FIELD POETRY PRIZE, Oberlin College Press/FIELD, 10 N. Professor St., Oberlin OH 44074-1095. (440)775-8408. Fax: (440)775-8124. E-mail: oc.press@oberlin.edu. Website: www.oberlin.edu/~ocpress. **Contact:** Linda Slocum, managing editor. Offered annually for unpublished work. "The FIELD Poetry Prize contest seeks to encourage the finest in contemporary poetry writing." No simultaneous submissions. Open to any writer. Deadline: Submit in May only. Guidelines for SASE. Charges $22 fee, which includes a 1-year subscription. Prize: $1,000 and book published in Oberlin College Press's FIELD Poetry Series.

FIVE POINTS JAMES DICKEY PRIZE FOR POETRY, Five Points, Georgia State University University Plaza, Atlanta GA 30303-3083. (404)651-0071. Fax: (404)651-3167. E-mail: msexton@gsu.edu. Website: www.webdelsol.com/Five_Points. **Contact:** Megan Sexton. Offered annually for unpublished poetry. Deadline: November 30. Guidelines for SASE. Charges $12 fee (includes 1 year subscription). Prize: $1,000 plus publication.

THE 49th PARALLEL POETRY AWARD, *Bellingham Review*, Mail Stop 9053, Western Washington University, Bellingham WA 98225. (360)650-4863. E-mail: bhreview@cc.wwu.edu. Website: www.wwu.edu/~bhreview/. **Contact:** Brenda Miller. Estab. 1977. Offered annually for unpublished poetry. Deadline: January 5-March 5. Guidelines for SASE. Prize: 1st-$1,000 and publication; 2nd-$300; 3rd-$200; all finalists considered for publication, all entrants receive subscription.

FOUR WAY BOOKS POETRY PRIZES, Four Way Books, P.O. Box 535, Village Station, New York NY 10014. (212)619-1105. Fax: (212)406-1352. E-mail: four_way_editors@yahoo.com. Website: www.fourwaybooks.com. **Contact:** K. Clarke, contest coordinator. Four Way runs different prizes annually. Guidelines for SASE or on website. Deadline: March 31. Prize: Cash honorarium and book publication.

N: ROBERT FROST POETRY AWARD, The Robert Frost Foundation, Heritage Place, 439 S. Union, Lawrence MA 01843. (978)725-8828. Fax: (978)725-8828. E-mail: mejaneiro@aol.com. Website: www.frostfoundation.org. **Contact:** Mary Ellen Janeiro. Offered annually for unpublished work "to recognize poets writing today in the tradition of Frost and other American greats." "Poems should be written in the spirit of Frost, as interpreted by the poet's knowledge of Frost's poetry, life, persona, etc." More than one poem may be entered. Open to any writer. Deadline: September 1. Guidelines for SASE. Charges $10 fee/poem. Prize: $1,000.

N: ALLEN GINSBERG POETRY AWARDS, The Poetry Center at Passaic County Community College, One College Blvd., Paterson NJ 07505-1179. (973)684-6555. Fax: (973)684-5843. E-mail: mgillan@pccc.cc.nj.us. Website: www.pccc.cc.nj.us/poetry. **Contact:** Maria Mazziotti Gillan, executive director. Offered annually for unpublished poetry "to honor Allen Ginsberg's contribution to American literature." The college retains first publication rights. Open to any writer. Deadline: April 1. Guidelines for SASE. Charges Charges $13, which covers the cost of a subscription to *The Paterson Literary Review*. Prize: $1,000.

N: GIVAL PRESS CHAPBOOK COMPETITION, Gival Press, LLC, P.O. Box 3812, Arlington VA 22203. (703)351-0079. Fax: (703)351-0079. E-mail: givalpress@yahoo.com. Website: www.givalpress.com. **Contact:** Robert L. Giron. Offered annually for previously published or unpublished poetry. The competition seeks to award well-written poetry in English. Guidelines for SASE or by e-mail. Deadline: December 15. Charges $15. Prize: $500 plus publication in a limited run.

GLIMMER TRAIN'S APRIL POETRY OPEN, Glimmer Train Press, 710 SW Madison St., #504, Portland OR 97205. (503)221-0836. E-mail: info@glimmertrain.com. Website: www.glimmertrain.com. **Contact:** Linda Swanson-Davies. Submissions must be unpublished and may be entered in other contests. There are no subject, form, or length restrictions. "Name, address and phone number need to appear on all submitted poems." Winners contacted by September 1. Include SASE for results. Deadline: April 30. Charges $10 for up to 3 poems (sent together). Prize: 1st-$500, publication in *Glimmer Train Stories* and 20 copies of that issue; 2nd-$250; 3rd-$100.

GLIMMER TRAIN'S OCTOBER POETRY OPEN, Glimmer Train Press, 710 SW Madison St., #504, Portland OR 97205. (503)221-0836. E-mail: info@glimmertrain.com. Website: www.glimmertrain.com. **Contact:** Linda Swanson-Davies. Submissions must be unpublished and may be entered in other contests. There are no subject, form, or length restrictions. "Name, address and phone number need to appear on all submitted poems." Winners contacted by March 1. Include SASE for results. Deadline: October 31. Charges $10 fee for up to 3 poems (sent together). Prize: 1st-$500, publication in *Glimmer Train Stories* and 20 copies of that issue; 2nd-$250; 3rd-$100.

N **GOVERNOR GENERAL'S LITERARY AWARD FOR POETRY**, Canada Council for the Arts, 350 Albert St., P.O. Box 1047, Ottawa, Ontario K1P 5V8, Canada. (613)566-4414 ext. 5576. Fax: (613)566-4410. E-mail: joanne.larocque-poirier@canadacouncil.ca. Website: www.canadacouncil.ca. **Contact:** Joanne Larocque-Poirier. Offered for the best English-language and the best French-language work of poetry by a Canadian published September 1, 2001, to September 30, 2002. Publishers submit titles for consideration. Deadline: April or August 2002, depending on the book's publication date. Prize: $15,000.

N **GREEN ROSE PRIZE IN POETRY**, *New Issues Poetry & Prose*, Department of English, Western Michigan University, 1903 W. Michigan Ave., Kalamazoo MI 49008-5331. (616)387-8185. Fax: (616)387-2562. E-mail: herbert.scott@wmich.edu. Website: www.wmich.edu/newissues. **Contact:** Herbert Scott, editor. Offered annually for unpublished poetry. The university will publish a book of poems by a poet writing in English who has published one or more full-length books of poetry. Guidelines for SASE or on website. *New Issues Poetry & Prose* obtains rights for first publication. Book is copyrighted in author's name. Deadline: September 30. Charges $20 fee. Prize: $1,000 and publication of book. Author also receives 10% of the printed edition.

GROLIER POETRY PRIZE, Grolier Poetry Book Shop, Inc., & Ellen LaForge Memorial Poetry Foundation, Inc., 6 Plympton St., Cambridge MA 02138. (617)547-4648. Fax: (617)547-4230. E-mail: grolierpoetrybookshop@compuserve .com. Website: www.grolierpoetrybookshop.com. **Contact:** Ms. Louisa Solano. Estab. 1973. Offered annually for previously unpublished work to encourage and recognize developing writers. Open to all poets who have not published a book (vanity, small press, trade or chapbook). Opens January 15. Guidelines must be followed; send SASE. Also poems of each winner and four runners-up will be published in the *Grolier Poetry Prize Annual*. Deadline: May 1. Charges $7 fee. Prize: Honorarium of $200 for each of the co-winners.

N **VIOLET REED HAAS POETRY CONTEST**, Snake Nation Press, 110 #2 W. Force St., Valdosta GA 31601. (229)244-0752. E-mail: jeana@snakenationpress.org. Website: www.snakenationpress.org. **Contact:** Jean Arambula. Offered annually for poetry mss of 50-75 pages. Deadline: April 15. Charges $10 fee. Prize: $500 and publication.

N **THE BEATRICE HAWLEY AWARD**, Alice James Poetry Cooperative, 238 Main St., Farmington ME 04938. (207)778-7071. E-mail: ajb@umf.main.edu. Website: www.umf.main.edu/~ajb. **Contact:** April Ossmann. Offered annually for unpublished poetry. Open ot US residents only. Deadline: December 1. Guidelines for SASE. Charges $20. Prize: Publication and $2,000.

CECIL HEMLEY MEMORIAL AWARD, Poetry Society of America, 15 Gramercy Park S., New York NY 10003. (212)254-9628. Fax: (212)673-2352. E-mail: brett@poetrysociety.org. Website: www.poetrysociety.org. **Contact:** Brett Lauer, programs associate. Offered for unpublished lyric poems on a philosophical theme. Open to PSA members only. Deadline: December 21. Guidelines for SASE. Prize: $500.

THE BESS HOKIN PRIZE, *Poetry*, 60 W. Walton St., Chicago IL 60610. (312)255-3703. E-mail: poetry@poetrymagazine.org. Website: www.poetrymagazine.org. **Contact:** Joseph Parisi, editor. Offered annually for poems published in *Poetry* during the preceding year (October-September). *Poetry* buys all rights to the poems published in the magazine. Copyrights are returned to the authors on request. Any writer may submit poems to *Poetry*. Guidelines for SASE. Prize: $500.

N **HONICKMAN/APR FIRST BOOK PRIZE**, The American Poetry Review, 1721 Walnut St., Philadelphia PA 19103. (215)496-0439. Fax: (215)569-0808. Website: www.aprweb.org. Offered annually for a poet's first unpublished book-length manuscript. Judging is by a different distinguished poet each year. Past judges include Adrienne Rich, Robert Creeley and Louise Gluck. Open to any writer. Deadline: October 31. Guidelines for SASE. Charges $20 fee. Prize: Publication by APR (distrubution by Copper Canyon Press through Consortium), $3,000 cash prize, $1,000 to support a book tour.

FIRMAN HOUGHTON AWARD, New England Poetry Club, 11 Puritan Rd., Arlington MA 02476-7710. **Contact:** Virginia Thayer. Offered annually for a lyric poem worthy of the former NEPC President. Deadline: June 30. Guidelines for SASE. Charges nonmembers $10 for 3 poems. Prize: $250.

N INDIANA REVIEW POETRY CONTEST, *Indiana Review*, BH 465/Indiana University, Bloomington IN 47405-7103. (812)855-3439. Fax: (812)855-4253. E-mail: inreview@indiana.edu. Website: www.indiana.edu/~inreview/ir.html. **Contact:** Shannon Gibney. Offered annually for unpublished work. Judged by guest judges; David St. John judged the 2001 contest. Open to any writer. Fifteen-page maximum (no minimum). Deadline: Early April. Guidelines for SASE. Charges $10 fee (includes prize issue). Prize: $1,000. Judged by Guest judges. David St. John judged the 2001 contest.

N INTERNATIONAL NARRATIVE CONTEST, Poets & Patrons, 6850 River Road Dr., 2C, Oak Forest IL 60452. (708)687-1998. **Contact:** Judy Korzenko, contest chair. Offered annually for unpublished narrative poetry. Open to any writer. Deadline: September 1. Guidelines for SASE. Prize: 1st-$75; 2nd-$25.

N INTERNATIONAL TANKA SPLENDOR AWARDS, AHA Books, P.O. Box 1250, Gualala CA 95445-1250. Fax: (707)884-1853. E-mail: ahabooks@mcn.org. Website: www.AHAPOETRY.com. This contest has been moved to the website.

IOWA POETRY PRIZES, University of Iowa Press, 119 W. Park Rd., Iowa City IA 52242. (319)335-2000. Fax: (319)335-2055. E-mail: rhonda-wetjen@uiowa.edu. Website: www.uiowa.edu/~ipress. **Contact:** Sharon Rebouche. Offered annually to encourage poets and their work. Submit manuscripts in April; put name on title page only. Open to writers of English (US citizens or not). Manuscripts will not be returned. Previous winners are not eligible. Deadline: April. Charges $15 fee.

N IRA LEE BENNETT HOPKINS PROMISING POET AWARD, International Reading Association, P.O. Box 8139, Newark DE 19714-8139. (302)731-1600. Fax: (302)731-1051. E-mail: exec@reading.org. Website: www.reading.org. Offered every 3 years to a promising new poet of children's poetry (for children and young adults up to grade 12) who has published no more than 2 books. Deadline: December 1. Guidelines for SASE. Prize: $500.

RANDALL JARRELL POETRY PRIZE, North Carolina Writers' Network, 3501 Highway 54 West, Studio C, Chapel Hill NC 27516. E-mail: mail@ncwriters.org. Website: www.ncwriters.org. **Contact:** Whitney Vaughan, program coordinator. Offered annually for unpublished work "to honor Randall Jarrell and his life at UNC-Greensboro by recognizing the best poetry submitted. Deadline: November 1. Charges $7 fee. Prize: $1,000 and publication in *Parnassus: Poetry in Review*.

THE JUNIPER PRIZE, University of Massachusetts, Amherst MA 01003. (413)545-2217. Website: www.umass.edu/umpress. Estab. 1964. Offered for poetry manuscripts by previously unpublished authors. Deadline: September 30. Charges $10 fee.

KALLIOPE'S ANNUAL SUE SANIEL ELKIND POETRY CONTEST, *Kalliope, a journal of women's literature and art*, 3939 Roosevelt Blvd., Jacksonville FL 32205. (904)381-3511. Website: www.fccj.org.kalliope. **Contact:** Mary Sue Koeppel. Offered annually for unpublished work. "Poetry may be in any style and on any subject. Maximum poem length is 50 lines. Only unpublished poems are eligible." No limit on number of poems entered by any one poet. The winning poem is published as are the finalists' poems. Copyright then returns to the authors. Deadline: November 1. Guidelines for SASE. Charges $4/poem or $10 for 3 poems. Prize: $1,000, publication of poem in *Kalliope*.

BARBARA MANDIGO KELLY PEACE POETRY AWARDS, Nuclear Age Peace Foundation, PMB 121, 1187 Coast Village Rd., Suite 1, Santa Barbara CA 93108-2794. Fax: (805)568-0466. E-mail: wagingpeace@napf.org. Website: www.wagingpeace.org. **Contact:** Chris Pizzinat. Offered annually for unpublished poems "to encourage poets to explore and illuminate positive visions of peace and the human spirit." Guidelines for SASE or on website. The Nuclear Age Peace Foundation reserves the right to publish and distribute the award-winning poems. Deadline: Postmarked by July 1. Charges $5/poem, $10 for 2-3 poems; no fee for youth entries. Prize: Adult-$1,000; youth (13-18)-$200; youth (12 and under)-$200.

THE GEORGE KENT PRIZE, *Poetry*, 60 W. Walton St., Chicago IL 60610. (312)255-3703. E-mail: poetry@poetrymagazine.org. Website: www.poetrymagazine.org. **Contact:** Joseph Parisi, editor. Offered annually for poems by an Illinois author published in *Poetry* during the preceding year (October-September). *Poetry* buys all rights to the poems published in the magazine. Copyrights are returned to the authors on request. Any writer may submit poems to *Poetry*. Guidelines for SASE. Prize: $500.

N THE JANE KENYON CHAPBOOK AWARD, Alice James Poetry Cooperative, 238 Main St., Farmington ME 04938. (207)778-7071. E-mail: ajb@umf.main.edu. Website: www.umf.main.edu/~ajb. **Contact:** April Ossmann. Offered every two years for unpublished poetry. Open to poets living in New England. Deadline: June 15. Guidelines for SASE. Charges $12 fee. Prize: Publication and $500.

(HELEN AND LAURA KROUT MEMORIAL) OHIOANA POETRY AWARD, Ohioana Library Association, 274 E. First Ave., Columbus OH 45201. (614)466-3831. Fax: (614)728-6974. E-mail: ohioana@sloma.state.oh.us. Website: www.oplin.lib.oh.us/OHIOANA/. **Contact:** Linda R. Hengst. Offered annually "to an individual whose body of published work has made, and continues to make, a significant contribution to poetry and through whose work, interest in poetry has been developed." Recipient must have been born in Ohio or lived in Ohio at least 5 years. Deadline: December 31. Guidelines for SASE. Prize: $1,000.

[N] THE LADY MACDUFF POETRY CONTEST (formerly The New Millennium Poetry Book Competition), P.O. Box 563, Hackensack NJ 07602-0563. (201)342-4455. Fax: (201)342-7396. E-mail: rexdalepublishco@cs.com. Website: www.rexdalepublishing.com. **Contact:** Elaine Rexdale. Offered annually for poetry written in English. Open to any writer. Deadline: November 30. Guidelines for SASE. Charges $25 fee. Prize: Grand-$500, publication and 20 copies; 1st-$100.

[N] [■] GERALD LAMPERT MEMORIAL AWARD, The League of Canadian Poets, 54 Wolseley St., Suite 204, Toronto, Ontario M5T 1A5, Canada. (416)504-1657. Fax: (416)504-0096. E-mail: league@ican.net. Website: www.poets.ca. **Contact:** Sandra Drzewiecki. Offered annually for a first book of poetry by a Canadian poet published in the preceding year. Guidelines for SASE and on website. Deadline: December 31. Charges $15 fee. Prize: $1,000.

THE JAMES LAUGHLIN AWARD, The Academy of American Poets, 584 Broadway, Suite 1208, New York NY 10012-3250. (212)274-0343. Fax: (212)274-9427. E-mail: academy@poets.org. Website: www.poets.org. **Contact:** Awards Director. Offered annually for a manuscript of original poetry, in English, by a poet who has already published one book of poems in a standard edition (40 pages or more in length and 500 or more copies). Only manuscripts that have come under contract with a US publisher between May 1 of the preceding year and April 30 of the year of the deadline are eligible. Deadline: April 30. Guidelines for SASE. Prize: $5,000 and the Academy will purchase at least 9,000 hardcover copies for distribution.

THE LEDGE ANNUAL POETRY CHAPBOOK CONTEST, *The Ledge Magazine*, 78-44 80th St., Glendale NY 11385. **Contact:** Timothy Monaghan. Offered annually to publish an outstanding collection of poems. Open to any writer. Deadline: October 31. Guidelines for SASE. Charges $12 fee. Prize: $1,000, publication of chapbook and 50 copies; all entrants receive a copy of winning chapbook.

THE LEDGE POETRY AWARD, *The Ledge Magazine*, 78-44 80th St., Glendale NY 11385. **Contact:** Timothy Monaghan. Offered annually for an unpublished poem of exceptional quality and significance. All poems considered for publication in the magazine. Open to any writer. Deadline: April 30. Guidelines for SASE. Charges $10 for 3 poems; $3/additional poem ($13 subscription gains free entry for the first three poems). Prize: $1,000 and publication in *The Ledge Magazine*.

[N] LENA-MILES WEVER TODD POETRY SERIES, Pleiades Press & Winthrop University, Dept. of English, Central Missouri State University, Warrensburg MO 64093. (660)543-8106. Fax: (660)543-8544. E-mail: kdp8106@cmsu2.cmsu.edu. **Contact:** Kevin Prufer. Offered annually for an unpublished book of poetry by an American or Canadian poet. Guidelines for SASE or by e-mail. The winning book is copyrighted by the author and Pleiades Press. Deadline: Generally March 31; e-mail for firm deadline. Charges $15, which includes a copy of the winning book. Prize: $1,000 and publication of winning book in paperback edition. Distribution through Louisiana State University Press.

THE LEVINSON PRIZE, *Poetry*, 60 W. Walton St., Chicago IL 60610. (312)255-3703. E-mail: poetry@poetrymagazine.org. Website: www.poetrymagazine.org. **Contact:** Joseph Parisi, editor. Offered annually for poems published in *Poetry* during the preceding year (October-September). *Poetry* buys all rights to the poems published in the magazine. Copyrights are returned to the authors on request. Any writer may submit poems to *Poetry*. Guidelines for SASE. Prize: $500.

[N] THE LARRY LEVIS PRIZE FOR POETRY, *Prairie Schooner*, 201 Andrews Hall, P.O. Box 880334, Lincoln NE 68588-0334. (402)472-0911. Fax: (402)472-9771. E-mail: eflanagan2@unl.edu. Website: www.unl.edu/schooner/psmain.htm. **Contact:** Hilda Raz. Offered annually for poetry published in *Prairie Schooner* in the previous year. Prize: $1,000.

THE RUTH LILLY POETRY PRIZE, The Modern Poetry Association, 60 W. Walton St., Chicago IL 60610-3305. E-mail: poetry@poetrymagazine.org. Website: www.poetrymagazine.org. **Contact:** Joseph Parisi. Estab. 1986. Offered annually to poet whose accomplishments in the field of poetry warrant extraordinary recognition. No applicants or nominations are accepted. Deadline: Varies. Prize: $100,000.

[N] LITERAL LATTÉ POETRY AWARD, *Literal Latté*, 61 E. Eighth St., Suite 240, New York NY 10003. (212)260-5532. E-mail: LitLatte@aol.com. Website: www.literal-latte.com. **Contact:** Jenine Bockman. Offered annually for unpublished poetry. Deadline: July 15. Guidelines for SASE. Charges $10 for 6 poems or $15 for 6 poems plus a 1-year subscription. Prize: 1st-$1,000; 2nd-$300; 3rd-$200; winners published in *Literal Latté*. Open to any writer.

N FRANCES LOCKE MEMORIAL POETRY AWARD, The Bitter Oleander Press, 4983 Tall Oaks Dr., Fayetteville NY 13066-9776. (315)637-3047. Fax: (315)637-5056. E-mail: bones44@ix.netcom.com. Website: www.bitteroleander.com. **Contact:** Paul B. Roth. Offered annually for unpublished, imaginative poetry. Open to any writer. Deadline: June 15. Guidelines for SASE. Charges $10 for 5 poems, $2 for each additional poem. Prize: $1,000 and 5 copies of issue.

LOUISIANA LITERATURE PRIZE FOR POETRY, Louisiana Literature, SLU—Box 792, Southeastern Louisiana University, Hammond LA 70402. (504)549-5022. Fax: (504)549-5021. E-mail: lalit@selu.edu. Website: www.selu.edu/orgs/lalit/. **Contact:** Jack Bedell, contest director. Estab. 1984. Offered annually for unpublished poetry. All entries considered for publication. Deadline: April 1. Guidelines for SASE. Charges $12 fee. Prize: $400.

N LOUISE LOUIS/EMILY F. BOURNE STUDENT POETRY AWARD, Poetry Society of America, 15 Gramercy Park S., New York NY 10003. (212)254-9628. Fax: (212)673-2352. Website: www.poetrysociety.org. **Contact:** Brett Lauer, programs associate. Offered annually for unpublished work to promote excellence in student poetry. Open to American high school or preparatory school students (grades 9 to 12). Guidelines for SASE and on website. Judged by prominent American poets. Deadline: December 21. Charges $1 for a student submitting a single entry; $20 for a high school submitting unlimited number of its students' poems. Prize: $250.

N ✿ PAT LOWTHER MEMORIAL AWARD, 54 Wolseley St., Toronto, Ontario M5T 1A5, Canada. (416)504-1657. Fax: (416)504-0096. E-mail: league@ican.net. Website: www.poets.ca. **Contact:** Edita Petrauskaite. Estab. 1966. Offered annually to promote new Canadian poetry/poets and also to recognize exceptional work in each category. Submissions to be published in the preceding year (awards). Enquiries from publishers welcome. Open to Canadians living at home and abroad. The candidate must be a Canadian citizen or landed imigrant, though the publisher need not be Canadian. Call, write, fax or e-mail for rules. Charges $15 fee/title.

LYRIC POETRY AWARD, Poetry Society of America, 15 Gramercy Park S., New York NY 10003. (212)254-9628. Fax: (212)673-2352. E-mail: brett@poetrysociety.org. Website: www.poetrysociety.org. **Contact:** Brett Lauer, programs associate. Offered annually for unpublished work to promote excellence in lyric poetry. Line limit 50. Open to PSA members only. Deadline: December 21. Guidelines for SASE. Prize: $500.

NAOMI LONG MADGETT POETRY AWARD, Lotus Press, Inc., P.O. Box 21607, Detroit MI 48221. (313)861-1280. Fax: (313)861-4740. E-mail: lotuspress@aol.com. **Contact:** Constance Withers. Offered annually to recognize an outstanding unpublished poetry manuscript by an African-American. Guidelines for SASE or by e-mail. Deadline: April 1-June 1. Charges $15 fee. Prize: $500 and publication by Lotus Press.

THE MALAHAT REVIEW LONG POEM PRIZE, *The Malahat Review*, Box 1700 STNCSC, Victoria, British Columbia V8W 2Y2, Canada. E-mail: malahat@uvic.ca (queries only). Website: web.uvic.ca/malahat. **Contact:** Marlene Cookshaw. Offered every two years to unpublished long poems. Preliminary reading by editorial board; final judging by the editor and 2 recognized poets. Obtains first world rights. After publication rights revert to the author. Open to any writer. Deadline: March 1. Guidelines for SASE. Charges $30 fee (includes a one-year subscription to the *Malahat*, published quarterly). Prize: $400, plus payment for publication ($30/page).

THE LENORE MARSHALL POETRY PRIZE, The Nation and The Academy of American Poets, 584 Broadway, Suite 1208, New York NY 10012. (212)274-0343. E-mail: academy@poets.org. Website: www.poets.org. **Contact:** Awards Director. Offered for book of poems published in US during previous year and nominated by the publisher. Deadline: June 1. Guidelines for SASE. Prize: $10,000.

LUCILLE MEDWICK MEMORIAL AWARD, Poetry Society of America, 15 Gramercy Park S., New York NY 10003. (212)254-9628. Fax: (212)673-2352. E-mail: brett@poetrysociety.org. Website: www.poetrysociety.org. **Contact:** Brett Lauer, programs associate. Original poem in any form on a humanitarian theme. Guidelines for SASE. Guidelines subject to change. Open to PSA members only. Deadline: December 21. Prize: $500.

MID-LIST PRESS FIRST SERIES AWARD FOR POETRY, Mid-List Press, 4324 12th Ave. S., Minneapolis MN 55407-3218. Fax: (612)823-8387. E-mail: guide@midlist.org. Website: www.midlist.org. **Contact:** Lane Stiles, senior editor. Estab. 1990. Offered annually for unpublished book of poetry to encourage new poets. Guidelines for SASE or on website. Contest is open to any writer who has never published a book of poetry. "We do not consider a chapbook to be a book of poetry." Deadline: February 1. Charges $20 fee. Prize: Publication and an advance against royalties.

MISSISSIPPI VALLEY NON-PROFIT POETRY CONTEST, P.O. Box 3188, Rock Island IL 61204-3188. (309)359-1057. **Contact:** Max Molleston, chairman. Estab. 1972. Unpublished poetry: Adult general, student division, Mississippi Valley, senior citizen, religious, rhyming, jazz, humorous, haiku, history and ethnic. Up to 5 poems may be submitted with a limit of 50 lines/poem. Deadline: April 1. Charges $5 fee, $3 for students.

MORSE POETRY PRIZE, Northeastern University English Deptment, 406 Holmes Hall, Boston MA 02115. (617)437-2512. Website: www.casdn.neu.edu/~english/morse.htm. **Contact:** Guy Rotella. Offered annually for previously published poetry, book-length manuscripts of first or second books. Deadline: September 15. Charges $15 fee. Prize: $1,000 and publication by Northeastern University Press.

KATHRYN A. MORTON PRIZE IN POETRY, Sarabande Books, P.O. Box 4456, Louisville KY 40204. (502)458-4028. Fax: (502)458-4065. E-mail: sarabandeb@aol.com. Website: www.SarabandeBooks.org. **Contact:** Kirby Gann, managing editor. Offered annually to publish an outstanding collection of poetry. All finalists considered for publication. Deadline: January 1-February 15. Guidelines for SASE. Charges $20 fee. Prize: $2,000 and publication under standard royalty contract.

SHEILA MOTTON AWARD, New England Poetry Club, 11 Puritan Rd., Arlington MA 02476-7710. **Contact:** Virginia Thayer. For a poetry book published in the last two years. Send 2 copies of the book and $10 entry fee. Prize: $500.

N **MOVING WORDS**, Arlington County Cultural Affairs Division, Ellipse Arts Center, 4350 N. Fairfax Dr., Arlington VA 22203. (703)228-7710. E-mail: oblong@erols.com. Website: www.arlingtonarts.org. **Contact:** Kim Roberts. Offered annually for published and unpublished poetry. Open only to writers who live, work or maintain a studio in Arlington, VA. Deadline: January 31. Guidelines for SASE. Prize: Publication on bus posters and website; $100 honorarium for 6 adult winners (a separate contest for students is also held); and public reading at the Ellipse Arts Center in Arlington, VA.

N **ERIKA MUMFORD PRIZE**, New England Poetry Club, 11 Puritan Rd., Arlington MA 02476-7710. **Contact:** Virginia Thayer. Offered annually for a poem in any form about foreign culture or travel. Deadline: June 30. Guidelines for SASE. Charges nonmembers $5/poem or $10 for 3 poems. Prize: $250.

NATIONAL POETRY BOOK AWARD, Salmon Run Press, P.O. Box 672130, Chugiak AK 99567-2130. (907)688-4268. Fax: (907)688-4268. E-mail: salmonrp@aol.com. **Contact:** John Smelcer. Offered annually to previously published or unpublished poetry. "Each year we invite poets nationwide to send their 68-96 page poetry manuscript. Individual poems may have been previously published, but the manuscript must be unpublished." Poems may be on any subject/style. Acquires one-time rights. Open to any writer. Deadline: December 31. Guidelines for SASE. Charges $10 fee. Prize: $1,000, publication of ms (minimum 500 copies), advertising in national literary magazines (*Poets & Writer*, etc.); arrangements for national reviews with approximately 50-100 promotional copies sent.

NATIONAL WRITERS ASSOCIATION POETRY CONTEST, The National Writers Association, 3140 S. Peoria, #295, Aurora CO 80014. (303)841-0246. Fax: Fax:(303)841-2607. **Contact:** Sandy Whelchel, director. Annual contest "to encourage the writing of poetry, an important form of individual expression but with a limited commercial market." Guidelines for SASE. Charges $10 fee. Prize: 1st-$100; 2nd-$50; 3rd-$25.

HOWARD NEMEROV SONNET AWARD, *The Formalist: A Journal of Metrical Poetry*, 320 Hunter Dr., Evansville IN 47711. **Contact:** Mona Baer. Offered annually for an unpublished sonnet to encourage poetic craftsmanship and to honor the memory of the late Howard Nemerov, third US Poet Laureate. Final judge for year 2001: X.J. Kennedy. Acquires first North American serial rights for those sonnets chosen for publication. Upon publication all rights revert to the author. Open to the international community of writers. Deadline: June 15. Guidelines for SASE. Charges $3/sonnet fee. Prize: $1,000 and publication in *The Formalist*; 11 other finalists also published.

N **NEW ISSUES FIRST BOOK OF POETRY PRIZE**, *New Issues Poetry & Prose*, Department of English, Western Michigan University, 1903 W. Michigan Ave., Kalamazoo MI 49008-5331. (616)387-8185. Fax: (616)387-2562. E-mail: herbert.scott@wmich.edu. Website: www.wmich.edu/newissues. **Contact:** Herbert Scott, editor. Offered annually for publication of a first book of poems by a poet writing in English who has not previously published a full-length collection of poems in an edition of 500 or more copies. *New Issues Poetry & Prose* obtains rights for first publication. Book is copyrighted in author's name. Guidelines for SASE or on website. Deadline: November 30. Charges $15. Prize: $1,000 and publication of book. Author also receives 10% of the printed edition.

N **THE NEW LETTERS POETRY AWARD**, *New Letters*, 5101 Rockhill Rd., Kansas City MO 64110. (816)235-1168. Fax: (816)235-2611. E-mail: newletters@umkc.edu. Website: www.umkc.edu/newletters. **Contact:** Aleatha Ezra or Mary Ellen Buck. Offered annually for unpublished work to discover and reward new and upcoming writers. Buys first North American serial rights. Open to any writer. Deadline: Third week of May. Guidelines for SASE. Charges $10 fee. Prize: 1st-$1,000 and publication in *New Letters*; two runners-up will receive a one-year subscription and will be considered for publication.

THE JOHN FREDERICK NIMS MEMORIAL PRIZE, *Poetry*, 60 W. Walton St., Chicago IL 60610. (312)255-3703. E-mail: poetry@poetrymagazine.org. Website: www.poetrymagazine.org. **Contact:** Joseph Parisi, editor. Offered annually for poems published in *Poetry* during the preceding year (October-September). Judged by the editors of *Poetry*. *Poetry* buys all rights to the poems published in the magazine. Copyrights are returned to the authors on request. Any writer may submit poems to *Poetry*. Guidelines for SASE. Prize: $500.

NLAPW INTERNATIONAL POETRY CONTEST, The National League of American Pen Women (Palomar Branch), 11929 Caminito Corriente, San Diego CA 92128. E-mail: helensherry@aol.com. **Contact:** Helen J. Sherry. Offered annually for unpublished work. All proceeds from this contest provide an annual scholarship for a student entering college in the fields of art, letters or music. Categories: Haiku (any style) and Poety (any style, 30 line limit). Open to any writer. Deadline: First Friday in March. Guidelines for SASE. Charges $5/poem or $5 for 2 haiku. Prize: $50, $25, $10 and honorable mentions in each category. Winning poems will be published in a chapbook.

THE FRANK O'HARA AWARD CHAPBOOK COMPETITION, Thorngate Road, Campus Box 4240, English Dept., Illinois State University, Normal IL 61790-4240. (309)438-7705. Fax: (309)438-5414. E-mail: jmelled@ilstu.edu. **Contact:** Jim Elledge, director. Offered annually for published or unpublished poetry "to recognize excellence in poetry by gays, lesbians and bisexuals. Entrants may be beginners, emerging poets or those with a national reputation. Poems may be formal, free verse, post-modern, prose poems, etc." Deadline: February 1. Guidelines for SASE. Charges $15/ ms fee. Prize: $500 and publication of the winning ms; author also receives 25 copies of the chapbook.

THE OHIO STATE UNIVERSITY PRESS/THE JOURNAL AWARD IN POETRY, The Ohio State University Press and The Journal, 1070 Carmack, Columbus OH 43210. (614)292-6930. Fax: (614)292-2065. E-mail: ohiostatepress @osu.edu. Website: www.ohiostatepress.org. **Contact:** David Citino, poetry editor. Offered annually for unpublished work, minimum of 48 pages of original poetry. Deadline: Entries accepted September 1-30. Charges $20 fee. Prize: $1,000 and publication.

ORION PRIZE FOR POETRY, Poetry Forever, P.O. Box 68018, Hamilton, Ontario L8M 3M7, Canada. (905)312-1779. Fax: (905)312-8285. Offered for poetry to fund the publication of a full-size collection by Ottawa poet Marty Flomen (1942-1997). Open to any writer. Deadline: June 15. Guidelines for SASE. Charges $3/poem fee. Prize: $100 minimum.

NATALIE ORNISH POETRY AWARD, The Texas Institute of Letters, Southwest Texas State University, San Marcos TX 78666. (512)245-2428. Fax: (512)245-7462. E-mail: mb13@swt.edu. Website: www.English.swt.edu/css/ TIL/rules.htm. **Contact:** Mark Busby. Offered annually for the best book of poems published January 1-December 31 of previous year. Poet must have been born in Texas, have lived in the state at some time for at least two consecutive years, or subject matter is associated with the state. Deadline: January 3. Guidelines for SASE. Prize: $1,000.

N **GUY OWEN POETRY PRIZE**, *Southern Poetry Review*, English Department, CPCC, Charlotte NC 28235. (704)330-6275. **Contact:** Ken McLaurin, editor. Offered annually for the best unpublished poem submitted in an open competition. Given in memory of Guy Owen, a poet, fiction writer and founder of *Southern Poetry Review*. Submit 3-5 poems with SASE. All submissions considered for publication. Deadline: Submissions accepted in April only. Charges $10 fee, which includes one-year subscription to *Southern Poetry Review* to begin with the Winter issue, containing the winning poem. Prize: $500 and publication in *Southern Poetry Review*.

N **THE PATERSON POETRY PRIZE**, The Poetry Center at Passaic County Community College, One College Blvd., Paterson NJ 07505-6555. (973)684-6555. Fax: (973)684-5843. E-mail: mgillan@pccc.cc.nj.us. Website: www.pcc c.cc.nj.us/poetry. **Contact:** Maria Mazziotti Gillan, director. Offered annually for a book of poetry published in the previous year. Deadline: February 1. Guidelines for SASE. Prize: $1,000.

PAUMANOK POETRY AWARD, Visiting Writers Program, SUNY Farmingdale, SUNY Farmingdale/Knapp Hall, Route 110, Farmingdale NY 11735. Fax: (516)420-2051. E-mail: brownml@farmingdale.edu. Website: www.farmingdal e.edu/CampusPages/ArtsSciences/EnglishHumanities/paward.html. **Contact:** Margery L. Brown, director, Visiting Writers Program. Offered annually for published or unpublished poems. Send cover letter, 1-paragraph bio, 3-5 poems (name and address on each poem). Include SASE for notification of winners. (Send photocopies only; manuscripts will not be returned. Deadline: September 15. Charges $12 fee, payable to SUNY Farmingdale VWP. Prize: 1st-$1,000 plus expenses for a reading in 2002-2003 series; runners-up(2)-$500 plus expenses for a reading in series.

N **PEARL POETRY PRIZE**, Pearl Editions, 3030 E. Second St., Long Beach CA 90803. (562)434-4523. Fax: (562)434-4523. E-mail: mjohn5150@aol.com. Website: www.pearlmag.com. **Contact:** Marilyn Johnson, editor/publisher. Offered annually "to provide unpublished poets with further opportunity to publish their poetry in book-form and find a larger audience for their work." Manuscripts must be original works written in English. Guidelines for SASE or on website. Deadline: July 15. Charges $20. Prize: $1,000 and publication by Pearl Editions.

PEREGRINE POETRY PRIZE, *Peregrine*, the literary journal of Amherst Writers & Artists, P.O. Box 1076, Amherst MA 01004-1076. E-mail: awapress@aol.com. Website: www.amherstwriters.com. **Contact:** Nancy Rose. Offered annually for unpublished poetry. "We seek writing that is honest, unpretentious and memorable." Entrants who reside in Western Massachusetts are also eligible for the "Best of the Nest" Prize. Open to any writer. Deadline: April 1. Guidelines for SASE. Charges $10 fee. Prize: $500, plus publication in *Peregrine*.

PHILBRICK POETRY AWARD, Providence Athenaeum, 251 Benefit St., Providence RI 02903. (401)421-6970. Fax: (401)421-2860. E-mail: leetw@lori.state.ri.us. Website: providenceathenaeum.org. **Contact:** Lee Teverow. Offered annually for New England poets who have not yet published a book. Previous publication of individual poems in journals or anthologies is allowed. Judged by nationally-known poets; Stanley Moss is the 2002 judge. Deadline: June 15-October 15. Guidelines for SASE. Charges $5 fee. Prize: $500, publication of winning manuscript as a chapbook and a public reading at Providence Athenaeum with the final judge/award presenter.

THE RICHARD PHILLIPS POETRY PRIZE, The Phillips Publishing Co., 719 E. Delaware St., Siloam Springs AR 72761-3725. **Contact:** Richard Phillips, Jr. Offered annually to give a modest financial reward to emerging poets who have not yet established themselves sufficiently to generate appropriate compensation for their work. Open to all poets. "There are no anthologies to buy. No strings attached. Simply put, the poet who enters the best manuscript will win the prize of $1,000 and will be published in September." Recent winners: Patricia Lang (Schhenectdy, NY) 2000, Clark Doane (Colcord, OK) 2001. Deadline: Postmarked by January 31. Guidelines for SASE. Charges $15 fee. Prize: $1,000 and publication.

POET'S CORNER AWARD, Broken Jaw Press, Box 596 Stn. A, Fredericton, New Brunswick E3B 5A6, Canada. (506)454-5127. Fax: (506)454-5127. E-mail: jblades@nbnet.nb.ca. Website: www.brokenjaw.com. Offered annually to recognize the best book-length manuscript by a Canadian poet. Deadline: December 31. Guidelines for SASE. Charges $20 fee (which includes copy of winning book upon publication). Prize: Publication of poetry ms.

POETIC LICENCE CONTEST FOR CANADIAN YOUTH, League of Canadian Poets, 54 Wolseley St., Toronto, Ontario M5T 1A5, Canada. (416)504-1657. Fax: (416)504-0096. E-mail: league@ican.net. Website: www.poets.ca. Offered annually for unpublished work to seek and encourage new poetic talent in two categories: Grades 7-9 and 10-12. Open to Canadian citizens and landed immigrants only. Guidelines for SASE or on website. Deadline: March 1. Charges $5 fee/poem. Prize: 1st-$500, 2nd-$350, 3rd-$250.

THE POETRY CENTER BOOK AWARD, The Poetry Center, San Francisco State University 1600 Holloway Ave., San Francisco CA 94132-9901. (415)338-2227. Fax: (415)338-0966. E-mail: newlit@sfsu.edu. Website: www.sfsu.edu/~newlit/welcome.htm. **Contact:** Steve Dickison, director. Estab. 1980. Offered annually for books of poetry and chapbooks, published in year of the prize. "Prize given for an extraordinary book of American poetry." Please include a cover letter noting author name, book title(s), name of person issuing check, and check number. Will not consider anthologies or translations. Deadline: December 31. Charges $10/book fee. Prize: $500 and an invitation to read in the Poetry Center Reading Series.

POETRY PUBLICATION, The PEN (Poetry Explosion Newsletter), The Poet Band Co., Box 4725, Pittsburgh PA 15206. (412)886-1114. **Contact:** Arthur C. Ford, owner/poet. Estab. 1984. Send maximum of 5 poems. Enclose $1 for reading fee. Use rhyme and non-rhyming verse. Maximum lines: 40. Prose maximum: 200-300 words. Allow 1 month for response. Sample copy $4. Send SASE for more information. Quarterly newsletter (*The Pen*) issued April, July, October and January. Subscriptions are $20 (yearly) or $38 for 2 years.

POETRY 2002 INTERNATIONAL POETRY COMPETITION, *Atlanta Review*, P.O. Box 8248, Atlanta GA 31106. E-mail: contest@atlantareview.com. Website: www.atlantareview.com. **Contact:** Dan Veach. Offered annually for unpublished poetry. Provides prizes and unique international recognition for poets as *Atlanta Review* appears in 120 countries. Guidelines for SASE or by e-mail. Open to all poets. Acquires first North American serial rights only—copyright returns to poet. Deadline: May 5 (first Friday in May). Charges $5/first poem; $2/each additional poem. Prize: 1st-$2,002; 2nd-$500; 3rd-$250. Also: 50 International Merit Awards (free issue and certificate) and many entrants are published in *Atlanta Review*.

POETRY WRITER'S CONTEST, No Noun-Sense, 147-2211 No. 4 Road, Richmond British Columbia V6X 3X1, Canada. (604)825-8861. Fax: (604)214-1306. E-mail: editor@webprospects.com. Website: www.nonounsense.com. **Contact:** Erin Berringer. Offered annually for unpublished work to promote poetry and poetry writers. Guidelines on website. Open to any writer. Deadline: March 21. Charges $8. Prize: 1st-$100; 2nd-$50; 3rd-$25. Winner and four honourable mentions will be published on the No Noun-Sense website, along with their bios.

RAINMAKER AWARDS IN POETRY, ZONE 3, Austin Peay State University, P.O. Box 4565, Clarksville TN 37044. (931)221-7031. Fax: (931)221-7393. E-mail: zone3@apsu01.apsu.edu. **Contact:** Susan Wallace, managing editor. Offered annually for unpublished poetry. Previous judges include Carolyn Forché, Marge Piercy, Howard Nemerov and William Stafford. Open to any poet. Deadline: January 1. Guidelines for SASE. Charges $8 fee (includes 1-year subscription). Prize: 1st-$500, 2nd-$300, 3rd-$100.

N LEVIS READING PRIZE, Virginia Commonwealth University, Dept. of English, P.O. Box 842005, Richmond VA 23284-2005. (804)828-1329. Fax: (804)828-8684. E-mail: eng_grad@vcu.edu. Website: www.has.vcu.edu/eng/grad/Levis_Prize.htm. **Contact:** Jeff Lodge. Offered annually for books of poetry published in the previous year to encourage poets early in their careers. The entry must be the writer's first or second published book of poetry. Previously published books in other genres, or previously published chapbooks, do not count as books for this purpose. Deadline: January 15. Guidelines for SASE. Prize: $1,000 honorarium (when funds permit) and an expense-paid trip to Richmond to present a public reading.

RED ROCK POETRY AWARD, Red Rock Review, Community College of Southern Nevada, English Dept., 3200 E. Cheyenne Ave., North Las Vegas NV 89030. (702)651-4094. E-mail: rich_logsdon@ccsn.nevada.edu. Website: www.ccsn.nevada.edu/english/redrockreview/default.html. **Contact:** Rich Logsdon. Offered annually for unpublished poetry. Open to any writer. Deadline: October 31. Guidelines for SASE. Charges $6 for 3 poems. Prize: $500.

N RIVER CITY WRITING AWARDS IN POETRY, The University of Memphis/Hohenberg Foundation, Department of English, Memphis TN 38152. (901)678-4591. Fax: (901)678-2226. Website: www.people.memphis.edu/~riverci ty. **Contact:** Thomas Russell. Offered annually for unpublished poem of 2 pages maximum. Guidelines for SASE or on website. Deadline: March 1. Prize: 1st-$1,000; 2nd and 3rd-publication and 1-year subscription.

N RIVER STYX 2001 INTERNATIONAL POETRY CONTEST, River Styx Magazine, 634 N. Grand Blvd., 12th Floor, St. Louis MO 63103. (314)533-4541. Fax: (314)533-3345. Website: www.riverstyx.org. **Contact:** Richard Newman, editor; Carrie Robb, managing editor. Offered annually for unpublished poetry. Poets may send up to 3 poems, not more than 14 pages. Open to any writer. Deadline: May 31. Guidelines for SASE. Charges $20 reading fee, which include a one-year subscription (3 issues). Prize: $1,000 and publication in August issue.

NICHOLAS ROERICH POETRY PRIZE, Story Line Press, Three Oaks Farm, P.O. Box 1240, Ashland OR 97520-0055. (541)512-8792. Fax: (541)512-8793. E-mail: mail@storylinepress.com. Website: www.storylinepress.com. **Contact:** Roerich Prize Coordinator. Estab. 1988. Offered annually for full-length book of poetry. Any writer who has not previously published a full-length collection of poetry (48 pages or more) in English is eligible to apply. Guidelines for SASE or on website. Deadline: May 1-October 31. Charges $20 fee. Prize: $1,000, publication, and reading at the Nicholas Roerich Museum in New York.

ANNA DAVIDSON ROSENBERG AWARD FOR POEMS ON THE JEWISH EXPERIENCE, Judah L. Magnes Museum, 2911 Russell St., Berkeley CA 94705. **Contact:** Paula Friedman. Offered annually for unpublished work to encourage poetry of/on/from the Jewish experience. Deadline for requesting mandatory entry forms is July 15; deadline for receipt of poems is August 31. Guidelines and entry form for SASE; forms sent out after April 15. Submissions must include entry form. Charges $2 fee/up to 3 poems. Prize: 1st-$100; 2nd-$50; 3rd-$25; New/Emerging Poet Prize-$25; Youth Award-$25; also, Silver(Senior) Award and honorable mentions. All winners and honorable mentions receive certificates, and winning poems are read in an awards reading at the museum.

N BENJAMIN SALTMAN POETRY AWARD, Red Hen Press, P.O. Box 3537, Granada Hills CA 91394. (818)831-0649. Fax: (818)831-6659. E-mail: editors@redhen.org. Website: www.redhen.org. **Contact:** Kate Gale. Offered annually for unpublished work "to publish a winning book of poetry." Open to any writer. Deadline: October 31. Guidelines for SASE. Charges $15 fee. Prize: $1,000 and publication.

THE SANDBURG-LIVESAY ANTHOLOGY CONTEST, Mekler & Deahl, Publishers, 237 Prospect St., S, Hamilton, Ontario L8M 2Z6, Canada. (905)312-1779. Fax: (905)312-8285. E-mail: james@meklerdeahl.com. Website: www.meklerdeahl.com. Offered annually for published or unpublished poetry (up to 70 lines). Writers retain all rights. Open to any writer. Deadline: October 31. Charges $12 fee (US); maximum 10 entries. Prize: 1st-$250 (US) and anthology publication; 2nd-$150 (US) and anthology publication; 3rd-$100 (US) and anthology publication. All entrants receive a copy of the published anthology, entrants with poetry in the anthology receive 2 copies.

N SASKATCHEWAN POETRY AWARD, Saskatchewan Book Awards Inc., Box 1921, Regina, Saskatchewan S4P 3E1, Canada. (306)569-1585. Fax: (306)569-4187. E-mail: sk.bookawards@dlcwest.com. Website: www.bookawards.sk.ca. **Contact:** Joyce Wells, executive director. Offered annually for work published October 1, 2001, to Sept. 14, 2002. This award is presented to a Saskatchewan author for the best book of poetry, judged on the quality of writing. Deadline: First deadline: July 31; final deadline: September 14. Guidelines for SASE. Charges $15 (Canadian). Prize: $1,500.

N SAY THE WORD, Arlington County Cultural Affairs Division, Ellipse Arts Center, 4350 N. Fairfax Dr., Arlington VA 22203. (703)228-7710. E-mail: oblong@erols.com. Website: www.arlingtonarts.org. **Contact:** Kim Roberts. Offered annually for unpublished poetry. "Theme for competition changes annually; all poems must be on subjects relating to the theme. Past themes have included: 'Ekphrasis: Poems on the Visual Arts,' 'Cityscape: Poems on the Urban Experience' and 'Smorgasbord: Poems About Food.'" Open to US residents only. Deadline: November 30. Guidelines for SASE. Charges $5 for up to 5 poems. Prize: $500 plus publication in *Poet Lore* for top winner; publication for three runners-up; winners invited to read at annual reading/wine tasting, "Read Between the Wines" in May of each year.

THE HELEN SCHAIBLE INTERNATIONAL SHAKESPEAREAN/PETRARCHAN SONNET CONTEST, Poets' Club of Chicago, 1212 S. Michigan Ave., Chicago IL 60605. **Contact:** Tom Roby, president. Estab. 1954. Offered annually for original and unpublished Shakespearean or Petrarchan sonnets. One entry per author. Submit two copies, typed and doublespaced; one with name and address, one without. Send SASE for winners list. Deadline: September 1. Prize: 1st-$50, 2nd-$35, 3rd-$15.

[N] SLAPERING HOL PRESS CHAPBOOK COMPETITION, The Hudson Valley Writers' Center, 300 Riverside Dr., Sleepy Hollow NY 10591. (914)332-5953. Fax: (914)332-4825. E-mail: info@writerscenter.org. Website: www.writerscenter.org. **Contact:** Stephanie Strickland or Margo Stever, co-editors. The annual competition is open to poets who have not published a book or chapbook, though individual poems may have already appeared. Limit: 16-20 pages. The press was created in 1990 to provide publishing opportunities for emerging poets. Judged by a nationally known poet. Deadline: May 15. Guidelines for SASE. Charges $10 fee. Prize: $500, publication of chapbook and a reading at The Hudson Valley Writers' Center.

SLIPSTREAM ANNUAL POETRY CHAPBOOK COMPETITION, Slipstream, Box 2071, Niagara Falls NY 14301. (716)282-2616 after 5 P.M. EST. E-mail: editors@slipstreampress.org. Website: www.slipstreampress.org. **Contact:** Dan Sicoli, director. Offered annually to help promote a poet whose work is often overlooked or ignored. Open to any writer. Deadline: December 1. Guidelines for SASE. Charges $10 fee. Prize: $1,000 and 50 copies of published chapbook.

PEREGRINE SMITH POETRY CONTEST, Gibbs Smith, Publisher, P.O. Box 667, Layton UT 84041. (801)544-9800. Fax: (801)544-5582. E-mail: info@gibbs-smith.com. Website: www.gibbs-smith.com. **Contact:** Gail Yngve, poetry editor; Suzanne Taylor, children's editor; Madge Baird, V.P. editorial. Offered annually to recognize and publish a previously unpublished work. Submissions accepted only during the month of April. Deadline: April 30. Guidelines for SASE. Charges $20 fee. Prize: $500 and publication.

THE SOW'S EAR CHAPBOOK PRIZE, The Sow's Ear Poetry Review, 19535 Pleasant View Dr., Abingdon VA 24211-6827. (540)628-2651. E-mail: richman@preferred.com. **Contact:** Larry K Richman, contest director. Estab. 1988. Offered for poetry mss of 24-26 pages. Guidelines for SASE or by e-mail. Deadline: Submit March-April. Charges $10 fee. Prize: 1st-$1,000, 25 copies and distribution to subscribers; 2nd-$200; 3rd-$100.

THE SOW'S EAR POETRY PRIZE, The Sow's Ear Poetry Review, 19535 Pleasant View Dr., Abingdon VA 24211-6827. (540)628-2651. E-mail: richman@preferred.com. **Contact:** Larry K. Richman, contest director. Estab. 1988. Offered for previously unpublished poetry. Guidelines for SASE or by e-mail. All submissions considered for publication. Deadline: Submit September-October. Charges $2 fee/poem. Prize: $1,000, $250, $100 and publication, plus option of publication for 20-25 finalists.

ANN STANFORD POETRY PRIZE, The Southern California Anthology, co Master of Professional Writing Program, WPH 404, U.S.C., Los Angeles CA 90089-4034. (213)740-3252. Website: www.usc.edu/dept/LAS/mpw. **Contact:** James Ragan, contest director. Estab. 1988. Offered annually for previously unpublished poetry to honor excellence in poetry in memory of poet and teacher Ann Stanford. Submit cover sheet with name, address, phone number and titles of the 5 poems entered. Deadline: April 15. Guidelines for SASE. Charges $10 fee. Prize: 1st-$1,000; 2nd-$200; 3rd-$100. Winning poems are published in *The Southern California Anthology* and all entrants receive a free issue.

[N] THE EDWARD STANLEY AWARD, *Prairie Schooner*, 201 Andrews Hall, P.O. Box 880334, Lincoln NE 68588-0334. (402)472-0911. Fax: (402)472-9771. E-mail: eflanagan2@unl.edu. Website: www.unl.edu/schooner/psmain.htm. **Contact:** Hilda Raz. Offered annually for poetry published in *Prairie Schooner* in the previous year. Prize: $1,000.

THE AGNES LYNCH STARRETT POETRY PRIZE, University of Pittsburgh Press, 3347 Forbes Ave., Pittsburgh PA 15261. Website: www.pitt.edu/~press. **Contact:** Melanie Shrauder. Estab. 1980. Series Editor: Ed Ochester. Offered annually for first book of poetry for poets who have not had a full-length book published. Mandatory guidelines for SASE. Deadline: March and April only. Charges $20 fee. Prize: $5,000.

sub-TERRAIN POETRY CONTEST, sub-TERRAIN Magazine, P.O. Box 3008 MPO, Vancouver, British Columbia V6B 3X5, Canada. (604)876-8710. Fax: (604)879-2667. E-mail: subter@portal.ca. Website: www.anvilpress.com. Offered annually for unpublished poetry; theme to be announced in summer issue. Deadline: August 1-January 31. Guidelines for SASE. Charges $15 fee, 4 poem limit. Prize: $250, publication in spring issue and 1-year subscription to *sub-TERRAIN*.

[N] HOLLIS SUMMERS POETRY PRIZE, Ohio University Press, Scott Quadrangle, Athens OH 45701. (740)593-1155. Fax: (740)593-4536. Website: www.ohio.edu/oupress. **Contact:** David Sanders. Offered annually for unpublished poetry books. Books will be eligible if individual poems or sections have been published previously. Open to any writer. Deadline: October 31. Guidelines for SASE. Charges $15 fee. Prize: $500 and publication of the manuscript in book form.

☒ MAY SWENSON POETRY AWARD, Utah State University Press, 7800 Old Main Hill, Logan UT 84322-7800. (435)797-1362. Fax: (435)797-0313. E-mail: MSpooner@upress.usu.edu. Website: www.usu.edu/usupress. **Contact:** Michael Spooner. Offered annually for unpublished works in honor of May Swenson, one of America's greatest poets. Entries are screened by 6 professional writers and teachers. The finalists are judged by a nationally known poet. Former judges include: John Hollander, Mary Oliver, Richard Howard, and Mark Doty. Open to any writer. Deadline: September 30. Guidelines for SASE. Charges $25 fee. Prize: $1,000, publication of manuscript, and royalties.

TIDEPOOL PRIZE FOR POETRY, Poetry Forever, P.O. Box 68018, Hamilton, Ontario L8M 3M7, Canada. (905)312-1779. Fax: (905)312-8285. Offered for poetry to fund the publication of a full-size collection by Hamilton poet Herb Barrett (1912-1995). Open to any writer. Deadline: July 15. Guidelines for SASE. Charges $3/poem fee. Prize: $100 minimum.

THE EUNICE TIETJENS MEMORIAL PRIZE, *Poetry*, 60 W. Walton St., Chicago IL 60610. (312)255-3703. E-mail: poetry@poetrymagazine.org. Website: www.poetrymagazine.org. **Contact:** Joseph Parisi, editor. Offered annually for poems published in *Poetry* during the preceding year (October-September). *Poetry* buys all rights to the poems published in the magazine. Copyrights are returned to the authors on request. Any writer may submit poems to *Poetry*. Guidelines for SASE. Prize: $200.

☒ TRANSCONTINENTAL POETRY AWARD, Pavement Saw Press, P.O. Box 6291, Columbus OH 43206. (614)263-7115. E-mail: info@pavementsaw.org. Website: pavementsaw.org. **Contact:** David Baratier, editor. Offered annually for a first book of poetry. Judged by Editor David Baratier and a guest judge (2001 judge David Bromige). Open to any writer. Deadline: August 15. Guidelines for SASE. Charges $15 fee. Prize: $1,500, 25 copies for judge's choice, standard royalty contract for editor's choice.

☒ KATE TUFTS DISCOVERY AWARD, Claremont Graduate University, 160 E. 10th St., Harper B7, Claremont CA 91711-6165. (909)621-8974. Fax: (909)621-8390. Website: www.cgu.edu/commun/tuftsent.html. **Contact:** Betty Terrell, awards coordinator. Estab. 1993. Offered annually for a first or very early work by a poet of genuine promise. Entries must be either a published book or a printer's proof or a book-length ms completed Sept. 15, 2001-Sept. 15, 2002. Open to US residents only. Guidelines for SASE or on website. Deadline: Sept. 15. Prize: $10,000.

☒ KINGSLEY TUFTS POETRY AWARD, Claremont Graduate University, 160 E. 10th St., Harper B7, Claremont CA 91711-6165. (909)621-8974. Fax: (909)621-8390. Website: www.cgu.edu/commun/tuftsent.html. **Contact:** Betty Terrell, awards coordinator. Estab. 1992. Offered annually "for a work by an emerging poet, one who is past the very beginning but who has not yet reached the acknowledged pinnacle of his or her career." Guidelines for SASE or on website. Deadline: Sept. 15. Prize: $100,000.

UNION LEAGUE CIVIC AND ARTS POETRY PRIZE, *Poetry*, 60 W. Walton St., Chicago IL 60610. (312)255-3703. E-mail: poetry@poetrymagazine.org. Website: www.poetrymagazine.org. **Contact:** Joseph Parisi, editor. Offered annually for poems published in *Poetry* during the preceding year (October-September). *Poetry* buys all rights to the poems published in the magazine. Copyrights are returned to the authors on request. Any writer may submit poems to *Poetry*. Guidelines for SASE. Prize: $1,000.

DANIEL VAROUJAN AWARD, New England Poetry Club, 11 Puritan Rd., Arlington MA 02476-7710. **Contact:** Virginia Thayer. Offered annually for "an unpublished poem worthy of Daniel Varoujan, a poet killed by the Turks at the onset of the first genocide of this century which decimated three-fourths of the Armenian population." Send poems in duplicate. Open to any writer. Deadline: June 30. Guidelines for SASE. Charges $10 for 3 entries. Prize: $500.

☒ CHAD WALSH POETRY PRIZE, *Beloit Poetry Journal*, 24 Berry Cove Rd., Lamoine ME 04605-4617. (207)667-5598. **Contact:** Marion K. Stocking. Offered annually to honor the memory of poet Chad Walsh, a founder of the *Beloit Poetry Journal*. The editors select a strong poem or group of poems from the poems published in the journal that year. Prize: $3,000.

THE WASHINGTON PRIZE, The Word Works, Inc., P.O. Box 42164, Washington DC 20015. E-mail: editor@word worksdc.com. Website: www.wordworksdc.com. **Contact:** Miles David Moore. Offered annually "for the best full-length poetry manuscript (48-64 pp.) submitted to the Word Works each year. The Washington Prize contest is the only forum in which we consider unsolicited manuscripts." Submissions accepted in the month of February. Acquires first and subsequent English-language publication rights. Open to any American writer. Deadline: March 1 (postmark). Guidelines for SASE. Charges $20 fee. Prize: $1,500 and book publication; all entrants receive a copy of the winning book.

WHITE PINE PRESS POETRY PRIZE, White Pine Press, P.O. Box 236, Buffalo NY 14201. E-mail: wpine@whitepi ne.org. Website: www.whitepine.org. **Contact:** Elaine LaMattina, managing editor. Offered annually for previously published or unpublished poets. Manuscript: Up to 96 pages of original work; translations are not eligible. Poems may have appeared in magazines or limited-edition chapbooks. "We hold rights until the book is out of print; then rights revert to the author. With previously published work, the author is responsible for obtaining permission for publication by White Pine Press." Open to any US citizen. Deadline: December 15. Guidelines for SASE. Charges $20 fee. Prize: $1,000 and publication.

THE WALT WHITMAN AWARD, The Academy of American Poets, 584 Broadway, Suite 1208, New York NY 10012-3250. (212)274-0343. Fax: (212)274-9427. E-mail: academy@poets.org. Website: www.poets.org. **Contact:** Awards Director. Offered annually to publish and support a poet's first book. Submissions must be in English by a single poet. Translations are not eligible. Contestants must be living citizens of the US and have neither published nor committed to publish a volume of poetry 40 pages or more in length in an edition of 500 or more copies. Deadline: September 15-November 15. Guidelines for SASE. Charges $20 fee. Prize: $5,000, a residency for one month at the Vermont Studio Center and publication by Louisiana State University Press.

WICK POETRY CHAPBOOK SERIES 'OPEN' COMPETITION, Wick Poetry Program, Dept. of English, Kent State University, P.O. Box 5190, Kent OH 44242-0001. (330)672-2067. Fax: (330)672-2567. E-mail: wickpoet@kent.e du. Website: dept.kent.edu/english/wick/wickpoetry.htm. **Contact:** Maggie Anderson, director. Offered annually for a chapbook of poems by a poet currently living in Ohio. Deadline: October 31. Guidelines for SASE. Prize: Publication of the chapbook by the Kent State University Press.

WICK POETRY CHAPBOOK SERIES 'STUDENT' COMPETITION, Wick Poetry Program, Dept. of English, Kent State University, P.O. Box 5190, Kent OH 44242-0001. (330)672-2067. Fax: (330)672-2567. E-mail: wickpoet@ke nt.edu. Website: dept.kent.edu/english/wick/wickpoetry.htm. **Contact:** Maggie Anderson, coordinator. Offered annually for publication of a chapbook of poems by a poet currently enrolled in an Ohio college or university. Deadline: October 31. Guidelines for SASE. Prize: Publication of the chapbook by the Kent State University Press.

STAN AND TOM WICK POETRY PRIZE, Wick Poetry Program, Dept. of English, Kent State University, P.O. Box 5190, Kent OH 44242-0001. (330)672-2067. Fax: (330)672-2567. E-mail: wickpoet@kent.edu. Website: dept.kent.edu/ english/wick/wickpoetry.htm. **Contact:** Maggie Anderson, coordinator. Open to anyone writing in English who has not previously published a full-length book of poems (a volume of 48 pages or more published in an edition of 500 or more copies). Deadline: May 1. Guidelines for SASE. Charges $15 fee. Prize: $2,000 and publication by the Kent State University Press.

THE RICHARD WILBUR AWARD, The University of Evansville Press, University of Evansville, Evansville IN 47722. (812)479-2963. **Contact:** The Editors. Offered in even-numbered years for an unpublished poetry collection. Deadline: December 1, 2002. Guidelines for SASE. Charges $20 fee. Prize: $1,000 and publication by the University of Evansville Press.

WILLIAM CARLOS WILLIAMS AWARD, Poetry Society of America, 15 Gramercy Park S, New York NY 10003. (212)254-9628. Fax: (212)673-2352. Website: www.poetrysociety.org. **Contact:** Brett Lauer, programs associate. Offered annually for a book of poetry published by a small press, non-profit or university press. Winning books are distributed to PSA members upon request and while supplies last. Deadline: December 21. Guidelines for SASE. Charges $10 fee. Prize: $500-1,000.

ROBERT H. WINNER MEMORIAL AWARD, Poetry Society of America, 15 Gramercy Park S, New York NY 10003. (212)254-9628. Fax: (212)673-2352. E-mail: brett@poetrysociety.org. Website: www.poetrysociety.org. **Contact:** Brett Lauer, programs associate. Recognizing and rewarding the work of someone in midlife. Open to poets over 40, still unpublished or with one book. Deadline: December 21. Guidelines for SASE. Charges $5 fee for nonmembers; free to PSA members. Prize: $2,500.

THE J. HOWARD AND BARBARA M.J. WOOD PRIZE, *Poetry*, 60 W. Walton St., Chicago IL 60610. (312)255-3703. E-mail: poetry@poetrymagazine.org. Website: www.poetrymagazine.org. **Contact:** Joseph Parisi, editor. Offered annually for poems published in *Poetry* during the preceding year (October-September). *Poetry* buys all rights to the poems published in the magazine. Copyrights are returned to the authors on request. Any writer may submit poems to *Poetry*. Guidelines for SASE. Prize: $3,000.

THE WRITER MAGAZINE/EMILY DICKINSON AWARD, Poetry Society of America, 15 Gramercy Park S, New York NY 10003. (212)254-9628. Fax: (212)673-2352. E-mail: brett@poetrysociety.org. Website: www.poetrysociety.org. **Contact:** Brett Lauer, programs associate. Offered annually for a poem inspired by Emily Dickinson, though not necessarily in her style. Guidelines for SASE; guidelines subject to change. Open to PSA members only. Deadline: December 21. Prize: $250.

N: WRITERS' JOURNAL POETRY CONTEST, Val-Tech Media, Inc., P.O. Box 394, Perham MN 56573. (218)346-7921. Fax: (218)346-7924. E-mail: writersjournal@wadena.net. Website: www.writersjournal.com. **Contact:** Esther M. Leiper. Offered for previously unpublished poetry. Deadline: April 30, August 30, December 30. Guidelines for SASE. Charges $2 fee first poem; $1 each thereafter. Prize: 1st-$25; 1st, 2nd, 3rd prize and selected honorable mention winners will be published in *Writers' Journal* magazine.

YALE SERIES OF YOUNGER POETS, Yale University Press, P.O. Box 209040, New Haven CT 06520-9040. Website: www.yale.edu/yup. **Contact:** Poetry Editor. Offered annually for a first book of poetry by poet under the age of 40. Deadline: Submit during February. Guidelines for SASE. Charges $15 fee. Prize: Winning manuscript is published by Yale University Press under royalty contact.

N. PHYLLIS SMART YOUNG PRIZE IN POETRY, *The Madison Review*, Department of English, 600 N. Park St., Madison WI 53706. (608)263-3374. Website: mendota.english.wisc.edu/~MadRev. **Contact:** Poetry Editor. Offered annually for unpublished work. "Awarded to the best poems submitted, out of a field of around 500 submissions yearly. The purpose of the prize is to award good poets." Submissions must consist of 3 poems. All contes entries are considered as submissions to *The Madison Review*. Simultaneous submissions allowed if noted as such. Guidelines on website. Deadline: September 30. Charges $5 fee. Prize: $500 and publication in the spring issue.

Playwriting & Scriptwriting

ALBERTA PLAYWRITING COMPETITION, Alberta Playwrights' Network, 1134 Eighth Ave. SW, 2nd Floor, Calgary, Alberta T2P 1J5, Canada. (403)269-8564. Fax: (403)265-6773. E-mail: apn@nucleus.com. Website: www.nucleus.com/ŒEapc. Offered annually for unproduced plays with full-length and Discovery categories. Discovery is open only to previously unproduced playwrights. Open only to residents of Alberta. Deadline: January 15. Charges $40 fee (Canadian). Prize: In each category: $3,500 written critique, workshop of winning play, reading of winning plays at a Showcase Conference.

N. AMERICAN DREAMER SCRIPTWRITING COMPETITION, American Dreamer ifi, P.O. Box 20457, Seattle WA 98102. (206)325-0451. Fax: (206)320-7724. E-mail: 2001AD@ADfilmworks.com. Website: ADfilmworks.com. Offered annually for unpublished original scripts. This is essentially the first "Revisions Competition." We give you the opportunity to make improvements to your work and to be evaluated on the merits of this work before you are placed in competition. This is a prime opportunity for writers to receive feedback and critiques on their writing. Open to all writers. Guidelines for SASE. Charges $30 fee. Prize: Winner receives $1,000. All contestants receive critique of initial submission.

N. AMERICAN RENEGADE PLAYWRITING CONTEST, American Renegade Theatre Co., 11136 Magnolia Blvd., North Hollywood CA 91601. (818)763-1834. Fax: (818)763-8082. E-mail: luckenbachj@hotmail.com. Website: www.americanrenegade.com. **Contact:** D.A. Cox. Offered annually for unpublished work to find and produce new playwrights. Guidelines on website. Open to any writer. Deadline: December 1. Charges $20 fee. Prize: $500 and guaranteed production under standard writers guild contract.

ANNUAL INTERNATIONAL ONE PAGE PLAY COMPETITION, Lamia Ink!, P.O. Box 202, Prince Street Station, New York NY 10012. **Contact:** Cortland Jessup, founder/artistic director. Offered annually for previously published or unpublished one-page plays. Acquires "the rights to publish in our magazine and to be read or performed at the prize awarding festival." Playwright retains copyright. Deadline: March 15. Guidelines for SASE. Charges $2/ play or $5⁄3 plays. Prize: $200, staged reading and publication of 12 finalists.

N. ANNUAL NATIONAL PLAYWRITING CONTEST, Wichita State University, School of Performing Arts, 1845 Fairmount, Wichita KS 67260-0153. (316)978-3368. Fax: (316)978-3951. E-mail: kiralyfa@twsuvm.uc.twsu.edu. **Contact:** Bela Kiralyfalvi, contest director. Offered annually for full-length plays (minimum of 90 minutes playing time) or 2-3 short plays on related themes (minimum 90 minutes, playing time). Deadline: February 15. Guidelines for SASE. Prize: Production by the Wichita State University Theatre. Winner announced April 15.

N. BARBARA ANTON PLAYWRITING AWARD, Florida Studio Theatre, 1241 N. Palm Ave., Sarasota FL 34236. (941)366-9017. Fax: (941)955-4137. E-mail: james@fst2000.org. Website: www.fst2000.org. **Contact:** James Ashford. Offered annually to a playwright of proven promise. Prize: Residency at Florida Studio Theatre and $1,000 stipend.

N. THE ARKANSAS REPERTORY THEATRE COMPETITION FOR NEW AMERICAN COMEDY, Arkansas Repertory Theatre, P.O. Box 110, Little Rock AR 72203-0110. (501)378-0445. Website: www.therep.org. **Contact:** Brad Mooy, literary manager. Offered every two years for unpublished, unproduced, full-length comedies (no musicals or children's plays). Scripts may be submitted with the recommendation of an agent or theater professional only. Must be at least 65 pages, with minimal set requirements and a cast limit of 12. One entry per playwright. Open to US citizens only. Deadline: December 31, 2001; notification March 2002. Prize: $10,000, a staged reading and transportation.

AURICLE AWARD, Plays on Tape, P.O. Box 152, Powell Butte OR 97753-0152. (541)447-7033. Fax: (541)416-0525. E-mail: theatre@playsontape.com. Website: www.playsontape.com. **Contact:** Bev Friesen. Annual contest to make available on tape and CD stage plays and to discover stage plays that have the components for audio production. Open to previously published and unpublished plays. Guidelines for SASE or on website. "We're looking for stageplay writers and radio-play writers. The concentration is on the adaptability of the stage play to audio. All writers encouraged regardless of résumé. We would like more minority submissions." Submit in any form: Recycled paper, floppy disk, e-mail. Deadline: December 31. Charges $5 fee. Prize: $100 award, then if the winning entry is audio published, an additional $500 plus royalty agreement.

AUSTIN HEART OF FILM FESTIVAL FEATURE LENGTH SCREENPLAY COMPETITION, 1604 Nueces, Austin TX 78701. (512)478-4795. Fax: (512)478-6205. E-mail: austinfilm@aol.com. Website: www.austinfilmfestival.c om. **Contact:** BJ Burrow, competition director. Offered annually for unpublished screenplays. The Austin Film Festival is looking for quality screenplays which will be read by industry professionals. Two competitions: Adult/Family Category and Comedy Category. Guidelines for SASE or call 1-800-310-3378. The writer must hold the rights when submitted; it must be original work. The screenplay must be between 90 and 120 pages. It must be in standard screenplay format (industry standard). Deadline: May 15. Charges $40 entry fee. Prize: $5,000 in each category.

BABYLON PLAYERS 'WORLD PREMIERE' PLAYWRITING CONTEST, Babylon Players, 386 High Point Dr., Edwardsville IL 62025. E-mail: contest@babylonplayers.org. Website: www.babylonplayers.org. Offered annually for unpublished work in 2 categories: One-Act Plays and Full-Length Plays. One full-length and one one-act play will be selected each year. Additional plays, or "runners-up" plays, may be chosen for production, but only one prize for each category will be given. Material must be original, unproduced and unpublished. Plays must utilize a simple set and common props. One-acts may range from 15 to 60 minutes; full-length plays should be over 1:45 with intermission. No period costumes or special effects. No more than six characters. Content/language should be acceptable to a general audience. All rights remain with the author. Open to any writer. Include SASE for return of materials and for a list of winners. E-mail any queries. Deadline: April 30. Guidelines for SASE. Prize: Full-length plays: $150 and production by Babylon Players; for one-acts, $100 and production.

BAKER'S PLAYS HIGH SCHOOL PLAYWRITING CONTEST, Baker's Plays, P.O. Box 699222, Quincy MA 02269-9222. (617)745-0805. Fax: (617)745-9891. E-mail: help@bakersplays.com. Website: www.bakersplays.com. **Contact:** John B. Welch, editor. Offered annually for unpublished work about the "high school experience," but can be about any subject, so long as the play can be reasonably produced on the high school stage. Plays may be of any length. Plays must be accompanied by the signature of a sponsoring high school drama or English teacher, and it is recommended that the play receive a production or a public reading prior to the submission. Multiple submissions and co-authored scripts are welcome. Teachers may not submit a student's work. The manuscript must be firmly bound, typed and come with SASE that includes enough postage to cover the return of the manuscript. Plays that do not come with an SASE will not be returned. Do not send originals; copies only. Deadline: January 31. Guidelines for SASE. Prize: 1st-$500 and publication; 2nd-$250; 3rd-$100.

N BAY AREA PLAYWRIGHTS FESTIVAL, The Playwrights Foundation, P.O. Box 460357, San Francisco CA 94146. (415)263-3986. E-mail: bayplays@best.com. **Contact:** Arturo Catricala or Amy Mueller, artistic directors. Offered annually for unpublished plays to encourage development of a new work. Unproduced full-length plays only. Open to any writer. Deadline: February 15. Guidelines for SASE. Prize: Small stipend and a professionally staged reading.

THE BEVERLY HILLS THEATRE GUILD—PLAY COMPETITION FOR CHILDREN'S THEATRE: THE MARILYN HALL AWARDS, 2815 N. Beachwood Dr., Los Angeles CA 90068-1923. (213)465-2703. **Contact:** Competition Coordinator. Offered annually for unpublished, theatrical works suitable for the grades in 2 designated categories. Category I: Plays for grades 6-8 (middle school), approximately 60 minutes or less; Category II: Plays for grades 3-5 (upper elementary), approximately 30 minutes or less. Authors may enter up to 2 scripts, 1 in each category. Plays must be written in Standard English. They may be original, adaptations, or translations. Musicals are not eligible. Authors must be US citizens or legal residents. Co-authorship permissable. Deadline: Entries must be postmarked January 15-February 28. Guidelines for SASE. Prize: Category I-$750; Category II-$250.

THE BEVERLY HILLS THEATRE GUILD-JULIE HARRIS PLAYWRIGHT AWARD COMPETITION, 2815 N. Beachwood Drive, Los Angeles CA 90068-1923. (213)465-2703. **Contact:** Competition Coordinator. Estab. 1978. "Annual contest to discover new dramatists and to encourage established and aspiring playwrights to develop quality plays for the theatre." Original full-length plays, unpublished, unproduced and not currently under option. Plays must be written in English, no translations from foreign languages, adaptations from other media, or musicals are eligible. Also offers additional competition for plays written for children's theatre. Application and guidelines required, send SASE. Open to any writer who is a US citizen or legal resident. Co-authorships permissable. Deadline: Entries accepted August 1-November 1. Prize: 1st-$5,000; 2nd-$2,500; 3rd-$1,500.

N BIENNIAL PROMISING PLAYWRIGHT AWARD, Colonial Players, Inc., Box 2167, Annapolis MD 21404. (410)263-0533. **Contact:** Frances Marchand. Offered every 2 years for unpublished full-length plays and adaptations. Open to any aspiring playwright residing in any of the states descendant from the original 13 colonies (Connecticut, Delaware, Georgia, Maryland, Massachusetts, New Hampshire, New Jersey, New York, North Carolina, Pennsylvania,

Rhode Island, South Carolina and Virginia), West Virginia, or Washington, DC. Deadline: December 31. Guidelines for SASE. Prize: Production and $750 cash award. Colonial Players, Inc., reserves the right to premiere the play on a royalty-free basis within two years after the cash award is presented.

WALDO M. & GRACE C. BONDERMAN IUPUI/IRT NATIONAL YOUTH THEATRE PLAYWRITING COMPETITION AND DEVELOPMENT WORKSHOP, 114 Red Oak Dr., Avon IN 46123. (317)274-2095. Fax: (317)278-1025. E-mail: dwebb@iupui.edu. Website: www.iupui.edu/~comstudy/playsym/symwork.html. **Contact:** Dorothy Webb. Offered every 2 years for unpublished plays to encourage writers to create artistic scripts for young audiences. "It provides a forum through which each playwright receives constructive criticism and the support of a development team consisting of a professional director and dramaturg. Plays will be cast from professional and experienced area actors." Guidelines for SASE or on website. "Plays should be intended for young audiences 1st grade through high school (no play is expected to appeal to all ages simultaneously). Playwrights must suggest the appropriate age category on official entry form. Deadline: September 1, 2002 (postmarked), received by Sept. 8, 2002. Prize: Awards will be presented to up to 10 finalists. In addition to the development work, 4 cash awards of $1,000 each will be presented to the 4 playwrights whose plays are selected for development.

N **RICHARD & BETTY BURDICK NEW PLAY FESTIVAL**, Florida Studio Theatre, 1241 N. Palm Ave., Sarasota FL 34236. (941)366-9017. Fax: (941)955-4137. E-mail: james@fst2000.org. Website: www.fst2000.org. **Contact:** James Ashford. Offered annually for unpublished plays. "All submissions to *Florida Studio Theatre* are considered for this festival. It is a developmental process followed by workshop productions of three new plays by writers from around the country." Anyone wishing to submit a full-length play should first send a cover letter, synopsis, 5-10 pages of sample dialogue and a SASE. *Florida Studio Theatre* reserves the right to produce the premiere full production. Open to any writer. Deadline: End of January. Guidelines for SASE. Prize: Development and workshop production, including housing and stipend while in Sarasota.

CALIFORNIA YOUNG PLAYWRIGHTS CONTEST, Playwrights Project, 450 B St., Suite 1020, San Diego CA 92101-8093. (619)239-8222. Fax: (619)239-8225. E-mail: write@playwrightsproject.com. Website: www.playwrightsproject.com. **Contact:** Cecelia Kouma, managing director. Offered annually for previously unpublished plays by young writers to stimulate young people to create dramatic works, and to nurture promising writers. Scripts must be a minimum of 10 standard typewritten pages; send 2 copies. Scripts will not be returned. All entrants receive detailed evaluation letter. Writers must be California residents under age 19 as of the deadline date. Deadline: April 1. Guidelines for SASE. Prize: Professional production of 3-5 winning plays at the Old Globe Theatre in San Diego, plus royalty.

JANE CHAMBERS PLAYWRITING AWARD, Women and Theatre Program of Association for Theatre in Higher Education (WTP/ATHE), Meadows School of the Arts, Southern Methodist University, P.O. Box 750356, Dallas TX 75275-0356. **Contact:** Gretchen Smith, coordinator. Estab. 1983. Offered annually to recognize a woman playwright who has written a play with a feminist perspective, a majority of roles for women, and which experiments with the dramatic form. Notification: June 15. Synopses of both winners sent to all TCG-affiliated theatres. "Writer must be female. A recommendation from a theatre professional is helpful, but not required." Deadline: February 1. Guidelines for SASE. Prize: $1,000. Student award: $250.

CHARLOTTE FESTIVAL/NEW PLAYS IN AMERICA, Charlotte Repertory Theatre, 129 W. Trade St., Charlotte NC 28202-2143. Website: www.charlotterep.org. **Contact:** Carol Bellamy, literary associate. Four plays selected for each festival. Must be full scripts, no one-acts or musicals. Must not have had any previous professional production. Scripts *must be bound* and include SASE if need to be returned. No cassettes, international reply coupons or videos accepted. Deadline: Accepted all year. Prize: Staged reading of script, transportation to festival, small honorarium for expenses.

CLEVELAND PUBLIC THEATRE NEW PLAYS FESTIVAL, Cleveland Public Theatre, 6415 Detroit Ave., Cleveland OH 44102-3011. (216)631-2727 ext. 350. Fax: (216)631-2575. E-mail: cpt@en.com. Website: www.clevelandartists.net/cpt. **Contact:** Clyde Simon, literary manager. Estab. 1983 Annual (January) festival of staged readings of 8-15 alternative, experimental, poetic, political work, and plays by women, people of color, gays/lesbians. "We accept both full-length and one-acts, but emphasize shorter works, simple set, 10 actor cast maximum. Deadline: September 1. Guidelines for SASE. Charges $10 fee.

N **COE COLLEGE PLAYWRITING FESTIVAL**, Coe College, 1220 First Ave. NE, Cedar Rapids IA 52402-5092. (319)399-8624. Fax: (319)399-8557. E-mail: swolvert@coe.edu. Website: www.public.coe.edu/departments/theatre/. **Contact:** Susan Wolverton. Estab. 1993. Offered biennially for unpublished work to provide a venue for new works for the stage. "There is usually a theme for the festival. We are interested in full-length productions, *not* one acts or musicals. There are no specific criteria although a current résumé and synopsis is requested." Open to any writer. Deadline: Before June 1. Notified by September 1. Guidelines for SASE. Prize: $325, plus 1-week residency as guest artist with airfare, room and board provided.

N **THE COLUMBUS SCREENPLAY DISCOVERY AWARDS**, 433 N. Camden Dr. #600, Beverly Hills CA 90210. (310)288-1882. Fax: (310)475-0193. E-mail: awards@hollywoodawards.com. Website: www.HollywoodAwards

.com. **Contact:** Carlos de Abreu. Monthly and annual contest "to discover new screenplay writers." Judged by reputable industry professionals (producers, development executives, story analysts). Writer must give option to purchase if selected. Open to any writer. Deadline: November 1. Guidelines for SASE. Charges $55 fee. Prize: Options up to $10,000, plus professional development guidance, software and access to agents, producers and studios.

N: DAYTON PLAYHOUSE FUTUREFEST, The Dayton Playhouse, 1301 E. Siebenthaler Ave., Dayton OH 45414-5357. (937)333-7469. Fax: (937)277-9539. **Contact:** Fran Pesch, theater manager. "Three plays selected for full productions, three for readings at July FutureFest weekend; the six authors will be given travel and lodging to attend the festival." Guidelines for SASE. Guidelines can also be faxed. Deadline: October 30. Prize: $1,000 and $100 to the other 5 playwrights.

DRAMARAMA PLAYWRIGHTING COMPETITION, Playwright's Center of San Francisco, P.O. Box 460466, San Francisco CA 94146-0466. (415)626-4603. Fax: (415)863-0901. **Contact:** Dr. S.B. Kominars. Annual contest for previously unpublished and unproduced plays. Two categories: Short Plays (under one hour) and Full-Length Plays (over one hour). Open to any writer, but "staged readings" will not be considered. Deadline: March 15, 2002. Guidelines for SASE. Charges $25 fee. Prize: $500 for winning play in each category.

DRURY UNIVERSITY ONE-ACT PLAY CONTEST, Drury University, 900 N. Benton Ave., Springfield MO 65802-3344. E-mail: sasher@drury.edu. Website: www.drury.edu/Academics/PLAYATT.html. **Contact:** Sandy Asher. Offered in even-numbered years for unpublished and professionally unproduced plays. One play per playwright. Guidelines for SASE or by e-mail. Deadline: December 1.

DUBUQUE FINE ARTS PLAYERS ANNUAL ONE-ACT PLAYWRITING CONTEST, 330 Clarke Dr., Dubuque IA 52001. (319)588-0646. E-mail: snakelady@mwci.net. Website: community.ia.com/ic/OneActPlayContest. **Contact:** Jennie G. Stabenow, contest coordinator. Annual competition since 1977 for previously unpublished, unproduced plays. Adaptations must be of playwright's own work or of a work in the public domain. No children's plays or musicals. No scripts over 35 pages or 40 minutes performance time. Two copies of manuscript required. Script readers' review sheets available. "Concentrate on character, relationships, and a good story." Buys rights to first full-stage production and subsequent local video rights. Deadline: January 31; reports by June 30. Guidelines for SASE. Charges $10/play. Prize: $600, $300, $200, plus possible full production of play.

EMERGING PLAYWRIGHT'S AWARD, Urban Stages, 17 E. 47th St., New York NY 10017. E-mail: urbanstages@aol.com. Website: www.mint.net/urbanstages. **Contact:** T.L. Reilly, producing director. Estab. 1983. Submissions required to be unproduced in New York City. Send script, letter of introduction, production history, author's name, résumé and SASE. Submissions accepted year-round. Plays selected in August and January for award consideration. One submission per person. Prize: $500 and New York production.

N: ESSENTIAL THEATRE PLAYWRITING AWARD, The Essential Theatre, 995 Greenwood Ave. #6, Atlanta GA 30306. (404)876-8471. E-mail: pmhardy@aol.com. **Contact:** Peter Hardy. Offered annually for unproduced, full-length plays by Georgia writers. No limitations as to subject matter. Deadline: June 1. Prize: $400 and full production.

SHUBERT FENDRICH MEMORIAL PLAYWRITING CONTEST, Pioneer Drama Service, Inc., P.O. Box 4267, Englewood CO 80155. (303)779-4035. Fax: (303)779-4315. E-mail: playwrights@pioneerdrama.com. Website: www.pioneerdrama.com. **Contact:** Beth Somers, assistant editor. Offered annually for unpublished but previously produced submissions to encourage the development of quality theatrical material for educational and community theater. Rights acquired only if published. People already published by Pioneer Drama are not eligible. Deadline: March 1. Guidelines for SASE. Prize: $1,000 royalty advance, publication.

FESTIVAL OF FIRSTS, City of Carmel-by-the-Sea-Community and Cultural Dept., P.O. Box 1950, Carmel CA 93921-1950. (831)624-3996. Fax: (831)624-0147. **Contact:** Brian Donoghue, award director. Offered annually for unpublished plays to recognize and foster the art of playwriting. Deadline: June 15-August 31. Guidelines for SASE. Charges $15/script. Prize: Up to $1,000.

N: FLORIDA PLAYWRIGHTS FESTIVAL, Florida Studio Theatre, 1241 N. Palm Ave., Sarasota FL 34236. (941)366-9017. Fax: (941)955-4137. E-mail: james@fst2000.org. Website: www.fst2000.org. **Contact:** James Ashford. Offered annually (late July/early August) for full-length plays. Send complete script. Two plays are chosen for the festival; each play rehearses for 2 weeks before the festival and receives one public performance. Deadline: Submissions accepted year-round. Prize: Participation in rehearsal and rewrite process, public performance, travel, housing, small stipend.

FULL-LENGTH PLAY COMPETITION, West Coast Ensemble, P.O. Box 38728, Los Angeles CA 90038. (323)876-9337. Fax: (323)876-8916. Website: www.wcensemble.org. **Contact:** Les Hanson, artistic director. Offered annually "to nurture, support and encourage" unpublished playwrights. Permission to present the play is granted if work is selected as finalist. Deadline: December 31. Guidelines for SASE. Prize: $500 and presentation of play.

JOHN GASSNER MEMORIAL PLAYWRITING COMPETITION, New England Theatre Conference, Northeastern University, 360 Huntington Ave., Boston MA 02115. E-mail: info@netconline.org. Website: www.netconline.org. **Contact:** Clinton Campbell, managing director. Offered annually to unpublished full-length plays and scripts. Open to New England residents and NETC members. Playwrights living outside New England may participate by joining NETC. Deadline: April 15. Guidelines for SASE. Charges $10 fee. Prize: 1st-$1,000; 2nd-$500.

GILMAN & GONZALEZ-FALLA THEATER FOUNDATION AWARD, 109 E. 64th St., New York NY 10021. (212)734-5132. Fax: (212)734-9606. E-mail: soncel@aol.com. **Contact:** Celso Gonzalez-Falle, vice president. Offered annually for body of work to encourage the creative elements in the American musical theater. The lyricist, book writer or composer should have a work produced in the US in either a commercial theater or a professional not-for-profit theater. Two letters of recommendation from professionals involved in the theatre are required. Open to US residents and American citizens. Deadline: December 31. Guidelines for SASE. Prize: $25,000.

GOVERNOR GENERAL'S LITERARY AWARD FOR DRAMA, Canada Council for the Arts, 350 Albert St., P.O. Box 1047, Ottawa, Ontario K1P 5V8, Canada. (613)566-4414 ext. 5576. Fax: (613)566-4410. E-mail: joanne.larocque-poirier@canadacouncil.ca. Website: www.canadacouncil.ca. **Contact:** Joanne Larocque-Poirier. Offered for the best English-language and the best French-language work of drama by a Canadian published September 1, 2001, to September 30, 2002. Publishers submit titles for consideration. Deadline: April or August 2002, depending on the book's publication date. Prize: $15,000.

GREAT PLAINS PLAY CONTEST, University Theatre of the University of Kansas, 317 Murphy Hall, Lawrence KS 66045-2176. (785)864-2696. Fax: (785)864-5251. E-mail: dunruh@ukans.edu. **Contact:** Delbert Unruh, director. Offered annually to encourage development and production of full-length dramatic works or musicals about life on the Great Plains. Plays must be full-length, original work or original adaptation that has been professionally produced or not been produced more than twice by amateur or educational companies. Acquires right to publish winning works in anthology. Open to any writer. Deadline: September 1. Guidelines for SASE. Prize: $500 Development Award, $2,000 Production Award (production at University Theatre and $500 for travel and housing during production).

GREAT PLATTE RIVER PLAYWRIGHTS FESTIVAL, University of Nebraska at Kearney, Theatre Department, 2506 12th Ave., Kearney NE 68849-5260. (308)865-8406. Fax: (308)865-8806. E-mail: garrisonj@unk.edu. **Contact:** Jack Garrison. "The purpose of GPRPF is to develop original scripts and encourage playwrights to work in regional settings. Full-length or one-act dramas and comedies, plays for young audiences and musicals will be considered. The contest is open to entry by any writer; however, submissions are restricted to unproduced, unpublished, original works - works in progress are strongly encouraged. Playwrights may submit more than one entry. The Festival reserves the rights to development and premiere production of the winning plays without payment of royalties." SASE required if return of scripts is desired. Selections will be announced by July 31. Deadline: January 1-April 1. Prize: Cash awards, production of script(s), free lodging and travel stipend.

PAUL GREEN PLAYWRIGHTS PRIZE, North Carolina Writers' Network, 3501 Hwy. 54 W., Studio C, Chapel Hill NC 27516. (919)967-9540. Fax: (919)929-0535. E-mail: mail@ncwriters.org. Website: www.ncwriters.org. **Contact:** Whitney Vaughan, program coordinator. Offered annually for unpublished submissions to honor a playwright, held in recognition of Paul Green, North Carolina's dramatist laureate and Pulitzer Prize-winning playwright. Open to any writer. Deadline: September 30. Guidelines for SASE. Charges $10 ($7.50 for NCWN members). Prize: $500.

HARVEST FESTIVAL OF NEW AMERICAN PLAYS, State Theater Company, 719 Congress Ave., Austin TX 78701. (512)692-0509. **Contact:** Michelle Polgar. Offered annually for unpublished full-length original plays and adaptations. No one-acts, musicals or plays for young audiences. Open to American playwrights. Deadline: April 1. Guidelines for SASE. Prize: 4-8 plays receive rehearsed readings over a one-month period. Selected playwrights receive stipend, travel, housing to attend rehearsals and festival. Plays will be considered for full production the following season.

W. KEITH HEDRICK PLAYWRITING CONTEST, Hudson River Classics Inc., P.O. Box 940, Hudson NY 12534. (518)851-7244. Fax: (518)822-1480. **Contact:** Jan M. Grice. Offered annually for unpublished work. Playwrights must be from New York State or the Northeast. Deadline: May 1. Guidelines for SASE. Charges $5 fee. Prize: $500 and a reading of the play by professional actors in the season following the contest.

HENRICO THEATRE COMPANY ONE-ACT PLAYWRITING COMPETITION, Henrico Recreation & Parks, P.O. Box 27032, Richmond VA 23273. (804)501-5138. Fax: (804)501-5284. E-mail: per22@co.henrico.va.us. Website: www.co.henrico.va.us/rec. **Contact:** Amy A. Perdue. Offered annually for previously unpublished or unproduced plays or musicals to produce new dramatic works in 1-act form. "Scripts with small casts and simpler sets given preference. Controversial themes and excessive language should be avoided. Deadline: July 1. Guidelines for SASE. Prize: Winner-$300; runner-up-$200. Winning entries may be produced; videotape sent to author.

HISPANIC PLAYWRIGHTS' DIVISION SOUTHWEST FESTIVAL OF NEW PLAYS,, Stages Repertory Theatre, 3201 Allen Pkwy., Suite 101, Houston TX 77019. (713)527-0220. Fax: (713)527-8669. **Contact:** Rob Bundy.

Offered annually to provide an outlet for playwrights of Hispanic/Latino heritage. Open to full-length plays, musicals and series of related shorts. Guidelines for SASE or on website. Winners notified in May. Deadline: October 1-February 15. Prize: 1st-reading by professional actors; runners-up(2)-selected scenes read.

HISPANIC PLAYWRIGHTS' PROJECT, South Coast Repertory Theatre, P.O. Box 2197, Costa Mesa CA 92628-2197. (714)708-5500 ext. 5405. Fax: (714)545-0391. E-mail: juliette@scr.org. Website: www.scr.org. **Contact:** Juliette Carrillo. Offered annually for unpublished plays to develop work by Latino writers across the US. Guidelines for SASE or call for a brochure and leave address. Deadline: January 15. Prize: Workshop or reading of the play.

HUDSON RIVER CLASSICS ANNUAL CONTEST, Hudson River Classics Inc., P.O. Box 940, Hudson NY 12534. (518)851-7244. Fax: (518)828-1480. **Contact:** Jan M. Grice. Offered annually for unpublished playwrights. Writers must be from the Northeastern US. Deadline: February 1-May 1. Guidelines for SASE. Charges $5 fee. Prize: $500 and concert reading of winning play.

JEWEL BOX THEATRE PLAYWRIGHTING COMPETITION, Jewel Box Theatre, 3700 N. Walker, Oklahoma City OK 73118-7099. (405)521-1786. **Contact:** Charles Tweed, production director. Estab. 1982. Offered annually for full-length plays. Send SASE in October for guidelines. Deadline: January 15. Prize: $500.

THE KENNEDY CENTER FUND FOR NEW AMERICAN PLAYS, J.F. Kennedy Center for the Performing Arts, Washington DC 20566. (202)416-8024. Fax: (202)416-8205. E-mail: rsfoster@kennedy-center.org. Website: kennedy-center.org/fnap. **Contact:** Rebecca Foster, manager, theater programming. Estab. 1988. Offered for previously unproduced work. "Program objectives: To encourage playwrights to write, and nonprofit professional theaters to produce new American plays; to ease the financial burdens of nonprofit professional theater organizations producing new plays; to provide a playwright with a better production of the play than the producing theater would normally be able to accomplish." Nonprofit professional theater organizations can mail in name and address to be placed on the mailing list or check website. Submissions and funding proposals only through the producing theater. Production grants are given to theaters to underwrite specific or extraordinary expenses relating to: Creative support, actor support and production support. Development grants are given to theaters to underwrite expenses for a reading and workshop of a new play in development. Deadline: Early May. Prize: Production grant-$10,000; development grant, $2,500; a few encouragement grants of $2,500 may be given to promising playwrights chosen from the submitted proposals.

MARC A. KLEIN PLAYWRITING AWARD FOR STUDENTS, Department of Theater Arts, Case Western Reserve University, 10900 Euclid Ave., Cleveland OH 44106-7077. (216)368-4868. Fax: (216)368-5184. E-mail: ksg@p o.cwru.edu. Website: www.cwru.edu/artsci/thtr/website/theahome.htm. **Contact:** Ron Wilson, Reading Committee chair. Estab. 1975. Offered annually for an unpublished, professionally unproduced full-length play, or evening of related short plays, by a student at an American college or university. Deadline: May 15. Prize: $1,000, which includes $500 to cover residency expenses; production.

KUMU KAHUA/UHM THEATRE DEPARTMENT PLAYWRITING CONTEST, Kumu Kahua Theatre Inc./ University of Hawaii at Manoa, Department of Theatre and Dance, 46 Merchant St., Honolulu HI 96813. (808)536-4222. Fax: (808)536-4226. **Contact:** Harry Wong III. Offered annually for unpublished work to honor full-length and short plays. Guidelines available every September. First 2 categories open to residents and nonresidents. For Hawaii Prize, plays must be set in Hawaii or deal with some aspect of the Hawaiian experience. For Pacific Rim prize, plays must deal with Hawaii or the Pacific Islands, Pacific Rim or Pacific/Asian/American experience—short plays only considered in 3rd category. Deadline: January 1. Prize: $500 (Hawaii Prize); $400 (Pacific Rim); $200 (Resident).

N L.A. DESIGNERS' THEATRE-COMMISSIONS, L.A. Designers' Theatre, P.O. Box 1883, Studio City CA 91614-0883. (323)650-9600-(323)654-2700 T.D.D. Fax: (323)654-3260. E-mail: ladesigners@juno.com. **Contact:** Richard Niederberg, artistic director. Quarterly contest "to promote new work and push it onto the conveyor belt to filmed or videotaped entertainment." All submissions must be registered with copyright office and be unpublished by "major" publishers. Material will *not* be returned. "Do not submit anything that will not fit in a #10 envelope." "No rules, no fees, no entry forms. Just present an *idea* that can be commissioned into a full work." Proposals for works not yet completed are encouraged. Open to any writer. Deadline: March 15, June 15, September 15, December 15. Guidelines for SASE. Prize: Production or publication of the work in the Los Angeles market. "We only want 'first refusal.' If you are picked, we negotiate royalties with the writer."

LOVE CREEK ANNUAL SHORT PLAY FESTIVAL, Love Creek Productions, co Granville, 162 Nesbit St., Weehawken NJ 07087-6817. E-mail: creekread@aol.com. **Contact:** Cynthia Granville-Callahan, festival manager. Estab. 1985. Annual festival for unpublished plays, unproduced in New York in the previous year, under 40 minutes, at least 2 characters, larger casts preferred. "We established the Festival as a playwriting competition in which scripts are judged on their merits in performance." All entries must specify "festival" on envelope and must include letter giving permission to produce script, if chosen, and stating whether equity showcase is acceptable. "We are giving strong preference to scripts featuring females in major roles in casts which are predominantly female. Deadline: Ongoing. Guidelines for SASE. Prize: Cash prize awarded to winner.

LOVE CREEK MINI FESTIVALS, Love Creek Productions, co Granville, 162 Nesbit St., Weehawken NJ 07087-6817. E-mail: creekread@aol.com. **Contact:** Cynthia Granville-Callahan, festival literary manager. "The Mini Festivals are an outgrowth of our annual Short Play Festival in which we produce scripts concerning a particular issue or theme which our artistic staff selects according to current needs, interests and concerns of our members, audiences and playwrights submitting to our Short Play Festival throughout the year." Considers scripts unpublished, unproduced in New York City in past year, under 40 minutes, at least 2 characters, larger casts preferred. Submissions must list name of festival on envelope and must include letter giving permission to produce script, if chosen, and stating whether equity showcase is acceptable. Finalists receive a mini-showcase production in New York City. Write for upcoming themes. "We are giving strong preference to scripts featuring females in major roles in casts which are predominantly female. Deadline: Ongoing. Guidelines for SASE. Prize: Winner of overall festival series receives a cash prize.

MAXIM MAZUMDAR NEW PLAY COMPETITION, Alleyway Theatre, One Curtain Up Alley, Buffalo NY 14202-1911. (716)852-2600. Fax: (716)852-2266. E-mail: email@alleyway.com. Website: alleyway.com. **Contact:** Joanna Brown, literary manager. Estab. 1990. Annual competition. Full Length: Not less than 90 minutes, no more than 10 performers. One-Act: Less than 40 minutes, no more than 6 performers. Children's plays. Musicals must be accompanied by audio tape. Finalists announced October 1. "Playwrights may submit work directly. There is no entry form. Annual playwright's fee $5; may submit one in each category, but pay only one fee. Please specify if submission is to be included in competition." "Alleyway Theatre must receive first production credit in subsequent printings and productions." Deadline: July 1. Prize: Full length-$400, travel plus lodging, production and royalties; One-act-$100, production plus royalties.

McLAREN MEMORIAL COMEDY PLAYWRITING COMPETITION, Midland Community Theatre, 2000 W. Wadley, Midland TX 79705. (915)682-2544. Fax: (915)682-6136. E-mail: alatheajim@aol.com. Website: www.mctmidland.org. **Contact:** Alathea Blischke, McLaren co-chair. Estab. 1990. Offered annually for full-length and one-act comedies for adults, teens or children. Work must not have received professional production. Deadline: December 1-January 31. Charges $10 fee/play. Prize: $300 for best full-length play; $100 for best one-act play; staged readings for 3 finalists.

MILL MOUNTAIN THEATRE NEW PLAY COMPETITION, Mill Mountain Theatre, Center in the Square, 1 Market Square, 2nd Floor, Roanoke VA 24011-1437. (540)342-5749. Fax: (540)342-5745. E-mail: outreach@millmountain.org. Website: www.millmountain.org. **Contact:** New Play Competition Coordinator. Estab. 1985. Offered annually for previously unpublished and unproduced plays by US residents, both full-length and one-acts for up to 10 cast members; musicals and solo pieces also accepted. Plays must be agent submitted—or have the recommendation of a director, literary manager or dramaturg. Deadline: Submit between October 1, 2001, and January 1, 2002. Guidelines for SASE. Prize: $1,000, staged reading and possible full production; travel stipend and housing for limited residency.

MOVING ARTS PREMIERE ONE-ACT COMPETITION, Moving Arts, 514 S. Spring St., Los Angeles CA 90013-2304. (213)622-8906. Fax: (213)622-8946. E-mail: treynichols@movingarts.org. Website: www.movingarts.org. **Contact:** Trey Nichols, literary director. Offered annually for unproduced one-act plays and "is designed to foster the continued development of one-act plays." All playwrights are eligible except Moving Arts resident artists. Deadline: February 28 (postmark). Guidelines for SASE. Charges $10 fee/script. Prize: 1st-$200 plus a full production with a 4-8 week run. 2nd and 3rd-program mention and possible production.

MUSICAL STAIRS, West Coast Ensemble, P.O. Box 38728, Los Angeles CA 90038. (323)876-9337. Fax: (323)876-8916. **Contact:** Les Hanson. Offered annually for unpublished writers "to nurture, support and encourage musical creators." Permission to present the musical is granted if work is selected as finalist. Deadline: June 30. Prize: $500 and presentation of musical.

NANTUCKET SHORT PLAY COMPETITION AND FESTIVAL, Nantucket Theatrical Productions, Box 2177, Nantucket MA 02584. (508)228-5002. **Contact:** Jim Patrick. Offered annually for unpublished plays to "seek the highest quality of playwriting distilled into a short play format." Selected plays receive staged readings. Plays must be less than 40 pages. Deadline: January 1. Charges $8 fee. Prize: $200 plus staged readings.

N NATIONAL AUDIO DRAMA SCRIPT COMPETITION, National Audio Theatre Festivals, 115 Dikeman St., Hempstead NY 11150. (516)483-8321. Fax: (516)538-7583. Website: www.natf.org. **Contact:** Sue Zizza. Offered annually for unpublished radio scripts. "NATF is particularly interested in stories that deserve to be told because they enlighten, intrigue or simply make us laugh out loud. Contemporary scripts with strong female roles, multi-cultural casting and diverse viewpoints will be favorably received." Preferred length is 25 minutes. Guidelines on website. Open to any writer. NATF will have the right to produce the scripts for the NATF Live Performance Workshop; however, NATF makes no commitment to produce any script. The authors will retain all other rights to their work. Deadline: November 15. Charges $25 fee (US currency only please). Prize: $800 split between 2-4 authors and free workshop production participation.

N NATIONAL CANADIAN ONE-ACT PLAYWRITING COMPETITION, Ottawa Little Theatre, 400 King Edward Ave., Ottawa, Ontario K1N 7M7, Canada. (613)233-8948. Fax: (613)233-8027. E-mail: olt@sympatico.ca.

Website: www.o-l-t.com. **Contact:** Elizabeth Holden, office manager. Estab. 1913. Purpose is "to encourage literary and dramatic talent in Canada." Guidelines for #10 SASE with Canadian postage or #10 SAE with 1 IRC. Deadline: January-May. Prize: $1,000, $700, $500.

NATIONAL CHILDREN'S THEATRE FESTIVAL, Actors' Playhouse at the Miracle Theatre, 280 Miracle Mile, Coral Gables FL 33134. (305)444-9293. Fax: (305)444-4181. Website: www.actorsplayhouse.org. **Contact:** Earl Maulding. Offered annually for unpublished musicals for young audiences. Target age is between 5-12. Script length should be 45-60 minutes. Maximum of 8 actors to play any number of roles. Settings which lend themselves to simplified scenery. Bilingual (English/Spanish) scripts are welcomed. Call for guidelines. Open to any writer. Deadline: August 1. Charges $10 fee. Prize: 1st-full production, $500.

NATIONAL HISPANIC PLAYWRITING AWARD, Arizona Theatre Co. in affiliation with Centro Cultural Mexicano, 40 E. 14th St., Tucson AZ 85701. (520)884-8210. Fax: (520)628-9129. E-mail: ERomero@aztheatreco.org. Website: www.aztheatreco.org. **Contact:** Elaine Romero, playwright-in-residence. Offered annually for unproduced, unpublished plays over 50 pages in length. "The plays may be in English, bilingual or in Spanish (with English translation). The award recognizes exceptional full-length plays by Hispanic playwrights on any subject." Open to Hispanic playwrights currently residing in the US, its territories, and/or Mexico. Deadline: October 31. Guidelines for SASE. Prize: $1,000 and possible inclusion in ATC's Genesis New Play Reading Series.

NATIONAL ONE-ACT PLAYWRITING COMPETITION, Little Theatre of Alexandria, 600 Wolfe St., Alexandria VA 22314. (703)683-5778. Fax: (703)683-1378. E-mail: ltlthtre@erols. **Contact:** Carolyn Winters, chairman. Estab. 1978. Offered annually to encourage original writing for theatre. Submissions must be original, unpublished, unproduced one-act stage plays. "We usually produce top two or three winners. Deadline: Submit scripts for year 2002 contest from January 1-May 31, 2002. Guidelines for SASE. Charges $20/play fee; 2 play limit. Prize: 1st-$350, 2nd-$250, 3rd-$150.

NATIONAL TEN-MINUTE PLAY CONTEST, Actors Theatre of Louisville, 316 W. Main St., Louisville KY 40202-4218. (502)584-1265. E-mail: tpalmer@actorstheatre.org. Website: www.actorstheatre.org. **Contact:** Tanya Palmer, literary manager. Offered annually for previously professionally unproduced ten-minute plays (10 pages or less). "Entries must *not* have had an Equity or Equity-waiver production." One submission per playwright. Scripts are not returned. Please write or call for submission guidelines. Open to US residents. Deadline: Postmarked by December 1. Prize: $1,000.

N NATIONAL THEATRE ARTIST RESIDENCY PROGRAM, Theatre Communications Group, 355 Lexington Ave., New York NY 10017. (212)697-5230. Fax: (212)983-4847. E-mail: grants@tcg.org. **Contact:** Fran Kumin. Offered annually. The National Theatre Artist Residency Program has been designed to foster both new and expanded relationships between theatres and individual artists. Deadline: To be determined. Prize: Grants of $25,000; $50,000; $100,000 depending on the category. Matching funds are also available.

N NEW AMERICAN COMEDY WORKSHOP, Ukiah Players Theatre, 1041 Low Gap Rd., Ukiah CA 95482. (707)462-1210. **Contact:** Michael Ducharme. Offered every 2 years to playwrights seeking to develop their unproduced, full-length comedies into funnier, stronger scripts. Two scripts will be chosen for staged readings; one of these will be chosen for full production. Deadline: November 30 of odd-numbered years. Guidelines for SASE. Prize: Playwrights chosen for readings will receive a $25 royalty per performance. The playwright chosen for full production will receive a $50 royalty per performance, travel (up to $500) to Ukiah for a one-week workshop/rehearsal, lodging and per diem.

NEW CENTURY WRITER AWARDS (SCREENWRITING), 32 Alfred St., Suite B, New Haven CT 06512-3927. (203)469-8824. Fax: (203)468-0333. E-mail: newcenturywriter@yahoo.com. Website: www.newcenturywriter.org. **Contact:** Jason J. Marchi, executive director. Offered annually for previously unproduced work or work with a limited publication or production history to discover emerging writers of screenplays, stage plays, TV scripts, TV movie scripts and musicals. All genres. Winners announced August/September. Guidelines/entry form for #10 SAE. All entrants receive 1-year subscription to *The Anvil*, an educational newsletter for writers. Open to all writers, both non-produced and those with limited production history. Call if in doubt about your eligibility. Tips: "We seek to encourage writers with cash awards and to connect writers to our numerous alliance companies in the film production and publishing industries. We also produce a popular reading series in New York City of works selected from annual finalists. Please call for application package—all submission details are included." Deadline: March 15. Charges $30 entry fee. Prize: 1st-$5,000; 2nd-$2,000; 3rd-$1,000; 4th-10th-$250.

NEW VOICE SERIES, Remembrance Through the Performing Arts, P.O. Box 162446, Austin TX 78716. E-mail: RemPerArts@aol.com. **Contact:** Marla Dean Macdonald, director of new play development. Offered annually "to find talented central Texas playwrights who are in the early stages of script development. We develop these scripts on the page through a Work In Progress production." Playwrights need to send script, bio and a script-size SASE. Open to central Texas playwrights only. Deadline: Ongoing. Prize: Free development of their play with our company and representation of their play to theaters nationally for world premiers.

NEW WORKS FOR THE STAGE, COE College Theatre Arts Department, 1220 First Ave. NE, Cedar Rapids IA 52402. (319)399-8624. Fax: (319)399-8557. E-mail: swolvert@coe.edu. Website: www.public.coe.edu/departments/ theatre. **Contact:** Susan Wolverton. Offered every 2 years (odd years) "to encourage new work, to provide an interdisciplinary forum for the discussion of issues found in new work, to offer playwright contact with theater professionals who can provide response to new work." Full-length, original unpublished and unproduced scripts only. No musicals, adaptations, translations or collaborations. Submit one-page synopsis, résumé and SASE if the script is to be returned. Deadline: June 1. Prize: $325 plus travel, room and board for residency at the college.

NEW YORK CITY PUBLIC SCHOOL PLAYWRITING CONTEST (formerly New York High School Playwriting Contest), Young Playwrights Inc., 321 W. 44th St., Suite 906, New York NY 10036. (212)307-1140. Fax: (212)307-1454. E-mail: writeaplay@aol.com. Website: http://youngplaywrights.org. Offered annually for plays by NYC public school students only. Deadline: April 1. Guidelines for SASE. Prize: Cash prizes, staged readings, certificates, books and records.

'THE NEXT STAGE' NEW PLAY READING FESTIVAL, The Cleveland Play House, P.O. Box 1989, Cleveland OH 44106-0189. Fax: (216)795-7005. E-mail: sgordon@clevelandplayhouse.com. Website: www.clevelandplayhouse.c om. **Contact:** Seth Gordon, director of new play development. Offered annually for unpublished/unproduced submissions. "'The Next Stage' is our annual new play reading series. Up to six writers are brought to our theater for two weeks of rehearsal/development. The plays are then given public staged readings, and at least one is chosen for a full production in the upcoming season. Deadline: Ongoing. Guidelines for SASE. Prize: Staged reading of play, travel and housing, consideration for full production. Writers sign a six-month option for production of script.

DON AND GEE NICHOLL FELLOWSHIPS IN SCREENWRITING, Academy of Motion Picture Arts & Sciences, 8949 Wilshire Blvd., Beverly Hills CA 90211-1972. (310)247-3059. E-mail: nicholl@oscars.org. Website: www.oscars.org/nicholl. **Contact:** Greg Beal, program coordinator. Estab. 1985. Offered annually for unproduced screenplays to identify talented new screenwriters. Guidelines for SASE, available January 1-April 30. Recipients announced late October. Open to writers who have not earned more than $5,000 writing for films or TV. Deadline: May 1. Charges $30 fee. Prize: $30,000 in fellowships (up to 5/year).

OGLEBAY INSTITUTE TOWNGATE THEATRE PLAYWRITING CONTEST, Oglebay Institute, Stifel Fine Arts Center 1330 National Rd., Wheeling WV 26003. (304)242-7700. **Contact:** Kate Crosbie. Estab. 1976. Offered annually for unpublished works. "All full-length *non-musical* plays that have never been professionally produced or published are eligible." Open to any writer. Deadline: January 1; winner announced May 31. Guidelines for SASE. Prize: Run of play and cash award.

N **OPUS MAGNUM DISCOVERY AWARD**, Christopher Columbus Society, 433 N. Camden Dr. #600, Beverly Hills CA 90210. (310)288-1881. Fax: (310)288-0257. E-mail: awards@hollywoodawards.com. Website: screenwriters.c om. **Contact:** Carlos de Abreu, president. Annual award to discover new authors with books/manuscripts that can be optioned for features or TV movies. Judged by entertainment industry story analysts and producers. Deadline: December 1. Guidelines for SASE. Charges $75 fee. Prize: Option moneys to winner, up to $10,000.

MILDRED & ALBERT PANOWSKI PLAYWRITING AWARD, Forest A. Roberts Theatre, Northern Michigan University, Marquette MI 49855-5364. (906)227-2559. Fax: (906)227-2567. Website: www.nmu.edu/theatre. **Contact:** (Ms.) J. Love, award coordinator. Estab. 1977. Offered annually for unpublished, unproduced, full-length plays. Guidelines and application for SASE. Deadline: August 15-November 19. Prize: $2,000, a fully-mounted production and transportation to Marquette to serve as Artist-in-Residence the week of the show.

N **PEACE PLAYWRITING CONTEST**, Goshen College, 1700 S. Main, Goshen IN 46526. (219)535-7393. Fax: (219)535-7660. E-mail: douglc@goshen.edu. **Contact:** Douglas L. Caskey, director of theater. Offered every 2 years for unpublished work dealing with social issues and other issues related to the broader theme of peace. Open to any writer. Deadline: December 31, 2001. Guidelines for SASE. Prize: 1st-$500, production, room and board to attend rehearsals and/or production; 2nd-$100, possible production.

PERISHABLE THEATRE'S WOMEN'S PLAYWRITING FESTIVAL, P.O. Box 23132, Providence RI 02903. (401)331-2695. Fax: (401)331-7811. E-mail: info@perishable.org. Website: www.perishable.org. **Contact:** Vanessa Gilbert, associate artistic director. Offered annually for unpublished, one-act plays (up to 30 minutes in length when fully produced) to encourage women playwrights. Judged by reading committee, the Festival Director and the artistic director of the theater. Open to women playwrights exclusively. Deadline: December 15. Guidelines for SASE. Charges $5 fee per playwright (limit 2 plays per playwright). Prize: $500 and travel to Providence.

N **PETERSON EMERGING PLAYWRIGHT COMPETITION**, Catawba College Thearte Arts Department, 2300 W. Innes St., Salisbury NC 28144. (704)637-4771. Fax: (704)637-4207. E-mail: jepperso@catawba.edu. Website: www.catawba.edu. **Contact:** Jim Epperson, chair. Offered annually for unpublished work "to assist emerging playwrights in the development of new scripts, hopefully leading to professional production. Competition is open to all subject matter except children's plays. Playwrights may submit more than one entry." Open to any writer. Deadline:

February 15. Guidelines for SASE. Prize: Production of the winning play at Catawba College; $2,000 cash award; transportation to and from Catawba College for rewrites and performance; lodging and food while in residence; professional response to the performance of the play.

ROBERT J. PICKERING AWARD FOR PLAYWRIGHTING EXCELLENCE, Coldwater Community Theater, co 89 Division, Coldwater MI 49036. (517)279-7963. Fax: (517)279-8095. **Contact:** J. Richard Colbeck, committee chairperson. Estab. 1982. Previously unproduced monetarily. "To encourage playwrights to submit their work, to present a previously unproduced play in full production." Submit script with SASE. "We reserve right to produce winning script. Deadline: End of year. Guidelines for SASE. Prize: 1st-$300, 2nd-$100, 3rd-$50.

PILGRIM PROJECT GRANTS, 156 Fifth, #400, New York NY 10010. (212)627-2288. Fax: (212)627-2184. **Contact:** Davida Goldman. Grants for a reading, workshop production or full production of plays that deal with questions of moral significance. Deadline: Ongoing. Guidelines for SASE. Prize: Grants of $1,000-7,000.

PLAYHOUSE ON THE SQUARE NEW PLAY COMPETITION, Playhouse on the Square, 51 S. Cooper, Memphis TN 38104. **Contact:** Jackie Nichols. Submissions required to be unproduced. Deadline: April 1. Guidelines for SASE. Prize: $500 and production.

PLAYWRIGHT DISCOVERY PROGRAM, VSA Arts Connection, 1300 Connecticut Ave. NW, Suite 700, Washington DC 20036. (202)628-2800. Fax: (202)737-0725. E-mail: playwright@vsarts.org. Website: www.vsarts.org. **Contact:** Dani Fox, special events manager. Invites students with and without disabilities (grades 6-12) to submit a one-act play that documents the experience of living with a disability. Two plays will be selected for production at the John F. Kennedy Center for the Performing Arts. Deadline: May 15. Guidelines for SASE. Prize: Monetary award and a trip to Washington D.C. to view the production or staged reading.

N! PRIME TIME TELEVISION COMPETITION, Austin Film Festival, 1604 Nueces, Austin TX 78701. (512)478-4795. Fax: (512)478-6205. E-mail: austinfilm@aol.com. Website: www.austinfilmfestival.com. **Contact:** BJ Burrow. Offered annually for unpublished work to discover talented television writers and introduce their work to production companies. Categories: Drama and Sitcom. Contest open to writers who do not earn a living writing for television or film. Deadline: March 15. Guidelines for SASE. Charges $25. Prize: $1,500 in each category.

N! PRINCESS GRACE AWARDS PLAYWRIGHT FELLOWSHIP, Princess Grace Foundation—USA, 150 E. 58th St., 21st Floor, New York NY 10155. (212)317-1470. Fax: (212)317-1473. E-mail: pgfusa@pgfusa.com. Website: www.pgfusa.com. **Contact:** Ms. Toby E. Boshak, executive director. Offered annually for unpublished submissions to support playwright through residency program with New Dramatists, Inc., located in New York City. Entrants must be US citizens or have US status. Deadline: March 31. Guidelines for SASE. Prize: $7,500 plus residency with New Dramatists, Inc., in New York City.

N! PUTTIN' ON THE RITZ, ONE-ACT PLAY CONTEST, Puttin' On the Ritz, Inc., 915 White Horse Pike, Oaklyn NJ 08107. (856)858-5230. Fax: (856)858-0812. E-mail: srcoar@aol.com. Website: www.puttinontheritz.org. **Contact:** Stephen R. Coar, outreach director/new play festival director. Offered annually "to encourage playwrights by the production of their new works. We especially encourage playwrights from the New Jersey/Philadelphia region." "We receive about 125 plays, and of those, produce three or four." Plays that have been professionally produced will not be considered. "Plays that run 40 minutes or less preferred. Plays without a SASE will not be returned." Open to any writer. Deadline: January 31. Prize: Production of selected plays.

ROCHESTER PLAYWRIGHT FESTIVAL, Midwest Theatre Network, 5031 Tongen Ave. NW, Rochester MN 55901. (507)281-1472. E-mail: sweens@uswest.net. **Contact:** Joan Sween, executive director. Offered every two years for unpublished submissions to support emerging playwrights. No categories, but entries are considered for production by various types of theaters: Community theater, dinner theater, issues theater, satiric/new format theater, children's theater, musical theater. Entry form required. Guidelines and entry form for SASE. No fee for first entry. Subsequent entries by same author, $10 fee. Open to any writer. Prize: Full production, travel stipend, accomodations, plus $300 cash prize.

N! RICHARD RODGERS AWARDS IN MUSICAL THEATER, American Academy of Arts and Letters, 633 W. 155th St., New York NY 10032-7599. (212)368-5900. Fax: (212)491-4615. **Contact:** Lydia Kaim. Estab. 1978. The Richard Rodgers Awards subsidize full productions, studio productions and staged readings by nonprofit theaters in New York City of works by American composers and writers who are not already established in the field of musical theater. Guidelines and application for SASE. Deadline: November 1.

THE LOIS AND RICHARD ROSENTHAL NEW PLAY PRIZE, Cincinnati Playhouse in the Park, Box 6537, Cincinnati OH 45206-0537. (513)345-2242. Website: www.cincyplay.com. **Contact:** Literary Associate. Annual award for playwrights and musical playwrights. "The Lois and Richard Rosenthal New Play Prize was established in 1987 to encourage the development of new plays that are original, theatrical, strong in character and dialogue, and make a significant contribution to the literature of American theatre. Residents of Cincinnati, the Rosenthals are committed to supporting arts organizations and social agencies that are innovative and that foster social change." Plays must be full-length in any style: Comedy, drama, musical, etc. Translations, adaptations, individual one-acts and any play previously submitted for the Rosenthal Prize are not eligible. Collaborations are welcome, in which case prize benefits are shared. Plays must be unpublished prior to submission and may not have received a full-scale, professional production. Plays that have had a workshop, reading or non-professional production are still eligible. Playwrights with past production experience are especially encouraged to submit new work. Submit a two-page maximum abstract of the play including title, character breakdown, story synopsis and playwright information (bio or résumé). Also include up to 5 pages of sample dialogue. If submitting a musical, please include a tape or CD of selections from the score. All abstracts and dialogue samples will be read. From these, selected manuscripts will be solicited. Do not send a manuscript with or instead of the abstract. Unsolicited manuscripts will not be read. Submitted materials, including tapes and CDs,will be returned only if a SAE with adequate postage is provided. Only one submission per playwright/year. Deadline: July 1-December 31. Prize: A full production at Cincinnati Playhouse in the Park as part of the annual season and regional and national promotion; and $10,000 award plus travel and residency expenses for the Cincinnati rehearsal period.

THE SCREENWRITER'S PROJECT, Cyclone Entertainment Group/Cyclone Productions, P.O. Box 148849, Chicago IL 60614-8849. (773)665-7600. Fax: (773)665-7660. E-mail: cycprod@aol.com or cyclone@cyclone-entertainment.com. Website: www.cyclone-entertainment.com. **Contact:** Lee Alan, director. Offered annually to give both experienced and first-time writers the opportunity to begin a career as a screenwriter. Cyclone Productions Inc. intends to produce the finest of submissions to The Screenwriter's Project. Deadline: August 1. Guidelines for SASE. Charges $40 fee for July 1 deadline; $45 for August 1 deadline; $50 fee for September 1 deadline. Prize: Three $5,000 grants.

SIENA COLLEGE INTERNATIONAL PLAYWRIGHTS COMPETITION, Siena College Theatre Program, 515 Loudon Rd., Loudonville NY 12211-1462. (518)783-2381. Fax: (518)783-4293. E-mail: maciag@siena.edu. Website: www.siena.edu/theatre. **Contact:** Gary Maciag, director of theatre. Offered every 2 years for unpublished plays "to allow students to explore production collaboration with the playwright. In addition, it provides the playwright an important development opportunity. Plays should be previously unproduced, unpublished, full-length, non-musicals and free of copyright and royalty restrictions. Plays should require unit set or minimal changes and be suitable for a college-age cast of 3-10. There is a required 6-week residency." Guidelines for SASE. Guidelines are available after November 1 in odd-numbered years. Winning playwright must agree that the Siena production will be the world premiere of the play. Deadline: February 1 to June 30 in even-numbered years. Prize: $2,000 honorarium; up to $1,000 to cover expenses for required residency; full production of winning script.

DOROTHY SILVER PLAYWRITING COMPETITION, The Eugene S. & Blanche R. Halle Theatre of the Jewish Community Center, 3505 Mayfield Rd., Cleveland Heights OH 44118. (216)382-4000 ext. 274. Fax: (216)382-5401. E-mail: halletheatre@clerejcc.org. **Contact:** Amy Kenerup, administrative director. Estab. 1948. All entries must be original works, not previously produced, suitable for a full-length presentation; directly concerned with the Jewish experience. Deadline: June 15. Prize: Cash award plus staged reading.

SOUTHEASTERN THEATRE CONFERENCE NEW PLAY PROJECT, P.O. Box 9868, Greensboro NC 27429. (910)272-3645. Fax: (910)272-8810. Website: www.setc.org. **Contact:** Susan Sharp. Offered annually for the discovery, development and publicizing of worthy new unproduced plays and playwrights. Eligibility limited to members of 10 state SETC Region: AL, FL, GA, KY, MS, NC, SC, TN, VA or WV. Bound full-length or two related one-acts under single cover (one submission only). No musicals or children's plays. Deadline: March 1-June 1. Guidelines for SASE. Prize: $1,000, staged reading at SETC Convention, expenses paid trip to convention and preferred consideration for National Playwrights Conference.

SOUTHERN APPALACHIAN PLAYWRIGHTS' CONFERENCE, Southern Appalachian Repertory Theatre, P.O. Box 1720, Mars Hill NC 28754. (828)689-1384. Fax: (828)689-1272. E-mail: SART@mhc.edu. Website: www.sartheatre.com. **Contact:** Deborah R. Austin, managing director. Offered annually for unpublished, unproduced plays to promote the development of new plays. All plays are considered for later production with honorarium provided for the playwright. Deadline: October 31 (postmark). Guidelines for SASE. Prize: 5 playwrights are invited for readings in late March, room and board provided.

SOUTHERN PLAYWRIGHTS COMPETITION, Jacksonville State University 700 Pelham Rd. N., Jacksonville AL 36265-1602. (256)782-5411. Fax: (256)782-5441. E-mail: swhitton@jsucc.jsu.edu. Website: www.jsu.edu/depart/english/southpla.htm. **Contact:** Steven J. Whitton. Estab. 1988. Offered annually to identify and encourage the best of Southern playwriting. Playwrights must be a native or resident of AL, AR, FL, GA, KY, LA, MO, NC, SC, TN, TX, VA or WV. Deadline: February 15. Guidelines for SASE. Prize: $1,000 and production of the play.

SOUTHWEST THEATRE ASSOCIATION NATIONAL NEW PLAY CONTEST, Southwest Theatre Association, University of Texas at Arlington, Box 19103, Theatre Arts Program, Arlington TX 76019-0103. E-mail: gaupp@uta.edu. Website: www.southwest-theater.com. **Contact:** Andrew Gaupp, co-chair. Annual contest for unpublished, unproduced work to promote the writing and production of new one-act or full-length plays. No musicals, translations, adaptations of previously produced or published work, or children's plays. Guidelines for SASE or by e-mail. Open to writers who reside in the US. One entry per writer. Deadline: March 15. Charges $10. Prize: $200 honorarium, a reading at the annual SWTA conference, complimentary registration at conference, one-year membership in SWTA, award plaque and possibility of excerpt publication in the professional journal of SWTA.

⚡ SPIRITUAL THEATER INTERNATIONAL NEW PLAYWRIGHT AWARDS, Spiritual Theater International, P.O. Box 538, Littleton CO 80160. E-mail: info@spiritualtheater.com. Website: www.spiritualtheater.com. **Contact:** Carl Anderson. Offered annually for unpublished plays. "Spiritual Theater International is dedicated exclusively to bringing uplifting, positive stories to the stage. Our ideal submission tells an uplifting story with vivid characters in compelling situations. We do not accept violent or sexually explicit material. Every year we showcase our best new works at the STI Denver Theater Festival, where a panel of industry judges selects one new play for full production." Guidelines for SASE or on website. Acquires all rights. Open to any writer. Deadline: February 1. Prize: 1st-full production and $1,000; 2nd-$750; 3rd-$500.

STANLEY DRAMA AWARD, Dept. of Theatre Wagner College, One Campus Rd., Staten Island NY 10301. (718)390-3157. Fax: (718)390-3323. **Contact:** Tanya Sweet, director. Offered for original full-length stage plays, musicals or one-act play sequences that have not been professionally produced or received trade book publication. Deadline: October 1. Guidelines for SASE. Prize: $2,000.

⚡ TCG/METROPOLITAN LIFE FOUNDATION EXTENDED COLLABORATION GRANTS, Theatre Communications Group Inc., 355 Lexington Ave., New York NY 10017-6603. (212)697-5230. Fax: (212)983-4847. E-mail: grants@tcg.org. Website: www.tcg.org. **Contact:** Emilya Cachapero, director of artistic programs. Program is "designed to allow writers to work collaboratively with other artists for a period beyond the sponsoring theatre's normal preproduction and rehearsal schedule. Grants of $5,000 will be awarded 2 times in 2002. Only artistic leaders of TCG Constituent member theatres can apply on behalf of the writer. Applications will be mailed to TCG Constituent Theatres."

TEXAS PLAYWRIGHT'S DIVISION, Stages Repertory Theatre, 3201 Allen Pkwy., Suite 101, Houston TX 77019. (713)527-0220. Fax: (713)527-8669. Website: www.stagestheatre.com. **Contact:** Rob Bundy, artistic director. Offered annually to provide an outlet for unpublished Texas playwrights. Guidelines for SASE or on website. Writer must be a current or previous resident of Texas, or the play must be set in Texas or have a Texas theme. Deadline: October 1-February 15. Prize: A reading by professional actors and prizes awarded.

⚡ THEATRE BC'S ANNUAL CANADIAN NATIONAL PLAYWRITING COMPETITION, Theatre BC, P.O. Box 2031, Nanaimo, British Columbia V9R 6X6, Canada. (250)714-0203. Fax: (250)714-0213. E-mail: pwc@theatrebc.org. Website: www.theatrebc.org. **Contact:** Robb Mowbray, executive director. Offered annually to unpublished plays "to promote the development and production of previously unproduced new plays (no musicals) at all levels of theater. Categories: Full-Length (2 acts or longer); One-Act (less than 60 minutes); and an open Special Merit (juror's discretion). Guidelines for SASE or on website. Winners are also invited to New Play Festival: 18 hours with a professional dramaturg, registrant actors and a public reading in Kamloops (every spring). Production and publishing rights remain with the playwright. Open to Canadian residents. All submissions are made under pseudonyms. E-mail inquiries welcome. Deadline: Fourth Monday in July. Charges $35/entry and optional $25 for written critique. Prize: Full-Length-$1,500; One-Act-$1,000; Special Merit-$750.

⚡ THEATRE CONSPIRACY ANNUAL NEW PLAY CONTEST, Theatre Conspiracy, 10091 McGregor Blvd., Ft. Myers FL 33919. (941)936-3239. Fax: (941)936-0510. E-mail: theatreconspiracy@prodigy.net. **Contact:** Bill Taylor, award director. Offered annually for unpublished full-length plays with 8 or less characters and simple production demands. Open to any writer. Deadline: November 30. Guidelines for SASE. Charges $5 fee. Prize: $500 and full production.

⚡ THEATRE PEI NEW VOICES PLAYWRITING AWARDS, P.E.I. Council of the Arts, 115 Richmond St., Charlottetown, Prince Edward Island C1A 1H7, Canada. (902)368-4410. Fax: (902)368-4418. E-mail: theatre@isn.net. **Contact:** Robert MacLean, artistic director. Offered annually. Open to individuals who have been resident of Prince Edward Island at least 6-12 months preceding the deadline for entries. Deadline: February 15. Guidelines for SASE. Charges $5 fee. Prize: Monetary.

⚡ THEATRE RESIDENCY PROGRAM FOR PLAYWRIGHTS, National Endowment for the Arts/Theatre Communications Group, 355 Lexington Ave., New York NY 10017. (212)697-5230. E-mail: grants@tcg.org. **Contact:** Emilya Cachapero. Offered annually to recognize that theatre institutions want to support and provide homes for artists, and that artists have a reciprocal role to play in helping to strengthen theaters. In both programs the writers need to be connected to theatres. The application guidelines detail the specific requirements. Application is downloadable at www.tcg.org. Deadline: March. Prize: $25,000 awarded directly to the playwright with $5,000 in support for the host theatre. Travel funds available for the playwright.

⚡ THEATREFEST REGIONAL PLAYWRITING CONTEST, Theatrefest, Montclair State University, Upper Montclair NJ 07043. (973)655-7071. Fax: (973)655-5335. E-mail: kellyl@mail.montclair.edu. Website: www.montclair.edu. **Contact:** John Wooten, artistic director. Offered annually for unpublished work to encourage and nurture the work of American dramatists. Open to any writer in the tri-state area (New Jersey, New York, Connecticut). Deadline: January 7. Guidelines for SASE. Prize: 1st-$1,500 and equity production; runners-up(2)-$500. Theatrefest has option to re-option play after production at Theatrefest.

N THUNDERBIRD FILMS SCREENPLAY COMPETITION, Thunderbird Films, 214 Riverside Dr. #112, New York NY 10025. (212)352-4498. Website: home.att.net/thunderbirdfilms. **Contact:** Eric Stannard. Offered annually for unpublished work to encourage, promote and reward writers of original, well-crafted screenplays. Open to any writer. Deadline: Varies. Guidelines for SASE. Charges $40 fee. Prize: $1,000 and possible option by Thunderbird Films.

TRUSTUS PLAYWRIGHTS' FESTIVAL, Trustus Theatre, Box 11721, Columbia SC 29211-1721. (803)254-9732. Fax: (803)771-9153. E-mail: trustus@trustus.org. Website: www.trustus.org. **Contact:** Jon Tuttle, literary manager. Offered annually for professionally unproduced full-length plays; cast limit of 8; prefer challenging, innovative dramas and comedies; no musicals, plays for young audiences or "hillbilly" southern shows. Guidelines and application for SASE. Deadline: March 1; no submissions before January 1. Prize: Public staged-reading and $250, followed after a one-year development period by full production, $500, plus travel/accommodations to attend opening.

UNICORN THEATRE NEW PLAY DEVELOPMENT, (formerly Unicorn Theatre National Playwrights' Award), Unicorn Theatre, 3828 Main St., Kansas City MO 64111. (816)531-7529 ext. 18. Fax: (816)531-0421. Website: www.unicorntheatre.org. **Contact:** Herman Wilson, literary assistant. Offered annually to encourage and assist the development of an unpublished and unproduced play. Acquires 2% subsidiary rights of future productions for a 5-year period. Deadline: Ongoing. Guidelines for SASE. Prize: $1,000 and production.

N UNIVERSITY OF ALABAMA NEW PLAYWRIGHTS PROGRAM, P.O. Box 870239, Tuscaloosa AL 35487-0239. (205)348-9032. Fax: (205)348-9048. E-mail: pcastagn@woodsquad.as.ua.edu. Website: www.as.ua.edu/theatre/npp.htm. Estab. 1982. Director/Dramaturg: Dr. Paul C. Castagno. Full-length plays for mainstage; experimental plays for B stage. Workshops and small musicals can be proposed. Queries responded to quickly. Competitive stipend. Development process includes readings, visitations, and possible complete productions with faculty director and dramaturg. Up to 6 months assessment time. Deadline: Submit August-March, by October for Janus Fest in January. Guidelines for SASE.

N UNIVERSITY OF BRITISH COLUMBIA'S CREATIVE WRITING RESIDENCY PRIZE IN STAGEPLAY, Prism International, Buch E462, 1866 Main Mall, University of British Columbia, Vancouver, British Columbia V6T 1Z1, Canada. (604)822-2514. Fax: (604)822-3616. E-mail: prism@interchange.ubc.ca. Website: www.arts.ubc.ca/prism. **Contact:** Editor. Offered in even years to award the best in contemporary drama. Buys first North American serial rights (included in payment of prize). Deadline: April 30. Charges $50. Prize: One month writer-in-residency at UBC, to the value of $25,000 plus expenses; and a public performance of the play.

N VERMONT PLAYWRIGHT'S AWARD, The Valley Players, P.O. Box 441, Waitsfield VT 05673. (802)496-3751. E-mail: valleyplayers@madriver.com. Website: www.valleyplayers.com. **Contact:** Jennifer Howard, chair. Offered annually for unpublished nonmusical, full-length play suitable for production by a community theater group to encourage development of playwrights in Vermont, New Hampshire and Maine. Deadline: February 1. Prize: $1,000.

N THE HERMAN VOADEN NATIONAL PLAYWRITING COMPETITION, Drama Department, Queen's University, Kingston, Ontario K7L 3N6, Canada. (613)533-2104. E-mail: hannac@post.queensu.ca. Website: www.queensu.ca/drama. **Contact:** Carol Anne Hanna. Offered every 2 years for unpublished plays to discover and develop new Canadian plays. See website for deadlines, guidelines. Open to Canadian citizens or landed immigrants. Charges $30 entry fee. Prize: $3,000, $2,000 and $1,000. 1st- and 2nd-prize winners are offered a one-week workshop and public reading by professional director and cast. The 3rd-prize winner will be offered a one-day workshop. The three authors will be playrwrights-in-residence for the rehearsal and reading period.

N VSA ARTS PLAYWRIGHT DISCOVERY AWARD, VSA arts, John F. Kennedy Center for the Performing Arts, 1300 Connecticut Ave. NW, Suite 700, Washington DC 20036. (202)628-2800. Fax: (202)737-0725. E-mail: playwright@vsarts.org. Website: www.vsarts.org. **Contact:** Dani Fox, events manager. Offered annually for unpublished work. "Students grades 6-12 are invited to submit an original one-act script that examines the experience of living with a disability. The award challenges student writers with and without disabilities to create a one-act script about their own life, or about experiences in the life of another person or fictional character." Authors must be US citizens or permanent residents of the US. Guidelines for SASE, by e-mail or on website. Deadline: Varies, usually in mid-May. Prize: Monetary award along with an expense-paid trip to the Kennedy Center in Washington DC to see their scripts performed live.

WEST COAST ENSEMBLE FULL-PLAY COMPETITION, West Coast Ensemble, P.O. Box 38728, Los Angeles CA 90038. (323)876-9337. Fax: (323)876-8916. **Contact:** Les Hanson, artistic director. Estab. 1982. Offered annually for unpublished plays in Southern California. No musicals or children's plays for full-play competition. No restrictions on subject matter. Deadline: December 31.

JACKIE WHITE MEMORIAL NATIONAL CHILDREN'S PLAYWRITING CONTEST, Columbia Entertainment Co., 309 Parkade, Columbia MO 65202. (573)874-5628. **Contact:** Betsy Phillips, director. Offered annually for unpublished plays. "Searching for good scripts suitable for audiences of all ages to be performed by the 25-40 students, grade 6-9, in our theater school. Deadline: June 1. Guidelines for SASE. Charges $10 fee. Prize: $250, full production and travel expenses to see production; company reserves the right to grant prize money without production.

WICHITA STATE UNIVERSITY PLAYWRITING CONTEST, University Theatre, Wichita State University, Wichita KS 67260-0153. (316)978-3360. Fax: (316)978-3202. E-mail: kiralyfa@twsuvm.uc.twsu.edu. Website: www.fin earts.twsu.edu/performing/theatre.asp. **Contact:** Bela Kiralyfalvi. Estab. 1974. Offered for unpublished, unproduced full-length or 2-3 short plays of at least 90 minutes playing time. No musicals or children's plays. Contestants must be graduate or undergraduate students in a US college or university. Deadline: February 15. Guidelines for SASE. Prize: Production of winning play (ACTF) and expenses-paid trip for playwright to see final rehearsals and/or performances.

YEAR END SERIES (YES) NEW PLAY FESTIVAL, Department of Theatre, Nunn Dr., Northern Kentucky University, Highland Heights KY 41099-1007. (606)572-6362. Fax: (606)572-6057. E-mail: forman@nku.edu. **Contact:** Sandra Forman, project director. Offered in even years for unpublished full-length plays and musicals. Open to all writers. Deadline: October 31. Guidelines for SASE. Prize: $500 and an expense-paid visit to Northern Kentucky University to see the play produced.

N: YOUNG CONNECTICUT PLAYWRIGHTS FESTIVAL, Maxwell Anderson Playwrights Series, P.O. Box 671, West Redding CT 06896. (203)938-2770. **Contact:** Bruce Post. Offered annually for unpublished plays to offer recognition and encouragement to young playwrights. Open to Connecticut residents ages 12-19. Deadline: April 3. Guidelines for SASE. Prize: Awards ceremony, professionally staged reading for 4 finalists.

YOUNG PLAYWRIGHTS FESTIVAL, Young Playwrights Inc., Suite 906, 321 W. 44th St., New York NY 10036. (212)307-1140. Fax: (212)307-1454. E-mail: writeaplay@aol.com. Website: http://youngplaywrights.org. **Contact:** Literary Department. Offered annually for stage plays (no musicals, screenplays or adaptations). Writers ages 18 or younger (as of deadline) are invited to send scripts. Deadline: December 1. Guidelines for SASE. Prize: Winning plays will be performed in professional Off Broadway production.

ANNA ZORNIO MEMORIAL CHILDREN'S THEATRE PLAYWRIGHTING AWARD, University of New Hampshire, Dept. of Theatre and Dance, PCAC, 30 College Rd., Durham NH 03824-3538. (603)862-2919. Fax: (603)862-0298. E-mail: jbrinker@cisunix.unh.edu. Website: www.unh.edu/theatre-dance. **Contact:** Julie Brinker. Offered annually for unpublished well-written plays or musicals appropriate for young audiences with a maximum length of 60 minutes. Guidelines and entry forms for SASE. May submit more than one play, but not more than three. Open to all playwrights in US and Canada. All ages are invited to participate. Deadline: September 1. Prize: Up to $1,000 to winning playwright(s) and public production by the UNH Theatre for Youth Program.

Journalism

N: THE AMERICAN LEGION FOURTH ESTATE AWARD, The American Legion, 700 N. Pennsylvania, Indianapolis IN 46206. (317)630-1253. Fax: (317)630-1368. E-mail: PR@legion.org. Website: www.legion.org. Offered annually for journalistic works published the previous calendar year. "Subject matter must deal with a topic or issue of national interest or concern. Entry must include cover letter explaining entry, and any documention or evidence of the entry's impact on the community, state or nation. No printed entry form." Guidelines for SASE or on website. Judged by a volunteer panel of four practicing print or broadcast journalists and/or educators judges the entries. Judges submit their recommendation to the National Public Relations Commission for final approval. Deadline: January 31. Prize: $2,000 stipend to defray expenses of recipient accepting the award at The American Legion National Convention in September.

AMY WRITING AWARDS, The Amy Foundation, P.O. Box 16091, Lansing MI 48901. (517)323-6233. Fax: (517)323-7293. E-mail: amyfoundtn@aol.com. Website: www.amyfound.org. **Contact:** James Russell, president. Estab. 1985. Offered annually for nonfiction articles containing scripture published in the previous calendar year in the secular media. Deadline: January 31. Prize: $10,000, $5,000, $4,000, $3,000, $2,000 and 10 prizes of $1,000.

ATLANTIC JOURNALISM AWARDS, School of Journalism, University of King's College, 6350 Coburg Rd., Halifax, Nova Scotia B3H 2A1, Canada. (902)422-1271 ext. 150. Fax: (902)425-8183. E-mail: pamela.herod@ukings.ns. ca. Website: http://aja.ukings.ns.ca. **Contact:** Stephen Kimber or Pamela Herod. Offered annually to recognize excellence and achievement by journalists in Atlantic Canada. Guidelines and entry forms available via mail request, or website (download entry form). Entries are usually nominated by editors, news directors, etc. Freelancers are eligible to enter. "We request permission from winning entrants to publish their work on our website. It is not published without their consent." The competition is open to any journalist living in Atlantic Canada whose entry was originally published or broadcast during the previous year in Atlantic Canada. Deadline: January 15. Prize: A plaque presented at an awards dinner.

N AVENTIS PASTEUR MEDAL FOR EXCELLENCE IN HEALTH RESEARCH JOURNALISM, Canadians for Health Research, P.O. Box 126, Westmount, Quebec H3Z 2T1, Canada. (514)398-7478. Fax: (514)398-8361. E-mail: info@chrcrm.org. Website: www.chrcrm.org. **Contact:** Linda Bazinet. Offered annually for work published the previous calendar year in Canadian newspapers or magazines. Applicants must have demonstrated an interest and effort in reporting health research issues within Canada. Guidelines for SASE or on website. Deadline: Late February (date TBD). Prize: $2,500 and a medal.

N ERIK BARNOUW AWARD, Organization of American Historians, 112 N. Bryan Ave., Bloomington IN 47408-4199. (812)855-9852. Fax: (812)855-0696. E-mail: awards@oah.org. Website: www.oah.org. **Contact:** Kara Hamm. One or two awards are given annually in recognition of outstanding reporting or programming on network or cable television, or in documentary film, concerned with American history, the study of American history, and/or the promotion of history. Entries must have been released the year of the contest. Deadline: December 1. Guidelines for SASE. Prize: Certificate.

N THE WHITMAN BASSOW AWARD, Overseas Press Club of America, 40 W. 45th St., New York NY 10036. (212)626-9220. Fax: (212)626-9210. Website: www.opcofamerica.org. **Contact:** Sonya Fry, executive director. Offered annually for best reporting in any medium on international environmental issues. Work must be published by US-based publications or broadcast. Deadline: January 29. Charges $100 fee. Prize: Certificate and $1,000.

N MIKE BERGER AWARD, Columbia University Graduate School of Journalism, 2950 Broadway, New York NY 10027-7004. (212)854-5047. Fax: (212)854-3148. Website: www.jrn.columbia.edu. **Contact:** Jonnet Abeles. Offered annually honoring "human interest reporting about the daily life of New York City in the traditions of the late Meyer 'Mike' Berger. Deadline: February 15. Guidelines for SASE. Prize: Cash prize.

N THE WORTH BINGHAM PRIZE, The Worth Bingham Memorial Fund, 1616 H ST. NW, Third Floor, Washington DC 20006. (202)737-3700. Fax: (202)737-0530. E-mail: susan@icfj.org. **Contact:** Susan Talaly, project director. Offered annually to articles published during the year of the award. "The Prize honors newspaper or magazine investigative reporting of stories of national significance where the public interest is being ill-served. Entries may include a single story, a related series of stories or up to three unrelated stories. Deadline: January 4. Guidelines for SASE. Prize: $10,000.

N HEYWOOD BROUN AWARD, The Newspaper Guild-CWA, 501 Third St. NW, Washington DC 20001-2797. (202)434-7173. Fax: (202)434-1472. E-mail: azipser@cwa-union.org. Website: www.newsguild.org. **Contact:** Andy Zipser. Offered annually for works published the previous year. "This annual competition is intended to encourage and recognize individual journalistic achievement by members of the working media, particularly if it helps right a wrong or correct an injustice. First consideration will be given to entries on behalf of individuals or teams of no more than two. Deadline: Last Friday in January. Guidelines for SASE. Prize: Plaque and $5,000.

N ⬛ CANADIAN FOREST SERVICE JOURNALISM AWARDS, Canadian Forest Service/National Resources Canada, c/o CSWA, P.O. Box 75, Station A, Toronto, Ontario M5W 1A2, Canada. (416)408-4566. Fax: (416)408-1044. E-mail: cswa@interlog.com. Website: www.interlog.com/~cswa. **Contact:** Andy F. Visser-deVries. Offered annually for work published in Canadian publications the previous calendar year to recognize outstanding journalism that promotes public awareness of forests and issues surrounding forests in Canada. Two categories: Newspaper and magazine. Material becomes property of Canadian Forest Service; mss will not be returned. Deadline: February 15. Guidelines for SASE. Prize: $1,000 and a plaque for each category.

N HARRY CHAPIN MEDIA AWARDS, World Hunger Year, 505 Eighth Ave., Suite 2100, New York NY 10018-6582. (212)629-8850 ext. 122. Fax: (212)465-9274. E-mail: media@worldhungeryear.org. Website: www.worldhungeryear.org. **Contact:** Lisa Ann Batitto. Estab. 1982. Open to works published the previous calendar year. Critical issues of domestic and world hunger, poverty and development (newspaper, periodical, TV, radio, photojournalism, books). Deadline: mid-January. Guidelines for SASE. Charges $25 for 1 entry, $40 for 2 entries or $50 for 3-5 entries. Prize: Several prizes from $1,000-2,500.

CONGRESSIONAL FELLOWSHIP PROGRAM, American Political Science Association, 1527 New Hampshire Ave. NW, Washington DC 20036-1206. (202)483-2512. Fax: (202)483-2657. E-mail: amdonald@apsanet.org. Website: www.apsanet.org/about/CFP/. **Contact:** Allison MacDonald. Offered annually for professional journalists who have 2-10 years of full-time professional experience in newspaper, magazine, radio or television reporting at time of application to learn more about the legislative process through direct participation. Visit our website for deadlines. Open to journalists and scholars. Prize: $35,000 and travel allowance for 3 weeks' orientation and legislation aide assignments December through August.

N FREEDOM OF THE PRESS AWARD, National Press Club, General Manager's Office, National Press Club, National Press Building, Washington DC 20045. (202)662-8744. E-mail: jbooze@npcpress.org. Website: npc.press.org. **Contact:** Joann Booze. Offered annually "to recognize members of the news media who have, through the publishing or broadcasting of news, promoted or helped to protect the freedom of the press" during the previous calendar year.

Categories: A US journalist or team for work published or broadcast in the US; a foreign journalist or team for work published or broadcast in their home country. Guidelines on website. Open to professional journalists. Deadline: April 1. Prize: $1,000 in each category.

ROBIN GOLDSTEIN AWARD FOR WASHINGTON REGIONAL REPORTING, National Press Foundation, National Press Bldg., Washington DC 20045. (202)662-8744. E-mail: jbooze@npcpress.org. Website: npc.press.org. **Contact:** Joann Booze. Offered annually for a Washington newspaper correspondent "who best exemplifies the standards set by the late Robin Goldstein, who established the Washington bureaus of the Asbury Park (NJ) Press and the Orange County (CA) Register. Working alone in each bureau, Goldstein proved that one dedicated reporter can do it all for the hometown readers—news, features, enterprise, analysis and columns. This contest honors reporters who demonstrate excellence and versatility in covering Washington from a local angle." Guidelines on website. Deadline: April 1. Prize: $1,000.

THE GREAT AMERICAN TENNIS WRITING AWARDS, Tennis Week, 341 Madison Ave., New York NY 10017. (212)808-4750. Fax: (212)983-6302. E-mail: tennisweek@tennisweek.com. Website: www.tennisweek.com. **Contact:** Heather Holland, managing editor. Estab. 1974. Category 1: Unpublished manuscript by an aspiring journalist with no previous national byline. Category 2: Unpublished manuscript by a non-tennis journalist. Category 3: Unpublished manuscript by a tennis journalist. Categories 4-6: Published tennis-related articles and book award. Deadline: December 15.

O. HENRY AWARD, The Texas Institute of Letters, Southwest Texas State University, San Marcos TX 78666. (512)245-2428. Fax: (512)245-7462. E-mail: mb13@swt.edu. Website: www.English.swt.edu/css/TIL/rules.htm. **Contact:** Mark Busby, secretary. Offered annually for work published January 1-December 31 of previous year to recognize the best-written work of journalism appearing in a magazine or weekly newspaper. Judged by a panel chosen by the TIL Council. Writer must have been born in Texas, have lived in Texas for at least two consecutive years at some time, or the subject matter of the work should be associated with Texas. Deadline: January 3. Guidelines for SASE. Prize: $1,000.

N EDWIN M. HOOD AWARD FOR DIPLOMATIC CORRESPONDENCE, National Press Club, General Manager's Office, National Press Club, National Press Building, Washington DC 20045. (202)662-8744. E-mail: jbooze@npcpress.org. Website: npc.press.org. **Contact:** Joann Booze. Offered annually to recognize excellence in reporting on diplomatic and foreign policy issues. Categories: Newspaper and broadcast. Guidelines on website. Deadline: April 1. Prize: $500 in each category.

N ICIJ AWARD FOR OUTSTANDING INTERNATIONAL INVESTIGATIVE REPORTING, International Consortium of Investigative Journalists, The Center for Public Integrity, 910 17th St. NW, Seventh Floor, Washington DC 20006. (202)466-1300. Fax: (202)466-1101. Website: www.icij.org. **Contact:** Maud Beelman. Offered annually for stories published between June 1, 2001, and June 1, 2002. Works produced in print, broadcast and online media are eligible; books are not eligible. Work must be on a transnational topic of world significance. Guidelines for SASE or on website. Deadline: July 15, 2002. Prize: 1st-$20,000; up to 5 finalist awards of $1,000 each.

INVESTIGATIVE JOURNALISM GRANT, The Fund For Investigative Journalism, P.O. Box 40339, Washington DC 20016. (202)362-0260. E-mail: fundfij@aol.com. Website: www.fij.org. **Contact:** John Hyde. Offered 3 times/year for original investigative newspaper and magazine stories, radio and TV documentaries, books and media criticism. Guidelines on website or by e-mail. The Fund also offers an annual $25,000 FIJ Book Prize in November for the best book chosen by the board during the year. Deadline: February 1, June 1 and October 1. Prize: Grants of $500-10,000.

N THE IOWA AWARD/THE TIM McGINNIS AWARD, The Iowa Review, 308 EPB, University of Iowa, Iowa City IA 52242. (319)335-0462. E-mail: iowa-review@uiowa.edu. Website: www.uiowa.edu/~iareview. **Contact:** David Hamilton. Offered annually for work already published in our magazine, usually within the previous year. The Iowa Award is a judge's choice of the best work of the year. The McGinnis Award is the editors' choice of a work that usually expresses an off-beat and (we hope) sophisticated sense of humor. Guidelines for SASE or on website. No entry form. Prize: $1,000 for Iowa Award; $500 for McGinnis Award.

N ANSON JONES, M.D. AWARD, Texas Medical Association, 401 W. 15th St., Austin TX 78701-1680. (512)370-1381. Fax: (512)370-1629. E-mail: allison.griffin@texmed.org. Website: www.texmed.org. **Contact:** Allison Griffin, media relations manager. Offered annually "to the media of Texas for excellence in communicating health information to the public." Open only to Texas media or writers published in Texas. Deadline: January 15. Guidelines for SASE. Prize: $1,000 for winners of each of the 6 categories.

DONALD E. KEYHOE JOURNALISM AWARD, Fund for UFO Research, P.O. Box 20815, Alexandria VA 22320-1815. (703)684-6032. Fax: (703)684-6032. E-mail: fufor@fufor.org. Website: www.fufor.com. **Contact:** Don Berliner, chairman. Estab. 1979. Offered annually for the best article or story published or broadcast in a newspaper, magazine, TV or radio news outlet during the previous calendar year. Prize: Separate awards for print and broadcast media; also makes unscheduled cash awards for published works on UFO phenomena research or public education.

N **ROBERT L. KOZIK AWARD FOR ENVIRONMENTAL REPORTING**, National Press Foundation, General Manager's Office, National Press Club, National Press Building, Washington DC 20045. (202)662-8744. E-mail: jbooze@npcpress.org. Website: npc.press.org. **Contact:** Joann Booze. Offered annually to recognize excellence in environmental reporting at the local, national or international level that impacted or prompted action to remedy an environmental situation. Categories: Print and broadcast. Guidelines on website. Deadline: April 1. Prize: $500 and Kozik medal in each category.

HERB LAMPERT STUDENT WRITING AWARD, Canadian Science Writers' Association, P.O. Box 75, Station A, Toronto, Ontario M5W 1A2, Canada. (416)408-4566. E-mail: cswa@interlog.com. Website: www.interlog.com/~cswa. Contest/Award Director: Andy F. Visser-deVries. Offered annually to any student science writer who has an article published in a student or other newspaper or magazine or aired on a radio or TV station in Canada. Open to any Canadian resident or citizen. Deadline: February 15. Guidelines for SASE. Prize: $750 for print and broadcast winners.

LIVINGSTON AWARDS FOR YOUNG JOURNALISTS, Mollie Parnis Livingston Foundation, Wallace House, 620 Oxford, Ann Arbor MI 48104. (734)998-7575. Fax: (734)998-7979. E-mail: LivingstonAwards@umich.edu. Website: www.livawards.org. **Contact:** Charles Eisendrath. Offered annually for journalism published January 1-December 31 the previous year to recognize and further develop the abilities of young journalists. Includes print, online and broadcast. Guidelines on website. Judges include Mike Wallace, Ellen Goodman and Tom Brokaw. Open to journalists who are 34 years or younger as of December 31 of previous year and whose work appears in US controlled print or broadcast media. Prize: 3-$10,000: 1 each for local reporting, national reporting and international reporting.

N **FELIX MORLEY JOURNALISM COMPETITION**, Institute for Humane Studies, 3401 N. Fairfax Dr., Suite 440, Arlington VA 22201-4432. 1-800-697-8799. Fax: (703)993-4890. E-mail: dalban@gmu.edu. Website: www.theihs.org. **Contact:** Dan Alban. Offered annually for nonfiction published July 1, 2000-December 31, 2001, to reward young writers who effectively address individual rights and free markets in their work. Writers must be either full-time students or under age 25 as of the deadline. Prize: 1st-$2,500; 2nd-$1,000; 3rd-$750; and $250 to several runners-up.

N **ROBERT T. MORSE AWARD**, American Psychiatric Association, 1400 K St. NW, Washington DC 20005. (202)682-6141. Fax: (202)682-6255. E-mail: sfoster@psych.org. Website: www.psych.org. **Contact:** Sharon Foster. Offered annually for work published August 1-July 31. Recognizes outstanding achievements in media coverage of mental illness and psychiatric treatment. Deadline: August 1. Guidelines for SASE. Prize: $1,000 and a plaque.

FRANK LUTHER MOTT-KAPPA TAU ALPHA RESEARCH AWARD IN JOURNALISM, University of Missouri School of Journalism, Columbia MO 65211. (573)882-7685. E-mail: ktahq@showme.missouri.edu. Website: www.missouri.edu/~KTAHQ. **Contact:** Dr. Keith Sanders, executive director, Kappa Tau Alpha. Offered annually for best researched book in mass communication. Submit 6 copies; no forms required. Deadline: December 6. Prize: $1,000.

N **NATIONAL MAGAZINE AWARDS**, National Magazine Awards Foundation, 109 Vanderhoof Ave., Suite 207, Toronto, Ontario M4G 2H7, Canada. (416)422-1358. Fax: (416)422-3762. E-mail: nmaf@interlog.com. Website: www.nmaf.net. **Contact:** Pat Kendall. Offered annually for work by Canadian citizens or landed immigrants published in a Canadian magazine during the previous calendar year. 21 categories for written work, additional awards for photos and artwork. Guidelines for 8½×11 SASE. Deadline: Second Monday in January (January 14, 2002). Charges $50 per entry. Prize: President's Medal, $3,000; Gold, $1,500; Silver, $500.

NATIONAL PRESS CLUB CONSUMER JOURNALISM AWARDS, National Press Club, National Press Bldg., Washington DC 20045. (202)662-8744. E-mail: jbooze@npcpress.org. Website: npc.press.org. **Contact:** Joann Booze. Offered annually to recognize excellence in reporting on consumer topics in the following categories: Newspapers, periodicals, television and radio. Entries must have been published/broadcast in the previous calendar year. Include a letter detailing how the piece or series resulted in action by consumers, the government, the community or an individual. Guidelines on website. Deadline: April 1. Prize: $500 for each category.

N **NATIONAL PRESS CLUB JOSEPH D. RYLE AWARD FOR EXCELLENCE IN WRITING ON THE PROBLEMS OF GERIATRICS**, National Press Club, General Manager's Office, National Press Club, National Press Building, Washington DC 20045. (202)662-8744. E-mail: jbooze@npcpress.org. Website: npc.press.org. **Contact:** Joann Booze. Offered annually for work published in the previous year. This award emphasizes excellence and objectivity in coverage of the problems faced by the elderly. Guidelines on website. Open to professional print journalists. Deadline: April 1. Prize: $2,000.

N **NATIONAL PRESS CLUB ONLINE JOURNALISM AWARD**, National Press Club, General Manager's Office, National Press Club, National Press Building, Washington DC 20045. (202)662-8744. E-mail: jbooze@npcpress.org. Website: npc.press.org. **Contact:** Joanne Booze. Offered annually to recognize the most significant contributions to journalism by the online media in two categories: Best Journalism Site (this award honors the best journalistic use of the online medium); and Distinguished Online Contribution (this award goes to the best individual contribution to public service using online technology). Guidelines on website. Deadline: April 1. Prize: $1,000 in each category.

N NATIONAL PRESS CLUB SANDY HUME MEMORIAL AWARD FOR EXCELLENCE IN POLITICAL JOURNALISM, National Press Club, General Manager's Office, National Press Club, National Press Building, Washington DC 20045. (202)662-8744. E-mail: jbooze@npcpress.org. Website: npc.press.org. **Contact:** Joann Booze. Offered annually for work published in the previous calendar year. "This award honors excellence and objectivity in political coverage by reporters 34 years old or younger. Named in memory of Sandy Hume, the reporter for *The Hill* who broke the story of the aborted 1997 coup against House Speaker Newt Gingrich, this prize can be awarded for a single story of great distinction or for continuing coverage of one political topic." Guidelines on website. Open to professional journalists 34 or younger. Deadline: April 1. Prize: $1,000.

NATIONAL PRESS CLUB WASHINGTON CORRESPONDENCE AWARDS, National Press Club, National Press Bldg., Washington DC 20045. (202)662-8744. E-mail: jbooze@npcpress.org. Website: npc.press.org. **Contact:** Joann Booze. Offered annually to honor the work of reporters who cover Washington for the benefit of the hometown audience. "This award is for a single report or series on one topic, not for national reporting, nor for a body of work. Entrants must demonstrate a clear knowledge of how Washington works and what it means to the folks back home." Guidelines on webiste. Deadline: April 1. Prize: $1,000.

NEWSLETTER JOURNALISM AWARD, National Press Club, National Press Bldg., Washington DC 20045. (202)662-8744. E-mail: jbooze@npcpress.org. Website: npc.press.org. **Contact:** Joann Booze. Offered annually to acknowledge excellence in newsletter journalism in 2 categories: Best analytical or interpretive reporting piece or best exclusive story. Entries must be published by an independent newsletter and serve the audience and mission of the newsletter. Guidelines on website. Deadline: April 1. Prize: $2,000 for each category.

ALICIA PATTERSON JOURNALISM FELLOWSHIP, Alicia Patterson Foundation, 1730 Pennsylvania Ave. NW, Suite 850, Washington DC 20006. (202)393-5995. Fax: (301)951-8512. E-mail: apfengel@charm.net. Website: www.aliciapatterson.org. **Contact:** Margaret Engel. Offered annually for previously published submissions to give 8-10 fulltime print journalists or photojournalists a year of in-depth research and reporting. Applicants must have 5 years of professional print journalism experience and be US citizens. Fellows write 4 magazine-length pieces for the *Alicia Patterson Reporter*, a quarterly magazine, during their fellowship year. Fellows must take a year's leave from their jobs, but may do other freelance articles during the year. Write, call, fax or check website for applications. Deadline: October 1. Prize: $35,000 stipend for calendar year.

N THE POPE AWARD FOR INVESTIGATIVE JOURNALISM, The Pope Foundation, 700 White Plains Rd., Scarsdale NY 10583. **Contact:** Catherine E. Pope, director. Offered annually to journalists who have been working for a minimum of 10 years. Deadline: November 1. Guidelines for SASE. Prize: 3 awards of $15,000 each.

PRINT MEDIA AWARD, International Reading Association, P.O. Box 8139, Newark DE 19714-8139. (302)731-1600 ext. 293. Fax: (302)731-1057. E-mail: jbutler@reading.org. Website: www.reading.org. **Contact:** Janet Butler. Offered annually for journalism published January 1-December 31 to recognize outstanding reporting in newspapers, magazines and wire services. Open to professional journalists. Deadline: January 15. Prize: Awards certificate, announced at annual convention.

THE PULLIAM JOURNALISM FELLOWSHIPS, The Indianapolis Star, a Gannet Co. publication, P.O. Box 145, Indianapolis IN 46206-0145. (317)444-6001 or (800)669-7827. Fax: (317)444-6750. E-mail: Russel.Pulliam@starnews.com. Website: www.starnews.com/pjf. **Contact:** Russell B. Pulliam. Offered annually as an intensive 10-week summer "training school" for college students with firm commitments to, and solid training in, newspaper journalism. "Call or e-mail us, and we'll send an application packet." Deadline: March 1. Prize: $5,775 for 10-week session, June-August.

THE MADELINE DANE ROSS AWARD, Overseas Press Club of America, 40 W. 45th St., New York NY 10036. (212)626-9220. Fax: (212)626-9210. E-mail: sonya@opcofamerica.org. Website: www.opcofamerica.org. **Contact:** Sonya Fry, executive director. Offered annually for best international reporting in any medium showing a concern for the human condition. Work must be published by US-based publications or broadcast. Deadline: Late January; date changes each year. Charges $100 fee. Prize: Certificate and $1,000.

N ARTHUR ROWSE AWARD FOR PRESS CRITICISM, General Manager's Office, National Press Club, National Press Building, Washington DC 20045. (202)662-8744. E-mail: jbooze@npcpress.org. Website: npc.press.org. **Contact:** Joann Booze. Offered annually for work published or broadcast the previous calendar year. "This award, sponsored by former *US News & World Report* reporter Arthur Rowse, honors excellence in examining the role and work of the news media. Categories: Single entry (1. Newspapers, magazines, newsletters and online; 2. Television and radio; 3. Books)and body of work (1. Newspapers, magazines, newsletters and online; 2. Television and radio). Guidelines on website. Open to professional journalists (with the exception of those entering as book authors). Deadline: April 1. Prize: $1,000 in each category.

N SCIENCE IN SOCIETY AWARD, National Association of Science Writers, Inc., P.O. Box 294, Greenlawn NY 11740. (516)757-5564. E-mail: diane@nasw.org. Website: www.nasw.org. **Contact:** Diane McGurgan. Offered annually for investigative or interpretive reporting about the sciences and their impact for good and bad. Six categories:

Newspaper, magazine, television, radio, book and Internet. Material may be a single article or broadcast or a series. Works must have been first published or broadcast in North America between June 1, 2001, and May 31, 2002; books must have a 2001 copyright date and may have been published any time that year. Deadline: July 1. Guidelines for SASE. Prize: $1,000 and a Certificate of Recognition.

[N] SCIENCE IN SOCIETY JOURNALISM AWARDS, Canadian Science Writers' Association, P.O. Box 75, Station A, Toronto, Ontario M5W 1A2, Canada. (416)408-4566. Fax: (416)408-1044. E-mail: cswa@interlog.com. Website: www.interlog.com/Œcswa. **Contact:** Andy F. Visser-deVries. Offered annually for work published/aired January 1-December 31 of previous year to recognize outstanding contributions to science journalism in all media. Three newspaper, 3 magazine, 2 TV, 2 radio, 1 special publication, student sciences writing award (Herb Lampert Student Writing Award). Each Material becomes property of CSWA. Does not return manuscripts. Open to Canadian citizens or residents of Canada. Deadline: January 31. Guidelines for SASE. Prize: $1,000 and a plaque.

SOVEREIGN AWARD, OUTSTANDING NEWSPAPER STORY, OUTSTANDING FEATURE STORY, The Jockey Club of Canada, P.O. Box 156, Rexdale, Ontario M9W 5L2, Canada. (416)675-7756. Fax: (416)675-6378. E-mail: tjcc@ftn.net. **Contact:** Bridget Bimm, executive director. Estab. 1973. Offered annually to recognize outstanding achievement in the area of Canadian thoroughbred racing journalism published November 1-October 31 of the previous year. Newspaper Story: Appeared in a newspaper by a racing columnist on Canadian Racing subject matter. Outstanding Feature Story: Appeared in a magazine book or newspaper, written as feature story on Canadian Racing subject matter. There is no nominating process other than the writer submitting no more than 1 entry per category. A copy of the newspaper article or magazine story must be provided along with a 3.25" disk containing the story in an ASCII style format. Deadline: October 31.

THE TEN BEST 'CENSORED' STORIES OF 2001, Project Censored—Sonoma State University, Rohnert Park CA 94928. (707)664-2500. Fax: (707)664-2108. E-mail: censored@sonoma.edu. Website: www.sonoma.edu/projectcens ored/. **Contact:** Peter Phillips, director. Offered for current published, nonfiction stories of national social significance that have been overlooked or under-reported by the news media. Peter Phillips and Project Censored choose 25 stories that have been underreported to make up *Censored: The News That Didn't Make the News and Why*, published by Seven Stories Press. Deadline: October 1.

THE LAWRENCE WADE JOURNALISM FELLOWSHIP, The Heritage Foundation, 214 Massachusetts Ave. NE, Washington DC 20002. (202)546-4400. Fax: (202)546-6979. E-mail: sheila.myles@heritage.org. **Contact:** Sheila Myles. Offered annually to award a journalism student who best exemplifies the high ideals and standards of the late Lawrence Wade. Applicants must be enrolled full-time in an accredited college or university. Guidelines for SASE. Prize: $1,000 and 10-week salaried internship at the Heritage Foundation.

STANLEY WALKER JOURNALISM AWARD, The Texas Institute of Letters, Southwest Texas State University, San Marcos TX 78666. (512)245-2428. Fax: (512)245-7462. E-mail: mb13@swt.edu. Website: www.English.swt.edu/css/TIL/rules.htm. **Contact:** Mark Busby. Offered annually for work published January 1-December 31 of previous year to recognize the best writing appearing in a daily newspaper. Writer must have been born in Texas, or must have lived in the state for two consecutive years at some time, or the subject matter of the article must be associated with the state. Deadline: January 3. Guidelines for SASE. Prize: $1,000.

EDWARD WEINTAL PRIZE FOR DIPLOMATIC REPORTING, Georgetown University Inst. for the Study of Diplomacy, 1316 36th St. NW, Washington DC 20007. (202)965-5735 ext. 3010. Fax: (202)965-5811. E-mail: dolgas@gunet.georgetown.edu. Website: data.georgetown.edu/sfs/programs/isd. **Contact:** Charles Dolgas, contest/award director. Offered annually to honor previously published journalists whose work reflects initiative, hard digging and bold thinking in the coverage of American diplomacy and foreign policy. Writer should place name on award mailing list to receive notice of nominations being sought. "Nominations are made by the editor on the basis of a specific story or series or on the basis of a journalist's overall news coverage." Deadline: mid-January. Prize: $5,000.

Writing for Children & Young Adults

[icon] THE GEOFFREY BILSON AWARD FOR HISTORICAL FICTION FOR YOUNG PEOPLE, The Canadian Children's Book Centre, 40 Orchard View Blvd., Suit 101, Toronto, Ontario M4R 1B9, Canada. (416)975-0010. Fax: (416)975-8970. E-mail: ccbc@sympatico.ca. Website: www3.sympatico.ca/ccbc or www.bookweek.net. **Contact:** (Ms.) Hadley Dyer. Offered annually for a previously published "outstanding work of historical fiction for young people by a Canadian author." Open to Canadian citizens and residents of Canada for at least two years. Prize: $1,000 and a certificate.

IRMA S. AND JAMES H. BLACK AWARD, Bank Street College of Education, 610 W. 112th St., New York NY 10025. (212)875-4450. Fax: (212)875-4558. E-mail: lindag@bnkst.edu. Website: streetcat.bnkst.edu/html/isb.html.

Contact: Linda Greengrass, director. Estab. 1972. Offered annually for a book for young children, for excellence of both text and illustrations. Entries must have been published during the previous calendar year. Deadline: January 1 after book is published.

BOOK PUBLISHERS OF TEXAS AWARD FOR CHILDREN'S OR YOUNG PEOPLE'S BOOK, The Texas Institute of Letters, Southwest Texas State University, San Marcos TX 78666. (512)245-2428. Fax: (512)245-7462. E-mail: mb13@swt.edu. Website: www.English.swt.edu/css/TIL/rules.htm. **Contact:** Mark Busby. Offered annually for work published January 1-December 31 of previous year to recognize the best book for children or young people. Writer must have been born in Texas or have lived in the state for at least two consecutive years at one time, or the subject matter is associated with the state. Deadline: January 3. Guidelines for SASE. Prize: $1,000.

N BRANT POINT PRIZE, What's Inside Press, P.O. Box 18203, Beverly Hills CA 90209. (800)269-7757. Fax: (800)856-2160. E-mail: bpp@whatsinsidepress.com. Website: brantpointprize.com. Offered annually for unpublished work to recognize excellence and imagination amongst children's writers. Stories must encompass a specific theme, which changes anually. 100% of entry fees go to a charity that benefits abused and neglected youths. Deadline: Changes annually; check website. Charges $10 tax-deductible donation to charity. Prize: Publishing contract, Tiffany & Co. pens, cash prizes.

MARGUERITE DE ANGELI PRIZE, Delacorte Press Books for Young Readers, Random House, Inc., 1540 Broadway, New York NY 10036. (212)782-9000. Fax: (212)782-9452. Website: www.randomhouse.com/kids. **Contact:** Diana Capriotti, editor. Estab. 1992. Offered annually for unpublished fiction manuscript suitable for readers 7-10 years of age, set in North America, either contemporary or historical. Deadline: April 1-June 30. Guidelines for SASE. Prize: $1,500 in cash, publication and $3,500 advance against royalties; world rights acquired.

DELACORTE PRESS PRIZE FOR A FIRST YOUNG ADULT NOVEL, Delacorte Press, 1540 Broadway, New York NY 10036. (212)354-6500. Fax: (212)782-9452. Website: www.randomhouse.com/kids. Offered annually "to encourage the writing of contemporary young adult fiction." Open to US and Canadian writers who have not previously published a young adult novel. Buys world rights to winning manuscript. Deadline: October 1-December 31 (postmark). Guidelines for SASE. Prize: $1,500 cash, publication and $6,000 advance against royalties.

GOLDEN KITE AWARDS, Society of Children's Book Writers and Illustrators (SCBWI), 8271 Beverly Blvd., Los Angeles CA 90048. (323)782-1010. E-mail: scbwi@scbwi.org. Website: www.scbwi.org. **Contact:** Mercedes Coats, coordinator. Estab. 1973. Offered annually for children's fiction, nonfiction and picture illustration books by SCBWI members published in the calendar year. Deadline: December 15.

N ⚓ GOVERNOR GENERAL'S LITERARY AWARD FOR CHILDREN'S LITERATURE, Canada Council for the Arts, 350 Albert St., P.O. Box 1047, Ottawa, Ontario K1P 5V8, Canada. (613)566-4414 ext. 5576. Fax: (613)566-4410. E-mail: joanne.larocque-poirier@canadacouncil.ca. Website: www.canadacouncil.ca. **Contact:** Joanne Larocque-Poirier. Offered for the best English-language and the best French-language works of children's literature by a Canadian in 2 categories: Text and illustration. Books must have been published September 1, 2001, to September 30, 2002. Publishers submit titles for consideration. Deadline: April or August 2002, depending on the book's publication date. Prize: $15,000.

HIGHLIGHTS FOR CHILDREN FICTION CONTEST, Highlights for Children, 803 Church St., Honesdale PA 18431-1824. Website: www.highlightsforchildren.com. **Contact:** Marileta Robinson, senior editor. Offered for stories for children ages 2-12; category varies each year. Stories should be limited to 900 words for older readers, 500 words for younger readers. No crime or violence, please. Specify that manuscript is a contest entry. Deadline: Postmarked January 1-February 28. Guidelines for SASE. Prize: $1,000 to 3 winners.

INTERNATIONAL READING ASSOCIATION CHILDREN'S BOOK AWARDS, International Reading Association, P.O. Box 8139, Newark DE 19714-8139. (302)731-1600 ext. 293. Fax: (302)731-1057. Website: www.reading.org. **Contact:** Janet Butler. Offered annually for an author's first or second published book in three categories: Primary (preschool-age 8) intermediate (ages 9-13); and young adult (ages 14-17). To recognize newly published authors who show unusual promise in the children's book field. Guidelines and deadlines for SASE. Prize: $500 and a medal for each category.

N CORETTA SCOTT KING BOOK AWARD, Coretta Scott King Task Force, American Library Association, 50 E. Huron St., Chicago IL 60611. (800)545-2433. Fax: (312)280-3256. E-mail: olos@ala.org. Website: www.ala.org/

N INDICATES THAT the listing is new to this edition. New markets are often more receptive to freelance submissions.

olos/awards.html. **Contact:** Tanga Morris. Offered annually for children's books by African American authors and/or illustrators published the previous year. Three categories: Preschool-grade 4; grades 5-8; grades 9-12. Deadline: December 1. Guidelines for SASE.

VICKY METCALF BODY OF WORK AWARD, Canadian Authors Association, Box 419, 320 S. Shores Rd., Campbellford, Ontario K0L 1L0, Canada. (705)653-0323. Fax: (705)653-0593. E-mail: canauth@redden.on.ca. Website: www.canauthors.org. **Contact:** Alec McEachern. Offered annually for a Canadian author who has published a minimum of 4 books inspirational to young people. Guidelines for IRCs. Deadline: December 31. Prize: $10,000.

VICKY METCALF SHORT STORY AWARD, Canadian Authors Association, Box 419, 320 S. Shores Rd., Campbellford, Ontario K0L 1L1, Canada. (705)653-0323. Fax: (705)653-0593. E-mail: canauth@redden.on.ca. Website: www.canauthors.org. **Contact:** Alec McEachern. Offered annually for a Canadian author of a short story for children. Guidelines for IRCs. Deadline: December 31. Prize: $3,000.

MILKWEED PRIZE FOR CHILDREN'S LITERATURE, Milkweed Editions, 1011 Washington Ave. S, Suite 300, Minneapolis MN 55415. (612)332-3192. Fax: (612)215-2550. Website: www.milkweed.org. **Contact:** Elisabeth Fitz, first reader. Estab. 1993. Annual prize for unpublished works. "Milkweed is looking for a novel intended for readers aged 8-13. Manuscripts should be of high literary quality and must be double-spaced, 90-200 pages in length. The Milkweed Prize for Children's Literature will be awarded to the best manuscript for children ages 8-13 that Milkweed accepts for publication during each calendar year by a writer not previously published by Milkweed Editions." Must send SASE for guidelines, both for regular children's submission policies and for the announcement of the restructured contest. Catalog for $1.50 postage. Prize: $10,000 advance on royalties agreed upon at the time of acceptance.

THE NATIONAL CHAPTER OF CANADA IODE VIOLET DOWNEY BOOK AWARD, National Chapter of Canada IODE, 40 Orchard View Blvd., Suite 254, Toronto, Ontario M4R 1B9, Canada. (416)487-4416. Fax: (416)487-4417. Website: www.iodecanada.ca. **Contact:** Sandra Connery, contest/award director. Offered annually for children's books of at least 500 words. Entries must have appeared in print January 1-December 31. Open to Canadian citizens only. Deadline: December 31. Guidelines for SASE. Prize: $3,000 (Canadian funds).

NATIONAL JEWISH BOOK AWARD—CHILDREN'S PICTURE BOOK, Marcia and Louis Posner Award, Jewish Book Council, 15 E. 26th St., New York NY 10010. (212)532-4949, ext. 397. **Contact:** Carolyn Hessel, director. Author and illustrator of a children's book on a Jewish theme. Deadline: November 30.

(ALICE WOOD MEMORIAL) OHIOANA AWARD FOR CHILDREN'S LITERATURE,, Ohioana Library Association, 274 E. First Ave., Columbus OH 43201. (614)466-3831. Fax: (614)728-6974. E-mail: ohioana@sloma.state. oh.us. Website: www.oplin.lib.oh.us/OHIOANA/. **Contact:** Linda R. Hengst. Offered to an author whose body of work has made, and continues to make, a significant contribution to literature for children or young adults and through their work as a writer, teacher, administrator or through community service, interest in children's literature has been encouraged and children have become involved with reading. Nomination forms for SASE. Recipient must have been born in Ohio or lived in Ohio at least 5 years. Deadline: December 31. Prize: $1,000.

PATERSON PRIZE FOR BOOKS FOR YOUNG PEOPLE, The Poetry Center at Passaic County Community College, One College Blvd., Paterson NJ 07505-1179. (973)684-6555. Fax: (973)684-5843. E-mail: mgillan@pccc.cc.nj. us. Website: www.pccc.cc.nj.us/poetry. **Contact:** Maria Mazziotti Gillan, director. Offered annually for books published the previous calendar year. Three categories: Pre-kindergarten-grade 3; grades 4-6; and grades 7-12. Open to any writer. Deadline: April 1. Guidelines for SASE. Prize: $500 in each category.

PEN/NORMA KLEIN AWARD, PEN American Center, 568 Broadway, New York NY 10012. (212)334-1660. Fax: (212)334-2181. E-mail: jm@pen.org. **Contact:** John Morrone. Offered triennially to recognize an emerging voice of literary merit among American writers of children's fiction. *Candidates may not nominate themselves.* Next award is 2002. Deadline: December 15. Guidelines for SASE. Prize: $3,000.

PEN/PHYLLIS NAYLOR WORKING WRITER FELLOWSHIP, PEN American Center, 568 Broadway, New York NY 10012. (212)334-1660. Fax: (212)334-2181. E-mail: jm@pen.org. **Contact:** John Morrone. Offered annually to a "writer of children's or young-adult fiction in financial need, who has published at least 2 books, and no more than 3, in the past 10 years, which may have been well reviewed and warmly received by literary critics, but which have not generated sufficient income to support the author." Writers must be nominated by an editor or fellow writer. Deadline: January 31. Prize: $5,000.

PRIX ALVINE-BELISLE, Association pour L'avancement des sciences et des techniques de la documentation, ASTED Inc., 3414 av. Parc #202, Montreal, Quebec, H2X 2H5 Canada. (514)281-5012. Fax: (514)281-8219. E-mail: lcabral@asted.org. Website: www.asted.org. **Contact:** Louis Cabral, executive director. Offered annually for work published the previous year before the award to promote authors of French youth literature in Canada. Deadline: April 1. Prize: $500.

[N] [icon] SASKATCHEWAN CHILDREN'S LITERATURE AWARD, Saskatchewan Book Awards Inc., Box 1921, Regina, Saskatchewan S4P 3E1, Canada. (306)569-1585. Fax: (306)569-4187. E-mail: sk.bookawards@dlcwest.com. Website: www.bookawards.sk.ca. **Contact:** Joyce Wells, executive director. Offered annually for work published October 1, 2001, to Sept. 14, 2002. This award is presented to a Saskatchewan author for the best book of children's or young adult's literature, judged on the quality of writing. Deadline: First deadline: July 31; final deadline: September 14. Guidelines for SASE. Charges $15 (Canadian). Prize: $1,500.

[N] SYDNEY TAYLOR BOOK AWARD, Association of Jewish Libraries, 3729 Meadowbrook Blvd., University Heights OH 44118. (216)321-7179. Website: www.jewishlibraries.org. **Contact:** L. Silver, chair. Offered annually for work published in the year of the award. "Given to distinguished contributions to Jewish literature for children. One award for older readers, one for younger." Publishers submit books. Deadline: December 31. Guidelines for SASE. Prize: Certificate, cash award and gold seal for cover of winning book.

TEDDY AWARD FOR BEST CHILDREN'S BOOK, Writers' League of Texas (formerly the Austin Writers' League), 1501 W. Fifth St., Suite E-2, Austin TX 78703. (512)499-8914. Fax: (512)499-0441. E-mail: awl@writersleague.org. Website: www.writersleague.org. **Contact:** Jim Bob McMillan, director. Offered annually for work published January 1, 2001-March 31, 2002. Honors an outstanding book for children published by a member of the Writers' League of Texas. Writer's League of Texas dues may accompany entry fee. Deadline: May 1. Guidelines for SASE. Charges $10 fee. Prize: $1,000 and trophy.

WORK-IN-PROGRESS GRANT, Society of Children's Book Writers and Illustrators (SCBWI) and Judy Blume, 8271 Beverly Blvd., Los Angeles CA 90048. (323)782-1010. E-mail: scbwi@scbwi.org. Website: www.scbwi.org. Two grants—one designated specifically for a contemporary novel for young people—to assist SCBWI members in the completion of a specific project. Open to SCBWI members only. Deadline: March 1. Guidelines for SASE.

[N] WRITING FOR CHILDREN COMPETITION, No Noun-Sense, 147-2211 No. 4 Road, Richmond British Columbia V6X 3X1, Canada. (604)825-8861. Fax: (604)214-1306. E-mail: editor@webprospects.com. Website: www.nonounsense.com. **Contact:** Erin Berringer. Offered annually for unpublished work to promote the art or writing for children. Guidelines on website. Open to any writer. Deadline: May 21. Charges $10. Prize: 1st-$200; 2nd-$50; 3rd-$25. Winner and four honourable mentions will be published on the No Noun-Sense website, along with their bios.

[icon] WRITING FOR CHILDREN COMPETITION, The Writers' Union of Canada, 40 Wellington St. E., Third Floor, Toronto, Ontario M5E 1C7. (416)703-8982 ext. 223. Fax: (416)504-7656. E-mail: twuc@the-wire.com. Website: www.writersunion.ca. **Contact:** Caroline Sin. Offered annually "to discover developing Canadian writers of unpublished children's/young adult fiction or nonfiction." Open to Canadian citizens or landed immigrants who have not been published in book format and who do not currently have a contract with a publisher. Deadline: April 23. Charges $15 entry fee. Prize: $1,500; the winner and 11 finalists' pieces will be submitted to a Canadian publisher of children's books.

Translation

ASF TRANSLATION PRIZE, The American-Scandinavian Foundation, 50 Park Ave., New York NY 10016-3007. (212)879-9779. Fax: (212)249-3444. E-mail: agyongy@amscan.org. Website: www.amscan.org. **Contact:** Adrienne Gyongy. Offered annually to a translation of Scandinavian literature into English of a Nordic author born within last 200 years. "The Prize is for an outstanding English translation of poetry, fiction, drama or literary prose originally written in Danish, Finnish, Icelandic, Norwegian or Swedish that has not been previously published in the English language." Deadline: June 1. Guidelines for SASE. Prize: $2,000, publication of an excerpt in an issue of *Scandinavian Review* and a commemorative bronze medallion; the Inger Sjöberg Prize of $500.

FELLOWSHIPS FOR TRANSLATORS, National Endowment for the Arts, Nancy Hanks Center, 1100 Pennsylvania Ave. NW, Washington DC 20506-0001. (202)682-5428. Website: www.arts.gov. **Contact:** Heritage and Preservation Division. "Grants are available to published translators of literature for projects that involve specific translation of prose (fiction, creative nonfiction and drama) or poetry (including verse drama) from other languages into English. We encourage translations of writers and of work which are insufficiently represented in English translation." Guidelines on website or by phone request. Deadline: Poetry: March 11, 2002; Prose: March 2003 (date to be determined). Prize: Grants are for $10,000 or $20,000, depending on the length and scope of the project.

SOEURETTE DIEHL FRASER TRANSLATION AWARD, The Texas Institute of Letters, Southwest Texas State University, San Marcos TX 78666. (512)245-2428. Fax: (512)245-7462. E-mail: mb13@swt.edu. Website: www.English.swt.edu/css/TIL/rules.htm. **Contact:** Mark Busby. Offered annually for work published January 1-December 31 of previous year to recognize the best translation of a literary book into English. Translator must have been born in Texas or have lived in the state for at least two consecutive years at some time. Deadline: January 3. Guidelines for SASE. Prize: $1,000.

GERMAN PRIZE FOR LITERARY TRANSLATION, American Translators Association, 225 Reinekers Lane, Suite 590, Alexandria VA 22314. (703)683-6100. Fax: (703)683-6122. E-mail: ata@atanet.org. Website: www.atanet.org. **Contact:** Jo Anne Englebert. Offered in odd-numbered years for previously published book translated from German to English. In even-numbered years, the Lewis Galentiere Prize is awarded for translations other than German to English. Deadline: April 15. Prize: $1,000, a certificate of recognition and up to $500 toward expenses for attending the ATA Annual Conference.

N **⏎** **JOHN GLASSCO TRANSLATION PRIZE**, Association des traducteurs et traductrices littéraires du Canada, Condordia University - SB 335, 1455, boul, de Maisonneuve ouest, Montréal, Québec H3G 1M8, Canada. (514)849-8540. E-mail: altegro@rocler.qc.ca. Website: www.geocities.com/ltac_attlc/. Estab. 1981. Offered annually for a translator's *first* book-length literary translation into French or English, published in Canada during the previous calendar year. The translator must be a Canadian citizen or landed immigrant. Eligible genres include fiction, creative nonfiction, poetry, published plays and children's books. Write for application form. Deadline: June 30. Prize: $1,000.

N **⏎** **GOVERNOR GENERAL'S LITERARY AWARD FOR TRANSLATION**, Canada Council for the Arts, 350 Albert St., P.O. Box 1047, Ottawa, Ontario K1P 5V8, Canada. (613)566-4414 ext. 5576. Fax: (613)566-4410. E-mail: joanne.larocque-poirier@canadacouncil.ca. Website: www.canadacouncil.ca. **Contact:** Joanne Larocque-Poirier. Offered for the best English-language and the best French-language work of translation by a Canadian published September 1, 2001, to September 30, 2002. Publishers submit titles for consideration. Deadline: April or August 2002, depending on the book's publication date. Prize: $15,000.

THE HAROLD MORTON LANDON TRANSLATION AWARD, The Academy of American Poets, 584 Broadway, Suite 1208, New York NY 10012-3250. (212)274-0343. Fax: (212)274-9427. E-mail: academy@poets.org. Website: www.poets.org. **Contact:** Awards Director. Offered annually to recognize a published translation of poetry from any language into English. Open to living US citizens. Anthologies by a number of translators are ineligible. Deadline: December 31. Guidelines for SASE. Prize: $1,000.

N **LOCKERT LIBRARY OF POETRY IN TRANSLATION**, Princeton University Press, 41 William St., Princeton NJ 03540. Fax: (609)258-6305. Website: www.pup.princeton.edu. **Contact:** Fred Appel, assistant editor. Book-length poetry translation of a single poet.

PEN/BOOK-OF-THE-MONTH CLUB TRANSLATION PRIZE, PEN American Center, 568 Broadway, New York NY 10012. (212)334-1660. Fax: (212)334-2181. E-mail: jm@pen.org. **Contact:** John Morrone. Offered for a literary book-length translation into English published in the calendar year. No technical, scientific or reference books. Publishers, agents or translators may submit 3 copies of each eligible title. Deadline: December 15. Prize: $3,000.

THE RAIZISS/DE PALCHI TRANSLATION FELLOWSHIP, The Academy of American Poets, 584 Broadway, Suite 1208, New York NY 10012-3250. (212)274-0343. Fax: (212)274-9427. E-mail: academy@poets.org. Website: www.poets.org. **Contact:** Awards Director. Offered in even-numbered years to recognize outstanding unpublished translations of modern Italian poetry into English. Applicants must verify permission to translate the poems or that the poems are in the public domain. Open to any US citizen. Deadline: September 1-November 1, 2002. Guidelines for SASE. Prize: $20,000 and a one-month residency at the American Academy in Rome.

LOIS ROTH AWARD FOR A TRANSLATION OF A LITERARY WORK, Modern Language Association, 26 Broadway, Third Floor, New York NY 10004-1789. (646)576-5141. Fax: (646)458-0030. E-mail: awards@mla.org. Website: www.mla.org. **Contact:** Coordinator of Book Prizes. Offered every 2 years (odd years) for an outstanding translation into English of a book-length literary work published the previous year. Translators need not be members of the MLA. Deadline: April 1. Guidelines for SASE. Prize: $1,000 and a certificate.

ALDO AND JEANNE SCAGLIONE PRIZE FOR A TRANSLATION OF A LITERARY WORK, Modern Language Association, 26 Broadway, Third Floor, New York NY 10004-1789. (646)576-5141. Fax: (646)458-0030. E-mail: awards@mla.org. Website: www.mla.org. **Contact:** Coordinator of Book Prizes. Offered in even-numbered years for the translation of a book-length literary work appearing in print during the previous year. Translators need not be members of the MLA. Deadline: May 1. Guidelines for SASE. Prize: $2,000 and a certificate.

ALDO AND JEANNE SCAGLIONE PRIZE FOR A TRANSLATION OF A SCHOLARLY STUDY OF LITERATURE, Modern Language Association, 26 Broadway, Third Floor, New York NY 10004-1789. (646)576-5141. Fax: (646)458-0030. E-mail: awards@mla.org. Website: www.mla.org. **Contact:** Coordinator of Book Prizes. Offered in odd-numbered years "for an outstanding translation into English of a book-length work of literary history, literary criticism, philology or literary theory published during the previous biennium." Translators need not be members of the MLA. Deadline: May 1. Guidelines for SASE. Prize: $2,000 and a certificate.

STUDENT TRANSLATION PRIZE, American Translators Association, 225 Reinekers Lane, Suite 590, Alexandria VA 22314. (703)683-6100. Fax: (703)683-6122. E-mail: ata@atanet.org. **Contact:** Jo Anne

Englebert. Support is granted for a promising project to an unpublished student enrolled in a translation program at a US college or university. Must be sponsored by a faculty member. Deadline: April 15. Prize: $500 and up to $500 toward expenses for attending the ATA Annual Conference.

Multiple Writing Areas

[N] AKRON MANUSCRIPT CLUB WRITER'S CONTEST, Akron Manuscript Club, Akron University, Falls Writer's Workshop & Taylor Memorial Library, P.O. Box 1101, Cuyahoga Falls OH 44223-0101. (330)923-2094. E-mail: mmlop@aol.com. **Contact:** M.M. LoPiccolo, contest director. Estab. 1929. Offered annually for previously unpublished stories to provide critique, encouragement and some financial help to authors in 3 categories. Guidelines for SASE. Get current deadlines before submitting. Open to any writer. Deadline: March. Charges $25 entry/critique fee. Prize: 1st-$50, according to funding; 2nd and 3rd-certificates. Get current guidelines before submitting.

AMELIA STUDENT AWARD, Amelia Magazine, 329 E St., Bakersfield CA 93304. (805)323-4064. Fax: (805)323-5326. E-mail: amelia@lightspeed.net. Website: www.ameliamagazine.net. **Contact:** Frederick A. Raborg, Jr., editor. Offered annually for previously unpublished poems, essays and short stories by high school students and undergraduates. One entry per student. Each high school entry should be signed by a parent, guardian *or* teacher to verify originality; include scholastic biography. No entry fee; however, if guidelines and sample are required, please send SASE with $3 handling charge. Deadline: May 15. Prize: $500.

[N] AMERICAN LITERARY REVIEW CONTEST, American Literary Review, P.O. Box 311307, University of North Texas, Denton TX 76203-1307. (940)565-2755. E-mail: americanliteraryreview@yahoo.com. Website: www.engl. unt.edu/alr. **Contact:** Managing Editor. Offered annually for unpublished work. This contest alternates annually between poetry and fiction. Open to any writer. Deadline: varies each year. Guidelines for SASE. Charges $10 entry fee. Prize: $500 and publication.

[N] ANNUAL U.S. MARITIME LITERATURE AWARDS, 222 Main St., Box 190, Annapolis MD 21401. E-mail: sailr@pyramid3.net. Website: www.maritimeamerica.com. Offered annually for unpublished short stories (nonfiction), poetry, limericks and environmental essays. All entries must include a U.S. geographical maritime location and theme. The term "maritime" may include both freshwater and saltwater bodies such as lakes, creeks, coastlines, ports, oceans, etc. Themes may include fishing, tragedy, discovery, adventure, weather, romance, kayaking, environment, diving, etc. Three divisions: Adult (18 and older); students ages 13-17; and students under age 13. Guidelines on website at www.usmaritimeawards.com/aausm.htm. Deadline: December 31 (postmark). Prize: Short story: $100; poetry: $100; essay: $100; limerick: $25.

ARIZONA AUTHORS' ASSOCIATION ANNUAL NATIONAL LITERARY CONTEST, Arizona Authors' Association, P.O. Box 87857, Phoenix AZ 85080-7857. (623)780-0053. Fax: (623)780-0468. E-mail: vijaya@vijayascha rtz.com. Website: home.rmci.net/vijayaschartz/azauthors.htm. **Contact:** Tony Heathcotte, contest coordinator. Offered annually for previously unpublished poetry, short stories, essays and articles. New awards for published books in fiction, anthology, nonfiction and children's. Winners announced at an Award Banquet in Phoenix in November, and short pieces published in Arizona Literary Magazine. Deadline: July 1. Charges $10 fee for poetry, $15 for short stories and essays, and $30 for books. Prize: 1st-prize unpublished novel wins publication in e-book and print-on-demand by 1stbooks.com. All winners interviewed on Book Crazy Radio, Phoenix.

[N] ART COOP TRAVELING FELLOWSHIP, Cottonwood Art Co-operative, 725 Ashland, Houston TX 77007-1424. E-mail: art_coop@yahoo.com. Website: www.geocities.com/art_coop. **Contact:** Victor Gonzalez. For most recent information, please visit website or write for guidelines with SASE. Submit cover letter explaining project and location, anticipated budget, bio, and publications list. Submit 3-50 page portfolio of fiction or creative nonfiction, 10-20 pages of poetry, or slides of visual artwork with SASE. Open to any writer. Deadline: May 1. Charges $20. Prize: Cash award to be determined and publication to support serious, aspiring poets, essayists, fiction writers and visual artists in completing a project that requires travel.

THE ART OF MUSIC ANNUAL WRITING CONTEST, Piano Press, P.O. Box 85, Del Mar CA 92014-0085. (858)481-5650. Fax: (858)755-1104. E-mail: pianopress@aol.com. Website: www.pianopress.com. **Contact:** Elizabeth C. Axford, M.A. Offered annually for unpublished work. Categories are: Essay Contest (ages 4-12, 13-17, and 18 and over), Short Story Contest (ages 4-12, 13-17, and 18 and over) and Poetry Contest (ages 4-12, 13-17, and 18 and over); nine total winners. All writings must be in music-related topics. The purpose of the contest is to promote the art of music through writing. Acquires one-time rights. All entries must be accompanied by an entry form indicating category and age; parent signature is required of all writers under age 18. Poems may be of any length and in any style; essays and short stories should not exceed five double-spaced, typewritten pages. All entries shall be previously unpublished and the original work of the author. Guidelines and entry form for SASE or by e-mail. Deadline: June 30. Charges $20 fee. Prize: Medal, certificate, publication in the annual anthology/chapbook and copies of the book.

AWP AWARD SERIES, Associated Writing Programs, Tallwood House, Mail Stop 1E3, George Mason University, Fairfax VA 22030. (703)993-4301. Fax: (703)993-4302. E-mail: awp@gmu.edu. Website: http://awpwriter.org. **Contact:** Katherine Perry. Offered annually to foster new literary talent. Categories: Poetry, short fiction, creative nonfiction and novel. Guidelines for SASE and on website. Open to any writer. Deadline: Must be postmarked January 1-February 28. Charges $20 for nonmembers, $10 for members. Prize: Cash honorarium (novel-$10,000; other categories-$2,000) and publication by a participating press.

BAKELESS LITERARY PUBLICATION PRIZES, Bread Loaf Writers' Conference, Middlebury College, Middleburg VT 05753. (802)443-2018. Fax: (802)443-2087. E-mail: bakeless@middlebury.edu. Website: www.middlebury.edu/~blwc. **Contact:** Ian Pounds, contest director. Offered annually for unpublished authors of poetry, fiction and creative nonfiction. Open to all writing in English who have not yet published a book in their entry's genre. Deadline: October 1-November 15. Guidelines for SASE. Charges $10 fee. Prize: Publication of book-length ms by Houghton Mifflin and a fellowship to attend the Bread Loaf Writers' Conference.

EMILY CLARK BALCH AWARD, Virginia Quarterly Review, 1 West Range, P.O. Box 400223, Charlottesville VA 22904-4233. (804)924-3124. Fax: (804)924-1397. Website: www.virginia.edu/vqr. **Contact:** Staige D. Blackford, editor. Best short story/poetry accepted and published by the *Virginia Quarterly Review* during a calendar year. No deadline.

N. BLACK WARRIOR REVIEW LITERARY AWARD, *Black Warrior Review*, P.O. Box 862936, Tuscaloosa AL 35486. (205)348-4518. Website: www.webdelsol.com/bwr. **Contact:** Ander Monson, editor. Offered annually to the best work of fiction and best poem published in *Black Warrior Review* each year. Different judges every year. 1999-2000 judges were Tom Franklin for fiction and Nancy Eimers for poetry. *Black Warrior Review* buys first rights. Guidelines for SASE. Prize: $500 and recognition in Fall/Winter Issue.

N. THE BOSTON AUTHORS CLUB BOOK AWARDS, The Boston Authors Club, 45 Chiltern Rd., Weston MA 02493. (781)235-6995. E-mail: AdrienneRichard@MediaOne.net. **Contact:** Adrienne Richard. Offered annually for books published the previous year. Two awards are given, one for trade books of fiction, non-fiction or poetry, and the second for children's books. Authors must live or have lived within 100 miles of Boston. Deadline: January 1. Prize: Certificate and honorarioum of $500 in each category.

BYLINE MAGAZINE AWARDS, P.O. Box 130596, Edmond OK 73013-0001. (405)348-5591. E-mail: bylinemp@flash.net. Website: www.bylinemag.com. **Contact:** Marcia Preston, award director. Contest includes several monthly contests, open to anyone, in various categories that include fiction, nonfiction, poetry and children's literature, an annual poetry chapbook award which is open to any poet and an annual ByLine Short Fiction and Poetry Award open only to our subscribers. For chapbook award and Subscriber Awards, publication constitutes part of the prize, and winners grant first North American rights to ByLine. Deadline: Varies. Charges $3-5 for monthly contests and $15 for chapbook contest. Prize: Monthly contests-cash and listing in magazine; chapbook award-publication of chapbook, 50 copies and $200; ByLine Short Fiction and Poetry Award-$250 in each category, plus publication in the magazine.

CANADIAN AUTHORS ASSOCIATION AWARDS PROGRAM, P.O. Box 419, Campbellford, Ontario K0L 1L0, Canada. (705)653-0323. Fax: (705)653-0593. E-mail: canauth@redden.on.ca. Website: www.canauthors.org. **Contact:** Alec McEachern. Offered annually for short stories, fiction, poetry, history, biography books inspirational to young people, short stories for children and to promising writers under age 30. Entrants must be Canadians by birth, naturalized Canadians or landed immigrants. Deadline: Varies. Guidelines for SASE. Prize: Prizes range from air travel for two to $10,000.

CANADIAN HISTORICAL ASSOCIATION AWARDS, Canadian Historical Association, 395 Wellington, Ottawa, Ontario K1A 0N3, Canada. (613)233-7885. Fax: (613)567-3110. E-mail: cha-shc@archives.ca. Website: www.cha-shc.ca. **Contact:** Joanne Mineault. Offered annually. Categories: Regional history, Canadian history, history (not Canadian), women's history (published articles, English or French), doctoral dissertations. Open to Canadian writers. Deadline: Varies. Guidelines for SASE. Prize: Certificates of merit-$1,000.

N. CHICAGO LITERARY AWARD, Left Field Press/Another Chicago Magazine, 3709 N. Kenmore, Chicago IL 60613-2905. E-mail: editors@anotherchicagomag.com. Website: www.anotherchicagomag.com. **Contact:** Editors. Offered annually for unpublished works to recognize excellence in poetry and fiction. Guidelines for SASE and on website. Buys first North American serial rights. Open to any writer. Deadline: December 15. Charges $10 fee. Prize: $1,000 and publication.

CHICKEN SOUP FOR THE WRITER'S SOUL WRITING CONTEST, P.O. Box 30880, Santa Barbara CA 93130. Fax: (805) 563-2945. Website: www.chickensoup.com. Estab. 2000. Offered for original, unpublished non-fiction works that are uplifting, inspiring and present a positive viewpoint. Essays, short stories and poems of up to 1,200 words will be considered. Guidelines for SASE or on website. Open to US residents 18 and older. The winner will be chosen by a panel of independent judges. Deadline: March 1. Prize: The chosen winner will receive (a) paid entrance to the Maui Writer's Conference, (b) Roundtrip ticket to Maui, Hawaii, coach fare, (c) 4 nights and 5 days hotel accomodations at the Outrigger Hotel, Maui, Hawaii, (d) shuttle transportation to and from airport, (e) your story will be considered for publication in an upcoming Chicken Soup for the Soul book.

[N] THE CITY OF VANCOUVER BOOK AWARD, Office of Cultural Affairs, 453 W. 12th Ave., Vancouver, British Columbia V5Y 1V4, Canada. (604)873-7487. Fax: (604)871-6048. E-mail: oca@city.vancouver.bc.ca. Website: www.city.vancouver.bc.ca/oca. Offered annually for books published the previous year which exhibit excellence in 1 or more of 4 categories: Content, illustration, design and format. The book must contribute significantly to the appreciation and understanding of the city of Vancouver and heighten awareness of one or more of the following: Vancouver's history, the city's unique character or achievements of the city's residents. The book may be fiction, nonfiction, poetry or drama written for adults or children and may deal with any aspects of the city: History, geography, current affairs or the arts. Guidelines on website. Prize: $2,000.

CNW/FLORIDA STATE WRITING COMPETITION, Florida Freelance Writers Association, P.O. Box A, North Stratford NH 03590-0167. (603)922-8338. Fax: (603)922-8339. E-mail: contest@writers-editors.com. Website: www.writers-editors.com. **Contact:** Dana Cassell, executive director. Subject areas include: Adult articles, adult short stories, writing for children, novels, poetry; categories within these areas vary from year to year. Entry fees vary from year to year; in 2001 were $3-20. Open to any writer. Deadline: March 15. Guidelines for SASE. Prize: Cash, certificates.

COLORADO BOOK AWARDS, Colorado Center for the Book, 2123 Downing, Denver CO 80205. (303)839-8320. Fax: (303)839-8319. E-mail: ccftb@compuserve.com. Website: www.ColoradoBook.org. **Contact:** Christiane H. Citron, executive director. Offered annually for work published by December of previous year or current calendar year. The purpose is to champion all Colorado authors and in particular to honor the award winners and a reputation for Colorado as a state whose people promote and support reading, writing and literacy through books. The categories are children, young adult, fiction, nonfiction & poetry, guidebooks, romance. Open to authors who reside or have resided in Colorado. Guidelines for SASE. Charges $40 fee. Prize: $350 in each category and an annual gala event where winners are honored.

COMMONWEALTH CLUB OF CALIFORNIA BOOK AWARDS, 595 Market St., San Francisco CA 94105. (415)597-4846. Fax: (415)597-6729. E-mail: blane@commonwealthclub.org. Website: www.commonwealthclub.org. **Contact:** Barbara Lane. Estab. 1931. Offered annually for published submissions appearing in print January 1-December 31 of the previous year. "Purpose of award is the encouragement and production of literature in California. Categories include: fiction, nonfiction, poetry, first work of fiction, juvenile ages up to 10, juvenile 11-16, notable contribution to publishing and Californiana." Can be nominated by publisher as well. Open to California residents (or residents at time of publication). Deadline: January 31. Guidelines for SASE. Prize: Medals and cash prizes to be awarded at publicized event.

[N] COMPACT FICTION/SHORT POEM COMPETITION, *Pottersfield Portfolio*, P.O. Box 40, Station A, Sydney, Nova Scotia B1P 6G9, Canada. Website: www.pportfolio.com. **Contact:** Lars Willum. Offered annually for unpublished work: Stories of 1,500 words or less and poems of 20 lines or less. Maximum of 2 stories or 3 poems per author. Buys first Canadian serial rights; copyright remains with author. Guidelines for SASE or on website. Deadline: May 1. Charges $20 for the first entry, $5 for each subsequent entry in the same category. Prize: $200 for the best story and the best poem, publication and a 1-year subscription to *Pottersfield Portfolio*.

VIOLET CROWN BOOK AWARDS, Writers' League of Texas (formerly the Austin Writers' League), 1501 W. Fifth St., Suite E-2, Austin TX 78703. (512)499-8914. Fax: (512)499-0441. E-mail: awl@writersleague.org. Website: www.writersleague.org. **Contact:** Jim Bob McMillan, director. Offered annually for work published July 1, 2001-June 30, 2002. Honors three outstanding books published in fiction, nonfiction and literary categories by Writers' League of Texas members. Membership dues may accompany entry fee. Deadline: June 30. Guidelines for SASE. Charges $10 fee. Prize: 3 $1,000 prizes and trophies.

[N] CWW ANNUAL AWARDS COMPETITION, Council for Wisconsin Writers, P.O. Box 55322, Madison WI 53705. Offered annually for work published by Wisconsin writers the previous calendar year. Thirteen awards: Major/life achievement, short fiction, scholarly book, short nonfiction, nonfiction book, juvenile fiction book, children's picture book, poetry book, fiction book, outdoor writing, juevnile nonfiction book, drama (produced), outstanding service to Wisconsin writers. Open to Wiscconsin residents. Deadline: January 15. Guidelines for SASE. Charges $25 fee for nonmembers, $10 for members. Prize: $500-1,500 and certificate.

[N] DANA AWARDS IN THE NOVEL, SHORT FICTION AND POETRY, 7207 Townsend Forest Court, Browns Summit NC 27214-9634. (336)656-7009. E-mail: danaawards@pipeline.com. Website: danaawards.home.pipeline.com. **Contact:** Mary Elizabeth Parker, chair. Offered annually for unpublished work. Purpose is monetary award for work that has not been previously published or awarded in any way. Exceptions would be work published for family/friends only. Works previously published online are not eligible. Three awards: Novel: For the first 50 pages of a novel completed or in progress. Short fiction: Short fiction (no memoirs) up to 10,000 words. Poetry: For best group of five poems based on exellence of all five (no light verse, no single poem over 100 lines). "Contest is open to writers who are 16 or older and who write in English. Most submissions are from authors in their late 20s through 60s." Deadline: October 31 (postmark). Charges $20 fee per novel entry, $10 fee per short fiction or poetry entry. Prize: $1,000 in each category.

DOG WRITERS ASSOCIATION OF AMERICA ANNUAL WRITING CONTEST, Dog Writers Association of America, PMB 309, 3809 Plaza #107, Oceanside CA 92056-4265. (760)630-3828. E-mail: liz-palika@home.com. Website: www.dwaa.org. **Contact:** Liz Palika, contest chair. Offered annually for submissions published between September 2000-September 2001 in the following categories: Newspaper Articles, Books, Poems, Mystery, Club Newsletters, Videos and Children's Books. Deadline: September 1. Guidelines for SASE. Charges $10-12 fee. Prize: Plaques and cash awards.

N **EL DORADO WRITERS' GUILD ANNUAL WRITING CONTEST**, El Doraldo Writers' Guild, P.O. Box 1266, El Dorado CA 95623-1266. E-mail: theacorn@visto.com. **Contact:** Kirk Colvin. Offered annually for unpublished work in two categories: Prose (fiction or nonfiction) to a maximum of 4,000 words; and poetry to a maximum of 40 lines. Winning entries will appear in the contest edition of *The Acorn* (the quarterly publication of the El Dorado Writers' Guild). Upon publication, all rights revert to the author. Members of the guild are not eligible for the contest. Deadline: November 1. Guidelines for SASE. Charges $8 for prose, $8 for up to 3 poems. Prize: For each category: 1st-$100; 2nd-$50; 3rd-$20; honorable mention(2)-$10.

EMERGING LESBIAN WRITERS FUND AWARD, ASTRAEA National Lesbian Action Foundation, 116 E. 16th St., 7th Floor, New York NY 10003. (212)529-8021. Fax: (212)982-3321. E-mail: info@astraea.org. Website: www.astraea.org. **Contact:** Christine Lipat, senior program officer. Offered annually to encourage and support the work of new lesbian writers of fiction and poetry. Guidelines for SASE or on website. Entrants must be a lesbian writer of either fiction or poetry, a US resident, work includes some lesbian content, at least one piece of writing (in any genre) has been published in a newspaper, magazine, journal, anthology or professional website, and not more than one book. (Published work may be in any discipline; self-published books are not included in the one book maximum.) Deadline: International Women's Day, March 8. Charges $5 fee. Prize: $10,000 grants.

EXPLORATIONS PRIZES FOR LITERATURE, UAS Explorations, University of Alaska Southeast, 11120 Glacier High, Juneau AK 99801. (907)465-6418 (message only). Fax: (907)465-6406. E-mail: art.petersen@uas.alaska.edu. Website: www.geocities.com/artpetersen. **Contact:** Art Petersen, editor. Offered annually to provide a venue for poets and writers of prose fiction across Alaska, the US, Canada, England and Europe. Guidelines for SASE, by e-mail and on website. Open to any writer. Deadline: May 15. Charges $6 for 1-2 poems, $3 for each additional poem; $6/story. Prize: 1st-$1,000, 2nd-$500, 3rd(2)-$100.

N **THE VIRGINIA FAULKNER AWARD FOR EXCELLENCE IN WRITING**, *Prairie Schooner*, 201 Andrews Hall, P.O. Box 880334, Lincoln NE 68588-0334. (402)472-0911. Fax: (402)472-9771. E-mail: eflanagan2@unl.edu. Website: www.unl.edu/schooner/psmain.htm. **Contact:** Hilda Raz. Offered annually for work published in *Prairie Schooner* in the previous year. Prize: $1,000.

N **MILES FRANKLIN LITERARY AWARD**, Arts Management Pty. Ltd., Station House L. 4, 790 George St., Sydney NSW 2000, Australia. 61-2-9212-5066. Fax: 61-2-9211-7762. E-mail: claudia@artsmanagement.com.au. **Contact:** Claudia Crosariol. Offered annually for work published for the first time the year preceding the award. "The award is for a novel or play of the highest literary merit for the year, which presents Australian life in any of its phases. Biographies, collections of short stories or children's books are not eligible for the award." Guidelines for SAE with 1 IRC. Open to writers of any nationality. Deadline: Mid-December. Prize: $28,000 (Australian).

N **GEORGIA STATE UNIVERSITY REVIEW WRITING CONTEST**, Georgia State University Review, Georgia State University Plaza, Campus Box 1894, Atlanta GA 30303-3083. (404)651-4804. Fax: (404)651-1710. **Contact:** Katie Chaple, editor. Offered annually "to publish the most promising work of up-and-coming writers of poetry (3-5 poems, none over 50 lines) and fiction (8,000 word limit)." Fiction and poetry editors subject to change annually. Rights revert to writer upon publication. Deadline: January 31. Guidelines for SASE. Charges $10 fee. Prize: $1,000 to winner of each category, plus a copy of winning issue to each paid submission.

THE GREENSBORO REVIEW LITERARY AWARD IN FICTION AND POETRY, *The Greensboro Review*, English Department, 134 McIver Bldg., P.O. Box 6170, Greensboro NC 27402-6170. (336)334-5459. E-mail: jlclark@uncg.edu. Website: www.uncg.edu/eng/mfa. **Contact:** Jim Clark, editor. Offered annually for fiction and poetry recognizing the best work published in the spring issue of *The Greensboro Review*. Sample copy for $5. Deadline: September 15.

N **GULF COAST POETRY & SHORT FICTION PRIZE**, *Gulf Coast*, English Department, University of Houston, Houston TX 77204-3012. (713)743-3223. Website: www.gulfcoast.uh.edu. **Contact:** Pablo Peschiera, managing editor. Offered annually for poetry and short stories. Open to any writer. Deadline: February 15. Guidelines for SASE. Charges $15 fee, which includes subscription. Prize: $300 each for best poem and short story and publication in *Gulf Coast*.

HACKNEY LITERARY AWARDS, Writing Today, Box 549003/Birmingham-Southern College, Birmingham AL 35254. (205)226-4921. E-mail: dcwilson@bsc.edu. Website: www.bsc.edu/. **Contact:** D.C. Wilson. Estab. 1969. Offered annually for unpublished novels, short stories (maximum 5,000 words) and poetry (50 line limit). Guidelines on website or for SASE. Deadline: September 30 (novels), December 31 (short stories). Charges $25 entry fee for novels, $10 for short stories and poetry. Prize: $5,000 for each category.

N HEART ANNUAL POETRY AND SHORT FICTION AWARD, HEArt—Human Equity Through Art, P.O. Box 81038, Pittsburgh PA 15217-0538. (412)244-0122. Fax: (412)244-0210. E-mail: lesanne@ix.netcom.com. Website: trfn.clpgh.org/heart/. **Contact:** Leslie Anne Mcilroy. Offered annually for unpublished work "to encourage poets and writers to use their work as a means of confronting discrimination and promoting social justice; and to give voice and recognition to quality contemporary activist literature." Open to any writer. Deadline: December 31. Guidelines for SASE. Charges $15 (includes winning issue) or $21 (includes 1-year subscription). Prize: $500 and publication in each category (poetry and short fiction).

N ROBERT F. KENNEDY BOOK AWARDS, 1367 Connecticut Ave., NW, Suite 200, Washington DC 20036. (202)463-7575. Fax: (202)463-6606. E-mail: info@rfkmemorial.org. Website: www.rfkmemorial.org. **Contact:** Book Award Director. Offered annually for work published the previous year "which most faithfully and forcefully reflects Robert Kennedy's purposes—his concern for the poor and the powerless, his struggle for honest and even-handed justice, his conviction that a decent society must assure all young people a fair chance, and his faith that a free democracy can act to remedy disparities of power and opportunity. Deadline: January 31. Charges $25 fee. Prize: Grand Prize winner-$2,500 and a bust of Robert F. Kennedy.

LARRY LEVIS EDITORS' PRIZE IN POETRY/THE MISSOURI REVIEW EDITOR'S PRIZE IN FICTION & ESSAY, *The Missouri Review*, 1507 Hillcrest Hall, Columbia MO 65211. (573)882-4474. Fax: (573)884-4671. Website: www.missourireview.org. **Contact:** Hoa Ngo. Offered annually for unpublished work in 3 categories: Fiction, essay and poetry. Guidelines for SASE after June. Deadline: October 15. Charges $15 fee (includes a 1 year subscription). Prize: Fiction and poetry winners-$1,500 and publication in the spring issue; essay winner-$1,000 and publication; 3 finalists in each category receive a minimum of $100.

N THE HUGH J. LUKE AWARD, *Prairie Schooner*, 201 Andrews Hall, P.O. Box 880334, Lincoln NE 68588-0334. (402)472-0911. Fax: (402)472-9771. E-mail: eflanagan2@unl.edu. Website: www.unl.edu/schooner/psmain.htm. **Contact:** Hilda Raz. Offered annually for work published in *Prairie Schooner* in the previous year. Prize: $250.

N ☘ BRENDA MACDONALD RICHES FIRST BOOK AWARD, Saskatchewan Book Awards Inc., Box 1921, Regina, Saskatchewan S4P 3E1, Canada. (306)569-1585. Fax: (306)569-4187. E-mail: sk.bookawards@dlcwest.com. Website: www.bookawards.sk.ca. **Contact:** Joyce Wells, executive director. Offered annually for work published October 1, 2001, to September 14, 2002. This award is presented to a Saskatchewan author for the best first book, judged on the quality of writing. Books from the following categories will be considered: Children's; drama; fiction (short fiction by a single author, novellas, novels); nonfiction (all categories of nonfiction writing except cookbooks, directories, how-to books or bibliographies of minimal critical content); poetry. Deadline: First deadline: July 31; final deadline: September 14. Guidelines for SASE. Charges $15 (Canadian). Prize: $1,500.

MAMMOTH PRESS AWARDS, 7 S. Juniata St., DuBois PA 15801. E-mail: guidlines@mammothbooks.com (guidelines only); info@mammothbooks.com (all other questions). Website: www.mammothbooks.com. **Contact:** Antonio Vallone. Offered annually for unpublished works. Prose manuscripts may be a collection of essays or a single long work of creative nonfiction, a collection of stories or novellas or a novel. Poetry manuscripts may be a collection of poems or a single long poem. Translations are acceptable. "Manuscripts as a whole must not have been previously published. Some or all of each manuscript may have appeared in periodicals, chapbooks, anthologies or other venues. These must be identified. Authors are responsible for securing permissions." Guidelines for SASE or by e-mail. Deadline: Prose March 1-Aug. 31; poetry Sept. 1-Feb. 28. Charges $20 fee. Prize: $750 advance against royalties, standard royalty contract and publication.

☘ MANITOBA WRITING AND PUBLISHING AWARDS, c/o Manitoba Writers Guild, 206-100 Arthur St., Winnipeg, Manitoba R3B 1H3, Canada. (204)942-6134. Fax: (204)942-5754. E-mail: mbwriter@escape.ca. Website: www.mbwriter.mb.ca. **Contact:** Robyn Maharaj. Offered annually: The McNally Robinson Book of Year Award (adult); The McNally Robinson Book for Young People Awards (8 and under and 9 and older); The John Hirsch Award for Most Promising Manitoba Writer; The Mary Scorer Award for Best Book by a Manitoba Publisher; The Carol Shields Award; The Eileen Sykes McTavish Award for Best First Book; The Margaret Laurence Award for Fiction; The Alexander Kennedy Award for Non-Fiction; two Book Publishers Awards; and the biennial Les Prix Litteraires. Guidelines and submission forms available upon request. Open to Manitoba writers only. Deadline: December 1 (books published December 1-31 will be accepted until mid-January). Prize: Several prizes up to $3,000 (Canadian).

N MARTEN BEQUEST TRAVELLING SCHOLARSHIPS, Arts Management Pty. Ltd., Station House L. 4, 790 George St., Sydney NSW 2000, Australia. 61-2-9212-5066. Fax: 61-2-9211-7762. E-mail: claudia@artsmanagement

.com.au. **Contact:** Claudia Crosariol, assistant director. Offered in even years for prose and poetry by authors ages 21-35. Applicants must be Australian-born. Guidelines for SAE with 1 IRC. Deadline: Last Friday in October. Prize: $18,000 (Australian).

MASTERS LITERARY AWARDS, Center Press, P.O. Box 17897, Encino CA 91416. E-mail: usa11@usa.net. Website: http://members.nbci.com/CenterPress. **Contact:** Scott A. Sonders, managing editor. Offered annually and quarterly for work published within 2 years (preferred) and unpublished work (accepted). Fiction, 15 page maximum; poetry, 5 pages or 150 lines maximum; and nonfiction, 10 pages maximum. "A selection of winning entries will appear in our national literary publication." Winners also appear on the Internet. Center Press retains one-time publishing rights to selected winners. Deadline: March 15, June 15, August 15, December 15. Guidelines for SASE. Charges $15 reading/administration fee. Prize: 4 quarterly honorable mentions from which is selected one yearly Grand Prize of $1,000.

N MATURE WOMEN SCHOLARSHIP AWARD, The National League of American Pen Women, Inc., 1300 17th St., NW, Washington DC 20036. Fax: (202)452-6868. **Contact:** Dr. Wanda A. Rider, president. Offered in even numbered years to women 35 and over. Classifications include: Art, letters, music composition. Send SASE for rules (available after August). Prize: $1,000 in each classification.

MID-LIST PRESS FIRST SERIES AWARDS, Mid-List Press, 4324 12th Ave. S, Minneapolis MN 55407-3218. (612)822-3733. Fax: (612)823-8387. E-mail: guide@midlist.org. Website: www.midlist.org. **Contact:** Lane Stiles. Offered annually for unpublished works in four categories: Creative nonfiction, short fiction, poetry and novels. Guidelines for SASE or online at website. Deadline: Varies. Charges $20. Prize: An advance against royalties and publication.

MIDLAND AUTHORS AWARD, Society of Midland Authors, P.O. Box 10419, Chicago IL 60610-0419. E-mail: writercc@aol.com. Website: www.midlandauthors.org. **Contact:** Carol Jean Carlson. Offered annually for published fiction, nonfiction, poetry, biography, children's fiction and children's nonfiction. Authors must reside in the states of IL, IN, IA, KS, MI, MN, MS, NE, ND, SD, WI or OH. Guidelines and submission at website. Deadline: March 1. Prize: Monetary award given to winner in each category.

N THE MILTON CENTER POSTGRADUATE FELLOWSHIP, The Milton Center, 3100 McCormick Ave., Wichita KS 67213. (316)942-4291 ext. 226. Fax: (316)942-4483. E-mail: miltonc@newmanu.edu. **Contact:** Essie Sappenfield, program director. Offered annually to new writers of Christian commitment to complete their first book-length manuscript of fiction, poetry or creative nonfiction. The Milton Center exists to encourage work by writers who seek to animate the Christian imagination, foster intellectual integrity and explore the human condition with honesty and compassion. "Write well and have mature work habits. Don't worry about doctrinal matters, counting Christian symbols, etc. What you believe will automatically show up in your writing." Deadline: March 15. Guidelines for SASE. Charges $15 fee. Prize: Stipend of $1,225/month, residency in Wichita September-May. Two fellowships awarded each year.

N JENNY McKEAN/MOORE VISITING WRITER, English Dept., George Washington University, Washington DC 20052. (202)994-6180. Fax: (202)994-7915. E-mail: dmca@gwu.edu. Website: www.gwu.edu/~english. **Contact:** David McAleavey. Offered annually to provide one-year visiting writers to teach one G.W. course and one free community workshop each semester. Guidelines for SASE or on website. This contest seeks someone specializing in a different genre each year; for 2002-2003 we will seek someone in creative nonfiction; in 2003-2004 a poet; in 2004-2005 a fiction writer. Deadline: November 15. Prize: Annual stipend approximately $48,000 plus reduced-rent townhouse (not guaranteed).

NATIONAL LOOKING GLASS CHAPBOOK COMPETITION, Pudding House Publications, 60 N. Main St., Johnstown OH 43031. (740)967-6060. E-mail: pudding@johnstown.net. Website: www.puddinghouse.com. **Contact:** Jennifer Bosveld. Offered twice/year for "a collection of poems, short short stories, or other creative writing that represents our editorial slant: Popular culture, social justice, psychological, etc. Submissions might be themed or not." Guidelines for SASE or on website. Past winners include Rebecca Baggett, Willie Abraham Howard Jr., Michael Day, Bill Noble, William Keener, Mark Taksa, Ron Moran and many others. Deadline: June 30, September 30. Charges $10 fee. Prize: $100, publication of chapbook, 20 free books, 10 more for the reviewer of the author's choice.

THE NEBRASKA REVIEW AWARDS IN FICTION, POETRY AND CREATIVE NONFICTION, *The Nebraska Review*, FAB 212, University of Nebraska-Omaha, Omaha NE 68182-0324. (402)554-3159. E-mail: jreed@unomaha.edu. **Contact:** Susan Aizenberg (poetry), James Reed (fiction) or John Price (creative nonfiction). Estab. 1973. Offered annually for previously unpublished fiction, creative nonfiction and a poem or group of poems. Deadline: November 30. Charges $15 fee (includes a subscription to *The Nebraska Review*). Prize: $500 for each category.

NEW MILLENNIUM WRITINGS AWARD, New Millennium Writings Journal, P.O. Box 2463, Knoxville TN 37901. (865)428-0389. E-mail: donwill@aol.com. Website: www.mach2.com. **Contact:** Don Williams, director. Offered twice annually for unpublished fiction, poetry, essays or nonfiction prose, to encourage new fiction writers, poets and essayists and bring them to attention of publishing industry. Entrants receive an issue of *NMW* in which winners appear.

Deadline: January 31, June 15. Guidelines for SASE. Charges $15 fee. Prize: Fiction-$1,000; Poetry-$1,000; Essay or nonfiction prose-$1,000; winners and runners-up published in *NMW* and at www.mach2.com; 25 honorable mentions listed.

NEW WRITERS AWARDS, Great Lakes Colleges Association New Writers Awards, English Dept., Denison University, Granville OH 43023. (740)587-5740. Fax: (740)587-5680. E-mail: krumholz@denison.edu. Website: www.glca.org. **Contact:** Prof. Linda Krumholz, award director. Offered annually to the best first book of poetry and the best first book of fiction among those submitted by publishers. An honorarium of at least $300 will be guaranteed the author by each of the colleges they visit. Open to any first book of poetry or fiction submitted by a publisher. Deadline: February 28. Guidelines for SASE. Prize: Winning authors tour the GLCA colleges, where they will participate in whatever activities they and the college deem appropriate.

NIMROD, The University of Tulsa, 600 S. College, Tulsa OK 74104-3189. (918)631-3080. Fax: (918)631-3033. E-mail: nimrod@utulsa.edu. Website: www.utulsa.edu/nimrod. **Contact:** Francine Ringold, editor. Offered annually for unpublished fiction and poetry for Katherine Anne Porter Prize for Fiction and Pablo Neruda Prize for Poetry. Theme issue in the spring. *Nimrod*/Hardman Awards issue in the fall. For contest or theme issue guidelines send SASE. Open to any writer. Deadline: April 20. Charges $20 fee, includes 2 issues. Prize: 1st-$2,000 in each genre; 2nd-$1,000.

N: NLAPW VIRGINIA LIEBELER BIENNIAL GRANTS FOR MATURE WOMEN, National League of American Pen Women Inc., 1300 17th St. NW, Washington DC 20036-1973. (202)785-1997. **Contact:** Mary Jane Hillery. Offered in even years for career enhancement in the creative arts. Three categories: Art, letters and music. Open to women 35 and over who are US citizens. Deadline: October 1 of odd-numbered years. Guidelines for SASE. Charges $8. Prize: $1,000 grant in each category.

OHIOANA BOOK AWARDS, Ohioana Library Association, 274 E. First Ave., Columbus OH 43201-3673. (614)466-3831. Fax: (614)728-6974. E-mail: ohioana@sloma.state.oh.us. Website: www.oplin.lib.oh.us/OHIOANA. **Contact:** Linda Hengst, director. Offered annually to bring national attention to Ohio authors and their books (published in the last two years). Categories: Fiction, nonfiction, juvenile, poetry, and books about Ohio or an Ohioan. Writers must have been born in Ohio or lived in Ohio for at least 5 years. Deadline: December 31. Guidelines for SASE.

KENNETH PATCHEN COMPETITION, Pig Iron Press, P.O. Box 237, Youngstown OH 44501. (330)747-6932. Fax: (330)747-0599. E-mail: pigironpress@cboss.com. **Contact:** Jim Villani. Offered biannually for unpublished poetry or fiction (except for individual works published in magazines/journals). Alternates between poetry and fiction. Deadline: December 31. Guidelines for SASE. Charges $10 fee. Prize: Trade paperback publication in an edition of 1,000 copies, 20 copies to author, and $500.

N: PEACE WRITING INTERNATIONAL WRITING AWARDS, Consortium of Peace Research, Education & Development, 2582 Jimmie, Fayettville AR 72703-3420. (501)442-4600. E-mail: jbennet@uark.edu. Website: comp.uark.edu/~jbennet. **Contact:** Dick Bennett. Offered annually for unpublished work. "PeaceWriting encourages writing about international nonviolent peacemaking and peacemakers. PeaceWriting seeks book manuscripts about the causes, consequences and solutions to violence and war, and about the ideas and practices of nonviolent peacemaking and the lives of nonviolent peacemakers." Categories include: Nonfiction prose, novels, collections of short stories, collections of poetry, collections of short plays and works for young people. Open to any writer. Enclose SASE for manuscript return. Deadline: December 1. Guidelines for SASE. Prize: $500 for best nonfiction; $500 for best imaginative work; and $500 for best work for young people.

PEN CENTER USA WEST ANNUAL LITERARY AWARDS, PEN Center USA West, 672 S. Lafayette Park Place, #41, Los Angeles CA 90057. (213)365-8500. Fax: (213)365-9616. E-mail: pen@pen-usa-west.org. Website: www.pen-usa-west.org. **Contact:** Bill Kraines, executive director. Offered annually for fiction, nonfiction, poetry, children's literature or translation published January 1-December 31 of the current year. Open to authors west of the Mississippi River. Deadline: December 31. Guidelines for SASE. Charges $20 fee. Prize: $1,000.

PEN WRITING AWARDS FOR PRISONERS, PEN American Center, 568 Broadway, New York NY 10012. (212)334-1660. Fax: (212)334-2181. E-mail: pen@echonyc.com. Website: www.pen.org. Offered annually to the authors of the best poetry, plays, short fiction and nonfiction received from prison writers in the US. Deadline: Submit January 1-September 1. Guidelines for SASE. Prize: 1st-$100; 2nd-$50; 3rd-$25 (in each category).

N: PENMANSHIP, A CREATIVE ARTS CALENDAR, P.O. Box 2475, Staunton VA 24402. E-mail: penmanship@hotmail.com. **Contact:** Sheredia Norris, assistant director. Offered to all artists; unpublished and previously published work welcomed. Three categories: Poetry, short stories and photography/artwork. Submissions are not returned unless requested. Send SASE and request for list of winning contributors. Deadline: September 1. Guidelines for SASE. Charges $10 fee. Prize: One winner in each category. Winners receive a contributor copy, certificate of notability and the following: Poetry-$100; short story-$150; photography/artwork-$250.

N: PENMANSHIP, BROADSIDE SERIES, P.O. Box 2475, Staunton VA 24402. E-mail: penmanship@hotmail.c om. **Contact:** Sheredia Norris, assistant director. Unpublished and previously published poems and short stories wel- comed. Include SASE for return of submissions. Open to any writer. Penmanship buys first rights, one-time rights and second serial rights. Winners list published online and will be sent to applicants that send SASE and request for a list of winning contributors. Deadline: September 1. Guidelines for SASE. Charges $5 entry fee. Prize: Winner receives 5 contributor copies, a certificate of notability and $100.

POSTCARD STORY COMPETITION, The Writers' Union of Canada, 40 Wellington St. E., Third Floor, Toronto, Ontario M5E 1C7, Canada. (416)703-8982. Fax: (416)504-7656. E-mail: twuc@the-wire.com. Website: www.w ritersunion.ca. **Contact:** Caroline Sin. Offered annually for original and unpublished fiction, nonfiction, prose, verse, dialogue, etc. with a maximum 250 words in length. Open to Canadian citizens or landed immigrants only. Deadline: February 14. Guidelines for SASE. Charges $5/entry fee. Prize: $500.

THE PRESIDIO LA BAHIA AWARD, Sons of the Republic of Texas, 1717 Eighth St., Bay City TX 77414. (979)245-6644. Fax: (979)244-3819. E-mail: srttexas@srttexas.org. Website: www.srttexas.org. **Contact:** Melinda Wil- liams. Offered annually "to promote suitable preservation of relics, appropriate dissemination of data, and research into our Texas heritage, with particular attention to the Spanish Colonial period." Deadline: June 1-September 30. Guidelines for SASE. Prize: $2,000 total; 1st-minimum of $1,200, 2nd and 3rd prizes at the discretion of the judges.

QUINCY WRITER'S GUILD ANNUAL CREATIVE WRITING CONTEST, Quincy Writer's Guild, P.O. Box 433, Quincy IL 62306-0433. E-mail: chillebr@adams.net. Website: www.quincylibrary.org/guild.htm. **Contact:** Carol Hillebrenner, contest coordinator. Categories include serious poetry, light poetry, nonfiction, fiction. "No identification should appear on manuscripts, but send a separate 3×5 card for each entry with name, address, phone number, e-mail address, word count, and title of work." Only for previously unpublished work: Serious or light poetry (2 page/poem maximum), fiction (2,000 words maximum), nonfiction (2,000 words maximum). Guidelines for SASE or by e-mail. Period of Contest: January 1-April Charges $2/poem; $4/fiction or nonfiction. Prize: Cash prizes.

QWF LITERARY AWARDS, (formerly QSPELL), Quebec Writers' Federation, 1200 Atwater Ave., Montreal, Quebec H3Z 1X4, Canada. (514)933-0878. Fax: (514)934-2485. E-mail: qspell@total.net. Website: www.qwf.org. **Con- tact:** Diana McNeill. Offered annually for a book published October 1-September 30 to honor excellence in English- language writing in Quebec. Categories: Fiction, nonfiction, poetry and First Book and translation. Author must have resided in Quebec for 3 of the past 5 years. Deadline: May 31 for books and August 15 for books and finished proofs. Guidelines for SASE. Charges $10/title. Prize: $2,000 in each category; $1,000-First Book.

N: REGINA BOOK AWARD, Saskatchewan Book Awards Inc., Box 1921, Regina, Saskatchewan S4P 3E1, Canada. (306)569-1585. Fax: (306)569-4187. E-mail: sk.bookawards@dlcwest.com. Website: www.bookawards.sk.ca. **Contact:** Joyce Wells, executive director. Offered annually for work published October 1, 2001, to September 14, 2002. In recognition of the vitality of the literary community in Regina, this award is presented to a Regina author for the best book, judged on the quality of writing. Books from the following categories will be considered: Children's; drama; fiction (short fiction by a single author, novellas, novels); nonfiction (all categories of nonfiction writing except cook- books, directories, how-to books or bibliographies of minimal critical content); poetry. Deadline: First deadline: July 31; final deadline: September 14. Guidelines for SASE. Charges $15 (Canadian). Prize: $1,500.

N: MARY ROBERTS RINEHART FUND, MSN 3E4 English Department, George Mason University, 4400 Univer- sity Dr., Fairfax VA 22030-4444. (703)993-1180. E-mail: bgompert@gmu.edu. Website: www.gmu.edu/departments/ writing. **Contact:** Barbara Gomperts, graduate studies coordinator. Offered annually for unpublished authors "who, in order to finish projected work, need financial assistance otherwise unavailable." Grants by nomination to unpublished creative writers for fiction, poetry and nonfiction with a strong narrative quality. Submissions must include nominating letter from person in appropriate field. Deadline: November 30. Guidelines for SASE. Prize: Approximately $2,000.

SUMMERFIELD G. ROBERTS AWARD, Sons of the Republic of Texas, 1717 Eighth St., Bay City TX 77414. (979)245-6644. Fax: (979)244-3819. E-mail: srttexas@srttexas.org. Website: www.srttexas.org. **Contact:** Melinda Wil- liams. Offered annually for submissions published during the previous calendar year "to encourage literary effort and research about historical events and personalities during the days of the Republic of Texas, 1836-1846, and to stimulate interest in the period. Deadline: January 15. Prize: $2,500.

BRUCE P. ROSSLEY LITERARY AWARD, 96 Inc., P.O. Box 15558, Boston MA 02215. (617) 267-0543. Fax: (617)262-3568. **Contact:** Vera Gold, executive director. Offered in even years to give greater recognition to a writer of merit. In addition to writing, accomplishments in the fields of teaching and community service are considered. Nomina- tions accepted August 1-September 30. "The 96 Inc. Bruce P. Rossley Literary Awards will be presented next in 2004. We are revising guidelines with input from our 60-member committee (available in 2003)." Any writer may be nomi- nated, but the focus is merit and those writers who have been under-recognized. Deadline: September 30. Charges $10 fee. Prize: $1,000.

N̄ **SASKATCHEWAN BOOK OF THE YEAR AWARD**, Saskatchewan Book Awards Inc., Box 1921, Regina, Saskatchewan S4P 3E1, Canada. (306)569-1585. Fax: (306)569-4187. E-mail: sk.bookawards@dlcwest.com. Website: www.bookawards.sk.ca. **Contact:** Joyce Wells, executive director. Offered annually for work published October 1, 2001, to September 14, 2002. This award is presented to a Saskatchewan author for the best book, judged on the quality of writing. Books from the following categories will be considered: Children's; drama; fiction (short fiction by a single author, novellas, novels); nonfiction (all categories of nonfiction writing except cookbooks, directories, how-to books or bibliographies of minimal critical content); poetry. Deadline: First deadline: July 31; final deadline: September 14. Guidelines for SASE. Charges $15 (Canadian). Prize: $1,500.

N̄ **SASKATOON BOOK AWARD**, Saskatchewan Book Awards Inc., Box 1921, Regina, Saskatchewan S4P 3E1, Canada. (306)569-1585. Fax: (306)569-4187. E-mail: sk.bookawards@dlcwest.com. Website: www.bookawards.sk .ca. **Contact:** Joyce Wells, executive director. Offered annually for work published October 1, 2001, to September 14, 2002. In recognition of the vitality of the literary community in Saskatoon, this award is presented to a Saskatoon author for the best book, judged on the quality of writing. Books from the following categories will be considered: Children's; drama; fiction (short fiction by a single author, novellas, novels); nonfiction (all categories of nonfiction writing except cookbooks, directories, how-to books or bibliographies of minimal critical content); poetry. Deadline: First deadline: July 31; final deadline: September 14. Guidelines for SASE. Charges $15 (Canadian). Prize: $1,500.

SHORT GRAIN WRITING CONTEST, Grain Magazine, P.O. Box 1154, Regina, Saskatchewan S4P 3B4, Canada. (306)244-2828. Fax: (306)244-0255. E-mail: grain.mag@sk.sympatico.ca. Website: www.skwriter.com/grain. **Contact:** Jennifer Still. Contest Director: Elizabeth Philips. Offered annually for unpublished dramatic monologues, postcard stories (narrative fiction) and prose (lyric) poetry and nonfiction creative prose. Maximum length for short entries, 500 words; Long Grain of Truth (nonfiction), 5,000 words or less. Guidelines for SAE and IRC or Canadian stamps. All entrants receive a one-year subscription to *Grain*. *Grain* purchases first Canadian serial rights only; copyright remains with the author. Open to any writer. No fax or e-mail submissions. Deadline: January 31. Charges $22 fee for 2 entries, plus $5 for additional entries; US and international entries $22, plus $4 postage in US funds (non-Canadian). Prize: Three prizes of $500.

✦ SHORT PROSE COMPETITION FOR DEVELOPING WRITERS, The Writers' Union of Canada, 40 Wellington St. E., Third Floor, Toronto, Ontario M5E 1C7, Canada. (416)703-8982 ext. 223. Fax: (416)504-7656. E-mail: twuc@the-wire.com. Website: www.writersunion.ca. **Contact:** Caroline Sin. Offered annually "to discover developing Canadian writers of unpublished prose fiction and nonfiction." Length: 2,500 words max. Open to Canadian citizens or landed immigrants who have not been published in book format and who do not currently have a contract with a publisher. Deadline: November 3. Guidelines for SASE. Charges $25 entry fee. Prize: $2,500 and publication in *Books in Canada* (a Canadian literary journal).

N̄ THE BERNICE SLOTE AWARD, *Prairie Schooner*, 201 Andrews Hall, PO Box 880334, Lincoln NE 68588-0334. (402)472-0911. Fax: (402)472-9771. E-mail: eflanagan2@unl.edu. Website: www.unl.edu/schooner/psmain.htm. **Contact:** Hilda Raz. Offered annually for the best work by a beginning writer published in *Prairie Schooner* in the previous year. Prize: $500.

N̄ SNAKE NATION REVIEW, Snake Nation Press, 110 #2 W. Force St., Valdosta GA 31601. (229)244-0752. E-mail: jeana@snakenationpress.org. Website: www.snakenationpress.org. **Contact:** Jean Arambula. Offered 3 times/year to offer good, well-written literature to the public and to give unpublished/underpublished writers a chance to see their work. Open to any writer. Deadline: March 15. Guidelines for SASE. Charges $5/story, $1/poem. Prize: Stories: $300, $200, $100. Poems: $100, $75, $50. Art/photos: $100.

SOUTHWEST REVIEW AWARDS, Southern Methodist University, 307 Fondren Library West, P.O. Box 750374, Dallas TX 75275-0374. (214)768-1036. Fax: (214)768-1408. E-mail: swr@mail.smu.edu. **Contact:** Elizabeth Mills. "The $1,000 John H. McGinnis Memorial Award is given each year for fiction and nonfiction that has been published in the *Southwest Review* in the previous year. Stories or articles are not submitted directly for the award, but simply for publication in the magazine. The Elizabeth Matchett Stover Award, an annual prize of $200, is awarded to the author of the best poem or group of poems published in the magazine during the preceding year."

WALLACE STEGNER FELLOWSHIPS, Creative Writing Program, Stanford University, Dept. of English, Stanford CA 94305-2087. (650)723-2637. Fax: (650)723-3679. E-mail: gay.pierce@leland.stanford.edu. Website: www.stanford. edu/dept/english/cw/. **Contact:** Gay Pierce, program administrator. Offered annually for a two-year residency at Stanford for emerging writers to attend the Stegner workshop to practice and perfect their craft under the guidance of the creative writing faculty. Guidelines available. Deadline: December 1. Charges $40 fee. Prize: Living stipend (currently $18,000/year) and required workshop tuition of $6,000/year.

sub-TERRAIN MAGAZINE AWARDS, *sub-TERRAIN Magazine*, 175 E. Broadway, #204A, Vancouver, British Columbia V5T 1W2, Canada. (604)876-8710. Fax: (604)879-2667. E-mail: subter@portal.ca. Website: www.anvilpress. com. **Contact:** Brian Kaufman, managing editor. Offered annually for nonfiction, poems, short stories and photography.

Contests include the *sub-Terrain* Creative Nonfiction Writing Contest, Poetry Contest and Annual Short Story Contest. The magazine acquires one-time rights only; after publication rights revert to the author. Deadline: Varies. Charges $15 fee, which includes a subscription to the magazine. Prize: Cash and publication.

N: TENNESSEE WRITERS ALLIANCE LITERARY COMPETITION, Tennessee Writers Alliance, P.O. Box 120396, Nashville TN 37212. (615)831-0072. **Contact:** Dawn Phariss, executive director. Offered annually for unpublished novels and poetry. Membership open to all, regardless of residence, for $25/year, $15/year for students. Acquires rights to publish once. Deadline: June 15. Guidelines for SASE. Charges $10 fee for members, $15 fee for nonmembers. Prize: 1st-$500, 2nd-$250, 3rd-$100.

N: TORONTO BOOK AWARD, City of Toronto c/o Toronto Protocol, 100 Queen St. W, 10th Floor, West Tower, City Hall, Toronto Ontario M5H 2N2, Canada. (416)392-8191. Fax: (416)392-1247. Website: www.city.toronto.com. **Contact:** Bev Kurmey. Offered annually for previously published fiction, nonfiction or juvenile books that are "evocative of Toronto." Deadline: February 28. Guidelines for SASE. Prize: Awards total $15,000.

N: MARK TWAIN AWARD FOR SHORT FICTION, *Red Rock Review*/Community College of Southern Nevada, English Department, 3200 E. Cheyenne Ave., N. Las Vegas NV 89030. (702)651-4094. Fax: (702)651-4339. E-mail: rich_logsdon@ccsn.nevada.edu. Website: www.ccsn.nevada.edu/english/redrockreview/default.html. **Contact:** Rich Logsdon, editor. Offered annually for unpublished fiction to emerging writers of fiction and poetry. Deadline: October 31. Charges $10 fee. Prize: $1,000.

N: THE BRONWEN WALLACE MEMORIAL AWARD, The Writers' Trust of Canada, 40 Wellington St. E, Suite 300, Toronto, Ontario M5E 1C7, Canada. (416)504-8222. Fax: (416)504-9090. E-mail: info@writerstrust.com. Website: www.writerstrust.com. **Contact:** Candice Cartier. Presented annually to a Canadian writer under the age of 35 who is not yet published in book form. The award, which alternates each year between poetry and short fiction, was established in memory of poet Bronwen Wallace. Prize: $1,000.

WESTERN HERITAGE AWARDS, National Cowboy & Western Heritage Museum, 1700 NE 63rd, Oklahoma City OK 73111. (405)478-6404. Fax: (405)478-4714. E-mail: editor@nationalcowboymuseum.org. Website: www.nationalco wboymuseum.org. **Contact:** M.J. VanDeventer, publications director. Offered annually for excellence in representation of great stories of the American West published January 1-December 31. Competition includes seven literary categories: Nonfiction; Western Novel; Juvenile Book; Art Book; Short Story; Poetry Book; and Magazine Article.

WESTERN MAGAZINE AWARDS, Western Magazine Awards Foundation, Main Post Office, Box 2131, Vancouver, British Columbia V6B 3T8, Canada. (604)669-3717. Fax: (604)669-3701. E-mail: wma@direct.ca. Website: www.westernmagazineawards.com. **Contact:** Bryan Pike. Offered annually for magazine work published January 1-December 31 of previous calendar year. Entry categories include business, culture, science, technology and medicine, entertainment, fiction, political issues, and much more. Guidelines for SASE or on website. Applicant must be Canadian citizen, landed immigrant, or fulltime resident. The work must have been published in a magazine whose main editorial office is in Western Canada, the Northwest Territories and Yukon. Deadline: February 23. Charges $27 for work in magazines with circulation under 20,000; $35 for work in magazines with circulation over 20,000. Prize: $500.

N: WESTMORELAND SHORT STORY & POETRY CONTEST, Westmoreland Arts & Heritage Festival, RD2, Box 355A, Latrobe PA 15650-9415. (724)834-7474. Fax: (724)834-2717. E-mail: info@artsandheritage.com. Website: www.artsandheritage.com. **Contact:** Donnie A. Gutherie. Offered annually for unpublished work. Writers are encouraged to submit short stories from all genres. The purpose of the contest is to provide writers varied competition in two categories: Short story and poetry. Entries must be 4,000 words or less. No erotica or pornography. Deadline: March 2. Guidelines for SASE. Charges $10 fee/story, $10 fee/two poems. Prize: Publication on the festival website, a reading at the festival, and cash prizes from $75-200.

N: WIND MAGAZINE CONTESTS, Wind Magazine, P.O. Box 24548, Lexington KY 40524. (859)277-6849. Website: www.wind.wind.org. **Contact:** Chris Green, editor. Offered annually for unpublished poems, chapbooks and short stories. Deadline: March 1 for poems, July 30 for short stories, October 31 for chapbooks. Guidelines for SASE. Charges $3/poem, $10/short story and $15/chapbook. Prize: $500 and publication in *Wind Magazine* for winning poem and short story; $100 plus 25 copies of published book for winning chapbook. All finalists receive a one-year subscription to the magazine. Enclose SASE for results.

WINNERS' CIRCLE INTERNATIONAL WRITING CONTEST, Canadian Authors Association, Metropolitan Toronto Branch, 33 Springbank Ave., Scarborough, Ontario M1N 1G2, Canada. (416)698-8687. Fax: (416)698-8687. E-mail: caamtb@inforamp.net. **Contact:** Bill Belfontaine. Offered annually to encourage new short stories which help authors to get published. First publishing rights required but copyright owned by writer. SAE plus 90 cents postage for "How to Write a Short Story" booklet. Registration and rules only, send SASE. Deadline: July 1-November 30. Charges $20 fee, payable to Canadian Authors Association. Prize: Grand Prize-$500, 1st-$200, 2nd-$150, 3rd $100 and 16 honorary mention winners in short stories. Winners of cash prizes and honorary mentions published in Winners' Circle Anthology.

■ **WRITERS GUILD OF ALBERTA AWARDS**, Writers Guild of Alberta, Percy Page Centre, 11759 Groat Rd., Edmonton, Alberta T5M 3K6, Canada. (708)422-8174. Fax: (702)422-2663. E-mail: wga@oanet.com. Website: www.writersguild.ab.ca. **Contact:** Norma Locke, executive director. Offers the following awards: Henry Kreisel Award for Best First Book; Wilfred Eggleston Award for Nonfiction; Georges Bugnet Award for Fiction (novel); Howard O'Hagan Award for Short Fiction; Stephan G. Stephansson Award for Poetry; R. Ross Annett Award for Children's Literature; Gwen Pharis Ringwood Award for Drama; and Isabel Miller Young Writers Award (poetry or fiction); John Whyte Essay Competition. Eligible books will have been published anywhere in the world between January 1 and December 31. The authors must have been residents of Alberta for at least 12 of the 18 months prior to Dec. 31. Unpublished manuscripts, except in the drama category, are not eligible. Anthologies are not eligible. Full-length radio plays which have been published in anthologies are eligible. Works may be submitted by authors, publishers or any interested parties. Deadline: December 31. Guidelines for SASE. Prize: Winning authors will receive $1,000 and a leather-bound copy of their book; the Isabel Miller Young Writers Award offers prizes of $300, $200 and $100.

Arts Councils & Foundations

ARIZONA COMMISSION ON THE ARTS FELLOWSHIP IN CREATIVE WRITING, Arizona Commission on the Arts, 417 W. Roosevelt, Phoenix AZ 85018. (602)255-5882. Fax: (602)256-0282. E-mail: general@ArizonaArts.o rg. Website: az.arts.asu.edu/artscomm. **Contact:** Jill Bernstein, literature director. Offered annually for previously published or unpublished fiction or poetry written within the last three years. Guidelines for SASE or by e-mail. Open to Arizona writers 18 years or older. Deadline: September 15, 2001 (fiction); mid-September 2002 (poetry). Prize: $5,000-7,500.

ARTIST ASSISTANCE FELLOWSHIP, Minnesota State Arts Board, Park Square Court 400 Sibley St., Suite 200, St. Paul MN 55101-1928. (651)215-1600 or (800)866-2787. Fax: (651)215-1602. E-mail: amy.frimpong@arts.state.mn.us. Website: www.arts.state.mn.us. **Contact:** Amy Frimpong. Literary categories include prose, poetry, playwriting and screenwriting. Open to Minnesota residents. Prize: Annual fellowships of $8,000 to be used for time, materials, living expenses.

ARTIST FELLOWSHIP, Japan Foundation, 39th Floor, 152 W. 57th St., New York NY 10019. (212)489-0299. Fax: (212)489-0409. E-mail: yuika_goto@jfny.org. Website: www.jfny.org/. **Contact:** Yuika Goto. Offered annually. "Contact us in September by mail or fax. Keep in mind that this is an international competition. Due to the breadth of the application pool only four artists are selected for awards in the US. Applicants need not submit a writing sample, but if one is submitted it must be brief. Three letters of recommendation must be submitted from peers. One letter will double as a letter of affiliation, which must be submitted by a *Japan-based* (not necessarily an ethnic Japanese) peer artist. The applicant must present a concise and cogent project objective and must be a professional writer/artist with accessible qualifications, i.e., a list of major works or publications." Deadline: December 1.

ARTIST FELLOWSHIP AWARDS, Wisconsin Arts Board, 101 E. Wilson St. 1st Floor, Madison WI 53702. (608)266-0190. Fax: (608)267-0380. E-mail: artsboard@arts.state.wi.us. Website: www.arts.state.wi.us. **Contact:** Mark Fraire, director. Offered every two years (even years), rewarding outstanding, professionally active Wisconsin artists by supporting their continued development, enabling them to create new work, complete work in progress, or pursue activities which contribute to their artistic growth. If the deadline falls on a weekend, the deadline is extended to the following Monday. Contact the Arts Board for an application and guidelines. The Arts Board requires permission to use the work sample, or a portion thereof, for publicity or educational purposes. Contest open to professionally active artists who have resided in Wisconsin 1 year prior to application. Artists who are full-time students pursuing a degree in the fine arts at the time of application are not eligible. Deadline: September 15. Prize: $8,000 fellowship awarded to eight Wisconsin writers.

■ **ARTISTS FELLOWSHIP PROGRAM IN POETRY & PROSE**, Illinois Art Council, 100 W. Randolph, Suite 10-500, Chicago IL 60601. (312)814-6790. Fax: (312)814-1471. E-mail: susan@arts.state.il.us. Website: www.state.il.us/agency/iac. **Contact:** Susan Eleuterio, program manager, literature. Offered annually for Illinois writers of exceptional talent to enable them to pursue their artistic goals. Applicant must have been a resident of Illinois for at least one year prior to the deadline. Guidlines for SASE. Deadline: December 1. Prize: Non-matching award of $7,000; finalist award of $700.

ARTISTS' FELLOWSHIPS, New York Foundation for the Arts, 155 Avenue of the Americas, 14th Floor, New York NY 10013-1507. (212)366-6900 ext. 217. E-mail: nyfaafp@nyfa.org. Website: www.nyfa.org. **Contact:** Artists' Fellowships. "Artists' Fellowships are cash grants of $7,000 awarded in 16 disciplines on a biannual rotation. Fiction and Playwriting will be reviewed in 2001-2002. Nonfiction Literature and Poetry will be the literature disciplines under review in 2002-2003. Awards are based upon the recommendations of peer panels and are not project support. The fellowship may be used by each recipient as she/he sees fit. Call for application in July. Deadlines in October. Results announced in April. The New York Foundation for the Arts supports artists at all stages of their careers and from diverse backgrounds." All applicants must be 18 years of age and a New York resident for two years prior to the time of application. Deadline: October. Prize: Grants of $7,000.

ARTS RECOGNITION AND TALENT SEARCH, National Foundation for Advancement in the Arts, 800 Brickell Ave., Suite 500, Miami FL 33131. (305)377-1140 or (800)970-ARTS. Fax: (305)377-1149. E-mail: nfaa@nfaa.org. Website: www.ARTSawards.org. **Contact:** Estela Carmona, programs coordinator. Estab. 1981. For achievements in dance, music, jazz, photography, theater, film & videos, visual art, voice and writing. Applications available on website or by phone request. Deadline: Early-June 1 ($25 fee); regular-October 1 ($35 fee). Prize: Exceptionally talented young artists have access to an award package totaling up to $800,000, $3 million in scholarship opportunities and the chance to be named Presidential Scholars in the Arts.

GEORGE BENNETT FELLOWSHIP, Phillips Exeter Academy, 20 Main St., Exeter NH 03833-2460. Website: www.exeter.edu. **Contact:** Charles Pratt, coordinator, selection committee. Estab. 1968. Annual award for Fellow and family "to provide time and freedom from material considerations to a person seriously contemplating or pursuing a career as a writer. Applicants should have a manuscript in progress which they intend to complete during the fellowship period." Guidelines for SASE or on website. The committee favors writers who have not yet published a book with a major publisher. Residence at the Academy during the Fellowship period required. Deadline: December 1. Prize: Annual award of $6,000 stipend, room and board.

BUSH ARTIST FELLOWS PROGRAM, The Bush Foundation, E-900 First National Bank Bldg., 332 Minnesota St., St. Paul MN 55101. (800)605-7315. Website: www.bushfoundation.org. **Contact:** Kathi Polley. Estab. 1976. Award for Minnesota, North Dakota, South Dakota, and western Wisconsin residents 25 years or older (students are not eligible) "to buy 12-18 months of time for the applicant to further his/her own work." All application categories rotate on a two year cycle. Publishing, performance and/or option requirements for eligibility. Applications available August 2002. Deadline: October. Prize: Up to 15 fellowships/year, $40,000 each.

N. CREATIVITY FELLOWSHIP, Northwood University, Alden B. Dow Creativity Center, 4000 Whiting Drive, Midland MI 48640-2398. (989)837-4478. Fax: (989)837-4468. E-mail: creativity@northwood.edu. Website: www.north wood.edu/abd. **Contact:** Award Director. Estab. 1979. Ten-week summer residency for individuals in any field who wish to pursue new and creative ideas that have potential impact in their fields. No accommodations for family/pets. Write for guidelines or check website. Authors must be US citizens. Deadline: December 31 (postmarked).

DOCTORAL DISSERTATION FELLOWSHIPS IN JEWISH STUDIES, National Foundation for Jewish Culture, 330 7th Ave., 21st Floor, New York NY 10001. (212)629-0500 ext. 205. Fax: (212)629-0508. E-mail: KBistrong@je wishculture.org. Website: www.jewishculture.org. **Contact:** Kim Bistrong, associate program director, grants and awards. Offered annually to students. Deadline varies, usually early January. Open to students who have completed their course work and need funding for research in order to write their dissertation thesis or a Ph.D. in a Jewish field of study. Guidelines for SASE. Prize: $7,000-$10,000 grant.

FELLOWSHIP, William Morris Society in the US, P.O. Box 53263, Washington DC 20009. E-mail: us@morrissociety. org. Website: www.morrissociety.org. **Contact:** Mark Samuels Lasner. Offered annually "to promote study of the life and work of William Morris (1834-96), British poet, designer and socialist. Award may be for research or a creative project." Curriculum vitae, 1-page proposal and two letters of recommendation required for application. Applicants must be US citizens or permanent residents. Deadline: December 1. Prize: Up to $1,000, multiple, partial awards possible.

FELLOWSHIP-LITERATURE, Alabama State Council on the Arts, 201 Monroe St., Montgomery AL 36130. (334)242-4076 ext. 224. Fax: (334)240-3269. E-mail: randy@arts.state.al.us. Website: www.arts.state.al.us. **Contact:** Randy Shoults. Literature Fellowship offered every year, for previously published or unpublished work to set aside time to create and to improve skills. Two-year Alabama residency required. Guidelines available. Deadline: March 1. Prize: $10,000 or $5,000.

FELLOWSHIPS, DC Commission on the Arts & Humanities, 410 Eighth St. NW, Washington DC 20004. (202)724-5613. E-mail: dcart@dc.gov. Website: dcarts.dc.gov. **Contact:** Sandra Maddox Barton. Offered biannually to reward excellence in an artistic endeavor. "Visit the website for updated deadline information and guidelines." Writers must be residents of the District of Columbia for at least one year prior to application date. Deadline: Early June. Prize: Fellowship of $5,000.

FELLOWSHIPS (LITERATURE), RI State Council on the Arts, 83 Park St., Sixth Floor, Providence RI 02903. (401)222-3880. Fax: (401)222-3018. E-mail: info@risca.state.ri.us. Website: www.risca.state.ri.us. **Contact:** Fellowship Coordinator. Offered every year for previously published or unpublished works in the categories of poetry, fiction, and playwriting/screenwriting. Open to Rhode Island residents only. Deadline: April 1, 2002. Guidelines for SASE. Prize: $5,000 fellowship; $1,000 runner-up.

FELLOWSHIPS FOR CREATIVE WRITERS, National Endowment for the Arts Literature Program, Nancy Hanks Center, 1100 Pennsylvania Ave. NW, Washington DC 20506-0001. (202)682-5428. Website: www.arts.gov. **Contact:** Amy Stolls. "Fellowships in prose (fiction and creative nonfiction) and poetry are available to creative writers of exceptional talent. Fellowships enable recipients to set aside time for writing, research, travel and general career advancement." Guidelines on website or by phone request. Deadline: Poetry: March 11, 2002; fiction and creative nonfiction: March 2003 (date to be determined). Prize: Grants are for $20,000.

FELLOWSHIPS TO ASSIST RESEARCH AND ARTISTIC CREATION, John Simon Guggenheim Memorial Foundation, 90 Park Ave., New York NY 10016. (212)687-4470. Fax: (212)697-3248. E-mail: fellowships@gf.org. Website: www.gf.org. Offered annually to assist scholars and artists to engage in research in any field of knowledge and creation in any of the arts, under the freest possible conditions and irrespective of race, color, or creed. Application form is required. Deadline: October 1.

FLORIDA INDIVIDUAL ARTIST FELLOWSHIPS, Florida Department of State, Division of Cultural Affairs, The Capitol, Tallahassee FL 32399-0250. (850)487-2980. Fax: (850)922-5259. E-mail: vohlsson@mail.dos.state.fl.us. Website: www.dos.state.fl.us. **Contact:** Valerie Ohlsson, arts administrator. Open to Florida writers only. Deadline: February. Prize: $5,000 each for fiction, poetry and children's literature.

GAP (GRANTS FOR ARTIST PROJECTS); FELLOWSHIP, Artist Trust, 1402 Third Ave, Suite 404, Seattle WA 98101-2118. (206)467-8734. Fax: (206)467-9633. E-mail: heather@artisttrust.org. Website: www.artisttrust.org. **Contact:** Heather Dwyer, program director. "The GAP is awarded to 70 artists, including writers, per year. The award is meant to help finance a specific project, which can be in very early stages or near completion. Literature fellowships are offered every other year, and approximately six literature fellowships are awarded. The award is made on the basis of work of the past five years." Fulltime students are not eligible. Open to Washington state residents only. Guidelines for SASE. Prize: Fellowship, $5,500; GAP, up to $1,400.

HAWAI'I AWARD FOR LITERATURE, State Foundation on Culture and the Arts, 44 Merchant St., Honolulu HI 96813. (808)586-0306. Fax: (808)586-0308. E-mail: sfca@sfca.state.hi.us. Website: www.state.hi.us/sfca. **Contact:** Hawai'i Literary Arts Council (Box 11213, Honolulu HI 96828-0213). "The annual award honors the lifetime achievement of a writer whose work is important to Hawai'i and/or Hawai'i's people." Nominations are a public process; inquiries should be directed to the Hawai'i Literary Arts Council at address listed. "Cumulative work is considered. Self nominations are allowed, but not usual. Fiction, poetry, drama, certain types of nonfiction, screenwriting and song lyrics are considered. The award is not intended to recognize conventional academic writing and reportage, nor is it intended to recognize more commercial types of writing, e.g., advertising copy, tourist guides, and how-to manuals." Deadline: November. Prize: Governor's reception and cash award.

THE HODDER FELLOWSHIP, The Council of the Humanities, Joseph Henry House, Princeton University, Princeton NJ 08544. (609)258-4717. Fax: (609)258-2783. E-mail: humcounc@princeton.edu. Website: www.princeton.edu/~humc ounc/. **Contact:** Cass Garner. The Hodder Fellowship is awarded to a humanist in the early stages of a career for the pursuit of independent work at Princeton in the humanities. The recipient has usually written one book and is working on a second. Preference is given to applicants outside of academia. "The Fellowship is designed specifically to identify and nurture extraordinary potential rather than to honor distinguished achievement." Candidates for the Ph.D. are not eligible. Submit résumé, sample of work (up to 10 pages), proposal and SASE. Deadline: November 1. Prize: Approximately $46,500 stipend.

N: INDIVIDUAL ARTIST FELLOWSHIPS/MINI-FELLOWSHIPS, Kansas Arts Commission, 700 SW Jackson, Suite 1004, Topeka KS 66603-3761. (785)296-3335. Fax: (785)296-4989. E-mail: kac@arts.state.ks.us. Website: arts.state.ks.us. **Contact:** Jean Denney. Offered annually for Kansas artists, both published and unpublished. Fellowships are offered in 10 artistic disciplines, rotating five disciplines every other year, and are awarded based on artistic merit. The fellowship disciplines are: Music composition, choreography, film/video, interdisciplinary/performance art, playwriting, fiction, poetry, two-dimensional visiual art, three-dimensional visual art, and crafts. Mini-fellowships (up to 12) are awarded to emerging artists in the same 10 disciplines. Guidelines on website. Deadline: Varies. Prize: Fellowship: $5,000. Mini-fellowship: $500.

INDIVIDUAL ARTISTS FELLOWSHIPS, Nebraska Arts Council, 3838 Davenport St., Omaha NE 68131-2329. (402)595-2122. Fax: (402)595-2334. E-mail: swise@nebraskaartscouncil.org. Website: www.nebraskaartscouncil.org. **Contact:** Suzanne Wise. Estab. 1991. Offered every three years (literature alternates with other disciplines) to recognize exemplary achievements by originating artists in their fields of endeavor and support the contributions made by Nebraska artists to the quality of life in this state. "Generally, distinguished achievement awards are $5,000 and merit awards are $1,000-2,000. Funds available are announced in September prior to the deadline." Must be a resident of Nebraska for at least 2 years prior to submission date; 18 years of age; not enrolled in an undergraduate, graduate or certificate-granting program in English, creative writing, literature, or related field. Deadline: November 15, 2001. Prize: $5,000 and merit awards are $1,000-2,000.

JOSEPH HENRY JACKSON AWARD, The San Francisco Foundation, Administered by Intersection for the Arts, 446 Valencia St., San Francisco CA 94103. (415)626-2787. Fax: (415)626-1636. E-mail: info@theintersection.org.

Contact: Kevin B. Chen, program director. Estab. 1965. Offered annually for unpublished, work-in-progress fiction (novel or short story), nonfiction or poetry by an author age 20-35, with 3-year consecutive residency in northern California or Nevada prior to submission. Deadline: November 15-January 31. Guidelines for SASE.

N EZRA JACK KEATS MEMORIAL FELLOWSHIP, Ezra Jack Keats Foundation (funding) awarded through Kerlan Collection, University of Minnesota, 113 Andersen Library, 222 21st Ave. S, Minneapolis MN 55455. (612)624-4576. Fax: (612)625-5525. E-mail: CLRC@tc.umn.edu. Website: special.lib.umn.edu/clrc/. **Contact:** Library Assistant. Purpose is "to award a talented writer and/or illustrator of children's books who wishes to use Kerlan Collection for the furtherance of his or her artistic development. Special consideration will be given to someone who would find it difficult to finance the visit to the Kerlan Collection." Open to any writer. Deadline: May 1. Guidelines for SASE. Prize: $1,500 for travel to study at Kerlan Collection.

KENTUCKY ARTS COUNCILS FELLOWSHIPS IN WRITING, Kentucky Arts Council, Old Capitol Annex, 300 W. Broadway, Frankfort KY 40601. (502)564-3757 or toll free (888)833-2787. Fax: (502)564-2839. E-mail: lori.mea dows@mail.state.ky.us. Website: www.kyarts.org. **Contact:** Lori Meadows. Offered in even-numbered years for devel opment/artist's work. Guidelines for SASE (3 months before deadline). Must be Kentucky resident. Deadline: September 15, 2002. Prize: $5,000.

MONEY FOR WOMEN, Barbara Deming Memorial Fund, Inc., P.O. Box 630125, The Bronx NY 10463. **Contact:** Susan Pliner. "Small grants to individual feminists in art, fiction, nonfiction and poetry, whose work addresses women's concerns and/or speaks for peace and justice from a feminist perspective." Guidelines and required entry forms for SASE. "The Fund does not give educational assistance, monies for personal study or loans, monies for dissertation, research projects, or self-publication, grants for group projects, business ventures, or emergency funds for hardships." Open to citizens of the US or Canada. The fund also offers two awards, the "Gertrude Stein Award" for outstanding works by a lesbian and the "Fannie Lou Hamer Award" for work which combats racism and celebrates women of color. No special application necessary for these 2 awards. Recipients will be chosen from all the proposals. Deadline: Decem ber 31 and June 30. Prize: Grants up to $1,500.

LARRY NEAL WRITERS' COMPETITION, DC Commission on the Arts and Humanities, 410 Eighth St., NW 5th Floor, Washington DC 20004. (202)724-1475. Fax: (202)727-4135. E-mail: lionellt@hotmail.com. Website: www.ca paccess.org/dccah. **Contact:** Lionell C. Thomas, grants and legislative officer. Thomas, grants and legislative officer. Offered annually for unpublished poetry, fiction, essay and dramatic writing. Call or visit website for current deadlines. Open to Washington DC residents only. Prize: Cash awards.

NEW HAMPSHIRE INDIVIDUAL ARTISTS' FELLOWSHIPS, New Hampshire State Council on the Arts, 40 N. Main St., Concord NH 03301-4974. (603)271-2789. Fax: (603)271-3584. Website: www.state.nh.us/nharts. **Contact:** Audrey V. Sylvester. Estab. 1982. Offered to recognize artistic excellence and professional commitment. Open to New Hampshire residents 18 and older; no full-time students. Deadline: First Friday in May.

PEW FELLOWSHIPS IN THE ARTS, The University of the Arts, 230 S. Broad St., Suite 1003, Philadelphia PA 19102. (215)875-2285. Fax: (215)875-2276. Website: www.pewarts.org. **Contact:** Melissa Franklin, director. Offered annually to provide financial support directly to artists so that they may have the opportunity to dedicate themselves wholly to the development of their artwork for up to two years. Areas of interest have included fiction, creative nonfiction, poetry, playwriting and screenwriting. Call for guidelines or view from the website. Entrants must be 25 or older and have been Pennsylvania residents of Bucks, Chester, Delaware, Montgomery or Philadelphia counties for two years or longer. Current students are not eligible. Deadline: December. Prize: $50,000 fellowship.

JAMES D. PHELAN LITERARY AWARD, The San Francisco Foundation, administered by Intersection for the Arts, 446 Valencia St., San Francisco CA 94103. (415)626-2787. Fax: (415)626-1636. E-mail: info@theintersection.org. **Contact:** Kevin B. Chen, program director. Estab. 1965. Offered annually for unpublished, work-in-progress fiction, nonfiction, short story, poetry or drama by a California-born author age 20-35. Deadline: November 15-January 31. Guidelines for SASE.

REQUEST FOR PROPOSAL, Rhode Island State Council on the Arts, 83 Park St. Suite 6, Providence RI 02903-1037. (401)277-3880. Fax: (401)521-1351. E-mail: randy@risca.state.ri.us. Website: www.risca.state.ri.us. **Contact:** Randall Rosenbaum, executive director. "Request for Proposal grants enable an artist to create new work and/or complete works-in-progress by providing direct financial assistance. By encouraging significant development in the work of an individual artist, these grants recognize the central contribution artists make to the creative environment of Rhode Island." Guidelines for 9×12 SASE. Open to Rhode Island residents age 18 or older; students not eligible. Deadline: October 1 and April 1. Prize: Non-matching grants of $1,500-4,000.

SEATTLE ARTISTS PROGRAM, Seattle Arts Commission, 312 First Ave. N., Second Floor, Seattle WA 98109. (206)684-7171. Fax: (206)684-7172. Website: www.pan.ci.seattle.wa.us/seattle/sac/home.htm. **Contact:** Irene Gomez, project manager. Offered every 2 years. Next literary deadline will be in 2002. The Seattle Artists Program commissions new works by emerging, mid-career or established individual artists based in Seattle. Literary and performing arts disciplines are funded in alternating years. Decided through open, competitive peer-panel review process and subject to approval by the full Commission. Applicants must be residents of or maintain studio space in the city of Seattle, Washington. Guidelines available in May. Deadline: July. Prize: Award amounts are $7,500 and $2,000.

STUDENT RESEARCH GRANT, the Society for the Scientific Study of Sexuality, P.O. Box 416, Allentown PA 18105-0416. (610)530-2483. Fax: (610)530-2485. E-mail: thesociety@inetmail.att.net. Website: www.sexscience.org. **Contact:** Ilsa Lottes. Offered twice a year for unpublished works. "The student research grant award is granted twice yearly to help support graduate student research on a variety of sexually related topics." Guidelines and entry forms for SASE. Open to students pursuing graduate study. Deadline: February 1 and September 1. Prize: $750.

TRILLIUM BOOK AWARD/PRIX TRILLIUM, Ontario Ministry of Citizenship, Culture and Recreation, 400 University Ave., 5th Floor, Toronto, Ontario M7A 2R9, Canada. (416)314-7786. Fax: (416)314-7460. Website: www.gov. on.ca/MCZCR. **Contact:** Edward Yanofsky, cultural industries officer. Offered annually for work previously published January 1-December 31. This is the Ontario government's annual literary award. There are 2 categories—an English language category and a French language category. Publishers submit books on behalf of authors. Authors must have been Ontario residents 3 of the last 5 years. Deadline: mid-December. Prize: The winning author in each category receives $12,000; the winning publisher in each category receives $2,500.

UCROSS FOUNDATION RESIDENCY, 30 Big Red Lane, Clearmont WY 82835. (307)737-2291. Fax: (307)737-2322. E-mail: ucross@wyoming.com. **Contact:** Sharon Dynak, executive director. Eight concurrent positions open for artists-in-residence in various disciplines (includes writers, visual artists, music, humanities, natural sciences) extending from 2 weeks-2 months. No charge for room, board or studio space. Deadline: March 1 and October 1. Charges $20 application fee.

VERMONT ARTS COUNCIL, 136 State St., Drawer 33, Montpelier VT 05633-6001. (802)828-3291. Fax: (802)828-3363. E-mail: mbailey@arts.vca.state.vt.us. Website: www.vermontartscouncil.org. **Contact:** Michele Bailey. Offered quarterly for previously published or unpublished works. Opportunity Grants are for specific projects of writers (poetry, playwriters, fiction, nonfiction) as well as not-for-profit presses. Also available are Artist Development funds to provide technical assistance for Vermont writers. Write or call for entry information. Open to Vermont residents only. Prize: $250-5,000.

WRITERS FELLOWSHIPS, NC Arts Council, Dept. of Cultural Resources, Raleigh NC 27699-4632. (919)715-1519. Website: www.ncarts.org. **Contact:** Deborah McGill, literature director. Offered every 2 years "to serve writers of fiction, poetry, literary nonfiction and literary translation in North Carolina and to recognize the contribution they make to this state's creative environment." Write for guidelines. Writer must have been a resident of NC for at least a year as of the application deadline and may not be enrolled in any degree-granting program at the time of application. Deadline: November 1, 2002. Prize: We offer 11 $8,000 grants every 2 years.

WRITERSMARKET.COM at http://www.WritersMarket.com features streamlined searches, personalized market information as well as new markets, daily updates and more.

Are You Ready to Write Better and Get Paid For What You Write?

At **Writer's Digest School,** we want you to have both a "flair for words" *and* the marketing know-how it takes to give your writing the best shot at publication. That's why you'll work with a professional, published writer who has already mastered the rules of the game firsthand. A savvy mentor who can show you, through detailed critiques of the writing assignments you send in, how to effectively target your work and get it into the hands of the right editor.

Whether you write articles or short stories, nonfiction or novels, **Writer's Digest School** has a course that's right for you. Each provides a wealth of expertise and one goal: helping you break into the writing market.

So if you're serious about getting published, you owe it to yourself to check out **Writer's Digest School**. To find out more about us, simply fill out and return the card below. There's absolutely no obligation!

Course descriptions on the back ➡

Send Me Free Information!

I want to write better and sell more with the help of the professionals at **Writer's Digest School**. Send me free information about the course I've checked below:

☐ Novel Writing Workshop
☐ Writing & Selling Nonfiction Articles
☐ Writer's Digest Criticism Service
☐ Getting Started in Writing

☐ Writing & Selling Short Stories
☐ Writing Your Life Stories
☐ The Elements of Effective Writing
☐ Marketing Your Nonfiction Book
☐ Screenwriting Workshop

Name _____

Address _____

City _____State _____ ZIP _____

Phone: (Day) (_____)_____ (Eve.) (_____)_____

Email Address _____

To get your package even sooner, call 1-800-759-0963
Outside the U.S. call 1-513-531-2690 ext. 342

IWMXX1X2

Novel Writing Workshop: Iron out your plot, create your main characters, develop a dramatic background, and complete the opening scenes and summary of your novel's complete story. Plus, you'll pinpoint potential publishers for your type of book.

NEW! **Getting Started in Writing:** From short fiction and novels to articles and nonfiction books, we'll help you discover where your natural writing talents lie.

Writing & Selling Short Stories: Learn how to create believable characters, write vivid, true-to-life dialogue, fill your scenes with conflict, and keep your readers on the edge of their seats.

Writing & Selling Nonfiction Articles: Master the components for effective article writing and selling. You'll learn how to choose attention-grabbing topics, conduct stirring interviews, write compelling query letters, and slant a single article for a variety of publications.

Writing Your Life Stories: Learn how to weave the important events of your personal or family's history into a heartfelt story. You'll plan a writing strategy, complete a dateline of events, and discover how to combine factual events with narrative flow.

Writer's Digest Criticism Service: Have an experienced, published writer review your manuscripts before you submit them for pay. Whether you write books, articles, short stories or poetry, you'll get professional, objective feedback on what's working well, what needs strengthening, and which markets you should pursue.

The Elements of Effective Writing: Discover how to conquer the pesky grammar and usage problems that hold so many writers back. You'll refresh your basic English composition skills through step-by-step lessons and writing exercises designed to help keep your manuscripts out of the rejection pile.

Marketing Your Nonfiction Book: You'll work with your mentor to create a book proposal that you can send directly to a publisher, develop and refine your book idea, write a chapter-by-chapter outline of your subject, line up your sources and information, write sample chapters, and complete your query letter.

Screenwriting Workshop: Learn to write for the silver screen! Work step by step with a professional screenwriter to craft your script, find out how to research the right agent or producer for your work, and get indispensable information about the Hollywood submission process.

Get America's #1 Writing Resource Delivered to Your Door—and Save!

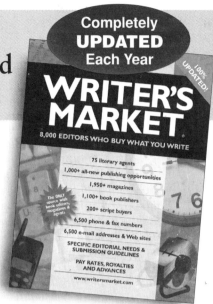

Finding the right markets for your work is crucial to your success. With constant changes in the publishing industry, staying informed as to who, where and why is a challenge. That's why every year the most savvy writers turn to the new edition of *Writer's Market* for the most up-to-date information on the people and places that will get their work published and sold (contact information for more than 8,000 editors is included). You'll also find a list of literary and script agents, interviews with today's hot authors, examples of query letters that editors loved—and hated, and sure-fire tips from industry pros which will further increase publishing opportunities.

2003 Writer's Market will be published and ready for shipment in August 2002.

Through this special offer, you can reserve your 2003 *Writer's Market* at the 2002 price—just $29.99. Order today and save!

Turn over for more books to help you write better and get published! ➤

OPEN HERE TO SAVE ON YOUR 2003 WRITER'S MARKET

More Great Books to Help You Sell Your Work!

Latest Edition!
2002 Novel & Short Story Writer's Market
edited by Anne Bowling

Discover buyers hungry for your work! You'll find the names, addresses, pay rates and editorial needs of thousands of fiction publishers. Plus, loads of helpful articles and informative interviews with professionals who know what it takes to get published!
#10756-K/$24.99/690 p/pb *Available December 2001*

Totally Updated! **2002 Guide to Literary Agents**
edited by Rachel Vater

Enhance your chances of publishing success by teaming up with an agent! You'll find more than 500 listings of literary and script agents, plus valuable information about how to choose the right agent to represent your work.
#10758-K/$22.99/370 p/pb *Available December 2001*

2002 Children's Writers & Illustrator's Market
edited by Alice Pope

As a writer, illustrator or photographer in the children's and young adult markets, this is your single-most important resource! Inside you'll find up-to-date listings of agents and representatives, magazine and book publishers, contests and awards, game and puzzle manufacturers, script buyers, toy companies, and more! And, you'll get advice on using the Internet to your best advantage, examples of great query letters, and interviews with industry experts.
#10757-K/$23.99/400 p/pb

Too Lazy to Work, Too Nervous to Steal
by John Clausen

Turn your love of writing into a moneymaking business! Clausen's funny, friendly writing style will entertain, inspire and prepare you to achieve your dreams of becoming a successful freelancer. And, you'll learn how your life experiences, friends, hobbies and skills all come into play to enhance your career.
#10732-K/$19.99/256 p/hc

NEW!
Roget's Thesaurus of Phrases
by Barbara Ann Kipfer, Ph.D.

Sure, you go to the thesaurus when you need a synonym for a word, but now you can do the same for a phrase! Need to know a different way to say "crowning achievement" or "budget deficit?" Look no further than Kipfer's indispensable reference. You'll make your own writing precise and colorful, with more than 10,000 multi-word entries and example lists!
#10734-K/$22.99/432 p/hc

Resources

Publications

In addition to newsletters and publications from local and national organizations, there are trade publications, books, and directories which offer valuable information about writing and about marketing your manuscripts and understanding the business side of publishing. Some also list employment agencies that specialize in placing publishing professionals, and some announce actual freelance opportunities.

TRADE MAGAZINES

ADVERTISING AGE, Crain Communications Inc., 740 N. Rush St., Chicago IL 60611. (312)649-5200. *Weekly magazine covering advertising in magazines, trade journals and business.*

AMERICAN JOURNALISM REVIEW, 1117 Journalism Bldg. University of Maryland, College Park MD 20742-7111. (301)405-8803. *10 issues/year magazine for journalists and communications professionals.*

DAILY VARIETY, Daily Variety Ltd./Cahners Publishing Co., 5700 Wilshire Blvd., Suite 120, Los Angeles CA 90036. (323)857-6600. *Trade publication on the entertainment industry, with helpful information for screenwriters.*

EDITOR & PUBLISHER, The Editor & Publisher Co., 770 Broadway, New York NY 10003-9595. (888)313-5530. *Weekly magazine covering the newspaper publishing industry.*

FOLIO:, Cowles Business Media, 11 Riverbend Dr. South, P.O. Box 4272, Stamford CT 06907-0272. (203)358-9900. *Monthly magazine covering the magazine publishing industry.*

GIFTS & DECORATIVE ACCESSORIES, Cahners Publishing Co., 345 Hudson St., 4th Floor, New York NY 10014. (212)519-7200. *Monthly magazine covering greeting cards among other subjects, with an annual buyer's directory in September.*

HORN BOOK MAGAZINE, 56 Roland St., Suite 200, Boston MA 02129. (617)628-0225. *Bimonthly magazine covering children's literature.*

PARTY & PAPER RETAILER, 4 Ward Corp., 107 Mill Plain Rd., Suite 204, Danbury CT 06811. (203)730-4090. *Monthly magazine covering the greeting card and gift industry.*

POETS & WRITERS INC., 72 Spring St., New York NY 10012. (212)226-3586. *Bimonthly magazine, primarily for literary writers and poets.*

PUBLISHERS WEEKLY, Bowker Magazine Group, Cahners Publishing Co., 245 W. 17th St., 6th Floor, New York NY 10011. (212)645-0067. *Weekly magazine covering the book publishing industry.*

TRAVELWRITER MARKETLETTER, P.O. 1782, Springfield VA 22151-0782 (253)399-6270. *Monthly newsletter for travel writers with market listings as well as trip information.*

THE WRITER, Kalmach Publishing, 210127 Crossroads Circle, Waukesha WI 58187. (617)423-3157. *Monthly writers' magazine.*

WRITER'S DIGEST, 1507 Dana Ave., Cincinnati OH 45207. (800)888-6880. *Monthly writers' magazine.*

BOOKS AND DIRECTORIES

AV MARKET PLACE, R.R. Bowker, A Reed Reference Publishing Co., 121 Chanlon Rd., New Providence NJ 07974. (908)464-6800.

BACON'S NEWSPAPER & MAGAZINE DIRECTORIES, Bacon's Information Inc., 332 S. Michigan Ave., Suite 900, Chicago IL 60604. (312)922-2400.

THE COMPLETE BOOK OF SCRIPTWRITING, by J. Michael Straczynski, Writer's Digest Books, 1507 Dana Ave., Cincinnati OH 45207. (800)289-0963.

THE COMPLETE GUIDE TO LITERARY CONTESTS, compiled by Literary Fountain, Prometheus Books, 59 John Glenn Dr., Amherst NY 14228-2197. (716)691-0133.

THE COMPLETE GUIDE TO SELF PUBLISHING, by Marilyn and Tom Ross, Writer's Digest Books, 1507 Dana Ave., Cincinnati OH 45207. (800)289-0963.

DRAMATISTS SOURCEBOOK, edited by Kathy Sova, Theatre Communications Group, Inc., 355 Lexington Ave., 4th Floor, New York NY 10017. (212)697-5230.

EDITORS ON EDITING: What Writers Need to Know About What Editors Do, edited by Gerald Gross, Grove/Atlantic Press, 841 Broadway, New York NY 10003.

FORMATTING & SUBMITTING YOUR MANUSCRIPT, by Jack and Glenda Neff, Don Prues and the editors of *Writer's Market*, Writer's Digest Books, 1507 Dana Ave., Cincinnati OH 45207. (800)289-0963.

GRANTS AND AWARDS AVAILABLE TO AMERICAN WRITERS, PEN American Center, 568 Broadway, New York NY 10012. (212)334-1660.

GUIDE TO LITERARY AGENTS, edited by Rachel Vater. Writer's Digest Books, 1507 Dana Ave., Cincinnati OH 45207. (800)289-0963.

HOW TO WRITE IRRESISTIBLE QUERY LETTERS, by Lisa Collier Cool, Writer's Digest Books, 1507 Dana Ave., Cincinnati OH 45207. (800)289-0963.

INTERNATIONAL DIRECTORY OF LITTLE MAGAZINES & SMALL PRESSES, edited by Len Fulton, Dustbooks, P.O. Box 100, Paradise CA 95967. (530)877-6110.

JUMP START YOUR BOOK SALES: A MONEY-MAKING GUIDE FOR AUTHORS, INDEPENDENT PUBLISHERS AND SMALL PRESSES, by Marilyn & Tom Ross, Writer's Digest Books, 1507 Dana Ave., Cincinnati OH 45207. (800)289-0963.

LITERARY MARKET PLACE and INTERNATIONAL LITERARY MARKET PLACE, R.R. Bowker, A Reed Reference Publishing Co., 121 Chanlon Rd., New Providence NJ 07974. (908)464-6800.

MAGAZINE WRITING THAT SELLS, by Don McKinney, Writer's Digest Books, 1507 Dana Ave., Cincinnati OH 45207. (800)289-0963.

MY BIG SOURCEBOOK, 66 Canal Center Plaza, Suite 200, Alexandria VA 22314-5507. (703)683-0683.

NATIONAL WRITERS UNION GUIDE TO FREELANCE RATES & STANDARD PRACTICE, by Alexander Kopelman, distributed by Writer's Digest Books, 1507 Dana Ave., Cincinnati OH 45207. (800)289-0963.

ONLINE MARKETS FOR WRITERS: Where and How to Sell Your Writing on the Internet, by Anthony Tedesco with Paul Tedesco, Owl Books/Henry Holt, 61 E. Eighth St., Suite 272, New York NY 10003. (212)353-0455. E-mail: anthony@marketsforwriters.com.

STANDARD DIRECTORY OF ADVERTISING AGENCIES, National Register Publishing, A Reed Reference Publishing Co., 121 Chanlon Rd., New Providence NJ 07974. (908)464-6800.

SUCCESSFUL SCRIPTWRITING, by Jurgen Wolff and Kerry Cox, Writer's Digest Books, 1507 Dana Ave., Cincinnati OH 45207. (800)289-0963.

THE WRITER'S GUIDE TO BOOK EDITORS, PUBLISHERS & LITERARY AGENTS, by Jeff Herman, Prima Publishing, 3000 Lava Ridge Ct., Roseville CA 95661. (800)632-8676.

WRITER'S ONLINE MARKETPLACE, by Debbie Ridpath Ohi, Writer's Digest Books, 1507 Dana Ave., Cincinnati OH 45207. (800)289-0963.

WRITER'S MARKET COMPANION, by Joe Fiertag and Mary Carmen Cupito, Writer's Digest Books, 1507 Dana Ave., Cincinnati OH 45207. (800)289-0963.

Websites

The Internet provides a wealth of information for writers. The number of websites devoted to writing and publishing is vast and continues to expand. Below is a short—and thus incomplete—list of websites that offer information and hypertext links to other pertinent sites relating to writing and publishing. Because the Internet is such an amorphous, evolving, mutable entity with website addresses launching, crashing and changing daily, some of these addresses may be obsolete by the time this book goes to print. But this list does give you a few starting points for your online journey. If, in the course of your electronic ventures, you find additional websites of interest, please let us know by e-mailing us at writersmarket@fwpubs.com.

Link sites

Books A to Z: www.booksatoz.com

Information on publications, services and leads to other useful websites, including areas for book research, production services, self-publishing, bookstores, organizations, and publishers.

Books and Writing Online: www.interzone.com/Books/books.html

A collection of sources directing you to other sites on the Web, this is a good place to jump to other areas with information pertaining to writing, literature and publishing.

Bookwire: www.bookwire.com

A gateway to finding information about publishers, booksellers, libraries, authors, reviews, and awards. Also offers information about frequently asked publishing questions and answers, a calendar of events, a mailing list, and other helpful resources.

Pilot-search: www.pilot-search.com

This search engine features more than 11,000 literary links. Writing advice is given, and information is posted on workshops, fellowships, and literary job openings.

Publishers' Catalogues Home Page: www.lights.com/publisher

A mammoth link collection of publishers around the world arranged geographically. This site is one of the most comprehensive directories of publishers on the Internet.

Zuzu's Petals Literary Resource: www.zuzu.com

Contains more than 10,000 organized links to helpful resources for writers, researchers, and others. Zuzu's Petals also publishes an electronic quarterly.

Miscellaneous

Delphi Forum: www.delphi.com

This site hosts forums on many topics including writing and publishing. Just type "writing" in the search bar, and you'll find 30 pages where you can talk about your craft.

Freelance Online: www.freelanceonline.com

A directory of and resource center for freelancers in the field of communications. Jobs, message boards, a searchable directory of over 700 freelancers, frequently asked questions, resources, and networking for beginning freelancers. The FAQ for freelancers has lots of useful information catalogued and linked especially for freelancing beginners.

Novel Advice: www.noveladvice.com

A cyber-journal devoted to the craft of writing. This site offers advice, online courses on the craft of writing (for a fee), and an extensive list of research resources.

Internet Entertainment Network: HollywoodNetwork.com

This site covers everything in Hollywood whether it's dealmaking, music, screenwriting, or profiles of agents and Hollywood executives.

ShawGuides: www.shawguides.com

Searchable database of writers' conferences.

United States Postal Service: www.usps.com

Domestic and international postage rate calculator, stamp ordering, zip code look-up, express mail tracking, etc.

Multiple services

Authorlink: www.authorlink.com

An information and news service for editors, literary agents, and writers. Showcasing and matching quality manuscripts to publishers' needs, this site also contains interviews with editors and agents, publishing industry news, links and writer's guidelines.

Book Zone: www.bookzone.com

A catalog source for books, audio books, and more, with links to other publishing opportunities, diversions and distractions such as news, classifieds, contests, magazines and trade groups.

BookWeb: www.ambook.org

This ABA site offers books news, markets, discussions groups, events, resources, and other book-related information.

Children's Writing Resource Center: www.write4kids.com

Presented by Children's Book Insider, The Newsletter for Children's Writers. *Offers information on numerous aspects of publishing and children's literature, such as an InfoCenter, a Research Center, results of various surveys, and secrets on getting published.*

Creative Freelancers: www.freelancers.com

A meeting spot for freelancers and employers. Writers post their résumés for free, and employers post job listings in writing, editing, proofreading, etc.

Editor & Publisher: www.mediainfo.com

The Internet source for Editor & Publisher, *this site provides up-to-date industry news, with other opportunities such as a research area and bookstore, a calendar of events, and classifieds.*

International Online Writers Association (IOWA): www.project-iowa.org/

This site includes resources, events calendar, and research aids.

Online Markets for Writers: www.marketsforwriters.com

Site rooted in groundbreaking book, Online Markets for Writers: Where And How To Sell Your Writing On The Internet *(Owl Books/Henry Holt & Co.), offering online market information, interviews, extensive resources, and advice from expert contributors including the National Writers Union (NWU) and the American Society of Journalists and Authors (ASJA).*

RoseDog.com: www.rosedog.com

This site is for readers, writers, agents, and publishers. Post excerpts from your unpublished work at no cost, to be reviewed by agents and publishers.

Small Publisher Association of North America (SPAN): www.SPANnet.org
This site includes membership information, publishing events and calendar, links, book sales, and other services.

Writer's Toolbox: www.writerstoolbox.com
Feataures resources for fiction writers, journalists, technical writers, and screenwriters.

Research

AcqWeb: www.library.vanderbilt.edu/law/acqs/acqs.html
Although geared toward librarians and researchers, AcqWeb provides reference information useful to writers, such as library catalogs, bibliographic services, Books in Print, and other web reference resources.

The Currency Site Historical Tables, Current Rates and Forecasts for World Currencies: www.oanda.com
Find current names for the world's currencies and exchange rates.

The Electronic Newsstand: www.enews.com
One of the largest directories of magazines on the Web. The Electronic Newsstand not only provides links to their magazines, but also tracks the content of many major magazines on a continually updated basis. It also allows users to customize their own newsstands to view only the magazines of their choice.

FindLaw: www.findlaw.com
Contains information on landmark legal decisions, and includes legal publishers and state and local bar association information.

InfoNation: www.un.org/Pubs/CyberSchoolBus/infonation/e_infonation.htm
A two-step database that allows you to view and compare the most up-to-date statistical data for the Member States of the United Nations.

Information Please Almanac: www.infoplease.com
General reference.

International Trademark Association: www.inta.org
Check the correct spelling of nearly 4,000 trademarks and service marks, and get the correct generic term.

Library of Congress: http://lcweb.loc.gov/homepage/lchp.html
Provides access to Library of Congress catalogues and other research vehicles, including full access to bills under consideration in the U.S. House of Representatives and Senate.

Media Resource Service: www.mediaresource.org
This service provided by the Scientific Research Society helps writers find reputable sources of scientific information at no charge.

Mediafinder: www.oxbridge.com
Contains basic facts about 100,000 publications.

Newswise: www.newswise.com
A comprehensive database of news releases from top institutions engaged in scientific, medical, liberal arts and business research.

The Polling Report: www.pollingreport.com
Includes recent public opinion poll results from leading U.S. polling firms on politics, business, social issues, news events, sports and entertainment.

ProfNet: www.profnet.com

Contains names of 6,000 news and information officers at colleges and universities, corporations, think tanks, national labs, medical centers, nonprofits, and PR agencies courtesy of this PR Newswire service.

Publishing Law Center: www.publaw.com
Links and articles about intellectual property and other legal issues.

SharpWriter.com: www.sharpwriter.com
Dictionaries, encyclopedic references, grammar tips.

World Factbook: www.odci.gov/cia/publications/factbook/index.html
Includes facts on every country in the world, on subjects from population to exports.

World Wide Web Acronym and Abbreviation Server: www.ucc.ie/acronyms/acro.html
Research to find the names behind the acronyms or the acronyms for the names.

Writer's Digest: www.writersdigest.com
This site includes information about writing books and magazine pieces from Writer's Digest. *It also has a huge, searchable database of writer's guidelines from thousands of publishers.*

Retail

Amazon.com: www.amazon.com
Calling itself "A bookstore too big for the physical world," Amazon.com has more than 3 million books available on their website at discounted prices, plus a personal notification service of new releases, reader reviews, bestseller, and suggested book information.

Barnes and Noble Online: www.barnesandnoble.com or www.bn.com
The world's largest bookstore chain's website contains 600,000 in-stock titles at discount prices as well as personalized recommendations, online events with authors, and book forum access for members.

Master Freelancer: www.masterfreelancer.com
Products and services for freelance writers.

Writers' organizations

Artslynx: International Writing Resources: www.artslynx.org/writing
The site lists organizations for writers and poets and links to relevant writing-related sites.

Children's Book Council: www.cbcbooks.org
A great resource for all facets of children's books. Has a beginner's guide to children's writing, a bimonthly theme-based showcase, and a monthly rundown of upcoming titles written by CBC members.

Freedom Forum Online: www.freedomforum.org
An excellent place to keep up on the state of journalism, nationally and internationally.

HTML Writers Guild: www.hwg.org
An international organization of Web authors. For non-members, there is access to information on Web writing-financial, marketing, and design aspects, as well as html and new technology resources.

International Journalists' Network: www.ijnet.org
This is the International Center for Journalists' online source for media assistance, journalism training opportunities, and media directories. You'll find a list of Codes of Ethics, as well as information on fellowships and awards.

Society for Technical Communication: www.stc.org
Access to salary surveys, STC grants and loans information, and recommended books.

Organizations

Whether you write nonfiction or science fiction, self-help or short stories, there are national organizations representing your field as a whole or representing their members in court. Hundreds more smaller, local groups are providing assistance from paragraph to paragraph. There is an organization—probably several—to suit your needs.

ACADEMY OF AMERICAN POETS, 584 Broadway, Suite 1208, New York NY 10012-3250. (212)274-0343. Fax: (212)274-9427. Website: www.poets.org. Contact: Michael Smith.

AMERICAN BOOK PRODUCERS ASSOCIATION, 156 Fifth Ave., New York NY 10010. (212)645-2368. Fax: (212)989-7542. E-mail: office@ABPAonline.org. Website: www.abpaonline.org.

AMERICAN MEDICAL WRITERS ASSOCIATION, 40 W. Gude Dr., Suite 101, Rockville MD 20850-1199. (301)294-5303.

AMERICAN SOCIETY OF JOURNALISTS AND AUTHORS (ASJA), 1501 Broadway, Suite 302, New York NY 10036. (212)997-0947. Fax: (212)768-7414. E-mail: asja@compuserve.com. Website: www.asja.org. Executive Director: Brett Harvey.

AMERICAN TRANSLATORS ASSOCIATION, 225 Reinekers Lane, Suite 590, Alexandria VA 22314-0214. (703)683-6100. Website: www.atanet.org.

ASIAN AMERICAN WRITERS' WORKSHOP, 16 W. 32nd St., Suite 10A, New York NY 10001. (212)494-0061. Fax: (212)494-0062. Website: www.aaww.org.

ASSOCIATED WRITING PROGRAMS, Tallwood House MSN1E3, George Mason University, Fairfax VA 22030. (703)993-4301. Fax: (703)993-4302. E-mail: awp@gmu.edu.

ASSOCIATION OF AUTHORS' REPRESENTATIVES, P.O. Box 237201 Ansonia Station, New York NY 10003. Website: www.aar-online.org.

ASSOCIATION OF DESK-TOP PUBLISHERS, 3401-A800 Adams Ave., San Diego CA 92116-2490. (619)563-9714.

THE AUTHORS GUILD, 31 E. 28th St., 10th Floor, New York NY 10016. (212)563-5904.

THE AUTHORS LEAGUE OF AMERICA, INC., 31 E. 28th St., 10th Floor, New York NY 10016. (212)564-8350.

CANADIAN AUTHORS ASSOCIATION, P.O. Box 419, Campbellford, Ontario K0L 1L0, Canada. (705)653-0323. Fax: (705)653-0593. E-mail: canauth@redden.on.ca. Website: www.Canauthors.org. Contact: Alec McEachern.

THE DRAMATISTS GUILD, 1501 Broadway, Suite 701, New York NY 10036-5601. (212)398-9366. Fax: (212)944-0420. Website: www.dramatistsguild.com.

EDITORIAL FREELANCERS ASSOCIATION, 71 W. 23rd St., Suite 1910, New York NY 10010. (212)929-5400. Fax: (212)929-5439. E-mail: info@the-efa.org. Website: www.THE-EFA.org.

EDUCATION WRITERS ASSOCIATION, 1331 H. St. NW, Suite 307, Washington DC 20005. (202)637-9700. Fax: (202)637-9707. E-mail: ewa@ewa.org. Website: www.ewa.org.

INTERNATIONAL ASSOCIATION OF BUSINESS COMMUNICATORS, One Hallidie Plaza, Suite 600, San Francisco CA 94102. (415)544-4700 or (800)776-4222. Website: www.iabc.com.

INTERNATIONAL ASSOCIATION OF CRIME WRITERS INC., North American Branch, P.O. Box 8674, New York NY 10116-8674. (212)243-8966. Fax: (815)361-1477. Contact: Mary A. Frisque

INTERNATIONAL TELEVISION ASSOCIATION, Raybourn Group International, 9202 N. Meridian St., Suite 200, Indianapolis IN 46260-1810. (800)362-2546. Fax: (317)571-5603. E-mail: jhiler@itva.org. Website: www.itva.org.

INTERNATIONAL WOMEN'S WRITING GUILD, Box 810, Gracie Station, New York NY 10028-0082. (212)737-7536. Website: www.iwwg.com. Executive Director: Hannelore Hahn.

MYSTERY WRITERS OF AMERICA, INC., 17 E. 47th St., 6th Floor, New York NY 10017. (212)888-8171. Fax: (212)888-8107. E-mail: mwa_org@earthlink.net. Website: www.mysterywriters.net. President: Donald E. Westlake. Executive Director: Priscilla Ridgeway.

NATIONAL ASSOCIATION OF SCIENCE WRITERS, Box 294, Greenlawn NY 11740. (631)757-5664.

NATIONAL WRITERS ASSOCIATION, 3140 S. Peoria, #295PMB, Aurora CO 80014. (303)841-0246. Fax: (303)751-8593

NATIONAL WRITERS UNION, 113 University Place, 6th Floor, New York NY 10003. (212) 254-0279. Fax: (212) 254-0673. E-mail: nwu@nwu.org. Website: www.nwu.org. Contact: Karen Ford.

NEW DRAMATISTS, 424 W. 44th St., New York NY 10036. (212)757-6960.

NOVELISTS, INC., P.O. Box 1166, Mission KS 66222-0166. Website: www.ninc.com

PEN AMERICAN CENTER, 568 Broadway, New York NY 10012. (212)334-1660.

POETRY SOCIETY OF AMERICA, 15 Gramercy Park, New York NY 10003. (212)254-9628. Website: www.poetry society.org

POETS & WRITERS, 72 Spring St., New York NY 10012. (212)226-3586. Fax: (212)226-3963. Website: www.pw.org.

PUBLIC RELATIONS SOCIETY OF AMERICA, 33 Irving Place, New York NY 10003. (212)995-2230.

ROMANCE WRITERS OF AMERICA, 3707 FM 1960 W., Suite 55, Houston TX 77068. (281)440-6885. Fax: (281)440-7510. Website: www.rwanational.com. Executive Director: Allison Kelley.

SCIENCE FICTION AND FANTASY WRITERS OF AMERICA, INC., P.O. Box 877, Chestertown MD 21620. 352 La Guardia Place, #632, New York NY 10012-1428. New York NY 10012-1428. Website: www.sfwa.org/org/sfwa_info.htm. President: Norman Spinrad. Executive Director: Jane Jewell.

SOCIETY OF AMERICAN BUSINESS EDITORS & WRITERS, University of Missouri, School of Journalism, 76 Gannett Hall, Columbia MO 65211. (573)882-7862. Fax: (573)884-1372. Website: www.sabew.org. Contact: Carolyn Guniss, executive director.

SOCIETY OF AMERICAN TRAVEL WRITERS, 1500 Sunday Dr., Suite 102, Raleigh NC 27607. (919)787-5181.

SOCIETY OF CHILDREN'S BOOK WRITERS AND ILLUSTRATORS, 8271 Beverly Blvd., Los Angeles CA 90048. (323)782-1010. Fax: (323)782-1892. Website: www.scbwi.org. President: Stephen Mooser. Executive Director: Lin Oliver.

SOCIETY OF PROFESSIONAL JOURNALISTS, 3909 N. Meridian St., Indianapolis IN 46208. (317)927-8000. Fax: (317)920-4789. Website: www.spj.org.

VOLUNTEER LAWYERS FOR THE ARTS, One E. 53rd St., 6th Floor, New York NY 10022. (212)319-2787. Fax: (212)752-6575.

WESTERN WRITERS OF AMERICA, % James Crutchfield, Secretary-Treasurer, 1012 Fair St., Franklin TN 37064.

WOMEN WRITING THE WEST, 8547 E. Arapahoe Rd., J541, Greenwood CO 80112-1436. (303)674-5450.

WRITERS GUILD OF ALBERTA, 11759 Groat Rd., Edmonton, Alberta, T5M 3K6, Canada. (780)422-8174.

WRITERS GUILD OF AMERICA, East Chapter: 555 W. 57th St., New York NY 10019, (212)767-7800; West Chapter: 7000 W. Third St., Los Angeles CA 90048, (323)951-4000. Website: www.wga.org.

Glossary

Key to symbols and abbreviations appears on the front and back inside covers.

Advance. A sum of money a publisher pays a writer prior to the publication of a book. It is usually paid in installments, such as one-half on signing the contract; one-half on delivery of a complete and satisfactory manuscript. The advance is paid against the royalty money that will be earned by the book.

Advertorial. Advertising presented in such a way as to resemble editorial material. Information may be the same as that contained in an editorial feature, but it is paid for or supplied by an advertiser and the word "advertisement" appears at the top of the page.

Agent. A liason between a writer and editor or publisher. An agent shops a manuscript around, receiving a commission when the manuscript is accepted. Agents usually take a 10-15% fee from the advance and royalties, 10-20% if a co-agent is involved, such as in the sale of dramatic rights.

All rights. See Rights and the Writer in the Minding the Details article.

Anthology. A collection of selected writings by various authors or a gathering of works by one author.

Assignment. Editor asks a writer to produce a specific article for an agreed-upon fee.

Auction. Publishers sometimes bid for the acquisition of a book manuscript that has excellent sales prospects. The bids are for the amount of the author's advance, advertising and promotional expenses, royalty percentage, etc. Auctions are conducted by agents.

Avant-garde. Writing that is innovative in form, style or subject, often considered difficult and challenging.

B&W. Abbreviation for black and white photographs.

Backlist. A publisher's list of its books that were not published during the current season, but that are still in print.

Belles lettres. A term used to describe fine or literary writing—writing more to entertain than to inform or instruct.

Bimonthly. Every two months. See also *semimonthly*.

Bio. A sentence or brief paragraph about the writer. It can appear at the bottom of the first or last page of a writer's article or short story or on a contributor's page.

Biweekly. Every two weeks.

Boilerplate. A standardized contract. When an editor says "our standard contract," he means the boilerplate with no changes. Writers should be aware that most authors and/or agents make many changes on the boilerplate.

Book packager. Draws all elements of a book together, from the initial concept to writing and marketing strategies, then sells the book package to a book publisher. Also known as book producer or book developer.

Business size envelope. Also known as a #10 envelope, it is the standard size used in sending business correspondence.

Byline. Name of the author appearing with the published piece.

Category fiction. A term used to include all various labels attached to types of fiction. See also *genre*.

CD-ROM. Compact Disc-Read Only Memory. A computer information storage medium capable of holding enormous amounts of data. Information on a CD-ROM cannot be deleted. A computer user must have a CD-ROM drive to access a CD-ROM.

Chapbook. A small booklet, usually paperback, of poetry, ballads or tales.

Circulation. The number of subscribers to a magazine.

Clean copy. A manuscript free of errors, cross-outs, wrinkles or smudges.

Clips. Samples, usually from newspapers or magazines, of your *published* work.

Coffee table book. An oversize book, heavily illustrated.

Column inch. The amount of space contained in one inch of a typeset column.

Commercial novels. Novels designed to appeal to a broad audience. These are often broken down into categories such as western, mystery and romance. See also *genre*.

Commissioned work. See *assignment*.

Concept. A statement that summarizes a screenplay or teleplay—before the outline or treatment is written.

Confessional. Genre of fiction essay in which the author or first-person narrator confesses something shocking or embarassing.

Contact sheet. A sheet of photographic paper on which negatives are transferred so you can see the entire roll of shots placed together on one sheet of paper without making separate, individual prints.

Contributor's copies. Copies of the issues of magazines sent to the author in which the author's work appears.

Cooperative publishing. See *co-publishing*.

Co-publishing. Arrangement where author and publisher share publication costs and profits of a book. Also known as *cooperative publishing*. See also *subsidy publisher*.

Copyediting. Editing a manuscript for grammar, punctuation and printing style, not subject content.

Copyright. A means to protect an author's work. See Copyright in the Minding the Details section.

Cover letter. A brief letter, accompanying a complete manuscript, especially useful if responding to an editor's request for a manuscript. A cover letter may also accompany a book proposal. A cover letter is *not* a query letter; see Targeting Your Ideas in the Getting Published section.

Creative nonfiction. Nofictional writing that uses an innovative approach to the subject and creative language.

CV. Curriculum vita. A brief listing of qualifications and career accomplishments.

Derivative works. A work that has been translated, adapted, abridged, condensed, annotated or otherwise produced by altering a previously created work. Before producing a derivative work, it is necessary to secure the written permission of the copyright owner of the original piece.

Desktop publishing. A publishing system designed for a personal computer. The system is capable of typesetting, some illustration, layout, design and printing—so that the final piece can be distributed and/or sold.

Docudrama. A fictional film rendition of recent newsmaking events and people.

Eclectic. Publication features a variety of different writing styles of genres.

Electronic submission. A submission made by modem or on computer disk.

El-hi. Elementary to high school.

E-mail. Electronic mail. Mail generated on a computer and delivered over a computer network to a specific individual or group of individuals. To send or receive e-mail, a user must have an account with an online service, which provides an e-mail address and electronic mailbox.

Erotica. Fiction or art that is sexually oriented.

Experimental. See *avant-garde.*

Fair use. A provision of the copyright law that says short passages from copyrighted material may be used without infringing on the owner's rights.

Feature. An article giving the reader information of human interest rather than news. Also used by magazines to indicate a lead article or distinctive department.

Filler. A short item used by an editor to "fill" out a newspaper column or magazine page. It could be a timeless news item, a joke, an anecdote, some light verse or short humor, puzzle, etc.

First North American serial rights. See Rights and the Writer in the Minding the Details article.

First-person point of view. In nonfiction, the author reports from his or her own perspective; in fiction, the narrator tells the story from his or her point of view. This viewpoint makes frequent use of "I," or occasionally, "we."

Formula story. Familiar theme treated in a predictable plot structure—such as boy meets girl, boy loses girl, boy gets girl.

Frontlist. A publisher's list of its books that are new to the current season.

Galleys. The first typeset version of a manuscript that has not yet been divided into pages.

Genre. Refers either to a general classification of writing, such as the novel or the poem, or to the categories within those classifications, such as the problem novel or the sonnet. Genre fiction describes commercial novels, such as mysteries, romances and science fiction. Also called category fiction.

Ghostwriter. A writer who puts into literary form an article, speech, story or book based on another person's ideas or knowledge.

Gift book. A book designed as a gift item. Often small in size with few illustrations and placed close to a bookstore's checkout as an "impulse" buy, gift books tend to be written to a specific niche, such as golfers, mothers, etc.

Glossy. A black and white photograph with a shiny surface as opposed to one with a non-shiny matte finish.

Gothic novel. A fiction category or genre in which the central character is usually a beautiful young girl, the setting an old mansion or castle, and there is a handsome hero and a real menace, either natural or supernatural.

Graphic novel. An adaptation of a novel in graphic form, long comic strip or heavily illustrated story, of 40 pages or more, produced in paperback form.

Hard copy. The printed copy of a computer's output.

Hardware. All the mechanically-integrated components of a computer that are not software. Circuit boards, transistors and the machines that are the actual computer are the hardware.

High-lo. Material written for newer readers, generally adults, with a *high* interest level and *low* reading ability.

Home page. The first page of a World Wide Web document.

Honorarium. Token payment—small amount of money, or a byline and copies of the publication.

How-to. Books and magazine articles offering a combination of information and advice in describing how something can be accomplished. Subjects range widely from hobbies to psychology.

Hypertext. Words or groups of words in an electronic document that are linked to other text, such as a definition or a related document. Hypertext can also be linked to illustrations.

Illustrations. May be photographs, old engravings, artwork. Usually paid for separately from the manuscript. See also *package sale.*

Imprint. Name applied to a publisher's specific line or lines of books (e.g., Avon Eos is an imprint of HarperCollins).

Interactive. A type of computer interface that takes user input, such as answers to computer-generated questions, and then acts upon that input.

Interactive fiction. Works of fiction in book or computer software format in which the reader determines the path the story will take. The reader chooses from several alternatives at the end of a "chapter," and thus determines the structure of the story. Interactive fiction features multiple plots and endings.

Internet. A worldwide network of computers that offers access to a wide variety of electronic resources.

Invasion of privacy. Writing about persons (even though truthfully) without their consent.

Kill fee. Fee for a complete article that was assigned but which was subsequently cancelled.

Lead time. The time between the acquisition of a manuscript by an editor and its actual publication.

Libel. A false accusation or any published statement or presentation that tends to expose another to public contempt, ridicule, etc. Defenses are truth; fair comment on a matter of public interest; and privileged communication—such as a report of legal proceedings or client's communication to a lawyer.

List royalty. A royalty payment based on a percentage of a book's retail (or "list") price. Compare *net royalty.*

Literary fiction. The general category of serious, non-formulaic, intelligent fiction.

Little magazine. Publications of limited circulation, usually on literary or political subject matter.

LORT. An acronym for League of Resident Theatres. Letters from A to D follow LORT and designate the size of the theater.

Magalog. Mail order catalog with how-to articles pertaining to the items for sale.

Mainstream fiction. Fiction that transcends popular novel categories such as mystery, romance and science fiction. Using conventional methods, this kind of fiction tells stories about people and their conflicts with greater depth of characterization, background, etc., than the more narrowly focused genre novels.

Mass market. Nonspecialized books of wide appeal directed toward a large audience. Smaller and more cheaply produced than trade paperbacks, they are found in many non-bookstore outlets, such as drug stores or supermarkets.

Memoir. A narrative recounting a writer's (or fictional narrator's) personal or family history.

Microcomputer. A small computer system capable of performing various specific tasks with data it receives. Personal computers are microcomputers.

Midlist. Those titles on a publisher's list that are not expected to be big sellers, but are expected to have limited sales. Midlist books are mainstream, not literary, scholarly or genre, and are usually written by new or unknown writers.

Model release. A paper signed by the subject of a photograph (or the subject's guardian, if a juvenile) giving the photographer permission to use the photograph, editorially or for advertising purposes or for some specific purpose as stated.

Modem. A device used to transmit data from one computer to another via telephone lines.

Monograph. A detailed and documented scholarly study concerning a single subject.

Multimedia. Computers and software capable of integrating text, sound, photographic-quality images, animation and video.

Multiple submissions. Sending more than one poem, gag or greeting card idea at the same time. This term is often used synonymously with simultaneous submission.

Narrative nonfiction. A narrative presentation of actual events.

Narrative poem. Poetry that tells a story. One of the three main genres of poetry (the others being dramatic poetry and lyric poetry).

Net royalty. A royalty payment based on the amount of money a book publisher receives on the sale of a book after booksellers' discounts, special sales discounts and returns. Compare list royalty.

Network. A group of computers electronically linked to share information and resources.

New Age. A "fringe" topic that has become increasingly mainstream. Formerly New Age included UFOs and occult phenomena. The term has evolved to include more general topics such as psychology, religion and health, but emphasizing the mystical, spiritual or alternative aspects.

Newsbreak. A brief, late-breaking news story added to the front page of a newspaper at press time or a magazine news item of importance to readers.

Nostalgia. A genre of reminiscence, recalling sentimental events or products of the past.

Novella. A short novel, or a long short story; 7,000 to 15,000 words approximately. Also known as a novelette.

Novelization. A novel created from the script of a popular movie, usually called a movie "tie-in" and published in paperback.

On spec. An editor expresses an interest in a proposed article idea and agrees to consider the finished piece for publication "on speculation." The editor is under no obligation to buy the finished manuscript.

One-shot feature. As applies to syndicates, single feature article for syndicate to sell; as contrasted with article series or regular columns syndicated.

One-time rights. See Rights and the Writer in the Minding the Details article.

Online Service. Computer networks accessed via modem. These services provide users with various resources, such as electronic mail, news, weather, special interest groups and shopping. Examples of such providers include America Online and CompuServe.

Outline. A summary of a book's contents in 5 to 15 double-spaced pages; often in the form of chapter headings with a descriptive sentence or two under each one to show the scope of the book. A screenplay's or teleplay's outline is a scene-by-scene narrative description of the story (10-15 pages for a ½-hour teleplay; 15-25 pages for a 1-hour teleplay; 25-40 pages for a 90-minute teleplay; 40-60 pages for a 2-hour feature film or teleplay).

Over-the-transom. Describes the submission of unsolicited material by a freelance writer.

Package sale. The editor buys manuscript and photos as a "package" and pays for them with one check.

Page rate. Some magazines pay for material at a fixed rate per published page, rather than per word.

Parallel submission. A strategy of developing several articles from one unit of research for submission to similar magazines. This strategy differs from simultaneous or multiple submission, where the same article is marketed to several magazines at the same time.

Parody. The conscious imitation of a work, usually with the intent to ridicule or make fun of the work.

Payment on acceptance. The editor sends you a check for your article, story or poem as soon as he decides to publish it.

Payment on publication. The editor doesn't send you a check for your material until it is published.

Pen name. The use of a name other than your legal name on articles, stories or books when you wish to remain anonymous. Simply notify your post office and bank that you are using the name so that you'll receive mail and/or checks in that name. Also called a pseudonym.

Photo feature. Feature in which the emphasis is on the photographs rather than on accompanying written material.

Plagiarism. Passing off as one's own the expression of ideas and words of another writer.

Potboiler. Refers to writing projects a freelance writer does to "keep the pot boiling" while working on major articles— quick projects to bring in money with little time or effort. These may be fillers such as anecdotes or how-to tips, but could be short articles or stories.

Proofreading. Close reading and correction of a manuscript's typographical errors.

Proposal. A summary of a proposed book submitted to a publisher, particularly used for nonfiction manuscripts. A proposal often contains an individualized cover letter, one-page overview of the book, marketing information, competitive books, author information, chapter-by-chapter outline, 2-3 sample chapters and attachments (if relevant) such as magazine articles about the topic and articles you have written (particularly on the proposed topic).

Proscenium. The area of the stage in front of the curtain.

Prospectus. A preliminary written description of a book or article, usually one page in length.

Pseudonym. See *pen name*.

Public domain. Material that was either never copyrighted or whose copyright term has expired.

Query. A letter to an editor intended to raise interest in an article you propose to write.

Release. A statement that your idea is original, has never been sold to anyone else and that you are selling the negotiated rights to the idea upon payment.

Remainders. Copies of a book that are slow to sell and can be purchased from the publisher at a reduced price. Depending on the author's book contract, a reduced royalty or no royalty is paid on remainder books.

Reporting time. The time it takes for an editor to report to the author on his/her query or manuscript.

Reprint rights. See Rights and the Writer in the Minding the Details article.

Round-up article. Comments from, or interviews with, a number of celebrities or experts on a single theme.

Royalties, standard hardcover book. 10% of the retail price on the first 5,000 copies sold; 12½% on the next 5,000; 15% thereafter.

Royalties, standard mass paperback book. 4 to 8% of the retail price on the first 150,000 copies sold.

Royalties, standard trade paperback book. No less than 6% of list price on the first 20,000 copies; 7½% thereafter.

Scanning. A process through which letter-quality printed text or artwork is read by a computer scanner and converted into workable data.

Screenplay. Script for a film intended to be shown in theaters.

Self-publishing. In this arrangement, the author keeps all income derived from the book, but he pays for its manufacturing, production and marketing.

Semimonthly. Twice per month.

Semiweekly. Twice per week.

Serial. Published periodically, such as a newspaper or magazine.

Serial fiction. Fiction published in a magazine in installments, often broken off at a suspenseful spot.

Series fiction. A sequence of novels featuring the same characters.

Short-short. A complete short story of 1,500 words maximum, and around 250 words minimum.

Sidebar. A feature presented as a companion to a straight news report (or main magazine article) giving sidelights on human-interest aspects or sometimes elucidating just one aspect of the story.

Similar submission. See *parallel submission*.

Simultaneous submissions. Sending the same article, story or poem to several publishers at the same time. Some publishers refuse to consider such submissions.

Slant. The approach or style of a story or article that will appeal to readers of a specific magazine. For example, a magazine may always use stories with an upbeat ending.

Slice-of-life vignette. A short fiction piece intended to realistically depict an interesting moment of everyday living.

Slides. Usually called transparencies by editors looking for color photographs.

Slush pile. The stack of unsolicited or misdirected manuscripts received by an editor or book publisher.

Software. The computer programs that control computer hardware, usually run from a disk drive of some sort. Computers need software in order to run. These can be word processors, games, spreadsheets, etc.

Speculation. The editor agrees to look at the author's manuscript with no assurance that it will be bought.

Style. The way in which something is written—for example, short, punchy sentences or flowing narrative.

Subsidiary rights. All those rights, other than book publishing rights included in a book contract—such as paperback, book club, movie rights, etc.

Subsidy publisher. A book publisher who charges the author for the cost to typeset and print his book, the jacket, etc. as opposed to a royalty publisher who pays the author.

Synopsis. A brief summary of a story, novel or play. As part of a book proposal, it is a comprehensive summary condensed in a page or page and a half, single-spaced. See also *outline*.

Tabloid Newspaper format publication on about half the size of the regular newspaper page, such as *The Star*.

Tagline. A caption for a photo or a comment added to a filler.

Tearsheet. Page from a magazine or newspaper containing your printed story, article, poem or ad.

Teleplay. A play written for or performed on television.

TOC. Table of Contents.

Trade. Either a hardcover or paperback book; subject matter frequently concerns a special interest. Books are directed toward the layperson rather than the professional.

Transparencies. Positive color slides; not color prints.

Treatment. Synopsis of a television or film script (40-60 pages for a 2-hour feature film or teleplay).

Unsolicited manuscript. A story, article, poem or book that an editor did not specifically ask to see.

Vanity publisher. See *subsidy publisher*.

Word processor. A computer program that allows for easy, flexible manipulation and output of printed copy.

World Wide Web (WWW). An Internet resource that utilizes hypertext to access information. It also supports formatted text, illustrations and sounds, depending on the user's computer capabilities.

Work-for-hire. See Copyright in the Minding the Details article.

YA. Young adult books.

Book Publisher Subject Index

This index will help you find publishers that consider books on specific subjects—the subjects you choose to write about. Remember that a publisher may be listed here only under a general subject category such as Art and Architecture, while the company publishes *only* art history or how-to books. Be sure to consult each company's detailed individual listing, its book catalog and several of its books before you send your query or proposal. The page number of the detailed listing is provided for your convenience.

FICTION

Adventure: Adventure 340; Alligator 128; Atheneum Bks for Yng Rdrs 136; Bantam Doubeday Dell Bks for Yng Rdrs 140; Berkley Pub Grp 144; Bethany 145; Book Creations 360; Borealis 341; Boyds Mills 148; Bristol Fashion 151; Caitlin 343; Clarion 164; Cloud Peak 165; Cormorant 344; Covenant Comm 169; Dial Bks for Yng Rdrs 175; Doubleday 176; Dutton 178; Electric Works 181; Fort Ross 189; Front Street 191; Geringer Bks 192; Hawk 201; Hendriks, FP 348; Holiday House 207; Holt Bks for Yng Rdrs 208; Houghton Mifflin Bks for Children 208; Little, Brown Childrn's Bks 230; Lobster 350; McElderry, Margaret 237; Milkweeds for Yng Rdrs 241; Minstrel 242; Moose Enterprise 351; Multnomah Publishers, Inc. 245; Nelson, Tommy 247; New Victoria 249; One World Bks 256; Onjinjin-kta 256; Owen, Richard 259; Paradise Cay 261; Picasso 353; Piñata 268; Putnam's Sons, G.P. 275; Ragweed 354; Random House Trade 277; Review & Herald 280; Rising Tide 281; River Oak 281; Scrivenery 289; Soho 296; Steel Pr Pub 301; Tor 310; Turnstone 357; Turtle Bks 312; Vandamere 322; Whitman, Albert 330; Windstorm Creative 334

Comic books: Edutainment 180; Insomniac 349; One World Bks 256; Picasso 353

Confession: Cormorant 344; Doubleday 176; One World Bks 256; Random House Trade 277; Soft Skull 296; Via Dolorosa 323; Willowgate 333

Erotica: Alligator 128; Arsenal Pulp 340; Autonomedia 137; Circlet 163; Gay Sunshine/Leyland 192; Guernica 347; Herodias 204; iPublish.com 218; Kensington 223; New American 247; New Victoria 249; One World Bks 256; Picasso 353; Vandamere 322; Willowgate 333; Windstorm Creative 334

Ethnic: Alligator 128; Arcade 133; Arsenal Pulp 340; Arte Publico 135; Atheneum Bks for Yng Rdrs 136; Borealis 341; Boyds Mills 148; Branden 149; Cormorant 344; Coteau 345; Doubleday 176; Dufour 178; Electric Works 181; HarperCollins [UK] 347; Hill, Lawrence 206; Houghton Mifflin Bks for Children 208; Insomniac 349; Interlink 216; Kensington 223; Lee & Low 228; Little, Brown Childrn's Bks 230; New American 247; One World Bks 256; Really Great 278; Red Hen 278; River City 281; Seal 290; Snowapple 355; Soho 296; Spinsters Ink 298; Third World 308; Turnstone 357; Turtle Bks 312; UCLA Amer Indian Studies Ctr 313; Whitman, Albert 330; Willowgate 333

Experimental: Arsenal Pulp 340; Atheneum Bks for Yng Rdrs 136; Autonomedia 137; Beach Holme 341; Coach House 344; Cormorant 344; Doubleday 176; Electric Works 181; Empyreal 346; Gay Sunshine/Leyland 192; Grove/Atlantic 197; House of Anansi 348; Insomniac 349; Livingston 231; McClelland&Stewart 350; Random House Trade 277; Red Hen 278; Scrivenery 289; Snowapple 355; Soft Skull 296; Stone Bridge 303; Tesseract 356; Turnstone 357; Univ of Illinois 316; Via Dolorosa 323; Willowgate 333; Windstorm Creative 334; York 359

Fantasy: Ace 124; Allisone 128; Atheneum Bks for Yng Rdrs 136; Baen 139; Bantam Doubeday Dell Bks for Yng Rdrs 140; Bookworld/Blue Star 148; Brucedale 342; Circlet 163; Cloud Peak 165; Coteau 345; Covenant Comm 169; Del Rey 174; Dial Bks for Yng Rdrs 175; Edge 346; Electric Works 181; Eos 182; Fort Ross 189; Front Street 191; Geringer Bks 192; Greenwillow 195; Hawk 201; Hendriks, FP 348; Herodias 204; Holt Bks for Yng Rdrs 208; Humanitas 348; iPublish.com 218; Little, Brown Childrn's Bks 230; McElderry, Margaret 237; Milkweeds for Yng Rdrs 241; Minstrel 242; Morrow/Avon 244; Naiad 245; New American 247; New Victoria 249; Onjinjinkta 256; Overlook Press, The 259; Picasso 353; Random House Trade 277; Rising Tide 281; River Oak 281; ROC Bks 282; Simon & Schuster Bks for Yng Rdrs 293; Snowapple 355; St. Martin's 300; Steel Pr Pub 301; Stone Bridge 303; Tesseract 356; Timberwolf 309; Tor 310; Turtle Bks 312; Warner Aspect 326; Warner Books 326; Whitman, Albert 330; Willowgate 333; Windstorm Creative 334; Wizards of the Coast 335; Write Way 336

Feminist: Alligator 128; Arsenal Pulp 340; Autonomedia 137; Brucedale 342; Cleis 164; Cormorant 344; Coteau 345; Doubleday 176; Ediciones Nuevo Espacio 179; Empyreal 346; Four Walls Eight Windows 190; Front Street 191; Guernica 347; HarperCollins [UK] 347; House of Anansi 348; Little, Brown Childrn's Bks 230; New Victoria 249; Picasso 353; Red Hen 278; Seal 290; Snowapple 355; Soho 296; Third World 308; Turnstone 357; Willowgate 333

Gay/lesbian: Alligator 128; Arsenal Pulp 340; Autonomedia 137; Circlet 163; Cleis 164; Cormorant 344; Coteau

345; Doubleday 176; Empyreal 346; Four Walls Eight Windows 190; Guernica 347; Hill Street 206; House of Anansi 348; Insomniac 349; Kensington 223; Little, Brown Children's Bks 230; Naiad 245; Picasso 353; Really Great 278; Red Hen 278; River City 281; Seal 290; Spinsters Ink 298; Stone Bridge 303; Stonewall Inn 303; Willowgate 333; Windstorm Creative 334

Gothic: Atheneum Bks for Yng Rdrs 136; Electric Works 181; Love Spell 233; Picasso 353; Steel Pr Pub 301; Turnstone 357; Willowgate 333; Windstorm Creative 334; Wizards of the Coast 335

Hi-lo: Willowgate 333

Historical: Academy Chicago 124; Adventure 340; Alexander 127; Arcade 133; Atheneum Bks for Yng Rdrs 136; Ballantine 140; Barbour 141; Beil, Frederic 143; Berkley Pub Grp 144; Bethany 145; Book Creations 360; Borealis 341; Boyds Mills 148; Brucedale 342; Caitlin 343; Carolrhoda 156; Christian Pub/Horizon Bks. 162; Clarion 164; Cloud Peak 165; Cormorant 344; Coteau 345; Covenant Comm 169; Cross Cultural 170; Discovery Enter 176; Doubleday 176; Dry Bones 178; Dufour 178; Dutton 178; Ediciones Nuevo Espacio 179; Editions la Liberte 346; Electric Works 181; Faith Kids 185; Forge 188; Front Street 191; Gay Sunshine/Leyland 192; Hawk 201; Herodias 204; Hill Street 206; Holiday House 207; Holt Bks for Yng Rdrs 208; Houghton Mifflin Bks for Children 208; Kensington 223; Leisure 228; Little, Brown Children's Bks 230; Lobster 350; Love Spell 233; Lyons 234; MacAdam/Cage 234; McClelland&Stewart 350; McElderry, Margaret 237; Milkweeds for Yng Rdrs 241; Moose Enterprise 351; Multnomah Publishers, Inc. 245; Narwhal 246; Nautical & Aviation 246; Naval Inst 246; New American 247; New England Pr 248; New Victoria 249; One World Bks 256; Pelican 264; Philomel Books 267; Picasso 353; Pineapple 268; Pippin 269; Pleasant Company 270; Ragweed 354; Random House Trade 277; Red Hen 278; Review & Herald 280; Rising Tide 281; River City 281; River Oak 281; Saxon House Canada 355; Scrivenery 289; Silver Moon 293; Simon & Schuster Bks for Yng Rdrs 293; Snowapple 355; Soft Skull 296; Soho 296; St. Martin's 300; Steel Pr Pub 301; Third World 308; Tor 310; Turtle Bks 312; Via Dolorosa 323; White Mane 330; Whitman, Albert 330; Willowgate 333; Windstorm Creative 334

Horror: Adventure 340; Alligator 128; Atheneum Bks for Yng Rdrs 136; Cloud Peak 165; Design Image Grp 175; Electric Works 181; Forge 188; Fort Ross 189; Front Street 191; Hawk 201; Kensington 223; Leisure 228; Moose Enterprise 351; New American 247; Picasso 353; Random House Bks for Yng Rdrs 277; Random House Trade 277; Rising Tide 281; ROC Bks 282; St. Martin's 300; Steel Pr Pub 301; Tor 310; Vista 324; Warner Books 326; Willowgate 333; Write Way 336

Humor: Adventure 340; Arcade 133; Atheneum Bks for Yng Rdrs 136; Bantam Doubeday Dell Bks for Yng Rdrs 140; Barbour 141; Boyds Mills 148; Brucedale 342; Caitlin 343; Cartwheel 157; Christian Pub/Horizon Bks. 162; Clarion 164; Cloud Peak 165; Coastal Carolina 165; Cormorant 344; Coteau 345; Covenant Comm 169; Doubleday 176; Dry Bones 178; Electric Works 181; Front Street 191; Geringer Bks 192; Greenwillow 195; Hawk 201; Hendriks, FP 348; Hill Street 206; Holt Bks for Yng Rdrs 208; Houghton Mifflin Bks for Children 208; Insomniac 349; iPublish.com 218; Little, Brown Childrn's Bks 230; McClelland&Stewart 350; Meriwether 239; Milkweeds for Yng Rdrs 241; Minstrel 242; Moose Enterprise 351; Multnomah Publishers, Inc. 245; New Victoria 249; One World Bks 256; Onjinjinkta 256; Picasso 353; Pippin 269; Random House Trade 277; Review & Herald 280; Rising Tide 281; River Oak 281; Simon & Schuster Bks for Yng Rdrs 293; Steel Pr Pub 301; Turnstone 357; Vandamere 322; Whitman, Albert 330; Willowgate 333; Windstorm Creative 334

Juvenile: Adventure 340; Albury 127; Annick 340; Baker 139; Bantam Doubeday Dell Bks for Yng Rdrs 140; Barron's 141; Bethany 145; Boyds Mills 148; Brucedale 342; Candlewick 154; CandyCane 155; Carolrhoda 156; Cartwheel 157; Cloud Peak 165; Coastal Carolina 165; Cook Comm 168; Coteau 345; Covenant Comm 169; Cricket 170; Dial Bks for Yng Rdrs 175; Down East 177; Editions la Liberte 346; Eerdmans Bks for Yng Rdrs 180; Electric Works 181; Faith Kids 185; Farrar Straus & Giroux Bks for Yng Rdrs 185; Forward Movement 189; Front Street 191; Geringer Bks 192; Godine, David 194; Greene Bark 195; HarperCollins [UK] 347; Hawk 201; Hendriks, FP 348; Herodias 204; Houghton Mifflin Bks for Children 208; ImaJinn 213; Jones Univ, Bob 221; Kar-Ben 222; Knopf & Crown Bks for Yng Rdrs, Alfred 224; Levin, Arthur 229; Little, Brown Childrn's Bks 230; Lobster 350; Maupin 236; Minstrel 242; Moose Enterprise 351; Narwhal 246; Nelson, Tommy 247; New Canaan 248; Pauline 263; Peachtree 264; Pelican 264; Picasso 353; Piñata 268; Playhouse 270; Pleasant Company 270; Ragweed 354; Random House Bks for Yng Rdrs 277; Review & Herald 280; Salina Bookshelf 285; Scholastic Canada 355; Scholastic Inc. 288; Scholastic Pr 288; Seedling 290; Simon & Schuster Bks for Yng Rdrs 293; Soundprints 296; Third World 308; Tidewater 309; Tingley, Megan 310; Tradewind 356; Unity House 314; Viking Childrn's 323; Walker 325; What's Inside 329; White Mane 330

Literary: Alligator 128; Arcade 133; Arsenal Pulp 340; Arte Publico 135; Autonomedia 137; Baker 139; Beach Holme 341; Beil, Frederic 143; Berkley Pub Grp 144; Borealis 341; Bridge Works 150; Broken Jaw 342; Brucedale 342; Carroll & Graf 156; Cleis 164; Coach House 344; Coffee House 165; Cormorant 344; Coteau 345; Covenant Comm 169; Dial Pr 175; Doubleday 176; Dufour 178; Dutton 178; ECW 345; Ediciones Nuevo Espacio 179; Editions la Liberte 346; Electric Works 181; Empyreal 346; Farrar, Straus & Giroux Paperbacks 186; Front Street 191; Geringer Bks 192; Godine, David 194; Goose Lane 347; Graywolf 195; Greenwillow 195; Grove/Atlantic 197; Guernica 347; HarperCollins [UK] 347; Hawk 201; Herodias 204; Hill Street 206; Houghton Mifflin 209; Houghton Mifflin Bks for Children 208; House of Anansi 348; Insomniac 349; Knopf & Crown Bks for Yng Rdrs, Alfred 224; Latin Amer Lit Rev 227; Little, Brown 231; Livingston 231; Loft 232; Longstreet 232; MacAdam/Cage 234; Mariner 236; McClelland&Stewart 350; Milkweed 240; NeWest 351; New American 247; Norton, WW 253; One World Bks 256; Overlook Press, The 259; Peachtree 264; Permanent/Second Chance 265; Picador USA 267; Picasso 353; Pineapple 268; Putnam's Sons, G.P. 275; Really Great 278; Red Hen 278; Rising Tide 281; River City 281; Ruminator 283; Sarabande 286; Saxon House Canada 355; Scribner 289; Scrivenery 289; Seal 290; Seven Stories 291; Snowapple 355; Soft Skull 296; Soho 296; Southern Methodist Univ 297; St. Martin's 300; Steel Pr Pub 301; Stonewall Inn 303; Story Line 303; Third World

Inc. 245; Nelson, Tommy 247; New Canaan 248; Norton, WW 253; One World Bks 256; Onjinjinkta 256; Picasso 353; Pineapple 268; Really Great 278; Revere, Fleming 280; Review & Herald 280; River City 281; River Oak 281; Scrivenery 289; Tidewater 309; Turtle Bks 312; UCLA Amer Indian Studies Ctr 313; Willowgate 333

Religious: Allisone 128; Ambassador; Artemis Creations; Baker Books 139; Barbour 141; Branden 149; Broadman & Holman 151; Candycane 155; Christian Pub/Horizon Bks 162; Covenant Comm 169; Cross Cultural 170; Doubleday 176; Doubleday Religious 176; Dry Bones 178; Electric Works 181; Faith Kids 185; Hill Street 206; Kar-Ben Copies 222; Kregel 225; Multnomah 245; Nelson, Tommy 247; New Canaan Publishing 248; Norton, W.W. 253; Onjinjinkta 256; Picasso 353; Revell, Fleming H. 280; Review and Herald 280; River Oak 281; UCLA Amer Indian Studies Ctr 313

Romance: Adventure 340; Alligator 128; Avalon Bks 138; Barbour 141; Berkley Pub Grp 144; Borealis 341; Brucedale 342; Covenant Comm 169; Cross Cultural 170; Ediciones Nuevo Espacio 179; Electric Works 181; Fort Ross 189; Front Street 191; Humanitas 348; ImaJinn 213; iPublish.com 218; Kensington 223; Leisure 228; Morrow/Avon 244; Multnomah Publishers, Inc. 245; New American 247; New Victoria 249; One World Bks 256; Picasso 353; Ponder 353; Rising Tide 281; River Oak 281; Scholastic Inc. 288; Silhouette 292; Steel Pr Pub 301; Stenhouse 302; Thorndike 309; Tyndale House 313; Warner Books 326; Willowgate 333; Zebra 338

Science fiction: Ace 124; Adventure 340; Alexander 127; Alligator 128; Atheneum Bks for Yng Rdrs 136; Autonomedia 137; Baen 139; Carroll & Graf 156; Circlet 163; Cloud Peak 165; Covenant Comm 169; Cross Cultural 170; Crossquarter 170; Del Rey 174; Dry Bones 178; Edge 346; Electric Works 181; Eos 182; Fort Ross 189; Front Street 191; Gay Sunshine/Leyland 192; Hawk 201; Hendriks, FP 348; iPublish.com 218; Little, Brown Childrn's Bks 230; Love Spell 233; Minstrel 242; Moose Enterprise 351; Morrow/Avon 244; New American 247; New Victoria 249; Picasso 353; Rising Tide 281; ROC Bks 282; Simon & Schuster Bks for Yng Rdrs 293; St. Martin's 300; Steel Pr Pub 301; Tesseract 356; Timberwolf 309; Tor 310; Warner Aspect 326; Warner Books 326; Wesleyan Univ 328; Willowgate 333; Windstorm Creative 334; Wizards of the Coast 335; Write Way 336

Short story collections: Adventure 340; Allisone 128; Arcade 133; Arsenal Pulp 340; Autonomedia 137; Barbour 141; Borealis 341; Breakaway 150; Bridge Works 150; Brucedale 342; Caitlin 343; Circlet 163; Coffee House 165; Cormorant 344; Coteau 345; Doubleday 176; Dufour 178; Dutton 178; ECW 345; Ediciones Nuevo Espacio 179; Editions la Liberte 346; Electric Works 181; Empyreal 346; Godine, David 194; Goose Lane 347; HarperCollins [UK] 347; House of Anansi 348; Humanitas 348; Latin Amer Lit Rev 227; Livingston 231; Loft 232; Lyons 234; McClelland&Stewart 350; Moose Enterprise 351; Naiad 245; One World Bks 256; Red Hen 278; River City 281; Ronsdale 354; Sarabande 286; Scrivenery 289; Snowapple 355; Soft Skull 296; Southern Methodist Univ 297; Tesseract 356; Third World 308; Turnstone 357; Via Dolorosa 323; Vintage Anchor 324; Vista 324; Willowgate 333; Wizards of the Coast 335; Zoland 338

Spiritual (New Age, etc.): Allisone 128; Berkley Pub Grp 144; Christian Pub/Horizon Bks. 162; Coteau 345; Covenant Comm 169; Electric Works 181; Hampton Roads 198; Imagination Store 213; Llewellyn 231; Onjinjinkta 256; Picasso 353; River Oak 281

Sports: Breakaway 150; Coteau 345; Electric Works 181; Hill Street 206; Holt Bks for Yng Rdrs 208; Lyons 234; Paradise Cay 261; Picasso 353; River Oak 281; Turtle Bks 312; Willowgate 333

Suspense: Adventure 340; Alligator 128; Arcade 133; Atheneum Bks for Yng Rdrs 136; Bantam Doubeday Dell Bks for Yng Rdrs 140; Berkley Pub Grp 144; Carroll & Graf 156; Clarion 164; Cloud Peak 165; Covenant Comm 169; Doubleday 176; Dunne, Thomas 178; Dutton 178; ECW 345; Ediciones Nuevo Espacio 179; Electric Works 181; Forge 188; Fort Ross 189; Hawk 201; Holt Bks for Yng Rdrs 208; Houghton Mifflin Bks for Children 208; Insomniac 349; Intercontinental 216; Kensington 223; Little, Brown Childrn's Bks 230; Meriwether 239; Minstrel 242; Morrow/Avon 244; Multnomah Publishers, Inc. 245; Mysterious 245; New American 247; Oaklea 254; One World Bks 256; Onjinjinkta 256; Picasso 353; Putnam's Sons, G.P. 275; Random House Trade 277; Rising Tide 281; Salvo 285; Scribner 289; Scrivenery 289; Soho 296; St. Martin's 300; Steel Pr Pub 301; Timberwolf 309; Vandamere 322; Viking Childrn's 323; Warner Books 326

Translation: Breakaway 150; Cormorant 344; Ediciones Nuevo Espacio 179; Electric Works 181; Gay Sunshine/Leyland 192; Grove/Atlantic 197; Guernica 347; Herodias 204; Latin Amer Lit Rev 227; Scrivenery 289; Via Dolorosa 323

Western: Adventure 340; Alexander 127; Atheneum Bks for Yng Rdrs 136; Avalon Bks 138; Barbour 141; Berkley Pub Grp 144; Book Creations 360; Cloud Peak 165; Electric Works 181; Kensington 223; Leisure 228; Moose Enterprise 351; Multnomah Publishers, Inc. 245; New American 247; New Victoria 249; River Oak 281; St. Martin's 300; Thorndike 309; Turtle Bks 312

Young adult: Adventure 340; Albury 127; Annick 340; Baker 139; Bantam Doubeday Dell Bks for Yng Rdrs 140; Beach Holme 341; Berkley Pub Grp 144; Bethany 145; Borealis 341; Boyds Mills 148; Brucedale 342; Caitlin 343; Christian Pub/Horizon Bks. 162; Chronicle Bks for Children 163; Coastal Carolina 165; Coteau 345; Covenant Comm 169; Dial Bks for Yng Rdrs 175; Ediciones Nuevo Espacio 179; Editions la Liberte 346; Eerdmans Bks for Yng Rdrs 180; Electric Works 181; Farrar Straus & Giroux Bks for Yng Rdrs 185; Front Street 191; Geringer Bks 192; HarperCollins [UK] 347; Hawk 201; Hendriks, FP 348; Herodias 204; Holt Bks for Yng Rdrs 208; Houghton Mifflin Bks for Children 208; Jones Univ, Bob 221; Knopf & Crown Bks for Yng Rdrs, Alfred 224; Listen & Live 230; Little, Brown Childrn's Bks 230; Lobster 350; McElderry, Margaret 237; Moose Enterprise 351; Narwhal 246; New Canaan 248; Orchard 257; Peachtree 264; Picasso 353; Piñata 268; Puffin 275; Ragweed 354; Random House Bks for Yng Rdrs 277; Scholastic Canada 355; Scholastic Pr 288; Simon & Schuster Bks for Yng Rdrs 293; Snowapple 355; Third World

308; Tingley, Megan 310; Unity House 314; Viking Childrn's 323; What's Inside 329; Windstorm Creative 334

NONFICTION

Agriculture/horticulture: American Press 131; Boyds Mills 148; Breakout 150; Broadcast Interview 151; Burford 153; Camino 154; Chelsea Green 160; Chemical Pub 160; Cornell Univ 168; Dover 177; Electric Works 181; Fernwood 346; Green Nature 195; Hancock House 198; Haworth 201; Hobar 207; Houghton Mifflin Bks for Children 208; Idyll Arbor 212; Krieger 225; Libraries Unlimited 229; Loompanics 233; Lyons 234; McClelland&Stewart 350; Norton, WW 253; Ohio Univ 255; Plexus 270; Purdue Univ 275; Purich 354; Reference Service 279; RFF Pr 281; Ronin 282; Stipes 302; Texas A&M Univ 308; Univ of Idaho 315; Univ of Nebraska 317; Univ of North Texas 318; Walsworth 325; Weidner & Sons 327; Windward 334

Alternative lifestyles: Hunter House 211; Ronin Pub 282; Sterling 302

Americana: Adams Media 124; Addicus 125; Adventure 340; Ancestry 132; Arkansas Research 134; Atheneum Bks for Yng Rdrs 136; Berkshire 144; Black Dog & Levanthal 145; Blair, John 146; Bluewood 147; Boston Mills 342; Bowling Green St Univ 148; Branden 149; Breakout 150; Brevet 150; Broadcast Interview 151; Camino 154; Capstone 155; Caxton 157; Chelsea House 160; Christian Pub/Horizon Bks. 162; Clarion 164; Clear Light 164; Cloud Peak 165; Cumberland House 171; Denali 174; Dial Pr 175; Doubleday 176; Dover 177; Down East 177; Eakin/Sunbelt 179; Editions la Liberte 346; Electric Works 181; Excelsior Cee 184; Fordham Univ 188; Godine, David 194; Golden West 194; Heritage Bks 204; HiddenSpring 205; High Plains 205; Hill Street 206; History Bank 361; Holiday House 207; Houghton Mifflin Bks for Children 208; Iconografix, Inc. 212; Kensington 223; Ketz, Louise B 361; Krause 224; Kurian, George 361; Layla 362; Lee, J&L 228; Lehigh Univ 228; Lion 230; Loft 232; Longstreet 232; Loompanics 233; Lyons 234; MBI 236; McDonald & Woodward 237; Michigan State Univ 240; Mustang 245; Mystic Seaport 245; Narwhal 246; New England Pub Assoc 362; Northeastern Univ 252; Ohio Univ 255; One World Bks 256; Onjinjinkta 256; Overmountain 259; Pacific Bks 260; Pelican 264; Picasso 353; Picton 268; Pleasant Company 270; Pruett 274; Purdue Univ 275; Random House Trade 277; Reference Pr Int'l 279; Reynolds, Morgan 280; Santa Monica 286; Sarpedon 286; Saxon House Canada 355; Scrivenery 289; Seal 290; Sergeant Kirkland's 291; Shoreline 355; Southern Illinois Univ 297; Sun Bks/Sun Pub 304; TCU 307; TowleHouse 310; Truman State Univ 312; TwoDot 313; UCLA Amer Indian Studies Ctr 313; Univ of Idaho 315; Univ of Illinois 316; Univ of New Mexico 317; Univ of North Carolina 318; Univ of North Texas 318; Univ of Oklahoma 318; Univ of Pennsylvania 318; Univ of Tennessee 319; Univ of Univ of Arkansas 315; Univ Pr of Kansas 320; Univ Pr of Kentucky 320; Univ Pr of Mississippi 320; Univ Pr of New England 321; Upney Editions 357; Vandamere 322; Vanderbilt Univ 322; Vernon 362; Viking Studio 324; Vintage Images 324; Voyageur 325; Washington State Univ Pr 326; Westcliffe 328; Westernlore 329; Yale Univ 337

Animals: Abdo 123; Adams Media 124; Adventure 340; Atheneum Bks for Yng Rdrs 136; Ballantine 140; Barron's 141; Benefactory 143; Beyond Words 145; Black Dog & Levanthal 145; Blackbirch 146; Boyds Mills 148; Burford 153; Capstone 155; Cartwheel 157; Charlesbridge (Trade) 159; Chelsea House 160; Children's Pr 161; Chronicle Bks for Children 163; Conari 167; Dawn Pub 173; Dimi Pr 175; Dover 177; Dutton Children's Bks 179; Editions la Liberte 346; Electric Works 181; Epicenter 182; Front Street 191; Gollehon 194; Green Nature 195; Half Halt 198; Hancock House 198; Herodias 204; Hobar 207; Houghton Mifflin Bks for Children 208; Inner Traditions 215; Jones Univ, Bob 221; Kensington 223; Kesend, Michael 223; Krieger 225; Little, Brown Childrn's Bks 230; Lone Pine 350; Lyons 234; McClelland&Stewart 350; McDonald & Woodward 237; Millbrook 241; Mountain Pr 244; New American 247; Northword 253; Ohio Univ 255; Orchard 257; Owen, Richard 259; Perigee 265; Picasso 353; Pineapple 268; Pippin 269; Putnam's Sons, G.P. 275; Random House Bks for Yng Rdrs 277; Review & Herald 280; Sasquatch 287; Seedling 290; Simon & Schuster Bks for Yng Rdrs 293; Soundprints 296; Square One 299; Sterling 302; Storey 303; Trafalgar Square 311; Turtle Bks 312; Univ of Illinois 316; Univ of Nebraska 317; Weidner & Sons 327; Westcliffe 328; Whitecap 359; Whitman, Albert 330; Willow Creek 333; Windswept House 334; Windward 334

Anthropology/archaeology: Algora 127; American Press 131; Autonomedia 137; Baker 139; Baywood 142; Bergin & Garvey 144; Blackbirch 146; Bluewood 147; Breakout 150; Broadman & Holman 151; Burnham 153; Chelsea House 160; Children's Pr 161; Clear Light 164; Common Courage 166; Cornell Univ 168; Cross Cultural 170; CSLI 171; Denali 174; Doubleday 176; Dover 177; Editions la Liberte 346; Electric Works 181; Encounter Bks 182; Fernwood 346; Fordham Univ 188; Gollehon 194; Greenwood Pub Grp 196; Gruyter, Aldine de 197; Harcourt Inc., Trade 199; Hawk 201; HiddenSpring 205; Horsdal&Schubart 348; Houghton Mifflin Bks for Children 208; House of Anansi 348; Iser 349; Island 219; Johnson 221; Kent State Univ 223; LadybugPress 225; Libraries Unlimited 229; Loompanics 233; Lyons 234; McDonald & Woodward 237; Millbrook 241; Minnesota Hist Soc 241; Narwhal 246; New England Pub Assoc 362; New York Univ 250; Northern Illinois Univ 252; Northland 253; Ohio Univ 255; Onjinjinkta 256; Oryx 257; Oxford Univ 259; Pennsylvania Hist and Museum Comm 264; Press at the Maryland Hist Soc 272; Pruett 274; Quest Books 276; Red Hen 278; Review & Herald 280; Rose 282; Schenkman 288; Sergeant Kirkland's 291; Stanford Univ 301; Sun Bks/Sun Pub 304; Sunbelt 304; Texas A&M Univ 308; Third World 308; UCLA Amer Indian Studies Ctr 313; Univ of Alabama 314; Univ of Idaho 315; Univ of Iowa 316; Univ of Nebraska 317; Univ of Nevada 317; Univ of New Mexico 317; Univ of North Carolina 318; Univ of Pennsylvania 318; Univ of Tennessee 319; Univ of Texas 319; Univ Pr of Kansas 320; Vanderbilt Univ 322; Vintage Anchor 324; Washington State Univ Pr 326; Weatherhill 327; Westernlore 329; Westminster John Knox 329; White Cliffs 329; Whitman, Albert 330; Yale Univ 337

Art/architecture: Abrams 123; Allworth 128; American Press 131; Arsenal Pulp 340; Art Direction 134; Atheneum Bks for Yng Rdrs 136; Autonomedia 137; Barron's 141; Beil, Frederic 143; Black Dog & Levanthal 145; Blackbirch 146; Blizzard 341; Bluewood 147; Boston Mills 342; Bowling Green St Univ 148; Branden 149; Brewers 150; Bucknell Univ 152; Bulfinch 152; Camino 154; Chelsea Green 160; Chicago Review 161; Children's Pr 161;

Kansas 320; Univ Pr of Kentucky 320; Univ Pr of Mississippi 320; Univ Pr of New England 321; University of South Carolina 319; Upney Editions 357; Utah State Univ 321; Vandamere 322; Vanderbilt Univ 322; Vanwell 358; Vehicule 358; Via Dolorosa 323; Viking 323; Vintage Anchor 324; Walker 325; Warner Books 326; Washington State Univ Pr 326; Watts, Franklin 327; Wesleyan Univ 328; Westernlore 329; Westminster John Knox 329; White Cliffs 329; Wiley & Sons, John 332; Windstorm Creative 334; Windswept House 334; Wish 335; Wonderland 363; Yale Univ 337; Zoland 338; Zondervan 338

Booklets: Bureau for At-Risk Youth 153; Speech Bin 298

Business/economics: Adams Blake 125; Adams Media 124; Addicus 125; Aktrin 126; Algora 127; Allworth 128; America West 129; American Bar 129; American Coll of Phys Exec 130; American Press 131; Ardsley 134; Aslan 135; ATL 137; Atheneum Bks for Yng Rdrs 136; Auburn 137; Autonomedia 137; Barricade 141; Barron's 141; Behr 142; Berkley Pub Grp 144; Betterway 145; Bloomberg 146; Bluewood 147; Brevet 150; Broadcast Interview 151; Broadman & Holman 151; Broadway 152; Bryant & Dillon 152; Canadian Plains 343; Career Pr 155; Carroll & Graf 156; Cato 157; Consortium 167; Contemporary Bks 167; Cornell Univ 168; Cross Cultural 170; Crown Business 171; Cypress 172; Cypress 172; Dearborn 174; Doubleday 176; Eakin/Sunbelt 179; ECW 345; Edutainment 180; Electric Works 181; Encounter Bks 182; Entrepreneur 182; Executive Excellence 184; Fairleigh Dickinson Univ 185; Fell, Frederick 186; Fernwood 346; Fort Ross 189; Forum Pub 189; Free Pr 190; Gifted Educ 193; Glenlake 193; Gollehon 194; Graduate Grp 194; Greenwood Pub Grp 196; HarperCollins [UK] 347; HarperInformation 200; Harvard Bus Sch 200; Hawk 201; Haworth 201; HiddenSpring 205; High Tide 205; Hobar 207; Holmes & Meier 208; Hungry Minds (Business) 211; ILR 213; Impact Publications 214; Information Today 214; Insomniac 349; Int'l Wealth Success 217; Island 219; iPublish.com 218; Jain 219; Jameson 220; Jewish Lights 220; Jist Works 220; Kensington 223; Ketz, Louise B 361; Klein, B 224; Kurian, George 361; LadybugPress 225; Lebhar-Friedman 227; Libraries Unlimited 229; Listen & Live 230; Loft 232; Maximum Pr 236; McClelland&Stewart 350; McFarland 237; McGraw-Hill Ryerson 351; McGregor 238; Metamorphous 239; Michigan State Univ 240; Morrow/Avon 244; NavPress 247; New England Pub Assoc 362; New Society 351; New World Library 250; New York Univ 250; Nichols 251; Nolo.com 251; Norbry 352; Northfield 253; Norton, WW 253; Oaklea 254; Oasis 254; Ohio State Univ 255; Oliver 255; Oryx 257; Oxford Univ 259; Palgrave 261; Pearson PTR Canada 352; Perigee 265; Peterson's 266; Pilgrim 268; Planning/Communications 269; Praeger 271; Precept 272; Prima 273; Productive 353; Purdue Univ 275; Putnam's Sons, G.P. 275; Quorom 277; Random House Trade 277; Reference Pr Int'l 279; Reference Service 279; Regnery 279; Reynolds, Morgan 280; RFF Pr 281; Ronin 282; Salem 285; Sasquatch 287; Sourcebooks 296; Square One 299; St. Martin's 300; Stanford Univ 301; Starbust 301; Stipes 302; Stone Bridge 303; Stylus 304; Success 304; Sun Bks/Sun Pub 304; Systems Co 306; Tarcher 306; Ten Speed 307; Texas A&M Univ 308; Thompson Educ Pub 356; Todd 310; Tower 310; Transnational 311; Trinity Fndtn 311; Triumph 312; Univ of Pennsylvania 318; University of Calgary Press 357; Verso 322; VGM Career 323; Viking 323; Vintage Anchor 324; Walsworth 325; Warner Books 326; Weidner & Sons 327; Windsor 333; Windstorm Creative 334; Wonderland 363; Yale Univ 337

Child guidance/parenting: Adams Media 124; Aslan 135; Baker 139; Ballantine 140; Barbour 141; Barron's 141; Behr 142; Bergin & Garvey 144; Berkley Pub Grp 144; Bethany 145; Beyond Words 145; Broadway 152; Bureau for At-Risk Youth 153; Cambridge Educ 154; Camino 154; Capstone 155; Celestial Arts 158; Charles Pr 158; Chicago Review 161; Child Welfare League 161; Childswork/Childsplay 161; Christian Pub/Horizon Bks. 162; City & Co 164; Conari 167; Concordia 167; Consortium 167; Cook Comm 168; Covenant Comm 169; Doubleday Religious 176; Editions la Liberte 346; Electric Works 181; Encounter Bks 182; Farrar, Straus & Giroux Paperbacks 186; Fell, Frederick 186; Free Spirit 190; Gifted Educ 193; Gifted Psych 193; Greenwood Pub Grp 196; Guilford 197; Harbor Pr 199; Harcourt Inc., Trade 199; HarperInformation 200; Harvard Common 200; Hawk 201; Haworth 201; Hazelden 202; Health Comm 202; Heinemann 203; Hendriks, FP 348; Hensley 204; HiddenSpring 205; Humanics Learning 210; Humanics Pub Grp 210; Impact Publishers, Inc. 214; Inner Traditions 215; Iron Gate 219; Kensington 223; LadybugPress 225; Lamppost 362; Lobster 350; Magni 234; McClelland&Stewart 350; Meadowbrook 238; Moody 242; Multnomah Publishers, Inc. 245; NavPress 247; New American 247; New England Pub Assoc 362; New Hope 249; New Horizon 249; New Society 351; Newmarket 250; Northfield 253; Norton, WW 253; Novalis 352; Paragon House 261; Parlay Int'l 262; Pauline 263; Perigee 265; Phi Delta Kappa 267; Picasso 353; Prima 273; Prufrock 274; Putnam's Sons, G.P. 275; Revere, Fleming 280; Review & Herald 280; River City 281; Seal 290; Sourcebooks 296; Square One 299; Starbust 301; Success 304; Tarcher 306; Taylor 306; Ten Speed 307; Tyndale House 313; Viking 323; Vintage Anchor 324; Vista 324; Weidner & Sons 327; Western Psych Services 328; Westminster John Knox 329; Williamson 332; Workman 336

Coffeetable book: A&B Pub Grp 123; Addax 125; Arcadia 133; Bentley 143; Beyond Words 145; Black Dog & Levanthal 145; Boston Mills 342; Brassey's 149; Broadman & Holman 151; Bulfinch 152; Chronicle 163; Clear Light 164; Coteau 345; Covenant Comm 169; Cross Cultural 170; Dana Pr 172; David, Jonathan 173; Dover 177; Epicenter 182; Excelsior Cee 184; Farcountry 361; Godine, David 194; Harcourt Inc., Trade 199; HarperInformation 200; Herodias 204; High Tide 205; Hill Street 206; History Bank 361; Iconografix, Inc. 212; Ideals Pub 212; Jacobs, Lee 219; Lark 226; Layla 362; Lebhar-Friedman 227; Loft 232; Longstreet 232; Lynx Images 350; MBI 236; McClelland-&Stewart 350; McDonald & Woodward 237; Minnesota Hist Soc 241; Monacelli 242; Multnomah Publishers, Inc. 245; Newmarket 250; Northland 253; Northword 253; Orange Frazer 257; Overmountain 259; PBC Int'l 263; Pelican 264; Picasso 353; Plexus 272; PressForward 272; ProStar 274; Revere, Fleming 280; River City 281; Schreiber 289; Sta-Kris 300; Sunbelt 304; Texas State Hist Assoc 308; Triumph 312; TwoDot 313; Vandamere 322; Vernon 362; Voyageur 325; Walsworth 325; Weatherhill 327; Westcliffe 328; Whitecap 359; Willow Creek 333; Wonderland 363

Communications: Battelle 142; Baywood 142; Focal 187; GATF 191; Oak Knoll 254; Tiare 309; Univ of Alabama 314

217; Kamehameha 222; Krieger 225; Kurian, George 361; Langenscheidt 226; Learning Pub 227; Lebhar-Friedman 227; Legacy 228; Libraries Unlimited 229; Maisonneuve 235; Mariner 236; Maupin 236; McClelland&Stewart 350; Metamorphous 239; Modern Lang Assoc 242; Neal-Schuman 247; New Canaan 248; New Hope 249; New Society 351; Nichols 251; Norbry 352; Nova 254; Novalis 352; Oasis 254; Octameron 255; Ohio State Univ 255; Orange Frazer 257; Oryx 257; Palgrave 261; Pencil Point 264; Peterson's 266; Phi Delta Kappa 267; Picasso 353; Planning/ Communications 269; Plexus 270; Presses de l'Université de Montreal 353; PressForward 272; Prima 273; Prometheus 273; Prufrock 274; Publicom 362; Puffin 275; Reference Pr Int'l 279; Reference Service 279; Review & Herald 280; Sagamore 284; Salina Bookshelf 285; Schaffer, Frank 287; Scholastic Professional 289; Scribner 289; Shaw 291; Shoreline 355; Silver Moon 293; Social Science Educ Consort 295; Somerville House 362; Speech Bin 298; Spence 298; St. Anthony 299; Standard 300; Starbust 301; Steel Pr Pub 301; Stylus 304; Sun Bks/Sun Pub 304; Teaching & Learning 307; Texas Western 308; Third World 308; Thompson Educ Pub 356; Trilobyte Press & Multimedia 356; Trinity Fndtn 311; Turtle Bks 312; Vandamere 322; Vanderbilt Univ 322; Via Dolorosa 323; Vintage Anchor 324; Walch, J. Weston 325; Wall & Emerson 358; Watts, Franklin 327; Weidner & Sons 327; Western Psych Services 328; Westminster John Knox 329; Windstorm Creative 334; Wonderland 363; Yale Univ 337

Entertainment/games: Bristol Pub 151; Dover 177; Lisa Drew 177; Facts on File 184; McFarland & Co 237; Meriwether 239; Minstrel 242; Piccadilly 267; Popular culture 270; Speech Bin 298; Standard 300; Sterling 302; Univ of Nevada 317

Ethnic: Arkansas Research 134; Arsenal Pulp 340; Arte Publico 135; Aslan 135; Avisson 139; Barricade 141; Behrman 143; Bethany 145; Blue Poppy 147; Bowling Green St Univ 148; Boyds Mills 148; Bryant & Dillon 152; Bucknell Univ 152; Camino 154; Carolrhoda 156; Chelsea House 160; Chicago Review 161; Children's Pr 161; Clear Light 164; Cleis 164; Coastal Carolina 165; Common Courage 166; Conari 167; Cornell Univ 168; Coteau 345; Course Crafters 360; Cross Cultural 170; David, Jonathan 173; Denali 174; Doubleday 176; Eakin/Sunbelt 179; Electric Works 181; Encounter Bks 182; Epicenter 182; Fell, Frederick 186; Feminist Pr at CUNY 186; Fernwood 346; Front Street 191; Guernica 347; Hachai 198; Hancock House 198; Harcourt Inc., Trade 199; Heritage Bks 204; Heyday 205; Hidden-Spring 205; Hill, Lawrence 206; Hippocrene 206; Holmes & Meier 208; Houghton Mifflin Bks for Children 208; Humanics Learning 210; Inner Traditions 215; Int'l Scholars 217; Iser 349; Knopf & Crown Bks for Yng Rdrs, Alfred 224; Kurian, George 361; Lake Claremont 225; Lee & Low 228; Lerner 229; Libraries Unlimited 229; Lion 230; Little, Brown Childrn's Bks 230; Locust Hill 231; Louisiana State Univ 233; Maisonneuve 235; McDonald & Woodward 237; McFarland 237; McGregor 238; Michigan State Univ 240; Millbrook 241; Minnesota Hist Soc 241; Mitchell Lane 242; Naturegraph 246; NeWest 351; New American 247; New England Pub Assoc 362; New World Library 250; New York Univ 250; Northland 253; Ohio Univ 255; Oliver 255; One World Bks 256; Overmountain 259; Palgrave 261; Passeggiata 262; Pelican 264; Picasso 353; Piñata 268; Pruett 274; Purich 354; Really Great 278; Red Hen 278; Reference Service 279; Republic of Texas 279; River City 281; Rosen Publishing Group, The 282; Rutgers Univ 283; Salem 285; Salina Bookshelf 285; Schenkman 288; Scribner 289; Seal 290; Shoreline 355; Simon & Schuster Bks for Yng Rdrs 293; South End 297; Stanford Univ 301; Sterling 302; Stone Bridge 303; Temple Univ 307; Third World 308; Thompson Educ Pub 356; Todd 310; Tuttle 312; UCLA Amer Indian Studies Ctr 313; Univ of Idaho 315; Univ of Nevada 317; Univ of New Mexico 317; Univ of North Texas 318; Univ of Oklahoma 318; Univ of Tennessee 319; Univ of Texas 319; Univ Pr of Kentucky 320; Univ Pr of Mississippi 320; Vanderbilt Univ 322; Vintage Anchor 324; Walsworth 325; Washington State Univ Pr 326; Wesleyan Univ 328; Westminster John Knox 329; White Cliffs 329; Whitman, Albert 330; Williamson 332; YMAA 337

Fashion/beauty: Owen, Richard 259; Quite Specific 276; Storey 303

Feminism: Cleis 164; New Victoria 249; Spinsters Ink 298; Vehicule 358

Film/cinema/stage: Allworth 128; Betterway 145; Bryant & Dillon 152; Dee, Ivan 174; Fairleigh Dickinson Univ 185; Fell, Frederick 186; Focal Pr 187; Guernica 347; Heinemann 203; Limelight 229; Lone Eagle 232; McFarland 237; Meriwether 239; Overlook Press, The 259; Piccadilly 267; Players 269; Precept 272; Quite Specific 276; Rutgers Univ 283; Santa Monica 286; Scarecrow 287; Smith & Kraus 295; Univ of Texas 319; Wesleyan Univ 328

Gardening: Adams Media 124; Black Dog & Levanthal 145; Boston Mills 342; Breakout 150; Bulfinch 152; Burford 153; Camino 154; Chelsea Green 160; Chicago Review 161; Chronicle 163; City & Co 164; Coastal Carolina 165; Conari 167; Countryman 169; Creative Homeowner 170; Electric Works 181; Front Street 191; Godine, David 194; Gollehon 194; HarperCollins [UK] 347; HiddenSpring 205; Hill Street 206; Hobar 207; Hobby House 207; Home Planners 208; Houghton Mifflin 209; Houghton Mifflin Bks for Children 208; Interweave 218; Kesend, Michael 223; Lamppost 362; Lark 226; Layla 362; Lone Pine 350; Longstreet 232; Lyons 234; McClelland&Stewart 350; North Point 252; Northland 253; Ohio Univ 255; Owen, Richard 259; PBC Int'l 263; Pearson PTR Canada 352; Pineapple 268; Plexus 270; Prairie Oak 271; Reference Pr Int'l 279; River City 281; Ronin 282; Sasquatch 287; Starbust 301; Steller 356; Sterling 302; Storey 303; Taylor 306; Ten Speed 307; Tricycle 311; Univ of New Mexico 317; Univ of North Carolina 318; Vernon 362; Weatherhill 327; Weidner & Sons 327; Westcliffe 328; Whitecap 359; Whitman, Albert 330; Willow Creek 333; Windward 334; Wonderland 363; Workman 336

Gay/lesbian: Alligator 128; Alyson 128; American Counseling 130; Arsenal Pulp 340; Aslan 135; Autonomedia 137; Barricade 141; Berkley Pub Grp 144; Broadway 152; Broken Jaw 342; Celestial Arts 158; Chelsea House 160; Cleis 164; Common Courage 166; Conari 167; Cornell Univ 168; ECW 345; Educator's Int'l 180; Feminist Pr at CUNY 186; Fernwood 346; Front Street 191; Gay Sunshine/Leyland 192; Guernica 347; Guilford 197; Harcourt Inc., Trade 199; HarperCollins [UK] 347; Haworth 201; Hazelden 202; Heinemann 203; HiddenSpring 205; Hill Street 206; House of Anansi 348; Insomniac 349; Kensington 223; LadybugPress 225; Little, Brown Childrn's Bks 230; Maisonneuve 235; McClelland&Stewart 350; New England Pub Assoc 362; New Harbinger 248; New Victoria 249; New York Univ

362; New Harbinger 248; New Hope 249; New Horizon 249; New World Library 250; Newmarket 250; Norton, WW 253; Oliver 255; Onjinjinkta 256; Oryx 257; Oxford Univ 259; Pacific Pr Pub Assoc 260; Parlay Int'l 262; Pathfinder 263; Peachtree 264; Pearson PTR Canada 352; Perigee 265; Perspectives 266; Pilgrim 268; Plexus 270; Precept 272; Presses de l'Université de Montreal 353; PressForward 272; Prima 273; Prometheus 273; Purdue Univ 275; Putnam's Sons, G.P. 275; Quest Books 276; Random House Trade 277; Reference Service 279; Regnery 279; Review & Herald 280; River City 281; Ronin 282; Rosen Publishing Group, The 282; Running Pr 283; Rutgers Univ 283; Sagamore 284; Salem 285; Santa Monica 286; Scribner 289; Shoreline 355; Slack 294; South End 297; Speech Bin 298; Starbust 301; Sterling 302; Storey 303; Sun Bks/Sun Pub 304; Systems Co 306; Tarcher 306; Taylor 306; Temple Univ 307; Ten Speed 307; Texas Western 308; Third World 308; Todd 310; Tricycle 311; Trilobyte Press & Multimedia 356; Triumph 312; Tuttle 312; Twenty-First Century 313; UCLA Amer Indian Studies Ctr 313; Unity House 314; Univ of North Carolina 318; Univ Pr of Mississippi 320; University of Calgary Press 357; Vandamere 322; Vanderbilt Univ 322; VGM Career 323; Viking 323; Vintage Anchor 324; Vista 324; Volcano 325; Walker 325; Wall & Emerson 358; Warner Books 326; Weidner & Sons 327; Whitman, Albert 330; Whitson 331; Wish 335; Woodbine House 335; Woodland 335; Workman 336; Yale Univ 337; YMAA 337

Hi-lo: Cambridge Educ 154; Rising Tide 281

History: A&B Pub Grp 123; Abdo 123; Academy Chicago 124; Adams Media 124; Adventure 340; Alexander 127; Algora 127; American Press 131; Appalachian Mtn Club 133; Arcade 133; Arcadia 133; Arkansas Research 134; Aronson, Jason 134; Arsenal Pulp 340; Atheneum Bks for Yng Rdrs 136; Autonomedia 137; Aviation 138; Avisson 139; Aztex 139; Barricade 141; Beil, Frederic 143; Berkley Pub Grp 144; Berkshire 144; Blackbirch 146; Blair, John 146; Bluewood 147; Borealis 341; Boston Mills 342; Bowling Green St Univ 148; Boyds Mills 148; Branden 149; Brassey's 149; Breakout 150; Brevet 150; Brewers 150; Bridge Works 150; Bristol Fashion 151; Broadcast Interview 151; Broadman & Holman 151; Broadway 152; Broken Jaw 342; Brucedale 342; Bryant & Dillon 152; Bucknell Univ 152; Caitlin 343; Camino 154; Canadian Educ 343; Canadian Library 343; Canadian Plains 343; Capstone 155; Carroll & Graf 156; Cartwheel 157; Catholic Univ of America 157; Caxton 157; Centerstream 158; CHA 344; Charlesbridge (Trade) 159; Chatham 159; Chelsea House 160; Chicago Review 161; Children's Pr 161; Clarion 164; Clear Light 164; Cloud Peak 165; Coastal Carolina 165; Common Courage 166; Conari 167; Consortium 167; Cook Comm 168; Cormorant 344; Cornell Univ 168; Coteau 345; Countryman 169; Covenant Comm 169; CQ 169; Cross Cultural 170; Cumberland House 171; Dante Univ 172; Darlington 173; Davis Pub 173; Dee, Ivan 174; Denali 174; Dial Pr 175; Doubleday 176; Dover 177; Down East 177; Drew, Lisa 177; Dry Bones 178; Dufour 178; Dunne, Thomas 178; Dutton Children's Bks 179; Eakin/Sunbelt 179; ECW 345; Editions la Liberte 346; Edutainment 180; Eerdmans, William 181; Electric Works 181; Elephant 181; Encounter Bks 182; Epicenter 182; Excalibur 183; Excelsior Cee 184; Facts on File 184; Fairleigh Dickinson Univ 185; Feminist Pr at CUNY 186; Fernwood 346; Flying Bks 187; Fordham Univ 188; Foreign Policy 188; Four Walls Eight Windows 190; Front Street 191; Gem Guides 192; GGC 192; Globe Pequot 193; Golden West 194; Goose Lane 347; Greenhaven 195; Greenwood Pub Grp 196; Grove/Atlantic 197; Guernica 347; Hancock House 198; Harcourt Inc., Trade 199; HarperCollins [UK] 347; Hawk 201; Heritage Bks 204; Heyday 205; HiddenSpring 205; High Plains 205; Hill, Lawrence 206; Hill Street 206; Hippocrene 206; History Bank 361; Holiday House 207; Holmes & Meier 208; Horsdal&Schubart 348; Houghton Mifflin 209; Houghton Mifflin Bks for Children 208; House of Anansi 348; Howell Pr 209; Humanitas 348; Iconografix, Inc. 212; Ideals Pub 212; ILR 213; Inner Traditions 215; Int'l Scholars 217; Iser 349; Jacobs, Lee 219; Jameson 220; Jewish Lights 220; Johnson 221; Jones Univ, Bob 221; Judaica 221; Kamehameha 222; Kensington 223; Kent State Univ 223; Kesend, Michael 223; Ketz, Louise B 361; Knopf & Crown Bks for Yng Rdrs, Alfred 224; Krieger 225; Kurian, George 361; Lake Claremont 225; Lambrecht 350; Layla 362; Lee, J&L 228; Lehigh Univ 228; Lerner 229; Libraries Unlimited 229; Limelight 229; Lion 230; Little, Brown 231; Little, Brown Childrn's Bks 230; Lobster 350; Loft 232; Longstreet 232; Louisiana State Univ 233; Loyola 233; Lynx Images 350; Lyons 234; Madison 234; Maisonneuve 235; Mariner 236; MBI 236; McClelland&Stewart 350; McDonald & Woodward 237; McElderry, Margaret 237; McFarland 237; McGraw-Hill Ryerson 351; McGregor 238; Michigan State Univ 240; Millbrook 241; Minnesota Hist Soc 241; Momentum 242; Moose Enterprise 351; Morningside 243; Morrow, William, 243; Morrow/Avon 244; Mountain Pr 244; Mystic Seaport 245; Narwhal 246; Naval Inst 246; NeWest 351; New England Pr 248; New England Pub Assoc 362; New Victoria 249; New York Univ 250; Newjoy 250; Newmarket 250; Nodin 251; North Carolina Div of Archives 251; North Point 252; Northeastern Univ 252; Northern Illinois Univ 252; Northland 253; Norton, WW 253; Ohio State Univ 255; Ohio Univ 255; Oliver 255; One World Bks 256; Onjinjinkta 256; Orange Frazer 257; Orchard 257; Oryx 257; Osprey 258; Overlook Press, The 259; Overmountain 259; Owen, Richard 259; Oxford Univ 259; Palgrave 261; Pantheon 261; Parkway 262; Passeggiata 262; Peachtree 264; Pelican 264; Pennsylvania Hist and Museum Comm 264; Permanent/Second Chance 265; Picasso 353; Picton 268; Pineapple 268; Pippin 269; Pleasant Company 270; Plexus 270; Pocket 270; Praeger 271; Prairie Oak 271; Presidio 272; Press at the Maryland Hist Soc 272; Presses de l'Université de Montreal 353; Prima 273; Prometheus 273; ProStar 274; Pruett 274; Puffin 275; Purdue Univ 275; Purich 354; Quite Specific 276; Random House Bks for Yng Rdrs 277; Random House Trade 277; Really Great 278; Reference Service 279; Regnery 279; Republic of Texas 279; Review & Herald 280; Reynolds, Morgan 280; RFF Pr 281; River City 281; Ronsdale 354; Ruminator 283; Rutgers Univ 283; Salem 285; Sandlapper 285; Sarpedon 286; Sasquatch 287; Saxon House Canada 355; Schenkman 288; Schocken 288; Scholastic Canada 355; Schreiber 289; Scribner 289; Scrivenery 289; Seaworthy 290; Sergeant Kirkland's 291; Shoreline 355; Silver Moon 293; Simon & Schuster Bks for Yng Rdrs 293; Social Science Educ Consort 295; South End 297; Southfarm 298; St. Anthony 299; St. Augustine's 299; St. Bede's 299; Stackpole 300; Stanford Univ 301; Steel Pr Pub 301; Steller 356; Sun Bks/Sun Pub 304; Sunbelt 304; Talese, Nan 306; Taylor 306; Temple Univ 307; Texas A&M Univ 308; Texas State Hist Assoc 308; Texas Western 308; Third World 308; Tidewater 309; TowleHouse 310; Trinity Fndtn 311; Trinity Pr Int'l 312; Truman State Univ 312; Turtle Bks 312; Twenty-First Century 313; TwoDot 313; UCLA Amer Indian Studies Ctr 313; Univ of Akron 314; Univ of Alabama 314; Univ of Alberta 357; Univ of California 315; Univ of Georgia 315; Univ of Idaho 315; Univ of Illinois 316; Univ of Iowa 316; Univ of Maine 316;

Univ of Missouri 317; Univ of Nebraska 317; Univ of Nevada 317; Univ of New Mexico 317; Univ of North Carolina 318; Univ of North Texas 318; Univ of Oklahoma 318; Univ of Pennsylvania 318; Univ of Tennessee 319; Univ of Texas 319; Univ of Univ of Arkansas 315; Univ Pr of Kansas 320; Univ Pr of Kentucky 320; Univ Pr of Mississippi 320; University of South Carolina 319; Upney Editions 357; Utah State Univ 321; Vandamere 322; Vanderbilt Univ 322; Vanwell 358; Vehicule 358; Vernon 362; Verso 322; Via Dolorosa 323; Viking 323; Vintage Anchor 324; Voyageur 325; Walch, J. Weston 325; Walker 325; Walsworth 325; Warner Books 326; Washington State Univ Pr 326; Watts, Franklin 327; Weatherhill 327; Wescott Cove 328; Wesleyan Univ 328; Westcliffe 328; Westernlore 329; Westminster John Knox 329; WestWinds 329; White Mane 330; Whitecap 359; Whitman, Albert 330; Whitson 331; Wiener, Markus 331; Wiley & Sons, John 332; Williamson 332; Windstorm Creative 334; Windswept House 334; Wonderland 363; Yale Univ 337; YMAA 337; Yucca Tree 337; Zondervan 338

Hobby: Adams Media 124; American Quilter's 131; Ancestry 132; Arkansas Research 134; Aviation 138; Bale 140; Barron's 141; Betterway 145; Black Dog & Levanthal 145; Breakout 150; Brewers 150; Broadcast Interview 151; Burford 153; Carstens 156; Charlton 344; Chelsea House 160; Chicago Review 161; Children's Pr 161; Conari 167; Creative Homeowner 170; C&T 153; Dover 177; Editions la Liberte 346; Edutainment 180; Electric Works 181; Excelsior Cee 184; Fell, Frederick 186; Gem Guides 192; Gollehon 194; Green Nature 195; Gryphon Pub 197; HarperInformation 200; Hawk 201; Hobby House 207; House of Collectibles 209; Iconografix, Inc. 212; Interweave 218; Iron Gate 219; Jacobs, Lee 219; Kalmbach 222; Kensington 223; Kesend, Michael 223; Klein, B 224; Krause 224; Lark 226; Legacy 228; Little, Brown Childrn's Bks 230; Lyons 234; MBI 236; McClelland&Stewart 350; Millbrook 241; Mustang 245; No Starch 251; North Light 252; Northland 253; Norton, WW 253; Osprey 258; Pathfinder 263; PBC Int'l 263; Perigee 265; Picasso 353; Picton 268; Popular Woodworking 271; Productive 353; Reference Pr Int'l 279; Scholastic Canada 355; Scrivenery 289; Seaworthy 290; Somerville House 362; Square One 299; Steel Pr Pub 301; Sterling 302; Success 304; Viking Studio 324; Voyageur 325; Weidner & Sons 327; Wescott Cove 328; Whitman, Albert 330

How-to: Abdo 123; Adams Blake 125; Adams Media 124; Addicus 125; Adventure 340; Alexander 127; Allisone 128; Allworth 128; American Bar 129; American Correctional 130; American Quilter's 131; Amherst 132; Ancestry 132; Appalachian Mtn Club 133; Arkansas Research 134; ASA 135; Aslan 135; Aviation 138; Aztex 139; Ballantine 140; Barricade 141; Behr 142; Bentley 143; Berkley Pub Grp 144; Bethany 145; Betterway 145; Beyond Words 145; Black Dog & Levanthal 145; Bloomberg 146; Breakout 150; Bristol Fashion 151; Broadcast Interview 151; Bryant & Dillon 152; Burford 153; Camino 154; Career Pr 155; CCC 158; Celestial Arts 158; CHA 344; Chelsea Green 160; Chemical Pub 160; Chicago Review 161; Chitra 162; Christian Pub/Horizon Bks. 162; Cloud Peak 165; Coaches Choice 165; Concordia 167; Consortium 167; Contemporary Bks 167; Cornell Maritime 168; Countryman 169; Craftsman 169; Creative Homeowner 170; Crossquarter 170; C&T 153; Cumberland House 171; David, Jonathan 173; Dearborn 174; Do-It-Yourself 176; Doubleday/Image 177; Dover 177; Edutainment 180; Electric Works 181; Empire 182; Excelsior Cee 184; Fell, Frederick 186; Focal Pr 187; Fodor's 188; Foster, Walter 190; Gatf Press 191; Gay Sunshine/Leyland 192; GGC 192; Gollehon 194; Green Nature 195; Group Pub 196; Gryphon House 197; Half Halt 198; Hampton Roads 198; Hancock House 198; Hanser Gardner 199; Harbor Pr 199; HarperInformation 200; HarperSanFrancisco 200; Hawk 201; Hazelden 202; Health Pr 202; Health Prof Pr 203; Heinemann 203; Heritage Bks 204; HiddenSpring 205; Hobar 207; Hobby House 207; Home Planners 208; House of Collectibles 209; Human Kinetics 210; Humanics Learning 210; Hungry Minds (Business) 211; Hungry Minds (Education) 211; Ideals Pub 212; Imagination Store 213; Information Today 214; Interweave 218; Int'l Wealth Success 217; Iron Gate 219; iPublish.com 218; Jacobs, Lee 219; Jist Works 220; Kalmbach 222; Kensington 223; Kesend, Michael 223; Klein, B 224; Krause 224; Lamppost 362; Lark 226; Layla 362; Lebhar-Friedman 227; Limelight 229; Lion 230; Llewellyn 231; Loft 232; Lone Eagle 232; Loompanics 233; Lyons 234; Magni 234; Marlor 236; Maupin 236; Maximum Pr 236; MBI 236; McClelland&Stewart 350; McGraw-Hill Ryerson 351; McGregor 238; Meadowbrook 238; Menasha 239; Meriwether 239; Metamorphous 239; Midknight Club 240; Morrow, William, 243; Morrow/Avon 244; Mountain N'Air 244; Mountain Pr 244; Mountaineers 244; Mustang 245; Mystic Seaport 245; Narwhal 246; Naturegraph 246; New American 247; New England Pub Assoc 362; New Horizon 249; New Society 351; No Starch 251; Nolo.com 251; North Light 252; Nova 254; Oak Knoll 254; Oaklea 254; Oasis 254; One on One 256; One World Bks 256; Open Road 256; Orchises 257; Pacific Pr Pub Assoc 260; Paladin 260; Paradise Cay 261; Perigee 265; Perspectives 266; Phi Delta Kappa 267; Picasso 353; Pineapple 268; Pleasant Company 270; Plexus 270; Popular Woodworking 271; Possibility 271; Productive 353; ProStar 274; Prufrock 274; Quill Driver/Word Dancer 276; Quite Specific 276; Ragged Mountain Press 277; Reference Pr Int'l 279; Revere, Fleming 280; Rocky Mtn 354; Running Pr 283; Safari 284; Santa Monica 286; Scholastic Canada 355; Scrivenery 289; Silman-James 293; Sourcebooks 296; Speech Bin 298; Square One 299; Starbust 301; Steel Pr Pub 301; Sterling 302; Stoeger 302; Stone Bridge 303; Success 304; Sun Bks/Sun Pub 304; Sunbelt 304; Systems Co 306; Tarcher 306; Ten Speed 307; Tiare 309; Todd 310; Tricycle 311; Trilobyte Press & Multimedia 356; Turtle Pr 312; Van Der Plas 321; Weatherhill 327; Wescott Cove 328; Westminster John Knox 329; Whitehorse 330; Wilderness 332; Willow Creek 333; Wilshire 333; Windsor 333; Windstorm Creative 334; Wise, Michael 331; Wonderland 363; Workman 336; Writer's Digest 336; YMAA 337

House and Home:: Betterway 145; Creative Homeowner 170; Home Planners 208; Pantheon 261; Sourcebooks 296; Sterling 302; Storey 303; Taylor 306; Warner Bks 326

Humanities: Dante Univ of America Pr 172; Free Pr 190; Greenwood 196; Greenwood Pub Grp 196; Aldine de Gruyter 197; Learning Pub 227; Roxbury 283; Stanford Univ 301; Univ of Arkansas 315; Zondervan 338

Humor: Adams Media 124; Adams Media 124; Adventure 340; Albury 127; Andrews McMeel 133; Arsenal Pulp 340; Aslan 135; Atheneum Bks for Yng Rdrs 136; Ballantine 140; Barbour 141; Black Dog & Levanthal 145; Brewers 150; Broadcast Interview 151; Broadman & Holman 151; Brucedale 342; CCC 158; Christian Pub/Horizon Bks. 162; Cloud Peak 165; College Board 166; Common Courage 166; Concordia 167; Consortium 167; Covenant Comm 169;

Cross Cultural 170; Cumberland House 171; David, Jonathan 173; Doubleday 176; Doubleday/Image 177; Dover 177; Dutton 178; ECW 345; Electric Works 181; Empire 182; Entrepreneur 182; Epicenter 182; Excelsior Cee 184; Front Street 191; Future Horizons 191; Gifted Psych 193; Gollehon 194; Hill Street 206; Holiday House 207; Houghton Mifflin Bks for Children 208; Insomniac 349; iPublish.com 218; Jacobs, Lee 219; Kensington 223; Lamppost 362; Layla 362; Lebhar-Friedman 227; Limelight 229; Longstreet 232; McClelland&Stewart 350; Meadowbrook 238; Menasha 239; Meriwether 239; Multnomah Publishers, Inc. 245; Mustang 245; Novalis 352; One World Bks 256; Onjinjinkta 256; Orange Frazer 257; Orchises 257; Owen, Richard 259; Paladin 260; Peachtree 264; Picasso 353; Piccadilly 267; Pippin 269; Pocket 270; Price Stern Sloan 273; Ragged Mountain Press 277; Ragweed 354; Random House Trade 277; Republic of Texas 279; Review & Herald 280; River Oak 281; Rutledge Hill 283; Sandlapper 285; Santa Monica 286; Schreiber 289; Shoreline 355; Smith, Gibbs 295; Sound & Vision 355; Steel Pr Pub 301; Sterling 302; Sun Bks/Sun Pub 304; Ten Speed 307; TowleHouse 310; Triumph 312; Vintage Images 324; Warner Books 326; Weatherhill 327; Wescott Cove 328; Westminster John Knox 329; Willow Creek 333; Windstorm Creative 334; Wonderland 363; Workman 336

Illustrated book: A Cappella 122; A&B Pub Grp 123; Abrams 123; Adams Media 124; Arsenal Pulp 340; Baker 139; Barbour 141; Beil, Frederic 143; Betterway 145; Black Dog & Levanthal 145; Blackbirch 146; Bluewood 147; Boston Mills 342; Branden 149; Broadway 152; Broken Jaw 342; Brucedale 342; Bulfinch 152; Burford 153; Canadian Plains 343; Chatham 159; Chronicle Bks for Children 163; City & Co 164; Collectors 166; Common Courage 166; Consortium 167; Covenant Comm 169; Creative Homeowner 170; C&T 153; Cypress 172; Darlington 173; David, Jonathan 173; Davis Pub 173; Dial Bks for Yng Rdrs 175; Doubleday/Image 177; Dover 177; Edutainment 180; Electric Works 181; Farcountry 361; Fodor's 188; Fort Ross 189; Front Street 191; Godine, David 194; Golden West 194; Goose Lane 347; Green Nature 195; Hampton Roads 198; Harcourt Inc., Trade 199; Hill Street 206; History Bank 361; Hobar 207; Holt Bks for Yng Rdrs 208; Houghton Mifflin Bks for Children 208; Humanics Pub Grp 210; Hungry Minds (Business) 211; Iconografix, Inc. 212; Inst of Police Tech & Mgmt 215; Jacobs, Lee 219; Jay Jo 220; Jewish Lights 220; Kalmbach 222; Kensington 223; Krause 224; Kurian, George 361; Lamppost 362; Lark 226; Layla 362; Lebhar-Friedman 227; Lee & Low 228; Limelight 229; Lobster 350; Longstreet 232; MBI 236; McClelland&Stewart 350; McDonald & Woodward 237; Merriam 239; Minnesota Hist Soc 241; Multnomah Publishers, Inc. 245; New England Pr 248; New Society 351; Northland 253; Northword 253; Novalis 352; Orange Frazer 257; Orchard 257; Osprey 258; Owen, Richard 259; Paradise Cay 261; PBC Int'l 263; Pelican 264; Pennsylvania Hist and Museum Comm 264; Philomel Books 267; Picador USA 267; Picasso 353; Pippin 269; Plexus 270; Popular Woodworking 271; Press at the Maryland Hist Soc 272; ProStar 274; Puffin 275; Quest Books 276; Ragweed 354; Random House Trade 277; Reference Pr Int'l 279; River City 281; Sandlapper 285; Santa Monica 286; Saxon House Canada 355; Seaworthy 290; Smith, Gibbs 295; Soundprints 296; Sourcebooks 296; Speech Bin 298; Sta-Kris 300; Standard 300; Sun Bks/Sun Pub 304; Texas State Hist Assoc 308; Third World 308; Tidewater 309; Triumph 312; Truman State Univ 312; Turtle Bks 312; Univ of New Mexico 317; University of South Carolina 319; Vandamere 322; Vernon 362; Verso 322; Vintage Images 324; Weatherhill 327; Welcome Enterprises 328; Wescott Cove 328; Westcliffe 328; Westminster John Knox 329; Whitman, Albert 330; Willow Creek 333; Windstorm Creative 334; Windswept House 334; Windward 334; Wonderland 363; Yale Univ 337

Juvenile books: Abdo 123; Abingdon 123; Addax 125; Adventure 340; Alaska NW 126; Annick 340; Arte Publico 135; ATL 137; Atheneum Bks for Yng Rdrs 136; Augsburg 137; Baker 139; Bantam Doubeday Dell Bks for Yng Rdrs 140; Barbour 141; Barron's 141; Behrman 143; Beil, Frederic 143; Benefactory 143; Beyond Words 145; Blackbirch 146; Borealis 341; Boyds Mills 148; Branden 149; Broadman & Holman 151; Brucedale 342; Butte 153; Camino 154; Candlewick 154; Capstone 155; Carolrhoda 156; Cartwheel 157; Caxton 157; Charlesbridge (School) 159; Charlesbridge (Trade) 159; Chelsea House 160; Chicago Review 161; Child Welfare League 161; Children's Pr 161; Christian Ed. 162; Chronicle Bks for Children 163; Clarion 164; Cloud Peak 165; Concordia 167; Cook Comm 168; Course Crafters 360; Covenant Comm 169; Cricket 170; David, Jonathan 173; Dawn Pub 173; Dial Bks for Yng Rdrs 175; Dover 177; Down East 177; Editions la Liberte 346; Eerdmans Bks for Yng Rdrs 180; Eerdmans, William 181; Electric Works 181; Evan-Moor Educ 183; Faith Kids 185; Forward Movement 189; Free Spirit 190; Front Street 191; Future Horizons 191; Gifted Psych 193; Godine, David 194; Greenhaven 195; Group Pub 196; Hachai 198; Harcourt Inc., Trade 199; HarperCollins [UK] 347; Hawk 201; Herodias 204; Highsmith 206; History Bank 361; Holt Bks for Yng Rdrs 208; Houghton Mifflin 209; Houghton Mifflin Bks for Children 208; Humanics Pub Grp 210; Impact Publishers, Inc. 214; Inner Traditions 215; Jay Jo 220; Jewish Lights 220; Jones Univ, Bob 221; Judaica 221; Kamehameha 222; Kar-Ben 222; Knopf & Crown Bks for Yng Rdrs, Alfred 224; Lamppost 362; Lark 226; Latin Amer Lit Rev 227; Layla 362; Lee & Low 228; Lerner 229; Little, Brown Childrn's Bks 230; Little Simon 230; Lobster 350; Marlor 236; McElderry, Margaret 237; Millbrook 241; Minstrel 242; Mitchell Lane 242; Moody 242; Moose Enterprise 351; Morehouse 243; Mountaineers 244; Multnomah Publishers, Inc. 245; Narwhal 246; Nelson, Tommy 247; New Canaan 248; New Hope 249; New Horizon 249; Northland 253; Northword 253; Novalis 352; Oliver 255; Onjinjinkta 256; Orchard 257; Overmountain 259; Owen, Richard 259; Oxford Univ 259; Pacific Pr Pub Assoc 260; Pauline 263; Peachtree 264; Pelican 264; Perspectives 266; Philomel Books 267; Picasso 353; Piñata 268; Pippin 269; Players 269; Pleasant Company 270; Press at the Maryland Hist Soc 272; Price Stern Sloan 273; Prometheus 273; Puffin 275; Ragweed 354; Random House Bks for Yng Rdrs 277; Red Hen 278; Review & Herald 280; Ronsdale 354; Rosen Publishing Group, The 282; Running Pr 283; Salina Bookshelf 285; Sandlapper 285; Scholastic Canada 355; Scholastic Inc. 288; Schreiber 289; Seedling 290; Simon & Schuster Bks for Yng Rdrs 293; Somerville House 362; Soundprints 296; Speech Bin 298; Standard 300; Sterling 302; Success 304; Teaching & Learning 307; Third World 308; Tidewater 309; Tingley, Megan 310; Tricycle 311; Turtle Bks 312; Twenty-First Century 313; Univ of New Mexico 317; Vanwell 358; Vernon 362; Walker 325; Watts, Franklin 327; Welcome Enterprises 328; WestWinds 329; White Mane 330; Whitecap 359; Whitman, Albert 330; Wiley & Sons, John 332; Windstorm Creative 334; Windswept House 334; Wish 335; Zondervan 338

Labor: Amacom 129; Battelle 142; Baywood 142; BNA 147; Brevet 150; ILR 213; Intercultural 216; Michigan State Univ 240; Temple Univ 307

Vanwell 358; Vintage Anchor 324; Walsworth 325; White Mane 330; Yale Univ 337; Yucca Tree 337

Money/finance: Adams Blake 125; Adams Media 124; Algora 127; Amacom 129; American Bar 129; ATL 137; Bale 140; Barbour 141; Betterway 145; Bloomberg 146; Broadcast Interview 151; Broadway 152; Bryant & Dillon 152; Cambridge Educ 154; Career Pr 155; Cato 157; Chelsea Green 160; Conari 167; Contemporary Bks 167; Crown Business 171; Cypress 172; Dearborn 174; Doubleday 176; Doubleday Religious 176; ECW 345; Electric Works 181; Fell, Frederick 186; Forum Pub 189; Glenlake 193; Gollehon 194; Graduate Grp 194; HarperCollins [UK] 347; HarperInformation 200; Hawk 201; Haworth 201; Hay House 201; Hensley 204; HiddenSpring 205; Hungry Minds (Business) 211; Insomniac 349; Int'l Scholars 217; iPublish.com 218; Jacobs, Lee 219; Kensington 223; Lamppost 362; Lebhar-Friedman 227; Loompanics 233; Magni 234; McClelland&Stewart 350; McGraw-Hill Ryerson 351; McGregor 238; Moody 242; New American 247; New England Pub Assoc 362; New World Library 250; Nolo.com 251; Northfield 253; Oasis 254; Oxford Univ 259; Paladin 260; Palgrave 261; Parlay Int'l 262; Perigee 265; Picasso 353; Planning/ Communications 269; Productive 353; Reference Pr Int'l 279; Regnery 279; Reynolds, Morgan 280; River Oak 281; Schreiber 289; Sourcebooks 296; Square One 299; Starbust 301; Success 304; Sun Bks/Sun Pub 304; Systems Co 306; Ten Speed 307; Todd 310; Urban Land Inst 321; Windsor 333; Windstorm Creative 334; Wonderland 363

Multicultural: Arsenal Pulp 340; Aslan 135; Autonomedia 137; Bluewood 147; Broadway 152; Canadian Educ 343; Capstone 155; Charlesbridge (School) 159; Charlesbridge (Trade) 159; Chelsea House 160; Chicago Review 161; Children's Pr 161; Chronicle Bks for Children 163; Cloud Peak 165; Common Courage 166; Conari 167; Course Crafters 360; Cross Cultural 170; David, Jonathan 173; Denali 174; Ediciones Nuevo Espacio 179; Electric Works 181; Encounter Bks 182; Facts on File 184; Feminist Pr at CUNY 186; Fernwood 346; Gifted Psych 193; Guernica 347; Harcourt Inc., Trade 199; HiddenSpring 205; Highsmith 206; Hill, Lawrence 206; Hippocrene 206; Insomniac 349; Iser 349; Judson 222; Kaya 222; Kensington 223; Kurian, George 361; LadybugPress 225; Lee & Low 228; Millbrook 241; Mitchell Lane 242; New England Pub Assoc 362; New Hope 249; Novalis 352; Ohio State Univ 255; One World Bks 256; Oryx 257; Palgrave 261; Paragon House 261; Passeggiata 262; Pelican 264; Picasso 353; River City 281; Rosen Publishing Group, The 282; Rutgers Univ 283; Schreiber 289; Seal 290; Silver Moon 293; Sun Bks/Sun Pub 304; Thompson Educ Pub 356; Turtle Bks 312; UCLA Amer Indian Studies Ctr 313; Univ of Nebraska 317; Univ of New Mexico 317; Univ of North Carolina 318; Vanderbilt Univ 322; Via Dolorosa 323; Volcano 325; Watts, Franklin 327; Western Psych Services 328; Westminster John Knox 329

Multimedia: ATL 137; Baker 139; Broadcast Interview 151; Charles River 159; Course Crafters 360; Covenant Comm 169; Electric Works 181; Entrepreneur 182; GGC 192; Granite 194; Group Pub 196; Harcourt Inc., Trade 199; Hazelden 202; Human Kinetics 210; Information Today 214; Iron Gate 219; Jist Works 220; Lebhar-Friedman 227; Listen & Live 230; Lynx Images 350; Norby 352; Picasso 353; Quite Specific 276; Reference Pr Int'l 279; Review & Herald 280; River City 281; River Oak 281; SAE Int'l 284; Schreiber 289; Serendipity Systems 291; Slack 294; Sourcebooks 296; Univ of New Mexico 317; Univ of North Carolina 318; Westminster John Knox 329; YMAA 337

Music/dance: A Cappella 122; Abingdon 123; Algora 127; Allworth 128; American Press 131; A-R 123; Arsenal Pulp 340; Aslan 135; Atheneum Bks for Yng Rdrs 136; Betterway 145; Bold Strummer 148; Branden 149; Cadence Jazz 154; Cartwheel 157; Centerstream 158; Chelsea House 160; Chicago Review 161; Children's Pr 161; City & Co 164; Consortium 167; Cornell Univ 168; Dover 177; Editions la Liberte 346; Electric Works 181; Empire 182; Fairleigh Dickinson Univ 185; Feminist Pr at CUNY 186; Greenwood Pub Grp 196; Guernica 347; HiddenSpring 205; Houghton Mifflin Bks for Children 208; Humanics Learning 210; Inner Traditions 215; Libraries Unlimited 229; Limelight 229; Louisiana State Univ 233; McClelland&Stewart 350; McFarland 237; Meriwether 239; Norton, WW 253; Onjinjinkta 256; Owen, Richard 259; Oxford Univ 259; Palgrave 261; Pelican 264; Pencil Point 264; Popular Culture Ink 270; PRB Prod 272; Quest Books 276; Random House Trade 277; River City 281; Salem 285; Santa Monica 286; Saxon House Canada 355; Schenkman 288; Soft Skull 296; Sound & Vision 355; Stipes 302; Tiare 309; Univ of Illinois 316; Univ of New Mexico 317; Univ of North Carolina 318; Univ Pr of Mississippi 320; Univ Pr of New England 321; Vanderbilt Univ 322; Vernon 362; Viking 323; Walker 325; Weatherhill 327; Wesleyan Univ 328; White Cliffs 329; Whitman, Albert 330; Writer's Digest 336; Yale Univ 337

Nature/environment: Abrams 123; Adams Media 124; Adirondack 125; Adventure 340; Alaska NW 126; Algora 127; Allisone 128; American Water Works 131; Appalachian Mtn Club 133; Arcade 133; ATL 137; Atheneum Bks for Yng Rdrs 136; Autonomedia 137; Backcountry 139; Barricade 141; Baywood 142; Beachway 142; Benefactory 143; Berkshire 144; Blackbirch 146; Blair, John 146; Boston Mills 342; Boyds Mills 148; Brucedale 342; Burford 153; Canadian Plains 343; Capstone 155; Carolrhoda 156; Cartwheel 157; Charlesbridge (School) 159; Charlesbridge (Trade) 159; Chatham 159; Chelsea Green 160; Chelsea House 160; Chemical Pub 160; Chicago Review 161; Children's Pr 161; Chronicle 163; Chronicle Bks for Children 163; City & Co 164; Clarion 164; Clear Light 164; Coastal Carolina 165; Common Courage 166; Conari 167; Consortium 167; Countryman 169; Cross Cultural 170; Crossquarter 170; Dawn Pub 173; Dimi Pr 175; Doubleday 176; Dover 177; Down East 177; Dutton Children's Bks 179; Editions la Liberte 346; Electric Works 181; Encounter Bks 182; Epicenter 182; Fernwood 346; Findhorn 187; Four Walls Eight Windows 190; Gem Guides 192; Globe Pequot 193; Godine, David 194; Goose Lane 347; Green Nature 195; Hancock House 198; HarperCollins [UK] 347; Hawk 201; Hay House 201; Henry Pr, Joseph 204; Heyday 205; HiddenSpring 205; High Plains 205; Hill Street 206; Hobar 207; Horsdal&Schubart 348; Houghton Mifflin 209; Houghton Mifflin Bks for Children 208; Humanics Learning 210; Imagination Store 213; Inner Traditions 215; Island 219; Jewish Lights 220; Johnson 221; Kensington 223; Kesend, Michael 223; Knopf & Crown Bks for Yng Rdrs, Alfred 224; Krieger 225; Lake Claremont 225; Lark 226; Lawrence, Merloyd 227; Lerner 229; Little, Brown 231; Little, Brown Childrn's Bks 230; Llewellyn 231; Lone Pine 350; Longstreet 232; Lynx Images 350; Lyons 234; McClelland&Stewart 350; McDonald & Woodward 237; Milkweed 240; Millbrook 241; Mountain N'Air 244; Mountain Pr 244; Mountaineers 244; Naturegraph 246; New England Pr 248; New England Pub Assoc 362; New Horizon 249; New Society 351; New World Library 250; North Point 252; Northland 253; Northword 253; Norton, WW 253; Novalis 352; Oasis 254; Ohio Univ

255; Oliver 255; Onjinjinkta 256; Orange Frazer 257; Orchard 257; Overmountain 259; Owen, Richard 259; Oxford Univ 259; Pacific Pr Pub Assoc 260; Paragon House 261; Perigee 265; Pilgrim 268; Pineapple 268; Pippin 269; Plexus 270; PressForward 272; ProStar 274; Pruett 274; Putnam's Sons, G.P. 275; Quest Books 276; Ragged Mountain Press 277; Random House Bks for Yng Rdrs 277; Random House Trade 277; Republic of Texas 279; Review & Herald 280; RFF Pr 281; Rocky Mtn 354; Ronsdale 354; Ruminator 283; Rutgers Univ 283; Sagamore 284; Salem 285; Sasquatch 287; Scholastic Canada 355; Scribner 289; Scrivenery 289; Seal 290; Sierra Club 292; Simon & Schuster Bks for Yng Rdrs 293; Smith, Gibbs 295; Somerville House 362; Soundprints 296; South End 297; Southern Illinois Univ 297; Square One 299; Stackpole 300; Stanford Univ 301; Starbust 301; Steller 356; Stipes 302; Storey 303; Sun Bks/Sun Pub 304; Sunbelt 304; Systems Co 306; Tarcher 306; Ten Speed 307; Texas A&M Univ 308; Texas Western 308; Tricycle 311; Turnstone 357; Turtle Bks 312; Twenty-First Century 313; Univ of Alberta 357; Univ of California 315; Univ of Georgia 315; Univ of Idaho 315; Univ of Iowa 316; Univ of Nebraska 317; Univ of Nevada 317; Univ of New Mexico 317; Univ of North Carolina 318; Univ of North Texas 318; Univ of Texas 319; Univ of Univ of Arkansas 315; Univ Pr of Colorado 320; Univ Pr of Kansas 320; Univ Pr of New England 321; Vanderbilt Univ 322; Venture 322; Vernon 362; VGM Career 323; Vintage Anchor 324; Voyageur 325; Walker 325; Washington State Univ Pr 326; Watts, Franklin 327; Weatherhill 327; Weidner & Sons 327; Westcliffe 328; Whitecap 359; Whitman, Albert 330; Wilderness 332; Williamson 332; Willow Creek 333; Windswept House 334; Windward 334; Zoland 338

Philosophy: Alba 127; Algora 127; Allisone 128; Aronson, Jason 134; Asian Humanities 135; Austin & Winfield 137; Autonomedia 137; Behrman 143; Bookworld/Blue Star 148; Breakout 150; Broadman & Holman 151; Bucknell Univ 152; Canadian Educ 343; Catholic Univ of America 157; Clear Light 164; Cormorant 344; Cornell Univ 168; Cross Cultural 170; Crossquarter 170; Diogenes 176; Doubleday 176; Doubleday/Image 177; Dover 177; Dry Bones 178; Duquesne Univ 178; Educator's Int'l 180; Eerdmans, William 181; Electric Works 181; Encounter Bks 182; Fairleigh Dickinson Univ 185; Fernwood 346; Fordham Univ 188; Front Street 191; Gifted Educ 193; Greenwood Pub Grp 196; Guernica 347; Guilford 197; Harcourt Inc., Trade 199; Hawk 201; Hay House 201; Herodias 204; HiddenSpring 205; Hohm 207; Holmes 208; House of Anansi 348; Humanics Pub Grp 210; Humanitas 348; Imagination Store 213; Inner Traditions 215; Inst of Psych Res 349; Int'l Scholars 217; Jain 219; Jewish Lights 220; Kensington 223; Kurian, George 361; Libraries Unlimited 229; Loft 232; Maisonneuve 235; Mariner 236; McClelland&Stewart 350; Midknight Club 240; New England Pub Assoc 362; New Society 351; Northern Illinois Univ 252; Novalis 352; Ohio Univ 255; One World Bks 256; Onjinjinkta 256; Oxford Univ 259; Palgrave 261; Paragon House 261; Paulist 263; Picador USA 267; Presses de l'Université de Montreal 353; Prometheus 273; Purdue Univ 275; Quest Books 276; Review & Herald 280; Salem 285; Saxon House Canada 355; Schenkman 288; Schocken 288; Scribner 289; Scrivenery 289; Soft Skull 296; South End 297; Spence 298; St. Augustine's 299; St. Bede's 299; Stanford Univ 301; Steel Pr Pub 301; Stone Bridge 303; Stonewall Inn 303; Sun Bks/Sun Pub 304; Swedenborg 305; Talese, Nan 306; Tarcher 306; Third World 308; Trinity Fndtn 311; Turtle Pr 312; Tuttle 312; Unity House 314; Univ of Alberta 357; Univ of Illinois 316; Univ of North Carolina 318; Univ of Scranton 319; Univ Pr of Kansas 320; University of Calgary Press 357; Vanderbilt Univ 322; Verso 362; Via Dolorosa 323; Viking 323; Viking Studio 324; Vintage Anchor 324; Wall & Emerson 358; Wesleyan Univ 328; Westminster John Knox 329; Windstorm Creative 334; Wisdom 334; Yale Univ 337; YMAA 337

Photography: Allworth 128; Amherst 132; Atheneum Bks for Yng Rdrs 136; Beyond Words 145; Black Dog & Levanthal 145; Boston Mills 342; Branden 149; Brucedale 342; Bulfinch 152; Caitlin 343; Chronicle 163; Clarion 164; Clear Light 164; Coastal Carolina 165; Collectors 166; Dover 177; Edutainment 180; Electric Works 181; Epicenter 182; Focal Pr 187; Godine, David 194; Herodias 204; High Tide 205; Hudson Hills 210; Humanitas 348; Iconografix, Inc. 212; Jacobs, Lee 219; Kurian, George 361; Layla 362; Longstreet 232; Louisiana State Univ 233; MBI 236; McClelland&Stewart 350; Minnesota Hist Soc 241; Monacelli 242; Northland 253; Norton, WW 253; Orange Frazer 257; Overmountain 259; PBC Int'l 263; Phaidon 267; Random House Trade 277; Really Great 278; Reference Pr Int'l 279; River City 281; Stackpole 300; Temple Univ 307; Texas A&M Univ 308; Univ of New Mexico 317; Univ of North Carolina 318; Univ Pr of Mississippi 320; Vandamere 322; Vernon 362; Viking Studio 324; Vintage Images 324; Weatherhill 327; Westcliffe 328; Whitman, Albert 330; Wonderland 363; Writer's Digest 336; Zoland 338

Psychology: Adams Media 124; Addicus 125; Alba 127; Algora 127; American Counseling 130; American Press 131; Aronson, Jason 134; Asian Humanities 135; Aslan 135; Atheneum Bks for Yng Rdrs 136; Avisson 139; Baker 139; Barricade 141; Baywood 142; Berkley Pub Grp 144; Bethany 145; Beyond Words 145; Breakout 150; Broadcast Interview 151; Broadway 152; Bucknell Univ 152; Burnham 153; Carroll & Graf 156; Celestial Arts 158; Charles Pr 158; Childswork/Childsplay 161; Conari 167; Consortium 167; Contemporary Bks 167; Cornell Univ 168; Cross Cultural 170; Cypress 172; Dana Pr 172; Dial Pr 175; Diogenes 176; Doubleday/Image 177; Duquesne Univ 178; Dutton 178; Editions la Liberte 346; Educator's Int'l 180; Eerdmans, William 181; Electric Works 181; Encounter Bks 182; Fairleigh Dickinson Univ 185; Free Spirit 190; Gifted Educ 193; Gifted Psych 193; Gollehon 194; Greenwood Pub Grp 196; Gruyter, Aldine de 197; Guernica 347; Guilford 197; Harbor Pr 199; Harcourt Inc., Trade 199; HarperSanFrancisco 200; Hatherleigh 201; Haworth 201; Hay House 201; Hazelden 202; Health Comm 202; Health Prof Pr 203; Henry Pr, Joseph 204; HiddenSpring 205; High Tide 205; Human Kinetics 210; Humanics Learning 210; Humanics Pub Grp 210; Idyll Arbor 212; Impact Publishers, Inc. 214; Inner Traditions 215; Inst of Psych Res 349; Int'l Scholars 217; Jacobs, Lee 219; Kensington 223; Larson/PBPF 226; Lawrence, Merloyd 227; Learning Pub 227; Libraries Unlimited 229; Llewellyn 231; Loompanics 233; Maisonneuve 235; McClelland&Stewart 350; Metamorphous 239; Morrow/Avon 244; New American 247; New Harbinger 248; New Horizon 249; New World Library 250; New York Univ 250; Norton, WW 253; Oaklea 254; One World Bks 256; Onjinjinkta 256; Oxford Univ 259; Parkway 262; Pathfinder 263; Perigee 265; Perspectives 266; Praeger 271; Presses de l'Université de Montreal 353; PressForward 272; Prima 273; Prometheus 273; Quest Books 276; Random House Trade 277; Ronin 282; Safer Society 284; Salem 285; Schenkman 288; Scribner 289; Sourcebooks 296; Square One 299; Stanford Univ 301; Starbust 301; Steel Pr Pub 301; Sun Bks/Sun Pub 304; Swedenborg 305; Tarcher 306; Third World 308; Unity House 314; Vintage Anchor 324; Warner Books 326; Weidner & Sons 327; Western Psych Services 328; Westminster John Knox 329; Wildcat Canyon 331; Wiley & Sons, John 332;

Williamson 332; Wilshire 333; Windstorm Creative 334; Wisdom 334; Wonderland 363; Yale Univ 337

Real estate:: Dearborn 174; Starburst 301

Recreation: Abrams 123; Adirondack 125; Alaska NW 126; Appalachian Mtn Club 133; Atheneum Bks for Yng Rdrs 136; Aviation 138; Backcountry 139; Beachway 142; Berkshire 144; Betterway 145; Boston Mills 342; Broadcast Interview 151; Burford 153; Capstone 155; Career Pr 155; Cartwheel 157; Chelsea House 160; Chicago Review 161; Chronicle 163; City & Co 164; Coastal Carolina 165; Countryman 169; Cumberland House 171; Denali 174; Down East 177; Electric Works 181; Epicenter 182; Facts on File 184; Farcountry 361; Gem Guides 192; Globe Pequot 193; Hawk 201; Heyday 205; Hill Street 206; Horsdal&Schubart 348; Houghton Mifflin Bks for Children 208; House of Collectibles 209; Human Kinetics 210; Idyll Arbor 212; Iser 349; Jacobs, Lee 219; Johnson 221; Kensington 223; Krause 224; Layla 362; Lebhar-Friedman 227; Lion 230; Little, Brown Childrn's Bks 230; Lone Pine 350; Lyons 234; McClelland&Stewart 350; McFarland 237; Menasha 239; Meriwether 239; Mountain N'Air 244; Mountaineers 244; Mustang 245; One World Bks 256; Orange Frazer 257; Owen, Richard 259; Paradise Cay 261; Peachtree 264; Picasso 353; Plexus 270; Pruett 274; Ragged Mountain Press 277; Rocky Mtn 354; Running Pr 283; Sagamore 284; Sasquatch 287; Scholastic Canada 355; Stackpole 300; Starbust 301; Sterling 302; Stipes 302; Sunbelt 304; Ten Speed 307; Triumph 312; Univ of Idaho 315; Van Der Plas 321; Venture 322; Whitecap 359; Whitman, Albert 330; Wilderness 332; Willow Creek 333; Windward 334; World Leisure 336

Reference: A Cappella 122; Abingdon 123; Adams Media 124; Adirondack 125; Aegis 126; Aktrin 126; Alba 127; Alexander 127; Allworth 128; AMG 132; American Bar 129; American Correctional 130; American Counseling 130; American Nurses 130; American Quilter's 131; Ancestry 132; Arkansas Research 134; Arte Publico 135; ASM 136; Asian Humanities 135; ATL 137; Austin & Winfield 137; Avisson 139; Baker 139; Barbour 141; Barricade 141; Behrman 143; Beil, Frederic 143; Berkley Pub Grp 144; Bethany 145; Betterway 145; Black Dog & Levanthal 145; Blackbirch 146; Bloomberg 146; BNA 147; Borealis 341; Bowling Green St Univ 148; Branden 149; Brassey's 149; Bristol Fashion 151; Broadcast Interview 151; Broadman & Holman 151; Broadway 152; Brucedale 342; Cadence Jazz 154; Canadian Library 343; Career Pr 155; Carroll & Graf 156; Carswell Thomson 343; Celestial Arts 158; Charles River 159; Charlton 344; Chelsea Green 160; Chemical Pub 160; Children's Pr 161; Christian Pub/Horizon Bks. 162; City & Co 164; Coaches Choice 165; Collectors 166; College Board 166; Common Courage 166; Consortium 167; Contemporary Bks 167; Cornell Univ 168; Coteau 345; Course Crafters 360; Covenant Comm 169; CQ 169; Cross Cultural 170; Cumberland House 171; Dante Univ 172; Darlington 173; David, Jonathan 173; Dearborn 174; Denali 174; Doubleday Religious 176; Doubleday/Image 177; Dry Bones 178; Dutton 178; Ediciones Nuevo Espacio 179; Eerdmans, William 181; Electric Works 181; Empire 182; Encounter Bks 182; Entrepreneur 182; Facts on File 184; Fairleigh Dickinson Univ 185; Fairview 185; Fell, Frederick 186; Ferguson 186; Fernwood 346; Fire Engineering Bks 187; Focal Pr 187; Foreign Policy 188; Forward Movement 189; Gatf Press 191; GGC 192; Gifted Educ 193; Gifted Psych 193; Graduate Grp 194; Greenwood Pr 196; Greenwood Pub Grp 196; Gryphon Pub 197; Hancock House 198; Harcourt Inc., Trade 199; HarperInformation 200; HarperSanFrancisco 200; Hatherleigh 201; Haworth 201; Health Pr 202; Health Prof Pr 203; Hein & Co. 203; Heinemann 203; Hendrickson 203; Heritage Bks 204; Highsmith 206; Hill, Lawrence 206; Hippocrene 206; History Bank 361; Hobar 207; Hobby House 207; Holmes & Meier 208; Home Planners 208; Houghton Mifflin 209; House of Collectibles 209; Human Kinetics 210; Hungry Minds (Business) 211; Hungry Minds (Education) 211; Ibex 212; Idyll Arbor 212; Impact Publications 214; Information Today 214; Inst of Police Tech & Mgmt 215; Intercultural 216; Int'l Med 217; Int'l Scholars 217; Iron Gate 219; ISTE 217; Iser 349; Island 219; Jacobs, Lee 219; Jain 219; Jewish Lights 220; Jist Works 220; Kamehameha 222; Kensington 223; Ketz, Louise B 361; Klein, B 224; Krause 224; Kregel 225; Krieger 225; Kurian, George 361; Langenscheidt 226; Lawyers & Judges 227; Learning Pub 227; Lebhar-Friedman 227; Lee, J&L 228; Lehigh Univ 228; Libraries Unlimited 229; Lippincott 230; Locust Hill 231; Lone Eagle 232; Longstreet 232; Loompanics 233; Lyons 234; Madison 234; Marine Techniques 235; McClelland&Stewart 350; McFarland 237; McGraw-Hill Ryerson 351; Meadowbrook 238; Medical Physics 238; Meriwether 239; Merriam 239; Metamorphous 239; Meyerbooks 240; Minnesota Hist Soc 241; Mystic Seaport 245; Narwhal 246; Nautical & Aviation 246; NavPress 247; Neal-Schuman 247; Nelson Pub, Thomas 247; New American 247; New England Pub Assoc 362; Nichols 251; No Starch 251; Nolo.com 251; Norton, WW 253; Novalis 352; Oasis 254; Octameron 255; Ohio Univ 255; Orange Frazer 257; Orchises 257; Oryx 257; Osborne Media Group 258; Our Sunday Visitor 258; Oxford Univ 259; Pacific Bks 260; Paladin 260; Palgrave 261; Paradise Cay 261; Paragon House 261; Parlay Int'l 262; Pencil Point 264; Pennsylvania Hist and Museum Comm 264; Perigee 265; Phi Delta Kappa 267; Picton 268; Pineapple 268; Plexus 270; Pocket 270; Popular Culture Ink 270; Precept 272; Presses de l'Université de Montreal 353; Prestwick 273; Productive 353; Prometheus 273; Purich 354; Quill Driver/Word Dancer 276; Quite Specific 276; Reference Pr Int'l 279; Reference Service 279; Review & Herald 280; RFF Pr 281; Ronin 282; Rose 282; Rosen Publishing Group, The 282; Rutgers Univ 283; SAE Int'l 284; Sagamore 284; Salem 285; Sandlapper 285; Santa Monica 286; Sasquatch 287; Scarecrow 287; Schreiber 289; Seaworthy 290; Serendipity Systems 291; Sergeant Kirkland's 291; Sheed & Ward 292; Silman-James 293; Sourcebooks 296; Southern Illinois Univ 297; Speech Bin 298; Square One 299; St. Martin's 300; Standard 300; Sterling 302; Stoeger 302; Stone Bridge 303; Sun Bks/Sun Pub 304; Sunbelt 304; Ten Speed 307; Texas State Hist Assoc 308; Third World 308; Tidewater 309; Todd 310; Tower 310; Transnational 311; Trilobyte Press & Multimedia 356; UCLA Amer Indian Studies Ctr 313; Unity House 314; Univ of Idaho 315; Univ of Illinois 316; Univ of Nebraska 317; Univ Pr of Kentucky 320; Upney Editions 357; Utah State Univ 321; Vandamere 322; Vanwell 358; Via Dolorosa 323; Walker 325; Wall & Emerson 358; Warner Books 326; Weatherhill 327; Weidner & Sons 327; Wescott Cove 328; Westcliffe 328; Westminster John Knox 329; White Mane 330; Whitehorse 330; Wiley & Sons, John 332; Willow Creek 333; Windstorm Creative 334; Wisdom 334; Wish 335; Wonderland 363; Woodbine House 335; Wordware 335; Writer's Digest 336; Yale Univ 337; York 359; Zondervan 338

Regional: Adams Media 124; Addicus 125; Adirondack 125; Alexander 127; Appalachian Mtn Club 133; Arcadia 133; Arkansas Research 134; Arsenal Pulp 340; Arte Publico 135; Avalon Travel 138; Avisson 139; Berkshire 144;

Black Dog & Levanthal 145; Blair, John 146; Borealis 341; Boston Mills 342; Bowling Green St Univ 148; Broken Jaw 342; Caitlin 343; Camino 154; Canadian Plains 343; Caxton 157; Chatham 159; Chelsea Green 160; Chelsea House 160; Chicago Review 161; Chronicle 163; City & Co 164; Clear Light 164; Cornell Univ 168; Coteau 345; Countryman 169; Cumberland House 171; Denali 174; Down East 177; Dry Bones 178; Eakin/Sunbelt 179; ECW 345; Eerdmans, William 181; Electric Works 181; Epicenter 182; Farcountry 361; Fernwood 346; Fordham Univ 188; Gem Guides 192; Globe Pequot 193; Goose Lane 347; Guernica 347; Hancock House 198; Heritage Bks 204; Heyday 205; HiddenSpring 205; High Plains 205; Hill Street 206; Holmes & Meier 208; Horsdal&Schubart 348; Houghton Mifflin Bks for Children 208; Howell Pr 209; Hunter Pub 211; Iser 349; Jameson 220; Johnson 221; Kamehameha 222; Kensington 223; Kent State Univ 223; Lake Claremont 225; Lambrecht 350; Lebhar-Friedman 227; Lee, J&L 228; Loft 232; Lone Pine 350; Longstreet 232; Louisiana State Univ 233; Loyola 233; McBooks 237; McGregor 238; Michigan State Univ 240; Minnesota Hist Soc 241; Mountain Pr 244; Mountaineers 244; New England Pr 248; New Society 351; New York Univ 250; Nodin 251; North Carolina Div of Archives 251; Northeastern Univ 252; Northern Illinois Univ 252; Northland 253; Ohio State Univ 255; Ohio Univ 255; Onjinjinkta 256; Orange Frazer 257; Oregon State Univ 257; Overlook Press, The 259; Overmountain 259; Pacific Bks 260; Palgrave 261; Parkway 262; Passeggiata 262; Pelican 264; Pennsylvania Hist and Museum Comm 264; Pineapple 268; Plexus 270; Prairie Oak 271; Pruett 274; Purdue Univ 275; Quill Driver/Word Dancer 276; Really Great 278; Republic of Texas 279; River City 281; Rocky Mtn 354; Ronsdale 354; Rutgers Univ 283; Sandlapper 285; Sasquatch 287; Seaworthy 290; Shoreline 355; Smith, Gibbs 295; Square One 299; Steller 356; Stoneydale 303; Sun Bks/Sun Pub 304; Sunbelt 304; Syracuse Univ 305; TCU 307; Temple Univ 307; Texas A&M Univ 308; Texas Western 308; Third World 308; Three Forks 309; Tidewater 309; TowleHouse 310; Turtle Bks 312; TwoDot 313; Univ of Akron 314; Univ of Alberta 357; Univ of Georgia 315; Univ of Idaho 315; Univ of Illinois 316; Univ of Maine 316; Univ of Missouri 317; Univ of Nevada 317; Univ of New Mexico 317; Univ of North Carolina 318; Univ of North Texas 318; Univ of Oklahoma 318; Univ of Scranton 319; Univ of Tennessee 319; Univ of Texas 319; Univ of Univ of Arkansas 315; Univ Pr of Colorado 320; Univ Pr of Kansas 320; Univ Pr of Kentucky 320; Univ Pr of Mississippi 320; Univ Pr of New England 321; University of South Carolina 319; Utah State Univ 321; Vandamere 322; Vanwell 358; Vehicule 358; Vernon 362; Vintage Anchor 324; Voyageur 325; Washington State Univ Pr 326; Weatherhill 327; Wescott Cove 328; Westcliffe 328; Westernlore 329; WestWinds 329; Whitecap 359; Windswept House 334; Zoland 338

Religion: Abingdon 123; ACTA 124; Alba 127; Albury 127; Alexander 127; Algora 127; Allisone 128; AMG 132; American Counseling 130; Aronson, Jason 134; Asian Humanities 135; Aslan 135; Atheneum Bks for Yng Rdrs 136; Augsburg 137; Autonomedia 137; Baker 139; Ballantine 140; Barbour 141; Behrman 143; Bethany 145; Bookworld/Blue Star 148; Breakout 150; Broadcast Interview 151; Broadman & Holman 151; Bucknell Univ 152; Canadian Educ 343; Catholic Univ of America 157; Chalice 158; Charles Pr 158; Chelsea House 160; Chosen Bks 162; Christian Ed. 162; Christian Pub/Horizon Bks. 162; College Pr 166; Conari 167; Concordia 167; Cook Comm 168; Cornell Univ 168; Covenant Comm 169; Cross Cultural 170; Crossquarter 170; Crossway 171; David, Jonathan 173; Doubleday 176; Doubleday Religious 176; Doubleday/Image 177; Dover 177; Dry Bones 178; Duquesne Univ 178; Eerdmans, William 181; Electric Works 181; Encounter Bks 182; Facts on File 184; Faith Kids 185; Fordham Univ 188; Fortress 189; Forward Movement 189; Green Nature 195; Greenwood Pub Grp 196; Group Pub 196; Guernica 347; Hachai 198; Harcourt Inc., Trade 199; HarperCollins [UK] 347; HarperSanFrancisco 200; Hendrickson 203; Hensley 204; Hidden-Spring 205; Hohm 207; Holmes 208; Inner Traditions 215; Innisfree 215; Insomniac 349; Int'l Scholars 217; Jain 219; Jewish Lights 220; Jones Univ, Bob 221; Judaica 221; Judson 222; Kar-Ben 222; Kindred 349; Kregel 225; Kurian, George 361; Larson/PBPF 226; Legacy 228; Libraries Unlimited 229; Liguori 229; Loft 232; Loyola 233; Magnus 235; McClelland&Stewart 350; Meriwether 239; Midknight Club 240; Moody 242; More, Thomas 243; Morehouse 243; Multnomah Publishers, Inc. 245; NavPress 247; Nelson Pub, Thomas 247; Nelson, Tommy 247; New Canaan 248; New Hope 249; New World Library 250; New York Univ 250; North Point 252; Northfield 253; Norton, WW 253; Novalis 352; Onjinjinkta 256; Our Sunday Visitor 258; Oxford Univ 259; Pacific Pr Pub Assoc 260; Palgrave 261; Paraclete 261; Paragon House 261; Pauline 263; Paulist 263; Pelican 264; Picasso 353; Pilgrim 268; Prometheus 273; Putnam's Sons, G.P. 275; Quest Books 276; Random House Trade 277; Reference Service 279; Resurrection 279; Revere, Fleming 280; Review & Herald 280; River Oak 281; Rose 282; Rosen Publishing Group, The 282; Rutgers Univ 283; Saxon House Canada 355; Scarecrow 287; Schreiber 289; Scribner 289; Sheed & Ward 292; Shoreline 355; Skinner House 294; Spence 298; Square One 299; St. Anthony 299; St. Augustine's 299; St. Bede's 299; Standard 300; Stanford Univ 301; Starbust 301; Sun Bks/Sun Pub 304; Swedenborg 305; Tarcher 306; Third World 308; TowleHouse 310; Trinity Fndtn 311; Trinity Pr Int'l 312; Tuttle 312; Tyndale House 313; UCLA Amer Indian Studies Ctr 313; Unity House 314; Univ of Alabama 314; Univ of Nebraska 317; Univ of New Mexico 317; Univ of North Carolina 318; Univ of Scranton 319; Univ of Tennessee 319; University of South Carolina 319; Via Dolorosa 323; Weatherhill 327; Westminster John Knox 329; White Stone Circle 330; Whitman, Albert 330; Wisdom 334; Yale Univ 337; Zondervan 338

Scholarly: Baywood 142; Beacon Pr 142; BNA 147; Bucknell Univ 152; Burnham 153; Catholic Univ 157; Cato Inst 157; Cornell Univ 168; Dante Univ of America Pr 172; de Gruyter, Aldine 197; Duquesne Univ 178; Fairleigh Dickinson 185; Focal 187; Greenwood 196; Greenwood Pub Grp 196; Harvard Bus School 200; Haworth 201; Int'l Scholars 217; Johnson 221; Kent State Univ 223; Knopf, Alfred 224; Lehigh Univ 228; McFarland & Co 237; Michigan State Univ 240; Minnesota Hist Soc 241; Morehouse 243; Northeastern Univ 252; Ohio State Univ 255; Oregon State Univ 257; Pacific Bks 260; Passeggiata 262; Phi Delta Kappa 267; Pilgrim 268; Praeger 271; Purdue Univ 275; Scarecrow 287; Schenkman 288; St. Martin's 300; Stanford Univ 301; Stylus 304; TCU Press 307; Texas State Hist Assoc 308; Texas Western 308; Univ of Akron 314; Univ of Alabama 314; Univ of Alberta 357; Univ of Calgary 357; Univ of California 315; Univ of Illinois 316; Univ of Maine 316; Univ of Missouri 317; Univ of New Mexico 317; Univ of Pennsylvania 318; Univ of Tennessee 319; Univ of Texas 319; Univ Pr of Colorado 320; Univ Pr of Kansas 320; Univ Pr of Kentucky 320; Univ Pr of Mississippi 320; Utah State Univ Pr 321; Vanderbilt Univ 322; Venture 322; Wesleyan Univ 328; Westernlore 329; Whitston 331; Yale Univ 337; York 359

Science/technology: Adams Media 124; Algora 127; American Astronautical 129; American Chemical 130; American Press 131; American Water Works 131; ATL 137; Atheneum Bks for Yng Rdrs 136; Battelle 142; Blackbirch 146; Bluewood 147; Breakout 150; Brewers 150; Cambridge Educ 154; Capstone 155; Carolrhoda 156; Cartwheel 157; Charlesbridge (School) 159; Charlesbridge (Trade) 159; Chelsea House 160; Chemical Pub 160; Chemtec 344; Children's Pr 161; Chronicle Bks for Children 163; Common Courage 166; Conari 167; Consortium 167; Cornell Univ 168; CSLI 171; Dana Pr 172; Dimi Pr 175; Doubleday 176; Dover 177; Dutton 178; Dutton Children's Bks 179; Editions la Liberte 346; Electric Works 181; Encounter Bks 182; Forge 188; Four Walls Eight Windows 190; Gem Guides 192; Gifted Educ 193; Green Nature 195; Harcourt Inc., Trade 199; Hendriks, FP 348; Henry Pr, Joseph 204; HiddenSpring 205; Hobar 207; Holiday House 207; Houghton Mifflin Bks for Children 208; House of Anansi 348; Humanics Learning 210; Humanitas 348; Information Today 214; Inst of Psych Res 349; Int'l Scholars 217; Island 219; Johnson 221; Kalmbach 222; Ketz, Louise B 361; Knopf & Crown Bks for Yng Rdrs, Alfred 224; Krieger 225; Lehigh Univ 228; Lerner 229; Libraries Unlimited 229; Little, Brown 231; Little, Brown Childrn's Bks 230; Loft 232; Loompanics 233; Lyons 234; McClelland&Stewart 350; McDonald & Woodward 237; Metamorphous 239; Millbrook 241; Mountain Pr 244; Naturegraph 246; Naval Inst 246; New Canaan 248; New England Pub Assoc 362; Norton, WW 253; Oliver 255; Oregon State Univ 257; Oryx 257; Owen, Richard 259; Oxford Univ 259; Paladin 260; Pantheon 261; Pencil Point 264; Perfection Learning 265; Pippin 269; Plexus 270; Precept 272; Purdue Univ 275; Putnam's Sons, G.P. 275; Quest Books 276; Random House Bks for Yng Rdrs 277; Reference Service 279; RFF Pr 281; Rose 282; Rosen Publishing Group, The 282; Running Pr 283; Salem 285; Salina Bookshelf 285; Scholastic Canada 355; Schreiber 289; Scribner 289; Scrivenery 289; Sky Pub Corp 294; Somerville House 362; South End 297; Stanford Univ 301; Steel Pr Pub 301; Sterling 302; Stipes 302; Swedenborg 305; Systems Co 306; Teaching & Learning 307; Ten Speed 307; Texas Western 308; Tricycle 311; Trilobyte Press & Multimedia 356; Trinity Fndtn 311; Twenty-First Century 313; Univ of Akron 314; Univ of Maine 316; Univ of New Mexico 317; Univ of Oklahoma 318; Univ of Texas 319; Univelt 314; Vintage Anchor 324; Walch, J. Weston 325; Walker 325; Wall & Emerson 358; Watts, Franklin 327; Weidner & Sons 327; Whitman, Albert 330; Wiley & Sons, John 332; Williamson 332; Windward 334; Yale Univ 337

Self-help: ACTA 124; Adams Media 124; Addicus 125; Adventure 340; Albury 127; Alexander 127; Alligator 128; Allisone 128; Arkansas Research 134; Aslan 135; Atheneum Bks for Yng Rdrs 136; Augsburg 137; Avisson 139; Baker 139; Ballantine 140; Barricade 141; Behr 142; Berkley Pub Grp 144; Bethany 145; Betterway 145; Beyond Words 145; Blue Poppy 147; Breakout 150; Broadcast Interview 151; Broadman & Holman 151; Broken Jaw 342; Bryant & Dillon 152; Career Pr 155; Carroll & Graf 156; CCC 158; Celestial Arts 158; Chelsea Green 160; Christian Pub/Horizon Bks. 162; Conari 167; Consortium 167; Contemporary Bks 167; Crossquarter 170; Cypress 172; Dana Pr 172; David, Jonathan 173; Do-It-Yourself 176; Doubleday Religious 176; Doubleday/Image 177; Dutton 178; Edutainment 180; Electric Works 181; Entrepreneur 182; Evans 183; Excelsior Cee 184; Executive Excellence 184; Fairview 185; Fell, Frederick 186; Findhorn 187; Forward Movement 189; Free Spirit 190; Future Horizons 191; GGC 192; Gifted Psych 193; Gollehon 194; Guilford 197; Hampton Roads 198; Harbor Pr 199; HarperCollins [UK] 347; HarperInformation 200; HarperSanFrancisco 200; Hatherleigh 201; Hawk 201; Hay House 201; Hazelden 202; Health Comm 202; Health Pr 202; Health Prof Pr 203; Hendriks, FP 348; Herodias 204; HiddenSpring 205; Hohm 207; Holmes 208; Houghton Mifflin 209; Human Kinetics 210; Humanics Pub Grp 210; Hungry Minds (Business) 211; Hungry Minds (Education) 211; Ideals Pub 212; Imagination Store 213; Impact Publications 214; Impact Publishers, Inc. 214; Information Today 214; Inner Traditions 215; Insomniac 349; Int'l Wealth Success 217; iPublish.com 218; Jewish Lights 220; Jist Works 220; Kensington 223; Kesend, Michael 223; Klein, B 224; Lamppost 362; Lebhar-Friedman 227; Liguori 229; Listen & Live 230; Llewellyn 231; Lobster 350; Loompanics 233; Magni 234; Marine Techniques 235; McClelland&Stewart 350; Metamorphous 239; Midknight Club 240; More, Thomas 243; Morrow/Avon 244; Mustang 245; NavPress 247; Nelson Pub, Thomas 247; New American 247; New Harbinger 248; New Horizon 249; New Society 351; New World Library 250; Newmarket 250; Nolo.com 251; Norton, WW 253; Nova 254; Novalis 352; Oaklea 254; One on One 256; One World Bks 256; Onjinjinkta 256; Pacific Pr Pub Assoc 260; Parlay Int'l 262; Pathfinder 263; Pauline 263; Paulist 263; Peachtree 264; Pelican 264; Perigee 265; Perspectives 266; Picasso 353; Planning/Communications 269; Possibility 271; PressForward 272; Prima 273; Productive 353; Prometheus 273; Putnam's Sons, G.P. 275; Quest Books 276; Random House Trade 277; Resurrection 279; Revere, Fleming 280; Review & Herald 280; River City 281; River Oak 281; Ronin 282; Rosen Publishing Group, The 282; Running Pr 283; Safer Society 284; Schenkman 288; Scrivenery 289; Skinner House 294; Sourcebooks 296; Square One 299; St. Martin's 300; Sta-Kris 300; Starbust 301; Steel Pr Pub 301; Success 304; Sun Bks/Sun Pub 304; Swedenborg 305; Systems Co 306; Tarcher 306; Ten Speed 307; Third World 308; Todd 310; Tricycle 311; Trilobyte Press & Multimedia 356; Turtle Pr 312; Tuttle 312; Tyndale House 313; Unity House 314; Via Dolorosa 323; Volcano 325; Walker 325; Warner Books 326; Weatherhill 327; Western Psych Services 328; Westminster John Knox 329; Wildcat Canyon 331; Wilshire 333; Windstorm Creative 334; Wisdom 334; Wonderland 363; World Leisure 336; YMAA 337; Zondervan 338

Sex: Arsenal Pulp 340; Aslan 135; Autonomedia 137; Breakout 150; Broadway 152; Conari 167; David, Jonathan 173; Doubleday Religious 176; ECW 345; Fernwood 346; Guernica 347; HarperInformation 200; Hazelden 202; Health Comm 202; HiddenSpring 205; High Tide 205; Imagination Store 213; Inner Traditions 215; Kensington 223; Lobster 350; Magni 234; Paragon House 261; Perigee 265; Picasso 353; Quest Books 276; Rose 282; Seal 290; Sheed & Ward 292; St. Anthony 299; St. Bede's 299

Social sciences: Burnham 153; Cambridge Educ 154; Free Pr 190; Greenwood 196; Greenwood Pub Grp 196; Merloyd Lawrence 227; Northern Illinois Univ 252; Oryx 257; Pilgrim 268; Purdue Univ 275; Roxbury 283; Stanford Univ 301; Texas Western 308; Univ of California 315; Univ of Missouri 317; J. Weston Walch 325; Whitston 331

Sociology: Algora 127; American Counseling 130; American Press 131; Arsenal Pulp 340; Atheneum Bks for Yng Rdrs 136; Austin & Winfield 137; Barricade 141; Baywood 142; Bethany 145; Branden 149; Bucknell Univ 152; Burnham 153; Canadian Educ 343; Canadian Plains 343; Cato 157; Charles Pr 158; Chelsea House 160; Child Welfare

League 161; Cleis 164; Conari 167; Consortium 167; Cornell Univ 168; Cross Cultural 170; Diogenes 176; Doubleday 176; Editions la Liberte 346; Eerdmans, William 181; Electric Works 181; Encounter Bks 182; Fairleigh Dickinson Univ 185; Feminist Pr at CUNY 186; Fernwood 346; Fordham Univ 188; Free Spirit 190; Greenwood Pub Grp 196; Gruyter, Aldine de 197; Guilford 197; Harcourt Inc., Trade 199; HarperInformation 200; Haworth 201; Hay House 201; HiddenSpring 205; House of Anansi 348; ILR 213; Int'l Scholars 217; Iser 349; LadybugPress 225; Learning Pub 227; Libraries Unlimited 229; Louisiana State Univ 233; Maisonneuve 235; Mariner 236; McClelland&Stewart 350; McFarland 237; Metamorphous 239; New York Univ 250; Ohio State Univ 255; Ohio Univ 255; Onjinjinkta 256; Oxford Univ 259; Palgrave 261; Paragon House 261; Pathfinder 263; Perspectives 266; Planning/Communications 269; Praeger 271; Presses de l'Université de Montreal 353; Purdue Univ 275; Random House Trade 277; Reference Service 279; Roxbury 283; Rutgers Univ 283; Salem 285; Schenkman 288; South End 297; Spence 298; Stanford Univ 301; Stonewall Inn 303; Sun Bks/Sun Pub 304; Talese, Nan 306; Temple Univ 307; Third World 308; Thompson Educ Pub 356; UCLA Amer Indian Studies Ctr 313; Univ of Alberta 357; Univ of Illinois 316; Univ of Pennsylvania 318; Univ of Scranton 319; Univ Pr of Kansas 320; Vehicule 358; Venture 322; Verso 322; Vintage Anchor 324; Watts, Franklin 327; Weatherhill 327; Westminster John Knox 329; Yale Univ 337

Software: Adams Blake 125; American Bar 129; American Water Works 131; A-R 123; Branden 149; Career Pub 155; Cypress 172; Doubleday 176; Educator's Int'l 180; Electric Works 181; Glenlake 193; ISTE 217; Jist Works 220; Neal-Schuman 247; No Starch 251; Norbry 352; Nova 254; One on One 256; Osborne Media Group 258; Productive 353; SAS 286; Serendipity Systems 291; Steel Pr Pub 301; Sybex 305; Windsor 333

Spiritual: ACTA 124; Alba 127; Allisone 128; AMG 132; Asian Humanities 135; Aslan 135; Augsburg 137; Beyond Words 145; Broadman & Holman 151; Broadway 152; Chalice 158; Charles Pr 158; Christian Pub/Horizon Bks. 162; Common Courage 166; Conari 167; Covenant Comm 169; Cross Cultural 170; Crossway 171; Doubleday Religious 176; Electric Works 181; Fell, Frederick 186; Findhorn 187; Front Street 191; Hampton Roads 198; Harcourt Inc., Trade 199; HarperInformation 200; HarperSanFrancisco 200; Hazelden 202; Humanics Pub Grp 210; Imagination Store 213; Inner Traditions 215; iPublish.com 218; Kregel 225; Larson/PBPF 226; Liguori 229; Loyola 233; Midknight Club 240; Moody 242; More, Thomas 243; NavPress 247; Nelson Pub, Thomas 247; Novalis 352; Oaklea 254; Onjinjinkta 256; Palgrave 261; Perigee 265; Quest Books 276; River Oak 281; Ronin 282; Rose 282; Santa Monica 286; Sheed & Ward 292; Square One 299; St. Bede's 299; Univ of New Mexico 317; Via Dolorosa 323; Warner Books 326; Westminster John Knox 329; White Stone Circle 330; YMAA 337

Sports: Abdo 123; Adams Media 124; Addax 125; Adirondack 125; Alaska NW 126; American Press 131; Arcadia 133; Archway 134; Atheneum Bks for Yng Rdrs 136; Avisson 139; Backcountry 139; Barron's 141; Beachway 142; Bentley 143; Black Dog & Levanthal 145; Blackbirch 146; Bluewood 147; Boston Mills 342; Bowling Green St Univ 148; Boyds Mills 148; Brassey's 149; Brassey's Sports 149; Broadway 152; Burford 153; Capstone 155; Carolrhoda 156; Carroll & Graf 156; Cartwheel 157; Chelsea House 160; Children's Pr 161; City & Co 164; Cloud Peak 165; Coaches Choice 165; Contemporary Bks 167; Coteau 345; Cumberland House 171; David, Jonathan 173; Doubleday 176; Dover 177; Down East 177; Eakin/Sunbelt 179; ECW 345; Electric Works 181; Facts on File 184; Fernwood 346; Greenwood Pub Grp 196; Half Halt 198; Harcourt Inc., Trade 199; Hendriks, FP 348; Hill Street 206; History Bank 361; Houghton Mifflin Bks for Children 208; Human Kinetics 210; Hungry Minds (Business) 211; Jones Univ, Bob 221; Kensington 223; Kesend, Michael 223; Ketz, Louise B 361; Krause 224; LadybugPress 225; Lerner 229; Lion 230; Little, Brown 231; Little, Brown Childrn's Bks 230; Longstreet 232; Lyons 234; McClelland&Stewart 350; McFarland 237; McGregor 238; Menasha 239; Millbrook 241; Momentum 242; Morrow/Avon 244; Mountaineers 244; Mustang 245; New American 247; New York Univ 250; Nodin 251; North Point 252; Norton, WW 253; Orange Frazer 257; Owen, Richard 259; Paradise Cay 261; Pelican 264; Perigee 265; Picasso 353; Prairie Oak 271; Prima 273; Pruett 274; Putnam's Sons, G.P. 275; Ragged Mountain Press 277; Random House Bks for Yng Rdrs 277; Random House Trade 277; Republic of Texas 279; River City 281; Rutledge Hill 283; Santa Monica 286; Sasquatch 287; Scarecrow 287; Scholastic Canada 355; Seaworthy 290; Somerville House 362; Sourcebooks 296; Square One 299; St. Martin's 300; Stackpole 300; Sterling 302; Stoeger 302; Stoneydale 303; Taylor 306; Thompson Educ Pub 356; TowleHouse 310; Triumph 312; Turtle Pr 312; Univ of Illinois 316; Univ of Nebraska 317; Van Der Plas 321; Vernon 362; Walker 325; Walsworth 325; Warner Books 326; Westcliffe 328; Whitman, Albert 330; Willow Creek 333; Windward 334; Wish 335; Workman 336; World Leisure 336; YMAA 337

Technical: Adams Blake 125; American Bar 129; American Chemical 130; American Coll of Phys Exec 130; American Correctional 130; American Nurses 130; American Press 131; American Quilter's 131; ASA 135; ASM 136; ATL 137; Austin & Winfield 137; Aviation 138; Baywood 142; Bentley 143; Bloomberg 146; Blue Poppy 147; Branden 149; Breakout 150; Brevet 150; Broadcast Interview 151; Canadian Plains 343; Charles River 159; Chelsea Green 160; Chemtec 344; Consortium 167; Cornell Maritime 168; Craftsman 169; CSLI 171; Cypress 172; Darlington 173; DBS Prod 174; Dry Bones 178; Electric Works 181; Empire 182; Fire Engineering Bks 187; Focal Pr 187; Fort Ross 189; Gatf Press 191; GGC 192; Green Nature 195; Guilford 197; Hancock House 198; Hanser Gardner 199; Harcourt Inc., Trade 199; Hatherleigh 201; Henry Pr, Joseph 204; History Bank 361; Hobar 207; Human Kinetics 210; Hungry Minds (Business) 211; Idyll Arbor 212; Information Today 214; Inst of Police Tech & Mgmt 215; Interweave 218; ISTE 217; Jacobs, Lee 219; Krause 224; Krieger 225; Lebhar-Friedman 227; Loft 232; Lone Eagle 232; Loompanics 233; Marine Techniques 235; Maximum Pr 236; McFarland 237; Medical Physics 238; Merriam 239; Metal Powder 239; Metamorphous 239; Neal-Schuman 247; Nichols 251; No Starch 251; Nova 254; One on One 256; Orchises 257; Osborne Media Group 258; Oxford Univ 259; Pacific Bks 260; Paradise Cay 261; Parkway 262; Parlay Int'l 262; Pencil Point 264; Pennsylvania Hist and Museum Comm 264; Planners 269; Precept 272; Productive 353; ProStar 274; Purich 354; Reference Pr Int'l 279; RFF Pr 281; SAE Int'l 284; SAS 286; Sams 285; Seaworthy 290; Silman-James 293; Sky Pub Corp 294; Society of Manuf Eng 295; Sourcebooks 296; Steel Pr Pub 301; Stipes 302; Sun Bks/Sun Pub 304; Sybex

305; Systems Co 306; Texas Western 308; Tiare 309; Transnational 311; Univ of Idaho 315; Urban Land Inst 321; Van Der Plas 321; Weidner & Sons 327; Windsor 333; Wordware 335

Textbook: Abingdon 123; Alba 127; AMG 132; American Coll of Phys Exec 130; American Correctional 130; American Counseling 130; American Nurses 130; American Press 131; Anchorage 132; APDG 133; Ardsley 134; Art Direction 134; ASM 136; Asian Humanities 135; ATL 137; Austin & Winfield 137; Avisson 139; Baker 139; Barron's 141; Behrman 143; Bellwether-Cross 143; Blue Poppy 147; Bowling Green St Univ 148; Branden 149; Brassey's 149; Broadcast Interview 151; Broadman & Holman 151; Butte 153; Canadian Educ 343; Canadian Library 343; Canadian Plains 343; Career Pub 155; CHA 344; Chalice 158; Charlesbridge (School) 159; Chemtec 344; Christian Pub/Horizon Bks. 162; College Pr 166; Common Courage 166; Consortium 167; Cornell Univ 168; Course Crafters 360; CQ 169; Cross Cultural 170; CSLI 171; Cypress 172; DBS Prod 174; Dearborn 174; Dover 177; Educator's Int'l 180; Eerdmans, William 181; Empire 182; ETC 183; Excelsior Cee 184; Fernwood 346; Fire Engineering Bks 187; Focal Pr 187; Fordham Univ 188; Foreign Policy 188; Free Pr 190; Gatf Press 191; GGC 192; Gifted Educ 193; Gifted Psych 193; Gleason Grp 361; Greenwood Pub Grp 196; Group Pub 196; Gruyter, Aldine de 197; Guilford 197; Hanser Gardner 199; Hartman 200; Haworth 201; Health Pr 202; Health Prof Pr 203; Hendriks, FP 348; History Bank 361; Hobar 207; Human Kinetics 210; Ibex 212; Icon Editions 212; Idyll Arbor 212; Imaginart 213; Inst of Police Tech & Mgmt 215; Inst of Psych Res 349; Interstate 218; Int'l Med 217; Int'l Scholars 217; Island 219; Jacobs, Lee 219; Jain 219; Jist Works 220; Judaica 221; Kamehameha 222; Krieger 225; Latin Amer Lit Rev 227; Learning Pub 227; Lebhar-Friedman 227; Libraries Unlimited 229; Lippincott 230; Loft 232; Medical Physics 238; Meriwether 239; Metal Powder 239; Metamorphous 239; Neal-Schuman 247; Norbry 352; Oasis 254; Orange Frazer 257; Orchises 257; Oxford Univ 259; Pacific Bks 260; Paradise Cay 261; Paragon House 261; Paulist 263; Pencil Point 264; Picton 268; Plexus 270; PRB Prod 272; Precept 272; Presses de l'Université de Montreal 353; Prestwick 273; Prufrock 274; Publicom 362; Purich 354; Quite Specific 276; Review & Herald 280; RFF Pr 281; Rosen Publishing Group, The 282; Roxbury 283; SAE Int'l 284; SAS 286; Sagamore 284; Salina Bookshelf 285; Sandlapper 285; Schenkman 288; Schreiber 289; Silman-James 293; Slack 294; Smith, Gibbs 295; Society of Manuf Eng 295; Sourcebooks 296; Southern Illinois Univ 297; Speech Bin 298; St. Augustine's 299; St. Bede's 299; St. Martin's 300; Stanford Univ 301; Stipes 302; Systems Co 306; Third World 308; Thompson Educ Pub 356; Transnational 311; Trilobyte Press & Multimedia 356; Trinity Fndtn 311; Trinity Pr Int'l 312; Truman State Univ 312; Univ of Alberta 357; Univ of Idaho 315; Univ of Nebraska 317; Utah State Univ 321; Vanderbilt Univ 322; Venture 322; Via Dolorosa 323; Wall & Emerson 358; Weidner & Sons 327; Wesleyan Univ 328; Westminster John Knox 329; White Cliffs 329; Wiener, Markus 331; Wisdom 334; Wordware 335; Yale Univ 337; York 359; Zondervan 338

Translation: Algora 127; AMG 132; Aronson, Jason 134; Arte Publico 135; Autonomedia 137; Barron's 141; Broadcast Interview 151; Chatham 159; Cornell Univ 168; Course Crafters 360; Cross Cultural 170; Dante Univ 172; Doubleday 176; Dover 177; Dry Bones 178; Dufour 178; Ediciones Nuevo Espacio 179; Eerdmans, William 181; Electric Works 181; ETC 183; Feminist Pr at CUNY 186; Fernwood 346; Fordham Univ 188; Free Pr 190; Gifted Psych 193; Guernica 347; Harcourt Inc., Trade 199; Harvard Common 200; Herodias 204; Hohm 207; Holmes & Meier 208; Inst of Psych Res 349; Iser 349; Johnson 221; Kamehameha 222; Latin Amer Lit Rev 227; Maisonneuve 235; MBI 236; McClelland&Stewart 350; Mountaineers 244; Northern Illinois Univ 252; Pacific Bks 260; Palgrave 261; Passeggiata 262; Presses de l'Université de Montreal 353; Quite Specific 276; Schreiber 289; Scrivenery 289; St. Bede's 299; Stone Bridge 303; Univ of Alabama 314; Univ of California 315; Univ of Illinois 316; Univ of Nebraska 317; Univ of New Mexico 317; Univ of North Carolina 318; Univ of Texas 319; Vernon 362; Via Dolorosa 323; Vintage Anchor 324; Weatherhill 327; Zoland 338

Transportation ASA 135; Aviation Publishers (PA) 138; Aztex 139; Bentley 143; Boston Mills 342; Bristol Fashion 151; Howell Pr 209; Iconografix 212; Kalmbach 222; Lerner 229; MBI 236; WW Norton 253; Possibility 271

Travel: Academy Chicago 124; Adirondack 125; Alaska NW 126; Alexander 127; Algora 127; Arcade 133; Arsenal Pulp 340; Atheneum Bks for Yng Rdrs 136; Avalon Travel 138; Barron's 141; Beachway 142; Berkshire 144; Black Dog & Levanthal 145; Blackbirch 146; Blair, John 146; Boston Mills 342; Boyds Mills 148; Breakout 150; Broadway 152; Burford 153; Camino 154; Chelsea House 160; City & Co 164; Conari 167; Coteau 345; Countryman 169; Cross Cultural 170; Cumberland House 171; Dover 177; Electric Works 181; Farcountry 361; Fodor's 188; Gem Guides 192; Gifted Psych 193; Globe Pequot 193; Green Nature 195; Grove/Atlantic 197; Harcourt Inc., Trade 199; HarperCollins [UK] 347; Harvard Common 200; Hellgate 203; Heyday 205; HiddenSpring 205; Hill Street 206; Hippocrene 206; Houghton Mifflin 209; Houghton Mifflin Bks for Children 208; Hunter Pub 211; Iconografix, Inc. 212; Ideals Pub 212; Impact Publications 214; Johnson 221; Kensington 223; Kesend, Michael 223; Kurian, George 361; Lake Claremont 225; Langenscheidt 226; Lebhar-Friedman 227; Lobster 350; Lonely Planet 232; Lynx Images 350; Lyons 234; Marlor 236; McClelland&Stewart 350; McDonald & Woodward 237; Menasha 239; Momentum 242; Mountain N'Air 244; Mountaineers 244; Mustang 245; Newjoy 250; Nodin 251; North Point 252; Northland 253; Norton, WW 253; Ohio Univ 255; One World Bks 256; Open Road 256; Orange Frazer 257; Pantheon 261; Paradise Cay 261; Passport 262; PBC Int'l 263; Pelican 264; Pennsylvania Hist and Museum Comm 264; Prairie Oak 271; ProStar 274; Pruett 274; Putnam's Sons, G.P. 275; Quest Books 276; Really Great 278; Red Hen 278; Republic of Texas 279; River City 281; Rocky Mtn 354; Ruminator 283; Rutledge Hill 283; Santa Monica 286; Sasquatch 287; Seal 290; Seaworthy 290; Shoreline 355; Soho 296; Square One 299; Steller 355; Stone Bridge 303; Sun Bks/Sun Pub 304; Sunbelt 304; Todd 310; Turnstone 357; Univ of New Mexico 317; University of Calgary Press 357; Upney Editions 357; Van Der Plas 321; Vernon 362; Vintage Anchor 324; Weatherhill 327; Wescott Cove 328; Westcliffe 328; Whitecap 359; Whitehorse 330; Whitman, Albert 330; Willow Creek 333; Workman 336; World Leisure 336; Zoland 338

True crime: Addicus 125; Ballantine 140; Berkley Pub Grp 144; Carroll & Graf 156; Kensington 223; McGregor 238; St. Martin's 300

General Index

This index lists every market appearing in the book; use it to find specific companies you wish to approach. Markets that appeared in the 2001 edition of *Writer's Market*, but are not included in this edition are identified by a two-letter code explaining why the market was omitted: (**ED**)—Editorial Decision, (**NS**)—Not Accepting Submissions, (**NR**)—No or Late Response to Listing Request, (**OB**)—Out of Business, (**RR**)—Removed by Market's Request, (**UC**)—Unable to Contact, (**RP**)—Business Restructured or Purchased, (**NP**)—No Longer Pays in Copies Only, (**SR**)—Subsidy/Royalty Publisher, (**UF**)—Uncertain Future, (**Web**)—a listing that appears on our website at www.WritersMarket.com

GENERAL INDEX